DISEASES
of the
NERVOUS SYSTEM

DISEASES

of the

NERVOUS SYSTEM

In Infancy, Childhood and Adolescence

Sixth Edition

By

FRANK R. FORD, M.D.

Baltimore, Maryland

CHARLES C THOMAS · PUBLISHER

Springfield · Illinois · U.S.A.

Published and Distributed Throughout the World by

CHARLES C THOMAS • PUBLISHER

BANNERSTONE HOUSE

301-327 East Lawrence Avenue, Springfield, Illinois, U.S.A.

© *1937, 1945, 1952, 1960, 1966 and 1973, by* CHARLES C THOMAS • PUBLISHER

Library of Congress Catalog Card Number 73-4018

ISBN 0-398-02845-1

First Edition, August, 1937

Second Edition, First Printing, March, 1945

Second Edition, Second Printing, May, 1946

Third Edition, April, 1952

Fourth Edition, January, 1960

Fifth Edition, June, 1966

Sixth Edition, October 1973

With THOMAS BOOKS careful attention is given to all details of manufacturing and design. It is the Publisher's desire to present books that are satisfactory as to their physical qualities and artistic possibilities and appropriate for their particular use. Thomas Books will be true to those laws of quality that assure a good name and good will.

Library of Congress Cataloging in Publication Data

Ford, Frank Rodolph, 1893-
    Diseases of the nervous system in infancy, childhood, and adolescence.
    1. Pediatric neurology. 2. Adolescence. I. Title.
[DNLM: 1. Nervous system diseases—In adolescence.
2. Nervous system diseases—In infancy and childhood.
WS340 F699d 1973]
RJ486.F6 1973   618.9'28   73-4018
ISBN 0-398-02845-1

Printed in the United States of America

C-1

CONTENTS

CHAPTER I

PRENATAL DISEASES AND DEVELOPMENTAL
DEFECTS OF THE NERVOUS SYSTEM

Page

CHAPTER II

HEREDOFAMILIAL AND DEGENERATIVE DISEASES OF THE NERVOUS SYSTEM

CHAPTER III

INFECTIONS AND PARASITIC INVASIONS OF
THE NERVOUS SYSTEM

CHAPTER IV

INTOXICATIONS, METABOLIC AND ENDROCINE DISORDERS, DIETARY DEFICIENCIES AND ALLERGIES INVOLVING THE NERVOUS SYSTEM

CHAPTER V

VASCULAR LESIONS AND CIRCULATORY DISORDERS
OF THE NERVOUS SYSTEM

CHAPTER VI

NEOPLASMS AND RELATED CONDITIONS INVOLVING THE NERVOUS SYSTEM

CHAPTER VII

INJURIES OF THE NERVOUS SYSTEM
BY PHYSICAL AGENTS

CHAPTER VIII

THE EPILEPSIES AND PAROXYSMAL DISORDERS
OF THE NERVOUS SYSTEM

CHAPTER IX

DISEASES OF THE AUTONOMIC SYSTEM

CHAPTER X

DISEASES OF THE MUSCLES

DISEASES
of the
NERVOUS SYSTEM

Chapter I

PRENATAL DISEASES AND DEVELOPMENTAL DEFECTS OF THE NERVOUS SYSTEM

INTRODUCTION.—We may divide the abnormalities of the nervous system which arise before birth into two chief groups. In one, some part of the nervous system is absent, or incompletely formed, and it is evident that we are not dealing with destruction as a result of injury or disease, but with a defect of development. In the second group, we find evidence that the nervous system has developed up to a certain point and that destruction of nervous tissue has then taken place. It is not always easy to separate these two groups, for injuries inflicted during the course of development may not only destroy the affected structure, but may inhibit the development of closely related structures. The defects of development, apparently, are much more common than the intrauterine diseases. The former group will be discussed first.

We shall learn in the following pages that there is a great variety of defects of the nervous system, and scarcely any portion of the brain or spinal cord is exempt. It may be said that deficiency of fetal activity during pregnancy or cessation of fetal movements are strongly suggestive of deficient development or injury during intrauterine life.

The clinical pictures presented by such defects are of great diversity, but some characteristics of the whole group may be mentioned. For example, it is obvious that the condition should be present at birth. Moreover, in contrast to the familial degenerations, the disease does not run a definitely progressive course. A history of similar defects in relatives or ascendants is sometimes elicited. The diagnosis is strengthened if we discover no evidence of birth injury or of illness during early infancy which might suggest the onset of a post-natal disease of the nervous system. Unfortunately, the situation is not so simple as these statements might indicate. In many cases of defective development of the cerebral cortex, basal ganglia of the forebrain and perhaps other suprasegmental structures, the symptoms do not become evident until several months after birth, for these structures are not fully functional in the new-born infant, and the absence of their influence is, therefore, not apparent. We may say then that a symptom-free interval following birth is not against the diagnosis of defective development of the suprasegmental structures of the nervous system. Defective nervous systems may react excessively to mild birth trauma, often giving rise to unjustified suspicions of birth injury. The situation is further complicated by the extraordinary sensitiveness of these children to intoxications and infections. Mild fevers and other illnesses may cause outspoken exacerbations of nervous symptoms, and even bring new symptoms to light, so that the physician may be misled into the belief that the disease of the nervous system resulted from the illness. Certain severe cases of cortical agenesis are often associated with chronic disturbances of nutrition leading to cachexia and death, thus suggesting a progressive process. It is evident, therefore, that the symptoms of prenatal defects of the nervous system may be modified during early infancy by a number of factors. On one hand, we have the child's natural tendency to develop and acquire new reactions; on the other, we have the tendency for defects of suprasegmental structures to become more and more evident as the time approaches at which these structures should develop their proper control of the segmental apparatus. We must also take into consideration the excessive reactions of a crippled nervous system to injuries, toxins and infections, and the limited resistance of defective neurons to the stress and strain of life.

Little is known of the causes of defective development of the nervous system. It is probably correct to state that the most prevalent point of view is that which attributes these conditions to an abnormal germ plasm. Morbid heredity is certainly the most obvious factor in certain cases. For example, we may mention the occasional recurrence of several instances of spina bifida or of cerebral aplasia in the same family. In most cases of congenital defect of the nervous system, however, the family history is negative, and, in general, the evidence of morbid heredity is not nearly so convincing as it is in cases of progressive degeneration of the nervous system.

A second possibility has been emphasized by the work of several embryologists. A number of defects of development of the nervous system have been produced by various procedures, such as pricking certain areas of a fertilized egg with a needle, placing it in solutions of different types, or by keeping it in an ice box for brief intervals. The last-named experiment is of great interest, for it has been possible to show by this means that local defects of development may be produced by a temporary inhibition of embryonic oxygenation. Stockard states that each organ develops in a definite sequence, and has a certain period of maximum growth. If during the period in which a certain organ is developing most rapidly the metabolism of the embryo is inhibited by cold, or by being placed in some unfavorable medium, the organ will never have an opportunity to attain its proper growth, and will be defective or rudimentary. By careful timing, Stockard has been able to produce defects of almost any organ. Ingalls reports similar experiments. Pregnant mice were placed in a chamber under very low oxygen tension at various stages of pregnancy. Various defects of development were produced in the fetus depending upon the time at which the anoxia was induced. Thus, it is said that during the first week of intrauterine life, cyclopia is to be expected, conjoined twins about the second week, ectromelia at the third week, tracheoesophageal fistula at the fourth, nuclear cataract of the lens at the fifth, hare lip at the sixth and cleft palate at the seventh. It is possible, therefore, that spontaneous defects of development may be the result of transient reduction of embryonic metabolism or hypoxia.

This theory is especially appealing in cases in which there is no evidence of morbid heredity and particularly in those in which the anatomical findings seem to indicate that the development of the nervous system has stopped abruptly at a certain stage of fetal life.

Ferris, a biologist, has shown that after ovulation the mammalian ova remain in a condition to be fertilized for only a few hours. He believes that human ovulation usually occurs in the afternoon. If intercourse occurs more than 8 hours later, the ovum can rarely be fertilized. If fertilization occurs after 8 hours a defective fetus is almost certain to result. The author refers to Mall's work who showed that aborted ova and embryos are usually malformed, and suggests that malformed products of conception are aborted as a rule early in embryonic life. Occasionally a malformed baby is carried in the mother's uterus long enough to be born alive.

Hertig and Shea have found evidence that if ovulation is delayed until the 15th day or later in the menstrual cycle the ovum is not apt to be fertilized or if fertilized will give rise to a defective embryo.

Nicholson has demonstrated that sperm motility and viability may be preserved for 6 days after sexual intercourse.

Bourne and Benirschke studied 1,500 placentas and umbilical cords and found that one umbilical artery was lacking in 15. They studied 113 infants who lacked one umbilical artery. Some 65 infants were stillborn or died shortly after birth. Of these 91 per cent displayed malformations of many different kinds. Only 48 infants survived and 29 per cent showed congenital abnormalities. Froehlich and Fujikura report a similar study.

Bain *et al.* describe sirenomelia and monomelia with renal agenesis and nodular changes in the amnion. In sirenomelia or mermaid fetus there is fusion of the legs to form a single extremity. In monomelia there is merely a single leg which shows no indication that it is formed as a result of fusion of two legs. There is always dysplasia of the urinary tract and resulting oligohydramnios. The features are flattened and the hands are large and flattened. In some cases there is only one umbilical artery.

Rausen *et al.* describe the transplacental transfusion syndrome q.v. This occurs in identical twins. Arteriovenous communications develop shunting blood from one twin into the circulation of the other. As a result one twin becomes anemic and retarded in development and the other becomes polycythemic.

Benirschke describes abnormalities of the placenta. He includes in addition to the placental transfusion syndrome and the loss of one artery of the umbilical cord several others. The umbilical cord sometimes inserts on the margin of the placenta and in rare instances into the membranes. The fetal blood vessels then pass within the membranes towards the placenta. If this area lies over the internal os they may rupture when the membranes are torn during labor and the fetus may be rapidly exsanguinated. In circumvallate placenta the membranes are folded over the margin of the placenta. The membranes dissect off the underlying villous tissue. Hemorrhage may cause fetal death. Infarcts of the placenta are apt to occur in toxemias. The fetus may be defective or die. Arteriovenous aneurysm in the placenta is known as chorangioma. Angiomas may be found in the baby. Fetal growth may be retarded and cardiac hypertrophy and hydramnios may occur. Various viruses, especially the rubella virus and the cytomegalic virus, may cause lesions in the placenta. The defects in babies of mothers who have rubella may be due in part to the damage to the placenta. Bacterial infections of the fetus may occur especially if the membranes rupture before labor begins. The fetus may aspirate the bacteria and develop pneumonia and otitis may occur sometimes leading to meningitis.

Abaci and Aterman state that 41 per cent of early abortions terminating pregnancies of 6 to 12 weeks are associated with microscopic changes in the placenta characteristic of hydatidiform mole. No normal embryos were found. In 20 per cent subchorionic hematomas were found with fibrotic changes of placental villi.

Defective implantation of the ovum may lead to malformation of the baby or stillbirth. The products of extrauterine pregnancy are often malformed.

Heredofamilial diseases of the nervous system are not associated with demonstrable abnormalities of the chromosomes. The defect, therefore, is attributed to abnormalities at the molecular level. In 1958, Jerome Lejune of Paris discovered that mongols have an extra chromosome. This discovery was followed by extensive investigations which have made it evident that certain defects of development are associated with demonstrable abnormalities of the chromosomes.

Recent studies with improved technique have revealed that a normal individual has forty-six chromosomes. There are twenty-two pairs of non-sex chromosomes, or autosomes, and one pair of sex chromosomes. In females, the sex chromosomes are large and are represented by XX. The male has a large chromosome, X and a small one, Y. It is now possible to distinguish the autosomes which are numbered in pairs. The autosomes are numbered from one to twenty-two pairs and the two sex chromosomes make up the normal number of forty-six.

The chromosomes are distinguished by their length and by the position of the centromere. They are arranged in seven groups: 1-3 A, 4-5 B, 6-12 C, 13-15 D, 16-18 E, 19-20 F, and 21-22 G. The X chromosomes are not given a number or letter but are usually placed with the G group. The Y chromosome resembles the G group in size and morphology.

Some individuals have more than forty-six chromosomes and some less. It is suggested that during the division of the germ cells, chromosome breakage may occur and a portion of a chromosome may be lost. This is termed *deletion*. Exchange of unequal fragments may result in abnormally large chromosomes. This is termed *translocation*. If, during the process of division of the germ cell, both halves of a chromosome are located in one daughter cell, this is termed *non-disjunction*.

In mongolism, there are usually forty-seven chromosomes. The pair of chromosomes numbered 21 is found to be associated with a third of equal size. This is termed a *trisomy*.

In Turner's syndrome, there are only forty-five chromosomes, and only one sex chromosome. This constitution is represented as XO. Females who have only the single sex chromosome may display abnormalities such as hemophilia and color blindness, which are sex-linked and appear, as a rule, only in the male. The absence of the second sex chromosome permits this latent abnormality to become evident.

In Klinefelter's syndrome, one often finds forty-seven chromosomes as a result of an extra sex chromosome. This is represented as XXY. Ferguson-Smith *et al.*, however, found two patients presenting the picture of Klinefelter's syndrome who had forty-eight chromosomes and a sex chromosome constitution of XXXY. Barr *et al.* describes the XXXXY chromosome syndrome.

Fraser *et al.* found mentally defective females with a sex chromosome constitution of XXX and forty-seven chromosomes. A very few cases of the XYY sex chromosome constitution have been discovered. There are forty-seven chromosomes. The subjects are males and sexually defective or mentally backward.

In some patients there may be more than one chromosome pattern in different cells. This is spoken of as a mosaic pattern. Klevitt discusses many such conditions. This is attributed to non-disjunction occurring during cell division in the early stages of embryonic growth. It is believed that if the normal cells are more numerous than the abnormal cells, the individual may be normal.

Sulzman states that tissue cultures were possible in 25 cases of spontaneous human abortion. Gross abnormalities of the chromosomes were found in 16. Trisomy was found in 6 cases, sex chromosome monosomy in 5 cases and triploidy in 5 cases. No chromosomal abnormalities were found in the products of 15 therapeutic abortions.

It is said that in some instances a sex-linked disease is found in females with a normal XX sex chromosomal pattern. The Lyon hypothesis proposes that this may be explained by the assumption that one of the X chromosomes is genetically inactive during the mitotic interphase and that genetic information is transmitted only by the other X chromosome. The inactive X chromosome is believed to be represented by the sex chromatin body (Barr body) which is most easily demonstrated by the study of the buccal smear. The female has this body and the male does not so the female is termed chromatin positive and the male chromatin negative.

As this work has progressed, it has become evident that chromosomal abnormalities may be found in individuals who appear to be normal so that the significance of such abnormalities is not entirely clear. It should be said in this connection that the methods of counting and identifying the chromosomes are not yet so accurate that one can be sure that chromosome anomalies are not present when they cannot be demonstrated.

A review of recent studies in cytogenetics by Dr. Havelock Thompson illustrates the complexities which are coming to light and makes it clear that this field is now one for specialists who devote their entire time to the subject.

Certain viruses and other organisms may be conveyed to the fetus by the mother's blood stream through the placenta. We may mention German measles, toxoplasmosis, syphilis, malaria, listerosis, smallpox, cytomegalic disease, Coxsackie virus infection, poliomyelitis, herpes encephalitis, and equine encephalitis. No doubt other diseases may damage the fetus. Coffee found that during the epidemic of influenza in Dublin, in 1957, the incidence of congenital malformations was greatly increased when the mother contracted the disease in the first three months of pregnancy. Bacteria may penetrate the membranes by way of the cervix and thus reach the placenta and the fetus.

Toxic and metabolic disorders of the mother may result in congenital defects of the baby. Babies of diabetic mothers are apt to have malformations of the nervous system. The incidence is eight times as high as in children of non-diabetic mothers. The defects point to disturbances of embryonic development before the tenth week of gestation. It has been found that abnormal serum protein levels, especially in the alpha and beta globulins, are associated with abortions, premature children, and defects of development. Abnormal hemoglobins should be mentioned in this connection. Deficiency of vitamins, especially folic acid due to deficient diet, or to the administration of aminopterin, a folic acid antagonist, may result in congenital defects in the baby. Deficiency of certain minerals including manganese may cause similar defects, it is claimed.

In 1961, a great increase of congenital malformations was observed in Germany. These children often had no arms or legs and sometimes other defects of development. Several thousands of children were affected. Small numbers of such children were discovered in England and in Italy. There was reason to believe that the use of thalidomide, a sedative drug, was responsible when used in the early weeks of pregnancy. No doubt, other drugs have a similar effect.

The ingestion of large amounts of quinine during pregnancy may cause deafness and blindness in the baby.

Roentgenotherapy over the pregnant uterus is a well-known cause of damage to the child's nervous system.

Falls or blows which injure the pregnant uterus are occasionally responsible for fetal damage.

An attempt at an anatomical classification of the defects of development of the nervous system is presented in tabular form below.

CLASSIFICATION OF CONGENITAL DEFECTS OF THE CENTRAL NERVOUS SYSTEM

I. *Defects associated with defective closure of midline structures*
   A. *Cerebral dysplasias with cranium bifidum*
      a. *Complete cranioschisis.*—In this condition the vault of the skull

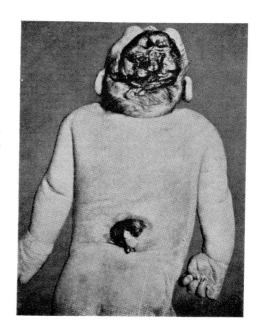

Fig. 1. Anencephalus with canium bifidum and spina bifida. (From Grinker and Sahs, Neurology.)

is absent. The brain is completely exposed, and more or less defective. Several types are described. In anencephaly the forebrain and the midbrain are absent, and are represented by a spongy mass of incompletely differentiated tissue, the area cerebro-vasculosa. The hindbrain is more or less complete. In hemicephaly the forebrain is absent, but the midbrain is completely or partially formed. In exencephaly parts of the hemispheres are present, and the diencephalon is fairly well developed.

b. *Meningoencephalocele.*—There is a defect in the skull through which protrudes a portion of the brain which may or may not contain a part of the ventricular system. The hernia is covered by meninges and skin. The brain may be defective.

c. *Meningocele.*—Only the meninges are found in the sac in this type. The brain may be defective.

d. *Cranium bifidum occultum.*—There is no sac in this type, but the bone is defective, and there is often some alteration in the overlying skin such as a "port wine" stain.

e. *Porencephaly.*—Here we have a cleft or defect opening upon the surface of the cerebral cortex and lined by well formed convolutions which connects by a small opening with the ventricular system. Such defects are bilateral and essentially symmetrical. They are believed to be due to defective closure of the neural tube. Yakovlev and Wadsworth employ the term *schizencephaly*. In most instances the cerebral defects found in association with cranium bifidum seem to be of this type.

B. *Myelodysplasia with spina bifida*

a. *Complete rachischisis.*—The neural tube has never closed. The spinal cord is spread out like a ribbon and fully exposed. As a rule there is no sac. The cord is always grossly defective, and it may be impossible to find any nerve cells or fibers at the level of the lesion.

b. *Meningomyelocele.*—In this condition there is a sac composed of skin and meninges, which contains the spinal cord or its roots firmly adherent to the inner wall.

c. *Meningocele.*—In this type the sac does not contain nerve roots or the cord.

d. *Spina bifida occulta.*—There is no external sac, but the laminae of vertebrae are defective, and the overlying skin is usually marked by an abnormal growth of hair or some other peculiarity. The neural tube has closed, but the cord is sometimes imperfectly developed.

e. *Congenital dermal sinuses.*—These are narrow openings in the skin which extend from the midline of the back to the spinal meninges. They are usually found in the sacral regions, and are regarded by Mallory as evidence of incomplete closure of the caudal end of the neural tube.

II. *Alobar and lobar holoprosencephaly* (DeMeyer)

Alobar

a. Cyclops with only one midline eye and one midline ventricle, absence of olfactory bulbs and tracts and median cleft palate and lip.

b. Cebocephaly with only one midline ventricle, absence of olfactory bulbs and tracts, median cleft palate and lip, but two eyes which may be imperfectly formed.

Lobar

c. Arhinoencephaly with absence of olfactory bulbs and tracts and testicular deficiency.

III. *Miscellaneous defects of development of the nervous system.*

a. *Absence of the corpus callosum.*—This defect rarely occurs except in association with some other anomalies. The gyrus fornicatus is usually absent. Fusion of the frontal hemispheres and absence of the falx are sometimes associated.

b. *Heterotopias.*—This term is applied to malformations due to failure of the neurons to migrate normally during development. As a result, we find nuclear masses in the white matter. These neurons are usually of embryonic type and often separated from the surrounding tissues by a zone of glia cells. Such conditions rarely exist alone.

c. *Cortical ageneses.*—This group embraces a number of conditions. Here we place agyria or lissencephaly *pachygyria* in which the cortical pattern is simplified and incompletely formed, and *microgyria* where the pattern is too complex. The histological structure of the cortex is of fetal type, and the projection and association tracts are small and incompletely developed. In other cases, the cortical pattern is normal, but there are histological defects in the cortex and motor tracts. Freeman refers to these cases as *cerebral* glioses since there is an isomorphous gliosis which he regards as an accompaniment of defect of development not a reaction to degeneration.

d. *Agenesis of the white matter.*

e. *Defects in the basal ganglia.*—This group includes the *status marmoratus* of the lenticular nuclei and related conditions.

f. *Defects of the cerebellum.*—Unilateral and bilateral defects are described which are associated with deficient development of pons and olives.

g. *Defects of the cranial nerve nuclei.*—The nuclei are either absent or small and atrophic. The term *nuclear aplasia* is often employed.

h. *Defects of the spinal cord.*—Here we might place status dysraphicus and diplomyelia.

i. *Neurenteric cysts.*—Neurenteric cysts are believed to be due to persistence of the neurenteric canal and Bremer believes that a delay in the regression of the neurenteric canal may be responsible for diplomyelia and disatematomyelia.

j. *Defects of mechanisms of special senses.*—Defects of the visual, olfactory and auditory apparatus are described. These, as a rule, involve the whole mechanism. For example, if the optic nerves are absent, the secondary visual neurons, and even the cortical centers, will be deficient, or incompletely developed.

IV. *Hypertrophies*

a. *Macrocephaly.*—The brain is larger than normal, and shows a very complex cortical pattern. There is an abundance of neurons and myelinated fibers. There is also often extensive gliosis.

b. *Hemihypertrophy.*—Hemihypertrophy of the body is sometimes associated with unilateral hypertrophy of the brain.

V. *Defects of development of the cerebrospinal fluid system with hydrocephalus*

a. *Defects of the aqueduct*

b. *Defective formation of the foramina of the fourth ventricle*

c. *Defective formation of the subarachnoid spaces and cisternae*

BIBLIOGRAPHY

Abaci, F. and Alterman, K.: Changes in the placenta and embyro in early spontaneous abortion. Amer. Jour. Obstet. and Gynec., **102**:252, 1968.

Adams, J. M. et al.: Viral infections in embryo. Jour. of Dis. of Children, **29**:109, 1956.

Aita, J. A.: Neurocutaneous disease. Springfield, Thomas, 1966.

Bain, A. D. et al.: Sirenomelia and monomelia with renal agenesis and amnion nodosum. Arch. of Dis. of Childh., **35**:250, 1960.

Benda, C. E.: Developmental Disorders of Mentation and Cerebral Palsies. New York, Grune and Stratton, 1952.

Benirschke, K.: Pathological aspects of the human placenta. Triangle, **8**:143, 1967.

———: Routes and types of infection in the fetus and newborn. Am. J. Dis. Child., **99**:714, 1960.

Blanc, W. A.: Amniotic infection syndrome. J. Pediat., **59**:473, 1961.

Bourne, G. L. and Benirschke, K.: Absence of one umbilical artery. Arch. Dis. Childhood, **35**:534, 1960.

———: Absent umbilical artery. Review of 113 cases. Arch. Dis. Childhood, **35**:534, 1960.

COFFEE, V. P. *et al.:* Maternal influenza and congenital deformities. Lancet, i:935, 1959.

COHEN, S. S.: Recent advances in the chemistry of inheritance. Jour. of Pediat. **60**:586, 1962.

DAUBE, J. R. AND CHOU, S. M.: Lissencephaly. Neurology, **16**:179, 1966.

DEKABAN, A. AND MAGEE, K. R.: Neurologic abnormalities in infants of diabetic mothers. Neurology, **8**:193, 1958.

DEMEYER, W., *et al.:* Familial alobar holoprosencephaly with median cleft lip and palate. Neurology, **13**:913, 1963.

DE MORSIER, G.: Etudes sur les dystrophies cranio-encephaliques, Ageneste des lobes olfactifs et des commissures calleuse et anterieure. La dysplasie olfacto-genitale. Schwetz Arch. Neurol. Psychiat., **74**:309, 1954.

DRISCOLL, S. G. *et al.:* Neonatal deaths among infants of diabetic mothers. Postmortem findings in 95 infants. Am. J. Dis. Child., **100**:818, 1960.

DUKE-ELDER, S.: System of Ophthalmology vol. 7. C. V. Mosby Co., St. Louis, 1962.

EMIG, O. R.: Inflammation of the placenta. Obstet. & Gynec., **17**:743, 1961.

EVANS, T. N. AND BROWN, G. C.: Viral infection and congenital anomaly. Am. J. Obst. & Gynec., **87**:749, 1963.

FARRIS, E. J.: Human ovulation and fertility. Lippincott, Philadelphia, 1956.

FERGUSON-SMITH, M. A.: Chromosome abnormalities with congenital disease. Mod. Med., March 6, 1961, p. 77.

FITZGERALD, P. A. M. F.: Defective development of the cerebral cortex involving symmetrical bilateral areas. Contributions to Embryology No. 176. Carnegie Inst. of Washington, D.C., 1940.

FORD, C. E.: The cytogenic basis of sex development. Am. J. Obst. & Gynec., **82**:1154, 1961.

FRANCOIS, J.: Chromosome abnormalities and ophthalmology. Jour. Ped. Ophth., **1**:17, 1964.

————: Heredity in ophthalmology. C. V. Mosby Co., St. Louis, 1961.

FROEHLICH, L. A. AND FUJIKURA, T.: Significance of a single umbilical artery. Amer. Jour. Obstet. Gynec., **94**:274, 1966.

GARCIA, A. G. P.: Fetal infection in virus diseases. Pediatrics, **32**:895, 1963.

GORLIN, R. J.: Chromosomal abnormalities and oral anomalies. Jour. Dent. Res., **42**:1297, 1963.

GRUENWALD, P. *et al.:* Abruptio and premature separation of the placenta. Amer. Jour. Obstet. and Gynec., **102**:604, 1968.

HANAWAY, J. *et al.:* Pachygyria: relation of findings to modern embryologic concepts. Neurologu., **18**:791, 1968.

HERSKOWITX, I. H.: Genetics. Little, Brown and Co., Boston, 1962.

HERTIG, A. T. AND SHEA, S. M.: Delayed ovulation and defective embryos. Pro. Amer. Soc. Clin. Path., September, 1966.

HSIA, D. Y. Y.: Recent advances in biochemical detection of heterozygous carriers in hereditary diseases. Metabolism, **9**:301, 1960.

INGALLS, T. H.: Causes and prevention of developmental defects. J.A.M.A., **161**:1047, 1956.

JOSEPH, M. C.: Thalidomide and congenital abnormalities. Develop. Med. & Child Neurol., **4**:338, 1962.

KALLMAN, F. J. *et al.:* Genetic aspects of primary eunuchoidism. Amer. Jour. Ment. Defic., **48**:203, 1944.

KLEVIT, H. D.: Sex chromosomes in abnormal sexual differentiation. Am. J. Med. Sc., **243**:790, 1962.

KOCH, G.: Neue Ergebnisse der klinischen und genetischen Schwachsinnsforschung. Ärtzliche Forschung, **17**:Heft 1, 1963.

————: Erworbene und erbliche Schwachsinnszustände Die Medizinsche Welt. **161**, No. 37.

————: Metabolisch und chromosomal bedingte Schwachsinnszustände Artztliche Forschung 1961, No. 15.

LECK, I. M. AND MILLAR, E. L. M.: Cause of thalidomide toxicity. Brit. Med. J., **5296**:16, 1962.

LEJEUNE, J., *et al.:* Etudes des chromosomes somatique de neuf enfants mongoliens. C. R. Acad. Sci., Paris, **248**:1721, 1959.

————: Le mongolisme trisomie degressive. Ann. Genet. (Par.) , 2:1, 1960.

LENA, W.: Medical Genetics. Univ. of Chicago Press, 1963.

LENNOX, B.: Chromosomes for beginners. Lancet, i:1046, 1961.

LEWENTHAL, H. *et al.*: Single umbilical artery. Israel. Med. Jour., 3:899, 1967.

LYON, M. F.: Sex chromatin and gene action in mammalin X chromosome. Amer. Jour. Hum. Genet., 14:135, 1962.

MACKLIN, M. T.: The role of heredity in disease. Medicine, 14:1, 1935.

MARBURG, O.: So-called agenesia of the corpus callosum. Arch. Neurol. & Psychiat., 61:297, 1949.

McKENNA, A. J.: Hypoplasia of the optic nerves. Read before the Canad. Ophthal. Soc., June 14, 1966.

MILLER, J. Q.: Lissencephaly in two siblings. Neurology, 13:841, 1963.

MINKOWSKI, M.: Prenatal neuropathologic changes leading to neurologic or mental disorders. Proc. of the first International Congress of Neuropath. Rome, September 1952.

NAEF, R. W.: Clinical features of porencephaly. Arch. of Neurol. and Psychiat., 80:133, 1958.

NICHOLSON, R.: Vitality of spermatozoa in the endocervical canal. Fertil. and Steril., 16:758, 1965.

NORMAN, R. M. AND GREENFIELD, J. G.: Neuropathology. Edward Arnold, London, 1958.

OVERZIER, C.: Classification of intersexuality. Triangle, 8:32, 1967.

PENROSE, L. S.: Genetics of anencephaly. Jour. Ment. Defic. Res. 1957, 1:4.

POLANI, P. E.: Sex anomalies due to chromosome errors. Postgrad. Med., 38:281, 1962.

SCHULL, W. J.: The cause of congenital malformations. Clin. Obst. & Gynec., 4:365, 1961.

SOKOLANSKY, G.: Zur Anatomie und Physiologie des Nervensystems der Anencephalie. Ztschr. f. d. ges. Neurol. u. Psychiat., 118:532, 1929.

STERNBERG, H.: Ueber Splatbildungen des medullarrhes bei jungen menschlichen Embryonen, ein Beitrag zur Entstehung der Anencephalie und Rachischisis Virchows. Arch. f. path. Anat., 272:335, 1929.

STOCKARD, C. R.: Developmental rate and structural expression; an experimental study of twins, double monsters and single deformities and the interaction among embryonic organs during their origin and development. Am. J. Anat., 28:115, 1920-21.

SULZMAN, A. E.: Chromosomal aberrations in spontaneous human abortions. New England Jour. Med., 272:811, 1965.

TAUSSIG, H. B.: A stuly of the German outbreak of phocomelia. J.A.M.A., June 30, 1962.

THIEDE, H. A. AND METCALFE, S.: Chromosomes and human pregnancy wastage. Amer. Jour. Obstet. and Gynec. 96:1132, 1966.

THOMPSON, H.: Abnormalities of autosomal chromosomes associated with human disease. Amer. Jour. Med. Sci., 250:718, 1965.

TONDURY, G.: Aetiological factors in human malformations. Triangle, vol. 7, p. 90, 1965.

WAGGONER, R. W. *et al.*: Agenesis of the white matter with idiocy. Amer. Jour. Ment. Defic., 47:20, 1942.

WALSH, F. B.: Clinical Neuroophthalmology. 2nd Ed. Baltimore, Williams and Wilkins, 1957.

YAKOVLEV, P. I. AND WADSWORTH, R. D.: Schizencephalies. A study of congenital clefts in the cerebral mantle. J. Neuropath. & Exp. Neurol., 5:116 and 169, 1946.

ZELLWEGER, H.: Genetic aspects of neurological disease. Arch. of Int. Med., 115:387, 1965.

THE MODE OF INHERITANCE OF CONGENITAL DEFECTS OF THE NERVOUS SYSTEM

Macklin, in a review of the role of heredity in disease, has given in summary the evidence for the inheritance of congenital defects of the nervous system. She points out that the occurrence of the same developmental anomaly in more than one child of a family, and often in several generations, could scarcely be the result of an environmental factor. The presence of the same malformation in both identical twins is not unusual, but it is almost unknown for only one identical twin to be affected, or for both fraternal twins to be afflicted in the same manner. Since identical twins have the same hereditary influences, and fraternal twins dissimilar heredity but identical prenatal influences otherwise, it is obvious that these facts point very strongly to the conclusion that heredity is the most important factor in many of the congenital defects of the nervous system.

The mechanisms by which such malformations are transmitted will not be discussed at this point, for they will be outlined in Chapter II, in the section dealing with progressive degenerations of the nervous system. It may be said, however, that, when they are inherited, congenital defects are apparently dependent upon recessive rather than upon dominant factors, and that, consequently, the hereditary nature is not always evident unless a complete study is made of the family tree.

CEREBRAL DYSPLASIA WITH CRANIUM BIFIDUM

Definition.—A defect of the brain associated with a defective closure of the skull usually in the midline. This is, of course, analogous to spina bifida with myelodysplasia.

Pathological Anatomy.—The grosser defects of the brain, such as anencephaly, need not be described, since they are incompatible with life and of only embryological interest, but the milder types of cranium bifidum, such as meningocele, meningoencephalocele and cranium bifidum occultum, will be described in brief. The skull, as a rule, is rather small, that is, the capacity of the cranial cavity is diminished and the forehead may recede. The defect in the bone is usually but not always in the sagittal plane, and most frequently either frontal or occipital. There is a rough parallelism between the defect in bone and the defect in the brain. In *meningoencephalocele,* the hernia contains a portion of the brain and, usually, some part of the ventricular system, although in some cases solid masses of nervous tissue have been found. It is covered with meninges and skin which may be normal or atrophic. In some cases, the sac contains choroid plexus and the ventricle is occluded as it passes through the opening in the bone with the result that the sac grows rapidly and is apt to rupture. The meningoencephalocele, in our experience, usually arises from some portion of the brain-stem. A common site is the roof of the fourth ventricle passing posteriorly under the cerebellum. This is usually associated with cervical spina bifida. In other cases, the vermis of the cerebellum is absent, and the sac separates the cerebellar hemispheres which are usually very small. In a third type, the sac arises from the roof of the third ventricle and passes posteriorly above the cerebellum. All of these are frequently associated with hydrocephalus. In *meningocele* the sac is formed of meninges and covered with skin. The aperture in the skull is, as a rule, relatively small. In rare instances a meningocele or meningoencephalocele protrudes into one orbit. *Cranium bifidum occultum* should be mentioned. In this condition there is, of course, no hernia or sac.

A number of defects are found in the brain in cases of cranium bifidum including microgyria and defects in the corpus callosum. The standard defect, however, has been shown by Yakovlev and Wadsworth and by Benda to be bilateral, true *porencephaly*. These writers prefer to term this condition *schizencephaly*. Here we find bilateral, usually symmetrical clefts in the dorsolateral walls of the hemispheres which penetrate to the ventricles. They are lined with gray matter and the external openings are covered by a membrane. In some cases there is no hydrocephalus. In other cases hydrocephalus is associated and the clefts are distended and enlarged. It is clear that this process is the expression of failure of the neural tube to close and it is therefore analogous to myelodysplasia such as we find in spina bifida. It should be mentioned that sequestration dermoids and epidermoids may be found in the cranial defect.

We must distinguish these conditions from secondary conditions which simulate them. For example, in severe types of congenital hydrocephalus, the increased intracranial pressure may eventually produce local destruction of the skull with the formation of small meningoencephaloceles. These may occur in any part of the cranium, and are not confined to the midline.

Clinical Features.—In cranium bifidum with meningocele or meningoencephalocele, we find a soft, rounded or lobulated tumor. Rarely it may be pedunculated. It may be large or small, and usually grows steadily in size. With few exceptions, it is found in the midline of the cranium. The occipital and frontal regions are the sites of predilection. The tumor may protrude at the root of the nose through a defect between the frontal bones and the cribriform plate or through a median defect in the frontal bone. In some cases, the tumor presents in the nasal cavity, the orbit, the mouth or the pharynx. In rare instances, the sac may be found on the lateral aspects of the cranium usually near a suture line. In the occipital region, it may extend through the posterior fontanel, the foramen magnum, or through a median defect in the occipital bone. Occipital meningoceles may be associated with spina bifida of the upper cervical spine. The sac may be covered by normal skin or by only a thin membrane. In some instances, there is a central cicatrix. Pressure upon the tumor causes the fontanels to bulge, and may cause loss of consciousness and disturbances of respiration. If the tumor can be reduced, the defect in the bone may be palpable. Unless the opening into the cranium is small a pulsation synchronous with the pulse is always palpable. Dr. Hoyt has showed us a case in which an encephalocele at the base of the skull caused the optic chiasm and

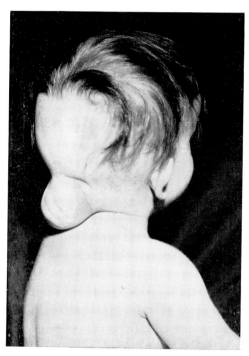

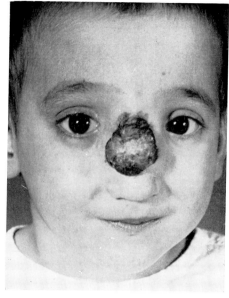

Fɪɢ. 3. Child with encephalocele protruding into nose from anterior fossa.

Fɪɢ. 2. Suboccipital meningocele with hydrocephalus. The tumor was removed but the hydrocephalus continued to progress.

the hypothalamus to appear in the pharynx where they were exposed by a defect in the soft palate.

The writer has observed three cases in which defects of the cranium without sac formation were associated with cerebral defects. In two cases, the defect was frontal, and the child was mentally defective and showed spastic diplegia. In the third, the child was born blind, and showed defect in the occipital lobes and a posterior defect in the bone.

Mental defects of various grades of severity and cerebral palsies are very common. Hydrocephalus is present in the majority of cases. Spina bifida is also a very common complication. Club-foot, hare-lip and cleft-palate may also occur.

Diagnosis.—The commonest condition which may be mistaken for the condition under consideration is cephalhematoma. Hematomas may be recognized by their situation which is usually over one parietal bone well away from the suture lines, by the absence of pulsation, by their gradual absorption, and by the rim of periosteal new bone which forms about the margins after a few weeks. Moreover, there is no defect in the underlying bone. Abscesses under the scalp should not give rise to any confusion with cranium bifidum, for aspiration will reveal pus. Occasionally, we find a

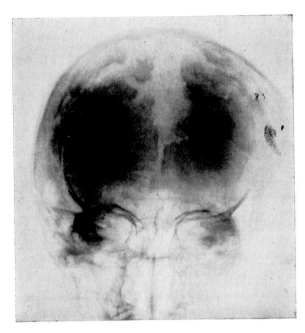

Fig. 4. Roentgenogram of the skull in cranium bifidum with defective development of the brain. No meningocele. (By the courtesy of Dr. Dandy. Lewis' Practice of Surgery. W. F. Prior Co. 1932.)

congenital tumor, such as a hemangioma or glioma, associated with a defect in the skull and resembling, in its gross appearance, a meningoencephalocele. It has been stated that meningocele may be distinguished from meningoencephalocele by transillumination, since the former is translucent and the latter opaque, but this test is not conclusive, for the brain tissue may be so thin that the light shows through it. In case of doubt, the sac may be injected with air, or ventriculography may be performed. The presence or absence of hydrocephalus may be determined by the same procedure.

Prognosis.—These tumors often grow larger, especially if hydrocephalus is present. Eventually, some of them rupture, or become infected, causing death from meningitis. Death may also result from hydrocephalus. In many cases, if not in the majority of cases, the child dies before the end of the first year.

Treatment.—Every effort should be made to prevent rupture or infection of the sac. It should be dusted with antiseptic powder and covered with sterile gauze. Fluids should be reduced to a minimum. Simple meningoceles may be excised successfully in many cases, but there is always danger of the development of hydrocephalus after operation, even if it has not existed before. Penfield has advanced evidence to show that the sac has some power of absorption and, therefore advises that it be preserved. His operation is mentioned briefly under spina bifida. It seems best to advise against operation in cases complicated by hydrocephalus, and in cases in which there is serious defect of the brain.

CASE HISTORY.—*Congenital cortical blindness associated with defect in the bone overlying the occipital lobes. One sibling had cortical blindness, and two cousins were also blind from birth. Probably cranium bifidum occultum with defective development of the occipital lobes.*

V. M., school-girl, 16 years of age, was first seen on July 12, 1934. The history was elicited that the child had been born at full term by normal, spontaneous delivery. There was no cyanosis nor other symptoms of birth injury. A large defect was noted in the bone in the region of the posterior fontanel which did not close. The child was also delicate, and cried almost constantly for more than a year, but did not seem to be ill. At the age of eight months, she was discovered to be totally blind, although the optic-nerve heads were normal, and the pupils reacted well to light. The child walked at 11 months of age, and talked at about the same time. The patient's only sibling died at the age of six weeks of diphtheria. He had seemed to be quite normal in every respect before the fatal illness, except for the fact that he seemed to be blind. His pupils reacted to light and the optic nerve heads appeared to be normal. Two paternal cousins, both girls, were also born blind.

Examination revealed a very slender, delicate, young girl, whose intelligence was at least average. There was a long, broad defect in the cranial bones, extending from the region of the posterior fontanel to the vertex, and the posterior part of the cranial cavity was small. There was no hernia, and no defect in the overlying skin. The pupils were equal and circular, and reacted well to light. There was some error of refraction, but the optic-nerve heads were normal in every respect, and the retinae and maculae were also normal. Vision was absent. There were the usual "searching movements" of the eyes. The examination of the other cranial nerves was entirely negative. The patient's skeletal system was small, and the hands, especially, were poorly developed, resembling those of a child of eight years. The musculature was very slender, and muscle tone was much diminished, so that the feet could be placed behind the head and the fingers and wrists hyperextended. There was, however, no disturbance of motility, sensibility or reflexes.

BIBLIOGRAPHY

BENDA, C. E.: *Loc-cit.*

DANDY, W. E.: An operative treatment for certain cases of meningocele. Arch. Ophth. 2:123, 1929.

DAVIS, C. H. AND ALEXANDER, E.: Congenital nasofrontal encephalomeningoceles and teratomas. J. Neurosurg. 16:365, 1959.

INGRAHAM, F. D.: Spina bifida and cranium bifidum. Cambridge, Harvard Univ. Press, 1943.

PENFIELD, W. AND CONE, W.: Spina bifida and cranium bifidum, results of plastic repair of meningocele and myelomeningocele by a new method. J.A.M.A. 98:455, 1932.

SUWANWELA, C. AND HONGSAPRABHAS, C.: Frontoethmoidal encephalomeningocele. Jour. Neurosurg. 25:172, 1966.

THOMS, H.: Family prevalence in anencephaly; report of a case. J.A.M.A. 70:10, 1918.

YAKOVLEV, P. I. AND WADSWORTH, R. C.: Schizencephalies I. J. Neuropath. and Exp. Neurol. 5:116, 1946.

————: Schizencephalies II. J. Neuropath. and Exp. Neurol. 5:169, 1946.

FAMILIAL ALOBAR AND LOBAR HOLOPROSENCEPHALY
(DEMEYER)

This condition may be familial. It is characterized by a series of deformities ranging from cyclopia which is the most severe to arhinencephaly
which is the least severe.

Cyclopia is characterized by the presence of a single eye in the middle of
the forehead which may be found on careful examination to be composed
of two eyes which are fused together. The head is small. The nose may be
absent or defective. There is a median cleft lip and median cleft palate.
The child is often stillborn and rarely survives long. It is completely helpless and no evidence of mental activity is found.

At post-mortem examination the brain is very small. The lateral ventricles are replaced by a single, dilated midline ventricle. Sulci and convolutions may be present. The olfactory bulbs and tracts are absent. The posterior parts of the brain may be relatively normal.

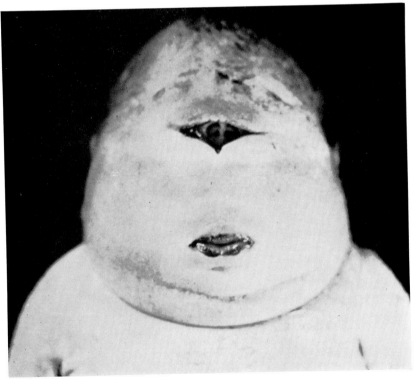

Fig. 5. Cyclops showing appearance of one eye in center of the forehead. Absence of
the nose. There was only one midline ventricle and the brain was extremely small. (By
the courtesy of Dr. Charles Lutterll.)

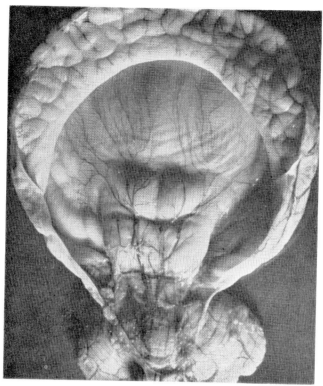

Fig. 6. Holoprosencephaly. The unpaired brain and the basal ganglia are demonstrated. (From Grinker and Sahs, Neurology. Thomas, 1966.)

Cybocephaly is characterized by profound mental deficiency. There is little or no motor function. The eyes are set closely together and may be imperfectly formed. Colobomata may be present. A median cleft lip and median cleft palate are found. The nose is imperfectly formed. There is a single midline ventricle as in cyclopia so these conditions are classified as alobar holoprosencephaly. Some of these patients have a normal chromosomal constitution but some have 47 chromosomes and the 13-15 trisomy. These are apt to have polydactylism.

Arhinencephaly is the least severe condition. There are two hemispheres and two lateral ventricles so it is termed lobar holoprosencephaly. There are bilateral lateral cleft lips and cleft palates. The brain may be grossly normal except for the absence of the olfactory bulbs and olfactory tracts. In males, the testicles may fail to develop properly. This is attributed to lack of gonadotropic stimulation. Some have a normal chromosomal constitution and some the 13-15 trisomy.

BIBLIOGRAPHY

DeMeyer, W. *et al.*: Familial alobar holoprosencephaly with median cleft lip and palate. Neurology, **13**:913, 1963.

De Morsier, G.: Median cranioencephalic dysraphias and olfactogenital dysplasia. World Neurol. **3**:485, 1962.

Nowakowski, H. and Lenz, W.: Genetic aspects in male hypogonadism. Recent. Progr. Hormone Res. **17**:53, 1961.

Haworth, J. C.: Cebocephaly with endocrine dysgenesis. Jour. Pediat. **59**:726, 1961.

Miller, J. Q. *et al.*: A specific congenital brain defect (Arhinencephaly) in 13-15 trisomy. New England Jour. Med. **268**:120, 1963.

CONGENITAL SPASTIC DIPLEGIA

Definition.—The term diplegia means merely bilateral paralysis, but the author employs it in the restricted sense given by Freud. According to this definition, congenital spastic diplegia applies to those cases of congenital bilateral paralysis and spasticity in which the legs are more severely affected than the arms. Congenital double hemiplegia is, therefore, excluded, for in this case the disability is more severe in the arms, and paraplegia is also excluded since the arms are not affected at all. It must be admitted, however, that very severe diplegias are not easy to distinguish from double hemiplegias, and mild diplegias merge imperceptibly with the paraplegias. Nevertheless, there are many cases of diplegia which cannot be termed either double hemiplegia or paraplegia, and which require the recognition of a third group.

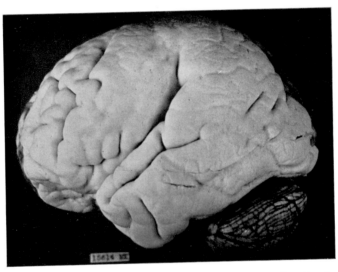

Fig. 7. Brain of an infant suffering from diplegia showing defective development of the cortex and absence of Rolandic fissure and adjacent sulci. The defects were bilateral and symmetrical. (Described in detail by Fitzgerald, P. A.: Contributions to Embryology, No. 176, Carnegie Institution of Washington, August 15, 1940.)

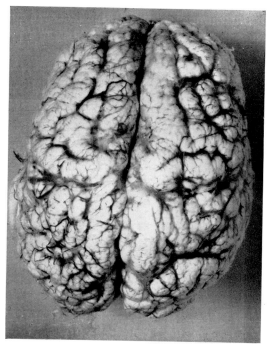

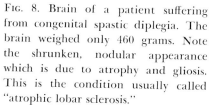

Fig. 8. Brain of a patient suffering from congenital spastic diplegia. The brain weighed only 460 grams. Note the shrunken, nodular appearance which is due to atrophy and gliosis. This is the condition usually called "atrophic lobar sclerosis."

Pathological Anatomy.—The anatomical substratum is not always the same, and several pathological processes are described. One of the commonest conditions is usually termed *atrophic lobar sclerosis*. Buzzard and Greenfield give the following description: "Macroscopically, the chief appearance is that of atrophy, either localized or affecting to a greater or less extent the whole brain substance. In slight cases, the convolutions when stripped of their meninges appear normal, but examination with a hand lens reveals here and there minute depressions or scar-like puckerings. The surface may have a finely worm-eaten appearance. In some advanced cases, the convolution is represented by a thin leaf of fibrous substance, the so-called parchment-like convolution. The parts of the mid-brain and hindbrain associated with the sclerosed areas fail to develop, and the cerebral peduncles are small. Microscopically, the condition is one of neuroglia overgrowth associated with degeneration of the neuron substance. The process appears to affect primarily the deeper layers of the cortex, and spread thence to the underlying white matter and to the superficial layers of the cortex. The vessels are affected showing perivascular neuroglial sclerosis, dilatation of the adventitial lymph spaces with granular corpuscles and some degree of periarteritis. The ependyma is involved, and may proliferate and show glandular masses which penetrate more or less deeply into the tissue around the ventricle." Secondary degeneration is found in the pyramidal and other fiber tracts. The interpretation of this condition is not clear. Collier and Greenfield seem to regard it as the result of a degenerative process which is active in utero.

In other cases, we encounter malformations and defects of development. These may be gross as in microgyria and pachygyria, or demonstrable only upon careful microscopic study. The following descriptions are derived chiefly from Freeman. In *pachygyria,* the cortical pattern is simplified with few and shallow sulci and broad convolutions. Since the primary fissures appear during the third month, the secondary fissures during the fifth month, and the smaller sulci during the seventh month, it is often possible to give an approximate date to the interruption of development. The microscopic structure of the cortex is quite abnormal. As a rule, the cortex shows only four layers of cells in place of the usual six layers, and these layers are irregularly arranged as in the primitive cortex before lamination occurs. There is also often a tendency to columnar arrangement, which is also a characteristic of the fetal cortex. Very frequently, a layer of cells is seen just below the meninges, the external granule layer, which should disappear by the end of the seventh month. Between the cortex and the white matter is usually a zone of relatively undifferentiated tissue in which few nerve cells are found, and which shows very little myelin. The white matter is thin, and perhaps, incompletely myelinated. Heterotopic nodules composed of immature nerve cells may be found scattered in the white matter indicating incomplete migration. The pyramidal tracts are not degenerated, but may be incompletely myelinated or merely smaller than normal. Usually the changes in the pyramidal tracts are more evident in the lumbar region than in the upper segments of the cord. In *Microgyria,* on the other hand, the convolutional pattern is very complex, and an abnormal number

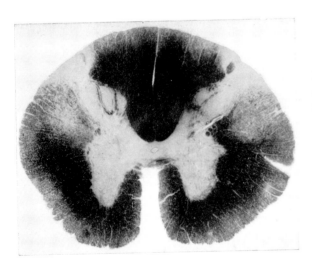

FIG. 9. "Atrophic lobar sclerosis." Section of the spinal cord showing degeneration of the pyramidal tracts, and of the spinocerebellar tracts. There was loss of cells in Clarke's columns, and of anterior horn motor cells with degeneration in the motor roots.

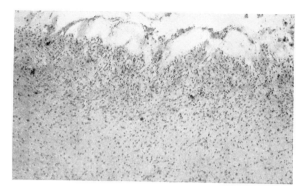

Fig. 10. Imperfectly developed cerebral cortex in full term infant. The surface is nodular and irregular, hence the term status verrucosus. There is proliferation of glial fibers, poverty of nerve cells, immaturity of nerve cells and loss of the normal architecture.

of sulci are present. This condition is usually confined to small areas of the cortex, often symmetrically placed in corresponding regions of the hemispheres. Wart-like nodules may be seen, which have been termed status verrucosus. The sulci are often abnormally shallow. As a rule, the cortex shows not more than four cell layers, but the architecture is, usually, more nearly normal than in pachygyria. Heterotopias in the white matter are very common. The ganglion cells are often immature, show vesicular nuclei and few processes. Abnormally large cells may be found. The myelination of the white matter may be complete or defective.

In other cases, the brain is apparently normal in its gross appearance. The cortical pattern is not defective in any way, but the brain is apt to be somewhat smaller than normal and is often strikingly firm. Microscopic examination reveals numerous abnormalities. There is always a generalized reduction in nerve cells and nerve fibers, but the myelin sheaths are usually well preserved. There is often irregularity in the arrangement of the cortical cells, and immature giant cells are found. Glial cells are not increased, but glial fibers are often present in enormous numbers. These are laid down along normal architectual lines, being most prominent in the middle layers of the cortex, but are also found in the white matter. Glial fibers are numerous beneath the ependyma, where they form nodules which project into the ventricles and under the pia to which they are often united. Freeman terms gliosis of this type isomorphous gliosis, and regards it as evidence of a developmental abnormality rather than a reaction to degeneration. These findings may be generalized, or may be confined to one hemisphere, to restricted areas of the cortex, or to the brainstem and basal ganglia. In some cases, Freeman describes fine lipoid droplets scattered throughout the brain and contained, as a rule, in microglia cells. This, no doubt, indicates a degenerative process which may well be superimposed upon a defect of development. It is possible that it is merely an expression of immaturity, since fat is found in the brain during myelination.

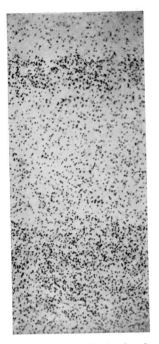

FIG. 11. Imperfectly developed cortex in full term infant. Poverty of nerve cells in the supra-granular layers of the cortex.

In summary, we may say that the brains of patients suffering from congenital diplegia fall into three principal groups: (1) Those which show evidence of a diffuse degenerative process or atrophic lobar sclerosis. (2) Those which show gross malformations or defects of development. (3) Those which are normal in their gross appearance, but show defects of development on microscopic examination. In the writer's experience, defects of development have been just about as frequent as the condition termed atrophic lobar sclerosis.

Etiology.—We must conclude, from the variety of the pathological findings, that congenital diplegia is not always due to the same cause, and it seems necessary to consider the etiology in relation to the two principal anatomical types: atrophic lobar sclerosis and various defects of development.

The former is, perhaps, not so constant in its characteristics that we are justified in assuming that it is always the result of any specific cause, and at least three possibilities must be considered among the etiological factors: asphyxia at birth, cerebral hemorrhage at birth, and degenerative or toxic processes operating in utero. There is a great difference of opinion among the leading authorities on the relative importance of these various factors. Recently a number of writers have stressed the importance of asphyxia at birth and this factor may be more important than we have realized in the past. It is difficult to evaluate, however, since many babies are deeply asphyxiated without ill effects. The use of nitrous oxide for delivery is thought to offer a possible means of asphyxia of the baby. It is also known that roentgenotherapy of the pelvis during pregnancy may produce a diplegic child. As regards the role of intracranial hemorrhage at birth, the diffuse nature of the pathologic process in atrophic lobar sclerosis makes it very difficult to imagine any connection.

The cause of the defects or malformations of the nervous system often found in diplegia is also obscure. Morbid inheritance is, undoubtedly, responsible in some cases, for studies by Böök and Hanhart, as well as many others, have revealed that spastic diplegia with mental deficiency is sometimes inherited as a simple recessive characteristic, and several cases in identical twins have been described. The writer has observed diplegia in a pair of identical twins, and, also, in two siblings, the younger of whom was delivered by Caesarean section, because birth injury was suspected in the case of the first child. Prematurity has been stressed as a cause of diplegia, but not more than one-third of all diplegics are premature, and most premature children eventually attain a normal development of the nervous system. Possibly, transient interference with oxygenation of the fetus may play a part in the defects of development, for Stockard has shown that it is possible to eliminate certain organs or parts of organs by placing fertilized eggs in the ice box for carefully timed periods. If the mother has German measles during the first two months of pregnancy, the child is apt to have diplegia as well as congenital heart disease and congenital cataracts. Cases have been discovered in which abnormalities of the chromosomes seem to be responsible.

Clinical Features.—Congenital diplegia is the commonest of the cerebral palsies of infancy, and several hundred cases have been observed at the Harriet Lane Home. In 1925, the writer made a study of over 200 cases of this type which were found among about 50,000 case records. Neurologists who deal with adult patients find congenital diplegia very unusual, no doubt because only a few of the patients so afflicted survive until adult life.

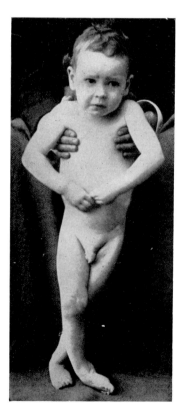

The clinical picture is subject to considerable variation depending upon the severity of the condition. In the most severe diplegias, the condition is evident at birth. In the first few days of life, there are symptoms which suggest birth injury, such as cyanosis, feeble crying and inability to nurse. The head may be small and the fontanels below average size. The extremities are very rigid, the head often retracted and the trunk arched backward. Often, it is possible to support the child by the head and heels. Both tonic and clonic spasms of the muscles occur. In somewhat less than one-third of all cases, the child is premature, and this fact may tend to obscure the symptoms for a time. Aplasia of the optic nerves is sometimes seen especially when the frontal lobes are defective. The tendon reflexes are usually increased, although the rigidity may be so severe that they may be elicited only with difficulty. Any stimu-

Fig. 12. Photograph of a patient suffering from congenital spastic diplegia.

lus may induce generalized reactions of the trunk and extremities. The tonic neck reflexes are often strongly developed. Indeed, in some cases the picture is that of decerebrate rigidity. It is of interest that the legs are often flexed rather than extended as is the rule in the less severe diplegias. The course of diplegia of this type is very brief as a rule. The rigidity grows more and more severe, so that it suggests a progressive process. Nutrition is maintained with great difficulty and these children often become emaciated. Temperature regulation is unstable, and fever often develops without any apparent cause. There is little resistance to infection. Such children are also sensitive to drugs, and we have observed two instances in which death followed the instillation of homatropine in the eyes. As a rule, the child does not survive the first year.

In other instances, the child is regarded as normal until several months after birth. It is then noted that the head is not maintained properly and that no progress is being made in sitting or standing. When the child is placed on the feet, the legs grow rigid and are strongly adducted, so that they assume the "scissors" position, and there is also a tendency to stand on the toes, arch the back and retract the head. When the child cries, the entire bodily musculature becomes rigid, but there may be no increase in muscle tone when the child is at rest. The tendon reflexes are increased, and there is usually an ankle clonus. Later, it becomes evident that there is a bilateral Babinski response. At first, it is not evident that the arms are affected, but, later it is discovered that they are also affected to some degree. Month by month, the symptoms become more and more obvious, in such a way as to suggest a progressive process. The rigidity seems to increase, and it soon is evident that more or less mental defect is present. Convulsive seizures and petit mal occur in approximately one-quarter of all cases. Speech is delayed, and almost always imperfect. Often, the child will begin to make some steps at about the age of four or five years, but the gait is spastic and clumsy. In other cases, the child may never walk. It is of interest that the delay in walking is not entirely due to weakness and spasticity, for often the child will be unable to walk when the legs are strong enough for the purpose. There is in such cases some defect in equilibrium which suggests a delay in the development of the righting reflexes. It has frequently been pointed out that the greatest disability lies in the spasticity and that there may be little actual weakness. There is never any loss of sensibility, and sphincter control is eventually acquired except when there is profound mental defect. The head is often below the average size and, indeed, general development is usually below par. Nutrition is often a problem, and digestive disorders are common. As a rule, the child dies during childhood of some intercurrent infection.

The mildest types of diplegia show merely some spasticity of the legs, especially at the ankle joints, and a tendency to talipes equinus. There is clumsiness of the hands, which is shown chiefly in writing and in fastening buttons. Some degree of mental defect is usually present, but this may be mild. The mental condition, of course, is not always comparable to the motor condition. As a rule, the mild types of diplegia are not recognized until relatively late in childhood. The prognosis as regards life is much better in the mild types, and such patients often survive into adult life. Striking peculiarities of development are seen in those patients who live a number of years. The legs are small and short, the pelvis relatively small, and the arms and shoulders much larger, but not so large as the neck which is usually developed normally and so appears disproportionately large.

The reaction of some cases of diplegia to acute infections, intoxications and convulsions is so striking as to require discussion. It has been mentioned above that the instillation of a few drops of atropine in the eyes may lead to fatal poisoning. Temperature regulation is unstable, and these children may react with high fever to relatively mild infections. At the same time, there may be a definite increase in the symptoms and even in the physical signs, and signs previously latent may become apparent. The spasticity and pathological reflexes are often increased; tremors, incoordination and choreiform movements may appear, and bulbar disturbances are sometimes seen. A series of convulsions, or some operative procedure under anesthesia may produce similar results. Sometimes, such physical signs appear during the course of an intercurrent illness in mentally defective children who have shown no motor symptoms previously. It seems justifiable to state that defective nervous systems are far more sensitive to infections and intoxications than the normal nervous system.

The syndromes described above may be combined with extra-pyramidal syndromes, with congenital ataxia of cerebellar type, with athetosis, with bulbar or pseudobulbar palsy, with optic atrophy, and with other congenital defects which will be taken up below. Perloff and Nodine describe four

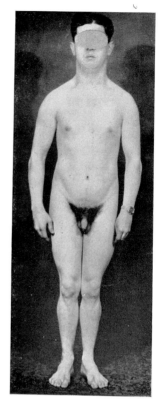

Fig. 13. Congenital spastic diplegia in an adult showing the poor development of the legs and pelvis, somewhat better development of the arms and shoulders and a thick muscular neck. The patient is only 5 feet tall and is very childish. K 56744

patients with congenital quadriplegia who developed sexual precocity associated with an excessive excretion of androgens.

Diagnosis.—The recognition of the syndrome of diplegia is relatively easy. From double hemiplegia it is distinguished by the greater severity of the symptoms in the legs than in the arms, and from cerebral paraplegia by the presence of some degree of weakness in the upper extremities.

Progressive degenerative processes are distinguished by the continued progression of the symptoms, and, often, by the presence of similar cases in other members of the family. Prolonged observation may be necessary in certain cases. The encephalitides and encephalopathies are usually recognized by the history of an acute onset, but great difficulty in the interpretation of the history is often encountered. These children often react so excessively to acute infections, that in case the parents have not noted any abnormality before the illness, they may be convinced that the neurological condition had its inception long after birth.

Prognosis.—The prognosis depends very largely upon the severity of the condition. In the most severe cases, the symptoms usually seem to increase, and the child usually dies within a few months or years. Less severe types admit to some degree of apparent improvement during childhood, although this is probably merely an expression of natural development. Soon, however, the condition becomes stationary. In mild cases, the patient may reach adult life, and even become self-supporting if given proper training.

Treatment.—If the child's mental condition is profoundly defective, treatment should not be attempted since nothing can be accomplished. If, however, the mental development is nearly normal, or even fairly good, every effort should be made to improve motility and to make the most of the child's mental powers. Exercises and passive movements are indicated. Most authorities recommend surgical measures to overcome excessive muscle spasm and deformity. We are accustomed to advise stretching under anesthesia, operative lengthening of the tendons and partial section of the peripheral nerves as described by Stoffel. After deformity has been reduced, and proper muscle balance attained, we begin exercises and massage. Braces may be necessary. Various drugs have been recommended in the treatment of such cases. Curare, myanisin and prostigmine are mentioned. It is very doubtful if any of these are of real value.

The treatment of the convulsions is discussed under epilepsy. The mental condition should be estimated as accurately as possible, and training appropriate to the child's capacity should be given.

BIBLIOGRAPHY

ALPERS, B. J. AND MARCOVITZ, E.: Pathologic background of cerebral diplegia. Am. J. Dis. Child. 55:356, 1938.

BENDA, C. E.: Developmental Disorders of Mentation and Cerebral Palsies. New York, Grune and Stratton, 1952.

Böök, J. A.: A genetic and neuropsychiatric investigation of a North Swedish population. Acts genet., **4**, 1953.

Collier, J. S.: The pathogenesis of cerebral diplegia. Brain, **47**:1, 1924.

———: Cerebral diplegia. Brain **22**:373, 1899.

FitzGerald, P. A. M. F.: Defective development of the cerebral cortex involving symmetrical bilateral areas. Contributions to Embryology No. 176. Carnegie Inst. of Washington, 1940.

Ford, F. R.: Cerebral birth injuries and their results. Medicine **5**:121, 1926.

Freud, S.: Die infantile Cerebrallähmung. Spec. Path. u. Ther., Nothnagel, IX, Wien, 1897.

Friedman, A. P. and Courville, C. B.: Atrophic lobar sclerosis of early childhood. Report of two cases with particular reference to their asphyxial etiology. Bull. Los Angeles Neurol. Soc. **6**:32, 1941.

Hanhart, E.: Eine Sippe mit einfach-rezessiver Diplegia spastica infantils aus einem Schweizer Inzuchtgebiet. Erbartz, 1936, Vol. 11.

Hohmann, H.: Die diplegia spastica infantilis hereditaria. Nervenarzt **28**:323, 1957.

Hyman, C. H.: The Stoffel operation for spastic paralysis with a report of 24 cases. Surg. Gynec. & Obst. **36**:613, 1923.

Ironsides, R.: Cerebral diplegia. Its classification and prognosis. Proc. Roy. Soc. Med. **25**:578, sec. Neurol., 1932.

Miller, J. Q.: Lissencephaly in 2 siblings. Neurology **13**:841, 1963.

Paskin, H. A. and Stone, T. T.: Familial spastic paralysis. Arch. of Neurol. and Psychiat. **30**:481, 1933.

Perloff, W. H. and Nodine, J. H.: Association of congenital spastic quadriplegia and androgenic precocity in four patients. J. Clin. Endocrinol. **10**:721, 1950.

Russell, E. M.: Cerebral palsy in twins. Arch. Dis. Childhood **36**:328, 1961.

Stiefler, G.: Littlescher krankheit bei geschwestern und bei zwilligen. Jour. Psychol. Neurol. **37**:362, 1928.

CONGENITAL SPASTIC PARAPLEGIA

Definition.—This condition is closely related to the congenital spastic diplegia just described, and, probably, represents merely an abortive form. It is, therefore, a cerebral paraplegia.

Pathological Anatomy.—This is, apparently, identical with that of the diplegias, but only that portion of the corticospinal motor system which supplies the lumbar enlargement is affected.

Etiology.—The problem of etiology is discussed under congenital diplegia.

Clinical Features.—Pure paraplegias without any involvement of the arms are very rare, but are encountered occasionally. As a rule, there is very moderate mental defect, and indeed, it is well known that the mental condition may be quite normal. As a rule, the weakness and spasticity are greatest at the ankle joint, and the knee and hip joints are less severely affected. In mild cases, only the calf muscles are involved. Talipes equinus is almost invariably present.

Diagnosis.—This condition must be distinguished from the various types of congenital spinal paraplegias such as those due to birth injury and to defects of the spinal cord. Disturbances of sphincter control, or loss of sensibility favor a spinal lesion, and the absence of such signs, the presence of mental defect, microcephaly or convulsions favor a cerebral origin.

Prognosis.—As a rule, the prognosis is much better than in diplegia. The expectation of life is greater, and the degree of permanent disability is much less.

Treatment.—This is discussed under congenital spastic diplegia.

BIBLIOGRAPHY

(See Congenital Spastic Diplegia)

CONGENITAL DOUBLE HEMIPLEGIA

Definition.—This is a bilateral paralysis with spasticity involving the arms more severely than the legs and often associated with pseudobulbar palsy and mental defect of high grade.

Pathological Anatomy.—The anatomical lesions are not uniform. We may find such malformations as have been described above, such as microgyria, pachygyria and various types of defect of development, as well as atrophic lobar sclerosis. In many cases, however, we find bilateral porencephaly, which is usually of the type attributed to defective development, or "true porencephaly," rather than the secondary type due to birth injury and vascular lesions. True porencephaly is usually a narrow slit or a funnel-shaped cavity in the cerebral hemisphere, the apex of which communicates with the lateral ventricle. As a rule, the lesions are near the fissure of Sylvius in the distribution of the middle cerebral artery. Usually an identical defect is found in the opposite hemisphere. The sides of the cavity are formed by well-developed convolutions which dip down smoothly and which often have a radial arrangement. Microgyria, hydrocephalus and other malformations may be associated. The piaärachnoid is not thickened or adherent, and covers the defect in the brain. Benda states that true porencephaly is a cleft formation due to failure of the neural tube to close. He employs the term *Schizencephaly.* In other cases, lesions which suggest the end results of birth injury are found. These are described under that title.

Etiology.—It is impossible to speak with confidence about the relative importance of the various causes of congenital double hemiplegia. Developmental defects play a part, and birth injury is probably much more important than in the diplegias.

Clinical Features.—Congenital double hemiplegia is a rare condition in the writer's experience, and is not always easily distinguishable from congenital spastic diplegia. As a rule, the patient is quite helpless and severely demented, but, in some instances, the disability is relatively mild. When the disability is pronounced, the symptoms are usually apparent from birth, but, when it is less severe, the parents may not realize that the child is defective for a number of months. Bulbar palsy, or more correctly, pseudobulbar palsy, is almost always present. This is described under the appropriate title. Convulsive seizures are very common. In some cases, there are involuntary movements such as tremor or athetosis. The mental state is usually grossly defective.

Diagnosis.—This syndrome is to be distinguished from congenital diplegia by the greater involvement of the arms and of the bulbar muscles. Some idea of the nature of the pathological process may be obtained by air encephalography. For example, porencephaly may be clearly demonstrated. Such procedures are of only academic interest, for they can scarcely be of benefit to the patient.

Prognosis.—This depends upon the severity of the condition, for little tendency to improvement can be expected.

Treatment.—This is discussed under diplegia.

BIBLIOGRAPHY

CRAIG, W. McK. AND KERNOHAN, J. W.: Cerebral cysts. J.A.M.A. **102**:5, 1934.

DYKE, C. G., DAVIDOFF, L. AND MASSON, C.: Cerebral atrophy with homolateral hemihypertrophy of the skull and sinuses. Arch. Neurol. & Psychiat. **29**:412, 1933.

FORD, F. R.: Cerebral birth injuries and their results. Medicine **5**:121, 1926.

GLOBUS, J. H.: A contribution to the histopathology of porencephalus. Arch. Neurol. & Psychiat. **6**:652, 1921.

LECOUNT, E. R. AND SEMERAK, C. B.: Porencephaly. Arch. Neurol. & Psychiat. **14**:465 (full references), 1925.

MAY, W. P.: Microgyria and its effects on other parts of the central nervous system. Brain **43**:26, 1920.

CONGENITAL HEMIPLEGIA

Definition.—The significance of this term is obvious.

Pathological Anatomy.—A number of different lesions have been described. The so-called "false porencephaly" is not uncommon. This is merely a cyst due to a destructive lesion. Central and peripheral types are described. In the peripheral types, there is a cavity in the cortex and subcortical white matter. This is lined by a thin membrane, composed of glia and connective tissue, and, in most cases, does not communicate with the ventricle, being separated from the ventricular lumen by the ependyma. The cavity is often crossed by trabeculae. The convolutions are cut across irregularly, and show dense gliosis near the margins of the defect. Usually, the meninges are adherent and thickened. The fluid may be yellow or clear and the wall may show pigmentation. In the central type, which has been described by Schwartz, the cavity is found just outside the ventricle and opens neither into the ventricle nor into the subarachnoid space. Such lesions are ascribed to hemorrhage, thrombosis of cerebral arteries, embolism and traumatic softenings such as result from birth injury. In other cases, we find local *atrophy* and *gliosis* of the cortex, in which the convolutions are shrunken and unduly firm. The cortical pattern, however, is normal and the sulci deep and wide. In microscopic examination, we find loss of nerve cells in the cortex, and atrophy of the subcortical white matter associated with proliferation of glia. The overlying piäärachnoid is usually thickened and adherent, and there may be a pigmented layer of fibrous tissue beneath the dura. In rare cases, the so-called *cerebral hemiatrophy* is found. In this condition, the two hemispheres are unequally developed. The cortical pattern on the affected side may be normal or of primitive type. There may be reduction of cells in the cortex and of the white matter, and a diffuse proliferation of the fibrous glia. The writer has studied the pathological lesions in nine cases of congenital hemiplegia. In three of these cases, there was a cavity in the opposite hemisphere, i.e., porencephaly, which involved the motor cortex or the internal capsule. In all three cases, the condition was believed to be a false porencephaly, probably the result of a vascular lesion. In three other cases, there was local atrophy and sclerosis of the cortex, with thickening and accumulation of fluid within the piäärachnoid. In the remaining three cases, there was evidence of an old subdural blood clot, as shown by thickening and pigmentation of the inner surface of the dura, and atrophy of the underlying cortex. The probabilities seem to point to a birth injury in all of these cases.

As a result of gross lesions in one hemisphere, at or before birth, the opposite cerebellar hemisphere and pons, as well as the homolateral lenticular nucleus, are smaller than normal. When the hemisphere is reduced in bulk, the cranium is flattened on the affected side, for the infantile skull is so plastic that it is moulded by the brain. Sometimes, the bone overlying the lesion is two or three times its normal thickness. In other cases, meningeal cysts or porencephalic cavities cause undue prominence and even thinning of the cranial vault overlying the lesion.

Etiology.—The writer believes that cerebral birth injury is the most frequent cause of congenital hemiplegia, but, undoubtedly, other causes enter into its production. Intrauterine injury or disease is probably rare, but is known to occur, and defects of development may be confined to one hemisphere, although they are, as a rule, bilateral. We have seen congenital hemiplegia in identical twins. In one twin, the hemiplegia was on the right and in the other, it was on the left. One would imagine that the ovum must have been damaged before it separated into two parts. The history is given below.

Clinical Features.—Congenital hemiplegia is not very uncommon, although not nearly so frequent as diplegia. It is unusual to find a definite facial palsy, although there may be some asymmetry.

In the writer's experience, flaccidity of the paralyzed limbs is relatively more frequent in congenital hemiplegias than among those occurring later in life. In such cases, we find striking underdevelopment of the hand and less evident underdevelopment of the arm and leg. The hand is of childish appearance, but it is not in any way deformed. Due to the shortening of

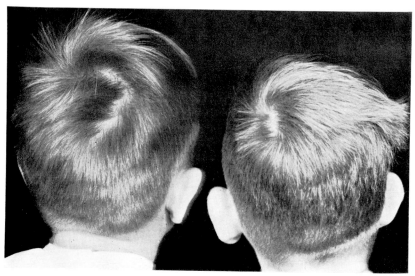

Fig. 14. Cowlick revolves clockwise in one twin and counter clockwise in the other twin.

the leg, the pelvis may be tilted and the spine may show a postural curve. Such hemiplegias may be mild or severe. The tendon reflexes are usually somewhat increased on the affected side, but this is never so striking as in spastic paralysis. There is, usually, a Babinski sign, but rarely clonus.

In other cases, the paralytic limbs are very spastic. Since the muscle spasm develops when the bones are very plastic, extreme deformity of the hand is produced.

In almost all cases, there is mental deficiency, but this, on the average, is not so severe as in the diplegias. Convulsive seizures, however, are more frequent than in diplegia, and occur in about 40 or 50 per cent of all cases. These are, as a rule, confined to the affected side, but may either extend to the opposite side or even be general from the first. Not infrequently, the paralysis is increased for a time after the convulsion. If the paralysis is on the right side, there is often some disturbance of speech. Apparently, true aphasia does not occur, but speech may be delayed or childish for long periods. Unilateral athetosis is often associated with the hemiplegia. Mirror movements are sometimes seen. Movement of one hand may be invariably associated with similar movements of the other hand. Hemianopia and cortical sensory loss are often present though they of course cannot be demonstrated early in life. Loss of opticokinetic nystagmus when the drum is revolved to the side of the lesion may be found when hemianopia is not demonstrable.

Even severe hemiplegias of congenital origin may not be apparent until the child is several months of age.

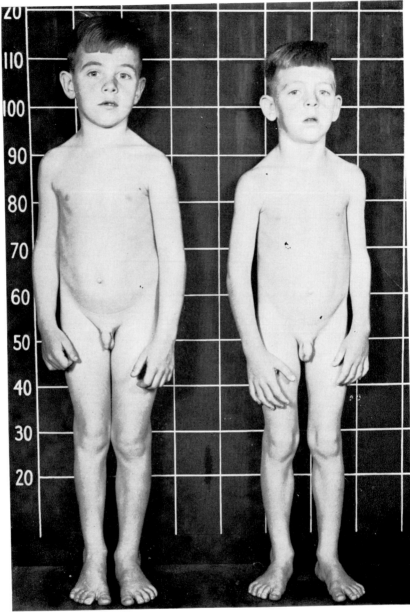

Fig. 15. Identical twins showing defective development of arm and leg on right side in one and on the left side in the other. Bodily development is deficient in one twin.

Diagnosis.—The diagnosis depends upon the history of a hemiplegia which reveals itself within a few months after birth without any immediately preceding cause. As a rule, defective development of the paralytic limbs indicates that paralysis began very early in life.

The etiological diagnosis is not always easy. If syphilis, neoplasm and abscess can be ruled out, we are forced to depend upon the history of birth to decide whether this is the result of birth injury or of some prenatal process.

Ventriculography or encephalography will give some idea of the gross anatomical changes. In an infant, porencephaly may be demonstrated by transillumination in some cases.

Prognosis.—The prognosis depends chiefly upon the severity of the injury of the nervous system. Little improvement is to be expected. The presence of convulsions makes the outlook unfavorable, for deterioration often occurs in such cases.

Treatment.—The usual treatment includes exercises, physiotherapy and anticonvulsive medication if there are seizures. Some writers, including Keats, believe that if the right arm is affected in a right handed child and the child is somewhat uncertain about which arm should be selected as the dominant arm, disorders of speech and behavior may result and convulsions may be induced. It is advised that no effort should be made to improve the function of the affected arm and the child be trained to use the left arm. In some cases, it is claimed, the affected arm should be immobilized.

Some authorities recommend the removal of the affected hemisphere when convulsions are frequent and the child's behavior is troublesome. The thalamus and caudate nucleus are spared and care must be taken to avoid injury to the hippocampus. The arteries which supply these structures must be saved. It is claimed that seizures are greatly reduced by this procedure and the mental state improves. The paralysis of the affected side is not increased, it is said, and speech disturbances are not aggravated regardless of which hemisphere is removed. Every effort is made to make sure that the better hemisphere is intact before operation.

Griffith discusses possible bad results of hemispherectomy and proposes modifications of the operation.

CASE HISTORIES (Ped. A-39097 and Ped. A-38865).—*Identical twins were found to have congenital hemiplegia in one case on the right side and in the other on the left.*

In October 1944 twin boys, William and James, were born to Mrs. K. after an uneventful pregnancy. This was not an unexpected event for twins were common on both sides of the family. There was only one placenta and the examination of the foetal membranes led to the belief that these were identical twins, a conclusion which was subsequently strengthened by the identical appearance of the children. The twins were the product of the eighth pregnancy, the preceding pregnancies resulting in normal children.

James did not grow as well as his brother and early in childhood it was evident that there was a striking difference in bodily statue. The defective bodily development of one of a pair of identical twins is discussed on page 179 and may be due to vascular abnormalities in the placenta resulting in deficient blood supply to one twin.

James, the first born, seems to have had no illnesses except for a series of three convulsions at the age of one year.

Both were rather slow in the development of motor reactions. They sat up at about one year and did not walk alone until the age of three or four years. When they were about a year old it was noticed that William did not use his right arm well and that James had difficulty with his left arm. Soon it became evident that the corresponding legs were also affected.

On examination the boys presented an almost identical appearance. William was somewhat larger than James, however. There were the usual signs of hemiplegia of moderate degree with spasticity and increase of the tendon reflexes. In the case of William this was on the right side and in James it was on the left. The severity of the hemiplegia was approximately the same. William had a cow-lick in which the hair seemed to revolve in clockwise fashion, whereas, James's cow-lick revolved counterclockwise. Mental deficiency of moderate degree was apparent in both children.

Electroencephalograms revealed a focus of abnormal waves in the parietal region of each child on the side opposite the hemiplegia. Air encephalograms showed dilatation of the anterior and middle part of lateral ventricle on the side opposite the hemiplegia. It is of interest that the deformity of the ventricles was exactly the same in the two cases.

BIBLIOGRAPHY

ALPERS, B. J. AND DEAR, R. B.: Hemiatrophy of the brain. J. Nerv. & Ment. Dis. 89:653, 1939.

BASSER, L. S.: Hemiplegia of early onset. The faculty of speech with special reference to the effect of hemispherectomy. Brain 85:427, 1962.

CAIRNS, H.: Hemispherectomy in the treatment of infantile hemiplegia. Lancet 2:411, 1951.

FRENCH, L. A. et al.: Cerebral hemispherectomy for control of intractible convulsive seizures. J. Neurol. 12:154, 1955.

GRIFFITH, H. B.: Cerebral hemispherectomy for infantile hemiplegia. Ann. Roy. Coll. Surg. Engl. 41:183, 1967.

HASSIN, G. B.: Crossed atrophy of the cerebellum: Pathologic study of a case. Arch. Neurol. & Psychiat. 33:917, 1935.

JOSEPHY, H.: Cerebral hemiatrophy. J. Neuropath. & Exp. Neurol. 4:250, 1945.

KEATS, S.: The child with hemiplegia. Am. J. Dis. Child. 89:421, 1955.

KRYNAUW, A.: Infantile hemiplegia treated by removing one cerebral hemisphere. J. Neurol., Neurosurg. and Psychiat. 13:243, 1950.

MCFIE, J.: Effects of hemispherectomy on intellectual functioning in cases of infantile hemiplegia. J. Neurol., Neurosurg. & Psychiat. 24:240, 1961.

MCLAURIN, R. L.: Parietal cephaloceles. Neurology 14:764, 1964.

MOTT, F. W. AND TREGOLD, A. F.: Hemiatrophy of the brain and its results on the cerebellum, medulla and spinal cord. Brain 22:239, 1900.

NAEF, R. W.: Clinical features of porencephaly: A review of 32 cases. Arch. Neurol. & Psychiat. 80:133, 1958.

Papez, J. W. and Vonderahe, A. R.: Infantile cerebral palsy of hemiplegic type. J. Neuropath. & Exp. Neurol. 6:244, 1947.

CONGENITAL (CEREBRAL) MONOPLEGIA

Definition.—This term, of course, refers to congenital paralysis of only one extremity.

Pathological Anatomy.—The anatomical findings are similar to those just described under congenital hemiplegia. The lesions, however, do not involve the entire motor cortex or pyramidal tract, but affect only that part which is concerned with the control of the affected limb.

Etiology.—The etiological factors would seem to be very much the same as those of congenital hemiplegia.

Clinical Features.—Pure monoplegias are very rare, and it is usual for the other limb on the same side of the body to be at least slightly affected. Thus, we find all gradations between hemiplegia and pure monoplegia. The commonest syndrome is the faciobrachial monoplegia in which the arm and hand are involved and there is a mild central weakness of the face. In other cases the leg is paralyzed and the arm and the face escape more or less completely. This type is in my experience usually due to birth injury. Congenital monoplegias are usually associated with spasticity of the affected muscles, but in some instances the muscles are flaccid.

The diagnosis, prognosis and treatment are discussed under Congenital Hemiplegia.

BIBLIOGRAPHY

(See Congenital Hemiplegia)

CONGENITAL PSEUDOBULBAR PALSY

Definition.—Congenital bulbar palsy of suprasegmental type associated with certain phenomena due to release of bulbar reflexes. This may exist alone, or may be associated with double hemiplegia.

Pathological Anatomy.—No adequate anatomical studies have been made. Oppenheim attributed this syndrome to microgyria or to porencephaly, involving the lower part of the central convolutions on both sides, but this view seems to have been based entirely upon theoretical considerations. Most authorities regard pseudobulbar palsy as due to interruption of the corticobulbar motor tracts on both sides, but it has been claimed that lesions within the lenticular nuclei are also very important in this syndrome.

Etiology.—Little or nothing is known of the causes involved in this condition, but, presumably, they are the same as those in other congenital palsies.

Clinical Features.—The essential features include weakness of the muscles supplied by the bulbar nuclei causing difficulty in swallowing, phonation and articulation. The face, jaws and even the extraocular muscles may also be involved. The affected muscles show no outspoken atrophy and the electrical reactions are quite normal. The reflexes are exaggerated, and certain abnormal reflexes may be elicited. For example, the jaw jerk is often increased, and even a jaw clonus may be elicited. The pharyngeal reflex may also be increased. Stimulation of the lips or tongue may produce reflex movements of sucking, chewing and swallowing, which are termed the "feeding reflex." Volitional movements of the face are reduced or abolished, but, when the child weeps or laughs, the facial movements are grossly exaggerated. In fact, laughing, and, more frequently, weeping, occur with very little provocation, and in an explosive fashion in such a way as to indicate release of the mechanisms underlying the expression of emotion. One gains the impression that such reactions are not necessarily expressive of the patient's mood. If the ocular movements are affected, the palsies are of supranuclear type, that is, there is paralysis of conjugate movement in one or more planes without squint or diplopia. In such cases, the patient's eyes may turn in the direction of a loud noise or of a bright light in a reflex fashion. Vestibular stimulation causes strong conjugate deviation in the appropriate direction, but no nystagmus, since the quick phase is lacking.

Often there is some degree of diplegia and, not infrequently, there are also athetoid movements which suggest involvement of the basal ganglia.

Worster-Drought studied eighty-two cases of suprabulbar palsy and found that more than one case was present in seven families.

Diagnosis.—This depends upon the presence of the signs and symptoms noted above.

Prognosis.—As a rule, there is no improvement, and the prognosis depends upon the degree of disability.

Treatment.—Speech training may be tried, but, as a rule, gives disappointing results.

CASE HISTORY.—*Paralysis of the face, jaws and bulbar muscles with spasticity, increased reflexes and exaggeration of emotional reactions existing from birth. Peculiar formation of the jaws.*

D. E. H. was born at full term of healthy parents. There was no evidence of birth injury. From the first, there was difficulty in nursing and in swallowing, and constant drooling of saliva. Later, it became evident that the child could not chew properly, could not articulate clearly and could not move the lips as other children do. Fluids were taken with greater difficulty. A large part would flow out of the mouth, some from the nose, and there was almost always coughing and strangling. Solid food could not be taken. Nutrition was, naturally, a problem. However, the child sat up, and walked at the usual time, and showed no striking disorder of motility of the extremities except for some little clumsiness of the hands. His behavior was regarded as normal, and he seemed to understand what was said to him as well as other children.

Examination at the age of 10 years revealed poor development and nutrition. He behaved well during the examination, and seemed to understand everything said to him, but one gained the impression that there was a mild degree of mental deficiency. The lower jaw presented an interesting deformity. The angle of the jaw was more obtuse than usual, and the rami formed a more acute angle than in the normal jaw, causing the mandible to be very narrow. The lower jaw teeth lay inside those of the maxilla, and the lower incisors were inside the uppers so that teeth could not be approximated. These peculiarities were regarded as the result of defective development secondary to the lack of normal muscular activity. The pupils and ocular movements were normal. The eyelids and forehead were also capable of proper movement. The mouth and lips, however, could not be moved at all. The child could not show the teeth, whistle or even move the lips. The mouth was constantly open, and saliva flowed down over the chin. When the lips were stimulated, however, active movements of the lips and tongue developed which were suggestive of sucking. When the child laughed or cried, exaggerated movements of the face appeared which were appropriate to the emotion. The jaws were usually open, and could not be closed voluntarily or moved otherwise. Movements could be produced by stimulation of the lips and tongue, and the jaw jerk was definitely exaggerated. The masseters and temporal muscles were small but not atrophic, and exhibited increased tone. The tongue was small, and moved only when the lips were stimulated. Articulation and phonation were impossible. An attempt to take some water caused coughing and regurgitation from the nose. Most of the water flowed from the mouth which remained open. The pharyngeal reflex was exaggerated, and could be produced by merely touching the lips or tip of the tongue. The sternomastoids and trapezii were small and somewhat spastic but were not atrophic, and contracted fairly well. The musculature of the body and extremities was slender, probably as a result of poor nutrition, but there was no definite weakness or outspoken spasticity. The child could dress himself and walk normally. There was no increase in the tendon reflexes, no ankle clonus and no Babinski.

BIBLIOGRAPHY

OPPENHEIM, H. U.: Wesen und Localisation der Kongenitalen und Infantilen Pseudobulbär-parlyse. J. F. Psycho. u. Neurol. 18:293, 1911.
PERITZ, G.: Pseudobulbär und Bulbär-paralysen des Kindersalters. Berlin, 1902.
WORSTER-DROUGHT, C.: Suprabulbar palsies. Jour. Laryng. and Otology 70:453, 1965.

CONGENITAL BULBAR PALSY

Congenital bulbar palsy is very rare. Bosma *et al.* have published a very careful study of two cases in unrelated girls of 15 and 5 years whose condition was essentially the same. The family history was negative in each case.

It was noted in infancy that the children could not nurse at the breast and bottle feeding was difficult. At 2 or 3 years it was noted that there was constant drooling and inability to articulate. The arms and legs were clumsy.

Examination revealed that the mouth was open and the lips could not be closed firmly. Food and saliva could not be retained in the mouth. The smile was transverse. The jaw could be moved in the vertical plane, but could not be protruded or moved laterally. The tongue could not be protruded beyond the lips and could not be moved laterally. The tip of the tongue could not be elevated. Food had to be placed beneath the teeth by the finger. Articulation was almost impossible. No significant atrophy of the tongue or jaw muscles is mentioned and the jaw jerk was said to be normal. The voice was nasal at times. The patient could not feel where a bolus of food was located in her mouth. The shape of objects in the mouth was not recognized. The corneal reflexes were reduced.

There was mild ataxia of all four extremities. This was more severe in the left hand than elsewhere. The ataxia was apparently due to loss of proprioception. Pain sense was reduced everywhere. The intelligence quotient was between 80 and 95.

CASE HISTORY.—*Congenital bulbar palsy.*

L. C. was seen at the age of 3 years. She was born at full term by spontaneous delivery. Birth weight was 8 lbs. 12 oz. She seemed to be quite healthy and was not jaundiced or cyanotic. Her mother had bronchitis from the fourth month to the sixth month of pregnancy. The parents and her two sisters were quite normal.

When the child was very young the mother discovered that she could not swallow properly. She would choke on her feedings. She had always drooled. She had much difficulty in chewing. There were no movements of her face. She could not protrude her tongue and could not talk.

She started to walk at 13 months, but was unsteady and had many falls. She was clumsy when using her hands and could not put a cookie in her mouth until she was 18 months old. Her mental development was considered to be normal. She never had seizures or spasms.

On examination, her vision seemed to be clear. The eyes were moved freely in all planes. There was no nystagmus. The face was symmetrical, but no movement was present. Her mouth was open and she could not close her lips properly so she drooled constantly. Her jaw could be moved up and down, but not laterally. Her tongue could not be protruded or pressed into her cheeks. She could not articulate. Her voice was nasal and weak.

She was slightly unsteady on her feet and her arms and hands were slightly clumsy. There was apparently some reduction of proprioception. The tendon reflexes were normal.

The child was seen again at the age of 6 years. There was no material improvement in her condition. Unfortunately sensory function within the oral cavity was not tested. Psychometric tests revealed normal intelligence. She had a pleasant personality.

BIBLIOGRAPHY

BOSMA, J. *et al.:* Impairment of somesthetic perception and motor function in oral and phayrngeal area. Neurology **17:**649, 1967.

CONGENITAL ATONIC DIPLEGIA

Definition.—This syndrome includes extreme hypotonia and weakness of the muscles, inability to walk or stand, profound mental defect and, often, incoordination.

Pathological Anatomy.—Little or nothing is known of the anatomical substratum of atonic diplegia. Foerster found atrophy of the frontal lobes in two cases, but does not mention microscopic examination. Others have, on theoretical grounds, assumed a defect in the cerebellum.

Etiology.—Van Rossum reports this condition in a brother and sister whose parents were closely related. Freiberg describes five cases of this condition including two brothers. There was no evidence of birth injury in any case and the parents were all healthy.

Clinical Features.—As a rule, the child is abnormally still during the first few weeks after birth and, at first, there may be some difficulty in breathing or in nursing. The chest may be retracted during inspiration in such a way as to suggest amyotonia congenita. Later, perhaps at about the end of the second or third month, the child becomes more active, and moves the extremities about in bed very freely. There is, however, no progress in learning to hold up the head or to sit up. Speech is delayed, or more frequently is never developed, and it is usually evident at an early age that the child

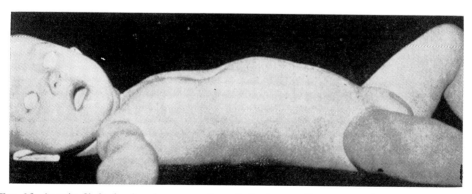

FIG. 16. Atonic diplegia showing retraction of the lower ribs as a result of the profound loss of muscle tone. The tendon reflexes were present, electrical reactions were normal and biopsy revealed normal muscle fibers. The child was profoundly deficient in mental development.

is mentally defective. Even after the child has reached an age when standing should be possible the head cannot be sustained and the trunk cannot be held in an upright position. Several writers have described a reaction which they consider peculiar to atonic diplegia. This is elicited by lifting the child by placing the hands around the trunk. The child's legs will then become rigid, being flexed at the hip and flexed or extended at the knee. In Clark's case, clonic movements of the legs occurred under these conditions. No doubt, this reaction is the expression of a postural reflex. The most characteristic feature of this syndrome is the great loss of muscle tone, which permits an extraordinary range of passive movement of the extremities. The feet may be placed behind the head, the hands and feet may be hyperextended to an abnormal degree, and the spine is, also, unduly flexible. Lateral movement at the knee joints is possible as a result of relaxation of the ligaments and capsules of the joints. In several cases, there has been some associated deformity such as congenital dislocation of the hips, herniae and the various types of kyphoscoliosis which are, no doubt, also results of the loss of muscle tone. On palpation, the muscles are very soft and can scarcely be distinguished from the subcutaneous fat, but there is no outspoken atrophy. Almost all case reports mention the presence of incoordination, which is described as resembling cerebellar ataxia. There is never any paralysis, but the strength is always feeble. Loss of muscle tone may make it difficult to elicit the tendon reflexes. In a few instances, the plantar reflex has been found to be extensor or equivocal, but is, usually, stated to be normal. The electrical reactions are always normal. Except for some relaxation of the facial muscles, the cranial nerves are not affected. In a few instances, epilepsy has developed.

Cases of this type are not very uncommon and I have studied a number of them. When the motor disturbances are severe, the mental condition is apparently always profoundly defective. Milder cases also occur which are associated with less evident mental defect.

Allan *et al.* studied a family in which severe mental deficiency was associated with weak, flaccid muscles and mild muscular atrophy probably due to disuse.

Diagnosis.—The principal conditions to be considered in the differential diagnosis are amyotonia congentia, congenital laxity of the ligaments, mongolism, congenital chorea, congenital cerebellar ataxia, and rickets. The presence of mental defect, of active tendon reflexes, of normal electrical reactions, and the peculiar reaction when the child is suspended, should make it possible to rule out amyotonia congenita. Rickets should be recognized by the presence of the bone lesions, and mongolism by the characteristic facies and other appearances. The differentiation from cerebellar ataxia and from chorea is not so easy. In congenital chorea, the involuntary

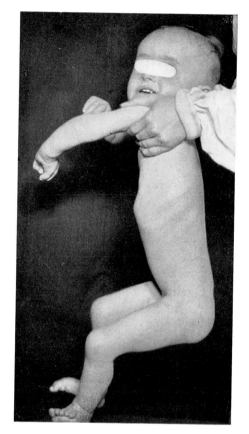

Fig. 17. Same child a few months after the previous picture was taken showing the characteristic postural reflex. When the child is suspended by the examiner's hands, the legs become flexed at the hip and knee and very rigid although they are always quite flaccid under other circumstances.

movements are more prominent, and in cerebellar ataxia, the incoördination should over-shadow the other features. Both syndromes may include loss of tone, but this should not be so extreme as in atonic diplegia.

Prognosis.—There may be a limited amount of improvement if the condition is not very severe.

Treatment.—No treatment is indicated in severe cases, but, if the mental condition is fair, exercises may be given and orthopedic measures may be used to prevent deformity.

BIBLIOGRAPHY

Allan, W. C. *et al.:* Familial mental deficiency with muscular weakness and atrophy. Am. J. Ment. Def. **48**:325, 1944.

Batten, F. E. and von Wyss, W. H.: The atonic form of cerebral diplegia. Brit. J. Child. Dis.**12**:65, 1915.

Clark, I. P.: Infantile cerebro-cerebellar diplegia of flaccid, atonic-astasic type. Am. J. Dis. Child. **5**:424, 1912.

Davidson, C. and Weiss, M. M.: Muscular hypotonia associated with congenital heart disease. Am. J. Dis. Child. **37**:359, 1929.

Dunn, H. G. *et al.:* Benign congenital hypotonia with chromosomal anomaly. Pediatrics **28**:4, 1961.

FEARNSIDES, E. G.: A case of the atonic form of cerebral diplegia. Brit. J. Child. Dis. **12**:166, 1915.

FOERSTER, O.: Der atonisch-astatische typhus der infantilen cerebrallähmung. Deutsch. Arch. f. klin. Med. **98**:216, 1909.

FREIBERG, H.: Prognose des atonisch-astatischen Symphom-Komplex bei der cerebralen Kinder-lähmung Arch fur Psych. u. Nerven krankheiten. **98**:264, 1932-33.

ROSSUM, A. VAN: Foerster's Atonic-Astatic Syndrome. Recent Neurological Research. Elsevier 1959.

SYNDROME OF HYPOTONIA, HYPOMENTIA, HYPOGONADISM AND OBESITY

The Prader-Willi Syndrome

Zellweger and Schneider have reviewed 93 cases of this condition of which 14 were personally studied and 79 were collected from the literature. In only one instance were two cases discovered in one family. Boys are affected more frequently than girls, the ratio being 5 boys to 2 girls.

The symptoms date from birth and in some instances it is noted that fetal movements in utero are feeble. The infants are hypotonic or atonic and display little or no spontaneous motor activity. The reflexes are absent. Temperature control may be defective for a time. Swallowing is difficult and tube feeding may be required. After some months, there is greater motor activity and the reflexes may be elicited. The difficulty in swallowing disappears. Weakness and loss of muscle tone persist, however.

Bodily growth is deficient. The head is dolicocephalic. The palate shows a high arch. The upper lip is triangular in shape and rises to an apex in the midline. The hands and feet are small.

During the second half of the first year or later an excessive appetite develops. The children beg for food and will eat as long as they are fed. Great obesity develops and the Pickwickian syndrome may result.

Most of the children are able to walk between the second and fourth year, but in rare instances they never are able to walk. Speech is delayed and imperfect. The intelligence quotient ranges between 20 and 87. Some patients display labile emotional reactions and temper tantrums.

The penis and testicles are always imperfectly developed. One or both testicles are often undescended. Adults are sterile. Biopsies of the testicles in childhood show no abnormalities. The gonadotropins are usually normal or diminished, but are rarely increased. Sexual development in the female is sometimes imperfect.

The bone age is delayed as a rule. Diabetes develops in about one third of all cases, sometimes before the age of 5 years. It is said that it does not cause loss of weight or acidosis. It does not respond to insulin but the oral hypoglycemic drugs are effective. It is usually mild and easily controlled. However, two patients died of the complications of diabetes in adult life.

Air studies and electroencephalograms are almost always normal. The

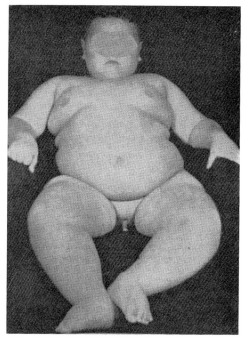

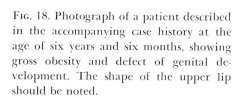

FIG. 18. Photograph of a patient described in the accompanying case history at the age of six years and six months, showing gross obesity and defect of genital development. The shape of the upper lip should be noted.

chromosomal constitution is normal except in a few cases. Muscle biopsy shows normal fibers or slender fibers. Two patients died at the ages of five and seven years as a result of the Pickwickian syndrome. One post-mortem study revealed no anatomical change in the nervous system or in the glands of internal secretion.

CASE HISTORY (Ped. A 11914).—*Extreme muscular weakness and loss of muscle tone in infancy. Mental deficiency. Gross obesity. Left testicle undescended. No improvement at the age of 10 years.*

D. S. was born at full term by spontaneous delivery. He had measles, pertussis and chickenpox early in life. His family attributed his symptoms to these illnesses. However, he was never able to walk, stand or even sit up. He began to get obese at the age of three years.

He was first examined at the age of six years and six months in 1933. His behavior was infantile and his speech was that of a child who was just starting to talk. He was extremely obese. He could not walk, stand or sit without support. He was able to move his arms and legs feebly. He could feed himself with a great effort, but could do no more. The muscles were covered with a thick layer of fat and could not be felt. They seemed to be small and soft and were certainly atonic. The tendon reflexes were sluggish if present at all. He had no obvious difficulty in breathing.

The penis was very small and the left testicle could not be felt in the scrotum or in the canal. The right testicle was small.

Many examinations were made. The electromyogram was normal. A muscle biopsy showed a great deal of fat in and around the muscle but no changes in the muscle fibers. An electroencephalogram was normal. Many biochemical studies were made without positive results.

The patient was seen again at the age of 10 years. There was no change in the neurological condition. No further development of the genital organs was found.

When the child was examined, in 1933, at the age of six years and six months, it was suspected that he was suffering from either amyotonia congenita or the Werdnig-Hoffmann muscular atrophy. After reading Dr. Zellweger's article and reviewing the patient's chart, it was quite evident that he was suffering from the condition described above.

BIBLIOGRAPHY

Dunn, H. S., Ford, D. K., Ausberg, N. and Miller, J. R.: Benign congenital hypotonia with chromosomal anomaly. Pediatrics 28:578, 1961.

Gorlin, R. J. and Sedano, H.: Prader-Willi Syndrome. Modern Medicine, August 12, p. 106, 1968.

Prader, A., Labhart, A. and Willi, H.: Ein syndrome von Adipositas, Kleinwuchs, Kryptochismus and Oligophrenie nach myatonicartigen Zustand im neuborenalter. Schweiz. Med. Wchnschr. 86:1260, 1956.

Schneider, H. J. and Zellweger, H.: Fome fruste of the Prader-Willi syndrome. Helvetia Paediatric a Acta 23:128, 1968.

Zellweger, H. and Schneider, H. J.: Syndrome of hypotonia, hypomentia-hypogonadism or Prader-Willi Syndrome. Amer. Jour. Dis. Child. 115:588, 1968.

Zellweger, H. U., Smith, J. W. and Cusminsky, M.: Muscular hypotonia in infancy. Diagnosis and differentiation. Rev. Canad. Biol. 21:599, 1962.

MENTAL DEFICIENCY WITH CONGENITAL ICHTHYOSIS AND SPASTICITY (SJÖGREN)

Sjögren describes twenty-eight cases of this condition. With only three exceptions all of these patients were born in the county of Västerbotten in the north of Sweden. The disease is believed to be inherited as a recessive characteristic, and affects both sexes.

Congenital mental deficiency is constantly present and most patients are classified as idiots and the rest as imbeciles. There is no progression in this condition, it is said.

The second cardinal symptom is weakness and spasticity of the extremities. The legs are involved more severely than the arms. Some of the patients were unable to walk.

The ichthyosis is present at birth and is not progressive. It is termed ichthyosiform erythrodermia.

In three cases, degeneration of the pigmented epithelium of the macula and its surroundings was discovered.

No post-mortem examinations have been made, up to the present time, it is said. Biochemical examinations were made in two cases with negative results.

No abortive cases were discovered and the incidence of neurological disorders among parents and siblings is not increased.

Sjögren has collected a number of case reports describing patients with neurological disorders and ichthyosis or xeroderma but these seem to be heterogenous and all differ in some respect from the case described above.

BIBLIOGRAPHY

BAAR, H. S. *et al.:* The Sjögren-Larsson syndrome. J. Maine M.A. **51:**189, 1960.

BLUMEL, J. *et al.:* Spastic quadriplegia combined with congenital ichthyosiform erythroderma and oligophrenia. Amer. Jour. Dis. Child. 96:724, 1958.

HEIJER, A. AND REED, W. B.: Sjögren-Larsson syndrome. Arch. Dermat. 92:545, 1965.

SJÖGREN, T. AND LARSSON, T.: Oligophrenia in combination with congenital ichthyosis and spastic disorders. Acta Psychiat. et Neurol. Scand. suppl. 113, Vol. 32, 1957.

WILLIAMS, R. D. B. AND TANG, I. L.: Mental defect, quadriplegia and ichthyosis. Am. J. Dis. Child. **100:**924, 1960.

SYNDROME OF RUD

This syndrome includes dry, scaling, hyperkeratotic skin, i.e. ichthyosis vulgaris which is most evident on the extensor surfaces of the extremities, the knees and elbows. This grows more severe during childhood. There is mental deficiency and epilepsy. Bodily growth is deficient. Sexual development is defective.

BIBLIOGRAPHY

MacGILLIVARY, R. C.: The syndrome of Rud. Amer. Jour. Ment. Deficiency, **59:**67, 1954.

AGENESIS OF THE WHITE MATTER WITH IDIOCY

Waggoner *et al.* reported a study of a girl who suffered from congenital idiocy with an intelligence quotient of 10 who had severe motor defects and was unable to walk without support. The optic discs were very white. She died in convulsions. There were eleven children in her family and five of her siblings suffered from the same symptoms. The affected children were all female. The parents were normal and no history of consanguinity was elicited.

At post-mortem examination the brain was small and weighed only 940 grams. The convolutions were rather broad. The cortex was thick. The cortical neurons were poorly developed and they were not arranged in proper position though the layers of the cortex could be recognized. There was no myelination of the cerebral white matter except for the pathways of the motor, visual and auditory systems. Even in these systems myelination was scanty. The number of axons was grossly reduced. Extensive gliosis was present. The cerebellum and the brain stem were more completely developed.

BIBLIOGRAPHY

WAGGONER, R. W. *et al.:* Agenesis of the white matter with idiocy. Amer. Jour. Ment. Deficiency, 47:20, 1942.

XERODERMA PIGMENTOSUM WITH INVOLVEMENT
OF THE NERVOUS SYSTEM

This is inherited as an autosomal trait. Exposure of the skin to sunlight causes progressive changes in the skin. In the first stage there is erythema, freckles and pigmentation. In the second stage, there is telangiectasis, atrophy with scars, granulations and verrucous excrescences. Entropion, ectropion, synblepharon, corneal ulceration and atrophy of the iris may result. In the third stage, malignant growths may appear including squamous cell carcinoma, basal cell carcinoma, malignant melanomas, angiosarcomas and keratoacanthomas. This stage may develop before the age of 5 years.

A progressive process develops in the nervous system early in life possibly before birth. Microcephaly is present. Mental deterioration occurs early. There are convulsions, spastic paraplegia, cerebellar ataxia, difficulty in speech, choreoathetosis and deafness.

Bodily growth is deficient. The gonads are incompletely developed. The patients have little resistance to infection. Various abnormalities have been found in the blood, especially elevation of the serum alpha globulins but perhaps none of them are constantly found. Reed *et al.* studied the cause of the sensitivity to light and concluded that the deoxyribonucleic acid of the cells of the skin is damaged and the repair which occurs in normal individuals does not occur.

Post-mortem examination of the nervous system reveals a small brain with atrophy of the cortex of the cerebrum and cerebellum. The ventricles are dilated. The cerebral cortex is thick and poorly demarcated. There is loss of neurons. Swollen axons are seen. There is also loss of neurons in the cerebellum and brain stem. Calcium deposits are seen in the brain. The posterior columns of the spinal cord may show demyelination.

BIBLIOGRAPHY

AITA, J. A.: Neurocutaneous Diseases. Thomas, Springfield, p. 35, 1966.
BENDA, C.: Developmental Disorders of Mentation and Cerebral Palsies. New York, Grune and Stratton, 1952, p. 192.
DE SANCTIS, C. AND CACCHIONE, A.: Xerodermic mental deficiency. Riv. sper. Freniat., 1932, Vol. 56.
————: L'idiozia xerodermica. Riv. sper. Freniat., 56:269, 1932.
EL-HEFNAWI, H. *et al.*: Blood studies in xeroderma pigmentosum. Brit. J. Dermat., 74:214, 1962.
ELSÄSSER, G.: Xerodermic idiocy. Arch. Dermato und Syph., 188:651, 1950.
EWING, J. A.: The association of oligophrenia and dyskeratoses. Am. J. Ment. Def., 1955, Vol. 60.
KATZENELLENBOGEN, I.: Xeroderma pigmentosa. Acta Med. Orient., 6:117, 1947.
LARMANDE, A. AND TIMSIT, E.: A propos de 20 cas de xeroderma pigmentosum. Concilium Ophthalmologicum, 3:1643, 1954.
LAUBENTHAL, F.: Uber einige Sonderformen des "angeborenen Schwachsinns." Ztschr. f. d. ges. Neurol. und Psychiat. 1938, Vol. 163.

PISANI, D. AND CACCHIONE, A.: Xerodermic idiocy. Riv. sper. Freniat., 1935, Vol. **58.**

REED, W. B. *et al.:* Xeroderma pigmentosum. J.A.M.A., **207:**2073, 1969.

SILBERSTEIN, A. G.: Xeroderma pigmentosa with mental deficiency. Am. J. Dis. Child., **55:**784, 1938.

STRIAN, F.: Xerodermatic idiocy of de Sanctis-Cacchione syndrome. Deutsche Ztschr. Nervenh, **189:**218, 1966.

WALSH, F.: Neuroophthalmology. 2nd Ed. 1957, p. 950. Baltimore, Williams and Wilkins Co.

CONGENITAL ATHETOSIS, CHOREA AND RIGIDITY

Definition.—There are several syndromes originating in intrauterine life which are usually attributed to defects of the basal ganglia of the forebrain. All of these present disorders of muscle tone, and, in most instances, involuntary movements are a prominent feature. The classical syndromes are connected with one another by transitional cases, and others are complicated by signs of disease of the pyramidal tracts, so that a great variety of clinical pictures are possible. For purposes of description, however, we shall present the following types: (1) Congenital double athetosis. (2) Congenital double chorea. (3) Congenital rigidity (extrapyramidal) without involuntary movements. (4) The group characterized by atypical movements. (5) The group complicated by paralysis, spasticity and other symptoms.

Pathological Anatomy.—The most important contributions to the anatomical basis of these syndromes have been made by the Vogts and their followers. In a number of cases of double athetosis, they have found that

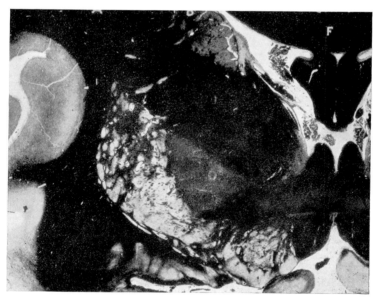

FIG. 19. Status marmoratus. The putamen and the caudate nucleus are broken up into small nests of cells separated by bundles of myelinated fibers. (Jakob. Arch. of Neurol. and Psychiat. 1925, Vol. 13, p. 611.)

the lateral and dorsal portions of the putamen and some parts of the caudate nucleus are broken up into small nuclear masses separated by a network of fine, myelinated, nerve fibers. The remaining portions of the striatum show loss of nerve cells and proliferation of glial cells and fibers. In almost all cases, lesions are found elsewhere, especially in the cerebral cortex and thalamus. In the sections stained by Weigert's method, the alternating light and dark areas in the putamen and caudate nucleus present a marbled appearance, and the Vogts, therefore, have termed this condition *status marmoratus*. It is necessary to point out that neither the nature nor the site of the lesion in congenital double athetosis is constant and a variety of anatomical changes have been described.

The Vogts have also found status marmoratus in cases of congenital choreoathetosis and in cases of congenital rigidity of extrapyramidal type in which involuntary movements are absent.

Bielschowski has made some anatomical studies upon cases of unilateral athetosis and hemiplegia which seem to be of prenatal origin. He finds

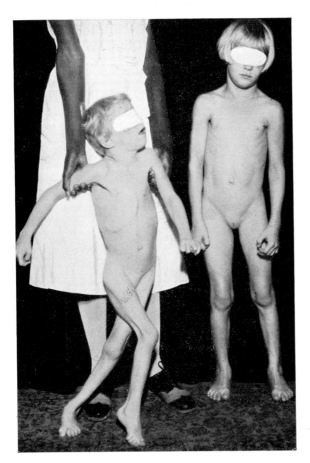

Fig. 20. Congenital double athetosis in two little girls who are believed to be identical twins. The symptoms are very severe in one twin but mild in the other who appears quite normal in the photograph.

cerebral hemiatrophy with selective degeneration of the motor cortex, especially involving the third cellular layer and shrinking of the striatum.

Etiology.—Since this condition, i.e. status marmoratus, has been found in several stillborn children, it has been regarded as a defect of development or as the result of some intrauterine process. Several authors, however, have been led to hold divergent views. Some writers attribute this condition to asphyxia and Benda believes it is due to stasis in the vein of Galen system. Löwenberg and Malamud state that their clinical observations and anatomical studies indicate that the status marmoratus is usually acquired as a result of infantile encephalitis, and that it may be a progressive rather than a stationary process. The reader should consult the references given below for a discussion of the complex problems which are involved in the interpretation of the anatomical findings. From my own observations, however, I am convinced that in the common congenital double athetosis

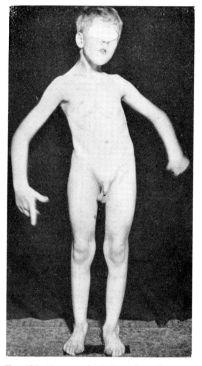

Fig. 21. Congenital double athetosis showing peculiar postures of the arms and hands and torsion of the neck. The child's mental development was normal.

there is no tendency to progression whatsoever. We have followed a number of cases of this type from infancy to adult life. It should be pointed out that kernicterus is one of the causes of double athetosis, though the anatomical changes are quite different from those of status marmoratus. Unilateral athetosis is sometimes associated with hemiplegia due to birth injury. Patzig found congenital double athetosis and status marmoratus in 14 members of a family. He suggests that this is an hereditary disorder.

Clinical Features.—*Congenital double athetosis* is usually not recognized until the child is several months old, although in severe cases symptoms may be observed within a few weeks after birth. The mother usually first notices that the child assumes strange postures and that the musculature becomes rigid when the child is handled. Involuntary movements are not easily recognized during infancy, but, except in very mild cases, they should be apparent by the end of the first year. There is delay in holding up the head, sitting up and walking. Speech is delayed and imperfect, and in severe cases there may be difficulty in swallowing. When the syndrome is fully developed, we find fluctuating changes in muscle tone. At one time, the muscles may be rigid, but at other times, relaxed. Posture is always changing in athetosis but, nevertheless, there is a tendency for certain positions to recur so that they may be regarded as typical. For example, the fingers are frequently hyper-extended and abducted, the wrist flexed, the forearm pronated, the arm retracted, the toes dorsally extended and the foot plantar flexed and inverted. The head is often retracted and rotated to one side as in spasmodic torticollis although the thoracic and lumbar spine rarely show the distortion which is characteristic of dystonia musculorum deformans. In bilateral athetosis, the involuntary movements involve the entire bodily musculature although they are usually most striking in the face and hands. A constant succession of grimaces passes over the face. The mouth may be opened and the tongue protruded. Slow, wormlike movements occur in the fingers and arms. The trunk and the proximal segments of the limbs do not escape but are not affected to the same degree. The movements are accentuated by voluntary efforts and nervous tension such as that produced by the approach of the examiner and are reduced or abolished by relaxation. They are absent during sleep. Voluntary movements are always disturbed and in severe cases coordinated movements are impossible. Any attempt to perform such acts as the finger-nose test may result in contraction of numerous muscles in the arm and even other parts of the body, so the whole limb becomes rigid and only random movements result. Apparently, there is an abnormal spread of innervation. As a result of the constant movements of the limbs, the muscles may become strikingly hypertrophied, so that these children often present an exceptional muscular development. Speech is grossly distorted and often cannot be understood. Deglutition is also frequently impaired. The gait is much altered and the involuntary movements are always accentuated when the patient is walking. Uncontrollable laughter and crying may occur. The tendon reflexes may be difficult to obtain. Owing to the tendency to spontaneous dorsal extension of the toes, the plantar reflex cannot be tested satisfactorily. Mental development is often more or less deficient, but the defect is, as a rule, less than one would at first suppose, for the distorted facial expression and the difficulty in speech make it easy to underestimate the child's intelligence.

In mild and moderately severe cases, the child eventually learns to walk and talk, although these functions may not be acquired until the end of the fifth year. During childhood, there is an apparent improvement, for there is constant progress in coördination which, of course, may be due, in part, to the natural course of development. Before puberty, however, improvement ceases, and thereafter the condition remains stationary. These statements apply only to moderately severe cases. In very severe congenital athetosis, the child's condition may seem to grow worse, and nutrition may be maintained with great difficulty. Such children are apt to die in cachexia or after trivial infections. Convulsive seizures may develop, although they do not constitute an essential or even a common feature of the syndrome. We have seen several of these patients who have had no voluntary power to elevate or depress the eyes though these movements were produced by vestibular stimulation. Lesny states that between the ages of 6 and 10 years the clinical manifestations of congenital athetosis may change. Tension athetosis may appear. This is a condition in which any voluntary movement causes generalized rigidity. In other cases, chorea or torsion spasm may develop. Hemiballismus sometimes occurs. I have seen one patient with congenital double athetosis who eventually developed syringomyelia and another whose case was complicated by spasmodic torticollis after some years.

Congenital Chorea.—It is less common than athetosis. In some cases, the movements resemble those of Sydenham's chorea, but usually the involuntary movements partake of the nature of athetosis, so that the term choreoathetosis is, perhaps, more suitable. Cases falling midway between these two syndromes are not uncommon. In the true syndrome of congenital chorea, involuntary movements are usually absent or inconspicuous during infancy. The muscles, however, are atonic, so that amyotonia congenita may be suspected. The child is slow to sit up and to hold up the head. The feet may be placed behind the head, and the hands and feet may be hyperextended to an unnatural degree. After six months or more, the involuntary movements become evident. These are sudden, jerky and irregular, as in Sydenham's chorea. Disturbances of speech, difficulty in swallowing and facial grimaces may be prominent. Mental development varies as it does in congenital athetosis. Any disturbance of the child's routine may cause a great exacerbation of the symptoms. It is not unusual to see such results following tonsillectomy or orthopedic operations. After a brief rest, the child may be restored to the original condition.

Congenital Rigidity.—In certain cases there are no involuntary movements and only excessive muscular rigidity is present. Posture, however, is usually distorted. The picture may suggest congenital spastic diplegia, but the rigidity presents none of the features of true spasticity, such as increase of tendon reflexes, ankle clonus and the Babinski sign. The muscle spasm is often apparent early in life, for such conditions are usually severe, but tends to grow more intense during the first two years. Stimuli of various types, such as handling the child, sudden noises and bright lights, are apt to accentuate the rigidity. Tonic fits are very common. In these the head is retracted, the arms flexed and the legs extended. Bulbar symptoms are present in most cases. The tendon reflexes may be normal or may be apparently absent as a result of the intense rigidity. Recently De Lange has described cases of muscular hypertrophy with rigidity and with pronounced mental defect. Widespread lesions of various types were found in the brains.

Cases with Atypical Movements.—In a number of cases we find atypical and bizarre movements and postures which do not lend themselves readily to analysis. There is, in general, some increase in muscle tone, but the group is so heterogeneous that it is impossible to generalize. Some cases present postures suggestive of those seen in dystonia musculorum deformans; others exhibit myoclonic movements, and others show difficulty in relaxing the grasp, such as is seen in Thomsen's disease. Tremors associated with rigidity are sometimes observed. In certain instances, there is a striking awkwardness, unlike any well-known type of ataxia, to which Collier has applied the name maladroitness.

Cases of Involuntary Movements Complicated by Spasticity, etc.—We have already mentioned that hemiplegia of prenatal origin is apt to be associated with unilateral athetosis, and that, in some cases of congenital spastic diplegia, mild athetoid movements may occur, especially when the child is laboring under any mental stress or excitement. It is evident that we sometimes encounter defects of development which involve both the pyramidal tracts and the extrapyramidal system.

Treatment.—No satisfactory treatment is known. It is recommended that treatment be instituted early and that the instructor should proceed slowly. Simple movements are learned first and then more and more complex ones. Such training is time consuming, and can scarcely be expected to produce useful results except in mild cases. Several surgical procedures have been advocated. Tenotomies and peripheral nerve sections, as in the Stoffel operation, may be of some value in cases characterized by persistent deformity. Bucy and Buchanan have removed a small cortical area corresponding to part of Brodmann's area 6. The athetosis was relieved. Putnam has performed anterior and anterolateral cordotomy, in the hope of interrupting extrapyramidal motor tracts. The movements were either diminished or abolished, and only mild paresis and transient disturbances of sphincter control resulted.

At present, operation upon the brain or spinal cord is still in an experimental stage and cannot be advised as a routine procedure. In mild cases, re-education should be tried, and deformities should be treated by proper orthopedic measures. Various drugs are recommended such as curare and myanesin. I have never seen striking improvement result.

BIBLIOGRAPHY

ALEXANDER, L.: The fundamental types of histopathologic changes encountered in cases of athetosis and paralysis agitans. Research Publ. Nerv. and Mentl. Dis., 21:334, 1941.

BENDA, C. E.: Developmental Disorders of Mentation and Cerebral Palsies. New York, Grune and Stratton, 1952.

BUCY, P. C. AND BUCHANAN, D. N.: Athetosis. Brain, **55**:476, 1932.

DE LANGE, C.: Two cases of congenital anomalies of the brain. Am. J. Dis. Child., **53**:429, 1937.

————: Congenital hypertrophy of the muscles, extrapyramidal motor disturbances and mental deficiency. Am. J. Dis. Child., **48**:243, 1934.

DENNY-BROWN, D.: Diseases of the basal ganglia. Oxford M., **VI**:261, 1945.

KRYENBERG, G.: Status dysmyelinisatus des pallidum bei congenitalen bilateralen athetosis. Zetschr. f. d. ges. Neurol. u. Psychiat., **132**:806, 1931.

LESNY, I.: The development of athetosis. Develop. Med. Child Neurol., **10**:441, 1968.

LÖWENBERG, K. AND MALAMUD, W.: Status marmoratus. Etiology and manner of development. Arch. Neurol. & Psychiat., **29**:104, 1933.

PATZIG, B.: Erbbiologie und erbpathologie des gehirns. Handbuch der Erbbiologie des Menschen. **vol. 5**, part 1, Berlin, Springer, 1939.

PUTNAM, T. J.: Treatment of athetosis and dystonia by section of extrapyramidal motor tracts. Arch. Neurol. & Psychiat., **29**:504, 1933.

VOGT, C. u. O.: Zur Lehre der Erkrankungen des Striären Systems. Jour. f. Physiol. u. Neurol., **25**:631, 1920.

————: Jour. f. Physiol. u. Neurol., **31**:256, 1925.

CONGENITAL CEREBELLAR ATAXIA

Definition.—Incoördination and other symptoms of cerebellar involvement of congenital origin.

Pathological Anatomy.—A number of anatomical studies have been made and a variety of defects are found. In some instances, the cerebellum may be represented by small nodules of deformed folia on either side, the vermis and hemispheres being absent. The inferior olives and the basis pontis are always defective, but the substantia nigra may be hypertrophied. The vermis may be absent without any gross defect of the hemispheres. Deficient development of the vermis may be found in several members of a family. Benda regards the cases in which the vermis is absent as examples of true rachischisis. Unilateral defects are also well known in which one hemisphere and part of the vermis are absent. Cases have been described in which the cerebellum was very small but symmetrically formed, and Freeman mentions microgyria of the cerebellar cortex with disordered architecture both in the cortex and white matter. Defects in the cerebral hemispheres are often associated.

Etiology.—The anatomical findings seem to point unmistakably to defects of development.

Clinical Features.—In uncomplicated cases, nothing is noted, as a rule, until the child begins to reach for objects. It is then observed that there is

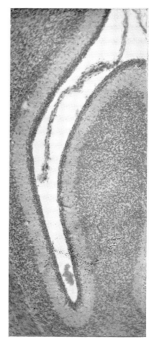

FIG. 22. Section of cerebellum of foetal appearance in full term infant. The granular cells still lie on the surface.

an intention tremor of the hands. Such children are late in holding up the head, in sitting up, and in standing and walking. Even when the pelvis is held firmly in the examiner's hands, the trunk can not be held erect and falls from side to side. Later, when the child begins to walk, it falls frequently, and sways from side to side as if sense of balance were defective. Strength may be very good, and muscle tone, as judged by passive movement, may be normal or nearly normal, although the difficulty in maintaining posture reveals a loss of postural tone. The rhythm of speech is often affected and may be of scanning or staccato type, but articulation is distinct as a rule. Nystagmus is usually absent. The tendon reflexes are generally quite normal. The intention tremor is always grossly increased by stress of emotion. In uncomplicated cases, mental development is quite normal.

It must be mentioned that gross defects of the cerebellum have been found unexpectedly at autopsy in subjects who have shown no clinical evidence of cerebellar deficiency.

Cerebellar ataxia may be associated with diplegia, both spastic and flaccid, with congenital chorea and mental defect. Norman describes a case of cerebellar agenesis in which progressive degeneration occurred later. Volpe reports a case of cerebellar ataxia with hypogonadotrophic eunuchoidism. Biemond describes a syndrome including brachydactyly, nystagmus and cerebellar ataxia in four generations. Mental deficiency and squints were associated.

Joubert, *et al.* describe a familial type of agenesis of the vermis associated with ataxia, abnormal eye movements, mental deficiency and episodes of hyperpnea.

Diagnosis.—We must consider in the differential diagnosis atonic diplegia, progressive degenerations of the cerebellum, ataxia following acute infections, cerebellar abscesses, tumors and tuberculomas. The degenerative processes offer the most difficult problem, but may be distinguished by their progressive course and often, by a history of other cases in the family. Ataxia due to encephalopathy should develop rather suddenly in association with an acute illness, while tumors, abscesses and tuberculomas usually run such a rapid course that they can scarcely be confused with congenital cerebellar defects for long. Atonic diplegia should be distinguished by the greater loss of muscle tone, the less evident incoördination and the greater defect of mentality. Following a debilitating illness which has not involved the nervous system, a child who has learned to walk recently may be very unsteady for a time and have to learn to walk again. (See Congenital Apraxia and Agnosia and also Congenital Maladroitness.)

Prognosis.—Uncomplicated cerebellar defect is not incompatible with prolonged life. If the symptoms are severe, there will probably be some disability throughout life, but, as a rule, there is apparent improvement year by year. In mild cases, there may be almost complete recovery. Batten has stated that, if there is no complicating cerebral lesion, substantial improvement may be expected, but that if cerebral defects are present the outlook is unfavorable.

Treatment.—Most writers recommend systematic exercises to develop coördination. Building blocks and other toys are useful during infancy, and walking machines are used to encourage the child to walk. In the writer's experience, most of these patients have improved without any special exercises.

BIBLIOGRAPHY

BAKER, R. C. AND GRAVES, G. O.: Cerebellar agenesis. Arch. Neurol. & Psychiat., **25:**547 (numerous references) , 1931.
BATTEN, F.: Ataxia in childhood. Brain, **28:**484, 1905.
BIEMOND, A.: Brachydactylie, nystagmus encerebellaire ataxie als familiain syndrom. Nederl T Geneesk, **78:**1423, 1934.
DE HAEME: Agenesie partielle du vermis due cervelet a caractere familial. Acta neurol. et psychiat. belg. 1955, vol. 55, p. 622.
JOUBERT, M. *et al.:* Familial agenesis of the cerebellar vermis. A syndrome of episodic hyperpnea, abnormal eye movements, ataxia and retardation. Neurology, **19:**813, 1969.
NORMAN, R. M. AND ULRICH, H.: Cerebellar hypoplasia associated with systemic degeneration in early life. Jour. Neurol. Neurosurg. and Psychiat., **21:**159, 1958.
RUBENSTEIN, H. S. AND FREEMAN, W.: Cerebellar agenesis. J. Nerv. & Ment. Dis., **92:**489, 1940.
SCHERER, H. J.: Beiträge zur pathologischen Anatomie des Kleinhirns; genuine Kleinhirn-atrophie. Ztschr. f. d. ges. Neurol. u. Psychiat., **145:**335, 1933.
VOLPE, R. *et al.:* Familial hypogonadotrophic eunuchoidism with cerebellar ataxia. Jour. Clin. Endocr., **23:**107, 1963.

DEVELOPMENTAL APRAXIA AND AGNOSIA

Walton *et al.* have published a study of five children who were thought to be excessively clumsy. A very complete and careful investigation revealed that these children were suffering from developmental abnormalities. Three children were found to have apraxia, one had apraxia and tactile agnosia and one had a disorder of the body image. No doubt, such conditions escape recognition in many instances.

These authors regard these conditions as developmental disorders comparable to the developmental disorders of speech.

BIBLIOGRAPHY

WALTON, S. N. *et al.:* Clumsy children. A study of developmental apraxia and agnosia. Brain, **85:**603, 1962.

CONGENITAL MALADROITNESS

It is well known that mentally deficient children are slow to learn to walk and to learn to perform complex motor activities. In some cases, however, they eventually become very agile.

A somewhat similar condition is occasionally encountered in children of normal mentality. They are slow to walk, slow to learn to tie shoe laces and to dress themselves. They cannot ride a bicycle nor play baseball. I have observed this condition more often in boys than in girls. Some of these children are lazy and dislike to exert themselves. They usually become obese. Others are intellectually inclined and spend most of their time reading. In some instances, the child avoids outdoor games because he finds he cannot compete with other boys of his age and gets so discouraged that he stops trying. Some children make persistent efforts to improve their athletic skill despite their handicaps. These children may acquire strong muscles but the other children, who take no exercise, have flabby, poorly developed muscles.

One might expect to find ataxia on examination but standard tests reveal no true ataxia. The station and gait are usually normal. The finger-nose and heel-knee tests are well performed. More complex movements, especially those which the child has never attempted before, cannot be properly performed.

It is of interest that having spent much time and effort in learning a certain activity, such as riding a bicycle, the child may eventually perform normally. Certain games, such as baseball or basketball, in which complex, highly coördinated movements must be made in rapid succession are always behond the capacity of these children. They are usually not handicapped in adult life for they choose a business in which muscular coördination is not important.

The real defect seems to be difficulty in learning complex motor reactions. Possibly this is a developmental defect. Lack of proper exercise plays an important role which is probably secondary in most instances, however.

CONGENITAL DEFECTS OF THE CRANIAL NERVES

Definition.—It seems best to discuss all the congenital defects in the domain of the cranial nerves at this point, for our knowledge of their anatomical basis and causation is inadequate for a more accurate classification. As regards the purely motor defects, it is always possible that the muscle may be defective rather than the nerve supply. Defects of the skeletal muscles are discussed under that title, although some of them are probably closely related to the conditions described at this point.

Pathological Anatomy.—Very little is known about the anatomical basis of these conditions. In congenital paralysis of motor nerves, absence or defective development of the nucleus has been found, and some authors describe findings that indicate a selective degeneration of the nerve. The corresponding muscles may be absent or atrophic.

Defects of the nerves subserving special senses such as the optic, the olfactory and the auditory are often associated with more or less aplasia of the central pathways and cortical centers of these nerves.

Etiology.—The anatomical findings and the tendency of such conditions to appear in several members of the family indicate that either defects of development proper or intrauterine degenerative processes are usually responsible. Probably a multiplicity of factors enter into the causation of this group of conditions.

Clinical Features.—Any of the twelve pairs of cranial nerves may be defective from birth. These palsies may be unilateral or bilateral; they may involve only one nerve or several nerves, and are often associated with other malformations and peculiarities of development. It is of interest that motor defects are most frequent, and that defects of sensory nerves, other than those of special sensibility, are not described so far as the writer can discover. We have already stated that in many although not in the majority of cases several members of a family are affected in the same way. Such defects, as a rule, remain stationary throughout life.

In a few cases, the *olfactory bulbs* have been discovered to be rudimentary or even absent, giving rise to congenital anosmia.

Probably the *oculomotor* nerve is defective more frequently than any other. The commonest example is congenital weakness of the levator palpebrae resulting in ptosis of the lid. This may be either so slight as almost to escape notice or so complete that the pupil is always covered. The mild forms are most common, and, as a rule, the condition is unilateral. The other muscles supplied by the third nerve are not affected in most instances, but sometimes the elevators are also deficient. If the pupil is allowed to remain covered during childhood, amblyopia expanopsia will result.

In a few rare cases, it is impossible to lift the lid by voluntary effort, but when the patient moves the jaw the eyelid lifts spontaneously. The absurd term *jaw winking* has been applied to this phenomenon. It is also termed the Marcus-Gunn syndrome. As a rule the lid lifts when the jaw is opened and closes when the jaw is closed, but the converse is also seen. In some cases, protrusion or lateral movements of the jaw are effective in opening the eyelid. Dr. Walsh has told me of a case of congenital ptosis in which moving the tongue, swallowing and contracting the sternomastoid muscles will cause the lid to lift but movements of the jaws have no effect. I have seen one case in which swallowing causes the lid to lift. Inability to elevate the eye is found in some cases. Dr. Walsh has showed me a little girl of 4 years who had congenital ptosis of the right eyelid, paralysis of the superior, inferior and internal recti and inferior oblique muscles. The pupil was normal. Opening of the mouth and deviation of the chin to the left caused the eyelid to lift.

In a number of instances, complete paralysis of all muscles innervated by the third nerve on one or both sides has been present from birth. The weakness may be restricted to the extraocular muscles, or the pupil may be paralyzed also.

Bielschowski has described a very peculiar anomaly in certain types of congenital paralysis of the third nerve. In such cases there is, of course, ptosis of the lid and dilation of the pupil with loss of light reflex. Every few seconds, however, the lid will begin to quiver and finally will lift spontaneously. At the same time, the pupil contracts strongly. After a short time, the lid closes again and the pupil dilates. This cycle is then repeated. In certain cases these phenomena are induced or inhibited by lateral movements of the eyes. The condition is called *cyclic oculomotor paralysis.*

Richter describes *alternate day squint.* This condition may be present at birth or may develop early in infancy. It may persist for years. Some 33 cases have been discovered. The squint is usually internal. It is present one day and absent the next day. Plastic operation on the extraocular muscles is usually effective.

Congenital palsies of the *sixth nerves* are not infrequently encountered. In some cases it is difficult to distinguish this condition from non-paralytic squints with internal strabismus. Occasionally one sees a child in whom one external rectus, usually the left external rectus, is fibrotic and inelastic so that the eye cannot be abducted. When the attempt is made to adduct the eye, the bulb is retracted. This is termed *Duane's syndrome.* It may be bilateral and is sometimes seen in more than one member of a family. The superior oblique sheath syndrome is described. It is said that the muscle

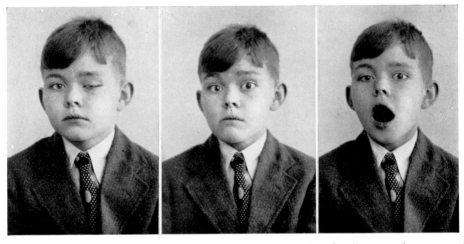

Fig. 23. "Jaw Winking" showing how the lid is elevated when jaw is opened or protruded. (By courtesy of Drs. Walsh and Little.)

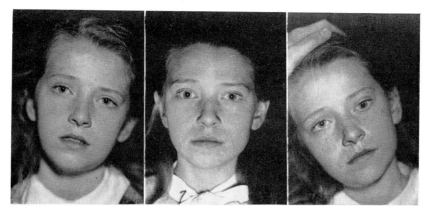

Fig. 24. Head tilting (A) due to paralysis of the right superior oblique muscles. When the head is straightened (B) the eyes appear approximately straight but by means of the diplopiates the right eye may be shown to be extorted with respect to the left eye. When the head is passively tilted to the right (C) a vertical divergence occurs with the right eye uppermost, allegedly due to overaction of the right superior rectus. (Cogan: *Neurology of the Ocular Muscles.* Thomas, Springfield, 1948.)

contracts well and depresses the eye when it is in adduction, but because of the tightness of the sheath, the eye cannot be elevated when it is in adduction. Removal of the sheath gives relief. This is a congenital condition.

I have seen two children with Dr. Walsh who from birth had almost complete ptosis of the upper eyelids and only minimal movement of the eyes with good vision, normally pupillary reactions and normal optic discs.

In general, it may be said that congenital ophthalmoplegias do not give rise to double vision if the patient is allowed to move the head at will. Vicarious attitudes of the head may result from the effort to avoid diplopia. The rule simply stated is that the face is moved in the direction of action of the weak muscle. Thus when the face is rotated to the right one expects to find weakness of the right external rectus or the left internal rectus. When the superior or inferior rectus or one of the obliques is affected, a more complex alteration of posture results with the face turned upwards or downwards, a bit to one side and the head tilted to one shoulder. In such cases, to which the term *ocular torticollis* is applied, it is often difficult to determine what muscle is at fault. This complex subject is discussed in the references given below. Ocular torticollis apparently rarely leads to contractures of the muscles of the neck or to gross structural changes in the bones. In rare cases, the child finds it impossible to secure single vision no matter how the head is turned. In such cases, the head may be held in such a position as to separate the visual images as far as possible and aid in suppressing the false image. The deviation of the head is then the opposite of the usual one. Congenital nystagmus may also lead to abnormal positions of the head which is rotated in the direction of the quick component of the nystagmus.

The writer has observed two cases of a rare and obscure type of congenital exophthalmos, which seems to be due to atonia of the extraocular muscles. When the lids are open, the bulbs are strikingly proptosed, but they may be pushed back into the orbits with ease either by the examiner's finger or by the closure of the lids. They may also be forced out of the orbit without difficulty. This condition may be associated with progressive loss of vision, probably due to stretching of the optic nerves. Ocular movements are not definitely limited. We have seen this condition only in Negroes.

We have also observed a man who has the ability to protrude either eye well out of the orbit so that the lids close behind it and the insertions of the recti are evident. He can retract the eye into its proper position at will. It would seem that the eye is pulled forward by the obliques and withdrawn by the recti. Dr. Walsh informs me that a patient who had exactly the same ability was subjected to post-mortem examination. Two separate superior oblique muscles were found in each orbit. The inferior oblique muscles were bifid near their termination and had two separate insertions.

Congenital inequality of the pupils is very common, and outspoken anisocoria is not very rare. As a rule, such pupils show normal reflexes.

Congenitally immobile pupils simulating Argyll Robertson pupils must be mentioned because of their practical importance. These pupils are in the writer's experience usually somewhat irregular and often unequal. The light reaction is absent, and the contraction during accommodation is minimal or lost. The writer has examined three patients who showed these pupillary disturbances. In all three, complete examinations and full investigation of the history revealed no evidence whatever of syphilis. One of these patients came of a family of ten siblings, and six of the ten had the same peculiarity, according to the physicians who examined them. These pupils do not show the myatonic phenomena described by Adie.

The *fifth nerve* is rarely defective, but a few instances of defects of the muscles of mastication are on record. I have examined one child in whom the jaw muscles were almost completely absent, only thin sheets of muscles being found in place of the temporals and masseters. The jaws did not move laterally, and could be closed with great difficulty. There was an interesting malformation of the mandible which was very narrow, and which presented an abnormal curve so that the incisor teeth were separated by at least one centimeter when the back teeth were approximated. The patient also had a mild paresis of the bulbar muscles. Another patient mentioned below showed lack of lateral movement of the jaws, due to absence of the pterygoids. Hewson reports a case in which congenital trigeminal anesthesia was found.

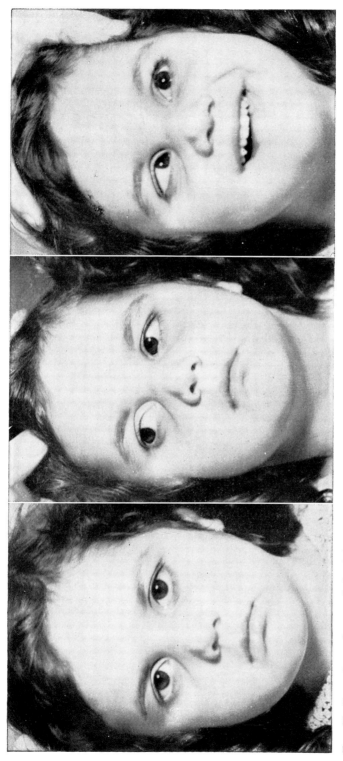

Fig. 25. Duane's syndrome of the left eye. The mother and maternal grandmother also showed the defect which was present in five members of three generations (Laughlin). (From Walsh: *Neuro-Ophthalmology,* courtesy the Williams and Wilkins Company.)

Micrognathia may be mentioned here. In this condition, the mandible is small and detracted and there is as a rule difficulty in swallowing and in breathing because the pharynx is obstructed by the tongue. There is shortening of the genioglossi muscles in some instances and perhaps, cleft palate.

Congenital weakness of the facial muscles. This condition is well known but rare. As a rule, it is bilateral but it may also be unilateral. In most instances the entire facial musculature is affected, but in some instances certain muscles escape. The skin is drawn smoothly over the face and as a rule shows no wrinkles. There is no sagging of the face as is seen in seventh nerve palsies. In fact, the skin is not easily moved over the subcutaneous tissues. Evidently the muscles are replaced by connective tissue. Frequently the patient's condition escapes recognition for a number of years. Occasionally more than one case of this type is found in the same family. Dr. Arthur King has given me the history of a family in which this condition was traced through three generations and involved five individuals including three females and two males. It is not unusual for malformations of the external ear to be associated. H. M. Thomas once described congenital facial paralysis in two brothers who also had congenital deafness and malformations of the external ears. In several cases of this type, the temporal bone has shown complete absence of the facial canal. Such defects may be associated with club feet, defects of the pectoral muscles, syndactylism, defects of the digits and mental deficiency. I have seen several cases in which the platysma muscle is missing on one side. When the child cries, the corner

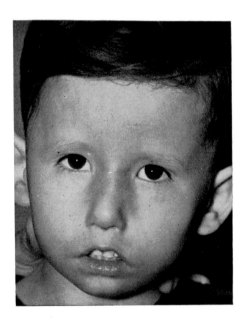

Fig. 26. Showing congenital bilateral facial paralysis in a child of three years. There was also paralysis of the external recti, of the tongue and the pterygoid muscles.

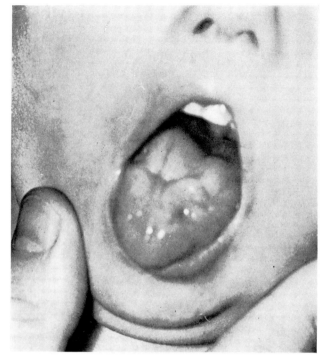

FIG. 27. Photograph of same child showing atrophy of tongue.

of the mouth draws down on the normal side but not on the side on which the muscle is missing. When the child smiles, there is no apparent asymmetry of the face. I have learned of the case of an otherwise normal little girl whose voluntary facial movements are quite normal but has *no emotional movements* of the *face* whatever.

There are also cases in which *voluntary movements* are *lacking* but the face moves in an exaggerated fashion in association with emotional reactions. This condition is usually a part of congenital pseudobulbar palsy q.v.

The *Möbius syndrome* is sometimes termed aplasia of the sixth and seventh nerves, but it seems to be a more complex condition. In my experience, the most common clinical picture is as follows: There is loss of lateral deviation of the eyes and sometimes loss of convergence as well. As a rule, vertical movements of the eyes are preserved and there is no ptosis of the lids. In some cases there is an internal squint. Congenital facial paralysis is a constant feature. The face does not sag, as one expects in acquired facial paralysis. As a rule, the facial paralysis is bilateral and complete but the lower part of the face may be spared and the paralysis may be unilateral. There is usually loss of lateral movement of the mandible so grinding movements of the jaw are lost but vertical movements are preserved. The tongue is usually atrophic. This condition is illustrated in Figure 26. In some cases there is no lacrimation when the child cries, thus indicating a neurogenic condition. Other anomalies such as paralysis of the pharynx may be associated. Van Allen found only a few fragments of muscle fibers in the face, but discovered that the left external rectus was normal grossly and histologically. It is suggested that supranuclear lesions are important in the ocular palsies. Two recent anatomical studies may be mentioned. Richter found a defect in the facial nucleus in a case of unilateral congenital facial paralysis. Riggs described a case in which there was congenital paralysis of both sides of the face, of both external recti and of both sides of the tongue. He found defects in the corresponding nuclei at post-morten examination. I have seen two cases of the Möbius syndrome in which there were clubbed feet, deficient development of the legs below the knees and mental deficiency. An abstract of one case is given below. This patient was completely deaf.

Congenital deafness is treated separately under the title deaf-mutism.

The *pharynx* and *larynx* are sometimes paralyzed at birth, and the *tongue* may be atrophic and paralytic on one or both sides. It should be kept in mind that obstruction of the esophagus and the trachea may be caused by compression due to anomalies of the great vessels such as the right subclavian and the innominate arteries. A double aortic arch may also cause such symptoms. Most of these conditions may be relieved by operation. Another condition which may simulate congenital bulbar palsy is esophago-tracheal fistula. Congenital bulbar palsy is a very rare condition. We have recently seen one case in which only the pharynx and the soft palate were paralyzed and the tongue and vocal cords escaped. Chapple states that if the baby's head is tilted to one side in utero the laryngeal nerves may be compressed with resulting laryngeal palsy. The sternomastoids and trapezii are not infrequently small or even absent. This condition is discussed with defects of the skeletal muscles.

Various combinations of the above-mentioned defects may occur. Fry and Kasak mention a little girl who showed congenital facial paralysis, complete loss of lateral movements of the eyes, loss of lateral movements of the jaws, atrophy and weakness of the tongue, weakness of the soft palate, absence of the left pectoral muscle and left breast, and absence of the terminal joint of the left forefinger. The writer has studied the case of a patient who was born with paralysis of the orbicularis of the lids, both external recti, the pterygoids and the tongue. Batten mentions the case of a child with congenital paralysis of the face, jaws and pharynx.

CASE HISTORY.—*Möbius syndrome with mental deficiency, clubbed feet, deficient development of the legs below the knees and bilateral deafness.*

C. A. P. was examined at the Rosewood State Hospital by the courtesy of Dr. Harry G. Butler, at the age of 15 years. He was born with clubbed feet which required operation. He was mentally defective and his intelligence quotient was estimated at 36. He had never been able to talk, and seemed to be completely deaf. The electroencephalogram was interpreted to be mildly abnormal. Slight cerebral atrophy was found on air study.

On examination bodily growth is below average for his age, but he is properly nourished. He seems to be cooperative, but is unable to hear what is said to him. He does not try to form words. The pupils react to light. He can rotate his eyes upward and downward, but no movements are possible in the horizontal plane. There is no squint or ptosis of the lids. No movement of either side of the face is possible. The face is very smooth and there is no sagging. When he tries to close his eyes, the bulbs roll up. The mandible moves well in the vertical plane but there is no lateral movement. The tongue is atrophic.

He walks well, but there is no action at the ankles. The thighs are well formed and seem to display proper strength. The legs below the knees are poorly developed and the feet are very small. Scars of operation are seen on the ankles. The knee jerks are active, but no ankle jerks are elicited. Sexual development is at least normal.

BIBLIOGRAPHY

BATTEN, F. E.: Congenital affection of the sixth, seventh and twelfth cranial nuclei. Brain, **28**:359, 1905.

CHAPPLE, C. C.: A duosyndrome of laryngeal nerve. Am. J. Dis. Child., **91**:14, 1956.

EVANS, P. R.: Nuclear agenesis. Möbius syndrome. Congenital facial diplegia syndrome. Arch. Dis. Childhood, **30**:237, 1955.

FALLS, H. F. *et al.:* Three cases of Marcus Gunn phenomenon in two generations. Amer. Jour. Ophthal., **32**:53, 1949.

FRY, F. R. AND KASAK, M.: Congenital facial paralysis. Arch. Neurol. & Psychiat., **2**:638, 1919.

GOLDFARB, C.: Familial congenital lateral rectus palsy with retraction. Dis. Nerv. Syst., **25**:17, 1964.

GREBE, H.: Aniridia et oligophrenia, un syndrome hereditaire. J. Genet. Hum., **3**:269, 1954.

HENDERSON, J. L.: Congenital facial paralysis. Clinical features, pathology and etiology. Brain, **62**:381, 1939.

HEWSON, G. E.: Congenital trigeminal anesthesia. Brit. J. Ophthal., **47**:308, 1963.

HOEFNAGEL, D. AND PENRY, J. K.: Partial facial paralysis in young children. New England J. M., **262**:1126, 1960.

JAMES, ALLEN: The superior oblique tendon sheath syndrome. Strabismus Symposium 11. C. V. Mosby, 1958, p. 410.

LEES, F.: Congenital static familial ophthalmoplegia. Jour. Neurol. Neurosurg. Psychiat., **23**:46, 1960.

NEURATH, R.: Zur Frage der Angebornen Functionsdefekte in Gebiete der Hirnnerven. München med. Wchnschr., **54**:1224, 1907.

NISENSON, A.: Receding chin and glossoptosis. A cause of respiratory difficulty in infants. J. Pediat., **32**:397, 1948.

———, ISAACSON, A. AND GRANT, S.: Mask like face with associated congenital anomalies. J. Pediat., **46**:255, 1955.

PALMER, E. D.: Dysphagia lusoria. Ann. Int. Med., **42**:1173, 1955.

PITNER, S. E. *et al.:* Observations of pathology of Möbius syndrome. Jour. Neurol. Neurosurg. and Psychiat., **28**:362, 1965.

RICHTER, C. P.: Clock-mechanism esotropia in children. Alternate day squint. Johns Hopkins Med. Jour., **122**:218, 1968.

RICHTER, R. B.: The anatomical basis of congenital facial paralysis. Meeting of the Amer. Assoc. of Neuropathologists, Atlantic City, June 16, 1957.

RIGGS, E. H.: The anatomical basis of congenital facial paralysis. Meeting of the Amer. Assoc. of Neuropathologists, Atlantic City, June 16, 1957.

RODIN, F. H. *et al.*: Hereditary congenital ptosis. Amer. Jour. Ophthal., 18:213, 1935.

SMITH, E. I.: Ocular torticollis. Brit. M. J., 1:416, 1935.

SPATZ, H.: Klinischer u. anatomischer Beitrag zu den angebornen Beweglichkeitsdefekten im Hirnnervenbereich. Ztschr. f. Kinderhlk., 51:579, 1931.

STEVENS, H.: Cyclic oculomotor paralysis. Neurology, 15:556, 1965.

THOMAS, H. M.: Congenital facial paralysis. J. Nerv. & Ment. Dis., 25:571, 1898.

VAN ALLEN, M. W. AND BLODI, F. C.: Neurologic aspects of the Möbius syndrome. Neurology, 10:249, 1960.

VAN DER WEIL, H. J.: Hereditary congenital facial paralysis. Acta Genet. Statist. Med., 7:348, 1957.

WAARDENBERG, P. J.: Colobomas and aniridia associated with oligophrenia. Ned. T. Geneesh., 78:1695, 1934.

WARTENBERG, R.: Winking-jaw phenomenon. Arch. Neurol. & Psychiat., 59:734, 1948.

WALSH, F. B.: *Loc. cit.*, p. 346.

WHITE, J. W.: Head tilting and turning of ocular origin. Am. J. Surg., 4:77, 1928.

ZAPPERT, J.: Ueber Infantilen Kernschwund. Ergebn. d. inn Med. u. Kinderh., 5:305, 1910.

CONGENITAL DEFECTS OF THE OPTIC NERVE AND RETINA

A number of developmental abnormalities of the optic nerve and retina have been described and some of these deserve consideration at this point. Defects of the bulb, cornea, iris and lens will be omitted since these are strictly ophthalmological problems.

Coloboma is the result of failure of closure of the fetal cleft of the optic vesicle and therefore analogous to spina bifida in which the neural tube has failed to close. As one might expect the defect lies in the line running from the center of the disc downward and inward to the inferior margin of the pupil. Such defects may involve the iris and optic nerve as well as the retina and choroid. They may be bilateral or unilateral. They appear as white patches of variable extent surrounded as a rule by a zone of pigmentation. In most cases the retinal vessels pass over the defect. Some colobomas lie in the periphery of the retina and others lie near the nerve head or in the nerve head. The degree to which vision is affected depends upon the position and extent of the lesion. Various other malformations such as microphthalmia may be associated. Angelman describes four infants with colobomas all of whom had congenital defects of the brain and three, in addition, congenital defects in the heart. It seems to be firmly established that colobomas are inherited and it is claimed that the mode of inheritance is suggestive of a recessive Mendelian characteristic. Dr. Walsh has recently showed me an example of the rare *hole in the optic nerve head*. This is a little rounded pit sharply defined and containing some pigment. There is usually a caecocentral scotoma with reduction of central vision.

Sjögren and Larsson studied a number of patients in Sweden who displayed microphthalmos or anophthalmos as well as mental deficiency. They found this condition to be inherited as a partially sex-linked recessive characteristic with a reduced penetrance.

Sjögren describes a form of mental deficiency associated with congenital cataracts.

Mental deficiency may be found in association with *aniridia* and Gillespie has found cerebellar ataxia and mental deficiency in association with aniridia. *Pseudoglioma of the retina* is discussed elsewhere.

Congenital aplasia of the *optic nerve* is a rare condition manifest by a small white disc with sharply defined margins. Vision is either absent or greatly diminished. If vision is present, it is confined to the central fields and there are no scotomas. There may be nystagmus or searching movements of the eyes. The condition is bilateral and nonprogressive. Thompson has traced this condition through six generations of a family. In this instance, the defect was inherited as a dominant characteristic but apparently it may be inherited according to other laws. A similar condition is found in association with gross developmental defects of the brain, especially defects of the frontal lobes. McKenna states that the ingestion of large amounts of quinine during pregnancy may cause aplasia of the optic nerves and congenital blindness.

In *anencephaly* according to Mann, the optic nerves contain no nerve fibers and the retinae are devoid of ganglion cells though the rods and cones are present.

The *congenital blindness of Leber seems to be* inherited as a recessive characteristic. We have seen several affected children in one family. In our experience, most of the children are completely blind. The pupils do not react to light. Ophthalmoscopic examination reveals no visible abnormalities of the retinae or optic nerves. The electroretinogram, however, shows no electrical activity whatever in the retina. Searching movements of the eyes are not present.

In some cases, vision is not completely lost though it is always grossly reduced. Searching movements are noted shortly after birth. The electroretinogram usually shows no electrical activity.

Between eight and fourteen years, pigment deposits usually appear in the periphery of the retinae.

Mental deficiency, convulsions, deafness, cataracts and keratoconus may complicate the picture.

A number of minor anomalies of the optic discs occur. One of the commonest is due to *myelination* of the *retinal nerve fibers*. These are seen as fan-shaped white areas lying as a rule above or below the disc in one or

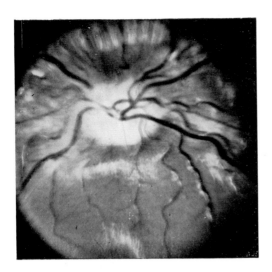

FIG. 28. Photograph of the optic disc showing a condition of congenital origin resembling papilledema. The light streaks are due to the retinal reflex and not to exudate. Hyperopia is associated. (By courtesy of Dr. Walsh.)

both eyes, and only rarely in the periphery of the retina. These areas present well defined striations following the course of the retinal nerve fibers and are easily recognized by this characteristic. Except for a scotoma corresponding to the site of the lesion, there is no loss of vision. Rarely one observes very large areas of myelinated fibers in the retinae which are associated with gross defects in the visual fields and loss of vision. Occasionally one sees *white veils* of *glial tissue* lying on or near the disc. These seem to be of congenital origin and are to be distinguished from glioses due to previous inflammatory processes. The disc may be irregular in outline or oval rather than circular. In some cases the disc is elevated and of mushroom shape presenting the *appearance* of *papilledema* at first glance. It is not unusual to see *hyperemic discs* in association with *hyperopia*. A very rare anomaly is termed *tilting of the discs*. Here the surface of the discs is inclined at an abnormal angle with the retina. A crescent is usually present. The reason for mentioning this very rare condition is that it is associated with defects in the temporal fields of vision which may lead to an erroneous diagnosis of compression of the chiasm. Tilted discs may also be associated with loss of the upper halves of the visual fields. Bergmeister's papilla, i.e., a mass of tissue deposited on the optic disc, may be mistaken for papilledema. It is due to failure of absorption of the embryonic hyaloid canal. Other remnants of the same structure are shreds of tissue on the optic disc, a cyst on the disc, strand of tissue extending from the disc to the lens sometimes associated with a posterior capsular cataract and a strand of tissue attached to the posterior aspect of the lens.

Various defects in the retina and choroid are recognized. In *choroideremia,* the whole choroid is absent and the fundus presents a glistening white appearance. Usually a small area in the region of the macula is spared. Both eyes are affected and the patient is night blind. Various types of *macular dystrophy* are described. They have been termed colobomas although the resemblance is probably superficial. Naturally there are central scotomas corresponding to the defect. In some cases macular dystrophy is sporadic and in others it is inherited. Malformations of the hands and feet may be associated. Bests hereditary macular dystrophy is a dominant characteristic. Despite the fact that there are large and apparently destructive lesions in the maculae, central vision may be normal or nearly normal. The lesion is often just below the fovea. Such defects must be distinguished from various acquired degenerations of the macula. In *albinism* and perhaps in *congenital nystagmus* deficiency of retinal pigment is responsible for the reduction of vision and nystagmus.

Congenital night blindness, i.e., an abnormal reduction of vision in reduced illumination, is well known in such diseases as pigmentary degeneration of the retinae but may occur in an individual with normal fundi and good vision in proper illumination. Bell states that it is inherited as a dominant, recessive or sex-linked recessive character.

Buphthalmos is characterized by enlargement of the eyeball, optic atrophy and increased intraocular tension. It is regarded as a result of congenital glaucoma due to defective development of the drainage system and is therefore analogous to congenital hydrocephalus with which it is sometimes associated. It has been shown that buphthalmos is inherited and behaves as a simple recessive characteristic. It is sometimes found in association with facial nevus, facial hemiatrophy and with von Recklinghausen's neurofibromatosis, as well as Lowe's syndrome. It must be distinguished from megalocornea in which the intraocular pressure is not increased.

A condition known as *retrolental fibroplasia* should be mentioned here. It is said to occur in 16 per cent of premature babies whose birth weight is less than 3 lbs. and in 8 per cent of babies whose birth weight is between 3 and 4 lbs. Owens and Owens have shown that this process begins as a rule between the ages of three and five weeks. There is an angiomatous dilatation of the retinal vessels with edema and detachments of the retinae. The retinal folds come forward, invade the vitreous and finally fuse, forming a fibrous membrane behind the lens. The process has become complete as a rule by the age of four months and there is then a dense white opacity behind the lens of one, or more frequently both eyes. Ciliary processes are evident over the periphery of this mass. Dr. Owens tells me that in about 50 per cent of cases, the process halts in the early stages and eventually regresses so the child is left with good vision. In some cases, however, some scarring remains and this may result in displacement of the maculae and eccentric fixation. Various cerebral defects may be associated such as congenital cerebral diplegia, and convulsions are not unusual. Ingram and Kerr found six diplegics in a study of twenty-one cases of retrolental fibroplasia. Glaucoma may result.

Recent work has shown that the administration of oxygen in high concentrations plays the major role in the production of fibroplasia lentis. Only rarely is a baby found with this condition who has not been in an oxygen chamber. Newborn experimental animals will develop retinolental fibroplasia if kept in oxygen for a time. Developmental defects of the brain may be associated. Patz states that the vascular pattern of the brain is not altered by exposure to excessive oxygen so it seems that the cerebral defects are not due to the same process as the retinal lesions. Patz states that in addition to testing the arterial blood oxygen level the retinae should be examined frequently. If the retinal vessels are constricted, the oxygen level in the incubator should be reduced at once. Dr. Robert M. Forrester states that retrolental fibroplasia is not due to exposure to high oxygen levels and the damage is done when the child is removed from the oxygen-rich environment, for a high degree of oxygen dependence has been induced. He states that retrolental fibroplasia can occur in an infant suffering from hypoxia if oxygen is not administered.

Children with retrolental fibroplasia frequently develop enophthalmos. It has been suggested that this is a result of their habit of pressing their knuckles into their eyes which eventually causes traumatic atrophy of the orbital fat.

Numerous other anomalies are described in the following references.

Sclerocornea, a congenital condition, may be associated with deformities of the ears, scar-like lesions in the skin and defects in the nervous system causing cerebellar ataxia and nystagmus. The cornea may be opaque and bluish. There may be bulging of the cornea. One or both eyes may be affected. Veirs and Brown describe congenital miosis in three generations of a family. They believe that the dilator of the pupil was partially or completely absent.

CASE HISTORY (Ped. 95029).—*Child of 5½ years with congenital aplasia of the optic nerves but no other evidence of defective development of the nervous system.*

A. McC. was born at full term by normal delivery. Her early development was satisfactory except for the absence of any evidence of vision. She walked and talked at the usual age. No illnesses or infectious diseases occurred during infancy. The family history was entirely negative as regards recent generations.

At the age of 5½ years the child was examined at Johns Hopkins Hospital. She was somewhat small for her age but otherwise well developed. Her intelligence seemed to be normal and she coöperated well in the examinations. The pupils were of moderate size and with very strong illumination gave a minimal light reaction. Vision at most was restricted to the ability to detect a strong light thrown into her eyes. The discs were very small, not more than half the usual size, and very pale. The disc margins were sharply defined. No lesions were discovered in the retinae. Ocular movements were of full range and there were spontaneous sweeping movements of the eyes, the "searching movements" of the blind. The other cranial nerves were normal. Motility, sensibility and the reflexes were all in order. Roentgenographic studies and the usual laboratory procedures gave only negative results.

Case History (No. 623474).—*Congenital blindness with loss of light reflex and discs and retinae of normal appearance. Leber's congenital amaurosis.*

A. D. T., a boy of 2 years, was examined in consultation in the Wilmer Institute in November 1952. It had been discovered that he was quite blind when he was only a few months old. His birth had been normal in every way and no evidence of intracranial birth injury had been observed. The mother's health had been good during pregnancy. The family history was quite negative for visual disturbances. The patient had been a bit slow in learning to walk but this was attributed to his defective vision.

The neurological examination was quite negative except for the evidences of blindness. The pupils were large but circular and equal. No light reflex could be elicited. The optic nerve heads were of normal color and shape. No abnormal appearances could be discovered in the retinae. There was no nystagmus and no searching movements.

The possibility of compression of the optic chiasm by a neoplasm was considered. Roentgenograms of the skull were quite negative. The spinal fluid was normal in all respects. All pneumoencephalograms revealed only normal appearances. An electroretinogram performed in another clinic is said to have shown abnormalities suggesting that the lesions were in the retinae.

Case History.—*Leber's congenital blindness with mental deficiency in three siblings.*

By the courtesy of Dr. Harry G. Butler I have examined three siblings at the Rosewood State Hospital. B. N. L. is now 18 years old. He was found to be blind at birth and it was soon evident that he was mentally deficient. He is subject to temper tantrums and bangs his head. He bites his fingers but does not mutilate them. He is not toilet trained. He cannot talk or understand. When he was 6 years old, ophthalmological examination revealed normal optic fundi though the patient was blind and the pupils did not react to light. The electroencephalogram showed diffuse spikes. The electroretinogram showed no activity.

On examination he is deficient in bodily growth, but nutrition is very good. He does not respond when addressed and so is either deaf or unable to understand. He sits with his legs crossed so each foot is beneath the knee of the opposite leg and rocks back and forth. When disturbed, he begins to breathe rapidly. There is bilateral enophthalmos and the orbits seem to be too large for the bulbs. This seems to be explained by his habit of rubbing his eyes with his knuckles. The pupils show no light reflex. Many small pigment deposits are seen in the retinae. There are constant searching movements of the eyes.

He stands and walks unsteadily. The arms and hands are fairly well developed, but the legs below the knees are very slender and the feet are small. The tendon reflexes in the arms are not increased, but the knee and ankle jerks are rather brisk. There is no ankle clonus and no Babinski signs.

J. L., a sister of 20 years and M. R. L., a sister of 13 years, display exactly the same abnormalities. Several other siblings are regarded as normal but are somewhat backward in school work.

BIBLIOGRAPHY

ALSTROM, C. H. AND OLSON, O.: Heredoretinopathia congenitalis monohybrida recessiva. autosomalis. Hereditas, 43:178, 1957.
———: Heredoretinopathia congenitalis autosomalis. Hereditas, 43, 1957.
ANGELMAN, H.: Syndrome of coloboma with multiple congenital abnormalities in infancy. Brit. Med. J., i:1212, 1961.
BEDELL, A. J.: Clinical significance of congenital changes in the optic disc. J.A.M.A., 151:95, 1953.
BELL, J.: Treasury of Human Inheritance. Eug. Lab. Mem. XXIII Anomalies and Diseases of the Eyes. Part 1. Congenital stationary night blindness. 11:104, 1922.
BEST, F.: Uber eine hereditäre Maculaaffektion. Beitrage zur Vererbungslehre. Ztschr. Augenheilk, 13:199, 1905.
BETTMAN, J. W. AND CLEASBY, B. W.: Congenital glaucoma. Pediatrics, 32:420, 1963.
CARROLL, F. D. AND HAIG, C.: Congenital stationary night blindness without ophthalmoscopic or other abnormalities. Arch. Ophth., 50:35, 1953.
COHEN, J. et al.: Evaluation of retrolental fibroplasia. Am. J. Ophth., 57:41, 1964.
DEKABAN, A. AND CARR, R.: Congenital amaurosis of retinal origin. Arch. of Neurol., 14:294, 1966.
GILLESPIE, F. D.: Aniridia, cerebellar ataxia and oligophrenia in siblings. Arch. of Ophthal., 73:338, 1965.
GOLDSTEIN, J. E. AND COGAN, D.: Sclerocornea and associated congenital anomalies. Arch. Ophthal., 67:761, 1962.
GREBE, H.: Aniridia et oligophrenia, un syndrome hereditaire. Jour. Genet. Hum., 3:269, 1954.
HALBERTSMA, K. T. N.: Pseudoatrophie du nerf optique chez nouveaus-nes. Arch. d'ophth., 1:699, 1937.
HOYT, W. F. AND POINT, M. E.: Pseudopapilledema. J.A.M.A., 181:191, 1962.
INGALLS, T. H.: Epidemiology of encephalo-ophthalmic dysplasia. J.A.M.A., 138:261, 1948.
INGRAM, T. T. AND KERR, J. D.: The association of retrolental fibroplasia with cerebral diplegia. Arch. Dis. Child., 29:282, 1954.
———: Diplegia in retrolental fibroplasia. Arch. Dis. Childhood, 29:282, 1954.
IVERSON, H. A.: Hereditary (congenital) optic atrophy. Arch. of Ophthal., 59:850, 1958.
LANMAN, L. P. et al.: Retrolental fibroplasia and oxygen therapy. J.A.M.A., 155:223, 1954.
LEBER, T.: Ueber anomale Formen der Retinitis pigmentosa. Arch. f. Ophthalmologie. 1870-1871 Bd. 16-17, p. 314-341.
MANN, I.: Developmental Abnormalities of the Eye. Cambridge University Press, 1937.
McKENNA, A. J.: Hypoplasia of the optic nerves. Read before the Canad. Ophth. Soc. June 14, 1966.
OWENS, W. C AND OWENS, E. U.: Retrolental fibroplasia in premature infants. Am. J. Ophth., 32:1, 1949.

PATZ, A.: The role of oxygen in retrolental fibroplasia. J. Mt. Sinai Hospital, 3:6, 1954.

————: New role of the ophthalmologist in prevention of retrolental fibroplasia. Arch. of Ophthal., **78**:565, 1967.

SHAW, M. W. *et al.*: Congenital aniridia. Amer. Jour. Hum. Genet., **12**:389, 1960.

SJÖGREN, T.: Klinische und vererubungsmedizinische Untersuchungen uber Oligophrenia mit kongenitaler Katarakt. Ztschr. Neurol., **152**, 1935.

———— AND LARSSON, T.: Microphthalmos and anophthalmos with or without coincident oligophrenia. Acta Psychiat. et Neurol. Suppl., **56**, 1949.

TERRY, T. L.: Extreme prematurity and fibroplastic overgrowth of persistent vascular sheath behind each crystalline lens. Am. J. Ophth., **25**:203, 1942.

THOMPSON, A. H. AND CASHELL, G. T. W.: A pedigree of congenital optic atrophy embracing 16 affected in 6 generations. Proc. Roy. Soc. Med. London, **28**:1415, 1935.

VEIRS, E. R. AND BROWN, W.: Congenital miosis. Arch. of Ophthal., **65**:59, 1961.

WAARDENBERG, P. J.: Colobomas and aniridia associated with oligophrenia. Ned. T. Geneesh., **78**:1695, 1934.

WALSH, F. B.: *Loc. cit.*

CONGENITAL (HEREDITARY) NYSTAGMUS

Definition.—An hereditary nystagmus, which begins shortly after birth and persists throughout life.

Pathological Anatomy.—Nettleship suggests that there may be a congenital lack of pigmentation of the retinal epithelium in the region of the macula, but no post-mortem examinations have been made and the anatomical basis is still unknown.

Clinical Features.—Nettleship has found that in some stocks nystagmus is limited to males, but is directly transmitted only by females, behaving in this regard as if it were dependent upon a sex-linked recessive factor. In another group of pedigrees, the disease is transmitted by either sex, and affects females almost as frequently as males. In this second type, the nystagmus is frequently associated with oscillation of the head, which is rare or absent in the first group.

In some instances, it is claimed that the presence of nystagmus has been noted at birth. This has been reported in several cases in which the mother came of tainted stock and, therefore, examined the child at once. In most cases, perhaps, it is not noticed until the third or fourth months. Vision is almost invariably defective ranging on an average from 10/20 to 5/20. This is due, in part to the presence of an error of refraction usually hyperopic astigmatism, but sometimes myopic astigmatism. In very few cases, there is emmetropia and nearly normal vision. Nettleship has emphasized the connection between congenital nystagmus and pale pigmentation of the eye. He finds that the iris is usually blue or gray, and may present the picture of partial albinism. However, in several of his cases, the iris was brown. In some instances, the retinae show a visible lack of pigmentation, but this is not constant or even usual. The nystagmus is almost always rapid, bilateral, synchronous and equal in the two eyes. Moreover, when the eyes are in the primary position, it is horizontal and of pendular type, that is, the movements are of equal speed in either direction. On lateral deviation of the eyes, the nystagmus is of greater amplitude and rhythmical rather than pendular. The head movements are also horizontal and of about the same frequency as the nystagmus. These have been thought to be compensatory and to neutralize to some extent the ocular movements. Congenital vertical nystagmus is described. As the child grows older, there is a tendency for the nystagmus to diminish, and the head movements may apparently disappear.

Diagnosis.—The essential elements in the diagnosis may be given as follows: (1) The presence of nystagmus very early in life, before the sixth month at the latest. (2) The positive family history. (3) The elimination of other causes. No doubt, sporadic cases occur, and we have studied several cases which seemed to be typical except for the absence of a positive family history.

We must distinguish this type of congenital nystagmus from types due to congenital amblyopia, which is due to defects of the optic nerve, central scotomas, opacities in the media, microphthalmos, coloboma, pigmentary degenerations of the retinae, etc. The "searching movements" of blind eyes should be distinguished with ease since these movements are slow, irregular and of large amplitude. Spasmus nutans is most likely to be confused with congenital nystagmus for it is associated with head movements. However, spasmus nutans appear as a rule between the fourth and twelfth months, is often more pronounced in one eye or is confined to one eye, the head movements are not compensatory for the nystagmus and lastly, recovery invariably occurs, usually before the end of the third year.

Prognosis.—The nystagmus often becomes less conspicuous but rarely ceases. The head movements may diminish or apparently cease after some years.

Treatment.—The error of refraction should be corrected, but no other therapeutic measures are of established value.

BIBLIOGRAPHY

ALLEN, W.: Primary hereditary nystagmus. Jour. Hered., **33**:454, 1942.

COX, RONALD A.: Congenital head-nodding and nystagmus. Arch. Ophth., **15**:1032-1036, 1936.

FORSYTHE, W.: Congenital hereditary vertical nystagmus. J. Neurol., Neurosurg. & Psychiat., **18**:196, 1955.

NETTLESHIP, E.: On some cases of hereditary nystagmus. Tr. Ophth. Soc. U. Kingdom, London, **31**:159, 1911.

WALSH, F. B.: *Loc. cit.*

YAWGER, N. S.: Familial head-nystagmus in four generations associated with ocular nystagmus. J.A.M.A., **69**:773, 1917.

ALBINISM

Ocular albinism is manifest by white eyebrows and eyelashes, pink or pale gray irides, lack of pigment of the retinae, defective development of the maculae, rapid pendular nystagmus, myopia, frequent blinking, blepharospasm and photophobia due to transparency of the irides. Vision is usually defective. This is an inherited condition which may be recessive, sexlinked recessive or a dominant trait.

Total albinism is also described. Margolis reports the study of 14 individuals in a family of 5 generations who displayed total albinism involving the skin, hair and eyes, who were congenitally deaf and therefore mutes. Lack of pigment in the sensory cells of the labyrinths may have been responsible for the deafness. This was a sex-linked condition manifest only in the males but conveyed by the females.

Tietz also studied a family in which there was albinism of the skin and hair and blue eyes who were also deaf mutes. This was found to be a dominant condition. Some white cats with blue eyes are also congenitally deaf.

Other writers mention colobomata of the iris, absence of the sphincter of the iris with fixed pupils, extraocular muscle palsies and cataracts. Mental deficiency, sterility and anosmia are also mentioned.

Fitzpatrick has shown that albinism is due to lack of an enzyme, tyrosinase, in the melanocytes of the skin. These cells are present but do not contain the enzyme so tyrosin cannot be converted into melanin.

CASE HISTORY.—*Albinism with reduced vision, congenital nystagmus and mental deficiency*

J. L. S., a colored albino, was seen by the courtesy of Dr. Harry Butler. His mother was also an albino. A brother is a partial albino and mentally deficient. He has always had poor vision and nystagmus.

He was unable to get along at school. This was due to poor vision and to constant fighting with other pupils. It seems that he was not quarrelsome, but when he was teased, he would fight.

The intelligence quotient was estimated at 60. Ophthalmological examination revealed vision of 5/200 using both eyes. There was incomplete pigmentation of the retinae and of the irises. There was congenital nystagmus due to high grade myopia.

On examination the patient is well developed and muscular. He is cheerful and cooperative.

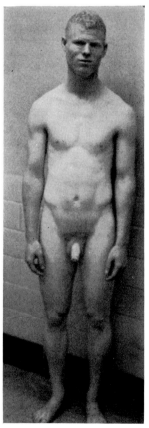

FIG. 29. Negro albino who is mentally deficient and has white skin, grayish white hair, pale gray irises, defective pigmentation of the retinae and vision of 5/200 with both eyes open.

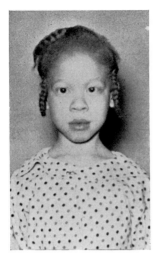

Fig. 30. Albino colored girl with congenital optic nystagmus. It is of interest that her 2 sisters are albinos and have nystagmus and that her 3 brothers are quite black and have no nystagmus. In her father's family all the males are black and the females albinos. (By the courtesy of Dr. Walsh.)

The hair is a very pale yellow, curly and thick. His eyelashes and eyebrows are also pale. The irides are pale gray. His body skin is very white. His sense of smell is intact. Hearing is good. Vision is reduced as mentioned above and he has pendular nystagmus of large amplitude.

There is no weakness, atrophy, tremor or ataxia. Speech is clear. No loss of sensibility is found. The station is steady and the gait is normal. The tendon reflexes are in order and the plantar reflexes are normal.

BIBLIOGRAPHY

CLARK, C. P.: Albinism with coexisting anomalies of the central nervous system. Trans. Amer. Ophthal. Soc., 42:250, 1944.

COCKAYNE, A. E.: Inherited abnormalities of the skin. Oxford Press. London, 1933, p. 78.

FITZPATRICK, T. B. AND LERNER, A. B.: Pigment and pigment tumors. Biochemical basis of human melanin pigmentation. A.M.A. Arch. Dermat., 69:133, 1954.

MARGOLIS, E.: Sex-linked deaf mutism associated with total albinism. Acta genet., 12:12, 1962.

PEARSON, K. et al.: Monograph on albinism in man. Biometric Series. Dulav. Co., London, 1911.

SORSBY, A.: Clinical Genetics. Mosby, St. Louis, p. 181, 1953.

TIETZ, W.: Syndrome of deaf-mutism associated with albinism. Amer. Jour. Genet., 15:259, 1963.

GILLESPIE, F. D.: Ocular albinism. A family with female carriers. Arch. of Ophthal., 66:774, 1961.

ZIPRKOWSKI, L.: Recessive total albinism and congenital deaf-mutism. Arch. Derm., 89:151, 1964.

————: Partial albinism and deaf-mutism due to a recessive sex linked gene. Arch. of Derm., 86:530, 1962.

CONGENITAL LACK OF LATERAL GAZE

(or Congenital Oculomotor Apraxia-Cogan)

Cogan has described a condition found in infants which he terms oculomotor apraxia. He has studied four cases and in one instance has kept the patient under observation up to the age of nine and a half years.

When the child is observed, spontaneous ocular movements are seen which appear to be normal, but when the child is asked to look to one side, for example to the right, it seems impossible for him to do so. He turns his face to the right so that the eyes are soon carried by the movement of the head into a position of left lateral deviation within the orbits. The turning of the head continues until, as a result of this excessive movement the eyes are finally passively brought to bear on the desired point. They remain fixed on this point while the head returns to such a position that the eyes finally attain the primary position. Thus, it seems that voluntary lateral movements of the eyes depend entirely upon movements of the head. This reaction occurs very rapidly and is not easy to analyse. Cogan has employed moving pictures to demonstrate it. Movements of the eyes in the vertical plane are not effected. This reaction occurs only in the horizontal plane.

Vestibular stimulation, it is said, causes tonic deviation of the eyes and not nystagmus. Opticokinetic nystagmus is lacking in the horizontal plane but present in the vertical plane.

This condition seems to be very similar to that described by Gordon Holmes as loss of volitional movements of the eyes and quite different from ocular apraxia as described by Holmes.

Cogan states that these children are slow to walk. Later in life, they are unable to make quick turns with proper facility and have difficulty in reading. This condition may be associated with other evidences of defective development of the nervous system or may occur as an isolated anomaly. I have seen one case in which there was associated loss of equilibrium and cerebellar ataxia. This child developed the ability to move her eyes to either side at the age of six years, though the movement was jerky and difficult. She was found to have no vestibular reflexes. A sibling who was mentally defective and had similar loss of lateral gaze was found at post-mortem examination to have absence of the vermis of the cerebellum.

BIBLIOGRAPHY

COGAN, D. C.: Oculomotor apraxia. Am. J. Ophth., **36**:433, 1953.
HOLMES, G. AND SMITH, S.: A case of bilateral motor apraxia. Brit. Med. J., **i**:437, 1916.
HOLMES, G.: The cerebral integration of ocular movements. Brit. Med. J., **ii**: 107, 1938.
REED, H. AND ISRAELS, S.: Congenital ocular motor apraxia. Brit. J. Ophth., **40**:444, 1956.

SPASMUS NUTANS

Definition.—A condition found only in infants and characterized by nystagmus head nodding and deviation of the head to one side. It is claimed that recovery invariably occurs without sequelae.

Etiology.—The cause of this condition is not entirely clear. Many writers, however, lay great stress on the fact that these children have almost without exception been kept in a dark room. It has been suggested that lack of light stimulation results in delayed development of optic fixation and hence, in nystagmus. Deficiencies of vitamins A and D have been also regarded as important. We have seen three cases in one family.

Clinical Features.—This condition is now rarely seen though, if one may judge by the literature, it was once very common. It is found, as a rule, between the ages of four and eighteen months and affects the two sexes alike.

Negro children seem to be especially prone to this disease. Sometimes the child has been kept in a dark room but in our experience this is not always true. The onset is usually in winter months.

Any one of the three cardinal symptoms may precede the others and may persist after the others have disappeared. The nystagmus may be horizontal, vertical, rotary or mixed. It may affect either one eye or both eyes. The rate is rapid and the amplitude is usually small. Fixation may increase the nystagmus but diminish the head movements.

The head nodding is usually inconstant occurring for a few seconds, ceasing and then returning. It is reduced or abolished by covering the eyes. Since it is absent when the child is lying down, the child must be placed in an upright position to demonstrate the nodding. It is generally agreed that the nodding bears no constant relation to the nystagmus in direction or rate so it cannot be compensatory.

In perhaps half of all cases, the child tilts the head to one side so the eyes must be deviated to permit fixation. The reason for this is not apparent.

The optic fundi seem to be normal. Syringing the ears with cold water has no effect on the nystagmus.

Diagnosis.—The diagnosis rests upon the presence of the three cardinal symptoms, the nystagmus which is often unilateral, the head nodding and the tilting of the head. It is found between the ages of four and eighteen months.

Congenital nystagmus is most apt to be confused with spasmus nutans. In this disease several members of the family are often affected and there is no tendency to improvement. The head movements are compensatory for the nystagmus. The nystagmus is often noted at birth or shortly after.

Prognosis.—The disease usually begins in the winter months and recovery usually occurs during the next summer. Almost invariably the symptoms have disappeared by the end of the second year. No sequelae are described. Dr. Walsh and I have seen one case in which the symptoms were still present at the age of four and a half years though they were less pronounced than they had been at one time.

Treatment.—The child should have sunlight, fresh air and abundant vitamins.

BIBLIOGRAPHY

Cox, R.: Congenital head nodding and nystagmus. Arch. Ophth., 15:1032, 1936.

Herrman, C.: Head shaking with nystagmus in infants. Am. J. Dis. Child., 16:180, 1918.

Hoefnagel, D. and Riery, B.: Spasmus nutans. Develop. Med. Child Neurol., 10:32, 1968.

Østerberg, G.: Spasmus nutans. Acta Ophth. Scandinav., 15:547, 1932.

Patersen, D. and Ellis, R. W. B.: Spasmus nutans as associated with defective lighting in the home. Lancet, 2:736, 1931.

Walsh, F. B.: *Loc. cit.*

HEREDITARY MYOKYMIA

This term is applied to spontaneous twitchings of small bundles of muscle fibers which are irregular in rate and extent and usually undulatory. Since such twitchings are not associated with atrophy of the muscles they have been termed benign in contrast to true spontaneous fasciculations which are often indicative of degeneration of the motor neurons.

Denny-Brown and Pennybacker have made a very helpful electromyographic study of these muscular twitchings. They show that true spontaneous fasciculations represent the single impulse contraction of those muscle fibers innervated by a single anterior horn motor neuron. Such contractions are most striking in cases of progressive spinal muscular atrophy. Myokymia, on the other hand, is evidenced by a short burst of action potentials rather than a single response. The physiological basis of myokymia is not yet known.

Myokymia has been known for many years. It is agreed that it does not cause any disability. It seems to be a static condition. Although it is rarely recognized in childhood, possibly because the subcutaneous fat is so thick, it is probably present throughout life. There is usually no history of myokymia in more than one member of a family, but Sheaff has studied a family in which the father and four sons were all affected. McKusick refers to a family in which multiple members are affected. This is apparently a dominant disease. History No. 917242.

The chief reason for mentioning this harmless condition is that it may be recognized and not confused with the true fasciculations which are so often ominous. The absence of muscular atrophy is of value in differential diagnosis. The diagnosis may be made by electromyographic study. Biopsy of a bit of muscle will show normal muscle fibers.

Denny-Brown and Foley describe another type of benign fasciculations which is associated with muscular cramps and is due to reduction of the serum sodium resulting from profuse diuresis or excessive sweating. This is manifest in the electromyogram by a single diphasic action potential of variable shape. Nervous tension seems to cause muscular twitchings, probably as a result of over-ventilation and loss of carbon dioxide.

BIBLIOGRAPHY

DENNY-BROWN, D. AND FOLEY, J. M.: Myokymia and benign fasciculations of muscular cramps. Tr. A. Am. Physicians, **61**:88, 1948.

———— AND PENNYBACKER, J. B.: Fibrillation and fasciculation in voluntary muscles. Brain, **61**:311, 1938.

McKUSIACK, V.: Mendelian Inheritance in Man. Johns Hopkins Press, Baltimore, 1966, p. 90, note 1577.

SHEAFF, H. M.: Hereditary myokymia. Arch. Neurol. & Psychiat., **68**:236, 1952.

HEREDITARY CHIN QUIVERING

In 1930, Frey published the result of a study of 100 persons all of whom were descendants of a single ancestor. Five generations were included. In 55 of these individuals, quivering of the muscles of the chin was present. As a rule, this began at birth and continued throughout life. In some, the quivering was constant, but in others, it would be observed only when the patient was emotionally disturbed. No other neurological disturbances were noted. The patients enjoyed good health. In 1938, Ganner published a second study including 33 cases in two families including five generations.

I have seen several cases of this peculiar condition and in one case, I was able to secure a history that chin quivering had been present in the previous generation. Dr. Lawson Wilkins has told me of a family in which this trait has been traced through three generations.

BIBLIOGRAPHY

Frey, E.: Ein streng dominant erbliches Kinnmuskelzittern. Duet. Ztschr. Nervenh. Bd. 115, s.9, 1930.
Ganner, H.: Erbliches Kinnzittern in eines Tiroler Tolschaft. Ztschr. ges. Neurol. u. Psychiat., 161:259, 1938.
Grossman, B. J.: Trembling of the chin. Pediatrics, 19:453, 1957.
Wadlington, W. B.: Familial trembling of the chin. Jour. Pediat., 53:316, 1958.

CONGENITAL INTERNAL HYDROCEPHALUS

Definition.—In its broad sense, hydrocephalus indicates merely the accumulation of fluid within the head. It is usually employed in a restricted sense, however, to apply to cases in which the fluid is under increased pressure as a result of obstruction of some part of the cerebrospinal fluid channels. Internal hydrocephalus indicates the accumulation of fluid under pressure in the ventricles of the brain.

Circulation of Cerebrospinal Fluid.—Much of our present knowledge of this subject is due to the fundamental work of Dandy and Weed.* These authors have demonstrated that the cerebrospinal fluid is produced almost entirely by the choroid plexuses, although it is possible that fluid originating from the perivascular spaces of the cortical vessels may contribute a small component. The fluid formed in the lateral ventricles flows through the foramina of Monro into the third ventricle, where it is increased by the contribution of the plexus of that ventricle and then passes through the aqueduct into the fourth ventricle. Here, another choroid plexus adds its component, and the fluid then flows into the cisterna magna through the foramina of Luschka and the foramen of Magendie. From the cisterna, the pathway leads anteriorly under the base and then up over the convexity

---

* It is only fair to say that the basic facts were established by Key and Retzius in 1876.

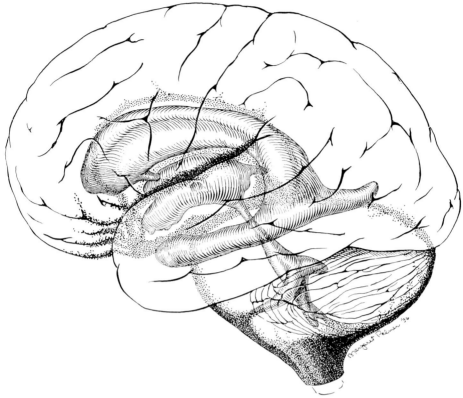

CHART 1. Diagram illustrating the relations of the ventricular system and subarachnoid spaces. (Redrawn from Dandy.)

in the sulci between the cortical convolutions. Weed has presented evidence to prove that the fluid is absorbed into the dural sinuses by way of the arachnoidal villi.

Pathological Anatomy.—The head is always greatly enlarged and of characteristic shape. The fontanels are of great size and the sutures separated. The cranial bones are very thin. The cortex of the brain shows flattening of the convolutions, and on section is found to be abnormally thin. The ventricular system is greatly dilated, and the septum lucidum stretched or torn. The choroid plexus almost invariably shows some degree of atrophy. These changes are, of course, the result of the accumulation of fluid in the ventricles under increased pressure.

The great distention of the ventricles and thinning of the cerebral cortex may in some instances cause rupture into the subarachnoid space. Pennybacker and Russell state that this is most apt to occur in the posterior part of the lateral ventricle between the fornix and the forceps. In some cases, the arachnoid is also ruptured, causing external hydrocephalus and perhaps, collapse of the cortex. Torkildsen reports cases in which the third ventricle ruptured either anteriorly or posteriorly. Rupture of the ependyma may lead to the formation of false diverticulae extending into the white matter. These may cause hemiplegia.

The cranial bones, especially those of the vault, are very thin and the sutures slow to close. The fontanels are very wide. Often, wormian bones form in the fontanels. Craniolacunae, the so-called lukenschadel are often seen. These seem to be regarded as developmental defects. False meningoceles may develop as a result of thinning of the bones and increased intracranial pressure. These must be distinguished from true meningoceles.

Our understanding of the mechanism by which this process is produced is almost entirely due to the brilliant work of Dandy, whose first contribution appeared in 1913. A great deal of important information had been accumulated before this date, but this was ill-correlated and imperfectly understood. Dandy has shown that almost all cases of hydrocephalus result from obstruction at some point in the cerebrospinal fluid pathways. In some cases, the obstruction is in the iter; in others, at the foramina of exit of the fourth ventricle, and, in a third type, in the cisternae of the basilar meninges. The first two types are termed non-communicating hydrocephalus, because dye injected into the ventricles is not recovered in the spinal fluid upon lumbar puncture. The third type is called communicating hydrocephalus, because dye introduced by ventricular puncture appears at once in the lumbar cul-de-sac.

Several types of lesions may be found in the aqueduct of Sylvius. In some cases, the canal has apparently never been properly formed. The sec-

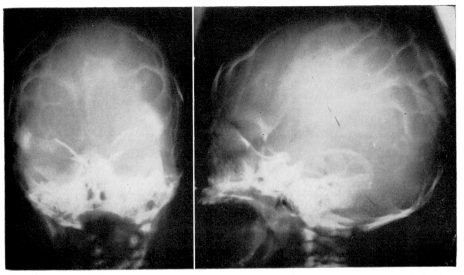

FIG. 31. Luckenschadel in an infant with a meningocele but no enlargement of the head. Ped. No. B-5667. (By the courtesy of Dr. Teasdall.)

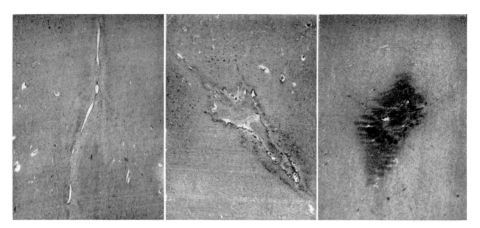

Fig. 32. Showing changes in the aqueduct of three different types. The first on the left has evidently never been properly formed and is represented by a narrow slit which is discontinuous in serial sections. The second seems to have been well formed and later occluded by proliferation of glial tissue. In both cases, however, there was hydrocephalus from birth. In the third illustration the aqueduct was closed by an inflammatory process and hydrocephalus developed as a result.

tions reveal merely a few strands of ependymal cells. There may be several small channels and minute cysts lined with ependyma, but these do not form a continuous canal. The term *atresia* is employed in such cases. Various types of spina bifida are often associated. In other cases, the aqueduct is well formed, but has been occluded. We have observed cases in which the obstruction was due to proliferation of the ependyma, and others in which a nodule of glial tissue had closed the canal. We may term this *gliosis* of the aqueduct. In rare cases, a thin, transparent membrane is found stretching across the canal, which is well formed and of large caliber. These lesions are described in articles by Dandy and others. In such cases, the hydrocephalus is limited to the lateral and third ventricles, and the fourth ventricle is not distended.

The foramina of Luschka and Magendie are the site of the obstruction in about one third of all cases of non-communicating hydrocephalus. The fourth ventricle is as much distended as the other parts of the ventricular system. Dandy has found two conditions in such cases. In one, the roof of the fourth ventricle is thin and transparent, but contains no openings, and, in the other, he finds thickening of the meninges and obliteration of the cisterna magna. It is probable that in the first case we are dealing with a failure of the foramina to develop, and, in the second case, with a similar failure of the cisterna magna to form. This has been termed the Dandy-Walker syndrome. In some instances, the middle and posterior parts of the cerebellar vermis are missing and the cerebellum is separated into two parts. This is regarded as a true cerebellar rachischisis.

Dandy was the first to offer an explanation of communicating hydrocephalus which was formerly called idiopathic hydrocephalus. He was able to show by injections of dyes into the ventricular system, that there was an obstruction to the circulation of cerebrospinal fluid under the base of the brain, so that the sulci over the convexity of the hemisphere could not be filled. Dandy has mentioned the possibility of intrauterine meningitis, but is inclined to believe that in most cases of congenital origin the arachnoid spaces have failed to develop. Since it is believed that the subarachnoid spaces are formed as a result of splitting of a solid mantle of mesenchyme which surrounds the developing brain, it seems quite possible that the interruption of this process at various stages might explain not only the communicating hydrocephalus, but even the non-communicating type in which the cisterna magna is absent. Russell thinks that meningeal hemorrhage at birth may be responsible in some cases. In a few cases occlusion of one foramen of Monro has caused dilatation of the lateral ventricle on the same side.

In certain cases of hydrocephalus, one finds the Arnold-Chiari malformation, q.v. *Spina bifida* q.v. is also very commonly associated. Cranium bifidum, absence of the corpus callosum, bilateral porencephaly, absence of the vermis of the cerebellum, malformations of the cerebral cortex and hydranencephaly q.v. are all found in association with hydrocephalus.

Certain bony anomalies which may cause hydrocephalus in infancy should be mentioned here. Platybasia is a well-known example and is often associated with other anomalies such as oxycephaly and the Klippel-Feil deformity. Chondrodystrophy is another condition and osteopetrosis is a third. The mechanism by which hydrocephalus is produced in such conditions is not entirely clear. It has been suggested that the posterior fossa is malformed or too small and the flow of fluids is thus interrupted.

So far the discussion has been limited to hydrocephalus due to obstruction and consequent failure of absorption of the cerebrospinal fluid. There is no doubt that congenital hydrocephalus is almost always of this type. A few cases have been reported in which hydrocephalus has been found in association with hypertrophy of the choroid plexus and it is believed that the hydrocephalus is due to increased production of cerebrospinal fluid in such instances. A case of this type is given in abstract below.

An excellent paper has been written by Dorothy Russell in which a complete discussion of the pathology of congenital hydrocephalus is given.

Etiology.—We must conclude therefore that congenital hydrocephalus is due to obstruction of the circulation of the cerebrospinal fluid at any part in its course, chiefly as a result of defective development of the proper channels and that in consequence of this obstruction, the fluid accumulates under pressure causing dilatation of the ventricular system with atrophy of the brain and enlargement of the head. Granholm and Radberg believe that organization of meningeal hemorrhage due to birth injury is the commonest cause of congenital communicating hydrocephalus.

Occasionally there is a history of other cases of hydrocephalus in the family. Bichers and Adams report a case of atresia of the aqueduct and state that there was a history of 6 other cases in the family in two generations. All of these were in males. Gellman states that seven cases are on record in which both of a pair of identical twins had congenital hydrocephalus. Edwards points out that sex linked hydrocephalus has been found in seven families. In three instances post-mortem examination revealed stenosis of the aqueduct.

Clinical Features.—In very severe cases, the child may die *in utero,* or the head may be so large at term that birth is impossible. In the majority of

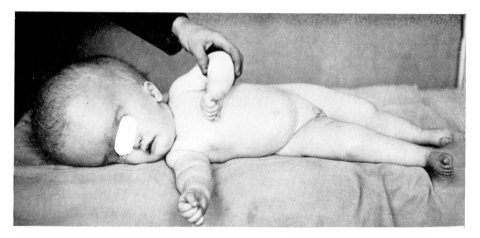

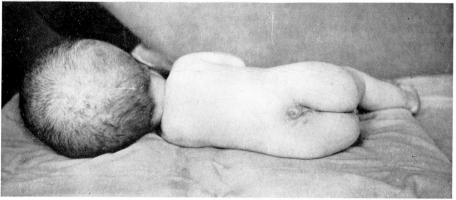

Fig. 33. Front and back views of a case of severe congenital hydrocephalus with spina bifida. The child was quite blind from optic atrophy and the extremities were weak and spastic. The tonic neck reflexes of Magnus were easily elicited as is suggested in the upper photograph. (By courtesy of Dr. Dandy.)

cases, the head is of normal size at birth, or only slightly enlarged. Dandy has shown that the ventricles may be greatly dilated in a newborn baby whose head is of approximately normal size. No doubt, the intrauterine pressure tends to present expansion of the skull. When the child is two or three months old, however, it is noted that the head is enlarging at an abnormal rate. In place of growing about one half inch a month in circumference, the head may expand one or two inches during this period. At the same time, the fontanels are found to be rather tense and show no tendency to close, the sutures are widened and the veins of the scalp are much distended. The head soon assumes a very characteristic shape with uniform increase in the vertical, lateral and anteroposterior diameters. The roof of the orbit is depressed, causing the bulbs to be pushed downward and outward. Roentgenograms reveal atrophy of the skull with "digital markings" over the vault, separation of the sutures and widening of the fontanels. Wormian bones may form in the suture line. In both, the communicating type and the type due to obstruction at the foramina of the fourth ventricle, the measurement from the spinous process of the second vertebra to

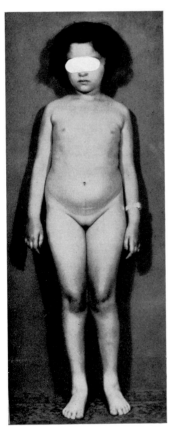

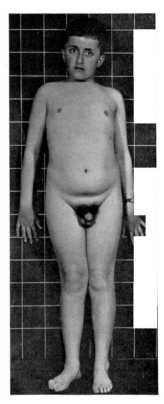

Fig. 34. (left) Photograph of a child of nine years whose head grew with abnormal rapidity in early infancy. After the first year the process became arrested and there were no symptoms until a few months before the patient came under observation, when violent headaches and vomiting developed, followed by reduction of vision. There was high grade papilledema. Ventriculographic study and operation revealed obstructive hydrocephalus which was apparently of congenital origin.

Fig. 35. (right) This child suffered from congenital internal hydrocephalus. At the age of two years third ventriculostomy was performed. At the age of nine years sexual development began. Photograph was made at age of 12 years.

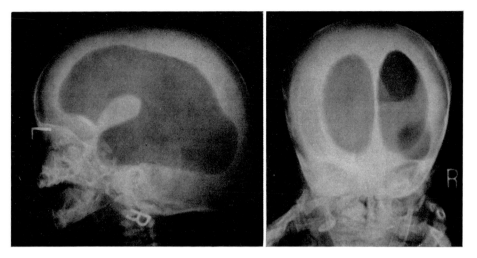

Fig. 36. Ventriculogram in a case of congenital hydrocephalus early in infancy.

the inion is increased, showing that the posterior fossa shares in the general enlargement. Since this distance is not increased in hydrocephalus due to obstruction of the aqueduct, the site of the lesion may sometimes be determined by inspection.

Obstruction of the foramen of Monro causes dilatation of the lateral ventricle on one side. This may result in bulging of the temple.

In some cases in which the head is very heavy and the bones soft and plastic the shape of the head may be moulded by pressure on the pillow so it may become flattened on the sides or asymmetrical.

We have already mentioned that a large variety of congenital defects may be associated with congenital hydrocephalus. The most common abnormalities seen in this connection are midline cranial and spinal defects associated with meningocele and, often malformations of the nervous system, such as spina bifida and cranium bifidum. The Arnold-Chiari deformity and platybasia should be mentioned here. Hydrocephalus is also associated with certain bony conditions such as osteopetrosis and with chondrodystrophia.

Sajid and Copple describe familial aqueductal stenosis associated with basilar impression.

A number of nervous symptoms result. The child is usually lethargic and dull, lying quietly in bed with little interest in its surroundings. If the process is rapid, there may be papilledema, but this is unusual, for the skull expands so easily that the intracranial pressure is never greatly elevated. Optic atrophy is the rule, but in mild cases this is incomplete or even absent. The bulbs may be displaced downward as a result of depression of the roof of the orbit. Sixth nerve palsies are sometimes seen. Inability to look up is present in some cases and may be associated with retraction of the upper lids. The legs are often spastic, and the arms may also be affected in the same manner, although usually not so severely as the legs. The tendon reflexes are moderately increased, and, in some cases, extensor reactions on plantar stimulation are elicited. In certain cases, cerebellar ataxia is present and may be more striking than the spasticity. I have observed this especially in cases in which hydrocephalus has followed meningitis. The child often cannot hold up the head because of the great weight of the fluid it contains. Convulsions are not uncommon. Nevertheless, children with heads of great size and atrophy of the cortex of high degree may show extraordinarily few neurological disturbances. They may learn to walk and talk and display evidences of moderate intellectual development.

The writer has been interested to observe a striking development of auditory memory in children who are quite blind and helpless. One child, whose head was enormous and whose cortex was found to be about one centimeter thick at autopsy, could recognize a large number of relatives by their voice, recite some fifty nursery rhymes without error, and rarely failed to remember the names of numerous physicians who examined him.

It is not unusual for obesity to occur often in association with delay in sexual development. Rarely sexual precocity is observed. No doubt, these phenomena are a result of damage to the hypothalamus.

If the progress of the disease is rapid, the child will often die during the first year of intercurrent infection or malnutrition, but in some cases the process seems to become arrested or partially arrested, and the patient may survive for indefinite periods. No doubt atrophy of the choroid plexus is responsible. In such cases, the child may go through life with more or less mental defect, optic atrophy and spastic paraparesis. Schick and Matson state that complete arrest of hydrocephalus is probably very rare, and, in most cases in which this diagnosis is made, there is a slow progression of the process.

It should be mentioned that ventricular puncture may be followed by a sudden aggravation of the symptoms due presumably to increased secretion of cerebrospinal fluid. Such a reaction is often difficult to control and may be fatal. Probably it can occur only in those cases in which the choroid plexus has not become grossly atrophic.

In rare cases, the symptoms of congenital hydrocephalus may be delayed until late childhood. We have observed the sudden development of signs of increased intracranial pressure in children of various ages, in whom, during infancy, the head was very slightly enlarged, who were somewhat slow in learning to walk, but who showed no signs nor symptoms sufficient to justify the diagnosis of hydrocephalus during the first few years of life. At operation, or autopsy, in such cases, the lesions are found to be identical

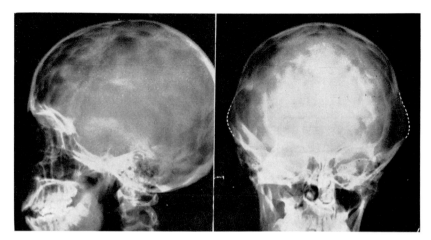

Fig. 37. Hydocephalus developing in childhood due to atresia of the aqueduct. All the sutures were firmly fused except the sphenoid temporal so the temples bulged out though the rest of the skull did not distend.

with those of congenital hydrocephalus. We have found occlusion of the aqueduct, closure of the foramina of the fourth ventricle and the Arnold-Chiari malformation in cases in which the onset of symptoms was delayed sometimes as late as the sixteenth year. We must assume, apparently, that the obstruction was incomplete at first and later as a result of fibrosis became complete or that a compensation or equilibrium between absorption and secretion was established for a time and that this later broke down. The cases in which the aqueduct becomes closed are often designated by the term *stricture of the aqueduct*. The symptoms are much more severe in such cases in which pressure develops after the cranial sutures are united and papilledema and vomiting often occur. This is, no doubt, due to the fact that the skull cannot expand, and the intracranial pressure reaches a much higher level than it does in the hydrocephalus of infants.

Guillaume and Roge state that in 15 young patients with hydrocephalus there were 4 who had small stature, 1 with gigantism, 4 with obesity, 4 with delayed puberty, 2 with absent secondary sexual characteristics, 3 with menstrual irregularity, 2 with glycosuria and 1 with diabetes insipidus and sleep disturbance. Precocious puberty may also be associated with hydrocephalus.

Diagnosis.—Congenital hydrocephalus should always be considered in the case of an infant with a large head. If one cannot be sure of the diagnosis when the child is first seen, further observation and repeated measurements of the head will soon reveal whether or not abnormal growth of the cranium is taking place. One should always keep in mind the possibility of brain tumor, abscess of the brain, intracranial granuloma, thrombosis of the dural sinuses, toxoplasmosis, subdural hematoma, syphilitic meningitis, chronic basilar meningitis, ependymitis, rickets, macrocephaly and chondro-dystrophia. Hydrocephalus may also occur in osteogenesis imperfecta, osteo-petrosis, basilar impression and chondrodystrophy. The so-called *pseudo-hydrocephalus* may be confusing. This term is applied to a condition seen in some premature babies whose heads grew with great rapidity during a pe-riod between the second and the eighth months after birth. During this time, a striking disproportion may be apparent between the size of the head and the body so hydrocephalus is suspected. After the eighth month, this disproportion rapidly diminishes and is said to disappear before the third year. Ventriculography, of course, offers an easy means to determine the presence or absence of hydrocephalus though it does not necessarily reveal the cause. The test is not without danger and should be made only by a neurosurgeon. Usually only a bubble of air is injected and this is moved about by posturing the head so as to outline the ventricles. The possibility of Arnold-Chiari deformity must always be kept in mind especially when there is a meningomyelocele.

It should not be forgotten that symptoms of hydrocephalus may appear or may be aggravated years after birth in such a way as to suggest brain tumor.

Treatment.—Dandy devised a number of surgical procedures for the re-lief of hydrocephalus. In cases of non-communicating hydrocephalus he opened the posterior part of the third ventricle for it was found that it was difficult to restore the aqueduct or the foramina of the fourth ventri-cle. In communicating hydrocephalus he would remove the choroid plex-uses of the lateral ventricles. Though excellent results were attained in cer-tain cases, such procedures failed completely as a rule.

In recent years, rubber or polyethylene catheters, or Torkildsen tubes, have been employed. Ingraham and Matson describe these methods fully. In cases in which the obstruction is in the aqueduct or posterior part of the third ventricle, the tube is carried from the lateral ventricle into the cis-terna magna. This is sometimes unsatisfactory in infants when the sub-arachnoid spaces are imperfectly developed. In such cases a long tube may be carried down the back and inserted in the ureter. In cases of communi-cating hydrocephalus, a tube may be placed in the spinal canal and the oth-er end placed in the ureter. When the spinal fluid is drained into the ureter, the child loses salt and must be given 2 grams of sodium chloride a day. When the foramina of Monro are obstructed, both ventricles must be drained or the septum pellucidum punctured. Harsh suggests that in fe-males drainage may be made into the Fallopian tube. Dr. George Smith has placed the tube in the gall bladder. The tube may be placed in the jugular vein and pushed into the right side of the heart.

Emory and Hilton state that treatment of hydrocephalus by shunting the excess cerebrospinal fluid into the heart by means of the Spitz-Holter valve leads to occlusion of the veins entering the heart, thrombus formation around the catheter, or on the wall of the atrium, local carditis, pulmonary emboli, mycotic aneurysms, periarteritis and intimal degeneration. Meningitis and pneumonia are also mentioned.

These operations are frequently successful for a time but there is reason to think that the tubes are apt to become obstructed eventually. It should be mentioned that operation for hydrocephalus may result in subdural hematoma, possibly because the release of pressure in the ventricles causes the brain to collapse and fall away from the dura so the veins connecting the cortex and the dural sinuses may be stretched and ruptured.

Moseley, *et al.* describe thickening of the skull when a patient with hydrocephalus has effective shunting. The sutures may close prematurely. If the shunt then fails to function, a dangerous situation may develop.

In cases in which the hydrocephalus is a result of the Arnold-Chiari deformity, the posterior margin of the foramen magnum and the arches of the first four laminae are removed. In platybasia, a similar operation is advised. Perhaps operations of this type might be helpful in chondrodystrophia and osteopetrosis, though in chondrodystrophy, the hydrocephalus is apt to become arrested eventually.

CASE HISTORY (Path. 14946. U-72729).—*Child of five months developed rapidly progressive hydrocephalus. Operation disclosed bilateral hypertrophy of the choroid plexus of the lateral ventricles without any obstruction of the cerebrospinal fluid system.*

I. C. was born at full term by normal labor. He seemed to be quite healthy, until the age of 5 months, when his head began to grow at an abnormal rate. He became irritable and ceased to make progress in holding up his head. It is of interest that a maternal aunt had two children who died in infancy with very large heads.

Examination on September 11, 1936, when the child was 6 months old, revealed a typically hydrocephalic head which measured 45.5 cm in occipitofrontal circumference. The fontanels were abnormally wide and tense. Neurological examination was otherwise negative. Dye injected into the spinal subarachnoid space was recovered promptly from both lateral ventricles and the dye was excreted in the urine just as rapidly as in a normal baby. Apparently there was no obstruction and absorption was normal.

Operation disclosed great masses of choroid plexus in both lateral ventricles. These were removed as completely as possible but hemorrhage occurred and the child died. Post-mortem examination revealed that the entire ventricular system including the aqueduct and the fourth ventricle was uniformly dilated. There was no obstruction in any part of the system. The choroid plexus was tremendously hypertrophied and had apparently caused hydrocephalus by excessive secretion.

BIBLIOGRAPHY

ANDERSON, F. M.: Subdural hematoma as complication of operation for hydrocephalus. Pediatrics, **10**:11, 1952.

BENDA, C. E.: The Dandy-Walker syndrome. So-called atresia of the foramen of Magendie. J. Neuropath. Exp. Neurol., **13**:14, 1954.

BICKERS, D. S. AND ADAMS, R. D.: Hereditary stenosis of the aqueduct of Sylvius as a cause of congenital hydrocephalus. Brain, **72**:246, 1949.

CHONG-SANG, K. *et al.:* Primary amenorrhea secondary to non-communicating hydrocephalus. Neurology, **19**:533, 1969.

CROSBY, R., MOSBERG, W. AND SMITH, G.: Intrauterine meningitis as a cause of hydrocephalus. J. Pediat., **39**:94, 1951.

D'AGOSTINO, A. N. *et al.:* The Walker-Dandy syndrome. Jour. Neuropath. and Exp. Neurol., **22**:450, 1963.

DANDY, W. E. AND BLACKFAN, K. D.: An experimental and clinical study of internal hydrocephalus, J.A.M.A., **61**:2216, 1913.

————: Internal hydrocephalus, an experimental, clinical and pathological study. Am. J. Dis. Child., **8**:406, 1914.

————: Internal hydrocephalus. Am. J. Dis. Child., **8**:569, 1918.

————: Extirpation of the choroid plexus of the lateral ventricles in communicating hydrocephalus. Ann. Surg., **68**:569, 1918.

————: Experimental hydrocephalus. Ann. Surg., **70**:129, 1919.

————: Diagnosis and treatment of hydrocephalus due to occlusion of the foramina of Magendie and Lushka. Surg. Gynec. & Obst., **32**:112, 1921.

————: Diagnosis and treatment of hydrocephalus resulting from strictures of the aqueduct of Sylvius. Surg. Gynec. & Obst., **31**:340, 1920.

————: The cause of the so-called idiopathic hydrocephalus. Bull. Johns Hopkins Hosp., **32**:57, 1921.

————: Operative procedure for hydrocephalus. Bull. Johns Hopkins Hosp., **33**:189, 1932.

DAVIS, L. E.: Physiologic study of the choroid plexus; a case of villous hypertrophy. J. M. Research, **44**:521, 1924.

D'ERRICO, A.: Surgical procedure for hydrocephalus associated with spinal bifida. Surgery, **4**:856-866, 1938.

EDWARDS, J. H.: Sex-linked Hydrocephalus: Report of a family with 15 affected members. Arch. Dis. Childhood, **36**:481, 486, 1961.

————: The syndrome of sex-linked hydrocephalus. Arch. of Dis. Childh., **36**:486, 1961.

EMORY, J. L. AND HILTON, H. B.: Complications of ventriculoauriculostomy. Surgery, **50**:309, 1961.

GELLMAN, V.: Congenital hydrocephalus in monovular twins. Arch. of Dis. Childh., **34**:274, 1959.

GRANHOLM, L. AND RADBERG, C.: Congenital communicating hydrocephalus. Jour. Neurosurgery, **20**:338, 1963.

GUILLAUME, J. AND ROGE, R.: Troubles neuroendocriniens et hydrocephalie chronique. Rev. Neurol., **82**:424, 1950.

HARSH, G. R.: Peritoneal shunt for hydrocephalus utilizing the fimbria of the Fallopian tube. J. Neurosurg., **11**:284, 1954.

HOLT, E. AND McINTOSH, R.: Diseases of Infancy and Childhood. New York, Appleton-Century, p. 136, 1940.

INGRAHAM, F. D. AND MATSON, D. D.: Neurosurgery of Infancy and Childhood. Springfield, Thomas, 1954.

KAHN, E. A. AND LAUROS, J. T.: Hydrocephalus from overproduction of cerebrospinal fluid. J. Neurosurg., **9**:59, 1952. (one case cured)

KERNOHAN, J. W.: Cortical anomalies, ventricular heterotopies and occlusion of the aqueduct of Sylvius. Arch. Neurol. & Psychiat., **23**:460, 1930.

KEY AND RETZIUSS: Onatomie des Nerven systems und des Bindesgewebe. P. A. Norstedt & söner, Stockholm, 1876.

LAURENCE, K. M. AND COATES, S.: The natural course of hydrocephalus. Arch. Dis. Childhood, **37**:345, 1962.

————: Neurological and intellectual sequelae of hydrocephalus. Archives of Neurology, **20**:73, 1969.

LICHTENSTEIN, B. W.: Distant neuroanatomic complications of spina bifida. Hydrocephalus, Arnold-Chiari deformity, stenosis of the aqueduct of Sylvius, *etc.* Pathogenesis and pathology. Arch. Neurol. & Psychiat., **47**:195, 1942.

LIST, C. F.: Neurologic syndromes accompanying developmental anomalies of the occipital bone, atlas, and axis. Arch. Neurol. & Psychiat., **45**:577, 1941.

MATSON, D. D.: Hydrocephalus in a premature infant caused by papilloma of the choroid plexus. J. Neurosurg., **10**:416, 1953.

McCONNELL, A. A. AND PARKER, H. L.: Deformity of hind-brain associated with internal hydrocephalus. Its relation to Arnold-Chiari malformation. Brain, **61**:415-429, 1938.

MOSELEY, H. F. *et al.:* Hyperostosis cranii ex vacuo. Radiology, **87**:1105, 1966.

NUSSEY, A. M.: Osteopetrosis. Arch. Dis. Child., **13**:161, 1938.

OGRYZLO, M. A.: The Arnold-Chiari malformation. Arch. Neurol. & Psychiat., **48**:30, 1942.

OVERTON, M. C., III AND SNODGRASS, S. R.: Ventriculo-venous shunts in infantile hydrocephalus. Jour. Neurosurg., **23**:517, 1965.

PENNYBACKER, J. AND RUSSELL, D.: Spontaneous rupture in hydrocephalus with subtentorial cyst formation. J. Neurol. & Psychiat., **6**:38, 1943.

ROBACK, H. N. AND GERSTLE, M. L.: Congenital atresia and stenosis of the aqueduct of Sylvius. Arch. Neurol. & Psychiat., **36**:248, 1936.

RUSSELL, D.: Observations on the pathology of hydrocephalus. Medical Research Council Special report series No. 265. London, His Majesty's Stat. Off., 1949.

RUSSELL, D. S. AND DONALD, C.: The mechanism of hydrocephalus in spina bifida (Arnold-Chiari malformation) . Brain, **58**:203, 1935.

RUSSELL, D. AND NORTHFIELD, D. W. C.: False diverticulae of the lateral ventricle causing hemiplegia in internal hydrocephalus. Brain, **62**:311, 1939.

SAJID, M. H. AND COPPLE, P. J.: Familial aqueductal stenosis and basilar impression. Neurology, **18**:260, 1968.

SCHICK, R. W. AND MATSON, D. D.: What is arrested hydrocephalus? J. Pediat., **58**:791, 1961.

SHELDON, W. D., PARKER, H. L. AND KERNOHAN, J. W.: Occlusion of the aqueduct of Sylvius. Arch. Neurol. & Psychiat., **23**:1183, 1930.

SPERLING, D. R., *et al.:* Cor pulmonale in hydrocephalic drainage. Am. J. Dis. Child., **107**:308, 1964.

TORKILDSEN, A.: Ventriculocisternostomy. A palliative operation in different types of non-communicating hydrocephalus. Oslo, Johan Grundt Tanum Forlag, 1947.

————: Spontaneous rupture of the cerebral ventricles. J. Neurosurg., **5**:327, 1948.

HYDRANENCEPHALY

Definition.—A condition in which the cerebral cortex is absent at birth though the cranium and meninges are intact.

Etiology.—Several theories have been advanced to explain this condition. Since there is almost always progressive enlargement of the head, the aqueduct is usually occluded and there are remnants of the cortex at the base, it has been suggested that it is merely congenital hydrocephalus which has run its course in utero. It is assumed that the intrauterine pressure has pre-

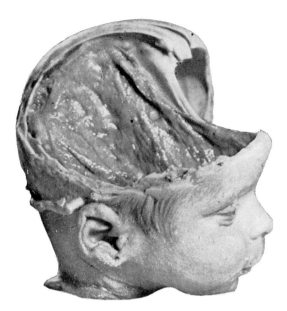
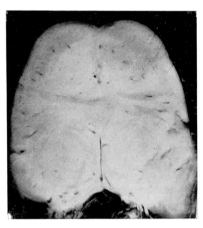

Fig. 38. Photograph of the head of a child with hydranencephaly and section through the midbrain (Path. 12146). The skull and meninges were intact. The cortex was represented by a transparent membrane composed of glial fibers. On the left side this membrane was intact, but on the right it had ruptured and collapsed. The basal portions of the frontal, temporal and occipital lobes were partially preserved. The third ventricle could be distinguished. The corpora striata were absent but the thalami and the hypothalamus were present. The brain stem was small and the pyramids and peduncles imperfectly developed. The cerebellum was small and its cortex immature. The aqueduct was plugged by a mass of glial tissue. Sections of the spinal cord revealed that the pyramidal tracts were absent.

vented the enlargement of the head before birth. Others regard this condition as a developmental defect and have termed it schizencephaly. It has also been interpreted as a form of bilateral porencephaly resulting from great vascular lesions. Possibly the cause is not always the same.

Pathological Anatomy.—The meninges are intact. The cerebral cortex is represented by a thin, transparent membrane composed of glial cells and fibers except for the base of the frontal, temporal and occipital lobes which are in a better state of preservation. Islands of cortex are sometimes found elsewhere. The corpora striata are absent, but the thalami though small are almost invariably present. The third ventricle is present. The brain stem is preserved though the descending tracts may be absent. The optic nerves appear to be atrophic but are present. The other cranial nerves are preserved. The cerebellum is usually grossly intact. The cerebral arteries are small but it is stated that they may be seen to pulsate at operation. The cranium is filled with clear fluid which may in some cases contain a slight excess of protein. The choroid plexus is preserved. There is atresia of the aqueduct in many cases. The adrenal glands are small.

Lindenberg and Swanson report a study of 5 cases in which extensive softening of the brain occurred in infancy. The softening was confined to the tissue supplied by the anterior and middle cerebral arteries. The suggestion is made that swelling of the brain resulted in compression of the carotid arteries and the resulting softening. At post-mortem examination the brains resembled those of babies with hydranencephaly. The carotid arteries were not occluded.

Clinical Features.—The head is usually of normal size and shape at birth but may be somewhat enlarged. During the first week or two, the baby is almost always regarded as normal. Nursing, breathing and movements of the extremities may seem to be normal. Hamby mentions the case of a child with hydranencephaly who was adopted at the age of one week after being declared by a pediatrician to be a normal baby. Within a short time, however, it becomes evident that the child is grossly defective. The extremities grow rigid, there are tonic fits and tremors. The tendon reflexes become brisk. The Moro reflex grows too active. Incoordinate movements of the eyes are seen. The baby is very irritable and may cry for hours at a time. Temperature control may be defective. No normal voluntary movements are ever seen. The pupils may react to light but there is never any evidence of vision. The optic discs may appear to be normal or may be small and

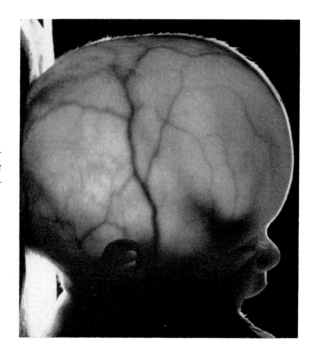

Fig. 39. (B-7518) Hydranenceph-aly. Transillumination of the skull. (By courtesy of Dr. William Faeth and Dr. David Clark.)

pale. The head begins to enlarge within a few weeks or months. Hamby has observed two cases in one family.

Halsey *et al.* report a study of 11 cases and emphasize the persistence of infantile reactions such as the Moro reflex, the grasp reflex and the stepping reflex. They also describe a form of rigidity suggestive of bilateral hemiplegia which they term dystonia.

The cracked pot sound is easily elicited. Subdural puncture yields clear spinal fluid when the needle has penetrated only a few millimeters beyond the meninges. The electroencephalogram reveals absence of electrical activity except over any island of cortex which may remain. Ventricular air injection makes the diagnosis clear for the whole cranium is filled with air and no cortex is visible. Hamby points out that a very simple and helpful test is transillumination of the head. The whole cranium lights up and only the falx is visible.

Prognosis.—These children rarely live more than a few weeks or a month or two, but Hamby mentions one which lived for three and a half years.

BIBLIOGRAPHY

ALEXANDER, E. *et al.*: Hydranencephaly. Observations on transillumination of the heads of infants. Arch. Neurol. & Psychiat., **76**:578, 1956.

YAKOLEV, E. H.: Schizencephalies. J. Neuropath. & Exp. Neurol., **5**:116, 1946.

COHN, R. AND NEWMAN, M.: Porencephaly. J. Neuropath. & Exp. Neurol., **5**:257, 1946.

HALSEY, J. H. *et al.*: Chronic decerebrate state in infancy. Arch. of Neurol., **19**:339, 1968.

HAMBY, W. B., KRAUSS, R. AND BESWICK, W.: Hydranencephaly. Clinical diagnosis. Pediatrics, **6**:371, 1950.

JOHNSON, E. AND WARNER, M.: Total absence of the cerebral hemispheres. J. Pediat., **38**:69, 1951.

LINDENBERG, R. AND SWANSON, P. D.: Infantile hydranencephaly: A report of 5 cases of infantile infarction of both cerebral hemispheres in infancy. Brain, **90**:839, 1967.

MARBURG, O. AND CASAMAJOR, L.: Phlebostasis and phlebothrombosis in the newborn. Arch. Neurol. & Psychiat., **52**:170, 1944.

OLIVE, J. T. AND DUSHANE, J. W.: Hydranencephaly. Am. J. Dis. Child., **85**:43, 1953.

SHURTLEFF, B.: Transillumination of the skull in infants. Am. J. Dis. Child., **107**:14, 1964.

WATSON, E. H.: Hydranencephaly. Report of two cases which combine the features of hydrocephalus and anencephaly. Am. J. Dis. Child., **67**:282, 1944.

THE ARNOLD-CHIARI MALFORMATION

Definition.—This is a downward displacement of the hindbrain with herniation of the medulla and cerebellum into the cervical canal. It is believed to be of intrauterine origin.

Pathological Anatomy.—A tongue-like process composed of cerebellum and medulla containing the inferior part of the fourth ventricle projects through the foramen magnum into the cervical canal. The hindbrain is elongated. These structures are sometimes packed so tightly into the spinal canal that there is obstruction to the outflow of the cerebrospinal fluid from the fourth ventricle and hydrocephalus may result. Compression of the medulla and the spinal cord may also occur in some instances. The last four cranial nerves may be stretched and the cervical spinal nerve roots as well. The cervical roots slope upward to their foramina of exit in place of downward as is usual. Hydromyelia is sometimes found. In some cases there is spina bifida often with meningomyelocele. The conus is usually fixed in the sacrum as a result of the spina bifida, and the cord has not ascended as it normally does in early life. The cauda equina is very short and the lumbar roots pass horizontally to the corresponding intervertebral foramina.

Lichtenstein has claimed that the descent of the hindbrain into the cervical canal is due to anchoring of the conus in the sacrum by the spina bifida with resulting traction on the hindbrain as the spinal column grows longer. This is a very attractive hypothesis, for it offers an acceptable explanation for the anatomical findings in most cases. Russell however, objects that the Arnold-Chiari deformity is not found in every case in which the spinal cord is tethered in the sacrum by spina bifida, and spina bifida is not clinically demonstrable in all cases of Arnold-Chiari deformity. None of the last mentioned cases seem to have had complete post-mortem examination, however. Gardner suggests that it is the pressure from above due to hydrocephalus which is the chief cause of the descent of the hindbrain. Feigin describes three cases in which the colliculi formed a conical projection backward overlying the pons and the cerebellum. He believes that this represents a malformation similar to the deformity of the cerebellum and medulla.

Clinical Features.—The most common clinical manifestations of the Arnold-Chiari deformity is congenital internal hydrocephalus. The association of spina bifida with congenital hydrocephalus is strongly suggestive of this condition. Russell states that in her experience the Arnold-Chiari deformity is invariably found when hydrocephalus is associated with meningomyelocele.

Occasionally, congenital hydrocephalus occurs in this condition, without any clinical or roentgenographic evidence of spina bifida.

Russell states that the hydrocephalus is of the communicating type, but Gardner states that it is usually obstructive. He says that air injected in the spinal subarachnoid space stops at the foramen magnum and does not reach the ventricles. Lichtenstein describes stenosis of the aqueduct in one case. MacFarlane and Maloney found obstruction of the aqueduct in 10 cases due to a congenital malformation and in 9 cases the hydrocephalus was due to compression of the posterior part of the fourth ventricle.

In some cases, the hydrocephalus does not develop in infancy but is delayed until the sutures of the skull have fused. As a result, the head is not

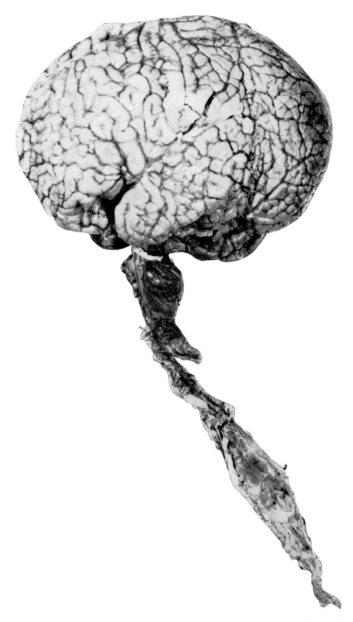

Fig. 40. Congenital hydrocephalus with Arnold-Chiari deformity and meningomyelocele. The deformity extended down to the fifth cervical vertebra and almost all of the cerebellum was within the spinal canal. (By the courtesy of Dr. Arthur King.)

enlarged and the hydrocephalus is manifest merely by headache and papil-ledema.

In cases such as those of Bucy and Lichtenstein, and Swanson and Finch-er, there is no evidence of increased intracranial pressure.

In certain cases, there has been evidence of damage to the medulla or upper segments of the spinal cord resulting in varying degrees of tetraple-gia. Several possible causes must be mentioned. There may be compression of the neuraxis by the wedging of the tissues into the narrow canal possibly aggravated by distention of the fourth ventricle when hydrocephalus is present. Stretching of the cord might also play a role. Bony deformities of the foramen magnum associated with platybasia may also be responsible. Syringomyelic cavities are sometimes found at this level and developmental defects of the cord associated with spina bifida and Klippel-Feil deformity. Since decompression often gives good results, it seems that compression is sometimes responsible. Palsies of the last four cranial nerves due to a stretching may be mentioned at this point.

Cerebellar ataxia and increased intracranial pressure may be the only clinical manifestations of this condition. We have observed cerebellar ataxia with vertical nystagmus and papilledema in two children. The onset was at the ages of 11 and 14 years. No evidence of spina bifida was present. Excellent results were obtained by operation.

In addition to spina bifida and cranium bifidum which are so often found in association with the Arnold-Chiari deformity, various other bony anomalies such as platybasia, deformities of the foramen magnum and the Klippel-Feil deformity may also occur.

Treatment.—The posterior margin of the foramen magnum and the arches of the first four vertebrae are removed. In some instances, the hydro-cephalus is relieved and evidences of compression of the spinal cord may disappear. In general, neurosurgeons report favorable results as regards the symptoms due to compression.

CASE HISTORY (No. 399309).—*Girl of 16 years with delayed sexual de-velopment showed unsteadiness, ataxia and nystagmus. Arnold-Chiari de-formity found at operation. Excellent result.*

E. S., a girl of 16 years, was admitted to the hospital on October 3, 1946. Some 18 months before she had begun to complain of headaches and at about the same time began to vomit frequently. During the next few months she became increasingly unsteady on her feet and somewhat clum-sy in the use of her hands. There were no other complaints but it was elicited that the child had never menstruated.

On examination the patient appeared to be somewhat immature for her age and showed no signs of puberty. Her mental status was quite nor-mal, however. The optic nerve heads showed no suggestion of papilledema. With the eyes in the primary position there was a spontaneous vertical nystagmus. Deviation upward or downward caused vertical nystagmus of large amplitude with the slow phase to the mid-position. Lateral deviation caused horizontal and rotary nystagmus with the slow phase to the mid-point. There was gross ataxia of cerebellar type in the legs and mild ataxia of the arms. Station and gait were both unsteady. The knee jerks and other tendon reflexes were rather brisk, but the plantar responses were in flexion.

Roentgenograms of the spine were negative. A ventriculogram revealed moderate dilation of the lateral, third and fourth ventricles.

On October 4, the posterior fossa was explored. The typical Arnold-Chiari deformity was discovered. The posterior rim of the foramen magnum and the upper four laminae were removed. The child made a good recovery from the operation and soon began to improve.

On December 2, 1946, she was examined again. The headaches and vomiting had ceased. She was unsteady only when running. A very slight nystagmus was still seen.

BIBLIOGRAPHY

BUCY, P. AND LICHTENSTEIN, B. W.: Arnold-Chiari deformity in an adult without obvious cause. Arch. Neurol. & Psychiat., **55**:162, 1946.

DANIEL, P. M. AND STRICH, S. J.: Some observations on the congenital deformity of the nervous system known as the Arnold-Chiari malformation. J. Neuropath. & Exp. Neurol., **17**:255, 1958.

FEIGIN, I.: Arnold-Chiari malformation with associated analogous malformation of the midbrain. Neurology, **6**:22, 1956.

GARDNER, W. J. AND GOODALL, R. J.: Surgical treatment of the Arnold-Chiari malformation in adults. J. Neurosurg., **7**:199, 1950.

LICHTENSTEIN, B. W.: Distant neuroanatomic complications of spina bifida hydrocephalus, Arnold-Chiari deformity, stenosis of the aqueduct of Sylvius, etc. Arch. Neurol. & Psychiat., **47**:195, 1942.

————: Cervical syringomyelia and syringomyelia-like states associated with Arnold-Chiari deformity and platybasia. Arch. Neurol. & Psychiat., **49**:881, 1943.

MACFARLANE, A. AND MALONEY, A.: Appearance of the aqueduct and relationship to hydrocephalus in Arnold-Chiari malformation. Brain, **80**:479, 1957.

McCONNELL, A. A. AND PARKER, H. L.: A deformity of the hind-brain associated with internal hydrocephalus. Brain, **61**:415, 1938.

PEACH, B.: Arnold-Chiari Malformation: Morphogenesis. Arch. of Neurol., **12**:527, 1965.

RUSSELL, D. S. AND DONALD, C.: The mechanism of internal hydrocephalus in spina bifida. Brain, **58**:203, 1935.

RUSSELL, D. S.: Observations on the pathology of hydrocephalus. Special Report Series Medical Research Council No. 265. London, His Majesty's Stationery Office, 1949.

SWANSON, H. S. AND FINCHER, E. F.: Arnold-Chiari deformity without bony anomalies or hydrocephalus. J. Neurosurg., **6**:314, 1949.

CONGENITAL EXTERNAL HYDROCEPHALUS

Since this term means merely a condition in which fluid accumulates over the surface of the brain, it may be applied to a number of pathological states of varying origin.

Dandy has shown how external hydrocephalus may develop from internal hydrocephalus of the communicating type. This occurs only when the basal cisternae are patent, but the sulci and branches of the subarachnoid spaces over the cortex are occluded. Fluid accumulates, therefore, in the cisterna chiasmatica which soon begins to bulge and extend laterally. Finally, large cystic extensions develop over the lateral surfaces of the hemisphere, which may be extensive enough to compress the lateral walls of the cortex and deform the ventricles. In many cases, the pressure becomes so great that the delicate arachnoid membrane ruptures with escape of fluid into the subdural space. The fluid cannot be absorbed from this location and continues to accumulate, finally causing the brain to be pushed down upon the base of the skull. In the same way, the pressure slowly causes the cranium to expand. As a result, the delicate veins which extend from the cortex to the longitudinal sinus are greatly stretched and, if the process is very rapid, may rupture, giving rise to serious bleeding into the subdural space. Dandy has found that this condition may follow operations upon the third ventricle intended to relieve congenital hydrocephalus, since the operative opening permits the fluid to enter the subdural space.

In these conditions, the intracranial pressure is elevated and the head expands rapidly, as it does in the common internal hydrocephalus. Defective development of the brain will not cause external hydrocephalus, for the cranium merely accommodates itself to the size of the brain, and microcephaly results. When the brain atrophies, however, after the skull is fully formed, great lakes of fluid may form over the cortex, giving rise to hydrocephalus ex vacuo. In such cases, there is no increase in pressure, and the fluid accumulates merely to compensate for loss of brain substance.

BIBLIOGRAPHY

(See Internal Hydrocephalus)

AGENESIS OF THE CORPUS CALLOSUM

Definition.—Defective development of the corpus callosum, the great commissure which connects the two hemispheres of the brain.

Pathological Anatomy.—According to Marburg, this condition is characterized by absence of the corpus callosum, the anterior commissure, the psalterium and the septum pellucidum. The gyrus cinguli is absent or inadequately developed. These structures are quite absent in cases of complete agenesis and incompletely formed in partial agenesis. Marburg states that all of these structures develop from the commissural plate. Since this plate is formed in the first fourteen days after conception, agenesis of the corpus callosum must be determined during this period. Marburg states that it is possible to distinguish cases of true agenesis from those cases in which vascular lesions and other destructive processes are responsible.

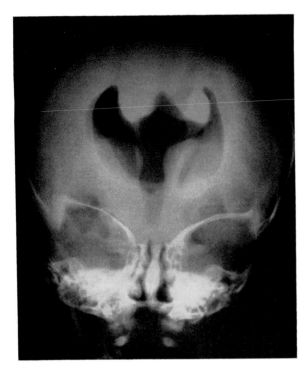

Fig. 41. Ventricles in agenesis of the corpus callosum.

A number of defects in the brain are found in association with agenesis of the corpus callosum. In a few instances the cerebral hemispheres are not separated but fused into a single structure. There is only one ventricle in the forebrain and the hippocampal structures are found in the midsagittal plane.

Porencephaly, hydrocephalus, microgyria and various heterotopias are described. In a large percentage of cases of interhemispheral lipomas, the corpus collosum is found to be defective.

Etiology.—This condition is regarded as a defect of development. There is evidence that it is inherited.

Clinical Features.—It is estimated that in a series of 1000 ventriculograms, agenesis of the corpus callosum will be found two or three times. The symptoms are not in any way characteristic. In fact, it is possible that the defect in the corpus callosum causes no symptoms whatever and the patients' complaints are due to the associated anomalies. Mental deficiency is almost always present but may be mild or severe. Convulsions are very common. They may appear years after birth. Major, minor and focal seizures are described. In some instances, there is spastic diplegia, hemiparesis, athetosis, optic atrophy, colobomata of the iris or the optic nerve. Hydrocephalus is common. Microcephaly and hypertelorism are mentioned. Precocious puberty has been noted. Defective bodily growth is described. In one of our cases, a dimple connected with a dermal sinus was found in the occipital region (Ped. No. B-2976).

Diagnosis.—The diagnosis cannot be made by history of clinical examination. Ventriculography is necessary. Five features of the ventriculogram are stressed by Carpenter and Druckemiller. (1) Dorsal extension and dilatation of the third ventricle. (2) Marked separation of the lateral ventricles. (3) Dilatation of the posterior horns of the lateral ventricles. (4) Angular dorsal margins of the lateral ventricles. (5) Concave mesial borders of the lateral ventricles. It should be said that Davidoff and Dykes were the first to point out the typical characteristics of the ventricles in this condition. Apparently, arteriograms and electroencephalograms are not helpful in making this diagnosis.

Treatment.—No treatment is possible except medication for the convulsions.

CASE HISTORY.—*Agenesis of the corpus callosum with colobomata of the retinae in a child of one year with frequent convulsions, and little or no motor or mental development.*

L. W. was seen at the age of one year. He had been born at full term by normal delivery after an uncomplicated pregnancy. Birth weight was 8 lbs 12 oz.

There was scarcely any evidence of motor reactions or of mental development. There seemed to be no vision. At 2 months convulsive seizures developed. The seizures recurred frequently and could not be controlled by medication.

An electroencephalogram revealed no significant abnormalities. An air study showed the typical picture of agenesis of the corpus callosum. Dr. Frank Walsh found colobomata of the retinae.

On examination at the age of one year, the nutrition and bodily growth were adequate. The head was not abnormal in shape or size. There were no spontaneous movements. When the child was disturbed, mass movements of the extremities appeared. These were similar to the mass movements of normal infants. The tendon reflexes were present but sluggish. The grasp reflexes were active and tonic neck reflexes were present. The child could not sit up or hold up the head. She did not try to talk and did not respond in any way when addressed.

BIBLIOGRAPHY

CARPENTER, M. AND DRUCKEMILLER, W.: Agenesis of the corpus callosum diagnosed during life. Arch. Neurol. & Psychiat., **69**:305, 1953.

DAVIDOFF, L. AND DYKE, G.: Agenesis of the corpus callosum. Diagnosis by encephalography. Am. J. Roentgenol., **32**:1, 1934.

LICHTENSTEIN, B. W. AND MALONEY, J. E.: Malformation of the forebrain with comments on the dorsal cyst, the corpus callosum and the hippocampal structures. J. Neuropath. and Exp. Neurol., **13**:117, 1954.

List, C., Holt, J. and Everett, M.: Lipoma of the corpus callosum. Am. J. Roentgenol., **55**:125, 1946.

Loeser, J. D. and Alvord, E. C.: Clinicopathological correlations in agenesis of the corpus callosum. Neurology, **18**:745, 1968.

Marburg, O.: So-called agenesia of the corpus callosum. Arch. Neurol. & Psychiat., **61**:297, 1949.

Menkes, J. H. *et al.*: Hereditary partial agenesis of the corpus callosum. Arch. Neurol., **11**:198, 1964.

Mosberg, W. H. and Voris, H. C.: An unusual congenital anomaly of the brain. Agenesis of the corpus callosum, absence of the septum pellucidum and fusion of the cerebral hemispheres. J. Neuropath. & Exp. Neurol., **13**:369, 1954.

Zelleger, H.: Agenesia corporis callosi. Helv. paediat Acta, **7**:136, 1952.

CONGENITAL MENTAL DEFECTS

Heredofamilial Mental Deficiency

Definition.—Under this heading, we shall discuss only those types of mental defect which result from imperfect or deficient development of the brain, excluding those cases associated with birth injury, vascular lesions, progressive disease of the nervous system and the congenital cerebral palsies.

Pathological Anatomy.—The brain is usually definitely below the average size and weight, but the gross appearances are not constant. Sometimes, the weight may be within normal limits or even exceed the average. The pattern of the cortical convolutions may be quite normal. As a rule, however, there is a tendency to a simplified convolutional pattern which may be taken to indicate imperfect development of the cortex. The secondary sulci may be absent, and, frequently, the insula is partially exposed. Pachygyria and microgyria are common, and irregularities and malformations of the cortex are seen. The essential lesions are found only on histological examination. In all cases, there is a definite reduction in the number of cortical neurons, and, frequently, the architecture of the cortex is abnormal so that the various strata can scarcely be distinguished. The neurons are frequently incompletely developed, and resemble neuroblasts in some ways. It seems to be generally agreed that the most striking defects are found in the granular and supragranular layers of cells. In most cases, there are also very definite defects in the cortical nerve fibers, especially the outer line of Baillarger, the radial bundles and the tangential fibers. The reduction of neurons and nerve fibers is believed to be more or less directly proportional to the degree of mental defect. Status dysraphicus may be associated. Benda has made a careful study of a series of brains recently. This description applies to the cases which seem to depend upon morbid inheritance. These are sometimes termed oligophrenias. Freytag and Lindenberg analyse the anatomical changes found in the brains of 359 patients who had been in the Rosewood State Hospital where mentally deficient patients are treated.

Etiology.—In most instances, amentia seems to represent an heredofamilial defect of development. Many family histories support this belief and the anatomical findings lend much weight to this theory.

It is stated that severe mental deficiency is apt to be inherited as a recessive characteristic but mild mental deficiency is often a dominant trait.

Clinical Features.—The incidence of amentia is very difficult to estimate with accuracy, and, probably, most of the figures given in official statistics fall very short of the truth. Undoubtedly, mental defect is more common in certain races than in others, and there is also a definite connection between the incidence of amentia and industrial, social and hygienic conditions. Tredgold gives figures to show that in England and Wales, there were 138,529 mentally deficient persons in 1906. Since the population was about 34,349,435, at the time, the average incidence of amentia was 4.03 per thousand. The minimum incidence was 1.1 and the maximum 4.68 per thousand in the various districts investigated. The milder degrees of deficiency are much more frequent than the severe types. Tredgold estimates that out of every 10,000 persons in England and Wales, there were: 2 idiots, 7 imbeciles and 29 feebleminded (morons). It is generally agreed that males are affect-

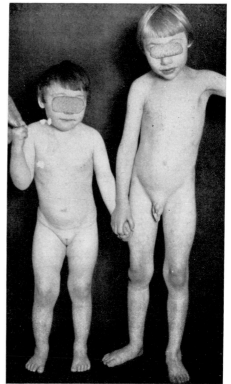

FIG. 42. Congenital mental defect with mild microcephaly in two siblings. A third child is also affected in the same way. (By the courtesy of Dr. Peckham.)

ed more frequently than females, the ratio being three to two. The primary, or developmental amentia, is of course the commonest type, and constitutes about 90 per cent of the whole group.

Amentia occurs in every possible degree from a complete lack of all forms of mental development to defects so mild that it is impossible to separate them from the lowest level of normal intelligence. The term idiot is applied to persons presenting the greatest degree of defect. A committee of the Royal College of Physicians of London has defined an *idiot* as a person so deeply defective in mind from birth that he is unable to guard himself against common physical dangers. An *imbecile* is defined as one who is incapable of earning a living, but is capable of guarding himself against common dangers, and a *feebleminded* person (or *moron*) is capable of earning a living under favorable circumstances, but is incapable of competing on equal terms with his normal fellows, or of managing himself and his affairs with ordinary prudence. Terman classifies mental defect according to the intelligence quotient as follows: Definitely feebleminded, below 70; borderline deficiency, 70 to 80; dull, 80 to 90. Kuhlman gives a more detailed classification. He defines idiots as those whose I.Q. is between 24 and 0; imbeciles, 25 to 49; morons, 50 to 74; borderline, 75 to 84; dull, 85 to 94; average, 95 to 104.

The behavior of defective children is of many different types. It may be said, in general, that their abnormality is shown not only by their failure to develop normal biological reactions, but also by their tendency to abnormal reactions. In the most severe cases (low grade idiots), it is usually noticed that the child is abnormal during the first few months of life. Frequently, the child is apathetic, never moving unless disturbed, and showing no reactions to the mother's voice nor to bright objects such as attract the normal infant's eyes. When the child is taken into the mother's arms, it does not respond by vigorous movements as does the normal infant, but remains quite still and relaxed. Sometimes, the child will not nurse. The mouth is often open and there may be a constant drolling of saliva. In other cases, there are constant gaping movements of the jaws, rolling of the eyes, constant fretfulness and monotonous crying. Epileptic seizures of various types are very common. Petit mal is very easily overlooked at this age. Such children may never rise above the level of a vegetative existence. They may remain quite helpless all their life.

Children suffering from a milder degree of amentia may not show such unmistakable evidences of mental defect during infancy. They are merely slow in learning to hold up the head, sit up, stand, walk and talk. From an early age, however, they are restless and irritable, prone to digestive disturbances and to malnutrition. Later in life, they show a constant and senseless activity, rushing about the room seemingly attracted by every object upon which their eyes fall. Whatever they pick up they throw down at once, and go off to something else. Any change in their environment, or even the presence of a stranger, causes great agitation, screaming and evidences of fear. Their attention cannot be held for more than a moment. One gains the impression that there is a great defect in inhibition. Convulsions are common. These children are very destructive, and seem to enjoy breaking everything within their reach. They are usually incontinent and dirty in their habits. Many of them will eat objects unfit for food, and are often poisoned by their habit of sucking lead paint from their beds. As a rule, the facial expression is so idiotic that the diagnosis can be made as soon as the child is seen. Facial grimaces, drooling of saliva and protrusion of the tongue are commonly present. Speech is defective, and there is little evidence of the child's comprehending what is said to it. These children are scarcely capable of responding to training except in the most limited way.

The milder types of mental defect rarely attract attention during infancy or early childhood, and it is only when the child reaches school and fails to make proper progress that the parents are forced to accept the fact that the child is abnormal. Such children may be restless and irritable as the type described above, although never, of course, to the same extreme degree, but in many cases they are placid and obedient. They may have relatively normal personalities despite their lack of intellect. These children will be quite content with a few toys and play quietly all day in the manner of younger children. They are often very popular among their playmates since they will let the more aggressive children have their way. They are usually clumsy and slow to acquire manual dexterity, but in some cases may be trained to perform some useful task and to contribute toward their own support. If left to their own resources they will always get into trouble, but if shielded and guarded from evil influences they may enjoy a relatively happy life.

We must now describe some of the characteristics which are more or less common to all types and degrees of feeblemindedness. Motor disturbances of a special type are not at all uncommon. Frequently the child is slow to learn to walk but eventually develops a great deal of agility and seems to have no real motor disorder. Repetitious tic-like movements of the face and extremities are common among the defectives and may, at times, arouse suspicions of chorea. As a rule, such movements are greatly accentuated when the child is frightened or disturbed, and much less evident when the child is quiet. After operations, such as tonsillectomy, violent motor unrest may be observed in children who have never shown similar symptoms before. Speech is delayed and imperfect. As a rule, the speech defect is proportional to the degree of mental deficiency. Some idiots can express themselves only by grunts and inarticulate sounds. Milder degrees of feeblemindedness are not incompatible with almost normal speech. The different types of speech defect correspond, according to Wyllie, with the different stages in the development of the speech of a normal child. In some cases, only a few nouns are acquired. Other children can form short sentences more or less correctly. Frequently, there is a tendency to omit certain consonants and to substitute vowels or other consonants for them. Thus "D" may be employed for "T." Vowels are formed more correctly as a rule. This type of speech has been termed idioglossia, for it may be quite incomprehensible to one who is not familiar with the child and so resembles an individual language. It seems best, however, to reserve the term idioglossia for the speech defect which is associated with deficient appreciation of the significance of sounds, i.e., congenital word deafness, and not to apply it to speech defects arising from lack of intelligence. Stammering, lisping, dysarthria and many other types of defective speech are found among the mental defectives.

The sense perceptions of the feebleminded cannot be studied successfully, for cooperation is always uncertain. As a rule, their reactions to sensory stimuli are sluggish or defective. It is often stated that deafness, color blindness, etc., are very common.

The mental reactions of feebleminded children are characteristic. For example, there is no power of sustained attention. In some cases, the child may respond quickly to almost any stimulus, but it is distracted almost at once to something else. Others fail to notice all but the most intense stimuli. The child's capacity for adjusting to new situations is very deficient as a rule. He cannot form new habits or meet new conditions. His judgment, originality, capacity for abstract thought, etc., are obviously defective or nonexistent. His emotions are simple and transient. Memory, on the other hand, when the child has grasped the problem, is often astonishingly good. Many parents are convinced that their child cannot be defective because of his capacity to recite nursery rhymes and perform other feats of memory. The sense of responsibility and of right or wrong, or "moral sense" are poorly developed as a rule. Sexual development is usually limited but morons may lead an active sex life and may produce large numbers of children.

The physical development of defective children is in many cases, if not in most cases, abnormal. As a rule, they are below the average in stature and in nutrition. Dentition is delayed. It is stated that various factors which injure the nervous system may also interrupt the formation of tooth enamel. Study of the enamel may throw some light on the time at which the nervous system was involved. Occasional cases are seen, however, in which the child is above the average size, and is rather precocious in physical development (Ped. A 20037). Mental defectives have very little resistance to disease as a rule, and many fail to reach adult life. Many physical peculiarities have been observed and are often termed stigmata of degeneration. The face is almost always peculiar either in its formation or in its expression. The ears are frequently malformed. Epicanthus, coloboma, squints, cataracts, etc., are found in the eyes. The tongue is often fissured and may show hypertrophied papillae. The head is usually somewhat below normal size and may be asymmetrical or malformed in a variety of ways. The fontanels close early. The hard palate is often narrow and high-arched, and the teeth irregular and prone to decay. Numerous anomalies of development are found in the heart, the blood vessels and gastrointestinal tracts. Congenital cystic kidney, horseshoe kidney and extrophy of the bladder are sometimes found. Hypospadias and undescended testicles are common. Moles, naevi, extra mammae, defects of hair formation and of skin are also described.

Diagnosis.—In the case of children who are severely defective, there is usually no difficulty in making the diagnosis, and the condition may often be recognized or suspected very early in infancy. In many instances, however, the physician may be unable to arrive at a definite opinion until the child has been examined repeatedly. Some children are so willful and spoiled that it is impossible to secure proper cooperation in the examination, others are retarded as a result of prolonged illness, and still others are so handicapped by defects of special senses or abnormalities of motility that the examiner cannot successfully establish proper contact with them. A very large number of factors must be taken into consideration, such as race, language, early training and social background. The Binet and other intelligence tests are of great value and, when properly employed with a full understanding of their limitations, give reliable results. Unfortunately, such tests are frequently over-emphasized, and it is not a very unusual experience to discover the diagnosis and prognosis based upon these tests alone eventually turn out to be entirely erroneous and misleading. The opinion of an experienced observer is of more importance than the result of any test. The child's adaptation to life as a whole, behavior at home, at school, and in the clinic must be carefully investigated and judiciously estimated before any substantial conclusions can be reached. The facial expression is often very revealing. The so-called stigmata of degeneration are sometimes helpful but should not be over-emphasized, for they may be found in people of average or even exceptional mental attainments. Kennedy finds that the mentally deficient children have a diminished cerebral metabolic rate.

Klinkerfuss *et al.* state that 90 per cent of children with hyperkinetic behavior have abnormal electroencephalograms. Most of them have non-specific slow frequencies.

Prognosis.—The prognosis depends almost entirely upon the degree of mental defect. Children with severe mental defects attain their full development early; their progress is slow and lasts only a short time. Milder defects permit a higher level of development, but there is always a fixed limit beyond which it is impossible for the child to progress. In general, therefore, we may say that the prognosis is unfavorable for improvement, and that a defective child will always remain defective. Indeed, intellectual deficiency seems to become more and more obvious as the child grows older and the demands of life become more and more exacting. In justice to the morons or high-grade feebleminded, we must point out that they supply a large part of the unskilled labor for the industrial world, performing the most fatiguing and monotonous tasks. We owe them our gratitude.

Treatment.—The management of these children is sometimes a difficult problem. If we are quite sure that the child is grossly defective and will never be able to make a living under any circumstances, the parents should be advised to place it in an institution suitable to their means and make provisions for its care after their death. Defectives of a higher grade should receive special training of industrial type so as to fit them to engage in some gainful occupation. The financial status of the family should always be considered and every effort be made to secure the child's future. Unfortunately, many parents are unwisely led to exhaust their savings in providing special training for children who cannot profit in any way. Great care should be taken to prevent defectives from reproducing.

It should be mentioned that it has been claimed that the administration of glutamic acid has a stimulating effect on the mental condition of defective children. It is said that the effect does not persist after the drug is withdrawn. Some writers have estimated that the intelligence quotient may be increased by 10 per cent. It is claimed that chlorpromazine is helpful in cases in which the child is aggressive and excessively active. Miltown and rauwolfia have similar effects.

Burks states that the children with hyperkinetic behavior who have normal electroencephalograms improve dramatically on amphetamine, whereas, those with abnormal electroencephalograms, improve moderately under the same therapy. However, Ney reports the case of a child who developed hallucinations when given this drug.

BIBLIOGRAPHY

ALBERT, K. AND WAELSCH, H.: Preliminary report on the effect of glutamic acid administration in mentally retarded children. J. Nerv. & Ment. Dis., 104:263, 1946.

ANDERSON, W. W.: The hyperkinetic child. Neurology, 13:968, 1963.

ASHBY, W. R. AND STEWART, R. M.: Size in mental deficiency. J. Neurol. & Psychopath., 13:303, 1933.

———: Brain of the mental defective; a study of morphology in its relation to intelligence. J. Neurol. & Psychopath., 14:217, 1934.

BENDA, C. E.: Developmental Disorders of Mentation and Cerebral Palsies. New York, Grune and Stratton, 1952.

———: The familial imbecile or oligoencephaly as a morbid entity. Am. J. Ment. Def., **49**:32, 1944.

BERRY, R. J. A. AND NORMAN, R. M.: Cerebral structure and mental function as illustrated by a study of four defective brains. J. Neurol. & Psychopath., **14**:289, 1934.

BURKS, H. F.: Effects of amphetamine therapy on hyperkinetic children. Arch. of Gen. Psychiat., **11**:604, 1964.

DUGDALE, R. C.: The Juke Family. New York, Putnam, 1910.

FREYTAG, E. AND LINDENBERG, R.: Neuropathological findings in patients of a hospital for the mentally deficient. A survey of 359 cases. Johns Hopkins Hospital Medical Journal, **121**:379, 1967.

GODDARD, H. H.: The Kallikak Family. New York, The Macmillan Co., 1912.

———: Feeblemindedness; Its Causes and Consequences. New York, The Macmillan Co., 1923.

GORDON, R. G., NORMAN, R. M. AND BERRY, R. J. A.: Neurological abnormalities, their occurrence and significance as illustrated at an examination of 500 mental defectives. J. Neurol. & Psychopath., **14**:97, 1933.

HUNT, B. R. *et al.*: Chlorpromazine in the treatment of severe emotional disorders of children. Am. J. Dis., **91**:268, 1956.

KENNEDY, C.: The cerebral metabolic rate in mentally retarded children. Arch. of Neurol., **16**:55, 1967.

KLINKERFUSS, G. H. *et al.*: Encephalographic abnormalities of children with hyperkinetic behavior. Neurology, **15**:883, 1965.

KOCH, G.: Erworbene und erbliche Schwachsinnszustände. Die Medizinische Welt. No. 37, 1961, **15**, August 10, 1961.

———: Erworbene und erbliche Schwachsinnszustände Die Medizinische Welt. No. 37, 1961.

LEVIN, P.: Restlessness in children. Arch. Neurol. & Psychiat., **39**:764, 1938.

NEY, P. G.: Psychosis in a child associated with amphetamine administration. Canad. Med. Assoc. Jour., **97**:1026, 1967.

Stoke Park Monographs on Mental Deficiency and Other Problems of the Human Brain and Mind. London, Macmillan and Co., 1933.

TREDGOLD, A. F.: Textbook of Mental Deficiency. Baltimore, Williams and Wilkins Co., 1956.

WALSH, F. B.: *Loc. cit.*

WILDENSKOV, H. O.: Investigation into the Cause of Mental Deficiency. Oxford Univ. Press, 1934.

ZELLWEGER, H.: Genetic aspects of mental retardation. Arch. Int. Med., **111**:165, 1963.

DELAY OF DEVELOPMENT IN INFANTS DUE TO SENSORY DEPRIVATION (Krieger and Sargent)

In a study of 35 malnourished children between the ages of 5 months and 2 years, Krieger and Sargent discovered 19 who seemed to suffer from sensory deprivation. By this term the authors mean lack of stimulation such as kissing, fondling, teaching the use of toys and playing with and talking to the child.

Lack of such stimulation results in retardation of mental development, apathy and indifference. Defective bodily growth is found in such children and may be due to lack of proper nutrition.

The authors describe a peculiar posture which was found in 10 of the 19 children. The arms were held in flexion at the elbows and in external rotation and abduction at the shoulders. The hands are pronated and are often held beside the head or behind it. The fingers are sometimes flexed. The legs may be abducted and flexed at the hips and knees.

Treatment, of course, includes proper nutrition and maximal stimulation. The posture becomes normal after treatment.

BIBLIOGRAPHY

KRIEGER, I. AND SARGENT, D. A.: A postural sign in the sensory deprivation syndrome in infants. Jour. of Pediat., **70**:332, 1967.

POWELL, G. F. *et al.:* Emotional deprivation and growth retardation simulating idiopathic hypopituitarism. New England Jour. Med., **276**:1271, 1967.

MICROCEPHALY

Definition.—At this point, we shall discuss only the "true microcephaly" which may be regarded as a defect of development characterized by a very small head of peculiar shape, by mental deficiency and other characteristics which will be described below in more detail. This condition is to be distinguished from the primary amentias and congenital diplegias in which the head is often somewhat below the average size, but never so small as that of the true microcephaly and from the relative microcephaly which may result from severe cerebral lesions occurring in early infancy.

Pathological Anatomy.—The brain is very much smaller than normal and often weighs less than 1000 grams when growth is complete. As a rule, the occipital lobes do not cover the cerebellum, so the general appearance of the nervous system suggests that of the lower animals. The convolutional pattern is often simplified and only the primary sulci are present. This has been termed the macrogyric or agyric type. In other types, i.e., the microgyric, the gyri are more numerous than normal. The nerve cells are often imperfectly developed and deficient in number. The fiber tracts are small. As a rule, no evidence of inflammation or degeneration can be found. These statements apply to true microcephaly which is genetically determined. A great variety of processes may cause microcephaly, however. Benda lists cystic degeneration which he regards as a result of a birth injury, pachygyria, agyria and lisencephaly, lobar agenes and porencephaly or schizencephaly. Jervis described two cases of a special type of microcephaly and gives in abstract five more cases found in the literature. These children showed in addition to microcephaly, idiocy, increased muscle tone and choreoathetoid movements. There were conspicuous deposits of calcium in the basal ganglia, cerebellum and cerebral cortex with demyelination of the centrum ovale, accumulation of lipoid material and increased glial reaction.

Etiology.—It is generally agreed that true microcephaly represents an arrest of development, for the appearances of the brain often resemble very closely that of the fetus of the third or fourth month. It seems to be clear that this is an inherited condition. Thus, Benda has found five cases in two generations of one family. Dannenberger found five microcephalics among nine children. Benda states that Frey found four cases in a family of eight children. Whitney found four cases of microcephalic twins and seven cases in one family. Brushfield and Wyatt and Tredgold also mention familial cases. Van den Bosch has made an extensive study of five families in Holland in which many microcephalic idiots were found. He believes that this condition is due to a rare recessive gene and in small villages in isolated districts where all families are interrelated, this condition is most likely to appear. McKusick *et al.* describe hereditary microcephaly associated with chorioretinopathy.

Clinical Features.—Usually, the parents are quite healthy. Very frequently, there are several children in the family affected. In a number of cases, identical twins have shown microcephaly of the same degree. If one of a pair of dissimilar twins is affected, the other may be microcephalic or may be normal. The child's head is, as a rule, abnormally small at birth, and the fontanels may be more or less completely closed. The abnormality, however, is not so striking in early infancy as it is later in life, for growth of the head is very slow indeed. Thus, at birth the head may measure $12\frac{1}{2}$ inches in circumference, as compared with the normal of 13 inches. At six months, when it should measure 16 inches, it is only 13 or 14 inches, and at one year, it may be only 14 or $14\frac{1}{2}$ inches when it should be 18 inches. The maximum circumference attained is always below 17 inches. In addition to the small size of the head, its shape is also peculiar. The forehead is narrow and recedes sharply, the occiput is flattened, and the lateral aspects of the head slope up to the vertex which is somewhat pointed. The features and jaws are usually well formed, and the contrast between the small cranium and the well-developed face is very striking. The bodily development is, as a rule, below the average, although this may not be apparent during infancy. Dentition is usually not delayed although it is in the other types of amentia.

Walking is delayed and in severe cases may always be defective. Speech is delayed and imperfect. Many of these children never learn to talk. There are convulsions in perhaps about one-third of all cases. Frequently, there is a marked hypertonus of the muscles during early childhood but true spasticity is rare. As a rule, the hypertonus passes off later. It has been suggested by Thompson that this is merely an exaggeration of the normal hypertonus of

Fig. 43. Outspoken microcephaly with mental defect but no diplegia. (By the courtesy of Dr. Holt.)

newborn children, and represents backward development rather than a defect of the pyramidal tracts.

There is a great deal of variation in the mental condition, but as a rule there is severe amentia. Most of the children are restless, irritable and destructive. Others may possess a relatively good disposition and may be able to perform useful tasks. It is sometimes astonishing how much intelligence may reside in a very small brain.

Diagnosis.—The diagnosis depends upon the peculiar shape of the head, its small size and the premature closure of the fontanels, as well as the absence of any evidence of cerebral injury or of disease in early infancy. In cases in which the mother has already borne one or more microcephalic children, the attempt has been made to diagnose the condition in utero by means of roentgenography, but this is actually difficult or impossible, for the head is usually of normal or nearly normal size during intrauterine life.

Prognosis.—The outlook depends entirely upon the degree of deficiency for no improvement can be expected. Most of these children die early in life, for they are very delicate and succumb easily to infections.

Treatment.—Microcephaly should be treated as the other types of primary amentia.

BIBLIOGRAPHY

BENDA, C. E.: Developmental Disorders of Mentation and Cerebral Palsies. New York, Grune and Stratton, 1952.

BRUSHFIELD, A. AND WYATT, W.: Microcephaly. Brit. J. Dis. Child., **23**:265, 1927.

COWIE, V.: The genetics and sub-classification of microcephaly. Jour. Ment. Defic. Res., **4**:42, 1960.

DANNENBERGER, A.: Die Mikrokephalen Familie Becker in Bürgel. Sommer's Klinik für psych. nerv. Kranhk., **7**:27, 1912.

FREEMAN, W.: Microcephaly and diffuse gliosis. Brain, **50**:188, 1927.

GREENFIELD, J. G. AND WOLFSOHN, J. M.: Microcephalia vera: A study of two brains illustrating the agyric form and the complex microgyric form. Arch. Neurol. & Psychiat., **33**:1296, 1935.

JERVIS, G. A.: Microcephaly with extensive calcium deposits and demyelination. Neuropath. & Exp. Neurol., **13**:318, 1954.

KLOEPFER, H. W. *et al.*: Manifestations of a recessive gene for microcephaly in a population isolate. Jour. Genet. Hum., **13**:52, 1964.

KOCH, G.: Genetics of microcephaly in man. Acta Genet. Med. (Roma) , **8**:75, 1959.

MAYER, C. U. REISCH, O.: Klinische studien an zwei mikrocephalen. Arch. f. Psychiat., **89**:662 (references) , 1930.

McKUSICK, V. *et al.*: Chorioretinopathy with hereditary microcephaly. Arch. of Ophthal., **75**:597, 1966.

TREDGOLD, A. F.: Mental Deficiency, London. Balliere, Tindall and Cox.

VAN DEN BOSCH, J.: Microcephalic children from consanguineous marriages. Nederl. tidjschr. Geneesk., **99**:3773, 1955.

WHITNEY, E. A.: Microcephaly. Med. J. & Rec., **130**:158, 1929; **135**:166, 1932.

MACROCEPHALY

Definition.—This rare condition is characterized by an abnormally large brain and by mental deficiency. It is regarded as a type of hypertrophy or hyperplasia of the brain. The occasional occurrence of two cases in one family suggests that it may be a familial condition. A secondary type occurs in which the enlargement of the brain is due to some progressive pathological process.

Pathological Anatomy.—Primary type. The brain is very large and heavy. In one instance it is said to have weighed 2850 grams. Externally the cerebral hemispheres show a convolutional pattern of great complexity. The primary fissures may be identified in most cases, however. On section the cortex is very thick and the subcortical white matter firm. The brain stem, cerebellum and basal ganglia are not hypertrophied. Benda states the spinal cord may be enlarged. The results of microscopic examination are not uniform.

Kinnier Wilson described two cases in 1934. One was that of a child of 2½ years whose brain weighed 1644 grams and the other a child of 3¼ years whose brain weighed 1502. The cortex in the first case was very cellular. The nerve cells were sometimes rounded and of abnormal shape. Some cells showed vacuoles and the Nissl bodies did not stain. The neurofibrillar network seemed to be incomplete. Apparently no changes were found in the white matter or in the glial cells.

Kastein describes five cases. In one group there is thickening of the cortex but the white matter is reduced. In other groups, the proportion of gray and white matter is normal. His histological description includes thickening of the cortex with large ganglion cells and numerous heterotopias. A diffuse increase of glial cells is mentioned. There are also heterotopias in the cerebellum, he states.

Apley and Symons report two cases in children who died of intercurrent infection. The brain of one weighed 1450 grams and that of the other, who was fifteen months old, 1770 grams. Histological examination by Norman is said to have revealed no abnormalities.

Benda described two cases. The brains weighed 2615 grams and 2060 grams. In the first case both white and gray matter were proportionally increased. There were some abnormal neurons but no gliosis. The cord was enlarged and there was syringomyelia. A recent meningoencephalitis made the interpretation of the histological changes impossible. In the second case the gray and white matter were both increased. The first layer of the cortex showed gliosis. The lower layers of the cortex showed large masses of nerve cells crowded together. The ependyma contained wart like prominences. The Bielschowsky stain revealed abnormalities of the fibrillary structures in cells with displacement of the nuclei. Dennis *et al.* have found five cases of macrocephaly in cases of chondrodystrophy.

Weil reports a somewhat different condition in a boy of seven years. The cerebral hemispheres were enlarged and this enlargement was attributed to the increased size of the astrocytes which were, however, not more numerous than usual. A gliomatous process, termed glioblastomatosis, was found in the brain stem, cerebellum, thalamus and upper part of the spinal cord. The motor cortex was not well developed and the boy's musculature was slender. The brother had a very large head. Weil suggests that there was an inherited tendency towards hypertrophy of the brain which eventually developed into a neoplastic process. Several similar cases are described.

So far, we have been speaking about developmental anomalies. If a pathological process causes swelling of the brain so early in life that the sutures of the skull are not closed and the head may expand, *secondary macrocephaly* may occur. Degenerations of the white matter may be responsible. Schilder's disease q.v. should be mentioned and the spongy degeneration of the white matter of Canavan q.v. Crome has published a description of secondary macrocephaly in which the white matter was soft and contained cavities due to myelin destruction. There was loss of cells in the cortex and gliosis. Many hyaline bodies were found under the pia, the ependyma and around the blood vessels. They showed the staining reactions of fibrin. Alexander had previously published a similar case with the onset of 8 months. The head measured 50 cm in circumference and at postmortem the brain weighed 1200 grams. There were numerous hyaline bodies such as Crome observed but minimal demyelination. The metachromatic leucoencephalopathy of Greenfield also causes enlargement of the head. Lipoidoses may cause similar macrocephaly. When children suffering from infantile cerebroretinal degenerations live longer than usual, the white matter may degenerate and the brain may become swollen. Steegmann and Karnosh report the case of a child who died at the age of 29 months whose brain weighed 2300 grams. We have seen one case in which a little girl's head was enormously enlarged because of innumerable tape worm cysts in the brain. There was no hydrocephalus. Primary gliosis of the brain q.v. may cause a similar picture.

Clinical Features.—Macrocephaly is more frequent in males than in females. In some instances, more than one case of macrocephaly is found in the same family. This seems to be a sexlinked recessive condition. The head is often larger than normal at birth, but in most cases it does not seem to have been large enough to attract attention. However, the fontanels are open more widely than normal. Soon after birth the head begins to grow rapidly, and this naturally leads to the diagnosis of hydrocephalus. The fontanels remain patent beyond the usual period. The general physical development is often somewhat retarded. The stature is small and delicate. The muscles are described as slender and weak. Movements are less vigorous than those of a normal infant. Within a few weeks or months, it becomes evident that mental development is defective. The child does not seem to notice its surroundings, fails to recognize the parents and displays an abnormal lack of responsiveness. The head is not sustained at the proper time, there is no progress in learning to stand or walk, and speech is delayed or perhaps never acquired. Most of these children are idiots or imbeciles. They usually learn to walk and to make their wants known by a few words, but can rarely learn to care for themselves. In about 50 per cent of cases, there are recurrent convulsions. Their legs are short and poorly developed.

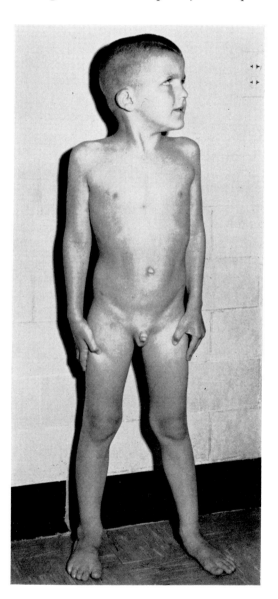

FIG. 44. Macrocephaly, at 6 years, primary type, showing large head of normal shape, short bodily growth and small stiff legs.

There is a tendency to hold the hands in an odd position in full extension at the wrist and strong flexion of the fingers. Optic atrophy does not seem to occur in the primary type.

It is stated by Campbell that the shape of the head is identical with that found in hydrocephalus, and it is certainly true that the general appearance is very similar. As may be seen from the accompanying illustration, however, in some cases the head does not show the lateral bulging or depression of the roof of the orbits so characteristic of hydrocephalus. It seems fair to say that the shape of the cranium is not abnormal. The abnormality lies entirely in the excessive size. The face is usually very large and the features coarse so there is no disproportion between the face and the cranium as there is in hydrocephalus. Roentgenograms show no digital markings over the vault even after the cranial sutures have closed. There is never any increased intracranial pressure. These statements apply only to the primary type of macrocephaly. In secondary macrocephaly, the symptoms depend upon the nature of the disease.

Unilateral hypertrophy of the brain is found in some cases of *general hemihypertrophy*. Mental deficiency is also found in some of these cases. Apparently, there have been no microscopic studies of such brains, and the actual nature of the condition is unknown. As a rule, the larger half of the brain is still within normal limits. Riley and Smith report a study of a family in which several members had macrocephaly pseudopapilledema and multiple hemangiomas. There was no loss of vision or mental change.

Diagnosis.—The essential points in the diagnosis are as follows: (1) The symmetrical enlargement of the head. (2) Evidences of defective development of the nervous system such as mental retardation, delay in the acquisition of motor functions and convulsions. (3) The exclusion of hydrocephalus, brain tumor, subdural hematoma and other conditions which might cause enlargement of the head. It is doubtful whether the clinical diagnosis can be established without ventriculography.

Prognosis.—The symptoms as a rule remain stationary, showing no tendency to progress nor to recede. However, most macrocephalic patients die as a result of convulsions or of intercurrent infection before adult life.

Treatment.—See Primary Amentia.

BIBLIOGRAPHY

ALEXANDER, W. S.: Progressive fibrinoid degeneration of the fibrillary astrocytes associated with mental retardation in a hydrocephalic infant. Brain, 72:373, 1949.

APLEY, J. AND SYMONS, M.: Megalencephaly. A report of two cases. Arch. Dis. Child., 22:172, 1947.

ARONSON, S. M. AND RABINER, A.: Hydrocephalus associated with lipoidosis of the central nervous system. Joint Meeting of Philadelphia Neurological Soc., New York Neurological Soc., and New York Academy of Med. April 21, 1955.

BENDA, C. E.: Developmental Disorders of Mentation and Cerebral Palsies. New York, Grune and Stratton, 1952, p. 200.

CAMPBELL, A. W.: Cerebral sclerosis. Hypertrophy of the brain. Brain, **28**:396, 1905.

CANAVAN, M. M.: Schilder's encephalitis periaxialis diffuse (macrocephaly). Arch. Neurol. & Psychiat., **25**:299, 1931.

CROME, L.: Megalencephaly associated with hyaline panneuropathy. Brain, **76**:215, 1953.

DENNIS, J. P. *et al.*: Megalencephaly and internal hydrocephalus and other neurological aspects of achondroplasia. Brain, **84**:427, 1961.

GESELL, A.: Hemihypertrophy and mental defect. Arch. Neurol. & Psychiat., **6**:400, 1921.

HABERLIN, J. H.: A case of hypertrophy of the brain. J.A.M.A., **46**:1988, 1906.

KASTEIN, G. W.: Megalencephalie 111 Congres Neurologique Internat. Copenhague, 21-25 About 1939, Copenhague, Einar Munksgaard, 1939.

PETER, K. AND SCHLUETER, K.: Ueber Maglencephalie als Grundlage der Idiotie. Ztschr. f. d. ges. Neur. und Psychiat., **108**:21, 1927.

RILEY, H. D., JR. AND SMITH, W. R.: Macrocephaly, pseudopapilledema and multiple hemangiomata. Pediatrics, **26**:293, 1960.

STEEGMANN, A. T. AND KARNOSH, L. J.: Infantile amaurotic idiocy with megalocephaly and atrophic cerebellum. Am. J. Insanity, **93**:1413, 1936.

WEIL, A.: Megalencephaly with diffuse glioblastomatosis of the brain stem and cerebellum. Arch. Neurol. & Psychiat., **30**:795, 1934.

WIGELSEWORTH, J. AND WATSON, G. A.: The brain of a macrocephalic epileptic. Brain, **36**:31, 1913.

WILSON, S. A. K.: Megalencephaly. J. Neurol. & Psychopath., **14**:193, 1934.

CONGENITAL DEAFNESS AND DEAF-MUTISM

Definition.—There are several types of congenital deafness which will be described briefly below. Needless to say, children who are born deaf or acquire deafness early in childhood, fail to develop normal speech and are called deaf-mutes.

Etiology.—The causes of congenital deafness are not very clear and no doubt a multiplicity of factors enter into its production. In some types, several members of a family are affected, and it is logical to ascribe the condition to an inherited defect of development or perhaps a familial degenerative process which occurs in utero. Congenital deafness is associated with cretinism, in some cases, and in others, with pigmentary degeneration of the retina. Feeblemindedness and numerous other signs of defective development are not uncommon among deaf-mutes. It has been shown that inbreeding among affected families increases the incidence of deafness. The administration of quinine to the mother to induce labor may cause deafness in the child and this possibility is supported by experimental investigations. There is little clinical evidence, however, to show that quinine is a common cause of congenital deafness. German measles in the mother during the first four months of pregnancy may be responsible. Kernicterus may also result in deafness.

Pathological Anatomy.—Fraser has reviewed the anatomical findings in various types of congenital deafness. He finds that in the type of Siebenmann, which is associated with cretinism, there are constant changes in the middle ear and bony capsule of the labyrinth, whereas the inner ear and eighth nerve are usually normal. Some authorities believe that the defective development of the cretin brain plays a part in this type of congenital deafness. In a rare type described by Michel, the labyrinth and eighth nerve are defective or absent, but the middle ear is normal. In the type of Alexander, the membranous labyrinth, its bony capsule and the eighth nerve are defective. Deafness associated with pigmentary degeneration of the retina has been described by numerous writers. Fraser states that the outstanding anatomical findings in such cases include changes in the blood vessels, defective development of the sensory epithelium of the labyrinth, and atrophy of the cochlear and vestibular ganglia. These changes have been compared with the changes in the retina and there seems to be a rather close analogy. The type of congenital deafness described by Scheibe is apparently the most common. Alexander states that about 70 per cent of all cases of congenital deaf-mutism belong in this group. Here we find severe defects in the cochlea and sacculus, but the canals and the utricle are usually normal. The cochlear branch of the eighth nerve and the ganglion are atrophic. The middle ear is usually normal. One post-mortem examination of a child whose deafness was attributed to German measles is said to have shown total absence of any differentiation of the primitive cells to form the organ of Corti.

Clinical Features.—The so-called endemic deafness which is associated with cretinism was once very prevalent in certain parts of the world such as Switzerland where goiter was common. Frequently, several members of a family were affected. It is stated that only about 25 per cent of all cretins have normal hearing; that 45 per cent have slight deafness; 25 per cent severe deafness and about 5 per cent absolute deafness. As a rule, the deafness is proportional to the mental condition, and absolute deafness is most frequent in the most severe cases of idiocy. Generally, the deafness is present at birth, but in some instances it is not noted for years. Endemic deafness is usually of the middle ear or conduction type and the vestibular reactions are usually preserved.

In the type associated with pigmentary degeneration of the retina, there is almost always a definite family history of similar conditions in siblings or ascendants. Reduction of vision is, of course, present and there is almost invariably mental defect. This is a nerve type of deafness and the vestibular reactions are absent or greatly reduced.

Scheibe's sacculo-cochlear degeneration is also a familial disease and gives rise to a nerve type of deafness. The vestibular reactions are preserved, however, for the semicircular canals are not affected.

Waardenburg has described a syndrome including deaf-mutism, hypertelorism, heterochromic iridis and a lock of white hair in the frontal region. There is a heredofamilial condition.

Dr. Emanuel Margolis has reported fourteen cases of total albinism and deaf-mutism in three generations of a large Jewish family. All of the patients were males.

Jervell *et al.* and Levine *et al.* have reported cases of deaf-mutism of congenital origin in which there was heart disease with syncopal attacks and sudden death in siblings.

Bart and Pumphrey describe a familial type of congenital deafness characterized by thickened skin over the knuckles and by white fingernails. Nockeman reports another type of congenital deafness associated with constricting bands about the fingers and hyperkeratosis of the palms. Fourman and Fourman found a type of hereditary deafness associated with ear-pits and Marshall found congenital deafness associated with anhidrotic ectodermal dysphasia.

Congenital syphilis apparently rarely causes deafness at birth. Thus, among 82 deaf-mutes in the Edinburgh Royal Institution for the Education of the Deaf and Dumb, there were found only three positive Wassermann reactions and one doubtful reaction. Other studies have given comparable results, so that we may conclude that congenital syphilis is responsible for deaf-mutism in less than 5 per cent of all cases.

It is not clear at present how frequent is the deafness due to German measles in the mother. Clayton-Jones states that in a school of 18 deaf children a history of German measles in the mother before the end of the fourth month was obtained in 8 instances. This is said to be a nerve type of deafness.

McKenna has shown that the ingestion of large amounts of quinine during pregancy may cause either congenital deafness or aplasia of the optic nerves.

Regardless of the type of deafness, it may be noted very early in life that the child does not react to sounds as the normal infant does, but it is always very difficult to be sure that this is due to deafness and not to mental defect. Later, however, it is observed that the voice is not normal and that its cries are monotonous and fail to show the variation in pitch that one expects. Finally, there is no progress in learning to talk and no evidence of understanding the mother's speech. Mental development in fields not dependent upon speech may be relatively normal, but general intellectual progress is always more or less retarded by the deafness. Personality changes often arise as a result of the difficult psychological situation which the child faces. It must be borne in mind that total deafness is not necessary for the development of deaf-mutism. Indeed, most deaf-mutes have the power of appreciating loud sounds.

Ewing has made a study of several children who were thought to be suffering from congenital aphasia and whose hearing was believed to be normal. When the entire range of hearing was tested, it was found that there was selective deafness for high tones. Certain components of speech were inaudible to these children and were, therefore, misformed or replaced by other sounds giving rise to a type of speech resembling idioglossia which is described in connection with congenital word deafness. Simple methods of testing hearing revealed no evidence of deafness in these children.

Some deaf-mutes show loss of vestibular function when the usual tests are made by rotation and irrigation of the ear. As a rule, however, they walk quite steadily and even in the dark show no apparent loss of equilibrium. Apparently muscle sense and vision have been utilized to compensate for the loss of vestibular function. It must be mentioned that patients who have bilateral loss of vestibular function may be completely disoriented under water where vision and muscle sense are useless. They should, therefore, be forbidden to dive or to swim under water.

Diagnosis.—The diagnosis is based on the demonstration of high grade deafness in a child of normal or of adequate intelligence. The essential studies, therefore, include the determination of auditory acuity and of intelligence. It is not always easy to distinguish between a child who is partially deaf and whose development has been retarded as a result of the deafness and a child who is mentally deficient and hence, unresponsive to sounds.

The whole range of hearing must be tested, for selective defects in the auditory scale seem to be important in some cases. When the child can be tested by the audiometer, no difficulties arise as a rule. In the past, it has been almost impossible to form any idea of the auditory acuity of young children. Recently Richter, Bordley and Hardy have devised a method which is said to give accurate results even in small children. This is based on the development of conditioned reflexes. The child is taught to associate the note of the audiometer with a disagreeable stimulus. When such a note is appreciated, therefore, an emotional reaction occurs which is manifest by a change in skin resistance. It is said that this method is not difficult to apply and does not demand too much time.

Treatment.—Much can be done for these children by speech training and instruction in lip reading. Training should be begun as soon as possible.

BIBLIOGRAPHY

BART, R. S. AND PUMPHREY, R. E.: Knuckle pads, leukonychia and deafness. New England Jour. Med., 276:202, 1967.

BORDLEY, J. AND HARDY, W. G.: A study of objective audiometry with the use of a psychogalvanic response. Ann. Otol., Rhino. and Laryngol., **58**:751, 1949.

——— AND RICHTER, C. P.: Audiometry with the use of galvanic skin resistance response. Bull. Johns Hopkins Hospital, **82**:569, 1948.

CLAYTON-JONES, E.: Rubella as a cause of congenital deafness in England. Lancet, 1:56, 1947.

DiGEORGE, A. M. *et al.:* Waardenburg's syndrome. J. Pediat., 57:649, 1960.

EWING, A. W. G.: Aphasia in Children. London, Oxford Press, 1930.

FOURMAN, P. AND FOURMAN, J.: Hereditary deafness in a family with ear pits. Brit. Med. Jour. 1955, ii, p. 1354.

FRASER, G. R.: Sex-linked recessive congenital deafness and the excess of males in profound childhood deafness. Ann. Hum. Genet., 29:171, 1965.

————: Profound childhood deafness. Jour. Med. Genet., 1:118, 1964.

FRASER, J. S.: Pathological and clinical aspects of deaf-mutism. J. Laryngol. & Otol., 37:13, etc., 1922.

HOPKINS, L. A.: Congenital deafness and other defects following German measles in the mother. Am. J. Dis. Child., 72:377, 1946.

JERVELL, O. AND LANGE-NIELSON, F.: Congenital deaf-mutism, functional heart disease with prolongation of QT interval and sudden death. Am. Heart J., 54:59, 1957.

LEVINE, S. A. AND WOODWORTH, C. R.: Congenital deaf-mutism, prolonged QT interval, syncopal attacks and sudden death. New England J. Med., 259:412, 1958.

LOVE, J. K.: Deaf-mutism. J. Laryng. & Otol., 36:29, 1921.

MARGOLIS, E.: A new hereditary syndrome. Sex-limited deaf mutism associated with total albinism. Acta Genet. Basel, 12:12, 1962.

MARSHALL, D.: Ectodermal dysplasia report of kindred with ocular abnormalities and hearing defect. Amer. Jour. Ophthal., 45:143, 1958.

McKENNA, A. J.: Hypoplasia of the optic nerves. Read before the Canad. Ophthal. Soc., June 14, 1966.

MOHR, J. AND MAGEROY, K.: Sex-linked deafness of a possibly new type. Acta Genet. Statist., 10:54, 1960.

NOCKEMANN, P. F.: Erbliche hornhautuerdickerung mit schnurfurrchen an fingern und zehen und innerohrschuerhovigkett. Medsche Welt, 37:1894, 1961.

ORMEROD, F. C.: The pathology of congenital deafness. Jour. Laryng., 74:919, 1960.

THOULD, A. K. AND SCOWEN, E. F.: The syndrome of congenital deafness and simple goiter. J. Endocrinol., 30:69, 1964.

WEST, R. A.: The effect of quinine upon the auditory nerve. Am. J. Obst. & Gynec., 36:241, 1938.

ZIPRKOWSKI, L. AND ADAM, A.: Recessive total albinism and congenital deaf mutism. Arch. of Derm., 89:151, 1964.

DEVELOPMENTAL DISORDERS OF SPEECH

Our ability to master languages varies within wide limits. One individual may acquire a number of languages with ease and another who is not less intelligent in other respects or less industrious may never be able to express himself with facility even in his native tongue. It is well known that certain children whose intellectual development is normal may be so grossly deficient in speech development that their condition exceeds the bounds of normal variation and must be considered pathological. In recent years a number of studies have been made of backward students in our public schools and it has been shown that specific, selective defects of various elements of speech are relatively common. Orton has taken an active part in these studies and draws very close analogies between these developmental disorders and the aphasias of adult life. Other authorities, who employ a more strictly psychological approach, deny the existence in any pure form of several types Orton distinguishes. For descriptive purposes, Orton's classification is very convenient and may be given in tabular form as follows:

1—Developmental word deafness
2—Developmental word blindness
3—Developmental motor aphasia
4—Developmental agraphia
5—Stuttering and stammering

These syndromes are found in all grades of severity ranging from slight departures from the normal to complete inability to learn to read or write. They are found in pure forms and also in combined or mixed forms. We exclude, of course, cases in which the speech disorder is due to intellectual deficiency or to simple motor or sensory defects such as deafness or paralysis.

Many writers have called attention to the striking association between developmental speech disorders and a tendency to left-handedness. According to Orton, disorders of speech are not frequent in children who have been strongly left-handed from infancy and have been allowed to use their left hands as they wished, but are especially frequent in children who have been compelled to learn to write with their right hand despite their preference for the left hand and in children who have been slow to select a dominant hand or are uncertain about its choice. He attributes these conditions to disturbances resulting from the failure to develop proper cerebral dominance. Whether this theory is correct or not it is evident that we are dealing with a delayed or deficient development of function of the cerebral speech mechanisms and that this is often associated with some uncertainty in the selection of a dominant hand.

Developmental word deafness, developmental word blindness and stuttering are so common and have been the subject of so many studies that they are considered below in some detail. The other syndromes being less important will be mentioned more briefly at this point.

Developmental agraphia is a term which is applied to delay in learning to write. The writing may be merely abnormally slow, so slow as to constitute an obstacle to advancement in school. In such cases the letters may be formed perfectly and spelling may be fairly good. In most cases, however, writing is irregular or even quite illegible and spelling is grossly defective. Some of these children show the tendency to reversals and will write "was" for "saw" or "b" for "d." They may be able to write mirror fashion more easily than in the usual way and are frequently able to write with the left hand better than with the right even when they are regarded as right-handed. This condition is often associated with word blindness but may exist in a pure form.

Developmental motor aphasia is a term applied to a condition in which the child cannot learn to articulate clearly but has no simple motor disorder and understands the spoken word without difficulty. Consonants are difficult for these children but vowels are much easier. Often the child can form isolated consonants well but cannot connect them to form words. Such children frequently improve very rapidly even without special training but are apt to show certain minor speech defects such as a lisp or traces of other childish speech characteristics. It is claimed that the children can recognize their errors in articulation in contrast to the children suffering from developmental word deafness whom they resemble in some respects.

BIBLIOGRAPHY

BENTON, C. D. *et al.:* Dyslexia and dominance. Jour. pediat. Ophthal., 2:53, 1965.
FAIGEL, H. C.: Language disability. Amer. Jour. Dis. Child., 110:258, 1965.
ORTON, S. T.: Reading, Writing and Speech Problems in Children. New York, W. W. Norton & Co., 1937.

DEVELOPMENTAL WORD DEAFNESS AND IDIOGLOSSIA

Definition.—This rare condition is also sometimes termed congenital auditory imperception. It may be defined as an inability to understand spoken speech with at least potentially normal mentality and without deafness. As a result of the difficulty in appreciating the significance of sounds, speech is delayed and imperfect. Developmental word deafness occurs in all degrees of severity varying from inability to grasp the meaning of sounds of all types to defects so mild that they can scarcely be regarded as abnormal. This condition is found more often in boys than in girls, and in a large proportion of cases there is a history of similar symptoms in other members of the family.

Pathological Anatomy.—Apparently, no anatomical studies have been made. It is not known whether there is a defect of development in the cerebral cortex or not.

Etiology.—The fact that several children in the same family may be affected suggests that the condition is inherited.

Clinical Features.—The child is always brought to the physician because of delay in learning to speak and because of failure to heed what is said to him. In some cases there is practically no attempt at speech, but usually the child develops a language of its own which is termed *idioglossia.* This has a superficial resemblance to "baby talk." The chief abnormality is found upon analysis to be due to imperfect formation of consonants. Only a few consonants are employed, and these are substituted for those which are lacking whenever they are required. As a rule, *b, p, t, d,* and *w* are employed most frequently, and *f, v, th, s, sh,* and *z* are lacking. Often *t* and *d* are substituted for one another. The vowels are well formed. In uncomplicated cases, the grammatical structure of the sentence is correct, the sentence is complete and every syllable is represented by a sound. In this respect, idioglossia differs from baby talk. The words are often delivered very rapidly so that the effect is that of a flood of meaningless jabber. No matter how much training the child receives, the words are never properly formed. The behavior of these children is normal except for some sensitiveness due to consciousness of their disability. The contrast between their intelligent appearance and their infantile type of speech is often very striking. When it is possible to test hearing properly, it is found to be good. The most characteristic feature of this condition is the more or less complete inability to understand what is said when the speaker's lips are concealed. The child hears but the words have no significance. Many of these children have learned to read lips to a certain extent and, hence, often appear to understand simple words and sentences. They are quick to grasp the meaning of gestures and signs. The difficulty in speech is undoubtedly secondary to the defect in the receptive functions.

Diagnosis.—The diagnosis depends upon the following features: (1) The defect in speech as described above. (2) The presence of normal hearing. The whole range of hearing must be tested. (3) The presence of normal or nearly normal intelligence. (4) The inability to understand speech when the speaker's lips are concealed.

Prognosis.—There is a tendency to improvement and most authorities state that training is helpful. The outlook would seem to depend upon the severity of the defect and upon the child's intelligence.

Treatment.—Special training in lip reading is recommended.

BIBLIOGRAPHY

CREAK, E. M.: A case of partial deafness, simulating congenital auditory imperception. J. Neurol. & Psychopath., 13:133, 1932.

EWING, A. W. G.: Aphasia in Children. London, Oxford Press, 1930.

HALL, B. S. AND HALL, B. M.: Auditory imperception, illustrated by description of three cases. J. Neurol. & Psychopath., 11:304, 1931.

KARLIN, I. W.: Congenital verbal auditory agnosia. Pediatrics, 7:60, 1951.

MORRISON, A. G.: Congenital word deafness, with some observations on the accompanying idioglossia. J. Neurol. & Psychopath., 11:28, 1930.

WORSTER-DROUGHT, C. AND ALLEN, I. M.: Congenital auditory imperception (congenital word deafness). The investigation of a case by Head's Method. J. Neurol. & Psychopath., 9:289, 1929.

————: Congenital auditory imperception and its relation to idioglossia and other speech defects. J. Neurol. & Psychopath., 10:193, 1930.

DEVELOPMENTAL WORD BLINDNESS AND MIRROR WRITING

Definition.—Certain children are unable to make proper progress in learning to write and to read although their application, their vision and their intelligence are quite normal. It has been shown that in many cases the difficulty lies in the child's inability to learn the meaning of graphic symbols, and the condition has, therefore, been termed congenital word blindness. It is frequently possible to discover several cases of word blindness in the same family, and sometimes members of several generations may be affected. This is a very common condition and has become a serious problem in schools in which modern methods of teaching are employed. The terms developmental dyslexia and specific dyslexia are also employed.

Pathological Anatomy.—No post-mortem examinations have been made. It is not known whether there is a defect of development in the cerebral cortex or not.

Etiology.—In an extensive genetic and statistical study, Hallgren shows that this condition is inherited as a dominant characteristic. It is four times as common in boys as in girls.

In 1964, Macdonald Critchley published a valuable analysis of developmental dyslexia. He describes the steps by which our present concept of this condition was reached, the clinical manifestations, the methods of examination by which a diagnosis may be made, the many divergent views, especially those of the school psychologists and psychiatrists, the methods of treatment and the end results. He holds firmly to the view that developmental dyslexia is a specific entity and not a result of a constellation of factors. He doubts that there is any organic defect in the nervous system.

Clinical Features.—As a rule, the child is considered to be normal in every respect until he enters school. It is then found that it is impossible for him to learn to read and write. Such children find it especially difficult to distinguish between certain letters, such as "b" and "d," "p" and "q" and "n" and "u," in which the form of the letter is similar but its orientation is different. The same difficulty in orientation is evident in their tendency to read "saw" for "was" and "ton" for "not." In the same way the sequence of letters may be confused and the child may read "form" for "from." Spelling is almost always grossly defective especially spelling of written words. It is of interest that these children often have no difficulty in recognizing numerals and may do well in arithmetic although the same tendency to reversals may cause confusion. The teacher is apt to regard the child as merely stupid or lazy, and it is very probable that many if not most cases of this condition are unrecognized. The child's normal capacity in other branches of school work, however, should arouse suspicions of the true nature of the disability. These children have no difficulty, as a rule, in grasping anything that is said to them, and they learn to talk with average facility. Some of these children learn to read music readily and may become accomplished musicians.

Some very interesting and characteristic features of this condition appear in the attempts at writing. Many of the children are left-handed and others are apparently ambidextrous. When trying to write with the right hand they are prone to misspell, omit or reduplicate letters. Letters, syllables or even whole words may be reversed in sequence and letters may be written backwards. Thus "cat" becomes "tac" and "dog" becomes "god." This transposition of words, i.e. writing from right to left, is called mirror writing. As a rule, it is found in only a fragmentary form when the right hand is employed. One gains the impression that the orientation of the words is indifferent to the child. When the pencil is taken in the left hand, however, some of these children write mirrorwise consistently. In most cases, this writing is performed with ease. Moreover, the child can read either type of writing with the same degree of ease, although the average individual cannot read the reversed script without the aid of a mirror.

Critchley has explained the mirror writing as follows: When a child first begins to learn to write, the movements performed in copying the given characters become stored in the mind as memories of muscle movements. Certain movements, the child learns, produce a certain letter. The natural movements for the left hand are the mirrored counterpart of the right hand. Hence, it would be natural for children to write mirror-fashion with the left hand were this tendency not corrected by their visual memory of the correct orientation of the word. Critchley's conclusion, therefore, is that the mirror writing with the left hand is merely another expression of the fundamental defect, namely, lack of visual memories, which permits the kinesthetic memories of muscle movements to act independently.

Studies by Gates and by other American authorities have revealed that dominance of the left hand is not so important in these cases as the dominance of the left eye. Left-eyed children instinctively move their eyes from right to left. Failure to develop proper ocular movements from left to right is among the most important causes of difficulty in reading. Photographic studies of ocular movements during reading have shown that these children's eyes make irregular movements back and forth with many pauses for fixation, whereas the normal child makes few pauses and the eyes move in steady progression from left to right. It is claimed by Gates that there is no sharply defined clinical entity corresponding to the concept of congenital word blindness and that the difficulties in reading encountered among school children are of many different types. Hermann states that these children show uncertainty in discrimination between right and left and in naming fingers. He suggests that there is an inherited impairment of the sense of direction in space.

Mehegan and Dreifuss studied 17 children who had reading difficulty and normal intelligence, but displayed abnormal motility with increased reflexes, Babinski signs, abnormal movements and abnormalities in the electroencephalogram.

In three valuable papers Goldberg analyzes the various factors responsible for developmental dyslexia. He points out that fetal anoxia was present in a definite percentage of cases. He also reports a study of 25 children suffering from this condition. In 7 cases electroencephalographic study revealed slow activity and occasional sharp waves in the parieto-occipital area.

Diagnosis.—Monroe has given an elaborate analysis of the various factors to be considered in determining the cause of difficulty in reading. We must consider mental deficiency first of all. If general intelligence is adequate, the visual functions must be investigated. Not only visual acuity should be tested but the ability to discriminate visual patterns and the spatial orientation of visual patterns. Auditory factors are also important for some children do not distinguish speech sounds properly or do not grasp the temporal sequence in which the various sounds occur. The ocular movements must also be studied for certain children whose muscle balance is normal cannot fix adequately or acquire proper left to right movements necessary for reading. This is especially true as regards left-eyed children. Monroe also points out the importance of vocabulary in learning to read and of proper methods of instruction. The emotional nature and personality of the child should be considered. Evidently adequate analysis of the cause of difficulty in reading requires the services of an expert.

Mirror writing is not restricted to cases of word blindness. It is also found in a fragmentary form in mental defectives, in some cases of right hemiplegia and also to some extent in normal children who are learning to write.

Prognosis.—The prognosis depends upon the child's intelligence, the severity of the defect and the skill of the teacher. There is usually slow improvement even in severe cases.

Treatment.—This is a problem for the expert teacher. The methods employed depend upon the nature of the disability and must be varied to meet individual needs. In general the child must be taught in the old fashioned way, learning the letters of the alphabet first and then words and sentences.

BIBLIOGRAPHY

BETTMAN, J. W.: Cerebral dominance in developmental dyslexia. Arch. of Ophthal., **78**:722, 1967.
CRITCHLEY, MacD.: Some defects of reading and writing in children; Their association with word-blindness and mirror-writing. J. State Med., **35**:217, 1927.
———: The significance of mirror-writing. Proc. Roy. Soc. Med., **20**:397, Sec. of Neurol., 1927.
———: Developmental Dyslexia. Springfield, Thomas, 1964.
DREW, A. L.: A neurological appraisal of familial congenital word blindness. Brain, **79**:440, 1956.
GATES, A.: The Improvement of Reading. New York, Macmillan Co., 1935.
GOLDBERG, H. K.: The ophthalmologist looks at the reading problem. Amer. Jour. Ophthal., **67**:47, 1959.
GOLDBERG, H. K.: The disabled reader. Jour. Pediatric Ophthal., 1968, February, p. 11.
———: The role of brain damage in congenital dyslexia. Amer. Jour. Ophthal., **50**:586, 1960.

HALLGREN, B.: Specific dyslexia. Acta Psychiat. et Neurol. Suppl. 65, Copenhagen, 1950.

HERMANN, K.: Congenital word blindness. Poor readers in the light of Gerstmann's syndrome. Acta Psychiat. et Neurol. Scand. Suppl. 108, 1956, p. 177.

MEHEGAN, C. C. AND DREIFUSS, F. E.: A neurological study of reading difficulty. Virginia Med. Mth., 94:453, 1967.

MONROE, M.: Children Who Cannot Write. Univ. of Chicago Press, 1932.

ORTON, S. T.: Word blindness in school children. Arch. Neurol. & Psychiat., 14:581, 1925.

TAFT, L. T. AND COHEN, H. J.: Reading disability. Bull. New York Acad. Med., 44:478, 1968.

STUTTERING AND STAMMERING

Definition.—Most authors define stammering as a disorder of speech in which utterance is arrested for a time by spasm or incoördination of the muscles of speech, and stuttering as a disorder in which there is repetition of the initial consonant. Others regard the two terms as synonymous.

Pathological Anatomy.—No anatomical changes have ever been demonstrated in the nervous system and, in view of the tendency to recovery, it is unlikely that any lesions are present.

Clinical Features.—Since stuttering and stammering are disorders of essentially the same nature, they will be considered together. They begin in almost all cases between the ages of 2 and 10 years. Orton states that they begin as a rule when speech is first attained or when the child first learns to write, that is, between the second and third years or between the sixth and eighth years. Boys are affected more frequently than girls and in certain cases there is evidence that the trait is inherited. In many cases the child is left-handed or shows some tendency to left-handedness. These disorders are commonly associated with neurotic personalities.

Before considering the nature of these conditions a few words must be said about *the physiology of normal speech*. The vowel sounds are produced by vibrations of the vocal cords set up by a current of air expelled from the lungs. The note is determined by the position and tension of the cords and by the resonance of the nasal and oral chambers. The vowel sounds are represented in English as A E I O U. The consonants are produced by interruption of the column of air exhaled from the lungs by the tongue and the palate: K H CH G Y R N. The consonants D B G M N V L R the lips: P B M. (2) Those produced by the tip of the tongue and upper teeth: TH S Z. (3) Those produced by the anterior part of the tongue and the palate: T D SH N L. (4) Those produced by the posterior part of the tongue and the palate: K H CH G Y R N. The consonants D B G M N L R are accompanied by vowel sounds but the others include no laryngeal elements. The soft palate is open during the formation of NM and NG so these sounds have nasal resonance but all other sounds in English are produced with the nasal chambers excluded by closure of the soft palate.

The stutterer forms the initial consonant several times, thus "C C C Cat."

The consonant "C" is formed properly as a rule, but the vowel sound "A" is impossible for a moment. Apparently the oral mechanisms function at once, but the laryngeal and respiratory mechanisms do not cooperate at first to form the vowel which should follow. Most authors attribute this to "spasm," and there are frequently facial grimaces and even movements of the head and extremities during the subject's violent efforts to form the word. The word is usually formed eventually in an explosive fashion. The stammerer fails to expel a proper blast from the lungs and therefore cannot make any sounds at all for a time. He may even try to speak when inhaling. Clearly, in both cases, there is a failure of cooperation between the oral mechanisms by which the consonants are formed and the laryngeal mechanisms by which vowel sounds are produced and the flow of air controlled. It is of interest that the subject can sing or whisper normally in most cases. Stuttering and stammering are inconstant as a rule, and are profoundly modified by psychological factors. The child is apt to have less difficulty with speech when calm and more difficulty when subjected to nervous strain of any type, but no general rule can be given.

These conditions are frequently found in children who display other neurotic trends, such as enuresis, night terrors, temper tantrums, digestive disorders and tics. It has been frequently pointed out that to force a left-handed child to learn to write with the right hand may induce stuttering. It is also claimed that stuttering can often be traced to emotional shocks and that the element of imitation is evident in many cases. The consensus of opinion seems to be that these disorders are the result of psychological factors. Orton, however, states that if these children are studied early in life, emotional disorders are not found and believes that their prevalence in older children is a result of the speech disorder rather than a cause. He claims that all cases fall into four groups: (1) Those in which there has been an enforced shift from the left to the right hand. (2) Those who have been slow in selecting a master hand. (3) Those in whom there is a history of stuttering in other members of the family. (4) A small group in whom no good explanation can be found. Orton concludes that a failure to develop proper cerebral dominance is to blame.

Prognosis.—In many instances, these disorders eventually disappear spontaneously, frequently when the subject becomes established in life and acquires a certain amount of self confidence. In other instances, despite excellent intelligence and the most expert care, the disorder persists throughout life. A prognosis should be given with considerable reserve.

Diagnosis.—The diagnosis is usually obvious but in certain cases the existence of neurological disorders or other complicating factors may cause some doubt about the nature of the speech defect.

Treatment.—Many different methods of treatment are recommended and it is evident that none of them are entirely satisfactory. It is recommended that every effort should be made to maintain the child's physical condition at the highest possible level and that all sources of emotional stress and strain should be fully investigated and eliminated as far as possible. The child is then given exercise in proper breathing and taught to form each sound separately and then in combination so as to make words. If the child is slow to select a dominant hand or is definitely left-handed and has been taught to write with the right hand, he should be retrained to use the left. If his dominant hand is in doubt, he should be aided to make a proper choice. Every effort should be made to keep the child from becoming self conscious and from developing feelings of inferiority. The care of an expert teacher is advised since improper training may accentuate the condition. I believe it unwise to add to these children's burdens by subjecting them to psychoanalysis.

CONGENITAL COLOR BLINDNESS

Definition.—A congenital inability to perceive colors which occurs most commonly in an incomplete or partial form.

Pathological Anatomy.—The anatomical basis of this defect is unknown but there is some reason to believe that the retinae are at fault.

Clinical Features.—Partial color blindness is very common, being present in at least 3 per cent of all males. In females it occurs in only about 0.2 per cent. This peculiarity is definitely inherited and is transmitted as a rule according to the law of a sex-linked recessive characteristic. It is believed that females are affected only when the pathological gene is inherited from both parents. Males do not transmit the defect directly but unaffected females convey it to their sons.

The proper classification of color blindness is a matter of great difficulty for there is no agreement about the nature of color vision. The following outline seems to be the simplest. The commonest form of color blindness is the so-called red-green blindness. On analysis, this is found to be due to inability to perceive either red or green. *Green blindness* is manifest by the confusion of red with green and by difficulty in perceiving a green mark on a gray background. In *red blindness,* the patient makes the same mistakes with red and green and cannot see a red mark superimposed on a gray background. *Blue blindness* is very rare. The subject sees only reds and greens and confuses blue with either. *Complete color blindness* is also very rare. It is said that the patient sees only black and white with the intermediate shades of gray. As a rule, amblyopia, photophobia, central scotoma and nystagmus are associated but it is claimed that complete color blindness may exist with normal visual acuity. This is inherited as a recessive characteristic.

Color blindness is almost invariably an isolated defect and there is no apparent tendency for it to be associated with mental deficiency or other abnormalities. It has been present in persons of remarkable intellectual powers. The brief outline given above gives no idea of the complexity of the subject and the reader is advised to consult the references for an adequate presentation of the facts.

Diagnosis.—The diagnosis is based upon the subject's inability to distinguish between colors and upon the absence of any significant defect in visual acuity or in the visual fields. Holmgren's colored worsteds are most commonly employed in routine tests but must be supplemented by more elaborate methods for satisfactory results. Stilling's pseudo-isochromatic plates are very useful.

BIBLIOGRAPHY

BELL, J.: Color-blindness. Treasury of Human Inheritance, Vol. 11, Part 11, Cambridge University Press, 1926.
HARRISON, R. *et al.*: Congenital total color blindness. Arch. of Ophthal., **64**:685, 1960.
SCHIÖTZ: Color-blind females. Brit. J. Ophth., 4:345, 1920.
WALSH, F. B.: *Loc. cit.*

CONGENITAL UNIVERSAL INDIFFERENCE TO PAIN

Definition.—A state of indifference to pain which is apparently of congenital origin and which differs in some respects from true analgesia. It is similar to the condition produced by bilateral frontal lobotomy in which pain is felt but the patient ignores it.

Pathological Anatomy.—Baxter and Olszewski report a post-mortem examination of the nervous system in which no anatomical abnormalities were discovered. Magee describes another post-mortem study of the brain in this condition. He found only slight pallor of the subcallosal fasciculus. Dr. Victor McKusick has made a study of the chromosomes of these patients and no abnormality was found.

Clinical Features.—As a rule, the parents notice by the beginning of the third year that the child does not cry when injured and seems indifferent to blows or falls. Cuts, burns, bruises and even fractures of the bones may result from the child's failure to guard against injury. As a rule such children do not complain of their mishaps and will continue to run around and play despite the presence of conditions which would cause severe pain in the normal child. In our experience, examination reveals no analgesia or thermanesthesia. The child always names correctly any stimulus applied but shows no sign of pain and makes no complaint. We have found no psychogalvanic reaction to potentially painful stimuli. One child seemed to be sensitive to pain of visceral origin for attacks of acute pyelitis made her scream and she struggled when her ureters were catheterized. In another case, an attack of appendicitis followed by peritonitis was not associated with any evidence of pain whatever. We have found no evidence to suggest hysteria or masochism in our cases and no tendency to mental deficiency.

Three cases of this type have been studied at the Harriet Lane Home for Children and references to several similar cases are given below. Walsh describes three cases of this condition.

Diagnosis.—The diagnosis is based upon the indifference to potentially painful stimuli and upon the absence of true analgesia. Syringomyelia and defects in the spinal cord should always be considered for these are the commonest causes of analgesia in childhood. Hysteria should be kept in mind as a possibility. (See Congenital and familial anesthesia of Biemond and Chromosome trisomy of group 13-15 in generalized congenital analgesia.)

Prognosis.—There is no tendency to develop any other neurological abnormalities but the children are prone to injure themselves and are frequently in the hospital. Some patients have enjoyed successful careers and have lived to middle age.

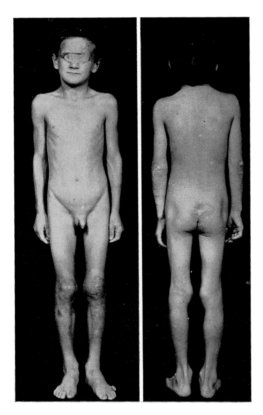

Fig. 45. Photograph of the child whose case is described below. Note the scar of the large burn over the sacrum and also many smaller scars.

Treatment.—The children should be trained to avoid injuries and their peculiar condition should be explained to them.

CASE HISTORY (Ped. A-4143).—*Boy of nine years who had sustained numerous injuries including fractures of the bones, extensive burns and injury to the cornea which seemed to cause him no discomfort. No objective evidence of disease of the nervous system found on examination except for mild congenital word blindness.*

W. S. was the first child in a family of four siblings. His birth and early development were normal. The family history was unimportant. At an early age it was noted that he did not seem to notice injuries as other children do. The usual falls and blows did not cause him to cry or show signs of pain. As an infant he developed the habit of biting his fingers and, when he acquired teeth, he would bite his fingers until they bled so that they eventually became scarred and deformed. At the age of two years he broke his left fibula, but continued to walk about as before, giving no sign of pain. When he was five years old sand was thrown into his left eye and the cornea was scratched and ulcerated. He made no complaint of this and it was not until several days later that his mother noticed his eye was inflamed and took him to an ophthalmologist. A dense corneal scar resulted which caused reduction of vision. At the age of five and one half years he was taken to a hospital because of a large swelling on the dorsum of the left foot. This was not tender and seemed to cause him no discomfort so the physicians were inclined to believe that it was some form of edema. Roentgenographic examination, however, disclosed a fracture of the first metatarsal bone and it was discovered that some time previously a large rock had been dropped on his foot. At the age of eight years the mother discovered a large sore over the buttocks which the child had not mentioned. He was taken to a hospital where an ulcerated lesion was found over the sacrum measuring two by three inches and also large lesions over both buttocks and over the posterior aspects of the thighs which resembled burns. It was discovered that several days before the boy had been sitting on a hot steam radiator. The lesions were covered with necrotic tissue so they were cleaned with a sharp knife and scrubbed with alcohol. It is stated that the child made no complaint during these procedures and showed no sign of pain. The child's body was covered with a great variety of scars and inquiry disclosed that he was frequently involved in fights with his playmates and would come home dripping with blood from lacerations due to being struck with sticks and stones. While fighting he would protrude his tongue between his teeth and bite it until it bled. As a result his tongue was much scarred. During this period roentgenograms of the feet revealed that he had an old fracture of the second metatarsal bone of the right foot. It was never discovered when this happened for the child had never mentioned it and did not remember the incident. A few months later the child was again admitted to the hospital because of a deep cut just above the left knee which had opened into the patellar bursa. This healed slowly and some weeks later he was admitted to the Harriet Lane Home for further study at the age of 9 years.

Examination revealed astonishingly little. The child was covered with scars of innumerable injuries, cuts, burns and excoriations. He was a bit below the average height for his age but his weight was proportional to his height. His intelligence was at least average. Neurological examination revealed that the cranial nerves, motility and the reflexes were all in order. The child could appreciate all types of sensory stimuli including light touch, warm and cool, pin prick, etc. The threshold was not elevated for any form of sensibility. However, the child was quite indifferent to such painful procedures as squeezing the tendo Achilles, pressing upon the supraorbital nerve, pinching the neck, squeezing the testicles and thrusting a pin deeply into the tissues. If asked if these tests caused pain, he would reply indifferently, "No," or "A little," or occasionally, "Yes," but never protested or showed signs of pain. There was no change in pulse rate or pupils. No psychogalvanic reaction to pain was elicited. Psychiatric study revealed that the intelligence quotient was 104. The child was right-handed, right-legged, and right-eyed. There was a specific reading defect with a tendency to reversals of the "was" for "saw" type. Personality study disclosed no abnormal trends. His fighting was apparently due to his courage in resisting bullies rather than any pugnacity on his part. Vasomotor reactions were normal in the extremities. All laboratory studies including the Wassermann and spinal fluid examinations were quite normal.

At the age of 10 years the child became ill and was taken to the hospital. He made no complaint of pain or of any local symptoms. Examination revealed a soft mass in the lower abdomen, but no local tenderness and no muscle spasm. There was a fever ranging between 102° and 104°F. and moderate leucocytosis. A peritoneal cyst of some type was suspected and exploration was performed. A large abscess was found in the peritoneum containing more than 100 cc of pus from which the colon bacillus was cultivated. It was concluded by the surgeon that the abscess was due to the rupture of an inflamed appendix. His convalescence was uneventful.

BIBLIOGRAPHY

ARBUSE, D., CANTOR, M. AND BARENBERG, P.: Congenital indifference to pain. J. Pediat., **35:**221, 1949.

BAXTER, D. W. AND OLSZEWSKI, J.: Congenital universal insensitivity to pain. Brain, **83:**381, 1960.

BOURLAND, A. AND WINKELMANN, R. K.: Study of cutaneous innervation in congenital anesthesia. Arch. of Neurol., **14:**223, 1966.

BOYD, D. A. AND NIE, L. W.: Congenital universal indifference to pain. Arch. Neurol. & Psychiat., **61:**402, 1949.

CRITCHLEY, McD.: Some aspects of pain. Brit. M. J., **ii:**891, 1934.

DEARBORN, G.: A case of congenital anesthesia. J. Nerv. Ment. Dis., **75:**612, 1931.

ERVIN, F. R.: Hereditary insensitivity to pain. Trans. Amer. Neurol. Ass., **86:**70, 1960.

FORD, F. R. AND WILKINS, L.: Congenital universal indifference to pain. Bull. John Hopkins Hospital, **62:**448, 1938.

FREEMAN, W. AND WATTS, J. W.: Pain of organic disease relieved by prefrontal lobotomy. Lancet, **i:**953, 1946.

MAGEE, K. R.: Congenital indifference to pain. Arch. of Neurol., 9:635, 1963.

McMURRAY, G. A.: Experimental study of a case of insensitivity to pain. Arch. Neurol. & Psychiat., 64:650, 1950.

OGDEN, T. E. *et al.*: Some sensory syndromes in children: indifference to pain and sensory neuropathy. Jour. Neurol. Neurosurg. & Psychiat., 1959, 22:267.

OLSZEWSKI, J.: Post-mortem examination of the nervous system in a case of congenital insensitiveness to pain. Meeting of the Canadian Neurological Soc. Toronto, June 12, 1958.

SCHILDER, P. AND STENGEL, E.: Asymbolia for pain. Arch. Neurol. & Psychiat., 25:598, 1931.

SWANSON, A. G.: Congenital insensitivity to pain with anhydrosis. Arch. of Neurol. 8:299, 1963.

WALSH, F. B.: Clinical Neuroophthalmology. Williams and Wilkins, p. 437, 1957.

CONGENITAL AND FAMILIAL ANESTHESIA (BIEMOND)

Biemond has studied two twins of eleven years. The girl's mental status was better than average and she seems to have had no motor disorders. There was extensive loss of sensibility. Pain was lost. The sense of touch and the appreciation of differences in temperature were both diminished. Stereognosis was not lost. The tendon reflexes were absent.

The other twin, a boy, was deaf and dumb. He had been considered mentally deficient but this was found to be incorrect. The tendon reflexes could not be elicited. The boy seemed to display the same loss of sensibility found in his sister's case. He died and post-mortem examination was made. The posterior root ganglia displayed deficient development and similar defects were found in the Gasserian ganglia. The posterior roots were defective and the posterior horns of the spinal gray matter as well. The posterior columns of the cord were deficient. The spinothalamic tracts could not be found. This condition seems to have been regarded as a defect of development. We have had one case in which the anatomical findings were essentially the same as those described by Biemond.

Swanson *et al.* report the study of brothers of twelve and fourteen years who could not feel pain or distinguish hot and cold. They did not sweat. Both had evidence of numerous injuries to the joints and soft tissues. The boy of twelve years died suddenly of a febrile illness. At post-mortem examination revealed complete absence of the finely myelinated fibers which form Lissauer's tract in the spinal cord, scarcity of finely myelinated fibers of the dorsal roots and lack of the small nerve cells in the dorsal root ganglia. The dura mater showed 2 full length clefts on the dorsal and central aspects.

I am informed that one or more children have been observed in London who display the same symptoms described above.

This condition must be distinguished from congenital universal indifference to pain q.v. from which it differs in some respects from syringomyelia and from generalized congenital analgesia with trisomy 13-15. Hereditary degeneration of the sensory nerve roots q.v. is a progressive process and is rarely seen in infancy.

Pinsky and Digeorge and Vasella *et al.* describe *congenital sensory neuropathy with anhidrosis.* Vassella states that these children may bite off the tip of the tongue and mutilate themselves.

BIBLIOGRAPHY

BIEMOND, A.: Investigation of the brain in a case of congenital and familial analgesia. 11th International Congress of Neuropathology. London, Sept. 1955.

PINSKY, L. AND DIGEORGE, A. M.: Congenital familial sensory neuropathy with anhidrosis. Jour. Pediat., **68:**1, 1966.

SWANSON, A. G. *et al.:* Anatomic changes in congenital insensitivity to pain. Arch. Neurol., **12:**12, 1965.

VASSELLA, H. M. *et al.:* Congenital sensory neuropathy with anhidrosis. Arch. Dis. Childh., **43:**124, 1968.

CRANIOSTENOSES—OXYCEPHALY, ACROBRACHYCEPHALY AND SCAPHOCEPHALY

Definition.—Virchow coined the term craniostenosis to apply to a certain group of malformations of the skull in which premature synostosis of two or more cranial bones occurs causing increased intracranial pressure and other symptoms. There are probably a number of such conditions, but we need discuss only the three types mentioned above, trigonocephaly and the craniofacial dysostosis of Crouzon which seems to belong to this group.

Etiology.—Park and Powers have advanced a great deal of evidence to show that these conditions are dependent upon defects in the germ plasm. There is sometimes a history of several cases in one family. This fact and the association of other defects of development such as syndactylism point unmistakably to a developmental anomaly.

Pathological Anatomy.—Before taking up the mechanism by which these conditions are produced, it is necessary to review the most important facts regarding the development of the skull in infancy. At birth in full-term infants, the membranous bones of the vault are still slightly separated although their margins are in apposition at some points. There is no bony union as may easily be determined by palpation. The anterior and posterior fontanels are still patent. Between the sixth month and end of the first year, the sutures of the vault are closed in the sense that the margins become serrated and begin to interlock, although roentgenographic examination reveals that the bones are not actually fused. The anterior fontanel closes between the fourteenth and the twenty-second months, and the posterior fontanel by the second month, under normal conditions. During childhood, it is still possible for the skull to grow, for the margins of the bones are not actually fused. The sutures are interlocked so firmly by the age of 10 years, however, that increased intracranial pressure causes little or no enlargement of the head. Usually but not invariably, the suture lines slowly disappear during middle age and eventually no anatomical evidence remains to show that the bones of the vault have ever been distinct.

In the various conditions under consideration, the cranial bones are united prematurely becoming fused before birth or during infancy. The line of union disappears completely or is marked by a bony ridge. Suture lines as seen in a normal skull are never found. This process is called synostosis. Since the skull cannot expand normally to accommodate the growing brain, the intracranial pressure becomes increased causing digital markings on the inner table of the skull. Virchow formulated the principle that when synostosis of two cranial bones occurs prematurely, normal growth is inhibited in a direction perpendicular to the obliterated suture line and that compensatory growth takes place in other directions. Evidently, a number of possible malformations may be expected depending upon the suture or sutures involved.

Park and Powers have presented a somewhat different point of view. They state that the primary cause is defective growth of the mesenchyme in which the bone is formed. The bones formed in such tissue are therefore smaller than normal and make contact with one another too soon. It is also necessary to assume, according to this theory, that the tissue which occupies the suture line and has the property of resisting ossification is defective and that, as soon as the bones become approximated, they fuse.

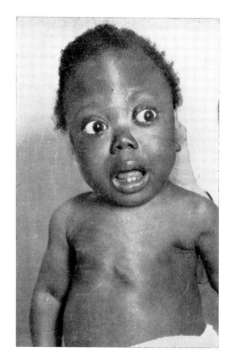

FIG. 46. Case of oxycephaly showing the narrow, high forehead running up to an apex at the vertex and the exophthalmos. There was advanced "convolutional atrophy" in the roentgenograms of the head and the coronal and sagittal sutures were absent.

Clinical Features Oxycephaly.—Grieg, who has made a very complete study of this condition, distinguishes three types: (1) True oxycephaly which is congenital and dependent upon general craniofacial synostosis. This is often associated with syndactylism and other deformities of the extremities. (2) Delayed oxycephaly which may appear at any time during the period in which the brain is growing and is never associated with deformities. (3) False oxycephaly which is a localized synostosis due to incidental diseases of the cranial bones.

The most striking feature of this condition is the great height of the skull which slopes gradually up to a point at the vertex. The skull is flattened laterally as well as anteroposteriorly, the forehead receding and the occiput flat. A bony prominence is sometimes seen in the region of the bregma. The superciliary ridges are inconspicuous, as are the temporal ridges and depressions. The nose is frequently deflected to one side. The malar bones may be flattened. The hard palate is shortened and high arched. In all well developed cases, the eyeballs are protruding and the exophthalmos may be so severe that it is impossible for the patient to close the lids. Frequently, there is a divergent squint. The transverse axis of the orbit seems to slope so that the outer canthus is always lower than the inner canthus. Vision is reduced or lost in some severe cases, and ophthalmoscopic examination reveals optic atrophy or papilledema. It is generally stated that the optic atrophy is of the secondary type, and it is believed to be the result

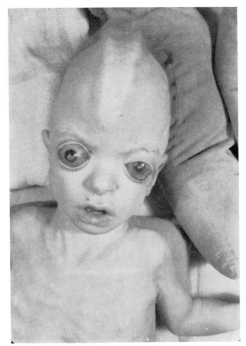

Fig. 47. Case of oxycephaly with spina bifida, hypospadia and syndactylism. (By the courtesy of Dr. H. G. Butler.)

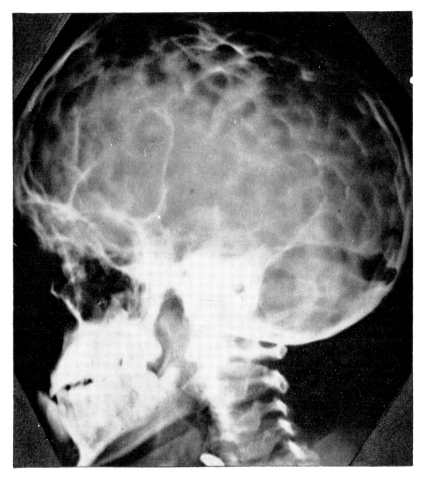

Fig. 48. Roentgenograms of the skull showing high vertex, convolutional markings and absence of suture lines. (From Walsh: Neuro-Ophthalmology, courtesy the Williams and Wilkins Company.)

of previous papilledema. Some authors, however, describe primary optic atrophy. In many instances, total blindness eventually results although this outcome is not invariable. It is stated that if papilledema occurs, it always appears during the early years of childhood when the growth of the brain is most rapid and that if the child reaches the tenth year with normal vision, no fears of optic atrophy need be entertained. Some ophthalmologists describe constriction of the superior parts of the visual fields due, it is believed, to tension on the optic nerves resulting from depression of the base of the skull which forces the nerves against the lower margin of the optic foramina. We have observed papilledema only in occasional cases and suspect that stretching of the nerves may be a common cause of the atrophy.

Errors of refraction are common, especially myopia. Sense of smell may also be lost or impaired, and deafness is described although so rarely that we are not forced to regard it as more than accidentally associated with oxycephaly. It has often been stated that mental development is not inhibited in this condition, and it is true that many patients seem to enjoy normal intelligence. However, in severe cases, there is very frequently a definite intellectual deficit. In this connection it must be kept in mind that loss of vision early in life may be responsible for a certain amount of mental retardation. The patients complain of severe and frequent headaches, and there is often some obstruction of the nasal passages due to the malformation of the nasal bones. Convulsions occur in some cases.

We have observed one very unusual case in a boy of four years. He displayed bilateral papilledema and increased spinal fluid pressure. The head was of normal size and shape and the ventricular system was completely normal. Roentgenograms of the skull showed no suture lines. Channels were cut through the skull to permit expansion and this procedure resulted in disappearance of the papilledema and enlargement of the head. Histological study of the bone removed revealed no evidence of suture lines.

In association with true congenital oxycephaly and never with any other type, we find, in many cases, certain characteristic deformities of the extremities. These usually take the form of syndactylism. The phalanges may be joined with their fellows of the same fingers with partial or complete absence of the joints, or they may be fused laterally with phalanges of adjacent fingers. In the same way, the phalanges may be fused with the metacarpal (or metatarsal) bones, and the metacarpals (or metatarsals) with one another. These deformities are always bilateral and essentially symmetrical. The hands are more severely affected than the feet. In general, the malformations are most marked in the distal joints, but in several cases it has been found that the elbow joints were defective so that complete extension was impossible. The combination of synostosis of the cranium and syndactylism is termed Apert's syndrome. Several different types are described which differ chiefly in the type of deformity found in the extremities.

Roentgenograms of the skull reveal the malformations already described. In addition the coronal and sagittal sutures are seen to be synostosed. Other sutures may be involved as well, but premature closure of the sagittal and coronal sutures seems to be essential for the development of oxycephaly. The middle and posterior fossae are deeper than usual and shortened in the anteroposterior diameter. The orbits are found to be very shallow and oblique. The frontal sinuses are small or absent and the antra may be reduced. The so-called "convolutional atrophy" of the cranial vault

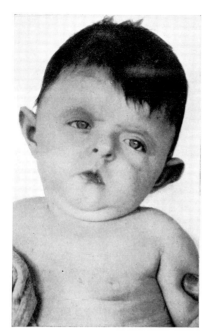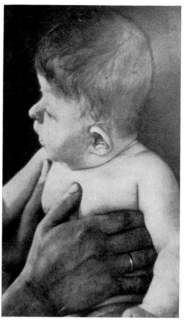

FIG. 49. Acrobrachycephaly, front and lateral views. Showing flattening of the head anteroposteriorly and broadening laterally. (After Park and Powers. Am. J. Dis. Child., 20:234, 1920.)

is always present and usually developed to a high degree. Grieg states that the diploe are absent. Platybasia may be associated.

A few patients have come to autopsy. The brains always show evidences of compression such as flattening of the convolutions and obliteration of the sulci. No other lesions are constant. The cerebrospinal fluid is present in reduced amount. Hydrocephalus is a rare complication. When hydrocephalus is found, there is usually also platybasia.

Usually, oxycephaly occurs sporadically and no history of morbid heredity can be obtained. In a few cases, however, one or more siblings have been affected and the disease has been traced through three generations.

It is believed that the peculiar shape of the head, that is, the narrowness and lack of depth, is due to the premature closure of the sagittal and coronal sutures and that the extraordinary height of the vault is due to compensatory expansion of the brain upward, since it cannot expand laterally or in the anteroposterior diameter. Sooner or later, as Grieg has shown, all the cranial sutures become closed and increased intracranial pressure develops. This gives rise to papilledema followed by secondary optic atrophy, to headache, to reduction of the depth of the orbits causing exophthalmos, and to "digital markings" of the vault.

Acrobrachycephaly.—This term is applied to a condition very similar to oxycephaly; so similar, in fact, that some authors have confused the two. The head is flattened in the anteroposterior plane, and the vault is also abnormally high just as in oxycephaly. The most striking difference lies in the breadth of the head which, as we have stated above, is reduced in oxycephaly, but which is greatly increased in acrobrachycephaly. The forehead is excessively broad, and the root of the nose is also widened so that the eyes are placed very far apart. The exophthalmos, optic atrophy, strabismus and other features which have been described above in connection with oxycephaly may also occur in acrobrachycephaly, but since the skull can expand freely in a lateral direction, evidences of increased intracranial pressure are less striking as a rule. The peculiar deformities of the fingers and toes also occur not infrequently in the latter condition.

Roentgenograms of the skull may reveal some "digital markings" over the vault. The coronal suture is synostosed more or less completely, but the sagittal suture and the fontanels remain open in many cases long after they should be closed. Wormian bones may be found in the fontanels or sutures. It is evident that the deformity is due to the premature closure of the coronal suture and that the skull has expanded both laterally and vertically because growth in the anteroposterior plane is impossible.

Scaphocephaly.—This is an incomplete craniostenosis as is acrobrachycephaly. The head is flattened laterally and the vertex is unduly high. The characteristic feature is the excessive length of the anteroposterior diamiter. The forehead bulges, the occiput is very full and the fontanels are tense or bulging. The coronal suture may be widened. When the fontanels close, their site may be marked by a bony prominence. Optic atrophy is

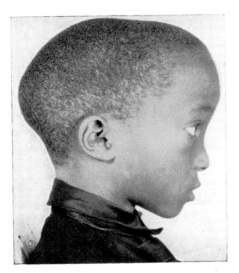

Fig. 50. Scaphocephaly showing increase in the anteroposterior diameter. The head is flattened laterally.

rather uncommon and may occur when the capacity of the cranium is not reduced. In such cases, it is possible that the optic nerves are stretched as a result of the increased anteroposterior diameter of the skull. Some degree of exophthalmos, divergent squint, papilledema and optic atrophy may be associated as in the other varieties of craniostenosis described above. Deformities of the extremities are excessively rare. Park and Powers have, however, described a child in whom scaphocephaly was associated with deformity of the elbow joints so that complete extension was impossible, and give an abstract of a case reported by Küttner in which the thumbs and great toes were slightly deformed. The child studied by Park and Powers also had a rudimentary tail.

Roentgenograms reveal the usual "convolutional markings" over the vault as well as synostosis of the sagittal suture. The deformity of the skull may be explained by the premature closure of this suture, for the head cannot expand laterally and must grow vertically and in the anteroposterior plane.

In November 1954, we observed a little girl (Ped. B-15064) who was then 13 months old. She had been born prematurely at 8 months and was slightly retarded in both mental and motor development. Her head was 45 cm in occipitofrontal circumference. There was no exophthalmos and no change in the optic discs. The sagittal suture was completely closed and fused with a small ridge overlying it. The other sutures were normal. The spinal fluid pressure was 100 mm water. The head was perfectly normal in shape and not flattened laterally as one might expect. At the age of 23 months, her head was still 45 cm in circumference, and there was a suggestion of papilledema. Apparently the sagittal suture fused prematurely, but long after birth. This is apparently a case of the condition described by Grieg as delayed craniostenosis.

Trigonocephaly.—This condition is said to be responsible for 9 per cent of the craniostenoses. It is due to the premature closure of the metopic suture. This suture begins to close in normal infants towards the end of the first year, but is not fully closed until sometime in the second year. The fully developed picture of trigonocephaly is seen only when the suture is closed at birth or soon after birth. The child's forehead is very narrow and the biparietal diameter of the skull is increased. A vertical ridge is seen in the midline of the forehead. The eyes are close together. There is no increase of intracranial pressure but mental deficiency was evident in 6 of 18 cases reported by Anderson *et al.* It is suggested that the frontal lobes are compressed. The family history is negative. Roentgenograms are important in the diagnosis. The treatment is similar to that of the other craniostenoses.

Craniofacial Dysostosis of Crouzon.—There is synostosis of the coronal, sagittal and lamboid sutures, brachycephaly with vertical elongation, increased widths and reduced anteroposterior diameter. There are frontal bosses, and pronounced digital markings. The orbits are shallow and external squint as well as exophthalmos. Hyperteliorism is often present. There may be papilledema. Optic atrophy may be secondary to papilledema or to compression of the nerves by bony proliferation in the optic canals. The nose is beaked and the base of the nose is broad. The maxillae are hypoplastic and the mandible relatively large. The palate may be high arched or cleft. The lower lip protrudes. There may be deafness due to middle ear or external auditory canal defects.

Diagnosis.—The following points are most important in the diagnosis: (1) Various types of malformations of the skull as described above. (2) Evidences of increased intracranial pressure such as headache, "digital markings" of the vault, exophthalmos and papilledema or optic atrophy. (3) Synostosis of one or more cranial sutures.

Hydrocephalus may easily be confused with the craniostenoses for the cranial bones are thin and soft in this condition, and the head may be moulded into various shapes by the pressure of the pillow and possibly in some instances by local differences in intracranial pressure. Brain tumor, abscess and other conditions causing increased intracranial pressure should be eliminated easily by the absence of the characteristic cranial malformations. If the clinical signs are inconclusive, the diagnosis may be established by ventriculography, but the conditions under consideration present such a characteristic appearance that there is rarely any need for such a procedure. Oxycephaly has been confused with microcephaly, for in both conditions the head may be pointed and the sutures prematurely closed. However, there is no papilledema or exophthalmos in microcephaly, and the total capacity of the cranium is much less than in oxycephaly. Moreover, microcephaly is frequently associated with idiocy and spastic paralysis.

When fusion of the sutures is delayed until childhood as in the two cases mentioned above the diagnosis may be more difficult for the characteristic deformities of the skull may not be evident.

Treatment.—Operation is often necessary to prevent optic atrophy, mental deterioration and progressive exophthalmos. Moreover, the appearance of the head may be improved. Ingraham states that early operation is required and that when this is performed before the end of the first year, the results are excellent. Channels are cut through the bone on either side of the affected suture and are lined with polyethylene film to prevent healing. Orbital decompression is sometimes required and the nasal passages may need to be opened.

CASE HISTORY (1135331).—*Congenital trigonocephalus and buphthalmos. Mild mental deficiency.*

I was requested to see this child of 23 months by Dr. Frank Otenasek. Birth was at full term after an uncomplicated pregnancy. Delivery was not difficult. The child was in good condition. Birth weight was 7 lbs. 2 oz. The child stood alone at 9 months and walked at 12 months. The child was unable to form words at 23 months. The family history was negative.

At birth the child was noted to have large eyes and a diagnosis of buphthalmos was soon made. Operation was performed at 2 months on both eyes in the hope of reducing the intraocular pressure. This operation was effective at first but at 6 months a second operation was required on the left eye. The child seemed to have photophobia and there was a constant over-flow of tears.

The skull was malformed. The forehead was very narrow and a vertical ridge was evident in the midline of the forehead. There was increase of the biparietal width of the skull. The circumference of the head was 49 cm and that of the chest was 51 cm. The corneae were a bit cloudy. The x-rays of the skull showed a premature fusion of the metopic suture. No other anomalies were discovered. There was no motor disorder.

BIBLIOGRAPHY

ANDERSON, F. N. *et al.:* Trigonocephaly. Jour. of Neurosurg., **19**:723, 1962.

———— AND GEIGER, L.: Craniosynostosis. Jour. Neurosurg., **22**:229, 1965.

BLANK, C. E.: Apert's syndrome. Ann. Hum. Genet., **24**:151, 1960.

BRONFENBRENNER, A. N.: Oxycephaly as a pathogenetic entity. Am. J. Dis. Child., **42**:837, 1931.

CROUZON, Q.: Dysostose cranio-facilae hereditaire. Bull. et. mém. Soc. méd. d. hôp. de Paris, **33**:545, 1912.

DOCK, G.: Oxycephaly and exophthalmos. Contributions to Med. and Biol. Research., **1**:433, 1919.

DUNN, F. H.: Apert's acroencephalosyndactylism. Radiology, **78**:738, 1962.

FARBER, H. K. AND TOWNE, E. B.: Early operation in premature cranial synostosis for prevention of blindness and other sequelae. J. Pediat., **22**:286, 1943.

FLETCHER, H. M.: On oxycephaly. Quart. J. Med., **4**:385, 1910.

FLIPPEN, J. H.: Cranio-facial dysostosis of Crouzon. Pediatrics, **5**:91, 1950. Report of a case in which the malformation occurred in four generations.

GORLIN, R. J. AND SEDANO, H.: Acrocephalosyndactyly (Apert's syndrome). Modern Medicine, November 17, 1969, p. 235.

————: Craniofacial dystosis. Modern Medicine, **Vol. 37**, No. 14, p. 134, 1969.

GRIEG, D.: Oxycephaly. Edinburgh M. J., **33**:N.S.P. 189, 1926.

INGRAHAM, F., ALEXANDER, E. AND MATSON, D.: Clinical studies in craniostenosis. Surgery, **24**:518, 1948.

KELLN, E. E. AND GORLIN, R. J., *et al.:* Oral manifestations of Crouzon's disease. Oral Surg., Oral Med. & Oral Path., **13**:1233, 1960.

MANN, I.: A theory of the embryology of oxycephaly. Trans. Ophth. Soc. United Kingdom, **55**:279, 1935.

McLAURIN, R. L. AND MATSON, D. D.: Importance of early surgical treatment of craniosynostosis. Pediatrics, **10**:637, 1952.

MOUNT, L. A.: Premature closure of the sutures of the cranial vault. New York State J. Med., **47**:270, 1947.

PARK, E. A. AND POWERS, G. F.: Acrocephaly and scaphocephaly with symmetrically distributed malformations of the extremities. Am. J. Dis. Child., **20**:234, 1920.

SHILLER, J. G.: Craniofacial dysostosis of Crouzon. Pediatrics, **23**:107, 1959.

SIMMONS, D. R. AND PEYTON, W. T.: Premature closure of the cranial sutures. J. Pediat., **31**:528, 1947.

VERGER, P. *et al.*: Acrocephalosyndactylia, Apert's syndrome. Arch. franc. pediat. **19**:91, 1962.

WALSH, F. B.: *Loc. cit.*

WEYGANDT: Der Geisteszustand bei Turmschädel. Deutsch. Ztschr. f. Nervenheilk, **63**:495, 1921.

WOODHALL, B.: Oxycephaly. J. Pediat., **20**:585, 1942.

CLEIDOCRANIAL DYSOSTOSIS

This is a rare condition commonly found in several members of a family and often appearing in two or more generations. It is characterized by absence of the middle portions of the clavicles, by increased width of the forehead and sometimes by defects in the midline of the cranium, mental defect and spastic paralysis.

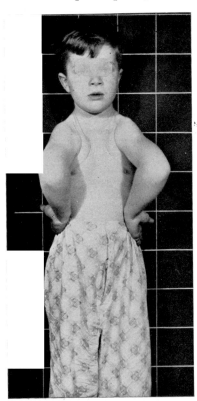

FIG. 51. Cleidocranial dysostosis showing great range of movement of the shoulders. There is a defect in the frontal bone concealed by a lock of hair.

The diagnosis is made very easily if the nature of the condition suspected in the abnormal range of movement of the shoulders is quite characteristic. The child can approximate the shoulders in front of the chest, and the range of passive movement of the scapulae is limited only by the length of the muscles. The head is very broad and somewhat flattened in the anteroposterior diameter. Ossification in the midline is delayed or defective. Thus, the metopic and sagittal sutures may remain open much longer than the usual period and the anterior fontanel may never close. There is no evidence of increased intracranial pressure as in oxycephaly or acrobrachycephaly, however. The pubic bones may be incompletely formed. Convulsions may occur.

The object in presenting this condition which is usually regarded as an orthopedic problem is to call attention to the abnormalities of the nervous system which are sometimes associated. Mental defect of various degrees is not infrequent in patients presenting this bony abnormality, and in some cases there is also paralysis and spasticity. Hemiplegia is described, but the most frequent type of paralysis seems to be spastic paraplegia of cerebral type. In several cases large cavities have been found in the occipital or frontal lobes of the brain, and in other instances agenesis of the cortex has been discovered at autopsy. Stewart has described agenesis of the gyrus cinguli and anterior half of the corpus callosum. The frontal lobes were small and very narrow. During life, the patient had been mentally defective and had exhibited the signs of spastic paraparesis.

BIBLIOGRAPHY

GORLIN, R. J. AND SEDANO, H.: Cleidocranial dystosis. Modern Medicine, March 25, 1968, p. 150.
KLEMMER, R. N. AND COOPER, H. B.: Cleidocranial dysostosis. Am. J. Roentgenol., **26**:710, 1931.
LEVIN, E. J.: Cleidocranial dysostosis. New York Jour. Med., **63**:1562, 1963.
STEWART, R. M.: The nervous system in cleidocranial dysostosis. J. Neurol. & Psychopath., **9**:217, 1929.

BASILAR IMPRESSION

Definition.—A deformity of the base of the skull described below. This is also called platybasia.

Pathological Anatomy.—The essential feature is the upward displacement of the base of the posterior fossa, i.e. the basilar and condylar portions of the occipital bone. As a result, the posterior fossa is reduced in capacity and otherwise deformed. The foramen magnum may be narrowed. The odontoid process may project into the spinal canal. The atlas may be fused with the occipital bone and a partial or complete Klippel-Feil syndrome may be found.

The cerebellum may be compressed and the tonsils forced into the spinal canal. The medulla may also be subjected to bony compression. Hydrocephalus may result from occlusion of the aqueduct or obliteration of the basilar cisternae. The Arnold-Chiari deformity is not uncommon. The cranial nerves of the posterior fossa may also be involved by pressure. Hydromyelia and syringomyelia may be associated.

Etiology.—It is stated that this deformity may be a result of rickets, osteomalacia and Paget's disease, but in most instances it probably represents a primary defect of development. Bull *et al.* point out that in many instances this is a familial condition genetically determined. Osteogenesis imperfecta, with brittle bones, deafness and blue sclerae, may be associated with basilar impression.

Clinical Features.—The child's head is rather long and its vertical diameter is reduced. The neck appears to be shortened and movements of the head may be limited by abnormalities of the upper cervical vertebrae. Roentgenograms of the skull from the lateral aspect are diagnostic. The basilar angle, i.e. the inclination of the clivus, is reduced, the lips of the foramen magnum are turned up and posterior fossa is enlongated and thin walled. A line drawn from the dorsal lip of the foramen magnum to the dorsal margin of the hard palate falls below the apex of the odontoid process, whereas in normal skulls the line always falls above. Views of the base reveals stenosis of the foramen magnum in most cases. Not infrequently one finds digital markings of the vault which indicate the presence of hydrocephalus. Various deformities of the atlas and axis may be found.

Various signs and symptoms referable to the nervous system are found in many, but not in all, cases. Weakness and spasticity of the extremities may result from pressure on the pyramids. In one such case, I was unable to discover any disturbance of sensibility. Clinical signs and symptoms characteristic of syringomyelia may occur and the typical cavities in the cord have been discovered at autopsy though the relation of the bony deformities to the lesions in the spinal cord is not clear. Cerebellar ataxia, unsteadiness of gait and nystagmus are common and the cranial nerves, especially those which make their exit from the posterior fossa are frequently involved. Sixth nerve palsies are found in many instances. In one of our cases, there was fifth nerve neuralgia. Papilledema and other signs of increased intracranial pressure are unusually present and are believed to result from obstruction of the circulation of the cerebrospinal fluid leading to hydrocephalus. In young children the head may grow very large. The Queckenstedt test may reveal partial or complete obstruction of the spinal canal. The neurological manifestations are rarely discovered in infancy but appear later during childhood, adolescence or even later. Once they are established they are apt to be progressive.

Sajid and Copple describe familial basilar impression and aqueductal stenosis.

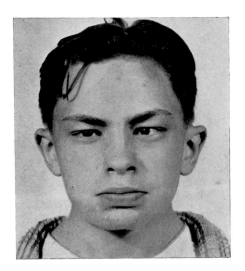

FIG. 52. Basilar impression in a boy of 17 years showing short neck, flattened head and internal squint.

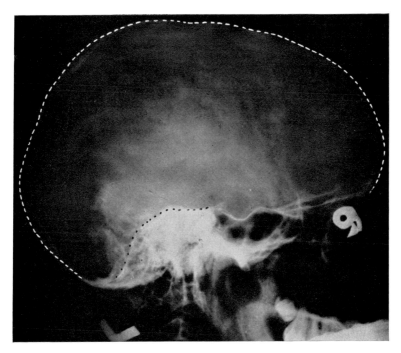

Fig. 53. Roentgenographic appearances of basilar impression. Skull of boy shown in preceding photograph. Slope of the clivus is shown by line of black dots. Note deformity of the posterior fossa and diminution of the vertical diameter of the skull.

Diagnosis.—The diagnosis depends upon the demonstration by roentgenography of the characteristic deformities of the skull.

Treatment.—Decompression of the posterior fossa and removal of the laminae of the upper four cervical vertebrae with the posterior lip of the foramen magnum are recommended. In our small experience, this operation has relieved the increased intracranial pressure when such was present, but its effect on the neurological disorders has not been striking.

BIBLIOGRAPHY

Bezi, I.:Assimilation of the atlas and compression of the medulla. Arch. Path., **12**:333, 1931.

Bull, J. W., Nixon, W. L. and Pratt, R. T.: Radiological criteria and familial occurrence of primary basilar impression. Brain, **78**:229, 1955.

Chamberlain, W. E.: Basilar impression (platybasia), a bizarre developmental anomaly of the occipital bone and upper cervical spine with striking and misleading neurological manifestations. Yale J. Biol. & Med., **11**:487, 1939.

Driesen, W. et al.: Results of surgical treatment of basilar impression. Acta neurochir., **15**:83, 1966.

Ebenius, B.: The roentgen appearance in four cases of basilar impression. Acta Radiol. Scand., **15**:652, 1934.

Gustafson, W. A. and Oldberg, E.: Neurologic significance of platybasia. Arch. Neurol. & Psychiat., **44**:1184, 1940.

HURWITZ, L. J. AND McSWENEY, R. R.: Basilar impression and osteogenesis imperfecta in a family. Brain, **83**:138, 1960.

LIST, C. F.: Neurologic syndromes accompanying developmental anomalies of the occipital bone, atlas and axis. Arch. Neurol. & Psychiat., **45**:577, 1941.

SAJID, M. H. AND COPPLE, P. J.: Familial aqueductal stenosis and basilar impression. Neurology, **18**:260, 1968.

OCULAR HYPERTELORISM

In 1924, Grieg called attention to a rare form of cranio-facial deformity which he called ocular hypertelorism because of the excessive distance between the eyes. Since then, a number of cases have been reported, and it has become evident that in a mild form the condition is not extremely rare. The appearance of the child is so characteristic that the diagnosis may be made at a glance. The eyes, as I have just said, are set very far apart; the bridge of the nose is therefore very broad and, in some cases, flattened; the orbits diverge to an abnormal degree frequently producing an external

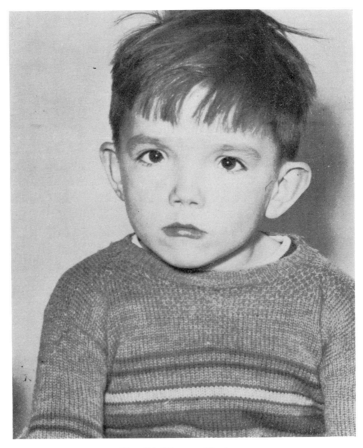

FIG. 54. Hyperteliorism.

squint, and the forehead is marked by a vertical groove extending upward from the root of the nose. The head is often brachycephalic, the occiput flattened and the temporal regions bulging. Grieg shows that the deformity is the result of malformation of that part of the sphenoid bone which is laid down in cartilage. The greater wings are very small and the lesser wings very large, so that the latter are actually larger than the former. Mental deficiency of various degrees is associated in most cases, but some children in whom the deformity is mild, may show normal intelligence. In contrast to the craniostenoses, there is no increase in intracranial pressure in hypertelorism and the sutures of the vault show no synostosis. Syndactylism has not been described, but in Grieg's cases the hands were broad and fat and the fingers short and blunt. In one case, hypertelorism was unilateral. The deformity has been traced through three generations of one family, but in most instances the condition is sporadic. Convulsions may occur. This condition is found in association with a number of developmental defects and deformities.

BIBLIOGRAPHY

ABERNATHY, D. A.: Hypertelorism in several generations. Arch. Dis. Child., 2:361, 1927.
ALLEN, F. M. B.: Hypertelorism without mental defect. Arch. Dis. Child., 1:172, 1926.
BRAITHWAITE, J. V. C.: The relation of hypertelorism to mongolism. Arch. Dis. Child., 1:369, 1926.
BROWN, A. AND HARPER, R. K.: Craniofacial dysostosis. The significance of ocular hypertelorism. Quart. J. Med., 15:171, 1946.
DRUMMOND, W. B.: Hypertelorism. Arch. Dis. Child., 1:167, 1926.
GRIEG, D. M.: Hypertelorism. Edinburgh M. J., 31:560, 1924.
LIGHTWOOD, R. C. AND SHELDON, W. P. H.: Hypertelorism, a unilateral case. Arch. Dis. Child., 3:170, 1928.
OGILVIE, A. G. AND POSEL, M. M.: Scaphocephaly, Oxycephaly and Hypertelorism. Arch. Dis. Child., 2:146, 1927.
WALSH, F. B.: *Loc. cit.*

THE MEDIAN CLEFT FACE SYNDROME (DEMYER)

DeMyer shows that ocular hypertelorism is often associated with other facial anomalies. He mentions: (1) A low, V-shaped frontal hairline. (2) Cranium bifidum occulta. (3) Primary telecanthus, i.e. increased separation of the medial canthi. (4) Median cleft nose. (5) Median cleft upper lip. (6) Median cleft palate. He reviews 25 cases which he divides into 4 groups depending upon the number of developmental anomalies associated with ocular hypertelorism.

There is little evidence of genetic influence. Intelligence is not often reduced. Thus, in 25 cases reviewed only 2 cases of severe mental deficiency were found and only 3 cases of mild mental deficiency. In contrast, hypotelorism is more or less constantly associated with amentia.

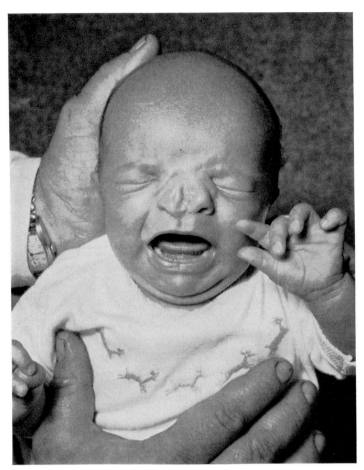

FIG. 55. Median cleft face syndrome. At 4 months. Lip and palate are not cleft, but piltrum is too broad. Above root of nose is a depression indicating cranium bifidum occlutum. (From DeMyer, W. The median cleft face syndrome. Neurology 1967, Vol. 17, 1961.)

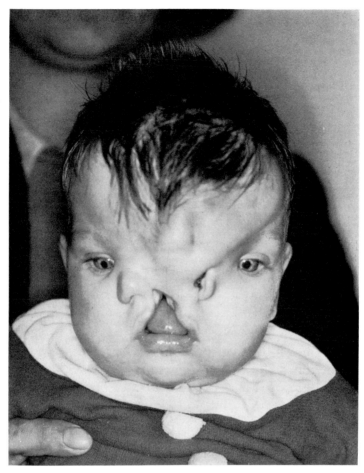

Fig. 56. Median cleft face syndrome. At 2 years 5 months. No philtrum or prolabium. Medial canthus overlaps conjunctiva so patient has hyperteliorism and primary telecanthus. (From DeMyer, W. The median cleft face syndrome. Neurology 1967, Vol. 17, 1961.)

BIBLIOGRAPHY

DeMYER, W.: The median cleft face syndrome: Differential diagnosis of cranium bifidum occultum hyperteliorism and median cleft nose, lip and palate. Neurology, **17**:961, 1967.

POPLITEAL PTERYGIUM SYNDROME

In this condition there is a web of skin extending from the ischial tuberosity to heel. There is defective development of the digits and syndactyly. Talipes equinivarus occurs. The eyelids may be connected by adhesions. Undescended testicles, cleft scrotum, inguinal hernia, absence of the labia majora and infantile uterus are described. The thighs may be united by a web. There is a cleft palate or cleft lip and cleft palate. Pits are sometimes found in the lower lips.

BIBLIOGRAPHY

CHAMPION, R. AND CREGAN, J. C. F.: Congenital popliteal webbing in siblings. Jour. Bone and Joint Surg., **41B**:355, 1959.
GORLIN, R. J. AND SEDANO, H.: Popliteal pterygium syndrome. Modern Medicine, January 13, 1969, p. 144.

WAARDENBURG'S SYNDROME

This is a heredofamilial condition. The abnormalities include unilateral or bilateral nerve deafness, a white forelock, heterochromia of the irides or pale blue irides, hypertelorism with widely spaced eyes and broadening of the base of the nose, confluence of the eyebrows, hypertrichosis of the medial ends of the eyebrows and sometimes partial albinism. All of the characteristic features are not to be expected in each patient.

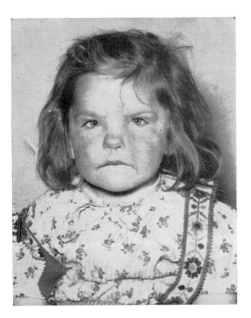

FIG. 57. Hypertelorism. This photograph was published to illustrate hypertelorism. The child is a deaf mute and has a lock of white hair in the frontal region which is not evident in the photograph. There is also heterochronia iridis. Her brother displays the same anomalies. This must be an example of Waardenburg's syndrome. (By the courtesy of Dr. Walsh.)

There may be mottled pigment changes in the peripheral parts of the retinae. The uvula may be absent. The mouth may be small.

Gladstone describes various types of heterochromia of the iris. He mentions three types, simple, complicated and sympathetic.

BIBLIOGRAPHY

CAMPBELL, B., CAMPBELL, N. AND SWIFT, S.: Recognition of Waardenburg's syndrome. Arch. Dermat., **86**:718, 1962.

DiGEORGE, A. M. *et al.:* Waardenburg's syndrome. J. Pediat., **57**:649, 1960.

GLADSTONE, R. M.: Development and significance of heterochromia of the iris. Neurology, **21**:184, 1969.

HANSEN, A. C. *et al.:* Waardenburg's syndrome. Jour. Nat. Med. Ass., **57**:8, 1965.

WAARDENBURG, P. J.: A new syndrome combining developmental anomalies of the eyelids, eyebrows, and nose root with pigmentary defects in the iris, head hair and congenital deafness. Am. J. Human Genet., **3**:195, 1951.

MANDIBULOFACIAL DYSOSTOSIS AND OCULOAURICULOVERTEBRAL DYSPLASIA

(Treacher Collins and Goldenhar's Syndromes)

This is an inherited condition, for it may be found in more than one generation of a family. It is mentioned here because it may be associated with severe degrees of mental deficiency. One of the most characteristic features is the slanting of the lid slits downward and outward. There is often notching of the eyelids. The cilia may be absent medial to the notch in the lid. The external ears are grossly malformed and imperfectly formed supernumerary ears are often found anterior to their proper location. The external auditory canals may be absent. Congenital sinuses may be found between the ears and the corners of the mouth. The hair distribution may be atypical and tongue shaped processes may extend to the cheeks. The maxillae and mandible are imperfectly formed and there is malocclusion

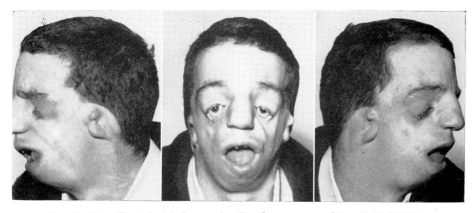

FIG. 58. Mandibulofacial dysostosis. (By the courtesy of Dr. F. B. Walsh.)

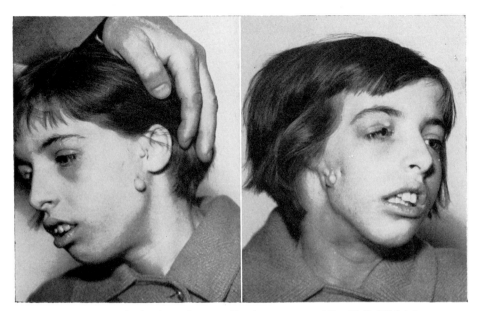

Fig. 59. Goldenhar's syndrome. (By the courtesy of Dr. F. B. Walsh.)

of the teeth. Roentgenographic study often reveals defects in the temporal bones and the auditory canals may be absent. Both the middle and inner ears may be defective. Many patients are deaf. The malar bones are often absent. In one of our patients the arches of the first two vertebrae were absent. Absence of fingers is mentioned. Unilateral types have been observed.

Gorlin *et al.* describe oculoauriculovertebral dysplasia sometimes termed Goldenhar's syndrome in which there are auricular appendices and pretragal blind fistulas as in mandibulofacial dysostosis but also epibulbar dermoids, vertebral anomalies and hemifacial microsomia.

BIBLIOGRAPHY

Collins, E. T.: Case of symmetrical congenital notches in the outer part of each lid and defective development of the malar bones. Tr. Ophthal. Soc. United King., 20:190, 1900.

Franceschetti, A. and Klein, D.: Mandibulofacial dysostosis. Acta Ophthal., 27:143, 1949.

Gorlin *et al.:* Oculoauriculovertebral dysplasia. J. Pediat., 63:991, 1963.

Gorlin, R. J. and Sedano, H.: Mandibulofacial dysostosis. Modern Medicine, March 11, 1968, p. 148.

Hoefnagel, D.: Dyscephalia mandibulo-oculo-facialis. Arch. of Dis. Childh., 40:57, 1965.

Hurwitz, P.: Mandibulofacial dysostosis. Arch. Ophth., 51:69, 1954.

Hunt, P. and Smith, D.: Mandibulofacial dysostosis. Pediatrics, 15:195, 1955.

Jancar, J.: Mandibulofacial dysostosis. J. Irish M. A., 48:145, 1961.

Marden, P. M. *et al.:* Congenital anomalies in the newborn infant. Jour. Pediat., 64:357, 1964.

ROTHMUND'S AND THOMPSON'S SYNDROMES

This is a familial developmental defect. It is said that 42 of 46 cases are familial. The patient's bodily growth is deficient and there may be sexual infantilism. During infancy there is a red, tense swelling of the face which eventually ends in atrophy, pigmentation and telangiectasia. The ears, forearms and hands are affected in the same way. Sunlight causes a strong reaction which seems to aggravate the process. Carcinoma may result. The teeth and nails are often defective. The corneae are small. Cataracts may develop. Microcephaly and mental deficiency are associated. This is thought to be inherited as a recessive condition.

It seems that the condition is static except for the process in the skin which is progressive.

We have seen only one case of this condition.

BIBLIOGRAPHY

TAYLOR, W. B.: Rothmund's syndrome-Thompson's syndrome. Arch. Dermat., 75:236, 1957.
THOMPSON, M. S.: Poikloderma congenita. Brit. J. Dermat. & Syph., 48:221, 1936.

ORODIGITOFACIAL DYSOSTOSIS

Syndrome of Papillon-League and Psaume

Papillon-League and Psaume first described this condition. They made observations on eight patients. Gorlin *et al.* describe an additional number of patients so that now about twenty-two are on record. It has been suggested that the condition is inherited as a dominant trait which is lethal in males for all of the patients are females.

Mental deficiency is associated with anomalies of development. There are hypertrophied buccal frenuli. Pseudoclefts involve the mandible, the tongue, the maxilla and the palate. The lateral incisor teeth may be missing. The alar cartilages of the nose may be defective. The canthi are malformed. The base of the skull is hypoplastic. The root of the nose is broad. Milia of the ears and face are common in the first three years. There may be syndactyly of the fingers. The skin is stated to be granular and there is frontal alopecia. A tremor of the hands is seen in some patients. Subdural hygroma and porencephalic cysts have been found. Ruess *et al.* suspect that there are chromosomal abnormalities.

BIBLIOGRAPHY

DOEGE, T. C. *et al.*: Studies of a family with the oral-facial-digital syndrome. New Eng. Jour. Med., 271:1073, 1964.
GORLIN, R. J. AND SEDANO, H.: Oral-facial-digital syndrome. Modern Medicine, 1969, vol. 37, No. 5, p. 164.
———— *et al.*: Hypertrophied frenuli, oligophrenia, familial trembling and anomalies of the hand. New England J. Med., 264:486, 1961.
———— AND PSAUME, J.: Orodigitofacial dysostosis. J. Pediat., 61:520, 1962.
PAPILLON-LEAGUE AND PSAUME, J.: Dismorphie des freins buccaux. Actualities odonto-stomatol., 25:7, 1954.
RUESS, A. L. *et al.*: Oro-facial-digital syndrome with associated chromosomal abnormalities. Pediatrics, 27:985, 1962.

CONGENITAL FAMILIAL PANCYTOPENIA WITH MULTIPLE CONGENITAL ANOMALIES

In 1926, Franconi described three siblings suffering from this condition. Since then, about thirty cases of this syndrome have been reported. A recessive gene is suspected.

Usually, there is a patchy brown pigmentation of the skin due to deposits of melanin. The patients are dwarfs and mentally deficient. Microcephaly,

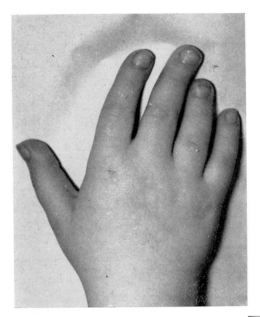

FIG. 60. This shows the typical hand with syndactyly and clinodactyly. (From Gorlin, R. J. and Psaume, J.: Orodigitofacial dysostosis. J. Pediat., **61**:520, 1962.

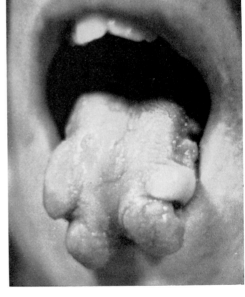

FIG. 61. This shows the clefts in the tongue. (From Gorlin, R. J. and Psaume, J.: Orodigitofacial dysostosis. J. Pediat., **61**:520, 1962.)

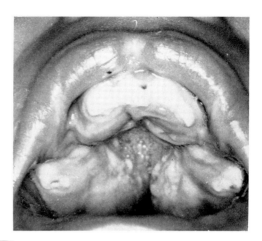

FIG. 62. This shows the defect in the upper lip, the bilateral clefts in the alveolar processes and the cleft in the palate. (From Gorlin, R. J. and Psaume, J.: Orodigitofacial dysostosis. J. Pediat., **61**:520, 1962.)

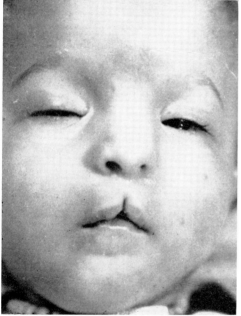

FIG. 63. This shows the cleft in the upper lip, mild hypoplasia of the alar cartilages and dystopia canthorum. (From Gorlin, R. J. and Psaume, J.: Orodigitofacial dysostosis. J. Pediat., **61**:520, 1962.)

deficient sexual development, squints, abnormalities of the thumbs, absence of the radius and renal malformations are described. Abnormalities of the thumbs are almost constant.

There is anemia, reduction of the white cells of the blood, and decrease of platelets. The bone marrow is hypoplastic. Death usually results from hemorrhage within the cranium or from the bowel.

BIBLIOGRAPHY

FRANCONI, H.: Familiäre infantile perniziosartige Anämie. Jahrb. f. Kinderh., **117**:257, 1927.
DAWSON, J. P.: Congenital pancytopenia associated with multiple congenital anomalies. Pediatrics, **15**:325, 1955.

McDonald, R. and Goldschmidt, B.: Pancytopenia with congenital defects. Arch. Dis. Childhood, 35:367, 1960.

MICROPHTHALMOS AND ANOPHTHALMOS WITH MENTAL DEFICIENCY

Sjögren and Larsson studied 130 cases of blindness in Sweden, in which anophthalmos or microphthalmos was responsible. These diseases were the cause of 8 per cent of all cases of blindness in school children.

In fifty-eight cases, there was profound mental deficiency. Epilepsy was common in these patients. Skeletal anomalies were found including clubfoot, flatfoot, kyphosis and kyphoscoliosis. Microcephaly was rare. Spastic diplegia was found in five cases.

It was determined that this condition was inherited probably in a partially sex-linked recessive manner with incomplete penetrance.

Case History.—*Microphthalmia, small head, mental deficiency and sexual infantilism.*

W. H. W. was seen by the courtesy of Dr. Butler at the Rosewood Training School. He had been found to be mentally defective early in childhood and was noted to have a small head and small eyes. He could not walk until he was 3 years old. His intelligence quotient was estimated at 30. The electroencephalogram was described as disorganized.

On examination the patient was tall and slender. The arms were long and the legs were even longer so the trunk appeared short. The head was small and measured 50 cm in circumference. There was bilateral microphthalmia. There was a coloboma of the right iris and a cataract in the right eye. The left cornea showed a dense scar. There were irregular nystagmoid movements of the eyes probably due to loss of vision. Speech was defective, but he could understand what was said to him and was able to cooperate.

The station was unsteady and the gait also unsteady. There was ataxia in the heel-knee tests and increased tone of the legs. The knee and ankle jerks were increased and there were bilateral Babinski signs. The scrotum was small. No testicles could be felt. The penis was infantile.

The patient's proportions were thought to be due to eunuchoidism. The combination of microphthalmia and mental deficiency has been described by Sjögren and Larsson.

BIBLIOGRAPHY

Sjögren, T. and Larsson, T.: Acta Psychiatrica et Neurologica. Scand. Suppl., 56, 1949.

CENTROFACIAL LENTIGINOSIS

In this condition many freckles appear in infancy. These are clustered in the center of the face about the nose, forehead and upper lip. There is non-progressive mental deficiency and convulsive seizures. Motor defects of various types are described. One case is reported in which the lentigenes were unilateral and there was hemiplegia. It is believed that this is an inherited condition, but the mode of transmission is uncertain.

CASE HISTORY.—*Centrofacial lentiginosis in a girl of 26 years.*

M. A. M. was born at term after an uncomplicated pregnancy by normal delivery. Birth weight was 7 lbs and 14 oz. Her family were all of normal intelligence. She was noted to have freckles on her face in infancy. It was soon realized that she suffered from gross mental deficiency. Her intelligence quotient could not be estimated. She could never talk or understand what was said to her. She began to have convulsions at the age of one year. She had congenital dislocation of the left hip and her abdomen was always distended because of Hirschsprung's disease.

On examination the patient was poorly developed and sparely nourished. Her head was small and the occiput was flattened. There were many freckles over the bridge of the nose, the center of the forehead, the upper lip and the cheeks adjacent to the nose. She was unable to cooperate and was resistent. The sexual development was defective. The abdomen was greatly distended. The left leg was shorter than the right as a result of the dislocation of the hip and it was difficult for her to walk. Her neck was webbed. The tendon reflexes were all present and the plantar reflexes were obscured by voluntary resistence.

BIBLIOGRAPHY

AITA, J. A.: Neurocutaneous Diseases. Thomas, Springfield, 1966.
SCHIFFER, K. H. AND WEBER, G.: Relationship between disorders of skin and the central nervous system. Dermatologie und Venerologie, **Vol. IV,** 1960, p. 1103.
STUART, C. E.: Unilateral lentigenes with hemiparesis. Brit. Jour. Dermat., **76:**492, 1964.

CRYPTOPHTHALMIA SYNDROME

This is an autosomal recessive trait. One or both eyes are covered with skin. The conjunctival sac is obliterated. The lens may be absent, hypoplastic, displaced or calcified. In unilateral cases, the opposite eye may show microphthalmia, epibulbar dermoid, or coloboma of the lid. The hair may cover the temples. The nostrils may be notched. The upper part of the ears may be attached to the scalp. The external auditory canals are narrow and the occicles may be malformed. Conduction deafness is present. Cleft lip and cleft palate are often present. Laryngeal atresia may be found. The tongue may be tied. Syndactyly of both hands and feet is often seen. Umbilical hernia is common. A number of urogenital defects are described including undescended testicles, hypospadias, pseudohermaphroditism, chordee, micropenis and agenesis of a kidney. Mental deficiency is often present.

BIBLIOGRAPHY

Gorlin, R. J. and Sedano, H.: Cryptophthalmia syndrome. Modern Medicine, November 3, 1969, p. 156.

PSEUDOGLIOMA OF THE RETINAE WITH MENTAL DEFICIENCY

Heine was the first to describe this condition. He published a study of two brothers in 1925. Since then, papers have been published by Dahlberg-Parrow, Forssman and Reichel. It is inherited as a sex-linked recessive trait, and all the patients are males.

It is said that the condition is congenital and all the characteristic features are present at birth. The mental deficiency is severe. There are apparently no typical motor disturbances.

The eyeballs are small. The anterior chambers are shallow. The iris is atrophied and there are synechiae around the pupils. The vitreum is filled with grayish white vascularized tissue. Secondary cataracts may occur. The patients are blind.

BIBLIOGRAPHY

Dahlberg-Parrow, R.: Congenital sex-linked pseudoglioma and grave mental deficiency. Acta Ophth. Scandinav., 34:250, 1956.

Forssman, H.: Mental deficiency and pseudoglioma. Amer. Jour. Ment. Defic., 64:984, 1960.

————: Mental deficiency and pseudoglioma, a syndrome inherited as a sex-linked recessive. J. Ment. Def., 64:984, 1960.

Heine, L.: Über das familäre Auftreten von Pseudoglioma congenitum bei zwei Brüdern. Zeitschrift für Augenheilkunde, 56:155, 1925.

Reichel, C.: Über familiares Auftreten angeborner Pseudogliome. Archiv. f. Kinderheilkunde, 162:290, 1960.

Warberg, M. et al.: Norrie's disease. Acta Genet. Statist. Med., 15:103, 1965.

————: Norrie's disease. Acta Ophthal., 39:757, 1961.

————: Norrie's disease. Acta Ophthal., 41:134, 1963.

SCLEROCORNEA AND ASSOCIATED ANOMALIES

This is a congenital condition. The cornea is more or less opaque and resembles the sclera. There may be conical cornea and glaucoma may develop. Such changes may be unilateral or bilateral. Malformations of the ears are often present. Linear streaks in the skin may be found which resemble scleroderma. There are malformations of the bones and deformities of the skull. The maxilla may be imperfectly developed. The testicles may be deficient.

The central nervous system does not escape. Defects in the brain and cerebellum are mentioned. I have seen only one case of this condition.

BIBLIOGRAPHY

Goldstein, J. E. and Cogan, D. G.: Sclerocornea and associated congenital anomalies. Arch. Ophthal., 67:761, 1962.

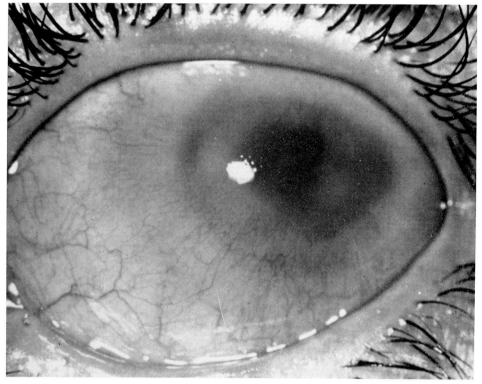

FIG. 64. Sclerocornea (Goldstein, J. E. and Cogan, D. G.: Arch. Ophth. **67**:761, 1962).

THE POPLITEAL PTERYGIUM SYNDROME

Large webs are found extending from the heels to the ischial tuberosities which limit the movements of the legs. The digits may show defective development. There may be club feet, and syndactylism. Filiform adhesions may hold the eyelids together. Undescended testicles, cleft scrotum, absence of the scrotum, absence of the labia majora, infantile uterus and a web between the thighs may be present. There may be hare lip and cleft palate. Pits in the lower lip are sometimes associated.

BIBLIOGRAPHY

GORLIN, R. J. and SEDANO, H.: The popliteal pterygium syndrome. Modern Medicine, Jan. 13, 1969, p. 144.

COCKAYNE'S SYNDROME

In 1936, Cockayne described a condition in two siblings. These children were dwarfs. There was pigmentary degeneration of the retinae and deafness. The symptoms began in the second year and the children seemed to be normal during infancy. Kyphosis with disproportionately long extremities and large hands and feet are mentioned. There is lack of subcutaneous fat. Development of the genitals is defective. The liver and spleen may be enlarged. Prognathism, sunken eyes and a thin nose give these children a senile appearance. The skin is sensitive to sunlight, and becomes pigmented and scarred. Optic atrophy, cataract, cold blue extremities, unsteady gait, thickened bones and mental deficiency are all characteristic symptoms. The intelligence tests indicate that these children are idiots. Their behavior is better than one would expect, however.

Few cases have been described. McDonald *et al.* found three children suffering from this condition in a family of five. One post-mortem examination was made. The brain was normally formed. Many patches of demyelination were found in the subcortical white matter, the brainstem and the spinal cord. There was also loss of neurons. Areas of necrosis and calcification were discovered in the brain and associated with thrombi in the arteries. There was also granulation tissue in the cerebral cortex.

One child had a chromosomal study with negative results. No metabolic abnormality could be demonstrated.

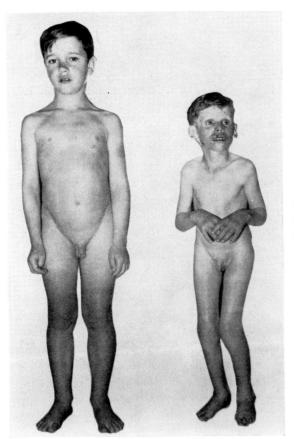

Fig. 65. Patient of ten years and nine months with normal boy of same age.

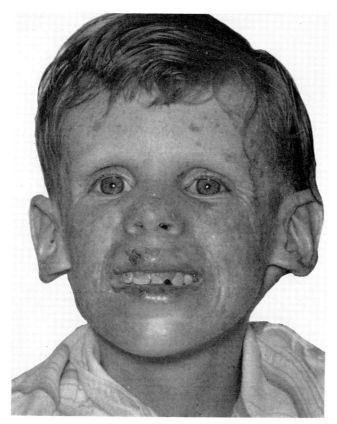

FIG. 65A. Same patient's face. (MacDonald, W. B. *et al.*: Cockayne's syndrome. Pediatrics, 25:997, 1960.)

BIBLIOGRAPHY

COCKAYNE, E. A.: Dwarfism with retinal atrophy and deafness. Arch. Dis. Childhood 11:1, 1936; 21:52, 1946.

LIEBERMAN, W. J. *et al.*: Cockayne's disease. Amer. Jour. Ophthal., 52:116, 1961.

PADDISON, R. M. *et al.*: Cockayne's syndrome. Derm. Trop., 2:195, 1963.

McDONALD, W. B. *et al.*: Cockayne's syndrome. A heredofamilial disorder of growth and development. Pediatrics, 25:997, 1960.

NEILL, C. A. AND DINGWELL, M. M.: A syndrome resembling progyria. Arch. Dis. Childhood, 25:52, 1950.

WILKINS, L.: The Diagnosis and Treatment of Endocrine Disorders of Childhood and Adolescence. Thomas, Springfield, 1950, p. 137.

INCONTINENTIA PIGMENTI
(THE BLOCH-SULZBERGER SYNDROME)

This is a rare disease. The cause is unknown. More than one case may occur in a family. Of 216 cases recorded, only six were in males. It has been suggested that in males, the trait causes intrauterine death.

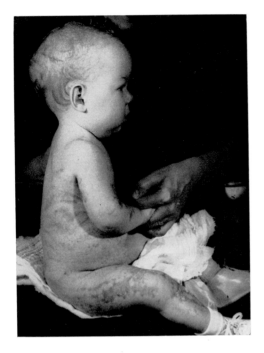

Fig. 66. Incontinenti pigmenti showing the pattern of the pigment deposits in the skin. (From Gorlin, R. J. and Anderson, J. A.: Characteristic dentition in incontinenti pigmenti. J. Pediat., 57:78, 1960.)

Cutaneous lesions are prominent. Erythema with vesiculation occurs in nearly 50 per cent of cases shortly after birth. The lesions are on the flexor surfaces of the extremities and lateral aspect of the trunk. After several months, they are followed by verrucous lesions and then by pigmented streaks of brown or slate color. These streaks may have a pattern resembling the veins in marble. Eosinophilia is often pronounced.

Delayed and imperfect dentition is common. The teeth may be conical; the nails defective, and the hair is scanty. Growth is defective. Osseous deformities are described.

The nervous system does not escape. Mental deficiency is present with microcephaly or hydrocephalus. Paralyses occur which are usually spastic. Convulsions are common. There may be optic atrophy, squints, cataracts, corneal opacities, nystagmus and blue sclerae. Retrobulbar glioma has been found.

Case History.—*Incontinentia pigmenti.*

By the courtesy of Dr. Harry G. Butler, J. M. F. was seen at the Rosewood State Hospital. He was born at term. At birth it was noted that he had pigmented areas on the left side of the trunk. It was evident that he was mentally deficient early in life and his intelligence quotient was estimated at 37 per cent. He was never able to walk or talk. At 6 months he had a few convulsions.

On examination at the age of 6 years a large erythematous lesion was seen on the right cheek and a smaller one on the chin. Curved lines of brownish pigmentation were seen on the left side of the trunk which followed the course of the ribs. There were rounded brown areas in the folds of the elbows and behind the right knee. On the forearms were hyperkeratotic areas.

The arms were very thin. They were held in flexion at the elbows. The wrists were also held in flexion. There was scarcely any tone in the muscles on passive movement, but the tendon reflexes were present.

The legs were very thin. They were kept in extension at the hip and knee, but the feet were held in flexion. The tendon reflexes were rather brisk and the great toes came up on plantar stimulation.

BIBLIOGRAPHY

GORLIN, R. J. AND SEDANO, H.: Incontinentia pigmenti. Modern Medicine, June 17, 1968, p. 162.
———— AND ANDERSON, J. A.: Characteristic dentition in incontinentia pigmenti. J. Pediat., **57**:78, 1960.
HABER, H.: The Bloch-Sulzberger syndrome (Incontinentia pigmenti). Brit. Jour. Derm., **64**:129, 1952.
KAUSTE, O. AND PAARELA, M.: Incontinentia pigmenti. Ann. paediat. Fenniae., **7**:79, 1961.
LENZ, W.: On genetics of incontinentia pigmenti. Ann. paediat., **19**:149, 1961.
MENDELSOHN, R. S. *et al.:* Incontinentia pigmenti. A.M.A. J. Dis. Child., **97**:348, 1959.

HALLERMAN-STRIEFF SYNDROME OR DYSCEPHALY WITH CONGENITAL CATARACTS

Fall and Schull report six cases of this condition and state that twenty-seven cases are recorded. The nose is beaked and the chin receded so the term bird face is employed. There is microbrachycephaly. The temporo-mandibular joints are displaced forward. The mouth is small. Dental anomalies occur. Atrophy of the skin, deficient hair, and congenital cataracts are characteristic. The child may be a dwarf, and mental deficiency is common. Microphthalmia sometimes occurs. This condition is sometimes termed the syndrome of Francois.

BIBLIOGRAPHY

FALLS, H. F. AND SCHULL, W. J.: The Hallerman-Strieff syndrome. A.M.A. Arch. Ophth., **63**:409, 1960.
GORLIN, R. J. AND SEDANO, H.: The Hallerman-Strieff syndrome. Modern Medicine 1959, **vol. 37,** No. 17, p. 146.
CARONES, A. V.: The dyscephalic syndrome of Francois. Ophthalmologica, **142**:510, 1961.

THE LEOPARD SYNDROME

This is inherited as an autosomal dominant trait with high penetrance. At birth or shortly afterwards numerous dark moles are seen. They are found on the trunk, neck, scalp, palms, soles and genitalia and rarely on the face. A few cafe au lait spots may be found.

Congenital cardiovascular abnormalities are common. Pulmonary stenosis

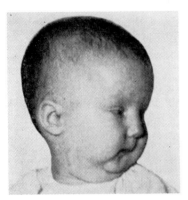

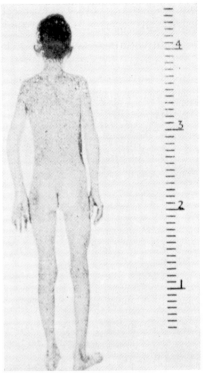

Fig. 67. Typical face associated with the Hallerman-Streiff syndrome with beaked nose and underdeveloped mandible. (From Falls, H. F. and Schull, W. J.: A.M.A. Arch. Ophth., **83**:409, 1960.)

Fig. 68. Photograph of patient illustrating multiple symmetrical moles with psychic and somatic infantilism and genital hypoplasia. (Moynahan, E. J.: Pro. Roy Soc. of Med., **55**:959, 1962.)

may be found and also subaortic stenosis. Various abnormalities of the electrocardiogram are described.

The bodily growth may be retarded. Pectus excavatum and pectus carinatum are seen. There may be kyphosis, winging of the scapulae, ocular hypertelorism and mandibular prognathism.

Nerve deafness sometimes occurs. Childish behavior is described. Sexual development is defective. The females have hypoplastic ovaries; males hypospadias and often undescended testicles.

BIBLIOGRAPHY

Gorlin, R. J. and Sedano, H.: The leopard syndrome. Modern Medicine 1969, **vol. 37,** No. 9, p. 178.

Mpynahan, E. J.: Multiple symmetrical moles with psychic and somatic infantilism. Proc. Roy. Soc. Med., **55**:959, 1962.

GARDNER'S SYNDROME WITH MENTAL DEFICIENCY

This syndrome includes multiple epidermoid cysts over the scalp and trunk as well as fibromas, lipomas, fibrosarcomas and osteomas arising in the mandible, maxilla and nasal sinuses, supernumerary teeth with impaction of teeth, irregular islands of increased bone density in the maxilla and mandible and multiple polyps of the intestine which may become malignant. In some patients only a few of the characteristic features are present so the outlines of this condition are not well established. It is clear that this is an autosomal dominant condition with complete penetrance.

The epidermoid cysts are usually apparent early in life. The intestinal polyps may not be evident until the age of 40 to 60 years.

Mental deficiency and convulsive seizures are not standard features of this disease and are not mentioned in some articles.

Turcot *et al.* report cases in which malignant intracranial growths such as medulloblastomas and glioblastomas are associated with intestinal polyposis in the same family.

CASE HISTORY.—*Gardner's syndrome with mental deficiency, and convulsions.*

J. D. W. was seen at the Rosewood State Hospital by the courtesy of Dr. Harry G. Butler. He was always backward in development. He did not walk until he was 3 years old and did not form words until he was 4 years old. He was found to be mentally defective when he was a small child. He was subject to convulsive seizures in early childhood.

When he was admitted to the hospital he would sit for hours rolling his head from side to side. He walked with bent knees. His intelligence quotient was estimated at 21 and 25 per cent. X-rays of the skull and chest showed no abnormalities. An area of sclerosis was found on the mandible. X-rays of the long bones showed nothing of significance. Multiple tumors were found on the trunk and head.

On examination the patient was of short stature. He was slightly obese. Muscular development was very good. He was able to form words indistinctly and could understand short simple sentences as a rule.

There were a large number of rounded tumors over the scalp. Many of these were about 2.0 cm in diameter and were elevated about 1.0 cm. They were firm and covered with normal skin. They proved to be epidermoids. One tumor which sprang from the left side of the head was about 8.0 cm in its longest diameter and was covered with soft wrinkled skin. It was very soft. It did not transilluminate. This seemed to be a fibroma. Another somewhat smaller one arose from the left side of the neck. It was fairly firm and contained some small hard nodules. On the left side of the trunk there was a pigmented tumor and a similar pigmented tumor was seen on the back in the lumbar region. These tumors were not tender. Many scars showed where tumors had been removed.

The pupils were equal and reacted to light. The optic fundi appeared to be normal. He could see but vision could not be estimated. There was no ptosis of the lids. The ocular movements were non-comitant, but no limitation of movement was found. Irregular nystagmoid movements were present. Otherwise the cranial nerves seemed to be in order. The pa-

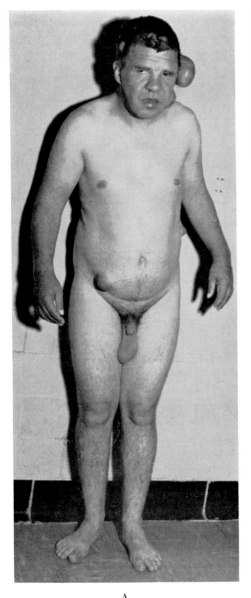

A

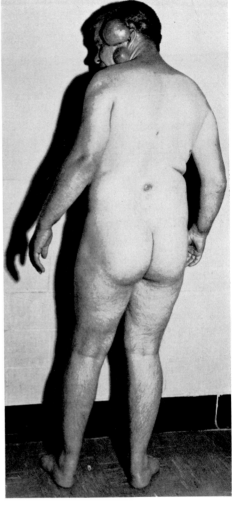

B

FIG. 69. A and B. Gardner's syndrome showing many epidermoid cysts over scalp and
body and large fibroma moluscum near left
ear and another just below the mandible.

tient could walk and stand without difficulty. He had good strength. No
tremor or ataxia was evident. The tendon reflexes were all in order and
the plantar reflexes were normal.

BIBLIOGRAPHY

DUNCAN, B. R.: Gardner's syndrome. Need for early diagnosis. Jour. Pediat., 72:497, 1968.
FADER, M. *et al.*: Gardner's syndrome: Intestinal polyposis, osteomas, sebacious cysts and a new
dental discovery. Oral Surgery, 15:153, 1962.

GARDNER, E. J. AND RICHARDS, R. C.: Multiple cutaneous and subcutaneous lesions occurring simultaneously with hereditary polyposis and osteomatosis. Amer. Jour. Human Genet., **5**:139, 1953.

————: Follow up study of a family group exhibiting dominant inheritance for a syndrome including intestinal polyps, osteomas, fibromas and epidermoid cysts. Amer. Jour. Human. Genet., **14**:376, 1962.

GORLIN, R. J. AND CHAUDHRY, A. P.: Multiple osteomatoses, fibromas, lipomas, fibrosarcomas of of the skin, and mesentery, epidermoid inclusion cysts of the skin, leiomyomas and multiple intestinal polyposis. A heritable disorder of connective tissue. New England Jour. Med., **263**:1151, 1960.

———— AND SEDANO, H.: Gardner's syndrome. Modern Medicine, May 6, 1968, p. 173.

TURCOT, J. *et al.:* Malignant tumors of the central nervous system associated with familial polyptosis of the colon. Dis. of colon and rectum, **2**:465, 1959.

LIPODYSTROPHIC MUSCULAR HYPERTROPHY

Senior states that a number of cases of this condition have been described under various titles including leprechaunism. It may be present at birth or develop early in childhood. Several familial cases are known so it is believed to be the expression of a recessive trait. Both sexes are affected. The children are rather tall. There is complete loss of subcutaneous fat

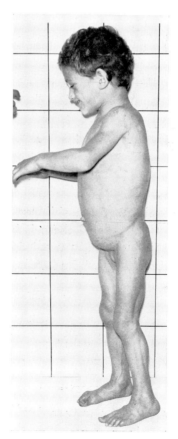

FIG. 70. Lipodystrophic muscular hypertrophy. (From Senior, B.: Arch. Dis. Childhood, **36**:426, 1961.)

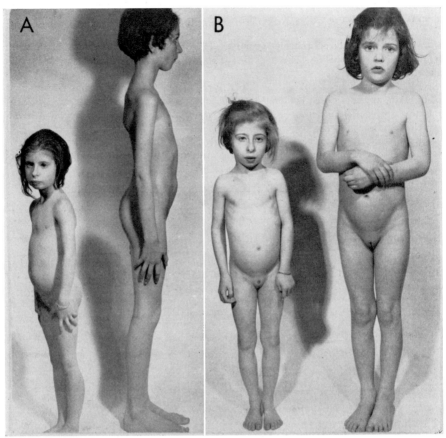

Fig. 71. A and B. Bird-headed dwarfs. A. Patient of eight years and nine months with normal child of same age. B. Patient's sister of seven years and normal girl of same age. (By the courtesy of Dr. J. A. Black. Low birth-weight dwarfs. Arch. Dis. Child., **36**:633, 1961.)

and abdominal fat, so the children present an emaciated appearance. The abdomen is enlarged and there is hepatomegaly. The liver function is deficient. The fasting blood sugar is low but diabetes may develop. The muscles are hypertrophied. The hands and feet are too large. The genital organs are increased in size. Senior's patient, a girl, had enlarged cystic ovaries and enlarged clitoris. Mental retardation is characteristic.

BIBLIOGRAPHY

Senior, R.: Lipodystrophic muscular hypertrophy. Arch. Dis. Childhood, 36:426, 1961.
——— and Gellis, S. S.: Syndromes of total and partial lipodystrophy. Pediatrics, **33**:593, 1964.

BIRD-HEADED AND OTHER LOW BIRTH-WEIGHT DWARFS

Bird-headed dwarfs have a beak-like nose, receding chin, and slender bodies. The cranial cavity is reduced in size. Their height is reduced. They are mentally defective and their intelligence may decline as they grow older. More than one case may occur in a family. Their birth weight is less than four and a half pounds as a rule.

Black mentions three other types of dwarfs whose weight at birth is low. There is a type characterized by snub noses. The bridge of the nose is flat. A recessive type is said to be associated with mental deficiency, but a dominant type is not inconsistent with normal intelligence.

In a third type, attributed to damage in early pregnancy, there is defective development of one side of the body. The mandible is small. A history of bleeding early in pregnancy is often elicited.

The fourth type, attributed to damage late in pregnancy, is found in one of twins. There is defective bodily growth and mental deficiency. The placenta may show infarcts or defective implantation.

BIBLIOGRAPHY

BLACK, J.: Low birth weight dwarfism. Arch. Dis. Childhood, **36**:633, 1961.
SECKEL, H. P. G.: Bird-headed Dwarfs. Thomas, Springfield, 1959.

THE TRANSPLACENTAL TRANSFUSION SYNDROME OF IDENTICAL TWINS

It is said that the twins are always monozygous, the placenta is usually diamniotic but always monochorionic. Arteriovenous anastomoses in the

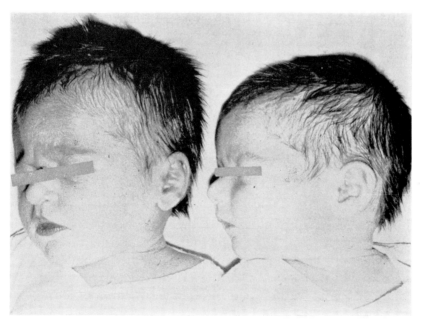

FIG. 72. Placental transfusion syndrome. Twins who survived showing difference in development. (From Rausen *et al*. Courtesy of Pediatrics, **66**:613, 1965, C. V. Mosby Co., St. Louis, Missouri.)

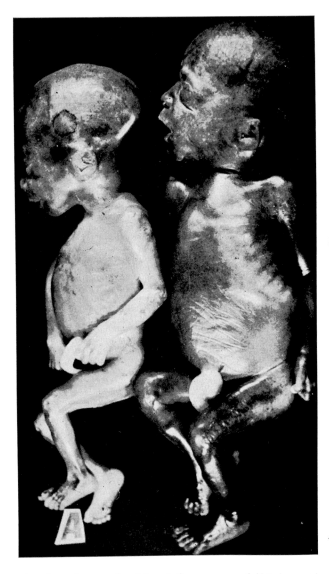

Fig. 73. Placental transfusion syndrome. Twins who died shortly after birth showing differences in color and in development. (From Rausen *et al.* Jour. of Pediatrics, **66:**613, 1956, C. V. Mosby Co., St. Louis, Missouri.)

chorion shunt the blood from one child into the circulation of the other. One child is anemic and the other polycythemic.

The polycythemic twin is cyanotic. There is respiratory distress due to cardiac overload, pulmonary hypertension, increased volume of the blood and increased blood viscosity. The heart is enlarged. Hydramnios is almost constant. Blood must be drawn to prevent heart failure. Bilirubinemia is increased due to increased hemolysis and exchange transfusion may be required. Digitalis may be needed.

The anemic twin is pale, feeble and poorly developed. Immediate transfusion may be necessary. Fluids may be required to combat dehydration. Defective growth and development are often noted if the child survives.

Rausen found 19 cases of the transfusion syndrome among 130 twin pregnancies. In 10 instances both twins died in the perinatal period. Most were stillborn and weighed less than 500 gm. In 5 instances, one of the twins survived and in 4 cases, both twins lived.

BIBLIOGRAPHY

Behrman, S. J.: Hazards of twin pregnancies. Post-Grad. Med., **38**:72, 1965.
Kresky, B.: Transplacental transfusion syndrome. Clin. Pediat., **3**:600, 1964.
Rausen, A. R. *et al.:* Twin transfusion syndrome. Jour. Pediat., **66**:613, 1965.

RUBENSTEIN'S SYNDROME

Mental deficiency, defective bodily growth, broad thumbs and great toes, undescended testicles and sexual deficiency.

In 1963, Rubenstein and Taybi published a study of seven children. There were five boys and two girls. Bodily growth was so deficient they might be termed dwarfs. The head was small. The nose was often beak-like. There was an antimongolian slant of the lid slits. The ears were low set. The mandible was poorly developed. The sternum was depressed. The most constant and characteristic feature was broadening of the thumbs and great toes. The bone age was retarded. An excessive growth of hair was found over the back of the neck and shoulders. These children were all mentally defective and the intelligence quotient ranged between 18 and 80. Motor development was slow. Respiratory infections and allergies were common. Errors of refraction associated with squints were often present. Cataracts were found in a few cases. The boys' testicles were undescended. In an 18-year-old boy I have seen the penis and scrotum were infantile.

No metabolic or chromosomal abnormalities could be found. The electroencephalogram usually showed diffuse abnormalities. The electrocardiogram was normal. No relative or ancestor displayed the same condition, but members of one child's father's family were said to have broad thumbs.

Case History.—*Rubenstein's syndrome in a boy of 9 years.*

By the courtesy of Dr. Harry G. Butler I have seen a boy of 9 years at the Rosewood Training School. Birth was at term after a 10 hour difficult labor. Birth weight was 5 lbs 11 oz. He was kept in oxygen for 10 hours. Motor development was slow. His mental development was slow and deficient. He was never able to attend school.

It was said that his parents were normal, but some of his father's family were said to have deformities of the hands and feet. This would seem to be of no significance for the patient was believed to be illegitimate.

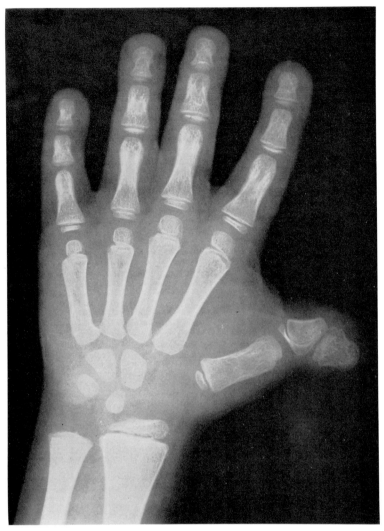

Fig. 74. Rubenstein's syndrome showing deformity of the thumb. (Courtesy of Dr. Harry Butler.)

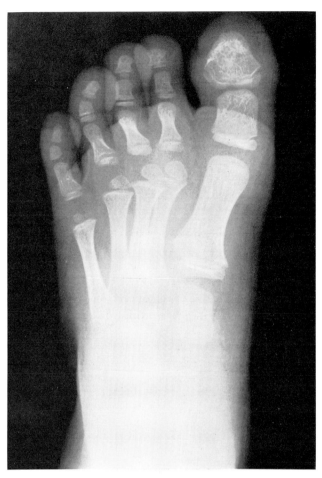

FIG. 75. Rubenstein's syndrome showing deformity of the great toe. (Courtesy of Dr. Harry Butler.)

On examination, the boy is about the size of a normal boy of 4 years. He is adequately nourished. He seems to be cheerful and can understand simple sentences. He will usually do as requested though his attention is poor. His articulation is only slightly imperfect and one can understand him.

His head is not abnormal in shape, but measures only 47 cm in circumference. There is no squint or limitation of ocular movement. The face is symmetrical and moves normally. The ears are set low. The nose is not beak-like. The hairline comes down nearly to the eyebrows. The palate is high arched. There is an excess of hair over the back of the neck and shoulders. One cannot say that the eyebrows are abnormal. There is a slight antimongolian slant to the lid slits.

The muscles are of proper bulk and tone. Strength is not definitely reduced. There is mild pectus excavatum. The arms and legs are short but proportional to the height. The thumbs are extraordinarily broadened and the great toes are also broadened. The left thumb is curved to the radial side. The 3rd and 4th fingers are webbed. The spine is straight. The penis is infantile. The scrotum is poorly developed and no testicles can be felt. His intelligence quotient is estimated at 50. He walks unsteadily. The knee and ankle jerks are active, but no clonus or Babinski sign is found. The electroencephalogram shows diffuse abnormalities.

CASE HISTORY.—*Rubenstein's syndrome in a boy of 18 years.*

Dr. Butler has also shown me a boy of 18 years. It is said that the pregnancy was complicated by elevation of the blood pressure and edema. Caesarian section was performed. Birth weight was 7 lbs 12 oz. The pa-

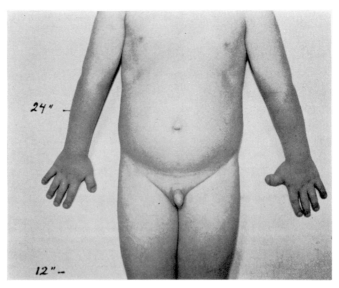

FIG. 76. Rubenstein's syndrome. Showing broad thumbs and small scrotum which contains no testicles. (By the courtesy of Dr. Harry G. Butler.)

tient was slow in mental and motor development. He sat up at 18 months, stood at 3 or 4 years and walked with much difficulty in 4 or 5 years. He never learned to talk. He was never toilet trained. The family history is said to be negative.

At 17 years it was found that there was detachment of the retina of the left eye. Operation was not successful. A few months later, a cataract was found in the right eye.

On examination the patient's nutrition is adequate. He seems to hear and will, at times, do as requested. He does not form words. His bodily growth is grossly reduced, so he may be termed a dwarf. His head is characterized by a very narrow forehead. His eyebrows are arched to an unusual degree. He keeps his eyes shut, probably because of photophobia. His eyes are both inflamed. His nose is beak-like. The ears are low set. The mandible is inadequately developed. The palate shows a high arch. There is

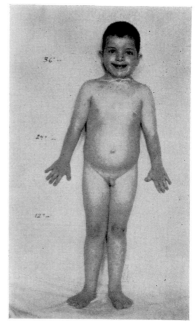

Fig. 77. Rubenstein's syndrome showing defective bodily growth. He is 8 years old and 42 inches tall. (By the courtesy of Dr. Harry G. Butler.)

an excess of hair over the posterior aspect of the shoulders and the forearms.

The patient sits with his head and body bent forward. His scapulae are displaced forward and there seems to be shortening of the pectorals so the scapulae cannot be placed in proper position and the arms cannot be externally rotated well. This seems to be due to maintaining this position for years. The right shoulder is higher than the left. There is pronounced pectus excavatum. The thumbs are greatly broadened and the great toes are too broad and too long. There is a long thoracic kyphos with some rotation of the spine. The muscles below the knee are rather slender, but the other muscles are not obviously reduced in size. The penis is infantile and the tiny scrotum contains no testicles. He cannot walk safely without support. The tendon reflexes are active, but there is no Babinski sign. X-rays show spina bifida occulta at S 1. The T 4-5 vertebrae are fused. The intelligence quotient is estimated at 18.

BIBLIOGRAPHY

Rubenstein, J. H. and Taybi, H.: Broad thumbs and great toes and facial abnormalities. Amer. Jour. Dis. Child., 105:588, 1963.

Coffin, G. S.: Brachydactyly, peculiar facies, and mental retardation. Amer. Jour. Dis. Child., 108:351, 1964.

PROGERIA AND WERNER'S SYNDROME

This strange condition has been described by Hutchinson and Gilford. The children are apparently normal at birth, but some months later, growth ceases and a senile appearance develops. The nose becomes thin and beak-like; the chin recedes; the hair falls out. The skin becomes wrinkled and atrophic. The subcutaneous fat disappears. The nails grow brittle. Growth ceases early and the patients are drawfs. The face is small and the head appears to be large by contrast though it is really slighlty small. There are frontal and parietal bosses. The viens of the scalp are prominent. The ears are not properly developed. Periarticular fibrosis develops around the joints limiting extension. The child stands with the knees separated. This has been termed the horse riding stance. Roentgenographic studies reveal osteoporosis. The terminal phalanges are pointed. The skull is thin and the anterior fontanel may fail to close. The nasal sinuses are not completely developed. Mental deterioration begins early. Arteriosclerosis and calcification of the blood vessels develop rapidly. These children often die of cerebral vascular lesions or coronary occlusion before adolescence. It is thought that this may be an autosomal recessive condition.

Atkins reports a case of this condition and states that this is the 23rd case reported. He also states that these patients usually die before puberty.

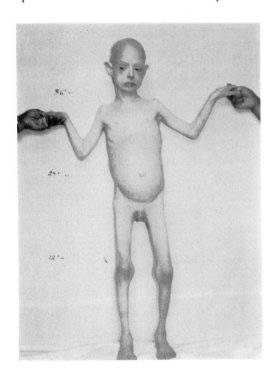

Fig. 78. Progeria.

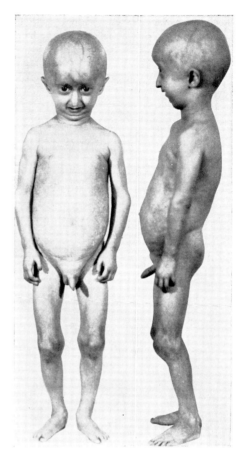

FIG. 79. Photograph of a child with progeria. (From Wilkins, L.: The Diagnosis and Treatment of Endocrine Disorders in Childhood and Adolescence, Thomas, 3rd Ed.)

At post-mortem examination he found no significant abnormality of the glands of internal secretion, except for the testicles which were immature. There was extensive arteriosclerosis involving the aorta and the coronary arteries. A myocardial infarction was the cause of death. The brain was greatly congested. A softening was found in the left frontal lobe. The muscles were histologically normal. There was an increase of hyaline material in the deeper layers of the skin.

In Werner's syndrome the symptoms are similar, but the onset is said to be shortly after puberty. This is a familial disease. The patients appear to develop senility prematurely. There is scleropoikiloderma, cataracts, blue sclerotics, diabetes, genital atrophy, vascular disease and osteoporosis.

BIBLIOGRAPHY

ATKINS, L.: Progyria. New England Jour. Med., **250**:1065, 1954.
EPSTEIN, C. J. *et al.*: Werner's syndrome. Medicine, **45**:177, 1966.
GABR, M. *et al.*: Progyria, a pathologic study. Jour. Pediat., **57**:70, 1960.

GILFORD, H.: Progyria, a form of senilism. Practitioner, **73**:188, 1904.

GORLIN, R. J. AND SEDANO, H.: Progeria. Modern Medicine, July 29, 1968, p. 62.

HUTCHINSON, J.: Congenital absence of hair and mammary glands with atrophic condition of the skin and its appendages in a boy whose mother had been almost wholly bald from alopecia areata since the age of six. Trans. Soc. Med.-Chir., **69**:473, 1886.

PETROHELOS, M.: Werner's syndrome. Amer. Jour. Ophthal., **56**:941, 1963.

TALBOT, N. B. *et al.*: Progeria. Clinical, metabolic and pathologic studies on a patient. Am. J. Dis. Child., **69**:267, 1945.

CONGENITAL DEFECTS DUE TO THE USE OF THALIDOMIDE BY THE MOTHER

It has been estimated that since 1959, 3500 to 4000 babies have been born in Germany whose arms or legs or both arms and legs are partially or completely absent. A smaller number of such cases have been discovered in other European countries, in England, and in this country. There is strong evidence that the use of thalidomide, a sedative drug, in the first two months of pregnancy is responsible.

The hands and feet may be attached to the body by a remnant of the

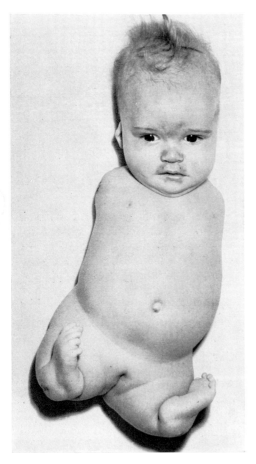

FIG. 80. Photograph of infant showing typical deformities attributed to thalidomide. (Joseph, M. C.: Thalidomide and congenital deformities. Develop. Abnormal. Child Neurol., 4:338, 1962.)

limb or may be missing. If present, the feet may be externally rotated and polydactyly and syndactyly may be present. Atresia of the esophagus, hydronephrosis and posterior choanal atresia may occur. An angioma is often seen on the forehead and nose.

It is said that the arms will be defective if the drug is given between the thirty-ninth and forty-first day after the last menstrual period. The legs are defective if the drug is taken between the forty-first and forty-fourth day. Stenosis of the rectum occurs when the drug is used between the fifty-fourth and fifty-fifth day.

Dr. Bengt Barr of Karolinska Institute, Stockholm points out that deafness due to atresia of the external auditory canal is not uncommon even when the extremities are not malformed. Deafness is associated with malformation of the ears. Facial paralysis on one or both sides, paralysis of the soft palate and various types of oculomotor muscle palsies are all found.

BIBLIOGRAPHY

JOSEPH, M. C.: Thalidomide and congenital deformities. Develop. Med. & Child Neurol., 4:338, 1962.

SPIERS, A. L.: Thalidomide and congenital abnormalities. Lancet, i:303, 1962.

TAUSSIG, H.: A study of the German outbreak of phocomelia. J.A.M.A., 180:1106, 1962.

OTHER DRUGS WHICH MAY DAMAGE THE FETUS WHEN INGESTED BY THE MOTHER

Kelsey estimates that less than 1 per cent of congenital malformations are due to drugs used by the mother. Sutherland and Light state that in addition to thalidomide, which causes fetal malformations in almost every case when it is taken between the 34th and the 45th day after the last menses, many other drugs are known to have untoward effects on the fetus or are suspected of having such effects.

Drugs used to combat malignancy are under suspicion. It is said that aminopterin is known to cause abortion and malformations. Methotrexate has similar effects. One instance in which busulfan and d-mercaptopurine and another in which chlorambucil were given suggest that these drugs have the same effects.

Androgenic steroids may cause masculization of female fetuses and thus, female pseudohermaphroditism. The corticosteroids apparently cause cleft palate in rare instances. Prednisolone may increase the incidence of abortions and stillbirths.

Tetracycline may cause pigmentation and prevent formation of the enamel of the teeth of the fetus when ingested by the mother. Retarded skeletal growth may result. Streptomycin may injure the inner ear of the fetus. Chloromycetin may cause aplastic anemia and many other serious effects. Carter and Wilson studied the cases of 85 women who received various antibiotics in the first 12 weeks of pregnancy. Twelve had malformed babies, and 13 had miscarriages.

Vitamin D, if taken in excessive amounts during pregnancy, may cause hypercalcemia and supravalvular stenosis of the aorta as well as other defects involving the heart. Supravalvular stenosis of the aorta leads to mental deficiency and a characteristic elfin face. In girls breast development may begin as early as 8 years, for vitamin D may increase estrogen secretion. Large doses of vitamin K may cause fetal jaundice and kernicterus.

Reserpine may cause nasal obstruction, difficulty in respiration and anorexia. One infant suffered from hypertonus, inactivity and hypothermia. Thiazides may cause thrombocytopenia and jaundice. Hexamethonium may cause paralytic ileus in the fetus. Sedatives may cause failure of respiration in the newborn infant.

Dicumerol may cause hemorrhage and death in the fetus, but it is said that heparin is safe.

Quinine may cause abortion and thrombocytopenia. McKenna reports 4 cases of congenital hypoplasia of the optic nerves. In one of these cases, there was also congenital deafness and in 2 cases, mental deficiency. The mothers had taken toxic doses of quinine in the early weeks of pregnancy to induce abortion. He also reports 2 cases of congenital deafness in which the drug was taken at the end of the first trimester. Vision was not affected in these 2 children.

The use of antithyroid drugs during pregnancy may cause goiter and thyroid deficiency in the fetus.

There is evidence that preludin and tolbutamide may damage the fetus but proof is lacking.

Nicholson states that aminopterin should never be given during pregnancy for it may cause abortion and malformation of the fetus.

Narcotic addiction in the mother may cause withdrawal symptoms in the infant shortly after birth which may be severe and even fatal.

Robert A. Good states that potassium depleting agents given during pregnancy may cause fatal damage to the kidneys which may prove fatal in infancy or in adult life.

I have seen a child who was born with gross malformations including amentia, cranium bifidum and cleft face whose mother had taken isoniazid during the first half of the pregnancy.

BIBLIOGRAPHY

CARTER, M. P. AND WILSON, F.: Antibiotics in early pregnancy and congenital malformations. Develop. Med. Child. Neurol., 7:353, 1965.

GOOD, R. A.: Fatal kidney defects due to potassium depleting agents. Modern Medicine, November 4, 1968, p. 43.

KELSEY, F. O.: Drugs in pregnancy. Minn. Med., 48:175, 1965.

LITCHFIELD, J. T.: Drug toxicity in the human fetus and newborn child. Appl. Ther., **9**:922, 1967.

McKENNA, A. J.: Hypoplasia of the optic nerves. Read before the Canad. Ophthal. Soc., June 14, 1966.

MILUNSKY, A. *et al.*: Methotrexate-induced congenital malformations. Jour. Pediat., **72**:790, 1968.

NICHOLSON, H. O.: Cytotoxic drugs in pregnancy. Jour. Obstet. Gynaec. Brit. Comwlth., **75**:307, 1968.

SUTHERLAND, J. M. AND LIGHT, I. J.: The effects of drugs upon the developing fetus. Pediat. Clin. North Amer., **12**:781, 1965.

TAYLOR, R.: Outcome for foetus of mothers receiving prednisolone during pregnancy. Lancet, i:117, 1968.

WARRELL, D. W. *et al.*: Maternal exposure to potential tetratogens. Jour. Amer. Med. Ass., **202**: 1065, 1967.

CONGENITAL ABSENCE OF ARMS AND HANDS

I have had the opportunity of examining a girl who was born without arms or hands. In each axilla was found a small shaft of bone about 2.0 cm long which was covered with skin and capped by a minute nail. Nothing was elicited in the history to explain this condition.

When the patient was very young her parents gave her toys which she could handle with her toes. As a result of courage, determination and intelligence she developed astonishing skill in the use of her feet. When I examined her, she was able to dress herself, to fasten buttons, to brush her teeth, comb her hair and use her feet almost as well as the average individual can use the hands. She shook hands with a firm grasp of her right foot. She was leading a useful life training other handicapped people to overcome their disability.

THE PIERRE ROBIN SYNDROME AND ASSOCIATED ANOMALIES

Pierre Robin syndrome includes defective development of the mandible, with receding chin, cleft palate, and a tendency for the tongue to fall back into the pharynx. Anomalies of the fingers and toes, as well as cardiac defects and deafness, may be present.

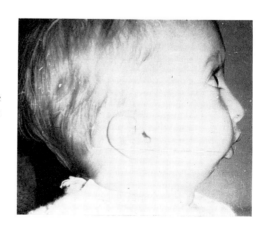

FIG. 81. Photograph of a child with the Pierre Robin Syndrome. (From Smith, L.: A.M.A. Arch. of Ophthal., **63**:984, 1960.)

In some cases there may be cleft palate, respiratory distress, stridor, cyanosis, indrawing of the lower ribs and sternum and occasionally opisthotonos. Survivors may be stunted in growth and mental deficiency may result. Congenital heart disease, microcephaly and accessory auricles may be associated.

Smith, Cavanaugh and Stowe found ocular defects in four of seven patients with this condition. Congenital glaucoma was found in two patients; bilateral retinal disinsertions with retinal detachment in one, and severe myopia in another.

McEvitt states that when respiratory distress is present, tracheostomy is indicated. The tube should be removed when the jaw has grown enough to

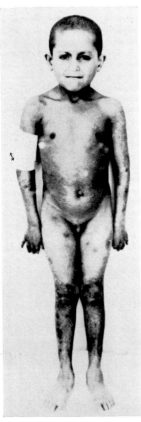

Fig. 82. Photograph of patient. From congenital generalized melanolucoderma associated with hypodontia, hypotrichosis, stunted growth and mental retardation. (By Berlin, C.: Dermatologia, **123**:227, 1961.)

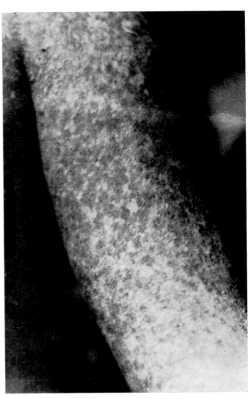

Fig. 83. Photograph of the patient's skin. From congenital generalized melanolucoderma associated with hypodontia, hypotrichosis, stunted growth and mental retardation. (By Berlin, C.: Dermatologia, **123**:227, 1961.)

allow the mouth to accommodate the tongue. He found that the tube could be removed from the age of four and a half to eighteen months.

BIBLIOGRAPHY

DENNISON, W. M.: The Pierre Robin syndrome. Pediatrics, **36**:336, 1965.
McEVITT, W. G.: Micrognathia and its management. Plastic Reconstr. Surg., **41**:450, 1968.
SMITH, J. L., CAVANAUGH, J. A. AND STOWE, F. C.: Ocular manifestations of Pierre Robin syndrome. A.M.A. Arch. Ophth., **63**:984, 1960.

FAMILIAL GENERALIZED MELANOLEUCODERMA WITH MENTAL DEFICIENCY AND DEFECTIVE BODILY GROWTH (BERLIN)

Berlin describes four siblings (two boys and two girls) who displayed dry, thin skin, mottled with brown, gray, yellow and white spots. These children were of dwarfish stature with thin legs, flat noses and defective development of the teeth. Hyperkeratosis of the palms and soles of the feet is mentioned. Mentality was defective. The boys had defective development of the penis and testicles, and were sexually impotent. The girls showed normal sexual development.

BIBLIOGRAPHY

BERLIN, C.: Congenital generalized melanoleucoderma with hypodontia, hypotrichosis, stunted growth, mental retardation occurring in two brothers and two sisters. Dermatologica, **123**:227, 1961.

PRIMARY ACANTHOSIS NIGRICANS

Acanthosis nigricans occurs most frequently in adults and is often associated with malignancy. A rare condition termed primary acanthosis nigricans which is not associated with malignancy may develop in childhood and even in infancy. It is believed to be inherited as a dominant characteristic. Brownish pigmentation is found in the axillae, the neck, face, shoulders and groins. A number of developmental defects may be associated including mental deficiency, convulsions, spastic paralysis and endocrine abnormalities. This seems to be a nonprogressive condition.

CASE HISTORY.—*Primary acanthosis nigricans associated with many defects of development.*

J. A. G. was seen at the Rosewood State Hospital by the courtesy of Dr. Harry Butler. He was admitted at the age of 8 years. He had always been mentally defective. He had never been able to form words or understand what was said to him. He could not walk, dress himself, or feed himself. He had convulsions at 6 months. He was noted to be sexually precocious at an early age. Brown pigmentation was noted on his chest at an early age.

On examination, he was unable to cooperate in any way. Dark pigmentation was seen over the chest, shoulders, neck, face and axillae. Large cysts were found on the eyelids which were termed hydrocystomata. The

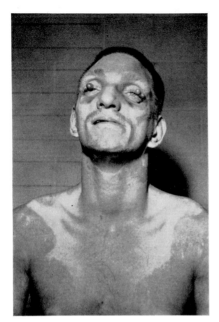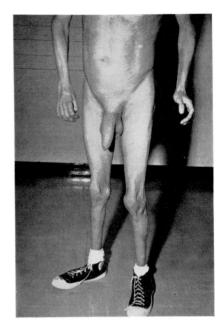

FIG. 84. Acanthosis nigricane showing malformations described in the case history.

patient was sparely nourished and muscular development was poor. There was a full range of active and passive movement at the shoulders and elbows. There was scarcely any movement at the wrist joints and there was also limitation of movement at the finger joints which showed bony thickening. The tendon reflexes were slightly increased.

The legs and thighs were too small and short. It was evident that the bones and muscles were both incompletely developed. Spasticity was present at the hips and knees and the knee jerks were greatly increased. At the ankles there was almost complete loss of active and passive movement. The ankle jerks were difficult to elicit. No Babinski sign was found. The penis was 6 inches long when completely soft and flaccid. The testicles were well developed.

BIBLIOGRAPHY

BUTTERWORTH, T. AND STREAM, L. P.: Clinical Genodermatology. Williams and Wilkins, p. 45, 1962.

WARIN, R. P. AND WOLSKE, M. M.: Juvenile acanthosis nigricans in twins with spastic paralysis. Pro. Roy. Soc. Med., **55**:303, 1963.

AITA, J. A.: Neurologic manifestations of general diseases. C. C Thomas, 1964, p. 886.

BORJESON'S SYNDROME

Borjeson *et al.* describe a family in which the males displayed a syndrome including severe mental deficiency, convulsions, deficient sexual development, obesity, reduced basal metabolic rate, swelling of the subcutaneous tissues of the face, narrow palpebral fissures and large ears.

BIBLIOGRAPHY

BORJESON, M. *et al.:* An X linked recessively inherited syndrome characterized by grave mental deficiency, epilepsy, and endocrine disorder. Acta Med. Scand., **171**:13, 1962.

CONGENITAL HEMIHYPERTROPHY

This process may involve one entire side of the body or may be confined to one part. It usually ends abruptly at the midline. It is evident at birth, but may become more striking at puberty. Males are affected more frequently than females. Mental deficiency is present in a large percentage of cases. The adrenal gland and the kidney are often enlarged. Varicosities in the leg, the groin and the lower part of the thigh are seen in some cases. The bones are lengthened and thickened. Gorlin points out that the tongue, teeth, uvula, maxilla, mandible and the palate may be hypertrophied. Hypospadias and cryptorchism are sometimes found.

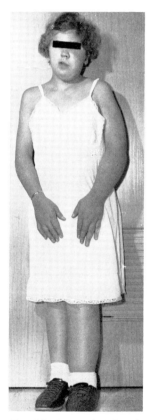

Precocious puberty may occur with increase of urinary gonadotropins and retarded bone age. The incidence of embryonic malignancy is increased.

The skull is often enlarged on one side, and in certain cases, it has been found that the brain is also enlarged.

There is no evidence that this condition is inherited.

Moffie describes a case of hemihypertrophy of the face which was associated with enlargement of the homolateral cerebral hemisphere and with epilepsy.

Celesia *et al.* report the case of a 15-year-old girl suffering from congenital muscular hypertrophy of the right leg. At 12 years she developed weakness of dorsal movement at the right ankle. At 13 years she developed myotonia of the right leg. Muscle biopsies revealed evidence of a myopathic type, possibly myotonic in type.

Congenital enlargement of one or more limbs may occur in neurofibromatosis, hemangioma, lymphangioma and in association with Wilms tumor.

Fig. 85. Congenital hemihypertrophy. (From Gorlin, R. J. and Meskin, L. H.: Congenital hemihypertrophy. J. Pediat., **61**:870, 1962.)

BIBLIOGRAPHY

CELESIA, G. G. *et al.:* Monomelic myopathy. Arch of Neurol., **17**:69, 1967.

FRAUMENI, J. F.: Wilms tumor and congenital hemihypertrophy. Pediatrics, **40**:886, 1967.

GESELL, A.: Hemihypertrophy and mental defect. Arch. Neurol. & Psychiat., **6**:400, 1921.

GORLIN, R. J. AND MESKIN, L. H.: Congenital Hemihypertrophy. Jour. of Pediat., **61**:870, 1962.

MOFFIE, D.: Een geval hemihypertrophia faciei. Maandschroft voor Kindergeneeskunde, **22**:3, 330, 1954.

REED, E. A.: Congenital total hemihypertrophy. Arch. of Neuro. and Psychiat., **14**:824, 1925.

SILVER, H. K.: Asymmetry, short stature, and variations in sexual development. Amer. Jour. Dis. Child., **107**:495, 1964.

THE CHEDIAK-HIGASHI SYNDROME

This is a familial condition which affects both males and females. The symptoms appear early in childhood. The skin is fair and the hair is blond. There is photophobia, which is sometimes attributed to ocular albinism. The liver and spleen are enlarged. Mental deterioration develops. Congenital heart disease is common. The lymph nodes are swollen. These children are prone to frequent infections. The lymphocytes display eosinophilic inclusions. There is anemia and pancytopenia; leukemia may develop. The children die early, usually before the age of seven years.

At post-mortem examination, the brain and all the internal organs are infiltrated by lymphocytes and abnormal cells.

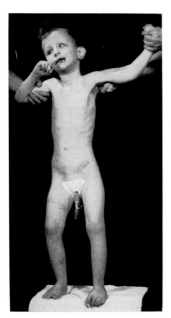

FIG. 86. Child suffering from the focal dermal hypoplasia syndrome. (From Gorlin, R. J. *et al.*: The focal dermal hypoplasia syndrome. Acta Dermato-Venereologica, **43**:421, 1963.)

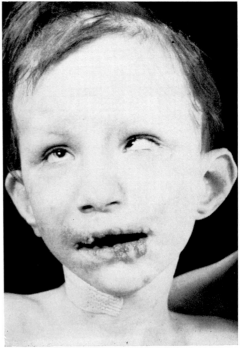

FIG. 87. Showing papillomas of the lips and squints. (From Gorlin, R. J.: Focal dermal hypoplasia syndrome. Acta Dermato-Venereologica, **43**:421, 1963.)

BIBLIOGRAPHY

DONOHUE, W. L. AND BRAIN, H. W.: The Chediak-Higashi syndrome. Pediatrics, **20**:416, 1957.

SPENCER, W. H. AND HOGAN, M. J.: Ocular manifestations of Chediak-Higashi syndrome. Am. J. Ophth., **50**:1197, 1960.

WINDHORST, D. B. *et al.*: Chediak-Higashi syndrome. Hereditary gigantism of cytoplasmic organelles. Science, **151**:81, 1966.

THE FOCAL DERMAL HYPOPLASIA SYNDROME

About thirteen cases of this condition have been reported. Twelve cases were in females. It seems to be due to a dominant gene with incomplete penetrance, which is probably lethal in males, as a rule.

According to Gorlin, the syndrome is manifest by focal areas in which the dermis is absent and the subcutaneous fat herniates, hypohidrosis, telangiectasia, linear pigmentation, focal alopecia, multiple papillomas of the mucosa and skin located especially on the lips and the vulva, syndactyly, polydactyly and absence of fingers and toes, colobomas of the iris and choroid, various squints, microphthalmos, dental anomalies and scoliosis. In some instances, there is gross mental deficiency and motor disorders, so the child is unable to stand or walk.

No chromosomal abnormalities have been found.

BIBLIOGRAPHY

GORLIN, R. J. *et al.*: Focal Dermal Hypoplasia Syndrome. Acta Dermato-Venereologica., **43**:421, 1963.

——— AND SEDANO, H.: Focal dermal hypoplasia syndrome. Modern Medicine, Vol. 37, No. 16, p. 112, 1969.

LEPRECHAUNISM

Patterson and Watkins review four cases of this condition and publish another one of their own. Donohue and Evans each studied two female siblings. Birth weight was always low; nutrition was deficient, and tube feeding was required. The nose was broad. The skin was loose. There was muscular wasting and the bone age was retarded. Mental deficiency was present. The clitoris was enlarged and breasts contained gland tissue. The ovaries were enlarged and cystic. One child died at forty-six days, one at sixty-nine days, and one before the age of two years. One was alive at six years.

The patient studied by Patterson and Watkins is a boy. His face is grotesque; his nose is broad and there is hair on his face. The hands and feet are too large, and the skin of the hands show large folds termed cutis gyrata. There is loss of subcutaneous fat and atrophy of the muscles. Nutrition is deficient and bodily growth is retarded. His mental development is deficient and his intelligence quotient has been estimated at 50 per cent.

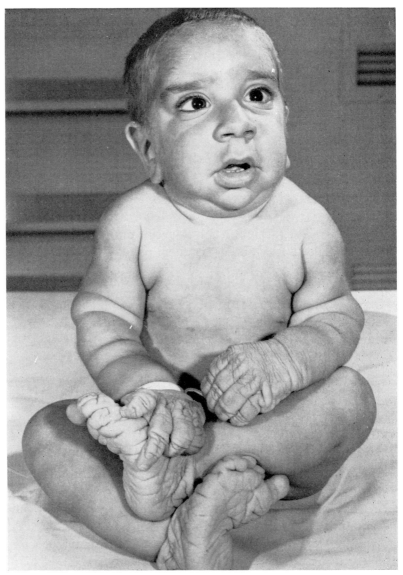

FIG. 88. Child at age of three years nine months. (Patterson, J. H. and Watkins, W. L.: Leprechaunism in a male infant. J. Pediat., **60**:730, 1962.)

The penis and testicles are enlarged, and the prostate is also large. Pubic hair appeared at one year.

The bone age is retarded. There is epiphyseal and metaphyseal dystrophy. The serum alkaline phosphatase is reduced. Mild generalized aminoaciduria was present.

The child was alive at the age of three years and nine months. He was unable to walk and could form only a word or two.

BIBLIOGRAPHY

DEKABAN, A.: Metabolic and chromosomal studies in leprechaunism. Arch. Dis. Childh., **40**:632, 1965.

DOHOHUE, W. L.: Dysendocrinism. J. Pediat., **32**:739, 1948.

————, AND UCHIDA, I.: Leprechaunism. J. Pediat., **45**:505, 1954.

EVANS, P. R.: Leprechaunism. Arch. Dis. Childhood, **30**:479, 1955.

PATTERSON, J. H. AND WATKINS, W. L.: Leprechaunism in male infant. J. Pediat., **60**:730, 1962.

SALMON, M. A. AND WEBB, J. N.: Dystrophic changes associated with lephechaunism in male infant. Arch. Dis. Childh., **38**:530, 1963.

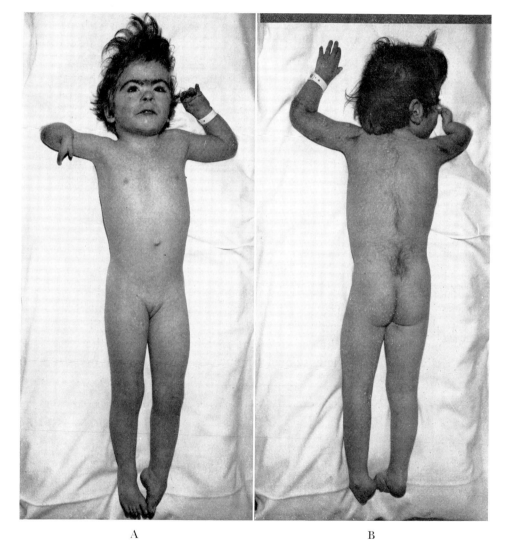

A   B

FIG. 89. A and B. Photograph of child at five and one-half years. (Ptacek, L. J., Opitz, J. M., Smith, D. W., Gerritsen, T. and Waisman, H. A.: The Cornelia de Lange syndrome. J. Pediat., **63**:1000, 1963.)

THE CORNELIA DE LANGE SYNDROME

This condition was described by De Lange, in 1933. In 1963, Ptacek *et al.* found about sixteen cases in medical literature and added six carefully studied cases of their own. In 1964, Opitz showed the evidence indicated that an autosomal recessive trait is responsible.

The condition is present in infancy. The appearance of the child is so characteristic that it may be recognized at a glance. The hands and feet are small and the hands are grossly defective. One or more fingers may be absent or there may be no hands and defective development of the forearm. There is a simian crease in the palm of the hand if there is any hand. Muscle tone is increased at first, but is later reduced. The head is small, but broad. The cry is described as a feeble, low-pitched growl. The facial appearance is characteristic: the jaw is small; the nose is small with anteverted nostrils; the eyebrows are heavy and meet in the midline; the lips are thin, with a small beak at the middle of the upper lip and a corresponding notch in the lower lip. There is an excess of body hair, marbled skin, and hypoplastic nipples and umbilicus. The genitals are imperfectly developed. Bodily growth is defective. Osseous maturation is retarded. There is profound mental deficiency. A number of ocular defects are mentioned, including optic atrophy.

These children fail to thrive and gain weight. There is little resistance to infections and death usually occurs in childhood.

There is a normocytic, normochromic anemia in many cases. There is an inability to concentrate urine. Hypogammaglobulinemia is found. Hypoaminoaciduria is found, though the plasma amino acids are within the normal range. Studies of the chromosomes have revealed no abnormality.

One post-mortem examination revealed a small brain which was not grossly malformed, but showed deficient myelination. All of the viscera except the liver showed deficient development.

BIBLIOGRAPHY

ABERFIELD, D. C. *et al.*: De Lange's Amsterdam Dwarfs syndrome. Developmental Med. and Child Neurol., 7:35, 1965.
DE LANGE, C.: Sur un nouveau de degeneration. Arch. de med. d. enf., 36:713, 1933.
OPITZ, J. M.: Editorial comments on the etiology of the Cornelia De Lange syndrome. Yearbook of Pediatrics 1964-1965. Editor, S. S. Gellis, Year Book Medical Publishers, Chicago, 1964.
PTACEK, L. J., OPTIZ, J. M., SMITH, D. W., GERRITSEN, T. AND WAISMAN, H. A.: The Cornelia De Lange syndrome. J. Pediat., 63:1000, 1963.
SCHLESINGER, B. *et al.*: Typus degenerativus Amstelodamenis. Arch. Dis. Childhood, 38:349.

CEREBRAL GIGANTISM IN CHILDHOOD

Sotos *et al.* describe five children who, at birth, are long, and grow too rapidly, in both height and weight, during the first four years of life.

Their weight, height and bone age are two to four years in advance of normal. After the age of four years, their rate of growth diminishes, but their measurements remain above normal.

The face shows a downward, lateral slant of the eyes, high, prominent forehead, and depression of the bridge of the nose. The palate is high arched. The head is a bit too large. The arms are long and their span equals or exceeds the height. The hands and feet are very large.

Mental deficiency is present, and the children are clumsy in their gait, and indeed, in all movements. The cerebral ventricles were dilated in three cases, but there is no progressive hydrocephalus or obstruction of the ventricular system. Sexual development is not accelerated.

The authors have been unable to find any evidence of eosinophil adenoma of the pituitary gland, or indeed, any endocrine disorder. There is nothing to suggest that the condition is inherited. The standard signs of neurofibromatosis are lacking.

BIBLIOGRAPHY

Sotos, J. F. *et al.:* Cerebral gigantism in childhood. A syndrome of excessively rapid growth with acromegalic features and non-progressive neurologic disorder. New England J. Med., **271:**109, 1964.
Stephenson, J. N. *et al.:* Cerebral gigantism. Pediatrics, 41:130, 1968.

CHONDRODYSTROPHY (ACHONDROPLASIA)

This well-known condition is the expression of a congenital defect of development of the cartilaginous bones. The characteristic features include the very short arms and legs, the relatively longer but still shortened trunk, the increased lumbar lordosis, the divergence of the fingers causing the so-called trident hand, and the large head. Mild grades of mental defect are frequently associated. These dwarfs are very muscular and active. They frequently become circus acrobats and midget wrestlers. It is said that they are very active in their sexual life.

There is some difference of opinion about the type of inheritance. Mc-Kusick states that in classical achondroplasia the inheritance is that of a dominant trait.

The head is broad and the circumference is increased. Its height is also greater than normal and the forehead often bulges. The bridge of the nose is flattened. The base of the skull is shortened as Virchow showed. This is due to defective development of the bones which form the base of the skull leading to premature union. The term tribasic synostosis has been applied to this peculiarity. Since the bones of the base are not membranous bones, as are the bones of the vault, but arise from cartilage, the tribasic synostosis may be regarded as a part of the general defect of bony development. It has been known for many years that the patient's intelligence is usually in inverse ratio to the size of the head, but no understanding of this seeming paradox was possible until Jensen called attention to the possibility of hydrocephalus. In 1921, Dandy was able to demonstrate by means of his method of ventriculography that the enlarged head of chondrodystrophy is in some cases at least associated with dilatation of the cerebral ventricles. This hydrocephalus differs from other types in that its development is slow and seems to cease spontaneously. Dandy found no obstruction to the flow of cerebrospinal fluid, and air injected into the spinal canal passed into the ventricles and up over the cortex. He cannot offer any satisfactory explanation for the hydrocephalus, but suggests that it may be due to the shortened base of the skull which might cause kinking of the aqueduct or obstruction of the cisternae at the base. It has been suggested that the base of the skull may eventually yield to the pressure and expand to such an extent that the hydrocephalus is relieved. Dennis *et al.* show that

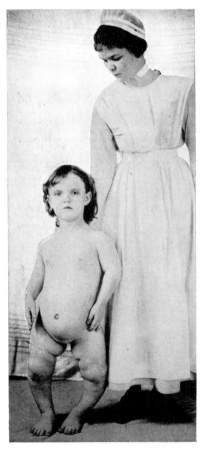

Fig. 90. Chondrodystrophy with hydrocephalus.

megalencephaly is also found in association with achondroplasia and report five cases in which the head was enlarged but there was no hydrocephalus.

The roentgenographic changes in the bones are diagnostic. The long bones are shortened and curved. The epiphyseal ends show knob-like enlargements and irregular deformities. The sacroiliac notch is very small. The foramen magnum is small. A number of these patients eventually develop paraplegia. As a rule this occurs in adult life rather than in childhood. Vogel and Osborne state that the spinal canal in these children is narrow and there is scarcely any subarachnoid space. In some instances a wedge shaped vertebra is found between the twelfth thoracic and the second lumbar vertebra. This leads to osteophyte formation with compression of the cord, the spinal nerve roots or possibly the nutritive arteries. The only remedy is an extensive laminectomy. Spillane mentions that paraplegia may also result from herniation of an intervertebral disc in these patients.

A condition described by McKusick as the cartilage hair syndrome must be distinguished. The patients are dwarfs with short extremities presenting the appearance of chondrodystrophy. The head is normal, however, and there is no bulging of the forehead. There is inability to extend the elbows fully. The hair is sparce, fine, fragile and of light color. There may be megalocolon. Mental condition is normal. This is inherited as a recessive trait.

The Ellis-van Creveld syndrome also presents some similarities to chondrodystrophy. The patients are short limbed dwarfs. They display polydactyly, knock knees, defective nails and teeth, mild epispadias, hydrocolpos and cardiac defects. A single atrium may be found. Malformations of the chest and weakness of the walls of the bronchi are mentioned. Either the cardiac defect or the difficulty in respiration may cause death in infancy. Mental deficiency is described but may not be an integral part of the condition. Inheritance is recessive.

McKusick also describes other conditions which have at least a superficial resemblance to chondrodystrophy including spondyloepiphyseal dysplasia, pycnodysostosis, and diastrophic dwarfism.

BIBLIOGRAPHY

DANDY, W. E.: Hydrocephalus in chondrodystrophy. Bull. Johns Hopkins Hosp., 32:1, 1921.

DENNIS, J. P. *et al.*: Megalencephaly and internal hydrocephalus and other neurological aspects of achondroplasia. Brain, 84:427, 1961.

DUVOISIN, R. C. AND YAHR, M. D.: Compressive spinal cord and root syndromes in achondroplastic dwarfs. Neurology, 12:202, 1962.

EPSTEIN, J. A. AND MALIS, L. I.: Compression of the spinal cord and cauda equina in achondroplastic dwarfs. Neurology, 5:875, 1955.

FREUND, E.: Spastic paraplegia in achondroplasia. Arch. Surg., 27:859, 1933.

GORLIN, R. J. AND SEDANO, H.: The Ellis-van Creveld syndrome. Modern Medicine, Dec. 2, 1968, p. 108.

McKUSICK, V. A. *et al.*: The Ellis-van Creveld syndrome. Bull. Johns Hopkins Hosp., 115:306, 1964.

———— *et al.*: Cartilage-hair hypoplasia. Bull. Johns Hopkins Hosp., 116:285, 1965.

————: Heritable Disorders of Connective Tissue. 3rd Ed. C. V. Mosby Co., 1966.

POTTER, E. L. *et al.*: Chondrodystrophy fetalis. Amer. Jour. Obst. and Gyn., 56:790, 1948.

SPILLANE, J. D.: Three cases of achondroplasia with neurological complications. J. Neurol., Neurosurg. & Psychiat., 15:246, 1952.

VOGEL, A. AND OSBORNE, R. L.: Lesions of the spinal cord in achondroplasia. Arch. Neurol. & Psychiat., 61:644, 1949.

CHONDRODYSTROPHIA CALCIFICANS CONGENITA OF CONRADI

This rare condition occurs in infancy. There is often congenital dislocation of the hips and club feet. Bodily development is defective so the children are dwarfs. The scalp is bald or covered with sparce hair. Congenital cataracts are often present. The joints are rigid and usually fixed in flexion. The muscles undergo atrophy. Mental deficiency is often present.

In infancy a characteristic picture is seen in roentgenograms of the bones. The carpal and tarsal bones are stippled by many small, calcified deposits. Similar deposits are seen in the epiphyses of the long bones, sacrum, pelvis and sternum. The trachea may show similar deposits. After the third year the characteristic changes in the bones are no longer present.

A post-mortem study made by Coughlin on a 2-month-old baby revealed in addition to the roentgenographic changes, fibrosis of the periarticular tissues and filling of the joint spaces by vascular connective tissue.

Various congenital abnormalities such as congenital heart disease and cleft palate are associated with this condition. Not many of these children survive the first few years of life. The inheritance is thought to be that of an autosomal recessive.

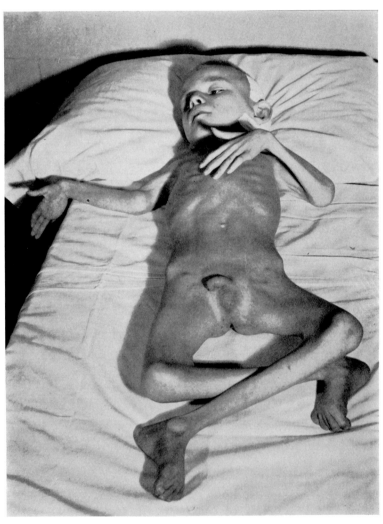

Fig. 91. Child suffering from chondrodystrophia congenita calcificans showing fixation of the joints in flexion. (By the courtesy of Dr. Robert Zwireckie and Dr. Harry Butler.)

CASE HISTORY.—*Chondrodystrophia calcificans congenita.*

A. B. was seen at the Rosewood Training School by the courtesy of Dr. Harry G. Butler. He was 8 years old at the time. The child was born prematurely at 8 months. A sibling born earlier suffered from the same condition as the patient and died at 35 months. The patient was found to have club feet and congenital dislocation of the hips. He was unable to move his arms or legs and was soon discovered to be mentally deficient. His bodily growth was deficient.

Roentgenographic examinations revealed irregular spotty calcific densities in the epiphyses and a diagnosis of chrondrodystrophia calcificans congenita was made. His intelligence quotient was estimated at 1.

On examination at the age of 8 years, the patient was a dwarf being no larger than a child of 3 years. His head was not abnormal in shape, but measured only 45 cm in circumference. It was evident that he could not talk or understand. There was scarcely any hair on his head. Dilated veins were evident over the scalp and the body. There was an internal squint. Cataracts were seen in both eyes. The arms above the elbows and the thighs were shortened as compared with the distal segments of the extremities. The arms were fixed at the shoulders and at the elbows they were fixed in flexion. The hips were fixed in flexion and external rotation, and the knees were fixed in flexion. The feet were held in dorsal flexion. The muscles were all extremely slender. Neither active or passive movements were possible at the joints. Except for the knee jerks, which were easily elicited, no tendon reflexes were elicited. The roentgenographic examinations of the bones revealed none of the characteristic changes which were present early in infancy.

BIBLIOGRAPHY

BAROVSKY, M. P. AND ARENDT, J.: Chondrodystrophy calcificans congenita. Jour. of Ped., **24**:558, 1944.

CONRADI, E.: Vorzeitiges Aufreten von Knochen-und eigenartigen Verkalungs Verlungskernen bei chondrodystrophie fötalis hypoplastica. Jahrb. f. Kinderh., **80**:35, 1914.

COUGHLIN, E. J. Jr.: Chondrodystrophia calcificans congenita. Jour. Bone and Joint Surg., **32A**:938, 1950.

LIGHTWOOD, R. C.: Congenital defect with strippled epiphyses. Pro. Roy. Soc. Med., **24**:564, 1930-31.

RAAP, G.: Chondrodystrophia calcificans congenita. Amer. Jour. Roentgenol., **49**:77, 1943.

MELNICK, J. C.: Chondrodystrophia calcificans congenita. Amer. Jour. Dis. Child., **110**:218, 1965.

THE WEIL-MARCHESANI SYNDROME

This condition is evidenced by a short, dwarfish stature and by short stubby fingers. The lenses are small and tend to be spherical. They are often dislocated and cataracts and glaucoma frequently develop. The head is round. The nose is pug shaped and the bridge of the nose is flattened. Mental deficiency is present. This is regarded as a dominant characteristic with low penetrance.

BIBLIOGRAPHY

KLOEPFER, H. W. AND ROSENTHAL, J. W.: Possible genetic carriers in spherophakia-brachymorphia syndrome. Amer. Jour. Human Genet., 7:398, 1955.

MARCHESANI, O.: Brachydaktylie und angeborne Kugellinse als Systemerkrankung. Klin. Monatsbl. Augenh., 103:392, 1938.

PLEONOSTEOSE OF LERI

This condition is characterized by short stature and by short arms and legs as well as short thick hands and feet. The palmar pads are thickened.

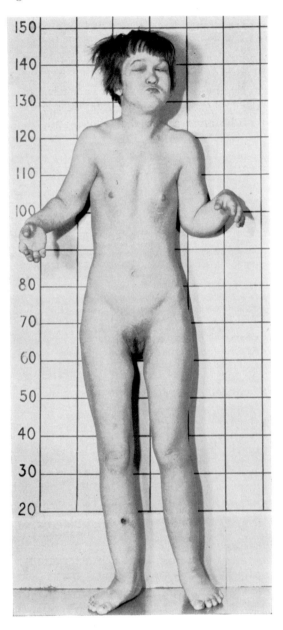

A

FIG. 92. A and B. Pleonostosis of Leri. Showing dwarfish stature, short arms and legs, small hands with thick palms and thick short fingers. The eyelids droop. She is mentally deficient.

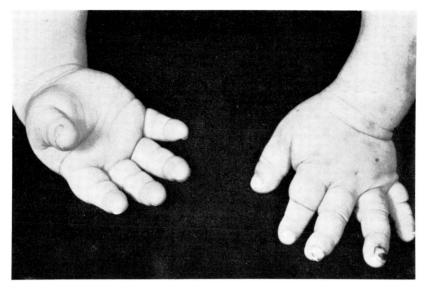

B

There is limitation of movement at the wrists, elbows and sometimes the knees, hips and spine. The fingers are very thick and short and display contractures in flexion. The legs are not usually affected as severely as the arms and hands, but the gait is described as abnormal. Drooping eyelids are often present. In some instances a mongoloid face is evident. Dr. McKusick suggests that the limitation of movement is due to connective tissue proliferation and thickening of the capsules of the joints.

Roentgenograms reveal a small sella tursica and large nasal sinuses as well as shortening of the bones of the hands and feet.

These features are not present at birth but become evident gradually. Mental deficiency is present in some cases. It is believed that this condition is inherited as an autosomal dominant. A parent and several children may be affected. Many cases are described in the European literature.

CASE HISTORY.—*Pleonosteose of Leri with some unusual features.*

C. M. was born by difficult delivery. She was kept in oxygen for 24 hours. She had episodes of cyanosis during the first few weeks of life. Her development was slow. It was evident early in life that she was mentally backward. The eyelids always drooped and there was congenital nystagmus.

She was admitted to the Rosewood Hospital where I saw her by the courtesy of Dr. Harry Butler. X-rays of the skull showed a minute sella and large nasal sinus. The intelligence quotient was estimated at 25.

On examination the patient did not talk or seem to understand. She was no taller than a child of 10 years though she was 20 years old. Her head was rather round. The cheeks were so fat her nose seemed to be partly buried. The bridge of the nose was depressed. The eyelids showed almost complete ptosis, and she could see only out of a narrow slit below the left upper lid. There was congenital nystagmus of the pendular type. She had high grade myopia which was no doubt the cause of the nystagmus.

The trunk was small and no larger than that of a child. The sternum was depressed, i.e. pectus excavatum. The back was straight. The nipples were very small and there was no breast tissue.

The arms were short. Extension at the elbows was limited. The wrists were fixed in flexion. The hands were small, broad and thick. The fingers were extremely short and thick. They were held in flexion.

The legs were short. The feet were very short and the toes were thickened. The patient walked with a staggering gait and seemed to be in danger of falling. The tendon reflexes were brisk in both the arms and legs. Ankle clonus was present on both sides and the plantar reflexes were suggestive of Babinski signs.

BIBLIOGRAPHY

McKusick, V.: Heritable Disorders of Connective Tissue. Thomas, Springfield, p. 303, 1960.
Rukavina, J. G. *et al.:* Leri's pleonosteose. Jour. Bone and Joint Surgery, **41A:**397, 1959.
Watson-Jones, R.: Leri's pleonosteose. Jour. Bone and Joint Surgery, **31B:**560, 1949.

DIASTROPHIC DWARFISM

About 50 cases of this condition had been reported in 1969. It is sometimes confused with achondroplasia. The child is a dwarf. The arms and legs are very short and the trunk is also short. There is cervical kyphoscoliosis which is often apparent at birth and is progressive during the first years. The thumb and the great toe are widely separated from the other digits and permit an excessive range of movement. The feet are supinated and adducted. The fingers are short and are held in extension at the interphalangeal joints. The hands are deviated to the ulnar side. The peripheral joints are stiff. Posterior dislocation of the ulnar and subluxation of the knees occur. There is progressive degeneration of the hip joints. At first the ears are spoken of as cystic and hemorrhagic. The hemorrhages are absorbed and later plates of bone are found in the ears. There is often cleft palate and the bridge of the nose may be depressed. This is an autosomal recessive trait. Roentgenograms show delayed development of the epiphyses which are flattened. The metaphyses of the long bones show severe changes. The second, third and fourth cervical vertebrae are described as keel shaped and there is severe cervical kyphosis and subluxation. The thoracic and lumbar vertebrae are of normal height.

BIBLIOGRAPHY

Gorlin, R. and Sedano, H.: Diastrophic dwarfism. Modern Medicine, February 24, 1969, p. 202.
Paul, S. S. *et al.:* Diastrophic dwarfism. Clin. Pediat., 4:95, 1965.

ARACHNODACTYLY

This condition, also termed Marfan's disease, is apparently an inherited developmental abnormality. It seems to be transmitted as a simple dominant characteristic. The typical features are as follows. The patient is tall, as a rule, but slender and poorly developed. The fingers and toes are abnormally long and slender, hence, the name arachnodactyly. The musculature is slender, weak and atonic. The ligaments are apt to be relaxed. The joints admit an excessive range of movement, and effusions may occur in the joints. Various deformities of the spine such as kyphosis and scoliosis are mentioned in association with deformities of the chest such as pigeon and funnel breast. The feet are often flat. Hernias are common. Heart disease is a frequent finding. The heart may be enlarged and loud murmurs may

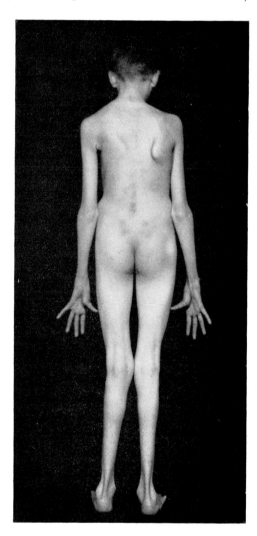

Fig. 93. Case of arachnodactyly. Note long slender extremities and especially the long fingers. The patient had scoliosis and congenital heart disease. (U-107527)

be audible. Defects in the interauricular septum have been found at post-mortem examination. One of the commonest findings is dilatation of the aorta which may cause deficiency of the aortic valves. This seems to be due to lack of proper elastic tissue in the aorta which may also lead to dissecting aneurysm. Congenital cystic disease of the lung is an uncommon finding. A remarkable feature of this condition is bilateral dislocation of the lens which is found in a very large percentage of all cases. It is said that the dislocation is usually upward. When the eyes are moved, the irides display a tremulous movement since they are not supported by the lenses. It is not unusual for glaucoma to result. Myopia is common and keratoconus and blue sclerae are mentioned. Retinal detachment is not unusual. The heads of these patients are dolichocephalic. The ears are large and stand out from the head. The face is long and narrow and the arch of the palate high. The subcutaneous fat is usually but not always sparse. White striae are seen on the skin and once we have seen extensive brown pigmentation covering one thigh and hip. Mental deficiency is not a real feature of this syndrome. Abortive cases of this condition are common in affected families.

Bacchus claims that the acid mucopolysaccharides of the serum are increased and the seromucoids are diminished. He thinks these findings are of diagnostic value. Sjoersma *et al.* state that there is an increased excretion of hydroxyproline in the urine.

The fingers and toes show the typical changes at birth and the diagnosis may be made very early. Amyotonia may be suspected in infancy. The deformities of the spine and chest develop later when the child begins to walk and are probably due to the inadequate support afforded by the weak musculature. Pneumonia and heart failure seem to be the commonest causes of death and infant mortality is said to be high. Chromosomal studies have shown no consistent abnormalities.

BIBLIOGRAPHY

BACCHUS, H.: Seromucoid and acid mucopolysaccharide values in Marfan's syndrome. J. Lab. & Clin. Med., **55**:221, 1960.

BERENSON, G. S. AND GREER, J. C.: Heart disease in hereditary syndromes. Arch. Int. Med., **111**:58, 1963.

BLACK, H. AND LANDAY, L. H.: Marfan's syndrome, a familial disorder. Am. J. Dis. Child., **89**:414, 1955.

ETTER, L. E. AND GLOVER, L. P.: Arachnodactyly complicated by dislocated lens and death from rupture of dissecting aneurysm. J.A.M.A., **123**:88, 1943.

FUTCHER, H. P. AND SOUTHWORTH, H.: Arachnodacyly and its medical complications. Arch. Int. Med., **61**:693, 1938.

GOLDEN, R. L. AND LAKIN, H.: The form fruste in Marfan's syndrome. New England J. Med., **260**:797, 1959.

GORLIN, R. J. AND SEDANO, H.: Marfan's syndrome. Modern Medicine, December 15, 1969, p. 138.

LUTMAN, F. C. AND NEEL, J. V.: Inheritance of arachnodactyly, ectopia lentis and other congenital anomalies. Arch. Ophth., **41**:276, 1949.

McKusick, V. A.: Heritable Disorders of Connective Tissue. St. Louis, C. V. Mosby Co., 1956.

Sjoerdsma, A. *et al.:* Increased excretion of hydroxyproline in Marfan's syndrome. Lancet, 2:994, 1958.

Stewart, R. M.: A case of arachnodactyly. Arch. Dis. Child., 14:64, 1939.

Traisman, H. and Johnson, F.: Arachnodactyly associated with aneurysm of the aorta. Am. J. Dis. Child., 87:156, 1954.

Walsh, F. B.: *Loc. cit.*

MYELODYSPLASIA WITH SPINA BIFIDA

Definition.—A type of defective development of the spinal cord associated with corresponding defect in the overlying vertebral laminae.

Etiology.—This condition is obviously a defect of development and, since the neural tube should be closed by the end of third week of fetal life and the bony canal from the first cervical to the fourth sacral vertebra by the end of the eleventh week, it is evident that the factors which govern its occurrence are operative very early in intrauterine life. In a few instances more than one case has been found in the same family, so there is some evidence for the assumption that spina bifida is due to a germ plasm defect. It has been suggested that defective implantation of the ovum may be responsible, but no proof has been offered to substantiate this theory. In 1968, D. H. Paget published a valuable study of these conditions with a new classification.

Pathological Anatomy.—A large number of different types of spina bifida are described, but only the common types need be discussed. The defect is most frequently found in the lumbar or lumbosacral segments. The sacral and upper cervical regions are infrequently affected and the lower cervical and thoracic segments are very rarely affected.

1. *Complete Rachischisis.*—This is the most severe type, for the neural tube lies open and exposed for a number of segments. The spinal cord is represented by a flattened, red, velvet-like ribbon which lies in a groove formed by the bifid vertebral laminae. The meninges are developed beneath the cord and pass laterally into a zone of parchment-like skin which blends with the normal skin around the margin of the lesion. There is often no sac, but in the more localized cases fluid may accumulate beneath the cord and so cause it to protrude to some extent. There is a tendency for the skin and meninges to grow over the lesion which not uncommonly leads to the mistaken impression that one is dealing with a meningocele. The exposed surface of the cord may show remnants of ependyma. In many cases the nervous tissues have not differentiated and nothing to suggest the structure of the spinal cord can be found in the region of the lesion. In others, we may distinguish nerve cells and nerve fibers. There is always paralysis of the legs.

2. *Meningomyelocele.*—In this type, we find a soft, rounded tumor con-

taining the spinal cord or its roots. The neural groove has closed, but the cord has retained its connection with the surface ectoderm so that it is attached firmly to the sac wall. The sac is formed of parchment-like skin and meninges and the fluid lies ventral to the cord. Despite the fact that the neural groove has closed, the cord may be imperfectly developed or injured by traction and adhesions so that paralysis is almost invariably present. There may be pronounced distention of the central canal of the cord which extends for many segments above the lesion. When this condition is very severe the cord may be reduced to a thin walled sac and its neural elements completely destroyed. Most authors regard this as a distinct type and term it *meningomyelocystocele*, but according to Keiller, it is merely an exaggeration of the hydromyelia which occurs in meningomyelocele and meningocele.

3. *Meningocele.*—Here we find an external swelling with normal skin or more frequently with thin atrophic skin which has often been compared to parchment. Within the skin we find a sac composed of the meninges. The dura and arachnoid may be fused so that the sac has a single wall, or may be separated by fluid so that we find a double sac. Penfield has made a careful study of the sac wall, and describes an inner layer composed of loose meshed tissue containing numerous spaces and irregular clumps of cells in intimate contact with the blood vessels. He compares these cells to those of the arachnoid, and has shown by injections of phenolphthalein

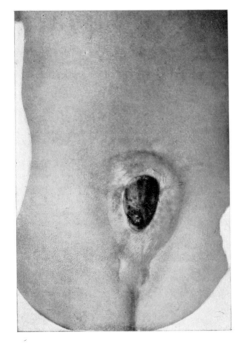

Fig. 94. Rachischisis. The central groove represents the open neural tube. The child's legs were of course paralytic. (By the courtesy of Dr. Peckham.)

that the sac wall is capable of absorbing fluids. The cord and the spinal nerve roots are usually normal, but may be injured or defective as in spina bifida occulta.

4. *Spina bifida occulta.*—There is no external sac, but the laminae of the vertebrae are defective and the site of the lesion may be marked by changes in the overlying skin, such as abnormal growth of hair, a dimple, a deposit of fat or telangiectases. The neural tube is closed. In the vast majority of these cases there is no neurological disturbance, but in certain cases there is some degree of paralysis. In such cases a mass of fibrous tissue is found attached to the posterior surface of the spinal cord and fused with the meninges. This usually extends into the defect in the laminae and anchors the cord firmly to the spine. At the same level, there is often gliosis in the posterior columns and central gray matter, and the central canal may be dilated. As a result of the adhesions between the spinal cord and the spine, the cord does not ascend during growth as it normally does, and the conus may be found several vertebrae below its usual position.

In some cases of spina bifida and spina bifida occulta, progressive gliosis may develop and one or more cavities sometimes appear in the gray matter so that the picture is very similar to that of the common type of syringomyelia.

Spina bifida is frequently associated with hydrocephalus. When hydrocephalus is associated with meningomyelocele, the Arnold-Chiari deformity is usually present. This association is not common in cases of meningocele. Cranium bifidum may be found in cases of spina bifida and is regarded as evidence of the same defect at a higher level. Numerous other deformities may complicate the picture such as extrophy of the bladder, syndactylism of the toes, paralytic and nonparalytic club feet, cleft palate and harelip. Teratomas and congenital tumors of various types may be present.

Clinical Features.—This is perhaps the commonest of the gross developmental defects of the nervous system and it has been estimated that it occurs once in a thousand births.

Myelodysplasia associated with lumbosacral spina bifida or spina bifida occulta gives rise to paralysis in the myotomes corresponding to the segments involved. Usually, the muscles of the calf and foot are atrophied and weak or paralyzed. The extensors of the knee and flexors of the hip are rarely affected, but in a number of cases the extensors of the hip and flexors of the knee are involved, although not to the same extent as the muscles below the knee. The affected muscles are flaccid. If the paralysis is extensive there are sometimes contractures maintaining flexion at the hip and extension at the knee. Various types of clubfoot are common, such as pes cavus, equinus, varus and calcaneus. The great toe is frequently dorsi-

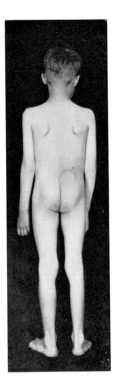

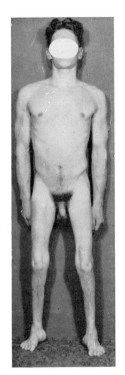

FIG. 95. Boy of 7 years who has been incontinent since birth as a result of myelodysplasia and spina bifida occulta involving chiefly the sacral segments of the cord. The right calf and right foot are smaller than the left. Right ankle jerk absent. Anesthesia over S. 3, 4, and 5 bilaterally. Disorders of bladder control characteristic of lesions in the conus. Presacral sympathectomy performed at the age of 6 years reduced residual urine from 200 cc. to 60 cc and abolished dribbling. The tumor to the right of the intergluteal fold is thought to be a meningocele or a lipoma.

FIG. 96. Myelodysplasia with spina bifida occulta showing defective development of the legs and pelvis as contrasted with the excellent development of the shoulders, arms and chest.

flexed. The ankle jerks are usually absent, the knee jerks are usually present and active, and the hamstring jerks may be present or absent. The electrical reactions are frequently altered, but the complete reaction of degeneration is not a common finding. Usually one obtains no response to electrical stimuli from completely paralytic muscles and finds quantitative diminution of electrical irritability in paretic muscles. Fascicular twitchings are rarely seen. These disturbances are in general bilateral and symmetrical, but there are numerous exceptions to this rule. The tendency is to a segmental distribution of the paralyses.

Sensory disturbances are difficult to demonstrate in infants and young children and are in general less pronounced than the paralyses. Frequently, analgesia and thermanesthesia may be found over the feet and ankles, and in many cases this sensory loss extends up over the posterior surface of the legs and thighs to the buttocks and perineum. Tactile sensibility is not involved to the same extent as pain sense, but in some cases complete cutaneous anesthesia is present. Proprioceptive sensibility is usually not affected unless the symptoms are severe. In general, the distribution of the sensory disturbances is of the segmental type, but in some cases it may resemble that of peripheral nerve lesions or even the "stocking" anesthesia of polyneuritis. It is the rule for the sensory loss to be bilateral and symmetrical, although in some exceptional cases the anesthesia may be confined to one side.

The feet and ankles are cold and cyanotic. Trophic disturbances are common. Ulcerations develop on the balls of the feet, the buttocks and the perineum. These may eventually penetrate deeply. The bones of the toes may become necrotic and be discharged bit by bit through the perforating ulcers. The toe nails may become opaque and thickened and finally drop off.

Disturbances of sphincter control are usually present unless the symptoms are very mild. If the legs are paralyzed, there is apt to be complete incontinence. In a few cases, especially when the lesion is chiefly confined to the conus, loss of sphincter control may be the only evidence of myelodysplasia. The anus is relaxed and the rectum may protrude. Residual urine results. Attacks of cystitis are characteristic. The residual urine may increase and eventually retention of urine in adolescence or even adult life may make the diagnosis clear.

Symptoms are evident at birth if the defect is a severe one. If only mild disturbances are present, they may not be detected until later in childhood. During early childhood, the child may seem to be making some progress in the development of motility, but this is probably only apparent and due to normal development, for later in life there is a tendency for the symptoms to increase to a limited extent. This may be the result of gliosis in the cord, but it is more probable, as I have suggested above, that it is due to the fact that the cord is adherent to the sac so that it may be stretched and traumatized by flexion of the spine. In fact, extensive paralysis has followed violent flexion of the back. We have observed one patient with spina bifida and the usual congenital atrophic palsies of the muscles supplied by the sacral segments of the cord. Later in life, he acquired spastic paralysis of the muscles supplied by the lumbar segments of the cord. We were inclined to attribute this later development to stretching of the spinal cord in the thoracic region. If the child survives, the lower extremities fail to develop, and the patient presents a very striking picture later in life with large muscular shoulders and trunk tapering down to a small pelvis and tiny legs.

Lawrence and Tew state that 70 per cent of the children who have myelocele or encephalocele are

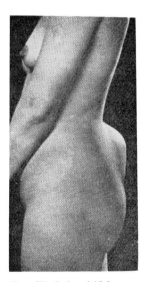

Fig. 97. Spina bifida occulta with overlying pad of fat which extended into the epidural space and compressed the cauda equina. (From Grinker and Sahs, Neurology, Thomas, 1966.)

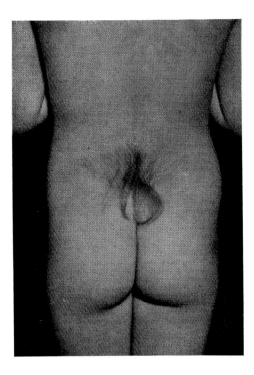

Fig. 98. Tuft of hair over area of spina bifida occulta. There was weakness of dorsiflexion of the left foot and spina bifida occulta in the second to the fifth lumbar vertebrae inclusive. (From Grinker and Sahs, Neurology, Thomas, 1966.)

moderately to severely disabled and have mental deficiency, whereas those with meningocele are not disabled and are of normal intelligence.

Spina bifida in the upper cervical segments is sometimes associated with defective development of the cerebellum and posterior columns of the spinal cord. Cerebellar ataxia may be present and weakness and spasticity of the legs and arms. Sensory disturbances are apt to be confined to the upper cervical dermatomes and pain and thermal sensibility are usually affected more than tactile sensibility.

When the cervical enlargement is involved, an interesting clinical picture is found which is very similar to that of syringomyelia. There is apt to be weakness and muscular atrophy in the arms, especially the forearms and hands. The fingers show trophic changes with ulcerations and loss of the terminal phalanges. If the legs are affected, the paralysis is of the spastic type with increased tendon reflexes and extensor plantar responses. In some instances, this condition becomes progressive giving rise eventually to tetraplegia as in the case of Turnbull. It would seem that a progressive process, perhaps a gliosis, develops on the basis of a congenital defect.

Amacher *et al.* describe meningocele on the anterior aspect of the sacrum. The sac presses on the rectum and bladder causing constipation and difficulty in urination. Involvement of the lumbar and sacral roots may cause sensory loss and mild weakness of the muscles they supply with loss of sphincter control. Intermittent elevation of intracranial pressure may occur due to compression of the sac. Roentgenograms of the sacrum reveal the opening in the anterior aspect of the sacrum which may be similar to that seen in cases of neurofibroma of the sacral roots. It is stated that abdominal excision is a safe and effective procedure.

Diagnosis.—When a sac is present there is rarely any difficulty in establishing the diagnosis. The situation of the tumor in the midline, usually in the lumbosacral region, the fluctuation on palpation and the translucency when tested with a flashlight, make the differentiation from other congenital tumors very easy. Moreover, pressure on the sac will cause bulging of the fontanels thus demonstrating its connection with the spinal subarachnoic spaces. Congenital lipomas must be differentiated. They may present as a soft mass over the sacrum and may be associated with spina bifida. If the lipoma involves the cauda as it may one may well think of myelodysplasia. The clinical differentiation of meningocele and meningomyelocele is not always easy. In meningocele the sac is usually perfectly translucent and pedunculated. The defect in the vertebrae is relatively small and paralysis is absent. In meningomyelocele, which is much the commoner, the sac is less translucent. The defect in the spine is often a large one and paralysis is often present. Electrical stimulation of the sac wall may cause movements of the legs if the nervous elements it contains are capable of functioning.

When there is congenital paralysis of the legs but no sac, the distinction between spina bifida occulta and other injuries or defects of the spinal cord may be difficult. Myelodysplasia is indicated by defects in the vertebral arches on palpation or roentgenographic study and by various abnormalities at the skin overlying the defect. It must be kept in mind that the laminae of the lumbosacral vertebrae are usually incompletely ossified until about the eighth year, so that the roentgenological diagnosis of spina bifida in childhood requires adequate knowledge of the normal standard for each age. Moreover, about 6 or 8 per cent of the population show spina bifida of some degree without any symptoms referable to the nervous system. Such defects involve L5 and sometimes L4. There may be a few tufts of coarse dark hair in this region or merely a pad of subcutaneous fat. In some cases, there is a large area of brown pigmentation or a "port wine" stain. Care must be taken to recognize the so-called mongolian spot which is a brownish or bluish area seen in the sacral region in mongolian and negro babies at birth. This is also sometimes seen in white babies. It is of no importance and soon disappears. Injury to the spinal cord during birth may cause some confusion. This is usually the result of difficult breech delivery and most commonly occurs in the thoracic segments. There is no muscular atrophy and the neurological signs are those of paraplegia-in-extension or more frequently, paraplegia-in-flexion. Amyotonia congenita must also be considered in the differential diagnosis. The weakness in this condition is usually more widely distributed and the loss of muscle tone is conspicuous. Sensory loss and trophic disturbances are absent.

Numerous authors have described nocturnal enuresis in association with a small defect of the laminae. Such defects are very common in normal children, and it scarcely seems justifiable to attach any importance to them unless there is some persistent disturbance of sphincter control during the day as well as at night.

Prognosis.—In most cases the sac slowly increases in size, and if the overlying skin is healthy it may attain extraordinary dimensions. The chief dangers are rupture and infection. Sudden rupture with escape of large quantities of spinal fluid may cause death in convulsions, and slow leaking is almost always followed by meningitis. In a few cases of meningocele the sac may shrink and eventually disappear spontaneously. The presence of a sac, however, justifies an unfavorable prognosis for death usually occurs in infancy. In giving a prognosis in cases of spina bifida occulta with neurological symptoms, the possibility of progression of the symptoms should be kept in mind. The association of hydrocephalus obviously justifies a bad prognosis. In children who have difficulty in emptying the bladder, urinary tract infections are a constant danger.

Treatment.—In spina bifida, the only treatment is surgical. If the sac is thin and rupture seems imminent, operation should be performed at once. If the sac is well covered by skin and there is no reason to expect rupture, it is best to defer operation until after the third year. The presence of paralysis or of definite hydrocephalus constitute contraindications for operation. The usual procedure is to excise the sac. Operation cannot relieve paralysis, although it may help to prevent increase in paralysis by freeing the cord from adhesions which probably cause some injury by traction, and by removal of deposits of fat which cause compression. However, the dissection of the roots and cord usually causes more or less damage, and the possible future benefits are balanced by the very real and immediate increase in symptoms.

In *spina bifida occulta,* operation is justified in many instances especially if there is any evidence of progression of the symptoms. It must be kept in mind that one may find tumors of congenital origin, or lipomas, or cysts or, indeed, something associated with the bony defect by mere accident.

BIBLIOGRAPHY

AMACHER, A. L. *et al.:* Anterior sacral meningocele. Surg. Gynec. Obstet., **126**:986, 1968.
BASSETT, R. C.: The neurologic defect associated with lipomas of the cauda equina. Ann. Surg., **131**:109, 1950.

BUCY, P. C. AND HAYMOND, H. E.: Lumbosacral teratoma associated with spina bifida occulta. Ann. J. Path., **8**:338, 1932.

DITTRICH, R. J.: Lumbosacral spina bifida occulta. Surg. Gynec. & Obst., **53**:378, 1931.

FAWCITT, J.: Some radiological aspects of congenital anomalies of the spine in childhood and infancy. Proc. Roy. Soc. Med., **52**:331, 1959.

GOZZANO, M.: A case of cervicodorsal spina bifida occulta with trophic and sensory disturbances and cervical hypertrichosis. Arch. Neurol. & Psychiat., **15**:702, 1926.

INGRAHAM, F. D.: Spina Bifida and Cranium Bifidum. Cambridge. Harvard Univ. Press, 1943.

KEILLER, V.: A contribution to the anatomy of spina bifida. Brain, 45:31, 1922.

LAURENCE, K. M.: Natural history of spina bifida. Arch. Dis. Childhood, **39**:41, 1964.

——— AND TEW, B. J.: Follow up of 65 survivors from 425 cases of spina bifida born in South Wales between 1956 and 1962. Develop. Med. Child. Neurol., 1967, **vol. 9,** Suppl. 13, p. 1.

MATSON, D. D.: Surgical treatment of birth defects involving the nervous system. J. Chronic Dis., **10**:131, 1959.

MERTZ, H. O.: Posterior spinal fusion defects and nervous dysfunction of the urinary tract. J. Urol., **24**:41, 1930.

McNAB, G. H.: Discussion on problems of spina bifida cystica. Proc. Roy. Soc. Med., **50**:738, 1957.

PADGET, D. H.: Spina bifida and embryonic neuroschisis. Johns Hopkins Med. Jour., **123**:233, 1968.

PENFIELD, W. AND CONE, W.: Spina bifida and cranium bifidum, results of plastic repair of meningocele and myelomeningocele by a new method. J.A.M.A., **98**:455, 1932.

RUSSELL, D. S. AND DONALD, C. B.: The mechanism of internal hydrocephalus in spina bifida. Brain, **58**:203, 1935.

SPILLER, W.: Myelodysplasia and spina bifida occulta. Am. J. Med. Sci., **151**:469, 1916.

TURNBULL, F. A.: Syringomyelic complications of spina bifida. Brain, **56**:304, 1933.

WEIL, A. AND WARREN, B. M.: Duplication of the spinal cord with spina bifida and syringomyelia. Arch. Path., **20**:882, 1935.

STATUS DYSRAPHICUS

A number of writers describe status dysraphicus, a concept which includes myelodysplasia associated with spina bifida and indeed, all defects of development of the spinal cord associated with defective closure of the neural tube. If we exclude the well known types associated with spina bifida we may offer the following description.

Benda states that the spinal cord may show absence of the posterior septum with an open cleft. The central canal may be dilated suggesting hydromyelia or congenital syringomyelia or the canal may be duplicated. Anomalies of the central gray matter are seen including persistence of an undifferentiated mantle zone. Ectopic deposits of gray matter are seen. There may be asymmetry, absence or distortion of the anterior or posterior horns of the gray matter. These findings are regarded as results of defective development. Since mental defect is usually associated various cerebral anomalies are also found.

The clinical findings may be most evident in the cervical segments or in the lumbosacral region. The manifestations are chiefly developmental anomalies which are believed to be secondary to the defects in the spinal cord. The muscles may be wasted and small. The skeleton shows innumerable anomalies. The bones of the affected extremities are often shortened. The fingers and toes may be malformed. Syndactylism is described. There are various deformities of the chest including funnel chest and chicken breast. The scapulae are often winged or displaced. Kyphoscoliosis is frequently present. Trophic changes are seen in the nails and in the skin. The hands and feet may be cold and cyanotic. Ulcers may develop. The growth of hair may be anomalous. The eyebrows may be asymmetrical. There may be heterochromia iridis. The ears may be malformed. Girls' breasts and nipples are often asymmetrical. The genital organs may show defective development. Mental defect is usually present and often severe. Roentgenograms of the spine may show spina bifida occulta.

BIBLIOGRAPHY

ANDERSON, F. M.: Occult spinal dysraphism. Jour. Pediat., **73**:163, 1968.
BENDA, C. F.: Developmental Disorders of Mentation and Cerebral Palsies. New York, Grune and Stratton, 1952, p. 61.
BREMER, F. W.: Die pathologisch-anatomische Bergundung des status dysraphicus. Deutsch. Ztschr. Nervenheilk, **99**:104, 1927.

MYELODYSPLASIA WITH KLIPPEL-FEIL SYNDROME

Definition.—This term designates a malformation of the cervical spine in which the vertebrae are reduced in number and sometimes completely fused into one mass of bone. Spina bifida is usually present and in a number of cases neurological disorders as described below.

Pathological Anatomy.—In typical cases, the cervical spine is replaced by a solid mass of bone in which perhaps three or four vertebral elements can be distinguished. The axis and atlas are usually included and often apparently the upper thoracic vertebrae. The length of the neck is so much reduced that the thorax ascends almost to the base of the skull. The posterior wall of the spinal canal is almost always absent or defective for some distance below the skull giving rise to spina bifida occulta.

Clinical Features.—Gunderson *et al.* describe three basic types. Type 1 is inherited as an autosomal dominant trait, type 2 as an autosomal recessive trait and type 3 as an autosomal dominant trait.

The child appears to have no neck whatever for the head rests directly on the trunk. The hair of the head extends posteriorly below the biacromial line as a rule. Both passive and active movements of the neck are limited by the bony deformities. As a rule, lateral movements and rotation on the longitudinal axis are almost completely abolished, but some movement in the anteroposterior plane is possible. Frequently, the head is rotated so as to present the picture of torticollis. Scoliosis and kyphosis are very common. The nipples are lowered. In some cases, there have been disturbances in breathing and in swallowing due, no doubt, to mechanical factors. The scapulae are always elevated in relation to the chest, but in certain cases, such as those of Critchley and du Toit, one scapula is much larger than the other so that the appearance is that of Sprengel's deformity.

Some very interesting neurological syndromes have been described in cases of the Klippel-Feil deformity. Signs and symptoms of a lesion of the spinal cord in the cervical region may be apparent very early in life, as in the case of Critchley in which the left arm and leg were weak and under-developed. No doubt, such symptoms are the result of defective development of the spinal cord which is associated with cervical spina bifida. After a number of years, these symptoms may progress until tetraplegia results. This was true not only of the case of Critchley but of the cases reported by du Toit and Guillain. These authors attribute the paralysis to syringo-myelia which they believe developed upon a basis of a congenital defect. Internal squint, nystagmus, chorioretinal atrophy, bifid uvela and high pal-ate may occur. In a number of instances, this deformity has been associated with "mirror movements," q.v.

Illingworth described attacks of unconsciousness in this syndrome, pos-sibly as a result of compression of the vertebral arteries by masses of bone.

Everberg *et al.* describe Wildervanck's syndrome in which the Klippel-

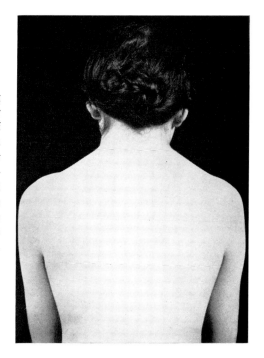

FIG. 99. Klippel-Feil syndrome in a young girl. Note the short neck and low hair line. There is defective development of the right thumb and absence of certain muscles in the thenar eminence. Mirror movement of the hands present since in-fancy. Roentgenograms of the cervical spine reveal that there are only five cervical vertebrae and a fragment of one more. The laminae of the first three are defective. The father has a similar neck.

Feil syndrome is associated with deafness, abducens paralysis and retraction of the eyeball.

Mental deficiency has been present in some cases of the Klippel-Feil deformity but not in the majority. Congenital deafness and congenital squints are also described.

Diagnosis.—The shortening of the neck, the lowering of the hair line and the limitation of movement of the head are enough to indicate the diagnosis. Roentgenographic studies of the cervical spine are conclusive. The shortening of the neck and fusion of the cervical vertebrae are the essential features of this condition, and neurological disturbances may be present or absent.

Prognosis.—The deformity does not change during life, but progressive paraplegia may develop after a number of years as stated above.

Treatment.—If there is evidence of compression of the cord and the symptoms are progressive laminectomy may be justified.

BIBLIOGRAPHY

BAUMAN, G. I.: Absence of the cervical spine, Klippel-Feil syndrome. J.A.M.A., **98**:129, 1931.

CRITCHLEY, McD.: Sprengel's deformity with paraplegia. Brit. J. Surg., **14**:243, 1926.

DU TOIT, F.: A case of congenital elevation of the scapula with defect of the cervical spine associated with syringomyella. Brain, 54:421, 1931.

ERSKINE, C. A.: Congenital cervical synostosis (Klippel-Feil syndrome). Acta Radiol., **17**:480, 1936.

EVERBERG, G. *et al.:* Wildervanck's syndrome: Klippel-Feil's syndrome with deafness and retraction of the eyeball. Brit. J. Radiol., **36**:562, 1963.

GORLIN, R. J. AND SEDANO, H.: The Klippel-Feil syndrome. Modern Medicine, Jan. 27, 1969, p. 146.

GUILLAIN, G. AND MOLLARET, P.: Syndrome de Klippel-Feil avec quadriplégie spasmodique. Rev. Neurol., 1:436, 1931.

GUNDERSON, C. H. AND SOLITARE, G. B.: The pathologic basis of mirror movements associated with cervical fusion. Fifteenth annual meeting of the American Academy of Neurology, Minneapolis, Minn., April 25, 1963.

——— AND GREENSPAN, R. H.: The Klippel-Feil syndrome. Medicine, **46**:491, 1967.

ILLINGWORTH, R. S.: Attacks of unconsciousness in association with fused cervical vertebrae. Arch. Dis. Childhood, **31**:8, 1956.

LUBS, H. A. *et al.:* Genetic reevaluation of fused cervical vertebrae. Clin. Res., **11**:179, 1963.

MICHIE, M. I. AND CLARK, M.: Neurological syndromes associated with cerevical and craniocervical anomalies. Arch. of Neurol., **18**:241, 1968.

STEPIEN, B.: Tetraparesie chez une maladie avec anomalie congénitale de la colonne vertebrale. Rev. Neurol., **239**, 1933.

MYELODYSPLASIA WITH CONGENITAL ABSENCE OF THE SACRUM AND LUMBAR SPINE

Seven cases of this condition are now on record. The legs, thighs and buttocks are very small. No voluntary movements are possible and there is incontinence. The thighs are fixed in flexion, internal rotation and extreme abduction. The knees are flexed and there is a fibrous web in the popliteal space. The feet show various deformities, but are usually fixed in dorsal flexion. The child sits with the feet beneath the buttocks. The 12th thoracic vertebra is too prominent and no spine can be felt below this point. No sacrum can be felt. The pelvis is unstable. It is too narrow. Cutaneous sensibility is usually present over the thighs, but is diminished in the legs and lost in the feet. No trophic changes are seen in the skin. The genital organs are usually not malformed. Since these children are said to go to school, their mentality is apparently not greatly impaired.

Roentgenographic study reveals absence of the lumbar vertebrae, sacrum and coccyx. The ilia are approximated and the 12th thoracic vertebra rests on them. The bones of the legs and the joints are well formed but show osteoporosis.

Five bilateral amputations of the legs were performed just below the trochanters, and four legs were dissected. No muscle tissue was found. The soft tissues were composed of lobules of fat surrounded by fibrous septa. The arteries were narrow but otherwise normal. Subcutaneous nerve fibers were found which were presumed to be sensory fibers. The skin was thin.

A post-mortem examination was performed on one patient. The lumbar spine was absent except for a 1st lumbar vertebra and a rudimentary 2nd lumbar vertebra. The spinal cord ended at the level of the body of the 7th thoracic vertebra. There was no lumbosacral plexus and no lumbosacral enlargement. Small nerves extended down to the 2nd sacral vertebra.

The legs were amputated and the children's bodies were fitted into a plastic bucket to which aluminum legs were fastened. They could walk by swinging the body.

CASE HISTORY.—*Congenital myelodysplasia with absence of lumbar spine and sacrum.*

C. E. was seen at the age of 4 years by the courtesy of Dr. Fred Kader. She was born without any sacrum and the ilia were loosely joined. The first lumbar vertebra was well formed but the second lumbar vertebra was only partially developed. The remaining lumbar vertebrae was completely absent. There was some power of flexion at the hip joints, but no other movement of the legs or thighs were possible. A draining fistula opened just below the second lumbar vertebra. No muscle could be felt in the legs below the knees and little if any in the thighs or buttocks. The hip and knee joints were held in about 50 degrees flexion by strong fibrous webs. There was recognition of pin prick over the anterior aspect of the thighs but none below the knees. There was complete incontinence. The tendon reflexes were all absent. When the child was seated, the lower end of the spinal column rested on the ilia.

When held up by the arms, the child could walk with bent legs using the flexors of the hips to advance the legs. She had an excellent sense of balance and could walk on her hands with ease. The intelligence quotient was estimated at 120.

BIBLIOGRAPHY

FRANTZ, C. H. AND AITKEN, G. T.: Complete absence of the lumbar spine and sacrum. Jour. of Bone and Joint Surg., **49A**:1531, 1967.

RUSSELL, H. E. *et al.:* Congenital absence of the sacrum and lumbar vertebrae. Jour. of Bone and Joint Surg., **45A**:501, 1963.

MYELODYSPLASIA WITH ABSENCE OF THE SACRUM

Definition.—In this condition the sacrum and coccyx are absent and there is usually defective development of the sacral or lumbosacral segments of the spinal cord.

Etiology.—Kucera states that in 5 of the 9 cases of agenesis of the sacrum discovered in Czechoslovakia between 1959 and 1966 the mother had been exposed to organic fat solvents. See Abnormalities of Children Born of Diabetic Mothers.

Pathological Anatomy.—The sacrum and the coccyx are absent and consequently the iliac wings are brought more closely together and are almost vertical. The pelvis is narrow. Various defects in higher levels of the spinal column may be associated, and deformities of the feet which are regarded as due to paralysis are usually present. No adequate studies of the nervous system in such cases have been made.

Clinical Features.—More than twenty cases of this condition have been reported. It may affect either sex, and may occur in more than one member of a family. The normal prominences of the buttocks are lost and the intergluteal fold is also absent. Palpation reveals soft tissue where the sacrum should be. Roentgenographic examination reveals the defects described above. Dislocation of the hips is not uncommon. Neurological symptoms are almost invariably present. There is loss of control of the bladder and rectum and paralysis and anesthesia in the distribution of the sacral or lower lumbosacral segments. The gluteal muscles and the hamstrings are most commonly paralyzed but the calf muscles may also be involved.

BIBLIOGRAPHY

HAMSA, W. R.: Congenital absence of the sacrum. Arch. Surg., **30**:657, 1935.

KUCERA, J.: Exposure to fat solvents. A possible cause of sacral agenesis in man. Jour. Pediat., **72**:857, 1968.

MIRROR MOVEMENTS

In this condition the patient cannot dissociate the movements of the two hands and every movement of the right hand is more or less exactly imitated by the left hand. A case is reported in which the patient was unable to climb a ladder since every time a rung was released by the right hand the left hand also opened. The legs were not affected as a rule but Dr. Douglas Buchannan has told me of a child who with a defect in the thoracic spine had mirror movements of the legs. This condition is always present from birth and persists through life although it becomes less apparent as the patient grows older.

The anatomical basis of this condition is unknown though several theories have been suggested. It has been imagined that the pyramidal tracts may both arise in one hemisphere so identical stimuli may be sent to the muscles on either side of the body. Since a large percentage of cases of mirror movements are associated with the Klippel-Feil syndrome in which a defect of development of the cervical cord is often present it would seem more logical to assume that there has been a defect in the decussation of the pyramidal tracts and impulses which should be distributed to only one side of the body are distributed to both sides. Gunderson and Solitare report two cases in which the cervical cord was partially split. Avery and Rentfro describe a case almost identical with that of Gunderson and Solitare.

Haerer and Currier report a case in which a patient who had had mirror movements all his life developed a complete hemiplegia. It was noted that he could not move the paralysed hand voluntarily, but that movements of the unaffected hand caused mirror movements in the paralysed hand.

Freiman *et al.* report the study of a family in which nine members showed mental deficiency, mirror movements, left-handedness and in one case agenesis of the corpus callosum. Inheritance was dominant.

It seems to be agreed that this is a dominant condition with reduced penetrance. Cases have been found in three generations of a family.

BIBLIOGRAPHY

AVERY, L. N. AND RENTFRO, C. C.: The Klippel-Feil syndrome. Arch. of Neurol. and Psychiat., **36**:1068, 1936.

CRAWFORD, C.: Report of a family showing mirror movements. Aust. Ann. Med., **9**:176, 1960.

FREIMAN, I. S. et al.: A hereditary syndrome characterized by mirror movements, left-handedness and organic mental defect. Trans. Amer. Neurol. Ass., **74**:224, 1949.

GUNDERSON, C. H. AND SOLITARE, G. B.: Mirror movements in patients with the Klippel-Feil syndrome. Arch. of Neurol., **18**:675, 1968.

GUTTMAN, E. et al.: Persistent mirror movements as a heredofamilial disorder. Jour. Neurol. and Psychiat., **2**:13, 1939.

HAERER, A. F. AND CURRIER, R. D.: Mirror movements. Neurology, **16**:757, 1966.

REGLI et al.: Hereditary mirror movements. Arch. of Neurol., **16**:620, 1967.

SMITH, C. K.: Mirror movements without spinal defect. Amer. Jour. Dis. Child., **73**:175, 1947.

SPINAL EXTRADURAL CYST WITH KYPHOSIS DORSALIS JUVENILIS

Definition.—These cysts seem to be evaginations of the dura which are filled with spinal fluid. They compress the spinal cord in the thoracic region. Apparently they are always associated with kyphosis and the changes in the spine termed kyphosis dorsalis juvenilis.

Pathological Anatomy.—Usually only one cyst is found lying dorsal to the dura. In a few instances, more than one cyst is present. A pedicle attaches the cyst to a spinal nerve root. Histological study indicates that the cyst wall is composed of dura and is lined with a membrane resembling the arachnoid. Often it is possible to demonstrate a communication between the cyst and the spinal subarachnoid space.

Clinical Features.—The onset occurs as a rule between the ages of 12 and 16 years and boys are affected more frequently than girls. The initial complaint may be either spastic paraplegia or spinal curvature. Often both features are present when the patient is first seen. The weakness of the legs may advance slowly or rapidly. In some instances, there have been spontaneous remissions, and it is often noted that bed rest will sometimes result in pronounced improvement. Root pains are rarely severe and often absent. Loss of cutaneous sensibility is not pronounced, as a rule, but the posterior columns of the cord may be severely affected. The control of the bladder and rectum is affected only in the late stages. In most instances in which the lesion is located in the mid-thoracic portion of the spinal canal, the knee and ankle jerks are exaggerated and Babinski's sign is present. In the rare instances in which the cyst is in the lumbar region, the knee jerks may be reduced.

The spine usually displays a rounded kyphos in the upper thoracic region. Roentgenograms show rounding of the anterior-superior and antero-inferior corners of the vertebrae in the thoracic region. There is some reduction of density in the anterior part of the vertebral body. The intervertebral disc may prolapse into the vertebra. Eventually there may be partial collapse of the anterior part of the vertebra which then assumes a wedge shape. The kyphosis is a result of this process. These changes just described are characteristic of a condition termed kyphosis dorsalis juvenilis. Only a few children suffering from this spinal condition have extradural cysts, but according to Cloward and Bucy, the children who have cysts of this particular type always show evidences of kyphosis dorsalis juvenilis in mild or severe form.

When a cyst is present certain additional changes are seen in the spine. The spinal canal is enlarged at the level of the lesion which is usually that of the sixth, seventh, eighth and ninth thoracic vertebrae. The pedicles may be eroded and there is sometimes erosion of the posterior surface of the vertebrae so that the intervertebral discs, which are more resistant, stand out like ridges.

Spinal puncture may reveal some increase of protein in the spinal fluid but this is not constant, it is said. The manometric tests may also be negative or positive. The myelogram, however, is said to be quite reliable.

Treatment.—It is advised that the cyst be removed as soon as possible. The operation is apparently not difficult and the results are good.

BIBLIOGRAPHY

Cloward, R. B. and Bucy, P. C.: Extradural cyst and kyphosis dorsalis juvenilis. Am. J. Roentgenol., **38**:681, 1937.
Nugent, G. R. *et al.*: Spinal extradural cysts. Neurology, **9**:397, 1959.
Wise, B. L. and Foster, J. J.: Congenital spinal extradural cyst. J. Neurosurg., **12**:42, 1955.

CONGENITAL DERMAL SINUSES

Definition.—These are narrow openings in the skin lined with stratified epithelium which extend from the midline of the back toward the neuraxis and often into the meninges. They are thought to be due to defects in the closure of the neural tube.

Pathological Anatomy.—These sinuses are found most commonly in the sacral region but may occur at any level of the spine. They sometimes are found in the occiput and rarely at the vertex or in the forehead at the root of the nose. They lead upwards and inwards. In some cases, the sinus contains hair, but usually they are lined with simple squamous epithelium without hair follicles or glands. In some cases there is a cyst which does not communicate with the skin. In other cases the sinus arising in the skin terminates before it reaches the meninges. Others pass from the skin, through a defect in the spinal laminae or between the laminae into the spinal canal. In the same way, the occipital sinuses penetrate the occiput into the posterior fossa. It is not unusual for dermoid and epidermoid cysts to be found in the cranium or the spinal canal in association with dermal sinuses which penetrate to the tumor and frequently convey infection.

Clinical Features.—The opening of the sinus in the skin is marked by a slight prominence with a central depression, the so-called dimple. Surrounding this there may be some change in the skin such as pigmentation, hairiness or port wine stain. Roentgenograms may reveal a defect in the underlying bone. A narrow channel may be found in the occipital bone and sometimes one finds a defect in the spinal laminae. In rare instances there is leakage of spinal fluid from the sinus. In such cases infection is very common and purulent discharge may be seen.

Such dimples are not uncommon in the sacral region. Probably only very few of them penetrate to the nervous system.

Obviously if there are evidences of intracranial or spinal neoplasm or of infection, neurosurgical intervention is indicated. If there is drainage of spinal fluid, the sinus should be removed at once. Probably discharge of pus from a dermal sinus justifies operation. The surgeon should be prepared to follow the sinus tract into the nervous system if necessary.

A careful search should be made for dermal sinuses in all cases of tumors of the posterior fossa and of the cauda equina as well as in all cases of pyogenic meningitis especially if the meningitis is recurrent and the staphylococcus aureus is responsible. Since the dimple may be inconspicuous it may be necessary to shave the back of the head and examine the scalp under a strong light.

Treatment.—Walker and Bucy recommend that as soon as the diagnosis is made the sinus should be removed. If infection has already developed, the sinus should be extirpated and drainage instituted.

CASE HISTORY (K-62816).—*Congenital sacral cyst with spina bifida and cutaneous dimple. Abortive attack of meningitis at age of 14 years. Later, progressive paraplegia. Operation. Removal of cyst. Recovery.*

E. R. had always been healthy and active. She learned to walk and to control the bladder at the usual age. At the age of 14 years, however, she had a febrile illness characterized by pain in the back, stiffness of the neck, headache and vomiting. The illness lasted only a few days but the pain in the back and legs persisted and within a few weeks she began to notice difficulty in walking and delay in passing urine. The symptoms slowly grew worse and almost a year after the onset, she was unable to walk without support.

Examination revealed a well nourished and well developed girl of 15 years. There was a mild thoracic scoliosis to the right and the right scapula was elevated apparently due to fibrosis and contracture of the upper third of the trapezius. The legs were well developed in general but the muscles of the buttocks, the hamstrings and calves were soft and slightly wasted. There was great weakness but not paralysis of all movements at the ankle, of flexion at the knee and of abduction and extension at the hip. There was also some difficulty in retaining urine but no complete incontinence. Cutaneous anesthesia was found over the buttocks and the posterior surface of the thighs extending down in a narrow band to the ankles. The ankle jerks were lost. A defect was palpable in the lower lumbar and upper sacral laminae and a small dimple was found at the level of the first sacral vertebra. Roentgenograms showed extensive defects in the bones. There was spina bifida in the lower lumbar and upper sacral vertebrae and also in the cervical segments. Only five certical vertebrae were present. Several ribs were united near the spine and the right scapula was of abnormal shape and smaller than the left.

Injection of air into the spinal canal with the hips elevated revealed an obstruction of the canal at the top of the sacrum. Operation revealed a large cyst within the dura in the upper part of the sacral canal which compressed the roots of the cauda equina. This lay directly under the dimple in the skin. The lining of the cyst was inflamed, but there was no pus. The cyst was removed and the patient improved rapidly. A few months later she was able to walk almost normally and had regained control of the bladder.

CASE HISTORY.—*Congenital dermal sinus. At the age of 14 months the child began to have fever and soon developed increased lumbar lordosis and rigidity of the spine. Operation revealed an infected epidermoid tumor in the spinal canal.*

M. J. B., a little girl of 16 months, was seen on August 12, 1958. She was born at full term by normal delivery. The mother's health had been good during the pregnancy. The child seemed to be normal in every way except for the presence of a small red spot in the lumbosacral region with a small dimple in the middle. No fluid escaped from this opening.

At the age of 14 months, the mother noted that the dimple was swollen. She pressed some material from it. About the same time, the child began to be fretful and irritable. She lost weight and did not sleep well. The child's back became increasingly rigid and was curved backward. She continued to be active and played with the other children though with less than her usual vigor.

At the age of 16 months, examination revealed a temperature of 102°F., but the child seemed to be only moderately ill. Her posture was remarkable. The trunk was rigid and the lumbar lordosis was greatly increased. The whole upper part of the trunk was strongly extended. The child could not be induced to bend the back or even the neck. When picking an object up from the floor, she would squat down to reach it so as to avoid bending the back. When placed on her side on the couch, her trunk was so strongly retracted that her head almost reached the buttocks so the posture was that of opisthotonos. Placed on her back, the lumbar and thoracic spine did not touch the couch. Kernig's sign was present on both sides.

A cutaneous angioma of 1.0 cm in diameter was found in the midline at the level of the fifth lumbar vertebra. A small dimple was seen in the center but no fluid could be expressed. A small nodule was felt lying below the dimple in the subcutaneous tissue. Roentgenograms revealed a small defect in the lamina of the fifth lumbar vertebra.

The gait was normal except for the rigidity of the spine. No weakness was found in the legs. The tendon reflexes were all in order. No sensory loss could be demonstrated. The cranial nerves were not involved.

Operation was performed by Dr. Frank Otenasek. The dermal sinus was found to extend down to a long epidermoid tumor within the dura. This extended up to the first lumbar vertebra. No compression of the conus or the cauda was evident. The tumor contained pus but no pus was seen in the meninges. B. proteus was cultivated from the tumor.

BIBLIOGRAPHY

BUCY, P. C. AND WALKER, A. E.: Congenital dermal sinuses, a source of spinal and meningeal infection and subdural abscess. Brain, **57**:401, 1934.

HAMILTON, J. G.: Case of dermal sinus of nose with frontal suppuration. J. Neurol. Neurosurg. & Psychiat., **23**:239, 1960.

MATSON, D. D. AND INGRAHAM, F. D.: Intracranial complications of congenital dermal sinuses. Pediatrics, **8**:463, 1952.

—— AND JERVA, M. J.: Recurrent meningitis associated with congenital lumbosacral sinus tract. Jour. Neurosurg., **25**:288, 1966.

MOISE, T. S.: Staphylococcus meningitis secondary to a congenital sacral sinus. Surg. Gynec. & Obst., **42**:394, 1926.

MOUNT, L. A.: Congenital dermal sinuses as a cause of meningitis, intraspinal abscess and intracranial abscess. J.A.M.A., **139**:1263, 1949.

SACHS, E. AND HORRAX, G.: Cervical and lumbar pilonidal sinus communicating with intraspinal dermoids. J. Neurosurg., **6**:97, 1949.

DIPLOMYELIA AND DIASTEMATOMYELIA

Diplomyelia.—This term refers to doubling or duplication of the spinal cord. The condition is found in the lower part of the cord and rarely if ever extends above the midthoracic region. In many cases there is an associated bony abnormality of the spine or extremities. In approximately half of all cases there is spina bifida. This is usually of the occult variety but meningoceles may also occur. Club feet of various types are described.

There is no constant disturbance of function associated with diplomyelia. Apparently the two spinal cords may serve as effectively as one. In some cases there are other malformations of the cord such as are found in association with spina bifida which of course cause the usual symptoms. Tumors of congenital origin may coexist.

In **diastematomyelia** there is a cleft in the spinal cord which splits the cord in the midline and extends only a segment or two as a rule. Each part of the cord is surrounded by a complete dural sac. A bony septum lies between the two parts. These children often have some difficulty in walking. There may be bilateral or unilateral weakness or possibly diffuse weakness and spasticity of the legs. Difficulty in the control of the bladder and trophic ulcerations of the feet are sometimes seen. There may be a tuft of hair or a pad of fat on the back and spina bifida is usually found. Roentgenograms may reveal the bony septum and permit a preoperative diagnosis. Pantopaque injections reveal two separate streams of the dye.

Matson *et al.* advise removal of the dural septum as well as the bony spur. They state that there is progression of symptoms if this is not done. Not much improvement is to be expected in the symptoms which have developed before operation, however.

Bremer believes that this condition is due to delayed regression of the neurenteric canal and points out that in some cases a neurenteric cyst is found in the spinal canal lying between the two portions of the cord.

BIBLIOGRAPHY

BREMER, J. L.: Dorsal intestinal fistula; accessory neurenteric canal: diastematomyelia. Arch. Path., **54**:132, 1952.

COHEN, J. AND SLEDGE, C. B.: Diastematomyelia. Embryologic interpretation. Am. J. Dis. Child., 100:257, 1960.

DALE, A. J. D.: Diastematomyelia. Arch. of Neurol., 20:309, 1969.

HERREN, R. Y. AND EDWARDS, J. E.: Diplomyelia. Arch. Path., 30:1203, 1940.

MATSON, D., WOODS, R., CAMPBELL, J. AND INGRAHAM, F. D.: Diastematomyelia (Congenital clefts of the cord) diagnosis and treatment.

MICHAEL, C. C. *et al.:* Diastematomyelia. Survey of 24 cases submitted to laminectomy. Arch. of Dis. Childh., 39:125, 1964.

NEUHAUSER, E., WITTENBORG, M. AND DEHLINGER, K.: Diastematomyelia. Transfixation of the cord or cauda equina with congenital anomalies of the spine. Radiology, 54:659, 1950.

———: Pediatrics, 6:98, 1950.

PERRET, G.: Symptoms and diagnosis of diastematomyelia. Neurology, 10:51, 1960.

CYSTS, MALFORMATIONS AND NEOPLASMS ARISING FROM REMNANTS OF THE NEURENTERIC CANAL

The neurenteric canal is a short tube evident in early embryonic life which connects the primitive alimentary canal with the central canal of the spinal cord at its caudal extremity. Under normal circumstances this structure disappears very soon. According to Bremer, however, it may persist longer than it should and thereby cause defects in midline structures. It may also be present at the time of birth. Teratomas may arise from remnants of this structure, it is believed. Bremer states that the tip of the coccyx is the site of the former neurenteric canal but that malformations at other levels may be due to ectopic or accessory neurenteric canals.

In the case of Keen and Coplin, a fistula was found arising in the posterior wall of the rectum, passing through the sacrum between the roots of the cauda and ending in the skin where it was surrounded by a fatty tumor. This would seem to represent a persisting neurenteric canal. In a case described by Lucksch the stomach and intestines opened at several points into the floor of a large myelomeningocele and in another case of the same author, there was a single tract extending from the esophagus into a myelocele. In these cases the tracts penetrated between separated halves of the spinal cord. Bremer considers them to represent accessory neurenteric canals. Such conditions are often mistaken for anterior meningoceles.

Saunders has published a report of a case of diastematomyelia with intestinal herniation into the defect. There was both anterior and posterior spina bifida. Kahn and Lemmen describe a similar case. Bremer regards diplomyelia and diastematomyelia as results of delay in the disappearance of the neurenteric canal. The canal usually disappears eventually but leaves defects of development in midline structures.

Hansmann deals with trigeminal teratomas between the rectum and the sacrum and also within the lumbosacral canal. He believes that these tumors arise from remnants of the neurenteric canal. He states that they usually remain quiescent for a time and then may start to grow rapidly. They do not as a rule give rise to distant metastases and often may be removed by the surgeon.

Ingraham and Matson mention briefly a case of great interest which is published in more detail by Holcomb and Matson. The patient was a boy of 4 years and 4 months. The chief complaint was difficulty in breathing. There were no neurological signs or symptoms. Roentgenograms revealed a mass in the upper right chest. There was spina bifida in the lower cervical and upper thoracic vertebrae. A large circular defect was seen in the body of the third thoracic vertebra. The spinal canal was widened at this level. Laminectomy was performed and the dural sac was found to be twice normal width. The cord appeared to be normal but some nerve roots on the right were atrophic. A stalk about 0.5 cm in diameter was attached to the anterior surface of the cord and passed through the anterior dura and the opening in the vertebra. The stalk was divided. Later, the mass in the chest was removed. It proved to be a cyst containing viscid, mucoid material. The wall of the cyst was formed of pseudostratified columnar epithelium, a loose submucosa and two thick layers of smooth muscle. It was interpreted as fetal intestinal tract. The authors attribute this anomaly to the persistence of an accessory neurenteric canal. They point out that if the cyst had matured and eventually produced acid gastric juice, it might have caused serious damage.

BIBLIOGRAPHY

BREMER, J. L.: Dorsal intestinal fistula; accessory neurenteric canal; Diastematomyelia. Arch. Path., **54**:132, 1952.

HANSMANN, G. H.: A congenital cystic tumor of the neurenteric canal. Surg. Gynec. & Obst., **42**:124, 1926.

HOLCOMB, G. W., JR. AND MATSON, D. D.: Thoracic cyst. Surgery, **35**:115, 1954.

INGRAHAM, F. D. AND MATSON, D. D.: Neurosurgery of Infancy and Childhood. Springfield, Thomas, 1954, p. 26.

KAHN, E. A. AND LEMMEN, L. J.: Unusual congenital anomalies of neurosurgical interest in infants and children. J. Neurosurg., **7**:544, 1950.

LEVIN, P. AND ANTIN, S. P.: Intraspinal neurenteric cyst in the cervical area. Neurology, **14**:727, 1964.

LUCKSCH, F.: Uber myeloschisis mit abnormer Darmausmundung. Ztschr. Heil., **24**:143, 1903.

MOES, C. A. F. AND HENDRICK, E. B.: Diastematomyelia. J. Pediat., **63**:238, 1963.

SAUNDERS, R. L.: Combined anterior and posterior spina bifida in a living neonatal female. Anat. Rec., **87**:255, 1943.

AMYOTONIA CONGENITA

Definition.—A congenital condition characterized by profound generalized muscular weakness and by striking loss of muscle tone. It is now evident that this is merely a syndrome which may be caused by a number of diseases but is usually due to the Werdnig-Hoffmann spinal muscular atrophy.

Pathological Anatomy.—Oppenheim believed that amyotonia is due to defective development of the muscles but this view was soon challenged.

Many studies, among which should be mentioned those of Greenfield and Stern and Grinker, have made it clear that in most infants who display this syndrome the muscular atrophy is the result of the degeneration of the motor cells in the anterior horns of the spinal cord. The question then arises whether or not amyotonia exists as a distinct disease or is merely a variety of the Werdnig-Hoffmann spinal muscular atrophy which begins in utero. The fine monograph of Brandt, as well as the anatomical studies mentioned above, offers strong evidence to prove we are dealing in most instances with only one disease.

Clinical Features.—The features of amyotonia congenita which have been stressed in diagnosis may be tabulated as follows: (1) The presence of symptoms at birth. (2) The striking loss of muscle tone, which it is claimed, outweighs the weakness. (3) The lack of definite progression of the symptoms. (4) The loss of tendon reflexes. (5) The absence of any history of similar conditions in the family. It has become evident that none of these criteria are reliable. Almost invariably prolonged observation reveals that there is definite progression in the symptoms. There are many instances in which more than one sibling is affected. The symptoms may not be evident at birth and may appear in the next few weeks. It seems to be correct to state that clinically as well as anatomically there is no basis for a differentiation between amyotonia and the Werdnig-Hoffmann muscular atrophy.

Diagnosis.—Brandt's differential diagnosis includes a large number of conditions which must be considered. Some of these are common and some rare. (1) Werdnig-Hoffmann spinal muscular atrophy is the essential basis of this syndrome. (2) Myopathies of various types including infantile dystrophy, myotonic dystrophy, and the strange myopathy described by Turner. (3) Congenital laxity of the ligaments. (4) Congenital universal muscular hypoplasia of Krabbe and the congenital non-progressive myopathy of Shy and Magee. (5) Congenital myasthenia of Levin. (6) Congenital defects of the nervous system which cause loss of tone such as atonic diplegia, congenital chorea and cerebellar ataxia. (7) Mongolism. (8) Arachnodactyly. (9) Von Gierke's disease. (10) Polyneuritis. (11) Osteogenesis imperfecta. (12) Nemaline myopathy should be included. (13) Hypotonia, hypomentia, hypogonadism and obesity of Zellweger. (14) Muscular hypotonia due to rickets, wasting illnesses of various types.

Brandt emphasizes the value of muscle biopsy and of the electromyogram in differential diagnosis.

Prognosis.—Obviously the prognosis depends upon the diagnosis. Few children who present the syndrome of amyotonia survive very long. Turner's cases ran a benign course and the patients were able to lead an active life. Such cases must be very rare.

Treatment.—Only symptomatic treatment is possible.

BIBLIOGRAPHY

BRANDT, S.: Werdnig-Hoffmann's Infantile Progressive Muscular Atrophy. Ejnar Munksgaard, Copenhagen, 1950.

BURDICK, WM., WHIPPLE, D. V. AND FREEMAN, W.: Amytonia congenita of Oppenheim. Am. J. Dis. Child., **69**:295, 1945.

COLLIER, J. AND HOLMES, G.: The pathological examination of two cases of amyotonia congenita with clinical description of a fresh case. Brain, **32**:269, 1909.

CONEL, L. LeR.: Distribution of the affected nerve cells in a case of amyotonia congenita. Arch. Neurol. & Psychiat., **40**:337, 1938.

FABER, H. K.: Amyotonia congenita: A survey of known cases with report of three new cases. Am. J. Dis. Child., **13**:305, 1917.

FORBUS, W. AND WOLF, F. S.: Amyotonia congenita in identical twins. Bull. Johns Hopkins Hosp., **47**:309, 1930.

FREEMAN, W.: The motor cortex in amyotonia congenita. J. Neuropath. & Exp. Neurol., **5**:207, 1946.

GREENFIELD, J. G. AND STERN, R. O.: The anatomical identity of the Werdnig-Hoffmann and Oppenheim forms of infantile muscular atrophy. Brain, **50**:652, 1927.

GRINKER, R. R.: The pathology of amyotonia congenita. Arch. Neurol. & Psychiat., **18**:982 (full references), 1927.

MILHORAT, A. T. AND WOLFF, H. G.: V-Metabolism of creatine and creatinine in myotonia congenita, myotonia atrophica, amyotonia congenita, dystonia musculorum deformans and paralysis agitans. *Ibid.*, **40**:680, 1938.

TURNER, J. W. A.: The relationship between amyotonia congenita and congenital myopathy. Brain, **63**:163, 1940.

————: On amyotonia congenita. Brain, **72**:25, 1949.

CONGENITAL ANOMALIES OF THE FACE WITH NEUROLOGIC DEFECTS

The Clover Leaf Cranium

The child has hydrocephalus but due to premature fusion of some of the cranial sutures, the head does not enlarge. A large meningoencephalo-

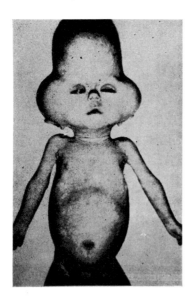

FIG. 100. Cloverleaf cranium. (From Aita, J. A. Congenital facial Anomalies with Neurologic Defects. Springfield, Thomas, 1969. Originally published by Liebaldt, G. Ergebn. Allg. Path. 1964, vol. 45, p. 23. Permission to republish from Dr. Aita.)

cele projects from the top of the head in the midline and two more from the temporal regions which extend downward and anteriorly into the cheeks which appear to be very fat. These are covered by thin bone with digitations and lacunae. The ears lie at the level of the chin. Proptosis is often present. These children do not live long.

BIBLIOGRAPHY

LIEBALDT, H.: On pathoanatomy of clover leaf cranium syndrome. Dysostosen. Wiedemann, H. R. Editor. Stuttgart: Gustav Fischer, 1966.

Craniotelencephalic Dysplasia

There is craniostenosis with premature closure of the metopic, coronal and sagittal sutures. There is bulging in the frontal region and protuberance of the frontal squamosa. Hypertelorism is present. There is mental deficiency.

BIBLIOGRAPHY

JABBOUR, J. AND TAYBI, H.: Craniotelencephalic dysplasia. Amer. Jour. Dis. Child., **108**:627, 1964.

Acrocephalosyndactyly of Apert

There is brachycephaly, fusion of the coronal suture, prominent digital markings, flat occiput, exophthalmos, antimongoloid slant of the lid slits, short beaked nose with depressed base, small maxilla, cleft palate, increased intracranial pressure, mental deficiency, seizures, various developmental defects of the brain and syndactylism.

BIBLIOGRAPHY

BLANK, C. E.: Apert's syndrome. Ann. Hum. Genet., **24**:151, 1960.

Craniocarpotarsal Dystrophy or the Whistling Face Syndrome

There is a broad short forehead, deep set eyes, hypertelorism, epicanthus, blepharophimosis, broad nasal bridge, small nostrils, immobile face which is flat with full cheeks, small mouth with puckered lips, long upper lip, deformities of the ears, small tongue, ulnar deviation of the hands, talipes equinovarus, restricted movements of the joints, unequal length of the legs, scoliosis and sometimes mental deficiency.

BIBLIOGRAPHY

BURIAN, F.: The whistling face characteristic. Brit. Jour. Plast. Surg., **16**:140, 1963.

Dyscraniopygophalangea or Ulrich Syndrome

There is brachycephaly or acrocephaly, blepharophimosis, microphthalmia or anophthalmia, hypertelorism, squint, small mandible, large or small mouth, polydactyly, genital defects, cardiac defects and various developmental defects of the brain.

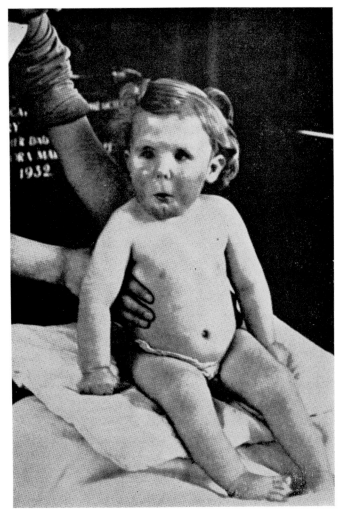

Fig. 101. Whistling Face. (From Aita, J. A. Congenital Facial Anomalies with Neurologic Defects. Springfield, Thomas, 1969. Originally published by Freeman, E. A. and Sheldon, J. H. Arch. Dis. Child., 1938, vol. 13, p. 277. Permission received from Dr. Aita.)

BIBLIOGRAPHY

Weber, J. W. and Schwartz, Z. H.: Typus Rostockiensis. Helvet. Pediat. Acta, **15**:163, 1960.

Blepharophimosis, Myopathy and Joint Contractures

There is blepharophimosis, depressed nasal bridge, deep set eyes, immobile face, pursed lips, low hairline, long eyelashes in multiple rows, hypoplasia of the maxilla, cleft palate, low set ears, high-pitched voice, myotonia, replacement of muscles with fat and connective tissue, contractures of the joints, prominence of the sternum, short stature and mental deficiency.

BIBLIOGRAPHY

Marden, P. M. and Walker, W. A.: A new generalized connective tissue syndrome. Amer. Jour. Dis. Child., 112:225, 1966.

Otocephaly or Syndrome of Microstomia, Agnathia and Synotia

Aplasia of the mandible, tongue and ears, transverse facial cleft, anophthalmos, aplastic ears meet near the midline, a small opening leads to the pharynx and congenital defects of the heart. This is a lethal condition.

BIBLIOGRAPHY

Johnson, W. W. and Cook, J. B.: Agnathia associated with pharyngeal atresia and hydramnios. Arch. of Pediat., 78:211, 1961.

Craniometaphyseal Dysplasia or Pyles Disease

Diffuse symmetrical hyperostosis of the skull, obliteration of the sutures, delayed closure of fontanels, hypertelorism, sometimes exophthalmos, obliteration of nasal sinuses, cranial nerve palsies and compression of carotid arteries, mental deficiency, elongated tibias and femurs and genu valgum.

BIBLIOGRAPHY

Millard, D. R. *et al.*: Pyles disease. Amer. Jour. Surg., 113:615, 1967.

Metaphyseal Dysostosis of Jansen

Irregular cystic metaphyseal segments of tubular bones, shortening of the legs, muscular atrophy, joint contractures, exophthalmos, hypertelorism, flat nose, large mouth, brachycephalic head and mental deficiency.

BIBLIOGRAPHY

Rubin, P.: Dynamic Classification of Bone Dysplasias, Year Book, Chicago, 1964.

Borjeson-Forssman-Lehman Syndrome

X linked recessive transmission confined to males, short stature, hypometabolism, hypogonadalism, genu valgum, microcephaly, mental deficiency, epilepsy, large ears, fatty swollen face and narrow palpebral fissures. The brain shows reduction of neurons and gliosis.

BIBLIOGRAPHY

Barr, H. S.: Borjeson-Forssman-Lehman syndrome. Jour. Ment. Defic. Res., 9:125, 1965.

Dwarfism with Telangiectatic Erythemia or Bloom's Syndrome

The face and nose are too large, the mandible is too small, the front teeth are large, the ears are prominent, muscular development is poor, mental deficiency is present, there is telangiectasia with atrophy and pigmentation of the skin, sensitive to light, cafe au lait spots, ichthyosis, acanthosis nigricans in some, dwarfish stature, small birth weight, syndactyly and extra digits.

BIBLIOGRAPHY

LANDAU, J. W. *et al.:* Bloom dwarf. Arch. Derma., **19:**687, 1966.

Hemifacial Microsomia or Otomandibular Dysostosis

There are unilateral defects with microtia, atresia of the external auditory canal, macrostoma and defective development of the mandibular ramus and condyle. Deficient development of the maxilla and mastoid process is common. Brachial pits and ear tags between the mouth and ear, facial and jaw muscles are weak and pulmonary agenesis is recorded.

BIBLIOGRAPHY

WILSON, T. G.: Hemifacial microsomia. Jour. Laryng., **72:**238, 1958.

Russell Dwarf

High bossed and broad forehead, beaked nose, small triangular face, small mandible, high arched palate, mouth shape of inverted B, philtrum drawn up, overhanging upper lip, low birth weight, dwarf, short arms, high-pitched voice and delayed bone development. Mental deficiency.

BIBLIOGRAPHY

CHAPTAL, J. *et al.:* Congenital dwarfism, Russell type. Pediatrie, **21:**710, 1966.

Gingival Hyperplasia and Hypertrichosis

Overgrowth of gums in childhood, profuse hair growth, coarse features, protruding lips, large nose and ears, mental deficiency, and epilepsy in some cases.

BIBLIOGRAPHY

SNYDER, C. H.: Gingival hypertrophy and hirsutism. Jour. of Pediat., **67:**499, 1945.

Rieger's Syndrome

Hypoplasia of the iris, anterior synechiae to cornea, slit-like pupils, optic atrophy, broad face, small maxilla, prognathism, partial anodentia, peg shaped teeth, myotonic dystrophy and syringomyelia in some cases.

BIBLIOGRAPHY

BUSCH, G. *et al.:* Rieger's syndrome. Klin. Monatsbl. Augenheilk., **136:**512, 1960.

Facioskeletal Dysplasia or Smith's Syndrome

Microcephaly, ptosis of the lids, epicanthus, broad nose with anteverted nostrils, broad alveolus of maxilla, small mandible, high arched palate, large low set ears, mental deficiency, hypotonia, low birth weight, failure to thrive, defective genitalia in males, but not in females, simian palmar creases, pedal syndactyly, short neck and autosomal recessive inheritance.

BIBLIOGRAPHY

PINSKY, L. AND DiGEORGE, A. M.: Smith's syndrome. Jour. Pediat., **66**:1049, 1965.

Bilateral Renal Agenesis or Potter's Syndrome

Aligohydramnios, pulmonary hypoplasia, flat hands, wrinkled skin, anorectal malformations, external male genitalia with ovaries but no testicles, hypertelorism, epicanthus, small mandible, low set ears, crease below lower lip, gross defects in nervous system with hydrocephalus and meningocele.

BIBLIOGRAPHY

AITA, J. A.: Congenital Facial Anomalies with Neurologic Defects. Springfield, Thomas, 1969.
MUIR, C. S.: Bilateral renal agenesis. Brit. Jour. Urol., **32**:39, 1960.

NEUROCUTANEOUS DISEASES

Diffuse Cortico-Meningeal Angiomatosis.—This is inherited as a recessive characteristic restricted to males. The symptoms become evident early in life. There are vascular skin nevi resembling livido racemosa or cutis marmorata. Convulsions, mental deficiency, pyramidal and extrapyramidal syndromes are associated. The process is slowly progressive.

Giant Hemangioma With Thrombocytopenia.—This condition is present at birth. Large cavernous hemangiomata are found which often grow during infancy. They bleed easily. Anemia and thrombocytopenia as well as purpura develop. Petechial and confluent hemorrhages occur in the nervous system.

Disseminated Systemic Hemangiomatosis.—This process is present at birth. There are numerous hemangiomas. The skin and the central nervous system are both involved. The skull and the vertebrae may be invaded also. Angiomas of the retinae are sometimes found. The viscera, larynx and muscles are sometimes affected.

Malignant Papulosis.—Pale reddish or yellow papules appear which become umbilicated in the center. They recur in repeated attacks. They are found chiefly on the trunk. There are progressive cerebral and spinal symptoms due to necrotizing arteritis and thrombosis involving chiefly the small vessels.

Urticaria Pigmentosa or Mastocytosis.—Flat brownish macules appear in infancy which itch severely. They are composed of mast cells. When they are irritated, urticaria develops and it is believed there is a release of histamine. Headache, flushing and nausea and vomiting result. There may be hypotension and syncope.

Keratosis Follicularis.—Papules covered with brownish crusts occur in childhood which gradually extend over the body and face. Mental deterioration develops with convulsions, cerebellar ataxia and polyneuritis.

Lipoid Proteinosis.—Polymorphous eruptions of yellow papules develop in childhood with hyperkeratotic plaques and ulcers. Yellow white infiltrations develop in the mucous membranes. Convulsions occur with mental deterioration. Congenital indifference to pain is described. Calcification occurs in the brain, especially in the hippocampal gyri. There may be increased retinal pigmentation, macular exudates, tortuosity of the retinal vessels and malformations of the optic discs. There may be hoarseness, difficulty in swallowing and shortness of breath.

Keratosis Palmoplantaris.—This is a recessive condition which occurs in childhood. There is extensive cornification of the palms and soles. Dysplasia of the nails, ears, digits, and teeth are found. Mental deficiency, convulsions and calcification of the dura are described. There may be defective growth of the body and genital organs.

Cutis Verticisa Gyrata.—This is an overgrowth of the scalp which causes corrugated folds and furrows. There is mental deficiency, convulsions and psychoses.

Dyskeratosis Congenita.—This is a recessive condition. The symptoms may be present at birth. There is reticular pigmentation, telangiectasia, atrophic changes in the skin, leucoplakia in the oral mucosa, dystrophy of the nails, hyperhidrosis of the palmar and plantar surfaces. Microcephaly and mental deficiency are associated.

Basal Cell Nevus.—This is an inherited condition, apparently a dominant trait. The symptoms are present at birth or in infancy. There are hundreds of pin head to 5.0 mm papules or pedunculated lesions on the face and in the axillae. There may be malformations of the brain, mental deficiency and calcifications of the dura. Medulloblastoma may develop. There may be cysts in the mandible, anomalies of the ribs and vertebrae, prognathism and hypertelorism.

Epidermolysis Bullosa Dystrophica.—This is a recessive trait. The symptoms are present at birth. There are vesicles and bullae with scarring and pigmentation. The nails and teeth are dystrophic. Mental deficiency and defects of motor development may be associated.

Linear Nevus Sebaceous of Jadassohn.—This is an inherited condition. Yellowish nevi are found over the forehead and nose. Biopsy reveals sebaceous glands and sweat glands. Malignant growth may develop. Squints, mental deficiency and convulsions occur.

BIBLIOGRAPHY

Aita, J. A.: Neurocutaneous Diseases. Springfield, Thomas, 1966.
Berg, J. M. and Windrath-Scott, A.: Cutis verticis gyrata. Jour. Ment. Defic. Res., 6:75, 1962.
Burke, E. C. *et al.*: Disseminated hemangiomatosis. Amer. Jour. Child., **108**:418, 1964.

DIVRY, P. AND VAN BOGAERT, L.: A familial disease characterized by a diffuse non-calcified corti-comeningeal angiomatosis and progressive demyelination. Neurol. Neurosurg. and Psychiat., 9:41, 1946.

FEUERSTEIN, R. C. AND MIMS, L. C.: Linear nevus sebaceous of face. Amer. Jour. Dis. Child., 675, 1962.

GORLIN, R. J.: Multiple basal cell nevi syndrome. Cancer, 18:89, 1965.

——— et al.: Syndrome of palmar-plantar hyperkeratosis. Jour. Pediat., 65:895, 1964.

GROSS, B. C. et al.: Hereditary urticaria pigmentosa. Arch. Dermat., 90:401, 1964.

HOMER, R. S.: Cutaneous mastocytosis. Arch. of Dermat., 89:610, 1964.

KEMENY, P. et al.: Fatal case of giant hemangioma with thrombocytopenia and bleeding. Ann. Paediat., 200:257, 1963.

LEWIS, I. C. et al.: Epidermolysis bullosa in newborn. Arch. of Dis. of Childh., 30:277, 1955.

McCUSKER, J. et al.: Lipoid proteinosis. Amer. Jour. Path., 40:599, 1962.

MILGROM, H. et al.: Dyskeratosis congenita. Arch. Dermat., 89:345, 1964.

PASTRAS, T. et al.: Mastocytosis. Amer. Jour. Med. Sci., 244:510, 1962.

PENDLEBURY, A. S.: Darier's disease. Nurs. Times, 60:449, 1964.

SUGARMAN, G. I. AND REED, W. B.: Two unusual eurocutaneous disorders with facial cutaneous signs. Arch. of Neurol., 21:242, 1969.

ULTMAN, J. E.: Clinical, cytologic and biochemical studies in systemic mast cell disease. Ann. Int. Med., 61:326, 1964.

WINKELMAN, R. K. et al.: Malignant papulosis of the skin and cerebrumach. of Dermat., 87:54, 1963.

DEFECTS OF DEVELOPMENT DUE TO ABNORMALITIES OF THE CHROMOSOMES

Mongolian Idiocy

Definition.—This is a type of congenital mental defect, or amentia, associated with certain physical peculiarities, such as obliquity of the lid-slits, a peculiar cast of countenance, etc. These appearances bear a superficial resemblance to the facies of the Mongol race, hence the name.

Pathologic Anatomy.—The brains are always below the average size and weight, but not as small as those of the true microcephalics. The cortical pattern is usually simplified, the sulci shallow and the convolutions broad. It is not unusual to find gross asymmetries of the hemispheres, cerebellum or brain-stem. On section, the cortex is very thin. Nerve cells are few in number and often of primitive type. The fibers are thin and myelin scanty. Heterotopias are described. There is no gliosis or evidence of inflammation or degeneration in uncomplicated cases, but the blood vessels show thickening and hyaline changes in their walls very early in life. Occasionally, a mongoloid may live until middle age. In such cases, there may be progressive dementia superimposed upon the original amentia and spasticity of the extremities. At post-mortem examination, the brain shows degenerative changes with many Alzheimer plaques.

Donaldson states that Brushfield's spots occur in 85 per cent of all mongoloids and are due to thinning of the iris. Similar but less distinct spots occur in normal individuals but are not due to such pronounced thinning of the iris.

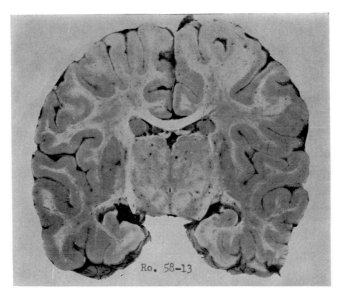

Fig. 102. Brain of a mongoloid showing characteristic enlargement of thalami and massa intermedia. The brain was smaller than normal. (By the courtesy of Dr. Richard Lindenberg.)

In 1959, Lejune found that mongoloids have 47 chromosomes rather than the usual number of 46. This discovery has been verified repeatedly. The extra chromosome is an autosomal one. Usually, three identical chromosomes are found in place of the normal pair numbered 21. This is termed a trisomy.

It is believed that an elderly mother who has a mongoloid child usually has a normal chromosomal constitution. During the division of the germ cell, two number 21 chromosomes are deposited in one daughter cell and none in the other. If the daughter cell containing two 21 chromosomes is fertilized by a sperm cell which contributes another chromosome 21 the fertilized cell will contain three 21 chromosomes and develop into a mongoloid child.

The risk of another mongoloid child is small. There is reason to believe that the children of elderly fathers show a higher incidence of mongolism than children of younger men.

As a rule, when a young mother has a mongoloid child, she is a carrier. Her chromosome count seems to be 45. This is because one of her number 21 chromosomes is adherent to the number 13-15 group and thus is not counted. During division of the germ cell, one daughter cell may receive this combined chromosome and a normal chromosome 21. When fertilized and another chromosome 21 is added by the sperm cell, there will be in effect three chromosomes 21 and a mongoloid child will result though chromosomal counts show only 46 chromosomes. Such a mother may produce a normal child or a carrier. One third of her children will be mongols.

The father may also be the carrier. In this case, the translocation is apt to be between the chromosome group 21-22 and group 21.

The possibility that radiation of the mother may play a role in the occurrence of mongolism in the infant has been mentioned.

Penrose states that mosaicism is found in one case of twenty mongoloids, and that in such cases, intelligence is better than in the common mongoloids and may even be normal.

Lejune has found evidence of a metabolic abnormality in mongolism. In fifteen mongols none were found to excrete normal amounts of 5-hydroxy-indole-acetic acid, indole-acetic acid or zanthurenic acid which are by-products of tryptophan. He suspects that the content of serotonin in the brain is reduced for this substance is a link in the chain between tryptophan and 5-hydroxy-indole-acetic acid.

O'Brien and Groshek also found diminished excretion of xanthurenic acid. They suggest that there is a specific abnormality of hydroxykynurenin transaminase metabolism.

Clinical Features.—It has been estimated that mongolism is the cause of from five to ten per cent of all defectives in England, although some authors have claimed an even higher incidence. In Germany, however, the proportion seems to be lower and is placed at about one per cent. If one of a pair of identical twins is affected, the other is sure to be affected also, whereas, only one of a pair of dissimilar twins is ever affected. The diagnosis may often be made at birth, for these children present a characteristic appearance, which is more easy to recognize than to describe. The cranium is small and brachycephalic. The features also are small and the whole face somewhat flat. The palpebral fissures are narrow and oblique, their outer angle slanting upward. Epicanthus is common. The nose is small, short, and flat. The tongue protrudes between the lips but is not so large as that of the cretin. After the third or fourth year it usually becomes deeply fissured. The rhinopharynx is often small, and a moderate amount of adenoid tissue causes obstruction and mouth-breathing. Myopia, squints, and nystagmus are common. In infancy mongols display small white spots arranged in a circle at the junction of the outer and middle thirds of the irides. These are termed Brushfield's spots. They seem to be invariably present in mongols during infancy though they disappear later in life. Such spots may also occur occasionally in normal individuals. Cullen and Butler find that keratoconus occurs in more than five per cent of these patients and may develop acutely. Blindness also occurs in almost five per cent. This is usually due to cataracts which cause uveitis when they become hypermature or un-successful operations for cataracts. Acute keratoconus may also cause loss of vision. Cataracts are almost invariably found after the age of 17 years and may appear as early as the eighth year. The teeth are small and irregu-larly formed. In many cases, there is some deformity of the external ears which often stand out from the skull. The extremities are somewhat small and short as compared with the trunk. The hands are short and the fingers thick and stubby. The little finger is often only about half the length of the ring finger and is curved inward.

These children often have a single transverse crease in the palms of the hands. This is termed the simian crease. Club feet of various types may oc-cur. The great toes are widely separated from the small toes and a trans-verse crease may be found on the soles of the feet. A very constant and characteristic feature is muscular hypotonia and relaxation of the liga-ments. The child's heels may be placed behind the head with ease, and pe-culiar positions are often assumed which would be difficult or impossible for the normal infant. The kyphoscoliosis and tendency to umbilical her-nia which we see so often may also be regarded as the result of poor muscle tone. Congenital defects of various organs are described. Cardiac malfor-mations are not unusual. The genital organs are frequently imperfectly de-veloped. Paraplegia is a rare complication.

As they get older the characteristic features become less evident.

In the lumbosacral region, one finds irregular areas of bluish or brownish pigmentation, the so-called mongolian spots. These disappear early in child-hood. Similar spots may be found in normal children in rare instances. It is said that leukemia occurs more frequently than among other children.

These children are usually somewhat below the average size at birth, and since they grow very slowly their defective development becomes more ob-vious during childhood. They are abnormally placid and inert during infan-cy, lying still for hours without crying or complaining. One gains the im-pression that they are insensitive to discomfort. Temperature control may be imperfect in infancy. The sutures of the skull may be slow to close. The frontal sinuses are often absent. Within a few months, it is evident that they are not making proper progress. There is always delay in holding up the head, sitting up, standing and walking. In many cases the mongolian idiot does not walk until the fifth year, and the average age of learning to walk is over three years. Only a few fail to walk eventually. Muscular co-ordination is always defective. These children are awkward and clumsy, their movements resembling those of younger children. Their speech is al-ways delayed and imperfect. In a few cases they never develop intelligible speech. In the average case, the child makes some effort to talk by the end of the third year. There is a tendency to misform certain consonants such

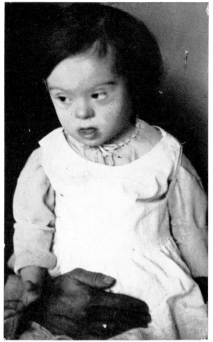

Fig. 103. Mongolian idiot showing the characteristic facial expression with open mouth and slanting eyes. (By the courtesy of Dr. Holt. Diseases of Infancy and Childhood, Appleton 1934.)

as *s, th, y* and *z,* giving rise to a lalling speech. The intellectual level varies in different individuals, but the range of variation is not great. Most mongolians are classified as imbeciles and many are idiots. Very few reach a mental age of six years. The average intelligence quotient is between 35 and 50. They are often fairly docile and good natured, playing contentedly with their toys and giving their parents very little trouble.

Walter *et al.* state that in 2.0 per cent of cases there are grand mal convulsions.

Cant reports the case of a girl whose appearance was that of a mongol but whose intelligence was normal.

Diagnosis.—Cretinism, achondroplasia, rickets and simple mental defects must be distinguished from mongolian idiocy. The differentiation from congenital cretinism is not always easy for these conditions have much in common. However, in the cretin the skin is very dry, cold, scaly and wrinkled to a degree not usually seen in mongolism. Moreover, the characteristic obliquity of the lid-slits is absent and the lids are puffy and swollen. The tongue is much larger in the cretin and does not show the fissures. An important point in the diagnosis of cretinism is the long delay in ossification of the epiphyses which is not found in mongolism. In case of doubt, thyroid substance may be tried, for this should make a profound change in the cretin and is without effect upon the mongol. Rickets should be distinguished with ease by the characteristic bony changes. Achondroplasia should offer no difficulty for these children, although small, are very muscular and active, and in most cases possess normal or nearly normal mentality. From the other types of amentia, mongolism may be distinguished by the peculiarities of physical development.

Hall states that newborn mongoloid infants usually have 6 of the 10 signs of this disorder. (1) The flat profile. (2) The absent Morto reflex. (3) Muscular hypotonia. (4) Oblique lid slits. (5) Excess skin at the back of the neck. (6) Hyperflexible joints. (7) Dysplastic pelvis which is broader than normal and shortened in vertical height. (8) Dysplastic ear. (9) Dysplastic phalanx of the fifth finger. (10) Simian crease of the palm. Study of the chromosomes has, of course, great value in establishing the diagnosis.

Prognosis.—The outlook for improvement is very gloomy. Few mongoloids attain a mental age of 6 years and it is unusual for them to learn to read. They are, therefore, always a care to their parents, cannot support themselves or even care for themselves in the home. Their resistance to disease is very deficient. Few live to adult life, and many die in early childhood of respiratory infections or heart failure. Later in childhood tuberculosis is very common.

Treatment.—Nothing can be done for these children beyond proper hygienic care and such training as they can assimilate. Their capabilities are rarely such that they can profit by expert instruction.

BIBLIOGRAPHY

Brousseau, K.: Mongolism, a Study of the Physical and Mental Characteristics of Mongolian Imbeciles. Revised by H. G. Brainerd. Baltimore, William & Wilkins Co., 1928.

Cant, W. H. P. *et al.:* Girl of mongoloid appearance and normal intelligence. J. Ment. Sc., 99:560, 1953.

Carter, C. O. *et al.:* Prediction of mongolism. Lancet, ii:678, 1960.

Cullen, J. F.: Blindness in mongolism (Down's syndrome). Brit. J. Ophth., 47:331, 1963.

Cullen, J. and Butler, H. G.: Mongolism (Down's syndrome) and keratoconus. Brit. J. Ophth., 47:321, 1963.

Donaldson, D. D.: Significance of spotting of the iris in mongoloids (Brushfield's spots). Arch. of Ophthal., 65:26, 1961.

Fraccaro, M. *et al.:* Chromosomal abnormalities in father and mongol child. Lancet, i:274, 1960.

Gordon, R. G. and Roberts, J. A. F.: Paraplegia and mongolism in twins. Arch. Dis. Childhood, 13:79, 1938.

Hall, B.: Mongolism in newborn infants. Clin. Pediat., 5:4, 1966.

Ingalls, T. H.: The cause and prevention of developmental defects. J.A.M.A., 161:1047, 1956.

Jacobs, P., Baikie, A. G. Court, Brown, W. M. and Strong, A. J.: The somatic chromosomes in mongolism. Lancet, 7075:710, 1959.

Jenkins, R. L.: Etiology of mongolism. Am. J. Dis. Child., 45:506, 1933.

Lejune, J., Gautier, M. and Turpin, R.: Etude des chromosomes somatique de neuf enfants mongoliens. C. R. Acad. Sci. (Paris), 248:1721, 1959.

Lejune, J.: Le mongolisme, trisomie degressive. Ann. Genet., 2:1, 1960.

Macklin, M. T.: Mongolian idiocy; the manner of its inheritance. Am. J. Med. Sc., 178:315, 1929.

MITCHELL, A. G.: Mongolism in the Negro. J.A.M.A., **99**:2105, 1932.

MORRIS, J. V. AND MacGILLIVERAY, R. C.: Mongolism in one of twins. J. Ment. Sc., **99**:557, 1953.

O'BRIEN, D. AND GROSHEK, A.: Tryptophan metabolism in mongoloids. Arch. Dis. Childhood, **37**:17, 1962.

PENROSE, L. S.: Paternal age in mongolism. Lancet, i:1101, 1962.

————: Familial studies on palmar patterns in relation to mongolism. Pro. VIII Int. Congr. Genet., p. 412, 1949.

POLANI, P. E. *et al.*: A Mongol girl with 46 chromosomes. Lancet, **i**: 721, 1960.

ROWE, R. D.: Cardiac malformations in mongolism. Amer. Heart Jour., **64**:567, 1962.

SIGLER, A. T. *et al.*: Radiation exposure in parents of children with mongolism. Bull. Johns Hopkins Hospital, **117**:374, 1965.

UCHIDA, I. A. AND CURTIS, E. J.: Possible association of maternal radiation and mongolism. Lancet, ii:848, 1961.

WALLIS, H. R.: The significance of Brushfield's spots in diagnosis of mongolism in infancy. Arch. Dis. Child., **26**:495, 1951.

WALSH, F. B.: *Loc. cit.*

WALTER, R. D., YEAGER, C. L. AND RUBIN, H. K.: Mongolism and convulsive seizures. Arch. of Neurol. and Psychiat., **74**:559, 1955.

WARNER, R.: Mongolism in one of twins and in another sibling. Report of a case. Am. J. Dis. Child., **78**:573, 1949.

Ovarian Agenesis with Deficient Bodily Growth and Sometimes Mental Deficiency or Turner's Syndrome

In 1938, Turner described this condition. The ovaries are completely absent and are represented only by a narrow ridge in the broad ligaments.

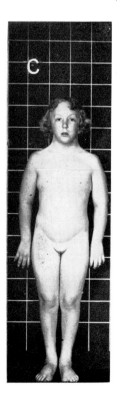

FIG. 104. Ovarian agenesis with deficient bodily growth, mental deficiency, webbed neck, defective sexual development and co-arctation of the aorta. (From Wilkins, L.: The diagnosis and treatment of endocrine disorders in childhood and adolescence. Thomas, 3rd Ed.)

The nipples, breasts, labia, vagina and uterus are infantile, but pubic hair is present. The patients are dwarfs. A webbed neck is often present. Coarctation of the aorta is frequently found, usually in association with the webbed neck. Mental deficiency is present in a large percentage of cases. These children may have myopia, glaucoma and detachment of the retina.

These patients are chromatin negative. As a rule, they have only forty-five chromosomes and one sex chromosome represented as XO. The follicle stimulating hormone is increased after the age of twelve years, but the 17 keto-steroids are normal. Females who have the XO sex chromosome constitution may display such sex-linked recessive diseases as hemophilia, for the absence of the second X chromosome permits such conditions to become evident.

Rainier-Pope *et al.* state that in addition to coarctation of the aorta, pulmonary stenosis, ventricular septal defect, patent ductus arteriosus and aortic valvular stenosis may be found.

Redondo states that multiple intestinal telangiectases are found and may cause serious hemorrhages.

Henkin states that in chromatin negative Turner's syndrome the patient can taste salt and sweet, but not sour and bitter. Olfactory function is deficient for all odors.

There may be other anomalies including low set ears, cubitus valgus, lymphedema of the legs, delayed maturation of the bones, anomalies of the cervical spine, elevation of the blood pressure and atrophy of the skin. Mosaic patterns of the chromosomes such as XO/XX, XO/XY, XO/XXY, XO/XXX and XO/XX/XXX are known.

The developmental anomalies seen in Turner's syndrome have been described in males. The testicles are absent or incompletely developed. Mental deficiency is often present. Cardiac malformations are described. Ocular anomalies such as ptosis of the lids, bilateral epicanthus and hypertelorism may be found. The buccal smear shows absence of the sex chromatin. There are 46 chromosomes with a normal XY component.

Migeon and Whitehouse have published a study of a sister and a brother who had webbed necks, widely spaced nipples, bony rarefaction, mental deficiency but no genital abnormality. The chromatin bodies and gross chromosomal pattern were normal. They also studied two brothers whose chromosomes were grossly normal and who were chromatin negative who displayed webbed necks, aortic stenosis and undescended testicles. They suggest that these conditions may be due to an autosomal point mutation.

BIBLIOGRAPHY

ALBRIGHT, F. *et al.*: A syndrome characterized by primary ovarian insufficiency and decreased stature. Amer. Jour. Med. Sci., **204**:625, 1942.

BLOISE, W. *et al.:* Gonadal dysgenesis (Turner's) with male phenotype and XO chromosomal constitution. Lancet, **ii:**1059, 1960.

CARON, P. *et al.:* Turner's syndrome in males. Henry Ford Hosp. Med. Bull., **12:**121, 1964.

EDWARDS, J. H. *et al.:* A new trisomic syndrome. Lancet, **i:**787, 1960.

FERGUSON-SMITH, M. A.: Chromosome abnormalities with congenital diseases. Mod. Med., March 6, 1961, p. 77.

FUTTERWEIT, W. *et al.:* Multiple congenital defects in a 12 year old boy with cryptorchidism (Male Turner's syndrome). Metabolism, **10:**1074, 1961.

HELLER, R. H.: The Turner phenotype in the male. Jour. Pediat., **66:**48, 1965.

HENKIN, R. I.: Abnormalities of taste and olfaction in patients with chromatin negative gonadal dysgenesis. Jour. Clin. Endocr., **27:**1436, 1967.

McCONNELL, T. S. *et al.:* XO/XX/XY mosaicism in female with Turner's syndrome. Obstet. and Gynec., **31:**53, 1968.

MIGEON, B. R. AND WHITEHOUSE, D.: Familial occurrence of the somatic phenotype of Turner's syndrome. Johns Hopkins Medical Jour., **120:**78, 1967.

POLONI, P. E.: Sex anomalies and abnormalities of sex chromosomes. Pro. Roy. Soc. Med., **54:**899, 1961.

————: Turner's syndrome and allied conditions. Brit. Med. Bull., **17:**200, 1961.

RAINIER-POPE, C. R. *et al.:* Cardiac defects in Turner's syndrome. Pediatrics, **33:**919, 1964.

REDONDO, D.: Multiple telangiectases of the intestines in Turner's syndrome. Surgery, **61:**285, 1967.

STEICKER, D. D. *et al.:* Turner's syndrome in the male. Jour. Pediat., **58:**321, 1961.

TURNER, H. H.: Syndrome of infantilism, congenital webbed neck and cubitus valgus. Endocrinology, **23:**566, 1938.

VANDYKE, H. E. *et al.:* Probable deletion of the short arm of chromosome 18. Amer. Jour. Hum. Genet., **16:**364, 1964.

WILKINS, L.: The Diagnosis and Treatment of Endocrine Disorders of Childhood and Adolescence. 2nd Ed. Springfield, Thomas.

Mental Deficiency Associated with the XXX Sex Chromosome Anomaly

Jacobs studied a female who had infantile breasts, labia, vagina and uterus. She started to menstruate at the age of fourteen years. The menses became irregular and then ceased. Her bodily growth was within normal limits. Her mentality is not mentioned. The gonadotropins in the urine were increased. The somatic cells showed double chromatin bodies. She had forty-seven chromosomes and three sex chromosomes, XXX. The authors speak of the superfemale, but one might consider the term misleading.

Fraser *et al.* studied 595 mentally deficient females in an institution. Among these they found four patients who were subject to convulsions and were also mentally defective. Apparently their physical development was not remarkable. They had normal menstrual periods and at least one had borne a healthy child. All were chromatin positive and frequently two sex chromatin bodies were found. Studies of the chromosomes revealed that they had forty-seven. There were three sex chromosomes, XXX.

BIBLIOGRAPHY

BARR, M. L. AND CARR, D. H.: Sex chromatin, sex chromosomes and sex anomalies. Canad. Med. Ass. Jour., **83:**979, 1960.

FRASER, J. *et al.:* The XXX chromosome syndrome. Lancet, **ii:**626, 1960.

HAMERTON, J. L. *et al.*: Sex chromosome abnormalities in a population of mentally defective children. Brit. Med. Jour., **5273**:220, 1962.
HAYWARD, M. D.: Chromosomes in pediatrics. Postgrad. Med. Jour., **37**:268, 1961.
JACOBS, P. A. *et al.*: Evidence for the existence of the human superfemale. Lancet, **ii**:423, 1959.
MCLEAN, N. *et al.*: Sex chromosome abnormalities among 4514 mental defectives. Lancet, **i**:293, 1962.

Testicular Deficiency or Klinefelter's Syndrome

In 1942, Klinefelter and his associates described a condition of testicular deficiency in which the seminiferous tubules, Sertoli cells and germinal epithelium were absent, and the interstitial cells were abundant. The testicles were small. The penis was of normal, or nearly normal, size and pubic hair was present. In many cases there was gynecomastia. The patients were sometimes tall and slender and of eunuchoid proportions, but were sometimes obese. The sperm cells were absent and the patients sterile. Mental deficiency was present in a number of these patients. Later investigations showed that some of these patients were chromatin positive and had forty-seven chromosomes with a sex constitution of XXY. The excretion of pituitary gonadotropins was increased.

Ferguson-Smith and his associates have found two patients who presented

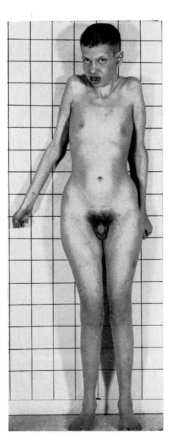

Fig. 105. The XXXY syndrome showing tall slender body, defective development of penis and testicles, feminine proportions and facial expression of mental deficiency. (From Ferguson-Smith, M. S.: Amentia and Microorchidism associated with the XXXY Sex Chromosome Constitution. Lancet ii:184, 1960.)

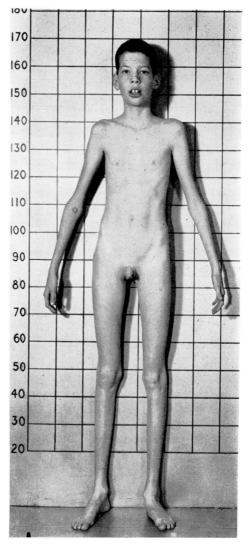

FIG. 106. Boy of 13 years with the XXXY syndrome. (By the courtesy of Dr. Hector Garcia *et al.*: XXYY Syndrome in prepubertal male. Johns Hopkins Med. Jour. 1967, vol. 121, p. 31.)

the usual picture of Klinefelter's syndrome and were grossly defective in mental development. They were tall and slender and of eunuchoid proportions. The penis and testicles were infantile. Two sex chromatin bodies were found in most somatic cells. They had forty-eight chromosomes and a sex chromosome constitution of XXXY.

Barr *et al.* describe the defects found in the XXXXY chromosome anomaly. The buccal smear reveals three chromatin bodies, and there are forty-nine chromosomes. The mental defect is severe, the testicles may be undescended, various skeletal malformations are found, and squints, cleft palate, ocular hypertelorism and other defects are mentioned.

Stimson describes a condition characterized by a XXYY sex chromosome constitution. He states that there is a eunuchoid bodily build, small testicles, long arms and legs, prognothism and acrocyanosis of the legs.

Lipsett, *et al.* find that the production of testosterone in chromatin positive patients is reduced. The administration of human chorionic gonadotropin does not restore normal production. Testosterone may be given.

Sexual chromosomal mosaics are found such as XX/XX, XXY/XY, XO/XY/XXY, XO/XY/XY, XY/XXY/XXYY and XXXY/XXXXY.

Garcia *et al.* have reported the case of a boy of 13 years who had the XXYY karotype. He was 170 cm tall and weighed only 35 kilos. His arms and legs were too long and thin. His face was narrow and the upper incisor teeth protruded causing malocclusion. There was mild pectus excavatum. A systolic bruit was heard over the heart. The penis was minute and the testicles were extremely small.

His behavior was childish. The intelligence quotient was between 60 and 70. The 17 ketosteroid excretion, gonadotropins, plasma bound iodine and plasma testosterone determinations were all within normal levels. The electroencephalogram and electrocardiogram were normal. The buccal smear was positive for Barr bodies. The karotype was XXYY as stated above.

Recently the XYY chromosomal constitution has been found in murderers and other criminals guilty of crimes of violence and it has been suspected that the personality of these individuals is such as to lead to violence.

BIBLIOGRAPHY

BARR, M. L. *et al.*: Defects in the XXXXY chromosome anomaly. Canad. M. A. J., **87**:891, 1962.

ELLIS, J. R. *et al.*: A male with XXXY chromosomes. Ann. Hum. Genet., **25**:145, 1961.

FERGUSON-SMITH, M. A. AND JOHNSON, A. W.: Chromosome abnormalities in certain diseases of man. Ann. Int. Med., **53**:359, 1960.

FERGUSON-SMITH, M. A., JOHNSON, A. W. AND HANDMAKER, S. D.: Primary amentia and microorchidism associated with the XXXY chromosome constitution. Lancet, **ii**:184, 1960.

———: Klinefelter's syndrome. Lancet, **ii**:167, 1957.

FRASER, J. H. *et al.*: Case of XXXXY Klinefelter's syndrome. Lancet, **ii**:1064, 1961.

GARCIA, H. O. *et al.*: XXYY syndrome in a prepubertal male. Johns Hopkins Med. Four., **121**:31, 1967.

KLINEFELTER, H. F., REIFENSTEIN, E. C. AND ALBRIGHT, F.: Syndrome characterized by gynecomastia, aspermatogenesis without Lydigism and increased excretion of follicle stimulating hormone. J. Clin. Endocrinol., **2**:615, 1942.

LIPSETT, M. B. *et al.*: Testosterone production in chromatin positive Klinefelter's syndrome. Jour. Clin. Endocr., **25**:1027, 1965.

STIMSON, C. W.: Meeting of the American Academy on Mental Retardation. Staten Island, N. Y., December 1963.

The Cat Cry Syndrome
(Deletion of Short Arm of Chromosome 5)

This syndrome is manifest by severe mental deficiency. Bodily growth is defective. There is microcephaly and a moon-like face. The ears are low set. The mandible is poorly developed. Palmar creases have an abnormal pattern. The most characteristic feature of this condition is said to be the child's peculiar cry which is said to resemble the cry of a cat. This is attributed to laryngeal malacia. There is a chromosomal abnormality. A portion of the short arm of one of the number 5 chromosomes is deleted.

BIBLIOGRAPHY

LEJEUNE, J. *et al.:* Segregation familiale d'une translocation 3-13 maladie du cri du chat. C. R. Acad. Sci. Paris, **258**:5766, 1964.

KAJII, T. *et al.:* Cri du chat syndrome. Arch. of Dis. Childh., **41**:97, 1966.

THOMPSON, H.: Abnormalities of autosomal chromosomes associated with human disease. Amer. Jour. Med. Sci., **vol. 250,** 1965.

MACINTYRE, M. N. *et al.:* The cat cry syndrome. Amer. Jour. Dis. Child., **108**:538, 1964.

Generalized Congenital Analgesia with Trisomy 13-15

Becak, Becak and Schmidt report the study of two unrelated boys of three and seven years who were unable to appreciate pain, though other modalities of sensibility were intact. They mention that a brother of one patient had the same condition. They also mention that two more siblings of a third family had congenital analgesia.

Both of the boys were mentally deficient. Both had extensive ulcerations of the skin. Though the skin was white, there was a melanoid substance in the skin and a similar substance was excreted in the urine. One boy had repeated fractures of the bones causing deformities and one had osteomyelitis.

Both boys were chromatin negative and had an XY sex chromosome constitution. One had a mosaic of forty-six, forty-seven and forty-eight chromosomes and one forty-six and forty-seven chromosomes. In each case, the extra chromosomes were derived from the 13-15 group and attached to the 21-22 group.

BIBLIOGRAPHY

BECAK, W., BECAK, M. L. AND SCHMIDT, B. J.: Chromosome trisomy of group 13-15 in two cases of generalized congenital analgesia. Lancet, **i**:664, 1963.

Trisomy 13-15

Townes *et al.* and Lubs *et al.* describe the 13-15 trisomy. Many abnormalities are mentioned, including cataracts, colobomas, defects in the heart, low-set ears, polydactyly, flexion of the fingers and hands, open sagittal suture of the skull, rockerbottom feet, defects of the diaphragm, obstruction of the bladder neck, esophageal dilatation, hypospadias, undescended testicles, dilatation of the cerebral ventricles, cerebellar defects and wormian bones. Smith mentions deafness, microphthalmia, cleft palate and harelip.

Cebocephaly in which there is only one midline forebrain ventricle, me-

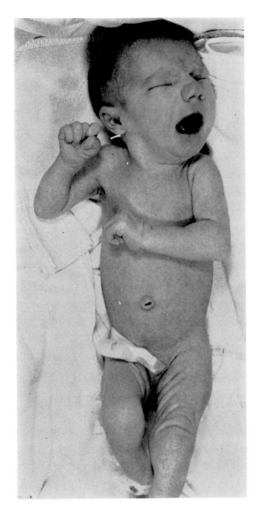

Fig. 107. Trisomy 13-15 showing broad nose, a typical feature. (By the courtesy of Dr. H. G. Butler.)

dian cleft lip and palate and sometimes absence of the testicles has been associated several times with the 13-15 trisomy.

CASE HISTORY.—*Trisomy 13-15 with clinical findings and anatomical examination of the nervous system.*

By the courtesy of Dr. Harry Butler I am able to give the history of an infant suffering from the 13-15 trisomy. The baby was grossly defective in mental development and was subject to convulsions. There was muscular hypotonia, but the tendon reflexes were present. The head was too small and the forehead was narrow. The bridge of the nose was broad and end of the nose was bulbous. The ears were large and there was a tag of skin in front of the left ear. The palate was high and narrow. The hands were soft and pudgy and the fingers tapered. The feet were also soft and puffy. There was an excess of hair between the eyes. No abnormality of the heart or eyes could be demonstrated.

The examination of the brain by Dr. Richard Lindenberg revealed that the hemispheres and cerebellum were small. The brain weighed only 720 grams. The genu and splenium of the corpus callosum were missing and the middle portion was thin. The lateral ventricles had the bull's horn shape typical of agenesis of the corpus callosum. The convolutions of the brain were primitive and the mass of white matter was greatly reduced. Ammon's horn appeared to be normal. Sclerosis of the lobuli of the cerebellum was evident. No defect was found in the midbrain, pons or medulla.

BIBLIOGRAPHY

CONEN, P. E. *et al.:* Multiple developmental anomalies and trisomy of a 13-15 group chromosome. Canad. Med. Jour., **87:**709, 1962.
HAWWORTH, J. C. *et al.:* Cebocephaly with endocrine dysgenesis. Jour. of Pediat., **59:**726, 1961.
LEE, C. S. N. *et al.:* The Di trisomy syndrome. Bull. Johns Hopkins Hosp., **118:**374, 1966.
LUBS, A. *et al.:* Trisomy 13-15. Clinical syndrome. Lancet, **ii:**1001, 1961.
MILLER, J. Q.: A specific congenital brain defect (arhinencephaly) in 13-15 trisomy. New England Jour. Med., **268:**120, 1963.
SMITH, D. W.: Trisomy 13-15. J. Pediat., **62:**326, 1963.
TOWNES, P. L. *et al.:* Trisomy 13-15. J. Pediat., **60:**528, 1962.

Trisomy 18

According to German *et al.* and Smith *et al.,* trisomy 18 is associated with many defects of development. The children's birth weight is about 2200 gm, even if born at term. Parts of the brain are absent. Spasticity is a regular feature. Cataracts and aplasia of the optic nerves are common. Intraventricular septal defects of the heart, patent ductus arteriosus and coarctation of the aorta are mentioned. Eventration of the diaphragm, hepatitis, ileal diverticula, ectopic pancreatic tissue and renal malformations are common. The joints are fixed in flexion. The fingers are clenched. The nails are defective and abnormal palmar creases are found. The bridge of the nose is wide. They live for an average of about seventy-six days.

Townes *et al.* describe a defect in the heart with an opening in the intraventricular septum and valvular pulmonic stenosis. The brain was small and the frontal lobes and the cerebellar vermis defective. Polycystic kidneys and ovarian hypoplasia were found. The eyelids could not be closed and the corneas were dry and scarred.

BIBLIOGRAPHY

TOWNES, P. L. *et al.:* Cardiac defect in trisomy 17-18. J. Pediat., **62:**703, 1963.
GERMAN, J. L. *et al.:* Autosomal trisomy of group 16-18. J. Pediat., **60:**503, 1962.
GORLIN, R. J. AND SEDANO, H.: Trisomy 18 syndrome (E syndrome). Modern Medicine, December 1, 1969, p. 124.
SMITH, D. W. *et al.:* The No. 18 trisomy. J. Pediat., **60:**513, 1962.

Scarpa, F. J. and Borgaonkar, D. S.: A V communis defect in trisomy E 1 (17-) . Bull. Johns Hopkins Hosp., 118:395, 1966.

Syndrome of the Ring Chromosome E

A few cases have been reported in which individuals have been found to have a ring chromosome E (deletion of the tip of the long and short arms). Various defects of development have been found including mental deficiency, hypertelorism, epicanthus, auditory atresia with deafness, webbed neck and deformities of the fingers and toes.

The parents and siblings are usually normal.

Case History.—*Syndrome of the ring chromosome E (deletion of the tip of the long and short arm).*

The patient was found to be mentally deficient early in life. She formed a few words imperfectly at the age of 2 years. The intelligence quotient was estimated at 43 per cent. The electroencephalogram revealed mild disorganization but no seizure discharges.

She is somewhat below average height. Her nutrition is normal. Her muscular development is very good. She does not always understand what is said to her and can form only short imperfect sentences. There are small ear pits on each side but the ears are not otherwise malformed. Her facial features are not abnormal. There are no abnormalities of the skin. The arches of the feet are rather high. Sexual development is normal.

No neurological abnormalities of any kind could be found. Study of the chromosomes revealed a ring chromosome E.

BIBLIOGRAPHY

Gripenberg, V.: The cytological behavior of a human ring chromosome. Chrosoma, 20:284, 1967.
Thompson, H.: Abnormalities of the autosomal chromosomes. Amer. Jour. Med. Sci., 250:718, 1965.
DeGrouchy, J.: Ring chromosome. Jour. Pediat., 66:414, 1965.

The Short Y Chromosome Syndrome

Abnormalities in the Y chromosome have been discovered a number of times. This chromosome may be too long or too short. In some instances the individual seems to suffer no ill effects from this abnormality. Nakagome refers to a girl who had a short Y chromosome and showed defective sexual development and an enlarged clitoris. He reports a study of a boy who had the same defect who was mentally defective and had diminished muscle tone. A case I have observed is given in abstract below.

Case History.—*Mental deficiency in a boy who shows the bodily characteristics of arachnodactyly. Short Y chromosome syndrome.*

D. E. K. was found to be mentally deficient when he was very young. He was never able to talk clearly. His intelligence quotient was found to

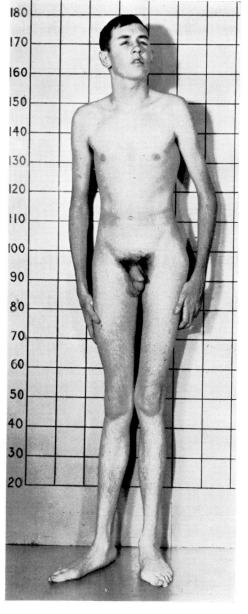

FIG. 108. The Short Y chromosome syndrome. There is severe mental deficiency. The fingers and arms and legs are very long and slender as in arachnodactyly.

be 15 per cent. There were no convulsions. Roentgenograms of the skull and chest were normal. The electroencephalogram was normal.

An examination at the age of 19 years revealed that he was very tall and slender. His arms and legs were very long and the fingers and toes were also extremely long and slender. The muscles were poorly developed and muscle tone was reduced. He had knock knees and flat feet. Strength was below average. He was clumsy but there was no real ataxia. Some limitation of extension at the elbows was noted. The tendon reflexes were present and there was no Babinski sign. The penis was of average size, but curved to the left as a result of fibrosis. The testicles were of average size and firm. There was no gynecomastia.

Homocytinuria was considered, but no homocystine was found in the urine. Ophthalmological examination revealed nothing of significance. The lenses were not dislocated. None of the cardiovascular abnormalities which are found in arachnodactyly were present. Study of the chromosomes revealed that the Y chromosome was short. This patient was seen by the courtesy of Dr. Harry Butler.

BIBLIOGRAPHY

NAKAGOME, Y.: A mentally retarded boy with a minute Y chromosome. Jour. Pediat., **67**:1163, 1965.

MULDAL, S. AND OCKEY, C. H.: Deletion of Y chromosome in a family with muscular dystrophy and hypospadias. Brit. Med. Jour., **5274**:291, 1962.

Pyknodystoris

This is an autosomal recessive condition. The patients are of short stature. The head is enlarged and the frontal and occipital regions bulge. The sutures of the skull are wide and slow to close. The bones are sclerotic and fragile so multiple fractures occur. There is a double row of front teeth in some cases. The mandible is small. The fingers present a drumstick appearance, though the ends of the terminal phalanges are narrow. Mental deficiency may be present. Chromosomal studies reveal deletion of the short arm of the group G chromosomes.

BIBLIOGRAPHY

ELMORE, S. M. *et al.*: Pycnodysostosis with a familial chromosomal anomaly. Amer. Jour. Med., **40**:273, 1966.

GORLIN, R. J. AND SEDANO, H.: Pycnodysostosis. Modern Medicine, April 22, 1968, p. 172.

NANCE, W. E. AND ENGEL, E.: Pyknodysostosis. Science, **155**:692, 1967.

Other Chromosomal Defects

Aita describes chromosome defects including 1-3, 4-5, 6-12, other 13-15, 16, other 17-18 and other 21-22 defects. A great number of malformations occur in these conditions, but in many instances no well defined clinical syndrome can be distinguished and the results of the chromosome defect cannot be predicted.

BIBLIOGRAPHY

AITA, J. A.: Congenital Facial Anomalies with Neurologic Defects. Thomas, Springfield, 1969.

GORLIN, R. J. AND SEDANO, H.: Trisomy D 1 (13 trisomy). Modern Medicine, **vol. 37**, No. 10, p. 240, 1969.

Chapter II

HEREDOFAMILIAL AND DEGENERATIVE DISEASES
OF THE NERVOUS SYSTEM

I**NTRODUCTION.**—The degenerations of the nervous system present an almost unlimited variety of manifestations, but there are, nonetheless, certain characteristics of the group as a whole which may be mentioned by way of definition. First we may state that the victims of these diseases are almost always quite normal at birth. This fact is of importance in distinguishing the degenerations from the congenital defects, which may also be inherited. Moreover, the symptoms once they have appeared are almost invariably progressive. If an adequate history is secured, we generally discover that some relative, a sibling, cousin or ascendant, has suffered from similar or identical symptoms. In some cases it is impossible to elicit such a history. As a rule this is merely the result of an incomplete investigation or deliberate withholding of the facts, but sporadic cases seem to occur from time to time. There is a striking tendency for the onset to occur at approximately the same age in siblings and in their cousins, but it is not unusual for the age of onset to vary in different generations. In many cases the disease seems to begin earlier in each successive generation. This fact has been termed the *law of anticipation*. As a rule, the onset is so insidious that the parents are unable to assign a date to the first departure from health.

In recent years, as a result of the development of improved methods of biochemical study, a number of the diseases formerly termed degenerative have been found to be due to metabolic disorders and should, therefore, be discussed in Chapter IV.

No satisfactory classification of the degenerations of the nervous system has ever been offered. The chief difficulties seem to be due to the fact that such diseases are found in almost infinite variety and that no two families ever show absolutely identical symptoms. Indeed, it is not unusual for siblings to present somewhat different clinical pictures. The typical, or classical, syndromes are relatively rare and are as a rule closely connected by transitional cases. Abortive forms of most of these diseases are well known. Moreover, more or less identical conditions may seem to be inherited according to different laws in different families. It is impossible to say, therefore, how many diseases are included in this group. We may regard the typical "diseases" which are customarily described as syndromes more or less arbitrarily selected which are chiefly of didactic value. Nevertheless, certain large groups may be distinguished with confidence, and it is, moreover, necessary to offer some classification for the orientation of the reader, so a tentative outline has been constructed below.

The significance of this outline will be somewhat clearer if we devote a few words to the historical aspects of the subject. All the diffuse cerebral degenerations were formerly included under the term of "cerebral sclerosis." From time to time various disease entities have been described and separated from this large heterogeneous group. Thus in 1887, Sachs published a clinical and pathological study of the infantile cerebromacular degeneration which he regarded as a congenital defect of development and called amaurotic family idiocy. Warren Tay had described the retinal changes six years earlier. Later studies revealed that this disease is, in fact, a progressive degenerative process characterized by specific cellular pathology with deposits of lipoid products in the nerve cells. In more recent years the Vogts, Spielmeyer and others have shown that there is a juvenile form of the disease in which the lesions are almost identical with those of the infantile form. Bielschowski has described a late infantile form of amaurotic idiocy and Kufs a type which begins between the fifteenth and twenty-fifth years. Except for the infantile form of Tay and Sachs which is of course characterized by the cherry-red spot in the macula, these types are all associated with some type of pigmentary degeneration of the retina. In fact, the ascendants of these patients may exhibit the retinal lesions alone so it is believed that some types of pigmentary degeneration of the retina represent an abortive form of cerebroretinal degeneration. This group of diseases is characterized by a specific histological process and by the combination of cerebral and retinal degeneration. Biochemical studies have revealed that these conditions are due to disorders of metabolism and they are termed the *lipidoses*. They are discussed in Chapter IV.

Another group of diseases must now be mentioned for they present some features which suggest a close relationship to the cerebroretinal degenerations. In some cases of Niemann-Pick disease there are degenerations in the brain associated with deposits of lipoid droplets in the nerve cells so that the histological picture is nearly identical with that of amaurotic idiocy. The lipoid deposits are said to be composed chiefly of lecithin and sphingomyelins. In infantile Gaucher's there are also similar lipoid deposits in the nerve cells but these are composed of cerebrosides especially kerasin. Similar histological changes are found in the remarkable condition termed gargoylism or Hurler's syndrome in which there are many developmental defects including deformities of the skull and bones. In Christian-Schuller disease cholesterol and its esters are found. In none of these is the process confined to the nervous system as it is in the cerebroretinal degenerations. These conditions are now included in the group of lipidoses and discussed in Chapter IV.

Still another group of conditions is linked with the cerebroretinal degenerations by the presence of similar pigmentary degenerations of the retina. Here we must mention the Laurence-Moon-Biedl syndrome, progressive cerebellar ataxia, progressive spastic paraplegia, progressive muscular atrophy, progressive nuclear ophthalmoplegia, progressive deafness, etc. These are all familial in many cases. Little is known about the pathological anatomy, but it may be said that in the few post-mortem examinations which have been made no lipoid deposits have been found in the nervous system.

In 1885, Pelizaeus described another type of "cerebral sclerosis." At first the condition was regarded as a defect of myelination but later it was recognized as a very slowly progressive degeneration of the white matter. In 1912, Schilder published his study of a similar condition characterized by demyelination in the cerebral hemispheres. This condition he termed encephalitis periaxialis diffusa. Since then a number of similar "cerebral scleroses" have come to light. Scholz, Krabbe, Balo and Greenfield have described various clinical and anatomical pictures. A condition termed central pontine myelinolysis has been described by Adams *et al.* The essential process is a single, large, symmetrical area of demyelination in the rostral part of the pons. Mathieson and Olszewski report a case of this condition in a child of nine years. The cause is unknown. Dr. Robert Zwirecki tells me that he has found this condition has followed the use of aureomycin in several cases.

Marchiafava's disease is characterized by symmetrical demyelination of the middle fibers of the corpus callosum, the anterior commissure, the central white matter, the optic chiasm and the middle cerebellar peduncles. It has not been described in children, to my knowledge. It has also become apparent that the so-called neuromyelitis optica and disseminated sclerosis exhibit certain similarities to these conditions. This group is a very heterogenous one for there is a great deal of variation in the clinical picture, in the course of the disease and in the gross appearances and degree of destructiveness of the lesions in the nervous system. Most of these conditions are clearly familial, some of them are occasionally familial and others, for example, disseminated sclerosis, are possibly never familial. The only reason for grouping them together is that the histological changes are, at least in their incipiency, of the same nature in all. The first change is always destruction of myelin and such conditions are frequently termed *demyelinating diseases*. Seitelberger states that the demyelinating diseases are all autoimmune diseases. Recent work has led to the conclusion that there are two different groups of conditions among these demyelinating diseases. In one group we find disseminated sclerosis, Schilder's disease, Balo's encephalitis concentrica and neuromyelitis optica. Here normally formed myelin is destroyed in some unknown manner. These diseases are usually not familial.

In a second group, we find progressive metachromatic leucoencephalopathy of Greenfield, the cerebral sclerosis of Scholz, infantile cerebral sclerosis of Krabbe and the Pelizaeus-Merzbacher disease. These conditions are termed *leucodystrophies*. A congenital defect of enzyme activity is suspected, i.e. an inborn error of metabolism. It may be significant that all of these conditions are familial. They are described in Chapter IV.

Another group of diffuse cerebral degenerations involves chiefly the gray matter. Unfortunately analysis of this group has not progressed very far. Recently, Alpers, van Bogaert and several others have described fairly uniform lesions in a small number of cases, but there are probably many other processes still undifferentiated.

There are several other degenerative processes which involve the basal ganglia of the forebrain more or less selectively. Perhaps the best known and most thoroughly studied of these is Huntington's chorea which is associated with lesions in the lenticular nuclei and cerebral cortex. A well known condition is the so-called dystonia musculorum deformans which seems to be restricted to subjects of Jewish blood. Only a few postmortem studies have been made of this disease and the anatomical changes do not seem to be distinctive. It may be said, however, that there is no cirrhosis of the liver and so it is not merely a form of hepatolenticular degeneration. The Vogts have also described demyelination of the fibers of the lenticular nuclei in certain cases of progressive double athetosis and have offered the name of status demyelinisatus for this condition. It is not at all certain that this condition represents a disease entity. Indeed, it seems to be regarded by most authorities as merely a pathological reaction which may occur in several diseases. Several neurologists have published cases of pigmentation and degeneration of the globus pallidus and substantia nigra occurring, as a rule, in several members of a family, but whether this is a clearly defined condition or not is still uncertain. In general, apart from the hepatolenticular degeneration which is now known to be due to an abnormality of copper metabolism, little is known of the degenerations of the basal ganglia and the interrelationship of the various conditions mentioned above remains obscure.

When we turn to the hereditary ataxias, we find even greater confusion. Friedreich, Marie and others have described certain syndromes which have since been known by their names, but there is little or no reason to believe that these conditions represent separate and distinct diseases since they are connected by transitional, abortive and atypical cases in such a way that it is impossible to say where one ends and the other begins. In the same way the various family spastic paraplegias and the spinal muscular atrophies are linked together. Rhein's excellent article reveals very clearly the profusion of types which may be found in this group. In the following outline, therefore, the writer has not attempted to distinguish different diseases but has given merely the possible groups of symptoms with their corresponding anatomical processes. The outline is consequently of value only for descriptive purposes.

Among the degenerations of the peripheral nerves, hypertrophic interstitial neuritis has at least a distinctive histological picture, and possibly represents a disease entity. Peroneal muscular atrophy, however, may occur in association with other conditions such as hereditary spastic paraplegia, so that it may have some relation to the large group of spinal degenerations mentioned above.

Among the myoclonus epilepsies are found certain cases in which deposits of amyloid-like bodies in the nerve cells give rise to a distinctive histological picture. Freeman considers this a specific pathological process. Unfortunately other types of myoclonus epilepsy present entirely different lesions.

CLASSIFICATION OF THE HEREDOFAMILIAL AND DEGENERATIVE DISEASES OF THE NERVOUS SYSTEM

A. Abiotrophies with diffuse and focal degeneration affecting chiefly the white matter.

  1. Massive focal lesions in the cerebral white matter involving the myelin sheath first and causing softening later.
  Encephalitis periaxialis diffusa of Schilder.

  2. Large, spherical lesions composed of concentric globes of demyelination separated by zones of intact myelin.
  Encephalitis periaxialis concentrica of Balo.

  3. Focal degenerations of both the optic nerves and spinal cord involving the gray matter as well as the white matter and sometimes causing complete softening.
  Neuromyelitis optica.

  4. Focal degenerations involving both white and gray matter chiefly in the spinal cord and brain-stem, but also in the cerebral hemispheres with myelin destruction and dense gliosis but without softening and without great injury of the axis cylinders.
  Chronic disseminated sclerosis.

  5. Disseminated areas of encephalomalacia resulting in cavity formation involving primarily the subcortical white matter but later invading and destroying the cortex.
  Disseminated encephalomalacia with cavity formation.

B. Abiotrophies involving the cerebral gray matter.
   Degeneration of the cerebral gray matter of Alpers.
C. Abiotrophies with selective degeneration of certain parts of the nervous system.
   1. Involving chiefly the basal ganglia of the forebrain.
      a. *Dystonia musculorum deformans.*
      b. *Status demyelinisatus of the Vogts.*
      c. *Pigmentary degeneration of the globus pallidus and substantia nigra of Spatz and Hallervorden.*
      d. *Juvenile paralysis agitans of Hunt.*
      e. *Huntington's chorea.*
   2. Involving chiefly the fiber tracts of the spinal cord, cerebellar apparatus and motor nuclei of the brain-stem and spinal cord.
      a. *Hereditary cerebellar ataxia of Friedreich* (Spinocerebellar, corticospinal and dorsal spinal tracts).
      b. *Hereditary cerebellar ataxia with spasticity* (Spinocerebellar and corticospinal tracts).
      c. *Hereditary degeneration of the cerebellar cortex in childhood with mental deficiency.*
      d. *Hereditary spastic paraplegia* (Corticospinal tracts).
      e. *Hereditary amytrophic lateral sclerosis* (Corticospinal tracts and anterior horn motor cells).
      f. *Spinal muscular atrophies* (Motor cells of anterior horns).
      g. *Hereditary ataxia with muscular atrophy.*
      h. *Hereditary bulbar palsies* (Motor nuclei of the bulb).
   3. Involving chiefly the spinal nerve roots.
      a. *Peroneal muscular atrophy of Charcot-Marie and Tooth* (Motor roots).
      b. *Peroneal atrophy with sensory loss of England and Denny-Brown* (Motor and sensory roots).
      c. *Hereditary degeneration of the sensory nerve roots of Hicks and Denny-Brown* (Selective sensory root degeneration).
      d. *Hypertrophic interstitial polyneuritis* (Proliferation of the sheath of Schwann).
   4. Involving chiefly the retinae and optic nerves.
      a. *Hereditary optic atrophy* (Papillomacular fibers).
      b. *Retrobulbar neuritis and optic neuritis* (Demyelination of the optic nerve with and without edema of the papilla).
      c. *Pigmentary degeneration of the retina* (Degeneration of the retinal ganglion cells).
      d. *Hereditary degeneration of the macula* (Degeneration of the macula).

D. Degenerations of the nervous system characterized by deposits of amyloid-like bodies in the ganglion cells.
   Hereditary myoclonus epilepsy of Unverricht.

BIBLIOGRAPHY

ADAMS, R. D. *et al.*: Central pontine myelinolysis. Arch. Neurol. & Psychiat., **81**:154, 1959.

AITA, J. A.: Neurologic manifestations of general diseases. Thomas, Springfield, 1964.

BIELSCHOWSKI, M.: Entwurf eines Systems der Heredodegenerationen. J. f. Psychol. u. Neurol. bd., **24**:48, 1919.

BRAIN, W. R. AND GREENFIELD, J. G.: Late infantile metachromatic leucoencephalopathy. Brain, **73**:291, 1950.

COLE, M. *et al.*: Central pontine myelinolysis. Neurology, **14**:165, 1964.

FERRARO, A.: Primary demyelinating processes of the central nervous system. An attempt at unification and classification. Arch. Neurol. & Psychiat., **37**:1100, 1937.

GREENFIELD, J. G.: Neuropathology. Edward Arnold Ltd., London, 1958.

JELLIFFE, S. E.: Parts of the central nervous system which tend to exhibit morbid recessive or dominant characters. Arch. Neurol. & Psychiat., **12**:380, 1924.

KING, L. S. AND MEECHAN, M. C.: Degeneration of the corpus callosum (Marchiafava's disease). Arch. Neurol. & Psychiat., **36**:547, 1936.

MACCHI, G.: Les maladies demyelinisantes: situation de la sclerose en plaques vis a vis de leur classement. Third International Congress of Neuropathology. Brussels, July 21-28, 1957.

MATHIESON, G. AND OLSZEWSKI, J.: Central pontine myelinolysis with other cerebral changes. Neurology, **10**:345, 1960.

NORMAN, R. M.: Diffuse progressive metachromatic leucoencephalopathy. Brain, **70**:234, 1947.

PAGUIRIGAN, A. AND LEFKEN, E. B.: Central pontine myelinolysis. Neurology, **19**:1007, 1969.

POSER, C. M.: Leucodystrophy an example of demyelinating disease. The Third International Congress of Neuropathology. Brussels, July 21-28, 1957.

SEITELBERGER, F.: Autoimmunological aspects of cerebral disease. Path. europ., **2**:233, 1967.

STADLER, H. E. *et al.*: Heredofamilial infantile cerebral degeneration. The relationship of systemic factors to the pathogenicity. J. Pediat., **44**:364, 1954.

WALSH, F. B.: Clinical Neuroophthalmology. 2nd Ed. Williams and Wilkins, Baltimore, 1957.

THE INHERITANCE OF HEREDOFAMILIAL DISEASES OF THE NERVOUS SYSTEM

Before discussing the inheritance of diseases of the nervous system it is necessary to give a brief outline of the laws governing the transmission of personal characteristics in general. According to the Mendelian theory, unit characteristics are transmitted in simple mathematical ratios. As a result of extensive genetic and cytological studies, it has been established that the factors, or genes, conveying inherited characteristics reside in the chromosomes of the germ cells. These structures are components of the nuclei and are found in a number of morphologically identical, homologous pairs. It has been shown that the normal number of chromosomes is 46. The ovum contains 46 chromosomes originally, but during the divisions termed meiosis which occurs in two stages four daughter cells result each of which contains only 23 chromosomes. Only one cell matures and the other 3 cells termed polar bodies degenerate. In the male the four cells resulting from meiosis all mature to form sperm cells but each contains only 23 chromosomes. When fertilization occurs, the union of the sperm and the ovum restores the proper number of 46 chromosomes half of which are derived from the ovum and half from the sperm. It is believed that each characteristic of the offspring is thus determined by two genes. Subjects receiving identical genes from each parent are termed *homozygous* and those who have unlike genes, *heterozygous*. Some genes always give rise to the characteristics which they convey and are therefore termed *dominant*. Others are latent unless they are paired with identical genes and are, hence, called *recessive*. Some genes are contained within the same chromosome, which determines sex and the characteristics which they convey will, therefore, be *sex-linked* or limited.

These facts may be made clear by the following illustration. If we may represent a dominant characteristic by X and a recessive characteristic by Y, the mating of a homozygous subject exhibiting the dominant character with a homozygous subject exhibiting the recessive characteristic may be expressed as the mating of XX and YY. The offspring will all be represented by XY, and since X is dominant they will show only the characteristics of parent XX and none of parent XY. Matings between such heterozygous subjects as XY will produce several combinations. In about 25 per cent we will obtain XX, another 25 per cent YY and in 50 per cent XY. Thus, 75 per cent of the offspring will exhibit the dominant characteristic represented by X, but only 25 per cent of these will be homozygous. Only 25 per cent will present the characteristic represented by Y. Obviously a recessive characteristic may remain latent for many generations, for it never becomes apparent unless genes conveying this trait are inherited from both parents. In cases in which the particular characteristic is very rare, the chances of this happening are small, so that it may occur only once in a long family tree. Since no history of any similar trait in previous generations or in collaterals may be discoverable, it may not be realized that there is any hereditary factor involved. In some families a dominant trait does not always appear as often as one might expect. The concept of *penetrance* has been developed in regard to such cases. It is assumed that although the individual in question has the genetic constitution which should give rise to the trait, the penetrance is incomplete and the defect does not become evident.

Pathological genes may cause severe disease in one individual and only minor symptoms in another. It is said that the *expressivity* of the gene varies. Von Recklinghausen's disease may be offered as an example.

BIBLIOGRAPHY

From ZELLWEGER, H.: Genetic aspects of neurological disease. Arch. of Int. Med., **115**:387, 1965.

Selection of Neurological Conditions With Single Major Gene Inheritance

Autosomal Dominant Inheritance
 Huntington's chorea
 Neurofibromatosis
 Epiloia
 Von Hippel-Lindau's disease
 Familial migraine
 Familial tremor
 Hereditary cerebellar ataxia with spasticity
 Amyotrophic lateral sclerosis
 Progressive ophthalmoplegia
 Myotonia congenita Thomsen
 Myotonic muscular dystrophy
 Myopathia distalis tarda
 Nemaline-central core myopathy
 Adynamia episodica hereditaria Gamstorp
Autosomal Dominant and/or Recessive Inheritance
 Disseminated sclerosis
 Cerebromacular degeneration type Spielmeyer-Vogt
 Metachromatic leukodystrophy (R)
 Dystonia musculorum deformans
 Olivopontocerebellar atrophy
 Friedreich's ataxia
 Hereditary spastic paraplegia (D)
 Hereditary spastic paraplegia with sensory neuropathy
 Hereditary sensory neuropathy
 Syringomyelia
 Hypertrophic polyneuritis Déjérine-Sotta
 Peroneal muscular atrophy Charcot-Marie-Tooth (D)
 Progressive muscular atrophy (R)
 Facioscapulohumeral form of muscular dystrophy (D)
 Familial periodic paralysis
Autosomal Recessive Inheritance
 Diffuse cerebral sclerosis, type Krabbe
 Diffuse cerebral sclerosis, type Pelizaeus-Merzbacher (X)
 Hallervorden-Spatz disease
 Hepatolenticular degeneration
 Amaurotic idiocy
 Niemann-Pick's disease
 Heredopathia atactica polyneuritiformis Refsum

  Ataxia telangiectasia
  Phenylketonuria
  Hartnup's disease
  Maple syrup disease
  Gargoylism (X)
  Familial microcephaly
  Werdnig-Hoffmann's disease
  Limb-girdle type muscular dystrophy
  Pseudohypertrophic muscular dystrophy (X)
  Muscular glycogenosis type Pompe
  Muscular glycogenosis type McArdle
X-Linked Recessive Inheritance
  Diffuse cerebral sclerosis type Pelizaeus-Merzbacher
  Diffuse cerebral sclerosis type Scholz
  Gargoylism
  Oculocerebrorenal syndrome of Lowe
  Neurohypophyseal diabetes insipidus
  Familial hydrocephalus
  Friedreich's ataxia (rare)
  Spastic paraplegia (rare)
  Peroneal muscular atrophy (rare)
  Pseudohypertrophic muscular dystrophy of Duchenne
  Familial nystagmus
  Color blindness
      (R)—Predominantly autosomal recessive
      (D)—Predominantly autosomal dominant
      (E)—Predominantly X-linked recessive
Sex-linked characteristics are distributed in a more complex manner. In most animals, the female possesses two sex chromosomes which we may term XX, and the male one X chromosome, and another of different morphology which is called Y and which seems to have little genetic importance. In dealing with a sex-linked recessive characteristic, five possible combinations may be observed. If we designate the recessive character as X', these possibilities may be expressed as follows: (1) Mating between a normal female, XX, and a male who exhibits the characteristic in an overt form X'Y, will produce female children X'X and the male children XY. Neither the males nor the females will exhibit the character indicated by X', for this is recessive when paired with X. The females will, however, convey this trait to their children and are therefore termed *carriers*. (2) Mating between carrier females XX', and normal males, XY, will give rise to male children, X'Y and XY, and female children XX and X'X. That is, half of the sons will exhibit the trait, and half of the daughters will con-

vey it. (3) Mating between XX′, or a carrier mother, and X′Y, and affected father, will give rise to sons X′Y and XY and daughters XX′ and X′X′. In other words, half of the sons will be affected and half will escape; half of the daughters will be affected and all will be carriers. (4) When an affected female mates with a normal male, i.e., X′X′ and XY, all the sons will be affected X′Y and all the daughters, XX′, carriers. (5) Mating of an affected female with an affected male, or X′X′ with X′Y, will produce only affected children, X′X′ and X′Y. It may be seen from a consideration of these possibilities, that sex-linked recessive traits are present in an overt form only in males in most cases and are transmitted directly only by females. Males cannot transmit such traits directly, but their daughters may transmit it to their grandsons. Females never show such traits except when they possess two identical genes conveying the characteristic from both sides of the family. Sex-linked dominant characteristics are transmitted in exactly the same manner although the characteristic is always manifest by every individual possessing one of the genes in question.

Choroideremia illustrates sex-linked *intermediate inheritance*. The affected males show extensive changes in the retinae and lose their vision. The females, who transmit the disease, show milder changes in the retinae but retain good vision.

There are many more possibilities than are indicated by this brief discussion. Investigations in this field have become so technical as to be almost incomprehensible to all but the specialist. Recent work suggests that the cytoplasm is also important in inheritance. The occurrence of the hinny as apart from the mule has been cited in this connection.

With these facts in mind, we may pass on to the consideration of the mode of inheritance of pathological traits or, more specifically, the inheritance of diseases of the nervous system. There is abundant evidence that many diseases of the human nervous system are transmitted according to Mendelian laws, but in most instances, the analysis of the family tree brings to light a number of apparent discrepancies and irregularities which offer considerable difficulty in interpretation. For example, the Mendelian ratios are rarely approximated with even reasonable accuracy, as contrasted with the results attained in the breeding of plants and simpler organisms. No doubt, the small families which human beings produce and the difficulties usually encountered in securing all the facts are responsible in large part for these discrepancies. Another source of confusion which, however, offers no real difficulty, is the occurrence of several cases of a given disease in a group of siblings despite the absence of any history of the same condition in ancestors. For example, infantile amaurotic idiocy almost invariably behaves in this manner and gives the impression that the disease arises anew in each case. In reality, however, this is merely what one might expect of a recessive characteristic which is dependent upon genes having a small incidence in the population, and it is only when two such genes are brought together by chance in the same individual that the disease assumes an overt form. It is much more difficult to explain the fact that some diseases may behave as dominant characteristics in one family and as recessives in another. Two possible solutions may be offered. The simplest is that we are in reality dealing with two distinct diseases which happen to give rise to identical symptoms. The other explanation is that the disease is dependent upon several pathological genes which may be so closely attached to one another in the chromosome that they usually act as a unit but may, under certain conditions, become separated, so that a given individual might possess an incomplete set of these pathological genes which would require union with the complimentary genes to produce the disease in an overt form. The disease might behave as a dominant characteristic before the genes became separated and after they were separated, as a recessive trait. In the rare cases in which the mode of inheritance of a given disease seems to change during several generations of the same family, it seems necessary to assume that we are dealing with several pathological genes which become split or dissociated in the manner mentioned above.

It must be kept in mind that a family may inherit two separate and distinct morbid genes. We have recently seen some members of a family afflicted with congenital cataracts and progressive cerebellar ataxia. Analysis of the family history made it clear that these individuals were the result of union of a person inheriting congenital cataracts and another whose family was subject to progressive cerebellar ataxia.

No explanation for the origin of hereditary diseases of the nervous system can be offered. Spontaneous variations or mutations have been observed in experimental animals in the course of investigations in genetics, and these variations are known to be transmitted to the offspring. No doubt, the morbid factors responsible for heredofamilial diseases arise in the same way.

It is believed that cytoplasmic inheritance occurs and depends upon discrete hereditary particles. Work on this non-chromosomal genetic mechanism is just starting.

BIBLIOGRAPHY

Aita, J. A.: Neurologic manifestations of general diseases. Thomas, Springfield, 1964.

Barker, L. F. *et al.:* Heredity in Nervous and Mental Disease. A series of investigations and reports by The Association for Research in Nervous and Mental Diseases. New York, Paul Hoeber, Inc., 1923.

Bell, J. *et al.:* Treasury of Human Inheritance. Cambridge University Press. Various volumes.

Cohen, S. S.: Recent advances in the chemistry of inheritance. Jour. Pediat., **60**:586, 1962.

Duke-Elder, S.: System of Ophthalmology. C. V. Mosby Co., St. Louis, 1962.

Francois, J.: Chromosome abnormalities and ophthalmology. Jour. of Pediat. Ophthal., 1:5, 1964.

HERSKOWITZ, I. H.: Genetics. Little, Brown and Co., Boston, 1962.

LENA, W.: Medical Genetics. Univ. of Chicago Press, 1963.

MACKLIN, M. T.: The rôle of heredity in disease. Medicine, 14:1, 1935.

McKUSICK, V.: A catalog X-linked traits in man. Jour. genet. hum., 11:51, 1962.

————: On the X chromosome of man. Washington, Amer. Inst. Biol. Sci., 1964.

————: Mendelian Inheritance in Man. Johns Hopkins Press, 1966.

MORGAN, T. H.: The Physical Basis of Heredity. Philadelphia, J. B. Lippincott and Co., 1919.

PRATT, R. T. C.: The genetics of neurological disorders. Oxford Univ. Press, London, 1967.

SONNEBORN, T. M.: Beyond the gene. American Scientists, 37:33, 1949.

STERN, C.: Anomalies of genetic origin. Pediatrics, 5:325, 1950.

STOCKARD, C. R.: The Physical Basis of Personality. New York, W. W. Norton Co., 1931.

WAARDENBURG, P. J., FRANCESCHETTI, A. AND KLEIN, D.: Genetics and Ophthalmology. Springfield, Thomas, 1961, 2 vols.

ZELLWEGER, H.: Genetic aspects of neurological disease. Arch. of Int. Med., 115:387, 1965.

ENCEPHALITIS PERIAXIALIS DIFFUSA OF SCHILDER

Definition.—This disease is characterized by massive lesions in the sub-cortical white matter of the cerebral hemispheres involving primarily the myelin, and eventually causing actual softening sometimes.

Pathological Anatomy.—One or both hemispheres of the brain may be swollen and there is often evidence of increased intracranial pressure, such as flattening of the cortical convolutions or herniation of the cerebellum into the foramen magnum. On section, lesions of extraordinary size are seen which are confined to the white matter of the hemispheres. These lesions are soft and spongy. A gelatinous fluid oozes from the cut surface and this may be shown to consist largely of fat-laden phagocytes and lipoid granules. The spongy tissue is a recticulum of glial fibers. In the central portion of well advanced lesions the tissue is completely destroyed and cavities appear. The lesions may extend from the frontal to the occipital pole of the brain, involving almost all the white matter of one or both hemispheres. They are not restricted to any particular lobes. In some cases there

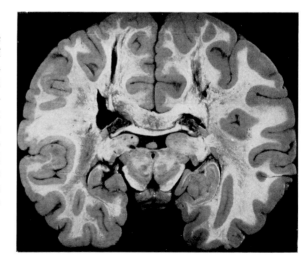

FIG. 109. Section through the cerebral hemispheres in a case of Schilder's disease showing the extensive lesions in the subcortical white matter involving the paracentral lobules most severely but also extending into the corpus callosum, the parietal and temporal lobes. It should be noted that the fibers are spared. In the most advanced positions of the lesions the tissue is completely broken down.

is a suggestion of bilateral symmetry in the process, but this is never exact and often there is no symmetry whatever. Wherever the lesions approach the cortex, they are sharply defined by a thin layer of preserved white matter, the arcuate fibers, whereas, the inner margins of the lesions are usually indefinite and merge gradually with normal tissue. This rule is subject to some exceptions and, in certain cases, the arcuate fibers are destroyed and the cortex may be somewhat affected. Usually there are no lesions in the brain-stem, the cerebellum, the spinal cord or the basal ganglia, but in a number of cases these structures are also involved. In the writer's experience, the lesions in the brain-stem, cerebellum and spinal cord are very small and are apt to be quite numerous. They are found in the gray matter as well as in the white matter and cannot be distinguished in any way from the fresh plaques of disseminated sclerosis. The association of such small disseminated lesions with the massive lesions of the cerebral hemispheres might suggest a very close relationship between disseminated sclerosis and Schilder's disease.

Histological examination reveals that the process begins with the destruction of the myelin sheath. The microglia cells proliferate, become phagocytic and take up the products of myelin disintegration, conveying this material to the perivascular sheaths of the small blood vessels. The granules in the phagocytes are composed of esters of cholesterol. The axis cylinders may be destroyed to some extent but do not seem to suffer as much as the myelin sheath. The astrocytes proliferate and form thick, branching processes, often becoming giant cells with two nuclei. In many lesions the process seems to stop at this point, leaving a reticulum of glial fibers filled with fat-laden phagocytes. In the most severe lesions, however, the glial fibers also undergo degeneration, eventually losing their processes and becoming vastly swollen. Large cavities may result under such circumstances. The

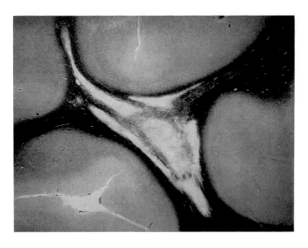

Fig. 110. Schilder's disease. Section of the cortex stained by the Weigert method showing how the process spares the cortex and the arcuate fibers immediately beneath.

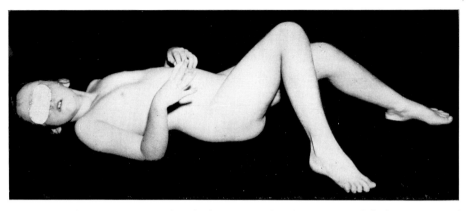

FIG. 111. Schilder's disease in a girl of nine years. The child is quite blind but the pupils react well to light. There is beginning papilledema but the ventriculograms are normal. Bilateral hemiplegia with strong spasm of the flexor muscles in right arm and both legs and athetoid movements of the right arm.

oligodendroglia are always affected. They show acute swelling and finally mucinoid degeneration, so that amorphous deposits of material giving the staining reactions of mucin are found in and about the lesions. In some cases, a few small blood vessels may be found surrounded by a number of lymphocytes infiltrating the perivascular sheath, but there is rarely any outspoken evidence of an inflammatory process and the cellular reaction is not more than can be explained by a degenerative process. It is stated that old lesions may become very dense and firm as a result of gliosis, but we have seen only the fresh and soft lesions. In most cases, especially those in which small disseminated lesions are found in the brain-stem and spinal cord, the cranial nerves may be demyelinated. In one case which the writer has studied, both eighth nerves were completely demyelinated. The optic nerves and the chiasm, however, are most frequently affected. We have seen papilledema due to increased intracranial pressure exactly the same as that associated with intracranial tumors, demyelination of the optic nerves and chiasm and demyelination of the optic nerves with edema of the papillae. Some of the changes in the optic nerves seem to be identical with those found in disseminated sclerosis. The meninges show nothing of interest. At most, a few lymphocytes may be found in the arachnoidal trabeculae and about the small blood vessels. Smith *et al.* state that chemical studies show depletion of the phospholipids and partial esterification of the cholesterol. The plasmalogens of the white matter were reduced in an amount greater than other phospholipids. Nelson *et al.* describe the findings revealed by electron microscopy.

Recent investigations of Schilder's material have led to the conclusion that his cases were heterogenous and some were really examples of meta-chromatic leucodystrophy.

Clinical Features.—This disease is usually sporadic but familial cases are reported. Possibly some of the familial cases would be placed in another category if they were studied more carefully.

The disease may develop at any age, but is perhaps most common in childhood. The two sexes are affected with equal frequency. The onset is not in any way characteristic. The first descriptions undoubtedly gave a false impression in that too much emphasis was placed upon the development of cortical blindness among the first symptoms. The disease not infrequently does develop in this way, producing first homonymous hemianopia and finally cortical blindness, but in my experience it more frequently begins with disturbances of motility. We have seen hemiplegia, brachial monoplegia, bilateral hemiplegia, cortical paraplegia and complete decerebrate rigidity. The extension of the process into the other parts of the brain is to be expected sooner or later. When the temporal lobes are both involved we find cortical deafness. Aphasia and apraxia are also common in the later stages of the disease. Involvement of the parietal lobe produces ataxia and cortical anesthesia. Convulsive seizures of various types may occur and constitute a very striking feature of some cases. Eventually mental deterioration becomes apparent and rapidly advances to complete dementia unless death puts a halt to the process. There is often loss of control of the emotional reactions with forced screaming, weeping or even laughter. Later, apathy, stupor and finally coma ensue. The optic nerves may escape injury, but more frequently they show definite changes. We have seen retrobulbar neuritis with temporal pallor and central scotomas, optic neuritis with edema of the disc and central scotomas and also true papilledema. Sixth nerve palsies are relatively common and seem to be due to increased intracranial pressure rather than to demyelination of the nerve. The other cranial nerves are rarely affected, but in one case we have observed complete bilateral deafness dependent upon demyelination of the eighth nerves. The bulbar muscles are frequently affected, but this is usually a pseudobulbar palsy associated with double hemiplegia rather than a result of a local process in the bulb. In most cases, the symptoms point to the cerebral hemispheres, but in certain cases which are characterized by multiple small plaques in the brain-stem, cerebellum and spinal cord, there may be cerebellar ataxia, intention tremor, scanning speech, nystagmus and paraplegia of spinal origin. Eventually, all cerebral function seems to be abolished. The child is completely paralyzed, incontinent and demented. Speech is lost and there seems to be blindness and deafness. Terminal coma is usual.

A remarkable feature of this disease must be emphasized since it may be of diagnostic value. In a small percentage of all cases there are signs and symptoms of increased intracranial pressure such as headache, vomiting, papilledema, palsy of one or both sixth nerves and slowing of the pulse and respiration. Symonds has suggested that the apparent papilledema seen in many cases is not a result of increased intracranial pressure but merely a local change in the optic nerve head, i.e. optic neuritis. This interpretation is correct in most cases, but there can be no doubt that true papilledema resulting from increased intracranial pressure does occur. The second case given below may be mentioned in this connection.

The course of the disease is usually subacute and averages about a year. We have seen one patient die within two weeks of the onset and a case is reported in which death resulted within eight days. It is claimed that some patients have lived ten years or more. As a rule, the symptoms are steadily progressive and show no tendency to recede once they are established. In some cases, the process seems to advance by a series of exacerbations, however, and in one case abstracted below, there was definite improvement for a time following an especially acute episode.

The spinal fluid is usually under increased pressure. There may be some increase in protein and a moderate increase in lymphocytes. There is rarely any fever and examination of the blood shows no leucocytosis.

Diagnosis.—It is very difficult to make the diagnosis during life, for other demyelinating and degenerative processes may cause almost exactly the same picture.

Prognosis.—As a rule, death results within one or two years after the onset. Remissions are described and it is claimed that the disease may become arrested for long periods. The prognosis is, however, always very bad if not entirely hopeless.

Treatment.—No effective treatment is known.

CASE HISTORY (U-19806. Path. 10500).—*Boy of two years developed internal squint; later, sudden weakness of the left leg. Incomplete recovery in six weeks. At two years and 10 months, sudden right hemiplegia with gradual improvement in next few weeks. Then progressive weakness, irritability, incontinence, dementia, stupor and finally death after operation at the age of theee years. Post-mortem examination revealed typical lesions of encephalitis periaxialis diffusa.*

D. B. was the second child of healty parents. One sibling, eighteen months older than the patient, was healthy and the family history was quite negative so far as could be learned. The patient enjoyed a good health until the age of two years when his mother noticed that his left eye turned inward. There were no other symptoms at that time, but a few months later the child suddenly fell to the floor and was unconscious for an hour. The next day it was noticed that his left leg was paralysed. The weakness gradually diminished and in six weeks the child could walk with only a slight limp. However, some weeks after this both legs seemed to grow stiff and the child began to walk on his toes in a spastic fashion. At the age of two years and 10 months he suddenly fell to the floor with a right hemiplegia. He was not unconscious and had no convulsions. There was some slight improvement, but the child was never able to walk after this episode. He soon began to grow weaker and finally could not sit up. Mental deterioration and irritability became evident. Speech was impaired and there was incontinence.

The child was examined for the first time at the age of three years. There was evident loss of weight and his general physical condition was very poor. His behavior indicated definite dementia, for it was difficult for him to grasp the simplest directions. At times he screamed without apparent cause and there was a great deal of irritability and restlessness. The cranial nerves were normal so far as could be determined, except for a left sixth nerve palsy. The pupillary reflexes were active, the optic nerve heads presented a normal appearance and there was certainly no gross loss of vision, although no proper tests of the fields were possible. The legs were spastic and almost completely paralysed. The child could not stand or walk. Indeed, it was impossible for the patient to sit up without support. The arms were weak and clumsy but not spastic. Speech was so much impaired that it was incomprehensible. There was double incontinence. The tendon reflexes were all exaggerated and there was a bilateral ankle clonus and Babinski reaction. The spinal fluid contained only five lymphocytes per cubic millimeter. The globulin test was negative and the pressure was not increased. The Wassermann test was negative.

The child rapidly grew worse, and soon sank into a stupor. The posterior fossa was explored but nothing to explain the patient's symptoms was found. Consciousness was not regained after the operation and the patient died the next day.

Post-mortem examination revealed the characteristic lesions of encephalitis periaxialis diffusa. There was gross and extensive lesions in both frontal and parietal lobes. The most advanced lesions were found in the superior portions of the hemispheres where the white matter of the paracentral lobules was involved, and the tissue was reduced to a spongy glial reticulum. The process was beginning to invade the temporal lobes and the occipital white matter showed well marked changes which must have caused some defects in the visual field. The corpus callosum was much softened. The internal capsules, the brainstem, cerebellum and grey matter, including the basal ganglia of the forebrain, were all intact. Histological examination revealed the usual changes.

The sudden onset of the paralyses with definite improvement, in at least the first instance, is of great interest and is rather difficult to understand in view of the anatomical changes.

CASE HISTORY (U-11887. Path. 9830).—*A boy of 14 years developed internal squint, intense headache, weakness and spasticity involving both legs and the left arm, pseudobulbar palsy, bilateral papilledema and bradycardia within the course of six weeks. Death resulted from failure of respiration due to compression of the medulla. Post-mortem examination revealed encephalitis periaxialis diffusa.*

O. W., schoolboy of 14 years, was admitted to the neurosurgical service of Dr. Walter Dandy on May 3, 1927. The complaints were headache and paralysis of the legs. About the middle of March the patient had begun to complain of severe headaches which were accompanied by vomiting. Soon vision because impaired, apparently because of diplopia. In April the left arm became weak and then the left leg was affected. A week or more later the right leg was also involved, so the patient could not walk. At about the same time difficulty in swallowing appeared and articulation became indistinct. Control of the bladder then became impaired and the patient voided involuntarily at times. On the first of May he was beginning to grow stuporous and was brought into the hospital.

Examination revealed a well developed, well nourished boy of 14 years. He was semistuporous and could not cooperate in the examination. When disturbed he screamed loudly in an explosive fashion. Pulse was between 50 and 60. Temperature normal. Respiration 20. The pupils were equal and reacted well. Vision could not be tested. Bilateral papilledema of 3 diopters was found with large and small hemorrhages and some exudate. There was paralysis of both sixth nerves and weakness of the soft palate, pharynx and tongue. The jaw jerk was increased. The left arm was weak and spastic, being held in the position of flexion usually seen in hemiplegia. Both legs were spastic and almost completely paralysed. The muscles of the trunk and spine were very rigid. The patient voided into the bed from time to time but the bladder was not distended. Sensibility could not be tested owing to the patient's mental condition, but it was evident that he could appreciate painful stimuli. All the tendon reflexes were grossly exaggerated in the legs and in the left arm. There was a bilateral extensor plantar response and ankle clonus. The abdominal reflexes were abolished.

Two days later the respirations fell to 12 per minute and the pulse rate to 30. Ventricular puncture was performed and clear fluid under great pressure was released. The pulse and respiration returned at once to normal, but within an hour both respiration and the pulse grew slow again and finally ceased.

Post-mortem examination revealed flattening of the convolutions and a well marked cerebellar pressure cone, with herniation of the medulla into the foramen magnum. There was great swelling of the right hemisphere which had caused herniation under the falx and displacement of the falx to the left. The right hemisphere contained two massive lesions occupying the white matter of the frontal, parietal and occipital lobes. The left hemisphere revealed only one very large lesion in the frontal lobe and a small one under the gyrus fusiforms. These were very soft and spongy. The most advanced lesions involved the white matter of the paracentral lobules and hence, were probably responsible for the paralysis of the legs and loss of control of the bladder. The optic nerves showed merely the usual changes of papilledema. Histologically, the lesions were quite typical. The striking feature of this case is the great increase of intracranial pressure which was due to the swelling of the right hemisphere and which led to death as a result of compression of the medulla by herniation into the foramen magnum.

BIBLIOGRAPHY

BOUMAN, L.: Encephalitis periaxialis diffusa. Brain, **47**:453, 1924.

————: Diffuse Sclerosis (Encephalitis periaxialis diffusa). John Wright and Sons, Bristol, 1934.

COLLIER, J. AND GREENFIELD, J. G.: Encephalitis periaxialis of Schilder. Brain, **47**:489, 1924.

FORD, F. R. AND BUMSTEAD, J. H.: Encephalitis periaxialis diffusa of Schilder. Bull. Johns Hopkins Hosp., **44**:443, 1929.

GASUL, B. M.: Schilder's disease: review of the literature and report of a case. Am. J. Dis. Child., **39**:595, 1930.

NELSON, E. *et al.:* Electron microscopic and histochemical studies in diffuse sclerosis (sudanophil type). Neurology, **12**:896, 1962.

POSER, C. M. AND VAN BOGAERT, L.: Natural history and evolution of the concept of Schilder's diffuse sclerosis. Acta psychiat. scand., **31**:285, 1956.

————: Diffuse-disseminated sclerosis in the adult. Jour. Neuropath. and Exp. Neurol., **16**:61, 1957.

SCHALTENBRAND, G.: Encephalitis periaxialis diffusa (Schilder). A case report with clinical and anatomic studies. Arch. Neurol. & Psychiat., **18**:944, 1927.

SCHILDER, P.: Zur Kenntnis der sogenannten diffusen Sclerose. Ztschr. f. d. ges. Neurol. u. Psychiat., **10**:1, 1912.

SMITH, J. K. *et al.:* A case of sudanophilic diffuse sclerosis with study of the brain lipids. Neurology, **11**:395, 1961.

STEWART, T. G., GREENFIELD, J. G. AND BLANDY, M. A.: Encephalitis periaxialis diffusa. Report of three cases with pathological examinations. Brain, **50**:1, 1927.

SYMONDS, C. P.: A contribution to the clinical study of Schilder's encephalitis. Brain, **51**:24, 1928.

URECHIA, C. I., MIHELESCU, S. AND ELEKES, N.: L'encéphalite périaxiale diffuse type Schilder. Encéphale, **19**:617, 1924. (Cases with bronze skin.)

WALSH, F. B.: *Loc. cit.*

ENCEPHALITIS PERIAXIALIS CONCENTRICA OF BALO

Definition.—This extraordinary condition is characterized by the peculiar lesions in the cerebral white matter described below and by clinical features similar to those of Schilder's disease, to which this disease is believed to be closely related.

Pathological Anatomy.—One section of the brain, the central white matter shows one or more large lesions which are roughly circular and are composed of alternating stripes of white and gray which form concentric circles. The outermost stripes are usually wider than the inner ones. They are interrupted where they impinge upon the cortex and the arcuate fibers are spared, as in Schilder's disease. Histological examination reveals that the gray stripes represent zones of degeneration and that the white stripes are composed of normal tissue. By serial sections it may be shown that these

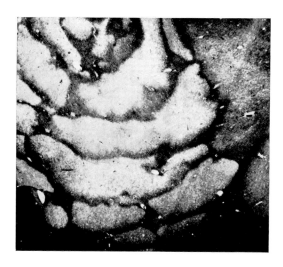

Fig. 112. Encephalitis periaxialis concentrica showing concentric zones of demyelination. (By the courtesy of Dr. Halsy Barker.)

circles are segments of globes, each of which surrounds a smaller globe and is, in turn, encompassed by a larger one forming in this way a structure comparable to that of an onion. In the center of each lesion is always found a small blood vessel. In the degenerated zones the myelin is destroyed and there are numerous microglia cells loaded with lipoid granules. Giant astrocytes are seen, as in Schilder's disease. The axis cylinders are preserved to a large extent. The basal ganglia, the cortex, brainstem and spinal cord are uninjured. Small areas of demyelination identical with those of disseminated sclerosis are sometimes found. In the neighborhood of the lesions, the adventitial sheaths of the small vessels are distended with lymphocytes and fat-laden phagocytes. The granules within the microglial cells stain with sudan red and are believed to be esters of cholesterol. The microscopic picture, therefore, apart from the gross form of the lesions, is identical with that of encephalitis periaxialis diffusa.

Spatz has attempted to explain these peculiar lesions on the basis of Liesegang's phenomenon, which is a colloidal reaction illustrated in the following experiment. If a mass of celloidin containing potassium bichromate is placed in a solution of silver nitrate, silver chromate will be deposited in the form of concentric rings. Spatz suggests by analogy that in encephalitis periaxialis concentrica we are dealing with a toxin, or a lipolytic ferment, which diffuses into the brain tissue from a small vessel and which is opposed by an antibody of some type, with the result that only alternating zones of myelin are destroyed. He further suggests that encephalitis periaxialis diffusa and disseminated sclerosis may be due to similar lipoid-destroying substances and that, in the former, this agent may diffuse into the brain from the ventricular system rather than from the blood vessels.

Clinical Features.—The disease seems to develop at any age and affects either sex. It begins as a rule with focal signs of a cerebral lesion such as hemiparesis, aphasia or hemianopia. These symptoms increase in severity and soon evidences of additional lesions appear. Bilateral hemiplegia with pseudobulbar palsy is often present at the end. Mental functions are unaltered in the early stages, but later the patient becomes forgetful, dull, stuporous and finally sinks into a terminal coma. Convulsive phenomena may occur and papilledema and other signs of increased intracranial pressure are frequent. The duration of the illness varies from a few weeks to a year. The diagnosis cannot be made during life and hence all reported cases have been fatal.

BIBLIOGRAPHY

BALO, J.: Encephalitis periaxialis concentrica. Arch. Neurol. & Psychiat., **19**:242, 1928.
BEHR, W.: Concentric sclerosis. Deutsch. Ztschr. Nervenh., **164**:480, 1950.
SPATZ, H. AND HALLERVORDEN, J.: Über die konzentrische Sklerose und die physikalischchemischen Faktoren bei der Ausbreitung von Entmarkungsprozessen. Arch. f. Psychiat., **98**:641, 1933.
SPATZ, H.: Über Leukoencephalitis concentrica. Allg. Ztschr. f. Psychiat. Bd., **95**:367, 1931.

CONGENITAL DEMYELINATING ENCEPHALOPATHY (MACKAY)

Mackay describes three cases in unrelated children in which the symptoms dated from birth. There were mental deficiency, convulsions and spasticity of the extremities. Death occurred at two, three and fourteen years. In two cases it was evident that the process was progressive. In the older child the process was apparently stationary. The anatomical changes included extensive demyelination of the cerebral white matter and also to some extent of the cortex with partial destruction of the axis cylinders. Gliosis was minimal and there was no evidence of an inflammatory process.

There are many varieties of such demyelinating processes. This one is mentioned to illustrate the fact that such conditions may be present at birth.

BIBLIOGRAPHY

MACKAY, R. P.: Congenital demyelinating encephalopathy. Arch. Neurol. & Psychiat., **43**:111, 1940.

DELANGE'S SYNDROME

DeLange has described the clinical and anatomical condition of three infants all of whom showed essentially the same picture and gives in abstract the findings in a case previously reported by Bruck. These children showed exceptionally large muscles and are described as resembling midget wrestlers. There was fluctuating rigidity of the trunk and extremities with retraction of the head. The tendon reflexes were not increased. The head was small and mental development was defective. They all died early.

At post-mortem, the cortex showed polygyria and microgyria. Numerous cavities, old and new, were found in the central white matter. The striatum and the corticospinal tracts had failed to develop. DeLange believes that this is a degenerative process which starts in intrauterine life.

BIBLIOGRAPHY

BRUCK, F.: Ueber einen Fall von congenitales Macroglosse conbinirt mit allegemeiner wahrer Muskelhypertrophie und Idiotie. Deutsch. med. Wchnschr., **15**:229, 1889.

DELANGE, C.: Congenital hypertrophy of the muscles, extrapyramidal motor disturbances and mental deficiency. Am. J. Dis. Child., **48**:243, 1934.

NEUROMYELITIS OPTICA

Definition.—There is an ill-defined group of conditions characterized clinically by optic neuritis and acute transverse myelitis and anatomically by disseminated areas of demyelination and often actual softening in the spinal cord and optic nerves. The lesions differ from those of disseminated sclerosis in their greater severity for they may cause complete tissue necrosis and cavity formation. No satisfactory name has yet been offered for this group of cases. Acute disseminated encephalomyelitis, disseminated encephalomyelomalacia and acute disseminated sclerosis are terms which have been applied to such conditions, but have also been applied to very different processes. Some cases in which the spinal lesions are very severe are called progressive necrosis of the spinal cord or necrotizing myelitis. The writer prefers to use the term neuromyelitis optica and to define it by the following description based upon several cases which he has studied.

Pathological Anatomy.—The lesions are found in the brain, the optic nerves and the spinal cord. The *spinal cord* is usually very severely affected. The lesions begin as small areas of demyelination in the white matter. Later, several lesions may coalesce, forming large, soft areas and frequently involving the gray matter. Eventually, the spinal cord may be completely liquefied for a large part of its length. The appearance of the cord, in such cases, resembles that resulting from extensive infarction but no changes in the blood vessels are to be found. The *optic nerves* are more or less completely demyelinated. Here the lesions are almost identical with those of disseminated sclerosis. If the process is confined to the proximal parts of the nerves or to the chiasm, the papilla shows only atrophy, but if the demyelination extends close to the bulb there is outspoken edema of the disc, i.e., optic neuritis. Rönne claims that only edema is found anterior to the cribriform plate. Apparently an active process in the distal third of the optic nerve which of course contains the central retinal vein, is apt to cause compression of that vessel and edema of the disc. Thus, retrobulbar neuritis and optic neuritis of this type are essentially the same and differ only in location and extent. One sometimes finds a number of small lesions in the *brain* which is, however, not severely damaged. There may be a few small areas of demyelination in the subcortical white matter. Where these approach the cortex they are apt to spare the arcuate fibers as do the lesions of Schilder's disease. A few small vessels may be surrounded by lymphocytes but there is nothing to suggest an inflammatory process and the only cellular reaction of any consequence is the proliferation of the astrocytes and of the microglia which become phagocytic and take up the broken down myelin.

Clinical Features.—This disease is apparently not restricted to subjects of any special age group, but is perhaps more common among children than among adults. As a rule it is a sporadic condition but McAlpine describes familial cases. In our experience girls have been affected more frequently than boys, but this is not mentioned by other authors.

The cardinal symptoms are transverse myelitis and optic neuritis. These may appear simultaneously or either may antedate the other. In our experience, loss of vision has usually been the first symptom. This may appear without any prodromata but is sometimes preceded by pain in and about the bulb. One or both eyes may be affected, but bilateral, simultaneous involvement is typical. On examination, a large central scotoma is usually found. The optic nerve head may appear quite normal at first or may show only mild congestion. As a rule, however, it is definitely swollen and edema-

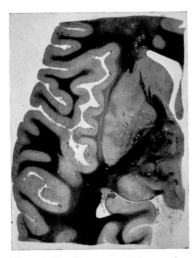

Fig. 113. Neuromyelitis optica. Horizontal section through the hemisphere. There are two small oval lesions in the white matter just lateral to the optic radiation. A smaller lesion is seen in the corpus callosum. (By the courtesy of Dr. Adolf Meyer.)

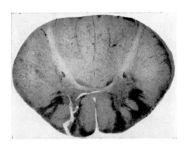

Fig. 114. Neuromyelitis optica. Section through the thoracic cord showing almost complete demyelination but no softening. Both white matter and gray matter are affected. Just below this level the cord was completely liquefied and just above this level, the lesions were discrete and involved only the white matter.

tous. The veins are engorged, hemorrhages are seen over the disc and white patches of exudate appear. The appearances are exactly the same as those of true papilledema due to increased intracranial pressure. After a few weeks, these changes begin to recede and leave either a diffuse pallor or a more or less definite temporal pallor. The loss of vision develops, as a rule, very rapidly. Within a few days after the onset the affected eye may be quite blind. The central scotoma, usually an absolute scotoma, enlarges, and the peripheral fields become constricted in most cases. Field defects of other types are rare, but we have seen bitemporal hemianopia indicating a lesion in the chiasm. Homonymous hemianopia is very unusual. The course of optic neuritis of this type is relatively brief, averaging perhaps several weeks to two or three months. There may be astonishing recovery. Patients who have been quite blind for more than a week may recover normal or nearly normal vision. Usually, however, recovery is only partial and in some cases the patient remains blind. Repeated attacks are very apt to occur and eventually vision is lost in most cases.

I have seen a little girl who was nearly blind in each eye. She described pleasing visual hallucinations which she could see at any time she wished. She liked to play the guitar and often saw scenes in which people were playing guitars.

The myelitis may precede the optic neuritis, may occur simultaneously or may follow after months or years. The onset is usually relatively acute and may be accompanied by some fever. Any level of the cord may be affected. The process is probably always a disseminated one, but the clinical signs usually indicate a transverse lesion. This is complete, as a rule, and frequently ascends rapidly for a time. In most cases there is complete paraplegia with anesthesia and loss of control of the bladder and rectum within the course of a new days. Paraplegia-in-extension, paraplegia-in-flexion and flaccid paraplegia with loss of tendon reflexes may all occur. The last usually indicates complete destruction of the lower segments of the cord. Several times we have observed definite cervical rigidity and Kernig's sign at the onset, and there is frequently some little local rigidity of the spine corresponding roughly to the level of the lesion. Definite root pains may also occur in such cases. The process may become arrested at any stage. In a number of cases death results from paralysis of respiration or from infection of the urinary tract. If the patient survives there may be much more improvement than one would have believed possible. Repeated attacks result in permanent paraplegia.

Symptoms referable to the brain are rare and mild, but we have observed them in several instances. The child may become drowsy and complain of headache, vertigo and diplopia. Convulsions sometimes occur. We have seen hemiparesis only once and have never observed cerebellar ataxia. The absence of cerebellar signs may be of some value in distinguishing this disease from disseminated sclerosis. Bulbar palsy occurred in one of our cases, and palsies of the sixth nerves are mentioned. Nystagmus seems to be very rare. Apparently definite signs of increased intracranial pressure have not been observed.

Some authorities state that there are no recurrences in this condition, but in our experience remissions and exacerbations are typical.

The spinal fluid usually contains between 20 and 50 lymphocytes, but a few leucocytes may be present in the early stages of the myelitis. In most cases, the cells disappear within a few weeks. In one case in which there was extensive softening of the spinal cord, there were several hundred cells in the spinal fluid some of which were leucocytes. No doubt these cells represented a reaction to the necrotic material rather than an evidence of an infectious process, for at post-mortem examination there were no inflammatory phenomena whatever. Twice we have observed in the myelogram evidences of partial obstruction at the level of an acute lesion which we attributed to swelling of the cord. Later, the myelogram was normal.

Diagnosis.—The diagnosis can scarcely be made without the presence of both the cardinal signs, optic neuritis and myelitis. When both of these signs are present and other causes such as the encephalomyelitis of measles and vaccinia can be ruled out, the diagnosis of neuromyelitis optica seems to be justified. In our experience, a tendency to recurrences is very characteristic and we believe that this disease may be strongly suspected in cases of recurrent transverse myelitis even without optic neuritis. Once or twice the tentative diagnosis of neuromyelitis, made on the basis of optic neuritis for which no cause could be found, has been confirmed by the subsequent development of myelitis. We believe, therefore, that the development of either myelitis or optic neuritis in childhood without demonstrable cause should suggest the possibility of this condition. Measles and vaccinia may of course give rise to myelitis and optic neuritis but in such cases the diagnosis is usually obvious, but disseminated sclerosis, especially acute disseminated sclerosis, offers a very difficult problem in differential diagnosis. The presence of radicular pains, the frequency of optic neuritis in contrast to retrobulbar neuritis, the greater loss of vision, the absence of cerebellar signs and the greater severity of the damage to the spinal cord, however, all favor the diagnosis of neuromyelitis optica. In children under ten years, disseminated sclerosis is unlikely. However, it is quite possible that these two diseases are really of essentially the same nature and that the condition described above is merely an atypical form of disseminated sclerosis, so that any distinction is purely arbitrary.

Prognosis.—The patient usually survives the first attack of myelitis and indeed, often makes a complete or nearly complete recovery. Even severe optic neuritis admits of substantial recovery of vision. The ultimate prognosis, however, seems to be unfavorable if not quite bad. As a rule the symptoms recur within a few months or years and eventually blindness and permanent paraplegia may be expected. Death is apt to result from paralysis of respiration or from intercurrent infection.

Treatment.—There is no specific treatment. Proper nursing care is essential to prevent bed sores and the bladder should be handled with the greatest care to prevent infection of the urinary tract.

CASE HISTORY—1 (U-45338-Ped. 79864-Path. 12822)—*Girl of nine years became blind within the course of a few days. About five days later, partial paralysis of the left leg, then paraplegia with retention of urine. Ascending paralysis and anesthesia finally involving the arms. Stupor and death from pyelitis after an illness of about six weeks. Post-mortem examination revealed the lesions of neuromyelitis optica.*

M. H. B., a girl of nine years, developed nausea and vomiting about August 25, 1932. These symptoms lasted only two days and then the child seemed to be as well as ever. On August 31, she complained that she could not see distinctly and within a few days she was almost completely blind. September 5, she said that her left leg felt "asleep" and it was found that there was partial paralysis of this leg. A few days later both legs were weak and she could not stand or walk. On September 12 she could not sit up without support and was incontinent of urine.

September 13, the patient was admitted to the hospital. She was found to be a thin, frail little girl who was rather irritable but showed no other mental disturbance. The pupils were dilated and reacted only very slightly to light. The optic nerve heads were elevated about 2 diopters, definitely edematous and congested. The retinal veins were somewhat dilated and tortuous. No hemorrhages or exudate were seen. Vision was lost in both eyes. The changes in the optic discs were similar to those of mild papilledema but were not severe enough to explain the complete loss of vision, so it was evident that more severe changes were present behind the papillae. The other cranial nerves were normal. The legs were quite paralysed and very flaccid. The abdominal muscles were also paralysed and the lower spinal muscles as well. The intercostal muscles were not affected. There was retention of urine with overflow incontinence. Complete anesthesia, including all modalities of sensibility, was found up to the umbilicus and some hypesthesia was present up to an indefinite level at about the nipple line. The knee and ankle jerks were present but feeble and the plantar reflexes were extensor. The abdominal reflexes were lost. No disturbances of motility or sensibility were found in the arms. There was a mild but definite cervical rigidity. The temperature ranged between 90° and 100° F. and the pulse between 80 and 130.

The Wassermann reaction in the blood was negative. The spinal fluid contained 60 cells of which 80 per cent were leukocytes and 20 per cent lymphocytes. There was an excess of globulin. The Wassermann test of the spinal fluid was also negative. The Queckenstedt test was negative. W. B. C. of 12000. Hb. 90 per cent. R. B. C. 4,500,000. Roentgenograms of the skull and spine negative. Urine negative.

The course was slowly down hill. The optic nerve heads became more and more elevated for a few weeks and then slowly began to recede, becoming pale and atrophic. The weakness slowly extended upward finally causing partial paralysis of the intercostal muscles, so that respiration was entirely abdominal. Finally the intrinsic muscles of the hands became weak and then the forearms were affected. The anesthesia extended upwards, parallel to the paralysis. All reflexes were lost except for the biceps jerk on either side. Spinal puncture on September 17 revealed 1300 cells, among which were phagocytes, leucocytes and lymphocytes. There were also a few red blood cells. Slowly the patient became stuporous and then comatose. The urinary tract became infected and finally the patient died on October 16, 1932.

Post-mortem examination revealed terminal pneumonia and an extensive infection of the genitourinary tract. The brain showed no gross abnormality. The spinal cord was reduced to a semifluid consistency in the lumbar and sacral segments. Scattered translucent areas in the posterior and lateral columns were seen in the thoracic and cervical segments. Histological examination revealed complete softening and disintegration of the lumbar and sacral segments. In the thoracic region, especially in the lower segments, there were disseminated areas of softening involving both the white and the gray matter which at some levels caused complete demyelination. Only the glial framework was preserved. In the cervical segments, the lesions were less severe and more discrete, and affected only the white matter. The myelin sheath was destroyed and the lesions were densely infiltrated with microglial cells loaded with lipoid products. A number of hypertrophied astrocytes were seen, some of which possessed two nuclei and thick branching processes. The axis cylinders were preserved to a large extent but were partially destroyed in the central parts of severe lesions. There was no perivascular infiltration except for the collections of phagocytes about the vessels. A few small lesions were found up as high as the decussation of the pyramidal tracts, but the medulla, pons and midbrain were not involved. The spinal nerve roots showed demyelination in the lower segments of the cord but were unchanged in the cervical and upper thoracic segments. The lumbar and sacral plexuses showed only a few degenerated fibers and the cervical plexus was normal.

The cerebellum showed no changes whatever, but the brain revealed a number of small areas of demyelination. These were confined to the subcortical white matter and were most numerous in the occipital lobes. The largest was not more than a centimeter in diameter. Where they approached the cortex they were sharply defined and did not involve the arcuate fibers, but in other directions they faded out gradually. The histological characteristics were identical with those of the lesions in the cervical cord. The myelin sheath was destroyed and the lesions were infiltrated with microglial phagocytes which were distended with lipoid products. No gliosis was found, but giant astrocytes with thick processes and often two nuclei were observed. There were no inflammatory phenomena. The optic nerves were extensively demyelinated and the chiasm was also demyelinated. The optic tracts were spared. The changes in the optic discs were indistinguishable from those of papilledema with atrophy, for the demyelination apparently had not extended anterior to the cribriform plate.

BIBLIOGRAPHY

BECK, G.: A case of diffuse myelitis associated with optic neuritis. Brain, **50**:687, 1927.

DAVISON, C. AND BROCK, S.: Subacute necrotic myelopathy. J. Neuropath. & Exp. Neurol., **3**:271, 1944.

HOFFMAN, H. L.: Acute necrotic myelopathy. Brain, **78**:377, 1955.

JAFFE, D. AND FREEMAN, W.: Spinal necrosis and softening of obscure origin. Arch. Neurol. & Psychiat., **49**:683, 1943.

McALPINE, D.: Familial neuromyelitis optica. Brain, **61**:430, 1938.

MILAN, SHERMITTE JR., ET HOROWITZ: La neuropticomyelite aigue; observation anatomico-clinique. Rev. neurol., **2**:257, 1931.

MILLER, H. AND EVANS, M.: Prognosis in acute disseminated encephalomyelitis with a note on neuromyelitis. Quart. J. Med., **22**:347, 1953.

MOERSCH, F. P. AND KERNOHAN, J. W.: Progressive necrosis of the spinal cord. Arch. Neurol. & Psychiat., **31**:504, 1934.

WALSH, F. B.: Neuromyelitis optica. An anatomical-pathological study of one case. Clinical studies of three additional cases. Bull. Johns Hopkins Hosp., **56**:183, 1935.

DISSEMINATED SCLEROSIS

Definition.—This is a disease of unknown etiology and a chronic remitting course, which is characterized by the development of disseminated

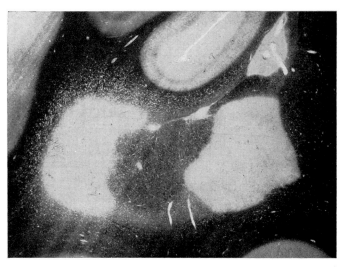

FIG. 115. Disseminated sclerosis. Small sharply defined plaques just beneath the cortex. These are old and the seat of dense gliosis.

areas of myelin destruction throughout the neuraxis, which obey no apparent law of distribution and which lead eventually to dense gliosis. They involve both the gray and white matter and never cause softening, cavity formation or extensive secondary degeneration.

Pathological Anatomy.—Externally, the brain and spinal cord show no gross abnormalities, but on palpation small areas of induration may usually be discovered. On section many large and small lesions are seen in all parts of the central nervous system. These are called *plaques*. They are dull gray or grayish red and seem more translucent than the surrounding tissues. Histological examination reveals that these areas are found in both white and gray matter and show no decided preference for any structures. Numerous plaques are always present in the central white matter of the cerebral hemispheres, the cortex, basal ganglia of the forebrain, the midbrains, pons and medulla. Many are found just under the ependyma of the ventricular system. The spinal cord shows a large number of foci. The cerebellum may be involved, but as a rule is not greatly damaged. The optic nerves are frequently attacked and less commonly sclerotic plaques are found in other cranial or spinal nerves. The lesions vary from a few millimeters to several centimeters in diameter and are quite irregular in shape. They bear no constant relation to the blood vessels although in many cases the earliest changes are in close relation to a small vessel. They are never of uniform age and fresh lesions may be found close beside very old lesions. In the most recent foci, the myelin sheaths are in process of disintegration and droplets of lipoid material are seen lying between the fibers or contained within phagocytic microglial cells. The axis cylinders may seem to be quite normal or may show some swelling or irregularity, but they are always in a better state of preservation than the myelin sheaths. The blood vessels in the region of the lesion may be unchanged or their adventitial sheath may be

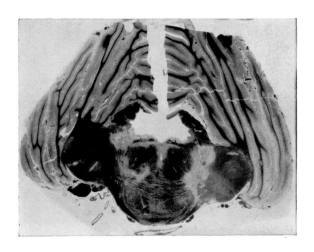

Fig. 116. Disseminated sclerosis. Fresher lesions in the pons involving both white and gray matter.

Fig. 117. Disseminated sclerosis. Plaque involving the posterior horn and the lateral column of the spinal cord.

distended with lymphocytes or fat-laden phagocytes. The granules in the phagocytes stain with sudan red. In the plaque and about its periphery there is usually beginning proliferation of the fibrous glial cells. Older plaques show no myelin or products of myelin destruction, but are represented by a dense network of glial fibers through which penetrate a number of naked axis cylinders. It is characteristic of this disease that there is little secondary degeneration and that the ganglion cells included in the lesions seem to suffer little damage.

Bornstein states that the addition of serum of a patient suffering from multiple sclerosis to a tissue culture of nervous tissue causes destruction of the myelin, whereas, the use of serum from normal persons has no such effect. When the multiple sclerosis serum is washed out of the culture, the myelin regenerates again.

Clinical Features.—There is little reason to believe that morbid heredity plays any part in this disease and it is rare to find two cases in one family. The so-called familial cases usually are shown by post-mortem examination to be of a very different nature, i.e., familial spinocerebellar ataxias. Males and females are affected alike. The disease is rarely recognized in childhood and its description is omitted from most textbooks of pediatrics. The writer, however, has seen several children who developed definite symptoms between the ages of nine and fifteen years and who subsequently ran a course quite typical of disseminated sclerosis. Among adults there are three common forms of onset: (1) With cerebellar symptoms; (2) With paraplegia; (3) With retrobulbar neuritis. In children we have seen the last type most frequently.

Arnouts states that he has found 178 cases in the literature in which a diagnosis of disseminated sclerosis had been made in childhood. In ten instances, this diagnosis had been verified at post-mortem examination. Arnouts adds another case with post-mortem examination. Van Bogaert describes a case in which the onset was at twelve years and the anatomical changes were typical.

Relative or absolute central scotomas develop very rapidly, so the child may be nearly blind within a few days. If the lesion is near the chiasm, the optic disc is quite normal or, at most, may show merely slight congestion, but if the plaque is in the nerve close to the cribriform plate the disc may become definitely edematous. The last is uncommon, however. In any case, within a few weeks, congestion and edema disappear and the nerve head grows pale, especially on the temporal side in the region of the papillomacular bundle. Vision improves as the process recedes and may be quite normal later, even when the temporal side of the disc is very pale. These changes may be confined to one eye or may affect both in succession at variable intervals. The simultaneous involvement of both eyes is unusual. Repeated attacks occur in many cases.

Kennedy and Carter found that of thirty children who had had optic neuritis, seven developed multiple sclerosis. In five, this disease became evident within three weeks and two years; within twelve years in one, and sixteen years in another.

In many cases, the child now enjoys a remission of months or even years, during which health seems to be completely restored. In other cases the disease runs a progressive course and one symptom rapidly succeeds another. Weakness and spasticity are usually early symptoms. As a rule, there is spastic paraparesis, but hemiplegia or monoplegia also occur. The onset of such hemiplegias may be so abrupt as to suggest a cerebral vascular lesion. The tendon reflexes are increased, ankle clonus is easily elicited and the plantar responses are of the extensor type. The abdominal reflexes may be lost in disseminated sclerosis, although this symptom is probably not so constant as many authors claim. In rare cases in which the cervical or lumbar enlargement is the site of a rapidly developing process, the paralysis may be of the flaccid type for a while and the reflexes may be reduced or abolished. Even in such cases spasticity usually develops later. Ataxia is also a very common symptom, and in most cases it is of the cerebellar type. The intention tremor is very characteristic. Ataxias due to loss of proprioceptive sensibility are also not uncommon. In many cases ataxia develops suddenly in one arm so that this limb is quite useless within a few days after the onset. Numbness and paresthesias are usually present to some extent, but cutaneous anesthesia is very rare. However, it is not uncommon to find a high degree of astereognosis, loss of sense of position, vibration and two-point discrimination. As a result of the weakness and ataxia the gait becomes altered. All combinations of the cerebellar, sensory and spastic gait may occur, but in most cases cerebellar incoordination is most prominent. The base is broad, the patient staggers from side to side and there are coarse oscillations of the head and trunk. Station is unsteady and the Romberg sign may be present. Speech is often altered in a characteristic manner. The syllables are produced slowly and separately with a rhythmical accentuation which is described as scanning or staccato speech. Articulation may also be indistinct but there is rarely as much slurring as in general paresis. Phonation and deglutition are usually not severely impaired. Nystagmus is a very common and characteristic sign. It is, as a rule, horizontal, rhythmical, synchronous in both eyes and brought out best by lateral deviation. Diplopia is common but usually transient. Anterior internuclear ophthalmoplegia is not uncommon in disseminated sclerosis and is a very typical sign. On the attempt at lateral gaze in this condition the abducting eye moves out well but shows nystagmoid oscillations, whereas the adducting eye cannot move beyond the midline. Convergence is preserved. This condition may be unilateral or bilateral. It is attributed to a lesion in the medial longitudinal fasciculus. There is rarely more than a mild degree of deafness but the appreciation of high tones may be considerably impaired. Some patients are subject to severe recurrent attacks of vertigo which may last for several weeks and are accompanied by vomiting. These attacks are probably due to the development of plaques in the medulla. Transient disturbances of sphincter control may occur from time to time and eventually some patients become entirely incontinent. Paresthesias of three different types are seen. In the common type, they are present constantly for weeks or months. In another type, we seem to be dealing with a discharge of sensory mechanisms for the paresthesias appear in brief paroxysms and extend over one side of the body or into one extremity. The third type is described as Lhermitte's sign. Here bending the head forward induces tingling, often described as resembling a gentle electric shock, which spreads down the back and into the extremities.

It is an old observation that hysterical symptoms are sometimes seen in the early stages of this disease and often obscure the real nature of the illness for a time. No doubt, the frequency of such symptoms has been much exaggerated, for it is easy to understand how variable symptoms in an emotionally unstable patient may erroneously be attributed to hysteria. There can be no doubt, however, that symptoms which may be relieved by suggestion occur not infrequently in this disease. In advanced cases of disseminated sclerosis, a mild dementia is commonly found. The patient becomes apathetic, childish and abnormally content with invalidism. There is sometimes a quiet euphoria with facile laughter. More rarely, irritability and impulsive misbehavior are prominent.

The course of the disease is not always the same. In young patients, the process usually advances by a series of acute subacute exacerbations, each one followed by a more or less complete remission. Each exacerbation, however, leaves some degree of permanent disability and it is the gradual accumulation of such residua that causes the progressive advance of the disease. All the symptoms may advance or recede at the same time or one symptom may develop while others are disappearing. In some patients, on the contrary, the course is slowly progressive and no improvement is ever observed. This gradual progression is rare in young persons. As a rule, the disease is afebrile. There is no leucocytosis unless there is some complicating infection.

The absence of certain symptoms is no less characteristic of disseminated sclerosis than the presence of others. For example, pain, other than that due to over-strain of weak muscles, very rarely occurs although trigeminal neuralgia, i.e., tic douloureux, is described in adults. Complete cutaneous anesthesia is practically never found. Muscular atrophy, except for that due to disuse, is rare, and well marked fascicular twitchings are exceptional. Complete blindness, complete dementia, complete loss of function of cranial nerves and complete paralysis, are all at least uncommon. Convulsive seizures, focal or general, and petit mal are so rare that it has been suggested that they are due merely to the chance combination of epilepsy and disseminated sclerosis. Wilson and MacBride, however, have published seven cases in which convulsions occurred. I have seen a small number of cases in which local tonic fits occurred. These were usually mild and sometimes minimal. There was no alteration of consciousness during such attacks. Mild sensory discharges also occur. The rarity of these features is probably due to the fact that the plaques of disseminated sclerosis are not so destructive as the lesions of some other diseases and do not cause much irritation. Anderman *et al.* describe paroxysmal attacks of dysarthria and ataxia of ten to twenty seconds' duration which they ascribe to sudden disturbances in the cerebellar mechanism. Zeldowicz describes sudden, recurrent attacks of paralysis, involving the legs more frequently than the arms, of a few minutes' duration. Uveitis occurs occasionally in patients who have characteristic signs and symptoms of disseminated sclerosis, but we have never established the diagnosis by post-mortem examination.

The terminal stage in this disease is quite different from the earlier stages. The patient is grossly demented or completely unconscious. Motor functions are lost. The patient is helpless. The muscles are wasted and atonic. Contractures are always present. The tendon reflexes are lost. There is complete incontinence. Vision is lost. Multiple cranial nerve palsies are evident.

Acute disseminated sclerosis is described. This seems to give rise to the same symptoms seen in the chronic relapsing type, but the symptoms are more severe. The course is brief and death may occur within a few months. It seems that the lesions are similar to those of the chronic type, but are more destructive.

Mackey *et al.* describe benign forms of multiple sclerosis. They state that some cases cease to progress after a time leaving the patient only partially disabled. I have seen a patient who had only spasticity at the left ankle who had no additional symptoms for 20 years and then developed rapidly advancing symptoms and was completely helpless. At postmortem examination innumerable typical plaques were found throughout the nervous system. They also mention cases in which the patient makes a complete recovery and remains well thereafter. I have seen a girl who had severe symptoms at the age of 12 years. She improved and made a complete recovery. Re-examination after 14 years revealed no evidence of disease. A third type is described in which no signs or symptoms of this disease are discovered but when the patient died of some other illness, typical lesions are found at post-mortem examination.

The spinal fluid may be quite normal, but during a period in which the disease is active, there is sometimes a moderate increase in lymphocytes and a positive globulin reaction. Rarely, the cell count may rise to sixty, eighty or one hundred per cubic millimeter. A paretic gold curve has been considered to be characteristic by some authors but this is inconstant. Bronsky states that the gamma globulin is increased in the spinal fluid and the albumin is reduced in those cases in which the gold curve is abnormal. The partition of the serum proteins is normal.

Namerow describes the study of a patient who had retrobulbar neuritis due to multiple sclerosis. It was found that vision deteriorated when the body temperature was elevated whether the elevation was spontaneous or induced.

Diagnosis.—In our experience, the development of central scotomas during childhood without apparent cause should always arouse suspicions of disseminated sclerosis. The family history is, of course, important in ruling out Leber's optic atrophy and other inherited conditions. If the visual disturbances improve or disappear after a few weeks and then, after a remission of years or months, symptoms referable to the cerebellar apparatus or the pyramidal tracts develop which also show a tendency to remissions and exacerbations, the diagnosis would seem to be justified. It has been pointed out above that the absence of certain symptoms is also important. The most important conditions to be considered in differential diagnosis are disseminated encephalomyelitis, Leber's optic atrophy, the hereditary ataxias, Schilder's disease, neuromyelitis optica and the rare Pelizaeus-Merzbacher disease. Acute disseminated encephalomyelitis usually follows an acute illness such as measles, is associated with fever and the active phase lasts only a short time. The symptoms do not recur. The hereditary ataxias are distinguished by a positive family history and by a steadily and slowly progressive course. Leber's optic atrophy is also hereditary and, as a rule, the symptoms are all referable to the eyes. Pelizaeus-Merzbacher disease is very slowly progressive and begins in many cases in early childhood. The family history is positive, but it is said that there are remissions in some cases. Schilder's disease, as a rule, runs a more rapid course than disseminated sclerosis, is marked by signs of massive cerebral lesions rather than of spinal lesions and does not commonly cause cerebellar ataxia. Neuromyelitis optica is marked by more severe and more acute lesions in the spinal cord and usually produces definite swelling of the optic nerves rather than retrobulbar neuritis. It is estimated that from one third to three fourths of all patients with unexplained retrobulbar neuritis eventually develop unmistakable evidences of disseminated sclerosis, and some authorities claim that this is the outcome in every case. In my experience these figures are much too high.

Prognosis.—The outlook is unfavorable, but not absolutely bad, for although most cases progress to complete disability within a few years, every neurologist of experience has observed instances in which the disease has remained stationary for long periods. The prognosis as regards the duration of life is reasonably good for this disease rarely kills promptly or directly.

Treatment.—It is scarcely worthwhile to describe the many methods of treatment which have been advocated. Suffice it to say that no remedies are known which are capable of modifying the course of the disease in the slightest degree.

CASE HISTORY (U-40053).—*Girl of ten years developed bilateral central scotomas of brief duration. At twelve years paresthesias and ataxia of arms and legs. Recovery in six months. At thirteen years, return of scotomas for a month and diplopia. At fourteen years scanning speech. Later, intention tremor and ataxic gait. At age of fifteen years, there was euphoria, temporal pallor of optic nerve heads, nystagmus, scanning speech, intention tremor, cerebellar gait, increased tendon reflexes, extensor plantar responses and loss of abdominal reflexes.*

R. B., a girl of ten years, developed bilateral central scotomas without apparent cause. Vision was greatly reduced for about two weeks and then gradually returned to normal. There were no further symptoms until the age of twelve years when numbness developed in the last two digits of the left hand. A month later the right hand was affected in the same way. Soon after this both arms became clumsy and tremulous. The patient dropped things from her hands and could not use her knife and fork. Her gait was very unsteady at this time. Within six months all these symptoms had disappeared once more. At the age of thirteen years, central scotomas developed again in both eyes. This time vision was much reduced for a month and temporal pallor of the optic discs was found some weeks later. Diplopia appeared shortly afterwards. The patient has not been free from symptoms since. At the age of fourteen years speech became impaired, and six months later the hands grew tremulous and gait unsteady. The patient could not hold a glass to her lips or write her name. Spontaneous flexor spasms began to occur in both legs.

The last examination at the age of fifteen years revealed some apathy and a mild euphoria but no definite intellectual deterioration. Vision was 10/20 in both eyes. The visual fields were normal, but there was definite pallor of the temporal side of both optic nerve heads. The left eye could not be fully abducted and there was diplopia in the left fields. On deviation to either side a coarse horizontal nystagmus was produced. When sitting up with the arms outstretched the trunk was unsteady and the arms oscillated unduly. There was a typical and very violent intention tremor on either side and outspoken dysdiadochokinesis. The legs were spastic and somewhat weak, left more than the right. The heel-knee test revealed severe ataxia on both sides. The station was unsteady and the patient required support when the eyes were closed. The gait showed typical cerebellar ataxia with oscillation of the head and trunk as well as spasticity. The speech was not greatly altered, but showed some tendency to scanning. Sensibility was intact except for complete loss of vibratory sense in the left leg below the pelvis and almost complete loss on the right. The tendon reflexes were universally increased and the knee and ankle jerks were greatly exaggerated. The abdominal reflexes were not elicited. Both plantar responses were typically extensor and there was bilateral ankle clonus.

BIBLIOGRAPHY

ADIE, W. J.: The aetiology and symptomatology of disseminated sclerosis. Brit. M. J., 2:997, 1932.

————: Discussion on disseminated sclerosis. Brit. M. A. Meeting Sec. Neurol. Brit. M. J., 2:269, 1932.

ANDERMANN, F., COSGROVE, J., LLOYD SMITH, D. AND WALTERS, A. M.: Paroxysmal dysarthria and ataxia in multiple sclerosih. Neurology, 9:211, 1959.

ARNOUTS, CH.: La sclérose en plaques chez l'enfant. Acta Neurol. et Psychiat. Belg., 59:796, 1959.

BORNSTEIN, M. B.: Tissue culture approach to demyelinative disorders. Nat. Canc. Inst. Monogr., 1963, No. 11.

————: A myelin-destroying factor in the blood of patients suffering from multiple sclerosis. Trans. Tissue Culture Assn., June, 1962, Washington, D. C.

BRAIN, W. R.: Disseminated sclerosis—A critical review. Quart. J. Med., 23:343, 1930. (Full references.)

BREGER, B. C. AND LEOPOLD, I. H.: Incidence of uveitis in multiple sclerosis. Amer. Jour. Ophthal., 62:540, 1966.

BRONSKY, D. et al.: Partition of the proteins in multiple sclerosis. J. Lab. Clin. Med., 56:382, 1960.

CARTER, H. R.: Multiple sclerosis in childhood. Am. J. Dis. Child., 71:138, 1946.

DRAKE, W. E. AND MACRAE, D.: Epilepsy in multiple sclerosis. Neurology, 11:810, 1961.

GALL, J. C. et al.: Multiple sclerosis in children. Pediatrics, 21:703, 1958.

HASSIN, G. B. AND BASSOE, P.: Multiple degenerative softenings versus multiple sclerosis. Arch. Neurol. & Psychiat., 7:613, 1922.

ISLER, W.: Multiple sclerosis in childhood. Helvet. paediat. acta, 16:412, 1961.

KENNEDY, C. AND CARTER, S.: Optic neuritis in multiple sclerosis. Pediatrics, 28:377, 1961.

LOW, N. L. AND CARTER, S.: Multiple sclerosis in children. Pediatrics, 18:24, 1956.

MACKAY, R. P. AND HIRANO, A.: Forms of benign multiple sclerosis. Arch. of Neurol., 17:588, 1967.

MARBURG, O.: Die Sogenannte "akute multiple Sklerose" (Encephalitis periaxialis scleroticans). Jahrb. f. Psychiat. u. Neurol., 27:211, 1906.

MOYA, G.: Familial cases of multiple sclerosis. Acta Neurol. et Psychiat. Belg., 62:40, 1962.

NAMEROW, N. S.: Circadian temperature rhythm and vision in multiple sclerosis. Neurology, 18:417, 1968.

PRATT, R., COMPSTON, N. AND McALPINE, D.: Familial incidence of disseminated sclerosis. Brain, 74:191, 1951.

RAWSON, M. D. AND GOLDFARB, G.: Treatment of acute retrobulbar neuritis with corticotropin. Lancet, 2:1044, 1966.

SCHUMACHER, G. et al.: Symposium on multiple sclerosis and demyelinating diseases. Am. J. Med., 12:499, 1952.

SPILLER, W. G.: The subacute form of multiple sclerosis. Arch. Neurol. & Psychiat., 1:219, 1919.

SYMONDS, C. P.: The pathological anatomy of disseminated sclerosis, Brain, 47:36, 1924.

VAN BOGAERT, L. ET MATTHYS, ET.: La sclerose en plaques chez L'enfant. Acta Neurol. et Psychiat. Belg., 59:815, 1959.

WALSH, F. B.: *Loc. cit.*

ZELDOWICZ, L.: Early signs of multiple sclerosis. Canad. M. A. J., 84:937, 1961.

RETROBULBAR NEURITIS

Definition.—Under this title we shall discuss: (1) The relatively common type of retrobulbar optic neuritis without edema of the disc which develops without apparent cause in young adults and less commonly in adolescents; and (2) The less common but apparently closely related condition in which there is definite swelling of the optic nerve head in addition to the disturbances of vision. Both of these conditions are frequently associated with disseminated sclerosis, neuromyelitis optica and Schilder's disease, but also occur without any other symptoms whatever. It is understood that the following discussion does not include papilledema due to increased intracranial pressure, or the forms of optic neuritis, or retrobulbar neuritis, of known etiology such as those due to lead poisoning, thallium, wood alcohol, vitamin deficiency, syphilis, meningitis or acute infectious diseases. Moreover, the various types of neuroretinitis, or papillitis, where the process is anterior to the cribriform plate are omitted.

Pathological Anatomy.—The anatomical process in retrobulbar neuritis is apparently identical with that so commonly associated with disseminated sclerosis. The optic nerve is the seat of a patchy demyelination. This process calls forth an extensive reaction of the microglia with phagocytosis of the products of lipoid destruction and later proliferation of the astrocytes causing dense gliosis. The axis cylinders are not injured to the same extent as the myelin and hence there is little or no secondary degeneration. If the process is confined to the proximal two-thirds of the optic nerve, there is no immediate change in the optic papilla and it is only after several weeks that optic atrophy becomes apparent. This is apt to be most evident on the temporal side of the disc. In certain cases, there is outspoken edema of the optic papilla in addition to the demyelination behind the cribriform plate. Apparently, this is due to the extension of the process peripherally into the distal third of the optic nerve which contains the central retinal vein and compression of this vein by the swelling of the tissues which accompanies the acute stages of the demyelination. In such cases, the edema of the optic disc is identical anatomically with the edema seen in cases of tumor of the brain.

Etiology.—I may say at once that the cause is unknown. If one follows patients suffering from retrobulbar neuritis for a period of years, a number of them will eventually develop evidences of disseminated sclerosis or other demyelinating disease. I do not believe, however, that we are justified in making a diagnosis of disseminated sclerosis on the basis of retrobulbar neuritis.

Clinical Features.—*Retrobulbar neuritis without edema of the disc* is most common during early adult life, but we have also observed a number of cases in adolescents and even in children. As a rule, the first symptom is blurring of vision in one or both eyes, but in some cases there is pain in and above the affected eye and discomfort is produced by ocular movements for a few days. The reduction of vision is very rapid in most instances and frequently it may be impossible for the patient to read within two or three days after the onset. The process is usually unilateral and involvement of the second eye, if it occurs, is apt to be deferred for weeks or months. On examination the pupils are usually found to be equal and circular. They may react equally to light, but the pupil of the affected eye is frequently a bit sluggish and tends to expand rapidly even when the light is still directed into the pupil. This is called a rebounding pupil. Central vision is found to be grossly reduced or abolished. The visual fields are usually normal in outline but central scotoma is almost always present. This is usually relative at first and later becomes absolute. The absolute scotoma is surrounded in most cases by a relative scotoma. Scotomas are occasionally found in the peripheral field of vision. In a few cases, the visual fields indicate that the process has extended into the chiasm, for we may have more or less definite bitemporal hemianopia often associated with central scotomas. Homonymous hemianopias are very rare. The optic disc at the onset may be perfectly normal but in many instances it shows slight congestion and some little haziness of the margins. Later, pallor appears, which is always most evident on the temporal side of the disc where the papillomacular bundle lies. This is usually evident in from two to four weeks. Strangely enough this pallor bears no apparent relation to the disturbances of vision. The patient may regain normal vision despite the fact that there is persisting pallor of the temporal side of the disc. There is a strong tendency for recovery in retrobulbar neuritis of this type. Usually within a few weeks, vision begins to improve. The scotoma may contract and finally disappear, leaving central vision of 10/20 or even 20/20. Rarely, if ever, does the patient lose vision permanently in the first attack, but it is not unusual for some reduction of vision to persist. Unfortunately, the prognosis is not as cheerful as these statements might indicate, for there is a strong tendency for the trouble to recur. When disturbances of vision recur, they again tend to affect the central portions of the fields, but the form and size of the scotomas vary from time to time, indicating that the process is not always located in exactly the same spot. In some instances, there are repeated attacks at brief intervals. In others, the recurrences appear at long intervals of many years. Again the patient may recover and have no further symptoms at any time. Vision may be extremely dim for several years and yet may improve to a useful level. It is impossible to say with confidence at the present time just how many of these patients finally succumb to disseminated sclerosis, but the longer they are kept under observation, the higher the incidence becomes. Retrobulbar neuritis also occurs in association with Schilder's disease and in neuromyelitis optica, but much less commonly than in disseminated sclerosis.

Retrobulbar neuritis with edema of the disc behaves in very much the same way as retrobulbar neuritis without edema. It is probably correct to state that the process seems to be somewhat more rapid and more severe and tends to involve both eyes at the same time. It is not unusual to see complete loss of vision develop within two days or less, in one or both eyes. As a rule, definite central scotomas are found which are almost always absolute. These may appear before the optic discs show definite edema. The peripheral fields of vision may be spared, but usually there is definite constriction of the outlines of the fields and, in most cases, vision is either lost or reduced to mere light perception at some stage of the process. In a few cases we have seen the lower half of the visual field completely lost and rarely the upper half of the field is involved first. The swelling of the papilla may be mild or severe. In most cases it is morphologically identical with that seen in cases of increased intracranial pressure. There may be great congestion and tortuosity of the retinal veins, hemorrhages over the disc and adjacent retina, deposits of exudate, obliteration of the physiological cupping and of the disc margins. In a small percentage of cases, blindness results from the first attack, but in most, good vision is restored after a few weeks. The writer has seen complete recovery of vision in an eye which had been blind for nearly a week. There is a striking tendency to recurrence. Some of these patients have several attacks of optic neuritis during a period of months and are apt to become quite blind. Others have no recurrences in the next few years. Striking improvement may occur after vision has been very dim for several years. In a large percentage of these children symptoms referable to the spinal cord or brain appear within a few months after the onset. The syndrome most commonly observed is that of neuromyelitis optica but the neurological picture is subject to considerable variation.

In both types of optic neuritis mentioned above, there may be a little increase in the protein of the spinal fluid and a slight pleocytosis during the active stage of the disease.

Diagnosis.—Retrobulbar neuritis without edema of the discs must be distinguished from that due to various poisons such as lead, arsenic, thallium and organic toxins such as methyl alcohol and from the retrobulbar neuritis which occurs in acute disseminated encephalomyelitis. It is rarely associated with neurosyphilis. In many cases adenomas of the hypophysis and neoplasms pressing upon the intracranial portion of the optic nerve, give rise to central scotomas and simulate for a time the condition described above. The value of roentgenograms of the sella is therefore obvious and the possibility of neoplasm should always be considered even when the roentgenograms are quite negative. Leber's optic atrophy may cause a condition which is not easily distinguished from the retrobulbar neuritis described above. A full family history, therefore, is important.

When there is edema of the optic nerve head, the first consideration is naturally to rule out tumor of the brain and other conditions giving rise to increased intracranial pressure. In such cases, however, the edema of the optic disc precedes the reduction of vision by a relatively long interval, and the fields of vision are reduced gradually by concentric constriction, the central portions of the fields being involved very late.

Prognosis.—The prognosis in typical cases of retrobulbar neuritis without edema of the disc is not unfavorable and it is unusual for gross impairment of vision to persist. It must be kept in mind that recurrences develop in many cases and that disseminated sclerosis may appear even after an interval of many years. In most cases, useful vision persists for long periods.

In the writer's experience the outlook in retrobulbar neuritis with edema of the disc is less favorable. In many cases the patient has become blind within a few years after the onset. When lesions develop in other parts of the nervous system these are apt to be severe and destructive and give rise to the picture of acute disseminated sclerosis or neuromyelitis optica in most cases.

Treatment.—It may be said very briefly that there is no treatment of established value.

BIBLIOGRAPHY

KENNEDY, C. AND CARROLL, F. D.: Optic neuritis in children. Tr. Am. Acad. Ophth., **64**:700, 1960.

RÖNNE, H.: Neuritis retrobulbaris. Kurzes Handbuch der Ophthalmologie, **5**:645, Berlin, Springer, 1930.

WALSH, F. B.: Neuromyelitis optica. An anatomical-pathological study of one case. Clinical studies of three additional cases. Bull. Johns Hopkins Hosp., **56**:183, 1935.

————: *Loc. cit.*

WOODS, A. AND ROWLAND, W. M.: Etiological study of a series of optic neuropathies. J.A.M.A., **97**:375, 1931.

DISSEMINATED ENCEPHALOMALACIA WITH CAVITY FORMATION

Definition.—This is a condition of obscure etiology, apparently peculiar to infancy, in which multiple softenings develop in the subcortical white matter giving rise eventually to cavities.

Etiology.—Stevenson and McGown have described seven cases of this condition but offer no final conclusions as regards it cause. In these cases the symptoms were evident at birth or soon afterwards. In my cases, the onset was definitely postnatal. Sternberg is inclined to think birth trauma is to blame. Courville attributes the cystic cavities to hemorrhages in the cerebral white matter resulting from anoxia at birth. Winkelmann and Moore describe one case and compare it to "swayback" in newborn lambs. Baker and Noran report another case which they believe represents the end stage of equine encephalomyelitis. Benda states that all of these cases are not necessarily the result of the same cause and thinks that birth injury is sometimes responsible. I believe that this is a degenerative process with certain similarities to Schilder's disease. Lumsden's careful study of this condition is of great interest.

In one of my cases, the onset was associated with a severe attack of pyelitis; in another, the patient had a brief febrile illness 3 weeks before the first obvious neurological signs appeared and in the third case, nothing to suggest infection was elicited in the history. No evidence of morbid heredity was to be found in the family history in these cases. The anatomical changes are not those of vascular disease or inflammation. It is more likely that we are dealing with a degenerative process of distinctive character which presents certain resemblances to Schilder's disease. The paper of Crome and Williams seems to favor this view for they show that this is a familial disease.

Pathological Anatomy.—In three cases which the writer studied, the brain was grossly shrunken and there was an excess of fluid in the subdural space. In one instance, there was a subdural hematoma which was well organized and about 0.5 cm thick overlying the right hemisphere, but in the other two cases the meninges were normal. There were no thrombi in the dural sinuses. The convolutions of the cortex were very soft and shrunken, being separated by wide and deep sulci. On section innumerable cavities were found in all parts of either hemisphere. These varied in size from gross cysts 2 or 3 cm in diameter to those so small they were just visible. The smaller ones were confined to the white matter of the cortical convolutions, but the larger lesions which were also probably the older lesions, extended into the cortex which was, in some places, entirely destroyed and also penetrated deeply into the central white matter of the hemisphere. The fresher lesions contained necrotic tissue and were not sharply outlined, but the older lesions were filled with clear fluid and showed a rough fibrous capsule. A number of the large lesions communicated with the ventricular system through large defects in the ependyma, but none of them opened into the subarachnoid space. No cavities were found in the basal ganglia of the forebrain, in the brainstem or spinal cord, but in one case there were large lesions in the lateral hemispheres of the cerebellum. Histological examination revealed that the earliest

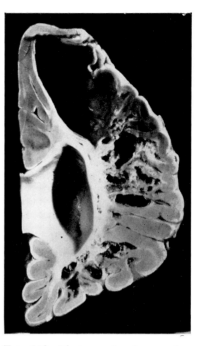

Fig. 118. Photograph of a section through the frontal lobe of the child whose history is given below. There is a very large cavity lined by rough fibrous tissue in the upper portion of the lobe. This is separated from the pia by only a thin layer of glial tissue. Below this smaller and fresher cavities are seen, involving the white matter and beginning to destory the cortex.

changes were those of degeneration of the myelin with proliferation of the microglia and astrocytes. The latter showed thick processes and sometimes two nuclei and the former were distended with the debris of broken down myelin. Later, the cerebral tissue was entirely destroyed and a ragged cavity resulted which was crossed by fibrous trabeculae. Eventually, a cavity filled with clear fluid resulted. The walls of the cavity were formed of a membrane composed of glial fibers and connective tissue. The tissues surrounding such cavities were shrunken and the small blood vessels were all surrounded by large spaces usually filled with microglial phagocytes. Astrocytes were present in large numbers and degenerative changes of mild degree were found in the nerve cells and fibers. The descending fiber tracts from the cortex were all completely, or nearly completely, degenerated and in one case there was scarcely any normal myelin to be found in the brain. The pyramidal tracts invariably showed secondary degeneration. No lesions were found in the basal ganglia, the brain-stem or the spinal cord except those resulting from secondary degeneration of the fiber tracts.

Nothing could be found to indicate the existence of an inflammatory process. No lymphocytes were present and there was no cellular reaction save the proliferation of the microglia and the astrocytes. The arteries and veins, large and small, were histologically normal and free of thrombi.

Clinical Features.—The onset was indicated by convulsions in each instance, and these were followed by paralysis, rigidity and stupor. In one case, there was a hemiplegia which was followed by hemiplegia on the other side some five weeks later. In another case, the symptoms seem to have indicated bilateral lesions from the beginning. The course was always progressive and marked by recurrent convulsions and increasing paralysis and rigidity. In one case, there were two definitely apoplectic episodes which suggested vascular lesions of the brain, but in the other two cases, the progress of the symptoms was more uniform. Eventually, the children showed signs of almost complete loss of cerebral function, being apparently deaf, blind, completely rigid and apparently unconscious. There was always fever at the onset and, thereafter, only some irregular elevation of temperature associated with convulsions or with the more acute cerebral episodes. The spinal fluid never showed any lymphocytes, but in one case there were a few hundred red cells in the fluid at one time and later a number of white cells. It was believed that the cellular reaction was due to the softenings and not to any inflammatory process. The Wassermann reaction was always negative in the blood and spinal fluid.

The course varied between 2 months and 18 months. In the latter case the child died of typhoid fever after being reduced to a vegetative condition for a number of months.

Diagnosis.—It does not seem possible to make the diagnosis upon clinical grounds at present. The symptoms described above should suggest this possibility, however, and the demonstration by ventriculography of multiple cavities in the brain, as in the case of Dr. Murray described below, should offer strong confirmatory evidence.

Prognosis.—In the writer's experience, this condition has been definitely progressive and always fatal.

Treatment.—Only symptomatic treatment can be advised at present.

CASE HISTORY (Psych. Path. 889).—*Child of five months developed severe pyelitis associated with vomiting, convulsions, muscular rigidity and deep coma. During the next four months the child was rigid, had frequent convulsions and remained unconscious. Post-mortem examination: Numer-*

ous cavities in the brain involving not only the subcortical white matter but the cortex as well.

J. B., who had previously enjoyed excellent health, developed a sudden illness at the age of five months. This was initiated by vomiting and convulsions which were soon followed by coma and by general muscular rigidity. The temperature varied between 102° and 105° F. The urine contained large quantities of pus and cultures showed B. coli. The white count was 22,000. Blood culture negative.

During the following weeks clonic twitchings, convulsions and muscular rigidity persisted. There was no sign of returning consciousness. As a rule the child maintained a more or less fixed position. The left leg was strongly extended, the right leg flexed. The arms were flexed and the fingers clenched. The head deviated to the right and the eyes to the left. All the tendon reflexes were increased and there was a bilateral ankle clonus, although the tendon reflexes had been absent at the onset. The optic discs were hyperemic but not edematous. Respiration was irregular at times and cyanosis was observed on several occasions. The pus quickly disappeared from the urine and there was never any significant retention of nitrogen. Blood pressure was 98/45. Temperature ranged between 99° and 106° F.

Some 3 months after the onset, the temperature and white count had returned to normal. There was no return of consciousness, but the child could nurse from a bottle. When bathed or otherwise disturbed, she was apt to have convulsions. When left alone, she remained in the position described above. Irregular nystagmoid movements of the eyes were present at times. The child seemed to be blind, but the optic nerve heads were not atrophic and the pupils reacted to light. The reflexes were as before.

The spinal fluid was at first clear and contained only the usual number of lymphocytes. There was no increase in globulin and the sugar content was within normal limits. Wassermann reaction in the blood and spinal fluid was negative. Later, about the end of the second week, a large number of red cells appeared in the spinal fluid and the fluid showed slight xanthochromia. About a month after the onset numbers of white cells appeared. Still later the fluid became normal. There were never any leucocytes and never more than 25 lymphocytes at any time.

Ventriculography was performed twice: Once some four weeks after the onset, and again 10 weeks after the onset. The first ventriculogram showed merely mild dilatation of the ventricular system. The second showed an enormous cavity in the left frontal lobe and a smaller cavity in the right frontal lobe. The brain was grossly atrophic and the entire ventricular system dilated.

Death occurred about four months after the onset.

Post-mortem examination revealed innumerable cavities in all lobes of either hemisphere which destroyed almost all the subcortical white matter and a large part of the cerebral cortex. The brain weighed only 380 grams. The cavities ranged in size from those just visible to the naked eye to others which measured 2 cm or more in diameter. Some of these were lined with a rough membrane and were quite empty. In others the tissue was not entirely destroyed and there was a spongy reticulum such as is seen in Schilder's disease. The lesions seemed to have developed first in the subcortical white matter, often at the base of a convolution and then extended peripherally into the cortex so that in the most advanced lesions only a thin layer of glia remained attached to the pia mater. The cerebellum showed large lesions in the dorsal parts of either hemisphere. The ventricular system was grossly distended and in several places there were wide openings between the cavities and the ventricles. No cavities were found in the basal ganglia or in the brainstem. The large and small arteries were quite normal. There were no thrombi in the cortical veins.

Microscopic examination revealed that the first part of the process involved destruction of the myelin with phagocytosis of the debris by microglia and a strong proliferation of the astrocytes. Later, the astrocytes were also destroyed and after a time the connective tissue trabeculae accompanying the blood vessels were also broken down, leaving a cavity filled with liquefied tissue or cerebrospinal fluid if the cavity communicated with the ventricles. This was lined with a rough membrane composed of connective tissue and glial fibers. The surrounding tissues were shrunken, containing large lacunae about the blood vessels which were often filled with phagocytes. There was also marked proliferation of astrocytes. There were no signs of an inflammatory process and no hemorrhage or changes in the blood vessels. All descending tracts from the brain showed complete secondary degeneration. There was almost universal loss of myelin in the cerebral white matter. In some regions the cortex was fairly well preserved, but in many areas it was completely destroyed and a thin layer of glial fibers adherent to the pia was all that remained.[1]

BIBLIOGRAPHY

ALPERS, B. J., FARMER, R. A. AND YASKIN, E. H.: Infantile encephalomalacia with multiple cavity formation. Arch. Neurol. & Psychiat., 76:229, 1956.

BENDA, C. E.: The late effects of cerebral birth injuries. Medicine, 24:71, 1945.

COURVILLE, C. B.: Central hemorrhagic encephalopathy. Neurology, 10:70, 1960.

CROME, L.: Multilocular cystic encephalopathy of infancy. J. Neurol., Neurosurg. & Psychiat., 1958, vol. 21, p. 146.

——— AND WILLIAMS, C.: The problem of familial multilocular encephalomalacia. Acta Paediat., 49:175, 1960.

LUMSDEN, C. E.: Multiple cystic softenings of the brain in the newborn. J. Neuropath. & Exp. Neurol., 9:119, 1950.

NORAN, H. H. AND BAKER, A. B.: Western equine encephalomyelitis. The pathogenesis of the lesions. J. Neuropath. & Exp. Neurol., 4:269, 1945.

STERNBERG, C.: Multiple Hoelnbildungen in Grosshirn als Folgen des Geburtstrauma. Beitr. z. path. Anat. u. z. allg. Path., 84:521, 1930.

STEVENSON, L. D. AND McGOWN, L. E.: Encephalomalacia with cavity formation in infants. Arch. Path., 34:286, 1942.

---

[1] This case is presented by permission of Dr. Marjorie F. Murray of Cooperstown, N. Y. The brain was studied in Dr. Meyer's laboratory at the Phipps Psychiatric Institute.

WINKELMANN, N. W. AND MOORE, M. T.: Progressive degenerative encephalopathy. Arch. Neurol. & Psychiat., 48:54, 1942.

DEGENERATION OF THE CEREBRAL GRAY MATTER

Definition.—A condition characterized by degeneration of the cerebral cortex and gray matter of the forebrain and brain stem. The clinical features include myoclonus, convulsions, choreoathetosis, cerebellar ataxia, progressive rigidity and dementia. This disease is sometimes familial.

Pathological Anatomy.—On gross examination, the brain may show cortical atrophy which is irregularly distributed and sometimes more pronounced on one side than the other. On histological examination, it is found that there is extensive loss of cells in the cerebral cortex with some myelin destruction and even areas of necrosis. The process seems to begin in the third and fourth cortical layers. The astrocytes are increased and the microglial cells show phagocytic activity in some instances. The subcortical white matter is not primarily affected and is separated from the lesions by a relatively intact lamina multiforms. Similar changes are found in the lenticular nuclei and thalami. The hypothalamus and the substantia nigra may also be involved. In some instances, the dentate nuclei, inferior olives and the cerebellar cortex are affected. In most cases, disorganization of the cytoarchitecture of the cortex is found and this is regarded as indicating defective development in fetal life.

Clinical Features.—This disease is sometimes inherited, for we have seen the disease in two siblings whose great uncle probably had the same condition. The onset is in infancy or early childhood, as a rule, before the age of six years. In several instances, it has been noted that development was retarded before the actual onset of progressive symptoms.

In two of our cases, the onset was marked by head-dropping spells, but soon myoclonic contractions of the arms were added. Convulsions, both general and unilateral, also appeared early in the course. The myoclonus slowly grew more constant and severe. The convulsions showed a tendency to occur in groups. Choreoathetoid movements were usually seen at one stage of the disease but were never strongly developed and eventually disappeared. Cerebellar ataxia was occasionally observed. Muscular rigidity was a constant feature. This began as a rule on one side but soon became bilateral. In some instances, contractures developed and the extremities were fixed in a position of flexion. Progressive mental deterioration paralleled the motor changes. Speech was soon lost. Vision then failed though the pupils continued to react to light and the optic nerve heads showed no pallor. The child seemed to be deaf. Finally status epilepticus would appear and eventually death would occur in such an episode.

Infantile and juvenile cases may be distinguished. The onset in the infantile type is always before the end of the first year and death occurs be-

Fig. 119. Progressive degeneration of the cerebral cortex showing how deeper layers of the cortex are reduced to spongy glial tissue devoid of nerve cells.

fore the age of three years. The diagnosis is often impossible. In the juvenile cases, the onset is between four and six years and death occurs as a rule between 8 and 19 years. The clinical picture is more distinctive in such cases.

Diagnosis.—The cardinal symptoms seem to include myoclonus, convulsions, choreoathetosis, ataxia, mental deterioration, deafness, blindness and death in status epilepticus. Myoclonus epilepsy must be distinguished.

Prognosis.—Apparently the disease is always fatal.

Treatment.—None.

CASE HISTORY (Ped. A-24278. Path. 19848).—*Boy of six years developed head dropping spells and myoclonus. Later, convulsions appeared. Right hemiplegia. Death in status epilepticus. Post-mortem examination revealed. degeneration of the cerebral gray matter.*

G. T., the fourth child of a family, was always retarded. He did not walk until he was two years old and first started to talk at the age of three years. His speech was always imperfect. The first three children of the family were quite healthy. The fifth child was affected in the same manner as the patient and her history is given below. The first three children were by the first husband and the patient and the fifth child were children of the second husband. It is of interest that a maternal great uncle died in status epilepticus at the age of 20 years.

When the patient was six years old, he began to have sudden seizures in which his head would drop forward on his chest for a moment. He might fall in these attacks. Soon after this he developed clonic movements of the arms which would occur many times every day. These continued and grew more frequent. There was ataxia and choreo-athetosis. His mental condition seemed to be growing worse. When he was eight years old he began to have generalized convulsions. These also grew more frequent and finally he fell into status epilepticus and was brought to the Harriet Lane Home.

When admitted to the hospital on December 27, 1945, the child was deeply unconscious and was showing constant clonic movements of the right arm and leg. The tendon reflexes were depressed on the right side. Physical examination disclosed nothing else of importance. The spinal fluid was quite normal. Roentgenograms of the skull were also negative. An electroencephalogram was reported to show a totally irregular pattern with a suggestion of spike and wave formation. Blood chemical studies showed no significant abnormalities. A ventriculogram disclosed no changes in the ventricles.

With medication of various types, the convulsions were stopped. The patient slowly regained consciousness and for a time was able to walk and talk though both were difficult. Later he developed right hemiplegia and some hemiparesis on the left. There was clear evidence of mental deterioration. Occasional clonic twitchings were seen on the right side. Finally in March 1946, the myoclonic movements grew continuous and bilateral. The child seemed to be deaf, blind and stuporous. Medication had little effect and the child died in status epilepticus on March 19, 1946, three months after entering the hospital and about two years after the onset of his symptoms. He was then eight years old.

Post-mortem examination revealed the same condition which has been described above. There was extensive degeneration of nerve cells in the cerebral cortex, thalami, lenticular nuclei, cortex of the cerebellum, dentate nuclei and gray matter of the brain stem.

CASE HISTORY (Ped. A-51076. Path. 20732).—*Girl of six years developed head dropping spells and myoclonic twitchings. Later convulsions appeared and then hemiplegia. Death occurred in status epilepticus. Post-mortem examination revealed degeneration of the cerebral gray matter.*

M. T., the younger sister of G. T. whose case history is given above, was also retarded in development for she did not walk until she was two years old and talked imperfectly at three years. She was always clumsy and mentally backward. In April 1946, at the age of six years, she began to have head-dropping spells and shortly after this myoclonic movements of the arms appeared just as they had in the case of her brother. There was mild choreo-athetosis and ataxia. In June she began to have attacks in which she would grow rigid and unconscious and fall backwards. These continued and the myoclonic twitchings grew more constant. On March 21, 1947, she began to have violent convulsions in rapid succession involving the left side, and was brought to the Harriet Lane Home on the same day.

On examination the child was seen to be in status epilepticus with constant clonic movements involving the left arm, leg and face. The diaphragm was also involved. Medication was effective in reducing these and in a few days the child was much improved. She remained dull and disoriented, however, and showed hemiparesis on the left. Laboratory studies of the blood and spinal fluid revealed nothing abnormal. Roentgenograms of the head were negative. Ventriculograms revealed normal ventricles. The electroencephalogram was reported to show totally irregular waves. A month later she went into status but once more was relieved. The myoclonic movements continued, however, and on August 14, 1947 she died in status epilepticus at the age of nearly eight years, her illness having lasted 16 months.

At post-mortem examination her brain showed the same process that was found in her brother's brain.

CASE HISTORY (Ped. 83173-Path. 14380).—*Convulsions beginning at age of six months with myoclonus and progressive deterioration. At 16 months blind, deaf and helpless. Death in convulsions. Post-mortem examination. Intense atrophy of cortical gray matter greater on the right than on the left.*

M. J., aged six months, began to have convulsive seizures without apparent cause. At first these were associated with fever and were regarded as febrile convulsions, but soon it became evident that seizures also occurred without any preceding illness. The convulsions became more frequent and more severe. Many of them were confined to the left side. Myoclonic twitchings were seen from time to time. These were more frequent on the left but were also seen on the right. Before the end of the first year it was clear that the child was deteriorating. She seemed to be blind and did not respond to auditory stimuli. She could no longer hold up her head or sit up without support. There was occasional vomiting and some loss of weight.

At the age of 14 months the child was taken into the hospital. She was fairly well nourished and developed. Temperature was normal. There was no evidence of any mental development and, so far as could be determined, the child was deaf and blind. There was no attempt at speech. The optic fundi, however, showed no pathological changes and the pupils reacted to light. There was some general muscular rigidity and the tendon reflexes were increased. Ankle clonus was elicited on both sides. Plantar reflexes were normal. The urine was normal. Blood counts revealed only slight anemia. Roentgenograms of the bones and spectroscopic analysis of the blood revealed no evidence of lead poisoning. The spinal fluid was quite normal. Ventriculography revealed that the right lateral ventricle was somewhat dilated.

The course was progressively downhill. The convulsions continued and there was frequent vomiting. Finally the child died in a series of violent seizures at the age of 16 months.

Post-mortem examination revealed a healthy condition of the organs except for the nervous system. The brain was somewhat atrophic, especially the right hemisphere, so that there was a good deal of clear fluid in the subdural space. Brain weight was only 700 grams. The cortical gray matter of the right hemisphere was very soft and shrunken. In the left hemisphere there was little if any atrophy apparent in the gross. The white matter and basal ganglia seemed to be normal. The entire vascular system was normal. Histological studies showed extraordinary loss of neurons in the cortex of the right hemisphere. This was almost universal and complete, but seemed to be most advanced in the third and fourth cortical layers. The cortex was represented by a spongy reticulum of glial tissue which was traversed in places by bundles of nerve fibers which were relatively well preserved. There was a moderate proliferation of microglial cells containing lipoid products, but no infiltration of lymphocytes or plasma cells. In general, there was no evidence of disease of the blood vessels. In the left hemisphere, the process was just beginning but seemed to be similar to that in the right hemisphere. The nerve cells of the left cerebral cortex were reduced in number and much shrunken in size. The reaction of the astrocytes was still very moderate but a number of fat-containing microglial cells were seen. The white matter of both hemispheres seemed to be intact and the basal ganglia showed no definite alteration. The cortex of the cerebellum was definitely involved. There was marked loss of Purkinje cells and the cells of the superficial molecular layer were almost all destroyed.

BIBLIOGRAPHY

ALPERS, B. J.: Diffuse progressive degeneration of the cerebral gray matter. Arch. Neurol. & Psychiat., 25:469, 1931.

BLACKWOOD, W. *et al.*: Diffuse cerebral degeneration in infancy (Alpers disease). Arch. Dis. Childhood, 38:193, 1963.

CHRISTENSEN, E. AND KRABBE, K. H.: Poliodystrophia cerebri progressiva (infantilis). Arch. Neurol. & Psychiat., 61:28, 1949.

FORD, F. R., LIVINGSTON, S. AND PRYLES, F.: Degeneration of the cerebral gray matter with convulsions, myoclonus, cerebellar ataxia, choreoathetosis, spasticity, dementia and death in status epilepticus. Differentiation of infantile and juvenile types. Pediat., 39:33, 1951.

FREEDOM, L.: Cerebral Birth Palsies. (Really a case of progressive cerebral degeneration.) Arch. Neurol. & Psychiat., 26:524, 1931.

MORSE, WM. I., 2ND.: Hereditary myoclonus epilepsy. Two cases with pathological findings. Bull. Johns Hopkins Hospital, 84:116, 1949.

WOLF, A. *et al.*, WOLF, A. AND COWEN, D.: Cerebral atrophies and encephalomalacias of infancy and childhood. Res. Ass. Nerv. and Ment. Dis., 34:199, 1954.

FAMILIAL CALCIFICATION OF THE BASAL GANGLIA AND DENTATE NUCLEI OF FAHR

Many cases of this condition have been described by various authors. Melchior describes the study of two families in each of which several children were affected early in life. He states that the condition is progressive and familial. Both sexes are affected.

The symptoms begin early in life. Bodily development is reduced. The head is dolicocephalic and the cranium is small. There is always mental deficiency. Spasticity and weakness of the extremities are present and the legs are poorly developed. Athetoid movements are sometimes seen, but the pyramidal tract signs are more striking. Sexual development is not especially defective. The course is progressive. Calcium metabolism is normal. No damage to the abdominal viscera is found. Roentgenograms show calcification of the basal ganglia of the forebrain and dentate nuclei of the cerebellum.

Post-mortem examination shows that the brain is small. There are always dense deposits of calcium in the lenticular nuclei and the dentate nuclei of the cerebellum. Smaller deposits may be found in other parts of the brain. The calcium is deposited in the walls of the small blood vessels. The vessels are occluded with softening in the tissue they supply. This process is restricted to the brain.

Muenter and Whisant state that there are 5 conditions in which calcium is deposited in the basal ganglia. (1) Hereditary cases. (2) Following an acute injury such as anoxia or encephalitis. (3) As a part of some disease such as tuberous sclerosis or neurofibromatosis. (4) Hypoparathyroidism. (5) Without discoverable cause.

CASE HISTORY.—*Familial calcification of the cerebral vessels in an adolescent girl.*

C. C. was seen in the Rosewood Training School by the courtesy of Dr. Harry Butler. It was said that her development had always been slow. She did not hold her head up until she was 18 months old and did not walk at all until she was 3 years old. She had never walked normally. She had never learned to talk. Her parents were first cousins.

Her behavior was destructive. She was incontinent. Intelligence quotient was estimated at 6. She walked on her toes with much difficulty. X-rays of the skull revealed dense deposits of calcium in the basal ganglia and dentate nuclei of the cerebellum. An air study showed normal ventricles, but an excess of air over the cortex. The serum calcium was 9.9 and the phosphorus 2.7.

On examination the patient was unable to cooperate. She did not form words, but made inarticulate sounds at times. Her nutrition was adequate. Her breasts were fairly well developed and she had pubic hair. Her head was broad, but the cranium was small. The cranial nerves were apparently in order. Her arms were strong, but the reflexes were brisk. No involuntary movements were seen. The legs were poorly developed and spastic. The tendons of Achilles were shortened. The knee and ankle jerks were increased and Babinski signs were found on both sides.

BIBLIOGRAPHY

ACEVEDO, S.: Familial idiopathic symmetrical calcification of the basal nuclei of the cerebrum. Acta neurol. latinoam., **9**:222, 1963.

CHAVANY, J. A., VAN BOGAERT, L. AND HOUDART, R.: Extrapyramidal aspects of Fahr's idiopathic nonarteriosclerotic intracerebral calcification. Monatschr. f. Psychiat. u. Neurol., **117**:77, 1949.

FOLEY, J.: Calcification of the corpus striatum and dentate nuceli occurring in a family. J. Neurol., Neurosurg. & Psychiat., 14:253, 1951.

FRITZSCHE, R.: Eine familiär auftretended Form von Oligophrenie mit röntgenologisch nachweisbaren symmetrischen Kalkablagerumgen in Gehirn, besonders in den Stammganglien. Schweiz. Arch. f. Neurol. u. Psychiat., 35:1, 1935.

KING, A. B. AND GOULD, D.: Symmetrical calcification in the cerebellum. Am. J. Roentgenol., 67:562, 1952.

MELCHIOR, J. C. *et al.*: Familial idiopathic cerebral calcification in childhood. A.M.A. J. Dis. Child., 99:787, 1960.

MUENTER, M. D. WHISNANT, J. P.: Basal ganglia calcification, hypoparathyroidism and extrapyramidal motor manifestations. Neurology, 18:1075, 1968.

VOLLAND, W.: Intracerebral vascular calcifications: Idiopathic form with preponderant extrapyramidal disease picture. Arch. f. Psychiat., 111:5, 1940.

FAMILIAL DIFFUSE CALCIFICATION OF THE CEREBRAL CORTEX

Geylin and Penfield have described a condition in a father and four children in which calcium deposits are found in the cerebral cortex and not in the basal ganglia and dentate nuclei as in the condition described by Fahr and others.

This condition is manifest by mental deterioration beginning in the first few months of life and by convulsions of various types. Weakness of one extremity was observed but usually disappeared after a time.

Roentgenograms of the skull revealed deposits of calcium in the cerebral cortex. Operation in one case showed that the deposits of calcium were located at the junction of the gray matter and white matter in the depths of the sulci. In cross section the process had a horseshoe shape. Histological examination revealed that the small blood vessels were surrounded by sleeves of calcium which invaded the vessel wall and caused occlusion. Dense glial proliferation was found in this region.

Bowman has reported the study of another family suffering from the same condition.

BIBLIOGRAPHY

GEYLIN, H. R. AND PENFIELD, W.: Cerebral calcification epilepsy. Arch. of Neurol. and Psychiat. 21:1020, 1929.

BOWMAN, M. S.: Familial occurrence of idiopathic calcification of cerebral capillaries. Amer. Jour. Path., 30:87, 1954.

NEUROLOGICAL CONDITIONS ASSOCIATED WITH PIGMENTARY CHANGES IN THE RETINAE

I have described the various types of cerebroretinal degenerations. These are believed to depend upon a specific pathological process marked by the accumulation of certain lipoids in the nerve cells. In most of these types there are pigmentary deposits associated with the retinal degeneration. This characteristic serves to link these cases with a number of ill-defined diseases which have only one feature in common, namely the presence of pigmentary degeneration of the retina. It is not my intention to imply that these conditions are actually due to the same process or that they are even necessarily closely related. Very little is known of the pathological anatomy. It seems useful, however, to discuss these cases together at this point. Franceschetti, Francois and Babel discuss all of these conditions in detail.

Stewart has described *cerebellar ataxia* in two sisters associated with pigmentary degeneration of the retina and mental deficiency.

Froment, Binnet and Colrat have studied a family in which both *cerebellar ataxia* and *spastic paraplegia* have developed in association with pigmentary degeneration of the retina in several generations. The neurological picture was not unlike that of disseminated sclerosis.

Conca describes two cases of pigmentary degeneration associated with neurological signs similar to those found in *Friedreich's ataxia*. A larger group of cases in which both pigmentary degeneration of the retinae and macular degeneration were found in association with Friedreich's ataxia are described by Franceschetti and Klein.

Clauss found progressive *spastic paraplegia* in association with *deafness* and pigmentary degeneration.

Muscular atrophy and *flaccid* paralysis are described by Ruggeri in a patient who also showed pigmentary degeneration of the retina, deafness and mental deterioration.

According to von Stock, *dementia* without neurological signs may occur in association with pigmentary degeneration of the retina and may run a rapid course.

Alstrom *et al.* describe a condition manifest by *retinal degeneration* with loss of *central vision, obesity, diabetes mellitus* and *nerve deafness*. This is a recessive condition. Polydactyly, mental deficiency and defective genital development were absent.

Biemond has described another syndrome resembling the Laurence-Moon-Biedl syndrome. There is *coloboma* of the *iris, mental deficiency, obesity, deficient sexual development* and *syndactylism*.

Flynn and Aird describe a family afflicted with *cataracts, pigmentary degeneration of the retinae, nerve deafness, ataxia, peripheral neuropathy* and *convulsions. Dementia* occurs eventually. The skin shows atrophy and ulcerations. There is baldness and decay of the teeth.

In 1959 Woodworth *et al.* described 4 cases in one family of *progressive ataxia* and *loss* of *vision*. In one patient the onset of symptoms was at 5 years and death occurred at 10 years. In another, the onset was at 15 years and in a third case, the onset was at 15 years. Post-mortem examination revealed optic atrophy, loss of cells in the retinae, degeneration of the lateral geniculate body, cerebellar cortex and inferior olive nucleus as well as the spinocerebellar tracts.

In 1966, Carpenter and Schumacher reported a family in which 4 individuals showed *progressive spasticity, loss* of *vision* and *involuntary movements*. The onset of symptoms in the father was at 25 years, but in the children the onset was at 11 months, 14 months and 16 months. Post-mortem examination revealed atrophy of the pons, and cerebellum with great loss of cells in the inferior olives. Pigmentary deposits in the retinae were found. The children all died between 16 and 31 months.

Weiner, L. P., Konigsmark *et al.* reported a study of a family of six generations in which 27 members developed *loss* of *vision, ataxia, difficulty* in *speech* and later, *athetosis*. Two children developed symptoms at 12 years and died at 15 and 16 years. Post-mortem examination revealed olivoponto-

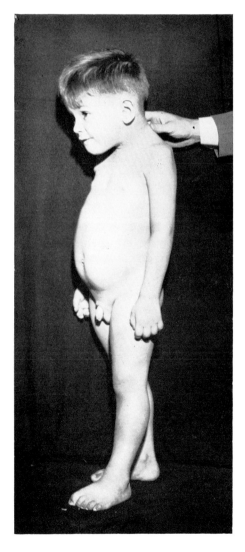

FIG. 120. Progressive muscular atrophy, nerve deafness, pigmentary degeneration of the retina, bulbar palsy and mental deterioration in brothers. Muscles of neck, shoulders and upper arms are seen to be atrophic.

cerebellar atrophy with loss of cells in the inferior olives, in the basis pontis, cerebellar cortex and substantia nigra. The spinal cord was normal. The retinae showed complete loss of ganglion cells and pigment deposits.

Baker *et al.* describe a family in which muscular atrophy of peripheral distribution, ataxia and pigmentary degeneration of the retinae developed in adolescence and diabetes later in life. Ten members of the family were affected in four generations.

Degeneration of the *globus pallidus* and *substantia nigra* with progressive muscular rigidity and pigmentary degeneration of the retina is described by Winkelmann.

Barnard and Scholz have reported cases in which *progressive nuclear ophthalmoplegia* was associated with pigmentary changes in the retina.

Hutchinson states that the original cases of Laurence and Moon eventually developed spastic paraplegia.

Refsum *et al.* describe the condition of four children who developed between the ages of four and seven years *deafness* of nerve type, atypical retinitis pigmentosa with night blindness, ichthyosis, *ataxia of cerebellar type, polyneuritis* with loss of the deep reflexes, increase of the protein content of the spinal fluid but no mental deterioration. The polyneuritis does not run a slowly progressive course, but advances by acute exacerbations which are followed by gradual improvement. Cammermeyer finds on postmortem examination hypertrophic interstitial polyneuropathy with neural muscular atrophy, retrograde atrophy of the ventral horns of the cord and secondary atrophy of the fasciculi gracili, deposits of fat in the peripheral nerves and meninges, degenerations of the brain-stem tracts with demyelination, atrophy of the inferior olives and reactive changes in the sympathetic ganglia. A possible relationship to hypertrophic interstitial polyneuritis q.v. is thus suggested. Richterich *et al.* discovered an abnormal fatty acid, phytanic acid in the plasma and urine in large amounts in a seven year old girl who was suffering from this disease. This acid is found only in minute amounts in normal individuals. This disease is believed to be inherited as an autosomal recessive character.

Eldjarn, L. *et al.* have shown that a diet free of chlorophyll and of foods which might contain phytol, phytanic acid or their precursers will reduce the phytanic acid of the blood and cause clinical improvement.

Kornzweig and Bassen describe a progressive process in a brother and sister, children of first cousins, who developed pigmentary changes in the retinae. In the case of the girl the maculae were involved but the boy developed merely a ring scotoma. About the age of eleven years, these children developed *weakness, wasting* of the *shoulder girdle muscles, ataxia, loss of tendon reflexes, peripheral sensory loss* and slight *deafness.* Mental changes were not noted. A remarkable feature of these cases were the changes in the red blood cells which were attributed to *acanthocytosis*. Both had *celiac disease* in infancy. Electroretinograms revealed no electrical activity. Schwartz *et al.* describe similar cases and point out that fats and fatty acids are not properly absorbed, there is deficiency of beta-lipoprotein in the serum, and reduced concentrations of total lipids, triglycerides, cholesterol and all phospholipids in the serum.

Levine *et al.* describe a family in which muscular weakness, loss of tendon reflexes, and involuntary movements sometimes beginning early in life were associated with acanthrocytosis. There was no pigmentary degeneration of the retinae and no abnormality of the alpha or beta lipoproteins was found.

Bergstet *et al.* describe a condition in which spasticity and ataxia are associated with central retinal degeneration and loss of vestibular function. The disease may begin at the sixth year and is inherited as an autosomal dominant trait.

Singer *et al.* describe a child, born of second cousins, who displayed the changes in the blood and in the nervous system but no lesions in the retinae.

Strobas *et al.* describe symmetrical calcium deposits in the basal ganglia with familial ataxia and pigmentary degeneration of the retinae.

Jequier *et al.* describe a family suffering from *spastic paraplegia,* associated with *peripheral loss* of *sensibility* leading to *trophic ulcerations* and *retinal degeneration.*

Kjellin describes a family with *spastic paraplegia, amyotrophy, mental deterioration* and *central retinal degeneration.*

Drachman reports 4 cases in all of which there was external ophthalmoplegia, optic atrophy, hearing loss, abnormal vestibular function, dysphagia, dysphonia, hyporeflexia, elevation of the spinal protein, abnormalities of the electroencephalogram, and defects in cardiac conduction. In some cases but not in all there was proximal myopathy, retinal pigmentary degeneration, peripheral neuropathy, corticospinal signs, and cerebellar signs. Retinal degeneration was found in 3 cases. These 4 patients were unrelated.

CASE HISTORY (Ped. A-22287).—*Progressive muscular atrophy, pigmentary degeneration of the retina, bulbar palsy and deafness beginning at the age of 18 mos. and ending in death at the age of four years. An older brother had similar symptoms.*

J. K. was apparently healthy until the age of 18 months. It was then noticed that he was growing deaf. Later the child seemed to be losing his vision. When he was about three years old, it became evident that his arms and neck were growing weak.

Examination at the age of three years (See Fig. 90) revealed extensive weakness and atrophy of the muscles of the neck, shoulders, arms and upper half of the trunk. A few fascicular twitchings were seen. The tendon reflexes of the arms were absent. The legs were not involved. No loss of sensibility was discovered. The visual fields were concentrically constricted and the periphery of the retinae showed the usual picture of pigmentary degeneration. The optic discs were pale. Pronounced deafness of nerve type was present on either side. The child was restless and uncooperative, and the examiners were convinced that there was mental deterioration. Laboratory studies gave no other information.

The symptoms increased. Strength, vision and hearing steadily declined. Bulbar palsy developed and the child choked on his food and died at the age of four years.

His older brother (H. K. Ped. A-22267) developed similar symptoms at the age of three years. His disease ran a slower course and at the age of seven years he was still living though hearing and vision were greatly reduced. No history could be elicited of any similar symptoms in other members of the family.

CASE HISTORY (K-71179).—*Girl of nine years developed ptosis of both eyelids and later bilateral and symmetrical limitation of ocular movements without loss of pupillary reactions. Pigmentary degeneration of the retina.*

L. S. was apparently normal until the age of nine years. At that age the mother noticed that her right eyelid was drooping. Later the left lid was affected in the same manner.

Examination at the age of 12 years revealed bilateral ptosis of the eyelids and limitation of elevation of the lids. Pigmentary changes in the periphery of the retinae were observed. Ophthalmological and neurological examination were otherwise negative. The injection of prostigmine was ineffectual.

Reexamination at the age of 15 years showed increase of the ptosis of the lids and definite limitation of all ocular movements on both sides. The pupils still reacted well and central vision was preserved. No history of any similar symptoms in other members of the family could be elicited.

CASE HISTORY (No. 506562) .—*Girl of eight years with pigmentary degeneration of retinae, progressive deafness, spasticity of the legs, mental deficiency and defective bodily growth.*

J. B. was seen first on Feb. 17, 1950, when she was eight years old. Her birth and early development were said to have been normal. When she was nine months old, however, it was discovered that her legs were stiff and weak. She was unable to walk until the age of three years and had never walked normally. When she was about five years old, her speech, which had been regarded as normal, became indistinct and it was discovered that she was deaf in both ears. High tones were lost and repeated tests by audiometer revealed slow progression in the deafness. She was always small for her age and backward mentally. She was sensitive, timorous and restless.

On examination the child was about the size of an average girl of four years. She was restless, irritable and easily frightened. Her behavior was similar to that of a child of two years. Vision was estimated at 20/30 in either eye. The optic discs showed only mild pallor, but in the periphery of the retinae there were many deposits of pigment of irregular shape. The fields could not be outlined. Hearing was much reduced in both ears and the otologists estimated it at 20 per cent. The other cranial nerves seemed to be in order.

The arms were moved freely without ataxia or tremor. Tone of the muscles was slightly increased and the tendon reflexes rather brisk. The gait was that of a spastic paraparesis. The tendon reflexes in the legs were increased and the plantar responses extensor.

No history of any similar symptoms in other members of the family could be elicited. One brother of six years was said to be quite normal, but his retinae have not yet been examined.

Case History (No. 1202810).—*At 3 or 4 years loss of appetite with under-nutrition, and slowing of bodily growth. At 8 years, progressive ptosis of the lids and palsies of the extraocular muscles. Deposits of pigment in the retinae. Excess of protein in the spinal fluid with xanthochromia.*

M. McM. was seen on June 15, 1966 at the age of 11 years. Birth was at term and delivery normal. She walked early and talked early though there was always a slight dysarthria. The family history was completely negative.

She was a vigorous child who grew rapidly and gained weight properly until the age of 3 or 4 years. She then lost her appetite. After this she did not grow or gain weight normally. Nutrition was impaired. Her physical activities diminished.

At 8 years, her eyelids began to droop and progressive palsies of the extraocular muscles began. The spinal fluid was examined in March 1966. The total protein was 150 mgs and there was some xanthochromia.

The child's intelligence remained normal. She made A grades at school. Her personality did not change. She remained good humored and well behaved. She had no motor disorder and could play the piano with facility.

On examination the child was of small stature for her age. She was poorly nourished. She seemed to be younger than her given age. The pupils were normal. Central vision and the fields of vision were normal. Color vision was intact. The retinae showed round, dark gray pigment deposits but no pallor of the discs or narrowing of the arteries. The eyelids drooped so as to touch the pupils and could not be properly elevated. There was scarcely any elevation of the eyes. Depression was only slightly reduced. On attempt at lateral gaze, the abducting eye moved well, but the the adducting eye scarcely moved at all. No convergence could be elicited. The remaining cranial nerves were all in order.

The muscles were small, slender and poorly developed probably as a result of disuse and undernutrition. Strength seemed to be proportional to the muscle bulk. No tremor or ataxia were found. No loss of sensibility. The tendon reflexes were in order and the plantar reflexes were normal.

The electroretinogram was interpreted as normal. The electromyogram was also normal. The electroencephalogram showed diffuse abnormalities but no focal changes. The air study showed no definite abnormalities. The spinal fluid was xanthochromic but contained only 66 mgs of protein.

CASE HISTORY.—*Mental deficiency, gross loss of vision due to retinal degeneration, defective bodily growth, defective sexual development, loss of tendon reflexes in arms and loss of ankle jerks, gross atrophy of the hands and defective development of the feet.*

By the courtesy of Dr. Harry Butler I have seen a patient whose mental condition and bodily development had always been defective. She had had little vision for years. She had never menstruated.

On examination at the age of 28 years her intelligence quotient was estimated at 30. She could hear and was able to cooperate in the examination. She spoke with only a little dysarthria. She was no taller than a child of 8 years. Her arms and legs were slender, but her abdomen was fat. There was a vigorous growth of hair on her head which extended down on the cheeks in front of the ears. The eyebrows were bushy and met in the midline. There was no deformity of the skull. The palate was high arched and narrow. The neck was short but not webbed. Over the epigastrium there was a faint reddish area suggesting an angioma. Patches of hair were seen on the dorsum of the wrists and on the legs just below the knees. No axillary hair was seen. There was sparse pubic hair. The nipples were fairly developed, but the breasts were scarcely visible or palpable.

The muscles of the extremities were slender. The fingers were very thin, but not short. The intrinsic muscles of the hands were grossly atrophied and powerless. The tendon reflexes were lost in the arms and at the ankles. The feet were very small. She walked with difficulty.

The pupils reacted feebly to light. Vision was reduced to light perception. The optic discs were pale, the retinal vessels narrow and the retinae were atrophic with a little pigment near the maculae.

CASE HISTORY.—*Pigmentary degeneration of the retinae, progressive loss of vision, progressive deafness, increasing loss of equilibrium and mental deficiency.*

T. B., a boy of 9 years was admitted to Rosewood Training School where he was seen by the courtesy of Dr. Butler. He was found to be mentally defective with an intelligence quotient of 24. There was gradual loss of vision, increasing deafness and progressive loss of equilibrium.

On examination the patient's bodily development was below average. His head was 56 cm in circumference. He could not cooperate in the examination, but did not resist. He seemed to be totally blind and deaf.

The pupils did not react to light. Cataracts prevented a view of the retinae. A previous examination had revealed pigmentary degeneration of the retinae. There was an external squint of non-paralytic type.

The musculature was poorly developed. The tendon reflexes in the arms were active. The knee and ankle jerks were brisk. Plantar reflexes were normal. The station and gait were very unsteady.

The picture was thought to resemble that described by Hallgren.

BIBLIOGRAPHY

ALEXANDER, W. S.: Phytanic acid in Refsum's syndrome. Jour. Neurol., Neurosurg. and Psychiat., **29**:412, 1966.

ALLAN, W. AND HERNDON, C. N.: Retinitis pigmentosa and apparently sex linked idiocy. Jour. Hered., **35**:40, 1944.

ALSTROM, C. H. *et al.:* Retinal degeneration combined with obesity, diabetes mellitus and neurogenous deafness. Acta psychiatrica et neurologica., Sup. 129, vol. 34, 1959.

BAKER, R. N. *et al.:* Hereditary muscular atrophy with ataxia, retinitis pigmentosa and diabetes mellitus. Neurology, **18**:942, 1968.

BARNARD, R. I. AND SCHOLZ, R. O.: Ophthalmoplegia and retinal degeneration. Am. J. Ophth., **27**:621, 1944.

BASSEN, F. E. AND KORNZWEIG, A. L.: Malformations of the erythrocytes in case of atypical retinitis pigmentosa. Blood, **5**:381, 1950.

BERGSTET, M. *et al.:* Hereditary spastic ataxia with central retinal degeneration and vestibular impairment. Neurology, **12**:124, 1962.

BLUMEL, J. AND KNIKER, W. T.: Laurence Moon Biedl syndrome (Biemond syndrome) . Review of the literature and report of five cases. Texas Rep. Biol. Med., **17**:391, 1959.

BONNET, P. ET COLRAT, A.: Lesions maculaires et troubles nerveux hereditaries. Bull. de la Soc. d'Ophth. de Paris. 333, June, 1934.

CAMMERMEYER, J.: Neuropathological changes in hereditary neuropathies. Manifestations of the syndrome heredopathia atactica polyneuritiformis. J. Neuropath. & Exp. Neurol., **15**:340, 1956.

CARPENTER, S. AND SCHUMACHER, G. A.: Familial infantile cerebellar atrophy associated with retinal degeneration. Arch. of Neurol., **14**:82, 1966.

CLAUSS, O.: Ueber hereditäre cerebellare ataxie in Verbindung mit Pigmentdegeneration der Retina und Degeneration des n. cochlearis. Ztschr. f. d. ges. Neurol. u. Psychiat., **93**:294, 1924.

DRACHMAN, D. A.: Ophthalmoplegia plus. Arch. of Neurol., **18**:654, 1968.

EDSTRÖM, R. *et al.:* Refsum's disease. Three siblings and one autopsy. Acta Psychiat. et Neurol. Scandinav., **30**:40, 1959.

ELDJARN, L. *et al.:* Dietary effects on serum phytanic acid levels and on clinical manifestations in heredopathia atactica polyneuritiformis. Lancet, **i**:691, 1966.

FLYNN, P. AND AIRD, R. B.: A neuroectodermal syndrome of dominant inheritance. Jour. Neurol. Sci., **2**:161, 1965.

FOSTER, J. B. AND INGRAM, T. T. S.: A familial cerebromacular degeneration and ataxia. Jour. Neurol. Neurosurg. and Psychiat., **25**:63, 1962.

FRANCESCHETTI, A., FRANCOIS, J. AND BABEL, J.: Les Heredo-degenerescences chorio-retiniennes. Paris. Masson et Cie, 1963, Vols. I and II.

——— AND KLEIN, D.: Heredoataxies par degenerescence spino-pontocerebelleuse Les manifestations tapeto-retiniennes. Rev. Oto-neuro-ophthal., **20**:109, 1948.

FROMENT, J., BONNET, P. ET COLRAT, Heredo-degenerations retinienne et spino-cerebelleuse. Jour. de Med. de Lyons, **18**:153, 1937.

GORDON, N. AND HUDSON, R. E.: Refsum's syndrome. Brain, **82**:41, 1959.

HALLGREN, B.: Retinitis pigmentosa combined with congenital deafness, with vestibulo-cerebellar ataxia and mental abnormality. Acta Psychiat. et Neurol. Scandinav. Suppl. 138, Vol. 34, 1959.

HUTCHISON, J.: On retinitis pigmentosa and allied affections as illustrating the laws of heredity, Ophth. Rev., **1**:2 and 26, 1882.

JAEGER, B. V. *et al.:* Occurrence of retinal pigmentation, ophthalmoplegia, ataxia, deafness and heart block. Amer. Jour. Med., **29:**888, 1960.

JAMPEL, R. S. *et al.:* Ophthalmoplegia and retinal degeneration associated with spinocerebellar ataxia. Arch. of Ophthal., **66:**247, 1961.

JEQUIER, M. *et al.:* Paraplegie familiale et degenerescence tapeto-retinienne. Confin. Neurol., **6:**277, 1945.

KJELLIN, K.: Familial spastic paraplegia with amyotrophy, oligophrenia and central retinal degeneration. Arch. of Neurol., **1:**133, 1959.

KLOEPFER, H. W. *et al.:* The hereditary syndrome of congenital deafness and retinitis pigmentosa. Laryngoscope, **76:**850, 1966.

KORNZWEIG, A. L. AND BASSEN, F. A.: Retinitis pigmentosa, acanthocytosis and heredodegenerative neuromuscular disease. Arch. Ophth., **58:**183, 1957.

LAURENCE, J. Z. AND MOON, R. C.: Four cases of retinitis pigmentosa occurring in the same family and accompanied by general imperfections of development. Ophth. Rev., **11:**32, 1866.

LEVINE, I. M. *et al.:* Hereditary neurological disease with acanthocytosis. Arch. of Neurol., **19:**403, 1968.

OLIVER, G. L. AND McFARLANE, D. C.: Congenital trichomegaly with associated pigmentary degeneration of the retina, dwarfism and mental retardation. Arch. of Ophthal., **74:**169, 1965.

REFSUM, S.: Heredopathia atactica polyneuritiformis. World Neurol., **1:**334, 1960.

REFSUM, S., SALOMONSEN, L. AND SKATVEDT, M.: Heredopathia atactica polyneuritiformis in children. J. Pediat., **35:**335, 1949.

REICHERT, T.: Retinitis pigmentosa und Multiple Sklerose. Klin. Monatbly. f. Augenheilk. Bd., **91:**163, 1933.

RICHTERICH, R. *et al.:* Refsum's syndrome. Ein angeborner Defekt im Lipid-Stoffwechsel. Klin. Wschr., **41:**800, 1963.

———— *et al.:* Refsum's disease. Formal genetics Humangenetik., **1:**333, 1965.

RUGGERI, R.: Su una complessa complessa sindrome famigliare L'eredodegenerazione acustico-ottico-cerebro-spinale. Ped. Rev., **48:**117, 1940.

SCHWARTZ, J. F.: The Bassen-Kornzweig syndrome. Arch. Neurol., **8:**438, 1963.

SINGER, K., FISHER, B. AND PERLSTEIN, M.: Acanthocytosis. A genetic malformation. Blood, **7:**577, 1952.

SOBREVILLA, L. A. *et al.:* Demyelinating central nervous system disease. Macular atrophy, and acanthocytosis. (Bassen-Kornzweiz syndrome) Amer. Jour. Med., **37:**821, 1964.

STEINBERG, D. *et al.:* Studies on the metabolic error in Refsum's disease. Jour. Clin. Invest., **46:**313, 1967.

———— *et al.:* Refsum's disease. Ann. Int. Med., **66:**365, 1967.

STEWART, R. M.: Amentia, familial cerebellar diplegia and retinitis pigmentosa. Proc. Roy. Soc. Med., **30:**849, 1937.

STROBAS, R. R. *et al.:* Symmetrical calcification of the basal ganglia with familial ataxia and pigmentary degeneration of the retinae. Brain, **80:**313, 1957.

TEMTANY, S. A.: Carpenter's syndrome. Jour. Pediat., **69:**111, 1966.

VON STOCK, W.: Ueber eine bis jetzt noch nicht beschriebene Form der familiar auftretenden Netzhautdegeneration bei gleichzeitger Verblondung. Klin. Monatbl. f. Augenheilk., **46:**225, 1908.

WALSH, F. B.: *Loc. cit.*

WEINER, L. P., KONIGSMARK, B. W. *et al.:* Hereditary olivopontocerebellar atrophy with retinal degeneration. Arch. of Neurol., **16:**364, 1967.

WINKELMANN, N. W.: Progressive pallidal degeneration. Arch. Neurol. & Psychiat., **27:**1, 1932.

WOODWORTH, J. A. *et al.:* A composite of hereditary ataxias. Arch. of Int. Med., **104:**594, 1959.

ZONCA, G.: Eredo Atassia cerebellospinale e alterazioni retiniche. Atti. Congs. Soc. Oftalm. Ital., 721, 1938.

PIGMENTARY DEGENERATION OF THE RETINA

Definition.—This condition is primarily an ophthalmological problem but deserves mention in any discussion of neurological diseases because of the not infrequent association of epilepsy, mental defect and other symptoms referable to the central nervous system.

Pathological Anatomy.—The process begins in the outer layers of the retina with degeneration of the rods and cones. The blood vessels are affected early and become severely constricted. Later the ganglion cells degenerate and finally the fibers of the optic nerve. The pigment epithelium reacts by production of large masses of brown pigment. No description is available of cerebral lesions.

Clinical Features.—The disease is strongly hereditary and has been traced through numerous generations. Several types are described which are transmitted differently. Thus, the morbid factor may be dominant, recessive or sex-linked recessive.

The onset may occur early in life. Symptoms may be present soon after birth, or may be delayed until middle age. The first complaint is of night blindness. The patient may be quite unable to find his way in twilight although vision is very good when the sun is shining brightly. The peripheral field of vision is affected before the central part and the patient may notice that objects have to be brought directly before the eyes before they become visible. Ophthalmoscopic examination reveals characteristic appearances. The optic nerve head shows more or less pallor, depending upon the stage of the disease. The retinal vessels are very narrow and often grayish or yellow. As a result of absorption of retinal pigment, the choroidal vessels are exposed. The most striking feature is the presence of large deposits of dark brown or black pigment. These deposits are irregular in size and shape but are often roughly triangular and connected by fine pigmented

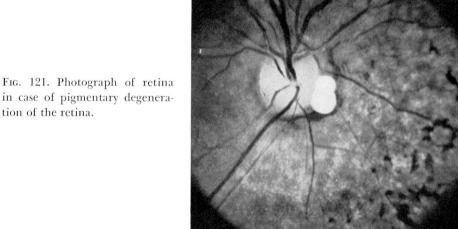

FIG. 121. Photograph of retina in case of pigmentary degeneration of the retina.

lines. Their shape has often been compared to that of the bone corpuscles. The pigmentation is most intense in a zone midway between the extreme periphery of the retina and the region of the macula. It often seems to follow the course of the blood vessels and is superficially situated so that it overlies the retinal arteries. The macular region is the last part of the retina to be involved. The process is almost always bilateral and symmetrical. The disturbances of vision correspond to the retinal lesions. Vision is lost first in the intermediate zone, causing a ring scotoma centering about the macula. Later, the peripheral fields are involved and last of all central blindness develops. The course of the disease is a very slow one and complete amaurosis rarely develops before middle age. There are no remissions. Hyaline bodies may appear in the optic discs and may be mistaken for papilledema.

In some cases, there may be no abnormal pigmentation, although the visual disturbances and the course of the disease are quite typical. The pigment may be formed later or may never appear. It is generally believed that such cases are properly classified as atypical varieties of pigmentary degeneration. Alström describes 175 cases in which there was blindness or gross loss of vision very early in infancy. As a rule, any vision present was gradually lost. Central vision was lost early. In most cases there were pigment deposits in the periphery of the retinae when the child was first seen but in some cases the optic fundi appeared to be normal for some years. Electroretinographic studies showed that the process was due to changes in the retinae. Genetic studies indicated that the disease is a recessive process with complete penetrance. No other neurological symptoms occur and there are no mental changes.

Other types are described in which the process begins in the region of the macula and gives rise to a central scotoma. In fact, there are so many varieties of this disease that it is difficult to determine its limits. The term *retinitis punctata albescens* is applied to a condition in which there are numerous white dots scattered over the retina and in some cases deposits of pigment also. Most authorities regard this is an atypical variety of pigmentary degeneration. Another similar condition is *tapetoretinal degeneration*. This is marked by the same white dots chiefly in the macular region, associated with pigment deposits, central scotomas, narrowing of the retinal vessels and night blindness. Some cases of the so-called *choroideremia*, i.e. absence of the choroid, are believed to represent the end stage of pigmentary degeneration of the retina. In this condition, the males lose their vision. The females show changes in the retinae, but retain good vision. This is termed intermediate sex-linked inheritance. Posterior polar cataracts often develop after some years and glaucoma is an occasional complication. Nystagmus is rather rare.

Hallgren studied 177 subjects who suffered from retinitis pigmentosa associated with congenital deafness and loss of equilibrium which was attributed to loss of vestibular function. About a quarter of these patients were mentally defective. A single recessive gene seemed to be responsible.

Senior *et al.* describe a familial disease of childhood in which there is progressive renal failure and loss of vision. One child was blind from birth. Other children had dim vision. The ophthalmoscopic examination revealed fine pigmentation in the equatorial region of the retinae, but the electroretinogram showed extensive abnormalities. A diagnosis of tapetoretinal degeneration was made. Two children died of uremia. Histological study showed loss of visual cells in the retinae. The parents had good vision but the mother's electroretinogram showed abnormalities.

Numerous congenital anomalies are associated with this disease. For example, I may mention deaf-mutism, mental deficiency and epilepsy. There are also a variety of progressive degenerations of the nervous system associated with pigmentary changes in the retina. These are mentioned in the preceding pages.

Diagnosis.—The diagnosis depends upon the history and upon the ophthalmoscopic examination. Syphilitic retinitis should always be kept in mind. It is said that electroretinographic study is helpful in diagnosis. Before any lesions can be seen with the ophthalmoscope, this test may show loss of electrical activity in the retinae.

Prognosis.—The disease is usually steadily progressive but the rate of progression is subject to great variation. Some patients become blind in infancy and others may retain useful vision to an advanced age.

Treatment.—No treatment is of any value.

BIBLIOGRAPHY

ALSTRÖM, C. H.: Heredo-retinopathia congenitalis. Hereditas 43, Lund, 1957.
BELL, J.: Treasury of Human Inheritance. Part 1. Retinitis pigmentosa and allied diseases. Cambridge Univ. Press, 1922.
DUKE-ELDER, W. S.: Textbook of Ophthalmology. St. Louis, Mosby, Vol. 3, p. 2765.
FRANCESCHETTI, A., FRANCOIS, J., AND BABEL, J.: Heredo-degenerescences chorio-retiniennes. Masson et C. Editeurs, Paris, 1963.
HALLGREN, B.: Retinitis pigmentosa combined with congenital deafness-vestibulo-cerebellar ataxia and mental abnormality in a proportion of cases. Acta Psychiat. et Neurol. Scandinav. Suppl. 138, Vol. 34, 1959.
SENIOR, B. *et al.*: Familial oculorenal dystrophy. Am. J. Ophth., **52**:625, 1961.
WALSH, F. B.: *Loc. cit.*

FAMILIAL DEGENERATION OF THE MACULAE

In the preceding sections, certain familial diseases have been discussed in which degenerative changes in the retina, more especially in the macula, are associated with widespread cerebral degeneration. These conditions are termed cerebroretinal degenerations. Similar degenerative processes may oc-

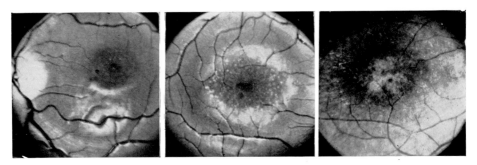

Fig. 122. Photographs illustrating three stages in the development of macular degeneration. The illustration on the left shows the earliest stage; the middle shows a more advanced condition in an older sibling and the illustration on the right reveals a further advance for the degeneration is now extending beyond the central portion of the retina. (By the courtesy of Dr. Walsh.)

cur in the macula without any corresponding involvement of the central nervous system, and one of these will be described at this point.

As a rule, the first symptoms appear between the ages of 12 and 20 years. Both sexes are affected in most families. Usually, the symptoms are confined to the children of one generation and the ascendants are usually healthy. The development of a relative central scotoma is the first evidence of the disease. This slowly grows larger and eventually becomes absolute. The peripheral fields of vision are preserved for many years at least and, although the disease is undoubtedly a progressive one, there seems to be a tendency for it to become arrested before complete blindness occurs. There may be some reduction of central vision before any retinal lesions are visible, or conversely, ophthalmoscopically demonstrable lesions may precede any reduction of vision. As a rule, however, yellowish gray spots appear in the region of the maculae early in the course of the disease. Small white or gray deposits resembling in size the common drusen bodies are soon seen surrounding these lesions. Later, small amorphous granules of brown pigment appear in the perimacular region. Still later, the macula is completely atrophic and of a yellow-gray color. The atrophic area varies between 1/2 and 2 disc diameters. It is surrounded by a zone of brown pigment deposits which may eventually extend out towards the periphery. The patients may be active both mentally and physically and apparently never show any evidence of cerebral degeneration.

It is said that the earlier in life the retinal lesions appear, the more likely it is that cerebral degeneration will occur. Cerebral damage rarely develops in patients whose symptoms begin after the age of puberty, it is claimed.

This condition must be distinguished from congenital defects such as colobomata and from local inflammatory processes involving the maculae. The last are usually unilateral.

CASE HISTORY (Wil.-1386).—*Girl of 15 years who noticed loss of central vision one year before. No other symptoms. Macular degeneration found on examination. One sister and one brother show same lesions. One brother has normal vision.*

S. M., school girl of 15 years, noticed gradual reduction of vision in both eyes about one year ago. Peripheral vision was not affected. The process slowly grew worse and worse and now the child cannot see to read. There have been no other symptoms whatever. Mental condition is perfectly normal.

Examination reveals a well developed, well nourished child of the given age. The pupils are equal and circular and react well to light and during accommodation. Central vision is reduced to about 20/100 in either eye. The outlines of the visual fields are normal, but there is a large absolute and relative central scotoma which extends towards the blind spot on the temporal side. Ophthalmoscopic examination reveals small circular areas of degeneration in both maculae about twice the size of the optic disc. The retina is pale in this region and is speckled with fine brown pigment granules. About this area are numerous fine, gleaming, white deposits in the retina. The peripheral retina is apparently normal. The optic nerve head is slightly pale on the temporal side in the region of the papillomacular bundle. Neurological examination is quite negative except for the ophthalmological findings.

The patient's parents and ascendants are said to have had normal vision. She is one of four siblings. The eldest, a girl of 26 years, has suffered from loss of central vision for about 10 years, but has not developed any other symptoms and still has good peripheral vision. The second child, a boy of 24 years, enjoys normal vision. The third child, a boy now 22 years old, shows exactly the same disturbances in vision as the patient and also the same changes in the maculae. The process has advanced further, however, and his central vision is only 4/100 in either eye (Wil.-1376). No history of disturbances of vision in collaterals can be elicited, although the family has investigated this matter very carefully.

BIBLIOGRAPHY

DAVIS, C. T. AND HOLLENHORST, R. W.: Hereditary degeneration of the macula occurring in five generations. Amer. Jour. Ophthal., **39**:637, 1955.
SORSBY, A.: The dystrophies of the macula. Brit. J. Ophth., **24**:469, 1940.
WALSH, F. B.: *Loc. cit.*
WRIGHT, R. E.: Familial macular degeneration. Brit. J. Ophth., **19**:160, 1935.

THE LAURENCE-MOON-BIEDL SYNDROME

Definition.—A syndrome characterized by pigmentary degeneration of the retinae, mental deficiency, obesity, defective sexual development and often polydactylism. There is much variation in the clinical picture and the limits of this syndrome are indefinite.

Pathological Anatomy.—Scarcely anything is known of the morbid anatomy. Few post-mortem examinations have been made and these apparently did not reveal any striking changes in the nervous system. The pituitary gland shows some abnormalities as do the sex glands (Griffiths).

Clinical Features.—This condition is found in both sexes being somewhat more frequent in males. It is familial as a rule and is usually attributed to a recessive factor though its behavior is not always consistent with recessive inheritance.

It is stated that the pigmentary changes in the retinae are typical of pigmentary degeneration in only about fifteen per cent of cases. In the others, the deposits are very fine and atypical in distribution so that they may appear uniformly scattered over the retina or may center at the macula. The nerve head may be pale and the retina may show extensive degeneration. Cataracts are not common but there is usually optic nystagmus and squints of various types are described. The course seems to be steadily progressive. Deafness is found in some cases.

The obesity is often appearent early in childhood. The fat is deposited on the trunk and proximal portions of the extremities. The abdomen and

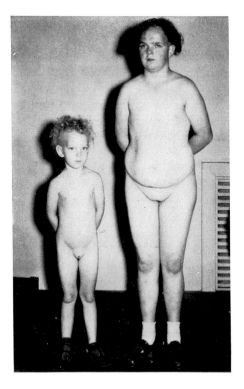

Fig. 123. Laurence-Moon-Biedl syndrome in two sisters, 5 and 20 years of age, respectively. Both were almost completely blind and both exhibited pigmentary degeneration of the retinae. The hair distribution is similar in both patients and an unusual variation of this syndrome. (J. H. 265857; R. H. 265858.) (From Walsh: Neuro-Ophthalmology, courtesy the Williams and Wilkins Company.)

hips are especially affected. The genitals remain infantile and girls do not menstruate. Body hair is usually absent. In two sisters we have observed the scalp hair was very scanty and fine. Diabetes insipidus is described but is uncommon. Bodily growth may be greatly reduced and some patients remain dwarfs. Polydactylism is a typical feature but occurs in only a small percentage of cases. The females eventually develop osteoporosis due to lack of sex gland function.

Mental deficiency is almost always present and is sometimes severe. The mental changes are not apparently progressive in my experience and one gains the impression that they are due to a defect of development rather than to a progressive degeneration of the brain.

Diagnosis.—The diagnosis is made on the basis of the syndrome described above.

Prognosis.—The disease does not seem to shorten life more than mental defects of other types. Vision progressively declines, however.

Treatment.—The generally accepted view is that no treatment is helpful.

CASE HISTORIES (No. 265857 and 265858).—*Sisters displaying dwarfism, sexual infantilism, mental deficiency, and pigmentary degeneration of the retinae.*

J. H. and R. H. are sisters. There was night blindness from early childhood. Mental development was deficient in both. Bodily growth was much retarded. A maternal uncle is said to have shown similar defects.

These patients were brought to Johns Hopkins Hospital when J. H. was 20 years old and her sister, R. H. was five years of age. J. H. was very dull and slow. Her behavior was similar to that of a child of three or four years. Her appearance is seen in the accompanying illustration. She displayed an excess of fat over the abdomen, hips and thighs. The skin was very soft and smooth. There was no body hair. The hair of the scalp was very fine and absent over the frontal region. No pubic or axillary hair was evident. The genitalia were infantile. No malformation of the hands was present but the fingers tapered. She was 57½ inches tall. Vision was reduced to counting fingers. The retinae displayed extensive deposits of pigment and extensive atrophy. A diagnosis of atypical pigmentary degeneration was made by Dr. Walsh. Gleaming deposits were seen in the vitreous, the so-called synchysis scintillans. Roentgenograms of the skull revealed no abnormalities. Estimation of the follicle stimulating hormones revealed that they were diminished. No polyuria was found.

The little sister showed the same changes in the retinae and was almost completely blind. She was also mentally deficient.

BIBLIOGRAPHY

BOWEN, P.: The Laurence-Moon-Syndrome. Arch. of Int. Med., **116**:598, 1965.
CICCARELLI, E. AND VESELL, E. S.: Laurence-Moon-Biedl Syndrome. Am. J. Dis. Child., **101**:519, 1961.

GRIFFITHS, G. M.: The Laurence-Moon-Biedl Syndrome. J. Neurol. & Psychiat., 1:1, 1938 (post-mortem examination).

LURIE, L. A. AND LEVY, S.: The Laurence-Moon-Biedl Syndrome. J. Pediat., 21:793, 1942.

ROSS, C. F., CROME, L. AND MACKENZIE, D. Y.: The Laurence-Moon-Biedl Syndrome. J. Path. & Bact., 72:161, 1956.

SORSBY, A., AVERY, H. AND COCKAYNE, A. E.: Obesity, hypogenitalism, mental retardation, polydactyly and retinal pigmentation. Quart. J. Med., 8:51, 1939.

WALSH, F. B.: *Loc. cit.*

DYSTONIA MUSCULORUM DEFORMANS

Definition.—Dystonia is a syndrome which may be caused by a number of different diseases including epidemic encephalitis and hepatolenticular degeneration. Among the causes of this condition, however, there seems to be an ill-defined disease confined largely to subjects of Russian-Jewish descent and constituting, according to Davison and Goodhart, a specific clinical entity. This disease has also been termed *dystonia lenticularis, torsion spasm, dysbasia lordotica* and *torsion dystonia.*

Pathological Anatomy.—Davison and Goodhart have performed post-mortem examinations upon four patients of Jewish-Russian descent who were suffering from the "idiopathic" degenerative type of the disease. They describe widespread degenerative changes affecting the putamen and caudate nuclei most severely. The dentate nuclei were also constantly involved. Milder changes were found in the thalamus, the substantia nigra and the cerebral cortex. There was nothing specific in the histological picture but it was possible to rule out hepatolenticular degeneration, epidemic encephalitis and other well known diseases of the basal ganglia.

Clinical Features.—This disease is most frequently found in Russian Jews, but more or less typical cases have been described in members of other races. Most cases, perhaps, appear sporadically, but in several instances two or more siblings have been affected and the disease may also involve more than one generation. Johnson *et al.* studied a family of 121 individuals in four generations. Nine cases of dystonia were discovered and seven probable cases. In a study of the literature, they found eighteen families in which dystonia had occurred in more than one generation.

In 1966 Larsson and Sjögren published a very complete study of 121 cases of dystonia from Sweden. They describe the myostatic type as well as the hyperkinetic type. They find this disease is transmitted as an autosomal monohybrid dominant.

If one may judge from the cases described in medical literature there is considerable variation in the symptoms and course of this disease. No doubt a number of different diseases have been included under the title of dystonia, especially epidemic encephalitis and hepatolenticular degeneration, which are known to give rise at times to very similar pictures. In our experience, however, the symptoms have been very uniform and the following description is based almost entirely on the writer's observations. The onset is gradual and appears in most cases between the ages of five and ten years. It is said that either involuntary movements or distorted postures may constitute the first symptoms. In the writer's experience, the most common initial sign has been a persistent hypertonus of certain muscles of the calf producing plantar flexion, inversion and adduction of the foot. Eventually, the foot may develop a rather characteristic deformity which has been termed the talon or semilunar foot. The plantar surface is strikingly concave so as to produce a type of pes cavus and the toes are held strongly in plantar flexion and adduction. Soon after the foot is affected, the thigh is fixed in flexion at the hip and later in adduction. The knee is extended. These changes usually begin on one side and later become bilateral. At first, this posture is only evident when the patient is standing or walking. The child may run well at first. The fixed postures are due to muscle spasm which is almost constant during waking hours, but which disappears during sleep and when the patient is completely relaxed. One of the most typical features of this disease is the increased lumbar lordosis which is apparent when the patient tries to stand or walk. To a large extent, this is due to the flexion of the hips which tilts the pelvis forward and compels the patient to hyperextend the spine in order to hold the body upright. This causes the buttocks to protrude. For

Fig. 124. Dystonia musculorum deformans in a child of 9 years showing the deformity of the left foot and slight spasm of the flexors of the left hip which are the commonest of the initial symptoms. There is only slight lordosis. (By the courtesy of Dr. Seliger.)

the same reason, that is because of the flexion of the hips, the patient must walk with the knees bent. Later, the muscles of the trunk are involved, causing other deformities of the spine. Torticollis appears eventually. Usually, the arms are affected later than the legs. Often there is adduction and internal rotation at the shoulder, extension at the elbow, pronation of the forearm and flexion at the wrist. Sometimes there is flexion in place of extension of the elbow. The feet sometimes present a characteristic appearance. They are held in the equinus position and the soles are turned in, i.e. supinated. The toes are flexed and the soles are flexed in a smooth curve. This is termed the semilunar foot.

The deformities are due not only to muscle spasm but, to a certain degree, to relaxation of other muscle groups. On palpation, we may find both atonic and hypertonic muscles, although hypertonia is probably always predominant. The distorted postures are usually more or less fixed from the first but they are accentuated by activity, such as walking. This is especially true of the lordosis. Eventually, the limbs become fixed by contractures and secondary changes in the bones and joints appear in due time.

Wechsler and Brock point out that in some cases no involuntary movements are found, and only the rigidity and deformities described above are present.

In most cases of dystonia there are widespread and powerful involuntary movements. In my experience, these have first appeared several years after the onset, usually about the time the arms become involved. In their general character they are similar to the mobile spasm of athetosis, for they are slow, irregular and often appear in successive waves. They are accompanied by a great increase in muscle tone. In contrast to the movements of athetosis, they spare the face, the fingers and the speech organs and involve the proximal segments of the limbs, the neck and the trunk. When the patient is asleep or completely relaxed, movements are absent in all cases, but any effort or emotional reaction induces them at once. Walking seems to produce the most active movements. It is often accompanied by the most bizarre gyrations of the trunk, head, arms and legs. These movements are too complex to be analyzed when they are fully developed, but when they are relatively mild it may be seen that they are such as to accentuate the postures described above. Thus, the effort to grip the examiner's hand will often cause a powerful flexion of the hips, which forces the patient's knees up against the body, strong extension of the elbow and internal rotation at the shoulder. It is impossible to carry out coordinated voluntary movements because of the excitation of the muscle spasm which may actually produce a result just the opposite of that intended. Thus, it is not unusual for the attempt to carry food to the mouth to result in strong extension of the arm which actually carries the food to arm's length. Certain postures seem to give rise to intense muscle spasm and violent movements when the disease is well advanced. Patrick describes the case of a boy who could neither sit nor lie on his back, for both positions produced powerful opisthotonos and extension of the spine. Consequently, he was forced to sleep in a kneeling position. Two of the writer's patients have also been forced to sleep on the face with the knees drawn up. The deformities and movements are perhaps both an expression of one and the same disorder, i.e. muscle spasm, which is in the one case persistent and in the other transient. So far as can be determined there is no paralysis or even any loss of power in the muscles until secondary wasting from undernutrition and disuse occur. Some writers have, however, described true muscular atrophy associated with degeneration of the anterior horn motor cells of the spinal cord.

The tendon reflexes are sometimes elicited with difficulty, but it is generally agreed that they are almost always present if proper relaxation can be secured. The plantar reflex is normal. No clonus can be elicited. Sensibility is not affected. The sphincter control is preserved. In the early stages of the disease, the mental condition is always normal, but after a number of years there may be evidence of deterioration. Dystonia is regarded as a progressive disease, but there is not always constant progression. There may, indeed, be steady increase of the symptoms. In other cases the patient's condition may remain stationary for long periods. There may be an astonishing degree of improvement which may be maintained for at least ten years. Such fluctuations in the course of the disease are usually unexplained.

A remarkable feature of many cases is the pronounced influence of psychological factors upon the symptoms. When the child is distressed for any reason the movements may be increased to an extraordinary extent and when the situation has become adjusted the patient may be so much improved, that one may be led to suspect that the diagnosis was incorrect and that all the symptoms were hysterical. However, I have never seen complete disappearance of symptoms.

Diagnosis.—The diagnosis is based upon the clinical picture described above, and upon absence of any features in the history or examination to suggest other degenerative diseases of the basal ganglia, epidemic encephalitis, hysteria or hepatolenticular degeneration. The diagnosis is strengthened if the patient is of Jewish race and if the family history is positive.

Prognosis.—There is no hope of recovery and the disease is almost always progressive. In rare cases, it is claimed, the disease remains stationary for years. Eventually, the patients become confined to bed, where they may linger on for many years. In my experience, the patients are ambulatory for from three to five years, and sometimes for many years.

Treatment.—Orthopedic procedures, such as tenotomies and the application of casts, are quite useless and often add to the patients' discomfort, but it is unusual for a patient to escape such mistreatment.

Cooper states that the placement of lesions in the mesial globus pallidus, ventrolateral nucleus of the thalamus and other structures in that region have caused long standing abolition of dystonia in 70 per cent of cases without any significant untoward results.

The patients usually require sedatives for sleep, since they are often kept awake by the movements.

CASE HISTORY.—*Little girl of nine years developed muscular spasms of the left leg causing inversion of the foot. Shortly after this the left hip became flexed and then adduction of the left thigh developed. Three years later the right leg was affected in a similar manner, and there were extensive involuntary movements involving not only the legs but the arms and trunk. Emotional instability and irritability. Pronounced loss of weight.*

E. J., a girl aged nine years of Hebrew parentage, began to walk so clumsily that her parents took her to a physician. It was found that she had a persisting spasm of certain muscles of the left leg, causing inversion and extension of the foot. Shortly after this it was noticed that a similar condition existed at the left hip, producing a constant partial flexion. At this stage there were no involuntary movements. Various ineffectual methods of treatment were tried, but after some months the abnormal postures were even more severe than before and a tendency to adduction of the hip was noticed. The child's condition at this time is shown in the accompanying illustration. Within two years it was evident that the right leg was beginning to be affected just as the left leg had been, and three years after the onset the muscular spasm was almost symmetrical. The child could not stand without some support to help in balancing. Both hips were strongly flexed, the thighs were adducted, the knees flexed to a certain degree and the feet inverted. The lumbar lordosis was greatly increased when the child assumed a standing posture. Every effort now produced widespread muscular spasm almost identical with that of athetosis. The trunk was twisted as well as the hips, shoulders and arms. The arms, however, showed no tendency to assume any special posture. The face was not affected and speech was normal. When the child was asleep or even completely relaxed the muscle spasm disappeared completely. There was very striking loss of weight by this time despite an adequate diet, but no cause could be found for this on medical examination. The child's intelligence was apparently quite normal for she made good progress in her studies, but she had grown very irritable and unstable so that one was led to suspect the beginning of mental changes. No evidence of cirrhosis of the liver could be discovered and there was no pericorneal pigmentation.

The next year, that is the fourth year of her illness, she was almost entirely helpless and could feed herself only with the greatest difficulty. She had no control over the legs whatever, for any effort produced a violent spasm of the muscles which drew her knees up to her abdomen and caused the thighs to cross. The arms were more apt to be extended than flexed although they were not fixed in any constant posture. Frequently the attempt to convey an object to her mouth would induce a stronger contraction of the extensors than of the flexors, so that the forearm would be violently extended for some moments. The face, the fingers, the ocular muscles and the bulbar muscles were still spared. The child was exhausted by the violent muscular spasms and was now very miserable and much emaciated. The child eventually became bedridden and died.

BIBLIOGRAPHY

BURMAN, M. S.: Therapeutic use of curare and erythroidine hydrochloride for spastic and dystonic states. Arch. Neurol. & Psychiat., **41**:307, 1939.

COOPER, I. S.: Dystonia musculorum deformans alleviated by chemopallidectomy. Arch. Neurol. & Psychiat., **81**:5, 1959.

———: Clinical and physiologic implications of thalamic surgery for dystonia. Bull. New York Acad. Med., **41**:870, 1965.

DAVISON, C. AND GOODHART, S. P.: Dystonia musculorum deformans. A clinicopathologic study. Arch. Neurol. & Psychiat., **29**:1108, 1933 and **39**:939, 1938.

GARLAND, H.: Torsion spasm. A case report. J. Neurol. & Psychopath., **12**:193, 1932.

GOODHART, S. P. AND KRAUSE, W. M.: On the deformity of the foot in dystonia musculorum. Arch. Neurol. & Psychiat., **11**:436, 1932.

HERZ, E.: Dystonia pathology and conclusions. Arch. Neurol. & Psychiat., **52**:20, 1944.

HUNT, J. R.: The progressive torsion spasm of childhood (dystonia musculorum deformans). J.A.M.A., **67**:1430, 1916.

JOHNSON, W. *et al.*: Studies on dystonia musculorum deformans. Arch. Neurol., **7**:301, 1962.

KOCK, G.: Krankheiten mit vorwiegender Beteilgung des extrapyramidalen Systems Humangenetik. P. E. Becker, Georg Thieme, Stuttgart, 1966.

LARSSON, T. AND SJÖGREN, T.: Dystonia musculorum deformans. Acta Neurol. Scand. Sup. 17, Vol. 42, 1966.

———: Dystonia musculorum deformans. Proc. Second Internat. Cong. of Human Genetics. Rome, Sept. 6, 1961.

MENDEL, K.: Torsiondystonie (dystonia musculorum deformans). Monatschr. f. Psychiat. u. Neurol., **46**:309, 1919.

PATRICK, H. T.: A case of dystonia musculorum deformans. Arch. Neurol. & Psychiat., **7**:541, 1922.

PUTNAM, T. J.: The treatment of athetosis and dystonia by section of the extrapyramidal motor tracts. Arch. Neurol. & Psychiat., **29**:504, 1933.

TAYLOR, E. W.: Dystonia lenticularis (dystonia musculorum deformans). Arch. Neurol. & Psychiat., **4**:417, 1920.

WECHSLER, I. S. AND BROCK, S.: Dystonia musculorum deformans with special reference to a myostatic form and the occurrence of decerebrate rigidity phenomena. A study of six cases. Arch. Neurol. & Psychiat., **8**:538, 1922.

ZEMAN, W. *et al.*: Idiopathic dystonia musculorum deformans. Neurology, **10**:1068, 1960.

STATUS DEMYELINISATUS OF THE VOGTS

Definition.—A progressive degenerative process largely confined to the lenticular nuclei in which demyelination is the most conspicuous change. It is, at present, very questionable whether this should be regarded as a disease entity or whether it is merely a pathological change which may occur in several diseases.

Pathological Anatomy.—This condition was first described by Cecile and Oscar Vogt, who regarded it as the expression of a progressive degenerative process. In two cases they found almost complete demyelination of all the nerve fibers of the lenticular nuclei. Both the striofugal and pallido fugal fiber tracts were degenerated. The cellular changes were not so conspicuous and there were no important lesions in other parts of the nervous system. The liver was always normal. Other pathologists have confirmed these findings, although they have sometimes discovered more extensive changes.

Clinical Features.—The disease usually begins early in infancy and more than one case may develop in the same family. The first feature to attract attention is usually generalized muscular rigidity which is followed by involuntary movements of athetoid type. The symptoms slowly increase, and before long tonic convulsions supervene. These are easily provoked by handling the child or by other stimuli, and also occur without apparent cause. If the child learns to walk and talk, these functions are eventually lost. Finally, after some years the child becomes quite helpless. The extremities are rigidly fixed by contractures and by intense muscle spasm. The involuntary movements have now ceased. It is difficult to determine whether the child is demented or not, since the motor disturbances offer such obstacles to any communication. There seems to be apparent dementia in most cases, however, and there is certainly loss of control of emotional reactions. Death occurs as a rule between the ages of five and fifteen years.

Diagnosis.—It is scarcely possible to make a diagnosis during life unless post-mortem examination has revealed the typical histological changes in a relative, but the clinical picture described above should suggest status demyelinisatus as one of the possibilities.

Prognosis.—The disease is apparently always progressive and fatal.

Treatment.—No specific treatment is known.

BIBLIOGRAPHY

BIELSCHOWSKI, M.: Weitere Bemerkungen zur normalen und pathologischen Histologie des striären Systems. J. f. Psychol. u. Neurol., **23**:233, 1921-22.

JAKOB, A.: The anatomy, clinical syndromes and physiology of the extrapyramidal system. Arch. Neurol. & Psychiat., **13**:596, 1925.

VOGT, C. u. O.: Zur Lehre der Erkankungen des striären Systems. J. f. Psychol. u. Neurol., **25**:631, 1920.

PIGMENTARY DEGENERATION OF THE GLOBUS PALLIDUS AND SUBSTANTIA NIGRA (HALLERVORDEN-SPATZ DISEASE)

Definition.—A familial disease characterized clinically by progressive symptoms of extrapyramidal character and anatomically by apparently specific histological changes including deposits of iron containing pigments in the pallidum which stain it a deep brown.

Pathological Anatomy.—The most striking feature is the intense pigmentation of the pallidum and substantia nigra which is very evident in the gross. Histological studies reveal that this is the result of deposits of granules which contain iron. These are found in the glial cells, tissue spaces and in the neurons. There is mild proliferation of the fibrous glia. Spatz found no serious loss of neurons or demyelinations but Kalinowsky describes degeneration of the neurons and loss of myelinated fibers. Similar changes are usually found in the cortex, the cerebellum and other parts of the brain but these are never so severe as those in the pallidum or substantia nigra.

Clinical Features.—The first complete study was made by Spatz and Hallervorden. They observed a family of nine children, five of whom developed a progressive disease of the nervous system between the ages of eight and ten years. The legs became rigid and the feet deformed. Later, athetosis appeared in one child but not in the others. Speech was always affected and sooner or later dementia developed. In the last stages of the disease, the muscles became strikingly wasted. The tendon reflexes were increased and a Babinski sign could be elicited, but the rigidity was predominantly of extrapyramidal type. Post-mortem examination was secured in two cases.

Kalinowsky has made very similar observations. There were four children in the family and three males developed symptoms between the age of nine and ten years. The sister remained well. Progressively increasing rigidity of the legs was noticed first which was associated with pes equinus. Later the arms became rigid also. In one patient bilateral athetosis developed, but in the other two there was a rhythmical tremor of Parkinsonian type. Speech became explosive and monotonous and uncontrollable laughter and weeping developed. Vision was reduced but not lost. The optic discs became pale, especially on the temporal sides. At the end, the child was quite helpless with the legs fixed by muscle spasm in flexion at the hip and knee with adduction at the hip. The feet were in pes cavus position. All the tendon reflexes were exaggerated and the plantar reflex was equivocal. The disease terminated in severe dementia and death.

Diagnosis.—The essential features of this condition seem to be progressive muscular rigidity affecting several members of a family, and beginning at the age of eight or ten years, which may be associated with rhythmical tremor, with athetosis or with no involuntary movements whatever. Later, mild signs referable to the pyramidal tracts appear. Finally there is dementia and death.

The clinical picture is scarcely specific enough to justify the diagnosis during life. We should, however, consider this condition in the differential diagnosis of all progressive familial diseases characterized by extrapyramidal syndromes.

Prognosis.—The disease has progressed to a fatal issue in all reported cases.

Treatment.—None is known.

BIBLIOGRAPHY

DeMeyer, W. *et al.:* Familial spasticity, hyperkinesia and dementia. Acta neuropath., 4:28, 1964.
Gross, H. *et al.:* Ueber eine spätinfantile Form der Hallervorden-Spatzschen Krankheit. Dtsch. Ztschr. Nervenheilk., **176:**77, 1957.

HALLERVORDEN, J.: Ueber eine familiäre Erkrankung im extrapyramidalen System. Ztschr. f. Nervenheilk., **81**:204, 1924.

———— UND SPATZ, H.: Eigenartige Erkrankung im extrapyramidalen System mit besonderer Beteiligung des Globus pallidus und der Substantia nigra. Ztsch. f. d. ges. Neurol. u. Psychiat., **79**:41, 1922.

KALINOWSKY, L.: Familiäre Erkankung mit besonderer Beteiligung der Stammganglien. Monatschr. f. Psychiat. u. Neurol., **66**:168, 1927.

MEYER, A.: Neuropathology. GREENFIELD, J. G., London, Edward Arnold, Ltd., 1958, p. 525.

NETSKY, M. G., SPIRO, D. AND ZIMMERMAN, H. M.: Hallervorden-Spatz disease and dystonia. J. Neuropath. & Exp. Neurol., **10**:125, 1951.

VAN BOGAERT, L.: Cerebral Lipidoses. Springfield, Thomas, 1957.

INFANTILE NEUROAXONAL DYSTROPHY

This is a familial condition. Girls seem to be affected more often than boys. It is believed to be inherited as a recessive trait. The children are apparently normal in infancy. The onset usually occurs between 18 months and 2 years. The children may never be able to talk or walk. There is gradually progressive deterioration in motor and mental functions. Generalized weakness occurs. In some children there is spasticity, but in others flaccidity is found. The arms may be spastic and the legs flaccid with loss of knee and ankle jerks. There are usually bilateral Babinski signs. An atonic bladder with retention eventually develops. Tonic neck reflexes may occur. Involuntary movements are sometimes seen. Seizures of various types and myoclonic movements occur in some cases. The pin may not feel sharp over the body and extremities, but is usually felt on the face. Nystagmus is a standard finding. The optic discs become pale and vision may be lost. Some children become deaf. Inability to swallow may require tube feeding. Death usually occurs by the age of 12 years.

The conduction time of the peripheral nerves is normal. The electromyogram shows signs of partial denervation. The electroencephalogram shows fast activity with superimposed spikes. The spinal fluid is normal.

The brain shows extensive changes. The neurons swell and the cytoplasm becomes homogenous. The neurofibrils are lost. The nuclei are displaced to the periphery of the cell and degenerates. Swellings develop on the dendrites which are termed spheroids. They vary in size between 10 μ and 100 μ. They are found to be composed of lipoglycoprotein and contain ribonucleic acid. The process causes demyelination of the pallidum which is not pigmented. The nuclei of the brain stem, the thalamus, the cerebellum and the nuclei of the columns of Gall and Burdach are all involved. Similar changes in the posterior horns of the cord and posterior roots cause degeneration of the posterior columns. The optic pathways may be atrophic. Sandbank found hypertrophied histiocytes containing homogenous eosinophil material in the cytoplasm in the spleen. Cowan found similar deposits in the kidneys and lymph nodes. Hedley-Whyte *et al.* describe characteristic alterations in the terminal axones and synaptic endings in an electron microscopic study.

BIBLIOGRAPHY

COWAN, D. AND OLMSTEAD, E. V.: Infantile neuroaxonal dystrophy. Jour. Neuropath. and Exp. Neurol., 22:175, 1963.

CROME, L. AND WELLER, S. D.: Infantile neuroaxonal dystrophy. Arch. of Dis. Childh., 40:502, 1965.

HEDLEY-WHYTE, E. T. *et al.*: Infantile neuroaxonal dystrophy. Neurology, 18:891, 1968.

HERMAN, M. M. *et al.*: Electron microscopic observations in infantile neuroaxonal dystrophy. Archives of Neurology, 20:19, 1969.

HUTTENLOCHER, P. R. AND GILES, F. H.: Infantile neuroaxonal dystrophy. Neurology, 17:1174, 1967.

INDRAVASU, S. AND DEXTER, R. A.: Infantile neuronal dystrophy and its relation to Hallervorden-Spatz disease. Neurology, 18:693, 1968.

NAKAI, H. *et al.*: Seitelberger's spastic amaurotic axonal idiocy. Pediatrics, 25:441, 1960.

RABINOWICZ, TH. AND WILDI, E.: Spastic amaurotic axonal idiocy. Cerebral Lipidoses. Van Bogaert, L., Thomas, Springfield, p. 34, 1957.

SANDBANK, V.: Infantile neuroaxonal dystrophy. Arch. of Neurol., 12:155, 1965.

SEITELBERGER, F. AND GROSS, H.: Ueber eine spatinfantile Form der Hallervorder-Spatzschen Krankheit. Dtsch. Ztschr. Nervenheilk., 176:104, 1957.

JUVENILE PARALYSIS AGITANS OF HUNT

Definition.—This is a slowly progressive Parkinsonian syndrome occurring either sporadically or in certain families and, according to Hunt, dependent upon a selective degeneration of the large cells of the lenticular nuclei.

Pathological Anatomy.—The brain is normal externally and no gross lesions are seen on section. Histological examination reveals degeneration and disappearance of the large cells of the globus pallidus. Some of the large cells of the putamen and caudate are affected in the same way. The substantia nigra is essentially normal. There is no evidence of inflammation or of vascular lesions. These statements are based on two autopsies, one by Hunt and one by van Bogaert. The liver was normal in both instances.

Clinical Features.—Most cases have occurred sporadically but there is said to be a familial element in several of the reported cases. The symptoms begin, as a rule, before the age of fifteen years. Tremor is first observed. This is typical of the Parkinsonian syndrome, being quite rhythmical and diminished by volitional movement. The tremor begins in one extremity and slowly extends until it is generalized. Later rigidity develops. The mask-like face, posture of flexion, bradykinesis, monotonous voice, dysarthria, and alteration of gait all develop eventually. The course is very slow but always progressive. Most of the patients are still able to walk twenty years after the onset. Mental changes are not prominent. The prognosis is bad and the patients eventually become helpless. Dr. David Clark once showed me a girl with a Parkinsonian syndrome of extremely slow evolution whose father had a similar neurological condition and at post-mortem examination showed loss of the large cells of the lenticular nuclei as described by Hunt.

BIBLIOGRAPHY

HUNT, J. R.: Progressive atrophy of the globus pallidus. Brain, **40**:58, 1917.
VAN BOGAERT, L.: Contribution clinique et anatomique à l'étude de la paralysie agitanta, juvenile primitive. Rev. Neurol., **2**:315, 1930.
————: Aspects cliniques et pathologiques des atrophies pallidales et pallidoluysiennes. Jour. Neurol. Neurosurg. and Psychiat., **9**:125, 1946.

HUNTINGTON'S CHOREA

Definition.—A chronic progressive type of chorea associated with mental deterioration and inherited by both sexes as a dominant characteristic.

Pathological Anatomy.—The brain is somewhat shrunken especially in the frontal lobes. The cortical neurons are reduced in number and the white matter is wasted. There are constant and severe degenerative changes in the lenticular and caudate nuclei where the ganglion cells are largely destroyed and replaced by glial cells. The process seems to be most intense in the putamen.

A recent article by Myrianthopoulos points out that no biochemical basis has yet been found for this disease and it is still impossible to anticipate whether or not an individual will develop this disease until the characteristic symptoms appear.

Clinical Features.—The history of this disease offers a remarkable illustration of the hereditary transmission of disease of the nervous system for it has been possible to trace the condition in the United States through many generations to its origin in three brothers who migrated into the country from England in the seventeenth century. Both sexes are affected and either may transmit the disease. Approximately half of the offsprings are affected when one parent carries the diseased germ plasm. The disease is never latent, it is claimed, and behaves as a dominant characteristic with almost complete penetrance.

The symptoms usually appear between 30 and 45 years but in a number of cases members of the affected families have exhibited symptoms in childhood. Cases are on record in which the first signs of the disease appeared as early as 4 years and death resulted before 10 years. Either dementia or chorea may constitute the first symptoms but as a rule choreic movements are well developed before any mental symptoms are noticed. The movements are similar to those of Sydenham's chorea but certain differences are apparent. If the patient is observed carefully in the early stages of the disease, it may be seen that the movements are abnormal only in that they are exaggerated. For example, the grimaces represent the natural play of expression over the face but each movement is so gross as to give a very different impression. The movements of the arms and hands are likewise often merely exaggerated gestures. Later, of course, the movements become so rapid and violent and their amplitude becomes so great that it is impossible to analyse them. Incoordination is not apparent at first but later is so severe that the patient is reduced to a helpless condition. Bulbar disorders are especially troublesome in many cases. Speech is lost and there is eventually inability to swallow. Eventually, the patient must be restrained to prevent injury for the violent movements result in constant trauma. The mental disturbances include irritability, emotional instability and finally complete dementia. Delusions and states of excitement may occur and asocial acts requiring commitment are not infrequent.

In a few cases, the choreic movements are not associated with definite deterioration and less frequently, the disease is manifest by only mental disorders. Sporadic cases are described which are clinically quite typical.

In most instances, however, in which neurological symptoms appear before the age of 10 years there is rigidity and tremor such as are found in the Parkinsonian syndrome. Chorea is absent. Convulsive seizures occur early in life and mental deterioration begins early also. The duration of this condition averages 8 years. At post-mortem examination the typical lesions of Huntington's chorea are found. In a recent review Myrianthopoulos states that 28 cases of this type have now been published.

Diagnosis.—The diagnosis depends upon the clinical symptoms of chronic progressive chorea with dementia and upon the family history. We must always consider the possibility of other degenerative processes which may give rise to similar symptoms.

Pincus, J. H. and Chutorian, A., describe a familial type of chorea which is not progressive and is not associated with mental deterioration.

Gath and Vinje find that air studies reveal widening of the ventricular bodies.

Prognosis.—The course of the disease is progressive and death results as a rule in from 10 to 15 years after the onset. Rare cases are described in which the symptoms are said to have become stationary for long periods. The affected individuals may be expected to transmit the disease to half of their children. The disease cannot be transmitted by unaffected parents.

Treatment.—No form of treatment is effective. Members of affected families should be advised against having children. It is claimed that rauwolfia will reduce the movements and stereotactically produced lesions in the pallidum may control the movements.

CASE HISTORY (No. 6317779).—*Huntington's chorea with onset at the age of 8 years. The disease was traced back for three generations on the maternal side.*

R. N. was brought to Johns Hopkins Hospital on February 17, 1953 at the age of 17 years. His father stated that the boy had seemed to be quite normal until he was 8 years old. It was noticed that he was unable to play baseball with the other boys because he had grown clumsy. Restless movements of the extremities were present. Mental changes were also evident and possibly had preceded the motor disturbances for the child failed the first grade at school. There was gradual progression of the motor disturbances. The boy's behavior had never been a problem.

The patient's mother developed chorea at the age of 20 years and died in an institution at the age of 35 years. A maternal aunt also died of the same disease. The patient's mother's mother had the same condition and died in an institution.

On examination the patient was well developed and nourished. He was cheerful and cooperative but slow to grasp what was expected of him. It was evident that he was somewhat deteriorated. There were generalized choreic movements of the face, trunk and all four extremities. No weakness or wasting of the muscles was present. Coordination was somewhat impaired in the extremities. Speech was indistinct and the rhythm was irregular. The station was unsteady. The gait was irregular and jerky. No loss of sensibility could be found. The reflexes were all in order except for "hung up" knee jerks.

BIBLIOGRAPHY

BELL, J.: Treasury of Human Inheritance. Part 1, Huntington's chorea. Cambridge University Press, 1934.

BITTENBENDER, J. B. AND QUADFASEL, F. A.: Rigid and akinetic forms of Huntington's chorea. Arch. Neurol. 7:275, 1962.

BRION, S. AND COMOY, C.: Rigidity and Huntington's chorea. Rev. Neurol., 112:813, 1965.

BYERS, R. K. AND DODGE, J. A.: Huntington's chorea in children. Neurology, 17:587, 1967.

CAMPBELL, A. M. G. et al.: The rigid form of Huntington's disease. Neurol., Neurosurg. & Psychiat., 24:71, 1961.

DAVENPORT, C. B. AND MUNCEY, E. B.: Huntington's chorea in relation to heredity and eugenics. Am. J. Insan., 73:195, 1916-17.

DUNLAP, C. B. AND MEYER, A.: Structural changes in Huntington's chorea. Brain, 50:631, 1927.

GATH, I. AND VINJE, B.: Pneumoencephalographic findings in Huntington's chorea. Neurology, 18:991, 1968.

HANSOTIA, P. et al.: Juvenile Huntington's chorea. Neurology, 18:217, 1968.

JERVIS, G. A.: Huntington's chorea in childhood. Arch. of Neurol., 9:50, 1963.

MARKHAM, C. H. AND KNOX, J. W.: Huntington's chorea in childhood. Jour. Pediat., 67:46, 1965.

MYRIANTHOPOULOS, N. C.: Review Article, Huntington's chorea. Jour. Med. Genet., 3:298, 1966.

OEPEN, H.: Paroxysmal disturbances in Huntington's chorea. Arch. Psychiat., 204:245, 1963.

OSLER, WM.: Remarks on the varieties of chronic chorea and a report upon two families of the hereditary form with one autopsy. J. Nerv. & Ment. Dis., 18:97, 1893.

OWENSBY, N. M.: Huntington's chorea in a twin child. J. Nerv. & Ment. Dis., 61:466, 1925.

PINCUS, J. H. AND CHUTORIAN, A.: Familial benign chorea. Trans. Amer. Neurol. Ass., 1966.

REISCH, O.: Studies of a Huntington family. A contribution to the symptomatology of different stages of Huntington's chorea. Arch. f. Psychiat., 86:327, 1929.

ROSANOFF, A. F. AND HANDY, L. M.: Huntington's chorea in twins. Arch. Neurol. & Psychiat., 33:839, 1935.

TRIDON, P. et al.: Infantile form of Huntington's chorea. Rev. Neurol., 110:531, 1964.

VESSIE, P. R.: Transmission of Huntington's chorea for 300 years. J. Nerv. & Ment. Dis., **76**:553, 1932.

DEGENERATION OF THE SUBTHALAMIC BODIES

In 1960, Malmud and Demmy reported the study of three patients who showed complex involuntary movements. One was an adult, but two were children. The children developed symptoms at the ages of five and six years. The movements were described as choreiform or choreoathetoid but some of them resembled ballism, for the limbs were flung about in a throwing movement. The process was slowly progressive. Mental deterioration became evident eventually, and there were pronounced emotional disturbances.

At post-mortem examination it was found that the subthalamic bodies were selectively degenerated. No lesions were found in any of the other nuclei of the extrapyramidal motor system. Lesions resembling those seen in Wernicke's encephalopathy were found in the mammillary bodies and the periaqueductal nuclei. These were attributed to malnutrition and were not considered to be a part of the basic process.

BIBLIOGRAPHY

MALMUD, N. AND DEMMY, N.: Degeneration of the subthalamic bodies. J. Neuropath. & Exp. Neurol., **19**:96, 1960.
MEZAROS, A.: Chronischer progressiver Choreoballismus. Ztschr. ges Neurol. u. Psychiat., **173**:461, 1941.
TITECA, J. AND VAN BOGAERT, L.: Heredodegenerative Hemiballism. Brain, **69**:251, 1946.

PHOTOSENSITIVITY WITH PROGRESSIVE DEMENTIA

Kloepfer reports a familial condition affecting seven children in a large family. Inheritance was recessive. Mental retardation was evident very early in life. In childhood exposure to sunlight caused blistering of the skin. There was progressive dementia and after adolescence loss of vision occurred.

Post-mortem study revealed loss of nerve cells and subcortical demyelination.

BIBLIOGRAPHY

KLOEPFER, H. W.: Progress report on study of a type of progressive juvenile dementia with oligophrenia and erythema. Proc. X Internat. Congr. Genetics, **2**:146, 1958.

A FAMILIAL SYNDROME MANIFEST BY ATHETOSIS, LOSS OF MUSCLE TONE, MENTAL DETERIORATION AND FEBRILE EPISODES WITH LOSS OF CONSCIOUSNESS (HARVEY)

Harvey, Haworth and Lorber describe a family in which the father and five children were affected. Apparently, the children seem to be normal in infancy. There are recurrent febrile episodes with unconsciousness. Following these illnesses, various neurological signs become apparent. There is athetosis, loss of muscle tone, loss of tendon reflexes, extensor plantar responses and mental deterioration. The disease thus seems to advance as a result of these episodes. Limited improvement may follow. There is no progression in the symptoms when the child is afebrile. The child may be unconscious for weeks and confused for months. One child died during a period of unconsciousness. No anatomical studies have been made.

Laboratory studies have been made without much result. The Wassermann reaction, air encephalogram, tests of liver function, spinal fluid examinations and tests for toxoplasmosis have been uniformly negative.

Attention is called to the cases of Miller and Gibbons. These authors reported twelve attacks of encephalopathy in three siblings between the ages of 11 and 14 years. Ten of these followed attacks of common upper respiratory tract infections and one was associated with acute follicular tonsilitis. Complete recovery occurred in each instance.

BIBLIOGRAPHY

Harvey, C. C., Haworth, J. C. and Lorber, J.: A new heredofamilial neurological syndrome. Arch. Dis. Child., 30:338, 1955.

Miller, H. G. and Gibbons, J. L.: Familial recurrent encephalomyelitis. Ann. Int. Med., 40:755, 1954.

THE CLASSIFICATION OF THE HEREDITARY CEREBELLAR ATAXIAS

A great many articles have been written about the various degenerative processes affecting the cerebellar apparatus in general and about the spinocerebellar ataxias in particular. Greenfield's splendid monograph offers a very careful analysis of this voluminous and confusing literature. These conditions are sometimes termed system degenerations for there is a tendency for certain structures to be selectively involved. In a broad general way, we may distinguish the following conditions:

The *hereditary spinocerebellar ataxias*. Hereditary ataxia in childhood is almost without exception of this type. Degeneration of the spinocerebellar tracts is the essential process but in certain cases there is also degeneration of the pyramidal tracts, the posterior columns of the cord and the posterior spinal nerve roots.

The *olivopontocerebellar atrophy*. This condition rarely develops during childhood. However, Carter and Sukavajana, and Franceschetti and Kline report cases of cerebello-olivary degeneration in children. Here we seem to be dealing with degeneration of the cortico-ponto-cerebellar system, i.e., the afferent pathway connecting the cerebral cortex with the cerebellum.

Cortical cerebellar atrophy. This is usually a disease of elderly subjects but Jervis and others have described cases in young siblings.

Degeneration of the dentate nuclei. Ramsy Hunt has described degeneration of the efferent system of the cerebellum, i.e., the dentate nuclei and the superior peduncles, under the term of dyssynergia cerebellaris progressiva. Gilbert's cases may belong in this category.

It should be pointed out that these processes eventually become more extensive so it is difficult to cling to the concept of a system degeneration. Thus, in Friedreich's ataxia, possibly the best known of the spinocerebellar ataxias, there is eventually mental deterioration, degeneration of brain stem structures, optic atrophy and even interstitial myocarditis.

Sutherland describes a familial type of spinocerebellar ataxia associated with loss of the light reflex of the pupils. Malamud reports a study of a family in which cerebellar ataxia was followed by the development of extrapyramidal signs. Woodworth described a familial disorder in which there were features of olivopontocerebellar atrophy, Leber's optic atrophy and Friedreich's ataxia.

BIBLIOGRAPHY

GILBERT, G. J. *et al.*: Familial myoclonus and ataxia. Neurology, **13**:365, 1963.

GREENFIELD, J. G.: The Spinocerebellar Degenerations. Springfield, Thomas, 1954.

HUNT, J. R.: Dyssynergia cerebellaris progressiva. Brain, **37**:247, 1914.

MALAMUD, N. AND COHEN, P.: Unusual form of cerebellar ataxia with sex-linked inheritance. Neurology, **8**:261, 1958.

SUTHERLAND, J. M. *et al.*: Atrophie spinocerebelleuse familiale avec mydriase fixe. Rev. Neurol., **108**:439, 1963.

WOODWORTH, J. A. *et al.*: A composite of hereditary ataxias. A familial disorder with features of olivopontocerebellar atrophy. Leber's optic atrophy and Friedreich's ataxia. Arch. Int. Med., **104**:594, 1959.

HEREDITARY CEREBELLAR ATAXIA OF FRIEDREICH

Definition.—A well known heredofamilial disease of the nervous system characterized by progressive degeneration of the spinocerebellar tracts, the corticospinal tracts and the posterior columns of the cord.

Pathological Anatomy.—Little can be discovered in the gross examination of the nervous system. In some cases, however, it is stated, the cerebellum is abnormally small and often the spinal cord seems to be more slender than normal. Microscopic investigation reveals demyelination and very dense gliosis in the posterior columns throughout their entire length. The anterolateral white matter in the region of the pyramidal tracts is affected in a similar fashion, but, as a rule, the process is not so complete as in the posterior column. A constant finding is the degeneration of both the anterior and the posterior spinocerebellar tracts. The posterior root fibers may show some degeneration which must be responsible for the loss of tendon reflexes. There is also severe loss of cells in the column of Clarke. Usually, no degeneration is found in the cerebellum proper despite its apparent shrinking, but mild degenerative changes have been described in the Purkinje cells. The degeneration of the pyramidal tracts can rarely be traced above the medulla. Detailed examination of the nervous system in advanced cases may reveal degenerations of the nuclei of the medulla, especially the vestibular nuclei, and mild changes in the cerebellum and its peduncles. The corpus Luysi and the pallidum may show degenerative changes.

Greenfield points out that in some cases in which dementia develops in spinocerebellar ataxia loss of nerve cells and gliosis are found in the cerebral cortex at autopsy.

Interstitial myocarditis is a very common finding.

Clinical Features.—The disease is definitely hereditary as well as familial and may, in many instances, be traced back for a number of generations. It occurs in both males and females, though somewhat more frequently in the former than the latter, and may be transmitted by either sex, and by normal as well as affected individuals. As a rule, the age of onset is roughly the same in members of the same generation, although it may vary within wide limits in different generations. The mode of transmission is obscure and it can scarcely be reconciled with any simple Mendelian law. Some authors postulate two morbid factors, one of which is dominant and one recessive. Macklin states it may be dominant but is usually recessive.

The first symptoms occur as a rule during childhood, but the onset is usually so insidious that it is impossible to assign a definite date to the beginning of the illness. We frequently elicit a history that the child was slow in learning to walk, or that the child was always clumsy, but it is not unusual to find that early development was quite normal in every respect.

The disturbances in gait are almost always the first symptoms to attract attention. There is a tendency to stagger and to fall. Naturally, the child cannot keep pace with playmates and is not good at games. There is difficulty in learning to write and it may be noticed soon that the child cannot handle a fork or spoon without spilling the food. Later, speech grows jerky and indistinct. The most striking early symptoms, therefore, are unsteadiness of gait, ataxia of the arms and disturbances in speech.

Examination in a typical and well advanced case may show little or nothing in the domain of the cranial nerves. Eventually, however, there will be found a rhythmical nystagmus on lateral deviation. Bulbar disturbances, if present at all, appear very late. Certain deformities are typical. The spine is almost always curved, a mild thoracic scoliosis being most common. The feet show as a rule a very high arch, pes cavus, and hammer toe. The great toes are flexed at the distal joint and hyperextended at the proximal joint. This deformity of the feet seems to be due to loss of muscle tone which causes dropping of the anterior part. This dropping causes tension on the tendons of the long extensors of the toes so that the toes are extended at the proximal joint. The extension at the proximal joints in turn causes tension on the flexor tendons and flexion of the middle and terminal joints of the toes. If the anterior part of the foot is passively lifted the position of the toes is corrected and the height of the longitudinal arch is diminished. If deformities appear early in life, they may produce frightful distortions after a number of years. The muscles may be somewhat wasted when the disease is of long standing, but at first they are quite normal and strength is very good. Muscle tone is almost always reduced when tested by passive movements and postural tone is especially affected. Incoordination is the most striking symptom. There are two elements in this: a cerebellar ataxia and ataxia due to degeneration of the posterior columns. Usually the former is predominant. There is always more ataxia in the legs than in the arms. The gait may be very unsteady when the heel-knee test is only mildly ataxic. The patient sways and reels as in other types of cerebellar ataxia, walks with a broad base and places the feet irregularly. Station is unsteady and Romberg's sign may be present. Oscillations of the head are seen. Speech is much impaired. It is often explosive and of irregular rhythm. Articulation may be so defective as to be incomprehensible. Irregular movements which seem to be involuntary may appear late in the course of the disease. These are described as choreiform movements but, in most cases, they seem to be merely an expression of the profound incoordination and are not entirely involuntary. Sense of position and of passive movement of the toes is lost or impaired and vibratory sense may be lost eventually. Two-point sense and stereognosis may be lost or diminished in the fingers. There is no loss of simple forms of cutaneous sensibility. The knee jerks and, indeed, all the tendon reflexes in the legs are lost very early in the course of the disease. Later the biceps and triceps jerks disappear. The plantar response is extensor in the typical cases, but this sign may be delayed for a number of years.

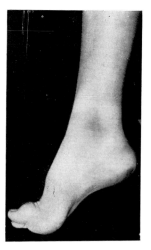

In the terminal stage of the disease, the patient is quite helpless and bedridden. The body is terribly deformed as a result of severe scoliosis. The muscles may be atrophied. Speech is lost or incomprehensible. High grade dementia has developed. Optic atrophy may appear. See hereditary cerebellar ataxia with spasticity. Incontinence is apt to be present, either from actual loss of sphincter control or perhaps from inattention to the sphincters. This stage is usually deferred until late in life but, if the disease begins in infancy and happens to advance rapid-

FIG. 125. Typical foot of Friedreich's ataxia.

ly, the patient may be bedridden before the age of twenty years or even by the age of puberty. Electrocardiograms in some instances show evidences of myocardial damage but clinical symptoms of cardiac weakness are not common.

Diabetes is not unusual in Friedrich's ataxia. See familial conditions in which juvenile diabetes is associated with diabetes insipidus, optic atrophy, nerve deafness and other syndromes.

Diagnosis.—The diagnosis is dependent upon the slowly progressive course, the positive family history and upon the following physical signs: (1) Signs of cerebellar ataxia such as the cerebellar gait, ataxia in finger-nose and heel-knee tests, the disturbance in speech, and nystagmus. (2) Signs of involvement of the posterior columns of the spinal cord such as loss of various types of proprioceptive sensibility, a tabetic type of ataxia and Romberg's sign. (3) Signs of disease of the pyramidal tracts which may be so masked by the other lesions that only a bilateral extensor response can be elicited. (4) Loss of tendon reflexes. (5) Characteristic deformities of the feet and spine. (6) Terminal dementia, bulbar disturbances and incontinence.

Prognosis.—The disease usually progresses steadily to complete disability. Certain abortive cases, however, seem to become arrested at almost any stage and others progress so slowly that the patient dies before disability is complete. Some aid in the prognosis may be obtained from the history of the disease in other members of the family and the estimated rate of progress in the past as well as from the age of onset.

Treatment.—No specific treatment is possible, but every means should be employed to maintain the patient's nutrition and general health at the highest possible level. Exercises and out door life are very helpful. In some cases orthopedic procedures are indicated.

BIBLIOGRAPHY

ALPERS, B. J. AND WAGGONER, R. W.: Extraneural and neural anomalies in Friedreich's ataxia. Arch. Neurol. & Psychiat., 21:47, 1929.
BAKER, A. B.: Friedreich's ataxia—A clinical and pathological study. Am. J. Path., 10:113, 1934.
BOYER, S. H. *et al.*: Cardiac aspects of Friedreich's ataxia. Circulation, 25:493, 1962.
FRIEDREICH, N.: Ueber degenerative Atrophie der spinalen Hinterstränge. Virchows Arch. f. Path. Anat., 26:391, 1863.
———: Ueber Ataxie mit bensonderer Berücksichtigung der hereditaren Formen. Virchows Arch. f. Path. Anat., 68:145, 1876.
GREENFIELD, J. G.: The Spino-cerebellar Degenerations. Springfield, Thomas, 1954.
HECK, A. F.: Heart disease in Friedreich's ataxia. Neurology, 13:587, 596, 1963.
HOLMES, G.: An attempt to classify cerebellar disease with a note on Marie's hereditary cerebellar ataxia. Brain, 30:545, 1907.
MANNING, G. W.: Cardiac manifestations in Friedreich's ataxia. Am. Heart J., 39:799, 1950.
NADAS, A. *et al.*: Cardiac manifestations of Friedreich's ataxia. New England J. Med., 244:239, 1951.
WALSH, F. B.: *Loc. cit.*

WINKELMANN, N. W. AND ECKEL, J. L.: Histopathologic findings in a case of Friedreich's ataxia. Arch. Neurol. & Psychiat., 13:37, 1925.

The Roussy-Levy Syndrome

This is an inherited disease, but the type of inheritance varies in different families. It begins as a rule in childhood. There is pes cavus and loss of tendon reflexes in the legs and reduction of tendon reflexes in the arms. There is atrophy of the muscles below the knees and even of those of the lower third of the thighs. The small muscles of the hands may atrophy causing the claw hand. The gait is unsteady and there is ataxia of the legs. The disease does not advance rapidly and may become stationary. Some patients are not really handicapped.

Some authorities regard this condition as a form of Friedreich's ataxia and others believe it is a combination of peroneal muscular atrophy and Friedreich's ataxia.

BIBLIOGRAPHY

GREENFIELD, J. G.: The Spino-cerebellar Degenerations. Springfield, Thomas, p. 31, 1954.

HEREDITARY CEREBELLAR ATAXIA WITH SPASTICITY AND OPTIC ATROPHY (BEHR'S SYNDROME)

Definition.—Certain hereditary ataxias have been described from time to time which differ from the type described by Friedreich in certain respects, such as the presence of spasticity and the early development of optic atrophy. The names of Marie, Gordon Holmes and Sangar Brown are associated with these cases. These ill defined conditions occur almost invariably in adult life. Behr, Takashima and Leeuwen and van Bogaert, however, describe similar cases in childhood.

Pathological Anatomy.—There is presumably degeneration of the spino-cerebellar tracts, the pyramidal tracts and the optic nerves.

Clinical Features.—The disease is familial and often hereditary. As a rule it affects both males and females. The symptoms begin early in childhood. The onset is gradual and the progression very slow. Difficulty in gait is usually the first symptom, and this is followed by ataxia of the arms, disturbances of vision with optic atrophy and spasticity of the legs. The tendon reflexes are not reduced or lost as in Friedreich's ataxia but are increased and there may be bilateral ankle clonus and Babinski's sign. It is probable that absence of degeneration of the posterior roots permits the spasticity to appear. Dysphagia and bulbar disturbances may develop later. There may be oculomotor palsies and ptosis of the lids. Mental deterioration may occur after years.

Diagnosis.—The essential features in the diagnosis are: (1) The positive family history. (2) The insidious onset and slow course. (3) The presence of ataxia of cerebellar type, of spasticity of the legs with increased tendon reflexes and clonus, the early onset of optic atrophy and occasional palsies of the extraocular muscles. (4) The absence of the deformities of Freidreich's disease, of nystagmus and of the signs and symptoms of degeneration of the posterior columns of the spinal cord.

Prognosis.—The disease usually progresses slowly until the patient is quite helpless and demented, but it may become arrested.

Treatment.—No specific treatment is known.

BIBLIOGRAPHY

ANDRÉ-VAN LEEUWEN AND VAN BOGAERT, L.: Hereditary ataxia with optic atrophy of the retrobulbar neuritis type and latent pallido-luysian degeneration. Brain, **72**:340, 1949.

BEHR, C.: Die komplizierte hereditärfamiliare Optikusatrophie des Kindesalters. Klinische Monatsblätter f. Augen heilkunde., **47**:138, 1909.

BJÖRK, A. *et al.*: Retinal degeneration in hereditary ataxia. J. Neurol., Neurosurg. & Psychiat., **19**:186, 1956.

FRANCESCHETTI, A.: Atrophie optique infantile associee a des troubles generaux (Syndrom de Behr) Schwetz Med. Wschr., **21**:285, 1940.

FRANCESCHETTI, A. AND KLEIN, D.: Heredoataxies par degenerescence spino-ponto-cerebelleuse. Les manifestations tapeto-retiniennes. Rev. Oto-neuro-ophthal., **20**:109, 1948.

TAKASHIMA, S.: Sechs Fälle der komplizierten hereditär-familiären Optikusatrophie die Kindesallers (Behr) Klin. Monatsbl. f. Augenh. 1913, n.f. xvl, s714.

VAN BOGAERT, L.: Premier observation anatomo-clinique de L'atrophie heredofamiliale complique de Behr. Bull. Acad. Roy. Med. Belg., **7**:218, 1942.

WALKER, J.: Disorders of esophageal motility in a family with hereditary spastic ataxia. Neurology, **19**:1212, 1969.

WALSH, F. B.: *Loc. cit.*

FAMILIAL DEGENERATION OF THE CEREBELLAR CORTEX WITH MENTAL DEFICIENCY IN CHILDHOOD

Norman has reported this condition in two families, three siblings being affected in one family, and two in the other. Jervis studied three siblings with the same condition and Scherer reports two more cases also in siblings. It is evident that this is a familial disease, therefore, and it is suggested that it is inherited as a recessive characteristic.

The symptoms are evident very early in childhood. A variable degree of mental deficiency is present. Cerebellar ataxia and nystagmus are observed very early in life. There seem to be no other symptoms. There is no deterioration in the patient's mental condition, it is claimed. The ataxia may progress or may seem to be stationary.

Post-mortem examination may reveal that the cerebral hemispheres are small and the cortical pattern simple, but there is no evidence of any progressive degeneration. The cerebellum shows gross atrophy. Histological study reveals extensive degeneration of the granular layer with less severe changes in the Purkinje cells. The Golgi cells are still present. The white matter and the dentate nuclei are not involved but the inferior olives may show changes. All authorities regard this as a degenerative process and not as a defect of development. More than half a dozen post-mortem examinations are recorded.

BIBLIOGRAPHY

GROB, E.: Case of primary, systematic cerebellar cortical atrophy with familial congenital cerebellar syndrome. Deutsche Ztschr. Nervenh., **182**:362, 1961.

JERVIS, G. A.: Early familial cerebellar degeneration. J. Nerv. & Ment. Dis., **111**:398, 1950.

LAMY, M. *et al.*: L'ataxie cerebelleuse hereditaire de l'enfance. Arch. franc. Pediat., **20**:5, 1963.

NORMAN, R. M.: Primary degeneration of the granular layer of the cerebellum: An unusual form of familial cerebellar atrophy occurring in early life. Brain, **63**:365, 1940.

SCHERER, H. J.: Beiträge zur pathologischen Anatomie des Kleinhirns. Ztschr. f. d. ges. Neu. u. Psychiat. bd., **145**:335, 1933.

HEREDITARY OLIVOPONTOCEREBELLAR ATROPHY OF CHILDHOOD WITH RELATED CONDITIONS

Carter and Sukavajana studied a family of nineteen children of whom several developed disturbances of gait, ataxia, tremors and speech difficulty late in childhood. The disease was progressive. It was apparently derived from the father who had the same symptoms, though the onset, in this case, was in adult life. Six males were affected and one female.

In the late stages of the disease, generalized muscular rigidity developed and mental deterioration became evident.

Post-mortem examination revealed profound cerebellar atrophy with degeneration of the olivary nuclei and substantia nigra. The changes were more severe in the cerebellum than in the pontine nuclei. Diffuse atrophy of the cerebral cortex was present.

Franceschetti and Klein describe hereditary spino-ponto-cerebellar ataxia with pigmentary degeneration of the retinae or macular degeneration.

CASE HISTORY (Unit. No. 1199436-Path. No. 35195).—*Olivopontocerebellar atrophy in a child of 2 years.*

D. G. was born at term by normal delivery. Birth weight was 6 lbs. She did well as an infant. She sat up at 6 months. Single words were formed at one year. She did not walk until she was 18 months old. The family history was negative for all diseases of the nervous system.

At the age of 20 months, the child began to become unsteady. Soon she could not sit alone. Then it became evident that her arms and legs were clumsy.

At the age of 25 months she was admitted to the hospital. Her head measured 49.5 in circumference. She was well nourished and developed. Her mental state seemed to be normal. There was gross ataxia of the arms and legs which seemed to be of cerebellar type. The child could not walk, stand or even sit up without support. There was no nystagmus.

The spinal fluid was normal. A number of neurosurgical tests were performed but nothing was found. All the standard tests for metabolic disorders were made with negative results. An air study revealed an excess of air beneath the tentorium. The fourth ventricle was dilated, but the third

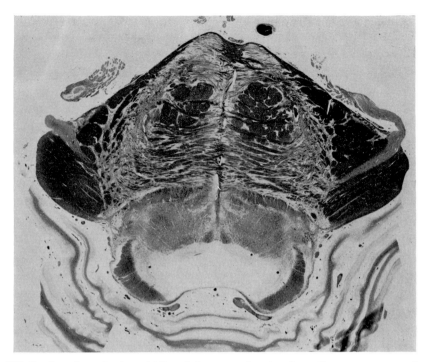

Fig. 126. Section through the middle of the pons showing loss of gray matter, and transverse fibers. The middle cerbellar peduncle is reduced in volume. The tegmentum and longitudinal fibers of the basis pontis are preserved. (By the courtesy of Dr. Bruce W. Konigsmark.)

and lateral ventricles were of normal size and no excess of air was seen over the cortex of the cerebral hemispheres.

The child was sent home, but soon developed pneumonia and died. Post-mortem examination revealed no gross changes in the cerebral hemispheres. The cerebellum was only 2/3 of its proper size. Histological examination revealed an almost total loss of Purkinje's cells in the cerebellar cortex and loss of granule cells. The white matter was thin. Half of the cells of the dentate nuclei were lost. The inferior olives and the accessory olives showed loss of cells. The arcuate nuclei were also involved. There was no degeneration of the long tracts in the spinal cord. There was gross loss of the gray matter in the pons and also loss of transverse fibers. The middle cerebellar peduncles were reduced in volume. The tegmentum and fibers of the basis pontis were preserved. I am indebted to Dr. Bruce W. Konigsmark for the anatomical findings.

BIBLIOGRAPHY

CARTER, H. R. AND SUKAVAJANA, C.: Familial cerebello-olivary degeneration with late development of rigidity and dementia. Neurology, 6:876, 1956.

FRANCESCHETTI, A. AND KLEIN, D.: Heredoataxies par degenerscence spino-ponto-cerebelleuse. Les manifestations tapeto-retiniennes. Rev. Oto-neuro-ophthal., 20:109, 1948.

OTHER TYPES OF HEREDITARY ATAXIA IN CHILDHOOD

Sjögren and Garland and Moorhouse call attention to a rare syndrome, of which about twenty cases are on record, which is manifest by cerebellar ataxia, mild mental defect, defective bodily growth, kyphoscoliosis, talipes valgus, deformities of the digits and in some instances pyramidal tract signs. Cataract is often the first sign of the disease and may appear early in childhood. It is believed that a single recessive gene is responsible. The process advances very slowly. Alter *et al.* report four cases of this disease in a family of colored children and review the literature. The only information about the anatomical changes in the nervous system is derived from a cortical biopsy studied by Marinesco. He describes changes in the nerve cells which are regarded as indicating a slow, chronic degenerative process.

Franceschetti *et al.* describe two types of infantile familial cerebellar ataxia. In one type there is external ophthalmoplegia, and, in the other, there is congenital cataract.

Gilbert *et al.* describe a familial type of cerebellar ataxia associated with myoclonus which begins in early childhood. They believe that the symptoms are due to degenerative changes in the dentate nuclei of the cerebellum.

Mathews and Rundle and Volpe describe familial progressive cerebellar ataxia with absence of sexual development and progressive dementia. The failure of sexual development was thought to be due to lack of gonadotropic stimulation.

Sylvester has reported a family suffering from progressive ataxia in which there was optic atrophy, deafness and muscular atrophy.

Mathews describes a family with progressive ataxia, deaf-mutism and muscular wasting.

Thoren has published a study of a family in which progressive ataxia of cerebellar type was associated with diabetes and with optic atrophy.

Tyce has reported cerebellar ataxia associated with mental deficiency and esophageal achalasia.

Hill and Sherman describe acute, brief episodes of cerebellar ataxia with complete spontaneous recovery in five generations of a family. The symptoms were most severe in childhood but persisted throughout life. Inheritance was that of a Mendelian dominant trait. No biochemical abnormality was found. No cutaneous eruption was associated.

White describes a familial condition inherited as an autosomal dominant trait in which recurrent attacks of nystagmus, vertigo and ataxia begin in childhood. In most cases there is improvement in adult life and in some cases the symptoms cease.

It should be kept in mind that generalized diseases of the central nervous system may give rise to cerebellar symptoms early in their evolution. Thus the juvenile cerebroretinal degeneration often causes pronounced cerebellar ataxia in the early stages. In some instances degeneration of the white matter may cause early ataxia of cerebellar type. The rare Pelizaeus-Merzbacher disease may be mentioned in this connection. The condition reported by Refsum *et al.*, heredopathia atactica polyneuritiformis, is manifested by cerebellar ataxia in addition to other signs.

BIBLIOGRAPHY

ALTER, M. *et al.:* Cerebellar ataxia, congenital cataracts and retarded somatic and mental maturation. Neurology, **12**:836, 1962.

ANDERSON, B.: Marinesco-Sjögren syndrome. Devel. Med. and Child. Neurol., **7**:249, 1965.

FRANCESCHETTI, A., MOSIER, G. AND KLEIN, D.: Über eine neue mit Ophthalmoplegia externa progressiva kambienierte infantale Form von zerebellaren Heredo-ataxie bei vier Geschinstern. Arch. d. J. Klaus-Stiftung f. Vererb. Suppl. 20, 1945, p. 59.

HILL, W. AND SHERMAN, H.: Acute intermittent familial cerebellar ataxia. Arch. of Neurol., **18**:350, 1968.

FRANCESCHETTI, A., MARTY, F. AND KLEIN, D.: Un syndrome rare: Heredoataxie avec cataracte congenitale et retard mental. Confina neurol., **16**:271, 1956.

GARLAND, H. AND MOORHOUSE, D.: An extremely rare recessive hereditary syndrome including cerebellar ataxia, oligophrenia, cataracts and other features. J. Neurol., Neurosurg. & Psychiat., **16**:110, 1953.

GILBERT, G. J. *et al.:* Familial myoclonus and ataxia. Neurology, **13**:365, 1963.

MARINESCO, G. *et al.:* Novelle maladie familiale caracterisee par une cataract congenitale et arret du development somato-neuro-physique. L'Enchephale, **26**:97, 1931.

MATHEWS, B. W. AND RUNDLE, A.: Familial cerebellar ataxia and hypogonadism. Brain, **87**:463, 1964.

———: Familial ataxia, deaf-mutism and muscular wasting. Jour. Neurol. Neurosurg. and Psychiat., **13**:307, 1950.

SJÖGREN, T.: Hereditary congenital spinocerebellar ataxia accompanied by congenital cataract and oligophrenia. Confina Neurologica, **10**:293, 1950.

THOREN, C.: Diabetes mellitus in Freidrich's ataxia. Acta paediat., Vol. 51, Sup. 135, p. 239, 1962.

TODOROV, A.: Le syndrome de Marinesco-Sjögren: premiere etude anatomoclinique. Jour. Hum. Genet., **14**:197, 1965.

TYCE, F. A. AND BROUGH, W.: The appearance of an undescribed syndrome. Psychiat. Res. Rep. Amer. Psychiat. Ass., **15**:73, 1962.

WHITE, J. C.: Familial periodic nystagmus, vertigo and ataxia. Arch. of Neurol., **20**:276, 1969.

BIEMOND'S POSTERIOR COLUMN ATAXIA

Biemond described, in 1951, a family in which the father, a paternal uncle, and four children developed progressive degeneration of the posterior columns of the spinal cord with ataxia.

Post-mortem examination of the father's nervous system revealed degeneration restricted to the posterior columns of the spinal cord and the posterior spinal nerve roots. There was loss of Purkinje cells in some of the cerebellar folia.

BIBLIOGRAPHY

BIEMOND, A.: Les degenerations spino-cerebelleuses. Folia Psych. Neurol. et Neurochir. Neerlandica, **54**:216, 1951.

PROGRESSIVE HEREDITARY SPASTIC PARAPLEGIA

Definition.—This is an heredofamilial degenerative disease characterized by degeneration of the pyramidal tracts and clinically by progressive spastic paraplegia. In the late stages the picture is apt to be complicated by signs referable to other parts of the nervous system such as ataxia, optic atrophy, dementia or wasting of the muscles. No doubt, several diseases may give rise to progressive paraplegia. Rhein's article reveals the existence of innumerable complications which may develop in such cases.

Pathological Anatomy.—The pyramidal tracts are always severely degenerated and the site of a dense gliosis. The degeneration is most complete in the lumbar segments and becomes less and less intense as the sections are made higher in the cord. Frequently it is impossible to find degeneration above the cervical enlargement and it is rare to trace it above the medulla. There may be mild changes in the giant pyramidal cells of the cortex, especially in the leg centers, but in other respects the brain is usually normal. In some cases, degeneration may be found in the posterior columns, the spinocerebellar tracts and even in the motor cells of the spinal gray matter, but in uncomplicated cases the lesions are confined to the pyramidal tracts.

Clinical Features.—The disease is strongly hereditary in most cases and may be traced back through a number of generations. Sporadic cases are, however, sometimes seen. The mode of inheritance is not always the same. In some families, both males and females may be affected and both may transmit the disease to their children. In one family which the writer has studied, the disease was confined to males and was transmitted only by unaffected females, thus indicating that it was dependent upon a sex-linked recessive factor. Cross and McKusick state that this condition may be inherited as a dominant, recessive or a sex-linked recessive disease.

The symptoms may begin at any age, but in the juvenile type are apt to occur between the first and tenth years. The onset is gradual and the progress of the disease is very slow. Often it is discovered that the child is slow in learning to walk and may never walk quite normally. After a time it is apparent that the gait is stiff and awkward. The child stumbles and falls frequently, tires quickly and cannot run as normal children do. On examination in the early stages of the disease we usually find merely increased knee and ankle jerks and, perhaps, a little spasticity. Strength may seem to be within normal limits at first. The spasticity is always greatest at the ankle joint and the ankle jerk is increased before the knee jerk is altered. There is a tendency to walking on the toes and to pes equinus, and claw toes. The Babinski sign may be negative. No sensory disturbances are evident, the sphincter control is normal and there is no muscular atrophy. Slowly the spasticity grows more severe and extends higher and higher. Muscular weak-

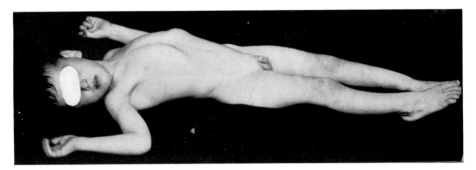

F<small>IG</small>. 127. Hereditary spastic paraplegia. At this time there was paraplegia-in-extension. Later, paraplegia-in-flexion developed.

ness now becomes apparent. The legs are apt to be spastic at all joints and the patient cannot lift the feet from the ground in walking, but must shuffle them forward. There may also be a tendency of scissors gait due to adductor spasm. Ankle clonus is easily elicited and the plantar response is definitely extensor. Later, the patient is unable to walk and the legs are stiffly extended as in paraplegia-in-extension. After some years, paraplegia-in-flexion may develop. By this time, the legs have become almost completely paralyzed, the lower half of the trunk is also stiff and weak, the arms have become spastic and clumsy, and the tendon reflexes are exaggerated. If the disease has been present from early life, the legs are strikingly underdeveloped and may seem only a little longer than the arms. The pelvis is also very small as compared with the shoulders.

In the late stages of the disease there is apt to be definite dementia, optic atrophy (see hereditary cerebellar ataxia with spasticity), wasting of the muscles, loss of sensibility, and ataxia. The control of the sphincters is not disturbed until late. Bulbar palsy or pseudobulbar palsy with loss of emotional control may occur. In some families atrophy of the muscles distal to the elbows and knees appears eventually in such a way as to suggest that peroneal muscular atrophy has been engrafted upon the spastic paraplegia.

Diagnosis.—The most important features in the diagnosis may be stated as follows: (1) The family history of similar cases in ascendants, collaterals or siblings. (2) A progressive spastic paraplegia of insidious onset and slow course. (3) The absence at first of loss of sensibility, muscular atrophy, ataxia, dementia, loss of sphincter control and visual disturbances. (4) The absence of any other explanation for the symptoms. If the family history is positive we are evidently dealing with some form of heredo-familial degeneration, but if this is negative, we must exert great care to rule out diseases which admit of treatment, such as spinal cord neoplasm, neurosyphilis and tuberculous spondylitis.

Prognosis.—The symptoms may be expected to advance slowly until the patient is completely incapacitated. The progress is very slow, as a rule, and many of these patients live to an advanced age. In some cases, especially where the arms are not affected until very late, the patient can make a living or at least contribute to his support by bench work of various types.

Treatment.—Various orthopedic measures may be helpful in enabling the patient to get about. Many of them can walk with crutches or braces even after the legs are paralyzed. There is no known treatment which exerts any effect upon the course of the disease.

CASE HISTORY (Ped. 63961).—*Boy of five years who developed weakness and spasticity of the legs in infancy. First paraplegia-in-extension, then paraplegia-in-flexion with finally atrophy of the peroneal group of muscles. Uncle, affected in same way at early age, shows more advanced symptoms at age of 20 years. Disease inherited as a sex-linked recessive.*

C. O., a boy of five years, was never able to walk. While he was still an infant it was noted that his legs were stiff and weak. These symptoms slowly grew more pronounced and when he was seen for the first time, the legs were very spastic and fixed firmly in extension. The arms were used freely, the cranial nerves were all in order, there was no disturbance of control of the bladder and no loss of sensibility. The plantar reflexes were extensor, there was a bilateral ankle clonus and increased knee and ankle jerks. The legs were not so well developed as the arms, but the difference was slight. No atrophy of the muscles was seen.

When seen two years later, at the age of seven years, the patient's condition was unchanged except that paraplegia-in-extension had now given way to paraplegia-in-flexion. The legs were flexed at the hip, knee and ankle and stimuli applied below the knee caused triple flexion. The feet showed beginning equinovarus.

Next year, there was, in addition to the above findings, some atrophy in the calves involving especially the peroneal muscles and causing flaccidity of the ankle joints and reduction of the ankle jerks. The difference in the development of the legs as contrasted with that of the arms was more obvious. The patient's mental development was definitely below par although the absence of schooling made the evaluation of this factor difficult. Vision was somewhat reduced, apparently due to myopic astigmatism, for the optic nerves showed no pallor.

The patient's uncle was also examined at the age of 20 years. He showed a condition identical with that of the patient, but at a later stage of its evolution. The legs were obviously small as contrasted with the arms. They were spastic at the hip and knee but very flaccid at the ankle joint. Strong flexor spasms occurred at the hip and knee. There was talipes equinovarus of high grade. Electrical reactions were almost entirely absent in the peroneal groups of muscles. The knee jerks were increased but the ankle jerks were absent. The plantar reactions were absent. There was no loss of sensibility, no disturbances in the control of the bladder and no evident dementia. The cranial nerves were all in order.

Among the siblings of the maternal great-grandmother there were four brothers who were all affected by symptoms identical with those of the patient. Of three sisters in this family, none was abnormal. The first sister had only one daughter who was normal, but gave birth to two afflicted sons. The second sister, the great-grandmother of the patient, had three children, two afflicted sons and a healthy daughter. The third sister had five sons, only one of whom was afflicted. The healthy grandmother had nine children in all; four of these were sons and all but the third were affected. The five daughters were, of course, healthy. Between these five daughters, siblings of the patient's mother, there have been 13 children. All of them are said to have been normal except patient, but there is some doubt about the accuracy of this information since the family resents the efforts of the social workers who have been trying to induce them to practice birth control, and have repeatedly refused information about the younger children. Evidently the disease is a sex-linked characteristic since it is seen only in the males and yet is transmitted by females. The males, of course, are never able to reproduce.

BIBLIOGRAPHY

AAGENAES, O.: Hereditary spastic paraplegia. Acta Psychiat. et Neurol. Scandinav., **34**:489, 1959.

APPEL, L. AND VAN BOGAERT, L.: Studies on familial spastic paraplegia. Acta neurol. et psychiat. belg., **52**:129, 1952.

RHEIN, J. H. W.: Family spastic paralysis. J. Nerv. & Ment. Dis., **44**:113, 1914. (Full References.)

SCHWARTZ, G. A.: Hereditary (familial) spastic paraplegia. Arch. Neurol. & Psychiat., **68**:655, 1952.

———— AND CHAN-NAO, LIU: Hereditary (Familial) Spastic paraplegia. Arch. of Neurol. & Psychiat., **75**:144, 1956.

STRUMPELL, A.: Uber eine bestimmte Form Der primaren combinirten Systemer krankung des Ruckenmarks. Arch. f. Psychiat. Nervenkr., **17**:217, 1886.

OTHER TYPES OF PROGRESSIVE SPASTIC PARAPLEGIA

Progressive spastic paraplegia is a syndrome which occurs in many different diseases. The process may be confined to the spinal cord, to the brain or may involve both the cord and the brain.

Van Bogaert has published a description of the findings in four different families. In one family the onset was in the first 3 years of life. There was progressive paraplegia and dementia. Degenerative changes were found in the brain and spinal cord. A second family in which dementia was associated with progressive spastic paralysis, showed similar but less severe degenerations. The third family in which the onset was at adolescence had optic atrophy as well as spastic paraplegia. The fourth family showed the spinal cord degenerations described by Strümpel.

Dick and Stevenson report the study of a family in which hereditary spastic paraplegia was associated with extrapyramidal signs.

Cross and McKusick found three types of familial spastic paraplegia in their study of the Amish. One type termed the Mast syndrome showed spastic paraplegia, mild choreoathetoid movements, minimal ataxia, dysarthria and severe dementia. In the Troyer syndrome, there was spastic paraplegia, dysarthria, mild ataxia and atrophy of the hands and feet. There was no dementia. In the Hershberger syndrome, there was variable spasticity of the legs, and severe mental deterioration.

BIBLIOGRAPHY

Dick, A. P. and Stevenson, C. J.: Hereditary spastic paraplegia. Report of a family with associated extrapyramidal signs. Lancet, i:921, 1953.
Van Bogaert, L.: Etude genetique sur les paraplegies spasmodiques familiales. Jour. Genet. Hum., 1:6, 1952.
Cross, H. E. and McKusick, V. A.: Survey of neurological disorders in a genetic isolate. Neurology, 17:743, 1967.

HEREDITARY AMYOTROPHIC LATERAL SCLEROSIS

Definition.—This is a rare heredofamilial disease characterized by degeneration of the pyramidal tracts and of the motor cells of the spinal gray matter. The clinical picture is similar to that of the common type of amyotrophic lateral sclerosis which develops in late middle age, and which is usually neither hereditary nor familial.

Pathological Anatomy.—It is doubtful whether the anatomical basis of a typical case has ever been studied. Maas, however, performed a post-mortem examination on a child who had nystagmus in addition to the characteristic features. He found, as might be expected, degeneration of the pyramidal tracts and of the motor cells of the anterior horns.

Clinical Features.—Several siblings may develop the disease and it is not unusual to discover that similar symptoms have occurred in previous generations. Both male and females are affected. The onset is between five and fifteen years in the type of disease under consideration, although the same picture may occur at any age. Either spasticity or muscular atrophy may be the first sign. The affected muscles show fascicular twitchings. These may appear before wasting is apparent but are soon followed by definite atrophy, which slowly grows more and more severe. The atrophy may begin in any group of muscles but is often first seen in the hands whence it extends to the forearms, arms, and shoulder girdle muscles. Not infrequently the bulbar nuclei are affected, causing atrophy of the tongue, and soft palate. The voice becomes hoarse, speech becomes nasal and indistinct and swallowing is impaired. Van Bogaert who has reviewed this subject distinguishes cases in which the bulbar palsy is the first symptom and cases in which the skeletal muscles are the first to be involved. Rarely are the motor nuclei of the third, fourth, fifth, sixth and seventh nerves affected. Spasticity almost always begins in the legs and may antedate the atrophy, so that for a time the picture is that of progressive spastic paraplegia. Both the spasticity and the atrophy are usually roughly symmetrical, but this rule is not without exceptions for the symptoms may be entirely confined to one side for long periods. If the child lives long enough, the atrophy extends so that the legs eventually become wasted and flaccid. The presence of pyramidal tract damage may be suspected in many cases by the fact that the tendon reflexes remain active even in muscles which are grossly wasted. Clonus may be elicited in most cases at some stage of the disease and Babinski's sign is usually present. If the process is relatively rapid, as it may be, a typical reaction of degeneration can be elicited, in the atrophic muscles but frequently it advances so slowly that there are never enough denervated muscle fibers present to give a typical reaction. The electromyogram shows fibrillations and spontaneous fasciculations and when muscle atrophy is advanced, a marked reduction of potentials on maximum contraction. Disturbances of sensibility aside from pains due to fatigue and to cramps in the muscles are not seen in uncomplicated cases. Sphincter control is retained until the terminal stages and dementia is absent or a very late symptom, but loss of control of the emotional reactions frequently appears early in the course of the disease.

Staal and Went report a study of a family of 15 children whose parents were closely related. Seven of these children developed the clinical picture of amyotrophic lateral sclerosis beginning at about the age of 10 years and ending fatally between 9 and 21 years later. Slowly progressive dementia was associated.

Diagnosis.—The diagnosis depends upon the signs of degeneration of both the pyramidal tracts and the lower motor neurons and upon the family history. When the family history is negative and only spasticity is present, we must rule out other diseases of the spinal cord. When both atrophy and spasticity are present, the diagnosis is simpler. The presence of widespread spontaneous fasciculations is characteristic.

Prognosis.—The prognosis is unfavorable though in some cases the symptoms have remained stationary for long periods. In the writer's small experience with cases of this type they have progressed much more rapidly than most other types of heredofamilial degeneration of the nervous system. Death frequently occurs from bulbar palsy or respiratory failure and terminal pneumonia.

Treatment.—No effective treatment is known.

BIBLIOGRAPHY

Brown, C. H.: Infantile amyotrophic lateral sclerosis of the family type. J. Nerv. & Ment. Dis., **21**:707, 1894.

Espinosa, R. E. *et al.:* Hereditary amyotrophic lateral sclerosis. Neurology, **12**:1, 1962.

FEARNSIDES, E. G.: Familial lateral sclerosis with amyotrophy. Proc. Roy. Soc. Med. London, Sec. of Neurol., **5**:143, 1912.

GORDON, R. G. AND DELICATI, J. L.: The occurrence of amyotrophic lateral sclerosis in children. J. Neurol. & Psychopath., **9**:30, 1928.

GRALAND, H. G. AND ASHLEY, C. E.: Hereditary spastic paraplegia with amyotrophy and pes cavus. Jour. Neurol., Neurosurg. and Psychiat., **13**:130, 1950.

GREEN, J. B.: Familial amyotrophic lateral sclerosis. Neurology, **10**:960, 1960.

HOLMES, G.: Family spastic paralysis associated with amyotrophy. Rev. Neurol. & Psychiat., **3**:256, 1905.

MAAS, O.: Zur Kenntnis der familiaren Nervenkrankheiten. Deutsche Ztschr. f. Nervenh., **41**:237, 1911.

REFSUM, S. AND SKILLICORN, S. A.: Amyotrophic familial spastic paraplegia. Neurology, **4**:40, 1954.

VAN BOGAERT, L.: La sclerose laterale amyotrophique et la paralysie bulbaire progressive chez l'enfant. Rev. Neurol., **i**:180, 1925.

WERDNIG-HOFFMANN INFANTILE SPINAL MUSCULAR ATROPHY

Definition.—This is a heredofamilial disease of infancy characterized by progressive degeneration of the motor cells of the spinal gray matter and clinically by muscular atrophy and paralysis.

Pathological Anatomy.—The process seems to start in the lumbosacral segments of the cord. The motor cells of the anterior horns are diminished in number. Some cells are small and shrunken. Others are swollen and show displacement of the nucelus and loss of Nissl bodies as in the axon reaction. Such cells gradually disappear without neuronophagia or gliosis. The

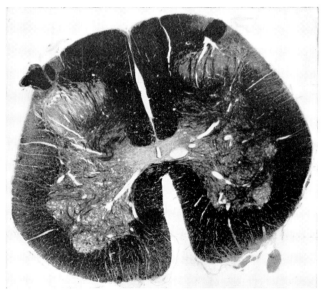

FIG. 128. Section of spinal cord in Werdnig-Hoffmann muscular atrophy showing well myelinated posterior roots and absence of myelination of anterior roots.

anterior roots are small and demyelinated, whereas, the posterior roots are well preserved. The nuclei of the cranial nerves show similar changes but these are, as a rule, less severe. Freeman has stated that the large cells of the motor cortex are lost but this has been disputed.

The muscle fibers are of two types. Numerous very small fibers are seen arranged in rather discrete bundles and also a few rather large fibers. No motor end plates are found on the smaller fibers. The transverse striations are usually present in both large and small fibers. There is little accumulation of fat in these muscles and not much increase of connective tissue.

Clinical Features.—In those cases which were formerly attributed to *amyotonia congenita,* there is often evidence that the process started in utero. The mother frequently states that fetal movements were feeble throughout pregnancy or having been vigorous at one time, diminished as term approached. At birth or within a few weeks after birth, the baby shows pronounced generalized muscular weakness and striking loss of tone. An abnormal range of movement is present at all joints. The feet may be placed behind the head with ease. The fingers may be hyper-extended so as to touch the wrist and the toes may be placed in contact with the anterior aspect of the ankle. There is some spontaneous movement of the extremities especially of the fingers and toes. Little movement is found at the proximal joints especially in the legs which seem to be completely paralyzed. This selectivity is more apparent than real for the proximal muscles act at a certain mechanical disadvantage. The chest does not expand but on the contrary is retracted during inspiration. Breathing is entirely diaphragmat-

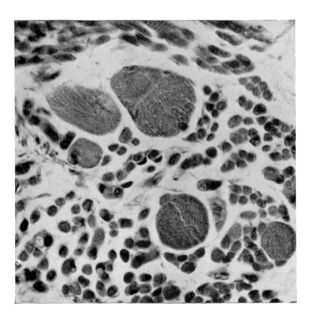

Fig. 129. Section of muscle from case of Werdnig-Hoffmann muscular atrophy showing large and small fibers.

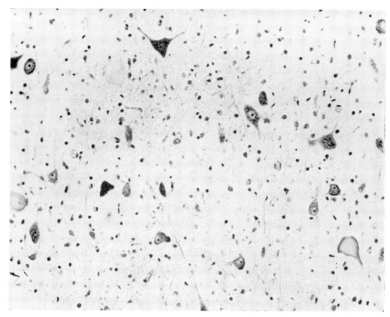

FIG. 130. Section through the facial nucleus showing a few normal cells, cells that are shrunken and stained deeply, cells that are swollen and have lost their granule and ghost cells which are scarcely visible. (By the courtesy of Dr. David Clark.)

ic. The diaphragm seems to enjoy a relative immunity to the process. The muscles are small and soft and are difficult to distinguish from the subcutaneous fat. These children cannot cough strongly enough to bring up mucus and the cry is a feeble one. The muscles of the neck, trunk and spine are affected as are those of the extremities. As a rule the muscles supplied by the cranial nerves are not severely affected at first but the face is often slightly immobile. The tongue may be weak and fasciculations and eventually atrophy may become evident. The tendon reflexes are always lost or at least grossly reduced.

Brandt states that in 66 per cent of all cases the weakness is evident before the end of the first six months but in some cases the child may not be affected before the end of the first year and may have learned to walk before the symptoms began. Such cases have always been recognized as examples of *Werdnig-Hoffmann muscular atrophy*. If the child has learned to sit up, he does not sit as steadily as before. If there has been any progress in learning to stand or walk, this ability is soon lost. The legs become weak and flabby. The weakness seems to begin in the gluteals and the pelvic girdle muscles. It extends into the thighs, shoulders, legs and forearms. The trunk is affected and the child cannot hold up the head. The abdominal and intercostal muscles are involved late and movement of the fingers and toes is lost last of all. Atonia is less evident than it is in the cases of earlier onset. Contractures soon appear and then deformities. The bulbar nuclei may be involved before death. The tendon reflexes which are present at first are eventually lost.

There is no sensory loss, no mental disturbance and no striking evidences of loss of sphincter control.

Males and females are affected alike and the disease is thought to be inherited as a recessive characteristic. Several siblings are apt to be affected in the same family but the disease can rarely be traced to previous generations.

Diagnosis.—The features of diagnostic importance may be summarized as follows: (1) A history of similar symptoms in a sibling. (2) The onset of progressive weakness and wasting of the muscles before the end of the first year. (3) Fascicular twitchings in the tongue and possibly in the skeletal muscles. (4) A subacute course resulting in death, as a rule, before the end of the fifth year. (5) The absence of all signs except those referable to degeneration of the lower motor neurons. (6) Evidences in the electromyogram and in muscle biopsy that the process is neurogenic. The list of conditions to be considered in differential diagnosis is a long one. It is given in the article on amyotonia congenita q.v. Suffice it to say that the differentiation of myopathy is the chief problem.

The electromyographic study is important in diagnosis. Spontaneous fibrillations, which represent the contraction of single muscle fibers and can be seen only in the tongue, are evidenced in the electromyogram by single potentials of a duration of one to two milliseconds and of an amplitude of 50 to 100 microvolts. There are also spontaneous fasciculations, which are visible in the skeletal muscles and represent the contraction of all the muscle fibers innervated by a single motor neuron or a motor unit. Between

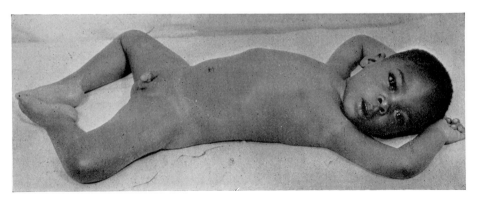

Fig. 131. Case of amyotonia, i.e. Werdnig-Hoffmann muscular atrophy of early onset, showing typical posture.

100 and 200 muscle fibers are contained in such a unit. They occur at an irregular rate between one in five seconds and two in one second. When the atrophy of the muscle is advanced, there is a great reduction of the number of potentials on maximal contraction.

Prognosis.—The prognosis is hopeless. Brandt states that half of the children are dead within one year and eighty per cent, within four years. He mentions one patient who survived in a helpless state for twenty years. The course is more rapid in the patients whose symptoms are noted soon after birth, it seems. When the onset is later, the course may be slower and the child may live several years. Death is usually due to pulmonary infection to which these children are especially prone.

Treatment.—This is merely symptomatic.

BIBLIOGRAPHY

BATTEN, F. E. AND HOLMES, G.: Progressive spinal muscular atrophy of infants. Brain, **35**:38, 1912.

BRANDT, S.: Werdnig-Hoffmann's infantile progressive muscular atrophy. Ejnar Munksgaard, Copenhagen, 1950.

BYERS, R. K. AND BANKER, B. Q.: Infantile muscular atrophy. Arch. of Neurol., **5**:140, 1961.

GREENFIELD, J. G. AND STERN, R. O.: The anatomical identity of the Werdnig-Hoffmann and the Oppenheim forms of infantile muscular atrophy. Brain, **50**:652, 1927.

GRINKER, R. R.: The pathology of amyotonia congenita. A discussion of its relation to infantile muscular atrophy. Arch. Neurol. & Psychiat., **18**:982, 1927.

HANHART, E.: Progressive infantile muscular atrophy of the spinal cord (Werdnig-Hoffmann disease) as a simple recessive sublethal mutation on the basis of 29 cases in 14 families. Helvet. paediat. acta, **1**:110, 1945.

ZELLWEGER, H. AND SCHNEIDER, H.: A new variant of spinal muscular atrophy. Neurology, **19**:865, 1969.

HEREDITARY JUVENILE MUSCULAR ATROPHY

Kugelberg and Welander have published 12 cases of progressive spinal muscular atrophy in children. These occurred in 6 families sometimes in more than one generation. Both males and females were affected. It was concluded that the disease depends upon a recessive gene which was not sex-linked.

The age of onset varied between 2 and 17 years. The large muscles of the buttocks and thighs were always affected first so the child could not arise from a squatting position or go up stairs. Later, the muscles about the shoulder were affected so the child could not lift the arms. Still later the muscles of the forearms became involved but the hands were spared until very late in the course. The muscles of the calves were also involved only in the terminal stage. The trunk muscles remained strong for a long time. The muscles supplied by the cranial nerves were all spared except for the sternomastoids which might grow weak. Sphincter control was not affected. Sensibility remains normal and mentality was never impaired. No evidence of pyramidal tract damage was found. Pes cavus and pes equinus were noted.

The authors point out that a diagnosis of progressive muscular dystrophy is always made until a complete study is performed. Fasciculations are seen in the affected muscles and this is the most significant sign in the clinical examination. Muscle biopsy and electromyograms reveal clear evidence of degeneration of the spinal neurons.

The course is very slow. Two subjects were unable to walk 8 to 9 years after the onset. Seven could still walk 20 years after the beginning of the disease. The patients can use their hands well enough to feed themselves and usually can earn a living.

Aberfeld and Namba describe a variant of this disease in which bulbar palsy and ophthalmoplegia develop.

As regards diagnosis, differentiation from progressive muscular dystrophy seems to be the chief problem.

CASE HISTORY (No. 765595).—*Mother and two children with hereditary, juvenile muscular atrophy.*

The mother was examined at the age of 38 years. When she was about 5 years old, it was noticed that she had many falls and could not run like the other girls of her age. She had much difficulty in going up stairs. There was extremely slow progression in her symptoms so that when she was first examined at the age of 38 years, she had just reached the point at which she could not do her housework. She had been conscious of twitching of the muscles for some years. Early in life, she developed pes cavus.

On examination there was diffuse wasting and weakness of all the skeletal muscles. The weakness was perhaps greatest at the proximal joints of the legs for she could not arise from a squatting position. She could stand on her toes only with great effort. The tendon reflexes were all present though sluggish. Spontaneous fasciculations were seen in the muscles. The muscles supplied by the cranial nerves were spared. The pes cavus had been corrected by operation.

The patient stated that her grandmother had pes cavus. Two of the patient's daughters, aged 3 and 13 years were quite healthy. One daughter at the age of 7 years had pes cavus and weakness of the proximal muscles of the lower extremities. Fasciculations were present. A son, at the age of 12 years, showed exactly the same findings.

Biopsy of muscle of the mother revealed patchy areas of atrophy characteristic of neurogenic atrophy. The spinal fluid was quite normal.

BIBLIOGRAPHY

ABERFELD, D. C. AND NAMBA, T.: Progressive ophthalmoplegia in Kugelberg-Welander disease. Arch. of Neurol., **20**:253, 1969.

ARMSTRONG, R. M. *et al.*: Familial proximal spinal muscular atrophy. Arch. of Neurol., **14**:208, 1966.

BROWN, M. R.: Inheritance of progressive muscular atrophy as a dominant trait. New England Jour. Med., **262**:1280, 1960.

CASTELLOTTI, V. AND SCARLATO, G.: Amyotrophy of Wohlfart-Kugelberg-Welander type. Sistema Nervoso., **18**:315, 1966.

FURUKAWA, T. *et al.*: Kugelberg-Welander disease. Neurology, **19**:156, 1968.

GATH, I. *et al.*: Myopathic electromyographic changes correlated with histopathology in Wohlfart-Kugelberg-Welander disease. Neurology, **19**:344, 1969.

KUGELBERG, E. AND WELANDER, L.: Heredofamilial juvenile muscular atrophy simulating muscular dystrophy. Arch. Neurol. & Psychiat., **75**:500, 1956.

MAGEE, K. R. AND WELANDER, L.: Heredofamilial juvenile muscular atrophy simulating muscular dystrophy. Arch. Neurol. & Psychiat., **2**:677, 1960.

SMITH, J. B. AND PATEL, A.: The Wohlfart-Kugelberg-Welander disease. Neurology, **15**:469, 1965.

SPIRA, R.: Neurogenic familial girdle type muscular atrophy. Confin. Neurol., **23**:245, 1963.

TSUKAGOSHI, H. *et al.*: Kugelberg-Welander syndrome. Arch. Neurol., **14**:378, 1966.

WOHLFART, G.: Hereditary proximal spinal muscular atrophy. A clinical entity simulating muscular dystrophy. Acta Psychiat. **30**:395, 1955.

HEREDITARY ATAXIA WITH MUSCULAR ATROPHY

Definition.—This disease has been termed "hereditary areflexic dystasia" by Roussy and Lévy and an abortive type of Friedreich's ataxia by others. It seems to present some of the features of the hereditary ataxias and of progressive neural muscular atrophy.

Pathological Anatomy.—Spiller found degeneration of the posterior columns, the pyramidal tracts and the spinocerebellar tracts as well as the lumbosacral nerve roots.

Clinical Features.—The disease is transmitted from generation to generation and affects either sex. In some families the onset is earlier in each succeeding generation. Disturbances in gait are usually noted first and may appear between the ages of five years and seventeen years. The gait seems to be mildly ataxic chiefly due to degeneration of the posterior columns. Some wasting of the calves becomes evident and, as a rule, this is confined to the lower third of the leg. The intrinsic muscles of the hands may be grossly wasted early in the course. The feet show both pes cavus and claw toes. In some cases there is kyphoscoliosis. Muscular pains and cramps occur in the legs. The knee and ankle jerks are lost.

Diagnosis.—The diagnosis depends upon the following features: (1) The positive family history. (2) Early onset and progressive course. (3) Signs of ataxia. (4) Wasting of the distal part of the calves and of the hands and loss of knee jerks. (5) Deformities of the feet and often kyphoscoliosis. (6) There is no optic atrophy and no mental deterioration.

Prognosis.—The prognosis is not entirely unfavorable because of the tendency of the disease to slow progression and spontaneous arrest.

Treatment.—None is known.

BIBLIOGRAPHY

BRUGSCH, H. G. AND HAUPTMANN, A.: Familial occurrence of Friedreich's ataxia with Charcot-Marie-Tooth's neurol muscular atrophy. Bull. New England Med. Center, **6**:42, 1944.

Papow, A.: Une famille atteinte d'une forme particulière de maladie héréditaire. Rev. Neurol., 2:447, 1932.

Roussy, G. et Lévy, G.: Sept cas d'une maladie familiale particulière. Rev. Neurol., 1:427, 1926.

Spiller, W. G.: Friedreich's ataxia. J. Nerv. & Ment. Dis., 37:411, 1910.

van Bogaert, L. et Borremans, P.: Etude d'une famille présentant la maladie familiale particulière de Roussy-Lévy. Rev. Neurol., 2:529, 1932.

HEREDITARY BULBAR PALSY

Definition.—A chronic progressive paralysis of the muscles innervated by the bulbar nuclei occurring in a familial and also in a sporadic form. This is termed the Fazio-Londe type of bulbar palsy.

Pathological Anatomy.—Gomes *et al.* published a post-mortem study of the nervous system in this disease, in 1962. Apparently, this was the first such study made. They found loss of nerve cells in the third, fourth, sixth, seventh, tenth and twelfth cranial nerve nuclei. They state that the findings are identical with those of the Werdnig-Hoffmann spinal muscular atrophy.

Clinical Features.—This is a very rare condition and only a few typical cases have been described. The onset occurs early or late in childhood and often begins with weakness of the muscles of the forehead and orbicularis oculi. The course is progressive and eventually all the facial muscles are involved, the tongue becomes atrophied and paralytic, the jaws, the soft palate, the pharynx and larynx are involved in turn. In some instances, the levator palpebrae and the muscles supplied by the third, fourth and sixth nerves which rotate the bulbs are involved so that ophthalmoplegia develops. These palsies are associated with loss of muscle tone and atrophy so

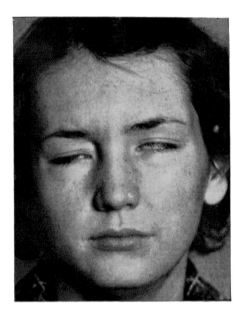

Fig. 132. Case of progressive bulbar palsy showing paralysis of the orbiculares.

the lips protrude causing the so-called "tapir-mouth." The reaction of degeneration may be elicited in affected muscles at some time in the course of the disease. Fine fibrillary twitchings are almost always to be seen in the tongue.

In some cases, the bulbar palsy is followed by progressive spinal muscular or amyotrophic lateral sclerosis. Van Bogaert has described this condition.

Diagnosis.—This depends upon the symptoms and positive family history as well as upon the exclusion of other causes. The electrical reactions may help in ruling out myopathy and myasthenia gravis. The injection of prostigmine may also help in the exclusion of myasthenia gravis.

Prognosis.—This is unfavorable. The course is said to be rapid in some cases.

Treatment.—No known treatment is of any avail.

BIBLIOGRAPHY

GOMEZ, M. R. *et al.:* Progressive bulbar paralysis in childhood (Fazio-Londe Disease) . Report of a case with pathologic evidence of nuclear atrophy. Arch. Neurol., **6:**317, 1962.

LONDE, P.: Paralysie bulbaire, progressive infantile et familiale. Rev. de Med., **13:**1020, 1893.

PAULIAN, D. E.: Contributions cliniques a l'etude de la paralysie bulbaire infantile familiale. Rev. Neurol., **38:**275, 1922.

VAN BOGAERT, L.: La sclerose laterale amyotrophique et la paralysie bulbaire progressive chez l'enfant. Rev. Neurol., **1:**180, 1925.

PERONEAL MUSCULAR ATROPHY

Definition.—A relatively common heredofamilial degenerative process involving the peripheral nerves and causing atrophy of certain muscle groups, notably the peroneal muscles of the leg. This disease is also called the neural, neuritic or the Charcot-Marie-Tooth muscular atrophy.

Pathological Anatomy.—The earliest lesions are found in the muscular branches of the peroneal nerves which become shrunken and degenerated. Later, the motor fibers of all the nerve trunks supplying the distal parts of the extremities are affected. Only mild changes are found in the motor cells of the spinal gray matter. In some advanced cases slight degeneration is demonstrable in the pyramidal tracts and posterior columns. The changes in the muscles are entirely secondary. In a recent review of the post-mortem examinations which have been made in this disease, Denny-Brown states that the process is essentially one of degeneration of the spinal nerve roots, the motor roots being as a rule selectively involved.

Clinical Features.—As a rule, the disease is easily traced through several generations and involves several siblings or cousins, but sometimes an entirely negative family history is elicited. Males and females are affected alike and either may transmit the disease to their children. According to Macklin this disease may be inherited as a dominant, recessive or sex-linked recessive.

The symptoms usually develop between five and fifteen years, but may be deferred until the third decade. The feet are inverted very early in the course of the disease, as a result of weakness of the peroneal muscles. Later, the anterior tibial group of muscles is affected and foot-drop appears, so that the child walks with a slapping, steppage gait. There is usually a well-developed deformity of the foot by the time this stage is reached. There is pes equinovarus, pes cavus and claw toes. The peroneal muscles are atrophied and the anterior tibial muscle group is also reduced. Fibrillary twitchings are rarely seen but have been described. Later, the gastrocnemius and the calf muscles are affected. The intrinsic muscles of the hands are involved somewhat later than the peroneal muscles and, by the time the calves are severely wasted, there is beginning atrophy of the forearms. There is

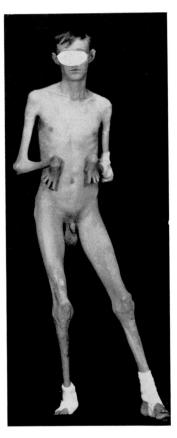

a tendency for the atrophy to spare the thighs, hips, upper arms and shoulders, so that it is only in well advanced cases that there is outspoken wasting proximal to the knees and elbows. In moderately advanced cases the patient's appearance is distinctive. The shoulders, hips and trunk are well developed and muscular and the upper arms and thighs are at least relatively normal, but the hands, forearms and legs are very slender. The contrast between the plump thighs and the slender legs with their claw toes has given rise to the term "ostrich legs." Eventually, the muscles below the knees may disappear completely and no electrical reactions whatever can be elicited. In fact, it is unusual to discover a typical reaction of degeneration. These patients are often able to walk fairly well even after all power at the ankle joint has been lost, since they use the leg just as an artificial leg is used. The tendon reflexes are lost eventually. First, the ankle jerk is reduced and then lost; next, the knee jerk is abolished, and finally, the reflexes in the arms disappear. Some patients complain of pains in the extremities, but these are usually merely the result of excessive strain upon the weak muscles and unsupported joints. It is unusual to find any definite loss of sensibility. In almost all cases, however, there are pronounced

Fig. 133. Peroneal muscular atrophy showing extreme atrophy of the distal muscle groups and deformities of hands and feet.

vasomotor disturbances, such as cyanosis and coldness of the extremities. Ataxia is not seen. The weakness and atrophy are symmetrically disturbed and usually equal on the two sides. I have seen several patients in whom one leg was involved several years before the other. In one patient, the left arm and leg were involved for 5 years before the right side was affected. Dr. John O'Connor has showed me a patient in whom the left leg alone had been atrophic for many years. His family was examined. It was found that the disease was present in three generations. In most instances, the process was bilateral and symmetrical, but in several patients it involved only the left leg, remaining localized for many years. The peripheral nerves are neither thickened nor tender. The plantar reflexes are eventually lost but are never of the extensor variety. The mental condition is normal. Sphincter control is preserved.

Recently, England and Denny-Brown have made a careful study of a large family in which peroneal muscular atrophy is frequently associated with extensive loss of cutaneous sensibility in the legs, perforating ulcers of the feet and atrophy of the bones of the feet leading to pes cavus at first and later to gross deformities. The family consists of 303 members in 7 generations, some 57 members being affected. In the more severe cases the onset is usually between the ages of 5 and 10 years. It is inherited as a dominant characteristic. This condition seems to link the common peroneal muscular atrophy with the rare condition which has been termed familial syringomyelia which Denny-Brown terms familial radicular neuropathy and I have ventured to term hereditary degeneration of the sensory nerve roots. This is described in the following section.

In some families, additional symptoms may develop such as optic atrophy and ataxia revealing apparent relationship with other degenerative processes in the nervous system (see hereditary cerebellar ataxia with spasticity).

Gibson describes a familial disease in which peroneal atrophy was associated with mental deficiency.

Kaeser describes a familial disease which begins with peroneal atrophy which is then followed by atrophy of the shoulder girdle muscles and then by bulbar palsy. Degeneration of the motor nuclei is found at post-mortem examination.

Dyck and Lambert describe a condition characterized by the clinical picture of the Charcot-Marie-Tooth disease in which hypertrophic changes are found in the peripheral nerves.

Diagnosis.—The essential features in the diagnosis may be summarized as follows: (1) The positive family history. (2) The weakness and atrophy which begin in the peroneal group of muscles and slowly extend to other muscles of the calf, hand, forearm, and later to the thigh and upper arm.

(3) The very slow course. In differential diagnosis we must consider distal dystrophy, various types of chronic polyneuritis including amyloid disease, hypertrophic interstitial polyneuritis, and the muscular atrophy with ataxia of Roussy and Lévy. These conditions are discussed elsewhere.

Haase and Shy, in a study of biopsy material, find evidences of myopathy as well as neurogenic atrophy. No doubt, distal myopathies are sometimes mistakenly placed in this category.

Prognosis.—The condition almost always progresses throughout life but the advance is often so slow that many patients claim that it is actually stationary. Unless the onset is very early or the disease advances with unusual rapidity, the patient will probably be able to get about until late in life.

Treatment.—No specific measures are known, but various palliative procedures are of value. Braces and supports for the ankle and foot are often helpful.

CASE HISTORY (No. 824328).—*Two brothers were found to be very deaf early in infancy. By the age of eighteen months, they showed slowly progressive wasting of the distal muscles of the extremities. There was also defective vision which seemed to run a slowly progressive course.*

R. L. and his brother, W. L., were found to be deaf when they were very young. It was presumed that their deafness was congenital. They could hear loud sounds but not words. Careful studies of their hearing revealed that their deafness was not very severe, but they had never been able to learn to understand spoken speech. Both had learned to read lips imperfectly.

It was evident early in life that the brothers had poor vision, and it later became evident that vision was failing. Examination at the ages of twenty-one and twenty-three years revealed pale optic discs and vision of 20/200. The retinae showed no changes. The fields of vision were concentrically constricted and there seemed to be minute central scotomas which involved much of the fixation point.

There was atrophy and gross weakness of the intrinsic muscles of the hands and the forearms were also moderately wasted. The muscles below the knee were severely atrophied and there was little power at the ankles. At the knee, strength was moderately reduced, and at the hips, strength was fairly good. No loss of sensibility could be found. The knee jerks were present but the ankle jerks were lost. The biceps and triceps reflexes were feeble. The picture was that of the Charcot-Marie-Tooth peroneal muscular atrophy.

The brothers were intelligent and well adjusted. Their handicaps did not seem to disturb them. Despite the difficulty in reading and in understanding what was said to them, they were able to get through high school. Rosenberg and Chutorian have republished a study of these brothers.

BIBLIOGRAPHY

BELL, J.: Treasury of Human Inheritance, Vol. 4, Part II. On the peroneal type of muscular atrophy. Cambridge University Press, 1935.

CHARCOT, J. M. ET MARIE, P.: Sur une forme particulière d'atrophie musculaire progressive souvent familiale débutante par les pieds et les jambes et atteignant plus tard les mains. Rev. de med., 6:97, 1886.

DYCK, P. J. AND LAMBERT, E. H.: Lower motor and primary sensory neuron diseases with peroneal muscular atrophy. Arch. of Neurol., 18:603, 619, 1968.

ENGLAND, A. C. AND DENNY-BROWN, D.: Severe sensory changes and atrophic disorders in peroneal muscular atrophy. Arch. Neurol. & Psychiat., 67:1, 1952.

GIBSON, R.: Peroneal muscular atrophy with mental defect and myopathy in siblings. Brit. Med. Jour., ii:1281, 1956.

HAASE, G. R. AND SHY, G. M.: Pathological changes in muscle from patients with peroneal muscular atrophy. Brain, 83:631, 1960.

MEADOWS, J. C. AND MARSDEN, C. D.: Scapuloperoneal amyotrophy. Archives of Neurology, 20:9, 1969.

MILHORAT, A. T.: Progressive muscular atrophy of peroneal type associated with atrophy of the optic nerves. Arch. Neurol. & Psychiat., 50:279, 1943.

ROSENBERG, R. N. AND CHUTORIAN, A.: Familial opticoacoustic nerve degeneration and polyneuropathy. Neurology, 17:327, 1967.

SYMONDS, C. P. AND SHAW, M. E.: Familial claw-foot with absent tendon-jerks. A "Forme Fruste" of the Charcot-Marie-Tooth disease. Brain, 49:387, 1926.

TOOTH, H. H.: The peroneal type of progressive muscular atrophy. A thesis for the degree of M.D. in the University of Cambridge. London, H. K. Lewis, 1886.

HEREDITARY DEGENERATION OF THE SENSORY NERVE ROOTS
Hereditary perforating ulcer of the foot—Hicks
Hereditary sensory radicular neuropathy—Denny-Brown

Definition.—A rare disease characterized by perforating ulcers and analgesia of the feet leading to atrophy of the bones of the feet and deformities. This condition is sometimes sporadic but may be familial. It has been termed familial syringomyelia.

Pathological Anatomy.—In 1951, Denny-Brown published the results of a careful post-mortem examination of a patient who came from the family originally studied by Hicks. He found advanced degeneration of the posterior spinal nerve roots, the posterior root ganglia and the sensory nerves. These changes were most severe in the sacral and lower lumbar roots. Amyloid deposits, which were considered to be secondary, were found in the posterior root ganglia. Degeneration of the posterior columns of the spinal cord was present and was thought to be secondary to the degeneration of the posterior roots. Degeneration of the cochlear and vestibular nuclei was found. The muscles showed no changes. No evidence of syringomyelia was found.

Clinical Features.—The clinical picture is well illustrated in the family described by Hicks. In 1922, Hicks published a study of a family of 34 members, including four generations, of whom 10 suffered from this condition. The onset was usually early in adult life but in other families the onset is sometimes early in childhood. First, a callus appears on one of the toes, and, later, a perforating ulcer develops. Soon the bones of the feet become atrophic and fragmented and are discharged bit by bit as sequestra. Gross deformities of the feet result. Pain and thermal sensibility are lost in the feet very early but this sensory loss rarely extends above the knees. Usually there is no weakness or atrophy of the muscles but the ankle jerks are soon lost and the knee jerks may disappear later. Sharp, brief pains occur not only in the legs but throughout the body. These resemble lightening pains of tabes dorsalis but the Wassermann test is always negative.

Loss of sensibility and ulcerations may eventually occur in the hands. Ataxia of the legs may develop after many years but this is apparently never severe. Vibratory sense is said to be preserved. Loss of control of the bladder is rare. The symptoms usually progress very slowly. In some cases which are clinically similar the onset is early in childhood and the course rather rapid. In the family studied by Hicks bilateral nerve deafness sometimes occurred but this feature is missing in other families. It must be pointed out that this condition is often sporadic. In the family of Hicks the disease seemed to be inherited as a Mendelian dominant character.

Prognosis.—The disease is apparently always progressive and in many cases it is necessary eventually to amputate the feet.

Diagnosis.—The diagnosis is based upon the clinical features described above. The distal distribution of the sensory loss and the absence of muscular wasting and paralysis are evidence against syringomyelia. A positive family history strongly supports the diagnosis.

BIBLIOGRAPHY

CLARKE, J. M. AND GROVES, E. W. H.: Syringomyelia (sacro-lumbar type) occurring in a brother and sister. Brit. Med. J., ii:737, 1909.

DENNY-BROWN, D.: Hereditary sensory radicular neuropathy. J. Neurol., Neurosurg. & Psychiat., 14:237, 1951.

GRANGER, M. E.: Sensory neuropathy with ulcerative mutilating acropathy. Neurology, 10:725, 1960.

HELLER, I. H. AND ROBB, P.: Hereditary sensory neuropathy. Neurology, 5:15, 1955.

HICKS, E. P.: Hereditary perforating ulcer of the foot. Lancet, i:319, 1922.

JOHNSON, R. H. AND SPALDING, J. M. K.: Progressive sensory neuropathy in children. Jour. Neurol., Neurosurg. & Psychiat., 27:125, 1964.

KHALIFEH, R. R. AND ZELLWEGER, H.: Hereditary sensory neuropathy with spinal cord disease. Neurology, 13:405, 1963.

KUROIWA, Y. et al.: Hereditary sensory neuropathy. Neurology, 14:574, 1964.

MANDELL, A. J. AND SMITH, C. K.: Hereditary sensory radicular neuropathy. Neurology, 10:627, 1960.

PARKS, H. AND STAPLES, O. S.: Two cases of Morvan's syndrome of uncertain cause. Arch. Int. Med., 75:75, 1945.

van Bogaert, L.: Histopathologic study of familial symmetrical mutilating arthropathy. Acta neurol. et psychiat. belg., **53**:37, 1953.

Walker, C. H. M.: Sensory radicular neuropathy. Great Ormond St. Jour. 1955-56 No. 10, p. 72.

HYPERTROPHIC INTERSTITIAL POLYNEURITIS

Definition.—This is a rare heredofamilial disease characterized by proliferation of the neurilemmal sheath of the peripheral nerves with subsequent degeneration of the nerve fibers and clinical symptoms of polyneuritis. Certain studies indicate that this is not a well defined condition.

Pathological Anatomy.—Studies by De Bruyn and Stern lead to the following conclusions about the nature of the anatomical process: (1) "Hypertrophy of the peripheral nerves, ganglia and spinal roots depending on two factors: One, an increase in the interstitial tissue; the other, which is peculiar to the disease, a proliferation of the sheath of Schwann with concomitant demyelination of nerve fibers. The proliferation of the cells of the sheath of Schwann gives rise to concentric layers of cells surrounding the axis cylinder resembling in cross section an onion bulb. The myelin sheath is usually destroyed but the axis cylinders often escape. (2) An associated degeneration of the posterior columns of the spinal cord, the relation of which to the lesions in the nerves and nerve roots may be consecutive, though this has not yet been definitely decided. . . ." Navasquez and Trebble state that reexamination of the material of De Bruyn and Stern revealed that amyloid deposits were present in the nerve sheaths.

Cammermeyer has shown that in the condition described by Refsum as heredopathia atactica polyneuritiformis changes are present in the peripheral nerves similar to those described above. It seems to be evident, therefore, that the histological features of hypertrophic interstitial polyneuritis are not entirely specific.

Clinical Features.—A number of sporadic cases have been reported, but as a rule several members of a family are affected and the disease may appear in more than one generation. Males and females are both affected. It is inherited as either a dominant or recessive factor.

The onset may occur in childhood and usually some evidence of the disease appears before the age of twenty years, although there are exceptions to this rule. Foot drop is the first sign to attract attention in most cases. This is, of course, due to atrophy and paralysis of the anterior tibial group of muscles. Later, the other muscles below the knees, hands and the forearms are affected. Sharp stabbing pains are said to occur and before long there may be cutaneous anesthesia over the feet and ankles, and even, perhaps, over the hands and wrists. Sometimes, a few fibrillary twitchings are seen in the affected muscles. Usually, the upper arms and thighs are not affected until very late in the course of the disease and the shoulders and hips are not affected at all. So far, the description has been quite consistent with that of the common peroneal muscular atrophy, but other symptoms have been described which are never seen in that disease. For example, there may be ataxia of the legs apparently due to degeneration of the posterior columns of the spinal cord. Kyphoscoliosis was observed in one of the first cases reported and has been seen subsequently. Nystagmus is mentioned although its anatomical basis is obscure. The pupils are said to be very small in some cases, perhaps as a result of degeneration of sympathetic fibers in the first thoracic nerve roots. Some cases are complicated by the presence of Argyll Robertson pupils. Bilateral Babinski signs and cerebellar ataxia are mentioned by some observers. Symonds and Blackwood offer evidence to prove that the spinal cord may be compressed. Possibly this is due to thickening of the nerve roots. The most characteristic feature of this condition, however, is the palpable thickening of the peripheral nerve trunks. In some cases these are so much enlarged that they may be felt under the skin like heavy cords or ropes, but in other cases the hypertrophy is not evident clinically and is found unexpectedly at post-mortem examination.

Gold *et al.* describe the study of 3 sisters with hypertrophic interstitial neuropathy and cataracts.

Diagnosis.—A recent study is that of Bedford and James, who found eight cases in five generations of a family. The diagnosis was made by biopsy of a nerve trunk. These authors stress the onset early in childhood, the extremely slow progression, the distal atrophy of the muscles of the extremities, minimal cutaneous sensory loss, more pronounced loss of proprioception causing ataxia of the legs, the loss of tendon reflexes and the normal pupils. In this family the disease behaved as a dominant. The diagnosis depends upon the family history, the weakness and atrophy of the distal muscle groups, the palpable thickening of the peripheral nerve trunks. Radicular pains, ataxia, nystagmus, myosis and kyphoscoliosis may be present or absent. If the diagnosis is in doubt, removal of a segment of thickened nerve should be conclusive. In differential diagnosis one must keep in mind peroneal muscular atrophy, distal dystrophy, amyloid disease of the nerves, leprosy, von Recklinghausen's neurofibromatosis and the hereditary ataxia with muscular atrophy of Roussy and Lévy.

Prognosis.—The course is so slow that many patients are able to walk until late in life, but are, nevertheless, somewhat incapacitated. There is apparently no hope of recovery.

Treatment.—No effective therapy is known but every effort should be made to prevent contractures and deformities.

CASE HISTORY.—*Pains in the legs and deformity of the feet early in childhood. Loss of tendon reflexes and reduction of sensibility in the legs. Gross thickening of the peripheral nerves. One brother and two nephews have the same condition.*

H. K., a man of twenty-nine years, was seen on March 21, 1960. He stated that his feet had been deformed since he was a small child. The deformity had been increasing slowly. Even in childhood he would scream with pain in his legs. These pains had persisted. They were described as sudden, sharp and brief, resembling the lightening pains of tabes dorsalis. His gait had become unsteady. He had no constant symptoms in his arms or hands, but had noted that if he turned his head to either side, the arm on that side would get numb.

His brother had exactly the same symptoms since he was a child. His brother's two children were affected in the same fashion. No one in the family had any digestive disturbances and all were in vigorous health except for the neurological process.

On examination, the cranial nerves were all in order. The pupils were of normal size and shape and reacted normally. The neck was not rigid. Turning the head to one side caused the arm on that side to feel numb. Pressure over the brachial plexus also caused numbness in the corresponding arm.

The arms and hands were strong and no atrophy was seen. The tendon reflexes were very sluggish. No loss of sensibility could be demonstrated. The nerve trunks above the elbows were grossly thickened and very firm. The ulnar nerves seemed to be 1.0 thick.

The station was slightly unsteady. The gait was ataxic. The thighs were muscular and strong. The legs below the knees were slender especially in the distal third. The muscles were firm and there was only a little weakness at the ankles. The heel-knee tests showed ataxia. The feet showed high arches and claw toes. I could not elicit the knee or ankle jerks but the plantar reflexes were normal. There was cutaneous hypesthesia over the outer aspect of the feet and ankles. Sense of passive movement of the toes and vibratory senses were reduced. The peroneal nerves were grossly thickened.

BIBLIOGRAPHY

ANDERMANN, F. *et al.:* Observations on hypertrophic neuropathy of Dejerine and Sottas. Neurology, **12:**712, 1962.

AUSTIN, J. H.: Observations on the syndrome of hypertrophic neuritis. Medicine, **35:**187, 1956.

BEDFORD, P. D. AND JAMES, F. E.: A family with the progressive hypertrophic polyneuritis of Dejerine and Sottas. J. Neurol., Neurosurg. & Psychiat., **19:**46, 1956.

BIELSCHOWSKY, M.: Familiare hypertrophische Neuritis und Neurofibromatose. J. f. Psychol. and Neurol., **29:**192, 1922.

CAMMERMEYER, J.: Neuropathological changes in hereditary neuropathies: Manifestations of the syndrome heredopathia atactica polyneuritiformis. J. Neuropath. & Exper. Neurol., **15:**340, 1956.

CROFT, P. B. AND WADIA, N. H.: Familial hypertrophic polyneuritis. Neurology, **7:**356, 1957.

De Bruyn, R. S. and Stern, R. O.: Hypertrophic polyneuritis of Dejerine and Sottas. Brain, 52:84, 1929.

Dejerine, J. et Sottas, J.: Sur la nevrite interstitielle hypertrophique et progressive de l'enfance. Nouv. Icon. d. l'Salpet., 5-11:63, 1893.

De Navasquez, S. and Trebble, H. A.: A case of primary generalized amyloid disease with involvement of the peripheral nerves. Brain, 61:116, 1938.

Garcin, R. et al.: Electron microscopic study of peripheral nerve tissue by biopsy in hypertrophic neuritis of Dejerine-Sottas. Rev. Neurol., 115:917, 1966.

Gold, G. N. et al.: Hypertrophic interstitial neuropathy and cataracts. Neurology, 18:526, 1968.

Harris, W. and Newcombe, W. D.: A case of relapsing interstitial hypertrophic polyneuritis. Brain, 52:108, 1929.

Krüche, W.: Zur Histopathologie der neuralen Muckelatrophie der hypertrophischen Neuritis und Neurofibromatose. Arch. f. Psychiat., 115:180, 1942.

Nattrass, F. J.: Recurrent hypertrophic neuritis. J. Neurol. & Psychopath., 2:159, 1921.

Symonds, C. P. and Blackwood, W.: Spinal cord compression in hypertrophic neuritis. Brain, 85:251, 1962.

RECURRENT HEREDOFAMILIAL BRACHIAL PLEXUS NEURITIS AND MONONEURITIS

Dreschfeld was the first to describe this condition. His paper was published in 1887. Taylor, in 1960, traced this disease through five generations of a family of 119 members. He found that twenty-four members were affected. He stated that this disease was inherited as an autosomal dominant gene with a high degree of penetrance.

In 1961, Jacob, Andermann, and Robb published a study of seven patients in two unrelated families. The onset of symptoms occurred at two years, five years, nine years, eighteen years, twenty-one years and twenty-seven years. Males and females were affected alike. Five patients had two attacks of neuritis, one had three attacks, and one had only one attack. Thus, there were fourteen attacks in seven patients. The usual symptoms were pain, weakness, atrophy of the muscles, loss of tendon reflexes and loss of sensibility. The findings on examination usually indicated that the roots of the brachial plexus were involved though in other instances the peripheral nerves were affected. There were eight attacks of right brachial plexus neuritis, two attacks of bilateral brachial plexus neuritis and only one case in which the left brachial plexus was affected alone. Two attacks of mild lumbosacral neuritis associated with brachial plexus neuritis are mentioned. The tenth cranial nerves were involved twice, the median nerve once and the radial nerve once. The onset was acute as a rule with severe pain. Gradual improvement began after a time and led to partial or complete recovery in most instances. The spinal fluid was normal. No porphyrins were found in the urine.

In one of the two families there was a tendency to small bodily growth and to facial asymmetry. Angioma, cleft palate and epicanthal folds were found in this family.

The cause of this condition is unknown. The authors point out that the symptoms are similar to those of allergic neuritis associated with serum sickness, but no evidence of allergy was discovered in their cases except for a tendency to hay fever in one patient. Pregnancy seemed to precipitate the symptoms.

CASE HISTORY.—*Repeated episodes of neuritis of peripheral nerves and brachial plexus neuritis beginning at the age of 14 years.*

J. De V. had an episode at age of 14 years during which there was pain, numbness and weakness in one leg and then in the other. She recalls that her tongue deviated to one side. There was recovery within two weeks.

About 6 months later, the symptoms recurred but did not last more than a few weeks. There was complete recovery.

At the age of 17 years, she had pains, numbness and weakness in both arms and both legs. The tendon reflexes were lost. There was recovery again.

Some months later, a fourth episode occurred. This was very severe, and she could not walk. Both legs and both arms were affected. She recovered completely except for some persisting weakness of the left hand.

After that she had tingling in the hands and face at times, but no disabling symptoms.

At the age of 26 years she developed pain in the right shoulder and soon could not elevate that arm at the shoulder. Within 8 days, it was possible to lift the arm with great effort.

It is of interest that a maternal aunt had episodes of pains and weakness in the arms during adolescence but recovered and had no such symptoms later in life.

On examination the right scapula is displaced laterally. The vertebral border stands out from the chest wall. Elevation of the scapula is preserved but adduction and rotation are very weak. At the shoulder joint, there is weakness in adduction, abduction and both internal and external rotation. At the elbow joint, there is weakness of flexion, but extension is strong. The biceps and radial reflexes are absent, but the triceps reflex is present. There is an area of reduced cutaneous sensibility on the outer aspect of the arm just below the deltoid muscle. The intrinsic muscles of the left hand are wasted and weak. Nothing else can be found. The cranial nerves are in order and there are no neurological disorders in the legs. The nerve trunks are not thickened.

BIBLIOGRAPHY

DRESCHFELD, J.: Some of the rarer forms of muscular atrophy. Brain, 9:178, 1887.
JACOB, J. C., ANDERMANN, F. AND ROBB, J. P.: Heredofamilial neuritis with brachial predilection. Neurology, 11:1025, 1961.
TAYLOR, R.: Heredofamilial mononeuritis with brachial predilection. Brain, 83:113, 1960.

RECURRENT POLYNEURITIS

The first case of this condition was reported in 1894, and since then, a number of isolated cases have appeared in medical literature. The cause is completely obscure. More than one case may be discovered in a family. The enlargement of the nerve trunks has suggested a relationship to hypertrophic interstitial polyneuritis.

In 1958, Austin analyzed thirty cases from the literature and added two cases of his own, which were carefully studied. In two families, he found more than one patient with this condition. The onset is usually early in life. Repeated attacks occur at intervals of months or years. The signs of distal polyneuropathy develop slowly over a period of months in most cases. On an average, the symptoms reach their worst within five months. Then improvement sets in and within about seven months, recovery occurs. In most cases there is completely recovery. Four patients have died. There is no pain as a rule and sensory disturbances are not prominent. The third, sixth, seventh, ninth and tenth cranial nerves may be affected. The sphincters usually escape. The spinal fluid protein is increased. In eleven patients, Austin found that the peripheral nerves had been enlarged. During recovery the nerves tended to return to their normal size.

Austin studied biopsies of peripheral nerves. There was edema in the subperineural space and between the bundles of nerve fibers. Harris and Newcomb performed a post-mortem study. They mention edema and nodules due to proliferation of the sheath of Schwann causing the onion bulb appearance seen in hypertrophic interstitial polyneuritis.

Austin found that corticosteroids seemed to cause improvement within a few days. The symptoms would recur promptly if the drug were withdrawn. This medication seemed to have no curative effect and merely suppressed the symptoms while it was being administered.

Other types of recurrent polyneuritis must be distinguished such as polyneuritis with porphyria q.v., allergic polyneuritis q.v., acute infectious polyneuritis q.v. and the heredofamilial brachial plexus neuritis of Taylor, q.v.

CASE HISTORY.—*Attacks of distal motor polyneuritis at ten years and at fourteen years ending in complete recovery. A third attack occurred at seventeen years. The peripheral nerves were thickened.*

C. M., a girl of seventeen years, was seen in April, 1962. There was a history of an illness at the age of ten years in which there was weakness of the arms and legs. The ankles were especially weak. There was no pain. Double vision was present for a short time. A careful study revealed no demonstrable cause for the symptoms. The patient recovered completely within a few months.

At the age of fourteen years, a second episode of the same type developed. Both the arms and the legs were involved. The weakness was not so great as it was in the first episode and recovery was more rapid.

In February 1962, at the age of seventeen years, the symptoms recurred for the third time. There was slow, progressive weakness of the arms and the legs. There was difficulty in walking, in writing and in fastening buttons. For a short time there was double vision, and also difficulty in swallowing with a tendency to get fluids up the nose. The voice was altered. There was no pain in the extremities.

These episodes were not preceded by any fever or illness. There were no signs of an allergic reaction. No serums or vaccines had been injected. There were no abdominal pains or mental changes. The urine was never discolored. The family history was said to be negative.

On examination the patient was slender and sparely nourished. No abnormalities of the cranial nerves were found. Possibly the voice was slightly nasal.

The arms were slender and poorly developed. The hands were small. Strength was slightly reduced at the shoulder and elbow joints. The grips were feeble and the intrinsic muscles of the hands were very weak. I could not be sure of any atrophy of the muscles. The tendon reflexes were lost. No loss of sensibility could be demonstrated. The ulnar nerves were grossly enlarged and very firm.

The legs showed better development than the arms. There was slight weakness at the hip and knee joints. The patient could arise from a chair without help of her arms, but could not arise from a squatting position. There was gross weakness of dorsal movement at the ankle and toe joints. Plantar movement was stronger but the patient could not stand on her toes even when both feet were used. The knee and ankle jerks were absent. Plantar responses were normal. The arches of both feet were high. No loss of any kind of sensibility could be demonstrated. The calves were not tender. The peripheral nerves were greatly enlarged.

The symptoms quickly receded on steroid therapy. The nerve trunks diminished in size.

In December 1962, the patient was still free of symptoms.

BIBLIOGRAPHY

Austin, H.: Recurrent polyneuropathies and their corticosteroid treatment. Brain, **81**:157, 1958.

Harris, W. and Newcomb, W. D.: A case of relapsing interstitial hypertrophic neuritis. Brain, **52**:108, 1929.

Ungley, C. C.: Recurrent polyneuritis. J. Neurol. & Psychopath., **14**:15, 1933.

HEREDITARY OPTIC ATROPHY
Leber's Optic Atrophy and Other Types

Definition.—This is an heredofamilial disease characterized by selective degeneration of the papillomacular bundle of the optic nerve.

Pathological Anatomy.—Kwittken and Barest have performed a complete study of the nervous system of a patient who suffered from Leber's optic atrophy. They found atrophy and degeneration of the ganglion cells of the retina and some atrophy of the inner nuclear layer. There was degeneration of the nerve fibers in the optic nerve, chiasm and optic tracts in the central region where the fibers for macular vision lie. Both geniculate bodies were shrunken and showed atrophy of cells. The optic radiation showed slight demyelination but the calcarine cortex was not altered. The changes in the geniculate bodies were attributed to transneuronal degeneration.

Very slight degeneration in the posterior columns of the spinal cord and peripheral nerves was attributed to the malnutrition which developed before the patient died.

Clinical Features.—*Leber's Optic Atrophy.* The disease is frequently found in several members of a family and may be traced through a number of generations. The first descriptions stated that it is confined to males and transmitted directly only by females so that it behaves as a sex-linked recessive characteristic. It has become evident more recently, however, that the disease may occur in females and may be transmitted in several ways. Macklin states it may be sex-linked recessive, simple recessive or dominant.

The onset of symptoms is usually at puberty but it may occur as early as five years or as late as middle age. Vision deteriorates very rapidly for a few weeks or months and it is usual for it to remain essentially stationary thereafter, though in some instances there may be a very gradual deterioration ending in blindness eventually. The ophthalmological picture is a very characteristic one. Bilateral central scotomas of large size are always present. These are usually absolute in the center and relative in the periphery. One eye may be affected a few weeks before the other, but both eyes are eventually involved. The periphery of the visual fields may be of normal extent, may be symmetrically constricted or show sector defects. In the first month the optic discs are usually congested and mildly edematous. Later these changes disappear and atrophy is seen. This is most marked on the temporal border of the optic discs, due to a more severe injury of the papillomacular bundle. The retinae show no changes. Many patients think that their vision has actually improved after the acute process has ceased, but it is generally believed that such improvement is merely apparent and due to a better utilization of the peripheral fields.

Numerous associated symptoms are described. Leber mentions that his patients often suffered from periodic headaches, vomiting, nervousness, vertigo, weakness and palpitation. Subsequent studies revealed that recurrent convulsions were frequently associated. Thus, Nettleship found nine instances in which epilepsy occurred in a family affected with Leber's disease. Various grades of mental defect have also been frequently described. Cramps in the calf muscles and paresthesias of different types are also common. Merritt's patient had club-feet which were inherited from the mother.

Ferguson and Critchley report four cases in one of which epilepsy and mental defect were associated, and in another pyramidal tract degeneration, ataxia and loss of proprioceptive sensibility. These authors also mention disturbances of speech and abnormal postures. I have observed congenital athetosis in one member of an affected family.

Went and Bruyn describe cases in which athetosis and spasticity were associated.

Wilson and his associates mention patients with Leber's optic atrophy with motor neuron disease, extrapyramidal symptoms, cerebellar and posterior column ataxia and transverse myelitis. He emphasizes burning pain in the lower part of the back and scoliosis. He speaks of cases without optic atrophy. He has made studies of the cyanide metabolism and states that it is possible that this disease is due to inability to detoxicate cyanides.

Another type of hereditary optic atrophy has been described by Kjer and others. We have seen three families in which this condition is prevalent. In one family five members were affected in three generations. In the second family four members were afflicted in two generations. In the third, eight cases were found in three generations. Both males and females are affected and Kjer claims that the mode of inheritance is that of a dominant characteristic. The defect of vision is recognized at about the age of 6 years as a rule. A small scotoma between the blind spot and the point of fixation is the first finding. At this time, there is temporal pallor of the discs. There is extremely slow progression. In adult life, central vision is greatly reduced and may be no more than 5/200. It seems that vision is never completely lost. The most obvious difference between this condition and Leber's optic atrophy is that the sudden and dramatic reduction of vision characteristic of the latter is missing and the progression is so slow that many individuals do not realize that vision is actually failing.

Leeuwen and van Bogaert distinguish three types of optic atrophy associated with hereditary ataxia. In one type there is a central scotoma and bitemporal pallor of the optic nerve heads. The scotoma usually appears early in life, but the peripheral fields may not be greatly reduced for many years. A second type, which also develops early, is characterized by diffuse pallor and rapid loss of vision which may result in blindness. The third type which is less sharply defined than the first two, is manifest by concentric constriction of the fields of vision, moderate reduction of central vision and slow progression. The optic atrophy may precede the other symptoms. These authors state that the same types of optic atrophy occur in familial spastic paralysis and the Charcot-Marie-Tooth muscular atrophy. Björk *et al.* state that in some cases, the lesion is not in the optic nerves but is in the retinae. Such lesions may be difficult to demonstrate with the ophthalmoscope but are demonstrable by electroretinography. In rare instances the neurological evidences of familial ataxia may be associated with pigmentary degeneration, macular degeneration or albescens punctata retinitis. Franceschetti and Klein describe such cases.

Diagnosis.—The diagnosis depends chiefly upon the family history since in many cases the picture is merely that of retrobulbar neuritis which might be due to many causes. Females are rarely affected in Leber's type but are affected frequently in Kjer's type.

Prognosis.—In Leber's disease as a rule vision declines very rapidly for weeks or months and then limited improvement, or apparent improvement, may ensue. Thereafter vision may remain at a low level for many years or there may be a gradual failure with complete blindness. It has been claimed that recovery of normal vision may occur but it is difficult to see how the diagnosis could be established in such cases. In Kjer's type progression is very slow.

Treatment.—None is effective.

CASE HISTORY.—*Central scotomas appearing at about the age of six or eight years in four generations of a family. Both sexes affected. Very slow progression of loss of vision. Temporal pallor of optic discs. Kjer's hereditary optic atrophy.*

S. C. was seen at the age of ten years in consultation with Dr. Walsh. For several years, it had been suspected that his vision was defective. Examination revealed the vision of each eye was reduced to 10/50. There were small central scotomas, but the outlines of the fields were full. There was very slight pallor of the temporal sides of the optic discs.

The family history was of great interest. The great-grandfather, the grandfather, the father, two uncles, one aunt and three first cousins, all on the father's side of the family, were found to have failing vision early in life. The failure of vision progressed very slowly and the peripheral fields were never involved. No one in the family became blind, even in old age.

The father was also examined. His optic discs showed pronounced temporal pallor. Vision was 20/300 and there were large central scotomas.

There were no neurological abnormalities to be found in the father or the patient. No history of any neurological symptoms were elicited in regard to other members of the family. No mental deterioration occurred in this family.

BIBLIOGRAPHY

ADAMS, *et al.:* Further clinical and pathological observations on Leber's optic atrophy. Brain, **89:**15, 1966.

ANDRE-VAN LEEUWEN AND VAN BOGAERT, L.: Hereditary ataxia with optic atrophy of the retrobulbar neuritis type and latent pallido-luysian degeneration. Brain, **72:**340, 1949.

BEHR, C.: Die komplizierte hereditärfamiliare Optikusatrophie des Kindesalters. Klinische Monatsblätter f. Augenheilkunde, **47:**138, 1909.

BELL, J.: Hereditary optic atrophy. Treasury of Human Inheritance, Vol. 2, Cambridge Univ. Press, 1931.

Björk, A. *et al.:* Retinal degeneration in hereditary ataxia. J. Neurol., Neurosurg. & Psychiat. **19:**186, 1965.

Bruyn, G. W. and Went, L. N.: A sex-linked heredodegenerative neurological disorder associated with Leber's optic atrophy. Part 1. Clinical studies. Jour. Neurol, Sci., 1:59, 1964.

Ferguson, F. R. and Critchley, M.: Leber's optic atrophy and its relationship with the heredofamilial ataxias. J. Neurol. & Psychopath., **9:**120, 1928.

Kjer, P.: Hereditary infantile optic atrophy with dominant transmission. Danish Med. Bull., 3:135, 1956.

Kwittken, J. and Barest, H. D.: The neuropathology of hereditary optic atrophy (Leber's disease). The first complete anatomic study. Am. J. Path., **34:**185, 1958.

Leber, Th.: Uber hereditare u. congenital angelagte Sehenervenleiden. Arch. f. Ophth., **17:**249, 1871.

Merritt, H. H.: Hereditary optic atrophy. Arch. Neurol. & Psychiat., **24:**775, 1930. (Full references.)

Taylor, J. and Holmes, G.: Two families with several members in each suffering from optic atrophy. Tr. Ophth. Soc. U. Kingdom, **33:**95, 1913.

Walsh, F. B.: *Loc. cit.*

Went, L. N.: A sex-linked heredo-degenerative neurological disorder associated with Lebers optic atrophy. Acta genet. Basl., **14:**220, 1964.

Wilson, J.: Skeletal manifestations of Leber's optic atrophy. A possible disorder of cyanide metabolism. Ann. Physical Med., **8:**91, 1965.

———: Leber's hereditary optic atrophy. A possible defect of cyanide metabolism. Clin. Sci., **29:**505, 1965.

———: Leber's hereditary optic atrophy. Brain, **86:**347, 1963.

HYALINE BODIES IN THE OPTIC NERVE HEAD

Various deposits in the optic nerve heads are sometimes seen. These are spoken of as hyaline bodies, drusen bodies and concretions. These are amorphous deposits containing calcium. It is stated that they may occur as a familial anomaly and also in such diseases as retinitis pigmentosa, tuberose sclerosis and angioid streaks of the retina. They are as a rule multiple, rounded, grayish bodies of semitranslucent appearance. In the early stages of this process, the deposits may be so deeply placed that they are not visible and the swollen discs may simulate true papilledema very closely. Even experienced observers may be led to suspect intracranial neoplasm. Later, in most instances, the hyaline bodies become visible. Often there is eventually constriction of the visual fields which begins in the inferior nasal quadrants. Optic atrophy may result. Sudden loss of vision may occur probably as a result of compression and occlusion of the central retinal artery. We have examined one family in which the two daughters had papilledema without any hyaline bodies or defects in the fields. Their mother had papilledema with large hyaline bodies and defects in the inferior nasal quadrants. After a few years small hyaline bodies became visible in the daughters' optic discs. Dr. Frank B. Walsh and Dr. John Chamber have recently reported a series of such cases in which an erroneous diagnosis of brain tumor had been made.

Case History (No. 566854).—*Child of seven years eight months began to lose vision in both eyes. Bilateral papilledema diagnosed. Ventriculo-*

gram revealed nothing significant. Neurological examination negative.
Hyaline bodies of the optic nerve heads found subsequently.

J. R., a previously healthy girl of 6 years, was found on routine test at school to have 20/20 vision in each eye. This test was made in November 1949. In February 1950, vision was found to be 20/30. In October 1950, vision was down to 20/70 in each eye. An ophthalmologist found concentric constriction of the visual fields and bilateral papilledema with beginning optic atrophy. The neurological examination was entirely negative. There were no complaints of headache, vomiting, dizziness or other symptoms suggestive of increased intracranial pressure.

Roentgenograms of the skull revealed no abnormalities. Ventriculograms revealed nothing of significance. Other studies did not help.

Examination at the age of seven years and eight months revealed only concentrically constricted fields of vision and reduction of central vision. The optic nerve heads were elevated and ill-defined. The cups were obscured. The veins were engorged and tortuous. The color was distinctly pale. In the margins of the discs were hyaline, amorphous bodies embedded in the nerve fibers. These were seen well on the right but were more numerous on the left. Otherwise the cranial nerves, motility, sensibility and the reflexes were all in order. No mental changes were present.

Dr. Walsh examined the patient and agreed with the diagnosis of hyaline bodies in the optic nerve heads.

BIBLIOGRAPHY

CHAMBERS, J. W. AND WALSH, F. B.: Hyaline bodies in the optic discs. Report of ten cases exemplifying importance in neurological diagnosis. Brain, 74:95, 1951.
RUCKER, C. W.: Defects in the visual fields produced by hyaline bodies in the optic discs. Arch. Ophth., 32:56, 1944.

THE MYOTONIC PUPIL (Adie's Syndrome)

The myotonic pupil is rarely observed in children, but a brief description is justified. The cause is unknown. It is usually unilateral. The pupil is almost always dilated, but circular. The size of the pupil is so great that one would imagine that the constrictors are damaged but the dilator fibers are intact so maximal dilatation occurs. Ruttner has found degeneration of the ciliary body in one case and it seems probable that the lesion is in that structure.

The size of the pupil varies for no apparent reason. The direct reaction to light is apparently lost, but if the patient stays in a bright light for a time, it slowly contracts. In the same way, the pupil fails to contract during accommodation though after prolonged fixation for possibly five minutes on a near object, it will often diminish in size. Having contracted in this way, it expands very slowly. Eventually, there is often loss of accommodation and total internal ophthalmoplegia. It is claimed that a drop of 2.5

per cent mecholyl will make the affected pupil contract, but not the normal pupil.

In some cases the knee jerks cannot be elicited. This is not easy to understand for there is no evidence of damage to either the motor or sensory pathways. Hardin and Gay discuss this problem. They suggest that the spinal synapses are blocked. I have seen this condition in father and a six-year-old daughter. See acquired segmental hypohidrosis with tonic pupils.

BIBLIOGRAPHY

Adie, W. J.: Tonic pupils and absent tendon reflexes. A benign disorder sui generis. Brain, **55**:928, 1932.

Hardin, W. B. and Gay, A. J.: The phenomenon of benign areflexoa. Neurology, **15**:613, 1965.

Laties, A. M. and Scheie, H. G.: Adie's syndrome. Arch. of Ophthal., **74**:458, 1965.

Levy, R.: The tendon reflexes in the Holmes-Adie syndrome. Neurology, **17**:1213, 1967.

Petajan, J. H. *et al.:* Progressive sudomotor denervation and Adie's syndrome. Neurology, **15**:172, 1965.

Rudolf, G. de M.: Tonic pupils with absent tendon reflexes in mother and daughter. Jour Neurol. and Psychopath., **16**:367, 1936.

Ruttner, F.: Tonic pupil: Clinical and anatomical investigation. Monatschr. f. Psychiat. u. Neurol., **114**:265, 1947.

Walsh, F. B.: Clinical Neuroophthalmology, 2nd Ed. Williams & Wilkins, 1957, p. 164.

HEREDITARY TREMOR

Definition.—This term refers to an inherited tremor which begins as a rule early in life and progresses very slowly indeed. This condition is regarded as a monosymptomatic heredofamilial degenerative process. It is possible that we are dealing with more than one condition. In some cases which seem to be quite static, a congenital defect of the nervous system may be responsible. Other names which have been employed are *inherited tremor* and *essential tremor*.

Pathological Anatomy.—The anatomical basis of this condition is unknown.

Clinical Features.—In many cases, the tremor may be traced through several generations, and, frequently, a number of children in a family are affected. In other families, only one child may be affected. As a rule, the family tree suggests that we are dealing with a dominant characteristic. Both males and females are subject to this condition, and either may transmit it. Critchley states that the tremor may begin in infancy or may even be present at birth. There is a tendency for the tremor to begin earlier in each generation. I have seen a number of children under the age of five years who displayed well-developed tremors. There is no doubt, however, that the tremor often becomes more evident during puberty, especially in girls. This fact may be related to the profound psychological and physiological readjustments which occur at this time. The tremor is rhythmical. It is increased by movement, and is strikingly accentuated by emotional reactions, fatigue and by similar factors. The tremor is also evident when the hands are outstretched. It is absent when the patient is relaxed and when the limbs are supported. It is always most evident in the hands, but may involve the head and the tongue. It is rarely seen in the legs. Coordination is disturbed much less than one would expect from the amplitude of the tremor, but, as a rule, there is difficulty in writing, and in all movements which require exact coordination. Strength is normal. The gait and station are unaffected. There is no rigidity of the muscles or slowing of movement. Articulation is affected eventually. The mental condition usually remains normal.

I have seen a young woman who had tremor of the hands all her life. She came from a South American country in which large families were the rule. Her mother had 20 children of whom 16 were affected. The descendants of the original Spanish conquerors have managed to maintain themselves as distinct clans of related families in this particular country. This lady's clan numbered several hundreds of persons. A large percentage of all of these relatives exhibited tremor of the hands.

Diagnosis.—The diagnosis depends upon the development of tremor early in life without other symptoms, upon the very slow progression and, especially, upon the family history. It is present at rest and also in the finger-nose test. Though it is usually a tremor of small amplitude, under the influence of emotion, it may become large. It begins in the hands and later involves the head and perhaps speech. The legs are spared in most cases.

Prognosis.—There is no hope of recovery, but these patients learn to make the best of their condition and are handicapped less than one would expect. Their inability to write properly makes it hard for them to get through school.

Treatment.—No treatment is advised.

BIBLIOGRAPHY

CRITCHLEY, McD.: Neurologic changes in the aged. Res. Nerv. Ment. Dis., **35**:198, 1956.
————: Observations on essential (heredofamilial) tremor. Brain, **72**:113, 1949.
DAVIS, C. H. AND KUNKLE, E. C.: Benign essential (Heredo-familial) tremor. Arch. Int. Med., **87**:808, 1951.
JAGER, B. V.: Hereditary tremor. Arch. Int. Med., **95**:788, 1953.
LARSSON, T. AND SJÖGREN, T.: Essential tremor. Acta Psychiat. et Neurol. Scandinav. Suppl. 144. Vol. **36**, 1960.

THE MYOCLONUS EPILEPSIES

Myoclonus epilepsy is merely a syndrome which may be produced by a variety of organic diseases of the brain. Watson and Denny-Brown and Symonds have published illuminating papers about this syndrome.

It should be said first of all that in *common epilepsy* there are often a few myoclonic contractions especially in the mornings. These are often not troublesome enough to cause the patient to mention them.

In *paramyoclonus multiplex,* q.v. myoclonus dominates the picture but according to Symonds there are occasional convulsions in most cases, but no clear evidence of progressive disease other than some mental deterioration which occurs late in the course. Symonds regards this condition as a form of epilepsy and his view is supported by post-mortem examinations which reveal no significant lesions in the brain.

Lafora and Glueck have described a *familial, progressive myoclonus epilepsy* which is associated with deposits in the ganglion cells termed Lafora bodies. It has been stated that these are composed of amyloid, but it is now thought they are formed by mucoproteins. These deposits have been found in the retinae as well as in the brain.

Such cases are rare but Freeman and Harriman and Millar have published descriptions of similar cases. It is stated that there is no degeneration of the nerve cells or white matter. The onset of symptoms occurs in childhood or at puberty and is marked by petit mal or convulsions. The seizures become infrequent later in life. Myoclonic shocks soon appear and slowly become more frequent and violent. These contractions involved chiefly the proximal portions of the extremities and the muscles of the trunk. They are arrhythmic and asynchronous. Active and passive movements aggravate the myoclonus. Sleep reduces or abolishes the movements. Mental deterioration becomes evident early in the course of the disease and advances finally to dementia. After some years cerebellar ataxia appears and then extrapyramidal rigidity. The terminal state is that of generalized rigidity in flexion, bulbar palsy, dementia and stupor. The course is as a rule between 10 and 20 years. This is transmitted as an autosomal recessive disease.

Unverricht described a familial type of myoclonus and epilepsy which was not associated with dementia. This seems to have been an autosomal recessive trait. Lundborg also reported cases of progressive myoclonic epilepsy some of which were associated with dementia and some were not.

Ramsy Hunt reported a study of 6 patients who suffered from myoclonus and intention tremor. Four of the 6 had convulsions. The other 2 who were twins had no convulsions. Post-mortem examination of one of the twins revealed degeneration of the dentate nuclei of the cerebellum as well as the degeneration of the tracts in the spinal cord seen in Friedreich's ataxia. Hunt uses the term dyssynergia cerebellaris myoclonica.

Novelletto states that the familial myoclonic epilepsy of Unverricht and Lundborg includes at least two separate disorders. One of these is the condition described by Lafora and Glueck. The other is the condition described by Hunt.

It is often said that the commonest cause of the syndrome of myoclonus epilepsy is *juvenile cerebroretinal degeneration,* q.v. It must be kept in mind that the typical retinal lesions are not always evident.

The *subacute inclusion body encephalitis* of Dawson is another cause of both convulsions and myoclonus.

Degeneration of the cerebral gray matter, q.v. causes progressive deterioration with convulsions and myoclonus.

Myoclonus epilepsy is said to be manifest in the electroencephalogram by diphasic or polyphasic spikes of high voltage. These are universal and asynchronous. A volley of spikes is associated with a myoclonic contraction. There are also slow waves of 3 per second which are more prominent in the later stages of the disease.

BIBLIOGRAPHY

FREEMAN, W.: Neuropathology. Philadelphia, W. B. Saunders Co., 1933, p. 268.

GILBERT, G. J. *et al.:* Familial myoclonus and ataxia. Neurology, **13**:365, 1963.

HARRIMAN, D. G. F. AND MILLAR, J. H.: Progressive familial myoclonic epilepsy. Brain, **78**:325, 1955.

HODSKINS, M. B. AND YAKOLEV, P. I.: Anatomico-clinical observations on myoclonus in epileptics and on related symptom complexes. Am. J. Psychiat., **9**:827, 1930.

HUNT, J. R.: Dyssynergia cerebellaris myoclonica. Brain, **44**:490, 1921.

JANEWAY, R. *et al.:* Progressive myoclonus epilepsy with Lafora inclusion bodies. Arch of Neurol., **16**:565, 1967.

LAFORA, G. R. AND GLUECK, B.: Beitrag zur Histopathologie der myoklonischen Epilepsie. Ztschr. Neurol. u. Psychiat. Bd., **6**:1, 1911.

LUNGBORG, H.: Die progressive Myoclonus-epilepsie. Upsala, 1903.

———: Der Erbang der progressiven Myoklonus-Epilepsie. Ztschr. f. ges. Neurol. u. Psychiat., **9**:353, 1912.

MUSKENS, L. J. J.: Epilepsy. Baltimore, Wm. Wood and Co., 1928.

NOAD, K. B. AND LANCE, J. W.: Familial myoclonic epilepsy associated with cerebellar disturbance. Brain, **83**:618, 1960.

NOVELLETTO, A.: Problemes actuels de la myoclonie-epilepsie progressive de Unverricht-Lundborg. Rev. billiographique et critique. Encephale., **47**:223, 1958.

ROIZIN, L. AND FERRARO, A.: Myoclonus epilepsy. J. Neuropath. & Exp. Neurol., **1**:297, 1942.

SCHOU, H. I.: Myoklonus-Epilepsie mit eigentumlichen Gehirnveranderungen. Ztschr. f. d. ges Neurol. u. Psychiat., **95**:12, 1925. (References to other pathological studies.)

SCHWARZ, G. A.: Lafora's disease. Arch. of Neurol., **12**:172, 1965.

SYMONDS, SIR C.: Myoclonus. Med. J. Australia, May, 765, 1954.

UNVERRICHT, H.: Über familiäre Myoclonie. Deutsche Ztschr. f. Nervenh., **7**:32, 1895.

WATSON, C. W. AND DENNY-BROWN, D.: Myoclonus epilepsy as a symptom of diffuse neuronal disease. Arch. Neurol. & Psychiat., **70**:151, 1953.

WOHLFART, G. AND HÖÖK, O.: Clinical analysis of myoclonus epilepsy, myoclonic cerebellar dyssynergy and hepatolenticular degeneration. Acta psychiat. et neurol. Scand., **26**:219, 1951.

YANOFF, M. AND SCHWARZ, G. A.: Retinal pathology of Lafora's disease. A form of glycoprotein mucopolysaccharide dystrophy. Trans. Amer. Acad. Ophthal., **69**:701, 1965.

YOKOI, S. *et al.:* Studies in myoclonus epilepsy (Lafora body form). Arch. of Neurol., **19**:15, 1968.

PARAMYOCLONUS MULTIPLEX

Definition.—An ill-defined disease which is characterized by myoclonic contractions. Symonds regards it as a form of epilepsy.

Pathological Anatomy.—Post-mortem examinations of nervous system by Friedreich and by Hunt are said to have revealed no definite anatomical changes. Symonds mentions a case in which Greenfield was able to find no lesions in the nervous system.

Clinical Features.—The disease is found in males more frequently than in females. It seems to be sporadic more often than familial but several cases have been found in the same family. Little is known about the mode of inheritance. The onset is usually in middle age but it may occur as early as the fifth year and cases are described in which the symptoms were present in infancy. The disease is characterized by sudden shock-like contractions of the muscles of very brief duration resembling the reaction to an electric shock. At first, merely a few bundles of muscle fibers are affected so that contractions might be called fascicular, but, later, whole groups of muscles take part in the contractions. At the onset, there is little or no movement of the extremities, but, later, when the contractions have become more violent, the patient may be thrown to the ground or even out of bed. The contractions occur at irregular intervals and are bilateral but not synchronous in the affected muscles. They may occur at any rate. At certain times, the contractions may be rhythmic. As a rule, the proximal muscles of the arms and shoulder muscles are affected first but eventually all the skeletal muscles are involved. It has been stated that the deltoid, trapezius, biceps, pectorals, brachioradialis, quadriceps and semitendinosus are often selectively affected. The diaphragm may show myoclonus. The face and bulbar muscles are among the last to be involved. There is no weakness or atrophy. When the movements are constant and violent, the patient may be helpless and unable to talk, but when the movements are absent there may be no disability whatever. The movements are induced by active or passive stretching of the muscles. They are reduced or abolished by sleep. At times the patient may be free of the movements and at other times myoclonus may be frequent or constant. Symonds speaks of myoclonus status. When the condition is advanced, the attempt to elicit the tendon reflexes may induce violent contractions so the reflexes seem to be increased. The myoclonus slowly grows more and more severe and, after a number of years, the patient is apt to be quite helpless for the violent contractions distort all volitional activity.

Mental deterioration is apparently prominent in the later stages of the disease but may not be present for many years. Most authorities now agree that myoclonus is due to cerebral discharges. Sharp spikes are found in the electroencephalogram. These are universal and synchronous. It is believed that they arise from a deeply seated focus, possibly the thalamus. Symonds points out that in many cases convulsions eventually develop. Often, epilepsy is found in other members of the family. Symonds regards myoclonus as a special form of epilepsy.

Diagnosis.—The differential diagnosis is not easy without prolonged observation. The chief problem is to differentiate this disease from the various types of myoclonus epilepsy, q.v. These are progressive organic diseases of the nervous system which eventually give rise to muscular rigidity, ataxia and other physical signs of organic disease. In paramyoclonus multiplex, we have only the myoclonus and perhaps, terminal mental changes.

Prognosis.—The prognosis is hopeless as regards recovery but the course is so slow that the patient may be active until old age.

Treatment.—No specific therapy has been discovered but anticonvulsive medication should be tried.

> Case History (U-141965).—*Boy of five years developed clonic contractions of proximal muscles of the arms and shoulders. Gradual increase in symptoms. Three maternal cousins developed same trouble at age of six years.*
>
> W. L., a previously healthy boy, developed sudden irregular muscular contractions of the arms and shoulders at the age of five years. These were increased by excitement but persisted to some extent throughout the day no matter what the child was doing. They were not present during sleep. The symptoms grew more severe so that, at the age of 12 years, the contractions were beginning to involve the muscles of the hips and thighs and caused his gait to be irregular and jerky. In other respects the child seemed to be quite healthy and did well at school. Three maternal cousins are said to have developed the same symptoms at the age of six years and have slowly grown worse. These cousins are all boys. The mother and father have no neurological symptoms. There is no history of convulsions in the patient or in his relatives.
>
> The patient was examined at the age of 12 years. He was well nourished and developed, and seemed to be intelligent and good humored. No neurological phenomena were found except for the myoclonic contractions. These were found chiefly in the pectorals, the trapezius, quadriceps and abdominal muscles on both sides. They were very sudden, brief contractions which were quite irregular and asynchronous on the two sides. They were powerful enough to move the arms and neck and to interrupt the rhythm of the gait. The myoclonus was not altered by volitional activity but was increased by excitement. The muscles were firm and strength was good. No atrophy was found. The tendon reflexes were active. Electrical reactions were normal. The cranial nerves were not affected.

BIBLIOGRAPHY

Biemond, A.: Paramyoclonus multiplex. Psychiat. Neurol. Neurochir. (Amst.), **66**:270, 1963.

Friedreich, N.: Paramyoclonus multiplex. Virchow's Archiv. f. path. Anat., **86**:421, 1881.

Hunt, J. R.: A contribution to the pathology of paramyoclonus multiplex. J. Nerv. & Ment. Dis., **30**:408, 1903.

LINDMULDER, F. G.: Familial myoclonus occurring in three successive generations. J. Nerv. & Ment. Dis., 77:489, 1933.
SYMONDS, SIR C.: Myoclonus. Med. J. Australia, May, 765, 1954.

FAMILIAL MYOCLONUS AND ATAXIA (GILBERT)
Dyssynergia cerebellaris myoclonica (Hunt)

In 1921, Ramsy Hunt published a study of six patients, all of whom displayed myoclonus and intention tremor. In four instances, the patients were subject to convulsions; in the other patients, who were twins, there were no convulsions, but signs of Friedreich's ataxia were present. One of the twins was found on post-mortem examination to have degeneration of the dentate nuclei of the cerebellum as well as evidences of Friedreich's ataxia.

In 1963, Gilbert *et al.* published a study of eight patients in five generations of a family. Four of the patients were examined and found to have intention tremor and myoclonus. These patients were not subject to convulsions and there was no mental deterioration. The onset was early in childhood and the course was of very slow progression. The spinal fluid of two patients contained an excess of uric acid. No post-mortem examination was made. An autosomal dominant gene with incomplete penetrance seemed to be responsible.

Jacobs has described a family also suffering from myoclonus and cerebellar ataxia and states that inheritance is that of an autosomal dominant gene of incomplete penetrance.

May and White describe a familial process manifest by cerebellar ataxia, myoclonus and nerve deafness transmitted by an autosomal dominant gene.

BIBLIOGRAPHY

GILBERT, G. J., McENTEE, W. J. AND GLASER, G. H.: Familial myoclonus and ataxia. Neurology, 13:365, 1963.
HUNT, J. R.: Dyssynergia cerebellaris myoclonica. Brain, 44:490, 1921.
JACOBS, H.: Myoclonus and ataxia occurring in a family. Jour. Neurol. Neurosurg. and Psychiat., 28:272. 1965.
MAY, D. L. AND WHITE, H. H.: Familial myoclonus, cerebellar ataxia and deafness. Arch. of Neurol., 19:331, 1968.

MYOCLONIC ENCEPHALOPATHY OF INFANTS (KINSBOURNE)
The Dancing Eyes Syndrome

In 1962, Kinsbourne published a paper about six children who had been studied on the service of Dr. Paul Sandifer. There were three girls and three boys. The onset of symptoms was between nine and twenty months. The children showed jerky movements of the head, eyes, trunk and extremities. The movements were increased by activity. Gross ataxia was always present and the children could scarcely walk or even stand. In some cases, the movements of the eyes consisted of irregular, jerky, vertical movements, which were not always in unison. The eyelids and sometimes the eyebrows moved with the eyes. Other children showed irregular unsustained lateral nystagmus.

The spinal fluid was always normal. Repeated electroencephalograms showed no abnormalities. One child had ventriculography, an air encephalogram and brain biopsy with completely negative results. The electromyogram, however, always showed either single myoclonic action potentials or bursts of action potentials.

Without treatment, active symptoms ceased in one child at the age of seven years, but she remained clumsy in her movements. Her speech was defective and her intelligence quotient was only 60.

The other five children were treated with steroids with excellent effects. Dr. Sandifer states that $7\frac{1}{2}$ units of ACTH always gave relief of the symptoms; whereas, 5 units might be inadequate. For a time, withdrawal or even reduction of the medication led to return of the symptoms but after five to seven years it was possible to stop treatment without untoward results.

In two cases, the onset of symptoms followed an upper respiratory infection. In one case there was a gastrointestinal infection before the symptoms began, and in one case, a triple vaccine had been administered. In two cases, there was no apparent precipitating cause.

By the courtesy of Dr. David Clark, I am able to mention our experience with three children studied at Johns Hopkins Hospital who seemed to be suffering from the same condition described by Dr. Kinsbourne. The onset of symptoms was always between the ages of one and three years. The family history was negative. The children showed jerky movements of the head, eyes, extremities and trunk. These movements might be absent when the child was asleep. They were increased by activity. The eye movements were rapid, irregular and random. The term opsoclonus was applied. Coordination was grossly impaired. The children could not walk or stand, and the arms were extremely clumsy. Oscillations of the head and trunk were evident when the child tried to stand or walk. When the symptoms were severe, the children did not talk. A striking feature was intense irritability which made it difficult to examine the children.

The spinal fluid was always normal. Air encephalograms showed no abnormalities. The electroencephalograms revealed no significant changes. No metabolic abnormalities have been discovered.

Adequate doses of steroids always relieved the symptoms. When the medication was withdrawn, or even reduced, the symptoms returned at once and were as severe as they were before medication. Two of our patients could tolerate withdrawal of treatment after the age of five years, but one was moderately dull. A third child is still under treatment at the age of three years.

In a number of cases this disease has been found in association with neuroblastoma q.v. It may be the first evidence of neuroblastoma.

No postmortem studies have been made in children, but two histological studies in adults showed lymphocytic infiltrations in the brain stem.

Dyken and Kolar found a plasma cell pleocytosis in the spinal fluid and both qualitative and quantitative changes in the IgG immunoglobulins.

CASE HISTORY (No. 1077502).—*L. C., a girl of twelve months, developed jerky movements of the eyes, head, extremities and trunk with gross ataxia. There was extreme irritability. At thirty months, steroids were given with relief of symptoms. At thirty-four months, the steroids were reduced and the symptoms returned. Resumption of medication controlled the symptoms once more.*

L. C. was born at term, by normal delivery, after an uncomplicated pregnancy. At three months she was able to turn over; at five months, she sat up; at eight months she could stand; at ten months she could walk alone, and at eleven months she could form six or eight words.

At twelve months, following a head cold with otitis, she began to display jerky movements of the eyes, head, extremities and trunk. She became so ataxic she could not walk or use her arms. When she was on her feet, there were oscillations of the head and trunk. These movements would stop during sleep. They were aggravated by any activity. The ocular movements were described as rapid, irregular and non-concomitant. The child ceased to speak. She was intensely irritable and resented being disturbed in any way, so it was almost impossible to examine her.

Roentgenograms of the skull and chest, electroencephalograms, and spinal fluid studies revealed nothing of significance. Two air encephalograms were performed with negative results.

The child was brought to Johns Hopkins Hospital at the age of thirty months where she displayed all the symptoms described above. She was placed on metacortin and the symptoms gradually disappeared. She was able to stand, walk, and talk, and her behavior was quite normal. However, she became obese and developed body hair and acne.

At the age of thirty-four months, the medication was reduced. The obesity diminished, but the symptoms rapidly returned and were just as severe as before. At the age of thirty-five months, the steroids were administered again and the neurological symptoms soon began to recede.

(This note is given by the courtesy of Dr. David Clark and Dr. John Allan.)

BIBLIOGRAPHY

CHRISTOFF, N.: Myoclonic encephalopathy of infants. Arch. of Neurol., 21:229, 1969.
DYKEN, P. AND KOLAR, O.: Dancing eyes, dancing feet: Infantile polymyoclonia. Brain, **91**:305, 1968.

KINSBOURNE, M.: Myoclonic encephalopathy in infants. J. Neurol., Neurosurg. & Psychiat., 25:271, 1962.
SANDIFER, P.: Personal communication.

SUBACUTE INFANTILE NECROTIZING ENCEPHALOMYELOPATHY

Definition.—A disease of infants resembling in its anatomical and clinical features Wernicke's encephalopathy but differing in its more chronic course and the absence of any evidence of vitamine deficiency.

Etiology.—It has been suggested that we may be dealing with an inborn defect of metabolism and that these children may be unable to utilize thiamine. Two cases have been observed in siblings whose parents were first cousins.

Pincus *et al.* found evidence that the conversion of thiamine pyrophosphate to thiamine triphosphate is inhibited.

Pathological Anatomy.—The lesions are symmetrically placed in the walls of the third ventricle, the periaqueductal gray matter and the floor of the fourth ventricle. Characteristically a thin layer of subependymal tissue is spared. The nuclei of the cranial nerves are involved. In some instances the thalamus, subthalamus, substantia nigra, red nucleus, colliculi, inferior olive and dentate nuclei are damaged. The optic chiasm and tracts may be demyelinated. The mammillary bodies may be spared though they are usually involved in true Wernicke's encephalopathy. In two of Richter's three cases there was focal necrosis in the caudate nucleus and putamen and in

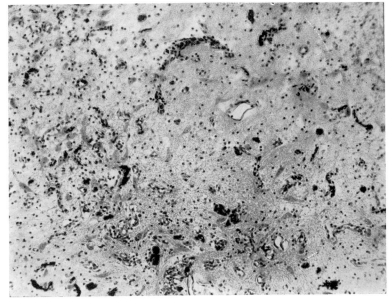

Fig. 134. A disease resembling Wernick's encephalopathy. Histological appearance of the lesion in the substantia nigra. (By the courtesy of Dr. David Clark.)

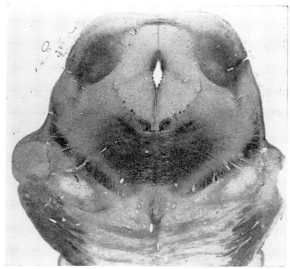

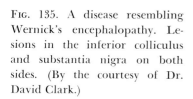

Fig. 135. A disease resembling Wernick's encephalopathy. Lesions in the inferior colliculus and substantia nigra on both sides. (By the courtesy of Dr. David Clark.)

one of his cases there were irregularly distributed foci of necrosis in the cortices of the cerebrum and cerebellum as well as in the cerebral white matter. In Leigh's case, the posterior columns of the cord were damaged and in our case the anterior gray matter of the first five cervical segments was involved. Microscopically, the lesions are areas of rarifaction with extensive loss of neurons though an occasional nerve cell is preserved. The myelin is destroyed but the axis cylinders are less severely affected. There are many fine glial fibers but no proliferation of astrocytes. A characteristic feature is the presence of dilated, congested and tortuous capillaries, but few hemorrhages. The process is more chronic than the typical Wernicke's encephalopathy in which hemorrhages are more plentiful.

Richter emphasizes the differences between this condition and Wernicke's encephalopathy.

Dr. David Clark has studied two brothers, J. D. G. (No. 905014) and J. G. (1001246), whose symptoms began at four months and subsequently came to post-mortem examination. The lesions in the brain stem were characteristic of the disease under discussion but there were also extensive lesions in the cerebral white matter involving especially the central white matter of the cerebral convolutions.

Clinical Features.—Feigin and Wolf report three cases with post-mortem examinations. Leigh has described one case which is accepted by Feigin and Wolf as being representative of the condition they describe. Richter has also published three cases in all of which post-mortem examinations were made. Cases have been seen in Boston and we have had one case which will be mentioned briefly below. The age of onset was always before the end of the first year. In some cases, the diet has been quite adequate and vitamines have been given. Vomiting and refusal of food often mark the onset of the illness. Growth and nutrition may be normal or defective. The neurological symptoms include weakness, tremor, ataxia, rigidity of the extremities, Babinski signs, ocular palsies, nystagmus, loss of vision and deafness. The course seems to be progressive to a fatal termination. Death occurred before the end of the first year in five cases and in three cases at 13 and 16 months and four years.

A juvenile form has been reported with onset around 3 years and death by 13 years in 3 siblings.

Paterson and Carmichael describe a family of 12 siblings of which 10 were affected by a disease similar to the one under discussion.

Hardman *et al.* describe a case in which the onset was in late adolescence, and the course was slow.

Diagnosis.—It is doubtful if the diagnosis can be made on clinical grounds at present.

Prognosis.—This seems to be unfavorable at present.

Treatment.—No treatment is known. Apparently vitamines are not effective.

CASE HISTORY (Ped. B-5346—Path. 24642).—*Child of 2 months began to vomit, lost vision, grew weak and ataxic. Death from respiratory failure. Post-mortem examination.*

K. L. M. was born at full term by induced labor at the end of a normal pregnancy. Birth weight was 7 pounds and 12 ounces. There was no cyanosis or jaundice and the child seemed to be healthy in all respects. She was breast fed for 2 weeks and then placed on a formula with supplementary vitamines A, B, C, D, and E. Appetite was good and the child's growth and nutrition were excellent. Two siblings of 16 months and 3 years were healthy.

At the age of 2 months the child began to vomit and to refuse her food. Soon her mother suspected that her vision was failing. There were peculiar movements of the eyes and also abnormal movements of the extremities. The child had been holding up her head for a time and now lost this ability. She ceased to cry properly and merely whined.

Examination in the Harriet Lane revealed a well-nourished and developed baby of two and one-half months. The temperature was normal; respiration 20; pulse 120. There were no signs of recent weight loss or dehydration. The anterior fontanel was open but not bulging. The child was a bit sluggish. At times there were random movements of the eyes which were regarded as searching movements. The pupils were small and showed little reaction to light. The child did not follow a light or even fix a light. The optic discs were extremely pale. It was thought that the baby could hear. The extremities were atonic but were moved with some freedom. Tremor of the hands was noted. The tendon reflexes were normal in the legs. Percussion of the biceps tendons caused the triceps to contract. Plantar stimulation caused the great toe to go up. The child could not hold up the head and could not sit up.

Laboratory studies including blood chemistries and blood counts showed nothing of interest. The electrocardiogram showed normal waves. Roentgenograms of the skull revealed no abnormality.

The vomiting persisted. The child became lethargic. She developed a cough. On October 1, rales were heard in the chest and aspiration pneumonia was suspected. She was better on the next day but then she died rather suddenly from failure of respiration.

The post-mortem examination showed a small amount of gastric fluid in the bronchi. The abdominal and thoracic viscera were all healthy. I am indebted to Dr. David Clark for information about the condition of the nervous system. In the gross no definite lesions were seen. Microscopic study, however, revealed a number of lesions which were typical of those described by Feigin and Wolf. These were symmetrically placed in the substantia nigra, inferior colliculi, medial and superior vestibular nuclei, alae cinereae, and reticular substance at the level of the seventh nerve nuclei. The anterior gray matter of the first five cervical segments of the cord was involved. The optic tracts were completely demyelinated and in status spongiosus.

BIBLIOGRAPHY

DUNN, H. G. AND DOLMAN, C. L.: Necrotizing encephalomyelopathy. Neurology, **19**:536, 1969.

FEIGIN, I. AND WOLF, A.: A disease of infants resembling chronic Wernicke's encephalopathy. J. Pediat., **45**:243, 1954.

GREENHOUSE, A. H. AND SCHNECK, S. A.: Subacute necrotizing encephalopathy. Neurology, **18**:1, 1968.

HARDMAN, LTC. J. M. *et al.*: Subacute necrotizing encephalopathy in late adolescence. Arch. of Neurol., **18**:478, 1968.

LAKKE, J. P. W. F. *et al.*: Infantile necrotizing encephalopathy. Arch. of Neurol., **16**:227, 1967.

LEIGH, D.: Subacute necrotizing encephalomyelopathy in an infant. J. Neurol., Neurosurg. & Psychiat., **14**:216, 1951.

NAMIKI, H.: Subacute necrotizing encephalopathy. Arch. Neurol., vol. 12, p. 12, 98, 1965.

PATERSON, D. AND CARMICHAEL, E. A.: A form of familial cerebral degeneration chiefly affecting the lenticular nuclei. Brain, **47**:207, 1924.

PETERSON, R. D. A. *et al.*: Necrotizing encephalopathy with predilection for the brainstem. Trans. Amer. Neurol. Ass., **89**:104, 1964.

PINCUS, J. H. *et al.*: Enzyme inhibiting factor in subacute necrotizing encephalomyelopathy. Neurology, **19**:841, 1969.

REYE, R. D. K.: Subacute necrotizing encephalomyelitis in infancy. J. Path. & Bact., **79**:165, 1960.

RICHTER, R. B.: Infantile subacute necrotizing encephalopathy with predilection for the brain stem. J. Neuropath. & Exp. Neurol., **16**:281, 1957.

————: Infantile subacute necrotizing encephalopathy; its relationship to Vernicke's encephalopathy. Neurology, **18**:1125, 1969.

ROBINSON, F. *et al.*: Necrotizing encephalomyelopathy of childhood. Neurology, **17**:472, 1967.

TOM, M. I. AND REWCASTLE, N. B.: Infantile subacute necrotizing encephalopathy. Neurology, **12**:624, 1962.

YASHON, D. AND JANE, J. A.: Subacute necrotizing encephalomyelopathy of infancy and childhood. Jour. Clin. Path., **20**:28, 1967.

EPILEPSY OF PRENATAL ONSET

A strange condition has been described by Badr-el-Din in three sibships of closely related families. Convulsions occur in the fifth month of intra-uterine life. The convulsions recur after birth and there is progressive mental deterioration, spasticity and myoclonus. Death occurs within a year and a half. This is believed to be a simple recessive disorder.

BIBLIOGRAPHY

Badr-el-Din, M. K.: A familial convulsive disorder with an unusual onset during intra-uterine life. Jour. Pediat., **56**:655, 1960.

HEREDITARY NERVE DEAFNESS

Definition.—This is a rare condition characterized by progressive deafness of nerve type. It is transmitted in some cases through several generations.

Pathological Anatomy.—The anatomical basis of this disease is unknown, but it is generally assumed that there must be a selective degeneration of the auditory fibers of the eighth nerve or of the labyrinth.

Clinical Features.—This subject receives scant mention in most textbooks but progressive nerve deafness in childhood has been mentioned by Alexander and Manasse. It is probable, however, that these authors are dealing with a variety of diseases since the details of their cases are not always the same. We have studied two families in which progressive nerve deafness was prevalent. In one of these families the deafness did not begin until adult life, but in the other, the deafness was usually apparent at the age of about six years. Both males and females were affected and the disease was transmitted by either sex. It was transmitted by unaffected individuals and therefore must have been dependent upon a recessive factor. The symptoms were few. The deafness began insidiously and progressed slowly and steadily. Complete loss of hearing usually occurred at the age of thirty. There was tinnitus aurium in most cases, but no loss of equilibrium or paroxysms of vertigo. The vestibular reactions were always normal. Audiometer records showed that the highest tones were lost first and the lowest tones were the last to go. There were no changes in the retinae.

It is well known that progressive deafness may occur in association with pigmentary degeneration of the retina. This is also a familial disease. Progressive deafness also occurs in certain patients with hereditary degeneration of the sensory neurons, q.v. and rarely in peroneal muscular atrophy.

A rare type of deafness is associated with hereditary nephritis. The deafness is apparent by the age of ten years and hematuria is often present in the first weeks of life. Lenticonus may be associated. This is a partially sex-linked disease. Females are rarely affected. It is termed Alport's syndrome.

Schafer *et al.* describe a familial disease manifest by nephropathy and nerve deafness. Convulsions and mental deficiency are present in some cases. A defect in amino acid metabolism is associated. The concentration of L proline in the plasma is increased and there may be excretion of proline, hydroxyproline and glycine in the urine.

Diagnosis.—Several conditions must be considered in the differential diagnosis. Otosclerosis is perhaps the commonest type of progressive familial deafness. This rarely begins before the age of puberty, but Alexander and others have reported cases in which some degree of deafness was apparent in childhood. In such cases, the deafness is of middle ear type until very late in the course of the disease. The diagnosis is based upon the family history, the character of the deafness and the absence of other causes.

Certain types of deafness which have been mentioned under the head of congenital deafness, q.v. may be incomplete at first and later become complete. In such cases we are probably dealing with a progressive degeneration of defective organs. This is apparently not infrequently true of the type of deafness associated with pigmentary degeneration of the retina.

A case of hereditary nerve deafness is abstracted below.

Prognosis.—The disease apparently always progresses to complete loss of hearing, but so far as the writer can learn, is not associated with other symptoms.

Treatment.—None.

CASE HISTORY (K-39229).—*Progressive nerve deafness beginning at the age of six years. Family history of deafness in ascendants, collaterals and siblings, occurring in both males and females and transmitted by both.*

K. L., healthy boy of six years, noticed gradually increasing deafness without other symptoms except for a slight tinnitus at times. There was no otitis and no vertigo or disturbance of equilibrium. The deafness slowly grew worse and after several years, the patient could not hear conversations over the telephone. At the age of 24 years, he was almost completely deaf except for a few notes in the lowest part of the scale. The audiometer curves were almost exactly parallel in the two ears. The vestibular reactions were normal and there was no clinical evidence of loss of equilibrium. Otological and neurological examinations were quite negative except for the deafness. Wassermann test negative.

The patient's paternal grandfather suffered from progressive deafness and was completely deaf at the age of 30 years. His deafness is said to have begun when he was still a child. The patient's father and one paternal uncle were also completely deaf at the ages of 30 and 35 respectively. One paternal uncle and three paternal aunts had normal hearing. In the patient's generation four other subjects were affected. His brother was very deaf at the age of 14 years but another brother and one sister were spared. Four first cousins, three males and one female were affected. One of these cousins was the son of a paternal aunt who had good hearing. It is evident, therefore, that the disease affected males most frequently, but also affected females as well and that it might be transmitted by either sex and by unaffected individuals.

BIBLIOGRAPHY

ALEXANDER, G.: Die Ohrenkrankheiten im Kindersalter, p. 24, Leipsig, Verlag von F. C. W. Vogel, 1912.
LIVINGOOD, W. C.: Psychogenic deafness. Arch. Environ. Hlth., 7:415, 1963.
MANASSE, P.: Über progressive Labyrinthare Schwerhorigkeit, p. 49, Wiesbaden, 1906.
SCHAFER, I. *et al.*: Familial hyperprolinemia. New England J. Med., **267**:51, 1962.
WILLIAMSON, D. A. J.: Alport's syndrome of hereditary nephritis with deafness. Lancet, **2**:1321, 1961.

MENIERE'S SYNDROME

This condition is so rare in childhood that it does not require more than a very brief discussion. The essential symptom is vertigo which occurs in sudden paroxysms and which is identical in character with that produced by strong stimulation of the vestibular apparatus. This vertigo is associated with vomiting, pallor and profuse sweating. The subject is unable to stand without support. Syncope may occur in the more severe attacks. Spontaneous nystagmus is usually present and the patient complains that there is apparent movement of objects. The duration of such seizures is variable. Some last only a few minutes and others several hours. The onset is as a rule sudden and without warning. Once the seizures begin, they are apt to occur with increasing frequency for years, although prolonged remissions are observed. As a rule these seizures are associated with tinnitus aurium and with slowly progressive deafness in one or both ears. One ear may be affected alone for long periods. The cause of the disease and its anatomical basis are still unknown though a few post-mortem examinations have revealed hydrops of the membranous labyrinth. There is no evidence that heredity plays any significant role. It seems to be accepted that the disease must involve the eighth nerve or labyrinth. No doubt the process is a specific one for other types of progressive deafness do not give rise to such paroxysms of vertigo. Dr. Dandy has shown that section of the vestibular portion of the eighth nerve will prevent the seizures. He is able to destroy the vestibular portion of the nerve without injury to the auditory portion in most cases. The vestibular reflexes are abolished by this operation, of course. If one nerve is sectioned, there is unsteadiness of gait and difficulty in visual fixation when the head is in motion for about three months but after this period there is adequate compensation. If both nerves are sectioned, however, there is prolonged and probably permanent unsteadiness and difficulty in visual fixation. It is claimed that ultrasound may be used to destroy the vestibular apparatus by an endaural approach. The cochlear function is not impaired.

CASE HISTORY (No. 135837).—*Girl of four years was found to have no function in the right labyrinth. At six years violent attacks of vertigo at frequent intervals. Operative relief by section of the right eighth nerve at the age of 15 years.*

M. G. M., a girl of four years, was found to be completely deaf in the right ear. There was also loss of vestibular reflexes. Repeated examinations gave the same results.

At six years, she began to have frequent, prolonged and extremely severe attacks of rotary vertigo. In some attacks she lost consciousness apparently because of syncope.

At the age of 15 years, the vestibular fibers of the left eighth nerve were sectioned by Dr. Dandy. The vertigo persisted. Then a week later, the whole right eighth nerve was sectioned. The vertigo stopped and when she was 32 years old she was seen again. She had had no vertigo since the right eighth nerve was sectioned, but she was unsteady and had to walk with caution.

BIBLIOGRAPHY

ARIAGNO, R. P.: Meniere's disease: Treatment with ultrasound. A.M.A. Arch. Otol., **71**:573, 1960.

CROWE, S.: Meniere's disease. Study based upon examinations made before and after intracranial division of the vestibular nerve. Medicine, **17**:1, 1938.

DANDY, W. E.: Meniere's disease. Symptoms, objective findings and treatment in forty-two cases. Arch. Otol., **20**:1, 1934.

FORD, F. R.: A clinical classification of vestibular disorders. Bull. Johns Hopkins Hospital, **87**:299, 1950.

———— AND WALSH, F.: Clinical observations upon the importance of the vestibular reflexes in ocular movements. Bull. Johns Hopkins Hosp., **58**:80, 1936.

HARRISON, M. S.: Vertigo in childhood. J. Laryng. & Otol., **76**:610, 1962.

PROGRESSIVE FACIAL HEMIATROPHY

Definition.—A condition characterized by progressive wasting of the tissues of the face including the skin, subcutaneous fat, connective tissue, cartilage, bones and muscles. A few cases are described in which the condition was bilateral.

Pathological Anatomy.—Only a few post-mortem examinations have been made and the results of these have been inconsistent. In addition to the wasting of the tissues mentioned above, some observers have found proliferation of connective tissue in the fifth nerve and others have found lesions in the brain stem. In some cases, areas of necrosis are found in the brain and calcium deposits are mentioned.

Etiology.—The cause of this condition is quite obscure. Some authors mention infectious diseases, traumatism, local infections in the face or jaws or lesions of the peripheral nerves or brain. Others impressed by the occurrence of more than one case in a family believe that morbid heredity is to blame and regard it as a dominant condition.

Some writers think that loss of "trophic" influence due to lesions of the

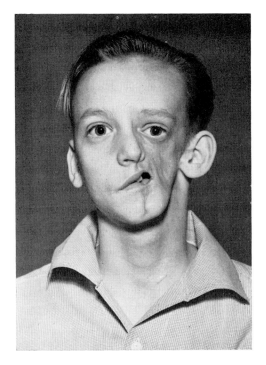

Fig. 136. Case of facial hemiatrophy in a boy of 16 years 10 years after the onset. (By the courtesy of Dr. Robert E. Cook.)

fifth nerve or cervical sympathetic nerve is responsible. Cassirer regards facial hemiatrophy as a local form of scleroderma.

Clinical Features.—The process usually begins early in life and may be well marked in childhood or even in infancy. I have seen a case in which the facial asymmetry was apparent at birth. The maxilla is often first affected and the shrinking of the bone causes the cheek to sink in and the upper teeth to be elevated. The mandible is involved later as is the frontal bone. The subcutaneous tissues waste rapidly and the skin becomes thin and wrinkled. The muscles also grow smaller but as a rule show no loss of strength. The blood vessels become superficial as a result of loss of subcutaneous tissues. The skin usually remains soft but may become adherent to the subcutaneous tissues and inelastic as in scleroderma. Sometimes, the affected skin is pigmented. The hair in the frontal region may fall out or turn white. The process is restricted to the domain of the fifth nerve as a rule but may extend beyond these limits. We have seen a case in a child in which one side of the tongue was atrophied and the inferior rectus was fibrotic and prevented elevation of the eye. In this case, the leg and thigh were atrophied, and the skin over the foot and ankle was thickened, as in scleroderma. This condition may be associated with localized scleroderma, i.e. morphea. The viscera may be involved and lesions in the heart, kidneys, lungs and intestines are described.

Cases are described in which the atrophy eventually involved both sides of the face. A rare condition termed total hemiatrophy is sometimes described in which one entire side of the body is affected. Syringomyelia and other diseases of the nervous system are occasionally found in association with facial hemiatrophy.

It is of interest that in a small percentage of cases, convulsive seizures have occurred. Thus Wartenberg mentions four cases of generalized seizures and four cases of focal seizures. Archimbault and Fromm discovered three more cases of generalized seizures and we have observed convulsions in one case of our own. Merritt *et al.* have recently reported two cases in which focal convulsions occurred on the side opposite the facial atrophy and in which deposits of calcium were found in the brain. As a rule the seizures develop some years after the atrophy has become well established. Hemiparesis may develop still later. Migraine may also occur in this condition and facial neuralgia is described as a symptom which may precede the atrophy. Rarely facial atrophy is associated with facial paralysis or signs of loss of function of the fifth nerve. Several writers describe signs which they interpret to indicate that the cervical sympathetic nerve is affected.

The condition seems to progress slowly during a period of years. It never seems to become complete and some remnants of the facial bones are present after many years. Walsh describes a congenital facial hemiatrophy which is non-progressive and is extremely rare.

By the courtesy of Dr. Frank B. Walsh I have seen a little girl of 5 years who had microcephaly and was mentally deficient. There was bilateral ptosis of the eyelids and heterochromia of the irides. Movements of the eyes were normal. One side of the face showed defective development, but she did not show the characteristics of progressive facial hemiatrophy.

Treatment.—No successful treatment is known. Various measures are employed by plastic surgeons including transplantation of fat to fill out the affected cheek and artificial dentures to preserve occlusion of the teeth.

BIBLIOGRAPHY

ARCHIMBAULT, L. AND FROMM, N. K.: Progressive facial hemiatrophy. Arch. Neurol. & Psychiat., **27**:529, 1932.

FINESILVER, B. AND ROSOW, H. M.: Total hemiatrophy. J.A.M.A., **110**:366, 1938.

FRANCESCHETTI, A. *et al.*: L'importance du facteur heredo-degeneratif dans l'hemiatrophie faciale progressive. Schweiz Arch. Neurol. Psychiat., **71**:311, 1953.

MERRITT, K. K., FABER, H. K. AND BRUCH, H.: Progressive facial hemiatrophy. A report of 2 cases with cerebral calcification. J. Pediat., **10**:374, 1937.

WALSH, F. B.: Facial hemiatrophy. A report of two cases. Am. J. Ophth., **22**:1, 1939.

WARTENBERG, R.: Zur Klinik und Pathogenese der Hemiatrophia faciei prog. Arch. f. Psychiat., **74**:602, 1925.

Chapter III

INFECTIONS AND PARASITIC INVASIONS OF THE NERVOUS SYSTEM

INTRODUCTION.—The last two decades have greatly enriched our knowledge of the inflammatory diseases of the central nervous system. If one refers to standard textbooks of twenty or thirty years ago, one will find an astonishing paucity of information as contrasted with the wealth of detailed studies available at present. No doubt the world wide epidemic of encephalitis was largely instrumental in arousing general interest in this field and the constant advance in the perfection of histological technique has enabled more accurate differentiation of pathological processes. At the same time, there have been important advances in the field of bacteriology and experimental medicine, especially in regard to the properties of the filterable viruses.

The writer has attempted to construct a classification of the infectious diseases of the nervous system with the object of offering the reader a means of rapid orientation. The scheme is based primarily upon etiology and secondarily upon the pathological anatomy. In the outline given below only those diseases are included in which there is reason to believe that the etiological agent has actually invaded the nervous system. Neurological conditions due to the effects of bacterial toxins are discussed in Chapter V.

A. *Diseases Due to Filterable Viruses*

Diffuse but relatively selective inflammatory processes involving chiefly the gray matter with ganglion cell destruction, perivascular and tissue lymphocytic infiltration and mild microgliosis.

   a. Chiefly in the diencephalon and midbrain—*Epidemic encephalitis,* Type A.

   b. More diffuse in the brain-stem, cortex and spinal cord—*Epidemic encephalitis,* Type B, *Australian "X"* disease and *Equine encephalomyelitis.*

   c. Chiefly in the medulla—*Rabies.*

   d. Chiefly in the spinal gray matter—*Acute anterior poliomyelitis.*

   e. Chiefly in the ganglia of the posterior spinal roots—*Herpes zoster.*

   f. Chiefly in the meninges—*Choriomeningitis.*

   g. Swollen nerve cells with nuclear and cytoplasmic inclusion bodies, areas of necrosis granulomas and calcium deposits—*Cytomegalic inclusion disease.*

404

B. *Group Lying between Viruses and Rickettsiae*
  Lymphogranuloma venereum. Psittacosis and trachoma fall into same group.

C. *Involvement of the Nervous System by Rickettsiae*
  Perivascular granulomata with proliferation of vascular endothelium and small softenings. *Typhus fever, Tick-bite fever* and *Tsutsugamushi fever.*

D. *Bacterial Infections Involving the Nervous System*
  Abscesses of the brain and spinal cord, multiple or single, meningitis and ependymitis, generalized and local, septic embolism and thrombosis with infarctions.

E. *Invasion of the Nervous System by Acid-Fast Bacteria*
  a. Granulomata and meningitis—*Tuberculosis.*
  b. Infiltrations of peripheral nerve trunks—*Leprosy.*

F. *Invasion of the Nervous System by Fungi*
  a. Granulomata, abscess and meningitis—*Actinomycosis.*
  b. Granulomata and meningitis—*Coccidiosis.*
  c. Meningitis and cortical cysts—*Torulosis.*
  d. Granulomata and meningitis—*Other fungi.*

G. *Invasion of the Nervous System by Spirochetes and Related Organisms*
  a. Meningitis, granulomata, vascular infiltrations with occlusion and infarctions, invasion of the nerve trunks and parenchymatous degenerations of the brain and spinal cord—*Syphilis.*
  b. Meningitis—*Relapsing Fever, Weil's Disease and Rat Bite Fever.*

H. *Involvement of the Nervous System by Protozoa*
  a. Occlusion of the cerebral arterioles by red cells laden with parasites with perivascular necroses and microgliosis—*Malaria.*
  b. Miliary granulomata with small areas of necrosis. Hydrocephalus and retinal lesions—*Toxoplasmosis.*
  c. Perivascular lymphocytic infiltration with mild toxic alterations of the neurons and infiltration of the meninges—*African trypanosomiasis.*
  d. Perivascular granulomata developing into cyst-like structures filled with organisms—*American trypanosomiasis.*

I. *Invasion of the Nervous System by Parasitic Worms*
  a. Single or multiple cysts in the nervous system—*Cysticercosis* and *Echinococcosis.*
  b. Deposit of embryos in cerebral vessels with inflammatory reaction in the brain and meninges—*Trichinosis.*
  c. Deposits of ova in brain sometimes causing granulomatous masses—*Schistosomiasis Japonica and Schistosomiasis Westermani.*

d. Deposits of embryos in eye and central nervous system. Toxocara canis and felis.

DISEASES DUE TO FILTERABLE VIRUSES

Viruses are minute organisms which are so small that they cannot be visualized by the standard microscope. They may be photographed by means of the electromicroscope, however. It is found that they are usually globoid bodies ranging in diameter from 7 mμ to 150 mμ. They differ in several respects from common bacteria. The viruses are obligate parasites and will not grow on common culture media. In most instances, they may be cultivated in tissue cultures and on fertilized egg yolk. Various laboratory animals are susceptible. Viruses produce immunity and specific antibodies in the serum by means of which they may be differentiated. At present no antibiotics or other drugs are known which are effective against viruses though immune sera and vaccines are of value in certain instances. Certain viruses may be crystallized without loss of potency. The virus which causes poliomyelitis is a member of this group. Many virus infections are derived from reservoirs in wild and domestic animals. Thus, rabies is often acquired from dogs, choriomeningitis from mice, equine encephalitis from horses, B virus infection from monkeys and louping ill from sheep. Other viruses seem to be transmitted from man to man. For example poliomyelitis has never been found in nature apart from man. In 1965 *Viral and Rickettsial Infections of Man,* 4th edition, was published. The editors were Horsfall and Tamm. Many authorities wrote articles and all available information about these conditions was included.

A number of viruses are neurotrophic and some have a selective effect on certain nervous structures. One may mention poliomyelitis which destroys the motor cells of the spinal cord and brain stem, rabies which involves the bulbar nuclei, epidemic encephalitis of von Economo which in the late stages selectively destroys the substantia nigra, choriomeningitis which is usually restricted to the meninges and louping ill which involves the cerebellum. Encephalomyocarditis seems to select the brain and the heart muscle. Other infections seem to involve the nervous system secondarily. One may mention mumps which is primarily a form of parotitis but may involve the nervous system.

Certain types of virus infection are transmitted by mosquitos and ticks. They are termed the arthropod-borne encephalitides. In this group are included the St. Louis encephalitis, the Japanese encephalitis, the Australian X disease, the western and eastern equine encephalomyelitis, the Murray Valley encephalitis and the Russian spring and summer encephalitis. Such diseases are prevalent in the summer months. Others, such as poliomyelitis, are transmitted by droplet or fecal infection through the respiratory or gastrointestinal tracts and may be spread by healthy carriers. At least one, i.e. rabies, is conveyed by biting.

Characteristically, virus infections of the central nervous system are acute, self-limited diseases. Only one, i.e. the European encephalitis of von Economo, seems to have a chronic progressive phase. Only one i.e. rabies, is invariably fatal once the symptoms have begun.

The common types of virus infection of the central nervous system are described separately below. Some of the rarer types are mentioned briefly at this point and are described fully in the references given below.

Heath discusses the progress that is being made in finding effective agents to combat diseases due to virus infections.

It is claimed that a specific form of virus encephalitis is found in Russia which is termed the *spring* and *summer encephalitis,* and affects forest workers. It is said that this is transmitted by ticks.

In 1951, the so-called *Murray Valley encephalitis* appeared in Australia. This disease seemed to have a special predilection for children as did the Australian X disease. It is said that both upper and lower motor neuron palsies resulted. The virus is similar to that of the Japanese encephalitis, it is said.

The virus of *louping ill* which causes cerebellar encephalitis in sheep may also infect man. The onset is indicated by fever and headache which develop a few days after exposure. The fever may last a week and then there is apt to be an afebrile period of one or two weeks. The second phase of the disease then supervenes with headache, fever, vomiting, drowsiness, tremor and ataxia. The neck is rigid. There may be cranial nerve palsies. Papilledema is mentioned. The spinal fluid contains from 50 to 500 lymphocytes. Complete recovery is expected within two weeks. The diagnosis may be made by the demonstration of antibodies in the serum during convalescence.

B virus infection, which seems to be a disease of monkeys, has caused a fatal type of ascending myelitis in laboratory workers in a few instances.

Cat-scratch disease is a result of scratching or biting by an apparently healthy cat. It is most common in childhood. An indolent lesion in the skin results. Within one to three weeks, the regional lymph nodes become involved. They may suppurate with the production of steril pus. There is fever, erythema nodosum, cytopenic purpura, lymphedema, pharyngeal angina, and rarely cerebral thrombophlebitis.

There may be involvement of the nervous system within 6 weeks with encephalitis manifest by convulsions, coma and tremors, ataxia and Babinski signs. Myelitis and radiculitis are described. The spinal fluid may contain an excess of cells and protein. The neurological symptoms last only for 2 to 18 days. Recovery is apparently always complete. The organism responsible has never been identified. It is said the patients are sensitive to an antigen made from the affected lymph nodes.

I have seen a boy of 10 years who had an acute encephalitis with 165 lymphocytes in the spinal fluid. Two weeks before the onset of his illness, he had been bitten in the face by his dog which, at the time, was suffering from a form of canine encephalitis termed *hard pad disease* which is believed to be due to the distemper virus. About a week after the onset of the encephalitis, the palms of the boy's hands and the soles of the feet became indurated and roughened. Karzon states that antibodies against canine distemper are found in the sera of almost all human adults and that after the age of two years the percentage of persons with these antibodies rises rapidly.

It has been found that a benign form of asceptic meningitis is due to a previously unrecognized virus, which is termed the Giles virus. The diagnosis cannot be made on clinical grounds.

A form of meningoencephalitis is described which is thought to be due to the virus of *lymphogranuloma venereum*.

Walton reports a case of meningitis due to *psittacosis*. The organism was isolated. Minute coccobacillary bodies were found in the cytoplasm of cells in the meninges. It is believed that the organisms which cause trachoma, lymphogranuloma venereum and psittacosis constitute a distinct group.

TABLE I.—VIRUSES WHICH INVOLVE THE NERVOUS SYSTEM

Enteroviruses
  Poliomyelitis viruses
  Coxsackie viruses
  Echo viruses
  Encephalomyocarditis virus
Arboviruses
  Equine encephalitis virus, Eastern
  Equine encephalitis virus, Western
  St. Louis encephalitis virus
  Japanese encephalitis virus
Myxoviruses
  Mumps virus
  Measles virus
Poxviruses
  Variola virus
  Vaccinia virus
Herpesviruses
  Herpes simplex virus
  Varicella-Zoster virus
  Cytomegalic virus
Unclassified Viruses
  Rubella virus
  Exanthem subitum virus
  Rabies virus
  Lymphocytic meningitis virus

They stand midway between the viruses and the rickettsiae. Aureomycin and tylosin tartrate are effective against them.

Friedlander states that two to eighteen days before the onset of jaundice, in cases of *virus hepatitis,* there may be symptoms of encephalitis, meningitis, myelitis and polyneuritis. The spinal fluid may contain an excess of cells or may be normal.

Mella states that this disease damages the chromosomes and it is possible that this may have teratogenic effects.

BIBLIOGRAPHY

AITA, J. A.: Neurologic Manifestations of General Diseases. Springfield, Thomas, 1964.

BOYD, G. AND CRAIG, G.: Bacillus as a cause of cat-scratch disease. J. Pediat., 59:313, 1961.

Current advances and concepts in virology. Physicians Bulletin. Eli Lilly and Co., 24:67, 1959.

DANIELS, W. AND McMURRAY, F. G.: Cat scratch disease. J.A.M.A., 154:1247, 1954.

DAVISON, G., NEUBAUER, C. AND HURST, E. W.: Meningoencephalitis in man due to louping ill virus. Lancet, 2:453, 1948.

ENDERS, J.: Present status of etiologic discovery in virus diseases. Ann. Int. Med., 45:331, 1956.

FIELDS, W. S. AND BLATTNER, R. J.: Viral Encephalitis. Springfield, Thomas, 1958.

FORBES, J. A.: Clinical aspects of meningoencephalitis. Med. J. Australia, 1:567, 1963.

FRIEDLANDER, W. J.: Neurologic prodromes to virus hepatitis. Neurology, 6:574, 1956.

HAYMAKER, W. *et al.:* Viral Encephalitis. Springfield, Thomas, 1958, p. 106.

HEATH, R. B.: The chemotherapy of virus diseases. Practitioner, 199:644, 1967.

HORSFALL, F. L. AND TAMM, I.: Viral and Rickettsial Infections of Man. 4th Ed. Philadelphia, J. B. Lippincott, 1965.

JERVIS, K. AND HIGGINS, J.: Russian spring and summer encephalitis. J. Neuropath. & Exp. Neurol., 21:1, 1943.

KARZON, D. T.: Distemper virus antibodies in human serum. Pediatrics, 16:809, 1955.

———— *et al.:* Isolation of Echo virus type 6 during outbreak of seasonal aseptic meningitis. J.A.M.A., 162:1298, 1956.

LEDINGHAM, J. C. G.: Studies on virus problems. III. The elementary bodies in virus infections. Bull. Johns Hopkins Hosp., 57:32, 1935.

LKEINMAN, H. *et al.:* Asceptic meningitis due to the Giles virus. Lancet, i:62, 1964.

LYON, G. *et al.:* The acute encephalopathies of obscure origin in infants and children. Brain, 84:680, 1961.

MELLA, B.: Chromosomal damage associated with infectious hepatitis. Neurology, 18:741, 1968.

PETTE, H.: Infection and the nervous system. Proc. German Neurological Soc. Arch. Neurol. & Psychiat., 24:1064, 1930. (Discussion by Spielmeyer, *et al.*)

POLLEN, R. H.: Cat-scratch encephalitis. Neurology, 18:1034, 1968.

RIVERS, T. M.: The relation of filterable viruses to diseases of the nervous system. Arch. Neurol. & Psychiat., 28:757, 1932.

————: Filterable Viruses. Baltimore, Williams and Wilkins Co., 1928.

————: Pathologic and immunologic problems in the virus field. Am. J. Med. Sc., 190:435, 1935.

RIVERS, T.: Viral and Rickettsial Infections of Man. Philadelphia, J. B. Lippincott, 1948.

RIVERS, T. M. AND SCHWENTKER, F. F.: Louping ill in man. J. Exp. Med., 59:669, 1934.

RIVERS, T. M. AND SCOTT, T. F. M.: Meningitis in man caused by a filterable virus. Science, 81:439, 1935.

ROBERTSON, E. G. *et al.:* Murray Valley encephalitis. Med. J. Australia, i:1, 100, 103 and 107, 1952.

SABIN, A. B.: Neurotropic virus diseases of man. J. Pediat., 19:445, 1941.

——— AND ARING, C.: Meningoencephalitis in man caused by the virus of lymphogranuloma venereum. J.A.M.A., **120**:1376, 1942.

——— AND HURST, E. W.: Studies on the B virus. IV. Histopathology of the experimental disease in the Rhesus monkeys and rabbits. Brit. J. Exp. Path., **16**:133, 1935.

——— AND WRIGHT, W. M.: Acute ascending myelitis following a monkey bite with the isolation of a virus capable of reproducing the disease. J. Exp. Med., **59**:115, 1934.

SAUNDERS, M.: Cultivation of the viruses. A critical review. Arch. Path., **28**:541, 1939.

SMITH, M. G., LENNETTE, E. H. AND REAMES, H. R.: Isolation of the virus of herpes simplex and demonstration of intranuclear inclusions in a case of acute encephalitis. Am. J. Path., **17**:55, 1941.

STEINER, M. M. *et al.*: Encephalopathy in cat-scratch disease. J. Pediat., **62**:514, 1963.

STEVENS, H.: Cat scratch encephalitis. Am. J. Dis. Child., **84**:218, 1952.

THOMPSON, T. E. AND MILLER, K. F.: Cat scratch encephalitis. Ann. Int. Med., **39**:146, 1953.

WALTON, K. W.: Pathology of a case of psittacosis showing intracytoplasmic inclusions in the meninges. J. Path. & Bact., **68**:565, 1954.

WALSH, F. B.: Clinical Neuroophthalmology, 2nd. Ed. Baltimore, Williams and Wilkins, 1957.

WEBSTER, L. T.: Classification of primary encephalitides of man according to virus etiology. J.A.M.A., **116**:2840, 1941.

———: Japanese B encephalitis virus: Its differentiation from the St. Louis encephalitis virus and relationship to louping ill. J. Exp. Med., **67**:609, 1938.

WILLIAMS, M. G.: Virus infections of the skin. Modern Medicine, November 21, 1966, p. 88.

ZARAFONETIS, C. J. D.: Meningoencephalitis in lymphogranuloma venereum. New England Jour. Med., **230**:567, 1944.

LETHARGIC ENCEPHALITIS OF VON ECONOMO OR EPIDEMIC ENCEPHALITIS, TYPE A

Terminology.—Von Economo proposed the term "lethargic encephalitis" because of the frequent occurrence of profound lethargy or somnolence. Other writers have preferred to designate the condition as epidemic encephalitis, since lethargy is not invariably present. Several writers have suggested that the European type of the disease be called epidemic encephalitis, Type A, and the Japanese and Australian types be termed Type B.

Etiology.—Despite numerous investigations the cause of epidemic encephalitis is still unknown. It is hard to avoid the conclusion, however, that it is due to a filterable virus for it presents so many of the characteristics of virus diseases.

Pathological Anatomy.—The brain in acute cases is edematous and congested. Histological examination shows dilatation of the small vessels and capillaries. Their adventitial spaces are distended with lymphocytes and sometimes leucocytes and plasma cells. There is a diffuse change in the nerve cells, most of which show some chromatolysis. Some cells are more severely altered than others and are undergoing neuronophagia. Thrombosis of small veins and arteries sometimes occurs causing minute softenings. The meningeal reaction is mild but there may be areas of dense lymphocytic infiltration. It is generally agreed that the process is most intense in the gray matter and that it is especially severe and constant in the substantia nigra, lenticular nucleus and nuclei of the brain-stem. The subthalamic region is usually affected.

In chronic cases of long standing, the pathological picture is very different. The walls of the blood vessels of the brain-stem show marked changes. The adventitia is much thickened and calcium may be deposited in the media. The neurons are diminished in number and some of them may be undergoing necrosis. The loss of cells is most evident in the substantia nigra and globus pallidus but is not in any sense confined to these structures. The loss of cells in the substantia nigra is especially characteristic of the cases in which the Parkinsonian syndrome has developed. In most sections the process seems to be purely degenerative but most observers are agreed that isolated foci of active inflammation may be found even in cases of long standing.

Epidemiology.—The disease was first properly described by von Economo in Vienna in 1917 but similar cases had been observed in Roumania in 1915 and 1916. Apparently sporadic cases were observed in several European countries at this time but received little attention. In 1918, however, the disease attained epidemic proportions and swept throughout Europe, England and the United States although the number of cases was still small. In 1919, 1920 and 1921, the disease was prevalent in almost all parts of the world and thousands of cases occurred in all civilized countries. The highest incidence was reached in 1920. In 1922 and 1923 the world epidemic reached a low level despite the occurrence of several local outbreaks. A second peak was reached in 1924, when the incidence was especially high in the British Isles and Germany. It has been estimated that not less than

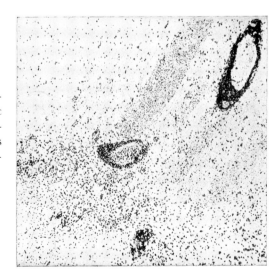

Fig. 137. Section through the brain-stem in an acute case of epidemic encephalitis showing intense perivascular infiltrations with lymphocytes and a diffuse cellular reaction throughout the parenchyma.

100,000 cases occurred between 1917 and 1929. Since then, no important outbreaks have developed but sporadic cases have been seen occasionally in all countries, Espir and Spalding report three cases recently observed in England.

Epidemic encephalitis is a disease of the winter months. As a rule the beginning of an epidemic is indicated by an increasing number of cases during October, November and December. The peak of the epidemic is reached in most cases in the late winter or early spring.

No age is exempt from encephalitis but the greatest incidence is in the second and third decades. Young children and even infants are often affected.

Clinical Features.—The disease is commonly divided into several stages: (1) The acute phase of which several types are recognized. This may be absent or so mild as to escape notice. (2) A period of relative well-being or remission. This may approach recovery and may last for a number of years. In some cases it is absent and the acute phase merges imperceptibly with the chronic stage of the disease. (3) The chronic phase of the disease in which a large number of new and characteristic symptoms develop insidiously and progress slowly over a period of years. The appearance of these late sequelae may be the first evidence of the disease to attract attention.

Acute Stage of Epidemic Encephalitis

I may begin by describing the picture seen in 1919 and 1920 although at present the acute symptoms observed at that time seem to be very unusual.

The onset is either abrupt or gradual, varying to some extent with the severity of the epidemic. In the majority of cases there are prodromal symptoms, some of which point to invasion of the nervous system and some of which are merely indicative of a systemic infection.

I shall distinguish several types of acute encephalitis: (1) The somnolent-ophthalmoplegic type. (2) The type marked by excitement and involuntary movements, often called the hyperkinetic type. (3) The form marked by early development of symptoms of the Parkinsonian syndrome. (4) Fulminating cases. (5) Abortive cases.

The Somnolent-Ophthalmoplegic Type.—The somnolence which gave rise to the name lethargic encephalitis is very characteristic. The child lies as if in deep stupor for days without spontaneous activity. Frequently the stupor is only apparent for the patient may be aroused easily and will then respond quite coherently, relapsing into somnolence as soon as the examiner departs. One gains the impression that the apparent stupor is nearly allied to sleep and the term somnolence is, therefore, applicable. True stupor and even coma, of course, occur in many cases. The second characteristic feature is the presence of extraocular palsies. The third nerve is most frequently affected but the fourth and sixth are also involved very commonly. These palsies are usually bilateral but often incomplete. For example, there may be ptosis of the eyelid alone or the internal rectus may be involved without other evidence of a third nerve lesion. Diplopia is almost constant as is ptosis of the lids. Such palsies may be permanent or transient. The pupils are often dilated and sometimes inactive to light. The contraction during accommodation is frequently impaired or lost. Optic neuritis and even retrobulbar neuritis are described but seem to be rare. Several types of nystagmus are noted. Facial palsies stand next to the oculomotor palsies in order of frequency. These are usually incomplete and transient. Trismus is observed in a number of cases but is rarely so severe as to suggest tetanus. Actual paralysis of the extremities is rare and, if present, is of brief duration, but mild hemiparesis and monoplegias are sometimes seen. The tendon reflexes are sometimes increased and sometimes diminished but in general are not significantly affected. During deep stupor or coma the plantar reflexes are commonly extensor. At the onset, there is not infrequently mild cervical rigidity but pronounced evidence of meningeal irritation is not a characteristic feature of this disease. Radicular pains, local hyperesthesias and neuralgias are prominent in certain cases. Convulsions are unusual and when present are usually focal rather than general. Involuntary movements are less prominent in this type than in the hyperkinetic type but myoclonus and tremors are often observed. These will be described later. It is not unusual to observe incontinence but this is apparently due in most cases to the patient's stuporous condition rather than to actual paralysis of the sphincters. Fever is usually brief and the temperature becomes normal before the

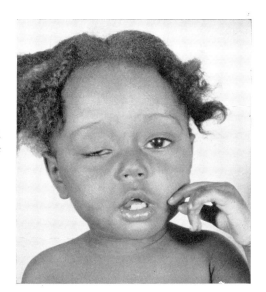

Fig. 138. Epidemic encephalitis. Residual oculomotor palsies after the acute stage of the disease.

acute stage comes to an end. There is no characteristic temperature curve and the temperature does not parallel the somnolence.

The duration of this type of the disease varies between a few days and several weeks or even months. The onset is, as a rule, less acute than that of the hyperkinetic form and the immediate mortality is lower. Von Economo regards this type as the basic type of the disease.

The Hyperkinetic Type.—The onset is usually more abrupt, often marked by high fever and delirium. The characteristic symptoms are almost the opposite of those described above. In place of lethargy and immobility, there is excitement, restlessness and insomnia. Various types of delirium may occur. There is confusion and disorientation, as a rule, with anxiety and apprehension. Hallucinations are not unusual. In many cases there are stabbing pains in the extremities which are usually attributed to irritation of the spinal roots.

Involuntary movements are common. These are usually choreiform and may be very violent. In a considerable percentage of cases there are myoclonic twitchings. These are usually but not invariably associated with lancinating pains. The oculomotor palsies so characteristic of the lethargic type are less common in the hyperkinetic type. The mortality is relatively high in this type probably due to the difficulty in maintaining proper nutrition and in securing adequate rest. The course is sometimes a brief one lasting only a few days but, as a rule, the over-activity lasts a number of weeks or more. In certain instances, the hyperkinesis disappears after a short time and is replaced by the more common somnolence and lethargy.

Acute Parkinsonian Type.—We shall learn in discussing the chronic phases of the disease that the Parkinsonian syndrome is one of the most typical sequels of epidemic encephalitis. In the acute stage this syndrome is less common and when present is rarely fully developed. However, in certain cases the patient shows a striking immobility, lying for many hours without any change of position or movement of the face even when fully conscious. The face is relaxed and the natural folds and wrinkles are smoothed out. Even during conversation there is little or no play of expression on the face. When addressed, the patient will turn the eyes to the examiner but will not move the head. All movements are slow and weak. Frequently the movement is arrested before its object is attained. In many cases there is a rhythmical tremor provoked by movement. Speech is slow, low pitched and monotonous. Muscle tone is not always increased as it is in the chronic Parkinsonian syndrome but in some cases a striking rigidity and spasticity of the muscles is present, so that the limbs may remain in any position in which they are placed.

Fulminating Cases.—In most of the large epidemics, especially when the epidemic had reached its peak, a certain number of hyperacute or fulminating cases were seen which might cause death within twelve hours or less. In some of these the picture was that of somnolence with oculomotor palsies or of hyperkinesis and the case was peculiar only in the extraordinarily rapid development of the symptoms. In others, the picture was that of sudden loss of consciousness with or without hemiplegia or convulsions. Some cases are marked by rapidly developing bulbar palsy.

Abortive Cases.—During epidemics, a great variety of mild and transient manifestations are observed which apparently represent abortive types of the disease. In some cases, the patients are very drowsy for a few days or weeks but are not conscious of any other departure from health and continue to lead their usual life. Transient visual disturbances such as diplopia or loss of accommodation, localized myoclonic movements, mild bulbar disturbances, neuralgic pains, headache, insomnia and restlessness are all observed as the manifestations of abortive cases.

Laboratory Findings.—As a rule, there is a moderate increase in the number of white cells ranging from 15,000 to 30,000 with a slight increase in the percentage of the polymorphonuclear leucocytes. The red count is usually normal or only slightly diminished. The chemical constituents of the blood usually show no departure from normal.

The spinal fluid was usually described as quite normal in the early stages of the epidemic but, as a rule, there is a moderate increase in lymphocytes ranging from 20 to 100 and rarely exceeding 200. In very acute cases there may be a few polymorphonuclear leucocytes. The globulin tests are usually faintly positive and sugar is normal. After two weeks, the spinal fluid is usually normal or at most shows some globulin. The fluid contains blood in only exceptional cases.

Residua of the Acute Stage.—The commonest objective residua are various types of oculomotor palsies such as have been described above. These often disappear completely or partially but in some instances remain unchanged throughout life. Disturbances of pupillary reflexes, especially loss of contraction during accommodation, are often seen either with palsies of the oculomotor nerves or alone. Optic atrophy is described but must be rare. The facial palsies rarely persist. Weakness or paralysis of the extremities is sometimes seen and seems to be somewhat more common among infants than among older children. It is unusual to discover typical cerebral palsies associated with spasticity, extensor responses and ankle clonus, however. In most cases there is merely weakness and tremor associated with some increase of reflexes and muscular rigidity, suggesting that we are dealing with the manifestations of a beginning Parkinsonian syndrome as well as mild injury of the pyramidal tract. However, the writer has seen children who had encephalitis early in life in whom there remained muscular rigidity with bilateral Babinski phenomena and ankle clonus, together with more typical symptoms. Definite signs of cerebellar ataxia are very rare but tremors which are increased during volitional movement are not unusual. As a rule, these are rhythmical and also present at rest, so that they are not typical of cerebellar disease. Choreic syndromes, both unilateral and bilateral may persist. The myoclonic movements sometimes continue for months or years after the acute stage.

Mental disturbances are even more common than objective signs. In infants, profound mental defect may remain but, as a rule, there is more alteration of behavior and of personality than loss of intelligence. There is restlessness, difficulty in concentration, irritability, emotional instability and vague hypochondriacal trends.

Remissions.—In a certain number of cases, perhaps about 30 or 40 per cent, the acute phase is followed by a period of relative well-being which may amount to complete, if temporary, recovery or may be complicated by such residua as have just been mentioned above. Such partial or complete remissions may last for several years before they are terminated by the development of *sequelae*. The writer has seen a patient who developed a Parkinsonian syndrome twenty-four years after a very mild acute attack of encephalitis. During the interval, the patient enjoyed excellent health and showed no residua. Such cases are, however, exceptional and the average duration of remissions is probably not more than a few months or two or three years.

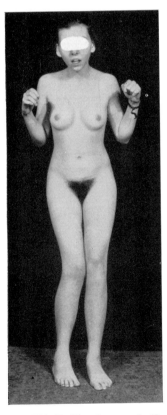

Fig. 139. Epidemic encephalitis. Parkinsonian syndrome in chronic phase of the disease. Symptoms are bilateral in this case.

Chronic Stage of Epidemic Encephalitis

General Discussion.—Most of the children who survived an attack of encephalitis during the early epidemic of 1919 and 1920 seemed at that time to bid fair to make a complete recovery. Some were quite well within a few months and others showed residua which seemed to be slowly diminishing. Only a few had suffered damage to the nervous system which seemed to be irreparable. This relatively optimistic prospect was soon abandoned, however, for during the next few years, it was observed that many of the patients who had seemed to recover began to develop new symptoms of unusual type and it became evident that the disease had a second phase which was even more serious than the first. The onset of this second or chronic phase is not marked by a return or an increase of the symptoms of the acute stage but by the gradual development of symptoms of an entirely different order, many of which are quite characteristic and are rarely if ever seen in any other disease of the central nervous system.

The symptoms of the chronic stage in most cases advance slowly and uniformly without fever or other signs of chronic infection. The spinal fluid is almost always quite normal in the chronic stage of the disease or at most shows merely some increase of globulin. There is no constant leucocytosis.

Parkinsonian Syndrome.—This is one of the most striking and most frequent syndromes seen in the late stages of epidemic encephalitis. It is unusual in children under ten years but is not uncommon in older children. The onset is very slow and the course almost always progressive until the patient becomes quite helpless and bed-ridden. In brief, it is characterized by an altered posture with flexion of the trunk and extremities, by muscular rigidity of a definite type with cogwheel phenomenon, by slowness of all movements, expressionless face, rhythmical tremor at rest and absence of arm-swinging in gait.

It is of great interest that these children can usually run better than they can walk and we have observed children who could not stand without sup-

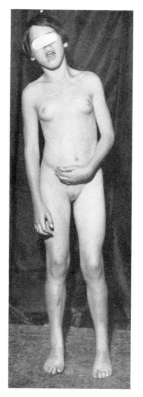

Fig. 140. Chronic epidemic encephalitis with unilateral (left) Parkinsonian syndrome and severe changes in personality.

port and yet could dance actively and even gracefully. In some cases the children show great variation in their symptoms during the twenty-four hours. During the day they may seem to be quite helpless and when placed on their feet will walk with great difficulty but at night they may get out of bed and run about the ward in a manner which one would not have deemed possible. The expressionless face is sometimes replaced by a rigid smile, the jaws are often widely opened, and may be dislocated, the tongue protruded and the head retracted. The rigidity may become so severe eventually that the child is virtually paralyzed and quite helpless. The extremities will remain in any position in which they are placed by the examiner. In such states progressive cachexia is very apt to develop and often leads to a fatal termination.

Bradykinesias.—These are slow movements of large amplitude which occur at a rate of 15 to 20 per minute. We have observed a case in which the movements began in the right latissimus dorsi and gradually developed during a number of months until almost all the muscles on that side of the body were affected. The right arm would be extended and retracted, the leg abducted and extended and the trunk bent to the right side. The rate was perfectly rhythmical. In this case there was a typical acute onset which was followed at once by the involuntary movements. These persisted unchanged for seven years when the patient passed from our observation.

Dystonic Syndromes.—Certain alterations of posture are not at all uncommon. The head may be tilted to one side and rotated to the opposite side as in the common spasmodic torticollis. The spine may be twisted and curved and the hips and shoulders held in asymmetrical postures. It is usually possible for the child to overcome the muscle spasm for a time, but the deformity almost always recurs very promptly. In many cases, the spasm will disappear when the child lies down and relaxes and it also seems to be increased by voluntary effort or emotional stress. Such cases are frequently termed dystonias, although we have never seen in epidemic encephalitis the lordosis or "dromedary gait" which are considered typical of dystonia musculorum deformans. In several instances the symptoms under discussion were associated with masklike face, rhythmical tremor, rigidity of the muscles and other signs of the Parkinsonian syndrome.

Tremors.—These are in most cases associated with the Parkinsonian syndrome and we find a rhythmical tremor of the hands which is usually increased when hands are held outstretched and inhibited by voluntary movement. Some of these tremors are atypical and we may find the tremor increases in amplitude in the finger-nose test. The movements may involve the lips, face, eyelids, jaws and other parts of the body but are most common in the hands. Typical "intention" tremors are rare in encephalitis.

Tic-like Movements.—It is of great interest that repetitive movements such as we have been accustomed to regard as psychogenic tics are not infrequent in the chronic stage of encephalitis. These movements may be very simple or very complex. Persistent bilateral blepharospasm is not uncommon. The child may merely twitch the mouth or wink one eyelid repeatedly or an elaborate sequence of movements may occur. We have seen one boy of nine years who went through the following motions a great many times in the course of every day. He would first begin to breathe very deeply and rapidly, then he would bring the radial margin of his hands several times to his mouth as if "saluting." After this movement was carried out four or five times he would elevate his hand and make movements as if waving "goodbye." During this period he always showed evidences of anger and would sometimes foam at the mouth. He would strike or kick anyone who came near at such moments. These tic-like movements may persist for years but in our experience tend to cease eventually. The mechanism of their production is not at all clear. Undoubtedly, they are results of the disease but they resemble psychogenic tics very closely.

Oculogyric Crises.—A very remarkable group of symptoms are included under the term of oculogyric crises. These are almost diagnostic of epidemic encephalitis, for they are excessively rare in other diseases of the nervous system. They are relatively late phenomena in most cases and may first appear several years after the onset. A Parkinsonian syndrome is usually associated. The attacks seem to be periodic in many instances but never preserve a definite rhythm. The incidence is undoubtedly modified by fatigue and by emotional factors. At the beginning of the attack, there may be a fixed stare for a few moments. Then the eyes roll upwards or to one side and are fixed in that position, so that the patient cannot depress them fully although they may be moved about to a limited degree. The spasm of the muscles may be very painful and the patient's face is often expressive of pain. Various grimaces are often associated and there may be rotation of the head backwards or to one side and distortion of the trunk. The mouth may be forced open and the tongue protruded as in one of our

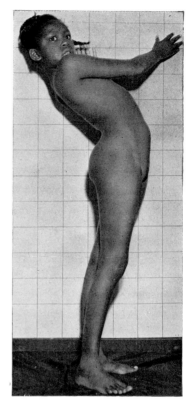

Fig. 141. Bradykinesia. Every few seconds the child's trunk is drawn backwards so she would fall if not supported. Thirty years later, the patient's condition was unchanged.

patients. The duration of the attack varies between several minutes and several hours. Usually, the symptoms are relieved as soon as the patient relaxes completely or falls asleep. Most patients lie down as soon as the spasm develops. This condition has persisted for many years in a number of our patients and seems to show no tendency to spontaneous recovery. Large doses of artane give some symptomatic relief.

Disturbances of Respiration.—A great variety of disturbances in the rate and rhythm of respiration occur during the chronic phase of the disease. These are, perhaps, just as distinctive as the oculogyric crises described above and, like them, develop in recurrent attacks. Most frequently the patient begins to breathe more and more rapidly and deeply until after a few minutes respiration has become very violent, the mouth is widely opened and all the accessory muscles are employed, so that the patient is the picture of distress. After minutes or a few hours, the disturbance slowly subsides. In some cases, the excessive ventilation of the lungs leads to tetany and prolonged apnea may follow the attack to such a degree as to cause cyanosis and even convulsions. Less commonly there are attacks of Cheyne-Stokes respiration, alternating attacks of deep and shallow breathing, sighing, yawning, sniffing, coughing, spitting, breath-holding spells and innumerable other variations. During the attacks there may be strange and distorted postures of the body, striking facial grimaces and involuntary movements. Such attacks may occur spontaneously but are frequently provoked by trivial altercations and seem to be associated with an emotional reaction in almost every case. Such attacks have usually ceased spontaneously after a few months or years, in my experience, and are most apt to develop during the early phases of the chronic stage of the disease.

Progressive Muscular Atrophy.—A number of writers describe progressive muscular atrophy which may simulate the common spinal atrophy or even amyotrophic lateral sclerosis. Bulbar palsy is sometimes associated. These conditions may begin years or months after the acute phase of the disease and run a slowly progressive course to a fatal termination. There are active fibrillary and fascicular twitchings in the muscles with pronounced atrophy, alteration of the electrical reactions and loss of tendon reflexes. Wimmer has described a number of cases of this type. The wasting may begin in any part of the musculature, but in our experience has appeared most frequently in the cervical segments affecting the arms or the hands and often the muscles of the neck first of all. It is usually bilateral but may be unilateral. In some cases the legs exhibit spasticity and increased tendon reflexes. The diagnosis is obviously uncertain for there is often no way of excluding the common type of progressive spinal muscular atrophy. In certain cases, the signs of a Parkinsonian syndrome are associated or some other characteristic feature is present which permits a satisfactory diagnosis to be made. Wimmer has found loss of motor cells in the spinal cord with degeneration of the pyramidal tracts and small foci in which the adventitia of the vessels is infiltrated with lymphocytes.

Convulsive Phenomena.—Convulsions are among the less frequent results of this disease, although they have been described by several writers. They may appear within a few months of the onset or may be delayed for several years. General convulsions with tonic and clonic contractions are most common, but we may also have petit mal and focal attacks. Several authors have described purely *tonic* seizures or tetanoid attacks in which consciousness may remain clear and in which the hands and feet may assume the postures seen in the carpopedal spasm of tetany. These seizures have been attributed to discharges originating in the basal ganglia.

Disturbances of Sleep.—We have already mentioned the characteristic *somnolence* of the acute phase and the less common *insomnia*. These symptoms may persist for long periods and are not uncommon in some degree in the chronic stages of the disease. *Reversal of sleep rhythm* is a frequent and typical feature of encephalitis especially in children. The patient may be sluggish or drowsy during the daylight hours and usually spends most of the time in sleep but as night approaches becomes more and more active and restless. About midnight or later the child may be wildly excited, laughing and screaming and in constant ill-directed activity. As day dawns this over-activity slowly diminishes and the child finally falls asleep just at the time when under normal conditions it should be awakening. These symptoms may develop during convalescence from the acute stage of the disease or among the sequelae several months after the onset, but in our experience are most commonly seen in cases of subacute or chronic type in which the more acute phase has been mild or absent. They frequently constitute the first evidence of the disease to attract attention. As a rule, reversal of sleep is a transient phenomenon and eventually disappears.

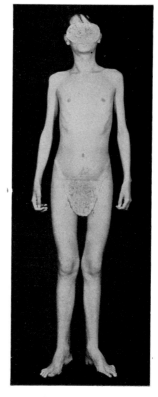

FIG. 142. Progressive muscular atrophy beginning five years after an acute attack of epidemic encephalitis. The muscles of the shoulders, arms, hands, chest and calves show atrophy and fascicular twitchings.

Disturbances of the Autonomic System.—Numerous symptoms of chronic encephalitis fall into this group. Excessive salivation is perhaps the most common and is found in a large percentage of all cases of Parkinsonism. Frequently the saliva is collected in the mouth because the patient fails to swallow but there can be no doubt that there is an actual excess of saliva in many cases. Facial seborrhea of extraordinary degree may occur and a moderately greasy face is common in the Parkinsonian syndromes.

Disturbances of Metabolism and Development.—The most frequent symptom complex of this group is that of pathological obesity with drowsiness and apathy. In some cases there is polyuria and polydipsia and even failure of genital development and hypotrichosis, so that the complete or nearly complete syndrome of Fröhlich may appear. These symptoms usually develop in children over five years of age during convalescence after the acute stage of the disease.

Progressive cachexia is not uncommon especially in the more severe Parkinsonian syndromes. It is apparently more or less independent of the food intake and is usually attributed to a disturbance of metabolism. No doubt, this cachexia as well as the Fröhlich's syndrome are the result of lesions in the infundibulum and hypothalamus.

Precocious puberty has been mentioned by a number of writers. We have had a child of eleven years under observation who exhibited excessive development of the genitalia with hypertrichosis and extraordinary eroticism. There was also a typical Parkinsonian syndrome and the history of the acute phase of the disease was so characteristic that there could be no doubt of the diagnosis.

Glycosuria of transient nature has been observed a number of times and is generally attributed to lesions in the brain-stem or diencephalon.

Mental Disturbances.—Encephalitis causes very severe psychic changes in children in a large percentage of all cases. In infants mental development is often completely arrested and idiocy or imbecility may result.

In children over ten years of age we frequently see pronounced slowing of mental processes or at least slowing of response which is associated with the Parkinsonian syndrome, as a rule. There is usually only moderate reduction of intelligence but a good deal of emotional instability and difficulty in concentration. They often show vague hypochrondriacal trends and sometimes delusions of a somatic nature.

The most characteristic mental disturbances, however, occur in children between the ages of three and ten years. As in older children, there is in most cases no marked reduction of intelligence but personality changes of a profound nature frequently result. The Parkinsonian syndrome may be associated but in most cases physical signs are absent or trivial. These children are very destructive and impulsive. Any impulse which occurs to them is at once translated into action. Their misdeeds are not planned but are the result of the temptation of the moment. The natural inhibitions and fear of consequence which restrain us all from injudicious misbehavior seem to be lacking in these children. Without any thought of punishment, they will steal, lie, destroy property, set fire and commit various sexual offenses. They usually make no attempt to evade detection and when reproached with their conduct will reply that they could not help it. They may exhibit exaggerated remorse for their offense which, however, does not prevent further misdeeds. An important factor in these behavior disorders is the emotional instability. The child's mood changes in response to the slightest stimulus. At times, sudden explosive outbursts of anger occur which seem to be entirely unmotivated. For example, we may mention the case of a little boy of nine years who was brought to the hospital by his father because he had become too dangerous to keep at home. Among other atrocities, he had attempted to kill his baby brother with a carving knife, had set fire to the house and had inflicted a deep cut on his mother's neck with a piece of glass. Under observation, he was found to undergo a spontaneous series of emotional reactions. He would make advances to the nurses and attempt to embrace them. A moment later, he would become furiously angry and foam at the mouth. He would bite or strike anyone within his reach at such moments, and on several occasions, was found to be beating a comatose patient over the head with a shoe. Such reactions suggest very strongly the "sham-rage" of Cannon and Bard, which is produced in animals by operations designed to release the hypothalamus from cortical control. Some children show excessive eroticism and precocious sexual reactions. We have seen a boy of eleven years who was committed because he had been molesting little girls. He masturbated almost constantly throughout the day, and, at night, would steal into the female ward and get into bed with adult women. The strong feeling of shame associated with the sexual life in childhood seems to be quite lacking in these children.

In some instances these children inflicted terrible mutilations on themselves. M. S. had epidemic encephalitis with the typical picture of somnolence at the age of 10 years. After this illness which lasted 7 weeks, her behavior became abnormal. She was emotionally unstable and could not be controlled. Respiratory tics developed. She had an insatiable appetite and became extremely obese. Strong sexual desires developed which she sought to gratify at every opportunity. She bit off all her fingers and ate them and some of her toes. Finally she gouged out her right eye and ate it. She seemed to have complete analgesia for when the surgeons repaired her mutilations, she showed no sign of pain, though no anesthesia was used. Once she forced a coin into the empty right orbit. Infection resulted and septic cavernous sinus thrombosis and meningitis caused her death.

Diagnosis.—This is based on the clinical features for no laboratory tests are available to establish the diagnosis. In the acute phase the picture may be similar to that of other neurotrophic virus infections. The absence of serological evidence of infection with other viruses may be of importance. The development of a chronic phase of the disease and the characteristic features of this phase often make it possible to be sure of the diagnosis.

Prognosis.—The mortality in the acute phase varied between 10 and 20 per cent in most epidemics. However, a large percentage of patients who survived the acute stage eventually passed into the second chronic phase of the disease and developed Parkinsonian syndromes or other disabling sequelae.

Treatment.—It may be said briefly that there is no specific treatment known for this disease. Victims of the Parkinsonian syndrome are usually able to take large doses of the alkaloids of belladonna or related drugs and often derive considerable benefit from them. Various operations have been developed which are intended to reduce the rigidity or the tremor. The motor cortex and the motor pathways in the cervical cord have been attacked. At present lesions are being produced in the region of the globus pallidus or thalamus. The results are sometimes good and sometimes bad.

BIBLIOGRAPHY

General articles

HALL, A. J.: Epidemic Encephalitis, Bristol, 1924.

PARSONS, A. C. AND MacNALTY, A. S.: Report on Encephalitis Lethargica. Reports on Public Health and Medical Subjects, No. 11. His Majesty's Stationery Office, 1922. London.

VON ECONOMO, C.: Encephalitis Lethargica, Its Sequelae and Treatment. Oxford Press, 1931.

Epidemiology

MacNALTY, A. S.: Epidemic Diseases of the Central Nervous System. London, Faber and Gwyer, 1927.

NEAL, J. *et al.*: Epidemic Encephalitis, Etiology, Epidemiology and Treatment. Report of the Matheson Commission, Columbia Univ. Press. New York, 1929. Second Report 1932. Third Report 1939.

Etiology

ESPIR, L. M. E. AND SPALDING, J. M. K.: Three recent cases of encephalitis lethargica. Brit. Med. J., i:1141, 1956.

FLEXNER, A.: Epidemic encephalitis and allied conditions. J.A.M.A., **81**:1688, 1923; obvious and obscure infections of the central nervous system. J.A.M.A., **91**:21, 1928.

NEAL, J. *et al.*: (See above) .

ZINSSER, H.: The present state of knowledge regarding epidemic encephalitis. Arch. Path., **6**:271, 1928.

Pathological anatomy

BUZZARD, E. F. AND GREENFIELD, J. G.: Lethargic encephalitis; its sequelae and morbid anatomy. Brain, **42**:305, 1919.

EAVES, E. C. AND CROLL, M. M.: Pituitary and hypothalamic region in chronic epidemic encephalitis. Brain, **53**:56, 1930.

HOHMAN, L. B.: Histopathology of post-encephalitis parkinsonian syndrome. Bull. Johns Hopkins Hosp., **36**:403, 1925.

McKINLEY, J. C. AND GOWAN, L. R.: Neuron destruction in post-encephalitis parkinsonism. Arch. Neurol. & Psychiat., **15**:1, 1926.

Acute symptoms

HAPP, W. M. AND MASON, V. R.: Epidemic encephalitis. Bull. Johns Hopkins Hosp., **32**:136, 1921.

JENKINS, ALBERTA: Epidemic encephalitis with cerebellar symptoms. Arch. Neurol. & Psychiat., **22**:469, 1929.

NEAL, J. B.: Experience with more than 100 cases of epidemic encephalitis in children. J.A.M.A., **77**:121, 1921.

WINTHER, K.: Les affections du nerf optique dans l'encéphalite épidémique. Acta psychiat. et neurol., **3**:165, 1928.

Chronic stage—General articles
PARSONS, A. C.: Report of an inquiry into the After-Histories of Persons Attacked by Encephalitis Lethargica. Reports on Public Health and Medical Subjects, No. 49. His Majesty's Stationery Office, 1928, London.
WIMMER, A.: Chronic Epidemic Encephalitis, London, Wm. Heinemann, 1928.

Parkinsonian syndrome
PARSONS, A. C.: (See above).
WIMMER, A.: (See above).

Dystonic syndromes
BROCK, S. AND MARGARETTEN, I.: Pyramidal and extrapyramidal system involvement in epidemic encephalitis. Arch. Neurol. & Psychiat., **8**:660, 1922.

Bradykinesias
LEVY, G.: Contribution à l'étude des manifestations tardives de l'encéphalite épidémique. Paris, 1923.

Disturbances of respiration
JELLIFFE, S. E.: Post-encephalitic respiratory syndromes. Arch. Neurol. & Psychiat., **17**:627, 1927.
TURNER, W. A. AND CRITCHLEY, McD.: Respiratory disorders in epidemic encephalitis. Brain, **48**:72, 1925.

Ocular Phenomena
HALL, A. J.: Chronic epidemic encephalitis with especial reference to ocular attacks. Brit. Med. J., **2**:833, 1931.
JELLIFFE, S. E.: Psychologic components in post-encephalitis. Oculogyric crises. Arch. Neurol. & Psychiat., **21**:491, 1929.
KENNEDY, F.: Ocular disturbances in epidemic encephalitis. Arch. Ophth., **1**:346, 1929.
WALSH, F. B.: *Loc. cit.*
WIMMER, A.: Tonic fits (oculogyric crises) in chronic epidemic encephalitis. Acta Psychiat. et Neurol. Scand., **1**:173, 1926.

Muscular atrophy
WIMMER, A. AND NEAL, A. V.: Les amyotrophies systematisées dans l'encéphalite épidémique chronique. Acta Psychiat. et Neurol., **3**:319, 1928.

Epilepsy
WIMMER, A.: Epilepsy in chronic epidemic encephalitis. Acta Psychiat. et Neurol., **3**:267, 1928.

Disorders of sleep
HAPP, W. M. AND BLACKFAN, K. D.: Insomnia following acute encephalitis in children. J.A.M.A., **175**:1337, 1920.

Disturbances of the autonomic system
KENNEDY, F., DAVIS, T. AND HYSLOP, G.: Contribution to the symptomatology of epidemic encephalitis. Arch. Neurol. & Psychiat., **8**:40, 1922.

Disturbances of metabolism
FORD, F. R. AND GUILD, H.: Precocious puberty following measles encephalomyelitis and epidemic encephalitis. Bull. Johns Hopkins Hosp., **60**:192, 1937.

LANG, W. J.: Postencephalitic Fröhlich's syndrome. J. Nerv. & Ment. Dis., 67:120, 1928.

WALSH, T. G.: Postencephalitic obesity. J.A.M.A., 87:305, 1926.

Mental disturbances

ANDERSON, G.: The sequelae of epidemic encephalitis in childhood with notes on prognosis as regards complete recovery. Quart. J. Med., 16:173, 1922, 1923.

BOND, E. AND APPEL, K. E.: Treatment of behavior disorders following encephalitis. Commonwealth Fund Publication, 1931.

BOND, E. D. AND SMITH, L. H.: Postencephalitic behavior disorders. A ten year review. Am. J. Psychiat., 92:17, 1935.

EBAUGH, F. G.: Neuropsychiatric sequelae of acute encephalitis in children. Am. J. Dis. Child., 15:89, 1923.

GIBBS, C. E.: Behavior disorders in children suffering from chronic epidemic encephalitis; clinical course in relation to signs of persisting organic pathology. Am. J. Psychiat., 9:619, 1930.

GOODHART, S. P. AND SAVITSKY, N.: Self-mutilation in chronic encephalitis, evulsion of both eyeballs and extraction of teeth. Am. J. Med. Sc., 185:674, 1933.

HOHMAN, L.: Post-encephalitic behavior disorders in children. Bull. Johns Hopkins Hosp., 33:372, 1922.

KENNEDY, R.: Prognosis of sequelae of epidemic encephalitis in children. Am. J. Dis. Child., 28:158, 1924.

PATTERSON, D. AND SPENCE, J.: Encephalitis in children. Lancet, 11:491, 1921.

SHERMAN, M. AND BEVERLY, B.: The factor of deterioration in children showing behavior difficulties after epidemic encephalitis. Arch. Neurol. & Psychiat., 10:329, 1923.

STEVENSON, M. M.: The life history of epidemic encephalitis in the child. Arch. Dis. Child., 3:57, 1928.

EPIDEMIC ENCEPHALITIS, TYPE B

Terminology.—It has been suggested that the Japanese encephalitis be termed encephalitis B to distinguish it from the Euoprean type of von Economo which may be called encephalitis A. Since the St. Louis encephalitis is apparently identical in its clinical and anatomical features with the Japanese type it may also be called encephalitis B. It seems to be established, however, that the virus recovered in St. Louis is not identical with the Japanese virus. These viruses fall into the group of Arbor viruses or arthropod borne viruses.

Etiology.—Experimental work indicates that the etiological agent is a filterable virus. Apparently both the Japanese and American types may be transmitted to experimental animals. The Japanese state that mice, guinea pigs and rabbits are susceptible and several workers have infected monkeys with inoculations of brain emulsions from the St. Louis material. It is said that the disease in monkeys is similar both clinically and anatomically to that in humans. Webster has isolated a filterable virus from the nervous system of patients in St. Louis. The investigators of the St. Louis epidemic claim that the Japanese and American viruses may be distinguished by their serological reactions. At present this seems to be the only evidence that the diseases are not actually identical.

Epidemiology.—Since 1871 there have been small epidemics of an acute disease of the central nervous system, in Japan, which was not epidemic meningitis and resembled in its general character encephalitis B. It was not until the large epidemics of 1912, 1919, 1924, and 1929, however, that adequate studies were made and the true nature of the condition recognized. In addition to these large epidemics of many thousands of cases, a certain number of sporadic cases occur every year, so the disease may be said to be endemic in Japan. This disease is also prevalent in other parts of the Pacific area.

In the summer of 1933, an epidemic of 1,100 cases of acute encephalitis appeared in St. Louis, Missouri, and the surrounding territory. The clinical features of this disease were practically identical with those of the Japanese encephalitis. The first cases appeared in July and the last in October. In 1934, small outbreaks occurred in Illinois, Ohio and Indiana. A second epidemic of 431 cases developed in St. Louis, in 1937, and during the same summer a few cases were observed in California. Other epidemics have occurred since then in the Western and Middle Western States.

Epidemics usually begin in the summer during July or August and soon reach their maximum. During September and October the incidence declines rapidly and later in the year the disease is very unusual. Sporadic cases follow the same laws. It has been observed that very hot and dry seasons have coincided with severe epidemics. Storms and heavy rainfall apparently exert some influence in halting the progress of epidemics. The disease is believed to be transmitted by mosquitoes from birds to man and by mites from bird to bird.

The Japanese encephalitis is more prevalent in children than in adults. Lewis *et al.* found that 50 of their 66 patients were under 16 years of age and 28 were under 9 years. The St. Louis encephalitis, on the contrary, is more frequent and more severe in elderly persons. Only 6 per cent of all cases of this disease occur in subjects under the age of 10 years.

Males are affected slightly more frequently than females. Farmers and persons living in rural districts suffer more than the urban population. The incubation period is uncertain.

Pathological Anatomy.—Gross examination reveals intense congestion of the brain and meninges with more or less edema and often minute hemorrhages in the cortex, basal ganglia and spinal gray matter. The meninges show an intense infiltration with lymphocytes and leucocytes as well as congestion and edema. Minute extravasations of red blood corpuscles are found in the neighborhood of the small vessels. In the central nervous system the adventitia sheaths of the small vessels are distended with lymphocytes and polymorphonuclear leucocytes. There are sometimes hyaline changes in the muscularis and later deposits of calcium and iron are found in the vessel wall. There is a diffuse infiltration of the cerebral tissues with lymphocytes and in very acute cases with leucocytes, and a moderate re-action of the microglia which take up broken down lipoid products. The infiltrations are most marked in the basal ganglia and brain-stem but are al-so found in the cerebral cortex, the thalamus and hypothalamus, the dentate nuclei of the cerebellum and the spinal gray matter. Many small cellular foci are found which resemble miliary abscesses. These are most numerous in the cortex and basal ganglia. Foci composed of glial cells are very numerous in the brain-stem. A characteristic feature is the presence of many small areas of necrosis which are more numerous and more widely scattered than in encephalitis type A. In rare cases small cavities may result. Widespread injury of the neurons is always found which seems to be of two types: that often seen in severe intoxications and that associated with local inflammatory lesions. However, there seems to be no tendency for this disease to cause complete or nearly complete destruction of the neurons in any special region. More or less degeneration of the white matter is usually found especially in the internal capsule and pyramidal tracts. In summary, we may state that in comparison with encephalitis type A, the process is more acute and more generalized, that it is associated with a more severe meningeal reaction, that hemorrhages and areas of necrosis are more fre-quent, that the cortex and the spinal cord are more severely injured and that there is no tendency to destroy selectively the substantia nigra and the oculomotor nuclei. The tendency in the Japanese variety of encephalitis to involve the cerebellum seems to be distinctive since this is apparently not true of the St. Louis encephalitis. These differences are apparently quanti-tative rather than qualitative and are perhaps not always sufficient to per-mit the differential diagnosis to be made with certainty upon anatomical grounds alone.

The lesions in the other organs are not distinctive in any way.

Clinical Features.—The following description applies to both the Japa-nese and the American cases.

Several types of onset are recognized. In type I the onset is abrupt with-out definite prodromata. There is headache, fever up to 40°C. and perhaps chills, nausea, signs of intense meningeal irritation, pains in the back and extremities, convulsions in many cases, tremors and soon drowsiness, de-lirium and loss of consciousness. In some instances paralysis of apoplectic onset constitutes the first symptom and this is followed at once by coma or stupor. In type II, the onset is more gradual and there is a definite period of invasion lasting for from one to four days. The prodromal symptoms include headache, fever, mild respiratory or gastrointestinal symptoms, pains in the extremities, photophobia and conjunctivitis. Then just when the patient seems to be recovering the fever rises, the headache suddenly becomes severe and cerebral symptoms develop as in type I. In a third type, definite nervous symptoms never develop. There is merely headache and fever with perhaps slight cervical rigidity. The diagnosis of such abortive cases depends upon the demonstration of an increased cell count in the spinal fluid.

In the characteristic cases, restlessness and delirium develop within one or two days after the onset of the fever. This slowly passes over into stupor or coma. Cervical rigidity is usually found within a few hours and soon there are intense signs of meningeal irritation. The musculature becomes very rigid, tremors and fibrillary twitchings appear. Trismus may suggest tetanus. In some cases there are transient cerebral palsies such as hemiplegia, monoplegia or bilateral paralysis. Death from hyperpyrexia, paralysis of respiration or pneumonia may occur between three days and two weeks. If the patient survives this period, the fever declines, the stupor lifts and convalescence is soon established.

Certain groups of symptoms will now be discussed in more detail. The *fever* usually rises gradually for three or four days and begins to diminish between the fifth and eighth day. It usually falls by lysis but in certain cases termination by crisis has been observed. Various irregular types of fever are also seen, some of which are probably due to secondary infection. In a few cases the fever may return after an apyrexial period in association with an exacerbation of symptoms. Rarely the fever may last for several months.

Psychic disturbances are almost constant. As a rule, there is clouding of consciousness with more or less restlessness. This stage often merges slowly into stupor or coma. Delirium with hallucinations is also observed. The somnolence of type A encephalitis is apparently not seen. Cataleptic stupors are mentioned and there is often depression associated with the confusion. As a rule, the psychic disturbances last between one and two weeks.

Signs of meningeal irritation constitute a cardinal group of symptoms. Cervical rigidity, Kernig's sign, hyperesthesia, pains in the back and extremities and severe headache are practically always present to some degree and are often so intense that the diagnosis of meningococcic meningitis may be suspected.

Muscular rigidity is also very constant, appearing in the first few days of the illness and lasting for a month or more. It appears to be composed of several elements such as the rigidity of meningeal irritation, true spasticity and extrapyramidal tract rigidity. This rigidity is most often generalized but may be confined to one extremity or involve the arm and leg on one side. It is stated that a mild Parkinsonian syndrome is not uncommon in the acute stage of the disease. This slowly disappears during convalescence. Trismus is seen in perhaps four per cent of all cases.

Involuntary movements are frequently seen during the acute stages of the disease. These are usually in the form of rhythmical clonic contractions of the jaws, face, tongue, abdomen and extremities. They may appear during the febrile period or during convalescence. Finer fibrillary twitchings are also observed and rhythmical tremors of the extremities, eyelids and tongue sometimes occur. Choreic and athetoid movements are very rare.

Mild and transient paralyses are very frequent during the acute stages of the illness. Hemiplegia is most common but monoplegia and bilateral hemiplegia also occur. These are, as a rule, associated with spasticity, increased tendon reflexes and Babinski phenomenon. Bulbar palsies are relatively common and paralysis of respiration has been seen in several cases. In some cases palsies with atrophy of the muscles and loss of tendon reflexes have been observed. Retention of urine or incontinence is not unusual but is rarely persistent. The tendon reflexes are altered in various ways. As a rule, they are increased during the early stages of the illness and diminished during convalescence. In only rare instances are they grossly exaggerated. The abdominal reflexes are usually lost.

The pupils are often unequal and may be dilated or contracted. They usually react to light, however. Diplopia may occur during the onset but is rare later, and ptosis of the lids, squints and ocular palsies are very unusual. There is frequently some hyperemia of the optic nerve heads, but papilledema, optic neuritis and optic atrophy are not described.

Disturbances of the autonomic system such as seborrhea, excessive salivation, sweating and disturbances of water metabolism are very unusual in encephalitis B in contrast to their frequency in encephalitis A.

The course of the disease is a relatively brief one. It may be divided into the following stages: (1) Prodromal period which lasts two or three days, as a rule. (2) The period of stupor and delirium of five days to two weeks. (3) Convalescence of relatively brief duration. The acute stage of the disease is less than three weeks as a rule.

Encephalitis B may be subdivided into the following types: (1) Fulminating cases. (2) The common acute cases. (3) Abortive cases. (4) Prolonged cases. (5) Cases characterized by remissions and exacerbations. The fulminating cases may terminate within 24 hours or even less. The onset is usually very abrupt and is often marked by chills. The patient sinks into coma and dies within a few hours. The common acute type does not require further description. In a few instances, despite a relatively sudden and severe onset, recovery may ensue within two or three days. By analogy with poliomyelitis we would expect that in some instances the process would not go beyond the prodromal stage. It has apparently been impossible to recognize instances of this kind in Japan but they are described by students of the epidemic in St. Louis. Kaneko and Aoki have observed cases in which the fever and stupor lasted several months and eventually terminated in death. They also mention several cases in which after a period of freedom from symptoms, both the fever and stupor returned.

Residua.—It has often been stated that serious residua are rarely found in the Japanese encephalitis. According to Lewis *et al.* this is untrue. They estimate that about one fifth of their patients will have permanent damage to the nervous system. They mention hemiplegia, hemiparesis, aphasia, cerebellar ataxia, tremor, mental deterioration, and even idiocy.

It seems to be the opinion of the majority of the Japanese observers that encephalitis B is not followed by the development of new symptoms after the acute stage is over and that the Parkinsonian syndrome rarely, if ever, results. This statement must be made with some hesitation, for the existence of both types of encephalitis in Japan introduces a possible source of error.

In 1938 Bredeck *et al.* published the results of a restudy of the victims of the 1933 epidemic in St. Louis. They found that 66 per cent of the patients were quite well. Only about 5 per cent showed any objective signs of injury to the nervous system. These signs included disorders of speech, reduction of vision, deafness and in a few instances disturbances in gait. Mild psychic disturbances were common residua, however. Loss of memory, irritability and drowsiness were most frequent. No progressive sequelae were found.

Laboratory Findings.—The white blood cells are always increased and range between 10,000 and 35,000 with an average of 15,000. The increase is chiefly in the polymorphonuclear leucocytes, for the lymphocytes may be relatively or even absolutely decreased. In some cases, the red count is increased to between 5,500,000 to 6,500,000 during the earlier stages of the disease but soon diminishes to normal or slightly below normal levels.

The spinal fluid is under increased pressure ranging as a rule between 150 and 250 mm of water. There are usually between 30 and 250 mononuclear cells per cubic millimeter. In about 80 per cent of cases the spinal fluid is clear; in around 17 per cent, opalescent and in a very few cases it is cloudy. The appearance of the fluid is not explained by the cell count, for cloudy fluids may show low counts. The protein is increased between

0.02 and 0.7 per cent and the globulin reaction is always positive. No constant changes in the sugar content are reported.

Diagnosis.—The clinical picture in these two diseases is apparently identical. In fact, it is not always possible to distinguish them from other types of encephalitis and from various kinds of lymphocytic meningitis on clinical grounds. The diagnosis depends upon the demonstration of a rising titer of antibodies against one or the other of these viruses during convalescence or the demonstration of the virus.

Prognosis.—In Japan the mortality has always been relatively high. The average death rate ranges between 33 and 60 per cent but in certain instances has exceeded 70 per cent. In St. Louis the mortality was about 20 per cent. Apparently residua are uncommon in the St. Louis encephalitis but in children at least they are common and sometimes severe in the Japanese encephalitis. At present there is no evidence that chronic progressive process, such as was seen following von Economo's disease, exists in either the St. Louis or Japanese types.

Prophylaxis and Treatment.—No specific therapy is yet available. Mosquito control is most important in prevention of the disease. A vaccine has been produced which is said to give protection.

BIBLIOGRAPHY

ARING, C. D.: Prognosis in Japanese B encephalitis. Arch. Neurol. & Psychiat., **62**:758, 1949.

BREDECK, J. F. *et al.*: Follow up of the 1933 St. Louis epidemic of encephalitis. J.A.M.A., **111**:15, 1938.

CASALS, J. AND CLARKE, D. H.: The Arborviruses. Viral and Rickettsial Infections of Man. Edited by Horsfall, F. L. and Tamm, I. J. B. Lippincott Co., 4th Ed., 1965, p. 583.

HAYMAKER, W. AND SABIN, A. B.: Topographic distribution of lesions in central nervous system in Japanese B encephalitis. Arch. Neurol. & Psychiat., **57**:673, 1947.

HEMPELMAN, T. C.: The symptoms and diagnosis of encephalitis (1933 St. Louis Epidemic). J.A.M.A., **103**:733, 1934.

KANEKO, R. U. AOKI, Y.: Ueber die Encephalitis Epidemica in Japan. Ergbn. d. inn. Med. u. Kinderh., **34**:342, 1928.

KOKERNOT, R. H. *et al.*: The 1952 outbreak of encephalitis in California. California Med., **79**:73, 1953.

LEAKE, J. P., MUSSON, E. K. AND CHOPE, H. D.: Epidemiology of epidemic encephalitis, St. Louis type, J.A.M.A., **103**:728, 1934.

LEWIS, L. *et al.*: Japanese B encephalitis: Clinical observations in an outbreak on Okinawa Shima. Arch. Neurol. & Psychiat., **57**:430, 1947.

McCORDOCK, H. A. AND GRAY, S. H.: Pathologic changes of the St. Louis type of epidemic encephalitis, J.A.M.A., **103**:822, 1934.

RICHTER, R. W. AND SHIMOJYO, S.: Neurologic sequelae of Japanese B encephalitis. Neurology, **11**:553, 1961.

WEBSTER, L. T. AND FITE, G. L.: Virus encountered in the study of material from the cases of encephalitis in St. Louis and Kansas City epidemic of 1933. Science, **78**:463, 1933.

WEIL, A.: Histopathology of the central nervous system in epidemic encephalitis (St. Louis epidemic). Arch. Neurol. & Psychiat., **32**:458, 1934.

Zentay, D. J. and Basman, J.: Epidemic encephalitis type B in children. J. Pediat., **14**:323, 1939.

ENCEPHALOMYELITIS DUE TO THE VIRUS OF EQUINE ENCEPHALITIS

Etiology.—The epidemic encephalomyelitis of horses has been shown to be a virus infection. Two varieties are known, the eastern and the western. Man is susceptible to both. These are termed Arbor viruses or arthropod borne viruses.

Epidemiology.—Both the equine and the human cases occur chiefly in the summer months and human cases usually appear within a district in which the equine disease is prevalent. The virus of western equine encephalomyelitis is found in birds as well as horses. It is believed at present that the virus is conveyed from bird to bird by mites and from birds to mammals by mosquitoes. The disease among horses is known to have appeared from time to time for at least seventy years, but it was only in 1938 that it was established that man is susceptible. During that year a small number of cases of acute encephalitis in Massachusetts and Rhode Island were shown to be due to the infection with the eastern virus. In some seventy per cent of all cases the victim was under ten years of age. Several smaller epidemics have appeared in various parts of the country since then. In 1955 four additional cases were recognized in Massachusetts.

In 1938 several epidemics appeared in the western states which were traced to the western virus. In the west adults were predominantly affected. In 1941 a large epidemic of nearly three thousand cases developed in North Dakota, Minnesota, South Dakota, Montana, Nebraska and Manitoba. Among 509 cases in Manitoba there were 27 cases in children under one year of age. It is claimed that this disease is prevalent in South America and in Russia. An epidemic of this disease occurred in New Jersey, in the Fall of 1959. Thirty-two persons died. By the study of immune bodies in the serum, it was discovered that many mild cases occurred in which the diagnosis could not have been suspected.

Pathological Anatomy.—The brain is frequently congested and petechial hemorrhages may be seen in the cortex. Histological examination reveals intense perivascular and parenchymatous infiltrations with lymphocytes and even leucocytes. There is also a striking proliferation of the astrocytes. Perivascular demyelination and even necrosis are found in both the white and gray matter. It seems to be agreed that the process is more destructive than other types of virus encephalitis. All parts of the brain and cord may be affected but the basal ganglia and the midbrain are most severely involved. This description applies to the eastern type. The lesions in the western type are less destructive.

Herzon *et al.* describe the anatomical changes in the brain of a child who died several years after an attack of western equine encephalomyelitis. They mention atrophy of the brain most evident in the white matter and some wasting of the cerebral cortex in the depths of the sulci. There were glial scars with basophilic deposits. These were most numerous in the subcortical white matter and in the thalamus. In the neighborhood of these scars were microglial nodules and perivascular infiltrations. The last were regarded as indicating continuing activity of the virus.

Clinical Features.—In the Massachusetts epidemic, the nervous symptoms were often preceded by prodromata, such as fever and headache which soon receded and were followed within twenty-four to thirty-six hours by acute cerebral symptoms. These began abruptly with headache, vomiting, drowsiness, muscular twitchings and convulsions. The onset seems to have been especially fulminating in infants. Within a few hours, the child was apt to be stuporous. Muscular rigidity, retraction of the head, Kernig's sign and trismus were usually present. The tendon reflexes were often absent and the plantar responses extensor. The temperature rose to 104° or 106°F. Drowsiness deepened into stupor and then into coma. Death in fatal cases occurred between the second and tenth day. Focal signs were not conspicuous but facial palsy, nystagmus, ptosis of the eyelids and signs indicative of pyramidal tract damage were observed. In non-fatal cases, the acute stage of the disease seemed to be terminated by the twentieth day.

In the western type of the disease, the onset seems to have been somewhat less abrupt and the symptoms less severe. The temperature was often only moderately elevated and the child might be merely lethargic rather than stuporous. The course also seems to have been a bit briefer. Medovy states that the virus of the western type may pass through the placenta and infect the baby in utero.

In the eastern type there is leucocytosis of 18,000 to 60,000. The spinal fluid is said to contain between 200 and 2,000 cells per cmm which are chiefly neutrophils at first but later become predominantly lymphocytes. In the western type, the leucocytosis is only moderate and there are rarely over 200 cells in the spinal fluid.

Diagnosis.—The diagnosis cannot be made on purely clinical grounds. Equine encephalomyelitis should always be considered whenever acute encephalitis appears in a district in which an epidemic among horses is in progress. If the child survives specific antibodies appear in the blood serum within two weeks after the acute illness has ended. It should be pointed out, however, that antibodies may be found in the blood of individuals who are not known to have had encephalitis. If it can be shown that antibodies have appeared or increased during the illness, the test would seem to be conclusive. If the child dies, the virus may be recovered in the brain and identified by proper laboratory procedures.

Zeifert *et al.* found no consistent correlation between the electroencephalographic findings and the patient's clinical state during or after the acute illness.

Prognosis.—In the Massachusetts epidemic of 1938, the death rate among children seems to have been around 75 per cent. Of those who survived a large percentage showed evidences of serious brain damage. Mental deficiency, deafness, blindness, loss of speech, hemiplegia or bilateral spastic paralysis were all observed. Ventriculography performed some months after the illness revealed gross atrophy of the brain. Webster reports two cases in adults in which the diagnosis was made by serological studies in which complete recovery occurred.

In the Manitoba epidemic, the mortality among children was low and it has been estimated that not more than 10 per cent of all patients suffering from the western type die in the acute stages. Medovy who observed the Manitoba epidemic describes the same residua as were seen in Massachusetts.

Finlay reports that in infants who have survived either the Western equine encephalitis or the St. Louis encephalitis, the incidence of serious sequelae is not high. In children between the ages of 5 and 14 years, only seven per cent have neurological signs and nineteen per cent had emotional and mental disturbances.

Treatment.—No effective treatment is known. A potent vaccine has been devised for immunization.

BIBLIOGRAPHY

CASALS, J. AND CLARKE, D. H.: Western Equine Encephalitis Virus. Viral and Rickettsial Infections in Man. Edited by Horsfall, F. L. and Tamm, I. J. B. Lippincott Co., 4th Ed., 1965.

———— AND ————: Eastern Equine Encephalitis Virus. Viral and Rickettsial Infections in Man. Edited by Horsfall, F. L. and Tamm, I., J. B. Lippincott Co., 4th Ed., 1965.

DAVIS, W. A.: Birds and mosquitoes as hosts for virus of eastern equine encephalomyelitis. Am. J. Hyg. (Sec. C), 32:45, 1940.

FARBER, S., HILL, A., CONNERLEY, M. L. AND DINGLE, J. H.: Eastern equine encephalomyelitis. J.A.M.A., 114:1725, 1940.

FINLEY, K. H.: Western equine and St. Louis encephalitis. Preliminary report of clinical follow up. Neurology, 5:223, 1955.

FOTHERGILL, L. D., DINGLE, J. H., FARBER, S. AND CONNERLEY, M. L.: Human encephalitis caused by the virus of the eastern type of equine encephalomyelitis. New England J. Med., 219:411, 1938.

FULTON, J. S. AND BURTON, A. N.: After effects of western equine encephalomyelitis. Canad. M. A. J., 69:268, 1953.

GETTING, V. A.: Equine encephalomyelitis in Massachusetts. New England J. Med., 224:999, 1941.

HAMMON, W. McD.: The arthropod borne virus encephalitides. Am. J. Trop. Med., 28:515, 1948.

HERZON, H., SHELTON, J. T. AND BRUYN, H. B.: Sequelae of western equine and other arthropod-borne encephalitis. Neurology, 1958, vol. 7, p. 535.

LEAKE, J. P.: An epidemic of infectious encephalitis. Pub. Health Reps., 56:1902, 1941.

MEDOVY, H.: Western equine encephalomyelitis in infants. J. Pediat., 22:308, 1943.

————: Human equine encephalomyelitis in Saskatchewan. Am. J. Dis. Child., 79:942, 1950.

MULDER, D.: Western equine encephalitis. 1949 epidemic in Colorado. Dis. Nerv. Sys., 12:259, 1951.

NORAN, H. H. AND BAKER, A. B.: Western equine encephalitis. The pathogenesis of the lesions. J. Neuropath. & Exp. Neurol., 4:269, 1945.

WEBSTER, H. DEF.: Eastern equine encephalomyelitis in Massachusetts. Report of 2 cases diagnosed serologically with complete clinical recovery. New England J. Med., 255:267, 1956.

WEBSTER, L. T. AND WRIGHT, F. H.: Recovery of the virus of eastern equine encephalomyelitis from brain tissues of human cases of encephalitis. Science, 88:305, 1938.

WEIL, A. AND BRESLICH, P. J.: Histopathology of the central nervous system in the North Dakota epidemic encephalitis. J. Neuropathol. & Exper. Neurol., 1:49, 1942.

WINTER, W. D. JR.: Eastern equine encephalomyelitis in Massachusetts in 1955. New England J. Med., 255:262, 1956.

ZEIFERT, M. et al.: The electroencephalogram following Western and St. Louis encephalitis. Neurology, 12:311, 1962.

CALIFORNIA ENCEPHALITIS

In 1964 it was found that a type of virus encephalitis existed in California. It is now known that this disease is endemic in California, Minnesota, Iowa, Illinois, Indiana, Ohio, Michigan, North Carolina and Florida. It is transmitted by mosquitoes and maintained in squirrels and rabbits.

It occurs in children between the ages of 4 and 11 years. It causes meningitis and encephalitis with headache, fever, nausea, vomiting and abdominal pain. It lasts one to four days. Sequelae are rare and only one fatal case is reported. Inapparent infections are believed to be more common than clinically recognizable cases.

Chun *et al.* describe the follow up in 35 children who had this disease. The only severe sequel was persistent hemiparesis in one child. Two children had recurrent seizures and two had an intelligence quotient below average.

Mathews *et al.* performed complete psychological tests on children following this disease and found that they did not differ from normal children of the same age group.

BIBLIOGRAPHY

JOHNSON, K. P. et al.: California encephalitis. Neurology, 18:250, 1968.

CHUN, R. W. M. et al.: California arborvirus encephalitis in children. Neurology, 18: 369, 1908.

MATHEWS, C. G. et al.: Psychological sequelae in children following California arbor virus encephalitis. Neurology, 18:1023, 1968.

GRABOW, J. D. et al.: Electroencephalogram and clinical sequelae of California arbovirus encephalitis. Neurology, 19:394, 1969.

AUSTRALIAN X DISEASE

Etiology.—The clinical and anatomical characteristics of this disease indicate a very close relationship to encephalitis type B. It may be transmitted to the sheep, calf and horse by the injection of filtered emulsions of nervous tissue. All authorities agree that this is a virus encephalitis and Burnet and Perdrau state that the virus closely resembles that of louping ill.

Epidemiology.—Small epidemics of this disease developed during 1917 and 1918 in Australia especially in New South Wales, Queensland and Victoria. Since then a few cases of the same type have been observed from time to time. The disease always appears during the warm season between January and April. The age incidence is almost identical with that of Heine-Medin disease. Various domestic animals are said to have been visited by an epidemic of encephalitis at the same time.

Pathological Anatomy.—The lesions do not require detailed description for they are apparently almost identical with those of epidemic encephalitis type B. They are most severe in the cerebral cortex, basal ganglia, dentate nuclei of the cerebellum, dorsal regions of the pons and medulla and the gray matter of the spinal cord.

Clinical Features.—Fifty per cent of the patients are under five years of age but young adults are sometimes affected. Males suffer twice as frequently as females. The onset is relatively abrupt, although there are often mild prodromal symptoms such as headache, weakness and pains in various parts of the body. Within a few hours, fever, vomiting and delirium occur. Later the child lapses into deep stupor or coma. There is usually general rigidity of the muscles and signs of meningeal irritation are prominent. Con-

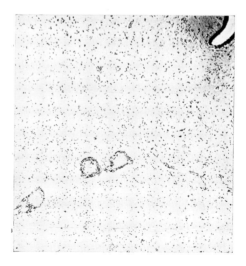

FIG. 143. Australian X disease. Section through the brain stem showing perivascular infiltrations similar to those of epidemic encephalitis.

vulsions are among the common symptoms. Oculomotor palsies and, indeed, all cranial nerve palsies are rare, although dysphagia and bulbar disturbances are sometimes seen. Paralysis of the extremities is very unusual and, if present, is merely transient, as a rule. The fever ranges between 101°F. and 105°F. In fulminating cases, death often results within twenty-four hours. The average duration of the acute symptoms in cases of a favorable nature is between one and two weeks. Death is due in most instances to hyperpyrexia or to involvement of the bulb.

The spinal fluid shows a mononuclear pleocytosis of moderate degree and a slight increase of protein.

Diagnosis.—The clinical picture seems to be indistinguishable from that of epidemic encephalitis type B. Apparently there are no serological tests available for diagnosis.

Prognosis.—The mortality is very high, averaging about 70 per cent. Those who survive, however, almost always make complete recoveries. In a few cases persisting weakness with atrophy of the muscles and loss of reflexes are seen and one or two mild hemiplegias have been observed. Mental defect following this disease has been reported in a few cases.

Treatment.—No effective treatment has yet been devised.

BIBLIOGRAPHY

BREINL, A.: Clinical, pathological and experimental observations of the mysterious disease. A clinically aberrant form of acute poliomyelitis. M. J. Australia, 5:209, 1918.

BURNET, F. M.: Louping ill virus as a possible cause of the X disease epidemics of 1917-1918. M. J. Australia, i:679, 1934.

CLELAND, J. B. AND CAMPBELL, A. W.: Acute encephalomyelitis; a clinical and experimental investigation of an Australian epidemic. Brit. M. J., 1:663, 1919.

KNEEBONE, J. LeM. AND CLELAND, J. B.: Acute encephalitis (X disease) at Broken Hill, probable successful transmission to sheep. Australian J. Exp. Biol. & Med. Sc., 3:119, 1926.

PERDRAU, J. R.: The Australian epidemic of encephalomyelitis (X disease). J. Path. & Bact., 42:59, 1936.

ACUTE ANTERIOR POLIOMYELITIS

Terminology.—This condition is commonly designated as infantile paralysis but since innumerable types of paralysis are seen in infancy, it seems preferable to employ the title given above. It is also called Heine-Medin disease.

Etiology.—It is scarcely profitable to discuss the many investigations which have been made to determine the cause of this disease. The infection may be transmitted to monkeys in series by intracerebral injection of filtrates of emulsions of the diseased spinal cord and, therefore, belongs in the group of diseases due to the filterable viruses. Recent studies have revealed that there are at least three viruses which are immunologically distinct, the Brunhilde, the Lansing and the Leon. Immunity to one does not confer immunity to another. They are very small viruses measuring between 8 and 17 mμ when visualized by the electronic microscope. The Brun-hilde strain is responsible for a large percentage of all cases of poliomyeli-tis. They are classified as enteroviruses with the Echo and Coxsackie viruses. The complex relationships of these viruses and similar viruses are discussed by Jungeblut. In October 1955, Dr. C. E. Schwerdt and Dr. F. L. Schaffer announced that they had succeeded in crystallizing the virus of poliomyeli-tis without destroying its potency.

Pathological Anatomy.—Post-mortem examination of patients who have died in the acute stages of the disease reveal more or less congestion and in-flammation of the meninges and on section a few minute hemorrhages may be found in the gray matter of the spinal cord. The gross changes, how-ever, are inconspicuous. Microscopic study shows that the most striking le-sions are confined to the gray matter, particularly the anterior horns of the spinal cord and the motor nuclei of the cranial nerves. Usually the cervical and lumbo-sacral enlargements are most severely affected. The process is ir-regularly distributed and usually asymmetrical. In affected segments of the cord, the anterior horn motor cells always show some degree of degenera-tion. In severe lesions, all the cells may be necrotic or absent, depending up-on the duration of the disease. Many cells show acidophilic inclusion bodies. Other cells are less severely injured and some show merely mild chromatolysis which may well be reversible. Corresponding to the lesions there is found more or less degeneration of the motor nerve fibers in the spinal nerve roots and peripheral nerve trunks. The motor nuclei of the brain-stem are affected exactly in the same way as the spinal gray matter.

As a rule, there is little actual destruction of neurons except in the seg-mental motor apparatus, but in some instances there is definite loss of gan-

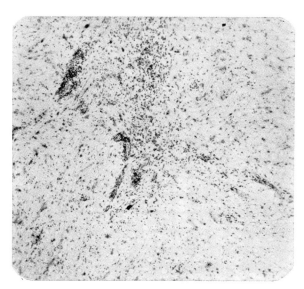

Fig. 144. Acute anterior polio-myelitis. Section through the spinal cord during the acute stage of the disease showing in-tense reaction in the anterior gray matter. (By the courtesy of Dr. Paul Levin.)

glion cells in the substantia nigra, and to a lesser extent in the basal ganglia, the hypothalamic region and in the cerebellar nuclei as well as various nuclear structures in the brain-stem. The cerebral cortex is never grossly damaged but Bodian has pointed out that there is a tendency for the motor area to be selectively involved to some extent. The cerebellar cortex likewise escapes severe damage. There is not infrequently some loss of cells in the posterior horns of the spinal gray matter and in Clarke's column but never to such a degree as in the anterior horn.

Inflammatory lesions, on the other hand, are widespread throughout the nervous system. The meninges at the base of the brain, around the brain-stem and the spinal cord are infiltrated with lymphocytes especially in the regions about small vessels. In the anterior spinal gray matter, the adventitia of all the vessels is distended by cuffs of lymphocytes, leucocytes and phagocytes of various types. Diffuse infiltration of the parenchyma by the same cells is also present. There are numerous microglial cells, many of which have taken up lipoid products or are phagocytizing necrotic neurons. The astrocytes frequently shows loss of processes, swelling and finally necrosis. The small blood vessels are distended and erythrocytes may be found in the tissues surrounding them. Frequently the endothelium is swollen and perhaps proliferated. Local edema is usually described. In the regions where the process is most intense, the tissue may be actually broken down with the formation of small softenings and areas of cystic degeneration. Similar but less intense evidences of inflammation are found in the posterior gray matter of the cord, in the white matter, the brain-stem and, indeed, in almost all parts of the central nervous system. The ganglia of the posterior spinal roots are often infiltrated with lymphocytes. Feigin finds areas of inflammation in the white matter in acute cases and in more chronic cases areas in which there is loss of myelin and axons.

Steegman and Davis describe widespread lesions in the nervous system which they attribute to anoxia.

After the acute stages have passed, the anatomical changes are not less characteristic. Fairly sharply defined lesions are found in the anterior horns of the spinal gray matter which are much shrunken. There is loss of the motor cells and extensive scar formation composed both of glial fibers and connective tissue. Small cysts may be present. The anterior spinal roots are atrophic and corresponding secondary degeneration is found in the muscles. As a rule, no lesions of any consequence are found outside of the segmental motor apparatus, but the pyramidal tract may seem somewhat shrunken when there are extensive lesions in the gray matter on the same side. Warburg has found small foci of perivascular lymphocytic infiltration, presumably indicating an active inflammatory reaction up to 309 days after the onset.

In addition to the lesions in the nervous system, there is a generalized hyperplasia of the lymphatic system throughout the body and the changes in the abdominal viscera which are seen in all acute infections. The reaction of the lymphatic tissues of the upper respiratory and intestinal tracts have received most attention since these structures are regarded by some authorities as the probable portals of entry of the virus. Lesions are described in the heart muscle.

The virus is found with great constancy in the spinal cord and sometimes in the cerebral hemispheres. It has also been recovered from the intestines, feces and abdominal lymph nodes and from washings of the nasopharynx. Recently it has been demonstrated in the blood stream before it enters the nervous system. It is of interest that the virus may be recovered from the nasal secretions or intestinal tract of healthy persons who have been in contact with the disease and of those patients who have had only minor illnesses or abortive forms of the disease without paralysis.

The infection is believed to gain access to the body through the nasopharynx or the gastro-intestinal tract. Monkeys may be infected successfully by either route.

Epidemiology.—Poliomyelitis occurs in epidemic, sporadic and endemic forms. It is very widely distributed and apparently exists to some degree in every part of the world. No race is immune. In the United States, it is most prevalent in certain regions such as Vermont, New York, New Jersey, Nevada and Minnesota. In these States the annual mean rate varies between 10 and 14 per 100,000. In Colorado and Utah, however, the mean rate per 100,000 is only 1.5. From time to time extensive epidemics have occurred which have been confined, as a rule, to temperate climates. North Europe, Northern United States, Canada, New Zealand, Australia and South Africa have suffered from largest epidemics. Thousands of cases occur in such epidemics but the incidence among the general population is low, rarely reaching 1 per cent. In the United States, with a population of about 160 millions, there were 35,953 cases in 1953 and 38,734 cases in 1954. There is a very distinct seasonal variation in poliomyelitis. More than three-fourths of the sporadic cases occur during the summer between June and October and all the epidemics have prevailed during the warm months. The incidence of poliomyelitis in sparsely populated rural districts is usually greater than that in large cities. This statement applies chiefly to epidemic poliomyelitis but a similar tendency in endemic forms has been noted.

The disease is obviously contagious but the precise method of its dissemination is not entirely clear. In the past, it has been generally believed that it is transmitted by droplet infection not only by persons who are actually ill but by patients in the prodromal stages and by healthy carriers. The infection was thought to gain entrance to the body through the nasopharynx.

More recently, evidence has been accumulated which indicates that the gastro-intestinal tract is a more important portal of entry. The virus has been found frequently in feces and in sewage. Several small epidemics have seemed to be milk-borne though this still is considered exceptional. Contaminated food is now under suspicion. Stillerman and Fischer have found evidence that recent tonsillectomy seems to render children more susceptible to poliomyelitis and especially to bulbar poliomyelitis. Recently evidence has been discovered which indicates that children given protective inoculations against pertussis and diphtheria show an increased incidence of poliomyelitis in the next four weeks. In many instances the paralysis occurred in the extremity in which the inoculation was given. No evidence that the virus exists in any animal but man has ever been discovered.

Children between the ages of two and four years are most susceptible to poliomyelitis and the disease is unusual in early infancy and in adult life although no age confers absolute immunity. It has been shown that the blood serum of convalescents and of a large percentage of adults, who have never suffered from poliomyelitis in a recognizable form, contains antibodies capable of protecting monkeys from a fatal dose of the virus. The theory has been advanced that immunity may be due to abortive forms of the disease which are so mild as to escape detection, and it has been estimated that such subclinical infections are one hundred times as common as the overt infections. When the mother has poliomyelitis near term the infant may develop the disease. At least four instances are on record in which an abortion occurred following an attack of poliomyelitis and the virus was recovered from the fetus.

The incubation period is believed to vary between seven and fourteen days. This estimate is based chiefly upon cases in which exposure to infection is known to have occurred for a limited period. The interval between the first and second cases in the same family is usually shorter, being often from one to six days.

Clinical Features

Acute Stage.—There seems to be at least three well-recognized types of *onset*. In the majority of cases there are *prodromal symptoms* such as fever, headache, vomiting, diarrhea or constipation and sometimes catarrhal inflammation of the upper respiratory passages. These are usually mild but may be alarming. In some epidemics, gastro-intestinal symptoms are most prominent; in others, inflammation of the upper respiratory tract. There is nothing specific or characteristic about the prodromal stage. The temperature rises slowly, usually reaching its peak in the afternoon and showing a tendency to drop in the morning. After from one to three days, symptoms referable to the central nervous system then appear. In a smaller percentage of cases, a remission of one or two days follows the initial symptoms. The child is afebrile and seems to be recovering when the temperature rises again and paralysis supervenes. The temperature chart in such cases shows two distinct periods of fever and the picturesque but inaccurate term of "dromedary" fever has been employed in reference to the two "humps." The third type of onset is characterized by the absence of prodromal symptoms and by the abrupt appearance of paralysis. This group is relatively rare but its existence seems to be established although it has been questioned by some observers.

The *invasion of the central nervous system* is marked by headache, pain in the back and along the course of the nerve trunks, tenderness of the muscles and nerves, Kernig's sign and rigidity of the entire spinal column. The temperature has usually reached 100°F. or 103°F. but may be higher. There is usually drowsiness and apathy but in some cases, irritability is observed or irritability alternating with drowsiness. Sometimes the drowsiness deepens into stupor or in fatal cases into coma. Delirium is rare. Convulsions may occur especially in infants but have not been frequent in recent epidemics. Within a short time, signs and symptoms indicative of involvement of the segmental motor apparatus develop. These are first irritative and later destructive. First we find in some cases twitchings of the muscles and perhaps transient increase of tendon reflexes. Local pain and tenderness may develop in the same segments, probably due to irritation of the posterior gray matter or posterior root ganglia. Later, the reflexes are diminished or lost and weakness and then paralysis develop. The paralysis usually appears on the first, second or third day of the illness but it may, as we have stated above, appear at the onset or in certain instances be delayed until the seventh or eighth day. Frequently, it reaches its maximum within a few hours but less commonly it advances for several days. In some cases, the paralysis begins in the legs and ascends slowly. In rare instances after remaining stationary for several days or weeks, the paralysis will begin to extend once more. In the early stages of the disease, one may discover mild signs suggestive of pyramidal tract damage, such as ankle clonus or even Babinski's phenomenon. Ataxia of one arm or leg may be present for a time. Mild sensory disturbances are sometimes found if one looks for them carefully. In some cases localized or generalized sweating has been a prominent feature but this is not constant enough to be of diagnostic importance. The fever lasts, as a rule, between four and five days and falls by lysis rather than by crisis. In some cases, a slight elevation of temperature persists for several weeks. The temperature may have reached normal before the development of the paralysis is complete or even before the paralysis appears. The prostration and drowsiness may continue or may even increase for several days after the fever has ceased. The acute stages of the disease, therefore, do not coincide with the febrile period. Peabody, Draper and Dochez define the acute stage as the period elapsing between the onset of paralysis and the disappearance of spinal rigidity. If we adopt this definition, the duration of the acute stage is found to vary from one to four weeks.

Since so much has been written, recently, about the prevalence and significance of muscle spasm in this disease and so many erroneous conclusions have been drawn it is well to point out that Pollock *et al.* have been unable to find any muscle spasm apart from that due to meningeal irritation in a careful study of 30 cases.

Special Types.—A number of different types of the disease are described, but every author employs a different classification and there is so much overlapping of the various types that no outline is quite staisfactory. The writer prefers the following classification which refers, of course, only to the acute stages of the disease:

1. Carrier state without symptoms.

2. Abortive type.—In this group we find merely constitutional symptoms as seen in the prodromal stages of the typical cases but no definite symptoms of invasion of the central nervous system develop.

3. Non-paralytic or meningeal type.—Here we find the constitutional symptoms of the first group with additional signs of central nervous system invasion without, however, an appreciable degree of paralysis. There is fever and drowsiness and signs of meningeal irritation are often conspicuous. There is an increase of cells in the spinal fluid.

4. Spinal type.—This group embraces the classical forms of the disease.

5. Brain-stem type.—We include in this group all cases in which the symptoms point to involvement of the medulla, pons or mid-brain. These may occur alone or may be combined with spinal symptoms.

6. Cerebral type.—This term has been employed to refer to: (1) Cases of Heine-Medin disease associated with profound stupor, both with and without spinal palsies. (2) Cases of hemiplegia of acute febrile onset without spinal palsies, i.e. Strümpell's polioencephalitis.

7. Ataxia or cerebellar type.—Cases characterized by ataxia with and without spinal palsies.

Several other syndromes have been ascribed to the virus of poliomyelitis such as polyneuritis and transverse myelitis. The writer rejects these and, in addition, the so-called cerebellar types and acute hemiplegias.

We shall pass now to a more detailed description of the types mentioned above.

The *carrier state*. It has been estimated that 75 per cent of the individuals who nurse children suffering from acute poliomyelitis are carriers and carry the virus in their intestinal tract.

The *abortive cases* present merely the symptoms already described as prodromata. Paul has pointed out that they seem to correspond in character and in time of occurrence to the first "hump" of the "dromedary" type. The frequency of abortive cases has been variously estimated. Some authorities believe that they are more frequent than the paralytic cases but all estimates are of necessity inaccurate, for the diagnosis has been established with certainty in very few instances. Such cases, however, are of great theoretical importance, for they confer immunity upon the patient and probably are the means of transmitting the infection to others. This diagnosis can be established only by the demonstration of the virus or by serological proof that the patient's immunity has increased during the illness. It may be suspected, however, when mild febrile illnesses develop in children who have been exposed to infection during epidemics.

The *non-paralytic or meningeal cases* are sometimes included among the abortive cases but the present writer prefers to distinguish two groups. The constitutional symptoms may be just as severe as in the cases eventuating in paralysis. There may be severe pain, cervical rigidity and Kernig's sign and the usual changes in the spinal fluid, drowsiness, apathy and even semi-stupor are not uncommon. Some writers include in this group cases in which there are alterations of the tendon reflexes and even some degree of muscular weakness. It is evident, therefore, that the non-paralytic cases differ from the paralytic cases chiefly in degree. The incidence of these cases is relatively high in certain epidemics and apparently low in others, so that no reasonably accurate estimate can be given. The diagnosis is a bit easier than that of the abortive cases for we have signs of meningeal irritation at least to indicate that the nervous system is involved, but it can be established only by the laboratory procedures mentioned above in connection with the abortive cases. Unquestionably the so-called benign lymphocytic meningitis and various types of virus encephalitis have been frequently confused with non-paralytic poliomyelitis.

I have already described the general symptoms of the *common spinal type* of poliomyelitis and I shall, therefore, confine the discussion to the paralyses at this point. The distribution is irregular and almost always distinctly asymmetrical. In the vast majority of cases the arms or the legs are affected. This might be expected since it was stated above that the lesions are most constant in the cervical and lumbosacral enlargements of the cord. The palsies are, of course, of all grades of severity varying from transient weakness which is difficult to demonstrate and which soon recedes, to complete and permanent paralysis. The muscles are usually affected in groups corresponding approximately to the myotomes or muscles supplied by certain segments of the cord. As a rule, if one muscle is paralyzed, the other muscles which derive their innervation from the same segments are at least involved to some extent. In some cases the weakness is found only in a single group of muscles but in others several muscle groups may be affected which may receive their nerve supply from widely separated portions of the cord. Except for certain unusual cases which will be discussed below, the paralysis is always of the type associated with lesions of the lower motor neuron. It is associated with diminished consistency of the muscles, loss of tone on passive movement, diminution or abolition of tendon reflexes and finally atrophy. In the more severe palsies, the response to faradism is lost within two weeks and the reaction to galvanism becomes sluggish at the same time. Such palsies differ from those due to lesions of the peripheral nerves only in their distribution. The accompanying table gives the relative frequency of paralysis in various parts of the body.

There is a fairly definite tendency for the paralysis to involve certain muscles and to spare others, although the difference is merely one of degree. In the leg, it is found that the quadriceps femoris is perhaps most frequently affected and that the peroneals, the flexors of the foot and the extensors of the toes are also commonly involved. The muscles which act on the hip joint, such as the iliopsoas and the gluteals, are often selected. In the upper extremity, there seems to be a striking tendency for the proximal muscle groups to suffer more than the distal groups. Thus the deltoid is frequently paralysed and often fails to recover. In many cases this is associated with paralysis of the spinati, the flexors of the elbow and the supinators of the forearm, all of which derive their innervation from C-5-6. The picture is, therefore, similar to that of Erb's brachial plexus palsy. The flexors of the fingers and wrist are less apt to be affected than the extensors. Not infrequently there is paralysis of all muscles about the shoulder joint and upper arm. The intrinsic muscles of the hand are usually spared.

In the vast majority of fatal cases, death results from paralysis of the muscles of respiration, which however, seem to enjoy a relative immunity in most epidemics. The diaphragm is perhaps most important and is usual-

TABLE II—DISTRIBUTION OF PARALYSIS
(According to Wernstedt)

	No. Cases	Percentage
Leg	4,519	78.6
Arm	2,372	41.3
Trunk	1,601	27.8
Throat and neck	333	5.8
Cranial Nerve	767	13.8
Total No. of Cases	5,784	100

ly affected in association with severe paralyses of the arms and shoulder girdle muscle, since the phrenic nucleus lies in the third, fourth and fifth cervical segments. In cases of diaphragmatic paralysis, breathing is purely thoracic and the epigastrium is retracted with each inspiration. Firm pressure on the sides of the chest causes distress and perhaps cyanosis. Frequently, the accessory muscles of respiration are brought into play. If the intercostal muscles are affected in addition to the diaphragm, respiratory failure results. The intercostals are innervated by the thoracic segments, which, fortunately, are not often injured severely. Intercostal paralysis is not recognized so easily as paralysis of the diaphragm for normal respiration in childhood is predominantly abdominal. However, it may be noted that the chest does not expand and, on the contrary, the lower ribs and perhaps the intercostal spaces are retracted during inspiration. Pressure on the abdomen causes distress. Any weakness of the respiratory muscles may cause coarse rales in the chest and predisposes to broncho-pneumonia.

Sublethal anoxia may cause convulsions, delirium, stupor or coma. Should the patient survive there may be mental disturbances and even blindness of cortical origin as in other types of anoxia. Such symptoms are usually transient but may be permanent.

The abdominal muscles may be involved but estimates of the frequency of abdominal paralysis are subject to great variation. Such palsies are best recognized by a localized bulging of the abdominal wall when coughing, crying or attempting to sit up. Localized paralysis of the muscles which act on the spinal column is not often discovered in the acute stages, for movements of the neck and back cause severe pain, but later such palsies are not infrequently discovered and often give rise to severe deformities.

The sphincters are seldom affected for more than a short time. In some cases there is retention of urine requiring catheterization for several days but this rarely persists. Paralysis of the rectal sphincter is even more rare.

In certain cases, the paralysis begins in a localized group of muscles, in most cases, in the legs, and then rapidly extends in such a way as to suggest that the process is progressing upward along the spinal cord from segment to segment. Less frequently the paralysis descends. In some cases the respiratory muscles are involved within a few hours, for there is no interruption in the extension of the paralysis. Dolgopol and Cragan state that they have found myocarditis in 16 out of 92 cases of poliomyelitis. They state that cardiac symptoms may develop between the second and the fifth day of the illness and death from heart failure may result. Arterial hypertension may occur and hypertensive encephalopathy is sometimes seen. In some cases the hypertension is believed to be due to renal damage resulting from the excessive calcium in the urine and nephrocalcinosis.

During the acute stages of poliomyelitis there may be local or even generalized sweating. The former may well be correlated with lesions of the sympathetic cells in the spinal gray matter. Various vasomotor disturbances are also common. The affected limbs are frequently cold and show a purplish-blue mottling and even mild edema. Since these symptoms are almost invariably present in paralysed limbs, their connection with organic lesions of the autonomic system is doubtful. In a few cases, definite signs of paralysis of the cervical sympathetic nerve have been recorded. There may be myosis and drooping of the eyelid and unilateral sweating of the face in such instances. Weiman *et al.* state that they have observed papilledema with increase of spinal fluid pressure in 5 children suffering from poliomyelitis. The papilledema appeared between 11 and 48 days after the onset of the illness. In 3 cases the child had been in the respirator and had hypertension. The papilledema disappeared in all cases without ill effect. In one patient, a ventriculogram and a dural sinus venogram were both performed with negative results. Gardner *et al.* suggest that in such cases the increase of spinal fluid protein causes obstruction of the arachnoidal villi and external hydrocephalus. Inadequate respiration may cause accumulation of carbon dioxide and papilledema as seen in some cases of emphysema.

The *brain-stem* type of Heine-Medin disease selects the motor nuclei of the cranial nerves just as the spinal form involves the cells in the anterior gray matter. In certain epidemics the bulbar types of the disease have been unusually frequent or have even outnumbered the spinal types. MacNalty mentions the Broadstairs epidemic in 1926 in which there were 32 bulbar cases, 17 spinal and 6 mild or abortive. Brown described a small epidemic in which 15 bulbar cases occurred and a few abortive types but not a single instance of the common spinal type. In most instances there are spinal symptoms as well as symptoms referable to the brain-stem, but in some cases the symptoms are purely bulbar. Only one cranial nerve may be affected or there may be multiple palsies. As a rule, the symptoms are unilateral and severe but persisting paralysis is unusual. The facial nerve is most frequently affected. In some cases the whole distribution of the nerve is involved; in others only one branch, such as that which supplies the lips, the eyelid or the forehead and in others the affected muscles are irregularly distributed in a patchy fashion, so that a very characteristic picture results. Sixth nerve palsy represents the commonest type of ocular palsy but there may be ptosis and squints due to partial or complete paralysis of the third nerve and fourth nerve palsies are described. Paralysis of conjugate deviation is very rare. Nystagmus is sometimes described, but is probably due to muscular weakness as a rule. Another nerve not infrequently affected is the tenth. We find paralysis or weakness of the soft palate, the pharynx, the vocal cords and irregularities of pulse and respiration not explained by other causes. The voice may be nasal or hoarse and swallowing may be difficult. Paralysis of the sterno-mastoid and trapezius is attributed to involvement of the spinal nucleus of the eleventh nerve in the highest cervical segments. The muscles supplied by the fifth nerve are sometimes paralysed but this nerve is usually spared as is the twelfth. The special senses and sensory branches of the cranial nerves are not involved. The relative incidence of various cranial nerve palsies is given in the accompanying table.

Baker *et al.* state that there are three syndromes due to bulbar poliomyelitis: (1) That due to involvement of the cranial nerve nuclei which is described above. (2) That due to involvement of the respiratory center. (3) That due to involvement of the vasomotor and cardioregulatory centers.

Involvement of the respiratory centers causes fluctuation of the rate and depth of respiration, periodic breathing and increasing periods of apnea with final respiratory failure. Baker finds that the lesions responsible involve the small cells in the lateral reticular substance of the medulla.

Involvement of the vasomotor centers, which are believed to be located in the medial reticular region and formed of large cells, causes rapid and irregular pulse with small pulse pressure and falling blood pressure. The mortality is high in bulbar poliomyelitis, and has been estimated at 50 per cent.

Bosma has made a careful study of the various types of difficulty in swallowing which may occur in poliomyelitis. He distinguishes (1) Deficiencies of movement of the tongue-hyoid-larynx column. (2) Weakness of the muscles supporting the tongue and hyoid with impaired delivery of food into the pharynx. (3) Abnormal patency of the palatopharyngeal isthmus. (4) Obstruction of the hypopharyngeal sphincter possibly due to lack of action of the cricopharyngeus. (5) Abnormal penetration of the larynx. (6) Weakness of the pharyngeal constrictor. (7) Compression of the pharynx by malposition of the head and neck.

Before discussing the *cerebral cases* it should be said that delirium and stupor may occur as in any severe infection presumably as a result of intoxication and that restlessness, excitability and confusion as well as coma may result from anoxia when respiration is impaired. Peabody *et al.* give a very striking description of one type which they place in the group of

TABLE III—DISTRIBUTION OF CRANIAL NERVE PALSIES
(According to Wernstedt)

Facial muscles	314
Muscles of deglutition	245
Eye muscles	231
Speech muscles	121
Tongue muscles	43
Muscles of mastication	22
Total cases	767

"cases with deep stupor." These particular cases are usually complicated by palsies of the cranial nerves and often by the common spinal paralyses. The most striking feature is drowsiness which is an early and dominant symptom. The child lies motionless with "a peculiar waxy, mask-like immobility" of the face. The eyes may be open in a sort of coma-vigil but the patient usually shows no evidence of consciousness. In other cases, the eyelids are partially or completely closed. They are easily aroused and then at once sink back into their former state. The mental condition, therefore, seems to be more properly termed somnolence than stupor. The degree of somnolence bears no constant relation to the height of the fever or the severity of the constitutional symptoms. The drowsiness lasts, as a rule, from three to six days and then may clear rapidly or slowly. In one instance the child is said to have awakened as if from sleep and looked about in a bewildered way as if quite unconscious that she had been ill. During convalescence, interesting psychic changes have been noted. Emotional instability is often prominent. The child may cry without apparent reason and later laugh when attention is diverted by some trivial occurrence. In other cases, irritability has persisted for a long time. This description, it is evident, might well apply to typical cases of epidemic encephalitis. That they are really instances of the last-named disease and not of epidemic encephalitis is shown by the association of typical spinal paralyses.

The connection of cases of hemiplegia and other types of spastic paralysis with poliomyelitis is very doubtful. The cases characterized by fever and sudden hemiplegia with normal spinal fluid which were first described by Strümpell and attributed by him and by subsequent writers to localization of the virus of Heine-Medin disease in the motor cortex, cannot be accepted without very careful scrutiny. Such syndromes are undoubtedly due to several causes. They will be discussed in another section. Suffice it to say at this point that it does not seem justifiable to accept this diagnosis at present unless it is supported by the coexistence of typical spinal paralysis, unless the virus is recovered from the nervous system, or unless lesions are found at post-mortem examination which admit of no other interpretation. So far as can be discovered, no such evidence has ever been advanced. The writer, however, is not prepared to deny the existence of such cases. The changes in the spinal fluid are scarcely characteristic enough to be reliable and the existence of serological immunity is not conclusive unless it can be shown that it was greatly increased during the illness. It is admitted that in poliomyelitis there may be widespread inflammatory lesions in the brain and even in the motor cortex but no cases are yet described in which there was actual destruction of the cortical neurons or of the internal capsule sufficient to produce outspoken hemiplegia. As a matter of fact only a few post-mortem examinations have been described in Strümpell's type of infantile hemiplegia and these have usually revealed vascular lesions.

The *ataxic or "cerebellar" type* has been denied a separate classification by most recent writers. I have already stated that in some cases the common spinal palsies are accompanied by mild and transient ataxia and that it is not unusual for ataxia of cerebellar type to be observed in the cases in which the brainstem is involved. The seat of the lesions responsible for the ataxia is not certain. It may be in the pontine nuclei or in the cerebellar connections in the brainstem, but since the cells of Clarke's column are known to be affected in many cases, it seems probable that in the spinal type of the disease, at least the essential lesions are there. Acute cerebellar ataxia without any typical manifestations of poliomyelitis is probably never a result of Heine-Medin disease.

Relapses.—It is customary to regard as relapses the recurrences of paralysis which have been observed in a few instances between one week and three months after the beginning of the illness. Eshner has reviewed a small series of cases of this type. The relapse is usually but not always accompanied by fever and meningeal irritation. Since it has been claimed that the virus may remain in the spinal cord for at least three and a half months after the acute illness, it is probable that the relapse represents merely renewed activity of the infection and should be distinguished from reinfections.

Second Attacks.—Still has made a careful study of some nine cases in which second attacks apparently occurred. He points out that the interval between the attacks is always two years or more. He concludes that, as a rule, immunity is absolute after three months and before two years, but that after the second year, the immunity diminishes and the liability to another infection begins. Since it is now known that three viruses cause poliomyelitis and immunity to one does not confer immunity to the others, one is inclined to imagine that a second attack of poliomyelitis is apt to be due to infection with a second virus.

Laboratory Tests.—There is a constant leucocytosis ranging from 15,000 to 30,000 beginning in the prodromal stage and persisting for six weeks or more. This is due chiefly to an increase in the leucocytes which are 10 to 15 per cent above normal. The lymphocytes may be relatively diminished. In a few cases, the total white count has been normal or low due to reduction of lymphocytes but even here the leucocytes are at least relatively increased.

The spinal fluid rarely fails to show some abnormality. Early in the course of the disease before paralysis develops and during the first week, the cell count ranges, as a rule, between 50 and 100 per cm. In a few cases 500 or even 1,000 cells have been counted. In rare instances even when the paralysis is very extensive, the cell count may be no more than 10 or 12. Before and during the onset of the paralysis, the fluid may show a small percentage of leucocytes, but usually lymphocytes predominate throughout the entire course of the disease and leucocytes are rare after the first few days. After the second week, the cell count is usually normal. The globulin content of the spinal fluid obeys just the opposite law. During the first week, it is normal or only very slightly increased but it slowly increases and the increase may persist for several weeks or even two months. The spinal fluid protein may exceed 100 mgs per cent several months after the acute stage of the illness. The sugar content is usually within normal limits as are the chlorides. In a few cases a delicate fibrin film is formed when the fluid is allowed to stand.

Convalescence.—If the child survives, the paralysis, as a rule, remains unchanged for several days or weeks after the fever and more acute symptoms have subsided. Spontaneous improvement then begins and usually continues for a number of months. It is usually taught that the major part of the improvement may be expected within six months or less but that appreciable return of power may be observed in the second six months or even in the second year. No spontaneous tendency towards recovery may be expected after this time. Within a few weeks after the development of the paralysis, the affected muscles begin to show definite atrophy which reaches various grades of severity, depending upon the permanency and extent of the spinal lesions. The electrical reaction of degeneration is often found in such muscles. In some cases, the muscle may show atrophy for a time and then fill out with the recovery of function until it reaches its former development. In others, the muscle disappears almost completely. The reaction of degeneration eventually disappears. All the denervated muscle fibers have been absorbed and those which remain respond normally.

Chronic Stage.—The lack of muscle balance resulting from the paralyses and the plasticity of the bones during childhood lead to the development of innumerable types of *deformity*. These are primarily problems for the orthopedic surgeon and do not require full presentation here. If, for example, one set of muscles is paralysed and the opposing group is preserved, the limb will be displaced in the direction of pull of the stronger muscle group. Subsequently, the muscles which are preserved will be shortened and eventually undergo contracture. The ligaments and capsule of the joint will develop fibrous changes, so that movement is mechanically limited. The paralysed muscles are consequently placed under tension which is believed to exert an injurious effect upon them, so that their recovery is retarded or prevented. In severely paralysed limbs, the bones fail to grow and even undergo marked rarefaction and atrophy. There is pronounced decalcification of the bones of the paralytic limbs and increased excretion of the calcium in the urine. In rare instances, calculi may form in the urinary tract when the patient is recumbent for long periods. Weight bearing, of course, adds a great deal to the development of deformities. Deformities of the ankles, knees and hips are, perhaps, most common because of the strain imposed upon these bones by the body weight but severe and progressive scoliosis may result from paralysis of the extensors of the spine, shortening of one leg or in many cases from paralysis of the abdominal muscles on one side. Paralysis of the intercostal muscles sometimes results in gross deformities of the chest, especially since the introduction of the Drinker respirator which has made it possible to save the lives of many children with extensive weakness of the muscles of respiration. Deformities of various types also occur in the hand, arm and shoulder but less frequently than in the legs.

The atrophic muscles often show coarse twitchings which may be mistaken for spontaneous fasciculations and so taken to indicate a progressive process. Careful examination, however, reveals that these twitchings are present only when the muscles are contracting. Denny-Brown who terms them *contraction fasciculations* has explained them as follows: In a normal muscle the various bundles of fibers contract in such a sequence that the action of individual units is obscured and the muscle seems to contract as a whole. In cases in which there has been considerable loss of motor cells, however, these contractions are not fused but are revealed as separate contractions of individual groups of fibers. In my experience, such contraction fasciculations are very common indeed in long standing cases, but I have not been able to demonstrate them in cases of a few months' duration.

Delayed Loss of Power.—It has been pointed out by numerous authors that muscular power may actually diminish after the child has made a partial recovery and that muscles which have regained some of their strength may become completely paralysed. The development of such delayed increase in symptoms is attributed to excessive fatigue and strain imposed upon weak muscles, to over-stretching and to the development of deformities which places the affected muscles at a mechanical disadvantage. Such symptoms always develop after the child begins to walk. As a rule, injudicious exercises or neglect are chiefly to blame and proper treatment will minimize such symptoms.

Sequelae.—It is claimed that in rare instances, progressive muscular atrophy or amyotrophic lateral sclerosis may occur many years after an attack of acute anterior poliomyelitis. I have seen several cases in which this diagnosis has been made but, as a rule, whenever it has been possible to follow the patient for long periods, it has been discovered that the atrophy is not a progressive one and that the twitchings which have been taken for spontaneous fasciculations are in reality contraction fasciculations. I have seen just one case in which there seemed to be no doubt that progressive atrophy and weakness with spontaneous fasciculations developed in muscles which had been slightly damaged by poliomyelitis a number of years before. This patient ran a rapidly progressive course.

More frequently slight increase of the wasting and weakness of certain muscles occurs after one or two years which can scarcely be attributed to fatigue or mechanical factors. This may well be due to contraction of the fibrous scars formed in old lesions. It is always confined to affected muscles and never progresses to any great extent. The writer has observed this in the muscles of the hand in several cases.

Diagnosis.—In typical cases in which the paralysis is present when the child comes under observation, the diagnosis offers little or no difficulty as a rule. The fever, signs of meningeal irritation, flaccid palsies and the changes in the spinal fluid produce a very characteristic picture. Pseudo-paralysis due to injury or inflammation should be recognized with ease, since the limb is fixed by muscle spasm and is not flaccid. Meningitis is not associated with the same type of paralysis and the spinal fluid changes are usually quite different. Polyneuritis may be distinguished by the distribution of the palsies and the absence of pleocytosis in the spinal fluid.

In cases characterized by a meningeal reaction but no paralysis the diagnosis cannot be established without the help of the laboratory for the same clinical picture may result from many types of infection such as choriomeningitis, virus encephalitis of several kinds and even leptospiral infections. The list of causes of acute lymphatic meningitis is a long one. Fortunately inexpensive methods of demonstrating the antibodies in human serum against poliomyelitis in quantitative fashion have been developed recently. Tissue cultures are inoculated with all three viruses and the serum to be tested is added. The results are determined colorimetrically. In 1954 Salk *et al.* published a description of a simplified method of this type. A rising titer of antibodies against poliomyelitis during convalescence may make a diagnosis possible. The virus may be cultivated from the nasopharynx for a time and may be isolated from the stools for several weeks after the illness.

Prognosis.—We must consider several problems in this connection: (1) The prognosis for life. (2) The probability of paralysis. (3) The probability of recovery from paralysis.

The mortality has apparently varied within wide limits in various epidemics and is, as a rule, higher at the beginning of an epidemic than at the end. Moreover, it is believed to be higher in epidemic cases than in sporadic cases. If many abortive and non-paralytic cases are included, the mortality will obviously be lower than if only the fully developed cases are recognized. The reported mortalities have varied between 5 and 50 per cent averaging, as a rule, between 10 and 15 per cent. In the first year of life the mortality is relatively high; between the first and the tenth year, it is somewhat lower and then there is a gradual increase with advancing age.

In individual cases, it is very difficult to give an accurate prognosis. Since death is almost always due to paralysis of the muscles of respiration or weakness of respiration resulting in bronchopneumonia, we must consider any indication of respiratory weakness of very serious import. Severe initial symptoms do not indicate necessarily that paralysis will develop and mild prodromata may be followed by fatal paralysis. It has been claimed that relatively high cell counts in the spinal fluid during the stage of onset are of unfavorable significance. Death usually occurs between the third and seventh day, and after the second week the prognosis is good unless there is some serious complication.

No reliable figures are available about the incidence of paralysis. Neal concludes that among children whose symptoms are typical enough to make diagnosis possible, paralysis usually occurs in only about 25 per cent. Most authorities have placed the incidence much higher. The variations depend both upon the severity of the epidemic and the number of abortive cases recognized.

After paralysis has developed, it is not easy to know how much improvement to expect. In almost all cases there is a definite tendency towards recovery after the first few weeks which persists for six months or a year. Naturally, the prognosis in cases of widespread and complete paralysis is worse than that for localized and incomplete paralysis. Mild palsies often disappear completely or nearly completely. Wickman claimed 44 per cent recoveries but, as a rule, complete recoveries vary between 5 and 20 per cent. The usual result, of course, is partial recovery. It must be kept in mind that some muscles which have shown encouraging improvement during convalescence may lose power later when the child begins to walk as a result of stretching and over-strain.

Prevention of the Disease.—Obviously, strict isolation should be enforced, for there can be no doubt that the disease is contagious. It is usual to preserve quarantine for at least four weeks after the onset of the disease. All the usual precautions should be observed including the use of a gauze mask.

Many years ago, convalescent serum and pooled adult serum were given by intramuscular injection in the hope of preventing the disease or of halting it after it had begun. Both of these hopes proved to be vain. It was soon found that such sera had no curative effect and the protective effect was of such brief duration that it was of no practical value.

Later, Park, Brodie, and Kolmer developed vaccines made from emulsions of the spinal cord of infected monkeys. These efforts were doomed to failure for our knowledge of the disease at that time was not sufficient to make the production of a proper vaccine possible. A number of children developed poliomyelitis after being given vaccine which contained virulent virus and the work was given up for some years.

After this, attempts were made to prevent infection by spraying the nose with astringent solutions. This idea was a result of the theory that the virus gains entrance to the nervous system by way of the olfactory tract. Before the astringents were widely used, it was learned that the gastrointestinal tract was the usual portal of entry.

In 1953, many children were given injections of immune globulin during epidemics in the hope that this would have a more prolonged and powerful protective effect than pooled adult serum. The results seemed to indicate that the children gained a partial immunity for several weeks.

In recent years, a comprehensive and systematic study was organized with the purpose of developing a suitable vaccine. Many investigators took part in this work including Armstrong, Enders, Weller, Robbins, Horstmann, Salk, Sabin, Howe, Bodian and Morgan, as well as many others. Problems were solved one by one, and finally it became possible to produce a vaccine which promised to have all the necessary properties. In 1954, a vaccine was produced by Salk and was given to nearly half a million children. This vaccine could be produced in large amounts at relatively small cost. It contained all of the three viruses. It was grown on tissue culture of monkey kidneys so as to avoid the possibility of the paralytic accidents which may occur when emulsions of nervous tissue are injected. It was treated with formaldehyde in such a way as to ensure the death of the virus but to preserve the antigenic properties of the material. It was known that this vaccine would cause the development of antibodies against the viruses of poliomyelitis, but its value against the natural disease was, of course, uncertain.

In April 1955, the results of this great experiment were announced. The new vaccine proved to be harmless. No child developed poliomyelitis as a result of the inoculation. There were no serious reactions of any type. It was estimated that the vaccine was between 80 and 90 per cent effective against paralytic poliomyelitis. No child who was inoculated died of the disease.

In 1955, many thousands of children were given the vaccine but the program had to be abandoned when it was found that some improperly prepared vaccine contained living virus. It is estimated that 13,850 cases of paralytic poliomyelitis occurred.

In 1956, the vaccine was administered on a large scale and only 7,911 cases of paralytic poliomyelitis were discovered.

In 1957, only 2,159 cases of paralytic poliomyelitis occurred. It was stated that among 28,000,000 persons who had received all three inoculations only 63 cases of paralytic poliomyelitis occurred and not all of these were fully confirmed.

In 1959, there were 6,289 cases of paralytic poliomyelitis in this country, and in 1960, only 2,525 cases. In 1961, there were only 988 cases and in 1962, there were only 650 cases.

In 1962, the Sabin oral vaccine of living but attenuated virus was used on a large scale. The vaccine of Type I and Type II viruses proved to be harmless but a few cases of poliomyelitis developed in adults who had been given the Type III vaccine.

In 1963, only 431 cases of poliomyelitis were discovered. There were only 303 cases of paralytic poliomyelitis. Both the Salk and the Sabin vaccines were employed.

In 1964, only 121 cases of poliomyelitis were recognized in the entire nation. Less than ten patients died and there were less than 100 paralytic cases.

There were only 61 cases of paralytic poliomyelitis in the United States during the year of 1965.

In 1966, there were 102 cases of paralytic poliomyelitis in this country. The increase was chiefly due to an epidemic of 66 cases among unvaccinated children in Texas.

Plotkin *et al.* state that the administration of oral poliomyelitis virus to breast-fed newborn infants is not effective. This is especially true as regards the Type 1 virus. Antibodies in the colostrum apparently prevent infection with the attenuated virus.

Treatment.—The child should, of course, be kept in bed and given careful nursing care as in other infections. On the advent of paralysis, the affected limbs should be immobilized in such positions as will relax the paralysed muscles and stretch their antagonists. The immobilization of the limbs prevents deformities and contractures, favors recovery of affected muscles by preventing over-stretching and reduces pain. The best methods to accomplish this are described in Kendall's paper. Hot wet packs applied to the affected muscles seem to have some effect in relieving pain.

The advent of respiratory paralysis or bulbar palsy demands the services of an expert physician who has had proper training and adequate experience in the handling of such problems. The hospital must have the facilities required and the nursing staff must be especially trained.

Failure of respiration due to weakness of the intercostal muscles and diaphragm requires artificial respiration. The tank respirator is usually employed. The air should be humidified and aerosoles may be sprayed into the patient's throat to keep the secretions fluid. Frequent aspiration and bronchoscopy may be necessary to keep the airways patent. Repeated tests of the alveolar air or blood must be made to make sure that there is no hypoxia and to detect acidosis and alkalosis. If the patient is unable to synchronize breathing with the rhythm of the respirator, sedation or a curare-like substance may be used. Pneumonia and bronchitis must be guarded against and treated promptly. Some authorities advise the use of penicillin prophylactically. Everyone who comes into contact with the patient must wear sterile gowns, rubber gloves and gauze masks.

The development of bulbar palsy presents a number of additional problems. Respiration may fail as a result of damage to the respiratory mechanisms of the brain stem. The air passages may be obstructed as a result of accumulation of secretions or aspiration of vomitus. Paralysis of the abductors of the vocal cords or laryngeal spasm, falling backward of the paralysed tongue and trismus may obstruct the inflow of air. Pulmonary edema may result from cardiac weakness or loss of serum albumin. Tachycardia and failing blood pressure may occur as a result of involvement of the vasomotor and cardioregulatory mechanisms in the brain stem.

In addition to the measures mentioned in the preceding paragraphs, the following therapeutic measures are advised. Feeding should be by nasal tube. The patient should be nursed in the prone position, to favor postural drainage of secretions. Tracheotomy is required. A cuffed tracheotomy tube with positive pressure respiration is advised. The patient must be rotated frequently. Failure of the vasomotor mechanism is combatted by the administration of oxygen and by intravenous drip of norepinephrine, or by intramuscular injection of caffein sodium benzoate or desoxycorticosterone. Pulmonary edema may require transfusion of blood plasma, or the use of drugs, to improve cardiac action. If vomiting occurs, intravenous saline may be necessary to prevent dehydration and alkylosis. If intravenous fluids are given, potassium deficiency must be kept in mind.

One must be on the alert for gastrointestinal hemorrhages which may require transfusions. Hypertensive encephalopathy with convulsions is described and barbiturates and magnesium sulfate are recommended. Digitalis is said to be useful in cases marked by persistent tachycardia and cardiac weakness. Ice packs are mentioned in connection with hyperpyrexia. Gastric distention may require the use of the stomach pump.

During convalescence, the care of an expert orthopedic surgeon is required. Only the principles of treatment require discussion here. Most authorities stress the importance of *prolonged rest*. Deformities must be prevented by proper splints and braces. The affected muscles must be protected from over-stretching and excessive fatigue. As soon as the pain and tenderness have disappeared and not before, exercises, massage and passive movements should be begun. As a rule, the child is ready for such treatment about 3 to 5 weeks after the onset. Contracture of the normal muscles, shortening of the ligaments and fibrous changes in the joint capsules must be combatted by proper passive movements. Carefully supervised exercises are of the greatest importance. Each muscle should be exercised separately and great care should be taken to make sure that the muscle is not injured by excessive strain, that the antagonistic muscles are not developed and that trick movements are not substituted. The use of dry heat to improve the circulation before exercise is recommended and there are certain advantages to be gained by exercising in a warm pool. Skillful massage is undoubtedly of some value. If the muscles of the legs or of the trunk are affected caution must be exercised to prevent the child's walking too soon, since this will usually lead to the production of deformities.

Recently this view has been strongly opposed. It has been claimed immobilization is harmful and passive movements, massage and exercises should be instituted at once. The outcome of this controversy is uncertain at present. In reality the details of treatment are unimportant, provided contractures and deformities are prevented, and the final result depends upon the number and distribution of the neurons which suffer irreversible damage during the acute stage of the disease.

In bladder paralysis various drugs have been advocated to avoid the use of the catheter. Lawson and Garvey state that they have found furmethide more helpful than prostigmine and mecholyl chloride, both of which have also been recommended.

Measures useful in combatting the tendency to form renal calculi include passive and active exercises, frequent change of position, high fluid intake and acid-ash diet. Milk should be given in limited amounts. Testosterone and estrogen are said to be helpful.

If the muscles of respiration are seriously impaired, cor pulmonale may develop. Recurrent pulmonary infections often occur and the respirator may be required at times.

In the chronic state of the disease when all hope of further improvement of muscle power is abandoned, we must make the best of the situation as it exists. Numerous operative procedures are employed, such as tendon transplantations and fixation of joints by arthrodesis and other means. Braces and corsets are often necessary to prevent deformity. Some attempts have been made to relieve paralysis by transplantation of the distal end of a sound nerve into the proximal end of the nerve supplying a paralyzed muscle. The procedure is still in an experimental stage and the actual results so far secured in human cases have not been encouraging.

BIBLIOGRAPHY

General articles

JOHNSON, R. *et al.*: Infantile paralysis or acute poliomyelitis. J.A.M.A., **131**:1411, 1946.

NEAL, J. AND HARRINGTON, H. *et al.*: Poliomyelitis-International Committee for the Study of

Infantile Paralysis. Baltimore, Williams & Wilkins, 1932. (Full discussion and all aspects of subject, etiology, immunity, epidemiology, treatment and experimental data. Bibliography up to date.)

PEABODY, F. W., DRAPER, G. AND DOCHEZ, A. R.: A Clinical Study of Acute Poliomyelitis Monography of the Rockefeller Inst. No. 4, 1912. (Splendid clinical descriptions.)

SABIN, A. B. *et al.*: Symposium on poliomyelitis. J.A.M.A., **117**:267, etc., 1941.

Symposium on poliomyelitis. Amer. J. Med., **6**:538, 1949.

Poliomyelitis. International Poliomyelitis Congress. J. B. Lippincott Co., 1949.

Etiology

BODIAN, D. AND HORSTMAN, D. M.: The Polioviruses. Viral and Rickettsial Infections of Man. Edited by Horsfall, F. L. and Tamm, I., J. B. Lippincott Co., 4th Ed., 1965, p. 430.

FLEXNER, S. AND NOGUCHI, H.: Experiments on the cultivation of the micro-organism causing epidemic poliomyelitis. J. Exp. Med., **18**:461, 1913.

HOWE, H. A. AND BODIAN, D.: Neural Mechanisms in Poliomyelitis. The Commonwealth Fund. New York, Oxford Univ. Press, 1942.

JUNGEBLUT, C. W.: Problems of classification of poliomyelitis virus. Arch. Path., **52**:18, 1951.

POLLOCK, L. J. *et al.*: Absence of spasm during onset of paralysis in anterior poliomyelitis. Arch. Neurol. & Psychiat., **61**:288, 1949.

STILLERMAN, M. AND FISCHER, A.: Acute bulbar poliomyelitis following recent tonsilectomy and adenoidectomy. Am. J. Dis. Child., **56**:778, 1938.

Pathological anatomy

BAKER, A. B. AND CORNWALL, S.: Poliomyelitis—The cerebral hemisphere—The cerebellum. Arch. Neurol. & Psychiat., **71**:435, 1954.

————, MATZKE, H. A. AND BROWN, J. E.: Poliomyelitis. III. Bulbar Poliomyelitis. Arch. Neurol. & Psychiat., **63**:257, 1950.

DENNY-BROWN, D.: Effect of poliomyelitis on the function of the motor neuron. (An electro-myographic study.) Arch. Neurol. & Psychiat., **64**:141, 1950.

FEIGIN, I.: Lesions in the white matter in acute poliomyelitis. Neurology, **7**:399, 1957.

STEEGMAN, T. T. AND DAVIS, H. V.: Anoxic encephalopathy following poliomyelitis. Arch. Neurol. & Psychiat., **63**:774, 1950.

WARBURG, B.: Experimental poliomyelitis. Histology of the persistent lesions of the central nervous system. Arch. Neurol. & Psychiat., **25**:1191, 1931.

Epidemiology

BIRAND AND DEUTSCHMAN: Poliomyelitis. History of the Disease and of Research Concerning Its Epidemiology During Recent Years. Report. Health Section of Secretariat League of Nations, **14**:207, 1935.

MACNALTY, A. S.: Epidemic Diseases of the Central Nervous System. London, Faber and Gwyer, 1927.

In newborn infant and in fetus

ABRAMSON, H. *et al.*: Poliomyelitis in the newborn infant. J. Pediat., **43**:167, 1953.

BARSKY, P. AND BEALE, A. J.: Fetal poliomyelitis. J. Pediat. **51**:207, 1957.

SCHAEFFER, M., FOX, M. AND LI, C.: Intrauterine poliomyelitis infection. Report of a case. J.A.M.A., **155**:248, 1954.

Clinical features: Epidemics of bulbar type

BOSMA, J. F.: Residual disability of pharyngeal area resulting from poliomyelitis. J.A.M.A., **165**:216, 1957.

BROWN, W. G. S.: An epidemic of the bulbar type of poliomyelitis. Lancet, **2**:1287, 1931.

MOORE, E. W.: Fate of the face in poliomyelitis. Lancet, **i**:1092, 1952.

SMITH, H. B.: Anterior poliomyelitis, bulbar type. Report of six cases. Long Island M. J., **29**:105, 1929.

Potassium deficiency
LANS *et al.:* Potassium deficiency in bulbar poliomyelitis. J.A.M.A., **146:**1017, 1951.

Sensory loss
PLUM, F.: Sensory loss with poliomyelitis. Neurology, **6:**166, 1956.

Cerebral types
FORD, F. R. AND SCHAFFER, A. J.: The etiology of infantile (acquired) hemiplegia. Arch. Neurol. & Psychiat., **18:**323, 1927.
ROTHMAN, P. E.: Polioencephalitis. Am. J. Dis. Child., **42:**124, 1931.

Non-paralytic cases
LUCCHESI, P.: Non-paralytic poliomyelitis versus choriomeningitis. J.A.M.A., **108:**1494, 1937.

Relapses
ESHNER, A. A.: A possible second attack of acute anterior poliomyelitis in the same patient. Med. Rec., **78:**526, 1910.

Second attacks
QUIGLEY, T. B.: Second attacks of poliomyelitis. Review of the literature and report of a case. J.A.M.A., **102:**752, 1934.
STILL, G. F.: Second attacks of acute poliomyelitis and the minimal duration of immunity. Arch. Dis. Child., **5:**295, 1930.

Local paralysis in children after injections
MARTIN, J. K.: Local paralysis in children after injections. Arch. Dis. Child., **25:**1, 1950.

Changes in the heart
DOLGOPOL, V. B. AND CRAGAN, M. D.: Myocardial changes in poliomyelitis. Arch. Path., **46:**202, 1948.
ROSE, L. M.: Electrocardiographic changes in poliomyelitis in childhood. Brit. Heart J., **14:**391, 1952.

Changes in the bones
BENNETT, R. L.: Classification and treatment of early lateral deviations of the spine following acute anterior poliomyelitis. Arch. Phys. Med., **36:**9, 1955.
HASSIN, G. *et al.:* Roentgenographic bone changes in a case of poliomyelitis. J.A.M.A., **65:**1459, 1915.
————: Roentgenographic bone changes in a second case of old poliomyelitis. J.A.M.A., **85:**267, 1925.

Ocular disorders
GARDNER, W. J., SPITLER, D. K. AND WHITTEN, C.: Increased intracranial pressure caused by increased protein content of the cerebrospinal fluid. New Eng. J. Med., **250:**932, 1954.
MURRAY, R. G. AND WALSH, F. B.: Ocular abnormalities in poliomyelitis and their pathogenesis. Canad. M. J., **70:**141, 1954.
WALSH, F. B.: *Loc. cit.*
WEIMAN, C. G., McDOWELL, F. H. AND PLUM, F.: Papilledema in poliomyelitis. Arch. Neurol. & Psychiat., **722:**66, 1951.

Effects on bladder and intestines
SCHABERG, A. *et al.:* Upper gastrointestinal lesions in acute bulbar poliomyelitis. Gastroenterology, **27:**838, 1954.
TOOMEY, J. A.: The intestines and urinary bladder in poliomyelitis. Am. J. Dis. Child., **45:**1211, 1933.

Tests for antibodies against poliomyelitis
CAMPBELL, A. M. G. *et al.:* Late motor neuron degeneration following poliomyelitis. Neurology, **11:**1101, 1969.

SALK, J. E. *et al.:* Color indicator method for testing poliomyelitis virus infectivity. Am. J. Hyg., **60**:214, 1954.

Late increase in weakness
LOVETT, R. L.: The third year in infantile paralysis. J.A.M.A., **77**:1941, 1921.

Sequelae
POTTS, C. S.: A case of progressive muscular atrophy occurring in a man who had had acute poliomyelitis nineteen years previously. Univ. Pa. Med. Bull., **16**:31, 1903.
SALMON, L. A. AND RILEY, H. A.: The relation between progressive spinal atrophy and an antecedent attack of acute anterior poliomyelitis. Bull. Neurol. Inst. New York, **4**:35, 1935.

Treatment
CREEVY, C. AND TICHY, F.: Etiology and treatment of urinary lithiasis in severe poliomyelitis. Arch. Neurol. & Psychiat., **68**:539, 1952.
FORSTER, F. M.: Modern Therapy in Neurology. St. Louis, C. V. Mosby Co., 1957. (Article on treatment in Poliomyelitis by Baker, A. B., p. 133.)
LAWSON, R. B. AND GARVEY, F. K.: Paralysis of bladder in poliomyelitis. J.A.M.A., **135**:93, 1947.
Minnesota Poliomyelitis Research Commission: Bulbar form of poliomyelitis: Therapeutic measures. J.A.M.A., **135**:425, 1947.
NEAL, HARRINGTON *et al.:* (See above.)
STIMSON, P. M.: Some debated points in the treatment of acute poliomyelitis. J. Pediat., **36**:704, 1950.
NEFFSON, H.: Tracheotomy in bulbar poliomyelitis. Am. J. Med. Sci., **224**:465, 1952.
STEIGMAN, A. J.: Treatment of the acute phase of poliomyelitis. Am. J. Dis. Child., **87**:343. 1954.

Use of the Drinker respirator
LEGG, A. T.: The use of the Drinker respirator in the after care of infantile paralysis. J.A.M.A., **100**:647, 1933.
WILSON, J. L.: Acute anterior poliomyelitis; Treatment of the bulbar and high spinal forms. New England J. Med., **206**:887, 1932.

Orthopedic treatment
GHORMLEY, R. *et al.:* Evaluation of the Kenny treatment. J.A.M.A., **125**:466, 1944.
KENDALL, H. O. AND KENDALL, F. P.: Care during the recovery period in paralytic poliomyelitis. Public Health Bull. No. 242, April, 1938.

Prophylaxis
British Medical Research Council: Poliomyelitis and prophylactic inoculation. Lancet, **271**:1223, 1956.
BRODIE, M. AND PARK, W. H.: Active immunization against poliomyelitis. J.A.M.A., **105**:1089, 1935.
HAMMON, W. McD. *et al.:* Evaluation of gamma globulin as a prophylactic agent for poliomyelitis. J.A.M.A., **151**:1272, 1953.
KOLMER, J. A.: Successful method for vaccination against acute anterior poliomyelitis. Am. J. Med. Sci., **188**:510, 1934.
LEAKE, J. P.: Poliomyelitis following vaccination against this disease. J.A.M.A., **105**:2152, 1935.
PLOTKIN, S. A. *et al.:* Oral poliovirus vaccination in newborn African infants. Amer. Jour. Dis. Child., **111**:27, 1966.
SALK, J. E.: Active immunization against poliomyelitis. Am. J. Pub. Health, **44**:994, 1954.
SCHULTZ, E. W. AND GEBHARDT, L. P.: Zinc sulphate prophylaxis in poliomyelitis. J.A.M.A., **108**:2182, 1937.

DISEASES DUE TO COXSACKIE VIRUSES

Definition.—There are a number of closely related viruses which are apparently capable of causing a variety of brief illnesses. The name refers to the town where the first strains of the virus were discovered. They are classified with the poliomyelitis viruses and Echo viruses.

Etiology.—These viruses are very small and are said to average between 15 and 25 mμ in diameter. Suckling mice and hamsters are especially susceptible to these viruses. Some strains may be grown on tissue culture and egg embryo. About 15 different strains are known to exist and may be differentiated by complement fixation and neutralization tests.

These viruses have been found in many parts of the world in sewage, house flies, and stools of individuals especially children.

Pathological Anatomy.—Bozsik found at post-mortem examination of an infant dying of infection with Coxsackie B 3 virus meningitis most severe in the spinal meninges and inflammatory changes in the anterior spinal gray matter.

Clinical Features.—It is believed that group A viruses may cause *benign lymphocytic meningitis* which simulates non-paralytic poliomyelitis very closely. There is fever, headache, nausea, abdominal pain, cervical rigidity and vomiting. The temperature may reach 104°F and lasts three to nine days. There are rarely more than 100 cells in the spinal fluid. Complete recovery is expected. In some cases there is a recurrence of symptoms within a few days after apparent recovery. Grist and Roberts found changes in the spinal cord similar to those due to poliomyelitis in a child who died of paralysis due to Coxsackie A 7 virus.

Group B viruses are thought to be responsible for *epidemic myalgia* q.v. which is also termed Bornholm disease and pleurodynia. This condition is discussed elsewhere. It is probably a true myositis for Lepin found myositis in a biopsy specimen. Javett studied a small epidemic of myocarditis in infants. There were 10 cases in all of which 6 were fatal. At post-mortem examination encephalitis was found in addition to myocarditis. The B virus was recovered. Kirby and Evans found Coxsackie B virus in cases of acute lymphocytic meningitis simulating non-paralytic poliomyelitis. In the summer of 1956 an epidemic of several hundred cases appeared in Kansas. The symptoms included headache, cervical rigidity, pains in the muscles and joints, pleurodynia, nausea and vomiting. Orchitis, abdominal pain and pericarditis are described. Recovery was complete within 10 to 14 days. Coxsackie B 5 virus was found in the stools of a large percentage of cases. McLeod *et al.* describe 17 cases in children due to the same virus. Langdale-Smith *et al.* describe an epidemic in which 25 of 47 school children developed either Bornholm disease or meningoencephalitis during the summer months. Syverton found that of 113 subjects who presented the clinical picture of non-paralytic poliomyelitis, 61 were infected with the Coxsackie B 5 virus. Neonatal infections with Coxsackie virus B are described by Sussman and by Kibrick. The process seems to be generalized with evidence of the involvement of the heart as well as the nervous system. The mortality is high. There is reason to think that infection occurs in the uterus.

Australian workers have found another group of viruses which they term group C in cases of *encephalitis* which were mild and brief. They state that in mice this virus produces encephalitis without myositis.

Richardson and Leibovitz state that hand, foot and mouth disease occurs in children with stomatitis, a vesicular eruption on the hands and feet and a maculopapular eruption on the buttocks. This is attributed to infection with the Coxsackie A 16 virus.

Herpangia, a brief, febrile illness with vesicular pharyngitis is also attributed to a strain of Coxsackie virus and summer grippe is due to a related strain, it is claimed. Apparently many such infections are clinically latent.

Diagnosis.—The virus is found in the stools, blood and spinal fluid. Suckling mice and hamsters may be inoculated and the virus may be identified by neutralization and complement fixation tests.

Treatment.—None is available yet.

BIBLIOGRAPHY

ARTENSTEIN, M. S. *et al.*: Clinical and epidemiological features of Coxsackie group B virus infections. Ann. Int. Med., **63**:597, 1965.

BAIN, H. W. *et al.*: Epidemic pleurodynia due to Coxsackie B 5 virus. Interrelation of pleurodynia, benign pericarditis and aseptic meningitis. Pediatrics, **27**:889, 1961.

BOZSIK, G.: Histologic changes in the infantile nervous system after Coxsackie B 3 infection. Deutsch. Ztschr. Nervenh., **179**:564, 1959.

CHANG, T. W. AND WEINSTEIN, L.: Infections of nervous system by Coxsackie virus A-9. Bull. Tufts New England Med. Center, **6**:181, 1960.

CLARK, M. *et al.*: Seasonal aseptic meningitis caused by Coxsackie and Echo viruses. Canad. M. J., **81**:5, 1959.

CURNEN, E. C.: Immunology, Epidemiology and Clinical Aspects of Coxsackie Virus Infections. Second International Poliomyelitis Conference, Copenhagen, 1952.

DALLDORF, G. AND MELNICK, J. L.: The Coxsackie Viruses. Viral and Rickettsial Infections of Man. Edited by Horsfall, F. L. and Tamm, I. J. B. Lippincott Co. 4th Ed. 1965, p. 474.

——— AND GIFFORD, R.: Clinical and epidemiological observations of Coxsackie virus infections. New England J. Med., **244**:868, 1951.

GERMER, W. D.: Viruserkrankungen des Menchen. Stuttgart, Geo. Thieme, 1954.

GRIST, N. R. AND ROBERTS, G. B. S.: Paralysis due to Coxsackie A 7 virus. J. Path. & Bact., **84**:39, 1962.

JAVETT, S. N. *et al.*: Myocarditis in the newborn infant. Study of outbreak associated with Coxsackie group B virus. J. Pediat., **48**:1, 1956.

KIBRICK, S.: Severe generalized disease occurring in the newborn period and due to infection with Coxsackie virus group B. Pediatrics, **22**:857, 1958.

KIRBY, W. M. M. AND EVANS, C. A.: Tissue culture isolation of Coxsackie group B virus in aseptic meningitis. J.A.M.A., **159**:743, 1955.

LANGDALE-SMITH, H. G.: A localized epidemic of Bornholm disease and meningoencephalitis. Brit. Med. J., **i**:805, 1957.

LEPINE, P., DESSE, G. ET SAUTTER, V.: Myositis in case of Bornholm disease. Bull. Acad. Nation. Med., **5-6**:66, 1952.

LERNER, A. M. AND FINLAND, M.: Coxsackie viral infections. Arch. Int. Med., **108**:329, 1961.

——— *et al.*: Infections due to the Coxsackie virus. New England J. Med., **263**:1265, 1960.

MAGOFFIN, R. L. *et al.*: Association of Coxsackie viruses with illnesses resembling mild poliomyelitis. Pediatrics, **28**:602, 1961.

——— *et al.*: Poliomyelitis-like viral infections. Pediatrics, **28**:602, 1961.

McLEAN, D. M. *et al.*: Coxsackie B 5 virus as cause of neonatal encephalitis and myocarditis. Canad. Med. Ass. Jour., **85**:1046, 1961.

McLEOD, D. L. *et al.*: Clinical features of aseptic meningitis caused by Coxsackie B virus. Lancet, **ii**:701, 1956.

MEADOWS, S. R.: Hand, foot and mouth diseases. Arch. of Dis. Childh., **40**:560, 1965.

MELNICK, J. L. AND CURNEN, E. C.: Coxsackie Group in Viral and Rickettsial Infections of Man. 2nd Ed. Rivers. Baltimore, J. B. Lippincott, 1952.

MEYER, H. M. *et al.*: Central nervous system syndromes of viral etiology. Amer. Jour. Med., **29**:334, 1960.

MILLER, G. D. AND TINDALL, J. P.: Hand, foot and mouth disease. Jour. Amer. Med. Ass., **203**:827, 1968.

MOOSSY, J. AND GEER, J. C.: Encephalitis myocarditis and adrenal cortical necrosis in Coxsackie B 3 virus infection. Arch. Path., **70**:614, 1960.

NOGEN, A. G. AND LEPOW, M. L.: Enterovirus meningitis in very young infants. Pediatrics, **40**:617, 1967.

RAPMUND, G. *et al.*: Neonatal myocarditis and meningoencephalitis due to Coxsackie B virus. New England Med. Jour., **260**:819, 1959.

RICHARDSON, H. B. AND LEIBOVITZ, A.: Hand, foot and mouth disease in children. Jour. Pediat., **67**:6, 1965.

SASLAW, S. AND ANDERSON, G. R.: Aseptic meningitis and non-paralytic poliomyelitis. Arch. Int. Med., **107**:568, 1961.

STANLEY, N. F., DORMAN, D. C. AND PONSFORD, J.: Studies on Coxsackie viruses. Australian J. Exper. Biol. & Med. Sci., **31**:9, 1953.

SUSSMAN, M. L. *et al.*: Fatal Coxsackie group B virus infection in the newborn. Am. J. Dis. Child., **97**:483, 1959.

SYVERTON, J. T.: Epidemic aseptic meningitis due to Coxsackie B virus. J.A.M.A., **164**:2015, 1957.

WALKER, S. H. AND TOGO, Y.: Group B, Type 5 Coxsackie encephalitis. Am. J. Dis. Child., **105**:105, 1963.

WINSSER, J. AND ALTIERI, R. H.: Coxsackie virus group B. Am. J. M. Sci., **247**:269, 1964.

DISEASES DUE TO THE ECHO VIRUSES

These viruses belong to the group of enteric viruses as do the poliomyelitis and Coxsackie viruses. The name is derived from the original term enteric cytopathic human orphan viruses. There are believed to be at least twenty-four types, which may be distinguished by complement fixation or neutralization tests. They are small spherical organisms about 30 micra in diameter. Most of them can be grown on tissue culture.

Epidemic and sporadic infections occur most commonly in the late summer and fall. Children are more frequently affected than adults, and often, several children in one family become ill at about the same time. The most common neurological syndrome is *acute benign lymphocytic meningitis*. This is similar to the meningitis due to non-paralytic poliomyelitis and to the Coxsackie viruses. The cell count in the spinal fluid may be high or low. In some cases there is a macular or maculopapular eruption. Petechial lesions occur rarely. Mild signs of peripheral neuritis are mentioned. The virus may be recovered from the spinal fluid in some instances. Type 9 is often responsible.

In rare instances there is a clinical picture *resembling poliomyelitis,* with weakness or paralysis of muscles. These palsies are nearly always transient, but in a few cases, persistent paralysis has been observed. There seem to have been three fatal cases. Steigman and Lipton report such a case.

It is believed that a type of ataxic neuritis may result from infection with the Echo virus Type 1.

Bell *et al.* state that Echo virus 25 was isolated from 13 patients with meningitis. One had meningoencephalitis with brain damage and hydrocephalus and two had myocarditis between 1961 and 1964.

Minor febrile illnesses are described without evidence of involvement of the nervous system. Fever with cutaneous eruption, and attacks of gastroenteritis, with vomiting and diarrhea, are attributed to infections with these viruses. Upper respiratory tract infections also occur. It is believed that subclinical infections are common.

Diagnosis.—The symptoms are not specific and the diagnosis must be made by the recovery of the virus or by serological studies.

Treatment.—No specific treatment is available.

BIBLIOGRAPHY

BELL, E. J. *et al.:* Echo virus 25 infections in Scotland 1961-1964. Lancet, 2:464, 1965.

ECKERT, G. *et al.:* Aseptic meningitis due to ECHO virus type 18. Jour. Dis. Child., **99**:1, 1960.

ELVIN-LEWIS, M. AND MELNICK, J. L.: Echo 11 virus associated with aseptic meningitis. Proc. Soc. Exper. Biol. Med. **102**:647, 1959.

FOLEY, J. F. *et al.:* Paralytic disease due to infection with ECHO virus type 9. New England Jour. Med., **260**:924, 1959.

KARZON, D. T. *et al.:* An epidemic of aseptic meningitis due to ECHO virus type 6. Pediatrics aseptic meningitis due to ECHO 4 virus. Amer. Jour. Dis. Child., **101**:610, 1961.

KHOOBYARIAN, K. *et al.:* Some viral central nervous system diseases. J. Dis. Child., **98**:15, 1959.

LYLE, W. H.: An outbreak of disease believed to have been caused by Echo 9 virus. Ann. Int. Med., **51**:248, 1959.

MARCOLONGO, F.: Clinical manifestations of disease due to Echo viruses. Riv. Ist. sieroterap. ital., **35**:153, 1960.

MELNICK, J. L.: Echoviruses. Viral and Rickettsial Infections of Man. Edited by Horsfall, F. L. and Tamm, I. J. B. Lippincott Co. 4th Ed. 1965, p. 513.

MEYER, H. M. *et al.:* Central nervous system syndromes of viral etiology. Am. J. Med., **29**:334. 1960.

SABIN, A. B. AND WIGAND, R.: ECHO type 9 virus disease. Jour. Dis. Child., **96**:197, 1958.

SASLAW, S.: Aseptic meningitis syndrome. A.M.A. Arch. Int. Med., **105**:69, 1960.

SOLOMON, P. *et al.:* Epidemiologic, clinical and laboratory features of epidemic of Type 9 Echo virus meningitis. J. Pediat., **55**:609, 1959.

STEIGMAN, A. J. AND LIPTON, M. M.: Fatal bulbospinal paralytic poliomyelitis due to Echo 11 virus. J.A.M.A., **174**:178, 1960.

ENCEPHALOMYOCARDITIS

Definition.—A virus disease of apes and rodents which is widespread in nature and occasionally infects man. Cases have been reported from Chicago, Sandinavia, England, the Philippines and Germany.

Etiology.—The virus is a small one averaging about 25 mμ in diameter. It is one of a series of closely related viruses which includes the Columbia S K virus, the M M virus and the virus of Mengo encephalomyelitis. This virus may be grown on tissue culture and egg embryo. Most laboratory animals are susceptible.

Pathological Anatomy.—It is said that there is a diffuse encephalitis involving the cerebral hemispheres and the brain stem with perivascular round cell infiltrations, small hemorrhages and degeneration of the neurons. No detailed studies are available. The heart shows focal areas of degeneration and necrosis with round cell infiltrations. There is an intestitial pneumonia.

Clinical Features.—An epidemic in Manila was manifest by benign lymphocytic meningitis with headache, cervical rigidity, pharyngitis and clouding of consciousness lasting about three days and ending in complete recovery. There were apparently no symptoms referable to the heart. There were 50 to 500 cells in the spinal fluid. In Europe the virus has been found in children with encephalitis and lymphocytic meningitis.

In other cases there have been evidences of severe encephalitis and also myocarditis with circulatory failure. In some instances myocarditis is the problem and there is little or no evidence of encephalitis.

Diagnosis.—The occurrence of both encephalitis and myocarditis should suggest the diagnosis. The virus may be isolated from the blood, stools and the spinal fluid by the inoculation of egg embryos, mice and hamsters. During convalescence complement-fixation antibodies and agglutinins appear in the serum.

Treatment.—No treatment is available at present.

BIBLIOGRAPHY

BERKOVICH, S. *et al.:* Virologic studies in children with acute myocarditis. Amer. Jour. Dis. Child., **115**:207, 1968.
BRENNING, R.: Encephalomyocarditis. Acta Soc. Med. Upsalien, **56**:51, 1951.
GERMER, W. D.: Viruserkrankungen des Menchen. Thieme, Stuttgart, 1954.
RICHDORF, L. F.: Myocardial failure in children with brain involvement. Lancet, **i**:166, 1950.
SAPHIR, O.: Encephalomyocarditis. Circulation, **6**:843, 1952.
SCHMIDT, E.: Virus myocarditis. Am. J. Path., **24**:97, 1948.
SMADEL, J. E.: Research in virus disease. Bull. U.S. Army Med. Dept., **7**:795, 1947.
DICK, G. W.: Mengo encephalomyelitis. Lancet, **ii**:286, 1948.
GAJDUSEK, D. C.: Encephalomyocarditis virus infection in childhood. Pediatrics, **16**:902, 1955.
WARREN, J.: Encephalomyocarditis Viruses. Viral and Rickettsial Infections of Man. Edited by Horsfall, F. L. and Tamm, I. J. B. Lippincott Co., 4th Ed. 1965, p. 562.

EPIDEMIC HICCOUGH

Definition.—An epidemic disease manifest by fever and hiccough.

Etiology.—Little is known of the cause of this condition. There can be no doubt that it is an infection, however. The fact that epidemics of hiccough have sometimes occurred just preceding epidemics of encephalitis and the hiccough is a common symptom of encephalitis has led to the supposition that these two diseases are related and it has even been suggested that epidemic hiccough is an abortive type of encephalitis.

Epidemiology.—This disease first appeared in the autumn of 1919 in Egypt, Austria, Germany and Canada. In the following year it invaded France and there are said to have been at least 5,000 cases in Paris alone. England and Switzerland were visited by the disease in 1920 and a few cases appeared in the United States. Another epidemic developed in 1924 and thousands of cases were observed in England and America. The disease is almost confined to the winter months or the late autumn. It usually affects males of middle age or older and rarely occurs during childhood. It is mildly contagious. Sporadic cases probably occur.

Pathological Anatomy.—This is unknown.

Clinical Features.—The disease begins with a mild coryza and a slight elevation of temperature. The pulse is rather slow, as a rule. Within 24 to 48 hours, the patient begins to hiccough at frequent intervals. Rarely is there any vomiting. Other symptoms are absent. The hiccough may last only one day or may persist for a week. No complications or sequelae have been described. In Baltimore the disease was accompanied by local pains and areas of hyperesthesia corresponding roughly to the spinal dermatomes.

As a rule, no treatment is required. If the hiccough is very trying, sedatives may be given or carbon dioxide administered. The method of rebreathing the air of a paper bag until the carbon dioxide tension is elevated may be recommended.

BIBLIOGRAPHY

MacNalty, A. S.: Epidemic hiccup. Lancet, 2:62, 1929.

RABIES

Terminology.—This disease is also termed hydrophobia, lyssa and rage.

Etiology.—Rabies is usually the result of a bite of a rabid dog or cat although all animals are susceptible and may transmit the disease. The skunks of the Western plains are said to be subject to rabies and their bite is greatly feared by persons who sleep outdoors. In Russia it is said that the wolves are often responsible for transmitting the disease. Recent studies of an epidemic on the Island of Trinidad have indicated that the vampire bat may convey rabies. A case has been reported in which the disease followed vaccination against smallpox. It has been established that rabies is due to a rather large virus the diameter of which is estimated to vary between 100 and 150 mμ. Constantine has shown by experimental means that rabies may be acquired by airborne infection.

Pathological Anatomy.—In general, the anatomical process is similar to that of epidemic encephalitis. An acute inflammatory process is found in the gray matter of the brain-stem and certain segments of the spinal cord. The substantia nigra, red nucleus and central gray matter of the pons and medulla are most intensely affected, as a rule. In these regions the adventitia of the small vessels is infiltrated with lymphocytes, plasma cells and sometimes leucocytes and small hemorrhages may be seen. There is also a diffuse infiltration of the gray matter and in some regions the destruction of the myelin of the adjacent white matter. The neurons show chromatolysis or even complete necrosis. The microglial cells are transformed into rod cells or gitter cells and often form clusters, the so-called Babes tubercles. There is very little proliferation of the astrocytes, although degenerative changes may be found. The lesions in the spinal cord bear a certain relation to the site of the bite. It is claimed that spinal lesions are usually found at the level of the wound and that they are most intense on the same side. The posterior root ganglia are also inflamed, especially those which supply the area of the bite. It is believed that the virus enters the terminal branches of the cutaneous nerves and is transmitted along the nerve trunk to the spinal cord whence it extends to the brain. Degenerative changes without definite evidences of inflammation are found in the lenticular nuclei, the thalamus, cerebellum and parts of the spinal cord. The same statement applies to the cerebral cortex although the cornu Ammonis usually shows an inflammatory reaction. The inflammatory phenomena may be very intense and acute in cases in which the incubation period is short but when the latent period is prolonged, the process may be almost entirely degenerative. In one of our cases there were no inflammatory phenomena and no conspicuous degenerative changes in the nerve cells despite the presence of numerous Negri bodies. These bodies are a characteristic feature of the disease. They are rounded structures between 4 and 10 micra in diameter, which stain with acid dyes, and are found in the cytoplasm of the nerve cells of the hippocampus, cerebellum, spinal ganglia and cerebral cortex in about 90 per cent of all cases. As a rule, they are absent in regions in which the inflammatory process is pronounced. The virus is present in the nervous system.

In the cases of acute ascending myelitis due to rabies, the lesions are of essentially the same nature as those described above and quite different from those of encephalomyelitis which may follow the Pasteur treatment. Knutti has given a very careful description of the lesion in his case.

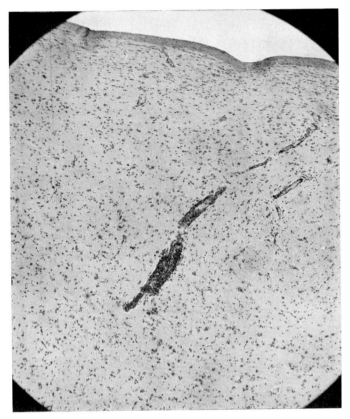

Fig. 145. Rabies showing perivascular infiltrations in the medulla.

Clinical Features.—Rabies or hydrophobia has never been a very common disease, and, in recent years, has become very rare as a result of the widespread use of the Pasteur treatment and of protective legislation. However, it is said to have been prevalent in Europe after World War I and a large number of cases occur in Russia every year. England, Ireland and Australia are almost free from the disease as a result of strict laws governing the importation of dogs. In the United States rabies is occasionally encountered, especially in the southern and western states. In New York City between 1926 and 1930 from 6,000 to 12,000 dog bites were reported to the Health Department every year and from 56 to 450 dogs were found to be rabid. As a result of the prompt application of the Pasteur treatment only 12 cases of human rabies have occurred during this period.

Only a small percentage of those bitten by a rabid animal develop the disease but the incidence depends upon the severity as well as upon the site of the wounds, being rather higher in multiple wounds and in those near the head. Wolf bites are more dangerous than dog bites it is said. In rabid dog bites the probability of rabies is less than 10 per cent, even if no treatment is given.

The incubation period varies within relatively wide limits. In general it is between 20 and 60 days, being shorter when the bite is on the head and longer when it is on the leg. The incubation period is also shortened in case of multiple wounds. Cases are reported in which the disease apparently remained latent in the nervous system for a year or more before giving rise to active symptoms.

Three stages of the disease are recognized. During the prodromal stage the child may have some symptoms in the region of the bite, such as pain or numbness. There may be drowsiness, headache and loss of appetite. The stage of excitement then appears. The child gradually grows restless and irritable. Noises and bright lights are distressing. Soon the child presents the picture of terror with staring eyes and foaming mouth. Violent convulsions occur as well as local twitchings. Periods of delirium may alternate with periods of lucidity. Cervical rigidity is usually severe. There may be involuntary movements of the extremities. The spasms of the pharynx and larynx, which are very painful and are precipitated by any effort to take food are characteristic. The name hydrophobia refers to these phenomena. Vomiting of bloody fluid and expectoration of blood-stained mucus may be seen. There is intense hyperesthesia and irritability, so that almost any stimulus may cause convulsions. The temperature may reach 105°F. but in a few cases the course is afebrile. After one to three days the paralytic stage develops. The child grows quiet and slowly lapses into coma. Death occurs within a few hours. The spinal fluid usually shows a few lymphocytes but in cases in which the incubation period is brief and the symptoms very acute, there may be as many as a thousand cells in the spinal fluid, many of them leucocytes. Globulin may be present or absent. Death is inevitable once the symptoms have developed.

In many cases of rabies there is some degree of paralysis, in the terminal stage of the disease, and, in certain instances, it is believed that rabies may cause acute ascending myelitis or disseminated myelitis. Such cases may run their course to a fatal termination without the pharyngeal spasms or excitement which are characteristic of hydrophobia. The case of Knutti is a well-studied example of this type. Some years ago an epidemic of paralytic rabies occurred on the Island of Trinidad. There were seventeen cases in all and ten of these were in children under the age of 15 years. The onset was usually acute with fever and headache. Frequently the symptoms began with burning and tingling in one foot or leg. After one to four days, weakness of the leg became apparent and developed rapidly into paralysis with loss of reflexes. The other leg and muscles of the trunk were soon paralyzed. Sphincter control was lost. After one or two more days, death resulted from paralysis of respiration. Loss of sensibility was often present over the lower part of the body. The temperature ranged from normal to 103°F. Profuse sweating was a constant feature. There were periods of delirium in most cases and usually stupor towards the end. The duration of the disease was from four to eight days and all cases terminated fatally. Hurst and Pawan, who describe this epidemic, discovered that many cattle on the island were affected with the same disease. The authors state that none of their patients gave any history of being bitten. They are inclined to believe that the disease was transmitted by the vampire bat, the bite of which may be overlooked. No doubt the diagnosis of rabies is rarely considered in cases of acute ascending myelitis and it is possible that this disease plays a larger part in the etiology of the myelitides than is realized at present.

In Florida, Texas and Pennsylvania, people have been bitten by insectivorous bats which were found to be infected with rabies. In most instances, the biting was due to picking up a sick bat and hence was not unprovoked. Infected bats have been found in Montana. Insectivorous bats do not recover from this infection but vampire bats become carriers.

Epidemics of rabies in cattle have occurred in South America and in Central America. At such times, vampire bats have been observed to be flying about during the day time, shrieking, fighting and biting the cattle. These bats have been found to be infected.

Diagnosis.—The diagnosis of the classical rabies offers no difficulty once the clinical picture is well developed. The history of a dog bite, the terror and excitement and, above all, the pharyngeal spasms are very distinctive. In some cases, the mental condition of the child is not typical, in that there may be merely stupor or delirium, so that tetanus may be suspected. In the latter there is usually trismus, and pharyngeal spasm is usually absent. Moreover, the incubation period of tetanus is usually less than two weeks and almost always less than three weeks if serum has not been given. Hysteria is easily differentiated by a short period of observation.

There seems to be no satisfactory method of recognizing the ascending myelitis which may sometimes be due to rabies, unless a definite history can be elicited of exposure to infection. The post-mortem findings are scarcely so characteristic as to permit a definite diagnosis unless supported by animal inoculation.

Prognosis.—A few cases have been reported in which it is claimed recovery occurred, but the diagnosis is open to doubt and it is generally believed that once the disease is established the patient is doomed. This statement applies to the rabies myelitis as well as to the classical hydrophobia.

It is claimed that when proper treatment is instituted promptly after the bite, substantial protection is attained. In treated patients, the mortality is not over 1.5 per cent and is even lower if we exclude cases in which there is undue delay in beginning treatment.

Prophylactic Treatment.—When a patient is bitten by an animal which is suspected of being mad, the animal must be secured and kept under observation so as to determine its condition. If the animal is killed the brain must be examined for the characteristic lesions.

If there is reason to believe the animal is rabid, the wound should be opened widely at once and thoroughly cauterized with phenol. It should then be washed with alcohol. Treatment should be administered as soon as possible for delay renders it less effective. Pasteur produced his virus by subdural inoculation of rabbits with brain emulsion of rabid dogs. This he called *street virus.* At the first inoculation the incubation period varied from 15 days to 20 days but with successive passages this was reduced to 7 days. This virus of uniform virulence he called the *fixed virus.* If now the spinal cord of the last rabbit is dried in a sterile jar, its virulence gradually diminishes and small quantities injected every day in a patient who has been bitten by a rabid animal will produce immunity before the disease develops. This method has been discarded for the use of attenuated virus is not without danger. Viruses which have been killed in some manner are now used. Two problems still await solution, however. Vaccination is not effective if the incubation period is less than 30 days for it seems to take 30 days for the vaccination to give protection. Paralytic accidents occur in rare instances, possibly once in 2,000 vaccinations. It is believed that this type of paralysis is due to the injection of emulsified nervous tissue. It is stated that a patient who is inoculated a second time is more apt to have such an accident than one who is inoculated for the first time.

A serum has been developed which, it is claimed, gives protection if given within 24 hours after the bite but is less effective if given later. This should be given at once, if the patient is not sensitive to serum.

A duck embryo vaccine has also been produced which should eliminate the danger of paralytic accidents. This should be used in addition to the serum. Fleming states that if the serum is administered, two supplemental doses of vaccine should be given ten and twenty days after the vaccination schedule is completed for the serum may suppress the response to the vaccine.

Compulsory vaccination of dogs is advised and individuals who work around animals may be given a small dose of duck embryo vaccine. If such an individual is subsequently bitten, only a single injection of vaccine is needed for proper protection.

BIBLIOGRAPHY

BASSOE, P. AND GRINKER, R. R.: Human rabies and rabies vaccine encephalomyelitis. Arch. Neurol. & Psychiat., **23**:1138, 1930.

BLATT, M.: Rabies in childhood. Arch. Neurol. & Psychiat., **21**:1218, 1929.

BLATT, M. L., HOFFMAN, S. J. AND SCHNEIDER, M.: Rabies. J.A.M.A., **111**:688, 1939.

BLATTNER, R. J.: Bats and rabies. J. Pediat., **46**:612, May, 1955.

CLOUGH, P.: Rabies in bats. Editorial. Ann. Int. Med., **42**:1330, 1955.

CONSTANTINE, D. G.: Spread of rabies by bats without biting. Publ. Health Repts., **77**:287, 1962.

DEAN, J. D.: Treatment of rabies. J. Med., **63**:3507, 1963.

FLEMING, D. S.: Evaluation of possible rabies. Minnesota Med., **45**:601, 1962.

DE VERTEUIL, E. AND URICH, F. W.: Study and control of paralytic rabies transmitted by bats in Trinidad. Tr. Roy. Soc. Trop. Med. and Hyg., **29**:317, 1935.

Editorial: Rabies. Some current problems and recent improvements in measures for its control. Ann. Int. Med., **34**:517, 1951.

HABEL, K.: Prophylaxis of rabies. Clin. Proc. Children's Hosp., **15**:190, 1959.

HURST, E. W. AND PAWAN, J. L.: An outbreak of rabies in Trinidad without history of bites and with the symptoms of an acute ascending myelitis. Lancet, **11**:622, 1931.

————: A further account of the Trinidad outbreak of acute rabic myelitis. Histology of the experimental disease. J. Path. & Bact., **35**:301, 1932.

JOHNSON, H. N.: Rabies Virus. Viral and Rickettsial Infections of Man. Edited by Horsfall, F. L. and Tamm, I. J. B. Lippincott Co. 4th Ed., p. 814, 1965.

KNUTTI, R. E.: Acute ascending paralysis and myelitis due to the virus of rabies. J.A.M.A., **93**:754, 1931.

KOUGH, R. H.: Attack on a human being by a rabid insectivorous bat. J.A.M.A., **155**:441, May 29, 1954.

League of Nations Health Organization: Report of International Conference on Rabies. Geneva, 1927.

LOWENBERG, K.: Rabies in man. Arch. Neurol. & Psychiat., **19**:638, 1928.

MORECKI, R. AND ZIMMERMAN, H. M.: Human rabies encephalitis. Arch. of Neurol., **20**:599, 1969.

PECK, F. B.: Duck embryo vaccine against rabies. J. Lab. & Clin. Med., **45**:679, 1955.

REISMAN, D., FOX, W. W., ALPERS, B. J. AND COOPER, D. A.: Hydrophobia. Report of two fatal cases with pathologic studies in one. Arch. Int. Med., **51**:643, 1933.

RICE, T. B.: Two human cases of rabies. J.A.M.A., **91**:1631, 1928.

SCHURKI, L. U. AND SPATZ, H.: Über die Anatomischen Veranderungen bei menschlichen Lyssa und ihr Beziehungen zu denen der Encephalitis epidemica. Ztschr. f. d. ges. Neurol. u. Psychiat., **97**:627, 1925.

STEVENSON, L. D. AND BERNTSEN, C. A.: Human rabies. J. Neuropath. & Exp. Neurol., **12**:169, 1953.

SULKIN, S. E. AND GREVE, M. J.: Human rabies caused by rat bite. Texas J. Med., **50**:620, August, 1954.

Texas Health Bulletin, Texas State Department of Health, Austin, **7**:13, August, 1954.

TIERKEL, E. S. AND SIKES, R. K.: Preexposure prophylaxis against rabies. Jour. Amer. Med. Ass., **201**:911, 1967.

VENTERS, H. D. *et al.*: Rabies in bats in Florida. Am. J. Pub. Health, **44**:182, January, 1954.

WITTE, E. J.: Bat rabies in Pennsylvania. Am. J. Pub. Health, **44**:186, February, 1954.

HERPES ZOSTER

Terminology.—This disease is also called shingles and zona.

Etiology.—Weller has shown that the virus of varicella and of herpes zoster are identical. It is believed that zoster is due either to reactivation of a latent varicella zoster virus or reintroduction of the virus into a partially immune subject.

Pathological Anatomy.—The most constant and severe lesions are found in the posterior root ganglia. Grossly the ganglia are found to be swollen and hyperemic. There may be small hemorrhages. Microscopic examination reveals lymphocytic infiltration of the tissues, especially about the small vessels. The sheath of the ganglion is also infiltrated. Some of the nerve cells are necrotic and some show milder degree of injury. After ten or twelve days degeneration of both the peripheral nerve fibers and the dorsal roots may be demonstrated. Later the acute reaction disappears, leaving loss of ganglion cells, degeneration of the nerve fibers and a dense glial scar. There may be a mild meningeal reaction. Denny-Brown *et al.* state that four findings are characteristic of herpes zoster. (1) A ganglionitis marked by pannecrosis of all or part of the ganglion with or without hemorrhage and by intense lymphocytic infiltration. This is always associated with characteristic vesicles in the corresponding dermatome. (2) Poliomyelitis which closely resembles the common acute anterior poliomyelitis but is readily distinguished by its unilaterality, segmental localization and greater involvement of the posterior horn, posterior root and dorsal spinal ganglion. (3) A relatively mild, localized leptomeningitis. (4) True peripheral mononeuritis, seen not only in the nerves distal to the ganglion but in the anterior nerve root both within the meninges and in the portion contiguous to the involved ganglion. Denny-Brown found at post-mortem examination of a case of "geniculate zoster" that the geniculate ganglion was not affected, though the facial nerve was involved in an inflammatory process.

In the patient of Thalheimer who died of encephalitis associated with herpes zoster, perivascular infiltrations were found in the cervical cord, brain-stem and lenticular nuclei but the substantia nigra was spared. In general the lesions were almost identical with those of epidemic encephalitis.

Clinical Features.—This disease is not uncommon in children and has been estimated to account for a little less than 1 per cent of all skin diseases in childhood. It occurs sporadically, as a rule, but a number of epidemics have been reported in the early summer and late autumn and it is sometimes possible to trace the infection to contact with another case.

The incubation period is usually between one and three weeks. The first symptom is usually pain which is accompanied by severe cutaneous hyperesthesia and corresponds in its distribution to one or more dermatomes. There is often slight fever and mild constitutional symptoms. The pain may be mild or very severe. After three or four days, or rarely as long as two weeks, a number of erythematous patches appear within the area of hyperesthesia and soon small vesicles filled with clear fluid develop upon this erythematous base. The vesicles soon become turbid and dry up, leaving crusted ulcerations. If secondary infection occurs, healing may be delayed and deep scars may occur. During the acute stages of the illness there may be very definite signs of meningeal irritation such as cervical rigidity and a positive Kernig's sign. The spinal fluid may contain an excess of lymphocytes and counts of over one hundred per cubic millimeter are recorded. The active phase of the disease lasts only a short time, usually a week or less. As a rule, the pain does not persist in children after the eruption has healed. The postherpetic neuralgia, which is so distressing in elderly patients, does not occur. Usually, the diagnosis may be made years after the illness by the presence of many clusters of small round scars and mild hyeresthesia corresponding to one or more dermatomes. It is of some interest that certain ganglia show a relative immunity to this disease. For example, we rarely find the eruption upon the extremities below the elbow or below the knee. As a rule, the lesions are found on the thorax, abdomen, neck, shoulders, thighs, buttocks or face. The lesions are usually unilateral and may involve from one to three dermatomes. More extensive eruptions are rare but in some cases a generalized cutaneous eruption resembling varicella appears some two or three days or more after the zoster. It is not very unusual for localized paralysis and atrophy of the muscles to develop. Such palsies are usually found in the muscles of the chest or abdomen corresponding to the distribution of the eruption. They are permanent in some instances. In a few cases zoster is associated with symptoms of irritation of the parietal peritoneum or pleura or even of the urinary bladder. R. Meyer *et al.* describe lesions in the bladder which are sometimes associated with neurogenic disorders of the bladder. Hiccough may occur in association

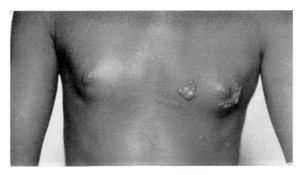

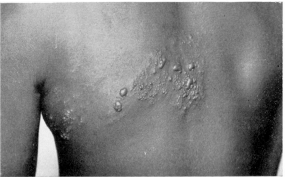

Fig. 146. Herpes zoster. Eruption is confined to the fifth thoracic dermatome.

with thoracic zoster. Arthritis is mentioned and it is stated that it is associated with swelling of the periarticular tissues and with troublesome limitation of movement.

Several cases of myelitis associated with zoster are described. These have usually been associated with myoclonus. Encephalitis is also mentioned and two fatal cases are reported. It is impossible to determine at present whether such cases represent encephalitis or myelitis due to the virus of herpes zoster or whether we are dealing with some other diseases of the nervous system which happen to be associated with symptomatic zoster.

The cranial nerves are not infrequently involved. The Gasserian ganglion is especially prone to this infection and the first branch of the fifth nerve is affected more frequently than the second or third. The eruption covers the upper eyelid, the conjunctiva and cornea and usually produces severe pain. As a result of the keratitis, there may be permanent scarring of the cornea. If severe anesthesia results, neuro-paralytic keratitis may ensue. Argyll Robertson pupil may result. We have seen one case of herpes zoster of the first division of the fifth nerve which was followed by the myotonic pupil described by Adie. In a few cases optic neuritis is associated with secondary atrophy and loss of vision. Paralysis of the third, fourth and sixth nerves is also described but is very rare. The third nerve is affected more often than the other nerves. It seems that the third nerve palsy is often delayed for a few weeks and that it is apt to regain function just as the seventh nerve does.

Any interesting type of facial palsy is associated with zoster of the concha of the ear, and of the external auditory canal and loss of taste. Less frequently the eruption is found over the anterior two-thirds of the tongue and the hard palate or the anterior pillars of the pharynx. Hunt has claimed that these symptoms are due to inflammation of the geniculate ganglion but Denny-Brown has shown that this is not always true. Rarely deafness and vertigo are associated. In some instances the herpetic facial palsy is mild and transient. In other cases it is severe and regeneration is slow. The crocodile syndrome may develop in such instances in association with other regeneration phenomena such as mass movements. Sometimes no regeneration occurs.

Engström and Wohlfart describe cases in which the 8th, 9th and 10th nerves were involved.

An attack of herpes zoster confers a degree of immunity but cases have been reported in which two or more attacks have occurred.

Diagnosis.—The eruption presents such a characteristic appearance that it may be recognized at sight, but it is sometimes very difficult to distinguish the primary type of the disease from the secondary or symptomatic type. The characteristics of the primary type have been described above and the presence of any signs or symptoms which cannot be reconciled with this picture should arouse suspicion of some other nervous disease.

Prognosis.—It is very unusual for any serious ill effects to persist from inflammation of the spinal ganglia. The palsies behave as do those of poliomyelitis and are apt to persist. Denny-Brown has shown that they are possibly due to damage to the anterior horn motor cells.

Herpes zoster of the Gasserian ganglion may cause permanent damage to the cornea and in some cases the facial palsy associated with "geniculate herpes" may persist. I have seen several cases of facial palsy associated with herpes of the ear which were followed by the development of the "syndrome of crocodile tears." After the facial nerve regenerated, there was profuse lacrimation from the homolateral eye whenever the patient took food in the mouth.

Treatment.—During the acute stage, the patient requires proper nursing care and analgesics may be needed for the pain. Every effort should be made to prevent infection of the vesicles which should be dusted with antiseptic powders. Aureomycin seems to prevent secondary infection and scarring.

BIBLIOGRAPHY

APPLEBAUM, E. *et al.*: Herpes zoster encephalitis. Am. J. Med., **32**:25, 1962.

BRAIN, W. R.: Zoster, varicella and encephalitis. Brit. M. J., 1:81, 1931.

BRUNELL, P. A. *et al.*: Herpes zoster in children. Amer. Jour. Dis. Child., **115**:422, 1968.

CARMODY, R. F.: Herpes zoster ophthalmicus complicated by ophthalmoplegia and exophthalmos. Arch. Ophth., **18**:707, 1937.

DENNY-BROWN, D., ADAMS, R. D. AND FITZGERALD, P. J.: Pathologic features of herpes zoster. A note on "geniculate herpes." Arch. Neurol. & Psychiat., **51**:216, 1944.

EDGERTON, A. E.: Herpes zoster ophthalmicus. Report of cases and review of the literature. Arch. Ophth., **34**:40, 1945.

ENGSTRÖM, H. AND WOHLFART, G.: Herpes zoster of the seventh, eighth, ninth and tenth cranial nerves. Arch. Neurol. & Psychiat., **62**:638, 1949.

GRANT, B. D.: Motor paralysis of extremities in herpes zoster. Bone and Joint Surg., **43**:885, 1961.

HEAD, H. AND CAMPBELL, A. W.: The pathology of herpes zoster. Brain, **23**:353, 1900.

HUNT, J. R.: The sensory field of the facial nerve; a further contribution to the symptomatology of the geniculate ganglion. Brain, **38**:418, 1915.

KENDELL, D.: Motor complications of herpes zoster. Brit. Med. Jour., 2:616, 1958.

LAWS, H. W.: Herpes zoster ophthalmicus complicated by contralateral hemiplegia. Arch. of Ophthal., **63**:273, 1960.

LIDSKY, M. D.: Herpes zoster encephalitis. Ann. Int. Med., **56**:779, 1962.

McALPINE, D. *et al.*: Acute demyelinizing disease complicating herpes zoster. Jour. Neurol. Neurosurg. and Psychiat., **22**:120, 1959.

McCORMICK, G. W.: Encephalitis associated with herpes zoster. J. Pediat., **30**:473, 1947.

MERSELIS, J. G. *et al.*: Disseminated herpes zoster. Arch. Int. Med., **113**:679, 1964.

MEYER, R. *et al.*: Herpes zoster involving the urinary bladder. New England J. Med., **260**:1062, 1959.

NACHMAN, A. R.: Neurologic complications of herpes zoster. Pediatrics, **7**:200, 1951.

PATON, L.: The trigeminal and its ocular lesions. Brit. J. Ophth., **10**:305, 1926.

SCHIFF, C. I. AND BRAIN, W. R.: Acute meningoencephalitis associated with herpes zoster. Lancet, 11:70, 1930.

SUGAR, O. AND BUCY, P. C.: Postherpetic trigeminal neuralgia. Arch. Neurol. & Psychiat., 65:131, 1951.

TAYLOR-ROBINSON, D.: Herpes zoster occurring in a patient with chickenpox. Brit. Med. Jour., 5187:1713, 1960.

THALHEIMER, W.: Herpes zoster: Central nervous system lesions similar to those of epidemic encephalitis. Arch. Neurol. & Psychiat., 12:73, 1924.

WALSH, F. B.: *Loc. cit.*

WELLER, T. H.: Varicella-Herpes Zoster Virus. Viral and Rickettsial Infections of Man. 4th Ed. Philadelphia, J. B. Lippincott Co., 1965.

WINKELMANN, R. K. *et al.*: Herpes zoster in children. J.A.M.A., 171:876, 1959.

NEURITIS OF THE FACIAL NERVE (OFTEN CALLED BELL'S PALSY)

Etiology.—In infants, Bell's palsy is rare and when it occurs is usually associated with otitis media due to common pyogenic organisms. In children, there is otitis in a fairly large percentage of all cases. In adults, otitis is rarely present but herpetic lesions may found in the external canal and the concha and possibly in other dermatomes. It seems, therefore, that bacterial infections are responsible sometimes in young persons and possibly viral infections, such as herpes zoster, in adults.

Dodge and Poskanzer tested the level of compliment-fixing antibody to varicella-zoster virus and also to herpes simplex virus in cases of Bell's palsy without vesicles. Their results were negative. Aitken and Brain found antibodies in nine patients to the varicella-zoster virus in cases of facial palsy associated with vesicles about the ear.

Pathological Anatomy.—Very few histological examinations have been made. These have shown a hemorrhagic interstitial neuritis involving that part of the nerve which lies in the temporal bone in close relation to the middle ear. Exploration has been performed in a number of cases and the nerve has been found to be swollen and inflamed.

Clinical Features.—As a rule, pain is the first symptom. This is localized usually in the ear but may radiate into the cheek or into the occiput. In some cases, the palsy precedes the pain. Within several hours or days it is noticed that the mouth is drawn to the opposite side and that the nasolabial fold is obliterated on the affected side. The eyelid cannot be closed. There may be some difficulty in forming labials and difficulty in eating due to accumulation of food in the cheek. Examination reveals loss of muscle tone on the affected side of the face. The forehead and cheek are smooth and relaxed. The patient is unable to wrinkle the forehead, close the eyelid or retract the corner of the mouth. All attempts at innervation make the weakness more apparent. Taste is often lost over the anterior two-thirds of the tongue. If the palsy is complete, the affected side of the face soon begins to sag and the lip and cheek may become edematous. The lower lid falls away from the bulbar conjunctiva and tears run down the cheek for the lacrimal punctum is no longer in position to collect them. These signs are not so evident in children as in adults. The nerve fibers which supply the lacrimal gland may be involved so the eye becomes dry and painful. As a rule, the pain ceases within a few days. At first the electrical reactions of the facial muscles are normal but after ten days partial or complete reaction of degeneration will be found if the nerve is undergoing degeneration. Bilateral facial paralysis is rare. Examinations of the ears, the nasal sinuses, the teeth as well as any other examinations which may be undertaken give, as a rule, negative results.

In most cases, signs of recovery appear within a few weeks. First there is some return of muscle tone and later power of movement develops. Recovery is apt to be prompt and complete if the palsy is partial. The prognosis is good if the electrical reactions remain normal. If paralysis has been complete and if reaction of degeneration is present, return of power is slow. In such cases, it is noted that when voluntary control returns, muscle tone is universally increased. Moreover, when the patient closes the affected eyelid, there is some movement of the mouth and forehead and conversely, showing the teeth causes narrowing of the palpebral fissure. In brief, it is impossible for the patient to innervate any part of the face without at the same time innervating all other muscles supplied by the facial nerve. Even the physiological blinking of the eyelid is associated with twitching of the mouth. These facts are most easily explained by the assumption that during the course of regeneration the motor fibers go astray and that certain fibers reach muscles which were formerly innervated by different fibers. For example, the effort to move the mouth results in the radiation of impulses into all parts of the face. It is apparent, therefore, that even after the nerve has regenerated, very definite disturbance of function may continue and striking asymmetry of the face may remain which is often erroneously interpreted as evidence of incomplete regeneration. It should be pointed out that the normal infant has mass movements of the face which should not be confused with the mass movements due to aberrant regeneration of the seventh nerve.

There is some variation in symptomatology, depending upon the site of the lesion. If the lesion is distal to the point at which the chorda tympani separates from the seventh nerve, taste is not affected. If the geniculate ganglion is involved, it is claimed that there is an herpetic eruption within the concha and external auditory canal. Certainly, the association of facial palsy with herpetic eruption in this region is not very rare. In some cases herpes zoster may be found over several cervical dermatomes at the same time, thus suggesting that we are dealing with true zoster and not symptomatic zoster. When the lesion is situated between the geniculate ganglion and the brain-stem, there is no overflow of tears for the lacrimal fibers are involved and the eye remains dry. The "syndrome of crocodile tears" may develop in such cases. In some instances after the facial nerve has regenerated the patient may notice a humming sound in the ear when the facial muscles are strongly contracted. This is, no doubt, due to straying of nerve fibers which formerly innervated the face into the stapedius muscle.

Diagnosis.—We may define Bell's palsy as a relatively benign type of facial nerve paralysis of obscure origin. Hence, the diagnosis must be made by exclusion. Syphilis should always be considered and the possibility of otitis and mastoiditis investigated. Tuberculous mastoiditis should be kept in mind and cholesteatoma of the temporal bone. Sarcoidosis may cause paralysis of the facial nerve especially in association with parotitis and uveitis. If the onset has been unusually slow, we should not forget to consider intracranial neoplasm, especially pontine glioma, neurofibroma and growths of the parotid gland. Bilateral facial palsies may occur in acute infectious polyneuritis. Bell's palsy is rare in infancy and facial paralysis at that age suggests the possibility of an intracranial neoplasm. Recurrent facial palsies may mark the onset of Melkersson's syndrome.

Prognosis.—If we can be relatively sure that the case belongs in the group under discussion, we may base the prognosis largely upon the severity of the lesion. The electrical reactions are of considerable value in this regard. If, after the palsy has been present two weeks, normal reactions are obtained, we may conclude in all probability that some return of function will appear within a short time and that recovery will be complete. If, on the other hand, there is a definite reaction of degeneration, it is certain that the return of function will be slow and that motility will not be quite normal if regeneration eventually becomes complete. Moreover, in a very few cases, regeneration fails to occur and the facial muscles atrophy completely, giving rise to extreme relaxation of the tissues and unsightly deformity.

The first sign of recovery is usually an improvement in muscle tone and often return of voluntary power precedes return of electrical irritability.

Treatment.—It is very doubtful whether treatment is of any value. Electrical stimulation or massage probably helps to improve the circulation but can have no influence upon regeneration. There is no proof that drugs are of any value. If the face is much relaxed, it may be supported by strips of adhesive. The eye should be protected by glasses when the patient is exposed to the wind and if the cornea becomes dry at night, it is probably best to keep the eyelid closed by a small pad. A saturated solution of boric acid may be used for conjunctivitis. If aberrant regeneration occurs, nothing can be done about it. In the British Isles otologists sometimes enlarge the bony canal because of the fear that swelling of the nerve may cause compression and interference with the circulation.

In the few cases in which the nerve fails to regenerate, it is possible to restore muscle tone by implanting some other motor nerve into the degenerated trunk of the facial nerve. The ninth, eleventh and twelfth have been employed. If such a procedure is contemplated, it should be carried out before the muscles have atrophied completely and by the end of the year if possible. British otologists sometimes place a nerve graft in the facial canal when the facial nerve has been destroyed in operation for mastoiditis.

Probably the presence of a response to galvanism may be regarded as evidence of the existence of muscle fibers. If the palsy is of very long duration and no muscle fibers are preserved, plastic surgery may diminish the deformity by turning back a strip of temporal muscle and attaching it to the angle of the mouth or by supporting the cheek by a subcutaneous strip of fascia or tantalum wire.

BIBLIOGRAPHY

AITKEN, R. S. AND BRAIN, R. T.: Facial palsy and infection with zoster virus. Lancet, **i**:19, 1933.
DODGE, P. R. AND POSKANZER, D. C.: Varicella-zoster and herpes simplex antibody responses in patients with Bell's palsy. Neurology, **12**:34, 1962.
HARRIS, W.: Neuritis and Neuralgia. London, Oxford Press, 1926.

MELKERSSON'S SYNDROME

This term is applied to a condition in which facial palsy of peripheral type is associated with swelling of the lips. In such cases there are repeated attacks of facial palsy which is apt to be bilateral though both sides may not be affected at the same time. Such palsies occur at intervals of several years, the first attack often occurring early in childhood.

These palsies seem to be severe and usually lead to degeneration of the nerve. In our experience there is always regeneration with mass movements and sometimes the syndrome of crocodile tears. In some instances, there is no particular swelling of the lips at the time of the paralysis. In other cases, the lips may swell coincidently with the onset of the paralysis and this swelling may persist for an indefinite period or it may recede gradually. Years after the paralysis has occurred the swelling may appear. If it recedes, it may recur repeatedly with or without the facial palsy. In most instances, the swelling is restricted to the lips. In some instances, however, the tongue, cheek and even the eyelids may be involved. A congenitally furrowed tongue is often seen in such cases. Two cases have been observed in one family. I believe that this diagnosis should be considered whenever repeated facial palsies of obscure origin are seen in a child. The facial swelling may not occur until several years later.

In the case of a young woman whom we have examined recently, the onset of the swelling was always marked by sudden, brief elevation of temperature to 103°F. or 104°F. She had had four attacks of facial palsy as a child and residua were evident on both sides of the face in the form of mass movements. Fever has not been present in other cases we have observed and is not mentioned in the literature.

The cause of this condition is quite obscure. The swelling of the lips has been attributed to angioneurotic edema. Plastic surgery is recommended when the swelling persists.

BIBLIOGRAPHY

KETTEL, K.: Melkersson's syndrome with report of five cases. Arch. Otol., **46**:341, 1947.

KUNSTADTER, R. H.: Melkersson's syndrome. Amer. Jour. Dis. Child., **110**:559, 1965.

LAYMAN, C. W.: Cheilitis granulomatosa and Melkersson-Rosenthal syndrome. Arch. Dermatol., **83**:112, 1961.

NEW, G. AND KIRCH, W. A.: Permanent enlargement of the lips and face associated with facial paralysis. J.A.M.A., **100**:1230, 1933.

SCOTT, G. A.: Melkersson's syndrome. Brit. Jour. Clin. Pract., **18**:415, 1964.

STEVENS, H.: Melkersson's syndrome. Neurology, **15**:263, 1965.

BENIGN SIXTH NERVE PALSIES IN CHILDREN

Knox, Clark and Schuster have described benign sixth nerve palsies in children. Twelve cases were studied during a 12 year period. The children were between the ages of 18 months and 15 years. It was suspected that a systemic viral disease was responsible in some cases and otitis media was suspected in other cases. All but two patients had had fever or respiratory tract illnesses one to three weeks before the onset of the abducens palsy. In all but one case the palsy began to clear up within three to six weeks and had disappeared by ten weeks. In one case nine months were required for complete recovery. The authors excluded all cases in which any abnormalities other than the sixth nerve palsy was present.

BIBLIOGRAPHY

KNOX, D. L., CLARK, D. B. AND SCHUSTER, F. F.: Benign sixth nerve palsies in children. Pediatrics, **40**:560, 1967.

OPSOCLONUS BODY TREMULOUSNESS AND BENIGN ENCEPHALITIS

Cogan describes a syndrome occurring after an illness resembling influenza with opsoclonus sometimes with blinking of the eyes, nystagmus, tremulous movements of the head, extremities and body, ataxia and myoclonus. There is headache, stiffness of the neck and an excess of cells in the spinal fluid. No virus has been demonstrated. The prognosis is good. Complete recovery occurs within a few weeks.

BIBLIOGRAPHY

COGAN, D. G.: Opsoclonus, body tremulousness and benign encephalitis. Arch. of Ophthal., **79**:545, 1968.

ACUTE LYMPHOCYTIC CHORIOMENINGITIS

Definition.—A type of meningitis due to a specific virus of acute onset, of brief course and favorable outcome characterized by a predominantly lymphocytic pleocytosis in the spinal fluid and by the absence of bacteria (Wallgren).

Etiology.—Rivers and Scott have shown that the spinal fluid contains a virus which produces meningitis in mice and other experimental animals. This virus is apparently identical with that discovered by Armstrong and Lillie in experimental animals. It is believed that the common house mouse develops the disease spontaneously and acts as a reservoir for the infection. This virus meningitis is known as choriomeningitis.

Baird and Rivers have shown that the virus cannot be found in every case of benign lymphocytic meningitis and it is difficult or impossible to differentiate by clinical means alone between the cases caused by the virus and those in which the virus cannot be demonstrated. A second virus meningitis giving rise to the same clinical picture has been discovered. This is termed pseudochoriomeningitis.

Pathological Anatomy.—Very few post-morten examinations have been made. Viets and Shields found lymphocytic infiltration of the meninges with slight involvement of the brain in one fatal case. Farmer and Janeway state that this disease is always a generalized infection and that interstitial pneumonia and necroses in the liver are invariably found at post-mortem examination.

Clinical Features.—This disease has been observed in almost all parts of the world. If one may judge from the number of cases reported in recent years, it is not uncommon. It appears, as a rule, in small epidemics but sporadic cases of identical nature are seen from time to time. Multiple cases in a family are not uncommon. I have seen four cases in a family of five children. Komrower *et al.* describe a case in the newborn baby of a mother who was also infected.

The clinical picture is singularly uniform. No age group is exempt but children are most frequently affected. The systemic phase of the disease is marked by an illness resembling influenza. This may terminate in a few days without the appearance of any neurological symptoms. Such cases are believed to constitute a large percentage of all infections with this virus. In other instances, meningitis follows in a few days. The onset is relatively abrupt and marked by headache, fever and vomiting. The usual signs of meningeal irritation such as cervical rigidity, Kernig's sign, hyperesthesia and dermatographism are always well marked and may be very severe. There is no tendency to somnolence in most cases but, on the contrary, there is irritability, insomnia and intense restlessness. The child often seems to be alarmingly ill despite the benign nature of the disease. In young children there may be convulsions. There may be mild papilledema or congestion of the optic nerve heads and in some cases sixth nerve palsies are described but, as a rule, the cranial nerves are spared and there are no signs of cortical injury. Nystagmus is mentioned by several writers. Palsies of the extremities are rare but Finlay *et al.* describe two cases in which paraplegia occurred. In some instances the throat is infected or inflamed but, as a rule, no evidence of infection outside of the nervous system can be found. The fever may reach 102°F. or 103°F. It is continuous or remittent. It usually ends by lysis at the end of the first week but may last two weeks or no more than two or three days.

The spinal fluid findings are characteristic. There is always increased pressure but, as a rule, the fluid is clear or at most faintly opalescent. Rarely it is definitely cloudy. The cell count ranges from 50 to 1,500. During the first few days the leucocytes may be predominant but later mononuclear cells constitute about 90 per cent of the total count. In many cases, however, the pleocytosis is of mononuclear type from the beginning. Film formation is rare but is described. The sugar and chloride content remain high, being either normal or nearly normal, thus constituting a helpful point in the differential diagnosis. It is said that the pleocytosis may persist to some degree for weeks after clinical recovery has occurred but as a rule the cell count drops to normal during the second or third week.

Howard has described two cases of fulminating hemorrhagic encephalitis with gross damage to the brain and spinal cord. The process involved proliferation of the vascular endothelium, and cellular infiltration of the vessels with hemorrhage and necrosis. The choroid plexuses were not involved and the meninges showed only focal accumulations of cells. The virus of choriomeningitis was demonstrated by the inoculation of guinea pigs. Colmore has collected 24 cases in which the process was severe. In 12 instances the patient died.

Diagnosis.—The clinical picture is not characteristic. The diagnosis is based upon the character of the spinal fluid findings, especially the predominance of mononuclear cells, the relatively high sugar and chloride content, the absence of any demonstrable organisms, upon the brief course and favorable outcome of the disease and upon the absence of otitis, mastoiditis, septic sore throat and other infections. The occurrence of other cases in the same locality strengthens the diagnosis. Farmer and Janeway state that three considerations are important in differentiating this condition from other types of lymphocytic meningitis. (1) A history of contact with mice. (2) Influenza like prodromata. (3) A cell count of over 600 in the spinal fluid. The virus can be demonstrated in the spinal fluid, according to Rivers, only during the first 10 days of the illness. After the 6th week of the disease, the patient's blood serum contains antibodies which will protect experimental animals from the virus. The presence of such antibodies in the serum is not diagnostic, apparently, for Armstrong found them in 11 per cent of individuals who gave no history of meningitis. The demonstration of a rising titer of antibodies during the first 6 weeks of convalescence should be conclusive, however. Non-paralytic cases of poliomyelitis may give rise to an almost identical clinical picture. Tuberculous meningitis is often differentiated with difficulty because of the similarity of the cellular reaction in the spinal fluid but in this condition the sugar and chloride content slowly fall and the course is steadily progressive to a fatal outcome. Mumps may produce lymphocytic meningitis without parotitis which may be confused with the condition under consideration unless the child is known to have been exposed to mumps. Other causes of lymphocytic meningitis such as herpes simplex, Coxsackie viruses, and infectious mononucleosis must be kept in mind. In the same way Weil's disease occasionally is manifest by lymphocytic meningitis and jaundice is absent. Epidemic encephalitis, especially the St. Louis type, may also be confused with benign lymphocytic meningitis although there is usually enough evidence of injury to the central nervous system to make the differential diagnosis.

Prognosis.—The outlook is very favorable for complete recovery. Sequelae are very rare. In one or two cases mental defect and epilepsy are said to have resulted.

Treatment.—No specific drugs are available for none of the sulfonamides or the new antibiotics seem to be effective against viruses.

BIBLIOGRAPHY

ADAIR, C., GAUL, R. AND SMADEL, J.: Aseptic meningitis. A disease of diverse etiology. Ann. Int. Med., **39:**675, 1953.

ARMSTRONG, C. AND DICKENS, P. F.: Benign lymphocytic choriomeningitis, a new disease entity. Pub. Health Rep., **50:**381, 1935.

———— AND LILLIE, R. D.: Experimental lymphocytic choriomeningitis of monkeys and mice produced by a virus encountered in study of the 1933 St. Louis epidemic of encephalitis. Pub. Health Rep., **49:**1019, 1934.

———— AND SWEET, L. K.: Lymphocytic choriomeningitis. Report of two cases with recovery of virus from gray mice trapped in two infected households. Pub. Health Rep., **54:**673, 1939.

BAIRD, R. D. AND RIVERS, T. M.: Relation of lymphocytic choriomeningitis to acute aseptic meningitis (Wallgren). Am. Pub. Health, **28:**47, 1938.

COLMORE, J. P.: Severe infections with the virus of choriomeningitis. J.A.M.A., **148:**1199, 1952.

DUMMER, C. M., LYON, R. A. AND STEVENSON, F. E.: Benign lymphocytic meningitis. J.A.M.A., **108:**633, 1937.

FARMER, T. W. AND JANEWAY, C. A.: Infection with the virus of choriomeningitis. Medicine, **21:**1, 1942.

FINLAY, G. M., ALCOCK, N. S. AND STERN, R. O.: The virus aetiology of one form of lympho-cytic meningitis. Lancet, 1:650, 1936.

HOWARD, M. E.: Infection with the virus of choriomeningitis in man. Yale J. Biol. & Med., 13:161, 1940.

KOMROWER, G. M., WILLIAMS, B. L. AND STONES, P. B.: Lymphocytic choriomeningitis in the newborn. Probable transplacental infection. Lancet, 1:697, 1956.

MacCALLUM, F. O., FINDLAY, C. M. AND SCOTT, T. M.: Pseudolymphocytic choriomeningitis. Brit. J. Exp. Pathol., 20:260, 1939.

RIVERS, T. M. AND, SCOTT, T. F. M.: Meningitis in man caused by a filterable virus. J. Exp. Med., 63:415, 1936.

VIETS, H. R. AND SHIELDS, W.: Acute lymphocytic meningitis. J.A.M.A., 108:375, 1937.

WALLGREN, A.: Une nouvelle maladie infectieuse du system nerveux central. Acta paediat., 4:158, 1925.

WARREN, J.: Lymphocytic Choriomeningitis Virus. Viral and Rickettsial Infections of Man. Edited by Horsfall, F. L. and Tamm, I. J. B. Lippincott Co. 4th Ed. 1965, p. 1166.

CHRONIC LYMPHOCYTIC MENINGITIS OF UNKNOWN ORIGIN

Definition.—A chronic lymphocytic meningitis of unknown origin and relapsing course.

Etiology.—The cause is unknown, but common bacteria seem to be ex-cluded. Skogland and Baker found antibodies in the blood serum against the virus of acute choriomeningitis in one case. We have been unable to demonstrate such antibodies in several cases.

Pathological Anatomy.—Baker describes the pathological changes in a fatal case. There were signs of a chronic meningoencephalitis and pro-nounced thickening of the meninges.

Clinical Features.—The onset is not marked by any alarming features. Headache and fever are usually the presenting symptoms. Signs of menin-geal irritation are present but not severe. The patient is not always ill enough to be confined to bed. The spinal fluid contains from 100 to 800 lymphocytes per cmm. The protein is greatly increased and may exceed 200 mgs per 100 cc. The spinal fluid sugar is low and may fall below 15 mgs per 100 cc. The blood shows only moderate leucocytosis. Physical signs re-ferable to the nervous system are mild and transient. Diplopia, tremor, nys-tagmus, increased tendon reflexes and transient Babinski sign are men-tioned. Mental processes may be slow and uncertain and delirium may occur.

The course is prolonged varying from several months to more than a year. The fever and cell count in the spinal fluid slowly decline. The pro-tein content of the fluid remains high for long periods and the sugar stays low. Exacerbations occur in certain cases at intervals of six or eight weeks. After the active symptoms have ceased the patients may be slow to regain their strength and vigor.

Treatment.—No specific treatment is known.

Prognosis.—In some cases the patients had not regained their health when the report was made a year or more after the onset. Others are known to be entirely well. Baker's case was fatal.

Diagnosis.—The diagnosis is made upon the clinical features described above and above all by the exclusion of other diseases such as tuberculous meningitis, torula infection, syphilis and other chronic infections of the meninges.

CASE HISTORY (Ped. 94733).—*Child of 4 years with chronic lymphocytic meningitis. Fever, signs of meningeal irritation and systemic symptoms slowly disappeared in the course of 2 months. The spinal fluid findings persisted for more than 5 months and there was still an increase of protein in the spinal fluid at the end of 15 months. Complete recovery.*

A. M. H., a colored girl of 4 years, was brought into the hospital on December 5, 1939. She had complained of headache for several weeks and had vomited repeatedly. Examination revealed evidences of recent loss of weight, fever ranging up to 103.2°F. and mild signs of meningeal irritation. The spinal fluid contained 470 cells of which 58 per cent were polymorphonuclear leucocytes, increased protein content and diminished sugar. Other examinations were negative.

During the next 30 days, the temperature rose to 103°F. on several occasions and then slowly fell to normal in the course of the next four or five days. In the next month similar rises of temperature occurred but these never exceeded 101°F. The child's general condition improved. She gained weight and the signs of meningeal irritation gradually disappeared. The alterations of the spinal fluid persisted. The polymorphonuclear leucocytes were replaced by lymphocytes. At the end of the second month the spinal fluid contained 508 lymphocytes per cmm and the Pandy reaction was 3 plus.

On February 6, 1940, approximately two months after the onset of the illness, the child was brought to Harriet Lane Home. Medical and neurological examinations were quite negative at that time. The child was kept under observation until April 25, 1940. During this period she remained free of symptoms and her temperature was normal. The cell count of the spinal fluid slowly decreased and shortly before discharge there were only 210 lymphocytes per cmm. The protein was 300 mgs per 100 cc. Sugar was at times as low as 59 mgs per 100 cc.

The patient was then followed in the out-patient department. Her health remained excellent. The spinal fluid on February 27, 1941, showed only 3 lymphocytes per 100 cc but the Pandy was still positive.

During her stay in the hospital a great many laboratory studies were made. Numerous Wassermann tests of the blood serum and spinal fluid were negative. Tuberculin tests were likewise negative. Guinea pig inoculations were ineffective. The serum was tested for agglutinins against all common bacteria with negative results. No antibodies against acute choriomeningitis were present. Cultures on many media were uniformly negative, and no organisms could be demonstrated by careful examination of stained smears of the spinal fluid.

BIBLIOGRAPHY

BAKER, A. B.: Chronic lymphocytic choriomeningitis. J. Neuropath. & Exp. Neurol., **6:**253, 1947.

SKOLAND, J. E. AND BAKER, A. B.: An unusual form of lymphocytic choriomeningitis. Arch. Neurol. & Psychiat., **42:**507, 1939.

VOGT, H.: Chronische Verlaufsform der bénignen lymphocytären Meningitis. Arch. f. klin. Med., **183:**501, 1938-39.

MUMPS MENINGOENCEPHALITIS

Etiology.—Mumps is due to a virus infection. The virus belongs to the family of myxoviruses in which the virus of measles and influenza also are included.

Pathological Anatomy.—Few adequate studies have been made of the anatomical changes in the nervous system. Almost all observers are agreed that in *meningitis* there is outspoken congestion and lymphocytic infiltration of the meninges. In some cases, polymorphonuclear cells have predominated. Various observers described the exudate as being gelatinous, fibrinous or purulent. Since the virus may be found in the spinal fluid it seems clear that this is a true virus meningitis.

Less is known of the anatomical changes found in mumps *encephalitis*. Bien mentions sharply defined areas of myelin destruction in the cerebral white matter with accumulation of fat-laden phagocytes in the perivascular spaces, but his description is scarcely full enough to establish the nature of the process. Wegelin has made a careful study of the nervous system of a child who died on the eighteenth day with typical symptoms of meningoencephalitis. He describes a rather intense inflammatory process with infiltrations of the perivascular spaces with lymphocytes and phagocytes, perivascular hemorrhages, perivascular demyelination, phagocytic alterations of the microglia and proliferation of the macroglia. The neurons showed only mild chromatolysis. The process was most intense in the brain-stem, especially around the aqueduct, the substantia nigra and the dorsal part of the medulla, but milder changes were found in all parts of the brain and spinal cord. Donohue reports a third study which revealed perivascular demyelination identical in all essentials with that found in measles. In 1955, Donohue added two more post-mortem studies in which perivascular myelinoclasis was found. Possibly cases such as Donohue describes are not due to local action of the virus but represent a different process similar to measles encephalitis.

Dr. J. R. Lindsay has examined the labyrinth of a patient who lost hearing after mumps. He found changes in the cochlear duct, with degeneration of the stria vascularis, organ of Corti, and the tectorial membrane of the basal coil. There was some degeneration of the peripheral cochlear neurons of the lower basal coil. Less severe changes were found in the vestibular system.

Nothing is known of the anatomical basis of the myelitis.

An interstitial inflammation is found in the salivary glands especially the parotid gland. Orchitis is often present in boys who have reached puberty. In girls the ovaries or breasts may be involved. Pancreatitis is rare but well known. In rare instances, the prostate, liver, spleen, thyroid, kidneys and heart may be involved.

Clinical Features.—Mumps may develop in persons of any age but it is somewhat more common in childhood than in adult life. The two sexes are affected with equal frequency but neurological complications are said to develop three times as frequently in males as in females. There is a great variation in the frequency with which the nervous system is involved. In some epidemics, almost all patients have shown evidence of a meningeal reaction but Brooks reports 1,059 cases at Camp Upton without a single instance of this type. Other estimates range between 1 per cent and 25 per cent. There seems to be no doubt that neurological disturbances are more frequent in epidemics, and especially in severe epidemics, than in the sporadic form of the disease.

In most instances, the neurological symptoms appear when the parotitis is at its height but they may be delayed until convalescence or may actually precede the parotitis. In an analysis of 19 cases of meningitis, Tailliens states that neurological complications developed after the parotitis was established in 10 cases; at the same time in 4 cases, and before in 5 cases. In the writer's experience, the cerebral symptoms have often developed coincidently with orchitis. We must also state that parotisis is not necessary for development of mumps meningitis. Wallgren has pointed out that the siblings or associates of children who are suffering from typical mumps may develop the usual meningeal symptoms without any clinical evidence of parotitis or orchitis. Serological studies have revealed that acute lymphocytic meningitis in children without parotitis is often due to the mumps virus.

The onset of mumps *"meningitis"* is marked by headache, drowsiness and vomiting which is followed by a sharp rise of temperature and in severe cases by stupor and convulsions. Signs of meningeal irritation are prominent and there is almost always well-marked cervical rigidity, Kernig's sign, tâche cérébrale, photophobia and hyperesthesia. The pupils may be dilated and are often unequal. The pulse is slow, as a rule. Such acute symptoms are of brief duration in most cases. Within a few days the child grows brighter, the meningeal signs diminish and disappear and recovery is complete within two weeks or more. In such cases a diagnosis of meningitis is made. Deafness is a well-known complication. It is discussed below.

In other cases, evidences of invasion of the brain or of the cranial nerves appear and the diagnosis of *"encephalitis"* is then made. Such cases are rare. The seventh nerve is involved with relative frequency. This may be due to extension of the inflammation from the parotid gland so as to involve the nerve in its peripheral course but in other cases it must be due to an intracranial lesion. The sixth nerve is not infrequently involved on one or both sides and the third nerve may also be affected. Cases of optic atrophy are described. Most of the cranial nerve lesions are of peripheral type but the writer has seen suprasegmental facial palsy and partial paralysis of the third nerve which seemed to be of nuclear type. Hemiplegia, hemianopia, hemianesthesia, conjugate deviation of the eyes, chorea, myoclonus and ataxia of cerebellar type are described but all of these are rare. In even the relatively severe cases in which definite signs of cerebral damage are seen, there is a strong tendency to recovery within a short time. Occasionally signs of cerebral damage or cranial nerve palsies may persist for months or may be even permanent. Prolonged deliria and personality disturbances with misbehavior such as occurs in epidemic encephalitis have been described in a few instances.

In exceptionally severe cases, such as are described in epidemics, the onset may be fulminating or even apoplectic so that the patient becomes unconscious within a very short time and dies within a day or more.

In many cases of mumps, the meningeal process is asymptomatic and is recognized only by changes in the spinal fluid.

The blood usually shows a relative lymphocytosis which may be compensated by a slight leucopenia so that the total white count may be normal or moderately increased. The spinal fluid in meningitis is under increased pressure and, as a rule, clear and colorless although cloudy or opalescent fluid is descibed. There is almost always a definite pleocytosis reaching several hundred cells or more. Counts up to 3,000 have been reported. The cells are usually all lymphocytes but there may be a few leucocytes as well and in exceptional cases leucocytes may predominate. The globulin reaction is positive but not strongly positive as a rule. In a few cases there has been enough fibrin present to form a film. The cells disappear from the fluid very slowly and the count usually returns to normal at about the end of the sixth week. In mumps encephalitis the cell count in the spinal fluid may be much lower and counts of 10 to 50 cells per cmm are reported.

Several cases of *myelitis* have been reported although no post-mortem examinations have been made. McKaig and Woltman describe the case of a girl of 16 years who developed paralysis and anesthesia below the second rib, loss of sphincter control and loss of all reflexes. These symptoms appeared for about a month after the onset of an attack of mumps. The spinal fluid contained only four cells and a little globulin. There was no improvement in the patient's condition after nineteen months. A similar case was published by Warrington. The lesions extended up to the level of the fifth cervical segment and the patient died, presumably of paralysis of respiration. In our case the patient made a substantial recovery.

In another small group of cases, the picture has resembled that of *polyneuritis* although McKaig and Woltman suggest that meningoradiculitis is a more probable diagnosis. In such cases there is usually paralysis of all four extremities but not of the trunk. There is no disturbance of sphincter control and, as a rule, no actual loss of cutaneous sensibility or tenderness of the muscles or nerves. The tendon reflexes are lost. Cranial nerve palsies are sometimes seen. Both facial nerves, the sixth, tenth and twelfth nerves have been affected in such cases. The diaphragm may be paralysed. These conditions develop somewhat later than the more common meningitis and have not been associated with a pleocytosis in the spinal fluid. Unless the patient dies of paralysis of respiration, complete recovery is to be expected. Cases of this type have been reported by Collens and Rabinowitz, Thompson and Revilliod. Holt mentions a similar case.

One or two cases of *local paralysis* with atrophy of the muscles and loss of reflexes have been reported. In a case mentioned by Dopter, the paralysis involved the muscles supplied by the fifth and sixth cervical segments and in a case of Janbon *et al.,* the paralysis was confined to the eighth cervical and first thoracic myotomes and there was paralysis of the cervical sympathetic nerve as well. Lennette describes similar local palsies. It is uncertain whether the lesions in such cases are in the spinal nerve roots or in the gray matter of the cord.

Deafness is a relatively common sequel of mumps. In most cases hearing is completely and permanently destroyed but in only about one-fourth of all cases are both ears affected. This complication develops, as a rule, during the first two weeks of the illness. It may be associated with meningitis or may represent the only evidence of involvement of the nervous system. In perhaps half of these cases, the hearing is suddenly lost without warning and no symptoms of irritation of the eighth nerve are present, but in other cases the onset is marked by tinnitus, vertigo, nystagmus, nausea and vomiting. The nystagmus, vertigo, nausea and vomiting last only a short time. The lack of equilibrium may persist for two months. The deafness, tinnitus and loss of vestibular reflexes may persist. Cases have been described in which deafness developed without mumps in children who had been exposed to mumps and it is thought that deafness may occur without parotitis just as meningitis may. It is believed by most authorities that an inflammatory process develops in the labyrinth, perhaps by extension along the eighth nerve from the meninges. It has been estimated that nearly 5 per cent of all deaf mutes owe their condition to an attack of mumps in childhood. Mumps keratitis occurs, in some instances, between the second and the eleventh day and usually affects only one eye. It is apt to clear up within one to four weeks.

The optic nerve may be affected. Cases of *optic neuritis,* neuro-retinitis, retrobulbar neuritis, papilledema and optic atrophy have been reported. Hydrocephalus is mentioned as a sequel of mumps by Sicard who attributed it to obliteration of the subarachnoid spaces by meningitis. Holowach claims that maternal mumps may cause chorioretinitis in the fetus.

Diagnosis.—The diagnosis depends upon the development of meningitis, deafness or other neurological syndromes described above, during or within a few weeks after the attack of mumps. Obviously, other coincidental conditions such as non-paralytic poliomyelitis, spirochetal meningitis, tuberculous meningitis, brain abscess and otitis media with mastoiditis or purulent labyrinthitis must also be kept in mind. If the child develops such symptoms without parotitis, it scarcely seems possible to establish the diagnosis on clinical grounds with certainty. The diagnosis can be established by showing a rising titer of antibodies during convalescence. A large percentage of cases of lymphocytic meningitis are found to be due to mumps when complement-fixation tests are employed. The virus may be isolated from the urine, saliva and spinal fluid often as early as the second day and culture on kidney cell tissue will permit a positive diagnosis within about three days.

Prognosis.—The outlook in meningitis is very favorable. The mortality is very low and complete recovery may be expected. Even where there are definite signs of cerebral lesions or paralysis of the cranial nerves, as in mumps encephalitis, recovery usually but not always ensues within a few weeks. In the so-called polyneuritis, death may result from paralysis of respiration but if the child survives, recovery is usually complete. In two cases which have been diagnosed ascending myelitis, there has been no improvement and death resulted in one. In our case abstracted below there was remarkable improvement. The prognosis is unfavorable in the deafness associated with mumps.

Treatment.—A live attenuated mumps virus vaccine has now been developed which produces immunity. A hyperimmune globulin has some value. Cortisone may reduce the severity of orchitis.

CASE HISTORY (U-135412).—*Complete transverse myelitis at T 4 appearing about 10 days after the onset of mumps and advancing slowly for two weeks in a girl of 15 years. Subsequent improvement.*

M. T. H. L., a previously healthy girl of 15 years, developed pain and swelling in the parotid regions on both sides on March 11, 1938. She had only a little headache and mild fever and stayed in bed only two days. She seemed to be quite well for a few days and then on March 21 she noticed that her feet were growing numb. During the next 10 days the numbness slowly ascended and her legs grew weak so that within a few days she could not walk. She soon became incontinent of urine and feces. There was never any pain in the back or legs. No headache and no vomiting. Temperature was normal.

Examination on April 5 revealed complete paralysis of the legs, abdominal and lower intercostal muscles. The cranial nerves were normal and the arms were not affected. Cutaneous anesthesia extended up to the nipple line and to a corresponding level behind. The knee and ankle jerks were present but diminished. No clonus. Bilateral extensor response on plantar stimulation. Complete incontinence.

The laboratory studies were quite negative except for the changes in the spinal fluid. This contained 100 lymphocytes per cmm and 37 mgs total protein. The Wassermann reaction was negative. The manometric tests showed no obstruction of the subarachnoid spaces. Roentgenograms of the spine and chest negative. The urine contained only a few white cells.

On April 7, the chest was weaker and the intercostals scarcely moved at all so respiration was slightly labored. Articulation was indistinct and swallowing difficult. The tongue deviated to the right. This date apparently marked the height of the paralysis for afterwards there was gradual improvement. On April 11, the chest was stronger and the bulbar symptoms had disappeared. The legs could be moved slightly and the tendon reflexes were becoming exaggerated. There was bilateral ankle clonus. The spinal fluid contained only 55 cells. On May 1, the bladder had become automatic. There was some power in all the muscles of the legs but the patient could not lift them from the bed. May 29, the patient could walk with some difficulty. There was good strength at all joints in the left leg. The right leg was somewhat weak at the hip and knee and almost completely paralysed at the ankle. Aside from a zone of anesthesia over the outer aspect of the right leg and foot the sensory disturbances had disappeared. The patient had regained control of the bladder. The spinal fluid still contained 25 lymphocytes per cmm. Discharged.

January 1939 the patient was reported to be recovered except for inability to dorsiflex the right ankle.

CASE HISTORY.—*Mumps at 2 years with bilateral swelling of the parotid glands and bilateral facial paralysis.*

R. D., a previously healthy child of 2 years, developed a fever of 101°F. of only 2 days duration. Both parotid glands became swollen and painful. At the height of the swelling of the glands, bilateral facial paralysis developed. This was of peripheral type. The child had been exposed to mumps shortly before the illness.

On examination 3 weeks after this illness, the child displayed incomplete bilateral facial paralysis. The salivary glands were not swollen or tender. No evidence of sarcoidosis could be found.

BIBLIOGRAPHY

AZIMI, P. H. *et al.:* Mumps meningoencephalitis in children. Jour. Amer. Med. Ass., **207:**509, 1969.

BIEN, G.: Encephalitis and mumps. Jahrb. f. Kinderh., **78:**619, 1913.

BRUYN, H. B., SEXTON, H. M. AND BRAINERD, H. D.: Mumps meningoencephalitis. California Med., **86:**153, 1957.

CASPARIS, H. R.: Cerebral complications of mumps. Am. J. Dis. Child., **28:**187, 1919.

COLLENS, W. S. AND RABINOWITZ, M. A.: Mumps polyneuritis, quadriplegia with bilateral facial paralysis. Arch. Int. Med., **41:**61, 1928.

DAVIDSON, W. L. *et al.:* Vaccination of adults with live attenuated mumps virus vaccine. Jour. Amer. Med. Ass., **201:**995, 1967.

DIENHARDT, F.: Mumps. Med. Sci. May 25, 1962, p. 827.

DONOHUE, W. L.: Pathology of mumps encephalitis. J. Pediat., **19:**42, 1941.

————, PLAYFAIR, F. D. AND WHITAKER, L.: Mumps encephalitis. Pathology and pathogenesis. J. Pediat., **47:**395, 1955.

FALK, W.: Mumps meningoencephalitis in children. Acta med. orient., **11:**220, 1952.

FEILING, A.: Mumps, a critical review. Quart. J. Med., **8:**255, 1914-15.

GRAZIA, G.: Neurologic complications in epidemic parotitis. Clin. Pediat., **43:**767, 1961.

HENDERSON, W.: Mumps meningoencephalitis. Lancet, **i:**386, 1952

HENLE, W. AND ENDERS, J. F.: Mumps Virus. Viral and Rickettsial Infections of Man. Edited by Horsfall, F. L. and Tamm, I. J. B. Lippincott Co., 4th Ed., 1965, p. 755.

HILLEMAN, M. R. *et al.:* Live attenuated mumps virus vaccine. New Engl. Jour. Med., **278:**227, 1968.

HOLOWACH, J.: Fetal chorioretinitis associated with maternal mumps. J. Pediat., **50:**689, 1957.

HOWARD, T.: Meningo-encephalitis as the only manifestation of mumps. Report of three cases. Am. J. Med. Sc., **158:**685, 1919.

HUBBARD, T.: Nerve deafness and mumps. Tr. Am. Otol. Soc., **13:**451, 1915.

JOHNSON, C. D. AND GOODPASTURE, E. W.: An investigation of the etiology of mumps. J. Exp. Med., **69:**1, 1934.

KRAVIS, L., SIGEL, M. AND HENLE, G.: Mumps meningoencephalitis with special reference to the use of complement fixation test in diagnosis. Pediatrics, **8:**204, 1955.

LENNETTE, E. H. *et al.:* Mumps virus infection simulating paralytic poliomyelitis. Pediatrics, **25:**788, 1960.

LEWIS, J. M. AND UTZ, J. P.: Orchitis, parotitis and meningoencephalitis. New England Med. Jour., **265:**776, 1961.

McKAIG, C. B. AND WOLTMAN, H. W.: Neurologic complications of epidemic parotitis. Report of a case of parotitis myelitis. Arch. Neurol. & Psychiat., **31:**794, 1934.

McKENZIE, D.: Labyrinthine deafness. Brit. Med. J., **2:**867, 1923.

MURRAY, H. G. *et al.:* Mumps meningoencephalitis. Brit. Med. Jour., **5189:**1850, 1960.

PADDOCK, B. W.: Mumps associated with meningitis in identical twins. Am. J. Dis. Child., **44:**565, 1932.

PITRES, A. ET MARCHAND, L.: Polynevrite post-ourlienne quadriplégique à forme pseudo-tabétique. Progrès. méd., 1922, p. 397.

RUSSELL, R. R. AND DONALD, J. C.: The neurologic complications of mumps. Brit. Med. Jour., **5087:**27, 1958.

SCHWARZ, G. A.: Meningoencephalomyelitis with epidemic parotitis. Arch. Neurol., **11:**453, 1964.

SICARD, J. A.: Hydrocéphalie acquise par méningite ourlienne. Rev. Neurol., **22:**706, 1914.

TAILLIENS, J.: La méningite ourlienne. Rev. Méd. de la Suisse Rom., **48:**420, 1928.

UTZ, J. P. *et al.:* The rapid diagnosis of mumps. New England J. Med., **257:**497, 1957.

WALLGREN, A.: Méningite ourlienne sans oreillons. Acta Paed., **6:**53, 1926-27.

WALSH, F. B.: *Loc. cit.*
WARRINGTON, W. B.: Acute generalized infective paralysis in adults. Clin. J., **43**:296, 1914.
WEGELIN, C.: Ueber Meningoencephalitis bei Mumps. Schweiz. med. Wochschr., **65**:249, 1935.
WOODWARD, J. H.: The ocular complications of mumps. Ann. Ophth., **16**:7, 1907.

ACUTE ENCEPHALITIS DUE TO THE VIRUS OF HERPES SIMPLEX

Definition.—Rare cases of fulminating and fatal encephalitis and more numerous cases of less severe meningoencephalitis are now believed to be due to the virus of herpes simplex.

Innes *et al.* state that a herpetic-like virus is found in Burkitt's lymphoma which causes a destructive process in experimental animals identical with herpetic encephalitis in children.

Pathological Anatomy.—Haymaker has shown that this disease presents distinctive anatomical changes. The brain is unusually soft. There are patchy areas of infiltration of the meninges with lymphocytes and histiocytes. The most destructive lesions are found in the cerebral cortex where large areas of degeneration and even necrosis are observed. Such lesions may be focal. The temporal lobes may be greatly swollen. In such regions the outer layers of the cortex are diffusely infiltrated with mononuclear cells and microglia. Numerous neuronophagic nodules are seen. The white matter is involved less severely and only as a rule where it approaches the cortical lesions. There is likewise little damage to the basal ganglia and the brain stem. The spinal cord escapes. Several observers have described intranuclear inclusion bodies in the neurons. These are large, acidophilic, slightly granular and spherical or irregular. The nucleus is greatly damaged. This is the type of inclusion body described by Cowdry as Type A.

The virus has been isolated and fully identified by Smith *et al.* and by Haymaker and others.

Clinical Features.—For a time only the fatal cases were recognized for the diagnosis could be made only by post-mortem examination. In these cases the onset is abrupt with fever and headache. Convulsions follow with delirium and coma. Temporal lobe symptoms are often present. Evidences of meningeal irritation seem to be constant and prominent features. The cranial nerves are frequently involved and signs of pyramidal tract damage are common. The temperature may reach 104°F. The spinal fluid contains an excess of lymphocytes ranging from 175 to 1000 per cmm. Death occurs between the sixth and the eleventh day.

Complement-fixation and neutralization tests are now available to measure the antibodies against herpes simplex. By such means it has been shown that benign cases of lymphocytic meningitis or meningoencephalitis occur and are apparently not extremely rare. The clinical picture is said to resemble that of choriomeningitis.

Infection with the herpes simplex virus may be acquired at birth when there are herpetic lesions on the mother's vulva. Premature infants are especially susceptible. A generalized infection may occur with involvement of the viscera but only slight damage to the brain. Infection after the first week of life causes encephalitis just as in adolescence and in early adult life. In such cases the abdominal viscera escape. Shearer and Finch describe the case of a boy of nine years who had seventeen organic psychoses with fever, headache, vomiting, confusion, agitation and disorientation in the course of three years. In each case he had an herpetic eruption on the lips, in the mouth and throat. The virus of simplex was recovered. During the illnesses, the electroencephalogram was abnormal. His intelligence quotient dropped from 83 to 68 after the first episode, but there was no deterioration during subsequent attacks.

Diagnosis.—The virus may occasionally be recovered from the spinal fluid. A rising titer of antibodies against the herpes simplex virus is the usual means of diagnosis in nonfatal cases. In fatal cases the virus is usually found in the brain and the anatomical changes are said to be characteristic. Balflour states that the lesions show well in the brain scan. Johnson *et al.* state that a precise diagnosis can be made only by the isolation of the virus and the identification by fluorescent antibody staining.

Treatment.—Bellanti states that the administration of 5-Iodo-2-deoxy-uridine may be beneficial.

BIBLIOGRAPHY

BALFLOUR, H. H. *et al.*: Brain scan in a patient with herpes simplex encephalitis. Jour. Pediat., **71**:404, 1967.

BECKER, W. B. *et al.*: Disseminated herpes simplex virus infection. Amer. Jour Dis. Child., **115**:1, 1968.

BELLANTI, J. A. *et al.*: Herpes simplex. Treatment with 5-iodo-2-deoxyuridine. Jour. Pediat., **72**:266, 1968.

BOOTH, C. B., OKAZAKI, H. AND GAULIN, J. C.: Acute inclusion encephalitis of the herpes simplex type. Neurology, **11**:619, 1961.

COWDRY, E. V.: The problem of intranuclear inclusions in virus diseases. Arch. Path., **18**:527, 1934.

DRACHMAN, D. A. AND ADAMS, R. D.: Acute herpes simplex encephalitis. Arch. Neurol., **7**:45, 1962.

FLORMAN, A. L. AND MINDLIN, R. L.: Generalized herpes simplex in eleven day old premature infant. Am. J. Dis. Child., **83**:481, 1952.

GAJDUSEK, D. *et al.*: Diagnosis of herpes simplex infections by complement-fixation test. J.A.M.A., **149**:235, 1952.

HARLAND, W. A. *et al.*: Herpes simplex in acute necrotizing encephalitis. Lancet, **2**:581, 1967.

HAYMAKER, W.: Pathology of herpes simplex encephalitis in man. Report of 3 cases. J. Neuropath. & Exper. Neurol., **8**:132, 1949.

INNES, J. R. M. *et al.*: Acute malacic and liquifying panencephalitis. Arch. of Neurol., **18**:563, 1968.

JOHNSON, R. T. *et al.*: Herpes simplex virus infections of the nervous system. Neurology, **18**:260, 1968.

KENNEY, T. D.: Intranuclear inclusions in infancy. Am. J. Pathol., **18**:799, 1942.

KERENYI, N. *et al.:* Herpes simplex encephalitis. Canad. Med. Ass. Jour., **81**:1011, 1959.

McKEE, A. P. *et al.:* Herpes simplex encephalitis. Southern Med. Jour., **61**:217, 1968.

MILLER, J. K. *et al.:* Herpes simplex encephalitis. Ann. Int. Med., **64**:92, 1966.

PIERCE, N. F. *et al.:* Encephalitis associated with herpes simplex infection presenting as a temporal lobe mass. Neurology, **14**:708, 1964.

RAWLS, W. E. *et al.:* Encephalitis associated with the herpes simplex virus. Ann. Int. Med., **64**:104, 1966.

ROSS, C. A. C. AND STEVENSON, J.: Herpes simplex meningoencephalitis. Lancet, **ii**:682, 1961.

SHEARER, M. L. AND FINCH, S. M.: Periodic organic psychosis associated with recurrent herpes simplex. New England J. Med., **271**:494, 1964.

SMITH, M., LENNETTE, E. H. AND REAMES, H. R.: Isolation of the virus of herpes simplex in a case of acute encephalitis. Am. J. Pathol., **17**:55, 1941.

WHITMAN, L., WALL, M. AND WARREN, J.: Herpes simplex encephalitis. A report of 2 fatal cases. J.A.M.A., **131**:1408, 1946.

WILDI, E.: Herpetic encephalitis of the newborn. Rev. Neurol., **84**:201, 1951.

WOLF, A. AND COWEN, D.: Perinatal infections of the central nervous system. J. Neuropath. & Exp. Neurol., **18**:191, 1959.

YOUNG, G. F.: Necrotizing encephalitis and chorioretinitis in young infant with rising herpes simplex antibodies. Arch. of Neurol., **13**:15, 1965.

ZUELZER, W. W. AND STULBERG, C. S.: Herpes simplex virus as the cause of fulminating visceral disease and hepatitis in infancy. Am. J. Dis. Child., **83**:421, 1952.

SUBACUTE SCLEROSING PANENCEPHALITIS

In several references given in the bibliography evidence is presented to show that this disease is due to a virus very similar to the measles virus.

Pathological Anatomy.—The brain shows no changes in the gross. There is only slight infiltration of the meninges. The cerebral cortex shows widespread perivascular infiltrations with plasma cells and lymphocytes. There is a variable degree of neuronal damage associated with a reaction of the astrocytes and microglia. A characteristic feature is the presence of acidophilic inclusion bodies in the nuceli which measure between 3 and 10 μ.

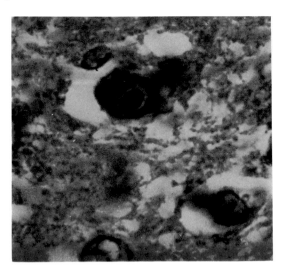

FIG. 147. Inclusion body in Dawson's encephalitis. (By the courtesy of Dr. Richard Lindenberg.)

These are of the type A described by Cowdry. The occipital and temporal lobes are usually affected more than the frontal lobes. The white matter of the hemispheres may show little damage or may be extensively degenerated. The thalami are severely affected but the lenticular nuclei show only mild changes. The nuclei of the brain stem may be involved. The spinal cord escapes and the cerebellum also as a rule though damage to the dentate nuclei is mentioned.

Clinical Features.—About 20 cases have been described. The age of onset is between 5 and 20 years. No familial cases are reported. Three stages of the disease are recognized. The first stage is characterized by mental deterioration and personality changes. Apathy and indifference are prominent and misbehavior is not a problem as a rule. There are often akinetic attacks and petit mal at this stage and convulsions occur occasionally.

The second stage is manifest by increasing mental deterioration and by involuntary movements of several types. The child is very dull. There is poverty of speech and often mutism. Swallowing is difficult. Myoclonic movements are characteristic. They are rhythmical movements of large amplitude, usually flexion in the arms and extension of the trunk. They are slower than the common myoclonic movements. They occur at intervals of 6 to 20 seconds. Torsion spasm, athetosis and choreiform movements are also typical of the second stage. A fine tremor resembling shivering is described.

The third stage is manifest by stupor and by decorticate rigidity. The involuntary movements have ceased. Signs of pyramidal tract damage may appear. In some instances there has been papilledema and cortical blindness is common. The course to a fatal termination averages about 2 to 4 months in younger children and a year or more in adolescents. Remissions are not uncommon and may last several months. The total protein content and the cell count in the spinal fluid may be normal but a paretic gold curve is usually found. The IgG is increased in the serum and spinal fluid. It is said that during the myoclonic movements of the second stage one finds rhythmical synchronous spikes in the electroencephalogram superimposed upon a basic rhythm which grows slower and slower and finally becomes disorganized and later when the torsion spasm develops there are long runs of high voltage waves. It has been thought that this pattern is diagnostic of inclusion encephalitis but this is doubtful.

Diagnosis.—The diagnosis is based on the clinical and laboratory findings.

Prognosis.—The outlook is very gloomy though there is some evidence that non-fatal cases may occur. Kurtzke describes a case diagnosed by brain biopsy in which the patient survived but was completely incapacitated.

Treatment.—No treatment is known. Antibiotics seem to be without value.

CASE HISTORY (No. 1199409).—*Subacute sclerosing leukoencephalopathy of Dawson in a child of 9 years with emotional disturbances, mental deterioration, myoclonic and choreic movements, and episodes during which she was out of contact.*

B. B., a girl of 9 years was healthy until the Fall of 1965. She then became emotional, irritable and had crying spells. She failed at school. There were recurrent episodes during which she would seem to be out of contact and would drool.

In the Spring of 1966, she began to have jerky movements of the shoulders. These soon became more frequent and extended so as to involve the arms and hands. She became clumsy in her movements. Before long the jerky movements became constant when she was awake. She could not walk, dress herself or feed herself. She refused food and lost 12 lbs.

On examination she was irritable and drowsy. She whimpered constantly. The cranial nerves were all in order. Involuntary movements were constant. The arms were suddenly adducted at the shoulders, flexed at the elbows and flexed at the wrist and finger joints. This posture was maintained for a second or two and then the arms were relaxed. There was no constant rigidity. The legs were moved restlessly in choreic fashion. There was no repetition of the same movement.

The spinal fluid contained 33 mgs of protein. There were no cells. The gold curve was 555553210. The Wassermann test was negative. The air study, brain scan and echo test were all negative. The electroencephalogram was abnormal with generalized slow waves and polyspikes. Brain biopsy revealed lesions typical of the subacute sclerosing leukoencephalopathy of Dawson.

BIBLIOGRAPHY

ADELS, B. R. *et al.*: Attempts to transmit subacute sclerosing panencephalitis. Neurology, **18**:30, 1968.

AKELAITIS, A. J. AND ZELDIS, L. J.: Encephalitis with intranuclear inclusion bodies. Arch. Neurol. & Psychiat., **47**:353, 1942.

BERMAN, P. H. *et al.*: Correlation of measles and subacute sclerosing panencephalitis. Neurology, **18**:91, 1968.

BOGAERT, L.: Sue une leucoencephalite sclerosante subaigue. Rev. Neurol., **87**:1, 1952.

BRAIN, R., GREENFIELD, G. AND RUSSELL, D.: Subacute inclusion encephalitis (Dawson type). Brain, **71**:365, 1948.

CLARK, N. S. AND BEST, P. V.: Subacute sclerosing inclusion body encephalitis. Arch. of Dis. Child., **39**:356, 1964.

COBB, W. AND HILL, D.: Electroencephalogram in subacute progressive encephalitis. Brain, **73**:392, 1950.

DAWSON, J. R.: Cellular inclusions in cerebral lesions of epidemic encephalitis. Arch. Neurol. & Psychiat., **31**:685, 1934.

FOLEY, J. AND WILLIAMS, D.: Inclusion encephalitis and its relation to subacute sclerosing leucoencephalopathy. Quart. J. Med., **22**:157, 1953.

GORDON, J. V.: Subacute inclusion encephalitis in South Australia. Med. J. Australia, i:118, 1963.

KURTZKE, J. F.: Inclusion body encephalitis. Non-fatal case. Neurology, **6**:317, 1956.

METZ, H. *et al.*: Subacute sclerosing pan-encephalitis. Arch. Dis. Childhood, **39**:554, 1964.

PETTE, H. AND DÖRING, G.: Ueber ein heimlische Panencephalomyelitis. Deutsche Ztschr. Nervenhk., **149**:7, 1939.

POSER, C. M. AND RADERMECKER, J.: Subacute sclerosing leucoencephalitis. J. Pediatrics, **50**:408, 1957.

SCHNECK, S. A.: Vaccination with measles and central nervous system disease. Neurology, **18**:78, 1968.

SEVER, J. L. AND ZEMAN, W.: Conference on measles virus and subacute sclerosing panencephalitis. Neurology, 1968, vol. 18, part 2, p. 1.

SHAW, C.: Electron microscopic observations in subacute sclerosing panencephalitis. Neurology, **18**:144, 1968.

SIMPSON, J. A.: Subacute inclusion-body encephalitis. Lancet, **ii**:685, 1961.

TIBBLES, J. A. R. *et al.*: Subacute inclusion encephalitis. Canad. M. A. J., **90**:401, 1964.

GENERALIZED CYTOMEGALIC INCLUSION DISEASE

Definition.—A disease of the fetus characterized by nuclear and cytoplasmic inclusions resembling those found in salivary gland disease of guinea pigs.

Etiology.—Wyatt claims on morphological grounds that this disease must be due to a necrotizing virus infection. It is believed that the infection takes place in utero and that the virus has an affinity for fetal tissues. Weller *et al.* have isolated a virus from three children believed to be suffering from this disease. This virus produced characteristic changes in the cells in tissue cultures. Antibodies against this virus were found in the blood of infants suffering from this disease and also in the blood of normal adults. The virus belongs to the herpes group.

Pathological Anatomy.—Wyatt *et al.* describe the characteristic morphological features of the disease as follows: The affected cells are often swollen and may measure up to 35 microns. The nuclear inclusions are huge, granular, acidophilic or metachromatic, usually single. There are never more than two in a single nucleus. They are surrounded by a pale halo. The cytoplasmic inclusions are numerous and frequently located in one portion of the cell. They are basophilic, uniform in size (2 to 4 microns in diameter) and spherical in shape. These inclusions are found largely in epithelial structures such as salivary glands, bronchial epithelium, liver, bile duct, renal tubular epithelium and less often in the adrenal glands, gastrointestinal epithelium, pancreas, thyroid and parathyroid. The brain may be severely damaged. An inflammatory process develops around the infected cells and a destructive effect is exerted on the tissues. In the nervous system the inclusion bodies are found chiefly in the astrocytes. Wyatt speaks of a granulomatous encephalitis.

Clinical Features.—It is claimed that more than 10 per cent of all babies dying in the first few weeks of life, whether stillborn, premature or full term, show on post-mortem examination the characteristic inclusions in the

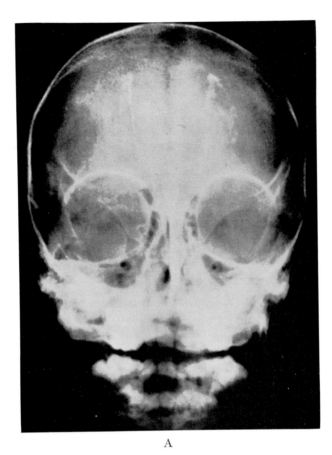

A

FIG. 148. Photograph of roentgenogram of the skull of a child suffering from cytomegalic disease showing periventricular calcification. There is microcephaly, enlargement of the ventricles, mental deficiency, convulsions and an abundance of cells in the urine containing typical inclusion bodies. (By the courtesy of Dr. Frank B. Walsh and Dr. Harry G. Butler.)

salivary glands. Death in these cases is due to various causes and the salivary gland virus disease is regarded as being latent. Wyatt states that in St. Louis post-mortem examinations show that about 1.0 per cent of newborn babies have a generalized form of this disease and lesions in the viscera. It was formerly held that the inclusions were incidental findings in infants dying of other causes, but Wyatt believes that the salivary gland virus is usually responsible for the infant's death when the viscera are extensively involved. Wyatt cites 66 cases of this generalized form which he has found in the literature and adds 6 cases of his own. Margileth found 104 cases in the literature in 1955 all of which were verified by post-mortem examina-

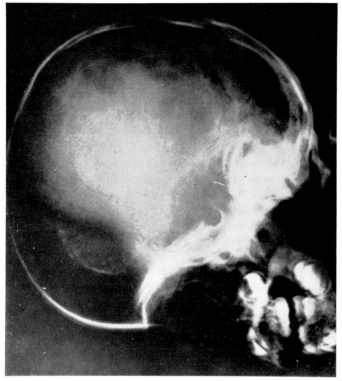

B

tion. This condition has been found in England, on the continent of Europe, in China, the Dutch Indies, Canada and the United States.

The process is essentially a disease of infancy and is acute or subacute. The symptoms are noted at birth or in the neonatal period in most instances. All organs may be involved, so the clinical picture varies. Margileth states that the usual symptoms resemble those of Rh incompatibility. There is often prematurity, jaundice, petechiae, purpura, hematemesis and melena. Hepatomegaly and splenomegaly are common. Microcephaly with mental defect and convulsions are often mentioned. There may be pneumonia, nephritis, ulcerative enteritis and hepatitis with cirrhosis and ascites. A second type occurs after the neonatal period but before the age of 5 years. These children die of a chronic debilitating illness and cytomegalic inclusions are found incidentally at post-mortem examination.

Brough *et al.* describe a generalized cutaneous eruption in newborn infants who are premature by weight. There are circular lesions varying from 2 to 7 mm in diameter slightly raised and dark blue to dark magenta. Sections reveal erythopoiesis. Some of these infants were found to be infected with the cytomegalic virus and some showed evidence of congenital rubella. The authors point out that erythropoietic activity is normally found in embryonic life.

My purpose in mentioning this condition is to call attention to the fact that the brain may be severely damaged. Kinney found lesions in the brain and Worth and Howard have described a fatal, fulminating case of generalized infection with encephalitis. Wyatt *et al.* report a case of encephalitis with typical histological findings in a boy of 13 weeks. In the gross hydrocephalus was evident. Disseminated inflammatory lesions were found in the subcortex, upper pontine region and in the thalami. Lymphocytes and plasma cells predominated in these lesions and were arranged in miliary groups. In the center of these cell clusters, which Wyatt terms granulomas, were found bloated astrocytes or microglial elements containing inclusion bodies. Heavy calcium deposits were found in the granulomas and in the walls of the blood vessels. Wyatt compares this condition to toxoplasmosis. Kidder and Campbell, Guy and Walter also report cases of encephalitis. Kernicterus is mentioned. There may be chorioretinitis resembling that seen in toxoplasmosis. Haymaker *et al.* describe a case in which the cerebral lesions were most severe in the periventricular tissues, the olfactory bulbs and the olfactory tract. Heavy deposits of calcium outlined the cerebral ventricles. Sackett and Ford describe two cases in which the cerebral ventricles were outlined by deposits of calcium which showed clearly in roentgenograms of the skull.

Wong and Warner state that this disease occurs in adults whose resistence is reduced by malignancy and other debilitating diseases.

Diagnosis.—Margileth states that Rh and A B O incompatibilities, sepsis, congenital syphilis and toxoplasmosis must be considered in differential diagnosis. A positive diagnosis may be established by the discovery of the cytomegalic inclusion cells from the renal tubules in the fresh urine or by biopsy of the liver or lung. Roentgenograms may show calcium deposits in the walls of the ventricles. Kluge *et al.* state that the virus may be recovered from the urine. In the neonatal period this is important in diagnosis, but in an older child, discovery of the virus may not be significant.

Prognosis.—The diagnosis has been made in most cases at post-mortem examination so the prognosis is unknown. A few patients have survived with microcephaly and mental defects. In the future as the diagnosis is made more often we may find the prognosis is less unfavorable than it appears to be now.

Treatment.—Margileth gave his patient, who survived with microcephaly, hemiplegia and mental deficiency, transfusions and suggests that possibly replacement transfusion at once may be the treatment of choice. The child was also given cortisone, gamma globulin and antibiotics.

BIBLIOGRAPHY

ALLEN, J. H.: Generalized cytomegalic inclusion disease with emphasis on roentgen diagnosis. Radiology, **71:**257, 1958.

AMROMIN, E. K.: Generalized salivary gland virus infection. Arch. Path., **56:**323, 1953.

BACALA, J. C. AND BURKE, R. J.: Generalized cytomegalic inclusion disease. J. Pediatrics, **43:**712, 1953.

BROUGH, A. J. *et al.:* Dermal erythropoiesis in neonatal infants. Pediatrics, **40:**627, 1967.

CAMPBELL, A. M.., GUY, J. AND WALTER, W. G.: Two cases of cytomegalic inclusion encephalitis. Arch. Dis. Child., **27:**507, 1952.

CROME, L.: Microgyria and cytomegalic inclusion disease in infancy. Jour. Clin. Path., **12:**427, 1959.

ELLIOTT, G. B. AND ELLIOTT, K. A.: Observations on cerebral cytomegalic disease of the fetus and newborn. Arch. Dis. Childhood, **37:**34, 1962.

EMANUEL, I. AND KENNY, G. E.: Cytomegalic inclusion disease of infancy. Pediatrics, **38:**957, 1966.

FISHER, E. R.: Cytomegalic inclusion disease in adult. New England Jour. Med., **258:**1036, 1958.

GUYTON, T. B. *et al.:* New observations in generalized cytomegalic inclusion disease. New England Jour. Med., **257:**803, 1957.

HANSHAW, J. B.: Cytomegalovirus complement-fixing antibody. New England Jour. Med., **275:**476, 1966.

HAYMAKER, W. *et al.:* Cerebral involvement with advanced periventricular calcification in generalized cytomegalic inclusion disease in the newborn. J. Neuropath. & Exp. Neurol. **13:**562, 1954.

HOOFT, C. AND DELBEKE, M. J.: Contribution to the study of cytomegalic inclusion disease. Arch. franc pediat. **17:**914, 1960.

KIDDER, L. A.: Cerebral and visceral inclusion disease of infancy. Am. J. Clin. Path., **22:**870, 1952.

KINNEY, T. D.: Intranuclear inclusions in infancy. Am. J. Path., **18:**799, 1942.

KLUGE, R. C. *et al.:* Cytomegalic inclusion disease of the newborn. Pediatrics, **25:**35, 1960.

MARGILETH, A.: The diagnosis and treatment of generalized cytomegalic inclusion disease of the newborn. Pediatrics, **15:**270, 1955.

McCRACKEN, G. H. JR. *et al.:* Congenital cytomegalic inclusion disease. Amer. Jour. Dis. Child., **117:**539, 1969.

McELFRESH, ARTHUR E. AND AREY, JAMES B.: Generalized cytomegalic inclusion disease. J. Pediat., **51:**146-156, 1957.

MERCER, R. D., LUSE, S. AND GUYTON, D. H.: Clinical diagnosis of generalized cytomegalic inclusion disease. Pediatrics, **1:**502, 1953.

NAEYE, R. L.: Cytomegalic inclusion disease. Amer. Jour. Clin. Path., **47:**738, 1967.

POTTER, E. L.: Placental transmission of viruses. Am. J. Obst. & Gyn., **74:**505, 1957.

SACKETT, G. L. AND FORD, M. M.: Cytomegalic inclusion disease with calcification outlining the cerebral ventricles. Am. J. Roentgenol., **76:**512, 1956.

SYMMERS, W. S.: Generalized cytomegalic inclusion body disease. Jour. Clin. Path., **13:**1, 1960.

WELLER, T. H.: Cytomegaloviruses. Viral and Rickettsial Infections of Man. Edited by Horsfall, F. L. and Tamm, I. J. B. Lippincott Co., 4th Ed., 1965, p. 926.

——— *et al.:* Isolation of intranuclear inclusion producing agents from infants with illnesses resembling cytomegalic inclusion disease. Proc. Soc. Exper. Biol. & Med., **94:**4, 1957.

——— AND HANSHAW, J. B.: Cytomegalic inclusion disease. New England J. Med., **266:**1233, 1962.

WOLF, A. AND COWEN, D.: Perinatal infections of the central nervous system. J. Neuropath. & Exp. Neurol., **18:**191, 1959.

WONG, T. AND WARNER, N. E.: Cytomegalic inclusion disease in adults. Arch. Path., **74:**403, 1962.

WORTH, W. AND HOWARD, H.: New features of inclusion disease in infancy. Am. J. Path., **26**:17, 1950.

WYATT, J., SAXON, J., LEE, R. AND PINKERTON, H.: Generalized cytomegalic inclusion disease. J. Pediatrics, **36**:271, 1950.

———— AND TRIBBY, W.: Granulomatous encephalitis in infancy. Arch. Path., **53**:103, 1952.

INFECTIOUS MONONUCLEOSIS

Etiology.—This is an acute infectious disease of unknown origin. It occurs in epidemic form in schools. It is believed to be due to a viral infection.

Pathological Anatomy.—The process is generalized with enlargement of the lymph nodes, the spleen and the lymphatic tissues of the pharynx. Perivascular infiltrations of normal and abnormal lymphocytes are found in all organs.

Clinical Features.—The disease may occur in infancy, but is more common in adolescence. The incubation period ranges between 4 and 14 days. The prodromal symptoms include low grade fever, mild headaches and sore throat. Nausea may occur. The febrile stage may last a week or two or more. The temperature may go up to 100° or 102°F or more. The clinical picture is usually fully developed by the seventh day. The cervical lymph nodes are enlarged and often the inguinal and axillary notes as well. Enlargement of the posterior cervical nodes is considered to be of diagnostic significance. The pharyngeal lymphatic tissue is involved and exudate is seen in the pharynx. Exanthematous lesions are seen on the soft palate. Edema of the eyelids may appear. The spleen is frequently enlarged. Jaundice sometimes occurs and the liver may be slightly enlarged. A variety of cutaneous eruptions may appear in some instances. Recovery is expected in from 2 to 4 weeks, but the patient may be debilitated for some weeks more.

In the first few days a neutrophil leucocytosis is present, but then the lymphocytes are increased and many abnormal lymphocytes appear. These abnormal cells have a foamy or vaculated cytoplasm and an oval or slightly lobulated nucleus. The total white count is between 10,000 and 20,000. The heterophil antibody titer is increased. After guinea pig kidney absorption, a titer of 1 to 14 is considered diagnostic.

Rupture of the spleen may cause death. Laryngeal edema is also a dangerous condition though a rare one. Hemolytic anemia and thrombocytopenic purpura may occur. Hepatitis is almost always present, but is rarely destructive. Cardiac and pulmonary involvement are known but rare.

It is now well known that the nervous system may be involved in this disease. The neurological process may appear within a few days of the onset or it may be delayed for several weeks. Perhaps the commonest syndrome is that of *lymphocytic meningitis*. This is, as a rule, an acute meningitis of brief duration and benign nature. It resembles the choriomeningitis very closely. There is rarely any sign of damage to the brain. Erwin *et al.* mention conjunctivitis, periorbital edema, uveitis, optic neuritis, papilledema and retinal hemorrhages as well as extraocular muscle palsies, ptosis and scotomas.

I have seen one case of *encephalitis*. There was high fever and convulsions with deep coma. The spinal fluid contained only 10 cells but the protein was high. Complete recovery followed.

Disseminated meningomyelitis also occurs. This is manifest by palsies of the extremities with loss of tendon reflexes and atrophy. There is also loss of sensibility. This process may extend into the brain stem and death may result from involvement of the respiratory mechanisms. There is usually a moderate increase of the mononuclear cells in the spinal fluid. Permanent disability may result. Post-mortem examination reveals a lymphocytic meningitis with infiltration of the spinal nerve roots. Petechial hemorrhages and small areas of degeneration are found in the spinal cord especially in the gray matter. Similar lesions are found in the brain stem.

Another syndrome is almost identical with that of *acute infectious polyneuritis* or the Guillain-Barre syndrome. In such cases we find rapidly developing and extensive paralysis with minimal sensory disturbances. The spinal fluid protein may reach high levels but there is no pleocytosis. Apparently this is a reversible process and if the patient survives there is apt to be complete, or nearly complete, recovery.

Silver *et al.* state that optic neuritis may occur and also localized neuritis of the peripheral nerves.

Bernstein and Wolf who have reviewed this subject state that the nervous system is involved in not more than 1 per cent of all cases and that in 85 per cent of all cases in which the nervous system is involved there is complete recovery. Very few cases are fatal.

Frenkel *et al.* find that cortisone exerts a favorable effect on the disease though antibiotics have no value.

Diagnosis.—The diagnosis depends on the clinical features described above, the presence of abnormal lymphocytes and the increase of the heterophil antibodies.

Prognosis.—The death rate is estimated at between 0.5 and 1.0 per cent. When severe polyneuritis develops the mortality is much greater and the disseminated meningomyelitis may also be fatal. Rupture of the spleen, laryngeal edema and purpura are serious complications. Treatment is merely symptomatic.

CASE HISTORY (No. 514627).—*Infectious mononucleosis followed by extensive paralysis of the extremities and a lymphocytic meningeal reaction.*

R. W., a young man of 18 years, developed a febrile illness in May 1949. His temperature soon reached 102.6°F., and later, 104°F. There was enlargement of the spleen and generalized lymph node enlargement. Heterophil antibodies were present, the blood contained 60 per cent large mononuclear cells and the study of the bone marrow revealed changes which were considered typical of infectious mononucleosis. The patient improved slowly but never regained his proper vigor.

About the first of July he began to complain of pain in his back and legs. These symptoms marked the onset of an extensive involvement of the nervous system which developed gradually during the next few weeks. During this month he ran a low grade fever. Soon there was paralysis of both legs and then loss of sensibility in the legs, paralysis of the face on both sides, involvement of the left hand and forearm and partial incontinence. The affected muscles rapidly wasted and the tendon reflexes were lost. The spinal fluid was tested repeatedly during this period. This cell count rose from 14 per cmm, on July 18, to 1,000 on July 29. The total protein reached a level of 625 mgs per 100 cc.

There was no particular change in the patient's condition during August. No new neurological findings appeared but he did not improve. His temperature continued to be slightly elevated in the afternoons. The spinal fluid cell count ranged around 100 and the total protein was around 150 mgs.

On September 19, he was admitted to Johns Hopkins Hospital. He was then much underweight and evidently chronically ill. The right pupil was smaller than the left. Both sides of the face were paralyzed. There was weakness and wasting of the muscles of the left hand, and forearm muscles. The left triceps was involved also. The finger reflexes and the triceps reflexes were lost. The shoulder girdle muscles on the right were paralyzed and the scapula winged. Both legs displayed complete paralysis with atrophy and loss of tone. The knee and ankle jerks were lost. The muscles of the chest and abdomen were not definitely involved. The patient was at times incontinent of urine and unaware that he had voided.

Cutaneous sensibility was greatly reduced or lost over both legs, thighs and buttocks with the exception of a small area around the coccyx where there was nearly normal sensibility. This sensory loss extended on the left up over the lower part of the abdomen. There was also sensory loss over the left hand and forearm sparing only the thumb and a narrow zone on the radial border of the forearm. The spinal fluid still showed an excess of lymphocytes and the protein was elevated.

This patient was seen in consultation with Dr. Nathan Herman.

CASE HISTORY (No. 601877).—*Boy of 17 years developed infectious mononucleosis. Rapidly became completely paralyzed in all skeletal muscles. Kept alive in the respirator. Almost complete recovery.*

F. M., a previously healthy boy of 17 years, developed a fever and headache on March 21, 1952. The next day he had a sore throat and began to vomit. There was no additional symptoms until March 26. On that day he noticed double vision and a feeling of numbness in his face and hands.

Neurological examination the next day revealed bilateral weakness of the sixth nerves and some weakness of the intrinsic muscles of the hands. On March 28, the patient displayed complete paralysis of the sixth nerves, right facial weakness, hoarseness of the voice, weakness of the soft palate, weakness of the abdominal muscles and retention of urine. The tendon reflexes were all reduced or absent. No loss of sensibility could be found.

The spinal fluid was quite normal in all respects. There was an excess of large lymphocytes in the blood and some atypical forms. The heterophil antibodies were present in high titer. The lymph nodes were all enlarged and the spleen could be felt. A diagnosis of infectious mononucleosis was made.

The patient's condition grew rapidly worse. On March 30, his respiration became weak and he was placed in the respirator. On the next day there was complete paralysis of all extremities, chest, abdomen, bladder, neck and all the muscles supplied by the cranial nerves. No evidence of intestinal peristalsis was present. The pupils still reacted to light and it was possible to lift the eyelids a few millimeters. This last was the only voluntary movement possible. His temperature was beginning to rise. On April 1, he was stuporous and soon became entirely unconscious. His temperature reached 102.4°F. There was cyanosis at times. On April 2, his temperature rose to 106°F. but soon began to fall. He remained in coma and there was no return of motor power.

On April 3, his temperature was falling and his mental condition was better. On the next day he could move his head a little. Improvement continued. Power returned in the extremities and in the muscles supplied by the cranial nerves. His muscles of respiration regained some power. On April 18, he was removed from the respirator. He was then able to void.

By the end of April he had regained some strength in all groups of muscles except for dorsiflexors of the left foot. The spinal fluid was tested again at this time and was found to contain 272 mgs of protein.

Improvement continued and in the summer of 1952, he was able to play lacrosse though there was still some weakness of dorsal movement at the left foot.

This patient was seen by the courtesy of Dr. Warde Allan.

BIBLIOGRAPHY

BAEHNER, R. L. AND SHULER, S. E.: Infectious mononucleosis in childhood. Clin. Pediat., **6**:393, 1967.

BENNETT, D. R. AND PETERS, H. A.: Acute cerebellar syndrome secondary to infectious mononucleosis. Ann. Int. Med., **55**:147, 1961.

BERCEL, N. A.: Infectious mononucleosis, encephalitis, epilepsy. Amer. Jour. Med. Sci., **224**:667, 1952.

BERNSTEIN, T. C. AND WOLFE, H. G.: Involvement of the nervous system in infectious mononucleosis. Ann. Int. Med., **33**:1120, 1950.

CUSTER, R. P. AND SMITH, E. B.: The pathology of infectious mononucleosis. Blood, **3**:830, 1948.

Davie, J. C. *et al.:* Infectious mononucleosis with fatal neuronitis. Arch. Neurol., **9**:265, 1963.

Dolgopol, V. B. and Husson, G. S.: Infectious mononucleosis with neurological complications. Arch. Int. Med., **83**:179, 1949.

Erwin, W., Weber, R. W. and Manning, R. T.: Complications of infectious mononucleosis. Am. J. M. Sc., **238**:699, 1959.

Fiese, M. J. *et al.:* Guillain-Barre syndrome in infectious mononucleosis. Arch. of Int. Med., **92**:438, 1953.

Frenkel, E. P. *et al.:* Meningoencephalitis in infectious mononucleosis. J.A.M.A., **162**:885, 1956.

Garvin, J. S.: Infectious mononucleosis with Guillain-Barre syndrome. J.A.M.A., **151**:293, 1953.

Hoagland, R. J.: Clinical manifestations of infectious mononucleosis. Modern Medicine, September 23, 1968, p. 170.

Hubler, W. L.: Infectious mononucleosis with predominantly neurologic manifestations. Proc. Mayo Clin., **26**:313, 1951.

Karpenski, F. E.: Neurologic manifestations of infectious mononucleosis in childhood. Pediatrics, **10**:265, 1952.

Nellhaus, G.: Isolated oculomotor nerve palsy in infectious mononucleosis. Neurology, **16**:221, 1966.

Nichols, W. W. and Athyreya, B.: Encephalitis with mononucleosis. Am. J. Dis. Child., **103**:72, 1962.

Peters, C. H., Widerman, A., Blumberg, A. and Ricker, W. A.: Neurologic manifestations of infectious mononucleosis. Arch. Int. Med., **80**:366, 1947.

Shechter, F. R. *et al.:* Retrobulbar neuritis. A complication of infectious mononucleosis. Am. J. Dis. Child., **89**:59, 1955.

Silver, H. K. *et al.:* Involvement of the central nervous system in infectious mononucleosis in childhood. Am. J. Dis. Child., **91**:490, 1956.

Slade, J. DeR.: Involvement of the central nervous system in infectious mononucleosis. New England M. J., **234**:753, 1946.

Thelander, H. E. and Shaw, F. B.: Infectious mononucleosis with special reference to cerebral complications. Am. J. Dis. Child., **61**:1131, 1941.

Thomsen, S. and Vintrup, B.: Six fatal cases of infectious mononucleosis complicated by central respiratory paralysis. Nord. med. (Hospitalstid), **4**:3295, 1939.

Walsh, F. C. *et al.:* Infectious mononucleosis encephalitis. Pediatrics, **13**:536, 1954.

BEHCET'S SYNDROME

This condition is most apt to occur in males either in adolescence or in early adult life. About 45 cases have been reported. McMenemey and Spillane isolated a virus from the eye and from the brain. This virus grew on the chorioallantoic membranes of fertile eggs and passed a Seitz E.K. pad filter. Antibodies against this virus were found in sera of patients suffering from Behcet's disease.

The course is chronic and relapsing. Ocular symptoms are characteristic. There is keratitis and uveitis as well as conjunctivitis. Hemorrhages into the vitreous occur. Vision may be lost in one or both eyes. Recurrent, painful ulcers develop in the mucous membranes, especially on the genitals and in the mouth. Erythema nodosum and other skin lesions are mentioned. The liver may be enlarged. There is apt to be low grade fever during the exacerbations. The course is chronic and relapsing.

The nervous system is involved in about 25 per cent of all cases. Cranial nerve palsies, brain stem lesions, spastic paralysis and cerebellar ataxia are described. The spinal fluid may contain hundreds of cells. Pallis and Fudge describe three syndromes: (1) A brain stem syndrome either episodic or progressive in irregular fashion leading to death from bulbar palsy. (2) A meningomyelitic syndrome manifest by recurrent attacks of paraplegia associated with fever, cervical rigidity and a polymorphonuclear pleocytosis in the spinal fluid. (3) A confusional syndrome which may progress to dementia with convulsions. Cases in which the nervous system is involved may be fatal. A diffuse meningeal reaction is described with perivascular infiltrations in the cerebral cortex, basal ganglia, brain stem, spinal cord and cerebellum. There are scattered softenings. Inflammatory changes are found in the iris, choroid, retina and optic nerve.

BIBLIOGRAPHY

BEHCET, H.: Ueber rezidivierende Aphthose durch ein Virus versachte Geschwure am Mund, am Auge und an den Genitalien. Dermat. Wchschr., **105**:1152, 1937.

BIENSTOCK, H. AND MARGULIES, E.: Behcet's syndrome. New England J. Med., **264**:1343, 1961.

FRANCE, R., BUCHANNAN, R., WILSON, M. AND SHELDON, M.: Relapsing iritis with recurrent ulcers of the mouth and genitalia. (Behcet's syndrome) Medicine, **30**:335, 1951.

MAMO, J. G. AND BAGHDASSARIAN, A.: Diagnosis of Behcet's disease. Arch. Ophth., **71**:4, 1964.

McMENEMEY, W. H. AND SPILLANE, J. D.: Observations on the mechanisms of neurological complications of Behcet's disease. Third International Congress of Neuropathology. Brussels, July 21-28, 1957.

WADIA, N. H. AND WILLIAMS, E.: Behcet's syndrome with neurological complications. Brain, **80**:59, 1957.

PALLIS, C. A. AND FUDGE, B. J.: The neurological complications of Behcet's syndrome. Arch. of Neurol. & Psychiat., **75**:1, 1956.

RUBENSTEIN, L. J. AND URICH, H.: Meningoencephalitis of Behcet's disease. Brain, **86**:151, 1963.

SILFVERSKOLD, B. P.: Recurrent uveitis (Behcet's syndrome) and encephalomyelomeningitis. Acta psychiat. et neurol. Scand., **26**:443, 1951.

THE ICELAND, OR AKUREYRI, DISEASE

In 1948 and 1949, there was an extensive epidemic of 465 cases of this disease in the town of Akureyri in northern Iceland which was reported by Sigurdsson *et al.* Similar but smaller epidemics have been discovered in New York state, Florida, Australia, Durban, Berlin and London.

The disease affects children as well as adults. The onset is usually insidious but may be acute. There is occipital headache, and low grade fever. Symptoms of upper respiratory tract infection or gastrointestinal symptoms are almost constantly present at the onset. Pains in the arms, legs, shoulders, and back are characteristic. The affected muscles are extremely tender. There is fatigue on the slightest exertion. In some cases, there is paresis of the muscles. One muscle may be affected or a whole group of muscles. The weak muscles are not always the tender muscles. The paresis begins about 2 days to 4 weeks after the onset of fever. The weakness may last for only a few days or for several months. Paralysis is rare. Weeks after the onset, a second group of muscles may develop weakness. There is said to be no wasting of the muscles. The tendon reflexes are usually present. There are also sensory changes and complaints of numbness, tingling and hyperesthesia are common. Actual reduction of cutaneous sensibility may be found. Nystagmus and diplopia are mentioned. There is rarely any true cervical rigidity. Relapses are very common. The cervical lymph nodes are often enlarged.

Emotional disturbances are characteristic. The patients are depressed and emotionally unstable. They cannot sleep well. Memory seems to be reduced.

No fatal cases are mentioned except by Chari and Swamy and the epidemic these authors report may well represent a disease very different from that described above.

Convalescence is prolonged. Sigurdsson examined a number of patients six years after the onset and found that very few considered themselves well. The chief complaints were aching of the muscles, fatigue and depression. However, it is said that all were working at their usual occupation except for one individual who had gastric ulcer.

A number of studies have been made to discover the etiological agent. Repeated tests have been made for the virus of poliomyelitis, Coxsackie disease, influenza, mumps and indeed, all the common viruses, without positive results. The spinal fluid is as a rule quite normal and in only a few instances has there been any increase of cells or of protein. Pellew and Miles inoculated some monkeys who developed infiltrations of the spinal nerve roots and myocarditis but could not transmit the infection to another series of monkeys. Ramsay *et al.* made electromyographic studies and found on volitional contraction the number of motor unit potentials was reduced and tended to occur in groups of 5 or 6. These findings were taken to indicate damage to the spinal cord but not degeneration of the anterior horn motor cells. The electroencephalogram revealed abnormalities of minor degree but the significance of these changes was regarded as uncertain. I see no mention made of muscle biopsy. Creatine excretion was increased. The white cells in the blood were sometimes diminished and sometimes increased.

BIBLIOGRAPHY

ACHESON, E. D.: A disease resembling poliomyelitis. Lancet, ii:1044, 1954.

————: The clinical syndrome variously called benign myalgic encephalomyelitis, Iceland disease and epidemic neuromyasthenia. Am. J. Med., 26:569, 1950.

CHARI, M. V. AND SWAMY, T. V.: Jamshedpur fever. Brit. Med. J., ii:1298, 1955.

PELLEW, R. A. AND MILES, J. A. R.: Disease resembling poliomyelitis in Adelaide. Med. J. Australia, ii:480, 1955.

RAMSAY, A. M. AND O'SULLIVAN, E.: Encephalomyelitis simulating poliomyelitis. Lancet, i:761, 1956.

SIGURDSSON, B. *et al.*: A disease epidemic in Iceland simulating poliomyelitis. Amer. Jour. Hyg., 52:222, 1950.

————: Clinical findings six years after outbreak of Akureyri disease. Lancet, i:766, 1956.

SUMNER, D. W.: Further outbreak of a disease simulating poliomyelitis. Lancet, i:764, 1956.
WHITE, D. N. *et al.*: Iceland disease. Neurology, 4:506, 1954.

MOLLARET'S MENINGITIS

A benign type of recurrent meningitis is described by Mollaret. This occurs at any age. The onset is acute with high fever. All the standard signs of meningitis develop, as well as muscular pains and tenderness. The symptoms reach their peak rapidly, usually within twelve hours, and then disappear within two or three days.

The spinal fluid contains thousands of cells if it is examined within twelve hours. There are lymphocytes and leucocytes, as well as large cells termed endothelial cells. These seem to be undergoing degeneration and disappear very rapidly. No organisms can be found in the fluid. The protein content is between 70 and 80 mgs.

The episodes of meningitis recur at intervals of weeks or months during a period of three or four years. Complete recovery is the rule.

Bruyn *et al.* state that the diagnosis must be made by exclusion.

BIBLIOGRAPHY

BRUYN, G. W., STRAATHOF, L. J. A. AND RAYMAKERS, G. M. J.: Mollaret's meningitis. Neurology, 12:745, 1962. Full references.

INFLUENZA

For a number of years cases of polyneuritis following a brief febrile illness have been ascribed to influenza without any proof of the nature of the initial illness. In the great epidemics, neurological symptoms have rarely been mentioned.

In the epidemic of Asian influenza of 1957, however, reports of numerous neurological symptoms were published. The Asian influenza virus is a variant of influenza virus A.

It seems that children were most apt to develop neurological disorders. Encephalitis was said to develop between the fourth and the tenth day after the onset with convulsions, coma, confusion and Babinski signs. Myelitis, radiculitis and polyneuritis were also described. The pathological changes in the nervous system were variable.

BIBLIOGRAPHY

ANDERSON, W. W.: Neurologic complications of Asian influenza. Neurology, 8:568, 1958.
BELL, W. E. *et al.*: Asian influenza as a cause of acute encephalitis. Neurology, 8:500, 1958.
BLATTNER, R. J.: Neurologic complications of Asian influenza. Jour. Pediat., 53:751, 1958.
COTTOM, D. G.: Acute cerebellar ataxia. Arch Dis. Child., 32:181, 1957.
FLEWETT, T. H. *et al.*: Influenzal encephalopathy and post-influenzal encephalitis. Lancet, 2:11, 1958.
GILMORE, L. K.: Asian influenza in children. Clin. Pro. Children's Hospital, 17:226, 1961.
HORNER, F. A.: Neurologic disorders after Asian influenza. New England Jour. Med., 258:983, 1958.

HOULT, J. G.: Influenzal encephalopathy and post-influenzal encephalitis. Brit. Med. Jour., **5108**:1311, 1958.

MELLMAN, W. J.: Influenza encephalitis. Jour. Pediat., **53**:292, 1958.

WELLS, C. C. *et al.*: Guillain-Barre syndrome and virus of Asian influenza. Arch. of Neurol. and Psychiat., **81**:699, 1959.

VIRUS HEPATITIS

Several viruses may cause hepatitis including not only the virus of acute infectious hepatitis, and that of the serum hepatitis but the yellow fever virus and the infectious mononucleosis virus.

The nervous system may be damaged as a result of hepatic failure or as a result of invasion of the nervous system by the virus. Neurological manifestations may occur before evidences of liver damage are present. Meningitis, lethargy, coma, delirium and focal cerebral syndromes are all described. Headache is often severe. The neck may be stiff and the cell count of the spinal fluid may be increased. In 15 per cent of cases perivascular infiltrations are found at post-mortem examination in the brain and meninges, so the diagnosis of meningoencephalitis is indicated.

Irritability and weakness are characteristic sequelae.

BIBLIOGRAPHY

FRIEDLANDER, W. J.: Neurologic signs and symptoms as a prodrome to virus hepatitis. Neurology, **6**:574, 1956.

LUCKE, B.: The pathology of fatal epidemic hepatitis. Amer. Jour. Path., **20**:471, 1944.

LUCKE, B. AND MALLORY, T.: The fulminant form of epidemic hepatitis. Amer. Jour. Path., **22**:867, 1946.

LEIBOWITZ, S. AND GORMAN, W. F.: Neuropsychiatric complications of viral hepatitis. New England Jour. Med., **246**:932, 1952.

STREIFLER, M. AND FELDMAN, S.: Encephalomyelitis in the preicteric stage of infectious hepatitis. Neurology, **3**:931, 1953.

WEINSTEIN, L. AND DAVISON, W. T.: Neurologic manifestations of the preicteric phase of infectious hepatitis. Amer. Practit., **1**:191, 1946.

NEUROLOGICAL COMPLICATIONS OF PRIMARY ATYPICAL PNEUMONIA

Primary atypical pneumonia may be due to a variety of viruses and not to a single specific virus. It should be mentioned that neurological syndromes may occur in association with this clinical picture. It is said that meningoencephalitis may develop between the third day and the thirtieth day after the onset of the pulmonary process. Myelitis, polyneuritis and the Guillain-Barre syndrome are described also. The mortality may be up to 30 per cent. Small focal hemorrhages, perivascular cellular reactions and perivascular demyelination are found at post-mortem examination.

BIBLIOGRAPHY

HOLMES, J. M.: Neurologic complications in atypical pneumonia. Brit. Med. Jour., **i**:218, 1947.

JACKSON, R. B.: Primary atypical pneumonia with associated encephalomyelitis. Neurology, **5**:356, 1955.

YESNICK, L.: Central nervous system complications of primary atypical pneumonia. Arch. of
    Int. Med., **97**:93, 1956.

COLORADO TICK FEVER

This disease is due to a virus infection and not to rickettsial infection as some tick fevers are. It is conveyed by wood ticks in the mountains of the West in the spring and early summer months. There is leukopenia and a maculo-papular rash. There is first a febrile episode of one to three days and then a remission of two or three days followed by a return of the fever and sometimes meningitis or encephalitis with stupor, delirium and convulsions. In a few cases the spinal fluid cell count and the protein are elevated. The neurological symptoms are more common in children. The disease is a benign one.

BIBLIOGRAPHY

BLATTNER, R. J.: Viral encephalitis. Adv. Pediatr., **12**:11, 1962.
ECKLUND, C. M.: Natural history of Colorado tick fever virus. Jour. Lancet, **74**:172, 1962.
FRASER, C. H.: Colorado tick fever encephalitis. Pediatrics, **29**:187, 1962.
SILVER, H. K.: Colorado tick fever. Jour. Dis. Child., **101**:30, 1961.

CATSCRATCH DISEASE

Children are the chief victims. The scratch or bite of a cat is responsible. An indolent skin lesion is soon seen and then within a week or two the regional lymph nodes are swollen. The swelling may recede or suppuration may occur.

Involvement of the nervous system may occur within 4 to 6 weeks after the primary lesion. Convulsions and coma develop. There may be stiffness of the neck and the spinal fluid cell count may be elevated. Tremors, ataxia and weakness of the muscles occur. The commonest clinical syndrome is encephalitis, but myelitis and radiculitis are described. The prognosis is favorable. The acute symptoms do not last over a week or two and residuals are rare.

The diagnosis may be established by intradermal skin tests and serological studies.

BIBLIOGRAPHY

ECKHEART, W. F. JR. AND LEVINE, A. I.: Corticosteroid therapy of catscratch disease. Arch. of
    Int. Med., **109**:463, 1962.
FOWLER, R. S. AND BAILEY, J. D.: Catscratch disease in childhood. Canad. Med. Ass. Jour.,
    84: 1358, 1961.
PAXTON, E. M. AND MCKEY, R. J.: Neurologic symptoms associated with catscratch disease.
    Pediatrics, **20**:13, 1957.
STEVENS, H.: Cat-scratch fever encephalitis. Amer. Jour. Dis. Child., **84**:218, 1952.
WEINSTEIN, L. AND MEADE, R. H.: Neurologic manifestations of catscratch disease. Amer. Jour.
    Med. Sci., **229**:500, 1955.

PSITTACOSIS (ORNITHOSIS)

This disease is contracted from birds but may be transmitted from one human patient to another. The clinical symptoms may be dominated by atypical pneumonia. Encephalitis and meningoencephalitis are well known neurological syndromes. Lethargy, delirium, edema of the optic discs, ataxia and involuntary movements may develop.

BIBLIOGRAPHY

DENMARK, J. C.: Encephalitis due to psittacosis. Brit. Med. Jour., **5060:**1531, 1957.
JANSSON, E.: Ornithosis in Helsinki. Ann. Med. Exp. Biol. Fenn., **38:**1, 1960.
THALABARD, J. AND GAUDIN, J.: Ornithosis, psittacosis and papilledema. Bull. Soc. Ophthal. Franc., **5:**400, 1961.

YELLOW FEVER

This disease is transmitted by a mosquito, aedes aegypti. There is intense hepatitis and nephrosis which cause widespread perivascular hemorrhages. There may be uremia, hypotension and cardiovascular collapse. Small hemorrhages may be found in the nervous system especially in the periventricular regions, the mammilary bodies, optic thalami and subthalamic bodies. The temporal lobe and cerebellum may also show hemorrhages.

There may be stupor or coma, delirium, convulsions, cranial nerve palsies and signs of focal cerebral lesions.

It is said that vaccines prepared from attenuated virus may be capable of causing meningitis and meningoencephalitis. This is most apt to occur in infants.

BIBLIOGRAPHY

BEET, E. A.: Encephalitis following yellow fever vaccination. Brit. Med. Jour., **i:**226, 1955.
ELTON, J. A.: Clinical pathology of yellow fever. Amer. Jour. Path., **25:**135, 1955.
FEITEL, M. *et al.:* Encephalitis folowing yellow fever vaccination. Pediatrics, **25:**956, 1960.

INVASION OF THE NERVOUS SYSTEM BY RICKETTSIAE

Involvement of the Nervous System in Typhus Fever

Etiology.—It is now generally accepted that this disease is due to infection by one of the group of rickettsiae, R. prowazeki.

The organism is a small coccoid or short bacillus-like body. These organisms cannot be cultivated on common media but it is claimed that they will live in tissue culture. Guinea pigs and other experimental animals are susceptible.

Epidemiology.—Two types of typhus fever are distinguished. The European type is transmitted by the body louse. It is prevalent in the Balkans and in central Europe. In this country it is found only in immigrants. An endemic type of typhus is found in the New World. This is believed to be transmitted by the common rat flea. The European type is not common in children, but the American type often affects children over the age of four years, though rare in infants.

Pathological Anatomy.—The brain is very hyperemic and edematous and numerous small hemorrhages are often seen in the meninges and gray matter of the hemispheres and brain-stem. Microscopic examination reveals very characteristic changes. Numerous miliary nodules are found in close relationship to the arterioles and capillaries. These are most abundant in the gray matter of the pons, the thalamus, lenticular and caudate nuclei, the dentate nuclei and molecular layer of the cerebellar cortex and in the second to the fifth layer of the cerebral cortex. These nodules are formed chiefly by hypertrophied microglial cells and by cells derived from the adventitia of the vessels. A few lymphocytes and plasma cells are also present. In the immediate neighborhood of the lesions there is some disintegration of the myelin sheaths, degeneration of the nerve cells and regressive changes in the astrocytes. The vessel in the central part of the lesion shows severe changes. The endothelium is swollen, the lumen often occluded and the vessel wall sometimes broken down. Small areas of infarction are sometimes seen as a result of the vascular lesions. These are usually in the gray matter. Numerous small vessels throughout the brain show adventitial infiltrations with lymphocytes but no other abnormalities. In addition there are mild evidences of toxic encephalopathy. The cranial nerves and the spinal nerve roots are often infiltrated and as a rule there is a patchy meningeal reaction. The organisms are seen as small round or elongated bodies within the swollen endothelial cells or the cells of the vascular adventitia usually within one of the granulomatous nodules described above. Lesions similar to those of the brain are found throughout the body. These are described in references given below.

Clinical Features.—Typhus fever occurs, as a rule, in winter months among the poor who live in crowded and unhygienic districts. It is apparently not so common in this country as it was formerly supposed to be. The onset is usually relatively acute, with fever, chills, pain in the back, headache and vomiting after an incubation period of about twelve days. The rash appears between the third and the fifth day on the flanks and in the axillae, soon spreading over the chest and body and becoming generalized. There is a fine dusky mottling of the skin and papular rose spots which later change to petechiae. The conjunctiva are injected and the eyelids edematous. The fever rises steadily during the first few days reaching its maximum at about the fifth day and frequently terminating by crisis at about the end of the second week. The white cells of the blood are not increased and there may be a mild leucopenia.

Neurological symptoms may dominate the picture. The neck is rigid. Delirium may be present from the onset. There is usually stupor and often coma in severe cases. During the febrile period or during convalescence, hemiplegia, hemiparesis, aphasia and other focal cerebral symptoms are not unusual. Jacksonian convulsions or generalized muscular twitchings occur. Bulbar palsy is common. The cranial nerves do not escape. Optic neuritis followed by optic atrophy is described and many observers have recorded neuritis of the facial, auditory and oculomotor nerves. Spinal cord lesions causing paraparesis and incontinence are mentioned. During convalescence various types of neuritis are common. In some cases this is of the generalized toxic type, but more frequently single nerves or groups of nerves are involved. Brachial plexus neuritis is not an infrequent complication. The sciatic, median, ulnar, axillary or musculocutaneous nerves may be selected.

The spinal fluid is usually normal during the first ten days but after this period, it usually contains an excess of protein and a few white cells. It may be bloody or xanthochromic.

Diagnosis.—The diagnosis depends upon the symptoms described above, residence in a district where the disease is present, the positive Weil-Felix reaction and the elimination of other diseases such as typhoid fever and malaria. The complement-fixation test is necessary to differentiate typhus from other rickettsial diseases. The organisms may be recovered from guinea pigs.

Prognosis.—In louse-borne typhus the mortality may be very high and varies between 15 and 60 per cent. Involvement of the nervous system is usual and residual neurological disorders are described. In the flea-borne disease the mortality is very low and complete recovery is expected.

Treatment.—A vaccine has been developed which, it is claimed, confers a degree of immunity. Paraaminobenzoic acid has been used in treatment. More recently aureomycin and chloromycetin have been found to be more effective, and excellent results are described.

BIBLIOGRAPHY

ASH, J. E. AND SPITZ, S.: The Pathology of Tropical Diseases. Philadelphia, W. B. Saunders, 1945, p. 30.

BASSOE, P.: The nervous system in typhus fever. (Abstracts of several Russian articles.) Practical Medicine. J. Nerv. & Ment. Dis., 171, 1922.

PETERSEN, J. C. et al.: Rickettsial diseases of childhood. Pediat., 30:495, 1944.

SNYDER, J. C.: Typhus Fever Rickettsiae. Viral and Rickettsial Infections of Man. Edited by Horsfall, F. L. and Tamm, I. J. B. Lippincott Co., 4th Ed., 1965, p. 1059.

WOLBACH, S. B., TODD, J. L. AND PALFREY, F. W.: The Etiology and Pathology of Typhus Fever. Harvard University Press, 1922. (Full references.)

YEOMANS, A. et al.: Therapeutic effect of paraaminobenzoic acid in louse-borne typhus fever. J.A.M.A., 126:349, 1944.

INVOLVEMENT OF THE NERVOUS SYSTEM IN TICK-BITE FEVER

Etiology.—The disease is believed to be due to infection with a form of rickettsia, termed by Wolbach, "Dermacentroxenus rickettsi," which is very similar to the organism which causes typhus fever. It is transmitted in the west by a tick, Dermacentor andersoni or venustus and in the east by the common dog tick, Dermacentor variabilis and, perhaps, by several other types of ticks. It is thought that rabbits, ground squirrels and other small rodents act as reservoirs for the disease. Larger mammals, either wild or domestic, are not susceptible.

Epidemiology.—This disease is closely related to typhus fever and has frequently been confused with typhus in the past. It was first recognized in the Rocky Mountains and only in recent years has it become evident that it is in reality widely distributed throughout the United States and Canada and is not infrequent along the Atlantic seaboard. The eastern form is peculiar in that it is usually associated with lesions in the nervous system, whereas such lesions rarely, if ever, are found in the western type of the disease.

Pathological Anatomy.—The pathological process in the nervous system is scarcely to be distinguished from that of typhus fever. We find the same changes in the small blood vessels, the miliary granulomata and the small focal necroses associated with occlusion of the arterioles. The latter, however, are situated chiefly in the white matter in contrast to those of typhus which are most numerous in the gray matter and at present this seems to constitute the chief difference in the processes. Rickettsiae are found in the lesions as in typhus fever.

Clinical Features.—The disease is confined to rural districts and it is most prevalent in summer and early fall. As a rule, it is possible to secure a history of tick bite shortly preceding the onset. Children are apparently very susceptible, for a large percentage of cases occurs in subjects under fifteen years of age. Several cases often develop in one family. The incubation period is relatively short, averaging three to eight days. The rash is almost identical with that of typhus fever but appears first on the wrists and ankles and involves the chest and body later. There is usually no local evidence of the tick bite and the regional lymph nodes are rarely enlarged. The spleen may be palpable. The fever rises to about 102°F. and at the end of a week may reach 105°F. In contrast to typhus fever in which the white cells are not increased, there is often a mild leucocytosis in tick fever. Neurological symptoms often occur early. There is lethargy or stupor which may alternate with restlessness, irritability or even violent delirium. In some cases, coma finally ensues. Signs of meningeal irritation are apparently more common than in typhus fever and are said to dominate the picture in 5 per cent of the cases. Tremors, convulsions, opisthotonos, and rigidity are described. In fatal cases death usually occurs in the second week. The spinal fluid may contain a slight excess of globulin and of white cells.

Diagnosis.—The diagnosis rests upon the history of being bitten by a tick shortly before the development of the clinical picture described above and upon the elimination of the other fevers. The Weil-Felix reaction is positive. The complement-fixation test is necessary for a precise diagnosis.

Prognosis.—The disease varies in its severity, being very fatal in the Bitter Root valley of Montana, where the mortality approximates 80 per cent, mild in Idaho where a mortality of around 5 per cent is reported and moderately fatal on the eastern seaboard, where between 20 per cent and 25 per cent of the cases are fatal. In most instances, recovery is complete if the patient survives. However, Thomas and Berlin mention cases in which mental changes, epilepsy, hemiplegia and paraplegia have persisted as lasting sequelae. Rosenblum *et al.* find neurological symptoms in 21 of 37 patients but physical signs in only 6 patients among the survivors.

Treatment.—The same methods are employed as in typhus fever.

BIBLIOGRAPHY

ATWOOD, E. L. *et al.*: A contribution to the epidemiology of Rocky Mountain spotted fever in the eastern United States. Amer. Jour. Trop. Med. Hyg., **14**:831, 1965.

CHALGREN, W. S. AND BAKER, A. B.: The nervous system in tropical disease. Medicine, **26**:395, 1947.

FLINN, L. B.: Paraaminobenzoic acid treatment of Rocky Mountain spotted fever. J.A.M.A., **132**:911, 1946.

HARRIS, P. N.: Histological study of a case of the eastern type of Rocky Mountain spotted fever. Am. J. Path., **9**:91, 1933.

LILLIE, R. D.: Pathology of the eastern type of Rocky Mountain spotted fever. Public Health Reports, **46**:2840, 1931.

PARKER, R. R.: Certain phases of the problem of Rocky Mountain fever. A summary of present information. Arch. Pathol., **15**:398, 1933.

ROSENBLUM, M., MASLAND, R. AND HARRELL, G.: Residual effects of Rickettsial disease on the central nervous system. Arch. Int. Med., **90**:444, 1952.

THOMAS, M. H. AND BERLIN, L.: Neurologic sequelae of Rocky Mountain spotted fever. Arch. Neurol. &. Psychiat., **60**:574, 1949.

WOODWARD, T. E. AND JACKSON, E. B.: Spotted Fever Rickettsiae. Viral and Rickettsial Infections of Man. J, Edited by Horsfall, F. L. and Tamm, I. J. B. Lippincott Co., 4th Ed., 1965, p. 1095.

INVOLVEMENT OF THE NERVOUS SYSTEM IN TSUTSUGAMUSHI FEVER

Etiology.—This disease, which is also known as scrub typhus, is another rickettsial disease due to infection by R. nipponica, or R. tsutsugamushi. It is conveyed by the bite of the larvae of the Kedani mite, Trombicula Akamushi, a parasite of rodents.

Epidemiology.—The disease is widely distributed in Japan, Malaya, Indochina, New Guinea, Sumatra, the Philippines and northern Australia. It is not seasonal.

Pathological Anatomy.—In many cases, there is a small eschar on the body which represents the bite of the mite. The lesions in general are almost identical with those found in other rickettsial diseases such as typhus and tick fever. They are found in close relation to the small blood vessels and are distributed throughout all the tissues of the body.

Clinical Features.—About a week after the patient has been bitten by the mite, the temperature begins to rise and the patient complains of headache and giddiness. There is apt to be enlargement of the lymph nodes which drain the region of the bite. The temperature as a rule rises each day reaching its maximum on about the fourth or fifth day and thereafter falling by lysis. On the seventh day a macular rash appears on the face, spreading to the chest, legs, forearms and trunk. Leucopenia is the rule. The conjunctivae are congested. There may be a general enlargement of the lymph nodes and tenderness of the liver and spleen. The pulse is rather slow.

Delirium is the commonest neurological feature and there is more apt to be insomnia than drowsiness. Mild signs of meningeal irritation may occur. Deafness is frequently mentioned. Squints are common. The retinal veins are usually engorged and retinal hemorrhages may be seen. Optic neuritis is described. Muscular twitching and even convulsions, dysphagia and dysarthria and either increase or reduction of the tendon reflexes may occur. Pains and paresthesias may be prominent. These are attributed to polyneuritis. The spinal fluid may show a slight increase of cells and of protein.

Diagnosis.—The presence of the eschar, the clinical features mentioned above and the geographical location will usually make the diagnosis evident. It is said that the blood serum agglutinates the O.X.K. strain of B. proteus. The inoculation of a rabbit or guinea pig with blood serum gives positive results. Only cross immunological studies give a clear differentiation from other rickettsial diseases.

Prognosis.—In some instances the disease is very fatal, but as a rule the mortality is less than 15 per cent. In those who survive there may be prolonged weakness with evidences of cardiac involvement and personality changes.

Treatment.—See treatment of typhus fever.

BIBLIOGRAPHY

MACHELLA, T. E. AND FORRESTER, J. S.: Mite or scrub typhus. Am. J. Med. Sc., **210**:38, 1945.

NOAD, K. AND HAYMAKER, W.: Neurological features of tsutsugamushi fever with especial reference to deafness. Brain, **76**:113, 1953.

RIPLEY, H. S.: Neuropsychiatric observations on tsutsugamushi fever. Arch. Neurol. & Psychiat., **56**:42, 1946.

TIERNEY, N. A.: Paraaminobenzoic acid in tsutsugamushi disease. J.A.M.A., **131**:280, 1946.

BACTERIAL INFECTIONS INVOLVING THE NERVOUS SYSTEM
Neurological Complications of Otitis Media and Nasal Sinus Infections

Though the intracranial infections resulting from otitis media and nasal sinus infections are less common than they once were, as a result of effective antibiotic therapy, such complications are still distressingly frequent. Brain abscess, meningitis, epidural abscess, petrositis, labyrinthitis, subdural empyema and septic dural sinus thrombosis are all characteristic of such infection. These conditions are described in the following pages.

Kiviranta states that recurrent otitis may be due to reduction of the serum gamma globulin.

Facial paralysis or Bell's palsy, q.v., is sometimes associated with pyogenic otitis media in infancy even when mastoid infection is absent.

Hoefnagel and Joseph state that oculosympathetic palsy may also occur in association with otitis media in children. The condition may be overlooked, for the drooping of the lid may not be striking, and in bright light, the pupil may be only slightly smaller than the normal one. There is no loss of sweating on the face. These authors believe that the sympathetic fibers which lie in the sheath of the carotid artery are involved in the carotid canal where they are separated from the tympanic cavity only by the anterior wall, which may be thin and may contain dehiscences. It is stated that recovery usually occurs within a few weeks, but in some instances, the condition is persistent.

BIBLIOGRAPHY

BIERMAN, W.: The diagnosis and treatment of Bell's palsy. J.A.M.A., **149**:253, 1952.

BLUESTONE, C. D. AND STEINER, R. E.: Intracranial complications of acute frontal sinusitis. Sth. Med. Jour., **58**:1, 1965.

BLUMENFELD, R. J. AND SKOLNIK, E. M.: Intracranial complications of sinus disease. Trans. Amer. Acad. Ophthal. and Otolaryngn., **70**:899, 1966.

HOEFNAGEL, D. AND JOSEPH, J. B.: Oculosympathetic palsy in otitis media. New England J. Med., **265**:475, 1961.

KIVIRANTA, U. K.: Recurring middle ear infection and serum proteins in children. Jour. Laryng., **81**:1253, 1967.

MARAN, A. G. C.: The cause of deafness in childhood. Jour. Laryng., **80**:495, 1966.

ABSCESS OF THE BRAIN

Etiology.—Abscess of the brain is usually due to the common pyogenic bacteria. Most frequently streptococci and pneumococci are found, but staphylococci and Bacillus coli are not unusual. Anaerobic organisms may be present.

Pathological Anatomy.—Greenfield and Buzzard describe three stages in the development of abscess of the brain: "(1) A stage resembling acute encephalitis in which there appear areas of softening and liquefaction. (2) These areas enlarge, merge into one another and tend to lose their red color; fully formed pus makes its appearance, at first in minute drops. (3) In the third stage the reaction in the surrounding brain tissue limits the abscess, a definite wall is formed and the surrounding encephalitis subsides. This stage may never be reached and the encephalitis may continue its spread until the death of the patient." The inner surface of the abscess wall is ragged and green or yellow. Microscopically, it is composed of degenerating leucocytes and fat-laden microglial cells, as well as fatty substances resulting from myelin destruction. Just outside this layer there may be a ring of calcification if the abscess is an old one. The next layer is chiefly composed of connective tissue and small blood vessels. In relatively recent abscesses this layer is very vascular. It contains numerous phagocytes and resembles granulation tissue but later it becomes very dense and fibrous. Only a few glial fibers are found in this zone. In the outermost zone the brain tissue is relatively intact. The blood vessels show proliferation of their adventitial sheaths which are infiltrated with leucocytes and lymphocytes and there may be dilatation of the vascular lumen with multiplication of the endothelial cells. The astrocytes are increased in numbers and show numerous thick processes which tend to lie parallel with the wall of the abscess. Nerve cells in this zone often show chromatolysis or degenerative changes. Very old abscesses often show a very dense wall which permits the entire sac to be shelled out like an encapsulated neoplasm, without rupture.

Abscesses due to penetration of the brain by a foreign body may be found in a chain-like series connected by a hemorrhagic tract, indicating the path of the infection. Abscesses due to fracture of the skull are usually associated with areas of softening which extend to the site of the fracture. In cases in which the infection has arisen from the mastoid, it is usually possible to find some alterations of the meninges and hyperemia of the cerebral tissue overlying the abscess. Such abscesses are single, as a rule, and are often very large. Frequently, there are smaller abscesses extending out from the walls of the larger abscess. These are evidently due to rupture of the capsule by increasing pressure with extension of the pus into the surrounding brain tissue. These extensions may become encapsulated in turn and rupture eventually just as the primary abscess ruptured. We shall see below that these facts are probably important in explaining the clinical course of some abscesses. In some cases, the abscess is very superficial. The pus collects in the subarachnoid space and invades the cortex only to a limited extent. Such superficial abscesses may be found on the surface of the temporal lobe but usually reach the Sylvian fissure before they are discovered. Multiple abscesses are, as a rule, due to infection conveyed by the blood stream. It is stated, however, that pulmonary infections which extend to the brain usually give rise to only one abscess and this is more often on the left than the right. The meninges may be quite normal or may show localized or generalized meningitis. Purulent ependymitis often results from rupture of the abscesses into the ventricle.

Clinical Features.—As a rule, there is a history of infection. Chronic otitis media is probably the most common cause but acute otitis media with or without complications, such as mastoiditis and sinus thrombosis, may also cause abscess. Suppurative processes in the lungs are notoriously prone to extend to the brain. A less common source of brain abscess is infection of the nasal sinuses. As a rule, it is the chronic sinus infection rather than the acute types which leads to abscess. Accidential opening of the dura in unskillful attempts to drain the sinus must also be mentioned. Brain abscesses may also follow fractures of the skull which open into the ear or nasal sinuses and offer a pathway for pyrogenic organisms to invade the brain, although meningitis is perhaps a more common sequel. Penetrating wounds caused by falling on nails or other sharp-pointed objects are occasional causes, for the infant's skull is too thin to afford much protection. Bacteremias, septicemias and pyemias are obvious causes of brain abscess. Brain abscess is common in certain types of congenital heart disease q.v. Abscess of the cerebellum may be due to the presence of a congenital dermal sinus which penetrates the dura and offers a pathway for infection. Rarely abscesses may follow acute infectious diseases, although no clinical evidence of a septic focus of infection is discovered. In some cases even the postmortem examination may throw no light on the portal of entry. A few instances of abscess in early infancy due to the colon bacillus are reported which seem to have been of prenatal origin.

The clinical signs and symptoms are often extraordinarily few and in many cases no evidence can be secured to justify the diagnosis, even when the case is reviewed in retrospect after the post-mortem examination. If the child is under observation when the process begins, the invasion of the brain is marked by fever, leucocytosis, malaise and anorexia, just as one would expect from septic infections in other parts of the body. Such symptoms are due to localized encephalitis. If the child is not under medical care during this period, it is evident that the symptoms may escape the notice of the parents and that later, when a history is taken, no information about the onset will be available. If the infection is very virulent or the child's resistance is poor, the abscess may extend very rapidly. The fever remains high, the leucocytosis continues and headache, vomiting, drowsiness and finally stupor ensue. Signs of increased intracranial pressure develop, as a rule, and the extension of the process into the ventricles or meninges produces purulent ependymitis or meningitis. Death may occur within two or three weeks after the onset. In less virulent infections, the course is very different. The abscess becomes surrounded by a dense wall and absorption of toxic products ceases. Fever, leucocytosis and other signs of infection then disappear. Indeed, the temperature is often subnormal. The symptoms now depend upon the size and location of the abscess. If it does not occlude the ventricular system or give rise to focal signs, the patient may appear to be quite well. There seems to be no doubt that the process may stop at this point in a few cases. The capsule grows thicker and eventually the infecting organisms die. Usually, however, increasing pressure within the abscess causes rupture of the capsule with extension of the pus into the surrounding tissues. This is marked by a recurrence of the fever and other evidences of infection, as well as by focal signs. If the abscess is near the surface, a meningeal reaction may occur. Sometimes this subsides within a short time, although the cell count in the spinal fluid may be elevated and some bacteria may be present. In other cases, purulent meningitis ensues. The extension of the pus may become encapsulated just as the first abscess and the signs of infection may disappear once more. Such remissions and exacerbations are characteristic of certain types of brain abscess. Eventually, death occurs from increased intracranial pressure, extension of the infection into the ventricles, the meninges or throughout the brain.

Abscesses resulting from blood borne infection may involve any part of the brain, although the frontal, occipital and temporal lobes are said to be their favorite sites. They are usually multiple and, hence, no description of the focal signs is possible. Abscesses arising from otitis media and its complications are found, as a rule, in either the temporal lobe or the cerebellum. The former are usually considered to be the more common. When the temporal lobe is the site of the lesion, focal signs are not always easy to demonstrate. Homonymous defects in the opposite visual fields usually occur eventually. The upper quadrants are usually involved first and later a complete homonymous hemianopia develops. Facial paresis is sometimes seen and it has been pointed out repeatedly that this is usually more apparent during emotional movements, such as weeping or laughing, than during voluntary movements of the face. Uncinate gyrus fits sometimes occur. The third nerve may be involved on the same side. In most cases there is some alteration of the contralateral tendon reflexes. They are, as a rule, diminished in relatively acute processes and increased in long-standing lesions. The plantar reflex is sometimes extensor, but hemiplegia is a very late sign and is rarely well developed. When the abscess is on the left, aphasia is common, especially if the posterior or middle part of the lobe is involved. As a rule, the most striking symptom is an inability to name familiar objects. The patient usually recognizes the nature of the object and can demonstrate its use, however. If the correct name is mentioned, the patient may recognize it at once. Later as the abscess expands, more global types of aphasia develop.

Symonds has described several cases of superficial abscess. He states that these usually produce no signs until they extend to the Sylvian fossa and involve the motor cortex. At this point there is a series of convulsions on the opposite side of the body followed by paralysis of cortical type and usually stupor or coma. If the lesion is on the left side, there may be aphasia. The spinal fluid contains, as a rule, a few lymphocytes but no pus or organisms.

Cerebellar abscesses, as a rule, give rise to fairly definite signs. There is hypotonia and cerebellar ataxia of the ipsilateral arm and later similar disturbances may be found in the leg. In very acute abscesses one may find very gross atonia and pronounced weakness, i.e., the so-called cerebellar asthenia. Nystagmus is a very important sign. This is chiefly horizontal and is most evident when the eyes are deviated towards the side of the lesion. The slow phase is always to the midline. If the patient is drowsy and does not fix well, the quick phase may be absent and we may discover only some difficulty in fixing objects on the side of the lesion. The eyes drift back towards the midline without any rhythmical movements. In acute abscesses the difficulty in lateral gaze may be mistaken for palsies of conjugate deviation. Suboccipital tenderness and headache are also significant of cerebellar lesions. Otogenous abscesses are not invariably confined to the temporal lobe and the cerebellum and may sometimes be found in the frontal or parietal lobes. We have seen a case in which infection of the sphenoid sinus led to abscess of the pituitary gland with fatal hypoglycemia associated with coma and convulsions.

Nelson *et al.* describe abscess of the pituitary gland secondary to sphenoid sinus infection with pituitary necrosis and death.

The spinal fluid does not always reveal the same changes. When the abscess is well encapsulated, the fluid may be quite normal. As a rule, however, we find from 18 to 100 cells, chiefly lymphocytes, normal sugar and chloride content and elevation of the proteins to between 50 and 150 mgm. If the abscess leaks from time to time, we may find a preponderance of leucocytes and even bacteria. If the cell count is not very high and the bacteria cannot be cultivated and especially if the sugar and chlorides are not much diminished, we are probably dealing with a transient meningeal reaction which will at least temporarily subside. Fall of the chlorides and sugar, and rapid rise of the polymorphonuclear leucocyte count indicate that purulent meningitis is impending.

Roentgenograms of the skull are important in some cases, for they may reveal evidences of mastoiditis or nasal sinus infection. In a few cases, such as those reported by Dandy, gas forming organisms give rise to pneumocephaly which is clearly revealed in the roentgenogram.

Diagnosis.—The most important diagnostic features may be summarized as follows: (1) The history of some preceding infection such as otitis media or of trauma. (2) General signs of infection such as fever and leucocytosis. (3) Signs of a focal cerebral lesion. (4) Signs of increased intracranial pressure. (5) Changes in the spinal fluid as described above. Unfortunately, many of these signs may be lacking. I have already stated above that in some cases no history of infection can be obtained. So long as the abscess is fully encapsulated, fever and leucocytosis may be absent. Focal signs are very difficult to elicit in an infant, especially such temporal lobe signs as hemianopia. Aphasia and unsteady gait are obviously impossible to demonstrate during this period. Even older children who are very ill or delirious frequently cannot cooperate enough to enable focal signs to be elicited. Signs of increased intracranial pressure may be delayed or absent. During early childhood the head may expand in response to pressure, so that in chronic abscesses one is apt to think of congenital hydrocephalus. In many cases the evidence of increased intracranial pressure is so marked that it does not seem justifiable to perform lumbar puncture and, hence, we can derive no information from the study of the spinal fluid. Moreover, the changes in the spinal fluid are variable and not always characteristic. The signs of abscess may be obscured by the presence of meningitis, lateral sinus thrombosis or labyrinthitis. We are forced, therefore, in many cases to rely largely upon objective diagnostic procedures such as pneumoventriculography and exploratory puncture of the brain with a hollow needle.

Prognosis.—The outlook is greatly improved since antibiotics and sulphonamides have been employed though brain abscess remains a serious condition. In only a very few cases does the process stop spontaneously and the pus become sterile. Surgical treatment is still unsatisfactory. Many months or even years after an abscess has been drained with apparent cure, it may become active again. Repeated operations may be required. If the infection is eventually eradicated, we still have to contend with a large cerebral lesion which may be associated with focal signs and very frequently gives rise to epilepsy. It is of interest that the scars resulting from old abscesses of the cerebellum do not seem to cause seizures of any type. The immediate mortality which was once between 80 and 100 per cent has fallen since the introduction of antibiotics to less than 50 per cent and would be much lower if all patients received prompt and efficient treatment.

Treatment.—Since this is a surgical problem, it need not be discussed in full. In acute abscesses which are not encapsulated, no surgical treatment is of any avail. After a well-formed abscess wall has developed, the pressure may be reduced from time to time by puncture, as Dandy has advised, or the abscess may be opened and drained. Abscesses with dense walls may, in some cases, be removed intact. Antibiotics and sulphonamides should be given both before and after operation for these drugs prevent the extension of the infection and combat meningitis. None of these drugs will sterilize an abscess and surgical methods are still required. Some surgeons instill antibiotics into the abscess after it has been opened. Some surgeons inject air into the abscess to determine its size and location. Thorotrast may be injected. This is taken up by the wall of the abscess and thereafter simple roentgenograms will reveal whether the abscess is expanding or contracting. The source of the infection which caused the abscess should be determined if possible and treated appropriately.

BIBLIOGRAPHY

BUCY, P.: Sulphanilamide in treatment of brain abscess and prevention of meningitis. J.A.M.A., 111:1639, 1938.

CAHILL, H. P.: The modern treatment of abscess of the brain. J.A.M.A., 102:273, 1934.

CODY, D. T. *et al.:* Diagnosis of latent brain abscess. Laryngoscope, 74:346, 1964.

COHEN, I.: Cerebral complications of putrid pleuropulmonary suppuration. Arch. Neurol. & Psychiat., 32:174, 1934.

———— AND DROOZ, R. B.: Brain abscess metastatic from the lung. Recovery following penicillin therapy and repeated aspiration. J. Neurosurg., 2:456, 1945.

DANDY, W. E.: Practice of Surgery, Dean Lewis, Hagerstown, Md.; W. F. Prior Co., 1932, Chapter 1, 12:365.

EVANS, W.: The pathology and etiology of brain abscess. Lancet, 1:1231, 1931.

KING, A. B., CONKLIN, S. D. AND COLLETTE, T.: Bacteroides infections. Ann. Int. Med., 37:761, 1952.

LISKE, E. AND WEIKERS, N. J.: Changing aspect of brain abscess. Neurology, 14:294, 1964.

MACEWEN, W.: Pyogenic Infective Diseases of the Brain and Spinal Cord, Meningitis, Abscess of the Brain, Infective Sinus Thrombosis. Glasgow, J. Maclehose & Sons, 1893.

MCGREAL, D. A.: Cerebral abscess in children. Canad. M. A. J., 86:261, 1962.

NEWLANDS, W. J.: Otogenic brain abscess. Laryng., 79:120, 1965.

ROBBINS, S. L.: Brain abscess associated with congenital heart disease. Arch. Int. Med., 75:279, 1945.

SANFORD, H. N.: Abscess of the brain in infants under 12 months of age. Am. J. Dis. Child., 35:256, 1928.

SYMONDS, C. P.: Some points in the diagnosis and localization of cerebral abscess. Proc. Roy. Soc. Med., 1927, 20:1139, Sec. Otology.

WALSH, F. B.: *Loc. cit.*

LOCALIZED NON-SUPPURATIVE ENCEPHALITIS ASSOCIATED WITH OTITIS

Symonds and others believe that invasion of the brain by pyogenic organisms does not always result in suppuration, but the process may become arrested in the stage of inflammation. Most of the cases reported have occurred in children who have had otitis with or without mastoiditis and other complications. The clinical picture is identical with that of brain abscess and the focal signs have usually pointed to the temporal lobe although in a few cases the cerebellum was involved. The spinal fluid shows changes identical with those associated with brain abscesses. On exploration, however, no pus can be found and the patient subsequently recovers or survives with slight residual signs of a focal lesion. It is, of course, possible that such patients really have abscesses which have not been discovered, but their continued good health is much against this supposition. Nielson suggests that the focal signs are due to thrombosis of the cortical veins.

No pathological-anatomical observations are yet available to support the concept of non-suppurative encephalitis, due to otitis.

The writer has observed several cases in which uncinate gyrus fits followed otitis and mastoiditis. The results of ventriculography and the benign course were strongly against the diagnosis of abscess and it is probable that these cases should be placed in this group.

BIBLIOGRAPHY

ADSON, A. W.: Pseudo-brain abscess. Surg. Clin. North America, 4:503, 1924.

ATKINSON, M.: Localized nonsuppurative encephalitis adjacent to a focus of infection in the skull. Arch. Neurol. & Psychiat., **41**:556, 1939.

BALLANTINE, H. T. AND SHEALY, C. N.: Role of radical surgery in treatment of abscess of the brain. Surg. Gynec. & Obst., **109**:370, 1959.

NELSON *et al.:* Neurological syndromes produced by sphenoid sinus abscess. Neurology, **17**:981, 1967.

SPERL, M. P. *et al.:* Observations on current therapy of abscess of the brain. A.M.A. Arch. Neurol. & Psychiat., **81**:439, 1959.

SYMONDS, C. P.: Localized non-suppurative encephalitis. Proc. Roy. Soc. Med., **20**:1142, 1927. Sec. Otology.

SEPTIC THROMBOSIS OF THE DURAL SINUSES

Definition.—Septic thrombosis of the lateral sinus is so closely associated with mastoiditis and otitis media that it seems best to discuss it at this point in connection with abscess of the brain and meningitis. Thrombosis of the superior longitudinal and straight sinuses is usually of the non-septic type and will be taken up in Chapter V whereas, septic thrombi are found, as a rule, in the lateral and cavernous sinuses and will be discussed at this point.

Etiology.—The lateral sinus is most commonly affected and in the vast majority of cases this is a sequel of otitis. Mastoiditis is frequently but not invariably associated. Involvement of the cavernous sinus is usually due to extension anteriorly of lateral sinus thrombosis but may also be due to infections of the face, orbit, maxilla, frontal bone, tonsils and pharynx. The longitudinal sinus is most frequently involved in septicemias and in meningitis but may also be involved as a result of infections of the scalp, frontal bone and nasal sinuses.

Pathological Anatomy.—The brain is edematous, as a rule, and the vessels of the meninges much distended. Hermorrhages may be present and in some cases there are extensive hemorrhagic infarcts. The affected sinus may be distended by blood clot which on section shows small purulent foci containing streptococci, staphylococci, pneumococci and their organisms or there may be no firm thrombus and the sinus may contain chiefly pus and fibrin. When the lateral sinus is involved, it is not unusual to find small foci of inflammation around the vessels of the temporal lobe and cerebellar hemisphere. When the cavernous sinus is affected, there are almost always abscesses in the orbit and frequently small abscesses and infarctions in the hypophysis. In either case, there may be meningitis, abscess of the brain and extradural abscess. Osteomyelitis of the base of the skull may be found. Frequently, there are evidences of septicemia and of embolism of the lungs or other viscera.

If the thrombus is confined to the lateral sinus and if there is no significant anomaly of the venous system, there is usually no serious disturbance of the circulation of the brain, although frequently hemorrhages and congestion may be found in the temporal and occipital lobes which were not suspected clinically. Woodhall has shown that it is not unusual to find that one lateral sinus is much smaller than the other. In such cases thrombosis of the larger sinus may cause extensive congestion and edema of the brain. In other cases, the torcular Herophili is absent, the superior longitudinal sinus empties directly into the right lateral sinus and the straight sinus into the left lateral sinus. Consequently occlusion of the right lateral sinus is apt to interrupt the venous drainage of the superior aspect of the hemispheres and occlusion of the left lateral sinus affects the central white matter and basal ganglia in the same way. In other cases unusual extension of the clot is responsible for serious circulatory disturbances. The thrombus may extend into the torcular causing obstruction of both lateral sinuses; into the petrosal and cavernous sinuses or into the jugular bulb thus blocking the collateral channels and preventing compensation. Bilateral thromboses in the lateral sinuses may likewise cause intense congestion of the brain. If we omit the possibilities of abscess and of meningitis, dural sinus thrombosis might be expected to cause increased intracranial pressure in at least five different ways: by distention of the vascular channels within the cranium, by edema of the brain and meninges, by hemorrhage, by preventing proper absorption of the cerebrospinal fluid into the venous system and by causing increased production of fluid as a result of congestion of the choroid plexus. Observations at operation and at post-mortem examination make it clear that the vessels are distended, that the brain and meninges are edematous, and hemorrhages and hemorrhagic infarctions are frequently present, but whether there is any disturbance in the secretion or in absorption of the spinal fluid is still uncertain. Symonds suspects that the fluid is not properly absorbed when the superior longitudinal sinus is involved.

Clinical Features.—The symptoms of sinus thrombosis are often difficult to detect and are not infrequently so much obscured by the other evidences of sepsis that the diagnosis is not made. The signs may be divided into two groups: (1) Those due to infection. (2) Those due to obstruction of the venous circulation of the brain.

Thrombosis of the Lateral Sinus.—With few exceptions, lateral sinus thrombosis is a sequel of otitis media and in most cases, but not in all, there is either acute or chronic mastoiditis. In about two-thirds of all cases there is a septic fever and in half there are chills. In some cases the course is afebrile. The blood culture is positive in less than half of all cases. Crowe has found the hemolytic streptococcus most common. The organisms in the blood stream are not always identical with those found in cultures from the middle ear and mastoid. Frequently one observes evidences of embolism and septicemia such as petechiae in the skin and mucous membranes, pulmonary infarction, abscess of the lung, purulent arthritis and abscesses of the muscles. The white cell count is increased, as a rule, but may be normal. It does not necessarily correspond to the height of the fever. The local signs may be inconspicuous or absent but in some cases we find edema over the mastoid bone, dilatation of the superficial veins, tenderness over the course of the internal jugular vein and even a palpable cord in the neck. In a few cases, paralysis of the ninth, tenth and eleventh nerves has been observed. This has been attributed to compression of the nerves by a thrombus in the jugular vein. Symonds states that a septic thrombus in the inferior petrosal sinus is a common cause of sixth nerve palsy; more frequent, he thinks, than petrositis. He also suspects that in rare instances the fifth nerve may be involved by thrombosis of the superior petrosal sinus. In such cases he suggests we are dealing with pressure palsies.

In about half of all cases there are signs or symptoms of increased intracranial pressure, such as generalized headaches, vomiting, diplopia, separation of the cranial sutures, bulging fontanels, drowsiness or stupor. Crowe found papilledema in approximately half of his cases and engorgement of the retinal veins in an additional twenty per cent. In some cases the papilledema is confined to the homolateral eye and it is usually greater on the side of the thrombus. When the papilledema is bilateral, it may be taken to indicate increased intracranial pressure but when unilateral, it probably indicates that there is an additional local factor such as obstruction of the drainage from the cavernous sinus due to extension of the clot to the petrosal sinuses or to the internal jugular vein. Papilledema of this type is often associated with striking engorgement of the retinal veins which may show hemorrhages along their course, but it does not differ so definitely from the papilledema due to tumor of the brain that the differentiation can be made with confidence. In the vast majority of cases, there are no definite focal signs indicative of a cerebral lesion. At most we may discover a mild facial paresis or a questionable Babinski sign on the opposite side. In rare cases, however, the thrombus may be unusually extensive or important anomalies of the dural sinuses may be present resulting in occlusion of the straight or longitudinal sinuses with paraplegia, hemiplegia or double hemiplegia. There is always stupor or coma in such cases and also signs of increased intracranial pressure.

Cases are reported in which both lateral sinuses have become thrombosed or in which it was deemed necessary to ligate both internal jugular veins. In such cases, there is usually great increase of intracranial pressure, especially if the occlusion occurs at approximately the same time on both sides. We have observed a patient (Path. 14106) in whom both lateral sinuses became thrombosed. There was intense headache, rapidly developing papilledema leading to blindness and death from increased intracranial pressure within three weeks.

Pulmonary embolism may result from dural sinus thrombosis. Emery has made a post-mortem examination of twenty-five cases of fatal pulmonary embolism in children.

We have observed lateral sinus thrombosis in association with otitis media which behaved in all respects like non-septic thrombosis. One such case is given in abstract below. Symonds has employed the term otitic hydrocephalus in connection with such cases.

The spinal fluid may be clear or may be xanthochromic. Red blood cells are usually present. The white cell count may be high or low depending upon the amount of meningeal reaction associated. The pressure is always elevated. Two tests are of value in demonstrating occlusion of the lateral sinus. Crowe's sign is elicited by pressing upon the internal jugular of the opposite side. A positive response is shown by dilatation of the veins of the face and scalp. Ayer's test is designed along similar lines. Spinal puncture is performed and a manometer is attached to the needle. Pressure on the opposite jugular vein is made. If the jugular vein or lateral sinus is really obstructed, this pressure will cause a pronounced rise in pressure. If these vessels are patent, no material rise of pressure will occur. Such tests must be interpreted with considerable caution because of the variation of the anatomy of the dural sinuses. False positive as well as false negative reactions may be elicited. The roentgenographic study of the skull is of some value in this regard for it has been shown that the relative size of the lateral sinuses may be estimated by the size of the bony channels in the skull.

Courville and Nielsen have described a series of cases in children in which focal convulsions developed during the course of acute otitis media. The convulsions were followed by hemiplegia which was sometimes of brief duration and sometimes persistent. They have suggested that these symptoms are due to extension of a thrombus into the veins draining the lateral aspect of the hemisphere. No doubt the thrombus extends from the lateral sinus by the inferior anastomotic vein to the veins of the cortex. Since these children survived the authors believe that abscess can be excluded. We have seen a number of cases of the same type.

Thrombosis of the Cavernous Sinus.—The cavernous sinus is involved most frequently as a result of extension anteriorly of a septic process in the lateral sinus and is, therefore, a result of otitis media and mastoiditis. It may also result from furuncles upon the face, erysipelas, osteomyelitis of the facial bones and jaws and purulent infection of the nasal sinuses and pharynx. It may occasionally be affected by non-septic thrombosis.

The clinical signs are very striking. There is first edema of the orbital tissues and eyelids, protrusion of the eyeball, congestion of the veins about the eye and often congestion and edema of the optic nerve head. Papilledema is not invariably present. Vision may be lost. The third, fourth and sixth nerves are usually paralysed and the upper branch of the fifth nerve may be affected as well. The sixth nerve is often involved first of all. As a rule, the process extends to the opposite side by way of the circular sinus within a few days and both eyes are then proptosed and immobile. In the septic type of cavernous sinus thrombosis, there are usually fever, chills, leucocytosis and often a positive blood culture. Meningitis usually supervenes before long. Necroses in the pituitary gland may occur and should the patient survive there may be evidences of pituitary deficiency. Jefferson points out that the exophthalmos and edema of the orbital tissues in cases of cavernous sinus infection are due to infection in the orbit and thromboses in the veins of the orbit. Occlusion of the cavernous sinus alone does not cause exophthalmos.

Diagnosis. *Lateral Sinus Thrombosis.*—The following features are important. (1) Otitis with or without mastoiditis. (2) Fever of septic type with or without chills persisting after the mastoid has been opened. (3) Positive blood cultures. (4) Signs of increased intracranial pressure. (5) Presence of Ayer's sign or Crowe's sign. (6) Bloody or xanthochromic spinal fluid. Unfortunately, none of these signs are always present or diagnostic of sinus thrombosis. Abscess of the brain is a frequent complication of lateral sinus thrombosis and sometimes cannot be excluded without ventriculography or exploration of the brain with a hollow needle. Spinal puncture may be performed to exclude meningitis. Recently the technique of demonstrating intracranial venous thromboses by the injection of radiopaque contrast media has been developed.

Cavernous Sinus Thrombosis.—The important signs are: (1) Exophthalmos. (2) Edema of the orbital tissues and conjunctiva. (3) Loss of ocular movements. (4) Papilledema in some cases. (5) Fever and leucocytosis. (6) Positive blood culture. (7) Signs of mastoiditis and otitis or of some other infection about the head. (8) Extension to the opposite eye within a few days. This condition must be distinguished from fistula between the cavernous sinus and the internal carotid artery which is usually traumatic and gives rise to a loud bruit and to pulsation of the bulb. The possibility of abscess, tumor or hemorrhages into the orbit must be considered. Syphilitic periostitis may give a similar picture which, however, develops, as a rule, more slowly.

Prognosis.—Before the introduction of sulfonamides and antibiotics the mortality in cases of lateral sinus thrombosis was nearly 30 per cent, though some surgeons gave much smaller figures. The outlook seems to have been greatly improved by the use of these drugs, though no accurate figures are available. Cavernous sinus infection was formerly a very serious condition and fatal nine times out of ten. By the use of antibiotics and the sulfonamides, however, the mortality has been reduced to about 30 per cent, if one may judge by case reports.

Treatment.—Most surgeons advise ligation of the jugular vein in lateral sinus thrombosis and drainage of the infected clot. Crowe advises simply mastoidectomy in all cases. Radical mastoidectomy is performed only if hearing is markedly impaired. If there is clinical evidence of septicemia, the sinus is exposed and opened if it appears to be infected. The clot is removed and the jugular vein ligated. I have seen cases in which the eleventh nerve was carelessly included in the ligature. In the absence of evidence of septicemia, it is not considered wise to open the sinus in most instances.

No satisfactory operation has been devised for the treatment of cavernous sinus thrombosis.

In all cases of septic dural sinus thrombosis, antibiotics or the sulfonamides should be given both before and after operation. Most authorities seem to prefer to employ both antibiotics and sulfadiazine together.

CASE HISTORY (U-43253).—*Typical case of "otitic hydrocephalus." (Symonds) Girl of 7 years developed otitis followed within a short time by headache, vomiting and papilledema. Cerebral ventricles small. Spinal fluid normal. Recovery after subtemporal decompression. Two years later mastoiditis, meningitis and death. Post-mortem revealed replacement of lateral sinus by fibrous cord.*

B. H., a previously healthy girl of 7 years, developed left otitis media on Christmas, 1931, following a mild febrile illness diagnosed influenza. The drum ruptured spontaneously and the ear drained for only a few days. There was no fever associated with the otitis. About a week after the ear ceased to drain, the child complained of headache and vomited several times. Vision became blurred and it was noticed that the left eye turned in. It was found that there was some deafness in the left ear.

Examination on January 28, 1932 revealed well-developed papilledema which was somewhat more severe on the left than on the right. The visual fields were concentrically constricted. There was a definite palsy of the left external rectus and probably slight weakness of the right external rectus. Audiometer readings showed moderate deafness on the left which involved all tones about equally. The caloric reactions were diminished in the left ear but normal on the right. Both ear drums were intact but both were retracted. There was no evidence of mastoiditis. The temperature was quite normal. Ventriculography revealed that the ventricles were of normal shape and perhaps a bit smaller than usual. The fluid was under great pressure but contained no cells. The Wassermann reaction of the spinal fluid and blood was negative. Dr. Dandy performed a subtemporal decompression on the right with the object of saving vision. The brain was under great tension but when the ventricles were tapped and the excess of fluid was also released from the subarachnoid spaces, the pressure was reduced. The decompression bulged for a time but the pressure slowly diminished and the papilledema soon began to recede. Vision improved and in March, 1932 was quite normal. The child seemed to be quite well for two years.

In February, 1934, the child developed otitis on the left once more. The drum was incised and there was a purulent discharge. The fever was not reduced, however, and signs of mastoiditis appeared. The mastoid was opened, and the child seemed to be better for two weeks. Then the temperature began to rise and signs of meningitis appeared. The decompression began to bulge and the child died.

Post-mortem examination revealed an acute purulent meningitis which was the cause of death. This was due to the pneumococcus. The left lateral sinus was found to be completely obliterated and transformed into a dense fibrous cord. It was the opinion of the pathologist that there had been thrombosis of this sinus two years before and that the clot had been organized and replaced by connective tissue.

CASE HISTORY (No. 485875. Path. 21794).—*Boy of 12 years developed bilateral otitis. Later, bilateral sixth nerve palsy without meningitis or hydrocephalus. Finally terminal meningitis. Post-mortem examination revealed thrombophlebitis of both inferior petrosal sinuses and osteomyelitis of the sphenoid bone.*

R. B., a colored boy of 12 years, was examined in the Otological Department on January 3, 1949. There was a history of bilateral otitis media. The right ear was still draining. There was a low grade fever and a suggestion of a right sixth nerve palsy. Mastoidectomy was performed and antibiotics administered. He was discharged in good condition.

On February 1, the patient returned with fever and drowsiness. There was complete paralysis of the right sixth nerve. The spinal fluid was normal but under slightly increased pressure. The Ayer test revealed a rather slow rise in pressure when the right jugular vein was compressed. The mastoid was explored again and the lateral sinus was found to be patent. Roentgenograms of the nasal sinuses and the base of the skull were negative. Antibiotics again gave relief of symptoms. The spinal fluid pressure became normal, but the sixth nerve palsy persisted.

On March 11, the patient returned a third time. Again he had fever and headache. Both external recti were completely paralyzed. The spinal fluid contained only 20 red cells. Ventriculographic study revealed normal ventricles. Roentgenograms of the skull and sinuses were again negative. Once more antibiotics relieved all the symptoms except for the palsies of the external recti.

On May 8, the patient was brought into the hospital in a moribund condition. He was in a stupor. The neck was rigid and retracted. The spinal fluid contained 37,000 white cells. He died the next day.

Post-mortem examination revealed extensive fresh pyogenic meningitis. There was thrombophlebitis of both inferior petrosal sinuses. The other dural sinuses showed no evidence that they had ever been occluded. The sphenoid sinus was full of pus and the sphenoid bone showed osteomyelitis.

We are inclined to believe that the child developed thrombophlebitis of the petrosal sinuses as a result of otitis and mastoiditis and that the sixth nerves were involved in their course through these sinuses, as Symonds has suggested. This seems probable because at the time the patient displayed bilateral sixth nerve palsies, there was no meningitis, hydrocephalus or lateral sinus occlusion and the spinal fluid pressure was elevated only to a moderate degree and then for a short time. There was no infection of the apex of the petrous bone.

BIBLIOGRAPHY

CHISHOLM, J. J. AND WATKINS, S. S.: Twelve cases of thrombosis of the cavernous sinus from a study of 50,000 surgical histories in Johns Hopkins Hospital. Arch. Surg., 1:483, 1920.

COURVILLE, C. AND NIELSEN, J. M.: Cerebral manifestations following acute otitis media in infancy and early childhood with particular reference to Jacksonian convulsions, conjugate deviation of the head and eyes and hemiplegia. Am. J. Dis. Child., 49:1, 1935.

———: Fatal complications of otitis media. Arch. Otolaryng., 19:451, 1934.

CROWE, S. J. AND DILL, J. L.: Thrombosis of the sigmoid or lateral sinus. Report of thirty cases. Arch. Surg., 29:705, 1934.

DANDY, W. E.: Cerebral (ventricular) hydrodynamic test for thrombosis of the lateral sinus. Arch. Otol., 19:297, 1934.

EDWARDS, E. A.: Anatomic variations of the cranial venous sinuses: Their relation to the effect of jugular compression in lumbar manometric tests. Arch. Neurol. & Psychiat., 26:801, 1931.

EMERY, J. L.: Pulmonary embolism in children. Arch. Dis. Childhood, 37:591, 1962.

FOX, S. L. AND WEST, G. B.: Thrombosis of the cavernous sinus. Newer concepts of its management and report of three cases. J.A.M.A., 134:1452, 1947.

FRENCKNER, P.: Sinography: A method of radiography in the diagnosis of sinus thrombosis. Proc. Roy. Soc. Med. Lond. December 4, 1936, Sc. Otol.

GARDINER, W. J.: Otitic sinus thrombosis causing intracranial hypertension. Arch. Otol., 30:253, 1939.

GOODHILL, V.: Penicillin treatment of cavernous sinus thrombosis. J.A.M.A., 125:28, 1944.

JEFFERSON, SIR G.: Concerning injuries, aneurysms and tumors involving the cavernous sinus. Trans. of the Ophthal. Soc., 73:117, 1953.

JOHNSTONE, D. F.: Cavernous sinus thrombosis treated with penicillin. Lancet, i:9, 1945.

ROSEN, S.: Thrombosis of the lateral sinus with metastasis; penicillin therapy; recovery. Arch. Otol., 42:416, 1945.

SYMONDS, C. P.: Discussion of cranial nerve palsies associated with otitis. Proc. Roy. Soc. Med., 37:387, 1944.

————: Intracranial thrombophlebitis. Ann. Roy. Col. Surg. Eng., **10**:347, 1952.

————: Otitic hydrocephalus. Neurology, **6**:681, 1956.

————: Otitic hydrocephalus. Brain, **54**:55, 1931.

————: Hydrocephalic and focal cerebral symptoms in relation to thrombophlebitis of the dural sinuses and cerebral veins. Brain, **60**:531, 1937.

TOBEY, G. L. AND AYER, J. B.: Dynamic studies on the cerebrospinal fluid in differential diagnosis of lateral sinus thrombosis. Arch. Otol., **2**:50, 1925.

WALSH, F. B.: Ocular signs of thrombosis of the intracranial venous sinuses. Arch. Ophth., **17**:46, 1937.

WHITE, J. W.: Penicillin therapy for thrombosis of the cavernous sinus in a fourteen month old child. Arch. Otol., **42**:147, 1945.

WOLF, J. W.: Thrombosis of the cavernous sinus with hemolytic streptococci bacteremia. Treatment by intravenous injection of sulfadiazine and penicillin with recovery. Arch. Otol., **40**:33, 1944.

WOODHALL, B.: Cranial venous sinuses correlation between skull markings and roentgenograms of the occipital bone. Arch. Surg., **33**:897, 1936.

————: Variations of the cranial venous sinuses in the region of the torcular Herophili. Arch. Surg., **33**:297, 1936.

————: Anatomy of the cranial blood sinuses with particular reference to the lateral sinuses. Laryngoscope, **49**:966, 1939.

SUBDURAL ABSCESS OF THE CRANIUM

Etiology.—This is an uncommon condition. It usually results from otitis and mastoiditis or from nasal sinusitis especially from chronic frontal sinus infection. It may also occur in pyogenic meningitis. Fracture of the skull is another cause.

Pathological Anatomy.—There is a purulent exudate under the dura and outside the arachnoid which extends over the lateral aspect of the hemisphere and sometimes over the base and vertex. It is not encapsulated. Leptomeningitis is found beneath this exudate. Softenings and hemorrhages are found in the cerebral cortex due to thrombosis of the small veins. Abscess of the brain, septic thrombosis of the dural sinuses, epidural abscess, leptomeningitis and osteomyelitis of the skull may be associated.

Clinical Features.—In most instances, this condition runs a rapid course to a fatal issue. The onset is usually preceded by evidence of otitis or of nasal sinus infection. Headache and fever then develop. Soon the neck grows rigid. Drowsiness and then stupor occur. Focal convulsions appear on the side opposite the lesion and are followed by hemiplegia or aphasia. Death often occurs within five days after the focal signs appear. Papilledema is rarely observed. The spinal fluid contains from 150 to 600 cells per cmm. Many of these are polymorphonuclear leucocytes. The spinal fluid protein is increased and the pressure is between 150 and 350 mm. water.

Diagnosis.—This condition is easily confused with abscess of the brain, local meningitis in the Sylvian fissure and with septic thrombosis of the superior longitudinal sinus. As a rule the diagnosis is not made until the skull is trephined.

Prognosis.—Most reported cases have been fatal.

Treatment.—The skull should be trephined and drainage established. Sulphonamides and antibiotics should be employed.

BIBLIOGRAPHY

COURVILLE, C. D.: Subdural empyema secondary to purulent frontal sinusitis. Arch. Otol., **39**:211, 1944.
HITCHCOCK, E.: Subdural empyema. Jour. Neurol., Neurosurg. and Psychiat., **27**:422, 1964.
KEITH, W. E.: Subdural empyema. J. Neurosurg., **6**:127, 1949.
KUBIK, C. S. AND ADAMS, R. D.: Subdural empyema. Brain, **66**:18, 1943.

SUBDURAL EFFUSIONS

It has recently come to light that in a large percentage of all cases of bacterial meningitis in babies, subdural collections of fluid accumulate. This fluid is xanthochromic or blood tinged and contains, as a rule, between 50 and 1000 mgs protein per 100 cc. Both red cells and white cells are present. Between 30 and 180 mgs of glucose per 100 cc. are usually found. Except in a very small percentage of cases no bacteria can be demonstrated. The fluid, therefore, is not pus as in subdural empyema, and not altered blood as in true subdural hematoma.

In rare instances, similar effusions may occur as a result of inflammation of the dura associated with otitis and mastoiditis, or pyogenic infections of the nasal sinuses. They may be occasionally associated with dural sinus thrombophlebitis. Smith states that compression of the brain by the effusion and by the subdural membrane may cause extensive laminar necrosis of the cerebral cortex and severe damage to the white matter.

Smith *et al.* suggest that inflammation of the archnoid may so alter its permeability as to permit transudation of fluid, cells and, rarely, bacteria into the subdural space. Once within the subdural space, the fluid may be absorbed slowly and may give rise to membrane formation.

It is advised that subdural puncture through the fontanel should be performed in all cases of meningitis in infants who do not get well promptly. If fluid is found repeated taps are indicated. If the fluid continues to accumulate, it may be necessary to trephine the skull and remove any membrane which may have formed.

BIBLIOGRAPHY

ARNOLD G.: Purulent and serous subdural effusions in course of purulent meningitis. J. Pediat., **39**:191, 1951.
BENSON, P. *et al.*: Prognosis of subdural effusions complicating pyogenic meningitis. J. Pediat., **57**:670, 1960.
McKAY, R. J., MORISSETTI, R. A., INGRAHAM, F. D. AND MATSON, D. D.: Collections of subdural fluid complicating meningitis due to Haemophilus influenzae. New Eng. J. Med., **242**:20, 1950.
RABE, E. F. *et al.*: Subdural collections of fluid in infants and children. Neurology, **18**:559, 1968.
PENFIELD, W. G.: Subdural effusion and internal hydrocephalus. Am. J. Dis. Child., **26**:383, 1923.

SMITH, J.: The pathology of influenza meningitis. Third International Congress of Neuropathology. Brussels, July 21-28, 1957.

SMITH, M., DORMONT, R. E. AND PRATHER, G. W.: Subdural effusions complicating bacterial meningitis. Pediatrics, 7:34, 1951.

ACUTE LABYRINTHITIS

Etiology.—Labyrinthitis is usually a complication of purulent otitis media or of meningitis. It is not an uncommon sequel of meningococcus meningitis, mumps and other acute infectious diseases. Tuberculous and syphilitic forms are well known.

Pathological Anatomy.—Two types of labyrinthitis are distinguished, the purulent and the "serous." In the former, the infection usually begins in the middle ear and extends into the labyrinth by way of the round or oval window. Later, the process may extend into the cranial cavity causing meningitis or abscess of the brain. In other cases, the infection extends centrifugally. Meningitis may result in infection of the labyrinth by way of the eighth nerve or the aqueduct of the cochlea. In either case, the inner ear is filled with pus and bacteria and the membranous labyrinth is destroyed. "Serous" labyrinthitis is a non-purulent inflammatory process which results as a rule from an infection in the meninges, the middle ear or the mastoid bone. It does not necessarily destroy the labyrinth as a purulent reaction does.

Clinical Features.—The onset of purulent labyrinthitis is marked by sudden and intense vertigo and usually by fever. These signs may develop in the course of either acute or chronic infections of the temporal bone. The patient is unable to stand or even to sit up, as a rule, and the least movement of the head provokes a great increase in the vertigo. Nausea and vomiting are almost invariably present. The patient lies by preference on the sound side of the head. Examination shows complete or nearly complete deafness in the affected ear. There is always spontaneous rotary and horizontal nystagmus, the slow phase of which is towards the side of the lesion. This is, of course, accentuated when the eyes are directed towards the opposite side. There is past-pointing to the side of the lesion. Not infrequently labyrinthitis is followed by meningitis or abscess of the brain.

"Serous" labyrinthitis is a relatively rare condition. There is apparently no satisfactory way of distinguishing the serous from the purulent form during the acute stage, but if the process subsides without complete destruction of the labyrinth, it is customary to assume that it was a "serous" labyrinthitis rather than a purulent inflammation.

When labyrinthitis results from extension of the infection into the inner ear during the course of meningitis, the signs and symptoms described above are sometimes obscured by the meningeal symptoms, and it is only when the patient is found to be deaf that the existence of labyrinthitis is recognized.

Purulent labyrinthitis results in complete deafness and loss of vestibular function. If it occurs before the fourth year and involves both ears, it invariably causes deaf-mutism. Between the fourth and seventh year, deaf-mutism may result, but is not constant. After the seventh year deaf-mutism is not to be expected unless the child is mentally deficient.

Diagnosis.—The diagnosis is based upon the development of sudden signs of irritation of the vestibular apparatus as described above in a patient suffering from meningitis, otitis or mastoiditis. The character of the nystagmus is of considerable value in distinguishing this condition from cerebellar abscess. In the latter, the nystagmus is of large amplitude and slow rate when the eyes are directed to the side of the lesion and is more rapid and of smaller amplitude when the eyes are directed to the opposite side. The slow phase of the nystagmus is always to the midline, i.e., the direction of the nystagmus is determined by the position of the eyes. There is no nystagmus when the eyes are directed towards a rest point near the midline. The nystagmus of labyrinthitis is spontaneous and constant. As stated above, the direction of vestibular nystagmus is not modified by change in position of the eyes. In cerebellar abscess, of course, we expect to find ataxia of the homolateral extremities and loss of muscle tone. Papilledema is usually present. Labyrinthitis due to mumps and no doubt, other virus infections must be distinguished.

Prognosis.—In the purulent type of labyrinthitis the prognosis is always very serious, since meningitis or abscess of the brain may result. If the child survives there is almost always complete loss of function of the affected ear. The "serous" type of labyrinthitis is very rare and does not always leave complete loss of function of the labyrinth.

Treatment.—Labyrinthitis following otitis is a surgical problem and the treatment cannot be fully discussed here. If there seems to be danger of extension of the infection into the meninges, the labyrinth must be opened and drained. Antibiotics and the sulfonamides should be administered.

BIBLIOGRAPHY

FRASER, J. S.: Pathological and clinical aspects of deaf-mutism. J. Laryngol. & Otol., **37**:57, 1922.
KERRISON, P. D.: Diseases of the Ear. Philadelphia, J. B. Lippincott Co., p. 292, 1930.

INFECTION OF THE PETROUS APEX

Etiology.—This is another complication of otitis and mastoiditis. It is not uncommon in childhood. Before the anatomical basis was established, it was customary to employ the term Gradenigo's syndrome. This syndrome comprises mastoiditis, pain in the face and paralysis of the homolateral sixth nerve.

Pathological Anatomy.—There is osteomyelitis of the apex of the petrous bone due to extension of the infection from the mastoid and middle ear. The inflammation penetrates the dura at this point, giving rise to a local meningitis which involves the sixth nerve and the gasserian ganglion.

Clinical Features.—The onset of symptoms is as a rule two to four weeks after the original otitis. Signs of mastoiditis are always present although in the chronic types of mastoiditis such signs may be inconspicuous. There may be fever, or temperature may be normal. The first symptom of Gradenigo's syndrome is usually pain which is localized not only in the mastoid region but in the face and especially in the eye and temple. There may be photophobia and lacrimation as well. If the pus ruptures through the cortex of the pyramid and escapes into the cranium under the dura there may be relief of pain for a time. Diplopia soon supervenes and before long it is possible to discover that the homolateral external rectus is paralysed or paretic. As a rule, there is no demonstrable anesthesia over the face but the corneal reflex may be reduced or abolished. In some cases, there is occipital pain which has been ascribed to irritation of the tentorial branch of the fifth nerve. In a few cases the seventh nerve is paralysed and sometimes there may be vertigo and tinnitus suggesting irritation of the labyrinth. Rarely the process extends to the jugular foramen and there is paralysis of the ninth, tenth and eleventh nerves. Symptoms of meningitis are often associated with Gradenigo's syndrome and a moderate increase of lymphocytes in the spinal fluid is often found even when clinical signs of meningitis are absent.

Diagnosis.—The diagnosis is based upon the association of sixth nerve palsy and pain in the distribution of the fifth nerve with mastoiditis. Stereoscopic roentgenograms of the base of the skull are helpful in the diagnosis. Symonds has recently stated that this same picture may result from infection of the inferior petrosal sinus.

Prognosis.—If treatment is neglected purulent meningitis will usually result, so this syndrome must always be regarded as of serious import. In cases in which the mastoid is opened promptly by a skillful surgeon, the outlook is not altogether unfavorable.

Treatment.—This is a surgical problem. Mastoidectomy is demanded at once. Recently surgeons have devised methods of draining the petrous apex, though the operation is difficult. Antibiotics and the sulfonamides serve to prevent the extension of the infection though they are not often completely effective unless drainage is secured.

BIBLIOGRAPHY

BARKER, L. F.: Gradenigo syndrome complicated by pneumococcic meningitis; recovery after intensive treatment with penicillin and sulfadiazine. Am. J. Med. Sc., **206:**701, 1943.

BAYLOR, J.: Suppuration of the petrous pyramid of the temporal bone. Internat. Clinics 1936, Vol. 11, series 46, p. 289.

Gradenigo, G.: A special syndrome of endocranial otitic complications (paralysis of the motor oculi externus of otitic origin). Ann. Otol. Rhin. & Laryng., 13:637, 1904.

Kopetsky, S. J. and Almour, R.: Suppuration of the petrous pyramid; pathology, symptomatology and surgical treatment. Ann. Otol. Rhin. & Laryng., 39:996, 1930; 40:157, 1931.

Sears, W. H.: Otogenic paralysis of the abducens with especial mention of isolated palsy associated with irritation of the gasserian ganglion. Ann. Otol. Rhin. & Laryng., 35:348, 1926-27.

PALSIES OF THE CRANIAL NERVES OF THE POSTERIOR FOSSA ASSOCIATED WITH CHRONIC OTITIS

Symonds has described a few cases of chronic otitis media in which palsies of the last four cranial nerves on one side developed a number of years after the onset of the infection. There was no evidence of mastoiditis and roentgenograms of the skull were negative. Collier has observed a small number of similar cases. At autopsy he has always found chronic osteomyelitis of the base of the skull and external pachymeningitis. Symonds has recently stated that septic thrombosis of the inferior petrosal sinus is a common cause of sixth nerve palsy and of the so-called Gradenigo's syndrome. He suggests that the posterior nerves may be involved by the same process.

It is well known that large cholesteatomas arising in the middle ear may erode the bone and eventually involve the nerves of the posterior fossa causing the syndrome described above. Since this process is a slow one, it rarely advances so far in childhood.

Thus, there are at least three possible explanations for the association of palsies of the nerves of the posterior fossa with chronic otitis.

BIBLIOGRAPHY

Collier, J.: Discussion of Symonds paper below.

Harris, W.: Polyneuritis Cranialis. Neuritis and Neuralgia, Oxford Press, p. 49, 1926.

Symonds, C. P.: Case of unilateral affection of cranial nerves, 9 to 12 associated with chronic otitis media. Proc. Roy. Soc. Med. Lond., 16: Sec. of Neurol. 53, 1923.

————: Discussion of cranial nerve palsies associated with otitis. Proc. Roy. Soc. Med., 37:387, 1944.

PURULENT MENINGITIS

Meningococcus Meningitis

Terminology.—This disease has also been called epidemic meningitis, cerebrospinal fever and spotted fever.

Etiology.—The meningococcus is a gram negative micrococcus which is found in the purulent exudate in the subarachnoid space and in certain cases in the blood stream and nasopharynx. It is sometimes termed the diplococcus intracellularis because it is often found within the cytoplasm of leucocytes. A number of strains of the meningococcus are distinguished which differ in their immunological reactions. Ninety per cent of the strains fall into two chief groups but two smaller groups are often described.

Epidemiology.—The disease is most prevalent in the northern temperate zone but is found in almost all parts of the world. No race seems to be immune. It exists in both epidemic and endemic forms. In all large cities a certain number of cases may be expected every year for the most fertile soil for the disease seems to be in crowded tenements and institutions where large numbers of people live in close contact. Epidemics recur at relatively long intervals which average, perhaps, ten years or more. Each one is followed by a gradually declining frequency until the average incidence is reached. Most epidemics begin in the winter or early spring and slowly subside as warm weather approaches.

Healthy carriers seem to be largely responsible for the dissemination of the disease. Under normal conditions the carrier rate is very small but it has been found that as epidemics develop, the carrier rate rises to 20 per cent or more and during severe epidemics it may reach 88 per cent.

Patients often harbor the meningococcus for long periods after their illness.

Children are more susceptible than adults and almost 50 per cent of all cases occur in children under the age of five years.

It is believed that the organism gains entrance to the body by way of the upper respiratory tract, for it may be recovered from the nasopharynx in a large percentage of cases during the prodromal period. In some cases the infection remains localized in the mucous membranes and the patient becomes a carrier. In other instances it invades the blood stream. In most cases, the organism reaches the meninges very promptly and sets up a purulent meningitis. If the blood stream infection is an overwhelming one, the so-called fulminating meningitis results, i.e., there is an acute septicemia with a terminal meningitis. If, on the other hand, only a few organisms reach the blood stream, the symptoms may be merely those of meningitis. Rarely the meningococcus may remain in the blood stream for weeks without giving rise to meningitis.

Pathological Anatomy.—The anatomical changes are essentially the same as those found in other types of purulent meningitis, differing only in degree. Several pathological pictures are distinguished, depending upon the duration and severity of the process. It is generally believed that the first lesions are found in the meninges around the sheaths of the small vessels. It has been claimed that the infection may also begin in the choroid plexus but the available evidence seems to indicate that this is a less common site than the meninges.

In the fulminating cases in which death takes place within a short time, the brain is intensely hyperemic and the subarachnoid spaces are distended by a serous exudate. Petechial hemorrhages may be found over the cortex and within the brain. Microscopic examination reveals numbers of leucocytes and lymphocytes in the leptomeninges, many of which contain meningococci. The convolutions are flattened and the ventricular system distended. The inflammatory process may extend along the adventitia of the cortical vessels but the brain is not directly involved aside from hyperemia, edema and minute hemorrhages.

In most cases, however, the patient survives long enough for the development of a purulent exudate. This is most abundant in the cisternae and basilar meninges but extends along the sulci over the convexity, throughout the ventricular system and into the spinal canal. There are more or less definite evidences of increased intracranial pressure and often hydrocephalus. The dural sinuses and cortical veins are sometimes occluded by thrombi and small infarctions in the cortex, usually of the hemorrhagic type, are not uncommon. Histological study reveals a fibrinopurulent exudate in the subarachnoid space and ventricular system. The process now begins to invade the cortex along the course of the penetrating vessels. The cells of the superficial layers show various stages of degeneration and both the astrocytes and microglia undergo proliferation and hyperplasia. The blood vessels are congested, their sheaths distended with leucocytes and red cells and the intima swollen and proliferated. A few leucocytes may be scattered diffusely throughout the tissues, especially in areas adjacent to the vessels. Multiple small cortical abscesses are sometimes found.

Wertham has stressed the frequency of focal areas of demyelination or even complete softening, not only in the cortex but in the deeper layers of the white matter and basal ganglia. These he regards as the result of changes in the small arteries. In some cases he has also found evidence of diffuse encephalitis which seems to develop primarily in the central portions of the brain and not by extension from the meninges.

Buchan *et al.* describe necrosis of the subcortical white matter in bacterial meningitis.

The cranial nerves may be infiltrated, especially the eighth and second nerves which are most severely injured. It has been shown that the infection sometimes extends along the sheath of the auditory nerve into the inner ear, causing a destructive labyrinthitis. Some authorities claim that optic neuritis may result from the same cause. Uveitis, choroiditis and even panophthalmitis with destruction of the bulb sometimes occur apparently as a result of metastatic infection by the blood stream.

In cases in which the infection persists for several months, we may see the end result of the process. The exudate has now disappeared. The pia-arachnoid, however, is milky or opaque and is often densely adherent to the cortex, so that it is impossible to strip the meninges without at the same time lacerating the cortex. Cysts filled with clear fluid may be found in the arachnoid. There is almost always hydrocephalus due to obstruction of the basilar cisternae. Shrinking and sclerosis of the cortical convolutions are often observed most frequently in the frontal and temporal regions. Sometimes the cortical lesions are localized, but often they are widespread or even generalized. Many of the cortical neurons have disappeared and there may be pronounced degeneration in the pyramidal tracts. The superficial layers of the cortex are the seat of a dense gliosis and may be intimately fused with the overlying meninges.

In the posterior basic or basilar meningitis, the inflammatory process is, as a rule, restricted to the basilar cisternae and is of a subacute or chronic type. The most striking finding is pronounced hydrocephalus which may reach a degree comparable with that of congenital hydrocephalus. Ependymitis may cause a similar picture.

The lesions in other organs such as the heart, the lungs and the joints are described in the reference given below.

Clinical Features: *different types.*—The onset of the disease is usually acute but may be either fulminating or very gradual. A number of different types are described but it must be kept in mind that such types are not actually distinct but are all connected by transitional cases. The following varieties will be distinguished: (1) Fulminating or hyper-acute cases; (2) Acute cases, which are, of course, most common; (3) Chronic and subacute cases; (4) Abortive cases; (5) Meningococcus septicemia without meningitis.

The *fulminating cases* are seen most frequently at the beginning of severe epidemics. The onset is very abrupt with intense headache, chills and high fever. In some instances, the disease begins in an almost apoplectic fashion, the victim falling suddenly to the ground without warning. There is usually extreme prostration or collapse with pallor and cyanosis leading rapidly to coma. In some cases, especially in those in which the infection is overwhelming, the temperature may be normal or even subnormal. A characteristic feature is the presence of petechiae and large purpuric spots in the skin. The common signs of meningeal irritation are often absent and the child may be flaccid rather than rigid. Hemiplegia and other evidences of focal cerebral lesions may develop suddenly probably as a result of purpuric lesions in the brain. The pulse is irregular, rapid and feeble. Respiration is usually rapid and shows various types of irregularity. Mace *et al.* state that a cranial bruit is often found in purulent meningitis in childhood. The spinal fluid may be quite clear at first but usually before the end, there is an excess of leucocytes. The meningococci are usually recovered in cultures and may sometimes be found in smears. They may be extracellular. Blood cultures are almost always positive and the organism may also be cultivated from the nasopharynx. Such cases are apparently the result of an overwhelming blood stream invasion with terminal meningitis.

The entire course may be less than twelve hours but averages between one and two days. Adrenal hemorrhage is often found in such cases at autopsy and this finding has been stressed as the cause of death. The term Waterhouse-Friderichsen syndrome is applied to such cases.

In the *common type* of meningococcic meningitis, the onset is acute but not so abrupt as in the cases just described. There may be prodromal symptoms such as vague malaise or catarrhal rhinitis, sore throat or cough lasting for a few days or even two weeks. In other cases, the patient has apparently enjoyed good health up to the very onset. The invasion of the nervous system is marked by headache and frequently by convulsions. The temperature rises to 104°F. within a few hours. In many cases, one or more chills occur at the onset of the fever. General hyperesthesia, rigidity of the spine and often opisthotonos develop within a few hours. The mental condition may be quite clear or there may be delirium. Stupor is not common at the onset of the moderately acute cases. The pulse is rapid, varying between 120 and 150, and may be irregular. Respiration may be either rapid or slow. Petechiae are common but purpura is unusual.

The course of untreated cases with acute onset is variable and for didactic purposes we may distinguish four types: (1) Prompt recovery; (2) Progressive course with fatal outcome; (3) Transition to a chronic or subacute type; (4) Course marked by exacerbations and remissions.

The most favorable cases run a course of from one to two weeks. Such an outcome is most frequent in instances in which effective treatment is given at the beginning.

In other cases, the disease runs a progressive course and terminates fatally within one or two weeks.

In some cases the course of the illness is marked by remissions and exacerbations. The patient seems to improve, the fever falls, the symptoms of meningitis diminish and the organisms may even disappear from the spinal fluid. After a few days, however, usually from three to six, the temperature rises once more, the symptoms become accentuated and abundant meningococci appear in the spinal fluid.

Worster-Drought and Kennedy distinguish between such *exacerbations* which they regard as fluctuations in the intensity of the infection and true *relapses*. They restrict the latter term to those cases in which the meningitis returns after an interval of several weeks during which the patient has been free of symptoms and the spinal fluid has been normal. True relapses are regarded by these authors as the result of a second invasion of the meninges by meningococci from the nasopharynx, for they have found that the cultures from the throat remain positive during the symptom-free interval. Such cases are apparently rare.

The disease presents some peculiarities in early infancy which must now

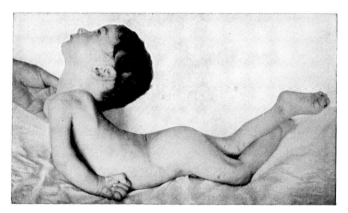

FIG. 149. Meningococcus meningitis. Basilar type showing intense opisthotonos.

be mentioned. According to Neal and Jackson, in infants the onset is less acute than in older children and diarrhea with greenish, slimy stools may attract more attention than the signs of meningeal irritation which are delayed and sometimes inconspicuous. Vomiting is not a constant symptom at the onset and hemorrhagic rashes are unusual. However, there is always an irregular fever and bulging of the fontanels is practically always present. Obstruction of the subarachnoid spaces and hydrocephalus are very common in infants. Subdural effusions develop in a large percentage of cases.

The *chronic type* of meningococcus meningitis, often called *chronic basilar meningitis* or *posterior basic meningitis,* gives rise to a clinical picture very different from those just described. It is seen, as a rule, in the sporadic type of the disease or in the wake of epidemics when the virulence of the disease is low. The onset is marked, as a rule, by only vague and indefinite symptoms. In some cases the parents cannot assign a definite date for the first symptoms but frequently there is a history of fever, anorexia and perhaps vomiting. Within a few weeks after this period, it is noted that the child is irritable and cries when disturbed. Soon the neck grows rigid and the head is retracted. Vomiting occurs from time to time without apparent cause and is usually of the projectile type. The head now begins to increase in size very rapidly, the fontanels bulge and the sutures are separated. The optic nerve heads may be congested or edematous but more frequently optic atrophy seems to develop without preceding papilledema. Palsies of the sixth nerves are common. The child is usually very apathetic or even semi-stuporous. General rigidity of the musculature is a striking feature. The child may be bent backwards in the form of an arc, i.e., in opisthotonos. The tendon reflexes are increased and there may be clonus and bilateral Babinski phenomenon. The course may be afebrile but is often marked by recurrent attacks of fever which are associated with exacerbations of symptoms and sometimes with convulsions. The disease steadily progresses. There is profound emaciation and cachexia leading to death from malnutrition or secondary infection. The spinal fluid is often quite normal but usually a mild pleocytosis is present with some increase in globulin. Organisms are rarely found, for the infection is confined to the basilar meninges. In some cases, however, purulent fluid containing organisms may be recovered from the ventricles. The course, as a rule, varies between two and five months but it is not unusual for the infection to become quiescent, so that the child may survive indefinitely with some degree of hydrocephalus, mental defect and loss of vision. The clinical picture is so typical that we may make a presumptive diagnosis from the symptoms alone, but an absolute diagnosis depends upon the recovery of the meningococcus, for other infections may give the same picture. To summarize the above description, it may be said that these cases are the result of an infection of low virulence which results in a subacute or chronic meningitis localized to the basilar meninges. The general symptoms of infection are mild and the clinical symptoms are chiefly those of hydrocephalus.

Among the *abortive cases* we must distinguish at least two types. In one variety, the patient complains of malaise, headache and perhaps pain in the back. There may be fever or even a mild chill. Meningococci are found in the nasopharynx but the symptoms disappear within a few hours and no signs of meningeal irritation ever develop. It is possible that these symptoms represent a beginning invasion of the blood stream which is checked at once. More definite cases are those in which a transient meningeal reaction occurs. The onset may be relatively severe with fever, chills, headache and vomiting. There is more or less rigidity of the spine but a rash is rare. The spinal fluid is clear and may at most contain a few leucocytes or lymphocytes. Organisms are usually absent but sometimes one or two may be found. These are always intracellular and only rarely can be cultivated. The blood culture is negative, as a rule, but positive results may be obtained from the nasopharynx. Within two or three days the symptoms have largely disappeared and recovery is rapid and complete. Worster-Drought and Kennedy distinguish between cases in which the symptoms disappear spontaneously or the true *abortive* cases and those in which the favorable course is the result of prompt treatment which they call *aborted* cases.

It is scarcely necessary to describe the *meningococcus septicemia* which is apparently not very uncommon in epidemics, for from the neurological point of view such cases are merely of theoretical importance. Suffice it to say that blood stream infections may persist for weeks without any evidence of meningitis. There is irregular fever, petechiae in the skin and often metastatic infections such as arthritis and endocarditis. The blood culture is positive. Meningitis may develop at any time.

Laboratory Findings.—The blood shows a constant leucocytosis averaging between 15,000 and 30,000. The polymorphonuclear leucocytes average between 80 and 85 per cent of the white count but may reach 95 to 98 per cent. In rare cases, leucopenia may be found. Often blood culture is positive on the first day of the illness.

The spinal fluid may be in certain instances normal or nearly normal on the first day. In some cases of the chronic basilar type of the disease, there is only a slight increase of cells. In almost all cases, however, there is a great increase in the cell count which ranges from a few hundred to many thousands. The fluid may be opalescent, cloudy, turbid or purulent, depending upon the number of cells it contains. Polymorphonuclear leucocytes usually predominate but the lymphocytes are also increased. In the later stages of the disease and in the more chronic types, the lymphocytes become relatively more numerous. The fluid is usually under increased pressure. The globulin and total proteins are increased and the latter may reach 500 mgs. per 100 cc. The fibrin is often increased and a film may form on standing. Sugar and chlorides are much diminished and the former may fall below 10 mgs. Sometimes Froin's syndrome with xanthochromia, increased protein and spontaneous coagulation may be found as a result of obstruction of the spinal canal. The Queckenstedt test is usually positive in such cases. The meningococci are often demonstrated with difficulty in smears of the spinal fluid but are recovered in most cases by proper cultural methods.

Cultures from the nasopharynx, the urine and from fluid aspirated from joints may be positive in certain cases. Organisms may also be demonstrated in the skin lesions.

Complications and Sequelae.—Pneumonia, usually broncho-pneumonia, occurs in a large percentage of cases, not only as a terminal event in fatal cases but even when the child seems to be making good progress toward recovery. Lobar pneumonia due to meningococci is described. In a few cases, endocarditis with vegetations and ulcerations of the heart valves has occurred. This may be associated with embolic phenomena and infarctions in various organs and is most frequent in cases of septicemia without meningitis. Pericarditis is very rare. Cystitis and pyelitis are common in certain epidemics but usually run a benign course and rarely result in pyonephrosis. Nephritis is also rare. The joints are involved not uncommonly. As a rule, the arthritis is multiple and the shoulders and knees are, perhaps, most frequently affected. There is local swelling and redness and often fluid in the joint. Aspiration yields a thin, purulent fluid which only rarely contains meningococci. The arthritis runs a relatively benign course and rarely results in joint destruction unless there is secondary infection. It may occur early or at the height of the illness. Duodenal ulcer may occur.

The most serious complications are referable to the *nervous* system. The pupils are often unequal and may be dilated or more frequently contracted, but oculomotor palsies are uncommon. Occasionally, sixth nerve paralysis may occur. The optic nerve head is usually normal or slightly congested, but papilledema is not uncommon and sometimes results in optic atrophy and blindness. In the chronic basilar type of meningococcus meningitis, optic atrophy develops in at least 50 per cent of all cases and is usually primary, that is, it is not preceded by any edema. In rare instances the infection actually invades the bulb, giving rise to optic neuritis, choreoretinitis, uveitis and even panophthalmitis with complete destruction of the eye. Fortunately, the last is usually unilateral. The eye may be invaded at any time during the course of the disease but, as a rule, this complication develops before the fourth day. Conjunctivitis and keratitis are relatively common.

The ear is also frequently affected and deafness is estimated to result in between 3 and 30 per cent of all cases. This develops early, usually between the third and fifth day. Two types are described. In one the deafness may develop suddenly and become quite complete, but substantial recovery occurs slowly during convalescence. More commonly the deafness is total, permanent and often bilateral. Both vestibular and cochlear branches of the eighth nerve are affected. This is due to labyrinthitis, but it is strange that the violent vertigo and other signs characteristic of acute labyrinthitis of other types are not observed.

Hydrocephalus is one of the commonest and most serious complications. In the early stages of the disease, hydrocephalus may result from the accumulation of thick exudate under the base of the brain or in the cisternae of the posterior fossa. Less frequently the aqueduct is occluded. If the exudate is absorbed, recovery may follow. Later in the disease, especially in the chronic basilar type and in some relapsing cases, the exudate becomes organized and a permanent obstruction results from the obliteration of the subarachnoid space or of the foramina of the fourth ventricle. If hydrocephalus develops suddenly there are usually relatively acute signs of increased intracranial pressure, such as headache, projectile vomiting, periodic breathing of various types and, perhaps, bradycardia. The last, however, is not constant, for the pulse often remains rapid. Dilatation of the retinal veins and papilledema may be present or absent. The symptoms are often obscured to such a degree by the other symptoms that the only reliable signs of hydrocephalus are the dilatation of the ventricles and enlargement of the head. In must be kept in mind that either communicating or noncommunicating hydrocephalus may exist and that although in the former the fluid recovered by spinal puncture is small in amount and of a different character from the ventricular fluid, in the latter, the spinal fluid may be abundant and identical with the ventricular fluid. In other cases, hydrocephalus develops more gradually and acute signs of increased intracranial pressure are absent. This is especially characteristic of the type which appears late in the course of the disease. The head gradually expands, optic atrophy and blindness develop and finally general weakness, spasticity and mental deterioration follow. In several cases we have seen outspoken cerebellar ataxia associated with hydrocephalus. No doubt the dilatation of the fourth ventricle is to blame.

Another common complication is subdural effusion. This develops, as a rule, early in the course of the illness. There may be bulging of the fontanels and convulsions, vomiting and focal neurological signs. Fever may continue, because of this complication, after the spinal fluid has become sterile. Subdural puncture yields yellow or blood tinged fluid which usually contains no bacteria. Repeated taps may be needed and, in rare instances, the formation of a false membrane may require operation.

In a few cases syndromes of cerebral origin develop, usually in the late stages of severe and protracted cases. Hemiplegia, monoplegia, aphasia and even cortical blindness are described. Often the symptoms are transient and disappear within a few days, but in some cases permanent disability results. The cause is apparently not always the same. In some instances, infarction of the cortex has been found associated with thrombosis of cortical arteries or perhaps more frequently due to extensive occlusion of the cortical veins. In others there is merely a local accumulation of exudate with inflammatory changes in the underlying cortex. Hemorrhages sometimes occur. Cerebral abscesses of large size are rare and usually due to secondary infection. The writer has observed one case in which serum was injected inadvertently into both paracentral lobules with the formation of large cysts and the production of cerebral paraplegia.

Syndromes referable to the spinal cord or spinal nerve roots are rare. In a few cases, paralysis of one or more extremities with atrophy of the muscles and loss of reflexes has been observed. Such symptoms usually develop suddenly and are more apt to occur in the later stages of the disease. Recovery is the rule. Wilkins has reported a case in which signs of a lesion of the cauda equina or of the conus followed meningococcus meningitis. The anatomical basis is not clear but infiltration of the spinal nerve roots and inflammatory changes in the superficial layers of the spinal cord have been found at autopsy. Only very rarely are the signs of a transverse lesion of the spinal cord observed. Apparently this is not due to a true transverse myelitis, but is the result of thrombosis and softening. In a number of cases severe neuritic pains appear in the back and extremities during convalescence in association with persisting rigidity of the spine. These symptoms have been attributed to inflammation of the spinal nerve roots and also to arthritis. Their precise origin is still uncertain.

In a few cases, we have seen persisting rigidity of the lumbar spine and legs without paralysis, loss of sensibility, changes in the reflexes or more than a little pain. The lumbar lordosis is abolished and the child walks with bent knees. The rigidity is quite unlike spasticity. In such cases, we have found that the cauda equina is bound firmly to the dura by dense adhesions. (E. W. U-118953) Occasionally, tumors of the cauda may cause exactly the same symptoms. Sometimes, fibrous thickening of the pia-arachnoid results in adhesions and the formation of cysts which may give rise to cerebral or spinal symptoms many months after the acute illness.

Diagnosis.—The diagnosis depends upon the clinical features I have described, and above all, upon the demonstration of the organism. The essential symptoms in the diagnosis are: the acute onset with headache, vomiting, prostration, fever and petechiae and the signs of meningeal irritation. The characteristic changes in the spinal fluid serve to eliminate the so-called meningism such as is found in almost any acute and severe infection. It must be remembered that the spinal fluid may be clear in the first few hours of the illness and also in certain cases where the infection is localized as in the chronic basilar type. Experienced clinicians may recognize the meningococcus in smears with considerable certainty, but absolute proof is dependent upon culture. Blood agar and blood broth are the most suitable culture media. The culture tubes should be warmed and inoculated directly by allowing the spinal fluid to drip into the tube. Rubber stoppers should then be inserted with the object of reducing the oxygen tension and the tubes incubated at once. The meningococci are very sensitive to temperature and may be killed by chilling. Colonies may be expected to appear within 24 to 48 hours. The organisms may also be found in the nasopharynx and in the blood in certain cases. They may be demonstrated in smears made from the scrapings of the petechiae.

Prognosis.—The mortality is much higher in epidemic cases than in the sporadic type of the disease and is higher during the first part and during the height of the epidemic than later when the virulence of the infection seems to decline. It is, of course, higher when treatment is begun late. Infants do not do so well as older children. Before the introduction of serum therapy the case fatality rate was between 50 and 80 per cent. The use of serum produced a striking reduction in these figures and the mortality then ranged between 20 and 40 per cent. At present, thanks to the introduction of the sulfonamides and antibiotics, the mortality is said to be less than 10 per cent.

The prognosis in individual cases is not easy and should always be guarded. Cases of the following types should always be considered unfavorable. (1) Cases in infants under one year of age. (2) Fulminating cases. (3) Cases in which treatment is begun late. (4) Cases complicated by hydrocephalus. (5) Cases in which the exudate is thick. (6) Cases in which there is unsatisfactory response to treatment.

In children over two years of age whose onset is not excessively violent, and who are properly treated at once, the outlook is favorable for prompt and complete recovery.

If the illness is severe or prolonged, the possibility of permanent injury to the nervous system should always be considered. An interesting study made by Slesinger of a series of cases in Pittsburgh between 1927 and 1932 should be mentioned in this connection. Some 84 cases were treated and there was an immediate mortality of 30 per cent. Of the 68 children who survived, 54 were apparently cured and 14 were discharged with some complication. In 1933, it was possible to re-examine 42 of these patients. It was found that 25 were in good condition, both mentally and physically, and showed no defects which could be attributed to the illness, but 17 showed various residua. Among the 42 re-examined, there were 3 children who had been discharged with hydrocephalus. In 2 cases, apparent recovery followed and in the other, the hydrocephalus eventually became arrested or at most slowly progressive. Among the 17 children with residua were 4 cases of deafness, 4 cases of mental deficiency, 3 cases of delayed speech, 1 case of complete blindness, 1 of arrested hydrocephalus, strabismus in 2 cases and focal epilepsy and spasticity of one leg in 1 case each. In 6 of these 17 children, no residua were noted upon discharge but on re-examination there was found delayed speech in 3 cases, deafness in 2 and mental defect in 1 case. Ross, in 1951, in reviewing the results, secured by sulfonamides and penicillin points out that there has been a definite reduction of the mortality rate but that the more modern drugs have not resulted in any striking reduction of neurological residua.

Prophylaxis.—As soon as the diagnosis can be made with a high degree of probability, the patient should be isolated and proper quarantine instituted. Since the infection is believed to be disseminated by droplet infection, gauze masks are essential. From a theoretical point of view, it might seem wise to isolate all carriers of the organisms but it has been found that the carrier rate is often so high that this is actually impossible and it is apparently not attempted by public health officials at present.

Greenberg and Cooper state that a somatic antigen vaccine prepared from 3 group A strains of Neisseria meningitidis is safe and effective.

Treatment.—Obviously general nursing care, as in all severe infections, is required. Various sedatives for the restlessness and excitement and analgesics for the pain may be indicated. The barbiturates have the disadvantage of depressing respiration, and we have used paraldehyde by mouth or by rectum. An ice bag applied to the head or spine may give some measure of relief. If the child is unable to take an adequate diet by mouth, gavage should be employed. Abundant fluids must be given. The bowels and bladder should be watched. Catheterization may be necessary. Every effort should be made to prevent bed sores.

We now have two effective means of treatment of meningococcic meningitis, antibiotics, especially penicillin, and sulfonamides. These may be employed separately or together. Penicillin may be given intramuscularly and intraspinously. Intramuscular injections may be given every three hours into the buttocks. The best dosage is still uncertain but at least a hundred thousand units may be given at each injection. Intramuscular injections are to be preferred since this route is so free from danger. Some authorities, however, insist that in severe cases intraspinal injections are required. Injections of 20,000 units may be given by the lumbar route twice a day or by cisternal injection if the spinal subarachnoid canal is obstructed. There is evidence that penicillin causes some irritation of the nerve roots and meninges so intraspinal medication should be avoided if possible. It is doubtful if the drug should ever be injected into the ventricles for it is known to damage the brain and cause convulsions.

In some cases, penicillin alone does not give satisfactory results and sulfonamides are required. These drugs are preferably given by mouth but may also be given by vein. Sulfadiazine is perhaps the most effective and some authorities think it is preferable to penicillin. In most clinics at the present time, penicillin and sulfonamides are used together.

In cases in which the child does not respond to treatment as expected, and in cases in which there are evidences of increased intracranial pressure, subdural puncture should be made to determine whether or not the child has subdural effusion. Repeated punctures may be required and, if membrane formation occurs, operative removal of the membrane may be necessary.

The Waterhouse-Friderichsen syndrome required the administration of cortisone or corticotropin and correction of any electrolyte changes which may develop. Norepinephrine is used to maintain the blood pressure.

BIBLIOGRAPHY

BANKS, H. S. AND McCARTNEY, J. E.: Meningococcic encephalitis. Lancet, 1:219, 1942.

BUCHAN, G. C. *et al.:* Diffuse necrosis of subcortical white matter associated with bacterial meningitis. Neurology, 19:1, 1969.

DANIELS, W. B.: Meningococcic bacteremia. Arch. Int. Med., 81:145, 1948.

DINGLE, J. H., THOMAS, L. AND MORTON, A. R.: Treatment of meningococcic meningitis and meningococcemia with sulfadiazine. J.A.M.A., 116:2666, 1941.

FINLAND, M., STRAUSS, E. AND PETERSON, O. L.: Sulfadiazine. J.A.M.A., 116:2641, 1942.

GREENBERG, L. AND COOPER, M. Y.: A somatic antigen vaccine for the prevention of meningococcal cerebrospinal meningitis. Bull. Wld. Hlth. Org., 33:21, 1965.

HODES, H. L. AND STRONG, P. S.: Treatment of meningococcic meningitis with sulfonamide. J.A.M.A., 119:691, 1942.

KAUFMAN, B. *et al.:* Statistical analysis of 242 cases of meningococcic meningitis. J. Pediat., **38**:705, 1951.

KERSKY, B. *et al.:* The incidence of neurologic residua in children after recovery from bacterial meningitis. Arch. of Pediat., **79**:63, 1962.

LOHREY, R. C. AND TOOMEY, J. A.: Epidemic meningitis and meningococcemia treated with penicillin. J. Pediat., **28**:86, 1946.

LONG, P. AND BLISS, E. A.: The Clinical and Experimental Use of Sulfanilimide, Sulphapyridine and Allied Compounds. New York, Macmillan Co., 1939.

LT. MACE, J. W. *et al.:* Cranial bruit in purulent meningitis in childhood. New England Jour. Med., **278**:1420, 1968.

MACNALTY, A. S.: Epidemic Diseases of the Central Nervous System. London, Faber & Gwyer, 1927.

McNEAL, W. J. AND PEASE, M. C.: Fulminant meningococcemia treated with penicillin calcium. Am. J. Dis. Child., **68**:30, 1944.

NEAL, J. B. AND JACKSON, H. W.: Epidemic meningitis in the first three months of life. J.A.M.A., **88**:1299, 1927.

O'CONNELL, J. E. A.: Clinical signs of meningeal irritation. Brain, **69**:9, 1946.

ROSS, A. T.: Meningococcic meningitis. Incidence of residua following serum, sulfonamide and sulfonamide-penicillin therapy. Arch. Neurol. & Psychiat., **67**:89, 1952.

ROTONDO, C. C. AND HANDELMAN, N. I.: Meningococcic meningitis. A report of multiple cases occurring in the same family. J. Pediat., **27**:576, 1945.

SCHWENTKER, F., GELMAN, S. AND LONG, P. H.: The treatment of meningococcic meningitis with sulphanilamide. J.A.M.A., **108**:1407, 1937.

SHAW, E. B. AND THELANDER, H. E.: Endemic cerebrospinal fever in childhood. J.A.M.A., **101**:746, 1933.

SLESINGER, H. A.: Complications and sequelae of meningococcic meningitis in infancy and childhood. Pa. Med. J., **36**:327, 1933.

SMITH, M., DORMONT, R. E. AND PRATHER, G. W.: Subdural effusions complicating bacterial meningitis. Pediatrics, **7**:34, 1951.

THORNER, M. W.: Modification of meningeal signs by concomitant hemiparesis. Arch. Neurol. & Psychiat., **59**:485, 1948.

WALSH, F. B.: *Loc. cit.*

WERTHAM, F.: The cerebral lesions in purulent meningitis. Arch. Neurol. & Psychiat., **26**:549, 1931.

WILLIAMS, H.: Meningococcic infections in infancy and childhood: Meningococcic septicemia with special reference to the adrenal apoplexy or the Waterhouse-Friderichsen syndrome. M. J. Australia, **1**:557, 1942.

WORSTER-DROUGHT, C. AND KENNEDY, A. M.: Cerebro-Spinal Fever, Etiology, Symptomatology, Diagnosis and Treatment of Epidemic Cerebro-Spinal Meningitis. London, A. & C. Black, Ltd., 1919.

Pneumococcus Meningitis

Etiology.—Several strains of pneumococcus may cause meningitis.

Pathological Anatomy.—The meningitis is characterized by a most abundant exudation of pus and fibrin which is often too tenacious to flow through the needle employed in spinal puncture. The process is sometimes peculiar in that it is most severe over the convexity of the cortex in contrast to other types of meningitis in which the exudate is most evident at the base. It is not unusual for the pus to be confined to some part of the subarachnoid space for a time, although it usually becomes generalized eventually.

Clinical Features.—This is a common type of meningitis in infancy and at the Harriet Lane Home about 10 per cent of all cases of acute meningitis occurring in children under three years of age are due to the pneumococcus. In half of these cases, the child is under six months of age. The meningitis is almost always secondary to definite pneumococcus infections elsewhere. In most cases, the disease begins with pneumonia and the meninges become infected as a result of pneumococcus bacteremia which so often occurs at the height of the pulmonary process. In a few cases, the meningitis precedes the development of clinical evidence of pneumonia and it may occur during convalescence, perhaps, in association with empyema. In some cases there are other signs of pneumococcic infection such as pericarditis or peritonitis. The organism, as a rule, may be recovered from the blood. Meningitis may be secondary to brain abscess. In older children, infection of the middle ear, mastoid bone or nasal sinuses may be responsible. Fractures and penetrating wounds of the skull should be mentioned. In older children, pneumococcus infection of the middle ear or mastoid bone is a common cause of meningitis. In such cases, the infection may extend directly into the cranial cavity and septicemia may be absent.

As a rule, the clinical symptoms of pneumococcus meningitis are merely the usual ones associated with any acute meningitis. However, in certain cases, the signs and symptoms may be atypical. Often, the process is confined for a time to the under surface of the temporal lobe, especially when the infection arises in the ear. From this point, it may extend into the Sylvian fissure where it causes convulsions, beginning in the opposite face and arm, which are apt to be followed by hemiplegia. In such instances, the spinal fluid may at first be quite normal. When the process is most intense over the convexity, as not infrequently happens, convulsions both general and focal may be the most striking symptoms at first, so that an abscess may seem to be the most likely diagnosis. In other cases in infants who are very ill with pneumonia, the meningitis may be obscured by the severity of the primary process in the lungs and may be found unexpectedly at post-mortem examination. Usually, however, the advent of meningitis during pneumonia is marked by sudden vomiting and convulsions promptly followed by stupor and by bulging of the fontanels. We have found subdural effusions in several cases of pneumococcic meningitis.

The course is almost always a very short one in untreated cases and only rarely does it last for more than a week. When the meningitis is circumscribed, however, the child may live for several weeks or even months. Pneumococcic meningitis has a tendency to recur repeatedly. Often this is due to the fact that the infection has become loculated in the meninges and so inaccessible to the drug employed. The meninges are often reinfected from a focus in the skull. Schneider and Thompson state that recurrent attacks of meningitis are sometimes a result of an unrecognized traumatic fistula opening into the nasal sinuses with cerebrospinal rhinorrhea.

Diagnosis.—The diagnosis may be suspected by the development of signs of meningitis during the course of pneumonia but is established only by the demonstration of the organisms in the spinal fluid where they are usually abundant. It must be kept in mind that the fluid may be clear for a time when the meningitis is circumscribed. Signs of meningeal irritation without any change in the spinal fluid may occur at the onset of pneumonia as in any other acute infection. These are attributed to intoxication rather than to bacterial invasion of the meninges and the term meningism is often employed to designate this picture. Puncture of the subdural spaces may be required to rule out subdural effusion.

Prognosis.—This condition was almost always fatal until the introduction of sulfonamides reduced the mortality to between 60 and 80 per cent. Penicillin seems to be even more effective and figures from case reports seem to indicate a mortality of around 45 per cent. In children who survive, there are often residua such as mental defect, hydrocephalus or hemiplegia, focal epilepsy, deafness and cranial nerve palsies.

Treatment.—Vigorous treatment with antibiotics and sulfadiazine is recommended. There is an advantage in employing several antibiotics, it is said. Some authorities recommend intradural administration of the medication, but others rely upon intramuscular injection and regard intradural injections as dangerous and unnecessary. Since pneumococcic meningitis is so often a result of infection of the ear, the nasal sinuses or the lung, a careful search should always be made for such foci and surgical drainage be carried out if possible. A. J. Johnson *et al.* state that intrathecal crystalline pancreatic desoxyribonuclease liquifies the thick exudate in the meninges and improves the prognosis.

BIBLIOGRAPHY

APPELBAUM, E. AND NELSON, J.: Penicillin treatment of pneumococcic meningitis. J.A.M.A., **128**:778, 1945.

DAVIDSON, L. T. AND WOLLSTEIN, W.: Pneumococcus meningitis in children with an analysis of 122 cases. Acta Paediat. Scan., **11**:367, 1930.

HODES, H. L., GIMBEL, H. S. AND BURNETT, G. W.: Treatment of pneumococcic meningitis with sulphapyridine and with its sodium salt. J.A.M.A., **113**:1614, 1939.

JOHNSON, A. J. *et al.*: Crystalline pancreatic desoxyribonuclease as an adjunct to the treatment of pneumococcal meningitis. New England J. Med., **260**:893, 1959.

SCHNEIDER, R. C. AND THOMPSON, J. M.: Traumatic cerebrospinal rhinorrhea as a source of recurrent meningitis. Ann. Surg., **145**:517, 1957.

SWEET, L. K. *et al.*: The treatment of pneumococcic meningitis with penicillin. J.A.M.A., **127**:263, 1945.

WARING, A. J. JR. AND SMITH, M. H. D.: Combined penicillin and sulfonamide therapy in the treatment of pneumococcic meningitis. J.A.M.A., **126**:418, 1944.

Meningitis Due to Staphylococci and Streptococci

Etiology.—A number of the pathogenic streptococci and staphylococci are capable of causing meningitis. Staphylococcus aureus and streptococcus hemolyticus are most common.

Pathological Anatomy.—There is nothing characteristic in the meningitis caused by these organisms. As a rule, however, the exudate is not so thick and contains less fibrin than in pneumococcus meningitis and drainage is, therefore, possible to some extent.

Clinical Features.—In newborn infants, this type of meningitis may follow infections of the umbilicus or rupture of an encephalocele or of the sac in spina bifida. Later in childhood, it may result from otitis media, mastoiditis and its complications, infections of the scalp, septicemia, erysipelas, furunculosis, fracture of the skull, lumbar puncture, osteomyelitis and surgical operations on the nasal sinuses or brain. In staphylococcus meningitis the back of the head and the trunk should always be examined for the presence of a dermal sinus which might be the portal of entry for the infection.

The clinical picture is merely that of an acute purulent meningitis and can scarcely be distinguished from meningococcus meningitis unless the organism is identified. The course is rapidly progressive, as a rule, but in some cases, especially in staphylococcus meningitis, may be protracted for a number of weeks. In such chronic cases, hydrocephalus may develop. Cerebral abscess is sometimes associated and we have seen thrombosis of the cerebral vessels with infarction of the cortex and hemiplegia.

The spinal fluid is always turbid and shows great numbers of pus cells and numerous organisms which are easily grown upon common media.

Diagnosis.—This depends upon the identification of the organism in the spinal fluid.

Prognosis.—Streptococcic meningitis was formerly almost always fatal. Penicillin has reduced the mortality to about one third if one may judge by recent case reports. Staphylococcic meningitis is still a very serious disease and even with modern treatment the outlook is not too cheerful.

Treatment.—It is important to search for the original focus of infection and to treat it suitably if possible. Since various strains of staphylococci and streptococci have different degrees of sensitiveness to chemotherapeutic agents, the organism must be tested to determine which antibiotic should be employed. The use of several antibiotics and perhaps sulfonamides as well is recommended. Erythromycin, carbomycin and bactracin are said to be effective against staphylococci resistant to other antibiotics.

BIBLIOGRAPHY

McCollum, W. D.: Cure of staphylococcic meningitis of otitic origin with penicillin. Arch. Otolaryngol., 40:514, 1944.

McCune, W. S. and Evans, J. M.: Intraventricular penicillin in the treatment of staphylococcic meningitis. J.A.M.A., 125:705, 1944.

White, W. I. *et al.:* Penicillin in the treatment of pneumococcal, meningococcal, streptococcal and staphylococcal meningitis. Am. J. Med. Sc., 210:1, 1945.

"Influenzal" Meningitis

Etiology.—The organism is sometimes termed the Pfeiffer bacillus after its discoverer, or B. influenzae, although it has no established relation to influenza. It is a small, short rod, the morphology of which is not distinctive. It grows only on special media such as blood agar. There are six types of this organism, it is claimed.

Pathological Anatomy.—The pathological process is not in any way characteristic, but there is a tendency to formation of a thick, fibrinopurulent exudate and of loculated pockets of pus in the basilar meninges, and in sulci over the cortex especially if the course is at all prolonged. The brain may be injured by arteritis and phlebitis which may cause softenings and hemorrhages. Superficial abscesses may occur and occasionally an intracerebral abscess. Subdural empyema occurs but subdural effusion is more common. Compression of the brain by the effusion and by the subdural membrane may cause necrosis of the cortex and damage to the underlying white matter.

Clinical Features.—This is not an uncommon type of meningitis in infants and, as a rule, nearly half a dozen are seen at the Harriet Lane Home every year. It has been estimated that about 20 per cent of all cases of purulent meningitis in childhood are due to B. influenzae. At least 80 per cent of these cases occur in infancy. The disease occurs sporadically and is not associated with influenza. The symptoms of meningitis are usually preceded by inflammation of the respiratory tract such as bronchitis, bronchopneumonia, or rhinopharyngitis with otitis. Rarely it is secondary to purulent arthritis or abscess. Such symptoms are not necessarily severe and may be overlooked. The course of the meningitis is usually very short and the onset relatively acute. The clinical picture does not differ in any essential from that due to other types of purulent meningitis. In a few cases, the disease may become subacute rather than acute and the course may be prolonged for four or five weeks, so that it resembles that of tuberculous meningitis. Relapses are not uncommon. If the child survives such an illness, there is apt to be some residua such as hemiplegia or mental defect. The spinal fluid is turbid and contains a great excess of leucocytes. The organisms are difficult to demonstrate in smears and do not grow on the ordinary culture media. They may be cultivated on blood agar, however. Many of the strains of the Pfeiffer bacillus which cause meningitis produce indol and Rivers has shown that in the absence of demonstrable organisms, the presence of indol in the spinal fluid is strong evidence that we are dealing with this organism. The organism may be found in the blood in a large percentage of cases.

Apparently subdural effusions are frequently associated with this type of meningitis. Such effusions contain small amounts of blood but, as a rule, no pus or bacteria. The mechanism by which they are produced is not clear. Frequently they may be controlled by repeated aspiration.

Diagnosis.—The diagnosis depends upon the study of the spinal fluid. The high cell count establishes the presence of meningitis and the recovery of the organism reveals the nature of the infection. Puncture of the subdural space is indicated if there is any ground for suspicion of subdural effusion.

Prognosis.—With prompt and adequate treatment the results are now good in most cases.

Treatment.—Various antibiotics are effective against this infection. Streptomycin and oxytetracycline are recommended. Sulfadiazine is usually employed at the same time.

BIBLIOGRAPHY

Koch, R. and Carson, M. J.: Management of Hemophilus influenzae type B meningitis. J. Pediat., **46**:18, 1955.

Logan, G. B. and Herrell, W. E.: Streptomycin in the treatment of influenzal meningitis of children. Proc. Staff Meet. Mayo Clin., **21**:393, 1946.

McKay, R. J., Morissette, R. A., Ingraham, F. D. and Matson, D. D.: Collections of subdural fluid complicating meningitis due to Haemophilus influenzae. New England J. Med., **242**:20, 1950.

Rivers, T. M.: Influenzal meningitis. Am. J. Dis. Child., **24**:102, 1922.

Sako, W., Stewart, C. A. and Fleet, J.: Treatment of influenzal meningitis with sulfadiazine. J.A.M.A., **119**:327, 1942.

Smith, J.: The pathology of influenza meningitis. Third International Congress of Neuropathology. Brussels, July 21-28, 1957.

Smith, M.: Influenzal meningitis. J.A.M.A., **130**:331, 1946.

INVOLVEMENT OF THE NERVOUS SYSTEM
IN BRUCELLOSIS

This disease is caused by three distinct organisms, Brucella melitensis, Brucella abortus and Brucella suis which are responsible for this disease in goats, cattle and pigs respectively. The caprine disease is prevalent in the Mediterranean area, Texas and California. This type of the disease is sometimes called Malta fever for it was first found on the island of that name. The disease of swine is found chiefly in Iowa and in Georgia and the bovine disease is widespread but possibly more prevalent in New York than elsewhere. The infection is acquired by using unpasteurized milk and butter and by eating inadequately cooked meat.

The incubation period is prolonged averaging between 5 and 15 weeks. There are at least three clinical types. The *undulant type* is characteristic of B. melitensis infection. The fever occurs in repeated episodes separated by remissions. This process may continue for many months. There is weakness, aching pains in the muscles, headache and insomnia. There is also a *malignant type* which is marked by high fever and delirium and may be fatal in a few weeks. A *chronic type* also occurs which is marked by weakness, debility, anemia, lack of energy and emotional instability. There may be only a slight rise of temperature in the afternoons. The variability of this disease makes a diagnosis on clinical grounds a matter of great difficulty.

In many cases there is no special localization of the disease and only constitutional symptoms are observed. A great variety of local manifestations are described, however. The liver and spleen may be enlarged. The lymph nodes may be swollen. The joints may show changes similar to those of rheumatic fever. Lesions in the bones are described. Zammit describes spondylitis which tends to heal in several months. Pleurisy, pericarditis, peritonitis, infections of the urinary tract and intestinal disturbances are all mentioned. Iritis, keratitis and retinal lesions are sometimes seen.

The diagnosis can be established only by the isolation of the organism from the blood, stool, urine or spinal fluid. Agglutination tests are of value if the titer is 1/160 or better and a skin test is employed.

The nervous system does not escape. Nichols has reviewed the neurological complications. He states that there is an inflammatory process in the adventitia of the blood vessels. Such vessels may become occluded or may rupture. There is also a meningeal reaction, usually diffuse, which may be either acute or chronic. In the chronic cases it becomes a granulomatous process. Hydrocephalus may result. The cranial nerves may be involved where they lie in the meninges at the base and the spinal nerve roots are also infiltrated. The spinal cord and the cerebral cortex are invaded by the inflammatory process and may be damaged by vascular occlusion and softening.

The neurological symptoms may appear in the acute stage of the disease, in the chronic phase or after a prolonged remission of possibly two years' duration. Headache and signs of meningeal irritation are present in most cases. Confusion, loss of memory and delirium may occur. Focal and general convulsions are described. The cranial nerves are often involved and it is said that the eighth nerves are damaged most frequently. Hemiplegia and aphasia are sometimes observed but paraplegia is more common. Pains and paresthesias in the legs are often mentioned and probably result from irritation of the spinal nerve roots. The knee and ankle jerks are often lost.

The spinal fluid may show no increase of cells but there is usually a pleocytosis of variable degree. Lymphocytes predominate. The protein content is increased. Organisms were isolated from the fluid in half of Nichols' cases.

Dihydrostreptomycin and sulfadiazine have been recommended but it is believed at present that the tetracycline drugs are most effective. Chloramphenicol is of value. Some authorities recommend that dihydrostreptomycin and one of the tetracycline drugs be used in combination. Dihydrostreptomycin must be employed with caution for I have seen a patient who became completely deaf while being treated with this drug. It is said that ACTH and cortisone are helpful if given in conjunction with the antibiotics.

BIBLIOGRAPHY

BRAUDE *et al.*: Aureomycin therapy in human brucellosis. J.A.M.A., **141**:831, 1949.

FINCHAM, R. W. *et al.*: Protean manifestations of nervous system brucellosis. J.A.M.A., **184**:269, 1963.

———: Nervous system brucellosis. J.A.M.A., **184**:269, 1963.

HAGEBUSCH, O. E. AND FREI, C. F.: Undulant fever in children. Am. J. Clin. Path., **11**:497, 1941.

McBRYDE, A., DANIEL, N. C. AND POSTON, M.: Brucella infection in children. J. Pediat., **4**:401, 1934.

NICHOLS, E.: Meningoencephalitis due to brucellosis with report of a case and review of the literature. Ann. Int. Med., **35**:673, 1951.

TREVER, R. W. *et al.*: Brucellosis. Arch. Int. Med., **103**:381, 1959.

ZAMMITT, F.: Undulant fever spondylitis. Brit. J. Radiol., **31**:683, 1958.

OTHER TYPES OF BACTERIAL MENINGITIS

Meningitis due to B. coli. An occasional case of meningitis due to this organism is observed in childhood, especially in infancy. Newborn infants may have meningitis apparently as a result of infection *in utero*. Pyelitis is probably the commonest cause. Evidences of blood stream infection are usually present, and hemorrhagic softenings and abscesses of the brain may occur. Infection of the sac in spina bifida is another cause of meningitis due to B. coli. Streptomycin is recommended and sulfonamides are effective.

Gonococcus meningitis. This is a rare condition. It may develop as a result of ophthalmia neonatorum, from ophthalmia acquired later in life or from vaginitis or urethritis. As a rule there is blood stream infection with polyarthritis and sometimes endocarditis. The organisms may be found in the blood. Sulfonamides and penicillin are effective.

Meningitis due to Salmonellae. A number of cases of meningitis due to these organisms in childhood have been observed. S. cholerae is possibly the commonest organism found in such cases. This infection is derived from hogs. S. typhimurium is derived from the mouse. Other strains are found in various domestic animals. As a rule there is enteritis followed by blood stream invasion and finally meningitis. Osteomyelitis, endocarditis and pyelitis may be present. Sulfonamides are said to be effective but it seems that chloramphenicol is the drug of choice.

Meningitis due to B. typhosus. Meningitis may occur in the course of typhoid fever. Both serous and purulent types are described. The onset of meningeal symptoms may occur early or late in the course of the illness. The organisms are usually found in the spinal fluid. In a few cases the meningitis seems to be primary and no intestinal lesions are evident. Chloramphenicol is the drug of choice.

Meningitis due to Listeriosis. This disease is due to infection by L. monocytogenes, a small, gram-positive rod. It occurs in cattle, sheep, rodents and certain fowls. It may also occur in man, especially in children in whom it may be fatal. It may cause a mild influenza-like illness or a generalized process with septicemia and meningitis. Epidemics may occur in man as well as in cattle. The bacillus may be isolated from the blood and spinal fluid. Monocytic cells are found in the spinal fluid. Penicillin and tetracycline drugs are effective. A form of this disease termed *infantile granulomatosis* is described. The infection may be found in an aborted fetus, in a premature baby and in an infant born at term. The process is generalized and almost invariably fatal. The mother is usually not ill but may recall a mild influenza-like illness.

Meningitis due to Pseudomonas aeruginosa or B. pyocyaneus. This is most apt to develop after spinal puncture for diagnosis, intrathecal injection of medication or spinal anesthesia. The organism is normally found in the human intestinal tract. The spinal fluid shows a greenish fluorescence when exposed to ultraviolet light. It is said that effective therapy depends upon the selection of a suitable antibiotic by sensitivity tests. In some cases polymixin must be used. Penicillin does not help.

Meningitis due to tularemia. This disease seems to be acquired from small animals especially the rabbit. The incubation period is between 4 and 10 days. There is often a primary lesion on the finger or conjunctiva. This appears as a red papule and then as a rule, gives place to an ulcer. The regional lymph nodes become swollen and then, in many cases, systemic symptoms appear. Pneumonia is usually present. Peritonitis is found in a large percentage of cases. Nodules develop in the liver and spleen. The essential lesions are not unlike tubercles. In some cases there is meningitis. This resembles tuberculous meningitis. There are several hundred lymphocytes in the spinal fluid. Streptomycin is said to be effective.

B. mucosus capsulatus or Friedländer's bacillus is a rare cause of meningitis in children. Sulfonamides and streptomycin are recommended.

Anthrax meningitis is described. This is a disease of cattle and sheep. It causes hemorrhagic meningitis which was invariably fatal until antibiotics were introduced. An antiserum is used and penicillin and other antibiotics such as aureomycin and terramycin are recommended. Very prompt treatment is essential.

Meningitis due to flavobacteria. Cabrera and Davis describe an epidemic of meningitis due to flavobacterium meningosepticum. Newborn and debilitated infants were especially susceptible. Of fourteen infants affected, ten died and four developed hydrocephalus. The usual antibiotics were ineffectual.

BIBLIOGRAPHY

BARRETT, G. S., RAMMALKAMP, C. H. AND WORCESTER, J.: Meningitis due to Escherichia coli. Am. J. Dis. Child., 63:41, 1942.

BEENE, M., HANSEN, A. AND FULTON, M.: Salmonella meningitis. Am. J. Dis. Child., 82:567, 1951.

BERMAN, P. H. *et al.:* Neonatal meningitis. Pediatrics, 38:6, 1966.

BRADFORD, W. L. AND KELLEY, H. W.: Gonococcic meningitis in the newborn infant with review of the literature. Am. J. Dis. Child., 46:543, 1933.

CABRERA, H. A. AND DAVIS, G. H.: Epidemic meningitis of the newborn caused by flavobacteria. Am. J. Dis. Child., 101:289, 1961.

CUTLER, M. AND CUTLER, P.: Pseudomonas meningitis. Am. Pract., 4:200, 1953.

DANIEL, W. A.: B. mucosus capsulatus (Friedländer) meningitis. Pediatrics, 3:3, 1949.

DAVID, J. K. AND OWENS, J. N.: Tularemic meningitis. Am. J. Dis. Child., 67:44, 1944.

DELTA, B. G. *et al.:* Listeria meningitis in newborn. Med. Ann. District of Columbia, 30:329, 1961.

DUFFY, P. E. *et al.:* Rhombencephalitis due to Listeria monocytogenes. Neurology, 14:1067, 1964.

FIELDS, W. S.: Tularemic meningitis. Arch. of Neurol. & Psychiat., 61:422, 1949.

GIBBENS, J.: Colon bacillus meningitis in newborn. Lancet, 1:1298, 1932.

GROOVER, R. V. *et al.:* Purulent meningitis in newborn infants. New England J. Med., 264:1115, 1961.

HAIGHT, T. H.: Anthrax meningitis. Am. J. Med. Sc., 224:57, 1952.

HENDERSON, L.: Salmonella meningitis. Am. J. Dis. Child., 75:351, 1948.

HOOD, M.: Listeriosis as an infection of pregnancy manifest in the newborn. Pediatrics, 27:390, 1961.

HOWE, C. *et al.:* Streptomycin treatment of tularemia. J.A.M.A., 132:195, 1946.

INSLEY, J. AND HUSSAIN, Z.: Listerial meningitis in infancy. Arch. Dis. Childhood, 39:278, 1964.

LILLIE, R. D. AND FRANCIS, E.: Pathology of tularemia in man. National Inst. of Health. Bull. no. 167, 1936.

NETER, E. R.: Salmonella cholerae suis meningitis. Arch. Int. Med., 73:425, 1944.

RADBILL, S. X. AND WESTON, W.: Typhoid fever in infants with special reference to typhoidal meningitis. Arch. Pediat., 43:160, 1926.

RADKE, R. AND CUNNINGHAM, G.: A case of meningitis due to pseudomonas aeruginosa (bacillus pyocyaneus). J. Pediat., 35:99, 1949.

SEELIGER, H. AND CHERRY, W. B.: Listeriosis. U.S. Public Health Monograph, 1957.

STEIN, H. AND EVANS, M.: Salmonella Bredeney meningitis. Am. J. Dis. Child., 84:457, 1952.

YU, J. S. AND GRAUAUG, A.: Hazard of neonatal purulent meningitis. Arch. Dis. Childhood, 38:391, 1963.

——— AND ———: Purulent meningitis in the neonatal period. Arch. Dis. Childhood, 38:391, 1963.

———: Neonatal meningitis. Clin. Pediat., 4:387, 1965.

ADHESIONS BETWEEN THE PIA AND ARACHNOID MEMBRANES AND SUBARACHNOID CYSTS

Terminology.—A number of terms are employed to designate the conditions described below. Many authors speak of arachnoiditis which is qualified by the term cystic, adhesive or circumscribed.

Definition.—Proliferation of the leptomeninges causing adhesions between the pia and arachnoid and cyst formation and resulting in various injuries to the nervous system. It should be pointed out that the neurological symptoms are supposedly a result of mechanical injury resulting from the cysts and adhesions and are not a direct result of the primary process such as meningitis or trauma which causes such cysts and adhesions.

Etiology.—It may be said at once that the etiology is obscure in most cases. It is well known, of course, that any of the common types of meningitis may result in adhesions between the pia and arachnoid and may be followed by hydrocephalus. It is claimed that local meningitis associated with otitis media may cause cysts in the posterior fossa and that in the same way local meningitis associated with infection of the sphenoid or ethmoid sinuses may cause cysts about the optic chiasm. Certain cases have been reported in which an acute lymphocytic meningitis of uncertain origin has been followed by extensive proliferation of the pia-arachnoid resulting in hydrocephalus or constriction of the spinal cord. The cases of Machella *et al.* and of Barker and Ford may be mentioned in this connection. The use of spinal anesthetics may be followed by adhesions between the pia and arachnoid and damage of the cord. Serum and antibacterial agents may be mentioned as possible causes. Winkelmann described cases in which detergents were employed to clean the apparatus used in spinal puncture and serious symptoms resulted from washing some of the material into the spinal canal. An extensive arachnoiditis followed with involvement of the cauda, the cord and finally hydrocephalus which was sometimes fatal.

Trauma is said to be an important etiological factor. It is stated that hemorrhage in the meninges may lead to the formation of cysts and adhesions.

Cysts and adhesions are also found in association with congenital hydrocephalus, the Arnold-Chiari malformation and syringomyelia. These are probably the result of incomplete formation of the subarachnoid spaces and are discussed under Congenital Hydrocephalus q.v. Robinson describes cysts in the middle fossa associated with defects in the temporal lobe and bulging of the temporal lobe.

These conditions must be distinguished from the lakes of fluid which overlie atrophic areas of the cerebral cortex and from the normal cisternae which are, of course, always filled with fluid. Parasitic and neoplastic cysts should cause no confusion.

Pathological Anatomy.—The diagnosis is often made at operation but few post-mortem examinations are recorded. Surgeons describe large or small cysts filled with clear fluid and surrounded by membranes resembling the arachnoid but somewhat thickened and opaque. These are found as a rule in locations in which the subarachnoid space is well developed as for example in the posterior fossa surrounding the cerebellum, around the optic chiasm and in the Sylvian fissure. Such cysts may compress the cerebral cortex or the cranial nerves. In the spinal canal the subarachnoid space may be obliterated for many segments and the cord appears to be constricted by the thickened membranes in certain cases. Cysts are also found in this location. Bits of tissue removed at operation for study usually show merely fibrosis but in some cases there is a mild inflammatory process. Often the pathologist reports normal meninges. In the case of Machella in which death occurred while the process was still active lymphocytic infiltrations as well as fibrous thickening of the meninges were found.

Clinical Features: Intracranial Conditions.—It is believed that this condition may develop at any age and that it is not less common in childhood than in other periods of life. In some cases the onset is preceded by some well known form of meningitis but in others there is merely a mild febrile illness of unknown origin or no illness at all.

Many cases are described in which the process is in the *posterior fossa*. In such instances, there are usually definite signs of increased intracranial pressure. There may also be signs of involvement of the cerebellum and palsies of the fifth, sixth and eighth nerves. Ventriculograms reveal hydrocephalus and operation discloses cysts and adhesions in the posterior fossa. This type is said to be closely associated with otitis media with or without mastoiditis.

In other cases, there are signs of involvement of the *optic chiasm* and optic nerves. In several reported cases there have been obesity and polyuria suggesting that the hypothalamus was involved. There may be evidence of increased intracranial pressure. Exploration reveals distention of the cisterna chiasmaticus and adhesions surrounding the optic chiasm. An association with ethmoiditis is claimed. In my opinion many cases described as arachnoiditis of the chiasm are really instances of retrobulbar neuritis. We have had only two cases in which progressive loss of temporal fields over a period of years led to exploration of the chiasm. Adhesions were found around the chiasm and when these were released, vision and the visual fields returned to normal.

Sometimes there are focal signs such as hemiplegia or local convulsions pointing to a lesion involving the motor cortex. The lateral ventricle is compressed. Exploration in such cases may expose a cyst in the *Sylvian fissure* with compression of the cerebral cortex.

Such cysts arising early in life may extend anterior to the temporal lobe with enlargement of the middle fossa, bulging of the temporal bone, elevation of the sphenoid ridge, erosion of the posterior wall of the orbit and pulsating exophthalmos.

In a few cases, similar cysts are described lying *between the hemispheres* above or anterior to the corpus callosum. Focal signs are not very evident in such cases and there is apt to be mental deterioration. The lesion must be located by ventriculography.

Spinal Conditions.—I can speak with more confidence about the spinal cases for I have followed several of them through the entire course of the illness. The onset is marked by fever and by the usual signs of a mild meningitis. The spinal fluid contains one hundred or more cells per cubic mm and most of these are lymphocytes. The fever lasts only about ten days. During the acute stage of the illness there may be lancinating pains suggesting irritation of the spinal nerve roots and even some weakness of the legs suggestive of involvement of the spinal cord. This weakness usually diminishes or disappears during the next few weeks but after a few weeks or months returns and gradually grows more severe. Examination at this stage discloses as a rule partial paraplegia with some loss of sensibility over the lower part of the body. The level of the lesion is indicated by radicular pains and paraesthesias which usually extend over a broad zone including several dermatomes. The upper level of the anesthesia is rarely sharply defined as it is in cases of spinal cord tumor. In some cases it is impossible to secure spinal fluid for the lumbar subarachnoid space has been obliterated. If fluid is obtained, it shows no increase of cells but may show an increase in protein. Manometric tests reveal partial or complete obstruction of the spinal canal. Lipidol is arrested at the level of the lesion and its lower border characteristically shows a serrated, irregular contour in contrast to the smooth lower border found in case of tumor. Operation discloses thickened, opaque pia-arachnoid which invests the cord very closely and constricts the spinal nerve roots. The subarachnoid space is obliterated. Small cysts may be seen in the meninges. The process may be localized or may extend over many segments of the cord. Evacuation of the cysts may result in improvement but in cases in which the meninges are diffusely thickened no surgical measures are of value. The symptoms tend to grow more severe for a number of months but eventually the process seems to become stationary so that the patient's condition may remain unchanged for years.

We have also observed cases in which there were no signs of damage to the spinal cord and the only finding was peculiar rigidity of the spine and hips which was certainly not true spasticity. The cauda was found to be fastened to the dura by adhesions in such cases.

Diagnosis.—If the symptoms follow an attack of meningitis, it would seem justifiable to suspect adhesions in the subarachnoid spaces. In many cases, however, there is nothing in the history or examination which points to the correct diagnosis. The lesion must be localized by clinical study and if necessary by ventriculography or by myelogram. The nature of the lesion can be established only by exploration. It should be kept in mind that observations made at operation are not always reliable and often a neoplasm may be found at a second operation when "arachnoiditis" was found before.

Prognosis.—In some cases, the evacuation or removal of a cyst is said to give relief of symptoms. In other cases, the cysts reform, and the symptoms return. Adhesions and thickenings of the meninges cannot be removed unless they are localized. If hydrocephalus is present it can rarely be relieved. Operation is therefore not satisfactory. It is generally agreed, however, that the course of this condition is less definitely progressive than that of a neoplasm and arrest of the process is apt to occur eventually.

Treatment.—If the lesion can be localized, it should be exposed and removed if possible.

BIBLIOGRAPHY

BARKER, L. F. AND FORD, F. R.: Chronic arachnoiditis obliterating the subarachnoid space. J.A.M.A., **109**:785, 1937.

CRAIG, W. McK. AND LILLIE, W. I.: Chiasm syndrome produced by chronic local arachnoiditis. Arch. Ophth., **5**:558, 1931.

DAVIS, L. E. AND HAVEN, H. A.: Clinicopathologic study of intracranial arachnoid membrane. J. Nerv. & Ment. Dis., **73**:129, 1931.

FRAZIER, C. H.: Cerebral pseudotumors. Arch. Neurol. & Psychiat., **24**:1117, 1930.

HEUER, G. AND VAIL, D. T.: Chronic cysternal arachnoiditis producing symptoms of involvement of the optic nerves and chiasm. Arch. Ophth., **5**:334, 1931.

HORRAX, G.: Generalized cisternal arachnoiditis simulating cerebellar tumor. Its surgical treatment and end results. Arch. Surg., **9**:95, 1924.

KATAGIRI, A.: Arachnoidal cyst of the cisterna ambiens. Neurology, **10**:783, 1960.

MACHELLA, T. E., WEINBERGER, L. M. AND LIPPINCOTT, S. W.: Lymphocytic choriomeningitis. Report of a fatal case with autopsy findings. Am. J. Med. Sci., **197**:617, 1939.

MACKAY, R. P.: Chronic adhesive spinal arachnoiditis. J.A.M.A., **112**:802, 1939.

McDONALD, J. V. AND COLGAN, J.: Arachnoidal cyst of the posterior fossa. Neurology, **14**:643, 1964.

ROBINSON, R. G.: Intracranial collections of fluid with local bulging of the skull. J. Neurosurg., **12**:345, 1955.

STOOKEY, B.: Adhesive spinal arachnoiditis simulating spinal cord tumor. Arch. Neurol. & Psychiat., **17**:1, 1927.

WALSHE, F. M. R.: Serous spinal meningitis. Med. Sc. Abst. & Rev., **1**:319, 1919-20.

WINKELMANN, N. W.: Neurological symptoms following accidental intraspinal detergent injection. Neurology, **2**:284, 1952.

ZEHNDER, M.: Subarachnoidalcysten des Gehirns. Zentralblt. f. Neurochir., **3**:100, 1938.

CEREBRAL EPENDYMITIS

Definition.—Acute and chronic ependymitis commonly occur in association with meningitis of various types and with abscess of the brain. In such cases the ependymitis is merely secondary and deserves no special discussion. In a few exceptional cases, however, acute ependymitis may be primary and the inflammation may remain localized within the ventricular system as a result of obstruction of the foramina of the fourth ventricle. Chronic forms of ependymitis are not excessively rare. The so-called granular ependymitis has been frequently described in various types of chronic disease of the brain. A primary form of obscure etiology is also well known.

Acute and Subacute Ependymitis.—The etiology is identical with that of meningitis, namely, syphilis, tuberculosis, infection with the meningococcus and various pyogenic organisms. The symptoms resemble those of brain abscess. There is headache, vomiting, drowsiness and vertigo. Sixth nerve palsies are common and papilledema may develop rapidly and become very severe. There is usually fever and leucocytosis. Signs of meningeal irritation may be present or absent depending upon whether there is extension of the inflammation to the meninges. The diagnosis depends upon the study of the cerebrospinal fluid. Lumbar puncture yields fluid which contains only a slight excess of cells and protein. Puncture of the cerebral ventricles, however, reveals cloudy or purulent fluid under great pressure containing many leucocytes, a high percentage of protein and often organisms. The treatment depends upon the etiology and, in general, is the same as that of meningitis.

Chronic Granular Ependymitis.—This is the commonest form of primary ependymitis. The ventricles are studded with small nodules and papules which are found to be the result of proliferation of the ependymal cells and of the subependymal glia. There may be evidences of chronic inflammation or the process may be purely hyperplastic. A number of etiological factors have been mentioned including syphilis, tuberculosis and other chronic diseases of the brain but in the primary form of granular ependymitis, the etiology is usually obscure. This condition may be found in cases of epilepsy, tuberosa sclerosis, dementia, praecox and is one of the causes of acquired hydrocephalus.

The only symptoms which we can attribute to this condition with confidence are those due to internal hydrocephalus which results whenever there is obstruction of the aqueduct or of the foramina of the cerebral ventricles by the ependymal proliferation. As a rule, there are no focal signs and the clinical picture is merely that of increased intracranial pressure. In long-standing cases, there may be spastic diplegia as a result of extreme atrophy of the cortex and papilledema eventually gives place to optic atrophy. In some cases, the foramen of Monro may be occluded, causing dilatation of one lateral ventricle. Hemiparesis and focal convulsions may be found in such cases and the picture may be identical with that of brain tumor. In some instances, the intracranial pressure eventually diminishes and the condition may become stationary or slowly progressive. We may find on examination merely optic atrophy, dementia or perhaps spasticity so that the disclosure of hydrocephalus by ventriculography is quite unexpected especially if the obstruction occurred so late that the head did not enlarge.

The diagnosis can scarcely be made upon clinical grounds. By means of Dandy's method of ventriculography and other tests which he has applied to the study of hydrocephalus, it is possible to determine the site at which the obstruction to the flow of cerebrospinal fluid is situated. The cause of the obstruction cannot be established unless it happens to be placed where it may be exposed at operation. Treatment is the same as that for other types of obstructive hydrocephalus.

> CASE HISTORY (Path. 12616).—*Progressive hydrocephalus beginning at the age of 16 months. Post-mortem examination revealed granular ependymitis which had caused obstruction of the foramina of the fourth ventricle.*
>
> D. W. was neglected by her ignorant and poverty stricken parents and as a result was always poorly nourished and ill. At an early age she developed rickets. At the age of 16 months her head suddenly began to grow with abnormal rapidity and the child began to vomit. Some time later she developed an acute upper respiratory infection and her condition soon grew so serious that she was brought to the hospital.
>
> Examination revealed an emaciated child whose head was greatly enlarged and of hydrocephalic shape. There was advanced craniotabes and deformity of the chest as well as the enlargement of the epiphyses usually seen in rickets. The child was moribund when admitted and died within a few hours from extensive bronchopneumonia.
>
> Post-mortem examination revealed in addition to severe rickets and bronchopneumonia, well-advanced hydrocephalus. The ependyma of the third and fourth ventricles was studded by innumerable elevations projecting upwards a millimeter or more. The aqueduct was dilated as were all cerebral ventricles. The foramina of the fourth ventricle were occluded by the granulations. Histological study revealed that these were formed by proliferation of the ependymal cells and contained a central core of glial fibers. There was no evidence of syphilis or of tuberculosis.

BIBLIOGRAPHY

GLOBUS, J. H. AND STRAUSS, I.: Subacute diffuse ependymitis, report of a case simulating tumor of the brain. Arch. Neurol. & Psychiat., **19**:623, 1928.

KERNOHAN, J. W. AND PARKER, H. L.: Stenosis of the aqueduct of Sylvius. Arch. Neurol. & Psychiat., **29**:538, 1933.

NELSON, S. H.: A case of chronic internal hydrocephalus due to ependymitis granularis. J. Neurol. & Psychopath., **7**:117, 1926-27.

MYELITIS AND ABSCESS OF THE CORD

Etiology.—The organisms may reach the cord by way of the blood stream as in septicemia and pyemia, by penetrating wounds or by direct extension from adjacent foci of infection. The staphylococci, streptococci and similar organisms are usually responsible.

Pathological Anatomy.—The spinal cord may be swollen, hyperemic and edematous at the level of the lesion or even completely softened. There is almost always meningitis either generalized or local. On section, the affected segments are usually found to be reduced to a purulent material, so that the white matter and gray matter cannot be distinguished. The process usually involves several segments and may extend throughout a large part of the cord. As a rule, it is spindle shaped and seems to begin in the central gray matter. Bacteria are almost always demonstrable in smears and cultures. As a rule, the areas in which the cord is completely broken down are surrounded by zones in which there is congestion and edema as well as small areas of necrosis. The small blood vessels are surrounded by cuffs of lymphocytes, leucocytes and microglial cells distended with lipoid granules. The tissues are also infiltrated diffusely with similar cells. It is very unusual for these lesions to be encapsulated but in a few cases fusiform abscesses have been discovered which are surrounded by a fibrous capsule similar to that of an abscess of the brain.

Clinical Features.—Myelitis of this type may develop in the course of septicemia of all types but is most commonly secondary to abscess of the lungs, osteomyelitis, infections of the genito-urinary tract, furuncles or other types of infection due to staphylococci and streptococci. It may also result from bacterial endocarditis and from secondary infections in the course of pneumonia, scarlet fever, typhoid fever and erysipelas.

The onset may be obscured by the presence of symptoms due to the primary infection. The development of myelitis is usually marked by pain in the back and the rapid development of paralysis of the legs. This is almost always flaccid and followed very shortly by retention of urine. The tendon reflexes are abolished and the plantar reflexes may be absent for a time although they often become extensor later. Sensibility is lost below the level of the lesion. Some degree of rigidity of the spine is present depending upon the amount of meningeal reaction. In some cases the process extends upwards rapidly.

The spinal fluid contains a variable number of leucocytes and lymphocytes. Protein is almost always increased. The manometric tests may show obstruction or the canal may be patent.

The course is relatively rapid as a rule. Bed sores develop despite the greatest care and death occurs from paralysis of respiration, meningitis or sepsis.

In the rare cases of abscess of the spinal cord the picture may be quite different and may resemble that of spinal cord tumor. The spinal canal may be obstructed by swelling of the cord and the spinal fluid may show the typical syndrome of Froin.

Diagnosis.—There is nothing specific in the neurological signs. The picture is merely that of a transverse myelitis of rapid onset developing in association with septicemia or with a suppurative process in some part of the body.

Prognosis.—Pyogenic myelitis is almost invariably fatal. Woltman and Adson have discovered twenty-eight cases of abscess of the spinal cord in medical literature. All of these were fatal but these authors report a single case of their own in which drainage of the abscess led to recovery.

Treatment.—Pyogenic myelitis has not responded to treatment in the past but it is possible that penicillin, streptomycin or the sulfonamides may be effective if given in time. Rarely an abscess of the cord can be drained.

CASE HISTORY (Ped. A-25989).—*Abscess of the spinal cord secondary to osteomyelitis. Complete transverse lesion at T 3. Operation and drainage. No return of function. Subsequently there was polyuria, low grade fever and decalcification of the bones of the legs.*

R. B. M., a boy of 4 years, developed pain and stiffness in the right hip joint in the spring of 1943. The symptoms slowly grew more severe. On July 22, he suddenly became ill with high fever and delirium. Later in the day, he had convulsions. The next morning he could not move his legs and his parents brought him to the Harriet Lane Home.

Examination revealed flaccid paralysis of both legs and of the muscles of the trunk up to the 3rd rib with corresponding anesthesia and retention of urine. There was only slight rigidity of the spine. The knee and ankle jerks were absent. Plantar responses were extensor. Numerous petechiae were found in the skin and mucous membranes. Temperature ranged between 40.8° and 38.0°C. and there was a pronounced leucocytosis. The spinal fluid contained 152 cells per cmm., most of which were lymphocytes. The Pandy reaction was 4 plus. Roentgenograms of the spine were negative but evidences of osteomyelitis were found in the right femur.

Operation revealed that the cord was greatly swollen at the 3rd thoracic segment. A longitudinal incision was made in the posterior aspect and about 2 cc of pus was evacuated. This pus contained staphylococci. Sulfathiazole was administered.

The child's general condition improved rapidly but there was no return of function of the spinal cord. For several months the tendon reflexes were absent and there was no sweating below the 3rd rib. During this time he ran a slight elevation of temperature and displayed a constant low grade polyuria both of which may have been due to the absence of sweat secretion. Spontaneous fractures developed in both legs and roentgenograms revealed severe decalcification of the bones of the legs.

BIBLIOGRAPHY

ARZT, P. K.: Abscess in the spinal cord. Arch. Neurol. & Psychiat., **51**:533, 1944.

BARNES, F. R.: A case of suppurative transverse myelitis. New England Med. J., **203**:725, 1930.

BUZZARD, E. F. AND GREENFIELD, J. G.: Pathology of the nervous system. New York, Paul Hoeber, p. 184, 1923.

WALKER, R. M. AND DYKE, S. C.: Abscess of the spinal cord. Lancet, **1**:1413, 1936.

WOLTMAN, H. W. AND ADSON, A. W.: Abscess of the spinal cord with report of a case with functional recovery after operation. Brain, **49**:193, 1926.

PYOGENIC INFECTIONS OF THE SPINAL EPIDURAL SPACE

Etiology.—The common pyogenic organisms are usually responsible, especially the staphylococci.

Pathological Anatomy.—Dandy has shown that the epidural space is restricted to the dorsal surface of the cord except in the lower sacral segments where it surrounds the cord completely. The epidural space is occupied chiefly by fat and loosely knit connective tissue. It is widest where the spinal cord is smallest, as in the thoracic region, and is thinnest where the cord is largest, as in the region of the cervical and lumbosacral enlargements. These anatomical relations, no doubt, explain why epidural infections are always situated on the dorsal surface of the cord and usually in the thoracic region.

Two distinct processes are recognized: the epidural abscess and the epidural granuloma. The abscess extends rapidly within the loose areola and fatty tissue of the epidural space, so that eventually the cord may be surrounded by pus for half its length or more. The infection apparently does not extend into the leptomeninges, but the cord is nevertheless severely affected. Allen and Kahn describe edema of the cord with areas of spongy rarefaction and softening in the posterior funiculi in their case. There was extensive degeneration in the long fiber tracts. Such lesions may be attributed to compression and to disturbances of circulation.

The granulomas are usually well localized and even at operations they may be mistaken for neoplasms. They are adherent to the posterior surface of the dura and may extend laterally for some distance. Microscopic examination reveals chronic granulation tissue studded with small abscesses. Staphylococci are usually abundant.

Clinical Features, Extradural Abscess.—The infection may reach the epidural space by the blood stream or by direct extension of local processes. Furunculosis is the commonest cause but phlebitis, osteomyelitis of the spine, infected bed sores and suppurative processes in the lungs and other organs are mentioned. Spinal puncture is a very rare cause.

The onset is marked by intense pain in the back which radiates along the course of the spinal nerve roots. This develops much more acutely and becomes much more severe than that of spinal cord tumor. Paralysis of the legs develops within three to nine days, as a rule. The paraplegia is of the flaccid type and is associated with loss of reflexes, anesthesia and loss of sphincter control. The paralysis is usually complete within one or two days after the onset and extends upward rapidly. There is always high fever, leucocytosis and other signs of infection. Rigidity of the spine and local tenderness are usually very striking features. The spinal fluid contains an excess of cells in most cases. Froin's syndrome is mentioned. Manometric test may reveal obstruction of the canal. In several cases pus has been obtained from the epidural space when lumbar puncture was attempted. Blood cultures are very frequently positive.

When the infection arises as a complication of osteomyelitis of the spine, the symptoms are at first merely those of osteomyelitis. The lumbar spine is most frequently affected and then the thoracic, cervical and sacral in the order given. In the cervical region the infection is said to involve the body of the vertebra but in other parts of the spine, the arch of the vertebra is the usual site of the infection. As a rule, there is a history of a blow on the back or of an injury of some type preceding the first symptoms. There may, of course, be osteomyelitic processes in other bones. In the acute cases we may expect high fever and chills but in the more chronic cases, there may be little fever. The spine is intensely rigid and any attempt to move causes severe pain. Local tenderness is present from the beginning and after about a week or ten days, swelling on one or both sides of the vertebral column can be discovered. If the epidural space is invaded now, the signs of epidural abscess described above will soon appear. Generalized meningitis may also develop as a result of invasion of the subarachnoid space. The vertebrae do not collapse as they do in Pott's disease but roentgenograms will often reveal foci of osteomyelitis, especially if the case is of relatively long standing.

Extradural Granuloma.—Only a few cases of extradural granuloma of this type have been described. In two of the cases which have come under the writer's observation, the granuloma was due to the direct extension of infection from a large furuncle which lay directly over it. In other cases, the organisms apparently reached the epidural space by means of the blood stream.

This course is quite different from that of extradural abscess and resembles that of spinal cord tumor. The onset, however, may be marked by the rather sudden development of root pains. After this there is usually a latent period of several weeks and then slowly increasing weakness of the legs is noted. The signs then point to compression of the cord, usually in the thoracic region. There is usually no evidence of infection, no special tenderness of the spine and no excess of cells in the spinal fluid which show the changes due to obstruction of the spinal canal. The usual tests for the patency of the spinal canal reveal a more or less complete block.

Diagnosis Extradural Abscess.—The diagnosis depends upon the rapid development of paraplegia which usually ascends, the rigidity of the spine, the signs of an acute septic infection, and most important of all, upon the discovery of pus in the epidural space. Evidences of osteomyelitis of the vertebrae or of blood stream infection may be taken as favoring this diagnosis. If pus is not obtained by puncture at the usual level, we may attempt to enter the epidural space at higher levels but if epidural abscess is seriously suspected, we must observe great care not to puncture the dura and convey the infection into the subarachnoid space.

Epidural Granuloma.—This diagnosis can scarcely be made unless there is a definite history of an infection just preceding the onset or unless the scar of a furuncle lies directly over the site of the lesion. In any event, the diagnosis is in doubt until it is verified by operation.

Prognosis.—The prognosis in cases of extradural abscess is very poor. Almost all cases have been fatal and paraplegia has usually persisted in patients who have survived. The extradural granulomas are more benign. The writer has seen three cases in which operation was successfully performed with substantial return of function.

Treatment.—The treatment is operative. Laminectomy and drainage of the epidural space is indicated in abscess and it is imperative that this be done at once before the infection has become so widespread that drainage is impossible. The epidural granulomas should be removed. Great care should be taken to avoid opening the dura and the wound should be drained for severe wound infections are apt to follow. Antibiotics or one of the sulfonamides should be administered.

CASE HISTORY (Ped. 96092).—*Girl of 4 years developed abscess of the spinal epidural space with paraplegia and loss of knee jerks. Operation and drainage. Gradual recovery despite invasion of the blood stream and multiple metastatic abscesses.*

E. F., a girl of 4 years, developed pain in the back and abdomen. The next day she was ill and refused to get out of bed. During the next few days she had some fever and on the seventh day, it was discovered that her legs were paralyzed. Retention of urine developed on the eighth day.

The child was brought to the hospital on the tenth day of her illness. She was dehydrated and very drowsy. Temperature was 40.4°C. Pulse 130.

There was a strongly positive Kernig sign but only slight cervical rigidity. The legs and the lower half of the trunk were paralyzed and the bladder was distended to the umbilicus. The knee and ankle jerks were absent on either side and the plantar reflexes feebly extensor. Partial anesthesia was found up to a level at about the umbilicus. The urine was negative except for the presence of acetone. White blood count 30,800. An attempt was made to perform lumbar puncture. No fluid was obtained but one drop of thick pus clung to the needle when it was withdrawn. Cisternal puncture yielded clear fluid containing 24 cells of which 20 were polymorphonuclear leucocytes. The temperature rose within a few hours to 40.8°C.

Operation was performed on the day following admission. The third and fourth lumbar laminae were removed and 25 cc. of pus welled out of the epidural space. Culture revealed hemolytic staphylococci. The next day the child seemed to be somewhat better and temperature was only 38°C.

On the ninth day after operation the temperature rose again. The knees were found to be swollen and aspiration yielded pus. Two days later incision was made and both knees were drained. The temperature fell but soon rose to 40.6°C. Blood culture now showed hemolytic staphylococci. The urine contained pus. Abscesses appeared on the gums and on the dorsum of the left hand. These were opened.

Two weeks after the laminectomy, the temperature was slowly falling, drainage from the spine had ceased and the knee joints were healing. The blood culture still showed a few colonies.

A week later the temperature was normal. The blood cultures were negative. There was no discharge from the spine or knee joints. The legs could be moved well except for some stiffness of the knees. The tendon reflexes were slightly increased, there was a bilateral ankle clonus and the plantar reactions were equivocal. The bladder functioned well and the urine was clear. Numerous transfusions were given during the course of the illness.

Five weeks after the laminectomy the child seemed to be well and there were no definite evidences of injury to the spinal cord. The primary focus of the infection was never definitely determined. Roentgenograms of the spine showed no evidence of osteomyelitis.

BIBLIOGRAPHY

ALLEN, S. S. AND KAHN, E. A.: Infections of the epidural space. J.A.M.A., **98**:875, 1932.

DANDY, W. E.: Abscesses and inflammatory tumors in the spinal epidural space. Arch. Surg., **13**:477, 1926.

FINDLAY, L. AND KEMP, F. H.: Osteomyelitis of the spine following lumbar puncture. Arch. Dis. Child., **18**:102, 1943.

GRANT, F. C.: Epidural spinal abscess. J.A.M.A., **128**:509, 1935.

MIXTER, W. J. AND WATTS, J. W.: Spinal epidural granuloma. New England J. Med., **204**:1335, 1931.

SCOVILLE, W. B. AND RASKIND, R. A.: Acute osteomyelitis of the cervical spine with spinal cord pressure: report of a case with surgical cure. Connecticut M. J., **7**:835, 1943.

TAYLOR, A. S. AND KENNEDY, R. F.: A case of extra-thecal abscess of the spinal cord. Arch. Neurol. & Psychiat., **9**:652, 1923.

WILENSKY, A. O.: Osteomyelitis of the vertebrae. Ann. Surg., **89**:561, 1929.

SPINAL SUBDURAL ABSCESS

This is an extremely rare condition. In 1948, Freedman and Alpers mentioned only eight cases including two of their own. This is a pyogenic infection often due to staphylococci. The pus lies beneath the dura and outside the arachnoid. Frequently the process extends over many segments of the spinal cord. The clinical picture is apparently almost identical with that of spinal epidural abscess.

BIBLIOGRAPHY

FREEDMAN, H. AND ALPERS, B. J.: Spinal subdural abscess. Arch. Neurol. & Psychiat., **60**:49, 1948.

MUFSON, J. AND SOLOMON, S.: Acute subdural spinal abscess. Arch. Neurol. & Psychiat., **67**:758, 1952.

INVASION OF THE NERVOUS SYSTEM IN SEPTICEMIA AND PYEMIA

Etiology.—A great variety of bacteria may produce blood stream infections and give rise to multiple lesions in the nervous system. I may mention streptococci, staphylococci, pneumococci, gonococci, meningococci, the colon bacillus, the Welch bacillus, the typhoid bacillus, various types of Brucella and many others. In the East, B. pestis causes a rapidly fatal form. Anthrax also causes an acute and fatal septicemia.

Pathological Anatomy.—The anatomical changes depend largely upon the virulence of the organism and the duration of the infection. One finds, as a rule, multiple small abscesses, small softenings due to bacterial emboli, petechial hemorrhages in focal collections of glial cells containing bacteria. Thromboses in the veins and dural sinuses are often present and these may cause hemorrhagic softenings and edema. Meningitis and ependymitis are commonly observed. In addition to these findings, which are attributed to inflammation and to circulatory disturbances, widespread degenerative changes are usually evident which may be ascribed to the effects of bacterial toxins. The nerve cells show cloudy swelling and there may be perivascular edema. Certain organisms produce specific effects. For example the Welch bacillus may cause gas edema and anthrax multiple hemorrhages.

Clinical Features.—It is impossible to give a description which will apply to all cases. In acute overwhelming infections, the patient passes into coma in a short time. There are convulsions, rigidity of the neck, hemiplegia and soon papilledema. Fever is of septic type. Petechiae are found in the skin. The spinal fluid may contain leucocytes, blood and bacteria. Death ensues in a few days.

More chronic and less severe bacteremias such as are seen in bacterial endocarditis (lenta) may produce repeated apoplectic episodes due to cerebral embolism. These episodes are usually mild as if the lesions were small. There also may be mild and transient lymphocytic meningitis and in some instances, subarachnoid hemorrhage due to rupture of a mycotic aneurysm.

Transient bacteremias due to pyogenic organisms may cause single or multiple abscesses of the brain or may even cause focal softenings. The same statement may be made as regards septicemias which are successfully treated by the modern drugs such as penicillin or sulfonamides.

If a child has more than one attack of septicemia or shows deficient resistance to bacterial infections, one must think of agammaglobulinemia. There is reason to believe that this condition is due to deficiency of plasma cells which are believed to form gamma globulin. Congenital agammaglobulinemia is inherited as a sexlinked recessive character, and is found only in boys. An acquired type develops in both males and females at about the time of puberty. In a third type, the symptoms develop between 4 and 12 weeks. At that time the gamma globulin derived from the mother has disappeared and there may be a delay before the baby can form his own antibodies. This type is transient. It appears that gamma globulins are necessary for protection against bacterial infections but not so important in the defense against viruses. A child lacking gamma globulin may have to have repeated injections of this material at regular intervals.

Stiehm and Fudenberg state that children given transfusions or gamma globulin may acquire antibodies to gamma globulin. This reaction may neutralize gamma globulin therapy.

Philippart *et al.* describe a chronic granulomatous disease which begins as a rule in the first 6 months of life. Dermatitis or adenitis are the first manifestations, but pneumonia, abscesses and meningitis soon occur. Staphylococcus aureus is usually to blame. A white cell enzyme deficiency is responsible. This enzyme enables leucocytes to kill bacteria. It is said that the nitro-blue tetrazolium dye test is most satisfactory in diagnosis. It is believed that this condition is inherited.

BIBLIOGRAPHY

CHALGREN, W. S. AND BAKER, A. B.: The nervous system in tropical disease. Medicine, **26**:395, 1947.

COURVILLE, C.: Pathology of the Nervous System, Mountain View, Cal., Pacific Press Pub. A., 1937, p. 81.

DIAMOND, I. B.: Changes in the brain in pyemia and septicemia. Arch. Neurol. & Psychiat., **20**:524, 1928.

FREEMAN, W.: Neuropathology. Philadelphia, Saunders, 1933, p. 120.

HAYMAKER, W.: Fatal infections of the central nervous system and meninges after tooth extraction. Am. J. Orthodontics and Oral Surg., **31**:117, 1945.

OGDEN, C. B.: Agammaglobulinemia. Pediatrics, **9**:722, 1952.

PHILIPPART, A. I. et al.: Chronic granulomatous disease of childhood. Jour. Pediat. Surg., **4**:85, 1969.

SOUTHARD, E. E. AND KEENE, C. W.: A study of brain infections with pneumococcus. J.A.M.A., **46**:13, 1906.

———: A study of acute hemorrhagic encephalitis; staphylococcus septicemia. Am. J. Med. Sc., **129**:475, 1905.

STIEHM, E. R. AND FUDENBERG, H. H.: Antibodies to gammaglobulin in infants and children exposed to isologous gamma-globulin. Pediatrics, **35**:229, 1965.

INVASION OF THE NERVOUS SYSTEM BY ACID-FAST BACTERIA

Tuberculosis of the Nervous System

Introduction

Etiology.—Tuberculosis is due to an acid fast bacillus, B. tuberculosis or Koch's bacillus. Several subvarieties exist such as the human type, the bovine and the avian.

Characteristics of Tuberculosis in Early Life.—It is generally believed that tuberculous infection is almost universal among civilized peoples and that in the vast majority of cases, it is acquired during childhood. Fortunately, in most instances, the disease remains latent during life although it is always possible that a latent infection may become active. In adult life and among older children, tuberculosis is almost always of this type, that is, it represents the activation of a chronic asymptomatic infection or a reinfection. The course is, therefore, modified by some degree of immunity. Among infants, however, and among younger children clinically active tuberculosis may follow immediately after the infection is acquired and runs a relatively rapid course, since there has been no pre-existing latent infection to stimulate the child's resistance.

It is believed that the most common source of infection is contact with infected persons and that the organisms are inhaled in droplets of sputum produced by coughing, sneezing and talking. Kissing is another cause of infection. The organisms may also be ingested by licking the dust from floors of rooms in which infected individuals have lived and by eating from inadequately cleaned dishes. Bovine tuberculosis is acquired by drinking milk of tuberculous cows. In rare cases, it is believed that tuberculosis may be acquired through the placenta.

When the bacilli enter the body, they may produce a local reaction or, perhaps, merely a minute lesion which escapes attention. The organisms then invade the lymphatic channels and extend to the regional lymph nodes where there is usually swelling and often caseation. If the patient's powers of resistance are high, there may be fibrosis and finally calcification and the infection may remain clinically latent. If, on the other hand, resistance is inadequate to cope with the infection, the lymphatic tissue may break down and the organisms may gain access to the circulation and extend to all parts of the body. The primary focus is almost always in the lungs, it is claimed, and the mediastinal lymph nodes are involved as a result. The site of the initial lesion seems to have little importance, however, in determining the location of the active lesions. Active tuberculosis during childhood is usually in the lungs and in the peri-bronchial and mediastinal lymph nodes. Tuberculous enteritis with extension to the mesenteric lymph nodes is another but less common form. Tuberculosis of the bones and joints, tuberculous otitis and mastoiditis, cervical adenitis and the various tuberculids, such as papulonecrotic tuberculids, lupus vulgaris, lichen scrofulosus and phlyctenular conjunctivitis are characteristic types of tuberculosis in childhood. Not infrequently tuberculosis becomes generalized during infancy and early childhood and produces miliary tuberculosis. We are concerned, however, only with tuberculosis of the nervous system of which the following types will be described: (1) Tuberculomas of the nervous system; (2) Tuberculous meningitis; (3) Tuberculous spondylitis; (4) Tuberculosis of the cranial bones.

For many years no special therapeutic measures were available for the control of tuberculosis. Rest and general hygienic measures were employed for treatment and isolation of active cases was relied upon to prevent the spread of the disease.

More recently attempts have been made to immunize children by the use of the B.C.G. vaccine of Calmette and Guerin. There is evidence that this vaccine is helpful but much difference of opinion still exists about its value.

Now several drugs are known to have therapeutic value in the treatment of this disease and surgical measures are being used more freely to remove active lesions. Modern treatment is described in the section on tuberculous meningitis q.v.

BIBLIOGRAPHY

HOLT, E. AND MCINTOSH, R.: Diseases of Infancy and Childhood. New York: D. Appleton & Co., p. 1022, 1933.

Tuberculomas of the Nervous System

Pathological Anatomy.—Tuberculomas may occur in any part of the nervous system. They are generally stated to be most frequent in the cerebellum and brain-stem, though this view has been disputed. They are often globular in shape but may be lobulated as a result of fusion of several small lesions. The center is usually yellow and caseous but the peripheral portions are, as a rule, pinkish-gray. They vary in size from a few millimeters in diameter to great masses three or four centimeters in diameter. Relatively fresh and rapidly growing tuberculomas seem to merge with the surrounding tissues but older lesions are well circumscribed by a fibrous capsule. It is not unusual to find several such lesions, especially if a careful search is made for them. Histological examination reveals that the central portions of the lesions are composed of caseous material. Surrounding the center is a zone of giant cells or epithelioid cells in which there is destruction of the nervous elements. Lymphocytes, plasma cells and even leucocytes are scattered through this region and there may be a moderate proliferation of fibroblasts which form a capsule. Tubercle bacilli are rarely demonstrable histologically. Beyond the second zone is a region in which degeneration of the neurons and nerve fibers is present. The small blood vessels are surrounded by lymphocytes and are often thrombosed. Numerous fat-laden microglial cells may be found in such regions and hypertrophied astrocytes. It is not unusual to find daughter tubercles surrounding the central mass, indicating extension of the process. In old lesions the capsule may be calcified but this is rare. If the lesion impinges upon the meninges, it is common to discover a localized meningitis. Apparently cerebral tubercles rarely break down to form abscesses. I have seen only two tuberculous abscesses of the brain.

A rather rare type of intracranial tuberculoma is described, as tuberculoma en plaque. This is a thin layer of caseous material involving the dura, the leptomeninges and the superficial portions of the cortex. Such lesions may be very extensive and overlie large areas of the brain. In a few cases tuberculomas, especially those of the cerebellum or temporal lobe, may be traced to tuberculous mastoiditis and otitis which has apparently extended directly through the dura into the nervous system. Frequently such processes are complicated by pyogenic infections and result in abscess formation. In the same way tuberculous spondylitis may result in tuberculoma of the spinal cord. As a rule, however, tuberculomas of the nervous system are the result of blood stream invasion and are secondary to a focus in the lungs or lymph nodes.

Clinical Features.—Tuberculomas of the brain are now relatively rare in the United States and it is stated that the large conglomerate tubercles which simulate neoplasm of the brain comprise less than 5 per cent of all intracranial masses. In the past, tuberculomas were apparently the most common type of intracranial tumor. In certain parts of the world, tuberculomas seem to be more frequent than in others. For example, in 1933 Garland and Armitage of Leeds found as a result of analysis of post-mortem records that 34 per cent of all their intracranial tumors were of tuberculous origin. In certain South American countries, cerebral tuberculomas are very common, it is said. The incidence may be somewhat greater in the Negro than in the white races and children are undoubtedly more frequently affected than adults.

The symptoms are not, as a rule, distinctive. The child may or may not show clinical evidences of tuberculosis elsewhere although post-mortem examination almost always reveals lesions in the lungs or lymph nodes. Syndromes referable to lesions of the cerebellum, the pons or the mid-brain are common, and hemiplegia and focal convulsions due to tuberculomas involving the cerebral cortex are not rare. In the writer's experience, tuberculomas occur anywhere in the cranium but are probably most frequent in the hemispheres. Signs of increased intracranial pressure are usually present by the time the disease is well developed. Usually there is a low grade fever but this is not constant. In many cases, there are mild and fluctuating signs of meningeal irritation which are associated with moderate pleocytosis in the spinal fluid. As a rule, these cells are chiefly of the lymphocytic series but leucocytes may predominate. Later, the spinal fluid may become negative or may show merely some increase of globulin.

The course is usually slowly progressive and it is unusual for a child to survive more than a year after the onset. Death may occur from increased intracranial pressure or from tuberculosis in other parts of the body, but, as a rule, the disease terminates in generalized tuberculous meningitis.

Tuberculoma en plaque is characterized, as a rule, by signs of focal cortical irritation such as Jacksonian fits of various types and, as a rule, by little or no paralysis or other physical signs. Increased intracranial pressure develops late and the disease runs a very slow course, sometimes lasting for five years or even more. This type of tuberculoma is very rare and most of the cases reported have been in adults.

Diagnosis.—It must be admitted that the diagnosis is often difficult and many tuberculomas are unexpectedly discovered at operation for suspected neoplasm of the brain. The most important points in the differential diag-

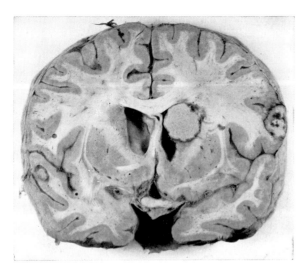

Fig. 150. Multiple tuberculomas of the brain. The largest one has destroyed the head of the caudate nucleus.

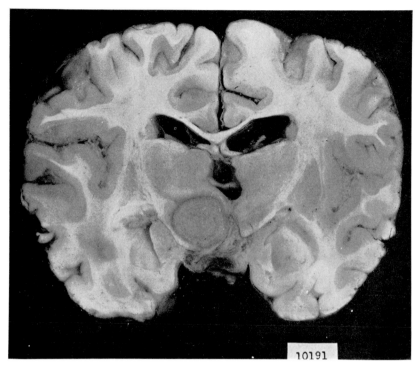

FIG. 151. Tuberculoma of midbrain causing Benedilt's syndrome, Path. 10191.

nosis are: (1) The history of exposure to tuberculosis; (2) Clinical evidences of tuberculosis in other parts of the body; (3) A positive intracutaneous tuberculin reaction in children under ten years; (4) Evidences of beginning meningeal reaction; (5) Signs of a focal lesion in the central nervous system; (6) Evidences of increased intracranial pressure.

Prognosis.—Sibley and O'Brien find that the prognosis in cerebral tuberculomas has improved in recent years since the antituberculous drugs have been employed. They report a mortality of 22 per cent in 102 patients.

Treatment.—If possible the tuberculoma should be removed surgically and antituberculous drugs administered.

CASE HISTORY (Ped. 54689—Path. 10191).—*Benedikt's syndrome in a child of 15 months due to large tuberculoma of the midbrain. Terminal tuberculous meningitis.*

E. W., a previously healthy colored boy of 15 months developed acute otitis media on the right side July 27, 1927. The discharge continued for four days and then ceased. On August 3, the right eyelid began to droop and the eye turned out. A few days later, the parents noticed a continuous tremor of the left arm and leg. The child slowly lost weight and took feedings badly.

September 21, the child was admitted to Harriet Lane. Examination revealed complete paralysis of the right third nerve and a coarse rhythmical tremor of the left arm and leg which was accentuated during movement but persisted during rest being absent only when the child was asleep. There was no papilledema or other neurological signs. Medical examination was negative. The spinal fluid contained 39 lymphocytes per cmm. and the Pandy test positive. The Wassermann reaction was negative in the blood and spinal fluid. Tuberculin test was negative with 0.1 mg. and positive with 1 mg. Urine negative. Temperature ranged between 37° and 38°C.

During the next few weeks the child seemed to improve. The spinal fluid was tested on September 30 and again on October 14 being quite normal each time. On December 6, however, the child's temperature began to rise and the signs of meningeal irritation developed. The spinal fluid then contained 240 cells, 75 per cent being lymphocytes. No tubercle bacilli were discovered. Roentgenograms of the lungs showed shadows about the hila. Bilateral papilledema finally developed and death occurred December 28.

Post-mortem examination revealed a large conglomerate tubercle in the mid-brain completely destroying the right red nucleus and the third nerve in its course through this nucleus. There was extensive meningitis of tuberculous type. The bovine organism was found to be responsible.

CASE HISTORY.—*Boy of 2 years developed focal convulsions on the right side, fever, loss of weight and signs of a pulmonary lesion. Post-mortem examination disclosed tuberculoma en plaque extending over the left motor cortex.*

T. B., a previously healthy colored boy of 2 years, began to have convulsive seizures in September 1938. These gradually became more frequent and severe. The child grew sluggish and listless. His appetite was poor and he lost weight rapidly. His mother was known to have tuberculosis.

Examination on October 12 revealed a well developed child who was very ill and had evidently lost much weight. He was semistuporous but irritable when aroused. Temperature ranged between 102° and 95°F. There was some enlargement of the cervical lymph nodes and signs of a lesion at the apex of the right lung. Neurological examination was negative. The cutaneous tuberculin test was strongly positive. Roentgenograms of the chest showed tuberculous changes in the apex of the right lung and miliary lesions also. The spinal fluid was examined five times. There was always a moderate increase in protein but only once was there an increase in cells.

From time to time there were series of convulsive seizures which always began in the right side of the face and in the right arm. Sometimes the seizure was localized but often it spread over the entire body. After a series of seizures the child would remain in deep stupor for several hours.

For several days after such attacks, the right arm and leg would be weak and atonic and the right plantar response would be extensor. The child's temperature rose to 105°F. and he died in coma on December 20, 1938.

Post-mortem examination revealed miliary tuberculosis in all the organs and a tuberculous cavity in the apex of the right lung. Over the lateral aspect of the left hemisphere was a yellowish plaque covering the pre-central and postcentral gyri and measuring 7 by 12 cm. On section this was found to be composed of many small tubercles which had become confluent. The plaque was 0.5 cm thick and involved the pia-arachnoid and the cortex which was largely destroyed. It dipped into the sulci and involved the base as well as the apex of each gyrus. There was no tuberculous meningitis but a few miliary tubercles were present in the meninges and brain.

BIBLIOGRAPHY

Armstrong, F. B. and Edwards, A. M.: Intracranial tuberculoma in Canada. Canad. M. A. J., **89**:56, 1963.

Garland, H. G. and Armitage, G.: Intracranial tuberculoma. Brit. J. Path. & Bact., **37**:461, 1933.

Obrrador, S. and Urquiza, P.: Value of streptomycin in treatment of intracranial tuberculoma. J. Neurol., Neurosurg. & Psychiat., **13**:66, 1950.

Pardee, I. and Knox, L. C.: Tuberculoma en plaque. Arch. Neurol. & Psychiat., **17**:231, 1927.

Sibley, W. A. and O'Brien, J. L.: Intracranial tuberculomas. J. Neurosurg., **6**:157, 1956.

———: Intracranial tuberculomas. Neurology, **6**:157, 1956.

Sinh, G. *et al.*: Pathogenesis of unusual intracranial tuberculomas. Jour. Neurosurg., **29**:149, 1968.

Van Wagenen, W. P.: Tuberculoma of the brain, its incidence among intracranial tumors and its surgical aspects. Arch. Neurol. & Psychiat., **17**:57, 1927.

Walsh, F. B.: *Loc. cit.*

Tuberculous Meningitis

Pathological Anatomy.—We must distinguish several types of tuberculous meningitis: (1) Generalized meningoencephalitis; (2) Generalized meningitis associated with solitary tubercle; (3) Localized meningitis which may be subacute or chronic; (4) Dr. Arthur King has given me particulars of a case of extensive chronic tuberculous pachymeningitis.

In tuberculous *meningoencephalitis,* the brain is very soft, the convolutions flattened and the meninges, especially those at the base and in the interpeduncular space, are opaque. In some cases, there is a thick greenish exudate in the meninges, extending downward under the pons and anteriorly to the chiasm and into the Sylvian fissure, but in others it is very difficult to discover any abnormality in the gross. Minute tubercles may often be seen at the base or in the Sylvian fissure. On section the ventricles are usually dilated and the ependyma thickened and red. Miliary nodules may be visible throughout the brain and even small areas of softening. Microscopic examination reveals a variable amount of exudate in the subarachnoid spaces, chiefly composed of mononuclear cells. In some cases this is diffuse but, as a rule, there are numerous small tubercles in relation to small vessels. Giant cells are not prominent in these but there are many lymphocytes, plasma cells, macrophages and fibroblasts. Usually there is little caseation. The adventitia of the cortical vessels is usually infiltrated with lymphocytes and other mononuclear cells. The cranial nerves may also be involved. Dr. Charles Luttrell has shown me a large tubercle in the third nerve. Throughout the brain are numerous minute foci composed of endothelial cells associated with lymphocytes and plasma cells. These surround small vessels which are often necrotic. About this area there is often a well-marked reaction of the glial elements. Freeman regards these as beginning miliary tubercles of embolic origin. Degenerative changes of the cerebral neurons and nerve fibers may be found. Apparently, this picture represents the result of a massive invasion of the blood stream with dissemination of the bacilli throughout the brain and leptomeninges.

The picture just described is uncommon. In most cases we find merely the alterations in the meninges and very little invasion of the brain. Rich has shown that a careful search will almost always reveal one or more tuberculomas which have apparently broken down and discharged the bacilli into the meninges.

The third type which is apparently very rare is characterized by a number of more or less discrete tubercles scattered along the branches of the meningeal vessels. These lesions seem to occur most frequently in the Rolandic or Sylvian fissure and are always sharply localized. In several cases, the vessels have become thrombosed with the production of cortical infarction. This process seems to indicate a high degree of resistance and is, as a rule, chronic.

The brains of children whose course has been prolonged by modern treatment are apt to show softenings due to occlusion of the blood vessels. It is said that the affected vessels are usually embedded in exudate. Extensive accumulations of exudate in the spinal meninges may eventually become organized with ingrowth of fibrous tissue and obstruction of the canal. The arteries may become occluded with softening of the cord.

Clinical Features.—This is the most common type of tuberculosis of the nervous system in childhood, and if we exclude epidemic meningococcic meningitis, tuberculosis is responsible for almost three-fourths of all cases of meningitis among children. Tuberculous meningitis is unusual before the age of six months and is most frequent during the second year of life although it may develop at any age. As a rule, it develops during the winter or early spring and not infrequently follows measles, pertussis or other acute illnesses. In many cases the infection may be traced to contact with a member of the household affected with tuberculosis, for tuberculous meningitis is almost always due to the human type of organism.

The onset may be relatively abrupt but, as a rule, is gradual and is preceded by prodromal symptoms for a few days such as lack of energy, loss of appetite, headache and vomiting. There is usually a slight elevation of temperature during this period.

Later symptoms which are definitely indicative of disease of the brain appear. The child begins to grow drowsy and irritable. The temperature slowly rises and may reach 101°F. In a few cases it remains subnormal for a time. The pulse is usually rapid. Both focal and general convulsions are common during this period. Signs of meningeal irritation are rarely prominent but mild cervical rigidity, hyperesthesia and photophobia may occur. Digestive disturbances such as vomiting and constipation are usual. The symptoms fluctuate in extraordinary fashion. Periods of irritability and screaming may alternate with apathy, drowsiness and stupor. Sometimes the child seems to be so much improved that recovery may be expected.

After a week or more, the patient sinks into a deep stupor and finally into coma. The temperature ranges between 102°F. and 106 F. The pulse is often slow and is characteristically irregular. The respiration is also irregular or periodic. The fontanels of infants bulge and there is almost always some change in the optic nerve heads. There may be merely dilatation of the retinal veins and congestion of the papilla or outspoken papilledema which may reach a height of several diopters. Tubercles are sometimes seen in the choroid if a careful search is made for them. The neck is rigid and Kernig's sign present, although those signs are rarely so pronounced as in purulent meningitis. Tâche cérébrale and other vasomotor phenomena may be observed. Various signs of involvement of the brain and cranial nerves are usual. The pupils are unequal in most cases and often dilated and fixed. Sixth nerve palsies and squints of other types are very common. Localized muscular twitchings, various automatic movements as well as focal and general convulsive seizures occur. Hemiparesis and cerebral monoplegias are frequently seen but, as a rule, are transient. Towards the end, the picture is often that of decerebrate rigidity and the tonic neck reflexes are often demonstrable. The entire course averages about three weeks in infants but is usually somewhat longer in older children. Since the course of this disease has been prolonged by modern treatment, certain complications have become more evident. Organization of exudate at the base of the brain sometimes results in obstruction of the subarachnoid channels and hydrocephalus. Focal lesions of the brain may develop due to occlusion of cerebral arteries. In the same way exudate in the spinal meninges may cause obstruction of the subarachnoid spaces and at the same time lead to invasion of the arteries and softening of the cord. Transverse cord lesions are not rare.

The spinal fluid shows only mild changes in the earliest stages of the disease but the changes grow more and more pronounced as the disease progresses. The pressure is increased and the fluid is clear or at most slightly opalescent. The cell count is relatively low at first but slowly rises to 100 or 200 or even higher. The cells are chiefly of the lymphocytic series in most cases but one occasionally encounters fluids in which the leucocytes are more numerous during the early stages of the disease. The globulin and total protein are greatly increased. Sugar estimations may give results within normal limits at the onset but the values slowly decrease and may reach 15 to 25 mgs before death. The concentrations of sodium and chloride in the serum and of chloride in the spinal fluid are almost invariably low. Rarely xanthochromia and the Froin syndrome occur. When the fluid is permitted to stand a while, a delicate fibrin film usually forms. Persistent examination of the fluid for tubercle bacilli will almost always reveal their presence. Examination of the film is the simplest method. If no film is present, alcohol may be added to the fluid so as to precipitate the proteins, the tube then centrifugalized and the precipitate examined in the usual manner. Inoculation of a guinea pig may give positive evidence of the presence of tubercle bacilli even when the organisms cannot be found in the precipitate.

As a rule, there is no leucocytosis in the early stages of the infection but towards the end the white blood count may reach 30,000. The intracutaneous tuberculin test is almost always strongly positive at the onset and during the early stages of the illness, but towards the end, it may become negative.

The more chronic and localized types of tuberculous meningitis are very rare and present little or nothing distinctive in the way of symptoms. There is usually some evidence of a focal process, such as localized convulsions, hemiparesis and other cortical syndromes. Signs of increased intracranial pressure are also frequently observed.

Diagnosis.—The following features are important in the diagnosis: (1) The history of exposure to infection; (2) Physical signs of tuberculous disease in the chest, bones or lymph nodes; (3) The clinical picture described above; (4) The tuberculin skin test; (5) The spinal fluid changes and, above all, the presence of tubercle bacilli. Any doubt about the diagnosis is soon resolved by the course.

Prognosis.—Before specific therapy was available this disease was fatal almost without exception. At present as a result of the use of modern drugs, it is claimed that 50 to 80 per cent or more of these children may be cured. Relapses are common, however. In some patients, extensive damage to the brain may make this therapeutic victory a hollow one.

Moreau *et al.* studied a number of children between the ages of 3 and 14 years one and a half years after apparent cure. Some 51, or 14 per cent, had neurological sequelae. Some 26 children had hemiplegia, 4 had paraplegia, 8 had ocular palsies, 2 had epilepsy and 21 had optic atrophy. Only 9 of these children were seriously disabled. There were also endocrine disturbances with obesity and amenorrhea in females. In males precocious puberty was observed. Calcium deposits in the brain and meninges are sometimes found if roentgenograms are made in such cases. Mooney finds ocular abnormalities in a very large percentage of patients who have been kept alive by proper therapy. He mentions choroidal tubercles, papilledema and optic atrophy. Choremis *et al.* found one or more epidermoid tumors in the spinal canal of 6 children between the ages of 7 and 12 years who had been treated for tuberculous meningitis between 3 and 7 years before. Many spinal punctures were made and a needle was used without a stylet. One tumor was found at the tenth thoracic segment. The others were all in the lumbar region. The authors believe that bits of epithelium were carried into the spinal canal by the needle and became implanted in the meninges.

Treatment.—Several drugs are now available for the treatment of tuberculous meningitis. (1) *Streptomycin* and *dihydrostreptomycin*. (2) The sulphones such as *promizole, promin* and *diasone*. (3) *Para-amino-salicylic acid*. (4) The derivatives of isonicotinic acid, such as *isoniazid, marsilid* and *aldinamide*. These drugs are used in combination for the tubercle bacilli are less apt to become resistant if two or more drugs are employed.

Streptomycin and dihydrostreptomycin are given by intramuscular injection. The average dosage is 0.5 gram per day for a child weighing 20 to 40 pounds and 1.0 gram for a child weighing 60 pounds. Streptomycin is apt to injure the vestibular apparatus and dihydrostreptomycin may cause deafness. It is claimed that if both drugs are used so that only half the usual dosage of each is employed, these untoward effects are largely eliminated. These drugs are withdrawn as soon as possible and it is best not to use them for more than four months continuously. It may be necessary to resume treatment after a time, however.

The isonicotinic derivatives are used in conjunction with streptomycin by many authorities. The oral dose is 3.0 to 10.0 mgs. per kilogram per day. Used alone drug resistance develops rapidly, but it is said that this does not happen when used with streptomycin. The chief toxic effects are excitement, dizziness, postural hypotension and increased tendon reflexes. Convulsions also occur especially in individuals who are prone to convulsions. Psychoses are mentioned. Peripheral neuritis is stressed by several writers, but it is claimed that the administration of B 6 will prevent neuritis. We have seen choreiform movements, myoclonus, and also torsion spasm which cleared up when the drug was withdrawn. One child of 2 years who took a number of his father's isoniazid tablets developed a series of convulsions and was in coma for some hours, but made a complete recovery (Ped. B-14955).

The sulfones are given by mouth. Promizole has been used most widely. It is given by mouth in divided doses. A total daily dosage of 0.25 to 0.50 gram is recommended. In larger dosage goiter and enlargement of the breasts may occur and leucopenia. This drug is often given together with streptomycin and is continued for long periods after the streptomycin is discontinued.

Para-amino-salicylic acid is given by mouth in doses of 0.5 gram per kilogram per day. It is employed as the sulfones are employed as an adjuvant. The toxic manifestations are largely gastrointestinal.

Kendig *et al.* advise the use of cortisone which prevents the formation of fibrinous exudate which may cause hydrocephalus and protect the organisms from the therapeutic drugs. Cortisone may activate the pulmonary process, however, and this effect must be combatted by the use of proper antituberculous drugs.

BIBLIOGRAPHY

BROOKER, W. D., FLETCHER, A. P. AND WILSON, R. R.: Spinal cord complications of tuberculous meningitis. Quart. J. Med., 23:275, 1954.

BUNN, P. A.: One hundred cases of miliary and meningeal tuberculosis treated with streptomycin. Am. J. M. Sc., 216:286, 1948.

CAIRNS, H. *et al.*: Treatment of tuberculous meningitis with streptomycin and intrathecal injections of tuberculin. J.A.M.A., 144:92, 1950.

CHEEK, D. B.: Electrolyte changes in tuberculous meningitis. Pediatrics, 18:218, 1956.

CHOREMIS, C. *et al.*: Intraspinal epidermoid tumors in patients treated for tuberculous meningitis. Lancet, ii:437, 1956.

COATES, E. O. *et al.*: Toxicity of isonicotinic acid hydrazines in pulmonary tuberculosis. Arch. Int. Med., 93:541, 1954.

DU MONT, F. *et al.*: Isoniazid (Isonicotinic acid hydrazide) in the treatment of miliary and meningeal tuberculosis. Am. Rev. Tuberc., 66:391, 1952.

FLATAU, E.: La Méningite tuberculeuse chronique diffuse. Encéphale, 23:578, 1928.

FREEMAN, W.: Neuropathology, Philadelphia, W. B. Saunders Co., 1933, p. 172.

HEMENWAY, J.: The constant presence of tubercle bacilli in the cerebrospinal fluid of tuberculous meningitis. Am. J. Dis. Child., 1:37, 1911.

KENDIG, E. L. *et al.*: Observations on the effect of cortisone treatment of tuberculous meningitis. Am. Rev. Tuberc., 73:99, 1956.

LEITCH, D. B.: Xanthochromia of the spinal fluid with complete coagulation in tuberculous meningitis. Am. J. Dis. Child., 15:348, 1918.

LORBER, J.: The incidence and nature of calcifications after tuberculous meningitis. Arch. Dis. Child., 27:542, 1952.

MEYERS, A. E.: A study of 105 cases of tuberculous meningitis. Am. J. Dis. Child., 9:427, 1915.

MOONEY, A. J.: Some ocular sequelae of tuberculous meningitis. Am. J. Ophth., 41:753, 1956.

MOREAU, R., BOUDIN, G. AND LHERMITTE, F.: Neurologic sequelae of tuberculous meningitis. Rev. Neurol., 90:678, 1954.

MORGAN, A. E.: A study of the blood in tuberculous meningitis. Am. J. Dis. Child., 11:224, 1916.

Rich, A. and McCordock, H. A.: The pathogenesis of tuberculous meningitis. Bull. Johns Hopkins Hosp., **52**:5, 1933.

Shane, S. J. and Riley, C.: Cortisone in the treatment of tuberculous meningitis. New England J. Med., **249**:829, 1953.

Walsh, F. B.: *Loc. cit.*

Tuberculous Spondylitis

Pathological Anatomy.—The process is believed to begin in the body of the vertebra and soon extends to the periosteum, the intervertebral discs and ligaments. From one to five adjacent vertebrae may be affected and in some cases there are several foci in the spine. As a result of weight bearing, the bodies of the vertebrae may collapse causing an angular kyphos. In a large percentage of all cases, the spinal cord or the spinal nerve roots are involved. This is apparently due to several causes. In most cases, abscess of the vertebral body extends into the epidural space and compresses the spinal cord. This would seem to be the most benign type of lesion and is probably responsible for a large percentage of cases in which recovery occurs. In other cases, the epidural space is invaded by tuberculous granulations which encircle the spinal cord and extend up and down for several segments. We have seen several cases in which this resulted from tuberculosis of the lamina without demonstrable involvement of the bodies of the vertebrae. The infection, as a rule, does not penetrate the dura but the cord is compressed and the blood supply is often affected, so that softening may occur. False membranes may be deposited on the inner side of the thickened dura. Rarely tubercles extend along the walls of the vessels and invade the leptomeninges and spinal cord. Generalized tuberculous meningitis may result or merely a localized meningomyelitis with tubercles in the subarachnoid space and periphery of the cord. Tuberculomas are rare in the cord. Bony compression of the cord may occur as a result of dislocation and deformity or of the displacement of a sequestrum backwards. Even after the active stages of the disease are passed the cord may be injured by sharp angulation of the vertebral canal or by rubbing against bony prominences. The spinal nerve roots are often involved by infiltration or by compression when there is collapse of the vertebrae.

Clinical Features.—Tuberculous spondylitis is most common between the ages of two and five years. It is unusual under two years and rare under six months. Males are somewhat more frequently affected than females. In some cases no other focus of tuberculosis can be found but, as a rule, spondylitis is secondary to some other lesion. Colored children are affected more frequently than white children in our experience.

The onset is usually gradual and is marked by pains in the distribution of the spinal nerve roots arising in the affected region of the spine. The pain is not necessarily felt in the back but is usually referred to the anterior surface of the body. Among other symptoms characteristic of the early stages of the disease are abnormalities of posture which result from fixation of the spine in positions adapted to relieve the pressure on the affected vertebrae, and peculiarities of motility due to the effort to avoid painful movements. The child walks very carefully with a rigid back and never runs or jumps. Sleep is broken by night cries which are apparently caused by relaxation of the muscle spasm and exacerbations of pain. There are usually constitutional symptoms, such as loss of weight, retarded growth, fatigue, and perhaps, afternoon rise of temperature. Later paraplegia or paraparesis may develop and spinal deformities of various types develop. Rounded curves are more common in the less acute cases and rapidly progressive processes usually cause sharp knuckles. In some cases, paralysis develops before other symptoms have been noticed. Cold abscesses not infrequently form about the vertebrae and sometimes extend into the abdominal or thoracic cavities or even point externally. A striking feature of cases of relatively long standing is shortening of the spine. This is due not only to collapse of vertebrae but to retardation of growth.

Certain features which are characteristic of disease at various levels of the spine may now be discussed. When the cervical spine is involved the pain is referred to the occiput or neck, if the lesion is in the upper segments, and into the arms and shoulders if the lesion is lower. The head is held very rigidly. It may be either flexed or extended and is sometimes tilted or rotated to one side. Sometimes the child will support the head with the hands. Collapse of the vertebrae and deformity occur relatively late for the cervical spine obviously does not bear as much weight as lower parts of the spinal column. Marked kyphosis is rare in the upper cervical spine but is not uncommon in the lower half. Examination usually reveals strong muscle spasm and the movements of the neck are limited more especially in rotation. If abscess forms it may drain into the retropharyngeal space or less commonly, laterally into the muscles of the neck.

When the lesion involves the thoracic spine the body is apt to be inclined forward and may be supported in this attitude by placing the hands on the knees. The lumbar lordosis may be diminished. The child walks with great caution often on the toes to avoid jars. When the upper thoracic vertebrae are affected, the shoulders are often elevated and squared. If abscess forms it drains into the posterior mediastinum and causes dyspnea and cyanosis.

Lesions in the lumbar spine usually cause increased lordosis. Psoas abscesses are typical and may cause psoas spasm with flexion of the hip.

It must be emphasized that paralysis due to compression of the cord by epidural tuberculous tissue may develop without deformity of the spine, without muscle spasm and even without demonstrable changes in the roentgenograms of the bones. We have found tuberculous disease of the laminae of the vertebrae in most cases of this type, but in other cases we could not find any evidence of tuberculous spondylitis.

In a very large percentage of all cases, there are symptoms referable to involvement of the spinal cord. Weakness and stiffness of the legs are usually the first symptoms to develop. Frequently, complete paraplegia does not result. It is only in the more severe cases that there is loss of control of the bladder and loss of cutaneous sensibility is often difficult to demonstrate. The upper level of the paralysis, as a rule, corresponds to the site of the kyphos, but in some instances the paralysis may extend above the deformity. It must be kept in mind that paraplegia may occur before the deformity appears and that it may even represent the only definite symptom of tuberculous spondylitis. When the lesion is below the lumbosacral enlargement, the paralysis is associated with atrophy, flaccidity and loss of reflexes.

The roentgenological examination is of the greatest importance in the diagnosis. Both lateral and antero-posterior views should be made and stereoscopic plates are very helpful. First there are seen destructive changes in the anterior part of the vertebral body, usually near the intervertebral disc. Later there is partial collapse of one or more vertebral bodies which assume a wedge shape. The intervertebral discs are reduced in thickness and may seem to disappear. As a result, deformity or angulation of the spine appears. Surrounding the affected vertebrae is usually a spindle-shaped shadow which represents the reaction in the tissues nearby. Expansion of such a shadow usually indicates the formation of an abscess.

Diagnosis.—The most important diagnostic features are: (1) Loss of weight and retarded growth; (2) Afternoon rise of temperature; (3) The clinical symptoms mentioned above, such as changes in gait, altered posture, night cries, etc.; (4) The demonstration of muscle spasm and limitation of movement and in advanced cases, deformity of the spine; (5) Positive intracutaneous tuberculin test; (6) The roentgenographic changes in the spine; (7) Evidences of tuberculosis elsewhere in the body; (8) Evidences of involvement of the spinal cord or spinal nerve roots. It must be emphasized that the absence of clinical signs and of roentgenographic evidence of tuberculous spondylitis does not eliminate the possibility of a local tuberculous process.

It is obviously of the greatest importance to make the diagnosis early before the deformity has appeared, since the result of treatment is much better in such cases. A number of other possibilities must always be kept in mind such as arthritis, crushing of the vertebra as a result of trauma, typhoid spine, melitensis infection and occasional cases of suipestifer infections, actinomycosis, blastomycosis and other rare infections. Neoplasms which invade and destroy the vertebrae may sometimes be mistaken for tuberculosis.

Prognosis.—Since the introduction of effective medication, the prognosis has become much better. Ginsburg states that the mortality has been reduced to between 1 and 4 per cent.

Treatment.—Early diagnosis is most important. Immobilization and proper medication are usually sufficient, but in some cases various surgical procedures are required.

CASE HISTORY (U-68957).—*Colored girl of 11 years developed pain in back after fall. Later fever and paraplegia with dysuria. Examination revealed signs of a local lesion at T. 5, but there was no rigidity of the spine and roentgenograms were negative. Operation disclosed tuberculous granulation tissue in the epidural space compressing the cord. The laminae of the vertebrae were involved by the infection.*

S. R., a previously healthy colored girl of 11 years, fell and struck her back in February, 1936. Shortly after this she began to complain of pain in the back between the scapulae. About the end of March she began to have some difficulty in walking and this increased until about the middle of April she was finally unable to walk. At the same time she developed difficulty in passing urine.

On May 2, she was admitted to the hospital. The temperature ranged between normal and 102°F. Pulse 100. General nutrition was fairly good. There was almost complete paralysis of both legs and marked weakness of the abdominal and spinal muscles. The lower intercostal muscles contracted feebly. Cutaneous sensibility was diminished but not lost below the nipple line. The knee and ankle jerks were brisk but not grossly exaggerated. No ankle clonus was elicited but there was a bilateral Babinski response. The abdominal reflexes were absent. There was slight tenderness over the spinous processes of the 4th and 5th thoracic vertebrae and a bit of muscle spasm could be palpated in the region. The spine moved freely as a whole and even strong flexion caused no pain. There was no kyphos. Several roentgenograms of the spine revealed no change in the vertebrae whatever. The mediastinal lymph nodes were somewhat enlarged. Spinal fluid examination revealed 20 lymphocytes per cmm, 100 mgs, total protein and a negative Wassermann test. The Queckenstedt test was positive. The intracutaneous tuberculin test was positive in dilution of 1/1000 but not in weaker dilutions.

On May 19, operation was performed. The laminae of the 4th and 5th thoracic vertebrae were removed and a mass of tuberculous granulation tissue was found on the dorsum of the cord in the epidural space. The dura was not opened but there was no evidence that the infection had penetrated beneath the dura. The laminae were softened and tubercles were found in the tissues overlying them. No sign of infection of the body of the vertebrae could be found. The granulation tissue extended vertically about 2 cm and seemed to be confined to the dorsal surface of the cord.

BIBLIOGRAPHY

Dott, N.: Skeletal traction and anterior decompression in management of Potts paraplegia. Edinburgh M. J., 54:620, 1947.

Ginsburg, S. *et al.*: The neurological complications of tuberculous spondylitis. Arch. of Neurol., 16:265, 1967.

Jones, R. and Lovett, R. W.: Orthopedic Surgery, Baltimore, Wm. Wood & Co., 1923, p. 201.

Tuberculosis of the Cranial Bones

Pathological Anatomy.—The infection usually gains access to the middle ear through the eustachian tube and is secondary to infection of the throat, cervical lymph nodes or lungs. It may, however, spread from more remote foci by way of the blood stream. In most cases, the process is a sluggish one but in others it progresses rapidly, invading the mastoid bone and the labyrinth. External pachymeningitis is not uncommon and eventually the dura may be penetrated with resulting meningitis or tuberculoma formation. The sigmoid sinus may be thrombosed. In a few cases, tuberculous osteomyelitis of the base of the skull in the anterior fossa has been observed. This is apparently due to extension of tuberculous processes in the sinuses and nasal bones.

Clinical Features.—It has already been stated that tuberculous otitis is usually secondary to lesions in the upper respiratory passages or the chest but may apparently be derived from remote foci. The onset is very gradual in most cases and is not accompanied by pain. There is a thin, watery discharge at first but this may later become purulent if secondary infection develops. There may be multiple perforations of the drum and later the whole drum may be destroyed. Hearing may be only slightly reduced in some cases but is often completely abolished. A very characteristic feature is the presence of paralysis of the seventh nerve which has been estimated to occur in 40 per cent of all cases.

Rarely tuberculosis may cause infection of one of the nasal sinuses and extend into the orbit or even into the cranium. We have observed cases in which paralysis of the third nerve occurred as a result of invasion of the orbit. Cases have been described in which the infection involved the sella and eventually damaged the optic chiasm and pituitary gland so as to simulate hypophyseal tumor.

The infection may extend through the dura causing tuberculous meningitis or solitary tubercle. The latter is most apt to be found in the cerebellar hemisphere or the temporal lobe. In cases complicated by pyogenic infections, abscess of the brain or purulent meningitis may result.

Diagnosis.—The diagnosis depends upon the evidences of tuberculosis elsewhere in the body, the slow course, absence of pain, the multiple perforations of the ear drum, the frequent presence of facial paralysis and, above all, upon the demonstration of tubercle bacilli in the secretions and granulations.

Prognosis.—This is unfavorable as a rule.

Treatment.—Therapeutic measures as in other types of tuberculosis are indicated and operation in specially selected cases.

BIBLIOGRAPHY

COLEMAN, C. C. AND MERIDETH, J. M.: Diffuse tuberculosis of the pituitary gland simulating tumor. Arch. Neurol. & Psychiat., **44**:1076, 1940.
DE VET, A. C.: Caries cranii. J. Neurosurg., **6**:269, 1949.
FLATAU, E.: Tuberkulose der Schadelbasis. Ztschr. f. d. ges. Neurol. u. Psychiat., **104**:365, 1926.

Sarcoidosis

Definition.—This is a generalized disease of unknown origin characterized anatomically by the development of hard tubercles and clinically by a variety of syndromes. The cutaneous lesions are termed Boeck's sarcoid or lupus pernio. The generalized form of the disease has been called lymphogranuloma benignum. The lesions in the bones are described under the term osteitis tuberculosa multiplex cystica. The combination of facial paralysis, uveitis and parotitis is called uveoparotid paralysis. Longcope employs the name sarcoidosis or Besnier-Boeck-Schuman disease.

Etiology.—The cause of this disease is not definitely established, but one cannot escape the conclusion that it is an infection. Patients suffering from sarcoidosis frequently develop active tuberculosis and because of this fact many authorities believe that the former is an atypical form of the latter. However, it is rarely possible to demonstrate the tubercle bacillus in typical lesions and in the majority of cases the cutaneous tuberculin test is negative.

Pathological Anatomy.—The characteristic lesion is the hard tubercle which is similar in size and general appearance to the common miliary tubercle of tuberculosis. The hard tubercle is composed of a mosaic of epithelioid cells which stain feebly. There is rarely any striking inflammatory reaction about this lesion and central necrosis is uncommon. Giant cells may occur but are not constant. The hard tubercles do not grow in size apparently but increase in number so that they may appear in the gross as large semitranslucent grayish masses. Occasionally they heal by a process of fibrosis. No micro-organisms are found. These lesions occur in all structures of the body but seem to be most common in the lymph nodes, lungs, spleen, skin, bones and uveal tract. They may involve the parotid and lacrimal glands, the cranial bones, meninges, cranial nerves and brain. The peripheral nerves may be infiltrated. Meyer *et al.* have reviewed fourteen cases in which the process had invaded the brain and the meninges. They describe two varieties. The commoner of these is a diffuse granulomatous leptomeningitis most severe at the base of the brain. This type involves the optic chiasm, cranial nerves and infundibulum and sometimes causes hydrocephalus. In some cases this process is acute and then may cause thrombosis of the cerebral vessels with softenings in the brain. The second variety is manifest by granulomatous masses in the brain as well as leptomeningitis and granular ependymitis. It is pointed out that the granulomas are usually perivascular.

Clinical Features.—The disease may occur at any age though it is most common in young adults. The systemic manifestations are mild. Fever is not constant or frequent even when the disease is generalized, though there may be brief elevations of temperature during acute episodes. There is rarely any considerable degree of anemia or leucocytosis. Eosinophilia, however, occurs in about one third of all cases. Loss of weight is rarely striking. A peculiar feature of this condition, mentioned by Longcope, is an increase of serum globulin. This is found in approximately half of all cases.

One of the most common and best known syndromes is that of *uveo-parotid paralysis* which includes uveitis, parotitis and facial paralysis. The uveitis may be unilateral or bilateral and mild or severe. The changes in the iris are indistinguishable from those of tuberculous iritis. The process may extend so as to involve the cornea, conjunctiva and even the retina and end in glaucoma with complete loss of vision. In more favorable cases, recovery without material reduction of vision may ensue. The parotitis is usually but not always bilateral. There is little or no pain or tenderness, the swelling is of moderate degree and the glands are firmer than in mumps. Suppuration does not occur. The lacrimal glands are often enlarged and nodules may appear in the eyelids. During the active stages of this process, there is apt to be a moderate degree of fever. Paralysis of one or both seventh nerves is present in most cases. This is of peripheral type and is believed to be due to involvement of the nerve in its passage through the parotid gland in most instances, though facial palsy may occur without demonstrable parotitis. The other cranial nerves are less commonly affected, but palsies of the fifth, eighth, ninth and tenth nerves are described. It is characteristic for these cranial nerve palsies to recede and then reappear. Retrobulbar neuritis and central scotoma may occur. White spots may develop in the choroid resembling tuberculous chorioretinitis. In some cases white masses appear which may extend forward into the vitreous. The optic nerve head may be involved by these masses. Polyneuritis and mononeuritis may occur. The involved nerves may be palpably thickened. Chronic granulomatous meningitis may develop in the basilar meninges causing optic atrophy, involvement of the optic chiasm and palsies of the third, fourth and sixth nerves. In some cases of this type there may be no sign of meningeal irritation and no cells in the spinal fluid. In more acute cases there may be a pleocytosis in the spinal fluid.

Masses of hard tubercles sometimes form in the meninges and cranial bones involving the sella turcica, hypophysis, optic chiasm, optic nerves, hypothalamus, cerebral peduncles and temporal lobes. Either primary optic atrophy or papilledema may result. Diabetes insipidus occurs. Walsh has reported cases of this type.

The lymph nodes are commonly involved. Both the superficial and internal nodes may be enlarged. The bronchial and mediastinal nodes are frequently affected. In some cases there may be large masses in the mediastinum which later disappear without treatment. The lungs may show disseminated lesions which in their roentgenographic appearances resemble miliary tuberculosis. Even extensive processes of this type may cause astonishingly few symptoms. Dyspnea is perhaps the most frequent complaint. This is due to pulmonary fibrosis, as a rule, and may be severe enough to cause cor pulmonale. An acute form of sarcoidosis is described with fever, bilateral enlargement of the hilar nodes, migratory polyarthritis and sometimes erythema nodosum. The heart may be involved, with fatal results. There may be heart block of various types and paroxysmal arrhythmias. The liver and spleen may be much enlarged so as to give rise to the picture of Banti's disease. One of the most typical processes is found in the bones. Multiple small areas of rarefaction appear in the phalanges of the fingers and toes which eventually form cysts. They are seen especially in the terminal portions of the bones and may cause palpable enlargement of the fingers. Sarcoidosis may give rise to hypercalcemia and renal insufficiency simulating the clinical picture of parathyroid tumor almost exactly.

The cutaneous manifestations are well known. The lesions are small or large, cutaneous or subcutaneous, nodules or infiltrations. In color they may be red, purple or brown. They are found most frequently in the skin of the face, nose, eyelids, ears and extremities. Sometimes they resemble erythema nodosum. A special variety is called lupus pernio because the lesions resemble chilblain. The cutaneous lesions usually heal leaving scarlike areas.

Krabbe mentions nodules in the skeletal muscles. We have seen infiltration of the muscles with miliary nodules and also a diffuse myositis with much atrophy.

Diagnosis.—The diagnosis depends upon the recognition of the syndromes described above and above all upon the microscopic study of cutaneous nodules or affected lymph nodes. It is known that a variety of conditions including beryllium intoxication, histoplasmosis and tuberculosis may cause granulomatous lesions similar to those of sarcoidosis, so the diagnosis cannot be made with complete confidence on the basis of histology alone. The roentgenographic appearances of the process in the lungs and bones are distinctive enough to be of value in the differential diagnosis. Active tuberculosis may of course complicate the picture. Symonds suggests that recurrent episodes with cranial nerve palsies, i.e., polyneuritis cranialis, are characteristic.

Hirsch *et al.* state that the Kveim test is valuable if it is properly performed. In this test, a suspension made from human sarcoid tissue is injected intracutaneously. A nodule appears at the site of the injection within two weeks. This is biopsied four to six weeks later. Sarcoid tubercles are found if the test is positive. In subacute cases of sarcoidosis, a positive reaction is found in 76 per cent. In more chronic cases and in cases in which the disease is inactive, the percentage of positive reactions is much smaller. In less than 5 per cent of patients suffering from other diseases are false positive tests secured.

Prognosis.—The tendency of sarcoidosis uncomplicated by tuberculosis is apparently to run a long course with remissions and exacerbations ending after years in recovery. The uveitis may result in permanent loss of vision, however. In a considerable percentage of cases active tuberculosis eventually develops and runs its usual course.

Treatment.—Antituberculous chemotherapy has apparently little value. Cortisone is said to be helpful in cases of subacute uveitis. Chloroquine is helpful in treating cutaneous lesions.

CASE HISTORY (U-195986).—*Case of sarcoidosis in a girl of 15 years with bilateral facial palsy and bilateral uveitis. Biopsy of lymph node revealed typical hard tubercles. Cutaneous tuberculin test positive in 1/100 dilution.*

B. T., a colored girl of 15 years, was seen for the first time on January 25, 1940. Two weeks before she had developed a right facial palsy and the left side of her face had become paralysed 4 days later. Examination revealed only bilateral paralysis of the face of peripheral type. The parotid glands were not swollen. The Wassermann test was negative in both the blood serum and the spinal fluid. No additional symptoms developed in the next few weeks and about the first of April, regeneration was apparent in the facial nerves.

On April 9, the patient developed pain in both eyes and vision began to fail. Examination revealed bilateral iritis. Vision was 20/30 and 25/50 respectively right and left. The iritis grew rapidly worse and intraocular tension rose so that various operative procedures became necessary. Paracentesis was performed several times, iridectomy gave unsatisfactory results and finally posterior sclerotomy was required. The last operation was performed in June 1940 and thereafter intraocular tension was reduced to approximately normal levels. Vision was at times reduced to 3/200 but gradually improved in the course of months so that in June 1941 it was 20/30 bilaterally.

Numerous studies were made during several admissions to the hospital. The roentgenographic studies of the lungs, heart, nasal sinuses and bones were entirely negative. There was no leucocytosis and no increase of the eosinophils of the blood. The Wassermann test was always negative in the blood and spinal fluid. The cutaneous tuberculin test was positive in a dilution of 1/100 but negative in weaker dilutions. The total protein of the blood serum was 8.3. The serum albumen was 3.2 and the globulin 5.1, indicating a definite increase of the globulin. A small inguinal lymph node was removed and on section showed lesions typical of sarcoidosis. A bit of iris was also examined and showed a granulomatous process which might be due to either tuberculosis or sarcoidosis. The Frei and Ito tests were negative. Temperature was always normal. No cutaneous lesions were ever evident and the parotid and lacrimal glands were never definitely enlarged or tender.

Since June 1941 the patient has remained well and shows no sign of her illness except for reduction of vision to 20/30 bilaterally.

BIBLIOGRAPHY

ALLISON, J. R.: Familial occurrence of sarcoidosis. Southern Med. Jour., **57**:27, 1964.

BASHOUR, F. A. *et al.:* Myocardial sarcoidosis. Dis. Chest, **53**:413, 1968.

BOWER, G.: Intrathoracic sarcoidosis. Dis. Chest, **44**:457, 1963.

COLOVER, J.: Sarcoidosis with involvement of the central nervous system. Brain, **71**:451, 1948.

CONE, R. B.: A review of Boeck's sarcoid. J. Pediat., **32**:629, 1948.

CONNOLLY, A. E.: Osteitis tuberculosa multiplex cystoides and sarcoid lesions. Brit. J. Radiol., **11**:25, 1938.

CRITCHLEY, McD. AND PHILLIPS, P.: Iridocyclitis, parotitis and polyneuritis. Lancet, **2**:906, 1924.

DYKEN, P. R.: Sarcoidosis of the skeletal muscle. Neurology, **12**:643, 1962.

EMIRGIL, C. *et al.:* Long term study of pulmonary sarcoidosis. Jour. Chron. Dis., **22**:69, 1969.

ERICKSON, T. C., ODOM, G. L. AND STERN, K.: Boeck's disease (sarcoid) of the central nervous system. Arch. Neurol. & Psychiat., **48**:613, 1942.

FEILING, A. AND VINER, G.: Iridocyclitis-parotitis-polyneuritis. J. Neurol. & Psychiat., **2**:353, 1921-22.

HINTERBUCHER, C. AND HINTERBUCHER, L.: Myopathic syndrome in muscular sarcoidosis. Brain, **87**:355, 1964.

HIRSCH, J. G. *et al.:* Kveim test for sarcoidosis. New England J. Med., **265**:827, 1961.

ISREAL, H. L.: The diagnosis of sarcoidosis. Ann. Int. Med., **68**:1323, 1968.

JAMES, D. G. *et al.:* Treatment of sarcoidosis. Lancet, **2**:526, 1967.

JEFFERSON, M.: Nervous signs in sarcoidosis. Brit. Med. J., **ii**:916, 1952.

———: Sarcoidosis of the nervous system, Brain, **80**:540, 1957.

KAPLAN, H.: Arthritis with sarcoidosis. Arch. Int. Med., **112**:924, 1963.

KRABBE, K.: Muscular localization of benign lymphogranulomatosis. Acta Med. Scand. Sup., **234**:193, 1949.

LONGSCOPE, W. T.: Sarcoidosis or Besnier-Boeck-Schumann disease. J.A.M.A., **117**:1321, 1941.

———: A study of sarcoidosis. Medicine, **31**:1, 1952.

——— AND PIERSON, W.: Boeck's sarcoid. Bull. Johns Hopkins Hosp., **60**:223, 1937.

MEYER, J., FOLEY, J. AND CAMPAGNA-PINTO, D.: Granulomatous angiitis of the meninges in sarcoidosis. Arch. Neurol. & Psychiat., **69**:587, 1953.

MORSE, S. I.: Treatment of chronic sarcoidosis. Am. J. Med., **30**:779, 1961.

PENNELL, W. H.: Boeck's sarcoid with involvement of the central nervous system. Arch. Neurol. & Psychiat., **66**:728, 1951.

POPPER, J. S. *et al.*: Sarcoid granuloma of the cerebellum. Neurology, **10**:942, 1960.

PORTER, G. H.: Sarcoid heart disease. New England J. Med., **263**:1350, 1960.

ROOS, B.: Cerebral manifestations of lymphogranulomatosis benign and uveoparotid fever. Acta med. Scandinav., **104**:123, 1940.

SILTZBACH, L. E. AND GREENBERG, G. M.: Childhood sarcoidosis. New England Jour. Med., December 5, 1968.

SILVERSTEIN, A. AND SILTZBACH, L. E.: Muscle involvement in sarcoidosis. Arch. of Neurol., **21**:235, 1969.

SILVERSTEIN, A. *et al.*: Neurologic sarcoidosis. Arch. of Neurol., **12**:1, 1965.

SKILLICORN, S. A. *et al.*: Intracranial Boeck's sarcoid tumor resembling a meningioma. J. Neurosurg., **12**:407, 1955.

SPILBERG, I. *et al.*: The arthritis of sarcoidosis. Arth. and Rheum., **12**:126, 1969.

SYMONDS, C.: Recurrent multiple cranial nerve palsies. J. Neurol., Neurosurg. & Psychiat., **21**:95, 1958.

TILLGREN, J.: Diabetes insipidus as a symptom of Schumann's disease. Brit. J. Dermat., **47**:223, 1935.

WALSH, F. B.: The ocular importance of sarcoid. Its relation to uveoparotid fever. Arch. Ophth., **21**:421, 1939.

WEIDERHOLT, W. C. AND SIEKERT, R. C.: Neurological manifestations of sarcoidosis. Neurology, **15**:1147, 1965.

LEPROSY

Etiology.—Leprosy is due to infection by an acid-fast bacillus discovered by Hansen, which is usually termed B. leprae. It is found in large numbers in lesions of certain types. In morphology the lepra bacillus resembles the tubercle bacillus.

Pathological Anatomy.—The nerve trunks show nodular thickenings as a result of proliferation of connective tissue and cellular infiltrations. Such lesions are almost invariably found in peripheral parts of the nerves, especially where the nerve is superficial and exposed to trauma. The bacilli are sometimes present in large numbers in the innermost lamellae of the perineurium and in the endoneural septa. They are contained, as a rule, within the so-called lepra cells which are surrounded by epithelioid cells, plasma cells and fibroblasts. Associated with these interstitial lesions is always some degree of degeneration of the nerve fibers which, however, does not have any qualitative relation to the interstitial change. Moreover, the number of bacilli is independent of the degree of tissue reaction. In some cases the reaction is relatively acute with active inflammatory reaction and edema, but, as a rule, the process is a chronic one and the thickening of the nerve is due chiefly to fibrosis. Some authorities describe a descending form of leprous neuritis, but it is generally agreed that the process usually begins in the terminal portions of the nerve and slowly ascends along the nerve trunk. Often the nerve seems to be invaded by extension of the infection from a cutaneous lesion, but it is probable that the bacilli may reach the nerve by way of the blood stream.

Distribution.—The disease has largely disappeared from Europe but a limited number of cases are still found in Norway, Sweden, Spain, Portugal and certain parts of France. It is very common in the Balkans. In Asia and Asia Minor the disease is prevalent and many thousands of cases are found in India, China and Siberia. Africa, especially central and east Africa and the Cameroons, is heavily infected. Many cases are also found in Iceland, Japan, Australia and the Philippines. In the United States, small numbers of cases are found in the Gulf region, the Pacific coast and the Great Lakes region.

Clinical Features.—Children are extremely susceptible to leprosy and the disease is not uncommon in childhood. Among the children of lepers who live with their parents, definite signs of the disease are found in about 4 per cent of the children under 4 years; in 19 per cent of the children between 4 and 8 years and in over 40 per cent of the children between 12 and 16 years. If the children are removed from their parents immediately after birth, the incidence of the disease is very low. The disease may develop early in infancy and the average age at which the diagnosis can be made is said to be somewhat over 5 years. Infection is believed to occur in the large majority of cases through the skin and an initial lesion is said to be demonstrable in 75 per cent of cases. In other children, it is probable that the organisms invade the nasal mucosa and reach the skin by way of the blood stream. It has been estimated that the average age of infection among the children of lepers is about 2 years and that the incubation period is between 3 and 4 years.

Lepromatous leprosy, formerly termed nodular leprosy, is a severe form of the disease which causes death within 15 years as a rule without treatment. A number of skin lesions are described but the most characteristic one is the nodule. These are red, elevated and firm. They are most conspicuous on the nose, cheeks, ears and forehead. They are not anesthetic. Histologically they are composed of granulation tissue which contains lepra cells and many bacilli. The nerves are not involved until late. The mucous membranes are ulcerated. The nose, pharynx, palate, larynx and trachea are involved. The testicles show degenerative changes. The liver, spleen, kidneys, adrenals and bone marrow show lepra cells and organisms. Amyloid deposits are often found in the viscera at post-mortem examination. There is keratitis, iritis and corneal ulceration in many cases. From time to time the lepra reaction, i.e. bouts of fever occur associated with flare-up of the lesions, is apt to occur. The lepromin reaction is usually negative.

The *tuberculoid type,* formerly called the maculoanesthetic type, is more benign and even untreated patients may survive for many years. This form may pass over into the lepromatous type, however. The standard skin lesion is the macule. These are partially depigmented, dry, roughened areas.

There is anihidrosis and soon anesthesia in such areas. Often biopsy shows only perivascular infiltration and bacilli are hard to find. Tuberculoid changes are present in some lesions. Involvement of the peripheral nerves is often the most conspicuous feature. The nerves are greatly thickened and lose their function soon. Sections reveal a granulomatous process with caseation and bacilli are found more easily than in the maculae. The nasal mucosa is involved but the other mucous membranes are apt to escape. Nasal scrapings may show no bacilli except during lepra reactions which do not occur so often as in the lepromatous cases. The eyes often escape damage though exposure keratitis may occur if the facial nerve is involved. There is little evidence of visceral damage. The lepromin reaction is positive but it should be kept in mind that this reaction is often positive in normal individuals.

The fifth nerve is frequently affected. Usually this is shown by patches of anesthesia over the forehead, the bridge of the nose and the cheeks. Rarely is the whole trigeminal distribution anesthetic. Not infrequently the anesthesia is bilateral and sometimes it is roughly symmetrical. Neuroparalytic keratitis may result. There is usually palpable thickening of the superficial nerve branches, especially of the superorbital nerve. Loss of function of the motor branch of the fifth nerve is rare. Localized palsies of the facial muscles are very common and characteristic. The eyelids are frequently partially or completely paralysed causing lagophthalmos and ectropion of the lower lid. The lips, especially the lower lip, are also frequently affected, causing striking eversion with much swelling. As a rule, only a few facial muscles are affected and the distribution of the paralysis is patchy. Complete paralysis of the whole facial nerve is uncommon. Loss of tone in the affected muscles is very prominent and the face is greatly disfigured as a result. The other cranial nerves are seldom involved. Oculomotor palsies are rare. The eighth, ninth, tenth, eleventh and twelfth nerves are spared, as a rule. Loss of taste, of smell, of vision and of hearing are all very common in advanced leprosy and are due in most cases to the extensive ulcerations of the mucous membranes.

Symptoms and signs referable to the spinal nerves begin in the distal parts of the extremities and progress proximally, as in other types of peripheral neuritis, but with this difference that the disturbances are not uniform and symmetrical as in common types of toxic polyneuritis but are patchy and incomplete, indicating involvement of individual nerves and even branches of individual nerves. The ulnar nerve in the arm and the common peroneal nerve in the leg are affected first, as a rule. Atrophy, weakness and loss of tone appear in the intrinsic muscles of the hands and feet and slowly give rise to various types of deformity. Simian hand and claw hand are very common. The atrophy is usually proportional to the loss of power. The tendon reflexes of paralytic muscles are lost. As a rule, the ankle jerk and finger reflexes are lost and the knee and biceps reflexes preserved. The plantar reflex is usually abolished and the abdominal reflexes preserved. There is never, apparently, any clonus or true Babinski phenomenon.

The disturbances of sensibility are of the same type as have been described above in discussing involvement of the fifth nerve. There is a tendency to irregular distribution of the anesthesia corresponding to the distribution of nerve branches. True dissociation does not occur but different modalities of sensation may be affected with different degrees of severity. Sense of passive movement, sense of position and vibratory sense are rarely affected to any appreciable degree. Pain is sometimes present, especially at the onset of relatively acute cases.

Various disorders of vasomotor and secretory function and trophic disturbances are almost constant and constitute characteristic features of the disease. The hands and feet are cold and blue. Sweat secretion is lost in the region of the macules and hair often falls out. The macules are usually devoid of pigment and atrophy of the skin is common. Dry necrosis of the fingers may occur but it is more common to find concentric atrophy of the small bones of the fingers and toes, so that the digit grows smaller and shorter, maintaining at the same time its original shape to some extent. The nail may remain attached to this stump of a finger or toe. Neuropathic joints are sometimes seen and even extensive decalcification of the bones producing extraordinary flexibility of the fingers.

Ulcerations are common and are of two types: those due to "trophic" disorders and those due to burns and injuries for the anesthesia makes these patients indifferent to such traumas.

An important feature is the nodular thickenings of the affected nerve trunks. Those most frequently found to be thickened are the ulnar nerve at the elbow, the great auricular nerve where it passes over the sternomastoid muscle, the superficial peroneal nerve at the knee and the supraorbital branch of the fifth nerve. Almost all superficial nerves may be palpated in some cases. Elliott, who has studied a number of leprous children in the United States, points out that slit lamp examination of the eyes may be helpful in diagnosis. He states that beading of the corneal nerves is very frequently found. There is also a punctate keratitis in some cases. Vascularization of the cornea at the limbus may occur and fine filaments are often seen in the anterior chamber which seem to arise from the posterior surface of the iris.

Diagnosis.—The most important clinical features in the diagnosis are the history of exposure, the typical cutaneous lesions and the peculiar type of neuritis with thickening of the affected nerve trunks. The demonstration of the bacilli, however, is necessary to establish the diagnosis when the clinical findings are not typical. Scrapings of the nodules and of the ulcerations of the mucous membranes are often positive but it is very difficult to demonstrate the organisms in the macules. In the nodular cases, the bacilli may be found in the blood stream during the febrile periods. The blood is citrated, centrifugalized and the sediment stained. Puncture of lymph nodes is advised by some authorities.

Prognosis.—The expectation of life among leprous children is brief but this is no doubt due in large part to the unsanitary conditions in which they are usually brought up. Nodular leprosy is apt to run a more rapid course than neuritic leprosy. The former is apt to lead to death within 15 years; the latter usually lasts longer. Spontaneous remissions are described. Early treatment exerts a favorable effect on the disease and numbers of patients have been freed of all manifestations of the disease for periods of several years.

Treatment.—Chaulmoogra oil and its derivatives have been employed for many years with doubtful results. More recently sulphone drugs such as promin and diasone have been used. It is said that these drugs cause gradual healing of the lesions though bacilli are still found years after treatment is started. Streptomycin is said to have some value. General hygienic measures are important and strict isolation for patients who have open lesions is imperative. Babies of leprous mothers should be removed from home immediately after birth.

BIBLIOGRAPHY

ARNOLD, H. L.: Modern Concepts of Leprosy. Springfield, Thomas, 1953.

ASH, J. E. AND SPITZ, S.: Pathology of Tropical Diseases. Philadelphia, W. B. Saunders Co., 1945.

ELLIOTT, D. C.: Leprosy, a disease of childhood. J. Pediat., 35:188, 1949.

FITE, G. L. AND GEMAR, F.: Regressive changes in leprosy under promin. South. M. J., **39**:277, 1946.

MONRAD-KROHN, G. H.: The Neurological Aspect of Leprosy. Christiania. Jacob Dybwad, 1923.

MUIR, E.: Preliminary report on diasone in leprosy. Internat. J. Leprosy, 12:1, 1944.

RODRIGUEZ, J. N.: Studies on early leprosy in children of lepers. Philippine J. Sc., 31:115, 1926.

ROSENBERG, R. N. AND LOVELACE, R. E.: Mononeuritis multiplex in lepromatous leprosy. Arch. of Neurol., 19:310, 1968.

SABIN, T. D.: Temperature-linked sensory loss in leprosy. Arch. of Neurol., 20:257, 1969.

WALSH, F. B.: *Loc cit.*

INVASION OF THE NERVOUS SYSTEM BY FUNGI

Actinomycosis

Etiology.—The organism is one of the fungi and is characterized by the formation of a radiating arrangement of mycelia. It is termed *"Actinomyces bovis"* since it is a common cause of disease in cattle.

Pathological Anatomy.—The nervous system is usually involved by direct extension from an infection about the head, although the organisms may also be transmitted by the blood stream from the caecum. In most cases there is a purulent leptomeningitis and the basilar meninges are infiltrated with leucocytes and a few lymphocytes and plasma cells. Localized pachymeningitis is described. Cerebral abscesses also occur and granulomatous masses. The fungi are usually found in large numbers in the meninges and in the pus of the abscesses. They are visible to the naked eye as small yellow granules sometimes termed "sulphur granules." The pus is said to have a characteristic rancid odor. Primary infections of the brain are very rare.

Clinical Features.—There are now more than forty cases on record in which the nervous system has been invaded by the ray fungus. The disease is almost confined to rural districts and is most common in herdsmen and cattle breeders. The primary lesion is usually in the skin or mucous membranes, most commonly about the face, mouth or neck, but it may also be found in the lungs or the abdominal cavity.

The invasion of the nervous system is marked by headache and signs of meningeal irritation which may be relatively mild for several weeks or even months. Slowly these symptoms become more and more severe, the patient becomes weaker and cachectic and finally sinks into stupor. If abscess forms, convulsions and even cerebral palsies may develop. The course of the disease is chronic and there is very little general reaction. The patient may not be confined to bed until late in the course of the disease. In many cases the temperature does not rise above 101°F. The spinal fluid usually contains several hundred cells per cubic millimeter and the count may rise to several thousand. About 70 to 80 per cent of these are polymorphonuclear leucocytes. The organisms have been discovered in the spinal fluid. The infection frequently involves the spine as do other fungus diseases and may give rise to a clinical picture which closely resembles Pott's disease with kyphosis, abscess formation and paraplegia.

Diagnosis.—The diagnosis should be considered whenever a chronic, low grade meningitis is found in association with phlegmons or other conditions which might be due to actinomycosis.

Prognosis.—Meningitis and abscess of the brain due to actinomycosis have always been fatal in the past. Perhaps, modern drugs will reduce the mortality.

Treatment.—Penicillin and other antibiotics are of value in local infections and in some instances surgical removal of the lesion is possible. The value of drugs in cases in which the central nervous system is invaded is uncertain.

BIBLIOGRAPHY

CANN, L. W. AND HOLLIS, G. J.: Case of actinomycotic cerebrospinal meningitis associated with actinomycosis. Lancet, 1:130, 1931.

ELLIS, R. W. B.: Actinomycosis in childhood. Arch. Dis. Childhood, 10:1, 1935.

MOERSCH, F. P.: Actinomycosis of the central nervous system. Arch. Neurol. & Psychiat., 7:745, 1922. (Full references.)
STEVENS, H.: Actinomycosis of the nervous system. Neurology, 3:761, 1953.

COCCIDIOSIS

Etiology.—The Coccidioides immitis exists in two forms. In nature it is a white mould with mycelia and chlamydospores. The parasitic form in man is a large spherical body with doubly refractile capsule which reproduces by endosporulation. This is of variable size but averages about 30 micra in diameter. Dickson believes that human infection is usually the result of inhalation of the chlamydospores.

Pathological Anatomy.—The lesions in the nervous system are very similar to those of tuberculosis. An acute meningitis is described which occurs as a part of a generalized disease. A chronic type of meningitis is also described in which the first symptoms are referable to the meninges. Miliary granulomas are found over the convexity and in the basal cisternae presenting the picture of tuberculous meningitis. Rarely one encounters granulomas in the brain resembling tuberculomas. Processes in the skull give rise to extradural abscesses and similar lesions in the spine cause epidural abscess or granuloma which may compress the spinal cord. The granulomata are composed of epithelioid and giant cells and eventually undergo liquefaction. The organisms may be recognized in sections and also cultivated. The lesions in the skin, bones, lungs and other tissues need not be described here.

Clinical Features.—The disease has been known since 1892 and hundreds of cases of various types have been studied. The vast majority of these have occurred among the residents of San Joaquin Valley in California but the disease has also been observed in South America.

Dickson has shown that the initial stage of the disease is an infection of the respiratory tract known as San Joaquin Valley fever. This resembles a common bronchitis or bronchopneumonia. In some instances lesions are found in the lungs, especially in the region of the hilum and in the upper lobes, which may be mistaken for pulmonary tuberculosis. Cavity formation is not rare. The organisms may be found in the sputum. A characteristic feature is the development of erythema nodosum between one and two weeks after the onset. As a rule, the pulmonary lesions heal within a few months. The primary lesion may sometimes occur in the skin, it is claimed. A small nodule forms which breaks down and is slow to heal.

This initial illness may end in several different ways. In the vast majority of cases, it ends in recovery as mentioned above. In rare cases, there is a generalized and fatal process resembling miliary tuberculosis which is fatal in a few weeks or months. A third type is a chronic granulomatous disease.

The most common neurological syndrome is that of meningitis developing in the terminal stage of the generalized form of the disease. The onset is gradual with headache and vomiting. There is fever of low grade, sweats, chills, mild leucocytosis and anemia with progressive loss of weight. Drowsiness, delirium and finally stupor appear. Signs of meningeal irritation are always present to some degree. There are apt to be evidences of increased intracranial pressure since hydrocephalus frequently occurs. The spinal fluid may contain several hundred lymphocytes. Film formation is mentioned. The organisms may be cultivated from the spinal fluid in an occasional case but negative cultures and smears do not exclude the diagnosis. The course is slower than that of tuberculous meningitis and death may be delayed for five months or more after the onset of meningeal symptoms.

Some cases have been observed in which a chronic type of meningitis developed as an isolated process without any evidence of the generalized disease. There have also been described cases of large cerebral granulomas giving rise to the picture of brain tumor and extradural spinal granulomas, resembling neoplasms of the cord in their clinical manifestations.

Diagnosis.—It is evident that the clinical features resemble those of tuberculosis very closely and the only satisfactory basis for the diagnosis is the demonstration of the organism in sections of cutaneous lesions or in cultures of the blood or spinal fluid. Complement-fixing antibodies may be demonstrated and the skin reaction may be of value. The history of residence in the San Joaquin Valley is, of course, important.

Prognosis.—The generalized form of the disease is apparently always fatal. No doubt some of the isolated granulomas may be removed successfully.

Treatment.—Recently it has been found that the administration of ethyl vanillate is of value in the treatment of early lesions. This drug is apparently not effective in the generalized forms of the disease or in meningitis. Isolated granulomas may be removed surgically.

BIBLIOGRAPHY

ABBOTT, K. H. AND CUTLER, O. I.: Chronic coccidioidal meningitis. Arch. Path., 21:320, 1936.

COURVILLE, C. B. AND ABBOTT, K. H.: Pathology of coccidioidal granuloma of the central nervous system and its envelopes. Bull. Los Angeles Neurol. Soc., 3:27, 1938.

DENNIS, J. L. AND HANSEN, A. E.: Coccidioidomycosis in children. Pediatrics, 14:481, 1954.

DICKSON, E. C. AND GIFFORD, M. A.: Coccidioides infections. Arch. Int. Med., 59:1029, 1937; Coccidioides infection. Arch. Int. Med., 61:853, 1938.

FIESE, M. J.: Treatment of coccidioidomycosis with ethyl vanillate. California Med., 80:349, 1954.

RAND, C. W.: Coccidioidal granuloma. A report of two cases simulating spinal cord tumor. Arch. Neurol. & Psychiat., 23:502, 1930.

RICHARDSON, H. B. *et al.*: Acute pulmonary coccidioidomycosis in children. Jour. of Pediat., 70:367, 1967.

STORTS, B. P.: Coccidioidal granuloma simulating brain tumor in a child of four years. J.A.M.A., 112:1334, 1939.

TORULOSIS

Etiology.—The *torula histolytica* is a yeast-like organism varying in diameter between 2 and 40 micra. It is round or oval in shape and often surrounded by a thick gelatinous capsule. It reproduces by budding, and does not form mycelium.

Pathological Anatomy.—The torula has a strong affinity for the nervous system and in half of the cases of this disease which are subjected to postmortem examination no lesions are found outside the nervous system. Nevertheless, it is believed that the portal of entry of the infection is either the lungs or the skin. The brain shows at necropsy a chronic meningitis most severe at the base and very similar to tuberculous meningitis. The fluid in the subarachnoid spaces is turbid and gelatinous, containing the organism in large numbers. The nervous tissue is often invaded. In the cortex are found cysts. The organisms penetrate along the perivascular spaces into the cortex from the subarachnoid space. They then proliferate distending the tissues and forming small cystic structures filled with a gelatinous material composed of the organisms and their capsules. There is very little reaction about such cysts, the glia does not proliferate and the nerve cells in the neighborhood show little or no change. In some cases lesions are found deep in the cortex and basal ganglia which seem to have arisen as a result of embolism. Freeman states that the smallest organisms are apt to provoke the formation of cysts with little or no reaction and that the largest organisms are those which provoke the greatest mesodermal reaction and are limited, as a rule, to the meninges.

Cox and Tolhurst describe torula infection in the lungs, lymphatic system, skin, mucous membranes, bones, joints and other tissues. They mention a generalized type. They point out that torulosis may be found in association with tuberculosis and also with Hodgkin's disease.

Clinical Features.—Torula infection may occur at any age and affects males and females alike. The onset is usually very gradual with headache, vomiting and drowsiness. The heads of infants may enlarge slowly as a result of hydrocephalus. Some degree of papilledema is almost always present and this may eventually lead to optic atrophy and reduction of vision. Cervical rigidity and Kernig's sign are almost always present but are usually not so severe as in purulent meningitis. In some cases, there is low grade fever and mild leucocytosis but other cases run their course without the usual signs of infection and systemic symptoms are rarely conspicuous. Hemiplegia or hemiparesis and other evidences of focal cerebral lesions may appear. The sixth nerves are frequently paralysed and the other cranial nerves are sometimes involved. Delirium is rare but drowsiness and stupor sometimes develop early. The course is a very slow one averaging more than three months. There may be temporary improvement but, in general, the disease progresses uninterruptedly. In the last stages emaciation is usually a striking feature. Anemia may be absent but sometimes develops in profoundly cachectic patients.

Neuhauser and Tucker and Campos describe cases in which infection apparently occurred before birth or at the time of birth. The organism was found in the mother's vagina. The symptoms were similar to those of toxoplasmosis. Hydrocephalus, intracranial calcifications, retinal lesions and enlargement of the liver and spleen are all mentioned.

The spinal fluid shows constant changes. The cell count ranges from 50 to 1,000. Mononuclear cells predominate but leucocytes may be present. Many organisms are usually seen in the counting chamber and may be recognized by their refractile capsules, although they are often mistaken for lymphocytes. Cultures are usually obtained on Sabouraud's medium. A very characteristic feature of the spinal fluid is the gelatinous deposit which forms in the bottom of the tube when the fluid is allowed to stand. In certain instances, the torula may be absent from the spinal fluid or may fail to grow on artificial culture media.

In only a few cases is there any clinical evidence of disease outside the

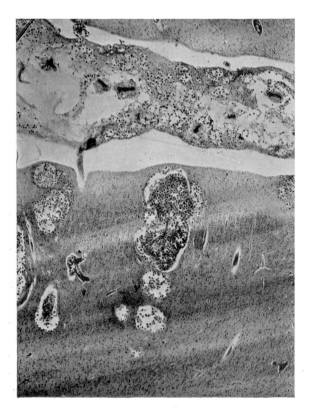

FIG. 152. Section of the cerebral cortex in the case abstracted below. The infection has penetrated the cortex along the perivascular spaces giving rise to cystlike structures in which innumerable organisms are seen. Similar nests of organisms are seen in the meninges. There is remarkably little reaction of the tissues.

central nervous system. Involvement of the lungs is sometimes seen. The lymph nodes may be enlarged. In generalized torula infection, the organisms may be found in the blood and urine and the liver and spleen may be enlarged. Torulae have been found in pus withdrawn from the liver and in cultures from the pharynx, tonsils and nasal sinuses. It must be kept in mind that torula infection may develop in connection with tuberculosis and it may be very difficult to distinguish the two processes during life.

Diagnosis.—It is difficult or practically impossible to establish the diagnosis without the demonstration of the causative organism. The majority of cases simulate tuberculous meningitis very closely. The insidious onset, evidences of meningeal irritation, low grade fever and increased cell count in the spinal fluid are all very suggestive and if there are signs of pulmonary infection in addition, the most capable clinician may be deceived. The course, however, is much longer than that of tuberculous meningitis. Brain abscesses may be suspected in other cases in which evidences of increased intracranial pressure, fever and signs of a focal cerebral lesion are combined and in some cases brain tumor may seem most likely, especially when the signs of meningeal irritation are over-shadowed by the increased intracranial pressure and when fever and leucocytosis are absent. The rare "tumor meningitis" or "sarcomatosis of the meninges" may cause almost identical pictures, for in this condition we have not only increased intracranial pressure but meningeal irritation and pleocytosis in the spinal fluid. We must, therefore, rely upon the demonstration of the organism in the spinal fluid, blood, urine, skin, lymph nodes or sputum. In a few cases sections of the meninges removed during exploration have permitted a correct diagnosis. This diagnosis should always be suspected in cases resembling tuberculous meningitis in which the course extends beyond six weeks.

Prognosis and Treatment.—No treatment has yet been found effective and the present belief is that all cases result fatally. Wilson and Duryea discuss the various drugs that have been used in this disease and report a case in which the intravenous administration of actidione, an antibiotic found in cultures of S. griseus, seemed to be effective. The patient seemed to be well 20 months after the onset. Others seem to have found this agent to be less effective. Amphotericin B may be rendered soluble by mixing it with sodium deoxycholate. The mixture is dry frozen and may be dissolved in water to be administered parenterally. It is claimed that several patients seem to have been greatly benefited by this drug.

CASE HISTORY (Path. 14948).—*Child of 4 years developed vomiting, convulsions and rigidity of the neck. Became stuporous and emaciated and died after 2 months. C.S.F. contained 400 cells and numerous torulae. Post-mortem exam revealed extensive lesions in brain, meninges and viscera.*

C. T. J., a previously healthy girl of 4 years, began to vomit about the middle of July 1936. A few days later she had a series of convulsions which were apparently generalized. After this she became drowsy and then stuporous. Temperature was normal.

Examination revealed striking loss of weight. The child was deeply stuporous and the neck, and indeed, the entire body musculature, rigid. The tendon reflexes were all sluggish and there was a bilateral extensor response. There was no evidence of vision or of hearing, but the optic nerve heads were normal in appearance and a sluggish light reflex was present. There was no anemia and no leucocytosis. Temperature was normal. The spinal fluid was cloudy and contained 400 cells which were chiefly lymphocytes. Torulae were present in large numbers in the smear and were easily cultivated on Sabouraud's media. The course was slowly progressive. The stupor deepened. The rigidity increased and the body and extremities assumed a position of flexion. Death occurred in a little more than 2 months after the onset.

Post-mortem examination revealed an extensive meningeal exudate composed of lymphocytes and numerous organisms. The cranial nerves at the base were embedded in this exudate. The cortex of the cerebrum and the cerebellum contained innumerable small cysts formed by masses of the organisms which had distended the tissues by proliferation. There was little if any reaction about these cysts. The bones of the base of the skull showed softened areas. In the lungs, spleen, kidneys and lymph nodes were similar deposits of the organisms. Rats and mice were inoculated and developed lesions identical with those of the patient.

BIBLIOGRAPHY

CAMPOS, J.: Congenital meningo-encephalitis due to torulosis neoformans. Rev. Clin. Inst. Lisb., **6**:87, 1954.

COLWELL, J. A.: Treatment of coccidioidomycosis with amphotericin. Ann. Int. Med., **50**:1028, 1959.

COX, L. B. AND TOLHURST, J. C.: Human Torulosis. A clinical, pathological and microbiological study with report of 13 cases. Melbourne Univ. Press, 1946.

DRUTZ, D. J. *et al.:* Treatment of disseminated mycotic infections. Amer. Jour. Med., September, 1968.

FIESE, M. J.: Coccidioidomycosis. Springfield, Thomas, 1958.

FREEMAN, W.: Torula infection of the central nervous system. J. f. Psychol. u. Neurol., **43**:236, 1931.

JONES, T. B.: Localized infection caused by yeast-like fungi with special references to spinal involvement. Surg. Gynec. & Obst., **50**:972, 1930.

MARTIN, W. J.: Cryptococcosis: Further observations and experience with amphotericin. A.M.A. Arch. Int. Med., **104**:4, 1959.

NEUHAUSER, E. B. AND TUCKER, A.: The roentgen changes produced by diffuse torulosis in the newborn. Am. J. Roentgenol., **59**:805, 1948.

REVES, D. L., BUTT, E. AND HAMMOCK, R. W.: Torula infection of the lungs and central nervous system. Report of six cases with three autopsies. Arch. Int. Med., **68**:57, 1941.

STEIN, H. E.: Disseminated coccidioidomycosis. Dis. Chest, **36**:136, 1959.

Stoddard, J. L. and Cutler, E. C.: Torula Infection in Man, Monograph 6, p. 1. New York, Rockefeller Inst., 1916.

Walsh, F. B. *Loc. cit.*

Wilson, H. and Duryea, A.: Cryptococcus meningitis (torulosis) treated with a new antibiotic Actidione. Arch. Neurol. & Psychiat., **66**:470, 1951.

INVASION OF THE NERVOUS SYSTEM IN OTHER FUNGUS INFECTIONS

In addition to those mentioned above, several other fungi may invade the central nervous system in rare instances. These will be mentioned briefly.

Nocardiosis.—This is a granulomatous disease formerly confused with tuberculosis and actinomycosis. The organism is believed to be derived from the soil. The infection may be the cause of chronic local granulomas but may invade the nervous system very early. The disease may occur in debilitated individuals as a terminal event. The organism may be cultivated easily and the colonies are distinctive. In the tissues the organisms take several forms. The local types are treated surgically and sulphonamides are said to be effective. When the nervous system is invaded, drugs are not effective.

Blastomyces dermatitidis.—This is a yeast-like organism varying in diameter from 7 to 20 micra. It has a highly refractile wall and reproduces by budding. Infections by this organism are rarely seen outside the United States. The commonest manifestation of this infection is a local dermatitis. In some instances a generalized and rapidly fatal disease develops, however. The lungs, lymph nodes and bones are involved and the process is not unlike tuberculosis. Meningitis and granulomata in the brain may also occur. Some of the granulomata are of large size and give rise to symptoms resembling those of brain tumor. This organism differs from the torula in that it provokes a strong reaction in the tissues. At present 2-hydroxystilbamadine is employed.

Paracoccidioides brasiliensis.—This is another yeast-like organism which is found chiefly in South America where it sometimes causes ulcerations in the mouth and on the face. It rarely produces a generalized infection with meningitis as a part of the picture. This organism is said to average about 30 micra in diameter and reproduces by multiple buds which grow out from all sides of the parent cell. Sulfonamides are recommended and must be given for long periods.

Histoplasma capsulatum.—This is a very small organism which measures between 1 and 4 micra in diameter. The capsule is thick. Though it reproduces by budding, few buds are seen in the tissues. This organism gives rise to an acute, generalized and fatal infection with fever, anemia, leucopenia and enlargement of the liver, spleen and lymph nodes. There is no special affinity for the nervous system, but cases of granulomatous meningitis are described. Uveitis may occur as an isolated process. Central vision is reduced. The macula becomes edematous. Then it becomes gray and cystic. Later, a dense white scar results. The skin test and complement-fixation are helpful in diagnosis. Amphotericin B is effective but toxic. Desensitization is helpful.

I have seen a case of histoplasmosis in which left hemiparesis occurred repeatedly during a period of several years in association with an increase of cells in the spinal fluid and another case in which typical lesions in the retinae were associated with recurrent facial paralysis with pain and swelling in the region of the parotid gland.

It has been established recently that benign infections with this organism are very common in the central portion of the Mississippi Valley but rare in the Southeastern Seaboard and the New England states. Furcolow found when studying an epidemic that infection seemed to be a result of contact with bird excreta. This process is usually asymptomatic and ends by producing multiple pulmonary scars with calcification. The differentiation from pulmonary tuberculosis is made by the demonstration of histoplasmin sensitivity and the negative tuberculin reaction. Ethyl vanillate is being tried but its value is uncertain. Sulfonamides are recommended and also amphotericin B.

Sporotrichum schenckii.—This organism is well known as a cause of chronic ulcerative lesions in the skin. Systemic invasion and meningitis have been described, however. There is a chronic meningitis with marked fibrosis but no giant cells. Small spores and fine filaments may be seen in the tissues and spinal fluid. Iodides are used in local infection but have no value in generalized infection.

Candida (monilia) albicans.—This organism is a common cause of thrush and may also invade the lungs. A few instances of meningitis are described.

Aspergillus.—This organism is sometimes found in corneal ulcers. Rarely it may invade the brain causing large granulomata which contain many small abscesses. The organism may be recognized by its long branching form and the blackish pigmentation.

Endomyces capsulatus.—This is a very small organism which may rarely cause granulomatous meningitis.

Mucor.—This organism is rarely pathogenic. It grows profusely on media containing sugar and infection occurs almost invariably in diabetics who are not properly regulated. Infection seems to start in the nasal sinuses and extend into the orbit causing exophthalmos and ophthalmoplegia. The cranium is then invaded with meningitis under the frontal lobes and extensive softenings due to invasion of the blood vessels. The organism forms large mycelial threads, aerial hyphae of large diameter and distinctive spore-bearing bodies. This condition may occur in infants.

BIBLIOGRAPHY

ALBAN, J.: Fungous infections in children. Post. Grad. Med., **42**:493, 1967.

ASH, J. E. AND SPITZ, S.: Pathology of Tropical Diseases, Philadelphia, Saunders, 1945.

BAKER, R. D.: Mucormycosis—A new disease. J.A.M.A., **163**:805, 1957.

BAUER, H. *et al.:* Cerebral mucormycosis. Am. J. Med., **18**:822, 1955.

BOSHES, L. M. *et al.:* Fungus infections of the central nervous system. Arch. Neurol. & Psychiat., **75**:175, 1956.

COOPER, R. A. AND GOLDSTEIN, E.: Histoplasmosis of the central nervous system. Am. J. Med., **35**:45, 1963.

FREEMAN, W.: Fungus infections of the central nervous system. Ann. Med., **6**:595, 1932.

FURCOLOW, M. L. *et al.:* Studies on an epidemic in Mexico, Missouri. New England J. Med., **264**:1226, 1961.

GASPAR, L.: Blastomycotic meningoencephalitis. Arch. Neurol. & Psychiat., **22**:475, 1929.

HARRIS, J. S.: Mucormycosis. Pediatrics, **16**:875, 1955.

HATHAWAY, B. M. AND MASON, K. N.: Recognition of nocardiosis. Am. J. Med., **32**:903, 1962.

HYSLOP, G., NEAL, J. B. AND KRAUS, W. M.: A case of sporotrichosis meningitis. Am. J. Med. Sc., **127**:726, 1926.

IAMS, A. M., TERREN, M. M. AND FLANAGAN, F. H.: Histoplasmosis in children. Review of the literature. Am. J. Dis. Child., **70**:229, 1945.

IYER, S., DODGE, P. AND ADAMS, R.: Two cases of aspergillus infection of the central nervous system. J. Neurol., Neurosurg. & Psychiat., **15**:152, 1952.

JACKSON, I. J. *et al.:* Solitary aspergillus granuloma of the brain. J. Neurosurg., **12**:53, 1953.

KING, A. B. AND COLLETTE, T.: Brain abscess due to cladosporium trichoides. Bull. Johns Hopkins Hosp., **91**:298, 1952.

KURREIN, F.: Cerebral mucormycosis. J. Clin. Path., **7**:144, 1954.

LARSEN, M. C. *et al.:* Nocardia asteroides infection. Arch. Int. Med., **103**:712, 1959.

LECOUNT, E. R.: Blastomycotic lesions of the brain. J. Nerv. & Ment. Dis., **36**:144, 1909.

LEINFELDER, J. T.: Ocular histoplasmosis. Surv. Ophthal., **12**:103, 1967.

LITTLE, J.: Amphotericin for infantile histoplasmosis. Pediatrics, **24**:1, 1959.

LOCKWOOD, W. R. *et al.:* Hydroxystilbamadine for blastomycosis. Ann. Int. Med., **57**:553, 1962.

LONG, E. L. AND WEISS, D. L.: Cerebral mucormycosis. Am. J. Med., **26**:625, 1959.

MAFFEI, W. E.: Mycoses of the nervous system. An. Fac. de. med. da Univ. de São Paulo, **19**:297, 1943.

MARTIN, F. P. *et al.:* Cerebral mucormycosis. J. Pediat., **44**:437, 1954.

MONITZ E. AND LOFF, R.: Aspergillose cerebrale. Press Med., **39**:273, 1931.

MORRIS, A. A., KALTZ, G. G. AND LOTSPEICH, E. S.: Ependymitis and meningitis due to candida (monilia) albicans. Arch. Neurol. & Psychiat., **54**:361, 1945.

MUKOYAMA, M. *et al.:* Aspergillosis of the central nervous system. Neurology, **19**:967, 1969.

PROCKOP, L. D. AND SILVA-HUTNER, M.: Cephalic mucormycosis. Arch. of Neurol., **17**:379, 1967.

RABIN, E. R.: Mucormycosis complicating burns. New England J. Med., **264**:1286, 1961.

RANKIN, J. AND JAVID, M.: Nocardiosis of the central nervous system. Neurology, **5**:815, 1955.

SALVIN, A. B.: Current concepts of diagnostic serology and skin hypersensitivity in the mycoses. Am. J. Med., **27**:97, 1959.

SHAPIRO, J. L., LUX, J. J. AND SPROFKIN, B. E.: Histoplasmosis of the central nervous system. Am. J. Path., **31**:319, 1955.

SKOOGLAND, J. E.: Meningitis caused by the higher fungi. New Orleans M. & Surg. J., **95**:334, 1943.

SPOFKIN, B. E. *et al.:* Histoplasmosis of the central nervous system. A case report of histoplasmosis meningitis. J. Neuropath. & Exp. Neurol., 14:288, 1955.
WEED, L. A. *et al.:* Nocardiosis. New England J. Med., 253:1137, 1955.

INVASION OF THE NERVOUS SYSTEM BY SPIROCHETES AND RELATED ORGANISMS

Congenital Syphilis of the Nervous System

Etiology.—Congenital syphilis is due to infection by the treponema pallidum which apparently penetrates the placenta and invades the foetal organism. It is not hereditary in the sense that it is conveyed by the germ plasm, but it is acquired *in utero* from a syphilitic mother. Since acquired syphilis rarely affects the nervous system during childhood, it does not seem necessary to discuss it at this point.

Pathological Anatomy.—With some exceptions, the pathological features of congenital syphilis of the central nervous system are identical with those of acquired syphilis. There are various types of meningitis, endarteritis, hydrocephalus, optic atrophy and parenchymatous processes, such as general paresis and tabes dorsalis. Large isolated gummata are very rare. Greenfield and Buzzard state that the process always starts in the meninges and perivascular spaces, usually at the base of the brain. Lymphocytic infiltration of the basilar meninges is almost invariably present in neurosyphilis, regardless of the type of the disease. If the process is an active one and extends rapidly throughout the meninges, acute syphilitic meningitis develops. Sluggish and more chronic processes are localized in the basilar meninges. In such cases the optic nerves may be infiltrated, giving rise to optic atrophy or the blood vessels may be involved, causing endarteritis and infarctions of the brain. If the subarachnoid spaces are obliterated by an adhesive process, the circulation of cerebrospinal fluid may be interrupted, causing hydrocephalus. In the same way, lymphocytic foci in the meninges may become enlarged and organized and may eventually become granulomatous masses or gummata. General paresis is usually regarded as the result of the invasion of the parenchyma of the brain by the treponema. The spinal cord is believed to be involved as the brain is. The process begins in the spinal meninges and may involve the spinal nerve roots, the spinal blood vessels or invade the periphery of the cord directly.

Acute diffuse syphilitic meningitis is not unlike other forms of meningitis. The meshes of the pia-arachnoid are filled with lymphocytes, phagocytes and plasma cells and in very acute processes, leucocytes may be present. The adventitia of the meningeal vessels is infiltrated with cells and the infiltrations extend along the perivascular spaces of the cortical blood vessels. In less acute types of meningitis, miliary gummata are found in the basilar meninges and in the sulci over the convexity. These are small nod-

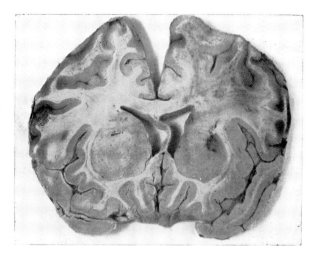

FIG. 153. Brain of the patient shown in Fig. 94 showing a small softening in the right putamen and another smaller lesion in the white matter above. More posteriorly there are larger lesions in the left lenticular nucleus and capsule; and softenings can be seen in the cortex.

ules composed of lymphocytes, fibroblasts and epithelioid cells. Giant cells may also be present. In such cases there is usually definite thickening of the meninges and the subarachnoid space may be obliterated in places. The cerebral blood vessels show inflammatory changes in the adventitia and the sheaths of the cranial nerves are infiltrated with lymphocytes. This process is apparently the cause of optic atrophy and of other cranial nerve lesions in neurosyphilis. Frequently the process invades the superficial layers of the cortex, and the meninges and the cortex are fused so intimately that it is difficult to find any demarcation between them. The dura is also involved in many cases and may become adherent to the arachnoid. In a few cases we have seen hemorrhagic pachymeningitis in infants which was apparently due to syphilis. The clot is 2 cm. or more thick and partially organized. The blood vessels within this tissue all show perivascular infiltrations of lymphocytes and other cells. In cases of hydrocephalus due to syphilis, basilar meningitis is always found which has caused obliteration of the subarachnoid spaces and obstruction of the flow of cerebrospinal fluid.

The cerebral vessels may be injured in several different ways. Usually there is infiltration of the adventitia, and to some extent of the media. The elastic lamellae become fragmented, the intima proliferates and finally may occlude the lumen of the vessel. Thromboses are very common. In other cases the vessel wall becomes weakened and ruptures or aneurysm formation results. Infarction of the brain is much more common than hemorrhage, however. Another type of syphilis of the cerebral vessels is accompanied by very little evidence of inflammation. The adventitia and intima proliferate, the elastic lamellae become reduplicated and eventually the lumen of the vessel is occluded. New capillaries are apt to develop and the cortex may become excessively vascular. This process involves only the very small blood vessels and the capillaries. It may result in excessive degenerative changes in the cortex.

Miliary gummata are common in neurosyphilis but large gummata are rare. These large gummata are superficially situated, as a rule, and appear as grayish or reddish masses which are adherent to the meninges. Histological studies reveal that they are composed of lymphocytes, plasma cells and giant cells with numerous fibroblasts. The cellular mass slowly becomes larger, blood vessels grow into it and finally the central portions become partially necrotic although the connective tissue framework is usually preserved.

In juvenile general paresis, meningeal and vascular lesions may both be present but the essential feature is a diffuse degenerative process in the cortex of the brain. The convolutions are shrunken, the sulci deep and wide and the ventricles dilated. On histological examination there is found extensive degeneration of the nerve cells and fibers of the cortex. The astrocytes are increased and the microglia are elongated forming the so-called rod cells. Freeman states that the lesions in juvenile paresis are always more destructive than those found in the severest cases of paresis in adults. The architecture of the cortex is altered and fat and iron may be present in large quantities. The cortical blood vessels show extensive accumulations of lymphocytes in their adventitial sheaths and there is frequently a patchy meningeal reaction. The cerebellum is also atrophic as a rule. The treponema pallidum is sometimes found in large numbers in the cortex.

In juvenile tabes dorsalis the posterior columns of the spinal cord are severely degenerated and the site of a dense fibrous gliosis. The changes in the posterior columns seem to be secondary to degeneration of the posterior spinal roots. The treponema is rarely found and the pathogenesis of tabes dorsalis is still a matter of dispute among neuropathologists.

If the nervous system is invaded early in foetal life, defects of development such as microgyria and simplified cortical patterns may be found in addition to the destructive processes just enumerated above. Such developmental anomalies are emphasized especially in cases of juvenile general paresis.

Clinical Features of Congenital Syphilis in General.—The incidence of congenital syphilis of all forms is subject to great variation, depending upon economic, social and racial factors. In the United States at the present time congenital syphilis is a rare disease and congenital neurosyphilis is very rare indeed. Public health measures and the liberal use of penicillin are no doubt responsible for the decreasing incidence of these conditions which were once so common.

It is generally stated that the effect of untreated syphilis upon reproduction gradually diminishes with the passage of time. Thus, after a woman has acquired syphilis, she may be sterile for a period, later there may be abortions, then still-births and finally a number of viable children who show less and less evidence of congenital syphilis. The last children may be quite healthy. It should be said, however, that this rule is not without exceptions and a syphilitic child may be interpolated anywhere in a series of apparently healthy infants. In large unselected groups of families in which the mother or both parents have syphilis, 25 to 80 per cent of the children are found to have congenital syphilis. Abortions and still-births are very common and it has been claimed that only from 9 to 23 per cent of the pregnancies in such families result in living, healthy children. Thorough treatment of a syphilitic woman before and during pregnancy will usually protect the child.

Third generation syphilis probably occurs but is extremely rare. In most instances, by the time congenital syphilitics become capable of reproduction, they are no longer able to communicate the disease.

The symptoms are extraordinarily numerous and diverse. In general, the earlier the manifestations of congenital syphilis appear, the more severe the infection. The common, early symptoms which correspond to the secondary lesions in acquired syphilis, include rhinitis, bullous skin eruptions and abnormalities of the skin and hair. Prematurity is very common. The spleen is frequently enlarged and the liver edge may be palpable. Jaundice may occur. The lymph nodes may be enlarged. Acute osteochondritis, often causing pseudo-paralysis, is not uncommon. Syphilitic dactylitis is very typical. Periostitis is well known. These symptoms are present in rare cases at birth but, as a rule, appear between the second and eighth week. It is exceptional for them to develop after the sixth month. The diagnosis must be made on the clinical signs, the roentgenograms of the bones and the his-

Fig. 154. Congenital syphilis. Hutchinson's teeth. (By the courtesy of Dr. Holt.)

tory, for the Wassermann reaction is unreliable until after the third month.

Many children with congenital syphilis show no clinical evidence of the disease during infancy. They may, however, develop symptoms at any time during childhood. These late symptoms correspond to the late symptoms of adults. Lesions of the bones, viscera, mucous membranes, eye and nervous systems are most common. Osteitis and periostitis may cause frontal bossing of the skull, saber shins, scaphoid scapulae, saddle nose, scoliosis and osteomyelitis. The first teeth are apt to be defective and to decay early, although they are not typical of syphilis. In the second set, the upper central incisors often show the peg shape and central notching described by Hutchinson and the molars may show the extra facets which have given rise to the term "mulberry molars." The spleen and liver are sometimes enlarged and jaundice and ascites may occur. Iritis may occur with or without keratitis. These children are usually anemic and delicate. They are undersized and poorly nourished. Their appearance is often infantile and the genital organs are sometimes poorly developed. These symptoms have been ascribed to syphilitic disease of the endocrine glands. The pituitary gland may be damaged.

Clinical Features of Congenital Neurosyphilis.—Jeans and Cooke found positive Wassermann reactions in the spinal fluid of 38 per cent of all white children under two years of age who were suffering from congenital syphilis. In only 8 per cent, however, were there any clinical evidences of active neurosyphilis. Among congenital syphilitics over 2 years of age, the percentage of positive spinal fluid Wassermann reactions was only 29 per cent but about 16 per cent of these children had serious lesions of the nervous system. In young adults with congenital syphilis, the nervous system is involved in only about 5 per cent and asymptomatic neurosyphilis is uncommon. Jeans and Cooke state that they have never seen a child develop neurosyphilis whose spinal fluid Wassermann reaction was negative during infancy. These facts may be explained as follows: The nervous system is invaded early, when the organisms are widely disseminated throughout the body, or not at all. During infancy, the nervous process is asymptomatic in most cases but it usually becomes clinically active some time in childhood or in adolescence. The mortality of neurosyphilis during childhood is much higher than that of the other forms of congenital syphilis, so the incidence gradually declines. Only a few of these children with neurosyphilis reach adult life. In general, it may be said that the nervous symptoms are in inverse proportion to the somatic symptoms. Thus, Jeans and Cooke found that only 11.5 per cent of the children with active neurosyphilis showed signs of active syphilis elsewhere, and, conversely, 72 per cent of the children with latent neurosyphilis had active lesions in other systems of the body.

The clinical types of congenital neurosyphilis cannot be separated into well-defined groups, for there is always some over-lapping. I shall describe various groups of symptoms below but it must be kept in mind that several groups may occur in the same patient.

Syphilitic Meningitis.—Meningitis is often the earliest clinical manifestation of congenital neurosyphilis. The symptoms develop on an average during the fourth and fifth months, but the same symptoms may occur at the end of the first month or as late as the end of the first year. There is usually some bulging of the fontanels, stiffness of the neck and mildly positive Kernig's sign. Fever may be absent or there may be a mild elevation of temperature. Convulsions are commonly present. The spinal fluid contains from 50 to 500 lymphocytes and the globulin is increased. The Wassermann reaction is positive. If treatment is begun early, the results are excellent.

If treatment is not given or is inadequate, the process may become chronic. Various cranial nerve palsies may occur. The seventh nerve is most frequently affected but the third, fourth and sixth nerves are also commonly involved. Signs of increased intracranial pressure may appear such as enlargement of the head, bulging of the fontanels, papilledema and vomiting. Optic atrophy may follow papilledema or may appear without preceding changes in the papillae. Hemiplegias and other cerebral syndromes may develop suddenly as a result of thrombosis of the cerebral vessels. If the child does not die promptly, blindness, paralysis and dementia eventually supervene.

Hydrocephalus.—In some cases hydrocephalus may be the only clinical

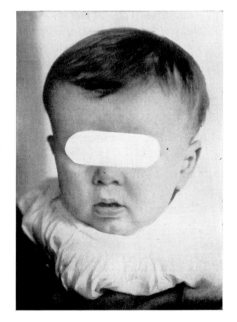

FIG. 155. Congenital syphilis with meningitis and mild hydrocephalus.

sign of neurosyphilis. The onset is usually between the fourth and the ninth month of life. Syphilitic hydrocephalus is rare at birth. The head does not grow as rapidly as it does in the common type of chronic congenital hydrocephalus. In most cases syphilitic hydrocephalus is complicated by optic atrophy or cranial nerve palsies. Syphilitic meningitis is always found at autopsy even when meningeal signs are absent. The obstruction seems to be in the basilar cisternae in most cases, so that the hydrocephalus is usually of the communicating type. Antisyphilitic treatment will not always relieve this condition, for the adhesions may remain after the inflammation has subsided. Some degree of hydrocephalus is found in about 30 per cent of all cases of syphilitic meningitis among infants. Syphilis is not an important factor in the severe chronic hydrocephalus of early infancy, however, for some years ago the author found only three cases which could be attributed to syphilis in a series of 100 autopsies performed upon infants with hydrocephalus.

Vascular Lesions of the Brain.—Focal cerebral lesions with apoplectic onset may rarely occur in congenital neurosyphilis. These are usually due to cerebral infarction resulting from syphilitic endarteritis. Cerebral infarction is not fatal unless a large artery is occluded or unless the brain-stem is involved. Such vascular accidents may occur without warning and may constitute the only clinical sign of neurosyphilis or they may be associated with evidences of meningitis or with cranial nerve palsies. They occur usually between one and two years and are rare after five years. Hemiplegia is the commonest syndrome but multiple lesions may occur causing double hemiplegia, cerebral paraplegia, monoplegia, hemianesthesia and aphasia. Eventually the child shows bilateral spasticity with speech disturbances and profound mental deterioration. Convulsions are common and often fail to respond to antisyphilitic treatment. In some cases there are no definite strokes but the symptoms advance gradually. This is probably due to many minute infarctions resulting from disease of the smaller vessels. Such cases are often confused with juvenile general paresis. The history of one or more strokes of paralysis and the definite signs of pyramidal tract injury should make the differentiation possible in most cases. However, it must be admitted that vascular lesions may complicate general paresis and that it is not always possible to make a satisfactory distinction between the various types of congenital neurosyphilis, even on anatomical grounds. Treatment is of no avail so far as the restoration of function is concerned but may serve to prevent further lesions. It is generally believed that cases which continue to advance despite adequate treatment are complicated by general paresis.

Intracranial Gummata.—Gummata large enough to produce symptoms of an intracranial tumor are rare and we have never verified the diagnosis

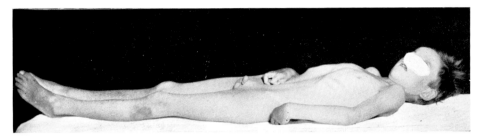

Fig. 156. Boy of 11 years suffering from congenital neurosyphilis of vascular type. The day before he was examined, he became unconscious and paralysed on the left side. Death occurred on the 4th day after many convulsions. Post-mortem examinations showed syphilitic endarteritis and an extensive fresh infarct in the right lenticular nucleus and capsule.

of intracranial gumma in childhood. In adults, gummata may cause signs and symptoms due to increased intracranial pressure, as well as hemiplegia and other signs of focal lesions in the brain. As a rule, the spinal fluid Wassermann reaction is positive and there is an increase in the cell count but I have seen several cases in which the spinal fluid was quite normal.

Juvenile General Paresis.—There is a great difference of opinion about the frequency of this type of congenital neurosyphilis. Jeans and Cooke consider it rare but Ferguson and Critchley estimate that 32 per cent of their cases of congenital neurosyphilis fall into this group and another 12 per cent into the group of tabo-paresis. As Jeans and Cooke point out, there is no general agreement about the criteria necessary for the diagnosis. Moreover, the incidence varies widely in different age groups. In the Harriet Lane Home and other pediatric hospitals, juvenile general paresis is rare but in the syphilis clinic of Johns Hopkins Hospital, where older children and young adults are treated, it constitutes a large percentage of all forms of congenital neurosyphilis. Certainly not all cases of dementia resulting from neurosyphilis should be considered paretic. I would restrict the clinical diagnosis to those cases of slowly progressive mental deterioration which are characterized by absence of focal signs and symptoms, by a strongly positive Wassermann reaction in the spinal fluid and by a striking resistance to antisyphilitic treatment. The onset is usually between the ages of 10 and 15 years but may occur as early as 4 years. There may be a history of skin lesions or other manifestations of congenital syphilis early in life, but very often the first evidence of the disease is the development of mental disturbances. Dullness, apathy and forgetfulness are among the first symptoms. School grades show a progressive falling off. The child grows untidy and is careless of personal hygiene. There may be irritability, restlessness, night terrors and temper tantrums but more often the child is not difficult to control. These children may, however, commit anti-social acts, such as stealing, in an impulsive way. The grandiose trends sometimes seen in adult paretics are rarely prominent, although such children may claim that they possess great quantities of candy or that their fathers are millionaires. Mild euphoria is very common. Delusions and hallucinations are rare. Speech soon becomes indistinct. Syllables are slurred and omitted and finally words are lost and the structure of the sentence is distorted. If the child has learned to write, this function is slowly lost. The gait becomes clumsy and unsteady. Coarse tremors of the hands and lips are seen. Focal or general convulsions are common but hemiplegia and similar cerebral insults are unusual. Symptoms and signs of tabes dorsalis may complicate the picture.

Examination may reveal the typical stigmata of congenital syphilis and in some cases there is deficient growth and even sexual infantilism. Sometimes, however, development is quite normal. The pupils may be large or small. The light reflex is usually absent and in many cases the contraction during accommodation is also lost. Optic atrophy is not uncommon. Coarse, irregular tremors are usually present. These affect especially the hands, lips and tongue. Speech is slurring and often unintelligible. Outspoken cerebellar ataxia is not infrequent. The tendon reflexes are usually increased but true spasticity is rather uncommon and the plantar reflexes are as a rule normal. In advanced cases, however, one may find spasticity and Babinski's sign. In some cases there is a complicating tabes dorsalis which results in loss of the tendon reflexes in the legs and in an additional type of ataxia.

The spinal fluid usually contains from 15 to 50 lymphocytes. Globulin tests are positive. The gold curve is usually of the paretic type. The Wassermann reaction is strongly positive in the blood and spinal fluid.

The course of the disease is slowly progressive. Finally, the child becomes completely demented, helpless, bed-ridden and cachectic. Death results from secondary infection and malnutrition. Treatment is even less effective than in general paresis of adults.

Juvenile Tabes Dorsalis.—This condition is rare, even rarer, in fact, than juvenile general paresis. The onset may occur as early as 5 years but is usually deferred until the age of 10 or 15 years. The symptoms are similar of those of adults. Incontinence is often the first evidence of the disease. Optic atrophy is very frequent. Lightning pains and gastric crises are described but are not so common as in adult tabetics. Charcot joints may occur. In examination we find Argyll Robertson pupils, optic atrophy, loss of knee and ankle jerks, positive Romberg sign and ataxic gait. The spinal fluid Wassermann is almost positive but the cell count may be low. The course is usually a very slow one and the disease may be stationary for long periods. In some cases general paresis develops in the terminal stage and in other cases the two diseases are combined from the beginning.

Other Types of Syphilis of the Spinal Cord.—The spinal cord may be involved in congenital neurosyphilis but it is unusual to observe spinal lesions without some evidence of cerebral damage. The commonest type of spinal syphilis is *meningomyelitis*. As the term implies, this process begins in the meninges and involves the cord and the spinal roots. There is usually pain of radicular type for some time preceding the other symptoms. This is usually in the thoracic dermatomes. Weakness of the legs then develops and increases slowly, eventually progressing to more or less complete paraplegia with retention of urine. The legs are usually first flaccid and later spastic. The loss of sensibility is usually less evident than the paralysis. Antisyphilitic treatment if given in time may arrest the process and cause great improvement. When this process is situated in the lumbosacral region, we may have radiculitis of the cauda equina in place of myelitis. Less commonly paraplegia develops suddenly without warning. In such cases treatment is of no avail. *Occlusion of a spinal artery* is usually to blame. We have not seen Erb's slowly progressive spastic paraplegia which is attributed to selective degeneration of the pyramidal tracts. Hypertrophic cervical pachymeningitis, a rare form of neurosyphilis in adults, apparently does not occur in childhood. Gummata of the spinal cord are practically unknown in childhood.

Argyll Robertson Pupil.—This sign is the most important single clinical evidence of neurosyphilis. It is very common in neurosyphilis of all types and exceptionally rare in other nervous diseases, so that its presence is almost diagnostic of the disease. The pupils are usually unequal and irregular. In most cases, they are small, but they may be dilated. The essential feature is the failure to react to light stimulation without loss of the contraction during accommodation. The Argyll Robertson pupil may be the only sign of neurosyphilis or it may be found in association with almost any other symptom. It is usually bilateral but may be unilateral. Its presence does not indicate active syphilis for, once developed, it is permanent whether the syphilitic process is arrested or not. The site of the lesion responsible for the loss of the light reflex is unknown. Slit lamp examination will usually reveal evidences of atrophy of the iris. In a large percentage of cases of juvenile general paresis all pupillary reactions are absent. Menninger states that this condition is characteristic of juvenile paresis and is rarely found in acquired paresis.

Paralysis of the Cranial Nerves.—The seventh nerves are most commonly affected, although any of the twelve pairs may be involved. Third nerve lesions are sometimes seen. This nerve may be involved alone or in company with the fourth and sixth nerves. In the latter instances, a meningeal process about the sphenoidal fissure or periostitis of the orbit is usually responsible. Orbital periostitis causes edema of the orbital tissues, exophthalmos and some degree of papilledema. In some cases there may be ptosis of the lid without other evidence of a third nerve palsy. Ingvar has shown that this is due to the fact that the fibers supplying the levator palpebrae are spread out over the surface of the third nerve and so may be involved by meningeal processes before the deeper lying fibers are affected. The other cranial nerves are less frequently affected. Cranial nerve lesions in congenital syphilis are usually due to meningitis but in some cases the nerves may be involved in their passage through the bony foramina of the base of the skull as a result of periostitis. In such cases the spinal fluid may be negative. The cranial nerves are also rarely affected as a result of vascular lesions in the brain stem.

Epilepsy.—Convulsions are common in all forms of cerebral syphilis. They may be the only clinical evidence of neurosyphilis. Such seizures may be general or focal or identical with the petit mal attacks of true epilepsy. Mental deterioration usually associated with the picture may be not unlike that of the so-called idiopathic epilepsy. However, the blood or spinal fluid Wassermann reaction is almost always positive unless the patient has been subjected to treatment. The convulsions may continue even after the Wassermann reaction has been rendered negative by treatment. No doubt, the scars resulting from the healed syphilitic lesions may in such cases serve as a focus of cortical irritation.

Deafness.—Deafness has long been known as a common sign of congenital syphilis. It begins between the ages of 10 and 15 years in most cases but may appear as early as the second year. It is almost always bilateral and often causes complete loss of hearing within a few months. Tinnitus and vertigo are usually present. Otitis is absent and the deafness is of the inner ear or nerve type. Antisyphilitic treatment is ineffective unless it is administered very early before hearing is grossly reduced. Cortisone may cause prompt improvement. Apparently deafness in congenital syphilis may be due either to involvement of the eighth nerves in the meninges or to syphilitic processes in the temporal bone.

Optic Atrophy.—Primary optic atrophy is common in congenital neurosyphilis. The onset may be at any age but it is rare before two years. The nerve head is diffusely pale and the edges sharply defined. The peripheral parts of the visual fields are affected first and central vision is preserved until the last in most cases, but a great variety of field defects may occur including central scotomas. Both eyes are apt to be affected and the prognosis is poor. Secondary optic atrophy may also occur following papilledema which results, as a rule, from hydrocephalus.

Interstitial Keratitis.—It has been estimated that in congenital syphilis interstitial keratitis occurs in about 40 per cent of all cases. It is only rarely seen in acquired syphilis. The onset is as a rule between 5 and 20 years. One or both eyes may be affected. The process is active for weeks or months and then improvement begins and may continue for a year or more. The onset is marked by pain in the eyes, photophobia and lacrimation. There is pericorneal congestion. Grayish opacities appear in the corneae which are termed maculae. These begin in the periphery and move centrally. Blood vessels grow into the corneae and may give them a reddish appearance. Iridocyclitis is often associated. Vision is grossly reduced for the corneae become opaque. After weeks or months, improvement sets in. The corneae begin to clear, and vision improves. The new blood vessels persist but no longer contain blood. Recurrences may occur.

It is said that satisfactory vision is attained in about 75 per cent of cases, but central opacities in the corneae may persist. Glaucoma and cataracts may develop and choroiditis is not unusual. The standard treatment seems to be penicillin and cortisone. Neurosyphilis of various types may be associated.

Tuberculous keratitis, corneal dystrophy and birth injury to the cornea must be distinguished. In Cogan's syndrome q.v. we find interstitial keratitis in association with progressive deafness, tinnitus and paroxysms of vertigo. Stevens reports a case in a boy of 10 years and Walsh describes a case in a girl of 19 years.

Choreoretinitis.—Many types of retinitis and choreoretinitis are ascribed to syphilis. The commonest is the so-called pepper and salt fundus. Tiny brown and yellow spots are evenly scattered over the entire retina. This condition is very rare in acquired syphilis and quite common in congenital syphilis, so that its presence is almost diagnostic of the latter. A more severe form is very similar in appearance to the common pigmentary degeneration of the retina. There are large irregular deposits of black or dark brown pigment in the peripheral parts of the retina. The blood vessels are small and the retina shows a pale yellowish-gray tint due to degenerative changes. The optic nerve may be atrophic or may show little change. Such lesions are often associated with interstitial keratitis.

The Relation of Congenital Syphilis to the Epilepsies, Mental Defects and Congenital Cerebral Palsies.—These symptoms, namely, convulsions, paralyses and mental deficiency, are well recognized manifestations of congenital neurosyphilis of various types. They are usually associated with other clinical evidences of syphilis and with a positive Wassermann reaction. A small number of cases of congenital neurosyphilis may always be found in any large group of defective children. The incidence in such groups has been variously estimated. Among epileptics and mental defectives confined in asylums and other institutions, positive Wassermann reactions are obtained in less than 10 per cent and among the congenital spastic palsies, the incidence of syphilis is even lower. Certain European writers, however, believe that the effects of syphilis are much more widespread than these figures indicate. They claim that syphilis in the parents may cause various defects in the children without the actual transmission of the disease, and that many defective children whose Wassermann reactions are negative and who have no stigmata of active syphilis are, nevertheless, victims of this disease. The symptoms are, therefore, to be attributed to injury to the germ-plasm. The subject is a large one and cannot be fully discussed here. The writer does not believe that it is justifiable to attribute congenital defects to syphilis unless there is serological or other evidence of active disease.

Diagnosis.—The diagnosis of congenital syphilis usually offers little difficulty. The most essential points to be considered may be summarized as follows: (1) The family history with special emphasis on abortions and stillbirths as well as evidences of congenital syphilis in siblings. (2) History of infancy with reference to prematurity, cutaneous eruptions. especially bullous lesions, rhinitis, etc. (3) Physical examination with search for the characteristic stigmata. (4) Bone lesions (roentgenograms). (5) Wassermann reaction.

The diagnosis of congenital neurosyphilis demands either typical clinical signs and symptoms or a positive Wassermann test in the spinal fluid. The spinal fluid examination is rendered doubly important because of the occurrence of asymptomatic neurosyphilis.

The Blood Wassermann Reaction.—It is generally accepted that the Wassermann reaction is not a reliable test for congenital syphilis before the end of the third month. A healthy infant whose mother has syphilis may yield a false positive reaction from the umbilical cord blood and a syphilitic infant may give a negative reaction. In many cases, however, syphilitic infants, especially those with active lesions, may give strongly positive reactions soon after birth. After the third month and before the end of the second year positive Wassermann reactions are almost invariably secured in congenital syphilis. Thus Jeans and Cooke found only one negative reaction among 488 syphilitic infants within these age limits. After the second year, positive reactions are not constant but the incidence is still over 90 per cent. Thus, it is evident that the Wassermann reaction is a much more reliable test for congenital syphilis than for acquired syphilis. A negative result in an untreated child is very strong evidence against syphilis and between the ages of three months and two years is almost conclusive.

Flocculation tests give essentially the same results. The Wassermann reaction in congenital syphilis is very resistant to treatment, even when the treatment is intensive and prolonged. The recognition that false positive Wassermann reactions are not rare has led to numerous efforts to find a more reliable test than the Wassermann complement-fixation test. Recently a treponema immobilization test has been developed. It is claimed that this test always gives reliable results but it is complicated and expensive.

Harner *et al.* state that the fluorescent treponemal antibody test is the most sensitive test for syphilis.

Spinal Fluid Examination.—Clinical evidence of congenital neurosyphilis is almost invariably accompanied by a positive Wassermann reaction in the spinal fluid after the fourth month of life. The reaction is in many cases not so strongly positive as in the blood and in some instances 0.8 cc to 1.0 cc of fluid must be used to secure complete fixation. The cell count is usually increased and a moderate number of lymphocytes are found, as a rule. If there is clinical evidence of meningitis the cell count may be very high, and in acute cases a large percentage of leucocytes may occur. The total protein content of the spinal fluid is usually increased and positive tests for globulin are secured. The glucose content is almost always quite normal but may be diminished in acute meningitis. Some authors place much emphasis upon the colloidal gold curve in the diagnosis of general paresis. The writer is inclined to believe that the so-called paretic curve is of very little value, for we have found it in a number of non-syphilitic nervous diseases and have not always found it in juvenile general paresis. Moderate increases in the cell count and positive globulin reactions in the spinal fluid of congenital syphilitics have little importance if the Wassermann reaction is negative. Jeans and Cooke have never observed clinical neurosyphilis in such cases, although they have kept a number under observation for years. The spinal fluid examination should be made, if possible, in every case of congenital syphilis coming under observation in infancy because of the high percentage of asymptomatic neurosyphilis in the first two years of life.

Prognosis.—The mortality among congenital syphilitics is estimated at from 25 to 50 per cent during the first two years. It is most important that all pregnant women suffering from syphilis should be treated thoroughly and as early as possible. Prompt and adequate treatment of the mother almost invariably protects the baby against infection. In general, adequate treatment may be expected to result in a great reduction of mortality except in the children with lesions in the nervous system in whom it remains relatively high. Injury to the central nervous system is irreparable. At best, treatment can only halt the progress of the disease. It can never restore the damaged tissues. Many children in whom the process has been arrested remain helpless invalids. In juvenile general paresis, little can be expected from the most intensive and prolonged treatment. The most favorable type of congenital neurosyphilis as regards treatment is meningitis. If treatment is begun before there is any serious damage to the central nervous system, the prognosis is relatively favorable. Vascular lesions, of course, do not respond, although further damage may be prevented. Deafness and optic atrophy are also resistant to treatment.

Jeans and Cooke, writing before the introduction of penicillin, found that the earlier treatment was initiated the quicker serological cure was attained. In a group of 32 cases of all types of congenital neurosyphilis in children under one year of age, they obtained serological cure in 20 after 6 months of treatment. In children over one year of age, only one out of 8 was cured in 6 months of treatment and only 14 out of 34 after a full year of treatment. Serological cure, of course, does not mean clinical cure, for many children so classified have permanent injury to the nervous system.

Treatment.—The heavy metals such as arsenic, bismuth and mercury are no longer used in the treatment of syphilis. Penicillin is employed almost exclusively though newer antibiotics are being tried. Fever therapy is still employed in the treatment of general paresis. It seems to be agreed that a baby with congenital syphilis should have at least 100,000 units of penicillin per kilogram. Holt recommends that this dosage be given in oil three times at intervals of 48 hours making a total dosage of 300,000 units per kilogram. Some preparations are on the market which are slowly absorbed and the total dose may be given by one injection. If aqueous penicillin is used injections are given at intervals of 3 hours until the total dosage is administered.

Untoward reactions of a serious nature are rarely seen as a result of penicillin. Herzheimer reactions may follow the first injection. It is sometimes advised that the initial dose should be a small one so as to avoid this reaction but it is not clear that this reaction is influenced by the size of the dose. Occasionally a child may become sensitive to penicillin. There is no proof that penicillin resistant strains of the treponema exist at present.

The children should be given repeated courses of treatment if the first is not effective. Neurosyphilis is relatively resistant to treatment. The clinical features of the case and the spinal fluid cell count are very important in determining the effect of the treatment. In many instances of congenital syphilis the Wassermann test remains persistently positive regardless of how much treatment is given. It is believed at present that such fixed reactions may be safely disregarded provided there is no other evidence of active disease.

The treatment of neurosyphilis is, of course, unsatisfactory not only because some forms are very resistant, but because irreparable damage has often been inflicted upon the nervous system before treatment is initiated. In general, it may be said that inflammatory processes respond well, whereas, degenerative processes are difficult to control.

General paresis, tabes dorsalis, primary optic atrophy and nerve deafness should be treated with a combination of penicillin and malaria. Tertian malaria is used for white patients and quartan for Negroes and for whites resistant to tertian malaria. Eight to twelve paroxysms are permitted and the penicillin is given during the febrile period. If the first course of treatment does not give satisfactory results a second course may be given in six months.

Therapy should not be restricted to antisyphilitic treatment. The child's general nutrition is of the greatest importance and should always receive careful attention. The weight chart must be followed with care. Urine must be examined at least once a month. Untoward effects of treatment should always be kept in mind.

The discovery of a case of congenital syphilis always demands the examination of all other members of the family. Syphilitic women should be advised against pregnancy and if pregnant should be treated intensively throughout pregnancy. Adequate treatment of the mother for the greater part of pregnancy usually results in a healthy child.

BIBLIOGRAPHY

BUZZARD, E. F. AND GREENFIELD, J. G.: Pathology of the Nervous System. New York, Paul B. Hoeber, 1923.

FERGUSON, F. R. AND CRITCHLEY, McD.: A clinical study of congenital neuro-syphilis. Brit. J. Child. Dis., 26:163, 1929.

FREEMAN, W.: Neuropathology. Philadelphia, W. B. Saunders Co., 1933.

GREEN, J.: The eye in hereditary syphilis. Am. J. Dis. Child., 20:29, 1920.

HAHN, R. D. *et al.:* Penicillin treatment of general paresis. A.M.A. Arch. Neurol. & Psychiat., 81:557, 1959.

HARNER, R. E.: The FTAABS test in late syphilis. Jour. Amer. Med. Ass., 203:545, 1968.

HASSIN, G.: Histology of the Peripheral and Central Nervous System. Baltimore, Wm. Wood & Co., 1933.

JEANS, P. C. AND COOKE, J. V.: Prepubescent Syphilis, Clinical Pediatrics. Vol. 17, New York, D. Appleton & Co., 1930.

JONES, E.: The symptoms and diagnosis of juvenile tabes. Brit. J. Child. Dis., 5:131, 1908.

KING, A. B.: Syphilis of the spinal cord. Am. J. Syph., Gonorrhea and Venereal Dis., 26:336, 1942.

MENNINGER, WM. C.: Juvenile General Paresis. Menninger Clinic Monograph Series. Baltimore, Williams and Wilkins Co., 1936.

MERRITT, H. H., ADAMS, R. D. AND SOLOMON, H. C.: Neurosyphilis. Oxford Univ. Press, 1946.

MILLER, M.: Hemorrhagic encephalopathy due to arsenic therapy. J.A.M.A., 97:161, 1931.

MOORE, J. E.: The Modern Treatment of Syphilis. Springfield, Ill., Charles C Thomas, 1933.

————: Penicillin in syphilis. Springfield, Charles C Thomas, 1946.

MOTT, F. W.: Notes on 22 cases of juvenile general paresis with 16 post-mortem examinations. Arch. Neurol., 1:250, 1899.

NEW, P. S. AND WELLS, C. E.: Cerebral toxicity associated with massive intravenous penicillin therapy. Neurology, 15:1053, 1965.

OELBAUM, M. H.: Hypopituitarism in male subject due to syphilis. Quart. J. Med., 21:249, 1952.

PARKER, H. L.: Juvenile tabes. Arch. Neurol. & Psychiat., 5:121, 1921.

PLATOU, R. *et al.:* Early congenital syphilis. Treatment of two hundred and fifty-two patients with penicillin. J.A.H.A., 133:10, 1947.

ROSE, E. K. *et al.:* Treatment of infantile congenital syphilis. Results with aqueous penicillin alone in sixty infants followed for two years. Am. J. Dis. Child., 77:729, 1949.

Rosenbaum, A. A.: Juvenile tabes dorsalis. Am. J. Dis. Child., 35:866, 1928.

Smith, F. R. Jr.: Late congenital syphilis; A study of the results of treatment in 267 patients. Bull. Johns Hopkins Hosp., 53:231, 1933.

Solomon, H. C. and M. H.: Syphilis of the Innocent. 1922, Washington, U. S. Inter-departmental Social Hygiene Board.

Stevens, H.: Cogan's syndrome. Arch. of Neurol. and Psychiat., 74:337, 1954.

Walsh, F. B.: Clinical Neuro-Ophthalmology. 2nd Ed. Baltimore, Williams and Wilkins, 1956. Maryland.

Watson, G. A.: The pathology and morbid histology of juvenile general paresis. Arch. Neurol. 2:621, 1903.

INVOLVEMENT OF THE NERVOUS SYSTEM
IN SPIROCHETAL DISEASES

Leptospirosis or Weil's Disease.—This is an acute infectious disease due to the Leptospira icterohemorrhagica, an organism frequently found in rats. This disease may occur sporadically or in small epidemics. It is rare in infants but not infrequent in older children.

The onset is marked by fever and digestive disturbances such as abdominal pain, constipation and vomiting. Muscle pains are also among the common symptoms. Jaundice is the most characteristic sign and usually appears on the third or fourth day. The urine is deeply colored and the stools clay colored. The van den Bergh reaction is usually direct at the height of the disease though later it may become biphasic or indirect. The liver is enlarged and the spleen may be palpable. As a rule the fever subsides after three or four days, but the general malaise persists for two weeks or more. The organism may be recovered from the blood by inoculation of a guinea pig. The disease occurs in mild and in severe forms. In the latter there are widespread hemorrhages, nephritis is apt to develop and the mortality is high. Conjunctival injection is usually striking in the early phases of the disease and uveitis may occur weeks or months after the acute stage is over.

My purpose in mentioning this disease is to call attention to the fact that the nervous system may be severely affected. Meningitis of lymphocytic type is said to occur in 10 per cent of all cases. In some instances, jaundice is absent and the diagnosis is impossible unless the causative organisms are demonstrated. Paraplegia has been described in five cases and it is claimed that polyneuritis may also occur. Penicillin is recommended. The organism may be cultivated on several media and agglutination tests are available.

We have observed two brothers (Ped. A-17277 and Ped. A-6026) one of whom suffered from the jaundice without meningeal involvement and the other exhibited lymphocytic meningitis without jaundice. The diagnosis was established by inoculation of a guinea pig.

Canicola Fever is said to be similar to Weil's disease but milder. It is acquired from dogs. Meningeal reactions are very common, it is said. Jaundice and conjunctival infection are not as common as in Weil's disease.

Relapsing Fever, a disease due to S. recurrentis and S. duttoni, the first being louse-borne and the second tick-borne. This disease is found in most parts of the world, being epidemic at times. The onset is marked by fever, headache, muscular pains, vomiting and bronchial symptoms. Jaundice may occur. This episode may last 4 or 5 days. A remission may then follow of 4 to 8 days' duration and this is apt to be followed by another febrile attack. From 2 to 10 febrile episodes may occur. Meningitis is present in a large majority of cases. The organisms are found in the spinal fluid and there is a lymphocytosis in the spinal fluid of variable degree. Injection of spinal fluid into mice will usually give positive results. There seems to be little evidence of encephalitis and in patients who survive there are few residua.

Swineherd's Disease.—This is an infection of hogs and cattle. It is due to the Leptospira pomona. In man the disease is manifest by mild systemic symptoms and a benign lymphocytic meningitis. It is said that iridocyclitis may occur as a late sequel to the acute illness. Ocular inflammation may occur a few weeks or even a year after the meningitis. It is said that penicillin is effective.

Rat-bite Fever is due to infection with S. morsus muris. There is usually an inflammatory reaction at the site of the bite and local lymphangitis. Some 10 to 20 days after the bite, a febrile illness develops which lasts 4 to 5 days. A remission of several days occurs and then another febrile period. Three of 10 paroxysms are usual. A great variety of nervous symptoms are described. These include convulsions, hemiparesis, cranial nerve palsies, spinal cord syndromes and peripheral neuritis. Apparently the organisms may reach all parts of the nervous system. Penicillin is an effective remedy for this disease.

BIBLIOGRAPHY

Ash, J. E. and Spitz, S.: Pathology of Tropical Diseases. Philadelphia, W. B. Saunders, 1945.

Ashe, W. F. *et al.:* Weil's disease. A complete review of the literature. Medicine, **20:**1945, 1941.

Chalgren, W. S. and Baker, A. B.: The nervous system in tropical disease. Medicine, **26:**395, 1947.

Coffey, J. H. *et al.:* Swineherd's disease. Aseptic meningitis due to leptospira pomona. J.A.M.A., **147:**949, 1951.

Joe, A. and Sangster, G.: Canicola fever. A report of three cases of meningitic type in human subjects. Edinburgh Med. J., **58:**140, 1951.

Russell, R. W. R.: Neurological aspects of leptospirosis. J. Neurol., Neurosurg. & Psychiat., **22:**143, 1959.

INVASION OF THE NERVOUS SYSTEM BY PROTOZOA

Malaria

Etiology.—Malaria, as it is known in temperate climates, rarely gives rise to any symptoms referable to the nervous system but the malignant tertian malaria of the tropics and semitropical countries not infrequently causes a great variety of nervous symptoms. The organism is called plasmodium falciparum. The infection is, of course, transmitted to man by the bite of infected mosquitoes.

Pathological Anatomy.—The brain has a strange leaden hue due to the black pigment produced by the parasites. Small petechial hemorrhages may be seen over the cortex. Histological examination reveals that the capillaries are distended by red cells containing the plasmodia in great numbers. The vascular endothelium may be swollen and small vessels are often completely occluded. Surrounding such vessels there is sometimes a small area of necrosis which is infiltrated with microglial cells and often contains blood. These lesions have been called "granulomata." Pigment granules are found not only in the lumen of the vessels and in the intimal cells but in the adventitia and in phagocytes within the adventitial sheath. A few lymphocytes and plasma cells may be found about the vessels. It is stated that the lesions are often most severe in the cerebellar cortex where the Purkinje cells are largely destroyed and a pronounced proliferation of the astrocytes occurs. The ganglion cells of the cerebral cortex suffer some damage but are rarely affected so severely as the Purkinje cells. The meninges may show infiltration with lymphocytes, plasma cells and macrophages.

Clinical Features.—The acute cerebral malaria is most common in children. Several types are described by various authors. One form is marked by a sudden onset of fever with or without a preceding chill. The child becomes delirious and then unconscious, often within an hour of the onset. The fever is very high and may reach 110°F. Cervical rigidity and Kernig's sign may be present. Convulsions are common. The picture is often very much like that of heat stroke. Death may occur within a very few hours. Focal cerebral signs may develop such as hemiplegia, aphasia or focal convulsions. The blood may or may not contain the parasites.

In the algid cases the onset may be marked by vomiting and prostration. Temperature may be normal or even subnormal. The pulse is feeble, respiration increased in rate and very shallow. Urine may be suppressed. Headache, delirium and convulsions occur. Finally the child sinks into coma and dies.

In the more chronic type of malaria infection neurological symptoms may appear without other evidences of general infection. Fever may be absent or there may be merely a brief rise of temperature just before nervous symptoms appear. Sudden hemiplegia and other cerebral syndromes are not uncommon in tropical countries. Focal convulsions may occur in the same way. They are preceded by fever of brief duration. Cases have been described in which transient paralysis occurred with a definite periodicity. The administration of quinine resulted in prompt recovery. Cerebellar and bulbar symptoms and ophthalmoplegias have also been reported and in rare cases, symptoms of multiple lesions in the nervous system which are said to resemble those of disseminated sclerosis.

The phenomena described above may be ascribed to occlusion of the small vessels by the plasmodia. Another group of symptoms may be regarded as arising from the chronic intoxication of malarial cachexia. In this group we include neuritis. Optic neuritis or papilledema may occur in association with cerebral malaria and the differentiation from brain abscess or tumor may be very difficult. Ophthalmoscopic examination reveals edema of the nerve head, retinal hemorrhages and patches of choreoretinitis. The visual fields may be concentrically constricted or there may be a central scotoma. The retinal vessels are believed to be occluded by the parasites in some cases. This condition must be distinguished from the amblyopia due to quinine poisoning. In the latter the disc is white and the retinal vessels are very narrow. Toxic deliria are common in the chronic infections or may follow severe acute attacks.

Diagnosis.—The chief points to be emphasized in the diagnosis are: (1) The presence of the parasites in the blood; (2) The periodicity of the symptoms; (3) The response to antimalarial drugs; (4) The enlargement of the spleen. It must be kept in mind, however, that repeated examinations are sometimes necessary to demonstrate the organisms and in the aestivoautumnal form, periodicity may not be conspicuous.

Prognosis.—The acute cerebral forms are very fatal and even with proper treatment, the mortality is sometimes as high as 50 per cent. If proper treatment is instituted before the patient is seriously ill, the prognosis is very favorable. The cerebral palsies are usually mild and tend to recover without severe residual symptoms.

Treatment.—The traditional treatment for malaria, of course, involves the use of quinine. This drug is not effective against the parasites in the tissues and, hence, will not prevent relapse in vivax malaria. Primaquine is said to destroy the organisms in the tissues but not in the blood. A combination of primaquine and chloroquine which eliminates the organisms in the blood is recommended. In falciparum malaria chloroquine alone is satisfactory. It is said that chloroquine may cause paralysis of accommodation. It may also cause edema of the corneae and rounded pigmented lesions in the maculae which cause persisting loss of central vision.

CHALGREN, W. S. AND BAKER, A. B.: The nervous system in tropical disease. Medicine, **26**:395, 1947.

EINHORN, N. H.: Tertian, quartan and mixed malarial infections. A survey of 334 cases in children. Am. J. Dis. Child., **73**:55, 1947.

EINHORN, N. H. AND TOMLINSON, W. J.: Aestivoautumnal malaria. A survey of 493 cases in children. Am. J. Dis. Child., **72**:137, 1946.

Myatt, A. and Coatney, G.: Present concepts and treatment of plasmodium vivax malaria. Arch. Int. Med., **93**:191, 1954.

Rigdon, R. H. and Fletcher, D. E.: Lesions in the brain associated with malaria. Arch. Neurol. & Psychiat., **53**:191, 1945.

Thompson, J. G. and Annecke, S.: Pathology of the central nervous system in malignant tertian malaria. J. Trop. Med., **29**:343, 1926.

Toxoplasmic Encephalitis

Etiology.—A form of encephalitis due to infection by a protozoan organism termed toxoplasma. This organism is about 6 or 7 micra in length and 2 to 4 micra in width and of crescentic, pyriform or oval shape. It contains a central nucleus.

It is claimed that this infection is common in small rodents and perhaps, in birds. Several cases of asymptomatic infection in young women have been discovered and there was evidence to show that the infection was acquired from pet dogs. Pork may contain the organism.

Pathological Anatomy.—There is a diffuse inflammatory process in the nervous system which seems to be most intense in the cerebral cortex, the basal ganglia and in the periventricular tissues. Miliary granulomas and small areas of necrosis are typical. These areas of necrosis may eventually result in cavities. Later, there is extensive gliosis and deposits of calcium are apt to appear. The meninges and the ependyma show miliary tubercles. Hydrocephalus is frequently present probably as a result of occlusion of the aqueduct by the ependymitis. Large lesions are often found in the retinae. The spinal cord may be involved. The organisms are found in the epithelioid cells of the granulomas, in the endothelial cells of the blood vessels and even in the neurons. They may also be found in large masses which are termed cysts. This description applies to the infantile cases.

Clinical Features.—The disease exists in all parts of the United States and has been reported from most parts of the world.

Several types are recognized: an encephalomyelitis of infants which seems to be of intrauterine origin and often runs a chronic course; an acute encephalitis in children between the ages of five and ten years; and an adult disease also acute which resembles in its clinical features typhus fever. There are also cases in which the only evidence of the disease is chorioretinitis and cases in which the process is latent and the diagnosis must be made by serological studies.

Cowen, Wolf and Paige have made extensive studies of the infantile type. The symptoms of the disease are almost always evident in the first few days of life. The commonest manifestations are hydrocephalus, convulsions, spasticity of the extremities and chorioretinitis. The last is most characteristic. The retinae show large white areas surrounded by dark deposits of pigment. It is stated that the lesions are focal, severe and extensive; that they usually involve both maculae and also peripheral parts of the retinae; that there is extensive connective tissue proliferation with heavy pigment deposits; that the media remain clear; that optic atrophy develops rapidly and that microphthalmos is commonly associated.

In some cases there is fever and the disease runs a rapid course terminating fatally in a few weeks. In others, the process becomes chronic and then inactive and the child may survive for an indefinite period. Such children show as a rule pronounced defects in mental development and in speech. There is apt to be hydrocephalus and some degree of spasticity of the extremities. Microcephaly may result in place of hydrocephalus. Optic atrophy and inactive lesions in the retinae are common. Convulsions occur in many instances. In a large percentage of all cases small disseminated deposits of calcium are demonstrable in the brain by roentgenographic examination. There seem to be no constant symptoms referable to the viscera but jaundice, enlargement of the spleen, pulmonary lesions and cutaneous eruptions are mentioned. The examination of the blood may reveal anemia and either a mild leucocytosis or leucopenia. The spinal fluid often contains an excess of protein and sometimes an excess of cells. The fluid may be xanthochromic. The organism has been found in the spinal fluid in two cases.

The mother of a child suffering from toxoplasmosis rarely recalls any serious departure from health during pregnancy. There may have been a mild febrile illness associated with enlargement of the lymph nodes. It is

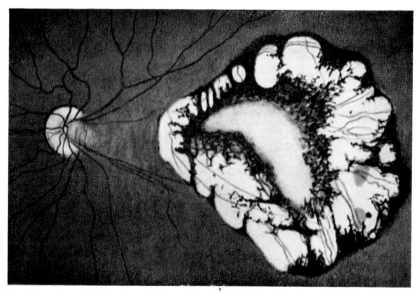

Fig. 157. Toxoplasmic chorioretinitis. (From Koch, Wolf, Cowen and Paige, Arch. of Ophthal. 1943, vol. 29, p. 1.)

of interest that Sabin states that having given birth to an infected child, the mother may expect subsequent children to be free from this infection.

We have observed several cases in adolescents who showed the typical retinal lesions and also the calcium deposits in the brain but who displayed only mild mental changes and no neurological disorders of any type. The process seemed to have been inactive since infancy.

Sabin describes two cases of acute encephalitis in boys of six and eight years. In the first case the child developed fever, headache and enlargement of the spleen and lymph nodes. Later, he became delirious and had convulsions. On the seventh day the spinal fluid contained 2200 cells, mostly lymphocytes. He died in coma on the thirtieth day. The toxoplasma was isolated from the brain and antibodies were demonstrated in the blood. In the second case, the symptoms were similar but less severe and the patient recovered within nine days. The diagnosis was made by the inoculation of mice with spinal fluid. Lelong *et al.* describe a study of acquired toxoplasmosis in 227 cases. The patients were mostly children between two and fifteen years. The disease was benign and no deaths resulted. In only one case was there evidence of meningitis. Enlargement of the lymph nodes was the most common symptom.

Pinkerton and Henderson report two cases of toxoplasmosis in adults in which the clinical picture resembled that of typhus or tick-bite fever. There was an acute onset with fever and chills. A maculopapular eruption covered the body. Pneumonia soon appeared and there were evidences of mild encephalitis. The organisms were found at post-mortem examination. It has been claimed recently that toxoplasmosis is a common cause of cho-

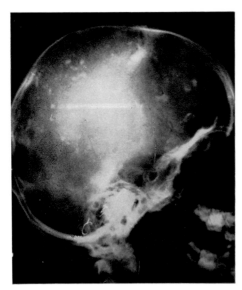

Fig. 158. Showing calcium deposits in the brain in a case of toxoplasmosis. (By the courtesy of Dr. Arthur King.)

rioretinitis which is not associated with any other symptoms or evidence of damage to the central nervous systems.

Diagnosis.—The diagnostic clinical features are hydrocephalus, chorio-retinopathy and intracranial calcium deposits. According to Sabin when all three of these findings are present toxoplasmosis is almost invariably the cause. He states, however, that the association of hydrocephalus, or cerebral defect without hydrocephalus, and chorioretinitis without calcium deposits in the brain does not suggest toxoplasmosis and is most apt to be due to a defect of development.

Sabin states that the diagnosis can be established completely only by laboratory methods. In the active stages of the disease the organisms may be demonstrated by the inoculation of mice or guinea pigs with blood or spinal fluid. Biopsy of lymph nodes sometimes gives positive results. Three serological tests are described: the skin test on human beings, the complement-fixation test and the *in vitro* dye test for the demonstration of toxoplasma neutralizing antibodies. These tests are all described in the references.

Sabin has found three infants with hydrocephalus, chorioretinitis and calcium deposits in the brain whose serological tests were negative for toxoplasmosis. At post-mortem examination these children were found to have many small softenings in the brain due to unusual changes in the blood vessels. The walls of the small blood vessels were thickened and filled with hyaline or amorphous acidophilic material. The lesions in the eyes were noninflammatory and atrophic. This condition has been termed *Sabin's encephalopathy.*

Prognosis.—Eichenwald has studied 150 infants suffering from congenital toxoplasmosis. He states that in one third of the cases there was an active infectious process. Only 12 per cent of these children died. The diagnosis was based upon laboratory studies and many relatively mild cases were included in the series. The classical triad was rare.

Among the survivors 90 per cent showed mental deficiency. Some 75 per cent suffered from spasticity and convulsions. In 50 per cent of cases there was impairment of vision.

No proper prognosis can be given for the acute encephalitis of childhood or for the generalized disease of adults. Not many cases of such conditions have been reported.

Treatment.—It has been shown that sulfonamides have some value in therapy. Recently pyrimethamine has been used successfully, it is claimed. Frenkel advises that both of these drugs be administered. It is claimed that spiramycin is effective in the treatment of retinal processes.

Eckerling *et al.* state that it is important to test for positive titers for toxoplasmosis in women who are suspected to have this condition before pregnancy. If the serological tests are positive, pyrimethamine and sulfona-mides are given before pregnancy and tetracycline and sulfonamides during the first pregnancy.

BIBLIOGRAPHY

CHODOS, J. B. *et al.*: Diagnosis of ocular toxoplasmosis. Canad. M. A. J., **88**:505, 1963.

CHODOS, J. B. AND HABEGGER-CHODOS, H. E.: Treatment of ocular toxoplasmosis with spiramycin. Arch. Ophth., **65**:401, 1961.

COWEN, D., WOLF, A. AND PAIGE, B. H.: Toxoplasmic encephalitis. Clinical diagnosis of infantile or congenital toxoplasmosis; survival beyond infancy. Arch. Neurol. & Psychiat., **48**:689, 1952.

ECKERLING, B. *et al.*: Toxoplasmosis a cause of infertility. Fertil. and Steril., **19**:883, 1968.

EICHENWALD, H. F.: The 67th Meeting of the Am. Pediat. Soc., June 17-19, 1957.

FRENKEL, J. K.: Dermal hypersensitivity to toxoplasma antigens. Proc. Soc. Exp. Biol. & Med., **68**:634, 1948.

FRENKEL, J. K. *et al.*: Chemotherapy of acute toxoplasmosis. J.A.M.A., **173**:1471, 1960.

KASS, E. *et al.*: Toxoplasmosis in human adult. Arch. Int. Med., **89**:759, 1952.

KOCH, F. L. P. WOLF, A., COWEN, D. AND PAIGE, B. H.: Toxoplasmic encephalomyelitis. Significance of ocular lesions in the diagnosis of infantile or congenital toxoplasmosis. Arch. of Ophthal., **29**:1, 1943.

LELONG, M. *et al.*: Acquired toxoplasmosis. A study of 227 cases. Arch. franc pediat., **17**:281, 1960.

PINKERTON, H. AND HENDERSON, R. G.: Adult toxoplasmosis. A previously unrecognized disease entity simulating the typhus spotted fever group. J.A.M.A., **116**:807, 1941.

PRIOR, J. A. *et al.*: Report of three cases with reference to asymptomatic toxoplasma parasitemia in young women. Arch. Int. Med., **92**:314, 1953.

RODNEY, M. B., MITCHELL, N., REDNER, B. AND TURIN, R.: Infantile toxoplasmosis. Pediatrics, **5**:649, 1950.

SABIN, A. B.: Human toxoplasmosis. Am. J. Ophth., **41**:600, 1956.

————: Toxoplasmic encephalitis in children. J.A.M.A., **116**:801, 1941.

SABIN, A. B. AND FELDMAN, H. A.: Dyes as chemical indicators of a new immunity phenomenon affecting a protozoan parasite (toxoplasma). Science, **108**:660, 1948.

————: Chorioretinopathy associated with other evidence of cerebral damage in childhood. A syndrome of unknown origin separable from toxoplasmosis. J. Pediat., **35**:296, 1949.

STEINER, G. AND KAUMP, D. H.: Infantile toxoplasmic encephalitis. J. Neuropath. and Exp. Neurol., **3**:36, 1944.

WALSH, F. B.: *Loc cit.*

WILDER, H. C.: Toxoplasma-like protozoa in chorioretinitis of adults. Am. J. Trop. Med. and Hygiene, **2**:417, 1952.

WOLF, A. AND COWEN, D.: Perinatal infections of the central nervous system. J. Neuropath. Exp. Neurol., **18**:191, 1959.

WOODS, A. C.: Chorioretinitis due to toxoplasmosis. Am. J. Ophth., **37**:163, 1954.

AFRICAN TRYPANOSOMIASIS

Etiology.—This is a specific infectious disease due to two distinct but closely related organisms; Trypanosoma gambiense and Trypanosoma rhodesiense. The disease is prevalent on the west coast of Africa, the Congo and in German East Africa where T. gambiense is found. A more virulent type of infection due to T. rhodesiense is found in Rhodesia.

The organism is a flagellated protozoan of the order of Binucleata. They are elongated, fusiform or fish-shaped and about 15 to 30 micra long and

1.5 to 2 micra wide. There is a central nucleus and a deeply staining chromatin body termed the micronucleus nearby. Near one end, which is less sharply pointed than the other, is a vaculoe and closely associated with this another chromatin body, the blepharoplast. From this end a long whip-like process arises which borders an undulating membrane attached to the body of the organism and extends to the opposite pole where it projects as a flagellum.

The T. gambiense is transmitted by the bite of the tsetse fly, or Glossina palpalis. The flies ingest the organism in the blood of infected animals, such as the antelope and other big game, which seem to act as a reservoir for the infection. The trypanosome undergoes a developmental cycle within the intestines of the fly and after a period of from 18 to 24 days, slender forms develop which pass forward into the salivary glands from which they may be injected beneath the skin by the fly's proboscis as it bites. In the case of T. rhodesiense, the Glossina morsitans seems to be the vector.

Pathological Anatomy.—At post-mortem examination it is usual to find a chronic inflammatory process in the lymphatic system and large numbers of the trypanosomes in the lymph nodes. The spleen and liver are enlarged. The brain shows no gross changes as a rule but the meninges are thickened and opaque. In some cases there is a mild hydrocephalus. Microscopic examination shows great numbers of lymphocytes within the perivascular spaces and meshes of the pia-arachnoid. Numerous trypanosomes are present. There are some changes of the cortical cells and perivascular demyelination is described. The blood vessels are not definitely altered and there are usually no hemorrhages or softenings. The spinal cord may reveal degeneration of the long tracts and reactive gliosis. Janssen *et al.* describe lesions in the peripheral nerves chiefly in the nerve roots. These lesions were attributed to toxins released during trypanolytic crises in most cases, but inflammatory lesions were also found. The patients had been treated with arsenic.

Clinical Features.—The course of the disease is usually divided into three stages: the incubation period, the febrile period and the terminal period in which the nervous symptoms dominate the picture. The symptoms may appear within ten days after the patient is bitten by an infected fly but the organisms may be present in the blood for months or even years before any serious departure from health is apparent. In Negroes, the incubation period is said to be longer than in Europeans who rapidly enter upon the second stage of the disease. This is marked by remittent fever which may reach 103°F. in the afternoon and fall to normal or even a subnormal level in the mornings. The lymph nodes soon become enlarged and the liver and spleen are palpable. During this period, the organisms may be found in the lymph nodes and in the circulating blood but not yet in the central nervous system. After months or even years the last stage develops. There is, at first, chiefly a change in personality, apathy, irritability, loss of interest and indifference. Later the patient may show tremors of the lips and tongue. The gait becomes weak and shuffling. Mild cervical rigidity and evidences of meningeal irritation appear. The patient finally becomes somnolent and cannot be aroused for more than brief periods. Eating becomes a great effort and the patient will go to sleep when the mouth is full of food. The somnolence is suggestive of that seen in epidemic encephalitis, for when the patient is aroused, the mind may be clear and questions may be answered correctly. There is progressive loss of weight and weakness. Convulsions may appear. Parkinsonian rigidity is said to occur. Hemiplegia is common. Cranial nerve palsies and optic atrophy are described. At last the patient becomes cachectic and dies in coma. The last stage rarely lasts more than a year.

Diagnosis.—The diagnosis depends upon the demonstration of the organism. In the early stages of the disease, these may be found in the fluid obtained by puncture of the swollen lymph nodes, and with more difficulty in smears of the blood. Some authorities recommend centrifugalizing 25 cc of citrated blood and examining the sediment for the trypanosomes. Inoculation of susceptible animals such as guinea pigs, white rats and monkeys is often successful. In the somnolent stage, it is usually easy to demonstrate the organisms in the spinal fluid.

Prognosis.—There is some hope of cure when treatment is begun while the disease is still in the first or second stage, but it has been almost uniformly fatal after the nervous system has been invaded.

Treatment.—A number of arsenical drugs have been employed, but at present tryparsamide is regarded as the most successful. This drug contains trivalent arsenic, has the property of penetrating the nervous system and is said to have a favorable effect upon the nervous symptoms. Bayer 205 has also been employed with success in recent years. Pentamidine is also used.

BIBLIOGRAPHY

BERTRAND, I., BABLET, J. ET SICE, A.: Lésions histologique des centres nerveux dans la trypanosomiase humaine. Ann. de l'Inst. Pasteur, 54:91, 1935.

HAWKINS, F. AND GREENFIELD, J. G.: Two autopsies of Rhodesiense sleeping sickness. Roy. Soc. Trop. Med. & Hyg., 35:155, 1941.

JANSSEN, P. et al.: Pathology of the peripheral nervous system in African trypanosomiasis. J. Neuropath. & Exp. Neurol., 15:269, 1956.

PEARCE, L.: Treatment of Trypanosomiasis with Tryparsamide. A Critical Review. Monograph of the Rockefeller Inst. No. 23, 1930.

AMERICAN TRYPANOSOMIASIS

Etiology.—This condition, sometimes termed Chagas' disease, is due to infection by the Trypanosoma cruzi which is transmitted by a blood sucking insect known as Lamus magistus. It is confined to South and Central America.

T. cruzi is a fusiform, flagellated organism about 20 micra long. It is distinguished from similar organisms by the presence of a very large micronucleus. In the febrile stage of the disease the parasites may be found in the blood stream but later they invade the cells of various tissues where they assume a rounded form resembling the Leishman-Donovan bodies, and undergo division. As a result of the continued multiplication of the organisms, the cells eventually become distended and finally rupture, discharging numerous flagellated parasites.

The vector, Lamus magistus, becomes infected by sucking the blood of affected animals. The organisms multiply in the intestinal tract of the insect and finally after some eight days small forms pass to the salivary glands whence they may be transmitted to the next animal bitten. Numerous domestic animals, including the cat, are susceptible and it is possible that such animals act as a reservoir for the infection. It has also been claimed that a certain armadillo harbors the parasite.

Pathological Anatomy.—The brain is studded with miliary granulomata. These are usually found near small vessels, the adventitial sheaths of which are infiltrated with lymphocytes. The organisms are found in the granulomata usually within microglial cells but also in astrocytes and even nerve cells. As stated above, they proliferate rapidly forming cyst-like structures which rupture and give rise to local inflammatory reactions. The lesions are found in every part of the brain but seem to be most numerous in the gray matter of the cortex, basal ganglia and nuclei of the brain-stem. A few organisms are found in the meninges accompanied by a patchy meningeal reaction. Numerous lesions of the same type are found in the heart, the skeletal muscles, the liver, spleen, the thyroid, the adrenal glands, the lymph nodes and the bone marrow.

Clinical Features.—The disease often begins acutely in the first year of life with fever, edema of the face, enlargement of the liver and spleen, palpable lymph nodes and swelling of the thyroid gland. In about half of all cases there are symptoms referable to the nervous system such as cervical rigidity, stupor, convulsions and strabismus. The organisms are said to be demonstrated with ease in the blood stream during this period. The mortality is relatively high but if the child survives, the fever usually recedes after two to four weeks and the disease enters upon a second or chronic stage.

In the chronic type of American trypanosomiasis, the chief symptoms are usually divided into three groups, those referable to the thyroid gland, to the heart and to the nervous system. The usual signs of hypothyroidism, such as the changes in the skin and hair, the puffy face, retardation of growth and mental deficiency are all present in a large percentage of cases. The thyroid gland is enlarged and firm. It has recently been stated that thyroid deficiency is not due to this disease and that Chagas was misled by the fact that thyroid deficiency was endemic in the region in which he made his studies. Various types of cardiac arrhythmia and weakness may occur. The liver and spleen are usually enlarged and there is general enlargement of all the superficial lymph nodes. Involvement of the adrenal gland may give rise to pictures similar to those of Addison's disease. Pronounced anemia may be present. The intestinal tract is involved. Peristalsis is reduced. The colon becomes dilated. The esophagus, stomach and small intestine may be affected in the same way. The ureters may also be involved.

Numerous neurological syndromes are described but the commonest picture seems to be that of cerebral diplegia with weakness and spasticity of the legs and to a lesser extent of the arms, with or without signs of bulbar palsy. There may be choreo-athetoid movements. Intelligence is almost always defective due not only to the involvement of the nervous system but to the thyroid deficiency as well. Focal syndromes, such as hemiplegias and aphasias, are described but seem to be uncommon. In many cases there are ocular palsies and squints which suggest nuclear lesions in the brain-stem. Convulsions both focal and general are not unusual. The disease seems to be slowly progressive as a rule but in some instances advances by acute febrile exacerbations which are often accompanied by delirium or stupor.

Diagnosis.—The diagnosis depends upon residence in regions where the disease is endemic, the history of a febrile illness in infancy, cardiac disturbances and the neurological picture described above. The enlargement of the liver, the spleen and the lymph nodes is characteristic. In the acute febrile types, the organisms may be found in smears of the blood. In more chronic cases, inoculation of guinea pigs with large amounts of blood may give positive results. Organisms may also be found in the cerebrospinal fluid and sometimes in fluid obtained from puncture of lymph nodes.

Prognosis.—The prognosis is apparently hopeless for recovery but the chronic phase may last for years.

Treatment.—Recent experiments have led to the view that L-furaltadone, a nitrofuran compound, may be curative. Thyroid substance may be employed in the cases showing cretinism.

BIBLIOGRAPHY

Ash, J. E. and Spitz, S.: Pathology of Tropical Diseases. Philadelphia, W. B. Saunders, 1945.

Ferreira-Santos, R.: Megacolon in Chagas' disease. Proc. Roy. Soc. Med., 54:1047, 1961.

Johnson, Carl: American Trypanosomiasis. Med. Clin. North America, 1943, p. 822.

Yorke, W.: Chagas' disease. Trop. Dis. Bull., 34:275, 1937.

AMOEBIC ABSCESS OF THE BRAIN

Amoebae are unicellular organisms of from 15 to 20 micra in diameter and composed of an outer clear zone and an inner granular zone which contains a nucleus and one or more vacuoles. They are capable of slow movement produced by streaming of the cytoplasm. Amoebae are classified as protozoa and are widespread in nature. The pathogenic type is an intestinal parasite called Entamoeba histolytica.

Infection is due to the ingestion of food which has been contaminated with fecal material of an infected individual. The amoebae localize in the walls of the large intestine and eventually cause ulcerative colitis and dysentery. In some cases, the amoebae are borne to the liver by the portal circulation and cause abscesses. About 50 cases are reported in which abscess of the brain occurred. Apparently the amoebae are carried to the brain by the circulation and pass through the capillaries of the lungs. Abscess of the brain rarely occurs except in association with liver abscess. The onset of cerebral symptoms is marked as a rule by convulsions. The course is said to be very rapid and usually ends in death within six to eight days. Rarely a patient may live for two weeks. The abscess is almost invariably found in the cerebral hemisphere rather than in the cerebellum or brain stem. Multiple abscesses may occur. The signs and symptoms are similar to those associated with the abscesses due to the common pyogenic organisms, but it is stated that meningitis is very rare and that the cell count is rarely increased in the spinal fluid. Amoebae do not produce a severe inflammatory process in the tissues and unless there is secondary infection with bacteria, amoebic abscesses are really areas of necrosis and liquefaction of the brain. The diagnosis may be suspected when cerebral symptoms develop in a patient suffering from amoebic abscess of the liver. Aureomycin and bacitracin are both said to be effective against the intestinal infection. Chloroquine disulphate has some value in liver abscess, it is said, and when this fails emetine may be used. Braley and Hamilton describe slowly progressive loss of central vision with an enlarging central scotoma due to a cystic retinal lesion at or near the fovea. The cyst is usually transparent. Anterior uveitis, hemorrhage and pigmentation are infrequent. They advise diiodohydroxyquin and chloroquine and then a second course of carbarsone. Iodochlorhydroxyquin is now recommended very strongly.

BIBLIOGRAPHY

ARMITAGE, F. L.: Amoebic abscess of the brain with notes of a case following amoebic abscess of the liver. J. Trop. Med., 22:69, 1919.

BRALEY, A. E. AND HAMILTON, H. E.: Central serous choroidosis associated with amebiasis. Arch. Ophth., 58:1, 1957.

TURNER, E. A.: Cerebral amoebic abscess treated by chemotherapy. J. Neurol., Neurosurg. & Psychiat., 11:291, 1948.

INVASION OF THE NERVOUS SYSTEM BY PARASITIC WORMS

Trichinosis

Etiology.—This disease is due to a small worm, the trichinella spiralis. All animals including man may serve as definitive and intermediate host. Larvae are released in the intestinal tract by the digestion of infected meat and attach themselves to the mucosa. Within twenty-four to forty-eight hours they become mature and the female being impregnated, discharges larvae into the intestinal lymphatics during the remaining period of her life which is estimated at thirty-five days. From the eighth to the twenty-fifth day, the larvae are found in the blood stream. The larvae which reach the skeletal muscles become encapsulated within a few weeks and remain capable of infecting another animal for years, though some die and become calcified. The larvae which reach other tissues fail to mature and soon disintegrate. Man is usually infected by eating inadequately cooked pork. The pig is infected by eating infested rats, it is believed.

Pathological Anatomy.—The larvae which are about 1.0 mm long set up an inflammatory process in all tissues. They become encysted only in striated muscles. There is focal inflammation and destruction of muscle fibers in the neighborhood of the parasites. The parasites begin to encyst on about the 35th day. The cyst wall may become calcified in from 6 to 18 months. In has been estimated that in fatal cases 50,000,000 parasites may be present in the body.

The brain, retinae, spinal cord and the meninges are involved. The parasites do not survive in such tissues but die and set up an inflammatory reaction. There are perivascular cellular infiltrations, petechial hemorrhages, softenings due to thromboses of small vessels and granulomatous nodules around dying parasites. These changes may cause irreversible damage to any part of the nervous system.

The parasites do not survive in the heart muscle but set up an inflammatory process which may result in serious myocarditis. The kidneys as well as the other organs are often damaged. It is claimed that the fetus may be infected.

Clinical Features.—It is stated that children are relatively immune to this disease but they are often infected and have the same symptoms that adults have. The disease is often divided into three stages. In the intestinal stage which includes the first seven days there may be vomiting, diarrhea and perhaps fever. Such symptoms are usually mild and no diagnosis is possible at this stage. It is said that the trichinae are not to be found in the stools.

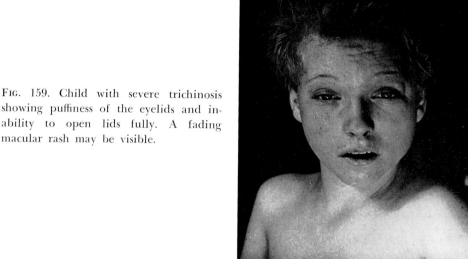

Fig. 159. Child with severe trichinosis showing puffiness of the eyelids and inability to open lids fully. A fading macular rash may be visible.

During the blood stream invasion, which begins on the seventh day, there is fever which may reach 104°F., leucocytosis, eosinophilia, urticaria, edema of the eyelids and face, headache and conjunctivitis. The muscles are swollen and tender. Stretching the muscles causes pain so shortening may occur. Not only the skeletal muscles are affected. The extra-ocular muscles, the muscles of mastication, the diaphragm and the tongue are all apt to be involved. A variable degree of weakness and paralysis results.

The nervous system may be affected severely. There are sometimes signs of meningeal irritation, apathy, delirium, coma and convulsions. Either paraplegia or hemiplegia may occur. Hemorrhages and other lesions may be seen in the retinae. Double vision and ocular palsies are sometimes seen. The tendon reflexes may be lost. The spinal fluid may contain an excess of cells or may be normal. Parasites may be found in the fluid.

The heart may fail as a result of myocardial damage. This may occur between the 4th and 8th weeks. If the patient survives the heart may remain weak. The kidneys are sometimes seriously affected. The urine is said to be dark in some cases. We have seen one case in which the renal damage resulted in fatal retention of potassium and paralysis.

The third stage, that of convalescence, begins between the 5th and 8th weeks. Complete recovery is usual but in some instances the muscles never regain their full strength and atrophy may persist. Lesions in the brain and spinal cord may be irreversible.

Diagnosis.—The diagnosis depends upon the clinical features described above and upon the demonstration of the parasites in the blood or in a bit of muscle excised for examination. Larvae may be found in the blood or spinal fluid in some instances between the 2nd and 4th weeks. An intradermal reaction to trichina antigen may be positive after the 17th day and a precipitin reaction after the 28th day. Calcified parasites may eventually be visible in roentgenograms of the muscles.

Prognosis.—The prognosis for life depends upon the severity of the infection. The mortality may be high if very large numbers of organisms are ingested. If the patient survives, the neurological symptoms usually, but not invariably, disappear. The skeletal muscles may show a variable degree of weakness and the heart may show persistent evidences of damage.

Treatment.—Drastic purging in the first few hours after ingestion of the meat has been advised. Thiabendazole is said to be very effective. Cortisone is said to relieve the fever, edema and muscular pain.

CASE HISTORY (Ped. 92316).—*Girl of 13 years developed diarrhea, pains in muscles, fever, cough, cutaneous eruption, edema of face and ankles and tachycardia. Almost complete loss of power of the muscles of the legs. Biopsy revealed many trichinae in muscles*

M. W., a previously healthy girl of 13 years, developed diarrhea and fever on April 25, 1935. Soon intense pains in the legs and back developed. An eruption resembling that of measles appeared and she began to cough. The neck and spine became so rigid that the doctor suspected meningitis and the patient was brought to Harriet Lane on March 17.

Examination disclosed a well developed girl of the given age who appeared to be very ill. The eyelids were slightly puffy and could not be opened fully. The ankles were slightly edematous. The jaws were stiff and movements were very painful. Speech was indistinct and the tongue swollen and sore. All the skeletal muscles were very tender and the muscles of the thighs and calves seemed to be a bit doughy on palpation. The legs were almost completely paralyzed. This was a true paralysis and not due to the pain the patient experienced on contracting her muscles. The knee jerks were absent. The heart was enlarged to the left and a systolic murmur was audible over the precordium. A fading macular rash was visible over the face and body. Temperature was 38°C. Respiration 24. Pulse 124. There were fine and coarse râles throughout the chest. Examination of the blood revealed 18 per cent eosinophils. Biopsy showed a large number of trichinae in the muscles. The spinal fluid was quite normal and did not contain an excess of cells or of globulin. Electrocardiogram gave low voltage curves and a pathological T wave.

The patient slowly improved. On March 26 the legs were somewhat stronger. The fever fell and the enlargement of the heart disappeared. The child was discharged a few weeks later quite well.

Additional investigations of the case disclosed that the family had been eating home-slaughtered meat for they lived on a farm and butchered their own hogs. There were five other members of the family besides the patient and all had definite eosinophilia ranging from 18 per cent to 44 per cent although none of them had any symptoms such as the patient showed.

BIBLIOGRAPHY

CONNER, L. A.: Atypical forms of trichiniasis. Ann. Int. Med., 3:353, 1929.

EVERS, L. B.: Manifestations of trichiniasis in the central nervous system. Report of a case with larvae in the spinal fluid. Arch. Int. Med., 63:949, 1939.

FOLEY, J. M.: Pathological changes in a case of encephalopathy due to trichinosis. Am. A. Neuropath. Ann. Meet. June 14, 1953.

GOLDSCHLAGER, A. I.: Trichinosis: A report of eight cases with skin and precipitin tests. Ann. Int. Med., 8:939, 1935.

GOULD, S. E.: Trichinosis, Springfield, Thomas, 1945.

HASSIN, G. B. AND DIAMOND, I. B.: Trichinosis encephalitis—Pathologic study. Arch. Neurol. & Psychiat., 15:34, 1926.

LABZOFFSKY, N. A. et al.: Fluorescent test for trichinosis. Canad. M. A. J., 90:920, 1964.

MERRITT, H. AND ROSENBAUM, M.: Involvement of the nervous system in trichiniasis. J.A.M.A., 106:1646, 1936.

MOST, H. AND ABLES, M. M.: Trichiniasis involving the nervous system. Arch. Neurol. & Psychiat., 37:589, 1937.

STANBURY, G. L. et al.: Treatment of trichinosis. Arch. Ophthal., 71:359, 1964.

Cysticerci

Etiology.—Cysticerci are the larval forms of tapeworms. Two varieties of tapeworms are commonly found in man; the taenia solium or pork tapeworm and taenia saginata or beef tapeworm. The adult worm lives in the human intestines so man is the definitive host. Ova are discharged in the feces. The ingestion of ova by an intermediate host such as the pig or cow is the next step in the life cycle. The ovum develops in the stomach into the embryo which works its way into the circulation and is carried to the various organs, most commonly the muscles, the subcutaneous tissues, the nervous system or the eye. The embryo then becomes encysted and forms the cysticercus. Ingestion of the cysticercus in inadequately cooked beef or pork leads to the development of the adult worm in the human intestines. Unfortunately man may occasionally become the intermediate host by eating food soiled with ova. Autogenous infection seems to be unusual and few patients with cysticercosis seem to harbor the adult worm in the intestines. Almost all cases of human cysticercosis are due to the taenia solium.

Pathological Anatomy.—As a rule, a large number of cysts are found within the cranium. They are situated most abundantly in the cortex of the brain and the meninges but may be found in any part of the nervous system, including the spinal cord. As a rule, the cysts vary from .5 cm to 2 or 3 cm in diameter. The cyst wall consists of three layers; an outer chitinous layer, a middle cellular layer and an inner parenchymatous layer composed of a network of refractile fibers. There is often a very intense reaction about the parasites. The meninges show marked fibrous thickening and evidences of chronic meningitis, which are especially severe at the base. Within the brain there are inflammatory changes about the cysts, perivascular infiltrations and endarteritis leading to thrombosis and infarctions. The anatomical changes are frequently mistaken for those of neurosyphilis. It is not unusual to find cysts within the ventricles either swimming freely or attached to the ependyma. If the ventricular system is occluded, hydrocephalus may occur. In some cases a number of cysts occur in groups resembling a bunch of grapes, the so-called racemose cysticercus, which may attain a great size. After a number of years the ova die and the cyst wall then becomes calcified. Cysts are not infrequently found in the eyes.

Clinical Features.—This disease is rare in this country and in most civilized countries in which there is compulsory inspection of meat. It is said, however, that it is still not uncommon in central and eastern Europe and especially in Mexico and in South America. In Germany and Poland the prevalence of the disease is no doubt due to the practice of eating raw pork.

As a rule, there are no constitutional symptoms during the invasion of the parasites but when the infection is a severe one, there may be fever pains and tenderness in the muscles and great weakness as in trichinosis. In such cases the cysts may be palpated beneath the skin and there is an increase in the eosinophil cells in the blood.

There is nothing characteristic in the neurological picture but it may be said that the findings almost invariably point to involvement of the brain. Convulsions either general or focal are among the commonest manifestations. Continuous local muscular twitchings are often described. Mild and transient focal signs such as hemiparesis, aphasia or hemianopia may occur often following convulsions and also more lasting focal signs. Evidences of involvement of the cerebellum, brain stem or spinal cord are also seen. Mental disturbances are common. There may be states of confusion, delirium and dementia. In a large number of cases there are evidences of increased intracranial pressure which is usually due to hydrocephalus, but may be due to swelling of the brain. Arana and Asenjo found hydrocephalus was often due to cysts in the fourth ventricle and posterior fossa. Floating cysticerci in the ventricular system may cause intermittent obstruction induced by sudden movements of the head with violent attacks of headache, nausea and vertigo, or even sudden death. There are often definite signs of meningeal irritation but these are rarely intense. The course is as a rule very slow and chronic, though acute cases leading to death in a few days are described.

The spinal fluid may contain an excess of cells reaching 300 in rare cases, but frequently the cell count is normal or only slightly increased. There is usually an excess of eosinophil cells in the blood at some stage of the dis-

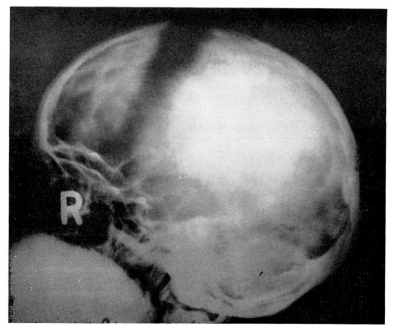

F<small>IG</small>. 160. Roentgenogram of the skull of child with cysticercosis of the brain causing enormous edema and separation of the cranial sutures. (By the courtesy of Dr. Charles Burklund.)

ease and in several cases numerous eosinophil cells have been found in the spinal fluid. It is claimed that positive complement-fixation reactions may be secured with echinococcus antigen.

Jacob and Mathews describe gross enlargement of the skeletal muscles due to a large number of cysts which were identified by biopsy.

Diagnosis.—This is not always easy. A history of tapeworm infestation is helpful and residence in a country where this infection is common is also important. The neurological symptoms include focal convulsions, signs of increased intracranial pressure, evidences of meningeal irritation and mental deterioration. The cysts may be felt in the muscles or subcutaneous tissues and identified by biopsy. In long standing cases, they may become calcified and visible in the roentgenograms of the head and muscles. An excess of eosinophil cells in the blood or spinal fluid is suggestive. Dixon has found the complement-fixation and skin tests of little value.

Prognosis.—Most authorities give a bad prognosis, but Dixon and Hargreaves state that only 8 per cent in their series of 284 cases resulted in death. Furthermore, less than 10 per cent of their living patients show mental deterioration. In cases in which the symptoms are severe, however, the outlook is gloomy.

Treatment.—No treatment is of any value. Surgery is of no avail for the cysts are almost always present in large numbers. Claims have been made that roentgenotherapy will destroy the parasites and relieve the symptoms.

CASE HISTORY (U-406716).—*Girl of eight years developed headache and vomiting. Later internal squint. Convulsions. Low grade fever. Mental confusion. On examination separation of the sutures, bilateral papilledema, left hemiparesis. Operation—innumerable cysts in brain i.e. cysticercosis.*

C. B., a little girl of eight years from Colombia, South America, was admitted to the Johns Hopkins Hospital on December 4, 1946. Some eight months before this time, she had begun to have headaches and to vomit from time to time. The more severe headaches were followed by drowsiness and delirium which lasted for a day or two days. Some four months before admission she developed an internal squint on the left side which later disappeared. Later, she had a convulsive seizure which was followed by twitching of the left hand. Throughout this illness there was a low grade fever ranging as a rule between 100° and 101°F. but at times reaching 102°F.

On examination the child showed signs of recent loss of weight and appeared to be chronically ill. Her temperature was 102.6°F. and pulse 140. The head was enlarged and the coronal suture was separated. She was confused and probably delirious and it was difficult to hold her attention for even a moment. The optic nerve heads were edematous, the elevation being measured at 4 or 5 diopters. Vision seemed to be grossly reduced. No other neurological signs were elicited except for a mild left hemiparesis with Babinski sign. At times there were clonic twitchings of the left hand.

The roentgenograms of the skull showed convolutional atrophy and gross separation of the sutures as shown in the accompanying illustration. Ventriculography, to our astonishment, revealed very small ventricles symmetrically placed. We had anticipated that there would be internal hydrocephalus. On December 15, Dr. Otenasek explored the right side. The brain was studded with innumerable, small, round, opalescent nodules of 2 or 3 mm. in diameter. Several of these were removed for biopsy and proved to be cysticercus cysts. The brain bulged so strongly that it was difficult to close the wound.

During convalescence the brain herniated through the decompression and the patient had several convulsions which required phenobarbital for their control. She was discharged January 24, 1947 without any definite improvement in her condition.

BIBLIOGRAPHY

ARANA, R. AND ASENJO, A.: Ventriculographic diagnosis of cysticercosis of the posterior fossa. J. Neurosurgery, 2:181, 1945.

ARMIJO, E. R. AND GONI, P. B.: Intracranial cysticercosis. Rev. Med. Hosp. General (Mexico), 30:317, 1967.

BECKER, B. AND JACOBSON, S.: Infestation of human brain with coenurus cerebralis. Report of three cases. Lancet, ii:198, 1951.

DIXON, H. B. F. AND HARGREAVES, W. H.: Cysticercosis (taenia solium). Further ten years' study covering 284 cases. Quart. J. Med., 13:107, 1944.

DOLGOPOL, V. B. AND NEUSTAEDTER, M.: Meningo-encephalitis caused by cysticercus cellulosa. Arch. Neurol. & Psychiat., 33:132, 1935.

JACOB, J. C. AND MATHEW, N. T.: Pseudohypertrophic myopathy in cysticercosis. Neurology, 18:767, 1968.

LOMBARDO, L. AND MATEOS, J. H.: Cerebral cysticercosis in Mexico. Neurology, 11:825, 1961.

OBRADOR, S.: Clinical aspects of cerebral cysticercosis. Arch. Neurol. & Psychiat., 59:457, 1948.

PERRY, I.: Cysticercus cysts of the brain: Report of a case with Jacksonian epilepsy. Arch. Neurol. & Psychiat., 35:862, 1936.

STEPIEN, L. J.: Cerebral cysticercosis in Poland. Jour. Neurosurg., 19:505, 1962.

ECHINOCOCCOSIS

Etiology.—The hydatid cyst is the larval form of an intestinal parasite, the taenia echinococcus. It is rather rare in the United States but is very common in Australia, New Zealand, Algiers, Tunis, Bulgaria, Roumania, Iceland, Uruguay and Argentina. In general the disease is most prevalent in countries in which hygiene is primitive, sheep raising is the chief industry and dogs are numerous.

The adult cestode is composed of four segments and varies from 3 to 6 mm in length. It is found in the intestines of the dog, wolf or jackal. From the point of view of human infection, the dog is the only host which needs to be considered. Each worm produces innumerable eggs and the intermediate host becomes infected by ingesting these eggs in contaminated food or water. Many species of wild and domestic animals may act as intermediate hosts, but the sheep, the ox and the pig are most commonly infected. Man is never a definitive host but may be an intermediate host. When the ovum arrives in the stomach, its chitinous shell is digested and the embryo is liberated. It then bores its way through the wall of the gut and enters a branch of the portal vein by which it is carried to the liver. Its journey is not ended here, however, and either by active migration or by the force of the blood stream, the parasite may eventually lodge in any tissue of the body. It has been estimated that 75 per cent of the parasites are found in the liver, 10 per cent in the lungs and 15 per cent in all other organs. The embryo once firmly lodged in the tissues becomes vacuolated and then vesicular. After about three weeks a small cyst is to be seen. This slowly expands and is surrounded by a well-marked inflammatory reaction. Fully developed cysts show an external hyaline layer which is laminated and elastic. An inner layer is composed of small nucleated masses embedded in a granular protoplasm. Within the cyst is a clear colorless fluid of slightly alkaline reaction and specific gravity between 1.008 and 1.015. Mature cysts show small thickenings of the internal or protoplasmic layer. These rapidly develop into the so-called brood capsules in which the scolices develop. The latter are formed by proliferation and evagination of the wall of the brood capsule. Eventually they become ovoid structures covered by a clear cuticle and capped by a single row of chitinous hooklets averaging 36 in number, as well as four sucking discs. The scolices are about 150 micra in length and hence, just visible to the unaided eye. It has been estimated that each cubic centimeter of the contents of a mature hydatid cyst contains 400,000 scolices. Within the intestinal tract of a dog or other definitive host, the scolices will develop into the adult worm and thus the cycle is repeated. It seems to be well-established as a result of experimental investigations that scolices may also give rise to cysts. Thus the rupture of a cyst into the peritoneum or pleural cavity or into a large vein may result in the dissemination of the parasites and the formation of a large number of cysts.

Pathological Anatomy.—Eventually the cysts may attain great size eroding bones and compressing the tissues. There is always more or less reaction of the surrounding tissues and often a dense fibrous membrane is formed. In the brain this membrane is very thin but where the cyst touches the meninges, a well formed fibrous capsule develops. Often there is some edema in the neighborhood of the parasite. Lymphocytes, plasma cells and eosinophil polymorphonuclear leucocytes are found. There is very little alteration of nerve cells or nerve fibers and such alterations as are found may be explained by pressure. The cyst may erode the skull or extend into the ventricular system causing hydrocephalus. The cerebral hemispheres are the favorite site of these parasites and it is rare to find the cerebellum involved.

Clinical Features.—Hydatid cysts of the nervous system may be primary or secondary. In the former case, they are derived from an embryo which has been carried by the blood stream from the intestines and through the liver and lungs to the nervous system. In the second case, they develop from scolices set free in the blood stream by rupture of a mature cyst. Such metastatic cysts are most apt to be found in the brain and are almost always multiple.

It is of interest that symptoms of hydatid cyst of the brain are at least seven times as frequent in children as in adults. Thus, Herrera-Vegas and Cranwell state that 27 of 31 cases of echinococcus cyst of the brain were found in children. The simplest explanation for this fact is that infestation usually takes place in childhood and that cysts of the brain will give rise to symptoms much earlier than those in other organs. In many cases there is also cystic disease of the liver or lungs.

The symptoms are similar to those of any other space occupying mass within the cranial cavity. Headache, vomiting and papilledema are usually present sooner or later, for the cysts eventually reach a large size. Focal signs may be present from the beginning or may be delayed. Hemiplegia, aphasia, ataxia and focal or general convulsions are common. It has been noted in many cases that the symptoms fluctuate from time to time, perhaps as a result of intermittent edema about the cyst. Unilateral bulging of the skull is very characteristic and is usually associated with pronounced thinning of the bone. On palpation over such regions the bone is found to be flexible and the feeling has been compared to that obtained by compressing a ping-pong ball. In a few cases the skull has been completely eroded and pulsating tumors may appear beneath the scalp. Roentgenograms of the skull may reveal evidences of increased intracranial pressure, as well as local bulging and atrophy of the vault, but the cyst is rarely visible unless it has undergone degeneration and calcification. The spinal fluid usually shows no characteristic changes but in a few instances has contained eosinophil cells. There is often a definite eosinophilia of the blood but as this depends upon the degree of absorption from the cyst, it is not always present.

Secondary cysts of the brain due to rupture of a cyst into the left side of the heart may produce violent symptoms due to multiple embolism and to anaphylaxis. Such reactions are associated with urticaria, erythema, gastrointestinal, respiratory and cardiac symptoms and may be fatal at once. Similar sensitization phenomena may occur as a result of rupture of a cyst into the ventricular system or meninges. A violent meningeal reaction may be expected in the latter case with high cell count and a large percentage of eosinophil leucocytes.

Suppuration of the cyst with the formation of a brain abscess has been observed in many cases and is very likely to follow exploratory puncture.

Hydatid disease may also involve the spinal cord as a result of localization within the vertebral column or in the spinal canal proper. Primary cysts of the spinal cord have not been observed but a number have been found in the epidural space. The roentgenographic appearances of hydatid disease of the bones resemble those of myeloma or simple bone cyst. There are multiple clear spaces with dark outlines but no proliferation of bone or subperiosteal reaction. Such lesions advance very slowly and rarely cause collapse of the vertebrae.

Diagnosis.—Symptoms of an intracranial tumor in a child in countries in which hydatid disease is prevalent should always suggest the diagnosis and careful investigation of the case for confirmatory evidences should then be made. The existence of eosinophilia in the blood is suggestive but not conclusive even when intestinal parasites can be excluded. Search for cysts of the liver or lungs is important and roentgenograms of the chest should always be made. Local thinning of the bones of the cranial vault is considered characteristic of cerebral hydatid disease. Casoni's cutaneous test is important. This is performed by injecting into the skin .3 cc of fresh hydatid cyst fluid which has been sterilized by passing through a Berkefeld filter. The fluid is obtained by puncture of a cyst in the lung or liver of a sheep. Positive reactions are manifest by local erythema and edema three to twelve hours later. It is claimed that a very large percentage of patients suffering from hydatid disease react positively. Death or suppuration of the cyst, however, prevents this reaction. If the cyst should be punctured with a hollow needle, we may expect to obtain the characteristic fluid containing scolices or at least hooklets, but this procedure must be strongly condemned, for it may be followed by dissemination of the disease, by anaphylactic phenomena and even by suppuration. Ventriculography may be necessary for accurate localization, but care must be exercised to avoid puncturing or rupture of the cyst.

Prognosis.—The prognosis is very unfavorable. Usually multiple cysts are found and there are numerous dangers in operation which will be mentioned below. The ultimate mortality of brain cysts is estimated at ninety per cent.

Treatment.—Dew recommends that a large exposure be made and that the cyst be evacuated very slowly with a very fine needle, great care being exercised to prevent any escape of the fluid. The cyst wall is then fixed by the injection of 1 or 2 per cent formalin without withdrawal of the needle and this is allowed to remain for five minutes. The cyst wall is then removed in toto and the skull is closed without drainage. It is important to prevent escape of fluid, for this may not only cause dissemination of the disease but may cause an immediate anaphylactic reaction.

Roentgenotherapy has been attempted with the object of killing the parasite, but in experimental animals the method has failed.

BIBLIOGRAPHY

ARANA-INIGUEZ, R.: Hydatid cysts of the brain. J. Neurosurg., 12:323, 1955.

COSACESCO, A. AND VEREANO, D.: Primary epidural hydatid cyst. (Lumbar spine) Presse. Med., 54:871, 1946.

DEW, H. R.: Hydatid Disease; Its Pathology, Diagnosis and Treatment. The Australian Medical Pub. Co., Ltd., 1928. (This monograph contains complete discussions of all phases of the disease and many references.)

LANGMAID, C. AND ROGERS, L.: Intracranial hydatids. Brain, 63:184, 1940.

MILLS, H. W.: Hydatid cyst in children. Surg. Gynec. & Obst., 42:585, 1926.

PHILLIPS, G.: Primary cerebral hydatid cysts. J. Neurol., Neurosurg. & Psychiat., 11:44, 1948.

RAYPORT, M. *et al.:* Vertebral echinococcosis. Jour. of Neurosurg., 21:647, 1964.

SCHISTOSOMIASIS

Schistosomiasis Japonica.—This disease is due to a fluke worm which lives in the liver of man and other mammals. Ova are discharged in the stools and wash into lakes where they become attached to a small snail and reach its liver. Eventually larvae are produced which being discharged from the snail attach themselves to the skin of persons swimming in the water.

These penetrate the skin and reach the liver where they mate and discharge ova into the portal circulation and bowel. Some ova get into the systemic circulation and lodge in all organs.

A febrile illness of several weeks' duration results with urticaria, cough, abdominal pains and cervical rigidity. The ova may be found in the stools and in submucous cysts revealed by the sigmoidoscope. Delirium and stupor may occur, and there may be signs of multiple cerebral and spinal lesions. Hemiplegia, ataxia, cranial nerve palsies and convulsions are described. Such symptoms are believed to be due to circulating ova which having gotten through the capillaries of the lungs have lodged in the brain as emboli. As a rule, these symptoms begin to diminish as the temperature falls. Fuadin, an antimony compound, is recommended.

Several cases are described in which focal cerebral lesions developed long after the febrile stage of the illness. The picture suggested brain tumor. In such instances, large granulomatous masses were found in the brain. These masses contained numbers of ova. It is believed that circulating larvae lodge in the cerebral veins and becoming mature produce masses of ova which lead to the formation of granulomata. Mansour and Reese describe generalized and localized myopathy.

Kane and Most state that S. mansoni and S. Haematobium behave in a very similar fashion but are apt to lodge in the spinal cord and cause transverse lesions.

Paragonimus Westermani.—The lung fluke worm is found in many parts of the world. Infection is due to the ingestion of infected crabs and crayfish. The larvae penetrate the intestinal wall and eventually reach the lungs and other tissues. It is apparently not uncommon for these larvae to reach the brain where they form granulomata and cysts full of ova. Convulsions, hemiplegias and other cerebral syndromes result. It is said that children are especially prone to these cerebral complications.

BIBLIOGRAPHY

Bird, A. V.: Acute spinal schistosomiasis. Neurology, 14:647, 1964.

Carroll, D. C.: Cerebral involvement in schistosomiasis japonica. Bull. Johns Hopkins Hosp., 78:219, 1946.

Chalgren, W. S. and Baker, A. B.: Nervous system in tropical disease. Medicine, 26:395, 1947.

Greenfield, J. G. and Prichard, B.: Cerebral involvement with schistosomiasis japonica. Brain, 60:361, 1937.

Kane, C. A. and Most, H.: Schistosomiasis of the central nervous system. Arch. Neurol. & Psychiat., 59:141, 1948.

Mansour, S. E. D. and Reese, H. H.: A previously unreported myopathy in schistosomiasis. Neurology, 14:355, 1964.

Mitsuno, T. *et al.*: Cerebral Paragonimiasis: A neurosurgical problem in the far East. J. Nerv. & Ment. Dis., 116:685, 1952.

Reeves, D. L. and Kerr, R. W.: Schistosomiasis japonica with intracerebral granuloma. Arch. Neurol. & Psychiat., 58:207, 1947.

NEMATODIASIS

Ascaris Lumbricoides.—The motile larvae emerge from the shells of the ova in the duodenum and invade the veins or lymphatics eventually reaching the lungs where most of them are filtered out from the blood stream and entering the alveoli migrate up the bronchi, into the esophagus and finally into the intestines where the adult worm lives. Some larvae pass through the pulmonary capillaries and are carried throughout the body lodging in various organs including the brain where they cause vascular lesions and inflammatory reactions. Beautyman and Woolf describe the case of a child who was found at post-mortem examination to have an inflammatory process in the brain stem. An ascaris larva was found in the thalamus. A variety of neurological symptoms are described in children infested with these worms which disappear when the worms are eliminated and are therefore attributed to toxins produced by the parasites.

Filaria.—Chalgren and Baker state that in cases of infection with Wuchereria bancrofti the adult worms are found in the lymphatics whereas the microfilaria circulate through the blood and lymph streams. These microfilaria seem to cause little damage to the tissues as a rule, but cases are described in which cerebral lesions developed and microfilaria were found in the brain or spinal fluid. Van Bogaert *et al.* have published cases in which Loa Loa filariasis caused severe encephalitis. These filaria sometimes get into the anterior part of the eye and float around in the aqueous.

Innes and Shoho state that a filarial worm, Setaria digitata, whose natural host is cattle, is a cause of paralysis in sheep, goats and horses in the East and may possibly cause paralysis in man. This parasite is conveyed by mosquitos. The microfilaria do not circulate in the blood stream but wander through the tissues causing linear softenings in the brain, meningitis and radiculitis.

Onchocercia volvolus, a filarial worm, found in West Africa is not found in the blood stream but localizes in the subcutaneous tissues especially about the head and in the eyes. An inflammatory process develops which results in blindness. The worm is transmitted by a gnat, Simulium damnosum.

Hookworms.—The larvae penetrate the skin, enter veins and are carried to the lungs. They then leave the pulmonary capillaries and get into the alveoli. Travelling up the bronchi they get into the gastrointestinal tract and eventually reach the duodenum. Apparently some of these parasites pass through the pulmonary capillaries and get into various organs.

Visceral Larvae Migrans. The larvae of the ascaris of the dog and cat of the genus toxocara. Infected dogs deposit the fertilized ova in the soil.

They become infective within 3 weeks. If they then enter the intestinal tract of man, they hatch out and become larvae. The larvae migrate through the intestinal wall and then into various organs. Their life cycle is never completed but they remain viable for a long time and migrate through the tissues causing eosinophilic granulomatous reactions. Children between the age of 2 to 4 years are most commonly infected. This is usually due to pica, i.e. eating infected dirt. There is fever, irritability, pallor, and loss of appetite. The liver is enlarged and the spleen may be enlarged. The lungs are involved and bronchitis and bronchopneumonia occur. Erythematous cutaneous eruptions develop. Convulsions are common. Many larvae are found in the brain. Granulomatous uveitis may develop. More than 200 cases have now been reported. Some of them have been fatal. Eosinophilia is always present. The white count may go up to 100,000 and 30 to 90 per cent of the cells may be eosinophils. The gamma globulin is increased. The only definitive diagnostic test is demonstration of the larvae in the tissues. Liver biopsy is often positive. The ova are not found in the stools. No treatment is curative. In children corticosteroids may give symptomatic relief in pneumonia. It is most important to prevent continued ingestion of contaminated soil.

In 1950 Wilder reported the study of 46 eyes removed from children between the ages of 3 and 13 years. In 20 of these cases a diagnosis of retinoblastoma had been made. In 2 cases the condition was bilateral. Eosinophil granuloma or eosinophilic abscess was found in all cases involving the retina and choroid. In 24 cases worms were found and in the other cases the histological process was identical. Since then the parasite has been identified as the larvae of toxocara canis. It is of interest that these children did not have the evidences of generalized infection which are described above and either no eosinophilia or slight eosinophilia is found.

CASE HISTORY (No. 726202).—*Girl of 7 years with eosinophilic granuloma in the right eye due to round worm.*

C. W., a little girl of 7 years, developed an internal squint of the right eye. On examination it was found that vision was grossly reduced in that eye. A large white mass was seen lying on the nasal side of the disc. Where this approached the disc it was 2 disc diameters wide and in the periphery it was 5 disc diameters wide. The retinal vessels were seen on the surface of the mass. It pushed forwards into vitreous 4 diopters. Three small white areas were seen in the upper temporal quadrant of the retina. There were some vitreous opacities. Neurological examination was negative as was the medical examination. Roentgenograms of the skull and orbit showed no abnormalities.

A diagnosis of retinoblastoma was made and the eye removed. An eosinophilic granuloma was found containing a worm.

BIBLIOGRAPHY

BEAUTYMAN, W. AND WOOLF, A. L.: An ascaris larva in the brain in association with acute anterior poliomyelitis. J. Path. & Bact., **63**:635, 1951.

BOURKE, G. M. AND YEATES, F. M.: Blindness due to household pets. Toxocara canis infestation. Med. J. Australia, **2**:12, 1961.

CHALGREN, W. S. AND BAKER, A. B.: The nervous system in tropical disease. Medicine, **26**:395, 1947.

DUGUID, I. M.: Ocular infestation by Toxocara. Brit. J. Ophth., **45**:789, 1961.

HEINER, D. C. AND KEVY, S. V.: Visceral larva migrans. New England J. Med., **254**:269, 1956.

INNES, J. AND SHOHO, C.: Cerebrospinal nematodiasis. Arch. Neurol. & Psychiat., **70**:325, 1953.

NICHOLS, R. L.: The etiology of visceral larva migrans. Jour. Parasitol., **42**:349, 1956.

SCHOCHET, S. S.: Human toxocara canis encephalopathy in a case of visceral larva migrans. Neurology, **17**:227, 1967.

SNYDER, C. H.: Features of visceral larva migrans. Pediatrics, **28**:85, 1961.

VAN BOGAERT, L. *et al.*: Encephalitis in Loa loa filariasis. J. Neurol., Neurosurg. & Psychiat., **18**:103, 1955.

WILDER, H. C.: Nematode enophthalmitis. Trans. Am. Acad. Ophth. & Otol., **55**:99, 1955.

ZINKHAM, W. H.: Visceral larvae migrans due to toxocara as a cause of eosinophilia. Johns Hopkins Med. Jour., **123**:41, 1968.

Chapter IV

INTOXICATIONS, METABOLIC AND ENDOCRINE DISORDERS, DIETARY DEFICIENCIES AND ALLERGIES INVOLVING THE NERVOUS SYSTEM

INTRODUCTION.—In this section I shall discuss the neurological conditions which result from the action of various toxins on the nervous system including endogenous, exogenous and bacterial toxins. Disorders of metabolism and of the glands of internal secretion are taken up next, and finally neurological conditions due to deficient diet and to allergy are discussed.

The most interesting condition among those due to infections is the disseminated encephalomyelitis which sometimes follows measles, vaccina, and other diseases. Marsden and Hurst have proposed the very suitable term perivascular myelinoclasis for this condition. There is no general agreement about the cause of these conditions and, hence, their classification is difficult. Several theories are prevalent at present. Since the histological nature of the lesions seems to be essentially the same whether the condition has followed measles, vaccinia or some other illness, it has been suggested that the process is due to a neurotropic virus which becomes activated by the primary infection or which invades the nervous system when the patient's resistance is reduced by illness. Unfortunately, for this theory, the hypothetical neurotropic virus has not been demonstrated. Some authorities believe that the virus of the original disease actually invades the nervous system. However, the pathological process is scarcely what one would expect under such circumstances and the virus is only rarely recovered from the brain. Another possibility is that the injury to the nervous system is due to toxins produced by the virus of the original infection which have the property of destroying the myelin of the nervous system. Lastly, some writers have advanced evidence to show that we are dealing with allergic reactions or the formation of antibodies which destroy myelin. This point of view developed from the study of paralysis following antirabies inoculation. The work of Rivers and Schwentker and more recently that of Kabat *et al.* and Morgan supports this theory. Ferraro and Roizin regard this process as an immunological allergic reaction to antigenic stimuli. Lumsden's study reveals that the lesions produced by injections of brain emulsion combined with an adjuvant are identical with those which are associated with measles. At this point it is of interest to refer to the observations of Vogel who found widespread focal demyelination in the cerebral white and gray matter in a patient who died of hemorrhagic pancreatitis. Vogel has produced demyelination in the nervous system of experimental animals by intracarotid injection of pancreatic lipase. He suggests that pancreatitis may liberate enzymes which get into the circulation and cause perivascular demyelination in the brain.

The following group of conditions seems to defy any attempt at intelligent classification. Sydenham's chorea apparently must be regarded as a toxic encephalopathy of more or less specific type but its anatomical basis is still very uncertain and many neuropathologists can discover no definite lesions whatever. The encephalopathy sometimes associated with pertussis is also very characteristic and, perhaps, specific. It has been attributed to vasomotor disturbances with some reason, to air embolism and to the action of a bacterial toxin. The last possibility would seem to be the most attractive at present. Other types of encephalopathy seem to be entirely non-specific for they may be associated with a great variety of clinical conditions and may result from non-bacterial as well as bacterial poisons. There is great difference of opinion about the significance of the so-called *toxic encephalopathy*. Some pathologists regard it as evidence of a serous encephalitis of very acute type in which the usual inflammatory phenomena have not yet appeared. This view can scarcely be supported at present and it seems clear that it is merely a result of injury to the nerve cells by various toxins. Some writers claim that this process may cause permanent injury to the brain and consequently persisting symptoms in children who survive the illness. Others state that the changes in the neurons are of no significance whatever. The writer is inclined to think that the lesions are analogous to the cloudy swelling of the kidneys and other viscera found in almost all acute and fatal illnesses and that they are probably the anatomical basis of delirium and stupor. These are usually reversible but may cause lasting damage in some instances.

Then we pass to toxic processes involving chiefly the peripheral nerves, or polyneuritis, due to infections. The more common types of intoxication of exogenous nature are discussed.

The next section deals with intoxications of various types, and disorders of metabolism. Here we find disorders of the liver and kidneys, the thyroid and parathyroid glands, hypoxia and carbon dioxide intoxication, disorders of carbohydrate metabolism, of lipid metabolism including the lipidoses and leucodystrophies, the mucopolysaccharidoses, the disorders of purine metabolism, the porphyrias, disorders of protein metabolism, vitamin deficiency, and all allergic conditions.

In addition to these conditions, most of which are well known, a number of studies have been made of small numbers of patients suffering from errors of metabolism which may be mentioned briefly at this point.

Richards and Rundle and Mathews have reported a study of a family of 13 siblings of whom 5 had mental retardation, defective sexual development, deafness, ataxia and peripheral muscle wasting. The symptoms progressed for a time and the process was then static. There was *ketoaciduria*.

Laster *et al.* and Rosenblum have described a familial disorder causing destructive lesions in the nervous system in early infancy with a fatal outcome. This is termed *sulfite oxidase deficiency*. The urine contains no inorganic sulphate, but large amounts of sulfite, S-sulpho-L-Cysteine and thiosulfate.

Worsley *et al.* describe a study of two brothers who developed at the age of two years ataxia, muscle twitching and intermittent hyperpnea. Mental deterioration developed. The scalp hair was lost. Death occurred about a month after the onset. Increase of lactic acid was found in the blood and renal aminoaciduria with lowered serum phosphate were found. Widespread necrotizing encephalopathy was found at post-mortem examination.

Baar and Hickman describe the condition of two siblings who developed slowly progressive mental deterioration with enlargement of the spleen. Death occurred at 4 years and 6 years. There were extensive lipid deposits in the cells of the liver, spleen, brain and spinal cord. This lipid was identified as inosine phosphatide. The term *Cephalin lipidosis* is used.

Crome *et al.* have studied female infants with congenital cataracts, convulsions, mental retardation and small stature. They died at 4 and 8 months. Post-mortem examination revealed renal tubular necrosis and encephalopathy. This is called *Crome's syndrome*.

Wolman *et al.* and Crocker *et al.* found a familial disease manifest by vomiting, diarrhea and progressive enlargement of the liver and spleen causing death between 2 and 4 months. Post-mortem study revealed xanthomatous deposits in all the tissues including the retinae and nervous system.

Hooft *et al.* studied a family in which two sisters showed retarded mental and physical development, an erythemato-squamous eruption, opaque finger nails and reduction of the serum lipids. This is termed *Hooft's disease*.

Arakawa *et al.* describe a condition evidenced by mental deficiency. Deficiency of formimino-transferase was discovered, Formiminoglutamic acid is excreted in the urine and causes a positive ferric chloride test.

Tangier disease is named from an island in the Chesapeake Bay in which the disease is prevalent. It is also termed analphalipoprotemia. It is manifest by enlargement of the tonsils which are of a yellowish color, enlargement of the liver, spleen and lymph nodes. These organs contain heavy deposits of esters of cholesterol. In some cases lipid deposits in the intestines also occur, which cause diarrhea. Slight corneal infiltration may occur. Some of these patients have recurrent attacks of polyneuritis with some improvement afterwards. The plasma cholesterol is reduced. The plasma alpha lipoproteins are greatly reduced or absent.

Feldman *et al.* reports a study of a family in which progressive ataxia occurred. Deposits of lipofuscin were found in the inferior olivary nucleus and cells of the liver. Hsia describes *idiopathic hyperlipemia*. This is an autosomal recessive condition giving rise to symptoms in childhood. There are repeated attacks of abdominal pain with rigidity of the abdomen and fever. They last from 1 to 4 days. There are soft yellow xanthomas on the knees, elbows, buttocks and thighs. Lipemia retinalis develops. Pancreatitis may occur. The blood vessels are obstructed by atheromatous plaques causing myocardial infarctions and cerebral vascular lesions. The serum is milky white. All the blood lipids are increased.

PRIMARY HYPERCHOLESTEREMIA

This is a dominant trait with incomplete penetrance. The onset is in childhood. There are xanthomas on the skin in about one quarter of the patients. There are also xanthomas in the tendons especially the tendons of Achilles and the tendons of the extensor muscles of the hands. Atheromatous plaques develop in the blood vessels in childhood especially in the coronary arteries, cerebral arteries and aortic valves. Xanthomatous deposits are found in the subcutaneous tissues. The serum cholesterol is constantly elevated but the serum is always clear and not milky white as in idiopathic hyperlipemia.

In 1959, Bigler and others described a clinical syndrome characterized by enlargement of the liver, mental deficiency, and defective physical development. Increased concentrations of triglycerides and phospholipids were found in the plasma.

In 1960, Coles and his associates published a paper concerning four siblings who were physically retarded and mentally deficient. A substance was found in the urine which was not fully identified, but was believed to be related to alloxan, an oxidation product of uric acid. An autosomal recessive gene was incriminated. This is termed the T substance anomaly.

Many inborn errors of aminoacid metabolism are now known. Some are very rare. Efron and Ampola have reviewed a number of such conditions. They distinguish cases in which defects in an enzyme system lead to an increase of aminoacids in the blood and tissues with aminoaciduria, disorders of non-essential amino acids and non-protein amino acids and conditions in which aminoaciduria is due to defective renal tubular reabsorption.

They point out that the identification of the aminoacid may be incorrect, that the finding of a biochemical abnormality may have no relation to the patients' symptoms, that not all aminoacidurias are significant, that many drugs and poisons cause renal tubular damage and aminoaciduria, that old contaminated urine may contain aminoacids though the fresh urine does not and acute illnesses of various types are not uncommonly associated with aminoaciduria. It is important that both the blood and urine should be tested for aminoacids.

The reader is advised to consult the original paper, The Aminoacidurias, by Efron, M. L. and Ampola, M. G., Pediatric Clinics of North America, 14:881, 1967. This contains the essential facts about the aminoacidurias. Some of the more common conditions are described in the text of Chapter IV.

Menkes *et al.* have studied a family in which an excess of glutamic acid was found in the plasma. There were five children, all boys, who developed a progressive and fatal process. The onset was in the first two months of life. The hair was white and brittle. Bodily growth was defective. Mental deterioration was rapid. Convulsions occurred frequently. Decerebrate rigidity and death usually ensued before the end of the second year. Two post-mortem examinations revealed extensive degeneration of the cerebral and cerebellar cortex and secondary degeneration of the white matter. Biochemical studies revealed only an excess of glutamic acid in the blood. This has been termed *Menkes disease.*

Stransky *et al.* describe a family in which 5 of 7 sibs had aminoaciduria with mental and physical deficiency, dwarfism, muscular dystrophy and osteoporosis.

Drummond *et al.* report a condition in which there is hypercalcemia and nephrocalcinosis associated with a defect in intestinal transport of tryptophane. Bacterial degradation of tryptophane causes indol production and thus indocanuria which on oxidation becomes indigo blue and causes the *blue diaper syndrome.*

Copps *et al.* describe a condition in two boys with physical and mental retardation in whom there was an increased urinary excretion of 3-4-dihydroxyphenylalanine.

Kromrower *et al.* describe a patient who secreted large amounts of kynurenine, hydroxykynurine and xanthurenic acid in the urine. This condition was termed *hydroxykynureninuria.*

Hypermethioninemia is described by Perry *et al.* in two females and one male infant who became somnolent and died in the third month. Hypoglycemia and a bleeding tendency developed. The children had a peculiar odor. Biochemical study revealed a marked elevation of methionine in the blood and urine.

Isovaleric acidemia is described. The onset of symptoms is in the first few months. The children have frequent episodes of lethargy and vomiting. These seem to be induced by upper respiratory tract infections. The

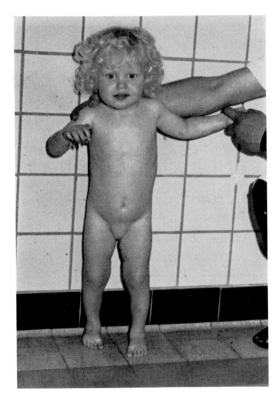

FIG. 161. Photograph of child described by Prof. C. Hooft *et al.* in article entitled Methionine Malabsorption Syndrome, Ann. Paediat. 1965, vol. 205, p. 73. As a result of treatment, the hair, which had been white, is now yellow.

lethargy may progress to coma with acidosis and ketonuria. These children have an offensive body odor described as resembling sweaty feet. They are mildly defective in both mental and motor development. They refuse milk, meat and eggs.

Isovaleric acid is increased in the blood and urine. Oral administration of leucine causes pronounced and sustained elevation of isovaleric acid in the blood and an increase of the body odor with lethargy and irritability. The enzyme isovaleryl coenzyme A dehydrogenase seems to be at fault. This condition seems to be inherited as a recessive trait.

Sidbury *et al.* describe a study of two families in which seven babies died in the first month of life. They had severe acidosis, dehydration, convulsions, sepsis and depressed bone marrow activity. Butyric acid and hexanoic acids were found in the blood and urine. The defect was thought to be due to the absence of the green acyl dehydrogenases. An odor resembling sweaty feet was noted and ascribed to the presence of butyric and hexanoic acids.

BIBLIOGRAPHY

AARLI, J. A.: Neurological manifestations in hyperlipidemia. Neurology, **18**:883, 1968.

AGUILAR, M. J. *et al.*: Kinky hair disease (Menkes disease). Jour. Neuropath. and Exp. Neurol., **25**:507, 1966.

AITA, J. A.: Neurologic Manifestations of General Diseases. Thomas, Springfield, 1964.

ALLAN, J. D. *et al.*: A disease probably hereditary characterized by severe mental deficiency and constant gross abnormality of amino acid metabolism. Lancet, **i**:182, 1958.

ALSTROM, C. H. *et al.*: Retinal degeneration combined with obesity, diabetes mellitus and neurogenic deafness. Acta Psychiat. Neuro. Scand., **34**: Suppl. 129, 1959.

ARAKAWA, T. *et al.*: Formiminotransferase deficiency. Ann. Paediat., **205**:1, 1965.

AUERBACH, V. H. *et al.*: Histidinemia. J. Pediat. **60**:487, 1962.

———— AND DiGEORGE, A. M.: Histidinemia. Rev. Neuro-Paediatria., **26**:105, 1963.

BAAR, H. S. AND GALINDO, J.: Borjeson-Forssman-Lehmann syndrome. Jour. Ment. Defic. Res., **9**:125, 1965.

———— AND HICKMAN, E. M.: Cephalin lipidosis. Acta Med. Scand., **155**:49, 1956.

BERLOW, S. *et al.*: Studies in histidinemia. Jour.-Lancet, **85**:241, 1965.

BIGLER, A. A. *et al.*: Inborn error of lipid metabolism. Pediatrics, **23**:644, 1959.

BROUGH, A. J. *et al.*: Dermal erythropoiesis in neonatal infants. Pediatrics, **40**:627, 1967.

BUDD, M. A. *et al.*: Isovaleric acidemia. New England Jour. Med., **277**:321, 1967.

CAMBELL, M.: The place of rubella in the aetiology of congenital heart disease. Brit. Med. Jour., **i**:691, 1961.

CARSON, N. A. S. AND NEILL, D. W.: Metabolic abnormalities detected in a survey of mentally backward individuals in North Ireland. Arch. Dis. Childhood, **37**:505, 1962.

CHILD, B. AND COOK, R. E.: Observations on a patient with defect in metabolism of glycine. International Congress of Pediatrics, Montreal, Canada, July 19, 1959.

COLES, H. M. T. *et al.*: T substance anomaly. Lancet, **ii**:1220, 1960.

COLOMBO, J. P. *et al.*: Congenital lysine intolerance with periodic ammonia intoxication. Lancet, **i**:1014, 1964.

CONTE, W. R., McCAMMON, C. S. AND CHRISTIE, A.: Congenital defects following maternal rubella. Am. J. Dis. Child., **70**:301, 1945.

COOPER, L. Z. *et al.*: Neonatal thrombocytopenic purpura and other manifestations of rubella contracted in utero. Amer. Jour. Dis. Child., **110**:416, 1965.

COPPS, S. C. *et al.*: Urinary excretion of 3-4-dihydroxyphenylalanine in two children of short stature with malnutrition. Jour. of Pediat., **62**:208, 1963.

CROCKER, A. C. *et al.*: Wolman's disease. Pediatrics, **35**:627, 1965.

CROME, L. *et al.*: Congenital cataracts, renal tubular necrosis and encephalopathy in two sisters. Arch. of Dis. Childh., **38**:505, 1963.

CUMMINGS, J. N. AND KREMER, M.: Biochemical Aspects of Neurological Disorders. Springfield, Thomas.

DENT, C. E. *et al.*: Symposium on inborn errors of metabolism. Am. J. Med. 22, 1957.

DESMOND, M. M. *et al.*: Congenital rubella encephalitis. Jour. Pediat., **71**:311, 1967.

DRUMMOND, K. N. *et al.*: The blue diaper syndrome. Hypercalcemia with nephrocalcinosis and indicanuria. Amer. Jour. Med., **37**:928, 1964.

EFRON, M. L. *et al.*: Familial hydroxyprolinemia. New England Jour. Med., **272**:1299, 1965.

————: Familial hyperprolinemia. New England Jour. Med., **272**:1243, 1965.

————: A simple chromatographic screening test for the detection of disorders of amino acid metabolism. New England Jour. Med., **270**:1278, 1964.

————: Aminoaciduria. New England Jour. Med., **272**:1058, 1965.

ELLIS, J. G.: Pulmonary artery stenosis—a frequent part of the congenital rubella syndrome. California Med., **105**:435, 1966.

ENGEL, W. E.: Neuropathy in Tangier disease. Arch. of Neurol., **17**:1, 1967.

ERICKSON, R. J.: Familial infantile lactic acidosis. Jour. Pediat., **66**:1004, 1965.

ERICKSON, C. A.: Rubella early in pregnancy causing congenital malformations of the eyes and heart. Ped., **25**:281, 1944.

FELDMAN, R. G. *et al.*: Familial intention tremor, ataxia and lipofuscinosis. Neurology, **19**:503, 1969.

FERRARO, A. AND ROIZIN, L.: Hyperergic encephalomyelitis following exanthematic diseases, infectious diseases and vaccination. J. Neuropath. & Exp. Neurol., **16**:423, 1957.

Francois, R.: Encephalopathie congenitale familiale associee a une anomalie du metabolisme de la tyrosine. Pediatric, 17:955, 1962.

Fredrickson, D. S.: Inheritance of high density lipoprotein deficiency. Jour. Clin. Invest., 43:228, 1964.

———— et al.: Tangier disease. Ann. Int. Med., 55:1016, 1961.

Friedmann, M. and Cohen, P.: Agenesis of the corpus callosum as a possible sequel to maternal rubella during pregnancy. Am. J. Dis. Child., 73:178, 1947.

Frimpter, G. W. et al.: Cystathioninuria. New England J. Med., 268:333, 1963.

Frimpter, G. W.: Cystathioninuria: nature of the defect. Science, 149:1095, 1965.

Garrell, D.: Metabolic effects associated with mental retardation. Amer. Jour. Dis. Child., 104:401, 1962.

Garrod, A. E.: Inborn errors of metabolism. The Croonian Lectures, Royal College of Physicians, 1908.

Gerritsen, T. and Waisman, H. A.: Hypersarcosinemia. An inborn error of metabolism. New England Jour. of Med., 1966.

Ghadimi, H. et al.: Inborn error of histidine metabolism. Pediatrics, 29:714, 1962.

————: A familiar disorder of histidine metabolism. New England J. Med., 265:221, 1961.

Gibson, S. and Lewis, K.: Congenital heart disease following maternal rubella during pregnancy. Am. J. Dis. Child., 83:317, 1952.

Gregg, N.: Congenital cataract following German measles in the mother. Trans. Ophth. Soc. Australia, 3:35, 1941.

Hamilton, J. B.: Rubella retinitis in Tasmania. Med. J. Australia, 2:418, 1948.

Hardy, J. B. and Sever, J. L.: Indirect inguinal hernia in congenital rubella. Jour. Pediat., 73:416, 1968.

Harris, H.: Cystathioninuria. Report on the 30th Ross Conference on Pediatrics Research. Ross Laboratory, 1959.

———— et al.: Cystathioninuria. Ann. Hum. Genet., 23:442, 1959.

Heggie, A. D. and Weir, W. C.: Rubella virus in mother and fetus. Pediatrics, 34:278, 1964.

Holmes, L. B. et al.: Isovaleric acidemia. A new genetic defect of leucine metabolism. Soc. for Pediat. Research, April 29, 1966.

Hooft, C. H. et al.: Methionine malabsorption syndrome. Ann. Paediat., 205:73, 1965.

Hooft, C. et al.: Methionine malabsorption in mentally defective child. Lancet, ii:20, 1964.

Hooft, C. et al.: Familial lipidaemia and retarded development without steatorrhoea. Helv. Paedat. Acta, 17:1, 1962.

Hopkins, L. A.: Congenital deafness and other defects following German measles in the mother. Am. J. Dis. Child., 72:377, 1947.

Hsia, D. Y. Y.: Inborn Errors of Metabolism. Year Book Publishers. 1959, p. 235.

Hsia, D. Y.: Tyrosinosis. Inborn Errors of Metabolism. Chicago, Year Book Publishers. 1960, p. 112.

Hudson, F. P. et al.: Experiences in detection and treatment of phenylketonuria. Pediatrics, 31:47, 1963.

Hurst, E. W.: Newer knowledge of virus diseases of the nervous system. Brain, 59:1, 1936.

Ingalls, T. H.: German measles and German measles in pregnancy. J. Dis. Child., 93:555, 1957.

Jackson, A. D. M. and Fisch, L.: Deafness following maternal rubella. Lancet, ii:1241, 1958.

Japson, J. B. and Smith, A. J.: Inborn error of metabolism with urinary excretion of hydroxy acids, ketoacids and aminoacids. Lancet, ii:1334, 1958.

Joseph, R. et al.: Maladie familiale associant des convulsions a debut tres precoce une hyper-albuminorachis et une hyperaminoaciduria. Arch. franc pediat., 15:374, 1958.

Kabat, E. A., Wolf, A. and Bezer, A. E.: Rapid production of acute disseminated encephalo-myelitis in monkeys by injection of heterologous and homologous brain tissues with adjuvant. J. Exp. Med., 85:117, 1947.

Kantor, H. I. and Strother, W. K.: Effects of maternal rubella. Am. J. Obst. & Gynec., 81:902, 1961.

KARMODY, C. S.: Asymptomatic material rubella and congenital deafness. Arch. of Otolaryng., 89:720, 1969.

KOCEN, R. S. *et al.*: Familial lipoprotein deficiency. Lancet, 1:1341, 1967.

KOCH, G.: Degenerative Entmarkungskrankheiten Humangenetik. P. E. Becker. Georg Thieme Stuttgart, 1966.

KORONES, S. B. *et al.*: Congenital rubella syndrome. New clinical aspects. Jour. Pediat., 67:166, 1965.

KROMROWER, G. *et al.*: A case of abnormal tryptophane metabolism probably due to a deficiency of kynureninase. Arch. Dis. Childh., 39:250, 1964.

KRUGMAN, S. AND WARD, R.: The rubella problem. J. Pediat., 44:489, 1954.

LA DU, B. N. *et al.*: Clinical and biochemical studies of two cases of histidinemia. Pediatrics, 32:216, 1963.

LAMY, M. *et al.*: Congenital absence of beta lipoproteins. Pediat., 31:277, 1963.

LASTER, L. *et al.*: A previously unrecognized disorder of metabolism of sulphur containing compounds. Jour. Clin. Invest., 46:1082, 1967.

LEVIN, B., MACAY, H. M. M. AND OBERHOLZER, V. G.: Argininosuccinic aciduria. Arch. Dis. Childhood, 36:622, 1961.

LOCK, F. R. *et al.*: Difficulties in diagnosis of congenital abnormalities: Experience in study of effect of rubella on pregnancy. J.A.M.A., 178:711, 1961.

LUMSDEN, C. E.: Experimental allergic encephalomyelitis. Brain, 72:198, 1949.

MATHEWS, W. B.: Familial ataxia deaf-mutism and muscular wasting. Jour. Neurol. and Psychiat., 13:307, 1950.

McMURRAY, W. C.: Genetic errors and mental retardation. Canad. M. A. J., 87:486, 1962.

MEDES, G.: A new error of tyrosonine metabolism. Biochem. J., 26:917, 1932.

MENKES, J. H. AND JERVIS, G. A.: Developmental retardation associated with an abnormality of tyrosine metabolism. Pediatrics, 28:399, 1961.

MENKES, J. H. *et al.*: A sex-linked recessive disorder with retardation of growth, peculiar hair and focal cerebellar and cerebral degeneration. Pediatrics, 29:764, 1962.

MENSER, M. A. *et al.*: A twenty-five year follow up of congenital rubella. Lancet, 2:1347, 1967.

MILLER, M. H. *et al.*: Audiological problems associated with maternal rubella. Laryngoscope, 79:417, 1969.

MONIF, G. R. G. AND SEVER, J. L.: Chronic infection of the central nervous system with rubella virus. Neurology, 16:111, 1966.

MONIF, G. R. G. *et al.*: Studies in congenital rubella. Bull. of the Johns Hopkins Hosp., 118:85, 1966.

MORGAN, I.: Allergic encephalomyelitis in monkeys in response to injection of normal monkey nervous tissue. J. Exp. Med., 85:131, 1947.

MOYNAHAN, E. J.: Familial congenital alopecia, epilepsy, mental retardation with unusual electroencephalograms. Proc. Roy Soc. Med., 55:411, 1962.

MURPHY, A. M. *et al.*: Rubella cataracts. Amer. Jour. Ophthal., 64:1109, 1967.

NYHAN, W. L. *et al.*: Idiopathic hyperglycinuria. Jour. Pediat., 62:540, 1963.

PAINE, R. S.: Evaluation of familial biochemically determined mental retardation in children with special reference to aminoaciduria. New England J. Med., 262:658, 1960.

PERERA, C. A.: Congenital cataracts following rubella in mother. Am. J. Ophth., 28:186, 1945.

PERRY, T. C. *et al.*: Hypermethioninemia. Pediatrics, 36:236, 1965.

PINEDA, R. G. *et al.*: Impact of the rubella epidemic on a clinic population. Amer. Jour. Obstet. and Gynec., 100:1139, 1968.

PLOTKIN, S. A. *et al.*: Some recently recognized manifestations of the rubella syndrome. Jour. Pediat., 67:182, 1965.

QUASTEL, J. H. AND QUASTEL, D. M. J.: The Chemistry of Brain Metabolism in Health and Disease. Springfield, Thomas, 1961.

REESE, A. B.: Congenital cataracts and other anomalies following German measles in mother. Am. J. Ophth., 27:483, 1944.

REICHLIN, S.: Neuroendocrinology. New England Med. Jour., **269**:1182, 1963.

RICHARDS, B. W.: A familial hormonal disease associated with mental deficiency, deaf-mutism and ataxia. J. Ment. Def. Res., **3**:33, 1959.

RIVERS, T. M.: Relation of filterable viruses to diseases of the nervous system. Arch. Neurol. & Psychiat., **28**:757, 1932.

————: Filterable Viruses. Baltimore, Williams & Wilkins Co., 1928.

RIVERS, T. M. AND SCHWENTKER, F. F.: Encephalomyelitis accompanied by myelin destruction experimentally produced in monkeys. J. Exper. Med., **61**:689, 1935.

ROSEMBLUM, W. I.: Neuropathologic changes in a case of sulfite oxidase deficiency. Neurology, **18**:1187, 1968.

RUSSELL, A. et al.: Hyperammoniaemia: a new instance of an inborn enzymatic defect of bio-synthesis of urea. Lancet, **ii**:699, 1962.

SCHAFER, I. A. et al.: Familial hyperprolanemia. New England J. Med., **267**:51, 1962.

SCRIVER, C. R. et al.: Hyper-beta-alaninemia associated with beta-aminoaciduria and gamma-aminobutyricaciduria somnolence and seizures. New England Jour. Med., **274**:635, 1966.

SELZER, G.: Virus isolation, inclusion bodies and chromosomes in rubella-infected human embryo. Lancet, **2**:336, 1963.

SIDBURY, J. B. et al.: Inborn error of short chain fatty acid metabolism. The sweaty feet syndrome. Jour. Pediat., **70**:8, 1967.

SMITH, A. J., AND STRANG, L. B.: Oasthouse urine disease. Arch. Dis. Childhood, **33**:109, 1958.

STRANSKY, E. et al.: Aminoaciduria with mental deficiency, dwarfism, muscular dystrophy, osteoporosis and acidosis. Philipp. Med. Ass. Jour., **38**:903, 1962.

SWAN, C. et al.: Congenital defects in infants following infectious diseases during pregnancy with special reference to the relationship between German measles and cataract, deaf-mutism, heart disease and microcephaly. M. J. Australia, **2**:201, 1943.

TADA, K. et al.: Congenital tryptophanuria with dwarfism. Tohoku Jour. Exp. Med., **80**:118, 1963.

TANAKA, K. et al.: Isovaleric acidemia. Pro. Nat. Acad. Sci., **56**:236, 1966.

TANAKA, K.: An hereditary disorder of leucine metabolism. Modern Medicine, May 23, 1966, p. 42.

TARTAKOW, I. J.: The teratogenicity of maternal rubella. J. Pediat., **66**:380, 1965.

VAN BUCHEM, F. S. P. et al.: Hyperostosis corticalis generalisata. Amer. Jour. Med., **33**:387, 1962.

WADA, Y. et al.: Hypervalinemia. Tohoku, Jour. Exp. Med., **81**:46, 1963.

WALSH, F. B.: *Loc. cit.*

WATTS, R. W. E.: Congenital abnormalities of amino acid metabolism. Devel. Med. Child. Neurol., **4**:405, 1962.

WELLER, T. H. AND NEVA, F. A.: Rubella Virus. Viral and Rickettsial Infections of Man. Ed. by Horsfall, F. L. and Tamm, I. J. B. Lippincott Co., 4th Ed. 1965, p. 802.

WOLMAN, M. et al.: Primary family xanthomatosis with calcification of the adrenals. Pediatrics, **28**:742, 1961.

WOODY, N. C.: Hyperlysinemia. Amer. Jour. Dis. Child., **108**:543, 1964.

WORSLEY, H. E. et al.: Lactic acidosis with necrotizing encephalopathy. Arch. of Dis. Childh., **40**:492, 1965.

ZINKHAM, W. H. et al.: Blood and bone marrow findings in congenital rubella. Jour. Pediat., **71**:512, 1967.

INTOXICATIONS DUE TO INFECTIONS

Disseminated Encephalomyelitis or Myelinoclasis Following Measles

Etiology.—Measles is due to a myxovirus in which group the viruses of influenza and mumps are included.

Pathological Anatomy.—The brain is usually congested at post-mortem examination and sometimes a few petechial hemorrhages may be seen over the cortex. On section many small yellowish-red lesions are seen in the white matter of the hemispheres, cerebellum, brain-stem and spinal cord. Histological examination reveals that these are all of essentially the same nature. In the center of each lesion lies a small vein which is much distended and often shows swelling of the endothelium and thickening of the adventitia. About the vessel is an area of more or less complete demyelination. The axis cylinders are usually not severely affected although Walthard has shown that they are sometimes partially degenerated in cases of long duration. The demyelinated area is thickly infiltrated with microglial cells which are distended with lipoid products. The same type of cell is found in the perivascular spaces where they may be accompanied by a few lymphocytes. Rarely red cells may be found in the adventitia of the vessels. About the margins of the lesions there is usually some proliferation of the astrocytes and also increase in glial fibers. In some regions two or more lesions may coalesce to form large areas of myelin destruction or even complete softening. The essential process, therefore, is merely that of perivascular myelin destruction with phagocytosis of the broken down lipoid products by the microglia. This is not always uniformly distributed throughout the neuraxis. It may be most intense in the brain, the spinal cord or the cerebellum. Dorothy Russell points out that perivenous hemorrhages may occur in this condition and states that this is the commonest cause of the so-called hemorrhagic leucoencephalitis. In some cases, Ferraro claims, there is in addition to these lesions a generalized swelling of the

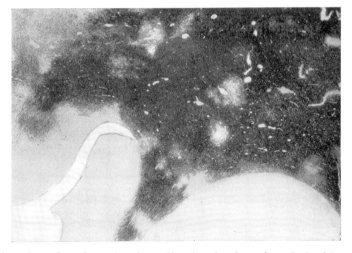

FIG. 162. Disseminated perivascular demyelination in the subcortical white matter in a case of measles encephalomyelitis. (Ferraro and Scheffer, Arch. of Neurol. and Psychiat. 1931, Vol. 25, p. 758.)

cortical cells which is described as toxic encephalopathy. In fact, Ferraro has published cases in which such changes were the only lesions demonstrable. Wohlwil, however, states the cellular changes described by Ferraro have no significance whatever. The meninges show very little, merely some edema and a few foci of lymphocytic infiltration.

Clinical Features.—It is probable that encephalomyelitis occurs in connection with measles more frequently than with any other infectious disease of childhood although the incidence is low even in measles. Hodes estimates that one child in 1200 with measles gets encephalomyelitis.

There is no obvious tendency to select either sex. Encephalomyelitis is most common between one and ten years but may occur at any age. As a rule, it is more apt to occur in severe cases of measles but there is no constant parallelism between the severity of the somatic symptoms and the occurrence of encephalomyelitis. Encephalomyelitis is rare in measles modified by gamma globulin but sometimes occurs.

A number of syndromes occur and it is necessary to discuss these separately for didactic purposes although there is, of course, much overlapping. I shall distinguish the following types: (1) Symptoms of diffuse cerebral involvement of brief duration, often termed "meningism." (2) Signs of multiple focal or diffuse lesions in the nervous system. (3) Signs of single focal cerebral lesions. (4) Cerebellar syndromes. (5) Spinal syndromes. (6) Optic neuritis.

Symptoms of Diffuse Cerebral Involvement of Brief Duration.—The onset is usually between the fourth and the sixth day of the eruption when the temperature has already begun to fall and the eruption to fade. Often the temperature may have been normal for twelve hours or more and convalescence may seem to have begun. At this period there is a sudden rise of

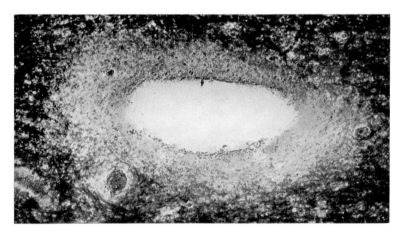

Fig. 163. Higher magnification of one of the lesions shown above.

temperature which may reach 105°F. and the child becomes very drowsy or even stuporous. In a few cases the nervous symptoms may occur at the height of the fever or even before the rash has appeared. The latter is very rare, however. Hodes suggests that in such cases we are dealing with direct effect of the virus infection. Cases have been reported in which the nervous symptoms were delayed until two or three weeks after the beginning of the illness. When the latent period is a very long one, some skepticism about the diagnosis is permissible.

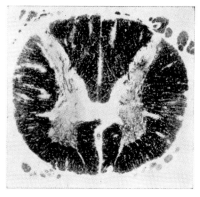

Fig. 164. Perivascular demyelination in the spinal cord. (Greenfield, Jour. of Path. and Bacteriol. 1930, Vol. 33, p. 456.)

The drowsiness may deepen into stupor or even coma. Headache, vomiting, dilatation of the pupils, muscular twitchings and even convulsions may appear within a few hours of the onset. There is almost invariably some cervical rigidity. The course is a very short one. Despite the alarming nature of the symptoms, the child may seem to be quite well within two or three days. Convalescence is, as a rule, uneventful, but in some cases there is a very striking irritability and lack of emotional control which may last several weeks.

The spinal fluid is under increased pressure and there is usually a moderate increase in the cell count ranging from 20 to 200. The cells are almost exclusively lymphocytes but a few polymorphonuclear leucocytes may be found, especially in the early stages of the illness. There is a moderate increase in the globulin and total protein content. The sugar is either normal or slightly decreased.

The characteristic features of this group of cases are the absence of definite focal signs and the prompt and complete recovery. Such cases are rarely reported but it is not unlikely that they are really the commonest of all.

This clinical picture is similar to the so-called *meningism* which may occur at the onset of almost any acute febrile illness in infancy. Denny-Brown finds edema of the brain at post-mortem examination in such cases and states that this may be severe enough to cause fatal herniation of the medulla when spinal puncture is performed. This edema is believed to be a result of a sudden drop in the serum electrolytes.

Signs of Multiple Focal or Diffuse Lesions in the Nervous System.—In certain cases there is definite evidence of a destructive process in the nervous system. The onset is identical with that described above. Indeed, the neurological picture is the same at first. The stupor is more profound or replaced by coma, however, and is of longer duration. Respiration is often slow or irregular and may be of the Cheyne-Stokes type. The optic nerve heads are usually congested and may show actual edema. The tendon reflexes are usually altered, being either increased or diminished. As a rule, the knee jerks are diminished or lost at first and become increased during convalescence. The plantar response is often of the extensor type on one or both sides. Retention of urine is common. As a rule, there is some diffuse muscular rigidity but in some cases, especially in those in which the onset is abrupt or fulminating, there may be complete atonia for a few days. There may be paresis of one or both sixth nerves but definite paralysis of the cranial nerves is rare. Sudden deafness of one ear is not uncommon. Sometimes weakness or paralysis of the bulbar muscles occurs. The child may die within a few days after the onset while still in deep coma. Usually, however, consciousness begins to return within a period of one or two weeks. A number of neurological signs and symptoms are now revealed. Most commonly there is paraparesis or paraplegia and only moderate weakness of the arms. Monoplegias and hemiplegias are uncommon. As a rule, the palsies are associated with some spasticity and the usual signs of involvement of the pyramidal tract, but it is not uncommon to find a few atrophic and flaccid muscles which suggest damage to the anterior horn cells in the spinal cord. Extensive paralyses with atrophy and permanent loss of reflexes are rare. In many cases there is pronounced ataxia which is usually of cerebellar type. Various tremors are not uncommon. One type is known as *acute tremor*. This is described as a rhythmical tremor of slow rate which affects the head, face and arms and which is often associated with muscular rigidity, slowness of movement and incoordination. Its anatomical basis is uncertain but most authorities attribute it to lesions in the basal ganglia of the forebrain. Choreic syndromes and athetosis are described. Several types of disturbance of speech may occur. Most often this is due to bulbar palsy but it may also be due to partial aphasia or to cerebellar involvement. Mental changes are almost invariably present for a time in severe cases. Most frequently, there is restlessness, irritability and loss of emotional control. There may be unmotivated screaming for days or weeks. The child may make use of the vilest language at its command. Sleep is irregular in most cases but prolonged somnolence may occur. These symptoms improve slowly during the next few weeks or months but may not disappear for years. Less commonly there is prolonged delirium and drowsiness. This is apt to be followed by definite defect of intelligence.

Signs of Single Focal Cerebral Lesions.—In some cases, hemiplegia, aphasia or hemianopia may follow measles. These syndromes may occur in association with other symptoms as described above or they may occur suddenly in an apoplectic fashion as if due to a gross vascular lesion. In the last case there are often convulsions on the affected sides and loss of consciousness for a time. The relation of such symptoms to the measles is not quite clear and it is probable that they result from non-specific lesions in the vessels which may occur as a result of many infectious diseases.

Cerebellar Syndromes.—It is not unusual to find during convalescence from measles all the usual signs of cerebellar ataxia including loss of muscle tone, scanning speech, nystagmus, intention tremor and typical gait. The cerebellar ataxia is usually bilateral but may be unilateral. As a rule, such symptoms are not evident during the acute stage of the disease and attract attention only during convalescence when the child begins to be more active. It sometimes happens that there is no suspicion of serious damage to the nervous system until the child is allowed out of bed for the first time and it is then found that he is unable to walk because of profound ataxia. Perfectly pure cerebellar syndromes are rare, but cerebellar ataxia is very often the most striking feature of measles encephalomyelitis. Indeed, measles is responsible for a large percentage of the so-called acute cerebellar ataxias. Griffith found 8 cases due to measles in his series of 31 cases of acute ataxia of childhood.

Spinal Syndromes.—It has been stated above that the spinal cord is frequently involved in the course of measles encephalomyelitis and it is not unusual to find paraplegia and retention of urine in association with stupor, convulsions and other symptoms referable to the cerebrum. In other cases, the patient's mind is quite clear and the symptoms point to the spinal cord alone. The picture may be that of a transverse myelitis, of disseminated myelitis or of an ascending myelitis. The paralysis is usually flaccid at first, the tendon reflexes are lost, the plantar response is extensor, there is retention of urine and more or less loss of sensibility over the lower part of the body. Usually the tendon reflexes return and eventually become increased as spasticity develops, but in a few cases of paralysis results in permanent loss of reflexes and atrophy of some muscles. The disturbances of sensibility usually disappear within a short time but the paralysis may be slow to improve and may persist to some degree for an indefinite period. In a few exceptional cases an acute ascending paralysis without sensory loss has occurred. The writer has also seen two cases in which there was merely paralysis and atrophy of certain muscles with loss of reflexes. These cases were so similar to the common infantile paralysis that the diagnosis would have been impossible had it not been for the appearance of the paralysis on the fourth day of the eruption. Death may result from ascending paralysis which causes paralysis of the muscles of respiration, from infection of the urinary tract or septic decubitus ulcers.

Optic Neuritis.—It is not unusual for the optic nerve heads to show mild

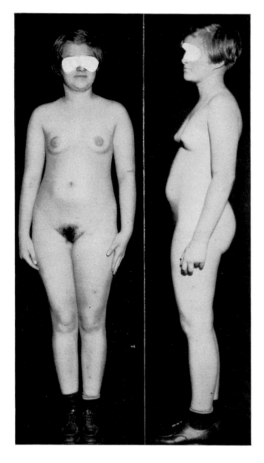

FIG. 165. (Ped. 99210). Showing premature development of secondary sexual characteristics following measles encephalomyelitis. The child was mentally deficient and subject to convulsions but the neurological examination was negative.

congestion and perhaps some edema during the acute stages of measles encephalomyelitis. Since the spinal fluid is often under increased pressure, some observers have regarded these changes as a result of cerebral edema. However, in some cases there is also reduction of vision and even transient blindness which may be taken to indicate optic neuritis. Two types are seen, the optic neuritis with edema of the disc and often hemorrhages and the retrobulbar neuritis with little or no change in the papilla. In both cases we find central scotomas. The prognosis is good.

Developmental Disorders.—Occasionally sexual precocity occurs following an attack of measles encephalitis. Obesity may be associated. Most such cases have been observed in girls, but Apley reports a very striking case of precocious puberty in a boy of four years.

Diagnosis.—The diagnosis is rarely difficult if the child is seen at the onset of nervous symptoms, for even if no history of measles can be obtained, the presence of a fading eruption should make the cause evident. The possibility of coincident poliomyelitis or tuberculous meningitis should be kept in mind. As a rule, the course of the disease makes the diagnosis evident in a short time. If the patient does not come under observation until years after the acute illness and a proper history cannot be elicited, the diagnosis can scarcely be established, for there are several other diseases which may give rise to identical symptoms. Hodes, Livingston and others have shown that during the acute stages of measles encephalitis there are abnormally slow, high voltage waves in all leads of the electroencephalogram. These abnormalities persist for a time after clinical recovery. The virus may be demonstrated in the urine within two days of the development of the rash Gresser and Katz have shown.

Prognosis.—The prognosis for life is relatively favorable and not more than 10 per cent of the patients die in the acute stages. Probably the actual mortality is lower, for many mild cases are not taken into consideration. Unfortunately, nearly half of the children who survive show more or less definite evidence of permanent damage to the central nervous system. If we may judge from the case reports found in the medical literature, paralysis, especially spastic paraplegia, is the commonest residuum and cerebellar ataxia is also very frequent, whereas mental changes and epilepsy are relatively rare. In our experience, based upon a number of cases which have been followed for from five to ten years, mental changes are most common of all and are found in nearly one third of the cases. As a rule, the mental changes are not very severe. There is moderate reduction of intelligence, more or less irritability and instability of mood. Epilepsy is not unusual.

Treatment.—Odessky *et al.* recommend the intramuscular injection of gamma globulin as soon as signs of encephalitis appear. The total dosage should not be less than 1.0 cc per pound of body weight. It is suggested that this be administered in three doses at intervals of 12 hours. Oxygen, anticonvulsive therapy and the proper control of fluid and electrolyte balance are all important. Antibiotics may be needed to prevent pneumonia. Miller advises the use of ACTH. If this process is an allergic one as many authorities believe, the use of this drug would seem to be quite logical. Allen believes such treatment is helpful. Hodes states that gamma globulin is ineffectual and ACTH and cortisone should not be used. Allen and Frank advise modifying measles in every case by the use of gamma globulin in the hope of preventing encephalitis.

Enders has developed a vaccine containing living virus which gives immunity and causes merely a mild illness. A vaccine containing a killed virus is being developed. It is claimed that active immunity against measles without dangerous reaction may be conferred by injection of modified measles virus and human immune globulin.

The present program is to give the child two injections of killed measles virus and then a third injection of attenuated virus.

CASE HISTORY (Ped. 8209).—*Measles encephalitis without focal signs. Child of six years developed convulsions on the fifth day of measles. Stuporous for several days. Cerebrospinal fluid contained 130 lymphocytes. Rapid recovery without residuum.*

W. E., boy of six years, was brought to Harriet Lane Home in stupor on the fifth day of an attack of measles. The onset of measles was attended by cough, coryza and conjunctivitis. The eruption appeared on the next day. On the third day he seemed somewhat better but the next evening he was miserable and cried all night. On the morning of the fifth day he had five general convulsions, became stuporous and was brought to the hospital.

Examination revealed a fading eruption over the body and general enlargement of the lymph nodes. The child was stuporous and could not be aroused for more than a moment. Temperature 98.6°F. The neck was not stiff and Kernig's sign was negative. Cerebrospinal fluid pressure increased. Globulin positive. Wassermann negative. No film formation. Cells 130, all mononuclear. W.B.C. 22,100.

The first night temperature rose to 101.2°F. but soon fell to normal. Rapid improvement ensued. On the ninth day cerebrospinal fluid showed 23 cells and the globulin was faintly positive. On the eleventh day, cells were only 8 and the globulin was negative. The patient was discharged on the twelfth day. He was seen again three weeks later and once more after two years. Recovery was complete.

CASE HISTORY (Ped. 18248).—*Measles encephalomyelitis with disseminated lesions in the brain and spinal cord. Child of five years and 10 months became stuporous during convalescence from measles. Six weeks later could not talk, sit up or hold up head. Gradual improvement but seven years later gait was still spastic, general convulsions were present and there were personality changes and reduction of intelligence.*

J. L., a boy of five years and ten months, had a severe attack of measles. He was in bed three days and then permitted to play about the house. About the sixth day he refused to eat, complained of headache and seemed very drowsy and ill. On the next day he became stuporous. The legs were drawn up and rigid. Three weeks after the onset he was brought to the hospital.

Examination revealed small pigmented areas over the body which were taken to be remnants of the eruption. He was very dull and querulous. There was a good deal of weakness of the arms and legs, especially marked on the right side. Both legs were slightly spastic. The left knee jerk was feeble, the right absent. Plantar reflexes extensor. Cerebrospinal fluid: cells 7, globulin 0, Wassermann negative. W.B.C. 9200.

Six weeks after the onset there was little improvement. The child still seemed mentally confused and mumbled incoherently. All four limbs could be moved but strength was very feeble. He could not sit up or hold up his head. There was no sphincter control.

Nine weeks after the onset, speech was nearly normal. The child could stand and walk but gait was spastic.

Seven years after the illness, the patient was reexamined. He was very restless and irritable and there was a fine tremor of the hands. For one year he had been having general convulsions with loss of consciousness. Gait was slightly spastic. Psychiatric examination revealed a mental age of ten years as against a chronological age of 13 years.

CASE HISTORY (H-7152).—*Single focal cerebral lesion following measles. Measles at the age of four years with sudden focal convulsions, coma, right hemiplegia and aphasia. Gradual recovery of speech, disappearance of hemiplegia but persistence of hemianopia. Focal convulsions recurred from time to time. Some mental defect and childish speech.*

E. K., a previously healthy child, developed a severe attack of measles at the age of 4 years. She was afebrile at the end of a week and seemed to be convalescing satisfactorily until the tenth day when she was suddenly seized with severe convulsions confined to the right side of the body and lapsed into coma. The convulsions lasted at intervals all that day and until noon of the following day. Late the next day she began to regain consciousness and soon it was evident that she had lost her speech and was completely paralysed on the right side. The hemiplegia disappeared within two months but speech returned very slowly. For several years she could use only a few words and formed only short sentences as a child might do who was just learning to talk. Later she learned to speak more fluently but her speech always resembled that of a child. About a year after the onset of the illness the patient began to have convulsive seizures which started on the right side and were usually confined to that side, although they sometimes became generalized. There were also periods of confusion without definite convulsions. These attacks were preceded by bright lights before the eyes which were seen only in the right visual fields. The attacks were diminished by luminal and bromides but could never be controlled satisfactorily.

Examination at the age of 11 years revealed a complete right homonymous hemianopia but no evidence of hemiplegia or hemianesthesia. The patient could read, write and understand what was said to her. However, she used short words and sentences and spoke with a childish lisp so that her speech would have been appropriate for a child of three or four years.

The patient has been seen at frequent intervals and is now a young woman of 18 years. There has been no further change in her condition. She still has focal attacks on the right side and still speaks with a childish accent. She is unable to do any remunerative work.

CASE HISTORY (Ped. 28523).—*Measles encephalomyelitis with severe cerebellar ataxia. Child of two years developed convulsions during the course of measles. During convalescence, gross ataxia of all extremities appeared with spasticity of left arm and leg. Gradual improvement but persisting mental defect, ataxia and petit mal.*

D. G., a girl of two years and six months, developed a severe attack of measles and was in bed for several weeks. About the end of the first week there were a number of convulsions. After these she was very ill and drowsy but no definite neurological symptoms were observed until she attempted to walk. It was then found that she could not control her arms and legs. About eight months after the illness she was brought to the hospital.

Examination revealed normal development and adequate nutrition. The cranial nerves were normal. Strength was slightly diminished in the left arm and leg and there was some spasticity and increase in the tendon reflexes on that side. The plantar reflex was extensor on both sides. The most striking finding, however, was a very marked ataxia of cerebellar type in all four extremities. The child could not stand without support. Blood and spinal fluid examinations were quite negative.

Reexamination 10 years after the onset revealed a well-nourished, well-developed girl of 13 years. She had been unable to pass the required tests in public school and was going to a special class. However, she was good natured and well behaved. Marked cerebellar ataxia was still present in arms and legs. The tendon reflexes in the legs were slightly increased and Babinski's sign was positive on both sides. For two months she had been subject to attacks of petit mal. Two years later there was no change. The petit mal continued.

CASE HISTORY.—*Case of measles myelitis resembling poliomyelitis. Boy of seven years developed severe case of measles followed by weakness and atrophy of left thigh and diminution of reflexes.*

J. S., healthy boy of seven years, developed a severe case of measles which confined him to bed for two weeks. The fever reached 105°F. but there was no delirium. The patient complained of pains in the legs but there was no paralysis and no loss of control of the bladder. At the end of two weeks he was allowed out of bed. It was then discovered that he limped very badly on the left leg and that that leg was very weak.

Examination revealed marked weakness of the extensors of the hip, the extensors of the knee, the hamstrings and the extensors of the ankle on the left. No loss of sensibility. Left knee and ankle jerks lost. Otherwise examination was negative.

Reexamination three months later revealed improvement but still a definite loss of power in the left leg. The calf and thigh were both somewhat atrophic. The weakness was most marked in the gluteus medius, gluteus maximus and hamstrings. The extensors of the ankle were slightly weak and the quadriceps also slightly weak. Tone was diminished in the affected muscles. The ankle jerk was diminished but present. No disturbance of sphincter control. No change in sensibility. Plantar reflex normal.

CASE HISTORY (U-65767).—*Measles myelitis with spastic paraplegia. Girl of four years developed paralysis of the legs, anesthesia of the lower half of the body and loss of sphincter control during a severe attack of measles. Gradual improvement in gait but persistent frequency and urgency of urination.*

M. B., healthy child of four years, had a severe attack of measles. On the sixth day of the illness she became incontinent and when she was able to get out of bed at the end of ten days, it was found that her legs were almost completely paralysed and that she could not walk or stand. No delirium or other cerebral symptoms were noted at any time. Examination revealed that the patient had partial anesthesia over the lower half of the body. There was gradual improvement in the strength of the legs and the patient could walk again within a year. She was entirely incontinent of both urine and feces during the day and night for about five years. After that she could retain the urine during the day but would wet the bed at night. Laxatives were apt to cause fecal incontinence. Ten years later she was able to walk almost normally.

Examination revealed moderate spasticity of the legs with increased tendon reflexes, ankle clonus and Babinski response. There was no demonstrable loss of sensibility. The bladder was found to show the disturbances found in disease of the pyramidal tracts.

CASE HISTORY (Ped. 87087).—*Measles encephalomyelitis associated with. prolonged stupor but followed by complete recovery except for retrobulbar neuritis, precocious puberty and some personality changes.*

C. J., a girl of nine years, developed measles December 31, 1933. She was not ill and on January 2, 1934, the rash was beginning to fade and her temperature was normal. On the next day she vomited and became drowsy, her temperature was found to be 105°F. and within a few hours she developed generalized movements of choreiform type and became delirious. There was severe trismus. The next day she was in a deep stupor. The stupor persisted for almost a full month and was associated with paralysis of the arms, legs and bulbar muscles. The patient was given food by gavage. She seemed to be totally blind. There was retention of urine.

At the end of a month, the stupor was beginning to clear, some movement returned in the left leg and later in the left arm. Some days after this there was return of power in the right arm and leg and then the bulbar palsy began to improve. Strength returned very rapidly and by March the child could take a few steps and could use her hands to feed herself. Speech was still altered but was easily comprehensible. Vision was present but the patient could scarcely distinguish her parents' faces. At this time she was intensely irritable and restless. The least provocation produced screaming spells and temper tantrums.

In April the child's general condition was much improved and she could walk and talk normally. She now began to menstruate and her breasts began to develop despite the fact that she was just 10 years old. There was frequent masturbation.

Examination on May 5, 1934, revealed a tall, slender girl of 10 years who was restless and irritable, but evidently of more than average intelligence. The changes of puberty were already well advanced, there was some axillary and pubic hair and the breasts were of adolescent type. The right pupil was slightly larger than the left and reacted less promptly. Vision in the right eye was 20/80 and in the left eye 20/20. There was a large central scotoma on the right which was absolute for color; no scotoma was found on the left. The right optic disc showed definite temporal pallor; the left showed slight temporal pallor. Neurological examination was otherwise negative.

In February, 1936, the child returned for examination. The vision in the right eye was now 20/50 and the scotoma had decreased in size. Her behavior was somewhat better and she was not so restless or irritable as before.

CASE HISTORY (U-63550).—*Boy of eight years developed bilateral retrobulbar neuritis with central scotomas on the sixth day of an attack of measles. Gradual improvement in the next six weeks. No other neurological findings.*

J. H., Jr., developed measles at the age of eight years. He did not seem to be very ill and would not stay in bed. On the sixth day, however, after he had seemed quite well for a day or two, he suddenly began to complain of headache and talked as if he were confused. He was never stuporous and showed no paralysis or loss of sphincter control. Two days later it was found that his vision was almost entirely lost, for he could not see his mother's hand when it was held before his face.

Three weeks after the onset, he seemed to be restored to health except for his loss of vision. He was taken to an ophthalmologist who found vision of the left eye 5/500 and of the right eye 1/500. There were large central scotomas on either side but the optic nerve heads were of normal color.

Vision improved rapidly after this so that six weeks after the onset vision of the right eye was 20/40 and of the left eye was 20/20. The scotoma on the right was smaller and that on the left had disappeared. There was moderate pallor of the temporal side of each optic disc. Neurological examination was entirely negative in other respects.

CASE HISTORY (Ped. 99210).—*Measles encephalitis with three weeks of somnolence in a girl of six and one-half years. Mental deficiency and personality changes evident on recovery, soon followed by recurrent convulsions. Secondary sexual characteristics began to develop four months after the onset of the illness.*

S. S., a girl of 10 years, was brought to the Harriet Lane Home for examination on October 9, 1936, because of convulsions and abnormal behavior. These symptoms had followed an attack of measles at the age of six and one-half years. She had been a healthy child before this illness and her mental development had been excellent. At the time the measles interrupted her progress she was leading her class of 55 children.

The measles occurred in March 1933. The child did not seem to be especially ill and the temperature reached normal on the fifth day. On the seventh day her temperature rose to 106°F., she had a series of violent general convulsions and became unconscious. The convulsions soon ceased but the patient remained in a state of somnolence for three weeks. As improvement took place it became apparent that profound mental changes had occurred. She was restless, irritable and destructive. It was impossible for her to learn and she had to be withdrawn from school. Convulsions occurred at intervals of two or three months. In July 1933, just four months after the measles and one month before she had attained the age of seven years her breasts began to develop rapidly and pubic and axillary hair appeared. A year later she began to menstruate and menstruation continued with only slight irregularity.

Physical examination revealed a well nourished girl of 10 years, slightly above the average height for her age, who was restless and distractible and laughed foolishly. The secondary sexual characteristics were well developed. Otherwise there were no physical abnormalities and detailed neurological examination was negative. The Binet test revealed an intelligence quotient of 61.

CASE HISTORY (Ped. A-5030).—*Measles encephalitis with muscular rigidity, tremor and slowing of movements constituting a mild acute Parkinsonian syndrome.*

W. L. M., previously healthy boy of three and one-half years, developed coryza and slight fever in December 1937. A few days later he developed a morbilliform rash and began to complain of headache. After six days the temperature declined to normal and the rash began to fade. The next day the child was drowsy and his speech was slow and indistinct. Shortly after this he could not form words and made merely inarticulate sounds. He had some difficulty in swallowing and drooled saliva. The right arm was held in flexion, there was tremor of both hands and gait was unsteady. During the period in which these symptoms were developing, which was about five days, the temperature was somewhat elevated.

The patient was brought to the hospital on about the seventh day after the neurological symptoms had first appeared. He was very restless and querulous. He talked constantly in a monotonous voice but articulation was so indistinct that it was impossible to understand him. He showed an almost constant rhythmical tremor of both hands only partially inhibited by movement and there was definite rigidity with cogwheel phenomenon demonstrable in both arms. The gait was uncertain and clumsy but probably not ataxic. The legs were also rigid and the knee and ankle jerks were exaggerated, being greater on the right than the left. The right plantar reflex was equivocal, the left was normal. Temperature was normal and the spinal fluid examination was quite negative.

The child improved rapidly and on January 20, the tremor had ceased, articulation was so clear that his words were easily comprehensible, the gait was better and the knee jerks were only slightly exaggerated.

CASE HISTORY (Path. 6378. Surg. 36118).—*Measles at 7 months followed by left hemiplegia. Focal epilspey on the left. Mental defect. Death at the age of 15 years. Post-mortem examination revealed old softening in the right hemisphere.*

A. McK. was a healthy baby until the age of 7 months. At that age she developed a severe attack of measles. Shortly after she seemed to have recovered, she suddenly fell to the floor and was found to have a left hemiplegia. Some power in the left arm and leg eventually returned and the child was able to walk, but the left arm was never useful. Her mental development was somewhat retarded. At the age of 4 years, the child began to have convulsive seizures which would begin on the left side, usually in the arm, and would eventually spread to the right side. These recurred from time to time and sometimes several would develop during one day. Operation was performed at the age of 10 years and the right hemisphere exposed by Dr. Dandy. There was a large defect in the superior convolution of the right temporal lobe which extended up along the fissure of Rolando involving the motor cortex and adjacent regions. This was due to thrombosis of the cortical branches of the right middle cerebral artery. The child was not benefited by operation and eventually died at the age of 15 years after a series of violent convulsions. Post-mortem examination of the brain revealed merely the lesions observed at operation.

BIBLIOGRAPHY

ALLEN, J. E.: The treatment of measles encephalitis. Pediatrics, **20**:87, 1957.

ALLEN, J. E. AND FRANK, D. J.: The use of gamma globulin in the treatment of measles encephalitis. Pediatrics, Jan., 1956.

APLEY, J.: Sexual precocity in boy after measles encephalitis. Arch. Dis. Child., **27**:584, 1952.

APPLEBAUM, E. *et al.*: Treatment of measles encephalitis with corticotropin. Jour. Dis. Child., **92**:147, 1956.

BARLOW, T.: On a case of early disseminated myelitis occurring in the exanthem stage of measles and fatal on the eleventh day of that disease. Med. Chirur. Trs., London, **70**:77, 1887.

BERGENFELDT, E.: Myelitis as a complication of measles. Acta Med. Scandinav. (in German), **61**:281, 1924.

BLAW, M. E. AND SHEEHAN, J. C.: Acute cerebellar syndromes of childhood. Neurology, **8**:538, 1958.

BOENHEIM, C.: Ueber nervöse Komplikationen bei spezifisch-kindlichen Infektionskrankheiten. Ergebn. d. inn. Med. u. Kinderh., **28**:598, 1925.

———: Zur Frage der nervösen Komplikationen bei spezifisch-kindlichen Infektionskrankheiten und Vaccination. Berl. klin. Wchnschr., **6**:1552, 1927.

BOX, C. R.: Acute ascending paralysis. Lancet, **1**:222, 1921.

BURNSTEINE, R. C. AND PAINE, R. S.: Residual encephalopathy following roseola infantum. J. Dis. Child., **98**:144, 1959.

DENNY-BROWN, D. E.: The changing pattern of neurologic medicine. New England J. Med., **246**:839, 1952.

FERRARO, A. AND SCHEFFER, I. H.: Toxic encephalopathy in measles. Arch. Neurol. & Psychiat., **27**:1209, 1932.

FORD, F. R. AND GUILD, M.: Precocious puberty after measles encephalomyelitis and epidemic encephalitis. Bull. Johns Hopkins Hosp., **60**:192, 1937.

FORD, F. R.: The nervous complications of measles, with a summary of the literature and publications of twelve additional case reports. Bull. Johns Hopkins Hosp., **43**:140, 1928.

GREENFIELD, J. G.: The pathology of measles encephalomyelitis. Brain, **52**:171, 1929.

GRESSER, I. AND KATZ, S.: Isolation of measles virus from urine. New England J. Med., **263**:452, 1960.

HALLIDAY, P. B.: Pre-eruptive neurological complications of the common contagious diseases, rubella, rubeola and varicella. J. Pediat., **36**:185, 1950.

HAMILTON, P. M. AND HANNA, R. J.: Encephalitis complicating measles: A report on 241 cases collected from the literature and 44 additional cases. Am. J. Dis. Child., **61**:483, 1941.

HODES, H. L. AND LIVINGSTON, S.: Electroencephalographic findings in measles encephalitis. J. Pediat., **36**:577, 1950.

HOYNE, A. L. AND SLOTKOWSKI, E. L.: Frequency of encephalitis as a complication of measles. Am. J. Dis. Child., **73**:554, 1947.

JACK, O.: Measles encephalitis. Jour. Pediat., **40**:383, 1952.

KARELITZ, M. *et al.*: Measles encephalitis. Pediatrics, **5**:599, 1950.

KARELITZ, S. AND EISENBERG, M.: Sequelae of measles encephalitis. Pediatrics, **27**:811, 1961.

KATZ, S. L. AND ENDERS, J. F.: Measles Virus. Viral and Rickettsial Infections of Man. Edited by Horsfall, F. L. and Tamm, I. J. B. Lippincott Co., 4th Ed., 1965, p. 784.

LITVAK, A. M., SANDS, I. J. AND GIBEL, H.: Encephalitis complicating measles. Report of 56 cases with follow up study of 32. Am. J. Dis. Child., **65**:265, 1943.

MALMUD, N.: Sequelae of postmeasles encephalomyelitis. A clinicopathologic study. Arch. Neurol. & Psychiat., **41**:943, 1939.

————: Encephalomyelitis complicating measles. Arch. Neurol. & Psychiat., **38**:1025, 1937.

MEYER, E. AND BYERS, R. K.: Measles encephalitis. Jour. Dis. Child., **84**:543, 1952.

MILLER, H.: Neurologic complications of acute specific fevers. Proc. Roy. Soc. Med., **49**:139, 1956.

MILLER, H. G.: Acute disseminated encephalomyelitis treated with acth. Brit. Med. J., **i**:177, 1953.

ODESSKY, L., BEDO, A. *et al.*: Therapeutic doses of gamma globulin in treatment of measles encephalitis. J. Pediat., **43**:536, 1953.

PAINE, R. S. AND BYERS, R. K.: Transverse myelopathy in childhood. Jour. Dis. Child., **85**:151, 1953.

REILLY, C. M. *et al.*: Measles vaccination in early infancy. New England J. Med., **265**:165, 1961.

ROZYCKI, T.: Measles encephalitis. Rhode Island Med. Jour., **50**:34, 1967.

RUSSELL, D.: The nosological unity of acute hemorrhagic leucoencephalopathy and acute disseminated encephalomyelitis. Brain, **78**:369, 1955.

SWANSON, B. E.: Measles meningoencephalitis. Jour. Dis. Child., **92**:272, 1956.

WALSH, F. B.: *Loc. cit.*

WALTHARD, K. M.: Spatstadium einer "Encephalitis" nach Masern Bemerkungen zur Histologie und Pathogenese. Ztschr. f. d. ges. Neurol. u. Psychiat., **124**:176, 1930.

WOHLWILL, F.: Review of Article by Ferraro and Scheffer. Zentralbl. f. d. ges. Neurol. u. Psychiat., **65**:238, 1932.

————: Über Encephalomyelitis bei Masern. Ztschr. f. d. ges. Neurol. u. Psychiat., **112**:20, 1928.

ENCEPHALOMYELITIS FOLLOWING GERMAN MEASLES

A number of cases of encephalomyelitis following German measles, or rubella, have been reported. According to Margolis who studied a large epidemic of this disease, one case of encephalomyelitis may occur in every 6,000 cases. The nervous symptoms began as a rule on the fourth day of the rash when the temperature rises and the leucopenia is replaced by a leu-cocytosis. Headache, stiffness of the neck and convulsions then develop and the child may pass into coma. The tendon reflexes are apt to be increased and Babinski's sign may be found. Unequal pupils are mentioned. The spinal fluid contains from 8 to 500 cells per cmm. The course is very brief and in three or four days the symptoms begin to recede. There were 4 deaths among the 14 patients in the series of Margolis. If the child survives the prognosis for recovery is excellent. Margolis mentions that one child still showed ataxia four months after the illness but can discover no other cases in which definite residua persisted.

Several post-mortem studies of the nervous system have been made. It seems to be agreed that there are perivascular infiltrations with lympho-cytes, plasma cells and even leucocytes and some mild changes in the neu-rons. These lesions are widely disseminated in both the gray and white mat-ter. No pronounced demyelination has yet been described so the process would seem to differ in this respect from that seen in measles encephalitis. The meninges show a mild reaction.

BIBLIOGRAPHY

BRIGGS, J. F.: Meningoencephalitis following rubella, 7:609, 1935.

BROCK, J. H. E.: Meningoencephalitis following German measles. Lancet, 2:1190, 1929.

CANTWELL, R. J.: Rubella encephalitis. Brit. Med. Jour., 5059:1471, 1957.

DAVISON, C.: Acute encephalomyelitis following German measles. Amer. Jour. Dis. Child., 55:496, 1938.

FRIEDFELD, L. AND DAVISON, C.: Acute encephalomyelitis following German measles. Am. J. Dis. Child., 55:496, 1938.

MARGOLIS, F. J., WILSON, J. L. AND TOP, F. H.: Post-Rubella encephalomyelitis. J. Pediat., 23:158, 1943.

MERRITT, H. H. AND KASKOFF, Y. D.: Encephalomyelitis following German measles. Am. J. Med. Sc., 191:690, 1936.

MITCHELL, W.: Neurologic and mental complications of rubella. Lancet, 2:1250, 1954.

SEVER, J. L. *et al.*: Isolation of the rubella virus. J.A.M.A., 182:663, 1962.

SIGURJONSSON, J.: Rubella and congenital deafness. Amer. Jour. Med. Sci., 242:712, 1961.

CONGENITAL RUBELLA (GERMAN MEASLES)

In 1941 Gregg, an Australian ophthalmologist published a paper in which he called attention to the association between German measles in the pregnant mother and defects of development in the baby. In 78 cases there were congenital cataracts and in 44 cases there were congenital defects of the heart. All of the children were mentally defective and most were of small stature and poorly nourished. With few exceptions there was a clear history of German measles in the first 2 months of pregnancy.

Karmody points out that congenital deafness may result from asympto-matic maternal rubella. The diagnosis is made by serological tests.

Two years later, Swan and his co-workers published a study of 49 cases of rubella which had occurred during pregnancy. In 25 cases the illness had occurred in the first two months and in every instance the child was defective. In 8 cases the disease developed in the third month and in just half of these was the child malformed. Of 16 children born of mothers whose illness developed after the third month, only 2 were defective. There were 31 children all told. Among these were 17 congenital defects of the heart, 14 ocular defects, 7 deaf-mutes and several cases of mental deficiency, microcephaly and hypospadias. Erickson has published a study of 11 cases of German measles in the first month of pregnancy in the United States. All of the children were defective. He found 9 cases of congenital cataract, 3 cases of microphthalmia, 2 cases of mental deficiency and no cardiac abnormalities. We have seen several instances of cataracts, congenital heart disease and spastic diplegia.

The congenital cataracts are of a special type. They are usually but not always bilateral. When the pupils are dilated, they appear as dense white discs with 6 radiating lines. There may be a clear zone peripheral to the density. Microphthalmia is usually present. The lens is small and the anterior chamber shallow. Buphthalmia is described. Loss of fixation causes nystagmus. Discussion is recommended as soon as possible. Changes in the retinae similar to those of pigmentary degeneration are described.

Congenital heart disease involves stenosis of the pulmonary artery at one or more sites in half of all cases. The defects include patent ductus arteriosus, pulmonary valvular stenosis, pulmonary infundibular stenosis, defects in the intraventricular septum and the tetrology of Fallot.

The deafness which is only partial in most cases is not associated with any defect in the drum or the external canal. There are said to be defects in the basal coil of the cochlea.

Not many detailed neurological examinations are published. Congenital diplegia occurs and mental deficiency is usually associated. Convulsions occur in many cases. Friedman and Cohen found defective development of the cerebral cortex, internal capsule and cerebellum and agenesis of corpus callosum.

Desmond *et al.* state that there is a generalized infection with the rubella virus in utero and the infection may be active for 4 to 6 months after birth. About 20 per cent of these babies die in infancy. There may be thrombocytopenia, anemia, hepatitis, pneumonia, rhinitis, otitis, enlargement of the spleen, congestive heart failure, diarrhea and deficient calcification of the skeleton as well as the skull which shows wide sutures. Zinkhan *et al.* state that the anemia is characterized by abnormally shaped red cells, normoblasts and reticulocytes. An odd finding is phagocytosis of the other blood cells by the reticulocytes.

Encephalitis may be evident at birth or may develop later. The anterior fontanel is bulging and there is an excess of protein in the spinal fluid. The child is lethargic, hypotonic and inactive. Some infants improve between 6 and 12 months. Bodily growth is defective. The circumference of the head is reduced. At post-mortem examination there is leptomeningitis, vasculitis, multiple areas of necrosis and perivascular calcification. The virus may be recovered from the urine, throat, intestinal tract and spinal fluid until the age of 6 months. Gamma globin should be given. Exposure to rubella during pregnancy requires the administration of gamma globulin at once. Ingalls advises that school girls should be exposed to the disease.

Brough *et al.* describe a generalized cutaneous eruption in newborn infants who are premature by weight. There are circular lesions varying from 2 to 7 mm in diameter slightly raised and dark blue to dark magenta. Sections show erythropoiesis. Some of the infants were found to be infected with the cytomegalic virus and some showed evidence of congenital rubella. The authors point out that erythropoietic activity is normally found in embryonic life.

Menser *et al.* find that a reexamination after twenty-five years shows that only five of fifty were mentally backward, only one was severely defective and only four were unable to work. Some were deaf and had cataracts as well as cardiac defects and some had genital defects. Seven of the eleven who had married had children.

ENCEPHALOMYELITIS FOLLOWING VACCINATION AGAINST VARIOLA

Epidemiology.—Attention was first directed to this condition in 1932 when small epidemics of encephalomyelitis appeared, which seemed to have a definite relation to vaccination against smallpox. Sporadic cases had undoubtedly been observed many years before this time but their true nature had not been recognized. The disease has been most prevalent in Holland, England, Germany and Austria. According to the report of the British Committee, about 115 cases had been observed in England up to November, 1930. In Holland approximately 146 cases were reported between 1922 and 1929. In Germany between 1927 and 1929 there were 67 cases and in Austria between 1925 and 1929 there were 81 cases. In other countries there have been a few sporadic cases or none at all. In the United States a number of cases have also been recognized. It is impossible to give any idea of the average incidence. In certain places at certain times more than one case has occurred in every thousand vaccinations and again several million vaccinations have been performed without the discovery of a single case of encephalomyelitis. In Holland between 1922 and 1927 the incidence was about one in 5,000. Recently five million persons were vaccinated in New York City because of an epidemic of smallpox. There were 45 cases of encephalitis. Death occurred in 4 cases. Complete recovery occurred in 38 cases and mild residua persisted in the others.

Encephalomyelitis has usually occurred during periods when many persons were being vaccinated to check an epidemic of smallpox. It follows primary vaccination much more frequently than secondary vaccination. The age incidence is of interest in that infants are almost immune and the vast majority of cases have occurred in children between 4 and 16 years. No age is entirely exempt, but after 30 years the disease is very rare. There is no evidence that this condition is contagious and no disease other than vaccinia has been connected with it. The source of the lymph seems to be of no importance, for in certain localities the use of several varieties of lymph may be followed by encephalomyelitis and the same lymphs may have proved innocuous in other regions. The two sexes are affected with equal frequency. In several cases two children of the same family have developed the disease at the same time, thus suggesting that individual susceptibility may be important. A history of allergy may be elicited.

Etiology.—This is discussed in the introduction to this chapter.

Pathological Anatomy.—The first adequate study of the anatomical changes in the nervous system were made by Turnbull and McIntosh who showed that the process was identical or nearly identical with that of the encephalomyelitis which sometimes follows measles and quite distinct from that of epidemic encephalitis and of acute poliomyelitis.

Clinical Features.—The incubation period is, as a rule, very constant and the symptoms first appear about 10 or 11 days after vaccination. Cases have been reported, however, in which the incubation period was reduced to 2 days or prolonged to 25 days. In cases which follow primary vaccination the onset is apt to appear somewhat earlier.

The local reaction is usually not remarkable in any way and generalized vaccinial eruptions have been noted in only one or two cases. It has been claimed that the disease may follow apparently unsuccessful vaccination.

The onset is rather abrupt, as a rule, and marked by headache, fever, drowsiness and vomiting. Convulsions are apt to occur especially in young subjects. Pain in the back, cervical rigidity and Kernig's sign are almost constant features in the first few days of illness. Within a few hours, the child may pass into stupor and then into coma. The objective neurological signs point to severe injury of the spinal cord. There is usually a bilateral Babinski response and in a large percentage of cases, flaccid paralysis of the legs with loss of tendon reflexes and retention of urine. Loss of sensibility is less common than paralysis but there may be complete anesthesia over the lower part of the body. Hemiplegia and other cerebral palsies are uncommon but have been described. The cranial nerves are not constantly affected. Mild congestion of the optic nerve heads is usually present and even transient papilledema may occur. Palsy of the sixth or of the oculomotor nerves is sometimes observed and bulbar disturbances are reported. Trismus is a common sign and may be so prominent as to suggest tetanus. The clinical picture therefore is very similar to that of measles encephalomyelitis, although in our experience it is somewhat more acute and the spinal cord is involved, as a rule, more intensely. Winkelman describes several cases in which damage to the spinal nerve roots seemed to result from vaccination.

The acute stage is relatively brief and usually lasts from one to two weeks. Convalescence is rapid. The stupor passes off and the palsies begin to recede. As a rule, the tendon reflexes return and eventually become exaggerated for a time. Relapses are mentioned by Greenberg and Appelbaum though they seem to be very unusual.

During the acute stage of the disease, the spinal fluid usually contains from 40 to 90 cells almost all of mononuclear type and there may be mild increase in protein. The cellular reaction is, therefore, less than one would expect from the intensity of the meningeal irritation. In a few cases, normal fluid has been found. The vaccine virus has been recovered from the spinal fluid in a few cases.

Diagnosis.—The diagnosis is based upon the development of the clinical picture described above within 2 to 25 days after vaccination against smallpox.

Prognosis.—The mortality has been very high and averages between 30 and 50 per cent. Death generally occurs between the fifteenth and eighteenth day and is usually associated with coma and bulbar palsy. In other cases, death results from bronchopneumonia, decubitus ulcers or infection of the urinary tract.

If the child survives, there is an astonishing tendency towards recovery and severe sequelae are exceptional. Recovery may be complete, even when there has been extensive paralysis. The writer has examined a girl who was completely paralysed in both legs and incontinent for four months but who had made a perfect recovery in the next few years. Great cavities, smoothly lined with epithelium, were present in her buttocks as a result of bed sores. Another child (Ped. 78594) showed all the signs and symptoms of a complete transverse lesion of the spinal cord with paraplegia-in-flexion for four months but recovered completely.

The writer has observed in three cases paraparesis associated with mild spasticity and increase of the knee jerks which had persisted for several years and promised to be permanent. In one of these children, there was mild mental defect, obesity and precocious development of the breasts at the age of 11 years. Miller mentions paraplegia, hemiplegia, radicular syndromes, dysarthria, epilepsy, and involuntary movements, but states that in few cases were any of these conditions found on reexamination several years later. He states that psychiatric sequelae were common.

In general it seems to be correct to state that in contrast with measles encephalomyelitis, the mortality in vaccinia encephalomyelitis is higher but that residua are less common, and rarely severe. When persisting nervous disorders are observed they are similar to those seen after measles encephalomyelitis although paraparesis is probably more common.

Prophylaxis.—Since infants are almost immune to this condition, vaccination should be performed before the age of one year. Children between the ages of 5 and 16 should not be vaccinated unless directly exposed to smallpox. The Minister of Health of England has recommended that only children in good health should be vaccinated and that it is preferable to make only one insertion unless protection is urgently required. In no circumstances should more than four insertions be made.

Treatment.—See Measles Encephalomyelitis. Special vaccinia-immune gamma globulin derived from the blood of persons recently vaccinated is recommended.

BIBLIOGRAPHY

FERRARO, A.: Pathology of demyelinating diseases as allergic reaction of the brain. Arch. Neurol. & Psychiat., 25:443, 1944.

FINLEY, K. H.: Pathogenesis of encephalitis occurring with vaccination, variola and measles. Arch. Neurol. & Psychiat., 37:505, 1937.

———: Perivenous changes of encephalitis associated with vaccination, variola and measles. Arch. Neurol. & Psychiat., 35:505, 1937.

GREENBERG, M. AND APPLEBAUM, E.: Post-vaccinial encephalitis. Report of 45 cases in New York City. Am. J. M. Sc., 216:565, 1948.

HURST, E. W.: Review of some recent observation on demyelination. Brain, 67:103, 1944.

JACOBS, H. *et al.*: Report of a case of postvaccinial encephalitis in a four-month-old child. J. Pediat., 35:94, 1949.

LUNDSTRÖM, R.: Vaccinia generalized. Treatment with gamma globulin. Pediatrics, 49:129, 1956.

McINTOSH, J.: Encephalomyelitis in virus infections and exanthemata. Brit. Med. J., 2:334, 1928.

MILLER, H. G.: Prognosis of neurologic illness following vaccination against smallpox. Arch. Neurol. & Psychiat., 69:695, 1953.

ROLLESTON, SIR H. *et al.*: Report of the Committee on Vaccination. London, His Majesty's Stationery Office, 1928.

———: Further Report of the Committee on Vaccination. London, His Majesty's Stationery Office, 1930.

SPILLANE, J. D. AND WELLS, C. E. C.: Neurology of Jennerian vaccination. Brain, 87:1, 1964.

THOMPSON, R.: The etiology of post-vaccinial encephalitis. Arch. Pathol., 12:601, 1931.

TURNBULL, H. M. AND McINTOSH, J.: Encephalomyelitis following vaccination. Brit. J. of Exper. Path., 7:181, 1926.

WALSH, F. B.: *Loc. cit.*

WILSON, R. E. AND FORD, F. R.: Nervous complications of variola, vaccinia and varicella. Bull. Johns Hopkins Hosp., 40:337, 1927.

WINKELMAN, N. W. JR.: Peripheral nerve and root disturbances following vaccination against smallpox. Arch. Neurol. & Psychiat., 62:421, 1949.

ENCEPHALITIS FOLLOWING VARIOLA

Etiology.—Several types of injury of the nervous system may occur as a result of smallpox. There may be direct invasion by pyogenic organisms causing meningitis or abscess, toxic encephalopathy or polyneuritis due to bacterial toxins, and disseminated encephalomyelitis as in vaccinia. It is with the last that we are concerned at this point.

Pathological Anatomy.—No adequate study was made before that of Marsden and Hurst. These authors found it impossible to distinguish upon histological grounds between the lesions resulting from smallpox and those associated with vaccinia, although in some cases the destruction of the spinal gray matter was somewhat more severe in the former.

Clinical Features.—Many cases of disease of the nervous system following variola may be found scattered through medical literature but until recent years there was no apparent uniformity in the symptoms. Thus, we find mention of hemiplegia and aphasia, paraplegia, bulbar palsy and purulent meningitis as well as polyneuritis and delirium. As a result of the work of McIntosh, Turnbull, Scarff, Hurst and Marsden, it is now known that the commonest neurological syndrome is that of disseminated encephalomyelitis.

The incidence of this condition is not uniform. Thus, Marsden and Hurst found seven typical cases as well as four atypical cases among 2,400 mild cases of smallpox observed between September, 1929 and February, 1930, but no further cases were seen in a series of 8,000 subsequent cases of smallpox. Many physicians of large experience have never observed a single case of encephalomyelitis following smallpox. Children seem to be more susceptible, for nine of the eleven cases of Marsden and Hurst occurred between the ages of eight and fifteen years. Most of these patients had never been vaccinated. The incidence of nervous symptoms bears no relation to the severity of the smallpox. In fact, the cases of Marsden and Hurst developed in a very mild type of the disease. Apparently, predisposition plays no importance in determining whether the nervous system will be affected or not, for not more than one case occurred in a single family.

The onset of nervous symptoms appeared between the fifth and the thirteenth day of the rash and usually between the seventh and eighth day. There is a sharp rise of temperature at the beginning and an irregular fever usually lasts for a week or more. Drowsiness, irritability, headache, pain in the back and vomiting are prominent among the early symptoms. Trismus is often very pronounced and may suggest tetanus. Signs of meningeal irritation are present as a rule in a mild form. Marsden and Hurst state that a very characteristic feature in their cases was sweating about the head and excessive salivation. The drowsiness may be replaced by coma in severe cases.

The spinal cord is almost always affected and paraplegia or paraparesis with loss of reflexes and retention of urine are common. Scattered palsies in the distribution of the branchial plexus are also sometimes seen. Bulbar palsy may occur either with paraplegia or alone. The other cranial nerves are not often affected but squints and facial palsies are mentioned. The stupor may last from one to two weeks. In a few cases which present the picture of myelitis, stupor is absent throughout. Death may result from bulbar palsy, failure of respiration, urinary tract infection, bronchopneumonia or infected bed sores.

After consciousness is restored there may be weakness of the legs or even paralysis, incoordination and disturbance of speech. Hurst and Marsden stress the last as a very characteristic feature. The speech is slow and monotonous with even spacing of the words and appears to require great effort on the part of the patient. Improvement may be slow. The paraplegia which is always of flaccid type at first usually becomes associated with spasticity eventually but certain muscles may remain toneless and finally become atrophic. Various mental disturbances may persist during convalescence such as irritability, restlessness and lack of emotional control. Delusions and hallucinations are mentioned.

In the first few days the spinal fluid may contain up to 50 per cent of leucocytes but after this the cells are almost all lymphocytes. The total cell count ranges between 10 and 500. Sugar and chlorides are normal. The fluid is sometimes stained with blood.

Diagnosis.—This depends upon the development of the picture described above or some part of the picture, occurring within two weeks after the development of the smallpox rash. Laboratory tests to establish the diagnosis of smallpox include the demonstration of inclusion bodies in material scraped from the base of the lesions, detection of antibodies in the patients' serum and isolation of the virus by tissue culture.

Prognosis.—Marsden and Hurst report four deaths out of their eleven cases. As a rule, those who survive make a complete or nearly complete recovery. Mild spastic paraparesis may persist but the incoordination and mental symptoms are said to disappear.

Treatment.—See Measles Encephalomyelitis. It is claimed that the administration of methisazone to subjects who have been exposed to smallpox will prevent the infection.

BIBLIOGRAPHY

BROUWER, B., DEJONGH, C. L. UND ROCHAT, R. R.: Über die Veranderongen un Zentralnerven-system Pocken. Deutsche Ztschr. f. Nervenh. Bd. 131:1, 1933.

DOWNIE, A. W.: The Poxvirus Group. Viral and Rickettsial Infections of Man. Edited by Horsfall, F. L. and Tamm, I. J. B. Lippincott Co., 4th Ed. 1965, p. 932.

McIntosh, J. and Scarff, R. W.: The histology of some virus infections of the central nervous system. Proc. Roy. Soc. Med. Sec. Path., **21**:705, 1927.

Marsden, J. P. and Hurst, E. W.: Acute perivascular myelinoclasis (acute disseminated encephalomyelitis) in smallpox. Brain, **55**:181, 1932.

Rice, R. M. and Carey, M. J.: Hemiplegia due to smallpox. J.A.M.A., **100**:817, 1933.

Rogers, K. D. and Harmuth, A. M.: Is it smallpox? General Practitioner, **15**:91, 1957.

Troup, A. G. and Hurst, E. W.: Disseminated encephalomyelitis following smallpox. Lancet, **1**:566, 1930.

ENCEPHALOMYELITIS FOLLOWING VARICELLA

Etiology.—Weller has shown that the virus of varicella and of herpes zoster are identical. It is believed zoster is due either to a reactivation of a latent varicella zoster virus or reintroduction of the virus into a partially immune subject.

Pathological Anatomy.—The only adequate descriptions of the anatomical process are those of Zimmerman and Yannet and van Bogaert. In brief, they found the perivascular demyelination already described in connection with the encephalomyelitis of measles and vaccinia. They also emphasize swelling and chromatolysis of the cortical neurons, i.e. a toxic encephalopathy such as Ferraro has found in measles. The importance of such changes is, of course, uncertain. Lander describes a very severe process with foci of demyelination and many hemorrhages in the white matter. Heppleston *et al.* emphasize changes in the blood vessels with swelling of the endothelium and inflammatory changes about the vessels.

Clinical Features.—Neurological symptoms are relatively rare in varicella but in recent years since a good deal of attention has been devoted to the subject, a number of cases of this nature have come to light so that there are now more than seventy-five on record. The onset occurs as a rule between three days and two weeks after the appearance of the rash and only in very rare instances do the neurological symptoms precede the eruption. In some cases, prodromata such as drowsiness, irritability and anorexia precede the more severe symptoms. Then vomiting, convulsions, stupor and delirium may develop abruptly. There is fever which usually ranges between 100° and 101°F. but which may exceed 105°F. Signs of meningeal irritation may be prominent but in our experience have usually been mild. After a few days or hours, the child begins to regain consciousness and numerous signs and symptoms indicative of injury to the brain, cerebellum and spinal cord become evident. Among the cerebral symptoms we find not only hemiparesis but acute tremor, ataxia and choreoathetoid movements. Relatively pure cerebellar syndromes are described, and seem to occur more frequently than the cerebral or spinal syndromes. The cranial nerves may be involved and ptosis of the eyelids, squints, optic neuritis, retrobulbar neuritis, facial palsy and palsies of the bulbar muscles are described. We have seen one case (Ped. 76333) in which severe unilateral optic neuritis with striking elevation of the disc occurred and which was associated with complete blindness in the affected eye. Jervis describes conjunctivitis and also phlyctenular lesions of the cornea with ulceration of the limbus and edema of the adjacent cornea. Subsequently, vision returned to normal and the disc showed only minimal changes. Various spinal syndromes are also described. We find disseminated myelitis, transverse myelitis, acute ascending spinal paralysis and purely motor disorders with atrophy of the muscles resembling poliomyelitis. Some writers describe polyneuritis. Paraplegia with spasticity is probably the commonest spinal syndrome. Spinal symptoms may occur alone or in association with cerebral symptoms. In general, we may say that the clinical picture is almost identical with that of measles encephalomyelitis. Varicella does not affect the nervous system as frequently as measles does and, as a rule, does not cause such severe injury. Only a few cases of fulminating and fatal types are reported.

The spinal fluid contains a slight excess of lymphocytes and a positive globulin reaction may be elicited.

Varicella pneumonia may cause cyanosis, dyspnea and tachycardia. Nodular pulmonary densities and prominent bronchovascular markings are seen.

Yuceoglu *et al.* describe acute glomerulonephritis which may cause reduction of renal function.

Diagnosis.—The diagnosis is based upon the development of the signs and symptoms described above within two weeks after an attack of varicella and upon the elimination of other causes. There is usually little difficulty in diagnosis.

Prognosis.—In most cases, the neurological disorders clear up rapidly and the mortality is low. Thus, in a series of twenty cases, there were only two deaths. In some instances, cerebellar ataxia, spastic paraparesis or mental defect has persisted.

Treatment.—See Measles Encephalomyelitis.

BIBLIOGRAPHY

APPELBAUM, E. *et al.*: Varicella encephalitis. Am. J. Med., 15:223, 1953.
GIBEL, H. *et al.*: Encephalitis complicating chickenpox. A.M.A. J. Dis. Child., 99:669, 1960.
HEPPLESTON, J. D., PEARCE, K. M. AND YATES, P. O.: Varicella encephalitis. Arch. Dis. Childhood, 34:318, 1959.
JERVEY, E. D. *et al.*: Ocular varicella with particular reference to kerato conjunctival lesions. Southern Med. Jour., 60:696, 1967.
KNYVETT, A. F.: The pulmonary lesions of chickenpox. Quart. Jour. Med., 35:313, 1966.
KRABBE, K. H.: Varicella-myelitis. Brain, 48:535, 1925.
LANDER, H.: Case of acute hemorrhagic leukoencephalitis complicating varicella. J. Path. & Bact., 70:157, 1955.
LEVIN, S.: Cerebellar ataxia following chickenpox. Lancet, i:1222, 1960.
LIPSETT, M. B. *et al.*: Hypothalamic syndrome following varicella. Amer. Jour. Med., 32:471, 1962.
McINTYRE, D. AND BEACH, H. L. W.: Acute encephalomyelitis complicating chickenpox. Brit. J. Child. Dis., 34:113, 1937.

Rotem, C. E.: Complications of chickenpox. Brit. Med. Jour., **5230**:944, 1961.

Schulte, F. J.: Uber die zerebralen Komplikationen bei Varizellen. Deutsch. Med. Wschr., **88**: 1836, 1963.

Underwood, A.: The neurological complications of varicella; a clinical and epidemiological study. Brit. J. Child. Dis., **32**:83, 1935.

van Bogaert, L.: Les manifestations nerveuses au cours des maladies eruptives. Rev. Neurol., **1**:150, 1933.

————: Histopathologische Studie über die Encephalitis nach Windpacken. Ztschr. f. d. ges. Neurol. u. Psychiat., **140**:201, 1932.

Walsh, F. B.: *Loc. cit.*

Welch, R. G.: Chickenpox and the Guillain-Barre syndrome. Arch. Dis. Child., **37**:557, 1962.

Weller, T. H.: Varicella-Herpes Zoster Virus. Viral and Rickettsial Infections of Man. 4th Ed. 1965, J. B. Lippincott Co., Philadelphia.

White, H. H.: Varicella myelopathy. New England Jour. Med., **266**:722, 1962.

Wilson, R. E. and Ford, F. R.: The nervous complications of variola, vaccinia and varicella. Bull. Johns Hopkins Hosp., **40**:337, 1927.

Yuceoglu, A. M. *et al.*: Acute glomerulonephritis as a complication of varicella. Jour. Amer. Med., Ass., **202**:879, 1967.

Zimmerman, H. M. and Yannet, H.: Non-suppurative encephalomyelitis accompanying chickenpox. Arch. Neurol. & Psychiat., **26**:322, 1931.

ENCEPHALOMYELITIS FOLLOWING VACCINATION AGAINST RABIES

Etiology.—The clinical and pathological features of this condition make it necessary to discuss it with the other types of perivascular myelinoclasis, despite its relationship to rabies.

This condition may develop in persons who have never been bitten by a rabid animal or exposed to rabies but who have, nevertheless, taken the Pasteur treatment. It is evident, therefore, that the treatment may be to blame. Experimental work has seemed to indicate that the injection of emulsified nervous tissue is responsible and it is believed that antibodies are set up by this procedure which are responsible for the damage to the nervous system. There are a number of obscure features however which are not yet elucidated. The incidence of the paralysis varies with the method employed in preparing the virus, being highest when large doses of fresh virus are employed and lowest when carbolized virus is used.

Pathological Anatomy.—According to Bassoe and Grinker and several other authorities, the lesions are exactly the same as those which have been described in the encephalomyelitis following measles. No Negri bodies have ever been found.

Stuart and Kraikorian have shown that some cases of acute ascending paralysis following antirabies vaccination are associated with alterations of the anterior horn cells indistinguishable from those found in Landry's paralysis of unknown origin. In such cases there is no myelin destruction, no proliferation of the glia and no evidences of inflammation.

Clinical Features.—This condition may occur in either sex and at any age but seems to be somewhat less frequent in children than in adults. It is very rare at present since carbolized virus is almost exclusively employed. In certain instances, when large doses of relatively fresh virus have been used, as many as 12 cases per thousand have been reported. The incubation period is in most cases between ten and seventeen days after the beginning of treatment but may be longer. We have seen one case otherwise typical in which the incubation period was four months. In general, the more severe cases appear earlier than the milder ones. Sometimes there are prodromal symptoms such as headaches, weakness and nausea. The actual onset is marked by fever and pains in the back and legs. Often there is headache and stupor. The most constant signs are weakness or paralysis of the legs with retention of urine and hypesthesia over the legs. The tendon reflexes are usually diminished or lost at first and may later become increased or remain absent. The plantar reflexes are often extensor. In a case which came under the writer's observation, the cervical and lumbosacral enlargements are both involved, causing weakness and atrophy of certain muscle groups in the arms and legs. Bulbar symptoms are described such as difficulty in swallowing and dysarthria. There is sometimes transient ptosis of the lids, oculomotor palsies and paralysis of the face. I have seen retrobulbar neuritis on both sides with a favorable outcome. Signs of meningeal irritation are often prominent for a few days. Neither the spasms of the pharynx nor the acute excitement so characteristic of rabies has ever been observed.

Several clinical syndromes have been described. (1) The disseminated encephalomyelitis mentioned above. (2) An ascending myelitis. (3) Transverse myelitis usually in the thoracic and lumbar segments. (4) A form simulating peripheral neuritis which affects the facial nerve most frequently.

The spinal fluid shows only a moderate pleocytosis and often a slight increase in globulin.

Diagnosis.—The diagnosis is based upon the development of the condition described above, following the Pasteur treatment.

Prognosis.—The mortality is about 15 per cent. In some cases death is due to paralysis of respiration as a result of ascending paralysis; in others, to infection of the urinary tract or to extensive decubitus ulcers. There is always a very marked tendency to improvement if the patient survives. The commonest sequel is weakness or atrophy of the legs. In one case the writer has seen residua which resembled those of poliomyelitis.

Treatment.—Since this is believed to be an allergic reaction, one might try ACTH or cortisone.

BIBLIOGRAPHY

Bassoe, P. and Grinker, R. R.: Human rabies and rabies vaccine encephalomyelitis. Clinico-pathologic study. Arch. Neurol. & Psychiat., **23**:1138, 1930.

BLATT, N. AND LEPPER, M.: Reactions following antirabies prophylaxis. Am. J. Dis. Child., **86**:395, 1953.
REMLINGER, P. *et al.:* Conference Internationale de la Rage. Suppl. Ann de l'Inst Pasteur, 1927.

THE NEUROLOGICAL COMPLICATIONS OF EXANTHEM SUBITUM

Rothman and Naiditch, in an interesting article, describe the neurological symptoms which may occur in this disease which reaches its highest incidence between the ages of 6 and 18 months. It is believed to be a result of a virus infection.

The onset is acute with fever which may reach 103°F. or even 105°F. Drowsiness, irritability, bulging of the fontanel and sometimes retraction of the head may occur. Convulsions are not unusual and may continue for hours. They may be generalized or local. Hemiplegia may follow the convulsions and the child may be stuporous or even comatose for a time. A macular rash usually appears on the third day and the temperature begins to fall about the same time the symptoms begin to clear up. Only rarely is there persistent hemiparesis but the child is often irritable and difficult to control for a time.

The spinal fluid is under increased pressure as a rule and in a few instances there has been a slight increase of protein and cells.

Moller has made a study of febrile convulsions to determine whether any special diseases predispose the patient to seizures. He reports that in 80 per cent of cases pharyngitis was responsible and exanthem subitum was second with 8 per cent.

It has been assumed in the past that the convulsions described above are febrile convulsions and the hemiplegias are merely post-convulsive phenomena. Rothman and Naiditch, however, suggest that the neurological symptoms are not fully explained by the fever and there may be a more specific effect on the brain. No anatomical studies of the brain are available.

BIBLIOGRAPHY

BURSTINE, R. C.: Residual encephalopathy following resola infantum. Jour. Dis. Child., **98**:144, 1959.
FABER, H. K. AND DICKEY, L. B.: The symptomatology of exanthem subitum. Arch. Pediat., **44**:491, 1927.
JOSEPH, R. *et al.:* Exanthema subitum and febrile convulsions. Ann. Pediat., **34**:86, 1958.
MOLLER, K. L.: Exanthem subitum and febrile convulsions. Acta Paediat., **45**:534, 1956.
OSKI, F. A.: Roseola infantum. Amer. Jour. Dis. Child., **101**:376, 1961.
ROTHMAN, P. E. AND NAIDITCH, M. J.: Nervous complications of exanthem subitum. California Med., **88**:39, 1958.

ENCEPHALOMYELITIS FOLLOWING SCARLET FEVER

Cerebral damage in association with scarlet fever is rare. However, cases of hemorrhagic encephalopathy, toxic encephalopathy and pyogenic infections of various types are described. Cerebral symptoms associated with acute glomerular nephritis which may follow scarlet fever may also be mentioned. Winkelmann described a case of acute disseminated encephalomyelitis associated with scarlet fever in a child of nine years. He considered the clinical and pathological changes very similar to those of measles encephalomyelitis. Ferraro has reported a case which is almost identical but ascribes the lesions to an allergic process.

BIBLIOGRAPHY

ELEY, R. C.: Neurological conditions in infants and children. J. Pediat., **9**:797, 1936.

FERRARO, A.: Allergic brain changes in post-scarlatinal encephalitis. J. Neuropath. & Exp. Neurol., **3**:239, 1944.

TOOMEY, J. A., DEMBO, L. H. AND McCONNELL, G.: Acute hemorrhagic encephalitis. Am. J. Dis. Child., **25**:98, 1923.

TOP, J. H. AND GORDON, J. E.: Central nervous system disease in the course of scarlet fever. J. Pediat., **11**:677, 1937.

WINKELMANN, N. W.: Scarlatinal encephalomyelitis. J. Neuropath. & Exp. Neurol., **1**:363, 1942.

ENCEPHALOMYELITIS FOLLOWING UNKNOWN INFECTIONS

Etiology.—Under this title the writer wishes to discuss those cases of disseminated encephalomyelitis or perivascular myelinoclasis, which are anatomically indistinguishable from the cases associated with measles and vaccinia but which occur after an obscure febrile illness or without any apparent cause. The cases of Miller and Gibbons suggest that even common upper respiratory tract infections may be responsible and that a constitutional factor may be important in some cases.

Pathological Anatomy.—Grinker and Greenfield state that the lesions are identical with those of vaccinia and of measles and encephalomyelitis.

Clinical Features.—This diagnosis has been employed so loosely and so many different clinical conditions have been included in this group that it becomes a matter of great difficulty to form any clear idea of the clinical picture. Some writers have described small epidemics of a mysterious disease of the nervous system which they wish to designate by the above title, but on careful analysis these cases seem to be too heterogeneous to justify the assumption of a common etiology. If we restrict the discussion to the few cases which have been verified by adequate post-mortem examination, we find that the symptoms are almost identical with the encephalomyelitis already described in connection with measles and vaccinia.

In most cases, the history is obtained of a brief febrile illness of unknown nature, often diagnosed influenza, which appeared several days or a week before the nervous symptoms. In most instances the symptoms indicate an infection of the respiratory tract. In the winter of 1956, however, I saw several children between the ages of 10 and 13 years who had episodes of vomiting and diarrhea of 24 hours' duration about two weeks before the onset of the neurological symptoms. In other instances the child has seemed to be quite well until the actual onset.

The first symptoms develop abruptly with fever, headache, pains in the back and vomiting. There is restlessness, irritability and later drowsiness and finally stupor. Moderate evidences of meningeal irritation are usually present. Paralysis of the legs or paraparesis are common and retention of urine may occur. There may be diplopia and transient squints but, as a rule, the cranial nerves are not severely affected. The optic nerve heads may be congested or actually edematous. The spinal fluid may be normal or may show moderate increase in cells and in protein. In brief, the clinical symptoms are identical with those of measles encephalomyelitis. The acute symptoms are of relatively brief duration. The fever begins to fall within a few days and the stupor soon clears. The physical signs may persist for several weeks or even remain permanently although there is a strong tendency towards recovery. Miller and Gibbons report twelve attacks of encephalomyelitis in three siblings between the ages of 11 and 14 years. Ten of these attacks followed common upper respiratory tract infections and one was associated with acute follicular tonsillitis. The symptoms included headache, vertigo, ataxia, drowsiness, stupor, coma, loss of tendon reflexes, extensor responses, nystagmus, diplopia, dysarthria, internal ophthalmoplegia and changes in mood and behavior. Fever, meningeal irritation and changes in the spinal fluid were mild and inconstant. Complete recovery occurred each time. The administration of ACTH seemed to cause improvement within twelve hours.

Alcock and Hoffman describe recurrent attacks of encephalomyelitis in childhood also. The clinical picture in their cases was similar to that described by Miller and Gibbons.

Diagnosis.—The diagnosis is difficult and usually remains in doubt unless it can be verified by post-mortem examination. It is based upon the development of the clinical picture of an acute encephalomyelitis or disseminated myelitis, such as follows measles or vaccinia, without antecedent illness or following a brief febrile illness of unknown nature. The absence of recurrences is against neuromyelitis optica and epidemic encephalitis is rendered at least unlikely by the absence of the late chronic sequelae, so characteristic of that disease.

Prognosis.—The mortality so far as can be determined at present is relatively low and probably is under 10 per cent. If the patient survives, there is gradual improvement for a number of months. McAlpine has made a study of the residua and mentions spastic paraparesis, Brown-Sequard syndromes, nystagmus, ataxia, hyperesthesia and moderate muscular atrophy of the legs.

CASE HISTORY (No. 1006008).—*Boy of ten years who had seven attacks of acute encephalomyelitis following various commonplace infections during the course of four years.*

R. W., a boy of ten years, had a head cold with otitis media on the left on September 5, 1961. On September 10, he complained of double vision, unsteadiness and numbness of the right side of the face and right arm. Examination revealed a right sixth nerve palsy, right facial weakness, unsteady station and gait, nystagmus, ataxia of the right arm and leg, and a scotoma in the lower temporal quadrant of the right eye field. The spinal fluid contained 1,000 cells, mostly lymphocytes. There were 86 mgs of protein in the spinal fluid. Cultures were sterile. An air study showed nothing abnormal. There was prompt improvement and he was discharged on October 5 in good condition.

The child remained well until the first of May, 1963. He then had a sore throat and head cold. Headaches, vomiting and stiffness of the neck developed. There was fever and drowsiness. These symptoms lasted seven days. He made a complete recovery.

About May 15, 1963, after he had been playing with a boy who had an illness with vomiting, the same symptoms flared up again. There were fifty cells in the spinal fluid. Spinal fluid cultures were negative. He was given 15 mgs prednisone a day. The symptoms cleared up quickly.

On November 30, 1963, he had diarrhea. On December 3, he developed fever, headache, nausea, and vomiting. His neck was stiff. He seemed to be drowsy and dull. The spinal fluid contained 100 cells and 94 were lymphocytes. Culture of the fluid was sterile. The sugar was 55 mgs. The symptoms receded rapidly.

In June, 1964, he had another episode similar to the previous ones. There was another in October and a third in January, 1965. There was headache, fever, vomiting and stiffness of the neck. Each episode lasted about a week. He has been given prednisone 15 mgs a day since November, 1963, but before the episode in June the mother had reduced the dosage to 5 mgs. During these episodes in 1964 and 1965, the mother did not give prednisone because of the vomiting.

In January, 1965, the patient was fourteen years old. In March, 1965, I was informed that there had been no additional episodes since January. The prednisone had been discontinued. His only problem was headache. He had had throbbing, frontal headaches with vomiting since the age of four years. Migraine was prevalent in the families of his mother and father. No neurological abnormalities could be found.

BIBLIOGRAPHY

ALCOCK, N. S. AND HOFFMAN, H. L.: Recurent encephalomyelitis in childhood. Arch. Dis. Childhood, **37**:40, 1962.

BROCK, S. AND DAVISON, C.: Acute demyelinating encephalitis following respiratory disease. Bull. of Neurological Inst. of New York, **6**:504, 1937.

Discussion on Encephalomyelitis. Proc. Roy. Soc. Med., **22**:1167, 1257, 1929.

GREENFIELD, J. G.: Disseminated encephalomyelitis. J. Path. & Bact., 33:453, 1930.

GRINKER, R. R. AND BASSOE, P.: Disseminated encephalomyelitis. Arch. Neurol. & Psychiat., 25:723, 1931.

McALPINE, D.: Acute disseminated encephalomyelitis—its sequelae and relationship to disseminated sclerosis. Lancet, 1:846 (ref.) , 1931.

MILLER, H. G. AND GIBBONS, J. L.: Familial recurrent encephalomyelitis. Ann. Int. Med., 40:755, 1954.

TURNBULL, H. M.: Encephalomyelitis in virus diseases and exanthemata. Brit. Med. J., 11:331, 1928.

ENCEPHALOPATHIES

Sydenham's Chorea and Rheumatic Fever

Etiology.—This disease is so commonly associated with rheumatic arthritis, endocarditis and pericarditis that it is usually regarded as another manifestation of the rheumatic infection. There is a strong suspicion that infection by the beta hemolytic streptococcus is responsible.

Pathological Anatomy.—The nature of the cerebral lesions has long been a subject of debate among neuropathologists and there is still no general agreement upon this problem. It is clear that any lesions which exist must be very mild and difficult to demonstrate, for many pathologists have failed to find them. It is scarcely conceivable that any considerable number of neurons are actually destroyed, for the disease almost invariably results in complete recovery. Perhaps, the most complete study has been made by Lewy, who describes the changes in eleven brains. In most of these cases death resulted within two weeks. In uncomplicated cases he found degenerative changes in the cells of the putamen and caudate with amoeboid transformation of the surrounding glial cells. In cases of longer standing there were lipoid deposits in the adventitial spaces. These lesions were not confined to the striatum but were also found in the cortex, substantia nigra and dentate nuclei of the cerebellum. No vascular lesions or inflammatory phenomena were found. Ziegler also describes diffuse degenerative changes. Colony and Malamud report a post-mortem examination which revealed diffuse degenerative process. However, Greenfield and Wolfsohn have found some extra-adventitial infiltration which they regard as evidence of a mild inflammatory reaction. Winkelmann and Eckel and Costero describe swelling of the endothelium of the small vessels of the brain, areas of softening in the gray matter, meningeal infiltrations, small nodules composed of glial cells and mesodermal elements and widespread changes in the nerve cells in cases of *acute rheumatic fever*. Bruetsch believes that this process may be chronic and cause vascular occlusion years later.

Clinical Features.—The disease is most frequent between the ages of six and nine years but may occur as early as three. It is unusual after the age of puberty, if we exclude the chorea gravidarum. Most authors agree that chorea is two or three times as common among girls as boys. Heredity plays a very indefinite role in this disease. Sometimes, it is true, several cases occur in the same family but such instances are not so common that we are justified in placing much emphasis upon them. Many authors state that chorea develops in sensitive, neurotic children who are often intellectually precocious. This is certainly correct in many instances but it is not uncommon to observe chorea in backward and even mentally defective children, so that it seems to be impossible to formulate any invariable rule.

The onset may be abrupt or gradual. In many cases it is stated that the symptoms follow a fright or some other emotional reaction. Since the symptoms are always accentuated by emotional disturbances, it is probable that such episodes merely bring to light a disease which already exists. Irritability, peevishness, headache and insomnia may precede the motor disturbances which constitute, of course, the most characteristic features of the disease.

Involuntary movements, incoordination, hypotonus and weakness may be given as the typical symptoms. In mild cases the child may seem to be merely restless and the movements are abnormal only in their persistence. Later they become violent and obviously pathological. They are quick, jerky, twitching movements which may bear a close resemblance to those termed psychogenic tics but differ from the latter in that the same movement is rarely exactly duplicated. The movements are at first of small amplitude but later may be very gross. Frequently the symptoms are more severe on one side than on the other or entirely confined to one side. The face, tongue, neck and trunk may be involved as well as the limbs. All natural gestures and movements of expression of the face are grossly exaggerated. When the child is lying down and completely relaxed, the movements are absent or diminished but any attempt to move or any emotional stimulus, even the entrance of the examiner into the room, may bring on the movements at once. During sleep the child is always still.

Voluntary movements are quite normal in mild cases but may be grossly distorted when the symptoms are severe. In the finger-nose test, for example, the arm often describes unnecessary flourishes before reaching the nose. When holding a glass of water to the mouth, the hand will suddenly relax and permit the glass to fall or a sudden jerk of the arm may send the glass across the room. The gait is severely affected. The legs are advanced in a jerky, incoordinate manner and the feet placed at irregular intervals. At times one leg will suddenly relax permitting the child to stumble or fall. The rhythm of the gait is broken by sudden movements of the trunk or legs. The arms are swung too widely and the head and trunk may oscillate irregularly. Speech is at first merely irregular in rhythm but later articulation becomes indistinct, so that it is difficult to understand the patient. Often the patient will not talk because it is so difficult to control the tongue.

Swallowing may be disturbed by incoordination of the tongue but true bulbar palsy is very rare.

Muscle tone is usually reduced. The range of passive movement is often much increased and the extremities may be placed in unnatural positions. When the arms are outstretched they oscillate unduly. The hands are often held in a curious position. The wrist is flexed and the fingers hyperextended at the proximal joints. When the arms are held above the head, the forearm is pronated. The tone of the trunk muscles is diminished and the patient cannot sit up steadily.

Strength is usually diminished and the least effort causes fatigue. Muscular contractions cannot be steadily sustained. For example, the grips may be firm for a moment but soon relax. The examiner may feel the patient's fingers tightening and relaxing every few moments. In some cases outspoken local weakness or hemiparesis may occur. This condition is not associated with spasticity or increased tendon reflexes but, on the contrary, with hypotonus and diminished reflexes.

The reflexes may be altered in several ways. Often the tendon reflexes are somewhat increased or at least brisk. In other cases, the muscular contraction is unduly prolonged and the leg remains in extension for several seconds. This reaction is very characteristic of chorea and is termed the hung-up knee jerk. In some cases, especially those in which weakness and hypotonus are pronounced, the tendon reflexes are diminished or abolished. A pendular reflex may be associated with hypotonus. The plantar reflex is almost always normal.

There are no disturbances of sensibility. The cranial nerves are rarely involved and except in the most severe cases, sphincter control is not affected.

Mental disturbances are usually present and may be mild or severe. These children are fretful, irritable and unstable. Insomnia is sometimes very troublesome and sleep is interrupted by night terrors and bad dreams. Emotional instability may be very marked. The child will often burst into tears with little or no cause. Fear and anger are easily aroused. Spontaneous laughter is less common. Any disturbance of the routine nursing care, the presence of a stranger or the approach of the examiner is sufficient to throw the child into a state of agitation and apprehension. In very severe cases, delirium sometimes occurs. This is marked by confusion, excitement and hallucinations. The latter are usually of a terrifying nature. The involuntary movements are usually very violent in such cases.

The course of the disease is variable. Mild cases may end in recovery within two or three months but severe attacks may persist for a year. In many cases, perhaps in most, there are recurrences every year for several years. The symptoms usually appear in the spring or early summer and disappear late in the fall and early winter months. Recovery may be incomplete between attacks. It is very unusual to have any manifestations of the disease persist after puberty. Parker and Lipschutz describe a case of chorea in which the movements were present for many years.

There is usually no elevation of temperature in chorea unless there is some complicating condition such as tonsillitis, arthritis or endocarditis. In severe cases, however, there may be fever in the absence of demonstrable complications. There is almost always more or less anemia and loss of weight. The leucocytes are not increased, as a rule, but eosinophilia up to 20 per cent may be found in certain cases. The spinal fluid is normal.

Warren and Chornyak describe the neurological disturbances seen in severe cases of *acute rheumatic fever*. They state that such symptoms may occur with little or no arthritis. The nervous system may be affected before, with or after the arthritis. There are usually few focal signs and the chief disturbances are mental. There may be hallucinations, panic states, phobias, delirium, restlessness and convulsions. Mental deterioration may result. The face may be mask-like. The spinal fluid may be normal or there may be a slight increase of cells and protein.

Complications.—Several other symptoms of the rheumatic infection are frequently associated with chorea. These may occur during the course of the disease, may precede or follow. Cardiac disease is the most important. Endocarditis is very common. This usually affects the mitral valve and may be mild or severe. Vegetative endocarditis with embolic phenomena has been repeatedly described but is actually rare. Signs of myocarditis, such as enlargement of the heart, may occur during acute attacks. Pericarditis is well known but unusual. In Baltimore serious cardiac symptoms are uncommon. Rheumatic arthritis is not unusual. In our experience it is usually mild and confined to one or two joints. Severe rheumatic polyarthritis is exceptional. Subcutaneous rheumatic nodules are sometimes seen and various other cutaneous eruptions such as erythema nodosum. Purpura is rare. Tonsillitis is present in many cases but its relation to chorea is problematical. Hyperpyrexia occurs occasionally with pericarditis or without cardiac symptoms.

Diagnosis.—This is rarely difficult but atypical cases may sometimes present confusing problems. Habit spasms and tics of neurotic children may be mistaken for chorea. Here the repetition of the same movement and absence of incoordination and of rheumatic symptoms usually enable the differentiation to be made. The fact that emotional instability and irritability are present in both cases may cause uncertainty for a while. In the acute phase of epidemic encephalitis, choreiform movements sometimes occur in association with excitement and insomnia. The movements are rarely quite typical, however, and the presence of oculomotor palsies, diplopia, reversal of sleep, tremors, myoclonus and pleocytosis in the spinal fluid should reveal the true diagnosis. Some children develop general movements very suggestive of chorea as an expression of nervous tension and agitation. This is especially true of young girls about the age of puberty. We have observed three cases in which the exciting cause was an illicit pregnancy. In each case the symptoms suddenly disappeared after the matter had been discussed with the parents. Incoordination is usually absent in hysterical conditions which simulate chorea. Mentally defective children may develop choreiform movements as a result of infectious diseases or following any painful or terrifying experience. We have seen such movements appear in several cases after various operative procedures. These persist for several weeks and then cease after the patient has resumed the usual routine of life.

Cases of chorea complicated by hemiparesis may offer difficult diagnostic problems if the typical movements are not apparent. The absence of spasticity and of increased tendon reflexes, extensor response and ankle clonus should arouse suspicions of chorea and the movements will be detected after further observation.

Prognosis.—It is very rare for uncomplicated chorea to cause death but cardiac involvement or exhaustion resulting from violent movements sometimes leads to a fatal issue. Hyperpyrexia is a rare cause of death. If the patient survives, the prognosis is excellent and complete recovery is to be expected. The parents should always be warned of the possibility of recurrent attacks, however. The mental symptoms may persist for a long time and, indeed, many children who have had chorea remain sensitive and unstable throughout life. In such cases, it is often impossible to distinguish the effects of the disease from the manifestations of a neurotic constitution. The personality plays an important role and the tendency of parents to spoil children who are ill must be kept in mind.

It is well known that some children who have been subject to attacks of chorea subsequently show a tendency to react by choreic movements to any nervous strain later in life or may even exhibit slight motor unrest habitually. It is very difficult to offer any explanation for such cases. There is never any fever or evidences of infection, speech is normal, coordination is usually unimpaired and the reflexes are always in order. It seems very unlikely, therefore, that there is any active process in the nervous system. Two possible explanations may be advanced; that the movements have become habitual by constant repetition or that the disease may have resulted in a mild but permanent injury to the brain.

Treatment.—Our rule is to keep the child in bed as long as the movements persist. It is essential that the environment should be quiet. The patient should be under the care of a nurse rather than of a relative. Visitors should be forbidden. Warm baths and other forms of hydrotherapy sometimes have a valuable sedative effect. Massage is often helpful. The heart should be examined from time to time.

When the child is so active that the proper rest cannot be secured by the simple measures outlined above, sedatives should be given. Phenobarbital has been very useful and may be given in full doses. Cortisone, it is claimed, is of definite value in the treatment of this disease. It is now recommended that beta hemolytic streptococci should be eliminated from the throat by therapeutic doses of penicillin and that thereafter for 5 years the patient should be given prophylactic doses by mouth every day. If the patient is sensitive to penicillin, sulphadiazine may be given or one of the tetracycline drugs.

BIBLIOGRAPHY

AINGER, L. E. *et al.*: Sydenham's chorea. Effects of hormone therapy. Am. J. Dis. Child., **89**:580, 1955.

BRAIN, W. R.: The position of the hand in chorea. Lancet, **1**:439, 1928.

BRUETSCH, W.: Chronic rheumatic brain disease. Am. J. Psychiat., **97**:276, 1940.

COLONY, H. S. AND MALAMUD, N.: Sydenham's chorea, a clinicopathologic study. Neurology, **6**:672, 1956.

COSTERO, L.: Cerebral lesions responsible for the death of patients with active rheumatic fever. Arch. Neurol. & Psychiat., **62**:48, 1949.

GREENFIELD, J. G. AND WOLFSOHN, J. M.: The pathology of Sydenham's chorea. Lancet, **2**:603, 1922.

LEWY, F. H.: Die Histopathologie der Choreatischen Erkrankungen. Ztschr. f. d. ges. Neurol. u. Psychiat., **85**:622, 1923.

PARKER, A. M. AND LIPSCHUTZ, E. W.: An unusual case of Sydenham's chorea of prolonged duration. New York J. Med., **58**:2834, 1958.

SHERMITTE, J. ET PAGNIEZ, P.: Anatomie et physiologie pathologique de la Chorie de Sydenham. L'Encéphale, **25**:24, 1930.

TARANTA, A.: Relation of isolated recurrences of Sydenham's chorea to preceding streptococcal infections. New England J. Med., **260**:1204, 1959.

THAYER, W. S.: An analysis of 808 cases of chorea with especial reference to cardiovascular manifestations. J.A.M.A., **47**:1352, 1906.

VON SANTHA, K.: Uber Gefassveranderungen im Zentralnervensystem bei Chorea Rheumatica. Virchow's Arch. f. Path. Anat., **287**:405, 1932.

WARREN, H. A. AND CHORNYAK, J.: Cerebral manifestations of acute rheumatic fever. Arch. Int. Med., **79**:589, 1947.

WINKELMANN, N. W. AND ECKEL, J. L.: The brain in acute rheumatic fever. Arch. Neurol. & Psychiat., **28**:844, 1932.

ZIEGLER, L. H.: Neuropathological findings in case of acute Sydenham's chorea. J. Nerv. & Ment. Dis., **65**:273, 1927.

PERTUSSIS ENCEPHALOPATHY

Etiology.—Little can be said about the causes of the various cerebral lesions described below except that directly or indirectly they are apparently a result of pertussis. There is no evidence that invasion of the nervous system by a neurotropic virus is to blame.

Pathological Anatomy.—The anatomical changes are not always the same and a number of different conditions have been found in the brain. Until recent years, it was customary to attribute the cerebral symptoms to hemorrhage but many writers have noted that hemorrhages are sometimes absent and even when present are not always extensive enough to explain the symptoms. Inflammatory processes have been described from time to time but the histological picture has not been consistent. Woolf and Caplin describe perivascular lymphocytic infiltrations in one case associated with disseminated areas of degeneration attributed to anoxia. In 1924 Husler and Spatz described a condition characterized by extensive degeneration of nerve cells in the cerebral cortex and since then their findings have been confirmed by several other pathologists.

Eleven patients dying at the Harriet Lane Home with pertussis encephalopathy have been subjected to adequate post-mortem examination. There was no clinical evidence of tetany in any case. Ten of these patients died within a few days of the onset of neurological symptoms and one lived for several months. In five cases, no lesions whatever were found.

In one case there was a massive hemorrhage in the subarachnoid spaces. In three cases, the cerebral vessels were intensely congested and innumerable minute hemorrhages were found scattered throughout the brain. Histological examination revealed that these were all confined to the perivascular spaces or to the tissues immediately surrounding the small vessels. There were no softenings or thromboses and no inflammatory phenomena. There seemed to be very little injury to the cortical cells or nerve fibers.

In one case, a widespread inflammatory process was discovered which affected all parts of the brain and even involved some segments of the spinal cord. Since there was a fresh bacterial endocarditis present, it is probable that the cerebral changes should be regarded as evidence of septicemia rather than direct effect of the pertussis.

In one case, in which the patient survived for six months, the picture was that described by Husler and Spatz. There was general symmetrical wasting of the cortex which was, perhaps, most obvious in the frontal lobes. On section the white matter was, perhaps, a bit atrophied, but the cortex was definitely thinner than normal. No vascular lesions were apparent. Histological study revealed an extraordinary loss of cortical nerve cells. This was universal but more severe in some regions than in others. In some areas there were scarcely any neurons to be found and the cortex was reduced to a mere spongy network of glia which was transversed by bundles of nerve fibers which were unexpectedly well-preserved. The cell loss was most severe in the third cortical layer and the giant pyramidal cells were for the most part intact. The glial reaction was not excessive but the astrocytes were swollen and their processes thickened. Numerous microglial cells filled with lipoid material were scattered throughout the tissues. Milder cell loss was found in the cerebellar cortex, in the basal ganglia and nuclei of the brainstem. The white matter showed some destruction of myelin but the damage was slight as compared with that of the gray matter. No degeneration was found in the pyramidal tracts.

The cerebral hemorrhages have been ascribed by many writers to the intense congestion of the brain produced by the violent paroxysms of coughing which occur in this disease. No doubt this is an important factor but since similar lesions are found in many other diseases, it seems more probable that injury to the cerebral vessels by bacterial toxins is responsible. Husler and Spatz regard the condition they describe as a result of a toxic degeneration of the cerebral neurons, and this theory seems to have been accepted by the majority of writers since their paper was published. It is of interest in this connection that pertussis vaccine seems to have neurotoxic properties for many cases are reported in which the administration of this vaccine was followed by cerebral damage. (See Toxic Encephalopathy.) Other authors have suggested that such lesions may be due to air emboli arising from rupture of the pulmonary alveoli during coughing or from vascular stasis or vasomotor disturbances, but no convincing proof has been offered to support such theories.

Clinical Features.—Pertussis is much more serious in infancy than later in childhood and almost all of the neurological complications occur, as a rule, before the age of two years. The neurological symptoms are not uniform but include a number of entirely different manifestations. This, in fact, might be expected from the preceding discussion of the pathological anatomy.

The commonest type of pertussis encephalopathy is characterized by the abrupt development of a series of convulsions. These may occur at almost any stage in the course of the disease but are most common at the height of the illness. The convulsions are very severe and frequent. As a rule they are generalized but may be focal or may involve either side alternately. There is usually high fever. The mortality is very high and often death ensues within a very few hours after the first convulsion. If the child does not die, various cerebral symptoms such as hemiplegia, monoplegia or diplegia may appear and stupor or drowsiness may persist for a number of days. Such conditions are most apt to follow a series of convulsions. Recurrent seizures may be followed by additional cerebral symptoms. The spinal fluid may be normal or blood-tinged. In such cases, it is impossible to predict the anatomical changes in the brain, for we may find no demonstrable lesions, multiple hemorrhages or the degenerative process described above. If the child survives, recovery may be complete. In some cases, however, hemiplegia or other focal cerebral signs persist.

In certain cases, the onset is much less abrupt and the course less rapid. A few weeks after the beginning of the cough, the child becomes drowsy and finally stuporous. The onset of symptoms is reported to have been delayed until the third month in a few cases. There are usually, but not always, convulsions. Some children show a constant twitching of small amplitude and rapid rate involving one or more extremities, which suggests the epilepsia partialis continua resulting from cortical inflammation. Finally, it is noted that the child's muscles are growing rigid and after some weeks there is almost complete immobility. The arms are flexed, as a rule, but one arm was extended in one of our cases. The legs are always stiffly extended or may be strongly adducted. The tendon reflexes may be exaggerated or reduced. Plantar stimulation in our experience has given normal results. On passive movement, strong muscle spasm is encountered. In some cases there is bulbar palsy and tube feeding may be required. There is usually complete loss of speech. The pupils react to light although the child may seem to be blind. We have seen pallor of the optic nerve heads in one case. In fatal cases the child may show no sign of consciousness for a number of months. In more favorable cases, the child is stuporous for several weeks and then begins to regain consciousness. Death is usually due to secondary infection. The spinal fluid shows a mild increase in lymphocytes during the first few weeks of the illness and is thereafter quite normal. Apparently the process is active for several weeks or even longer. We have studied three cases of this type. In two cases, death resulted between the fourth and the sixth month of the illness after the child had remained in a vegetative state and helpless. In such cases, the degenerative process described by Husler and Spatz is always found at post-mortem examination.

Diagnosis.—Loss of consciousness during a paroxysm of coughing may be merely due to tussive syncope though this is not common, but the development of convulsions during the course of pertussis should suggest either tetany or encephalopathy. Since the tetany may be due to alkalosis resulting

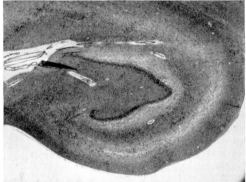

Fig. 166. Pertussis encephalopathy showing extensive loss of cells in the cerebral cortex.

Fig. 167. Pertussis encephalopathy showing loss of cells in the cornu Ammonis.

Fig. 168. Pertussis encephalopathy showing intense general muscular rigidity.

from loss of the acid contents of the stomach by frequent vomiting, the carbon dioxide combining power of the blood, as well as the calcium and phosphorus content, must be determined. If tetany can be ruled out, some form of encephalopathy is probably present. The hemorrhagic form is not easy to distinguish from the degenerative form at first, but the progressive course of the latter should make the differentiation easy after a few weeks' observation. The discovery of focal signs would seem to prove the presence of a local lesion but they may disappear without sequelae. The atrophy of the cortex which occurs in the degenerative form of encephalopathy may be demonstrated by spinal air injection within a few months after the onset, but in such cases the diagnosis can be made on clinical grounds much earlier.

Prognosis.—In cases in which there is a sudden onset of violent convulsions, the prognosis for life is poor, especially if the child is under one year of age. Focal signs develop such as hemiplegia, which may disappear, but the occurrence of general rigidity seems to be of ominous significance and, so far as we can determine, leads either to death or to serious and permanent disability.

Treatment.—Treatment is merely symptomatic.

BIBLIOGRAPHY

ARENDT, A.: Cerebral complications of pertussis. Arch. Path. Anat., 335:642, 1962.

ASKIN, J. A. AND ZIMMERMAN, H. M.: Encephalitis accompanying whooping cough. Am. J. Dis. Child., 38:97, 1929.

DOLGOPOL, V. B.: Changes in the brain in pertussis with convulsions. Arch. Neurol. & Psychiat., 46:477, 1941.

FORD, F. R.: Degeneration of the cerebral cortex in the course of pertussis. Am. J. Dis. Child., 37:1046, 1929.

HUSLER, J. U. AND SPATZ, H.: Die Keuchhusten-Eklampsie. Ztschr. J. Kinderh., 38:428, 1924.

JOCHIMS, J.: Ein Beitrag zur Keuchhusten-Encephalopathie. Ztschr. f. Kinderh., 45:326, 1928.

LAPIN, JOSEPH H.: Whooping Cough. Springfield, Thomas, 1943.

LITVAK, M., GIBEL, H., ROSENTHAL, S. AND ROSENBLATT, P.: Cerebral complications of pertussis. J. Pediat., **32**:357, 1948.

NEUBERGER, K.: Ueber die Pathogenese der Keuchhusten-Eklampsie. Klin. Wchnschr., **4**:113, 1925.

POWERS, G. F.: Tetany as a cause of convulsions in whooping cough. Am. J. Dis. Child., **30**:632, 1925.

RICH, A.: On the etiology and pathogenesis of whooping cough. Bull. Johns Hopkins Hosp., **51**:346, 1932.

SEARS, W. G.: Nervous complications of whooping cough. Brit. J. Child. Dis., **26**:178, 1929.

SINGER, L.: Ueber die Keuchhustenapoplexie. Ztschr. f. Kreislaufforsch., **20**:338, 1928.

WALSH, F. B.: *Loc. cit.*

WOOLF, A. L. AND CAPLIN, H.: Whooping cough encephalitis. Arch. Dis. Child., **31**:87, 1956.

ACUTE TOXIC ENCEPHALOPATHY

Definition.—An intoxication in which the effect is believed to be exerted directly upon the cerebral neurons. It is not easy to distinguish this condition sharply from *hemorrhagic encephalopathy* or *cerebral vascular lesions following acute infectious diseases.*

Etiology.—This is the result of acute and severe infections such as diphtheria, pneumonia, erysipelas, scarlet fever, influenza, yellow fever, dysentery and cholera. A great variety of drugs and poisons also cause encephalopathy. (See *Drugs* and *Poisons.*)

In such cases we must consider (1) The effect of the drug or toxin. (2) The effect of high fever. (3) Dehydration. (4) Changes in the blood chemistry such as hypoglycemia and alteration of the electrolyte balance. (5) Anoxia due to convulsion and other causes. Lyon *et al.* have made a careful study of these cases. Many possible factors are considered. They conclude that hypoxia plays a significant role and the initial injury may be a neurotoxin of bacterial origin which has not yet been identified.

Pathological Anatomy.—Brown and Symmers, in 1925, described a condition in children which was characterized by intense edema and congestion of the brain and by cloudy swelling of the neurons. There was no evidence of an inflammatory process and no significant glial reaction. The authors termed this acute serous encephalitis and regarded it as a fulminating form of encephalitis which causes death before the usual inflammatory lesions develop.

Grinker and Stone published a more extensive article in 1928 in which they included some thirteen cases. They found congestion and edema associated with swelling, chromatolysis, vacuolation and disintegration of the cortical neurons. Grinker stated that many nerve cells were necrotic and that only a few showed reversible changes. The small cerebral vessels showed, in addition to congestion, proliferation of the endothelium often so intense as to lead to occlusion of the lumen. There was no sign of inflammation and the glial reaction was restricted to swelling and degeneration. These authors regarded the changes as the result of an intoxication due to pneumonia and other infectious diseases and not as evidence of a primary encephalitis as did Brown and Symmers. Low in 1930 also described similar changes in the brain in association with severe infections.

There is much difference of opinion about the significance of these lesions. Certain pathologists have stated that they are merely artefacts due to post-mortem changes. Others believe that they are results of bacterial intoxication but that they are always reversible and never cause disability if the child survives. If the writer may be permitted to express an opinion, we have here the anatomical basis of delirium, stupor and convulsions which may develop during various acute and severe infections in infancy and early childhood. These lesions usually disappear without residuum but sometimes result in permanent damage to the brain. The process is a non-specific one which may be produced by many different diseases. It is the result of bacterial toxins and is not a fulminating encephalitis as Symmers thinks.

It is probable that acute toxic encephalopathy, hemorrhagic encephalopathy and what I have termed cerebral vascular lesions following acute infectious diseases are basically the same. All seem to be due to a variety of intoxications acting on the nervous system. If the nerve cells seem to be affected directly, we may speak of toxic encephalopathy. If the chief anatomical manifestation is hemorrhage, we speak of hemorrhagic encephalopathy. If extensive changes are found in the blood vessels causing small softenings, we may classify the case in the third category.

Clinical Features.—The neurological features are frequently obscured by the primary process which in my experience has usually been pneumonia, dysentery, scarlet fever or some other acute infectious disease. The onset is almost always abrupt with high fever, vomiting, convulsions and stupor. There is general muscular rigidity in most cases but occasionally the child is quite flaccid. Almost all writers speak of signs of meningeal irritation, but I am inclined to believe that the rigidity is of cerebral origin and that the rigidity of the cervical muscles is merely a part of the rigidity of the whole bodily musculature. The plantar reflexes are usually extensor and the tendon reflexes may be exaggerated or diminished. The pupils are often dilated and the light reflex sluggish. The optic nerve heads are sometimes normal and sometimes congested. The spinal fluid is under increased pressure as a rule and may contain a slight excess of globulin. It never contains a definite excess of cells. The urine shows albumin and casts and sometimes blood. In our experience the blood cultures have been negative. One gains the impression that the nervous system is involved with the other organs of the body as a result of an overwhelming intoxication and that it is not selectively affected.

The course is variable. In certain cases the neurological symptoms may disappear within a few hours. The convulsions cease, the rigidity disappears and consciousness is regained. The clinical picture is frequently termed *meningism* or *meningismus*. There are no sequelae in such cases. In more severe cases, which are fortunately not common, the neurological symptoms persist. The convulsions return at intervals for several days or even weeks and the child remains in stupor. We have observed cases of this type in which the child has subsequently remained mentally defective and apparently deaf and blind. The optic nerve heads show no pallor and the pupils react to light so the blindness is probably of cortical origin. In a few cases there has been weakness and spasticity on one or both sides. Speech is lost in children who have learned to talk and the child may be unable to walk or even sit up. During convalescence ventriculograms show diffuse and symmetrical dilatation of the ventricles and enlargement of the sulci of the cortex may be demonstrated by injection of air by the spinal route. In our experience some of these children remain defective although there is a tendency towards improvement. In the most severe cases the convulsions are very frequent and severe, the fever rises to 105°F. or more, the stupor deepens into coma and the child dies within a few hours or days. Mentally deficient children seem to be especially prone to develop toxic encephalopathy. No doubt, defective brains are more susceptible to such intoxications. In some of the very severe dysenteries polyneuritis may follow the encephalopathy thus adding weight to the theory of intoxication.

A number of cases of acute encephalopathy following the use of the pertussis vaccine have been reported. Byers and Moll describe 15 cases in children ranging from 5 to 18 months of age. These were observed during a period of 10 years. Doses of 20, 40 and 40 billion bacteria were administered. Six children reacted to the first dose, 3 to the second dose and 6 to the third dose. The acute phase of the disease lasted between 36 hours and 10 days. The onset occurred from 20 minutes to 72 hours after the injection. The symptoms included fever, restlessness, drowsiness, convulsions, and coma. There was often hemiplegia and at least once flaccid paralysis with bulbar palsy. One child made a good recovery, but residua persisted in the others. These children displayed mental defects, convulsions and cerebral palsies. In two cases there was blindness. In two there was decerebrate rigidity. Air studies revealed cortical atrophy in 6 cases. Two patients seemed to run a progressive course to death. Post-mortem examination in one patient is said to have revealed atrophy of the brain and gliosis. Toomey has collected 38 cases from various sources. He states that in 23 cases there was recovery. Globus and Kahn describe the post-mortem findings in one case. They state that the brain was very soft. The architecture of the cortex was lost. Cortical nerve cells were swollen and had no tigroid substance. There were many macrophages loaded with fat in the cortex. There were similar changes in the brain stem and cerebellum but these were much milder.

There was no inflammatory reaction and no vascular changes. The process was regarded as purely degenerative.

Knox *et al.* describe 12 cases in childhood in which a febrile illness with upper respiratory tract infection was followed by sixth nerve palsy within a few weeks and in which spontaneous recovery occurred in a few more weeks.

Diagnosis.—The diagnosis may be suspected whenever in the course of an acute infectious disease the child becomes stuporous or delirious and develops convulsions and muscular rigidity. Meningitis, abscess of the brain and dural sinus thrombosis are the conditions most likely to be confused with toxic encephalopathy, and it is not always easy to rule out these possibilities. During convalescence ventriculography will reveal symmetrical wasting of the brain in certain cases.

Prognosis.—If the neurological symptoms are of brief duration the prognosis is favorable for complete recovery. If the stupor and convulsions persist for a week or more the prognosis must be guarded for the child may be permanently disabled. Mental deficiency seems to be the commonest residuum and convulsions may also result. In very severe cases the child may show spasticity of the muscles.

Treatment.—The treatment is restricted to the proper management of the original disease and to the symptomatic treatment of the neurological symptoms. Phenobarbital and other sedatives may be given to control the convulsions.

BIBLIOGRAPHY

ALEXANDER, L. AND WU, T. T.: Cerebral changes in gastrointestinal infections with terminal cachexia. Arch. Neurol. & Psychiat., 33:72, 1935.
ANDERSON, A. I.: Report of five cases of acute encephalitis. Boston Med. & Surg. J., 189:177, 1932.
BROWN, C. L. AND SYMMERS, D.: Acute serous encephalitis. Am. J. Dis. Child., 29:174, 1925.
BYERS, R. K. AND MOLL, F. C.: Encephalopathy following prophylactic pertussis vaccination. Pediatrics, 1:437, 1948.
GLOBUS, J. AND KAHN, J.: Encephalopathy following pertussis vaccine prophylaxis. J.A.M.A., 141:507, 1949.
GRINKER, R. R. AND STONE, T. T.: Acute toxic encephalitis in childhood; clinicopathologic study. Arch. Neurol. & Psychiat., 20:244, 1928.
KNOX, D. L., CLARK, D. B. AND SCHUSTER, F.: Benign fever and sixth nerve palsy in children.
LOW, A. A.: Acute toxic (non-suppurative) encephalitis in children; clinicopathologic study. Arch. Neurol. & Psychiat., 23:696, 1930.
LYON, G., DODGE, P. R. AND ADAMS, R. D.: Acute encephalopathies of obscure origin in infants and children. Brain, 84:680, 1961.
THOMPSON, S. G. AND PANOS, T. C.: Shigellosis: pediatric aspects. Texas J. Med. 53:320, 1957.
TOOMEY, J. A.: Reactions to pertussis vaccine. J.A.M.A., 139:448, 1948.
WINKELMANN, N. W. AND ECKEL, J. L.: Endarteritis of the small cortical vessels in severe infections and toxemias. Arch. Neurol. & Psychiat., 21:863, 1929.
ZELLWEGER, H. AND IDRISS, H.: Encephalopathy in salmonella infections. Am. J. Dis. Child., 99:770, 1960.
ZIMMERMAN, H. M. AND YANNET, H.: Cerebral changes in pneumococcus septicemia. Report of a case with necropsy. J. Nerv. & Ment. Dis., 75:386, 1932.

NEUROPATHIES

POLYNEURITIS AND OTHER NEUROLOGICAL CONDITIONS DUE TO DIPHTHERIA

Definition.—A very common form of polyneuritis due to the toxin of Bacillus diphtheriae.

Pathological Anatomy.—The lesions are found in the peripheral nerves. It is generally taught that in diphtheritic polyneuritis the process is more diffuse and less definitely confined to the peripheral parts of the nerves than in neuritis due to other causes. The process is roughly symmetrical on the two sides and in most cases involves the nerves of the lower extremities more severely than those of the arms. The nerves may be slightly swollen or congested but gross alterations are usually inconspicuous. Histological preparations reveal that destruction of myelin is perhaps the earliest change. By means of the Weigert stain, it is seen that the medullary sheath is broken up to a large extent. In the Marchi stain one finds globular deposits of lipoid material lying in long chains within the nerve sheath. Many of these are contained within phagocytes but others lie between the nerve fibers. The cells composing the sheath of Schwann undergo proliferation and take up lipoid material and phagocytes also appear in the interstitial connective tissue. The axis cylinders are not injured so severely as the myelin sheaths but in sections stained by Bielschowski's method, it may be seen that they are swollen and irregular, showing spindle-shaped enlargements and varicosities or even granular degeneration in advanced cases. The proximal parts of the nerve trunks, the plexuses and the spinal nerve roots may show no definite changes. True inflammatory phenomena are lacking. A study by Fisher and Adams of 6 cases of diphtheritic polyneuritis revealed that the chief change was demyelination involving most severely the nerve fibers within the posterior root ganglia and in the adjacent portions of the spinal roots and peripheral nerves. Similar changes were found more peripherally in 2 cases. Wallerian degeneration was not prominent in any case. There was no evidence of an inflammatory or allergic process.

In some cases, the spinal cord seems to be quite normal, even when subjected to careful histological examination. As a rule, however, there is mild chromatolysis of the motor cells in the anterior horns and perhaps slight changes of a similar nature in other neurons in the gray matter. Interstitial myocarditis is a common finding.

Pathogenesis.—It seems to be established beyond reasonable doubt that diphtheritic polyneuritis is due to the production of a neurotropic toxin which is absorbed into the blood stream and carried throughout the body. It has been shown that the toxin is a protein.

Walshe has made a very illuminating analysis of the mechanism of diphtheritic paralysis as a result of a study of wounds infected by Bacillus diphtheriae. He shows that three types must be considered. (1) Local or regional palsies which are believed to result from local action of the toxin. The best example of this is the paralysis of the pharynx in the common pharyngeal diphtheria. Palsies due to the presence of the toxin in the blood stream which may be subdivided into two groups; (2) the generalized type or polyneuritis, and (3) the specific or selective type illustrated by the paralysis of the ciliary muscle which is peculiar to diphtheria. The first type develops much sooner than the generalized polyneuritis and its location depends, of course, upon the location of the infection. Thus, when infants develop diphtheritic infection of the umbilicus, the abdominal muscles may be paralyzed first. The paralysis of accommodation, however, develops regardless of the site of the infection and, therefore, represents the action of a blood-borne poison as does the generalized polyneuritis.

Clinical Features.—Diphtheria was at one time regarded as the commonest cause of polyneuritis in childhood. It is usually stated that some evidence of neuritis develops from 10 to 20 per cent of all cases of diphtheria. The incidence of paralysis does not depend entirely upon the severity of the disease for very extensive paralysis may follow relatively mild infections, especially if the diagnosis is not made and the patient is not properly treated.

The neurological features usually develop in a definite sequence. In severe cases there may be restlessness, confusion and delirium in the acute stages of the illness. In fatal cases there is usually coma. In the common pharyngeal type of diphtheria, one may observe a nasal voice and regurgitation of fluids through the nose between the fifth and twelfth day. This is due to paralysis of the soft palate. At the same time the constrictors of the pharynx may be affected causing difficulty in swallowing and the voice may become hoarse and finally may be lost. These symptoms are attributed to a local action of the toxin. Paralysis of this type is the first to develop and is not infrequently the only evidence of neuritis noted. These bulbar palsies usually begin to regress within ten days or two weeks. Apparently such palsies may result from infections too mild to cause generalized polyneuritis, for the pharyngeal paralysis may occur without general paralysis but the converse is quite rare.

During the third week, vision may become blurred as a result of paralysis of the ciliary muscle. In older children, it may be discovered that distant vision is clear but close vision is so indistinct that it is impossible to read. In some cases where the muscle is merely weak, the child may be able to read a few lines then can go no further for the weakened muscle soon fatigues. As a rule, these symptoms are not associated with other evidences of third nerve paralysis but in some cases the entire third nerve may be paralysed and the pupil dilated and immobile. Sometimes the contraction of the pupil during accommodation is lost but the light reflex is preserved. The sixth nerve is sometimes involved as are the facial and the hypoglossal.

The signs of polyneuritis are usually deferred until between the third and eighth week, and, therefore, may first appear after the paralysis of the pharynx has receded. We then may find muscular weakness with foot and wrist drop, loss of tendon reflexes, pains in the extremities, tenderness of the muscles and nerve trunks and hyperesthesia of the skin as well as some degree of hypesthesia. The sensory disturbances are usually less evident than the motor symptoms but in children old enough to cooperate, extensive paralysis is always associated with peripheral loss of sensibility of some degree. Complete anesthesia, however, is rare. Proprioception is sometimes severely affected and may be the cause of the ataxia which is sometimes described. The paralysis is, of course, most severe in the distal muscle groups as in other types of polyneuritis, but in severe cases the proximal muscle groups may be involved as well. Thus, in infants it is not unusual to find weakness of the neck so the head cannot be sustained and falls forward when the child is placed in a sitting position. The back may be weakened in the same manner. The most serious condition, however, is weakness of the muscles of respiration. In most cases this is due to paralysis of the phrenic nerve and some weakness of the intercostals. This is indicated by attacks of dyspnea. Later, the voice becomes very weak, the dyspnea becomes more constant and there is cyanosis of the lips. The breathing is of the thoracic type and is rapid and shallow. Myocardial weakness is a typical sign and is one of the common causes of a fatal outcome. Paralysis of the extremities usually reaches its height within a week or ten days after it first appears and lasts for a similar or greater period before it begins to recede slowly. As a rule, it lasts in all between two months and a year. In some cases, considerable muscular atrophy may result. Palsies of isolated nerves such as the ulnar nerve, the peroneus or the long thoracic are described but are rare. Some local factor must enter into such selective palsies. Loss of sphincter control is very rare.

In diphtheritic infections of unusual location, the symptoms are rather atypical. Thus, in primary laryngeal diphtheria, the fever and constitutional symptoms may be mild or lacking at first and the only symptoms are those of laryngeal paralysis or obstruction. Such cases may prove fatal within a very short time. Nasal diphtheria may also occur without severe constitutional symptoms. There is usually a blood-tinged nasal discharge which causes excoriation about the nostrils. Rare cases of diphtheritic infection of the umbilicus, of the vagina and of wounds are described. These are of interest in that they are sometimes associated with regional paralysis corresponding to the site of the infection.

The spinal fluid is clear and shows, as a rule, no increase of cells. There is, however, in most cases a definite increase in globulin which may reach high levels in some cases and lead to the erroneous diagnosis of the Guillain-Barré syndrome. The blood counts reveal a leucocytosis which is, in general, proportional to the severity of the illness. In fulminating cases, however, there may be reduction of the polymorphonuclear leucocytes. Anemia often develops.

Several neurological syndromes other than polyneuritis are described in connection with diphtheria. Hemiplegia and other signs pointing to lesions in the cerebral hemispheres are the most common. Rolleston has collected a number of cases of hemiplegia which developed during the course of diphtheria. He distinguishes two types: the transient and the persisting. The latter are almost certainly due to embolism of the cerebral arteries resulting from the discharge of minute fragments of mural thrombi from the heart. They are, as a rule, associated with dilatation of the heart, irregular pulse, enlargement of the liver and often with evidences of embolism in other organs. The onset is, of course, apoplectic. The transient palsies are not explained so easily. Rolleston has suggested that they may be due to very minute emboli or to uremic intoxication but spasm of the cerebral arteries has been regarded as a possible cause. Hinds, Howell and Ironsides have reported a case of hemiplegia in which there were multiple hemorrhages throughout the body and suggested that this was an instance of "hemorrhagic encephalitis." Cerebral lesions may also result from thrombosis due to injury to the vessel walls as in other severe infections. In a few cases diphtheria has been followed by incoordination of cerebellar type to which the name of acute cerebellar ataxia has been applied. The anatomical basis of this condition is unknown. Both Critchley and Globus have observed an acute choreic syndrome following diphtheria. Cardiac weakness is a common and serious complication. In fulminating cases heart failure may be the cause of death. The symptoms may develop suddenly with little warning. The electrocardiogram may reveal ventricular escape, prolonged QRS complex, intraventricular block, and AV dissociation.

Diagnosis.—If the child shows typical lesions in the pharynx, the diagnosis offers a few difficulties, as a rule, for the spreading membrane, the constitutional symptoms and the morphology of the organisms in a stained smear from the membrane usually permit the diagnosis to be made within a few hours, and this may be confirmed later by cultures. The most difficult cases are those in which the membrane is atypical or is situated in some inaccessible location such as the nose, the trachea or the larynx. In such cases, the diagnosis can be made only by demonstration of the organisms. Diphtheria is not likely in an immunized child. In some cases, children come under observation suffering from polyneuritis of several weeks' duration and no history of preceding diphtheria can be obtained. If we can elicit a history of pharyngeal paralysis, paralysis of accommodation, and later polyneuritis, we may be sure of the diagnosis even then, for the sequence of events in diphtheritic paralysis is very typical. If the patient is found to have virulent organisms in the throat the diagnosis is confirmed.

Prognosis.—The prognosis for the paralysis is, in general, favorable if the child survives. As a rule, there is complete recovery within a year even if the paralysis is severe and in mild cases of paralysis relatively prompt recovery may be expected. Exceptions to this rule are well known, however. The writer has examined a man of 54 years who suffered from a severe attack of diphtheria at the age of four years complicated by extensive paralysis from which he never recovered. When examined, he showed defective development of the extremities, especially the legs with small calf muscles and foot drop on the left, but the trunk, neck and shoulders were muscular and well developed. Both ankle jerks were absent. No disturbances of sensibility were found.

Prophylaxis.—Infants are now immunized by the injection of the alum precipitated toxoid. It is advised that four injections be given between the ages of 3 months and 18 months. This is believed to give prolonged protection. It is also advised that additional injections be given at the ages of 3, 6 and 9 years.

Treatment.—It is scarcely necessary to discuss the treatment of diphtheria. In brief it may be said that the most important measure is the administration of a potent antitoxin in full doses at the earliest possible moment. The child should be kept at complete rest and should receive the best nursing care. The indications for intubation or tracheotomy are described in all standard textbooks. Proper isolation is required until virulent bacilli disappear from the throat. Penicillin, erythromycin and the tetracycline drugs are said to be helpful. The paralysis does not require any special treatment, as a rule, except for proper rest. If the pharynx is paralysed, gavage may be required, and if respiration is involved, the Drinker respirator may be used advantageously. We have kept a child with paralysis of respiration alive for three months in the respirator. She eventually made a good recovery. If this machine is not obtainable, oxygen may help. Later, during convalescence, massage, passive movements and carefully supervised exercises are indicated. In some cases, light wire braces are required for the foot drop. Special care must be taken to avoid excessive exertion because of the danger of heart failure. The anemia may be treated by the administration of iron. When children are not seen until after the acute stage of the disease, there seems to be no indication for the administration of antitoxin, for the paralysis will not be affected in any way.

BIBLIOGRAPHY

BROWN, M.: Mechanisms involved in polyneuritis as exemplified in post-diphtheritic polyneuritis. Ann. Med., **36:**786, 1952.

BRÜCKNER: Akute Ataxie nach Diphtherie. Deutsche med. Wochnschr., **35:**1249, 1909.

CRITCHLEY, McD.: Post-diphtheritic chorea. Brit. J. Child. Dis., **21:**188, 1924.

DELP, M. H., SUTHERLAND, G. F. AND HASHINGER, E. H.: Postdiphtheritic polyneuritis. Report of five cases with albuminocytologic dissociation simulating Guillain-Barré syndrome. Ann. Int. Med., **24:**618, 1946.

DOLGOPOL, V. B. AND KATZ, S. H.: Encephalitis in diphtheria. Am. J. Dis. Child., **79:**640, 1950.

FISHER, C. M. AND ADAMS, R. D.: Diphtheritic polyneuritis. A pathological study. J. Neuropath. & Exp. Neurol., **15:**243, 1956.

GLOBUS, J. H.: Ueber Symptomatische Chorea bei Diphtherie. Ztschr. f. d. ges. Neurol. u. Psychiat., **85:**414, 1923.

IRONSIDES, R. AND HOWELL, H.: Cases of hemiplegia due to hemorrhagic encephalitis following diphtheria. Proc. Roy. Soc. of London, Sec. Dis. Child., **19:**3, 1925.

MORGAN, B. C.: Myocarditis in diphtheria. Pediatrics, **32:**549, 1963.

ROLLESTON, J. D.: Diphtheritic paralysis. Arch. Pediat., **30:**335, 1913.

————: Hemiplegia. Rev. Neurol. & Psychiat., **14:**145, 1916.

SEROG: Cerebellare ataxie nach Diphtherie. Med. Klin., **12:**1255, 1916.

WALSH, F. B.: *Loc. cit.*

WALSHE, F. M. R.: The pathogenesis of diphtheritic paralysis. Quart. J. Med., **12:**14, 1918.

ACRODYNIA

Definition.—This is a condition characterized by a cutaneous eruption, hyperesthesia, loss of muscle tone and psychic changes as described below. It is called erythredema, erythredema polyneuritis, pink disease, Swift's disease and Feer's vegetative neurosis.

Etiology.—The cause is not yet established. Many authorities believe that acrodynia is the result of some specific infection; others favor dietary deficiency and have suggested that lack of vitamin B may be responsible. The infection theory is supported by the occurrence of leucocytosis in most cases, by the occasional development of two cases in one family and the frequent but not invariable association of upper respiratory tract infections with the disease. The cutaneous lesions have been compared with those of pellagra by the adherents of the dietary deficiency theory but, as a rule, no history of an inadequate diet is elicited. It seems to be clear that chronic arsenic poisoning may give rise to symptoms which are distinguished with difficulty from those of acrodynia, but it scarcely seems likely that arsenic is a factor in many cases as has been suggested. Recently it has been suggested that mercury poisoning due to calomel is responsible. Calomel may be used in teething powders, diaper rinses, as a vermifuge, laxative and tonic. Mercurial ointments are also mentioned.

Pathological Anatomy.—There is no general agreement about the anatomical basis of this disease and only a few post-mortem examinations have been made by trained neuropathologists. The clinical signs and symptoms strongly suggest involvement of the peripheral nerves and Greenfield and Paterson, Kernohan and Kennedy and Wyllie and Stern have, indeed, found considerable myelin destruction in the nerves which they regard as evidence of a toxic neuritis. Some authors have been unable to find these changes and are skeptical of the existence of polyneuritis, but the weight of evidence, in the writer's opinion, seems to favor the existence of mild changes in the peripheral nerves. Orton and Bender believe that they found significant degeneration in the lateral horns of the spinal gray matter where the neurons of the sympathetic nerves lie. They describe minute hemorrhages and gliosis. Greenfield and Stern found chromatolysis of the anterior horn cells and proliferation of glial cells, although their description is not identical with that of Orton. Several writers have found lesions in the brain, in the cortex, the floor of the fourth ventricle and thalamus and the infundibulum, but these descriptions are not very convincing and no two writers report the same lesions.

Warthin studied the skin lesions very carefully. He states that there is edema, hyperkeratosis and proliferation of the reticuloendothelial cells in the corium and papillary layer which he thinks are very similar to the lesions in the early stage of pellagra.

There may be enlargement of the lymph nodes, bronchopneumonia, enteritis, either catarrhal or ulcerative, cloudy swelling and chronic passive congestion of the viscera.

Clinical Features.—The disease is apparently confined to children and infants and occurs between the age of four months and four years, as a rule, although cases have been described as early as six weeks and as late as fourteen years. There seems to be no definite racial or sexual predilection. Feer claims that there is a tendency for the disease to recur in certain localities and to avoid other localities but this feature has not been observed by others. In America, acrodynia is most prevalent in winter or spring but in Australia the majority of cases appear in the summer or autumn.

The onset may be abrupt but is more often gradual. The child becomes restless and irritable, sleep is disturbed and appetite fails. Often there is a mild elevation of temperature for a time. Such symptoms may exist for from one to three weeks before the more distinctive symptoms appear. In other cases, there is only a mild fever for several days associated with infection of the upper respiratory tract or perhaps without obvious cause. This is followed by a remission of several days or a week.

At the end of the second or third week, however, the cutaneous lesions have usually appeared. There is often a general erythema at first which covers the body as well as the extremities. Soon this fades to a large extent over the body but at the same time becomes more severe over the hands and feet. Usually only miliaria and sudaminal eruptions remain over the body.

The hands and feet are swollen, cold and dusky red, presenting an appearance which has been compared to raw beef. The lesions are most intense at the tips of the fingers and toes and slowly fade out over the wrists and ankles. Scattered papules of dark red may be seen over the hands and feet as well as bullae. Similar lesions are seen over the tip of the nose, the cheek bones and perhaps the ears. Later there is desquamation and large pieces of skin may exfoliate. Ulcerations are common over the fingers and toes. The finger and toe nails are often lost. Gangrene of the tips of the digits is described. The hair often falls out or is pulled out. Bower finds that if one hand is immersed in warm water the other extremities do not show the usual reflex increase of temperature. Many of these lesions are the result of trauma, for the eruption is very irritating and unless restrained, the child will scratch and bite the fingers until they are deeply lacerated. There is naturally secondary infection of the skin in many cases. The eruption undergoes fluctuations from time to time, fading and then returning without apparent cause.

The neurological symptoms are usually present by the time the cutaneous lesions are well developed. There is profound weakness of all extremities as a rule and virtual paralysis of the legs has been described, although it is rare. We have recently studied the case of a child (Ped. 94075) in which there was bilateral foot-drop and the usual signs of a severe polyneuritis. There was complete reaction of degeneration in the dorsiflexors of the toes and ankles. The weakness is accompanied by extreme loss of muscle tone which is out of proportion in many cases to the weakness. The tendon reflexes are usually greatly diminished and often lost. The muscles may be wasted. The muscles and nerves seem to be extremely tender and there is also definite cutaneous hyperesthesia. In some cases loss of sensibility of peripheral distribution is demonstrable. At this stage the picture is very distinctive. The child presents the appearance of utter misery, whining, crying and scratching constantly. There is no interest in toys or in food. Sleep is greatly disturbed. These children often assume a rather characteristic posture with the face down on the pillow and the knees drawn up under the body. It has often been said that the mental condition is normal but in the writer's opinion this is untrue, for some children have been semi-delirious or confused. In one case we have observed the constant repetition of a meaningless phrase. Convulsions are unusual and there are no clinical evidences of meningeal irritation. Generalized and profuse perspiration is a very characteristic feature of these conditions. This gives rise to a peculiar "mousy" odor which is considered distinctive.

Loss of appetite is almost constant and leads to emaciation but other gastrointestinal symptoms are not conspicuous, as a rule. Either diarrhea or constipation may occur, the latter being more frequent. Thirst is often excessive. There is often lacrimation, photophobia and conjunctivitis. Keratitis may occur. Gingivitis is not uncommon and ulcerations of the gums or cheeks are described. Excessive salivation is a very frequent symptom. Infections of the respiratory tract are common. Coryza, pharyngitis, tonsillitis, sinusitis, bronchitis and broncho-pneumonia are often described. The cervical lymph nodes are usually moderately enlarged. The spleen is rarely palpable. The pulse is constantly accelerated, ranging from 120 to 160. The blood pressure is elevated, as a rule, ranging from 100 to 130 mm. Hg. There is no fever unless there is a complicating infection.

The laboratory studies are not very helpful. The blood shows a constant leucocytosis ranging from 10,000 to 20,000. This may be due to an increase in leucocytes or there may be no change in differential formula. A mild secondary anemia may be present. Blood cultures are negative and cultures from the nose and throat are not productive of any constant result. The spinal fluid is normal as a rule but may contain an excess of globulin. Cobb has found changes in the long bones which were somewhat similar to those of infantile scurvy but which he did not consider specific. The urine shows a trace of albumin. Mercury may be found in the urine.

Diagnosis.—The diagnosis is usually made with ease if the symptoms are fully developed. The combination of cutaneous lesions, irritability, weakness, hypotonus, profuse sweating, drooling, tachycardia and hypertension in a child between the ages of four months and five years is distinctive. The posture is often characteristic, as is the expression of misery in the face.

Prognosis.—The mortality is usually given as approximately 10 per cent or less. The disease is frequently prolonged, however. In mild cases recovery may occur within four to six weeks but in more severe cases the disease may drag on for a year or more. The course is irregular and improvement gradual. In fatal cases death usually results from secondary infections such as broncho-pneumonia, pulmonary abscess, tuberculosis and various pyogenic infections. There are apparently no sequelae apart from the scars of the ulcerations.

Treatment.—No treatment is of proven value. Some authors recommend diets containing large amounts of vitamin B but most observers have found this to be valueless. Others have seen improvement follow removal of infected tonsils or treatment of an infected sinus. Wyllie and Stern have been led to believe that feeding liver is helpful. Others have recommended the use of mercury-vapor arc lamp. On the theory that mercury poisoning is responsible, BAL has been given and good results are claimed. Bower states that vasodilators such as hexamethonium give definite relief of symptoms.

The child should be given sedatives for insomnia and pain. It may be necessary to tie the hands to prevent scratching or to fasten on cotton gloves. Calamine lotion and other soothing applications may be used to relieve the itching and sensitiveness of the skin lesions. The diet should be abundant and should contain adequate amounts of the vitamins. If the child will not eat, gavage should be employed. Foci of infections should be treated.

BIBLIOGRAPHY

Bivings, L. and Lewis, G.: Acrodynia: A new treatment with BAL. J. Pediat., **32**:63, 1948.

Bowers, B. D.: Pink disease and its treatment with ganglion blocking agents. Quart. J. Med., **23**:215, 1954.

Byfield, A. H.: A polyneuritic syndrome resembling pellagra (acrodynia). Amer. J. Dis. Child., **20**:347, 1920.

Chamberlain, J. L. and Quillian, W. W.: The diagnosis and treatment of acrodynia. Clin. Pediat., **2**:439, 1963.

Cobb, C.: Acrodynia. Amer. J. Dis. Child., **46**:1076, 1923.

Elmore, S. E.: Ingestion of mercury as a probable cause of acrodynia. Pediatrics, **1**:643, 1948.

Fischer, A. E. and Hodes, H. L.: Subacute mercury poisoning (acrodynia) caused by protiodide of mercury. J. Pediat., **40**:143, 1952.

Orton, S. T. and Bender, L.: Lesions in the lateral horns of the spinal cord in acrodynia, pellagra and pernicious anemia. Bull. Neurol. Inst. N.Y., **1**:506, 1931.

Parsons, L. G.: Pink disease. Practitioner, **125**:146, 1930.

Paterson, D. and Greenfield, J. G.: Erythredema polyneuritis. Quart. J. Med., **17**:6, 1923-24.

Rodda, F. C.: Acrodynia. A clinical study of 17 cases. Am. J. Dis. Child., **30**:224, 1925.

Thursfield, J. H. and Paterson, D. H.: Dermato-polyneuritis (Acrodynia: Erythredema). Brit. J. Child. Dis., **19**:27, 1922.

Walsh, F. B.: *Loc. cit.*

Warthin, A. S.: The so-called acrodynia or erythredema (Swift's disease). Arch. Path., **1**:64, 1926; Swift's disease. Proc. Assn. for Research Nerv. & Ment. Dis., 1930, p. 9.

Weston, W.: Acrodynia. Arch. Ped., **37**:513, 1920.

Wyllie, W. G. and Stern, R. O.: Pink disease; Its morbid anatomy with a note on treatment. Arch. Dis. Child., **6**:137, 1931.

FAMILIAL HYPERTROPHIC POLYNEURITIS ASSOCIATED WITH A PARAPROTEIN IN THE SERUM (GIBBERD AND GAVRILESCU)

The clinical picture is that of a very slowly progressive polyneuritis similar in some respects to the familial hypertrophic polyneuritis of Dejerine and Sottas. A mother and son were studied. The family tree included 29 persons and 5 generations. Two members of previous generations were affected.

The son's symptoms began at the age of 15 years. There was generalized wasting of the muscles which was most severe in the distal muscles. There was great weakness of the intrinsic muscles of the hands and also severe weakness at the ankle and toe joints. His feet became deformed and several operations on the feet were required. The tendon reflexes were all reduced and the knee and ankle jerks were lost. No loss of sensibility was found except for slight reduction of vibratory sense. The peripheral nerve trunks were enlarged.

Biopsy of a peripheral nerve revealed demyelination and muscle biopsy showed only neurogenic atrophy. An abnormal protein was discovered by electrophoretic study. This migrated between the beta and the gamma globulins. It was present not only in the serum of the mother and son but in the spinal fluid and the urine.

BIBLIOGRAPHY

GIBBERD, F. B. AND GAVRILESCU, K.: A familial neuropathy associated with a paraprotein in the serum, cerebrospinal fluid and urine. Neurology, **16**:130, 1966.

ACUTE INFECTIVE POLYNEURITIS OF UNKNOWN ORIGIN AND THE SYNDROME OF OPHTHALMOPLEGIA, ATAXIA AND AREFLEXIA OF FISHER

Definition.—Under this title the writer includes certain cases in which a brief febrile illness is followed by a symmetrical paralysis of the extremities often involving the proximal muscle groups more than the distal groups and often associated with bilateral facial paralysis. Numerous names have been applied to this condition, such as polyneuritis with facial diplegia, infective neuronitis, polyradiculitis, myeloradiculo-polyneuritis, etc. The more acute and severe cases are identical with Landry's paralysis.

Etiology.—It is generally agreed that acute infective polyneuritis is due to an infection but the nature of the etiological agent is quite unknown. In fact, it is not improbable that several infections may enter into the production of this clinical picture. Bradford, Bashford and Wilson claimed in 1919 that they had isolated a filterable virus which was capable of reproducing the disease in monkeys but later this claim was withdrawn and no further positive results have been published. One gets the impression that we are dealing with an infection in the upper respiratory tract by an organism which produces a powerful neurotoxin. The assumption that a virus is responsible is not supported by good evidence. The most potent neurotoxins we know, namely those of botulism, tetanus and diphtheria, are all of bacterial origin.

Pathological Anatomy.—Only a few post-mortem examinations have been made and these have given somewhat divergent results. In almost all cases there has been definite degeneration of the peripheral nerves as in the common types of polyneuritis. In most cases, however, the degeneration has extended into the ventral and dorsal roots to an extent seldom observed in polyneuritis of the common variety, and the spinal gray matter and the dorsal root ganglia have also shown unusually severe changes. Thus, there is congestion of the small vessels, extensive chromatolysis of the neurons and accumulation of glial cells, not only in the spinal gray matter but in the motor nuclei of the cranial nerves. The central lesions, however, are not invariable for Gordon Holmes found only degeneration of the peripheral nerves in two of his cases. In cases of brief duration, only chromatolysis of the anterior horn motor cells is observed. Some observers mention striking changes in the pia-arachnoid such as edema, hyperemia, small hemorrhages and even cellular infiltrations, but others consider the meninges normal. Honeyman has recently reported four cases in which a careful histological study with modern methods revealed no significant changes in the nervous system. The evidence seems to indicate that we are dealing with the effect of a toxin upon the nervous system and that this condition is merely an atypical polyneuritis. It is well known that in some instances intracranial pressure is greatly increased. Since the ventricles are small as a rule, we have been inclined to attribute this to edema of the brain, but Denny-Brown found at post-mortem examination in one case that the Pacchionian villi were plugged by masses of amorphous material which he attributed to clots forming in the spinal fluid which contained large amounts of protein. Denny-Brown speaks of external hydrocephalus.

Clinical Features.—This disease may occur at any age. It is sporadic, as a rule, and no definite epidemics have been reported. There is no special predilection for either sex.

In most cases there is a mild febrile illness at the onset. The fever lasts a day or two and may be associated with headache, pains in the back and abdomen, vomiting and perhaps some prostration. Often there is an upper respiratory tract infection such as coryza, pharyngitis or bronchitis. Less commonly gastrointestinal symptoms occur. These symptoms have frequently been attributed to influenza but the evidence for this diagnosis is slender. In some cases these symptoms are absent or so mild that the parents fail to mention them. Only rarely is the child seriously ill. After the initial symptoms there is usually a latent period varying in duration from several days to several weeks during which the patient may seem to be quite well or may complain only of fatigue and weakness. The variation in the length of the latent period is so great that one often wonders whether the initial fever is actually related to the neurological symptoms which follow.

The onset of symptoms referable to the nervous system is usually relatively sudden. Within a day or even a few hours generalized muscular weakness develops to such a degree that the patient may be unable to walk or even move about in bed. In other cases the weakness may begin locally and extend slowly over a period of a week. The distribution of the palsies is peculiar in that they may seem to involve the proximal muscle groups more severely than the distal muscle groups. The muscles acting upon the hip joint are often the first to be affected, but the pelvic and shoulder girdle muscles, as well as those which act upon the elbow and knee joints, are also involved early. The muscles of the trunk, neck, back, abdomen and chest may be paralyzed. Sometimes, the distal groups of muscles are scarcely affected at all but usually they are weak, if not paralyzed. In less typical cases, the weakness is generalized or may even select the distal muscle groups as in the common polyneuritis. Later, muscular atrophy may develop but rarely becomes severe. One is sometimes astonished by the moderate degree of the atrophy even in cases of complete and long-standing paralysis. The tendon reflexes are, of course, lost or reduced. The paralysis of the intercostals may cause dyspnea and paralysis of respiration may occur when the diaphragm is also involved. Disturbances of sphincter control are not uncommon but are usually transient. A very typical and frequent feature is the bilateral paralysis of the facial nerve which is not, however, invariably present. This may be complete or partial and may appear simultaneously on the two sides, or one side of the face and then the other may be affected in succession. It is possible that the bilateral types of facial paralysis which sometimes occur without other symptoms may be abortive cases of infective polyneuritis.

It is not unusual for the bulbar muscles to be paralyzed but disturbances of vision, ocular palsies or loss of pupillary reactions are rare. In fact, the facial nerves are the only cranial nerves to be affected in most cases. Disturbances of sensibility are not prominent, as a rule, and it may be impossible to discover any definite anesthesia even in cases of several weeks' duration. In some cases, however, there is hypesthesia which corresponds in its distribution to distribution of the palsies. In cases in which the weakness is predominantly proximal, there may be anesthesia over the thighs, the upper arms and even the trunk, corresponding more to the dermatomes than to the areas supplied by peripheral nerves. When the palsies are distal, the hypesthesia is also distal. Pain is rarely severe but is usually present. Often the patient mentions only dull aching in the back and paresthesias. In the writer's experience, there is only mild tenderness of the muscles. The mental condition is quite normal, as a rule, and consciousness may be unaltered until death.

During the paralytic stage of the disease there is usually no significant elevation of temperature although a low grade fever is reported in some cases. Moderate leucocytosis is often found. There is usually tachycardia, however, which bears no relation to the temperature. Cardiac dilatation may occur. The spinal fluid is clear and contains no excess of cells as a rule. The protein content may be increased or normal. In some cases there is a great excess of protein and massive coagulation of the spinal fluid is described as in Froin's syndrome. The French neurologists regard the great excess of protein as characteristic of this group of cases to which the term Guillain-Barré syndrome is applied. The protein content of the spinal fluid may be normal during the acute stages of the disease and yet reach a very high level during convalescence. This sign is not specific, however, for similar increase in spinal fluid protein may occur in polyneuritis due to diphtheria and other common diseases.

In a small percentage of cases, there is increased intracranial pressure with papilledema. The spinal fluid pressure may reach 600 mm of water. The intracranial pressure may remain at a high level for several months and it may be necessary to perform subtemporal decompression to prevent loss of vision from secondary optic atrophy.

The course is variable. In most cases, the onset is abrupt and the symptoms advance rapidly for one or two weeks. If the patient survives, improvement is usually evident within one or two months. Less commonly, one sees cases in which the onset is less abrupt and the weakness grows slowly more severe for two or three months. Occasionally the paralysis may recede and then advance again. I have seen a few instances in which second attacks occurred. In fatal cases, death usually occurs within the first two weeks of the illness. Death is usually due to paralysis of the muscles of respiration. Respiration may suddenly cease in patients whose respiration had seemed strong up to that moment. Convalescence is in general somewhat more rapid than in other types of polyneuritis but may be protracted. Occasionally severe ataxia of cerebellar type may persist after the weakness has disappeared. Striking increase of tendon reflexes sometimes occurs during convalescence suggesting that the long tracts may have sustained some damage.

Ertel *et al.* describe four cases of the Guillain-Barré syndrome in which the serum sodium was significantly reduced. In two cases, the reduction of serum sodium was severe enough to cause symptoms. They found three similar cases described in medical literature and after their paper was presented in abstract, they were informed of three additional cases. They believe that the hyponatremia resulted from excessive release of the antidiuretic hormone.

It seems wise to discuss the so-called *Landry's paralysis* at this point. The term has been loosely applied to almost any type of acute ascending paralysis but in the narrow and more accurate sense indicates a massive rapidly developing flaccid paralysis, usually but not always ascending, which is not associated with outspoken disturbances of sensibility, with loss of sphincter control, disturbances of consciousness, fever or pleocytosis in the spinal fluid. It should be added that the anatomical changes are inconspicuous and as a rule one finds chromatolysis of the motor cells in the spinal cord or no anatomical alterations at all. It must be admitted that this clinical and anatomical picture may follow a number of infections and intoxication but in most cases the cause is quite obscure. The characteristic features of the cases under consideration correspond so closely to those described by Landry that it appears to be useless to devote a separate discussion to the latter. We may regard Landry's paralysis as exemplified by the more acute and fatal cases of acute infective polyneuritis.

Richter has published a case in which the diagnosis of Guillain-Barré syndrome was made which was characterized by severe ataxia due to loss of proprioception. At post-mortem examination, extensive degeneration in the posterior columns of the cord were found apparently secondary to degeneration of the posterior nerve roots.

Fisher has published cases of ophthalmoplegia, areflexia and ataxia which he suggests may be variants of acute infective polyneuritis. There is complete or nearly complete external ophthalmoplegia which in some cases seems to be of supranuclear type. The ataxia seems to be of cerebellar origin. The tendon reflexes are lost but there is no massive paralysis such as is seen in acute infective polyneuritis. The spinal fluid protein is moderately increased. The prognosis is good. One case in a boy is given below which seems to belong in this category. Smith and Walsh have published similar cases.

Diagnosis.—The diagnosis is based upon the history of a preceding febrile illness, the proximal distribution of the muscular palsies, the presence of bilateral facial paralysis, minimal or absent sensory changes, the increase of spinal fluid protein and the absence of any demonstrable cause for symptoms. Poliomyelitis is usually ruled out with ease because of the absence of significant elevation of temperature at the onset of the paralysis, the absence of signs of meningeal irritation, the normal cell count in the spinal fluid, and the symmetrical distribution of the palsies. There may be some difficulty in distinguishing this condition from other types of polyneuritis for none of the features mentioned above are constant or entirely peculiar to this condition. It should be stated that infectious mononucleosis may give rise to this same picture. The outlines of this group of cases will remain uncertain until the cause is discovered. In children who are seen during the period of convalescence, the picture may bear some resemblance to that of muscular dystrophy in that the pelvic girdle and hip muscles are chiefly affected although, of course, there is no hypertrophy of the calves. In one case in which a proper history could not be obtained at first, we were in doubt about the diagnosis until the child began to recover. Later a complete history was elicited and the diagnosis seemed to be evident.

Prognosis.—No accurate figures can be offered as regards the mortality. In one series of cases 20 per cent resulted fatally. The outlook in any individual case depends upon the site and severity of the paralysis and upon the rapidity with which it is developing. The chief danger seems to be paralysis of the muscles of respiration. Recovery has seemed to be rather rapid and complete in our experience and the patients have usually been completely restored to health within a year. Occasionally weakness of the extremities may persist and the patient may remain an invalid. When the facial nerve is completely degenerated, there is apt to be contracture and distortion of the face as a result, causing permanent disfigurement. One little girl who had this disease at the age of 5 months subsequently developed mass movements of the face with such distorted expressions that she was shunned by the other children. Another patient developed the syndrome of crocodile tears though mass movements of the face were not pronounced. In some cases there has been a moderate increase in the tendon reflexes during convalescence and in one case this was still demonstrable a year after the onset.

Treatment.—Since the cause is obscure, the treatment is merely symptomatic. It has been claimed that various drugs including cortisone and dimercaptopropanol have some therapeutic value, but this is doubtful. If respiration fails or bulbar palsy develops, artificial respiration and possibly tracheotomy are necessary. See treatment of bulbar palsy in poliomyelitis. During convalescence, massage, passive movements and controlled exercises are indicated.

CASE HISTORY (Ped. 83097).—*Child of nine years developed a mild upper respiratory tract infection followed by polyneuritis. During convalescence. cerebellar ataxia became evident and papilledema developed. Recovery.*

W. B., a boy of nine years, developed coryza, pharyngitis, cough and fever on November 18, 1947. These symptoms lasted some four days. On November 23, he complained of pains in the legs, back and neck. The muscles seemed to be tender. There was no fever at that time, but the pain and tenderness grew more severe and he became very weak.

On November 28, he was admitted to the Sydenham's Hospital. At that time he was having severe pains in the legs, back and neck. There was pronounced tenderness of the muscles. Bilateral, diffuse and symmetrical weakness of the muscles of the arms, legs and trunk was evident. The knee and ankle jerks were lost. The temperature was normal and remained normal thereafter. The urine was negative. The spinal fluid on repeated tests contained an excess of protein but no excess of cells. The blood culture was negative and the cultures from the throat revealed no significant organisms. The tuberculin test was negative. Roentgenograms of the chest revealed only a minimal infiltration of the right lung root. the blood pressure was 110/70.

On December 3, the spinal fluid pressure was found to be 280 mm water. The protein was elevated (Pandy 2 plus). There was only one cell per cmm.

On December 4, the child had a convulsion. On December 6, he complained of headache and examination of the optic nerve heads revealed beginning papilledema.

On December 11, the pain and tenderness were somewhat less severe. It was possible to determine that the weakness was most pronounced in the legs and greater in the distal muscles than in the proximal muscles. The tendon reflexes were still absent. There was no demonstrable loss of sensibility. Ataxia was now demonstrable in both the arms and legs and this seemed to be of cerebellar type. The papilledema was more pronounced than before. The blood pressure was 150/100.

On December 20, the child was admitted to Harriet Lane Home. In the next few days strength improved and the pain and tenderness diminished. The ataxia became more evident and the papilledema increased. The blood pressure remained between 150 and 140 systolic and 110 to 120 diastolic. Tests of renal function showed no definite reduction. The spinal fluid pressure remained elevated and the total protein was 124 mgs per 100 cc.

On January 2, 1948, it was evident that the child was recovering. There was only questionable weakness in the legs. The ataxia was diminishing for the child could walk alone though he still staggered. The knee and ankle jerks had not returned. The papilledema was receding and the headache had ceased. The blood pressure was lower, averaging about 125/80. Recovery was rapid.

CASE HISTORY.—*Boy of 10 years developed complete external ophthalmoplegia, and cerebellar ataxia with sluggish tendon reflexes following a brief illness with diarrhea. Complete recovery after some weeks.*

J. G., a previously healthy boy of 10 years, developed an illness associated with diarrhea about the 5th of January, 1956. He seemed to be well again within a few days.

About January 12, he complained of headache. The next day he vomited and complained of double vision. He became unsteady on his feet.

On January 17, he was examined. The child was mentally clear and cooperated well. Vision was normal and the fields full. No changes were seen in the optic discs. There was very slight bilateral ptosis of the lids. The pupils were rather large and possibly reacted somewhat sluggishly. There was diplopia but no obvious squint. Ocular movements were almost completely lost. Not more than 3 degrees of movement was possible in any plane. The cranial nerves seemed to be in order in other respects.

The station and gait were both unsteady. There was no gross weakness of the extremities but there was ataxia of cerebellar type in all four extremities. No sensory disturbances were found. The tendon reflexes were rather sluggish.

The pulse, temperature and blood pressure were all normal. Medical examinations revealed nothing of significance. The spinal fluid contained no increase of cells but the protein content was slightly elevated. Routine laboratory studies were all negative.

Soon the child began to improve. On February 10, there was no ataxia and he walked well. There was still weakness of right lateral gaze, but upward, downward and left lateral movements of the eyes were of almost full range. Complete recovery soon occurred.

BIBLIOGRAPHY

ARING, C. D. AND SABIN, A. B.: Fatal infectious polyneuritis during childhood, etc. Arch. Neurol. & Psychiat., **47**:938, 1942.

ARKWRIGHT, J. A.: Criticism of certain recent claims to have discovered and cultivated filter-passing viruses of trench fever and influenza. Brit. Med. J., **2**:233, 1919.

AYLETT, P.: Five cases of acute infective polyneuritis. Arch. Dis. Child., **29**:531, 1954.

BRADFORD, J. R., BASHFORD, E. F. AND WILSON, J. A.: Acute infective polyneuritis. Quart. J. Med., **12**:88, 1919.

BUCHSBAUM, H. W. AND GALLO, A. E. JR.: Polyneuritis, papilledema and lumboperitoneal shunt. Arch. of Neurol., **21**:253, 1969.

CASAMAJOR, L. AND ALPERT, G. R.: Guillain-Barré syndrome in children. Am. J. Dis. Child., **61**:99, 1941.

DENNY-BROWN, D. E.: The changing pattern of neurologic medicine. New England J. Med., **246**:839, 1952.

ERTEL, N. H. *et al.*: Hyponatremia in acute polyneuropathy. Arch. of Neurol., **17**:530, 1967.

FISHER, M.: An unusual variant of acute idiopathic polyneuritis (Syndrome of ophthalmoplegia ataxia and areflexia). New England J. Med., **255**:57, 1956.

FORD, F. R. AND WALSH, F. B.: Guillain-Barré syndrome (acute infective polyneuritis) with increased intracranial pressure and papilledema. Bull. Johns Hopkins Hosp., **73**:391, 1943.

GILLESPIE, J. B. AND FIELD, E. H.: Acute polyneuritis of uncertain origin. J. Pediat., **14**:363, 1939.

GILPIN, S. F., MOERSCH, F. P. AND KERNOHAN, J. W.: Polyneuritis. A clinical and pathologic study of a special group of cases frequently referred to as instances of neuronitis. Arch. Neurol. & Psych., **35**:937, 1936.

GOODWIN, R. F. AND POSER, C. M.: Ophthalmoplegia, ataxia and areflexia, Fisher's syndrome. J.A.M.A., **186**:258, 1963.

GUILLAIN, G.: Radiculoneuritis with acellular hyperalbuminosis of the cerebrospinal fluid. Arch. of Neurol. and Psychiat., **36**:975, 1936.

HECHT, M. S.: Acute infective polyneuritis in childhood. J. Pediat., **10**:743, 1937.

HOLMES, G.: Acute febrile polyneuritis. Brit. Med. J., **2**:37, 1917.

HONEYMAN, W. M.: Pathological study of a group of cases sometimes referred to as polyneuritis. Bull. of Neurological Inst. of New York, **6**:519, 1937.

KENNEDY, R. F.: Infective neuronitis. Arch. Neurol. & Psychiat., **2**:621, 1919.

LANDRY, J. B.: Note sur Paralysie ascendante aigue. Gaz. Hebd. de Med. Paris, 1859.

MARKLAND, L. D. AND RILEY, H. D.: Guillain-Barré syndrome in childhood. Clin. Pediat., **6**:162, 1967.

McFARLAND, H. R. AND HELLER, G. L.: Guillain-Barré disease complex. Arch. of Neurol., **14**:196, 1966.

MELNICK, S. C. AND FLEWETT, T. H.: Role of infection in the Guillain-Barré syndrome. Jour. Neurol. Neurosurg. and Psychiat., **27**:395, 1964.

NEWEY, J. A. AND LUBIN, R.: Corticotropin (ACTH) therapy in Guillain-Barré syndrome. J.A.M.A., **152**:137, 1953.

PATRICK, H. T.: Facial diplegia in multiple neuritis. J. Nerv. & Ment. Dis., **44**:322, 1916.

POSNER, J. B. *et al.*: Hyponatremia in acute polyneuropathy. Four cases with inappropriate secretion of antidiuretic hormone. Arch. of Neurol., **17**:530, 1967.

RICHTER, R. B.: The ataxic form of the Guillain-Barré syndrome. J. Neuropath. & Exp. Neurol., **21**:171, 1962.

SMITH, J. L. AND WALSH, F. B.: Syndrome of external ophthalmoplegia, ataxia and areflexia (Fisher). Arch. Ophth., **58**:109, 1957.

TAYLOR, E. W. AND MCDONALD, G. A.: The syndrome of polyneuritis with facial diplegia. Arch. Neurol. & Psychiat., 27:79, 1932.

VIETS, H. R.: Acute polyneuritis with facial diplegia. Arch. Neurol. & Psychiat., 17:794, 1927.

UVEITIS AND DEAFNESS WITH DEPIGMENTATION
OF HAIR AND SKIN

This is a very rare condition characterized by the triad of signs mentioned above. The cause is undetermined and there are no anatomical studies yet available. Even the clinical picture is vaguely outlined. The uveitis is usually bilateral and severe leading eventually in many instances to secondary glaucoma, phthisis bulbi and blindness. The course may be characterized by recurrent exacerbations and the process seems to be a progressive one during a period of months or perhaps years. The deafness is usually bilateral and is preceded by paroxysms of vertigo and tinnitus. After a number of such episodes the patient may remain completely deaf. In other cases deafness has been mild and transient so that one gains the impression that the prognosis for hearing is more favorable than for vision. The third group of symptoms, namely, loss of hair and depigmentation of the hair and skin is not always present. The eyelashes are said to turn white in a large percentage of cases, however. The depigmentation is the basis of the theory that these cases represent a state of sensitization to tissue pigments which leads to the destruction of the pigment bodies in the skin, hair, choroid and labyrinth. This condition is sometimes termed the Vogt-Koyanagi syndrome. In this connection two other syndromes should be mentioned. *Cogan's syndrome* is characterized by interstitial keratitis which is bilateral and fluctuating, and progressive bilateral nerve deafness which is associated with episodes of violent vertigo. Stevens reports a case in a boy of 10 years. Cody and Williams found periarteritis nodosa in this condition. *Harada's syndrome* includes exudative choroiditis with retinal detachment and an excess of cells in the spinal fluid. In some cases there are evidence of meningitis or encephalitis. Vitiligo, poliosis and deafness may occur.

CASE HISTORY (No. 141208).—Colored girl of 18 years complained of pain in her eyes. Little was to be found to explain her symptoms at first, but soon it became evident that she had bilateral uveitis. Vision declined and eventually glaucoma developed with opacity of the corneae and amaurosis. She began to complain of noises in her ears, of deafness and attacks of vertigo. The eyebrows and eyelashes became white and the eyelids and the skin about the eyes also lost their pigment. The hair in the parietal region was gray in patches and the frontal hair fell out.

Later, when she was 20 years old, there was some return of pigment in the skin and the frontal hair began to grow back. She was then completely blind. Her hearing was only moderately reduced and there was little tinnitus. She no longer had attacks of vertigo, but there was pronounced loss of function of the vestibular nerves which made her very unsteady. The process seemed to be inactive.

CASE HISTORY.—*Progressive nerve deafness began at 5 years followed at intervals by interstitial keratitis with photophobia, ocular palsies with ptosis, tremor of movement of the arms and unsteadiness.*

L. B. was regarded as a healthy boy until he was 5 years old. Then he was found to be deaf in both ears. This was found to be due to nerve deafness and to be slowly progressive. No vertigo was associated.

At 12 years, he was found to have interstitial keratitis and photophobia without loss of corneal reflexes. Serological tests for syphilis were negative.

At 13 years, it was discovered that there was limitation of ocular movements in all planes bilaterally with some ptosis of the lids. A few months later, he showed an intention tremor of both arms, but no static tremor. He was unable to write. He could walk steadily.

At the age of 14 years, he was slightly unsteady and could not stand on one foot with the eyes open. There was a little ataxia in the legs. The deafness had increased so even with a hearing aid in each ear, he could scarcely hear. His vision remained good. His bodily growth was inadequate for a boy of 14 years and his behavior was somewhat immature. No history of any condition resembling that of the patient could be elicited in the family. Studies for periarteritis were negative.

BIBLIOGRAPHY

CODY, D. T. AND WILLIAMS, H. L.: Cogan's syndrome. Pro. Mayo Clin., **37**:372, 1962.

COGAN, D. G.: The syndrome of non-syphilitic interstitial keratitis and vestibulo-aural symptoms. Arch. Ophth., **33**:144, 1945; also Arch. Ophth., **42**:42, 1949.

HAGUE, E. B.: Uveitis, dysacousia, alopecia, poliosis and vitiligo. A theory as to cause. Arch. Ophth., **31**:520, 1944.

PARKER, W. R.: Severe uveitis with associated alopecia, poliosis, vitiligo and deafness. A second review of the published records. Arch. Ophth., **24**:439, 1940.

RONES, B.: Uveitis with dysacousia, alopecia and poliosis. Arch. Ophthal., **7**:847, 1932.

STEVENS, H.: Cogan's syndrome (non-syphilitic interstitial keratitis with deafness). Arch. Neurol. & Psychiat., **71**:337, 1954.

POLYNEURITIS DUE TO OTHER INFECTIONS

Polyneuritis is seen as an occasional complication of almost all severe infections, so that it is impossible to give an exhaustive account of the possible causes. We may mention typhoid fever, typhus fever, bacillary dysentery, malaria, paratyphoid fever, influenza, dengue, scarlet fever, septicemia, pyogenic infections of various types, as well as the more specific types which have been described in the preceding pages. Mumps polyneuritis is mentioned under the nervous complications of mumps. A few cases of polyneuritis have been described in association with infectious hepatitis and with infectious mononucleosis. These are said to resemble acute infectious polyneuritis in their clinical characteristics.

In the more severe cases of typhoid fever, it is not unusual to find pains in the extremities and tenderness of the toes and calf muscles. The ankle jerks may be lost and even the knee jerks diminished or abolished. It is unusual, however, to find a fully developed picture of polyneuritis with paralysis of the distal muscle groups. More frequently we see local palsies of one ulnar or peroneal nerve which is presumably due to the general intoxication and prolonged compression of the nerve between the mattress and the bony prominence.

A word should be said about the importance of influenza in the production of polyneuritis. In most epidemics of this disease, polyneuritis has been rare but the diagnosis of polyneuritis following sporadic cases of influenza is made very frequently. It is not unlikely that this diagnosis is erroneous in many cases, for clinical features of influenza are scarcely so characteristic that a diagnosis can be made with certainty. It would seem preferable, therefore, for the present, to include these cases in the group of febrile polyneuritis of unknown origin until their relation to true influenza is more clearly understood.

All of the common pyogenic organisms may at times give rise to polyneuritis. Small epidemics of polyneuritis have been observed in association with enteritis due to staphylococcus infection. Septicemia, especially the acute and relapsing types due to streptococci, may cause extensive polyneuritis. It is possible that neuritis is not common in the more acute forms because the patient dies before the symptoms have time to develop. The writer has observed a case in which a large abscess resulting from an infected tooth was associated with rapidly advancing polyneuritis, bilateral facial palsy and bulbar disturbances. When the abscess was drained, the progress of the symptoms was arrested at once and the patient eventually made a complete recovery after many months. Cultures showed only staphylococci and streptococci and no diphtheria bacilli.

BIBLIOGRAPHY

Harris, W.: Neuritis and Neuralgia. Oxford Press, 1926.
Plough, I. C. and Ayerle, R. S.: The Guillain-Barré syndrome associated with acute hepatitis. New England Med. J., **249**:61, 1953.
Stewart, T. G.: Causation and symptomatology of multiple neuritis. Brit. Med. J., **2**:461, 1925. (Discussion.)
Wilson, G.: Differential diagnosis of neuritis and conditions simulating it with especial reference to influenzal multiple neuritis and ataxia. J.A.M.A., **80**:1443, 1923.
Zimmerman, H. J. and Lowry, C. F.: Guillain-Barré syndrome in infectious hepatitis. Ann. Int. Med., **26**:934, 1947.

CHRONIC POLYNEURITIS OF UNKNOWN ORIGIN

Many authors recognize a slowly progressive type of polyneuritis of unknown origin which may continue to advance for several years. Harris mentions the case of a girl of 15 years who developed weakness of all four limbs, the neck, face, jaws and even the tongue. After nine months the extremities were completely paralyzed, the tendon reflexes were lost but only moderate wasting of the muscles occurred. There was no sensory disturbance except for paresthesias. Despite change of climate and all forms of treatment, the progress of the disease continued for 18 months. Improvement then began and ended in recovery within two more years. Ten years later the patient was still in good health. Harris is inclined to attribute such cases to an unknown disturbance of metabolism. Batten refers to the case of a little girl of 3 years who developed during the course of three months almost complete paralysis of the arms and legs with wasting of the muscles and loss of reflexes. At this point, the disease ceased to progress and some improvement occurred. However, the symptoms soon began to advance again and about fourteen months after the onset, the child died. At postmortem examination there was found degeneration of the peripheral nerves and chromatolysis of the anterior horn cells which were attributed to an intoxication of unknown nature. Hyland and Russell have given a full account including a complete pathological report of a case which seems to belong in this group. Extensive degeneration of the peripheral nerves was found. In several cases there has been an unexplained dermatitis at the onset.

The diagnosis is made by exclusion of all recognized causes for polyneuritis. The prognosis is apparently fairly good. Harris states that it is especially good in the cases in which there are no sensory changes. Recovery may be delayed for several years. In certain cases, however, the disease progresses inexorably to death.

Treatment should be directed to the removal of all possible sources of poison and foci of infection and to secure free elimination by large amounts of fluids and saline cathartics.

CASE HISTORY (Ped. A-69660).—*Boy of seven years developed almost complete paralysis of all four extremities in the course of eight months with loss of tendon reflexes but no sensory disturbances. Improvement was first evident during the ninth month.*

C. B. P., a boy of seven years, began to notice weakness of his hands in November 1948. There was no illness of any type at this time. The weakness slowly grew worse and in January he could not handle small objects properly. In February there was weakness of the legs and about the first of March, he could not go up steps. There was never any fever, pain, numbness, difficulty in the control of the bladder or cranial nerve disturbance.

Examination in April revealed great weakness of all muscles of the upper extremities. The distal muscles were more severely affected than the proximal muscles. This same rule was observed in the legs for movements at the ankles especially dorsiflexion were very weak, at the knees not quite so weak and at the hips fairly strong. The child walked almost entirely by the use of his gluteals. The neck was weak but the chest, abdominal and spinal muscles were strong. The tendon reflexes were all lost. There was no tenderness, pain or sensory loss. The cranial nerves were all intact. A moderate increase of protein was found in the spinal fluid. Biopsy of a bit of muscle disclosed nothing very striking. Other laboratory and medical examinations disclosed nothing of moment.

In May the patient was reexamined. He had grown much worse. There was no power at the finger or wrist joints, little power at the elbow and just enough strength at the shoulder to lift the arm against gravity. He could not lift his head from the pillow. There was no power at the ankles and scarcely any at the knees. The gluteals at the hip were still able to contract with moderate strength. No new symptoms or signs had developed since the last examination.

In July the child was in almost exactly the same condition as in May. The only definite change was loss of power of abduction at the shoulder.

The child was given physiotherapy in the Children's Hospital School and late in August the report came that he had begun to show some improvement in the strength of the proximal muscles. In March 1953 we learned that the patient had finally made a complete recovery without residuum.

BIBLIOGRAPHY

BATTEN, F. E.: Diseases of Children. Garrod, Batten and Thursfield. London, Edward Arnold, p. 840, 1913.

HARRIS, W.: Toxic polyneuritis. Brain, 45:415, 1922.

HYLAND, H. H. AND RUSSELL, W. R.: Chronic progressive polyneuritis with report of a fatal case. Brain, 53:278, 1930.

TETANUS

Definition.—This condition is also called lockjaw. It is due to the action of an exotoxin produced by the tetanus bacillus and is characterized by recurrent tonic convulsions superimposed upon a persistent, generalized rigidity which involves the muscles of the jaws with especial severity. A local form is also recognized.

Etiology.—The organism, B. tetani, is widely distributed in the soil, especially fertilized soil, for it is found in the feces of the horse and of many other animals including man. It is a Gram positive, anaerobic bacillus which is actively motile and produces spores which are formed at one end of the bacillus, giving it the appearance of a drum stick. The spores are very resistant to heat, to drying and to various antibacterial agents and may survive for many years in dry places. It has been shown that the toxin is a complex protein.

Pathogenesis.—The nervous system is not invaded by the organism and the symptoms are due entirely to the exotoxin which the bacillus produces.

As a rule, B. tetani does not multiply within the tissues unless there is also present some foreign body or necrotic material and there is some evidence that other organisms are necessary for its growth. Puncture wounds and buried splinters offer favorable conditions for this infection. Such wounds may appear to be completely healed before the symptoms arise. It is generally believed that the toxin reaches the nervous system by extending along the nerve trunks in a proximal direction. Some investigators believe that it flows along perineural lymphatics; others, that it passes through the axis cylinders and others, that it is spread by way of tissue spaces. Apparently, the chief basis for this belief is the existence of local tetanus. Once within the central nervous system, the toxin is believed to diffuse rapidly upward and downward throughout the neuraxis causing generalized tetanus. These statements represent the usual teaching at the present time. Recently, however, J. J. Abel and his co-workers have advanced very convincing evidence against this point of view. Abel has shown that the toxin can reach the central nervous system only through the blood stream and that local tetanus is due to the direct action of the toxin upon the muscles. The toxin diffuses locally through lymphatic channels. The generalized muscular rigidity is of the same nature as the local rigidity. It is not affected by anesthetics or sedatives or even by section of the motor nerves, once it has become fully developed. This is therefore due to the action of the blood-borne toxin upon the musculature. The convulsive seizures and intense reflex activity seen in many cases represent the effects of the toxin upon the central nervous system. It is believed that these symptoms are due to the action of the toxin on the motor cells in the spinal cord for they may be produced by the injection of minute quantities of toxin into the anterior gray matter. Thus, according to Abel, we are dealing with three processes; a local lymphborne intoxication of the muscles, a generalized effect of the same nature due to blood-borne toxin and a third series of symptoms due to the action of the blood-borne toxin upon the anterior horn cells of the spinal cord.

Pathological Anatomy.—No definite anatomical changes have yet been demonstrated. Some writers mention hyperemia of the gray matter and even small hemorrhages which are probably agonal. Baker describes perinuclear chromatolysis and perivascular demyelination. Probably all of these changes are reversible.

Clinical Features.—In tropical countries and among certain races, tetanus of the newborn is very common as a result of infection of the stump of the umbilical cord. A few cases of this nature are still seen in this country. At present, the most frequent source of tetanus among children in this country is injury by the explosion of fireworks and injury by wadding of blank cartridges on national holidays. Other causes are puncture wounds due to splinters and nails which have lain in the ground, especially ma-

nured ground, infection of operative wounds by organisms contained in
catgut or dressings, automobile accidents in which dirt is ground into the
tissues, compound fractures, the injection of contaminated horse serum or
gelatin for hemostasis and the use of vaccines, especially anti-smallpox vaccine. The last is probably a less common cause than has been thought, for
many cases diagnosed as tetanus in the past were undoubtedly vaccinia encephalomyelitis. In some cases, the origin and site of the infection is obscure but since the organism is frequently found in the intestines, it is
probable that many of these cases of "idiopathic tetanus" are of intestinal
origin.

The incubation period averages about seven or eight days but may be
prolonged to several weeks or even months in cases in which antitoxin has
been administered. Rarely it is reduced to two or three days.

Two forms are distinguished: the *local* and the *general*. The former is
often termed ascending tetanus and the latter, descending tetanus. General
tetanus begins in some cases with restlessness, irritability, sweating and
tachycardia. Frequently the onset is insidious. The first distinctive symptom
is usually slight tightness or twitching of the muscles. In the vast majority
of cases the muscles of mastication are affected first causing *trismus* of
mild degree. However, the posterior cervical muscles and the abdominal
muscles may be affected very early, often apparently before the trismus has
been noticed. The tightness of the muscles grows progressively more severe.
At first the muscles may be stretched fairly well both voluntarily and passively. There is no increased tone evident on palpation. The jaws may fall
open more or less during sleep and sedatives, hypnotics and anesthetics may
cause complete relaxation. Pressure over the affected muscles and efforts to
stretch them cause much pain. Later the movements grow more and more
limited and finally a constant and intense rigidity develops so that the muscle cannot be stretched and feels as hard as wood on palpation. At this
point drugs have no influence. The rigidity gradually extends involving the
muscles of the spine, the abdomen and the chest. The legs grow rigid and
the arms are finally affected. The legs are fully extended, the head is retracted and the trunk is arched backwards into a position of *opisthotonos*.
The arms are flexed and the fingers clenched. The facial muscles are involved causing retraction of the angles of the mouth and the so-called *risus
sardonicus*. If the orbicularis oris is affected, the lips may be pursed. The
eyelids are partially closed and the eyebrows elevated as a result of contraction of the frontalis. The bulbar muscles are involved causing dysphagia,
aphonia and cyanosis. In many cases, dysphagia is among the earliest symptoms. The unstriated muscles do not escape. Involvement of the sphincters
may cause retention of urine and feces. Profuse sweats are common. Even-

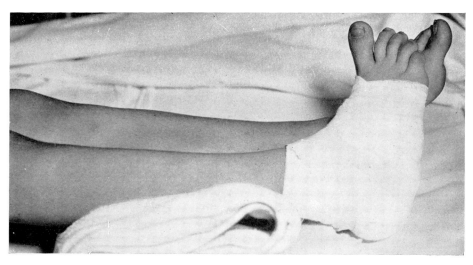

FIG. 169. Local tetanus showing tonic spasm of the anterior tibial group of muscles. The wound involved the tendons of these muscles.

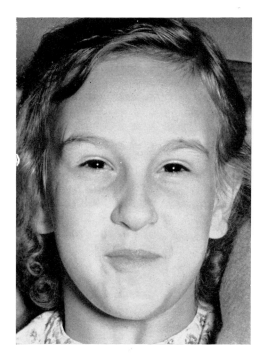

FIG. 170. Risus sardonicus of mild degree in tetanus. The child is recovering. Increased tone of all facial muscles is evident. She seems to be smiling.

tually rigidity of the muscles of respiration or involvement of the larynx may cause fatal asphyxia.

In many cases, but not in all, the toxin reaches the central nervous system and there are tonic seizures and evidences of increased reflex activity. The tendon reflexes are grossly exaggerated and the cutaneous reflexes are increased. A light tap upon a tendon may throw the limb into violent clonic contractions. Generalized tonic convulsions of the entire bodily musculature appear. These are mild at first but gradually become more frequent and more prolonged. They seem to be productive of much pain. Consciousness is not lost as a rule. Between the seizures there is usually persisting muscular rigidity so that relaxation is never complete. The seizures result in an exaggeration of the posture described above. They occur spontaneously and also in response to all types of sensory stimuli. When they are very frequent, the lightest touch or even an unexpected noise may provoke them. They are abolished by anesthetics and controlled by sedatives. Compression fractures of the vertebrae may result. Frequently fatal asphyxia occurs during such seizures for they may last for a number of minutes. Symptoms referable to the nervous system develop as a rule late and in only the more severe cases.

We have observed cases in which death was due to sudden failure of respiration without spasm of the muscles of respiration. Firor finds that this is the usual termination in experimental animals in which toxin has been injected into the anterior spinal gray matter. He thinks failure of the respiratory center is to blame.

The temperature may be quite normal but in some cases there is fever. The development of high fever is regarded as a bad prognostic sign. Terminal hyperpyrexia is common. A moderate leucocytosis is present. The spinal fluid may be under increased pressure but is otherwise normal.

The course is variable and in fatal cases death is rarely deferred more than three or four days after the onset of the symptoms. In some fulminating cases, death may result from asphyxia within a few hours of the onset. In the more favorable cases, the seizures grow less frequent and severe and the rigidity diminishes in the course of days. The trismus is often the last sign to disappear. Convalescence is slow for the child is usually exhausted and nutrition is impaired.

In the localized forms, the first symptoms are those of rigidity of the muscles in the neighborhood of the wound. As a rule, this rigidity is constant and not paroxysmal. The rigidity extends in most cases to several groups of muscles and frequently involves a whole limb. The lower extremities most often exhibit this form of the disease. The symptoms may gradually advance for from ten to twenty days and intense muscular rigidity may persist for from twenty to fifty days. Complete recovery may be delayed for many months. In favorable cases, the symptoms remain local but in other instances, the local symptoms are followed by generalized tetanus which runs the usual course. The tendon reflexes in the affected limb are first exaggerated and then lost as the rigidity becomes more intense. As a rule, the local tetanus is less serious than the general form. Its incubation period is longer and may exceed a month. Cases of local tetanus are most apt to occur in subjects who have received inadequate doses of antitoxin as a prophylactic measure.

A cephalic type of tetanus may result from infections of the face, neck or head. It begins, as a rule, with rigidity of the facial muscles on one or both sides or with involvement of the jaws or pharynx. It is said that actual paralysis of the facial muscles may follow and that rigidity of one side of the face may be associated with paralysis of the opposite side of the face. This may be true but it is not clear why tetanus of the facial muscles should behave so differently from that of other muscles. I have seen several cases of cephalic tetanus in which tonic spasm of one side of the face was mistaken for paralysis of the opposite side and it seems possible that errors of this nature have led to the belief that the facial nerve may be paralyzed. It is claimed that oculomotor paralysis and even paralysis of the pupil may result from infections involving the orbit and that palsies of the larynx and pharynx may occur when the site of infection is in the throat. Cephalic tetanus may remain localized or may be followed by generalized tetanus just as other forms of local tetanus. It is generally stated that the mortality is very high in cephalic tetanus but in our experience, it has been low in the local, cephalic tetanus. The facial spasm may remain more or less constant for several weeks before it begins to recede.

Tetanus neonatorum is characterized by a short incubation period of not more than five or six days. The first symptom is usually inability to nurse due to trismus. As a rule death results within a day or two. It is believed that the infection is usually localized in the stump of the umbilical cord although there is frequently no local evidence of inflammation.

The idiopathic tetanus in which the site of infection is not demonstrable is attributed to intestinal infection and is, therefore, often called splanchnic tetanus. Cases have occurred in association with intussusception or appendicitis and the bacilli have been recovered from the feces. Infections of the middle ear by way of a perforated ear drum are described.

Abortive cases are sometimes seen which are characterized by only transient trismus or rigidity of the neck.

One attack does not necessarily cause lasting immunity for cases in which recurrences or second attacks have occurred are described.

Diagnosis.—The diagnosis is not, as a rule, difficult. The history of a wound, the trismus, the opisthotonos, risus sardonicus and abdominal rigidity and the tonic muscular rigidity persisting between the paroxysms are characteristic. Strychnine poisoning is distinguished by the absence of rigidity between the paroxysms and the absence of striking trismus. The course is much shorter. Rabies is distinguished by the longer incubation period which is rarely less than two weeks, the striking excitement, the greater prominence of pharyngeal spasm and the infrequency of trismus. The history of being bitten by a dog or some other animal is, of course, of great significance. Meningitis may be recognized by the changes in the spinal fluid. It must be kept in mind that mild trismus may occur in epidemic encephalitis and in the encephalomyelitis of vaccinia and measles.

Prognosis.—Before the introduction of the antitoxin, the general mortality was about 90 per cent and in infants even higher. At present not more than 50 per cent of all cases are fatal. In the Harriet Lane Home only 6 of 19 cases in older children have been fatal. The prognosis is unfavorable in cases in which the incubation period is relatively brief and in cases characterized by hyperpyrexia. A more favorable prognosis may be given in cases in which antitoxin has been given for prophylaxis and in cases in which the symptoms remain localized.

Prevention of Tetanus.—It is recommended that infants be routinely immunized against tetanus by the injection of toxoid. Several injections are given at intervals of months, and additional injections in childhood are advised.

Puncture wounds in general, especially those contaminated by dirt or soil and those caused by blank cartridges or fireworks, are regarded as potential causes of tetanus. Such wounds should be carefully and completely treated by surgical excision, and infected tissue and foreign bodies removed if possible.

If the patient has been immunized by toxoid, another dose of toxoid should be given at once. This is expected to give protection within a week and antitoxic serum is not required.

If the patient has not been immunized by toxoid and is seen within twenty-four hours, or possibly forty-eight hours, antibiotics such as penicillin or terramycin will give protection, some authorities claim.

If the patient is not seen promptly and has not been immunized, antitoxin is required. Human tetanus hyperimmune gamma globulin is now on the market. It is recommended that 250 units be given intramuscularly. This is said to be almost completely devoid of allergic effects and does not convey serum hepatitis. It gives protection for a month, for it disappears from the patient's serum more slowly than the horse serum.

If human antitoxin is not available and serum is required, horse or bovine serum must be given, though fatal anaphylactic reactions are possible and serum neuritis is not rare. A skin test should be made; if this is negative, anaphylactic shock is not to be expected, but serum neuritis is still possible. It is usual to give 1500 Americal units, some of which should be injected about the wound. If evidences of allergy develop, adrenaline and cortisone are indicated.

Treatment.—Diaz-Rivera and his associates list the objectives in the treatment of tetanus: (1) The neutralization of the unfixed toxin. (2) The elimination of the source of the toxin. (3) The prevention of muscle spasm and convulsions. (4) The maintenance of proper hydration and electrolyte balance. (5) The maintenance of proper nutrition. (6) The maintenance of adequate respiration. (7) The prevention of pneumonia and other infections.

The wound should be treated surgically at once. Human tetanus hyperimmune gamma globulin is preferable to the horse or bovine serum for reasons given above, but the proper dosage has not yet been determined. The dosage of horse serum varies according to different authorities. Some recommend doses of 100,000 Americal units and some believe that doses of over 20,000 units are dangerous.

Various sedatives are recommended to diminish the convulsions and are undoubtedly of great value. Chloral, phenobarbital and others are used in very large doses. Many writers have obtained good results with magnesium sulphate injected intramuscularly, but this is not without danger. Recently avertin has been employed with excellent results. It is given by rectum in doses of 90 to 100 milligrams per kilogram of body weight in aqueous solution and may be repeated several times a day. The blood pressure should be watched for this drug may cause sudden hypotension and collapse. Firor claims that barbiturates cause a dangerous depression of the respiratory center and recommends paraldehyde as a sedative. Kelly and Laurence state that intravenous injections of chlorpromazine are effective in controlling the convulsions of tetanus. Tolseram is recommended. Jenkins and Luhn advise that if the process advances to convulsions, sedation should be regulated by intravenous drip of 0.4 per cent thiopental. The patient should be kept at such a level he will respond to stimulation, but will have no convulsions. The concentration can usually be reduced to 0.2 per cent within a day or two and eventually to 0.1 per cent.

Turner and Galloway have advocated that a patient suffering from severe tetanus be placed in a respirator and tracheotomy performed. Curare is then employed in a dosage sufficient to relax the muscles and permit the effective action of the respirator. Wright *et al.* agree that this type of therapy is especially helpful in tetanus neonatorum, but point out that it demands much skill.

Pascale *et al.* strongly recommend the use of hyperbaric oxygen and think the mortality rate may be greatly reduced by this treatment.

It is of the greatest importance that the patient be disturbed as little as possible. The room should be quiet and dark. No one but the nurses and physicians should be permitted to see the patient. The child must have proper feeding. In our experience the use of a nasal catheter has been very satisfactory. This is tied in place and not reinserted for each feeding.

BIBLIOGRAPHY

ABEL, J. J.: Researches on tetanus. I. On poisons and diseases and some experiments with the toxin of Bacillus Tetani. Science, 79:121, 1934.

ABEL, J. J. AND CHALIAN, W.: Researches on tetanus. VIII. At what point in the course of tetanus does antitetanus serum fail to save life? Bull. Johns Hopkins Hosp., 62:610, 1938.

ABEL, J. J., EVANS, E. A. JR. AND LEE, F. C.: Researches on tetanus. II. The toxin of B. tetani is not transported to the central nervous system by any component of the peripheral nerve trunks. Bull. Johns Hopkins Hosp., 56:84, 1935.

ABEL, J. J., HAMPIL, B. AND JONAS, A. F.: Researches on tetanus. III. Further experiments to prove that tetanus toxin is not carried in the peripheral nerves to the central nervous system. Bull. Johns Hopkins Hosp., 56:317, 1935.

ABEL, J. J. AND HAMPIL, B.: Researches on tetanus. IV. Some historical notes on tetanus and commentaries thereon. Bull. Johns Hopkins Hosp., 57:343, 1935.

ANWAR, A. A. AND TURNER, T. B.: Antibiotics in experimental tetanus. Bull. Johns Hopkins Hosp., 98:85, 1956.

BAKER, A. B.: Central nervous system in tetanus. J. Neuropath. & Exp. Neurol., 1:394, 1942.

BISHOP, J. M., DuBOSE, R. H. AND HAMLIN, F. E.: Otogenous tetanus. J.A.M.A., 98:1546, 1932.

CARTER, W. S. AND HOLDER, T. M.: The correct use of tetanus prophylaxis. Clin. Pediat., 2:657, 1963.

COX, C. A. *et al.*: Limitations of tetanus antitoxin. Brit. Med. J., 5369:1360, 1963.

DIAZ-RIVERA, R. S. *et al.*: The management of tetanus. J.A.M.A., 147:1635, 1951.

DIETRICH, H. F.: Tetanus in children. Am. J. Dis. Child., 59:693, 1940.

DIETRICH, H. F., KARSHNER, R. G. AND STEWART, S. F.: Tetanus and lesions of the spine in childhood. J. Bone & Joint Surg., 22:43, 1940.

ELLIS, M.: Human antitetanus serum in treatment of tetanus. Brit. Med. J., i:1123, 1963.

ELLIS, M.: Effect of human antitetanus serum. Brit. Med. J., 5338:1123, 1963.

FILLER, R. M. AND ELLERBECK, W.: Tetanus prophylaxis. J.A.M.A., 174:1, 1960.

FIROR, W. M., LAMONT, A. AND SHUMACKER, H. B.: Studies on the cause of death in tetanus. Ann. Surg., 3:478, 1949.

FLETCHER, W. M.: Tetanus Dolorosa and the relation of tetanus toxin to the sensory nerves and spinal ganglia. Brain, 26:383, 1903.

HEWITT, R. L. *et al.*: Diagnosis and treatment of tetanus. Arch. Surg., 88:768, 1964.

JENKINS, M. T. AND LUHN, N. R.: The management of tetanus. Anesthesiology, 23:690, 1962.

KELLY, R. E. AND LAURENCE, D. R.: Control of tetanus convulsions. Lancet, 270:118, 1956.

KLOT KLOETZEL, K.: Prognosis in severe tetanus. J.A.M.A., 185:559, 1963.

McCARROLL, J. R.: The prevention of tetanus. G. P. Kansas, 32:120, 1965.

McCOMB, J. A.: The prophylactic dose of homologous tetanus antitoxin. New England J. Med., 270:175, 1964.

McCOMB, J. A. AND DWYER, R. C.: Passive-active immunization with tetanus immune globulin (human). New England J. Med., 268:857, 1963.

NATION, N. S. *et al.:* Human hyperimmune globulin for tetanus. California Med., **98**:305, 1963.

PASCALE, L. R. *et al.:* Hyperbaric oxygen for tetanus. J.A.M.A., **189**:408, 1964.

RUBBO, S. D. AND SURI, J. C.: Human globulin for tetanus immunization. Brit. Med. J., **5297**:79, 1962.

SCHMIDT, R. *et al.:* Diagnostic and therapeutic clues in study of tetanus. Arch. Neurol. & Psychiat., **69**:55, 1953.

SLIMON, J. C.: Tetanus complicated by facial paralysis. Brit. Med. J., **2**:200, 1932.

TAYLOR, F. W.: Treatment of acute tetanus. J.A.M.A., **102**:895, 1934.

TURNER, V. C. AND GALLOWAY, T. C.: Tetanus treated as a respiratory problem. Arch. Surg., **58**:478, 1949.

WESTWATER, A. M.: A case of recurrent tetanus. Brit. Med. J., **i**:395, 1917.

WRIGHT, R. *et al.:* Respirator for tetanus neonatorum. Lancet, **ii**:678, 1961.

PARALYSIS DUE TO THE BITE OF THE WOOD TICK

Definition.—A type of rapidly ascending paralysis due to infestation by various ixodid ticks such as Dermacentor venustus, D. andersoni, D. varabilis in American and ixodes holocyclus in Australia.

Etiology.—This type of paralysis is always associated with the presence of the tick which is believed to secrete some powerful toxin causing paralysis. There is no evidence of infection. If the tick is placed upon experimental animals such as the dog, guinea pig or rabbit, paralysis may ensue. Sheep and other domestic animals are affected spontaneously.

In the eastern states the tick responsible is the common dog tick, Dermacentor variabilis, which also transmits tick fever. It is believed that only the female causes paralysis. They attach themselves and become engorged within 5 to 13 days. During this time they produce eggs. The males copulate with the females and fertilize the eggs. Within a day after full engorgement the females drop off. There is reason to believe that only females bearing fertilized eggs cause paralysis. Perhaps this is why ticks are abundant and paralysis rare. The tick season is from March to August in the eastern states. The most dangerous months are May, June and July.

Pathological Anatomy.—No anatomical lesions have been found despite careful examination of various laboratory animals which were paralysed by application of the tick.

Clinical Features.—During the last twenty years, numerous cases of paralysis of this type have been reported in the States of Idaho, Washington, Oregon and Montana. Some 30 cases had been reported in the eastern states in 1955. All were in children. Only one was fatal. In the western states 332 cases had been reported and the mortality rate was 11 per cent. It is also stated that the disease is prevalent in British Columbia, South Africa and Australia. Children are more subject to this condition than adults, and, in fact, most cases described in medical literature have occurred before puberty.

The onset is rather sudden. A child begins to walk unsteadily and to show signs of abnormal fatigue. Within a few hours there is motor paralysis which is apparently always of ascending type, involving, in turn, the legs, trunk, arms and bulb. In some cases ataxia is a prominent symptom. Lagos and Thies state that true ataxia is usually found in tick paralysis and report a case in which there was only ataxia without muscle weakness. The patient may be drowsy. In infants and young children there may be convulsions at the onset. Older children may complain of diplopia or blurring of vision but cranial nerve palsies are rare. Complaints of numbness in the face and extremities are mentioned but there seems to be no actual loss of sensibility. The control of the sphincters may be lost but is more frequently preserved. The tendon reflexes are diminished or abolished. Ross states that the toxin acts on the central nervous system for the paralysed muscles continue to respond to faradic stimulation of the peripheral nerve.

The tick is found attached to the nape of the neck, behind the ear, in the scalp or the groin. One finds an ecchymotic area at the site of attachment but there is no pain or other sensation to attract the patient's attention to that region. The incubation period, that is the time elapsing between the attachment of the tick and the development of paralysis, is said to vary between six and eight days. If the tick is detected and removed, improvement is apparent within a few hours and recovery will occur within a few days unless the child is already moribund. If the tick is not removed, death may result. In infants the end may come within twenty-four hours after the onset of paralysis but, in adults, a course of two weeks is not unusual. Death always results from paralysis of respiration. One attack is said to confer immunity.

The pulse is rapid and there may be moderate elevation of temperature. The leucocytes of the blood are increased and there may be an eosinophilia of 10 per cent.

Diagnosis.—The diagnosis depends upon the discovery of the tick in a patient afflicted with the type of paralysis described above.

Prognosis.—The outlook depends upon the age of the patient and upon the amount of toxin absorbed. The mortality is very high in infants, especially if the tick is not removed promptly.

Treatment.—It is most important to remove the tick at once. Otherwise treatment is symptomatic. If respiration fails or bulbar palsy develops, artificial respiration and possibly tracheotomy are required. (See treatment of bulbar palsy in poliomyelitis.)

CASE HISTORY (U.M.H. 201-189).—*Girl of 10 years developed generalized weakness, ataxia and loss of tendon reflexes. Some improvement in next few days. Prompt and complete recovery after removal of tick.*

H. M. B., a previously healthy girl of 10 years was brought into the hospital on July 28, 1952. The history stated that the previous morning she had gotten out of bed and fallen at once to the floor for her legs were too weak to support her. During that day she could not walk without support. When she reached the hospital the next day, she was found to be extremely weak in all four extremities but the legs were weaker than the arms. She could not walk without help and was apt to fall to the floor when she attempted to stand or walk. There was ataxia in all four extremities which was thought to be of cerebellar type. No alteration of sensibility could be found. The tendon reflexes were all absent. Medical examination was entirely negative. The laboratory tests revealed nothing of importance. The temperature reached 100°F. on the first day but soon fell to normal. The pulse, which was 100 at first, soon fell to 80. The spinal fluid was normal in all respects. The electrocardiogram showed sinus tachycardia and minor abnormalities difficult to interpret.

There was some improvement in the next few days. On July 31, there was no definite ataxia and strength was more nearly normal. The child could stand and walk. The tendon reflexes, however, were still absent.

On August 3, a very large tick was removed from the back of the child's head by a nurse who destroyed it before it could be identified. After this the child recovered completely within a very short time and soon was discharged from the hospital.

BIBLIOGRAPHY

ABBOTT, K. H.: Tick paralysis. Proc. Staff Meet. Mayo Clin., **18**:39, 1943.

ADLER, K.: Tick paralysis. Canad. Med. Ass., **94**:550, 1966.

BARNETT, E. J.: Wood tick paralysis in children. J.A.M.A., **109**:846, 1937.

BASSOE, P.: Paralysis of ascending type in an adult due to the bite of the wood tick. Arch. Neurol. & Psychiat., **11**:564, 1924. (Full references.)

COSTA, J. A.: Tick paralysis on the Atlantic seaboard. Am. J. Dis. Child., **83**:336, 1952.

LAGOS, J. C. AND THIES, R. E.: Tick paralysis without muscle weakness. Neurology, **21**:471, 1969.

MCCUE, C. M., STONE, J. B. AND SUTTON, L. E.: Three cases of tick (Dermacentor variabilis) paralysis in Virginia. Pediatrics, **1**:174, 1948.

ROSS, I. C.: An experimental study of tick paralysis in Australia. Parasitology, **18**:410, 1926.

SANZENBACHER, K. E. AND CONRAD, E.: Tick paralysis, a killer treatable neuropathy. Southern Med. Jour., **61**:764, 1968.

STANBURY, J. B. AND HUYCK, J. H.: Tick paralysis. Medicine, **24**:219, 1945.

SNAKE BITES

It is estimated that between 7,000 and 12,000 deaths from snake bite are reported in India every year and many deaths occur from this cause in Africa, Australia, South America and tropical countries. In the United States, only about 50 deaths a year are said to be caused by venomous snakes.

The venom of poisonous snakes contains several toxins each of which has a different effect. Each snake venom is composed of varying proportions of these toxins. Among the effects are hemorrhages, hemolysis, coagulation of the blood, damage to the tissues and paralysis. The venom of certain snakes including the various types of cobra, krait, sea snakes, the tiger snake of Australia and the coral snake of this country all contain large amounts of neuroparalytic toxin which is not unlike curare in its effects. It is estimated that the venom of the krait is so powerful that 1.5 mg. may be fatal to a man. It is because of this paralytic effect that snake bite is mentioned here.

The initial effect is said to be local pain followed by sleepiness and vomiting. The pulse becomes weak and rapid. The blood pressure falls. The patient is cold, pale and bathed in sweat. Muscular weakness develops within a short time and soon there is ascending weakness or paralysis. The patient remains conscious but sensibility is reduced. Soon respiration becomes labored and at last gasping. The arms are affected, the head falls forward, the jaw hangs open and salivation is profuse. The pupils become dilated and fixed to light. The eyelids droop. The soft palate is paralysed and articulation is impaired. Albumin and red cells are found in the urine. Death results from paralysis of respiration and failure of the heart action. Terminal convulsions may be due to anoxia. If the patient survives, complete recovery is to be expected, it is said.

If the bite is on an extremity, a ligature may be applied and suction employed to remove the poison after an incision has been made. Venesection may be helpful. Potassium permanganate is injected to fix the venom in the tissue. Antivenom is effective if given in time. Artificial respiration is advised. Recently it has been advised that after the ligature is applied, the limb should be placed in ice water for 5 minutes. The ligature is then removed. The limb is then kept in finely crushed ice for 24 hours. The patient must be kept warm at all times. The limb must be allowed to grow warm gradually. McCready and Wurzel state that the blood must be tested for hemolysis and defective coagulation. Fibrinogen may be needed to check hemorrhage. Transfusions and infusions of saline and dextrose may be required for shock. Antibiotics are needed for infection and antihistamines for venoms that release histamine.

BIBLIOGRAPHY

Boys, F. and Smith, H. M.: Poisonous Amphibians and Reptiles. Springfield, Thomas, 1959.

Chopra, R. and Chowhan, J.: Snake bites and their treatment in India. Indian Med. Gaz., **74:**422, 1939.

Hadidian, Z., Sarkar, N. K. et al.: A Panel on Venoms. Organic-Biochemistry-Pharmacology Comm. of Research and Development sec. of the American Drug Manufacturers Assn. Annual Meeting. Rye, New York, October 1957.

Kellaway, C.: The symptomatology and treatment of bites of Australian snakes. Med. J. Australia, **ii:**171, 1942.

McCready, T. and Wurzel, H.: Poisonous snake bites. J.A.M.A., **170:**268, 1959.

Porges, N.: Snake venoms, their biochemistry and mode of action. Science, **117:**47, 1953.

SNYDER, CLIFFORD C.: Treatment of snake bite. Modern Medicine, August 12, 1968, p. 30.
STAHNKE, H. L. *et al.:* The treatment of snake bite. Am. J. Trop. Med., 6:323, 1957.

SPIDER BITES

Several poisonous spiders are known. We may mention the Atrax formidabilis and the Atrax robustus of Australia and the Polybetes maculatus of South America. The monstrous tarantula, contrary to public belief, is not dangerous to man. The most dangerous of all spiders belong to the genus Latrodectus. They produce a powerful neurotoxin. These spiders are found on all the continents and in all 48 states of this country. Latrodectus mactans is the species most common in the United States. Its popular name is the *black widow*. This spider is a shiny black color with long slender legs and a bulbous abdomen upon which is found a yellow, orange or red spot shaped like an hourglass. The leg spread of the female may reach two inches. The male is much smaller and is not dangerous to man. This spider lives in outdoor privies, woodsheds, garages, barns, gardens and basements.

It is estimated that several hundred persons are bitten by this spider in this country every year and that a small percentage of these cases are fatal. Children are most likely to succumb. The bite is felt as a needle prick but in a few minutes severe pain begins at the site of the sting and spreads rapidly into the abdomen, back, thighs and chest. A large percentage of the victims are bitten on the penis or buttocks while seated on an outdoor toilet seat. The site of the bite is marked by a minute red spot which may be difficult to see. Within a short time there are systemic symptoms such as vomiting, sweating, changes in heart action, and possibly cyanosis. A low grade fever develops and there may be moderate leucocytosis. The urine may contain albumin and casts. Neurological symptoms are striking. The pain is agonizing, it is said, and may require morphine. Painful spasms of the muscles of the abdomen and legs develop. These occur with increasing frequency and are then replaced by intense rigidity. The rigidity of the abdomen has led to useless operations in some cases. Respiration may be involved. Priapism is described. There is often retention of urine. The tendon reflexes are exaggerated. Restlessness, anxiety and even delirium occur. The pain begins to diminish after 6 hours and ceases between 24 and 48 hours. If the patient survives, there is complete recovery.

The intravenous injection of calcium gluconate is regarded as the best treatment. Succinylcholine chloride is strongly recommended by Norfleet.

A brown spider is also dangerous. It is found from Kansas south to the Gulf Coast and from Tennessee west to Oklahoma, but less frequently in other parts of this country. It is described as having an oval body and is slightly smaller than the black widow. It has a dark spot shaped like a violin on its head. Its color varies from light fawn to dark brown. The scientific name is Loxoscleles Reclusus. After two to eight hours, severe pain begins. There is fever, chills, nausea, vomiting and itching. There is local tissue necrosis and running sores. All fatal cases have been in children. Fardon *et al.* advise that early excision of the site of the sting is the only effective treatment and prevents extensive sloughs.

We have seen one case in which a large spider stung a patient on the lower lid. The lids and the orbital tissues became greatly swollen so the eye was closed. Optic atrophy and loss of vision followed.

BIBLIOGRAPHY

BOGEN, E.: Arachnidism. Spider poisoning. Arch. Int. Med., **37**:623, 1926.

FARDON, D. W. *et al.*: The treatment of brown spider bite. Plast. Reconstr. Surg., **40**:482, 1967.

GREER, W. E. R.: Arachnidism. The effect of calcium gluconate. New England Med. J., **240**:5, 1949.

HOREN, W. P.: Arachnidism in the United States. J.A.M.A., **185**:839, 1963.

NORFLEET, E. K.: The use of succinylcholine chloride in black widow spider bite. J. Oklahoma State Med. A., **48**:77, 1955.

THORP, R. AND WOODSON, W.: The black widow, America's most poisonous spider. Univ. North Carolina Press, 1945.

BEE AND WASP STINGS

Occasionally one observes severe reactions to bee stings. Multiple stings are sometimes fatal, but even a single sting may cause a violent reaction and even death. Such reactions seem to be allergic. Some individuals exhibit within an hour or less swelling of the face, difficulty in breathing, itching and apprehension. In the more severe cases there may be, in addition, twitchings and spasms of the muscles, convulsions, anginal pains, cyanosis, vomiting, diarrhea, failure of respiration and loss of consciousness. This reaction may be regarded as an acute anaphylactic shock.

I have seen a patient who, on two occasions, immediately after being stung by a bee had such a severe reaction that he became unconscious. In each instance, within a week, he developed a moderately severe polyneuritis with bilateral foot drop, loss of angle jerk and sensory loss over the feet and ankles. He walked with difficulty for several months. There was complete recovery each time.

BIBLIOGRAPHY

ALLINGTON, H. AND R.: Insect bites. J.A.M.A., **155**:240, 1954.

BARNARD, J. H.: Allergic and pathologic findings in fifty insect-sting fatalities. Jour. Allergy, **40**:107, 1967.

HOWELL, J. D. AND KRAFT, B.: Bee and wasp stings. J. Indiana Med. A., **55**:749, 1962.

JEX-BLAKE, A. J.: Bee stings in Kenya Colony. Brit. Med. J., **ii**:241, 1942.

MARSHALL, T. K.: Wasp and bee stings. Practitioners, **178**:712 (June), 1957.

SCHENKEN, J. R., TAMISIEA, J. AND WINTER, F. D.: Hypersensitivity to bee sting: Report of fatal case and review of literature. Am. J. Clin. Path., **23**:1216, 1953.

VANSELOW, N. A.: Hypersensitivity to hymenoptera insects. Jour. Ark. Med. Soc., **63**:428, 1967.

WHITE, R.: Allergic reactions to stinging insects. Jour. La. Med. Soc., **120**:235, 1968.

SCORPION STINGS

Scorpions are members of the class Arachnida and are therefore related to spiders. Some of them possess a powerful neurotoxin which may be lethal. They are found in most tropical and subtropical parts of the world. They are especially troublesome in North Africa, India, Mexico and in the state of Arizona.

Scorpions vary in size between one inch and eight inches in length. These creatures have a flexible tail which contains poison glands and a sharp spine behind the tip of which the poison ducts open. The tail is brought forward over the scorpion's back in such a way as to sting anything before it.

It is estimated that 2500 persons are stung by scorpions in Arizona every year. Sixty-four deaths, mostly in childhood, are recorded, whereas only fifteen deaths are attributed to the rattlesnake and three to the black widow spider during the same period.

The ground scorpions of Arizona are not dangerous, but two bark scorpions are known to produce a lethal poison. These are the Centruoides sculpturatus and Centruoides gertschi. The sting of these scorpions causes a local burning or tingling sensation at once. This sensation travels up the arm or leg rapidly. No swelling or ecchymosis is seen at the site of the sting. Often the puncture wound is not visible. Soon there is spasm of the pharyngeal muscles and tongue. Great restlessness then begins. The child, for children are the usual victims, is never still for a moment and will get up on furniture, climb up on an adult or even try to climb the wall. Muscular twitchings develop and then powerful convulsions. Tonic spasms may bend the body backward or forward. Grotesque postures and violent movements of the extremities may appear. The child is often blind for 6 or 8 hours. Salivation is profuse. Delirium and stupor occur. Just before death the spasms subside, it is said.

A potent antiserum has been produced. When this is not available, it is recommended that a tourniquet be put around the extremity and an ice pack applied. After 5 minutes the tourniquet is released but the limb is kept in iced water for 2 hours. Sodium pentothal or sodium phenobarbital are injected intravenously.

BIBLIOGRAPHY

STAHNKE, H. L.: The Arizona scorpion problem. Arizona Med., **7** (3) :23, 1950.

VENOMOUS FISH

The *stingray* is a fish which may inject a powerful toxin by means of a caudal spine which may be thrust into its victims with considerable force. This spine has lateral grooves which contain the venom. The creature is found in shallow waters on the coast of this country and will sting bathers who are unfortunate enough to step on it.

Intense pain develops at the site of the wound within a few moments and may spread throughout the extremity and into the abdomen. Muscle spasm and even paralysis may occur. There is nausea, vomiting, bradycardia, cardiac arrhythmia, sweating, and diarrhea.

It is advised that a tourniquet be applied above the wound at once and the wound washed with cold salt water. The extremity is then placed in hot water for 30 minutes. The wound must be debrided, cleaned and closed. Penicillin and tetanus antitoxin are used. Novocain nerve block may be required to control the intense pain. Measures may be required for the relief of shock.

The *lionfish,* i.e. Pterosis radiata, a red and white tropical fish with long dorsal spines, injects a potent venom when touched. There is intense pain and swelling in the extremity. An individual who has been wounded by several spines may die in agony. No antidote is known.

The *stonefish* is found on the shores of the Pacific and Indian Oceans, the coasts of Australia, the Philippines and East Africa. It lies in shallow water partially buried in the sand. Waders are apt to step on it. Its sharp spines inject a potent venom which causes intense pain in the leg which rapidly extends to the groin and abdomen. Respiration is impaired. Convulsions and death may result within six hours. The leg may be paralysed completely. Treatment is symptomatic for no antitoxin is available.

Halstead states that many other fishes are capable of stinging. He mentions the spiny dogfish, the elephant fish, catfish, weever fish, scorpion fish, surgeonfish, dragonfish, star-gazers and many types of rays.

The box jellyfish, which lives in the waters around Australia, is said to possess long tentacles which inject a deadly venom which causes death within three minutes.

BIBLIOGRAPHY

HALSTEAD, B. W.: Dangerous Marine Animals. Cornell Maritime Press, Cambridge, Maryland, 1959.

RUSSELL, E. E.: Stingray injuries. A review and discussion of their treatment. Am. J. Med. Sc., **226**:611, 1953.

——— *et al.:* Studies on mechanism of death from stingray venom. Amer. Jour. Med. Sc., **235**:566, 1958.

INTOXICATIONS DUE TO EXOGENOUS POISONS
Lead Poisoning

Etiology.—Lead may be absorbed from the skin, inhaled through the lungs or ingested by way of the gastrointestinal tract. Infants have been poisoned as a result of the use of a lead nipple shield or by the application of powder or salve containing lead to the breast. The commonest cause of lead poisoning in our experience is a result of sucking or gnawing lead paint from toys or furniture. In infants this is, of course, to be expected as a part of the child's normal behavior but in older children, it is probably the expression of a perverted appetite, usually the result of a mental defect. Drinking water may be contaminated by the use of lead pipes or lead lined cisterns. Some years ago we saw a large number of cases in Baltimore which were traced to the use of discarded battery casings for fuel. The casings contained large amounts of lead and, when burned, gave off volatile compounds which caused poisoning by inhalation.

Pathological Anatomy.—In lead polyneuritis there is demyelination of the peripheral nerves as in other types of polyneuritis with some destruction of the axis cylinders. Apparently the anterior horn motor cells of the spinal cord also suffer considerable damage. These central lesions no doubt explain why recovery is not always complete in lead neuritis.

In lead encephalopathy, the brain is usually pale and edematous. The convolutions are flattened and herniation of the medulla is common. A few petechial hemorrhages may be seen but these are not so numerous or so constant as in arsenical encephalopathy. Blackman has made a very illuminating histological study. He finds the brain to be permeated by a serous exudate which is so abundant in some areas as to cause the tissues to be distended and spongy. The capillary vessels are damaged and even necrotic in some instances and a few small vessels show thrombi. Small hemorrhages and softenings are common. The neurons and nerve fibers suffer a variable degree of injury. As a rule, the cerebral cortex and the central white matter of the hemispheres are most severely affected but the cerebellum is constantly involved. Akelaitis points out that in some cases the ventricles are eventually dilated.

Almost all the organs suffer to some extent from lead poisoning and it scarcely seems necessary to detail all the lesions which have been described. The changes in the bones, however, are of so much clinical importance that they must be given in brief. A dense band between 2 and 4 mm wide is seen in roentgenograms which lies just beneath the proliferating zone of the epiphyseal cartilage. Park has shown that this is composed of parallel trabeculae which are composed chiefly of calcified intracellular substance containing large quantities of lead. Large numbers of giant cells are found between the trabeculae but osteoblasts are few. In normal bone these trabeculae of calcified cartilage are soon destroyed and replaced by true bone but in lead poisoning, they persist much longer and are much denser due to their lead content.

Lead is believed to exist in the circulation in the form of a soluble diphosphate. For some time after it is absorbed, it is to be found in all tissues of the body but more especially in the liver, brain and bones. Eventually, it comes to be stored almost entirely in the bones where it is relatively inert and causes no recognizable symptoms. It is, however, slowly liberated and excreted over a long period of time. If, however, acidosis develops or ill-judged efforts are made to remove the lead from the body, it may be mobilized suddenly into the blood stream giving rise to acute symptoms once more.

Clinical Features.—Lead poisoning is not rare in Baltimore at the present time. Between 1931 and December 31, 1956, there were 545 cases in this city and of these 109 were fatal. In most cases, lead poisoning is due to the ingestion of lead paint gnawed from toys or cribs. Acute infections and various conditions such as may lead to acidosis seem to play a role in precipitating the development of symptoms.

As a rule the lead is taken in small amounts over a long period. The symptoms, therefore, develop gradually in most instances. There is loss of weight, vomiting, weakness and anorexia. In many cases there is severe constipation and abdominal cramps. There is nothing very typical in the clinical picture at this stage and the diagnosis is, therefore, easily missed. Symptoms referable to the nervous system are frequently the first evidence of lead poisoning to attract attention. In children *lead encephalopathy* is much more common than polyneuritis. Holt states that in 36 cases of lead poisoning seen at Harriet Lane, there were 31 cases of encephalopathy and 5 cases of neuritis. The onset of encephalopathy is usually relatively abrupt with severe and repeated convulsions. These are usually generalized but may be focal. Sometimes focal attacks occur on both sides in irregular sequence. Transient palsies may follow each seizure. It is sometimes very difficult to control the convulsions and the children often die in a series of violent attacks despite every effort to control them. In the interval between the convulsions the child may be drowsy or even comatose, but states of excitement and delirium are also seen. Cervical rigidity is usually present but in the writer's opinion this is merely a part of a general muscular rigidity and is not to be regarded as evidence of meningeal irritation. Hemiplegia and other types of cerebral palsies are not infrequent and various involuntary and automatic movements are sometimes seen. Tremor of the hands is common. Occasionally one encounters an outspoken cerebellar syndrome manifest by a cerebellar gait as well as by ataxia of the arms and legs. The optic nerve heads are often greatly swollen and show hemorrhage and exudate. This picture seems to be due to papilledema resulting from edema of the brain. If decompression is performed, the brain may herniate through the opening for several months. These changes may be followed by optic atrophy and blindness. In other cases, retrobulbar neuritis is found and for a time the nerve heads may show no changes adequate to explain the loss of vision. Sonkin states that a reliable early sign of lead poisoning is in the presence of glistening, discrete gray deposits of lead in the retinae around the optic discs. Cranial nerve palsies are not especially common but we have seen ptosis of the lids, strabismus and facial palsies. If the fontanels are not closed they may be tense or bulging and the sutures separated.

The blood pressure is frequently somewhat elevated during the more acute stages. Temperature is usually normal or at most slightly elevated but terminal hyperpyrexia may occur and there is sometimes fever in association with convulsions. The spinal fluid always shows definite changes. The pressure is elevated and the protein is greatly increased. The Pandy test often reveals a dense cloud of globulin. The cell count is subject to considerable variation. In some cases there may be 100 or more lymphocytes and in others the count is normal or only slightly elevated. The average is perhaps about 10 to 20 cells.

The urine almost always contains albumin and in a large percentage of cases sugar as well.

Polyneuritis may complicate lead encephalopathy especially in older children and in some cases even extensive neuritis may occur without any cerebral symptoms whatever. As a rule, lead neuritis is not so selective in children as in adults and wrist-drop and foot-drop alone are rarely, if ever, seen. On the contrary, the paralysis involves all muscle groups, including both the flexors and extensors. The legs are usually more severely affected than the arms and the distal muscles more than the proximal ones. Moreover, there is often definite tenderness of the muscles and even some degree of anesthesia of peripheral type. Muscular cramps are very common. The tendon reflexes are lost, the ankle jerks being abolished first. The reaction of degeneration is to be expected in the affected muscles. The cranial nerves are usually spared but optic neuritis and optic atrophy may occur. The writer has recently seen a case in a child who had eaten paint. The extremities were completely paralyzed, the neck was weak, both facial nerves were paralysed, the bulbar muscles were involved and eventually paralysis of the intercostals and diaphragm led to death from failure of respiration.

The spinal fluid shows only slight changes as compared to those found in encephalopathy. The pressure is not definitely increased, the cell count is normal, as a rule, and the protein is only moderately increased.

Certain clinical features are common to all types of lead poisoning. One of the best known signs is the lead line of the gums. This is a bluish black zone on the margins of the gums or, perhaps, merely a number of fine dark spots which cannot be clearly seen without magnification. This is due to actual deposit of lead in the tissues and cannot be wiped off. The blood studies almost always reveal some degree of anemia. This may be mild or severe. Various types of immature red cells are seen in the smear but cells showing fine basophilic stippling are so numerous and so constant that they are regarded as of diagnostic importance. It must be emphasized that identical cells occur in other types of anemia and that they may be absent in lead poisoning. The leucocytes are not abnormal. Another feature of diagnostic significance which has attracted much attention recently is the lead line of the bones. This is a dense zone of from 2 to 4 mm width lying just beneath the zone of proliferating epiphyseal cartilage. It is most definite where growth is most active and is easily seen in roentgenograms of the ribs, the lower end of the femur and upper end of the humerus, the lower ends of the radius and ulna and at both ends of the tibia and fibula. In clear films it may be seen that this band is due to dense trabeculae lying parallel to the long axis of the bone and very close to one another. The borders of the shadows are not very sharply defined but shade off into normal bone. These slowly grow broader and less distinct. Other conditions may give rise to somewhat similar bands, such as arrested growth, healing rickets, large doses of viosterol and poisoning with phosphorus, and, perhaps, other heavy metals. Small dense shadows may be seen in roentgenograms of the abdomen in some cases which seem to be bits of lead in the intestines.

Diagnosis.—The diagnosis is based upon the history of eating paint or of exposure to lead poisoning from some other source, the clinical signs and symptoms of encephalopathy or less commonly polyneuritis, the basophilic stippling of the red cells, the lead line of the gums, the dense zone shown in roentgenograms of the bones and the demonstration of lead in the blood by the spectroscope. Chisolm and Harrison point out that coproporphyrin is increased in the urine and in acute cases of lead poisoning usually range between 500 and 1000 mg in twenty-four hours. It is said that if coproporphyrin is not present lead poisoning is unlikely. Renal glycosuria is common. Bradley, J. E., *et al.* claim, however, that the presence or absence of coproporphyrin in the urine is not important in the diagnosis of lead poisoning. The concentration of lead in the blood may be measured by either chemical or spectographic methods. Normal values are between 0 and 0.03 per 100 cc of blood. When the level reaches 0.1, symptoms may occur. A level of 0.3 usually indicates encephalopathy is imminent.

Whitaker states that the most satisfactory test is made by the administration of calcium disodium versenate and the subsequent determination of the lead content of the urine.

Lead encephalopathy should be suspected in all cases of convulsions in childhood in which the cause is not clear. In mentally defective children who might be expected to have convulsions as an expression of a cerebral defect, we must always consider the possibility of complicating lead poisoning, since such children often eat paint. If there is optic neuritis or other signs of increased intracranial pressure, brain tumor may be erroneously diagnosed, but the most common mistake in our experience is to confuse lead encephalopathy with tuberculous meningitis. The stupor, the rigidity and the excess of protein and cells in the spinal fluid make this mistake a relatively natural one to make, especially if the tuberculin test happens to be positive.

Prognosis.—The mortality is, in our experience, relatively high in lead encephalopathy. Holt states that 13 children out of 20 who were brought into the clinic in convulsions died within a short time. If the child survives, there is often permanent injury to the nervous system. Thus of the seven who survived in Holt's series of 20, two were idiots, three were more mildly defective, one seemed to be normal in mentality but showed difficulty in gait and only one seemed to be quite restored to health. We have also seen complete blindness result from optic atrophy following lead encephalopathy. Hemiplegia, bilateral weakness and spasticity may persist. Epilepsy is not an uncommon sequel. Jenkins and Mellins state that of 46 children suffering from acute lead poisoning, 13 died and subsequently 27 of the 33 survivors were found to be mentally retarded. Two years later, many of these children were examined again and half had improved but were still backward.

In polyneuritis, the outlook is much better if there is no complicating encephalopathy. There is, as a rule, slow but continued improvement which may eventually amount to recovery. Certain muscles, however, may never regain their power, probably due to destruction of the cell body in the spinal cord.

Treatment.—The treatment of lead encephalopathy may be divided into four parts: (1) The control of the convulsions. (2) The reduction of increased intracranial pressure. (3) The removal of lead from the blood stream. (4) The removal of lead from the body. The convulsions are very resistant to the usual sedative drugs such as phenobarbital and sometimes require general anesthetics.

At present, calcium disodium versenate is usually employed to remove the lead from the body. It is claimed that this drug chelates the lead stored in the body, and it gets into the blood stream in a non-toxic form, so it may be excreted. It is advised that the bowels must be cleaned out carefully, so as to prevent the absorption of lead from the intestinal tract before the chelating drug is employed. Rieders states that intravenous injection of the calcium disodium versenate is necessary and it should not be given by mouth.

Chisholm advises the use of Bal and edathamil calcium disodium.

Intravenous urea is now recommended to reduce intracranial pressure. Subtemporal decompression is employed in some cases. Even if no treatment is employed there will be gradual excretion of the lead over a period of months or years. It is, of course, of the greatest importance to prevent the further ingestion of lead.

In polyneuritis, the method of treatment is essentially the same. The efforts should be made to store the lead in the bones until the acute symptoms have disappeared. The usual measures for treatment of polyneuritis are indicated.

BIBLIOGRAPHY

Akelaitis, A. J.: Lead encephalopathy in children and adults. J. Nerv. & Ment. Dis., **93:**313, 1941.

Aub, J. C., Fairhall, L. T., Minot, A. S. and Reznikoff, P.: Lead poisoning. Medicine, **4:**1, 1925.

Blackman, S. S.: The lesions of lead encephalitis in children. Bull. Johns Hopkins Hospital, **61:**1, 1937.

Blumberg, H. and Scott, T. N. McN.: A thirty-minute spectrographic micro-method for the detection of pathologic lead in the peripheral blood. Bull. Johns Hopkins Hosp., **56:**32, 1935.

————: The quantitative spectrographic estimation of blood lead and its value in the diagnosis of lead poisoning. Bull. Johns Hopkins Hosp., **56:**276, 1935.

Bradley, J. E.: The incidence of abnormal blood levels of lead on a metropolitan pediatric clinic. J. Pediat., **49:**1, 1956.

Byers, R. K. and Lord, E. E.: Late effects of lead poisoning on mental development. Am. J. Dis. Child., **66:**471, 1943.

Byers, R. K. and Maloof, C.: Treatment of lead poisoning by calcium disodium versenate. Am. J. Dis. Child., **87:**559, 1954.

Chisolm, J. J. and Harrison, H. E.: The treatment of acute lead encephalopathy in children. Pediatrics, **19:**2, 1957.

————: The use of chelating agents in the treatment of acute and chronic lead intoxication. J. Pediat., **73:**1, 1908.

Cohen, G. J. and Ahrens, W. E.: Chronic lead poisoning. J. Pediat., **54:**271, 1959.

Deane, G. E. et al.: Use of BAL in treatment of acute lead encephalopathy. J. Pediat., **42:**409, 1953.

Elliot, M. M., Souther, S. P. and Park, E. A.: Transverse line in x-ray plates of the long bones of children. Bull. Johns Hopkins Hosp., **41:**364, 1927.

Ennis, J. M. and Harrison, H. E.: Treatment of lead encephalopathy with BAL. Pediatrics, **5:**853, 1950.

Goodwin, T. C.: Lead poisoning report of a case in a child with extensive paralysis. Bull. Johns Hopkins Hosp., **55:**347, 1934.

Greengard, J. et al.: Urea for lead encephalopathy. New England J. Med., **264:**1027, 1961.

————: Lead poisoning in childhood. Clin. Pediat., **5:**269, 1966.

Hunter, D. and Aub, J. C.: Lead studies: Effect of parathyroid hormone on excretion of lead and of calcium in patients suffering from lead poisoning. Quart. J. Med., **20:**123, 1927.

Jenkins, C. D. and Mellins, R. B.: Lead poisoning in children. Arch. Neurol. & Psychiat., **77:**70, 1957.

Karpinski, F. E. et al.: Calcium disodium versenate in therapy of lead encephalopathy. J. Pediat., **42:**687, 1953.

Park, E. A., Jackson, D. and Kajdi, L.: Shadows produced by lead in the x-ray pictures of the growing skeleton. Am. J. Dis. Child., **41:**485, 1931. (First read by Dr. Park at a meeting of the Pediatric Section of the N. Y. Academy of Medicine, Nov. 14, 1929.)

Popoff, N. and Weinberg, S.: Pathologic observations in lead encephalopathy. Neurology, **13:**101, 1963.

RIEDERS, F.: Current Concepts in the Therapy of Lead Poisoning. Chapter 16 in Metal-binding in Medicine. Philadelphia, J. B. Lippincott, 1960.

SHIPLEY, P. G., SCOTT, T. N. McN. AND BLUMBERG, H.: The spectrographic detection of lead in the blood as an aid to the clinical diagnosis of plumbism. Bull. Johns Hopkins Hosp., **51**:327, 1932.

SONKIN, N.: Retinal stippling with lead poisoning. New England J. Med., **269**:779, 1963.

WALSH, F. B.: *Loc. cit.*

WHITAKER, J. A. *et al.*: Early detection of lead poisoning. Pediatrics, **29**:384, 1962.

DRUGS AND POISONS

Only those substances which affect the nervous system are mentioned here. Since children are rarely exposed to the chemicals used in industry, these are omitted. Arsenic, lead, botulism, anticonvulsives, anesthetics, asphyxiating gases and vitamins are discussed elsewhere. Intoxication in childhood is usually the result of ingestion of drugs found in the medicine chest, the basement or the outhouse or less commonly improper medication by the physician. An enterprising child can find many lethal agents in the modern home. It is estimated that between 1940 and 1950, 3659 children under five years of age died in the United States from poisons found about the home.

It should be stated that drugs should be administered to infants with great care. When under the age of three months children lack the enzymes by which drugs are metabolized so that the drugs may accumulate in the body. Moreover the renal tubules are functionally immature and drugs may not be excreted properly.

Alcohol.—We have seen two children who drank a large quantity of whiskey which had been left within reach and were brought into the hospital in coma. Hypoglycemia may result and convulsions. Garrison reports the case of a child who was made seriously ill by sponging with isopropyl alcohol because of inhalation or absorption of the alcohol through the skin. The administration of insulin and glucose are recommended and the stomach should be emptied.

Aminophylline may cause restlessness, irritability, vomiting, convulsions and paralysis of respiration in children. Children under 3 years seem to be susceptible. Treatment by oxygen, intravenous fluids and antibiotics is advised.

Antiallergy Drugs.—We have seen one case in which a child took a large number of her mother's *benadryl* capsules. The face became flushed and the child became comatose within a short time. Repeated convulsions followed. For several weeks there were evidences of extensive cerebral damage with cortical blindness and stupor. Eventually there was complete recovery. Fatal cases are reported. Treatment is symptomatic.

Ethylene glycol, a common ingredient of commercial *antifreeze* solutions, is extremely poisonous. Thus, Friedman *et al.* state that two boys who drank 3 to 4 ounces of this material died and two, who took 1 to 2 ounces, recovered. Vomiting should be induced at once and the stomach lavaged with 1 to 5000 potassium permanganate. Acidosis may be controlled with parenteral bicarbonate. Peritoneal dialysis or hemodialysis may be helpful.

Antihypertensive drugs may cause postural hypotension and syncope. Diuril may cause depletion of potassium with the usual symptoms. Inversine may cause a flapping tremor and convulsions.

Antiinfectious Agents.—Streptomycin may cause damage to the vestibular system with vertigo and then lack of equilibrium due to loss of vestibular reflexes. Some patients seem to develop cerebellar ataxia as well as loss of equilibrium after large doses of streptomycin. Dihydrostreptomycin may cause deafness. The loss of hearing may be delayed for several weeks after the drug is discontinued. Neomycin, kanamycin and vancomycin may also destroy hearing. Isoniazid may cause tremors, ataxia, myoclonus, torsion spasm and polyneuritis. The prolonged administration of chloramphenicol is said to cause optic neuritis with optic atrophy. Central scotomas are characteristic. Altafur, one of the antimicrobial nitrofurans, causes palsies of the extraocular muscles, nystagmus, deafness, difficulty in speech and in swallowing and peripheral neuritis. Furadantine may, in some instances, cause severe polyneuritis.

Allergic reactions to penicillin are not rare. Anaphylactic shock is described. Arthralgia with urticaria is the most common in my experience. Polyneuritis, cranial nerve involvement, myelitis and diffuse encephalitis are described. The sciatic nerve may be damaged when the drug is injected into the buttock in such a way as to infiltrate the nerve. There is partial recovery as a rule but when this accident occurs in childhood, the result may be defective development of the affected leg.

Bloomer *et al.* have shown that large doses of penicillin administered to patients in uremia cause reduction of consciousness and generalized muscular twitchings suggesting status epilepticus.

Belladonna and its derivatives cause dilatation of the pupils, dryness of the mouth, flushing of the skin, excitement and delirium. The temperature may be elevated and the pulse rapid. Vivid hallucinations are characteristic. Occasionally healthy children of 10 years or more may become delirious when atropine is given as a cycloplegic. Infants, especially defective infants, may have severe reactions when homatropine is used to dilate the pupils. We have seen two deaths in such cases. Children may take laxative tablets containing atropine and may also eat berries such as the seeds of the jimson weed which contain the alkaloids. Excessive dosage with atropine for enuresis may cause poisoning. Gastric lavage is advised. Pilocarpine is helpful but does not relieve the cerebral symptoms. During the stage of excitement sedatives are indicated but later when depression has developed, stimulants may be required.

Benzedrine is used by ophthalmologists as a cycloplegic and in the home as a stimulant and as an inhalant to open the nasal passages. It is also used in narcolepsy. Taken in excess it causes excitement, tremors, vomiting, diarrhea, irregular heart action and dilatation of the pupils. Convulsions and coma may occur. We have seen two fatal cases. Treatment is apparently symptomatic.

It has been found that the excessive use of amphetamines with or without barbiturates which is now prevalent among young people will produce irreversible brain damage.

Boric acid, used so much for the ammonical dermatitis of infancy, may be absorbed from the mucous membranes and through broken skin. It causes a brillant red rash on the palms, soles and scrotum. There may be vomiting and diarrhea. Convulsions, rigidity and coma may occur. Boric acid is found in the urine in such cases and may be identified by dipping tumeric paper in the acidified urine. The paper turns pink or red when dried. Treatment includes fresh plasma or whole blood for shock and intravenous glucose to stimulate the urinary outflow. Convulsions may require sedation.

Camphor is used in mothballs, which a child may swallow. Confusion, excitement, hallucinations, convulsions and coma result. Death may be due to failure of respiration. Gastric lavage is recommended and sedation when required.

Chloroquine will cause reversible opacities of the corneae, and irreversible retinal lesions with central scotomas and contraction of the fields of vision. Myopathy is also described. It is claimed that when the drug is stopped, gradual recovery occurs.

Oral Contraceptive Pills.—Between 1962 and 1965, 962 children are reported to have ingested up to 22 contraceptive pills of their mother. Only 40 children became ill and vomited. The other children showed no ill effects.

Cleaning Fluids may cause serious symptoms. *Carbon tetrachloride* is used in the home to clean fabrics. It may cause diplopia, confusion, ataxia and coma. Several fatal cases are reported. Various anatomical lesions are described including perivascular demyelination, degeneration of the cerebellar cortex, optic atrophy and peripheral neuritis. Liver damage is apt to occur within 48 hours. Children are poisoned by drinking the chemical, by inhalation and by absorption when the material is used to remove adhesive tape. It should be mentioned that this same drug is used as a vermifuge. The stomach should be emptied and a saline laxative given. Otherwise treatment is symptomatic.

Cortisone and Related Drugs may cause obesity, hyperglycemia, salt and water retention, high blood pressure, polycythemia, purpura, osteoporosis, hirsutism, flabby musculature, defective bodily growth, gastric ulcer and psychoses. Bacterial infections may be activated. Some compounds, especially those containing fluorine such as triamcinolone and fluorocortisone, may cause extensive myopathy. Cataracts may develop if cortisone is given for long periods. Cerebral edema is described.

Steroids given for long periods in cases of rheumatoid arthritis seem to increase the incidence of arteritis manifest primarily in most cases by polyneuritis.

Digitalis poisoning is marked by vomiting, diarrhea, dizziness, green or yellow vision, slow and irregular pulse, convulsions and coma. Death may occur as a result of ventricular fibrillation. Treatment is symptomatic. *Squill* is rarely used as a cardiac tonic at present but is found in rat poison. The action seems to be like that of digitalis. Fortunately a large dose causes vomiting at once and the poison is thus eliminated.

Ferrous Sulphate may cause vomiting, bloody diarrhea, stupor and convulsions. The usual cause is the ingestion by the child of a large number of tablets. Several cases have been fatal. Gastric lavage is advised and transfusions. The administration of B vitamins and alpha-tocopherol is also advised.

Chronic Fluorine Poisoning occurs in areas in which the drinking water contains more than 4 parts per million of fluorine, Singh *et al.* state. The first effect is mottling of the enamel of the teeth. Later, the bones are involved. There may be kyphosis and destructive lesions in the hip joints. Still later, the nervous system may be damaged causing paresthesias and weakness of the legs.

Food Poisoning.—Botulism is discussed elsewhere. *Ergotism* may result from the use of bread made from rye infested by the fungus Claviceps purpura. In acute poisoning, i.e. the convulsive form, there is vomiting, diarrhea, coldness of the skin, confusion, excitement and then convulsions and coma. Death may occur within a short time. If the patient survives, there may be mental changes, cerebral palsies, and degenerations of the long tracts in the spinal cord. A gangrenous form is described which is manifest by gangrene of the fingers and toes and lesions in the viscera. Children may develop ergotism by taking their mothers' headache tablets which contain ergotamine tartrate. Vasodilators are recommended and atropine may reduce the vomiting. *Lathyrism* is due to the use of meal which is made from several varieties of vetches, chiefly the Lathyrus sativus and the L. cicera. Wheat contaminated by Vicia sativa may also be responsible. Lathyrism occurs chiefly in India where large numbers of cases may be seen during a famine. The symptoms appear to be those of degeneration of the lateral and posterior columns of the spinal cord. Occasionally the sweet pea, *Lathyrus odoratus,* is used for food. A toxic effect on the

mesodermal tissues results with aneurysm of the aorta, herniae and deformities of the bones. The toxic agent is believed to be B-aminopropi-
onitrile. *Mushroom* poisoning is almost always due to the Aminita genus,
either A. muscaria or the more deadly A. Phalloides. In the muscaria type
the symptoms are due to the alkaloid muscarine. They develop within an
hour or two. There is nausea, vomiting, diarrhea, contraction of the pupils,
coma and convulsions. Death may occur within a few hours. The prognosis
is good if atropine is given early for this is an effective antidote. In the
phalloides group, the symptoms appear between 6 and 15 hours after the
mushroom is eaten. There is abdominal pain, vomiting, diarrhea, dehydration and prostration. Vision is blurred and then lost. Paralysis of the extraocular muscles occurs. Jaundice and renal failure develop later. Death occurs in 5 to 8 days sometimes from uremia. More than 50 per cent of such
cases are fatal. No antidote is known. Apparently several toxins are present.
Elliott *et al.* recommend hemodialysis with an artificial kidney. They state
that an antitoxic serum is of doubtful value. *Mussel poisoning:* Certain
mussels, especially Mytilis edulis and Mytilis californianus, may become
toxic during the summer months. Mussel poisoning has been recognized for
many years in Europe, England, the Pacific region and North America, especially in California where in July 1927 there were 102 cases, a number of
which were fatal. Cooking does not destroy the poison which has a neuro-
paralytic effect resembling that of curare. The symptoms begin within 5 to
30 minutes after the mussels are ingested. Numbness of the fingers and toes
appears first. Within 6 hours this numbness has spread to the arms, legs and
neck and is followed by profound weakness and ataxia. The tendon reflexes may be lost. The mental condition is usually clear but some patients
are drowsy. Vomiting usually occurs but there is constipation rather than
diarrhea. The pulse and respiration are both accelerated. Death results in
about 15 per cent of all cases from paralysis of the muscles of respiration.
Emetics and purges are recommended. Caffeine is said to be helpful. Artificial respiration may keep the patient alive until recovery can occur. If the
patient survives, complete recovery may be expected within a few days. It
is said that 1.0 cc of an aqueous extract of the toxic mussels will kill a
mouse within a few minutes if injected into the peritoneum. No lesions are
found in the nervous system at post-mortem examination. The source of
the poison is not known. It has been suggested that it is derived from
plankton or other small organisms upon which the mussels feed. The flesh
of certain *fish,* such as the tropical *trigger fish* or Balistoides niger and its
relatives, is poisonous. There is tingling of the lips and tongue. Then swelling of the extremities with intense pains. Paralysis and loss of vision occur.
A strange symptom is reversal of thermal sensibility. Hot objects feel cold

and cold objects, hot. Meat which has been treated with *nicotinic acid* to preserve the red color may cause flushing, sweating, nausea and abdominal cramps. No lasting damage occurs.

Holscher and Natzschke state that when stored, the nitrites of fresh spinach may be converted into nitrates. Young infants given this material may develop methemaglobinemia due to nitrate poisoning. They advise the intravenous injection of 1 to 2 mgs of methylene blue per kilogram of body weight in a 1 per cent solution.

Ginger extract has been found to contain at times triorthocresylphosphate. Cresyl esters have also been found in cooking oils. The poison has a selective effect on the peripheral nerves and causes a severe polyneuritis. In some instances after the peripheral nerves have regenerated, the patient is found to have a spastic paraplegia showing that the long tracts in the spinal cord are also involved. Optic atrophy may occur. Koster and David state that eating large amounts of licorice may induce a pronounced elevation of the blood pressure which soon falls to a normal level when the licorice is no longer eaten.

Sniffing of vaporized plastic and model aeroplane cements can injure the liver, kidneys, brain and bone marrow. This practice is popular among adolescents. The symptoms are intoxication, exhilaration, disorientation and coma. No deaths are reported.

Insecticides contain a number of toxic materials. *Nicotine* may be absorbed through the skin as well as from the digestive tract. It causes nausea, salivation, abdominal pain, vomiting and diarrhea. Dizziness, confusion, and weakness occur. The pulse is slow, at first, but later becomes rapid. The blood pressure falls and respiration fails. Death in convulsions may occur within a very short time. The poison is destroyed rapidly in the body and artificial respiration may keep the patient alive until the critical period has passed. Treatment is otherwise symptomatic. *Fluorides* are also used in insecticides. They act upon the nervous system, the heart and gastrointestinal tract. Abdominal pain, vomiting, and diarrhea occur and are followed by falling blood pressure, convulsions and death. Death may result from failure of respiration or heart failure. Gastric lavage with calcium lactate, intravenous calcium lactate and calcium gluconate are recommended. Calcium or milk may be given by mouth to precipitate unabsorbed fluorides in the stomach. *Cyanides* are also used in fumigation to destroy insects or rodents. The gas may be inhaled. The symptoms occur almost at once with giddiness, headache, palpitation, hyperpnea, coma and convulsions. Death occurs within a short time. The diagnosis may usually be made by the odor of bitter almonds. The administration of pure oxygen and artificial respiration are advised. *Chlorinated hydrocarbons* such as paradichlorobenzene and benzene hexachloride have been used recently. These may be absorbed through the skin as well as through the respiratory tract and the stomach. They cause excitement, irritability, loss of equilibrium and convulsions. Barbiturates are required for sedation and intravenous calcium gluconate is recommended. The skin should be cleaned with soap and water if the drug has been applied to the skin and the stomach washed out if the drug has been ingested. Saline laxatives are used. *Organic phosphates* such as parathion and malathon are also used in insecticides. These drugs cause inhibition of cholinesterases and hence, cause accumulation of acetylcholine. There is headache, giddiness, blurring of vision, weakness, cramps of the muscles, nausea, diarrhea and discomfort in the chest. Sweating is profuse and salivation is mentioned. Cyanosis, pulmonary edema, convulsions and coma develop. Papilledema is mentioned. Failure of respiration may be the cause of death. Intravenous atropine is given at once. It is claimed that the administration of pyridine-2-aldoxime methiodide as well as atropine is effective. If ingestion is suspected, emesis should be induced. Oxygen or artificial respiration may be required. The emergency lasts from 24 to 48 hours. Gershon and Shaw state that prolonged exposure to organo-phosphorus insecticides cause depressive or schizophrenic reactions. Other insecticides such as *D.D.T.* and *its derivatives* methoxychlor, pyrethrum, rotenone, chlordane, toxaphene and lethanes should be treated with barbiturates for sedation, oxygen inhalations and saline catharsis for there are no antidotes.

Magnesium Sulphate is absorbed from the intestines but is usually excreted by the kidneys so rapidly that it does not accumulate. When given to reduce edema in nephritis, however, it may be retained and cause poisoning. The blood pressure falls, muscular paralysis occurs with death due to failure of respiration. The action is like that of curare but there is also an effect on the brain which may cause coma. Calcium is used as an antidote.

Metals.—Lead poisoning is discussed elsewhere. Arsenic is no longer a common cause of poisoning. Formerly, the injudicious use of drugs was largely responsible for arsenic poisoning. Now, arsphenamine, Fowler's solution, tryparsamide, acetarsone and similar drugs are rarely used and poisoning is usually due to the ingestion of rat poison, weed killers, and insecticides by children. Arsenic may be absorbed from the skin if it is left in contact too long. Acute poisoning causes vomiting, diarrhea, convulsions and collapse with death in a short time. Chronic poisoning causes a metallic taste in the mouth, puffy lids, abdominal pain, nausea, vomiting, polyneuritis with much pain and tenderness, pigmentation of the skin and sometimes herpes zoster. White lines appear on the nails. There is albumin in the urine. Abundant fluids and saline laxatives are indicated. The skin should be washed if contaminated. BAL, i.e. 2-3-dimercaptopropanol, is recommended to facilitate the removal of the drug from the body. *Thallium* is used as a depilatory in fungus infections of the scalp and is sometimes used as a rat poison. The ingestion of large doses causes vomiting, weakness of the extremities, convulsions, delirium, loss of hair, blindness and death in several days. Absorption from the skin causes less dramatic symptoms with polyneuritis and central scotomas. There may be night terrors and loss of hair. Saline cathartics, brewers yeast and BAL are recommended. *Mercury* is rarely given to a child except in the form of calomel. It is claimed by some investigators that calomel is the cause of acrodynia q.v. A condition resembling amyotrophic lateral sclerosis may develop, it is claimed. *Barium* is used in rat poisons. It causes powerful stimulation of the muscles both striated and smooth. There are severe abdominal cramps, vomiting, diarrhea, arterial hypertension, myocardial stimulation and finally death from cardiac arrest. Tremors and spasms of the muscles are followed by extensive paralysis. Death usually occurs within an hour, it is said. Barium enemas sometimes result in extensive deposits of barium crystals in the capillaries of the lungs. BAL is recommended. *Gold* is used in the treatment of rheumatoid arthritis. It has a number of toxic effects including puritis, stomatitis, exfoliative dermatitis, purpura hemorrhagica, hepatic and renal damage, agranulocytosis, peripheral neuritis and encephalitis. BAL is said to be the most effective therapeutic agent.

Naphthalene is used in mothballs which may be swallowed. It may cause hemoglobinuria, anemia and optic atrophy. Cataracts may result.

Narcotics such as *morphine* and its derivatives may cause constriction of the pupils, drowsiness passing into coma, shallow breathing, cold skin, slow weak pulse, vomiting and death from failure of respiration. Children are sensitive to such drugs. The stomach may be washed out and caffeine may be given or ephedrin. Artificial respiration may be required. Recently meperidine and methadon have been recommended. Recently nalorphine has been found to be a specific antidote against morphine and all morphine mimetic substances. Large doses of *codeine* may cause lethargy, cyanosis and convulsions. When codeine is given to suppress cough in measles, such symptoms may lead to the diagnosis of encephalitis.

Nitrites.—A number of infants have died of methemoglobinemia as a result of the use of bismuth subnitrate in diarrhea. Intestinal bacteria may convert the nitrates into nitrites. In such cases, there is postural hypotension and often syncope or convulsions. Nitrite poisoning has been observed in children who drank water from a well contaminated by nitrogenous fertilizers.

Phenolphthalein may cause acute disseminated encephalomyelitis, it is said. It is suggested that this is due to allergy, for the drug is not really toxic. The death of a two-year-old child is reported.

Nose Drops.—Tyzine, or *tetrahydrosoline hydrochloride,* a drug used in nose drops, may cause coma and shock if given in large doses.

Oils.—Machine oils sometimes contain triorthocresylphosphate and if ingested by mistake instead of castor oil may cause poisoning. See Ginger extract.

Phosphorus.—Yellow phosphorus is no longer used in matches but is found in roach powder and in rat poisons. It causes violent irritation of the gastrointestinal tract, destruction of the liver and also acts upon the muscles and the heart. Dr. David Clark has told me of such a case in which the child's stools burst into blue flames as soon as they were passed.

Poisonous Plants.—The reader is referred to a paper by William H. Wood, Jr., who lists 35 poisonous plants which grow in this country and may be eaten by children. A number of these are mentioned in the text of this article. *Morning Glory* seeds cause hallucinations and prolonged changes in personality.

Quinine and its derivatives may cause fever, vomiting, excitement, confusion and syncope. Respiration may be affected. If the patient survives, there may be deafness and optic atrophy. Often the optic discs are quite white and the retinal arteries mere threads. Central vision may be preserved though the fields do not exceed 5 degrees. Chloroquin may cause edema of the corneae which is reversible and pigmented lesions in the maculae which are rounded and characteristic. These lesions cause loss of central vision which persists. The retinal vessels are narrow. Polyneuritis may also occur. Knox has published cases in which quinine amblyopia was associated with

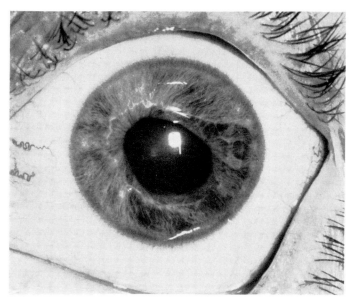

FIG. 171. Iris atrophy and toxic amblyopia due to quinine intoxication. Knox, D. L. and Palmer, C. A. L. Iris atrophy after quinine amblyopia. Read before the Meeting of the Wilmer Residents Meeting, Johns Hopkins Hospital, April 30, 1966.

atrophy of the irides. McKenna has described aplasia of the optic nerves and congenital deafness in children whose mothers took large doses of quinine early in pregnancy in the hope of inducing abortion.

Refrigerants.—A number of toxic gases are now used in electric refrigerators which sometimes leak with disastrous results. Among these materials is *methyl chloride*. This causes confusion, drowsiness, disturbances of vision, palsies of the ocular muscles, muscular twitchings and convulsions. *Methyl bromide* is also used as an insecticide. It causes confusion, disturbances of vision, stupor and convulsions. Cerebellar ataxia was a striking feature in one case we have seen.

Salicylates may cause serious symptoms in children even in some instances in which the dosage has not been excessive. The first symptoms are dizziness, ringing in the ears, deafness and hyperpnea. Later, there is acidosis with vomiting, hypoglycemia and bleeding from reduction of prothrombin. Finally coma, convulsions, fever and respiratory failure occur. Treatment includes abundant fluids with glucose to promote the excretion of the drug, measures to combat acidosis and vitamin K to prevent hemorrhage. Sedation may be required to stop convulsions and sponge baths to reduce temperature. Peritoneal dialysis is recommended for boric acid poisoning and exchange transfusion also. Robin states that alkylosis may occur at first with reduction of the serum potassium. The arterial pH must be measured. It should be remembered that oil of wintergreen may be absorbed by the skin. Cohen points out that salicylate poisoning may be mistaken for diabetic acidosis for the urine contains reducing bodies and there may be polyuria and acidosis.

Sedatives.—Barbiturates are found in the medicine cabinet in most homes today. Excessive dosage causes drowsiness, ataxia, unsteadiness, dilated pupils, diplopia, ptosis, dysarthria and often ocular palsies. There may be cyanosis. Respiration may be slow. Bilateral Babinski signs may appear. If death occurs early, it is usually due to failure of respiration; if late, it is apt to be due to pneumonia. Treatment is symptomatic. The stomach should be washed out. Respiratory stimulants are indicated and picrotoxin is recommended by some authorities. Megimide, which seems to be a central nervous system stimulant, is said to improve respiration and improve the state of consciousness. Oxygen and artificial respiration may be required. Bromides are discussed under anticonvulsive drugs.

Sudden withdrawal of sedatives such as barbiturates and glutethimide may cause convulsions and delirium.

Strychnine is found in tonics, purgatives and rat poisons. Tonic convulsions are typical symptoms. These are very violent and cause intense opisthotonos. They occur at intervals of 10 minutes or more and are followed by relaxation of the muscles. During the seizures respiration is interrupted so anoxia is always a problem. Reflex excitability is increased so any stimulus may provoke a seizure. Death results from failure of respiration. Unfortunately the patient is quite conscious so strychnine poisoning is a dreadful ordeal. The best treatment is said to be the intravenous injection of a quick acting barbiturate.

Tranquilizers.—A large percentage of patients treated with full doses of phenothiazine derivatives develop neurological syndromes if treated for more than a short time. Even one dose of moderate size may cause severe symptoms. The Parkinsonian syndrome with tremor, rigidity of the muscles and slowing of movement is, perhaps, the most common complication. Dyskinesias such as torticollis, facial spasms, dysarthria, labored breathing, opisthotonos, tortipelvis and oculogyric crises also occur. In addition, the patient may become very restless and present a picture not unlike chorea. Weakness, fatigue and apathy may develop. Drugs used for Parkinson's disease will usually relieve these symptoms. In an occasional case, such symptoms may be persistent, it is claimed.

Hill describes the findings in an infant of a schizophrenic mother who was treated with trifluoperazine. The child had a shrill cry, tremors, flexion at the wrist and proximal joints of the fingers and irregular respiration. There was gradual recovery. A second infant born after 26 months, had tremors and hypertonia for 6 months. He also made a good recovery.

Rauwolfia derivatives will cause the Parkinsonian syndrome, but not, as a rule, the other syndromes mentioned above. Marsilid, i.e. iproniazid, may cause liver damage, ataxia and myoclonus.

Vermifuges.—*Felix mas* is the standard remedy for tape worm. This drug may cause gastrointestinal symptoms, muscular cramps and convulsions. Respiration may be impaired and the heart action weakened. Death may result. If the patient survives there may be optic atrophy and loss of vision. Treatment is symptomatic. *Santonin,* another antihelmintic, is used for round worms. It may cause yellow vision, diarrhea and convulsions. *Chenopodium* may cause vomiting, deafness and in large doses coma and death. Carbon tetrachloride is used as a vermifuge also. It is mentioned above.

Principles of Treatment

Removal of the Drug from the Body.—If the drug is absorbed from the skin, as in case of the chlorinated hydrocarbon insecticides, the skin should be washed at once with soap and water. If the drug has been ingested, the stomach should be washed out by lavage or emptied by the induction of vomiting. Some drugs, as for example strychnine, may be neutralized in the stomach by tannic acid (tea) or by potassium permanganate. Powdered absorbent charcoal may be added to the water used for washing the stomach. Saline laxatives may be employed to empty the intestines. BAL may be used to promote excretion by the kidneys in poisoning by arsenic and mercury and calcium disodium versenate in treatment of lead poisoning.

Antidotes.—A few specific antidotes are available, such as atrophine for muscarine poisoning or poisoning due to the organic phosphates used as insecticides.

Symptomatic Therapy.—In many cases, only symptomatic therapy is possible. Intravenous barbiturates may be required for convulsions. Oxygen inhalations and artificial respiration may be helpful if respiration is impaired. Intravenous fluids and transfusions may be needed. Measures to combat acidosis are required in some cases such as salicylate poisoning. Antibiotics may be used to prevent pneumonia. Vitamin K or transfusion of blood may be required to stop bleeding in certain cases, for example salicylate poisoning. Dialysis by the artificial kidney may be helpful in removing the poison from the body. Bruton advises exchange transfusion in some instances in infants and young children.

BIBLIOGRAPHY

The British and American Pharmacopoeias, Toxicologies, and Pharmacologies.

Aring, C. D.: The systemic nervous affinity of triorthocresylophosphate. Brain, **65**:34, 1942.

Bain, K.: Accidental poisoning in young children. J. Pediat., **44**:616, 1954.

Barger, G.: Ergot and Ergotism. London, 1931.

Bernstein, S. et al.: Parathion poisoning in children. Jour. Med. Soc. New Jersey, **65**:199, 1968.

Black, R. L. et al.: Cataracts with long term steroids. J.A.M.A., **174**:166, 1960.

Bloomer, H. A. et al.: Penicillin induced encephalopathy in uremic patients. J.A.M.A., **200**:121, 1967.

Braver, D. A. et al.: Posterior subcapsular cataracts in corticosteroid treated children. Jour. Pediat., **69**:735, 1966.

Brown, I. A.: Chronic mercurialism. Arch. Neurol. & Psychiat., **72**:674, 1954.

Brozovsky, M. and Winkler, E. G.: Glue sniffing in children and adolescents. N. Y. St. Jour. Med., **65**:1984, 1965.

Bruton, O. C.: Exchange transfusion for poisoning in children. U. S. Army Forces Med. J., **9**:1128, 1958.

Chamberlain, P. H. et al.: Thallium poisoning. Pediatrics, **22**:1170, 1958.

Chen, K. K. and Rose, C. L.: Nitrite and thiosulfate therapy in cyanide poisoning. J.A.M.A., **149**:113, 1952.

Clark, W. M. et al.: Ferrous sulphate poisoning in infants. Am. J. Dis. Child., **88**:220, 1954.

Cocke, J. G. et al.: Optic neuritis with prolonged use of chloramphenicol. Jour. Pediat., **68**:27, 1966.

Cohen, A. S.: Differential diagnosis of salicylate intoxication and diabetic acidosis. New England J. Med., **254**:457, 1956.

Conn, J. W. et al.: Licorice-induced pseudoaldosteronism. Jour. Amer. Med. Ass., **205**:492, 1968.

Conney, A. H.: Drug metabolism and therapeutics. New England Jour. Med., **280**:653, 1969.

Cummings, L. H.: Hypoglycemia and convulsions in children following the ingestion of alcohol. J. Pediatrics, **58**:23, 1961.

Eadie, M. J. and Ferrier, T. M.: Chloroquine myopathy. Jour. Neurol. Neurosurg. and Psychiat., **29**:331, 1966.

Edwards, R. O.: Poisoning from plant ingestion. Jour. Fla. Med. Ass., **52**:875, 1965.

Ehrlich, R. M.: Neurologic complications in children on phenothiazine tranquilizers. Canad. M. A. J., **81**:241, 1959.

ELLIOTT, W. *et al.:* Hemodialysis for mushroom poisoning. Lancet, ii:630, 1961.

ELLIS, F. G.: Polyneuritis induced by nitrofurantoin (Furadantin) . Lancet, ii:1136, 1962.

FAIRWEATHER, M. J. *et al.:* Thallium poisoning in children. Texas State J. Med., 51:466, 1955.

FOX, M. J. AND JOCHIMSEN, E.: The danger of codeine over-dosage in children. Wisconsin Med. J., 52:487, 1953.

FRIEDMAN, E. A. *et al.:* Hazards of ethylene glycol ingestion. Am. J. Med., 32:891, 1962.

GARRISON, R. F.: Acute poisoning from the use of isopropyl alcohol in tepid sponging. J.A.M.A., 152:317, 1953.

GERSHON, S. AND SHAW, F. H.: Mental effects of insecticides. Lancet, i:1371, 1961.

GLASER, H. H. AND MASSENGALE, O. N.: Effects of glue sniffing in children. J.A.M.A., 181:300, 1962.

GLASSON, J. AND STELLING, F. H.: Poison in machine oil. Southern Med. J., 49:1325, 1956.

GOLDBLOOM, R. AND GOLDBLOOM, A.: Boric acid poisoning. J. Pediat., 43:631, 1953.

GOODMAN, L. AND GILMAN, A.: The Pharmacological Basis of Therapeutics. New York, Macmillan Co., 1941.

GROB, D. *et al.:* Death due to Parathion, an anticholinesterase insecticide. Ann. Int. Med., 31:899, 1949.

HARMAN, J. H.: Muscular wasting and corticosteroid therapy. Lancet, i:887, 1959.

HARTSHORN, E. A.: Physiological stated altering response to drugs. Drug. Intelligence, 3:1, 1969.

HAWKINS, J. E.: The ototoxicity of kanamycin. Ann. Otol. Rhin. & Laryng., 68:698, 1959.

HENDERSON, L. W. AND MERRILL, J. P.: Treatment of barbiturate intoxication. Ann. Int. Med., 64:876, 1966.

HILL, R. W. *et al.:* Extrapyramidal dysfunction in infant of schizophrenic mother. Jour. Pediat., 69:589, 1966.

HÖLSCHER, P. AND NATZSCHKA, J.: Methaemoglobinaemia in young infants due to nitrite in spinach. Germ. med. Moth., 9:325, 1964.

HOLT, L. E. AND HOLZ, P. H.: Value of charcoal antidote. J. Pediat., 63:306, 1963.

HOOD, T. R. AND WRIGHT, E.: Poisoning with the newer pesticide compounds. J. Kansas Med. Soc., 55:384, 1954.

HUANG, N. N. *et al.:* Visual disturbances in cystic fibrosis following chloramphenicol administration. Jour. Pediat., 68:32, 1966.

KENDALL, A. C.: Acute disseminated encephalomyelitis due to phenophthalein. Brit. Med. J., 1902:1461, 1954.

KNOX, D. *et al.:* Iris atrophy after quinine amblyopia. Arch. of Ophthal., 76:359, 1966.

KOSTER, M. AND DAVID, G. K.: Reversible severe hypertension due to licorice ingestion. New England Jour. Med., 278:1381, 1968.

LAWLER, H. J.: Aspirin poisoning in children. Rocky Mountain M. J., 50:326, 1953.

LINTON, A. L. *et al.:* Methods of forced diuresis and its application in barbiturate poisoning. Lancet, 2:377, 1967.

LLOYD, L. A. AND HILTZ, J. W.: Ocular complications of chloroquine therapy. Canad. Med. Ass. Jour., 92:508, 1965.

LOFTUS, L. R.: Peripheral neuropathy from chloroquine. Canad. M. A. J., 89:917, 1963.

LOUW, A. AND SONNE, L. M.: Megimide in the treatment of barbituric acid poisoning. Lancet, 271:961, 1956.

LUBY, E. D. AND DOMINO, E. F.: Glutethimide addiction. J.A.M.A., 181:46, 1962.

LUSE, S. A. AND WOOD, W. G.: The brain in fatal carbon tetrachloride poisoning. Arch. of Neurol., 17:304, 1967.

LYMAN, E. D.: Food poisoning due to nicotinic acid in the meat. Nebraska Med. J., 42:243, 1957.

MACLEAN, K. AND SCHURR, P. H.: Reversible amyotrophy complicating treatment with fluorocortisone. Lancet, i:701, 1959.

McCURDY, D. K. *et al.:* Renal tubular acidosis due to amphotericin B. New Eng. Jour. Med., 278:124, 1968.

McKENNA, A. J.: Hypoplasia of the optic nerves. Read before the Canad. Ophthal. Soc., June 14, 1966.

MELLANBY, E.: The experimental production and prevention of degeneration of the spinal cord. Brain, **54**:291 (lathyrism), 1931.

MEYER, K. F., SOMMER, H. AND SCHOENHOLZ, P.: Mussel poisoning. J. Preventive Med., **2**:365, 1928.

Modern Medicine, May 9, 1966, p. 28. The Pill. A new poison hazard.

MYERS, E. N. *et al.*: Salicylate ototoxicity. New Engl. Jour. Med., **273**:587, 1965.

OGLESBY, R. B. *et al.*: Cataracts with long-term steroid therapy. Arch. Ophth., **66**:519, 1961.

PONSETI, I. V. AND SHEPARD, R. S.: Lesions of the skeleton and other mesodermal tissues in rats fed sweet pea Lathyrus odoratus seeds. J. Bone & Joint Surg., **36**:1031, 1954.

RESSLER, C. *et al.*: The significance of two toxic substances involved in lathyrism. Science, **134**:188, 1961.

ROBERTSON, D. M. *et al.*: Ocular menifestations of digitalis toxicity. Arch. of Ophthal., **76**:640, 1966.

ROBIN, E. D. *et al.*: Salicylate intoxication with special reference to the development of hypo-kalemia. Am. J. Med., **26**:869, 1959.

ROUNDS, V. J.: Aminophylline poisoning. Pediatrics, **14**:528, 1954.

RUBIN, M. B., RECINOS, A., WASHINGTON, J. A. AND KOPPANYI, T.: Ingestion of poisons in children. Clin. Pro. Children's Hospital, Washington, D. C., **5**:57, 1949.

SAMUELS, A. S.: Acute chlorpromazine poisoning. Am. J. Psychiat., **113**:746, 1957.

SEGAR, W. E.: Peritoneal dialysis in the treatment of boric acid poisoning. New England J. Med., **262**:798, 1960.

SEMSCH, R. D.: Acute poisoning in children. Minnesota Med., **37**:862, 1954.

SHAH, S. R. A.: A note on some cases of lathyrism in a Punjab village. Indian Med. Gaz., **74**:385, 1939, Editorial: Lathyrism, p. 421.

SHAMBAUGH, G. E.: Ototoxic effect of dihydrostreptomycin. J.A.M.A., **170**:1657, 1959.

SINGH, A. *et al.*: A profile of endemic fluorosis. Medicine, **42**:229, 1963.

STANAGE, W. F. AND HENSKE, J. A.: Accidental ingestion of poisons by children. J. Pediat., **47**:470, 1955.

STEINBERG, V. L.: Neuropathy in rheumatoid disease. Brit. Med. J., **5186**:1600, 1960.

STEVENS, H. AND FORSTER, F.: Effect of carbon tetrachloride on the nervous system. Arch. Neurol. & Psychiat., **70**:635, 1953.

TRUEMNER, K. M.: Pulmonary emboli due to barium enema. J.A.M.A., **173**:1089, 1960.

WHISNANT, J. P. *et al.*: Chloroquine neuromyopathy. Proc. Staff Meet. Mayo Clin., **38**:501, 1963.

WHITE, B. H. AND DAESCHNER, C. W.: Aminophylline poisoning in children. J. Pediat., **49**:262, 1956.

WILLETT, R. W.: Peripheral neuropathy due to nitrofurantoin (Furadantin). Neurology, **13**:344, 1963.

WILLIAMS, R. S.: Triamcinolone myopathy. Lancet, **i**:688, 1959.

WINTERS, R. W. *et al.*: Disturbances of acid-base equilibrium in salicylate intoxication. Pediatrics, **23**:260, 1959.

WOOD, W. H.: Poisonous plants. J. Pediat., **50**:499, 1957.

FOOD POISONING

Botulism

Definition.—An acute and often fatal intoxication due to the ingestion of food containing the toxin of Clostridium botulinus and characterized by weakness, disturbances of vision, difficulty in swallowing and talking, constipation, subnormal temperature and rapid pulse.

Etiology.—Clostridium botulinus is a Gram-positive, spore bearing, anaerobic rod which is apparently rather widespread in nature and is found frequently in the soil. It is non-pathogenic but produces an exceptionally virulent neurotoxin. Botulism always results from the ingestion of preserved food which has not been completely sterilized and in which the organisms have multiplied with the production of toxin. As a rule, vegetables are to blame but the poison may also develop in canned meat. Commercially canned food is a rare source of botulism at present and almost without exception home canned food is responsible. The usual story is that such food is used as a cold salad without cooking, for boiling even a short time destroys the toxin. The spores are not easily killed but apparently cause no symptoms when taken by mouth. It has been claimed recently that infection of a wound by a special type of this organism, termed type E, may give rise to botulism. In 1963 a small number of cases of botulism developed in this country due to type E organism in smoked fish and canned tuna fish. It has been shown that the toxin is a protein.

Pathological Anatomy.—Various pathologists have described congestion and small hemorrhages in the central nervous system but it is probable that these are due to asphyxia and that there are no significant lesions in the nervous system. The toxin is believed to act upon the motor endplates or the neuromuscular junction. Cowdry has published a valuable study of this problem.

Clinical Features.—The contaminated food is often described as having a cheesy flavor. Since there is some production of gas, the container may be distended or the food full of bubbles. However, in a number of cases the victims do not notice any peculiarity of the food, especially when it is served with acid dressings which disguise the abnormal taste. Usually, several members of a family or a party who have consumed the same food are affected at the same time. A mere taste has caused death.

Symptoms appear, as a rule, between twelve and forty-eight hours after the infected food is consumed, most often about twenty-four hours. In perhaps a third of all cases there are gastrointestinal symptoms at the onset, such as nausea, vomiting and diarrhea, but in the majority of cases, constipation is present from the onset. The beginning of the neurological disorders is marked by the development of disturbances of vision and bulbar palsy simultaneously. Blurring of vision due to loss of accommodation, diplopia, ptosis of the lids and limitation of ocular movements are characteristic. The pupils may be dilated and fail to react to light but as a rule they are merely somewhat sluggish. Inability to swallow, weakness of the voice, difficulty in articulation, weakness of the jaws and face are all constantly found in well developed cases. Food may be regurgitated through the nose or may gain entrance into the larynx causing choking. The mouth is dry and saliva thick and scanty.

Within a very short time the skeletal muscles become involved. The head cannot be lifted from the pillow. The arms are affected more than the legs. Respiration becomes feeble and both the intercostals and the diaphragm are involved.

It has frequently been pointed out that these patients show abnormal fatigue rather than paralysis, so that a patient may be able to perform a movement once but not to repeat it. The intestines cease to function causing complete constipation and there is retention of urine. The pulse is rapid and weak. Profuse sweating is usually observed. As a rule there is no alteration of the tendon reflexes and no disturbance of sensibility or pain. The mental condition is unaltered in most instances but there may be terminal coma. The temperature is normal or subnormal unless the patient has pneumonia. The spinal fluid shows no change.

The course is brief. Death occurs in fatal cases, as a rule, between the fourth and eighth days as a result of paralysis of respiration, circulatory failure or pneumonia. Convalescence may be slow but if the patient survives, complete recovery always ensues.

Diagnosis.—The important elements in the diagnosis are the history of eating preserved food, the gastrointestinal symptoms, the development of disturbances of vision and bulbar palsy as described between 12 and 48 hours afterward followed shortly by weakness of all the skeletal muscles. The coincident illness of several persons who have eaten together shortly before is at least evidence of food poisoning. In the early stages of the disease, the toxin may be demonstrated by the injection of blood serum into a mouse. The toxin or bacilli may be found in the remains of the food. Acute exacerbations of myasthenia gravis simulate botulism most exactly. In this disease, the pupils always react well to light, prostigmin usually gives prompt relief and one would expect a history of previous symptoms.

Prognosis.—The mortality has varied in various outbreaks depending upon the amount of the toxin consumed but averages 50 per cent. If the patient can be kept alive improvement may be expected within one or two weeks.

Treatment.—This condition might be prevented by cooking all home preserved foods before eating. The antitoxin is no doubt of value but is rarely given in time to be very helpful. It is ineffective if given after symptoms have developed. Since there are several toxins polyvalent serum is required. Large doses such as 20,000 units are recommended by intramuscular or intravenous injection. The stomach should be washed out and every effort should be made by enemas and saline purges to empty the entire intestinal tract. The patient should be placed at complete rest as far as possible. Nasal tube feeding may be required. If respiration grows weak, oxygen may be administered. If a Drinker respirator is available, it may be used to great advantage. Antibiotics may be required to prevent pneumonia and

urinary tract infections. A toxoid is being developed which immunizes against all types of the organism.

BIBLIOGRAPHY

CAPRIO, F. S.: An outbreak of botulism in New Jersey. J.A.M.A., **106**:687, 1936.

COWDRY, E. V. AND NICHOLSON, F. M.: An histological study of the central nervous system in reference to botulinus poisoning. J. Exp. Med., **39**:827, 1924.

DAVIS, J. B. *et al.*: Clostridium botulinum in fatal wound infection. J.A.M.A., **146**:641, 1951.

DICKSON, E. C.: Botulism. Oxford Medicine, **5**:231, 1932.

DICKSON, E. C. AND SHEVKY, E.: Studies on the manner in which the toxin of Clostridium botulinum acts upon the body. The effect upon the autonomic nervous system. J. Exp. Med., **37**:711, 1923.

————: The effect upon the voluntary nervous system. J. Exp. Med., **38**:327, 1923.

EDMUNDS, C. W. AND LONG, P. H.: Contributions to pathology and physiology of botulism. J.A.M.A., **31**:542, 1923.

GUYTON, A. C. AND MCDONALD, M. A.: Physiology of botulinus toxin. Arch. Neurol. & Psychiat., **57**:578, 1947.

KOENIG, M. G. *et al.*: Type B botulism. Amer. Jour. Med., **42**:208, 1967.

THOMAS, C. G., KELEHER, M. AND MCKEE, A.: Botulinism; a complication of Clostridium botulinum wound infection. Arch. Path., **51**:623, 1951.

TYLER, H. R.: Antitoxin use in botulism. Arch. Neurol., **9**:652, 1963.

WALSH, F. B.: *Loc. cit.*

WHITTAKER, R. L. *et al.*: Treatment of type E botulism. Ann. Int. Med., **64**:448, 1964.

METABOLIC AND ENDOCRINE DISORDERS INVOLVING THE NERVOUS SYSTEM

Injury to the Central Nervous System Due to Anoxia and Oxygen Poisoning

Etiology.—Four chief types are distinguished: (1) Anoxia characterized by low oxygen tension in the arterial blood. A number of conditions may produce this, such as asphyxia at birth, strangulation, suffocation, drowning, nitrous oxide and other anesthetics, high altitude, obstruction of the respiratory passages, paralysis of respiration and various diseases of the lungs. (2) Anemic anoxia, in which inadequate amounts of hemoglobin are available to transport oxygen to the nervous system. Here we may place severe anemias, exsanguination, and carbon monoxide poisoning. (3) Stagnant anoxia which is due to defective circulation of the blood. In this category fall disorders of cardiac action and vascular obstructions of various types. (4) Histotoxic anoxia, in which the tissue cells are unable to use oxygen though an adequate supply is available. Potassium cyanide poisoning is given as an example and perhaps, hypoglycemia should be placed here.

The article by Hoff, Grenell and Fulton presents an instructive discussion of these conditions. Since the above list is by no means exhaustive, it is evident that many types of anoxia may occur. Not many are known to cause lasting damage to the nervous system. Asphyxia at birth is the most important problem though its rank among the causes of infantile cerebral

palsies and mental defects is still uncertain. The problem of anoxia at birth is discussed under cerebral birth injuries q.v. Poisoning by illuminating gas and exhaust gas, which is usually termed carbon monoxide poisoning, stands next in frequency, and cerebral damage under general anesthesia would seem to stand third. Haggard has made it clear that the effects of illuminating gas are not due entirely to carbon monoxide. He has shown that neuroblasts will grow in tissue cultures in the presence of 70 per cent carbon monoxide but the least trace of illuminating gas kills the cells at once.

Pure oxygen is used under increased pressure in the treatment of patients suffering from carbon monoxide poisoning, congenital heart disease and gas gangrene. It should be mentioned that excessive exposure to such high oxygen concentrations may result in hemorrhagic lesions in the lungs and convulsions.

Pathological Anatomy.—Courville's splendid monograph on the effects of anoxia on the nervous system makes it clear that a large variety of lesions may occur. The effects depend upon the severity of the anoxia, its duration and the time the patient survives. It is possible that all types of anoxia do not always cause the same damage. Courville discusses many types of anoxia but deals chiefly with that due to nitrous oxide anesthesia. If the patient dies within a few hours, one finds extreme congestion of the veins, edema and perivascular hemorrhages. It is suggested that there may also be constriction of the arterioles but the evidence for this is not complete. This process does not seem to be a very destructive one, but it may result in small perivascular areas of necrosis.

In patients who live several days, lesions are found which are more directly due to anoxia. The cerebral cortex is severely affected. There may be scattered loss of nerve cells, disseminated foci of softening and laminar softening usually in the deeper layers of the cortex. In some instances there may be subtotal disintegration of the cortex. This process is bilateral and to some extent symmetrical. It may be selective to some extent. In some instances the frontal lobes show the greatest damage but there is a tendency for the occipital lobes to be selected in a large percentage of cases. Softenings in the lenticular nuclei, especially in the globus pallidus are common and the thalamus may be involved. In the cerebellum the Purkinje cells are almost constantly damaged and the dentate nuclei may show lesions. Diffuse demyelination of the cerebral white matter is found in some instances. The brain stem and the spinal cord seem to escape serious damage. The retinae and the optic nerves are also spared.

After a time, possibly several weeks, a third process develops. Lesions appear which seem to be due to vascular occlusion. Courville seems to believe that these lesions may be very large. There is proliferation of the vascular

endothelium which may cause occlusion of the vessels and possibly softenings. Softenings in the subcortical white matter seem to be the most characteristic features of this delayed process. It should be said that these observations were made on the brains of adults and in most instances nitrous oxide anesthesia was responsible.

The experimental work of Morrison and others in which low oxygen tensions were employed led to the production of lesions so nearly identical with those given above that they need not be described. The same statement may be made as regards the work of Titrud and Haymaker, who studied the lesions produced by high altitude anoxia in aviators.

Courville and Marsh have recently described lesions in children's brains which they regard as residua of injuries suffered as a result of asphyxia at birth. These are discussed in the article on cerebral birth injuries.

Many studies have been made of the lesions in the nervous system found in cases of carbon monoxide poisoning. Necrosis of the anterior part of the lenticular nuclei seems to be more constant than in other types of anoxia, but in many instances there are also areas of necrosis in the cerebral cortex and cerebral white matter so that the picture is at least very similar to that seen in anoxia due to nitrous oxide. There is no obvious tendency for the occipital cortex to be affected which no doubt explains the fact that cortical blindness is rare. However, calcification of the blood vessels is stressed and it is rarely mentioned in other types of anoxia. The demyelination of the peripheral nerves so often described in carbon monoxide poisoning is not mentioned in cases of nitrous oxide poisoning.

Hallervorden found destructive lesions in the lenticular nuclei of fetuses whose mothers were exposed to carbon monoxide.

A number of studies have been made on the brains of patients dying after prolonged coma resulting from hypoglycemia. Extensive lesions are found in the cerebral cortex and also damage to the lenticular nuclei and the thalamus. The process is not unlike that attributed to anoxia.

Clinical Features.—It is estimated that cardiac arrest may cause lasting damage to the nervous system if it persists for three minutes or more. Interruption of respiration of only a few minutes' duration may also cause cerebral damage.

Anoxia may be produced in infancy and childhood in a number of ways. It may occur *in utero* as a result of separation of the placenta and at birth from various causes. These problems are discussed in connection with Cerebral Birth Injuries, q.v.

Asphyxia results from smoke inhalation, laryngospasm, obstruction of the bronchi by secretions, pneumonia, being shut in iceboxes, burying in caves, covering of the face by plastic bags, drowning, and in helpless babies, when the nose and mouth are covered by the pillow.

Illuminating gas, automobile exhaust gas, and fumes from coal furnaces may cause loss of consciousness and persisting damage to the nervous system. Anderson states that cardiac damage may occur from exposure to carbon monoxide inhalation. Convulsive seizures are thought to cause injury to the brain as a result of anoxia but other factors cannot be excluded. I have seen, on several occasions, breath-holding spells so severe that the child seemed to be dead and was resuscitated with difficulty, but no evidences of cerebral damage was apparent.

Transient cortical blindness may occur, in rare instances, as a result of extremely severe attacks of asthma.

Hypoxia due to paralysis of the muscles of respiration should be mentioned. This may occur in paralytic poliomyelitis, polyneuritis, myasthenia gravis and in the terminal state of muscular dystrophy.

Levy *et al.* describe the case of a boy of 3 years who had hypoxia and retention of carbon dioxide with pulmonary hypertension and cor pulmonale. Enlargement of the adenoids was thought to be responsible. Removal of the adenoids is said to have given relief of his symptoms.

Cardiac arrest is not a very uncommon cause of serious hypoxia. This may occur during any operation, but is most apt to occur during heart surgery. Björk and Hulquist discuss the death of eight children who had been subjected to deep hypothermia by extracorporeal cooling during open heart surgery. These deaths were all due to cerebral damage. In some cases, the lesions were chiefly in the cerebral cortex, the hippocampus, the cerebellum and thalamus. In others, the damage was chiefly in the globus pallidus. The former type was attributed to deficient blood flow and the latter to anoxia. These authors suggest that intravascular agglutination of blood cells may play an important role. Air embolism may occur during such operations.

Heart disease, especially congenital heart disease, may result in cerebral damage when the cyanosis is very severe as Mosberg has shown.

Anesthesia, especially nitrous oxide anesthesia, may have destructive effects on the nervous system even when the operation is brief and no failure of respiration or arrest of heart action is noted, as Courville has shown. Other types of anesthesia seem to cause such effects less frequently.

Drowning creates other problems in addition to hypoxia. Freshwater drowning causes dilution of the plasma, decrease of osmolarity, decrease of electrolytes, swelling of the red cells with hemolysis and decrease of blood viscosity. The arterial carbon dioxide pressure falls and acidosis occurs. Plasma potassium concentration decreases at first and then increases as the red cells break down.

Drowning in sea water, which is hypertonic to body fluids, causes reduction of the plasma volume. The arterial carbon dioxide pressure rises. Acidosis occurs. Plasma proteins, electrolytes, hemoglobin and osmolarity increase. The red cell size decreases. The blood becomes more viscous.

All forms of anoxia do not cause identical symptoms, but certain features are common to all types. The patient is usually in coma for a time. There may be generalized rigidity and convulsions. The pupils are dilated and Babinski signs are usually present. Respiration may fail. Courville states that if coma lasts twenty-four hours, the prognosis is grave.

About one third of all patients die without regaining consciousness. If the patient survives, evidences of damage to the nervous system may be present when consciousness is regained. Additional symptoms may develop after a delay of a few days or a week or two. Shillito describes a case in which the late symptoms appeared after an exceptionally long delay of nineteen days. In some instances, the patient seems to have no ill effects until the delayed symptoms appear. It is possible that these late symptoms are due to white matter damage.

In patients who survive, improvement may continue for months. Among the residuals, disturbances of vision are common. In our experience, cortical blindness with normal optic discs and active pupillary reflexes has occurred repeatedly as a result of nitrous oxide anesthesia. We have not observed damage to the optic nerves or retinae. Lamb states that if cardiac arrest lasts more than twenty-three minutes when the pharyngeal temperature is 16°C., the retinae will show anoxic damage. Mental defects, either severe or mild, are not unusual. There may be aphasia. Spasticity, weakness, tremor and ataxia sometimes occur. Polyneuritis is not rare in poisoning due to illuminating gas and automobile exhaust gas, but is not described in other types of anoxia.

Diagnosis.—The attending circumstances and the clinical symptoms usually make the diagnosis clear.

Prognosis.—It seems that most patients either die or make a complete recovery. Shillito states that in a follow up of 21,000 cases of carbon monoxide asphyxia, one third of the patients died promptly, only forty-three showed signs of damage to the brain on regaining consciousness and all recovered after weeks or months except for nine. Among the nine patients who suffered permanent damage to the nervous system in Shillito's study, five had a Parkinsonian syndrome.

Treatment.—It is of the greatest importance to see that the patient gets an abundant supply of oxygen at the earliest possible moment. It has been recommended recently that oxygen be administered under two atmospheres of pressure. Penicillin may be required to prevent pneumonia in patients who remain stuporous for days.

CASE HISTORY (A-62193).—*Severe asphyxia at the age of three months with rigidity and convulsions. Subsequently the child displayed spastic diplegia, mental defect, microcephaly and apparent blindness.*

S. O. seemed to be a normal child for the first three months of life. At the age of three months, she was found lying on her face in bed with her

head so covered that she could get no air. She was deeply cyanotic and unconscious. Artificial respiration was administered and after prolonged efforts the child was induced to breathe. She was then rigid and a number of convulsions occurred in the next few days. After that episode, the child made no progress and appeared to be grossly retarded.

On examination at the age of eight months the child's head was 16 inches in occipitofrontal circumference. The anterior fontanel was almost entirely closed. It was impossible for the child to sit up or even hold up the head firmly. There was generalized muscular rigidity, slightly greater on the left than the right. The tendon reflexes were brisk. No clonus elicited. The grasp reflexes were strong on both sides. Tonic neck reflexes were evident but not fully developed. There was no evidence of vision. and the child did not fix or follow a light. The pupils reacted fairly well, however, and the optic discs showed only a slight pallor. As a rule, the eyes were deviated to the right and downward.

Air encephalogram revealed dilatation of the ventricular system and a moderate accumulation of air over the cerebral cortex. The atrophy was slightly greater on the right side than the left.

CASE HISTORY (Ped. 90607).—*Child of eight years grew cyanotic during ether anesthesia. Later, unconsciousness, rigidity and convulsions. Severe mental changes resulted.*

S. K. was a healthy child and an excellent student. In March 1934, when he was eight years old, he developed appendicitis. Operation was performed under ether anesthesia. Shortly after the anesthetic was started, he grew cyanotic and stopped breathing. Artificial respiration was required. Later when he had been returned to bed, he was rigid and unconscious. Convulsions occurred at intervals for some hours. The next day he was conscious but could not speak. He did not recognize his parents for two weeks.

After this illness, he was never able to advance at school. He was unable to recall what he had studied and arithmetic was impossible for him. There was no motor disturbances or reduction of vision. His behavior was unchanged. There were no convulsions after the day of the operation.

CASE HISTORY.—*Circumcision performed on a healthy child of 22 months under nitrous oxide anesthesia. Cardiac arrest. Gross cerebral damage.*

S. W. was examined at the age of 3 years. His parents stated that his birth and early development were normal in every way. He sat up at 6 months and walked and talked at the age of one year. He had no scizures and no illnesses. He was regarded as a healthy vigorous child.

When he was 22 months old circumcision was performed under nitrous oxide anesthesia. The heart beat stopped. The chest was opened and cardiac massage was performed. It was estimated that the heart began to beat between 4 and 6 minutes after it had stopped. He did not regain consciousness and there were repeated convulsions in the next few days. He

was kept in the hospital for a month. During this period he showed little evidence of consciousness and was very rigid.

When the child was brought home he was inert and unresponsive. There was no evidence of vision. Rigidity was intense. When food was placed in his mouth he would swallow but he did not chew. There were frequent seizures. After some months there was limited improvement. He seemed to hear and apparently developed dim vision. A few spontaneous movements were seen. Dilantin reduced the seizures.

Examination at the age of 3 years revealed that the head was rather small. There was no ptosis or squint and the pupils reacted to light. The child would at times fix a light or follow a light. The optic discs appeared to be normal. The face was symmetrical. The head could not be held up and the child could not sit. Respiration was not altered. There was generalized rigidity. The arms were held in flexion at the elbow and the legs were flexed at the hip and knee. Little spontaneous movement was seen. Most movements were mass movements such as one sees in infancy when all four extremities are moved at once. The grasp reflexes were strong. No tonic neck reflexes were elicited. The Moro reflex was not demonstrable. The tendon reflexes were brisk and the great toes came up on plantar stimulation.

CASE HISTORY.—*Electric shock at thirteen years with loss of heart beat and respiration. Prolonged unconsciousness. Survival with loss of cortical vision and extrapyramidal motor syndrome.*

J. B. H. was a healthy boy of thirteen years, in September 1961. While working on a metal boat with an electric drill he received a shock which caused cessation of respiration and heart beat. External cardiac massage and artificial respiration were applied promptly, and then the chest was opened and the heart massaged directly. Ventricular fibrillation occurred but was stopped by the electric defibrillator. Spontaneous heart beat and respiration then developed. There were episodes of hyperthermia which were treated by ice packs.

The boy remained unconscious for several months. The level of consciousness slowly improved. Voluntary movements returned. He was completely blind for many months.

On May 22, 1964, examination revealed that the patient could understand most of what was said to him. He would try to do what was requested of him. His speech was grossly defective but his answers were responsive to questions and were comprehensible. Vision was grossly reduced and was estimated at 1/100. The fields of vision could not be outlined. The pupils were equal and reacted to light. The optic fundi showed no abnormalities. There was no squint, nystagmus, ptosis or limitation of ocular movement. There was some reduction of facial movements, when he smiled, the movements of the face were of large amplitude.

The patient could not stand or walk. There was generalized muscular rigidity with weakness and slowing of movement. No tremor or athetosis

but there were athetoid postures which were aggravated by muscular activity. The tendon reflexes were not increased and there was no Babinski sign or ankle clonus. No loss of sensibility could be demonstrated.

CASE HISTORY (No. 1146113).—*Post-operative failure of respiration in a boy of 8 years with cyanosis and convulsions. Prompt recovery. On 4th day delayed symptoms appeared with pyramidal disorders, aphasia, convulsions and neurogenic fever.*

R. T. S., a previously healthy boy of 8 years was seen by the courtesy of Dr. William T. McLean, Jr. He was operated upon on February 8, 1965 for acute appendicitis. The appendix was not ruptured and no untoward reaction was noted during the operation. Cyclopropane anesthesia was used.

He was taken to the recovery room at 10:40 a.m. At 11:00 he was found to be cyanotic and apneic. Respiration was established promptly, but at 12 a.m. he had a series of convulsions lasting 20 minutes. When he regained consciousness, he seemed to be blind for a short time.

After this he was apparently quite well until February 12. On that day, the 4th day after the operation, he was out of contact for 30 minutes. Then it was found his speech was impaired and there was weakness of the right arm and leg.

On February 14, he entered Johns Hopkins Hospital. He could understand what was said to him and would do as requested, but was unable to talk. He indicated Yes and No by lifting his right arm or the left arm respectively. The tendon reflexes were brisk and greater on the right than the left. The right plantar reflex was extensor and the left was equivocal. The right arm and leg were clumsy and weak. He could not protrude the tongue.

Convulsive seizures were frequent. The legs would be rigidly extended and the arms would be extended at the elbows with pronation and flexion at the wrists. Such episodes lasted 10 to 20 seconds. It was apparent that consciousness was not lost during these seizures. Episodes of fever developed. The temperature would reach 40 degrees C. Since no evidence of infection could be found, neurogenic fever was suspected. The extremities then developed constant rigidity holding them in the position described above.

The electroencephalogram revealed diffuse slow waves. Studies of the blood and spinal fluid were negative. A number of drugs were given in the hope of controlling the seizures but none were effective.

BIBLIOGRAPHY

ANDERSON, R. F. *et al.:* Myocardial toxicity from carbon monoxide poisoning. Ann. Int. Med., **67**:1172, 1967.

AUSTIN, W. H. AND RAND, P. W.: Drowning. Jour. Maine Med. Ass., **58**:58, 1967.

BJÖRK, V. O. AND HULQUIST, G.: Brain damage after hypothermia for open heart surgery. Thorax, **15**:284, 1960.

HALLERVORDEN, J.: Uber eine Kohlenoxydvergiftung im Fetalleben mit Entwicklungsstörung der Hirnrinde. Allg. Zeitschr. Psychiat., **124**:289, 1949.

LAMB, A.: Ocular changes during cardiac arrest. Brit. J. Ophth., 45:490, 1961.

LAWSON, D. D. *et al.:* Treatment of carbon monoxide poisoning. Lancet, i:800, 1961.

MOSSBERG, J. L.: Anoxia of the central nervous system in congenital heart disease. Am. J. Dis. Child., 78:28, 1949.

PLUMB, F. *et al.:* Neurologic deterioration after anoxia. Arch. Int. Med., 110:18, 1962.

POLLARD, H. S. *et al.:* Gas embolism in extracorporal cooling. J. Thorac. & Thorac. & Cardiovasc. Surg., 42:772, 1961.

REDDING, J. *et al.:* Resuscitation in drowning. J.A.M.A., Dec. 23, 1961.

TOMASHEFSKI, J. F. AND BILLINGS, C. E.: Therapy for carbon monoxide poisoning. Ohio State Med. J., 57:149, 1961.

Anoxic Type

See references under Cerebral Birth Injuries.

BURCHELL, H. B.: Reports of accidents from anoxia in aircraft. Air Surgeon's Bull., 1:20, 1944.

BINGEL, A. AND HAMPEL, E.: Spättod nach Erhängen. Ztschr. f. d. ges. Neurol. u. Psychiat. Bd. 1949, s. 640, 1934.

COURVILLE, C. B.: Asphyxia following nitrous oxide anesthesia. Medicine, 15:129, 1936.

———: Contribution to the Study of Cerebral Anoxia. Los Angeles, San Lucas Press, 1953.

———: Effects of drowning on brain observed after survival for six days. Bull. Los Angeles Neurol. Soc., 20:189, 1955.

COURVILLE, C. B. AND MARSH, C.: Neonatal asphyxia: Its residuals and production. Bull. Los Angeles Neurol. Soc., 9:121, 1944.

COURVILLE, C. AND NIELSEN, J. M.: Cerebral anoxia and convulsive disorders. Bull. Los Angeles Neurol. Soc., 18:59, 1953.

GEBAUER, P. W. AND COLEMAN, F. P.: Postanesthetic encephalopathy following cyclopropane. Ann. Surg., 107:481, 1938.

HADFIELD, C. F.: Discussion of late ether convulsions. Proc. Roy. Soc. Med. London, 21:1928.

HELWIG, F. C.: Histopathologic studies of the brain in delayed death following strangulation. South. M. J., 30:531, 1937.

HOFF, E. C., GRENFLL, R. G. AND FULTON, J. F.: Histopathology of the nervous system after exposure to high altitudes, hypoglycemia and other conditions associated with central anoxia. Medicine, 24:161, 1945.

LORHAN, P. H.: Convulsions during general anesthesia (ether). Arch. & Surg., 44:268, 1942.

MARESCH, R.: Ueber einen Fall von Kohlenoxydschädig des Kindes in der Gebärmutter. Wien. Med. Wchnsr., 1929.

MORRISON, L. R.: Histopathologic effect of anoxia on the central nervous system. Arch. Neurol. & Psychiat., 55:1, 1946.

STEEGMAN, A. T.: Encephalopathy following anesthesia. Arch. Neurol. & Psychiat., 41:955, 1939.

THORNER, M. W. AND LEWY, F. H.: The effects of repeated anoxia on the brain. J.A.M.A., 115:1595, 1940.

TITRUD, L. A. AND HAYMAKER, W.: Cerebral anoxia from high altitude asphyxia. Arch. Neurol. & Psychiat., 57:397, 1947.

UCKO, L. E.: A comparative study of asphyxiated and non-asphyxiated boys. Develop. Med. Child. Neurol., 7:643, 1965.

WALSH, F. B.: *Loc. cit.*

WEBER, F. P.: Complete mindlessness and cerebral diplegia after status convulsivus associated with Aether anesthesia. Brit. J. Child. Dis., 28:14, 1931.

Stagnant Type

GILDEA, E. F. AND COBB, S.: Effects of anemia on the cerebral cortex of the cat. Arch. Neurol. & Psychiat., 23:876, 1930.

NEUBUERGER, K. T.: Lesions of the human brain following circulatory arrest. J. Neuropath. & Exp. Neurol., 13:144, 1954.

Weinberger, L. M., Gibbon, M. H. and Gibbon, J. T.: Temporary arrest of the circulation of the central nervous system. Arch. Neurol. & Psychiat., **43**:615, 1940.

Anemic Type

Haggard, H. W.: Studies in carbon monoxide asphyxia. Growth of neuroblasts in the presence of carbon monoxide. Am. J. Physiol., **60**:244, 1922.

Levy, A. M. *et al.:* Hypertrophied adenoids causing pulmonary hypertension and severe congestive heart failure. New Eng. Jour. Med., **277**:506, 1967.

Sayers, R. R. and Davenport, S. J.: Review of carbon monoxide poisoning. Public Health Bull. **195**. United States Treasury Department, Public Health Service 1930.

Shillito, F. H., Drinker, C. K. and Shaughnessy, T. J.: Carbon monoxide poisoning. The problem of nervous and mental sequelae. J.A.M.A., **106**:669, 1936.

Wilson, G.: An unusual cortical change in carbon monoxide poisoning. Arch. Neurol. & Psychiat., **13**:191, 1925.

Wilson, G. and Winkelmann, N. W.: Multiple neuritis following carbon monoxide poisoning. J.A.M.A., **82**:1407, 1924.

Histotoxic Type

Ferraro, A.: Experimental toxic encephalomyelopathy: Diffuse sclerosis following subcutaneous injection of potassium cyanide. Psychiat. Quart., **7**:267, 1933.

Lawrence, R. D. Meyer, A. and Nevin, S.: The pathological changes in the brain in fatal hypoglycemia. Quart. J. Med., **11**:181, 1942.

NEUROLOGICAL COMPLICATIONS OF CHRONIC PULMONARY INSUFFICIENCY

Chronic pulmonary insufficiency may cause dyspnea, cyanosis, polycythemia and congestive heart failure. The oxygen content of the blood is reduced and the carbon dioxide content is increased. This condition may result from diseases of the lungs including emphysema and pulmonary fibrosis, weakness of the muscles of respiration due to poliomyelitis and other motor disorders, severe kyphoscoliosis and even extreme obesity. In the last condition, respiration is limited by the great excess of fat. It has been termed the Pickwickian syndrome for a character in Pickwick Papers displayed the same symptoms.

My purpose in mentioning this condition is to call attention to the fact that symptoms referable to the nervous system may be prominent.

Headache is often present and is sometimes severe. It is apt to be most troublesome at night.

Papilledema may develop. It may be evidenced only by venous congestion or may be severe with hemorrhages and exudates.

Disturbances of consciousness are common. Drowsiness is a standard symptom and in some cases progresses into stupor and even coma. The administration of oxygen aggravates the mental changes which are attributed to carbon dioxide intoxication.

Tremor of the fingers and larger muscular twitchings are described. The twitchings are induced by a firm muscular contraction. Cerebral vascular lesions may occur as a result of congestion and polycythemia.

I have seen one boy of 16 years, whose weight was 400 pounds, who showed cyanosis, drowsiness and bilateral papilledema. No definite abormalities were found in the brain at post-mortem examination.

The youngest patient we have seen with this condition (Ped. 1014435) was four years old. She was of small stature, but enormously obese, weighing 110 lbs.

Meyer *et al.* examined the brain of a patient who died of this condition. They found that the cerebral vessels were all dilated and congested but apparently there was no edema. They attributed the increase intracranial pressure to dilatation of the cerebral vessels.

Treatment.—Hyperventilation and bronchodilators are helpful. Artificial respiration may be required. Diuretics, digitalis and if necessary, bleeding, are advised. When obesity is responsible, reduction of weight gives relief.

BIBLIOGRAPHY

AUSTEN, F. K., CARMICHAEL, M. W. AND ADAMS, R. D.: Neurologic manifestations of chronic pulmonary insufficiency. New England J. Med., 257:579, 1957.

AUCHINCLOSS, J. H., JR., COOK, E. AND RENZETTI, A. D.: Clinical and physiological aspects of a case of obesity, polycythemia, and alveolar hypoventilation. J. Clin. Invest., 34:1537, 1955.

BURWELL, C. S., ROBIN, E. D., WHALEY, R. D. AND BICKELMANN, A. G.: Extreme obesity associated with alveolar hypoventilation—a Pickwickian syndrome. Am. J. Med., 21:811, 1956.

CARROLL, D.: A peculiar type of cardiopulmonary failure associated with obesity. Am. J. Med., 21:819, 1956.

CAYLER, G. G. et al.: Cardiorespiratory syndrome of obesity (Pickwickian syndrome) in children. Pediatrics, 27:237, 1961.

CONN, H. O.: Pulmonary emphysema simulating brain tumor. Am. J. Med., 22:524, 1957.

FADELL, E. J.: et al.: Fatty infiltration of respiratory muscles in the Pickwickian syndrome. New England Jour. Med., 266:861, 1962.

FINKELSTEIN, J. W. AND AVERY, M. E.: Pickwickian syndrome in children. Am. J. Dis. Child., 106:251, 1963.

MEYER, J. S. et al.: Cardiorespiratory syndrome of extreme obesity with papilledema. Neurology, 11:950, 1961.

O'REILLY, R. J.: The clinical recognition of carbon dioxide intoxication. Dis. Chest, 37:185, 1960.

TERZIAN, H.: Pickwick syndrome and narcolepsy. Rev. Neurol., 115:184, 1966.

WEIL, M. H. AND PRASAD, A. S.: Polycythemia of obesity: further studies of its mechanism and a report of two additional cases. Ann. Int. Med., 46:60, 1957.

NEUROLOGICAL CONDITIONS ASSOCIATED WITH DISORDERS OF THE LIVER

Introduction.—It has long been known that damage to the liver may be associated with symptoms referable to the nervous system. Acute and extensive necrosis of the liver is termed *acute yellow atrophy.* This condition may be caused by virus hepatitis and other infections and by poisons such as phosphorus, chloroform, bismuth, mesantoin and thiantoin. Excitement, delirium, hallucination, convulsions and choreiform movements are seen. Rigidity may develop. A typical posture is described in which the legs are

crossed and drawn up on the abdomen. The course is a rapid one ending in coma and death in a few days. Jaundice may not be obvious. The electro-encephalogram usually shows slow waves when the patient is in coma but it is said that these changes are not specific or constant.

In *chronic liver disease,* such as cirrhosis, the symptoms are less dramatic. There is quiet confusion with lethargy and sometimes convulsions passing into coma. The neurological signs include rigidity, a flapping tremor when the arms are outstretched, grimacing, increase of tendon reflexes and Babinski signs. The rigidity is of special character and is not identical with that of pyramidal tract disease or of the Parkinsonian syndrome. There may be lid lag and lid retraction without evidence of thyroid disease. In some cases, the patient may go in and out of coma several times. Jaundice is almost always present but may not be obvious. Bleeding from esophageal varices is common and ascites may occur. There is a characteristic odor said to resemble that of a skunk. The electroencephalogram shows bilateral, synchronous, high voltage waves of $1\frac{1}{2}$ to 3 per second while the patient is in coma.

The standard tests of liver function are not always helpful. It is claimed that the injection of radioactive rose bengal permits a more accurate estimate of liver function than other tests, and has much value in differential diagnosis. In contrast to Wilson's disease, the common diseases of the liver are not characterized by any disturbance of copper metabolism. Recently it has been claimed that the ammonia content of the blood is increased and it is suggested that liver coma is due to ammonia intoxication. Roberts *et al.* point out that reduction of plasma sodium and chloride may occur especially when ascites is present. Paracentesis may aggravate this condition.

Anatomical changes in the brain in cases of liver coma are not striking. Adams and Foley find a constant increase in the number of protoplasmic astrocytes. These cells are larger than normal and have a very large pale nucleus. They were described by Alzheimer many years ago. There are minimal changes in the neurons and nerve fibers.

Victor *et al.* state that repeated episodes of liver coma or episodes of liver encephalopathy without coma may cause irreversible symptoms including dementia, dysarthria, cerebellar ataxia, and choreoathetosis as well as rigidity and tremor. Lesions are found in the cerebral cortex, white matter, basal ganglia and cerebellar cortex which are similar to those of Wilson's disease.

Brown who has published a very complete description of the neurological conditions which occur in association with disease of the liver, points out that recurrent episodes may occur without coma in which pyramidal and extrapyramidal symptoms are seen. Recovery is apparently spontaneous.

Treatment is not satisfactory. McCann recommends the use of a per-

fusion apparatus to remove the ammonia from the blood. A plastic tube with a column of sodium-exchange resin within nylon mesh bolting is employed. Heparin is given and perfusion is begun by connecting the apparatus to a suitable artery and adjacent vein. About 70 per cent of the ammonia in a blood specimen is removed after a single passage through the resin. The antibiotics destroy the urea splitting bacteria in the bowel and reduce the absorption of ammonia. A low protein diet is advised.

Trey *et al.* find that exchange blood transfusion is a valuable form of treatment.

Thompson and Holmes state that immunizing injections of jack bean urease drastically reduces urea hydrolysis and the formation of ammonia and prevents episodes of hepatic coma.

Baltzan *et al.* discuss the effects of obstruction of the portal vein with porto-caval shunt. They state that the symptoms include recurrent bouts of coma, and a chronic progressive process with dysarthria, pyramidal tract signs, cerebellar ataxia and mental deterioration. Spongy degeneration of the cerebral cortex and superior cerebellar cortex are found at post-mortem examination. Changes in the liver are minimal. No evidence of abnormal copper metabolism is found. They suggest that this condition is due to toxic substances in the portal blood which is not detoxified by the liver since the liver is bypassed.

A well known and specific disease of the liver associated with damage to the brain is *hepatolenticular degeneration* or Wilson's disease. This is now known to be the expression of an inherited defect in copper metabolism. It is described below.

Kernicterus, a condition in which the lenticular nuclei are damaged and stained yellow, is found in cases of icterus gravis neonatorum due to Rh incompatibilities and also in other types of infantile jaundice due to infection and obstruction of the bile ducts. It occurs also in the *congenital, familial, non-hemolytic jaundice* described by Crigler.

Virus hepatitis should be mentioned. It is stated that 2 to 18 days before the appearance of jaundice neurological symptoms including encephalitis, meningitis, myelitis and polyneuritis may occur. Damage to the liver may cause other symptoms.

Brown has published a very complete analysis of all the available data regarding the cause of damage to the nervous system in disease of the liver. He points out that our knowledge is still very incomplete.

BIBLIOGRAPHY

ADAMS, R. D. AND FOLEY, J. M.: The neurological disorder associated with liver disease. Metabolic and toxic diseases of the nervous system. Res. Nerv. & Ment. Dis., **32**:198, 1953.
BALTZAN, M. A., OLESZEWSKI, J. AND ZERVAS, N.: Chronic porto-hepatic encephalopathy. J. Neuropath. & Exp. Neurol., **16**:410, 1957.

BATSON, B. E.: Neonatal hyperbilirubinemia. Clin. Obst. & Gynec., 5:85, 1962.

BERNSTEIN, J. AND BROWN, A. K.: Jaundice with sepsis in infancy. Pediatrics, 6:873, 1962.

CRANDALL, L. A. AND WEIL, A.: The pathology of central nervous system in diseases of the liver. Experiments with animals and with human material. Arch. Neurol. & Psychiat., 29:1066, 1933.

EISMAN, B. *et al.*: Studies in ammonia metabolism. Am. J. Med., 20:890, 1956.

ERGAS, M. AND WALLIS, K.: Kernicterus due to neonatal hepatitis. Ann. Paediat., 200:161, 1963.

FRIEDLANDER, W. J.: Neurologic prodromes to virus hepatitis. Neurology, 6:574, 1956.

JONES, P. N. AND CAPPS, R. B.: Management of hepatic coma. Med. Clin. North America, 48:37, 1964.

LEVIN, E. J.: Congenital biliary atresia with emphasis on the skeletal abnormalities. Radiology, 67:714, 1956.

McCANN, W. J.: Ion exchange for hepatic coma. New York State J. Med., 61:879, 1961.

McDONALD, R. AND DE LA HARPE, P. L.: Prognosis of hepatic coma in children. J. Pediat., 63:916, 1963.

OGILVIE, A. G. AND SPENCE, J. C.: Cholemia: A clinical study of nervous symptoms in liver atrophy. Arch. Dis. Child., 2:41, 1927.

READ, A. E. *et al.*: The neuropsychiatric syndromes associated with chronic liver disease and an extensive portal-systemic collateral circulation. Quart. Jour. Med., 36:135, 1967.

RIDDELL, A. G. AND McDERMOTT, W.: Hepatic coma. Lancet, i:1263, 1954.

ROBERTS, K. E. *et al.*: Electrolyte alterations in liver disease and hepatic coma. Med. Clin. North America, 40:901, 1956.

SHERLOCK, S. *et al.*: Portal systemic encephalopathy. Lancet, 6836:453, 1954.

SILEN, W. AND EISMAN, B.: The diagnosis and therapy of hepatic coma. Postgrad. Med., 28:445, 1960.

STOKES, J. F., OWEN, J. R. AND HOLMES, E. G.: Neurologic complications of infective hepatitis. Brit. M. J., 2:642, 1945.

STORMONT, J. M., MACKIE, J. E. AND DAVIDSON, C. S.: Observations on antibiotics in treatment of hepatic coma. New England J. Med., 259:1145, 1958.

SUMMERSKILL, W. H. J. AND MOLNAR, G. D.: Ocular signs in hepatic cirrhosis. New England J. Med., 266:1244, 1962.

SUMMERSKILL, W. H. J., WOLFF, STANLEY J. AND DAVIDSON, CHARLES S.: The management of hepatic coma in relation to protein withdrawal and certain specific measures. Am. J. Med., 23:59-76, 1957.

THOMPSON, A. AND HOLMES, A.: Immune inhibition of urea breakdown in patients with cirrhosis. Gastroenterology, 52:14, 1967.

TREY, C. *et al.*: Treatment of hepatic coma by exchange blood transfusion. New Eng. Jour. Med., 274:473, 1966.

VICTOR, M., ADAMS, R. D. AND COLE, M.: Neurological symptoms in chronic hepatic disease. Meeting of the American Neurological Association, Atlantic City, New Jersey, June 12-14, 1961.

WALSHE, J. M.: Observations on the symptomatology and pathogenesis of hepatic coma. Quart. J. Med., 20:421, 1951.

HEPATOLENTICULAR DEGENERATION

Definition.—In this group we place a neurological syndrome which is associated with a more or less specific degenerative process in the brain, involving chiefly the lenticular nucleus, and with cirrhosis of the liver. A zone of greenish pigmentation lying in the periphery of the cornea is a characteristic feature.

Etiology.—Biochemical studies have revealed that the serum ceruloplas-

min is deficient. The serum copper is reduced. The serum uric acid is diminished. Excessive amounts of copper are deposited in the liver, brain, kidneys and corneae. The urine contains an excess of copper. Intravenous radio-copper is excreted too rapidly and little is retained in the plasma. Evidences of abnormal renal tubular function are found with glycosuria and increased excretion of phosphates, amino acids, uric acid and calcium.

The usual interpretation of these findings is that the deficiency of ceruloplasmin is the primary defect. This protein, of course, binds most of the plasma copper in normal individuals, so when it is lacking, copper remains unbound and is taken up by the tissues and injures the liver, kidneys and brain. More recently cases of Wilson's disease have been found in which the ceruloplasmin is not reduced and other cases have come to light in which reduction of ceruloplasmin is found without any clinical symptoms.

O'Reilly has written a comprehensive discussion of the biochemical features of this condition and the numerous theories which have been advanced to explain its pathogenesis. The reader is advised to consult this paper.

Pathological Anatomy.—Wilson found bilateral cavitation in the putamen in his cases with very slight changes in other parts of the nervous system. In cases more recently recorded the lesions have not been so precisely localized. In only about half of all cases are gross lesions found in the putamen, but the process is always most severe in this region. There may be merely edema with degeneration of the neurons or a rarefaction of the tissue which is termed status spongiosus. Degenerative changes of the neurons are found also in the globus pallidus, the caudate, the dentate nucleus of the cerebellum and the cerebral cortex. There is always proliferation of the fibrous glia which often produces a dense capsule around the more severe lesions. Alzheimer's giant glial cells are regarded as more or less characteristic of this process. They are described as astrocytes showing large, pale nuclei with irregular outlines. Some cells contain two or more nuclei. Okinaka describes deposits of copper granules in the glial cells of the putamen. There may be hyaline changes in the walls of the small blood vessels and proliferation of capillaries is described. However, there is never any perivascular infiltration with lymphocytes or other evidences of inflammation and the vascular changes are not adequate to explain the lesions.

The liver is invariably injured. There is always a nodular cirrhosis which is not in itself characteristic. Hurst and Barnes, however, found an acute interstitial hepatitis in one case and suggest that it is the recurrence of such acute reactions which eventually leads to the cirrhosis. Copper granules are found in the liver cells according to Okinaka. Studies of the cornea have revealed that the pigmentation is due to deposits of fine golden yellow granules in Descemet's membrane. These granules are apparently composed

of copper. Copper deposits are found in the kidneys. Schaffner *et al.* state that the liver cells show glycogen degeneration of the nuclei, fine cytoplasmic fat droplets and lipofuscin pigment. Acid phosphatase activity is reduced and electron microscopy reveals an increased number of lysosomes. It is claimed that these changes are not found in other diseases of the liver. The renal tubules show focal areas of degeneration, sloughing and necrosis of the epithelial cells. Intracytoplasmic deposits of copper are found in these cells. No abnormalities are found in the glomeruli.

Clinical Features.—The disease frequently affects several members of one family, often two or more siblings, and may rarely occur in more than one generation. It is, therefore, definitely an heredofamilial disease. The mode of inheritance seems to be that of a recessive characteristic. The onset usually occurs in the first decade, but may be deferred to the second decade. The course is invariably progressive and often marked by exacerbations. Death usually occurs between the second and fifth years of the disease, but one case is said to have terminated in five weeks and another to have dragged on for eleven years.

Our conception of the disease has grown much broader in recent years and a number of different syndromes are now recognized in addition to that described by Wilson in 1912. In this type, which may be regarded as the *classical syndrome,* and is found characteristically in children of 10 to 15 years, bulbar disturbances are often among the first symptoms. Difficulty in articulation appears and is followed by dysphagia, hoarseness and weakness of the voice and later by difficulty in mastication. Such symptoms may be well advanced before any other neurological disturbances have developed. Eventually the patient loses the power of speech completely and may have to be fed through a tube. The face is usually fixed in a rigid smile and the mouth is widely opened so that saliva drools from the lips. Volitional movements of the face and jaws are possible but late in the course of the disease such movements become slow and weak. The appearance of the face is identical with that seen in children who have developed a Parkinsonian syndrome following epidemic encephalitis. In one of our patients, the capsules of the jaw joints became so stretched by this tendency to hold the mouth open that dislocations occurred whenever he yawned. Loss of emotional control and exaggeration of emotional reactions are usually present and, in the late stages of the disease, forced laughter and weeping may occur. The skeletal musculature invariably becomes rigid sooner or later and eventually this rigidity grows so intense that the patient is quite helpless, although true paralysis apparently does not occur. In most cases a cogwheel phenomenon may be elicited and it is evident that we are dealing with an extrapyramidal type of hypertonus which resembles that of the Parkinsonian syndrome very closely. Tremor is another constant sign. This

is coarse and rhythmical. It is present at rest but becomes accentuated when volitional movements are attempted and under the influence of emotional stress. It resembles, therefore, a combination of the tremor of the Parkinsonian syndrome and the intention tremor of disseminated sclerosis. Distorted postures are often present sometimes without involuntary movements. Ataxia is a rare symptom. The tendon reflexes are usually normal but Babinski signs sometimes are found. No alteration of sensibility has ever been found. It is difficult to estimate the frequency and severity of the mental changes. The loss of control of emotional reactions and the peculiar expression give the observer the impression of dementia which may be misleading. In the late stages of the disease it is impossible for the patients to make themselves understood and since they are quite helpless there is no way of determining their mental state. There can be no doubt that severe dementia develops in some instances and probably mild reduction of intelligence occurs in most cases. The disease is always progressive but apparently not always steadily progressive. In some of the cases reported by Barnes and in certain members of a family which the writer has studied, the disease advanced by a series of exacerbations. In other cases there seem to be no exacerbations and the disease advances steadily, sometimes slowly and sometimes rapidly. The course is apt to be slower in older patients. Eventually the patient becomes quite helpless and bedridden. Speech is lost, swallowing becomes impossible, in-

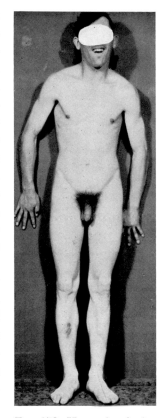

Fig. 172. Hepatolenticular degeneration. Photograph of a patient showing the fixed smile and open mouth. Unfortunately, his habitual posture is not evident for he is supporting himself against the wall. The ulcer on the right shin should be noted.

continence develops and death ensues. The pigmentation of the cornea and the symptoms referable to the cirrhosis of the liver will be discussed below.

It is evident from the description given above that the clinical picture of Wilson's disease is not identical with the Parkinsonian syndrome, although there are many features in common. A nearly pure *Parkinsonian syndrome* may, however, develop in the course of hepatolenticular degeneration.

Barnes and Hurst have reported cases in which bilateral athetoid movements were present and choreic movements have been mentioned by other observers. It is therefore necessary to include *progressive choreo-athetosis* among the possible manifestations of this disease.

One of the cases described by Barnes and Hurst was notable for the occurrence of tonic fits in the terminal stages. Growers, indeed, had described such seizures many years before and in one of Wimmer's cases there were similar seizures for five years before other symptoms developed. In the case of Barnes, the spasms were general and paroxysmal, persisting for about five seconds and recurring every fifteen seconds for some hours. They were superimposed upon a background of persisting muscular rigidity. Consciousness was preserved throughout the attacks, although speech was rendered impossible by fixation of the jaws. The arms were rigidly abducted, extended and overpronated; the legs abducted, slightly flexed at the hip and extended at the ankle; the back was strongly arched, the neck flexed and the jaw clenched. The expression was one of pain and anxiety. Any stimulus, such as an attempt at passive movement provoked or accentuated the spasms. The temperature was elevated and there was profuse sweating. Barnes states that the clinical picture resembled that of tetanus so closely that a physician seeing the patient for the first time would surely make that diagnosis. Such seizures seem to develop during acute exacerbations of the disease and if the child survives are apt to be followed by definite advance in the symptoms.

Myotonus is a very rare feature of this disease. Barnes mentions that one of the children in the family which he studied was often unable to relax the fingers after grasping the examiner's hand. *Myoclonus* is described.

Psychotic symptoms may be the first evidence of the disease. I have seen a girl of 13 years whose behavior suggested schizophrenia. Neurological signs of Wilson's disease developed later.

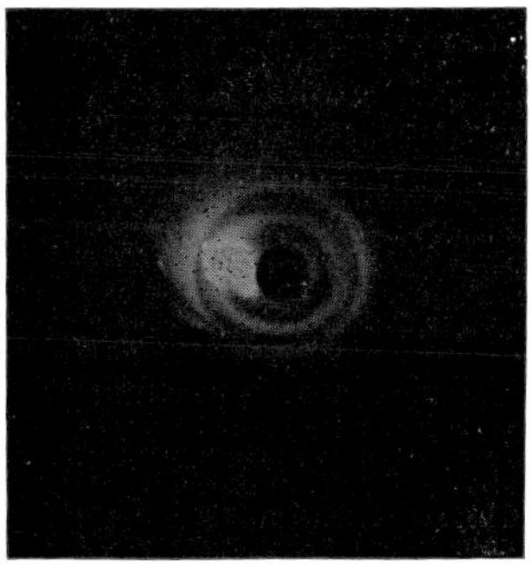

FIG. 173. Photograph of the cornea illuminated by a beam of light showing the Kayser-Fleischer zone of pigment in the periphery. The bright spot on the right is merely the reflection of the light. (By courtesy of Dr. Walsh.)

In Wilson's cases there was no clinical evidence of *cirrhosis of the liver* although well advanced changes were discovered at post-mortem examination. Subsequent experience has confirmed this rule that the cirrhosis is usually latent. Even the standard tests of liver function often give negative results. Silverberg and Gellis state that in children, the evidences of liver disease are usually more prominent than that in older subjects. It should be said that the disease may be manifest by cirrhosis alone or by cirrhosis with pericorneal pigmentation and that no neurological abnormalities may be evident during life and no lesions found in the brain at post-mortem examination. Barnes and Hurst, however, observed symptoms

of acute hepatitis as well as signs of cirrhosis in several members of the family which they studied. They described recurrent attacks of jaundice, vomiting and fever which are due, they believe, to acute attacks of interstitial hepatitis. In one case in which the patient died during such an attack, they found a condition resembling acute yellow atrophy of the liver. If the patient survives long enough, he may develop ascites, hematemesis, epistaxis and atrophy of the liver. At first the liver is enlarged and the edge is abnormally firm, but later it may become so shrunken that it is difficult to demonstrate any liver dullness, as in one of the writer's cases. No doubt the gastrointestinal disorders which some of these patients exhibit are a result of involvement of the liver.

During and immediately after the acute attacks of hepatitis and whenever clinical symptoms of cirrhosis of the liver are present, the standard tests of liver function, such as the bromsulphalein, cephalin flocculation and thymol turbidity test will often give positive results. In some cases osteomalacia occurs. Rosenoer and Mitchell mention osteochondritis of the spine, fragmentation of bone, osteochondritis dissecans as well as osteoporosis. Loose bodies in the joints are mentioned. Renal glycosuria may also occur and there may be an excess of calcium, phosphates and uric acid in the urine. These findings are attributed to damage to the renal tubules.

In some cases, especially in cases of long duration, there is a brownish pigmentation over the face, neck and extremities. Irregular splotches of pigmentation may be seen over the buttocks and body. The nail beds are bluish. Denny-Brown suggests that this pigmentation is due to deposits of copper in the skin.

The *pericorneal pigmentation* is one of the cardinal signs of this disease and perhaps the most important of all from the point of view of diagnosis. It appears to the naked eye as a narrow zone of greenish-gray or greenish-yellow overlying the outermost margin of the iris. As this zone grows more and more pronounced it slowly becomes golden. With the slit lamp it is seen to be composed of fine golden granules lying in Descemet's membrane on the posterior surface of the cornea. When this zone is very faint, it can be demonstrated only by the slit lamp. Rarely identical granules may be seen under the anterior capsule of the lens and a sunflower cataract is described (Walsh). Optic atrophy does not occur so far as the writer can learn in this condition. The pupillary reflexes are normal and palsies of the extraocular muscles are not observed. As a rule vision is clear and the retinae normal. It is said that the electroencephalogram is apt to show nonspecific changes.

McIntyre *et al.* report three cases of acute hemolytic reactions during

which large amounts of copper were excreted in the urine. They believe that the hemolysis was due to copper intoxication.

Diagnosis.—The essential features in the diagnosis may be summarized as follows: (1) The tendency for several members of a family to be affected. (2) The onset in the first or second decade. (3) The neurological symptoms described above which include tremor, muscular rigidity, altered posture, bulbar palsy and loss of control of emotional reactions. (4) The tendency to advance by exacerbations. (5) The Kayser-Fleischer ring of pericorneal pigmentation. (6) The cirrhosis of the liver which is usually latent but which may give rise to clinical signs and symptoms. (7) It is stated that increased excretion of amino acids and of copper in the urine is characteristic. The effect of 2,3-dimercaptopropanol, or BAL, which causes an even greater output of copper in the urine is also of diagnostic value.

Sternlieb and Scheinberg state that the diagnosis may be made with confidence if the ceruloplasmin in the serum is low and the liver biopsy shows an excessive amount of copper. Walshe and Briggs point out that ceruloplasmin is formed in the liver and diseases of the liver other than Wilson's disease may reduce the level of this substance in the serum. Cartwright states that the Kayser-Fleischer corneal ring is the only pathognomonic feature. It is claimed that heterozygous carriers may be detected by a decrease of ceruloplasmin synthesis. See Bearn and Sternlieb.

Prognosis.—The course of the disease without treatment seems to vary between a few weeks and a number of years and the outcome is always fatal. There is reason to believe at present that treatment will make the prognosis more favorable.

Treatment.—It is advised that repeated courses of BAL be given at intervals. The details of this treatment are not yet standardized. Denny-Brown gives 2.0 mgs per kilo by intramuscular injection twice a day for 10 days and repeats the course at intervals of 6 weeks to 6 months.

It is claimed that the progression of the neurological symptoms is halted and there is actual improvement. The pericorneal zone becomes grayish. Liver function may improve and jaundice clear up. The amino acids in the urine are not reduced, however.

Warnock and Neill urge that the diagnosis be made before symptoms develop by the study of siblings of affected individuals and that treatment be started at once. They describe the case of a boy of 16 years with signs of liver damage but no neurological symptoms who was treated for 4 years. All signs of hepatic dysfunction disappeared and no neurological disorders developed. Corboresin is being used in the hope it will prevent the absorption of copper from the gastrointestinal tract. Walshe states that the administration of penicillamine is more effective in causing excretion of copper than

BAL. D,L-penicillamine is said to be most effective. This drug may be given by mouth and causes no reaction. Versene, or ethylenediamine tetra-acetic acid, is being used for it will increase the excretion of copper. A preparation of ceruloplasmin is available and is being tried. Cumings states that the administration of potassium sulphide in 20 mgm doses by mouth reduces the absorption of copper.

Sternlieb and Scheinberg report that seven asymptomatic patients have been treated for periods up to five years and have developed no evidence of the disease. They advise a low copper diet containing less than 1.0 mgs of copper a day excluding foods with high copper diet such as liver, mushrooms, nuts and oysters, the administration of potassium sulfide to bind the ingested copper and the oral administration of penicillamine.

BIBLIOGRAPHY

AITA, J. A.: Neurologic manifestations of general diseases. Springfield, Thomas, 1964.

BARNES, S.: Hepatolenticular degeneration. Brain, **49**:36, 1926.

———— AND HURST, E. W.: Hepatolenticular degeneration. Brain, **48**:297, 1925.

BEARN, A. O.: Genetic and biochemical aspects of Wilson's disease. Amer. Jour. Med., **15**:442, 1953.

BROWN, I. A.: Liver Brain Relationships. Springfield, Thomas, 1957.

CARTRIGHT, G. E. *et al.:* A critical analysis of serum copper and ceruloplasmin concentrations in normal subjects, patients with Wilson's disease and relatives with Wilson's disease. Am. J. Med., **28**:555, 1960.

COOPER, A. M. *et al.:* Investigation of aminoaciduria in Wilson's disease. Demonstration of a defect in renal function. J. Clin. Invest., **29**:265, 1950.

CUMINGS, J. A.: The copper and iron content of the nervous system in normal and hepatolenticular degeneration. Brain, **71**:410, 1948.

CUMMINGS, J. N.: The effects of BAL in hepatolenticular degeneration. Brain, **74**:10, 1951.

————: Discussion of treatment of Wilson's disease. Proc. Roy. Soc. Med., **52**: (No. 1) Sec. Pediat., p. 62, 1959.

DENNY-BROWN, D.: Wilson's disease. New England J. Med., **270**:1149, 1964.

———— AND PORTER, H.: Effect of BAL (2,3-Dimercaptopropanol) on hepatolenticular degeneration. New England Med. J., **245**:917, 1951.

GOLDSTEIN, N. P. *et al.:* The treatment of Wilson's disease with D. L. Penicillamine. Neurology, **12**:231, 1962.

GREENFIELD, J. G., POYNTON, F. AND WALSHE, F. M. R.: On progressive lenticular degeneration. Quart. J. Med., **17**:385, 1924.

GRÜTER, W.: Hemolytic crises as early manifestations of Wilson's disease. Deutsche Ztschr. Nervenheilkunde., **179**:401, 1959.

HALL, H. C.: La Degénérescence hépato-lenticulaire. Paris. Masson and Cie, 1921.

HOMBURGER, F. AND KOZOL, H. L.: Hepatolenticular degeneration. J.A.M.A., **130**:6, 1946.

MATHEWS, W. B.: The absorption and excretion of radiocopper in Wilson's disease. J. Neurol., Neurosurg. & Psychiat., **17**:242, 1954.

McINTYRE, N. *et al.:* Hemolytic anemia in Wilson's disease. New England Jour. Med., **276**:439, 1967.

MUNCIE, W. AND LHERMITTE, J.: Hepatolenticular degeneration. Arch. Neurol. & Psychiat., **23**:750, 1930.

OKINAKA, S. *et al.:* The pathogenesis of hepatocerebral disease. Arch. Neurol. & Psychiat., **72**:573, 1954.

O'REILLY, S.: Problems in Wilson's disease. Neurology, **17**:137, 1967.

———— *et al.:* Iron metabolism in Wilson's disease. Neurology, **18**:634, 1968.

OSBORN, S. B. AND WALSHE, J. M.: Studies with radioactive copper in relation to the natural history of Wilson's disease. Lancet, **1**:346, 1967.

RICHMOND, J. *et al.:* Hepatolenticular degeneration treated by penicilliamine. Brain, **87**:619, 1964.

ROSENOER, V. M. AND MITCHELL, R. C.: Skeletal changes in Wilson's disease. Brit. J. Radiol., **32**:805, 1959.

SCHAFFNER, F. *et al.:* Liver cell changes in Wilson's disease. Am. J. Path., **41**:315, 1962.

SCHECHTER, M. AND JONES, C.: Hepatolenticular degeneration. Review of the literature and report of a case treated with dimercaprol. Arch. Int. Med., **91**:541, 1953.

SCHEINBERG, I. H. AND STERNLIEB, I.: The pathogenesis and clinical significance of liver disease in hepatolenticular degeneration. Med. Clin. North America, **44**:665, 1960.

SILVERBERG, M. AND GELLIS, S. S.: The liver in juvenile Wilson's disease. Pediatrics, **30**:402, 1962.

STERNLIEB, I. AND SCHEINBERG, I. H.: Tr. Am. Gastroenterological A. Annual Meeting, New York, July 1962.

STERNLIEB, I. *et al.:* Detection of heterozygous carrier of Wilson's disease gene. Jour. Clin. Invest., **40**:707, 1961.

TAPLIN, G. V. *et al.:* Development of a radioisotope tracer test for the differential diagnosis of jaundice. J. Louisiana Med. Soc., **109**:255, 1957.

THOMALLA, C.: Ein Fall von Torsionspasmus mit Sectionbefund. Ztschr. f. d. g. Neurol. u. Psychiat., **41**:s.311, 1918.

UZMAN, L. L.: On the relationship of urinary copper excretion to aminoaciduria in Wilson's disease. Am. J. Med. Sc., **226**:645, 1953.

———— AND DENNY-BROWN, D.: Aminoaciduria in hepatolenticular degeneration. Am. J. Med. Sc., **215**:599, 1948.

WALSH, F. B.: *Loc. cit.*

WALSHE, J. M.: Penicillamine. A new oral therapy for Wilson's disease. Am. J. Med., **21**:487, 1956.

————: Liver signs in Wilson's disease. Arch. Dis. Childhood, **37**:253, 1962.

———— AND BRIGGS, J.: Diagnosis of Wilson's disease. Lancet, **2**:263, 1962.

———— AND ————: Serum ceruloplasmin in liver disease. Lancet, **ii**:263, 1962.

WARNOCK, C. G. AND NEILL, D. W.: Dimercaprol in the pre-neurological stage of Wilson's disease. J. Neurol., Neurosurg. & Psychiat., **17**:70, 1954.

WILSON, S. A. K.: Progressive lenticular degeneration. Brain, **34**:295, 1912.

WIMMER, A.: Etudes sur les syndromes extrapyramidaux. Rex. Neurol., **37**:952, 1921.

KERNICTERUS WITH ICTERUS GRAVIS AND ERYTHROBLASTOSIS FETALIS

Definition.—A condition occurring in the first few days of life characterized by destruction of the lenticular and caudate nuclei which are deeply stained with bile pigments. Muscular rigidity and choreoathetoid movements result. Icterus gravis and erythroblastosis are usually associated. In most instances, Rh isoimmunization is responsible.

Etiology: Erythroblastosis.—It has been shown that if rabbits are injected with the blood of the Rhesus monkey, antibodies are formed which are termed anti-Rh agglutinins. This rabbit serum will agglutinate certain human bloods which are termed *Rh-positive.* Other human bloods are not agglutinated and are termed *Rh-negative.* It has been established that in more than 90 per cent of cases in which erythroblastosis develops, the mother is

Rh-negative and the father and the fetus are Rh-positive. It is believed that this condition is a result of immunization of the mother against Rh-positive blood. This may occur as a result of passage of the Rh-positive fetal blood through defects in the placenta or as a result of transfusions of Rh-positive blood. Apparently, transfusions given early in life may result in injury to the fetus years later. It is assumed that the anti-Rh agglutinins pass through the placenta to destroy the Rh-positive blood of the infant. Erythroblastosis does not always develop when an Rh-negative woman is impregnated by an Rh-positive man. Statistical studies indicate that about 12 per cent of all marriages will be between Rh-positive males and Rh-negative females. The incidence of erythroblastosis is, however, only about 0.1 per cent of all pregnancies. Several explanations have been offered for this discrepancy. (1) The placenta may not be permeable enough to permit the passage of the Rh factor from the fetus to the mother. (2) Several pregnancies may be required to build up the mother's antibodies. Erythroblastosis is rare in first pregnancies. (3) The mother apparently does not always have the ability to produce antibodies strong enough to induce recognizable symptoms in the child. (4) Males who inherit the Rh factor from only one parent and are, therefore, heterozygous do not transmit the Rh factor to all of their children and some of their children will be Rh-negative and so escape. Once erythroblastosis has developed in a family, subsequent children are apt to be affected with increasing severity, especially if the father is homozygous. It is now known that there are a number of Rh incompatibilities and not just one. The subject has become one for a specialist. Apparently, 85 per cent of all serious reactions are due to Rh incompatibility, but ABO incompatibility is apparently more common than was once believed. This seems to occur especially when the mother belongs to group O and the baby to group A or B. A small number of cases are due to other rare incompatibilities, it is claimed.

It is quite clear now that kernicterus may develop in association with jaundice in the newborn which is not complicated by erythroblastosis or due to Rh iso-immunization. Kernicterus is known to occur in cases of congenital atresia of the bile ducts, in jaundice due to sepsis, and in hereditary, non-hemolytic jaundice as described by Crigler. The neurological features of these cases seem to be identical with those found in kernicterus due to Rh incompatibility.

Pathological Anatomy.—Section of the brain reveals intense pigmentation of the lenticular and caudate nuclei and often less obvious discoloration of the corpus Luysi, the dentate nuclei, the mammillary bodies, the inferior olives, the cornu Ammonis and even the cortex. Sometimes the bulbar nuclei and the spinal gray matter are stained. As a rule, the nuclear

masses are exclusively affected. Petechiae and even large hemorrhages may occur. The meninges and the ependyma may also be stained yellow. Histological investigation reveals that the ganglion cells in the pigmented regions are severely injured. Many cells have completely disappeared and others show various degrees of disintegration. These changes seem to be most intense in the basal ganglia. The pigment is found not only in the ganglion cells but in large phagocytes and lying free in the interstitial tissue. In a few cases, pigmentation has been absent and only degenerations of the cells were found. It seems to be generally accepted that the pigmentation is merely secondary and that the bile is taken up by the cells after they become necrotic. The lesions described above are usually designated by the term "Kernicterus."

A few studies have been made of the brains of subjects who have survived the acute phase of this illness. As one might expect destructive lesions are found in the same nuclear structures which are involved in the active stage. It is pointed out that there is found in addition demyelination of the white matter of the brain and spinal cord. The optic nerves may be involved. There may be central necrosis of the liver lobules. The cause of the damage to the brain is not clear. Some authorities believe that it is a result of metabolic disturbances resulting from damage to the liver. Crigler's observations would seem to lend weight to this suggestion. Wiener thinks it is due to agglutination of red cells in the capillaries of the brain with resulting anoxia. Meriwether *et al.,* on the basis of histological studies, suggest that hypoxemia on the basis of anemia is responsible. However, Jervis of-

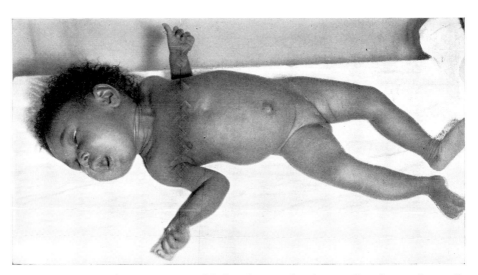

Fig. 174. Icterus gravis neonatorum with kernicterus showing swollen face and peculiar posture which was due to athetosis.

fers much evidence to prove that bilirubinemia is responsible for the damage to the nervous system. He suggests that the non-conjugated bilirubin is more toxic than the conjugated variety. Waters, and Brittin have produced kernicterus in experimental animals by injection of bilirubin.

Clinical Features.—Isolated cases of erythroblastosis are described, but if the disease has once made its appearance in a family, a high percentage of subsequent babies are apt to be affected. As a rule, the first child of a series has a better chance of escaping than the later ones. Males are said to be affected three times as often as females.

In icterus gravis, there may be no jaundice at birth although it is present in most instances. In any case, it is evident within a few days and rapidly becomes intense. The vernix caseosa is usually saffron yellow. Edema is usually present and most apparent in the face and neck. The liver and spleen are enlarged. The urine is scanty and contains large quantities of bile. The stools are bile stained. Anemia is almost invariably found. The red cells may be reduced to less than two million and the color index is increased. Numbers of nucleated red cells are seen. There is also leucocytosis with immature cells of every type. No constant changes in bleeding time or clotting time are found. The course is usually afebrile except for a terminal rise of temperature. Apparently the active process lasts about two weeks in most instances. Death may occur at any time during this period.

In a large percentage of all cases of icterus gravis there are evidences of *Kernicterus*. The child becomes apathetic and takes its feedings poorly. Restlessness, drowsiness and finally stupor ensue. Intense rigidity of the musculature is often seen with opisthotonos, trismus and spasms of the bulbar muscles. Tonic and clonic convulsions are frequently observed. The spinal fluid is deeply stained with bile pigments and may contain red cells. In the most severe cases, respiration becomes irregular, frothy blood stained sputum appears and the child may die in circulatory collapse. The onset of the neurological symptoms is usually between the second and the fifth day. Death may occur between the third and the seventh days. It is stated that the earlier the onset, the more severe the symptoms are apt to be. The symptoms may be so mild in some instances as to escape detection yet the child will subsequently display the typical sequelae. Only apathy, refusal to nurse or rolling of the eyes for a day or two may be noted. It is stated, however, that when the typical symptoms are observed, there is always lasting damage to the nervous system.

Gerrard has made a very careful study of the subsequent course of these children. He shows that the clinical changes and symptoms appear in a certain sequence. He described three syndromes: (1) The most severe form which is marked by intense rigidity similar to the so-called decorticate rigid-

ity, rolling of the eyes, profuse sweating and evidences of deficient temperature control. These patients always die in infancy. (2) A less severe form which results in rigidity with involuntary movements of the trunk as well as the extremities. The picture is said to resemble dystonia. There is no instability of the body temperature and the patients may survive, though they remain quite helpless. (3) The mildest form is fortunately the one most frequently encountered among children who survive the acute symptoms. Gerrard states that for a time the child seems to improve and by the age of 4 to 8 weeks may show only retraction of the head and rolling of the eyes. About the third month, however, weakness and hypotonia become apparent. The hypotonia is especially evident in the neck and arms. Within a few months restless movements are seen and by the end of the second year, these are apt to assume the character of chorea or athetosis. As these movements develop, the hypotonia recedes. The child often learns to walk between the ages of 2 and 3 years and at this time it is evident that there is ataxia and lack of equilibrium. Emotional control is deficient. In the next few years, there may be definite improvement. The involuntary movements and the ataxia may diminish though they do not as a rule disappear. Deafness, which is found in between 20 and 40 per cent of all cases, persists. This may be mild or severe. It is attributed to damage to the cochlear nuclei. Rosen regards this apparent deafness as a form of aphasia. Various disturbances of ocular movements are seen. Loss of upward gaze is described. Mental deficiency is usually present though a few children of normal intelligence are found in this group. The mental defect is often severe. Gerrard does not believe that mental deficiency without motor disturbances is ever due to kernicterus.

Churchill and Colfelt state that congenital athetosis associated with deafness and loss of upward gaze are strongly suggestive of kernicterus.

The first teeth may be stained a greenish color probably by bile pigments, and enamel may be defective. Cirrhosis of the liver may be discovered in childhood.

Diagnosis.—I must first mention the more common types of jaundice of the newborn. In all infants, the bile pigments of the blood increase very rapidly after birth and at the end of a few days, the blood may contain twenty times as much as at birth. In at least one third of all normal infants, clinical jaundice develops. After a week or more, this begins to diminish and the blood pigments reach a normal level at about the end of a month. This is regarded as *physiological jaundice.* It is more common and more severe as a rule in premature infants. *Congenital atresia* of the *bile ducts* gives rise to a severe and progressive obstructive jaundice causing death within two months. Giant cell transformation of the liver may cause the same picture. Other causes of icterus neonatorum are *sepsis, hepatitis*

and *congenital syphilis.* The *hemorrhagic diathesis* may also be associated with a moderate degree of jaundice.

It is stated that the administration of excessive doses of vitamin K to the newborn may cause jaundice and kernicterus. Crosse advises that not more than 10 mgs should be given a day if the infant is premature. Smith states that sulfisoxazole with penicillin may also cause kernicterus.

Arias *et al.* state that prolonged jaundice in infancy may be due to the presence in the mother's milk of pregnane 3 (alpha) 20 (beta) diol which inhibits glucuronyl transferase activity. It is said that kernicterus does not occur.

Fessas *et al.* state that deficiency of glucose 6 phosphate dehydrogenase may cause neonatal jaundice.

Batson describes a number of conditions which must be considered in differential diagnosis when jaundice appears in the newborn.

The diagnostic features of erythroblastosis seem to be as follows: (1) The mother is Rh negative and the father and baby Rh positive in 90 per cent of all cases. The Coombs' test on the cord blood is positive. (2) Several children in the family are usually affected. (3) There is anemia with numbers of immature cells of both the red and white series in the blood, jaundice, edema, enlargement of the liver and spleen and petechial hemorrhages. (4) The jaundice differs from the physiological type by its earlier onset, greater intensity, family incidence and high mortality rate. From that associated with sepsis by the absence of fever and the negative blood culture. From that due to syphilis by the absence of all evidences of congenital syphilis. From jaundice due to congenital atresia of the bile ducts and other forms of obstructive jaundice by the presence of bile in the stools and from hemorrhagic disease of the newborn by the greater prominence of jaundice, the lesser incidence of hemorrhage and the essentially normal bleeding and clotting times. (5) Neurological signs described above, i.e. kernicterus, may be associated. The various Rh incompatibilities must all be considered and the possibility of ABO and the rare incompatibilities investigated if Rh incompatibility is not present.

Van Praagh stresses the importance of early diagnosis for treatment must be begun early. The first signs are hypotonia, lethargy and poor sucking reflex. In the second stage which occurs within a few days, spasticity is the most important sign. This may be transient so the infant must be observed closely.

Wiener states that his own classification of the Rh-Hr types is the only satisfactory one.

Hoffmann and Hollander state that hydrops fetalis may be diagnosed by means of ultrasound.

Prognosis.—Kernicterus develops in about 20 per cent of all cases of

erythroblastosis. More than half of these children die in the first month while the process is still active. Apparently there is always lasting damage to the nervous system in children who survive. These statements apply, of course, to children who are not treated effectively. With modern treatment the prognosis is vastly better and the incidence of kernicterus is reduced to a very small percentage. This applies to the babies who are born alive. The percentage of stillborn babies has not been reduced.

Jacobs states that the infants of mothers who have had stillbirths or have given birth to babies who died of erythroblastosis during the neonatal period have small chance of survival. The outlook is better for babies whose mothers have had children who were only mildly affected.

Treatment.—Dr. V. J. Freda administers by intramuscular injection high titered anti-Rh gamma globulin to Rh-negative mothers who have given birth to their first Rh positive baby to destroy all antigenic red cells which have entered the circulation. It is hoped that this treatment will prevent antibody formation in later pregnancies. Of the 40 mothers treated in this manner, no one produced sensitizing antibodies between the 6th and 18th month.

Freda and Green *et al.* give detailed advice about the treatment of mothers who are Rh negative and are pregnant by Rh positive husbands. This problem is a highly specialized one and these papers should be read in the original. It is stated that the obstetric history, the probable zygosity of the father, the estimated fetal weight, the expected date of confinement, the antibody titer and spectrophotometry of the amniotic fluid should all be taken into consideration.

If the Rh antibody appears for the first time during pregnancy or reaches a critical level of 1:16, the infant is almost certain to be affected. If this level is not reached until one week before delivery, no fear need be entertained for the baby. If the critical level of antibody is exceeded before this time, amniocentesis must be performed repeatedly and treatment must be guided by the spectrophotometric study of the fluid. If the spectrophotometric tracing reaches a level of 3 plus, the baby must be given an intraperitoneal transfusion. If it does not exceed the level of plus 2, pregnancy may be allowed to go to 37 weeks and delivery must be induced at that time. If these indications do not develop, the pregnancy may be allowed to go to term.

Friesen *et al.* report the results of 100 intrauterine transfusions for erythroblastosis fetalis. Forty-seven fetuses were treated. One third of the 47 survived. There were 4 neonatal deaths and 27 deaths in utero. Hydrops fetalis was thought to be the cause of death in 16. Ten deaths were thought to be a direct result of the intrauterine transfusion. It was esti-

mated that the mortality among non-hydropic fetuses was estimated at more than 15 per cent for each transfusion. All but one infant among those who survived required exchange transfusions. All but one appeared to be developing normally.

Dunn states that exchange transfusion before the baby is 9 hours old is required only when Rh disease is clinically evident or when the cord blood hemoglobin value is less than 13.3 gm per 100 ml and the cord blood bilirubin is greater than 3.5 mgs per 100 ml.

Cremer *et al.* and Broughton *et al.* state that exposure to sunlight causes prompt reduction of the serum bilirubin. It is suggested that this method of treatment might be useful in preventing kernicterus.

Doolittle describes a technique to be used in delivery of mothers of a Rh positive child when she is Rh negative to prevent any of the infant's blood from entering the maternal circulation. He states that the placenta should be emptied as soon as possible. Intravenous oxytocin should not be given at delivery of the anterior shoulder. Every precaution is used to deliver an intact placenta. Using this technique he found that only 2 mothers developed anti-Rh antibodies among 153 delivered.

Peddle states that fetomaternal transfusion may occur during amniocentesis if the needle pierces the placenta and may cause or aggravate Rh isoimmunization.

Sussman and Berk have published a complete discussion of all phases of the problem of erythroblastosis fetalis. They confirm the belief that injection of 5 ml of high titered anti-Rh gamma globulin intramuscularly will prevent isoimmunization of a Rh negative mother of a Rh positive baby. It must be given within 72 hours after birth.

In dealing with ABO incompatibility when replacement transfusion is necessary it is advised that group O blood of the proper Rh type be used in which the anti-A and anti-B antibodies have been neurtalized by A and B substances.

BIBLIOGRAPHY

ALLISON, A. C.: Danger of vitamin K to the newborn. Lancet, i:669, 1955.

ARIAS, I. M. *et al.*: Prolonged neonatal unconjugated hyperbilirubinemia associated with breast feeding and a steroid, pregnane-3 (alpha) 20 (beta) diol in maternal milk that inhibits glucuronide formation in vitro. J. Clin. Invest., 43:2037, 1964.

ASCARI, W. Q. *et al.*: Rh (D) immune globulin (human). J.A.M.A., 205:1, 1968.

BATSON, B. E.: Neonatal hyperbilirubinemia. Clin. Obst. & Gynec., 5:85, 1962.

BIEMOND, A. AND VAN CREVELD, S.: Nuclear jaundice in neonatal (umbilical) sepsis with jaundice. Arch. Dis. Child., 12:173, 1937.

BISHOP, G. J. *et al.*: Clinical trial of one millitre of Rh o D globulin preventation of Rh immunization. Med. Jour. Aust., i:122, 1968.

BOGGS, T. R. *et al.*: Early recognition of Rh sensitization. Obst. & Gynec., 21:334, 1963.

BROUGHTON, P. M. G. *et al.*: Effect of blue light on hyperbilirubinemia. Arch. of Dis. Child., 40:666, 1965.

BROWN, I. A.: Liver Brain Relationships. Springfield, Thomas, 1957.

CAPPELL, D. F.: Mother-child incompatibility problem in relation to nervous sequelae of hemolytic disease of the newborn. Brain, 70:486, 1947.

CHURCHILL, J. A. AND COLFELT, R. H.: Etiologic factors in athetotic cerebral palsy. Arch. Neurol., 9:400, 1963.

CREMER, R. J. *et al.:* Influence of light on the hyperbilirubinemia of infants. Lancet, i:1094, 1958.

CROME, L.: Morphological nervous changes in survivors of severe jaundice of the newborn. J. Neurol., Neurosurg. & Psychiat., 18:17, 1955.

CROSSE, V. M. *et al.:* Kernicterus and prematurity. Arch. Dis. Childhood, 30:501, 1955.

DIAMOND, L. K., BLACKFAN, K. D. AND BATY, J. M.: Erythroblastosis fetalis and its association with universal edema of the fetus, Icterus gravis neonatorum and anemia of the newborn. J. Pediat., 1:269, 1932.

DOOLITTLE, J. E.: Are you preventing erythroblastosis? Mich. Med., 66:1569, 1967.

DUNN, P. M.: The unnecessary exchange transfusion; Jour. Pediat., 69:829, 1966.

EVANS, P. R. AND POLANI, P. E.: Neurological sequelae of Rh sensitization. Quart. J. Med., 19:129, 1950.

FESSAS, P. *et al.:* Neonatal jaundice in glucose 6 phosphate dehydrogenase deficient infants. Brit. Med. Jour., ii:1359, 1962.

FISHER, O. D.: Influence of selective induction of labor on mortality in haemolytic disease of the newborn. Brit. Med. J., 5019:615, 1957.

FITZGERALD, G. M., GREENFIELD, J. G. AND KOUNINE, B.: Neurological sequelae of "Kernicterus." Brain, 62:292, 1939.

FORSTER, F. M. AND McCORMACK, R. A.: Kernicterus unassociated with erythroblastosis fetalis. J. Neuropath. & Exp. Neurol., 3:379, 1944.

FREDA, V. J.: The Rh problem and a new concept of its management using amniocentesis and spectrophotometric scanning of the amniotic fluid. Amer. Jour. Obstet. Gynec., 92:341, 1965.

——— *et al.:* The use of Rh immunoglobulin in the prevention of Rh disease. Bull. Sloan Hosp. Wom. N. Y., 13:93, 1967.

FRIESEN, R. E. *et al.:* Experience with 100 intrauterine transfusions for erythroblastosis fetalis. Amer. Jour. Obst. Gynec., 97:343, 1967.

GARTNER, L. M. AND ARIAS, I. M.: Studies of prolonged neonatal jaundice in the breast-fed Infant. Jour. Pediat., 68:54, 1966.

GERRARD, J.: Kernicterus. Brain, 75:526, 1952.

GREEN, G. H. *et al.:* The place of foetal transfusion in haemolytic disease. Aust. N. Z. J. Obstet. Gynaec., 5:53, 1965.

HOFFMAN, D. AND HOLLANDER, H. J.: Diagnostik des hydrops fetus universalis mittels Ultraschall. Zbl. Cynak., 19:667, 1968.

HOLMES, G. E. *et al.:* Neonatal bilirubinemia in the production of long term neurological deficits. Amer. Jour. Dis. Child., 116:37, 1968.

HSIA, D. *et al.:* Studies on erythroblastosis due to ABO incompatibility. Pediatrics, 13:503, 1954.

HYMAN, C. B. *et al.:* Central nervous system abnormalities after neonatal hemolytic disease or hyperbilirubinemia. Amer. Jour. Dis. Child., 117:395, 1969.

JACOBS, W. M.: Prognosis of Rh-incompatible infants. Surg. Gynec. & Obst., 108:485, 1959.

JERVIS, G. A.: Constitutional non-hemolytic hyperbilirubinemia with findings resembling kernicterus. Arch. Neurol. & Psychiat., 81:55, 1959.

LANDE, L.: Kernicterus due to Rh sensitization. J. Pediat., 32:693, 1948.

LANDSTEINER, K. AND WIENER, A. S.: Agglutinable factor in human blood recognized by immune sera for rhesus blood. Proc. Soc. Exper. Biol. & Med., 43:223, 1940.

LITCHFIELD, H. R.: Erythroblastosis fetalis. J. Pediat., 27:353, 1945.

McELWIN, T. W. *et al.:* Management of Rh-sensitized pregnancy. Am. J. Obst. & Gynec., 84:476, 1962.

MERIWETHER, L. S. *et al.:* Kernicterus. Arch. Neurol. & Psychiat., 73:293, 1955.

MISENHIMER, H. R.: Prediction of erythroblastosis fetalis. Obst. & Gynec., 23:485, 1964.

OSE, T. *et al.:* Follow up study of exchange transfusion for hyperbilirubinemia in infants in Japan. Pediatrics, **40**:196, 1967.

PASACHOFF, H. D.: Congenital atresia of the bile ducts with erythroblastosis and kernicterus. Am. J. Dis. Child., **50**:1084, 1935.

PEDDLE, L. J.: Increase of antibody titer following amniocentesis. Amer. Jour. Obstet. and Gynec., **100**:567, 1968.

PLATOU, E.: Experiences with hemolytic disease of the newborn. Lancet, **75**:179, 1955.

QUEENAN, J. T. AND DOUGLAS, G.: Intrauterine transfusion. Obst. & Gynec., **25**:308, 1965.

ROSEN, J.: Rh child. Deaf or aphasic? J. Speech & Hearing Dis. **21**:481, 1956.

SCHNEIDER, J. *et al.:* Prevention of haemolytic disease of the newborn by anti-D serum given to the mother. German Med. Mth., **12**:570, 1967.

SHORTER, R. G. *et al.:* Hepatitis in the newborn infant. Proc. Staff Meet., Mayo Clin., **36**:148, 1961.

SMETANA, H. F.: Neonatal jaundice. Arch. of Path., **80**:553, 1965.

SMITH, C. A.: The newborn infant. J.A.M.A., **172**:433, 1960.

STENCHEVER, M. A. AND CIBILS, L. A.: Management of the Rh-sensitized patient. Amer. Jour. Obstet. and Gynec., **100**:554, 1968.

STIEHM, E. R. AND RYAN, J.: Breast milk jaundice. Amer. Jour. Dis. Child., **109**:212, 1965.

SUSSMAN, L. N. AND BERK, H.: The born and the unborn. Modern Medicine, Jan. 13, 1969, p. 86.

SWINYARD, C. A.: Kernicterus and Its Importance in Cerebral Palsy. Springfield, Thomas, 1961.

VAN PRAAGH, R.: Diagnosis of neonatal kernicterus. Pediatrics, **28**:870, 1961.

WALKER, W.: The management of haemolytic disease of the newborn. Brit. Med. Bull. **15**:123, 1959.

WATERS, W. J. AND BRITTIN, H. A.: Bilirubin encephalopathy. Pediatrics, **15**:45, 1955.

WIENER, A. S.: Nomenclature of the blood groups with special reference to the Rh-Hr types. Trans. N. Y. Acad. Sci., **29**:875, 1967.

WILIE, A. A.: Hemolytic disease of the newborn. Obst. & Gynec., **5**:17, 1955.

YANNET, H. AND ZIMMERMAN, H. M.: Cerebral sequelae of icterus gravis and their relation to kernicterus. Am. J. Dis. Child., **49**:418, 1935.

YLPPÖ, A.: Zur. Klinik und Aetiologie des familiären Icterus neonatorum gravis. Ztschr. f. Kinderh., **17**:334, 1918.

ZIMMERMAN, H. M. AND YANNET, H.: Kernicterus: Jaundice of the nuclear masses of the brain. Am. J. Dis. Child. **45**:740, 1933.

ZIPURSKY, A. AND ISRAELS, L. G.: Pathogenesis and prevention of Rh immunization. Canad Med. Ass. Jour., **97**:1245, 1967.

HEREDITARY NON-HEMOLYTIC JAUNDICE WITH KERNICTERUS
(Crigler's Kernicterus)

Dr. John F. Crigler, Jr., has showed me several cases of congenital non-hemolytic jaundice associated with kernicterus. These cases have been discovered in three families living in St. Mary's County, Maryland. The family T. includes 13 siblings of whom James T. (Ped. A-72501) and Lawrence T. (Ped. A-82072) are affected. The family H. includes 5 children. Three of these are affected: Thomas H. who died in another hospital, James H. who died at Johns Hopkins (Ped. A-67435. Path. 21574) and John H. (Ped. A-81451). The family M. is composed of 5 children. Only Lillian M. is affected (Ped. A-53938).

Genealogical investigation of these three families has revealed that they are all descendants of a couple named M. and represent the sixth genera-

tion. The children are all cousins, therefore, Dr. Crigler has not yet discovered the exact incidence of this disease in the earlier generations though it is clear that many cases occurred.

The disease is manifest at birth or within a few days by jaundice but the child is not really ill at that time. There is no anemia or evidence of blood destruction. There is bile in the stools. The tests for Rh incompatibility are always negative. The unconjugated serum bilirubin is always very high and there is a delay in the excretion of bilirubin. Liver function tests are otherwise quite negative. The enzyme glucuronyl transferase is lacking. The jaundice does not recede but persists during the life of the child.

Between the ages of one and three months, evidences of extrapyramidal disease appear. The child displays distorted postures and slow writhing movements characteristic of athetosis but motor activity is diminished nevertheless for normal motility is grossly reduced.

There is a variable degree of rigidity of the musculature. The face becomes expressionless. These symptoms progress slowly.

These children are very sensitive to infections and react with high fever to mild illness. The duration of their life depends in large part on the care with which they are nursed. Death invariably occurs between the ages of two weeks and eighteen months in our experience.

One post-mortem examination and several biopsies of the liver have been secured. The liver displays no definite anatomical changes in the first few weeks of life, but after the age of four months there may be periportal scarring. The brain shows kernicterus with deep staining of the cerebral cortex, the thalamus, corpus striatum, mammillary bodies, dentate nucleus and inferior olive.

BIBLIOGRAPHY

CHILDS, B.: The nature of indirect bilirubin. Bull. Johns Hopkins Hosp., **97**:333, 1955.
———— AND NAJJAR, V. A.: Familial nonhemolytic jaundice with kernicterus. Pediatrics, **18**:369, 1956.
CRIGLER, J. F. AND NAJJAR, V. A.: Congenital familial non-hemolytic jaundice with kernicterus. Pediatrics, **10**:169, 1952.
DOXIADIS, S. A. *et al.*: Enzyme deficiency and neonatal jaundice. Lancet, **i**:297, 1961.
ROSENTHAL, I. M. *et al.*: Congenital non-hemolytic jaundice with disease of the central nervous system. Pediatrics, **18**:378, 1956.
SUGAR, P.: Familial nonhemolytic jaundice with kernicterus. Arch. of Intern. Med., **108**:121, 1961.

DISORDERS OF RENAL FUNCTION

The Cerebral Symptoms of Renal Disease and Various Neurological Conditions Associated with Nephropathies

Etiology.—The kidneys may be damaged by a number of causes. Bacterial toxins and poisons of other types cause nephritis. Invasion of the kidneys by pyogenic organisms gives rise to pyelonephritis. Obstruction of the

urinary passages leads to hydronephrosis and eventually to renal failure. Vascular disease may also cause uremia. Heredofamilial types of nephritis are described.

Pathological Anatomy.—It seems unnecessary to discuss the various lesions found in the kidneys since we are concerned primarily with the nervous system. The lesions in the brain will be mentioned below.

Clinical Features.—Several clinical syndromes may result, directly or indirectly, from renal damage. One of the most interesting is the so-called *hypertensive encephalopathy* associated with *acute glomerular nephritis.* The hemolytic streptococcus is usually responsible. Since we are not concerned primarily with the problem of renal failure it is unnecessary to discuss it in detail. Suffice it to say that in acute glomerular nephritis, there is usually a definite history of preceding infection which is followed after a variable interval by edema of the eyelids and ankles, vomiting, headache and often diarrhea. The urine may be reduced in amount and as a rule contains albumin and blood. The excretion of phthalein may be reduced but is often quite normal. In only the very severe cases is there a significant degree of nitrogen retention. The temperature is often slightly elevated and anemia develops as the disease progresses.

In a certain percentage of cases, cerebral symptoms are prominent. There may be headache, vomiting, disturbances of vision, bradycardia, slowing of respiration, generalized or focal convulsions and stupor deepening into coma. The retinae may show papilledema with hemorrhages and patches of exudate. Transient hemiplegia and other focal cerebral syndromes may appear usually following focal convulsions. Vision may be merely reduced or there may be periods of complete amaurosis. The blood pressure is invariably elevated when these symptoms are present and the height of the pressure is said to parallel the severity of the symptoms. The systolic pressure is usually over 150 millimeters of mercury and may reach 250 millimeters. The spinal fluid pressure is also elevated and there may be an excess of globulin in the fluid although there is no change in the cellular content. The cerebral symptoms may occur without any reduction of phthalein excretion and without significant elevation of the nonprotein nitrogen in the blood. It is said to be essential for the diagnosis that there be a sudden and pronounced elevation of the blood pressure above its former level.

A number of authorities, including Blackfan and McAlpine, believe that the cerebral symptoms are not due to direct action of any excretory product upon the nervous system but result from hypertension and vasomotor disorders which so frequently are associated with renal disease. The signs of increased intracranial pressure they attribute to cerebral edema which they believe is due to vasomotor disturbances. The focal convulsions

and transient hemiplegias are regarded as indicative of localized vascular spasms. In the same way the amaurosis may be attributed to spasms of the retinal arteries or perhaps to similar disturbances in the occipital cortex.

McAlpine has pointed out that in some instances in which uremia occurs without hypertension we find only drowsiness passing into coma. The non-protein nitrogen of the blood is always much elevated before symptoms appear and there is even an approximate parallelism between the symptoms and the chemical findings in the blood. There are no signs of increased intracranial pressure and no cerebral palsies.

In the common type of uremia in which there is both hypertension and extreme elevation of the non-protein nitrogen, one may find the features of both of the conditions mentioned above.

In some cases of uremia muscular twitchings are prominent and resemble fasciculations very closely. Outspoken signs of tetany and convulsions are seen which are attributed to retention of phosphorus and alteration of the calcium-phosphorus ratio.

A rare complication is the sudden development of an acute widespread muscular paralysis. Recent investigations have led to the view that this syndrome may be due to either an accumulation of potassium in the blood or a lack of potassium. In the first case it is stated that the T wave in the electrocardiogram is elevated and in the second, it is depressed. The first condition is relieved by the administration of sodium chloride and the second, by potassium salts.

In more chronic types of renal insufficiency, arteriosclerosis is apt to develop and hemorrhages and softenings may occur in the brain. Some of these children fail to grow properly and are described as renal dwarfs. They may show bony changes ascribed to secondary hyperparathyroidism.

Types of familial nephropathy associated with degenerative processes in the nervous system should be mentioned. Lowe's syndrome, q.v. might be classified with these.

Marin and Tyler call attention to a rare hereditary interstitial nephritis which is usually fatal early in life. Nerve deafness is associated and two cases of polyneuritis have been noted.

Senior *et al.* describe a familial disease of children in which progressive renal failure is associated with loss of vision due to retinal degeneration.

Schafer *et al.* describe a familial disease manifest by nephropathy and nerve deafness. Convulsions and mental deficiency are present in some cases. A defect in amino acid metabolism is associated. The concentration of L proline in the plasma is increased and there may be excretion of proline, hydroxyproline and glycine in the urine. Selkoe reports a case of hyperprolinemia in which there was no renal damage.

McCance *et al.* describe a syndrome including mental deficiency, corneal

opacities, nystagmus, intention tremor, convulsions and renal failure ending in uremia. At post-mortem examination of one patient, no testicles were found. There were lesions in the cerebrum and cerebellum.

Herrmann *et al.* describe a family in which diabetes, nephropathy, deafness and progressive cerebral degeneration with cerebellar ataxia, focal seizures, hemiparesis and aphasia occurred. Myoclonus could be provoked by photic stimulation.

Rahman *et al.* describe a remarkable condition termed angiokeratoma corporis diffusum universale or hereditary dystopic lipidosis. This affects both males and females. A critical phase is described in childhood manifest by fever, pains and paresthesias in the hands and feet, protein and blood in the urine, abdominal pain and macular and papular lesions in the skin which prove to be small angiomas. The retinal and conjunctival veins are tortuous and there are corneal opacities. During this phase, the symptoms occur in acute crises.

The second phase is termed the quiescent phase. There is protein in the urine, renal function deteriorates, anhidrosis develops. The cutaneous lesions increase. The cutaneous lesions occur only in males.

The third phase is termed the accelerated phase. The kidneys become shrunken and the heart enlarges. Hypertension develops. Renal failure occurs and terminates in uremic coma. A sudanophil lipid is found in the heart muscle, blood vessels and the sympathetic neurons.

Gorlin and Sedano state that ceramide dihexoside and ceramide trihexoside are found in the tissues.

Cannon *et al.* state that Bartter's syndrome occurs most often in children between the ages of 3 months and 4 years. There is failure to grow, muscular weakness, salt craving, polyuria, polydipsia, dwarfism and mental deficiency. It is characterized by hypokalemic alkalosis, hyperaldosteronism, normal blood pressure, absence of edema and usually low blood sodium and chloride. Study of the kidneys reveals immature glomeruli and evidences of glomerulonephritis. More than one case may occur in a family.

Diagnosis.—The diagnosis depends upon the demonstration of renal damage and upon the presence of hypertension and of the cerebral symptoms mentioned above.

Prognosis.—The mortality depends upon the severity of the nephritis and averages between 10 and 30 per cent. If the patient survives, complete recovery may be expected, for the cerebral symptoms leave no residuum as a rule. The possibility of recurrences following subsequent infections must be kept in mind, however.

Treatment.—Complete rest in bed is important and infections should be treated with proper judgment. Special diets seem to have little value. The cerebral symptoms of acute glomerular nephritis, Blackfan claims, may be

relieved by the administration of magnesium sulphate. This drug may be given by mouth in large doses, as much as 30 to 60 cc of a 50 per cent solution of the crystalline salt being required every four hours in some cases. Diarrhea does not result, at first, but there is general dehydration, reduction of blood pressure and coincident improvement in the cerebral manifestations. The medication should be continued until the blood pressure is normal.

Hemodialysis and peritoneal dialysis have been employed recently and have prolonged many patients' lives. These methods are especially valuable when the renal function is expected to be regained.

Tyler states that hemodialysis and peritoneal dialysis may cause convulsions, encephalopathy and psychotic states as a result of rapid decrease in blood urea causing edema of the brain. In the same way rapid correction of the blood pH may accentuate the difference between the blood and spinal fluid pH because of the rapid movement of carbon dioxide and the slow movement of bicarbonate across membranes. Prolonged dialysis may cause polyneuritis probably due to removal of water soluable vitamins.

Rejection of a transplanted kidney may increase hypertension causing hypertensive encephalopathy. Treatment to suppress immunologic reaction to the transplant may depress the hematopoietic system and cause intracerebral hemorrhage. Necrosis of the transplant may cause toxic psychosis. If the transplant functions well, shifts in the electrolytes may induce seizures.

Friedman states that hemodialysis leads to anemia. The skin is pigmented by the deposit of urochrome. Patients develop arthritis, peptic ulcer, peripheral neuropathy and secondary hyperparathyroidism. Blood transfusions may cause hepatitis.

Lopez and Collins report the case of a girl of 12 years who had dialysis for renal failure. At post-mortem examination she had Wernicke's disease and central pontine myelinolysis.

Freeman *et al.* show that gynecomastia may result from hemodialysis.

BIBLIOGRAPHY

ALPORT, A. C.: Hereditary congenital hemorrhagic nephritis. Brit. Med. J., i:504, 1927.

ASBURY, A. K. *et al.*: Renal defect and polyneuropathy. Arch. Neurol., 8:413, 1963.

BAUM, F. C. JR. AND BAYER, J. F.: Familial nephrosis associated with deafness and congenital urinary tract anomalies in siblings. Jour. Pediat., 66:33, 1962.

BLACKFAN, K. D. AND McKHANN, G. F.: Acute glomerular nephritis in children: Treatment of the cerebral manifestations. J.A.M.A., 97:1052, 1931.

BROWN, M. R., CURRENS, J. H. AND MARCHAND, J. F.: Muscular paralysis and electrocardiographic abnormalities resulting from potassium loss in chronic nephritis. J.A.M.A., 124:545, 1944.

CANNON, P. J. *et al.*: Juxtaglomerular cells, hyperplasia and secondary hyperaldosteronism: Bartter's Syndrome. Medicine, 47:107, 1968.

FINCH, C. A., SAWYER, C. G. AND FLYNN, J. N.: The clinical syndrome of potassium intoxication. Am. J. Med., 1:337, 1946.

FREEMAN, R. M. *et al.*: Gynecomastia, an endocrinological complication of hemodialysis. Ann. Int. Med., **69**:67, 1968.

FRIEDMAN, E. A.: Dialysis therapy on a medical service. Minn. Med., **48**:1615, 1965.

GORLIN, R. J. AND SEDANO, H.: Angiokeratoma corporis diffusum. Modern Med., **37**:196, No. 7, 1969.

GUILD, H.: The prognosis of acute glomerular nephritis in childhood. Bull. Johns Hopkins Hosp., **48**:193, 1931.

HERRMANN, C. *et al.*: Hereditary photomyoclonus associated with diabetes, deafness, nephropathy, and cerebral dysfunction. Neurology, **14**:212, 1964.

LOPEZ, R. I. AND COLLINS, G. H.: Wernicke's encephalopathy. Neurology, **18**:248, 1968.

MADONICK, M. J. *et al.*: Pleocytosis and meningeal signs in uremia. Arch. Neurol. & Psychiat., **64**:431, 1950.

MARIN, O. S. M. AND TYLER, R.: Hereditary interstitial nephritis associated with polyneuropathy. Neurology, **11**:999, 1961.

MCALPINE, D.: The hypertensive cerebral attack. Brit. Med. J., **2**:990, 1935.

MCCANCE, R. A. *et al.*: The cerebro-ocular-renal dystrophies. Arch. Dis. Childhood, **35**:240, 1960.

MULROW, P. J. *et al.*: Hereditary nephritis. Report of a kindred. Amer. Jour. Med., **35**:737, 1963.

OPPENHEIMER, B. S. AND FISHBERG, A. M.: Hypertensive encephalopathy. Arch. Int. Med., **41**:264, 1928.

RAHMAN, A. N.: Ocular manifestations of hereditary dystopic lipidosis. Arch. Ophth., **69**:708, 1963.

———— *et al.*: Angiokeratoma corporis diffusum universale. Tr. A. Am. Physicians, **74**:366, 1961.

SCHAFER, I. *et al.*: Familial hyperprolinemia. New England J. Med., **267**:51, 1962.

SELKOE, D. J.: Familial hyperprolinemia with mental retardation. Neurology, **19**:494, 1969.

SENIOR, B. *et al.*: Familial oculorenal dystrophy. Am. J. Ophth., **52**:625, 1961.

TYLER, R. H.: Neurological complications of dialysis, transplantation and other forms of treatment of chronic uremia. Neurology, **15**:1081, 1965.

TYLER, H. R.: Neurological disorders in renal failure. Amer. Jour. Med., **44**:734, 1968.

WALSH, F. B.: *Loc. cit.*

WISE, O. *et al.*: Angiokeratoma diffusum. Quart. Jour. Med., **31**:177, 1962.

DISORDERS OF THE THYROID GLAND

Cretinism and Myxedema

Definition.—Cretinism is a state of defective development due to congenital deficiency of the secretion of the thyroid gland. It is found in endemic form in restricted regions and in sporadic form all over the world. The term myxedema is applied to acquired states of thyroid deficiency.

The thyroid hormones which are concerned with the well known functions of the thyroid gland are termed thyroxine and triiodothyronine. Munson has published a study of a substance termed thyocalcitonin which reduces the serum calcium and seems to be an antagonist of the parathyroid hormone. It is derived from the parafollicular cells.

Etiology.—The endemic cretinism is prevalent in certain mountainous regions such as the Alps, the Carpathians, the Pyrenees and the Himalayas, where goiter is very prevalent. It was also common at one time in the states bordering on the Great Lakes in this country. It is believed that endemic cretinism is due to lack of iodine in the soil. In Michigan, the incidence of goiter in school children, which was once 47 per cent, has fallen to 1.4 per

cent since iodized salt has been used. Hsia describes three types of familial cretinism each due to a different enzymatic defect in hormone synthesis. Acquired thyroid deficiency may also develop without apparent cause or may follow a severe illness. Very rarely acute thyroiditis may result in thyroid deficiency. The administration of excessive doses of antithyroid drugs, such as propylthiouracil, to the mother may cause thyroid deficiency and goiter in the baby. Greenman *et al.* state that the babies of mothers with thyroid deficiency should be observed very carefully for mental deficiency and congenital malformations are common. Operative removal of the gland is an obvious cause of thyroid deficiency. Secondary hypothyroidism occurs in pituitary deficiency.

Blizzard *et al.* state that circulating antithyroid antibodies were found in the scra of eleven of sixty-seven mothers of cretins. Only two mothers had known thyroid disease. Not all babies of mothers who have such antibodies are cretins, for some are normal.

Martin and Rento report cases in which babies of mothers who have taken excessive amounts of iodides during pregnancy may be born with goiters and may have the appearance of cretins.

Winter *et al.* state that chronic lymphocytic thyroiditis is a cause of juvenile thyroid deficiency.

Pathological Anatomy.—In sporadic cretinism the gland is either absent or is represented merely by a few small cyst-like structures suggesting a congenital failure of development. A colloid goiter is usually found in endemic cretinism.

The brain may be small or of normal size. There is no constant defect in the pattern of the convolutions. Histological examination, however, reveals some reduction of cells in the cortex and degenerative changes in the remaining ones. Some cells are small and atrophic and others are swollen and are undergoing chromatolysis. Marinesco claims that the reduction of cells is most evident in the fifth layer where the large pyramidal cells are found. He has also found iron deposits in the muscularis of the cerebral vessels and incrustations of a calcium-like material upon nerve cells. It is believed that the thyroid secretion is necessary for the complete development of the nervous system. In experiments on rats deprived of the thyroid gland, a reduction of the development of the dendrites and axons of the cerebral nerve cells may be demonstrated.

In myxedema, there are, of course, no developmental defects of the nervous system, but the neurons may be swollen or shrunken and show chromatolysis.

Price and Netsky describe granular bodies containing glycogen in the areas of focal degeneration in the cerebellar cortex, the posterior columns

and the dorsal root zone of the spinal cord. They measure between 10 and 50 μ. They term them myxedema bodies.

Dobson and Abrle state that changes in the sweat glands are almost always present in hypothyroidism. They find granular material in the large pale cells of the eccrine glands. The granules are no more than a few microns in diameter, globular in shape and surround small vacuoles.

Nickel *et al.* studied biopsy specimens of muscle and nerve of twenty-five patients suffering from myxedema. The nerves showed mucinoid deposits in the endoneurium and perineurium and mild degenerative changes in the myelin sheaths and axis cylinders. The muscles showed mucinoid deposits in the endomysium and perimysium, with some loss of cross striations of the muscle fibers, sarcoplasmic degeneration and increase of the nuclei.

Clinical Features.—The symptoms are not present at birth, for it is believed that the mother's thyroid gland protects the child for a brief period. It is only when a cretin is born of a woman with thyroid deficiency that the condition is recognizable in the first few weeks of life. It is stated, however, that physiological jaundice may last much longer than usual and may persist for 3 months. As a rule, it is noted between the sixth and twelfth month that the child is not growing properly and is showing no evidence of mental development. In severe cases, the diagnosis may be made by the end of the third or fourth month. The face is very typical. The lips are thick, the cheeks baggy, the eyelids thickened, the forehead wrinkled, the mouth usually opened and the thickened tongue protruding. The mucous membranes are often pale. The forehead is low and the base of the nose broadened. The fontanels may not close until the eighth year. Hair is coarse, scanty and dry. The body is small and in fully developed cases the child is always a dwarf. The abdomen protrudes and an umbilical hernia is common. Fatty pads are seen in the supraclavicular fossae, in the axillae and between the scapulae. The skin is thickened, dry and often scaly. Body temperature is below the normal and may not rise in response to infections as in normal children. The extremities are cold and often cyanotic. Pulse is slow. The heart is often enlarged. The heart sounds are feeble. The electrocardiogram shows reduced voltage of the QRS and T waves. Roentgenological studies reveal that the development of the centers of ossification is delayed and that the epiphyses of the long bones may fail to unite with the shafts for many years. The carpal and tarsal bones may not appear until the tenth year, although they should be present in normal infants of six months. Sexual development may be delayed and imperfect. Anemia is characteristic.

Numerous signs of defective development of the nervous system are evident. Intelligence is always definitely defective and unless proper treatment

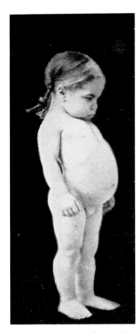

FIG. 175. Cretin. (By the courtesy of Dr. Holt.)

is instituted, the child will be an imbecile or an idiot. The behavior of cretins is quite different from that of the common restless, irritable idiots, for they are quiet, sluggish and frequently good-natured and contented. A large part of the day is spent in sleep. In general, their mental condition is that of normal children of half their age. If untreated, many of them never learn to talk or say at most a few childish words. Walking, standing and, indeed, all reactions are delayed. Their movements are very slow. The knee jerks may be elicited with difficulty and the movement of the leg is slow and of small amplitude. Convulsions do not occur. The spinal fluid is normal but for an excess of protein.

McGarrison, Naville and others have described congenital diplegia in cretins which is believed to be due to thyroid deficiency during intrauterine life. This is apparently most likely to be found in cretins whose mothers also suffer from hypothyroidism. Naville studied 1700 children between the ages of 5 and 8 years in the public schools of Geneva. In this group he found only 4 cases of congenital diplegia which could be attributed to the thyroid deficiency with probability, although there were 80 cases of diplegia not based on thyroid disease. There were, in addition, 12 cases of defective cerebral development other than diplegia which were probably due to thyroid deficiency.

Occasionally cases are seen in which symptoms of thyroid deficiency do not appear until the child is several years old. The child may have grown normally and may have seemed to develop mentally at the usual rate up to a certain point. Then growth becomes retarded and the mental condition remains unchanged or may even regress. The clinical manifestations are, of course, dependent largely upon the age at which the disease develops. The cause of infantile myxedema is not clear as a rule. The electroencephalogram is said to show generalized low voltage activity with predominantly slow alpha waves.

Jellinek and Kelly state that unsteady gait, nystagmus, ataxia of the extremities and slurred speech may occur in myxedema as well as deafness and peripheral neuropathy even when the signs of thyroid deficiency are not obvious.

Cremer, G. M., *et al.* describe ataxia of cerebellar origin in myxedema.

Nickel *et al.* found weakness of the proximal muscles of the extremities

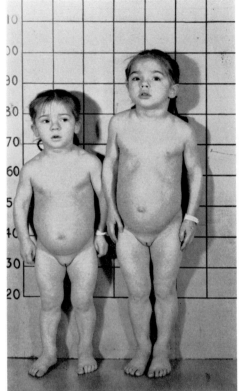

FIG. 176. Two sisters 5 and 8 years old who are cretins with mental deficiency, defective growth, large, firm muscles and brisk tendon reflexes. Debre Semelaigne syndrome. (By the courtesy of Dr. Victor McKusick.)

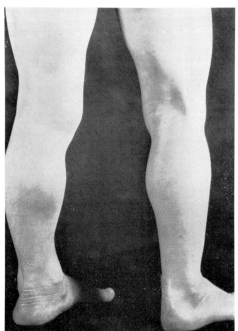

FIG. 177. Photograph of legs of 8 year old cretin showing large firm muscles.

which they attributed to myopathy and paresthesias and pains in the distal part of the extremities which were sometimes associated with some reduction of sensibility and were attributed to neuropathy.

Angel and Sash described myxedematous coma which is associated with reduced body temperature and sometimes slowing of respiration. They advise immediate treatment with a rapidly acting thyroid hormone such as triiodothyronine, warming the body and artificial ventilation. Antibiotics are given to prevent pneumonia.

Holvey *et al.* advise the immediate intravenous injection of sodium L-thyroxin. They state that the external warming of the patient should be avoided for it promotes vascular collapse.

In some cases of thyroid deficiency, the muscles are enlarged and abnormally firm. Muscle cramps are common. Muscular contractions are slow. Weakness and easy fatigue are characteristic. There is no myotonia. This is sometimes termed the *Debré Semelaigne syndrome.* Hypertrophia musculorum vera q.v. and De Lange's syndrome must be distinguished. In another syndrome, often called the *Hoffmann syndrome,* we find the symptoms mentioned above, though enlargement of the muscles is not always present, and in addition myotonic phenomena. Myotonic grasp, myotonia on percussion and myotonic electrical reactions are seen. The myotonia may be very severe. Myotonia congenita must be distinguished. All observers seem to agree that all of these muscular disorders are promptly relieved by the administration of thyroid extract in adequate dosage.

Van Geldern describes precocious puberty in hypothyroidism. He suggests that hypothyroidism may cause increased hypophyseal production of gonadotropic hormones as well as thyrotropic hormone.

Diagnosis.—The diagnosis depends upon the delay in growth, the mental retardation, the characteristic face, protuberant abdomen, the fatty swellings over the clavicles, the dry skin, scanty hair, low body temperature, the delay in ossification and the striking response to thyroid medication which usually is conclusive. There are obvious difficulties in the way of determination of the basal metabolism in infants, so that this test is not employed in infancy. The determination of the blood cholesterol is more useful. Before treatment it is usually between 250 and 350 mgs per 100 cc. Treatment reduces the cholesterol level promptly. If medication is withdrawn, the cholesterol level rises rapidly to between 300 and 600 mgs per 100 cc. It is claimed that the determination of the protein bound iodine is the most accurate test of thyroid function for the iodine content is always low in thyroid deficiency.

Radioactive iodine is now used to study the thyroid gland. A standard dose is given by mouth and the amount taken up by the gland is determined by the Geiger counter. Apparently patients whose gland is small or

absent take up little iodine but in goitrous cretins the gland is said to take up iodine more avidly than the normal gland. Cook and Man stress the importance of making the diagnosis at the earliest possible time. They find the determination of the butanol-extractable iodine very helpful. They point out the necessity of treating the mother during pregnancy should any suspicion of thyroid deficiency arise. The roentgenograms of the bones not only show delayed ossification, but as Wilkins has pointed out certain characteristic peculiarities. He describes multiple, irregular islets of ossification scattered over a large area. These islets enlarge and coalesce to form irregular porous or fluffy masses. The condition most apt to cause confusion with cretinism is mongolian idiocy. The latter may be recognized by the peculiar formation of the eyes and hands and striking reduction of muscle tone. Secondary hypothyroidism is described and is attributed to lack of the thyrotropic hormone of the pituitary gland. This condition may be recognized, it is stated, by the fact that there is a rise in the protein bound iodine following the administration of the thyrotropic hormone. This rise does not occur in primary hypothyroidism.

Prognosis.—There is no evidence of spontaneous improvement in cretinism and even if the patient lives to reach adult life, the mind and body will remain dwarfed. The administration of dry, powdered thyroid gland, by mouth, exerts a prompt and powerful effect but this, unfortunately, falls short of cure. However, if treatment is begun in the first year of life, these children may seem to develop normally. It is only when they are compared with other children of the same age that it is apparent that they are below par in their stature and mental attainments. Smith, D. W., *et al.* state that the response to treatment depends upon the age of the child when treatment is begun, the severity of the deficiency, and the adequacy of treatment. In some cases irreparable damage is done to the brain in utero.

Treatment.—Cretins are relatively sensitive to thyroid substance and will show diarrhea, irritability and profuse sweating as well as tachycardia if the dosage is too large. In infants, half a grain may be given each day to begin with and this increased or diminished as seems best. The highest dosage which is well tolerated is advised.

Hamburger states that the disappearance of overt signs of thyroid deficiency does not indicate that therapy is adequate and treatment must be controlled by tests of the protein-bound iodine or the butanol extractable iodine. In some cases in which mentality is seriously impaired and the prognosis is bad, treatment causes such irritability that it cannot be continued.

Myxedema coma should be treated by the administration of l-triiodothyronine preferably by intravenous drip. Tracheostomy and artificial ventilation may be necessary. Cortisol must be given and antibiotics as well. Body temperature is low, but some authorities warn against warming.

CASE HISTORIES (No. 1188730 and 1188731).—*Debre Semelaigne syndrome in two sisters who are cretins.*

Dora M. and Freda M. were seen on February 12, 1966 by the courtesy of Dr. Victor McKusick. Dora was 8 years old and Freda was 5 years old. When the children were a few months old, it was evident that they were not developing properly. They were treated for thyroid deficiency but the treatment was evidently inadequate for they did not improve.

On examination the children were dwarfs. The girl of 5 years was no larger than a normal child of 15 months and the child of 8 years was the size of a normal child of 3 years. There was pronounced mental defect. The older girl seemed to understand a few simple words. The younger girl did not show evidence of understanding what was said to her. Neither child talked. They were quiet and placid.

The skin was dry, scaly and cold. Hair was dry and scanty. Pads of fat were seen above the clavicles. The forehead was low and the lips thick. The abdomen protruded. The uptake of radioactive iodine was greatly reduced. No thyroid gland could be palpated.

The children both showed striking enlargement of the muscles which were also too firm and of rubbery consistency. All movements were slow. The gait was similar to that of an infant. It was noted that the children did not lift their toes enough when they walked probably because they could not do so in time. No myotonia could be elicited. The tendon reflexes were active. There was no Babinski sign and no ankle clonus.

BIBLIOGRAPHY

ANGEL, J. H. AND SASH, L.: Hypothermic coma in myxedema. Brit. Med. J., **5189**:1855, 1960.

ASTROM, K. E. *et al.:* Hypothyroid myopathy. Arch. of Neurol., **5**:472, 1961.

BIJVOET, O. L. M. *et al.:* Effects of calcitonin on patients with Paget's disease, thyrotoxicosis or hypercalcemia. Lancet, **i**:876, 1968.

BOWERS, C. Y. *et al.:* The myxedema reflex in infants and children with hypothyroidism. J. Pediat., **54**:46, 1959.

BLIZZARD, R. M. *et al.:* Maternal autoimmunization to thyroid. New England J. Med., **263**:327, 1960.

———— *et al.:* Maternal autoimmunization to thyroid as probable cause of antithyrotic cretinism. New England J. Med., **263**:327, 1960.

COOKE, R. E. AND MAN, E. B.: Management of hypothyroidism in infancy and childhood. Pediatrics, **17**:617, 1956.

CREMER, G. M. *et al.:* Myxedema and ataxia. Neurology, **19**:37, 1969.

CREVASSE, L. E. AND LOGUE, R. B.: Peripheral neuropathy in myxedema. Ann. Int. Med., **50**:1433, 1959.

CUMINGS, D. E.: Myxedema with Erbs limb girdle muscular dystrophy. Arch. of Int. Med., **109**:724, 1962.

DEBRÉ, R. AND SEMELAIGNE, G.. Syndrome of diffuse muscular hypertrophy in infants causing an athletic appearance. Its connection with congenital myxedema. Am. J. Dis. Child., **50**:1351, 1935.

DOBSON, R. L. AND ABRLE, D. C.: Changes in sweat glands in hypothyroidism. Jour. Investigative Dermatology, **37**:457, 1961.

GELDERN, VAN H. H.: Precocious puberty in hypothyroidism. Arch. Dis. Childhood, **37**:337, 1962.

GRABOW, J. D. AND CHOU, S. M.: Thyrotropin hormone deficiency. Arch. of Neurol., **19**:284, 1968.

GREENMAN, W.: Abnormal babies of hypothyroid mothers. New England J. Med., **267**:426, 1962.

HAMBURGER, R. N.: The regulation of thyroid dosage in a cretin. Connecticut Med., **26**:96, 1962.

HOLVEY, D. N. et al.: Thyroxin therapy for myxedema coma. Arch. Int. Med., 113:89, 1964.

HSIA, D. Y.: Inborn Errors of Metabolism. Chicago, Year Book Publishers, 1960.

JARCHO, L. W. AND RYLER, F. H.: Myxedema, pseudomyotonia and myotonia congenita. Arch. Int. Med., **102**:357, 1958.

JELLINEK, E. H.: Fits, faints, coma and dementia in myxedema. Lancet, 2:1010, 1962.

———— AND KELLY, R. E.: Cerebellar syndrome of myxedema. Lancet, **2**:225, 1960.

KERLEY, C. Q.: Cretinism. Arch. Pediat., **43**:94, 1926.

MANN, E. B., CULOTTA, C. S., SIEGFRIED, D. A. AND STILSON, C.: Serum precipitable iodines in recognition of cretinism. J. Pediat., **31**:154, 1947.

MARINESCO, C.: Lesions in Cong. Myxedema with Idiocy. L'Encéphale, **19**:265, 1924.

MARTIN, M. M. AND RENTO, R. D.: Exogenous iodide goiter in infants. J. Pediat., **61**:94, 1962.

McGARRISON, R.: The Thyroid Gland in Health and Disease. Baltimore, Wm. Wood & Co., p. 141, 1917.

MUNSON, P. L.: Thyocalcitonin: Experimental and clinical aspects. Triangle, **8**:89, 1967.

———— AND HIRSCH, P. F.: Discovery and pharmacologic evaluation of thyrocalcitonin. Amer. Jour. Med., **43**:678, 1967.

NAVILLE, F.: Congenital diplegia and thyroid disturbances in abnormal infants of Geneva. Schweiz. Arch. f. Neurol. u. Psychiat., **13**:559, 1923.

NICKEL, S. N. et al.: Myxedema neuropathy and myopathy. Neurology, **11**:125, 1961.

NICKERSO, J. F. et al.: Fatal myxedema with and without coma. Ann. Int. Med., **53**:475, 1960.

NIELSEN, P. E. AND RANLOV, P.: Management of myxedema coma. Acta Endocrinol., **45**: 353, 1964.

NORDQUIST, P. et al.: Myxedema coma and CO_2 narcosis. Acta Med. Scandinav., **166**:195, 1960.

NORRIS, F. H. AND PANNER, B. J.: Hypothyroid myopathy. Arch. Neurol., **14**:574, 1966.

PECHET, M. M. et al.: Regulation of bone resorption and formation. Amer. Jour. Med., **43**:696, 1967.

PONCHER, H. G.: Myotonia congenita and thyroid disease. Am. J. Dis. Child., **52**:1065, 1936.

PRICE, T. R. AND NETSKY, M. G.: Myxedema and ataxia. Neurology, **16**:957, 1966.

SANDERS, V.: Neurologic manifestations of myxedema. New England Jour. Med., **266**:547, 1962.

SMITH, DAVID W., BLIZZARD, ROBERT M. AND WILKINS, LAWSON: The mental prognosis in hypothyroidism of infancy and childhood. Pediatrics, **19**:1011-1021, 1957.

SMITH, R. N. AND LALJEE, H. C. K.: Thyrocalcitonin deficiency after treatment of thyroid disorders. Brit. Med. Jour., 4:589, 1967.

THOMASEN, E.: Myotonia. Thomasen's Disease. Paramyotonia and Dystrophia Myotonica. Copenhagen Univ., 1948.

THOMPSON, W. O., SILVENS, E. AND DAILEY, M. E.: Cerebrospinal fluid in myxedema. Arch. Int. Med., **44**:368, 1929.

WALSH, F. B.: *Loc. cit.*

WAYNE, E. J.: Hypothyroidism and the nervous system. J.A.M.A., **172**:1420, 1960.

WILKINS, L.: The rates of growth, osseous development and metabolic development in cretins as a guide to thyroid therapy. J. Pediat., **12**:429, 1938.

———— AND FLEISCHMANN, W.: The diagnosis of hypothyroidism in childhood. J.A.M.A., **116**:2459, 1941.

WINTER, J. et al.: The relationship of juvenile hypothyroidism to chronic lymphocytic thyroiditis. Jour. Pediat., **69**:709, 1966.

ZUCKERMAN, SIR S.: Hormones. Scientific American, **196**:76, 1957.

HYPERTHYROIDISM

Definition.—A syndrome described below associated with hyperplastic changes in the thyroid gland and attributed to excessive secretion of the thyroid hormone. There is some evidence that excessive secretion of thy-

rotropic hormone may be responsible for some cases of hyperthyroidism and possibly for exophthalmos without hyperthyroidism.

Etiology.—The cause is not clear. In a few cases, the symptoms have followed acute infections such as scarlet fever or pertussis but this is not a constant or even a frequent association. There seems to be a definite constitutional factor, for several members of the same family are not infrequently affected.

Pathological Anatomy.—In Graves' disease, the gland is large, firm and very vascular. Microscopic examination reveals that the acini are small, the epithelial cells are columnar and colloid is scanty. Toxic adenoma of the thyroid gland is rare in children though carcinoma is not uncommon. It is claimed that the brain may show edema and other changes suggestive of an intense intoxication. The muscles, however, are said to show lymphocytic infiltrations and it is claimed that there is swelling of the extraocular muscles associated with edema of the orbital tissues in some cases characterized by exophthalmos. Later the muscles may show fibrosis.

Clinical Features.—Most authors state that hyperthyroidism is very rare in children under fifteen years and exceptionally rare under the age of five years. It is said that it never occurs in boys before the age of ten years. In some parts of the country, however, this disease cannot be very rare, for Dinsmore reports 48 cases from Cleveland with the comment that in his experience hyperthyroidism is much more common in children than one would realize from the literature. It is uncommon but scarcely rare in Balti-

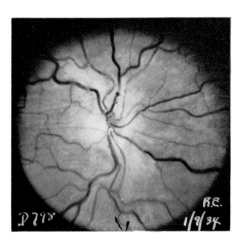

Fig. 178. Photograph of the retina showing papilledema in the case of exophthalmos in hyperthyroidism. (By the courtesy of Dr. Walsh.)

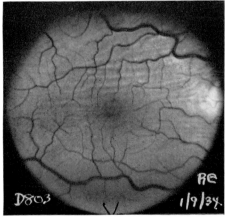

Fig. 179. Photograph of the same retina shown on left. There is edema and folding of the retina and great congestion of the retinal veins. Complete recovery followed decompression of the orbit. (By the courtesy of Dr. Walsh.)

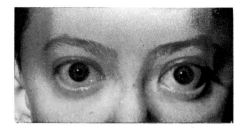

Fig. 180. Exophthalmos in hyperthyroidism.

more. We have seen a case in which the condition was congenital. The mother was suffering from thyroid deficiency. Javett *et al.* state that the infant of a woman suffering from thyrotoxicosis may be normal or may suffer from thyroid deficiency or hyperthyroidism. Goiter and exophthalmos are mentioned. If antithyroid medication is given during pregnancy, the baby will usually be normal.

The symptoms are not unlike those in adult life. There is restlessness, irritability, emotional instability, and enlargement of the gland. Loss of weight is not always present. There are often mild cardiac symptoms such as tachycardia, palpitation on exertion and rarely definite enlargement of the heart. The blood pressure, especially the systolic pressure, may be elevated.

Digestive disturbances such as diarrhea and, less commonly, vomiting are described. In many cases there is a striking tendency to precocious physical development so a child of 12 years may present the appearance of an average child of 16 or 18 years. Pigmentation is found in the periorbital region and in the creases of the palms. Neurological symptoms are also seen although most authors believe them to be less common than in adults. Exophthalmos is present to some degree in most well-developed cases. The hands are moist and sweating and flushing of the face are often noticeable. The hot hand is a helpful sign. The sign of von Graefe is often present. The tremor so characteristic of hyperthyroidism in adults is present only in a relatively small percentage of cases. Frequently, one sees movements of large amplitude which are very similar to those of chorea and which may be associated with a certain degree of incoordination. These occur so frequently that it seems improbable that they are the result of complicating Sydenham's chorea. Since they disappear after operation, it is probable that these movements are in some way a result of the altered thyroid activity. The musculature is not wasted except so far as the general undernutrition may be to blame, but there is often an appreciable degree of reduction of muscle tone as well as weakness and abnormal fatigue. The last may be so striking as to suggest the possibility of myasthenia gravis. Drooping of the jaw due to muscle weakness is seen.

Palsies of the extraocular muscles which are not unusual in adults are

rare in childhood. Such palsies may be due to inelasticity of muscles and are not always due to weakness of muscles. Retraction of the bulbs may result. Papilledema is sometimes associated with severe exophthalmos and central scotomas are sometimes found with changes in the optic nerve head suggestive of retrobulbar neuritis. The blood cholesterol is low being sometimes no more than 100 mgs per 100 cc. In general the disease is milder in children than in adults and in most cases can be controlled by conservative measures. This is especially true of the type which appears in girls just before puberty. Skanse and Nyman claim that thyrotoxicosis may increase the frequency of convulsive attacks in epilepsy and produce electroencephalographic abnormalities and major seizures in patients who do not have epilepsy or organic disease of the nervous system.

Connor describes thyroid crises in childhood. There is restlessness and agitation, low grade fever, rapid breathing, exophthalmos, enlargement of the thyroid gland and a wide pulse pressure. Treatment includes oxygen, cooling, sedation, chlorpromazine and an antithyroid drug must be given at once.

In adults it is believed that an acute form of muscular weakness occurs which involves the extraocular muscles and the skeletal muscles as well and simulates myasthenia gravis very closely. True myasthenia gravis, if one may make a diagnosis on the basis of the prostigmine test, may occur as a rather rare complication of thyrotoxicosis. A rare chronic or subacute form is described in which there is striking wasting of the muscles and active muscular twitchings which simulates amyotrophic lateral sclerosis or progressive muscular atrophy. Linder describes two cases in which hyperthyroidism was associated with attacks of periodic paralysis and diminished serum potassium. Thyroidectomy gave relief of all symptoms. Such pictures do not seem to occur in children.

Hed *et al.* studied seventeen patients suffering from thyrotoxic myopathy. They found that in the electromyogram all had diphasic potentials of 1 to 4 milliseconds duration and polyphasic potentials of 3 to 6 milliseconds. The amplitude varied between 100 microvolts and 3 millivolts. (They took these findings to indicate myopathy.) There were no fibrillations except in two cases in which there was reason to suspect peripheral neuritis.

Satoyoshi *et al.* describe a type of hyperthyroidism associated with periodic paralysis and low serum potassium. It is stated that effective treatment of the thyroid disease prevented the paralytic attacks. He also claimed that the administration of thiamine to these patients reduced the frequency of the paralytic attacks.

Diagnosis.—The diagnosis is not difficult when the clinical features are fully developed. The restlessness, emotional instability, loss of weight, tachycardia, exophthalmos, enlargement, vascularity and firmness of the

gland and, perhaps, reduction of the blood cholesterol level are the most important diagnostic criteria. The protein bound iodine in the blood is said to be increased. The uptake of radioactive iodine by the thyroid gland is also increased. The administration of 3,5,3-triiodothyronine is said to make it possible to discover latent cases of thyrotoxicosis for this drug suppresses the I^{131} uptake in patients with normal glands but not in those with thyrotoxicosis.

Prognosis.—The course is favorable as a rule and the mortality is low being well below 10 per cent in reported cases. Often the disease runs a very short course and the symptoms may disappear after a few weeks' treatment.

Treatment.—The child should be put to bed and placed at complete rest until the symptoms are greatly diminished or disappear. Iodine and propylthiouracil are employed. Some authorities rely upon such medical treatment. Others employ them merely in preparation for operation. The administration of radioactive iodine has been advised but seems to be difficult to control.

Hayles and Chaves-Carballo state that subtotal thyroidectomy is a more satisfactory treatment for exophthalmic goiter than medication in children.

BIBLIOGRAPHY

BARR, D. P. AND SHORR, E.: Treatment of Graves' disease with thiouracil. Ann. Int. Med., 23:754, 1945.

BRAIN, W. R.: Exophthalmic ophthalmoplegia. Quart. J. Med., 7:293, 1938.

COHEN, S. J. AND KING, F. H.: Relation between myasthenia gravis and exophthalmic goiter. Arch. Neurol. & Psychiat., 28:1338, 1932.

CONNOR, R. C. R.: Management of thyroid crisis. Lancet, ii:74, 1962.

DAY, R. M. AND CARROLL, F. D.: Optic nerve involvement associated with thyroid dysfunction. Arch. of Ophthal., 67:289, 1962.

DIAMOND, I. B.: Changes in the brain from thyrotoxicosis. Arch. Path., 26:297, 1938.

DINSMORE, R. S.: Hyperthyroidism in children. Surg. Gynec. & Obst., 42:172, 1926.

DUDGEON, L. S. AND URQUHART, A. L.: Lymphorrhages in the muscles in exophthalmic goiter. Brain, 49:182, 1926.

DUNLAP, H. F. AND KEPLER, E. J.: Occurrence of periodic paralysis in the course of exophthalmic goiter. Proc. Staff Meet., Mayo Clin., 6:272, 1931.

ENGEL, A. G.: Thyroid function and myasthenia gravis. Arch. of Neurol., 4:663, 1961.

———: Thyroid function and periodic paralysis. Amer. Jour. Med., 30:327, 1961.

HALES, I. B. AND DOBYNS, B. M.: The metabolism of triiodothyronine in Graves' disease. J. Clin. Endocrinol., 20:68, 1960.

HAYLES, A. B. AND CHAVES-CARBALLO, E.: Exophthalmic goiter in children. Mayo Clin. Pro., 40:889, 1965.

HED, R. *et al.*: Thyrotoxic myopathy. J. Neurol. Neurosurg. & Psychiat., 21:270, 1958.

HELMHOLTZ, H. F.: Exophthalmic goiter in childhood. J.A.M.A., 87:157, 1926.

HEUER, G. J.: The cerebral nerve disturbances in exophthalmic goiter. Am. J. Med. Sc., 151:339, 1916.

HUDSON, B. *et al.*: Aids to diagnosis of thyroid disorders. Aust. Ann. Med., 9:19, 1960.

JAVETT, A. N. *et al.*: Neonatal thyrotoxicosis. Pediatrics, 24:65, 1959.

KIRKEBY, K. *et al.*: Pigmentation in thyrotoxicosis. Acta Med. Scandinav., 174:257, 1963.

LAURENT, L. P. E.: Acute thyrotoxic bulbar palsy. Lancet, 1:87, 1944.

LINDER, M. A.: Periodic paralysis associated with hyperthyroidism. Ann. Int. Med., **43**:241, 1955.

LOGOTHETIS, J.: Neurologic and muscular manifestations of hyperthyroidism. Arch. of Neurol., **5**:533, 1961.

————: Acute thyrotoxic encephalomyopathy associated with low serum potassium. Amer. Jour. Med., **32**:631, 1962.

MARTIN, M. M. AND MATUS, R. N.: Neonatal exophthalmos with maternal thyrotoxicosis. Amer. Jour. Dis. Child., **111**:545, 1966.

MCEACHERN, D. AND ROSS, W. D.: Chronic thyrotoxic myopathy. Brain, **65**:181, 1942.

NAFFZIGER, C. H. AND JONES, O. W. JR.: Surgical treatment of progressive exophthalmos following thyroidectomy. J.A.M.A., **99**:638, 1932.

RIENHOFF, W.: Diseases of the Thyroid Gland. Practice of Surgery, Dean Lewis, Hagerstown, Maryland, W. F. Prior Co., 1929.

ROSENBERG, D. *et al.*: Neonatal hyperthyroidism. New England J. Med., **268**:292, 1963.

SATOYOSHI, E. *et al.*: Periodic paralysis in hyperthyroidism. Neurology, **13**:746, 1963.

————: Periodic paralysis. A study of carbohydrate and thiamine metabolism. Neurology, **13**:24, 1963.

————: Myopathy in thyrotoxicosis. Neurology, **13**:645, 1963.

SCHLEZINGER, N. S. AND CORIN, M. S.: Myasthenia gravis associated with hyperthyroidism in childhood. Neurology, **18**:1217, 1968.

SKANSE, B. AND NYMAN, E.: Thyrotoxicosis as a cause of cerebral dysrhythmia and convulsive seizures. Acta Endocrinol., **22**:246, 1956.

STOYOSHI, E. *et al.*: Periodic paralysis in hyperthyroidism. Neurology, **13**:746, 1963.

WALSH, F. B.: *Loc. cit.*

WEDD, A. AND PERMAR, H. H.: Ophthalmoplegia in Graves' disease. Am. J. Med. Sc., **175**:733, 1928.

WEICKHARDT, G. D. AND REDMOND, A. J.: Myasthenia gravis and hyperthyroidism. Ann. Int. Med., **52**:1246, 1960.

WHITE, C.: Foetus with congenital hereditary Graves' disease. J. Obst. & Gynec. Brit. Emp., **21**:231, 1912.

CARCINOMA OF THE THYROID GLAND

Carcinoma of the thyroid gland is not rare in childhood. There are several types. Some metastasize to the cervical lymph nodes and cervical lymphatics early. They also spread to the bones and lungs. Extensive metastases may exist for years without causing great deterioration of health or cachexia. As a rule thyroid function is not altered, but thyroid deficiency and hyperthyroidism are described. Cunliffe *et al.* report a case in a young girl in which the growth produced large quantities of calcitonin.

Early operation is advised which should be followed by irradiation. Radioactive iodine is not satisfactory.

BIBLIOGRAPHY

CUNLIFFE, W. J. *et al.*: A calcitonin secreting thyroid carcinoma. Lancet, **2**:63, 1968.

KENNEDY, R. L. J.: Carcinoma of the thyroid gland in children. Jour. Pediat., **7**:631, 1935.

DISORDERS OF THE PARATHYROID AND DISEASES OF THE BONES

Hypoparathyroidism and Hypocalcemia

Definition.—A condition due to deficient secretion of the parathyroid glands. The disease is characterized by certain disturbances in the metab-

olism of calcium and phosphorus, which may give rise to tetany and to convulsions.

Etiology.—The cause is usually obscure except in the cases in which the glands have been removed accidentally in operations upon the thyroid gland. Apparently the parathyroid glands may be injured by infections and may also be deficient or absent from birth. Familial cases are reported.

Pathological Anatomy.—The blood vessels show hyalinization and often deposits of calcium in their walls. Such changes are most evident in the caudate nucleus and the globus pallidus and in the dentate nucleus of the cerebellum but may be more extensive. Degeneration of the nerve cells is found in regions in which the changes in the blood vessels are most severe and is attributed to ischemia.

Dr. John Wagner once showed me the brain of a patient whose parathyroid glands had been removed fifteen years before, when an operation was performed on the thyroid gland. The brain was sectioned and roentgenograms were made of each section. The structure of the brain was beautifully revealed. The basal ganglia were densely impregnated. The dentate nuclei of the cerebellum were also very dense. The corona radiata was visualized by linear deposits as was the internal capsule. The inner margins of the cortical convolutions were outlined in the same way.

Clinical Features.—This condition may develop at any age in contrast to the infantile tetany which is a disease of infancy. It is, of course, relatively rare, but a number of cases have been discovered in childhood. It is claimed that the babies of mothers suffering from hyperparathyroidism, may show evidences of parathyroid deficiency at birth.

The major symptoms are tetany, convulsive seizures and neurological symptoms. The tetany is manifest by carpopedal spasms, tingling in the extremities, cramps and tremors. The peripheral nerves are too irritable. The signs of latent tetany are evident. Tetany may be induced by fevers, infections, gastrointestinal disturbances and by exertion.

A variety of seizures are described. They may be focal or generalized, and are often associated with loss of consciousness. It must be pointed out that patients do not react uniformly to parathyroid deficiency. Some patients will have no seizures when the calcium phosphorus ratio has reached a level at which other patients would invariably have seizures. Unfortunately, some patient's symptoms persist even when the metabolic disorder is corrected and anticonvulsive medication is not always effective.

These patients have ridged finger nails and defective teeth with lack of enamel. The hair may be lost and the skin rough. Cataracts develop. There is photophobia with blepharospasm. Conjunctivitis, especially phlyctenular conjunctivitis, is common. There may be abdominal pains and vomiting.

Symptoms referable to the nervous system are characteristic. There are changes in personality with irritability, emotional lability, and sometimes, dullness. Mental deterioration occurs. Organic psychoses are described. Chorea, athetosis, dystonia, Parkinsonian syndromes, torticollis and oculogyric crises develop in rare instances. Papilledema with increased intracranial pressure has been reported repeatedly.

Fungus infections, especially monilia, of the finger nails and tongue are common. Addison's disease and pernicious anemia may complicate the picture.

Gorlin and Sedano describe a syndrome which includes Addison's disease, hypothyroidism, hypoparathyroidism, moniliasis, pernicious anemia, juvenile cirrhosis and ovarian failure. Increased intercranial pressure with papilledema, intercranial calcification, convulsions, mental deterioration, muscle twitchings, cramps, tetany, abdominal pain, rigidity, keratoconjunctivitis, photophobia, cataracts and laryngospasm may occur. This is inherited as an autosomal recessive trait.

The bones characteristically show increased density. Deafness occurs and may be due to bony changes in the ears. Calcium deposits in the globus pallidus and caudate, as well as the dentate nucleus, are often found. It should be stated that similar deposits occur in other conditions and are not diagnostic of parathyroid deficiency. The neurological symptoms have no constant relation to such calcium deposits. Extensive calcification of the brain may not be associated with any symptoms and severe symptoms may occur without calcium deposits. The electroencephalogram shows nonspecific changes. The electrocardiogram shows an increase of the Q.T. interval.

The biochemical abnormalities may be summarized as follows: (1) The serum calcium is reduced. (2) The serum phosphorus is increased. (3) Excretion of calcium in the urine is diminished. (4) Excretion of phosphorus in the urine is increased. (5) The serum phosphatase is normal. (6) Parathormone is effective.

Albright has described a condition often termed *pseudohypoparathyroidism*. This is manifest by the same symptoms as true hypoparathyroidism but the parathyroid gland may be normal histologically and the patient does not respond to parathormone. It has been pointed out that these children are often of short stature and have rounded faces with a tendency to obesity. Mental deficiency is common and they sometimes have calcium deposits in the brain and subcutaneous tissues. Cataracts are common. Dentition is defective. A Parkinsonian syndrome develops in some cases. Chromatin-negative gonadal dysgenesis is common. They respond to dihydrotachysterol. Munson states that in two cases of pseudohypoparathyroidism the thyrocalcitonin has been found to be greatly increased.

Jancar describes a condition he terms pseudo-pseudo hypoparathyroidism.

These children are of short stature with obese, stocky bodies, broad or round faces, mental retardation and abnormal electroencephalograms. He points out that when the patient makes a fist the two central metacarpophalangeal joints are depressed. The serum calcium and phosphorus values are normal. Parathyroid hormone is not effective. He reviews fifty-one cases of this condition in the literature and adds a case of his own. Jancar's patient had one large acrocentric chromosome.

We have seen two children, a boy and a girl, who suffered from hypoparathyroidism with tetany, photophobia, moniliasis, diarrhea, Addison's disease, total alopecia, deficiency of the sex glands, diabetes, thyroid deficiency and in one case pernicious anemia. They were found to have antibodies against the adrenal and parathyroid glands and were thought to have autoimmune disease.

Diagnosis.—The diagnosis depends upon the clinical and metabolic features mentioned above and the absence of other causes for the symptoms. The response to parathormone is important. Other causes of hypocalcemia are infantile rickets, tetany of the newborn, alkalosis, steatorrhea, diarrhea and chronic renal insufficiency. It is claimed that magnesium deficiency may give rise to symptoms suggestive of tetany. See Disorders of Magnesium Metabolism.

Prognosis.—In mild cases, symptoms occur only in association with excessive exercise, gastrointestinal disturbances or infections and the child does not require constant treatment. In more severe cases, however, constant treatment is required and death often occurs in acute exacerbations as a result of convulsions or heart failure. Proper treatment relieves the tetany and the changes in the electrocardiogram disappear. The convulsions either cease completely or are much diminished as a rule. In some instances, however, the seizures persist even after the metabolic disorder has been corrected and may also fail to respond to anticonvulsive medication. The papilledema subsides slowly. On the other hand, the mental state is not restored to normal and the cataracts and the calcium deposits in the brain persist.

Treatment.—Collip's parathormone is a specific and if given in adequate doses restores the calcium and phosphorus values of the blood to their normal level. As a rule, it seems to lose its effect after prolonged administration. For treatment of a chronic state of parathyroid deficiency, therefore, other methods are necessary. It is recommended that a diet low in phosphorus be given and that calcium salts be administered. It has been shown that dihydrotachysterol, a substance closely related to vitamin D, is effective. This preparation may be given by mouth.

CASE HISTORY (No. 1070583).—*Familial hypoparathyroidism. Girl of eleven years with tetany, persistent seizures and chorea. Brother suffered from the same condition and died in convulsions.*

M. G., a girl of eleven years, was seen on December 14, 1963, by the courtesy of Dr. David Clark. When the child was fifteen months old, she had a convulsive seizure associated with fever. Additional seizures occurred in the following years usually associated with febrile illnesses. There were repeated attacks of tetany. At the age of nine years, a diagnosis of hypoparathyroidism was made, for the standard biochemical abnormalities were discovered. These were corrected without too much difficulty, and the child did well for a time.

When the patient was ten years old, she began to have frequent seizures, with loss of consciousness, which could not be controlled. As many as sixty seizures might occur every day. The child's mental condition deteriorated. Involuntary movements developed.

It should be said that an older brother had the same condition and died in convulsions; otherwise, the family history was negative.

The patient had a pneumoencephalogram which showed only slight enlargement of the ventricles and an arteriographic study which was normal. There were no calcium deposits in the brain. The electroencephalogram showed diffuse abnormalities.

On examination, the child was small but well nourished. She was very dull and not always in contact. There were constant generalized choreic movements. From time to time, her pupils would become dilated, her right arm would be rigidly extended, her face would turn to the left and she would become unconscious. Her respiration and pulse were very slow at such times.

Serum calcium and phosphorus were rigidly controlled without beneficial effect. Dilantin and other anticonvulsive drugs were ineffectual, and toxic effects developed when doses of even moderate size were given, making it necessary to withdraw the medication.

The patient showed the usual changes in the finger nails and the teeth. The hair appeared to be normal but there had been loss of hair at one time. The liver was enlarged and, at times, the spleen could be felt. There was anemia which was controlled by steroids.

BIBLIOGRAPHY

BENSON, P. F. AND PARSONS, V.: Hereditary hypoparathyroidism. Quart. Jour. Med., 33:197, 1964.

BLACKBURN, C. R. B.: Effects of hypocalcemia on the central nervous system. Rocky Mountain Med. J., 54:441, 1957.

BRONSKY, D. *et al.:* Idiopathic hypoparathyroidism and pseudohypoparathyroidism. Medicine, 37:317, 1958.

CANTAROW, A.: Chronic juvenile hypoparathyroidism. Arch. Pediat., 49:293, 1932.

COLLINS-WILLIAMS, C.: Idiopathic hypoparathyroidism with papilledema in a boy six years of age. Pediatrics, 5:998, 1950.

CRUZ, C. E. AND BARNETT, N.: Mental retardation in pseudo-pseudohypoparathyroidism. Amer. Jour. Ment. Defic., 67:381, 1962.

EATON, J. McK., J. D. AND LOVE, J. G.: Symmetric cerebral calcification, particularly of the basal ganglia. Arch. Neurol. & Psychiat., 41:921, 1939.

——— AND HAINES, S. F.: Parathyroid insufficiency with symmetrical cerebral calcification. J.A.M.A., 113:749, 1939.

EMERSON, K., WALSH, F. B. AND HOWARD, J. E.: Idiopathic hypoparathyroidism; a report of 2 cases. Ann. Int. Med., 14:1256, 1941.

FELITTI, V. J. AND MACFEE, L. L.: Recovery from symptoms in pseudohypoparathyroidism. Johns Hopkins Medical Jour., 123:271, 1968.

FOLEY, J.: Calcification of the corpus striatum and dentate nuclei occurring in a family. J. Neurol., Neurosurg. & Psychiat., 14:253, 1951.

FRAME, B. AND CARTER, S.: Pseudohypoparathyroidism. Neurology, 5:297, 1955.

GORLIN, R. J. AND SEDANO: Addison's disease, idiopathic familial, juvenile hypoparathyroidism, keratoconjunctivitis, and superficial moniliasis. Modern Medicine, October 20, 1969, p. 217.

HERMANS, P. E. *et al.:* Pseudo-pseudohypoparathyroidism. Mayo Clin. Proc., 39:81, 1964.

JANCAR, J.: Cerebro-metacarpo-metatarsal dystrophy (pseudo-pseudo hypoparathyroidism) with chromosomal anomaly. J. Med. Genet., 2:32, 1965.

LEVIN, P. *et al.:* Intracranial calcification and hypoparathyroidism. Neurology, 11:1076, 1961.

LOWENTHAL, A.: Fahr's intracerebral non-arteriosclerotic vascular calcification. A cerebral manifestation of disturbance of parathyroid function. Acta neurol. et Psychiat., 48:613, 1948.

MACBRIDE, C. M. AND SANDERS, T. E.: Tetany with increased intracranial pressure and papilledema. Tr. A. Am. Phys., 53:227, 1938.

McKINNEY, A. S.: Idiopathic hypoparathyroidism presenting as chorea. Neurology, 12:485, 1962.

MORSE, W. I. *et al.:* Familial hypoparathyroidism with pernicious anemia, steatorrhea and adrenal cortical insufficiency. New England Jour. Med., 264:1021, 1961.

MUNSON, P. L.: Thyocalcitonin: Experimental and clinical aspects. Triangle, 8:89, 1967.

NAEF, R. W. AND ADLE, E. H.: Idiopathic hypoparathyroidism. Report of a case. Ann. Int. Med., 50:495, 1959.

NICHOLS, F. L. *et al.:* Familial hypocalcemia, latent tetany and calcification of the basal ganglia. Amer. Jour. Med., 30:518, 1961.

RICHTER, P. L. AND CHUTORIAN, A. M.: Familial hypoparathyroidism. Neurology, 18:75, 1968.

ROBERTS, P. P.: Familial calcification of cerebral basal ganglia and its relation to hypoparathyroidism. Brain, 82:599, 1959.

SCHWARZ, G. AND BAHNER, F.: Die Genetik des Pseudo-hypoparathyreoidismus und des Pseudo-Pseudo-hypoparathyreoidismus. Dtsch. med. Wschr., 88:240, 1963.

SIMPSON, J. A.: Neurological manifestations of idiopathic hypoparathyroidism. Brain, 75:76, 1952.

SUGAR, O.: Central neurological complications of hypoparathyroidism. Arch. Neurol. & Psychiat., 70:86, 1953.

THORPE, E. S. JR.: Chronic tetany and chronic myelial stomatitis in child four and a half years old. Am. J. Dis. Child., 38:328, 1929.

WISE, B. AND HART, J.: Idiopathic hypoparathyroidism and pseudohypoparathyroidism. Arch. Neurol. & Psychiat., 68:78, 1952.

Hyperparathyroidism and Hypercalcemia

Definition.—A condition characterized by changes in the bones and by disturbances in the metabolism of calcium and phosphorus which are associated with adenoma of the parathyroid glands and attributed to excessive secretion of these glands.

Etiology.—Several cases may be found in some families thus suggesting that heredity plays an important role.

Pathological Anatomy.—One or more adenomata are found in the parathyroid glands, in most cases, but generalized hyperplasia of all parathyroid tissue may occur as well. The bones show general rarefaction and increased activity of the osteoclasts. Extensive proliferation of the fibrous tissue in the bone marrow develops which may give rise to cysts and may so injure

the marrow as to cause anemia. Benign tumors composed of giant cells with multiple nuclei may develop as a result of local proliferation of osteo-clasts. Deposits of calcium are found in the urinary tract and kidneys and sometimes in ligaments and cartilage.

Bischoff and Esslen describe myopathic changes with scattered fibers of reduced diameter, loss of transverse striations, and granular-vacuolar de-generation. The electromyogram showed evidences of myopathy.

Clinical Features.—The condition may occur at any age but is quite rare in childhood. Thus Gutman mentions two cases in which the symptoms be-gan between one and nine years and ten cases in which the onset was be-tween ten and nineteen years in a series of one hundred and fifteen cases. Ludwig states that primary hyperparathyroidism during pregnancy involves great danger to the baby. Half of these children die *in utero* or shortly af-ter birth, or display neonatal tetany or congenital hypoparathyroidism. Ex-cessive use of vitamin D during pregnancy may have a similar effect on the fetus.

The first symptoms are usually those of pains in the back and extremi-ties. Soon there is weakness and loss of tone of the muscles which may be so severe as to suggest myasthenia gravis or Addison's disease. In some cases, there is wasting of the muscles so the case may be mistaken for one of mus-cular dystrophy. The electrical irritability of the muscles and nerves is di-minished and the tendon reflexes diminished or lost. The gait becomes wad-dling or limping and ultimately the patient becomes quite helpless. The writer has observed a case in which the muscular weakness and loss of tone antedated the other symptoms by a period of two years and aroused suspi-cions of muscular dystrophy. Bradycardia and irregularities of cardiac rhythm occur and the QT interval in the electrocardiogram may be short-ened.

Moure states that in hypercalcemia the electroencephalogram shows dif-fusely slow activity with paroxysms of frontal dominant, generalized slow-ing. When the serum calcium was reduced, the record became more normal.

Bony changes may precede or follow the muscular weakness. Solitary or multiple swellings may be seen, especially in the jaws. Pathological frac-tures are common and gross deformities due to decalcification of the bones are characteristic, such as bowing of the legs, distortion of the chest, spine and pelvis. Growth may be so seriously affected that the child becomes a dwarf. We have observed a case in which such extensive changes occurred in the cervical spine as to compress the spinal cord. In a case reported by Al-bright *et al.*, the patient fractured the spine while lifting a heavy weight at the age of fifteen years and injured the spinal cord.

Gastrointestinal symptoms dominate the picture in some cases and there is usually progressive loss of weight, nausea, vomiting, constipation and

anorexia. Gastric ulcer is not unusual. Renal symptoms due to nephrolithiasis are present in many cases and there is often polyuria and polydipsia. Renal insufficiency without nephrolithiasis is not uncommon and may cause death from uremia. The blood pressure may be elevated and intracranial hemorrhage may occur. There is frequently secondary anemia. Pancreatitis and obstruction of the pancreatic duct may result from deposits of calcium in the pancreas. Both primary and secondary hyperparathyroidism may be associated with calcium deposits in the blood vessels which may cause cerebral or cardiac infarction.

The changes revealed in the bones by roentgenography are very typical. There is always general decalcification and osteoporosis except when the intake of calcium is abundant. In many but not all cases, there are likewise giant cell tumors and cysts which cause the spontaneous fractures of the bones. The skull shows a fine trabeculation and the tabes become indistinct. As a rule, it is thin or perhaps of normal thickness but in some few cases it has been grossly thickened so as to resemble that of Paget's disease. Thickening of the long bones is very rare. Joint disorders may suggest rheumatoid arthritis. Calcium is deposited in the synovial membrane and cartilage. Calcium is also deposited in the tendon sheaths. Subperiosteal erosion of the upper borders of the ribs may occur.

Walsh has shown that calcium crystals may be found in the conjunctivae adjacent to the corneae and an incomplete band keratopathy as well. These changes are demonstrated by the slit lamp.

There may be headache, drowsiness, apathy, deafness and in some instances psychoses. If the condition arises in childhood mental deficiency may result.

Reinfrank and Edwards describe the case of a child who had sudden symptoms including abdominal pain, drowsiness, lethargy, profound muscular weakness and constipation. The serum calcium was 21.8 mgs and the serum phosphorus 3.4 mgs. The blood urea nitrogen rose rapidly. A diagnosis of hypercalcemic crisis was made. A large parathyroid tumor was found and when this was removed, the child recovered rapidly. The authors state that in such cases, death may occur within a few hours. Gassman and Haas report two similar cases in which disorientation and hallucinations occurred. Both patients died.

The standard findings in the calcium phosphorus metabolism are as follows: (1) Increased serum calcium, usually over 12 mgm per 100 cc. (2) Diminished serum phosphorus except when there is severe loss of renal function. (3) Elevation of the alkaline phosphatase level in proportion to the degree of bone disease. (4) Increased excretion of calcium in the urine.

The tumor is palpable in only about 10 per cent of cases and, therefore, the absence of a palpable tumor in the neck is not against the diagnosis.

Diagnosis.—Albright, Aub and Bauer state that the disease may manifest itself by changes in the bones, renal failure or nephrolithiasis. The changes in the blood chemistry are most important in diagnosis. The high serum calcium, they claim, is responsible for the weakness and loss of muscle tone.

Other causes of hypercalcemia must be considered in differential diagnosis such as prolonged bed rest because of paralysis or fractured bones, excessive intake of vitamin D or dihydrotachysterol, destruction of bones by malignant neoplasms and sarcoidosis. Ingestion of excessive amounts of vitamin D by the mother during pregnancy may produce this condition in the baby. Idiopathic calcemia must be ruled out. Albright's syndrome or polyostotic fibrous dysplasia q.v. must be distinguished. It should be said that despite the extensive changes in the bones, calcium and phosphorus metabolism is not altered in this condition.

One must also keep in mind the secondary hyperparathyroidism found in cases of long standing renal failure, i.e. the so-called renal rickets. It should be pointed out that the serum calcium is not elevated in this condition.

Prognosis.—The prognosis depends largely upon the stage of the disease at which the diagnosis is made and the adenoma removed. If this is done very early, complete recovery may be expected, but if extensive deformities have already developed or serious renal injury occurred, little improvement can be expected. Psychoses may follow removal of the adenoma.

Treatment.—As soon as the diagnosis is made, operative removal of the growth is indicated. Roentgenotherapy is apparently ineffective.

BIBLIOGRAPHY

ADAMS, H. AND MURPHY, R.: Surgery for primary hyperparathyroidism. Surg. Gynec. & Obst., 116:45, 1963.

AITA, J. A.: Congenital Facial Anomalies with Neurologic Defects. Springfield, Thomas, 1969, p. 115.

ALBRIGHT, F., AUB, J. C. AND BAUER, W.: Hyperparathyroidism, a common and polymorphic condition as illustrated by seventeen proved cases from one clinic. J.A.M.A., 102:1276, 1934.

———: Hyperparathyroidism and renal disease. Tr. Am. A. Genito-Urin. Surg., 27:195, 1934.

ANSPACH, W. E. AND CLIFTON, W. M.: Hyperparathyroidism in children. Am. J. Dis. Child., 58:54, 1939.

BISCHOFF, A. AND ESSLEN, E.: Myopathy with primary hyperparathyroidism. Neurology, 15:64, 1965.

BURR, J. M. et al.: Sarcoidosis and hyperparathyroidism with hypercalcemia. New England Jour. Med., 261:1271, 1959.

BYWATERS, E. G. L.: Joint lesions in hyperparathyroidism. Ann. Rheum. Dis., 22:171, 1963.

COPE, O. et al.: Pancreatitis in hyperparathyroidism. Ann. Surg., 145:857, 1957.

CROME, L. AND SYLVESTER, P. E.: A case of severe hypercalcemia of infancy with an account of the neuropathological findings. Arch. Dis. Childhood, 35:620, 1960.

DODD, K., GRAUNARTH, H. AND RAPOPORT, S.: Hypercalcemia, nephropathy and encephalopathy following immobilization. Pediatrics, 6:124, 1950.

Editorial: Etiology of idiopathic hypercalcemia. Brit. Med. Jour., 5169:335, 1960.

GASSMAN, R. AND HAAS, H. G.: Acute parathyroidism due to adenoma of the parathyroid gland. Schweiz. med. Wschr., 90:67, 1960.

GREENBAUM, D. AND MASON, A. S.: A multiple familial parathyroid adenomata. Proc. Roy. Soc. Med., 53:903, 1960.

GREENE, J. A. AND SWANSON, L. W.: Psychosis in hypoparathyroidism. Ann. Int. Med., 14:1233, 1941.

GUTMAN, A. B., SWENSON, P. C. AND PARSONS, B.: The differential diagnosis of hyperparathyroidism. J.A.M.A., 103:87, 1934.

HARMON, M.: Parathyroid adenoma in child. Jour. Dis. Child., 91:313, 1956.

HILLMAN, D. A.: Neonatal familial primary hyperparathyroidism. New England Jour. Med., 270:483, 1964.

KARPATI, G. AND FRAME, B.: Neuropsychiatric disorders in primary hyperparathyroidism. A.M.A. Arch. of Neurol., 10:387, 1964.

KEYNES, W. M.: Symptoms of hyperparathyroidism. Brit. Med. J., 5221:239, 1961.

LUDWIG, G. D.: Hyperparathyroidism in pregnancy. New England J. Med., 267:637, 1962.

MIEHER, W. C. et al.: The diagnosis of hyperparathyroidism. Arch. Int. Med., 107:361, 1961.

MITCHELL, R. G.: The prognosis of idiopathic hypercalcemia of infants. Arch. of Dis. Childh., 35:383, 1960.

MIXTER, C. G. et al.: Pancreatitis with hyperparathyroidism. New England J. Med., 266:265, 1962.

MOURE, J. M. B.: The electroencephalogram in hypercalcemia. Arch. of Neurol., 17:34, 1967.

NOETZLI, M. AND STEINBACH, H. L.: Rib erosion in hyperparathyroidism. Am. J. Roentgenol., 87:1058, 1962.

O'BRIEN, D. AND PEPERS, T. D.: Idiopathic hypercalcemia of infancy. J.A.M.A., 173:1106, 1960.

REINFRANK, R. F. AND EDWARDS, T. L.: Hypercalcemic crisis in a child. J.A.M.A., 178:468, 1961.

SMITH, L. C. et al.: Hyperparathyroid crisis. Am. Surg., 29:761, 1963.

SNYDER, C. H.: Idiopathic hypercalcemia of infancy. J. Dis. Child., 96:376, 1958.

THOMAS, W. C. et al.: Hypercalcemic crisis due to hyperparathyroidism. Amer. Jour. Med., 24:229, 1958.

WALSH, F. B.: Loc. cit.

Hypercalcemia of Infancy

There is microcephaly or craniostenosis in some patients. The forehead is broad. Wide epicanthic folds, convergent squint, hyperteliorism, nystagmus, tortuous retinal vessels, band keratopathy and optic atrophy due to encroaching on the foramina occur. Papilledema may result from craniostenosis. The cheeks may be full. The chin is pointed. The mouth is wide with prominent upper lip which is longer than usual. The ears are low set.

There is deficient tone in the muscles but the tendon reflexes are increased. Mental deficiency is common. The stature is short. The birth weight is low.

Supervalvular stenosis of the aorta, pulmonary stenosis, hypoplasia of the thoracic aorta, or stenosis of other major arteries are often found. Syncope may result. Calcium deposits occur in the brain and kidneys. Uremia may occur. The serum calcium is elevated. There is no evidence of inheritance, as a rule, but Ehrhardt and Money report 2 cases in one family.

A calcium free diet and reduction of the intake of vitamin D are advised.

BIBLIOGRAPHY

AITA, J. A.: Congenital Facial Anomalies with Neurologic Defects. Springfield, Thomas, 1969, p. 115.

CROME, L. AND SYLVESTER, P. E.: Idiopathic hypercalcemia of infancy with an account of the neuropathological findings. Arch. of Dis. of Childhood, 35:620, 1960.

EHRHARDT, A. A. AND MONEY, J.: Hypercalcemia. A family study of psychologic functioning. Johns Hopkins Med. Jour., 121:14, 1967.

SNYDER, C. H.: Idiopathic hypercalcemia of infancy. Jour. Dis. Child., 96:376, 1958.

WALSH, F. B. AND HOWARD, J. E.: Hypercalcemia and band keratopathy. Jour. Clin. Endocrinol., 7:644, 1947.

GARCIA, R. E. *et al.*: Hypercalcemia and aortic stenosis. New England Med. Jour., 271:117, 1964.

Polyostotic Fibrous Dysplasia or Albright's Syndrome

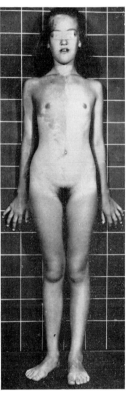

FIG. 181. Albright's disease in a girl of 8 years showing typical pigmentation over right face, body and arm and signs of precocious puberty. (By the courtesy of Dr. Lawson Wilkins.)

This condition is found, with rare exceptions, only in girls. Three characteristic groups of symptoms are described: (1) Changes in the bones. (2) Cutaneous pigmentation. (3) Endocrine disturbances, especially precocious puberty.

Patchy areas of rarefaction are seen in the long bones which have a superficial similarity to those of hyperparathyroidism. These are seen most often in the femur which often becomes bowed and may be the seat of a pathological fracture. The base of the skull shows a dense bony growth which may cause obliteration of the nasal sinuses, distortion of the features and even proptosis. The jaw may be enlarged in such a way as to suggest acromegaly. This bony process is not associated with any demonstrable abnormality of calcium or phosphorus metabolism.

The pigmentation appears in large areas which show a tendency to be limited to one side of the body, and to involve only one arm or leg. These areas are much larger than the cafe au lait patches of von Recklinghausen's disease though their color is approximately the same. They are evident in infancy as a rule and grow somewhat darker.

This condition is rare in boys. It is apparently not an inherited condition. Sexual precocity is a standard feature in girls. The menses may begin between

FIG. 182. (Ped. B-17374) Girl of 8 years. Precocious puberty with menses at 6 years, large pigmented areas on right side of trunk, lesions in long bones and dense bone at base of skull with progressing optic atrophy and partial blindness. Same subject as shown in Fig. 183.

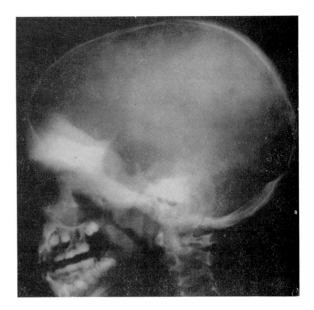

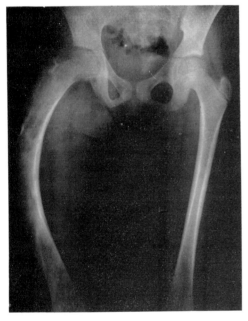

FIG. 183. Same subject as in Fig. 182 showing bending and characteristic lesions in right femur.

one and five years. Pubic and axillary hair then develop, and the breasts begin to grow. The external genitalia assume the adult form and may become hypertrophied. Bodily growth is accelerated but growth soon ceases for the epiphyses close early. Hyperthyroidism and insulin resistent diabetes may be associated.

One post-mortem examination revealed basophilic adenomas of the hypophysis, hyperplastic thyroid gland and mature cystic ovaries with no luteinization.

My object in mentioning this rather rare condition is to point out that the dense proliferation of bone at the base of the skull may cause compression of the optic chiasm and optic nerves with optic atrophy and loss of vision as well as deafness due to compression of the eighth nerves.

BIBLIOGRAPHY

ALBRIGHT, F.: Polyostotic fibrous dysplasia. J. Clin. Endocrinol. **7**:307, 1947.

BENEDICT, P. H.: Endocrine features of Albright's syndrome. Metabolism, **11**:30, 1962.

FALCONER, M. A.: Fibrous dysplasia of the bone with endocrine disorders and cutaneous pigmentation. Quart. J. Med. **11**:121, 1942.

GORLIN, R. J.: Albright's syndrome. Modern Medicine, April 8, 1968, p. 161.

HIBBS, R. F. AND RUSH, H. P.: Albright's syndrome. Ann. Int. Med., **37**:587, 1952.

STERNBERG, W. H. AND JOSEPH, V.: Osteodystrophia fibrosa with precocious puberty and exophthalmic goiter. Pathologic report of a case. Am. J. Dis. Child., **63**:748, 1942.

WARRICK, C.: Polyostotic fibrous dysplasia. Jour. Bone and Joint Surgery, **31B**:175, 1949.

PROGRESSIVE HEREDITARY DIAPHYSEAL DYSPLASIA OF ENGELMANN

Stegan and Peterson, writing in 1957, state that about twenty-one cases of this rare condition had been reported at that time. The essential features seem to be gross enlargement of the diaphyses and the skull. It is an heredofamilial disease presumably due to an abnormality of metabolism.

In children, the onset is between four and ten years. The process is slowly progressive. The chief complaints are weakness and difficulty in walking. The muscles undergo atrophy. There are often pains in the extremities. Exophthalmos and papilledema occur, possibly because of involvement of the orbits. Deafness is probably due to bony changes in the ear. The enlargement of the skull and the thickening of the long bones become obvious as the disease progresses. The patient stands with bent knees, and some eventually become unable to walk. Sexual dystrophy is mentioned in some cases. Mental deterioration may occur. The liver and spleen enlarge.

Roentgenograms show thickening and increased density of the diaphyses of the long bones and little change in the epiphyses. The process is usually symmetrical. Biopsies show thickening of the periosteum with increased formation of new bone. There is evidence of resorption of new bone with replacement by cancellous bone. Muscle biopsy may show areas of necrosis, presumably due to deficient blood supply for the arteries are tortuous and thickened and the lumen is narrow.

The only metabolic abnormality thus far discovered is an increase of alkaline phosphatase which is inconstant.

Differential diagnosis includes vitamin A intoxication, syphilis, infantile cortical hyperostosis, scurvy, rickets, melorheostosis, Paget's disease, hypophosphatasia, polyostotic fibrous dysplasia.

In addition to the child whose case is given in abstract below, we have seen a girl of 12 years, with exactly the same condition. She could not walk. The right optic disc was pale and vision was 20/70. The muscles showed atrophy. The arteries of the muscles showed thickening of their walls and calcium deposits in the media. The alkaline phosphatase was normal.

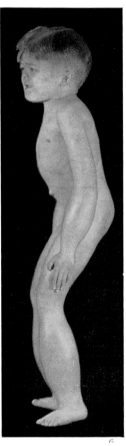

FIG. 184. Hereditary diaphyseal dysplasia showing extraordinary thickening of the skull and long bones. The cranial vault is almost an inch thick and there is bilateral papilledema.

CASE HISTORY (Microfilm 1714).—*Enormous thickening of the skull and of the shafts of the long bones beginning at one year of age. Increased intracranial pressure and papilledema. Exophthalmos. Deafness.*

C. W., a white boy of 4 years, was first seen in Harriet Lane in September 1927. He was the only child of normal parents. He began to walk at the age of one year and talked at 14 months. However, it was soon noted that his legs were becoming bowed and that he stood with bent knees. Soon it was seen that his head was becoming too large and the bones of his extremities were growing very thick. His gait became more difficult. His hearing was reduced. Tears overflowed from his eyes.

Examination revealed an extremely large head, 59.5 cm in occipitofrontal circumference, with widely opened fronto-parietal sutures. There was gross enlargement of the shafts of the long bones, though the hands and the feet appeared to be normal. The legs were bowed and the patient was forced to stand with bent knees. There was marked scoliosis and kyphosis. His mental condition was considered to be normal. Bilateral papilledema was discovered with mild optic atrophy but vision was 20/50 in each eye. Epiphora was noted on both sides. Hearing was grossly reduced and the external auditory canals were nearly occluded.

Roentgenograms of the skull revealed great thickening of the bones which were estimated to measure 2 inches thick over the vault. These

bones presented a mottled appearance with areas of both increased and diminished density. The cortex was irregular and ill-defined. New bone had been laid down in irregular trabeculae under the periosteum. The long bones were enormously enlarged in their middle portions, where the changes were similar to those seen in the skull. The hands and feet and the epiphyses presented a normal appearance. The spine and the pelvis were involved. Biopsy of the tibia revealed the loss of cortical lamination and the presence of thick trabeculae irregularly arranged. The marrow showed fibrous replacement. All the arteries were much thickened.

The serum calcium and serum phosphorus were estimated many times and normal values were invariably obtained. There was a tendency to retention of both calcium and phosphorus. The alkaline serum phosphatase was always elevated, readings of 24 to 27 units being usually reported. No anemia was found. Tests of renal function gave negative results. All possible tests for syphilis were performed repeatedly and these were invariably negative.

Ventricular puncture was performed and air injected. There was marked increase of intracranial pressure but the ventricles were small and symmetrical.

He was followed for many years. He was soon unable to walk or feed himself. At the age of 15 years, he had heart failure, but responded to digitalis. At the age of 27 he was found to have bilateral cataracts. When they were removed his vision was normal and the fields were normal. The optic discs were not pale. He died at the age of 40 years.

BIBLIOGRAPHY

BINGOLD, A. C.: Engelmann's disease. Brit. J. Surg., 37:266, 1950.

CLAWSON, D. K.: Progressive diaphyseal dysplasia (Engelmann's disease). Jour. Bone and Joint Surg., 46A:143, 1964.

COHEN, J. AND STATES, J. D.: Progressive diaphyseal dysplasia. Lab. Invest., 5:492, 1956.

ENGELMANN, G.: Ein Fall von Osteopathia hyperostotica (sclerotisans) multiplex infantilis. Fortschr. Geb. Röntgenstrahlen, 39:1101, 1929.

JACKSON, W. P. U., HANELIN, J. AND ALBRIGHT, F.: Metaphyseal dysplasia, epiphyseal dysplasia, diaphyseal dysplasia, and related conditions. III. Progressive diaphyseal dysplasia. Arch. Int. Med., 94:902, 1954.

LENNON, E. A. et al.: Engelmann's disease. Jour. Bone and Joint Surg., 43B:273, 1961.

MICHAELIS, L. S.: Engelmann's disease. Proc. Roy. Soc. Med. (Section of Orthopaedics), 42:271, 1949.

SEAR, H. R.: Engelmann's disease; osteopathia hyperostotica sclerotisans multiplex infantilis; report of a case. Brit. J. Radiol., 21:236, 1948.

STEGMAN, K. F. AND PETERSON, J. C.: Progressive hereditary diaphyseal dysplasia. Pediatrics, 20:966, 1957.

STEWART, H. B. AND COLE, E. R.: Progressive diaphyseal dysplasia (Engelmann's disease). J. Pediat., 48:482, 1956.

STRONGE, R. F. AND McDOWELL, H. B.: A case of Engelmann's disease. J. Bone & Joint Surg., 32B:38, 1950.

WALSH, F. B.: Loc. cit.

WYLLIE, W. G.: The occurrence in osteitis deformans of lesions of the central nervous system. Brain, 46:336, 1923.

CRANIOMETAPHYSEAL DYSOSTOSIS AND CRANIODIAPHYSEAL DYSOSTOSIS (PYLE'S DISEASE)

Craniometaphyseal dysostosis is an autosomal recessive condition. The nasal bridge is extremely broad and flattened. The maxillae and mandible are dense and enlarged. There is hyperteliorism. The nasal passages are obstructed by bony proliferation and the mouth must be kept open. The nasal sinuses are obliterated. The skull is thickened especially at the base. The optic nerves are often compressed causing optic atrophy and blindness. In the same way the eight nerves may be involved with deafness and facial paralysis may occur. There may be mental deficiency and delayed motor development. Headaches and vomiting develop. The metaphyses of the long bones show decreased density but the diaphyses show increased density. Similar changes are seen in the epiphyseal ends of the metacarpals and phalanges. The blood counts, serum alkaline phosphatase, calcium and phosphorus are normal.

A condition termed craniodiaphyseal dysostosis has most of the features just described. It is an autosomal recessive trait. There is severe mental deficiency. The ribs are widened and extremely dense. The clavicles are thickened in the midportions. The long bones are straight with a thin cortex.

BIBLIOGRAPHY

Gorlin, R. J. and Sedano, H.: Craniometaphyseal dysostosis and craniodiaphyseal dysostosis. Modern Medicine, 36:154, 1968.

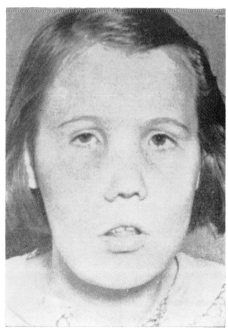

Fig. 185. Craniometaphyseal dysostosis. Note bony enlargement of the base of the nose which was completely obstructed. (By the courtesy of Dr. Frank B. Walsh.)

MILLARD, D. R. *et al.*: Craniofacial surgery in craniometaphyseal dysplasia. Amer. Jour. Surg., 113:615, 1967.

Fibrous Dysplasia of the Skull

Many cases of fibrous dysplasia or osteitis fibrosa of the skull have been reported. This condition may develop in childhood. The bone is thickened and softer than normal. It is composed of poorly calcified osteoid tissue which undergoes fibrous transformation. Large masses may form on the skull. Malignant changes may develop in such lesions. Meningiomata may cause similar gross appearances.

Sussin and Rosenberg report a study of 50 cases. They found optic atrophy in 8 often associated with exophthalmos, deafness in 4 cases in some of which the external canals were occluded and convulsions in 6 cases. No other neurological abnormalities were associated. Mental deficiency may result. A bone survey revealed lesions in other bones in only 3 cases.

The calcium and phosphorus of the serum were always normal. The alkaline phosphatase was increased in 14 cases.

> CASE HISTORY (U-127718).—*Osteitis fibrosa involving frontal bone and orbit on left at age of 10 years with compression of left optic nerve and exophthalmos.*
>
> E. N., a previously healthy girl of 10 years, began to have diplopia in the spring of 1934. Examination revealed slight displacement downward of the left bulb but the optic nerve head was of normal color and vision was good. In March 1937, however, it was found that vision in the left eye was reduced to 20/30. On December 17 of the same year vision was almost lost in the left eye and the child was brought to Dr. Dandy.

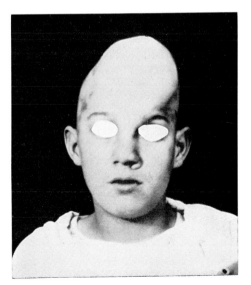

FIG. 186. Localized fibroosteitis cystica forming a large mass in the frontal bones in a boy of 13 years. The inner table of the skull was displaced inward but not eroded. Intellectual development was retarded and there were severe headaches but no papilledema. (By the courtesy of Dr. Dandy.)

Examination disclosed that the left eye was displaced downward for 6 mm and forward for 5 mm. The left pupil reacted slowly to light and vision was reduced in this eye to bare light perception. The disc was slightly pale. A large absolute central scotoma was found which extended outward to 40° leaving a narrow zone of color vision about its periphery. Ocular movements were of full range except for limitation of upward movements of the bulb. The left supraorbital ridge and indeed all bony structures about the left orbit seemed to be thickened, and roentgenograms showed increased thickness of the bones in the posterior and superior parts of the orbit. Dr. Dandy removed the roof of the orbit by the intracranial route and enlarged the optic foramen. The optic nerve was found to be compressed. January 6, 1938, there was some improvement in vision and the patient could count fingers.

BIBLIOGRAPHY

BASEK, M. M.: Fibrous dysplasia of the middle ear. Arch. of Otolaryng., 85:4, 1967.

CAHILL, P.: Fibrous dysplasia of the skull. Med. Jour. Aust., 2:843.

GASS, J. D. M.: Orbital and ocular involvement in fibrous dysplasia. Southern Med. Jour., 58:324, 1965.

LEEDS, N. AND SEAMAN, W. B.: Fibrous dysplasia of the skull. Radiology, 78:570, 1962.

SCHWARTZ, D. T. AND ALPORT, M.: Malignant change in fibrous dysplasia. Amer. Jour. Med. Sci., 247:1, 1964.

Osteogensis Imperfecta

The forehead is broad and there are bitemporal prominences. The head is broad. The occiput is described as overhanging. In severe forms the skull is membranous and soft at birth. The face is small. The sclerae are blue. Deafness of conduction type develops. Muscle tone is reduced and the ligaments are lax. Basilar impression may be found. Hydrocephalus occurs in some cases. The odontoid process may compress the spinal cord. The stature is small. The arms and legs are short. There is often scoliosis or kyphosis. The bones are fragile. The serum alkaline phosphatase is elevated. Hydrocephalus may develop and mental deficiency is present in some instances. This is believed to be an autosomal dominant condition.

BIBLIOGRAPHY

McKUSICK, V.: Heritable Disorders of Connective Tissues. Mosby, St. Louis, 1966.

Damage to the Nervous System in Osteopetrosis

The essential feature is the alteration of the bones which are dense, compact and homogenous. Nevertheless, the bones are very fragile and fractures occur with mild trauma. Deformities not unlike those of rickets result. The child may display a square forehead, clubbing of the ends of the long bones and pigeon breast. Anemia is usually present for the bone marrow is involved. As a rule, calcium and phosphorus are normal, but in some cases the calcium in the serum is decreased and tetany develops. Pincus,

et al. claim that there is hypermineralization of the bones and excessive excretion of phosphorus.

My purpose in calling attention to this condition is to point out that optic atrophy may occur. This may be either primary or secondary to papilledema. Exophthalmos squints and ocular palsies may occur. Nystagmus is usually due to defect in central vision early in life. Facial palsies which eventually become bilateral are common. It is odd that the facial weakness recedes and recurs. Deafness may be of the conduction type or due to involvement of the eighth nerve. The fifth nerves are also often involved with trigeminal neuralgia. Anosmia is not infrequent. The skull is often enlarged. This may be due to thickening of the bones or to hydrocephalus. Mental deficiency may occur though it is not always present. Convulsions are mentioned. The spinal fluid pressure may be increased.

Johnston *et al.* state that there are two types of osteopetrosis. One begins in childhood and is inherited as a recessive condition. This is termed the malignant form and leads to optic atrophy, cranial nerve palsies and enlargement of the liver and spleen. The patients die at an early age as a result of anemia and infection. A more benign form is inherited as a dominant trait. It becomes evident after the age of 15 years. In about half the cases there are no symptoms, but in others there may be fractures, osteomyelitis and cranial nerve palsies. The roentgenographic examination does not distinguish between these two forms.

No treatment is known.

CASE HISTORY (Ped. A-81365).—*Child of 23 months with primary optic atrophy, large head and thickening and increased density of the bones of the base of the skull. Diagnosis of osteopetrosis.*

P. D., a girl of 23 months, was brought to the hospital on October 27, 1950. At the age of three months the child had been found to be blind. She sat up at six months, walked at 15 months and formed single words at 20 months. She could not form proper sentences at 23 months and was still not toilet trained.

On examination the child was very restless and irritable. Her behavior was that of a younger child. She made repetitive movements as defective children do. The head measured 19½ inches in circumference and the chest 18½. The height was 34 inches. There was a prominence in the occipital region and the base of the nose was somewhat thickened. The pupils were dilated and did not react to light. The optic nerve heads were small and white. Otherwise the cranial nerves seemed to be in order. No disturbances of motility or changes in the reflexes were evident.

Roentgenograms of the skull revealed great density and thickening of the bones of the base of the skull. The maxilla was affected in the same way. The normal structure of these bones was lost. The ribs were thickened and somewhat sclerotic. The long bones were enlarged at the ends but not denser than usual. The serum calcium was 11.2 mgs. The phos-

phorus was 6.4 mgs. The alkaline phosphatase was 7.2 units. The Wassermann test was negative. The non-protein nitrogen was 44 mgs.

BIBLIOGRAPHY

ANTHONEY, B. W. AND POLLACK, H. C.: Marble bones with pathologic fracture and bilateral
optic atrophy in a negro child. Radiology, **38**:355, 1942.
JOHNSTON, C. C. *et al.:* Osteopetrosis. Medicine, **47**:149, 1968.
KLINTWORTH, G. K.: Neurologic manifestations of osteopetrosis. Neurology, **13**:512, 1963.
McCUNE, D. J. AND BRADLEY, C.: Osteopetrosis: Marble bones in an infant. Review of the litera-
ture. Am. J. Dis. Child., **48**:949, 1934.
NUSSEY, A. M.: Osteopetrosis. Arch. Dis. Child., **13**:161, 1938.
PINCUS, J. B. *et al.:* Juvenile osteopetrosis. Metabolic studies. Am. J. Dis. Child., **73**:458, 1947.
RISER, R. O.: Marble bones and optic atrophy. Am. J. Ophth., **24**:874, 1941.
TIPS, R. L. AND LYNCH, H. T.: Malignant congenital osteopetrosis resulting from a consanguine-
ous marriage. Acta Paediat., **51**:585, 1962.
WALSH, F. B.: *Loc. cit.*
WELFORD, N. T.: Facial paralysis associated with osteopetrosis. Jour. Pediat., **55**:67, 1959.

Hypophosphatasia with Inadequate Growth of the Skull Simulating Craniostenosis

This is a metabolic disorder of genetic origin. It seems to be inherited as
an autosomal recessive. It is said that the heterozygous carriers may be detected for their serum alkaline phosphatase is diminished though they have
no symptoms. The process may start *in utero* or early in infancy. Bodily
growth is defective. There may be scoliosis and deformities of the bones
resembling those of rickets. Zones of deficient calcification are seen in
roentgenograms which extend from the epiphyseal cartilage well into the
diaphysis.

The head is too small and the fontanels bulge. The eyes may be too
prominent and the sclerae may be blue. The appearance of the head may
suggest craniostenosis. Roentgenograms of the skull, however, do not reveal
closure of the sutures. The suture lines are marked by broad zones of fibrous tissue in which calcium has not been deposited. Calcium deposits may
cause renal damage. Deformities of the chest may impair respiration. Cyanosis is mentioned. Vomiting is common and convulsions are described.
These children rarely live more than a year. Cortisone has been used with
uncertain success.

Chemical studies reveal that the serum phosphorus is normal. Serum calcium may be increased or normal. The alkaline phosphatase is diminished.
There is an excess of phosphorylethenolamine in the urine. The diagnosis
seems to depend upon these chemical findings and upon the roentgenographic appearances of the bones.

BIBLIOGRAPHY

BLACKARD, W. G. *et al.:* Familial hypophosphatemia. New England Jour. Med., **266**:899, 1962.
FRASER, D.: Hypophosphatasia. Am. J. Med., **22**:730, 1957.

KELLSEY, D. C.: Hypophosphatasia and congenital bowing of the long bones. J.A.M.A., **179**:187, 1962.

McCANCE, R. A. *et al.:* Genetic, clinical, biochemical and pathological features of hypophosphatasia. Quart. J. Med., **25**:523, 1956.

RATHBUN, J. C. *et al.:* Hypophosphatasia. Arch. Dis. Child., **36**:540, 1961.

——— *et al:* Arch. Dis. Child., **36**:540, 1961.

SACHS, E. *et al.:* An unusual case of kyphotic paraplegia and hypophosphatasia. Jour. of Neurosurg., **17**:1005, 1960.

DISORDERS OF THE PANCREAS AND CARBOHYDRATE METABOLISM
Neurological Features of Diabetes Mellitus

Etiology.—The cause of diabetes is obscure. In a certain percentage of cases there is a distinct familial element, so that it is generally believed that an inherited constitutional factor is important. Harris suggests that diabetes may be due to several recessive genes. The milder cases of diabetes of late onset are due to a single morbid gene and the more severe cases of early onset may be due to a double inheritance of two pathological genes. Pancreatitis is a rare cause of diabetes.

Pathological Anatomy.—Dillon has studied the brains of patients dying in diabetic coma. He describes dilatation of the capillaries and acute degenerative changes in the neurons of the cortex, basal ganglia and brain stem. These he thinks are a result of anoxia.

Clinical Features.—The onset is usually insidious with loss of weight, weakness and excessive thirst. Often appetite is increased at first but later anorexia is apt to develop. Vomiting and other digestive disturbances are often prominent. Diminished resistance to infections such as is shown by repeated attacks of furunculosis or impetigo may be the first symptoms to attract attention. Pruritis, especially of the genitalia, may occur. If the child survives long enough, growth and development are greatly retarded.

Polyneuritis is not a common feature of diabetes in children. However, Rundles has described 8 cases developing between the ages of 17 and 20 years in a total series of 125 cases of diabetes of which he made a very careful study. He emphasizes a number of features of considerable interest. In addition to the common symptoms of polyneuritis, such as muscular weakness, tenderness and loss of tendon reflexes, he states that reduction or loss of pupillary light reflexes, disturbances of sphincter control similar to those seen in tabes and pronounced disturbances of the autonomic nervous system are common. Among the symptoms included in the last category he places dependent edema of the legs, loss of sweating in the legs, diarrhea and postural hypotension. *Retinopathy* is common and often becomes severe enough to cause blindness. Small red spots appear which are believed to be venous aneurysms. Later, hemorrhages and exudates are seen. The

veins become dilated and tortuous. Gross hemorrhages occur and massive gliosis is seen.

Schwartzman *et al.* analyzed 507 cases of diabetes in which the onset was before the end of the first year. In addition to polyuria and loss of weight, they describe mental and physical retardation and dwarfish stature. More than 12 per cent of these children had peripheral neuritis.

I have seen a dwarfish mentally deficient girl whose mother had diabetes and who had diabetes herself in infancy.

Hutchison and Kerr describe temporary diabetes in newborn infants. Of four children with this condition, three had cerebral damage with mental deficiency or spastic paralysis.

Cornblath describes 15 cases of transient diabetes in newborn infants. These children were underweight and quickly became dehydrated. Glycosuria was severe and the blood sugar was high exceeding 300 to 500 mgs. They responded to insulin properly. Ketosis was rare. Recovery occurred within 3 days to 18 months. None had permanent diabetes.

Various palsies of the cranial nerves may occur in adult diabetics but we have not seen them in children.

On the other hand, *diabetic coma* is common in juvenile diabetics. This frequently follows severe infections such as pneumonia, pyelitis, influenza or the consumption of large amounts of carbohydrate as in eating candy. Coma may be the first striking evidence of untreated diabetes. The onset is usually marked by apathy and drowsiness. Abdominal pain and vomiting are also frequent at the beginning. Slowly or suddenly the drowsiness deepens into stupor and then coma but convulsions do not occur. The lips are bright red and the face flushed. The skin is dry and the eyeballs soft on palpation. The breath usually smells of acetone and breathing is deep and rapid. Blood pressure is low. The urine shows a large amount of sugar and ketone bodies. The blood sugar is elevated and there is always a definite diminution of the alkali reserve. Repeated episodes of coma cause damage to the brain with loss of memory and personality changes. Fabrykant and Pacella state that some children suffering from labile diabetes show abnormal electroencephalographic records suggestive of epilepsy. These children have not only hypoglycemic episodes but pseudo-hypoglycemic attacks which are not associated with low blood sugar levels and not relieved by carbohydrates. They state that the administration of dilantin is helpful in such cases and makes it possible to control the diabetes more effectively. It should be mentioned that the administration of insulin may result in reduction of the serum potassium and cases are reported in which children have died of potassium deficiency with generalized paralysis while under treatment for diabetic coma. Cases of paralysis due to excessive accumula-

tion of potassium in the blood as a result of renal damage in long standing cases of diabetes are also described.

In certain cases, lipoid bodies accumulate in the blood, giving rise to the so-called *lipemia*. The cause of this is not entirely clear but it is no doubt due to the defective oxidation of fats. Lipemia is not confined to severe cases of diabetes but may be found in rare instances in relatively mild forms of the disease. It may be recognized, perhaps, most easily by the creamy color of the retinal vessels, the so-called lipemia retinalis. The blood serum is also of a creamy color and contains a great excess of fat. In idiopathic hyperlipemia the fasting serum may have the same creamy color. Cuppage states that extensive fat embolism may be found at post-mortem study in poorly regulated diabetics.

Unfortunately, degenerative changes often begin to appear late in childhood or at adolescence. These include retinopathy, cataracts, calcification of the arteries, arterial hypertension, renal damage and cardiac symptoms. These conditions are not always prevented by the most careful regulation.

Diabetic tabes scarcely ever occurs early in life. We have seen two adolescents, however, suffering from severe and prolonged juvenile diabetes whose pupils did not respond to light but contracted during accommodation. There was ataxia rather than weakness, loss of tendon reflexes, difficulty in emptying the bladder and in one case destructive changes in the ankle joint resembling those seen in tabes dorsalis. In such cases there is usually atrophy of the iris and iris pigment may be seen in the vitreous and on the anterior capsule of the lens.

Lipoatrophic diabetes: This rare condition may begin in adolescence. Boudin *et al.* describe a case with the onset at 14 years. It is believed to be inherited as an autosomal recessive. Subcutaneous fat is lost over the entire body. There is insulin resistant diabetes without ketosis. There is also hyperinsulinism, hepatomegaly progressing to portal cirrhosis, increased lipids in the blood and elevation of the basal metabolic rate without evidence of thyroid disease.

In Boudin's case, the blood pressure was 200/130. Exudates and hemorrhages were seen in the retinae. There was electrocardiographic evidence of cardiac ischemia. Pigmentation was seen in the axillae. Protein was found in the urine. There was tremor and dysarthria with loss of hearing. Involuntary movements were present with increased muscle tone. Mental deterioration developed. An air study revealed enlargement of the cortical sulci.

Maccario describes a condition associated with hyperglycemia but not with ketosis which causes coma and neurological symptoms which can be relieved by insulin and fluids. It is believed that this condition is due to hyperosmolarity of the serum which causes dehydration of the nerve cells.

Zitomer *et al.* describe diabetic gastric neuropathy which is a late complication, and is manifest by failure of the stomach to empty properly, lack of peristalsis and dilatation of duodenum.

Skin lesions are common in diabetes and may suggest the diagnosis. Pruritis and furunculosis are well known. Fungi such as candida may produce serious granulomatous infections especially in children. Reddish-yellow firm papules termed xanthoma diabeticorum occur in children and are usually found on the buttocks. Yellowish skin due to carotene may be seen on the palms and soles. Subcutaneous fat necrosis may occur on the thighs where insulin is injected.

Diagnosis.—The diagnosis of diabetes depends chiefly upon the demonstration of an excessively high blood sugar with or without ketosis and acidosis. It must be kept in mind that sugar may be absent from the urine and that the presence of reducing bodies in the urine is not significant unless it can be shown by proper tests that glucose is really present. The glucose tolerance test is most important. The administration of cortisone before the test is made makes it more delicate and latent cases of diabetes may be discovered. Renal diabetes is associated with a normal or low blood sugar. Alimentary glycosuria must always be considered. Galactosuria q.v. may cause jaundice, enlargement of the liver, cataracts and malnutrition. Cohen points out that salicylate poisoning may cause polyuria, acidosis, and reducing bodies in the urine and thus may simulate diabetic acidosis. Freedman *et al.* point out that when diabetes is associated with pronounced elevation of blood pressure, pheochromocytoma should be considered as well as thyrotoxicosis.

In the diagnosis of diabetic coma, the most important features are the acidosis, the hyperglycemia, the glycosuria and the dehydration. The differentiation of this type of coma from insulin shock is most important, since the treatment is radically different.

Prognosis.—Before the introduction of insulin, it was unusual for a child suffering from outspoken diabetes to survive more than a few months or years. With proper modern treatment, however, the outlook is much better and the disease may often be symptomatically controlled, so that the child may grow and develop normally. There seems, however to be no definite tendency in most cases towards actual recovery of function and proper diet and the use of insulin must be continued throughout life. Intercurrent infections often sharply reduce the sugar tolerance and are responsible for most of the fatalities at present. Degenerative changes often occur 10 to 15 years after the onset of the disease however. The prognosis of diabetic coma depends largely upon the precipitating cause and is much better in those cases due to breaking diet than in those due to infection. I have

observed the case of a child who was successfully revived from deep coma by the use of insulin no less than eleven times. No sequelae were observed.

Treatment.—The proper treatment of diabetes is outside the scope of this article. In brief, it consists of careful regulation of diet, control of infections and upon the use of insulin as required to keep the blood sugar at a normal level. Cullen states that the administration of atromid, a lipid reducing agent reduces exudates in 81 per cent of cases and improves vision in 43 per cent.

Coma demands large injections of insulin and subcutaneous or intravenous injection of normal salt solution to combat the dehydration. It is best to give repeated injections of relatively small amounts of insulin such as 10 to 25 units every half hour until the blood sugar is brought to normal limits. Later, when the blood sugar is nearly normal, glucose may be given intravenously to avoid hypoglycemia. Alkalis are of little value. Removal of the pituitary gland or section of the stalk are advised by some authors for severe retinopathy.

Kaye and Davidson state that oral agents are not suitable for the control of diabetes of childhood.

BIBLIOGRAPHY

BLUFARB, S. M. AND CARO, W. A.: Cutaneous manifestations of diabetes mellitus. Modern Medicine, Jan. 27, 1969, p. 59.

BOUDIN, G. *et al.:* Lipoatrophic diabetes with neurologic manifestations. Rev. Neurol., **109**:64, 1963.

COHEN, A. S.: Differential diagnosis of salicylate intoxication and diabetic acidosis. New England M. J., **254**:457, 1956.

CORNBLATH, M.: Transient diabetes in early infancy. Modern Medicine, October 10, 1966, p. 283.

CULLEN, J. F.: The treatment of diabetic retinopathy. Geriatrics, **23**:137, 1968.

CUPPAGE, F. E.: Fat embolism in diabetes. Am. J. Clin. Path., **40**:270, 1963.

DECKERT, T. *et al.:* Prognosis of proliferative retinopathy in juvenile diabetics. Diabetes, **16**:728, 1967.

DILLON, E. S., RIGGS, H. E. AND DYER, W. W.: Cerebral lesions in uncomplicated diabetic acidosis. Am. J. Med. Sc., **192**:360, 1936.

DREYFUS, P. M., HAKIM, S. AND ADAMS, R. D.: Diabetic ophthalmoplegia. Arch. Neurol. & Psychiat., **77**:337, 1957.

DONNELL, G. N. AND LANN, S. H.: Galactosuria. Pediatrics, **7**:503, 1951.

ELLENBERG, M.: Diabetic neuropathy of the upper extremities. Jour. Mt. Sinai Hosp., **35**:13, 1968.

FABRYKANT, M. AND PACELLA: Labile diabetes. Electronencephalographic status and effect of anticonvulsive therapy. Ann. Int. Med., **29**:860, 1948.

FIELD, R. A. *et al.:* Treatment of diabetic retinopathy. New England J. Med., **264**:689, 1961.

FREEDMAN, P.: Pheochromocytoma with diabetes. Quart. J. Med., **27**:307, 1958.

GAMSTORP, L. *et al.:* Peripheral neuropathy in juvenile diabetes. Diabetes, **15**:411, 1966.

GOODMAN, J. I.: Diabetic anhidrosis. Amer. Jour. Med., **41**:831, 1966.

HARDY, J.: Selective anterior hypophysectomy in the treatment of diabetic retinopathy. Jour. Amer. Med. Ass., **203**:73, 1968.

HUTCHISON, J. H. AND KERR, M. M.: Temporary neonatal diabetes. Brit. Med. J., **5302**:436, 1962.

JACKSON, R. L. *et al.:* Degenerative changes in young diabetic patients. Pediatrics, **5**:959, 1950.

JORDAN, R.: Neuritic manifestations of diabetes mellitus. Arch. Int. Med., **57**:307, 1936.

KAYE, R. AND DAVIDSON, M. H.: Limitations in the use of oral hypoglycemic agents in juvenile patients with diabetes. Jour. Pediat., **66**:844, 1965.

KOEHLIN, D.: Neurological symptoms in juvenile diabetes. Acta Pediat., **50**:205, 1961.

LAWRENCE, D. G. AND LOCKE, S.: Neuropathy in diabetic children. Brit. Med. J., **5333**:784, 1963.

MACCARIO, M.: Neurologic dysfunction associated with nonketosis. Arch. of Neurol., **19**:525, 1968.

MILLER, G. L.: Diabetes increases risk in pregnancy. Postgrad. Med., **43**:91, 1968.

RUNDLES, R. W.: Diabetic neuropathy. Medicine, 24:111, 1945.

SCHWARTZMAN, J. et al.: Diabetes mellitus in infants under one year of age. Am. J. Dis. Child., **74**:587, 1947.

STEINBERG, T. AND GWINUP, G.: Lipodystrophy. Diabetes, **16**:715, 1967.

WALSH, F. B.: *Loc. cit.*

WEINSTEIN, E. A. AND DOLGER, H.: External ocular muscle palsies occurring in diabetes mellitus. Arch. Neurol. & Psychiat., **60**:597, 1949.

WHITE, P.: Diabetes in Childhood and Adolescence. Philadelphia, Lea and Febiger, 1932.

ZITOMER, B. R. et al.: Gastric neuropathy in diabetes mellitus. Metabolism, 17:199, 1968.

ZORILLA, E. AND KOZAK, G. P.: Ophthalmoplegia in diabetes mellitus. Ann. Int. Med., **67**:968, 1967.

Abnormalities of Children of Diabetic Mothers

Driscoll *et al.* describe abnormalities found in 95 children of diabetic mothers who died 40 minutes to 3 months after birth. Most deaths occurred in the first 48 hours. They found a tendency to enlargement of the heart and diminished weight of the brain. Major defects of development were found in 20 infants and lethal defects in 16. Pneumonia was the commonest inflammatory process and was found in 24 infants. Hyaline membrane disease occurred in 71 children and caused death in 49. There were more vascular lesions than occur in the children of normal mothers. Intracranial hemorrhage was found in 32. Petechiae, subdural, subarachnoid and intraventricular hemorrhages are mentioned. Massive pulmonary hemorrhages were observed in 4 babies and large thromboses of pulmonary vessels in 3. Hyperplasia of the islands of Langerhans was found in 81 per cent. Gigantism, splanchnomegaly, jaundice, edema and obesity were found to be rare.

Despite the rarity of such conditions in Driscoll's studies, a number of gigantic babies weighing over 10 lbs have been observed. There is edema, jaundice, and obesity. Hypoglycemia is not unusual and in some instances causes severe symptoms. The serum potassium may be increased. Defects of the nervous system are common.

I have seen a boy of 17 years who weighed 10 lbs and 15 oz when delivered by Caesarian section 2 months before term because his mother who had diabetes was too ill to carry him any longer. He was obese, and jaundiced. The blood sugar was reduced. He showed spastic tetraplegia and was completely helpless. There was blindness due to optic atrophy. He was grossly deficient in mentality. He was subject to convulsions. An air study showed extensive atrophy of the brain.

Passarge and Lenz describe the syndrome of caudal regression of which 43 cases have been reported. This is manifest by agenesis of the sacrum and coccyx with small legs, deficient development of the muscles below the knees, club feet and webs behind the knees. It is found in about 1 per cent of the children of diabetic mothers. There is a good deal of variation in the clinical picture.

BIBLIOGRAPHY

BIX, H.: The relationship between maternal diabetes and giant babies. Amer. Jour. Obst. and Gynec., **29**:903, 1935.

DEKABAN, A. AND MAGEE, K. R.: Neurological abnormalities in infants of diabetic mothers. Neurology, **8**:193, 1958.

DRISCOLL, S. *et al.:* Neonatal deaths among infants of diabetic mothers. Amer. Jour. Dis. Child., **100**:818, 1960.

PASSARGE, E. AND LENZ, W.: The syndrome of caudal regression. Pediatrics, 1966, p. 537.

FAMILIAL CONDITIONS IN WHICH JUVENILE DIABETES MELLITUS IS ASSOCIATED WITH DIABETES INSIPIDUS, OPTIC ATROPHY, NERVE DEAFNESS AND OTHER SYNDROMES

We have seen two siblings of one family and two siblings of another family who had juvenile diabetes mellitus and progressive optic atrophy. Rose *et al.* has reviewed 18 cases of this condition found in medical literatue of whom 10 were deaf. He adds 7 cases of his own of whom 5 were deaf. It is believed that the optic atrophy is not due to diabetes, but is inherited as a separate condition. The optic atrophy is manifest by concentric constriction of the fields of vision and failure of central vision as well.

We have also seen two pairs of siblings of different families who had not only diabetes mellitus and optic atrophy, but diabetes insipidus as well. Rose describes 5 cases of this syndrome found in medical literature.

Rose also found 8 cases of diabetes mellitus associated with optic atrophy and the clinical picture of Frierich's ataxia.

Alstrom *et al.* describe a recessive condition manifest by diabetes mellitus, pigmentary degeneration of the retinae, obesity, and nerve deafness, but no mental deficiency, sexual deficiency or extra digits as in the Lawrence-Moon-Biedl syndrome.

Herrman *et al.* report a study of 5 generations of a family in which 14 members suffered from diabetes mellitus, photomyoclonus, deafness, nephropathy and a process in the nervous system causing dementia, ataxia and nystagmus. At post-mortem examination diffuse degeneration of the neurons was found. Some neurons were ballooned by deposits of neutral fats. In some cases the onset was in childhood.

BIBLIOGRAPHY

ALSTROM, C. H. *et al.:* Retinal degeneration combined with obesity, diabetes mellitus, and neurogenic deafness. Acta Psychiat. and Neurol. Scand., 1959, vol. 34, Sup. 129, p. 1.

HERRMAN, F. C. *et al.*: Hereditary photomyoclonus, associated with diabetes mellitus, deafness, nephropathy and cerebral dysfunction. Neurology, 14:212, 1964.

ROSE, F. C. *et al.*: The association of juvenile diabetes and optic atrophy. Quart. Jour. Med., 35:385, 1966.

SHAW, D. A. AND DUNCAN, L. J. P.: Optic atrophy and nerve deafness in diabetes mellitus. Jour. Neurol. and Psychiat., 21:47, 1958.

HYPOGLYCEMIA AND INSULIN SHOCK

Definition.—Reduction of blood sugar to pathological levels with the production of symptoms.

Etiology.—The amount of glucose in the blood is influenced by many factors. I shall merely mention some of the conditions under which hypoglycemia occurs. First it should be said that the mechanisms controlling the glucose content of the blood in the *newborn infant* are sometimes unstable and estimations of 40 to 50 mgs per cent are not unusual. In 1941 Potter, Seckel and Stryker collected 45 cases of *hyperplasia* and *hypertrophy* of the islets of the pancreas occurring in infants who were stillborn or died within the first few days of life. In 29 cases the mother had diabetes. The children may be unusually large at birth. Their blood sugar may drop precipitously in the first few days. *Adenoma* of the *islets* of the pancreas is rare in childhood and only about half a dozen cases are reported. *Insulin shock* in diabetic children is an obvious and common cause of hypoglycemia. Disease of the *adrenal glands* may reduce the blood sugar. *Liver damage* resulting from various causes may give rise to a hepatogenous type of hypoglycemia. It is well known that damage of the *pituitary gland* may cause low blood sugar. Suprasellar cysts are often responsible. *Renal glycosuria* is a rare cause. *Functional types* of hypoglycemia are not uncommon.

McQuarrie has described a familial type of hypoglycemia which seems to be inherited as a recessive characteristic. The ingestion of glucose induces hypoglycemia. ACTH is effective therapy.

Cochrane and his associates describe several cases of hypoglycemia in which the ingestion of lucine causes a profound fall in blood glucose. The onset is early in childhood and the symptoms are severe with convulsions and loss of consciousness. Mental deficiency may result. This is a familial disease.

Froesch and others have found a disorder of carbohydrate metabolism in seven members of a family. The administration of fructose results in an excessive and prolonged rise of fructose in the blood and a fall of blood glucose to levels as low as 10 mgs. Severe symptoms of hypoglycemia result. The condition seems to be transmitted as an autosomal recessive gene.

Lewis *et al.* describe a familial form of hypoglycemia which develops in infants during the night. This is a familial disease due to lack of glycogen

synthetase in the liver. It is advised that the child be given a midnight feeding. Hypoglycemia may occur in association with large neoplasms such as sarcomas and other non-pancreatic growths. Miller *et al.* found evidences of insulin in two such tumors.

Insulin shock therapy in the pregnant female may damage the brain of the fetus especially in the first fourteen weeks of gestation.

The ingestion of alcohol will cause hypoglycemia. Cummins reports two cases, one of which was fatal. Hypoglycemia is apt to be induced by alcohol if the liver is depleted of glycogen.

Knowbloch *et al.* state that damage to the nervous system in children suffering from hypoglycemia cannot always be attributed to the hypoglycemia. Many of these children have evidence of damage to the nervous system before hypoglycemic reactions occur. It is suggested that the cerebral defect may cause the hypoglycemia.

In early diabetes or in the prediabetic state, the glucose tolerance curve reveals hyperglycemia in the first three hours and then in the fourth and fifth hours drops to hypoglycemic levels.

Pathological Anatomy.—Severe and prolonged hypoglycemia may cause extensive damage to the cerebral cortex. It is said that the third and fifth layers of the cortex suffer most severely. There may be similar changes in the basal ganglia and in the cerebellum. The process is apparently not unlike that caused by anoxia. In fact, Courville states that they are identical. In a few instances in adults extensive degenerations have been found in the motor cells of the spinal cord and brain stem. These were cases of pancreatic adenoma.

Clinical Features.—Whatever the cause may be, the symptoms of hypoglycemia are always the same. They are apt to develop in recurrent, paroxysmal attacks. Premonitory symptoms such as hunger, pallor, sweating, tremor, restlessness, irritability, vertigo and diplopia are described. Nausea and vomiting may occur. The attack may terminate at this point, or the patient may become confused and incoherent. This state may then progress to stupor or even coma. Generalized and focal convulsions may develop. The pulse is rapid and the blood pressure low. The pupils may be dilated. The blood sugar may fall to 20 or 30 mgs per cent in such states.

Hypoglycemic stupor may last for hours or days. There is usually prompt recovery after glucose is administered but the symptoms may persist long after the blood sugar has been brought to a normal level. Mild attacks end in complete recovery. Very severe attacks may be fatal. Repeated attacks and even one severe attack may result in lasting damage to the nervous system. Mental changes seem to be the commonest residua. These may be mild or may reduce the patient to a state of profound dementia. Cerebellar

ataxia is described and muscular weakness and rigidity are sometimes seen. As a rule such signs are bilateral and symmetrical but hemiparesis is described. Some patients are subject to convulsions following a hypoglycemic episode.

A few cases are described in which extensive muscular atrophy has resulted from degeneration of the motor cells in the spinal cord. Mulder *et al.* and Rosner and Elsted describe neuropathy. Adenoma of the islets was found in most of these cases. It should be mentioned that in hypoglycemia due to overdosage of insulin, the serum potassium may be reduced with the production of flaccid paralysis of the muscles.

Diagnosis.—The diagnosis depends upon the clinical symptoms described above and the discovery that the blood sugar is 60 mgs per cent or less. Improvement following the administration of glucose is significant.

Hyperplasia of *the islets* of the pancreas is believed to be the cause of the hypoglycemia in children of diabetic mothers. It is said that this hyperplasia may also occur in the children of mothers who are in a pre-diabetic state. These children respond quickly to the administration of glucose and recover spontaneously as a rule in a few days.

In the rare cases of *adenoma* of the *pancreas,* the attacks may be induced by fasting and also by the ingestion of carbohydrates. The reaction occurs about 2 hours after eating and fasting of from 4 to 12 hours is usually sufficient to induce an attack. The glucose tolerance curve may be flat, average or high, but the sugar falls to hypoglycemic levels after 2 to 4 hours. In these cases there is danger of cerebral damage and even death. The symptoms tend to get progressively more severe. Adenomas of the pancreas may be only a part of a familial process in which parathyroid, pituitary and other glands may also be involved. This has been termed the Zollinger-Ellison syndrome.

In the familial type, described by McQuarrie, the ingestion of glucose seems to be responsible for the hypoglycemia. If a low carbohydrate diet does not control the symptoms, steroids may be administered.

In the leucine sensitive type, the children should be given minimal amounts of protein and a carbohydrate feeding thirty minutes after meals.

In cases such as those reported by Froesch, in which fructose induced the fall in blood sugar, the parents should be instructed to withhold food containing this substance.

In rare cases, *thyroid deficiency* may be associated with hypoglycemia possibly as a result of secondary changes in the adrenal glands. *Large growths* especially sarcomas may be associated with low blood sugar.

In the *hepatogenous cases* fasting is said to precipitate the attacks and the fasting blood sugar is low. The glucose tolerance test shows a pro-

nounced and prolonged rise with a fall to hypoglycemic levels after four hours. The administration of adrenalin causes no rise in the blood sugar. There are usually other signs of liver disease.

In *pituitary* and *adrenal* hypoglycemia, the glucose tolerance test does not always show a typical curve. The fasting blood sugar is apt to be low and there is a tendency for the sugar to be low 3 or 4 hours after the ingestion of glucose. Hypoglycemia induced by the injection of insulin lasts longer than the usual 60 to 90 minutes seen in the normal reaction. This test is not devoid of danger. One must depend upon other signs of pituitary and adrenal deficiency for the diagnosis.

Several types of *functional hypoglycemia* are described. One type seems to be due to *fever, vomiting* and *refusal* of *feedings*. Another is thought to be induced by *emotional reactions* in sensitive children. In these types carbohydrate metabolism is normal in between episodes.

Prognosis.—The outlook depends upon the cause of the condition. Functional hypoglycemia as a rule is not a serious condition though I have seen one case, in which vomiting, fever and refusal of food were responsible, with a blood sugar of 10 mgs and permanent damage to the brain. Adenoma of the pancreas is a very dangerous condition.

Treatment.—If the patient is seen in a state of hypoglycemic shock, the administration of glucose intravenously is indicated. Glucagon is strongly recommended. It is less likely to disturb proper control in unstable diabetics. It may be given intramuscularly or subcutaneously so that parents may inject it and thus avoid dangerous delay in treatment. No serious local or systemic reactions are described and no harmful effects result if the drug is given for some condition other than hypoglycemia. The cause of the condition must then be determined. Adenoma of the islets of the pancreas must be removed surgically. The type due to an excessive reaction to carbohydrate must be treated by a low carbohydrate, high fat, high protein diet. Other types are treated according to the underlying cause.

CASE HISTORY (Ped. A-92247).—*Boy of seven weeks developed upper respiratory tract infection, vomited and refused to eat. Convulsions and coma followed. Blood sugar of 10 mgs. Gross damage to the brain as a result.*

M. M., a baby of seven weeks, was admitted to the hospital in convulsions. The child had been born at full term, by normal delivery. There was no evidence of birth injury. His mother's health had been good during the pregnancy. He had been followed carefully by a pediatrician and was regarded as a healthy child. A few days before the child was admitted to the hospital, he had developed a fever and coryza. His throat was red. The child vomited repeatedly and refused to eat. On the third day of this illness, the child began to have convulsions and became comatose.

On examination, the child's skin was mottled and the pulse feeble.

Respiration was irregular. Almost constant twitching of the extremities was noted. There was generalized muscular rigidity. No evidence of consciousness was observed. The spinal fluid was normal in all respects. The blood sugar was found to be 10 mgs per cent and could not be brought to a normal level for almost eight hours. The child then began to improve. The convulsions ceased and some degree of consciousness returned. For a time, it was thought that the child was doing well.

In the next few months, it became evident that the child was not developing properly. He began to have convulsions again. He displayed no interest in his surroundings. At the age of six months, he was unable to sit up or even hold up his head. The tendon reflexes were all exaggerated. Movements of the extremities were similar to those of infants. There was no evidence of mental development. Frequent myoclonic contractions were evident, and the patient was said to have both tonic and clonic convulsions every day. Many tests of the blood sugar level were made and no tendency to hypoglycemia was found.

BIBLIOGRAPHY

BARRIS, R. W.: Pancreatic adenoma associated with neuromuscular disease. Ann. Int. Med., **38**:124, 1953.

BIX, H.: The relationship between maternal diabetes and giant children. Am. J. Obst. & Gynec., **29**:903, 1935.

BOLEY, S. J. *et al.*: Functioning pancreatic adenomas in infants and children. Surgery, **48**:592, 1960.

COCHRANE, W. A.: Idiopathic infantile hypoglycemia and leucine sensitivity. Metabolism, **9**:386, 1960.

———— *et al.*: Familial hypoglycemia precipitated by amino acids. J. Clin. Invest., **35**:411, 1956.

COLLE, F. AND ULSTROM, R. A.: Management of ketotic hypoglycemia. J. Pediat., **64**:632, 1964.

CONN, J. W. AND SELTZER, H. S.: Spontaneous hypoglycemia. Am. J. Med., **19**:460, 1955.

CORNBLATH, M. *et al.*: Low blood glucose in premature infants. Pediatrics, **32**:1007, 1963.

COURVILLE, C. B.: Late cerebral changes incident to severe hypoglycemia. Arch. Neurol. & Psychiat., **78**:1, 1957.

CREERY, R. D. G.: Hypoglycemia in the newborn. Developmental Med. and Child. Neurol., **8**:746, 1966.

CUMMINS, L. H.: Hypoglycemia and convulsions in children following alcohol ingestion. J. Pediat., **58**:23, 1961.

DANOWSKI, T. S. *et al.*: Endocrine adematosis or Zollinger-Ellison syndrome. Acta Med. Scandinav., **172**:559, 1962.

DANTA, G.: Hypoglycemic peripheral neuritis. Neurology, **21**:121, 1969.

DEKABAN, A. AND MOORE, W.: Neurological complications of idiopathic hypoglycemia in children. Acta neurol. scand., **43**:69, 1967.

DEKABAN, A. *et al.*: Familial idiopathic hypoglycemia. Arch. Neurol., **7**:529, 1962.

DUBE, A. H.: Late postprandial hypoglycemia. New England Jour. Med., **267**:438, 1962.

ELRICK, H. *et al.*: Glucagon treatment of insulin reactions. New England J. Med., **258**:476, 1958.

ETHERIDGE, J. E. AND MILLICHAP, J. G.: Hypoglycemia and seizures in childhood. Neurology, **14**:397, 1964.

FARQUHAR, J. M.: Hypoglycemia in newborn infants of diabetes. Arch. Dis. Child., **31**:203, 1956.

FEINBERG, D. H. *et al.*: Islet cell tumor epilepsy. Penn. Med., **70**:53, 1967.

FROESCH, E. R. *et al.*: Die hereditäre Fructose-Intoleranz eine bisher nicht bekannte kongenitale Stoffwechselstörung Schweiz. Med., **87**:1168, 1957.

GALL, J. C. AND BURKE, E. C.: Idiopathic hypoglycemosis. Proc. Staff Meet., Mayo Clin., **30**:477, 1955.

GARDINER, L. I. AND REYERSBACH, G.: Brain damage in juvenile diabetic patient as with insulin hypoglycemia. Pediatrics, **7**:210, 1951.

GRAY, S. H. AND FEEMSTER, L. C.: Compensatory hypertrophy and hyperplasia of the islands of Langerhans in the pancreas of a child born of a diabetic mother. Arch. Path., **1**:348, 1926.

HADDAD, H. M. *et al.:* Leucine induced hypoglycemia in infants. New England J. Med., **267**:1057, 1962.

HARDY, J. D.: Islet cell tumors. Amer. Jour. Med. Sci., **246**:218, 1963.

HARRIS, H.: Heredity in diabetes mellitus. Proc. Roy. Soc. Med., **42**:326, 1949.

HAWORTH, J. C. AND COODIN, F. J.: Idiopathic spontaneous hypoglycemia in children. Pediatrics, **25**:748, 1960.

HEBERDEN, P. AND FRIEDLANDER, F.: Hypoglycemic coma. Arch. Dis. Child., **30**:372, 1955.

KNOBLOCH, H. *et al.:* Prognostic and etiologic factors in hypoglycemia. Jour. Pediat., **70**:876, 1967.

LAWRENCE, R. D., MEYER, A. AND NEVIN, S.: The pathological changes in the brain in fatal hypoglycemia. Quart. J. Med., **11**:181, 1942.

LEVIN, B. *et al.:* Fructosaemia, an inborn error of metabolism. Arch. Dis. Childh., **38**:220, 1963.

LEWIS, G. M. *et al.:* Hypoglycemia due to an inherited enzyme deficiency. Arch. Dis. Childhood, **38**:40, 1963.

LIDZ, T. *et al.:* Muscular atrophy, and pseudologia fantastica associated with islet cell adenoma of the pancreas. Arch. Neurol. & Psychiat., **62**:304, 1949.

LUDIVINA, Y. *et al.:* Islet cell tumor in the neonate. Pediatrics, **41**:789, 1968.

MABRY, C. C. *et al.:* Leucine induced hypoglycemia. J. Pediat., **57**:526, 1960.

MALMUD, N. AND GROSH, L. C.: Hyperinsulinism and cerebral changes. Arch. Int. Med., **61**:579, 1938.

McQUARRIE, I.: Idiopathic spontaneously occurring hypoglycemia in infants. Am. J. Dis. Child., **87**:399, 1954.

MILLER, D. *et al.:* Hypoglycemia with non-pancreatic tumors. Ann. Surg., **150**:684, 1959.

MULDER, D. W. *et al.:* Hyperinsulin neuropathy. Neurology, **6**:627, 1956.

PILDES, R. *et al.:* The incidence of neonatal hypoglycemia. Jour. of Pediat., **70**:76, 1967.

POTTER, S. L., SECKEL, H. P. AND STRYKER, W. A.: Hypertrophy and hyperplasia of the islets of Langerhans of the fetus and newborn infant. Arch. Path., **31**:467, 1941.

RICHARDSON, J. E. AND RUSSELL, D. S.: Cerebral disease due to functioning islet cell tumors. Lancet, **ii**:1054, 1953.

ROSNER, L. AND ELSTAD, R.: The neuropathy of hypoglycemia. Neurology, **14**:1, 1964.

SCHULMAN, J. L. AND GREBEN, S. E.: The effect of glucagon on the blood glucose level and clinical state in the presence of marked insulin hypoglycemia. J. Clin. Invest., **36**:74, 1957.

SOBEL, D. E.: Fetal damage due to electric shock therapy, insulin coma, chlorpromazine or reserpine. Arch. Gen. Psychiat., **2**:606, 1960.

TOM, M. AND RICHARDSON, J.: Hypoglycemia from islet cell tumor of pancreas with amyotrophy and extensive degeneration of anterior horn cells. J. Neuropath. & Exp. Neurol., **10**:57, 1951.

WOLF, A., HARE, C. C. AND RIGGS, H. W.: Neurological manifestations in 2 patients with spontaneous hypoglycemia with necropsy report of a case with pancreatic island adenomata. Bull. Neurological Inst. of New York, **3**:232, 1933.

WOMACK, N. A., GNAGI, W. R. JR. AND GRAHAM, E. A.: Adenoma of the islands of Langerhans with hypoglycemia. Successful operative removal. J.A.M.A., **97**:831, 1932.

THE GLYCOGEN STORAGE DISEASES

Eleven types of glycogen storage disease are now described. There is always an accumulation of glycogen in one or more organs. The liver, heart, skeletal muscles and the nervous system may be involved more or less selec-

TABLE IV

Type	Name	Organs Affected	Glycogen Structure	Enzyme Deficiency
1.	Von Gierke's disease	Liver and kidneys	Normal	Glucose-6-phosphatase
2.	Pompe's disease	Generalized	Normal	Acid maltase
3.	Forbe's disease	Generalized	Limit dextrin	Amylo-1 6 transglucosidase debrancher
4.	Andersen's disease	Liver	Amylopectin type	Amylo-1 4 to 16 transglucosidase brancher
5.	McArdle's disease	Muscles	Normal	Muscle phosphorylase
6.	Her's disease	Liver	Normal	Liver phosphorylase
7.		Liver and skeletal muscles	Normal	Phosphoglucomutase two patients
8.		Liver	Normal	Phosphorylase one pateint
9.		Liver	Normal	Liver phosphorylase one patient
10.	Antopol's disease	Heart and muscles	Normal	Phosphoglucomutase in liver and muscles
11.	Hug's disease	Muscles and nervous system	Normal	Phosphofructokinase

tively. As a rule deficiency of an enzyme is at fault, but abnormal glycogens may be responsible.

Von Gierke's Disease or the Hepatic Form. In this condition, the liver is grossly enlarged. The spleen is not greatly increased in size. Bodily growth is defective, but there is often obesity. Attacks of hypoglycemia and acidosis with convulsions and coma are often the most striking manifestations. Adrenaline does not cause a proper rise in blood sugar. Fasting blood sugar is low and when glucose is administered, the blood sugar rises excessively and remains elevated for long periods. Neurological signs are absent. The muscles may be slender and weak but are not paralysed. Renal function is not impaired though the kidneys may be enlarged.

Fine *et al.* describe small yellow paramacular spots in the retinae of five children suffering type 1 glycogen disease. Vision was not reduced.

Biopsy reveals that there are glycogen deposits in the liver and kidneys. It has been shown that glucose 6-phosphatase is found in the liver in inadequate amounts. Several children may be affected in one family. The inheritance follows the recessive pattern. The children may die early in life or improve and live to adult life. In two post-mortem examinations hepatic adenomas have been found. Riddell and Davies have performed portacaval transposition in a case of type 1 glycogen storage disease with good results.

Pompe's Disease—a Generalized Type. In this condition, the heart is enlarged early in life and contains abundant deposits of glycogen. There is usually no bruit. Congenital heart disease is usually suspected. Cyanosis and dyspnea are the commonest symptoms. The liver is not enlarged except as a result of heart failure. The metabolic abnormalities described in the

hepatic type are not present. Deficiency of acid maltase is responsible. Rhabdomyomas of the heart have been found in several cases. In this type of glycogen storage disease death usually occurs before the end of the first year. Heart failure is the cause of death.

The muscles and the nervous system are both involved. The child is atonic and helpless. The expression suggests idiocy. The tendon reflexes are elicited with difficulty. Glycogen deposits are found in the muscles and in the central nervous system as well. A case of this type is given in abstract below.

Swaiman describes a case of late acid maltase deficiency whose only symptoms were due to a moderately severe myopathy resembling the Duchenne type of muscular dystrophy.

CASE HISTORY (Ped. A-68202. Path. 21653).—*Pompe's disease in a child of four months with profound generalized muscular weakness and loss of tone simulating amyotonia congenita. Death from heart failure. Post-mortem examination revealed deposits of glycogen in the heart, muscles and nerve cells of the brain and spinal cord.*

G. C., a child of four months, was admitted to the Harriet Lane Home on Jan. 24, 1949. He had always been a sluggish baby and was believed to be mentally deficient. His cry was weak and there was some difficulty in swallowing. For several weeks he had been vomiting repeatedly and had had diarrhea at times. He seemed to be getting weaker.

On examination profound generalized muscular weakness was found associated with marked reduction of muscular tone. Only feeble movements were observed in the extremities. The child could not sit up or even hold up the head. The facial muscles and the jaws were involved and swallowing was difficult. Respiration was rapid and weak but was chiefly intercostal. The tendon reflexes were elicited with difficulty if at all. The heart was enlarged in all diameters and the liver was also somewhat enlarged. It was not possible to gain any clear idea of the child's mental sta-

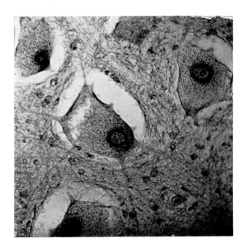

FIG. 187. Showing glycogen deposits in the anterior horn cells of the spinal cord. (By the courtesy of Dr. David Clark.)

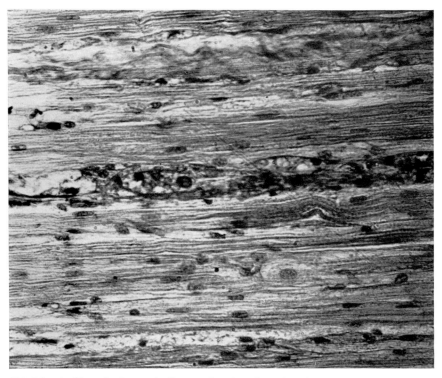

Fig. 188. Muscle fibers in Pompe's disease showing deposits of glycogen. (By the courtesy of Dr. David Clark.)

tus because of the lack of motor reactions. A number of diagnoses were entertained including amyotonia congenita, myasthenia gravis and congenital malformation of the heart. Dr. David B. Clark, however, made a diagnosis of von Pompe's disease. Prostigmine failed to produce any improvement in the motor reactions.

On the 16th day after admission the child became cyanotic and the pulse more rapid. He lapsed into coma and died on Feb. 10, 1949.

Post-mortem examination revealed enlargement of the heart, liver and kidneys. Histological study of these organs made the diagnosis of glycogen disease clear for they displayed all the usual changes. The finding of greatest interest was the extensive deposit of glycogen in the nervous system. The neurons of the brain and spinal cord were distended with glycogen granules so that the appearance of the cell was not unlike that of these seen in cerebroretinal degeneration where lipoid granules distend the neurons. The skeletal muscles also displayed infiltrations with glycogen.

A rare condition has been described by McArdle. His patient was a young man who had suffered all his life from pain and tenderness in the muscles

following exercise. These symptoms developed in the legs and thighs after walking only one hundred yards. Immediately after exercise the affected muscles would become shortened. Passive stretching of the shortened muscles would cause pain. After light exercise the symptoms would subside within a short time but more strenuous exercise might cause prolonged symptoms. The muscles were not wasted or weak. There was no pseudohypertrophy or myotonia. The reflexes were in order.

Various studies were made. The electromyogram revealed no electrical activity in the shortened muscles when they were at rest. No myoglobin was found in the urine. It was thought that the blood lactate and pyruvate did not rise after exercise as they do in a normal subject. The serum potassium rose, however. It was suspected that the muscles were unable to utilize glycogen in a normal manner.

Schmid and Mahler made a complete study of a patient whose symptoms were of long duration and more severe than those of the patient of McArdle. Exertion caused cramps and greater exertion caused myoglobinuria. It was found that the muscles contained five times the normal amount of glycogen which could not be converted to glucose. This was apparently due to lack of phosphorylase. Excessive exertion caused necrosis of the muscles and myoglobinuria. The administration of glucose prevented the symptoms. Glucogen was found to be helpful.

Schmid and Hammaker state that this disease is inherited as if it were due to a rare recessive autosomal gene.

Engel states that three stages may be distinguished in the type of this disease which begins in childhood: (1) In childhood, there is easy fatigue and dark urine. (2) In early adult life there are cramping pains and myoglobinuria. (3) In the fourth or fifth decade, there is progressive weakness and wasting of the muscles but no myoglobinuria.

He described two cases in which the disease began in the fourth and fifth decades. In one there was no phosphorylase, and in one only 35 per cent of the usual amount in the muscles. No excess of glycogen was found in the muscles. One patient had cramps in the muscles but no weakness and one had weakness and wasting, but no cramps.

I have seen two cases of this syndrome, both in boys. One case is given in abstract below.

Favara *et al.* describe familial recurrent paralytic episodes in children with myoglobinuria. One child died in the second episode. Phosphorylase activity in the muscles was increased.

CASE HISTORY (No. 718935).—The first symptoms were noted when A. S. was about 3 years old. His mother had taken him to the park and he ran around on the grass with the other children. Suddenly he began to scream

and said that his legs hurt. He could not walk and had to be carried home. Within a few hours he was well again. However, he was never able to play outdoor games with the other children and always complained of pains in his legs when he ran or walked even a short distance. The symptoms did not change materially as he grew older. He found that after exercise he had limitation of movement for the muscles would become shortened and tender. Stretching of the muscles caused severe pain. After walking the hamstrings and gluteals as well as the calves would be affected in this manner. He was fond of playing the piano and this exercise would cause his fingers to become flexed and the pectorals to become shortened so he could not elevate his arms. The urine was never discolored. The family history was negative for any condition resembling that of the patient.

Neurological examination revealed nothing except for the fact that the musculature was rather slender as one might expect since he had never been able to take proper exercise. The muscles were of normal consistency and strength. There was no myotonia. The tendon reflexes were quite normal. No lesions were found on the skin.

The pain, tenderness and shortening of the muscles described above were easily elicited by exercise under observation.

Unfortunately a complete examination could not be made. There was no myoglobin in the urine even after exercise. The electromyogram was normal. No metabolic study was made and no muscle biopsy was performed.

Hug's Disease. In this condition the liver may be slightly enlarged at first, but the enlargement recedes. There is some reduction of the liver phosphorylase. The children do not develop properly. Some learn to walk with difficulty and may even form a word or two for a time. There is gradual deterioration. Weakness, spasticity and paralysis develop terminating in decerebrate rigidity and dementia. A deficiency of phosphofructokinase is responsible. Hypoglycemia, lipemia and acidosis do not occur. Catecholamines are found in the urine.

At post-mortem examination the brain, cerebellum, brain stem and spinal cord contain deposits of glycogen and the muscles are involved in the same manner.

BIBLIOGRAPHY

McArdle's Diseases

DYKEN, M. L. *et al.*: An electromyographic diagnostic test in McArdle's disease. Neurology, **17**:45, 1967.

ENGEL, W. K.: Late onset type of skeletal muscle phosphorylase deficiency. New England J. Med., **268**:135, 1963.

FAVARA, B. E. *et al.*: Familial paroxysmal rhabdomyolysis in children. Amer. Jour. Med., **42**:196, 1967.

McARDLE, B.: Myopathy due to a defect in muscle glycogen breakdown. Clin. Sc., **10**:13, 1951.

ROWLAND, L. P. *et al.*: The clinical diagnosis of McArdle's disease. Neurology, **16**:93, 1966.

SCHMID, R. AND HAMMAKER, L.: The hereditary basis of McArdle's syndrome. New England J. Med., **264**:223, 1961.

——— AND MAHLER, R.: Chronic progressive myopathy with myoglobinuria. Demonstration of a glycogenolytic defect. J. Clin. Invest., **38**:2044, 1959.

SLOTWINER, P. *et al.:* Myopathy resembling McArdle's syndrome. Arch. of Neurol., **20**:586, 1969.

Other Types

CASTAIGNE, P. AND LHERMITTE, F.: Determinations nerveuses des glycogenoses. Fifth International Neurological Congress, Lisbon, 1953, **i**:271.

CLEMENT, D. H. AND GODMAN, G. C.: Glycogen disease resembling mongolism, cretinism and amyotonia. J. Pediat., **36**:11, 1950.

CORI, G. T. AND SCHULMAN, J. L.: Glycogen storage disease of the liver. 11 Enzyme studies. Pediatrics, **14**:646, 1954.

CREVELD, S. VAN: Glycogen disease. Medicine, **18**:1, 1939.

CROME, L. *et al.:* Neuropathological and neurochemical aspects of generalized glycogen storage disease. J. Neurol. Neurosurg. & Psychiat., **26**:422, 1963.

DI SANT'AGNESE, P. A. *et al.:* Glycogen disease of muscles. J. Pediat., **61**:438, 1962.

DI SANT'AGNESE, P. A., ANDERSEN, D. H. AND MASON, H. H.: Glycogen storage disease of the heart. Pediatrics, **6**:607, 1950.

EHLERS, K. H. AND ENGLE, M. A.: Glycogen storage disease of the myocardium. Amer. Heart Jour., **65**:145, 1963.

ELLIS, R. W. B. AND PAYNE, W. W.: Glycogen disease. Quart. J. Med., **5**:31, 1936.

FIELD, R. A.: Glycogen Deposition Disease. The Metabolic Basis of Inherited Disease. Stansbury, J. B., Wyngaarden, J. B. and Fredrickson, D. S. McGraw-Hill, New York, 2nd Ed., 1966.

FINE, R. N. *et al.:* Retinal changes in glycogen storage disease type 1. Amer. Jour. Dis. Child., **115**:328, 1968.

HSIA, D. Y.: Inborn Errors of Metabolism. Chicago, Year Book Publishers, 1960, p. 137.

HUG, G. *et al.:* Glycogen storage disease. Amer. Jour. Dis. Child., **111**:457, 1966.

KRIVIT, W. *et al.:* Glycogen storage disease primarily affecting the skeletal muscles and clinically resembling amyotonia. Pediatrics, **12**:165, 1953.

LAYZER, R. B. *et al.:* Muscle phosphofructokinase deficiency. Arch. of Neurol., **17**:512, 1967.

MEHRIZI, A. AND OPPENHEIMER, E. H.: Heart failure associated with an unusual deposition of glycogen in the myocardium. Bull. Johns Hopkins Hosp., **107**:329, 1960.

RIDDELL, A. G. AND DAVIES, R. P.: Portacaval transposition in the treatment of glycogen storage disease. Lancet, **ii**:1146, 1966.

SMITH, J. AND ZELLWEGER, H.: Muscular form of glycogenosis, type 11 Pompe. Neurology, **17**:537, 1967.

SWAIMAN, K. F. *et al.:* Late infantile acid maltase deficiency. Arch. of Neurology, **18**:642, 1968.

TARUI, S.: Phosphofructokinase deficiency in skeletal muscle. Biochem. Biophys. Res., **19**:517, 1965.

WILLIAMS, N. E. AND FIELD, J. B.: Low leukocyte phosphorylase in hepatic phosphorylase deficient glycogen storage disease. Jour. Clin. Invest., **40**:1841, 1961.

ZELLWEGER, H., DARK, A. AND HAIDAR, G. A.: Glycogen disease of the skeletal muscle. Pediatrics, **15**:715, 1955.

GALACTOSURIA WITH CATARACTS AND MENTAL DEFICIENCY

This condition is regarded as a constitutional defect of metabolism. The essential abnormality seems to be lack of an enzyme termed galactose-1-phospate-uridyl transferase which in normal individuals converts galactose phosphate into glucose phosphate. This enzyme is found in the liver and also in the red cells. It is believed that this disease is inherited as a recessive characteristic. The heterozygous carrier of the abnormal gene can be detected by means of the galactose tolerance test or by the decrease of P-gal-uridyl-transferase. About 30 cases had been reported in 1955.

Crome has made a post-mortem examination on a child suffering from this disease. He found microcephaly and multiple small foci of necrosis. The nerve cells showed chromatolysis. There was extensive gliosis in both the gray and white matter. The process seemed to involve all parts of the nervous system.

It is stated that at birth the child seems to be normal, but after a few days begins to vomit and becomes lethargic. Physiological jaundice may be prolonged. The liver and spleen become enlarged and ascites may develop. Hypoglycemic attacks may occur. Both physical and mental development are retarded. Cataracts develop. Osteoporosis is a feature. The urine contains albumin and also sugar which by proper analysis can be shown to be galactose. Aminoaciduria may occur. A portion of the sugar in the blood is found to be galactose. The child, if untreated, may die in infancy. Early and severe cases are described and also late cases which are less severe.

Wilhelm points out that milk allergy is difficult to distinguish and specific allergy tests are necessary to establish the correct diagnosis.

If milk is removed from the diet, the child's condition improves in striking fashion. Nutrition and growth become satisfactory. The cataracts, however, persist and surgery is required. The mental defect is, unfortunately, apt to remain. Pesch *et al.* state that the administration of progesterone causes an increase in the ability to oxidize galactose.

It has been suggested that a woman who has had a child suffering from galactosuria should be put on a galactose free diet in subsequent pregnancies.

The diagnosis may be made quickly by a modification of the Guthrie test for phenylketonuria. Galactose will inhibit the growth of a mutant strain of *E. coli.*

BIBLIOGRAPHY

CROME, L.: Galactosemia, pathology and neuropathology. Arch. Dis. Childhood, **37**:415, 1962.
————: Galactosemia with neuropathologic findings. Arch. Dis. Childhood, **37**:415, 1962.
DONNELL, G. N. *et al.*: Mental retardation with galactosemia. J. Pediat., **58**:836, 1961.
———— *et al.*: Growth and development of children with galactosemia. J. Pediat., **58**:836, 1961.
———— *et al.*: Enzymatic expression of heterozygosity in families of children with galactosemia. Pediatrics, **25**:572, 1960.
ISSELBACHER, K. *et al.*: The specific defect in galactosemia. Proc. Am. Pediat. Soc., May 9-11, 1956.
KOCH, R. *et al.*: Nutritional therapy of galactosemia. Clin. Pediat., **4**:571, 1965.
KOMROWER, G. M. *et al.*: A clinical and biochemical study of galactosemia. Arch. Dis. Child., **31**:254, 1956.
PESCH, A. L. *et al.*: Effects of progesterone in congenital galactosemia. J. Clin. Invest., **39**:178, 1960.
RITTER, J. A. AND CANNON, E.: Galactosuria with cataracts. New England J. Med., **252**:747, 1955.
TOWSEND, E. H. *et al.*: Galactosuria and its relation to Laennec's cirrhosis. Pediatrics, **7**:760, 1951.
WALKER, F. A. *et al.*: Galactosemia. Ann. Hum. Genet., **25**:287, 1962.
WILHELM, R. E.: Differentiation of chronic galactosemia and milk allergy in early childhood. J. Allergy, **28**:401, 1957.

DISORDERS OF LIPID METABOLISM

The Cerebral Lipidoses

Introduction.—There are a number of rare but well known diseases which are characterized by deposits of lipids in various tissues of the body including the central nervous system. Chemical studies have led to the theory that these conditions represent disorders of the metabolism of the lipids. Each disease is believed to represent a specific defect. The chemistry of the lipids is very complex and still imperfectly understood. The staining reactions are less reliable than one might wish. No doubt many of the statements made below will require modification in the future. The substances mentioned below are not found in increased amount in the blood stream and are believed to accumulate in the tissues as a result of defective activity of intracellular enzymes.

1. Cerebroretinal Degenerations—Tay-Sachs
   Disease
   Abdominal viscera — No increase of lipids
   Brain — Glycolipids gangliosides
2. Niemann-Pick's Disease
   Abdominal viscera — Glycerophosphatides
   Brain — Glycerophosphatides
3. Schüller-Christian Disease
   Abdominal viscera — Cholesterol esters
   Brain — Cholesterol esters
4. Gaucher's Disease
   Abdominal viscera — Kerasin, a galactosido-cerebroside and glycosido-cerebrosides
   Brain — Undetermined
5. Hurler's Syndrome
   Abdominal viscera — Controversial, Mucopolysaccharides? Glycolipids?
   Brain — Controversial

Other lipidoses which are not so well known should be mentioned here. Farber has described *lipogranulomatosis* which is discussed briefly below. Norman and others have studied a *familial cerebral lipidosis* which is already advanced at the time of birth. This is mentioned below. A reference given below, i.e., Cerebral Lipidoses, contains a number of important studies of these conditions. A condition termed *cephalin lipidosis* which has never been described before is reported.

The Leucodystrophies

Recent investigations have led to the conclusion that certain diseases formerly classified among the degenerations of the white matter are really disorders of lipid metabolism. These are familial conditions in contrast to the so-called sudanophil processes such as disseminated sclerosis and Schilder's disease which are not usually familial. The analysis of these cases is far from complete. It seems to be believed that a lack of specific enzyme

activity is responsible for a disorder of myelin metabolism. Seitelberger suggests that in Pelizaeus-Merzbacher disease we are dealing with a glycero-phosphatide dystrophy of the myelin sheath and in the cerebral scleroses of Scholz and Krabbe and the metachromatic type of Greenfield the process is a sphingolipid dystrophy. There is much difference of opinion about such matters.

BIBLIOGRAPHY

BIRD, A.: Lipidosis and the central nervous system. Brain, 71:434, 1948.

FRANCESCHETTI, A.: Les manifestations oculaires des troubles primative due metabolisme des lipids. Arquivos de Neuro-psiquiatria, 13:69, 1955.

HSIA, D. Y. Y.: Inborn errors of metabolism. Year Book Publishers Inc., Chicago, 1959.

————: Inborn errors of metabolism. New England J. Med., 262:1222, 1960.

PAGE, I. H.: The Chemistry of the Brain. Springfield, Thomas, 1937.

THANNHAUSER, S. J.: The lipidoses. Oxford Medicine, VI. part 2, p. 214.

————: Diseases of the nervous system associated with disturbances of lipide metabolism. Res. Nerv. & Ment. Dis., 32:238, 1953.

VAN BOGAERT, L.: Interet de l'etude des lipidoses pour la neuropathologie. La Presse Med., 45:587, 1937.

————: Editor of Cerebral Lipidoses, a Symposium. Antwerp, July 1955. Springfield, Thomas, 1957.

THE CEREBRAL LIPIDOSES

Cerebroretinal Degeneration—Subacute Infantile Form or Amaurotic Idiocy of Tay-Sachs

Definitions.—Obviously this is not a form of idiocy in the usual meaning of the term, but a progressive and uniformly fatal degeneration of the nervous system. It is with few exceptions restricted to subjects of Jewish race and characterized by specific histological changes as well as by fairly constant clinical features. It will be shown in the following pages that this disease is closely related to several other degenerative processes involving the retinae and central nervous system.

Pathological Anatomy.—The cerebrum usually shows no malformation or gross changes, but some pathologists have described a waxy consistency which may be due to the high lipoid content. The cerebellum is often very small and abnormally firm. Histological examination reveals universal changes in the ganglion cells throughout the entire central nervous system. The cells are swollen and their cystoplasm presents a finely granular, hyaline appearance. The nuclei are displaced to the periphery of the cell and eventually disintegrate. The Nissl bodies are found only in the area surrounding the nuclei and are reduced to very fine granules. The hematoxylin stains of Schaffer and Weigert reveal that the swelling is due to deposits of large and small droplets in the cytoplasm. The droplets are regarded as lipoids or pre-lipoids. The neurofibrils are intact at first but are displaced to the periphery of the cell. A very typical feature is the appearance of large balloon-like swellings upon the dendrites close to their origin. These may be as

large as the cell body. There is also demyelination which seems to be secondary to the destruction of the cells. The astrocytes undergo proliferation but this is not so extensive as the reaction of the microglia which become amoeboid and distended with the debris of cellular disintegration. There are no evidences of an inflammatory process and no significant changes in the blood vessels. The process in the retinae is identical with that in the brain. The ganglion cells, which are most numerous in the region of the macula, become swollen and loaded with lipoids, causing the retina to assume a dirty white appearance. The fovea contains no cells and remains transparent so that the choroidal blood vessels remain visible. As a result we see a small red spot surrounded by an edematous and necrotic zone of grayish white. The optic nerves show secondary degeneration. The deposits in the nerve cells are composed of the cerebral ganglioside G.M.2.

O'Brien finds that the component A of B.N. Acetylglucosaminidase and B.N. Acetylgalactosaminidase is totally lacking in the brain, liver, skin, kidney, blood plasma and leucocytes.

In certain instances in which the child survives longer than usual, there is massive degeneration of the white matter and swelling of the brain. The

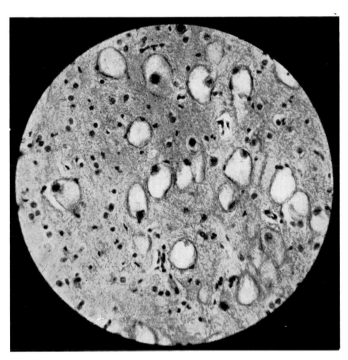

Fig. 189. Section showing great swelling of the cells in amaurotic idiocy. The Nissl bodies have disappeared and the nuclei are displaced to the periphery of the cell. By means of special stains it may be shown that these cells contain great quantities of lipoid products which form both fine and coarse globules throughout the cytoplasm of the cells.

degeneration of the nerve fibers is believed to be secondary to the destruction of the nerve cells. Aronson *et al.* point out that though the brain of children suffering from this disease is small and under average weight when the child dies within 14 months after the onset, when the child lives more than 24 months, the brain and consequently the head enlarges and increases in weight. One brain weighed 1830 gm. This increase in size is found to be due to glial hyperplasia. A mild internal hydrocephalus is also found and this is thought to be a result of meningeal fibrosis caused by the discharge of lipoid products into the subarachnoid spaces. In contrast to Niemann-Pick disease, the liver and spleen are not as a rule enlarged. Thannhauser states that these organs contain no excess of lipoids.

Aronson *et al.* announced in 1962 that nineteen children suffering from Tay-Sachs disease lacked the serum enzyme fructosel phosphate aldolase. Of fifty-two parents of these children, fifty-one showed lack of this enzyme and one had a diminished amount. The enzyme was lacking in eleven of nineteen grandparents and in four of twelve healthy siblings. Values were normal in all but three of seventy-one normal adults. In 1962, Bessman and Baldwin discovered imidazole aminoaciduria in these patients.

Clinical Features.—A few instances are recorded in which this disease has developed in gentiles. As a rule, however, it occurs only in Jews and especially those who came to this country from Poland and eastern Russia.

It is stated that when the disease occurs in gentiles, there is usually consanguinity, whereas in Jewish families, consanguinity is usually not evident. Heterozygous carriers of the abnormal gene may be identified, it is claimed, by vacuoles in the lymphocytes. Frequently, several siblings are affected, but it is very exceptional for more than one generation to be involved. As a rule the disease dies out in the same family in which it appears. Males and females are affected alike. No etiological factor is known other than morbid heredity and it is assumed that the disease is the expression of a defect in the germ plasm. The mode of inheritance is obviously recessive. Dr. Robert Cook has told me of a woman who changed husbands repeatedly in the hope of getting a healthy baby. To her dismay, four successive husbands produced four successive children with Tay-Sachs disease.

At birth and for several months thereafter, the children seem to be quite healthy. The first evidence of illness is sluggishness or apathy which is noted as a rule between the fourth and eighth months. The child ceases to fix objects with the eyes, does not notice the parents and in general takes no interest in its surroundings. Soon there is definite evidence of regression. Motor reactions which have been acquired are lost. The child ceases to sit up and later becomes unable to hold up the head. The muscles become soft and atonic and there is progressive loss of weight. It is now apparent, as a rule, that vision is lost or greatly reduced. Ophthalmoscopic examination

will reveal the diagnosis at once. The region of the fovea is marked in either eye by a bright red area which is described in the text books as a cherry red spot. Surrounding this is a grayish white zone of necrotic and edematous retina which makes the central red area stand out in striking contrast. The optic nerve head is somewhat pale, but the blood vessels are normal. This last feature is of value in ruling out occlusion of the central retinal artery. These changes are always bilateral and, as a rule, about equally advanced in either eye.

The symptoms progress slowly. Within a few months the child becomes entirely blind, demented and more or less completely helpless. In this second stage of the disease there is intense spasticity of the musculature and very active reflex phenomena. The tendon reflexes are grossly exaggerated, ankle clonus is easily elicited and there is a bilateral Babinski reaction. In some cases the posture is of interest. The arms are extended at the elbow, adducted at the shoulder, and flexed at the wrist. The forearm is pronated. The legs are extended and the head somewhat retracted in the later stages of this disease. The picture is, in general, that of decerebrate rigidity. Active tonic neck reflexes are usually present as are nursing and chewing reflexes. Loud noises and, in fact, almost any sudden stimulus will provoke reflex movements. Convulsive seizures of various types are common. These are general or local and perhaps tonic more frequently than clonic. As a rule there is bulbar, or perhaps more accurately, pseudobulbar palsy. Tube feeding is sometimes required. Phenomena suggestive of release of the emotional mechanisms have been described, such as explosive laughing, or crying. Searching movements of the eyes are observed, as in any other type of blindness and various types of true nystagmus which may be associated with rotary movements of the head. In the terminal stages the head may become very much enlarged. Throughout the course of the disease there is always increasing loss of weight so that the child becomes extraordinarily emaciated. The muscles become atrophic and the subcutaneous fat disappears so that eventually the extremities seem to be mere skin and bones. Gross deformities result as a consequence of contractures. The liver and spleen are not enlarged and there is no significant anemia. The disease is always fatal and ends, as a rule, between the second and third year, only a few children living beyond the third year.

Jampel and Quaglio have made a careful study of eye movements in this condition. They state that spontaneous or voluntary movements are the first to be lost, the following movements are lost next and vestibular reflex eye movements are the last to go.

We have seen a little colored boy (Ped. B-33706) who developed a progressive process in the nervous system at about the age of six months and died at the age of twenty months. The neurological findings were consistent

with infantile cerebromacular degeneration and the post-mortem examination of the brain showed lesions quite typical of this disease. The retinae did not show the usual cherry red spot but a round, intensely black deposit of pigment directly in the maculae. These were about half the size of the discs in diameter and closely resembled dots of India ink.

Diagnosis.—We should always think of this diagnosis in cases of progressive disturbances of vision developing between the second and twelfth months in Jewish children. The most important test in the diagnosis is the examination of the retinae. The cherry red spot is apparently always present when the disease is well advanced. However, a red spot of almost identical appearance is seen in some cases of Niemann-Pick and Gaucher's disease. Cortical biopsy should establish the diagnosis and rectal biopsy may also reveal nerve cells with the characteristic changes. The lymphocytes may show vacuoles which are thought to be of diagnostic significance. If the liver and spleen are enlarged and if there is high grade anemia, Niemann-Pick or Gaucher's disease should be suspected.

The demonstration of loss of the A component of B.N. Acetylglucosaminidase and B.N. Acetylgalactosaminidase establishes the diagnosis.

Prognosis.—Death always occurs between the end of the second and the fourth years. There is no evidence that recovery or even arrest of the disease is possible.

Treatment.—Parents who have had one child afflicted with this disease may be advised that a large proportion of all subsequent children will suffer from the same condition.

BIBLIOGRAPHY

ARONSON, S. M. *et al.*: Infantile amaurotic idiocy. Pediatrics, **26**:229, 1960.

——— AND RABINER, A.: Hydrocephalus associated with lipoidosis of the central nervous system. Proc. of the Philadelphia Neurological Soc., New York Neurol. Soc. and New York Academy of Med. Joint Meeting, April 21, 1955.

———: The megaloencephalic phase of infantile amaurotic familial idiocy. Arch. Neurol. & Psychiat., **79**:151, 1958.

BESSMAN, S. P. AND BALDWIN, R.: Imidazole aminoaciduria in cerebroretinal degeneration. Science, **135**:789, 1962.

BIELSCHOWSKY, M.: Zur Histopathologie u. Pathogenese der amaurotischen Idiotie mit besonderer Berücksichtigung der zerebellaren Veranderungen. J. f. Psychol. u. Neurol., **26**:123, 1921.

———: Amaurotische Idiotie und lipoidzellige Splenohepatomegalie. Jour. f. Psychol. u. Neurol., **36**:103, 1928.

DERWORT, A. AND DETERING, K.: Vacuolated lymphocytes in familial amaurotic idiocy and their significance. Nervenartz., **6**:19, 1959.

GOMEZ, C. J. *et al.*: Studies in Tay-Sachs disease. Jour. Neuropath. and Exp. Neurol., **22**:1, 1963.

HAMBURGER, R.: Lipoidzellige Splenohepatomegalie in Verbindung mit amaurotischer Idiotie. Jahrb. f. Kinderhk., **116**:41, 1927.

JAMPEL, R. S. AND QUAGLIO, N. D.: Eye movements in Tay-Sachs disease. Neurology, **14**:1013, 1964.

KOREY, S. R., GOMEZ, C. I., TERRY, R. D. *et al.*: Studies in Tay-Sachs disease. J. Neuropath. & Exp. Neurol., **22**:22-98, 1963.

MASSAKOWSKI, M. *et al.:* On the relationship of metachromatic leukodystrophy and amaurotic idiocy. Brain, 84:585, 1961.

NAKAI, H. AND LANDING, B. H.: Suggested use of rectal biopsy in diagnosis of neural lipidoses. Pediatrics, 26:225, 1960.

O'BRIEN, J.: Tay-Sachs disease. Generalized absence of a Beta D.N. Acetylhexosaminidase component. Science, August 15, 1969, p. 698.

PONCHER, II. G.: Lipoid histiocytosis. Am. J. Dis. Child., 42:77, 1931.

SACHS, B.: An arrested cerebral development with special reference to its cortical pathology. J. Nerv. & Ment. Dis., 15:541, 1887.

————: Amaurotic idiocy and general lipoid degeneration. Arch. Neurol. & Psychiat., 31:247, 1929. (Discussion by Strauss, etc.)

SCHAFFER, C.: The pathogenesis of amaurotic idiocy. Arch. Neurol. & Psychiat., 24:765, 1930.

SCHENCK, L. *et al.:* The startle response and serum enzyme profile in early detection of Tay-Sachs disease. Jour. Pediat., 65:749, 1964.

SLOME, D.: The genetic basis of amaurotic idiocy. J. Genet., 27:363, 1933.

TERRY, R. D. AND WEISS, M.: Studies in Tay-Sachs disease 11. Ultrastructure of the cerebrum. Jour. Neuropath. Exp. Neurol., 22:18, 1963.

THANNHAUSER, S. J.: Diseases of the nervous system associated with disturbances of lipide metabolism. Res. Nerv. & Ment. Dis., 32:238, 1953.

VAN BOGAERT, L.: Cerebral Lipidoses. Thomas, Springfield, Ill., 1957.

VOLK, B. W.: Ed., Tay-Sachs Disease. 1964, New York.

WALSH, F. B.: *Loc. cit.*

WYNBURN-MASON, R.: On some anomalous forms of amaurotic idiocy and their bearing on the relationship of the various types. Brit. J. Ophth., 27:145, 1943.

Heller's Infantile Dementia

Heller has described a type of progressive dementia which begins between the ages of two and four years. These children seem to be quite normal before the onset. The first symptoms include restlessness and emotional disturbances, especially evidences of anxiety. Attention declines and the child is slow to learn new things. Later, it becomes evident that actual regression is taking place. The child forgets what has been learned. Speech is gradually lost. Behavior becomes infantile. There is disobedience, irritability and negativism. Tics, repetitive and stereotyped movements appear. The child babbles like a baby and plays with his fingers and toes. Complete dementia develops within a few years. It is of interest that no weakness, tremor, rigidity or ataxia are described. The retinae are said to show no changes. The facial expression is said to be normal. Convulsions are not mentioned. There is never any improvement. Growth may be somewhat retarded.

We have seen a small number of such cases. The profound dementia without motor disorders, changes in vision or convulsions seems to be distinctive. In only one case was the diagnosis verified by biopsy of the cortex. In one interesting case which I have observed, the patient, a boy of 4 years, displayed the behavior of a normal, healthy, placid baby of 6 months though his motor functions were proper for his age.

My reason for mentioning this condition at this point is that Corberi de-

scribes two post-mortem examinations. Sections of the cerebral cortex, cerebellum and spinal cord were made. He states that a diffuse, lipoid cell degeneration of the cortical neurons was found which closely resembled that of amaurotic idiocy. It is hard to believe, however, that this syndrome is always due to the same anatomical process. Thus, Benda found in one case that the cortical neurons were small, disorganized and lacking in Nissl bodies and there was marginal gliosis with an occasional giant glial cell. He does not mention lipoid deposits in the cells. Malmud states that in four cases of this disease he found amaurotic idiocy without loss of vision in two cases at post-mortem examination and in two other cases he found degeneration of the corpus Luysi and the mammillary body and mammillothalamic tract. The process was bilateral and symmetrical. Siblings were involved. It is said that the chief problems in differential diagnosis are the childhood autism of Kanner and childhood schizophrenia, but I imagine other degenerative processes may cause similar pictures.

BIBLIOGRAPHY

BENDA, C. E.: Developmental Disorders of Mentation and Cerebral Palsies. Grune and Stratton, New York, 1952.

CHAPMAN, A. H.: Early infantile autism. J. Dis. Child., 99:783, 1960.

CORBERI, G.: Sindrome di regressione mentale infanto-giovanile. Revista di pathologia nervosa e mentale., 31:6, 1926.

HELLER, T.: Uber Dementia infantilis. Ztschr. f. die Erforschung und Behandlung des jungendl Schwachsinns., 2:17, 1908.

———: Uber Dementia infantilis. Ztschr. f. Kinderforsch., 37:661, 1930.

MALMUD, N.: Heller's disease and childhood schizophrenia. Am. J. Psychiat., 116:215, 1959.

REISER, D. E.: Psychoses of infancy and early childhood. New England J. Med., 269:844, 1963.

ZAPPERT, J.: Dementia infantilis (Heller). Ztschr. f. Kinderpsychiat., 4:161, 1938.

Cerebroretinal Degeneration—Early Juvenile (Late Infantile) Form of Bielschowski

A form of cerebroretinal degeneration has been studied by Bielschowski which begins at the age of three or four years and runs a relatively slow course as compared with the infantile type of the disease. The symptoms are similar in general but ataxia and other evidences of cerebellar degeneration are prominent, although they are not easily demonstrable in the infantile form. In most cases there is bilateral optic atrophy with or without narrowing of the retinal arteries. It has been stated that there are no lesions in the maculae in this type of cerebroretinal degeneration. Possibly this statement is due to the fact that it is not always easy to recognize minor alterations in the appearance of the maculae. Walsh states that there may be a dull red spot in the macular region and also mentions pigmentary degeneration of the retinae. In four cases verified by post-mortem examination we have observed the following lesions. In one case (Ped. A-67295) there was pallor of the discs and narrowing of the arteries. The patient's brother

displayed the same appearance of the discs but no narrowing of the arteries. In another child (Ped. A-68476) the discs were pale but the arteries normal. A faint grayish area was seen around the maculae. This patient's brother displayed slightly pale discs, a dull brownish red spot in the maculae and a dull gray area around it. In another case, which was typical clinically but not verified by post-mortem examination, there was the same brownish red spot and a faint, dull gray area around it. The discs and arteries appeared to be normal. The anatomical lesions are identical with those of the infantile type of the disease except for their more chronic nature. The prognosis is equally hopeless. This condition seems to form a link between the infantile and the juvenile forms. It is very rare. Rectal biopsy may reveal typical changes in the cells of the myenteric plexus and the lymphocytes may show vacuoles which are significant in diagnosis.

CASE HISTORY (Ped. A-67295).—*Late infantile cerebro-retinal degeneration beginning at age of three years with convulsions. Later, blindness and dementia. Brother had onset at three years and died at age of eight years. Post-mortem examination revealed typical lipoid cell degeneration. Optic atrophy but no retinal lesions.*

B. A. was seen at the age of eight years for the first time. Her parents stated that she was a normal child until the age of three years when she began to have sudden convulsive seizures. These continued and were resistant to medication. There was soon evidence of mental deterioration. Slowly the child lost the ability to talk and to walk. Later, it was discovered that she was blind.

Examination revealed fair development and nutrition. The child could hear but did not seem to understand. She could not articulate but made sounds like infants make. There was moderately severe generalized spasticity of the muscles with increased tendon reflexes and bilateral Babinski sign. All movements of the extremities were extremely ataxic. The child could not stand without help. There were restless movements of the arms and hands which resembled those seen in chorea. The pupils reacted to light though the optic nerve heads were slightly pale and the retinal arteries narrow. There were no changes seen in the region of the maculae and no pigment deposits in the retinae.

The patient's older brother developed symptoms at the age of three years and died at the age of eight years. He also exhibited convulsions, dementia, blindness and profound motor disturbances so that he was eventually helpless. A careful histological examination was made of the nervous system (at another hospital) which revealed the usual lipoid cell degeneration. This child showed only optic atrophy and no lesions developed in the retinae.

BIBLIOGRAPHY

BIELSCHOWSKI, M.: Ueber spatinfantile familiäre amaurotische Idiotie mit Kleinhirnsymptomen. Deutsche Ztschr. f. Nervenh., **50**:7, 1914.

FAWCETT, J. S. *et al.:* On the natural history of late infantile cerebromacular degeneration. Neurology, **16**:1130, 1966.

GREENFIELD, J. G. AND NEVIN, S.: Amaurotic idiocy. Study of a late infantile case. Trans. Ophth. Soc. United Kingdom, **53**:170, 1933.

HASSIN, G. B.: A case of amaurotic family idiocy. Late infantile type (Bielschowski). Arch. Neurol. & Psychiat., **16**:708, 1926.

PLUM, C. M. *et al.:* Juvenile amaurotic idiocy and vacuolated lymphocytes. Ann. Paed. Fenn., **6**:16, 1960.

SEITELBERGER, F. *et al.:* Spatinfantile amaurotische idiotie. Arch. Psychiat. Nervenkr., **196**:154, 1957.

VOLK, B. W. *et al.:* Late infantile amaurotic idiocy: Ultramicroscopic and histochemical studies. Arch. of Path., **78**:483, 1964.

WALSH, F. B.: *Loc. cit.*

Cerebroretinal Degeneration—Juvenile Form of Batten or Spielmeyer-Vogt

Definition.—This disease is not confined to persons of Jewish race and differs from the infantile type not only in its symptomatology but in the age of onset and course.

Pathological Anatomy.—The lesions of the juvenile type of cerebroretinal degeneration are essentially the same as those of the infantile form and hence do not require description. Greenfield and Holmes have made a complete study of the pathological changes. They state that the retinal lesions are of the same nature as those found in the infantile form of the disease but that the rods and cones are involved in addition to the ganglion cells, whereas in the infantile form only the ganglion cells are affected.

Bessman and Baldwin state that they find large amounts of carnosine, anserine, histadine and l-methylhistadine in the urine of patients suffering from the juvenile type of cerebroretinal degeneration. Three families were studied. It is of interest that siblings and parents who have no neurological symptoms also show the same aminoaciduria. In one family, two children have cerebroretinal degeneration. Both the father and the mother have the aminoaciduria. The father's brother also has aminoaciduria. He married a woman who did not have aminoaciduria. One of the children of this match has aminoaciduria but none have the nervous disorder. One wonders if the heterozygotes have the aminoaciduria and only the homozygotes have the nervous disease.

Seitelberger has described a pigment variant of juvenile amaurotic idiocy. In this condition the changes in the nerve cells are typical of the juvenile type of this disease but there are deposits of dark pigment in the microglia, in the perivascular spaces and scattered in the tissues. He refers to 3 other cases of the same type.

Clinical Features.—The disease is definitely familial and as a rule more than one child in a family is affected. In a certain percentage of cases, a history of similar symptoms in a previous generation may be elicited. Pig-

mentary degeneration of the retina alone may be found in a parent whose children exhibit the whole picture of cerebroretinal degeneration. Sjögren, who has published a very careful study of this condition, states that the facts indicate that it is dependent upon a recessive hereditary factor. Males and females are both affected with about the same frequency. It is inherited either as a dominant or as a recessive characteristic, Macklin says.

The onset occurs between the ages of three and ten years and, in most instances, between five and six years. The first symptom to attract attention is loss of vision in most cases, but sometimes mental disturbances appear first. The retinal lesions are apparently subject to considerable variation. Greenfield and Holmes, as well as several other authors describe a small pale area in the region of the macula which is speckled with fine dark brown pigment and surrounded by a reddish zone. The process is at first limited to the macula and perimacular regions. Later atrophic and pigmented areas develop in the periphery. According to Sjögren, however, it is not the rule for the process to be so sharply localized to the region of the macula, and if it happens to start here it soon becomes more extensive. He describes a picture very similar to that of the common pigmentary degeneration of the retina. First, yellowish gray areas of degeneration which show no pigment appear in the retinae. Later, pigment granules are deposited, being either very fine and dust-like or resembling in some cases the "bone corpuscles" of pigmentary degeneration. The optic nerve heads are yellowish gray and the retinal arteries are narrow. In a few instances vision has been definitely reduced for several years before any changes could be found in the retinae, but the typical changes almost always develop eventually. Cases are reported in which no changes were found in the retinae but it is not always clear that a careful examination was made. Posterior cortical cataracts may develop in the later stages of the disease. The loss of vision continues with relative rapidity and, as a rule, within one or two years after the onset the patient is either quite blind or nearly blind.

According to Sjögren the visual disturbances may be taken to represent the first stage of the disease which lasts on an average about two years. The beginning of the second stage is marked by the onset of convulsions, which are characterized by both tonic and clonic phases and are identical with those seen in common types of epilepsy. Convulsions recur from time to time during the subsequent course of the disease. Myoclonic twitchings are often prominent. Definite mental changes make their appearance at about this time. There is lack of emotional control, irritability, restlessness and in general personality changes rather than intellectual deterioration. Speech may begin to show some alterations such as stammering and repetition of words and syllables.

Later, definite mental deterioration develops which initiates Sjögren's

third stage. Attention, memory, and judgment are all impaired and the child quickly forgets whatever has been learned. The personality changes are more severe now. Spasmodic laughing and weeping appear. Speech is slow and monotonous and articulation may be very indistinct. The Parkinsonian syndrome begins to develop, with typical rigidity, slowing of movement, rhythmical tremors, stooping posture and dragging gait, with absence of arm swing. In some cases, both tremors of rest and intention tremors are present. The tendon reflexes are still in order.

A fourth stage is described in which dementia has reached the degree of idiocy. The child never speaks and takes no notice of its surroundings. The Parkinsonian syndrome has now developed to such a point that the patient is almost helpless and can walk only with help or not at all. Prolonged screaming and crying are common and there may be forced movements of the arms and body. The muscles now begin to waste but the tendon reflexes and electrical reactions are still normal. There may, however, be extensor plantar responses.

In the final or fifth stage of the disease the child is totally demented and paralytic. The patient lies in bed with the thighs flexed on the abdomen, the chin on the chest and the arms strongly flexed at the elbow. The muscles are now grossly atrophied and there may be a partial reaction of degeneration. The tendon reflexes are increased and the plantar reflexes are constantly of the extensor variety. Athetoid movements of the hands and feet may be present. The course varies between ten and fifteen years and death occurs in status epilepticus or from intercurrent infection. Cobb, Martin and Pampiglioe found high voltage, triphasic waves without constant focus but widespread and bilaterally synchronous in the electroencephalograms of 12 patients under 9 years of age who were suffering from juvenile cerebroretinal degeneration. Older patients did not show such waves. These writers believe that this electroencephalographic pattern is characteristic and important in establishing the diagnosis.

Diagnosis.—When all the typical features including the lesions in the retinae are present the diagnosis would not seem to be difficult. Congenital syphilis must always be considered, however. When only the retinal lesions are found and other symptoms have not yet appeared, one must distinguish familial degenerations of the maculae and pigmentary degeneration of the retina. When the retinal lesions are not present or are overlooked, there seems to be no means by which one can establish the diagnosis with confidence on clinical grounds. Cerebral degenerations of other types may produce essentially the same picture. Vacuoles may be found in the lymphocytes in some cases. Rectal biopsy may establish the diagnosis or cortical biopsy may be necessary.

Loken and Cyvin describe the case of a boy whose symptoms began at

the age of 6 years and whose clinical symptoms suggested juvenile amaurotic idiocy but the brain showed senile plaques and Alzheimer's fibrillary changes. His brother seems to have had the same condition.

Prognosis.—The disease runs a slowly progressive course and invariably ends in death after ten or fifteen years.

Treatment.—No effective treatment is known.

BIBLIOGRAPHY

ALLE, C.: The extracortical manifestations of cerebromacular degeneration. J. Neurol. & Psychopath., **14**:35.

BATTEN, F. E.: Cerebral degeneration with symmetrical changes in the maculae in two members of a family. Tr. Ophthal. Soc. Un. Kingdom, **23**:386, 1903.

——— AND MAYOU, M. S.: Family cerebral degeneration with macular changes. Pro. Roy. Soc. Med. (Sec. Ophthal.) , **8**:70, 1915.

BATTEN, R. D.: Two brothers with symmetrical disease of the macula commencing at the age of 14. Trans. Ophthal. Soc. U. Kingdom, **17**:48, 1897.

BESSMAN, S. P. AND BALDWIN, R.: Imidazole aminoaciduria in cerebromacular degeneration. Science, **135**:789, 1962.

COBB, W., MARTIN, F. AND PAMPIGLIONE, G.: Cerebral lipoidosis: An electroencephalographic study. Brain, **75**:343, 1952.

GREENFIELD, J. G. AND HOLMES, G.: The histology of juvenile amaurotic idiocy. Brain, **48**:183, 1925. (Full references.)

HARLEM, O. K.: Juvenile cerebroretinal degeneration. Amer. Jour. Dis. Child., **100**:918, 1960.

HOFFMAN, J.: Spielmeyer-Vogt disease. Am. J. Ophth., **42**:15, 1956.

JERVIS, G. A.: Juvenile amaurotic family idiocy. Am. J. Dis. Child., **61**:327, 1941.

LOKEN, C. AND CYVIN, K.: A case of clinical juvenile amaurotic idiocy with the histological picture of Alzheimer's disease. J. Neurol. Neurosurg. & Psychiat., **17**:211, 1954.

LUBIN, A. J. AND MARBURG, O.: Juvenile amaurotic idiocy. Arch. Neurol. & Psychiat., **49**:559, 1943.

NAKAI, H. AND LANDING, B. H.: Use of rectal biopsy in diagnosis of neural lipidoses. Pediatrics, **26**:225, 1960.

ODOR, D. L.: Juvenile amaurotic idiocy. An electron microscopic study. Neurology, **16**:496, 1966.

RAYNER, S.: Juvenile amaurotic idiocy in Sweden. Lund, 1962.

SEITELBERGER, F. AND SIMMA, K.: Aronson, S. M. and Volk, B. W. Cerebral Sphingolipidoses. Academic Press, New York, p. 29, 1962.

SJÖGREN, T.: Die juvenile amaurotische Idiotie. Hereditas, **14**:197, 1931.

WALSH, F. B.: *Loc. cit.*

WATSON, C. W. AND DENNY-BROWN, D.: Myoclonus epilepsy as a symptom of diffuse neuronal disease. Arch. Neurol. & Psychiat., **70**:151, 1953.

ZEMAN, W. AND DONAHUE, S.: Fine structure of lipid bodies in juvenile amaurotic idiocy. Acta Neuropath. Berlin, **3**:144, 1963.

——— AND HOFFMAN, J.: Juvenile and late forms of amaurotic idiocy in one family. Jour. Neurol. Neurosurg. and Psychiat., **25**:352, 1962.

Cerebroretinal Degeneration—Late Form of Kufs

This type of the disease begins as a rule between the fifteenth and twenty-fifth years and progresses very slowly. The most outstanding symptoms are mental deterioration and convulsions. Myoclonus may be prominent. Later, tremors, muscular rigidity and ataxia develop. The last is of cerebellar type. As a rule there is no loss of vision and the retinae seem to be normal. Kufs has presented evidence that this disease is closely related

to the common pigmentary degeneration of the retina. It is very common, he has found, to discover that one or more ascendants of the patient have had the typical retinal lesions but have never developed any mental or motor disturbances. The changes in the brain are said to be typical of cerebroretinal degeneration. Biopsy of the cerebral cortex or rectum may reveal typical cell changes.

Seitelberger and Simma report eight cases of late onset in which there are extraneuronal deposits of a lipopigment and term this the pigment variant of amaurotic idiocy.

BIBLIOGRAPHY

KUFS, H.: Über eine Spätform der amaurotischen Idiotie und ihre heredofamiliaren Grundlagen. Ztschr. f. d. ges. Neurol. u. Psychiat., **95**:169, 1925.
SEITELBERGER, F. AND SIMMA, K.: On the Pigment Variant of Amaurotic Idiocy in Cerebral Sphingolipidoses. p. 29, Eds. Aronson, S. M. and Volk, B. W., New York.
VAN BOGAERT, L.: Sur une forme familiale tres tardive de l'idiote amaurotique. Dtsch. Z. Nervenheilk., **168**:276, 1952.
————: Formes a evolution chronique de l'idiote amaurotique sans amaurose. Jour. Ment. Defic. Res., **4**:119, 1960.
————: Les idioties amaurotiques. Rev. Med. Liege, **17**:273, 1962.
WALSH, F. B.: *Loc. cit.*

Gaucher's Disease of Infancy

Definition.—A disease characterized by enlargement of the spleen and liver as a result of deposits of kerasin in the reticuloendothelial cells and by changes in other organs including the nervous system.

Etiology.—The disease is apt to affect several siblings in a family but is rarely traced to previous generations. It is familial, therefore, but not obviously hereditary. It is suggested that it is due to a simple recessive gene. In some instances the typical cells may be found in the bone marrow of a parent who is quite healthy. The present tendency is to regard this disease as the expression of a congenital defect of lipoid metabolism.

Brady *et al.* have found that there is a deficiency of glucocerebroside cleaving enzyme in the spleen of subjects suffering from Gaucher's disease.

Pathological Anatomy.—The spleen, liver, lymph nodes, bone marrow and sometimes other tissues are infiltrated by large round cells with one or more small nuclei. The cytoplasm of these cells is distended by accumulations of fine granules which do not stain easily and which are believed to be composed of kerasin, i.e. a galactosiderocerebroside, a glucosiderocerebroside and a glycolipid. The brain shows lesions of a different type which presents striking resemblances to those of amaurotic idiocy. The ganglion cells may be shrunken, but are often swollen and distended by granular deposits. The nucleus is displaced and the neurofibrils are removed to the periphery of the cell. Globular swellings are found on the dendrites. The granules do not give the same staining reactions as those of amaurotic idiocy. Barlow describes typical Gaucher's cells in the adventitia of the cerebral

vessels. Thannhauser states that cerebrosides are not found in excess in the brain so the process cannot be identical with that in the viscera. The mechanism responsible for the changes in the neurons is still unknown. The lipoid content of the blood is not increased.

Clinical Features.—The clinical manifestations of the acute infantile disease have been carefully described by Meyer. He states that the disease is found as a rule in people of European ancestry and has never been discovered in Jewish children. Several siblings are apt to be affected. The onset is as a rule about the fourth or fifth month but may be earlier or later. The first sign is usually enlargement of the spleen. Shortly after this the child's personality changes. There is apathy and slowing of movement. It is impossible to hold the child's attention. The eyes do not fix properly though the child is not blind and the optic fungi show no changes. Ocular palsies and squints are common. Ataxia develops. The face may be immobile or may show tic-like movements. There may be trismus. Convulsions sometimes occur. The mouth is held open. Later muscular rigidity develops with opisthotonos. Pseudobulbar phenomena are prominent with attacks of laryngospasm, stridor, difficulty in swallowing and trismus. There may be increase of the tendon reflexes and true spasticity. In the end there seems to be a form of decerebrate rigidity. Bouts of fever may occur which are not explained by infection. Anemia is not a typical feature and there is little if any cutaneous pigmentation. There may be wedge shaped pigmentation of the conjunctiva with the base close to the corneal margin. This has been regarded as a pathognomonic finding. The child loses weight rapidly and the course is steadily progressive to a fatal outcome. Death occurs in a stupor at about the tenth month and it is unusual for the child to live more than sixteen months.

As a rule, there are no characteristic changes in the optic fundi. Dr. Richard Tyler, however, has told me of a patient who was studied on the service of Dr. E. A. Carmichael at the National Hospital, Queen Square, London who had typical cherry red spots in the maculae. The symptoms began early in childhood. There were myoclonic movements, convulsions and reduction of vision. At the age of 8 years the cherry red spots were discovered and a diagnosis of juvenile cerebroretinal degeneration was made. At the age of 21 years a spontaneous fracture occurred in the left femur. Roentgenograms of the long bones showed thinning of the cortex and lack of proper trabeculation. Biopsy of the bone marrow showed changes typical of Gaucher's disease. The cherry red spots were still present. The patient's sister died at the age of 15 months. She had become blind and had cherry red spots in the retinae. The patient's father was one of 16 siblings of whom eight were females. All of the females except for the eldest died in infancy of unknown cause.

Roentgenographic changes in the bones are characteristic. The long bones show clubbing at the ends. The cortex is thin and irregular. There are patchy areas of rarefaction and also areas of condensation. Spontaneous fractures may occur and collapse of the vertebrae is described.

The disease occurs in older children and sometimes involves the nervous system as it does in infants. In children the course of the disease is slower than in infants. There is splenohepatomegaly, subicteric pigmentation of the exposed skin, hemorrhagic diathesis, hypochromic anemia, early leucopenia and thrombocytopenia.

An adult type of the disease is described in which there is enlargement of the spleen, anemia and pigmentation of the skin. The nervous system is affected occasionally. The patient may not be seriously handicapped.

Diagnosis.—The family history and the clinical features described above should suggest the diagnosis. Puncture of the spleen or aspiration of the bone marrow and histological examination of the tissue removed is the simplest way to establish the diagnosis. The splenic pulp should show the typical changes in the reticulocytes. Niemann-Pick disease is most difficult to distinguish from Gaucher's disease and studies of the staining reactions of the lipoid deposits are required to make the differential diagnosis. Syphilis may cause some confusion for it is a common cause of enlargement of the liver and spleen.

Prognosis.—All cases are believed to be fatal within a year or more.

Treatment.—No effective treatment is known.

BIBLIOGRAPHY

ADACHI, M. *et al.:* Fine structure of central nervous system in early infantile Gaucher's disease. Arch. Path., **83:**513, 1967.

BANKER, B. O. *et al.:* Infantile Gaucher's disease. Meeting of the Am. Neurol. A., Atlantic City, New Jersey, June 12-14, 1961.

BARLOW, C.: Neuropathological findings in a case of Gaucher's disease. J. Neuropath. & Exper. Neurol., **16:**239, 1957.

BRADY, R. O. *et al.:* Demonstration of a deficiency of glucocerebroside cleaving enzyme in Gaucher's disease. Jour. of Clin. Invest., **45:**1112, 1966.

CROCKER, A. C. AND LANDING, B. H.: Phosphatase studies in Gaucher's disease. Metabolism, **9:**341, 1960.

ESPINAS, O. E. AND FARIS, A. A.: Acute infantile Gaucher's disease in identical twins. Neurology, **19:**133, 1969.

GEDDES, A. K. AND MOORE, S.: Acute infantile Gaucher's disease. Jour. of Pediatrics, **43:**61, 1953.

GROEN, J.: The hereditary mechanism of Gaucher's disease. Blood, **3:**1238, 1948.

HERRLIN, K. M. AND HILLBORG, P. O.: Neurologic signs in juvenile form of Gaucher's disease. Acta Paediat. Scandinav., **51:**137, 1962.

HOFFMAN, S. J. AND MAKLER, M. I.: Gaucher's disease. Am. J. Dis. Child., **38:**775, 1929.

HSIA, D. Y. Y. *et al.:* Gaucher's disease. New Eng. Jour. Med., **261:**164, 1959.

KNUDSON, A. G. AND KAPLAN, W. D.: Genetics of the Sphingolipidoses in Cerebral Sphingolipidoses. Ed. Aronson, S. M. and Volk, B. W., 1962, p. 395, New York.

LINDAU, A.: Neure Auffassingen über die Pathologie der familiären amaurotischen Idiotie. Acta Psychiat. et Neurol., 5:167, 1930.

MEYER, R.: Syndrome neurologique et diagnostique clinique de la Maladie de Gaucher die nourissons. Rev. franc. pediat., 8:559, 1932.

REISS, O. AND KATO, K.: Gaucher's disease with especial reference to the roentgenology of the bones. Am. J. Dis. Child., 43:365, 1932.

RODGERS, C. L. AND JACKSON, S. H.: Acute infantile Gaucher's disease. Pediatrics, 7:53, 1951.

STRANSKY, E. AND DAVIS-LAWAS, D.: Gaucher's disease. Am. J. Dis. Child., 78:694, 1949.

UZMAN, L. L.: Polycerebrosides in Gaucher's disease. A.M.A. Arch. Path., 55:181, 1953.

VAN BOGAERT, L.: Cerebral Lipidoses. Thomas, Springfield, 1957.

WALSH, F. B.: *Loc. cit.*

Schuller-Christian Disease

Definition.—This is a disease characterized by destructive lesions in the membranous bones and in other tissues which contain foam cells filled with cholesterol esters and other elements as described below.

Etiology.—The cause is unknown and it is only in a few instances that there has been a tendency to a familial occurrence. Various interpretations have been offered for the lesions and it has been claimed that they are neoplastic or inflammatory. At present, however, chiefly as a result of the studies of Rowland, it is generally accepted that the disease is one of lipoid metabolism.

Pathological Anatomy.—The essential feature of the pathological process is the formation of deposits of lipoid containing cells, the so-called foam cells, with a cellular reaction composed chiefly of lymphocytes, eosinophils and plasma cells and finally proliferation of fibroblasts and scar formation. Such deposits are most common in the membranous bones but may occur in other tissues. The tuber cinereum is frequently involved and the orbits invaded causing the characteristic exophthalmos. Deposits also occur in the skin, mouth, larynx, bones of the skeleton, spleen, liver, lymph nodes, lungs and pleura. Davison describes a case in which there were widespread patches of demyelination in the central white matter of the brain with accumulation of fat-laden microglia phagocytes and of giant glial cells. A few typical foam cells were found. The axis cylinders were usually destroyed and in certain parts of the cortex the neurons were also degenerated. The tuber cinereum was severely affected in Davison's case. It is important to note that these lesions were chiefly found in the white matter and had no resemblance to those of the cerebromacular degenerations or those sometimes found in Niemann-Pick's disease, in both of which the ganglion cells show specific changes. Numerous other authors mention deposits in the dura and infiltrations about the cranial nerves at the base. Thannhauser finds that the cases of Teilum, Heine, Chiari and van Bogaert are of the same nature as that of Davison. The essential lesion in the brain, he states, is the lipide granuloma. This starts in the perivascular tissues and goes through stages of proliferation, granuloma formation, xanthoma forma-

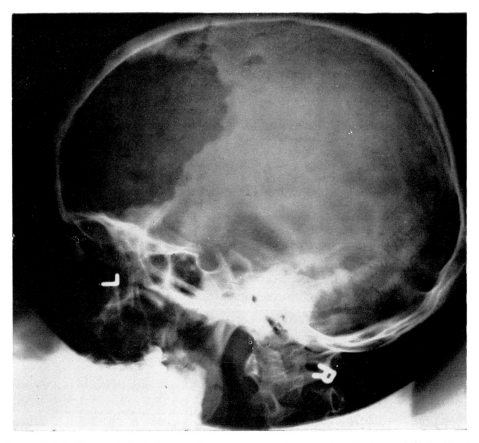

Fig. 190. Schuller-Christian's disease. Roentgenogram shows extensive bony defect. (C. H. 212855.) (Case 272) (From Walsh; Neuro-Ophthalmology, courtesy of the Williams and Wilkins Company.)

tion and finally reaches a fibrous phase. Cholesterol deposits are found in these granulomata. Such lesions are found almost exclusively in the white matter. They occur in the cerebral hemispheres, the brain stem and the cerebellum. Secondary degenerations may be found in the optic tracts, the pyramidal tracts, the cerebellar pathways and the long tracts of the spinal cord. Dr. David Clark has told me of a case in which the superior longitudinal sinus was obstructed causing hydrocephalus.

Clinical Features.—It is stated that the disease affects males more frequently than females, that it is not confined to members of any race and that it is only rarely familial. The vast majority of cases begin in childhood. The typical features are due to deposits of the xanthomatous cells in the skull giving rise to soft tumor-like swellings over the cranium, exophthalmos and diabetes insipidus. The last is often associated with other symptoms indicative of involvement of the tuber cinereum and hypophysis

such as failure of sexual development, obesity of specific type and even the fully developed Fröhlich's syndrome. Dwarfism is also described, probably as a result of injury of the anterior lobe of the hypophysis. The deposits in the orbits cause not only exophthalmos but paralysis of the extraocular muscles and optic atrophy. Mental retardation has been observed several times. The tumors of the skull are often associated with a palpable defect in the vault. Roentgenological studies reveal large irregular areas of destruction of the bone which usually show sharply defined edges and only rarely any new bone formation. Similar defects occur in the pelvic bones or bones of the extremities but these are not common. Lesions in the mastoid bone may cause aural discharge and deafness. Several types of skin lesions are described. The most typical are the small yellow nodules or so-called xanthomas found most frequently over the eyelids which show typical foam cells on section but yellowish or bronze discoloration of the skin is also mentioned. Minute red papules with a yellow center are characteristic and seborrheic dermatitis is common. Pruritis is sometimes present. The teeth are often imperfectly formed and may fall out spontaneously when the alveolar process is invaded. Stomatitis and gingivitis are very frequently observed but are not constant. There may be miliary lesions in the lungs leading to infiltrations which suggest fibrosis. Eventually cystic changes may develop giving rise to the term honeycomb lung. There is no increase of lipoids in the blood. Secondary anemia may occur and there is often a low grade fever.

Among the neurological signs optic atrophy is probably most common. This may be due to involvement of the optic nerves in the orbits or to compression of the chiasm. Other cranial nerves may be affected by deposits in the dura. In Davison's case there was bilateral spasticity, ataxia and cranial nerve palsies. Thannhauser states that the clinical syndrome includes impairment of vision, double vision, unsteadiness, weakness of the extremities with increased tendon reflexes and Babinski signs and difficulty in speech and swallowing.

The course is usually a slow one and remissions are described. Apparently the lesions undergo a gradual evolution and show a certain tendency to fibrosis and healing. Late in the course of the disease great loss of weight may occur and even terminal cachexia.

Van Bogaert *et al.* described, in 1937, a familial disease evidenced by slowly progressive cerebellar ataxia and myoclonus in adolescence and ending in bulbar palsy years later. Mental deterioration sometimes occurred. Characteristic features were xanthomata of the tendons, xanthelasma of the eyelids and cataracts. In some cases, the blood cholesterol was elevated. Massive deposits of cholesterol crystals were found in the white matter of the cerebellum and cerebral peduncles.

Philippart and van Bogaert state that the cholestanol is found in the central nervous system, the tendons and the serum and that this is a defect in cholestanol metabolism.

Diagnosis.—The diagnosis depends upon the characteristic triad of symptoms, exophthalmos, diabetes insipidus and defects in the skull, but several other features are important, such as the xanthomata over the skin. The loss of teeth and the stomatitis are also typical symptoms. Roentgenological studies of the skull, lungs and long bones are very helpful and biopsy should usually be conclusive.

Eosinophilic granuloma must be distinguished. This occurs at any age but is usually found in young persons. It is often manifest by a single lesion which may be located in the skull, rib, pelvis, mandible, long bones or vertebra. Sometimes the lesion is in the soft tissues. In younger patients there are sometimes multiple lesions and recurrence may occur. As the name implies the process is granulomatous and many eosinophil cells are present.

Another similar condition is termed the Letterer-Siwe disease. It is seen in infancy and early childhood. It is more acute and disseminated with a rapidly progressive course and high mortality. Local areas of destruction in the bones are found with ecchymoses, purpura, enlargement of the liver and spleen, pulmonary infiltration, leucopenia and thrombopenia. Bone marrow biopsy often reveals reticuloendothelial cells. Roentgenotherapy, corticosteroids and antifolic acid drugs are recommended.

Aarli lists the primary familial hyperlipidemias and the secondary hyperlipidemias. He points out that the neurological manifestations fall into two groups: (1) Those who have signs of sudden onset due to cerebral vascular occlusion resulting from atheromatous changes in the vessels or fat emboli and (2) Slowly progressive damage to the nervous system due to accumulation of lipid deposits in the nervous tissue.

Prognosis.—About one third of the cases are fatal but since many of these cases have been untreated, the mortality with proper therapy is probably much lower.

Treatment.—This is fully discussed by Sosman. Roentgen ray therapy is apparently effective in curing the local lesions and in improving the patient's general condition. The bony lesions often disappear completely under treatment. A low fat diet has been recommended but its value is still uncertain. Endocrine therapy has been tried. Extract of the posterior lobe of the pituitary body may be employed to reduce the diabetes insipidus and often aids in improving the patient's general condition as a result of improving sleep. Thyroid seems to be ineffective but insulin has some value in improving nutrition.

BIBLIOGRAPHY

Aarli, J. A.: Neurological manifestations in hyperlipidemia. Neurology, **18**:883, 1968.

Avioli, J. P. *et al.*: Chronic and sustained hypernatremia, absence of thirst, diabetes insipidus,

adrenocorticotropin insufficiency, resulting from widespread destruction of the hypothalamus. Ann. Int. Med., **56**:131, 1962.

CHIARI, H.: Ueber Veränderungen im Zentralnervensystem bei generalisierter Xanthomatose vom Typus Schüller-Christian. Virchow's Arch. f. path. Anat., **288**:527, 1938.

DAVISON, C.: Xanthomatosis and the central nervous system (Schüller-Christian syndrome), Arch. Neurol. & Psychiat., **30**:75, 1933. (Full references.)

————: Xanthomatosis and the central nervous system. Arch. Neurol. & Psychiat., **35**:629, 1936.

ELIAN, M. *et al.*: Neurological manifestations of general xanthomatosis. Neurology, **21**:115, 1969.

HAMILTON, W.: Congenital Letterer-Siwe disease. Scot. Med. Jour., **6**:575, 1961.

HEINE, J.: Beitrag zur Schüller-Christian'schen Krankheit und dessen beziehungen zur allegemeinen Xanthomatose. Zeigler's Beiträge zur Path. Anat., **94**:412, 1934.

KELLEY, J. H. AND MCMILLAN, J. T.: Eosinophilic granuloma of the bone. Ann. Surg., **156**:147, 1962.

MENKES, J. H. *et al.*: Cerebrotendinous xanthomatosis. Arch. of Neurol., **19**:47, 1968.

MÜLLER, D. AND ORTHNER, H.: Intracerebral lipid granulomatoses. Deutsche Ztschr. Nervenh., **187**:608, 1965.

OBERMAN, H. A.: Idiopathic histiocytosis: Clinicopathologic study of eosinophilic granuloma of bone, Hand-Schüller-Christian disease and Letterer-Siwe. Pediatrics, **28**:307, 1961.

PHILIPPART, M. AND VAN BOGAERT, L.: Cholestanosis (cerebrotendinosis xanthomatosis). Arch. of Neurol., Vol. 21, No. 6, p. 603, 1969.

ROGERS, D. L. AND BENSON, T. E.: Familial Letterer-Siwe disease. Jour. Pediat., **60**:550, 1962.

ROWLAND, R. S.: Xanthomatosis and the reticulo-endothelial system. Arch. Int. Med., **42**:611, 1928.

SHARBARO, J. L.: Eosinophilic granuloma of bone. J.A.M.A., **178**:706, 1961.

SOSMAN, M. C.: Xanthomatosis (Schüller-Christian syndrome lipoid histiocytosis). J.A.M.A., **98**:110, 1932. (Full references.)

TEILUM, G.: Cerebrale und viscerale xanthomatose mit diabetes isipidus. Ziegler's Beiträge zur Path. Anat., **106**:460, 1942.

THANNHAUSER, S. J.: Diseases of the nervous system associated with disturbances of lipide metabolism. Res. Nerv. & Ment. Dis., **32**:238, 1953.

VAN BOGAERT, L.: Cerebral Lipidoses. Thomas, Springfield, 1957.

———— SCHERER, H. J. ET EPSTEIN, E.: Une forme cerebrale de la cholesterinose généralisée. Paris, Masson, 1937.

————: Le cadre des xanthomatosis et leurs differents types. 2-Xanthomatoses secondaires. Rev. med. Liege, **17**:433, 1962.

WALSH, F. B.: *Loc. cit.*

NIEMANN-PICK DISEASE WITH DEGENERATION OF THE NERVOUS SYSTEM

Definition.—A familial disease occurring chiefly in subjects of Hebrew parentage associated with enlargement of the liver and spleen due to deposits of lipoids in these organs and sometimes with lesions in the nervous system similar to those of the cerebro-macular degenerations.

Etiology.—Nothing can be said about the cause of the disease beyond the fact that it is regarded as an example of defective lipoid metabolism. This seems to be an autosomal recessive trait. The heterozygous carriers cannot be detected at present.

Pathological Anatomy.—The essential features of this disease are the great enlargement of the liver and spleen which is due to the accumulation of lipoid containing cells, the so-called foam cells. These are believed to be

elements of the reticulo-endothelial system and the lipoid granules are said to be glycerophosphatides chiefly sphingomyelin. Less evident changes are found in other organs such as the adrenal, the pancreas, the heart muscle and the vascular endothelium. In a few cases the central nervous system is involved. Universal cellular degeneration is found with accumulation of lipoid products in the affected cells. These lipids have been found to be sphingomyelin.

Lowden *et al.* studied a child suffering from the slowly progressive or juvenile type of Niemann-Pick disease. They found that there was no increase of the sphingomyelin in the brain in contrast to the infantile brains. Two unidentified fatty acids were found in the sphingomyelin of the gray and white matter. Only 5 per cent of the expected amount of myelin was found in the white matter.

Clinical Features.—The disease is strongly racial in its incidence being confined almost exclusively to persons of Hebrew race. There is a tendency for several cases to appear in one family. Girls are affected more frequently than boys. The onset is usually between the third and sixth month of life.

The clinical manifestations include palpable enlargement of the liver and spleen, brown pigmentation of the skin and often a waxy pallor which is explained by severe anemia. Symptoms referable to the nervous system may be present or absent. When nervous symptoms occur, the first manifestation seems to be mental deterioration which progresses rapidly to complete dementia. Muscle tone is reduced and the tendon reflexes are lost. Finally all motor power is lost. The mouth stays open. The tongue protrudes. Vision and hearing are lost. The retinae show a cherry red spot surrounded by a gray area. Lipemia retinalis is rarely seen. There is rapid loss of weight and the child dies in cachexia.

Crocker has described four different types. (1) The classical infantile type described above. (2) The infantile type without involvement of the nervous system. (3) The juvenile type which progresses less rapidly. A case of this type is abstracted below. (4) A less clearly defined type beginning in adolescence. Terry *et al.* have described a rapidly progressive adult form as well. An atypical infantile form is described in which the onset is in the first month with vomiting, pigmentation of the skin and enlargement of the liver and spleen.

The case of a child with juvenile Niemann-Pick disease is given below in abstract. Her case is of interest in that the neurological symptoms dominated the picture. The onset was at 3 years and death occurred at 8 years. A chronic adult type is known but is very rare.

Diagnosis.—The diagnosis may be suspected in children of Jewish race who develop in the early months of life enlargement of the liver and

spleen. If symptoms suggestive of infantile cerebro-macular degeneration are added, the diagnosis is strengthened. Puncture of the spleen and the demonstration of the typical foam cells are conclusive. Vacuoles may be found in the cytoplasm of the lymphocytes.

Prognosis.—All reported cases in infants have resulted in death within a short time, usually before the third birthday.

Treatment.—No treatment is known. The spleen has been removed without lasting benefit. Sosman has recommended that roentgen ray therapy be tried.

CASE HISTORY (Path. 22677).—*Niemann-Pick disease with mental deterioration and myoclonus at 3 years. Later convulsive seizures of various types, loss of speech, complete dementia. Death at age of 8 years. Postmortem examination.*

J. N. was quite healthy until she was about 3 years of age. Then she became listless and apathetic. At 5 years she was extremely emotional and timid. Her speech became indistinct and she had little to say. There were sudden jerky movements of the arms and trunk. She began to stagger and walk into objects and coordination became impaired. Soon she began to have attacks in which she would become unconscious and then actual convulsions. Some of these seizures were generalized and some focal. The left side was often affected. There were also staring spells and drop-seizures. Later she displayed constant involuntary movements and was completely demented. She died at the age of 8 years.

Examination at the age of 7 years and 6 months revealed a girl who was well developed but grossly undernourished. She did not talk and did not respond to anything which was said to her. It was not possible for her to cooperate in the examination. There seemed to be profound dementia. The optic fundi examined under anesthesia showed no lesions. No involvement of the cranial nerves was discovered. There was constant myoclonic jerks, more violent on the left side but also on the right. Choreoathetoid movements were also evident on both sides. Spasticity was found on both sides but was more pronounced on the left. The tendon reflexes were all increased and there was a Babinski sign on each side.

The child died on September 25, 1950, at the age of 8 years. Postmortem examination revealed emaciation. The liver was slightly enlarged and the spleen moderately enlarged. The brain weighed 1100 grams and there was convolutional atrophy of moderate degree. Dr. H. Richard Tyler made a histological examination of the brain. He found involvement of the dentate nuclei of the cerebellum, some of the cranial nerve nuclei, especially the sixth nerve nuclei and the cerebral cortex. The cortex of the cerebellum was not involved. The neurons were enlarged and filled with deposits which did not stain with the common fat stains, and presented a coarsely reticulated appearance. The nuclei were displaced. Dr. Tyler considered these cells typical of those found in Niemann-Pick

disease. The changes in the cerebral cortex were most severe in the parietal region. The motor cortex was moderately affected and the occipital, frontal and orbital were slightly affected. The first, second and third layers of the cortex showed an increased number of astrocytes. There was satellitosis in the second layer and proliferation of the blood vessels. No gross loss of cells was evident. Dr. Stanton Eversole found foam cells in the spleen which he said were typical of Niemann-Pick disease.

In 1955 we learned that a younger sister of the patient had begun to show the same symptoms which the patient had displayed.

BIBLIOGRAPHY

BIELSCHOWSKI, M.: Amaurotische Idiotie und Lipoidzellige Splenohepatomegalie. J. f. Psychol. u. Neurol., 36:103, 1928.

CROCKER, A. C. AND FARBER, S.: Niemann-Pick disease; A review of 19 patients. Medicine, 37:1, 1958.

BRADY, R. O. *et al.:* The metabolism of sphingomyelin. II Evidence of an enzymatic deficiency in Niemann-Pick disease. Pro. Nat. Acad. Sci. U.S.A., 55:366, 1966.

CENTERWALL, W. R. AND WEBB, J. K. G.: A fatal familial syndrome in a south Indian family resembling the diseases of infantile Goucher and Niemann-Pick. Indian Jour. Child. Hlth., 12:723, 1963.

CROCKER, A. C.: The cerebral defect in Tay-Sachs disease and Niemann-Pick disease. Jour. Neurochem., 7:69, 1961.

FORSYTHE, W. I. *et al.:* Three cases of Niemann-Pick's disease in children. Arch. of Dis. Childh., 34:406, 1959.

HAMBURGER, R.: Lipoidzellige Splenohepatomegalie in Verbindung mit Amaurotischer Idiotie. Jahrb. f. Kinderh., 116:41, 1927.

HASSIN, G. B.: Niemann-Pick's disease; pathologic study of a case. Arch. Neurol. & Psychiat. 24:61, 1930.

KLENK, F.: Beitrage zur der lipoidsen Nieman-Pickscher und amaurotische idiotie. Ztschr. physiol. Chem., 262:238, 1939.

LOWDEN, J. A. *et al.:* The subacute form of Niemann-Pick disease. Arch. of Neurol., 17:230, 1967.

LUSE, S.: The Fine Structure of the Brain and Other Organs in Niemann-Pick Disease. Inborn Disorders of Sphingolipid Metabolism. Editors Aronson, S. M. and Volk, B. W. Pergamon Press, Oxford, p. 93, 1967.

MENTEN, M. L. AND WELTON, J. P.: Lipid analysis in case of Niemann-Pick disease. Am. J. Dis. Child., 72:720, 1946.

PHILIPART, M. AND MARTIN, L.: Niemann-Pick disease. Arch. of Neurol., 20:227, 1969.

PONCHER, H. G.: Lipoid cell histocytosis. Am. J. Dis. Child., 42:77, 1931.

SCHAFFER, C.: The pathogenesis of amaurotic idiocy. Neurol. & Psychiat., 24:765, 1930. (Study of case of Niemann-Pick disease.)

TERRY, R. D. *et al.:* Adult lipidosis resembling Niemann-Pick disease. Amer. Jour. Path., 30:263, 1954.

VAN BOGAERT, L.: Cerebral Lipidoses. Thomas, Springfield, 1957.

VIDEBAEK, A.: Niemann-Pick's disease. Acute and chronic. Acta Paediat. Uppsala, 37:355, 1949.

WALSH, F. B.: *Loc. cit.*

FAMILIAL NEUROVISCERAL LIPIDOSIS
(Generalized Gangliosidosis)

This condition has been described as Tay-Sachs disease with visceral involvement, a variant of Hurler's disease and pseudo-Hurler's disease. It is

now clear that it is a separate and distinct disease. It sometimes occurs in more than one member of the family. It runs a rapid course to a fatal termination. The symptoms may be present at birth or may begin within a few weeks after birth. Death has occurred in all nine reported cases before the age of two years.

There is generalized edema. The liver and spleen are enlarged. There are bony changes which resemble those of Hurler's disease. The head is often too large. Rapid deterioration of mental and motor functions occurs. A cherry-red spot may be seen in the maculae. There are vacuoles in the lymphocytes and foam cells are found in the bone marrow. Deposits of gangliosides are found in the cells of all tissues. The diagnosis depends on the biochemical studies. More recently it has been found that there are deposits of mucopolysaccharides in the tissues also. Thus this disease is a disorder of metabolism of the gangliosides and of the mucopolysaccharides.

Derry *et al.* report two cases they term infantile systemic lipidosis. They distinguish two types of this condition. Their cases are termed type II. The age of onset was around one year. There was no increase in size of the viscera or changes in the bones. There were lipid deposits in the liver, spleen, bone marrow and nerve cells. The lipid was the major monosialoganglioside of the brain. Gonatas and Gonatas have described this condition.

Type I is characterized by the development of neurological symptoms and enlargement of the viscera before the age of 5 months, lesions in the bones and facial features of Hurler's disease. The same lipids are found in the brain and viscera as in type II. This is the type described by O'Brien *et al.*

O'Brien gives a very complete description of this condition. He states that the ganglioside which accumulates in the brain and viscera is ganglioside G.M. and there are two mucopolysaccharides found in the viscera. One is similar to keratin sulphate and the other contains sialic acid though it is structurally similar to keratin sulphate.

BIBLIOGRAPHY

CRAIG, J. M. *et al.:* Metabolic neurovisceral disease. Am. J. Dis. Child., **98**:577, 1959.

DERRY, D. M. *et al.:* Late infantile systemic lipidosis. Major monosialogangliosidosis. Delineation of two types. Neurology, **18**:340, 1968.

GONATAS, N. K. AND GONATAS, J.: Ultrastructural and biochemical observations on a case of infantile lipidosis. Jour. Neuropath. and Exp. Neurol., **24**:318, 1965.

LANDING, B. H. *et al.:* Familial neurovisceral lipidosis. Am. J. Dis. Child., **108**:503, 1964.

NORMAN, R. M. *et al.:* Tay-Sachs disease with visceral involvement. J. Path. & Bact., **78**:409, 1959.

O'BRIEN *et al.:* Generalized gangliosidosis. Am. J. Dis. Child., **109**:338, 1965.

O'BRIEN, J.: Generalized gangliosidosis. Jour. Pediat., **75**:168, 1969.

CONGENITAL FAMILIAL CEREBRAL LIPOIDOSIS RESEMBLING INFANTILE CEREBRORETINAL DEGENERATION

Norman and Wood and Brown, Corner and Dodgson have reported the cases of two children who showed signs of gross cerebral damage at birth and died 17 days and 7 weeks after birth. There was no admixture of Jewish blood in the family. The children, who were siblings, could not nurse and had to be tube fed. The heads were very small. Respiration was irregular and temperature control deficient. Muscular rigidity was noted in one case. There was optic atrophy and the retinal vessels were very minute.

On the post-mortem examination there was an excess of fluid under the dura. The brain was grossly atrophied, and the cerebellum and brain stem also wasted. In Norman's case the brain weighed 87 gm and in Brown's case 65 gm. The grain was unusually firm. The cortical pattern was simplified. Histological study revealed that many of the nerve cells had been destroyed. Some were globular and contained lipoid deposits which stained a yellowish red with Scharlach R. These deposits were not soluble in ether, ethyl alcohol or chloroform, differing in this respect from the deposits in infantile cerebroretinal degeneration. The Nissl substance was lost and no neurofibrillae were seen. Such changes were found in the cerebral cortex, cerebellum, brain stem and basal ganglia. There was diffuse gliosis. Some of the astrocytes contained deposits of neutral fat. Myelination was defective. In the white matter were found crystals which were thought to be cholesterol. In the abdominal viscera were cells containing lipoid deposits which had the same staining reactions as those found in the cerebral neurons.

These cases are reported as examples of cerebral lipoidosis already well advanced at birth.

BIBLIOGRAPHY

BROWN, N. J., CORNER, B. D. AND DODGSON, M.: A second case in the same family of congenital familial cerebral lipoidosis resembling amaurotic idiocy. Arch. Dis. Childhood, **29**:48, 1954.

HAGBERG, B. *et al.:* Congenital amaurotic idiocy. Acta Paediat., **54**:116, 1965.

NORMAN, R. M. AND WOOD, N.: A congenital form of amaurotic idiocy. J. Neurol. & Psychiat., **4**:175, 1941.

LIPOGRANULOMATOSIS (FARBER)

Farber has performed post-mortem examinations upon two patients. One died at the age of 9 months and one at the age of 13 months. He examined a third patient at the age of 14 months. One of his post-mortem examinations was performed upon a girl. J. B. A-48912, who had been examined at the age of 8 months at the Harriet Lane Hospital. We have examined another child, J. R. C. B-41133, at the age of 18 months. Thus, four cases are on record.

Farber states that the symptoms are usually present at birth or shortly after birth. There is a hoarse cry, difficulty in feeding, difficulty in respiration, stiffness of the joints, with swelling and masses in the periarticular tissues suggestive of rheumatoid arthritis. There is often moderate enlargement of the liver, pigmentation of the skin and subcutaneous nodules. Cherry red spots have been observed in the maculae. These children do not live long. Two of Farber's patients were siblings. Roentgenograms show extensive deposits in and about the joints. There may be osteoporosis and erosion of the bones. Biopsy of the masses about the joints may permit a proper diagnosis and bone marrow aspiration is said to be helpful.

At post-mortem examination according to Farber there is involvement of the pleura, pericardium joints, periarticular tissues, liver, spleen, lymph nodes, alveolar walls and spaces of the lungs, gallbladder and nerve cells of the brain, spinal cord and ganglia.

The essential process is said to be a granulomatous mass containing foam cells. In the nervous system, it is said, the nerve cells contain lipoid granules and the picture resembles that of Tay-Sachs disease.

Uzman has made chemical analyses of the lipids. He finds fatty acids which are largely sphingomyelins. In his second paper Farber speaks of a lipo-glyco-peptide complex.

CASE HISTORY (B-41133).—At the age of 3½ months, J. B. C. began to vomit and to lose weight. Later, respiration became impaired. A mass was removed from a vocal cord and a tracheotomy tube was inserted. The joints became stiff and nodules developed at the joints.

At the age of 18 months the child was admitted to Harriet Lane Hospital. He was poorly developed and chronically ill. There were masses about the joints which were held rigidly in flexion. The neck was rigid and the face turned to the right. Masses were evident over the spinous processes of the lower thoracic and lumbar vertebrae. A soft swelling was present in the left lower eyelid. The lymph nodes were enlarged. A stricture was present in the trachea. The left hip and the right elbow were dislocated.

The child was almost completely unresponsive and immobile. The tendon reflexes were increased. There was a fine tremor of the hands. The pupils responded to light but the optic discs were pale. No lesions were seen in the retinae. Vertical oscillations of the eyes were observed. The protein of the spinal fluid was increased. The blood lipids were increased. Biopsy of a nodule from a tendon sheath revealed a granulomatous mass containing foam cells. Post-mortem examination revealed all the typical findings as described by Farber. Lipoid deposits were found in the cerebral neurons.

BIBLIOGRAPHY

Abul-Haj, S. K. *et al.*: Pathogenesis of Farber's disease. J. Pediat., **61**:221, 1962.

Farber, S.: A lipid metabolic disorder. Lipogranulomatosis. Tr. Am. Pediat. Soc., May 7-8-9, 1952.

Farber, S., Cohen, J. and Uzman, L. I.: Lipogranulomatosis. J. Mt. Sinai Hosp., **24**:816, 1957.

DYSTONIC JUVENILE IDIOCY WITHOUT AMAUROSIS

Elfenbein reports the study of a girl of 13 years who was found to have essentially the same condition as a 16-year-old boy previously reported by Kidd. Birth and early development were apparently normal. Between the ages of 4 and 6 years the patient developed an unsteady gait, ataxia, and difficulty in speech. She entered school at the age of 6 years and passed the first grade. She failed the second grade. Mental deterioration was evident. She became incontinent. Petit mal began at 13 years and then convulsions. Her 9 siblings were healthy, but 2 paternal first cousins had the same neurological condition as the patient and both died at the age of 13 years.

Examination revealed severe dementia. Speech was dysarthric. Vision was normal. The fields of vision were full. The optic fundi were normal. The pupils reacted well. Voluntary movements of the eyes were lost in the vertical plane, but vertical doll's head movements were full. Horizontal ocular movements were normal. The gait was unsteady. There were dystonic postures with increase of lumbar lordosis, abduction of the arms, flexion and pronation of the forearms and flexion of the fingers at the proximal joints, and extension at the middle and terminal joints. There was an intention tremor of the arms. The tendon reflexes were increased, but no Babinski sign was found.

The spinal fluid contained 73 mgs per cent of protein. An air study showed some enlargement of the ventricles and a subarachnoid fluid filled cyst above the sella. The electroencephalogram revealed a diffuse slowing and disorganization.

Bone marrow study revealed large foam cells and cells obtained by rectal biopsy showed similar appearances. Biopsy of the right frontal lobe showed an increase of astrocytes and microglia. There was no demyelination. The neurons showed cytoplasmic distention. They stained with oil red, sudan black and gave the PAS reaction. The Nissl substance was lost.

Electron microscopy revealed massive accumulations of polymorphous cytoplasmic bodies all of which had the same basic structure. It was concluded that this condition was the same as that described by Kidd and differed from other known conditions. A complete differential diagnosis is given. De Leon describes other cases.

BIBLIOGRAPHY

ELFENBEIN, I. B.: Dystonic juvenile idiocy without amaurosis. Johns Hopkins Med. Jour., **123**:205, 1968.

KIDD, M.: An electron microscopical study of a case of atypical cerebral lipidosis. Acta Neuropath. Berlin, **9**:70, 1967.

DE LEON, G. A.: Juvenile dystonic lipidosis. Johns Hopkins Medical Journal, **125**, No. 2:62, 1969.

THE LEUCODYSTROPHIES

Diffuse Progressive Metachromatic Leucoencephalopathy of Greenfield

Greenfield has recently described a condition in young children which he states is very similar to Schilder's periaxial encephalitis, but also differs in some essential respects. The brain is apt to be rather large and heavy at the upper limit of normal. The demyelination involves fiber tracts and systems rather than contiguous areas, selecting chiefly those fibers which are myelinated relatively late. Moreover, there is usually an almost complete loss of the oligodendroglia with formation of numerous masses of mucinoid material. The optic radiations and pyramidal tracts are mildly involved but there is no tendency to spare the arcuate fibers. The axis cylinders show very little change.

Granular deposits are found in the neurons which stain metachromatically. Austin claims that galactosphingosulfatides are present in increased amounts in the brain and that these substances stain strongly metachromatically. Hagberg *et al.* confirm these findings. Abraham and Lampert point out that the metachromatic deposits in the nerve cells have a characteristic distribution. The globus pallidus, thalamus, subthalamic nucleus, amygdaloid complex, lateral geniculate body, paraventricular hypothalamic nuclei and dentate nucleus are all involved. Selective lesions are found in the nuclei of the brain stem, but some nuclear masses such as the substantia nigra, the red nucleus, the dorsal nucleus of the vagus and the Edinger-Westphal nucleus are spared. The ganglion cells of the retinae contain metachromatic granules. The spinal cord shows involvement of both the anterior and posterior horn cells of the gray matter, the cells of Clark's column, the nucleus gracilis and nucleus cuneatus and the posterior root ganglia. Fogelson *et al.* describe lamellar inclusions in the oligodendroglial cells, demonstrable in electromicroscopic study.

Metachromatic staining granules are seen in the renal tubules, phagocytes in the portal tract of the liver, the gallbladder and perineural phagocytes. This disease is considered to be a familial disorder of lipid metabolism of the nervous system, i.e. a leucodystrophy. Dr. John S. O'Brian states that the cerebral tissue of these patients is difficient in sphingolipids containing the long-chain fatty acids.

Fig. 191

Fig. 191   Fig. 192

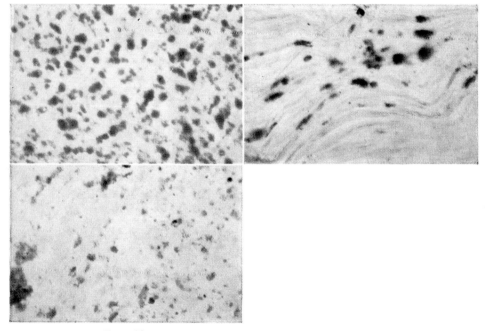

Fig. 193

Fig. 191. Metachromatic deposits in the brain.
Fig. 192. Metachromatic bodies in peripheral nerve.
Fig. 193. Metachromatic bodies in the urine. (All by the courtesy of Dr. David Clark.)

Clinical Findings.—Late infantile and juvenile cases are most common, but a few cases are reported in which the symptoms started in adolescence and adult life. This is a recessive disease. In the late infantile type the children are said to develop normally up to the second or early in the third year of life. Then motor disturbances develop with difficulty in walking and in the use of the arms. Ataxia is at least in part responsible for the motor disorder. Squints, ptosis of the lids and nystagmus are mentioned. In only one case out of the six thus far reported was there loss of vision. Convulsions occurred in two patients. Mental deterioration always occurs but only in the late stages of the disease. Eventually the child becomes helpless. The limbs are either rigid or flaccid. The tendon reflexes are lost but the plantar response are extensor. Bulbar symptoms develop in the terminal stages of the disease and lead to pulmonary infections. The head may be somewhat enlarged. A cherry red spot may appear in the maculae. The spinal fluid contains an excess of protein but there is no increase of cells. Death has occurred between the ages of two years and nine months and three years and one month. I have had one patient in whom the diagnosis was verified by post-mortem study, whose symptoms began at the age of six years and who lived to the age of seventeen years. Several children in the same family may be affected.

Dr. Feigin reports the study of the brain of a child who was congenitally defective in every way and died at the sixth week. At post-mortem examination the brain revealed an extensive metachromatic leucodystrophy.

Masters *et al.* describe a similar condition in two families in which megacolon with episodes of abdominal distention were observed.

Hoefnagel *et al.* review cases in which lesions were found in the endocrine glands, especially the adrenal glands. In some instances, there was bronzing of the skin, but this was not true of all cases. In Hoefnagel's case, the cortex of the adrenal gland was atrophied, the basophil cells of the pituitary gland had vanished and there was an interstitial cell tumor of the testis.

Diagnosis.—Austin states that the diagnosis may be made by examination of the urine. One or two drops of toluidine blue or methylene blue are added to a centrifugalized specimen and a drop is put on a slide. Granular bodies of various sizes are seen which stain metachromatically. If toluidine blue is used the color is a golden brown but methylene blue gives various shades of red. Under polarized light these bodies are doubly refractive. They seem to be identical with the granular bodies found in the kidney tubules. In the later stages of the disease, these bodies are abundant in the urine. Biopsy of the kidney will often reveal the correct diagnosis. Hagberg believes that biopsy of the sural nerve is a valuable diagnostic procedure.

Yudell *et al.* state that the demonstration of prolonged conduction time

in the peripheral nerves is helpful in diagnosis. They mention that sulfatase is lacking in the urine. We have found that the diagnosis can usually be made by biopsy of a sural nerve and the study of the urine for metachromatic bodies.

Hagberg *et al.* state that sulphatides are excreted in the urine of normal individuals but are greatly increased in the urine of patients suffering from metachromatic leucodystrophy.

BIBLIOGRAPHY

ABRAHAM, K. AND LAMPERT, P.: Intraneuronal lipid deposits in metachromatic leukodystrophy. Neurology, 13:686, 1963.

ALLEN, R. J. *et al.:* Metachromatic leukodystrophy. Pediatrics, 30:629, 1962.

AUSTIN, J. H.: The diagnosis of metachromatic diffuse cerebral sclerosis. Neurology, 7:415, 1957.

AUSTIN, J. H.: Metachromatic form of diffuse cerebral sclerosis. III. The significance of sulfatide and other lipid abnormalities in the white matter and kidney. Neurology, 10:470, 1960.

AUSTIN, J. *et al.:* Metachromatic leukodystrophy. Neurology, 18:225, 1968.

BRAIN, W. R. AND GREENFIELD, J. G.: Late infantile metachromatic leucoencephalopathy with primary degeneration of the interfascicular oligodendroglia. Brain, 73:291, 1950.

EINARSON, L., NEEL, A. V. AND STROMGREN, E.: On the problem of diffuse brain sclerosis with special reference to the familial forms. Acta Jutlandica, 16:1, 1944.

FEIGIN, I.: Demyelinating diseases with special emphasis on the metachromatic type. J. Neuropath. & Exp. Neurol., 18:156, 1959.

———: Diffuse cerebral sclerosis (metachromatic leukoencephalopathy). Amer. Jour. Path., 30:715, 1954.

FOGELSON, M. H. *et al.:* Oligodendroglial lamellar inclusions. Neurology, 19:150, 1968.

GREENFIELD, J. G.: A form of progressive cerebral sclerosis in infants associated with primary degeneration of the interfascicular glia. J. Neurol. & Psychopath., 13:289, 1933.

HAGBERG, B., SOURANDER, P. AND THOREN, L.: Peripheral nerve changes in the diagnosis of metachromatic leukodystrophy. Acta Paediat., 135:63, 1962.

HAGBERG, B., SOURANDER, P., SVENNERHOLM, L. AND VOSS, H.: Late infantile metachromatic leucodystrophy of gynetic type. Acta Pediat., 49:135, 1960.

HAGBERG, B. AND SVENNERHOLM, L.: Chemical studies in leucodystrophy. Acta Paediat., 49:690, 1960.

HOEFNAGEL, *et al.:* Diffuse cerebral sclerosis with endocrine abnormalities in young males. Brain, 85:553, 1962.

JERVIS, G.: Infantile metachromatic leukodystrophy. J. Neuropath. & Exp. Neurol., 19:323, 1960.

MASTERS, P. L. *et al.:* Familial leucodystrophy. Arch. Dis. Childh., 39:345, 1964.

NORMAN, R. M.: Diffuse progressive metachromatic leucoencephalopathy. Brain, 70:234, 1947.

——— AND TINGEY, A. H.: Metachromatic leucoencephalopathy, a form of lipidosis. Brain, 83:369, 1960.

SCHUTTA, H. S. *et al.:* A family study of the late infantile and juvenile forms of metachromatic leucodystrophy. Jour. Hum. Genet., 3:86, 1966.

THIEFFRY, S.: La leucodystrophie metachromatique infantile familiale. Pediatrie, 17:593, 1962.

VAN BOGAERT, L. AND DE WULF, A.: Diffuse progressive leukodystrophy in the adult. Arch. Neurol. and Psychiat., 42:1083, 1939.

YUDELL, A. *et al.:* The neuropathy of sulfatide liposis (metachromatic leukodystrophy). Neurology, 17:103, 1967.

The Metachromatic Leucoencephalopathy of Scholz
(Subacute Juvenile Form)

This is another diffuse, degeneration of the white matter similar in many ways to the other types described in this section. The deposits in the granule cells are said to stain metachromatically. This disease is classified as one of the leucodystrophies. This is a sex linked recessive disorder.

Scholz states that the symptoms begin during the eighth and tenth years with deafness which seems to be of cortical nature. This seems to be associated with aphasia of receptive or sensory type. Later, there is blindness also of cortical type although in some instances the optic nerve heads are a little pale. The pupillary reflexes are preserved, however. Later, usually within a year after the onset, the legs become weak and spastic and after a time the arms are also affected. Gradually the child becomes deteriorated and finally demented. Forced laughter and weeping are often observed and various involuntary movements such as chorea and athetosis appear. At the end the child is deaf, blind, demented and completely paralytic. Death terminates the disease after an illness varying from one to two years.

BIBLIOGRAPHY

BIELSCHOWSKY, M. AND HENNEBERG, R.: Über familiare diffuse Sklerose. J. f. Psychol. u. Neurol., **36**:131, 1928.

DIEZEL, P. B.: Histochemical findings in leucodystrophy (Degenerative diffuse sclerosis of the type Scholz, Bielschowsky and Henneberg). The Third International Congress of Neuropathology, Brussels, July 21-28, 1957.

SCHOLZ, W.: Klinische, path. anat. u. erbbiol. Untersuchungen bei familiarer diffuse Hirnsclerose im Kindersalter. Ztschr. f. d. ges. Neurol. u. Psychiat., **99**:651, 1925.

Familial Cerebral Sclerosis With Pigmentation of the
Skin and Atrophy of the Adrenal Glands

Lichtenstein and Rosenbluth and Peiffer published articles about this condition in 1959. Hoefnagel published another in 1962 and in 1964 Fanconi published an additional paper. Fanconi was able to review 10 cases in all. The patients were all males. The onset was in childhood. In some families several siblings were affected.

In 9 cases the adrenal glands were atrophied. In some cases clinical evidences of adrenal deficiency were noted. In 1 case the adrenal glands could not be found. In the case of Hoefnagel, there was no cutaneous pigmentation, but in all the other cases, there was pigmentation of the skin which was found to be due to melanin. Hoefnagel found loss of the basophil cells in the pituitary gland and an interstitial cell tumor in one testis.

In all cases there was extensive demyelination in the brain. In most cases, a diagnosis of Schilder's disease was made. Lichtenstein employs the term

Schilder's disease, but describes the globoid bodies characteristic of Krabbe's disease. Peiffer describes the metachromatic leucodystrophy of Scholz.

Vick and Moore state that this condition is a distinct syndrome. It is confined to young males and inherited as a sex linked recessive trait. The adrenal insufficiency precedes the neurological symptoms. The course is progressive and treatment of the adrenal deficiency does not prevent the progression of the neurological process.

BIBLIOGRAPHY

FANCONI, A. *et al.:* Morbus Addison mit hirnsklerose in kindesalter. Ein hereditares syndrom. mit X chromosomater vererbung. Helv. Paediat. Acta, **18**:480, 1964.

HOEFNAGEL, D. *et al.:* Diffuse cerebral sclerosis with endocrine abnormalities in young males. Brain, **85**:553, 1962.

LICHTENSTEIN, B. W. AND ROSENBLUTH, P. R.: Schilder's disease with melanoderma. Jour. Neuropath. and Exp. Neurol., **18**:384, 1959.

PEIFFER, J.: Über die metachromatischen leukodystrophien (typ. Scholz). Arch. Psychiat. Nervenkr., **199**:386, 1959.

VICK, N. A. AND MOORE, R. Y.: Diffuse sclerosis with adrenal insufficiency. Neurology, **18**:1066, 1968.

CEREBRAL SCLEROSIS OF PELIZAEUS-MERZBACHER
(Chronic Infantile Form)

Definition.—A heredofamilial disease characterized by chronic, progressive and diffuse degeneration of cerebral white matter and by the clinical symptoms described below. This disease is believed to be a leucodystrophy. Seitelberger suggests that Pelizaeus-Merzbacher disease may be a dystrophy of the myelin sheath due to a defect in glycerophosphatide metabolism (see van Bogaert). Other authorities classify it among the sudanophil leucodystrophies.

Pathological Anatomy.—The studies of Merzbacher led him to believe that the disease was the expression of failure of development and he therefore suggested the term aplasia axialis congenita. Spielmeyer, however, soon showed that Merzbacher was in error and that the process was in reality a very slowly progressive degeneration of the white matter. When the Weigert stain is employed there seems to be extensive demyelination, but by other methods it may be shown that the axons are covered by a thin layer of lipid material. This is found to be composed of sphingomyelins and cerebrosides. The glycerophosphatides are lost. The axons suffer little damage and secondary degeneration is rarely found. The process seems to begin near the ventricles and progress towards the cortex. A narrow zone of white matter beneath the cortex is preserved. Eventually almost all the white matter of the brain, cerebellum, brain-stem and spinal cord is more or less completely degenerated, but small perivascular areas, or "markinsuli," are

FIG. 194. Pelizaeus-Merzbacher disease. Diffuse, universal and symmetrical demyelination of the cerebral white matter with dense gliosis. No spongy areas as in Schilder's disease. The process begins near the ventricles and spreads towards the cortex. No microglial phagocytes or products of myelin degeneration seen. The clinical course extended over many years. A brother has the same symptoms. (By the courtesy of Dr. Adolf Meyer and Dr. Snediker.)

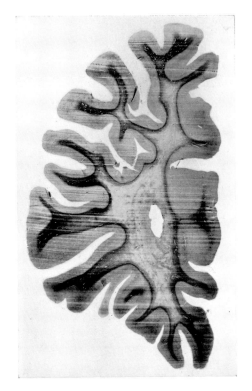

found in which the myelin is intact. There is extensive proliferation of the fibrous glial cells, causing increased density of the brain and giving rise to the term cerebral sclerosis. In the margins of advancing lesions the destroyed myelin is taken up by microglial cells. No evidence of an inflammatory process can be found. The gray matter shows very little change, as a rule, and the alterations described may well be merely secondary. As contrasted with the lesions in Schilder's disease, the process seems to be more widespread and it is also obviously more chronic. It does not seem to cause softening or cavitation.

Blackwood and Cumings have made a chemical analysis of the brain and find much reduction of the phospholipids and indeed, reduction of all lipids.

Clinical Features.—This disease is usually found in several members of a family and frequently may be traced through several generations. It is found chiefly in males but is not confined to them. Thus, among Merzbacher's fourteen patients, there were two females and twelve males. Unaffected females may transmit the disease and, in fact, the disease is usually thus transmitted. Apparently the morbid factor is sex-linked but behaves somewhat irregularly. Other cases are described in which the inheritance

was autosomal recessive or dominant though the histological picture was typical.

The symptoms usually begin early in infancy, at about the third month, but may occur later. There are rotary movements of the head and rotary nystagmus. Strangely enough these may disappear later. The next cardinal symptom is spasticity of the legs, which is followed after some years by a similar condition in the arms. The tendon reflexes are increased, there is ankle clonus and Babinski sign. Still later, ataxia develops which is of cerebellar type and is usually accompanied by a typical "intention tremor" and scanning speech. Somewhere about the end of the sixth year, it usually becomes evident that the child is becoming demented. Various involuntary movements may now appear such as choreoathetosis, tremors and grimacing. A more or less complete Parkinsonian syndrome is often observed with immobility of the face, cog-wheel resistance in the extremities, bradykinesis and a flexed posture. The weakness eventually develops into paralysis. Contractures result and lead to deformities such as scoliosis and pes cavus. Loss of sensibility is not observed. There may be some pallor of the optic nerve heads but this is not always to be expected. The clinical picture is not always the same and even in the same family a great deal of variation in the symptomatology may occur.

The course of this disease is extraordinarily slow so that, even after several years' observation, it may not be certain that it is progressing at all. A very remarkable feature which has often given rise to confusion with disseminated sclerosis is the occurrence of remissions or of temporary arrest of symptoms. The patients not infrequently survive until middle age despite the fact that the symptoms begin in infancy.

Diezel *et al.* describe two types of this disease which run a more rapid course. Two cases are described in brothers with onset of symptoms in the first few months of life and death within the first year. Another pair of brothers are reported in which the symptoms began at about 10 years and death occurred at 20 years. Post-mortem examinations revealed the typical lesions.

Thulin *et al.* describe the case of a child who had neurological symptoms at birth and died at the age of 3 years and 3 months. The examination of the nervous system revealed a process resembling the Pelizaeus-Merzbacher disease.

Diagnosis.—The principal conditions to be considered in differential diagnosis are congenital spastic diplegia and various degenerative processes. The first is non-progressive but when associated with cerebellar defects or with involuntary movements may be a source of confusion. The family history should be of great value in this respect since the defects of development are rarely so strongly hereditary as Pelizaeus-Merzbacher disease. It is

not always possible to distinguish this disease from progressive degenerative processes of other types since they exist in such variety. Despite the histological similarity of the two conditions it is easy, as a rule, to distinguish Schilder's disease from the disease under consideration, since in the former the course is rarely over a few years.

Fahmy *et al.* describe a familial condition in which the clinical picture resembled that of the Pelizaeus-Merzbacher disease, but the pathological lesions were different.

Prognosis.—There is no hope of recovery, but life is not greatly shortened, as a rule, if the patient receives proper nursing care.

Treatment.—This is merely symptomatic.

BIBLIOGRAPHY

BATTEN, F. E.: Unusual type of hereditary disease of the nervous system (Pelizaeus-Merzbacher disease). Brain, 36:341, 1914.

BLACKWOOD, W. AND CUMINGS, J. N.: A histological and chemical study of three cases of diffuse cerebral sclerosis. J. Neurol., Neurosurg. & Psychiat., 17:33, 1954.

CAMP, C. D. AND LOWENBERG, K.: An American family with Pelizaeus-Merzbacher disease. Arch. of Neurol. and Psychiat., 45:261, 1941.

DIEZEL, P. B. *et al.*: Leukodystrophy with orthochromatic decomposition products. Arch. Path. Anat., 338:371, 1965.

DIEZEL, P. B. AND HUTH, K.: Pelizaeus-Merzbacher disease with familial occurrence. Deutsche Ztschr. Nervenh., 184:264, 1963.

FAHMY, A. *et al.*: A new form of hereditary cerebral sclerosis. Arch. of Neurol., 20:468, 1969.

FERRARO, A.: The familial form of encephalitis periaxialis. J. Nerv. & Ment. Dis., 76:329, 1927.

MERZBACHER, L.: Eine eigenartige familiar-hereditäre Erkrankungsform. Ztschr. f. d. ges. Neurol. u. Psychiat., 3:1, 1910.

NISSENBAUM, C. *et al.*: Pelizaeus-Merzbacher disease. Infantile acute type. Ann. Paediat., 204:365, 1965.

PEIFFER, J. AND ZERBIN-RUDIN, E.: Zur Variationsbreite der Pelizaeus-Merzbacherschen Krankheit. Acta neuropath. Berl., 3:87, 1963.

PELIZAEUS, F.: Über eine eigentümliche Form spastische Lähmung mit Cerebralerscheinungen auf hereditärer Grundlage. Arch. f. Psych. u. Nervenkrankh., 16:698, 1885.

SCHEFTEL, Y.: Pelizaeus-Merzbacher disease. J. Nerv. & Ment. Dis., 74:175, 1931.

SPIELMEYER, W.: Der anatomische Befund bei einem zweiten Falle von Pelizaeus-Merzbacherscher Krankheit. Zentralbl. Neurol., 32:203, 1923.

THULIN, B. *et al.*: Demyelinating leukodystrophy with total cortical atrophy. Arch. Neurol., 18:113, 1968.

TYLER, H. R.: Pelizaeus-Merzbacher disease. Arch. of Neurol. and Psychiat., 80:162, 1958.

VAN BOGAERT, L.: Cerebral Lipidoses. Springfield, Thomas, 1957.

VON HAGEN, K. AND SULT, C. W.: Familial diffuse sclerosis (Pelizaeus-Merzbacher disease). Bull. Los Angeles Neurol. Soc., 4:23, 1939.

ZEMAN, W. *et al.*: Pelizaeus-Merzbacher disease. Jour. Neuropath. and Exp. Neurol., 23:334, 1964.

CEREBRAL SCLEROSIS OF KRABBE
(Acute Infantile Form)

This is a diffuse, rapidly progressive degeneration of the white matter. There are no metachromatic deposits but globoid bodies are a characteristic feature and myelin balls are seen. Blackwood and Cumings have made a

careful study of this condition and conclude that these bodies are deposits of kerasin which is one of the cerebrosides. This disease is classified as one of the leucodystrophies.

In the last stage of the disease, degeneration of the peripheral nerves is found with demyelination of the nerve sheaths and degeneration of the axons. It is inherited as a simple recessive disorder.

Krabbe studied some five cases all of which were very similar, if not identical. The disease is very strongly familial and several siblings are affected as a rule. They are always considered to be quite healthy at birth and it is only when the child has reached the age of from four to six months that symptoms appear. The child then begins to cry constantly, and without apparent cause. After a short time, this ceases and is followed by a state of apathy or stupor. At the same time the musculature grows rigid and this gradually increases until the child is rendered entirely helpless. From time to time tonic seizures develop in which the head is retracted, the arms flexed and the legs stiffly extended. Clonic convulsions may also occur. Such seizures are usually provoked by stimuli such as handling or washing, but also may be provoked by bright lights or loud noises. Eventually the child can no longer swallow and must be fed by gavage. There may be optic neuritis and later optic atrophy, but the child may become blind without any apparent change in the optic discs or loss of light reflex. Deafness may eventually supervene. Vomiting is frequent and is one of the causes of the progressive loss of weight. Toward the end of the disease, the rigidity of the muscles disappears and flaccid paralysis follows. It is unusual for the disease to last more than a year. The prognosis is apparently quite hopeless. Stadler *et al.* have studied the blood lipids in a number of cases of this type and in healthy siblings. They find a significant elevation of cholesterol and phosphatides, they state, in both patients and siblings.

BIBLIOGRAPHY

BLACKWOOD, W. AND CUMINGS, J. N.: A histological and chemical study of three cases of diffuse cerebral sclerosis. J. Neurol., Neurosurg. & Psychiat., **17**:33, 1954.

HAGBERG, H. *et al.*: Infantile globoid cell leucodystrophy. Neuropädiatrie, **1**:74, 1969.

HOGAN, G. R. *et al.*: The peripheral neuropathy of Krabbe's leukodystrophy. Neurology, **19**, 11:1094, 1969.

KASS, A.: Acute diffuse infantile sclerosis of the brain (Krabbe's disease). Acta paediat., **42**:73, 1953.

KRABBE, K.: A new form of diffuse brain sclerosis. Brain, **39**:74, 1916.

NELSON, E. *et al.*: Ultrastructural and chemical studies on Krabbe's disease. J. Neuropath. & Exp. Neurol., **22**:414, 1963.

NORMAN, R. M. *et al.*: Histological and chemical findings in Krabbe's leucodystrophy. Jour. of Neurol. Neurosurg. and Psychiat., **24**:223, 1961.

STADLER, H. E. *et al.*: Heredofamilial infantile cerebral degeneration. The relationship of systemic factors to the pathogenicity. J. Pediat., **44**:364, 1954.

VAN BOGAERT, L.: Cerebral Lipidoses. Springfield, Thomas, 1957.

SPONGY DEGENERATION OF THE NERVOUS SYSTEM IN INFANCY

Definition.—This is a familial leucodystrophy characterized by the presence of vacuoles in the central nervous system. It was first distinguished from the other leucodystrophies by van Bogaert and Bertrand, in 1949, though other cases had been published previously, under various titles. Banker *et al.* reviewed the subject fully in 1964. About thirty-one cases had been published at that time. Inheritance is recessive.

Feigin *et al.* state that spongy degeneration is a post-mortem artifact. They review seven cases. In three cases, they found the metabolic defect of maple sugar urine disease. In one case, they found lesions characteristic of subacute necrotizing encephalopathy. In three cases no specific cause was found. They refer to a case described by Chou and Waisman in which spongy degeneration was found in homocystinuria and another reported by Malamud in which phenylketonuria caused spongy degeneration.

Pathological Anatomy.—The brain is often increased in size and weight. The white matter is soft, gelatinous and discolored. The ventricles are often enlarged. On microscopic study, innumerable vacuoles are seen which vary in diameter from 15 micra to 200 micra. These are most numerous in the deeper layers of the cerebral cortex and the subcortical white matter, where extensive demyelination is found. The more central portions of the white matter are less severely involved. Loss of nerve cells may be pronounced. The astrocytes are increased and areas of gliosis are present. The basal ganglia, cerebellum, brain stem and spinal cord are also involved. There is reduction of all the brain lipids on chemical analysis.

Clinical Features.—It is of interest that the children have light complexions and blood or red hair, though their parents have dark hair and eyes. Their parents are usually Jewish people who, as a rule, originally came from Eastern Europe. Most of them lived in the Vilna-Kovno area of Lithuania and the adjacent area of Bialstok of Poland or in the Volyhnia region of the Ukraine. The inhabitants of these regions are all closely related.

The clinical features of this disease show little variation but are not so characteristic as to permit a diagnosis. The onset is at about the second or third month. They are flaccid at first and cannot hold up the head. Soon the flaccidity disappears and the muscles become spastic; optic atrophy and squints appear; tonic seizures with opisthotonos and also tonic-clonic seizures occur. Myoclonus is mentioned. Pseudobulbar palsy develops. Death occurs in decerebrate rigidity by the second year in most cases. One child died at eight years and nine months, and one child was alive at nine years.

The spinal fluid is usually normal. No abnormal substances have been found in the blood or urine.

Diagnosis.—Only brain biopsy or post-mortem examination permit a proper diagnosis.

Treatment.—None is known.

BIBLIOGRAPHY

BANKER, B. Q. *et al.:* Spongy degeneration of the central nervous system in infancy. Neurology, **14**:981, 1964.

BLACKWOOD, W. AND CUMINGS, J. N.: A histological and chemical study of three cases of diffuse cerebral sclerosis. J. Neurol., Neurosurg. & Psychiat., **17**:33, 1954.

VAN BOGAERT, L. AND BERTRAND, I.: Sur une idiotie familiale avec degenerescence spongiouse die nevraxe. Acta neurol. psychiat. belg., **49**:572, 1949.

BUCHANAN, D. S. AND DAVIS, R. L.: Spongy degeneration of the nervous system. Neurology, **15**:207, 1965.

CANAVAN, M. M.: Schilder's encephalitis diffusa. Arch. Neurol. & Psychiat., **25**:299, 1931.

CHOU, S. AND WAISMAN, H.: Spongy degeneration of the central nervous system. Case of homocystinuria. Arch. of Path., **79**:357, 1965.

FEIGIN, I. *et al.:* The infantile spongy degenerations. Neurology, **18**:153, 1968.

GLOBUS, J. H. AND STRAUSS, I.: Progressive degenerative subcortical encephalopathy. Arch. Neurol. & Psychiat., **20**:1190, 1928.

JERVIS, G. A.: Early infantile acute diffuse sclerosis of the brain. Am. J. Dis. Child., **64**:1055, 1942.

MALAMUD, N.: Neuropathology of phenylketonuria. Jour. Neuropath. and Exp. Neurol., **25**:254, 1966.

MEYER, J. E.: Über eine Ödemkrankheit des Zentralnervensystems im frühen Kindesalter. Arch. Psychiat. Nervenkr., **185**:35, 1950.

SACKS, O. *et al.:* Spongy degeneration of the white matter. Neurology, **15**:165, 1965.

VAN BOGAERT, L.: Familial spongy degeneration of the brain. Acta Psychiat. Scandinav., **39**:107, 1963.

WOLMAN, M.: The spongy type of diffuse cerebral sclerosis. Brain, **84**:243, 1961.

ZU RHEIN, G. M. *et al.:* Familial idiocy with spongy degeneration of the central nervous system of the van Bogaert-Bertrand type. Neurology, **10**:998, 1960.

MEGALOENCEPHALY WITH HYALINE PAN-NEUROPATHY
(Alexander's Disease)

Definition.—Another leucodystrophy characterized by deposits of hyaline material in the nervous system. Wohlwill found five cases in 1959. Inheritance is recessive.

Pathological Anatomy.—Crome states that the brain is usually larger and heavier than normal. He studied the brain of a child of two years and two months which weighed 1520 grams. There were large cavities in the white matter of the frontal and parietal lobes. The ventricles were dilated. There was degeneration of the myelin and axis cylinders, loss of nerve cells and gliosis of the cortex overlying the destructive lesions in the white matter. Innumerable elongated deposits termed hyaline bodies were found in the subpial cortex, arcuate fibers, marginal zones of the brain stem and spinal cord. These are grouped around blood vessels. Some were several hundred

micra in length and 80 micra in width. Others were very small. They were homogenous. Wohlwill studied these deposits and concluded that they were composed of glycolipids.

Clinical Features.—There is nothing distinctive in the clinical picture. Crome describes the case of a child who could never sit up or hold up the head. At four months, the child began to have seizures; soon there were screaming spells. At seven months, the child was taken to a hospital. The circumference of the head was 45 cm. It gradually increased to 53.7 cm. The spinal fluid protein varied between 20 and 46 mgs. An air study revealed what seemed to be porencephalic cavities in both hemispheres. The child became rigid and developed opisthotonos. Death occurred at two years and two months.

Diagnosis.—Only brain biopsy or post-mortem examination permit a diagnosis.

Treatment.—None.

BIBLIOGRAPHY

ADAMS, R. D. AND RICHARDSON, E. P. JR.: Demyelinative Diseases of the Human Nervous System. Chemical Pathology of the Nervous System. New York, Pergamon Press, 1961, p. 162.

ALEXANDER, W. S.: Progressive fibrinoid degeneration of fibrillary astrocytes associated with mental retardation in a hydrocephalic infant. Brain, 72:373, 1949.

CROME, L.: Megaloencephaly associated with hyaline pan-neuropathy. Brain, 76:215, 1953.

STEVENSON, L. D. AND VOGEL, F. S.: A case of macrocephaly with peculiar deposits throughout the brain and spinal cord. Ciencia, 12:71, 1952.

STEVENSON, L. D.: Discussion with Dr. Wohlwill. J. Neuropath. & Exp. Neurol., 16:130, 1957.

VOGEL, F. S. AND HALLERVORDEN, J.: Leucodystrophy with Rosenthal fiber formation. Acta Neuropath. Berl., 2:126, 1962.

WOHLWILL, F. J., BERNSTEIN, J. AND YAKOVLEV, P. I.: Dysmyelinogenic leukodystrophy. J. Neuropath. & Exp. Neurol., 18:359, 1959.

THE MUCOPOLYSACCHARIDOSES
Gargoylism or Hurler's Syndrome

Definition.—One of the mucopolysaccharidoses, which is characterized by dwarfism, deformities of the face and bones, changes in the viscera and mental deterioration.

Etiology.—This is a genetically determined disorder of mucopolysaccharide metabolism which behaves like a simple recessive trait. Several siblings may be affected, but the disease is not found in previous generations as a rule.

Pathological Anatomy.—A number of post-mortem examinations are reported. The brain, as a rule, is reduced in weight and the ventricles are often dilated. The neurons are almost universally swollen and contain granular deposits. There may be mild hypertrophic changes in the macroglia, but the microglia and oligodendroglia usually show little reaction. The cerebral cortex, basal ganglia, brain stem, cerebellum and spinal cord may be in-

volved. Fusiform swellings may be seen on the dendrites of the Purkinje's cells of the cerebellum. Extracellular deposits of granular material are sometimes found. The white matter may be thin and shrunken and rarely there are areas of demyelination. In a few cases an extraordinary thickening of the leptomeninges has been found. This thickening is due to proliferation of collagenous connective tissue which contains deposits of granular material. Subdural hematoma was found in Magee's case. The corneae show deposits in the middle and posterior layers. A variable degree of involvement of the viscera is found. The liver is usually enlarged and deposits are found in the cells. Similar infiltrations are described in some instances in the spleen, kidneys, heart, blood vessels, aorta, intestines, pancreas, and pituitary gland. The heart valves are thickened, and the coronary arteries are also involved. There is some doubt about the cause of the changes in the bones, but it has been claimed that they are secondary to deposits in the osteoblasts.

There has been much dispute about the nature of the deposits in the tissues, but at the present time most authorities seem to believe that they are composed of mucopolysaccharides. Chondroitin sulphate B and heparitin sulphate are found in the tissues and in the urine.

Clinical Finding.—In typical cases the patient is a dwarf. There is almost always a kyphos in the upper lumbar region. The head is relatively large in contrast to the small body. Its shape is not constant for it has been described as scaphocephalic, acrocephalic and macrocephalic. The distance from the ears to the vertex is increased. The face is termed grotesque. The nose is flattened, the root recedes and the nostrils flare widely. The hair of the head is coarse and abundant. The eyes are widely spaced. The lips are thick. The mouth is often open for there is nasal obstruction. The ears are set low. The neck is so short that the large head seems to sit on the shoulders. The extremities are short and the joints admit of only a limited range of movement. The hands are broad and the fingers short. The fingers are often held in partial flexion for they cannot be fully extended. The hand is often described as a trident hand. The little finger may be incurved. The child stands with bent knees and elbows. There is sometimes obvious enlargement of the ends of the long bones. The abdomen is protuberant and umbilical and inguinal hernias are common. A smooth enlargement of the liver and spleen is a typical feature. Sexual development usually remains infantile. In a large percentage of cases the corneas are opaque because of deposits in the posterior layers. These children may develop optic atrophy. Glaucoma occurs and internal squints are common. In a few patients whose corneas are clear and the retinae can be seen, pigmentary degeneration of the retinae is found. When the corneae are opaque, the electroretinogram may reveal degeneration of the retinae. Deafness may develop. There is

progressive mental deterioration in most cases. These children have increasing difficulty in walking and eventually cannot walk at all. Weakness and spasticity of the extremities appear and increased tendon reflexes and Babinski signs are then found. Convulsions sometimes occur. Very extensive changes are found in the roentgenograms of the bones. The sella turcica is elongated. The vertebrae show variations in size and shape. The kyphos is due to a wedge shaped lumbar vertebra which often has a hook like prominence on its anterior aspect. The bones of the extremities are abnormally short and irregularly thickened. The marrow cavity may be widened. The epiphyses are often grossly enlarged and irregular. The bones of the fingers are described as cone shaped. Malformation of the joints is apparently responsible for the limitation of movement. Cardiac murmurs are common and heart failure may occur. Older patients show excessive hirsutism. Skin lesions are said to be characteristic. Groups of small, white papules and nodules described as orange peel appearances are described. Histological examination reveals deposits of a mucopolysaccharide in parenchymal cells.

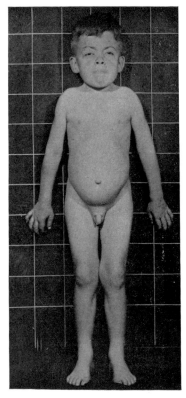

FIG. 195. Gargoylism in a boy of 7 years. He shows deficient bodily growth, mental defect, malformed head and face, protuberant abdomen, enlarged liver and spleen and typical changes in the cornea and bones.

These findings are apparently not present in infancy as a rule. It is said that these children may present a normal appearance for some months and may show no sign of mental deterioration. The mental changes and alteration of the face and bones usually become evident about the second or third year. The process is progressive. In most instances death occurs before the tenth year. Often heart failure or respiratory tract infection is the cause of death.

The spinal fluid is said to be normal. No excess of lipoids has been found in the blood. Reilly describes large, dark violet granules in the cytoplasm of the leukocytes. Karl Meyer *et al.* find that in gargoylism large quantities of sulfated mucopolysaccharides; chondroitin sulfate and heparitin sulfate are excreted in the urine every day. Neither of these substances is found in the urine of normal individuals.

Diagnosis.—When the whole picture is found the diagnosis is obvious.

In cases in which the syndrome is incomplete, a complete study may be required. The bony changes are very important in diagnosis. The disease may be confused with cretinism, congenital syphilis and Morquio's disease. It has been suggested that gargoylism is closely related to the last. The excretion of mucopolysaccharides in the urine may be of diagnostic value when the clinical features are not adequate to justify a positive diagnosis.

Prognosis.—The course is progressive and few patients live to be more than ten years old. Some may survive to middle age, however.

Treatment.—None.

BIBLIOGRAPHY

AEGERTER, E. E. AND KRESSLER, R. J.: Hurler's syndrome. J. Pediat., **12**:579, 1938.

ALEU, F. P. *et al.*: Electron microscopy of two cerebral biopsies in gargoylism. Jour. Neuropath. and Exp. Neurol., **24**:304, 1965.

ASHBY, W. R., STEWART, R. M. AND WATKINS, J. H.: Chondro-osteo-dystrophy of the Hurler type (Gargoylism). Brain, **60**:149, 1937.

ELLIS, R. W., SHELDON, W. AND CAPON, N. B.: Gargoylism, chondro-osteo-dystrophy, corneal opacities, hepatosplenomegaly and mental defect. Quart. J. Med., **5**:119, 1936.

HAMBRICK, G. W. AND SCHEIE, H. G.: Skin changes in Hurler's syndrome. Arch. Dermat., **85**:455, 1962.

HENDERSON, J. L.: Gargoylism: A review of the principal features with report of five cases. Arch. Dis. Childhood, **15**:201, 1940.

JERVIS, G. A.: Gargoylism (Lipochondrodystrophy): A study of ten cases with emphasis on the formes frustes of the disease. Arch. Neurol. & Psychiat., **63**:681, 1950.

LEVIN, S. AND KAPLAN, M. B.: Skin lesions in gargoylism. Am. J. Dis. Child., **99**:444, 1960.

LINDSAY, S., REILLY, W. A., GOTHAM, T. J. AND SKAHEN, R.: Gargoylism. Am. J. Dis. Child., **76**:239, 1948.

LINDSAY, S.: Cardiovascular system in gargoylism. Brit. Heart Jour., **12**:17, 1950.

LURIE, L. A. AND LEVY, S.: Gargoylism: Review of the literature and report of two cases. Am. J. Med. Sc., **208**:184, 1944.

MacGILLIVERAY, R. C.: Gargoylism. J. Ment. Sci., **98**:687, 1952.

MAGEE, K. R.: Leptomeningeal changes associated with lipochondrodystrophy (gargoylism). Arch. Neurol. & Psychiat., **63**:282, 1950.

McKUSICK, V.: Heritable Disorders of Connective Tissue. St. Louis, C. V. Mosby Co., 1956.

MEYER, K. *et al.*: Sulfated mucopolysaccharides of urine and organs in gargoylism. Proc. Soc. Exp. Biol. Med., **102**:587, 1959.

MITTWOCH, U.: Inclusions of mucopolysaccharide in lymphocytes of patients with gargoylism. Nature, **191**:1315, 1961.

REILLY, W. A.: The granules in the leucocytes in gargoylism. Am. J. Dis. Child., **62**:489, 1941.

REILLY, W. A. AND LINDSAY, S.: Gargoylism. Am. J. Dis. Child., **75**:595, 1948.

SMITH, E. B. *et al.*: Gargoylism. Ann. Int. Med., **36**:652, 1952.

STRAUSS, R. *et al.*: Gargoylism. A review of the literature and report of sixth autopsied case with chemical studies. Am. J. Clin. Path., **17**:671, 1947.

SEAR, H. R. AND MADDOX, J. K.: A case of Hurler's disease. M. J. Australia, **i**:488, 1945.

TERRY, K. AND LINKER, A.: Four forms of Hurler's syndrome. Proc. Soc. Exp. Biol., **115**:394, 1964.

THANNHAUSER, S. J. AND SCHMIDT, G.: Lipids and lipidoses. Physiol. Rev., **26**:275, 1946.

UZMAN, L. L.: Chemical nature of the storage substance in gargoylism. Arch. Path., **60**:308, 1955.

VAN BOGAERT, L.: Cerebral Lipidoses. Springfield, Thomas, 1957.

WALSH, F. B.: *Loc. cit.*

OTHER MUCOPOLYSACCHARIDOSES

Hunter's syndrome: The clinical picture is very similar to that of the Hurler's syndrome. The children are dwarfs. Their joints are stiff. They have the same grotesque faces as in Hurler's syndrome. The liver and spleen are enlarged. There is pigmentary degeneration of the retinae. There is an excess of hair over the body and grooved, ridged or nodular areas in the skin extending from the scapulae to the axillae. Chondroitin sulphate B and heparitin sulphate are excreted in excess. However, there is no clouding of the corneae and no lumbar gibbus. Mental deterioration is slower than in Hurler's syndrome. The inheritance is that of a sex-linked recessive trait.

Sanfilippo syndrome: In this condition bodily growth is not severely impaired. There is no great physical disability. Mental deterioration advances rapidly. There is no clouding of the corneae and the liver and spleen are only slightly enlarged. It is said that there is no cardiac damage. The patients live longer than in the syndromes mentioned above. Only heparitin sulphate is excreted in excess. The inheritance is that of an autosomal recessive.

Morquio's syndrome: These children are dwarfs. The vertebrae are flattened so their trunks are grossly shortened. They have barrel chests with pigeon breasts. They stand with their legs flexed at hip and knee and display knock knees. The corneae are cloudy. Mental deficiency is mild. Spastic paraplegia may result from compression of the spinal cord. This is an autosomal recessive condition. Only keratosulphate is excreted in excess.

Scheies syndrome: These children have a normal stature and often normal intelligence. Their joints are stiff. They have aortic valve involvement. Broad mouths are characteristic. The carpal tunnel syndrome may develop. This is inherited as an autosomal recessive trait. Chondroitin sulphate B is excreted in excess.

Maroteaux-Lamy syndrome: These children have normal intelligence. The bony changes are those of Hurler's syndrome. The liver and spleen are enlarged. Corneal opacities develop early. There is no cardiac involvement. Only chondroitin sulphate B is excreted in excess. This is believed to be an autosomal recessive trait.

BIBLIOGRAPHY

GORLIN, R. J. AND SEDANO, H.: The Morquino-Brailsford syndrome. Modern Medicine, June 3, 1968, p. 130.

HUNTER, C.: A rare disease in two brothers. Pro. Roy. Soc. Med., 10:104, 1917.

MAROTEAUX, P. AND LAMY, M.: Hurler's disease. Morquio's disease and related mucopolysaccharidoses. Jour. of Pediat., 67:312, 1965.

McKusick, V.: Heritable Disorders of Connective Tissue. 3rd Ed. 1966, C. V. Mosby Co. (abundant references.)

Morquio, M. H.: Sur une forme dystrophie osseuse familiale. Bull. Soc. Pediat. de Paris, **27**:145, 1929.

Sanfilippo, S. J. and Good, R. A.: A laboratory study of the Hurler's syndrome. Amer. Jour. Dis. Child., **102**:140, 1964.

Scheie, H. G. *et al.*: A newly recognized forme fruste of Hurler's disease. Amer. Jour. Ophthal., **53**:753, 1962.

Wallace, B. J. *et al.*: Mucopolysaccharidosis type III. Morphologic and biochemical studies of two siblings with the Sanfilippo syndrome. Arch. of Path., **82**:462, 1966.

DISORDERS OF PURINE METABOLISM
Hyperuricemia

This sex linked condition is restricted to males. The symptoms are evident early in infancy. There is mental deficiency of severe degree. Athetosis is a standard sign and there is spasticity of the legs with increased tendon reflexes and Babinski signs. Convulsions often occur in infancy. These children bite their fingers and lips so their front teeth may have to be drawn. The tonic neck reflexes are strongly developed in childhood.

Tophi, gouty arthritis and hematuria with uric acid crystals in the urine and renal calculi occur. Uremia may be fatal. The blood level of uric acid ranges from 8.7 mgs to 25.0 mgs. The excretion of uric acid in the urine in 24 hours may exceed 600 mgs, whereas in controls there is only one third as much excreted. Two hundred times of glycine is converted into uric acid as in normal individuals. The partition of amino acids in the urine is normal. Berman *et al.* believe that deficiency of the enzyme inosinate phosphoribosyl pyrophosphate transferase is responsible.

Nyhan *et al.* suggest that the levels of uric acid in the serum would not harm the nervous system of adults, but has an adverse effect on the development of the nervous system in the fetus.

Lindenberg found sclerosis of Ammon's horns, deficient development of the pyramidal tracts, cerebellar peduncles and pons. Another patient was found to have ectopic deposits of gray matter in the cerebral white matter. A third post-mortem examination failed to discover any anatomical abnormalities. In patients who die in uremia the usual lesions found in that condition are present.

Medication to reduce the serum uric acid may protect the kidneys, but have no effect on the neurological condition.

CASE HISTORY.—*Hyperuricemia in two brothers. Post-mortem examination of an uncle suffering from the same condition.*

By the courtesy of Dr. Harry Butler J. L. S. was examined at the Rosewood State Hospital at the age of 3 years and 6 months. He was born at term. Birth weight was 7 lbs and 12 oz. He was discovered to be mentally deficient when he was very young. He was subject to convulsions in infan-

cy. Involuntary movements were recognized soon. He was never able to sit up or crawl. He bit his lips and fingers. He never was able to talk or understand.

On examination his bodily development was below average. His head was somewhat small. No abnormalities of the cranial nerves were discovered, but there was a grayish area in the retinae in the region of the maculae. The upper lip had been bitten so it was much shortened. The chest was wide and deep in contrast to the small abdomen. The pelvis was narrow.

There were constant athetoid movements of the arms and head. The legs showed less movement and were usually held rigidly in extension. Muscle tone was sometimes increased and sometimes reduced. The child could make vigorous movements but these were clumsy. The tonic neck reflexes were easily elicited. There were bilateral grasp reflexes. The child could not sit up because this position induced strong extensor spasm. The tendon reflexes were increased. Plantar stimulation caused either flexion or extension of the toes. Small bony nodules were seen on the anterior aspect of the proximal end of the clavicles. No tophi were seen. The joints were not involved.

X-rays of the body revealed a large liver. The serum uric acid was 8.9 mgs. The partition of the amino acids in the urine was normal.

A brother, T. S., who was 26 months old, displayed exactly the same condition on examination. He was mentally deficient and could not talk or understand. He was subject to seizures. He showed athetoid movements and tonic neck reflexes. The tendon reflexes were increased. His chest was large. The grayish areas about the maculae were present. He had not bitten his lips. The level of uric acid in the blood was always elevated.

The half brother of the mother of these children was grossly deficient in mental development, had violent athetoid movements, was subject to convulsions, could never walk, feed himself or talk. He died at the age of 9 years of pneumonia. Post-mortem examination by Dr. Richard Lindenberg revealed a small brain weighing 1130 grams. There was bilateral sclerosis of Ammon's horns, cortical sclerosis of the cerebellum, small pons, small pyramidal tracts and small brachia conjunctiva.

CASE HISTORY (J. H. H. 857202 and 857203).—*Hyperuricemia in two brothers.*

By the courtesy of Dr. Harry Butler, M. A. W. was examined at the Rosewood State Hospital. Early in childhood it was found that he had involuntary movements. Soon it was evident that he was mentally deficient. He could never crawl, sit up or feed himself. He could not form words or understand. He bit his lips and fingers. As an infant he had convulsions. An older brother, E. D. W., had the same condition. The mother and father both had convulsions in infancy. No history of gout in the family is mentioned. When he was admitted to Rosewood he was found to have athetosis and was quite helpless. The tonic neck reflexes were

fully developed. He bit his lips and fingers so some front teeth had to be drawn. The intelligence quotient was less than 15 per cent. The uric acid in the serum was found to vary between 8.9 and 16.8 mgs. The excretion of uric acid in the urine was vastly increased and a greater part of glycine was converted into uric acid than in normal controls.

The urine was full of crystals and on cystoscopy the bladder was full of crystals. On one occasion, the ureters were obstructed. When the urine was made alkaline, the crystals were no longer a problem.

Examination on January 18, 1967 at the age of 9 years and 2 months revealed impaired nutrition. Bodily development was below average for his age. His head was 48.5 cm in circumference. His chest was broad and deep, but the abdomen was small and the pelvis narrow. No tophi or gouty arthritis was found.

He was unable to cooperate in the examination. He made inarticulate sounds and it was uncertain whether he could understand or not. There were constant violent athetoid movements involving all extremities, the trunk and neck with tonic extension of the trunk. Coordination was grossly impaired but he moved his extremities with considerable force. The tendon reflexes were sluggish. No Babinski signs were elicited. The tonic neck reflexes were no longer present. There were gray areas in the retinae in the region of the maculae. The hands and feet were padded to protect them against bruising by his violent movements.

The brother, E. D. W., was admitted to Rosewood at the age of 5½ years on February 11, 1960. He had exactly the same symptoms as M. A. W. There were mental deficiency, violent athetoid movements, and

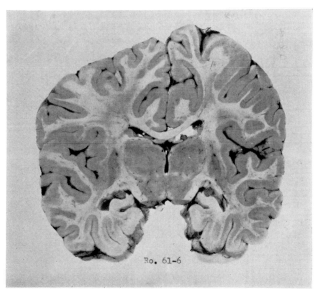

Fig. 196. Brain of child suffering from hyperuricemia showing sclerosis of Ammon's horns. (By the courtesy of Dr. Richard Lindenberg.)

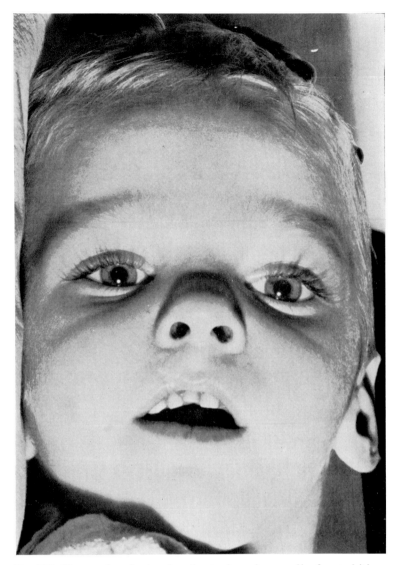

Fig. 197. Hyperuricemia showing shortening of upper lip due to biting.

tonic neck reflexes. He bit his lips and fingers. There were grayish areas in the regions of the maculae. The intelligence quotient could not be estimated. The serum uric acid was 14 mgs on one occasion and 18 mgs on another. The excretion of uric acid was greatly increased and he converted vastly more glycine into uric acid than normal individuals. The urine was full of crystals. He died on September 28, 1966 at the age of 12 years and 6 months of bronchopneumonia.

A post-mortem examination was performed at the National Institute of Health. Tophi were found in the ears. Two thirds of the lower lip

and the terminal joint of the left little finger were missing. Deposits of urates were found in the kidneys and in the auricular appendages of the heart. Ectopic deposits of gray matter were found in the cerebral white matter. No urates were found in the brain and no destructive lesions or developmental defects.

BIBLIOGRAPHY

BERMAN, P. H. *et al.:* Congenital hyperuricemia. Arch. of Neurology, **20**:44, 1969.
HOEFNAGEL, D. *et al.:* Hereditary choreoathetosis, self mutilation and hyperuricemia in young males. New England Jour. Med., **273**:130, 1965.
————: The syndrome of athetoid cerebral palsy, mental deficiency, self mutilation and hyperuricemia. Jour. Ment. Defic. Res., **9**:69, 1965.
LESCH, M. AND NYHAN, W.: A familial disorder of uric acid metabolism and central nervous system function. Amer. Jour. Med., **36**:561, 1964.
NYHAN, W. *et al.:* A familial disorder of uric acid metabolism and central nervous system function. Jour. of Pediat., **67**:257, 1965.
———— *et al.:* Genetics of X-linked disorder of uric acid metabolism. Pediat. Res., **1**:5, 1967.
PARTINGTON, M. W. AND HENNEN, B. K. E.: The Lesch-Nyhan syndrome. Devel. Med. Child. Neurol., **9**:563, 1967.
RILEY, L. D.: Gout and cerebral palsy in a three year old boy. Arch. of Dis. Childhood, **35**:293, 1960.
SASS, J. K. *et al.:* Juvenile gout with brain involvement. Arch. of Neurol., **13**:639, 1965.

THE PORPHYRIAS

A number of different porphyrias are known, but only the following types need be described.

Erythropoietic Porphyrias
    Congenital erythropoietic porphyria
    Erythropoietic protoporphyria
Hepatic Porphyrias
    Acute intermittent porphyria Swedish type
    Acute intermittent porphyria South African type.

Mixed forms and late forms are reported. They are described in the references given below.

BIBLIOGRAPHY

DEAN, G.: The Porphyrias. Philadelphia, Lippincott Co., 1963.
GOLDBERG, A. AND RIMINGTON, C.: Diseases of Porphyrin Metabolism. Springfield, Thomas, 1962.
Proceedings of the International Conference on the porphyrias. S. African Jour. Lab. and Clin. Med., **9**:143, 1963.

Congenital Erythropoietic (Photosensitive) Porphyria

The symptoms are evident early in life. Often the urine stains the diaper red. When the infant is exposed to sunlight extensive bullous lesions develop on the exposed areas which are termed hydroa aestivale. These bullae break down leaving ulcers which heal slowly. Extensive scarring results. Hypertrichosis develops. The teeth are pink or brown. The spleen may be enlarged. There is nearly always hemolysis. The reticulocytes are increased

and normoblasts are found. The bone marrow is hyperplastic. Examination under fluorescent light reveals the presence of porphyrins in the bone marrow. The urine is red.

If the urine is examined under a Woods light, red fluorescence is seen. The urine contains large amounts of uroporphyrin I and smaller amounts of coproporphyrin I. Porphobilinogen is not present. This appears to be a recessive condition.

BIBLIOGRAPHY

ALDRICH, R. A. *et al.*: A review of porphyrin metabolism. Amer. Jour. Med. Sci., **230**:675, 1955.
KENCH, R. *et al.*: Biochemical and pathological studies of congenital porphyria. Quart. Jour. Med., **22**:285, 1953.
SCHMID, R. *et al.*: Erythropoietic congenital porphyria. Blood, **10**:416, 1955.

Erythropoietic Protoporphyria

The onset is early in childhood. Exposure to sunlight causes itching, erythema and edema. Bullae never occur. The red cells show an increased content of protoporphyrins and coproporphyrins. The urinary excretion of porphyrins is normal. Fecal excretion of coproporphyrins and protoporphyrins may be increased. There are no neurological symptoms. This is inherited as a dominant condition.

BIBLIOGRAPHY

LYNCH, P. J. *et al.*: Erythropoietic protoporphyria. Arch. of Dermat., **92**:351, 1965.
PETERKA, E. S. *et al.*: Erythropoietic protoporphyria. Clinical and laboratory features in seven new cases. J.A.M.A., **193**:1036, 1965.
RIMINGTON, C. AND CRIPPS, D. J.: Biochemical and fluorescence-microscopy screening tests for erythropoietic protoporphyria. Lancet, i:624, 1965.

Swedish Type of Acute Intermittent Porphyria

Etiology.—This is an inborn error of porphyrin metabolism which is inherited as a dominant characteristic. The porphyrins are related to hemoglobin and to the pigment of the muscles. Their chemistry is very complex and is not fully understood. About 300 micrograms of a mixture of coproporphyrin I and coproporphyrin III are found in the urine of normal individuals every day. In this type of acute porphyria, the excretion of coproporphyrin III is increased and there is also excretion of products which are not found in the urine of normal persons such as porphobilinogen and uroporphyrin III. The source of these substances is not clearly established.

Peters *et al.* suggest that symptoms of porphyria are due to zinc, copper or other cation bloc of several metalloenzyme systems.

Pathological Anatomy.—Denny-Brown and Sciarra found patchy demyelination of the peripheral nerves with little damage to the axis cylinders. The anterior horn cells of the spinal cord showed the axon reaction. Hierons found loss of anterior horn cells in some cases. The long fiber

tracts of the spinal cord show as a rule no damage but Hierons found pronounced demyelination in one case. Denny-Brown and Sciarra mention small areas of demyelination around the small arterioles in the cerebral white matter. Hierons found more extensive changes in the brain including cell changes, demyelination and areas of softening without significant lesions in the blood vessels. Hierons believes that the process responsible for the mental changes is functional and reversible. Denny-Brown and Sciarra suggest that the lesions in the nervous system are due to ischemia presumably of vasomotor origin. London and Hierons think that anoxia and a direct effect of the metabolic disorder may be important also.

It seems to be agreed that the porphyrins are not directly toxic to the nervous system and that they are not found in abnormal amounts in the nervous system in acute porphyria.

Clinical Features.—The disease seems to have no predilection for any race for we have seen it in Negro as well as white children. Many cases are found in Scandinavia. The onset of symptoms may occur early in childhood.

There are recurrent attacks. The first symptom may be abdominal pain or mental disturbances. The polyneuritis, the third of the characteristic symptoms, develops a bit later.

The *abdominal pain* is usually located below the umbilicus and is colicky in character. It is associated with vomiting and usually with constipation. Roentgenography may show segmental distention of the bowel. There is often fever at the onset.

There are almost always *mental changes* which may be mild or severe. Irritability, restlessness, insomnia, delirium and finally coma are described. Psychotic behavior may obscure the diagnosis for a time. Hallucinations may occur. *Convulsions* are sometimes seen but are not common. Cortical blindness has been described.

Polyneuritis appears within a few days. Pain and hyperesthesia develop in the extremities. Often the child is so sensitive and so irritable that it is impossible to perform a proper examination. Soon muscular weakness appears. This has, as a rule, the distribution of the standard peripheral neuritis involving the distal muscles more severely than the proximal muscles. Actual loss of sensibility is not often demonstrated. Mason describes a case in which an ascending type of paralysis developed. Retention of urine is not uncommon. Bulbar palsy and oculomotor paralysis are mentioned. *Transient blindness* may occur and is attributed to spasm of the retinal arteries.

Hierons found increased ankle jerks, bilateral ankle clonus and bilateral extensor responses in one patient, and we have seen a patient in whom the diagnosis was fully established (No. 682626) who displayed fascicular

twitchings and brisk tendon reflexes rather than the standard picture of polyneuritis.

When the mental disturbances and the convulsions appear, the blood pressure rises. When the polyneuritis develops, the blood pressure usually falls to a lower level. Oliguria may occur during the acute episodes. In the case given below, evidences of both renal and hepatic damage were discovered after repeated attacks. Denny-Brown mentions necrosis of the renal tubules.

The acute symptoms may last for several weeks depending on the severity of the attack. The convulsions cease, the mental condition improves and the pains and hyperesthesia diminish though as a rule not as rapidly as the other symptoms. The muscular atrophy may persist. The skin may become slightly brown, but never blisters.

After an attack the patient may remain quite well except for residual palsies for months or years. In most cases additional episodes eventually occur.

One baby, born of a mother who was having an attack of acute porphyria at the time, excreted porphyrins for a few days and then showed no further signs of abnormal porphyrin metabolism. The baby was premature and rather dwarfish.

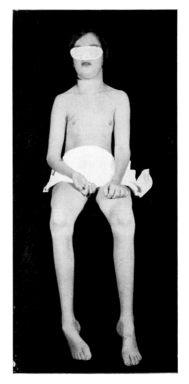

Fig. 198. Polyneuritis in a case of acute porphyrinuria showing bilateral foot drop, wasting of the hands and calves and slight edema of the face. This case is abstracted below.

It should be emphasized that these patients are sensitive to barbiturates. A small dose of phenobarbital may precipitate an acute attack or lead to a fatal exacerbation if administered during an attack. Pentothal anesthesia must be avoided. A sedative termed sedormid is also dangerous.

The spinal fluid is normal except for a slight increase in protein. The urine is characteristically red or brown. It is described as resembling port wine. The depth of the color varies from time to time and is apt to be deepest during an attack. The color may be normal at other times even when it contains porphyrins. Sometimes the urine is of normal color when it is passed and becomes red after standing a time. Spectroscopic tests show that the urine contains type III uroporphyrin, and porphobilinogen and abnormally large amounts of coproporphyrin III. Apparently the abnormal porphyrins are always present even when the patient is free of symptoms.

Diagnosis.—The diagnosis is based upon the abdominal pain, the mental confusion, convulsions, the polyneuritis, the dark skin and the discolored urine. The demonstration of the proper porphyrins in the urine should be conclusive. The Watson-Schwartz test for porphobilinogen is helpful. Porphyrins show red fluorescence under ultraviolet light and may be quickly demonstrated by this means in the urine. Ackner points out that the excretion of porphobilinogen is not always increased during acute attacks.

Paralytic myoglobinuria q.v. must be distinguished. During the acute stage this condition may be taken for acute nephritis. The pigment in the urine is thought to be blood. The abdominal pain may lead to a diagnosis of an acute surgical condition.

Prognosis.—The ultimate prognosis seems to be rather unfavorable for about half of the reported cases have ended fatally. Our patient whose case is described below eventually ceased to have attacks but showed evidences of visceral damage when last seen.

Treatment.—No specific treatment is known. We must rely on symptomatic therapy. Guild has used liver extract. Artificial hibernation has been suggested. Barbiturates must be avoided. Durst and Krembs seem to have found the administration of tetraethylammonium chloride helpful. Melby states that chlorpromazine has beneficial effects. Cortisone has been recommended. Gajdos and Gajdos-Torok state that intramuscular injections of adenosine-5-monophosphoric acid cause prompt improvement. Peters *et al.* find that dimercaptopropanol and ethylenediamine, chelating agents, are effective. They secured beneficial results in thirty-one of thirty-seven patients of whom twenty-four were suffering from acute hepatic porphyria.

It is claimed that retention of water, and hyponatremia occur and that restriction of fluid intake will relieve the coma, psychosis and convulsions. A respirator is required in certain cases.

CASE HISTORY (Ped. 82579).—*Recurrent attacks of abdominal pain, convulsions, hypertension, vomiting, constipation and porphyrinuria followed by polyneuritis in a young girl of eight years.*

K. S. was seen for the first time at the age of 10 years. It was stated in the history that she had been quite healthy until September, 1931 when she was about eight years old. At this time she complained of pain in the abdomen and had several convulsions during a period of a few days. Albumen was found in the urine which was somewhat discolored. The discoloration was attributed to blood and a diagnosis of nephritis was made. She soon recovered and remained well for over a year.

In January, 1933, the patient again complained of abdominal pain and began to vomit. She was removed at once to a hospital where she had a series of convulsions. The urine was discolored again but the kidney function tests were almost normal and there was only a trace of albumen.

Some days after the onset she developed severe pain and tenderness in the extremities and later wrist-drop and foot-drop. There was retention of urine for a week or more. The acute stages of this illness lasted only about 2 weeks and then the child slowly improved, so that she was able to walk and run about almost normally.

About the first of May, 1933, the same symptoms returned, namely, abdominal pains, convulsions and discoloration of the urine. She was admitted to Harriet Lane on May 12, 1933. Examination revealed a well-developed and well-nourished little girl of 10 years who was intensely irritable and screamed when she was disturbed. It was almost impossible to gain her cooperation but she was in good contact and not definitely delirious. The cranial nerves were quite normal. At the finger, toe, wrist and ankle joints there was complete paralysis. At the knee and elbow joints there was some power and at hip and shoulder strength was normal or nearly normal. The chest, neck, back and abdominal muscles seemed to be strong. There was retention of urine and at times incontinence. The musculature was wasted, especially that of the hands, the forearms and calves. Some of the wasting dated from the previous illness in January, 1933. The knee and ankle jerks were absent and the plantar reflexes were not elicited. There was evidently intense tenderness of the muscles of the arms and leg as well as cutaneous hyperesthesia. Cutaneous sensibility was not tested properly because of poor cooperation but there was evidently no complete anesthesia.

General medical examination revealed little. The heart was not enlarged but the blood pressure was 140/96. The pulse was accelerated averaging between 120 and 110. Temperature was normal. There was some muscle spasm and tenderness in the epigastrium.

Laboratory examinations, R.B.C. 5,290,000, Hb. 104 per cent. W.B.C. 11,450. Differential formula normal. Spinal fluid negative in every way. Urine showed a trace of albumen and a dark port wine colored pigment which was proved by spectroscopic and other tests to consist of porphyrins. The levulose test revealed some evidence of liver damage. The excretion of phenolphthalein was 45 per cent in two hours and the nonprotein nitrogen was elevated. Electrocardiograph revealed normal sinus rhythm.

In the next few weeks, the child slowly improved. There were no more convulsions. The irritability diminished and the child became cooperative. The blood pressure slowly fell to normal and the color of the urine became natural. The pulse rate also became normal. The hemoglobin, however, fell about 20 per cent despite the child's clinical improvement. Strength showed little change but the tenderness of the muscles disappeared and there was some return of power after a few months. She was discharged on July 10, 1933.

On October 31, 1933 the patient returned again. She had had a mild upper respiratory infection and shortly afterwards abdominal pain, nausea and vomiting. Examination revealed no definite change in the neuro-

logical condition. In fact, she was somewhat stronger than when last examined but the blood pressure was again elevated to 140/100, the urine was discolored and there was some tachycardia. These symptoms soon ceased and she was again discharged on November 29, 1933.

There was no return of symptoms until October 6, 1934 when she had an attack of diarrhea and fever. Pains in the abdomen, back and extremities soon developed. There was nausea and vomiting but no convulsions. The urine was of the same port wine shade. She was admitted to the hospital on the 10th. Examination revealed tachycardia varying between 100 and 120, violent heart action, a systolic murmur at the apex, blood pressure of 142/100 and a definite accentuation of the neurological signs. The arms and legs were very weak again and almost completely paralysed at the distal joints. The tendon reflexes were all lost. Respiration was entirely intercostal and fluoroscopic examination showed that the diaphragm did not act. The diarrhea was followed by intense constipation. The child was very drowsy at first and irritable as she had been before. Careful tests of sensibility revealed some hyperesthesia over the thighs, abdomen and perhaps the chest. The urine contained large quantities of porphyrin again and there was difficulty in voiding as well as incontinence. These symptoms gradually abated and by the end of the month the child seemed to be convalescent and the diaphragm was beginning to move again.

On December 16, 1934, there was once more a mild attack characterized by abdominal pain, nausea and vomiting but this lasted only a short time and did not add to the neurological symptoms.

On February 12, 1935, there was some pain in the abdomen and back, elevation of the blood pressure, difficulty in voiding, tachycardia and vomiting. The urine was discolored. Within a week, however, the child was as well as she had been before. She showed at that time severe atrophy of the distal muscle groups, diminished or lost tendon reflexes and some disturbances in cutaneous sensibility.

The patient was given large doses of liver extract. The attacks ceased and her neurological symptoms diminished.

In February 1953, when the patient was 30 years old, she displayed atrophy of the intrinsic muscles of the hands and some wasting of the legs below the knees. She was somewhat below average size. There had been no acute attacks for many years. She displayed evidences of renal and hepatic damage.

This patient has been studied by Dr. Harriet Guild.

The South African Type of Acute Intermittent Porphyria

Dean has studied a form of porphyria in South Africa. In a family of 434 adults he found 60 members who had inherited the disease. Of the 36 women affected, almost all were subject to abdominal pains. In 13 cases, there were acute attacks with paralysis. In 8 cases, the patient died. Among

24 men affected, only one had a paralytic attack and died. In more recent generations there were 21 children who had inherited the abnormality, but none of them had developed symptoms. All patients were descendants of a couple who married in 1688.

The South African disease differs in some respects from the Swedish type in that the skin becomes brown and is easily blistered and abraded. The porphobilinogen may be normal between attacks, but porphyrins are always increased in the feces. Acute attacks are induced by the use of barbiturates, chloroquine and sulphonamides. This is a dominant characteristic.

BIBLIOGRAPHY

ACKNER, B. *et al.:* Metabolite excretion in acute porphyria. Lancet, **i**:1256, 1961.

ALDRICH, R. A. *et al.:* Rev. of porphyrin metabolism with special reference to childhood. Am. J. Med. Sc., **320**:675, 1956.

CRIPPS, D. J. AND CURTIS, A. C.: Chloroquine in hepatic porphyria. Arch. Dermat., **86**:575, 1962.

DEAN, G. AND BARNES, H. D.: The inheritance of porphyria. Brit. Med. J., **ii**:89, 1955.

————: Porphyria. A family disease. South African Med. J., **30**:377, 1956.

————: The Porphyrias. J. B. Lippincott Co., Philadelphia, 1963.

DENNY-BROWN, D. AND SCIARRA, D.: Changes in the nervous system in acute porphyria. Brain, **68**:1, 1945.

DORBRINER, K., STRAIN, W. H. AND GUILD, H.: The excretion of porphyrins in congenital porphyria. J. Clin. Invest., **17**:761, 1938.

DOW, R. S.: Electroencephalographic findings in acute intermittent porphyria. Electroenceph. and Clin. Neurophysiol., **13**:425, 1961.

GOLDBERG, A.: Acute intermittent porphyria. Quart. Jour. Med., **28**:183, 1959.

HAEGER-ARONSON, B.: Various types of porphyria in Sweden. South African Jour. Lab. Clin. Med., **9**:288, 1963.

HIERONS, R.: Changes in the nervous system in acute porphyria. Brain, **80**:176, 1957.

LONDON, I. M.: Porphyrin metabolism and diseases of the nervous system. Res. Nerv. & Ment. Dis., **32**:392, 1953.

MARKOWITZ, M.: Acute intermittent porphyria. Ann. Int. Med., **41**:1170, 1954.

MARTIN, W. J. AND HECK, F. J.: Porphyrins and porphyria. Am. J. Med., **20**:239, 1956.

MASON, V. AND COURVILLE, C.: Acute ascending paralysis (Landry's paralysis) with acute idiopathic hematoporphyria. Arch. Neurol. & Psychiat., **25**:848, 1931.

MASON, V. R., COURVILLE, C. AND ZISKIND, R.: The porphyrins in human disease. Medicine, **12**:355, 1933.

MASON, V. R. AND FARNHAM, R. M.: Acute hematoporphyria. Arch. Int. Med., **47**:467, 1931.

MELBY, J. C.: Chlorpromazine in the treatment of porphyria. J.A.M.A., **162**:174, 1956.

PETERS, H. A. *et al.:* Therapy of acute, chronic and mixed hepatic porphyria with chelating agents. Neurology, **8**:621, 1958.

RICHARDS, F. F. AND BRINTON, D.: Peripheral neuropathy and the diagnosis of acute porphyria. Brain, **85**:657, 1962.

ROTHMAN, P. E.: Hematoporphyrinuria. Am. J. Dis. Child., **32**:219, 1926.

SCHMID, R. AND SCHWARTZ, S. *et al.:* Ciba Foundation Symposium on Porphyrin Biosynthesis and Metabolism. Little, Brown and Co., Boston, 1955.

WALDENSTRÖM, J. AND VAHLIQUIST, B.: Studies on the excretion of porphobilinogen in patients with so-called acute porphyria. Acta Med. Scand., **cxvii**:1, 1944.

——— AND HAEGER-ARONSON, B.: Patterns of human porphyria. Brit. Med. Jour., **5352**:272, 1963.
WALSH, F. B.: *Loc. cit.*
WATSON, C. J.: The problem of porphyria. New England Jour. Med., **263**:1205, 1960.

FAMILIAL METHEMOGLOBINEMIA WITH MENTAL DEFICIENCY

Familial methemoglobinemia is a rare condition. As a rule it is associated with no neurological disturbances. Worster-Drought, White and Sargent, however, have published the study of a family of three siblings all of whom were mentally deficient and showed various neurological disorders. These authors refer to two other cases in which mental deficiency was present.

Familial methemoglobinemia is believed to be inherited as a recessive trait. It has been traced through four generations. The most striking feature is cyanosis of lavender hue. This is evident at birth or in early infancy and persists throughout life. As a rule, there are no symptoms or at most merely dyspnea on exertion attributable to deficient oxygenation of the blood. Mild polycythemia is usually present. The methemoglobin may make up 20 or even 40 per cent of the blood pigment. The administration of methylene blue will cause the cyanosis to disappear and large doses of ascorbic acid have the same effect.

Worster-Drought *et al.* studied three children, siblings of 3, 7 and 8 years. Two were boys and one a girl. They were undersized and cyanotic. The cyanosis was most evident in the cheeks, lips, ears, roof of the mouth and hands. The skin had a brownish tinge. Methemoglobin made up from 12 to 26 per cent of their total blood pigment. There was mild polycythemia in each case. All of these children were slow to walk and to talk. Coordination was defective. The tendon reflexes were well reduced or absent. An internal squint was usually found. The intelligence quotient ranged from 20 to 47 per cent. A maternal cousin and a maternal grandfather were said to have been cyanotic. The children were treated by methylene blue by mouth. Two doses of 2 to 4 grains each were given on two days of each week. This was sufficient to abolish the cyanosis but had no effect on the children's mental condition.

The authors were unable to determine whether the mental deficiency was due to the prolonged anoxia or was inherited as a separate morbid trait.

Familial methemoglobinemia must be distinguished from that type due to poisons such as acetanilide, bismuth, subnitrate, aniline, sulphonamides, nitrophenol, nitrites and nitrates.

BIBLIOGRAPHY

WORSTER-DROUGHT, C., WHITE, J. C. AND SARGENT, F.: Familial, idiopathic methaemoglobinaemia associated with mental deficiency and neurological abnormalities. Brit. M. J., **2**:114, 1953.

DISORDERS OF PROTEIN METABOLISM

Phenylpyruvic Acid Dementia or Phenylketonuria

Definition.—A type of slowly progressive dementia in which phenylpyruvic acid is found in the urine. It is regarded as an inborn defect of metabolism.

Etiology.—The condition is inherited and is believed to depend upon a single recessive gene. Phenylpyruvic acid is always found in the urine though it is not a normal constituent of the urine. Phenylalanine is found in the blood in increased amounts and tyrosine is found in diminished amounts. It is believed that at least one defect in these patients is the inability to convert phenylalanine into tyrosine. It has been suggested that lack of a specific liver enzyme, phenylalanine hydroxylase, is responsible.

Hsia states that phenylalanine is normally converted to tyrosine by an enzyme, phenylalanine hydroxylase. This enzyme consists of two fractions. Fraction 1 is present only in the liver. It is deficient in phenylketonuria. An excessive accumulation of 1-phenylalanine occurs in the blood and tissues. The excessive phenylalanine is converted into phenylpyruvic acid by its transaminase. This substance is converted into phenyllactic acid, phenylacetic acid and phenylacetylglutamine and excreted in the urine. The urine also contains o-hydroxyphenylacetic acid, m-hydroxyphenylacetic acid and indole products derived from tyrosine and tryptophane. Tyrosine metabolism is inhibited and this is responsible for the reduction of pigment in the skin and hair of these patients. The adrenaline levels in the blood is low. The damage to the central nervous system is attributed to phenylalanine or one of its products.

Patients who display the clinical symptoms are believed to be homozygous. Heterozygous relatives may be shown to have lower capacities to metabolize phenylalanine than normal individuals according to Hsia and Driscoll.

Pathological Anatomy.—Alvord *et al.* found deficient myelination in the white matter of the brain in two siblings of 16 months and 5 years. Failure of myelination was most evident in the optic tracts and corticoponto-cerebellar system. The brains of three adults showed little. In one some demyelination was found in the optic chiasm. There was some gliosis and loss of cells as well as accumulation of fat around the blood vessels in all five brains. One would gather from these observations that there is a delay in myelination but eventually myelination becomes complete.

Josephy and Coquet *et al.* found minimal changes in post-mortem examination, but Benda found extensive demyelination of the central white matter in the brains of two patients who died at the ages of 21 years of tuber-

culosis. There were deposits of myelin balls and amyloid. Benda interpreted these findings to indicate a slowly progressive degeneration of the white matter.

Malmud and Gerstl *et al.* found that in young patients there were scattered, mild foci of spongy changes in the myelin, whereas, in older patients there was outspoken demyelination with abundant accumulation of sudanophil lipid material and intense gliosis.

Clinical Features.—The condition is said to be found in about 0.5 per cent of the inmates of any institution for the mentally deficient. It is not restricted to members of any special race but Jervis found no case among Jewish children.

Denniston reports a study of a family of seven children of a mother suffering from phenylketonuria. Five children were found to be mentally deficient. Three of these five were tested for phenylketonuria with negative results. Two children could not be examined.

The chief manifestation is mental deficiency. This is not evident in infancy as a rule but is usually discovered early in childhood. Clinical symptoms become apparent between three and five months of age. There is irritability, vomiting, eczema, a mousy odor and loss of interest in surroundings. The children are slow to learn to walk and usually never learn to form words. At best they may be able to form a few words. It seems clear that intelligence slowly declines so we should speak of dementia rather than oligophrenia. Most children are classified as idiots but many eventually become imbeciles. They are restless, aggressive, destructive and vicious in most though not in all cases. Jervis mentions two patients whose intelligence was normal.

Armstrong states that it is possible the damage to the nervous system occurs before the age of two years and thereafter, there is no progression in the process.

These children are of light complexion with light hair and blue eyes even when they come of dark skinned families. It is said that the lighter the child's complexion, the more severe the symptoms will be. Many of them are subject to eczema. They are said to have a characteristic odor described as musty, barnlike or horsy. Their features are attractive in childhood though this may not be true later in the course of the disease.

Repetitive movements such as occur in many types of mental deficiency, tremors, ataxia and athetosis all occur. Muscle tone may be increased or diminished. The tendon reflexes may be increased. The optic discs are usually normal. Bodily growth may be reduced but no clear evidences of endocrine disorder are seen. Sexual development is normal.

Prolongation of the RST complex is sometimes found in the electro-

cardiogram. Air injection may show slight dilatation of the cerebral ventricles.

Low *et al.* state that in infancy these children have spasms and the electroencephalogram shows multiple seizure foci. Older children have convulsions and focal or generalized spike discharges are seen in the electroencephalogram.

Feinberg and Fisch describe changes in the bones which are found in both treated and untreated children. There is metaphyseal cupping with calcified, sharply defined, perpendicular spicules that extend from the metaphyseal side of the epiphyseal plate into the columnar and proliferative zones of cartilage. Such striations may persist for years.

Diagnosis.—The diagnosis may be made by the examination of the urine and the clinical features of the case. A few drops of aqueous solution of ferric chloride are added to the acidified urine which then turns a dark green color. The color fades to a pale green within 15 minutes. This reaction is characteristic of phenylpyruvic acid.

The ferric chloride test cannot be made for the first 4 to 6 weeks of life. It is feared that mental changes may have occurred by that time. Dr. Robert Guthrie has devised a test which can be used in the first few days of life. Some of the baby's blood is put in a culture of B subtilis with thienylalanine, an inhibitor. If phenylalanine is present, the inhibitor will be counteracted. Irwin *et al.* state that the fluorometric test is the best method for routine hospital screening. Partington states that paper chromatography is also valuable and permits an early diagnosis.

Ghadimi has shown that histidinemia q.v. may cause a false positive response to the ferric chloride test and Hudson *et al.* have stated that false positive tests may also be due to tyrosinosis q.v. The determination of the level of phenylalanine in the serum is necessary for the definitive diagnosis. The heterozygous carrier may be identified by the phenylalanine tolerance test.

Prognosis.—The prognosis is unfavorable unless treatment is begun in infancy for there is progressive deterioration in the patient's condition. The final results in cases in which children are treated in infancy are not yet clear.

Treatment.—It is recommended that these children be given a diet very low in phenylalanine. This is usually a hydrolysate or casein from which most of the phenylalanine has been removed. These children require from 25 to 50 per kilogram of phenylalanine though the normal baby requires more. Horner and Streamer, Blainey and Gulliford and also Armstrong describe the results. It is said that limited improvement may occur in the mental condition of demented children. The improvement becomes evident as

a rule between the second and fifth week. After this some children regress and some remain static. A few have continued to improve. It is said that the seizures diminish and the abnormalities of the electroencephalogram diminish. The phenylpyruvic acid disappears from the urine. It is agreed that treatment must be begun early in infancy before irreversible damage occurs. Horner and Streamer state that a baby who showed no mental changes but a positive urine test was still normal after ten months of treatment. Woolf *et al.* state that phenylalanine must be maintained at a normal level in the blood for if it is reduced to an abnormally low level, physical growth and health will be impaired. These authors describe a proper diet for these children. Hypoglycemia and hypoproteinemia may occur if the child does not eat well. Partington states that after the fourth year the diet may be discontinued without fear of aggravation of the child's condition. This statement is denied by other authorities who urge diet be continued for 10 years. Solomons advises that the diet be terminated at about the age of seven years and finds that the children improve when this is done.

It seems that the light complexion is due to deficiency of tyrosine for when this material is administered, the hair and skin pigment is restored to normal.

BIBLIOGRAPHY

ALVORD, E. C. *et al.*: Neuropathological findings in phenylpyruvic oligophrenia. J. Neuropath. & Exp. Neurol., 9:298, 1950.

ARMSTRONG, M. D.: The relation of the biochemical abnormality to the development of the mental defect in phenylketonuria. Report of the twenty-third Ross Pediatric Research Conference, p. 28, 1956.

BEADLE, G. W.: Genes and the chemistry of the organism. American Scientist, 34:31, 1946.

BENDA, C. E.: Developmental Disorders of Mentation and Cerebral Palsies. Grune and Stratton, New York, 1952, p. 451.

BERMAN, P. W. *et al.*: Diet therapy for phenylketonuria. Pediatrics, 28:924, 1961.

———— *et al.*: Effectiveness of diet in phenylketonuria. Devel. Med. and Child Neurol., 9:411, 1967.

BERRY, H. K. *et al.*: Procedures for monitoring the low-phenylalanine diet in treatment of phenylketonuria. Jour. of Pediat., 67:609, 1965.

BICKEL, H. *et al.*: The influence of phenylalanine intake on phenylketonuria. Lancet, ii:812, 1953.

BLAINEY, J. D. AND GULLIFORD, R.: Phenylalanine restricted diet in the treatment of phenylketonuria. Arch. Dis. Child., 31:452, 1956.

CENTERWALL, W. R. *et al.*: Treatment of phenylketonuria. J. Pediat., 59:102, 1961.

DE MENIBUS, C. H. *et al.*: Children born of phenylketonuric women. Ann. Pediat., 43:477, 1967.

DENNISTON, J. C.: The children of mothers with phenylketonuria. J. Pediat., 63:461, 1963.

DOBSON, J. *et al.*: P. K. U. Collaborative study. New Eng. Jour. Med., 278:1142, 1968.

DODGE, P. R. *et al.*: Hypoglycemia complicating treatment of phenylketonuria with a phenylalanine deficient diet. New England J. Med., 260:1104, 1959.

FEINBERG, S. B. AND FISCH, R. O.: Roentgenographic bone findings in phenylketonuria. Radiology, 78:394, 1962.

FELLMAN, J. H.: Epinephrine metabolites and pigmentation in the central nervous system of phenylpyruvic oligophrenia. J. Neurol., Neurosurg. & Psychiat., 21:58, 1958.

FISCH, R. O. *et al.:* Twelve years of clinical experience with phenylketonuria. Neurology, **19**:659, 1969.

GERSTL, B. *et al.:* Lipid alterations in human brains in phenylketonuria. Neurology, **17**:51, 1967.

GHADIMI, H. *et al.:* Inborn error of histidine metabolism. Pediatrics, **29**:714, 1962.

GUTHRIE, R.: Phenylketonuria screening in newborns. Pediatrics, **32**:338, 1963.

HACKNEY, I. M. *et al.:* Phenylketonuria: mental development, behavior and termination of low phenylalanine diet. Jour. Pediat., **72**:645, 1968.

HORNER, F. A. AND STREAMER, C. W.: Treatment of phenylketonuria. J.A.M.A., **161**:1628, 1956.

HSIA, D. Y. AND DRISCOLL, K. W.: Detection of heterozygous carriers of phenylketonuria. Nature, **178**:1239, 1956.

HSIA, D. Y.: Inborn Errors of Metabolism. Year Book Pub., Chicago, 1960.

———: Phenylketonuria. Develop. Med. Child Neurol., **9**:531, 1967.

IRWIN, H. R. *et al.:* Blood phenylalanine levels of newborn infants. Calif. Med., **101**:331, 1964.

JERVIS, G. A.: Phenylpyruvic oligophrenia. A study of fifty cases. Arch. Neurol. & Psychiat., **38**:945, 1937.

JOSEPHY, H.: Phenylpyruvic oligophrenia. Illinois Med. J., **94**:2, 1948.

KNOX, W. E.: An evaluation of the treatment of phenylketonuria with diets low in phenylalanine. Pediatrics, **26**:1, 1960.

KOREY, S. R.: A possible mechanism in phenylpyruvic oligophrenia. Report of the twenty-third Ross Pediatric Research Conference, 34, 1956.

LOW, N. L., BOSMA, J. F. AND ARMSTRONG, M. D.: Studies on phenylketonuria. Arch. Neurol. & Psychiat., **77**:359, 1957.

LYMAN, F. L.: Phenylketonuria. Springfield, Thomas, 1963.

MABRY, C. C. *et al.:* Maternal phenylketonuria. New England J. Med., **269**:1404, 1963.

MALMUD, N.: Neuropathology of phenylketonuria. Jour. Neuropath. and Exp. Neurol., **25**:254, 1966.

MAUTNER, H. AND QUINN, K. V.: Phenylpyruvic oligophrenia. Ann Paediat., **172**:1, 1969.

McBEAN, M. S. AND STEPHENSON, J. B. P.: Treatment of classical phenylketonuria. Arch. of Dis. Childh., **43**:1, 1968.

MENKES, J. H.: Cerebral proteolipids in phenylketonuria. Neurology, **18**:1003, 1968.

MIYAMOTO, M. AND FITZPATRICK, T.: Phenylalanine related to hypopigmentation in phenylketonuria. Nature, **179**:199, 1957.

MONCRIEFF, A. AND WILKINSON, R. H.: Further experiences in treatment of phenylketonuria. Brit. Med. J., **i**:763, 1961.

PAINE, R. S.: The variability of manifestations of untreated patients with phenylketonuria Pediatrics, **20**:290, 1957.

PARTINGTON, M. W.: Phenylketonuria. Modern Medicine, December 6, 1965.

———: Early symptoms of phenylketonuria. Pediatrics, **27**:465, 1961.

SOLOMONS, G. *et al.:* Evaluation of the effects of terminating the diet in phenylketonuria. Jour. Pediat., **69**:596, 1966.

UMBARGER, B.: Phenylketonuria. Treatment. Am. J. Dis. Child., **100**:908, 1960.

WATSON, C. W. *et al.:* Electroencephalographic abnormalities in phenylpyruvic oligophrenia. Neurology, **18**:203, 1968.

WOOLF, L. I. *et al.:* The dietary treatment of phenylketonuria. Arch. Dis. Childhood, **33**:31, 1958.

HOMOCYSTINURIA

Definition.—An inborn error of metabolism inherited as an autosomal recessive trait and manifest by the excretion of excessive amounts of homocystin in the urine.

Pathological Anatomy.—Arterial and venous thromboses are found in various organs including the brain. The arteries are dilated and the media

show few muscle fibers separated by expansion of the intercellular ground substance. Softenings are found in the brain due to emboli as well as thrombi. There is an abnormal tendency to coagulation of the blood. A diffuse neuronal rarifaction in the outer layers of the cerebral cortex is mentioned.

Clinical Features.—These children appear to be normal at birth. The characteristic features develop gradually. They have fine hair, a malar flush, mottled skin and a shuffling gait. Dislocation of the lenses is almost constant but is not evident before the child is several years old unless special studies are performed. Buphthalmos may occur.

Osteoporosis develops causing fractures of the long bones and collapse of the vertebrae. The children develop knock knees, high arched feet, funnel chest and kyphoscoliosis. Arachnodactyly may occur. The range of movement of the joints is reduced.

Dunn *et al.* point out that even before the age of one year, hemiplegia and other cerebral syndromes often occur which are associated with and followed by convulsions. These are attributed to cerebral softenings. Mental deficiency is soon evident. Nervous tension is common.

The liver contains fat, but it is said that cirrhosis does not occur. Cystathionine synthetase activity is reduced in the liver.

Thirty-eight patients found among 20 families have been studied by Schimke and others of Dr. McKusiack's group.

Diagnosis.—The diagnosis depends on the clinical picture described above and above all on the demonstration of excessive amounts of homocystine in the urine by paper chromatography.

The chief problem is the differentiation of the Marfan syndrome. In this condition we find the long slender extremities and dislocation of the lenses, but the mental condition is normal, there is no tendency to thrombosis, the inheritance is dominant and there is no excess of homocystine in the urine.

CASE HISTORY.—*Homocystinuria with mental deficiency, convulsions and osteoporosis. Dislocation of the lenses was followed by increased intraocular pressure causing rupture of the right eye and progressive enlargement of the left bulb.*

By the courtesy of Dr. Harry G. Butler I have seen G. M., a child of 10 years and 9 months, at the Rosewood State Hospital. She was found to be mentally deficient in infancy. At 7 months she began to have convulsions. Petit mal also occurred. The lenses were found to be dislocated early in life. When she was 8 years old, a staphaloma of the right eye was found. The left hip was fractured at 9 years. A brother is said to have difficulty in speech. A sister shows mental deterioration. Another brother has convulsions.

When she was admitted at the age of 7 years she was found to be severely defective. The intelligence quotient was estimated at less than 30 per cent. The electroencephalogram was grossly abnormal. X-ray studies of the bones showed universal osteoporosis. The vertebrae were partially collapsed and flattened. Homocysteine was found in the urine.

On examination the child showed pronounced under nutrition. Her bodily development was deficient for her age. The muscles were all slender. The arms and legs seemed to be slightly longer than normal. The fingers were very long and too slender. The upper part of the sternum was depressed, but the lower part was too prominent. The ribs were retracted at the attachment of the diaphragm. The lumbar lordosis was reduced. The feet were flat and became pronated when she stood. Some pubic hair was present.

The right eye was represented by a small white nodule in the depths of the orbit. The bulb had evidently ruptured and the eye had shrunken. The left eye had become enlarged and the cornea was opaque. One would expect rupture of the left bulb soon.

The child did not try to talk, but made inarticulate sounds. She did not understand what was said to her and resisted examination. She could stand unsteadily and could walk with a staggering gait. The tendon reflexes were all brisk.

BIBLIOGRAPHY

CARSON, N. A. J. *et al.:* Homocystinuria. Jour. Pediat., **66**:565, 1965.
DUNN, H. G. *et al.:* Homocystinuria. Neurology, **16**:407, 1966.
SCHIMKE, R. N. *et al.:* Homocystinuria. Jour. Amer. Ass., **193**:711, 1965.

FAMILIAL AMYLOIDOSIS WITH SPECIAL INVOLVEMENT OF THE PERIPHERAL NERVES (ANDRADE)

Since this disease is said to begin in the second or third decade a brief note seems to be indicated. Andrade has studied 75 cases, all found in certain parts of Portugal. It is clearly a familial disease which affects both males and females. The course averages 7 to 10 years to a fatal outcome. Gastrointestinal disorders with diarrhea, loss of weight and weakness are very prominent. Nephrosis may result from renal damage. Cardiac symptoms are also described. The polyneuritis is evidenced by paresthesias and mild pains. Pains and thermal sensibility are reduced before tactile sensibility. Eventually there is wasting of the muscles, progressive weakness and loss of tendon reflexes. Trophic lesions in the feet are described. Apparently the peripheral nerves are not grossly thickened as a rule. The tongue is not usually enlarged. The pupils often show abnormalities. They may be small, irregular and inactive to light. We have seen internal ophthalmoplegia with large irregular pupils. Otherwise the cranial nerves seem to escape. Haberland describes a case in which there was confusion, disorientation and stupor. Post-mortem examination revealed deposits of amyloid in

the walls of the ventricles, in the tissues lining the subarachnoid spaces, the choroid plexuses, in the walls of the meningeal and cerebral vessels and in the cerebral cortex. Amyloid may be deposited in the orbits causing exophthalmos and in the vitreous causing dense opacities. The spinal fluid may contain a great excess of protein.

Munsat and Poussaint emphasize the diagnostic importance of chronic gastrointestinal symptoms, non-specific electrocardiographic changes, dysphonia, impotence, orthostatic hypotension, trophic ulcers and dyshidrosis.

Rukavina *et al.* report that the electrophoretic pattern of the serum proteins shows an abnormal peak between β and a^2 which they believe is diagnostic. Ultracentrifugalization reveals an increase of the lipoproteins in the serum in the S 25-40 and 20-25 fractions. The investigators believe this condition is an inherited abnormality of lipoprotein metabolism. Death occurs as a result of heart failure, intercurrent infection or cachexia.

The diagnosis is most easily established by biopsy of muscle and nerve. Biopsy of a gum and of the larynx have been employed and Fentem advises rectal biopsy.

Post-mortem examination reveals amyloid deposits in all the viscera. The peripheral nerves and the kidneys are most severely affected. There are deposits of amyloid in the nerve sheaths with degeneration of the nerve fibers. The pancreas and the heart are also severely involved, but the liver and spleen are not badly damaged.

This is one of the primary types of amyloidosis of which several are distinguished. Muckle and Wells describe a familial type of amyloidosis associated with recurrent attacks of urticaria and progressive deafness. The kidneys are apt to be involved. The authors regard this as a result of a dominant trait. Gafni *et al.* point out that amyloidosis is a standard feature in familial Mediterranean fever.

Secondary amyloidosis is found in cases of chronic illness such as osteomyelitis or tuberculosis of the bones. The deposits are found in the spleen, kidneys and liver. A nephrotic syndrome results with edema, albuminuria and casts in the urine.

BIBLIOGRAPHY

ANDRADE, C.: Familial atypical, generalized amyloidosis with special involvement of the peripheral nerves. Brain, 75:408, 1952.

ARAKI, S. *et al.*: Polyneuritic amyoloidosis in a Japanese family. Arch. of Neurol., 18:593, 1968.

FALLS, H. F. *et al.*: Ocular manifestations of hereditary primary amyloidosis. Arch. Ophth., 54:660, 1955.

FENTEM, P. H. *et al.*: Rectal biopsy in amyloidosis. Brit. Med. J., 5275:364, 1962.

FREDERIKSEN, T. *et al.*: Familial primary amyloidosis. Am. J. Med., 33:328, 1962.

GAFNI, J. *et al.*: Classification of inherited amyloidosis. Lancet, i:71, 1964.

———— *et al.*: The role of amyloidosis in familial Mediterranean fever. Israel. Jour. Med. Sci., 4:995, 1968.

HABERLAND, C.: Primary systemic amyloidosis. Cerebral involvement. J. Neuropath. & Exp. Neurol., 23:135, 1964.

HELLER, H. *et al.:* Classification of amyloidosis with special regard to the genetic types. Path. Microbiol., 27:833, 1964.

KANTARJIAN, A. AND DEJONG, R.: Familial primary amyloidosis with nervous system involvement. Neurology, 3:399, 1953.

KAUFMAN, H. E. AND THOMAS, L. B.: Vitreous opacities diagnostic of familial primary amyloidosis. New England J. Med., 261:1267, 1959.

KYLE, R. A. *et al.:* Value of rectal biopsy in the diagnosis of primary systemic amyloidosis. Amer. Jour. Med. Sc., 251:501, 1966.

MISSMAHL, H. P.: Rectal biopsy for amyloidosis. Germ. Med. Mth., 9:101, 1964.

MUCKLE, T. J. AND WELLS, M.: Urticaria, deafness and amyloidosis. Quart. J. Med., 31:235, 1962.

MUNSAT, T. L. AND POUSSAINT, A. F.: Clinical manifestations and diagnosis of amyloid polyneuropathy. Neurology, 12:413, 1962.

NAVASQUEZ, S. AND TREBBLE, H. A.: A case of primary generalized amyloid disease with involvement of the nerves. Brain, 61:116, 1938.

RUKAVINA, J. C. *et al.:* Primary systemic amyloidosis. A review. Medicine, 35:239, 1956.

SCHLESSINGER, A. *et al.:* Peripheral neuropathy in familial primary amyloidosis. Brain, 85:357, 1962.

SOHAR, E. *et al.:* Primary peri-reticular amyloidosis in Israel. Its relation to familial Mediterranean fever. Quart. Jour. Med., 32:211, 1963.

STRICH, S. J. AND WADE, G.: Primary amyloidosis. Lancet, ii:70, 1953.

SULLIVAN, J. F., WITCHELL, T. E., GHERARDI, G. J. AND LAAN, W. V.: Amyloid polyneuropathy. Neurology, 5:847, 1955.

A Syndrome Including Mental Deficiency, Loss of Muscle Tone, Hydrophthalmos, Cataracts and Organic Aciduria (Lowe)

This condition has been described by Lowe, Terry and MacLachlan and also by Bickel. It is regarded as an inborn error of metabolism. The children are excessively active. There is severe mental deficiency. Muscle tone is reduced and the tendon reflexes are sluggish. Vision is grossly reduced or lost because of hydrophthalmos and cataracts and searching movements of the eyes are apt to be present. There is intermittent fever of unknown origin possibly due to dehydration. The bones show changes suggestive of rickets or osteomalacia. Bodily growth is reduced. Emaciation develops. This is a sex linked recessive disease. The female heterozygotes have small cataracts.

Lowe *et al.* have made extensive metabolic studies. They find that there is acidosis and organic aciduria. The excretion of amino acids is increased. Ammonia production by the kidneys is diminished. The function of the renal tubules is impaired. Blood pressure is normal. Vitamin D and calcium lactate seem to control the decalcification of the bones. There may be scaphocephaly and defective development of the mandible. The ears are large and low set. The skin is pale and the hair blond. Death in convulsions results from renal failure.

Post-mortem examination reveals that the renal tubules contain proteinaceous material and are eventually destroyed. The glomeruli are damaged and interstitial fibrosis develops. The brain may show edema and neuronal degeneration, spongy degeneration, defects of development or no anatomical abnormality.

BIBLIOGRAPHY

BICKEL, H.: Hyperamino-aciduria in Lignac-Fanconi disease, in galactosuria and in an obscure syndrome. Arch. Dis. Child., **29**:224, 1954.

CHUTORIAN, A. AND ROLAND, L. P.: Lowe's syndrome. Neurology, **16**:115, 1966.

CROME, L. *et al.*: Congenital cataracts, renal tubular necrosis and encephalopathy in two sisters. Arch. Dis. Child., **38**:505, 1963.

DONNELL, G. N.: Oculo-cerebral-renal syndrome. Pro. Roy. Soc. Med., **54**:336, 1961.

LOWE, C. U., TERRY, M. AND MACLACHLAN, E. A.: Organic aciduria, decreased renal ammonia production, hydrophthalmos and mental retardation. Am. J. Dis. Child., **83**:164, 1952.

McCANCE, R. A. *et al.*: The cerebro-oculo, renal dystrophies, a new variant. Arch. of Dis. Childh., **35**:240, 1960.

RICHARDS, W. *et al.*: The oculo-cerebro renal-syndrome of Lowe. Amer. Jour. Dis. Child., **109**:185, 1965.

RICHARDS, W. *et al.*: The oculo-cerebro-renal syndrome of Lowe. Am. J. Dis. Child., **109**:185, 1965.

WILSON, W. A. *et al.*: Oculo-cerebral syndrome of Lowe. Arch. Ophth., **70**:5, 1963.

Hereditary Pellagra-Like Skin Eruption With Cerebellar Ataxia and Renal Aminoaciduria (Baron, Dent, *et al.*)

These authors describe a new clinical syndrome found in four of eight children of a first cousin marriage. The family name is Hartnup and this has been called Hartnup disease.

A cutaneous eruption, similar to that of pellagra, is the earliest and commonest symptom. This occurs in the early summer after exposure to sunlight. Ataxia, diplopia, apathy, depression, hallucinations and confusion occur. Nystagmus and increased tendon reflexes may persist between acute exacerbations. Hypoglycemia may complicate the picture. Pains in the extremities and back are common. Emotional disturbances are characteristic. The ataxia might occur as a result of infection, it is said. The older siblings displayed slowly progressive mental deterioration.

All of these children had gross renal aminoaciduria and the chromatogram is said to show a unique pattern. Indole-3-acetic acid was excreted in amounts ranging from 50 to 200 mgs a day. In addition, indican and indole-3-acetyl-glutamine were excreted in large amounts. The acidified urine might turn black on standing.

Milne and his associates have found that tryptophan is not absorbed from the intestines very well and a greater amount than normal is converted into indole derivatives. It is said that tryptophan may be metabolized in

several ways. The pathway which leads to the formation of nicotinic acid may be blocked. The enzyme tryptophan pyrolase may be lacking.

Halvorsen and Halvorsen state that the administration of nicotinamide controls the cutaneous eruption and the mental disturbances and prevents new episodes.

BIBLIOGRAPHY

BARON, N. D., DENT, C. E., HARRIS, H., HART, E. W. AND JEPSON, J. B.: Hereditary pellagra-like skin rash, temporary cerebellar ataxia, and renal aminoaciduria. Lancet, ii:421, 1956.

DENT, C. E.: Hartnup disease. Report of the twenty-third Ross Pediatric Research Conference. November 8-9, 1956.

HALVORSEN, K. AND HALVORSEN, S.: Diagnosis of Hartnup disease. Pediatrics, 31:29, 1963.

HERSOV, L. A. AND RODNIGHT, R.: Hartnup disease in psychiatric practice. J. Neurol., Neurosurg. & Psychiat., 23:40, 1960.

MILNE, M. D. *et al.*: The metabolic disorder in Hartnup disease. Quart. J. Med., 29:407, 1960.

SCRIVER, C. R.: Hartnup disease. New England Jour. Med., 273:530, 1965.

WONG, P. W. K. AND PILLAI, P. M.: Clinical and biochemical observations in two cases of Hartnup disease. Arch. of Dis. Childh., 41:383, 1966.

PROGRESSIVE FAMILIAL, INFANTILE CEREBRAL DYSFUNCTION ASSOCIATED WITH AN UNUSUAL URINARY SUBSTANCE (MAPLE SUGAR URINE DISEASE)

In 1954, Menkes, Hurst and Craig published a paper dealing with 4 siblings, 3 boys and a girl, who displayed a new clinical syndrome. There were also 2 female siblings in the family who were quite healthy. The parents and the collateral relatives were healthy.

The onset of symptoms was at 5 days in 3 patients and at 3 days in the other child. Death occurred at 11 days, 12 days, 14 days and 3 months. In all cases the babies became increasingly rigid. Respiration became irregular. In 2 cases there was convulsions. The Moro reflex was lost. Feeding was difficult. The rigidity was eventually associated with opisthotonos. The course was rapidly progressive. The spinal fluid was normal. One pneumoencephalogram showed apparent atrophy of the brain.

Two post-mortem examinations were made. The liver was enlarged in one case and the cells contained much glycogen. There was slight dilatation of the proximal portion of the convoluted tubules of the kidneys. The brain was edematous and weighed 650 gm (normal for age 412 gm.). Some fiber tracts in the pons showed defective myelination but there were no destructive lesions.

In a second case the brain weighed 515 gm whereas the normal weight at the child's age is 332 gm. The only abnormalities found were swelling of the astrocytes in the corona radiata and slight delay in myelination of the fiber tracts in the spinal cord.

Crome *et al.* examined the brain of an infant who lived longer than

most and died at fifteen months. They found status spongiosus in the white matter with destruction of the myelin and gliosis of the white matter.

The only specific finding in these cases was the odor of the urine which is said to have resembled that of maple sugar. The nature of the material responsible for this odor was not identified.

In a personal communication, Dr. Menkes tells me that since his paper was published ten more patients, who displayed the typical syndrome, have come to his attention. These children were found in five families.

In 1959, Menkes published an additional study of the urine of these children. He states that a mixture of alpha-keto acids, the most important of which is alpha-ketoisocaproic acid, is excreted in large quantities in the urine. He suggests that the disorder is due to impairment of the degradative metabolism of the branched-chain amino acids.

Morris *et al.* report the case of a child of sixteen months who had recurrent episodes of semicoma and ataxia associated with the excretion of large amounts of the branched-chain amino acids. At other times, the urine was normal. The child was quite normal at the age of forty-one months.

Dacis *et al.* state that the diagnosis of this disease may be made by the demonstration that the patient's leucocytes are unable to metabolize the branched-chain amino acids. The diagnosis may be made quickly by a modification of the Guthrie test for phenylketonuria. The branched-chain amino acids are tested for by the effect of their antagonist, 2-methylleucine or the growth of B subtilis.

Westall advises a diet containing minimal amounts of leucine, isoleucine and valine.

BIBLIOGRAPHY

BLACKWOOD, W. *et al.*: Diffuse cerebral degeneration in infancy. Arch. Dis. Childhood, **38**:193, 1963.

CROME, L., DUTTON, G. AND ROSS, C. S.: Maple syrup urine disease. J. Path. & Bact., **81**:379, 1961.

DACIS, J.: Maple sugar urine disease. Clin. Pediat., **3**:365, 1964.

DACIS, J., HUTZLER, J. AND LEVITZ, M.: The diagnosis of maple sugar urine disease. Pediatrics, **32**:234, 1963.

DIEZEL, P. B. AND MARTIN, K.: Maple syrup urine disease with familial occurrence. Arch. of Path. Anat., **337**:425, 1964.

LANE, M. R.: Maple syrup urine disease. J. Pediat., **58**:80, 1961.

LONSDALE, D. AND BARBER, D. H.: Maple syrup urine disease. New England Jour. Med., **271**:1338, 1964.

MENKES, J. H. AND SOLCHER, H.: Maple syrup disease. Arch. of Neurol., **16**:486, 1967.

MENKES, J. H.: Maple syrup disease. Isolation and identification of organic acids in the urine. Pediatrics, February, 1959, p. 348.

MENKES, J. H., HURST, P. L. AND CRAIG, J. M.: A new syndrome: Progressive familial, infantile cerebral dysfunction associated with an unusual urinary substance. Pediatrics, **14**:162, 1954.

MORRIS, M. D. *et al.*: Clinical and biochemical observations on an apparently nonfatal variant of branched-chain ketoaciduria. Pediatrics, **28**:918, 1961.

——— *et al.:* Late onset maple syrup urine disease. Jour. Lancet, **86**:149, 1966.

SNYDERMAN, S. E. *et al.:* Maple syrup urine disease with particular reference to dietotherapy. Pediatrics, **34**:454, 1964.

WESTALL, R. G.: Dietary treatment of children with maple syrup urine disease. Arch. Dis. Childhood, **38**:485, 1963.

——— *et al.:* Maple sugar urine disease. A.M.A. J. Dis. Child., **94**:771, 1957.

NEUROLOGICAL DISORDERS ASSOCIATED WITH INCREASE OR REDUCTION OF SERUM SODIUM

The *low sodium* syndrome is associated with symptoms referable to the gastrointestinal and cardiovascular systems, the kidneys and the central nervous system. Anorexia, lack of thirst, nausea, vomiting, abdominal cramps and diarrhea are common symptoms. Renal function may be impaired and uremia may result. Tachycardia, hypotension, syncope and collapse may occur. Twitching of the muscles and muscle cramps are well known. The nervous manifestations include drowsiness, apathy and confusion and finally coma and convulsions. There may be generalized muscular rigidity, retraction of the head, dilated pupils, increased tendon reflexes and Babinski signs. Apparently these neurological disturbances are reversible and if the child survives, there will be complete recovery. The serum sodium may be reduced to 12 or 20 meq per liter. The picture is, of course, modified by the state of hydration, the acid base equilibrium and the level of the other serum electrolytes.

Two types of sodium deficiency are recognized. The first is due to loss of sodium as a result of profuse sweating, vomiting, diarrhea and excessive diuresis such as may occur in cardiac edema when mercury diuretics are given to a patient maintained on a normal fluid intake and low salt regimen. If drainage of the cerebral ventricles into a ureter is established in a case of hydrocephalus, sodium deficiency will develop unless salt is given. The serum sodium is low in Addison's disease and it is said that children suffering from fibrocystic disease of the pancreas are especially apt to develop sodium deficiency during hot weather. Repeated thoracentesis and abdominal paracentesis will also reduce the serum sodium.

A second type of sodium deficiency is due to dilution of body fluids as a result of edema or the administration of fluids deficient in sodium. Excessive dosages of pitressin may cause retention of water and dilution of the serum electrolytes. Damage to the brain as a result of trauma, neurosurgical procedures and other processes may produce the same effects as excessive dosage of pitressin. Tap water enemas, especially in cases of megacolon, may have the same effect. I have seen a child suffering from psychogenic diabetes insipidus who, if permitted, would run to the water tap and drink so excessively that he would become unconscious and have convulsions.

When the child is suffering from sodium depletion, the administration of hypertonic saline is indicated. In the type due to dilution of body fluids, the treatment is not so simple. Saline should be given with caution after estimating the depletion, the dilution and the total body water. The possibility of pulmonary congestion should be kept in mind.

It is stated that in cases of Addison's disease, the legs flex at the knees in such a way that the patient cannot walk. The hamstrings are shortened. This seems to be a contracture of the tendons and not the muscles. Thorn suggests that this is in some manner connected with excessive deposits of sodium in the tendons.

In 1955 Harrison published some very important studies of dehydrated infants who had accumulated an *excess of sodium* in the body. The serum sodium level was 150 meq or more per liter. In the great majority of cases the infant was suffering from diarrhea. There was loss of water by the stools without corresponding loss of sodium. In some cases the administration of fluids containing too much sodium either by mouth or by intravenous injection seemed to be responsible for the condition or perhaps, merely aggravated the condition. Mere lack of proper fluids was possibly responsible in a few cases. In 1943, Luetscher and Blackman published some cases in which similar electrolyte disturbances were found apparently as a result of injury to the kidneys by sulfathiozole. Cooper has published evidence to indicate that hypernatremia and other types of electrolyte imbalance may result from injury to the hypothalmus by neurosurgical procedures or fractures of the skull.

My purpose in mentioning these observations is to call attention to the fact that excessive concentrations of sodium in the body may be associated with severe damage to the central nervous system. Thus, Harrison states that two thirds of his patients displayed neurological disorders which often dominated the picture. The initial symptoms were irritability, somnolence and increased muscle tone. As the symptoms progressed, there was muscular rigidity, increased tendon reflexes, opisthotonos, muscular twitchings and convulsions. Coma and respiratory depression followed. The spinal fluid contained an excess of protein but no increase of cells. Occasionally the fluid might contain blood. In all cases there was loss of weight but loss of skin turgor and evidences of impaired peripheral circulation were not always apparent. There was oliguria and sometimes anuria. The nonprotein nitrogen was increased. In many instances the serum calcium was reduced and potassium might also be reduced.

Turpin *et al.* point out that subdural hematomas may form when the brain shrinks in cases of hypernatremic dehydration.

In most cases the surviving children made complete recoveries but in

some instances there was permanent injury to the brain with mental deficiency and rigidity of the muscles. At post-mortem examination petechial hemorrhages may be found in the brain and there may also be disseminated areas of cellular degeneration.

Treatment is by the administration of hypotonic solutions of sodium chloride according to the child's needs. Other electrolyte imbalances should also be corrected. It should be kept in mind that the rapid replacement of fluids with intravenous glucose may cause water intoxication and convulsions. Swanson states that the administration of diamox is very helpful.

Occasionally by mistake strongly hypertonic solutions of sodium chloride may be given intravenously. As a result there may be vascular lesions which seem to be due to arterial thromboses. These may result in gangrene of the extremities and cerebral softenings.

BIBLIOGRAPHY

BLACKLIDGE, V. Y.: Treatment of hypernatremia in children. California Med., 95:219, 1961.

BRUCK, E. *et al.:* Pathogenesis and pathophysiology of hypertonic dehydration. Amer. Jour. Dis. Child., 115:122, 1968.

COOPER, I. S.: Disorders of electrolyte and water metabolism following brain surgery. J. Neurosurg., 10:389, 1953.

DEBRE, R. *et al.:* Metabolic significance of nervous symptoms due to attacks of vomiting with ketosis in children. J. Pediat., 48:409, 1956.

Editors Column: Enemas can be fatal. J. Pediat., 45:751, 1954.

EVANS, M. E.: The low salt syndrome in children during hot weather. J. Kansas Med. Soc., 55:125, 1954.

FEINBERG, I. AND HARRISON, H.: Hypernatremia in infants. Am. Pediat. Soc. May 3, 1954, Pediatrics.

FINBERG, L.: Pathogenesis of lesions in the nervous system in hypernatremic states. Pediatrics, 23:40, 1959.

LEITER, L., WESTON, R. AND GROSSMAN, J.: The low sodium syndrome. Bull. New York Acad. Med., 29:833, 1953.

LOGOTHETIS, J.: Neurologic effects of water and sodium disturbances. Postgrad. Med., 40:408, 1966.

LUETSCHER, J. AND BLACKMAN, S.: Severe injury to the kidneys and brain following sulfathiazole administration. High serum sodium and chloride levels and persistent brain damage. Ann. Int. Med., 18:741, 1943.

LUTTRELL, C. N. AND FINBERG, L.: Hemorrhagic encephalopathy induced by hypernatremia. A.M.A. Arch. Neurol. Psychiat., 81:424, 1959.

MACAULAY, D. AND WATSON, M.: Hypernatremia in infants as a cause of brain damage. Arch. of Disease in Childh., 42:485, 1967.

MATSON, D. D.: A new operation for treatment of communicating hydrocephalus. J. Neurosurg., 6:238, 1949.

MEYERS, G. B.: Abnormalities of body water, sodium, potassium and magnesium. Arch. Int. Med., 95:503, 1955.

RESNICK, M. E. *et al.:* Coma and convulsions due to compulsive water drinking. Neurology, 19:11:1125, 1969.

SKINNER, A. L. AND MOLL, F. C.: Hypernatremia with diarrhea in infants. Am. J. Dis. Child., 92:562, 1956.

SCHOOLMAN, H., DUBIN, A. AND HOFFMAN, W.: Clinical syndromes associated with hypernatremia. Arch. Int. Med., **95**:15, 1955.

SWANSON, A. G.: The effect of acetazoleamide (diamox) on encephalopathy induced by water excess and hypernatremia. Neurology, **10**:537, 1960.

THORN, G. W.: The Diagnosis and Treatment of Adrenal Insufficiency. Springfield, Thomas, 1949, p. 144.

TURPIN, R. *et al.:* Subdural hematoma in hypernatremic dehydration. Ann. Pediat., **36**:311, 1960.

WEIL, W. B. AND WALLACE, W. M.: Hypertonic dehydration in infancy. Pediatrics, **17**:171, 1956.

WELTI, W.: Delirium with low serum sodium. Arch. Neurol. & Psychiat., **76**:559, 1956.

WISE, B. L.: Neurogenic hyperosmolarity (Hypernatremia) . Neurology, **453**:12, 1962.

DISORDERS OF MAGNESIUM METABOLISM

There is reason to believe that variations in the magnesium content of the body may give rise to a number of symptoms. The normal content of magnesium in the serum is between 1.4 and 2.5 meq per liter, but since magnesium is chiefly an intracellular substance, the serum level gives very little information about its concentration in the body.

Magnesium deficiency it is claimed, may cause excitement, irritability, tremors, involuntary movements, cramps and convulsions. Davis *et al.* state that magnesium deficiency may cause convulsions in the first few days after birth. Carpopedal spasm and the standard signs of tetany may occur so this condition has been termed magnesium tetany. The administration of magnesium sulphate by mouth or by injection is said to give prompt relief of symptoms.

Magnesium deficiency may result from the use of magnesium free fluids in diarrheas, post-operative states and in the treatment of diabetic coma. It may also occur as a result of profuse diuresis such as occurs when cardiac edema is treated by mercury diuretics. It is seen in cases of lupus erythematosus, pancreatitis and in cases of nephrosis. Diets deficient in magnesium may in rare instances be responsible.

The diagnosis is not easy to establish. The serum magnesium level may be normal in such cases. It is recommended that magnesium be administered whenever the symptoms described above may develop in an individual who may have lost magnesium in the urine or may have had an inadequate intake.

Magnesium poisoning may cause lethargy progressing to coma, weakness or paralysis of the muscles, fall of blood pressure and failure of respiration. Depression of the heart action may be fatal. This condition may occur in renal disease especially if epsom salts are given, in states of dehydration, and in untreated diabetic acidosis. Oxalic acid poisoning is said to cause retention of magnesium. Efforts should be made to improve renal function and secure proper hydration. Calcium is used as an antagonist. The serum magnesium level is apt to be found to be about 6.0 meq per liter.

BIBLIOGRAPHY

BLACK, E. H. *et al.*: Neurologic manifestations of magnesium deficiency in infantile gastroenteritis and malnutrition. Arch. Dis. Childhood, 37:106, 1962.

DAVIS, J. A. *et al.*; Neonatal fits associated with hypomagnesaemia. Arch. Dis. Childh., 40:286,
1965.

FLINK, E. B.: Magnesium deficiency syndrome in man. J.A.M.A., 160:1406, 1956.

———— *et al.*: Evidence of clinical magnesium deficiency. Ann. Int. Med., 47:956, 1957.

HAYNES, B. W. *et al.*: Magnesium metabolism in surgical patients. Ann. Surg., 136:659, 1952.

MARTIN, H. E. *et al.*: Clinical studies of magnesium metabolism. Med. Clin. North. Am., 1157,
1952.

MEYERS, G. B.: Abnormalities of the body water, sodium, potassium and magnesium. Arch. Int.
Med., 95:503, 1955.

MILLER, J. F.: Tetany due to deficiency in magnesium. Am. J. Dis. Child., 67:117, 1944.

SUTTER, C. AND KLINGMAN, W. O.: Neurologic manifestations of magnesium depletion. Neurology,
5:691, 1955.

VALLEE, B. L. *et al.*: The magnesium-deficiency tetany syndrome in man. New England J. Med.,
262:155, 1960.

WONG, H. B. AND TEH, Y. E.: An association between serum magnesium and tremor and convulsions in infants and children. Lancet, 2:18, 1968.

NEUROLOGICAL CONDITIONS DUE TO DEFICIENT DIET

Introduction.—In 1907, Eijkman published a paper showing that polyneuritis similar to that of beriberi might be produced in fowls by a diet of
polished rice and that polyneuritis might be prevented or cured by adding
the polishings to the diet. Since then the connection of deficient diet with
polyneuritis has been established beyond doubt by numerous experimental
and clinical investigations. The hypothetical substance necessary for the
prevention of beriberi is apparently not one of the major constituents of
the food such as carbohydrates, fats and proteins but an accessory substance which is required in only very small amounts. This particular substance has been termed vitamin B_1 or the water soluble antineuritic vitamin.
It is found in yeast and wheat grains and many other foods.

Since the first observations were made a large number of "vitamins" have
been described. The terminology has become very complex since different
names are used by various writers for the same substance and the literature
has grown so confused that it is impossible for anyone but the specialist to
follow it intelligently. The writer will, therefore, make no attempt to cover the entire subject and will discuss only the facts which seem to be relatively clear.

BIBLIOGRAPHY

DENNY-BROWN, D.: Neurological conditions resulting from prolonged and severe dietary restriction. Medicine, 26:41, 1947.

EDDY, W. H. AND DALLDORF, G.: The Avitaminoses. Baltimore, Williams and Wilkins Co., 1937.

FISHBEIN, M. *et al.*: The Vitamins. Amer. Med. Assoc., Chicago, Ill., 1939.

SPILLANE, J. D.: Nutritional Disorders of the Nervous System. Baltimore, Williams and Wilkins
Co., 1947.

SMITH, D. A.: Nutritional neuropathies in civilian internment camp, Hong Kong. Brain, **69**:209, 1946.

VITAMIN A DEFICIENCY AND POISONING

Vitamin A is a primary alcohol which is found in nature in the form of fatty acid esters. Carotine, the yellow pigment of carrots and other vegetables, may be changed in the body into vitamin A. Vitamin A is found in cod liver oil, the liver oil of halibut and in butter, eggs, cream, and the liver and kidney of the animals we eat.

Deficiency of vitamin A is manifest often by night blindness which has been explained by the discovery that this vitamin is necessary for the formation of the visual purple, rhodopsin. There are also extensive changes in the skin with dryness, scaliness and hyperkeratosis of the hair follicles. The ocular changes include photophobia, dryness of the eye, yellowish white spots on the conjunctiva, i.e. Biot's spots, clouding of the cornea and eventually keratomalacia and perforation. Bass points out that the frequent diagnosis of milk allergy has resulted in many infants being kept on diets deficient in vitamin A. He states that mental and physical retardation results. The fontanel may bulge and cranial nerve lesions may develop. Anemia, hematuria, and gynecomastia may develop. The diagnosis is made by the history, by the night blindness, physical findings and the demonstration of a low blood level of vitamin A. It is said that the normal level in children is between 75 and 200 units per ml of plasma and that concentrations below 75 units are as a rule of clinical significance.

In this country defective absorption of vitamin A is more often responsible for symptoms than defective diet. Such conditions as cystic fibrosis of the pancreas, atresia of the bile ducts, coeliac disease and chronic dysentery are often responsible.

A number of cases of vitamin A poisoning have come to light in recent years. They are usually due to excessive dosage of concentrated preparations of the vitamin. The symptoms include irritability, drowsiness, anorexia, loss of hair, dry skin, itching, burning pains in the extremities associated with extreme tenderness, and hard tender lumps over the skull and extremities. There may be jaundice and enlargement of the liver and spleen. New deposits of bone are seen under the periosteum. The epiphyseal plate becomes prematurely vascularized and ossified and results in defective growth of the bones. Edema of the brain may result with enlargement of the head in infants and papilledema in older children. Recovery follows withdrawal of the drug it is said.

BIBLIOGRAPHY

BASS, M. H.: Relation of vitamin A intake to cerebrospinal fluid pressure. J. Mt. Sinai Hosp., **24**:713, 1957.

BLATTNER, R. J.: Vitamin A deficiency. Editorial. J. Pediat., **60**:953, 1962.
GERBER, A., RAAB, A. AND SOBEL, A.: Vitamin A poisoning in adults. Am. J. Med., **16**:729, 1954.
JOSEPHS, H. W.: Hypervitaminosis A and carotinemia. Am. J. Dis. Child., **67**:33, 1944.
KNUDSON, A. AND ROTHMAN, P.: Hypervitaminosis A. Am. J. Dis. Child., **85**:316, 1953.
TUDOR, R. B.: Chronic vitamin A poisoning. J. Lancet, **75**:372, 1955.

Infantile Tetany and Vitamin D Deficiency and Poisoning

Definition.—Tetany is a condition characterized by tonic spasms of the muscles of the extremities (carpopedal spasm) and of the larynx (laryngismus stridulus), by convulsive seizures and by abnormal irritability of the peripheral nerves. In the following discussion only infantile tetany will be treated. This is believed to be due to lack of vitamin D and is, therefore, a deficiency disease.

Etiology.—Tetany in infancy is almost always associated with definite signs of rickets. Thus, Holt states that in 293 cases of infantile tetany seen at Harriet Lane, only 3 failed to show definite evidence of rickets. In a very large percentage of cases, the development of symptoms was associated with an acute infection. The calcium of the blood plasma is invariably reduced in this form of tetany and it is to this factor that the irritability of the nerves is attributed. Without attempting to enter into a full discussion of the causes of rickets and tetany, it may be said in brief that these conditions are now attributed to *lack* of sunlight and to a diet which contains inadequate amounts of vitamin D. Two forms of vitamin D are known. One, of vegetable origin, is irradiated ergosterol and in its chemically pure form is known as calciferol. It has been named by the Council on Pharmacy and Chemistry, *viosterol*. The second form is 7-dehydrocholesterol which develops in the skin under the influence of the ultraviolet rays of sunlight. These substances are not abundant in our food but are found in fish oils, butter fat and to some extent in meat.

Pathological Anatomy.—In infantile tetany no lesions are found other than those due to rickets which need not be described here.

Clinical Features.—Tetany may occur even in the newborn but is very rare before the end of the third month. Between three months and one year, tetany was once very common and a small number of cases occur during the second year. Tetany is most prevalent in the winter and early spring. It is also more common in artificially fed infants and in Negro children and is especially frequent in children who have had insufficient care, no cod liver oil and inadequate sunlight. It has already been stated above that tetany is almost invariably associated with rickets although only a small percentage of children with rickets develop tetany. There is reason to believe that acute infections play an important role in precipitating active tetany. Holt quotes figures compiled by Guild to show that in 85

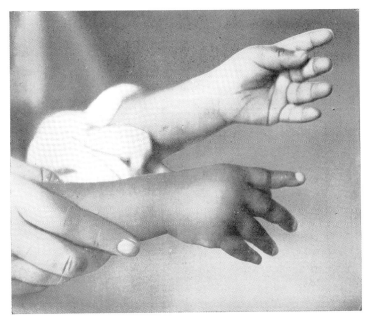

Fig. 199. Position of the hands in tetany. (By the courtesy of Dr. Holt.)

per cent of all cases seen at Harriet Lane, acute infections immediately preceded the development of active symptoms.

In the vast majority of cases, therefore, tetany appears in association with an acute infection in children who have already shown evidences of rickets. The so-called *carpopedal spasm* is one of the first and most constant signs of active tetany. This usually appears abruptly and affects the upper extremities first. The fingers are flexed at the proximal joints and extended at the distal joints and the thumbs are strongly adducted and opposed. The wrist may be flexed and sometimes the elbow. The feet also show flexion of the proximal joints of the toes and extension of the distal joints. The plantar surface of the foot is concave and the dorsum convex. The ankle may be slightly extended. Rarely the thighs are adducted. The face may show strong contraction of the muscles in cases in which the symptoms are severe. In general, the muscle spasm is symmetrical and affects only the distal groups of muscles. Except in very severe cases the proximal joints move freely. As a rule, some power of voluntary movement is preserved. The child can usually use the hands with some difficulty to grasp toys or food unless the spasm is so severe that it cannot be overcome. Once the patient's efforts have ceased the extremities return to their former posture. There is no alteration of consciousness whatever. If severe, the spasms are often very painful and the pain is increased if an attempt is made to overcome the spasm by passive movements. Carpopedal spasm, once it has developed,

is continuous for hours or even days, although it may vary in intensity from time to time. If it is prolonged, there may be edema of the extremities.

Laryngospasm is apparently due to tonic spasm of the muscles of the larynx and is analogous to carpopedal spasm. In fact, these conditions often occur simultaneously. The vocal cords are strongly adducted so that a crowing sound develops with each inspiration. In severe attacks there may be complete interruption of respiration and the child becomes cyanotic and may have convulsions or become unconscious. In some cases, only two or three "crows" are heard and then the child breathes normally until the attack returns. In other cases there may be some little inspiratory stridor for half an hour or more. Only very rarely does death result in such attacks. A large number of attacks may occur during one day.

Convulsions are probably the most common manifestation of active tetany. They are generalized, as a rule, and associated with loss of consciousness, so that they cannot be distinguished from those due to other causes. In some cases they occur with extraordinary frequency and severity. Usually they come in series. Sensory stimuli may seem to provoke them and Holt mentions a child on whom the application of cold water in bathing would invariably provoke a seizure. Unilateral convulsions have been observed in a number of cases. These may never involve the other side or may alternate involving first one side and then the other. We have seen transient hemiplegia follow repeated and severe attacks of a unilateral nature.

In infancy convulsions constitute the most constant evidence of tetany although they also occur at any age. Laryngospasm is practically confined to the first two years of life. Carpopedal spasm also occurs at any age but is most frequent in children over two years.

The signs of latent tetany are always present in children who show the symptoms mentioned above and often occur in children who have rickets but no symptoms of tetany. *Chvostek's sign* is a brief contraction of the facial muscles due to tapping the face over the seventh nerve. This sign is said to have little significance during the first week of life and after the fifth year. It must be kept in mind that it is always a quantitative test since even a normal nerve will react to a hard blow. Other nerves react in the same way to mechanical stimuli. The peroneal nerve may be tapped where it lies over the head of the fibula and the ulnar nerve at the elbow. *Trousseau's sign* is elicited by shutting off the circulation of the arm above the elbow by means of a bandage or the cuff of the blood pressure apparatus so that the radial pulse is obliterated. After a few moments the hand develops the typical carpal spasm. It is said that this sign may be absent even when tatany is well marked. *Erb's sign* is an increased irritability of the peripheral nerves to galvanic currents. Suffice it to say here that in the first six

months any opening contraction obtained with a current of less than five milliamperes whether anodal or cathodal, is positive evidence of tetany. Under five years of age a cathodal tetany, either opening or closing, with currents of less than five milliamperes is evidence of tetany. The value of these signs is not always easy to estimate. The electrical tests, especially, must be performed by an experienced examiner and the child's age must always be taken into consideration, for reactions indicative of tetany under six months may be quite normal after two years of age. The results vary with different examiners and also apparently vary spontaneously in the same child from day to day so that the tests must be repeated several times.

If rickets is present the muscles are poorly developed, atonic and weak. The child is slow to walk. The abdomen bulges due to loss of muscle tone. Usually the bony deformities overshadow the muscular weakness so one may not realize the disability is largely muscular.

At present it is believed that estimation of the blood calcium and phosphorus is the most accurate test for infantile tetany. In active tetany the blood calcium is almost always reduced from the normal value of about 10 milligrams per hundred cubic centimeters to less than 7.5 milligrams. The inorganic phosphorus is also usually reduced. Occasionally the phosphorus is normal (4 to 6 milligrams) or even higher. If the phosphorus is high, tetany may develop with a blood calcium level of 8 milligrams, whereas if the phosphorus is low, no signs of tetany appear until the calcium falls to 7 milligrams. In untreated cases, the product of calcium multiplied by phosphorus is usually below 40 and practically always below 45. In latent tetany there is also a reduction of blood calcium but the reduction is, as a rule, less marked and values ranging from 7.5 to 8.5 are usually obtained.

Diagnosis.—When the clinical picture is well developed and the signs of latent tetany are present, the diagnosis of infantile tetany is obvious but when the clinical symptoms are incompletely developed or complicated by other factors, there may be considerable difficulty in the diagnosis. Carpopedal spasm is quite characteristic and may be regarded as positive evidence of tetany, since it is not easily confused with any other common condition. It must be said, however, that tonic fits, especially if they are frequent and are not associated with any alteration of consciousness, may be mistaken for tetany. Tonic fits, as a rule, last only a few moments and are followed by complete relaxation, so that if this possibility is considered, the differentiation from tetany should be possible. Laryngospasm must be distinguished from congenital stridor, laryngitis of catarrhal type and from breath-holding spells. In congenital stridor, the stridor is noted early in life and is continuous showing no tendency to paroxysms. It is sometimes modified by the child's position. Laryngitis is associated with signs of respiratory tract inflammation, a barking cough, some fever and a hoarse voice. As a

rule, the common catarrhal laryngitis, or spasmodic croup, develops at night and lasts a few hours. Breath-holding spells should be recognized by the fact that there is no stridor. The child takes a deep breath and holds it until cyanosis may appear. These attacks are associated with evidence of anger or fright and occur in neurotic children. It is in cases in which convulsions are the only evidence of tetany, and especially when the situation is complicated by an acute infection, that the diagnosis is most difficult. In such cases the diagnosis depends upon the demonstration of one or more of the signs of latent tetany and upon the presence of a low serum calcium. The discovery of signs of rickets may be taken to strengthen the diagnosis of tetany and if the symptoms are controlled by the administration of calcium, we may regard it as confirmed.

As regards parathyroid tetany, it is most apt to occur after the usual age of infantile tetany, it is not associated with rickets, the calcium of the serum is low but the phosphorus is very high, antirachitic treatment is ineffective, but parathormone will relieve the symptoms. Tetany due to hyperventilation and gastric tetany are easily recognized and celiac disease is likewise to be recognized by the long history of indigestion and loss of fat from the bowels. The administration of large amounts of citrated blood may cause precipitation of ionized calcium and tetany.

Begum, R. *et al.* point out that mothers who give birth to babies with congenital rickets should be examined for malabsorption and secondary hyperparathyroidism.

The administration of excessive amounts of vitamin D may cause hypercalcemia and serious symptoms. There may be loss of appetite, vomiting, fatigue, and weakness of the muscles. Renal damage may occur and there may be deposits of calcium in the tissues. Such deposits may be seen in the conjunctiva. There is polyuria and the urine contains an excess of calcium. The ingestion of excessive amounts of vitamin D during pregnancy may cause supravalvular stenosis of the aorta and mental deficiency in the baby.

Prognosis.—Death may occur from recurrent convulsions, from asphyxia in prolonged laryngospasm or from some complicating condition. In some cases it has occurred suddenly without either of these symptoms and no adequate cause has been discovered at post-mortem examination. Figures quoted by Holt based upon an analysis of the Harriet Lane material by Guild indicate that a mortality of about 3 per cent may be expected from tetany alone. Possibly the mortality would be much higher in untreated cases. If the child survives, there is no reason to expect any sequelae. Apparently, the occurrence of convulsions in infantile tetany does not make it probable that the child will develop epilepsy later in life. However, it seems to be true that children with defective nervous systems develop convulsions more readily than normal children and in cases in which the tetany

is very mild and the convulsions are severe and prolonged and especially when the latter do not respond to treatment as readily as one might expect, the possibility should be considered that the child has not only tetany but a defective nervous system.

Treatment.—If children are properly protected against rickets by the administration of cod liver oil or viosterol and exposure to sunlight, tetany will not develop, except in exceptional circumstances. Prophylaxis is, therefore, most important.

If the child is seen in general convulsions, it will often be necessary to administer chloroform or some other general anesthetic. If severe laryngospasm, such as to cause alarming interference with respiration, is present, artificial respiration may be required. Chloral or morphine should be given. Calcium chloride is given by mouth. It should be effective within from four to six hours. Holt recommends an initial dose of 3 grams of the hydrated salt followed by 1 gram every four hours for twenty-four hours. Thereafter one gram three times a day is usually adequate. This should be continued for two weeks or more until antirachitic therapy has taken effect. Calcium gluconate may be given in place of the chloride. It has the advantage that it may be injected intramuscularly or intravenously so as to produce a more rapid effect. Holt suggests that viosterol should not be given until twenty-four hours after calcium has been begun, since it may increase the blood phosphorus and induce further symptoms. Thereafter, it must be continued in adequate doses of from 20 to 60 drops a day until cure is effected. A proper maintenance dose is then employed.

BIBLIOGRAPHY

BEGUM, R. *et al.:* Maternal malabsorption presenting as congenital rickets. Lancet, i:1048, 1968.
HELLMAN, A. M. AND ROTHSTEIN, J. L.: Low calcium tetany of the new born as a problem for the obstetrician. Am. J. Obst. & Gynec., 29:686, 1935.
HOLT, E. AND McINTOSH, R.: Diseases of Infancy and Childhood. Tenth Edition, p. 259, 1933.
WALSH, F. B.: *Loc. cit.*

Infantile Scurvy and Vitamin C Deficiency

Definition.—A disease of infants characterized by multiple hemorrhages especially subperiosteal hemorrhages, changes in the gums, in the bones, etc. Intracranial hemorrhage and various other neurological conditions may occur.

Etiology.—The disease is caused by a diet deficient in vitamin C, which is found most abundantly in citrus fruit, but is present in almost all fresh vegetables, raw meat and fish. Breast milk as a rule contains enough of this substance to prevent the development of symptoms, but under certain conditions such as improper diet and undernutrition, the milk may become so deficient in the antiscorbutic factor that scurvy develops. Cow's milk usu-

ally affords ample Vitamin C but its potency is rapidly destroyed by pasteurization, by boiling and by exposure to air. Vitamin C has been identified as cevitamic acid or ascorbic acid.

Pathological Anatomy.—The pathological changes outside of the nervous system need not be described in detail. Suffice it to say that the essential lesions are subperiosteal hemorrhages, hemorrhages in the skin, mucous membranes and changes in the bones, especially separation of the epiphyses. There is no definite anatomical changes in the blood vessels and the blood seems to coagulate normally. It has been claimed, however, that the bleeding is due to loss of the intracellular cement substance of the vascular endothelium.

The nervous system has received very little study but is affected in rare instances. The peripheral nerves may be involved by extravasations into the surrounding tissues or into the nerve sheath and in a few instances have been found to show well-marked degeneration. Hematoma of the orbit may cause exophthalmos and palsies of the third, fourth and sixth nerves. Subdural hematoma on one or both sides may occur. This may be complicated by subarachnoid hemorrhage.

Clinical Features.—The disease is found in infants fed on boiled milk, dried milk or even pasteurized milk, who have not been given orange juice,

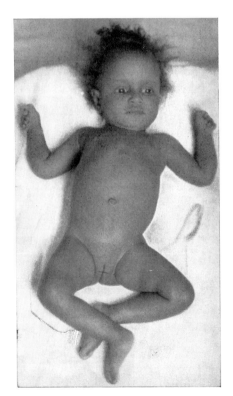

FIG. 200. Scurvy showing characteristic posture of the extremities.

tomato juice or other source of vitamin C, and in breast fed infants whose mothers take an inadequate amount of fresh fruit. It is more prevalent during winter months than in summer and is generally confined to the second six months of life. Scurvy is rare in infants under four months and over eighteen months of age. Some children seem to be abnormally susceptible to this condition and several cases may occur in a family despite the administration of moderate amounts of orange juice.

The onset may be sudden or insidious depending upon the degree of vitamin deficiency. The characteristic symptoms include tenderness of the extremities, swellings due to subcutaneous or subperiosteal hemorrhage, spongy swelling of the gums and hemorrhages in the skin and mucous membranes. The sharp projecting ridges of the ends of the ribs may be felt in some cases and are easily distinguished from the rounded beading of rickets. There is a typical posture in some cases with the legs semiflexed at hip and knee and external rotation of the thighs. The tenderness and perhaps epiphyseal separation often causes pseudo-paralysis. Fever is present in 75 per cent of all cases and may reach 103°F. In severe cases these is always secondary anemia and often loss of weight and anorexia. The urine frequently contains red cells. Rickets is a frequent complication of scurvy. Heart failure may occur and is a common cause of death.

The neurological features are frequently obscured by the tenderness of the extremities and in infants with severe scurvy, it is almost impossible to perform an adequate neurological examination. Stewart has discovered tenderness of the peripheral nerve trunks, weakness and hyperesthesias as well as diminution or increase of the tendon reflexes. These signs he regards as evidences of involvement of the nerve trunks. Such signs seem to be present in a fairly large percentage of cases, but their significance is not quite clear. It is of interest that the pain disappears very promptly after orange juice is given, so promptly, in fact, that it scarcely seems possible that the relief can be due to absorption of the subperiosteal hemorrhages. The commonest condition referable to the nervous system is subdural hematoma which is probably due to scurvy more frequently than most pediatricians realize. The symptoms of this condition are given elsewhere and need not be repeated here. Convulsions are also observed in a number of cases. Hemorrhages into the orbit are a relatively common and characteristic feature of scurvy. This, of course, causes exophthalmos and paralysis of the third, fourth and sixth nerves in many cases. Hemorrhage into the subarachnoid spaces is rare but has been observed in Harriet Lane.

Diagnosis.—The diagnosis depends upon the history of a diet deficient in vitamin C, the age of the subject, the tenderness of the extremities, the swollen, spongy gums and the hemorrhagic tendency. Roentgenological examination of the long bones is important, for scurvy may be mistaken for

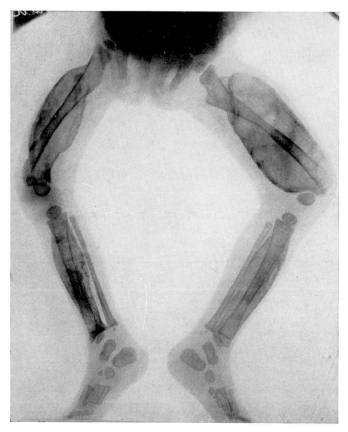

FIG. 201. Roentgenograms of the bones in an advanced case of scurvy showing great sub-periosteal hemorrhages. (By the courtesy of Dr. Holt.)

osteomyelitis, syphilitic osteochondritis, poliomyelitis and, above all, for arthritis. In advanced cases we find separation of the epiphyses and calcified subperiosteal hemorrhages. In early cases there may be atrophy of the trabeculae of the shaft of the long bones and broadening of the epiphyseal lines with a zone of rarefaction just beneath.

Prognosis.—In properly treated cases, the prognosis is good unless intracranial hemorrhage is present. Neglected children may die of secondary infection and hemorrhage.

Treatment.—Orange juice in doses of two to four ounces a day is usually sufficient and produces definite improvement within one or two days. Recovery usually follows with astonishing rapidity. If there is constant vomiting, the orange juice may be given by nasal drip. When an immediate effect is imperative, ascorbic acid may be given intravenously. It should be dissolved in sterile water and neutralized by one half its weight of sodium bicarbonate. Doses of 30 mgs or more may be used.

BIBLIOGRAPHY

HESS, A. F.: Scurvy, Past and Present. Philadelphia, J. B. Lippincott Co., 1920.

————: Focal degeneration of the spinal cord in a case of infantile scurvy. J. Infect. Dis., **23**:438, 1918.

MEYER, A. W. AND McCORMICK, L. M.: Studies on Scurvy. Stanford University Press, 1928.

PARK, E. A. AND JACKSON, D.: Congenital scurvy: A case report. J. Pediat., **7**:741, 1935.

————, GUILD, H. G., JACKSON, D. AND BOND, M.: The recognition of scurvy with especial reference to the early x-ray changes. Arch. Dis. Childhood, **10**:265, 1935.

SAMNIS, J. F.: A case of scurvy with cerebral hemorrhage. Arch. Pediat., **36**:279, 1919.

SHAPIRO, E. AND HURWITZ, S.: Hemorrhages of the brain and retina in scurvy. Arch. Pediat., **55**:327, 1938.

STEWART, R. M.: Clinical features of scorbutic neuritis. J. Neurol. & Psychopath., **6**:191, 1925.

SUTHERLAND, G. A.: On hematoma of the dura mater associated with scurvy in children. Brain, **17**:27, 1894.

WALSH, F. B. *Loc. cit.*

Infantile Beriberi, Wernicke's Hemorrhagic Encephalopathy and Vitamin B₁ Deficiency

Definition.—A disease of breast fed infants found chiefly in the Orient and in the West Indies and characterized by a combination of gastrointestinal, cerebral, neural and cardiac symptoms. It is believed to be due to deficient diet. In Japan it has been called breast-milk intoxication.

Etiology.—It is generally believed at present that beriberi represents the expression of a dietary deficiency. The lacking element is a water soluble substance termed vitamin B_1 which has been identified and in the pure form is called thiamine. It is present in relatively large amounts in yeast, whole grains, legumes and nuts and in smaller amounts in muscle and organ meats, milk and eggs. Apparently human milk is less rich in this substance than cow's milk. The amount available in breast milk depends largely upon the mother's diet. Beriberi does not develop, it is claimed, in persons taking a very low carbohydrate diet even though vitamin B_1 is taken in inadequate amounts. It is believed, therefore, that this substance is necessary only for proper carbohydrate metabolism.

Pathological Anatomy.—The peripheral symptoms are due to changes in the spinal nerves in which there is destruction of the myelin sheath and some loss of axis cylinders just as in other types of polyneuritis. These changes affect the proximal parts of the nerves as much as the peripheral parts and extend into the anterior and posterior roots. The posterior root ganglia are said to be severely affected. Degenerative changes are found in the motor cells of the anterior horns of the spinal cord and also in the sensory cells of the posterior horns.

The cerebral symptoms are associated with the process known as *Wernicke's hemorrhagic encephalopathy*. There are small foci of degeneration in the gray matter about the third ventricle, in the midbrain and often in

the pons. The white matter is less severely affected. As a rule there are many petechial hemorrhages. The structures most commonly affected include the thalamus, the hypothalamus, the mammillary bodies and the cranial nerve nuclei of the midbrain and pons.

Wolf and Feigin describe lesions in the brains of three young children similar to those seen in chronic cases of Wernicke's encephalopathy. No history of deficient diet was elicited thus suggesting the possibility that Wernicke's encephalopathy may occur from causes other than deficient diet.

The heart is said to show hydropic degeneration of the muscle fibers with edema and swelling of the collagen fibers.

Clinical Features.—This disease is very rare in this country or at least is rarely recognized but it is relatively common in the Philippine Islands, the West Indies and the Orient. Breast fed infants whose mothers are suffering from the disease are almost certain to be affected and it is also not unusual in the infants of mothers who are taking an improper diet who seem to be in relatively good health. Apparently, deficiency of vitamin B_1 is more dangerous in infancy than in adult life.

As a rule, the disease develops between one and three months of age. The child loses weight, but has no appetite, becomes restless, fretful and sleeps poorly. Vomiting is frequent and diarrhea is emphasized by some authorities as a constant symptom. In addition to the gastrointestinal disturbances there are three chief groups of symptoms, the cerebral, cardiac and polyneuritic. The onset of the *cerebral manifestations* is often abrupt. There is ptosis of the lids, nystagmus and various ocular palsies. There are also ataxia and choreiform movements. The patient cannot stand or even sit up if old enough to do so. The mental condition progresses from restlessness and irritability to confusion, stupor and coma. Convulsions are common and may lead to death in a few hours in the more fulminating cases. Generalized muscular rigidity with opisthotonos is seen in some instances. The *polyneuritis* which is so typical of beriberi in adults is much less prominent in infants. However, there is general muscular weakness in most cases, although actual palsies of the distal muscle groups are rarely mentioned. The knee and ankle jerks may be diminished or even lost. As a rule, the children are very sensitive and cry when they are handled, especially if the calf muscles are compressed. This seems to be a very characteristic feature and probably indicates a mild polyneuritis. Another typical symptom is alteration of the voice which may be merely hoarse or even lost as a result of tenth nerve palsy. *Cardiac weakness* is frequently present as in adults. The pulse is almost always rapid and there may be dilatation of the heart, cyanosis and edema of the extremities. In uncomplicated cases there is no fever. The spinal fluid shows no significant changes.

Retrobulbar neuritis with central scotomas and sometimes pigmentary changes in the maculae or actual optic atrophy may occur. The cause, however, is not clearly determined and it does not seem to be certain that this condition is due to B_1 deficiency.

Diagnosis.—The most important elements in the diagnosis are the history of the deficient diet in the mother, and the combination of gastrointestinal, cerebral, polyneuritic and cardiac symptoms as described above.

Prognosis.—In the acute cases, the prognosis is serious and the mortality is very high. Without prompt diagnosis and proper treatment, the outlook is unfavorable but it is claimed that the administration of vitamin B_1 in large amounts produces an immediate and very striking improvement unless the child is already moribund.

Treatment.—A proper diet containing adequate amounts of eggs, milk, meat and leguminous vegetables should be given. Thiamine chloride may be given in doses of from 5 to 20 mg daily. Some authorities give much larger doses. This drug may be given subcutaneously or intravenously if desired.

BIBLIOGRAPHY

ALCANTARA, V. C. AND DE OCAMPO, G.: The larynx in infantile beri beri. Arch. Otol., 30:389, 1939.

ALEXANDER, L.: Wernicke's disease. Am. J. Path., 16:61, 1940.

ANDREWS, V. L.: Infantile beri beri, Philippine. J. Sc., 7:67, 1912.

CAMPBELL, A. C. P. AND BIGGART, J. H.: Wernicke's encephalopathy. Its alcoholic and non-alcoholic incidence. J. Path. & Bact., 48:245, 1939.

DE WARDENER, H. E. AND LENNOX, B.: Cerebral beri beri (Wernicke's encephalopathy). Lancet, i:11, 1947.

HARIDAS, L.: Infantile beri beri in Singapore. Arch. Dis. Childhood, 22:23, 1947.

HASS, S. V.: Beri beri in late infancy, result of coeliac disease. Arch. Pediat., 46:467, 1929.

TANAKA, T.: So-called breast milk intoxication. Am. J. Dis. Child., 47:1286, 1934.

VEDDER, E. B.: The pathology of beri beri. J.A.M.A., 110:893, 1938.

WALSH, F. B.: *Loc. cit.*

WARING, J. I.: Beri beri in infants. Am. J. Dis. Child., 38:52, 1929.

WOLF, A. AND FEIGIN, M.: Chronic Wernicke's Encephalopathy in Children. American Assoc. of Neuropathologists. Meeting of June 14, 1953.

Pellagra

Definition.—Pellagra is a disease characterized by cutaneous eruptions, gastrointestinal disturbances and symptoms referable to the central nervous system.

Etiology.—It seems to be established that pellagra is due to a deficient diet for it is prevented or cured by a diet containing adequate amounts of fresh milk, meat, eggs and leguminous vegetables. Yeast is quite rich in this pellagra-preventing factor. Recently it has been shown that *nicotinic acid,* which is one of the constituents of the B complex, will cure pellagra very promptly, so that the present belief is that an inadequate intake of this substance is the essential cause of the disease.

Pathological Anatomy.—There are usually no gross changes in the nervous system. Histological examination reveals in many cases a striking loss of ganglion cells in the cerebral cortex. Others are swollen, the Nissl bodies have largely disappeared and the nucleus is displaced peripherally. These cortical changes have been termed "central neuritis" by Adolf Meyer. Some degeneration of the white matter is sometimes seen. The spinal cord shows degenerations in the lateral and posterior columns resembling in its distribution that of pernicious anemia but accompanied by a more pronounced gliosis. Even the peripheral nerves may exhibit some evidences of demyelination. The blood vessels throughout the nervous system are also involved. Fatty degeneration of the endothelium, thickening and hyaline changes of the media and new capillary formation are described. Apparently these changes are not so specific that they can be recognized with certainty.

Clinical Features.—Pellagra may occur at any age and is not uncommon in childhood although it seems to be rare in infancy. The disease was once frequent in the southern States but has been reported from every part of the United States. It is also prevalent in southern Europe, the Balkans, Asia Minor and Lower Egypt, China, the Philippine Islands, Mexico and Central and South America. Pellagra is a disease of the rural districts although it is not unknown in cities. The symptoms are apt to appear in the

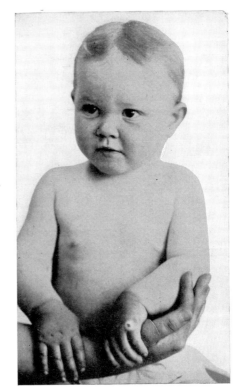

FIG. 202. Pellagra showing typical lesions over hands and wrists.

spring or summer months and in long-standing cases there is apt to be an exacerbation each spring and improvement during the late autumn or winter. With few exceptions the patients have taken a diet lacking in fresh milk, meat and vegetables and usually corn, i.e. maize, has been a principal article of diet. Usually they have lived in extreme poverty.

The gastrointestinal or cutaneous symptoms, are, as a rule, the first to attract attention. There may be anorexia and loss of weight. Diarrhea is usual and a number of watery stools may be passed each day. In other cases diarrhea alternates with constipation. Vomiting is unusual. The cutaneous eruption is seen on the exposed surfaces of the body and is no doubt increased by the action of sunlight. It begins as an erythema resembling sunburn and later exfoliation and desquamation follow. Brownish pigmentation may persist. As a rule, the eruption is quite dry and the skin rough and thickened but in some instances there may be vesicles and finally ulceration, especially if secondary infection takes place. The lesions are found over the dorsum and the hands and wrists, upon the feet and legs and the cheeks, bridge of the nose, forehead and neck. They may extend over the trunk as well. They are symmetrical on the two sides and sharply defined. Burning but no itching is mentioned. The tongue is red and sometimes dry and glazed. Stomatitis and gingivitis are often associated.

The nervous system is perhaps not affected so severely in children as in adults, but three groups of symptoms may be described: those referable to the brain, to the spinal cord and to the spinal nerves. The cerebral symptoms are unquestionably an integral part of the disease and are present to some extent in every well developed case of pellagra. In milder cases the children are merely dull, peevish and irritable. Their faces are expressive of anxiety, depression or apathy. They lack the spontaneous laughter and tireless energy of normal children. They can make no progress at school. There may be tremors of the hands, abnormal fatigue on exertion and unsteadiness of gait. In very severe cases, confusion, hallucinations and delirium occur. Death in coma may follow. Proper treatment causes the disappearance of the delirium, but in some cases the child is thereafter mentally backward.

In adults, pellagra is something associated with ataxia and spasticity of the legs which may be attributed to the lesions in the posterior and lateral columns of the spinal cord. Such symptoms are rare in children but are occasionally observed as in the case given below.

In other cases one finds signs of polyneuritis with weakness and atrophy of the legs, loss of tendon reflexes, pains and tenderness of the calves. It seems to be generally believed at present that polyneuritis is not an essential feature of pellagra but is due to an associated deficiency of vitamin B_1. In

tropical countries optic neuritis with central scotomas is described in association with other symptoms which suggest pellagra.

There is no fever in uncomplicated cases, except in the terminal stages. The blood shows some anemia and perhaps a relative lymphocytosis. Urine is normal. Gastric analysis usually reveals achlorhydria. The spinal fluid is normal or may show a slight excess of globulin.

The course is variable. In some cases the disease is acute or subacute ending in cachexia, dementia and death within a few months. In others, the course is chronic with exacerbations each spring persisting even without proper treatment for a number of years. There may be remissions of several years. The neurological symptoms do not fluctuate so much as the cutaneous and gastrointestinal symptoms and are apt to remain throughout the remissions.

Diagnosis.—The diagnosis depends upon the history of a defective diet and upon the three groups of symptoms: (1) The cutaneous eruption. (2) The gastrointestinal symptoms. (3) The symptoms referable to the nervous system. (4) In doubtful cases the response to treatment is of diagnostic importance.

Prognosis.—Apparently the prognosis is somewhat better in children than in adults and a favorable outcome may be expected if treatment is instituted before the case is far advanced. The gastrointestinal symptoms and the lesions of the skin and mucous membranes are promptly relieved by proper treatment. The symptoms referable to the nervous system and especially the mental changes respond more slowly to treatment and it is not unusual for some degree of mental deficiency to persist.

Treatment.—A diet containing an abundance of fresh milk, meat, eggs and vegetables should be given. Nicotinic acid should be administered in doses of 50 mgs or more every day. Since several vitamin deficiencies may occur together in the same patient, it is wise to give Brewer's yeast and perhaps, liver extract as well.

CASE HISTORY (Ped. 7806-Path. 4435).—*Child of three years developed cutaneous eruption over hands and forearms. This disappeared and returned next year. At age of five years eruption returned. Intractable diarrhea, mental confusion, spasticity and ataxia of legs, slurring speech, death.*

E. A. was a healthy infant. During the first two years he was given milk and did very well. Afterwards, he was given eggs, potatoes, cabbage, peas and rice. His diet was deficient in fresh meat and in milk. At the age of three years he developed an eruption over the hands and forearms which disappeared within a few months. There was some diarrhea at this time but the child is said to have been well in other respects. The next winter the same symptoms reappeared and again passed off after a few months.

When the child was five years and five months of age, the eruption returned for the third time. The backs of the hands and the dorsal surface of the forearms as well as the cheeks and the bridge of the nose became red and scaly. He began to complain of abdominal pain and had six to eight watery stools a day. Within a short time he developed screaming spells and seemed frightened most of the time. In March he became unable to walk, his speech became indistinct and he lost control of his bowels and bladder. For some months he was in a hospital but did not improve. He was brought to Harriet Lane.

Examination revealed that the skin of the forearms, hands, cheeks, and over the bridge of the nose was brown, thickened and scaly. The tongue and indeed all the mucous membranes were red and sore. The child was confused and cried almost constantly. There were coarse tremors of the lips, tongue and hands. The legs were spastic and ataxic. The child did not stand or walk without support. The tendon reflexes were exaggerated and there was bilateral ankle clonus and extensor plantar response. Speech was slurring. The stools were liquid. There was a secondary anemia but no leucocytosis. The spinal fluid was quite normal. Temperature remained essentially normal.

There was no improvement in the child's condition. Little was known about pellagra at that time and he was not given any special diet. In August his mental condition became worse, contractures developed in the legs and emaciation became extreme. He died in stupor. Post-mortem examination revealed the usual findings.

BIBLIOGRAPHY

DENTON, J.: Pathology of pellagra. Am. J. Trop. Med., **5**:173, 1925.

FINE, M. AND LACHMAN, G. S.: Retrobulbar neuritis in pellagra. Am. J. Ophthal., **20**:708, 1937.

GOLDBERGER, J.: Present status of our knowledge of the etiology of pellagra. Medicine, **5**:79, 1926.

McCOLLUM AND SYMMONDS: The Newer Knowledge of Nutrition. New York, The Macmillan Co., 1929.

MEYER, A.: On parenchymatous systemic degenerations mainly in the central nervous system. Brain, **24**:47, 1901.

PEARSON, G. H. J.: Central neuritis. Arch. Neurol. & Psychiat., **20**:366, 1928.

SPIES, T. D., WALKER, A. A. AND WOODS, A. W.: Pellagra in infancy and childhood. J.A.M.A., **113**:1481, 1939.

WALSH, F. B.: *Loc. cit.*

Vitamin B₆ Deficiency

Recent observations seem to indicate that lack of pyridoxine or vitamin B₆ may lead to serious symptoms. It was found that infants fed exclusively on a certain prepared milk formula would lose weight, become irritable, drowsy, confused and sometimes develop convulsions. A hypochromic, microcytic anemia sometimes occurred. Analysis of the formula led to the conclusion that it contained less pyridoxine than human milk. The pyridoxine had apparently been destroyed by the high temperature used in sterilization. The addition of pyridoxine to the formula relieved or prevented the

symptoms. It is also stated that a sensory neuritis may result from prolonged pyridoxine deficiency.

In 1954, Hunt described the case of a baby who had to have 2.0 mgs of pyridoxine a day to prevent convulsions. In 1961, Lombroso showed that a familial genetically determined disorder was responsible for this disorder.

BIBLIOGRAPHY

BEJSOVEC, M. *et al.:* Familial intrauterine convulsions in pyridoxine dependency. Arch of Dis. Childh., **42**:201, 1967.

COURSIN, D. B.: Convulsive seizures in infants with pyridoxine deficient diets. J.A.M.A., **154**:406, 1954.

GARTY, R. *et al.:* Pyridoxine-dependent convulsions in an infant. Arch. Dis. Childhood, **37**:21, 1962.

HUNT, A. D. *et al.:* Pyridoxine dependency: Report of a case of intractable convulsions controlled by pyridoxine. Pediatrics, **13**:140, 1954.

LOMBROSO, C. T.: Vitamine B_6 dependency in infants. Convulsions, irritability and hyperacousia. A familial and genetically determined disorder. Seventh Internat. Congress of Neurology, Rome, Sept. 10, 1961.

MARIE, J. *et al.:* Pyridoxine dependence. The first familial case. Rev. Neurol., **105**:406, 1961.

MOLONY, C. AND PARMELEE, A.: Convulsions in young infants as a result of pyridoxine deficiency. J.A.M.A., **154**:405, 1954.

SCRIVER, C. R.: Vitamin B_6 dependency and infantile convulsions. Pediatrics, **26**:62, 1960.

——— AND HUTCHINSON, J. H.: Vitamin B_6 deficiency syndrome in human infancy. Pediatrics, **31**:240, 1963.

SNYDERMAN, S. *et al.:* Pyridoxine deficiency in the human infant. J. Clin. Nutrition, **1**:200, 1953.

WALDINGER, C. AND BERG, R. B.: Pyridoxine dependency at birth. Pediatrics, **32**:161, 1963.

——— AND ———: Signs of pyridoxine dependency manifest at birth in siblings. Pediatrics, **32**:161, 1963.

Encephalopathy in Infants Recovering From Malnutrition (Kwashiorkor)

Kahn has reported 16 cases in Negro children of South Africa in which during recovery from severe malnutrition a neurological syndrome developed. Gerbasi has reported similar cases from Italy. Kahn's 16 cases were observed among many hundreds of cases of malnutrition for he states that 500 cases of infantile malnutrition pass through his wards every year.

This type of malnutrition is termed infantile pellagra, malignant malnutrition and kwashiokor. It is ascribed to a diet consisting mainly, or entirely, of cereals, and lacking animal proteins and milk. No doubt vitamin deficiency plays a role. The symptoms include retarded growth, edema, angular stomatitis, cheilosis and dermatitis. The hair of the head which in Negro children is black, thick and curly, becomes grayish-brown, thin and straight and the skin turns a light brown color. A diet including abundant quantities of cow's milk gives relief of these symptoms within three or four weeks. No neurological symptoms are observed in such patients except for irritability.

In rare instances infants, after between 6 days to several weeks of proper diet, develop a series of neurological symptoms. There are rhythmical tremors most evident in the arms and hands though in some cases the legs, neck, tongue, face and abdominal muscles are affected. The arms are held in flexion at the elbow and wrist and slightly abducted at the shoulder. Cogwheel rigidity is found in the extremities. The face has a vacant expression and the mouth often stays open. Myoclonus is sometimes seen. The spinal fluid is quite normal. There are no mental changes other than irritability. The tendon reflexes are usually increased.

The prognosis is said to be good and recovery is expected within a few weeks or months. One child, however, showed mild hemiparesis, mental retardation and convulsions three years after treatment.

The cause of this syndrome is obscure. Kahn and Falcke made rather extensive laboratory studies but found nothing which was not present in other malnourished children. The serum electrolytes were normal. There was a mild normochromic anemia. The serum albumin level was low and the serum globulin, high. Serum cholinesterase levels were high. Blood sugar was normal. The electroencephalogram revealed no abnormalities. It is of interest that the administration of abundant vitamins before the onset of the nervous symptoms had no protective value. The suspicion that hepatic encephalopathy might be responsible could not be verified.

Dr. Selma Snyderman has concluded that the deficiency is not due to lack of any specific amino acids but to lack of total nitrogen in the diet. Kwashiorkor in children of less than 6 months of age may have permanent intellectual impairment.

BIBLIOGRAPHY

CRAVIOTO, J. AND ROBLES, B.: Evolution of adaptive and motor behavior during rehabilitation from kwashiorkor. Amer. J. Orthop., **35:**449, 1965.

GERBASI, M.: L'anemia perniciosiforme del lattante. Helvet. pediat. acta., **5:**299, 1950.

KAHN, E.: A neurological syndrome in infants recovering from malnutrition. Arch. Dis. Child., **29:**256, 1954.

——— AND FALCKE, H. C.: A syndrome simulating encephalitis affecting children recovering from malnutrition (kwashiorkor) . J. Pediat., **49:**37, 1956.

STOCH, M. B. AND SMYTHE, P. M.: Infant undernutrition and brain growth. Arch. Dis. Childhood, **38:**546, 1963.

TROWELL, H. C.: Malignant malnutrition (kwashiorkor) . Tr. Roy. Soc. Trop. Med. and Hyg., **42:**417, 1949.

WILLIAMS, C. D.: Nutritional disease of childhood associated with a maize diet. Arch. Dis. Child., **8:**423, 1933.

THE MALABSORPTION SYNDROMES

These syndromes are caused by deficient digestion, absorption or utilization of food, as a result of intestinal disorders such as colitis, coeliac disease, sprue and others. The most constant symptoms include malnutrition,

easy fatigue, abdominal discomfort, loss of appetite, diarrhea, abdominal distention, edema and low blood pressure.

There may be steatorrhea, anemia, reduction of the blood proteins including the gamma globulins, reduction of prothrombin, blood calcium and magnesium.

The neurological manifestations include fatigue, weakness, loss of reflexes and polyneuritis. Subacute combined degeneration of the spinal cord may occur. Defective development and mental deficiency results in children. Tetany and hemorrhagic phenomena are described.

Dudrick *et al.* describe the technique of intravenous feeding in patients who cannot be fed by mouth.

BIBLIOGRAPHY

AITA, J. A.: Neurologic Manifestations of General Diseases. Springfield, Thomas, 1964, p. 339.

ADLERSBERG, D.: The malabsorption syndrome in man. Amer. Jour. Clin. Nutr., 8:166, 1960.

DUDRICK *et al.:* Long term total parenteral nutrition with growth development and positive nitrogen balance. Surgery, 64:134, 1968.

SENCER, W.: Neurologic manifestations of the malabsorption syndrome. J. Mt. Sinai Hosp., 24:331, 1957.

TEXTER, E. C.: The malabsorption syndrome. Jour. Mich. Med. Soc., 60:788, 1961.

WIRTS, C. W. AND GOLDSTEIN, F.: Gastroenterology. Modern Medicine, October 21, 1968, p. 93.

INVOLVEMENT OF THE NERVOUS SYSTEM IN ALLERGIC REACTIONS

Definition.—Several conditions are included in this discussion. (1) Cases in which neurological symptoms, usually lesions of the spinal nerve roots or peripheral nerves, follow the injection of sera for therapeutic purposes or less commonly for the purpose of producing immunity. It is claimed that cerebral symptoms, meningeal reactions and perhaps spinal syndromes may also result. (2) Cases in which neurological conditions, usually cerebral symptoms, occur without the injection of any foreign protein but are accompanied by allergic phenomena. (3) Cases in which paralysis, either acute ascending spinal paralysis or polyneuritis, follows the injection of foreign protein, especially typhoid vaccine, without any of the usual signs of allergy. (4) Cold allergies are rare. A brief case report is given below. A good deal of evidence has been accumulated to show that the perivascular demyelination of measles encephalomyelitis and of the related encephalomyelitides is a result of allergic processes. These conditions are, however, described elsewhere. Miller and Staunton have published a very complete and helpful review of these problems.

Etiology.—Certain sera have been blamed more frequently than others. For example among the 42 cases of neuritis collected by Allen, 26 resulted from the use of tetanus antitoxin, 4 from antidiphtheritic serum, 4 from

antistreptococcic serum, 3 from antipneumococcic serum and 3 from anti-scarlet fever serum. Such figures mean little, for certain sera are used more frequently than others. In only a few cases have vaccines been to blame. Apparently some cases, especially those in which the symptoms are cerebral, are the result of allergic reactions due to spontaneous sensitization to food, etc. In such cases we are probably dealing with a constitutional condition, for a family history of similar reaction is often elicited. No reason can be assigned for the special selection of the nervous system in these cases. Waksman and Adams have published experiments in which central or peripheral nervous tissue with adjuvants were injected into experimental animals. Rabbits injected with peripheral nervous tissue developed lesions only in the peripheral nerves. When injected with central nervous tissue, rabbits developed lesions in the brain and also in the peripheral nerves.

Pathological Anatomy.—There is little or no information available about the anatomical basis of these conditions. Hutinel has described cerebral edema and multiple meningeal hemorrhages in a case in which a violent meningeal reaction developed in the course of treatment for meningococcic meningitis, but the presence of meningitis, of course, makes the significance of such lesions uncertain. Some writers assume that the peripheral nerves are injured by the reaction of the surrounding tissues and that there is in such cases a perineural edema. In the same way the radicular lesions may be connected with the meningeal reaction. However, there is no apparent reason why the nervous tissues may not be directly affected. Kennedy claims that the cerebral symptoms that he has described are due to edema of the cerebral cortex. Experimental work has revealed that congestion and even minute hemorrhage in the nerves and spinal cord may be produced by violent allergic reactions.

Clinical Features.—We shall discuss first the cases in which the injection of sera of various types is apparently responsible. The usual picture may be outlined as follows. From five to twelve days after the serum is administered, most commonly between the seventh and ninth days, the patient develops the usual symptoms of serum sickness such as fever, pruritus, generalized urticaria, erythema or angioneurotic edema, pains in joints, adenitis, eosinophilia, leucopenia and, perhaps, headaches and vomiting. The eyelids may be swollen and the conjunctivae injected and edematous. The cornea may also be edematous. In some cases the retina is involved and the optic nerve head may be hyperemic or actually elevated. Vision may be blurred or reduced, but as a rule is promptly restored to normal. Shortly after this signs and symptoms referable to the nervous system may appear and rapidly reach their maximum intensity. There is often severe reaction at the site of injection and the entire arm or leg, as the case may be, is greatly swollen. The distribution of the paralysis is independent of the site

of the injection, at least to a large extent, for brachial plexus palsy may follow the injection of the serum into the thigh. Frequently serum has never been administered previously.

As a rule, the first manifestations are pains which follow the course of the spinal nerve roots. These are most common in the arms and shoulders and may be unilateral or bilateral. They may be confined to one or two dermatomes or may be widespread. Symptoms of meningeal irritation such as cervical rigidity, Kernig's sign and hyperesthesia are common. The nerve trunks are sensitive to pressure. Within a few days weakness or paralysis of the muscles appears and atrophy develops rather rapidly. The pain may last only a few days or may persist for several weeks. In more than half of all cases, the roots of the brachial plexus are involved. The muscles innervated by the fifth and sixth cervical segments are most frequently affected, so the palsy is of the Erb-Duchenne type. The deltoid, spinati, rhomboids, biceps, brachialis anticus, brachioradialis and often the supinators and extensors of the wrist are weak or paralyzed. In rare cases the lower roots of the plexus are affected. The tendon reflexes are, of course, lost, and the electrical reactions are altered according to the severity of the paralysis. Complete reaction of degeneration may develop. It is very difficult to demonstrate any objective loss of sensibility although paresthesia and hyperesthesia are almost invariably present. If the paralysis is extensive, one can usually find small areas of hypesthesia and analgesia. In such instances the clinical features seem to indicate involvement of the *roots* of the *plexus*. Allergic arthritis is often a complication.

In other cases, the picture is that of a *peripheral nerve lesion*. These are often but not always bilateral and symmetrical. The writer has observed a case in which the cutaneous branches of the femoral nerves were affected on both sides after the injection of anti-scarlet fever serum and another in which the cutaneous antibrachii medialis was involved following the use of antidiphtheritic serum. The latter was also bilateral. In neither case was there any motor loss. The nerves most commonly selected seem to be the radial, sciatic, peroneal, tibial, thoracalis longus and the axillary.

A small number of cases are described in which the symptoms were those of polyneuritis. These do not differ in any way from the more common types of polyneuritis except in the somewhat greater prominence of the sensory phenomena. I have observed one patient who on two separate occasions developed acute anaphylactic shock immediately after being stung by a bee. In each case he developed a mild polyneuritis within the next week. The polyneuritis lasted for several months. I have seen polyneuritis due to penicillin in two patients. One patient had two attacks. The symptoms were not very severe and in all cases there was gradual recovery.

A *meningeal reaction* is not infrequently observed in infants in connec-

tion with severe serum sickness. This is, of course, regardless of the type of serum employed and of the site of injection. In some cases there are general or focal convulsions. Vigorous intraspinous treatment for meningococcus meningitis may give rise to severe meningeal reactions apparently of allergic type. A number of injections are usually given without reaction and then after one more, violent symptoms appear. There may be a great increase in the rigidity, opisthotonos, coma and convulsions. The spinal fluid contains an excess of cells and is under great pressure but the organisms cannot be demonstrated and the sugar and chlorides are not reduced as one would expect were the symptoms due to an exacerbation of the meningitis. Moreover, the cells are chiefly those of the lymphocytic series. Death has resulted in a large percentage of such cases. Spinal cord damage must be extremely rare but several cases are described in which there was clinical evidence of transverse or disseminated lesions.

We have stated above that in some cases the symptoms may develop without the injection of foreign protein but there are nonetheless associated allergic phenomena such as urticaria, angioneurotic edema, hay fever and asthma. There is usually a long history of allergic manifestations and often a similar tendency can be demonstrated in the other members of the family. In most cases of this type the neurological symptoms have been of *cerebral origin*. Thus Foster Kennedy reports the case of a girl of two years who had repeated attacks of violent headache and convulsions in connection with giant urticaria. The child was found to be sensitive to milk and when placed on a milk-free diet was relieved of the attacks. In the case of a boy of eleven years, a prophylactic injection of anti-scarlet fever serum was followed on the fourth day by fever, headache, urticaria and signs of meningeal irritation. On the seventh day papilledema, aphasia and right hemianopia appeared. The spinal fluid was under great pressure but contained only 14 cells. Recovery was complete in four weeks. Several similar cases are described. A long history of symptoms of protein sensitization is usually secured and, as a rule, the symptoms have developed spontaneously although in a few instances they have followed the injection of sera or other foreign protein. Csermely described the case of a patient who developed urticaria on the third day after the injection of antitetanus serum and on the tenth day cerebral symptoms. Death occured on the fourteenth day and post-mortem examination revealed perivascular demyelination similar to that seen in measles encephalitis. Williams and Chafee describe a similar case. Park and Richardson have reviewed the literature dealing with cerebral complications of serum sickness. They find 11 cases previously reported and add 3 of their own. Hemiplegia and aphasia seem to be the commonest manifestations. They suggest that the cerebral vessels are primarily involved and the softenings in the brain are secondary. Meriwether

et al. report the case of a boy of 7 years who, following the injection of serum, developed a prompt anaphylactic reaction and some days later urticaria. The child became stuporous, rigid and developed athetoid movements. Death ensued. Post-mortem examination revealed degeneration in the cerebral white matter and in the basal ganglia perivascular myelin destruction and extensive cell destruction of ischemic type. Various cranial nerve lesions may occur in association with meningeal and cerebral reactions. Laryngeal palsies are sometimes seen.

Dr. Crowe informs me that he has seen six or more children who have developed bilateral deafness of nerve type following the administration of serum for various purposes. There is loss of vestibular reactions in most cases. The deafness has usually appeared in association with signs of serum sickness but is not as a rule associated with injury to the peripheral nerves. McCready has described a case of this type.

The writer has seen a case in which angioneurotic edema of the orbit developed very suddenly in a patient subject to urticaria. There was papilledema, loss of vision and paralysis of the third, fourth and sixth nerves, all of which soon disappeared.

A few cases have been described in which polyneuritis or acute ascending paralysis of Landry's type has followed the injection of foreign protein, notably typhoid vaccine. There is no loss of sphincter control and no loss of sensibility. Death results from paralysis of respiration or bulbar palsy. Since there is no evidence of allergy or at least the usual signs and symptoms are absent, the proper interpretation and classification of these cases is uncertain.

The cerebral damage which in rare instances follows the injection of *pertussis vaccine* is discussed under the term of *toxic encephalopathy* q.v. There seems to be no proof that this condition is due to allergy.

Diagnosis.—The diagnosis as regards the radicular and neuritic type is not difficult. The essential features are the history of injection of serum from five to twelve days before and the development of generalized signs of serum sickness just before the appearance of the neurological manifestations. So many cases of this type have been reported that the association of the neurological symptoms with the allergic reaction seems to be established. As regards the cerebral forms, the situation is not at all clear and it would seem best to scrutinize such cases very carefully before accepting the suggestion that they are really of allergic nature.

Prognosis.—As a rule, the prognosis is very good. The radicular and neural types run a benign course ending in recovery after weeks or months. In especially severe cases, the muscular atrophy may persist for long periods and may never entirely disappear. The cerebral symptoms usually disappear within a few weeks but after several attacks may become permanent. The

prognosis for life seems to be good except in the cases which follow intraspinous serotherapy. The mortality is high in this group.

Treatment.—During the acute stages of the condition, we must treat the allergic phenomena. Adrenaline has been used but no doubt cortisone is more valuable. Calamine lotion is helpful to reduce the itching. If there is evidence of increased intracranial pressure, repeated spinal puncture may be performed or dehydration may be attempted by intravenous urea.

Later the patient may require orthopedic treatment for the palsies. Instruction should be given to refuse further injections of sera unless the situation demands such treatment, in which cases great care must be exercised.

In cases in which the attacks occur spontaneously, the source of the sensitization should be investigated and the offending protein eliminated from the patient's environment. If this is impossible, desensitization must be attempted but always with great caution. Apparently this is a very difficult matter.

CASE HISTORY.—*Cold allergy in a boy of 8 years.*

V. H., a previously healthy boy of 8 years, ate some ice cream. Almost immediately his lips became swollen and his tongue was swollen so greatly that he could not articulate. Urticarial lesions extended over the entire body and extremities. He soon developed double vision, and it was found that both external recti were weak. The pupils were slightly too large and reacted sluggishly to light. There was no evidence of edema of the orbital tissues. He was given benadryl and the swelling of the lips and tongue receded and the urticaria cleared up. When he was examined a week after the onset the weakness of the external recti was still present and the pupils were still sluggish. It was found that the touch of an ice cube on the forearm caused urticaria and even the touch of a cool metal object caused the same reaction.

When seen again 2 weeks after the onset, there was complete loss of ocular movement in all planes bilaterally and a moderate degree of ptosis of the lids. The pupils did not react at all. Vision was still clear. Bilateral facial weakness of peripheral type was present. There was generalized weakness of the arms and legs without ataxia. No loss of sensibility was demonstrable. The tendon reflexes could not be elicited.

It is of interest that the patient's mother would get urticaria during childhood if she drank cold water.

About 3 weeks after the second examination, the child had made an almost complete recovery. The pupils were still slightly sluggish and the left was slightly greater than the right.

BIBLIOGRAPHY

BROWN, A. L.: Ocular manifestations in serum sickness. Am. J. Ophth., **8:**614, 1925.

CSERMELY, H.: Demyelinating encephalopathy following the use of antitetanus serum. Arch. Neurol. & Psych., **64:**676, 1950.

GAYLE, R. F. AND BOWEN, R. A.: Acute ascending myelitis following the administration of typhoid vaccine; report of a case with necropsy findings. J. Nerv. & Ment. Dis., **78**:221, 1933.

GORDON, A.: Motor paralysis of individual nerves following administration of prophylactic serums. J.A.M.A., **98**:1625, 1932.

KENNEDY, R. F.: Certain nervous complications following the use of therapeutic and prophylactic sera. Am. J. Med. Sc., **177**:555, 1929.

————: Cerebral symptoms induced by angioneurotic edema. Arch. Neurol. & Psychiat., **15**:28, 1926.

KRAUS, W. M. AND CHANEY, L. B.: Serum disease of the nervous system. Arch. Neurol. & Psychiat., **37**:1035, 1937.

McCREADY, P. B.: Inner ear deafness from tetanus antitoxin injection. Ann. Otol., Rhin. & Laryng., **47**:247, 1938.

MERIWETHER, L. S. *et al.*: Cerebral pathology following serum anaphylaxis. Arch. Neurol. & Psychiat., **73**:286, 1955.

MILLER, H. G. AND STANTON, J. B.: Neurological sequelae of prophylactic inoculation. Quart. J. Med., **23**:1, 1954.

PARK, A. M. AND RICHARDSON, J. C.: Cerebral complications of serum sickness. Neurology, **3**:277, 1953.

PLITMAN, G. I. AND GENDEL, B. R.: Serum neuritis. Ann. Int. Med., **41**:605, 1954.

WAKSMAN, B. H. AND ADAMS, R. D.: A comparative study of allergic neuritis in the rabbit, guinea pig and mouse. J. Neuropath. & Exp. Med., **15**:293, 1956.

WALSH, F. B.: *Loc. cit.*

WILLIAMS, H. W. AND CHAFEE, F. H.: Demyelinating encephalomyelitis in case of tetanus treated with antitoxin. New England J. Med., **264**:489, 1961.

YOUNG, F.: Peripheral nerve paralysis following use of various sera. J.A.M.A., **98**:1139, 1932.

Chapter V

VASCULAR LESIONS AND CIRCULATORY DISORDERS OF THE NERVOUS SYSTEM

I**NTRODUCTION.**—This chapter is devoted to the discussion of the conditions which give rise to vascular lesions of the nervous system, not only hemorrhage, thrombosis and embolism, but the more general circulatory disorders such as the anemias and conditions causing concentration and increased viscosity of the blood. The infections and intoxications which involve the nervous system indirectly by causing injury to the blood vessels or by altering the properties of the blood are included. Vascular anomalies and malformations are also discussed here. It has been a difficult matter to decide about the proper classification of some of these conditions and the writer is aware of certain disadvantages in the following arrangement.

BIBLIOGRAPHY

AITA, J. A.: Neurologic Manifestations of General Diseases. Springfield, Thomas, 1964.

BANKER, B. Q.: Cerebral vascular disease in infancy and childhood. Jour. Exp. Neurol., **20:**127, 1961.

LEVENS, A. J.: Strokes in children. Modern concepts in cerebrovascular disease. American Heart Ass., 1968, vol. 3, no. 4, p. 17.

SHILLITO, J.: Carotid arteritis—A cause of hemiplegia in childhood. Jour. of Neurosurg., **21:**540, 1964.

WALSH, F. B.: Clinical Neuroophthalmology, 2nd Ed., Baltimore, Williams and Wilkins, 1957.

WISOFF, H. F. AND ROTHBALLER, A. B.: Cerebral thrombosis in children. Arch. of Neurol., **4:**258, 1961.

DISORDERS DUE TO CHANGES IN THE BLOOD VESSELS

HEMORRHAGIC ENCEPHALOPATHY

Definition.—A condition characterized by multiple hemorrhages in the brain due to the presence of a circulating toxin which causes damage to the blood vessels or to the perivascular tissues. See *Toxic encephalopathy* and *Cerebral vascular lesions due to acute infectious diseases.*

Pathological Anatomy.—Several different processes are described by various authorities. The best known type is that due to arsphenamine. Here we find innumerable small hemorrhages surrounding the small blood vessels in the brain and the spinal cord. The usual interpretation offered is that the arsenic has damaged the capillary endothelium and as a result blood has leaked into the surrounding tissues.

Alpers describes a somewhat different condition which he finds in a large variety of intoxications. The essential lesion, he states, is a perivascular

966

necrosis. The blood seeps into this necrotic tissue from the surrounding capillaries with the production of ring hemorrhages. He states that the necrosis may be present without hemorrhage.

Adams *et al.* describe endothelial proliferation and necrosis of the vessel wall with fibrinous exudate in the perivascular tissues and large and small hemorrhages and softenings. This condition is designated as *acute necrotizing hemorrhagic encephalopathy*. The cause was not clear in Adams' cases.

Hurst and others have described *hemorrhagic leucoencephalitis*. In this condition there are acute and severe inflammatory changes in the cerebral white matter with involvement of the blood vessels, hemorrhages and extensive demyelination.

Perivascular hemorrhages are sometimes found in the so-called *perivenous myelinoclasis* which is associated with measles and other exanthemata. Dorothy Russell reports cases of this type and suggests that most cases reported as examples of hemorrhagic leucoencephalitis are really due to perivenous myelinoclasis. Hemorrhagic encephalopathy apparently did not occur in the great epidemic of influenza of 1918, but was discovered, in some cases, in the Asiatic influenza of 1957. McConkey and Daws studied four patients who developed cerebral symptoms following Asiatic influenza. The diagnosis was confirmed by a rise in antibody titers.

Many other causes for multiple hemorrhages in the brain are known, such as those due to true encephalitis, changes in the properties of the blood, septicemia, embolism and softenings due to thrombosis. These are described elsewhere.

Clinical Features.—Almost all acute infectious diseases are mentioned among the causes of hemorrhagic encephalopathy. Influenza, pneumonia of various types, especially the virus pneumonia, scarlet fever, diphtheria, pertussis, typhus fever, typhoid fever, and malaria are among those most frequently incriminated, but the complete list is a long one. Virus infections probably play an important role in such conditions. Various exogenous poisons may produce the same effects. Arsenical drugs, especially arsphenamine, carbon monoxide and hydrocyanic acid may be mentioned. Vitamin deficiency is also a possible cause.

It is not possible to delineate any typical clinical picture, but as a rule the onset is abrupt and marked by high fever, convulsions and coma. Muscular rigidity and bilateral Babinski signs are usually found. Bulbar symptoms may be present. If the patient survives, there may be spastic paraparesis, with ataxia, difficulty in control of the bladder, reduction of cutaneous sensibility and some mental changes. Adams and Kubik describe cases of acute necrotizing hemorrhagic myelopathy in which the process is confined to the spinal cord.

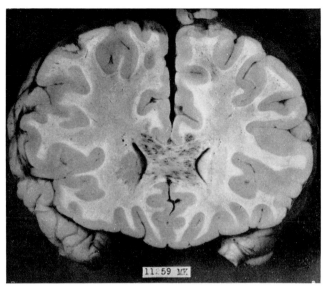

FIG. 203. Hemorrhagic encephalopathy showing multiple small hemorrhages in the corpus callosum and subcortical white matter.

In some cases there are petcchiae in the skin and perhaps a few red cells in the urine and in the spinal fluid.

The course of the illness is variable but as a rule the active stages of the illness last only a few days.

BIBLIOGRAPHY

ADAMS, R., CAMMERMEYER, J. AND DENNY-BROWN, D.: Acute necrotizing hemorrhagic encephalopathy. J. Neuropath. & Exp. Neurol., 8:1, 1949.

ADAMS, R. D. AND KUBIK, C.: Morbid anatomy of demyelinating diseases. Am. J. Med., 12:510, 1952.

ALPERS, B. J.: The so-called brain purpura or hemorrhagic encephalitis. Arch. Neurol. & Psychiat., 20:497, 1928.

BAKER, A. B.: Hemorrhagic encephalitis. Am. J. Path., 11:185, 1935.

GLOBUS, J. H. AND GINSBURG, S. W.: Pericapillary encephalorrhagia due to arsphenamine. Arch. Neurol. & Psychiat., 30:1226, 1933.

HENSON, R. A. AND RUSSELL, D.: Acute hemorrhagic leucoencephalitis. J. Path. & Bact., 54:227, 1942.

HURST, E. W.: Acute hemorrhagic leucoencephalitis. Med. J. Australia, ii:1, 1941.

IRONSIDES, R. AND HOWELL, H.: Case of hemiplegia due to hemorrhagic encephalitis following diphtheria. Proc. Roy. Soc. London, Sec. Dis. Child., 19:3, 1925.

McCONKEY, B. AND DAWS, R. A.: Neurologic disorders associated with Asian influenza. Lancet, ii:15, 1958.

RUSSELL, D.: The nosological unity of acute hemorrhagic leucoencephalopathy and acute disseminated encephalomyelitis. Brain, 78:369, 1955.

SHALLARD, B. AND LATHAM, O.: A case of acute haemorrhagic leucoencephalitis. Med. J. Australia, February 10, p. 145, 1945.

WALSH, F. B.: *Loc. cit.*

CEREBRAL VASCULAR LESIONS FOLLOWING ACUTE INFECTIOUS DISEASES

Definition.—Changes in the cerebral blood vessels associated with acute infectious diseases which may lead to circulatory disturbances and even softenings. See also *acute toxic encephalopathy* and *hemorrhagic encephalopathy*.

Etiology.—Almost any severe infection may be responsible but pertussis, pneumonia, scarlet fever, diphtheria, measles, dysentery, influenza, typhus fever, typhoid fever, meningitis and rheumatic fever are among the most common causes.

Pathological Anatomy.—It is well known that lesions in the walls of the systemic, as well as the cerebral, blood vessels are frequently found in almost all severe infectious diseases. One of the first extensive studies was that of Wiesel who investigated the arteries of 300 young subjects who died of diphtheria, influenza, pneumonia and typhoid fever. He found destructive lesions in the smooth muscle and the elastic tissue of the media of large and small arteries which sometimes resulted in necrosis. These changes did not reach their maximum until the 18th day or later and since there were no inflammatory phenomena, were attributed to bacterial toxins. These lesions were said to heal leaving small scars. They were said to be entirely non-specific. Innumerable other studies have been made. The smaller vessels are frequently found to show proliferation of the endothelium and even the walls of the capillaries are altered. Changes in the cerebral blood vessels in acute rheumatic fever are mentioned in the discussion of Sydenham's Chorea and Rheumatic Fever q.v.

The damage to the nervous system is apparently variable in degree and on the whole not as great as one might anticipate. There may be edema of the brain, minute hemorrhages and many small areas of partial or complete ischemia.

Dr. Vasile Von Llea performed a biopsy of the cerebral cortex in a girl of ten years who had hemiparesis and focal convulsions. He found inflammatory changes in the small and medium sized blood vessels. A muscle biopsy revealed the same vascular lesions. Subsequently, muscle biopsy was performed in thirty cases of epilepsy in childhood. In seven children there were inflammatory changes in the blood vessels. The authors believe that these lesions are of rheumatic origin.

Bilaloglu states that in addition to the cutaneous eruption, the painful joints and renal damage, patients suffering from Schönlein-Henoch syndrome may have arteriolitis and occlusion of the blood vessels with cerebral vascular lesions.

Occasionally one encounters large softenings in the brain due to thrombosis or embolism of a large vessel or even a massive hemorrhage. These are no doubt a result of the focal necroses in larger arteries which Wiesel described and of emboli due to mural thrombi in the heart.

Clinical Features.—It is impossible to outline a clear clinical picture. In cases in which the process is a diffuse one the commonest symptoms are delirium, stupor, coma and generalized rigidity often associated with convulsions. Focal signs are not conspicuous as a rule, but the Babinski sign may be present on both sides. Such symptoms are apt to appear during the height of the original illness but do not always terminate when the systemic symptoms disappear. The spinal fluid as a rule shows only a moderate increase of protein.

In other instances, the clinical symptoms are such as to indicate a single focal lesion of large size. Hemiplegia and aphasia are most common. The onset is almost invariably abrupt. Softenings or hemorrhages are found if the patient comes to post-mortem examination. In such instances, dehydration with increased viscosity of the blood may play a role in inducing thrombosis in either veins or arteries. Embolism resulting from fragments of mural thrombi formed in the heart is sometimes responsible.

I have seen a child of 6 years who had recovered from a severe attack of pneumonia a week before. He suddenly fell to the floor and was unconscious for a short time. On examination he displayed left hemiparesis and blindness of the right eye. There was occlusion of the right central retinal artery. The pulse of the right brachial artery was absent. It seemed that an embolus arising in the lung had broken into three parts which lodged in the right middle cerebral artery, the central retinal artery and the right brachial artery.

Diagnosis.—The diagnosis depends upon the association of the cerebral symptoms described above with acute infectious disease and the elimination of brain abscess, dural sinus thrombosis and meningitis. One cannot anticipate the histological nature of the process. A sudden hemiplegia is as a rule clear evidence of a large vascular lesion.

Prognosis.—This depends upon the amount of irreversible damage done to the brain and can scarcely be estimated in the early stages of the illness.

Treatment.—No specific treatment is possible.

BIBLIOGRAPHY

ALLBUTT, C.: Diseases of the Arteries, New York, Macmillan Co., 1915.

BILALOGLU, N.: Schönlein-Henoch syndrome. Clin. Pediat., 2:541, 1963.

BROWN, M. H.: Aortitis associated with systemic infections. Ann. Clin. Med., 5:353, 1926.

CAIRNS, H. AND RUSSELL, D. S.: Cerebral arteritis and phlebitis in pneumococcal meningitis. J. Path. & Bact., 58:649, 1946.

FROTHINGHAM, C.: The relation between acute infectious diseases and arterial lesions. Arch. Int. Med., **8**:153, 1911.

KLOTZ, O.: Diseases of the Media. Univ. Pitts. Med. School Publication, 1911.

MALLORY, F. B.: Infectious lesions of blood vessels. Boston City Hosp. Repts., p. 148, 1913.

NORAN, H. H., BAKER, A. B. AND LARSON, W. P.: Central nervous system in pneumonia: An experimental study. Arch. Neurol. & Psychiat., **58**:653, 1947.

NORAN, H. H. AND BAKER, A. B.: The central nervous system in pneumonia: A pathological study. Am. J. Path., **22**:579, 1946.

ROLLESTON, J. D.: Three cases of hemiplegia following scarlet fever. Arch. Neurol. & Psychiat., **6**:530, 1908.

———: Transient hemiplegia in diphtheria. Rev. Neurol. & Psychiat., **14**:145, 1916.

SHELDON, W. P. H.: Intracranial hemorrhage in infancy and childhood. Quart. J. Med., **20**:353, 1927.

SMITHIES, F.: Hemiplegia as complication of typhoid fever with report of a case. J.A.M.A., **49**:389, 1907.

TOWNSEND, S. R., CRAIG, R. L. AND BRAUNSTEIN, A. L.: Neurophilic leucocystosis in the spinal fluid associated with vascular accidents. Arch. Int. Med., **63**:848, 1939.

VON LLEA, VASILE et al.: Betrachtungen über die vaskuläre. Epilepsie bei Kindern Sonderdruck aus Psychiatrie, Neurologie und medizinische Psychologie 11 Jarhgang Heft, **5**:137.

WIESEL, J.: Die Erkrankungen Arterieller Gefasse im Verlaufe akuter Infektionen. Ztschr. f. Heilk. Abt. f. path. Anat., **27**:69, 1907.

WILLIAMS, E. M.: Typhoidal hemiplegia with report of three clinical cases and one with necropsy. Am. J. Med. Sc., **163**:677, 1912.

WINKELMANN, N. W. AND ECKEL, J. L.: Endarteritis in the small cortical vessels in severe infections and toxemias. Arch. Neurol. & Psychiat., **21**:863, 1929.

ACUTE INFANTILE HEMIPLEGIA OF OBSCURE ORIGIN

Definition.—I shall take up at this point the cases of sudden hemiplegia and other focal cerebral syndromes which develop without discoverable cause during infancy and early childhood and which have been described in the past by various terms, such as Marie-Strümpell encephalitis, polio-encephalitis, etc.

Pathological Anatomy.—Very few careful post-mortem examinations have been made and consequently little is known of the anatomical process. In one case, which will be described below, the writer found a large softening in the motor cortex which was due to thrombosis of the superficial branches of the middle cerebral artery. The cerebral arteries all showed thick intimal plaques composed of connective tissue and containing a good deal of fat. There were numerous areas of necrosis in the media and the muscular layers were reduced to one half of their proper thickness in certain regions. The elastic lamellae were swollen and in some places disintegrated completely. Reduplication of the elastic lamellae was also present. The adventitia was unaltered. In the right middle cerebral artery one of the plaques had broken down and thrombosis had resulted causing infarction in the corresponding area of the cortex. The arteries of the viscera showed similar but less severe changes. Several other autopsies have revealed

similar arterial lesions. The cases of Ghetti and of Tuthill may be mentioned in this connection. In a few cases of this type venous thromboses have been found. The anatomical evidence, therefore, points to vascular lesions as the cause of this condition, although it is still inadequate to justify the statement that vascular lesions are responsible in all cases. There is no anatomical evidence at present to support the theory of Strümpell that such cases represent the cerebral localization of the virus of epidemic poliomyelitis.

Kudo describes 8 cases in children between the age of 4 years and 13 years in whom hemiplegia developed. In some cases this developed gradually and in other cases the onset was abrupt. In one case, the left side and then the right side were involved. In all cases the circle of Willis was partially occluded, the internal carotid artery was almost always narrow and in 5 cases the basilar artery was narrowed. In all cases there were extensive collateral channels. These cases were all found in subjects of Japanese race.

Lhermitte *et al.* discuss hypoplasia of the internal carotid. This condition may be associated with ischemic accidents, hemorrhage due to aneurysm and extensive collateral vessel formation. Turnbull discusses agenesis of the internal carotid artery.

Clinical Features.—We have observed more than two hundred cases of this type at the Harriet Lane Home, so it is evident that it is not in any sense a rare condition. Boys and girls seem to be affected with equal frequency. The child is usually under six years and the condition is rare after ten years. In a large proportion of cases the child has been in excellent health for months or years before the onset and the neurological symptoms suddenly develop without warning. Otitis has preceded the neurological symptoms in some cases.

The clinical symptoms, as a rule, might be explained by a single gross vascular lesion of the brain. The child suddenly falls to the floor in a fit. The movements usually involve only one side of the body but may be bilateral. There is almost always loss of consciousness and frequently vomiting. The temperature may rise to 101° or 103°F. The convulsions recur for several hours or days and the child usually remains stuporous or comatose. Then the convulsions cease, the temperature falls to normal and the child slowly regains consciousness. It is then evident that there is hemiplegia, hemianopia or some other focal signs referable to a cerebral lesion.

The spinal fluid is, as a rule, quite negative. We have never found an excess of cells at the onset or within the next few days. In several cases, however, we have found a number of leucocytes in the spinal fluid during the second week of the illness. These we have been inclined to attribute to the meningeal reaction to necrotic tissue.

In the early stages of the illness, the affected hemisphere may be so swollen that ventriculographic study may suggest brain tumor. Later, of course, atrophy becomes evident. Arteriograms may reveal occlusion of one of the cerebral arteries or occasionally occlusion of the carotid artery.

Later the hemiplegic extremities become spastic and the usual deformities develop. The affected limbs do not develop as well as the normal limbs and years later may be very small and distorted. Tremor or athetosis may appear. In other cases the focal signs may largely or completely disappear. Unfortunately, in almost half of all cases convulsive seizures recur from time to time. They may be frequent or may occur at only long intervals. As a rule in such cases the seizures are confined to the affected side of the body or at least begin on that side. If the lesion is in the left hemisphere, speech may be delayed but unless the child's mental condition is seriously impaired, speech will be acquired eventually. There is usually some degree of mental defect but this is usually not very severe except in the cases characterized by frequent convulsive seizures. In such cases the child may become an idiot. In some instances the paralysis disappears a short time after the initial illness but reappears after each seizure in a transient form.

It is extremely unusual to observe a recurrence of the paralysis. I have never seen hemiplegia recur. Dr. David Clark, however, has told me of two cases in which there was a second episode with hemiplegia. Occasional cases of thrombosis of the internal carotid artery are seen in children between the ages of 5 and 12 years. Duffy *et al.*, Fisher, Stevens and Cabieses and Saldias report such cases and I have seen another which is given in abstract below.

Fowler reports two cases of basilar artery occlusion in childhood which, of course, caused the standard signs and symptoms. Dooley and Smith describe the case of a boy of 6 years who developed occlusion of the basilar artery.

Diagnosis.—The diagnosis depends upon the clinical picture described above and upon the elimination of other causes. It is usually necessary to follow the patient for some time to feel reasonably sure of the diagnosis. It is almost certain that a number of conditions give rise to this syndrome and no doubt more careful studies will eventually bring to light the various etiological factors.

Levens lists the following causes of strokes in children:

I. Acute Infantile Hemiplegia (Hemiplegia of Childhood)
   Idiopathic
   Other—Thrombotic, Embolic, etc.
II. Thrombosis
   Arterial (Brain and Neck)

      congenital cyanotic heart disease
      trauma to head and neck
      atlantoid compression
      structural defects of intima and media
      familial hypercholesterolemia
      arteritis
      infantile
      pulseless disease (Takayasu's Disease)
      tuberculous endarteritis
    extensions and complications
      mucormycosis
      neoplasm
      retropharyngeal abscess
  Venous and Venous Sinuses
    infectious
      meningitis
      brain abscess
      direct extension from nasal sinuses
      association with infectious disease or febrile illness
    non-infectious
      congenital heart disease
      dehydration
      neonatal
      Pickwickian Syndrome
    direct involvement
      leukemia
      neuroblastoma
III. Emboli
  Heart Disease
    congenital cyanotic
    rheumatic
    endocarditis, bacterial
      acute
      subacute
  Sepsis with Pneumonia or Lung Abscess
    fat
    air—exchange transfusion, i.v. infusion
    thromboembolic phenomena associated with exchange transfusions
    thromboembolic phenomena associated with homocystinuria
IV. Hemorrhage
  Bleeding Tendencies and Blood Dyscrasias
    hemorrhagic disease of the newborn

hemophilia

vitamin C deficiency

leukemia

thrombotic thrombocytopenic purpura

sickle cell anemia

Lupus Erythematosus; Periarteritis Nodosa

Uremia

Malignant Hypertension and Arteriosclerosis of Childhood

Arteriovenous Malformations and Aneurysms

Idiopathic

Prognosis.—The mortality is relatively low and very few children die in the acute stage. The outlook for recovery is, however, unfavorable. Severe hemiplegias rarely disappear completely although the child always recovers enough power to walk. The arm is usually useless, however. In about half of all cases epilepsy follows and mental deficiency of various grades is to be expected. Later in life it is possible to demonstrate cortical sensory loss and hemianopia in some cases.

Treatment.—There is no specific treatment. During the acute stages phenobarbital may be used to control the convulsions. Later we may employ the usual orthopedic treatment for hemiplegia and phenobarbital or dilantin for epilepsy if the seizures develop.

CASE HISTORY (Path. 9033-Ped. 47516).—*Sudden convulsive seizure in a healthy boy of three years and 11 months followed by stupor and left hemiplegia. Death. Post-mortem examination revealed fatty plaques in cerebral arteries with infarction in right cerebral cortex.*

J. B., a white boy of three years and 11 months, was the child of healthy parents. Two siblings were living and well. Growth and development had been normal in every way. At the age of six months the child had measles and scarlet fever occurred at two years. These illnesses were

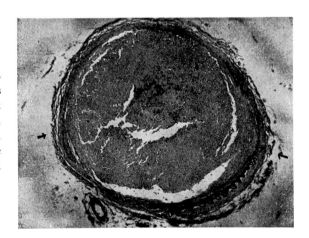

FIG. 204. Section through thrombus in the right middle cerebral artery. On the left the elastic tissue is destroyed and the muscularis is severely affected. The arrows point to broken down intimal plaques. (From Ford, F. R. and Schaffer, A. J. The etiology of infantile hemiplegia. Arch. of Neurol. and Psychiat. 1927, vol. 18, p. 323.)

very mild and were accompanied by no neurological symptoms. Prompt and complete recovery followed and the patient enjoyed a year of perfect health preceding the present illness. The day before the onset the child seemed to be irritable and would not eat his breakfast. He seemed to have a slight cold in the head. A few hours later two severe convulsive seizures developed in rapid succession. These involved the left side exclusively. The child remained unconscious and the next day was brought into the Harriet Lane Home.

Examination revealed a well-developed, well-nourished boy of the given age who was stuporous and restless. Temp. 100.5°F. Pulse 60. Resp. 20. Weight 38 lbs. 11 ozs. There was no rigidity of the neck. The ears were normal as were the throat, tonsils and chest. The skin showed no eruption. The head and eyes deviated to the right and the left arm and leg were flaccid and powerless. The tendon reflexes were about equal on the two sides but the right plantar reflex was flexor and the left, extensor. No clonus was elicited. The retinae were quite normal and there was no suggestion of papilledema. W.B.C. 10,600. Hb. 75 per cent. Spinal fluid: cells 2. Globulin 0. Wassermann reaction in blood and spinal fluid negative. Mastic curve 000000000.

The temperature rose to 103°F., the stupor deepened into coma and the child died on the third day of the illness.

Post-mortem examination revealed no disease of the viscera. The heart was not enlarged and the valves were smooth. There was a very mild bronchitis which did not extend to the terminal bronchi. The kidneys and liver were normal. Nothing was found to indicate syphilis.

The brain showed softening and swelling in the fronto-parietal region on the right which corresponded to the distribution of the cortical branches of the middle cerebral artery. On section it was found that the softening did not penetrate below the subcortical white matter and the internal capsule was intact as were the basal ganglia. A thrombus was found in the right middle cerebral artery just beyond the point where the penetrating branches to the capsule are given off. The intima of this artery showed numerous plaques of connective tissue which were infiltrated by deposits of lipoids. One of these had ulcerated and thrombosis had resulted. The media showed atrophy of the muscular layers and there was fragmentation and reduplication of the elastic lamellae. The adventitia was unchanged. There was nothing to suggest an inflammatory process and no signs of syphilis. The other cerebral arteries all showed the same changes but there were no more infarcts or thrombi. The visceral arteries showed beginning changes similar to those found in the cerebral arteries. The meninges were normal and the venous sinuses and veins were also normal.

The cause of the changes in the cerebral arteries remained obscure despite the most careful and complete post-mortem examination.

CASE HISTORY.—A previously healthy girl of 5 years, M. E., developed a severe headache in the right frontal region on June 26, 1957. A short time

later she vomited and seemed to be slightly drowsy. The next day she seemed to be better but on June 28, she was found to have weakness of the left arm and leg.

Neurological examination revealed left hemiparesis with increased tendon reflexes on the left side. There was a grasp reflex on the left. The right carotid pulse was reduced. Medical examinations gave negative results. An arteriogram was performed and it was found that the right internal carotid artery was obstructed just proximal to the bifurcation. A number of laboratory procedures were carried out but these need not be detailed for they reveal no evidence of any systemic disorder.

Anticoagulants were given. The child did well. Within two weeks the neurological signs had disappeared.

The child was examined on August 22 by the courtesy of Dr. Harold Stevens. She showed no neurological abnormalities at that time.

BIBLIOGRAPHY

CABIESES, F. AND SALDIAS, C.: Thrombosis of the internal carotid artery in a child. Neurology, **6**:677, 1956.

DAVIE, A. C. AND COXE, W.: Occlusive disease of the carotid artery in children. Arch. of Neurol., **17**:313, 1967.

DOOLEY, J. M. AND SMITH, K. R.: Occlusion of the basilar artery in a 6 year old boy. Neurology, **18**:1037, 1968.

DUFFY, P. E. *et al.:* Acute infantile hemiplegia secondary to spontaneous carotid thrombosis. Neurology, **7**:664, 1957.

FISHER, R. G. AND FRIEDMAN, K. R.: Carotid thrombosis in children. J.A.M.A., **170**:1918, 1959.

FORD, F. R. AND SCHAFFER, A. J.: The etiology of infantile (acquired) hemiplegia. Arch. Neurol. & Psychiat., **18**:323, 1927.

FOWLER, M.: Two cases of basilar artery occlusion in childhood. Arch. Dis. Childhood, **37**:78, 1962.

GHETTI, M.: Case of infantile hemiplegia. Brit. Med. J., **1**: Epitome 1, 1910.

IRISH, C. W.: Cerebral vascular lesions in new born infants and young children. J. Pediat., **15**:64, 1939.

KUDO, T.: Spontaneous occlusion of the circle of Willis. Neurology, **18**:485, 1968.

LEVENS, A. J.: Strokes in children. Modern concepts of cerebrovascular disease. Amer. Heart Ass., October 1968, vol. 111, No. 4, p. 17.

LHERMITTE, F. *et al.:* Hypoplasia of the internal carotic artery. Neurology, **18**:439, 1968.

MITCHELL, R. G.: Venous thrombosis in acute infantile hemiplegia. Arch. Dis. Childhood, **27**:95, 1952.

ROTHMAN, P. E.: Polioencephalitis. Am. J. Dis. Child., **42**:124, 1931.

STEVENS, H.: Carotid artery occlusion in childhood. Pediatrics, **23**:699, 1959.

TIZARD, J. P. M. *et al.:* Disturbances of sensation in children with hemiplegia. J.A.M.A., **155**:628, 1954.

TURNBULL, I.: Agenesis of the internal carotid artery. Neurology, **12**:598, 1962.

TUTHILL, C. R.: The elastic layer in cerebral vessels. Arch. Neurol. & Psychiat., **26**:268, 1931.

WYLLIE, W. G.: Acute infantile hemiplegia. Proc. Roy. Soc. Med. London, **41**:459, 1948.

THROMBOSIS OF THE DURAL SINUSES OF MARANTIC TYPE

Definition.—This type of dural sinus thrombosis is frequently termed marantic, primary, or nonseptic. It is not associated with demonstrable in-

vasion of the blood stream by bacteria. The septic thrombosis of the lateral sinus so frequently associated with mastoiditis is discussed in Chapter III.

Pathological Anatomy.—It must be kept in mind that the venous channels of the brain form innumerable anastomoses with one another and that occlusion of a limited segment of a cerebral vein or dural sinus frequently causes very little disturbance of the circulation. Unless the thrombosis is very extensive and causes obstruction of various collateral channels or unless there is an important anomaly in the formation of the vessels, actual softening does not result. When destructive lesions occur, they are usually extensive and accompanied by congestion, hemorrhage and widespread edema. For example, thromboses of the lateral sinuses cause no significant damage to the brain though increased intracranial pressure is not rare. Thrombosis of the superior longitudinal sinus may also cause little or no significant injury to the brain if the clot does not extend into the cerebral veins but when the clot is extensive and extends into the collaterals so as to cause interruption of the circulation of the superior portions of the hemispheres, we may find great congestion and hemorrhagic softening of the upper half of the frontal and parietal lobes with edema of the whole brain and evidences of increased intracranial pressure. We have seen two cases in which the superior longitudinal sinus was occluded by small meningiomas which caused no deformity of the ventricles but caused an accumulation of cerebrospinal fluid under high pressure. Thrombosis of the straight sinus and of the vein of Galen may also be compensated to some extent but the formation of extensive clots in these vessels usually causes hemorrhages and softening in the central white matter of the cerebral

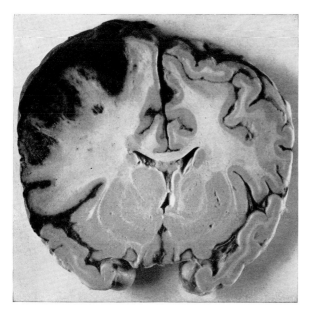

Fig. 205. Thrombosis of the longitudinal sinus extending into the cortical veins on the right and causing extensive softening in the cortex. (By the courtesy of Dr. Woodhall.)

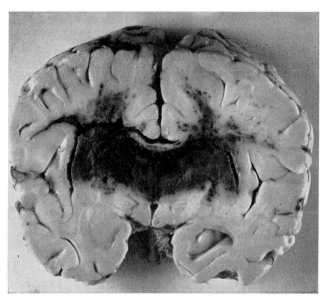

Fig. 206. Thrombosis of the straight sinus and the vein of Galen showing softening and hemorrhage in the basal ganglia and central parts of the hemispheres. (By the courtesy of Dr. Woodhall.)

hemispheres and basal ganglia with bleeding into the ventricles. Thrombosis of the cavernous sinus apparently always causes definite signs, but since this condition is almost always of septic type, the symptoms may be due to infection in the orbit in large part.

Etiology.—It is taught that primary dural sinus thrombosis is the result of three groups of factors: (1) Injury to the endothelium of the vessels by bacterial toxins and other poisons. (2) Changes in the blood which favor clotting, such as increased viscosity, concentration, anemia, etc. (3) Slowing of the blood stream due to cardiac weakness, etc. No doubt all of these factors are important.

This condition may follow a large number of diseases such as dysentery, diphtheria, prolonged diarrheas, anemias of various types, nutritional disturbances, wasting illness due to chronic infections such as tuberculosis, malignant growth, marasmus and cachexias of all kinds. Extensive burns may be responsible. Congenital heart disease and polycythemia may lead to dural sinus thrombosis. It is not unlikely that intravenous injections and transfusions may play a part in some cases. Puncture of the superior longitudinal sinus may be responsible, especially if there is anemia or some other condition favoring thrombosis. Barnett and Hyland mention head injuries and hyperpyrexia among the causes of dural sinus occlusion. Phillips finds that the fibrinogen in the blood is sometimes increased.

Clinical Features.—The age of onset is on an average about eight or nine

months and it is unusual to find sinus thrombosis of this type after the fourth year. Many authorities state that this condition occurs most frequently in the late summer and early fall probably because of the prevalence of diarrheas and nutritional disturbances at this time. The child is usually in poor general condition but is not always cachectic. Anemia is usually present but may be masked by concentration of the blood. We have found sickle cell anemia in several cases. Blood cultures are negative. The spinal fluid may be clear, xanthochromic or frankly bloody. There is rarely any striking increase of white cells but counts up to 30 lymphocytes may be found. The pressure is almost invariably increased and the protein content above the normal level.

The signs and symptoms associated with thrombosis of each sinus will now be discussed.

Thrombosis of the Superior Longitudinal Sinus.—It has been stated above that thrombi of limited extent may fail to produce significant disturbances of the circulation and hence, give rise to no symptoms. Even in more extensive thrombosis, clinical signs and symptoms are often absent or are obscured by other features of the illness. In other cases the onset may be abrupt and the symptoms severe. Sudden loss of consciousness and convulsions may mark the onset. The convulsions may be bilateral or unilateral at first but usually involve both sides eventually. In several cases we have observed fine clonic twitchings which were almost exactly rhythmical and which involved the arms and face as well as the legs. Muscular rigidity is almost invariably present and often the head is retracted. Signs of increased intracranial pressure develop, as a rule, very shortly after the onset. The fontanels bulge, vomiting develops and the optic nerve heads become edematous. Edema of the forehead and anterior part of the scalp may appear. In cases in which the thrombus is confined to the posterior part of the sinus, the superficial veins of the scalp may become distended. These veins emerge from the region of either the anterior or posterior fontanel, where they form a caput medusae and flow downward into the veins of the face and neck. Signs of focal cerebral lesions are frequently but not invariably observed. The most typical syndrome but not the most common is that of cerebral paraplegia with loss of voluntary control of the bladder which results from softening of the paracentral lobules. The arms may be involved to some extent. In most cases the symptoms are predominantly unilateral and hemiplegia is not uncommon. Puncture of the sinus may encounter much resistance and may fail to yield blood.

The ventricles are small at first due to edema, hemorrhage and congestion but later, if the child survives, become dilated due to the loss of tissue.

Woolf described the post-mortem findings in three cases in which fever, dehydration and suppuration in the head or neck were followed by convul-

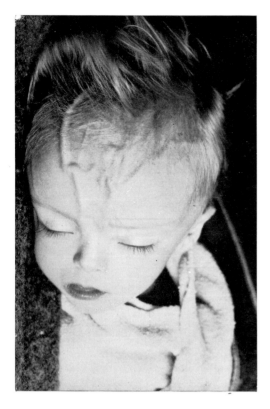

FIG. 207. Thrombosis of the posterior part of the longitudinal sinus of long duration showing collateral circulation.

sions, bilateral paralysis and coma. These children remained mentally defective and displayed a spastic diplegia. The lesions in the brain indicated thrombosis of the superior longitudinal sinus.

The marantic type of dural sinus thrombosis is found in the superior longitudinal sinus very frequently. It is believed that the numerous lacunae and fibrous septa in this sinus favor the development of thrombosis.

Emery performed post-mortem examinations on twenty-five children who died of pulmonary embolism. He found the usual causes were thrombosis of the dural sinuses, and of veins in the liver and nasopharynx.

Thrombosis of the Straight Sinus.—We have seen only a few cases of thrombosis of this sinus. If the thrombus is extensive enough to obstruct the blood flow from the great vein of Galen, the child may become comatose and rigid. There may be involuntary movements or convulsions. The intracranial pressure is greatly elevated within a short time and hemorrhage into the cerebral ventricles give rise to blood stained spinal fluid. The clinical picture seems to be that of decerebrate rigidity. Death occurs very promptly.

Thrombosis of the Cavernous and Lateral Sinuses.—Thrombosis of these sinuses is usually of septic-type and the subject is, therefore, discussed

in Chapter III. As a rule, non-septic thrombosis of one lateral sinus is either non-symptomatic or is manifest only by signs of increased intracranial pressure. Bilateral thrombosis causes intense intracranial pressure.

Diagnosis.—We should always consider the possibility of sinus thrombosis in the cases of infants who develop cerebral symptoms during the course of severe anemias, diarrheas, nutritional disturbances and cachexias. If convulsions, stupor, signs of increased intracranial pressure and perhaps cerebral palsies appear, sinus thrombosis should be suspected. The signs characteristic of occlusion of each sinus are taken up above. The conditions most difficult to distinguish from primary sinus thrombosis are abscess of the brain and subdural hematoma. Angiography by injection of diodrast into the carotid arteries does not always give clear visualization of the venous sinuses. Frenckner has employed the injection of a radiopaque substance into the sinuses to demonstrate thrombosis. He injects the dye through a trephine opening near the torcular Herophili. Ray *et al.* inject the dye in the anterior part of the superior longitudinal sinus. One does not always get adequate filling of the venous channels by these methods, but it is claimed that occlusion of the dural sinuses may be demonstrated.

Prognosis.—In cases of thrombosis of the superior longitudinal sinus in which the symptoms are fully developed and the diagnosis is, therefore, fairly clear, the outlook is very unfavorable and death almost invariably results. We have observed several cases, however, in which the diagnosis seemed to be established and in which the child survived. In one case the patient was left with hemiplegia, focal epilepsy and some mental defect, in another, there was moderate optic atrophy with reduction of vision and severe mental defect. It is impossible to give any estimate of the mortality or expectation of recovery since the diagnosis is so frequently uncertain.

Treatment.—Adequate amounts of fluid should be administered and every effort should be made to maintain the circulation. When there is greatly increased intracranial pressure and papilledema, subtemporal decompression may be the means of saving vision. Heparin has been employed to prevent extension of the clot but this drug must be used with considerable caution, for it is not easy to control. Dicumarol is also employed and seems to be a safer drug. Barnett and Hyland warn against the use of anticoagulants because of the danger of provoking hemorrhage.

CASE HISTORY (Path. 7835-Ped. 33643).—*Thrombosis of the superior longitudinal sinus with hemorrhagic infarction of superior portions of the hemispheres in infant with sickle cell anemia. Coma, spasticity of the legs, double Babinski response and signs of increased intracranial pressure.*

M. T., colored boy of 18 months, was seen for the first time December 28, 1923. He had been a healthy boy and had walked and talked at the age

of 15 months. Suddenly, two days before admission, he had begun to vomit and had become stuporous. His condition slowly grew worse and diarrhea developed.

Examination revealed a dehydrated child who showed signs of recent loss of weight. The fontanels were tense. The optic discs showed beginning edema. The legs were very spastic with increased tendon reflexes, bilateral ankle clonus and extensor response. Spinal puncture revealed blood-tinged fluid under increased pressure. Blood could not be obtained from the longitudinal sinus. The examination of the blood revealed the usual signs of sickle cell anemia. The stupor deepened into coma, respiration became of the Cheyne-Stokes type, the temperature rose from 99° to 104°F. and the child died in convulsions.

Post-mortem examination revealed a premortem thrombus in the superior longitudinal sinus with softening and hemorrhagic infiltration of the superior frontal and parietal lobes of the hemispheres. These changes extended almost to the fissure of Sylvius. There was also hemorrhage into the subarachnoid spaces over the superior and lateral surfaces of the brain which had spread to some extent into the basal cisternae. The brain was much swollen. The usual changes of sickle cell anemia were found in the blood-forming organs.

CASE HISTORY (Path. 13535-Ped. 86531).—*Child of 10 weeks with congenital strictures of the ureters and hydronephrosis, developed thrombosis of the straight sinus with hemorrhagic softenings about the ventricles and central portions of the hemispheres, decerebrate rigidity and death.*

R. R. began to vomit at the age of one week. It was noticed at the end of a month that his abdomen was distended.

Examination at the age of 10 weeks revealed an undernourished infant who was markedly dehydrated. There were large sausage-shaped masses felt in either flank and the kidneys were enlarged. Blood pressure was 170/120. N.P.N. 106 mgs. Urine showed albumen. The ureters were catheterized with some difficulty and the next day, bilateral nephrostomy was performed. A transfusion was given. The day after operation the child became comatose and developed general rigidity. The arms were flexed, the legs extended and the head retracted. The fontanels bulged. Cisternal puncture yielded yellow fluid containing 3000 red cells per cm. The pressure was greatly elevated. Death resulted a few hours later.

Post-mortem examination revealed thrombosis of the straight sinus and of the great vein of Galen. There was gross hemorrhage into the cerebral ventricles and areas of hemorrhagic softening about the ventricles which included the thalami and corpora striata. A little blood was found in the subarachnoid spaces. There was also bilateral hydroureter and hydronephrosis due to congenital stricture.

BIBLIOGRAPHY

ASKENASY, H. M. *et al.:* Thrombosis of the longitudinal sinus: Diagnosis by carotid angiography. Neurology, **12**:288, 1962.

BAILEY, O. T. AND HASS, G. M.: Dural sinus thrombosis in early life. 1—Clinical manifestations and extent of brain injuries. J. Pediat., 11:755, 1937.

BAILEY, O. T. AND HASS, G. M.: Dural sinus infection in early life. Recovery from acute thrombosis of superior longitudinal sinus and relation to certain acquired cerebral lesions in childhood. Brain, 60:293, 1937.

BARNETT, H. AND HYLAND, H.: Non-infective intracranial venous thrombosis. Brain, 76:36, 1953.

BEDFORD, T. H. B.: The great vein of Galen and the syndrome of increased intracranial pressure. Brain, 57:1, 1934.

BEST: Heparin and thrombosis. Brit. M. J., ii:977, 1938.

BYERS, R. K. AND HASS, G. M.: Thrombosis of the dural venous sinuses in infancy and in childhood. Am. J. Dis. Child., 45:1161, 1933.

DOYLE, J. B.: Obstruction of the longitudinal sinus. Arch. Neurol. & Psychiat., 18:374, 1927.

EDWARDS, E. A.: Anatomic variations of the cranial venous sinuses; their relation to the effect of jugular compression in lumbar manometric tests. Arch. Neurol. & Psychiat., 26:801, 1931.

EMERY, J. L.: Pulmonary embolism in children. Arch. Dis. Childhood, 37:591, 1962.

GARDNER, W. J.: Otitic sinus thrombosis causing intercranial hypertension. Arch. Otolaryng., 30:252, 1939.

HOLMES, G. AND SARGENT, P.: Injuries of the superior longitudinal sinus. Brit. Med. Jour., 2:493, 1915.

PHILIPS, G.: Cerebral thrombophlebitis and fibrinogen. B. J. Neurol., Neurosurg. & Psychiat., 11:263, 1948.

RAY, B. S., DUNBAR, H. S. AND DOTTER, C. T.: Dural sinus venography as an aide to diagnosis in intracranial disease. J. Neurosurg., 8:23, 1951.

SMITH, J. C.: Primary cerebral thrombophlebitis. J.A.M.A., 148:613, 1952.

SYMONDS, C. P.: Hydrocephalic and focal cerebral symptoms in relation to thrombophlebitis of the dural sinuses and cerebral veins. Brain, 60:531, 1938.

————: Otitic hydrocephalus. Neurology, 6:681, 1956.

WALSH, F. B.: Ocular signs of thrombosis of the intracranial venous sinuses. Arch. Ophth., 17:46, 1937.

WOODHALL, B.: Variations of the cranial venous sinuses in the region of the torcular herophili. Arch. Surg., 33:297, 1936.

WOODHALL, B.: Anatomy of the cranial blood sinuses with particular reference to the lateral. Laryngoscope, October 1939.

WOOLF, A. L.: The pathology of acute infantile cerebral diplegia. J. Ment. Sc., 101:610.

MALIGNANT HYPERTENSION AND ARTERIOSCLEROSIS OF CHILDHOOD

Etiology.—This is a variety of the so-called essential hypertension. Its precise origin is uncertain. Demonstrable evidences of renal insufficiency are usually not present until the terminal stages of the disease.

Pathological Anatomy.—There is always more or less advanced arteriolar sclerosis identical with that found in adults. The large arteries are often thickened and there may be atheroma of the aorta. Hypertrophy and dilatation of the heart are usually present. Contracted kidneys with ischemic atrophies, degenerations and necroses and similar but less severe changes in other organs are described. The brain usually shows many minute areas of necrosis due, no doubt, to the arteriolar sclerosis. Such lesions are probably

the cause of the diffuse atrophy of the brain which is so commonly found. In some cases there are also large hemorrhages or softenings due to damage to the cerebral arteries.

Clinical Features.—There seems to be little or no tendency to familial incidence and either sex is affected. The onset may be at any time after the age of six years. Severe and frequent headaches are usually the first symptoms and are often associated with vertigo and vomiting. Examination in the early stages of the disease reveals hypertension of various degrees. The systolic pressure may reach 250 mgs of mercury and the diastolic may be over 200. The urinalysis, blood chemistry and phenolphthalein test of renal function may all be normal. There may be little or no thickening of the peripheral arteries and only moderate enlargement of the heart at first. The optic nerve heads usually show outspoken swelling and often hemorrhages. In certain cases this is distinguished with difficulty from the papilledema due to brain tumor. As a rule, however, the retinal arteries are thickened and there are white patches of exudate in the retinae which make it evident that we are dealing with the so-called albuminuric retinitis. Apparently there may be two distinct processes seen in the fundi; papilledema due to increased intracranial pressure and "albuminuric retinitis" due to local changes in the retina which are probably a result of circulatory disturbances. The spinal fluid is under high pressure in some cases and may reach 500 mm of water. It may contain an excess of globulin and sometimes blood.

Symptoms referable to the nervous system are very prominent. Convulsions both general and focal are frequent. Transient or persistent hemiplegia, hemiparesis, aphasia and hemianopia may occur. It is believed that transient hemiplegias and focal convulsions are often due to vascular spasm and not to organic obstruction of the circulation. Such manifestations are attributed to hypertensive encephalopathy. The persistent hemiplegias are probably always due to actual hemorrhage or softenings. Griffith has emphasized the frequency of facial palsy of peripheral type and palsies of the sixth nerve are not uncommon. Fleeting amaurosis is observed.

The course is a rapid one and is often marked by relatively acute exacerbations. In the later stages of the disease nitrogen retention develops with all the evidences of renal insufficiency. There may be anemia, nosebleed and hemorrhages from the bowels. Death may occur from uremia, from heart failure or from cerebral hemorrhage.

It must be pointed out that all of the symptoms just enumerated may occur in various types of renal failure apparently as a result of the associated hypertension. Chronic nephritis with or without associated hyperparathy-

roidism may lead to extensive arteriosclerosis with cerebral and cardiac infarctions.

Diagnosis.—The diagnosis depends upon the elevation of the blood pressure, the thickenings of the peripheral arteries, enlargement of the heart, and upon the changes in the retinae. The last may usually be distinguished by an experienced physician from those due to brain tumor, for the thickening of the retinal arteries develops very early in malignant hypertension. Contrary to the popular impression, increased intracranial pressure due to brain tumor does not, as a rule, cause persistent elevation of the blood pressure. Ventriculography reveals a normal or slightly dilated ventricular system, but should be avoided if possible for puncture of the brain in this condition may cause serious intracranial hemorrhage.

The diagnosis of hypertension demands, of course, an understanding of the normal levels of the blood pressure at various ages. The following table gives the average values obtained by a number of investigators.

Age	Systolic	Diastolic
At birth	55 mm Hg.	40 mm Hg.
10th day	70	50
6th month	80	55
Before puberty	90-100	60-65
After puberty	100-110	65-70

If the diagnosis of hypertension is made, several possibilities must be considered. (1) Hypertension associated with renal insufficiency or damage to a renal artery. (2) Hypertension associated with coarctation of the aorta. (3) Hypertension associated with sudden and pronounced increase of intracranial pressure such as that due to hemorrhage, edema or sudden hydrocephalus. (4) Paroxysmal hypertension due to pheochromocytoma. Insley and Smallwood report four cases in children in which papilledema was present. (5) Benign hypertension at puberty which soon recedes. (6) Essential hypertension which is often malignant. (7) Hypertension in certain diseases such as acrodynia and lead poisoning. (8) Hypertensive encephalopathy due to over-dosage with ACTH or cortisone. (9) Hypertension due to excessive production of aldosterone with or without adrenal adenoma. (10) Hypertension with Cushing's syndrome. (11) Hypertension in hyperthyroidism. (12) Hypertension with congenital adrenal hyperplasia. (13) The pulseless disease of Takayashu.

In dealing with changes in the blood vessels of children one must keep in mind not only arteriosclerosis resulting from chronic nephritis and hypertension, but hyperparathyroidism, and periarteritis nodosa.

Prognosis.—The course of malignant hypertension in childhood is relatively brief and averages between one and five years.

Treatment.—No treatment is satisfactory. Diets are ineffective. Recently several operations have been devised for the relief of this condition. These involve in general section of the abdominal and thoracic sympathetic nerves. It cannot be said that any of these operations has been satisfactory but some brilliant results are claimed for each procedure and their ultimate value is still undetermined. Various drugs such as the rauwolfia alkaloids, veratrum veride and hexamethonium are now employed.

BIBLIOGRAPHY

ABT, A. P. AND FEINGOLD, B. P.: Blood pressure in infancy and childhood. Am. J. Dis. Child., **40**:1285, 1930.

AMBERG, S.: Hypertension in the young. Am. J. Dis. Child., **37**:335, 1929.

CARMAN, C. T. AND BRASHEAR, R. E.: Familial occurrence of pheochromocytoma. New England Jour. Med., **263**:419, 1960.

CLAUSEN, E. G.: Pheochromocytoma in children. Amer. Jour. Surg., **94**:409, 1957.

CRAIG, J.: Malignant hypertension in childhood. Arch. Dis. Child., **6**:157, 1931.

DANARAJ, T. J. AND ONG, W. H.: Primary arteritis (pulseless disease) of the abdominal aorta in children causing bilateral stenosis of the renal arteries and hypertension. Circulation, **20**:856, 1959.

FARQUAR, J. W.: Pheochromocytoma in childhood. Jour. Roy. Coll. Surg. Edinb., **3**:300, 1958.

GRANT, F. C.: The differential diagnosis of tumor of the brain. The importance of considering renal hypertension with choked disc. Arch. Neurol. & Psychiat., **27**:816, 1932.

GRIFFITH, J. Q.: Involvement of the facial nerve in malignant hypertension. Arch. Neurol. & Psychiat., **29**:1195, 1933.

GUILD, H. AND KINDELL, F.: Arteriosclerosis in childhood; report of 2 cases. Bull. Johns Hopkins Hosp., **62**:159, 1938.

HAGGERTY, R. J. *et al.:* Essential hypertension in infancy and childhood. J. Dis. Child., **92**:535, 1956.

HOLMAN, R. L.: Atherosclerosis. A pediatric nutrition problem? Am. J. Clin. Nutrition, **9**:565, 1961.

HUTCHINSON, R. AND MONCRIEFF, A.: Hypertension in children. Brit. J. Child. Dis., **27**:201, 1930.

INSLEY, J. AND SMALLWOOD, W. C.: Pheochromocytoma in children. Arch. Dis. Childhood, **37**:606, 1962.

JEWESBURY, E. C. O.: Atypical intracerebral hemorrhage. Brain, **70**:274, 1947.

KENNEDY, R. I. *et al.:* Malignant hypertension in a child. Cure following nephrectomy. Am. J. Dis. Child., **61**:128, 1941.

KRETCHMER, N. *et al.:* Primary aldosteronism in a nine-year-old child. Pediatrics, **23**:1115, 1959.

OLIVER, W. J. *et al.:* Hypertension in infancy and childhood. J. Michigan Med. Soc., **59**:82, 1960.

OSTER, J.: Arterial hypertension in a child cured by nephrectomy. Acta med. Scandinav., **128**:42, 1947.

PEPPER, H. P.: Malignant hypertension simulating brain tumor. Penn. Med. J., **35**:75, 1931.

SNYDER, C. H. AND VICK, E. H.: Hypertension in children caused by pheochromocytoma. Am. J. Dis. Child., **73**:581, 1947.

TAUSSIG, H. AND HECHT, M. S.: Studies concerning hypertension in childhood. Bull. Johns Hopkins Hosp., **62**:482, 1938.

TAUSSIG, H. AND REMSEN: Essential hypertension in a boy two years of age. Bull. Johns Hopkins Hosp., **57**:183, 1935.

TETVETAGLU, F. AND LEE, C.: Adrenal pheochromocytoma in a child—Review of 47 cases in children. Am. J. Dis. Child., **91**:365, 1956.
WALSH, F. B.: *Loc. cit.*

INVOLVEMENT OF THE NERVOUS SYSTEM IN PERIARTERITIS NODOSA

Etiology.—The cause is unknown. It was formerly believed that an infection must be to blame. Recently it has been suggested that this condition represents a sensitization phenomenon.

Pathological Anatomy.—The primary change is an inflammatory reaction in the muscularis of the smaller arteries which leads to necrosis. The process may extend into the intima causing reduction of the lumen and thrombosis or destruction of the vascular walls may lead to aneurysm formation with rupture and hemorrhage. The arteries of the kidneys, heart and gastrointestinal tract are affected most frequently but the peripheral nerves and the muscles are involved in nearly 20 per cent of the cases and the brain or spinal cord in somewhat less than 10 per cent. When the cutaneous vessels are affected, we may find ecchymoses or purpuric lesions.

The lesions in the nervous system seem to be softenings due to the changes in the arteries and are hence, similar to those in other organs. The damage to the spinal nerves are also apparently in most instances due to ischemia though it has been claimed that a true toxic polyneuritis may occur.

Clinical Features.—The disease is not common but is as frequent during childhood as at other ages. It is said to be four times as frequent in males as in females. The symptomatology is so diverse that it is almost impossible to give any adequate description.

The constitutional symptoms include fever which is usually irregular and may be remitting, tachycardia, weakness, emaciation and loss of weight. The blood may show a marked anemia with pronounced leucocytosis and often eosinophilia which may reach 50 per cent.

The kidneys are frequently affected and we often find nitrogen retention and blood, casts and albumin in the urine. Death from uremia is not uncommon. Arterial hypertension is present in a large percentage of cases. Cardiac symptoms are not as frequent as one might expect but there may be evidence of myocardial disease or even coronary thrombosis. Abdominal pains, vomiting, melena and other evidences of intestinal involvement are among the more common symptoms. Intestinal ulcerations are described. Pulmonary infections including bronchitis and pneumonia are common and may be responsible for death. Asthma may precede the other manifestations of the disease by several years. Polyarthritis may be the most striking evidence of the disease. The joints resemble those of acute rheumatic fever. Cutaneous eruptions are prominent in the so-called neurocutaneous

form of the disease. This type is relatively frequent in children and runs a somewhat longer course than the other types. There are areas of necrosis in the skin, erythematous lesions, hemorrhagic nodules and purpuric spots. In such cases there is also bleeding from the mucous membranes. Phlebitis may occur.

Pains in the extremities are among the more constant features and occur in nearly 40 per cent of cases. The muscles are soft, wasted and very tender. We have seen constant fascicular twitchings in one case which were intense enough to cause irregular movements of the fingers. *Palsies* of the *peripheral nerves,* especially the common peroneal, tibial, radial, median and ulner nerves are very common. In the writer's small experience, the peripheral nerves have been affected individually and one at a time so as to suggest multiple separate lesions of the nerves rather than a generalized toxic polyneuritis, but apparently cases of the latter occur. Cody and Williams found Cogan's syndrome in periarteritis nodosa. There is undoubtedly a myositis also in some cases and tenderness of the muscles may be found when the nerves are not involved.

The *central nervous* system is not infrequently involved. The commonest clinical picture is that of a cerebral vascular lesion with the abrupt onset of hemiplegia, aphasia or hemianopia. Convulsions may occur. In some cases there are evidently a great many lesions in the nervous system involving the brain stem, cerebellum and spinal cord as well as the brain. We have seen occlusion of both central retinal arteries. Subarachnoid hemorrhage is described and meningitis with a pronounced elevation of the spi-

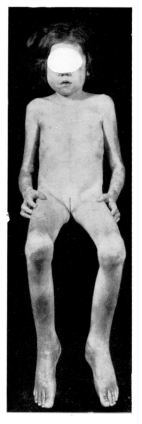

Fig. 208. Photograph of girl with periarteritis nodosa showing cutaneous eruption, edema of the face and legs and bilateral foot-droop. Thrombosis of the central retinal arteries caused complete blindness.

nal fluid cell count and increased protein content. Walsh describes small white exudates in the retinae arranged in a circular fashion around the disc. In the case of Runge and Melzer, there were bulbar disturbances, difficulty in speech, cerebellar ataxia, bilateral pyramidal tract lesions and mental changes.

Diagnosis.—The fever, eosinophilia, hypertension, progressive loss of renal function and damage to the peripheral nerves suggest the diagnosis,

which may be confirmed by biopsy of a bit of muscle. However, a negative biopsy is not conclusive evidence against the diagnosis.

Prognosis.—The mortality is undoubtedly high. Certainly, most cases in which the diagnosis has been established have resulted fatally, usually within a year or less.

Treatment.—Treatment is unsatisfactory. Cortisone and its derivatives may have some therapeutic value.

Frohnert and Sheps state that among patients treated with corticosteroid therapy the five year survival period rate was 48 per cent as compared with a rate of 13 per cent for untreated patients.

CASE HISTORY (Ped. A-56982).—*Child of eight years developed attacks with headache, fever and abdominal pain. Later, convulsions and finally right hemiplegia and aphasia. Finally hypertension and death in uremia. Post-mortem examination revealed periarteritis nodosa.*

E. T., a girl of eight years and five months, was admitted to Harriet Lane Home on August 17, 1947. One year before, she had begun to complain of headaches and abdominal pains. These symptoms recurred at frequent intervals until the date of admission. Some eight months before, it had been discovered that the child had fever during these attacks. As a rule, the temperature rose to 101°F. or 102°F. but once it reached 105°F. Some three months before admission, the child began to have convulsions. Several seizures occurred during a period of a week. After the last one, the child remained in coma for 10 days. When she regained consciousness it was found that there was right hemiplegia and aphasia. Some evidences of hemiplegia were found on the left side also. The hemiplegia diminished but the aphasia persisted. A blotchy erythematous eruption was seen on the face and body at times. Pains in the joints were now added to the other symptoms.

On examination the child was found to be much underweight. No cutaneous eruption was present. She understood what was said to her and would do as she was requested to do, though she could not talk. The cranial nerves were all in order except for a mild right facial weakness of central type. The optic fundi showed engorged veins with narrow arteries and a few small patches of white exudate scattered over the retinae. There was weakness and spasticity of the right arm, but no neurological signs could be made out in the right leg or on the left side. Irregular twitches were seen in the right hand. The liver and spleen were enlarged. The heart was also enlarged. The blood pressure was 155/110.

There was no anemia or leucocytosis. The blood W.R. was negative. The urine showed albumin 2 plus, casts and some red and white cells. The phthalein excretion was 51 per cent. The N.P.N. was 125 mgs.

The child grew rapidly worse. The N.P.N. rose gradually to 146. Cyanosis and edema developed and she died in uremia on August 29, about a year after the onset.

Post-mortem examination revealed the usual evidences of periarteritis nodosa, the kidneys, heart, spleen, liver and brain being most severely affected.

CASE HISTORY.—*Girl of 18 years developed peripheral nerve involvement in both arms. Periarteritis found on biopsy.*

M. F., a previously healthy girl of 18 years developed pain in both shoulders in March 1968. Later the pain in the shoulders ceased but pain developed in the left arm. She then found that there was weakness of extension at the left wrist and proximal joints of the digits.

Examination on May 2, 1968 revealed gross weakness in extension at the left wrist and proximal joints of the digits. There was some loss of cutaneous sensibility over the dorsal aspect of the left thumb and index finger. Nothing else was found. She had no fever and no evidence of visceral involvement was found in a routine examination at a hospital.

She was seen again on July 11. She stated that the pain had ceased. The weakness was still present. She had noted wasting of the long extensors of the left wrist and fingers. On examination the right arm displayed gross weakness of the spinati with some wasting. There was complete paralysis of extension of the left wrist and of extension at the proximal joints of the digits. There was 2.0 cm wasting of the left forearm.

Exploration of the left radial nerve just above the elbow revealed a segmental lesion of the radial nerve which was somewhat thickened and atrophy of the nerve below this level. The distal portion of the nerve did not respond to electrical stimulation. Biopsy of the sheath of the nerve and adjacent muscle showed typical changes of periarteritis nodosa. Biopsy of the sensory branch of the nerve showed merely degeneration.

BIBLIOGRAPHY

ARKIN, A.: A clinical and pathological study of periarteritis nodosa. Am. J. Path., 6:401, 1930.

BALO, J.: Ueber eine Haufung von Periarteritis Nodosa Fallen, nebst Beitragen zur Polyneuritis infolge von Periarteritis Nodosa. Virchows. Arch. f. Path. Anat., 259:773, 1926.

CODY, D. T. AND WILLIAMS, H. L.: Cogan's syndrome. Pro. Mayo Clin., 37:372, 1962.

DICKSON, W. E. C.: Polyarteritis acute nodosa and periarteritis nodosa. J. Path. & Bact., 12:31, 1908.

FROHNERT, P. P. AND SHEPS, S. G.: Long term follow-up study of periarteritis nodosa. Amer. Jour. Med., 43:8, 1967.

JOHANSMANN, R. J. AND ZEEK, P.: Periarteritis nodosa in week old infant. A.M.A. Arch. Path., 58:207, 1954.

KEITH, H. M. AND BAGGENSTOSS, A. H.: Primary arteritis (periarteritis nodosa) among children. J. Pediat., 18:494, 1941.

KERNOHAN, J. W. AND WOLTMAN, H. W.: Periarteritis nodosa: A clinicopathologic study with especial reference to the nervous system. Arch. Neurol. & Psychiat., 39:655, 1938.

LAMB, A. R.: Periarteritis Nodosa—A clinical and pathological review of the disease with a report of two cases. Arch. Int. Med., 14:481, 1914.

LOVELACE, R. E.: Mononeuritis multiplex in polyarteritis nodosa. Neurology, 14:434, 1964.

MALMUD, N.: A case of periarteritis nodosa with decerebrate rigidity and extensive encephalomalacia in a five year old child. J. Neuropath. & Exp. Neurol., 4:88, 1945.

MARIE, J. *et al.:* Periarteritis nodosa in infancy. Ann. Pediat., 8:26, 1961.

MILLER, H. G. AND DAILEY, R.: Clinical aspects of periarteritis nodosa. Quart. J. Med., **15**:255, 1946.

PARKER, G. W. AND BAHRD, M. G.: Periarteritis nodosa with report of a case. Ill. Med. J., **62**:367, 1932.

RICH, A. AND GREGORY, J. E.: The experimental demonstration that periarteritis nodosa is a manifestation of hypersensitivity. Bull. Johns Hopkins Hosp., **72**:65, 1943.

RICHARDSON, M.: Lasionen des Zentralnervensystems, beim Periarteritis Nodosa. Ztschr. f. d. ges. Neurol. u. Psychiat., **115**:626, 1928.

ROBERTS, F. B. AND FETTERMAN, G. H.: Polyarteritis nodosa in infants. J. Pediat., **63**:519, 1963.

ROTHSTEIN, J. L. AND WELT, S.: Periarteritis nodosa in childhood, report of two cases with necropsy observations. Abstracts of cases in the literature. Am. J. Dis. Child., **46**:1277, 1933.

RUNGE, R. AND MELZER, H.: Über Periarteritis Nodosa mit Starker Beteilung des Zentralnervensystems. J. f. Psychol. u. Neurol., **40**:298, 1930.

VINING, C. W.: A case of periarteritis nodosa with subsequent recovery. Arch. Dis. Child., **13**:31, 1938.

WALSH, F. B.: *Loc. cit.*

INVOLVEMENT OF THE NERVOUS SYSTEM IN SYSTEMIC LUPUS ERYTHEMATOSUS

Etiology.—The cause is unknown. Some authorities regard this condition as a sensitization phenomenon.

Pathological Anatomy.—Pathological alterations may be found in all of the organs of the body. According to Klemperer, Pollack and Baehr the basic process is a fibrinoid degeneration of the collagen; that is, the fibrous connective tissue, and all the lesions in the body may be explained in this way. The walls of the blood vessels are involved and it appears that most of the damage which occurs in the nervous system is due to vascular occlusion. Daily describes lesions in the walls of the blood vessels causing partial occlusion and sometimes thrombosis of vessels leading to areas of demyelination and even softening in the brain. Malamud and Saver describe similar lesions. Penn and Rowan describe cases in which softenings occurred in the spinal cord.

Clinical Features.—Half of all cases are said to begin between the ages of 10 and 20 years. Females are affected more frequently than males. The average course is about four years to a fatal termination. Remissions and exacerbations are often seen.

The commonest symptoms are fever, arthritis, cutaneous lesions and chronic nephritis. Fever is always present when the disease is in an active state. The arthritis is clinically very similar to rheumatoid arthritis and is sometimes very painful. The typical cutaneous eruption consists of small, discoid, erythematous lesions which result eventually in atrophy of the skin and pigmentation. They are often found on the nose and cheeks in the so-called butterfly distribution. In the disseminated variety they are distributed widely over the whole body. These lesions may appear in repeated crops and seem to be provoked by exposure to sunlight. It must be emphasized

that the cutaneous eruption is not always present in this condition and that the presence of typical cutaneous lesions does not justify the diagnosis of lupus erythematosus in the sense of a systemic disease. It must be mentioned that urticaria and thrombocytopenic purpura are sometimes seen and that ulcerations of the mucous membranes with hemorrhages may occur. Evidence of nephritis is present in a large percentage of all cases but hypertension is apparently not common. Pneumonia and fibrinous pleurisy are typical features of this disease. There may be verrucous endocarditis, fibrinous pericarditis and myocardial infarction. The liver may be enlarged and the spleen also. Generalized enlargement of the lymph nodes is often found. The usual blood picture is that of anemia and leucopenia. The serum globulin is often increased. Ross states that in lupus erythematosus the capillaries of the nail fold are thick and disorganized and run in horizontal and oblique directions. The number of capillaries is reduced.

My purpose in discussing this disease is to call attention to the fact that the nervous system is frequently involved. Tumulty and Harvey state that 25 per cent of all cases exhibit clear evidence of involvement of the brain. Convulsions either generalized or focal are not unusual. Hemiplegia with or without aphasia has been noted repeatedly. In my experience, the onset of such symptoms is sudden and the clinical features are suggestive of vascular occlusion. Mental disturbances are present in most cases in the terminal stages. Confusion, delirium and coma are seen. In some instances the spinal fluid contains an excess of lymphocytes and sometimes blood. We have not observed the peripheral nerve lesions which are seen so commonly in periarteritis nodosa, but peripheral neuritis is described. Goldberg and Chitanondh describe the case of a child who had three attacks of polyneuritis, the last of which was fatal. Post-mortem examination revealed the lesions of lupus erythematosus. They state that four other cases of the same condition have been reported. Piper reports a case in which softenings occurred in the spinal cord. Extensive myositis may occur. Siekert and Clark state that neurological disorders often appear before the systemic symptoms. They mention convulsions, subarachnoid hemorrhage, aphasia, paraplegia, hemiplegia vertigo, nystagmus, neuropathy, cortical blindness, chorea, hallucinations and various mental changes.

The retinae may display fluffy exudates and small hemorrhages as Maumenee has shown. A moderate degree of papilledema is not rare. In one instance we have observed thrombosis of the central retinal vein.

Lewis states that nephrosis associated with lupus may be recognized by a typical serum electrophoresis pattern. The serum albumin levels are less than 2 gm per 100 cc and the alpha-2-globulin concentration is normal.

Cortisone and hydrocortisone are the most useful drugs and are often

given for long periods. Various antimalaria drugs such as camoquin, i.e. amodiaquin hydrochloride and chloroquine arc recommended.

BIBLIOGRAPHY

BAILEY, A. A. *et al.:* Neuritis associated with systemic lupus crythematosus. New England Jour. Med., **253:**693, 1955.

COOK, C. *et al.:* Lupus erythematosus in children. Pediatrics, **26:**570, 1960.

COPELAND, G. D. *et al.:* Systemic lupus erythematosus. Amer. Jour. Med. Sc., **236:**318, 1958.

DAILY, D.: Central nervous system in acute lupus erythematosus. J. Nerv. & Ment. Dis., **102:**462, 1945.

DUBOIS, E. L. *et al.:* Clinical manifestations of systemic lupus erythematosus. J.A.M.A., **190:**104, 1964.

FULTON, W. H. AND DYKEN, P. R.: Neurological syndromes of systemic lupus erythematosus. Neurology, **14:**317, 1964.

GEISER, J. D.: Disseminated lupus erythematosus in children. Dermatologica, **124:**129, 1962.

GLASER, G.: Lesions of the central nervous system in disseminated lupus erythematosus. Arch. Neurol. & Psychiat., **67:**745, 1952.

GOLDBERG, M. AND CHITANONDH, H.: Polyneuritis with albumincytologic dissociation in the spinal fluid in systemic lupus erythematosus. Am. J. Med., **27:**342, 1959.

HARVEY, A. McG., SHULMAN, L. E., TUMULTY, P., CONLEY, C. L. AND SCHOENRICH, E.: Systemic lupus erythematosus. Medicine, **33:**291, 1954.

HEPTINSTALL, R. AND SOWRY, G.: Peripheral neuritis in lupus erythematosus. Brit. Med. J., **i:**525, 1952.

KLEMPERER, P., POLLACK, A. AND BAEHR, G.: The pathology of disseminated lupus erythematosus. Arch. Path., **32:**569, 1941.

————: Diffuse collagen disease. J.A.M.A., **119:**331, 1942.

LEWIS, F. N.: The diagnosis of lupoid nephrosis. Canad. M. A. J., **87:**584, 1962.

MALAMUD, N. AND SAVER, C.: Neuropathologic findings in disseminated lupus erythematosus. Arch. Neurol. & Psychiat., **71:**723, 1954.

MAUMENEE, A. E.: Retinal lesions in lupus erythematosus. Am. J. Ophth., **23:**971, 1940.

MEISLIN, A. AND ROTHFIELD, N.: Systemic lupus erythematosus in childhood. Pediatrics, **42:**37, 1968.

O'CONNOR, J. F.: Psychoses associated with systemic lupus erythematosus. Ann. Int. Med., **51:**526, 1959.

PENN, A. S. AND ROWAN, A. J.: Myelopathy in systemic lupus erythematous. Arch. of Neurol., **18:**337, 1968.

PIPER, P. G.: Disseminated lupus erythematosus with involvement of the spinal cord. J.A.M.A., **153:**215, 1953.

ROBINSON, R. C. V.: The use of camoquin in the treatment of discoid lupus erythematosus. Bull. School of Med. Univ. Maryland, **42:**14, 1957.

ROSS, J. B.: Nail fold capillaroscopy. Jour. Invest. Dermatol., **47:**282, 1966.

ROTHFIELD, N. F. AND PACE, N.: L.E. cell test. New England Jour. Med., **266:**535, 1962.

SIEGEL, M. *et al.:* Comparative study of rheumatoid arthritis and systemic lupus. New Eng. Jour. Med., **273:**893, 1965.

SIEKERT, R. G. AND CLARK, E. C.: Neurologic signs and symptoms as early manifestations of systemic lupus erythematosus. Neurology, **5:**84, 1955.

TUMULTY, P. A. AND HARVEY, A. McG.: The clinical course of disseminated lupus erythematosus. Bull. Johns Hopkins Hosp., **85:**47, 1949.

WALSH, F. B.: Clinical Neuro-ophthalmology. Williams and Wilkins Co., Baltimore, 1957, 2nd ed.

IDIOPATHIC HYPERLIPEMIA

These children have soft yellow papules on the knees, elbows and buttocks as well as on the trunk, face, thighs, hands and feet. These are

termed xanthomas. They are not found on the eyelids. Lipemia retinalis is often present. The serum is milky white and there is a great increase of all the lipids.

Attacks of abdominal pain are often the first manifestation. The abdomen is rigid and tender. There may be fever and leucocytosis. Such symptoms last from one to four days. Cerebral vascular lesions, angina, myocardial infarction and pancreatitis occur. Fatty plaques are found in the blood vessels and endocardium. This is an autosomal recessive disease.

BIBLIOGRAPHY

Hsia, D. Y.: Idiopathic Hyperlipemia. Inborn Errors of Metabolism. Year Book Publishers Inc., 1959, p. 230.

PRIMARY HYPERCHOLESTEREMIA

This condition differs from idiopathic hyperlipemia by the fact that the fasting serum is always clear. The serum cholesterol is increased. There are xanthomas in about a quarter of the patients. They involve the tendons of Achilles, the extensor tendons of the hands and the patella tendons. Atheromatous lesions in the blood vessels occur early and may cause cerebral lesions and coronary occlusions with a fatal outcome. The adventitial connective tissue cells take up cholesterol and become hyperplastic. All the arteries and the heart valves are involved. Xanthomas are found in the subcutaneous tissues. This is said to be a dominant trait with incomplete penetrance.

BIBLIOGRAPHY

Hsia, D. Y.: Primary Hypercholesteremia. Inborn Errors of Metabolism. Year Book Publishers. Inc., 1959, p. 235.

DISORDERS DUE TO CHANGES IN THE BLOOD

Hemorrhagic Disease of the Newborn

Definition.—A hemorrhagic diathesis of obscure origin limited to the first few weeks of life.

Etiology.—It has been pointed out that the blood count of the fetus is very high and that in the course of the first few days of extrauterine life, this is reduced to the normal level by means of rapid blood destruction which often gives rise to jaundice. The suggestion has been made that hemorrhagic disease of the newborn is in some way connected with this process. This theory is supported by the claim that in normal infants who show no tendency to hemorrhage, there is, nonetheless, a striking prolongation of the bleeding time for a few days after birth. Recently evidence has been presented to indicate that lack of prothrombin is responsible for the bleeding tendency. Since vitamin K seems to be a necessary element in the formation of prothrombin, it has been thought that lack of this substance in the mother's diet may be responsible for the hemorrhagic tendency in the baby.

It is believed that vitamin K deficiency causes a deficiency of four clotting factors. More often, it is claimed, a hemorrhagic tendency is due to anoxia or sepsis.

Pathological Anatomy.—Large and small hemorrhages are found in all the tissues, but most commonly in the subcutaneous tissues, the mucous membranes and the serous surfaces. In a few cases, gastrointestinal hemorrhages are associated with ulcerations. The nervous system is involved less frequently than other organs but in a large percentage of cases there are petechiae in the meninges and cortex. Less commonly massive intracranial hemorrhages occur. These may arise in the brain or in the meninges. Extensive subarachnoid hemorrhages may occur. There are also hemorrhages into the retinae.

Clinical Features.—This disease is not common, occurring in somewhat less than 1 per cent of all newborn babies. It affects either sex indifferently. The symptoms develop, as a rule, about the third or fourth day after birth but may be delayed until the second or third week. The hemorrhages are almost multiple. They may be first discovered in the subcutaneous tissues or mucous membranes. Bleeding from the umbilicus is common and melena is not infrequently the first symptom. Infrequently the hemorrhages may be first seen in the eye, the nose, mouth, genital organs and ears. There is a slow, constant oozing rather than sudden gushes of blood. Unless checked promptly, there may be great loss of blood causing profound anemia and collapse. Jaundice is frequently present and may be very deep. The temperature is variable, being high, low or normal. The urine may contain blood. There is always anemia and the clotting time is almost invariably prolonged, often being increased to ten minutes or even more.

In some cases there is intracranial hemorrhage. The symptoms are almost identical with those due to cerebral injury at birth. There may be stupor, vomiting, convulsions, muscular rigidity, cyanosis, bulging of the fontanels and altered blood in the spinal fluid. Almost always there are abundant evidences of a generalized hemorrhagic tendency by the time cerebral symptoms are apparent.

The course of the disease is relatively brief. The hemorrhages usually cease as suddenly as they begin and, as a rule, within four or five days new hemorrhages cease to develop. Relapses are rare.

Diagnosis.—When multiple hemorrhages occur in a newborn infant, we must consider three chief possibilities: sepsis, syphilis and hemorrhagic disease of the newborn. The last is the commonest. If there is no evidence of syphilis either in the mother or child, the blood culture is negative and nothing to suggest infection can be found, we are justified in making the diagnosis of hemorrhagic disease. The diagnosis is confirmed by prolongation of the clotting time. Holt claims that the measurement of the avail-

able prothrombin time by Quick's method is the most important diagnostic procedure. When signs of intracranial hemorrhage develop in association with hemorrhages elsewhere in the body, especially if the symptoms are somewhat delayed after birth, it would seem to be a logical assumption that hemorrhagic disease and not birth trauma is responsible for the intracranial bleeding. When cerebral symptoms occur alone, however, even if there is some delay in clotting of the blood, it may be a very difficult matter to evaluate the relative importance of these two factors. Some authorities consider hemorrhagic disease an important cause of intracranial hemorrhage, but others claim that it is exceptional for this disease to cause intracranial hemorrhage.

Edson *et al.* report the case of an infant who was born when her mother had abruptio placentae with large clots of blood over and below the placenta. The baby developed multiple hemorrhages and died. The plasma fibrinogen and other clotting factors were greatly reduced. This was attributed to intravascular coagulation.

Prognosis.—If proper treatment is begun at once, the prognosis is not unfavorable as regards survival. If intracranial hemorrhage has occurred, the possibility of permanent cerebral injury must be considered, however. Without treatment, it is said that the mortality is around 75 per cent.

Treatment.—Adult blood or blood serum exert a prompt effect in stopping the tendency to hemorrhage. Some authorities recommend the injection of 10 cc of citrated blood of one of the parents into the buttocks, but a transfusion of 5 to 8 cc of blood per pound of body weight is much more effective. The transfusion has the advantage of acting more promptly and of also relieving the anemia. Treatment should be given at the earliest possible moment. The administration of vitamin K is said to give prompt results. In some clinics this substance is administered routinely to the mothers before delivery in the hope of preventing hemorrhagic disease in the infant. There is some difference of opinion about the results.

It is claimed that the administration of excessive doses of vitamin K to the newborn infant may cause jaundice and kernicterus. Crosse advised that not over 10 mgs should be given a day if the infant is premature.

Dr. Aballi states that vitamin K deficiency is usually not responsible for hemorrhagic tendencies in the newborn. There is a defect in factor V, factor VII or in fibrinogen activity. He also states that the optimum dosage of vitamin K, when it is needed, is between 10 and 25 micrograms.

BIBLIOGRAPHY

ABALLI, A. J.: The fifty-seventh meeting of the Southern Medical Assn. New Orleans, January, 1964.

ALLISON, A. C.: Danger of vitamin K to newborn. Lancet, i:669, 1955.

BEVERIDGE, R. S.: Hemorrhagic disease of the newborn. Arch. Dis. Child., 3:39, 1928-39.

CROSSE, V. M. *et al.*: Kernicterus and prematurity. Arch. Dis. Childhood, **30**:501, 1955.

CRUIKSHANK, J. N.: Hemorrhages of the newborn. Lancet, **1**:836, 1923.

EDSON, J. R. *et al.*: Defibrination syndrome in an infant born after abruptio placentae. Jour. Pediat., **72**:342, 1968.

FOOTE, J. A.: Hemorrhagic tendency as a frequent cause of cranial hemorrhage of the newborn. Am. J. Dis. Child., **20**:18, 1920.

GREEN, R. M. AND SWIFT, J. G.: Hemorrhagic diseases of newborn. Boston Med. & Surg. J., **164**:454, 1911.

LAWSON, R. B.: Treatment of hypoprothrombinemia (hemorrhagic disease) of the newborn infant. J. Pediat., **18**:224, 1941.

PONCHER, H. G. AND PATO, K.: Treatment of hypoprothrombinemia hemorrhagica neonatorum. J.A.M.A., **115**:14, 1940.

RODDA, F. C.: Coagulation time of the blood of the newborn with special reference to cerebral hemorrhage. J.A.M.A., **75**:452, 1920; Am. J. Dis. Child., **19**:269, 1920.

SNELL, A. M. AND BUTT, H. R.: Supplementary report on vitamin K. J.A.M.A., **113**:2056, 1939.

VIETTI, T. J.: Vitamin K prophylaxis in the newborn. J.A.M.A., **176**:791, 1961.

WADDELL, W. W. JR. AND GUERRY, DU P.: Effect of vitamin K on clotting time of the prothrombin and blood with special reference to unnatural bleeding of the newly born. J.A.M.A., **112**:2259, 1939.

WARWICK, M.: Cerebral hemorrhage of newborn. Am. J. Med. Sc., **158**:95, 1919; Am. J. Dis. Child., **21**:448, 1921.

INVOLVEMENT OF THE NERVOUS SYSTEM IN THROMBOCYTOPENIC PURPURA

Definition.—This is a disease of childhood characterized by purpura, fever, reduction of the blood platelets and sometimes by hemorrhages into the nervous system and other organs.

Etiology.—The cause is entirely unknown and it is not unlikely that several different conditions are included in this group. No doubt, infections play a large role.

The bleeding is believed to be due to deficiency of the blood platelets and hence, to a change in the properties of the blood rather than injury to the blood vessels as in other conditions characterized by a hemorrhagic tendency.

Pathological Anatomy.—Hemorrhages may be found in the substance of the brain, in the meninges and in the ventricles. In some cases extensive hemorrhages are found which destroy whole lobes of the brain or even most of one hemisphere. Alpers considers these to be most common. In other cases there are numerous small punctate hemorrhages scattered throughout the cerebrum, brain-stem and under the ependyma of the ventricular system. The vessels in the region of the extravasations may show some swelling of the endothelium, but this is not universally present. Both large and small hemorrhages may occur in the same case. Bleeding into the subarachnoid spaces or the subdural space is relatively common and minute petechiae in the pia-arachnoid are found in almost all cases. In many instances, meningeal hemorrhage results from rupture of a cerebral hemorrhage into the ventricular system or into the subarachnoid spaces.

Clinical Features.—The disease is most common between the ages of 2 and 10 years and affects the two sexes alike. In some instances several members of a family have been affected. The disease is usually mild but severe and even fulminating cases may occur. Both small petechiae and large ecchymoses are seen in the skin and these develop in successive crops, appearing and slowly fading from time to time. In severe cases, there are hemorrhages from the bowels, the genito-urinary tract and the nose and throat. Such symptoms are often accompanied by fever, weakness and great prostration. The spleen may be enlarged. The course of the average case varies between one and six weeks but recurrences of the symptoms months or years later are well known. Intracranial hemorrhage is not unusual. The onset of neurological signs is usually delayed for from two or three days to three weeks after the appearance of cutaneous lesions. The symptoms vary with the location and extent of the bleeding. Massive hemorrhages usually cause headache, loss of consciousness, hemiplegia and convulsions. In many cases death results within a day or less. Subarachnoid hemorrhage gives rise to signs of increased intracranial pressure, signs of meningeal irritation and bloody spinal fluid. Bleeding confined to the subdural space may cause papilledema and other signs of increased intracranial pressure without producing any local signs whatever. Transient cerebral palsies and focal convulsions, which run a benign course, are probably due to petechial hemorrhages in the brain. In some instances retinal hemorrhages lead to disturbances of vision or even blindness. Dr. Walsh has told me of a newborn baby who had severe purpura but recovered in a short time. The mother had purpura but her symptoms had been largely controlled by removal of the spleen. Biglow and Graves describe lesions in peripheral nerves associated with thrombocytopenic purpura and primary hemorrhagic thrombocythemia. They state that the nerve may be compressed by hematoma or damage by hemorrhage within the nerve sheath.

In most cases there is definite reduction of the blood platelet count. The clotting time is normal or only moderately prolonged but the clot is flabby and nonretractile. The bleeding time is much prolonged and the tourniquet test is positive. Anemia is a constant feature when the bleeding tendency is pronounced.

In *thrombotic thrombocytopenic purpura,* the small vessels, arterioles, and venules are occluded by hyaline thrombi with the production of small hemorrhages and infarctions in all the tissues. In the brain the lesions are found chiefly in the cortex and nuclear structures. The disease is almost always fatal, it seems, and the course is on an average of one to two weeks. Neurological symptoms are very prominent. There is fever, weakness, irritability, delirium progressing to stupor and coma. Hemiplegia and other focal signs are very common. No treatment is known. The platelets are re-

duced in number. The bleeding time is prolonged, but the clotting time is normal. Hemolytic anemia is always present. The cuff test is positive.

Purpura of Henoch-Schoenlein: This is thought to be an anaphylactoid arteritis. It occurs most frequently in children between the ages of 3 to 7 years. Glomerulonephritis is common. The purpuric lesions occur in the skin and mucous membranes. There is gastrointestinal pain, hematemesis and bleeding from the bowel. There is blood in the urine. Joint pains occur. Cerebral symptoms such as hemiplegia, convulsions and coma sometimes occur. Subarachnoid hemorrhage is described. Hypertensive encephalopathy may result because of renal damage.

Diagnosis.—A simple classification of hemorrhagic diseases may be offered:

A—Due to changes in the blood.
  1. Thrombocytopenic Purpuras. Bleeding time prolonged. Clotting time normal.
    a—*Essential thrombocytopenic purpura.* Described above.
    b—*Secondary thrombocytopenic purpura.* This is due to drugs such as tridione, sulfonamides, infections, anemias, leukemias and many other factors.
    c—*Thrombotic thrombocytopenic purpura* or platelet thrombosis. This is mentioned above.
    d—A type of purpura of the newborn has been shown to be due to destruction of the infant's platelets by antibodies in the maternal blood.
  2. Other defects in the blood. Clotting time prolonged. Bleeding time normal.
    a—Lack of prothrombin
      i—Lack of vitamin K (?) *hemorrhagic disease of the newborn,* q.v.
      ii—*Familial hypoprothrombinemia*
      iii—Due to dicumarol and similar drugs
    b—Lack of thromboplastinogen or thromboplastin component, hemophilia, q.v.
    c—Congenital lack of fibrinogen
B—Due to changes in the blood vessels.
  1. Vitamin deficiency, *scurvy,* q.v.
  2. Toxic substances such as arsphenamine.
  3. Hereditary *pseudohemophilia,* possibly due to failure of the small vessels to retract.
  4. *Schölein-Henoch's purpura* possibly due to allergic reaction.

The diagnosis of essential thrombopenic purpura of childhood depends upon the elimination of other causes of purpura and upon the recognition of the clinical picture described above as well as upon the reduction of the blood platelets.

Prognosis.—It is difficult to gain a clear impression of the prognosis, for fatal cases are more apt to be reported than cases in which the patient recovered and in which consequently the diagnosis could not be established. The large hemorrhages into the substance of the cerebrum are apparently usually fatal but cases marked by hemiplegia, convulsions and even signs of increased intracranial pressure may run a benign course and end in recovery.

Treatment.—Transfusions are said to be of value in stopping the bleeding. Lumbar puncture may be employed in cases of subarachnoid hemorrhage but probably is not devoid of danger. In recurrent and chronic cases, splenectomy is recommended. Steroid therapy is advised.

CASE HISTORY (Ped. 97024).—*Child of seven weeks developed repeated intracranial hemorrhages into both the ventricular system and the sub-dural spaces. Subcutaneous petechiae and ecchymoses occurring in associ-ation with intracranial hemorrhages. Hydrocephalus. Death at the age of six months from thrombocytopenia purpura.*

T. W. was the first child of healthy young parents. The pregnancy was uneventful and birth and delivery were normal in every respect. The child was given proper doses of cod liver oil and orange juice. At the age of five weeks, the child began to cough and a nasal discharge was ob-served. These symptoms continued and two weeks later the child had a convulsion involving the right side. He was brought to the hospital on the same day.

Examination revealed a well developed and well nourished infant in deep stupor. There were convulsive movements on the right side of the body. A few subcutaneous hemorrhages were observed upon the scalp and abdomen. A loud systolic murmur was audible over the entire skull. The spinal fluid was grossly bloody as was fluid removed from the subdural space on either side. R.B.C. 1,860,000. Hemoglobin 51 per cent. Repeated spinal and subdural punctures showed diminishing amounts of blood. The intracranial bruit disappeared, the convulsions ceased and the child was discharged apparently well about five weeks later.

For some two weeks the child did well at home and then another crop of subcutaneous hemorrhages appeared and convulsions returned. The second examination revealed that the head had increased in circumfer-ence from 39.5 cm. to 44.0 cm. The fontanels were tense and there were bilateral 6th nerve palsies. Right hemiplegia was present. Numerous hem-orrhages were seen in the mucous membranes and subcutaneous tissues. The spinal fluid was now clear but bloody fluid was obtained from the subdural space. The platelet count in the blood smear was reduced, the bleeding time was prolonged and the tourniquet test, positive. Clotting time was within normal limits. The roentgenograms of the bones showed no signs of scurvy. Ventriculography revealed that the cerebral ventricles were grossly dilated. The Wassermann test in the blood and spinal fluid was negative in several tests. The child was discharged after about 2 months in the hospital. The bleeding had stopped but it was now evident that the child was mentally defective and the signs of right hemiplegia were still present.

For the next month the child did well and then was brought into the hospital for the third time because of bronchitis and convulsions. The head was now 48.5 cm. in circumference. There was papilledema and par-tial loss of vision. The spinal fluid contained much blood but no blood was found in the subdural spaces. Again the bleeding ceased and the child was discharged after a three weeks' stay in the hospital.

He was well for only a short time and then vomiting and convulsions recurred. The head was larger and the spinal fluid full of blood again.

Subcutaneous hemorrhages were present as on the previous admissions. He was discharged again without much improvement and readmitted within three weeks. On this occasion blood was found in the ventricular and subdural fluid, there were the usual signs of increased intracranial pressure, general spasticity of the musculature, numerous subcutaneous hemorrhages, vomiting and convulsions. The head was 53.0 cm in circumference. Death occurred the following day, at the age of six months.

Post-mortem examination revealed extensive destruction of the brain and large fresh blood clots in the cerebral ventricles and subdural spaces. There was gross dilatation of the ventricles. No sign of scurvy was found.

BIBLIOGRAPHY

ADAMS, R. D., CAMMERMEYER, J. AND FITZGERALD, P. J.: Neurological aspects of thrombocytic acroangiothrombosis. J. Neurol., Neurosurg. & Psychiat., 11:27, 1948.

ALPERS, B. J. AND DUANE, W. JR.: Intracranial hemorrhage in purpura hemorrhagica. J. Nerv. & Ment. Dis., 78:260, 1933.

BARONDESS, J. A.: Thrombotic thrombocytopenic purpura. Am. J. Med., 13:294, 1952.

BIGLOW, N. H. AND GRAVES, R. W.: Peripheral nerve lesions in hemorrhagic diseases. Arch. Neurol. & Psychiat., 68:819, 1952.

CHALGREN, W. S.: Neurologic complications in hemorrhagic disease. Neurology, 3:126, 1953.

GEIGER, A. J.: Purpura hemorrhagica with cerebrospinal hemorrhage. J.A.M.A., 102:1000, 1934.

LADWIG, H. A.: The central nervous system in thrombotic thrombocytopenic purpura. Neurology, 3:267, 1953.

LEWIS, I. C. AND PHILPOTT, M. G.: Neurological complications of Schönlein-Henoch syndrome. Arch. Dis. Child., 31:369, 1956.

MACWHINNEY, J. B. *et al.*: Thrombotic thrombocytopenic purpura in childhood. Blood, 19:181, 1962.

NERKIN, S. AND WIENER, J.: Schönlein-Henoch disease. Amer. Jour. Clin. Path., 33:55, 1960.

O'BRIEN, J. L. AND SIBLEY, W. A.: Neurological manifestations of thrombotic thrombocytopenic purpura. Neurology, 8:55, 1958.

SILVERSTEIN, A.: Thrombotic thrombocytopenic purpura. Arch. of Neurol., 18:358, 1968.

SINGER, K., BORNSTEIN, F. P. AND WILE, S. A.: Thrombotic thrombocytopenic purpura. Blood, 2:542, 1947.

WALKER, J. H. AND WALKER, W.: Idiopathic thrombocytopenic purpura. Arch. Dis. Child., 36:649, 1961.

WALSH, F. B.: *Loc. cit.*

WINTROBE, M. M.: Clinical Hematology. 3rd Ed., Philadelphia, Lea and Febiger, 1951.

INVOLVEMENT OF THE NERVOUS SYSTEM IN HEMOPHILIA

Etiology.—Hemophilia is a hereditary disease transmitted as a sex-linked recessive trait by the X chromosome. The males have the bleeding tendency and the females, as a rule, are carriers. A male with this disease, who has children by a normal woman, will have normal sons but his daughters will be carriers. The daughters born to a female carrier and a normal male have a 50 per cent chance of being carriers and the sons a 50 per cent chance of being hemophiliacs. Females who develop this disease are homozygous and have inherited the disease from both parents.

It seems to be agreed that the pathological bleeding is due to deficient

coagulation of the blood. It is now known that there are a number of factors necessary for proper coagulation. Some eleven are recognized. Two types of hemophilia are recognized: (1) Type A caused by deficiency of factor VIII, i.e. the antihemophilic factor. (2) Type B caused by deficiency of factor IX, or plasma thromboplastin component.

Another type of congenital bleeding diathesis, Willebrand's disease, or angiohemophilia, is inherited as a dominant characteristic. This is attributed to deficiency of factor VIII and to abnormalities of the capillaries.

Pathological Anatomy.—There are no anatomical findings other than hemorrhages and their results.

Clinical Features.—We have already stated that the active manifestations of the disease are confined almost exclusively to males and that we almost always obtain a history of similar symptoms in relatives. Bleeding is seldom noticed before the end of the first year but after this age the hemophiliac's life is usually punctuated by a series of hemorrhages. These are usually produced by minor trauma but may occur without apparent cause. The common sites of hemorrhage in order of frequency may be given as follows: Nose, joints, muscles, gastrointestinal tract, genitourinary tract, eye and nervous system. Cutaneous hemorrhages and petechiae such as are seen in purpura are uncommon. In hemophilia the hemorrhages are larger and, as a rule, deeply seated in the tissues. A pin prick may slowly ooze blood for many hours, so that even trivial wounds may be serious. Bullock and Fildes and more recently Seddons have made a study of the cases in which the nervous system was the site of hemorrhage. In some fourteen cases intracranial bleeding occurred into the hemisphere, the brain-stem, the ventricles, the subdural and subarachnoid spaces. In several cases, the spinal cord or the cauda equina were involved and in other cases bleeding into the tissues has compressed the trunks of the peripheral nerves. Lord mentions a case in which bleeding caused paralysis of the ulnar nerve and ischemic contracture of the muscles of the forearm and Seddons describes a case in which the femoral nerve was affected by a large hemorrhage under the iliopsoas muscle. The writer has observed two cases identical with that of Seddons.

Diagnosis.—The history of prolonged bleeding in the patient and in other members of the family is almost pathognomonic of this disease but the diagnosis may be established by the determination of the clotting time which is prolonged to twenty minutes or to more than an hour, whereas, the normal time is from three to six minutes. The bleeding time is, of course, normal. The platelet count is normal.

Willebrand's disease, which is sometimes termed *pseudohemophilia* or *angiohemophilia* affects either sex for it is inherited as a dominant trait. It is most troublesome in childhood. Symptoms may occur in the first few

weeks of life. There is capillary fragility, defective clot retraction, defective agglutination of platelets, morphologically abnormal platelets and prolonged bleeding time. Treatment is not satisfactory. Transfusions may be needed but may not stop the bleeding. The prognosis for life is favorable, however. Congenital afibrinogenemia must be considered in differential diagnosis. This is transmitted by a rare recessive gene.

Prognosis.—The prognosis is unfavorable and about half of all cases run their course to a fatal issue before the end of the seventh year. In a few mild cases, the tendency to bleeding has apparently ceased spontaneously.

Treatment.—Pressure will sometimes control superficial bleeding but for internal hemorrhage, transfusion is usually necessary. Plasma may be used in place of whole blood and antihemophilic globulin is now available. As a rule, this is effective but its influence lasts only a short time. Brinkhous *et al.* advise the use of a high potency glycine precipitated antihemophilic factor for classical hemophilia. No effective method of curing the underlying condition is yet known. Hemophiliacs must be protected against even the most trivial injury and surgical procedures are almost absolutely contraindicated. The patients should be forbidden to marry.

CASE HISTORY (U-47886).—*Boy of 14 years who had history of manifestations of hemophilia since birth, developed signs of a lesion in the left lumbar plexus coincidently with a palpable mass in the left lower quadrant.*

The patient, J. G., a Jewish boy of 14 years, had been under observation almost all his life. When 10 days old he was circumcised and prolonged hemorrhage resulted which was controlled only by the subcutaneous injection of blood. No further bleeding was noted until the age of 4 years and since then the patient has been admitted to the hospital 12 times because of hemorrhage. There have been hematuria, hemarthrosis and many attacks of subcutaneous hemorrhage. Such attacks have been relieved by transfusions and by the injection of horse serum. Clotting time has always been much prolonged but the platelet count has been normal. Several weeks before the patient was last seen he developed ecchymoses over the left thigh, the right arm and right shoulder. He was given a transfusion and bleeding stopped. Three weeks later he developed pain in the left thigh and left lower quadrant of the abdomen. Soon the anterior surface of the left thigh grew numb and he was unable to extend the knee.

Examination.—A mass was palpated in the left lower quadrant. There was strong psoas spasm which held the left thigh flexed upon the abdomen. The entire surface of the left thigh was much swollen and very tender. Passive movements at the hip and knee caused severe pain. Muscular power was good at the ankle and the flexors of the knee were strong. The

extensors of the knee seemed to be very weak but the muscles of the hip seemed to be strong, although there was so much pain that it was impossible to test strength satisfactorily. Cutaneous sensibility was greatly reduced over the entire anterior surface of the thigh and over the internal surface of the leg, down as far as the ankle and in the center of this region there was complete cutaneous anesthesia. The knee jerk was absent but the ankle jerk was active. These symptoms were attributed to a hemorrhage beneath the psoas muscle infiltrating the nerve trunks of the left lumbar plexus.

BIBLIOGRAPHY

ALAGILLE, D. AND CHARLAS, J.: Intracranial hemorrhage in hemophilic children. Arch. franc pediat., 23:795, 1966.

BRINKHOUS, K. M. *et al.*: A new high potency glycine precipitated antihemophilic factor concentrate. J.A.M.A., 205:613, 1968.

BULLOCK, W. AND FILDES, P.: Haemophilia. Treasury of Human Inheritance, University of London, 1911.

BUCHANNAN, J. C. AND LEAVELL, B. S.: Pseudohemophilia. Ann. Int. Med., 44:241, 1956.

HANDLEY, R. S. AND NUSSBRECHER, A. M.: Heredity in pseudohemophilia. Quart. J. Med., 4: new series, 1, 165, 1935.

LORD, J. B.: Hemophilia with Volkmann's syndrome. J.A.M.A., 87:406, 1926.

McELFRESH, A. E.: Hemophilia. J. Pediat., 51:474, 1957.

RUTHERFORD, W. J.: A pedigree of hemophilia. Brit. J. Child. Dis., 29:276, 1932.

SEDDONS, H. J.: Hemophilia as a cause of lesions in the nervous system. Brain, 53:306, 1930.

WALSH, F. B.: *Loc. cit.*

WINTROBE, M. M.: Clinical Hematology. 3rd Ed., Philadelphia, Lea and Febiger, 1951.

INVOLVEMENT OF THE NERVOUS SYSTEM IN ANEMIAS

Anemia is a common problem in childhood. The list of possible causes is a long one. Fortunately only a few types are apt to cause damage to the nervous system. *Anemias due to abnormal hemoglobins:* The hemoglobins are designated by the letters of the alphabet. Normal adult hemoglobin is designated A and fetal hemoglobin F. Certain abnormal hemoglobins are designated S, C, D, etc. These hemoglobins are distinguished by electrophoresis, chromatography and other special tests. As a rule, these diseases are inherited as simple recessive traits. The homozygous individuals display the diseases in its fully developed form and the heterozygous carriers may have minor symptoms.

In this country, *sickle cell* anemia is the chief problem. The abnormal hemoglobin is designated S. The homozygous patient is designated SS and the heterozygous carrier AS. The disease is restricted to the Negro race almost without exception. Symptoms frequently develop in infancy and childhood. The patients display a subicteric tint of the sclerae, deficient bodily growth, a palpable spleen, and mild anemia. Cutaneous ulcers which are slow to heal are common. Priapism due to thrombosis of the corpora cavernosa occurs in boys. From time to time, they have hemolytic crises

marked by fever, abdominal pain, pains in the bones and joints, swelling of the liver and spleen, jaundice and a rapid fall of the blood count. Such episodes may be precipitated by infections, hypoxia, anesthesia, transfusions and dehydration. Generalized embolism of bone marrow and fat globules may occur with fatal results. Hemorrhages and areas of necrosis in the bone marrow are thought to be responsible. Two other types of crises are described. In one there is pain in the extremities and abdomen, with fever and leucocytosis, so the picture suggests an acute abdominal emergency. There is no drop in the blood count. The cause is not clear. A third type of crisis is termed the aplastic crisis. The blood count drops and there is leucopenia. There is reduction of the chronic elevation of the serum bilirubin. Infection is thought to be the usual cause. Transfusions are required.

Changes in the bones are found. Radial striations are seen in the skull. The retinal veins may be tortuous.

Comer and Fred state that the pattern of the blood vessels of the conjunctiva in sickle cell disease is characteristic. The vessels are sharply defined, dark red, comma or corkscrew shaped and appear to be isolated from the conjunctival circulation. They are best seen in the lower bulbar conjunctiva.

Involvement of the nervous system is said to occur in one third of all cases. Convulsions are common. Subarachnoid hemorrhage is not unusual. Cerebral vascular lesions causing hemiplegia, disturbances of vision and speech are well known. Subdural hematoma occurs and also thrombosis of the dural sinuses. Hemorrhages in the retina and vitreus are found and vision may be lost as a result of occlusion of the central retinal artery. Mental changes may occur suddenly. Compression of the spinal cord or spinal nerve roots may result from collapse of vertebrae due to bone infarctions.

These symptoms are due to hemorrhages and softenings which are sometimes small and sometimes large. It is believed that the abnormal red cells obstruct the blood vessels. Fat and bone marrow embolism play a definite role. Heterozygous carriers may have hematuria or infarction of the spleen during flights at high altitude.

The diagnosis of sickle cell anemia and sickle cell trait may be made by observation of the red cells under reduced oxygen tension. The cells soon lose their normal shape and appear as elongated filamentous or crescentic shapes.

Treatment includes transfusions and antibiotics for these patients are subject to infections. Dr. Murayama has stated that a crisis may be relieved by the administration of oxygen under pressure, i.e. by hyperbaric oxygen.

Walsh states that sickle cell trait may be associated with tortuosity of the

retinal arteries and overfilling of the veins. There may be icterus of the sclerae and occasionally pallor of the optic discs.

Hemoglobin C disease is rare and does not give rise to severe symptoms as a rule. However, sickle cell hemoglobin C disease, represented as SC may cause tortuous veins in the retinae with hemorrhages and sometimes vascular occlusions. Vision may be seriously impaired. Extensive embolism of bone marrow elements and fat globules may occur as in sickle cell anemia.

Anemias Due to Other Causes.—*Pernicious anemia.* Reisner *et al.* describe four cases of pernicious anemia in two sets of siblings, and include an analysis of twelve cases collected from the literature. The children's ages, at the time the diagnosis was made, were between nine months and fourteen years. The diagnosis was made upon the presence of macrocytic anemia with megaloblastic bone marrow, the exclusion of other causes for this type of anemia, the response to specific treatment and the necessity for continued treatment to prevent relapse. In six cases of the sixteen, there was free acid in the gastric fluid. In these cases, however, absence of the intrinsic factor was demonstrated. It is of interest that in three of the cases studied by Reisner *et al.* there were neurological disorders typical of subacute combined degeneration of the spinal cord. The children showed ataxic gait, ataxia in the heel-knee test, weakness of the legs, loss of vibratory sense in the legs, loss of ankle jerks and either increase of or loss of the knee jerks. The Babinski sign was always present. Mental retardation was evident in two children. The neurological signs and symptoms were held in check by vitamin B12 and there was some improvement when treatment was instituted but this fell short of recovery. We have seen only one child with subacute combined degeneration of the cord and pernicious anemia (Ped. A. 34883). There was prompt but limited improvement on proper therapy.

Jadhav *et al.* describe vitamin B12 deficiency in South India in breast-fed infants of seven to nine months. It is manifest by apathy, failure of development, involuntary movements, excessive pigmentation of the skin and megaloblastic anemia. It is attributed to vitamin B12 deficiency in the mother during pregnancy and the puerperium.

Bassen and Kornzweig reported a rare type of abnormality of the red cells termed *acanthrocytosis* in 1950. Pointed projections are seen on the surface of the cells similar to pseudopods. These children have celiac disease early in life. This condition then disappears and they develop ataxia with evidences of damage to the posterior columns of the spinal cord. The tendon reflexes are lost. Athetoid movements of the arms appear and tremor of the head and hands. Pigmentary changes in the retinae are found.

The disease is inherited as a recessive trait. It has been found only in Jewish families. Biochemical abnormalities are characteristic. The serum cholesterol, carotenoids, vitamin A and the phospholipids are all reduced. The beta lipoproteins are absent.

Congenital pancytopenia might be mentioned. In this familial condition there is anemia, and reduction of the white cells and platelets. The skin is pigmented. The patients are dwarfs and mentally deficient. Many anomalies of development are found. This condition is described in Chapter I.

Halsted and Prasad describe cases of *iron deficiency anemia* in males in Iran and Egypt. There was deficient bodily growth, lack of sexual development, atrophy of the testicles and prostate gland, lack of facial and body hair as well as enlargement of the liver and spleen. The administration of ferrous sulphate relieved all the symptoms. It was found that *zinc deficiency* was also present. Treatment with zinc relieved the endocrine abnormalities but not the anemia. The complete relief afforded by iron was explained by the fact that commercial iron preparations contain zinc.

Graham and Cordano describe another type of anemia which occurs most frequently in children between the ages of 7 to 9 months. They suffered from diarrhea and were malnourished. They were fed on milk. A fall in serum ceruloplasmin levels occurred first and reduction of copper in the blood was then found. There was failure of iron absorption, neutropenia, leukopenia, demineralization of bone and defective erythrocyte production and survival. The administration of copper by mouth caused dramatic improvement.

CASE HISTORY (Ped. A-4643).—*Sickle cell anemia with right hemiplegia at the age of three years and left hemiplegia with pseudobulbar palsy at the age of six years.*

J. G., a Negro boy, was never very vigorous and was always poorly nourished. At the age of three years he suddenly developed right hemiplegia with loss of speech and for a short time was unconscious. He began to improve within a few weeks. Eventually he regained his speech and learned to walk with a hemiplegic gait. For some years no additional symptoms developed though several doctors told his mother he was anemic. At the age of six years he suddenly had another stroke in which his left side was paralysed. For several days he was unconscious and was very dull and confused for two weeks. After this second episode, he never regained his speech and had great difficulty in chewing and swallowing. He could not stand, walk or even sit up alone. His bladder emptied involuntarily.

Examination at the age of seven years, almost a year after the left side was affected, revealed a slender, poorly nourished colored boy who showed the usual signs of bilateral hemiplegia with severe spasticity of the extremities, increased tendon reflexes, extensor plantar responses, difficulty in swallowing, inability to articulate and increased jaw jerk. He could not

sit up without support. The heart was not enlarged but there was a loud systolic bruit over the whole precordium. Blood pressure was 100/80. Despite the fact that the patient had been treated for some months by transfusions and other methods of combatting anemia, the hemoglobin was only 54 per cent and the red cells numbered only 2,100,000. The smear showed the usual picture of sickle cell anemia. The Wassermann test was negative in the blood and spinal fluid. Roentgenograms of the bones showed the usual changes.

BIBLIOGRAPHY

ARENA, J. M.: Vascular accidents and hemiplegia in a patient with sickle cell anemia. Am. J. Dis. Child., **49**:722, 1935.

BALLARD, H. S. AND BONDAR, H.: Spontaneous subarachnoid hemorrhage in sickle cell anemia. Neurology, **7**:443, 1957.

BASSEN, F. A. AND KORNZWEIG, A. L.: Malformation of the erythrocytes in a case of retinitis pigmentosa. Blood, **5**:381, 1950.

BRIDGES, W. H.: Cerebral vascular disease accompanying sickle cell anemia. Am. J. Path., **15**:353, 1939.

CAPRILES, L. F.: Intracranial hypertension and iron deficiency anemia. Arch. Neurol., **9**:147, 1963.

COMER, P. B. AND FRED, H. L.: Diagnosis of sickle-cell disease by ophthalmoscopic inspection of the conjunctiva. New Engl. Jour. Med., **271**:544, 1964.

CORDANO, A. *et al.*: Copper deficiency in infancy. Pediatrics, **34**:324, 1964.

DIAMOND, M. P.: Five cases of sickle cell haemoglobin-C disease. Lancet, **2**:322, 1959.

GRAHAM, G. G. AND CORDANO, A.: Copper depletion and deficiency in the malnourished infant. The Johns Hopkins Med. Jour., **124**:139, 1969.

GREER, M. AND SCHOTLAND, D.: Abnormal hemoglobin as a cause of neurologic disease. Neurology, **12**:114, 1962.

HAEREM, A. T.: Blindness following massive gastrointestinal hemorrhage. Ann. Int. Med., **36**:883, 1952.

HALSTED, J. A. AND PRASAD, A. S.: Zinc deficiency in man. Israel Med. J., **22**:307, 1963.

HARDEN, A. S. JR.: Sickle cell anemia. Changes in vessels and in bones. Am. J. Dis. Child., **54**:1044, 1937.

HUGHES, J. G., DIGGS, L. W. AND GILLESPIE, C. E.: Involvement of the nervous system in sickle cell anemia. J. Pediat., **17**:166, 1940.

JADHAV, M. *et al.*: Vitamin B 12 deficiency in infants. Lancet, **ii**:903, 1962.

JOSEPHS, H. W.: Anemia of infancy and early childhood. Medicine, **15**:307, 1936.

KAMPMEIER, R. H.: Sickle cell anemia as a cause of cerebral vascular disease. Arch. Neurol. & Psychiat., **36**:1323, 1936.

LEIKIN, S. L.: Pernicious anemia in childhood. Pediatrics, **25**:91, 1960.

MAURAYAMA, M.: Treatment of sickle cell anemia crises by hyperbaric oxygen. Meeting of the Amer. Ass. Advancement of Science. Washington. January 1967.

PAULING, L. *et al.*: Sickle cell anemia, a molecular disease. Science, **110**:543, 1949.

PERLSTEIN, M. A. AND SINGER, K.: Acanthocytosis—A new hematologic neurologic syndrome. Trans. Chicago Neurol. Soc. Dec. 9, -1952.

REISNER, E., WOLFF, J., MCKAY, R. AND DOYLE, E.: Juvenile pernicious anemia. Pediatrics, **8**:88, 1951.

SCOTT, R. B. AND FERGUSON, A. D.: Studies in sickle cell anemia. Clin. Pediat., **5**:403, 1966.

SHELLEY, W. M. *et al.*: Bone marrow and fat embolism in sickle cell anemia and sickle cell hemoglobin disease. Am. J. M., **27**:647, 1959.

SINGER, K., FISHER, B. AND PERLSTEIN, M. A.: Acanthocytosis. A genetic erythrocyte malformation. Blood, **7**:577, 1952.

WALSH, F. B.: *Loc. cit.*

WATSON, R. J. *et al.*: Hand-foot syndrome in sicklemia. Pediatrics, **31**:975, 1963.

Wertham, F., Mitchell, N. and Angrist, A.: The brain in sickle cell anemia. Arch. Neurol. & Psychiat., **47**:752, 1942.

Wintrobe, M. M.: Clinical Hematology. 3rd Ed., Philadelphia, Lea and Febiger, 1951.

INVOLVEMENT OF THE NERVOUS SYSTEM IN CONGENITAL HEART DISEASE AND COARCTATION OF THE AORTA

It is beyond the scope of this article to discuss the numerous types of congenital defects of the heart which occur. They are fully described by Taussig.

Pathological Anatomy.—Congestion and petechiae are almost always found at post-mortem examination. Infarctions are common. These may be due to arterial occlusions resulting from thrombosis or embolism or possibly from increased viscosity of the blood due to polycythemia and anoxia. Venous occlusions and thrombosis of the dural sinuses occur. Diffuse demyelination such as one finds in various types of anoxia may be found. Multiple or single abscesses of the brain occur. Infected infarcts are described. Anoxia and circulatory disturbances, as well as various types of embolism, may occur during heart surgery. Vascular anomalies are often found including telangiectases and arteriovenous fistulae. Malformations of the brain are sometimes associated with congenital heart disease. Mongolism is not rare in such cases.

Tyler and Clark have published an instructive article about neurological complications found in 1,875 cases of congenital heart disease at Johns Hopkins Hospital. Such complications were found in 25 per cent of this series of cases.

Syncopal attacks with cyanosis and dyspnea occurred in 225 cases, often as a result of exertion or over-eating. These reactions were most common in the tetralogy of Fallot, truncus arteriosus and transposition.

Alter *et al.* point out that profuse sweating is often indicative of congestive heart failure.

Convulsions were noted in 109 cases most often in association with cyanosis and dyspnea. They were usually found in the same types of heart disease which cause syncopal attacks. Convulsions were more common in infancy than later in childhood.

Cerebral vascular lesions occurred in 72 cases. The incidence was highest in transposition, pulmonary stenosis, tetralogy of Fallot and Eisenmenger's syndrome. Arterial thromboses were found with softenings which occasionally became infected. Dural sinus thrombosis also occurs which may sometimes cause increased intracranial pressure. No doubt, polycythemia with increased viscosity of the blood is partly responsible for the thromboses. Hemiplegia, aphasia, athetosis and other cerebral syndromes occur. The retinal blood vessels are dilated and tortuous.

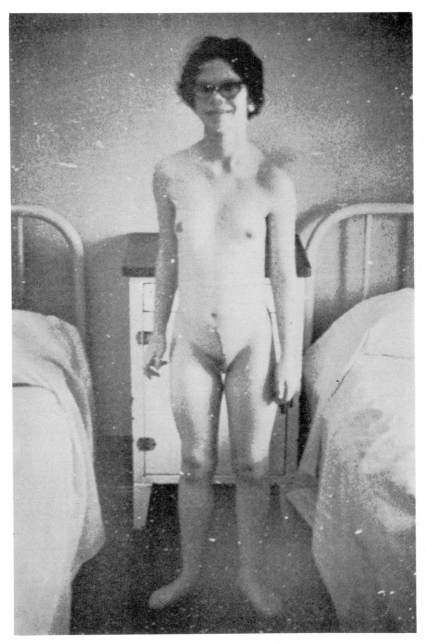

FIG. 209. Supravalvular stenosis of the aorta. There is dwarfish stature, full face, pointed chin, thick lips, broad mouth, large nostrils and malocclusion of the teeth. She is mentally deficient.

Mental deficiency was discovered in 107 cases. This was more common in the cyanotic types of heart disease. In some instances the cardiac defect was not directly responsible for the child's mental condition for in this group there were 15 mongols, 6 microcephalics and 6 patients with cataracts and deafness whose mothers had had German measles early in pregnancy.

Brain abscess was found in 27 cases and meningitis once. In all of these patients there was a condition present which permitted venous blood to by-pass the pulmonary capillary bed which is believed to remove bacteria from the blood stream. It is of interest that in pulmonary arteriovenous fistulae the incidence of brain abscess is also increased. Bacterial endocarditis occurs in congenital heart disease but only one case was discovered by Tyler and Clark. Aita states that 30 to 40 per cent of patients who have supra-valvular aortic stenosis have idiopathic hypercalcemia q.v.

Kalyanaraman *et al.* have performed electroencephalograms on 50 patients suffering from congenital heart disease. They find a small group in which the encephalogram is normal, and a larger group in which there are non-specific abnormalities. In 15 out of 50 cases paroxysmal abnormalities are found.

Oppenheimer found paradoxical embolism in 13 cases of transposition of the aorta and pulmonary artery. The ductus arteriosus was the source of emboli in another case. Arterial thrombosis was found in 6 more cases which was possibly due to emboli though no venous thrombosis was found. A number of operations have been devised by Blalock and others to correct some of these cardiac malformations. Cerebral embolism may occur during such procedures and also as a result of diagnostic study involving cardiac catheterization and angiography.

Currarino and Engle state that ligation of the subclavian artery in the Blalock-Taussig operation retards the longitudinal growth of the bones and decreases the thickness of the muscle mass of the arm in young patients.

Stephens studied 342 patients who had operation for congenital heart disease. Neurological abnormalities were present before operation in 14. Neurological complications appeared in 26 cases following operation. In some instances these were attributed to polycythemia causing cerebral thrombosis. Traction injuries of the brachial plexus and direct injury to the intrathoracic nerves were noted. Heart failure due to cardiac trauma is described. Hypothermia sometimes caused polyneuritis, and sometimes cerebral damage. Hypoxia resulted in convulsions and paralysis.

Other developmental anomalies should be mentioned. We have seen arteriovenous fistulae in the brain. Wyburn Mason describes compression of the spinal cord by dilated vessels in congenital heart disease. Tyler and Clark found 11 cases of deafness in their series and 4 cases of unilateral facial paralysis associated with malformation of the ear. It is pointed out

that bodily growth is deficient and weight is more severely reduced than height.

Fraser *et al.* describe a combination of congenital abnormalities including severe bilateral perceptive deafness, prolonged Q.T. interval in the electrocardiogram and syncopal attacks some of which are fatal and some of which end in recovery. It is suggested that the syncopal attacks may be due to Adams-Stokes episodes. This condition is said to be inherited as a recessive characteristic. The authors studied nine patients in six families. Three died in syncopal attacks. This condition is termed the Jervell and Lange-Nielsen syndrome.

Koury and Hawes describe pulmonary hypertension which occurs in children who live at high altitudes. There is dyspnea, cyanosis, polycythemia, enlargement of the heart and syncopal attacks.

In rare instances, primary polycythemia occurs in children. In such cases several members of the family may be affected.

Sclerema Neonatorum: This rare condition occurs only in newborn babies. The skin and subcutaneous tissues become indurated and hard. The affected areas are cold. The skin cannot be picked up in folds. It is difficult to penetrate with a needle. There is no edema. The loss of elasticity of the tissues may cause some limitation of movement. The process begins as a rule in the thighs, buttocks and calves but may extend over the entire body.

Circulatory deficiency is always present. Congenital heart disease or dehydration due to diarrhea or vomiting may be responsible. Biopsy of the skin and subcutaneous fat reveals no histological abnormalities. It has been claimed that solidification of the fat is responsible, but this theory is not universally accepted.

It is advised that proper hydration be maintained and the electrolytes be kept at a normal level. The local application of heat has no value. Cortisone has been suggested.

In most cases this condition is fatal as a result of the circulatory deficiency, but if recovery occurs, it is complete.

Lang *et al.* state that the illness resembling mononucleosis which may occur between 7 and 25 weeks after cardiopulmonary bypass in open heart surgery is due to infection by the cytomegalovirus.

CASE HISTORY (Ped. A-91253).—*Child of 7 months who was found to have congenital heart disease and arteriovenous fistulae on both sides of the brain.*

S. H., a colored baby of 7 months, was considered to be quite normal until he developed a febrile illness on January 29, 1952. He soon began to vomit and was brought into the Harriet Lane Home. Examination revealed bulging fontanels, cervical rigidity and high fever. The spinal fluid contained 3000 white cells. Cultures soon revealed that the child had

influenzal meningitis. Chloromycetin was given and the cultures became sterile on the third day.

The fontanels continued to bulge and a subdural effusion was found which was relieved by a few taps.

At this point, it was realized that another condition must be present. The fontanel continued to bulge though the effusion had disappeared and the spinal fluid was quite normal. The sutures of the skull were separated. The heart was enlarged and a systolic murmur was audible. Roentgenograms of the chest revealed a mass in the left upper mediastinum. An angiocardiogram was performed by means of the cephalic vein. Definite evidence of congenital heart disease was found though the exact nature of the malformation was not clear. The mass in the mediastinum

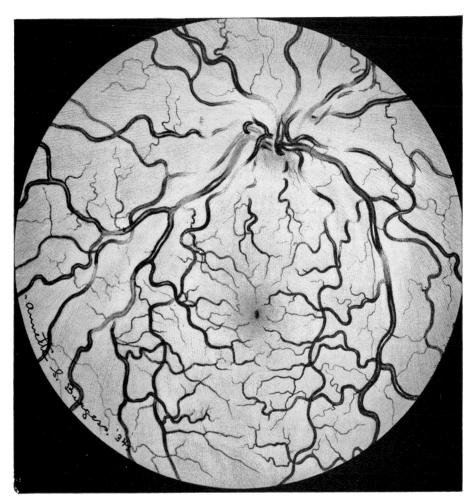

FIG. 210. Congenital heart disease. Note blurring of the disc amounting to papilledema. The uniformity of color in the veins and arteries is apparent. (From Walsh; Neuro-Ophthalmology, courtesy the Williams and Wilkins Company.)

proved to be a great venous lake. Since the dye seemed to reach both sides of the heart at the same time, it was conjectured that the vena cava might empty into both auricles.

Carotid arteriograms revealed gross dilatation of the carotid arteries. A great tangled mass of vessels was seen in the right temporal region. This mass seemed to be fed by branches of the middle cerebral artery and emptied into the right lateral sinus. A smaller vascular mass was seen on the left which seemed to drain into the left lateral sinus.

No neurological symptoms were evident. The child was sent home in good condition.

CASE HISTORY.—*Congenital heart disease with sclerema neonatorum.*

J. M. W. was born with severe congenital heart disease. There was cyanosis and periods of apnea. Examination revealed truncus arteriosus, interventricular septal defect and aortic stenosis. The skin of the thighs and calves was indurated and the subcutaneous tissues were also indurated. The skin could not be picked up in folds. The thighs and calves were very cool. There was no edema. Some limitation of movement was present due to the lack of elasticity of the tissues. Body temperature ranged from 92° to 94°.

BIBLIOGRAPHY

AITA, J. A.: Congenital Facial Anomalies with Neurologic Defects. Springfield, Thomas, 1969.

ALTER, B. P. *et al.*: Sweating in congenital heart disease. Pediatrics, 41:123, 1968.

AUERBACH, M. L. *et al.*: Benign familial polycythemia in childhood. Pediatrics, 21:54, 1958.

BERTHRONG, M. AND SABISTON, D. C.: Cerebral lesions in congenital heart disease. Bull. Johns Hopkins Hosp., 89:384, 1951.

BLALOCK, A. AND TAUSSIG, H. B.: The surgical treatment of malformations of the heart in which there is pulmonary stenosis or pulmonary atresia. J.A.M.A., 128:189, 1945.

CAMPBELL, M. AND EMANUEL, R.: Six cases of congenital complete heart block followed for 34-40 years. Brit. Heart Jour., 29:577, 1967.

CLARK, D. B. AND CLARK, E. S.: Brain abscess as a complication of congenital cardiac malformation. Tr. Am. Neurol. A., 177:73, 1952.

COHEN, M. M.: The central nervous system in congenital heart disease. Neurology, 10:452, 1960.

CURRARINO, G. AND ENGLE, M. E.: The effect of ligation of the subclavian artery on the bones and soft tissues of the arms. Jour. Pediat., 67:808, 1965.

ENGELKING, E.: Über familiäre Polyzythämie. Klin. Monatsbl. f. Augenh., 64:645, 1920.

FARAHMAND, F. *et al.*: Cranial bruit in ductus arteriosis. J. Pediat., 64:441, 1964.

FRASER, G. R. *et al.*: Deafness and cardiac abnormalities. Quart. J. Med., 33:361, 1964.

GARCIA, R. E. *et al.*: Hypercalcemia and aortic stenosis. New England J. M., 271:117, 1964.

HALBERTSMA, I.: Polycythemia in childhood. Am. J. Dis. Child., 46:1356, 1933.

HUGHES, W. E. AND HAMMOND, M. L.: Sclerema neonatorum. Jour. Pediat., 32:676, 1948.

JERVELL, O. AND LANGE-NIELSEN, F.: Congenital deaf-mutism, functional heart disease with prolongation of the Q T interval and sudden death. Am. Heart J., 54:59, 1957.

KALYANARAMAN, K. *et al.*: The electroencephalogram in congenital heart disease. Arch. of Neurology, 18:98, 1968.

KOURY, G. H. AND HAWES, C. R.: Pulmonary hypertension in children owing to residence at high altitudes. J. Pediat., 62:177, 1963.

LANG, C. AND LANG, D. J. *et al.*: Association of cytomegalic virus with the post-perfusion syndrome. New England Jour. Med., 278:1147, 1968.

LEACH, C. B.: Congenital heart disease. Clinical analysis of 75 cases from the Johns Hopkins Hospital. J. Pediat., 7:802, 1935.

LEVINE, S. A. AND WOODWORTH, C. R.: Congenital deaf-mutism, prolonged Q T interval, syncopal attacks and sudden death. New England J. Med., **259**:412, 1958.

MARTELLE, R. R. AND LINDE, L. M.: Cerebrovascular accidents with tetralogy of Fallot. Amer. Jour. Dis. Child., **101**:206, 1961.

MATSON, D. D. AND SALAM, M.: Brain abscesses in congenital heart disease. Pediatrics, **27**:772, 1961.

MOSSBERG, J. I.: Anoxia of the central nervous system in congenital heart disease. Am. J. Dis. Child., **78**:28, 1949.

NORA, J. J. *et al.:* Klippel-Feil syndrome with congenital heart disease. Am. Dis. Child., **102**:858, 1961.

OPPENHEIMER, E. H.: Arterial thrombosis (parodoxical embolis), in association with transposition of the great vessels. Johns Hopkins Med. Jour., **124**:202, 1969.

ROBBINS, S. L.: Brain abscess associated with congenital heart disease. Arch. Int. Med., **75**:279, 1945.

ROLAND, J.: Pulmonary arteriovenous fistulae. Brit. Heart J., **16**:34, 1954.

STEPHENS, J. W.: Neurological sequelae of congenital heart surgery. Arch. of Neurol., **7**:450, 1963.

TAUSSIG, H. B.: Congenital malformation of the heart. Holt and McIntosh. Dis. Child., 12th Ed. p. 576, 1953.

TYLER, H. R. AND CLARK, D. B.: Cerebrovascular accidents in patients with congenital heart disease. Arch. Neurol. & Psychiat., **77**:483, 1957.

TYLER, H. R. AND CLARK, D. B.: Incidence of neurological complications in congenital heart disease. Arch. Neurol. & Psychiat., **77**:17, 1957.

TYLER, H. R. AND CLARK, D. B.: Loss of consciousness and convulsions with congenital heart disease. Arch. Neurol. & Psychiat., **79**:506, 1958.

VOGLER, W. R. AND DORNEY, E. R.: Endocarditis in congenital heart disease. Am. Heart J., **64**:198, 1962.

WALSH, F. B.: *Loc. cit.*

WIELAND, W.: Weitere Untersuchungen über Polycythaemia vera im Kindesalter. Ztschr. f. Kinderh., **53**:703, 1932.

WILLIAMS, J. C. P., BARRATT-BOYES, B. G. AND LOWE, J. B.: Facies with supravalvular stenosis, Circulation, **24**:1311, 1961.

INVOLVEMENT OF THE NERVOUS SYSTEM IN BACTERIAL ENDOCARDITIS

Etiology.—Two types are described, the acute or malignant endocarditis and the subacute type. The former is due to the pneumococcus, the hemolytic streptococcus, the meningococcus and the gonococcus, as a rule, and is associated with pneumonia, erysipelas and septicemia. The latter is almost invariably due to streptococcus viridans, but may result from other types of streptococci, staphylococci and even the Pfeiffer bacillus.

Pathological Anatomy.—Diamond, who has made a careful study of 13 cases, states that the brain is always involved. He describes lesions of several types. The commonest of all is the miliary nodule found in relation to small vessels. These are composed of glial cells, lymphocytes, leucocytes, cells of the vascular adventitia and occasionally giant cells. They often contain bacteria. The vessel may be patent or occluded. There are also often miliary abscesses, areas of partial or complete softening due to embolism, petechial hemorrhages and inflammatory and degenerative hemorrhages in

the brain. The formation of mycotic aneurysms is not unusual. In a few cases, there is a definite subacute meningitis.

Clinical Features.—Subacute endocarditis is not common in children and rarely appears before the age of four years. It often develops upon a basis of previous rheumatic endocarditis or congenital malformation of the heart and may follow tonsillectomy, extraction of teeth or acute infections. The onset is insidious and marked by a slight fever, weakness and loss of weight. After a time embolic phenomena appear such as petechiae in the mucous membranes and skin. Later, there may be signs of infarction of the spleen or the liver. The urine contains a few red blood cells. Anemia develops and slowly increases. Symptoms referable to the heart are usually present eventually but may be absent for weeks or months. The fever gradually grows higher but is often interrupted by partial remissions. Chills are common in older children. The blood culture shows S. viridans in most cases although many cultures may be necessary before a positive one is obtained.

In the later stages of the disease, symptoms of cerebral embolism are common. Sudden hemiparesis, disturbances of speech and vision occur. As a rule we seem to be dealing with multiple small lesions rather than single massive lesions. I have seen sudden cerebellar ataxia and brainstem syndromes. These may recede for a time, only to be followed by additional cerebral insults. Embolism of the central retinal artery may occur. Jones and Siekert describe lesions in peripheral nerves due to embolism. In a few cases, aneurysms develop upon the arteries of the circle of Willis, causing focal signs such as compression of cranial nerves and finally rupturing with the production of subarachnoid hemorrhage. Similar aneurysms may be palpable under the skin along the course of the larger arteries. Death occurs after weeks or months. In one case, the writer has seen subacute meningitis develop among the first symptoms of the disease. This ended in recovery but was followed by hemiplegia and finally by the development of the complete picture of subacute bacterial endocarditis. Post-mortem examination confirmed the diagnosis. Toone has recently described a series of cases in which cerebral symptoms were the first manifestations of the disease. The malignant endocarditis runs a much more rapid course and often presents the picture of septicemia. Cardiac symptoms may not be evident and multiple abscesses are common.

Diagnosis.—The diagnosis may be very difficult in the early stages of the disease before the characteristic symptoms are present. The most important diagnostic features are the presence of embolic phenomena, signs of progressive endocarditis, and above all a positive blood culture for S. viridans.

The organisms must be found repeatedly to establish the diagnosis for contaminations are common.

Prognosis.—Just a few years ago, this disease was almost invariably fatal. Now by the use of penicillin, a large percentage of all patients may be cured; some writers claiming success in three cases out of four. It must be kept in mind, however, that some patients who survive the infection may nevertheless have suffered extensive and permanent damage to the brain as a result of embolism so the therapeutic victory is an empty one.

Treatment.—The sensitiveness of the organism to various antibacterial agents must be determined and the most effective drug employed. As a rule penicillin is the most important drug but it is usually combined with a mixture of streptomycin and dihydrostreptomycin. The administration of 2 to 5 million units of penicillin every day for 3 to 4 weeks is usually sufficient. This is the adult dosage and children should be given a dosage suitable for their weight. In some cases more prolonged medication is required. After the medication is terminated, blood cultures are indicated for a period of several months.

It is recommended that prophylactic injections of penicillin be given to a patient who has had bacterial endocarditis if extraction of a tooth or operation on the upper respiratory tract or urinary tract is required.

BIBLIOGRAPHY

ALPERS, B. J. AND GASKILL, H. S.: The pathological characteristics of embolic or metastatic encephalitis. J. Neuropath. & Exp. Neurol., **3**:210, 1944.

BELL, W. E. AND BUTLER, C.: Cerebral mycotic aneurysms in children. Neurology, **18**:81, 1968.

DAWSON, M. H. AND HUNTER, T. H.: Treatment of bacterial endocarditis with penicillin. J.A.M.A., **127**:129, 1945.

DIAMOND, I. B.: Brain changes in malignant endocarditis. Arch. Neurol. & Psychiat., **27**:1175, 1932.

JONES, H. R. AND SIEKERT, R. G.: Embolic mononeuropathy. Arch. of Neurology, **19**:535, 1968.

LEECH, C. B.: Streptococcus viridans endocarditis in children. Am. J. Med. Sc., **180**:621, 1930.

SANSBY, J. M. AND LARSON, L. M.: Acute bacterial endocarditis in infancy. Am. J. Dis. Child., **39**:1261, 1930.

THAYER, S.: Studies on bacterial infective endocarditis. Johns Hopkins Hospital Reports, **22**:1, 1926.

TOONE, E. C.: Cerebral manifestations of bacterial endocarditis. Ann. Int. Med., **14**:1551, 1941.

WINKELMAN, N. W. AND ECKEL, J. L.: The brain in bacterial endocarditis. Arch. Neurol. & Psychiat., **23**:1161, 1930.

WALSH, F. B.: *Loc. cit.*

EMBOLISM DUE TO RHEUMATIC HEART DISEASE

Cerebral embolism is not rare in rheumatic heart disease, especially when there is atrial fibrillation. Mural thrombi develop in the atria which do not contract fully. If the fibrillation reverts to normal rhythm spontaneously or as a result of medication, contraction of the atria may dislodge mural

thrombi and cause cerebral emboli often of large size. The middle cerebral artery is most frequently involved. The onset of symptoms is characteristically sudden. Softenings due to emboli are often hemorrhagic. Recurrent episodes are to be expected.

BIBLIOGRAPHY

AITA, J. A.: Neurologic Manifestations of General Diseases. Springfield, Thomas, 1964, p. 25.
DECOBAN, A.: Neurology of Infancy. Williams and Wilkins Co., 1959, p. 105.

FAT EMBOLISM OF THE BRAIN

Etiology.—In the great majority of cases, fat embolism results from fracture of one or more bones. The femur and other large bones are more apt to be the source of the emboli than smaller bones. The same result may follow extensive bruising of fat deposits or operations upon obese subjects, although such cases are exceptional. It has also been claimed that manipulation of stiff joints and similar orthopedic procedures may be responsible. Closed chest massage and exposure to low atmospheric pressure may both cause fat embolism. De Gutierrez-Mahoney believes that fat embolism is common in cases of head injury and suggests that the fat comes from the brain.

It is believed that the fat of the bone marrow is broken up and that the fat globules are forced into the venous sinuses as a result of the increased pressure resulting from hemorrhage. The emboli are borne to the heart and then to the lungs, where they lodge in the capillaries. Later many of them are forced through the capillaries of the lungs and get into the arteries by which they are carried to the brain, viscera and skin. It has been suggested that these emboli may add to their bulk by taking up the finely emulsified fat from the blood. Some writers believe that agglutination of the fat particles in the blood and consequently embolism may occur without trauma as a result of changes in the properties of the blood. Johnson and Svanborg believe that fat embolism is due to qualitative changes in the blood lipids and may be due to tissue damage of various types.

Pipkin states that in addition to mechanical obstruction of blood vessels, toxic symptoms result from hydrolysis of neutral fats into fatty acids. Petechial hemorrhages result and anemia.

Pathological Anatomy.—The lungs usually show multiple small hemorrhagic areas and histological examination with appropriate stains reveal that the capillaries are loaded with globules of fat. Emboli composed of cellular elements of the bone marrow may also be found in the lungs. The brain shows petechiae scattered throughout the hemispheres and brainstem. Each lesion surrounds a small arteriole or capillary which is filled by fat. Around the occluded vessel is an area of necrosis and the periphery of this

area is usually infiltrated by red cells, phagocytes and proliferating glial cells. Softenings are sometimes found in the lenticular nuclei. The other viscera show similar embolic lesions.

Clinical Features.—Following the injury, which we have stated above usually includes fracture of one or more large bones, the patient may seem to be as well as can be expected for days or hours. After between twelve hours to two or three days, the pulmonary symptoms develop with rapid respiration, rapid, feeble pulse, cough, cyanosis, blood-tinged sputum and fever. These symptoms mark the deposit of emboli in the lungs and heart. Maruyama and Little point out that roentgenograms of the chest show diffuse bilateral pulmonary densities similar to those seen in pulmonary edema. These are perihilar, nodular and basal. Some hours later, the emboli pass through the capillaries of the lungs and begin to reach the brain and other organs. The patient becomes restless, delirious, stuporous and finally comatose. Convulsions often occur and status epilepticus is described. Focal signs such as strabismus, hemiparesis, and localized twitchings may occur. Decerebrate rigidity is described. Many petechiae are usually seen over the chest and other parts of the body and in the conjunctiva and mucous membranes. We have seen multiple small white areas of necrosis in the retinae with flecks of hemorrhage due to embolism of the retinae. The urine and sputum may contain fat globules and they may even be found in the blood in some cases. Death almost always results when the symptoms are severe and the course is usually not more than four days. Adler and Peltier state that detection of lipuria and determination of serum lipase values are the most helpful tests.

Prognosis.—The outlook is very unfavorable when the signs are definite enough to justify the diagnosis. If the patient survives, there is usually complete recovery.

Diagnosis.—The diagnosis is based upon the fracture of one or more bones followed, after a latent period of a few hours or days, by pulmonary and cardiac disturbances and then by cerebral symptoms and by petechiae in the skin.

Treatment.—If the fracture involves the bones of an extremity, a tourniquet should be placed around the limb as soon as possible. The marrow cavity should then be opened and a drain inserted. The tourniquet may then be released. If the embolism arises in subcutaneous fat, a drain should be inserted. Usually these measures are carried out too late to be effective.

Pipkin advises elevation of the fractured limb. He states that fat may be dissolved by injections of 5 per cent alcohol in 5 per cent glucose. Oxygen should be administered and transfusions are indicated in some cases.

BIBLIOGRAPHY

ADLER, F. AND PELTIER, L. F.: Tests for fat embolism. Clin. Orthop. **21**:226, 1962.

BERRIGAN, T. J. *et al.*: Fat embolism. Amer. Jour. Roentgenol., **96**:967, 1966.

DE GUTIERREZ-MAHONEY, W.: The pathogenesis of traumatic unconsciousness. Importance of fat embolism. War. Med., **1**:816, 1941.

ELTING, A. W. AND MARTIN, C. E.: Fat embolism with a study of two fatal cases. Ann. Surg., **82**: 336, 1925.

FISHER, J. H.: Bone-marrow embolism. Arch. Path., **52**:315, 1951.

GAUSS, H.: The pathology of fat embolism. Arch. Surg., **9**:593, 1924.

GREENFIELD, J. G.: Discussion on fat embolism and the brain. Proc. Roy. Soc. Med., **1**:651, 1941.

HARRIS, R. I., PERRETT, T. S. AND MACLACHLIN, A.: Fat embolism. Ann. Surg., **110**:1095, 1939.

HAYMAKER, W. AND DAVISON, C.: Fatalities resulting from exposure to simulated high altitudes in decompression chambers. Jour. Neuropath. and Exp. Neurol., **9**:29, 1950.

JOHNSON, S. R. AND SVANBORG, A.: Investigations with regard to the pathogenesis of the so-called fat embolism. Ann. Surg., **144**:145, 1956.

MARUYAMA, Y. AND LITTLE, J. B.: Traumatic fat embolism. Radiology, **79**:945, 1962.

PIPKIN, G.: The early diagnosis and treatment of fat embolism. Clin. Orthop., **12**:171, 1958.

SCHNEIDER, R. C.: Fat embolism. A problem in differential diagnosis of cranio-cerebral trauma. J. Neurosurg., **9**:1, 1952.

SILVERSTEIN, A.: The significance of cerebral fat embolism. Neurology, **2**:292, 1952.

WALSH, F. B.: *Loc. cit.*

WERTZBERGER, J. J. AND PELTIER, L. F.: Fat embolism: The importance of arterial hypoxia. Surgery, **63**:626, 1968.

WHITAKER, J. C.: Traumatic fat embolism. Report of 2 cases with recovery. Arch. Surg., **39**:182, 1939.

AIR EMBOLISM OF THE NERVOUS SYSTEM

Etiology.—Air embolism may result from two causes: from the liberation of nitrogen in the blood stream due to sudden reduction of atmospheric pressure, i.e. caisson disease and from the introduction of air or other gases into the vascular system from without. The former cause need scarcely be considered, for it is almost exclusively confined to industrial accidents such as may occur among divers or among workmen who are employed in caissons under water. The latter type of air embolism occurs most frequently as a result of therapeutic accidents. Air which enters one of the peripheral veins causes symptoms mostly as a result of accumulation in the right side of the heart. Sudden death may result. To reach the brain in such cases, the air must pass through the pulmonary capillaries. This is called *venous embolism*. The entrance of air into the pulmonary veins, however, results in cerebral embolism very promptly. This is called *arterial embolism*. Injection of air into the pleural cavity with the object of causing artificial pneumothorax and various operations performed to induce collapse of the lung are the commonest causes of this condition. Puncture of the lung with a needle in the effort to drain empyema may cause embolism. Recently operations for congenital heart disease have in some instances given rise to this condition. Cases have been described following

craniotomies in the upright position, spinal encephalography, puncture and washing out of the antrum; intravenous injections, inflation of the Eustachian tube and injection of air into the retroperitoneal tissues to demonstrate neoplasms. Since there is reason to think that large amounts of air may be injected into the peripheral veins without ill effect, some of these case reports are not entirely convincing. Jacoby states that pneumoencephalography is especially hazardous in children. The air may get in the venous system and cause embolism.

Pathological Anatomy.—The lesions in the nervous system are not unlike those of fat embolism for many small areas of necrosis are found in relation to small arterioles. These are often infiltrated with blood giving the appearance of ring hemorrhages.

Clinical Features.—In most cases the patient has suddenly collapsed and fallen to the floor a few moments after some procedure such as irrigation of the antrum or injection of air into the pleural cavity has been begun. There is often unconsciousness for a time and convulsions may occur. Blindness is a common finding. We have observed hemiplegia and also double hemiplegia and hemianopia following various procedures intended to collapse the lung. Recently we observed the case of a little boy with congenital heart disease whose heart was catheterized during studies which were being made to determine the nature of his cardiac defect. He suddenly complained that he could not see and it was found that he also had right hemiplegia. When his eyes were examined an hour later, it was found that he was blind in the right eye. Vision returned to approximately a normal level within a few days and the hemiplegia diminished but did not disappear. Recently Walsh and Goldberg have pointed out that transient blindness is one of the commonest and most characteristic evidences of air embolism. This is apparently due to retinal damage. As a rule improvement begins within one or two days and there is a strong tendency to recovery, although in some cases permanent symptoms result. I know of one case in which air embolism caused such extensive cerebral damage that the patient never regained consciousness and lived for several months in a vegetative state.

Diagnosis.—Venous embolism causes a loud cardiac bruit with cyanosis, feeble pulse, falling blood pressure and syncope. Arterial embolism causes air in the retinal vessels, pallor of the tongue, marbling of the skin and air in the cerebral vessels demonstrable in roentgenograms.

Prognosis.—If the patient survives for a few days, there is little danger of death. There is always a strong tendency to improvement but when the cerebral symptoms are very severe, there is apt to be some residuum.

Treatment.—In venous embolism it is advised that the patient's head be lowered and the body placed in the left lateral position. If these measures

fail, the heart may be exposed and the air removed by massage or aspiration with a syringe. Oxygen should be administered. There seems to be no treatment for arterial embolism.

BIBLIOGRAPHY

COHEN, A. *et al.:* Air embolism. Ann. Int. Med., **35**:779, 1951.

GORDING, R.: Further investigation into the serious complications arising from puncture of maxillary antrum. Experimental researches on the effects of the introduction of air into the venous system. Acta Otol., **3**:160, 1921-22.

GROVE, W. E.: Mishaps in puncture and irrigation of maxillary sinus. Ann. Otol., Rhin. & Laryng., **31**:913, 1922.

HAMILTON, C. E. AND ROTHSTEIN, E.: Air embolism. J.A.M.A., **104**:2226, 1935.

JACOBY, *et al.:* Pneumoencephalography and air embolism. Simulated anesthetic death. Anesthesiology, **20**:336, 1959.

KING, A. B, AND OTENASEK, F. J.: Air embolism occurring during encephalography. J. Neurosurg., **5**:577, 1948.

NICHOLSON, M. J. AND CREHAN, J. P.: Emergency treatment of air embolism. Current Res. Anesth. Anal., **35**:634, 1956.

REYER, G. W. AND KOHL, H. W.: Air embolism complicating thoracic surgery. J.A.M.A., **87**:1626, 1926.

WALSH, F. B. AND GOLDBERG, H. K.: Blindness due to air embolism. J.A.M.A., **114**:654, 1940.

VASCULAR ANOMALIES INVOLVING THE NERVOUS SYSTEM

Introduction.—In recent years these interesting conditions have attracted widespread attention. A great deal of information about the symptoms course and pathological anatomy has been accumulated and a more satisfactory classification has been devised. If we exclude true neoplasms arising from the walls of the intracranial blood vessels, i.e. the hemangioblastomas, we may divide the vascular anomalies into the following groups: (1) Saccular aneurysms of the cerebral arteries. (2) Arteriovenous aneurysms or arteriovenous fistulae. (3) Venous angiomas. (4) Telangiectases. (5) Meningeal angiomatosis or the Sturge-Weber Syndrome. (6) Familial cerebellar ataxia with choreoathetosis, telangiectasia and infections of the respiratory tract. (7) The Klippel-Trenaunay-Weber syndrome. These conditions are believed to be congenital malformations or to arise upon a basis of defective development of the cerebral vascular system.

SACCULAR ANEURYSMS OF THE CEREBRAL ARTERIES

Pathological Anatomy.—These aneurysms are almost always small, rarely exceeding 2.0 cm in diameter. They are situated in most cases upon the carotid artery, the circle of Willis and somewhat less commonly in the posterior fossa upon the basilar or vertebral arteries. It is rare for such aneurysms to be found in the substance of the brain. In a large percentage of cases, multiple aneurysms are found. Several types may be distinguished: (1) Those attributed to congenital weakness of the vessel wall. It is usual in such cases to find that the muscular and elastic coats of the artery are

narrow or even lacking at the site of the lesion. These are relatively common. Dissecting aneurysms may result from the same defects in the arteries. (2) Those associated with coarctation of the aorta and hence, attributed to overloading of the cerebral circulation and, perhaps, to congenital weakness of the vessel wall as well. These are extremely rare but of great interest. (3) Those due to infected emboli, such as develop in the course of bacterial endocarditis. In these cases there is infarction of the vessel wall as well as a subacute inflammatory process. (4) Those due to local inflammatory and degenerative processes, such as syphilis and various infectious diseases. These are very rare in children. Wagenvoort *et al.* describe giant cell arteritis in children with aneurysm formation.

Clinical Features.—It must be admitted that saccular, intracranial aneurysms are rare in childhood but they occur even in infancy. They are found in the same sites and give rise to the same symptoms as in adults. Newcomb and Munns report the case of a baby who died 64 hours after birth of ruptured saccular aneurysm arising from the posterior communicating artery. The symptoms dated from birth. Symonds has given a very illuminating analysis of the manifestations of intracranial aneurysms. He divides these into three groups: (1) Local signs due to direct pressure of the aneurysm. (2) Signs due to rupture or leaking, i.e. subarachnoid hemorrhage. (3) Signs due to the disease causing the aneurysm.

Focal signs due to direct pressure of the aneurysmal sac occur in a large percentage of cases. The onset is usually abrupt with sudden local pain in

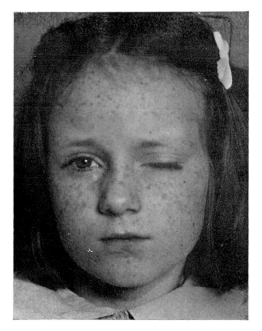

FIG. 211. Little girl with saccular aneurysm of the internal carotid artery compressing the left third nerve.

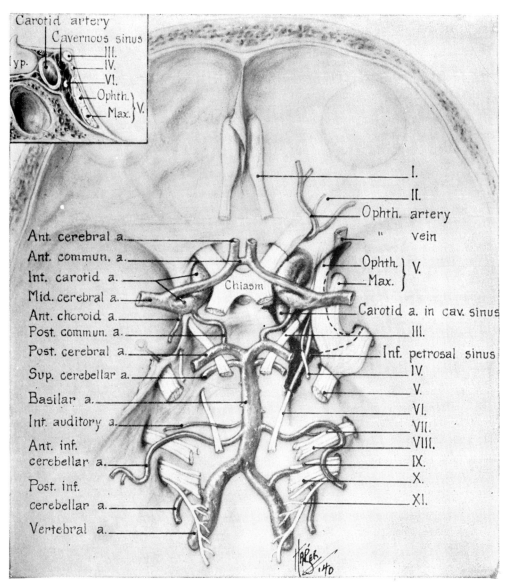

Carotid artery
Cavernous sinus
III.
IV.
VI.
Ophth.⎫
Max.⎬ V.
Typ.

I.
II.
Ophth. artery
"   vein
Ophth.⎫
Max.⎬ V.
Carotid a. in cav. sinus
III.
Inf. petrosal sinus
IV.
V.
VI.
VII.
VIII.
IX.
X.
XI.

Ant. cerebral a.
Ant. commun. a.
Int. carotid a.
Mid. cerebral a.
Ant. choroid a.
Post. commun. a.
Post. cerebral a.
Sup. cerebellar a.
Basilar a.
Int. auditory a.
Ant. inf. cerebellar a.
Post. inf. cerebellar a.
Vertebral a.

Chiasm

Fig. 212. Composite drawing of the regional anatomy of the base of the skull, cranial nerves, circle of Willis and cavernous sinus. (Drawing by Mrs. Paul Padget.) (From Walsh: Neuro-Ophthalmology, courtesy the Williams and Wilkins Company.)

the frontal or occipital region and palsies of one or more cranial nerves. If the sac is situated on the proximal part of the *internal carotid artery* the third nerve is most constantly paralysed and in some cases the fourth and sixth nerves as well. The first branch of the fifth nerve and sometimes the second and third branches are also affected. In aneurysms situated on the more distal part of the carotid, which are much less common, there is

apt to be compression of the lateral aspect of the optic chiasm with blindness in the homolateral eye and loss of temporal field of the opposite eye. If the lesion involves the *anterior cerebral* or *anterior communicating artery*, there may be compression of one optic nerve or of the chiasm. Dr. David Clark has told me of a case of unilateral optic atrophy, in a child of four years, in which operation revealed that the optic nerve was pushed upwards by a loupe of the carotid artery in such a way as to force it against the upper margin of the optic foramen. We have seen one case of aneurysm of the anterior communicating artery in which there was bitemporal hemianopia with neurogenic fever and somnolence due to compression of the hypothalamus. Aneurysms of the *middle cerebral artery* are apt to lie in the Sylvian fissure. They cause no symptoms as a rule before rupture. When the aneurysm arises from the *posterior communicating artery*, the third, fourth and sixth nerves are apt to be involved but the fifth is rarely affected. Not many aneurysms spring from the *posterior cerebral artery*. A few found at the base have compressed the third, fourth and sixth nerves. Aneurysms in the posterior fossa may be very large and compress the brain stem and the cranial nerves. Aneurysms of the *basilar artery* may cause hemiplegia or tetraplegia, bulbar palsy, ataxia and involvement of the cranial nerves which lie in the posterior fossa. Those which arise from the *vertebral artery* may compress the medulla and the last four cranial nerves.

In a very few cases, roentgenograms of the skull reveal shadows in the walls of saccular aneurysms. Sometimes thin semilunar plaques are seen which are considered typical but the diagnosis can rarely be made by such means. In a few instances the clinoid processes may be eroded by pressure of a carotid aneurysm.

A saccular aneurysm on the intracavernous part of the artery may rupture with the production of a carotid-cavernous fistula and pulsating exophthalmos.

We have repeatedly seen return of function of cranial nerves paralysed by pressure of an aneurysm, most often a carotid aneurysm. No doubt the sac has filled with blood clot and has shrunk when there was organization. We have seen two cases in which an aneurysm has developed in the first two years of life and then became inactive and calcified. One of these was exposed at operation at the age of 22 years. Third nerve palsies due to compression by a saccular aneurysm may be associated with no abnormalities of the pupil though the palsy may be complete in other respects. If return of function occurs, there is usually evidence of aberrant regeneration and mass movements of the muscles innervated by the third nerve.

Complete rupture of an intracranial aneurysm is fatal almost at once but leakage is not incompatible with life if the bleeding is arrested by the formation of a clot. In fact, it is usual for several leaks to occur before

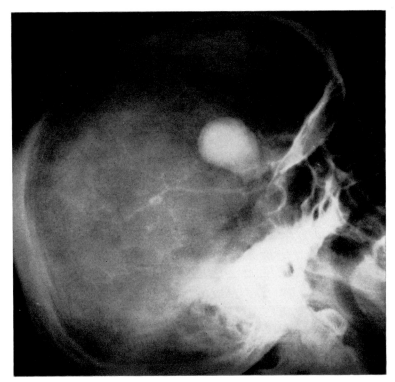

Fig. 213. Arteriogram of large aneurysm of the middle cerebral artery arising in the Sylvian fissure. The patient has coarctation of the aorta. The photographer has tilted the photograph at an unusual angle.

death. Leakage may occur following violent exertion or straining at stool or may seem to be spontaneous. The symptoms of partial rupture are those of subarachnoid hemorrhage. They may be divided into those due to: (1) Increase of intracranial pressure. (2) Meningeal irritation. (3) General systemic reaction. (4) Focal signs. (5) Changes in the retina. (6) Alterations of the spinal fluid due to admixture of blood. The onset is generally very sudden with severe headache, vomiting, loss of consciousness and often convulsions. The pulse is slow and slow, irregular respiration may occur. If the hemorrhage is a massive one, the patient may die promptly but if it is of moderate size and is arrested before the pressure causes death, the patient may remain unconscious for varying periods, ranging from a few hours to several days. During this period the head may be retracted, the legs extended and the arms fully extended, adducted and the forearms strongly pronated. Any stimulus may cause convulsive twitchings of the entire body and irregularity of respiration. We have also observed tonic fits. There is frequent vomiting. Cervical rigidity, Kernig's sign, photophobia and hyperesthesia are usually present but are rarely so severe as in purulent

meningitis. Herpes zoster may develop as a result of irritation of the posterior root ganglia by the blood. There is usually fever, which may reach 104°F. and leucocytosis. Bile pigments are increased in the blood and urine. The retinae often show typical changes. The veins are engorged and small flame-shaped hemorrhages are seen along their course in the retina. The edges of the optic disc may be indistinct or edematous but outspoken papilledema is uncommon. Massive circular hemorrhages on or near the disc, the so-called subhyaloid hemorrhages, are very characteristic. They may rupture into the vitreous and so obscure the retina. The careful work of Walsh has shown that the retinal hemorrhages are not due to distention of the optic nerve sheath as has been thought. They arise independently from small veins. It must be emphasized, however, that retinal lesions may be absent.

Hemorrhage may rupture the pia and tear into the cortex. This is most apt to happen in rupture of aneurysms of the *middle cerebral* artery which lie in the Sylvian fissure. The frontal and temporal lobes may be involved. Hemianopia results and faciobrachial monoplegia. Aphasia occurs when the left hemisphere is involved. Rarely rupture of a *posterior cerebral* aneurysm causes hemianopia. Leakage of an aneurysm on the *anterior part of the circle of Willis* may cause extravasations into one or both frontal lobes with hemiparesis or bilateral hemiparesis.

The spinal fluid contains a large amount of blood. The distribution of the blood is usually equal in the three tubes but if the puncture is made very promptly, the first tube may be clear and the fluid may grow progressively more bloody as it flows. No clotting occurs on standing. The color is pink or red during the first day but soon begins to turn yellow, brown or orange. When centrifugalized, the supernatant fluid is discolored and spectroscopic tests reveal the presence of hemoglobin and oxyhemoglobin, as well as bile pigments within a few hours after the onset of symptoms. The benzidine and van den Berg tests are also positive. The red cells are crenated. After two days white cells are present in increased proportion to the red cells. At first these are chiefly leucocytes but at the end of five days there are many large mononuclear cells and lymphocytes. At the end of a month, there may still be a few lymphocytes and some phagocytes containing fragments of red cells, although the pigment has disappeared from the fluid.

Troost *et al.* point out that in subarachnoid hemorrhage the spinal fluid sugar is reduced.

After the acute symptoms are over, the patient usually shows mental disturbances such as forgetfulness, irritability, and emotional instability for a time, in addition to any focal symptoms which may have occurred. Reduction of vision or blindness from intraocular hemorrhages may persist. In four cases I have seen hemiplegia appear suddenly between two and three weeks after the aneurysm has leaked. I have been inclined to attribute

this to the formation of a thrombus in the sac with extension into the artery from which it springs. We have observed two cases in which softening occurred in the distribution of the anterior cerebral arteries in which it was shown by arteriograms and by post-mortem examination that these arteries were quite patent. One might suppose that the formation of the aneurysm might have caused irritation of the vessel wall and spasmodic contraction sufficient to cause softening. In rare cases the blood sets up such a severe reaction in the meninges that obliteration of the subarachnoid spaces occurs and hydrocephalus results. I know of two instances in which the blood has broken through the arachnoid and caused a subdural hematoma. In a large percentage of cases repeated hemorrhages occur. More than one aneurysm may be responsible. If leakage occurs a second time at the same site, the blood may be confined by adhesions and the spinal fluid may remain clear.

Aneurysms due to bacterial endocarditis are accompanied by the usual signs of that disease, such as fever, cardiac symptoms, and embolic phenomena. Aneurysms may appear upon the peripheral arteries. In some cases the development of a cerebral aneurysm is preceded by sudden hemiplegia or other cerebral symptoms of apoplectic nature, which may be taken to indicate the impaction of an embolus in the affected vessel. Mycotic aneurysms may develop on the smaller branches of the intracranial arteries, which are rarely affected by congenital aneurysms.

Another type of intracranial aneurysm of great interest is that associated with congenital coarctation of the aorta. In this condition there is stenosis or complete occlusion of the aorta at the isthmus and the lower part of the body is supplied with arterial blood by anastomotic circulation through the internal mammary and intercostal arteries. The clinical features include dilatation and excessive pulsation of the carotid and subclavian arteries. Blood pressure is usually elevated in the brachial arteries. The heart is enlarged and there is a precordial bruit, due to dilatation of the aortic orifice. Over the back, between the scapulae and between the nipples, large subcutaneous arteries are palpable, which convey blood from above downward. The pulses in the abdominal aorta, femoral arteries and vessels of the legs are small or absent. If present, they show a delayed rise and fall as in aortic stenosis. Intermittent claudication is sometimes present in the legs and seems to indicate that the anastomotic circulation is not always adequate. There is very commonly cardiac decompensation. As a result of the overloading of the carotids and vertebrals, the pressure within the circle of Willis is elevated and this favors the development of aneurysm. Intracranial hemorrhage may also occur without aneurysm. Convulsions and syncopal attacks are described. Various deformities of the brain and circulatory apparatus are sometimes associated, such as congenital heart disease, mental

defects of various degrees, etc. The roentgenographic findings are characteristic. Plates taken in the oblique position show absence of the aortic
knob and dilatation of the ascending aorta. The heart is enlarged, especially the left ventricle, and there is often scalloping of the lower border of
the ribs due to dilatation of the intercostal arteries. A few instances of
coarctation of the aorta are described in which a transverse lesion of the
spinal cord developed. This may be due to compression of the spinal cord
by dilated arteries which are regarded as collaterals. These dilated arteries
may also exhibit saccular aneurysms which behave as do similar aneurysms
in the cranium.

Diagnosis.—It is scarcely possible to make the diagnosis until there has
been some leakage, but the appearance of palsies of the third, fourth and
sixth nerves of peripheral type in an otherwise healthy child should suggest
the possibility of saccular aneurysm, especially if the symptoms are of sudden onset and associated with pain. If there is evidence of coarctation of
the aorta or of bacterial endocarditis, the possibility of intracranial aneurysm should always be considered. Recurrent subarachnoid hemorrhage
without apparent cause is very typical. Arteriograms are of course essential
for diagnosis.

Prognosis.—If we omit from consideration mycotic aneurysms, it is
found that about 50 per cent of all patients die within a month or two of
the onset, but of those who survive this period only about 20 per cent die
in the next 10 years. Of the survivors only a very few display any considerable disability.

Treatment.—In case of subarachnoid hemorrhage the treatment should
be conservative. Nothing should be done which is not urgently required.
Spinal puncture is contraindicated for it may provoke further bleeding.
Complete rest is important and sedatives may be given as necessary. Several
weeks later operation is possible. Dandy has operated successfully upon a
number of aneurysms of the internal carotid artery. A ligature is placed
upon the artery in the neck and another ligature is placed distal to the aneurysm but proximal to the posterior communicating artery. The results
have been excellent. Anterior cerebral aneurysms may also be cured in
many instances. Aneurysms situated upon other arteries are not handled so
easily. Great skill and mature judgment are required in such operations for
the circulation of important parts of the brain may be interrupted with
the production of massive hemiplegias and other catastrophes.

CASE HISTORY (Ped. A-74726).—*Boy of five years who had subarachnoid
hermorrhage 19 days after a head injury. A second hemorrhage occurred
a month later. Arteriograms revealed a saccular aneurysm attached to the
right anterior cerebral artery. This was removed successfully.*

W. W., a boy of five years, fell out of an automobile on November 5,

1949. A long laceration in the left temporal and frontal region resulted but the skull was not fractured and no evidence of intracranial damage was detected during the five days he was kept in the hospital.

On November 24 he had a convulsion which lasted one hour. After this he had persisting headache and pain in the neck. He vomited several times. On November 29, there was a second convulsion.

He was admitted to Harriet Lane Home in the care of Dr. Harriet Guild. There it was found that he had mild papilledema in both eyes and paralysis of the left external rectus. The neck was rigid. Spinal puncture revealed xanthochromic fluid with some crenated red cells. In view of the history of trauma, trephine openings were made to eliminate the possibility of subdural hematoma but the results were negative. A ventriculogram was also negative.

On December 21, the child developed a violent headache and his neck became rigid once more. The spinal fluid contained fresh blood. Both external recti were weak. A series of arteriograms were made and a small saccular aneurysm was found on the anterior cerebral artery at the level of the genu of the corpus callosum. Dr. Otenasek exposed this at operation. Abundant evidences of hemorrhage were found and it seemed clear that this was the actual site of the hemorrhage. The aneurysm was removed without ill effect. The patient was soon free of symptoms.

CASE HISTORY (Path. 10333-Ped. 46577).—*Boy of eight years complained of headache and dizziness. Next morning was found in bed in convulsions. Later, semistupor, cervical rigidity, positive Kernig's sign, retinal hemorrhages and bloody spinal fluid. Death on third day. Ruptured saccular aneurysm of posterior communicating artery.*

G. M., boy of eight years, complained one day of headache and vertigo. These symptoms lasted only an hour or less and he seemed to be quite well the rest of the day. The next morning his parents found him in general convulsion in bed. Later in the morning he had another seizure without regaining consciousness in the intervening period. In the afternoon he showed some evidence of returning consciousness but at best he was still stuporous. He was able, however, to indicate that he had a severe headache. Vomiting occurred several times during the day.

Some 20 hours after the first convulsion, the child was brought to the hospital. He was in semi-coma, with head retracted and legs flexed. He could be partially aroused by painful stimuli but could not cooperate. Neck was rigid. Kernig's sign positive. Tendon reflexes all brisk but equal. Cranial nerves were negative. Numerous small flame-shaped hemorrhages could be seen along the course of the retinal veins, which were much engorged. No edema of the nerve head or subhyaloid hemorrhages. P. 60-76. T. 37.9°-37.2° C. R. 20-24. B.P. 118195. The spinal fluid contained a large quantity of blood which already showed some alteration.

The next day there was no definite change in his condition. On the third day after the onset, the pulse grew slow, respiration shallow, the lips became cyanotic and the child died in a terminal convulsion.

Post-mortem examination revealed distention of the subarachnoid space and cerebral ventricles with blood. This was traced to a small saccular aneurysm situated at the junction of the right posterior cerebral and posterior communicating arteries. This had ruptured and given rise to a fatal hemorrhage.

CASE HISTORY (U-104079. Path. 15257).—*Large saccular aneurysm of the right vertebral artery with compression of the brain stem causing suboccipital pain, diplopia, difficulty in swallowing and unsteadiness of gait in a girl of 17 years. Death after operation. Post-mortem examination.*

M. J. R., a previously healthy school girl of 17 years, developed severe pain in the right suboccipital region in September 1936. There was some rigidity of the neck at times. After two weeks these symptoms grew less severe and the pain became intermittent rather than constant. During the next few months she was free from symptoms but about the middle of March she began to notice double vision and difficulty in swallowing. She vomited once or twice. The pain returned and developed into a generalized headache. A few days later the patient became unsteady on her feet and found that she was apt to stagger to the right.

Examination disclosed a well developed young girl who was both cooperative and intelligent. There was no definite papilledema but both external recti were weak and there was diplopia in the lateral fields. Rhythmical nystagmus was evident on lateral deviation to right and left. The right half of the soft palate and the right vocal cord were weak and there was difficulty in swallowing. No ataxia of the extremities was found but the station and gait were both unsteady, the tendency being to fall to the right. Ventriculography disclosed bilateral hydrocephalus of moderate degree. Operation disclosed a large saccular aneurysm arising from the right vertebral artery and filled with blood clot. This mass which was 4 cm in diameter compressed the medulla and pons which were greatly deformed. There was no evidence that rupture had ever taken place. The patient failed to rally and died a few hours after the operation was completed. Post-mortem examination yielded no additional information. The aneurysm seemed to be of congenital origin.

CASE HISTORY (K-62768. Path. 14305).—*Sudden vomiting, loss of consciousness, convulsions, and left hemiplegia in a girl of 14 years. Death in four hours. Ruptured saccular aneurysm of the right middle cerebral artery found at post-mortem examination.*

F. McD., a previously healthy girl of 14 years, complained of sudden severe headache. She vomited a few minutes later and within one half hour became stuporous. Convulsive movements appeared on the left side and later became bilateral. Breathing grew slow and noisy. About three hours after the onset, she was brought to Johns Hopkins Hospital.

When first examined the patient was in deep coma. The pulse was 48 and respiration 12. The pupils were dilated and the retinal veins intensely congested. The left arm and leg were quite flaccid and apparently para-

lysed. Plantar responses were both extensor. No cervical rigidity was present. About 20 minutes after the patient was admitted, respiration ceased.

Post-mortem examination revealed an extensive subarachnoid hemorrhage which was traced to a ruptured saccular aneurysm in the right fissure of Sylvius. This arose from the middle cerebral artery. The hemorrhage had broken into the temporal and frontal lobes and had entered the lateral ventricle. There were no other lesions in the cerebral blood vessels and no endocarditis. The aneurysm seemed to be of congenital origin.

BIBLIOGRAPHY

BAKER, T. W. AND SHELDON, W. D.: Coarctation of the aorta with intermittent leakage of a congenital cerebral aneurysm. Am. J. Med. Sc., 191:626, 1936.

CLARKE, E. AND WALTON, J.: Subdural hematoma complicating intracranial aneurysm and angioma. Brain, 76:378, 1953.

DANDY, W. E.: Intracranial Arterial Aneurysms. Comstock Pub. Co., Ithaca, N. Y., 1944.

FORSTER, F. M. AND ALPERS, B. J.: Anatomical defects and pathological changes in congenital cerebral aneurysms. J. Neuropath. & Exp. Neurol., 4:146, 1945.

FOSTER, F. M. AND ALPERS, B. J.: Aneurysm of the circle of Willis associated with congenital polycystic disease of the kidneys. Arch. Neurol. & Psychiat., 50:669, 1943.

GOLDEN, J., ODOM, G. AND WOODHALL, B.: Subdural hematoma following subarachnoid hemorrhage. Arch. Neurol. & Psychiat., 69:486, 1953.

GRAEME-ROBERTSON, E.: Cerebral lesions due to intracranial aneurysms. Brain, 72:150, 1949.

GREEN, F. H. K.: "Congenital" aneurysm of the cerebral arteries. Quart. J. Med., 21:419, 1928.

HYLAND, H. H.: Prognosis in spontaneous subarachnoid hemorrhage. Arch. Neurol. & Psychiat., 63:61, 1950.

JEFFERSON, G.: Compression of the chiasm, optic nerves and optic tracts by intracranial aneurysms. Brain, 60:444, 1938.

———: On saccular aneurysms of the internal carotid artery in the cavernous sinus. Brit. J. Surg., 26:267, 1938.

LEVIN, P.: Intracranial aneurysms. Arch. Neurol. & Psychiat., 67:771, 1952.

LEY, A.: Compression of the optic nerve by fusiform aneurysm of the internal carotid artery. J. Neurol., Neurosurg. & Psychiat., 13:75, 1950.

LICHTENBERG, H. AND GALLAGHER, H. F.: Coarctation of the aorta: Anomaly of great vessels of the neck and intermittent leakage of a cerebral aneurysm diagnosed during life. Am. J. Dis. Child., 46:1253, 1933.

MADOW, L. AND ALPERS, B.: Aneurysm of the posterior communicating artery. Arch. Neurol. & Psychiat., 70:722, 1953.

NEWCOMB, A. L. AND MUNNS, G. F.: Rupture of an aneurysm of the circle of Willis in the newborn. Pediatrics, 3:769, 1949.

RADNER, S.: Vertebral angiography by catheterization. A new method employed in 221 cases. Acta Radiol. Suppl. LXXXVII. Stockholm 1951.

RICHARDSON, J. C. AND HYLAND, H. H.: Intracranial aneurysms. Medicine, 20:1, 1941.

SYMONDS, C. P.: Clinical study of intracranial aneurysms. Guy's Hosp. Rep., 73:159, 1923.

———: Spontaneous subarachnoid hemorrhage. Quart. J. Med., 18:93, 1924.

TALBOT, F. B.: Aneurysm of the middle cerebral artery in a child nine and one half years old. Contributions to Med. Biol. Research, 2:1004, 1919.

THOMPSON, R. A. AND PRIBRAM, F. W.: Infantile cerebral aneurysm associated with ophthalmoplegia and quadriparesis. Neurology, 19:785, 1969.

TROOST, B. T. et al.: Hypoglycorrhachia associated with subarachnoid hemorrhage. Arch. of Neurol., 19:438, 1968.

WAGENVOORT, C. A. et al.: Giant cell arteritis with aneurysm formation in children. Pediatrics, 32:861, 1963.

WALSH, F. B. AND HEDGES, T. R. JR.: Optic nerve sheath hemorrhage. Tr. Am. Acad. Ophth., Sept. 1950, p. 29.

WOLTMAN, H. W. AND SHELDEN, H. D.: Neurologic complications associated with congenital stenosis of the isthmus of the aorta. Arch. Neurol. & Psychiat., 17:303, 1927.

YASKIN, H. E. AND ALPERS, B. J.: Aneurysm of the vertebral artery. Arch. Neurol. & Psychiat., 51:271, 1944.

ARTERIOVENOUS FISTULAE

Pathological Anatomy.—We must distinguish between the acquired arteriovenous fistula which is due to rupture of a large artery into a vein and which is also always due to trauma, and the arteriovenous aneurysm or fistula which arises on a congenital basis. We may mention the communication between the internal carotid and the cavernous sinus which usually results from fracture of the skull as an example of the first type. So far as I can learn, this is the only situation in which traumatic arteriovenous fistula occurs within the cranial cavity. (See Arteriovenous fistula between the cavernous sinus and the Internal Carotid artery.)

The congenital arteriovenous aneurysm is composed of three parts: (1) A tangled mass of tortuous and greatly dilated veins which pulsate and contain bright arterial blood. (2) An enlarged artery which supplies the lesion. (3) An interposed bed of dilated vessels which occupy the position of the capillaries and through which numerous arteriovenous communications are

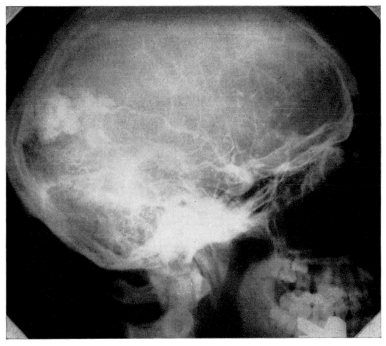

FIG. 214. Arteriogram showing an arteriovenous fistula in the occipital region. (By the courtesy of Dr. Arthur King.)

formed. An audible bruit and often a palpable thrill are present. Such lesions may be circumscribed as for example in the type in which the fistulae are found on the lateral aspect of the hemisphere between the middle cerebral artery and the adjacent veins. In many instances, however, the process is very extensive and innumerable fistulae are present. Since this is a developmental anomaly many variations and malformations of the vascular system are associated. The process gradually extends as a result of the progressive distention of the veins, and eventually the entire venous system of the brain and skull is enlarged. The veins are thought to become arterialized. Calcium may be deposited in the walls of the affected vessels. Thromboses occur and repeated hemorrhages.

Clinical Features.—The clinical features are often very distinctive. Since the lesions are most common in the distribution of the middle cerebral artery, the first symptoms are usually referable to the motor cortex. Focal and less commonly, general convulsions may be the only complaints for a number of years. These attacks occur at along intervals at first but slowly become more frequent and severe. Later, it is noticed that each seizure is followed by transient weakness or paralysis of the extremity in which the convulsion begins. For a time, complete recovery occurs each time but, eventually there is apt to be persisting hemiplegia. Of course, hemianopia, aphasia and other cerebral symptoms may occur in the same way. Dandy has described two cases in which the aneurysm arose from the vertebral artery and gave rise to the usual symptoms of a cerebral tumor. Intracranial hemorrhages are not common but may recur repeatedly. We have seen one patient who survived six severe hemorrhages during a period of ten years and finally died from the seventh. In a large percentage of all cases, papilledema eventually develops. In some instances, this is due to occlusion of the aqueduct by the aneurysm, but in other cases it seems probable that the distention of the cerebral veins by arterial blood is responsible for the increased intracranial pressure. Bilateral or unilateral exophthalmos of mild degree is described. The retinal veins often contain an admixture of venous blood and arterial blood so their color is brighter than normal. In addition to these features, some very striking and characteristic signs frequently occur. In many cases, the patient complains of a noise in the head. Ausculation over the cranium reveals a loud bruit, either confined to the period of cardiac systole or accentuated during systole. This sign is not constant and may be absent for long periods, so that the failure to demonstrate a bruit is not conclusive evidence against an arteriovenous communication. It is present, however, at some period during the course of a very large percentage of such cases. Another sign of diagnostic importance is dilatation of the veins of the scalp. This sign again is not constant and, if present, may not be evident until the head is shaved. In a few cases, one or

both carotid arteries are dilated and exaggerated pulsations may be observed. Compression of the carotid may stop the bruit. Cardiac dilatation and hypertrophy are described. Cyanosis may develop. Death may result from heart failure. The roentgenograms of the skull may be quite negative but in some cases shadows may be seen within the substance of the brain. These are apparently neither uniform nor characteristic. Often the diploic channels of the vault are dilated and the Rolandic vein may be so dilated as to cause a deep groove in the overlying bone. Crawford and Russell describe small arteriovenous aneurysms in the hemispheres and cerebellum of young people which gave rise to sudden and fatal intracranial hemorrhage.

A special group of cases has been brought to light recently by Wyburn-Mason in which a series of fistulae extended from the retina posteriorly along the optic nerve, optic tract and pulvinar to the dorsum of the midbrain and superior aspect of the cerebellum. The process is essentially a unilateral one though the midbrain may be involved on both sides. The onset of symptoms is frequently in childhood and the family history is negative. The most characteristic feature is the presence of arteriovenous fistulae in one retina though in some instances there is merely an increase in size and number of the retinal veins. Arteriovenous fistulae were present in the retina in 14 of the 20 cases described. According to Wyburn-Mason the presence of arteriovenous fistulae in the retina suggests the possibility of this intracranial process very strongly. Mild proptosis of the affected eye is common and this may be associated with pulsation. A bruit is usually evident over this eye. Often vascular naevi are present on the face and dilated veins are found in the lids and about the orbit. Hydrocephalus is present in most cases and in infants causes great enlargement of the head. Often the children are mentally defective and peculiar behavior is described. Various neurological signs are mentioned most of which refer to the optic pathways or the midbrain. Hemianopia and blindness in one or both eyes are common. The pupillary reflexes are often lost or altered. Partial or complete paralysis of the third nerve and loss of upward gaze are mentioned. Nystagmus and cerebellar ataxia occur. In some cases hemiplegia is present. Ventriculography reveals dilatation of the third and lateral ventricles. Carotid arteriograms often show nothing significant. The aneurysm seems to be fed, as a rule, by branches of the basilar artery so that injection of the vertebral is necessary for its demonstration.

The cases described by Alpers and Forster and by Jaeger and Forbes present hydrocephalus but none of the other neurological signs mentioned above. However, at autopsy an arteriovenous aneurysm was found in the midbrain and diencephalon which was fed by the posterior cerebral arteries and drained by the vein of Galen. Russell and Nevin have reported two

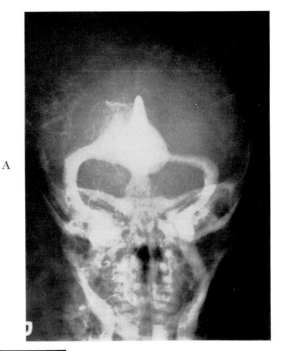

A

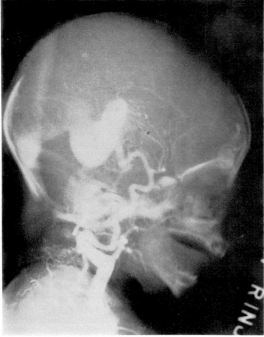

B

FIG. 215. Arteriovenous fistula between the anterior choroidal artery and the vein of Galen. There was enlargement of the heart and hydrocephalus. The arterial phase of the arteriogram is shown and then the venous phase which shows the great dilatation of the vein of Galen and the lateral sinuses. (By the courtesy of Dr. Frank Walsh.)

similar cases. The child whose picture is given in Figure 216 undoubtedly falls into this group. It is said that when the onset is in early infancy, the chief effect is congestive heart failure. When the onset is later, hydrocephalus is the most striking manifestation and then an intracranial bruit is heard. Later in childhood headaches are prominent.

We have several cases of arteriovenous fistulae involving the scalp, the skull and the dura and in most instances the cerebral cortex as well. Dandy has shown that these derive their arterial supply from the middle meningeal artery which is seen to be greatly dilated in roentgenograms of the skull. They may empty into the dural sinuses. The term *sinus pericranii* is sometimes applied. There is usually papilledema, hemianopia and often convulsions. In most cases the condition is bilateral. The veins of the scalp are dilated and angiomatous masses may be present. An intracranial bruit is usually audible.

Arteriovenous fistulae may also occur in the spinal cord and spinal column. It is rare, however, for a patient to have fistulae in both the brain and cord. One such case is given in the discussion of spinal vascular anomalies, q.v.

Diagnosis.—The history of focal convulsions, recurrent hemiplegia and signs of intracranial hemorrhage should always suggest the possibility of an intracranial arteriovenous aneurysm. If there is increased vascularity of the scalp and cranial vault and increased pulsations of one or both carotid arteries, the diagnosis is strengthened. Papilledema is often present. The systolic bruit is perhaps the most important diagnostic sign. This is often

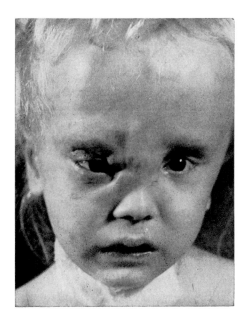

Fig. 216. Child of four years with hydrocephalus and loud intracranial bruit. There are dilated veins in and about the right orbit and over the scalp. The aneurysm did not fill when the carotid was injected showing it was fed by basilar system as in cases described by Wyburn-Mason. (Ped. A-50041.)

heard most clearly over the eyeballs. It must be stated, however, that the bruit is not always present and even when heard is not always significant of arteriovenous aneurysm, but if other typical signs and symptoms are present, the discovery of a systolic bruit is very strong evidence in favor of this diagnosis. The diagnosis may usually be made by arteriography. Blood drawn from the jugular vein may show a higher oxygen tension than normal.

Other causes of intracranial bruits may be mentioned at this point. In apparently healthy children between the ages of two and four years, a soft systolic bruit may be heard not infrequently. This is apt to disappear eventually though it has been known to persist in certain instances until adolescence. Though the cause of such murmurs is unknown, no significance is attached to them.

It is well known that intracranial bruits may occur in anemia and will disappear when the anemia is effectively treated.

Bruits arising in the heart or in the great vessels may be transmitted to the cranium in many cases.

Increased intracranial pressure may be responsible for occipital bruits. These are attributed to herniation of the medulla into the foramen magnum with kinking or compression of the vertebral arteries. Perhaps, this is also the cause of the bruit sometimes heard in congenital hydrocephalus.

Graphic recordings of the sounds over the heart, the large vessels and the cranium made simultaneously in connection with an electrocardiogram may make it possible to determine the origin of a bruit which is not easy to analyze with a stethoscope.

Prognosis.—The course of arteriovenous aneurysms is usually a slow one and often ten years will elapse after the first symptoms are noted before the development of serious disability. These lesions may become inactive in some cases for a number of years and in other instances their progress seems to become accelerated, repeated hemorrhages occur, intracranial pressure is elevated and death finally ensues from a massive extravasation.

Treatment.—Ligation of the arterial trunks which supply the aneurysm is sometimes possible and the whole mass of vessels may be removed. In most instances, however, the process is so extensive or in such a location that nothing can be done.

CASE HISTORY (U-65744).—*Transient right hemiplegia at seven years. Focal convulsions on right side beginning in index finger. Transient hemiplegia after convulsions. At age of 14 years headaches began. Loud intracranial bruit heard. At 16 years papilledema with retinal hemorrhages. Operation. Arteriovenous fistula between left middle cerebral artery and Rolandic vein.*

L. U. was regarded as a normal child until the age of seven years when she had a sudden right hemiplegia which disappeared within two days. No cause for this could be found and no diagnosis was made. Two years later the child began to have convulsive seizures which began with a feeling of numbness in the right index finger which quickly spread over the entire right side and was followed at once by twitching of the muscles. There was no loss of consciousness and the left side was never affected. After the seizures, which lasted about five minutes, the patient could not speak for ten minutes or more and there was partial paralysis of the right arm and leg for two to five days. The frequency of the attacks varied within wide limits. Sometimes there would be no attacks for several months and again, there might be two hundred in one month. There were no additional symptoms until the age of 14 years when the child began to complain of headaches and a throbbing in the head at times.

Examination revealed a well-developed girl who seemed to be at least of average intelligence for her age. There was a loud bruit heard over the entire left side of the cranium which was loudest during systole. This was most easily heard over the left eyeball. When the left carotid artery was compressed, the bruit ceased. The optic nerve heads showed some engorgement of the veins but no edema. The retinal arteries and veins were both rather dark in color. Vision and visual fields were normal. The cranial nerves were otherwise normal. The right arm was slightly weaker than the left but not definitely smaller than the left. There was no demonstrable disorder of motility of the right leg but the hand was used clumsily and stiffly. Speech was clear. Station steady and gait normal. No disorder of sensibility could be made out. The tendon reflexes were slightly more brisk on the right side, especially in the arm, but there was no clonus and no Babinski reflex. The heart was enlarged to the left and there was a systolic murmur at the base. This was transmitted into the neck. The hemoglobin was 120 per cent. There were no dilated veins over the scalp or face. Pulses in legs were strong and equal. Roentgenographic examination of the skull revealed a deep groove corresponding approximately to the location of the left Rolandic vein.

During the next two years the patient continued to have frequent seizures. The headaches became more frequent and severe and vomiting occurred at times. At the age of 16 years, the patient was brought into the hospital on the Neuro-Surgical Service of Dr. Dandy. There was then definite but low grade papilledema on both sides. The color of the retinal vessels was deeper than normal and suggested mild cyanosis. Operation disclosed an enormous dilatation of the left Rolandic vein which was filled with bright red blood and which pulsated with each heart beat. It was decided that one or more fistulae existed between the middle cerebral artery and this vein. Large tortuous vessels radiated both anteriorly and posteriorly from the Rolandic vein. It was not considered advisable to attempt to extirpate the lesion and the wound was closed.

In the next five years the patient had few seizures and only mild headaches. The decompression was always rather full. The bruit was constantly present. Sudden death occurred at the age of 25 years.

CASE HISTORY (1131870).—*Boy of ten days developed cyanosis. The heart and liver were enlarged. The pulse was 200. Congenital heart disease was suspected. A large arteriovenous fistula was found between the posterior cerebral artery and the vein of Galen.*

S. W., a boy of ten days, was admitted to Johns Hopkins Hospital on October 18, 1964, because of episodes of cyanosis and rapid breathing. Examination revealed cyanosis and enlargement of the heart and liver. The pulse was 200 and the respiration about 100. There was a precordial systolic bruit. Blood pressure was 100/40. The electrocardiogram indicated right ventricular hypertrophy. Congenital heart disease was suspected.

Cardiac catheterization revealed no evidence of malformation. Cerebral arteriograms revealed gross enlargement of the right internal carotid artery, the posterior communicating artery and the posterior cerebral artery. The last fed the enormously dilated vein of Galen through a choroidal artery. There was evidence of hydrocephalus.

At operation on October 23, a large artery was clipped which was thought to be the anterior choroidal artery and seemed to be feeding the vein of Galen. The filling of the vein of Galen was reduced, but respirations ceased on October 25. This case is presented by the courtesy of Dr. Frank B. Walsh.

BIBLIOGRAPHY

ALPERS, B. J. AND FORSTER, F. M.: Arteriovenous aneurysm of great cerebral vein and arteries of the circle of Willis. Arch. Neurol. & Psychiat., 54:181, 1945.

BASSETT, R. C.: Surgical experiences with arteriovenous anomalies of the brain. J. Neurosurg., 8:59, 1951.

BOLDREY, E. AND MILLER, E. R.: Arteriovenous fistula of the great vein of Galen and the circle of Willis. Report on two patients treated by ligation. Arch. Neurol. & Psychiat., 62:778, 1949.

CRAWFORD, J. V. AND RUSSELL, D.: Cryptic arteriovenous and venous hamartomas of the brain. J. Neurol. Neurosurg. & Psychiat., 19:1, 1956.

CUSHING, H. AND BAILEY, P.: Tumors Arising from Blood Vessels of the Brain. Baltimore, Charles C Thomas, 1928.

DANDY, W. E.: Arteriovenous aneurysm of the brain. Arch. Surg., 17:190, 1928.

———: Arteriovenous aneurysms of the scalp and face. Arch. Surg., 52:1, 1946.

GLATT, B. S. AND ROWE, R. D.: Cerebral arteriovenous fistula associated with congestive heart failure in the newborn. Pediatrics, 26:596, 1960.

HIRANO, A. AND TERRY, R. D.: Aneurysm of the vein of Galen. J. Neuropath. & Exp. Neurol., 17:424, 1958.

JAEGER, R. AND FORBES, R. P.: Bilateral congenital arteriovenous communications of the cerebral vessels. Arch. Neurol. & Psychiat., 55:591, 1946.

MOERSCH, F. P. AND KERNOHAN, J. W.: Cerebral arteriovenous aneurysms with report of a case. J. Nerv. & Ment. Dis., 74:137, 1931.

MONIZ, E. *et al.*: Aspect à l'épreuve encéphalographique des angiomes artérielles du cerveau dans la domaine de la carotide interne. Rev. Neurol., 2:165, 1932.

RUSSELL, D. S. AND NEVIN, S.: Aneurysm of the great vein of Galen causing internal hydrocephalus. J. Path. & Bact., 51:375, 1940.

SCHULTZ, E. C. AND HUSTON, W. A.: Arteriovenous aneurysm of the posterior fossa in an infant. J. Neurosurg., 13:211, 1956.

STERN, L. AND WIGLESWORTH, F. W.: Congestive heart failure secondary to cerebral arterio-venous aneurysm in the newborn infant. Amer. Jour. Dis. Child., 115:581, 1968.

SUGAR, O.: Pathological anatomy and angiography of intracranial vascular anomalies. J. Neuro-surg., 8:3, 1951.

VERBIEST, H.: Extracranial and cervical arteriovenous aneurysms of the carotid and vertebral arteries. Johns Hopkins Med. Jour., 122:350, 1968.

WALSH, F. Z.: *Loc. cit.*

WARD, C. E. AND HORTON, B. T.: Congenital arteriovenous fistulas in children. J. Pediat., 16:746, 1940.

WYBURN-MASON, R.: Arteriovenous aneurysm of the midbrain and retina with facial naevus and mental changes. Brain, 66:12, 1943.

VENOUS ANGIOMAS

Pathological Anatomy.—Several types of venous angiomas are recognized. Usually we find one or more dilated veins or varices which are abnormal, not only in their size but in their conformation and location. Simple varices, serpentine varices, cirsoid, racemose and plexiform varices are distinguished. As a rule, these are found in the meninges and cortex, although in some cases they may penetrate more deeply into the brain. They are almost invariably associated with more or less definite malformation of the brain, so that one often suspects that the symptoms, such as mental deficiency and epilepsy, may be due to the defective development of the brain rather than to the vascular abnormality. Certain venous angiomas which are usually termed cavernous angiomas form a large cluster or mass of vessels which may penetrate into the brain to the walls of the ventricular system. The differentiation from arteriovenous aneurysms is not always easy. In venous angiomas the communications between the arteries and the veins are capillaries and there is no pulsation or bruit. The dilated veins contain venous blood. In arteriovenous aneurysms, the communications between the arteries and veins are much larger than capillaries and consequently the blood in the distended veins is brighter. There is usually a bruit and pulsation. Venous angiomas are never entirely composed of vascular tissues and nerve cells or glial fibers may always be demonstrated between the loops of the veins. This characteristic serves to distinguish them from the true neoplasms or hemangioblastomas. Venous angiomas are regarded as congenital malformations of the vascular system which are probably present from birth.

Clinical Features.—These lesions usually give rise to symptoms very early in life, most frequently in infancy or early childhood. It is usually stated that the onset of symptoms is earlier in venous angiomas than in arteriovenous aneurysms although this rule is subject to exceptions. In some cases, symptoms have been noted soon after birth. The commonest clinical mani-

festation is focal epilepsy. Convulsions may occur at intervals during a period of many years without any other symptoms. In a large proportion of
cases, however, there is also mental deficiency or hemiplegia, hemianopia
and various other cerebral symptoms. The hemiplegia may be present from
birth or may develop in apoplectic fashion following a convulsive seizure.
Such hemiplegias are probably due to thromboses in the angiomas. Sometimes each convulsion is followed by transient hemiplegia which may eventually become permanent. We have also seen venous angiomas which involved the cerebellum and brain stem in which the clinical manifestations
were, of course, referable to those structures. There is never any bruit over
the cranium and only rarely any definite evidence of increased intracranial
pressure. In some instances, however, the angioma may be so situated as to
cause obstruction of the ventricular system and so give rise to hydrocephalus and papilledema. Venous angiomas also occur in the spinal cord but
rarely in association with similar anomalies in the brain. Cutaneous naevi
are found in a small percentage of cases. The roentgenographic study of
the cranium may reveal nothing or there may be deposits of calcium in the
lesion. The appearance of the calcified lesions is apparently not distinctive.
At most there are granular deposits or ill-defined shadows. The vault does
not show the dilatation of the vascular channels seen in the arteriovenous
fistulae. We have seen one case in which venous angioma in the posterior
part of the orbit caused intermittent exophthalmos. When the patient was
recumbent, her eye protruded. When she was upright, it receded so there
was enophthalmos. This case has been reported by Walsh and Dandy.
Thrombocytopenia may occur in association with very large angiomas.

Diagnosis.—The diagnosis of venous angioma of the brain is suggested
by a history of focal convulsions beginning early in life and associated
with transient or persistent hemiplegia or other focal signs. The absence of
an intracranial bruit and of excessive vascularity of the scalp and vault are
of value in distinguishing arteriovenous fistulae. The latter also frequently
cause increased intracranial pressure which is rare in venous angioma.

Prognosis.—Venous angiomas usually show no definite evidence of progression as do arteriovenous fistulae. If they happen to be so situated as to
cause hydrocephalus, the prognosis is, of course, unfavorable, and if there
are frequent convulsions there may be progressive mental deterioration. In
most cases, in our experience, these lesions have not caused death directly
although the span of life in defective children is, as a rule, not long.

Treatment.—The danger of serious hemorrhage makes it very difficult
and often impossible to remove these lesions by operation. It seems best to
leave them alone. Roentgenotherapy has been recommended by some authorities but the results do not seem to be satisfactory. Phenobarbital may
be of value in the control of the convulsions.

BIBLIOGRAPHY

Brock, S. and Dyke, C. C.: Venous and arteriovenous angioma of the brain. Bull. Neurol. Inst., 2:247, 1932.

Brock, S. and Wolf, A.: The pathology of cerebral angiomas; A study of nine cases. Bull. Neurol. Inst. N. Y., 4:144, 1935.

Cushing, H. and Bailey, P.: Tumors Arising from the Blood Vessels of the Brain. Baltimore, Charles C Thomas, 1928.

Delima, L. J. and Penzholz, H. A.: Case of intermittent exophthalmos. Jour. Neurosurg. and Psychiat., 31:81, 1968.

Walsh, F. B. and Dandy, W. E.: The pathogenesis of intermittent exophthalmos. Arch. Ophth., 32:1, 1944.

Worster-Drought, C. and Dickson, W. E. C.: Venous angioma of the cerebrum. J. Neurol. & Psychopath., 8:19, 1927-28.

TELANGIECTASES OF THE NERVOUS SYSTEM

Definition.—Telangiectases may be defined as vascular malformations composed of vessels having the structure of capillaries. They may occur in the skin, the mucous membranes and indeed, in all organs of the body. Michael and Levin describe telangiectases of the brain in several members of a family. When the telangiectases are extensive the term hereditary hemorrhagic telangiectasia is employed. This is inherited as a dominant trait.

Pathological Anatomy.—These lesions appear as bluish nodules which may reach a diameter of 5.0 cm or more. In most instances, several are found in the brain. They are located in the cerebral cortex, within the hemisphere and the cerebellum. Possibly almost half of all intracranial telangiectases are found in the pons. Histologically they are composed of a tangled mass of thin walled blood vessels of variable caliber. There is never any muscle or elastic tissue in the vessel wall. Glial fibers are found between the loops of vessels. Hemorrhage is usually present and some of the vessels are apt to be thrombosed. Calcium deposits are often found in these lesions. In some instances, one finds only a few dilated vessels which cause no symptoms unless they rupture.

Clinical Features.—Telangiectases often give rise to symptoms early in life. Focal convulsions are the commonest manifestations of those cases in which the lesion is in the cortex. Hemorrhage or thrombosis may cause hemiplegia or other focal signs. The diagnosis is very difficult. Michael and Levin point out that calcium deposits in the form of discrete granules are frequently seen in roentgenograms of the head and may be helpful in diagnosis. Telangiectases may be found in the skin or mucous membranes as well as the kidneys, intestines and lungs. A history of similar symptoms in other members of the family may be elicited.

The pontine telangiectases usually cause repeated episodes involving the

cranial nerve nuclei and long tracts. Usually there is incomplete recovery from each episode. Evidences of increased intracranial pressure are usually absent and if present, develop late in the course of the disease. The spinal fluid may be clear or bloody. Death is usually a result of hemorrhage. Teilman has made a study of 23 cases which he classifies as telangiectases of the pons and of 17 cases classified as cavernous hemangiomas. Pulmonary arteriovenous fistulae occur which may injure the nervous system by causing polycythemia, hypoxia, air emboli and brain abscess.

In the generalized hereditary telangiectasia, small vascular telangiectases are seen on the lips and tongue, but all parts of the body may be involved. Hemorrhages from the nose, the kidneys, gastrointestinal tract and bleeding in the brain may occur. The disease is inherited as a simple mendelian dominant.

BIBLIOGRAPHY

BAILEY, O. T. AND WOODARD, J. S.: Small vascular malformations of the brain. Their relation to unexpected death, hydrocephalus and mental deficiency. J. Neuropath. & Exp. Neurol., 18:98, 1959.

BEAN, W. B. AND RATHE, J.: Universal angiomatosis. Arch. of Int. Med., 112:869, 1963.

BIRD, R. M. AND JAQUES, W. E.: Vascular lesions of hereditary hemorrhagic telangiectasia. New Eng. Jour. Med., 260:597, 1959.

BIRD, R. M.: A family reunion. A study of hereditary hemorrhagic telangiectasis. New England J. Med., 257:105, 1957.

BOCZKO, M. L.: Neurologic implications of hereditary hemorrhagic telangiectasis. Jour. Nerv. and Ment. Dis., 139:525, 1964.

COURVILLE, C. B. et al.: Hereditary hemorrhagic telangiectasis and pulmonary arteriovenous aneurysm. Union med. Canada, 92:1135, 1963.

FOLEY, R. E. AND BOYD, D. P.: Pulmonary arteriovenous aneurysm. Surg. Clin. Amer., 41:801, 1961.

GORLIN, R. J. AND SEDANO, H.: Hereditary hemorrhagic telangiectasia. Modern Medicine, January 15, 1968, p. 142.

HARRISON, D. F. N.: Familial hemorrhagic telangiectasia. Quart. J. Med., 33:25, 1964.

KARLISH, A. J.: Hereditary hemorrhagic telangiectasia with arteriovenous aneurysm of the lung. Pro. Roy. Soc. Med., 56:170, 1963.

MARGOLIS, G. et al.: The role of small angiomatous malformations in the production of intracerebral hematomas. J. Neurosurg., 8:564, 1951.

MICHAEL, J. C. AND LEVIN, P.: Multiple telangiectases of the brain with discussion of the hereditary factors in their development. Arch. Neurol. & Psychiat., 36:514, 1936.

MOYER, J. H. et al.: Pulmonary arteriovenous fistula. Amer. Jour. Med., 32:417, 1962.

NAFFZIGER, H. C. AND STERN, W. E.: Brain abscess associated with pulmonary angiomatous malformation. Ann. Surg., 138:265, 1953.

QUICKEL, K. E. AND WHALEY, R. J.: Subarachnoid hemorrhage in a patient with hereditary telangiectasia. Neurology, 17:716, 1967.

RUSSELL, D. S. et al.: Discussion: The pathology of spontaneous intracranial hemorrhage. Proc. Roy. Soc. Med., 47:689, 1954.

SINGER, K. AND WOLFSON, W. Q.: Hereditary hemorrhagic telangiectasia. New England J. Med., 230:637, 1944.

TEILMAN, K.: Hemangiomas of the pons. Arch. Neurol. & Psychiat., 69:208, 1953.

WINTROBE, M. M.: Clinical Hematology. 3rd Ed. Philadelphia, Lea and Febiger, 1951.

THE STURGE-WEBER SYNDROME OR
MENINGEAL ANGIOMATOSIS

Definition.—This condition is characterized by facial nevus flammeus or port wine stain, convulsions, calcium deposits in the cerebral cortex of distinctive nature, and often buphthalmos, mental deficiency and hemiplegia.

Pathological Anatomy.—The lesions in the brain are found most frequently in the cortex of the occipital lobe but may extend over large areas of cortex. The process is almost always unilateral. Atrophy of the convolutions is evident in the gross. There is an excess of small thin walled vessels in the pia and also in some instances in the underlying cortex. In such regions the nerve cells and fibers are degenerated and replaced by neuroglia. Numerous small deposits of calcium are found in relation to the small blood vessels in the second and third layers of the cortex. It is generally believed that these calcium deposits are due to circulatory disturbances though this view has been opposed. Wohlwill and Yakolev emphasize the malformation of the blood vessels in the meninges, the degenerative changes in these vessels with calcium deposits in their walls and the degenerative changes in the cerebral cortex. They also point out that the viscera may be involved and mention angiomas of the intestines, lungs and ovary.

Clinical Features.—This condition is usually evidenced at birth by the presence of a nevus flammeus on one side of the face. This nevus almost

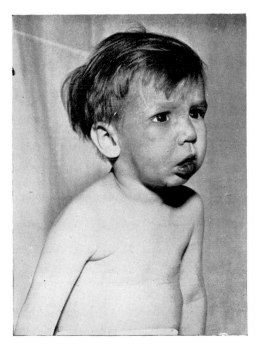

Fig. 217. Facial nevus covering the entire right side of the face. There are other features in this case not evident in the photograph. A nevus covers the right hand and forearm which are hypertrophied. The left leg is weak and spastic and the right eye shows mild buphthalmos. The patient is subject to convulsions beginning in that leg. No intracranial calcification is evident yet.

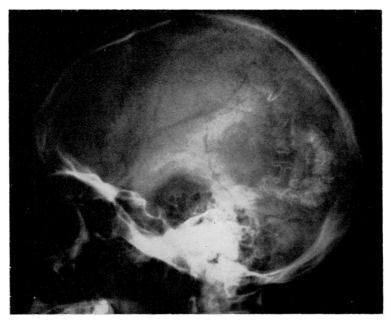

F𝗂ɢ. 218. Typical roentgenogram of the skull in a case of Sturge-Weber syndrome showing the typical layers of calcium in the occipital cortex. (By the courtesy of Dr. George W. Smith.)

invariably covers the forehead and may or may not extend into the cheek. It may extend into the other side of the forehead. The nevus may be faint at birth and grow more evident as the child becomes older. In one instance (No. 494196) the facial nevus was so vascular that severe hemorrhage occurred. In one of our cases (No. 173880) there was no facial nevus though the patient had convulsions and typical calcium deposits in the brain. Occasionally the nevus may extend over the homolateral side of the neck, chest and arm. In such cases the *arm* may become *hypertrophied*. The homolateral eye may be enlarged as a result of congenital glaucoma, i.e. *buphthalmos*. The iris of such an eye may remain blue though the normal eye is brown. It is believed that this condition is due to angiomatosis of the choroid which is not always easy to see on ophthalmoscopic examination. *Hemiplegia* is present in many cases and is found on the side opposite the nevus. It may be constant and severe or may appear for a short time after each convulsion. Often there is defective development of the affected extremities. *Hemianopia* is also frequently found but is often demonstrated with difficulty because of the patient's mental status.

With few exceptions these children are *mentally defective*. Their mental status may deteriorate, especially if convulsions are frequent. *Convulsions* are apparently a constant feature of this syndrome. They usually begin on

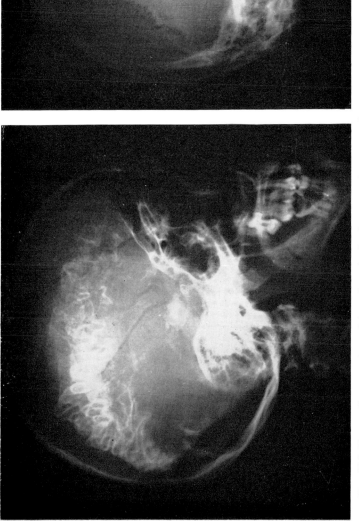

FIG. 219. Unusually extensive calcium deposits in the cortex in a case of Sturge-Weber syndrome. (By the courtesy of Dr. George Smith.)

the side opposite the nevus and may be confined to that side or become generalized. They are often resistant to anticonvulsive medication.

Roentgenograms of the head reveal distinctive *calcifications* in the cortex of the brain on the side of the nevus. These deposits form curved lines which follow the folds of the gyri and display as a rule a double contour. These lines are confined in most instances to a triangular area in the occipital region but in some instances, as shown in Figure 219, almost the whole surface of the hemisphere may be involved. In one of our cases no calcium deposits were seen in the roentgenograms at the age of 17 years though the case was otherwise typical (No. 522505).

The electroencephalogram shows slow waves as a rule but the pattern is not characteristic. Arteriograms have not proved helpful.

Diagnosis.—There is rarely any difficulty about the diagnosis. The facial nevus, convulsions, mental deficiency and characteristic deposits seen in the roentgenograms are distinctive.

Prognosis.—In some patients the condition remains essentially static for many years. Others, especially if convulsions are frequent, deteriorate slowly. We have seen a fatal intracranial hemorrhage in one case (No. Path. 20732).

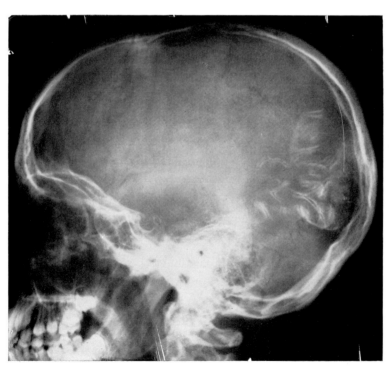

Fig. 220. Roentgenogram of skull of a boy of 12 years. He is subject to convulsions but has no angioma on face.

Treatment.—Anticonvulsive medication is usually required but is not always effective. Livingston finds that bromides and phenobarbital are most satisfactory. Dandy and Green have removed the affected parts of the cortex with good results.

BIBLIOGRAPHY

ALEXANDER, G. L. AND NORMAN, R. M.: The Sturge-Weber Syndrome. Baltimore, Williams and Wilkins, 1960.

FALKINBURG, L. W. *et al.*: Sturge-Weber-Demetri disease. Pediatrics, **22**:319, 1958.

GARDINER, P. A.: Eye lesions of Sturge-Weber syndrome. Develop. Med. Child. Neurol., **5**:647, 1963.

GREEN, J. R.: Encephalo-trigeminal angiomatosis. J. Neuropath. & Exp. Neurol., **4**:27, 1945.

HRNCHIAR, A. AND RINSLEY, D. D.: Sturge-Weber disease. Bull. Menninger Clin., **27**:233, 1963.

KRABBE, K. H.: Facial and meningeal angiomatosis associated with calcifications of the brain cortex. Arch. Neurol. & Psychiat., **32**:737, 1934.

LICHENSTEIN, B. W.: Sturge-Weber-Demetri syndrome. Arch. of Neurol. and Psychiat., **71**:291, 1954.

LIVINGSTON, S., EISNER, V., BROWN, W. AND BOKS, L.: The Sturge-Weber syndrome. Postgrad. Medicine, **19**:221, 1956.

MILLER, S. J. H.: Ophthalmic aspects of Sturge-Weber syndrome. Proc. Roy. Soc. Med., **56**:419, 1963.

MORGAN, G.: Pathology of Sturge-Weber syndrome. Proc. Roy. Soc. Med., **56**:422, 1963.

TYSON, H. H.: Nevus flammeus of the face and globe associated with glaucoma, vascular changes in the iris and calcified growth in the left occipital lobe with right homonymous hemianopia. Arch. Ophth., **8**:365, 1932.

WALSH, F. B.: Neuro-ophthalmology. Williams and Wilkins, 1947, p. 1094.

WEBER, F. PARKES: A note on the association of extensive haemangiomatous naevus of the skin with cerebral (meningeal) haemangioma, especially cases of facial vascular naevus with contralateral hemiplegia. Proc. Roy. Soc. Med. Sec. Neurol., **22**:431, 1929.

WOHLWILL, F. J. AND YAKOLEV, P. I.: Histopathology of meningo-facial angiomatosis. J. Neuropath. & Exp. Neurol., **16**:341, 1957.

THE KLIPPEL-TRENAUNAY-WEBER SYNDROME

This condition is apparently a variant of the Sturge-Weber syndrome. There are extensive cutaneous naevi flammei. Enlargement of the bones, especially the fingers, and muscles are characteristic. Superficial veins are enlarged and deeper angiomas or arteriovenous fistulae, which cause subcutaneous hemorrhages, are often present. Buphthalmos may be associated. Colobomata of the irides are described. Cerebral angiomata are found in some cases. This condition is said to be inherited as an irregular dominant.

BIBLIOGRAPHY

WAARDENBURG, P. J., FRANSCHETTI, A. AND KLEIN, O.: Genetics and Ophthalmology. 2:1381, Springfield, Thomas, 1961.

KLIPPEL, M. AND TRENAUNAY, R.: Du naevus variqueux osteohypertrophique. Arch. gen. Med., **77**:641, 1900.

SCHNYDER, U. W. *et al.*: Syndrome de Klippel-Trenaunay avec colobome irien atypique. Jour. Genet. Hum., 1956.

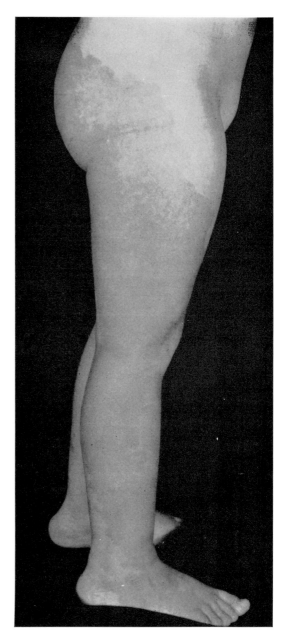

FIG. 221. Lateral view of the legs of a child with the Klippel-Trenauay-Weber syndrome showing the extensive nevus. (By the courtesy of Dr. Robert E. Cooke.)

CASE HISTORY (No. 1203071).—*Klippel-Trenaunay-Weber syndrome. Port wine stains on buttocks, thighs and legs, recurrent lumps on body of bluish color, enlargement of the left arm, left thumb, forefinger and middle finger. Episodes of sudden somnolence.*

J. M., a child of four and a half years, was born with extensive red

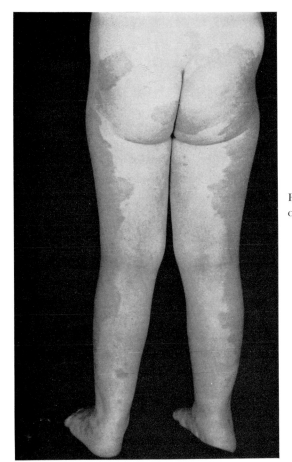

FIG. 222. Posterior view of the same child.

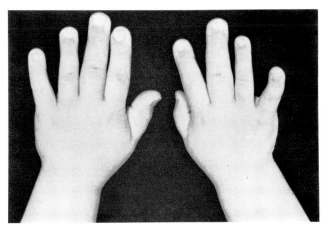

FIG. 223. The child's hands showing enlargement of the left thumb and two middle fingers.

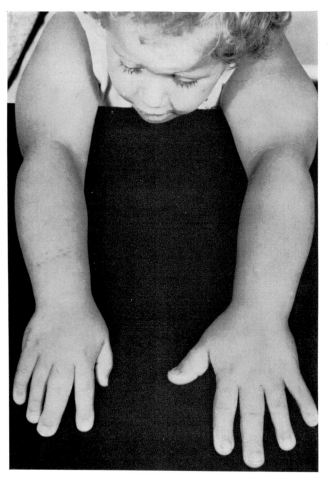

Fig. 224. View of the child's arms showing the greater length and size of the left arm and hand as contrasted with the right arm and hand.

nevi over the buttocks, thighs and legs. When she was a year old, a bluish lump developed on the neck. This disappeared after a time. At 18 months, a similar lump appeared on the right shoulder. This was removed. It was found to be a cystic mass containing old blood. It was believed to be an angioma. Several more such lumps developed, but all disappeared after a time. At 2 years, it was noted that the left arm was too large above the elbow and at 26 months, it was seen that some of the fingers of the left hand were growing too long. The child had a tendency to fall asleep suddenly.

The child had always been vigorous. She walked at 18 months. At a year she formed words and at 2 years sentences. Her intelligence was thought to be normal. She never had any seizures. X-ray studies of the bones were

reported to be normal. The parents and 2 brothers displayed no abnormalities. The family history was negative.

On examination the child was playful and cheerful. She was well developed and nourished. The left pupil measured 3 mm and the right, 4 mm. Both reacted well. The irides were of the same color. There were no changes in the optic discs or retinae. There was slight enophthalmos on the left. No ptosis of the lids, squint, nystagmus or reduction of ocular movement was found. No loss of sensibility on the face. No facial weakness. Hearing was good.

There were extensive nevi on the buttocks, thighs, legs and left foot. Small cafe au lait spots were seen over the right side of the chest near the axilla. Faint telangiectases were found over the left shoulder above the clavicle. The left arm was enlarged above the elbow. The tissues had a doughy consistency. No plexiform neuromas were felt. The right arm was slightly enlarged. The left forefinger, middle finger and thumb were strikingly enlarged being too long and too thick. The right thumb was also enlarged. Less conspicuous enlargements of the toes were seen.

On two occasions the child suddenly fell asleep but awakened spontaneously within a few minutes.

This child was seen by the courtesy of Dr. Robert Cook.

PROGESSIVE FAMILIAL CEREBELLAR ATAXIA AND CHOREOATHETOSIS WITH TELANGIECTASIA AND CHRONIC INFECTION OF THE RESPIRATORY TRACT

In 1941 Madame Louis-Bar published a case report in which progressive ataxia was associated with telangiectasia of the conjunctivae. No additional cases of this condition came to light for the next few years. In May of 1957, however, Wells and Shy published a study of two cases in sisters. In June, Boder and Sedgwick published seven cases and one case history with a post-mortem examination. In July Biemond described four cases in two sets of siblings with two post-mortem examinations and Centerwall and Miller submitted a paper for publication including a very careful and complete study of two patients with one post-mortem examination. Buchanan has observed three cases and I have seen one which is mentioned briefly below. Thus, there are 20 cases on record, 12 girls and 8 boys and 4 post-mortem examinations. Among the 20 patients there are 14 siblings. It seems that the disease is inherited as a simple recessive characteristic. In 1963 Boder was able to review 101 cases.

As a rule, the child is regarded as a normal baby. Often there is some delay in the development of motor reactions so the child may not walk until the age of 16 to 20 months.

Progressive motor disturbances become evident between the ages of 18 months and 3 years. The gait is affected first and the control of the arms is

involved later. Apparently either cerebellar ataxia or choreoathetosis may be the first manifestation. In some instances the ataxia is the initial symptom and the athetosis develops later. As a rule the ataxia is the greater problem. There is gradual increase in the symptoms. Intention tremor appears. Nystagmus and various disorders of ocular movement develop. Usually conjugate movements of the eyes show a tendency to halt and then resume their movement. On return to the primary position, there may be some oscillations during fixation. Smith and Cogan mention ocular apraxia as described by Cogan in their case. Speech is slow and scanning at first but later dysarthria becomes so severe that the child cannot be understood. Bulbar palsy occurs in the terminal state. There is drooling of saliva. The face is mask-like and the smile is slow to develop. The posture is altered. The head and trunk are inclined forward and the shoulders droop. Myoclonic movements may occur. The tendon reflexes are lost eventually. By the age of 8 or 10 years the child is unable to walk alone and is soon confined to a wheel chair. Contractures develop in the legs causing deformities of the feet. Mental deterioration occurs in at least one third of the patients. Bodily growth and sexual development are deficient. Growth is retarded.

At about the age of 2 or 3 years, telangiectases are evident on the bulbar

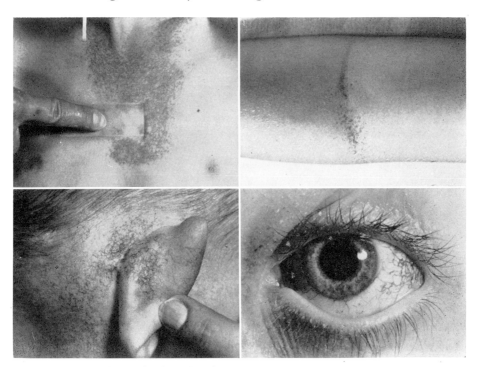

Fig. 225. Photographs of children showing telangiectasia on chest, in the fold of the elbow, the ear and the conjunctiva. (From Centerwall and Miller, Ataxia. Telangiectasia and Sinopulmonary Infections. A.M.A. Jour. of Dis. Child. 1958.)

conjunctivae. These are located on the exposed portion of the conjunctivae and do not quite touch the corneae. Later, telangiectases are seen on the ears, the eyelids, the bridge of the nose, the anterior aspect of the neck where it is exposed, the dorsum of the hands and feet, and folds of the elbows and knees (see Fig. 225). These small vessels are bright red as if filled with arterial blood. They gradually become more extensive and more evident. Centerwall and Miller exposed a patient to sunlight and ultraviolet light without causing any increase in the telangiectasia. Other skin lesions include cafe au lait spots. In the case of Madame Louis-Bar these were extensive and are described as fern-like areas on the chest, back and thighs. In other cases they have been small and inconspicuous. Dry skin and keratosis follicularis are mentioned. Boder and Sedgwick mention a lesion diagnosed adenoma sebaceum.

A cardinal feature of these cases is a tendency to repeated infections of the respiratory tract. This process eventually becomes chronic and leads to a fatal outcome. There is a chronic nasal discharge early in childhood and then attacks of nasal sinusitis, otitis media, bronchitis and pneumonia leading eventually to chronic bronchitis, pneumonia and bronchiectasis. The children lose weight, cease to grow and die. Various antibiotics are helpful and in some cases children have been helped by constant administration of these drugs. Death occurs as a rule at about the age of 12 years. Thus, each of Biemond's patients died at 12 years and this was also true of the patient of Centerwall and Miller. The child of Boder and Sedgwick died at 10 years and 6 months.

The post-mortem examination in the case of Boder and Sedgwick was performed by Courville. He found loss of Purkinje cells in the cerebellar cortex and widespread loss of granule and basket cells. There was slight damage to the dentate nuclei and cerebellar white matter. The blood vessels of the cerebellar meninges and the cerebellar white matter were enlarged and engorged. No other abnormalities were found in the nervous system. The ovaries were both absent.

Biemond found the same lesions in both of his post-mortem examinations. There was gross atrophy of the vermis of the cerebellum especially in the posterior part. In the pyramids, the uvula and the nodule there was narrowing of the granule layer and loss of Purkinje cells. Nothing else was found. He was unable to find any abnormalities of the blood vessels.

The nervous system in the case of Centerwall and Miller was studied by Courville. There were very large veins in the meninges of the cerebrum as well as the cerebellum. These vessels were especially enlarged in the basilar meninges. Large veins were also found in the fontanel centrum, parietal lobes, dentate nuclei and cerebellar white matter. In the cerebellar cortex there was loss of Purkinje cells and thinning of the granule layer (Fig.

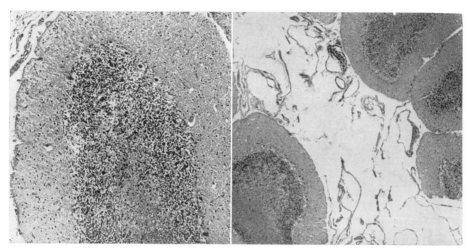

FIG. 226. Photographs showing large thin walled veins in the cerebellar meninges and also loss of Purkinje cells in the cerebellar cortex. (From Centerwall and Miller, Ataxia, Telangiectasia and Sinopulmonary Infections. A.M.A. Jour. of Dis. Child. 1958.)

226). The cells of the dentate nuclei showed pyknotic changes. Scattered loss of pyramidal cells was found in the frontal cortex especially in the central gyri. In the substantia nigra there was loss of pigmented cells and a fenestrated appearance of the tissue about the cells. In addition to the lesions in the cerebellum, demyelination of the posterior columns of the spinal cord and dorsal spinocerebellar tracts occurs. The peripheral nerves show fibrosis and fiber loss. The muscles show changes of uncertain origin. The pituitary gland shows odd changes with giant nuclei and vacuoles in the cytoplasm. The ovaries show agenesis. The breasts have no ductal or glandular tissue.

Terplan and Krauss found demyelinated hemosiderin-laden glial scars around capillaries and ectatic veins in the white matter with focal demyelination in the corpus callosum, brachia conjunctiva, and pontis, optic tract and medulla. Atrophy and gliosis of all cerebellar folia and dentates and demyelinization of the funiculi graciles were found.

The incidence of malignant processes developing in lymphoid tissues is increased. Lymphosarcoma occurs.

A number of writers describe deficiency of gamma globulin especially in patients who are prone to frequent and severe infections. Peterson *et al.* have studied the immune system in 8 patients. Two thymus biopsies showed a lack of Hassall's corpuscles. No thymus was found in 1 patient. The lymph nodes in 6 of 8 patients were abnormal and tonsillar tissue was deficient in all patients in which it was studied. All patients had an immunological deficit in response to homographs. The IgA content of the saliva is reduced or absent.

Pelc and Vis state that chromatographic study of the urine in all three of their patients revealed a peptide containing proline and hydroproline. This peptide was absent in the urine of their normal relatives.

CASE HISTORY.—*A. F., a child of 21 months, was examined in September 1952. He was born at full term and there was no cyanosis or jaundice. There was no Rh incompatibility. He had pneumonia at 11 months and shortly after this there was a convulsion. The family history was negative for all nervous diseases.*

The child did not walk until he was 14 months old and was very unsteady. His speech was disordered. Examination at the age of 21 months revealed striking unsteadiness of station and gait as well as generalized athetoid movements of the trunk and extremities. There was also pronounced incoordination of all four extremities. Speech was very imperfect. The cranial nerves were in order. The muscles were firm and strong and the tendon reflexes in order.

The child was seen again in August 1957 at the age of 6 years. He had had a number of severe respiratory tract infections but in general had done well. The parents stated that his eyes had become red during the last year. He was having trouble at school because of his writing but not because of his mental condition.

On examination the child displayed altered postures and involuntary movements typical of double athetosis and his coordination was greatly reduced in all four extremities. There was pronounced dysarthria. I could not say, however, that the neurological process had advanced since my first examination. The child was active all day and could run rapidly though clumsily. His mental condition was not definitely abnormal.

The conjunctivae appeared to be bright red. On close inspection many small, tortuous vessels were seen in the bulbar conjunctivae which did not quite touch the corneae. Similar dilated vessels were evident over the upper portions of both ears front and back and a few less evident vessels were seen in the lids and the bridge of the nose. On the back of the neck on the left side was a single line of small red dots. No changes were seen in the hands or feet. On the top of the shoulder on either side were old scars attributed by the parents to blisters due to exposure to sunlight in infancy. No further blisters had occurred though the boy was outdoors most of the time and his skin was tanned.

BIBLIOGRAPHY

BEVERIDGE, J.: Ataxia telangiectasia. Med. J. Australia, i:613, 1960.

BIEMOND, A.: Paleocerebellar atrophy with extrapyramidal manifestations in association with bronchiectases and telangiectasis of the conjunctiva bulbi as a familial syndrome. First International Congress of Neurological Sciences. Brussels, July 21-28, 1957.

BODER, E. AND SEDGWICK, R. P.: Ataxia telangiectasia. Pediatrics, 21:526, 1958.

BODER, E. AND SEDGWICK, R. P.: Ataxia-telangiectasia. Univ. South. California Med. Bull., 9:15, 1957.

BODER, E. AND SEDGWICK, R. P.: Ataxia telangiectasia. A review of 101 cases. Little Club Clin. Develop. Med., 8:110, 1963.

BOWDEN, D. H. *et al.*: Ataxia-telangiectasia. Jour. Neuropath. and Exp. Neurol., 22:549, 1963.

BUCHANAN, D. N.: Clinical presentation at the Twenty-fifth Anniversary Convention of the Department of Pediatrics, University of Chicago, October 13, 1956.

CENTERWALL, W. R. AND MILLER, M. M.: Ataxia, telangiectasia and sinopulmonary infections. A syndrome of slowly progressive deterioration in childhood. A.M.A. J. Dis. Child., 1958.

DUNN, H. G. *et al.*: Ataxia-telangiectasia. Canad. Med. Ass. Jour., 91:1106, 1964.

EISEN, A. H.: Immunologic deficiency in ataxia telangiectasia. New Eng. Jour. Med., 272:18, 1965.

FIREMAN, P. *et al.*: Ataxia-telangiectasia. Lancet, i:1193, 1964.

GORLIN, R. J. AND SEDANO, H.: Ataxia-telangiectasia. Modern Medicine, September 23, 1968, p. 164.

GUTMANN, L. AND LEMLI, L.: Ataxia-telangiectasia associated with hypogammaglobinemia. Arch. Neurol., 8:318, 1963.

JUNGO, O. *et al.:* Die chronische progressive cerebellare Ataxie mit Teleangiektasien. Helv. Paediat. Acta, 18:280, 1963.

LOUIS-BAR, MME.: Sur un syndrome progressif comprenant des télangiectasies capillaires cutanées et conjonctivales symétriques, a disposition naevoide et des troubles cérébelleux. Confina Neurol., 4:32, 1941.

McKUSICK, V. AND CROSS, H. E.: Ataxia telangiectasia and Swiss type agammaglobinemia. J.A.M.A., 195:739, 1966.

MILLER, S. J. AND GOODDY, W.: Madame Louis-Bar's syndrome. Brain, 87:581, 1954.

MOYNAHAN, E. J.: Ataxia-telangiectasia. Proc. Roy. Soc. Med., 56:727, 1963.

PAINE, R. S. AND EFRON, M. L.: Atypical variants of ataxia-telangiectasia syndrome. Develop. Med. Child. Med. Neurol., 5:14, 1963.

PELC, S. AND VIS, H.: Familial ataxia with ocular telangiectasias. Acta neurol. et psychiat. belg., 60:905, 1960.

PETERSON, R. D. A. *et al.*: Ataxia-telangiectasia syndrome. Lancet, i:1189, 1964.

PETERSON, R. D. A. *et al.:* Lymphoid tissue abnormalities associated with ataxia telangiectasia. Amer. Jour. Med., 41:342, 1966.

ROBINSON, A.: Ataxia-telangiectasia with craniostenosis. Arch. of Dis. Childh., 37:652, 1962.

SEDGWICK, R. P. AND BODER, E.: Progressive ataxia in childhood with particular reference to ataxia-telangiectasia. Neurology, 10:705, 1960.

SIEKERT, R. G., KEITH, H. M. AND DION, F. R.: Ataxia telangiectasia in children. Proc. Staff Meet. Mayo Clin., 34:581, 1959.

SMITH, L. AND COGAN, D.: Ataxia telangiectasia. Arch. Ophth., 62:364, 1959.

SOLITARE, G. B. AND LOPEZ, V. F.: Louis-Bar syndrome. Neurology, 17:23, 1967.

SOLITARE, G. B.: Louis-Bar's syndrome. Neurology, 18:1180, 1968.

TELLER, W. M. AND MILLICHAP, J. G.: The Louis-Bar syndrome. J.A.M.A., 175:779, 1961.

TERPLAN, K. L. AND KRAUSS, R. F.: Histopathologic brain changes in association with ataxia-telangiectasis. Neurology, 19:446, 1969.

PICKUP, J. D. AND PUGH, R. J.: Familial ataxia-telangiectasia. Arch. Dis. Childhood, 36:344, 1961.

PTACEK, L. J. *et al.*: Starch gel serum electrophoresis in ataxia telangiectasia. Proc. Am. Acad. Neurol. Denver, Colorado, April 1964.

UTIAN, H. L. AND PLIT, M.: Ataxia-telangiectasia. Jour. Neurol., Neurosurg. and Psychiat., 27:38, 1964.

WELLS, C. E. AND SHY, G. M.: Progressive familial choreoathetosis with telangiectasia. J. Neurol., Neurosurg. & Psychiat., 20:98, 1957.

WILLIAMS, H. E. *et al.*: Ataxia-telangiectasia. Arch. of Dermatol., 82:937, 1960.

YOUNG, R. R.: Ataxia-telangiectasia and the thymus. Trans. Amer. Neurol. Ass., 89:28, 1964. 89:28, 1964.

YOUNG, R. R. *et al.:* Abnormalities of serum gamma 1 A globulin and ataxia-telangiectasia. Medicine, 43:423, 1964.

ZELLWEGER, H. AND KHALIFEH, R. R.: Ataxia telangiectasia. Helv. Paediat. Acta, 18:267, 1963.

VASCULAR ANOMALIES INVOLVING THE SPINAL CORD

Pathological Anatomy.—These lesions are in general comparable to the corresponding ones of the brain. Thus we distinguish. (1) Arteriovenous fistulae. (2) Venous angiomas. (3) Telangiectases. The saccular aneurysms of the arteries found upon the circle of Willis are very rare in the spinal canal. These anomalies are apparently all of congenital origin.

Clinical Features.—Wyburn-Mason has recently made an illuminating study of the vascular anomalies of the spinal cord which is warmly recommended to the reader. In *arteriovenous fistulae* the process, he states, is apt to involve the anterior part of the cervical enlargement or the posterior part of the cord from the seventh cervical segment to the upper lumbar segments. The onset may be gradual or abrupt. The clinical signs may indicate compression of the cord or perhaps, thrombosis of a blood vessel with softening. In other cases there is hematomyelia with subarachnoid hemorrhage. Repeated acute episodes may occur. It is common for symptoms to appear before the age of 15 years but complete paraplegia may be delayed for many years. Spinal puncture may reveal evidences of obstruction of the spinal canal and blood is frequently found in the spinal fluid. If pantopaque is injected, the column of oil may show pulsation under the fluoroscope which is regarded as characteristic. Pigmented birth marks, cutaneous angiomas, spina bifida and lipomata may be present. Audible bruits do not seem to have been discovered in proven cases.

Venous angiomas involve almost invariably the lower half of the cord, rarely extending above the fifth thoracic segment. Males are affected more frequently than females, the proportion being three to one. The onset of symptoms is later than in arteriovenous fistulae for it is unusual for symptoms to appear during childhood. The process advances by acute episodes marked by severe root pains and evidences of damage to the lower part of the cord. There is usually spasticity of some muscles and atrophy of others. Pain and thermal sensibility are apt to be lost but touch and proprioception preserved. These episodes may be followed by pronounced improvement. In some cases naevi are seen in the skin. The spinal fluid is quite normal in one third of all cases, according to Wyburn-Mason and in two thirds there is an elevation of protein. In perhaps one fifth of all cases, there are evidences of obstruction of the spinal canal. Following an acute lesion there may be an increase of lymphocytes in the fluid for a time. Lipiodol injection may be helpful in the diagnosis for the droplets of oil may form sinuous curves which seem to outline the tortuous loops of the dilated veins.

Telangiectases are usually multiple being found in the cerebral cortex, pons and other parts of the body as well as in the spinal cord. They may be found at almost any level of the spinal cord. The typical clinical manifestation of this condition is sudden hematomyelia. Improvement may follow and additional acute episodes may occur. It is of interest that blood is apparently not found in the spinal fluid as in arteriovenous fistulae. Similar lesions are found in the epidural tissues and vertebrae where they give rise to spinal cord compression as a result of epidural hemorrhage. Cutaneous naevi are often associated.

Wyburn-Mason also mentions compression of the spinal cord in cases of *coarctation of the aorta* by dilated arteries which are regarded as collaterals. In a few instances saccular aneurysms are found on such arteries. A similar condition may also be found in *congenital heart disease.*

Diagnosis.—The features of diagnostic importance are given above. In general the most significant clinical characteristics of these conditions are the tendency to repeated sudden episodes indicating damage to the spinal cord, the occasional presence of blood in the spinal fluid, and the presence of cutaneous naevi. Other congenital anomalies such as spina bifida, lipomata, pigmented moles and congenital heart disease may be present. The use of lipiodol or of pantopaque is of much value in differential diagnosis for the opaque material may lie in characteristically curved and sinuous lines, or in cases of arteriovenous fistulae, may show pulsations which are typical. Spontaneous spinal subarachnoid hemorrhage, according to Wyburn-Mason, is almost invariably due to arteriovenous fistulae though it may occur also as a result of arterial anomalies associated with coarctation of the aorta. Spontaneous hematomyelia results from telangiectases and arteriovenous fistulae. In the former there is

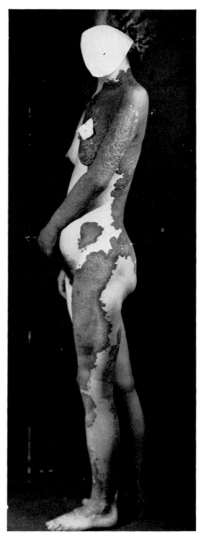

Fig. 227. Girl with extensive naevus who developed a malignant melanoma of the choroid. (Case of Dr. C. A. Young, by the courtesy of Dr. Walsh.)

no subarachnoid hemorrhage associated but in the latter blood is found in the spinal fluid in almost all cases. In angiomas which involve the vertebrae the dilated venous channels are usually evident in the roentgenograms of the spine. It must be pointed out that cutaneous naevi are not always significant of vascular anomalies of the spinal cord. They are, of course, often entirely absent in such conditions and may be present in cases of congenital malformation of the cord, neoplasms of congenital origin, syringomyelia and without any abnormality of the nervous system whatever.

Prognosis.—In general, the prognosis seems to be unfavorable.

Treatment.—Decompression of the cord without suture of the dura has been recommended but it is doubtful if this is of any value. Ligation of the vessels is apt to increase the paralysis. Deep roentgen ray therapy has been used but the effects are not striking and it may hasten the evolution of the lesion.

CASE HISTORY (U-53549).—*Multiple arteriovenous fistulae in brain and spinal cord. Paralysis of left leg at five years; subarachnoid hemorrhage at 11 years. Convulsions beginning at 14 years; complete paraplegia at 21 years. Examination showed mental deficiency, intracranial bruit, optic atrophy, upper right quadrantanopia, right central facial weakness, weakness and slight spasticity of right arm, speech defect and complete transverse lesion of the cord at T-10.*

D. N. was subject to repeated nosebleeds from early childhood, always from the left side of the nose. These were sometimes so severe that the nose had to be packed. Weakness and stiffness of the left leg was noted from the age of about five years and at the age of seven years, the mother observed that the left leg was smaller than the right. Frequency of urination was present from very early in life. At the age of 11 years the patient had a sudden illness marked by violent headache, vomiting, cervical rigidity, retraction of the head and stupor. For a time there was some fever. The child was in bed for 12 weeks but seemed to make a complete recovery. At the age of 14 years, about the time the menses began, the patient began to have petit mal and also nocturnal convulsions. These continued during the remaining years of the patient's life at variable intervals. During the twenty-first year, the patient suddenly developed complete paralysis of the left leg which was present one morning when she awakened. About three weeks later the right leg was paralysed in the same way and the patient became entirely incontinent and anesthetic below the waist. She was then brought to the hospital.

Examination disclosed a wealth of neurological findings. The patient was moderately deficient in her mental development and somewhat childish. The head was of normal size and shape. A small tumor presented in the left orbit just to the left of the root of the nose. This was soft and was much increased when the left jugular vein was compressed. When the left carotid artery was compressed, this tumor was much reduced in size.

A slight pulsation was palpable in the left bulb and there was a loud systolic bruit heard over both bulbs which was abolished by compression of the left carotid artery. Vision was normal in the right eye and only slightly reduced in the left eye but both optic nerve heads appeared a bit pale. A right upper quadrant defect of homonymous type was discovered in the visual fields. There was also a right facial weakness of central type but the remaining cranial nerves were normal. The left leg, thigh and buttock were much smaller than those on the right and the leg was also shorter as a whole. Indeed, in comparison with the development of the arms and shoulders, the pelvis and both legs were definitely underdeveloped. A postural curve of the spine was evident which was explained by the shortening of the left leg. Both legs were spastic, the left being more spastic than the right. All the muscles of the lower extremities were completely paralysed and the lower half of the abdominal muscles were also affected, so the umbilicus moved upward when the patient lifted the head. Complete anesthesia for all modalities of sensibility extended upward to a level of 2 cm below the umbilicus. All the tendon reflexes in the legs were increased, there was a bilateral Babinski sign and bilateral ankle clonus was elicited. Stimulation of the legs caused flexion of both legs at all joints. There was some little weakness of the right arm and slight spasticity. Roentgenograms of the skull revealed several globular shadows in the substance of the frontal, temporal and parietal lobes of the left hemisphere. The largest of these was near the Rolandic fissure and measured more than a centimeter in diameter.

The laminae of the seventh to the 10th thoracic vertebrae were removed and beneath the dura a mass of tangled vessels was found surrounding the spinal cord and also extending into the substance of the cord. These appeared to be veins but contained some admixture of arterial blood, for their color was bright red and they pulsated strongly. At the upper pole of this mass a very large artery was found which seemed to enter directly into the mass of distended veins. A palpable thrill was present at this point, though no bruit had been audible over the spine before operation. When the artery was ligated, the mass of vessels collapsed to a large extent and pulsations ceased. No return of function followed the operation and the patient died a few days later of pneumonia. Postmortem examination was refused.

BIBLIOGRAPHY

Antoni, N.: Spinal vascular malformations (angiomas) and myelomalacia. Neurology, **12**:795, 1962.

Bailey, P. and Bucy, P.: Cavernous hemangioma of the vertebrae. J.A.M.A., **92**:1748, 1929.

Buchanan, D. N. and Walker, A. E.: Vascular anomalies of the spinal cord in children. Am. J. Dis. Child., **61**:928, 1941.

Cobb, S.: Haemangioma of the spinal cord associated with skin naevi of the same metamere. Ann. Surg., **62**:641, 1915.

Henson, R. A. and Croft, P. B.: Spontaneous spinal subarachnoid hemorrhage. Quart. J. Med., **25**:52, 1956.

RAND, C. W.: Haemangioma of the spinal cord. Arch. Neurol. & Psychiat., **18**:755, 1927.

SARGENT, P.: Haemangioma of the pia mater causing compression paraplegia. Brain, **48**:259, 1929.

SPILLER, W. G. AND FRAZIER, C. H.: Telangiectases of the spinal cord. Arch. Neurol. & Psychiat., **10**:29, 1923.

WOLF, A. AND WILENS, S. L.: Multiple hemangiomas of the spinal cord with syringomyelia. Am. J. Path., **10**:545, 1934.

WYBURN-MASON, R.: The Vascular Abnormalities and Tumors of the Spinal Cord and Its Membranes. St. Louis, C. V. Mosby, 1944.

NEOPLASMS AND RELATED CONDITIONS INVOLVING THE NERVOUS SYSTEM

INTRACRANIAL NEOPLASMS

INTRODUCTION.—It was customary among the older pediatricians to regard brain tumors as great rarities in infancy and early childhood, but as a result of more intensive study and of the introduction of pneumoventriculography, which permits more accurate diagnosis, it is now clear that brain tumors are almost as common in childhood as in adult life. According to Cushing's figures, only one-sixth of all intracranial neoplasms occur before the age of fifteen years, but from our own experience, we would be inclined to consider this an underestimate. Gliomas constitute about 75 per cent of all intracranial tumors of childhood as compared with about 40 per cent among the tumors of adult life. Consequently, the chances of discovering a benign tumor at operation are relatively small. However, not all gliomas are of equal malignancy and excellent results may be obtained in certain types. In recent years Bailey has made a careful study of the glioma group and by means of the silver stains developed by Cajal and his followers has been enabled to distinguish a number of types which differ, not only in their histological characteristics but in their malignancy, localization, age incidence, sensitivity to radiation and in the clinical symptoms which they produce. A number of these types of glioma occur in childhood and these will be described in brief below. The remaining 25 per cent of intracranial tumors of childhood includes hypophyseal duct cysts, about 13 per cent; tuberculomas, about 5 per cent; pinealomas, about 4 per cent; and a few papillomas of the choroid plexus, hemangioblastomas, meningiomas, metastatic growths and various other unusual types. The acoustic nerve tumors, hypophyseal adenomas, meningiomas and certain gliomas which are not uncommon in adult life are rare before adolescence.

About 65 per cent of all brain tumors giving rise to symptoms before the age of fifteen are found in the cerebellum according to Cushing's figures. It is of interest that during adult life the percentage of cerebellar tumors steadily falls and that of cerebral growths slowly rises, so that in old age cerebellar tumors are rare. The most complete discussion of intracranial tumors of childhood is found in the monograph of Bailey, Buchanan and Bucy.

1065

BIBLIOGRAPHY

AITA, J. C.: Neurologic Manifestations of General Diseases. Springfield, Thomas, 1964.

ARNSTEIN, L. *et al.:* Case report and survey of brain tumors during the neonatal period. J. Neurosurg., **8**:315, 1951.

BACKUS, R. E. *et al.:* Seizures with intracranial tumors. Pediatrics, **29**:978, 1962.

BAILEY, P.: Further remarks concerning tumors of the glioma group. Bull. Johns Hopkins Hosp., **40**:354, 1927.

————: Intracranial Tumors. Springfield, Thomas, 1933.

BAILEY, P., BUCHANAN, D. N. AND BUCY, P. C.: Intracranial Tumors of Infancy and Childhood. University of Chicago Press, 1939.

BAILEY, P. AND CUSHING, H.: Tumors of the Glioma Group. Philadelphia, J. B. Lippincott Co., 1926.

BLACK, B. K. AND SMITH, D. E.: Nasal glioma. Arch. Neurol. & Psychiat., **46**:164, 1950.

CRITCHLEY, McD.: Brain tumors in children. Brit. J. Child. Dis., **22**:251, 1925.

CUNEO, H. M. AND RAND, C. W.: Brain Tumors of Childhood, Springfield, Thomas, 1952.

CUSHING, H.: Intracranial tumors of preadolescence. Am. J. Dis. Child., **33**:551, 1927.

DANDY, W. E.: The Brain. Practice of Surgery, Dean Lewis, **12**:1, 1945.

DAVIS, L.: Intracranial tumors of childhood. Wisconsin Med. J., **29**:429, 1930.

FESSARD, C.: Cerebral tumors in infancy. Amer. Jour. Dis. Child., **115**:302, 1968.

FRENCH, L. A.: Brain tumors in children. Minnesota Med., **31**:867, 1948.

GLASAUER, F. E. AND YUAN, R. H. P.: Intracranial tumors with extracranial metastases. J. Neurosurg., **20**:474, 1963.

GLOBUS, J. H., ZUCKER, J. M. AND RUBENSTEIN, J. M.: Tumors of the brain in children and adolescents. Am. J. Dis. Child., **65**:604, 1943.

KEITH, H. M., CRAIG, W. M. AND KERNOHAN, J. W.: Brain tumors in children. Pediatrics, **3**:839, 1949.

KERNOHAN, J. W. AND UIHLEIN, A.: Sarcomas of the Brain. Springfield, Thomas, 1962.

KINNEY, T. D. AND ADAMS, R. D.: Reticulum cell sarcoma of the brain. Arch. Neurol. & Psychiat., **50**:552, 1943.

LIEBNER, E. J. *et al.:* Posterior fossa tumors. Radiology, **82**:193, 1964.

MILLER, R. H., CRAIG, W. AND KERNOHAN, J.: Supratentorial tumors among children. Arch. Neurol. & Psychiat., **68**:797, 1952.

POLMETEER, F. E. AND KERNOHAN, J. W.: Meningeal gliomatosis. Arch. Neurol. & Psychiat., **57**:617, 1947.

RUSSELL, D. S.: Pathology of Tumors of the Nervous System. Baltimore, Williams and Wilkins Co., 1959.

SMITH, W. A. AND FINCHER, E. F.: Intracranial tumors in children. South. Med. J., **35**:547, 1942.

WALKER, A. E. AND HOPPLE, T. L.: Brain tumors in children. J. Pediat., **35**:671, 1949.

WALSH, F. B.: Clinical Neuroophthalmology, 2nd Ed. Baltimore, Williams and Wilkins, 1957.

CEREBELLAR NEOPLASMS

Clinical Features.—These may be discussed under several heads: (1) Evidence of increased intracranial pressure. (2) Cerebellar signs. (3) Signs due to pressure on adjacent structures.

The signs of increased intracranial pressure appear relatively early in cerebellar tumors and usually constitute the first evidence of the disease. Headache is almost always present. The pulse is slow. There is sudden projectile vomiting, often but not invariably without nausea and without relation to meals. This is due to compression of the medulla, either as a result of intracranial hypertension, which causes herniation into the foramen

magnum, or of direct compression by the tumor. In the first case it appears rather late and has no localizing value but in the latter case it may be among the first symptoms and then usually indicates a posterior fossa growth. Diplopia due to paresis of the sixth nerve is another evidence of increased intracranial pressure without localizing importance. Some degree of papil ledema is usually to be found by the time headaches have become severe. At first there is little or no disturbance of vision but when the edema has become pronounced there are recurrent attacks of blurring of vision and the fields become concentrically constricted as secondary atrophy develops. In some instances there is no papilledema even though there is ataxia and headache. In infants the sutures may give way and the head may expand in such a way as to suggest congenital hydrocephalus.

The first evidence of cerebellar involvement is usually unsteadiness of

TABLE IV.—TYPES OF NEOPLASM OF THE BRAIN AND THEIR USUAL LOCATION

Part of the Nervous System Affected	*Classification*
Cerebellum	Astrocytoma Medulloblastoma Hemangioblastoma
Fourth Ventricle	Ependymoma Papilloma of choroid plexus
Pons and Medulla	Spongioblastoma
Midbrain	Spongioblastoma Pinealoma Teratoma
Third Ventricle	Ependymoma Papilloma of the choroid plexus
Hypothalamus and Optic Chiasm	Colloid cyst Spongioblastoma Hypophyseal duct cyst Adenoma of hypophysis
Cerebral Hemispheres	Astrocytoma Astroblastoma Glioblastoma multiforme Meningioma Sarcoma of leptomeninges
Lateral Ventricles	Ependymoma Papilloma of the choroid plexus
Meninges, Diffuse, "Tumor Meningitis"	Medulloblastoma Sarcoma of leptomeninges Papilloma of the choroid plexus Ependymoma Pinealoma

gait which seems to be due to loss of equilibrium as well as to cerebellar ataxia. Cerebellar ataxia may not be pronounced until late in the course of the disease. Nystagmus is very common but not invariably present. It is chiefly horizontal and, if the growth is unilateral, it is usually of slower rate and larger amplitude when the eyes are directed to the side of the lesion. There is a rest position situated from ten to thirty degrees to the side opposite the lesion and the slow phase of the movement is always toward this point. Cerebellar nystagmus is a nystagmus of fixation and is diminished by covering the eyes. The fifth nerve may be compressed in the cerebellopontine angle, causing numbness of the face and loss of corneal reflex. Deafness, tinnitus and loss of vestibular reactions may indicate involvement of the eighth nerve. The seventh nerve is not often severely affected but facial paresis may be found. Late in the course of the disease compression of the brainstem causes respiratory disturbances, difficulty in swallowing, hoarseness of the voice, and bulbar speech. The pyramidal tracts may be affected causing spasticity of the limbs, weakness and incontinence. The head is often tilted to the side of the lesion and the chin rotated to the opposite side. Stiffness of the neck and suboccipital tenderness are important signs of posterior fossa lesions and may be present early in the disease. Apathy, drowsiness and finally stupor gradually ensue in case the pressure is not relieved. Tonic fits are not uncommon in the last stages and convulsive seizures of any type may occur. Webster and Weinberger state that the seizures must be due to cortical anoxia resulting from increased intracranial pressure.

There are two cerebellar syndromes due to neoplasm: (1) The syndrome of the hemisphere in which one finds nystagmus and cerebellar ataxia on the side of the lesion and (2) The syndrome of the vermis in which one finds loss of equilibrium or trunkal ataxia often without definite ataxia of the extremities or nystagmus.

It is sometimes very difficult to distinguish cerebellar tumors from supratentorial growths. Midline cerebellar tumors may cause no focal signs other than unsteadiness of station and gait. Unfortunately, increased intracranial pressure of high degree, whatever its cause, may give rise to the same symptoms. Thus, acute hydrocephalus and tumors in "silent areas" of the cortex or intraventricular tumors may be mistaken for cerebellar tumors. The chronological sequence in which these symptoms appear must be taken into consideration in attempting to evaluate them. If the loss of equilibrium and unsteadiness of gait appear before there is any evidence of increased intracranial pressure, they point to cerebellar tumor. If, on the other hand, these symptoms develop late, after headache and vomiting have been present for some months and after papilledema has given place to atrophy,

they are of no importance as focal signs. Another source of confusion is due to the fact that cerebellar tumors may cause symptoms such as obesity, polyuria and genital atrophy as a result of hydrocephalus and dilatation of the third ventricle. In such cases, especially if the patient is blind from secondary optic atrophy and if the sella shows changes as a result of increased intracranial pressure, cerebellar tumors may be mistaken for suprasellar cysts. The differential diagnosis again must be made largely upon the sequence in which the symptoms appear. In case of suprasellar cyst the loss of vision, obesity and polyuria occur very early and precede the symptoms of increased intracranial pressure. Moreover, the optic atrophy is usually of the primary type, the sella is often destroyed and in about 80 per cent of cases there is roentgenographic evidence of calcification in the tumor. If the symptoms are the result of cerebellar tumor with hydrocephalus, they appear late and the optic discs usually show evidences of preceding edema. The differential diagnosis between cerebellar tumor and acute hydrocephalus will be discussed in connection with the latter condition.

If the growth begins early in life before the sutures of the cranium are firmly closed the head will enlarge rapidly and assume an hydrocephalic shape. The position of the inion in relation to the altas is of great importance in determining the site of the tumor for the distance between these two points indicates the size of the posterior fossa. In longstanding cerebellar tumors the inion will be higher than normal and in cases in which the growth is above the posterior fossa the inion may be lower than it is in the normal child.

Roentgenographic studies show very little in cerebellar tumors. The appearances are merely those of increased intracranial pressure, i.e. "convolutional atrophy," separation of the sutures and mild atrophy of the clinoid processes. Calcification is not common in cerebellar tumors and is not easy to demonstrate if present.

If the clinical signs are inconclusive ventriculography should be performed. In cerebellar lesions the ventricles are symmetrically dilated; not only the lateral ventricles but the third ventricle as well. The fourth ventricle can rarely be demonstrated. It must be kept in mind that the ventricular system is normal at first and that it is only when the tumor has reached such a size that the fourth ventricle is obstructed that hydrocephalus appears.

Brust *et al.* describe a case in which a ventriculo-pleural shunt for a malignant growth led to metastases in the pleura.

McLaurin and Ford describe obstruction of the foramina of the fourth ventricle following one or more operations to remove cerebellar tumors. In some cases operation and removal of adhesions gives relief, but often a ventricular-jugular shunt is required.

BIBLIOGRAPHY

BAILEY, P.: Concerning cerebellar symptoms produced by suprasellar tumors. Arch. Neurol. & Psychiat., **11**:137, 1924.

BRUST, J. C. M. *et al.:* Glial tumor metastases through a ventriculo-pleural shunt. Arch. of Neurol., **18**:649, 1968.

CRITCHLEY, McD.: The diagnosis of cerebellar tumors in childhood. Brit. J. Child. Dis., **23**:165, 1926.

GOL, A. AND McKISSOCK, W.: Cerebellar astrocytomas. J. Neurosurg., **16**:287, 1959.

McLAURIN, R. L. AND FORD, L. E.: Obstruction following posterior fossa surgery. Johns Hopkins Med. Jour., **122**:309, 1968.

OPPENHEIMER, D. R.: Benign tumor of the cerebellum. J. Neurol., Neurosurg. & Psychiat., **18**:199, 1955.

WEBSTER, J. E. AND WEINBERGER, L. M.: Convulsions associated with tumors of the cerebellum. Arch. Neurol. & Psychiat., **43**:1163, 1940.

Astrocytomas

Pathological Anatomy.—This type of glioma is probably the commonest of all gliomas of childhood. It is situated in the great majority of cases in the hemisphere or vermis of the cerebellum but may occur in the cerebral hemisphere. As a rule, it contains one or more large cysts filled with yellow fluid which coagulates when withdrawn. The tumor may be merely a small mural nodule in the wall of the cyst. Solid astrocytomas also occur. The tumor tissue may be very soft or may be dense and fibrous. This depends upon the relative preponderance of fibrous and of protoplasmic astrocytes.

Clinical Features.—Boys and girls are affected with equal frequency. The onset of symptoms is usually before the fifteenth year. When the growth is situated in the cerebellar hemisphere there is ataxia of the homolateral extremities and, as a rule, nystagmus which is of larger amplitude and slower rate when the eyes are deviated to the side of the lesion. When the lesion is in the midline, equilibrium is affected first and there may be no ataxia of the extremities. It should be said, however, that occasionally even a large cerebellar astrocytoma may give rise to no focal signs and cannot be localized by clinical means. Papilledema may be present or absent. Roentgenograms of the skull may show enlargement of one or both sides of the posterior fossa and sometimes thinning of the bone. Ventriculograms show dilatation of the lateral and third ventricles when there is obstruction of the fourth ventricle. The course is relatively slow and in some cases the patient may survive for a number of years even without operation. Astrocytomas are somewhat more frequent than the medulloblastomas. The average survival period after operation is said to be six years and some patients in whom an apparently complete extirpation has been performed show no sign of recurrence for many years. Astrocytomas are the most benign of all gliomas of childhood. Matson states that of 34 children operated upon, 32 survived and were free of increased intracranial pressure. Some 24 were

completely asymptomatic or at most had mild ataxia and the remaining patients had persisting disabilities of some type, chiefly diminished vision, cranial nerve palsies and ataxia.

Treatment.—Radical removal of the growth by means of an incision through the vermis is advised. These growths, whether fibrous or protoplasmic, do not respond to radium or to roentgenotherapy. Indeed, preoperative radiation may cause death as a result of edema and swelling of the tumor.

BIBLIOGRAPHY

BUCY, P. C. AND THIEMAN, P. W.: Astrocytomas of the cerebellum. Arch. of Neurol., **18**:14, 1968.
CUSHING, H.: Experience with cerebellar astrocytomas. Critical review of 76 cases. Surg. Gynec. & Obst., **52**:129, 1931.
GOL, A.: Cerebellar astrocytomas in children. Am. J. Dis. Child., **106**:21, 1963.
MATSON, D. D.: Cerebellar astrocytoma in childhood. Pediatrics, **18**:150, 1956.

Medulloblastomas

Pathological Anatomy.—Tumors of this type are unfortunately almost as common as the astrocytomas. They seem to rise in the roof of the fourth ventricle and soon fill the ventricle. They are soft, friable tumors of great invasive power and rapid growth. The cells are round or spindle shaped with scanty cytoplasm and round nuclei with heavy chromatin network. They lie, as a rule, in structureless masses but may form pseudorosettes. By special stains neuroglial fibrillae may be demonstrated extending from both poles of the cells. These are short and of embryonic type but an occasional adult neuroglial fiber can be found. In nearly 15 per cent of cases these tumors are disseminated by the circulation of the cerebrospinal fluid and invade the subarachnoid spaces about the brain and spinal cord, involving the cranial nerves and compressing the cauda equina and cord. It is believed that these tumors arise from primitive undifferentiated cells of the neural ectoderm. They have been termed sarcomas in the past because of their cellular character.

Clinical Features.—These tumors develop early in childhood and usually cause symptoms between the third and sixth year but may occur later. King reports a case in which the symptoms develop in the neonatal period. Cushing states that these tumors are three times as common in boys as in girls. In many cases there is nothing characteristic in the clinical features. Evidences of increased intracranial pressure appear early and there may also be vomiting, vertigo and other symptoms due to direct pressure on the medulla. A typical group of symptoms, loss of equilibrium and staggering gait without ataxia in the extremities and with little if any nystagmus, is attributed to destruction of the posterior part of the cerebellar vermis and is termed the posterior-vermis syndrome. Air studies usually reveal obstruction of the fourth ventricle with internal hydrocephalus of the non-communi-

cating type, but we have seen cases in which a communicating type of hydrocephalus was discovered. In one the primary growth in the vermis was inconspicuous and the obstruction was under the base of the brain where it could not be demonstrated by the posterior fossa approach. The course is a rapid one and leads to death within a year in most instances.

In some cases deposits in the meninges may give rise to symptoms. This occurs most frequently after operation but may also occur before operation. In such cases there may be evidences of meningeal irritation. Cranial nerve palsies are often present. They are multiple and often symmetrical. The eighth nerves are involved early as are the fifth, but almost all the nerves may be involved before death. The spinal roots are frequently infiltrated, causing pains, tenderness of the spine and loss of reflexes. The spinal cord may be compressed and paraplegia may occur. Spinal puncture in such cases reveals yellow fluid often containing some admixture of blood. The cell count is very high, ranging from 20 to 200, including lymphocytes and tumor cells undergoing mitoses. The protein content is greatly increased but the spinal fluid sugar may be reduced or absent. Leavitt has reported the occurrence of a medulloblastoma in each of a pair of identical twins.

Treatment.—These tumors recur rapidly and the average duration of life is only a few months after operation. Deep roentgenotherapy has some value but as a rule only defers the fatal outcome. An occasional patient may live ten years or more as in the case given in abstract below.

CASE HISTORY (U-31726).—*Girl of nine years developed signs of a cerebellar tumor. Operation revealed a medulloblastoma invading fourth ventricle. This was removed as completely as possible. Substantial recovery. One year later, paraplegia developed due to many metastatic deposits in the spinal subarachnoid space. There was no return of cerebellar symptoms.*

M. R., a little girl of nine years, developed severe headaches and vomiting in January, 1930. These symptoms became more and more severe and in May the gait became unsteady and she began to complain of diplopia. In June she was admitted to the neurosurgical service of Dr. Dandy. There was bilateral papilledema, nystagmus, unsteadiness of station and gait. Operation disclosed a friable tumor filling the fourth ventricle and extending into the cerebellum above. This was removed and was found to be a medulloblastoma. The child improved rapidly and seemed to be quite well for almost exactly a year. In June, 1931, she began to complain of pain in the left thigh. Some weeks later the left leg grew weak and by the last of June she could not walk and had become incontinent. There was pain in both legs.

Examination revealed no signs of an intracranial lesion. The optic nerve heads were quite negative except for some slight residua of the old

papilledema. The other cranial nerves were also normal. The arms were used freely without weakness or ataxia. The legs, however, were very weak at all joints and very flaccid. The left quadriceps and flexors of the hip were quite paralysed but the other muscles all showed some power. The pain was most severe over the anterior surface of the left thigh corresponding to the distribution of the third and fourth lumbar roots. Some hypesthesia was demonstrable below the umbilicus but this was patchy except over the third and fourth lumbar dermatomes on the left where it was uniform and almost complete. The knee jerks were lost and the left ankle jerks as well. Plantar reflexes were extensor. Spinal fluid contained some 60 cells and a great excess of protein. The Queckenstedt test was positive.

Case History (Path. 7376–Ped. 34869).—*Boy of 15 months developed multiple palsies of the cranial nerves beginning with the right third and then both seventh nerves. Later all the cranial nerves were affected, there were symptoms of increased intracranial pressure and irritation of the meninges but never any paralysis of the extremities or change in the tendon reflexes. Many cells in the spinal fluid. Death some three months after onset. Postmortem: Small medulloblastoma in the fourth ventricle with extensive invasion of the basilar meninges and infiltration of the cranial nerves on both sides.*

W. T., white male child of 15 months, was brought to the Harriet Lane Home on January 21, 1923. He had always been well until 6 weeks before when the right eye began to turn out and the eyelid to drop. Two weeks later the right side of the face became paralysed and shortly afterwards, the left side of the face was also paralysed. Vomiting began about this time.

Examination revealed a child of the given age who seemed to be drowsy and irritable. The head was normal in shape and size. Vision seemed to be reduced but not lost. The optic fundi showed no pathological changes. There was complete paralysis of the right third nerve and the right pupil was therefore dilated and immobile. The left pupil reacted sluggishly but the bulb moved freely. Both seventh nerves were completely paralysed and the facial muscles showed reaction of degeneration. Hearing seemed to be lost in both ears. The other cranial nerves seemed to function normally. No disturbances of motility were found. The reflexes were all present and normal. The spinal fluid contained from 30 to 100 cells which were chiefly large lymphocytes or mononuclears. Some of these were thought to be tumor cells but could not be definitely identified. There was often a trace of blood in the fluid and the protein was greatly increased.

The patient continued to vomit and became greatly emaciated. The neck became stiff and Kernig's sign appeared, so that the picture was suggestive of chronic meningitis. The drowsiness deepened into stupor. Ulcers developed over both corneas due to anesthesia, the jaws became paralysed, the child became unable to swallow and then could not protrude

the tongue. Eventually, he seemed to have lost the function of the entire twelve pairs of cranial nerves. However, the extremities could still be moved freely, the tendon reflexes were active and the child responded to pin prick. Shortly after the end of the third month of the illness he died of pneumonia.

Post-mortem examination revealed a thin layer of neoplastic tissue extending over the entire base of the brain from the chiasm anteriorly to the medulla posteriorly and completely surrounding the brain-stem. The posterior surface of the spinal cord was also covered with this same tissue and the nerve roots of the cauda were encrusted with deposits. The fourth ventricle was completely filled with a soft, friable tumor which extended upwards into the roof nuclei of the cerebellum. Histological study revealed that the tumor was a typical medulloblastoma. It had infiltrated the cranial nerves and more or less completely destroyed them. It had spread throughout the subarachnoid spaces just as a meningitis does but had not invaded the brain or spinal cord.

CASE HISTORY (Path. 9252).—*Medulloblastoma causing purely meningeal syndrome in boy of three years and mistaken for meningococcic meningitis.*

R. B., a previously healthy boy of three years, developed unsteadiness of gait in March 1926. Shortly after this, he began to vomit and complained of headache. The unsteadiness became less obvious after a time but the vomiting continued. At times he was dull and seemed drowsy although he was also irritable and restless at other times.

May 3, 1926, some two months after the onset of the illness, he was brought to the hospital. Examination revealed slightly unsteady gait, slight cervical rigidity, diminished tendon reflexes, and normal optic fundi. Otherwise neurological and medical examinations were unproductive. His pulse and temperature remained normal. The spinal fluid contained from 60 to 1000 cells on various examinations, 80 per cent of these being mononuclear cells. There was a marked increase of protein. Examination of a smear was thought to show bacteria and a culture was made out of which grew numerous colonies of meningococci. The child was treated with antimeningococcus serum but grew steadily worse and died a week after he was admitted to the hospital. The diagnosis of medulloblastoma was seriously considered until the report of the culture of meningococcus was received from the laboratory. Post-mortem examination, however, revealed only a large medulloblastoma filling the fourth ventricle and extending throughout the subarachnoid spaces under the base and into the sulci over the cortex. The brain stem was surrounded by the growth. The cranial nerves were not infiltrated as in the case described above. There were no bacteria to be discovered in the meninges and no meningitis except for the reaction of the tumor.

CASE HISTORY (U-107538).—*Boy of nine years with headache, papillede-*

ma, nystagmus and head tilting. Medulloblastoma of fourth ventricle found at operation. Post-operative radiation. Quite well 10 years later.

F. M., a boy of nine years, was admitted to Johns Hopkins Hospital on May 7, 1937. The history was that of headache and vomiting of five months' duration. There had been loss of seven pounds weight. The parents had noticed that he held his head tilted to the left and his neck seemed to be stiff. No other symptoms could be elicited. The child had been under observation for some years since he had been exposed to tuberculosis and had been found to have a calcified lesion in the spleen which was believed to be a tuberculoma.

On examination the child was found to have bilateral papilledema of two diopters. There was a horizontal nystagmus on deviation to the right and left which was of cerebellar type. The head was tilted to the left and there was some little rigidity of the neck. Nothing else could be found on examination.

Ventriculography revealed evidences of obstruction in the posterior part of the fourth ventricle. Dr. Dandy explored the posterior fossa and discovered a friable tumor in the posterior part of the fourth ventricle spreading down over the posterior aspect of the medulla to the foramen magnum and filling the cisterna magna. This was removed completely except for a small process which penetrated the floor of the ventricle. The patient did well after operation and was given deep roentgenotherapy. Several series of radiations were given, the last series ending in November 1938.

Since then the child has remained quite free of symptoms though the back of his head is still bald from the depilatory effect of the roentgen rays. When last seen on March 10, 1947, neurological examination was entirely negative.

Histological study of the tumor revealed the typical characteristics of a medulloblastoma.

BIBLIOGRAPHY

BAILEY, P.: Further notes on cerebellar medulloblastomas. The effect of roentgen radiation. Am. J. Path., **6**:125, 1930.

BERG, L.: Hypoglycorrhachia of non-infectious origin. Diffuse meningeal neoplasia. Neurology, **3**:811, 1953.

CUSHING, H.: Experiences with cerebellar medulloblastomas. Critical review. Acta Path. et Microbiol. Scand., **7**:1, 1930.

CUSHING, H. AND BAILEY, P.: Medulloblastoma cerebelli; a common type of midcerebellar glioma of childhood. Arch. Neurol. & Psychiat., **14**:192, 1925.

FORD, F. R. AND FIROR, W.: "Sarcomatosis" of the leptomeninges. Bull. Johns Hopkins Hosp., **35**:65 and 108, 1924.

INGRAHAM, F., BAILEY, O. AND BARKER, W.: Medulloblastoma cerebelli. New England J. Med., **238**:171, 1948.

KING, A. B.: Medulloblastoma with onset during the neonatal period. J. Neurosurg., **10**:75, 1953.

LEAVITT, F. H.: Cerebellar tumors occurring in identical twins. Arch. Neurol. & Psychiat., **19**:617, 1928.

RAAF, J. AND KERNOHAN, J. W.: Relation of abnormal collections of cells in posterior medullary

velum of cerebellum to origin of medullobastoma. Arch. Neurol. & Psychiat., **52**:163, 1944. WALSH, F. B.: *Loc. cit.*

Hemangioblastomas

Pathological Anatomy.—These tumors are rare in childhood but are of such interest, that they may be mentioned. They arise in either the hemisphere or in the midline of the cerebellum, the former site being more common than the latter. In more than half of the cases the tumor is represented by a large cyst containing a small mural nodule of tumor. In other cases the growth is solid or contains only small cysts. Histologically several types are distinguished. Some are composed chiefly of capillaries; others are chiefly cellular and others contain large cavernous spaces. Between these vascular channels are found numerous fat-containing cells which are believed to arise from proliferation of the capillary endothelium. All types are distinguished by a characteristic connective tissue reticulum. Lindau has shown that many cerebellar tumors formerly classified as gliomatous cysts are in reality hemangioblastomas. The whole complex includes, in addition to the hemangioblastomas of the cerebellum and brain stem, retinal angiomas (which seem in most cases to be hemangioblastomas), hemangioblastomas of the spinal cord and spinal nerve roots associated often with syringomyelic cavities, epithelial cysts, angiomas and cystadenomas of the pancreas, cysts and angiomas of the liver, spleen and kidneys, tumors resembling hypernephromas of the kidneys, paragangliomas and adenomas of the adrenals, cystadenomas of the ovaries, cysts and adenomas of the

FIG. 228. A.P. (U. No. 262735) at age of 13 yrs. She had a hemangioblastoma of the left retina and signs of spinal and cerebellar growth. The deviation of the left eye was due to loss of vision. She was the sister of the patient, S.P. whose history is given on page 1079.

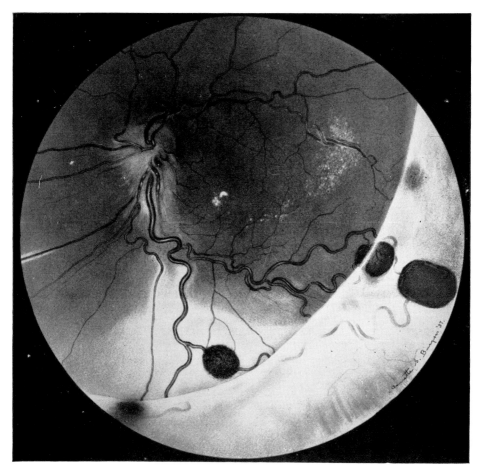

Fig. 229. The ophthalmoscopic picture in Dr. Coston's patient with Lindau's disease. Case 384. (From Walsh: Neuro-Ophthalmology, courtesy, the Williams and Wilkins Company.)

epididymis and in rare instances cutaneous naevi and cafe au lait spots. Only a very few hemangioblastomas have been found above the tentorium. Von Recklinghausen's disease has been found in association with this disease. Nibbelink reports a case in which a pheochromocytoma was associated.

Clinical Features.—The disease is apparently inherited and seems to behave as a simple dominant characteristic. A remarkable family history elicited from a patient of Dr. Otenasek is of interest in this connection. This history is given in abstract below. The onset is usually in early adult life but may occur in childhood. There are three chief symptom complexes.

The cerebellar hemangioblastomas cause increased pressure and the usual signs of cerebellar damage. The course is sometimes marked by fluctuations

possibly due to variations of pressure in the cyst and possibly to hemorrhage in some instances. Loss of proprioception and astereognosis and even sensory seizures in one arm or the other may be among the first symptoms of this condition and may lead to an erroneous diagnosis of a neoplasm in the parietal lobe. We know of five instances in which the parietal lobe has been explored. No doubt, these sensory disturbances indicate extension of the growth into the brain stem. Unless there are other manifestations present, such as retinal changes, it does not seem possible to make the diagnosis on clinical grounds before operation though a history of similar symptoms in another member of the family is suggestive. No doubt the injection of diodrast into the vertebral arteries would show an abnormal vascular pattern.

The retinal lesions are often so typical as to justify the diagnosis. One or both eyes may be affected. One sees large tortuous veins which often contain bright red blood and are accompanied by a large artery which shows beading and variations in caliber. These vessels lead to rounded nodules usually situated in the periphery of the retina where they may be difficult to see. Such masses are believed to be hemangioblastomas. They may be multiple. They are often associated with hemorrhages, exudates, detachment of the retina and glaucoma. The typical features of the process may be concealed by these secondary changes so the diagnosis cannot be established by ophthalmoscopic examination. Vision is eventually lost though not for a number of years as a rule.

The third group of symptoms are due to hemangioblastoma of the spinal cord. Wyburn-Mason states that the signs may indicate damage to the cervical cord, the lumbosacral enlargement or the cauda equina. Often there is a syringomyelic cavity associated which gives rise to the usual signs. The course of this condition is variable. It may be brief or prolonged. A great excess of protein in the spinal fluid is a typical finding. The cisternal fluid also contains much protein. Pantopaque injection reveals as a rule great tortuous veins lying in the spinal subarachnoid spaces. In a number of cases the spinal hemangioblastoma is found at autopsy having given rise to no symptoms during life. Levin states that in every case of Lindau's disease in which the spinal cord has been properly examined, a spinal tumor has been found.

The lesions in the abdominal viscera rarely give rise to any symptoms. The tumors of the kidneys which resemble hypernephromas are apparently not always malignant. Cutaneous naevi are rare but Wyburn-Mason describes a few instances in which they were observed.

The diagnosis depends upon the symptoms mentioned above. The history of retinal, spinal and posterior fossa tumors in a family as in the history given below is so typical as to admit of little doubt of the diagnosis.

It should be said, however, that in most instances the clinical picture is incomplete and the patient reveals signs of only cerebellar, spinal or retinal involvement. It is of interest that in several instances, polycythemia has been associated with cerebellar hemangioblastoma. Pheochromocytoma and paroxysmal hypertension are found in rare instances. It is said that in such cases the hemangioblastoma is apt to be found in the brain stem rather than in the cerebellum.

The cerebellar growths may be removed successfully and in a few instances successful operations have been performed on the spinal tumors. The great vascularity of these lesions, however, makes any operation difficult. Retinal hemangioblastomas may be benefited by the use of the electric cautery in some instances.

CASE HISTORY (U-461580).—*Loss of vision of the left eye at age of 10 years. Later, numbness over the right side of the chest and clumsiness of the right leg. At age of 29 years, developed paraparesis. On examination angiomatous changes in the left retina and signs of syringomyelia. Operation disclosed extensive angiomatous process in the spinal cord. Remarkable family history including 15 cases in three generations exhibiting various evidences of Lindau's disease.*

S. P. was discovered to have defective vision in the left eye at the age of 10 years. Examination disclosed an angiomatous process. Vision showed little change subsequently. At the age of 20 years he noticed a feeling of numbness over the right side of his chest. Somewhat later, the right leg became clumsy. At the age of 29 years his legs grew weak and a sense of numbness developed in both legs which spread slowly up to the chest.

On examination (May 20, 1948) no abnormalities are seen in the skin. In the left retina there are a number of large tortuous veins extending to the temporal side. Near the disc is a mass covered with white connective tissue which is connected with the dilated vessels. Vision is greatly reduced. The cranial nerves are otherwise intact. The legs are both somewhat weak and spastic with increased tendon reflexes. The right leg is very ataxic and there is slight ataxia in the left leg. Station is unsteady and gait ataxic and spastic. There is a zone of cutaneous anesthesia over the right side of the trunk extending from T6 to T8. Below this zone there is a reduction of pain and thermal sensibility on both sides of the body. Sense of position and passive movement of the toes are greatly reduced on the right side.

The spinal fluid contained 1540 mgs of protein per 100 cc. A pantopaque injection revealed the typical pattern of an angioma. Exploration exposed a very extensive series of dilated vessels over the posterior aspect of the cord extending over many segments. No tumor mass was discovered.

The patient's family history is of great interest. The abnormality, i.e. Lindau's disease, is traced back to Richard and Mary D. who lived in Bristol, Virginia, between 1810 and 1890. Little is known of this couple. They

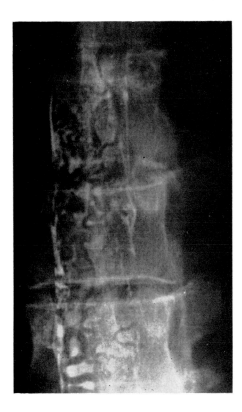

Fig. 230. Hemangioblastoma of the spinal cord. The tortuous veins are made evident by pantopaque injection. (By the courtesy of Dr. Arthur King.)

had six children, however, and two of these are known to have had symptoms strongly suggestive of the disease.

There were ten grandchildren and of these eight seem to have been affected. Laura M. (U. No. 646) was operated upon by Dr. Dandy and a cerebellar hemangioblastoma was found. Curry D. became blind and Dr. Frazier of Philadelphia found an inoperable intracranial tumor. Ronald D. was found at post-mortem examination to have a brain tumor and "carcinoma" of the kidney. Ethel D. was operated upon for a spinal cord tumor. Lucille D., the mother of our patient, grew blind in one eye and had numbness of one arm. She was operated upon by Dr. Coleman of Richmond, Virginia. Sidney D. seems to have displayed no symptoms but one of his three sons, who is mentioned below, was affected. This also seems to have been true of Pearl B. who is not known to have had any symptoms but whose daughter, mentioned below, was involved in the family misfortune. Another group of three siblings, Flora B., Mary B., and Lula B. all suffered from intense headaches and Flora lost her vision. Thus, the only two members of this generation who seem to have escaped transmitted the disease.

There were ten great grandchildren of Richard and Mary D. and of these, five, including our patient, are affected. He has four siblings. Doris P. and Edward P. are said to be alive and well. John P. (U. No.

64337) developed loss of vision of the left eye due to angiomatous changes, ataxia, papilledema, weakness and sensory loss in the left arm. A cerebellar hemangioblastoma was removed by Dr. Dandy. Ann P. (U. No. 262735) was seen at the age of 13 years (see Fig. 160). She displayed retinal angiomatosis, loss of proprioception in the left arm and unsteady gait. Operation was unsuccessful, and she died some years after Dr. Dandy had operated upon her. Another family of three siblings, children of Sidney D., includes only one instance of the disease. David D. (U. No. 300209) developed angioma of the retina and was operated upon in the Wilmer. One child of Laura D., mentioned above, seems to be well at present. Lois H. (U. No. 56444) daughter of Pearl B., mentioned above, was operated upon by Dr. Dandy who found a cystic hemangioblastoma of the cerebellum. There was also angiomatous changes in the retina.

In January 1960, we saw a child of six years, who was a great-great grandchild of the original couple, who was then suffering from a hemangioblastoma of the left retina.

It is evident, therefore, that this family is subject to three chief disorders: (1) Retinal angiomatous changes which must be due to hemangioblastoma though complete proof of the true nature of the retinal process is not yet established. (2) Cerebellar hemangioblastoma. (3) Spinal hemangioblastoma. In only one case is there a history of a lesion of the internal organs. Ronald D. is said to have had a carcinoma of the kidney. No skin lesions are mentioned. There can be no doubt that the family suffers from Lindau's disease.

The disease is found in both males and females and is transmitted by either sex. Two instances are recorded of individuals, who are not known to have had active symptoms, passing on the condition to their children. These were grandchildren of Richard and Mary D. and the other eight members of this generation had active manifestations. In the three generations of which we have knowledge there were 26 members and of these 15 were affected. Apparently the disease is transmitted as a dominant factor. I am indebted to Dr. Arthur King for many of the facts given above.

BIBLIOGRAPHY

BONEBRAKE, R. A. AND SIQUEIRA, E. B.: Familial occurrence of solitary hemangioblastoma of the cerebellum. Neurology, 14:733, 1964.

CARPENTER, G., SCHWARTZ, H. AND WALKER, A. E.: Neurogenic polycythemia. Ann. Int. Med., 19:470, 1943.

CHAPMAN, R. C. AND DIAZ-PEREZ, R.: Pheochromocytoma associated with cerebellar hemangioblastoma. J.A.M.A., 182:1014, 1962.

CHRISTOFERSON, L. A.: Von Hippel-Lindau's disease. J.A.M.A., 178:280, 1961.

CRAMER, F. AND KIMSEY, W.: The cerebellar hemangioblastomas. Arch. Neurol. & Psychiat., 67:237, 1952.

CUSHING, H. AND BAILEY, P.: Hemangiomas of the cerebellum and retina. Arch. Ophth., 57:447, 1928.

CUSHING, H. AND BAILEY, P.: Tumors Arising from the Blood Vessels of the Brain. Springfield, Charles C Thomas, 1928.

DANDY, W. E.: Venous abnormalities and angiomas of the brain. Arch. Surg., 17:715, 1928.

LEVIN, P. M.: Multiple hereditary hemangioblastomas of the nervous system. Arch. Neurol. & Psychiat., **36**:384, 1936.

LINDAU, A.: Studies über Kleinhirncysten. Acta Pathol. et Microbiol. Scandinav., Suppl. 1, 1926.

MELMON, K. L. AND ROSEN, S. W.: Lindau's disease. Amer. Jour. Med., **36**:595, 1964.

NIBBELINK, D. W. *et al.*: On the association of pheochromocytoma and cerebellar hemangioblastoma. Neurology, **19**:455, 1969.

OTENASEK, F. J. AND SILVER, M. L.: Spinal hemangiomas in Lindau's disease. J. Neurosurg., **18**:295, 1961.

VIETS, H. R.: An additional case of hemangioblastoma of the retina and cerebellum with a note on Lindlau's disease. J. Nerv. & Ment. Dis., **77**:457, 1933.

WALSH, F. B.: *Loc. cit.*

WOLF, A. AND LILENS, S. L.: Multiple hemangioblastoma of the spinal cord with syringomyelia. Am. J. Path., **10**:545, 1934.

WYBURN-MASON, R.: The Vascular Abnormalities and Tumors of the Spinal Cord and Its Membranes. St. Louis, C. V. Mosby, 1944.

NEOPLASMS OF CEREBRAL HEMISPHERES

Clinical Features.—We may subdivide the manifestations of cerebral tumors into: (1) Focal signs; (2) Signs of increased intracranial pressure. The latter have been described in connection with cerebellar tumors and need not be enumerated again. Increased intracranial pressure is almost always the result of hydrocephalus due to occlusions of some part of the ventricular system. The situation and size of the tumor, therefore, determine whether such signs appear early or late. Evidences of increased pressure are among the first symptoms in the majority of supratentorial tumors in children, but there are numerous exceptions to this rule. In infants, in whom the cranial sutures are not yet united, the head may expand as in the common congenital hydrocephalus and symptoms of pressure may never become evident.

Focal signs are usually very meager in very young children and infants, because of their inability to cooperate in many tests and because certain cortical areas have not become functionally active. Hemianopia, cortical anesthesia, aphasia and apraxia cannot be demonstrated. Even disturbances of gait and incoordination are demonstrated with great difficulty in young children and cannot be elicited infants. We are reduced, therefore, to depending upon disturbances of the motor system such as hemiplegia and focal convulsions. Even these signs, which would be of very definite significance in adults, must be interpreted with caution in infants for Jacksonian fits, followed by transient hemiplegia, may occur in the absence of any gross lesion in the corresponding cortical areas. In many cases the localization of intracranial lesions in infants can be established only by ventriculography.

In more mature children and adolescents, we may expect signs as in adults. These will be mentioned very briefly. In lesions of the right frontal lobe we may be unable to demonstrate any focal signs until the growth has

extended posteriorly to the motor area. Many writers, however, have emphasized the importance of early mental changes as indicative of lesions of the frontal lobes. Apathy, indifference, habit deterioration and euphoria are mentioned. There is a tendency to soil the clothes although sphincter control is not lost. However, such symptoms are so common in tumors placed in other parts of the brain that little or no stress can be placed upon them. A fine tremor is sometimes found in the hand hemolateral to the lesion. Nose rubbing and yawning are described. If the lesion involves the superior frontal convolutions, forced grasping and groping may be found on the opposite side. If the inferior surface is involved, we may discover unilateral optic atrophy or loss of sense of smell. If the left frontal lobe is the site of the lesion, motor aphasia may occur. Tumors involving the motor cortex usually cause focal convulsions which, in many cases, are followed by transient paralysis. Recovery may be complete at first but after numerous attacks some weakness persists which becomes more and more severe. If the growth is primarily subcortical, hemiplegia may develop without focal convulsions. Lesions in the parietal region may be expected to cause some degree of cortical anesthesia, such as astereognosis, loss of sense of passive movement, two point discrimination, etc. Hemiataxia and hypotonia are also to be expected. On the left side, especially if the lesion is in the inferior parietal convolution, we may find in addition sensory aphasia and, perhaps, apraxia. If convulsions occur, they are apt to be generalized. Occipital lobe tumors cause hemianopia of various types and, if on the left side, may cause word blindness. Temporal lobe lesions are sometimes associated with uncinate fits and often with defects in the upper quadrants of the opposite visual fields. However, the temporal and parietal lobes are relatively silent areas.

Tumors involving the corpus callosum give rise to no distinctive signs. Mental disturbances are apt to be prominent. Since the growth usually invades the hemispheres, there is apt to be hemiparesis on one or both sides and focal or general convulsions.

Tumors near the surface of the cortex in infants may cause local bulging of the skull and some growths may even erode the skull, appearing under the scalp. Local tenderness on percussion may be found but is not a reliable focal sign for it is often found over a dilated ventricle far from the site of the growth. Roentgenographic studies may reveal calcified tumors or erosion of the skull. Dilated vascular channels may be found overlying meningeal growths but this appearance must be interpreted with great caution. If the pineal body is visible, it may be displaced to the side opposite the growth. In general, roentgenography reveals only evidences of increased intracranial pressure.

False localizing signs should be mentioned. Tumors in the frontal lobe

may cause herniation of the brain through the tentorium resulting in pressure on a calcarine artery producing hemianopia. A tumor in one hemisphere may displace the brain stem so the cerebral peduncle on the opposite side may be forced against the edge of the tentorium so that ipsilateral hemiplegia may result. The medulla and tonsils of the cerebellum may be forced into the foramen magnum causing bulbar signs and symptoms.

Ventriculography by Dandy's method is of the greatest value in cases in which the focal signs are indefinite or absent. The homolateral ventricle is compressed and displaced and the contralateral ventricle is usually dilated or at least relatively enlarged. The third ventricle may be shifted also. These changes have been fully described by Dandy and the reader is referred to his articles.

In addition to the tumors described below, the benign cystic astrocytoma, the spongioblastoma and many others are found in the cerebral hemisphere.

BIBLIOGRAPHY

BAILEY, P. AND BUCY, P.: Astroblastomas of the brain. Acta Psychiatrica et Neurologica Scand., 5:439, 1930.

DANDY, W. E.: The localization or elimination of cerebral tumor by ventriculography. Surg. Gynec. & Obstet., 30:329, 1920.

MILLER, R. *et al.:* Supratentorial tumors among children. Arch. Neurol. & Psychiat., 68:797, 1952.

Glioblastoma Multiforme

Pathological Anatomy.—These tumors are highly malignant and grow rapidly. They are found chiefly in the cerebral hemispheres, often extending from one hemisphere into the other by way of the corpus callosum. Their structure is extremely varied. Spindle cells, round cells and giant cells are found. These cells are usually bipolar and show fine neuroglial fibrillae. Hemorrhages and areas of degeneration are very common. Numerous mitotic figures are seen. Compression of blood vessels may cause gross softenings. Fortunately, these tumors are uncommon and represent only about 9 per cent of the gliomas of childhood.

Clinical Features.—These growths are characterized by sudden onset and rapid course. Apoplectic phenomena may occur and may suggest a vascular lesion. Signs of increased intracranial pressure are usually severe. Since they are often found in the temporal or parietal lobe and extend deeply into the white matter, they often give rise to aphasia and apraxia.

Treatment.—These tumors cannot be removed completely by surgical means. Deep roentgenotherapy should be tried after partial removal and decompression but there is no hope for cure.

CASE HISTORY.—*Boy of 12 years developed convulsions on the left side without warning. These continued. Left hemiplegia developed and death*

occurred 22 hours after onset. Post-mortem examination revealed a glio-blastoma multiforme in right hemisphere which had given rise to a gross hemorrhage.

C. B., a previously healthy boy of 12 years, suddenly had a convulsion involving the left arm and leg. The boy was attending an entertainment at the time and had been in perfect health. He did not regain conscious-ness after this seizure and similar convulsions recurred during the next few hours. Later, the seizures became generalized and it was possible to demonstrate hemiplegia on the left between the attacks. The right optic nerve head showed some congestion but the left was normal. The left plantar reflex was extensor but the right was flexor. Blood pressure was 100/80. The spinal fluid contained blood. Finally, after 22 hours, the child died with rising pulse and temperature.

Post-mortem examination revealed extensive subarachnoid and intra-ventricular hemorrhage. This was traced to the right lateral ventricle which was compressed by a small vascular tumor arising in the region of the thalamus and compressing the internal capsule. The hemorrhage had arisen in this tumor and had broken into the ventricular system. The tu-mor showed the histological characteristics of glioblastoma multiforme.

BIBLIOGRAPHY

CAIRNS, H. AND RUSSELL, D. S.: Intracranial and spinal metastases in gliomas. Brain, 54:377, 1931.

GLOBUS, J. H. AND STRAUSS, I.: Spongioblastoma multiforme. Arch. Neurol. & Psychiat., 14:139, 1925.

KING, A. B. AND EISINGER, G.: May glioma multiforme be hereditary? Guthria Clin. Bull., 35:169, 1966.

MANGANIELLO, L. O.: Massive spontaneous hemorrhage in gliomas. J. Nerv. & Ment. Dis., 110:277, 1949.

Oligodendrogliomas

These tumors are not common in adults and are unusual in children. Nevertheless, a number have been reported in children of all ages. They are solid growths, circumscribed but not encapsulated, situated as a rule in the cerebral hemisphere or in the lateral ventricle. However, they may be found in almost any location. We have observed one in the hypothalamus and optic chiasm in a child of two years and another in the fourth ventri-cle, cerebellum and brain stem in a child of six. Histological examination shows the tumor is composed of cells with small round nuclei and scanty cytoplasm containing a clear zone around the nucleus. Specific stains make it possible to identify these cells as oligodendroglia. The tumor often con-tains deposits of calcium which may show in the roentgenograms of the skull and suggest the nature of the growth. Although these tumors are said to grow slowly they may spread throughout the ventricles and the meninges as more malignant growths do. It is difficult to remove them completely by operation and they do not seem to be sensitive to roentgenotherapy. The prognosis is therefore unfavorable.

BIBLIOGRAPHY

BERKHEISER, S. W.: Oligodendrogliomas in young age groups. J. Neurosurg., 13:170, 1956.

BLUMENFIELD, C. M. AND GARDNER, W. J.: Disseminated oligodendroglioma. Arch. Neurol. & Psychiat., 54:274, 1945.

DICKSON, W. E. C.: Oligodendroglioma of the floor of the third ventricle. Brain, 49:578, 1926.

GREENFIELD, J. C. AND ROBERTSON, E. G.: Cystic oligodendroglioma of the cerebral hemisphere and intraventricular oligodendroglioma. Brain, 56:247, 1933.

KRUEGER, E. AND KRUPP, G.: Oligodendrogliomas arising from the structures of the posterior fossa. Neurology, 2:461, 1952.

LOVE, J. G. AND CARMICHAEL, F. A.: Primary neoplasm of low grade malignancy (oligodendroglioma) in a child. Proc. Staff. Meet. Mayo Clinic, 12:454, 1937.

Neuroblastomas and Ganglioneuromas (of the Brain)

Pathological Anatomy.—Many different terms have been employed to designate this group of neoplasms for their true nature is still a matter of dispute and each author gives them a different name to indicate his conception of their histogenesis. We shall call those tumors containing ganglion cells of adult type, ganglioneuromas, and those containing chiefly neuroblasts, neuroblastomas. Penfield states that these tumors are not identical with those of peripheral origin, known by the same name, which seem to resemble the medulloblastomas. These growths are found in the floor of the third ventricle, in the temporal and in the parietal lobes and also in the cerebellum and spinal cord. They are formed of small, rounded cells with scanty cytoplasm which is almost devoid of Nissl bodies. The nuclei are large and clear and the nucleolus is very large and dark. The cells stain specifically with various silver stains. These tumors are relatively invasive as compared to the ganglioneuromas which are often encapsulated. The latter are composed of polygonal, or less commonly pyramidal, cells with definite Nissl substance and often neurofibrillae, although axons and dendrites are usually absent. There is often a well-formed connective tissue stroma. Both mature and immature cells of the glial series may be present. Indeed, many authors regard these growths as gliomas containing nerve cells. Courville believes that neuroblastomas are more common than they are generally believed to be and suggests that many of them are misinterpreted as spongioblastomas unipolare.

Clinical Features.—There is nothing in the clinical picture which permits the diagnosis to be made before operation. The ganglioneuromas are relatively benign and run a slow course. The neuroblastomas, however, may be malignant and may recur rapidly after operation. Both occur in children.

Treatment.—The encapsulated tumors should be removed, if possible. Radium or deep roentgenotherapy may be employed in inoperable cases.

BIBLIOGRAPHY

ALPERS, B. J. AND GRANT, F. C.: The ganglioneuromas of the central nervous system. Arch. Neurol. & Psychiat., **26**:501, 1931.

COURVILLE, C. B.: Ganglioglioma tumor of the central nervous system; review of the literature and report of two cases. Arch. Neurol. & Psychiat., **24**:439, 1930.

————: Gangliomas, a further report with special references to those of the temporal lobe. Arch. Neurol. & Psychiat., **25**:309, 1931.

KERNOHAN, J. W., LEARMONTH, J. R. AND DOYLE, J. B.: Neuroblastomas and gangliocytomas of the central nervous system. Brain, **60**:287, 1932.

STEEGMAN, A. T. AND WINER, B.: Temporal lobe epilepsy resulting from ganglioglioma. Neurology, **11**:406, 1961.

NEOPLASMS INVOLVING THE OPTIC NERVES AND CHIASM

Hypophyseal Duct Tumors

Pathological Anatomy.—These growths arise from embryonic remnants of the craniopharyngeal duct. They are composed of epithelial cells and are usually cystic or multicystic, although they may be solid. Their histological structure is subject to great variation and a number of different types are distinguished. Ingraham and Scott describe merely three types: (1) Mucoid epithelial cyst lined with ciliated columnar epithelium. (2)

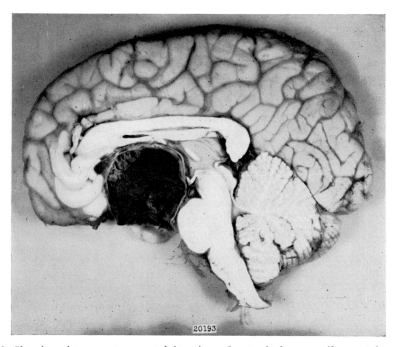

FIG. 231. Showing the appearance and location of a typical suprasellar cyst in a child. The cyst is filled with blood as a result of an attempt to drain it. (By the courtesy of Dr. Charles Burklund.)

Adamantinoma formed of tissue resembling a tooth bud. (3) Simple squamous cell tumor. The last is most common. Within the cysts is found a turbid fluid containing cholesterin crystals. Areas of calcification are frequently seen in the walls of the cysts. These tumors may arise within the sella but, as a rule, they are situated above in relation to the infundibulum and floor of the third ventricle. Some of them grow rapidly and reach a large size early in life; others cease to grow while they are still very small and become calcified remaining stationary throughout life. The majority of suprasellar tumors of childhood arise from the craniopharyngeal duct.

Clinical Features.—The onset may often be traced back to the fifth or sixth year and in half of all cases, definite disturbances are present before the age of fifteen years. The nature of the first symptoms depends upon the size and location of the tumor. If it is situated near the sella, signs of compression of the *optic chiasm* will appear first, but in many cases the growth is so placed as to invade the third ventricle, giving rise to hydrocephalus and to increased intracranial pressure as the first evidences of its presence. It is of interest that in adults these tumors are apt to cause primary optic atrophy but in children the rule is reversed and papilledema is more common. A great variety of visual disturbances may occur. If the

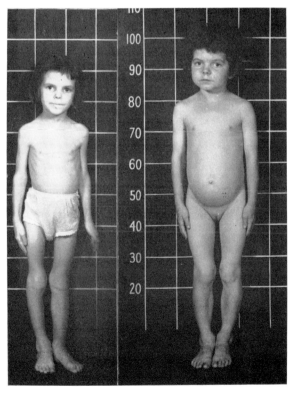

Fig. 232. Craniopharyngioma. Photograph at the left shows child at age 8 years. Her height was comparable to that of a child of 3 years. She was emaciated. The discs were pale. A calcium deposit was seen in the sella. Cortisone improved her nutrition but the optic atrophy progressed. The photograph on the right shows her appearance at the age of 11 years just before Dr. George Smith removed the growth successfully. Ped. A-91456.

chiasm and optic pathways are not directly involved, vision is not affected until the papilledema is beginning to recede and optic atrophy develops. In such cases, we find enlargement of the blind spots and gradual concentric constriction of the visual fields. In certain instances we may find complete blindness in cases in which the papilledema is relatively fresh and seems to be inadequate to cause such severe loss of vision. Two factors seem necessary to explain this condition, papilledema and direct pressure upon the optic nerves and chiasm. In other cases we find various defects of the visual fields due to compression of the chiasm, optic nerves or optic tracts. These are not so uniform as those due to adenomas of the pituitary gland, but, as a rule, there is a tendency to bitemporal defects of the visual fields. Such defects may begin in either the upper or the lower quadrants, and are usually asymmetrical, so that one eye may be nearly blind at a time when the other eye shows only a small quadrant defect. Scotomas may be found in the temporal fields, usually just central to the margin of the advancing quadrant defect. It is not at all unusual to find homonymous hemianopia due to compression of one optic tract. As a rule, when the chiasm or optic nerves are compressed by the tumor, we find primary optic atrophy but in rare cases there may be complete bitemporal hemianopia without any change in the color of the optic nerves. Diplopia may occur as a result of involvement of the third, fourth or sixth nerve. Beckman and Kubie have shown that in some cases it may also be due to heteronymous defects in the visual fields and impaired macular vision, causing fixation on non-corresponding points of the retinae.

Loss of sense of smell is sometimes found due to compression of the olfactory lobes. The growth may extend laterally, invading the under surface of the temporal lobes and causing uncinate fits; or it may extend backward to the cerebral peduncles, causing hemiparesis and spasticity and eventually decerebrate rigidity. In a few cases, thalamic syndromes and tremor or rigidity of Parkinsonian type have occurred and are attributed to invasion of the thalamus and lenticular nuclei. Cerebellar ataxia is described.

In the majority of cases, *metabolic* and *developmental changes* are present. These symptoms are probably of dual nature, including elements due to compression of the hypothalamus and others due to deficient secretion of the pars anterior of the pituitary gland. Growth is often strikingly retarded so that the child may be no taller than a sibling several years younger. The hair of the head is very fine and delicate and body hair is usually absent. The skin is soft and of very fine texture. The skeleton is slender and the fingers taper excessively. The penis and testicles in males are imperfectly developed and in girls, the breasts remain infantile and menstruation is delayed or absent. In most cases there is obesity of a characteristic

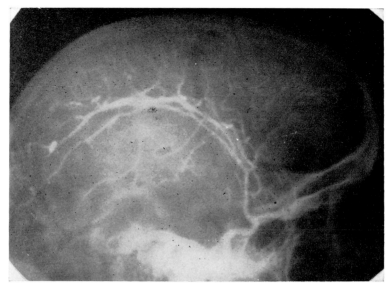

Fig. 233. Arteriogram in case of huge suprasellar cyst showing displacement of middle cerebral arteries. (By the courtesy of Dr. Arthur King.)

type in which the fat is deposited over the abdomen, shoulders, buttocks and thighs. The picture is, therefore, that of Frölich's syndrome. In other cases there is no adiposity and the most striking abnormalities are the failure of bodily growth and of sexual development. Erdheim, Barker and others have described cases of this type in which the hypophysis was evidently destroyed early in childhood. These dwarfs show delayed closure of the epiphyses as the cretins do but differ from them in that their intelligence is quite normal. Hypoglycemic attacks are not unusual in such cases. They sometimes occur spontaneously but may be induced by fasting. These patients are very sensitive to insulin. Coma due to adrenal crisis may also occur as a result of illness, vomiting, diarrhea or lack of food. In exceptional cases sexual precocity is observed in place of sexual dystrophy. We have observed two cases of this type and one is presented briefly below.

A few cases of Simmond's syndrome, or pituitary cachexia which is attributed to gross destruction of the hypophysis, are described in association with these tumors. The case of Frazier is of interest. Figure 186 shows a little girl suffering from a suprasellar cyst. Defective growth and impaired nutrition were the chief problems though there was mild optic atrophy and loss of temporal fields. She was subject to hypoglycemic episodes. As the growth expands and involves the frontal lobes and the hypothalamus, there may be mental changes including apathy, somnolence, difficulty in concentration, loss of memory, irritability and eventually stupor or coma.

In a very large percentage of all cases, roentgenograms of the *sella* reveal destruction of the clinoid processes. The picture is not exactly the same as that associated with adenoma of the hypophysis, in which the sella is usually expanded, for these cysts usually exert pressure from above and tend to flatten the sella. It must be admitted, however, that in some instances the growth lies in the sella and causes the same picture as an adenoma and that there may be no changes in the sella in other cases. A very characteristic feature in the roentgenogram is the presence of abnormal shadows lying just above the sella. These are due to areas of calcification in the wall of the cyst. They may be of almost any shape. It has been estimated that such shadows are found in more than 75 per cent of these tumors.

In one of our cases the cyst eroded into the sphenoid sinus and there

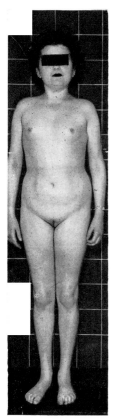

FIG. 234. Suprasellar cyst. Girl of 21 years showing defective bodily growth and sexual development. Size and weight were those of a 9 year old child. Mental development was normal. Case history is given in abstract. (Ped. 30135) (From Wilkins' Diagnosis and Treatment of Endocrine Disorders of Childhood and Adolescence. Thomas 1950.)

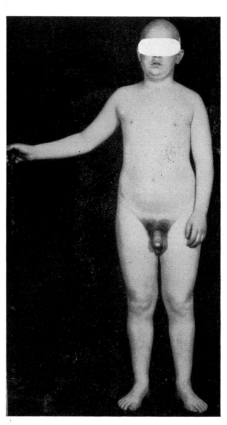

FIG. 235. Photograph of patient described in appended history at the age of 12 years showing obesity and premature sexual development. The head has been shaved in preparation for operation. An epithelial cyst above the sella was discovered.

were periodic discharges of cholesterol crystals and fluid from the nose. These discharges were associated with relief of headaches. Similar leaking into the meninges may cause repeated attacks of meningeal irritation.

The chronological order in which the signs and symptoms appear and their relative severity are subject to great variation. In some cases all the representative features are present; in others only one. The clinical course is also variable. Sometimes it is brief, but it may be prolonged and the patient's condition may remain almost stationary for many years.

Diagnosis.—The most significant features from the point of view of diagnosis are: (1) The evidence of compression of the optic chiasm. (2) The roentgenographic findings. (3) The developmental disorders. The differentiation of suprasellar cysts from adenoma of the hypophysis depends largely upon the age of onset and upon the roentgenographic changes. If all the characteristic features are present, the diagnosis offers no difficulty but the diagnosis may be very uncertain in case the child is blind when first examined or is too young to permit proper study of the fields of vision. In such cases we must rely chiefly upon the roentgenograms of the sella. If no changes are found in the sella, the diagnosis can scarcely be established upon clinical grounds, for it must be recalled that internal hydrocephalus alone may cause optic atrophy as well as obesity, polyuria and genital dystrophy. Ventriculography must be employed in doubtful cases. The third ventricle is distorted or obliterated in suprasellar tumors and is distended in hydrocephalus due to tumors of the posterior fossa or to congenital defects in the aqueduct. The developmental disorders are not reliable diagnostic criteria for they may occur without intracranial tumor. Indeed, tumor is a rather unusual cause of such syndromes.

Treatment.—These tumors offer very difficult surgical problems, for they are adherent to the infundibulum and often cannot be removed without grave injury to important structures. At least three types of reaction to operation are recognized, hyperthermia, hypoglycemia and polyuria. Sometimes relief may be secured by evacuation of the cyst. There is reason to believe that postoperative radiotherapy is of value. Replacement therapy is often needed after operation.

> CASE HISTORY (U. 104835).—*Boy of 10 years began to grow dull and somnolent. Later talkative and euphoric. Foolish joking. Headaches. Two convulsions. Excessive appetite, rapid gain in weight, rapid sexual development. Hypophyseal duct cyst extending into the right frontal lobe.*
>
> B. B., a white boy of 10 years, had always been quite healthy and rather large for his age. He was an excellent student and usually stood at the head of his class at school. In the fall of 1935, however, he began to lose interest and to fall behind in his work. He complained of headaches. In the spring of 1936 he grew sluggish and slept a large part of the day. In

the summer and fall he gradually became restless and overactive. He soon began to talk constantly in a foolish jocular manner. He teased his parents and playmates. Appetite grew to enormous proportions and he gained weight very rapidly so that in December he was 30 lbs. overweight. Genitalia began to develop and soon had assumed adult proportions. No polyuria noted. During this period he had two generalized convulsive seizures. In April 1937 he was brought to Dr. Dandy.

Examination revealed striking obesity and complete development of the genitalia as shown in Figure 189. The pubic hair was abundant and there was coarse hair over the legs but none over the chest, or in the axillae. The child was very restless and talked constantly in a jocular manner. He tried to pinch the nurses. The optic nerve heads showed a suggestion of early papilledema and there was possibly some little contraction of the temporal fields. Central vision was normal. Neurological examination was negative. Roentgenograms of the cranium showed separation of the sutures and destruction of the sella. At operation a large epithelial cyst was discovered above the sella filled with fluid containing cholesterol crystals. This had extended into the right frontal lobe.

CASE HISTORY (Ped. A-30135).—*Pituitary dwarf. Headache and vomiting began at the age of five years and thereafter growth was slow. At 15 years reduction of vision in the left eye, left hemiparesis and diabetes insipidus. Drainage of suprasellar cyst with relief of neurological symptoms. Growth remained defective and sexual organs infantile.*

B. S. was apparently a normal child until the age of five years. At that time she began to have headaches and to vomit frequently. The headaches continued and in the next few years, it became evident that she was not growing as she should. At the age of 15 years, she noticed that vision of the left eye was failing and that the left arm and leg were weak. There was an excessive thirst and a correspondingly increased urinary output. Roentgenographic study revealed shadows above the sella and a diagnosis of suprasellar cyst made. The cyst was drained. All the neurological symptoms disappeared, but growth was not accelerated and there was no evidence of sexual development. Her mental status was quite normal, however, and she made a good living playing juvenile parts on the stage.

At the age of 21 years, she came to Dr. Lawson Wilkins to whom I am indebted for the opportunity of seeing her. She was 53½ inches tall and weighed 78½ lbs. so that she was about as large as an average girl of 10 years. Her body was formed like that of a child with only a suggestion of feminine contours. There was scarcely any sign of development of the breasts or genitalia. The vagina and cervix were infantile. Subcutaneous fat was present but not excessive and of normal distribution. There was no body hair. The bone age was not quite up to the 16 year standard. Neurological examination was quite negative. The optic nerve heads were of good color and the visual fields were not restricted. Her intelligence was clearly normal for she was quick in her reactions and evidently capa-

ble of looking after her interests. Her manner was a curious mixture of childishness and sophistication. Her gestures were childish and her voice like that of a little girl. The casual observer would have regarded her as a precocious child of 10 years. The patient was insistent that she be made sexually mature. Stilbestrol caused her breasts to grow but did not cause bodily growth or the development of pubic hair. When testosterone was added to the medication pubic hair appeared and her height increased. Her bodily growth was soon halted by fusion of the epiphyses. However, she married and was able to lead a normal sexual life.

BIBLIOGRAPHY

BARKER, L. F.: A case of hypophyseal dwarfism. Endocrinology, **17**:647, 1933.

BECKMAN, J. W. AND KUBIE, L. S.: A clinical study of twenty-one cases of tumor of the hypophyseal stalk. Brain, **52**:127, 1929.

BENTON, J. W. *et al.:* The bobble-head doll syndrome. Report of a unique truncal tremor associated with third ventricular cyst and hydrocephalus in children. Neurology, **16**:725, 1966.

————: Diplopia without extra-ocular palsies caused by heteronymous defects in the visual fields associated with defective macular vision. Brain, **52**:317, 1929.

ERDHEIM, J.: Nanosomia pituitaria. Beitr. z. path. Anat. u. z. allg. Path., **62**:302, 1916.

FRAZIER, C. H.: Pituitary cachexia. Arch. Neurol. & Psychiat., **21**:1, 1929.

INGRAHAM, F. D. AND SCOTT, H. W.: Craniopharyngiomas in children. J. Pediat., **29**:95, 1946.

McKENZIE, K. G. AND SOSMAN, M. C.: The roentgenological diagnosis of craniopharyngeal pouch tumors. Am. J. Roentgenol., **11**:171, 1924.

NORTHFIELD, D. N. C.: Rathke pouch tumors. Brain, **80**:20, 1957.

VAN BOGAERT, L.: Thalamic and Parkinsonian types of infundibular tumors. Arch. Neurol. & Psychiat., **19**:377, 1928.

WALSH, F. B.: *Loc. cit.*

WHITE, J. C. AND COBB, S.: Psychological changes associated with giant pituitary neoplasms. Arch. Neurol. & Psychiat., **74**:383, 1955.

WORSTER-DROUGHT, C.: Dyspituitarism of the Lorain type, associated with pituitary cyst arising from Rathke's cleft and secondary lesions in hypothalamic region and ventricles. Brain, **50**:704, 1927.

Disorders of the Pituitary Gland

Introduction.—There are three types of cells in the anterior lobe of the pituitary gland; those containing alpha granules which stain with eosin, those containing basophil granules and those which contain no granules. The first two are termed chromophil cells and the last, chromophobe cells. Adenomas composed of each of these three cell types are recognized. The chromophobe adenomas are very common in adult life, the eosinophil adenomas are rare and basophil adenomas are almost always very minute so they can scarcely be termed tumors.

Extensive studies, both clinical and experimental, have been made upon the physiology of the pituitary gland in recent years and it is now believed that several hormones are elaborated in the anterior lobe. It is believed that they are all proteins. The *growth hormone* is believed to act directly upon the tissues of the body. It has been found that only growth hormone obtained from human pituitary glands is effective in man. Moon *et al.* have

shown that this hormone will stimulate the growth of human cells in tissue culture.

Rimoin, McKusick *et al.* describe a study of ateliosis or proportional dwarfism which was discovered to be a recessive characteristic. All the pituitary hormones were found to be present in proper amounts except for the growth hormone which was deficient. Mental and sexual development were normal. Several *gonadotrophic hormones* are distinguished and are thought to act indirectly by stimulating the ovaries or testes. There is reason to think that deficiency of the gonadotropic hormone may occur as an isolated defect. See Bibben, and Gordon and also Le Marquand. In the same way, hormones are described which act upon the *adrenal* and *thyroid* glands. Cushing's syndrome has been attributed to excessive secretion of corticotropin by basophilic adenomas causing adrenal cortical hyperplasia. Grabow and Chou describe thyroid deficiency due to absence of the thyrotropic hormone without evidence of deficiency of any other pituitary hormones.

The posterior lobe of the pituitary gland contains *vasopressin* and *oxytocin*. They are polypeptides in structure. Vasopressin has an antidiuretic effect and also elevates the blood pressure. Oxytocin has the property of causing smooth muscle to contract. There is some reason to think that these substances are produced in the hypothalamus and stored and possibly modified in the posterior lobe. The intermediate lobe, it is claimed, produces *intermedin* which stimulates melanocytes and increases pigmentation.

Harris describes the mechanisms by which the hypothalamus controls the activities of the pituitary gland and thus, indirectly, the other endocrine glands. It has been shown that various hormones, which are believed to be polypeptides, are elaborated in the hypothalamus and are carried to the pituitary gland by a portal system of veins which are richly supplied by nerve fibers. These hormones excite the pituitary gland to produce various hormones which act directly on the tissues or on the other glands of internal secretion. In turn, the hypothalamus is influenced by the level of hormones and possibly other substances in the blood stream.

Pituitary Deficiency.—The effects of partial destruction of the pituitary gland in childhood by suprasellar cyst or chromophobe adenoma are most evident in bodily growth and sexual development. Growth becomes extremely slow and the deficiency in growth becomes more evident as the child grows older. The skeletal proportions are normal and suitable for the child's age. Cartilaginous ossification is delayed and the epiphyses may fail to fuse until late in life. These children remain sexually infantile, no doubt, because of deficient gonadotropic hormone secretion. Obesity is sometimes present. Some of these children are subject to hypoglycemic attacks as a result of infection or lack of food. They may be weak and easily fatigued. Muscular development is defective. The output of the 17-keto-

steroids may be diminished but outspoken signs of secondary adrenal deficiency are not present as a rule. One would expect to find a low basal metabolic rate and elevation of the blood cholesterol as a result of secondary hypothyroidism but such findings are rare. It is of interest that mental development is usually normal in contrast to the thyroid dwarfs, i.e. cretins, whose mental development is profoundly defective. Lipemia retinalis is described.

More complete destruction of the pituitary gland causes a clinical picture which is sometimes termed Simmond's syndrome. Growth ceases. If the genital organs have developed, they become atrophic. There is no axillary or pubic hair. Cachexia may occur but is not always present. There is also, in some instances, low blood pressure, low body temperature, and dystrophic changes in the skin, hair and nails. Intolerance to cold, a low basal metabolic rate, decreased serum iodine, increased serum cholesterol, muscular weakness and dulling of mental reactions occur. These patients are sensitive to insulin, and develop hypoglycemia very easily. The serum sodium and chloride levels are low and the output of 17-ketosteroids is reduced. Infections, operations, vomiting, diarrhea and lack of food may lead to confusion, disorientation and coma. Such reactions are attributed to adrenal crises.

Pituitary Overactivity.—The only well established type of excessive secretory activity of the pituitary gland is found in cases of gigantism and acromegaly. These syndromes are believed to be due to excessive secretion of the growth hormone by eosinophil cells. Eosinophil adenoma, q.v., is usually present but it is believed that an increase of eosinophil cells without actual tumor formation may be responsible.

Recently evidence has been found that the pituitary gland may also secrete an excess of adrenocorticotropic hormone. In 1932, Cushing stated that small basophil adenomas of the pituitary gland cause a type of adrenal disorder now termed Cushing's syndrome. More recently it has been found that in many cases of this condition, there is evidence of adenoma of the pituitary when the adrenal disorder is discovered. In other cases, no evidence of adenoma can be found, though the level of adrenocorticotropic hormone in the blood is elevated, until after operation on the adrenal glands has been performed. The patient then develops adenoma of the pituitary gland and dark pigmentation of the skin. The secretion of the melanin stimulating hormone is also increased in such cases. As a rule chromophobe adenomas are found, but malignant tumors are also discovered occasionally.

Williams, E. D. *et al.* state that 11 cases are known in which carcinoma of the thyroid gland gave rise to Cushing's syndrome. Micic and Arsenijevic state that mediastinal tumors may be responsible.

There is reason to believe that hyperthyroidism is sometimes due to excessive stimulation by the pituitary gland which produces the thyrotropic hormone.

Several groups of symptoms must be distinguished in cases of pituitary adenoma. (1) Those due to excessive secretory activity as for example gigantism and acromegaly. (2) Those due to destruction of the secretory cells by chromophobe cells with the production of pituitary deficiency. (3) Those due to compression of the infundibulum and hypothalamus. Polyuria, polydipsia, somnolence and obesity may be mentioned here.

BIBLIOGRAPHY

ALLEN, E.: Sex and Internal Secretions. 2nd Ed. Baltimore, Williams and Wilkins, 1939.

BAAR, H. S.: Dysontogenetic pituitary cysts (Pituitary cachexia in childhood). Arch. Dis. Child., **22**:118, 1947.

BERCOVICI, B. AND EHRENFELD, E. N.: The significance of galactorrhea. J. Obst. & Gynec. Brit. Emp., **70**:295, 1963.

BIBEN, R. L. AND GORDAN, G. S.: Familial hypogonadotropic eunochoidism. Jour. Clin. Endocrin., **15**:931, 1955.

BROWN, J. *et al.*: Acanthosis nigricans and pituitary tumors. J.A.M.A., **198**:619, 1966.

CHEN, R. *et al.*: Cushings disease in a boy. Johns Hopkins Medical Jour., **125**:119, 1969.

CUSHING, H.: Basophil adenomas of the pituitary bodies and their clinical manifestations. Bull. Johns Hopkins Hosp., **50**:137, 1932.

DANDY, W. E. AND REICHERT, F.: Studies on experimental hypophysectomy; effect on maintenance of life. Bull. Johns Hopkins Hosp., **37**:1, 1925.

EVANS, H. M. AND LONG, J. A.: Characteristic effects upon growth, oestrus and ovulation induced by the intraperitoneal administration of fresh anterior hypophyseal substance. Proc. Nat. Acad. Sc., **8**:38, 1922.

FRASIER, S. D.: The serum growth hormone response to hypoglycemia in dwarfism. Jour. Pediat., **71**:625, 1967.

GRABOW, J. D. AND CHOU, S. M.: Thyrotropin hormone deficiency. Arch. of Neurol., **19**:284, 1968.

HARRIS, G. W.: The central nervous system and the endocrine glands. Triangle, **6**:242, 1964.

HENNEMAN, P. H. *et al.*: Effects of human growth hormone in man. J. Clin. Invest., **39**:1223, 1960.

HENNEMAN, P. H.: The effect of human growth hormone on growth of patients with hypopituitarism. Jour. Amer. Med. Ass., **205**:828, 1968.

LE MARQUAND, H. S.: Congenital hypogonadotropic hypogonadism in five members of a family. Pro. Roy. Soc. Med., **47**:442, 1954.

LI, C. H., EVANS, H. M. AND SIMPSON, M. E.: Isolation and properties of the anterior hypophyseal growth hormone. J. Biol. Chem., **159**:353, 1945.

MICIC, R. AND ARSENIJEVIC, M.: Cushing's syndrome caused by mediastinal tumor. Lancet, **2**:436, 1963.

MOON, H. D. *et al.*: Effect of somatotropin on cell growth. Endocrinology, **70**:31, 1962.

PUTNAM, T. J., BENEDICT, E. B. AND TEEL, H. M.: Experimental canine acromegaly produced by injection of anterior lobe pituitary extract. Arch. Surg., **18**:774, 1929.

REIFENSTEIN, E. C.: Endocrinology: A synopsis of normal and pathologic physiology, diagnostic procedures and therapy. Med. Clin. North America, 1232, September, 1944.

RIMOIN, D. L. AND McKUSICK, V. *et al.*: Growth hormone deficiency in man: An isolated recessively inherited defect. Science, **152**:1635, 1966.

SMITH, P. E.: Hypophysectomy and replacement therapy in the rat. Am. J. Anat., **45**:205, 1930.

————: The disabilities caused by hypophysectomy and their repair. The tuberal (hypothalamic) syndrome in the rat. J.A.M.A., **88**:158, 1927.

STEINER, M. M. AND BOGGS, J. D.: Absence of the pituitary gland in a 17 year old dwarf. Jour. Clin. Endocrin., **25**:1591, 1965.

TABATZNIK, B. AND RABINOWITZ, D.: Hyperglyceridemia and lipemia retinalis in hypopituitarism. Bull. Johns Hopkins Hosp., **107**:175, 1960.

VARIOUS AUTHORS: Glandular physiology and therapy. J.A.M.A., Chicago, 1942.

WALSH, F. B.: *Loc. cit.*

WILKINS, L.: The Diagnosis and Treatment of Endocrine Disorders in Childhood and Adolescence. Springfield, Thomas, 1950.

WILLIAMS, E. D. *et al.:* Thyroid carcinoma and Cushings syndrome. Jour. Clin. Path., **21**:129, 1968.

Chromophobe Adenomas

These tumors are very rare in childhood although relatively common in adult life. Only three or four children under the age of fifteen years are included in Cushing's large series. The growth is composed of epithelial cells which may be arranged in columns or in irregular masses without definite architecture. The cells contain no granules and are almost identical with the normal chromophobe cells of the anterior lobe.

The chromophobe adenomas rupture the capsule of the gland very early and compress the optic chiasm giving rise to bitemporal hemianopia and to other field defects. In most cases, but not in all, the upper temporal quadrants are involved first. The process advances in a clock-wise fashion, in the field of the right eye, and in anticlock-wise fashion, in the field of the left eye, so the upper nasal quadrants are the last to be lost. Scotomas may develop close to the point of fixation on the temporal side and extend in the same way frequently involving central vision. Primary optic atrophy is usually but not always present and papilledema is very rare. Disturbances of development are rare. Fröhlich's syndrome has been observed and Dott and Bailey mention one case of infantilism. The developmental and metabolic changes are described in the preceding section. Two cases of pituitary adenoma in children are given in abstract below. These symptoms are probably due to destruction of the chromophil cells by the pressure of the adenoma for the chromophobe cells are not regarded as possessing any secretory function. Eventually, the tumor extends upward into the third ventricle or laterally into the temporal lobe giving rise to increased intracranial pressure. The third, fourth and sixth nerves may be compressed by lateral expansion of the growth. Diplopia may occur as a result of fixation on noncorresponding points of the retinae as well as a result of palsies of the extraocular muscles. The roentgenological examination reveals "ballooning" of the sella at first. Later, the clinoid processes are destroyed and the picture is less typical. If the growth is extensive enough, the walls of the orbits may be eroded and if the growth is shrunken by roentgen therapy, pulsating exophthalmos may result. Cerebrospinal rhinorrhea may occur,

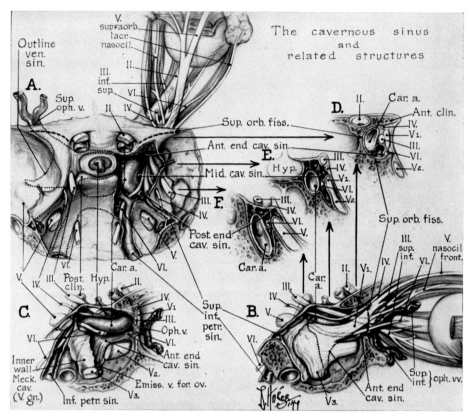

FIG. 236. Diagram illustrating the anatomical relations of the cavernous sinus and adjacent structures. (From Walsh. Arch. Ophth. 42:646, 1949.)

in the same way, as a result of erosion of the cribriform plate. Calcification is very rare in these tumors. Hemorrhage sometimes occurs into the adenoma causing sudden compression of the extraocular nerves and optic chiasm and in some cases subarachnoid hemorrhage. Unless the growth is very extensive, it may be removed successfully by a skillful surgeon. Roentgenotherapy gives excellent results in some cases but may injure the brain. Hormonal therapy is usually required after operation.

Salassa *et al.* state that among 122 patients with adrenocortical hyperplasia who had adrenalectomy performed becuase of Cushing's syndrome, twelve were found to have pituitary tumors either before or after operation. In one case, the pituitary tumor was malignant, but in the others, it was a chromophobe tumor. In these cases, the adrenalectomy is followed by deep pigmentation of the skin. Montgomery *et al.* report two cases of this type with carcinomas of the pituitary gland. Nelson *et al.* state that among ten patients having adrenalectomy for Cushing's syndrome, pituitary tu-

mors appeared in eight. All of these patients were deeply pigmented. Elevation of the plasma was found in five cases. In the other five cases, the pituitary gland had been radiated. No evidence of pituitary tumor was found in any of these cases before the adrenalectomy. Histological examination of the tumor was performed in two cases and in both chromophobe cells were found.

In a few instances, exploration of a patient who displays evidences of pituitary deficiency, compression of the chiasm and enlargement of the sella reveals that the sella is filled with a cyst with thin walls resembling the arachnoid membrane which is filled with clear fluid. Ciliated cells have been found in the wall of such cysts. The pituitary gland cannot be found in some instances. Robertson reports two cases of this condition. Calkins *et al.* describe an arachnoid cyst causing enlargement of the sella tursica.

CASE HISTORY (U-198213. Path. 16896).—*Boy of nine years developed headaches and mental disturbances. Later grew blind in right eye. Exploration at age of 13 years revealed large growth above sella. Death. Post-mortem examination disclosed chromophobe adenoma of the hypophysis extending under the entire base of the brain.*

D. K. began to have paroxysmal headaches at the age of nine years. These soon became more severe and more frequent and were associated with vomiting. At the age of 12 years, mental changes were noted. He grew irritable, untruthful and indolent. At school he could not concentrate on his work or remember what he had learned. It was discovered at this time that he was growing obese. He was given testosterone in large doses with the result that during the next few months his penis grew to nearly adult proportions. His mental condition grew slowly worse. About this time he lost vision in the right eye.

On April 23, 1940, at the age of 13 years, he was brought to the Harriet Lane Home. He was rather obese with large deposits of fat about the trunk and hips. The penis was large but the testicles small. Pubic hair was well developed and there was some hair in the axillae and on the upper lip. The patient was semistuporous and when aroused was irritable and unreasonable. Vision of the right eye was reduced to light perception. Vision of the left eye was intact. The optic discs were of normal appearance. Roentgenograms of the sella showed extensive erosion.

Exploration was performed by Dr. Dandy who found a large growth above the sella. No attempt to remove this was made. The patient slowly grew worse and died some weeks later. At post-mortem examination an enormous chromophobe adenoma of the hypophysis was found. This had extended under the brain and invaded all three cranial fossae. The brain stem and both frontal and temporal lobes were compressed by great masses of tumor. The cranial nerves at the base were embedded in the growth, and the right optic nerve was compressed and atrophic. Histological studies showed that the tumor was not malignant.

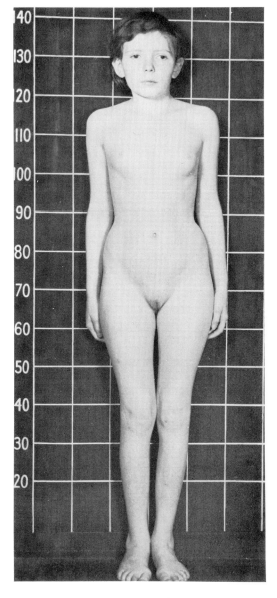

Fig. 237. Girl of 14 years who had had a chromophobe adenoma of the hypophysis removed at 11 years of age. Bodily growth had been deficient, nutrition was poor and sexual development was lacking.

CASE HISTORY (Ped. A-99152).—*Girl of 11 years developed headache, polyuria and failing vision. Soon there was paralysis at the left third nerve. At operation a large chromophobe adenoma of the hypophysis was removed. Vision improved promptly and there was evidence of regeneration of the third nerve some months later. Bodily growth was arrested however.*

This little girl is a patient of Dr. George Smith who kindly permitted me to see her. She was 11 years old when first seen. During the summer of

1951 she had been troubled by frontal headaches and noticed that she was drinking more water than usual. Soon she realized that her vision was failing. Later, in the summer, the left eyelid began to droop and she had double vision for a time.

When she was first examined in October she was a pale, slender little girl a bit smaller than most girls of her age. There was some pallor of the left optic nerve head. Vision of the right eye was 20/40 and that of the left eye 20/70. A large defect was found in the lower temporal quadrant of the left eye field. A complete left third nerve palsy was present. The sella turcica showed slight enlargement and there was perhaps a little erosion of the posterior clinoids.

Dr. George Smith operated and found a very large chromophobe adenoma of the hypophysis which was compressing the left optic nerve and had extended into the left middle fossa. This was removed successfully.

Vision began to improve before long. Soon vision of the right eye was 20/20 and that of the left eye 20/30. The field defect diminished. The third nerve did not improve so rapidly. In December 1952 the left pupil was still dilated and fixed. The left eye could be moved out well but not up or down. When the child tried to look up the eye was adducted. Efforts at adduction, elevation and depression all caused the lid to lift. Thus it was evident that faulty regeneration was in progress.

In December 1952, the child was almost 13 years old. Her bodily growth was not quite up to the average of a child of 10 years and she showed no sign of sexual development. Hormone therapy was instituted.

In May 1954 the condition of the left third nerve had not changed. Hormonal therapy had taken effect. She had grown larger and developed sexually. Her breasts were of adolescent size. She seemed to be in vigorous health.

BIBLIOGRAPHY

CALKINS, R. A. *et al.:* Intrasellar arachnoid diverticulum. Neurology, **18**:1037, 1968.

CUSHING, H.: The Pituitary Body and Its Disorders. Philadelphia, J. B. Lippincott Co., 1912.

DOTT, N. M. AND BAILEY, P.: Hypophyseal adenomata. Brit. J. Surg., **13**:314, 1925.

JEFFERSON, G.: Extrasellar extensions of pituitary adenomas. Proc. Roy. Soc. Med. London. sec. neurol., **33**:433, 1940.

McCONNELL, A. A. AND MOONEY, A. J.: On normal discs in patients with chiasmal lesions. Brain, **61**:37, 1938.

MEREDITH, J. M. *et al.:* Osteogenic sarcoma of skull following roentgen-ray therapy for benign pituitary tumor. Jour. Neurosurg., **17**:792, 1960.

MONTGOMERY, D. A. D. *et al.:* Pituitary tumors manifest after adrenalectomy for Cushing's syndrome. Lancet, **ii**:707, 1959.

NELSON, D. H., MEAKIN, J. W. AND THORN, G. W.: Acht-producing pituitary tumors following adrenalectomy for Cushing's syndrome. Ann. Int. Med., **52**:560, 1960.

ROBERTSON, G.: Pneumoencephalography. Springfield, Thomas, 1957, p. 230.

SALASSA, *et al.:* Pituitary tumors in patients with Cushing's syndrome. J. Clin. Endocrinol., **19**:1523, 1959.

WALSH, F. B.: Bilateral total ophthalmoplegia with adenoma of the pituitary gland. Arch. Ophth., **42**:646, 1949.

Eosinophil Adenomas

These tumors arise from the anterior lobe of the hypophysis and are formed of cells containing alpha granules which take eosin and other acid stains.

Two syndromes are associated with eosinophil adenomas: acromegaly

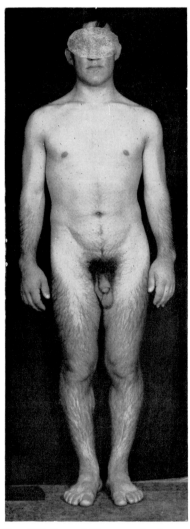 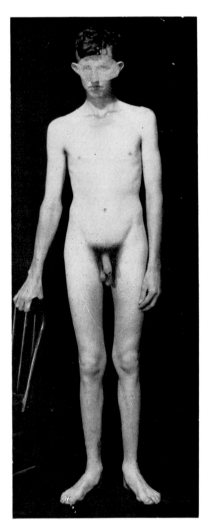

Fig. 238. Boy of 19 years who began to show acromegalic changes in hands, feet and features at the age of 17 years. Eosinophilic adenoma of the hypophysis removed successfully.

Fig. 239. Boy of 16 years who is 6 ft. 7 in. tall. The sella is not deformed and the visual fields are full. Probably a case of gigantism with eosinophilic changes in the hypophysis but no tumor.

and gigantism. In both, the most striking feature is the excessive growth of the bones. If the disease begins before the epiphyses are united, the bones grow uniformly and gigantism results; but if the epiphyses have already closed when the process develops, growth is thereby modified and acromegaly develops. In this condition there is extraordinary enlargement of the hands and feet; the lower jaw becomes unduly prominent and the features coarse and thickened. It is scarcely necessary to describe acromegaly in detail, for it probably never occurs during childhood and is rare in adolescence. Gigantism is an exceptionally rare disease. As a rule, the excessive growth begins about the age of puberty but in a few instances the patient has developed with abnormal rapidity during infancy. The arms and legs are abnormally long and the trunk is long and relatively slender. The hands and feet are of extraordinary size but are often well formed, in contrast to the thick, clumsy hands of the acromegalic. The conformation of the head and face is usually normal during childhood and for a time at least the features may preserve a childish appearance which is in ludicrous contrast to the patient's great height. Later, there is apt to be some tendency to the development of acromegalic characteristics, such as prognathism, spacing of the teeth, enlargement of the tongue and coarsening and thickening of the features. The sella turcica is much enlarged, in most cases but not in all, and there may be defects in the visual fields due to compression of the chiasm but often the latter are absent for eosinophil adenomas rarely attain a large size during childhood. In some cases no real tumor can be found but it is believed that there is always at least an increase in the number of eosinophil cells in the pars anterior. In many giants the muscles are large and strong. Sexual development may begin early and for a time their libido and potency may be excessive. There is usually an excessive development of the frontal sinuses and of the mastoid cells. In the cases of Behrens and Barr, the mastoid cells extended into the squamous portion of the temporal bone. Growth may continue long beyond the usual period, even to the age of twenty-five or thirty years, and delayed closure of the epiphyses may be demonstrable in roentgenograms of long bones. In some cases the basal metabolism is increased and there is often a tendency to hyperglycemia or even glycosuria. Hyperthyroidism and insulin resistant diabetes occur. Galactorrhea may occur. Richards states that conduction deafness occurs in acromegaly as a result of otosclerosis.

Later in life, the signs of acromegaly may be engrafted upon those of gigantism. The adenoma may finally attain a large size, compressing the chiasm and causing bitemporal field defects or blindness. Eventually the patient grows weak and may become helpless. The muscles become wasted. Scoliosis develops. Sexual powers are lost. Giants rarely reach an advanced age. This late deterioration is attributed to pituitary deficiency.

Greenwood *et al.* state that the plasma level of the growth hormone is increased in acromegaly. The implantation of radioactive gold or yttrium into the pituitary gland does not consistently reduce the level of the growth hormone, but alpha particle irradiation reduces the level of the growth hormone and is effective clinically.

There seems to be no other condition which simulates pituitary gigantism very closely except for Cerebral Gigantism in Childhood, q.v., as described by Sotos *et al.* It is of interest that so far as the writer can discover no cases of gigantism or of acromegly have been reported in association with neoplasms of the hypothalamus.

BIBLIOGRAPHY

ATKINSON, F. R. B.: The onset of acromegaly before 15 years of age. Brit. J. Child. Dis., **28**:12!, 1931.

BEHRENS, L. H. AND BARR, D. P.: Hyperpituitarism beginning in infancy. The alton giant. Endocrinology, **16**:120, 1932.

CRAWFORD, J. D. AND SOYKA, L. F.: Growth hormone. Practitioner, **192**:550, 1965.

CUSHING, H. AND DAVIDOFF, L. M.: The Pathological Findings in Four Autopsied Cases of Acromegaly with a Discussion of Their Significance. Monographs of the Rockefeller Institute, 1927, No. 22.

GREENWOOD, F. C. *et al.:* Plasma-growth hormone levels in untreated acromegaly and after radioactive implants into the pituitary. Lancet, **ii**:555, 1965.

KOZAK, G. P. *et al.:* Acromegaly pre and postpituitary irradiation. Metabolism, **15**:290, 1966.

LUFT, R. *et al.:* Studies on the pathogenesis of diabetes in acromegaly. Acta Endocr., **56**:593, 1967.

McCULLOUGH, E. P. AND HEWLETT, J. S.: Acromegaly associated with amyotrophic lateral sclerosis and acromegaly of amyotrophic type. J. Clin. Endocrinol., **7**:636, 1946.

RICHARDS, S.: Deafness in acromegaly. Jour. Laryng., **82**:1053, 1968.

WALSH, F. B.: *Loc. cit.*

Gliomas of the Chiasm and Intracranial Part of the Optic Nerves

Pathological Anatomy.—These tumors arise from the chiasm or from the adjacent wall of the third ventricle. They may extend forward along the optic nerve and even invade the orbit. They are largely restricted to childhood and the average age of Cushing's patients was about twelve years. In six of his eighteen cases of glioma of the chiasm there were evidences of von Recklinghausen's disease. Many of these growths are spongioblastomas. A large percentage of our patients have been under the age of five years when first seen.

Clinical Features.—These tumors grow very slowly and may not cause death for many years. The field defects are irregular and the nasal or central parts of the visual fields may be invaded very early. Central scotomas are not uncommon and may lead to the diagnosis of retrobulbar neuritis. Cushing has pointed out that, although there is a tendency to bitemporal hemianopia, a sharply defined vertical meridian is rare. The optic nerves usually show primary atrophy but there may be papilledema. In some cases

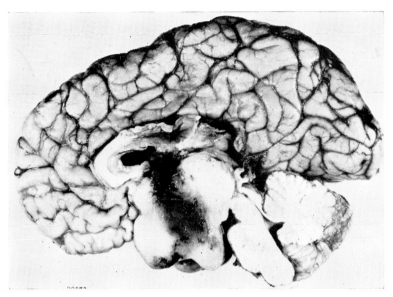

Fig. 240. Glioma of the optic chiasm and hypothalamus.

the nerve head is markedly elevated due to extension of the growth into the papilla and exophthalmos may develop. Lateral views of the sella seem to show an extension forward under the anterior clinoid processes. This is due to enlargement of the optic foramina which may be demonstrated in anteroposterior views. In some cases, the optic foramina extend into the sphenoid fissure. The sella is usually not eroded as the growth extends upward into the infundibulum and floor of the third ventricle. Polyuria, polydipsia and obesity are common. In some cases, especially when severe diabetes insipidus is present, there may be emaciation. Other symptoms are somnolence, low blood pressure, diminished basal metabolic rate, fever, or hypothermia. Nystagmus may be a prominent feature in some cases especially in young children. Cushing (1932) has described a very interesting case of a girl of 13 years who remained in a state of somnolence until disturbed, when she uttered piercing screams and attempted to bite and scratch anyone nearby. Cushing compares her condition to the sham rage reaction produced by Cannon in cats whose hypothalamus had been separated from the cerebral hemispheres. The tumor in this case was so situated as to produce the same result. We have observed precocious puberty in a little girl of 6 years.

CASE HISTORY.—*Vision of the right eye defective from infancy. Right optic disc pale and small. Left temporal field lost. Left optic disc slightly pale but of normal size. Very large glioma of optic chiasm found at operation.*

M. K., a girl of 7 years was born after 17 hours labor. When she was an infant, it was found that vision of the right eye was greatly diminished. There was vertical nystagmus in infancy which ceased later. At one year the right eye turned in. There was no history of headache or vomiting.

On examination the child's mental condition seemed to be normal. Bodily growth and nutrition seemed to be quite normal. The head was normal in size and shape. Vision of the right eye was reduced to 3/200. The left eye vision was 20/30. There was concentric constriction of the field of the right eye and loss of the temporal field of the left eye. The right optic disc was pale and abnormally small. The left optic disc was slightly pale but of normal size. The right eye turned in but there was a full range of movement of each eye. The left arm and hand were not developed as well as the right arm and leg but there was no weakness, spasticity or increase of tendon reflexes. No cutaneous or subcutaneous nodules. No cafe au lait spots.

The brain scan revealed a huge growth above the chiasm. This proved to be a glioma of the chiasm which was inoperable. It was believed that this growth was probably present before birth.

In a number of cases there are evidences of von Recklinghausen's disease, such as areas of pigmentation of the skin or multiple neurofibromata over the body.

If the growth is restricted to one optic nerve, operation is indicated. If the growth is more extensive radiation is recommended. Taveras *et al.* believe that radiation is effective.

BIBLIOGRAPHY

BAILEY, P. AND EISENHARDT, L.: Spongioblastomas of the brain. J. Comp. Neurol., **56**:391, 1932.

CUSHING, H.: Papers Related to the Pituitary Body, Hypothalamus and Parasympathetic Nervous System. Springfield, Thomas, 1932, p. 49.

CUSHING, H. AND MARTIN, P.: Primary gliomas of the chiasm and optic nerves in their intracranial portion. Arch. Ophth., **52**:209, 1923.

TAVERAS, J. M., MOUNT, L. A. AND WOOD, E. H.: The value of radiation therapy in the management of glioma of the optic nerves and chiasm. Radiology, **66**:518, 1956.

WALSH, F. B.: *Loc. cit.*

WYLLIE, W. G.: Primary tumors of the optic nerves and of the chiasma. J. Neurol. & Psychopath., **5**:209, 1924-25.

NEOPLASMS OF THE OPTIC NERVES AND ORBIT

Pathological Anatomy.—A large variety of tumors may occur in the orbit. Hemangiomas are probably the most numerous. In children, gliomas of the optic nerve are common. They may be primary in the orbit or extend into the orbit from the cranium. Meningiomas and sarcomas are not especially rare and neurofibromas, osteomas, lymphangiomas, aneurysms, dermoids, teratomas and cysts are described. The orbit may be invaded by other growths arising in the nasopharynx or nasal sinuses and may also be the site of metastatic deposits from neuroblastomas, sarcomas and chloromas.

Clinical Features.—Slowly progressive exophthalmos is the most constant and characteristic sign of tumor of the orbit and is usually the first sign to appear. Tumors which lie within the muscular cone displace the eye directly forward, but tumors situated in the more anterior parts of the orbit push the bulb in the opposite direction as well as forward. Thus, a mass above the bulb displaces the eye forward and downward and a tumor which lies medially displaces the bulb laterally as well as forward. There is frequently edema of the lids and conjunctiva but this sign may be absent when exophthalmos is pronounced.

Compression or infiltration of the optic nerve may cause loss of vision. Gliomas of the optic nerve may cause blindness before exophthalmos is noted and other tumors which lie near the apex of the orbit may produce the same effect, but as a rule loss of vision is a relatively late symptom. In most cases in which the nerve is compressed central vision fails before the peripheral fields are involved. Papilledema may be caused by orbital tumors and this is followed by optic atrophy. In other cases primary atrophy is found. The optic nerve heads may present a normal appearance even when vision is much reduced. Occasionally the tumor invades the optic papilla and is demonstrable by the ophthalmoscope. This is especially true of gliomas.

Diplopia and squints occur in many cases. These are due to at least three causes: involvement of the third, fourth or sixth nerves, infiltration of the extraocular muscles or mechanical displacement of the bulb by the mass. The upper branch of the fifth nerve is not uncommonly affected and the sympathetic fibers which supply the eye as well. If the growth extends into the inferior part of the orbit the second branch of the fifth nerve may be involved.

Roentgenograms of the orbits may show significant changes. In children the sutures may be widened. Gliomas of the optic nerves frequently cause enlargement of the optic foramen. Sarcomas erode the bone and meningiomas may cause thickening of the bones. Von Recklinghausen's disease of the orbit is sometimes associated with defects in the temporal bone. Osteomas are easily demonstrable in the roentgenogram. The most common malignant tumor of the orbit in early childhood is said to be rhabdomyoma, which was formerly termed sarcoma.

Diagnosis.—In differential diagnosis one must consider not only neoplasms but a great variety of other conditions. Meningoceles and encephaloceles are not rare. They are of course congenital and associated with a defect in the roof of the orbit. A number of inflammatory processes occur. Abscesses and cellulitis often due to extension of infection from the nasal sinuses may occur. We have seen tuberculosis of the orbit and granulomatous processes of unknown origin often called pseudotumor. Syphilitic

osteitis of the orbit is rare in children. Cavernous sinus thrombosis should also be mentioned at this point. Trauma may cause pulsating exophthalmos due to arteriovenous fistulae between the carotid artery and the cavernous sinus. Schüller-Christian disease may cause unilateral or bilateral exophthalmos. A diffuse thickening of bones of the orbit, i.e. osteitis fibrosa, is not unusual. Oxycephaly is another cause of bilateral exophthalmos. In this condition the orbits are shallow. Chloromatous deposits in the orbit are well known though not common. I should also mention exophthalmos due to thyroid disease and the so-called exophthalmic ophthalmoplegia which is rare in children. Hematomas of the orbit may occur in scurvy.

Treatment.—Surgical treatment is the method of choice. If the tumor cannot be properly exposed by the anterior approach or there is reason to believe it may extend into the cranium, Dandy's operation should be performed. If complete extirpation is not possible, roentgenotherapy may be tried.

CASE HISTORY (No. 873057).—*Hemangioma of orbit in child of 4 years.*

C. M., a little girl of 4 years, developed double vision on February 24, 1960. She had been known to have small angiomas of the left cheek and left upper lid since 1959. On examination on March 3, 1960, slight proptosis of the left eye was found with weakness of the external rectus and double vision. The optic disc was of normal color. Vision was 20/20 of the left eye. There were no defects of the visual field of the left eye. The intraocular pressure was not increased. No bruit could be heard. The right eye was normal and always remained normal.

On March 18, 1960, the left eye vision was 20/30. There was complete paralysis of the left external rectus and weakness of the internal rectus and superior oblique. The pupil was dilated and sluggish. The proptosis was more pronounced. The spinal fluid protein was not increased. An air study was performed and the ventricles were of normal size and shape.

On April 29, 1962, an angioma of the left lower lid was found. The pupil was sluggish. Vision was 20/20 right and 20/40 left. Every morning a little blood was seen in the conjunctiva of the left eye. The proptosis was very slight.

On July 22, 1963, vision of the left eye was 20/30. There was no weakness of the extraocular muscles and no diplopia. The proptosis was only 1.0 mm.

On April 9, 1965, vision of the left eye was 20/20 and the proptosis measured 4.0 mm. Slight pallor of the left optic disc was noted.

In August 1966, we heard that since the last examination the proptosis had varied between 2.0 mm and 7.0 mm. The angioma of the upper lid had vanished, but angiomas in the mouth had appeared.

On March 31, 1967, vision was 20/30 again. The disc was slightly pale. The left external rectus was weak again. The proptosis measured 8.0 mm.

A left carotid arteriogram was made. It could be seen that 3 branches of the ophthalmic artery were separated by a mass estimated at 2.0 cm in diameter. The mass was in the upper central part of the orbit. The pattern of the intercranial arteries was normal.

Dr. John Chambers operated by an extradural approach and removed the roof of the orbit. He found and removed an angioma measuring 1.6 cm in its greatest diameter. This was adherent to the surrounding structures and had evidently bled for there was yellow pigment around it. The child recovered with normal vision, normal fields, normal movement of the eyes and with prompt relief of the proptosis.

BIBLIOGRAPHY

CHUTORIAN, A. M. *et al.:* Optic gliomas in children. Neurology, 14:83, 1964.

DANDY, W. E.: Orbital tumors. Results following transcranial operative attack. Oskar Piest, New York, 1941.

DODGE, H. W. *et al.:* Gliomas of the optic nerve. Arch. Neurol. & Psychiat., 79:607, 1958.

HUDSON, A. C. *et al.:* Discussion on gliomas of the optic nerve. Proc. Roy. Soc. Med. Lon., 33:685, 1940.

ILIFF, C. AND H.: Tumors of the Eye and Adnexa. Springfield, Thomas, 1962.

INGALLS, R. C.: Tumors of the Orbit and Pseudotumors. Springfield, Thomas, 1953.

POSNER, M. AND HORRAX, G.: Tumors of the optic nerves. Long survival in three cases. Arch. Ophth., 40:56, 1948.

VERHOEFF, F. H.: Primary intraneural tumors (gliomas) of the optic nerves. Arch. Ophth., 51:120, 1922.

WALSH, F. B.: *Loc. cit.*

Gliomas of the Retina

Pathological Anatomy.—Grinker has described three chief groups of retinal gliomas. The *medullo-epitheliomas* are composed of primitive retinal epithelium but also contain neuro-epithelial rosettes and some retinoblasts. The *retinoblastomas* are comparable to the medulloblastomas of the brain and very malignant, metastasizing to the brain and distant parts of the body. They are formed of small, round, darkly staining cells packed closely together. *Neuroepitheliomas* are also found. These are characterized chiefly by the formation of true rosettes and are composed of cells closely resembling the normal rods and cones of the retina. McLean has described an *astrocytoma* of the retina.

Clinical Features.—These tumors may be present at birth and always develop before the age of 15 years. Several members of the same family may be affected. They are first seen as small nodules involving the retina or the optic nerve head, which rapidly extend forward and soon invade the anterior structures of the bulb. Later, the bulb ruptures and the whole orbit is soon filled with a fungating mass of tumor. Roentgenograms very frequently reveal calcium deposits in the orbit. In about 20 per cent of all cases these tumors are bilateral. The growth extends into the cranium and gives rise to tumor meningitis. The bones and the viscera are finally in-

volved. Inflammatory masses in the eye, i.e. the so-called pseudotumor retinae must be distinguished. Eosinophilic granuloma due to the embryonated ova of toxascaris canis may simulate retinoblastoma.

Treatment.—Removal of the entire contents of the orbit is indicated as soon as the diagnosis can be made and heavy radiation should then be employed. The prognosis is unfavorable, even if operation is performed early. The opposite eye should be carefully examined at frequent intervals. It is debatable whether it is justifiable to remove both eyes. It is said that a patient who survives a retinoblastoma may transmit the gene to half his children.

BIBLIOGRAPHY

CARBAJAL, V. M.: Metastases in retinoblastoma. Amer. Jour. Ophthal., **48**:47, 1959.
GRINKER, R.: Gliomas of the retina. Arch. Ophth., **5**:920, 1931.
MACKLIN, M. T.: Inheritance of retinoblastoma in Ohio. Arch. of Ophthal., **62**:842, 1959.
MANCHESTER, P. T., JR.: Retinoblastoma among offspring of adult survivors. Arch. of Ophthal., **65**:546, 1961.
McLEAN, J.: Astrocytoma of the retina. Arch. Ophth., **18**:255, 1937.
WALSH, F. B.: *Loc. cit.*
WILDER, H. C.: Nematod endophthalmitis. Tr. Am. Acad. Ophth., **55**:99, 1950.

NEOPLASMS OF THE THALAMUS AND CORPUS STRIATUM

Pathological Anatomy.—Gliomas such as astrocytomas and spongioblastomas may involve the thalamus and basal ganglia of the forebrain. The same structures may be invaded by ependymoma of the third ventricle. All of these tumors may occlude the ventricle and cause hydrocephalus and increased intracranial pressure.

Clinical Features.—These growths rarely produce the symptoms that one might expect. Unilateral sensory disturbances may be associated with neoplastic involvement of the thalamus but there are rarely any symptoms suggestive of the thalamic syndrome of Dejerine and Roussy. In the same way there may be choreoathetoid movements or tremor when the basal ganglia are involved but never a fully developed Parkinsonian syndrome or the whole picture of chorea or athetosis. Symptoms referable to the thalamus and lenticular nuclei are usually mild and overshadowed by spasticity and signs of increased intracranial pressure. Ody finds that the picture of partial decerebrate rigidity is most common. Sciarra and Sprofkin stress tremor, rigidity and slowing of movement.

CASE HISTORY (Path. 13866—U. 58061).—*Astrocytoma involving hypothalamus, thalamus, lenticular nucleus and optic chiasm in a boy of seven years with optic atrophy, athetosis and headaches.*

T. V. was found to have defective vision at the age of three years. He was given glasses which did not improve his vision. In other respects he seemed to be healthy. He was active and made good progress at school. At

the age of six years, he developed peculiar postures of the right arm and leg and some incoordination. A diagnosis of chorea was made. Some months later he began to have headaches and to vomit at times. The difficulty in the use of the right arm and leg became more pronounced and the left arm and leg were then affected in the same way. His gait became unsteady. Vision declined progressively.

Examination revealed a well-nourished, well-developed boy of seven years whose general appearance was not abnormal in any way. He cooperated intelligently in the examination and behaved well. Central vision was grossly reduced in both eyes. The right eye was nearly blind and the temporal fields of the left eye were obliterated. The nasal fields of the right eye were preserved, however. Both optic discs were pale but there was no evidence of old papilledema. Both sixth nerves were weak. The right arm was held in peculiar postures frequently being retracted behind the back with the elbow extended and the forearm pronated. The left arm showed similar postures but these were not so constant or so pronounced. There was no spasticity and no definite weakness but all movements showed definite incoordination apparently due to a type of mobile spasm. This was so severe on the right that the child used his left arm whenever possible. The gait was halting and irregular. No alteration of sensibility could be made out. The tendon reflexes were all normal. Roentgenograms of the skull were negative. Ventriculography was then performed. The lateral ventricles were dilated and the third ventricle was displaced upwards.

There was no polyuria or polydipsia. The child showed no somnolence. He continued to behave normally and there were no abnormal emotional reactions. Temperature ranged between 98.6° and 101.8°F. Pulse 100 to 130.

Dr. Dandy exposed the base of the third ventricle and the optic chiasm. A large, inoperable growth was found. The child died within a short time with temperature of 108°F.

Post-mortem examination revealed an infiltrating glioma containing small cysts which involved the infundibulum, the entire hypothalamus, the optic chiasm and optic nerves. The growth extended into the left orbit above the optic nerve. The lenticular nuclei were partially destroyed and the left thalamus was invaded. The growth showed the characteristics of a fibrillary astocytoma.

BIBLIOGRAPHY

BAILEY, P. AND EISENHARDT, L.: Spongioblastomas of the brain. J. Comp. Neurol., 56:391, 1932.

MCKISSOCK, W. AND PAINE, W. E.: Primary tumors of the thalamus. Brain, 81:41, 1958.

ODY, F.: Tumors of the basal ganglia. Arch. Neurol. & Psychiat., 27:249, 1932.

SCIARRA, D. AND SPROFKIN, B.: Symptoms and signs referable to the basal ganglia in brain tumor. Arch. Neurol. & Psychiat., 69:450, 1953.

WALSH, F. B.: *Loc. cit.*

WYLLIE, W. G.: Primary tumors of the optic nerves and of the chiasma. J. Neurol. & Psychopath., 5:209, 1924-25.

NEOPLASMS OF THE HYPOTHALAMUS AND INFUNDIBULUM

Pathological Anatomy.—Various gliomas such as the astrocytoma, spongioblastoma and glioblastoma occur in this region. Suprasellar cysts may invade the hypothalamus and pinealomas may also do so. The infundibuloma, a tumor containing vascular lakes and sinusoids, should also be mentioned. Several hamartomas, which are probably malformations rather than new growths, have been found in this region.

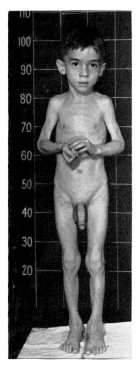

Fig. 241. Boy of 4 years showing sexual precocity. An astrocytoma was found in the hypothalamus. The case history is given in abstract. (Ped. 40034) (From Wilkins, Diagnosis and Treatment of Endocrine Disorders of Childhood and Adolescence, Thomas, 1950.)

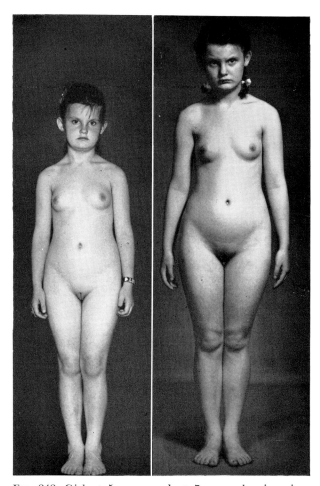

Fig. 242. Girl at 5 years and at 7 years showing signs of precocious puberty. Postmortem examination revealed a small mass of hyperplastic nervous tissue resembling that of the tuber cinereum which was attached to the right mammillary body. This may be termed a manartoma. (From Seckel, Scott and Benditt. Six examples of precocious sexual development. Am. J. Dis. Child., 1949, vol. 78, p. 484.)

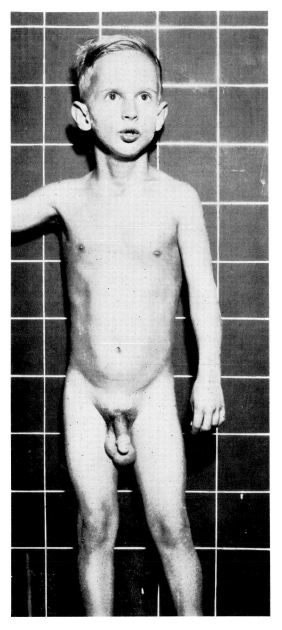

FIG. 243. Boy of 3½ years with large penis and large testicles who died suddenly in adrenal crisis. Postmortem revealed adrenal hyperplasia. Testicles contained much tissue resembling testicular interstital tissue or reticular zone of adrenal. As a rule in sexual precocity in boys due to adrenal hyperplasia the testicles are small. (Endocrine Disorders in Childhood and Adolescence, Thomas 1950.)

Clinical Features.—Although gross lesions are sometimes found in the hypothalamus without the associated symptoms one might expect, a rich and varied symptomatology is ascribed to processes in this region. These symptoms will be given very briefly. (1) *Diabetes insipidus* is very common. It is often associated with (2) *Adiposogenital dystrophy*. Obesity may occur without genital atrophy. Bodily growth may be reduced. Suprasellar cyst is the lesion most commonly found when this syndrome is due to neoplasm.

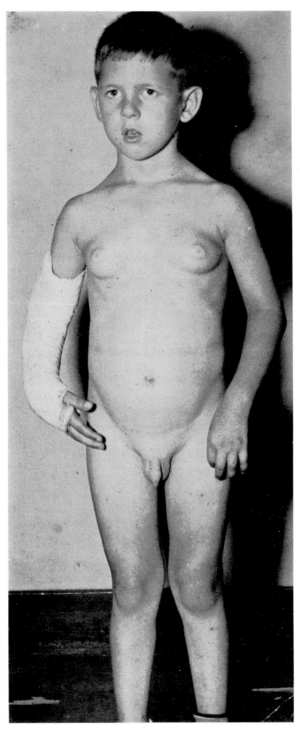

FIG. 244. Precocious growth of breasts in a boy due to feminizing tumor of the adrenal cortex.

(3) *Hyperthermia* may occur and may last for months. Persistent (4) *Somnolence* is observed and may be associated with low body temperature. (5) *Hyperglycemia* and glycosuria are described as a result of acute lesions. More chronic lesions are apt to be associated with (6) *Hypoglycemia* and sensitiveness to insulin. (7) *Precocious puberty* has been found in cases of neoplastic invasion of the hypothalamus many times. In such cases gliomas, hamartomas, infundibulomas, and occasionally suprasellar cysts are found. Precocious puberty is seen occasionally in cases of tuberose sclerosis and von Recklinghausen's disease. Ependymomas and even hydrocephalus may be responsible. Money and Hosta mention cases in which neoplasms or hamartomas of the hypothalamus have caused precocious puberty as well as laughing seizures. Constitutional precocity is not rare. It is seen more frequently in girls than in boys. In girls several cases may be found in one family, but in boys it may be traced through several generations. In rare instances sexual precocity results from interstitial cell tumors of the testis or from granulosa cell tumors of the ovary. Adrenal cortical tumor or hyperplasia may cause precocious puberty in boys but without enlargement of the testicles as a rule. In girls it may cause female pseudohermaphroditism. In rare instances precocious female sexual development may occur in boys. Precocious sexual development has been found following epidemic encephalitis, miliary tuberculosis, disseminated encephalomyelitis of measles, and meningitis. A few cases are known to be associated with growths of the liver. It is described in rare instances of thyroid deficiency. In Albright's disease precocious puberty is an essential feature of the disease. It is said that in the early stage of eosinophil adenoma of the pituitary precocious puberty may be evident. (8) The *sham-rage* of Cannon is stated to result when a lesion isolates the posterior hypothalamus from the brain. Cushing mentions a case in which glioma of the chiasm was responsible. (9) *Cachexia* and defective growth have been seen in some of our cases.

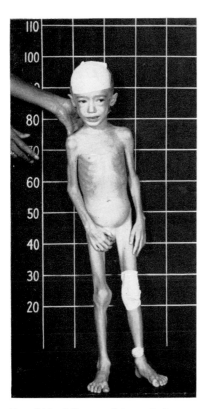

FIG. 245. Glioma of hypothalamus. Child is 5½ years old. Undernutrition is chief problem and led to diagnosis of anorexia nervosa at age of 4 years. Papilledema at 5½ permitted correct diagnosis, and this was verified by operation. (By the courtesy of Dr. Henry Seidel.)

CASE HISTORY (Ped. A-40034).—*Astrocytoma of the hypothalamus with precocious sexual development in a boy of four years.*

I. D. D. was just two years old when his mother noticed that his penis was growing too rapidly. When he was three years old, in the spring of 1944, he developed headaches and soon began to vomit. A few months later, it was observed that his head was enlarging. In the fall of 1944, the development of his genital organs was rapid and pubic hair appeared. His gait grew unsteady in February 1945.

The child was brought to Johns Hopkins Hospital on March 1, 1945. He was then four years old. His height and general bodily development were within normal limits. His head measured 20.1 in in occipital frontal circumference. There was some downy body hair and coarse hair in the pubic region. The penis was 10.0 cm long and the scrotum and testicles of approximately adult size. The bone age was slightly under five years. Roentgenograms of the head revealed only pressure markings of the vault. His mental state was quite normal. Neurological examination revealed only mild bilateral papilledema and unsteady gait.

Ventriculography revealed dilatation of the lateral ventricles but the third ventricle did not fill. At operation, Dr. Otenasek discovered a large growth filling the third ventricle which could not be removed completely. The tumor proved to be an astrocytoma. Some of the tumor tissue was implanted in immature mice for bioassay with negative results.

BIBLIOGRAPHY

CUSHING, H.: Papers Related to the Pituitary Body, Hypothalamus and Parasympathetic System. Thomas, Springfield, 1932, p. 49.

FULTON, J. F. AND BAILEY, P.: Tumors in the region of the third ventricle: Their diagnosis and relation to pathologic sleep. J. Nerv. & Ment. Dis., 69:1, 1929.

GLOBUS, J. H.: Infundibuloma: a tumor of neurohypophyseal origin. J. Neuropath. & Exper. Neurol., 1:59, 1942.

GLOBUS, J. H. AND STRAUSS, I. I.: Tumors of the brain with disturbance of temperature regulation. Arch. Neurol. & Psychiat., 25:506, 1931.

HAMPSON, J. G. AND MONEY, J.: Familial sexual precocity in girls. Psychosom. Med., 17:16, 1955.

HUNG, W. et al.: Precocious puberty in a boy with hepatoma. J. Pediat., 63:895, 1963.

JACOBSON, A. W. AND MACKLIN, M. T.: Hereditary sexual precocity in boys. Report of a family with 27 affected members. Pediatrics, 9:682, 1952.

JOLLY, H.: Sexual Precocity. Springfield, Thomas, 1955.

LE MARQUAND, H. S.: Pubertas praecox associated with tumor (hamartoma) in the floor of the third ventricle. Roy. Berkshire Hosp. Repts., 1934-35, p. 31.

LISS, L.: Pituicytoma, a tumor of the hypothalamus. Arch. Neurol. & Psychiat., 80:567, 1958.

MARCOUSE, P. M. et al.: Hamartoma of the hypothalamus. Jour. of Pediat., 43:301, 1953.

MONEY, J. AND HOSTA, G.: Laughing seizures with sexual precocity. The Johns Hopkins Medical Jour., 120:326, 1967.

NOVAK, E.: The constitutional type of female sexual precocity. Amer. Jour. Obstet. and Gynec., 47:20, 1944.

PAPEZ, J. W. AND ECKER, A.: Precocious puberty with hypothalamic infundibuloma. J. Neuropath. & Exp. Neurol., 6:15, 1947.

RUSH, H. P. et al.: Pubertas praecox. Endocrinology, 21:404, 1937.

SCHMIDT, E., HALLERVORDEN, J. AND SPATZ, H.: Die Entstehung der Hamartome und hypothalamus mit and ohne pubertas praecox. Deutsch. Ztschr. f. Nervenheilk., 177:235, 1958.

SECKEL, H. P. G. *et al.:* Six examples of precocious sexual development. Am. J. Dis. Child., **78**:484, 1949.

STOTIJN, C. P.: Precocious puberty and tumor of the hypothalamus. Jour. Nerv. and Ment. Dis., **111**:207, 1950.

THAMDRUP, E.: Precocious Sexual Development. Springfield, Thomas, 1961.

TROLAND, C. E. AND BROWN, C. A.: Precocious puberty of intracranial origin. J. Neurosurg. **5**:541, 1948.

VAN DER SAR, A. AND MOFFIE, D.: Precocious puberty due to hypothalamic hamartoma in negroid boy. Acta Psychiat. et Neurol. Scandinav. Sep. E, **35**:345, 1960.

WEINBERGER, L. M. AND GRANT, F. C.: Precocious puberty and tumors of the hypothalamus. Arch. Int. Med., **67**:762, 1941.

WHITE, P. T. AND ROSS, A. T.: Inanition syndrome in infants with anterior hypothalamic neoplasms. Neurology, **13**:974, 1963.

WILKINS, L.: The Diagnosis and Treatment of Endocrine Disorders in Childhood and Adolescence. Thomas, 1965, 3rd Ed.

NEOPLASMS INVOLVING THE BRAIN-STEM

Gliomas of the Brain-Stem

Pathological Anatomy.—The same types of glioma are found in the brain-stem as in other parts of the nervous system. The slow growing astrocytoma and spongioblastoma are most common but glioblastoma multiforme also occurs.

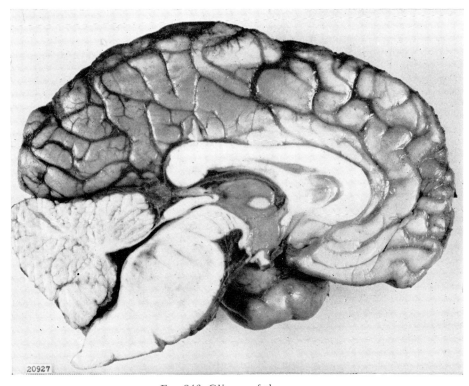

FIG. 246. Glioma of the pons.

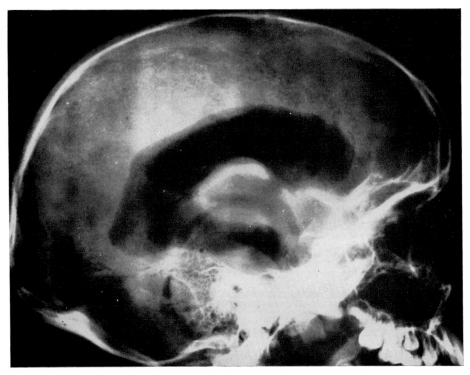

Fig. 247. Ventriculogram in case of glioma of the pons showing diffuse enlargement of the pons. (By the courtesy of Dr. Arthur King.)

Gliomas of the Pons.—These growths are unfortunately not uncommon in childhood. Their course is slow and the onset insidious. Pressure symptoms are delayed in most cases and death may occur before papilledema develops. The fifth, sixth, seventh and eighth cranial nerves are apt to be involved. Paralysis of lateral gaze is a typical sign. It is as a rule first unilateral and then bilateral. At this stage, all movements in the horizontal plane except convergence are lost but vertical movements of the eyes are preserved. Involvement of one or both sixth nerves of course complicates this picture. The palsies of the fifth and seventh nerves are apt to be incomplete for a time. Cerebellar ataxia of mild degree and unsteadiness of station and gait are often present. This is due no doubt to invasion of the pontocerebellar fibers or of the peduncle. Weakness or paralysis of the arms and legs is apt to become apparent before the end and Babinski's sign is found though the muscles usually remain flaccid. Retention of urine and incontinence are common. The lemniscus seems to be very resistant to pressure and sensory changes over the body are among the late symptoms. If the glioma is confined to one half of the pons, hemiplegia may be found associated with palsy of the sixth or seventh nerves on the opposite side. In

most cases, however, the glioma is diffuse and causes symptoms on both sides of the body. The old term for this condition, i.e. hypertrophy of the pons refers to the diffuse enlargement which is found at autopsy. Inexperienced pathologists frequently diagnose encephalitis on the gross appearance. We have been astonished in two instances to observe complete, spontaneous recovery in children who have presented the symptoms described above. In a few cases cavities are found in the cervical cord which give rise to misleading symptoms. In some cases roentgenotherapy gives at least temporary relief. Von Recklinghausen's disease is sometimes associated.

Gliomas of the Medulla.—Tumors in this region are characterized by vertigo and vomiting very early in their course. Disturbances in respiration, cardiac arrhythmia and difficulty in swallowing are among the early symptoms. Tenth nerve palsies cause weakness of the soft palate and hoarseness of the voice, increasing to aphonia and inspiratory stridor. The tongue may be paralyzed and atrophic. Usually the pyramidal tracts are involved eventually, and spasticity and weakness of the extremities with loss of sphincter control develops. Trigeminal pain and analgesia may result from involvement of the descending root of the fifth nerve. Death occurs suddenly, usually before signs of increased pressure develop. Primary tumors of the medulla are very rare, but gliomas of the pons frequently extend into the medulla.

Luse and Teitelbaum report the case of an infant who had a congenital glioma of the brain stem. They state that less than 10 congenital gliomas have been reported.

Gliomas of the Midbrain.—Midbrain gliomas give rise to a number of syndromes. Tumors in the region of the corpora quadrigemina produce the same symptoms which are found in connection with pineal tumors; namely, loss of associated upward movement of the eyes, loss of light reaction of the pupils, instability in the anteroposterior plane, some degree of cerebellar incoordination and spasticity of the limbs. Nystagmus and deafness are sometimes seen. Signs of increased intracranial pressure are severe and develop very early. Drowsiness may be more marked than the increased intracranial pressure would seem to explain.

If the tumor is in the tegmentum and involves the red nucleus, a coarse rhythmical tremor is found in the opposite arm and there is in most cases ipsilateral third nerve palsy; i.e. Benedikt's syndrome. If the superior cerebellar peduncle is involved, choreoathetoid movements may replace the tremor. Hemianesthesia and hemiparesis may occur. There may be paralysis of the muscles supplied by the fifth nerve. In some cases there is paralysis of emotional movements of the face on the opposite side.

Tumors in the more ventral part of the midbrain are apt to cause Web-

er's syndrome; that is, paralysis of the homolateral third nerve with hemiplegia on the opposite side. If both crura are involved, there may be tetraplegia.

CASE HISTORY (Path. 16457. Ped 58400) .—*Child of 11 years. Gradual development of bilateral palsies of the sixth and seventh nerves, loss of conjugate lateral movements, tetraplegia and retention of urine without papilledema. Glioma of the pons found at post-mortem examination.*

M. J., a colored boy of 11 years, began to grow weak in the right arm and leg in April 1939. A few weeks later his speech became indistinct and an internal squint appeared. Later the left arm and leg were affected. He began to have periods of uncontrollable weeping for no apparent reason. In the summer his parents noticed that, when he was asleep, his eyelids remained open. There were only occasional headaches.

On June 9, 1939, he was brought to the Harriet Lane Home. At this time he was drowsy and slow in his responses but would obey orders. There was evidence of recent loss of weight. All four extremities were very weak and he could not walk, stand or even sit up though some power of movement was present in all muscle groups. Muscle tone was diminished on passive movement, but the tendon reflexes were brisk and the plantar responses were of the extensor variety. The bladder was distended though he could pass small amounts of urine. The optic fundi were unchanged and the pupils reacted promptly to light. There was an internal squint, which seemed to be due to bilateral palsies of the external recti, but no ptosis of the eyelids was apparent. Movements of the eyes in the vertical plane were of full range but no lateral movements of the eyes could be elicited. There was therefore loss of lateral conjugate movements as well as palsies of the sixth nerves. Convergence was preserved. The face was weak on either side. The left orbicularis oculi and the right zygomaticus were completely paralysed though the other muscles showed some power of contraction. The jaws moved well. Hearing was intact. The patient could not protrude the tongue, but no atrophy was apparent. He swallowed with great difficulty. Articulation was lost.

The spinal fluid was quite normal and the Queckenstedt test negative. Roentgenograms of the chest and skull showed no abnormalities. The blood Wassermann test was negative.

The course was steadily downhill. The extremities became completely paralysed. The patient was soon unable to swallow and gavage was required. Respiration became irregular and finally on June 29, the patient became unconscious and died.

Post-mortem examination revealed an infiltrating glioma of the pons which contained several small cysts. The tumor contained both astrocytes and spongioblasts. All structures of the pons were infiltrated by the growth which had also extended into the right cerebral peduncle for a short distance. There was no hydrocephalus.

BIBLIOGRAPHY

ALPERS, B. J. AND WATTS, J. C.: Mesencephalic gliomas. Arch. Neurol. & Psychiat., **34**:1250, 1935.

ALPERS, B. J. AND YASKIN, J. C.: Gliomas of the pons; clinical and pathologic characteristics. Arch. Neurol. & Psychiat., **41**:435, 1939.

BAILEY, P. AND EISENHARDT, L.: Spongioblastomas of the brain. J. Comp. Neurol., **56**:391, 1932.

BROCK, S. AND NEEDLES, W.: Tumors of the brain-stem: A clinical study of five cases with autopsy findings. J. Nerv. & Ment. Dis., **72**:521, 1930.

BUCKLEY, R. C.: Pontine gliomas. A pathologic study and classification of twenty-five cases. Arch. Path., **9**:779, 1930.

COOPER, I. S., KERNOHAN, J. W. AND CRAIG, W. McK.: Tumors of the medulla oblongata. Arch. Neurol. & Psychiat., **67**:269, 1952.

HARE, C. C. AND WOLF, A.: Intramedullary tumors of the brain stem. Arch. Neurol. & Psychiat., **32**:1230, 1934.

LUSE, S. A. AND TEITELBAUM, S.: Congenital glioma of the brain stem. Arch. of Neurol., **18**:196, 1968.

NETSKY, M. AND STROBOS, R.: Neoplasms within the midbrain. Arch. Neurol. & Psychiat., **68**:116, 1952.

PILCHER, C.: Spongioblastoma polare of the pons; clinicopathologic study of eleven cases. Arch. Neurol. & Psychiat., **32**:1210, 1934.

WALSH, F. B.: *Loc. cit.*

Pineal Neoplasms

Pathological Anatomy.—Several types of neoplasms develop in this region. The most frequent are the pinealomas, which are composed of large globular cells with abundant cytoplasm and large round nucleolus. They sometimes have short processes ending in bulbous termination. Blepharoplasten may be demonstrated in the cytoplasm. These cells are divided into large masses by an abundant reticulum which contains small cells resembling lymphocytes. These tumors, thus, reproduce the structure of the adult pineal body very exactly. Pineoblastomas are described which resemble the cells of the pineal anlage. These are invasive and may extend into the third ventricle, the cerebellum and even break into the lateral ventricle through the occipital lobe. Teratomas and gliomas are also found in this region.

Clinical Features.—These may be divided into three groups: signs of increased intracranial pressure, focal neurological signs and developmental disturbances. The signs of increased intracranial pressure are apt to appear early, due to occlusion of the aqueduct from pressure above or filling of the posterior part of the third ventricle by the growth. Papilledema is present in practically every case. Compression of the upper part of the midbrain gives rise to very characteristic signs. Paralysis of upward associated ocular movements above the horizontal plane is perhaps the most typical and frequent early sign. This may be associated with paresis of one or both internal recti, with ptosis of the lids or with unequal pupils. Loss of convergence is also common. Later, conjugate movements in other planes may be lost. Sixth nerve palsies due to pressure may complicate the picture. The pupillary light reflexes are apt to be lost and the reaction during the accom-

modation may be preserved. The pupils are usually large and circular in contrast to the typical Argyll Robertson pupils found in neurosyphilis, which are, of course, usually small and irregular. Involvement of the inferior colliculi may cause deafness. One very characteristic feature is inability to preserve the balance in the anteroposterior plane when the eyes are closed. The patient tends to fall forwards or backwards. Cerebellar ataxia is often present, due to involvement of the superior cerebellar peduncles. Bilateral or unilateral spasticity and weakness of the limbs with increased tendon reflexes and Babinski's sign are not uncommon. If the growth extends laterally, it may involve the external geniculate body and cause hemianopia.

The developmental disorder is termed *macrogenitosomia praecox* or the *pineal syndrome*. The classical syndrome is confined exclusively to boys before the age of puberty. It is said that no case is recorded in which precocious puberty has occurred in a girl which was associated with a pinealoma. The penis and testicles rapidly assume adult proportions, the voice grows deep, the pubic, axillary and body hair appears and there is precocious growth and muscular development. In some cases there is a tendency

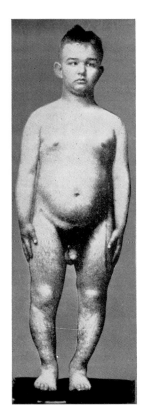

FIG. 248. The so-called pineal syndrome with outspoken p u b e r t a s praecox in a boy of seven years. Note obesity, hypertrichosis, complete development of the genital organs and internal strabismus. The growth was not a true pinealoma but a ganglioneuroma invading the floor of the third ventricle. (After Bailey and Horrax—Arch. of Neurol. and Psychiat. 1928, Vol. 19, p. 403.)

toward obesity. Pubertas praecox is not a common or characteristic sign of pineal tumors. In fact, it has been present in only a few cases in which the diagnosis of pinealoma was histologically verified. The intracranial tumors most commonly found in such cases are teratomas, gliomas and cysts. It is not clear how such tumors produce precocious puberty but several theories have been advanced which may be summarized as follows: (1) That the tumor (teratoma) contains sex gland tissue. (2) That the tumor secretes a hypothetical hormone of the pineal gland. (3) That the destruction of normal pineal function leads to precocious puberty. (4) That the essential lesion is in the hypothalamus and does not involve the pineal body in any way. The anatomical facts seem to support the last statement very strongly. It seems to be generally assumed that the hypothalamic growth causes excessive secretion of gonadotropic hormone by the hypophysis.

Some pineal tumors are calcified and, hence, may be visualized in roentgenograms of the cranium. Ventriculography reveals in the early stages of the growth merely dilatation of the lateral and third ventricles and obliteration of the supra-pineal recess. Later the posterior part of the third ventricle may be invaded and a filling defect may be demonstrated. Since these growths do not, as a rule, extend forward to the foramina of Monro, air will pass from one lateral ventricle to the other. The ventricular fluid is sometimes bloody when a very vascular tumor has invaded the ventricular system.

Occasionally, growths composed of pineal tissue are found in the anterior part of the third ventricle. These are usually extensions or implantations secondary to a growth arising in the pineal body. In some instances, however, the tumors seem to arise from cell rests in the anterior part of the ventricle and are termed ectopic pinealomas. The pineal body is intact in such cases. Such growths give rise to polyuria and eventually invade the chiasm so they may be mistaken for suprasellar cysts.

More malignant pinealomas give rise to a very different picture. These tumors extend throughout the ventricular system and deposits may be found even in the spinal meninges. The floor of the third ventricle is usually invaded first causing somnolence, polyuria and fluctuations of temperature. Signs of increased intracranial pressure are mild and develop late. Mental changes are prominent. The focal signs described above in connection with the less malignant pinealomas are absent. The spinal fluid shows a pleocytosis of 60 or 70 cells which resemble lymphocytes but which are no doubt derived from the tumor. Evidences of involvement of the spinal cord or cauda equina may appear late in the course. Dr. Muncie and I have reported cases of this type in which the pineal gland was found to be intact though the growth resembled a pinealoma. Mackay points out that such growths may arise from pineal cell rests in the floor of the third ventricle.

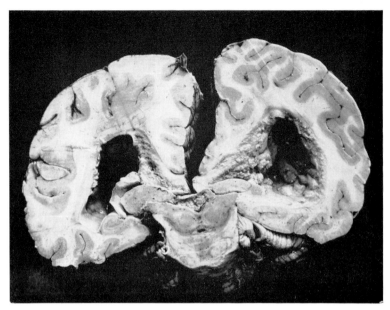

FIG. 249. Malignant pinealoma showing erosion of the ventricular walls.

Diagnosis.—The essential features of diagnostic importance are the early signs of increased intracranial pressure, dilatation of the pupils with loss of light reflex, inability to rotate eyes upward above horizontal plane, bilateral ptosis of the eyelids and instability in the anteroposterior plane. The developmental changes are rare and not reliable from a diagnostic point of view. If the patient presents signs of an intracranial tumor as well as precocious puberty the growth will probably be found involving the hypothalamus but the histology cannot be predicted. Ventriculography is often necessary to establish the exact location of the growth. For other causes of precocious puberty see Tumors of the Hypothalamus and Infundibulum.

Treatment.—Surgical exploration of this region is very difficult but Dandy has devised a method of approach by splitting the corpus callosum, which he has employed in several cases. All of these patients eventually died of recurrences of the growth. Roentgenotherapy is advised by Horrax. Decompression is performed to reduce the intracranial pressure or a Torkildsen tube is introduced.

CASE HISTORY (Path. 14788-Psych. 7519-Psych. Path. 925).—*Malignant pinealoma. Boy of 15 years developed headache. Ventricular system dilated. Exploration of posterior fossa negative. Relief of symptoms after deep roentgenotherapy. Two years later polyuria. Four years after onset, unsteadiness of gait, difficulty in speech and apraxia. Spinal fluid con-*

tained 60 cells and much protein. Progressive dementia and death. Post-mortem examination revealed growth which had destroyed the lining of the entire ventricular system.

W. S., a previously healthy boy of 15 years, developed a severe headache in April 1932. Examination is said to have shown questionable papilledema. The spinal fluid pressure was 210 mm water and contained 16 cells. Ventriculography was performed and showed the lateral and third ventricles to be dilated. It was thought that the child had a cerebellar tumor and the posterior fossa was explored with negative results. On the chance that he might have an undisclosed neoplasm, he was given two courses of deep roentgenotherapy. The symptoms receded and he returned to school. During the years 1933 and 1934 he did well at school. In August, 1934, he began to have polyuria. At the same time, he complained of fatigue and seemed to be irritable. Neurological and ophthalmological examinations were quite negative in October 1934, however. In December, 1935, the patient began to have difficulty in his gait and speech. He could grasp the meaning of only short sentences and could not express himself clearly for he often used inappropriate words. His gait was reeling but no ataxia or weakness could be demonstrated in the arms or legs. The spinal fluid contained 60 cells and the Pandy test was negative. In February, 1936, the child had two generalized convulsions and was stuporous for several hours. Ventriculography was performed again, but the ventricular system showed only moderate symmetrical dilatation. He soon became mentally disturbed alternating between periods of restlessness and irritability and periods of somnolence. When he was able to cooperate, he seemed to be completely apraxic. At this time he was admitted to the Phipps Psychiatric Clinic. Spinal puncture showed pressure of 220 mm. water, 70 cells resembling lymphocytes and protein of 450 mgs. The temperature fell to 96°F. by rectum at times. He died on May 9, 1936, just four years after the onset of symptoms.

Post-mortem examination disclosed that the tumor resembled a pinealoma but seemed to have arisen in the anterior part of the third ventricle. The pineal body was intact. The growth had extended throughout the entire ventricular system and had destroyed the ependyma and invaded the underlying brain. The central white matter of the hemispheres was invaded to some extent, the corpus callosum was destroyed in its inferior half, and the floor of the third ventricle was largely destroyed. The dilatation of the ventricles was largely due to erosion of their walls by the tumor.

CASE HISTORY (Ped. B-582).—*Boy of 9 years began to lose vision of the left eye. At 11 years developed headache and nausea. The left eye was found to be blind and the temporal field of the right eye was lost. The sella was somewhat enlarged. A typical pinealoma was found at operation.*

G. M., a previously healthy boy of 9 years, was found to have reduction of vision of the left eye. This was not considered important for the disc was of good color and vision was only moderately reduced being estimated at 20/30.

At the age of 11 years, however, he complained of frequent headaches and nausea. Vision was tested again and he was found to be blind in the left eye. He was brought to the hospital on March 9, 1953.

On examination the patient was well developed and nourished. No abnormalities of growth or development were evident. The left pupil was dilated and did not react directly to light. The consensual light reaction was sluggish. The right pupil reacted directly but not consensually. The left eye was quite blind. Vision of the right eye was 20/20 but the entire temporal field was lost up to the vertical meridian. The optic nerve heads showed a normal appearance. There was no suggestion of pallor. The left lid drooped slightly and there was some reduction of upward movement of the left eye. Some observers thought that there was slight reduction of sensibility over the sensory field of the right fifth nerve. Neurological examination was otherwise negative. Roentgenograms of the skull revealed that the sella was moderately enlarged. The clinoid processes were somewhat atrophic and the floor was depressed.

Exploration revealed a growth which had broken out of the sella and extended into the left middle fossa. The chiasm and the left optic nerve were surrounded and compressed. The gross appearances were suggestive of adenoma of the hypophysis but histological study revealed that it was a typical pinealoma. I am indebted to Dr. George Smith for this information.

BIBLIOGRAPHY

BAGGENSTOSS, A. H. AND LOVE, J. G.: Pinealomas. Arch. Neurol. & Psychiat., 41:1187, 1939.

DANDY, W. E.: Operation for removal of pineal tumors. Surg. Gynec. and Obst., 33:113, 1921.

FORD, F. R. AND MUNCIE, W.: Three cases of an unusual type of malignant tumor arising within the third ventricle and invading the walls of the ventricular system. Arch. Neurol. & Psychiat., 60:192, 1937.

FORD, F. R. AND GUILD, H.: Precocious puberty following measles encephalitis and epidemic encephalitis with a discussion of the relation of intracranial tumors and inflammatory processes to the syndrome of macrogenitosomia praecox. Bull. Johns Hopkins Hosp., 60:192, 1937.

FRIEDMAN, E. D. AND PLAUT, A.: Tumor of the pineal gland with meningeal and neural metastases. Arch. Neurol. & Psychiat., 33:1324, 1935.

HORRAX, G.: Treatment of tumors of the pineal body. Arch. Neurol. & Psychiat., 64:227, 1950.

————: Pineal pathology; further studies. Arch. Neurol. & Psychiat., 19:394, 1928.

————: Studies on the pineal gland. I. Experimental observations. Arch. Int. Med., 17:607, 1916.

————: Studies on the pineal gland. II. Clinical observations. Arch. Int. Med., 17:627, 1916.

————: The differential diagnosis of tumors primarily pineal and primarily pontine. Arch. Neurol. & Psychiat., 17:179, 1927.

————: Extirpation of a huge pinealoma from a patient with pubertas praecox. Arch. Neurol. & Psychiat., 37:385, 1937.

————: The eye signs in pineal tumors. J. Neurosurg., 3:15, 1946.

HORRAX, G. AND BAILEY, P.: Tumors of the pineal body. Arch. Neurol. & Psychiat., 13:423, 1925.

HORRAX, G. AND DANIELS, J. T.: The conservative treatment of pineal tumors. Surg. Clin. North America, 22:649, 1942.

HORRAX, G. AND WYATT, J. P.: Ectopic pinealomas in the chiasmal region. Report of 3 cases. J. Neurosurg., 4:309, 1947.

KAGEYAMA, N. AND BELSKY, R.: Ectopic pinealoma in chiasm region. Neurology, 11:318, 1961.

Landing, B. H.: Endocrine tumors in children. J. Florida M. A., **49**:479, 1962.

Mackay, R. P.: Pinealoma of diffuse ependymal origin. Arch. Neurol. & Psychiat., **42**:892, 1939.

Müller, R. and Wohlfart, G.: Intracranial teratomas and teratoid tumors. Acta psychiat. et Neurol., **22**:70, 1947.

Ringertz, N., Nordenstam, H. and Flyger, G.: Tumors of the pineal region. J. Neuropath. & Exper. Neurol., **13**:540, 1954.

Russell, W. O. and Sachs, E.: Pinealomas. Arch. Path., **35**:869, 1943.

Walsh, F. B.: *Loc. cit.*

Weinberger, L. M. and Grant, F. C.: Precocious puberty and tumor of the hypothalamus. Arch. Int. Med., **67**:762, 1941.

INTRAVENTRICULAR NEOPLASMS

Clinical Features.—Tumors within the ventricles produce no focal signs at first but give rise to symptoms of increased intracranial pressure. In some cases, especially when the tumor is movable, the symptoms fluctuate in striking fashion, so as to suggest that the intracranial pressure is not constantly elevated but varies within wide limits. It has been claimed that this phenomenon is characteristic of intraventricular tumors and that the fluctuation in pressure is due to a valve-like action of the tumor. The theory is that the tumor obstructs the outflow of cerebrospinal fluid from the ventricle until the pressure rises to the point that the tumor is displaced with discharge of fluid and relief of symptoms. The headache may be relieved in some cases by placing the head in certain positions. In the same way, stooping, straining, sudden movements and certain positions may cause paroxysmal headaches and vomiting. Presumably, the effort has resulted in wedging the tumor into a position which suddenly obstructs the flow of fluid, and since the cranium is a rigid, walled chamber filled with fluid, the pressure rises at once. It must be said that these symptoms are not peculiar to intraventricular tumors and have been described in pineal and cerebellar growths as well.

Tumors of the lateral ventricles cause only symptoms of increased intracranial pressure for a time but, later, when they force their way into the hemispheres, may cause symptoms such as hemiplegia, hemianesthesia or hemianopia, etc., just as do tumors primarily in the hemisphere.

Tumors within the third ventricle cause at first only signs of increased intracranial pressure but later will often produce a great variety of symptoms when they invade adjacent structures. Such tumors may extend into the hypothalamus and infundibulum causing symptoms which have been discussed above or they may extend laterally involving the optic thalami and lenticular nuclei. When the growth is situated in the posterior part of the ventricle, it may invade the superior part of the midbrain causing the pineal syndrome.

Tumors of the fourth ventricle may cause only signs of increased intracranial pressure at first but, as a rule, focal signs appear relatively early.

Vomiting often develops before there is outspoken papilledema. Subsequently signs and symptoms indicative of involvement of the cerebellum and pons appear.

A number of tumors are found in the cerebral ventricles. If we exclude gliomas arising in the brain and invading the ventricular system secondarily, we may mention the ependymomas, papillomas of the choroid plexus, and colloid cysts of the third ventricle. We must also mention the intraventricular growths which are found in tuberose sclerosis. Cysts of the cavum septi pellucidi may be included for convenience although they are, of course, not true neoplasms.

BIBLIOGRAPHY

DANDY, W. E.: Benign Tumors in the Third Ventricle of the Brain: Diagnosis and Treatment. Springfield, Ill., Charles C Thomas, 1933.

————: Benign, Encapsulated Tumors of the Lateral Ventricles of the Brain. Baltimore, Williams and Wilkins Co., 1934.

FULTON, J. F. AND BAILEY, P.: Tumors in the region of the third ventricle; their diagnosis and relation to pathologic sleep. J. Nerv. & Ment. Dis., **69**:1, 1929.

WEISENBERG, T. H.: Tumors of the third ventricle with the establishment of a symptom-complex. Brain, **33**:236, 1911.

EPENDYMOMAS

Pathological Anatomy.—These tumors are relatively rare but much more frequent in childhood than in adult life. The average age of the patients in the series of Fincher and Coon was 13 years at the time when they came under observation. They may be found in the lateral, third or fourth ventricles. They also occur in the central canal of the spinal cord. The tumor is partially encapsulated and may contain small cysts. Histological examination reveals a mosaic of polygonal cells with granular cytoplasm and large vesicular nuclei. Among these cells are seen small bodies in shape and size resembling bacilli, which stain like the blepharoplasten of normal ependymal cells. Calcified areas are often present.

Clinical Features.—These tumors grow slowly but there is nothing typical in the clinical picture. In rare cases they metastasize to the meninges. Fincher and Coon think that the shadows of calcified areas in the roentgenograms should suggest ependymoma, for shadows are rare in other cerebral tumors of childhood. They also state that fluid drawn from the cysts does not coagulate in contrast to the fluid of common gliomatous cysts. Bailey *et al.* state that the ependymomas of the fourth ventricle are apt to cause symptoms due to increased intracranial pressure, loss of equilibrium due to involvement of the posterior vermis of the cerebellum, vomiting, vertigo and respiratory disturbances due to pressure on the medulla, reduction of muscle tone, loss of reflexes and in the terminal stage, retraction of the head and tonic fits. The demonstration of an intraventricular tumor by ventriculography should always suggest ependymoma.

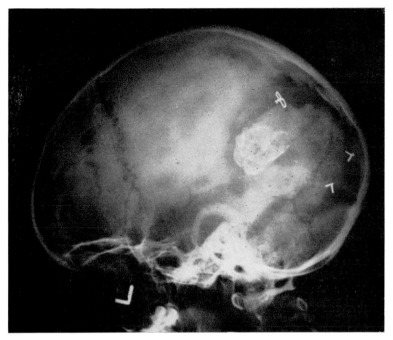

Fig. 250. Showing calcification in an ependymoma of the lateral ventricle.

Treatment.—These growths are often encapsulated and attached to the ventricular wall by a pedicle. If located in the lateral ventricle, they may often be removed completely. When situated within the fourth ventricle, the operation is very hazardous.

BIBLIOGRAPHY

BAILEY, P.: A study of tumors arising from ependymal cells. Arch. Neurol. & Psychiat., 11:1, 1924.

FINCHER, E. F. JR. AND COON, P. G.: Ependymomas; A clinical and pathologic study of eight cases. Arch. Neurol. & Psychiat., 22:19, 1929.

TÖNNIS, W. UND ZÜLCH, K. J.: Das Ependymoma der Gross hirnhemisphären im Jungendalter, Zentralbl. f. Neurochirur., 2:141, 1937.

WALSH, F. B.: *Loc. cit.*

Papillomas of the Choroid Plexus

Pathological Anatomy.—These growths are very rare and are somewhat more apt to be found in the fourth ventricle than the lateral or third ventricle. Their gross appearance is suggestive of a cauliflower for the surface is rough and nodular. In some cases there are large and small cysts. The cells are of epithelial type and surround a central core of connective tissue. Many of them are malignant. Papillomas must be distinguished from the rare hypertophies of the choroid plexuses which are mentioned in connection with congenital hydrocephalus q.v.

Clinical Features.—There is nothing very typical in the course or symptoms of these tumors and they cannot be distinguished from other intraventricular tumors before operation. Focal signs are often absent until late in the course of the disease. In rare cases, these tumors may metastasize to the meninges and ventricular surface. Dandy reports two cases of very malignant adenomas of the choroid plexus in infants.

Treatment.—Localization by ventriculography and operative removal.

BIBLIOGRAPHY

Cushing, H. and Davis, L. E.: Papillomas of the choroid plexus, with the report of six cases. Arch. Neurol. & Psychiat., **13**:681, 1925.

Dandy, W. E.: Benign Encapsulated Tumors of the Lateral Ventricles of the Brain. Williams and Wilkins Co., Baltimore, 1934, p. 28.

Fairburn, B.: Choroid plexus papilloma and its relation to hydrocephalus. J. Neurosurg., **17**:166, 1960.

Hall, G. W. and Fentress, T. L.: Papilloma choroideum with diffuse central nervous system metastases. J. Neurol. & Psychopath., **14**:108, 1933.

Solomon, C. I. and Friedman, J. J.: Tumors of the choroid plexus in childhood. Am. J. Dis. Child., **52**:114, 1936.

van Wagenen, W. R.: Papilloma of the choroid plexus. Report of two cases, one with removal of tumor at operation and one with seeding of tumor in ventricular system. Arch. Surg., **20**:199, 1930.

Colloid Cysts of the Third Ventricle

Pathological Anatomy.—These rare cysts are found only in the anterior part of the third ventricle where they are attached to the choroid plexus. Owing to their situation, they usually occlude the foramina of Monro. The walls are composed of flat or cuboidal epithelium surrounded by a thin fibrous capsule. In Bailey's case some of the epithelial cells were ciliated. Sometimes the cyst is trabeculated and in the gross appears to be multilocular. Thick, tenacious mucinoid material is contained within the cyst. This may be white or greenish. Bailey has suggested that these tumors arise from remnants of the paraphysis.

Clinical Features.—The symptoms seem to be due to constant or intermittent obstruction of the third ventricle. Kelly has recently made a very helpful analysis of the various symptoms which may occur.

In some cases one finds headaches and papilledema without any focal signs or characteristic features to suggest the proper diagnosis.

In other instances there are paroxysmal headaches with vomiting, transient amblyopia, unconsciousness and sometimes sudden death. Such attacks may be induced by flexion of the head. It is believed that these attacks are due to sudden obstruction of the foramina of Monro. The cyst must be movable. Prolonged freedom from symptoms may occur in such cases.

A third syndrome is characterized by progressive dementia. In some cases of this type there is no clinical evidence of increased intracranial pressure.

No doubt, the dementia is a result of atrophy of the cerebral cortex due to progressive hydrocephalus.

Kelly describes repeated attacks of weakness or paralysis of the legs. These may occur so suddenly that the patient falls to the ground. They are not associated with loss of consciousness or convulsive phenomena.

Despite the distention of the third ventricle, disturbances of metabolism are not described. False localizing signs are sometimes observed. Some of these may be a result of herniation through the tentorium but the cause of others is obscure. I know of two cases in which there was anesthesia in the sensory field of the fifth nerve.

Diagnosis.—The clinical features are not so characteristic that one can make a diagnosis with confidence. The ventriculogram is extremely helpful. One expects to find evidences of obstruction of the foramina of Monro and sometimes a small rounded tumor is visualized in the anterior part of the third ventricle.

Treatment.—Most surgeons prefer the anterior approach. The tumor is removed by tunneling through the frontal lobe. It is pointed out that pre-operative drainage of one lateral ventricle by a Torkildsen tube is apt to be disastrous unless the septum pellucidum has ruptured.

CASE HISTORY (U-33548).—*Girl of 10 years developed severe headaches in response to sneezing, straining. Later headaches were associated with stupor and once with a tonic spasm. Examination was quite negative. Colloid cyst found in third ventricle by ventriculography and successfully removed by Dr. Dandy.*

M. A. B., a girl of 10 years, developed recurrent headaches in March, 1930. These became more and more frequent, more severe and more prolonged. At first they occurred at intervals of about two months but later the interval was reduced to about two weeks. Vomiting accompanied the headaches and there was sometimes drowsiness. Coughing and straining as well as bending forward seemed to precipitate the attacks. In October there was an especially severe headache during which the child became unconscious and cyanotic. There was generalized muscular rigidity with retraction of the head and extension of the extremities for a time. Pulse was slow. The patient was brought to see Dr. Dandy on October 11, 1930.

Neurological examination was negative except for enlargement of the head which measured 55.5 cm. in the occipito-frontal circumference. The mother stated that the child had always had a large head. Roentgenograms of the cranium revealed definite evidence of long-standing increased intracranial pressure with convolutional markings and separation of the sutures. Ventriculography was performed. Well-marked hydrocephalus was found and a tumor was visualized in the anterior part of the third ventricle. At operation Dr. Dandy removed a small round cyst which was placed so as to obstruct both foramina of Monro. This contained a thick, green-

ish-brown material. The walls of the cyst were lined with flat and columnar epithelium and some of the cells showed cilia. The patient made a
complete recovery.

This case illustrates the absence of focal signs in tumors confined to the
ventricular system. The tumor which was of congenital origin had evidently given rise to a mild increase of intracranial pressure very early in
life for the mother had noted the enlargement of the head when the patient was a baby. This had caused well-marked dilatation of the ventricles
but no papilledema.

BIBLIOGRAPHY

BAILEY, P. AND FULTON, J. F.: *Loc. cit.,* case 3.

BULL, J. W. AND SUTTON, D.: The diagnosis of paraphyseal cyst. Brain, **72**:1949.

CAIRNS, H. AND MOSBERG, W.: Colloid cysts of the third ventricle. Surg. Gynec. & Obst., **92**:545,
1951.

DANDY, W. E.: Benign Tumors in the Third Ventricle. Springfield, Illinois, Charles C Thomas,
1933.

DRENNAN, A. M.: Impacted cyst in the third ventricle of the brain. Report of two cases. Brit.
Med. J., 2:47, 1929.

KELLY, R.: Colloid cysts of the third ventricle. Analysis of 29 cases. Brain, **74**:23, 1951.

McKISSOCK, W.: Surgical treatment of colloid cysts of the third ventricle. Brain, **74**:1, 1951.

SHUANGSHOTI, S. AND NETSKY, M. G.: Neuroepithelial (colloid) cysts of the nervous system.
Neurology, **16**:887, 1966.

Congenital Cysts of the Cavum Septi Pellucidi
and Cavum Vergae

The cavum septi pellucidi is a cavity sometimes found in the septum
pellucidum and is often termed the fifth ventricle. Verga's ventricle is a
space which may occur between the corpus collosum and the psalterium,
bounded laterally by the columns of the fornix. Both of these structures
are common in brains of infants but are usually obliterated in adult
brains. They may sometimes be found existing together and may even communicate with one another and with the ventricular system. In rare cases
these spaces become dilated with fluid and give rise to symptoms of brain
tumor. Dandy has described two instances of this nature, in one of which
there was a large cyst formed by the union of the cavum septi pellucidi
and the cavum Vergae, and in the other merely a cyst of the septum pellucidum. The latter condition occurred in a child who had always been
mentally backward and whose head had been abnormally large since birth.
At the age of four years and six months he had suddenly developed convulsions on the left side of the body and had become comatose. At times
the left arm was paralyzed and both plantar reflexes were extensor. Ventriculography revealed that the anterior horns of the lateral ventricles were
separated unduly, their medial walls were indented and the third ventricle
was compressed from above. The lesion was, therefore, just beneath the
corpus callosum. Because of his experience in the first case, Dandy diag-

nosed a cyst of the septum pellucidum. This was found and opened at operation. The child's convulsions ceased and his mental condition improved. Operation was performed on the right side and it was noted that the convolutional pattern of the cortex was distinctly abnormal.

Dandy states that the condition cannot at present be diagnosed upon clinical grounds but may be recognized by the characteristic alteration of the ventriculogram. Hydrocephalus may be present or absent. Tumors of the septum are sometimes found.

BIBLIOGRAPHY

CRAIG, W. McK., MILLER, R. H. AND HOLMAN, C. B.: Cysts of the septum pellucidum. Proc. Staff Meet. Mayo Clin., 28:330, 1953.

DANDY, W. E.: Congenital cerebral cysts of the cavum septi pellucidi and cavum vergae. Arch. Neurol. & Psychiat., 25:44, 1931.

FRENCH, J. D. AND BUCY, P. C.: Tumors of the septum pellucidum. J. Neurosurg., 5:433, 1918.

WOLF, A. AND BAMFORD, T. E.: Cavum septi pellucidi and cavum vergae. Bull. Neurological Inst. New York, 4:294, 1935.

PRIMARY NEOPLASMS OF THE MENINGES

Introduction.—It is believed that most of the primary growths of the meninges arise from the pia-arachnoid. The meningiomas of which a variety of histological types are recognized are occasionally found. They seem to be a bit more invasive in children than in adults and are sometimes termed sarcomas. There are also two rare tumors of the meninges which spread diffusely through the subarachnoid spaces. One of these is believed to arise from the lining cells of the leptomeninges or from the cells of the perivascular tissues and one from the chromatophore cells which are sometimes found in the meninges.

BIBLIOGRAPHY

BAILEY, P., CUSHING, H. AND EISENHARDT, L.: Angioblastic meningiomas. Arch. Path., 6:953, 1928.

BAILEY, P. AND BUCY, P. C.: The origin and nature of meningeal tumors. Am. J. Cancer, 15:15, 1931.

Meningiomas

Pathological Anatomy.—These tumors were formerly called dural endotheliomas, but in recent years Mallory and Penfield have claimed that the typical cell is similar to a fibroblast and therefore call them fibroblastomas. Bailey and Bucy, however, state that a number of cell types are found in such tumors and suggest a series of names descriptive of each type. It is perhaps simpler to call them by Cushing's non-committal term of *meningioma*. Almost all writers agree that they are of connective tissue origin and probably arise from the cell clusters of the arachnoid which penetrate the dura. They are attached to the inner aspect of the dura and arise in most cases near one of the dural sinuses. They are usually more or less spherical

and lobulated but may be flattened. Rarely they are cystic. The histology is subject to a great deal of variation and many different types are described. Some of these tumors are so vascular as to suggest angioma; others are relatively avascular. Psammoma bodies are common. Multiple tumors are sometimes found. A very characteristic feature is the tendency to invade the cranium and to produce hyperostosis. This occurs in about 15 per cent of all cases. The hyperplastic bone almost always contains tumor cells which may even extend through the outer table and form a mass under the scalp. Less frequently the bone is eroded and in children, local bulging is seen. Strangely enough they rarely penetrate the pia or invade the brain and never metastasize by the blood stream. Compression of blood vessels or invasion of venous channels may cause massive infarctions. There is a tendency for meningiomas of childhood to be more invasive than those of adult life and they are sometimes diagnosed as sarcomas. They are apt to recur after operation. In some cases they are found in association with neurofibromas and in such cases several members of a family are apt to be affected.

Clinical Features.—These tumors are rare before the age of fifteen years but are sometimes seen even in early childhood. Mendiratta *et al.* report a case in which a meningioma was present at birth and refer to two other cases found in medical literature. They are found more frequently over the convexity than at the base. Frontal and prefrontal locations are most common and temporal, occipital and parietal tumors occur in the given order. They are rare in the posterior fossa. Favorite sites for their attachment are: (1) From the anterior part of the falx and longitudinal sinus, causing focal convulsions starting in the leg, crural monoplegia and, if the growth straddles the falx as it sometimes does, cerebral paraplegia with loss of sphincter control. (2) From the orbital roof or the lesser wing of the sphenoid, causing palsies of the third, fourth and sixth nerves and upper branch of the fifth nerve. Optic atrophy may be associated. (3) From the floor of the middle fossa, giving rise to convulsions with uncinate gyrus phenomena, pain in the face from pressure on the Gasserian ganglion and if left-sided, aphasia. (4) From the olfactory groove causing anosmia and unilateral or bilateral optic atrophy. (5) Within the sheath of the optic nerve in either its orbital or its intracranial course causing unilateral exophthalmos and primary optic atrophy with free motility of the bulb. The growth may extend into the nerve head or cause detachment of the retina. A relatively large percentage of such growths occur in children. They may grow very slowly. (6) From the tuberculum sellae compressing the optic chiasm but causing as a rule no change in the clinoid processes. (7) In the posterior fossa in some instances and rarely within the cerebral ventricles where they are found to be attached to the choroid plexus.

The brain is compressed rather than invaded and hence, focal signs are, as a rule, rather late. Convulsions, either focal or general, are commonly the first evidence of the tumor. Later signs of increased intracranial pressure appear. The course is usually a slow one. The diagnosis can rarely be made before operation unless there is a definite hyperostosis of the cranium. In some cases, such as that of Frazier and Alpers, which occurred in a child at the age of six years, the extracranial mass may reach an enormous size, almost as large as the head itself with astonishingly few cerebral symptoms. A local increase in the vascularity of the cranium and especially dilatation of the groove of the middle meningeal artery is also very suggestive of meningioma. Sometimes the tumor itself is visible. Localization is often impossible without ventriculography or angiography. Treatment is purely surgical and, if the growth can be completely removed, the prognosis is favorable.

In rare cases, a small meningioma may occlude the superior longitudinal sinus and cause hydrocephalus by preventing the absorption of cerebrospinal fluid. In some such cases, the diagnosis can be made only by a venogram.

BIBLIOGRAPHY

ALPERS, B. J. AND HARROW, R.: Cranial hyperostosis associated with an overlying fibroblastoma. Arch. Neurol. & Psychiat., 28:339, 1932.

BAILEY, P. AND BUCY, P. C.: The origin and nature of the meningeal tumors. Am. J. Cancer, 15:15, 1921.

COSTON, T. O.: Primary tumor of the optic nerve. Arch. Ophth., 15:696, 1936.

CRAIG, W. McK.: Malignant intracranial endotheliomata. Surg. Gynec. & Obst., 45:760, 1927.

CUSHING, H.: The meningiomas (dural endotheliomas). Their source and favored seats of origin. Brain, 45:282, 1922.

CUSHING, H. AND EISENHARDT, L.: Meningiomas. Charles C Thomas, 1938.

DANDY, W. E.: Dural Endothelioma. Lewis, Practice of Surgery, 12:516.

FRAZIER, C. H. AND ALPERS, B. J.: Meningeal fibroblastomas of the cerebrum. A clinico-pathologic analysis of seventy-five cases. Arch. Neurol. & Psychiat., 29:935, 1933.

GARCIA, F.: Meningioma of the internal auditory meatus in a child of 3 years. J. Neurosurg., 13:215, 1956.

GLOBUS, J. H. *et al.*: Primary sarcomatous meningioma. J. Neuropath. & Exp. Neurol., 3:311, 1944.

MENDIRATTA, S. S. *et al.*: Congenital meningiomas. Neurology, 17:914, 1967.

NAGER, G. T.: Meningiomas Involving the Temporal Bone. Springfield, Thomas, 1963.

PENFIELD, W.: The encapsulated tumors of the nervous system. Surg. Gynec. and Obst., 45:178, 1927.

SPILLER, W. G.: Cranial hyperostosis associated with underlying meningeal fibroblastoma. Arch. Neurol. & Psychiat., 21:637, 1929.

WALSH, F. B.: *Loc. cit.*

Sarcomatosis of the Leptomeninges

Pathological Anatomy.—These tumors are believed to arise in the leptomeninx or in the perivascular spaces of the cortical blood vessels. They are termed sarcomas, peritheliomas, mesotheliomas and endotheliomas by vari-

ous writers. In some cases they do not form large masses but extend throughout the subarachnoid space and perivascular spaces just as an infection does. Indeed, the gross appearance of the brain is frequently such that the diagnosis of tuberculous meningitis is made. There is a good deal of variation in the appearance of the cells of tumors of this type but all of them are believed to be of connective tissue origin. Some of them are very malignant and infiltrate the brain and others are limited in their growth by the pia which they never penetrate.

Clinical Features.—These tumors are very rare and of more theoretical than practical interest. They occur at any age and several cases are described in children and even in infants. The clinical signs are not unlike those of the more common medulloblastoma for they give rise to signs of increased intracranial pressure, and sometimes to signs of meningeal irritation. The cranial nerves are frequently involved and signs indicative of local lesions in the brain are common. There are frequently pronounced mental disturbances. The course is relatively rapid in most cases. The spinal fluid may show no changes or there may be several hundred cells and greatly increased protein content. No doubt, the cells are derived from the tumor but they are usually reported as lymphocytes. In some cases there is no sugar in the spinal fluid. The clinical picture is frequently confused with that of tuberculous meningitis. Needless to say it is almost impossible to make the diagnosis during life though one might be justified in making a diagnosis of tumor meningitis. Treatment is entirely ineffectual.

BIBLIOGRAPHY

BAILEY, P.: Intracranial sarcomatous tumors of leptomeningeal origin. Arch. Surg., **18**:1359, 1929.

BERG, L.: Hypoglychorrhachia of non-infectious origin: diffuse meningeal neoplasia. Neurology, **3**:811, 1953.

HANBERRY, J. AND DUGGER, G.: Perithelial sarcoma of the brain. Arch. Neurol. & Psychiat., **71**:732, 1954.

LICHTENSTEIN, B. W. AND ETTLESON, A.: Diffuse mesothelioma of the leptomeninges. Arch. Path., **24**:497, 1937.

TOP, F. H. AND BROSIUS, W. L.: Diffuse sarcomatosis of the meninges. J. Pediat., **10**:27, 1937.

Primary Melanoblastosis of the Leptomeninges

Pathological Anatomy.—It is now well known that pigment-laden cells, the chromatophores, may be found in the pia-arachnoid of every normal brain, if diligent search is made for them. In some instances they are so numerous that the basilar meninges are stained black. In very rare, but interesting cases, malignant growths may arise from these cells producing a diffuse infiltration of the basilar meninges, so that the whole base of the brain is stained black. The cells extend by way of the subarachnoid spaces, infiltrate the cranial nerves and force their way into the perivascular spaces

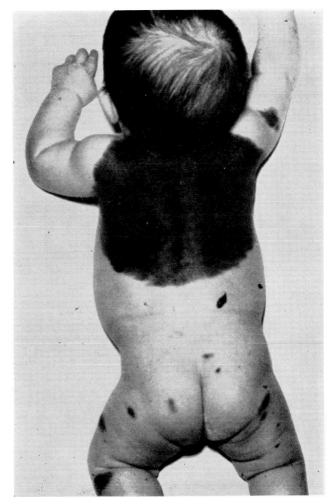

Fig. 251. Gigantic melanotic mole. (From Fox, H., Emery, J. L., Goodbody, R. A. and Yates, P. O. Neurocutaneous Melanosis. Arch of Disease in Childhood. 1964, vol. 39, p. 508. By permission of the authors, editor and publishers.)

of the cortex and brain-stem. The cisternae are finally obliterated, producing hydrocephalus and increased intracranial pressure. In some cases these tumors metastasize to parts of the body remote from the nervous system. Usually there are no large tumor masses and the process is a diffuse one.

Clinical Features.—The symptoms are those of "tumor meningitis." There are frequently psychic disturbances and changes of personality at the onset. Later there are symptoms of increased intracranial pressure such as headache and vomiting but the fundi may remain normal throughout the entire course of the disease. Palsies of the cranial nerves are usually ob-

served and several nerves may be involved on both sides, causing polyneuritis cranialis. In many cases there is some evidence of meningeal irritation. If the process extends into the spinal canal, there may be root pains and multiple or single lesions of the spinal cord. Pain in the back is very frequent.

Melanosis or melanoma of the leptomeninges is frequently associated with pigmentation of the skin. There may be merely areas of dark pigmentation, large or small or melanomas which may be benign or malignant. The large melanomas sometimes have the distribution of bathing trunks. About half of the malignant melanomas metastasize to the nervous system.

Various defects of development are described in such cases. Defective development of the brain and the cerebellum are described with mental defects and convulsions.

Pigmented cells may be demonstrated in some but not in all cases. There is apt to be xanthochromia and a great increase of white cells of various types. Protein is greatly increased. Dr. Arthur King has told me of a case in which the spinal fluid was of an inky black color. Melanin may be found in the urine in some cases.

BIBLIOGRAPHY

FARNELL, F. J. AND GLOBUS, J. H.: Primary melanoblastosis of the leptomeninges and brain. Arch. Neurol. & Psychiat., 25:803, 1931.

FISCHER, S.: Primary perivascular cerebral, cerebellar and leptomeningeal melanoma with predisposition to naevi verrucosi. Acta psychiat. scand., 31:21, 1956.

FOX, H. *et al.*: Neurocutaneous melanosis. Arch. of Dis. Childh., 39:508, 1964.

HOFFMAN, H. J. AND FREEMAN, A.: Primary malignant leptomeningeal melanoma in association with giant hairy nevi. Jour. Neurosurg., 26:62, 1967.

KING, A., CHAMBERS, J. AND GAREY, J.: Primary malignant melanomas of the spinal cord. Arch. Neurol. & Psychiat., 68:266, 1952.

REED, W. B. *et al.*: Giant pigmented nevi, melanoma and leptomeningeal melanocytosis. Arch. of Dermat., 91: 100, 1965.

PRIMARY NEOPLASMS OF THE SKULL

Introduction.—Among the growths arising within the walls of the cranium we may mention sarcomas, osteosarcomas, periosteal sarcomas, epidermoids, a few rare hemangiomas of the vault, osteomas of the cranium and nasal sinuses and osteochondromas of the base. The sarcomas of various types are most common. These always destroy the bone very rapidly and often cause a palpable tumor under the scalp. Pulsation transmitted from within the cranium may be noted, thus revealing that the bone has been eroded. In some cases new bone may be formed within the growth.

Osteomas of a variety of types are described. Some of these are merely small endostoses, which spring up from the base, often from the lesser wing of the sphenoid, the clinoid processes or the floor of the middle fossa.

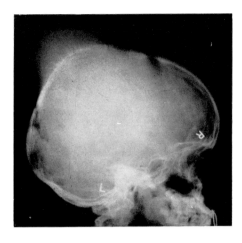

Fig. 252. Sarcoma of the skull.

Some are seen near the acoustic foramen. There are also massive bony tumors arising from the vault. These must be distinguished from the local form of osteitis fibrosa which is described elsewhere. Osteochondromas are found, as a rule, at the base of the skull but these are excessively rare. The osteomas of the nasal sinuses present such a distinctive picture that I shall devote a brief section to their description.

BIBLIOGRAPHY

HERTZ, H.: Haemangiomas of the skull. Papers dedicated to Dr. Poul Iversen. Rosenkilde and Bagger, Copenhagen, Nov. 20, 1949.

ROWBOTHAM, G. F.: Neoplasms that grow from bone-forming elements. Brit. J. Surg., **45**:123, 1957.

OSTEOMAS OF THE ACCESSORY NASAL SINUSES

Pathological Anatomy.—These tumors are rare but more than 200 cases have been described. They invariably arise in the accessory nasal sinuses. The frontal sinus is the site of origin in about 40 per cent of all cases and the ethmoids, antra and sphenoids are less frequently involved. These growths are composed of very dense bone with concentric lamellae and scanty Haversian canals. They are connected by a small pedicle with the bony wall of the sinus and consequently, as they expand, they carry the mucous membrane before them. The tumor is, therefore, always separated from healthy bone by the remnants of the mucous membrane and numerous mucoceles are usually found surrounding it. The orbit is frequently invaded and large masses of bone may extend into the cranial cavity. As a result of obstruction of drainage from the sinuses, infections and orbital abscesses are common. Despite their great density, some of these osteomas grow rapidly and show a tendency to recurrence if their removal is not complete.

Clinical Features.—We may restrict the discussion to osteomas arising in

the frontal and ethmoid sinuses, for these are the type most apt to cause neurological disturbances.

The frontal sinus osteomas appear as slowly growing bony tumors under the skin of the forehead, usually very close to the midline. Fifty per cent arc said to appear during adolescence or before. The growth, as a rule, extends into the roof of the orbit pressing the bulb downward, outward and forward, thus producing exophthalmos, diplopia, strabismus and, perhaps, edema of the orbit. Evidences of infection of the sinuses or orbital abscess may complicate the picture. In many cases the anterior fossa is invaded, giving rise to signs of compression of the frontal lobe and to increased intracranial pressure. In an interesting case described by Armitage, the tumor had penetrated into the anterior horn of the lateral ventricle and a communication had been formed between the nasal passages and the ventricle with leaking of cerebrospinal fluid from the nose and insufflation of air into the ventricular system. There were multiple mucoceles within the frontal lobe. The patient had been conscious of a splashing sound within his head at times which was no doubt produced by mixture of air and fluid in the ventricle.

Osteomas arising within the ethmoid sinuses also extend into the orbit but the invasion is more posterior than that of the frontal osteomas. Consequently, they push the eye forward rather than downward. They compress the optic nerve, causing optic atrophy and blindness and in the same way they involve the third, fourth and sixth nerves as they enter the sphenoidal fissure. Invasion of the cribriform plate is apt to cause anosmia. In most cases no bony tumor is palpable externally. Cushing has described four cases of this nature. Leakage of cerebrospinal fluid from the nose was observed as well as pneumocephaly. In one case a mucocele was found capping the tumor which had penetrated the frontal lobe.

Walsh and Harrison both describe cases of advanced osteomas with compression of the optic nerves and complete blindness. These were believed to have arisen in the sphenoid sinus.

Diagnosis.—The clinical signs described above may be suggestive of osteoma, especially if a firm tumor presents externally but the diagnosis rests chiefly upon the roentgenographic findings. The appearance of very dense nodular shadows in relation to the nasal sinuses should strongly suggest the diagnosis of osteoma. Care must be taken to distinguish the meningiomas, which often invade the skull and cause hyperostoses under the scalp.

Treatment.—Craniotomy and removal of the growth offers the only hope of relief but the mortality from infection has been very high in the past. No doubt the use of penicillin and sulfonamides will make the operation much safer. The nasal approach is not feasible for the dura is often penetrated by the tumor or torn at operation and such openings must be care-

fully closed with a facial transplant if meningitis or brain abscess is to be avoided.

CASE HISTORY (Path. 12654–U. 26258).—*Osteoma of the right frontal sinus, present at birth, causing exophthalmos on the right with optic atrophy. Gradual increase in symptoms. Death after operation.*

G. H. was noted to have undue prominence of the right eye at birth. She was otherwise healthy and grew and developed normally. Year by year the right eye seemed to protrude more and more. Vision in the right eye was reduced and finally edema of the tissues of the right orbit developed.

At the age of 14 years she came to the hospital for operation. The right eye was proptosed and the orbital and periorbital tissues much swollen. Vision in the right eye was only 10/200 and the disc was pale. Roentgenograms showed a dense shadow just above the right bulb which had displaced the inner table of the frontal bone inwards and the outer table anteriorly. The osteoma was removed with some difficulty. Infection developed requiring a second operation which proved fatal. At post-mortem the dura was found to be exceptionally vascular as if there were an angiomatous change present and several small fibromata were found upon the cranial nerves which suggested von Recklinghausen's disease.

BIBLIOGRAPHY

ARMITAGE, G.: Osteoma of the frontal sinus with particular reference to its intracranial complications and with report of a case. Brit. J. Surg., **13**:565, 1930-31.

CUSHING, H.: Experiences with orbito-ethmoidal osteomata having intra-cranial complications, with report of four cases. Surg. Gynec. & Obst., **44**:721, 1927.

HARRISON, W. J.: A case report of osteoma of the orbits resulting in bilateral optic atrophy. Am. J. Ophth., **25**:1233, 1942.

WALSH, F. B.: *Loc. cit.*

TUMORS OF THE GLOMUS JUGULARE

The glomus jugulare is one of a number of small bodies which are believed to be chemoreceptors. The largest of these is the carotid body. The glomus jugulare is very small and is situated on the dome of the jugular bulb within the temporal bone. It is composed of epithelioid cells in small alveolar clusters surrounded by delicate collagenous tissues. Almost one hundred neoplasms are reported which have arisen from the glomus jugulare. They present the same structure as the normal glomus.

The growth may begin in adolescence. The temporal bone is involved first. There is deafness, tinnitus, vertigo, discharge from the ear and often hemorrhage. Pulsation of the drum may be seen and a bruit may be heard over the mastoid bone. Vascular polyps present in the external canal and the diagnosis may be made by biopsy. The growth extends eventually into the posterior fossa and involves the ninth, tenth, eleventh and twelfth nerves. The fifth and sixth nerves may also be involved and the seventh

nerve is often damaged in its passage through the temporal bone. Ataxia and nystagmus are late signs and indicate involvement of the brain stem or cerebellum. Hydrocephalus occurs late if at all. In ten cases the carotid bodies were also involved. It is impossible to remove these growths except in the very earliest stages. They are apparently to some extent radiosensitive.

BIBLIOGRAPHY

ALFORD, B. R. AND GUILFORD, F. R.: Tumors of the glomus jugulare. Laryngoscope, **72**:765, 1962.

BICKERSTAFF, E. AND HOWELL, J. S.: Neurological importance of tumors of the glomus jugulare. Brain, **76**:567, 1953.

GORLIN, R. J. *et al.*: Multiple glomus tumors of the pseudocavernous hemangioma type. Arch. of Derm., **82**:776, 1960.

GUILD, S. R.: The glomus jugulare, a non-chromaffin paraganglion in man. Ann. Otol. Rhin. & Laryng., **62**:1045, 1953.

HENSON, R. A., CRAWFORD, J. V. AND CAVANAUGH, J. B.: Tumors of the glomus jugulare. J. Neurol., Neurosurg. & Psychiat., **16**:127, 1953.

LADENHEIM, J. C. AND SACHS, E.: Familial tumors of the glomus jugulare. Neurology, **11**:303, 1961.

SIKERT, R. G.: Neurologic manifestations of tumors of the glomus jugulare. Arch. Neurol. & Psychiat., **76**:1, 1956.

MALIGNANT TUMORS OF THE NASOPHARYNX

Pathological Anatomy.—A number of growths arise in the nasal sinuses, nasal passages and basilar portions of the skull which may be discussed conveniently at this point. In adult life carcinoma is found most frequently in this region but among children sarcomas of various types are more common. Lymphosarcomas, adenosarcomas and mixed cell sarcomas are described and some pathologists mention endotheliomas. All of these are infiltrating and locally malignant and some of them metastasize by the blood stream. Frequently these growths invade the cranium extending into the anterior or middle fossa and into the orbit by way of the sphenoid fissure. The cranial nerves are involved at their foramina of exit or by metastatic deposits in the cervical lymph nodes. Sometimes the growth strips the dura from the base and compresses the brain without invading it. Abscess of the brain or purulent meningitis may be associated.

Clinical Features.—These growths are rare during childhood but we have seen a small number between the ages of 6 and 15 years. The symptoms are subject to considerable variation but in at least one third of all cases the nervous system is involved. In a large percentage of cases the neurological symptoms are the first to appear and we have frequently found extensive palsies of the cranial nerves when no growth is apparent on nasopharyngeal examination.

One of the commonest types of malignant tumor arises near the opening of the Eustachian tube in the lateral pharyngeal wall, and extends under

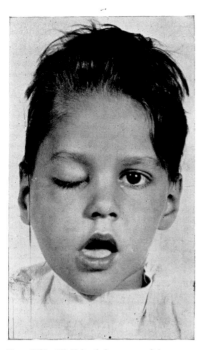

Fig. 253. Child of 4 years with nasopharyngeal carcinoma. He has palsies of cranial nerves 3, 4, 5, 6 and 7, occlusion of the Eustachian tube, infiltration of the soft palate by the growth and a firm mass under the angle of the jaw.

the mucous membrane. The second and third branches of the fifth nerve are involved early causing pain and numbness in the face. Deafness of conduction type soon appears due to occlusion of the Eustachian tube. The growth may involve the capsule of the jaw joint or may invade the pterygoid muscles causing deviation of the jaw. The levator veli palati is also frequently infiltrated causing immobilization of the soft palate. Next the growth invades the sphenoid fissure and the orbit involving the third, fourth and sixth nerves and causing exophthalmos and oculomotor palsies. The optic nerve may also be compressed and vision may be lost. In some cases the sella is invaded and one finds symptoms referable to the pituitary gland, the infundibulum and the optic chiasm. Loss of sense of smell is common but since the nasal passages are frequently occluded, its significance is not always clear. Frequently the ninth, tenth, eleventh and twelfth nerves are paralyzed. This may result from deposits in the lymph nodes of the retroparotid space or from involvement of the nerves in their foramina at the base of the skull. The temporal bone may be infiltrated causing nerve deafness and the Gasserian ganglion may be invaded by way of the foramen ovale. In my experience the facial nerve has been involved only once. In only rare cases are there large intracranial tumor masses and these are usually found in the middle fossa. The growth may often be palpated in the lateral pharyngeal wall where it invades the soft palate and enlarged lymph nodes are eventually found in the retroparotid space. Roentgenograms of the base of the skull are often helpful in the diagnosis for in many cases erosion of the base of the middle fossa is seen. Growths arising in the deeper portions of the parotid gland must be distinguished.

CASE HISTORY (Path. 12500—U. 42345).—*Boy of 11 years developed pain in right cheek, diplopia, nose bleed, headache, vomiting and finally loss of vision after 10 months. Examination showed involvement of cranial nerves 1, 2, 3, 4, 5, 6, 9, 10, 11 on the right. Complete blindness and optical atrophy. Spasticity and weakness of the left arm. Death. Post-mortem*

examination. Carcinoma of the nasopharynx invading base of the skull and involving the cranial nerves.

V. S., a schoolboy of 11 years, developed pain in the right cheek and upper jaw. Shortly after this he became deaf in the right ear. Still later there was diplopia and the right eyelid began to droop. Vision became impaired in the right eye. Several nosebleeds occurred and nasal obstruction developed on the right side. Violent headaches and vomiting appeared some six months after the onset and the child seemed to be drowsy and at times confused after this. The patient slowly grew weak and lost weight. Some nine months after the onset he became quite blind and bedfast. The left arm was now partially paralysed.

Examination about 10 months after the beginning of the illness revealed an undernourished pale boy of the given age who was semistuporous. There was a slight firm swelling in the right temporal region. No lymph nodes were palpable in the neck. There was complete loss of sense of smell. Vision was lost and the optic nerve heads showed complete primary optic atrophy. The right eye was slightly more prominent than the left, and there was complete paralysis of the right third, fourth and sixth nerves. There was anesthesia over the distribution of the right fifth nerve and the jaw deviated to the right apparently because of mechanical changes in the right jaw joint rather than paralysis of the motor root. There was loss of hearing in the right ear of conduction type. The right side of the soft palate, pharynx and larynx were paralysed. Definite weakness and spasticity was found in the left arm but there was only slight increase of tendon reflexes in the left leg. Nose and throat examination revealed some increase of adenoid tissue in the vault of the nasopharynx. A neoplasm was suspected but several bits of tissue removed for biopsy showed merely inflammatory changes. A few days later the child died.

Post-mortem examination revealed an extensive carcinoma infiltrating base of the skull, the nasopharynx and the maxilla. There was a large mass in the right middle fossa which had compressed the temporal lobe. The sella and the sphenoid sinus were destroyed and the hypophysis, the infundibulum and the optic chiasm were all destroyed by infiltration and compression. The right orbit was invaded and beginning invasion of the left orbit was evident. Tumor tissue was found under the mucous membranes on either side of the pharynx extending down into the retroparotid space on the right. The soft palate was infiltrated on the right and the opening of the Eustachian tube was occluded.

BIBLIOGRAPHY

CROWE, S. J. AND BAYLOR, J. W.: Benign and malignant growths of the nasopharynx and their treatment with radium. Arch. Surg., **6**:429, 1923.

GODTFRIEDSON, E.: Malignant nasopharyngeal tumors. Acta psychiatra et neurologica. Sup. XXXIX. 1-323, 1944.

TROTTER, W.: On certain clinically obscure malignant tumors of the nasopharyngeal wall. Brit. Med. J., **2**:1057, 1911.

WALSH, F. B.: Ophthalmologic signs of malignant nasopharyngeal tumours. Read before the Canadian Ophthalmological Soc., 1948.
WOLTMAN, H.: Malignant tumors of the nasopharynx with involvement of the nervous system. Arch. Neurol. & Psychiat., 8:412, 1922.

TUMORS OF THE OLFACTORY NEUROEPITHELIUM

Mendeloff reviews 20 cases of these tumors which have already been published and adds 6 cases of his own. These growths are composed of undifferentiated cells resembling neuroblasts. Rosettes are found in some instances. Two types are distinguished: (1) The olfactory neurocytoma which is not only locally invasive but gives rise to distant metastases. (2) The olfactory neuroepithelioma which is apparently only locally invasive. The precise origin of these growths is not established. It has been suggested that they arise in the olfactory epithelial cells, in the olfactory placode and in the organ of Jacobson.

The onset of symptoms may occur at any age. In one case symptoms developed at the age of 8 years. Among the 6 cases of Mendeloff, half of the patients came under observation in adolescence.

The first symptom is usually nasal obstruction or nosebleed. Anosmia is also an early symptom. The growths invade the nasal sinuses and the orbits and soon penetrate the base of the skull and extend into the frontal lobes.

Early operation and roentgenotherapy are advised and in some cases seem to have been successful. These growths are radiosensitive to some extent. They are always dangerous.

BIBLIOGRAPHY

MENDELOFF, J.: Olfactory neuroepithelial tumors. Cancer, 10:944, 1957.

NEOPLASMS ARISING FROM BLASTOMERIC DEFECTS

Introduction.—These tumors arise from nests of cells which have become misplaced during embryonic growth and, therefore, may be composed of tissues which have no place within the cranium under normal conditions. The commonest type is, perhaps, the epidermoid or pearly tumor of Cruveilhier. Differing from this only in the possession of the deeper layers of the skin, hair follicles and, perhaps, the sebaceous glands is the dermoid tumor, which seems to be somewhat rarer. If several different tissues, such as bone, teeth, muscle, etc., are included within the growth, it is termed a teratoma. Such tumors represent portions of a second individual and are in reality malformations which may, however, give rise to neoplasms. A few rare cases of intracranial lipoma have been reported and a number of chordomas or chordoblastomas, which are believed to represent malignant degeneration of remnants of the primitive notochord.

CHORDOBLASTOMAS

Pathological Anatomy.—These rare tumors arise from remnants of the primitive notochord which are found upon the clivus Blumenbachii in about 2 per cent of all autopsies. They are milky white with a translucent jelly-like appearance and nodular surface. They arise in the base of the sphenoid bone and may extend into the nasopharynx or orbits or upwards into the third ventricle. Histologically they are composed of vacuolated cells, arranged in cords or masses. The cells are of variable size and are widely separated by intracellular material, containing mucin. The same tumors may be found in the sacral spine and, indeed, at any level of the neuraxis.

Clinical Features.—These tumors sometimes involve the chiasm, causing bitemporal hemianopia. By extending backwards they cause pressure on the pons and peduncles, producing ataxia and paraparesis. In several cases, extension of the growth under the base has given rise to multiple cranial nerve palsies. Invasion of the nasopharynx is described. Roentgenographic examination of the base of the skull by means of plates under the patient's chin and the rays coming from the parietal region may reveal destruction of the sphenoid bone and at least suggest the diagnosis. Adenocarcinomas of the hypophysis may give rise to the same symptoms.

BIBLIOGRAPHY

BAILEY, P. AND BAGDASAR, B.: Intracranial chordoblastoma. Am. J. Path., 5:439, 1929.

BURROW, J. LEF. AND STEWART, M. J.: Malignant spheno-occipital chordoma. J. Neurol. & Psychopath., 4:205, 1923.

FOOTE, R. F. *et al.:* Chordoma in siblings. California Med., **88**:383, 1958.

HASS, G. M.: Chordomas of the cranium and cervical portion of the spine: Review of the literature with report of a case. Arch. Neurol. & Psychiat., **32**:300, 1934.

KAMRIN, R. P. *et al.:* Diagnosis and treatment of chordoma. J. Neurol., Neurosurg. & Psychiat., **27**:157, 1964.

POPPEN, J. L. AND KING, A. B.: Chordoma. Experience with thirteen cases. J. Neurosurg., **9**:139, 1952.

SASSIN, J. F. AND CHUTORIAN, A. M.: Intracranial chordoma in children. Arch. of Neurol., **17**:89, 1967.

STEWART, M. J. AND MORIN, J. E.: Chordoma; a review with report of a new sacrococcygeal case. J. Path. & Bact., **29**:41, 1926.

VAN WAGENEN, W. P.: Chordoblastoma of the basilar plate of the skull and eccordosis physaliphora spheno-occipitalis. Arch. Neurol. & Psychiat., **34**:548, 1935.

WALSH, F. B.: *Loc. cit.*

PEARLY TUMORS

Dermoids and Epidermoids

Pathological Anatomy.—These tumors are due to defects in embryonic development by which bits of squamous epithelium become detached from

the surface and implanted within the body. Those associated with dermal sinuses must be due to defective closure of the neural tube. Since these growths are of essentially the same type, it seems unnecessary to describe them separately.

The epidermoids resemble mother of pearl in the gross for the capsule is pure white with a pearly sheen. The walls are composed of epithelium and Bailey has described four layers: the stratum durum, stratum granulosum, stratum fibrosum and stratum cellulosum. The resemblance to the structure of the epidermis is very striking. These growths are filled with a scaly white debris containing cholesterol crystals and evidently derived from the accumulation of exfoliated cells of the lining membrane.

The dermoids may be brown or reddish. They differ from the epidermoids only in the possession of the deeper layers of the dermis in their capsule. Most of them contain hair and hair follicles as well as sebaceous glands. The content of these tumors is a yellow, greasy material. The capsule may become calcified.

Clinical Features.—These tumors grow slowly but may cause symptoms early in life. The clinical picture depends upon the location of the growth. They are found in a variety of sites.

In the *orbits* pearly tumors behave as any other tumor displacing the bulb and causing exophthalmos. In the *pericranium* they present as rounded masses in the scalp with erosion of the underlying bone from without inward. In the *diploe* they cause separation of the inner and outer tables of the skull.

In the *temporal bone* they are found in the petrous or at the injunction of the petrous and mastoid bone. They cause slowly progressive facial palsy, deafness and loss of vestibular reactions. The deafness is of middle ear type at first but later nerve deafness develops. Eventually these growths erode into the middle or posterior fossa. Erosion of the temporal bone may be demonstrated in roentgenograms of the base. They must be distinguished from cholesteatomatous masses developing in the middle ear as a result of ingrowth of stratified epithelium through longstanding perforation of the drum due to chronic otitis.

In the *region* of the *sella* and *fossa interpeduncularis*. In such cases there may be compression of the optic chiasm and symptoms suggesting suprasellar cyst. The clinoids may be thin and the sulcus chiastimaticus broader than normal. The optic foramina may be enlarged.

Others are found in the *meninges* under the *temporal lobe* or over the *lateral aspect* of the *hemisphere*. The growth may press deeply into the cortex causing hemiplegia and convulsions.

In the *cerebellopontine angle* with involvement of the fifth, sixth, seventh and eighth nerves. Pain in the face may be a feature.

Such tumors are sometimes found in the *roof* of the *third ventricle* and region of the *pineal body*. The symptoms may suggest a pinealoma.

A large percentage of pearly tumors are found in the *fourth ventricle* and *vermis* of the cerebellum where they cause increased intracranial pressure and cerebellar symptoms. Some are inside the occipital bone but outside the dura. These erode the bone. Of the intradural tumors in the posterior fossa about half are associated with dermal sinuses either complete or incomplete. If complete, the sinus extends from the skin to the tumor. The canal in the bone is usually narrow and oblique so it is not always demonstrated in roentgenograms of the skull. The sinus is evidenced in the skin by a dimple and by a small prominence. When the sinus is complete it may convey infection into the cranium causing abscess or meningitis. The staphylococcus aureus is the commonest organism found in such cases. Such infections may be the first sign of the growth for they may occur when the tumor is still very small.

Dermoids and epidermoids may rupture spontaneously and the meninges may be soiled by the contents of such tumors at operation. In such cases there may be shock and a severe reaction. The spinal fluid may be oily. The meningeal reaction may lead to fibrous adhesions and chronic hydrocephalus.

Pearly tumors are found in the *spinal canal,* most often in the lumbar

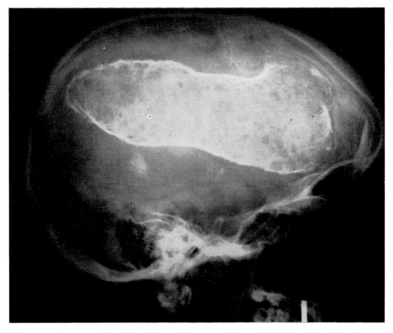

Fig. 254. Roentgenogram showing dermoid cyst with calcified wall. (By the courtesy of Dr. Walsh.)

region. They are often associated with sacral dermal sinuses which may convey infection into the canal. In rare instances there has been leakage of spinal fluid from such sinuses. I have seen one case in which rupture of the dermoid resulted in filling of the spinal subarachnoid space with sebaceous material. There was rigidity of the lumbar spine and hips but no weakness, sensory loss or change in the reflexes (see page 979 C.W.).

Choremis *et al.* found one or more epidermoid tumors in the spinal canal in 6 children between the ages of 7 and 12 years who had been treated for tuberculous meningitis between 3 and 7 years before. Many spinal punctures had been made and a needle was used without a stylet. One tumor was found at the tenth thoracic segment. The others were all in the lumbar region. The authors believe that bits of epithelium were carried into the spinal canal by the needle and become implanted in the meninges. Black and German describe a case in which an epidermoid tumor was found lying between the two halves of the cord which displayed diastematomyelia.

Treatment.—The only treatment is operative removal. Great care must be taken to avoid soiling of the meninges. It must be kept in mind that these tumors are often infected.

BIBLIOGRAPHY

BAILEY, P.: Cruveilhier's "Tumeurs perlées." Surg. Gynec. & Obst., **31**:390, 1920.

BLACK, S. P. AND GERMAN, W. J.: Four congenital tumors found at operation within the vertebral canal. J. Neurosurg., **7**:49, 1950.

BUCY, P. C.: Intradiploic epidermoid of the skull. Arch. Surg., **31**:190, 1935.

CAREY, P. C.: Epidermoid and dermoid tumors of the orbit. Brit. J. Ophth., **42**:225, 1958.

CHOREMIS, C. *et al.*: Intraspinal epidermoid tumors in patients treated for tuberculous meningitis. Lancet, **ii**:437, 1956.

CRITCHLEY, McD. AND FERGUSON, F. R.: The cerebrospinal epidermoids. Brain, **51**:334, 1928.

FLEMING, J. F. R. AND BOTTERELL, E. H.: Cranial dermoid and epidermoid tumors. Surg. Gynec. & Obst., **109**:403, 1959.

JEFFERSON, G. AND SMALLEY, A. A.: Progressive facial palsy produced by intratemporal epidermoids. J. Laryng. and Otol., **53**:417, 1938.

KAY, F. A. AND PACK, G. T.: Cholesteatoma of the brain. Report of a tumor of unusual size. Arch. Neurol. & Psychiat., **19**:446, 1928.

LOGUE, V. AND TILL, K.: Posterior fossa dermoid cysts with special reference to intracranial infection. J. Neurol., Neurosurg. & Psychiat., **15**:1, 1952.

LOVE, J. G. AND KERNOHAN, J. W.: Dermoid and epidermoid tumors of the central nervous system. J.A.M.A., **107**:1876, 1936.

MATSON, D. D. AND INGRAHAM, F. D.: Intracranial complications of congenital dermal sinuses. Pediatrics, **8**:463, 1952.

OLIVECRONA, H.: Suprasellar cholesteatomas. Brain, **55**:122, 1932.

TYTUS, J. S. AND PENNYBACKER, J.: Pearly tumors in relation to the central nervous system. J. Neurol., Neurosurg. & Psychiat., **19**:241, 1956.

WALSH, F. B.: *Loc. cit.*

LIPOMAS

Intracranial lipomas are very rare but more than sixty cases have been published. They seem to arise in the pia but may be imbedded deeply in the nervous system. As a rule, their structure is that of adipose tissue elsewhere in the body but lipoblastomas are also described. It is claimed that these growths are found most commonly between the superior portions of the hemispheres lying upon the corpus callosum. In the anteroposterior view roentgenograms of the skull often show symmetrical crescentic bands due to calcification in the walls of the lipoma. This picture seems to be characteristic. Arteriograms may show dilated arteries above the corpus callosum. They are also seen at the base of the brain, in the brain-stem and cerebellum. Nordkin *et al.* point out that in some instances subcutaneous lipomas at the vertex may be associated with lipomas of the corpus callosum. A slender stalk of the subcutaneous tumor may extend through the skull and connect with the intracranial mass.

In a large percentage of cases lipomas cause no symptoms and are found

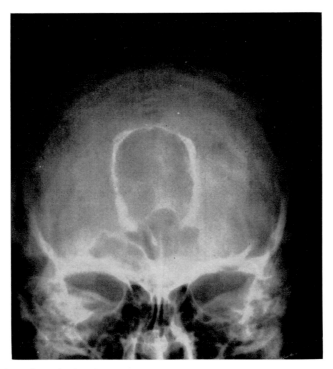

Fig. 255. Calcium deposits in the capsule of lipoma of the corpus callosum. The arteriogram showed dilated anterior cerebral arteries within the lipoma. The anterior horns of the ventricles were separated. The diagnosis was verified by Dr. George Smith.

unexpectedly in post-mortem examination. There is little evidence that intracranial lipomas expand as true neoplasms do. Their behavior suggests that they are to be regarded as malformations rather than neoplasms. When evidences of damage to the nervous system are found in such cases, they often seem to be due to associated malformations of the brain. The more embryonic type of lipoma, however, may show active growth and may behave as other neoplasms do.

It is stated that lipomas may grow larger if the patient gains weight and if the patient is put on a reducing diet, the lipoma may diminish and there may be some reduction of the symptoms.

Spinal lipomas are described under spinal cord tumors q.v.

BIBLIOGRAPHY

BAKER, A. B. AND ADAMS, J. M.: Lipomatosis of the central nervous system. Am. J. Cancer, 34:214, 1938.
EWING, J.: Neoplastic Diseases. 3rd Ed. Philadelphia, W. B. Saunders Co., 1928.
NORDIN, W. A., TESLUK, H. AND JONES, R. K.: Lipoma of the corpus callosum. Arch. Neurol. & Psychiat., 74:300, 1955.
SPERLING, S. J. AND ALPERS, B. J.: Lipoma and osteolipoma of the brain. J. Nerv. & Ment. Dis., 83:13, 1936.
SUTTON, D.: Radiologic diagnosis of lipoma of the corpus callosum. Brit. J. Radiol., 22:534, 1949.

TERATOMAS

These are very rare although a large number of cases have been described, probably because of their great interest. They may contain teeth, bone, hair, nails, skin and in fact parts of any organ of the body. It is evident, therefore, that they represent a part of a second individual and, hence, closely related to the monsters. Some of these tumors are not true new growths, but malignant changes may develop in teratomas and give rise to metastases. Teratomas may occur in almost any part of the cranium. They are sometimes seen in the pineal region, in the fourth ventricle and base of the skull. Since many contain bone or teeth, they are usually demonstrable in roentgenograms of the skull. Dr. Otenasek recently found a teratoma in the tip of the conus of the spinal cord in a boy who had been incontinent for years but had displayed no other neurological symptoms. The patient had red hair and red hair was also found in the teratoma.

BIBLIOGRAPHY

BUCY, P. C. AND BUCHANAN, D. N.: Teratoma of the spinal cord. Surg. Gynec. & Obst., 60:1137, 1935.
HOSOI, K.: Teratomas and teratoid tumors of the brain. Arch. Path., 9:1207, 1930.
INGRAHAM, F. D. AND BAILEY, O. T.: Cystic teratomas and teratoid tumors of the central nervous system in infancy and childhood. J. Neurosurg., 3:511, 1946.
LEVIN, P. M.: Glioblastoma arising in a hypothalamic teratoid and invading the neurohypophysis. J. Neuropath. & Exp. Neurol., 1:146, 1942.

METASTATIC NEOPLASMS OF THE BRAIN

Metastatic tumors of the brain are not infrequent in adult life but seem to be uncommon during childhood, probably because carcinoma, which is the commonest malignant growth in later life, is very rare in childhood. Daniel and Mathews state that in 95 girls between the ages of 12 and 21 years old who were operated upon fibroadenomas were found in 90, two had cystic mastitis, one had an intraductal papilloma, one a blue-domed cyst and one, a lipoma. There were no malignant growths though carcinoma does occur. However, sarcomas of various types, hypernephromas, chloromas and, indeed, almost all malignant neoplasms of childhood, may give rise to secondary growths in the brain as a result of cellular emboli conveyed by the blood stream. Tumors of the sympathetic system, which are discussed elsewhere, are not unusual causes of cerebral metastases.

It is important to recognize intracranial metastases so as to avoid useless operations. In every case in which there is reason to suspect an intracranial tumor, one should look for growths elsewhere in the body. Sometimes the primary growth has been destroyed by radium and, when intracranial metastases appear some months or years later, there may be no physical signs of their origin. In some cases a single cerebral metastasis may produce symptoms identical with a primary tumor of the brain but in most cases, multiple lesions are present. Symptoms which cannot be explained on the basis of one growth are always suggestive of metastases. In some cases, there are innumerable small deposits within the brain and meninges, which cause psychic disturbances without definite focal signs and often without evidences of intracranial hypertension until late in the course. Lymphomas of various types and sarcomas may extend into the subarachnoid spaces, giving rise to "tumor meningitis" with signs of meningeal irritation and pleocytosis in the spinal fluid and involvement of the cranial nerves and spinal nerve roots. Melanotic sarcomas may act in this way. We have seen one case in which a malignant growth lodged on the heart valve and caused extensive cerebral damage by throwing off showers of emboli composed of tumor cells. Roentgenograms of the skull will sometimes show multiple areas of bone absorption which may be sharply defined or indistinct and moth-eaten in appearance. It is very important to obtain roentgenograms of the chest for neoplasms extending by way of the blood stream often produce deposits in the lungs.

The behavior of cerebral metastases is unpredictable. In some instances, growth is rapid, but they may grow slowly. A sudden onset suggestive of embolism is rare. Focal symptoms may come and go in such a way as to suggest fluctuating circulatory disturbances. Focal seizures also occur. In rare instances, erosion of a blood vessel causes cerebral hemorrhage. Sometimes,

a metastatic deposit becomes necrotic and only a thin walled cyst is found at operation.

Ventriculograms may offer some difficulties of interpretation. There may be evidences of only one large tumor or the deposits may be so numerous and so small that the ventricular system is symmetrical. In some cases, multiple tumors may be demonstrated very clearly, however. The brain scan is often helpful.

BIBLIOGRAPHY

DANDY, W. E.: Metastatic Tumors. Practice of Surgery, Dean Lewis, **12**:669, 1945.

DANIEL, W. A. AND MATHEWS, M. D.: Breast tumors in adolescent girls. Pediatrics, **41**:743, 1968.

DODGE, H. W. JR., SAYRE, G. P. AND SVIEN, H. J.: Sugar content of the cerebrospinal fluid in diffuse neoplastic involvement of the meninges. Proc. Staff Meet. Mayo Clin., **27**:259, 1952.

GLOBUS, J. H. AND SELINSKY, H.: Metastatic tumors of the brain. Arch. Neurol. & Psychiat., **17**:481, 1927.

GRANT, F. C.: Intracranial malignant metastases. Ann. Surg., **84**:635, 1926.

KUFFER, F. *et al.*: Surgical complications in children undergoing cancer therapy. Ann. Surg., **167**:215, 1968.

LEVINSKY, W. J.: Spinal fluid sugar in meningeal tumor. New England Med. J., **268**:198, 1963.

McCORMACK, L. J., HAZARD, J. B., BELOVICH, D. AND GARDNER, W. J.: Identification of neoplastic cells in cerebrospinal fluid by a wet-film method. Cancer, **10**:1293, 1957.

McCORMACK, L. J., HAZARD, J. B., GARDNER, W. J. AND KLOTZ, J. G.: Cerebrospinal fluid changes in secondary carcinoma of meninges. Am. J. Clin. Path., **23**:470, 1953.

NAYLOR, B.: An exfoliative cytologic study of intracranial fluids. Neurology, **11**:560, 1961.

RAMIREZ, G. AND ANSFIELD, F.: Carcinoma of the breast in children. Arch. of Surgery, **96**:222, 1968.

SKOV-JENSEN, T. *et al.*: Malignant melanoma in children. Cancer, **19**:620, 1966.

SPRIGGS, A. I.: Malignant cells in cerebrospinal fluid. J. Clin. Path., **7**:122, 1954.

INCREASED INTRACRANIAL PRESSURE OF UNKNOWN ORIGIN

Definition.—This condition has been termed *pseudotumor cerebri, serous meningitis, Quincke's meningitis* and *arachnoiditis*. The essential feature is a pronounced increase of intracranial pressure which gives rise to all of the usual symptoms and signs, such as headache, vomiting, double vision, and papilledema, but for which none of the usual causes can be found. Occasionally headache is absent. Focal signs of cerebral damage are absent. Measurements of the spinal fluid pressure by spinal or ventricular puncture reveals moderate or pronounced elevation. The papilledema may be severe and prolonged so that optic atrophy may result. Ventriculograms reveal small or normal ventricles symmetrically placed. Hydrocephalus in the usual sense is thus ruled out. If the cerebral cortex is exposed at operation, one finds an excess of fluid in the subarachnoid spaces but release of this fluid and drainage of the ventricles does not reduce the intracranial pressure to the normal level. The cerebrospinal fluid is clear and does not contain an excess of cells or protein. It is abnormal only in its abundance and high pressure. Adolescent girls and young adult women are most frequently affected. Moore has published cases in children of 4, 6, 7½, 8 and 14 years.

The patients are sometimes rather obsese. Premenstrual edema aggravates the symptoms very definitely in some instances. Obviously cases of intracranial neoplasm will be sometimes included in this group by mistake.

Clinical Features.—The symptoms have already been outlined above by way of definition. It seems that these cases fall into two groups, an acute group of limited duration and a chronic type. In the first, the duration may be no more than a few weeks. Soon the symptoms begin to recede and the edema of the discs begins to diminish.

In rare cases, the condition is more persistent. After the first phase of the process, which seems to be exactly like that of the more acute cases, has passed the pressure does not fall to a normal level. The decompression continues to be firm and from time to time will bulge in alarming fashion. Dandy comments on the fact that this bulging may develop and disappear within a few minutes. As a rule, these patients do well. Even though it is clear that the intracranial pressure remains above the normal level, there is as a rule no tendency to the development of progressive optic atrophy. Possibly the decompression prevents the development of very high pressures which might produce this effect.

Not much can be said about the possible causes of this syndrome. It seems clear that there is an excess of fluid within the cranium which seems to lie within the brain as well as in the ventricles and meninges. In cases of brief duration I am confident that we are sometimes dealing with unsuspected dural sinus thrombosis. Such cases are common in infants and young children. If the onset of symptoms is preceded by otitis media, as in the cases termed otitic hydrocephalus by Symonds, sinus thrombosis is usually found. A case illustrating this possibility is given in abstract in the discussion of septic thrombosis of the dural sinuses. Arteriograms and venograms are helpful in establishing this diagnosis. Some types of toxic encephalopathy associated with edema of the brain following acute infections may give rise to a similar picture, and lead encephalopathy may also resemble the cases under consideration. Malignant hypertension and hypertension due to pheochromocytoma may cause papilledema. Rare causes of increased intracranial pressure are hypoparathyroidism, vitamin A poisoning, acute infectious polyneuritis, or the Guillain-Barre syndrome, Addison's disease, arteriovenous fistula and pulmonary emphysema. The last is associated with cyanosis, polycythemia, cor pulmonale, reduction of the oxygen content of the blood and increase of blood carbon dioxide. Headache and drowsiness are found in such cases as well as papilledema. Kyphoscoliosis, weakness of the muscles of respiration and excessive obesity may cause similar symptoms. Harris points out that elevation of the spinal fluid protein may cause increased intracranial pressure, as a result of communicating hydrocephalus, which is apparently produced by thickening of the meninges and possi-

bly obstruction of the Pacchioniam villi. When spinal fluid pressure is tested with a manometer which has been cleaned by detergents, fatal arachnoiditis may result with increased intracranial pressure. Nevertheless, it is evident that in most instances the cause is completely obscure. The origin of the chronic cases is even more mysterious. One might consider the possibility that we are dealing with a metabolic disorder involving retention of fluids.

Dees and McKay point out that pseudotumor cerebri may occur after prolonged treatment of children with adrenal steroids for asthma. The symptoms develop when the medication is stopped or reduced. The edema then recedes. We have recognized several cases of this type.

Lecks and Baker in a study of 17 cases state that in 2 cases soybean milk had been given to the child because of gastrointestinal allergy and 5 children had been receiving corticosteroids for prolonged periods.

O'Doherty states that tetracycline will cause acute benign increased intracranial pressure in older children. Lumbar puncture gives prompt and lasting relief.

Lubeck reports a case of iron deficiency anemia in a girl of fourteen years who developed papilledema with hemorrhages and exudates and a spinal fluid pressure of 280 mm. water. She recovered more rapidly when ferrous sulphate was administered. He states that the literature contained eleven other similar cases.

In my experience, death rarely results, though I have seen fatal rupture of the cortex when decompression was performed. Optic atrophy and loss of vision may result if the intracranial pressure is not properly controlled and mild pallor of the discs is apt to result whenever pronounced papilledema develops. Herniation of the cortex through the decompression often causes mild facial weakness on the opposite side and rupture of the cortex at operation may also cause focal signs. As a rule the patient makes essentially a complete recovery and the symptoms never recur.

No treatment is completely successful. Repeated spinal punctures with removal of spinal fluid has been performed for many years. In cases which do not yield to such treatment, subtemporal decompression is performed. More recently hypertonic saline and albumin have been given intravenously to reduce intracranial pressure but are not very effective. In 1958, intravenous injection of urea dissolved in 10 per cent invert sugar was recommended. This solution has a powerful dehydrating effect and reduces intracranial pressure promptly. The dangers include excessive dehydration, venous thrombosis, severe reactions in the tissues if the drug extravasates and uremia. It is claimed that a steroid, dexamethasone, is effective in reducing cerebral edema. The drug is given intravenously in 10.0 mgs dosage initially and then 4.0 mgs are given every six hours.

CASE HISTORY (U-129648 Sinai).—*Girl of 12 years with high grade increased intracranial pressure. Diagnosis of pseudotumor cerebri. Decompression. Prompt recovery.*

C. K., a girl of 12 years, was examined on November 14, 1955. The history was that of severe diffuse headaches for 2 weeks and of frequent vomiting for 4 days. There was no diplopia or other neurological symptoms. She had had no head injuries and no infections of any kind.

Examination revealed fresh, pronounced papilledema on both sides but no other neurological findings. She was not obese. The child was not dull or confused. The pulse was 68 and the blood pressure 110/66. Temperature was normal. The blood counts were normal. Roentgenograms of the skull revealed no abnormality. A ventriculogram was performed. The ventricles were small and symmetrical. Some difficulty was encountered in finding the ventricles.

A right subtemporal decompression was performed. The brain bulged so strongly that a small rupture of the cortex resulted. For a few days the child was extremely irritable and dull. Serum albumin was given in 100 cc. doses of 25 per cent solution. This had little effect. Vision was lost for about 4 days and then slowly returned to normal. This was regarded as a result of damage to the occipital lobes by the needle. The temperature was elevated for several days after the operation.

Soon the mental condition became normal. The papilledema receded. The subtemporal decompression which had bulged strongly became soft and the child was discharged from the hospital on November 27. Subsequently she remained well.

It is of interest that her first menstrual period was 2 months before the illness and she had her second period 2 days after she was admitted to the hospital.

CASE HISTORY (No. 662786).—*Girl of 13 years with severe and prolonged increased intracranial pressure. Diagnosis of pseudotumor made. Bilateral decompression required.*

C. W., a girl of 13 years, was first seen on January 25, 1954 in consultation with Dr. Otenasek. She had been troubled by severe headaches and frequent vomiting for 4 weeks and there had been diplopia for 3 weeks. Her menses had started 2 months before.

On examination the child was well developed and somewhat obese with much fat on the abdomen and thighs. The breasts and genitalia showed signs of puberty. The child was not dull or drowsy. Neurological examination revealed bilateral papilledema with hemorrhages which seemed to be fresh and paresis of the left external rectus. The spinal fluid pressure was measured at 230 mm water. The total protein content was 30 mg. A ventriculogram showed rather small ventricles symmetrically placed. For a time the child seemed to do well and the papilledema did not increase.

On February 15, however, it was found that the papilledema was increasing and fresh hemorrhages had developed. The headaches were severe again and the vomiting had returned. A second air study showed no

evidence of a neoplasm. The spinal fluid pressure was 270 mm. A right subtemporal decompression was performed. There was bulging of the decompression.

On March 27, the patient was admitted for the third time. The decompression was firm and tense. Fresh hemorrhages had appeared in the fundi. The spinal fluid pressure ranged from 290 to 360 mm. Repeated spinal punctures failed to reduce the intracranial pressure. On April 7, a left subtemporal decompression was performed.

After that the papilledema began to recede and the diplopia disappeared. There was still soft bulging of the decompressions. For more than a year after the second operation there was still some evidence of increased intracranial pressure as shown by soft bulging over the decompressions which varied in degree from time to time.

BIBLIOGRAPHY

BENSON, P. F. AND PHAROAH, P. O. D.: Benign intracranial hypertension due to adrenal steroid therapy. Guy's Hospital Rep., **109**:212, 1960.

CAPRILES, L. F.: Intracranial hypertension and iron-deficiency anemia. Arch. Neurol., **9**:147, 1963.

COHN, G. A.: Pseudotumor cerebri induced by steroids. J. Neurosurg., **20**:784, 1963.

CONN, H. O. *et al.:* Pulmonary emphysema simulating brain tumor. Am. J. Med., **22**:524, 1957.

DANDY, W. E.: Intracranial pressure without brain tumor. Ann. Surg., **106**:492, 1937.

DAVIDOFF, L. M.: Pseudotumor cerebri. Neurology, **6**:605, 1956.

DEES, S. AND McKAY, H. W.: Occurrence of pseudotumor cerebri during treatment of children with asthma by adrenal steroids. Pediatrics, **23**:1143, 1959.

DUNN, J., BAKER, G. S. AND WAGENER, H. P.: Pseudotumor cerebri. Proc. Staff Meet. Mayo Clinic, **30**:497, 1955.

ELKINS, C. AND RACK, F. J.: Cerebral pseudotumor or intracranial hypertension of unknown cause. New England J. Med., **244**:171, 1951.

FOLEY, J.: Benign forms of intracranial hypertension. Brain, **78**:1, 1955.

GREER, M.: Benign intracranial hypertension. Neurology, **13**:439, 1963.

————: Benign intracranial hypertension. Neurology, **13**:472, 1962.

————: Benign intracranial hypertension IV. Menarche. Neurology, **14**:569, 1964.

HARRIS, P.: Chronic progressive communicating hydrocephalus due to protein transudates from brain and spinal tumors. Development. Med. & Child Neurol., **4**:270, 1962.

JACOBSON, H. C. AND SHAPIRO, J. H.: Diagnosis of pseudotumor cerebri. Radiology, **82**:202, 1964.

JAVID, M.: Urea—The new use of an old agent. Surg. Clin. North America, **38**:907, 1958.

JEFFERSON, A.: A clinical correlation between encephalopathy and papilledema in Addison's disease. J. Neurol., Neurosurg. & Psychiat., **19**:21, 1956.

KREVSKY, S.: The bulging fontanelle syndrome following tetracycline administration. Mich. Med., **67**:597, 1968.

LECKS, H. L. AND BAKER, D.: Pseudotumor cerebri; an allergic phenomenon? Clin. Pediat., **4**:32, 1965.

LUBECK, M. J.: Papilledema caused by iron-deficiency anemia. Tr. Am. Acad. Ophth., **63**:306, 1959.

McALPINE, D.: Toxic hydrocephalus. Brain, **60**:180, 1937.

MOORE, R. B.: Pseudotumor. Pediatrics, **19**:266, 1957.

MORRICE, G. *et al.:* Vitamin A intoxication as a cause of pseudotumor cerebri. J.A.M.A., **173**:1802, 1960.

O'DOHERTY, N. J.: Acute benign intracranial hypertension in an infant receiving tetracycline. Develop. Med. Child. Neurol., **7**:677, 1965.

RYA, B. S. AND DUNBAR, H. S.: Thrombosis of dural venous sinuses as a cause of pseudotumor cerebri. Ann. Surg., **134**:376, 1951.

SAHS, E. G. AND HYNDMAN, O. R.: Intracranial hypertension of unknown cause, cerebral edema. Arch. Surg., **38**:428, 1939.

SIDELL, A. D. AND DALY, D. D.: The electroencephalogram in cases of benign intracranial hypertension. Neurology, **11**:413, 1961.

SYMONDS, C.: Otitic hydrocephalus. Neurology, **6**:681, 1956.

WAGENER, H. P.: Pseudotumor cerebri. Am. J. Med. Sc., **227**:214, 1954.

WALSH, F. B.: *Loc. cit.*

NEOPLASMS OF THE SPINAL CORD

Incidence.—Spinal cord tumors are uncommon in childhood and very rare in infancy. No large series of spinal tumors in childhood has been published and the statistics of various writers show great variation. Dandy's series of 36 verified spinal cord tumors include five cases in children under 15 years. Stookey found only eight cases in children under 12 years among 160 cases at all ages. Frazier and Elsberg observed a combined total of only five cases, despite their long experience. These discrepancies depend, no doubt, upon the source of the surgeons' material and the percentage of children included. In a study of the literature up to and including the year 1942, Hamby was able to discover a total of 214 cases of true neoplasms involving the spinal cord under the age of 15 years. Ross and Bailey have recently published a study of 13 cases of spinal cord tumors in childhood.

Pathological Anatomy.—In our experience, extradural sarcomas are most frequent in childhood. Most of these seem to arise in the epidural tissues and may extend for several segments along the cord. Others arise in the mediastinum or retro-peritoneal space and extend into the spinal canal by the intervertebral foramina or by erosion of the bone. Other sarcomas arise in the vertebrae and extend into the epidural space. Giant cell tumors of the spine of relatively benign type have been described. Less frequently,

TABLE V.—INCIDENCE OF SPINAL CORD TUMORS IN CHILDHOOD. Hamby.

	1933 Series		1943 Series		Total	
	NO.	PER CENT	NO.	PER CENT	NO.	PER CENT
Gliomas	23	23	21	18.4	44	20.6
Sarcomas	18	18	24	21	42	19.6
Dermoids	10	10	27	23.3	37	17.3
Neurinomas	7	7	16	14	23	10.7
Lipomas	7	7	3	2.6	10	4.7
Meningiomas	5	5	5	4.4	10	4.7
Chloromas	8	8	1	.9	9	4.2
Blood vessel tumors	2	2	5	4.4	7	3.3
Sympathetic tumors	4	4	2	1.8	6	2.8
Miscellaneous tumors	16	16	10	8.8	26	12.1
Total	100	100	114	99.6	214	100.0

we have found *neurofibromas*. There seems to be a manifestation of von Recklinghausen's disease in most cases. Intradural *meningiomas* which are so common among adults, are not common in childhood. *Gliomas* of the cord are, unfortunately, as common as the sarcomas. Some of these grow rapidly and seem to be very malignant and others grow slowly. They usually involve the posterior columns early. Ependymomas may arise in the central canal and extend for many segments along the cord. They are sometimes associated with syringomyelia. We have observed several cases in which *medulloblastomas* and other cellular *gliomas* of the brain have given rise to deposits in the spinal canal with compression of the spinal cord. In two cases, the spinal symptoms antedated the cerebral symptoms.

Kernohan has made a careful study of the gliomas of the spinal cord and reports that they fall into the same groups as the cerebral gliomas. He describes ependymomas, spongioblastomas, astroblastomas, medulloblastomas and ganglioneuromas. Unfortunately, he does not give the age incidence of the various types. There is good reason to believe that gliomas sometimes develop upon a basis of congenital defect. For example, we have seen several cases in which gliomas arose in association with myelodysplasia and spina bifida occulta.

A number of types of tumors are described which are to be ascribed to defects of development. Dermoids and epidermoids are sometimes encountered. These tumors may be associated with congenital dermal sinuses which offer a portal of entry for infection. Fulton and Kubie report two cases of teratomatous cysts containing mucous and ciliated cells. Wyburn-Mason has collected a number of cases of *hemangioblastomas* both within and without the dura which are frequently associated with cavities in the spinal cord similar to those of syringomyelia. Since these are often found in association with cerebellar hemangioblastomas and similar lesions in the retinae it is clear that they represent a manifestation of Lindau's disease. They rarely give rise to symptoms in childhood, however. A special type of neoplasm found in the sacral region is thought to arise from remnants of the neurenteric canal and others are found at any level of the cord which are termed chordomas and are thought to develop from the notochord.

Bassett describes lipomas of the cauda equina which are associated with fatty masses lying over the sacrum. These masses of fat are present at birth and may be mistaken for meningoceles. There is spina bifida. At operation the subcutaneous lipoma extends into the canal and penetrates the dura. It surrounds the roots of the cauda and the conus. Less commonly lipomas compress the cord and in some instances lie under the pia.

Clinical Features.—The first symptoms of *extramedullary spinal cord tumor* is in the vast majority of cases localized and persistent *pain* which is often associated with cutaneous hyperesthesia. This is due to compression

of a *spinal nerve root* and is naturally absent when the tumor is so situated that no roots are compressed. The distribution of the pain is that of the dermatome supplied by the affected root. As a rule, the pain is unilateral at first but may become bilateral later. It is increased, as a rule, by coughing, sneezing and straining at stool. In some cases there is pain and muscle spasm upon flexing the back but this is not severe, as a rule, unless the cauda equina is involved. Often the pain becomes much worse shortly after the patient falls asleep, so the child awakens crying with pain just as in tuberculous spondylitis. There may be some local tenderness of the vertebra at the level of the lesion but this is usually not very definite unless the growth has actually invaded the bone. Rarely can any anesthesia be found unless several roots happen to be involved, since the dermatomes overlap so extensively that involvement of one or even two roots causes no definite loss of sensibility.

If the lesion is above the lumbosacral enlargement, the next sign to appear is usually *spasticity* and *weakness* of the legs. As a rule, one leg is affected more than the other, but it rarely if ever happens that one leg is paralysed before the other is involved to some extent. Usually the difference in the degree of weakness is not great. In some cases spasticity never develops. This is especially true in cases in which the paralysis develops very rapidly or when the tumor is situated so as to compress the anterior surface of the cord. Before long there is some loss of *proprioceptive sensibility,* indicative of involvement of the posterior columns of the cords, which gives rise to ataxic gait and to Romberg's sign. About the same time, or perhaps a bit later, *cutaneous anesthesia* below the level of the lesion develops. This may begin in the dermatomes just below the level of the lesion and spread down but more commonly begins in the lower part of the body and extends slowly upward until it reaches the level of the pain. All modalities of sensibility are affected. Usually the anesthesia is unequal on the two sides of the body, and the more severe anesthesia is apt to be on the side opposite the weaker leg. Pains in the body below the level of the lesion, due to irritation of the spinothalamic tracts, are not prominent, and in most cases are absent. Burning, tingling or hot and cold sensations are, however, common. By the time definite anesthesia is present, there is apt to be some difficulty in passing urine and perhaps some difficulty in retaining it when the urge comes to void, but complete loss of *sphincter control* is a very late symptom of compression of the spinal cord. Loss of control of the bladder always occurs before rectal incontinence. Constipation is invariably present by the time the legs have become weak, however. As the growth continues to expand the legs become very spastic and are strongly extended. Eventually, if the pressure is not relieved, paraplegia-in-extension is followed by paraplegia-in-flexion when the interruption of conduction is almost com-

plete. There is now involuntary micturition, trophic changes in the skin and decubitus ulcerations will develop unless the patient is nursed with the greatest care.

Certain features characteristic of lesions at special levels of the cord will now be mentioned. If the tumor is *above the cervical enlargement,* the arms, as well as the legs, will be affected, and the entire bodily musculature will exhibit increased tone. The diaphragm and the intercostal muscles share in the paralysis, so paralysis of respiration may occur. Lesions anywhere above the first thoracic segment may cause Horner's syndrome. Lesions *in the cervical enlargement* spare the diaphragm but may cause paralysis of the arms and chest as well as the legs. In this region it is not unusual to find *paralysis* of certain muscle groups of the arms associated with *atrophy,* loss of tone and loss of reflexes. This is due to involvement of the motor roots or of the motor cells of the spinal gray matter. A partial or complete reaction of degeneration may be elicited in such muscles. Such paralysis is of segmental distribution, that is, it is confined to muscles which receive their innervation from certain segments of the cord, and its distribution at once reveals the exact location of the growth. Lesions *in the thoracic segments* of the cord spare the arms but cause spasticity and paralysis of the legs and of some parts of the spinal, abdominal and thoracic muscles, depending upon the segments involved. Segmental palsies are rarely demonstrable in lesions of the thoracic cord. When the lesion involves

TABLE VI.—TUMORS OF THE SPINAL CORD IN CHILDREN

No.	Type	Age	Clinical Features
U. 48036	Extra-dural sarcoma	14 yrs.	Involvement of lower cervical roots on both sides with brachial plexus palsies without paraplegia. Recovery after removal.
U. 36692	Extra-dural sarcoma	14 yrs.	Involvement of lower sacral roots on left by growth in epidural space. Recovery after removal and radiation.
H. 16666	Extra-dural sarcoma	14 yrs.	Compression of the cord at eighth thoracic segment. No improvement after incomplete removal.
U. 8625	Extra-dural sarcoma	10 yrs.	Sarcoma of mediastinum invading spinal canal and compressing cord at T.3.
S. 56380	Extra-dural sarcoma	11 yrs.	Compression of cord at L.1.
U. 25971	Extra-dural sarcoma	5 yrs.	Growth arising near kidney and invading spinal canal at L.2. Recurrent.
U. 10338	Extra-dural fibroma	14 yrs.	Mediastial growth invading spinal canal through intervertebral foramen at T.4.
U. 42015	Extra-dural neurofibroma	14 yrs.	Growth of the mediastinum invading canal at T.4.

No.	Type	Age	Clinical Features
U. 48036	Extra-dural neurofibroma	15 yrs.	Compression of the cord at C.6.
U. 31078½	Extra-dural osteoma	10 yrs.	Gradual compression of first cervical segment by bony growth of first vertebra.
U. 2517	Extra-dural chloroma	12 yrs	Compression of the cord at T.5 by chloroma. Blood count normal at first.
U. 17833	Intra-dural fibroblastoma	13 yrs.	Compression of the cord at T.7 by growth. Operation delayed by absence of sensory level, and by negative Queckenstedt and lipiodol tests until late in course.
Ped. 68608	Intra-dural neurofibroma	13 yrs.	Compression of C.1 by growth. No other symptoms but at post-mortem there were numerous tumors on cranial nerves.
U. 40970	Glioma	11 yrs.	Growth in center of cord at T.10.
U. 31132	Glioma (spongioblastoma?)	14 yrs.	Central growth at T.1.
U. 2413½	Glioma	5 yrs.	Central growth at T.7.
U. 27425	Glioma	7 yrs.	Slowly growing lesion filling entire lumbosacral enlargement and finally becoming calcified.
S. 58046	Glioma metastatic	6 yrs.	Cellular glioma involving base of 3rd ventricle and metastasizing into spinal canal and L.1.
U. 31726	Glioma metastatic medulloblastoma	9 yrs.	Growth of fourth ventricle metastasizing into spinal canal and compressing cord at L.1 and 2.
U. 33940	Ependymal glioma?	10 yrs.	This growth filled the subarachnoid space and ensheathed the cord and roots. Pain was only symptom for years. Began in lumbar canal but slowly extended up to cervical segments and caused paraplegia 10 years after first symptoms.
U. 53549	Arteriovenous fistula	5 yrs.	Recurrent attacks of paraplegia from age of 5 yrs. to 21 yrs.
C.W.	Dermoid cyst	8 yrs.	Peculiar muscle spasm in legs and lumbar spine without weakness, sensory disturbances or change in reflexes. Removal of tumor and recovery.
U. 111730	Extra-dural sarcoma	11 yrs.	Compression of fifth cervical segment and destruction of vertebrae. Complete recovery following laminectomy and deep roentgenotherapy. Metastases in the lungs a few months later. Death. Path. 1666.

the *lumbosacral enlargement,* only the legs and the sphincters are affected. If the lumbar segments are involved, the quadriceps may be flaccid and the knee jerks lost but the ankle jerks will be increased and the calf muscles spastic.

When the tumor involves the *cauda equina,* pain is usually very severe and persistent. It radiates down the posterior surface of the legs along the

course of the sciatic nerves. It is increased by flexion of the spine, coughing, sneezing, straining and by certain postures. For example, the patient
may be relatively comfortable when standing but may have intense pain
when lying or sitting. Some patients will be most comfortable when lying
on their side with their knees drawn up. There is never any spasticity and
paralysis develops relatively late. The tendon reflexes are lost eventually.
Loss of control of the bladder may develop relatively early in the course.
The anesthesia occupies a saddle-shaped area over the buttocks, the posteri-
or surface of the thighs and legs. When the lesion does not extend above
the second sacral roots, there is no paralysis and we find only disturbances
of control of the sphincters and anesthesia over the sacral dermatomes. *Intramedullary neoplasms,* such as gliomas or ependymomas, are apt to produce more striking segmental signs due to destruction of the gray matter.
The sensory loss as a rule begins just below the level of the lesion and
moves downward. Pyramidal tract signs are apt to be late. The clinical picture is similar to that of syringomyelia.

In certain cases of neoplasm of the cauda one can demonstrate no loss
of function whatever. Strength, sensibility and reflexes may be intact and
the patient may have no difficulty in controlling the bladder. Pain is usually
severe but may be mild. The most striking finding on examination is spasm
of the muscles of the knee, hip and lumbar spine which involves chiefly the
flexors. The lumbar lordosis is reduced and the patient walks with the knees
semiflexed. Less frequently the lumbar lordosis may be *increased.* The muscle spasm is quite unlike that of true spasticity and resembles that found
in tuberculous spondylitis or arthritis. Dr. George Bennett described this
syndrome in 1927.

The symptoms progress slowly in most cases and almost always steadily,
without definite remissions or exacerbations. Very rapid progress in the
symptoms suggests a malignant growth. Hemangiomas and arteriovenous
fistulae may cause repeated spinal palsies of sudden onset. The cysts described by Fulton and Kubie may also cause repeated attacks of paraplegia
with partial recovery. In the case of their second patient, paraplegia occurred at the ages of $2\frac{1}{2}$ years, 9 years, 12 years and 27 years of age. In the
first patient, sudden paraplegia occurred at the age of 2 years and operation
prevented recurrences. In this case spinal puncture yielded clear mucus resembling white of egg and containing a number of ciliated cells, for the
needle entered the cyst. The writer has seen one case of a similar cyst in
which paralysis developed at the age of 12 years and again at 32 years.
Cloward and Bucy describe cysts associated with kyphosis juvenilis dorsalis
q.v.

It is of interest that in certain cases neoplasms involving the vertebrae or

merely surrounding the vertebrae may cause sudden paraplegia without compression of the cord. It is believed that involvement of the blood supply leads to softening in such cases. Hodgkin's disease may behave in this manner.

The characteristic changes in the spinal fluid are termed Froin's syndrome. The fluid is yellow and contains a great excess of protein. It often clots spontaneously and contains few if any cells. These changes indicate complete obstruction of the spinal canal. When the obstruction is only partial, there may be only a moderate increase in protein. There is less increase in protein, as a rule, when the growth is extradural. Cushing and Ayer have shown that the protein may be increased above the tumor but never to the same degree as below the site of the tumor.

We must remember that symptoms may increase very definitely immediately after spinal puncture. When the growth is high enough to affect the muscles of respiration, we must therefore exercise great care lest sudden failure of respiration be induced. If spinal puncture is necessary in such cases, it should be done in the operating room, so that immediate operation is possible and facilities for artificial respiration are at hand.

Love *et al.* have reported two cases in which spinal cord tumor was associated with papilledema. In one case there was an ependymoma of the filum terminale and in the other an oligodendroglioma of the thoracic cord. In each case the intracranial pressure was elevated as measured by the manometer, there was internal hydrocephalus and the cerebrospinal fluid, ventricular and cisternal, contained an excess of protein, 160 and 180 mgs. In each case the papilledema receded promptly after the neoplasm was removed. Gardner *et al.* suggest that in such cases the increase of spinal fluid protein obstructs the arachnoidal villi and causes external hydrocephalus.

Nassar and Correll report four cases in which a spinal cord tumor caused subarachnoid hemorrhage. Among them was a boy of 15 years. They analyze 11 cases found in medical literature. Ependymomas were most apt to cause bleeding.

Roentgenograms of the spine may reveal evidences of the growth. There may be erosion of the vertebrae in malignant tumors and even benign growths may cause dilatation of the canal or enlargement of the intervertebral foramina. Roentgenograms of the lungs and bones are useful in discovering metastatic deposits.

Interesting metabolic changes occur after transverse lesions of the spinal cord. There is loss of nitrogen and calcium. The basal metabolic rate is reduced. Osseus atrophy develops. In males there is testicular atrophy and in females amenorrhea.

Diagnosis.—The following items are of the greatest importance in the diagnosis of primary neoplasms of the spinal cord:

1. The history. This is typically that of a slowly progressive lesion of the cord without definite exacerbations or remissions.

2. The demonstration of a single focal lesion of the cord; i.e. a sensory and motor level.

3. The presence of increased protein content of the spinal fluid, xanthochromia and spontaneous coagulation or merely increased protein content. The absence of such changes is not quite conclusive, however.

4. The presence of obstruction of the spinal subarachnoid space, as shown by the Queckenstedt test or pantopaque injection. Again this is not always present.

5. The exclusion of tuberculous spondylitis, syphilis and traumatic conditions by history, serology, roentgenographic studies, etc.

6. The absence of evidences of a malignant growth elsewhere in the body and of cerebral neoplasm which may have extended into the spinal canal.

We must not only recognize the presence of a tumor of the spinal cord but determine its exact location. The presence of atrophy of certain muscles with loss of reflexes and flaccidity is conclusive in this regard. If no segmental palsies are demonstrable, as is frequently the case, one must rely upon the upper level of the corticospinal motor signs, the level of root pain and the sensory level. It must be kept in mind that the sensory level may be far below the true level of the growth and is of little importance unless verified by some other localizing sign. If clinical signs are inconclusive, pantopaque injection may be necessary.

It is rarely possible to make a differential diagnosis between intramedullary and extramedullary tumor with certainty, although we may make a correct guess in most cases. The distinguishing features between intramedullary and extramedullary growths may be given as follows:

Intramedullary	*Extramedullary*
1. Sensory loss begins in a zone just below level of the lesion and is often dissociated. It moves downward.	1. Sensory loss begins well below in most cases and slowly extends up to level of lesion.
2. Pyramidal tract signs are late.	2. Pyramidal tract signs are early.
3. Lower motor neuron signs are often prominent.	3. Lower motor neuron signs are often absent.
4. Root pains are often absent.	4. Root pains are usually the first sign.
5. Spinal block develops late.	5. Spinal block develops early.

Prognosis.—The prognosis in general is unfavorable since so many spinal cord tumors causing symptoms during childhood are malignant. In cases of benign tumors, the outlook is very good, provided the operation is performed early and the cord is not traumatized.

Treatment.—If we can find no evidence of metastatic disease and there is a definite sensory or motor level with partial or complete obstruction of the spinal cord, operation is fully justified and should be carried out at once. Even if there is reason to suspect an intramedullary growth, it is best to operate nonetheless, since we can rarely be certain that the tumor is actually inoperable. Extramedullary tumors should be removed as fully as possible, even if it is evident that the growth is malignant. Intramedullary tumors can rarely be extirpated by surgical means but some of the ependymal gliomas of the central canal may be removed successfully. If the growth cannot be removed completely or seems to be malignant, deep roentgenotherapy should be tried.

CASE HISTORY.—*Child of eight years developed a peculiar gait. Muscle spasm of unusual type found in legs and lumbar spine, but there was no spasticity, weakness, sensory disturbance or change in the reflexes. Lipiodol test positive. Dermoid cyst filling the lumbar cul de sac found at operation. Recovery.*

C. W., a child of eight years, began to have difficulty in gait in the summer of 1938. His local physician was puzzled by the case and sent him to Dr. George Bennett by whose courtesy the writer was permitted to make a neurological examination. The child's gait was peculiar in that the legs were partially flexed at the hip and knee and the lumbar spine was somewhat flexed. It was possible for him to walk, however. The lumbar spine was held rigidly in partial flexion and powerful muscle spasm prevented any movement in the lumbar or lower thoracic spine. The legs showed muscle spasm at the hip and knee but this was not so intense as that of the spine. On passive movement at the hip or knee, the examiner encountered a resistance which was quite unlike spasticity and felt like that associated with arthritis. No pain was caused by such movements. There was no weakness or atrophy of the muscles, and no ataxia. The bowels and bladder were controlled normally but priapism was almost constant. The tendon reflexes were normal and the plantar responses flexor. No disturbance of sensibility could be made out. One might say, therefore, that there was no evidence of loss of function of the spinal cord or spinal nerve roots.

Lipiodol injection revealed an obstruction in the upper lumbar region of the spinal canal. Operation disclosed a dermoid cyst filling the entire lumbosacral subarachnoid space. This surrounded the spinal roots and the lumbosacral enlargement of the spinal cord as if it had been poured into the canal in a liquid form. With some difficulty the tumor was removed. The tumor had not invaded the cauda or indeed, compressed it severely. The child seemed to make a complete recovery and remained well.

BIBLIOGRAPHY

ADELSTEIN, L. J. AND PATTERSON, G. H.: Surgical treatment of ependymal glioma of the spinal cord. Arch. Surg., **30**:997, 1935.

BASSETT, R. C.: The neurologic deficit with lipomas of the cauda equina. Ann. Surg., **131**:109, 1950.

BAYNOR, R. B.: Papilledema associated with tumors of the spinal cord. Neurology, **19**:700, 1969.

BENNETT, G. E.: Tumors of the cauda equina and spinal cord; report of four cases in which marked spasm of the erector spinae and hamstring muscles was outstanding sign. J.A.M.A., **90**:1480, 1927.

BUCY, P. C. AND BUCHANAN, D. N.: Teratoma of the spinal cord. Surg. Gynec. & Obst., **60**:1137, 1935.

CLOWARD, R. B. AND BUCY, P.: Extradural cyst and kyphosis dorsalis juvenilis. Am. J. Roentgen., **38**:681, 1937.

COOPER, I. S. AND HOEN, T. I.: Metabolic disorders in paraplegics. Neurology, **2**:332, 1952.

COXE, W. S.: Tumors of the spinal cord in children. Am. Surg., **27**:62, 1961.

CRAIG, J. AND MITCHELL, A.: Spinal tumors in childhood. Arch. Dis. Child., **6**:11, 1931.

CROSBY, R., WAGNER, J. AND NICHOLS, P.: Intradural lipoma of the spinal cord. J. Neurosurg., **10**:81, 1953.

CROSS, S. W.: Concerning intraspinal dermoids and epidermoids with report of a case. J. Nerv. & Ment. Dis., **80**:274, 1934.

CUSHING, H. AND AYER, J. B.: Xanthochromia and increased protein in the spinal fluid above tumors of the cauda equina. Arch. Neurol. & Psychiat., **10**:167, 1923.

DANDY, W. E.: The diagnosis and localization of spinal cord tumors. Ann. Surg., **81**:223, 1925.

EHNI, G. AND LOVE, J. G.: Intraspinal lipomas. Arch. Neurol. & Psychiat., **53**:1, 1945.

ELSBERG, C.: Tumors of the Spinal Cord. New York, Paul B. Hoeber, 1925.

ELSBERG, C. A., DYKE, C. C. AND BREWER, E. D.: Symptoms and diagnosis of extra-dural cysts. Bull. Neurol. Inst. of New York, **3**:359, 1934.

FRAZIER, C.: Surgery of the Spine and Spinal Cord. D. Appleton-Century & Co., 1918.

GARDNER, W. J., SPITLER, D. K. AND WHITTEN, C.: Increased intracranial pressure caused by increased protein content of the cerebrospinal fluid. New England J. Med., **250**:932, 1954.

GESCHICTER, C. F. AND RIX, R. R.: Tumors of the spine with a consideration of Ewing's sarcoma. Arch. Surg., **36**:899, 1938.

HAMBY, W. B.: Tumors in the spinal canal in childhood. J. Nerv. & Ment. Dis., **81**:24, 1935.

———: Tumors in the spinal canal in childhood. Analysis of the literature. J. Neuropath. & Exp. Neurol., **3**:397, 1944.

HANSMAN, G. H.: A congenital tumor of the neurenteric canal with specific reference to its histology and pathological significance. Surg. Gynec. & Obst., **42**:124, 1926.

HESS, W. E.: Giant cell tumor of cervical spine. Jour. Bone and Joint Surg., **42A**:480, 1960.

INGRAHAM, F. D.: Intraspinal tumors in infancy and childhood. Am. J. Surg., **39**:342, 1938.

KEPLINGER, J. E. AND BUCY, P. C.: Giant cell tumors of the spine. Ann. Surg., **154**:648, 1961.

KERNOHAN, J. W., WOLTMAN, H. W. AND ADSON, A. W.: Intramedullary tumors of the spinal cord: A review of fifty-one cases with an attempt at histological classification. Arch. Neurol. & Psychiat., **25**:679, 1931.

———: Gliomas arising from the region of the cauda equina. Arch. Neurol. & Psychiat., **29**:287, 1933.

KERNOHAN, J. W.: Primary Tumors of the Spinal Cord and Intradural Filum Terminale. Cytology and Cellular Pathology of the Nervous System. **3**: Sec. xx, p. 991, New York, Paul Hoeber, 1932.

KUBIE, L. S. AND FULTON, J. F.: A clinical and pathological study of two teratomatous cysts of the spinal cord containing mucus and ciliated cells. Surg. Gynec. & Obst., **46**:297, 1928.

LOVE, J. G., WAGNER, H. P. AND WOLTMAN, H. W.: Tumors of the spinal cord associated with choking of the optic discs. Arch. Neurol. & Psychiat., **66**:171, 1951.

LOVE, J. G. AND DODGE, H. W.: Dumbbell (Hourglass) neurofibromas affecting the spinal cord. Proc. Staff Meet. Mayo Clin., **27**:249, 1952.

MAC CARTY, C. S. et al.: Sacro-coccygeal chordomas. Surg. Gynec. & Obstet., **113**:551, 1961.

MOSBERG, W.: Spinal tumors diagnosed during the first year of life. J. Neurosurg., **8**:220, 1951.

NASSAR, S. I. AND CORRELL, J. W.: Subarachnoid hemorrhage due to spinal cord tumors. Neurology, **18**:87, 1968.

NISENSON, A. AND PATTERSON, G. H.: Spinal cord tumors in childhood. A study of three cases of ependymoma. J. Pediat., **27**:315, 1945.

O'CONNELL, J. E. A.: Subarachnoid dissemination of spinal tumors. J. Neurol., Neurosurg. & Psychiat., **9**:55, 1946.

RAND, R. W. AND RAND, C. W.: Intraspinal Tumors of Childhood. Springfield, Thomas, 1959.

REWCASTLE, N. B. AND FRANCOEUR, J.: Teratomatous cysts of the spinal canal. Arch. Neurol., **11**:91, 1964.

RICHARDSON, F. L.: A report of 16 tumors of the spinal cord in children. The importance of spinal rigidity as an early sign of disease. J. Pediat., **57**:42, 1960.

ROSS, A. T. AND BAILEY, O. T.: Tumors arising within the spinal canal in children. Neurology, **3**:922, 1953.

SACHS, E. AND HORRAX, G.: Cervical and lumbar pilonidal sinus communicating with intraspinal dermoids. J. Neurosurg., **6**:97, 1949.

SCHWARTZ, H. G.: Congenital tumors of the spinal cord in infants. Ann. Surg., **136**:183, 1952.

SHENKLIN, H. A. AND ALPERS, B. J.: Clinical and pathologic features of gliomas of the spinal cord: A review of fifty-one cases with an attempt at histological classification. Arch. Neurol.

SLOOFF, J. E. *et al.*: Primary Intramedullary Tumors of the Spinal Cord and Filum Terminale. Philadelphia, W. B. Saunders Co., 1964.

STOOKEY, B.: Tumors of the spinal cord in childhood. Am. J. Dis. Child., **36**:1184, 1928.

————: Intradural spinal lipoma. Arch. Neurol. & Psychiat., **18**:16, 1927.

SYMONDS, C. P. AND MEADOWS, S. P.: Compression of the spinal cord in the neighbourhood of the foramen magnum. Brain, **60**:52, 1937.

TURNER, O. A.: Spinal extradural cyst. Arch. Neurol. & Psychiat., **58**:593, 1947.

WILLARD, DEF. P. AND NICHOLSON, J. F.: Giant cell tumor of the cervical spine. Ann. Surg., **107**:298, 1938.

WYBURN-MASON, R.: The Vascular Abnormalities and Tumours of the Spinal Cord and Its Membranes. St. Louis, C. V. Mosby, 1944.

SYRINGOMYELIA AND SPINAL GLIOSES

Definition.—Syringomyelia may be defined as a condition characterized by proliferation of glial fibers in the central portions of the spinal cord with destruction of the neurons, breaking down of the tissue and the formation of a cavity. When the same process involves the medulla oblongata, we speak of syringobulbia. This process seems to arise on a basis of defective development. Cavities within the spinal cord, due to trauma or vascular processes, are excluded.

Pathological Anatomy.—On palpation the spinal cord is usually found to be swollen and firm in some segments and atrophic and flattened, like an empty tube, in other segments. On section one or more cavities are apparent. These are most advanced as a rule in the region of the cervical enlargement but may extend in some cases into almost every segment of the spinal cord. Frequently they invade the medulla oblongata. In some cases this process begins in the lumbosacral enlargement rather than in the cervical region. Histological study reveals that the cavities involve first of all the gray matter near the central canal, the base of the posterior columns and the posterior horns. Later, they either invade the anterior gray matter and

the lateral columns or perhaps merely compress the structures. The cavities are always surrounded by a thick wall of dense glial fibers, and, indeed, in some segments, we may find only large areas of gliosis without cavity formation. There seems to be no doubt that the cavities are the result of necrosis of such areas of gliosis. Usually, the cavity communicates with the central canal. If multiple cavities are present, they may communicate with one another or be quite discrete. The cavities are usually lined by ragged glial fibers but in some cases ependymal cells are found which are probably derived from the central canal. Sometimes the cavity is distended with fluid and causes serious compression of the white matter with rapid progress of the symptoms. It is not very rare to find solid masses of tissue which seem to form a definite neoplasm. Poser states that among 245 cases in which a diagnosis of syringomyelia was made there were intramedullary tumors in 16 per cent. In 209 cases in which a diagnosis of intramedullary neoplasm was made, syringomyelia was found in 31 per cent. Ependymomas were most frequently associated but gliomas of various types were also found. Poser points out that syringomyelia is frequently associated with Lindau's disease and von Recklinghausen's neurofibromatosis.

In the medulla oblongata, the lesions are somewhat different. Usually there is a narrow slit-like cavity, extending laterally and anteriorly from the fourth ventricle and involving the nucleus ambiguus, the hypoglossal nucleus, the descending root of the fifth nerve and perhaps the tractus soliarius. Median slits are rare and it is also rare for such lesions to extend as high as the seventh nerve nucleus. Usually there is relatively less gliosis in the bulb.

The primitive cells of the glial series are found during early embryonic life in close relation to the central canal of the neural tube. Under normal conditions they migrate peripherally and differentiate into the various types of adult glia. It is believed that in syringomyelia, certain spongioblasts fail to migrate and to differentiate in this way and eventually begin to proliferate, forming dense areas of gliosis in the central portions of the cord. This theory is supported by the occasional presence of small groups of primitive glial cells in the neighborhood of the raphe and the central canal in spinal cords which are otherwise normal.

Clinical Features.—Males and females are affected with equal frequency, and it is very rare for more than one case to appear in the same family. Only in exceptional cases does syringomyelia give rise to outspoken disability before the age of twenty years; but it is not unusual to obtain from adults a history of mild symptoms early in childhood, which seems to indicate that the process begins very early, even though it does not attract attention until later. We have, however, seen several cases in which the child was seriously disabled before the age of fifteen years.

Cervical Syringomyelia.—This is, of course, the type most frequently encountered. The first group of symptoms to attract attention may be disorders of motility, loss of sensibility, deformities or the so-called trophic disturbances. In the writer's experience among children, the presenting symptom has usually been severe and rapidly progressive scoliosis. The various symptoms will now be taken up in order.

Disturbances of *motility* are due to the extension of the lesion into the anterior spinal gray matter, and, therefore, we find paralysis in association with atrophy of the muscles, loss of reflexes and flaccidity. Since the lesion is usually in the cervical enlargement, the hands or arms are the first to be affected in most cases. The intrinsic muscles of the hands are frequently involved early, causing various deformities of the fingers. The forearm is affected in the same way, and the muscles of the shoulder girdle and upper arm. Eventually the muscles of the neck, spine and chest become atrophic. These palsies may develop in almost any sequence. The muscular atrophy is almost never exactly symmetrical and may be unilateral for a number of years. It is not unusual to see fascicular twitchings in the affected muscles but these are rarely striking. The reaction of degeneration is unusual in its typical form but the affected muscles frequently show diminished electrical irritability. After the disease has become far advanced, the pyramidal tracts are involved, causing paraplegia and spasticity of the legs with loss of sphincter control eventually.

The disturbances of *sensibility* are apt to be unnoticed by the patient for long periods. Apparently, loss of pain sense does not attract attention so quickly as tactile anesthesia. In typical cases, there is some degree of analgesia and thermanesthesia without comparable loss of tactile sensibility. It must be admitted, however, that all modalities of cutaneous sensibility may be lost in certain areas. As a rule, however, the analgesia is more extensive than the tactile anesthesia. The distribution of the sensory loss is variable. If it is due to interruption of the dorsal commissure, it is bilateral, but if the lesion is in the posterior horn of the gray matter, the sensory loss is unilateral. Sometimes it has the distribution of a dermatome and in other cases it involves the hand or hand and forearm, presenting the so-called glove or sleeve anesthesia. In the common type of the disease, the anesthesia is confined to the dermatomes supplied by the cervical enlargement; that is, the arms, shoulders, neck and chest. Later, the process extends into the posterior columns of the cord and causes ataxia, loss of proprioceptive sensibility and unsteadiness of station and gait. Finally, sensory loss may develop over the lower half of the body when the spinothalamic tracts are involved. In a few cases, hemianesthesia appears early in the disease. Pain is not a striking symptom in most cases but sometimes there are severe pains of root distribution or even unilateral or bilateral pains in the lower

parts of the body, due to irritation of the spinothalamic tracts. Some of the pain seems to be due to the scoliosis, for it may be relieved by supporting the spine. Optic atrophy with defects in the fields of vision may occur as a result of colobomatous deformities, as a secondary effect of papilledema and as a primary process of uncertain origin.

Lumbosacral Syringomyelia.—This type is not common but not really rare. The findings on examination are the same as in the common cervical type but found in the legs rather than the arms and shoulders. Wasting of the anterior tibial group of muscles is often the first sign and the foot is often deformed as a result of weakness of the intrinsic muscles. The gluteals and hamstrings are usually involved later. Analgesia of the foot may result in perforating ulcers and loss of toes. The analgesia may be traced up the posterior aspect of the leg and thigh to the buttock and perineum. Often the process is well advanced in one leg before the other leg is involved.

Numerous *deformities* are associated with syringomyelia. Many of these are due to the defective muscle balance which results from the palsies. Deformities of the hands and fingers may be found with atrophy of the intrinsic muscles of the hands. Scoliosis is almost always present eventually and is frequently the first sign to attract attention. In the writer's experience, this is usually severe and progresses rapidly in children, probably because the child's bones are relatively soft and plastic. Such curves are first functional but soon become structural. Other bony deformities, such as spina bifida, absence of fingers, cervical ribs, and the Klippel-Feil syndrome, must be regarded as associated defects of development. Bremer has made a study of congenital anomalies associated with syringomyelia. He mentions malformations of the sternum, funnel chest, polymastia, differences in the size of the breasts, high arched palates, webbed fingers, hypospadias, malformed ears and peculiarities of hair distribution. In some cases changes develop in the joints which are apparently identical with the Charcot joints of tabes dorsalis. There is destruction of the cartilage and articular surfaces and relaxation of the capsule and ligaments, so that an abnormal range of movement is possible. In syringomyelia the joints of the upper extremity are affected rather than the knee and ankle joints, as in tabes dorsalis. We have seen few Charcot joints in children. The bones may also become decalcified, causing spontaneous fractures. Local overgrowth of bones may occur and the hand may resemble that of acromegaly.

Various changes in the skin and soft tissues are described, which are termed *trophic,* for lack of a better name. No doubt, they are the result of the analgesia which predisposes to trauma, and of vasomotor disturbances. The skin may be thick and horny or thin and glossy. The nails may become opaque and finally drop off. Ulcerations may occur on the fingers, causing

extensive loss of tissue. Edema of the hand is common, as well as cyanosis. In some cases, the muscles may suddenly become enlarged, so that they may appear to be hypertrophied.

Syringobulbia may result from the extension of the process from the cervical cord, or may be primary. While the disease is still confined to the cervical enlargement, there may be signs of destruction of the cervical sympathetic nerve, i.e., Horner's syndrome and in rare cases, evidences of irritation of the sympathetic nerve. The descending root of the fifth nerve may be affected early, causing analgesia and thermanesthesia of the face. This develops first in those portions of the fifth nerve area adjoining the dermatome of the second cervical root and progresses centrally, so that the lips and tip of the nose are the last to be affected. In one case of ours recurrent corneal ulcers began at the age of 8 years as the first evidence of syringobulbia. Nystagmus of rotary type is a common sign of invasion of the medulla and probably indicates involvement of the vestibular nuclei or of their tracts. The nucleus ambiguus and hypoglossal nucleus are characteristically affected. The tongue becomes atrophied and paralyzed on one or both sides. The soft palate and pharynx and the vocal cords are also often paralyzed. The facial nerve and the third and fourth nerves are spared, as a rule, but the sixth nerve may be involved. Vertigo or syncope may occur if the patient laughs, coughs or sneezes. When the highest cervical segments are affected, we find paralysis of the sternomastoids and trapezii, due to invasion of the spinal nucleus of the eleventh nerve.

In some cases of syringomyelia, a transverse lesion may develop. This may be due to the development of a true neoplasm, often an ependymoma, in the cavity. It is also claimed that mild trauma may sometimes cause hemorrhage into the syringomyelic cavity and sudden increase in symptoms. The writer is not convinced that this is a common complication, however. More frequently, the rapid development of symptoms seems to be due to the accumulation of fluid under pressure in the cavity. In such cases, improvement may occur later.

Hydrocephalus may be associated with syringobulbia and syringomyelia. The relationship is not very well understood, however. It has been suggested that the hydrocephalus is due to proliferation of glia about the aqueduct or occlusion of the foramina of the fourth ventricle by proliferation of the ependyma. The Arnold-Chiari malformation is found in some cases and platybasia as well.

Several authors have called attention to the occasional association of syringomyelia and von Recklinghausen's neurofibromatosis.

Diagnosis.—After the clinical picture is well developed, there is rarely any doubt about the diagnosis of syringomyelia. The essential clinical features are, of course, the slowly progressive atrophy of the muscles supplied

by the cervical enlargement, the dissociated anesthesia in the cervical dermatomes, the scoliosis and the "trophic" changes. When the disease begins in the lumbosacral enlargement, similar signs appear in the corresponding segments but the clinical picture is usually less typical. The conditions which are most apt to be confused with syringomyelia are progressive spinal muscular atrophy, leprosy, Raynaud's disease, cervical ribs with compression of the cervical nerve roots and neurosyphilis. The development of disturbances of sensibility makes it possible to rule out progressive spinal muscular atrophy. In leprosy the diagnosis is, as a rule, easily made by the presence of the thickened nerve trunks and the cutaneous lesions. Raynaud's disease remains confined to the distal parts of the extremities and is not accompanied by much analgesia or atrophy of the muscles. Cervical ribs may offer some difficulty in differentiation, especially since they may be associated with syringomyelia. However, in such cases the symptoms are found only in the forearms and hands and do not progress to involve the shoulder girdle or chest. There may be a certain degree of dissociation of sensibility in cervical ribs but complete loss of pain without loss of tactile sensibility does not occur. The various tests for patency of the spinal canal may be of some value in ruling out spinal neoplasms, since we do not find complete obstruction in syringomyelia, as a rule, although partial obstruction is not unusual. When dealing with a case of suspected syringomyelia we must always consider the possibility of associated malformations such as platybasia, Arnold-Chiari deformity, Klippel-Feil syndrome, cervical ribs and spina bifida.

Occasionally one encounters an individual who is insensitive to painful stimuli but not actually anesthetic. This condition seems to be a congenital peculiarity and is not associated with any objective signs of disease of the nervous system (see Congenital Insensitiveness to Pain).

Prognosis.—The prognosis is very unfavorable although the disease may progress so slowly that the patient may be active for many years. When symptoms appear early in life, the outlook is relatively serious, and complete disability may be expected before adult life is attained.

Treatment.—No satisfactory treatment has yet been devised. Numerous writers have claimed that radium or roentgenotherapy is of definite value in arresting the progress of the disease. When the cavity contains fluid under pressure, laminectomy and incision through the posterior columns may give dramatic relief, as in the case abstracted below. In cases in which there is no increase in pressure within the cavity, operation can cause only harm. If the symptoms are developing very rapidly, if there is severe pain and especially if there is evidence of partial obstruction of the spinal canal, laminectomy is probably justified.

McIlroy and Richardson state that dilatation of the cavity by fluid under

pressure and ependymoma should be kept in mind. They state that operation was performed on 24 patients. No patient improved, 8 patients showed no increase in their symptoms after operation but 7 patients continued to deteriorate.

CASE HISTORY (U. 27425).—*Slowly progressive central gliosis in the lumbosacral cord of a girl of 14 years. Negative Queckenstedt and lipiodol tests. Operation. Roentgenotherapy ineffective. Complete paraplegia after about ten years.*

D. M., a girl of 14 years, was first seen in 1927. Seven years before she had complained of numbness in the right foot and a tendency to retention of urine. These symptoms slowly grew more severe. Examination revealed analgesia and thermanesthesia over the outer side of the right foot, posterior part of the calf, thigh and the right buttock. The right ankle jerk was lost and there was a beginning deformity of the foot with high arch and claw toes. In 1928 the right foot became edematous and a performing ulcer developed under the great toe. There was some weakness of the dorsi flexors of the ankle. In 1929 the anesthesia had extended up to the level of the groin but dermatomes L3 and 4 on the anterior surface of the thigh still retained some sensibility. There was paralysis of all movements at the right ankle but no weakness at other joints. Queckenstedt test and lipiodol injection revealed no evidence of a spinal block. Spinal fluid was quite normal. Roentgenograms were negative. Exploration revealed a greatly swollen and indurated cord which felt cystic in places. The exposure was extended up to the 8th thoracic vertebra and the cord was still abnormal at that level. A bit of tissue removed from the posterior columns showed a dense mass of glial fibers. In the next few years the weakness slowly extended and three years after the operation the child was completely paralyzed in both legs and there was beginning involvement of the abdominal muscles. There was, of course, anesthesia and loss of control of the bladder and rectum.

CASE HISTORY (U. 2836).—*Boy of 13 years with long-standing weakness of left arm developed rapidly progressive spinal curvature and disturbances in gait. Dissociated anesthesia from T3 to L3 on right. Spasticity of the legs and weakness of soft palate and pharynx on left.*

R. C., a white boy of 13 years, was admitted to the hospital with the complaint of curvature of the spine and weakness of the left arm. The symptoms were first noticed about two years before, when his gait became impaired, but it was elicited from his mother that the child had not been able to use the left arm properly for a number of years. There had been a variable squint since the age of seven months and vision in the right eye had never been very good.

Examination revealed a well-nourished and well-developed boy with a pronounced scoliosis to the right with the apex in the midthoracic region. There was some rotation, so that the right side of the back was unduly prominent. The extensors of the spine were weak and somewhat wasted

on the left. The bones and muscles of the left arm and hand were some-what smaller than those of the right and the skin of the left hand rough and scaly. Strength was much diminished in all muscle groups of the left arm as was muscle tone. Both legs were weak and somewhat spastic; the left being weaker than the right. No ataxia was found. Sphincter control was normal. Over the right side of the body from the level of the third rib anteriorly to the knee and over a corresponding area behind, there was profound analgesia and thermanesthesia but tactile sensibility was not definitely affected. Sense of passive movement, posture, vibratory sense and stereognosis were all preserved. The tendon reflexes were all active and somewhat greater on the left than on the right. The plantar reflexes were both extensor, the left being more definitely pathological than the right. Ankle clonus elicited on left. The abdominal reflexes were dimin-ished on the left and not elicited on the right. Vision of the right eye was 5/70 but the optic nerve head was normal. This was considered due to amblyopia ex-ablepsia, for there was a concomitant internal squint of the right eye. There was definite weakness of the left side of the soft palate and superior constrictors of the pharynx. Cranial nerves were otherwise normal.

Complete studies, including Wassermann reaction of the blood and spinal fluid, Queckenstedt test, roentgenograms of the spine and routine medical studies, revealed nothing of importance.

The child has now been followed for nearly ten years. The scoliosis has developed, despite every effort to control it, and the patient is now quite helpless.

CASE HISTORY.—*Syringomyelia associated with congenital defects. Sudden development of hydrocephalus at the age of 16 years. Operative incision into cavity with release of fluid under pressure. Immediate cessation of headache and subsequent improvement in motor and sensory disturbances.*

H. D., schoolboy of 16 years, was born with certain defects, including hypospadias, supranumerary toes on both feet, high arched palate and an abnormally receding chin. Several years before the patient was first seen, his parents had noticed that he had some difficulty in the use of his arms and that the hands were becoming deformed. For a few weeks the patient had complained of severe headaches and had vomited suddenly without nausea on several occasions. He also complained of pain in the shoulders, arms and hands.

Examination revealed the deformities mentioned above. The optic nerve heads were somewhat congested but otherwise the cranial nerves were quite normal. The hands were very weak and there was pronounced atrophy of the intrinsic muscles with *main en griffe*. Analgesia and therm-anesthesia were found over the hands, the inner border of the forearm and arm and over the chest from the second rib to the nipple line. The legs were perhaps slightly weak and the knee and ankle jerks rather brisk, but the plantar reflexes were normal and there was no clonus. During the

next few days the headache continued and the optic discs showed increasing papilledema. The arms were almost powerless and the legs grew weaker, so that the patient could walk only with difficulty. Just a week after admission, the patient became stuporous, the pulse fell to 55 per minute, and hemorrhages appeared in the optic nerve heads. Laminectomy was performed. The cervical cord was pale and distended, so that it filled the canal tightly. An incision was made in the midline, which opened into a large central cavity lined with a rough membrane. Fluid spurted out under great pressure and the spinal cord became smaller and pinker. The headache was relieved at once and, in the course of the next week, the pains in the arms ceased and strength improved. When the patient was discharged, some weeks after operation, his hands were stronger, his legs seemed to be normal, the anesthesia was still present but less pronounced, and the papilledema had receded.

BIBLIOGRAPHY

ALPERS, B. J. AND COMROE, B. I.: Syringomyelia with choked disc. J. Nerv. & Ment. Dis., **75**:577, 1931.

BASSOE, P.: The coincidence of cervical ribs and syringomyelia. Arch. Neurol. & Psychiat., **4**:542, 1920.

BERMAN, E. J.: Syringomyelie in Kindesalter. Monatschr. f. Kinderh., **37**:1, 1927.

BREMER, F. H.: Klinische Untersuchungen zur Aetiologie, der Syringomyelie, der "status Dysphrecticus." Deutsche Ztschr. f. Nervenh., **95**:1, 1926.

CRITCHLEY, McD.: Sprengel's deformity with paraplegia. Brit. J. Surg., **14**:243, 1926.

DER TORT, F.: A case of congenital elevation of the scapula with defect of the cervical spine associated with syringomyelia. Brain, **54**:421, 1931.

DUFFY, P. E. AND ZITER, F. A.: Infantile syringomyelia. Neurology, **14**:500, 1962.

HAUSMAN, L.: Macrosoma in syringomyelia. Arch. Neurol. & Psychiat., **21**:228, 1929.

KOCH, G.: Syringomyelie Humangenetik. P. E. Becker, Georg Thieme, Stutgart, 1966.

McILROY, W. J. AND RICHARDSON, J. D.: Syringomyelia; a clinical review of 75 cases. Canad. Med. Ass. Jour., **93**:731, 1965.

POSER, C. M.: The Relationship Between Syringomyelia and Neoplasm. Springfield, Thomas, 1956.

VAN BOGAERT, L.: Syringomyelie biezwei Schwestern in einem der Fälle einer Kleinhirncyste. Ztschr. f. d. ges. Neurol. u. Psychiat., **149**:661, 1934.

WALSH, F. B.: *Loc. cit.*

WALSHE, F. M. R.: Syringomyelia in a child. Proc. Roy. Soc. Med. 1927, **20**: sec. neurol., p. 1246.

WOODS, A. H.: Removal of a tumor from the spinal cord in syringomyelia. Its histology and relationship with the ependyma. Arch. Neurol. & Psychiat., **20**:1250, 1928.

WYLLIE, W. G.: A case of unilateral bulbar lesions, probably syringobulbia, with special reference to the sensory pathways within the medulla. J. Neurol. & Psychopath., **4**:148, 1923-24.

NEOPLASMS OF THE SYMPATHETIC SYSTEM

Introduction.—Several types of tumors are believed to arise from the neuroblasts, which migrate from the neural crest during embryonic life to form the various components of the sympathetic system. Among these we may mention the neuroblastoma, the paraganglioma and the ganglioneu-

roma, representing successive steps in the differentiation of the chief cell type. These will be taken up in order.

Neuroblastoma.—These are composed chiefly of small cells with little cytoplasma and hyperchromatic nuclei. They are arranged in clumps and rosettes. Larger cells, either round or pear-shaped with vesicular nuclei, are also found, which resemble spongioblasts. They almost always arise in the suprarenal gland or in the retroperitoneal space.

Such tumors are not uncommon in childhood. More than half of them cause symptoms before the age of three and few are found after the age of fifteen years. The cardinal symptoms are fever, anemia, vomiting and abdominal tumor. Appendicitis or rheumatic fever may be suspected. Metastases may develop before the primary growth is apparent. In the Hutchinsonian type, metastatic deposits in the skull develop very early. Soft swellings are found over the cranium and exophthalmos of one or both eyes appears about the same time. Metastases may also develop in the lungs, the ribs and spine, and both the femur and humerus, but are not so frequent or so early as those in the cranium. The lymph nodes are involved, as a rule. In the Pepper type, metastases to the liver are the first to attract attention. The clinical course is a rapid one. In a large percentage of cases death occurs within two months of the onset, and it is rare for the child to live a year. Radium and roentgen ray therapy are useless and only one successful operation is recorded. Bill points out that spontaneous regression may occur. The malignant cells may disappear or may become mature.

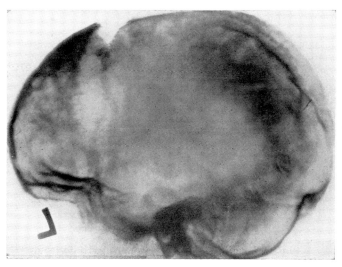

Fig. 256. Roentgenogram of the skull in a case of neuroblastoma with metastases to the brain and cranium showing typical motheaten appearance of the vault and separation of the sutures due to increased intracranial pressure.

Kaser and von Studnitz state that the excretion of vanillylmandelic acid, an end product of epinephrine and norepinephrine metabolism, is always greatly increased in the urine. They consider this a valuable aid in diagnosis.

As a rule, there are no symptoms referable to the destruction of the adrenal glands. Lewis and Geschickter, who have made a very valuable study of the subject, describe one case in which hemihypertrophy was found on the side of the tumor.

In a number of cases the dancing eyes syndrome of Kinsbourne has been found in association with neuroblastoma even though no metastatic lesions are found in the brain. See the dancing eyes syndrome.

Paraganglioma.—These tumors present a variable histological picture, but are all believed to arise from the chromaffin system; that is, from the carotid body, the medulla of the adrenal gland, the paravertebral sympathetic ganglia and the sympathetic system of the intestines. They are usually benign and solitary but may be multiple and malignant. Since such growths are relatively rare in childhood and do not metastasize to the nervous system, they do not require a detailed description. It is of interest, however, that those arising in the adrenal gland may be associated with the symptoms of Addison's disease, vasomotor instability which sometimes closely resembles Raynaud's disease, and either hypertension or hypotension. In a significant number of cases, multiple neurofibromatosis of von Recklinghausen is found. Glycosuria also occurs.

Ganglioneuroma.—In tumors of this group, we find, as a rule, large, well-formed ganglion cells as well as smaller neuroblasts. They are found at any age but are rare in children. Besides those which arise in the brain, which have been described elsewhere, there are others which arise in the sympathetic system, the adrenal gland or the peripheral nerves. Despite the presence of mature ganglion cells in these tumors, they may be malignant. Ganglioneuromas may be associated with chronic diarrhea. Greenberg and Gardner have found large amounts of norepinephrine and epinephrine in the tumors and in the urine. The diarrhea ceases when the tumor is removed.

BIBLIOGRAPHY

BILL, A. H.: Regression of neuroblastoma. Jour. of Pediat. Surg., 3:103, 1968.

DAVIDSON, *et al.:* Opsoclonus and neuroblastoma. New England Med. Jour. October 24, 1968, p. 948.

FRAUMENI, J. F.: Wilm's tumor and congenital hemihypertrophy. Modern Medicine, March 11, 1968, p. 105.

GREENBERG, R. E. AND GARDNER, L. I.: Chronic diarrhea associated with neural tumors. J. Clin. Invest., 39:1729, 1960.

KASER, A. AND VON STUDNITZ, W.: Urinary excretion of vanillylmandelic acid in sympathetic neuroblastoma. J. Dis. Child., 102:199, 1961.

Koop, C. E. and Hernandez, J. R.: Neuroblastoma; experience with 100 cases in children. Surgery, **56**:726, 1964.

Lewis, D. and Geschickter, C. F.: Tumors of the sympathetic system, neuroblastoma, paraganglioma, ganglioneuroma. Arch. Surg., **28**:16, 1934.

Perez, C. A.: Treatment of malignant sympathetic tumors in children. Pediatrics, **41**:452, 1968.

Priebe, C. J. and Clatworthy, H. W.: Neuroblastoma: evaluation of 90 children. Arch. of Surg., **95**:538, 1967.

Smith, R. A. *et al.:* Functionally active intrathoracic neuroblastoma. Arch. Dis. Childhood, **36**:82, 1961.

Solomon and Chutorian: Opsoclonus and ocult neuroblastoma. New England Med. Jour., **279**:475, 1968.

Visfeldt, J.: Treatment of neuroblastoma. Acta radiol. Stockh., **6**:421, 1967.

Williams, C. M. and Greer, M.: Diagnosis of neuroblastoma. J.A.M.A., **183**:836, 1963.

NEOPLASMS OF THE PERIPHERAL NERVES

With the exception of the neurofibromas of von Recklinghausen's disease, peripheral nerve neoplasms are rare in childhood. Solitary neurofibromas are sometimes found. Malignant growths are described which, in some instances, represent sarcomatous changes in neurofibromas. A full discussion of this subject is given in the following references.

BIBLIOGRAPHY

Penfield, W.: Encapsulated tumors of the nervous system. Surg. Gynec. & Obst., **45**:178, 1927.

Penfield, W.: Nelson's Loose Leaf Surgery. Chapter VI, **11**:303, 1927.

Stout, A. P.: Tumors of the peripheral nervous system. Atlas of Tumor Pathology, Armed Forces Institute of Pathology. Washington, D. C.

Foot, N. C.: Peripheral neurogenic tumors. Am. J. Clin. Path., **6**:1, 1936.

NEUROFIBROMATOSIS OF VON RECKLINGHAUSEN

Definition.—This is a condition characterized by multiple tumors springing from the sheaths of the spinal, cranial or sympathetic nerves, by cutaneous pigmentation and tumor formation, by abnormalities in the bones and frequently by evidences of defective development of the nervous system and other malformations. The complete picture is one of considerable complexity.

Etiology.—There is a strong tendency for the disease to recur in successive generations of affected families and it is, therefore, believed that it is the expression of an abnormal germ plasm. Frazier and Gardner have studied a family in which bilateral acoustic neurofibromata occurred. They found that this condition could be traced through five generations and behaved like a Mendelian dominant character but the expressivity is subject to great variation.

Pathological Anatomy.—The tumors attached to the nerve trunks have been studied very carefully by Penfield, who regards them as true connective tissue growths. They are composed for the most part of mature cells but in isolated areas proliferating fibroblasts may be found. Penfield claims

that these tumors may be distinguished from the solitary tumors of the eighth nerve, which they closely resemble, by the greater maturity of the cells of which they are composed and also by the fact that the nerve actually penetrates the growth. In the solitary tumors of the eighth nerve, the nerve lies in the capsule of the tumor and the growth is composed of fibroblasts. Hence, Penfield prefers to call the latter fibroblastomas.

The histology of the cutaneous tumors is the same as that of the tumors attached to the nerve trunks. In some cases, in which there are intracranial neurofibromas, we may also find meningeal growths which are identical in every way with the common meningiomas. Gliomata and areas of gliosis are not rare in such cases and in a large percentage of all cases of glioma of the optic chiasm, there is some evidence of von Recklinghausen's disease. Ependymomas may also occur. Numerous developmental defects are described below. Histological examination of the pigmented areas of the skin reveals melanin pigment in the deeper layers of the epidermis. The branches of the cutaneous nerves are thickened and clubbed in this region.

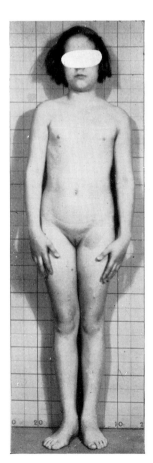

FIG. 257. Photograph of little girl of 10 years showing patches of cutaneous pigmentation and mollusca fibrosa. The child's complexion is much darker than that of her relatives. The cutaneous lesions were noted at the age of 2 years. At the age of 6 years scoliosis began to develop. This was arrested by operative fusion of several vertebrae in the thoracic region. Optic atrophy was found in the right eye several years later.

Clinical Features.—Frequently there are a few faint brownish areas on the skin at birth or early in infancy. Cutaneous or subcutaneous tumors are not evident as a rule so early. Certain deformities are often evident very early in life. These findings may become more obvious during childhood or may remain essentially static for years. In some instances the process becomes activated at puberty.

The *skin,* in most cases, reveals numerous areas of yellow or brown pigmentation. These are termed *café au lait spots.* These areas may be very large or small and are quite irregular in shape. It is said that they are especially characteristic in the axillae. There are also innumerable small, circular, brownish areas resembling freckles. Any part of the body surface may be affected. One must distinguish the *mongolian spot, i.e.,* and areas of brownish pigmentation in the lumbosacral region observed at birth in Mongolians, Negroes and rarely in white infants. This soon disappears. Associated with these areas of deeper pigmentation, the skin, as a whole may be rather darker than the patient's race and family would lead one to expect. In most cases there are numerous *cutaneous tumors* ranging from tiny papules, no more than a millimeter in diameter, to tumors of considerable weight and size. These are usually pigmented and soft. Some are pedunculated and hang from the skin in folds. Their arrangement follows no apparent rule. The term *fibroma molluscum* is employed.

The *subcutaneous tumors* are characteristic and almost constant features of this disease. They lie as a rule along the course of the nerve trunks where they may be felt and seen, resembling a string of large beads. They are rounded and movable to some extent and not attached to the skin. Usu-

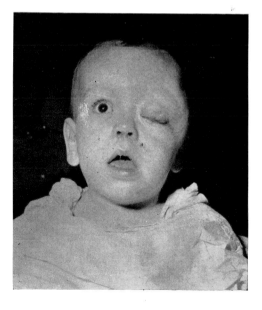

FIG. 258. Child with neurofibromatosis of orbit and lid. (See case history Ped. A 12105.)

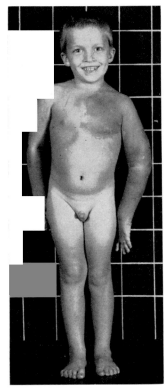

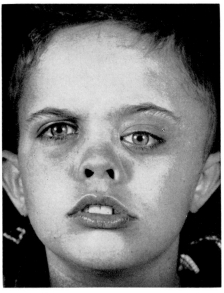

FIG. 260. Boy of 13 years with von Recklinghausen's disease. Left eye is displaced down and forward. Left temple bulges. Pulsating exophthalmos with bruit. Cyst in left middle fossa. Cafe au lait spots (See case history No. 505025).

FIG. 259. (A. 96714) von Recklinghausen's disease. Plexiform neuroma of the left arm with hypertrophy. Pigmentation of chest and arm. Soft, tender nerve trunks are felt in axilla and left arm.

ally they are not tender. In some instances, they are present in great numbers but occasionally only one or two are found. They are variable in size. Often none more than 1.0 or 2.0 in diameter are observed. In other instances large masses occur. The rate of growth is also subject to considerable variation. Often the tumors will seem to remain static for years and then in response to some unknown stimulus will begin to grow rapidly. As a rule, there is little interference with the function of the nerves to which the tumors are attached, but it is not unusual for the patient to complain of pain. In some cases, the nerve may be compressed or invaded in such a way as to cause paralysis. Such a case is given in abstract below. It is not unusual for neurofibromata to develop just outside the intervertebral canals where they may not be palpable. They may be associated with similar growths on the spinal nerve roots within the spinal canal. Such growths may

cause symptoms suggesting polyneuritis. Sarcomatous degeneration may occur. Indeed, it is not unusual for the more rapidly growing tumors to become malignant. It has been claimed with dubious justification that surgical removal of a growth may induce malignant changes in these tumors.

Extensive *plexiform growths* may occur extending diffusely through the tissues. These may occur over the cranium, causing "elephantiasis" of the scalp. Davis has described plexiform neuroma of the orbital tissues and eyelid with buphthalmos and glioma of the optic nerve and temporal lobe. A few similar cases have been reported and a photograph of a child with this condition is shown here. Rosendal points out that defects in the temporal bone and enlargement of the orbit are often associated with plexiform neuromas in this region. The sella is described as box-like. This is due to defective development of the sphenoid bone. Defects in the region of the lamboidal suture are well known. Bruwer described both pulsating and non-pulsating exophthalmos in von Recklinghausen's disease. In some cases this was due to defects in the posterior wall of the orbit with herniation of the tip of the temporal lobe. In other cases, it was due to the presence of a neurofibroma in the posterior part of the orbit. We have seen a case (No. 505025) in which the pulsating exophthalmos was found to be due to a large cyst in the middle fossa which had eroded the superior wall of the orbit. There was bulging of the skull in the temporal region. The child had other evidences of neurofibromatosis and his mother showed the cutaneous pigmentation and cutaneous and subcutaneous tumors. Robinson states that the cysts in the temporal fossa may be due to agenesis of the temporal lobe. In one case (Case History A. G.) in which there was plexiform neuroma of the lid, the orbit was grossly enlarged and there was pulsating enophthalmos. We have also seen a child with a large plexiform neuroma lying behind one ear and a defect in the occipital bone. Hypertrophy of an arm or a leg may result from an extensive plexiform neuroma. There is usually definite evidence of lymph stasis associated with these diffuse growths. Such cases may be confused with partial hemihypertrophies or hemangiomas.

Neurofibromata may also be attached to the *nerve roots* within the spinal canal. These may be found in association with the cutaneous manifestations or without any external evidence of the disease. The roots of the cauda equina are, perhaps, most often affected, but the spinal cord may be compressed as well. As a rule, there is a multiplicity of tumors but solitary growths of typical histology may occur.

The *cranial nerves* do not escape. In some instances, almost every nerve in the cranium may be affected. The symptoms in such cases are therefore very complex. Single tumors are most apt to be attached to the eighth nerve. The common acoustic neuroma of adult life is probably a special type of neurofibroma though it is rarely associated with the cutaneous signs. In

adolescence, bilateral neurofibromas of the eighth nerves may occur. These are well described by Revilla. The first symptom is usually deafness of nerve type. This advances slowly and eventually becomes complete. As a rule one ear is affected months or years before the other. The vestibular reactions are lost early, but as a rule there are no sudden paroxysms of vertigo such as are seen in Ménière's disease. Soon the homolateral side of the face feels numb and the corneal reflex may be lost. Slight paresis of the face, shown by reduction of spontaneous blinking develops but actual facial paralysis is rare. Diplopia due to sixth nerve palsy is a common and early sign. Soon unsteady station and gait and ataxia of the homolateral arm and leg appear due to compression of the cerebellum. Cerebellar nystagmus is a nearly constant sign. Papilledema may appear early or may never develop. Sometimes the internal auditory foramen is eroded and enlarged and this may be demonstrated in roentgenograms of the base of the skull. These bilateral acoustic neuromas of adolescence

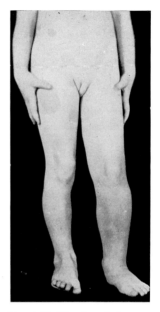

FIG. 261. Elephantiasis nervorum in von Recklinghausen's disease causing enlargement of the left leg resembling hypertrophy.

are often strongly familial. Revilla mentions the cases of sisters studied in this hospital in which there was a history of bilateral eighth nerve tumors in 35 members of their mother's family. This condition was traced back to the eighteenth century (U-335824). In half of these cases, there is cutaneous evidence of von Recklinghausen's disease. The onset of symptoms may occur as early as nine years. Occasionally, one observes unilateral acoustic neuromas in children or adolescents in association with von Recklinghausen's disease. Graig and Bjorksten describe isolated acoustic neuromas in children. Love describes a neurofibroma arising in the petrous bone and causing gradual deafness and facial palsy.

Tumors in the *chest* and *abdomen* are also a part of this picture. The nerves of the autonomic system seem to be involved. Large and small growths are found in the walls of the intestines and mediastinum. Cases of megacolon and giant appendix are described as well as papillary adenomatosis of the intestinal mucosa associated with neurofibromatosis of the splanchnic nerves or pelvic plexuses.

Walsh has given a very full account of the *ocular* manifestations of this disease. He mentions various lesions of the lids including fibroma molluscum, neurofibroma and plexiform neuroma. Congenital glaucoma, or

buphthalmos, is also described. Tumors may be found in the iris, the cornea, the retina, choroid, ciliary body and the optic nerve head. We have observed the appearance of pigmentary degeneration of the retina on one side in a boy who had neurofibromatosis.

In rare instances, one sees a chronic, slowly progressive process in the peripheral nerves in association with evidences of von Recklinghausen's disease. No tumors may be palpable on the affected nerve trunks. In such cases, neuromas will be found on the spinal nerve roots just outside the intervertebral canals. Such a case is given in abstract below.

Signs indicative of involvement of the optic chiasm in a case of von Recklinghausen's disease should always suggest the possibility of *glioma of the chiasm*. We have seen a child with bulging of the right temple, exophthalmos on the right, slightly pale optic discs, and only a little reduction of vision, who was found to have unilateral hydrocephalus, enlarged optic foramina, defects in the posterior wall of the orbit and a large glioma of the chiasm which had occluded the foramen of Monro. There were a few *café au lait* spots on the skin. Cushing described sham rage in a patient suffering from glioma of the chiasm and we have seen two patients who showed this same condition. We have also seen gliomatous cysts in the cerebellum and gliomas of the brain and spinal cord associated with multiple neurofibromatosis. Glioma of the pons may be mistaken for neurofibroma in the cerebellopontine angle. Scharenberg and Jones describe diffuse glioma of the brain in von Recklinghausen's disease. Lesions of the spinal cord in such cases may be due to an ependymoma arising in the central canal. Hemangiomas of various types may be found in the nervous system and meningiomas may be found in association with the typical neurofibromas. It is claimed that syringomyelia may occur in this disease. We have observed stricture of the aqueduct in one instance. Hemangiomas, lymphangiomas and lipomas occur in various places.

Various congenital defects of development of the skeleton occur, such as spina bifida occulta, and spina bifida with meningocele malformations of the fingers, congenital elevation of the scapula, asymmetries of the face and skull, and absence of long bones.

Lehman and Brooks have made a valuable study of the acquired bony changes. They emphasize that scoliosis is very common. This occurs in two types, a mild curve due in some cases to inequality in length of the legs and very severe kyphoscoliosis, which they are inclined to attribute to local bony changes. The affected vertebrae are infiltrated by plexiform neuroma as a rule. We have seen cases of paraplegia associated with the more severe scoliosis and are inclined to believe that this is due to stretching of the spinal cord. The long bones may be spongy and may show abnormally rapid growth. In other cases the bones may be shortened. There are rarefied areas

of bone absorption under the periosteum which resemble bone cysts and also pedunculated growths projecting from the surface of the long bones and covered with a thin shell of bone. These are ascribed by Brooks and Lehman to subperiosteal neurofibromas. The bones of the pelvis and skull may show rarefied areas of the same type. The writer has observed a case of intracranial neurofibromatosis, in which each of the innumerable meningeal tumors was penetrated by a bony projection from the inner table of the skull, so that the cranium resembled the interior of a cavern roofed with stalactites. Brooks and Lehman believe that the bony changes which they describe are characteristic and, hence, important in diagnosis.

In some cases of this disease there is *mental defect* which is not the result of intracranial neoplasms but seems to represent merely deficient development of the brain. It must be emphasized that this is not in any sense an invariable association for the mental condition may be normal. Convulsions are not rare. Many authors have described *disease* of the *glands* of *internal secretion* in this condition. Acromegaly is mentioned most commonly. It must be said, however, that this type of acromegaly is almost always atypical and frequently develops much too early to be convincing, since there is grave doubt whether true acromegaly ever appears before puberty. It seems more likely, as Brooks and Lehman state, that such developmental abnormalities are merely due to local disease of the bones and not to disorders of the endocrine system. However, myxedema and polyglandular syndromes have also been reported. Yakolev and Guthrie describe the case of a boy with premature development of the genitals in association with a mass in the third ventricle. Benda mentions a girl who displayed precocious puberty. Pheochromocytoma may occur in rare instances. The blood pressure may also be elevated as a result of compression of the renal artery by neurofibroma. Neuroblastomas and paragangliomas are sometimes found. Glomus tumors may occur in rare instances. These may be multiple, and, in some instances, are evident at birth. We have seen several cases in which carcinoma of the thyroid gland occurred in von Recklinghausen's disease.

Gorlin and Sedano describe a condition inherited as a dominant trait in which multiple plexiform neuromas, medulated nerve fibers of the corneae, pheochromacytoma and medullary carcinoma of the thyroid gland may occur at puberty. In some cases there is megacolon and neurofibromatous lesions of Auerbach's and Meissner's plexuses.

Lee and Abott report the study of a family of 17 members of whom 8 had neoplasms in the central nervous system. There were also defects of development and posterior cataracts. Three patients had peripheral neurofibromas and several had a few cafe au lait spots.

Diagnosis.—The cases characterized by typical cutaneous lesions or multiple subcutaneous nodules offer, as a rule, no difficulty in diagnosis since

their nature is evident at a glance. In the central type of the disease, however, such superficial lesions are often absent and the diagnosis cannot be made before operation. Changes in the bones seem to be more characteristic than was formerly realized and Brooks and Lehman place great stress on the roentgenograms of the bones in diagnosis. Dodge and Craig point out that solitary peripheral nerve tumors may occur and the diagnosis may be difficult.

Prognosis.—When the tumors are confined to the peripheral nerves, the outlook for life is very good and it is unusual to see a patient who is seriously disabled by this condition. The possibility of malignant changes must always be kept in mind, however. Intracranial or intraspinal tumors are very serious since they are often so numerous that they cannot be removed at operation. However, the writer has followed the case of one patient who had four craniotomies with removal of one or more growths each time and who survived for more than ten years after the first operation.

Treatment.—In view of the danger of provoking malignant changes in these growths, it is usually taught that therapy should be reduced to the minimum. Peripheral tumors should not be removed unless they cause unbearable pain or serious disability. Radium and roentgenotherapy have been used with little success. No general rule can be given as regards the treatment of intracranial growths. One often finds multiple growths, but frequently the symptoms are due to only one lesion and operation may result in years of relief.

CASE HISTORY.—*Girl of 13 years, with cutaneous pigmentation, fibroma molluscum and subcutaneous neurofibromas, began to grow very rapidly at the age of 10 years, developed scoliosis and changes in the bones of the face and extremities suggestive of acromegaly. Moderate mental deficiency.*

J. M., a white girl of 13 years, had never made proper progress at school. At the age of 10 years she began to grow very rapidly and soon was much taller than her older siblings. At the age of 12 years she began to complain of pain in her shoulder and her mother noticed that her back was crooked. The deformity increased rapidly.

Examination revealed that the patient was 5 ft. 9 in. tall (average for age and sex, 4 ft. 11 in.). The arms and legs were very long and slender but the hands and feet were large and the fingers and toes long and slender. The face at first glance was suggestive of acromegaly in that the mandible was elongated and the lower incisors were widely spaced. The tongue was not enlarged, the lips not thickened, the maxilla was unaffected and the supraorbital ridges were not unduly prominent. There was a severe kyphoscoliosis in the lower cervical and upper thoracic spine with marked rotation. The left shoulder was elevated and the head tilted to the right. The muscles of the left arm were somewhat wasted, strength

was diminished and tendon reflexes lost. This was due, no doubt, to compression of the spinal roots of the left brachial plexus in the kyphos. There were numerous coffee-colored areas of pigmentation over the body and extremities ranging from 1 mm to 3 mm in diameter. A large number of small, soft nodules were also found in the skin, some of which were pink and some brown. These were fibromata mollusca. Subcutaneous nodules were also felt. The breasts were almost fully developed and the external genitalia were of adult appearance. The visual fields were normal and the roentgenograms of the sella normal.

CASE HISTORY (Path. 11735-Ped. 68608).—*Girl of 13 years with multiple neurofibromas attached to the cranial and spinal (?) nerves but no peripheral signs of von Recklinghausen's disease.*

C. W., a girl of 13 years, was admitted to the Harriet Lane Home on November 11, 1930. There was a history of pain and stiffness of the neck for four weeks, difficulty in passing urine for two weeks and weakness of the right arm and leg for one week. The child had never been ill before. The family history was quite negative.

Examination revealed a well-formed, well-nourished girl whose skin showed no lesions of any type. There were signs of advancing puberty. The breasts were round and pubic hair was beginning to develop. The cranial nerves were intact. At times there was a suggestion of nystagmus on deviation to either side. Some fine twitchings of the tongue were seen. The optic discs were normal. Both legs were slightly weak and the right arm was very weak. Some weakness was also present in the neck, back, abdomen and shoulders. The affected muscles were not spastic. Indeed, there was some hypotonus. The gait showed chiefly weakness but there also seemed to be some loss of equilibrium. No definite ataxia. There was a tendency to retention of urine requiring catheterization at times. Cutaneous sensibility was much diminished over the right arm and over the trunk and neck on the right from the nipple line up to the chin. Below this zone sensibility seemed to be intact. On the left there was a corresponding zone of sensory loss but here it was much less severe. The tendon reflexes were not increased in the arms but the knee jerks were very brisk. The ankle jerks, however, were absent. The plantar response was extensor on either side. The abdominal reflexes were not elicited. The spinal fluid contained 12 cells. There was a great excess of protein and the globulin reaction was 4 plus.

The child grew steadily weaker. The hypesthesia became anesthesia and extended over the entire body below the chin. Death occurred on November 26, 1930, apparently as a result of paralysis of respiration.

Post-mortem examination revealed a large, soft tumor occupying the foramen magnum and compressing the posterior part of the first cervical segment of the spinal cord and the lower part of the medulla. There were also smaller tumors on the left seventh nerve, the right seventh

nerve, the left eighth nerve and a flat tumor attached to the dura near the internal acoustic foramen on the right. All of these showed the typical histological picture of neurofibroma. The spinal cord was not removed.

CASE HISTORY (Ped. A-12105).—*Child of three years with diffuse neuro-fibromatosis of the left eyelid and temporal tissues. Defect in the temporal bone and enlargement of the left middle fossa. Sutures of the left orbit separated. Areas of pigmentation of the skin.*

It was noticed at birth that the left upper eyelid was swollen and did not open, and that there was a soft swelling in the left temporal region. The child was brought to Harriet Lane several times during infancy and a diagnosis of meningocele was made. Operation was deferred repeatedly because of a persistent nasopharyngeal infection. On February 6, 1940, he was admitted once more.

Examination disclosed a well nourished and well developed boy of three years. His appearance is illustrated in Figure 258. The left eyelid was much thickened and spongy, and could not be opened. The bulb was not unduly prominent and moved freely. There was no pulsation of the bulb. In the temporal region, there was a soft swelling which seemed to merge with the swelling of the lid. A number of soft cords could be felt beneath the skin. A large defect was palpable in the temporal bone and the intracranial pulsation was transmitted through this. No neurofibromas were present over the body or extremities, but over the abdomen and back there were a small number of coffee-colored spots. A constant purulent nasal discharge was present.

Roentgenograms of the skull revealed separation of the sutures of the left orbit with enlargement of the orbit, a defect in the squamous portion of the temporal bone of about 3 cm in diameter and enlargement of the left middle fossa. A plexiform neuroma was found in the temporal region at operation. This was confined to the subcutaneous tissue and did not penetrate the skull. The middle fossa was opened and found to be grossly enlarged. The lesser wing of the sphenoid bone was displaced upward and tilted inwards toward the falx. No tumor was discovered in the cranium and the temporal lobe itself seemed to be enlarged. The eyelid was not explored.

CASE HISTORY (No. 505025).—*At 6 months the left eye began to be displaced forward and downward. The left temple bulged. Brown spots appeared over the abdomen and buttocks. At 13 years, pulsating exophthalmos and a faint bruit were discovered. Operation revealed a cyst in the left middle fossa and a defect in the wall of the orbit.*

W. L., a boy of 13 years, was examined on December 15, 1955. The history stated that at the age of 6 months it was noticed that his left eye was becoming more prominent. This deformity increased and brown spots developed over his abdomen and thighs. His mother had numerous brown spots over her body and also many cutaneous tumors.

On examination the child was well developed and nourished. His mental status seemed to be normal. The left eye was displaced forward and downward. The exophthalmometer showed 5 mm proptosis. See Figure 260. The left temple bulged. A faint bruit was heard over the left eye and some pulsation was observed. Vision was 20/30 and 20/70 right and left. The fields of vision were full and the optic discs normal. The cranial nerves were all in order. There were no disturbances of motility, senisibility or reflexes. A number of *café au lait* spots were found over the abdomen, buttocks and thighs but no cutaneous or subcutaneous tumors were present.

Roentgenograms revealed that the left middle fossa was enlarged and the sphenoidal ridge much elevated. There seemed to be a defect in the roof of the orbit.

Operation revealed a thin walled, transparent cyst lying anterior to the tip and medial to the left temporal lobe. This was removed. The walls of the cyst were composed of hyaline connective tissue. It contained yellow fluid.

On examination the mother was found to have numerous cafe au lait spots over the trunk and thighs as well as numerous cutaneous tumors, i.e. mollusca fibrosa.

CASE HISTORY (No. 421097).—*At age of 12 years wasting of the arms and legs began. At 15 years vocal cord paralysis developed. Later, bilateral facial paralysis. Biopsy of lesion on chest revealed plexiform neuroma.*

M. W., a boy of 17 years, was examined in Johns Hopkins Hospital on December 5, 1956. The history stated that the boy had always had an internal squint and that vision of the right eye had always been defective. A cyst of unknown nature was removed from his scalp at the age of 8 years. In 1951 at the age of 12 years, he began to show atrophy and wasting of the muscles of the right leg below the knee. Later, the left leg was involved in the same way, and soon his hands began to waste. In 1954, his voice began to get hoarse. On December 5, 1956, he was found unconscious on the floor. It was evident he had vomited. He was brought to the hospital. It was stated that his two siblings were quite normal and no member of the family had any condition similar to the patient's.

The boy regained consciousness by the time he arrived in the hospital. He was poorly developed and rather dull. The head was large and long. The pupils reacted to light and were equal and circular. The vision of the right eye was reduced to counting fingers but the left eye vision was 20/40. The right optic disc was pale and there was a lesion in the macula which appeared to be a staphyloma. Bilateral cataracts were present. There was complete paralysis of the left external rectus. On right lateral deviation irregular nystagmoid movements were seen. There was bilateral facial palsy of peripheral type. The hearing was not grossly reduced. The voice was hoarse and the vocal cords immobile in the cadaveric position.

There was wasting of the muscles below the knees and complete bilater-

al foot drop. The thighs were slightly wasted but the buttocks were not involved. The intrinsic muscles of the hands were wasted and weak. The tendon reflexes were lost in the legs and reduced in the arms. Cutaneous sensibility was somewhat reduced in the feet and fingers and there was also loss of proprioception in the fingers and toes. The nerve trunks were not thickened.

Two lesions were found on the skin, one in the right pectoral region and one in the right lumbar region. These were about 2.0 cm in diameter and slightly elevated. They were soft and covered by nodular skin. Small, soft cords could be felt in these lesions. On biopsy the pectoral lesion was found to be a plexiform neuroma. No subcutaneous nodules were found and no brown spots were seen on the skin.

The spinal fluid contained only 2 cells but the total protein was 485 mgs. The manometric tests showed no obstruction in the spinal canal.

Roentgenograms of the long bones revealed two cystic areas in the distal end of the right femur and a larger one in the distal end of the left femur. The internal auditory canals were both dilated. Air was injected and there seemed to be dilatation of the lateral ventricles and also of the anterior part of the third ventricle. There seemed to be a mass in the posterior part of the third ventricle.

Irrigation of the ears with ice water provoked no nystagmus or vertigo. The electroencephalogram showed only generalized slowing.

On November 1, 1958, the patient's condition was worse. There was bilateral involvement of the sixth and seventh nerves. Hearing was not definitely impaired. The voice was hoarse. Twitching of the tongue was evident. A large mass had appeared under the mandible on the left side of the neck. There was gross weakness and wasting of the hands, and of the legs, below the knees. The boy could not walk or stand. Loss of vibratory sense and loss of cutaneous sensibility were found in the legs, below the knees. The knee and ankle jerks were lost. The patient died on August 16, 1961.

Dr. David Clark examined the nervous system. He found hydrocephalus of moderate degree. Small areas of gliosis were found in each cerebellar hemisphere. There was a large neurofibroma on the right eighth nerve and a small one attached to the left eighth nerve. Another was found on the left third nerve, as well as the left seventh and ninth nerves. A meningioma en plaque was found on the falx. Almost all the spinal nerve roots were involved by tumors. Some of these were discrete nodules attached to the roots, but many were fusiform swellings which seemed to be growths within the nerve roots. As the roots passed through the intervertebral foramina, they became greatly enlarged and finally continuous with a large sarcomatous mass in the retroperitoneal space (Fig. 262).

CASE HISTORY (791363).—*A little boy was found to have bilateral optic atrophy at 2½ years. At 3 years, he began to have headaches. At 6 years, the child began to have minor seizures. At 8 years, examination revealed*

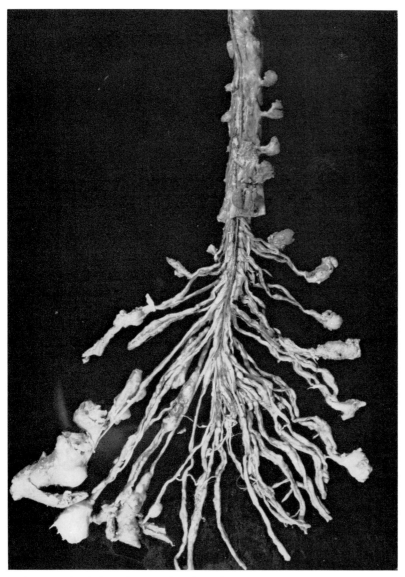

FIG. 262. Photograph of the spinal cord and cauda equina showing neurofibromata of the spinal nerve roots which terminate in a large sarcomatous mass in the retroperitoneal space. (By the courtesy of Dr. David Clark.)

cafe au lait spots, bilateral optic atrophy and gross reduction of vision. A glioma of the chiasm was found at operation.

M. F. was seen in consultation with Dr. Samuel Livingston on November 12, 1957. He was then 8 years old. His parents knew nothing of his family or his birth for he was an adopted child.

At the age of 2½ years it was suspected that his vision was not good and

examination led to a diagnosis of optic atrophy. Vision was estimated at 20/200 in each eye. A few months later a pneumoencephalogram was performed and the parents were informed that the ventricles were slightly enlarged and he might have arrested hydrocephalus. In the next 18 months several tests of vision were made and it was decided that his vision was not failing progressively. At this time he began to complain of headaches which recurred from time to time afterwards.

When he was 6 years old, he began to have minor seizures. In these he would throw his head back and make noises in his throat. His eyes would roll up. These seizures occurred in series of 4 to 9 attacks. When the patient was 7 years old, he had a convulsion.

On examination the child's head was slightly increased in circumference. It was not typically hydrocephalic in shape but the posterior portion was broad. There were numerous cafe au lait spots on the trunk. Vision was about 10/100 in the right eye and in the left eye was reduced to counting fingers at one foot. The boy's attention was so poor the fields could not be outlined. The optic discs showed advanced atrophy which seemed to be primary. Some irregular nystagmoid movements were seen. Otherwise the cranial nerves were in order. No disorders of motility or sensibility were found. The reflexes were all in order. The child seemed to be slightly backward in mental development.

Roentgenograms of the skull revealed calcium deposits above the sella. An air injection revealed that the third ventricle was pushed upwards and backwards. Exploration disclosed a large glioma of the optic chiasm which, of course, could not be removed. A small bit of tissue was removed and this established the diagnosis.

CASE HISTORY (Ped. A-2662. Path. 15681).—*Neurofibromatosis beginning at age of five years and associated with a large spongioblastoma in the base of the third ventricle giving rise to symptoms at the age of 11 years. Operation. Death. Post-mortem examination.*

N. S. was born at full term. He seemed to be a vigorous boy and developed rapidly. At the age of five years his mother noticed small tumors in the skin over his body and extremities and also numerous areas of brownish pigmentation. At the age of 11 years, he began to have difficulty in making his grades at school although he had done well before. He was over-active and distractible. His behavior was a problem and he was always joking in a foolish fashion. It was impossible for him to keep still or to concentrate. His I.Q. was 92. He soon began to complain of severe headaches and later of disturbances of vision. About the same time, he developed increased appetite and increased thirst and began to become obese. At the age of 13 years left hemiplegia developed in the course of several weeks. He began to vomit and was brought to Harriet Lane Home.

Examination disclosed an obese boy of the given age. Over the trunk and extremities there were innumerable small subcutaneous tumors ranging up to 0.5 cm in diameter and also a number of yellowish-brown areas. The skeleton was normal except for some increase in the dorsal curve of

the spine. He was over-active and his manner was overfriendly. There was bilateral papilledema of high grade with hemorrhages and exudate. Vision in the right eye was reduced to 4/400 but in the left eye was 20/30. The fields were constricted but showed no significant defects. The left arm and leg were weak and spastic. Roentgenograms showed destruction of the sella, convolutional atrophy of the vault, and separation of the sutures. Ventriculography disclosed a filling defect in the third ventricle. At operation, an inoperable growth was found in the third ventricle. Some days later the child died. Post-mortem examination showed a large infiltrating growth in the base of the third ventricle extending into the thalamus and the internal capsule on the right, anteriorly above the chiasm and posteriorly into the midbrain. The aqueduct and third ventricle were both obstructed. Histological examination indicated that the growth was a spongioblastoma.

CASE HISTORY (U-240243).—*Acoustic neuroma in a child of 14 years. Operation. At age of 19 years another neuroma was removed from the opposite side. No cutaneous signs of von Recklinghausen's disease.*

D. T., a girl of 14 years, began to walk unsteadily in the summer of 1941. She also noticed deafness in the left ear. These symptoms grew steadily worse. There was no headache and no diplopia. In September she came to Dr. Dandy.

Examination revealed bilateral papilledema of 3 diopters. There was horizontal nystagmus of cerebellar type on deviation to either side. The left corneal reflex was absent and the left side of the face somewhat numb. There was a slight left facial paresis. Cerebellar ataxia was observed in the left arm and leg with a tendency to stagger to the left. The left ear showed pronounced deafness though the low tones were preserved. Roentgenograms of the skull showed dilatation of the left internal auditory foramen. The patient's parents denied the existence of any similar cases in the family. There were no cutaneous signs of neurofibromatosis. Operation disclosed a typical acoustic neuroma attached to the left eighth nerve. It was removed successfully and the patient made an uneventful recovery with damage to the left seventh and eighth nerves. The tumor showed the typical histological picture.

Some five years later, the patient returned with symptoms of identical nature this time, however, were referable to the right side. Again an acoustic neuroma was found and removed. Unfortunately this rendered the patient completely deaf.

CASE HISTORY (U-444576).—*Boy of 16 years with many subcutaneous neurofibromata and bilateral foot drop.*

C. E. W., a boy of 16 years, noticed progressive weakness of his legs and increasing difficulty in gait in the fall of 1946. There was aching pain in both legs. Some months later he became conscious of many rounded nodules in his arms and legs which seemed to be growing larger. He came into the hospital on December 3, 1947.

Examination revealed a tall, well-developed boy who showed a striking indentation of the left side of the chest and a mild scoliosis in the thoracic region. There were a few faint brownish areas on the thighs and buttocks which were visible only in a strong light. No tumors were present in the skin. Under the skin were visible and palpable rounded tumors in great numbers. The largest of these were found in the popliteal spaces where they seemed to be 3 or 4 cm in diameter. These were very firm. The course of every nerve trunk was marked by a linear series of subcutaneous nodules. On an average these were about 1.0 to 2.0 cm in diameter. The muscles of the legs below the knees were wasted. Dorsal movement of the toes and feet was lost and there was bilateral foot drop. Plantar movement was very weak. The ankle jerks were lost. Sensibility was reduced in the sensory field of the sciatic nerves. Small nodules were seen in the irides with the slit-lamp. Later the patient developed severe abdominal pains and a number of masses were discovered in the abdomen.

CASE HISTORY.—*Cystic glioma removed from right parietal area at age of 7 years. At the age of 25 years, developed ataxia in the arms and legs. Neurofibromata removed from the cervical canal.*

V. C., a young woman of 26 years, was examined in consultation with Dr. Hugo Rizzili on February 28, 1957. She stated that 19 years before she had developed headaches and disturbances of vision. There was bilateral papilledema, left homonymous hemianopia and loss of proprioception in the left arm and leg. A cystic growth was removed from the right parietal region. This was regarded as a spongioblastoma. Post-operative radiation was given. The papilledema soon receded and the symptoms in the left arm and leg disappeared. The hemianopia persisted.

In November 1954 a fetal adenoma was removed from the thyroid gland and some subcutaneous tumors were also removed. These were said to be neurofibromata.

In November, 1956, the patient began to notice that she was growing unsteady on her feet and her arms and legs were growing clumsy. She could not fasten buttons. These symptoms advanced rapidly. She noticed some pains in her neck.

On examination the head was rather large and an operative defect was found in the right parietal region. The pupils were equal and reacted to light. Vision was 10/15 right and 10/20 left. There was an almost complete left homonymous hemianopia. The optic discs showed no gross changes. The cranial nerves were in order.

The station was unsteady and the gait unsteady and ataxic. There was no weakness of the arms or legs but there was definite ataxia of both the arms and the legs. Cutaneous sensibility was intact but sense of passive movement and position and vibratory sense were reduced in all four extremities. The tendon reflexes were not increased or reduced and the plantar responses were normal.

Numerous small tumors were seen over the skin which resembled fibromata mollusca and there was a typical café au lait spot on the left breast.

A myelogram revealed an obstruction at C1. At operation Dr. Rizzoli found bilateral neurofibromas protruding between the arches of C1 and C2. These tumors arose from the second cervical root and pushed the cord posteriorly so it was indented by the arch of the first cervical vertebra. In the neck these tumors measured 3.0 cm in diameter. Lower down another neurofibroma was found in the neck attached to the C4 root on the right.

CASE HISTORY (No. 1133493).—*Child of 6 years developed almost complete loss of function of the radial nerve in the course of 15 months. One small café au lait spot on the trunk. Operation revealed a schwannoma.*

D. S., a little girl of six years, was seen by the courtesy of Dr. David Clark. Some weakness of the extensors of the right wrist had been noted 15 months before. The process was progressive and when she was examined on December 5, 1964, it was found that there was complete paralysis of the long extensors of the fingers, thumb and wrist. The brachioradialis did not contract and there was some cutaneous hypesthesia over the sensory field of the radial nerve. There was no weakness of the triceps muscle and the triceps reflex was preserved. Nothing else could be found except for a small *café au lait* area on the right side of the trunk. No mass could be felt along the course of the radial nerve.

Operation revealed a fusiform enlargement of the radial nerve midway between the elbow and the shoulder. This was removed and proved to be a schwannoma.

No history of signs of von Recklinghausen's disease in the family was elicited.

CASE HISTORY (U-160788).—*Girl of four years developed progressive scoliosis. Pigmented areas in the skin appeared. Several years later the legs became weak. During traction at the age of 17 years, paraplegia occurred. At operation the spinal cord was found to be stretched over the spinal curvature.*

CASE HISTORY.—*Boy of 10 years, who had been blind in the left eye since the age of three years, developed a transverse lesion of the spinal cord. Family history of von Recklinghausen's disease. Meningiomas found in the orbit and the spinal canal.*

J. L. M., a boy of 10 years, was the fourth son of a patient who was afflicted with von Recklinghausen's disease. The father had slowly become deaf and helpless and had brown spots over his body. Three of the four sons including the patient exhibited signs of this disease. The patient's siblings were not examined.

At the age of three years the patient was found to be blind in the left eye and in the next few years the left eye had slowly protruded. Some two months before the patient was examined he had begun to develop weakness and numbness of his legs.

On examination the patient was found to have a number of small faintly brown splotches over his trunk and a few small subcutaneous nod-

ules over the abdomen. The left eye was proptosed about 4.0 mm and quite blind. The left pupil did not react directly to light and the optic nerve head was quite pale. Movements of the left bulb were restricted moderately in all planes. Hearing was not affected and the cranial nerves showed no other damage. The arms were not affected in any way. The legs were spastic and weak, the right being weaker than the left. The tendon reflexes were all increased and the plantar response was extensor on both sides. No definite loss of sensibility was found. The spine was straight and movements were not restricted.

Manometric tests revealed obstruction of the spinal canal. A meningioma was found in the upper thoracic level and removed successfully. At a second operation a meningioma was removed from the left orbit. No other neoplasms could be found.

CASE HISTORY (No. 795088).—*Progressive scoliosis at eight years with paraplegia some years later. Bilateral acoustic neuromas and probably. glioma of the chiasm. No cutaneous lesions.*

J. H. was seen at the age of eight years. The only complaint was progressive scoliosis. At about the age of thirteen years, he began to notice that his legs were weak and there was increasing difficulty in walking. Later, it was discovered that he was growing deaf in the right ear and the eyes were dancing.

Examination at the age of eighteen years revealed deafness of the right ear, apparently due to eighth nerve damage with nystagmus and damage to the fifth and seventh nerves as well. The optic discs showed mild papilledema, evidently of long duration. There was gross scoliosis, with shortening of the trunk. Weakness of the legs, with bilateral Babinski signs and brisk knee and ankle jerks, was present. Vision of the left eye was much reduced, though the right eye vision was good. There was mild proptosis on the left. No lesions were found in the skin. The father had a single *café au lait* area on his abdomen.

Operation was performed and an acoustic neuroma was removed from the posterior fossa on the right side. After this, there was complete deafness on the right, and paralysis of the face.

Some months later, the legs had grown weaker and the patient could no longer walk. The boy's vision had failed rapidly and was reduced to hand movements. The left eye was still somewhat proptosed. The left ear was almost completely deaf.

CASE HISTORY.—*Drooping of the right lid at the age of 6 years. Enophthalmos noted later. Plexiform neuroma of the upper lid. Enlargement of the right orbit.*

A. G. was a normal healthy boy, until the age of six years, when his parents noted that the right eyelid was beginning to droop. The parents were not conscious of any other abnormality.

When the boy was examined at the age of thirteen years, the upper lid was found to be thickened and drooped so as to cover part of the pupil.

There was striking enophthalmos with small pulsations but not bruit or thrill. The bulb might be pushed in very easily. One could feel a rounded defect in the squamous part of the right temporal bone. The right side of the face seemed to be slightly larger than the left. No other abnormalities were evident on examination.

Roentgenographic examination of the skull revealed the rounded defect in the right temporal bone and striking enlargement of the right orbit without evident defect in the wall of the orbit. The sphenoid ridge was elevated. The sella appeared to be normal. Biopsy of the lid revealed plexiform neuroma.

CASE HISTORY (1162393).—A little boy was seen at the age of 4 years. He had been quite healthy until 2 years before. He then began to lose weight and his growth had ceased. When examined at the age of 4 years, he was emaciated. He was no taller than a child of 3 years. There were several tumors on the skin and a large number of café au lait spots over the body. His behavior was abnormal for he would scream and fight if anyone touched him. It was believed that he had the sham rage syndrome. Biopsy of 2 skin tumors revealed that they were neurofibromata. His eyes were examined under anesthesia for he had severe photophobia. The optic discs were pale. His vision was reduced but could not be estimated exactly. An air study revealed evidences of a tumor mass in the region of the optic chiasm. The sella showed the anterior extension characteristic of glioma of the optic chiasm.

CASE HISTORY.—*Evidence of damage to lumbar plexus discovered at the age of 4 days. Two café au lait spots.*

T. B. was born at term by spontaneous delivery. Presentation was cephalic. He breathed well and took his feedings well. On the 4th day it was noted that he did not move his left leg properly.

Examination at 3 months revealed weakness of the flexors of the left hip and almost complete paralysis of the left quadriceps with loss of the left knee jerk. The hamstrings seemed to be shortened. There was a café au lait spot on the right knee.

He was seen again at the age of 9 years. He had been having severe headaches and also sudden sharp pains in the anterior aspect of the left thigh. Examination revealed no abnormality of the cranial nerves. The left leg was shorter than the right. The left quadriceps was grossly wasted. There was weakness in flexion at the hip and scarcely any power in the left quadriceps. The left knee jerk was lost. There was cutaneous anesthesia over the anterior aspect of the left thigh and over the inner aspect of the leg below the knee. There was a large café au lait spot on the right knee and another had appeared on the abdomen.

BIBLIOGRAPHY

ALLIBONE, E. C. *et al.:* Neurofibromatosis of the vertebral column. Arch. Dis. Childhood, **35:**153, 1960.

BJORKESTEN, G.: Unilateral acoustic tumors in children. Acta Neurol. et Psychiat. Scandinav.,
    32:1, 1957.
BIELSCHOWSKY, M.: Familiare hypertrophische neuritis und neurofibromatose. J.f. Psychol. u.
    Neurol., **29:**192, 1922.
BRUWER, A. J.: Neurofibromatosis with unilateral pulsating and non-pulsating exophthalmos.
    Arch. Ophth., **53:**1, 1955.
BUTTERWORTH, T. AND STREAM, L. P.: Clinical Genodermatology. Williams and Wilkins, 1962.
CAMPBELL, W. C.: Congenital hypertrophy. Report of a case with neurofibromatosis. Surg.
    Gynec. & Obst., **36:**699, 1923.
CHAPMAN, R. C., KEMP, V. E. AND TALIAFERRO, I.: Phaeochromocytoma associated with mul-
    tiple neurofibromatosis and intracranial hemangioma. Am. J. Med., **26:**883, 1959.
CRAIG, W. McK. *et al.:* Neurinomas in children. J. Neurosurg., **1:**505, 1954.
CROME, L.: Central neurofibromatosis. Arch. Dis. Childhood, **37:**640, 1962.
CROWE, F. W. *et al.:* Multiple Neurofibromatosis. Springfield, Thomas, 1956.
CUSHING, H.: Papers Related to the Pituitary Body, Hypothalamus and Parasympathetic System.
    Springfield, Thomas, 1932, p. 49.
D'AGOSTINO, A. N. *et al.:* Sarcomas of peripheral nerves and somatic tissues associated with
    multiple fibromatosis. Cancer, **16:**1015, 1963.
DAVIDOFF, L. M. *et al.:* Hereditary combined neurinomas and meningiomas. J. Neurosurg.,
    12:375, 1955.
DAVIS, F. A.: Plexiform neurofibromatosis of the orbit and globe with associated glioma of
    the optic nerve and brain. Arch. Ophth., **22:**761, 1939.
DAVIS, F. W., HULL, J. G. AND VARDELL, J. C.: Pheochromocytoma with neurofibromatosis. Am.
    J. Med., **8:**131, 1950.
DODGE, H. W. AND CRAIG, W. McK.: Benign peripheral nerve tumors. Minnesota Med., **40:**294,
    1957.
FINBY, N. AND BEGG, C. F.: Pheochromocytoma and neurofibromatosis. New York Jour. Med.,
    64:1010, 1964.
GARDNER, W. J. AND FRAZIER, C. H.: Bilateral acoustic neurofibromas: Survey of family of 5
    generations with bilateral deafness in 38 members. Arch. Neurol. & Psychiat., **23:**266, 1930.
GORDON, M. B.: An endocrine consideration of von Recklinghausen's disease. Report of a case
    associated with infantile myxedema. Endocrinology, **13:**553, 1929.
GORLIN, R. J. AND SEDANO, H.: Multiple mucosal neuromas, pheochromocytoma and medullary
    carcinoma of the thyroid. Modern Medicine, December 16, 1968, p. 146.
HEARD, G. AND PAYNE, E. E.: Scalloping of vertebral bodies in von Recklinghausen's disease.
    Jour. Neurol., Neurosurg. and Psychiat., **25:**345, 1962.
————: Malignant disease in von Recklinghausen's neurofibromatosis. Pro. Roy. Soc. Med.,
    56:502, 1963.
————: Nerve sheath tumors and von Recklinghausen's disease of nervous system. Ann. Roy.
    Coll. Surgeons England. **31:**229, 1962.
———— *et al.:* Cervical vertebral deformity in von Recklinghausen's disease of the nervous
    system. Jour. Bone and Joint Surg., **44B:**880, 1962.
HELMHOLZ, H. AND CUSHING, H.: Von Recklinghausen's disease. Bull. Johns Hopkins Hosp.,
    17:93, 1926.
JACKSON, A. H.: Three cases of multiple neurofibromatosis with malignant degeneration.
    J. Nerv. & Ment. Dis., **78:**581, 1933.
JOFFE, N.: Calvarial bone defects of lamboid suture in neurofibromatosis. Brit. Jour. Radiol.,
    38:23, 1965.
KIVOSHI, H.: Multiple neurofibromatosis (von Recklinghausen's disease) with special reference
    to malignant transformation. Arch. Surg., **22:**258, 1931.
KOCH, G.: Phakomatosen Humangenetik. P. E. Becker, Georg Thieme, Stutgart, 1966.
KOHOUT, E. AND STOUT, A. P.: Glomus tumors in children. Cancer, **14:**555, 1961.
KRÜCHE, W.: Zur Histopathologie der neuralen Muskalatrophie der hypertrophischen Neuritis
    und Neurofibromatose. Arch. f. Psychiat., **115:**180, 1942.

LAWS, J. W. AND PALLIS, C.: Spinal deformities in neurofibromatosis. Jour. Bone and Joint Surg., **45B**:674, 1963.

LEE, D. K. AND ABOTT, M. L.: Familial central nervous system neoplasia. Arch. of Neurology, **20**:154, 1969.

LEHMAN, E.: Recklinghausen's neurofibromatosis and the skeleton. Arch. Derm. & Syph., **14**:178, 1926.

———— AND BROOKS, B.: Bone changes in von Recklinghausen's neurofibromatosis. Surg. & Obst., **38**:587, 1924.

LICHTENSTEIN, B. W.: Neurofibromatosis. Arch. Neurol. & Psychiat., **62**:822, 1949.

LOVE, J. G.: Unilateral deafness—and progressive facial palsy due to intrapetrous neurofibroma. Prog. Staff Meet. Mayo Clin., **25**:228, 1950.

McKEON, F. AND FRAZER, M. J. L.: Neurofibromatosis with pathological fractures in newborn. Arch. of Dis. Childh., **36**:340, 1961.

MOORE, J. G.: Neonatal neurofibromatosis. Brit. Jour. Ophthal., **46**:682, 1962.

PARKES WEBER, F.: Periosteal neurofibromatosis with a short discussion of the whole subject of neurofibromatosis. Quart. J. Med., **23**:151, 1930.

PEARCE, J.: The central nervous system pathology in multiple neurofibromatosis. Neurology, **17**:691, 1967.

PENFIELD, W.: Encapsulated tumors of the nervous system, etc. Surg., Gynec. & Obst., **45**:178, 1927.

———— AND YOUNG, A. W.: Nature of von Recklinghausen's disease and the tumors associated with it. Arch. Neurol. & Psychiat., **23**:320, 1930.

PENIDO, J. R. *et al.:* Tumors of the vagus nerve. Proc. Staff Meet. Mayo Clin., **32**:239, 1957.

PEREA, V. D. AND GREGORY, L. J. JR.: Neurofibromatosis of the stomach. J.A.M.A., **182**:259, 1962.

PEYTON, W. T. AND SIMMONS, D. R.: Neurofibromatosis with defect in the wall of the orbit. Arch. Neurol. & Psychiat., **55**:248, 1946.

PREISER, S. AND DAVENPORT, C.: Multiple neurofibromatosis and its inheritance. Report of a case. Am. J. Med. Sc., **156**:507, 1918.

REVILLA, A. G.: Neurinomas of the cerebellopontine recess. Bull. Johns Hopkins Hosp., **80**:254, 1947.

ROBINSON, R.: Temporal lobe agenesis. Brain, **87**:87, 1964.

ROSENDAL, T.: Some cranial changes in Recklinghausen's neurofibromatosis. Acta radiol. Scand., **19**:373, 1938.

SCHARENBERG, K. AND JONAS, E.: Diffuse glioma of the brain in von Recklinghausen's disease. J. Neurosurg., **6**:269, 1956.

SCHLEGEL, G. G.: Neurofibromatosis and pheochromocytoma. Schweiz. Med. Wschr., **90**:31, 1960.

SINCLAIR, J. E. AND YANG, Y. H.: Ganglioneuromata of the spine associated with von Recklinghausen's disease. Jour. Neurosurg., **18**:115, 1961.

WALSH, F. B.: *Loc. cit.*

WILSON, J. S. AND ANDERSON, A. A.: Cutaneous and intestinal neurofibromatosis. Amer. Jour. Surg., **100**:761, 1960.

WINESTEIN, F.: Relation of von Recklinghausen's disease to giant growth and blastomatosis. J. Cancer Res., **8**:409, 1924.

WOLTER, J. R. *et al.:* Neurofibromatosis of the choroid. Amer. Jour. Ophthal., **54**:217, 1962.

YAKOVLEV, P. O. AND GUTHRIE, R. H.: Congenital ectodermoses. Arch. Neurol. & Psychiat., **26**:1145, 1931.

TUBEROSE SCLEROSIS OR EPILOIA

Definition.—This rare disease is manifest by multiple tumors and malformations involving the brain, skin and viscera. It, therefore, presents many analogies with the neurofibromatosis of von Recklinghausen.

Pathological Anatomy.—The convolutional pattern of the cerebral cortex may be altered by areas of microgyria or abnormally broad gyri, but is

usually normal. On careful inspection multiple yellowish-white areas, or plaques, are seen, which are unduly firm on palpation. Many small nodules project into the ventricles. Small cysts, intraventricular gliomas and angiomas are common. Histological examination reveals that the firm areas in the cortex are composed of masses of glial tissue. Many abnormal cells are found in such regions, some of which are of great size and are thought to be either malformed neuroblasts or spongioblasts. The cortex is incompletely developed and myelin sheaths are absent in the sclerotic areas. Stratification of cells is irregular and the cells are malformed or degenerated. The blood vessels may be calcified and various degenerative changes may occur as a result. Beneath these plaques the white matter may show defective myelination and may contain spongioblasts and other malformed glial cells. Calcium deposits are eventually laid down in these areas of the white matter. The ventricular nodules are said to be spongioblastomas and often contain dense deposits of calcium. Lesions in the cerebellum are uncommon. Retinal tumors and gliomatous plaques and cysts of the optic nerve head are common. The cortical tumors grow slowly if at all and should be regarded as glioses rather than gliomas. However, malignant and invasive growths may arise in such lesions and it is claimed that spongioneuroblastoma is especially apt to develop. Globus and Strauss found tuberose sclerosis in 3 of their 16 cases of glioblastoma multiforme. Tumors of the heart,

Fig. 263. Tuberose sclerosis in a girl of 15 years showing adenoma sebaceum over the cheeks. These lesions appeared at the age of three years. The next year vision became impaired in the left eye and an internal squint developed. At 14 years signs of increased intracranial pressure appeared. Dr. Dandy removed a glioma from the third ventricle. Several sclerotic areas were found in the cortex of the right frontal lobe during this operation. The evidences of increased intracranial pressure were relieved but the patient still shows progressive mental deterioration and has an occasional fit. (Dandy: Benign Tumors in the Third Ventricle. Thomas, 1933.)

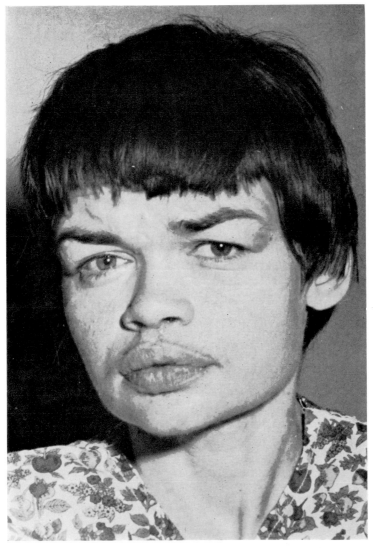

FIG. 264. Tuberose sclerosis showing coarse features and low forehead. There are adenoma sebaceum which do not show well in the photograph.

kidney, liver, pancreas and thyroid gland are often found. In certain instances these patients develop multiple cystic lesions in the lungs due to over-growth of connective tissue, smooth muscle and blood vessels. Crome finds endocardial fibroelastosis, a condition which may cause heart failure. In many cases, papules occur on the face which are termed *adenoma sebaceum*. However, these are chiefly composed of connective tissue and capillaries and contain few glandular elements. Various developmental defects are also found, such as congenital heart disease, hare-lip, spina bifida and

polydactylism. Dickerson has found that the cystic areas in the phalanges are really areas of fibrous replacement of bone surrounded by an abundant osteoid matrix. The dense plaques seen in the roentgenograms of the skull are found to be areas of osteosclerosis confined to the trabeculae of the diploic spaces.

Clinical Features.—The disease affects males and females alike. It is sometimes both familial and hereditary and has been traced through several generations. A dominant inheritance is claimed. Sporadic cases, however, are not uncommon. The children may be defective from early infancy or may develop normally up to the age of nine or ten years. Often the child is slow to walk or talk but seems to make some progress for a short time.

Epileptic phenomena are frequently the first evidences of the disease. They usually develop before the end of the second year. Minor attacks or focal twitchings without loss of consciousness occur. Aicardi states that infantile flexor spasms are common. Later the attacks grow more frequent and severe. There is a tendency for the seizures to be evenly spaced but long remissions are observed. Sooner or later, violent general convulsions develop. Fainting spells or periods of confusion and excitement may occur as equivalents.

Soon after the seizures begin usually before the sixth year, *psychic changes* become evident. The child becomes indifferent, ceases to learn, takes no interest in toys and shows all the evidences of mental deterioration. Very few patients retain a normal mentality. We have seen one patient, however, whose mentality was still normal in adult life though he had several of the classical signs of this condition. Among the psychotic symptoms, Critchley lists preoccupation, dissociation, apathy, motiveless excitement, catatonia, flexibilitas cereas, negativism, echolalia, bizarre attitudes and stereotype

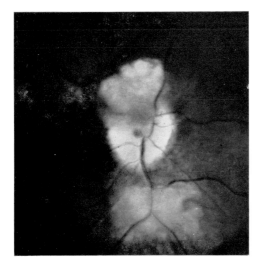

Fig. 265. Photograph of the retina showing nodular growth on the optic disc, probably a glioma, in the case shown in the preceding illustration. (By the courtesy of Dr. Walsh.)

movements. Fits of screaming and crying are common. Some patients may injure themselves or others.

Neurological manifestations are not very striking and in some cases none may be demonstrable. In younger children muscle tone may be diminished but later in life there may be rigidity. Restlessness is common and constant movements of the hands and fingers, often of very complex type, may be observed. Local pareses, with spasticity or with hypotonia, are sometimes present, but paralysis is rare. In all cases in which the symptoms are well-marked speech is more or less profoundly altered. Some children never talk, especially if the onset is early, and others become mute or dysarthric. An unusual complication is the development of increased intracranial pressure with papilledema. This is usually due to development of an intraventricular tumor, which causes occlusion of the ventricular system and hydrocephalus.

Pecularities of development have been mentioned above. Many subjects of this disease are below the average stature. Sexual infantilism is rare, it is said, and sexual precocity is not unusual. One might imagine that both of these conditions result from lesions in the hypothalamus. Cretchley has observed cases of simian hand, shortening of the little finger, malformations of the ears, hemihypertrophy, polydactylism, spina bifida, strabismus, myopia, and defects in the arrangements of the teeth, high arched palate, hare-lip, congenital heart disease, etc.

A very characteristic feature, which is not however constant, is the presence of *cutaneous lesions.* These usually appear during the first decade and are accentuated at the age of puberty. The commonest type, termed "adenoma sebaceum," are yellow, pink or red papules, varying from two or three millimeters in diameter to one centimeter. They are scattered over the cheeks and the bridge of the nose in the so-called butterfly distribution but may be found on the forehead and chin. Yakovlev and Guthrie also describe pedunculated skin polypi, subcutaneous nodules, local thickenings of the skin, termed shagreen skin, ichthyosis, pigmented warts, which may be covered with hair, naevi, café au lait spots and anemic areas. Nodules under the nail are often found. These lesions are similar to those seen in von Recklinghausen's disease, and it is believed that these diseases are closely related.

Van der Hoeve has emphasized the importance of *retinal tumors* which he calls phakomas. He describes small, round flat growths scattered over the retina and mushroom-like tumors springing from the optic nerve head. The latter often undergo cystic degeneration. The cysts may rupture, causing small hemorrhages. Optic atrophy may occur and congenital cataracts are described.

Eventually, the patient may become totally demented and the de-

mentia or the convulsions may necessitate the child's being placed in an institution for defectives. Most cases terminate fatally, either as a result of status epilepticus, tumor growth in the heart, viscera or brain, or of some terminal infection. Lesions in the heart may lead to heart failure. The cystic lesions in the lungs may cause serious embarrassment of respiration or even death. Pheochromocytoma is sometimes found.

In the fully developed form of the disease, cutaneous lesions, convulsions, and psychic changes are all present. A number of abortive types, however, occur. Thus, Critchley mentions cases of adenoma sebaceum alone, adenoma sebaceum with epilepsy but without mental deterioration, and visceral tumors of characteristic type, without other symptoms. It is evident, therefore, that the outlines of the disease are not very clearly defined.

Recently attention has been drawn to the presence of small areas of increased density in the skull which are often visible in the roentgenogram. The bones of the skeleton may show periosteal deposits, osteoporosis and punched-out area suggesting cysts. Calcium deposits are seen in the subcortical white matter and in the nodular tumors which lie in the walls of the ventricles.

Diagnosis.—The diagnosis during life depends upon the characteristic cutaneous manifestations, opacities in the skull and brain and tumors of

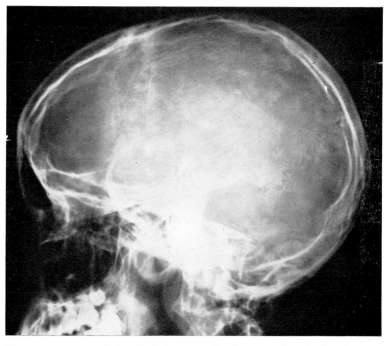

FIG. 266. Roentgenogram of the skull in case of tuberose sclerosis showing areas of increased density in the bone. (By the courtesy of Dr. David Clark.)

Fig. 267. Shagreen skin in case of tuberose sclerosis. (By the courtesy of Dr. Harry Butler.)

the retina for the cerebral symptoms are not so typical as to permit the disease to be distinguished from other progressive cerebral processes. The nodular growths which object into the ventricles may be demonstrated by ventriculography. The cysts in the lungs seem to be of diagnostic value. No doubt, tuberose sclerosis is frequently responsible for convulsions which are mistakenly attributed to epilepsy.

Prognosis.—Nothing can be done to halt the progress of the disease and death often occurs early in the second decade or before.

Treatment.—The usual sedative drugs may be employed for the convulsive seizures. If increased intracranial pressure or definite focal signs of a cerebral lesion appear, operation may be considered. Dr. Dandy has removed the growths from the ventricles in several cases with complete relief of signs and symptoms of increased intracranial pressure.

CASE HISTORY.—*Tuberose sclerosis in a 13-year-old girl.*

C. O. was examined at the age of 13 years. The child was born at term and seemed to be a healthy baby. Her early development was normal. At

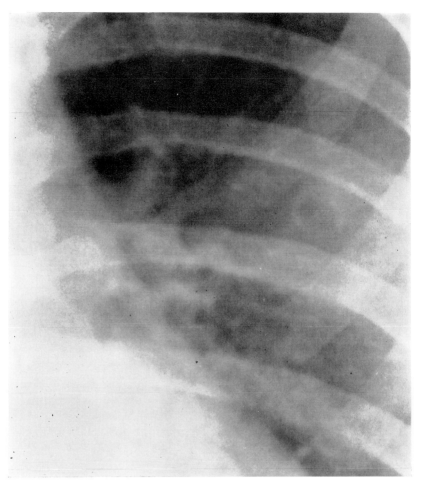

Fig. 268. Tuberose sclerosis showing multiple small cysts in the lung. (By the courtesy of Dr. Harry G. Butler.)

8 months, she was trying to walk and talk and could put a cookie in her mouth. At 20 months she walked well and had a number of words.

At 2 years she began to have seizures. She would develop a blank expression and her head and trunk would be rigidly extended. At such times she would not respond. Such attacks occurred every few minutes. They might last a few seconds or for 10 minutes. They could never be controlled by medication.

After the seizures began mental and motor deterioration became evident. By the age of 5 years she had ceased to talk and did not respond in any way to what was said to her. She was unsteady on her feet and if she fell could not get up. She would burn herself or injure herself in other ways, but showed no evidence of pain. She had to be fed and could not

chew her food. She never picked up objects or held them. She held her hands in front of her face and clapped them constantly.

At times she would weep for hours and at other times she would smile and giggle persistently.

When she was 9 years old, her breasts began to develop and pubic hair appeared. Menstruation began at 10 years.

X-rays of the head showed characteristic calcified deposits in the cerebral cortex and dense areas in the cranial vault.

On examination her bodily development was deficient. The capacity of the cranium was reduced. The lumbar lordosis was increased. She was adequately nourished. Her breasts were of adolescent character, and a good growth of pubic hair was evident. Small brownish papules were seen over the cheeks, i.e. adenoma sebaceum.

She did not try to form words or respond when spoken to. She staggered about clapping her hands in aimless fashion. It was evident that she could see for she would look at people. She smiled constantly. Every few minutes she would have a tonic seizure during which her eyes would blink and her head and trunk would be rigidly extended. She would fall backwards if not supported.

The muscles were very slender and there seemed to be a diffuse reduction of strength. The hands and feet were not fully developed. The tendon reflexes in the arms were active and the tendon reflexes in the legs were increased. Ankle clonus was present on both sides but the plantar reflexes were obscured by tickle responses.

BIBLIOGRAPHY

ACKERMANN, A. J.: Pulmonary and osseus manifestations of tuberous sclerosis. Amer. Jour. Roentgenol., 51:315, 1944.

AICARDI, J. et al.: Bourneville's tuberous sclerosis and infantile flexor spasms. Ann. Pediat., 42:770, 1966.

BAAR, H. S. AND GALINDO, J.: Pulmonary glomangiomata and hamartoma in tuberous sclerosis. Arch. of Path., 78:287, 1964.

BERLAND, H. I.: Roentgenological findings in tuberose sclerosis. Arch. Neurol. & Psychiat., 69:669, 1953.

CHAO, D. H.: Congenital neurocutaneous syndromes in childhood. Jour. Pediat., 55:447, 1959.

CRITCHLEY, McD. AND EARL, C. J. C.: Tuberose sclerosis and allied conditions. Brain, 55:311, 1932.

CROME, L.: Epiloia and endocardial fibroelastosis. Arch. Dis. Child., 29:136, 1954.

D'AGOSTINO, A. AND KERNOHAN, J. W.: Tuberous sclerosis complex. Jour. Neuropath. and Exp. Neurol., 21:79, 1962.

DAVIS, R. L. AND NELSON, E.: Unilateral ganglioneuroma in tubersclerotic brain. Jour. Neuropath. and Exp. Neurol., 20:571, 1961.

DAWSON, J.: Pulmonary tuberous sclerosis. Quart. J. Med., 23:113, 1954.

DE LA CRUZ AND LA VECK, G. D.: Tuberous sclerosis. Amer. Jour. Ment. Deficiency, 67:369, 1962.

DICKERSON, W. W.: The nature of certain osseus lesions in tuberous sclerosis. Arch. Neurol. & Psychiat., 73:525, 1955.

FREEMAN, W.: Tuberose sclerosis. Arch. Neurol. & Psychiat., 8:614, 1922.

GONZALEZ-ANGULO, A. et al.: Tuberous sclerosis. Arch. Otolaryng., 80:193, 1964.

GREENFIELD, J. G.: Neuropathology. Norman, R. M., Tuberose Sclerosis. Williams and Wilkins Co., Baltimore, 1958, p. 342.

HALL, G. S.: Tuberose sclerosis, rheostosis and neurofibromatosis. Quart. J. Med., 9:1, 1940.

——: Ocular manifestations of tuberose sclerosis. Quart. J. Med., 15:209, 1946.

HASEGAWA, J. AND IHRKE, R. E.: Tuberous sclerosis complex. J.A.M.A., 173:150, 1960.

HOLT, J. AND DICKERSON, W.: Osseous lesions of tuberous sclerosis. Radiology, 58:1, 1952.

JERVIS, G. A.: Spongioneuroblastoma and tuberous sclerosis. J. Neuropath. & Exp. Neurol., 13:105, 1954.

KESSEL, F. K.: Some radiologic and neurosurgical aspects of tuberous sclerosis. Acta Psychiat., et neurol., 24:499, 1949.

MARSHALL, D.: Tuberous sclerosis. New Eng. Jour. Med., 261:1102, 1959.

MORALES, J. B.: Congenital rhabdomyoma, tuberous sclerosis and splenic histocytosis. Arch. Path., 71:485, 1961.

NICKEL, W. R. AND REED, W. B.: Tuberous sclerosis. Arch. Derm., 85:209, 1962.

ROSS, A. T. AND DICKERSON, W. W.: Tuberose sclerosis. Arch. Neurol. & Psychiat., 50:233, 1943.

RUDNICK, P. A. *et al.*: Tuberous sclerosis complex and astrocytoma. J.A.M.A., 178:73, 1961.

SCHNITZER, B.: Tuberous sclerosis complex. Arch. of Path., 76:626, 1963.

VAN DER HOEVE, J.: Eye diseases in tuberose sclerosis and Recklinghausen's disease. Trans. Ophth. Soc. London, 43:534, 1923.

WALSH, F. B.: *Loc. cit.*

WOLFE, H. J. AND FOLEY, F. D.: Observations on tuberous sclerosis. Arch. of Path., 76:197, 1963.

YAKOVLEV, P. I. AND GUTHRIE, R. H.: Congenital ectodermoses in epileptic patients. Arch. Neurol. & Psychiat., 26:1145, 1931.

PRIMARY GLIOSIS OF THE BRAIN

Definition.—Gliosis of the brain either focal or diffuse which is not secondary to degeneration of the neurons and which does not constitute a true neoplasm.

Pathological Anatomy.—According to the descriptions of Foerster, von Santha and Nevin large areas of the brain are swollen, gray and firm. The thalamus, lenticular nucleus and brain stem are most commonly affected but large areas of the cortex may also be involved. Histological examination reveals that these areas are the seat of an excessive growth of glial fibers. In the cases of Foerster and von Santha the cells contained elongated nuclei lying parallel to one another and it was concluded that they were equivalent to the cells of the sheath of Schwann. Nevin and others describe many different types of glial cells including spongioblasts and astrocytes and conclude that the cells are all of the glia series. The increased mass of the brain usually results in increased intracranial pressure. Fissures and hemorrhages are found in various parts of the brain and there is some destruction of nerve fibers and neurons. The process is believed to arise upon a basis of blastomatous malformation of the glial tissue.

Clinical Features.—It is impossible to construct a clinical picture for few cases are described and the symptoms are not uniform. The onset may occur at any age but is frequently in childhood. Convulsive seizures are usually the first manifestations of the disease and may precede other symptoms

by an interval of years. Later there is progressive mental deterioration, signs of focal lesions in the brain appear and finally increased intracranial pressure develops. The course is subacute or chronic and death may be long deferred. In Foerster's case the child showed pigmented spots over the skin and neurofibromata so the diagnosis of von Recklinghausen's disease was made. These signs have not been present in other cases. It hardly seems possible to make the diagnosis during life.

BIBLIOGRAPHY

Foerster, O. and Gagel, O.: Zentrale diffuse Schwannose bei Recklinghausenschen Krankheit. Ztschr. f. d. ges. Neurol. u. Psychiat., 151:1, 1934.

Freeman, W.: Neuropathology. W. B. Saunders Co. 1933, p. 276.

Nevin, S.: Gliomatosis cerebri. Brain, 61:170, 1938 and J. Neurol. & Psychiat., 1: new series, 342, 1938.

van Santha, K.: Diffuse lemmoblastose des Zentralnervensystems. Ztschr. f. d. ges. Neurol. u. Psychiat., 154:763, 1936.

DIFFUSE HYPERTROPHY OF THE CEREBELLAR CORTEX

Oppenheimer reports two cases of this unusual condition and reviews ten more. The clinical picture is that of a posterior fossa neoplasm. At operation the cerebellum is enlarged. The material removed shows that the cortex of the cerebellum is thickened. Atypical nerve cells are found in the granular layer and medullated fibers in the molecular layer. The central white matter is reduced or absent. In some cases there are calcareous deposits in the walls of the capillaries. In other cases, small angiomatous nodules are seen. No neoplastic cells are seen. It seems that operation may be successful.

BIBLIOGRAPHY

Oppenheimer, D. R.: Benign tumor of the cerebellum. J. Neurol., Neurosurg. & Psychiat., 18:199, 1955.

INVOLVEMENT OF THE NERVOUS SYSTEM IN HODGKIN'S DISEASE

The nervous system is affected in a very large percentage of all cases of this disease and a great many papers have been published upon this subject in recent years. Three types of tissue are found in Hodgkin's disease, the paragranuloma, the granuloma and the sarcoma. The spinal cord is involved most frequently and, as a rule, the injury is caused by invasion of the spinal epidural space by lymphoblastic tissue and compression of the cord. This may result from extension of this tissue through the intervertebral foramina from affected lymph nodes of the abdomen or thorax or from deposits in the fascia or periosteum of the spine. In some cases, the cord is injured by the destruction and collapse of the vertebrae. It may be softened without compression when the blood supply is interrupted by

masses in the mediastinum surrounding the vertebrae. Primary deposits in the dura and epidural tissues are described. The peripheral nerves may be compressed in the pelvis or axilla by masses of affected lymph nodes. The sympathetic chain of ganglia are not uncommonly involved by the pressure of masses in the neck or thorax. In only a few cases is the lymphoid tissue found in the brain or meninges. It is sometimes stated that Hodgkin's sarcoma may invade the brain and may be found in the cerebellum or temporal lobe. I have seen cases in which the cortex was extensively involved and another in which deposits were found in the brain stem. The granuloma and the sarcoma are both prone to invade the base of the skull and cause cranial nerve lesions and diabetes insipidus. The growths usually remain outside the dura. The paragranuloma is not believed to involve the brain.

Cavanaugh *et al.* describe multiple foci of demyelination which become confluent and massive. The astrocytes showed micronuclei, abnormal mitoses and increased chromosome numbers but were not regarded as malignant. The anatomical changes resembled those found in Schilder's disease and the clinical symptoms were such as one might expect in that disease.

In rare instances, a diffuse meningeal reaction may occur in the course of this disease. In the case of (T. B.-U. 25979) a child who suffered from a very chronic type of Hodgkin's disease, with remissions and exacerbations, we have observed a transient meningeal reaction with fever lymphocytes in the spinal fluid (170 per cubic millimeter), the usual signs of meningeal irritation and at one time, deep stupor. For several days there was partial right hemiparesis and partial sensory aphasia. Complete recovery ensued within two weeks. This patient was subjected to a very careful study and no other cause for the symptoms could be found. Torula meningitis may occur in Hodgkin's disease and this possibility should always be kept in mind when a meningeal reaction occurs during the course of this disease.

The diagnosis depends upon the general symptoms of the disease, such as the enlargement of the superficial lymph nodes, masses in the thorax and abdomen, enlargement of the liver and spleen, lesions of the skin such as pruritus, pigmentation and herpes zoster, changes in the blood such as anemia, increase in the platelets and monocytes, sometimes eosinophilia and, perhaps, upon the presence of the characteristic Pel-Epstein fever. The removal of a lymph node should be conclusive if the typical changes are present. In the early stages there is simply hyperplasia of the lymphoid tissue but later we find eosinophils and a great variety of mononuclear and epithelioid cells with the giant polynuclear cells described by Reed. Deep roentgenotherapy or exposure to radium emanation usually gives temporary relief or at least some amelioration of the symptoms but the prognosis is always unfavorable. Nitrogen mustard gas is being tried at present.

BIBLIOGRAPHY

BARKER, L. F.: Severe acute meningo-encephalopathy of lymphogranulomatous origin occurring in course of Hodgkin's disease. Arch. Neurol. & Psychiat., **32**:1038, 1934.

CAVANAUGH, J. B. *et al.*: Cerebral demyelination with disorders of the reticuloendothelial system. Lancet, **ii**:524, 1959.

CHEVALIER, P. ET BERNARD, J.: La Maladie de Hodgkin; lymphogranulomatose maligne. Paris, Masson & Cie, 1932.

CONYBEARE, E. T.: Some features of Hodgkin's disease. Guy's Hosp. Repts., **83**:53, 1933.

DAWSON, P. J. AND HARRISON, C. V.: A clinicopathologic study of benign Hodgkin's disease. Jour. Clin. Pathol., **14**:219, 1961.

DOLMAN, C. L. AND CAIRNS, A. R. M.: Leukodystrophy associated with Hodgkin's disease. Neurology, **11**:349, 1961.

EGLESTON, J. C. AND HARTMANN, W. H.: Hodgkin's disease involving the spinal epidural space. Johns Hopkins Medical Jour., **123**:265, 1968.

EVANS, H. E. AND NYHAN, W. L.: Hodgkin's disease in children. Bull. Johns Hopkins Hosp., **114**:237, 1964.

GILLOT, F. *et al.*: Hodgkin's disease in a meningeal form. Pediatrics, **15**:697, 1960.

HARE, D. C. AND LEPPER, E. H.: Two cases of lymphogranulomatosis maligna; One with involvement of the vertebral periosteum. Lancet, **1**:334, 1932.

JOHNSON, J. M.: Hodgkin's disease with invasion of the spinal column; Pressure on the cauda equina and degeneration of the posterior columns of the cord. Penn. Med. J., **34**:877, 1931.

MELTON, E. I. AND MCNAMARA, W. L.: Hodgkin's disease involving the pituitary gland with diabetes insipidus. Ann. Int. Med., **25**:525, 1946.

MULLER, S. A.: Association of zoster and malignant disorders in children. Arch. of Derm., **96**:657, 1967.

PAULLIN, J. E.: The central nervous system manifestations of lymphogranuloma. Internat. Clin., **4**:192, Dec. 1931.

POYNTON, F. J. AND HARRIS, K. E.: A case of paraplegia in Hodgkin's disease. Lancet, **2**:903, 1930.

SHAPIRO, P. F.: Changes in the spinal cord in Hodgkin's disease. Arch. Neurol. & Psychiat., **24**:509, 1930.

SOHN, D. *et al.*: Neurologic manifestations of Hodgkin's disease. Arch. of Neurol., **17**:429, 1967.

SPARLING, H. J. AND ADAMS, R. D.: Primary Hodgkin's sarcoma of the brain. Arch. of Path., **42**:338, 1946.

STOLBERG, H. O. *et al.*: Hodgkin's disease of the lung. Am. J. Roentgenol., **92**:96, 1964.

ULTMANN, J. E. AND DELAFIELD, F.: Clinical features and diagnosis of Hodgkin's disease. Cancer, **19**:297, 1966.

VIETS, H. R. AND HUNTER, F. T.: Lymphoblastomatous involvement of the nervous system. Arch. Neurol. & Psychiat., **29**:1246, 1933.

WALSH, F. B.: *Loc. cit.*

WEIL, A.: Spinal cord changes in lymphogranulomatosis. Arch. Neurol. & Psychiat., **26**:1009, 1931.

JUVENILE XANTHOGRANULOMA, JUVENILE EOSINOPHILIC GRANULOMA AND LETTERER-SIWE DISEASE

Juvenile xanthogranuloma occurs in newborn babies and in infants. The process involves the upper lids. Masses in the orbit cause exophthalmos. Bony erosion of the upper and outer walls of the orbit may occur. The process is said to recede spontaneously.

Juvenile eosinophilic granuloma is usually a focal, single lesion with

many eosinophil cells. It may involve the skull, ribs, pelvis, mandible or long bones. It may also occur in the lungs. The lesions, however, may be multiple. Excision and x-ray therapy are usually effective, but recurrences are known.

The Letterer-Siwe disease is seen in infancy and early childhood. It is an acute and disseminated disease with high mortality. Destruction of bones, especially the skull is prominent. There are cutaneous ecchymoses, purpura, pulmonary infiltrations, enlargement of the liver and spleen, reduction of the white cells and platelets. X-ray therapy, antifolic acid compounds and corticosteroids are used.

BIBLIOGRAPHY

SBARBARO, J. L.: Eosinophilic granuloma of bone. J.A.M.A., **178**:706, 1961.

KELLEY, J. H. AND McMILLAN, J. T.: Eosinophilic granuloma of the bone. Ann. Surg., **156**:117, 1962.

ROGERS, D. L. AND BENSON, T. E.: Familial Letterer-Siwe disease. Jour. Pediat., **60**:550, 1962.

INVOLVEMENT OF THE NERVOUS SYSTEM IN HYPERPLASIAS OF THE WHITE BLOOD CELLS, LEUKEMIAS, CHLOROMAS AND MYELOMAS

Definition.—The terminology of this field is so confusing that it seems best to begin by offering a simple classification of the various conditions under discussion. The outline given by MacCallum is probably the most suitable. This has been slightly simplified.

A. Hyperplasias of the Lymphoid Tissues.
   a. With leukemic blood.
      (1) with swelling of lymphoid tissues and lymphoid infiltration of organs—*Acute and chronic lymphoid leukemias.*
      (2) with tumors originating in various situations and invading tissues—*Lymphoid chloroma.*
   b. Without leukemic blood.
      (3) with tumors involving the bone marrow—*Lymphoid myeloma.*
      (4) with regional invasive tumor-like growth—*Lymphosarcoma.*
B. Hyperplasia of the Myeloid Tissue.
   a. With leukemic blood.
      (5) with myeloid infiltration of tissues—*Acute and chronic myeloid leukemias.*
      (6) with tumors of myeloid tissues—*Myeloid chloroma.*
   b. Without leukemic blood.
      (7) with tumors of the bone marrow—*Myeloid myeloma.*
C. Hyperplasia of the Cells of the Monocytic Series.
      (8) with infiltration of the tissues and leukemic blood—*Acute and Chronic Monocytic Leukemias.*

Leukemias and Chloromas of Various Types.—So far as the nervous system is concerned, the symptoms of the various types of leukemia seem to be identical, and it seems to be generally held that the chloromas are merely local manifestations of leukemia. It is, therefore, permissible to discuss these conditions together, distinguishing merely between the acute and the more chronic forms. In the acute leukemias the onset is often so abrupt as to suggest an infection. Usually there are chills, fever, vomiting and pains throughout the body. The lymph nodes are often enlarged and other lymphoid tissues, such as the tonsils and adenoids, are swollen. The spleen is palpable in most cases. Ulcerative lesions, resembling those of scurvy, are found in the mouth. Both large and small hemorrhages in the skin and mucous membranes are prominent symptoms in the fulminating cases, and it is not unusual to have bleeding from the bowels. Cellular masses, chloromas, develop in various parts of the skeleton but are most frequently found in the skull and orbits. Infiltrations of the skin, causing nodular lesions and finally ulcerations are sometimes seen. These are designated by the unfortunate term *mycosis fungoides,* but may be regarded as merely local deposits of the leukemic cells.

In the more chronic types, the first symptoms noted are usually pallor, weakness, digestive disturbances and loss of weight. At the beginning, there may be no fever. The spleen is usually enlarged and the lymph nodes pal-

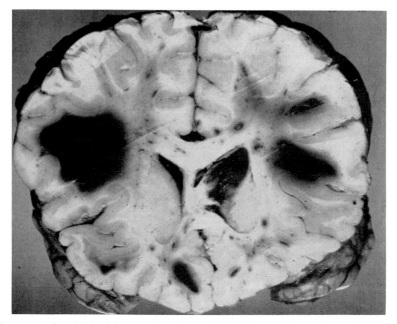

Fig. 269. Brain of a child of 4 years showing multiple hemorrhages due to leukemia. The course was only three weeks. (By the courtesy of Dr. Arthur King.)

pable but hemorrhages are usually not seen until the later stages of the disease. Symptoms referable to all systems of the body may eventually develop. Priapism is a fairly characteristic symptom and is attributed to infiltration of the corpora cavernosa. The skeleton may show lesions. Osteolysis, osteosclerosis, subperiosteal bone formation and transverse bands of diminished density may be found.

The nervous system is frequently involved in all forms of leukemia. The spinal cord is most often affected. As a rule, this is due to deposits of leukemic cells in the epidural space which compress the cord and interfere with the circulation. As a result, small areas of fenestration and softening appear and finally, if the condition continues, complete softening of the cord, which may be very extensive and involve many segments. Diffuse infiltration of the cord, with leukemic cells accompanied by a reactive gliosis, has been observed, and in a few instances hemorrhages and infarctions due to changes in the blood vessels. The cauda equina and spinal nerve roots, the lumbar and sacral plexuses and even the peripheral nerves may be infiltrated by the leukemic cells. The brain and the cerebral meninges are sometimes affected but less frequently than the spinal cord. Diffuse cellular infiltrations with reactive gliosis have been described, as well as massive deposits resembling neoplasms. Sometimes the subarachnoid spaces are invaded and then we may find evidences of leukemic meningitis with pathological cells in the spinal fluid. We have seen diffuse leukemic meningitis when the white blood cells had been brought under control by medication. Chloromatous deposits in the spine may cause destruction of the vertebrae and pictures resembling tuberculous spondylitis. Most frequently, however, the chloromas are found in the orbits and over the convexity of the skull. Leukemic retinitis with hemorrhages and plaques may cause severe visual disturbances. Involvement of the chiasm and optic nerves occurs in some instances and may simulate retrobulbar neuritis. Apparently leukemic deposits in the nerve sheath and region of the cavernous sinus are responsible. Palsies of the third, fourth and sixth nerves may occur. Diabetes insipidus may result from invasion of the infundibulum. Less commonly the labyrinth may be involved. In the fulminating forms of leukemia, there is a tendency for hemorrhages to develop in the nervous system just as in other tissues. Apoplectic phenomena, such as sudden hemiplegia, focal and general convulsions, and subarachnoid hemorrhages, are all described. Roberts *et al.* state that infiltration of the cardiac muscle by leukemic cells and hemorrhages are found frequently though as a rule only changes in the electrogram result.

Duke *et al.* describe microaneurysms in the retinae of patients suffering from chronic leukemia.

Richardson describes multiple areas of demyelination in the hemi-

spheres, as well as the cerebellum and brain stem. The nuclei of the oligo-dendroglia are enlarged and contain eosinophilic inclusions. Giant astro-cytes are seen with multiple nuclei. This condition, termed *multifocal leu-kocephalopathy*, is found in association with leukemia, malignant lympho-ma, sarcoidosis, carcinomatosis and miliary tuberculosis.

Particles resembling papova viruses have been found in cases of progres-sive multifocal leukoencephalopathy. The human wart virus belongs to this same group of viruses. These particles are found in the nuclei of the oligodendroglial cells.

The diagnosis is relatively easy if the clinical symptoms are typical and if large numbers of immature cells are in the blood. It must be kept in mind, however, that a few immature cells are often found in the circulat-ing blood of infants and young children, especially in various infections and anemias. The acute leukemias simulate septic infections very exactly in some cases and in more chronic forms we must always consider glandular fever, syphilis and tuberculosis. In aleukemic phases of the disease, the white cells may actually be reduced in numbers, but the presence of patho-logical cells is sufficient to suggest the diagnosis. Sometimes removal of a cellular deposit or an affected lymph node for histological study is neces-sary. The differentiation of the various types of leukemia depends upon the determination of the precise nature of the cells. If they are relatively mature, little difficulty is usually encountered, but when very primitive cells are discovered in the more acute types of leukemia, the differential diagno-sis is a difficult problem even for the most experienced hematologists.

No treatment has more than temporary value. In the more chronic types, deep roentgenotherapy will often give extraordinary relief for a while and may seem to restore the patient to health. Later, the symptoms recur and prove resistant to the same treatment. Recently several drugs have been em-ployed which have at least transient value. These include the nitrogen mus-tard gas, aminopterin and amethropterin. Cortisone is of value. Shanbrom *et al.* claim that the intraspinal injection of amethropterin is of value in the treatment of leukemic meningitis. There is evidence that leukemia may be a sequel of roentgen ray exposure. Even the apparently harmless irradi-ation during diagnostic pelvimetry may be responsible, it is suspected.

Kinlough and Robson state that eight patients with chronic leukemia had normal numbers of chromosomes. In two of four patients with chronic myeloid leukemia, an abnormally small Ph chromosome was found. No ab-normality was found in four patients with chronic lymphatic leukemia. In six of eight patients with acute leukemia, the chromosomes were normal. In two patients with acute myeloid leukemia, an extra chromosome was found.

Myelomas.—These growths are of several types. Some are composed

chiefly of myelocytes; others of myeloblasts, plasma cells, lymphoid cells or even erythroblasts. They all arise within the bone marrow, which is largely replaced by tumor tissue, and erode the bones, causing multiple fractures and deformities. No leukemic changes occur in the blood. The diagnosis depends chiefly upon the roentgenographic changes of the bones, anemia, and upon the presence of the so-called Bence Jones protein in the urine, which, however, is not constant. In acute cases, there may be fever and other symptoms suggestive of infection. The spinal cord and spinal nerve roots may be compressed as a result of neoplastic deposits or as a result of collapse of a vertebra. Intracranial metastases may occur. In a few instances polyneuritis has developed apparently as a result of a toxic or metabolic process for the nerves are not involved by the neoplastic process. I have seen two such cases. In one of these the neurological symptoms disappeared spontaneously though the patient succumbed eventually.

CASE HISTORY (Path. 14118-U. 61266).—*Boy of 14 years developed petechiae, enlargement of lymph nodes, hematuria and cyanosis. Leukemic changes in blood, sudden death due to massive hemorrhages in brain.*

B. T., a boy of 14 years, developed petechiae in the skin and mucous membranes. There was some loss of weight and progressive weakness. Two weeks later he developed hematuria and was brought into the hospital.

Examination revealed a pale, thin boy of the given age. There were numerous petechiae in the skin and mucous membranes, general enlargement of the lymph nodes, enlargement of the spleen and liver, hemorrhages and exudate in the retinae. R.B.C. 4,320,000. W.B.C. 820,000. About 90 per cent of the white cells were myeloblasts.

The next day the child showed striking cyanosis of the face, neck and chest above the nipple line. The superficial veins of the face and neck were engorged and the mediastinal dullness was increased. Hemorrhage into the mediastinum with compression of the superior vena cava was suspected. Shortly after this the child suddenly vomited, became unconscious and died.

Post-mortem examination revealed infiltration of all the organs with immature cells of the myeloid series. There was a large hemorrhage in the mediastinum. The brain contained a massive hemorrhage in the right frontal lobe and several smaller ones in the parietal region. The meninges, optic nerve sheath and retinae were infiltrated with myeloblasts.

CASE HISTORY (Path. 10953-U. 25157).—*Aleukemic leukemia in child of 12 years with compression of the spinal cord by extradural mass.*

H. K., a previously healthy boy of 12 years, began to complain of headache. He lost weight and developed a pasty color. About the same time he began to have pain in the back. This was followed by weakness of the legs and by difficulty in passing urine. Within a month there was complete paraplegia.

Examination 3 months after the onset revealed a pale, emaciated boy of 12 years. There was general enlargement of the lymph nodes. The legs were completely paralyzed and spastic and there was a sensory level at T6. The bladder was distended. Hb. 70 per cent. W.B.C. 5200. A differential was not made.

Operation by Dr. Dandy revealed a cellular mass of tumor at the level of the second thoracic vertebrae. This was extradural and was removed as completely as possible. The child failed to rally and died a few days later.

Post-mortem examination disclosed the changes in the bone marrow and other organs of lymphoid leukemia. The spinal cord had been compressed by a deposit of lymphoid cells in the extradural space.

CASE HISTORY (Path. 12819-U. 8625).—*Multiple myeloma in child of 10 years compressing the spinal cord and recurring after operation.*

E. B., a girl of 10 years, began to complain of pain in the back just beneath the right scapula in December, 1925. This slowly grew worse. In September, 1926, she began to walk unsteadily and was brought to the hospital.

Examination revealed spastic paraplegia with anesthesia up to the nipple line. There was some difficulty in emptying the bladder. Roentgenograms revealed a mass on the right side of the spine involving the 4th rib. The spinal fluid contained a great excess of protein and the Queckenstedt test was positive.

Operation by Dr. Dandy disclosed a tumor mass within the spinal canal continuous with a mass in the right mediastinum. Most of this was removed and the patient was given deep roentgenotherapy. The child was completely relieved of her symptoms until January, 1931. She then began to develop a kyphos at the level of the operation. Later root pain appeared and after more roentgenotherapy, which seemed to be ineffective, she was explored once more. The tumor was found to have recurred and the epidural space was filled with the growth. There was improvement again but later, sudden and complete paraplegia developed. The child died soon after.

Post-mortem examination disclosed multiple myelomata in all the vertebrae and in numerous ribs. The epidural space was filled with tumor masses for several segments above and below the site of operation.

BIBLIOGRAPHY

ALLEN, R. A. AND STRAATSMA, B. R.: Ocular invasion in leukemia. Arch. Ophthal., 66:490, 1961.

ASTRÖM, K. E. *et al.*: Progressive multifocal leukoencephalopathy. Brain, 81:93, 1958.

CLARKE, E.: Spinal cord involvement in multiple myelomatosis. Brain, 79:332, 1956.

DUKE, J. R. *et al.*: Retinal microaneurysms in leukemia. Brit. Jour. Ophthal., 52:368, 1968.

FITZGERALD, P. H. *et al.*: Chromosome defects in acute leukemia. J. Nat. Cancer Inst., 32:395, 1964.

HUTCHINSON, E. C. *et al.*: Neurologic complications of reticuloses. Brain, 81:75, 1958.

HYMAN, C. B. *et al.*: Central nervous system involvement by leukemia in children. Blood, 25:1, 1964.

KINLOUGH, M. A. AND ROBSON, H. N.: Chromosomes of patients with leukemia. Brit. Med. J., ii:1052, 1961.

LAURENCE, B. M.: Intracranial complications of leukemia treated with intrathecal amethopterin. Arch. Dis. Childhood, 36:107, 1961.

MOORE, R. Y. AND ODA, Y.: Malignant lymphoma with diffuse involvement of the peripheral nervous system. Neurology, 12:186, 1962.

MOORE, E. W. *et al.:* The central nervous system in acute leukemia. Arch. of Int. Med., 105:451, 1960.

NIERI, R. L. *et al.:* Central nervous system complications of leukemia. Mayo Clin. Proc., 43:70, 1968.

RHEIN, G. M. Z. AND CHOU, S.: Particles resembling papova viruses in human demyelination disease. Science, 148:1477, 1965.

RICHARDSON, E. P.: Multifocal leukoencephalopathy. New England J. Med., 265:815, 1961.

ROBERTS, W. C. *et al.:* The heart in acute leukemia.

SHANBROM, E. *et al.:* Aguent for leukemic encephalopathy. New England Med. J., 265:169, 1961.

———— AND FINCH, S. C.: The auditory manifestations of leukemia. Yale J. Biol. & Med., 31:144, 1958.

SILVERSTEIN, A.: Intracranial hemorrhage in patients with bleeding tendencies. Neurology, 11:310, 1961.

SHAW, R. K. *et al.:* Meningeal leukemia. Neurology, 10:834, 1960.

SCHUMACHER, H. R. *et al.:* Fungus infections and leukemia. Am. J. Med. Sci., 247:313, 1964.

SPARLING, H. J. *et al.:* Invasion of the nervous system by malignant lymphoma. Medicine, 26:285, 1947.

SULLIVAN, M. P.: Intracranial complications of leukemia in children. Pediatrics, 20:757, 1957.

Lymphatic Leukemia

DIAMOND, I. B.: Leukemia changes in the brain. A report of fourteen cases. Arch. Neurol. & Psychiat., 32:118, 1934.

FARBER, S. *et al.:* Temporary remissions in acute leukemia in children produced by folic acid antagonist aminopterin. New England J. Med., 238:787, 1948.

GOLDBACH, L. J.: Leukemic retinitis. Arch. Ophth., 10:808, 1933.

HAWKSLEY, J. C.: Lymphocytic leukemia causing pontine hemorrhage. Arch. Dis. Childhood, 7:29, 1932.

HOWELL, A. AND GOUGH, J.: Acute lymphatic leukemia with facial diplegia and double abducens palsy. Lancet, 1:723, 1932.

JEANS, V. AND COOKE, J. V.: Acute lymphatic leukemia in children. J.A.M.A., 101:432, 1933.

REESE, H. H. AND MIDDLETON, W. S.: Mechanical compression of the spinal cord by tumorous leukemic infiltration. J.A.M.A., 98:212, 1932.

SILVERMAN, F. N.: Skeletal lesions in leukemia. Am. J. Roentgenol., 59:819, 1948.

STEWART, A. *et al.:* Leukemia in children related to prenatal x-ray. Lancet, ii:447, 1956.

WALSH, F. B.: *Loc. cit.*

WELLS, C. E. AND SILVER, R. T.: Neurologic manifestations of leukemia. Ann. Int. Med., 46:439, 1957.

Myeloid Leukemia

BARKER, L. F.: Neutrophilic myelocytes in the cerebrospinal fluid of patients suffering from myeloid leukemia and their significance for the diagnosis of myeloleukemia infiltration of the leptomeninges. Southern Med. J., 14:437, 1921.

CRITCHLEY, McD. AND GREENFIELD, J. G.: Spinal symptoms in chloroma and leukemia. Brain, 53:11, 1930.

HARRIS, W.: Leukemia polyneuritis. Lancet, 1:122, 1921.

Chloroma

GOODALL, A. AND ALEXANDER, W. A.: Acute myelocythemia and chloroma. Quart. J. Med., **17:** 112, 1924.

HEISSEN, F.: Chlorom und Zentralnerven System. Ztschr. f. d. ges. Neurol. u. Psychiat., **95:**248, 1925.

ROTHSCHILD, H.: Chlorom der Dura mater mit atypischer Symptomatologie. Deutsche Ztsch. f. Nervenh., **91:**57, 1926.

Myeloma

CLARKE, E.: Cranial and intracranial myelomas. Brain, **77:**61, 1954.

DENKER, P. C. AND BROCK, S.: The generalized and vertebral forms of myeloma. Cerebral and spinal complications. Brain, **57:**291, 1934.

KURNICK, N. B. AND YOHALEM, S. B.: Peripheral neuritis complicating multiple myeloma. Arch. Neurol. & Psychiat., **59:**378, 1948.

SCHEINKER, I.: A new type of polyneuritis associated with plasma cell myeloma. Deutsch. Ztschr. f. Nervenh., **147:**247, 1938.

VICTOR, M. *et al.:* The neuropathology of multiple myeloma. J. Neurol. Neurosurg. & Psychiat., **21:**73, 1958.

———— *et al.:* Neuropathy of multiple myeloma. J. Neurol., Neurosurg. & Psychiat., **21:**73, 1958.

Chapter VII

INJURIES OF THE NERVOUS SYSTEM
BY PHYSICAL AGENTS

INTRODUCTION.—In the following pages trauma and other physical agents which may injure the nervous system will be discussed. Birth injury is, of course, most important and will be taken up first. Then the post-natal traumatic conditions are described. These require separate consideration since they fall into entirely different categories from the birth injuries. Neurological disorders due to compression resulting from bony malformations are then mentioned briefly and finally the effects of radium and roentgen rays, of lightning and electric shocks and of intense heat are considered. The last mentioned conditions are rare in childhood but are of considerable interest.

BIBLIOGRAPHY

AITA, J. A.: Neurologic Manifestations of General Diseases. Thomas, Springfield, 1964.
WALSH, F. B.: Clinical Neuro-ophthalmology, 2nd Ed. Baltimore, Williams and Wilkins, 1957.

BIRTH INJURIES

CEREBRAL BIRTH INJURIES

Due to Trauma and Anoxia

Introduction.—Despite the attention it has received, this subject is still imperfectly understood and an extraordinary difference of opinion still exists among various authorities in regard to several important aspects of this situation. Nevertheless, a great deal of substantial information has been accumulated. For example, we now have a number of careful and accurate descriptions of the fresh lesions in the brains of stillborn babies and a great deal has been learned of the causes which lead to their production. The symptoms of cerebral trauma at birth have likewise received careful study. On the other hand, there is no general agreement about the anatomical residua of cerebral birth injuries or about the syndromes which they may produce if the child survives. Some writers consider birth injury to be the principal cause of infantile cerebral palsy and others regard it as relatively unimportant.

Incidence.—There can be no doubt that intracranial hemorrhage has been very common among the new born. Post-mortem examinations of the brains of still born babies, or of babies dying within a few days after birth, have revealed a very high percentage of lesions attributable to trau-

ma during delivery. Thus, Spencer found intracranial hemorrhage in 40 per cent, DeLuca in 36 per cent, Schafer in 20 per cent, Archibald in 43 per cent, Warwick in 43 per cent and Pierson in 44 per cent. In children born by breech delivery and especially in premature children, the figures are even higher and sometimes approach 80 or even 90 per cent. These were all gross studies and it is probable that microscopic studies would have revealed many other lesions, no doubt, many due to anoxia. I am told that large hemorrhages are less common at present. It seems fair to conclude, however, that at least one third of all deaths within the first two weeks are due to birth injury. Clinical studies such as those of Pierson and Irving indicate that about 1 or 2 per cent of all babies die of cerebral birth injury.

The incidence of cerebral injury among children who survive is not easy to estimate. Clinical evidence of intracranial hemorrhage may be detected in approximately 2 or 3 per cent of all new born babies. The figures, of course, vary within wide limits depending upon the care with which the children are observed. Certain authors have performed routine spinal puncture upon a large series of infants. Sharpe reports that in 10 per cent of 500 new born babies, blood is found in the cerebrospinal fluid. A more careful study was made by Hines Roberts upon 423 colored babies. In 60 cases, or 14 per cent, he found blood in the fluid but in only 26, or 6 per cent, of these children were there any clinical signs of intracranial hemorrhage. The significance of such figures is not clear. On one hand, asymptomatic intracranial hemorrhage may be discovered but it is very difficult to distinguish between blood already in the spinal fluid and blood freshly drawn by the needle. Moreover, clear fluid does not exclude the possibility of intracranial hemorrhage as we have frequently had cause to remember. However, despite these possibilities of error, it seems probable that in addition to the 2 per cent or 3 per cent of new born babies who show clinical evidences of cerebral injury, there are a number of children who have asymptomatic intracranial hemorrhage and it is possible that this second group outnumbers the first.

The Causes of Cerebral Birth Injury.—There is no doubt that *trauma* and *hemorrhage* are of great importance among the causes of cerebral damage at birth. Obviously, any condition which increases the stress which the foetal head sustains in its passage through the birth canal will increase the chances of injury. Malformed and contracted pelves, rigid soft parts, precipitate or prolonged labor, the use of pituitrin, holding back the head during the second stage of labor, abnormal presentations, high forceps deliveries, breech extractions and over-large foetal heads are all common factors which lead to cerebral birth injury. First babies are most frequently injured. The purely obstetrical factors will not be discussed further, for they

are outside the scope of this article but the reader is referred to papers by Holland, Greenwood and Ehrenfest for an analysis of this phase of the subject.

Birth trauma differs from the common head injuries which occur later in life in that it is due to slow moulding and compression of the head and not to violent blows and shocks. Thus, bleeding over the convexity is attributed to over-riding of the parietal bones and tearing of the veins which empty into the longitudinal sinus. These veins are very fragile in the infant and unsupported by Pacchionian granulations as they are in the adult. Moreover, they extend between the relatively movable brain and their fixed attachment to the sinus. Ehrenfest has claimed that similar overlapping of the parietal and occipital bones may cause injury of the lateral sinus and its tributary veins.

Tearing of the dural septa is also a result of distortion of the foetal head. Since compression of the head is either in the antero-posterior or lateral diameter, or both, it is evident that there must be a compensatory increase in the vertical diameter. This change in configuration is resisted by the dural ligaments, the falx and the tentorium. If the tension is great enough they may be stretched and ruptured. Tears in the tentorium are very common and are usually found near the insertion of the falx. As a result, the straight sinus or some of its tributaries may be injured. If the antero-posterior diameter is increased, the falx may be torn. Greenwood thinks that the vertical diameter of the head is not increased in normal vertex presentations. On the contrary, it may be decreased as a result of over-riding of the parietal bones. The antero-posterior diameter is definitely lengthened, however. In brow presentations and breech extractions, he has shown that the vertical diameter is always increased. Crothers has pointed out that breech delivery imposes great strain upon the tentorium. The force of uterine contraction and manual suprapubic pressure both tend to compress the walls of the supratentorial chamber and consequently cause pressure on the tentorium from above, and the traction on the body, which when transmitted to the spinal cord and brain-stem, tends to draw the tentorium down.

Holland has shown that the multiple extravasations which occur in the distribution of the vein of Galen are due to elevation of the vertex. This vein extends between the fixed sinus and the movable brain. In the process of moulding, the vein may be sharply kinked and stretched. Temporary occlusion or even rupture may result. Holland has been able to demonstrate tears in the vein.

Schwartz has suggested that when the head of the baby is partly delivered it is exposed only to atmospheric pressure whereas the body may be subjected to a much greater pressure during uterine contractions. As a result

blood is forced into the great veins more especially the superior sagittal system with engorgement, stasis and possibly hemorrhage.

Norman takes a different view, and is supported by Rydberg. They believe that strong compression of the head interferes with the arterial blood flow and causes anemia of the brain.

Earle, Baldwin and Penfield emphasize herniation of the brain through the tentorium with compression of branches of the middle cerebral, posterior cerebral and anterior choroidal arteries against the edge of the tentorium.

Lindenberg has shown that in states of increased intracranial pressure due to trauma almost all of the major cerebral arteries may be compressed and occluded with resulting softenings.

It has been suggested that fragments of thrombi forming in the vessels of the umbilical cord or placenta may become detached and may be carried through the foramen ovale and to the brain where embolic softenings may result.

Yates examined the necks of sixty fetuses. He found significant evidences of damage in twenty-seven. In twenty-four cases, there was hemorrhage in the adventitia of one or both vertebral arteries. The thin-walled veins, which accompany the vertebral arteries in their canals, were found to be torn. In one case, the vertebral artery was occluded by a thrombus. Bruising and tearing of the spinal nerve roots was found in nine cases. The dura was sometimes torn and ligaments stretched or torn.

Brat states that the vacuum extractor is a safe and efficient replacement for forceps delivery.

Awon describes injuries inflicted by the vacuum extractor. He states that moulding occurs promptly and the parietal bones flare so the brain is exposed and the sagittal sinus may be ruptured and the falx may be torn.

For many years, the importance of *asphyxia* at birth has been a matter of debate. Some clinicians have pointed out that most babies are asphyxiated to some extent at birth and that even babies who are deeply asphyxiated may nevertheless suffer no injury to the nervous system. Other authorities have supported the theory that asphyxia may cause irreversible damage to the brain. In recent years the observations of Courville on nitrous oxide anesthesia, of Titrud and Haymaker on anoxia in aviators and of Morrison and others on anoxia in experimental animals have made it clear that sublethal anoxia may cause permanent cerebral damage. Schreiber, Farber and Clifford and others have insisted that anoxia at birth is a frequent cause of cerebral injury. They emphasize the frequency of apnea at birth in children who are subsequently found to be defective and stress the dangers of drugs and anesthetics which are now frequently employed to ease labor pains. Premature separation of the placenta, placenta praevia, infarc-

tion of the placenta, placental insufficiency from any cause, kinking or compression of the cord, maternal anemia, heart failure and pneumonia may all cause some degree of anoxia of the baby before birth. During delivery, it is well known that asphyxia may result from strong and lasting uterine contractions, compression of the umbilical cord, the use of nitrous oxide anesthesia, plugging of the infant's respiratory passages with mucus, hyaline membrane disease of the lungs, and narcosis of the infant due to the use of excessive amounts of barbiturates. Little shows that aplasia of the umbilical artery is often associated with congenital defects and Bourne and Benirschke find that absence of one umbilical artery is disastrous to the baby. Henderson *et al.* point out that infants delivered by Caesarian section are prone to aspirate blood and amniotic fluid and even regurgitated stomach contents. It must also be kept in mind that injury to the infant's brain resulting from trauma at birth may result in apnea. On the basis of experimental work it is claimed that a single exposure of an animal to an atmosphere of 6 per cent oxygen for 20 minutes may be enough to cause irreversible anatomical damage. Courville has shown that anoxia of only a few minutes in nitrous oxide anesthesia in adults may cause lasting cerebral injury. However, it is not clear just how sensitive to anoxia a baby's brain really is. As a result of experimental work Kabat states, "The ability of the newborn to achieve complete functional recovery following periods of complete arrest of the brain circulation (i.e. anoxia) is approximately 400 per cent greater than that of adults." Clinical observations of Wilson, Torrey and Johnson also indicate that a baby's nervous system is extremely tolerant of anoxia. The studies of Keith *et al.* lend no support to the belief that asphyxia causes any neurologic abnormality in babies who survive. This statement applies to premature as well as full-term infants. It should be pointed out that the baby *in utero* is normally cyanotic and the oxygen tension in the blood is extremely low. At present it is impossible to say how frequently the baby's brain is injured at birth by anoxia and what part this condition plays in the genesis of infantile cerebral palsies.

The proceedings of the fifty-seventh Ross Conference on Pediatric Research deals with Brain Damage in the Fetus and Newborn from Hypoxia and Asphyxia. A number of investigators discuss the clinical picture, the anatomical changes, the electroencephalographic findings and the biochemical changes which result.

Dr. David Clark has told me of two women who had partial separation of the placenta at the seventh month. In each case fetal movements had been normal up to that time. Then fetal movements were absent for a time. Later, the mothers were conscious of repeated episodes of violent fetal movements of a few minutes duration. After birth both babies were found to be grossly defective and subject to convulsions. It seems clear that

the babies were injured by intrauterine anoxia and developed intrauterine convulsions.

Compression of the thorax is a very important cause of cerebral congestion and venous extravasations. The blood is forced out of the large venous reservoirs of the chest and abdomen through the incompetent valves of the jugular veins into the head and neck. If the compression is severe and prolonged, an extraordinary picture may arise which is termed *traumatic asphyxia*. In this condition, intense cyanosis of the head and neck persists for several days and is associated with hemorrhages into the retinae, conjunctiva and meninges. Convulsions often occur. There may be transient loss of vision and sometimes some reduction of vision may persist.

Reynolds offers a very interesting study of the physiological changes which occur when the fetal circulation is converted into the neonatal circulation. He points out that it is essential for the systemic blood pressure to reach a proper level promptly after the first breath is taken. He also suggests that it would be wise to lower the delivered baby below the level of the placenta while it is still in the uterus before clamping the cord for this gives the baby as much as 20 to 30 per cent increase of blood volume.

A very important contributing cause of intracranial hemorrhage at birth is *prematurity*. Almost all writers agree that cerebral birth injury is much more frequent in the premature than among those infants born at term. Ylppö found cerebral lesions either large or small in 90 per cent of all premature infants he examined. He explains this fact by the great fragility of the blood vessels in immature children. By applying suction to the skin Ylppö showed that hemorrhage occurred in full term babies when a negative pressure of 520 mm Hg was reached but that in the premature, only 150 mm Hg pressure was needed to cause rupture of the veins. Ehrenfest has emphasized the thinness and fragility of the premature infant's skull. The jelly-like consistency of the premature brain must also predispose to injury. Levine and Gordon give a long list of the physiological deficiencies of premature babies which render them unable to respond effectively to the stress of delivery. It should also be mentioned that the birth canal is possibly not completely prepared for delivery in premature births.

Barnes states that there is as great a hazard in being born three weeks late as there is in being born three weeks too early. He states that the demands of the post-mature fetus for food and oxygen exceed the capacity of the placenta so there is serious malnutrition and high mortality as well as a high percentage of cerebral injury.

Rausen points out that monochorionic twins face serious hazards. Among 130 monochorionic twins, he found 19 cases in which arteriovenous anastomoses in the placenta resulted in an unequal distribution of blood. One twin became anemic and one polycythemic. The polycythemic twin is apt

to require venesection to prevent heart failure and possibly an exchange transfusion because of the increase of bilirubin in the blood. The anemic twin needs a transfusion and often fluids. In 10 instances both twins died, in 5 instances 1 twin survived and in 4 instances both twins lived.

Ozan and Gonzales describe the case of an infant which was apparently injured *in utero,* by a blow on the mother's abdomen. The child developed epilepsy.

Finster *et al.* state that during attempts to induce caudal anesthesia during labor an anesthetic was accidently injected into the fetus in four instances. Two infants died.

The importance of *hemorrhagic disease* in the causation of intracranial bleeding was first pointed out by Green. This factor has also been emphasized by Warwick, Foote, Cruikshank and others. Warwick found gross hemorrhages in the viscera of 8 out of her 18 cases and Rodda found multiple hemorrhages in 20 per cent of his cases. Other authors state that hemorrhagic disease of the new born is rarely associated with intracranial hemorrhage. Holt and Howland quote the figures of Ritter and Townsend. These authors found only 4 cases of intracranial hemorrhage in 240 cases of hemorrhagic disease. Fleming states that he has never seen symptoms of intracranial hemorrhage in a frank case of hemorrhagic disease. However, there are a number of cases described in pediatric literature in which the connection seems to be fully established and we have observed several cases at Harriet Lane.

The occurrence of intracranial hemorrhage in children who have been born by Caesarian section is often offered as proof that hemorrhage may occur without trauma but it must be kept in mind that some obstetricians deliver the baby through a very small incision in the uterus and even apply forceps for this purpose so that the possibility of trauma to the head is not entirely eliminated. Moreover, section is often performed after the mother has been in ineffectual labor for some time and the child may have sustained injury before operation.

Maternal diabetes and prediabetes place the baby in jeopardy. Diverse malformations of the fetus are said to result if the process begins early in fetal life. If the process begins later, the baby will be too big and there will be water retention, a Cushing-like appearance with hypertrichosis and hyperinsulinism. Such children are fragile and birth injuries are frequent among them.

Lipsitz and English state that the administration of magnesium sulphate to the mother to combat toxemia may cause weakness in the baby with a weak cry and difficulty in nursing and breathing. See congenital defects due to the use of thalidomide by the mother and other drugs which may damage the fetus when ingested by the mother.

Pathological Anatomy; Fresh Lesions.—*Gross Traumatic and Hemorrhagic Lesions.* There have been a number of excellent studies of the morbid anatomy in still born infants. Fractures of the cranium are sometimes seen but are not at all common. Ehrenfest has collected a number of cases and Fleming mentions 16 cases in his series. The frontal bones were involved in 9 cases; the parietal bones in 5 and the occipital and temporal bones in one case each. The fracture is almost always over the convexity where the bones are thin and relatively fragile. The base is, of course, very strong and rigid in comparison. Fractures are usually due to indentation of the skull by forceps and have been compared to the dents produced in a celluloid ping-pong ball by pressure. The linear fractures like those of adult life are rare. Associated with such depressed fractures there is usually compression of the underlying brain and often softening. The meninges may be lacerated and extradural and subdural hemorrhage may occur. The second, third, fourth and sixth cranial nerves may be lacerated in the orbit and hematoma of the orbit may be found.

In most cases there is no fracture of the skull but intracranial hemorrhages of various types are found. These are almost always of venous origin. Capon has made a careful study of the intracranial lesions in 80 postmortem examinations of infants dying shortly after birth. He gives the following summary:

"1. Small tentorial vessels coursing along the fibers of the tentorium may be torn; the blood then collects in a film upon the upper surface of the cerebellum or upon the upper tentorial surface draining posteriorly around the occipital lobes.

"2. The vena magna Galeni, which is frequently distorted during the moulding of the head, may rupture at the point where the straight sinus is formed. The blood collects posterior to the mesencephalon and drains downwards around the cerebellum, pons and medulla.

"3. The cerebral veins, near their terminations in the superior longitudinal sinus, may be injured. . . . The effused blood flows downwards in the subdural space. Usually the hemorrhage is unilateral but sometimes it is bilateral.

"4. Superior longitudinal sinus, transverse sinus and straight sinus. It is only in the most severe types of birth injury that such examples are found. The infant is almost invariably still-born.

"5. The internal cerebral veins, for instance the choroidal veins, may be damaged. These examples are rare and are found almost exclusively in still-born, premature infants. The blood collection may occupy the lateral, third and fourth ventricles; blood is also frequently found in these cases within the spinal membrane."

One may conclude from these statements that the hemorrhage is almost

always in the meninges rather than in the substance of the brain. The brain may, however, be injured as a result of compression by a large hematoma. If the bleeding is in the cisternae at the base, the blood usually diffuses throughout the subarachnoid spaces without causing local injury, but if the hemorrhage occurs at the vertex where the sulci are narrow and diffusion is restricted, compression and softening of the cortex is not uncommon. Blood in the subdural space is not absorbed so readily as in the subarachnoid space as I shall have occasion to mention later.

The relative infrequency of hemorrhage arising within the brain may be appreciated by the following figures. Weyhe found 35 cases in which there was hemorrhage into the brain in a series of 122 cases of intracranial hemorrhage in the new born. Spencer found only 1 case of hemorrhage in the brain in a series of some 90 cases. Warwick did not find any primary intracerebral hemorrhages but in two cases there was softening underlying a hematoma in the meninges. Other authors give similar figures. Schwartz, however, claims that if histological examination is made, cerebral lesions will be found very frequently. He has emphasized hemorrhages and areas of necrosis in the central white matter and basal ganglia of the forebrain. These lie close to the ventricles and are usually bilateral. They are ascribed to circulatory disturbances in the distribution of the vein of Galen. Schwartz claims that such lesions are characteristic of birth injury and gives very good illustrations of their development. Haller, Nesbitt and Anderson state that gross traumatic lesions are becoming rare in most obstetrical clinics as a result of more skillful technique in delivery.

Many brains of new infants show small, scattered foci of fat-laden phagocytes chiefly surrounding the small vessels. This condition was described by Virchow as *encephalitis congenita*. The significance of these findings has been a matter of debate ever since. Schwartz and other investigators regard them as evidence of birth injury but other pathologists state that they represent merely one step in the process of myelination and have no pathological significance.

The special sense organs are not infrequently involved. It has been estimated that from 20 to 50 per cent of all new born infants have small hemorrhages in the retinae. These may be associated with intracranial lesions or may be found in infants who are otherwise quite healthy. The inner ears of infants have been studied by Voss, who reports that hemorrhages are often found even when the temporal bone is not fractured.

Lesions Due to Anoxia.—There seem to be no adequate studies of fresh lesions in the baby's brain due to uncomplicated asphyxia. If we assume that they must be the same as are found in the brains of adults subjected to anoxia of various types, we may expect to find, according to Courville, in the first day or two congestion, edema and perivascular hemorrhages.

This process is not a very destructive one, but may cause perivascular necrosis. Somewhat later, one may find disseminated or focal lesions of variable severity in the cerebral cortex, especially in the deeper layers. The lenticular nuclei, thalami and the cortex of the cerebellum may be involved. Demyelination may be found in the cerebral white matter. Still later, softenings are apt to develop. These are attributed to occlusion of the blood vessels due to proliferation of the endothelium. Anderson believes that anoxia may be responsible for massive intraventricular hemorrhage. See Injury to the Central Nervous System Due to Anoxia. The brain stem suffers little damage and the spinal cord and spinal nerve roots seem to escape. No information seems to be available about possible damage to the retina or optic nerves.

Chronic Lesions.—Although a number of excellent studies have been made upon the fresh lesions due to birth injury, little is known about the anatomical sequelae which may result if the child survives. Numerous conditions have been ascribed to birth injury without any adequate evidence and there seems to be no general agreement among those best able to express an opinion.

First it may be said that small or moderately large hemorrhages into the subarachnoid spaces are probably absorbed promptly and usually give rise to no significant injury to the brain. This statement is confirmed by clinical observations upon new born babies who show blood in the spinal fluid but, nevertheless, recover promptly. The writer has injected blood into the meninges of puppies only to find it was absorbed very quickly with only transient symptoms. Levinson and Saphir have made a careful study of the meningeal reaction of hemorrhage among the new born and find that this is astonishingly mild. There seem to be rare instances, however, in which the blood is organized and the subarachnoid spaces are obliterated with the result that hydrocephalus is produced. In most instances in which subarachnoid hemorrhage and hydrocephalus are associated, I believe we are dealing with congenital hydrocephalus and the large head and fragile bones increased the incidence of birth injury. Whether large, diffuse subarachnoid hemorrhages may cause generalized atrophy of the brain as a result of pressure is, perhaps, still in doubt. Schwartz apparently believes that this is possible. The present writer has not been able to establish this connection. However, it is clear that *large hematomas* which compress the *cortex* may give rise to *local softenings*. The writer has studied several cases in which there was a definite history of birth injury and persisting cerebral palsies. At operation or post-mortem examination, local atrophy and sclerosis of the cortex were found associated with some thickening of the overlying pia-arachnoid. The following case may be regarded as typical of this condition.

CASE 16—Table 13 (Surg. 41660).—W. H., born by difficult, high forceps extraction. Head lacerated on the left and depressed fracture noted. Resuscitated with great difficulty. Spinal fluid bloody on several occasions. Right hemiplegia noted at age of several months. Focal convulsions on right side. Right arm and leg much smaller than left. Craniotomy on the left at age of 18 years revealed some delicate adhesions between the arachnoid and dura over the Sylvian fissure. The pia-arachnoid was thickened in this region and contained a few small cystic collections of yellow fluid. The convolutions bordering on the fissures of Sylvius and Rolando were atrophic and very firm. Microscopic examination of a bit of cortex and meninges revealed thickening and pigmentation of the meninges and atrophy and gliosis of the cortex.

Subdural hematomas apparently leave fairly characteristic changes even after a number of years. Here the blood is apt to be organized rather than absorbed. There is usually widespread atrophy of the cortex under such lesions with dilatation of the homolateral ventricle. Roentgenograms of the skull show enlargement of the middle fossa on the side of the lesion. The following case is representative:

CASE 5—Table 13 (Path. 7805-Surg. 51254).—A. F., born by long labor without instruments. On second day, the child developed a series of violent convulsions, bulging of fontanels and cyanosis. Spinal fluid nearly pure blood. Several months later right hemiplegia was noted. Right arm and leg never developed properly. Focal convulsions on right side since early childhood. Death at the age of 11 years. At post-mortem examination, the dura was much thickened over the entire convexity of the left hemisphere except for the frontal and occipital poles. Underlying the dura and strongly attached to it was a yellow membrane almost a centimeter thick, composed of fibrous tissue and containing numerous yellow granules. This was rather vascular. The pia-arachnoid was somewhat thickened and also attached to the subdural membrane. The cortex of the frontal, parietal and temporal lobes was reduced to less than a centimeter's thickness, showed extensive gliosis and almost complete loss of nerve cells. The left lateral ventricle was enormously dilated and there was some dilatation of the third ventricle. The pyramidal tract was degenerated.

The following case may be offered as an example of the *central type of porencephaly* described by Schwartz and attributed by him to circulatory disturbances in the distribution of the vein of Galen.

CASE HISTORY (Surg. 5089-Ped. 13824).—G. H., born by prolonged labor. Two doses of pituitrin were given. Shortly after birth the child became stuporous, rigid, vomited, refused to nurse and showed cyanosis and bulging fontanels. At five months there was bilateral generalized spasticity, bulbar palsy and some pallor of the optic discs. Death. Post-mortem ex-

amination revealed gross cavities in either hemisphere. These were elongated and placed just to the outer side of the lateral ventricles from which they were separated by a thin membrane representing the ependyma. They were lined with a rough, pigmented tissue composed of glia and connective tissue and crossed by numerous trabeculae containing small vessels. The lenticular nuceli and both pyramidal tracts were injured.

Hemorrhages and softenings in the subcortical tissues give rise to the more *common type of porencephaly*. In such cases a cyst is found just under the cortex which is atrophic and denser than normal. These lesions are usually unilateral and always asymmetrical. They are lined with a fibrous membrane and do not communicate directly with the ventricles as a rule. The following case may be given as illustration.

CASE 13—Table 13.—C. D. P. was born by prolonged but not abnormal labor. Deeply cyanotic at birth and resuscitated after hours' effort. Had convulsions for some days and could not nurse. Spinal fluid contained blood. At eight months paralysis of the left arm and leg were noted and at 13 years convulsions developed on the left side. Operation disclosed a tremendous cyst surrounding the posterior portion of the fissure of Sylvius. This was covered by atrophic and sclerotic cortex. The overlying meninges were normal. The cyst was lined by a rough membrane devoid of ependyma and did not communicate with the ventricle. There was much yellow pigment in the walls of the cyst.

Benda has recently made an important contribution to this subject. He describes the lesions in twenty-four brains which he regards as showing the late effects of cerebral birth injury. These were found in a total number of one hundred and thirty autopsies performed upon mentally deficient children. Three conditions are described: (1) Mantle sclerosis; (2) Cystic degeneration of the brain, and (3) Diffuse patchy devastation. In *mantle sclerosis* there is degeneration of the cortical layers with necrosis of the subcortical white matter. The white matter may present a status spongiosus in which small subcortical cysts are sometimes found. The gray matter is devoid of nerve cells which are replaced by gliosis. The leptomeningeal covering of the affected areas is greatly thickened. The subarachnoid spaces are fibrotic and contain enlarged vessels suspended in the fibrous meshwork. The pia is greatly thickened and tightly fused with the gliotic cortex. There are areas of calcification and residuals of old and more recent hemorrhages. The condition may affect parts of one lobe or a whole lobe or even one hemisphere. The condition is asymmetrical but may be bilateral. Benda thinks this process is a result of ischemic necrosis and possibly bruising of the brain. It is termed central porencephaly, encephaloclastic porencephaly, false porencephaly and central encephalomalacia.

Cystic degeneration is said to correspond to the central porencephaly of

Schwartz. There are numerous large and small cavities in the central white matter. The cortex and the white cores of the convolutions are not primarily involved. The cysts do not in the beginning communicate with the ventricles, though they may do so eventually. They are lined with glial fibers. This condition is attributed to occlusion of arteries, venous thromboses and dural sinus thrombosis. In 3 of 5 cases, the sagittal sinus was obliterated. It is termed also parchment atrophy of the brain, subcortical encephalomalacia and subcortical porencephaly.

Diffuse patchy devastation is characterized by diffuse, patchy destruction of the cortical layers, leptomeningeal fibrosis, brain atrophy with enlargement of the lateral ventricles and areas of central necrosis, cystic degeneration and demyelination. Status marmoratus may be found in parts of the basal ganglia. Benda states this third condition is due to ischemic or hemorrhagic necrosis which is more diffuse and less extensive than in the second condition described above. Earle, Baldwin and Penfield describe areas of gliosis and atrophy in the anterior and medial portions of the temporal lobes in patients subject to temporal lobe seizures. They attribute these lesions to compression resulting from herniation of the brain through the tentorial incisura at the time of birth.

Little has been written of the late effects of anoxia at birth. Courville and Marsh give the following tabulation of the residua which they attribute to this condition.

1. *General Alterations*
   a. Grossly normal brain but with scattered patches of cellular degeneration in cortex or corpus striatum.
   b. Cerebral and cerebellar atrophy with more or less uniform, minor, moderate or severe (walnut kernel brain) alterations in cortex.
   c. Marked irregular widespread cortical change usually associated with brain cysts or porencephaly.
2. *Local Changes*
   a. Focal cortical and subcortical lesions (microgyria brain cysts)
   b. Lobar lesions (lobar sclerosis, ulegyria, porencephaly)
   c. Hemisphere changes (agenesis)

Courville regards these conditions as residua of the acute lesions resulting from anoxia which are described above.

Banker and Larroche have made a study of the effects of anoxia on the brains of newborn babies. They consider softening of the periventricular white matter the most characteristic. They also mention a diffuse loss of cells in the cerebral cortex. They state that the periventricular lesions must interrupt the optic radiations and thus cause defects in the fields of vision.

Towbin states that in utero hypoxia causes hemorrhagic infarctions involving the periventricular white matter and basal ganglia. Whereas hy-

poxia during birth in full term babies causes damage in the cerebral cortex. The location of the lesions is determined by the gestational age.

Clinical Features, Acute Stage.—A number of careful clinical studies of cerebral birth injuries have been made by Cameron, Capon, Holland, Munro and Fleming, but except for a somewhat better understanding of certain physiological problems, these have contributed little to the descriptions of the older writers. In cases of severe cerebral injury such as may be caused by large intracranial hemorrhages, the child is usually stillborn. If less severe injuries are present, the child may be born alive but deeply asphysiated. In most cases the symptoms are present within a day after birth but in some cases they may be delayed for several days. When signs of intracranial hemorrhage appear after the end of the first week, it is always possible that some factor other than trauma is playing a major role.

First, it must be said that almost all babies show some degree of asphyxia at birth. This disappears as soon as respiration is established and has no clinical significance. More persistent asphyxia is a symptom of some abnormality, most commonly of cerebral injury.

It is usual to describe at least two clinical pictures. In the common type, there is either persistent or recurrent cyanosis. Respiration is disturbed, being slow, irregular or periodic. Periods of apnea may occur. As a result the lungs may not be properly expanded causing atelectasis. The child cries feebly or not at all and will not take the breast. In most cases the child is quite rigid, the head retracted and the hands clenched. It is apathetic or stuporous. This rigidity is usually generalized but may be more evident on one side or in one extremity. There are frequently local twitchings of the muscles which, as a rule, are irregular and may persist for hours at a time. Generalized twitchings and convulsions are common. Often handling the child or loud noises will induce rigidity and twitchings. The tendon reflexes are often increased but not invariably so and ankle clonus may be elicited on one side or both sides. The Moro reflex is usually absent at first but may later be active. The fontanels are usually tense or even bulging depending upon the degree of increased intracranial pressure. Out-spoken papilledema is rare but the retinal veins are sometimes definitely engorged and retinal hemorrhages are very common. The pupils are sometimes dilated, contracted or unequal. As a rule, a dilated pupil is taken to indicate a lesion at the base on the homolateral side, but it is questionable whether this sign is always significant in the newborn. Nystagmus is described. Squints are usually of no significance at this age unless they are associated with paralysis of oculomotor muscles. Hemorrhage in the orbit may cause exophthalmos. Little information may be gained from the pulse or temperature. Spinal puncture usually but not always reveals blood-tinged fluid which is under increased pressure. This condition is usually observed imme-

diately after birth but the same picture may develop later in association with delayed intracranial hemorrhage.

Burnard states that the ductus arteriosus remains patent causing a precordial bruit for only twenty-four hours after normal birth. In premature babies and in cases of full-term babies when there is asphyxia or respiratory distress, one may hear a rough, high-pitched bruit at the third or fourth interspace in the later part of systole for days. Burnard and James state that in severe asphyxia the heart progressively enlarges, dyspnea is the most prominent symptom and the lungs are congested. Left ventricular failure results.

Sugar may be found in the urine and suspicions of diabetes may be aroused. As a rule the glycosuria soon ceases.

The pallid asphyxia, so called, occurs only immediately after birth. As the name implies, the child is pale rather than blue. Moreover, it is flaccid rather than rigid. Frequently, it is impossible to induce respiration at all and if it is finally initiated, it is feeble, shallow and intermittent. The pulse is usually rapid and feeble and the temperature subnormal. The tendon reflexes are reduced or abolished and the Moro reflex absent. The fontanels are soft. Such children usually die within a very short time. Crothers believes that this picture indicates hemorrhage into the posterior fossa with injury of the medulla but Munro regards it as evidence of surgical shock. No doubt, both of these factors play important roles.

Many writers speak of cerebral palsies at birth but it is not easy to understand what these observations indicate. A number of instances have been recorded in which post-mortem examination unexpectedly revealed complete absence of both cerebral hemispheres in infants who had exhibited all the usual motor reactions of the newborn. It has been deduced, therefore, that the motility of the newborn is entirely reflex and dependent upon the spinal cord and brain-stem. Nevertheless, we sometimes see apparent paralysis of one or more extremities associated either with rigidity and twitchings or with flaccidity. In the writer's experience these signs disappear very quickly if the child survives and may or may not be followed by true cerebral paralysis months later. It is possible that the local rigidity represents cortical irritation equivalent to a focal convulsion with which it is indeed usually associated and that the flaccidity is an example of "shock" such as is seen in the flaccidity and loss of reflexes which are found for a few hours after acute hemiplegia of adults. It seems to be evident that the motor cortex is not entirely unresponsive to irritation in the newborn, even if its function is not essential to the infant's motor reactions.

Localized cyanosis of the face and neck may be seen in rare instances in the newborn without disturbance of respiration. This condition is identical with the so-called traumatic asphyxia and is due to severe compression of

the trunk which forces the blood from the large venous trunks of the chest and abdomen into the vessels of the head and neck. Apparently, distention of the capillaries causes transient vasomotor paralysis and petechial hemorrhages in the conjunctiva, retinae and meninges. After a few days the cyanosis gradually fades. This condition must be distinguished from the so-called harlequin color change in the newborn. These babies became blanched on the upper side of the body and red or cyanotic on the lower half. By changing the child's position the color pattern may be reversed. This condition is believed to have no clinical significance.

In fatal cases, the child usually dies within a few days. In case the child survives, the symptoms slowly or rapidly disappear, the rigidity diminishes, the twitching ceases, respiration and color improve and the child nurses better and cries normally. In a few instances, however, the child may remain in a precarious state for several weeks.

Kozinn *et al.* state that massive cephalohematoma is a dangerous condition and usually indicates a defect in coagulation of the blood.

Pressure on the cornea by forceps or by bony prominences of the pelvis may cause injury. The cornea is clouded for days but soon this clears to a large extent. It can then be seen that Descemet's membrane has been ruptured and strips of this membrane are lying in the anterior chamber. The posterior part of the cornea may remain hazy due to absorption of aqueous humor through the defect in the membrane.

Injuries to the third and sixth nerves at birth are sometimes seen. The sixth nerve is most frequently affected but third nerve lesions are not extremely rare. Palsy of the fourth nerve is rarely recognized. The nerves may be damaged as a result of intracranial hemorrhage, by pinching or callus formation in the sphenoid fissure or by hemorrhage in the orbit. In the last case there should be exophthalmos. I have seen one instance in which the third cranial nerve was damaged at birth and subsequently regenerated with the production of mass movements of the muscles supplied by that nerve. Congenital defects, squints, and Duane's syndrome must be distinguished.

The optic nerve may be damaged by compression in the orbit or in the cranium by hemorrhage or bony compression. Cases are reported in which the optic nerve was avulsed from the bulb. Hemorrhages in the retinae are common. These are more frequent in premature babies. As a rule they are small and lie in the nerve fiber layer. Such hemorrhages are usually absorbed rapidly and cause no great damage. Larger subhyaloid hemorrhages are sometimes seen, and may be a result of intracranial hemorrhage. These may cause lasting loss of vision.

Horner's syndrome is sometimes seen at birth. This is as a rule associated with injury to the lower roots of the brachial plexus but may occur alone.

In some instances the lesion is in the brain stem or cervical cord but it may also be due to pressure on the neck by forceps. If there is no improvement, the lesion is probably in the cervical cord or brain stem. If the condition persists more than a short time, the iris will not become pigmented when it should.

Dr. Edwin Broyles informs me that it is not unusual to see paralysis of one vocal cord in a newborn baby who has been delivered by forceps. He states recovery is to be expected. He regards this condition as a result of pressure on the throat by the forceps blade. Holinger attributes laryngeal and pharyngeal paralysis in the newborn to intracranial hemorrhage and cerebral agenesis. Chapple claims that tilting of the head to one side *in utero* causes compression of either the superior laryngeal or recurrent nerve or both with resulting palsies. Not much information is available about birth injuries of the brain stem, possibly because such lesions are usually fatal within a short time. Lebenson, however, describes a case in a newborn baby of Paranaud's syndrome. There was loss of upward gaze, deviation of the eyes downward, dilated pupils and retraction of the lids. The child eventually recovered. I have seen a child who following a difficult delivery displayed bilateral third nerve palsies and generalized spasticity. There was no regeneration of the nerves and I was inclined to believe that the nuclei were damaged in the midbrain.

Diagnosis.—The recognition of cerebral birth injury is easy when the symptoms are fully developed. The most important signs are cyanosis, stupor, refusal to nurse, feeble cry and bulging of the fontanels. There may be muscular rigidity and twitching or striking flaccidity. If spinal puncture reveals the presence of altered blood in the fluid, there can be little doubt of the diagnosis of intracranial hemorrhage. Some caution must, however, be exercised in the examination of the spinal fluid. First, it must be said that the absence of blood in the spinal fluid does not disprove the possibility of cerebral injury or even of an intracranial hemorrhage, for the blood may fail to reach the subarachnoid spaces. The mere presence of blood again is not conclusive, for bleeding may result from pricking a vein with the needle. We must be able to demonstrate *altered* blood. If the blood has been present in the subarachnoid spaces for a day or more, the following changes will occur: (1) The supernatant fluid after centrifugalization will be yellow or orange color and will give a positive benzidine test. (2) The red cells will be crenated and empty envelopes of red cells will be found, as well as hematoidin crystals. (3) There is an excess of white cells present including phagocytes containing hemoglobin. (4) The fluid is uniformly bloody and does not clear as it continues to flow. If, on the other hand, the blood is due to trauma caused by the needle, the supernatant fluid will be clear and gives a negative benzidine test, the red cells will be

normal and there will be no excess of white cells or phagocytes. As a rule, the fluid clears to some extent as the flow continues. We must also consider the so-called xanthochromia of the newborn which is apparently not uncommon in association with jaundice and which is almost constant in premature children. The fluid is usually only faintly yellow; there are no red cells or only a very few and no significant increase in white cells. Glaser has found the benzidine test to be negative. If we should be so unfortunate as to make a "bloody tap" in the presence of xanthochromia, the normal condition of the red cells and the negative benzidine test on the supernatant fluid should be sufficient to reveal the true situation. Even if we can convince ourselves that the blood was present in the subarachnoid spaces before spinal puncture was performed, we are not justified in concluding that there has been any significant injury to the brain. The possibility that the bleeding might be due to hemorrhagic disease of the newborn should be considered. In very rare cases, congenital angiomas and other vascular tumors may cause intracranial hemorrhage at birth.

The absence of clinical symptoms of birth injury does not disprove the possibility that injury may have occurred, for numerous cases are described in which serious lesions of the brain have been found at post-mortem examination which were not suspected during life.

Congenital defects of the brain are often difficult to distinguish from cerebral birth injuries. Defective infants may exhibit many of the symptoms regarded as evidence of birth injury such as cyanosis, inability to take the breast, feeble cry and rigidity or flaccidity. They usually show no evidence of increased pressure, however, such as bulging of the fontanels or changes in the eye-grounds and the spinal fluid is clear. The presence of associated malformations may be of value in the diagnosis.

Badr El Din describes a familial disease which gives rise to convulsions in utero and also shortly after delivery.

If the fontanels are very large, the circumference of the head increased or there is any sign of spina bifida, we should always consider congenital hydrocephalus which I believe predisposes to cerebral injury at birth.

Premature infants offer difficult problems in diagnosis. They are, of course, often very feeble and unable to nurse or cry. Moreover, they are usually cyanotic and almost always show xanthochromic spinal fluid. Since they are notoriously subject to birth injury and also frequently exhibit defects of cerebral development, the situation may become so complex that no satisfactory conclusions can be reached.

Persistent cyanosis in a newborn infant may, of course, be due to congenital heart disease as well as to the conditions mentioned above. There is also evidence that tetany may occur within a few days after birth and this diagnosis should be considered in cases of muscular rigidity and convul-

sions which are not associated with bulging fontanels or bloody spinal
fluid. It should also be mentioned that hemorrhage into the adrenal glands
at birth may cause profound prostration and flaccidity resembling in this
respect the pallid asphyxia described above.

Brown and Morgan give the following list of possible causes of cyanosis
of the newborn.

Causes Due to Pathological Condition of the Infant

1. Prematurity
2. Persistent thymus gland
3. Diaphragmatic hernia
4. Tracheo-esophageal fistula
5. Congenital cardiac malformation
6. Tongue swallowing
7. Pneumonia of the newborn
8. Tetany of the newborn
9. Sepsis of the newborn
10. Intracranial hemorrhage (spontaneous)

Causes Due to Accidents of Labor

1. Aspiration of mucus
2. Atelectasis
3. Prolapsed cord or cord around neck
4. Early separation of the placenta and low implantation of the placenta
5. Prolonged breech presentation with difficulty in delivering the after-coming head
6. Severe circulatory or toxic condition of mother or drugs, particularly morphine administered to mother during labor
7. Cerebral edema
8. Intracranial hemorrhage (traumatic)

Shey and Klein point out that the babies of mothers who are addicted to
narcotics may show severe withdrawal symptoms shortly after birth. Within
twenty-four hours, the baby becomes restless and irritable. There is a shrill
cry. They take little food and vomit what they take. Cyanosis, diarrhea,
lacrimation, salivation and sweating are described. The child may die in
convulsions. Opium derivatives must be administered or phenobarbital, and
then gradually withdrawn. The mother should be treated early in pregnancy. It is stated that even in intrauterine life, the fetal movements are increased when the mother requires her usual dose of narcotics. We have seen
similar reactions in infants of mothers who are excessively alcoholic.

Prognosis.—The mortality among children who exhibit definite evidence
of cerebral injury is high. According to Roberts, Fleming and Munro,
about half of these children die within the next few days and the writer's
experience is in complete agreement with these figures. If mild cases are not
recognized, the mortality is naturally higher, and if the children are observed with exceptional care, a lower mortality will be reported.

The prognosis for recovery in children who survive cerebral birth in-

juries is uncertain. Fleming states that there is no satisfactory way of determining whether the child will recover or will be permanently injured. The writer has reached the same conclusions. There is little information which bears directly on this problem, for very few studies have been made of the late results of cerebral birth injuries which are not open to serious criticism. Rydberg gives an unfavorable prognosis. He states that out of 41 children who had survived cerebral injury at birth, only 10 were quite normal. However, he includes among the sequelae 7 cases of squint which is, of course, most frequently nonparalytic. Moreover, his method of diagnosis and of excluding congenital defects of the nervous system is not entirely clear. Recent articles by other writers give a much more cheerful conclusion. Roberts has followed for a number of months a series of 48 children whose spinal fluid contained blood soon after birth. Only 14 of these children exhibited clinical symptoms of cerebral injury, however. When the article was published, Roberts stated that only one of the children was definitely abnormal and even in this case there was reason to suspect congenital syphilis. The period of observation was, perhaps, too brief to permit final conclusions. A second article by Roberts appeared in 1939. As a result of study of 19,052 consecutive deliveries, he stated that clinical evidence of intracranial hemorrhage is found in between 1 and 2 per cent of all newborn infants. Of the children who survive such hemorrhages, Roberts concludes that 75 per cent develop normally and that very few show spasticity. Munro has published the results in a series of 48 children who were observed from one to six years after birth and who were studied very carefully at birth. Only 7 of these were defective but some died of various diseases other than birth injury. Fleming of Glasgow has made a very valuable contribution to the subject. He has followed 33 children, who were known to have suffered birth injuries, for more than a year. Only 5 were defective. Recently Howard Smith has made a similar series of observations. He concludes that the presence or absence of blood in the spinal fluid has no prognostic importance. Among 20 children who showed clinical evidences of cerebral injury at birth, 6 died in a few days, 12 developed normally and 2 remained mentally subnormal. One of these 2 was "spastic." The writer's experience leads him to agree with Fleming and Roberts rather than with Rydberg. If we accept the figures given above, we may conclude that less than 15 per cent of the children who show definite signs of cerebral injury at birth, but nevertheless survive, may be expected to be defective later in life.

When the spinal puncture discloses blood-stained fluid but clinical signs of birth injury are absent, the prognosis is apparently very good. In our experience, these children have all survived and have remained well.

Treatment.—If the child fails to breathe at birth, the nose and throat

should be cleared of mucus and artificial respiration applied. Most obstetricians perform mouth to mouth insufflation but the Drinker respirator, if available, is helpful. Henderson has insisted on the use of carbon-dioxide-oxygen mixtures as a physiological stimulant, but the plasma carbon dioxide is already so high in asphyxiated infants that it seems very doubtful whether any good could be done by raising it higher. The more conservative obstetricians all condemn the violent methods of resuscitation such as compressing the chest or the swinging method of Schultze. If there is any reason to suspect shock, no unnecessary measures should be attempted. The child should be kept warm and given abundant fluids. If attacks of cyanosis occur from time to time, the administration of carbon-dioxide-oxygen mixture is recommended. Hodges *et al.* advise that a catheter be introduced into the respiratory passages and aspiration and oxygenation carried out as necessary. Oxygen should not be administered under more than a pressure of 40 cm of water. Westin advises treatment for pallid asphyxia with hypothermia or hypothermia plus oxygenated blood. Hutchinson *et al.* advise the use of hyperbaric oxygen.

Ewerbeck states that more intensive treatment is needed for asphyxia during or after delivery. Shock, hypovolemia and acidosis must be treated vigorously. Intravenous administration of 5 per cent glucose and serum 70 to 150 ml per kilogram of weight per day or more may be needed. Respiratory or metabolic acidosis should be treated effectively.

Srouji states that pneumothorax or pneumomediastinum are sometimes causes of neonatal respiratory distress. Positive pressure resuscitation seems to increase the incidence of this condition. Thoracostomy may be required.

A day or more after birth, spinal puncture may be performed, preferably with a hypodermic needle or similar small, sharp needle. This delay makes it possible to distinguish the altered blood of an intracranial hemorrhage from that due to a faulty puncture. If there is any blood in the fluid or if there is good reason to believe that there is intracranial hemorrhage, the clotting time of the blood should be determined. If this is definitely delayed, a transfusion should be performed or vitamin K given. When there is hemorrhage from the mucous membranes or cutaneous petechiae, the blood may be injected at once without waiting for the test of the clotting time. Sherman and Clatworthy state that gastrointestinal bleeding in newborn babies is rarely due to lesions that can be repaired by surgery and transfusions are the most effective treatment.

A number of writers claim that spinal drainage by repeated puncture is a valuable therapeutic measure. This they say is helpful in reducing the increased intracranial pressure and in removing blood from the meninges which may lead to a serious meningeal reaction. The writer is not convinced that all these claims are justified. It is clear that small or moderate amounts

of blood are usually absorbed promptly from the subarachnoid spaces and leave no appreciable ill-effects. Hemorrhages into the brain or the subdural space, of course, cannot be affected in any way by spinal puncture. This statement is also true of encapsulated hematomas in the subarachnoid spaces. It is possible, moreover, that the struggling of the infant during spinal puncture and the relief of pressure due to release of fluid may play a part in prolonging the bleeding or even in starting it again after it has stopped. The possibility of precipitating herniation of the medulla into the foramen magnum and causing paralysis of respiration must be kept in mind. Despite all these objections, there is no doubt that spinal puncture, if performed properly and with adequate judgment, is of value in reducing intracranial pressure and removing hemoglobin from the meninges. Obvious symptomatic improvement often follows the removal of 15 or 20 cc of bloodstained fluid.

In the writer's experience, there is rarely if ever any justification for a craniotomy in newborn infants. Such procedures are almost always fatal and can scarcely lead to any good, since by the time the hematoma can be localized and removed, injury to the brain has already occurred. Most conservative obstetricians oppose even operative procedures to relieve depressed fractures of the skull, pointing out that these almost always fill out quickly without operation. Others believe that it is best to elevate the bone as soon as the child's condition makes it feasible.

Clinical Features, Chronic Stage.—There are two chief questions which require consideration at this point: (1) What neurological syndromes represent the sequelae of cerebral birth injury? (2) What role does birth injury play in the causation of the infantile cerebral palsies, mental defects and epilepsies of childhood? There is certainly no adequate answer to either question to be found in medical literature. One group of writers believe that birth injury is the greatest single cause of cerebral abnormalities in childhood and another group regard it is relatively unimportant. If the first question could be answered, we would obviously have an approach to the solution of the second question, and a great deal has been written about the relation of birth injury to all of the common neurological conditions of childhood. Since cerebral diplegia (q.v.) is probably the commonest type of infantile cerebral palsy seen by the pediatrician, it becomes a matter of considerable importance to determine whether this is a result of birth injury or not. Osler and Gowers claimed that cerebral diplegia is almost invariably due to birth injury and, indeed, that it is the characteristic result of meningeal hemorrhage. The Continental neurologists as a whole have opposed this view. Freud published an important article in which he offered abundant evidence to show that diplegia is always the result of a prenatal process and that birth injury causes only hemiplegia, monoplegia and

bilateral hemiplegia. Collier reached the same conclusion. This is almost exactly the opposite of Osler's teaching.

The only direct approach to the elucidation of these problems would seem to be the careful study of a large group of children at birth and their re-examination years later when the final outcome can be determined. It seems strange that this has not been done in the past. Most studies have been made during the neonatal period while the child is still under the obstetrician's care or years later by neurologists who have little information about conditions at birth and, hence, have relied chiefly on theoretical considerations for diagnosis. The reason for such an unsatisfactory situation soon becomes apparent when one tries to fill in the missing links in the chain of evidence. When the diagnosis of cerebral injury is established beyond doubt at birth, the child either dies within a few days or makes an apparent recovery in most instances. Only a few children survive with definite residua. A large percentage of children who eventually are discovered to be defective have shown no definite evidence of injury at birth. It is evident, therefore, that it is a very difficult matter to obtain a direct answer to our questions. Recently some very important studies have been made. Fleming has studied 33 children who showed definite evidence of cerebral birth in-

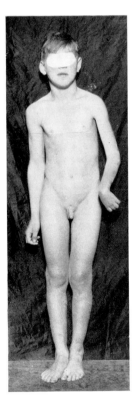

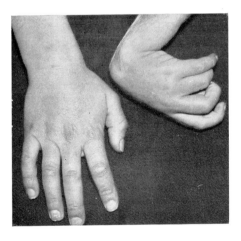

FIG. 270. Cerebral birth injury. Left hemiplegia with spasticity, deformity and defective development of the arm and leg.

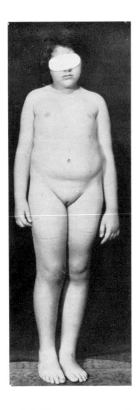

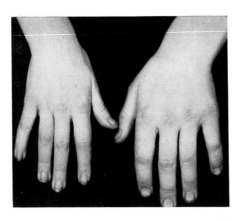

Fig. 271. Cerebral birth injury. Right hemiplegia with atonic muscles without deformity but with defective development of the arm.

jury and followed them for a year or more. Only 5 of these were definitely abnormal at the end of this period. The first child at the age of 20 months was mentally defective, made no attempt to walk or talk and exhibited spasticity and twitching of the left arm. Circumference of the head was 44 cm. The second child at one year of age was defective in mental development and could not walk or talk. No paralysis was detected. Head circumference was 46 cm. A third child showed hydrocephalus, optic atrophy, spasticity of the left arm and pronounced mental defect at two years of age. Head circumference was 62 cm. The fourth child at 14 months of age was definitely defective and exhibited athetoid movements of both arms, as well as spasticity of the right leg. The last child was microcephalic and idiotic. Optic atrophy and general rigidity were found. The child died at 2½ years and post-mortem revealed conditions which were regarded as indicating a prenatal process. Many other authors have published similar papers but since the connection of the neurologic disorder with birth is either not fully established or the late results are inadequately described, they need not be analyzed.

The writer has been interested for some years in determining the ultimate results of cerebral birth injury. For this purpose he has collected a

series of cases in which the diagnosis of cerebral injury was definitely established at birth and in which re-examination several years later was possible. Thirty-three of these children survived but showed definite residua. The writer believes that the diagnosis is correct in these cases, but it is very probable that many results of birth injury are omitted. Obviously, the more severely injured children are apt to die in infancy and are, therefore, not represented in the tables. It is likewise evident that the very mild injuries will often escape recognition at birth and that injuries which do not give rise to definite physical signs will attract no attention later in life, so that the child may be regarded as having made a complete recovery. The writer regards the cases here presented as characteristic of birth injury, even if all the possible results are not fully represented. If we assume that asphyxia at birth may cause diffuse damage to the brain, it is evident that the sequelae will be quite different from those listed here which are almost exclusively a result of focal lesions resulting presumably from trauma and hemorrhage.

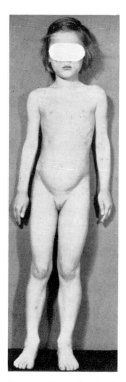

Fig. 272. Cerebral birth injury. Right crural monoplegia with defective development of the leg.

The analysis of these cases seems to justify the following conclusions: Hemiplegia is the commonest type of paralysis due to birth injury. This is either mild or severe. As a rule it is associated with definite spasticity, increased tendon reflexes, clonus and extensor response but in a number of cases, there has been striking hypotonus, i.e. flaccid hemiplegia. There is always underdevelopment of the affected arm and hand and less evident underdevelopment of the leg. Very evident differences in development of the extremities may appear even when there is very little disability. When there is much spasticity present, the affected hand is deformed to a degree not seen in hemiplegias developing later in life.

Monoplegias are also seen. Crural monoplegias are more frequent than brachial monoplegias. In either case there is apt to be slight involvement of the other limb on the corresponding side, so that it is sometimes difficult to say whether we are dealing with a hemiplegia of unequal distribution or a monoplegia with insignificant involvement of the other limb.

Four double hemiplegias were found, all of which were unequal on the two sides and associated with bulbar disturbances which should probably be termed pseudobulbar palsy. These, of course, resemble the congenital diplegias very closely.

In one case, both legs were affected but one was more severely involved than the other. This is the only case which resembled the congenital cerebral paraplegia.

In several cases, athetoid movements of mild degree were associated with bilateral or unilateral paralysis. The writer has observed no cases which could possibly be confused with the common congenital double athetosis.

Convulsive seizures were present in many cases. These were usually either confined to the affected limbs or began on the affected side becoming generalized later. The focal attacks might be associated with loss of consciousness or the mind might be clear and the attack might be represented by a few clonic movements in one extremity. One child had a few muscular twitchings every hour or more in the right arm. As a rule, a severe focal convulsion was followed by increased weakness of the affected limb. We have found only one case of focal convulsions without paralysis. It is of interest that the onset of the convulsions was sometimes delayed until ten or more years after birth.

Hemianopia was discovered only twice although it is probably often overlooked because of the difficulty in securing proper cooperation in the testing of the visual fields. We have seen several older children in whom hemianopia was discovered by accident. The hemianopia had never been noticed by the patient. There were no other neurological defects. We have been inclined to attribute this condition to cerebral birth injury though we have had no definite proof. We have seen one case in which spatial orientation and memory of topography were defective. Altitudinal hemianopia was associated. Hemianesthesia was discovered once but again is probably present in many cases.

The mental condition of these children has proved to be very interesting. The writer has formed the opinion that the usual finding is merely a mild or moderate deficiency in intelligence with little change in personality. The children are, as a rule, placid and good-natured. They play contentedly with their toys and get along well with their friends. They do not seem to show the constant, senseless activity so common in the congenitally defective children. In general, one gains the impression that the patient is a normal child laboring under a handicap rather than a totally abnormal, unreasonable creature. Two exceptions must be made to these statements. Some children are so spoiled that they make a very bad impression and in others repeated convulsions seem to lead to irritability and changes in personality. Obviously, the child's inherited trends must be taken into consideration.

In a number of cases, there is a tendency for the child's head to grow very rapidly in the first few weeks or months of life. Fleming has made similar observations. Some authors speak of this as hydrocephalus but the writer does not consider this term applicable, for in most cases the head

soon ceases to expand abnormally. It is probable that this sign is due to increased pressure resulting from large hemorrhage and is analogous to the rapid enlargement of the head in subdural hematoma. There is little evidence that actual obstruction of the pathways conveying the cerebrospinal fluid occurs. In the writer's opinion, when chronic hydrocephalus is associated with birth injury, the causal relation is more apt to be the opposite and it is the large head of congenital hydrocephalus which has led to injury during birth. In a number of children who sustain cerebral injury at birth, we have found at autopsy not only the lesions of birth injury but defects in the aqueduct and foramina of the fourth ventricle which are identical with those found in uncomplicated congenital hydrocephalus. In a small number of cases the child has become strikingly obese. Two possible explanations must be considered in such cases: (1) That there has been injury to the hypothalamus and the obesity is due to disordered metabolism. (2) That injury to the hemisphere has caused morbid hunger and led to excessive intake of food.

We have observed a few cases in which there was reason to believe that asphyxia at birth was responsible for extensive damage to the brain. One of these is given in abstract below. In these children we found relative microcephaly, generalized spasticity, i.e. spastic cerebral diplegia, mental deficiency and blindness of cortical type in most cases. Sometimes the optic nerve heads were pale but usually the pupils reacted to light despite the pallor of the discs. Air encephalography revealed atrophy of the cortex and symmetrical dilatation of the ventricular system. I cannot be sure that these children's condition is actually due to anoxia at birth but it seems possible that it is. The picture is of course a duplicate of the common cerebral diplegia with the additional feature of blindness. My present impression is that such cases are uncommon.

Diagnosis.—The diagnosis depends chiefly on the history of birth but in the writer's opinion, the character of the clinical picture is of distinct importance in the differential diagnosis. Thus, he believes that hemiplegia, monoplegia and asymmetrical palsies are more likely to be due to birth injury than to congenital defects of development. The distinction between double hemiplegia and severe diplegia is often difficult or impossible. These statements represent merely the author's opinion and are not generally accepted.

Prognosis.—The outlook for recovery is not very cheerful as a rule, for the disability often becomes more obvious as the child grows older and faces more difficult problems. This applies especially to the mental disturbances. A child who might seem nearly normal at the age of two years may prove later in life to be incapable of self-support. The development of

epilepsy makes the prognosis less favorable since deterioration may be associated. If there is hemiplegia, the spasticity often seems to grow more severe in the first few years of life and may slowly mould the plastic bones so as to produce progressive deformities. The deficient development of the affected limbs also becomes more striking later in life. However, mild palsies sometimes apparently diminish.

Treatment.—The palsies are treated as described under congenital diplegia (q.v.). Epilepsy is treated symptomatically in most cases. Some writers advise craniotomy preferably after ventriculography and removal of scars and cysts. If one hemisphere is grossly injured and seizures are frequent, it is sometimes advised that the entire hemisphere be removed. In the writer's opinion, good results are exceptional. Special training may be necessary for the mentally deficient and for speech defects.

CASE HISTORY (Ped. A-40592).—*Blindness and cerebral spastic diplegia in a child of eight months possibly due to anoxia at birth.*

S. W. was first seen at the age of eight months. The mother had been profoundly exsanguinated by repeated hemorrhages during delivery and placenta praevia was discovered. Transfusions were required. By mistake pure nitrous oxide without oxygen was administered for several minutes. At birth the baby was deeply asphyxiated and could not be induced to breathe for three quarters of an hour. Later, there was rigidity and a number of convulsions were observed in the next few days. Periods of apnea occurred. The eyes deviated to one side for a time and displayed jerky nystagmoid movements. The child subsequently showed defective development.

On examination the child was unable to sit up or even hold up the head. There was bilateral spasticity with increased tendon reflexes. The head was conspicuously small. There was no evidence of vision and the optic nerve heads were somewhat pale. The pupillary light reflexes were minimal.

At the age of four years the child had shown little change. She was still rigid and unable to stand or sit up. She could not talk. The optic nerve heads were very pale. No evidence of vision was found. The circumference of the head was 14¼ inches. An (air) encephalogram revealed extensive atrophy of the cerebral cortex and enlargement of the ventricles. This case is presented by the courtesy of Dr. Walsh.

CASE HISTORY (1187058).—*Labor of 18 hours. Breech presentation then discovered. Cesarean section performed. Evidence suggestive of spasmus nutans at 3 months. Small pale left optic disc. Vision of left eye reduced. Vision of the right eye fairly good and right optic disc not definitely pale or small.*

L. P., a child of 6 months was delivered by Cesarean section when breech presentation was discovered after 18 hours of unsuccessful labor.

The child seemed to be in good condition at birth. At 3 months, the mother noted rapid oscillations of the eyes. The left eye turned in at the same time. The mother noted head nodding and head tilting.

Examination at 6 months revealed a head of normal size and shape. The right pupil reacted well to light. The left pupil reacted less promptly. The left optic disc was pale and too small, but the right optic disc was of normal size and not definitely pale. There was an internal squint of the left eye and this eye did not move fully to the left. In bright light, nystagmoid movements developed which were chiefly horizontal. There was head nodding at times, but head tilting was not observed. Neurological examination was otherwise negative.

Neurosurgical examinations revealed no evidence of an intracranial neoplasm. It was concluded that the right optic nerve had been injured at birth.

BIBLIOGRAPHY

BANKER, B. Q. AND LARROCHE, J. C.: Neonatal anoxia and mental retardation. Arch. Neurol., 7:386, 1962.

EHRENFEST, H.: Birth Injuries of the Child. New York, D. Appleton & Co., 1922.

FORD, F. R.: Cerebral birth injuries and their results. Medicine, 5:121, 1926.

OZAN, H. A. AND GONZALES, A. A.: Post-traumatic fetal epilepsy. Neeurlogy, 13:541, 1963.

Pathological Anatomy

AWON, M. P.: The vacuum extractor. Experimental demonstration of distortion of the foetal skull. J. Obst. Gynaec. Brit. Cwith., 71:634, 1964.

BENDA, C. E.: The late effects of cerebral birth injuries. Medicine, 24:71, 1945.

CAPON, N. B.: Intracranial traumata in the newborn. J. Obst. & Gynec. Brit. Emp., 29:572, 1922.

COURVILLE, C. B.: Contribution to the Study of Cerebral Anoxia. San Lucas Press, Los Angeles, Calif., 1953.

COURVILLE, C. B. AND MARSH, C.: Neonatal asphyxia: Its encephalitis residuals and mechanism of their production. Bull. Los Angeles Neurol. Soc., 9:121, 1944.

CUSHING, H.: Concerning surgical intervention for the intracranial hemorrhage of the newborn. Am. J. Med. Sc., 130:563, 1905.

GREENWOOD, W. O.: The moulding of the foetal head and its consequences. J. Obst. & Gynec. Brit. Emp., 31:611, 1924.

HALLER, E. S., NESBITT, R. AND ANDERSON, G. W.: Clinical and pathologic concepts of gross intracranial hemorrhage in perinatal mortality. Obst. & Gynec. Surv., 11:179, 1956.

HAMMES, E. M.: Reaction of the meninges to blood. Arch. Neurol. & Psychiat., 52:505, 1945.

HOLLAND, E.: Cranial stress in foetus during labor and the effects of excessive stress on the intracranial contents. J. Obst. & Gynec. Brit. Emp., 29:549, 1922.

KABAT, H.: The greatest resistance of very young animals to arrest of brain circulation. Am. J. Physiol., 130:588, 1941.

KABAT, H., DENNIS, C. AND BAKER, A. B.: Recovery of function following arrest of brain circulation. Am. J. Physiol., 132:737, 1941.

LEVINSON, A. AND SAPHIR, O.: Meninges in intracranial hemorrhage of the newborn. Am. J. Dis. Child., 46:973, 1933.

LINDENBERG, R.: Compression of brain artereies as pathogenic factor for tissue necroses and their areas of predilection. J. Neuropath. & Exp. Neurol., 14:223, 1955.

NORMAN, R. M.: Bilateral atrophic lobar sclerosis following thrombosis of the superior longitudinal sinus. J. Neur. & Psychopath., 17:135, 1936.

NORMAN, R. M. *et al.*: Vascular mechanism of birth injury. Brain, 80:49, 1957.

PIERSON, R. N.: Spinal and cranial injuries of babies in breech deliveries. Surg. Gynec. & Obst., 37:790, 1923.

RAUSEN, A. E. *et al.*: The twin transfusion syndrome. Jour. Pediat., 66:613, 1965.

SCHWARTZ, P.: Erkrankungen des Zentralnervensystems nach traumatischer Geburtsschadigung anatomische Untersuchungen. Ztschr. f. d. ges. Neurol. u. Psychiat., 40:263, 1924.

SPENCER, H. R.: On visceral hemorrhages in still born children; Analysis of 130 autopsies, being a study of the causes of still birth. Tr. Obst. Soc. London, 33:203, 1892.

TOWBIN, A.: Cerebral hypoxic damage in fetus and newborn. Archives of Neurology, 20:35, 1969.

VOSS, O.: Geburtstrauma und Gehörorgan. Ztschr. f. Hals-, Nasen- u. Ohrenh. 6:182, 1923.

WALSH, H.: Development of children born prematurely with birth weights of 3 pounds or less. Med. Jour. Aust., 1:108, 1969.

WARWICK, M.: Cerebral hemorrhage in the newborn. Am. J. Med. Sc., 158:95, 1919.

————: Necropsy finding in newborn infants. Am. J. Dis. Child., 21:448, 1921.

WINDLE, W. F. AND BECKER, R. F.: Asphyxia neonatorum. An experimental study in the guinea pig. Am. J. Obst & Gynec., 45:183, 1943.

YATES, P. O.: Birth trauma to the vertebral arteries. Arch. Dis. Childh., 1959, p. 436.

————: Birth trauma to vertebral arteries. Arch. Pathol., 77:62, 1964.

YLPPÖ, A.: The origin of hemorrhage in the premature and the newborn. Ztschr. f. Kinderh., 38:32, 1924.

————: The pathology of premature babies. Klin. Wchnschr., 1:1241, 1922.

Clinical

BADR, EL-DIN: A familial convulsive disorder with an unusual onset during intrauterine life. Jour. Pediat., 56:655, 1960.

BANKER, B. Q.: The neuropathological effects of anoxia and hypoglycemia in the newborn. Develop. Med. Child. Neurol., 9:544, 1967.

BARNES, A. C.: The post-maturity syndrome. California Med., 85:289, 1956.

BIRDSONG, McL. AND EDMUNDS, J. E.: Harlequin color change of the newborn. Obst. & Gynec., 7:518, 1956.

BOURNE, G. L. AND BENIRSCHKE, K.: Absence of one umbilical artery. Arch. Dis. Childhood, 35:534, 1960.

BRANDER, T.: Cerebral defects in children delivered by caesarian section. Acta paediat. Scand., 23:145, 1938.

BRAT, TH.: Indication for and results of the use of the "ventouse obstetricale." Jour. Obstet. Gynaec. Brit. Cwlth., 72: 883, 1965.

BROWNE, J. C. McC.: Postmaturity effect on fetus. Am. J. Obst. & Gynec., 85:573, 1963.

BURNARD, E. D.: Precordial bruit after birth in asphyxiated infants. Proc. Roy. Soc. Med., 52 (No. 1) Sec. Pediat.:77, 1959.

BURNARD, E. D. AND JAMES, L. S.: Heart failure after neonatal asphyxia. Pediatrics, 28:545, 1961.

CAMPBELL, W. A. B. *et al.*: The effects of neonatal asphyxia on physical and mental development. Arch. Dis. Child., 25:351, 1950.

CHAPPLE, C. C.: A duosyndrome of laryngeal nerve. Am. J. Dis. Child., 91:14, 1956.

CLIFFORD, S. H.: Asphyxia of the fetus and the newborn infant. Am. J. Obst. & Gynec., 39:388, 1940.

CRAIG, W. S.: Intracranial hemorrhage in the newborn. Arch. Dis. Childh., 13:89, 1938.

CROTHERS, B.: Changes in pressure inside the foetal craniovertebral cavity. Surg. Gynec. & Obst., 37:790, 1923.

EARLE, K., BALDWIN, M. AND PENFIELD, W.: Incisural scleronis and temporal lobe seizures produced by hippocampal herniation at birth. Arch. Neurol. & Psychiat., 69:27, 1953.

EWERBECK, H.: Prevention of cerebral damage in the newborn. Dtsch. med. Wschr., 92:1485, 1967.

FABER, H. K.: Cerebral atrophy in children. J. Michigan State M. Soc., 41:221, 1942.

FINSTER, M. *et al.:* Accidental intoxication of the fetus with local anesthetic drug during caudal anesthesia. Amer. Jour. Obstet. Gynec., **92**:922, 1965.

FLEMING, G. B.: Paper on recognition and treatment of birth injuries in newly born. Brit. Med. J., **2**:481, 1931.

FLEMING, G. B. AND MORTON, E. D.: Meningeal hemorrhage in the newborn. Arch. Dis. Child., **5**:361, 1930.

GALLOWAY, W. H. *et al.:* Premature breech delivery. Amer. Jour. Obstet. and Gynec., **99**:975, 1967.

GOLDZIEHEN, M. A.: Syndrome of adrenal hemorrhage in the newborn. Endocrinology, **16**:165, 1932.

GOLLIN, H. A., M.D., ELLIS, A. H., M.D. AND EVANS, E. F., M.D. (University of Illinois, Chicago): The problem of the oversized fetus. Am. J. Obst. & Gynec., **75**:742-753, 1958.

GRUENWALD, P.: Asphyxia, trauma and shock at birth. Arch. of Pediat., **67**:103, 1950.

HEIMER, C. B. *et al.:* Neurological sequelae of premature birth. Am. J. Dis. Child., **108**:122, 1964.

HENDERSON, H. *et al.:* Oxygen studies of the cord blood of caesarian-born infants. Am. J. Obst. and Gynec., **73**:664, 1957.

HODGES, R. J. H. *et al.:* Endotracheal aspiration and oxygenation in resuscitation of the newborn. Brit. J. Anaesth., **32**:9, 1960.

HOLINGER, P. H.: The role of the laryngologist in resuscitation of the newborn infant. J.A.M.A., **159**:1338, 1955.

HUTCHINSON, J. H. *et al.:* Hyperbaric oxygen for apnea neonatorum. Lancet, **2**:1019, 1963.

IRVING, F. C.: Obstetrical aspect of intracranial hemorrhage. New England J. Med., **203**:499, 1930.

KEITH, H. M., NORVAL, M. A. AND HUNT, A. B.: Neurologic lesions in relation to the sequelae of birth injury. Neurology, **3**:139, 1953.

KEITH, H. M. AND GAGE, R. P.: Neurologic ills from birth complications. Pediatrics, **26**:616, 1960.

KOZINN, P. J. *et al.:* Massive hemorrhage under scalps of newborn babies. Amer. Jour. Dis. Child., **108**:413, 1964.

LEBENSON, J. E.: Paranaud's syndrome due to obstetrical trauma with recovery. Am. J. Ophth., **40**:738, 1954.

LEVINE, S. Z. AND GORDON, H.: Physiologic handicaps of the premature infant. Am. J. Dis. Child., **64**:274, 1942.

LIPSITZ, P. J. AND ENGLISH, I. C.: Hypermagnesemia in the newborn infant. Pediatrics, **40**:856, 1967.

LITTLE, W. A.: Umbilical artery aplasia. Obst. & Gynec., **17**:695, 1961.

LLOYD, R. I.: Birth injuries of the cornea and allied conditions. Trans. Am. Ophth. Soc., **35**:212, 1937.

MORGAN, E. A. AND BROWN, A.: Cyanosis of the newborn. J.A.M.A., **105**:1085, 1935.

MORRISON, L. R.: Histopathologic effect of anoxia on the central nervous system. Arch. Neurol. & Psychiat., **55**:1, 1946.

MUNRO, D.: Cranial and intracranial damage in the newborn; end results; study of 117 cases. South. Surg. Tr., **40**:393, 1927.

————: Symptomatology and immediate treatment of cranial and intracranial injury in newborn including intracranial hemorrhage. New England J. Med., **203**:502, 1930.

MUNDO-VALLARTA, J. AND ROBB, J. P.: A follow up study of newborn infants with perinatal complications. Neurology, **14**:413, 1964.

PATTEN, C. A. AND ALPERS, B. J.: Cerebral birth conditions with special reference to the factor of hemorrhage. Am. J. Psychiat., **12**:751, 1933.

PENFIELD, W. AND LIVINGSTON, S.: Birth injury: focal epilepsy and cortical excision. Pediatrics, August, 157, 1949.

PERLMUTTER, J.: Drug addiction in pregnant women. Amer. Jour. Obstet. and Gynec., **99**:569, 1967.

Report of the Fifty-seventh Ross Conference on Pediatr. Research. Brain Damage in the Fetus and Newborn from Hypoxia and Asphyxia. Puerto Rico, January 24-25, 1967.

REYNOLDS, S. R. M.: Changes in the circulation at birth. Modern Medicine, Nov. 15, 1957, p. 83.

ROBERTS, M. H.: The spinal fluid in the newborn with especial reference to intracranial hemorrhage. J.A.M.A., **85**:500, 1925.

————: Intracranial hemorrhage in the new born. J.A.M.A., **113**:280, 1939.

RYDBERG, E.: Cerebral injury in newborn children consequent on birth trauma. Acta. Path. et Microbiol. Scand., Suppl. x, 1932.

SCHIPKE, R. *et al.:* Acute subdural hemorrhage at birth. Pediatrics, **14**:468, 1954.

SCHREIBER, F.: Neurologic sequelae of paranatal asphyxia. J. Pediat., **16**:297, 1940.

SHANNON, W. R.: Cerebral injury in the newborn, its relation to constitution and the tetany syndrome. Am. J. Dis. Child., **48**:517, 1934.

SHERMAN, N. J. AND CLATWORTHY, H. W.: Gastrointestinal bleeding in neonates. Surgery, **62**:614, 1967.

SHEY, I. A. AND KLEIN, M. D.: The effects of maternal narcotic addiction on the newborn. Am. J. Obst. & Gynec., **71**:29, 1956.

SJOSTEDT, J. E.: The vacuum extractor and forceps in obstetrics. Acta obstet. gynec. scand., vol. 46, Suppl 10, p. 1, 1967.

SMITH, L. H.: Blood in the cerebrospinal fluid of the newborn. Its relation to prognosis. J. Obst. & Gynec., **28**:89, 1934.

SROUJI, M. N.: Pneumothorax and pneumomediastinum in the first three days of life. Jour. Pediat., **2**:410, 1967.

TITRUD, L. A. AND HAYMAKER, W.: Cerebral anoxia from high altitude asphyxiation. Arch. Neurol. & Psychiat., **57**:397, 1947.

VSDIN, G. L. AND WEIL, M. L.: Effects of apnea neonatorum on intellectual development. Pediatrics, **9**:387, 1952.

WALSH, F. B.: *Loc. cit.*

WESTIN, B. *et al.:* Neonatal asphyxia pallida treated with hypothermia alone or with hypothermia and transfusion of oxygenated blood. Surgery, **45**:868, 1959.

WILSON, R. A., TORREY, M. A. AND JOHNSON, K. S.: Initiation of respiration in asphyxia neonatorum. Surg. Gynec. Abst., **65**:601, 1937.

SPINAL BIRTH INJURIES

Introduction.—Very little attention was devoted to this subject until the publication of Crothers' paper in 1923. A number of isolated cases had been recognized before this time and spinal lesions were familiar to the obstetricians and pathologists, but neurologists and pediatricians apparently rarely took spinal birth injuries into consideration. It is of interest that Parrot published an excellent study of a case of spinal birth injury in 1870 which attracted little attention and was soon forgotten. In 1925, the writer published a series of six cases of complete transection of the spinal cord due to injury during delivery which had been studied on the pediatric service of John Howland. Crothers and Putnam collected all the material available on this subject in the form of a monograph which appeared in 1927. Twenty-eight cases were included.

Etiology.—Birth injuries of the spinal cord are unlike spinal injuries of any other type in that they are usually due to stretching of the cord and not to compression. Crothers has made a careful analysis of the anatomical factors involved. He points out that the spinal cord is very delicate and inelastic. It is attached below by the cauda equina and above by the roots of

the brachial plexus and medulla. The vertebral column of infants may be stretched very easily for the ligaments are elastic and the muscles delicate. Moreover, the dura is more elastic than in adults. Strong traction in the long axis of the body may therefore be expected to cause elongation of the spinal column and to stretch the spinal cord and its membranes. That this actually occurs seems to be established by the nature of the lesions found at autopsy. Spinal cord injuries almost always result from breech deliveries, especially difficult deliveries in which version and extraction are performed. Excessive traction on the trunk while the head is still firmly engaged in the pelvis is apparently responsible. The lesion is almost always in the lower cervical or thoracic segments.

In certain cases, paraplegia is associated with segmental palsies of one or both arms. This association admits of more than one interpretation. We might assume that stretching of the spinal cord results in tearing it from the cervical roots or that stretching of the plexus may cause avulsion of the roots from the cord with hematomyelia. In such cases it is possible that the lesion is not in the plexus at all but in the gray matter of the cervical enlargement. In Crothers' series there were 19 cases of spinal injury following breech delivery. In two of these there was an associated brachial plexus palsy of the Klumpke type with the cervical sympathetic syndrome. It is probable that in these cases traction on the cord had caused avulsion of the lower roots of the plexus with injury of the spinal gray matter. In one case of this type which the writer has followed for a number of years, there was no return of function, thus lending some support to the theory that the lesion is actually in the cord. Among Crothers' 7 cases of spinal birth injury which occurred in children whose heads presented, there were 4 cases in which brachial plexus palsies were also associated. These were all of the common type involving either the upper arm or the whole arm. No doubt the cervical roots had been avulsed from the cord with resulting hematomyelia. The post-mortem examination described by Boyer lends a great deal of support to this theory.

Pathological Anatomy.—In the general papers on the pathology of birth

Fig. 273. Rupture of the dura with separation of the ends by 2.0 cm. The cord was stretched and softened and infiltrated with blood. This is a result of breech delivery. (From Ford, F. R. Breech delivery in its possible relations to injury of the spinal cord. Arch. of Neurology and Psychiatry 1925, vol. 14, p. 742.)

injury, a number of lesions are described in the spinal canal such as large and small subdural and extradural hemorrhages, as well as petechial hemorrhages in the cord itself. Fractures and dislocations of the cervical spine are mentioned when delivery was effected under exceptionally difficult circumstances. We have seen 2 cases in which fracture dislocation of the axis on the atlas resulted in compression of the cervical cord. In the cases under consideration, especially those in which there is complete transection of the cord, a fairly specific type of lesion has usually been found. The vertebral column is usually intact. In a case reported by the writer, no injury whatever could be found in the spine despite careful study, but the dura was torn across, the ends being separated by an inch or more. Extensive hemorrhage was found at this point. The spinal cord was almost completely ruptured, being stretched until it was very thin. In Byers' case the dura was intact but the cord was completely severed. On section it is usually found that the hemorrhage extends into the central gray matter for several segments both above and below the lesion. If the child survives for several weeks, the dura and spinal cord are found to be adherent and the blood clot is organized so that the defect is filled with scar tissue. Ascending and descending degenerations are found in the spinal cord as in all spinal sections. The lesions are most frequent in the lower cervical and thoracic segments. It may be sharply localized or large parts of the cord may be destroyed by spreading hemorrhage.

Clinical Features.—Spinal injuries at birth are the result of breech deliveries in the majority of cases. There is usually a history of severe dystocia or of hasty delivery by version and extraction as an emergency measure, for conservative obstetricians avoid breech delivery if possible. If a truthful history can be obtained, it will usually be found that excessive force was applied. Several obstetricians have reported that they felt a "snap" as if something had given way while they were exerting traction.

The child may be regarded as normal at birth or may be profoundly shocked. In one case reported by the writer, the hemorrhage extended up the spinal canal and filled the cranial subarachnoid spaces giving rise to cerebral symptoms. Usually the spinal lesion is not recognized for several days, and then it is observed that the legs are flaccid and immobile. Retention of urine may be the first symptom to attract attention. Examination will now show that the legs are completely paralyzed and that the abdominal muscles are soft and bulge whenever the baby is held up. If the lesion is high enough, the intercostal muscles may fail to act. There is no evidence of sensibility over the lower half of the body. As a rule the tendon reflexes are abolished at first and spontaneous reflex movements are also absent. The bowels are obstinately constipated and do not move without enemata.

At first, there is a tendency to retention of urine and it may be necessary to catheterize the baby for several days. In about 20 per cent of all cases there are symptoms referable to the brachial plexus. This may be of the common Erb's upper arm type, the distal type of Klumpke or the whole arm type. The spinal column is usually clinically normal and, indeed, it is unusual to discover any roentgenographic evidence of spinal injury. The clinical symptoms just described indicate a complete physiological transection of the spinal cord in the first stage which is termed by Riddoch the stage of spinal shock. Almost all case reports in the literature refer to such severe injuries but undoubtedly there must be many milder injuries which do not attract attention.

In some cases, the child's condition remains unchanged and there is never any evidence of return of function of the lower segments of the spinal cord. The skin over the lower part of the body is dry and scaly. Bed sores and ulcerations develop rapidly and will not heal. The muscles waste away and severe contractures and deformities develop. Even the bones become rarefied and slender. The tendon reflexes do not appear and stimulation of the feet produces no response. The bladder remains distended and there is constant dribbling. Urinary tract infections are very common. This condition is incompatible with prolonged existence. Two possible explanations may be offered for the failure of the lower segments of the cord to function. The whole lower part of the cord may be injured or destroyed or it may have undergone isolation dystrophy as a result of separation from the higher segments and the effect of intoxications and infections.

As a rule, however, the clinical picture changes after a few weeks or months, even in cases in which the spinal cord has been completely severed. We now have the condition described by Riddoch as the stage of reflex activity, or paraplegia-in-flexion. The legs now begin to show evidences of returning tone. They are held in triple flexion at hip, knee and ankle and exhibit from time to time tonic spasms which involve chiefly the flexor mus-

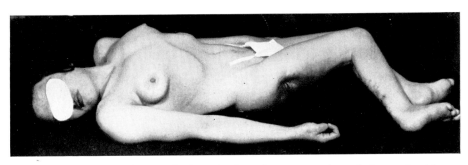

FIG. 274. Birth injury of the spinal cord. Complete transection of the cord with paraplegia-in-flexion, defective development of the legs and healed bed sores, in a girl of 20 years.

cles. These appear spontaneously but more especially in response to stimulation of the legs. The bladder now discharges urine at regular intervals and the constant dribbling is no longer present. Urine is apt to be discharged during the tonic spasms of the legs. From time to time there is profuse sweating over the lower half of the body, the condition of the skin is relatively normal and there is increased resistance to infection, so bed sores now begin to heal. On examination we will usually find that the tendon reflexes have returned. The hamstring reflexes are said to be the first to appear but the knee and ankle jerks are soon obtainable. Stimulation of the feet or legs will cause powerful flexion of the leg or the so-called flexion reflex. If this movement is bilateral and accompanied by sweating and discharge of urine, it is termed the mass reflex. It apparently represents an almost explosive discharge of all the functions of the lower fragment of the cord. If the lesion in the cord has destroyed several segments of the gray matter, its location will be marked, not only by the sensory level but by a group of atrophic toneless muscles which may show the reaction of degeneration and which fail to develop reflexes when the other muscles do. The longitudinal extent of the lesion may be estimated by the distribution of such segmental signs.

This second stage of reflex activity may continue unchanged for many years as illustrated in the case report appended. The condition may be temporarily or permanently abolished by infections of the respiratory or urinary tract or by sepsis due to bed sores. The reflexes rapidly disappear and the condition reverts to that seen in the first stage of spinal shock.

In cases in which the patient survives for a number of years, there is a striking failure of development of the affected part of the body. The feet preserve an infantile form.

In one patient who had an unusually high lesion, there was complete loss of sweating and of vasomotor reactions, so that temperature control was lost and the child had to be sponged several times a day in warm weather to reduce his temperature.

Diagnosis.—The diagnosis of spinal birth injury is indicated by a history of breech delivery or of excessive traction on the trunk during delivery, by the presence of altered blood in the spinal fluid, by immediate flaccid paralysis of the legs and lower part of the body, loss of reflexes and disturbances of sphincter control. Loss of sensibility may be demonstrated in some cases. Evidence of injury to the spinal column may be taken to strengthen the diagnosis. Later in life, we may expect to find in most cases the picture of paraplegia-in-flexion. During the first few weeks of life, spinal birth injury is most apt to be confused with amyotonia congenita or defective development of the cord associated with spina bifida occulta. Amyotonia congenita may be distinguished, as a rule, by the fact that the weak-

ness and hypotonia are generalized and not confined to the lower part of the body and by the absence of disturbances of sphincter control and of sensibility. Myelodysplasia is usually associated with some peculiarity of the skin over the sacral region such as naevi, abnormal hair formation or pads of fat and is always associated with defects in the spinal laminae. We have seen one instance in which a neuroblastoma caused a complete transverse lesion of the spinal cord in the first few days of life or possibly before birth. We believed that we were dealing with birth injury until the lesion was found at operation.

Prognosis.—The outlook depends entirely upon the severity of the injury. When the spinal cord is completely severed, there can be no improvement. Life is endangered by infections, especially urinary tract infections and in cases in which the lesion is high enough to cause paralysis of the intercostal muscles, pneumonia. Now with potent antibiotics available infections can be controlled so the life span may not be reduced. Mild injuries obviously may admit of some improvement.

Treatment.—During the early stages of spinal cord birth injury the child must be nursed very carefully and every effort made to prevent bed sores and urinary tract infection. Later various orthopedic measures may be useful just as in any other spinal injury.

CASE HISTORY (U-28961).—*Complete physiological transection of cord at birth due to breech extraction with paraplegia-in-flexion and survival for more than 20 years without any return of conduction in the cord.*

E. R., third child of healthy parents, was born by prolonged and difficult labor. Forceps were applied unsuccessfully and the child was finally delivered by version. Soon after birth it was noticed that the child did not move the legs. However, she nursed well and moved the arms actively. At first the legs were quite flaccid but later they assumed a position of flexion and developed some rigidity. The child held up the head at the usual time and talked well at 14 months but made no progress in learning to sit up or to move the legs. When the child was about two years old it was noticed that she voided moderate amounts of urine at regular intervals although before there had been constant dribbling.

Between the ages of five and twenty-two years the patient was under observation. Examination (see illustration) revealed defective development of the legs and feet of infantile appearance with round pads of fat on the soles. When the patient was held in a seated position a severe scoliosis appeared in the thoracic and lumbar segments and there was a rounded kyphos in the lumbar spine. These curves largely disappeared when the child was recumbent. The legs were usually held in partial flexion at hip and knee and on passive movement there was found to be well-marked increase of tone in the hamstrings and flexors of the hips. No voluntary power was present in the legs and the abdominal, and lower spinal mus-

cles were also paralyzed. The intercostal muscles did not contract and respiration was entirely diaphragmatic. From time to time spontaneous muscular spasms occurred in the legs and abdomen during which the legs were
strongly flexed upon the abdomen, there was some discharge of urine and
profuse perspiration appeared over the lower half of the body. The same
reaction might be obtained by stimulating the skin anywhere below the
nipple line, although this reaction was most easily elicited from the plantar surface of the feet. The knee and ankle jerks were not definitely elicited but the hamstring reflexes were active. Clonus could be elicited in the
hamstrings and dorsi-flexor of the ankles. Sensibility was completely lost
below the nipple line. The patient could recognize painful stimuli by
the reflex movements which they produced. There were scars of healed
decubitus ulcers over the hips and sacrum,

Medical examination and laboratory studies, including the Wassermann
and tuberculin tests, were negative. Roentgenograms showed only the deformities of the bones.

According to the last report, the patient was still alive at the age of 25
years. She had had numerous urinary tract infections, septic bed sores and
attacks of erysipelas.

CASE HISTORY.—*Breech extraction. Transverse lesion at C8 and T1.*

M. N. was delivered by breech extraction. During delivery the mother
heard two snaps. He weighed 9 lbs 6 oz. His head was large. He was very
white and did not breathe. Artificial respiration was carried out for 45
minutes before his diaphragm began to contract. His chest did not expand. This baby was the product of the mother's first pregnancy.

The child's arms were moved freely, but the hands showed no movement. His legs did not move and for a few weeks, no reflexes were present in the legs. For a time, there was constant dribbling of urine. The
dribbling stopped and he began to pass large amounts of urine at a time.
Pinching his leg would cause urination. He never sweated even during hot
weather. His temperature would go up to 104°F. in a hot room and would
fall within a few minutes to 96°F. if removed to a cool room. It was
found that pinching his legs would not make him cry, but pinching his
arms would do so.

On examination at the age of 5 months the child is well nourished. His
head is large, but probably not abnormal. The anterior fontanel is open,
but does not bulge. The cranial nerves are all in order, but the eyelids
droop and the pupils are very small.

There is no weakness of the neck, shoulder girdle muscles, or arms at
the shoulders or elbows. The wrists are held in extension due to weakness
of the long flexors. The intrinsic muscles of the hands show no movement.

The chest does not expand at all and during inspiration the chest is contracted. The diaphragm contracts vigorously. The abdominal muscles are
very flabby and do not contract. The abdominal reflexes are absent.

The legs are atonic. The tendon reflexes are very sluggish. Plantar stim-

ulation causes dorsiflexion of the toes and flexion at the ankle, knee and hip.

There seems to be analgesia over the legs and trunk up to the second rib. The office is hot but no moisture is seen or felt over the child's body.

Thus the transverse lesion at the eighth cervical and first thoracic segments of the spinal cord destroyed the innervation of the long flexors of the fingers and wrist and of the intrinsic muscles of the hands and the cervical sympathetic nerve fibers as well. Loss of motor and sensory function below the level of the lesion resulted. The reflex activity of the lower fragment of the cord remained at a low level. Lack of sweating seemed to be responsible for the loss of temperature control.

BIBLIOGRAPHY

BOYER, G. F.: The complete histopathological examination of the nervous system of an unusual case of obstetrical paralysis forty-one years after birth and review of the literature. Proc. Roy. Soc. Med. London, 5:31, 1911-12, Sec. Neurol.

BYERS, R. K.: Transection of the spinal cord in the newborn. Arch. Neurol. & Psychiat., 27:585, 1923.

CROTHERS, B.: Injury of the spinal cord in breech extractions as an important cause of foetal death and paraplegia in childhood. Am. J. Med. Sc., 165:94, 1923.

CROTHERS, B. AND PUTNAM, M. C.: Obstetrical injuries of the spinal cord. Medicine, 6:41, 1927.

FORD, F. R.: Breech delivery with special reference to infantile paraplegia. Arch. Neurol. & Psychiat., 14:742, 1925.

BIRTH INJURY OF THE BRACHIAL PLEXUS AND SPINAL NERVES

Etiology.—The common type of brachial plexus injury in which the fifth and sixth cervical roots are injured is believed to be due to stretching of the plexus as a result of strong traction on the shoulder in the delivery of the head in breech delivery, or of drawing of the head and neck away from the shoulders in the effort to deliver the shoulders in cephalic presentations. It is easily demonstrated in anatomical preparations that either of these maneuvers causes stretching of the upper roots of the plexus and that the fifth and sixth cervical roots may be torn without injury of the lower roots. More severe traction of the same type will give rise to paralysis of the whole arm. The cause of the distal type of brachial plexus palsy is not so clear. Sever has shown that forcible elevation and abduction of the arm will stretch the first thoracic and eighth cervical roots. This may occur if traction is made on the arm in delivering the trunk. It is also stated that pressure of the finger in the axilla will injure these same roots. Crothers has advanced the theory that traction on the trunk in breech delivery may result in avulsion of the lower roots from the cervical cord. In such cases the spinal cord is usually injured and it is possible that the essential lesion is in the spinal gray matter and not in the roots or trunks of the plexus.

Pathological Anatomy.—There is usually some hemorrhage about the

nerves and within the nerve sheath. As a rule, the injury seems to be due to tearing of the nerve sheath and to compression of the nerve fibers by hemorrhage and edema. In other cases, the nerves are completely ruptured and the ends separated, or the roots may be avulsed from the spinal cord with injury to the spinal gray matter.

The case of Boyer is of interest in this connection. At post-mortem examination of a woman who had suffered a severe injury to the brachial plexus at birth, it was found that the fifth and sixth cervical roots were reduced and the seventh was completely absent, having been avulsed from the cord. The posterior roots were not so severely affected as the anterior roots. The anterior horn of the spinal gray matter was completely destroyed in the seventh cervical segment and was much reduced for several segments above and below. There was degeneration of the uncrossed pyramidal tract on the affected side as well as the vestibulospinal tract, but the posterior columns and the crossed pyramidal tracts were not involved. The spinocerebellar tract was degenerated and could be traced into the vermis through the superior cerebellar peduncle. There was great thickening of the meninges at the site of the lesion. No symptoms referable to the leg were detected during childhood.

In the common upper arm type of brachial plexus palsy, which is called Erb's palsy, the lesion is usually found at the point where the fifth and sixth cervical roots unite to form the upper trunk. In the distal type of Klumpke, the lesion involves either the lower trunk formed by the union of the eighth cervical and first thoracic roots or the spinal gray matter of the corresponding segments. After some months there is found a dense mass of scar tissue which surrounds the nerve trunks and binds them together. This may constitute a serious obstacle to regeneration. In some cases, it has been impossible to demonstrate anatomical lesions despite the presence of definite paralysis of the arm.

Clinical Features.—The paralysis is present immediately after birth and should be noticed within a short time. With few exceptions it is unilateral but we have seen a small number of bilateral palsies. These have always been unequal in degree. Several types of paralysis are recognized, depending upon the site of the lesion.

Erb's upper arm plexus palsy is by far the commonest type. This is recognized at once by the characteristic posture of the arm. There is adduction and internal rotation at the shoulder, extension at the elbow and often pronation of the forearm and some degree of flexion of the wrist. This is, of course, due to paralysis and relaxation of certain muscle groups and unopposed action of their antagonists. There is paralysis of the deltoid, upper part of the pectoralis major and spinati which cause abduction and external rotation at the shoulder, of the biceps and brachialis anticus which flex

the elbow, and some weakness of the supinators and of the long extensors of the wrist. When the lesion is more proximal than usual, there may be weakness of the rhomboids. When the arm is passively abducted, it falls limply. In the same way it may be shown that the flexors of the elbow and external rotators of the shoulder are inactive. The Moro reflex may be of value in the demonstration of the paralysis. The grasping reflex is, however, intact although it will usually be found that the wrist is somewhat flexed when the child grips firmly. In relatively mild cases there is no weakness at the wrist whatever. The biceps and radial reflexes are abolished. As a rule, it is impossible to demonstrate any loss of sensibility. If the lesion is severe enough to cause the degeneration of the nerves, the faradic reaction will be lost after two weeks and the galvanic reaction will be slow; that is, the reaction of degeneration will be present in affected muscles. If recovery is delayed and the arm is not placed in a suitable position, contractures soon develop in the antagonists of the paralytic muscles; namely, the pectorals, the subscapularis and the pronators. Moreover, the head of the humerus becomes flattened and the end of the acromium process becomes depressed in such a way as to prevent complete abduction.

The distal type of brachial plexus palsy described by Klumpke is rarely seen. We have had five cases in a total of almost two hundred brachial plexus birth palsies. Case Ped. 48366 (M. V.) is a very typical one in which are found all the signs and symptoms enumerated below. Here the paralysis involves the intrinsic muscles of the hand with weakness of the long flexors of the wrist and fingers. In the writer's experience, there have usually been outspoken trophic disturbances such as edema of the hand, changes in the fingernails and even ulcerations. These are not seen in the upper arm type. The grasp reflex is, of course, absent. Loss of sensibility may sometimes be demonstrated in the hand. As a rule, the signs of paralysis of the cervical sympathetic nerve are evident. The pupil is smaller than the opposite one and the homolateral eyelid droops a bit, although it may be opened. In such cases it is usual for the iris to remain unpigmented for a long time. The writer has followed a case of this type for several years. For more than a year the affected iris was blue although the normal iris was deep brown. Later small brown areas of pigmentation appeared and after three years, pigmentation was complete except for a few small blue areas scattered irregularly over the iris. In this case there was no sign of recovery, so far as the paralysis of the hand was concerned, at the end of the eleventh year. If recovery does not occur, the hand will fail to develop as rapidly as it should and will show some deformity, usually a claw-hand resembling that of ulnar nerve palsy.

In some cases, we find complete paralysis of the entire arm. The reflexes are all lost, the muscles waste rapidly and there is often complete loss of

sensibility almost up to the shoulder. It is the extensive over-lapping of the cervical dermatomes which prevents loss of sensibility in the upper arm type of plexus palsy and when all the roots are involved, this is no longer possible and extensive anesthesia results. There is, of course, partial arrest of development of the affected arm which is most evident in the hand, but deformity is usually slight since there is no muscular action to produce it.

Several articles have called attention to paralysis of the diaphragm. This is always associated with brachial palsy on the same side. It is unilateral as a rule but bilateral cases are described. Since the phrenic nerve is derived from the third, fourth and fifth roots of the cervical and brachial plexuses, paralysis of the diaphragm is usually associated with the upper arm of plexus palsy. In unilateral paralysis of the diaphragm, the first symptom to attract attention is usually recurrent attacks of cyanosis. Examination will reveal that the costal margin makes a wider excursion on the affected side and that Litten's sign is absent. Shifting of the cardiac dullness to the affected side is apt to be found, since the mediastinum of infants is freely movable. The movement of half of the diaphragm seems to be largely ineffectual and breathing is therefore almost entirely thoracic. The thrust of the diaphragm may usually be felt just under the costal margin on the unaffected side and is, of course, absent on the affected side. Fluoroscopic examination is usually conclusive. By this means it is found that the affected side of the diaphragm is unusually high and that it rises during inspiration, whereas the normal side descends. The opposite movement occurs during expiration, thus giving rise to the term "seesaw movement." The affected lung usually fails to expand fully. Grave difficulty of respiration is usually found when both sides of the diaphragm are affected. The abdomen does not protrude during inspiration and breathing is entirely intercostal. Recovery is slow, as a rule, usually a matter of months, and cases have been reported in which diaphragmatic paralysis persisted for three years. Such children are subject to infections of the respiratory tract and to pneumonia from which they die very quickly. The chest may show a certain amount of deformity in cases of long standing.

Various bony injuries may be associated with brachial plexus palsies. For example, there may be fracture of the neck of the scapula, fracture of the clavicle, of the shaft of the humerus or separation of an epiphysis. In a relatively large percentage of cases there may be palpated a soft swelling in the supraclavicular fossa for some days after birth, which probably represents a hematoma at the site of the lesion in the plexus.

Regeneration of the nerve roots may result in mass movements in the muscles which were formerly paralyzed, but these are usually not very striking. Dr. Peter Robinson has showed me several interesting cases in which twitching of the deltoid or the biceps occurred during inspiration. He was

able to show that strong contractions of the arm would in some instances cause contraction of the diaphragm. These phenomena are apparently not unusual in cases of Erb's brachial plexus palsy in which extensive regeneration has occurred. It seems evident that regeneration of the fifth cervical root, which contains nerve fibers destined for the diaphragm by way of the phrenic nerve as well as fibers which innervate the deltoid and biceps muscles, has occurred in such a disorderly manner that these nerve fibers have become misdirected into the wrong muscles.

I have never seen evidence of injury to the lumbosacral plexus, though such injuries are described. The peripheral nerves are not frequently involved. The radial nerve may be damaged when the humerus is fractured and the axillary nerve when the shoulder is dislocated. Penn and Ross describe cases in newborn babies in which the sciatic nerve is damaged and circulatory changes are found in the buttocks which may cause ulceration and sloughing. These children had been given an injection into the umbilical cord. It is thought that this injection caused thrombosis of the inferior gluteal artery. Craig and Clark describe cases of obturator nerve damage in the newborn. They ascribe this to stretching the nerve as a result of extreme abduction of the thighs in utero.

Diagnosis.—The diagnosis is usually evident at a glance unless the palsy is of a very unusual type. The common Erb's palsy is easily recognized by the typical posture of the arm which is described above. The whole arm type can scarcely be confused with cerebral palsies since they cause, as a rule, twitching and rigidity rather than flaccidity. Even in the cases in which flaccid paralysis results from cerebral lesions at birth, there is usually some loss of function in the corresponding leg and outspoken cerebral disturbances. When the hand is affected, it may be difficult to be sure that the lesion is in the roots and not in the nerve trunks of the arm. The observation of associated paralysis of the cervical sympathetic nerve will make the true diagnosis evident. Care must always be taken to rule out pseudo-paralysis due to injury to the bones and joints. This is usually easy since in such cases the muscles are all rigid so as to immobilize the injured part, and no paralysis can be found. The posture of the arm is atypical, electrical reactions are normal and roentgenograms of the bones will usually reveal the nature of the lesion. Syphilitic osteitis and epiphysitis usually cause no difficulty in diagnosis, for they are rarely present at birth, but if the child comes under observation later and no information is available, we must rely on the roentgenograms and the Wassermann reaction to confirm the clinical impression. Falls on the shoulder may cause exactly the same condition as birth injury and by the same mechanism, namely, stretching of the brachial plexus. Moreover, poliomyelitis which happens to be confined

to the cervical enlargement, may produce a picture which cannot be distinguished from Erb's palsy on examination. The history is, of course, most important in the diagnosis of post-natal palsies. We have already stated above that cerebral lesions should be distinguished with ease from brachial plexus lesions, but it is sometimes very difficult to be sure that the injury does not involve the spinal gray matter rather than the roots of the plexus. This is especially true of the Klumpke type of palsy, the pathological anatomy of which is still obscure. If there are no disturbances of function in the legs, the differentiation may be impossible.

Prognosis.—In the common Erb's palsy, the outlook is good if the child is properly treated and more or less complete recovery usually occurs within a year. In some cases recovery occurs within a few weeks. The whole arm type is, of course, less favorable, but some function is apt to develop eventually. In the writer's small experience with the Klumpke palsy, the outlook is distinctly unfavorable.

Treatment.—The principles of treatment are very simple. The child's arm should be placed in a splint so designed that the paralyzed muscles are relaxed and their antagonists are stretched. This should not be delayed more than a few days. In the upper arm type of palsy, the proper position is abduction to 90 degrees and external rotation at the shoulder, flexion to 90 degrees at the elbow, full supination of the forearm and perhaps extension at the wrist. The forearm should point directly upward. At the end of two or three weeks the splint should be removed for a short time every day and gentle massage and passive movements given. When power begins to return, exercises should be attempted. Electrical treatment seems to have no value and serves to terrify the child. Operation is probably never justified. Mild injuries do not require operation and severe injuries usually involve avulsion of the roots from the cord and, therefore, make suture of the nerves impossible. It must be kept in mind that a great deal of damage can be done by clumsy dissection of the plexus and that the formation of scar tissue may add to the symptoms years after the operation.

Adler and Patterson take a different point of view. They advise prompt passive movements and exercises and state that braces may cause permanent deformity.

In neglected cases in which regeneration of the nerves has occurred but in which the development of contractures and deformities has prevented proper function, various operations are recommended. Thus, orthopedic surgeons recommend tenotomies to relieve the contractures and osteotomies for the bony malformations. For example in cases of Erb's palsy, the tendons of the subscapularis and pectorals may be sectioned and the tip of the

acromium removed. These matters are discussed in textbooks of orthopedic surgery to which the reader is referred.

BIBLIOGRAPHY

ADLER, J. B. AND PATTERSON, R. L.: Erb's palsy. Jour. Bone and Joint Surg., **49A**:1052, 1967.

BOYER, G. F.: Complete histopathological examination of the nervous system of an unusual case of obstetrical paralysis forty-one years after birth and a review of the pathology. Proc. Roy. Soc. Med. London, **5**:31, Sec. Neurol. 1911.

COMBES, M. A. *et al.*: Sciatic nerve injury in infants (intragluteal injections). J.A.M.A., **173**:116, 1960.

CRAIG, W. S. AND CLARK, J. M. P.: Obturator palsy in newborn. Arch. Dis. Childhood, **37**:661, 1962.

CRAIG, W. E. AND CLARK, J. M. P.: Peripheral nerve palsies in newly born. J. Obst. & Gynaec. Brit. Emp., **65**:229, 1958.

CRAIG, W. S. AND CLARK, J. M. P.: Obturator palsy in the newly born. Arch. Dis. Childhood, **37**:661, 1962.

FRANCE, N. E.: Unilateral diaphragmatic paralysis and Erb's palsy in the newborn. Arch. Dis. Childhood, **29**:357, 1954.

JONES, R. AND LOVETT, R. W.: Orthopedic Surgery. Wm. Wood & Co., Baltimore, 1923, p. 511.

PENN, A. AND ROSS, W. T.: Sciatic nerve palsy in newborn infants. South African Med. J., **29**:553, 1955.

ROBINSON, P. K.: Associated movements between limb and respiratory muscles as a sequel to brachial plexus birth injury. Bull. Johns Hopkins Hosp., **89**:21, 1951.

SAN AGUSTIN, M. *et al.*: Neonatal sciatic palsy after umbilical vessel injection. J. Pediat., **60**:408, 1962.

SEVER, J. W.: Obstetric paralysis. Am. J. Dis. Child., **12**:541, 1916.

TAYLOR, A. S.: Brachial Birth Palsy. Lewis, Practice of Surgery. Hagerstown, Maryland, W. F. Prior Co., **3**:Chap. 7.

TYSON, R. M. AND BOWMAN, J. E.: Paralysis of the diaphragm in the newborn. Am. J. Dis. Child., **46**:30, 1933.

VASSALOS, E. *et al.*: Brachial plexus paralysis in newborn. Amer. Jour. Obstet. and Gynec., **101**:554, 1968.

BIRTH INJURY OF THE FACIAL NERVE

Etiology.—The commonest cause of seventh nerve paralysis at birth seems to be compression of the nerve in its peripheral portion by forceps. No doubt prolonged pressure against the maternal pelvis may produce the same result. In a few cases it is due to fracture of the temporal bone, or, perhaps to hematoma in the posterior fossa.

Pathological Anatomy.—There seem to be no anatomical studies on this particular point.

Clinical Features.—Attention is usually attracted by the child's failure to close the eye on the affected side. When the child cries, the eyeball rolls up and the lid remains open. Moreover, the affected side of the mouth does not move under any circumstances. Even touching the cornea does not cause the lids to close, although the eyeball will roll upward and the opposite lids will close. If the lesion is a complete one there will often be some drooping of the affected cheek and sagging of the corner of the mouth. Nursing is

not especially disturbed, since the tongue is employed chiefly in this act. In some cases, only one group of the facial muscles are involved since the pressure has injured only a small branch of the nerve. Hence, we may see paralysis of the mouth without involvement of the eyelid or of the forehead and eye without weakness of the mouth. These facial palsies are usually mild. They begin to improve very quickly as a rule. Bilateral palsies are very rare.

If degeneration of the nerve occurs, return of power will be slow and mass movements will develop as a result of aberrant regeneration. If the lesion is proximal to the geniculate ganglion and the lacrimal fibers are interrupted, the eye will be dry during the stage of paralysis and regeneration of the nerve will lead to the crocodile tear syndrome.

Diagnosis.—We must distinguish palsies of the facial nerve due to injury in its extracranial course from those due to fractures of the temporal bone or hemorrhages in the posterior fossa. The differentiation is based on the marks of pressure over the face in the first case and upon the evidences of intracranial hemorrhage in the other cases. It is also necessary to consider congenital defects of the nerve or facial muscles. In defects of development, the paralysis is usually bilateral. It is frequently associated with defects in the ears or other deformities. The face does not sag as if there were fibrosis of the muscle. In such cases there is no improvement.

The writer has never seen a definite supranuclear facial palsy at birth and does not believe that lesions in the cerebral cortex or internal capsule at this age produce any evident disturbance of facial innervation.

Prognosis.—Recovery usually takes place within a few weeks, but if there is complete reaction of degeneration, that is, if the nerve is so badly injured as to degenerate, months may elapse before power returns. In rare instances, there is no return of function. No doubt, the lesions in such cases are of a different nature from those responsible for the usual benign palsies.

Treatment.—No treatment is required, as a rule, except protection of the eye by the use of boric ointment.

BIBLIOGRAPHY

HEPNER, W. R.: Some observations on facial paresis in the newborn infant: Etiology and incidence. Pediatrics, 8:494, 1951.

POST-NATAL TRAUMATIC CONDITIONS

Traumatic Lesions of the Brain and Cranial Nerves

Definition.—In this section I shall consider traumatic lesions of the brain such as contusions, lacerations, hemorrhages, edema and other injuries

with and without fracture of the skull. Injuries of the cranial nerves are also included.

Pathological Anatomy.—Many different lesions are described. The skull is often fractured but extensive cerebral damage may occur without fracture. Some authors offer elaborate classifications of the many possible varieties of fracture, but there seems to be little advantage in such distinctions. For practical purposes we may distinguish: (1) Simple fractures. (2) Depressed fractures in which the brain is penetrated or compressed by the inner table. (3) Compound fractures or fractures opening into the nasal sinuses or middle ear which offer a possible pathway for infection. (4) Penetrating wounds of the skull such as stab wounds or bullet wounds. It should be mentioned that fractures in general and stellate fractures in particular may be followed by absorption of the bone and disintegration of the dura so a large defect in the skull results.

The physical mechanisms involved in traumatic damage to the brain are discussed in some detail by Rowbotham and others but since these are rather complex and chiefly of theoretical interest, it does not seem necessary to describe them here. Suffice it to say that, except for cases in which the skull is penetrated, the injury is believed to result from linear or rotary acceleration and deceleration of the head causing the brain to move in relation to the skull and even parts of the brain to move in relation to other parts.

In many cases there are hemorrhagic areas visible on the surface of the brain. These may be situated directly beneath the site of the impact or may bear no obvious relation to the site of impact. The inferior surfaces of the frontal and temporal lobes are, perhaps, the most frequently involved by such lesions. On section, it is usually found that the lesions are funnel-shaped, being most extensive on the surface of the brain and diminishing towards an apex in the depths of the hemisphere. They may penetrate to the ventricle. Such lesions are termed *contusions*. They often result in softening of the affected tissues and porencephalic cavities. In violent injuries, the cortex and pia may be torn with the result that profuse hemorrhage occurs. The term *laceration* is applied here. The corpus callosum may be split. Large and small hemorrhages may be found in the cortex or in the central parts of the brain. A favorite site is in the brain stem near the aqueduct. In certain cases there may be a profusion of minute hemorrhages most numerous in the central white matter. One of the most common findings is subarachnoid hemorrhage due to tearing of the cortical veins or the tributaries of the dural sinuses. Subdural hemorrhage often of large size is not rare and is usually believed to be a result of tearing of the large veins which pass from the brain to the superior longitudinal sinus or to the lateral sinus. Extradural hemorrhage may result from rupture of the middle

meningeal artery, tearing of a dural sinus or from diploic veins. Hemorrhages may occur in the ventricular system. As a rule bleeding is of venous origin probably because their thick elastic walls and tortuous course protect the arteries from rupture. Lindeberg points out that in many head injuries there is increased intracranial pressure which leads to compression of cerebral arteries with softening as a result. He shows that the anterior, middle and posterior cerebral arteries are so compressed as well as the anterior choroidal, internal carotid and the superior and posterior inferior cerebellar arteries. In some cases, large amounts of clear fluid collect in the subdural spaces. The ventricles may be distended apparently as a result of an obstructive hydrocephalus. It is well known that edema develops following injury of the brain. As a rule this is most intense in and about the traumatized tissues but it is believed that in some instances a large part of the brain may become edematous. The frequency and clinical importance of such extensive edemas is at present a matter of dispute. Since there is often no correlation between the clinical picture and the anatomical changes, it is believed that trauma to the head may cause widespread disturbances in the cerebral neurons which are not anatomically demonstrable. Presumably this process is reversible. The term *concussion* is often used in this connection.

Strich describes extensive degeneration of the white matter attributed to stretching and tearing of the nerve fibers by shearing forces. Post-mortem examination reveals numerous retraction balls at the end of interrupted fibers, it is stated.

After a time, the necrotic tissue begins to undergo resolution, and hemorrhage to be absorbed. Microglia phagocytes filled with lipoid products and cellular debris appear in great numbers and the adventitia of the small blood vessels is filled with the same cells. The astrocytes proliferate and form dense scars in which they are aided by fibroblasts which grow out of the walls of the blood vessels and from the meninges. Small lesions are converted into scars but larger areas of necrosis may give rise to cavities. Adhesions may form in the subarachnoid spaces and even connect the brain with the dura. As such scars contract, there may be traction on the brain and blood vessels causing distortions of the cortex and ventricular system. Loss of tissue is compensated for by dilatation of the ventricles and by the formation of lakes of fluid in the subarachnoid spaces overlying the lesion.

In rare cases softening and breaking down of the tissues may be followed by rupture of small blood vessels running through this area causing the so-called *delayed traumatic apoplexy*, which may develop weeks after the original injury.

The cranial nerves are frequently injured in fractures of the base. The seventh and eighth nerves may be injured when the fracture runs through

the petrous bone. Hemorrhage in the labyrinth may occur. Fractures involving the orbit or the floor of the middle fossa may be associated with palsies of the third, fourth and sixth nerves. The optic nerve is not infrequently damaged. The sense of smell is sometimes lost after head injuries often when no fracture is present. This is thought to be due to avulsion of the olfactory fibers from the cribriform plate.

Compound fractures, penetration of the brain by foreign bodies and fractures which open into the nasal sinuses or middle ear may be followed by *meningitis* or by *abscess of the brain*. Fractures involving the nasal sinuses or ears may also result in leakage of cerebrospinal fluid if the dura is lacerated at the same time. In some instances, air may bubble into the cranium from the nasal sinuses causing pneumocephaly, q.v. We have seen one patient who suffered a fracture of the base of the skull which caused tearing of the lateral sinus. There was also traumatic softening of the base of the temporal lobe. Large pieces of cerebral cortex were washed into the lateral sinus and ultimately caused extensive pulmonary embolism. (No. 411644-Path. 23172) McMillan states that embolism of cerebral tissue occurs in 2 per cent of severe head injuries.

Lindenberg and Freytag state that blunt trauma to the head of infants of 5 months or less do not cause hemorrhages or necroses as in older subjects, but cause large tears in the white matter especially in the temporal and frontal lobes and microscopic tears in the crests of the convolutions of the convexity.

Clinical Features.—Violent blows on the head almost always result in immediate loss of consciousness. The face is pale, the pulse rapid and feeble, temperature subnormal, respiration shallow and the blood pressure low. This is the picture to which the term *concussion* is applied. Surgical *shock* which results from excessive hemorrhage or extensive injuries in any part of the body, causes almost exactly the same manifestations though as a rule consciousness is not so severely affected. Recently Denny-Brown and Russell have made some very instructive experimental studies of concussion. They find that it is due to sudden acceleration of the brain to a velocity of approximately 23 feet per second and that there is temporary loss of medullary reflexes resulting in fall of blood pressure and failure of respiration. There are no constant anatomical lesions. Concussion is a transient state. The patient either dies or soon begins to rally. Campbell states that shock rarely persists more than a few hours after head injury and when it does persist should suggest the possibility of an injury elsewhere in the body or loss of blood.

Sir Charles Symonds points out there are various degrees of concussion. The more severe types may be followed by persisting symptoms such as anxiety, irritability, difficulty in concentration, fatigue and impaired mem-

ory. He gives evidence to prove that there are changes in the nerve cells and fibers which may be reversible or persisting.

If the patient makes a prompt and complete recovery without residua, it is customary to assume that we were dealing with a physiological disorder, i.e., concussion, without anatomical damage to the brain. In more severe injuries, however, a series of clinical pictures occur which have been well described by Woodhall. The most important symptoms are changes in consciousness, pulse, temperature, respiration and blood pressure. Papilledema is not a common finding in head injuries and rarely appears before the third day so ophthalmoscopic examination is not very helpful as a rule. It is doubtful if spinal fluid pressure readings can be regarded as reliable guides to treatment. Woodhall describes four types of acute cerebral injuries. *In type one,* which is the mildest, consciousness is lost for only a few hours and complete consciousness is regained after a variable but relatively brief interval. The temperature, after an early drop, rises to about 101°F. or less and then slowly declines to normal within from 24 to 72 hours. The pulse follows the temperature. Respiration is not significantly affected. In this group of cases, the prognosis is good and no operation is required. *In type two,* the temperature rises to 101°F. or more. There is early or late bradycardia and often slowing of respiration. The patient is drowsy or even stuporous. These symptoms, according to Woodhall, indicate that intracranial pressure is increased but compensation is adequate. At any time, however, compensation may fail, the temperature rises rapidly, the pulse increases, respiration grows irregular and the patient may die if the intracranial pressure cannot be relieved. Such patients require careful observation. *In type three,* the picture is that of high, unremitting fever ranging from 102°F. to 103°F. with corresponding tachycardia and rapid irregular respiration. There is stupor or coma. The mortality is high in such cases. Woodhall thinks decompression is required as a rule. *In type four,* there is deep coma, rapidly rising temperature, pulse and respiration. Death usually occurs within a short time no matter what treatment is employed.

I believe it is fair to state that the majority of American authorities have held the view that after the stage of shock has passed off the symptoms and outcome are determined by the state of intracranial pressure if we may disregard focal signs for the moment. If there is no accumulation of blood or other fluids in the cranium, one would be forced to assume that the increase of pressure is due to edema of the brain. Recently this view has been opposed by a number of observers including Zierold, Russell and Browder who base their opinion chiefly on studies of the spinal fluid pressure variations. They state that intracranial pressure is rarely seriously elevated in cases of acute head injury and that, furthermore, there is no parallelism between the intracranial pressure and the pulse rate, tempera-

ture and state of consciousness. In fatal cases, they say increased intracranial pressure is not the cause of death. These investigators in general do not commit themselves by offering explanations for the symptoms. Their views, however, are of great importance since the standard treatment for acute head injuries involves such measures as dehydration and decompression, all of which are designed to reduce intracranial pressure. I scarcely feel competent to express an opinion in this controversy. It is evident, however, that in cases in which there are large intracranial hemorrhage or collections of fluid and in the occasional case in which decompression is followed by immediate and striking relief, that increased intracranial pressure is largely or entirely responsible for the symptoms. Perhaps, it would be fair to say that in cases in which there are no significant accumulations of blood or other fluid in the cranium, increased intracranial pressure is usually not the chief cause of the patient's symptoms.

Hemorrhage into the subarachnoid spaces causes not only signs of increased intracranial pressure but irritation of the meninges, often suggesting a mild meningitis. There is frequently pain and muscle spasm along the spinal column causing cervical rigidity and Kernig's sign. The retinal veins may become greatly dilated and both small and large hemorrhages appear over the disc and along the course of the retinal veins.

Massive venous hemorrhages into the subdural space may develop very rapidly as a result of rupture of veins overlying the cortex. These cause rapid rise in intracranial pressure and frequently focal signs such as hemiplegia. The clinical picture is almost identical with that of rupture of the middle meningeal artery which is described elsewhere.

In certain cases clear fluid collects very rapidly in the subdural spaces and causes pressure just as a hematoma might. No doubt this is cerebrospinal fluid. This subject is discussed more fully under subdural hydroma.

Signs of focal cerebral injuries are often very difficult to demonstrate during the period of unconsciousness. Localized convulsions, of course, indicate a lesion on the opposite side of the brain. The head and eyes always turn to the side opposite the lesion during a convulsion and this fact may be the only evidence of localization in convulsions due to hemorrhages in the frontal or occipital lobes. Hemiplegia may be detected by the loss of tone and diminution of tendon reflexes on the affected side as well as the presence of a Babinski sign. Absence of the abdominal reflexes on one side may be important. If the lesion involves the base of the brain, the homolateral pupil is dilated as a rule, and shows little if any light reflex either directly or consensually, although there may be no other signs of a third nerve lesion. Facial paralysis is usually evident by the loss of tone in the cheek and by failure of the affected side to move when the supraorbital nerve is compressed. Rowbotham states that immediate paralysis may be

due to (1) neural shock, (2) epileptic seizures, (3) compression by depressed bony fragments, (4) contusion, (5) laceration. The first two, he expects to disappear in 24 hours. Paralysis after an interval, he states, may be due to (1) compression by a surface hemorrhage, (2) external hydrocephalus, (3) edema, (4) arterial occlusion, (5) spreading venous thrombosis. He also mentions delayed traumatic intracerebral hemorrhage, and (6) abscess.

McLaurin and McBride state that intracerebral hematoma is found most frequently in the temporal lobe. When the immediate effects of the blow have passed off, the patient may have a lucid period of hours or days. Hemiplegia then becomes apparent and the level of consciousness may decline. The hematoma may become encapsulated and cause papilledema as a neoplasm does.

Hemiplegia may sometimes be associated with the so-called early spasticity from the onset and in such cases focal convulsions are apt to occur on the same side. Later, the hemiplegia may become flaccid and, if the patient survives, true and lasting spasticity may develop weeks later. Large hemorrhages above the tentorium may cause first contralateral hemiplegia from focal pressure on the motor cortex. Later, displacement of the hemispheres may force the cerebral peduncle against the edge of the tentorium with the production of homolateral hemiplegia. Finally decerebrate rigidity may appear which is believed to be due to herniation of the brain through the tentorium with compression of the midbrain.

In rare instances, hemorrhages involving the globus pallidus and putamen may cause bilateral or unilateral athetosis. Such symptoms may be transient or persisting. In the same way, hemorrhage into the corpus Luysi may cause hemiballismus.

Bleeding, or leakage of cerebrospinal fluid, from the nose or ears indicates fracture of the base. Fractures of the vault are often palpable or are demonstrable by roentgen rays. Unfortunately, many basilar fractures cannot be seen in roentgenograms of the skull. Ecchymoses and edema of the orbital tissues may indicate fracture of the orbit. It has been claimed recently that injuries of the hypothalamus may cause either retention or depletion of various electrolytes such as sodium, potassium and chlorides and either acidosis or alkylosis. Addisonian crises are mentioned. Daniel and Pritchard state that trauma may cause massive necrosis of the anterior lobe of the pituitary gland as a result of transection of the pituitary stalk with shock, elevation of the blood glucose, polyuria, decreased serum sodium and increased serum potassium..

Some peculiarities in the reaction of infants and young children to cerebral injuries may be mentioned at this point. It is not unusual to see rapid and complete recovery following states of deep stupor or coma which ap-

pear very ominous. In the same way, focal convulsions and hemiplegia may disappear rapidly and seem to have much less significance than in older children or in adults. Pickles describes such cases. It is easy for the inexperienced observer to take too serious a view of cerebral injuries in young children and to be misled into advising surgical procedures which are apt to be disastrous, since infants react very badly to operation.

Bodian describes 5 cases of bilateral loss of vision in children due to head injuries with loss of pupillary reactions and dilatation of the pupils in two cases and mid-dilatation and sluggish reaction to light in one in which complete recovery of vision occurred within 12 hours in all cases. In 1 case the loss of vision was unilateral.

Griffith and Dodge report 7 cases of bilateral blindness of brief duration in children due to head trauma with preservation of pupillary reactions with prompt and complete return of vision.

Hollenhorst and others describe unilateral blindness and optic atrophy developing during craniotomies when the patient is in the face down position. It seems that two factors are necessary; direct pressure on the bulb and low blood pressure. It is quite possible that this condition may occur in cases of head injury when the patient lies unconscious on the face for a time. Indirect injury to the optic nerve is also described. This may be due to displacement of the brain with traction on the nerve. Loss of vision is evident at once. Improvement may occur within three or four weeks. The impact is in the frontotemporal region on the side of the affected eye. Central scotomas, sector defects and loss of the lower quadrants result. The optic discs may be swollen within a few days and there may be hemorrhages in the retina, but within three weeks the optic disc is pale. Turner has described this condition. The chiasm may be injured by trauma and bitemporal hemianopia may result. In some cases of head injury, optic atrophy develops slowly during convalescence. This seems to be due to compression by callus or scar formation.

Frantzen *et al.* describe cases of occlusion of cerebral arteries following trauma to the head and neck. Fracture or dislocation of the cervical spine may cause occlusion of a vertebral artery with softening in the brain stem.

Improvement may be rapid or slow depending upon the severity and site of the lesions. The patient may be delirious, confused or semi-stuporous for weeks. There is usually headache and mild signs of pressure may continue for a time. Marked irritability, abnormal fatigue and inability to concentrate are characteristic. In this stage the evidences of focal injury become more evident. Hemiplegia or hemiparesis is, perhaps, most common, but hemianesthesia, hemianopia, aphasia and almost all possible cortical syndromes may occur. The cranial nerves may be affected. The third, fourth and sixth are sometimes involved in association with fractures

through the orbit. The optic nerve is also frequently injured in the same way with resulting atrophy and loss of vision. Loss of sense of smell may occur alone due to injury of the olfactory lobes at the base or avulsion of the olfactory filaments. The inner ear may be destroyed by hemorrhage into the temporal bone or the seventh and eighth nerves may be both involved by fractures invading their canals. Bleeding into the labyrinth may cause irritation with vestibular nystagmus and vertigo as well as deafness. In some instances, the labyrinth seems to remain in a state of excessive irritability and there may be head-movement vertigo or even spontaneous vertigo. The vestibular nerve may have to be sectioned to relieve those symptoms. Hough and Stuart describe the injuries which may occur in the middle ear in traumatic injuries to the head. Fractures of the bones of the maxilla or of the mandible sometimes injure the second or third branches of the fifth nerve. The first branch of the fifth nerve may be affected with the oculomotor nerves in the orbit. Injuries of the olfactory nerve are most common. The facial nerve is next most frequently affected and the optic nerve stands third in the list. Diabetes insipidus may follow head injuries presumably as a result of injury to the hypothalamus. Glycosuria may occur but is usually transient. We have seen one instance of the sham rage syndrome in a young girl who after a prolonged period of coma would bite or scratch anyone who approached her for several weeks.

In rare cases, there may be a sudden increase in focal symptoms or focal symptoms may develop weeks after the injury when the patient may seem to be well on the way to recovery. Coincidentally, there may be signs of increased pressure and meningeal irritation. It is found at operation or at autopsy that there has been a fresh hemorrhage into an old area of traumatic softening. It is believed that the bleeding is due to the fact that the softening of the tissues deprives the blood vessels of their usual support leading to distention and finally to rupture.

The focal signs and symptoms usually recede rapidly and it is unusual to find complete hemiplegia or complete loss of speech among the persisting sequelae. The mental disorders are as a rule more serious.

During convalescence there is, as a rule, restlessness and irritability. Amnesia is usual, both for the accident and for events immediately preceding the accident. The patient cannot endure bright lights, loud noises or, in fact, to be disturbed in any way. In typical cases persistent symptoms result. These are chiefly mental and affect the personality, as a rule, more than the intelligence. Headache is a common complaint. Behavior is usually altered. All degrees of abnormality exist, ranging from mild departures from normal, which are easily overlooked, to antisocial developments which require commitment to institutions for the insane. Mild disturbances are very frequent but the more severe manifestations are fortunately very

rare. The patient's inherited constitution and personality, as well as the influence of home life are, of course, very important in coloring and modifying the picture, but certain features stand out in such a way that they may be regarded as conditioned more or less directly by the organic lesions. Post-traumatic states in children are rarely complicated by the desire for compensation and by litigation as they are so frequently in adults, so that at least one confusing element is largely eliminated. Explosive outbreaks of temper, with little or no provocation, are among the more striking symptoms. Emotional instability is very prominent. Psychiatric examination reveals chiefly difficulty in attention and abnormal fatigue of the mental processes. Definite intellectual defect is sometimes found but is not so severe or so frequent as the behavior disorders. Local or general headaches and feelings of vertigo are usually mentioned by older children. The vertigo is often accentuated by movements of the head and by exertion. There is characteristically pronounced sensitiveness to noise and to the confusion of crowds and school rooms. Warm rooms and the heat of the sun may cause unpleasant symptoms. In some cases, there is a tendency to flushing or pallor or excessive sweating. Tremors may be observed. These are chiefly coarse and irregular and provoked by emotional stress and strain.

Diagnosis.—In acute cases there is rarely any doubt about the cause, although the exact nature of the lesion, its site and extent may present very difficult problems in diagnosis. For practical purposes, we must distinguish the element of shock or concussion, the signs of increased intracranial pressure and the evidences of destructive lesions in the brain. The signs and symptoms of these syndromes have been given above and need not be repeated. Some authorities recommend the use of spinal puncture to measure the intracranial pressure but the writer is inclined to agree with Dandy that it is safer to rely upon clinical observation. Later, a number of complications and sequelae may ensue such as abscess of the brain, meningitis, subdural hematoma, effusions into the subdural or subarachnoid spaces, delayed hemorrhage and pneumocephaly. These are described in subsequent sections.

A blow directly on the eye may cause edema of the orbital tissues and intraorbital hemorrhage. The pupil may be dilated and fixed and the pulse may be slow. These findings, of course, suggest intracranial hemorrhage. In many instances, however, the changes in the pupil are due to direct trauma to the iris and the bradycardia to the oculo-cardiac reflex.

It is often very difficult to evaluate the importance of a history of head trauma in a patient afflicted by epilepsy or other cerebral symptoms who is first seen long after the injury occurred. As a rule, we are justified in assuming that there was actual injury to the brain if the patient was completely unconscious for an hour or more immediately after the accident. A

history of vomiting, convulsions, paralysis, bleeding from the ears and roentgenological evidence of fracture of the skull also strengthen the diagnosis. If no severe symptoms followed immediately after the accident, it is very hazardous to place too much stress upon the injury but this rule cannot be followed blindly, for exceptions are not very unusual. Much help may be gained in such cases by ventriculography, for we often find localized dilatations of the ventricle or lakes of air over the cortex in patients who have had severe head injuries, even when clinical examination is quite negative. Caution is needed, however, to avoid over-stressing slight asymmetries which may be of no significance or which may be due to some other cause.

Treatment.—The reader should consult the references given below for a complete discussion of the proper treatment of acute head injuries. These cases present many problems requiring the mature judgment of a competent neurosurgeon and those not qualified by special training should refuse to accept the grave responsibility which their care entails. Suffice it to say here that in the first few hours when shock is present it is imperative to place the patient at complete rest and to avoid any procedures which are not necessary. The patient should be kept warm, fluids should be administered by rectum or by hypodermoclysis and morphine given if required with great caution so as not to obscure symptoms. Spinal puncture should be avoided and even roentgenograms of the head deferred. Operation is absolutely contraindicated except in those cases in which rapid deterioration in the patient's condition suggests the development of an intracranial hemorrhage. Rupture of the middle meningeal artery q.v. is a well known cause of such rapidly developing hemorrhages and demands immediate operation. Acute subdural hematoma should also be mentioned in this connection. Dr. John Chambers has found that in cases of acute subdural hematoma the bleeding often arises from veins which pass from the cortex to the lateral sinus. These veins may be cauterized. Later, after shock has disappeared, treatment need not be so conservative. A chart should be kept with careful observations of the patient's state of consciousness, pulse, temperature, respiration and blood pressure. If the patient does well, no treatment is required except for proper nursing care with attention to nutrition, the administration of proper fluids and the evacuation of the bowels and bladder. The serum electrolytes should be estimated and proper measures instituted to keep them within normal limits. The possibility of pneumonia and of infection of the urinary tract should be kept in mind and antibiotics should be given if required. In stuporous patients every effort should be made to prevent aspiration of saliva and to keep the respiratory passages from being obstructed by falling back of the tongue. If progress is unsatisfactory or the patient's condition grows worse, the possi-

bility of hemorrhage or accumulation of fluid in the cranium should be considered. In such cases, multiple trephine openings may be made in the skull preferably under local anesthesia and a needle inserted to make sure. If fluid or blood is encountered, drainage through the needle may be sufficient or operation may be required. If no fluid is found and the surgeon is convinced that intracranial pressure is elevated to a serious degree, several therapeutic measures are employed such as spinal puncture, dehydration or decompression. Objections may be made to all of these. Spinal puncture tends to induce herniation of the medulla and possibly favors intracranial hemorrhage. Subtemporal decompression is probably inadequate in some cases and, moreover, may lead to herniation of the brain through a small opening with cortical softening as a result. General anesthetics are of course to be avoided and local anesthesia employed if possible. Dehydration, whether produced by reducing fluids, by intravenous injection of sucrose or other hypertonic solutions or by rectal administration of magnesium sulphate, may have an adverse effect on the circulation. The wisdom of dehydration is still a matter of dispute on both theoretical and practical grounds.

Compound fractures should be treated as soon as the patient's condition permits. The wound should be cleaned, necrotic tissue removed and closure made without drainage. Pieces of bone and foreign bodies embedded in the brain should be removed promptly together with necrotic brain tissue and blood clots. In such cases and in cases in which there is leakage of spinal fluid or blood from the nose or ears, penicillin or sulfonamides should be administered to prevent infection.

After the acute stage has passed, operation is less hazardous, but the results are not always satisfactory. Paralysis and other focal signs may be relieved by the removal of a hematoma compressing the cortex but not infrequently the lesion is in the brain and operation gives no relief.

During convalescence the patient requires rest and quiet for a time, but it is very important to return to a normal routine as soon as possible so as to avoid any tendency to invalidism. Discipline should be firm and impersonal. Every effort should be made to avoid spoiling and bad habit formation. If there is much restlessness and irritability small doses of phenobarbital may be given.

It has been claimed that the common post-traumatic headache is very frequently found to be due to accumulation of small amounts of fluid under the dura and removal of this fluid through a trephine opening in the skull will give relief.

Traumatic cerebral palsies may be treated by physiotherapy and by appropriate orthopedic measures. Focal epilepsies resulting from trauma often fail to respond to phenobarbital and dilantin. Penfield and Foerster

claim excellent results from careful excision of the scar and removal of adhesions between the brain and meninges. Most surgeons are not so enthusiastic. No time limit can be set for the development of epilepsy for we have observed cases in which convulsions first appeared 20 years or more after the injury.

Prognosis.—The prognosis depends upon the severity of the injury and the skill of the physician. The mortality is greatly increased by radical surgery in the acute stages. Focal signs always tend to improve but there is always a possibility of epilepsy which may develop years after the injury. Alterations of personality and intellectual deficit are apt to persist. Injuries of the optic and auditory nerves usually fail to improve but the other cranial nerves show a strong tendency to recovery.

BIBLIOGRAPHY

BEEKMAN, F.: The end results of head injuries in children. Arch. Neurol. & Psychiat., **19**:955, 1928.

BLAU, A.: Mental changes following head trauma in children. Arch. Neurol. & Psychiat., **35**:723, 1936.

BODIAN, M.: Bilateral loss of vision due to head injuries in children with prompt and complete recoveries. New York State Jour. Med., **64**:916, 1964.

BROCK, S.: Injuries of the Brain and Spinal Cord. Baltimore, Williams and Wilkins, 1940.

BROWDER, J. AND MEYERS, R.: A revaluation of the treatment of head injuries. Ann. Surg., **110**:357, 1939.

BULLOCK, M. H. *et al.*: Injuries of the brain caused by penetration of the orbit. Minnesota Med., **42**:1408, 1959.

CAMPBELL, E. AND WHITFIELD, R.: The incidence and significance of shock in head injury. Ann. Surg., **138**:698, 1953.

CHAMBERS, J.: Acute subdural hematoma. J. Neurosurg., **8**:263, 1951.

COOPER, I. S.: Disorders of electrolyte and water metabolism following brain surgery. J. Neurosurg., **10**:389, 1953.

COURVILLE, C. B. AND PLATNER, C. D.: The etiology of traumatic meningitis. Bull. Los Angeles Neurol. Soc., **3**:150, 1938.

DANDY, W. E.: Cranial injuries and their effects. Dean Lewis, Practice of Surgery, **12**:265, 1945.

DANIEL, P. M. AND PRICHARD, M. M. L.: Traumatic infarction of the anterior lobe of the pituitary gland. Lancet, **ii**:927, 1959.

DENNY-BROWN, D.: Cerebral concussion. Physiol. Rev., **25**:296, 1945.

DENNY-BROWN, D. AND RUSSELL, R.: Experimental cerebral concussion. Brain, **64**:93, 1941.

DOTT, N. M., RUSSELL, W. R. AND TRAQUAIR, H. M.: Traumatic lesions of the optic chiasm. Brain, **58**:398, 1935.

EBAUGH, F. G. AND STRECKER, E. A.: Neuropsychiatric sequelae of cerebral trauma in children. Arch. Neurol. & Psychiat., **12**:443, 1924.

FRANTZEN, E., JACOBSEN, H. H. AND THERKELSEN, J.: Cerebral artery occlusion in children due to trauma to the head and neck. Neurology, **11**:695, 1961.

FURMAN, M. A.: Hearing loss caused by head injury. J. Occup. Med., **4**:399, 1962.

GRIFFITH, J. F. AND DODGE, P. R.: Transient blindness following head injury in children. New England Jour. Med., **278**:648, 1968.

HOLLENHORST, R. W., SVIEN, H. J. AND BENOIT, C. F.: Unilateral blindness occurring during anesthesia for neurosurgical operations. Arch. Ophth., **52**:819, 1954.

HOUGH, J. V. D. AND STUART, W. D.: Middle ear injuries in skull trauma. Laryngoscope, **78**:899, 1968.

IRELAND, J.: Fracture of the skull in children. Arch. Surg., **24**:23, 1932.

KEDDY, J. A.: Accidents in childhood. Canad. M.A.J., **91**:675, 1964.

LINDENBERG, R.: Compression of brain arteries as pathogenic factor for tissue necroses and their areas of predilection. J. Neuropath. & Exp. Neurol., **14**:223, 1955.

LINDENBERG, R.: Significance of the tentorium in head injuries from blunt force. Clinical Neurosurgery, **12**:129, 1966.

LINDENBERG, R. AND FREYTAG, E.: Morphology of brain lesions from blunt trauma in early infancy, Archives of Pathology, **87**:298, 1960.

LINDENBERG, R. AND FREYTAG, E.: The mechanism of cerebral contusion. A.M.A. Arch. Pathol., **69**:440, 1960.

LINDENBERG, R. *et al.*: Lesions of the corpus callosum following blunt mechanical trauma to the head. Am. J. Path., **31**:297, 1955.

McCONNELL, A. A.: The pathologic basis of post-traumatic syndrome. Brain, **76**:473, 1953.

McLAURIN, R. L. AND McBRIDE, B. H.: Traumatic intracerebral hematoma. Ann. Surg., **143**:294, 1956.

McMILLAN, J. B.: Emboli of cerebral tissue in the lungs following severe head injuries. Am. J. Path., **32**:405, 1956.

PICKLES, W.: Acute focal edema of the brain in children with head injuries. New England Jour. Med., **240**:92, 1949.

PORTER, R. J. AND MILLER, R. A.: Diabetes insipidus following closed head injury. J. Neurol., Neurosurg. & Psychiat., **11**:258, 1948.

RAND, C. W. AND COURVILLE, C. B.: Histologic changes in the brain in cases of fatal injury to the head. VII. Alterations in the nerve cells. Arch. Neurol. & Psychiat., **55**:79, 1946.

RICKHAM, P. P.: Head injuries in childhood. Helvet. chir. acta, **28**:560, 1961.

ROWBOTHAM, G. F.: Acute Injuries of the Head. Baltimore, Williams and Wilkins, 1945.

RUSSELL, W. R.: Cerebral involvement in head injury. Brain, **55**:549, 1932.

RUSSELL, W. R. AND SCHILLER, F.: Crushing injuries to the skull. J. Neurol., Neurosurg. & Psychiat., **12**:52, 1949.

SCHREIBER, M. S.: Some observations on certain head injuries of infants and children. Med. J. Australia, **2**:930, 1957.

SHAPIRO, P. AND JACKSON, H.: Swelling of the brain in cases of injury to the head. Arch. Surg., **38**:443, 1939.

STRICH, S. J.: Brain damage from closed head injuries. Lancet, **2**:443, 1961.

SYMONDS, C. P.: Prognosis in cerebral concussion and contusion. Lancet, **i**:854, 1930.

————: Delayed traumatic intracerebral hemorrhage. Brit. M. J., **i**:1048, 1940.

————: Concussion and its sequelae. Lancet, **i**:1, 1962.

TURNER, J. W. A.: Indirect injuries of the optic nerve. Brain, **66**:140, 1943.

WALKER, A. E.: Posttraumatic Epilepsy. Springfield, Illinois, Charles C Thomas, 1949.

WALSH, F. B.: *Loc. cit.*

WOODHALL, B.: Acute cerebral injuries, analysis of temperature, pulse and respiration curves. Arch. Surg., **33**:560, 1936.

ZIEROLD, A. A.: Intracranial pressure in head injuries. Arch. Surg., **31**:823, 1935.

EXTRADURAL HEMORRHAGE

Definition.—Hemorrhage between the skull and the dura. Some writers employ the term rupture of the middle meningeal artery for the bleeding usually arises from that artery. Since this is a surgical problem and not a neurological one, it will be discussed very briefly.

Pathological Anatomy.—The fracture usually involves the squamous part of the temporal bone lacerating the middle meningeal artery or some of its branches and causing extradural bleeding which serves to strip the

dura from the bone as it accumulates. As the dura is separated from the skull, numerous small vessels are torn and bleeding continues at an ever increasing rate. The lateral surface of the hemisphere is compressed very rapidly. Extradural hemorrhage may also result from laceration of the venous channels in the dura or from the diploic veins in fractures of the skull. In such cases it develops more slowly.

If the pressure is not promptly relieved, softenings may occur in the brain. There may be softening in the cortical and subcortical tissues directly below the hematoma and also softenings in the temporal and occipital cortex. Hemorrhages in the brain stem may occur and are no doubt responsible for the fatal outcome in some cases.

Clinical Features.—The typical history is that of an injury to the head sufficient to cause fracture of the skull which is followed by transient loss of consciousness. After a short time the patient regains consciousness and often seems relatively well for a time. In some cases, the initial injury is so severe that the patient never regains consciousness and the symptoms of the initial shock merge with those of the hemorrhage. Symptoms of increased intracranial pressure develop very rapidly. The patient complains of headache, vomits and then becomes drowsy and finally comatose. Focal convulsions appear on the side opposite the lesion beginning, as a rule, in the face and extending to the arm and leg. Hemiplegia often follows but may be obscured by the loss of consciousness. Hemianopia and cortical blindness may occur but are not easy to demonstrate for the patient is usually in a stupor when such symptoms develop. The homolateral pupil is usually dilated. The pulse and respiration grow slow, the temperature rises and the blood pressure is increased for a time. Later the respiration becomes irregular and the pulse becomes rapid and variable. Anemia may develop rapidly.

Rowbotham states that, "As drowiness develops, the pulse rate increases and the blood pressure rises. As unconsciousness deepens, the pressure rises and the pulse rate falls and may become as low as forty beats a minute. Occasionally the pulse rate remains high and never falls below normal. Finally, as the cerebral circulation becomes inadequate, the systemic circulation also fails, with the result that the blood pressure falls and the pulse becomes rapid and thready."

It must be said that the clinical picture is not always typical. Occasionally the lucid interval may be a matter of days or weeks rather than hours. The hemiplegia may be homolateral and so mislead the surgeon as to the site of the hemorrhage. King and Chambers describe 8 cases in which the onset of symptoms was delayed. Despite the great increase of intracranial pressure papilledema is rarely demonstrable.

If nothing is done to relieve the pressure the patient may develop general muscular rigidity and retraction of the head shortly before death, probably as a result of herniation through the tentorium. Campbell described several cases of extradural hematoma of the posterior fossa. These may be acute or subacute. There are evidences of increased intracranial pressure, and evidences of compression of the cerebellum and brain stem in most cases. Frequently there is a fracture line seen in the occipital bone. It is advised that when extradural hematoma is suspected and supratentorial hematoma is not found that the occipital bone be trephined. Matson states that extradural hemorrhage is not rare in infancy and is often of venous origin. Usually there is no fracture of the skull but the lamboidal suture may be separated. The bleeding into the extradural space may be so massive that anemia and shock may result. The baby is pale and cold. The pulse is feeble and the blood pressure falls rapidly. Transfusion as well as prompt operation are required.

Diagnosis.—The most important features from the point of view of diagnosis are: (1) The history of a severe blow upon the head with or without loss of consciousness. (2) Symptoms and signs of rapidly increasing intracranial pressure after a brief latent period. (3) Focal signs such as dilatation of the homolateral pupil and hemiplegia or muscular twitchings on the opposite side. These may be absent. (4) Roentgenographic evidence of a fracture through the squamous portion of the temporal bone is strong evidence of rupture of the middle meningeal artery. Woodhall has recently described aberrant forms of extradural hemorrhage and has pointed out the advisability of making bilateral trephine openings in the skull whenever this possibility is suggested. A blow upon the eye may cause dilatation of the pupil as a result of injury to the iris and bradycardia due to edema of the orbital tissues and the resulting oculo-cardiac reflex.

Prognosis.—This condition is a very serious one. The hemorrhage often develops so rapidly that the patient is moribund before operation can be performed. Apparently death always occurs in untreated cases. In some instances, the patient's life is saved by operation, but the brain has sustained so much damage that the patient exhibits permanent damage and may even remain in a vegetative state. Bilateral spasticity with pseudobulbar palsy and mental deficiency are sometimes seen.

Treatment.—Operation must be performed as soon as the diagnosis can be made, the artery ligated at the base and the hematoma evacuated.

BIBLIOGRAPHY

CAMPBELL, E., WHITFIELD, R. AND GREENWOOD, R.: Extradural hematomas of the posterior fossa. Ann. Surg., **138**:509, 1953.

COURVILLE, G. B. AND AMYES, E. W.: Late residual lesions of the brain consequent to dural hemorrhage. Bull. Los Angeles Neurol. Soc., **17**:163, 1952.

INGRAHAM, F. D., CAMPBELL, J. B. AND COHEN, J.: Extradural hematoma in infancy and child-hood. J.A.M.A., **140**:1010, 1949.

KING, A. AND CHAMBERS, J.: Delayed onset of symptoms due to extradural hematomas. Surgery, **31**:839, 1952.

McKENZIE, K. G.: Extradural hemorrhage. Brit. J. Surg., **26**:356, 1938.

WOODHALL, B., DEVINE, J. W. AND HART, D.: Homolateral dilatation of the pupil, homolateral paresis and bilateral muscular rigidity in the diagnosis of extradural hemorrhage. Surg. Gynec. & Obst., **72**:391, 1941.

ARTERIOVENOUS FISTULA BETWEEN THE CAVERNOUS SINUS AND THE INTERNAL CAROTID ARTERY

Definition.—This condition is almost always due to fracture of the base of the skull which causes rupture of the internal carotid artery where it lies within the cavernous sinus. The arterial blood is, therefore, introduced directly into the venous system causing gross distention of all the tributaries of the sinus and edema of the tissues. Rarely the same result is produced by rupture of a saccular aneurysm of the internal carotid artery in the cavernous sinus.

Clinical Features.—Immediately after the injury there is an audible bruit within the cranium which is sometimes so loud that it may be heard at a distance of several feet by the examiner. The orbital tissues become edematous and the veins about the orbit distended. The bulb protrudes and there is palpable and visible pulsation synchronous with the heart beat. The conjunctiva is edematous and the retinal veins are usually grossly distended. In most, but not all, cases there is definite papilledema. As a result of the edema of the tissues and of the exophthalmos, there is often paralysis of the extraocular muscles so that the eye becomes immobilized. Vision may be reduced. In some instances, this is due to hemorrhages in the retina. Optic atrophy frequently results. Glaucoma is sometimes observed and macular dystrophy may develop later. As a result of these changes vision is usually seriously impaired and is often lost eventually. The homolateral carotid artery eventually becomes dilated and shows larger pulsations than the contralateral artery. As a rule within a few weeks, there is exophthalmos on the side opposite the lesion and pulsation of this bulb which is, however, usually of smaller amplitude than that of the homolateral bulb. This is due to the presence of communications between the two cavernous sinuses which transmit the arterial blood into the opposite sinus under high pressure.

Diagnosis.—The diagnosis is made on the history of trauma, exophthalmos and pulsation of the bulb. It must be remembered that defects in the superior orbital plate will cause pulsating exophthalmos and that various types of hemangioma will give rise to the same symptoms. These conditions should be distinguished by the absence of trauma. Thrombosis of the cavernous sinus causes exophthalmos but not pulsation or an audible bruit. If

the exophthalmos and pulsation are about equal on the two sides, it may be difficult to determine the location of the communication. Pressure on the affected artery in the neck will usually stop the bruit in such cases and thereby reveal the side of the lesion.

Treatment.—Ligation of the internal carotid artery is recommended and usually results in great improvement, if not in cure, of the condition. Proper arteriographic studies should be made before the artery is ligated to make sure the anastomotic circulation is adequate, for in some cases defective development of the circle of Willis causes extensive softening of the hemisphere when the internal carotid is occluded. If ligation of the internal carotid artery of the neck is ineffective, Dandy recommends ligation of the artery within the cranium. He shows that cure of this condition depends upon thrombosis and is not directly dependent upon the ligation.

BIBLIOGRAPHY

DANDY, W. E.: Carotid-cavernous aneurysms (pulsating exophthalmos) . Zentralbl. f. Neurochirur., 2:77, 1937.
————: The treatment of carotid cavernous arteriovenous aneurysm. Ann. Surg., **102**:916, 1935.
DESCHWEINITZ, G.: Pulsating Exophthalmos. Philadelphia, W. B. Saunders Co., 1908.
LOCKE, C. E. JR.: Intracranial arteriovenous aneurysm. Ann. Surg., **80**:1, 1924.
WALSH, F. B.: *Loc. cit.*

CHRONIC SUBDURAL HEMATOMA

Definition.—This term refers to the formation of a blood clot beneath the dura mater. Formerly, this condition was designated as *hemorrhagic pachymeningitis,* for it was regarded incorrectly as the result of a chronic inflammation of the dura.

Etiology.—The causes of subdural hematoma are still imperfectly understood. Trauma is undoubtedly responsible for many, if not for the majority of cases in adults, but can scarcely be regarded as the most important cause in babies. It has been emphasized by a number of authors that this condition is almost invariably found in undernourished infants, especially those who have been cared for by charitable institutions and those who have been neglected. It is seen after debilitating illnesses, dysentery, typhoid, pneumonia and tuberculosis and in anemias and various cachectic states. Subdural hematoma is also sometimes associated with altered states of the blood which favor bleeding, such as scurvy and purpura and with conditions in which the vessels are abnormally fragile and such as prematurity and congenital syphilis. We have observed subdural hematoma several times in cases of progressive degeneration of the brain during infancy. In a few cases a history of birth injury is elicited. Smith and Crothers point out that subdural hematoma may result from spinal air injection. These authors show that in about one third of all spinal air injections in

children air gets into the subdural spaces. In such cases subdural fluid is often found. The fluid is apparently cerebrospinal fluid with a variable admixture of blood. In some cases, a typical subdural hematoma forms and must be treated in the usual manner. It is said that this complication is most frequently found when there is atrophy of the brain. It is suggested that when the air enters the subdural space, the brain falls away from the dura and the veins which extend from the cortex to the dural sinuses are stretched and may be torn. Turpin *et al.* point out that subdural hematomas may form when the brain shrinks in cases of hypernatremic dehydration.

Pathological Anatomy.—When the dura is exposed, a dark bluish discoloration is apparent and on incising the membranes a fluid collection of blood is disclosed. This is darker than venous blood and sometimes contains bile pigments as well as masses of fibrin. A thick, vascular membrane is often attached to the inner surface of the dura and histological examination reveals that this is formed of organized blood clot and contains many thin-walled vessels which have extended into it from the dura. An avascular membrane lies upon the surface of the arachnoid. At the periphery of the hematoma the inner and outer membranes fuse, completing the encapsulation of the clot. The situation of the hematoma is almost constant. As a rule, it covers almost the entire surface of the hemisphere from the frontal to the occipital pole and extends from the Sylvian fissure below almost up to the falx above. The outer membrane is usually firmly attached at its upper margin, so that it cannot be removed completely at this point. Not infrequently, bilateral hematomas are encountered. In a few instances the hematoma is found over the temporal lobe. Similar lesions in the posterior fossa are rare. In relatively fresh hematomas, the membranes are thin and delicate but in lesions of long standing, they may be very dense and fibrous and in a few cases have eventually become calcified.

It is generally accepted that the bleeding occurs from the small, thin-walled veins which extend from the surface of the convexity of the cortex to the dural sinuses especially the longitudinal sinus. It is reasonable to suppose that this may result from weakness of the vessels, from alteration of the properties of the blood or from mechanical injury to the vessels. These veins are very fragile in the infant and are not supported as they are in the adult by Pacchionian granulations. It is easy to imagine, therefore, that a sharp blow upon the head may cause displacement of the brain and rupture of such vessels. Another cause has not received the emphasis it deserves. Atrophy of the brain such as is found in progressive degenerations of the nervous system sometimes causes such shrinking and retraction of the cortex that the brain is no longer in contact with the inner surface of

the dura and the veins are consequently subjected to stretching and sometimes rupture. Courville states that underlying the hematoma there may be areas of softening in the cortex and subcortex, and occasionally central softening within the hemisphere. There may also be softening of the basilar surface of the temporal lobe and of the basilar and medial surfaces of the occipital lobe with hemorrhagic cysts in the brain stem.

The apparently progressive nature of subdural hematoma and the long latent interval between the injury and the appearance of symptoms are not fully understood. It has been suggested by Cushing and Putman that the fragile vessels which form on the under surface of the dura may rupture spontaneously and cause further bleeding. Peet and Kahn have claimed that the pressure of the clot causes congestion of the veins and a continuous transudation of plasma which adds to the bulk of the hematoma and by forcing the cortex away from the dura lead to stretching and rupture of small veins and additional bleeding. Gardner claims that the progressive behavior of this condition is due to an accession of tissue fluid which is drawn into the hematoma through the semipermeable membrane of the arachnoid as a result of the osmotic tension of the proteins of the altered blood within. Dandy, on the other hand, is not convinced that these hematomas actually grow in size and attributes the advance in symptoms to cerebral edema. It must be pointed out that blood in the subarachnoid spaces behaves very differently from blood in the subdural space, for it is not organized and is absorbed rapidly. It has never been possible to reproduce the typical subdural hematoma experimentally, despite numerous attempts. Rabe *et al.* have made a very complete study of an infant suffering from a traumatic subdural hematoma. After evacuation of the hematoma, albuminous fluid accumulated in the subdural space. The authors found that the albumin in this fluid was derived from the plasma and presumably from the vessels in the subdural membrane. They point out that the brain, after the hematoma is evacuated, does not fill the cranial cavity and the resulting space is soon filled with fluid. Eventually, the growth of the brain obliterates this space and recovery results.

Clinical Features.—We must distinguish two types of this condition: those in which only cerebral symptoms are found and those in which the cerebral symptoms are accompanied and, perhaps, over-shadowed by symptoms of some other illness. The latter occurs in undernourished and cachectic children, usually between the ages of four and eighteen months. Many of these children are suffering from some chronic infection and not a few have scurvy. The former, as a rule, is of traumatic origin and occurs at any age, in robust as well as in malnourished subjects. In some cases the child has fallen or been dropped in such a way as to strike the head. As a rule,

such injuries are relatively mild and cause either no loss of consciousness or only transient unconsciousness, but severe injuries are also followed by this condition.

The first symptoms are usually convulsions and vomiting. In infants, the fontanels soon begin to bulge, the veins of the scalp become distended, the sutures separate and the head enlarges rapidly. Even in unilateral hematomas, the head is usually symmetrical and resembles that seen in hydrocephalus, although local bulging is sometimes observed. It is stated by Peet and Kahn that the percussion note over the hematoma is very dull in contrast to the tympanitic note over a dilated ventricle. The optic fundi show dilated veins and retinal hemorrhages in at least half of the cases. The disc is often congested and slightly elevated but typical papilledema is not very common. Palsy of one or both sixth nerves is observed if the intracranial pressure is greatly elevated. As a rule, the other cranial nerves are not affected but nystagmoid movements are sometimes seen. Despite the fact that one hemisphere may be greatly compressed and displaced, hemiplegia and other signs of cortical damage are frequently absent. Moreover, the presence of hemiparesis is of little or no localizing value since it is frequently on the side of the hematoma. This is usually attributed to the displacement of the brain and compression of the opposite cerebral peduncle by the edge of the tentorium. The pupil of the homolateral eye may be dilated. This is apparently a result of herniation of the brain through the tentorium with pressure on the third nerve. There may be a slight rise in tempera-

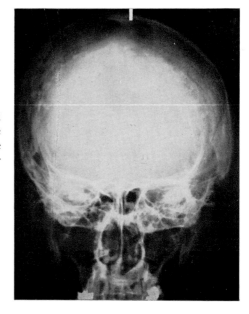

FIG. 275. Skull in old calcified subdural hematoma. The vault is elevated and the capacity of the skull is increased on the left side. Calcium deposits are seen under the dura.

ture each day and the white cells of the blood are often moderately increased. Anemia is often present. Older children, of course, complain of headache.

The course in untreated cases is apparently not always the same. In most instances the child grows steadily worse with vomiting, loss of weight and deepening stupor. The head slowly enlarges. Death occurs after weeks or months. There is good reason to believe, however, that in some instances hematomas may eventually be absorbed for, occasionally, one finds unexpectedly at operation or autopsy pigmented connective tissue under the dura which must be the remainder of an old blood clot. Sometimes such tissue becomes calcified and may be recognized in roentgenograms.

The spinal fluid is sometimes under increased pressure though in other cases the pressure is not increased. The fluid may be clear and the cell count normal. In infants, however, the fluid usually contains altered blood. Puncture of the hematoma yields fluid containing large amounts of altered blood pigment, fragments of red cells, bits of fibrin and phagocytes containing pigment. The fluid is usually dark red but after several aspirations may gradually become orange and then yellow.

Roentgenograms of the skull rarely show fracture. In infants and young children, there is almost always separation of the sutures. The vault never shows convolutional markings. If the pineal shadow is visible, it is apt to be displaced away from the hematoma. Ventriculograms reveal compression of the homolateral ventricle which is displaced towards the opposite side often to such a degree as to cross the midline.

Davidoff and Dyke describe roentgenographic changes in the skull due to hematomas of long standing. The pressure of the clot causes enlargement of the middle fossa. Later absorption of the hematoma leads to thickening of the skull and enlargement of the frontal and ethmoid sinuses, they claim. There is sometimes calcification of the membranes in such cases.

We have observed communicating hydrocephalus several times in infants with bilateral hematomas. This has usually become evident after the surgical removal of the hematoma and has resulted most often when infection of the hematoma had occurred. The explanation is not clear but one might suspect that the subarachnoid channels have become occluded.

Diagnosis.—Subdural hematoma should be considered in at least three situations: (1) In cases of unexplained cerebral symptoms following injuries of the head. (2) In all cases of increased intracranial pressure unless some other cause is apparent. (3) In cases in which cerebral symptoms follow wasting illnesses or scurvy. (4) After air encephalography especially in cases of cerebral atrophy. The chief symptoms are convulsions, fever, brisk reflexes, bulging of the fontanels, anemia, enlargement of the skull, hemorrhages in the retinae, hemiplegia and fracture of the skull. The chief

conditions which resemble subdural hematoma are brain tumor, cerebral abscess, hydrocephalus and subarachnoid hemorrhage. The differential diagnosis is not always easy to make upon clinical findings alone. If subdural hematoma is suspected, puncture of the subdural space will usually either establish or disprove the diagnosis. In infants, the puncture is easily made through the anterior fontanel but in older children whose fontanels have closed, trephine openings must be made. The ventriculograms also give fairly typical pictures, for the homolateral ventricle is uniformly compressed and displaced to the opposite side and the opposite ventricle is dilated. In bilateral hematomas, both ventricles are compressed and displaced mesially.

The differentiation of subdural hematoma and subarachnoid hemorrhage requires further discussion. If blood is recovered from the subdural space but the spinal fluid is clear, or conversely, if the spinal fluid is bloody and the subdural puncture yields nothing or merely a few drops of fluid, the diagnosis offers no difficulty; but when blood-stained fluid is obtained from both punctures, the origin of the bleeding is obscure. The history, however, offers some aid; for subarachnoid hemorrhage is usually due to rupture of an aneurysm of the circle of Willis. The onset is apoplectic or at least sudden and meningeal irritation is pronounced; whereas, the onset of chronic subdural hematoma is always insidious or slow, and meningeal irritation is much less evident or absent. The ventriculogram offers a more substantial differentiation, for it shows normal or dilated ventricles in subarachnoid hemorrhage and compressed ventricles in subdural hematomas.

Prognosis.—It is usually stated that about 50 per cent of all cases result in death from intercurrent infections but the prognosis depends so much upon the treatment and upon the illnesses with which the hematoma may be associated that no accurate figures can be given. Certainly, spontaneous recovery must be rare. Radical surgical treatment is accompanied by a very definite mortality but offers the best chance of cure. If aspiration alone is employed, a large majority of children who survive show permanent cerebral symptoms such as mental defect, epilepsy, cerebral palsies, optic atrophy and deafness. Rosenberg has estimated that 70 per cent remain abnormal but includes in his figures such conditions as enuresis and stuttering which may be of functional origin so that the outlook is not as bad as his figures would seem to indicate. Peet and Kahn feel that prompt and radical surgical treatment justifies a good prognosis for the future, if the child survives.

Treatment.—The usual treatment in the past has been repeated aspiration of the subdural spaces with a hollow needle. In all but a few cases, fluid soon reaccumulates. The course is prolonged under these conditions and the results are unsatisfactory. Peet and Kahn have claimed that simple

aspiration is effective in only relatively recent cases, for in cases of long standing, the inner membrane is so dense that the brain cannot expand, an empty space remains and fluid continues to accumulate. They insist, therefore, on turning down a bone flap and removing the membranes. A radical cure is thus obtained and it is believed that the incidence of mental defect and other evidences of permanent damage to the nervous system is greatly diminished as compared with that found in cases treated by aspiration. Ingraham and Heyl adopt a similar point of view. My own experience leads me to agree with these writers. Dandy advises craniotomy and removal of the hematoma.

BIBLIOGRAPHY

BULL, J. W. D.: The radiological diagnosis of chronic subdural hematoma. Proc. Roy. Soc. Med., 33:203, 1939. Sec. Neurol.

BURHAMS, C. W. AND GERSTENBERGER, H. J.: Internal hemorrhagic pachymeningitis in infancy. J.A.M.A., 80:604, 1923.

COLE, M. AND SPATZ, E.: Seizures with chronic subdural hematoma. New England J. Med., 265: 628, 1961.

COURVILLE, C. B.: Lesions in the brain complicating subdural and extradural hematomas. Neurology, 3:306, 1953.

CRITCHLEY, McD.: Calcified subdural hematoma. Proc. Roy. Soc. Med. London, 26:306, 1933. Sec. Neurol.

DANDY, W. E.: Subdural Hematoma. Lewis, Practice of Surgery, 12:295.

DAVIDOFF, L. M. AND DYKE, C. G.: Relapsing juvenile subdural hematoma. Bull. Neurol. Inst. of New York, 7:95, 1938.

———: Chronic subdural hematomas. A roentgenographic and pneumoencephalographic study. Bull. Neurol. Inst. of New York, 7:112, 1938.

FLEMING, H. W. AND JONES, O. W. JR.: Chronic subdural hematoma; simple drainage as a method of treatment. Report of eight cases. Surg. Gynec. & Obst., 54:81, 1932.

GARDNER, W. J.: Traumatic subdural hematoma with reference to the latent interval. Arch. Neurol. & Psychiat., 27:847, 1932.

INGRAHAM, F. D. AND HEYL, H. L.: Subdural hematoma in infancy and childhood. J.A.M.A., 112:198, 1939.

INGRAHAM, F. D. AND MATSON, D. D.: Subdural hematoma in infancy. J. Pediat., 24:1, 1944.

INGRAHAM, F. D. AND MATSON, D. D.: Subdural hematomas in infancy. Adv. Pediat., 4:231, 1949.

KAPLAN, A.: Chronic subdural hematoma; a study of eight cases with special reference to the state of the pupil. Brain, 54:430, 1931.

KUNKEL, P. AND DANDY, W. E.: Subdural hematoma. Diagnosis and treatment. Arch. Surg., 38:24, 1939.

MATSON, D. D.: Intracranial hemorrhage in infancy and childhood. Res. Nerv. & Ment. Dis., 34:59, 1954.

PEET, M. M. AND KAHN, E. A.: Subdural hematoma in infants. J.A.M.A., 98:1851, 1932.

PUTMAN, T. J. AND CUSHING, H.: Chronic subdural hematoma. Its pathology, relation to pachymeningitis hemorrhagica and surgical treatment. Arch. Surg., 11:329, 1925.

RABE, E. et al.: A study of subdural effusions in an infant. Neurology, 12:79, 1962.

ROSENBERG, O.: Die Pachymeningitis Hemorrhagica Interna in Kindersalter. Ergebn. d. inn. Med. u. Kinderh., 20:549, 1921.

RUSSELL, P. A.: Subdural haematoma in infancy. Brit. Med. Jour., 2:446, 1965.

SHULMAN, K. AND RANSOHOFF, J.: Subdural hematoma in children. Fate of children with retained membranes. J. Neurosurg., 18:175, 1961.

SMITH, H. V. AND CROTHERS, B.: Subdural fluid as a consequence of pneumoencephalography. Pediatrics, 5:375, 1950.

SUTHERLAND, G. A.: On hematoma of the dura mater associated with scurvy in children. Brain, 17:27, 1894.

SVIEN, H. J. AND GELETY, J. E.: Treatment of subdural hematoma. J. Neurosurg., 21:172, 1964.

TURPIN, R. *et al.*: Subdural hematomas in hypernatremic dehydration. Ann. Pediat., 36:311, 1960.

WALSH, F. B.: *Loc. cit.*

YASHON, D. *et al.*: Traumatic subdural hematoma of infancy. Arch. of Neurol., 18:370, 1968.

SUBDURAL HYDROMA (TRAUMATIC)

Definition.—The accumulation of cerebrospinal fluid under the dura as a result of head injury. Acute and chronic forms are recognized. This condition must be distinguished from subdural hematoma, subdural empyema and subdural effusions.

Etiology.—It is believed that a traumatic rupture of the arachnoid membrane may behave like a ball valve in that it permits the cerebrospinal fluid to flow into the subdural space but not to flow back into the subarachnoid spaces. The fluid is not readily absorbed in the subdural space, and may persist there for long periods. The transudation of tissue fluids adds to its volume and causes a gradual increase in the protein content.

Pathological Anatomy.—The fluid is found over the convexity of the brain beneath the dura. In acute cases the fluid is clear, or blood tinged, cerebrospinal fluid. In the more chronic cases, the fluid is yellow and contains a great excess of protein. It is claimed that there is no membrane formation. The brain is compressed and the ventricles deformed just as in subdural hematoma.

Clinical Features.—The clinical symptoms are not distinctive in any way. There is usually headache, drowsiness, vomiting and bradycardia. In most instances, a history of head injury may be elicited. Hemiparesis may be found but, as a rule, focal signs are not conspicuous. It seems to be correct to say that the clinical picture is identical with that of subdural hematoma.

We have seen one case of traumatic subdural hydroma of the posterior fossa in a child of 9 years. (No. 703674.) The clinical picture was decerebrate rigidity. Prompt recovery followed operation.

Diagnosis.—It is not possible to make the diagnosis on clinical grounds. However, this condition is one which must be considered whenever a patient has headache and evidences of increased intracranial pressure following an injury to the head. Puncture of the subdural space will establish the diagnosis.

Treatment.—As a rule tapping with a needle is sufficient to give relief; but if the fluid is very albuminous, it may be necessary to make an opening

in the skull and remove it completely. Cohen describes a case in which the fluid reaccumulated after each tapping.

BIBLIOGRAPHY

Cohen, I.: Chronic subdural accumulations of cerebrospinal fluid after cranial trauma. Arch. Neurol. & Psychiat., **18**:709, 1927.

Dandy, W. E.: Chronic subdural hydroma. Lewis, Practice of Surgery, **12**:306, 1932.

Haynes, W. G.: Subdural hygroma. War Med., **6**:34, 1944.

Naffziger, H. C.: Subdural fluid accumulations following head injuries. J.A.M.A., **82**:1751, 1924.

Rabe, E. F. *et al.*: Subdural collections of fluid in infants and children. Neurology, **18**:559, 1968.

Walsh, F. B.: *Loc. cit.*

TRAUMATIC SUBEPICRANIAL HYDROMA

Epstein, Epstein and Small describe a study of thirteen children suffering from this condition. Falls were responsible for the injury in twelve cases, and the blow of a baseball bat was the cause in one case. The skull is fractured and the dura and arachnoid lacerated. The periosteum is also lacerated so the cerebrospinal fluid escapes into the subepicranial space.

Swelling of the scalp may be evident within three hours or may be delayed until the sixth day. In some instances, the swelling may envelop the entire scalp. There is always fluctuation. There is no discoloration of the skin.

The swelling always disappeared by the sixteenth day, the authors state. No treatment is required. It is advised not to aspirate the fluid for fear of causing infection.

BIBLIOGRAPHY

Epstein, J., Epstein, B. and Small, M.: Subepicranial hydroma, a complication of head injuries. J. Pediat., **59**:562, 1961.

TRAUMATIC ARACHNOIDAL CYSTS

Definition.—An encapsulated collection of fluid in the pia-arachnoid due to head injury.

Etiology.—The mechanism by which the cyst is formed is not clear.

Pathological Anatomy.—The fluid is not in the subdural space but is enclosed in the pia-arachnoid. It is sometimes yellow and albuminous but in other cases is said to be identical with the cerebrospinal fluid. In such cases there must be some communication with the ventricles or subarachnoid spaces. The cyst is found directly below the point of impact. There may be porencephaly or atrophy of the brain, but in some instances there is only a small depression in the cortex due to pressure of the cyst. There is usually erosion of the inner table of the skull and in some instances a gross defect in the skull through which the cyst protrudes. Taveras and Ransohoff suggest that in such cases the arachnoid has herniated into the fracture and the bone is slowly eroded by pulsations of the brain.

Clinical Features.—The blow is always a severe one. There may be fracture of the skull but fracture is not always present. The only complaint in some cases is persistent, localized headache at the site of the impact. This is usually intense. Convulsions are present in some instances and hemiplegia and mental defect are mentioned. The last features are often due to injury to the brain, and not to the cyst.

After a time, roentgenograms will show erosion of the inner table due to the pressure of the cyst. In cases in which the bone is fractured, especially in cases of stellate fracture, the cyst may force its way through the skull and appear as a soft swelling under the scalp. Pneumoencephalography may reveal cerebral atrophy or porencephaly but the cyst does not fill as a rule. Injection of air directly into the cyst may be helpful.

Treatment.—Operation is advised with removal of the cyst and repair of the dura and skull when necessary. Operation gives prompt relief of the headache and it is said that it may also halt the convulsions in some instances.

BIBLIOGRAPHY

Lende, R. A. and Erickson, T. C.: Growing skull fractures in childhood. Jour. Neurosurg., **19**:479, 1961.

Taveras, J. M. and Ransohoff, J.: Leptomeningeal cysts of the brain following trauma with erosion of the skull. J. Neurosurg., **10**:233, 1953.

CEREBROSPINAL RHINORRHEA AND PNEUMOCEPHALY

Etiology.—Cerebrospinal rhinorrhea results as a rule from a fracture of the base of the anterior fossa which opens a communication between the subarachnoid space and the nasopharynx. Often a fracture of the cribiform plate or of the ethmoid, sphenoid or frontal sinus is responsible. A fracture through the petrous bone may cause a leakage of cerebrospinal fluid which may flow into the nasopharynx through the Eustachian tube.

Intracranial tumors and osteomas of the nasal sinuses may erode the base of the anterior fossa and cause rhinorrhea and even posterior fossa tumors may cause rhinorrhea as a result of increased intracranial pressure which may force cerebrospinal fluid through the foramina of the olfactory nerves. Even hydrocephalus without tumor may be responsible. Inflammatory processes usually in the nasal sinuses which erode the bone and the dura may produce the same result.

Kaufman has published cases in which nontraumatic, low pressure rhinorrhea seemed to be due to the persistence of the craniopharyngeal canal. In such cases the sella may be empty. Nasal encephaloceles may cause low pressure rhinorrhea.

Rhinorrhea may result in pneumocephaly when air gains access to the cranium through the fistula. In rare cases abscesses due to gas producing organisms may produce aeroceles in the brain. Subdural pneumocephaly

may occur without rhinorrhea if the fistula communicates with the subdural space but not the subarachnoid space.

Clinical Findings.—The history is usually elicited of an injury to the head which is not always severe. There is then headache similar to the spinal puncture headache and dripping of fluid from the nose. This may be clear and typical of cerebrospinal fluid, yellow or blood stained. In some cases it drips slowly and in small amounts so it may escape the notice of the patient and physician. In other cases gushes of fluid may occur when the head is bent forward or the patient strains.

Pneumocephaly may occur especially if the fistula is large. Air fills the subarachnoid spaces and the ventricles. Air in the subarachnoid spaces causes irritation of the meninges and a pleocytosis in the spinal fluid. The patient may notice a splashing sound in the head when it is moved and the physician may hear this sound by applying a stethoscope to the head and gently shaking it. Coughing or sneezing may force air into the cranium and cause intense headache or even loss of consciousness. In some cases the pia is ruptured and cavities develop in the brain full of air. These may well be due to traumatic softenings which may be enlarged by air under pressure due to coughing. The fistula acts like a ball valve.

Infection is always a danger and meningitis or brain abscesses may develop.

Diagnosis.—The fluid in the nose may be collected by having the patient hold the head forward so the fluid will drip from the nose. If glucose is found in the fluid, this is strong evidence that it is cerebrospinal fluid. Injection of a nonirritating dye such as indigo carmine into the spinal subarachnoid space or cisterna will cause the fluid in the nose to be stained.

Roentgenograms will reveal the presence or absence of air within the cranium and often the site of the fracture. Tomograms may be necessary.

The exact site of the fistula may be revealed by the injection of radioisotopes into the cisterna and a brain scan.

Prognosis.—Traumatic rhinorrhea will often heal spontaneously. In nontraumatic cases the prognosis depends on the cause.

Treatment.—If the fistula is found to be in such a place that surgical repair is possible the opening of the dura should be closed. If this is not possible the head may be placed between sandbags with the nose elevated. Medication may be necessary to prevent infection.

BIBLIOGRAPHY

BRISMAN, R. *et al.:* Cerebrospinal fluid rhinorrhea and the empty sella. Jour. Neurosurg., **31**:538, 1969.

DANDY, W. E.: Pneumocephalus (intracranial pneumatocele or areocele). Arch. Surg., **12**:949, 1926.

DI CHIRO, G. *et al.:* Isotope cisternography in the diagnosis and follow-up of cerebrospinal fluid rhinorrhea. Jour. of Neurol., Neurosurg. and Psychiat., **28**:522, 1968.

GRANT, F. C.: Intracranial aerocele following fracture. Surg. Gynec. & Obst., **36**:251, 1923.

HORRAX, G.: Intracranial aerocele following fractured skull. Ann. Surg., **73**:18, 1921.

KAUFMAN, H. H.: Nontraumatic cerebrospinal rhinorrhea. Arch. of Neurol., **21**:59, 1969.

LOCKE, C. E.: The spontaneous escape of cerebrospinal fluid through the nose. Arch. Neurol. & Psychiat., **15**:309, 1926.

MARKHAM, J. W.: Clinical features of pneumocephalus. Acta Neurochir., **16**:1, 1967.

MEALEY, J.: Chronic cerebrospinal fluid otorrhea. Report of a case associated with chronic infection of the ear. Neurology, **11**:996, 1961.

OMMAYA, A. K.: Cerebrospinal fluid rhinorrhea. Neurology, **14**:106, 1964.

OMMAYA, A. K. *et al.*: Non-traumatic cerebrospinal fluid rhinorrhea. Jour. Neurol., Neurosurg. and Psychiat., **31**:1968.

TRAUMATIC LESIONS OF THE SPINAL CORD

Etiology.—Injuries of the spinal cord due to trauma are almost always associated with fracture or dislocation of the spine. Indirect violence is most commonly to blame. Longitudinal compression of the spine by falls on the head or feet or by the imposition of heavy weight causes crushing of the vertebrae and dislocation with subsequent injury of the spinal cord. Direct injuries such as penetrating wounds are very rare in childhood.

Pathological Anatomy.—A few words must be said about the anatomical peculiarities of the vertebrae which determine, to a large extent, the site and character of traumatic injuries. The bodies of the vertebrae are composed of spongy bone which is compressed with relative ease as compared with the dense compact bone of which the neural arches are composed. Longitudinal compression, therefore, is apt to cause crushing of the body of the vertebra which then assumes a wedge shape with the apex pointing forward. If compression continues beyond this point, there is apt to be anterior dislocation of the upper vertebra. There are two levels of the spine where fractures and dislocations are most common. These are at the fifth and sixth cervical and at the twelfth thoracic and first lumbar vertebrae. Falls on the head or the impact of a heavy weight on the head will usually cause strong flexion of the neck and anterior fracture dislocation at C5 or C6. If the neck happens to be extended at the moment of injury, there may be fracture of the odontoid process or of the axis or atlas. The first and second cervical vertebrae represent, perhaps, the third most common site of spinal fracture. Forces which act upon the upper half of the trunk or the shoulders usually cause flexion and fracture dislocation of the twelfth thoracic or first lumbar vertebrae.

In rare but interesting cases, injuries to the spine cause no evident fracture at the time but in the following weeks or months, a delayed deformity will develop which indicates collapse of the vertebrae. The term "Kümmel's spine" is often applied to this condition. Its pathogenesis is still not quite clear. Most writers regard it as the result of traumatic hemorrhage into the body of the vertebra which interferes with the circulation and later causes necrosis of the bone. If the patient is permitted to walk, the weight

of the body will eventually crush the necrotic bone. We have studied one such case and found nothing but necrosis of the affected vertebra without any sign of infection.

Fractures and dislocations of the spinal column do not always cause injuries of the cord but, unfortunately, both such injuries are relatively common. When there is gross displacement of the bones, the cord is usually completely crushed, but in relatively mild injuries the gross lesions are chiefly confined to the central portions of the cord. On inspection the cord may show a fusiform swelling at the site of the lesion and there may be some extradural and intradural hemorrhage. On section we find hemorrhagic areas of necrosis involving the gray matter and the base of the posterior columns. These extend above and below the site of injury for several segments, growing smaller as they become more remote. They usually end in small circular lesions just posterior to the central canal. These lesions are filled with pulped nervous tissue and blood. If the patient survives long enough, cavities result which have a superficial resemblance to syringomyelia. McVeigh has shown that such lesions may be produced experimentally by pressure on the cord. The cord is pulped at the site of compression and the debris escapes by forcing its way through the central gray matter. Such a lesion is usually termed hematomyelia though this name has certain misleading implications.

In some cases one is puzzled to find a traumatic injury of the spinal cord though the most careful examination reveals no evidence of fracture or dislocation. In such cases one must consider the possibility of extrusion of an intervertebral disc or of dislocation of the vertebrae with spontaneous reduction.

Holmes and others have described cases in which the impact of high velocity bullets has caused areas of necrosis in the gray matter and posterior columns of the cord without penetrating into the spinal canal at all. Such lesions scarcely require consideration in this article but the reader will find the subject described in the appended references.

Clinical Features.—A large number of spinal cord syndromes may result from injuries but since these are surgical rather than strictly neurological problems, they will be discussed very briefly.

First, we may take up the lesions in the first and second cervical segments. These are the result of fracture-dislocation of the skull on the atlas and of fracture of the odontoid process. They may result from diving into a shallow pool and striking the head on the bottom, from hanging and even from mild injuries in play which snap the head backwards. If there is much displacement of the fragments and serious compression of the cord, death usually is almost instantaneous since the muscles of respiration are paralyzed. If the injury to the spinal cord is a mild one or develops gradu-

ally, there may be weakness of the entire bodily musculature and corresponding loss of sensibility extending up to the sensory field of the fifth nerve. We have studied the case of a boy who injured his neck in diving and developed slowly progressive paralysis in the next few months. When brought into the hospital he was quite paralytic except for the sterno-mastoids which were maintaining respiration with great difficulty. Death occurred within a few hours and at post-mortem examination, it was found that the atlas had been crushed and the odontoid process had forced its way into the foramen magnum compressing the decussation of the pyramids.

The more common fracture-dislocations at about the level of the fifth and sixth cervical vertebrae do not cause immediate death as a rule, even if the cord is completely crushed, since the lesion is just below the phrenic nucleus. There is paralysis of movements of all muscles except the diaphragm and those innervated by the cervical plexus. The sensory loss extends up to the second rib. As a rule, there is a narrow zone of hyperesthesia corresponding to the level of the lesion. The pupils are small and there may be slight drooping of both eyelids. In males, mild priapism is evident at first. For a time, there is abolition of all reflexes and retention of urine. Later, if the patient survives and is fortunate enough to escape serious infections, the reflexes may return and either paraplegia-in-flexion or paraplegia-in-extension may develop, depending upon the severity of the lesion. In a few cases, the injury involves the gray matter but not the ascending and descending tracts, so that we find only paralysis of the muscles innervated by the fifth and sixth cervical segments and some sensory loss, usually analgesia and thermanesthesia, in corresponding dermatomes. The hands, trunk and legs may be unaffected. The writer has seen two such cases in which no sensory loss could be found. The posture of the arms in such cases may be exactly that of the common brachial plexus birth palsy. When the lesion is somewhat lower and involves the seventh and eighth cervical segments, the posture of the arms is reversed. The arms are abducted and externally rotated at the shoulder, flexed at the elbow and the forearm is supinated. The sensory level, of course, follows the midline of the arm and involves all of the hand except the thumb and forefinger.

Fractures at the level of the twelfth thoracic and first lumbar vertebrae involve the conus and the cauda equina. We find a flaccid type of paralysis of the legs with atrophy of the muscles, loss of reflexes, inability to control the sphincters and sensory loss extending as a rule, up to about the level of Poupart's ligament. The exact level of the motor and sensory disturbances varies a good deal in different cases. It is unusual for the knee jerks to return and spasticity never develops. In three cases in which the lumbosacral enlargement was traumatized, we have seen extensive paralysis with atrophy and loss of reflexes but no demonstrable anesthesia whatever. In some in-

stances the roots are not damaged and injury to the conus is manifest by incontinence and sacral anesthesia.

In a few cases of fresh transections of the cord in the upper thoracic region we have seen a low grade polyuria and partial loss of temperature control. We have been inclined to attribute these symptoms to interruption of the nervous pathways controlling sweat secretion and vasomotor reactions over a large part of the body surface.

It was formerly taught that lesions within the spinal cord proper never caused pain, but certain observations of Gordon Holmes have established that acute traumatic lesions may be associated with intense pain referred to the legs and parts of the body below the level of the lesion. This pain is found only in incomplete lesions, and, as a rule, is confined to the side on which the injury is greatest. It is usually associated with hyperesthesia and has been compared, although perhaps without good reason, to the type of pain seen in lesions of the optic thalmus. The writer has seen a case of this type in which severe paroxysms often developed coincidentally with violent muscular spasms of the legs. The pain ceased in a few weeks as is the rule in such cases.

The writer has observed an interesting case of an infant suffering from severe cervical adenitis of several weeks' duration. During convalescence he attempted to sit up and at once fell back dead. Jones has advanced evidence from post-mortem and clinical studies to show that in such cases there may be decalcification of the atlas without osteomyelitis and that dislocation may result from abrupt movements of the head. The medulla is compressed and death occurs instantly. The cause of the changes in the bones is obscure. In one case in which the condition was recognized by roentgenographic study and proper precautions taken to prevent dislocation, the bones eventually developed their normal density.

Illingsworth has described sudden loss of consciousness in children who have congenital fusion of the cervical vertebrae. Fromm and Pitner describe progressive quadriparesis as a result of agenesis of the odontoid process leading to dislocations of the axis on the atlas.

Diagnosis.—The history of a fall or of some injury to the spine usually makes the *nature* of the injury obvious. It must be kept in mind that nursemaids or even parents will sometimes conceal the fact that the child has been allowed to fall because of fear of legal responsibility. Fractures and dislocations are almost always present to confirm the history. In rare instances, however, no bony lesions may be demonstrable, either clinically or roentgenologically. Moreover, the interpretation of roentgenograms may be difficult in some cases. Congenital defects of the vertebrae may simulate old fractures in that they may present the same wedge shape. The fifth lumbar vertebra is subject to so many morphological variations that it is

difficult to be sure that mild alterations are actually pathological. It may also be mentioned that it is difficult to study the seventh cervical and first thoracic vertebrae since lateral views are so hard to obtain. The *level of the lesion* is determined with ease in most cases by the neurological examination. When the lesion is in the lumbar spine, however, the neurological signs may be inadequate to distinguish between injury of the conus and of the cauda. It is the rule in such cases to assume that the conus is injured if the first lumbar vertebra is fractured and that the cauda is involved if the bony lesion is below this level. The *anatomical character* and *severity* of the lesion in the spinal cord frequently cannot be determined at once. If the paralysis is not complete at first, it is evident that we are dealing with a relatively mild injury, but if there is complete loss of conduction in the cord, it is impossible to say whether the cord is actually transected or whether there is merely a transient loss of function without complete anatomical destruction. Apart from laminectomy, there is no way of answering this question except by longer observation. If the stage of spinal shock is brief, that is, if the reflexes return after a relatively short time and if muscle tone on its return is found chiefly in the extensors, we are justified in suspecting that the lesion is incomplete. If signs of compression of the spinal cord develop weeks or months after an injury of the back, we may consider several possibilities. Kümmel's delayed traumatic spondylopathy should be kept in mind. This is associated with deformity of the spine due to collapse of a vertebra. Osteomyelitis and tuberculous spondylitis may also develop after trauma. The possibility of extrusion of an intervertebral disc should also be considered.

Prognosis.—Death in the first few hours may occur from paralysis of respiration, from shock or from associated injuries. After the first few days, the danger is chiefly from infected decubitus ulcers, infections of the urinary tract and pneumonia. Lesions high enough to weaken the muscles of respiration have a high mortality.

The prognosis as regards recovery depends upon the severity of the injury. If the lesion is only a partial one, there is always a striking return of function in the next few months. Jefferson considers loss of sensibility of much more serious import than paralysis. No improvement is to be expected after a year. When the cord is completely transected, no voluntary power will ever return. The most the patient can expect is the development of a paraplegia-in-flexion with automatic bladder and relative freedom from cutaneous ulcerations. Lesions of the cauda equina, however, behave more like those of peripheral nerves in that there is often slow improvement for long periods of time. Thus, in fractures of the first lumbar vertebra, signs due to damage to the spinal roots may recede while those due to injury to the conus may persist.

Treatment.—Since this is a surgical problem, treatment need not be discussed fully. If the patient is seen immediately after the accident, treatment for shock is often required. In the next few hours nothing should be done as a rule unless it is urgently required. Neurological examination can be made at once, however, and as soon as possible roentgenograms of the spine. If there is any reason to suspect that the cord is actually compressed by the bone, this condition should be corrected by appropriate surgical or orthopedic measures as soon as the patient's condition permits. Spinal manometric tests are considered to be very important by some authorities. As a rule, little is to be gained by early laminectomy since the injury reaches its greatest extent at once and the operation merely adds to the mortality. It is of greatest importance that the patient should receive careful nursing care and every effort should be made to prevent bed sores and infections of the urinary tract.

CASE HISTORY (Ped. A-6422). *Boy of 2 years developed complete paralysis of legs and trunk up to level of 3rd thoracic myotome with corresponding anesthesia as a result of an injury to the spine. Polyuria and hyperpyrexia without infection.*

W. D., a previously healthy boy of 2 years, was injured in an automobile accident on the 8th of March 1938. He was unconscious for a short time and it was later discovered that he was paralysed in both legs. There was loss of control of the bladder and loss of sensibility over the lower part of the body. Roentgenograms of the spine revealed no evidence of fracture or dislocation of the vertebrae but the 4th rib on the left was broken. After the injury, it was noticed that the child ran a continuous and irregular fever ranging from 37° to 40°C.

Examination on April 22, some five and a half weeks after the injury, revealed complete paralysis of the legs, abdomen and chest except for the upper intercostal muscles, indicating a level of about the 3rd thoracic monotome. Sensibility was lost below a corresponding level. The legs were not spastic, but showed some tone, chiefly in the flexor muscles. The knee and ankle jerks were present, and stimulation of the toes caused triple flexion, which was unilateral as a rule. Strong stimuli caused bilateral flexion. The bladder discharged urine spontaneously at regular intervals. Temperature ranged from 37° to 40°C. W.B.C. 6000. Urine contained no white cells. Roentgenograms of the spine negative.

It was soon found that the child's temperature varied with that of his environment and that the apparent fever was due to heavy bed clothes. By varying the coverings of his bed, his temperature could be kept at any level desired. The polyuria was of low grade and, no doubt, a result of the fact that sweating was absent over most of the body.

BIBLIOGRAPHY

ALEXANDER, E., MASLAND, R. AND HARRIS, C.: Anterior dislocation of the first cervical vertebra simulating cerebral birth injury in infancy. Am. J. Dis. Child., **85**:173, 1953.

BERKHEISER, E. J. AND SEIDLER, F.: Non-traumatic dislocation of the atlanto-axial joint. J.A.M.A., **96**:517, 1931.

BROOKS, T. P.: Dislocation of the cervical spine. Some predisposing causes. J.A.M.A., **104**:902, 1935.

DANDY, W. E.: Loose cartilage from intervertebral disc simulating tumor of the spinal cord. Arch. Surg., **19**:660, 1929.

FERNSTROM, U.: Protruded lumbar intervertebral discs in children. Acta chir. scand., **3**:71, 1956.

FORD, F. R.: Syncope, vertigo, and disturbances of vision resulting from intermittent obstruction of the vertebral arteries due to defect in the odontoid process and excess mobility of the second vertebra. Bull. Johns Hopkins Hosp., **91**:168, 1952.

FORD, F. R. AND CLARK, D.: Thrombosis of the basilar artery with softenings in the cerebellum and brain stem due to manipulation of the neck. Bull. Johns Hopkins Hosp., **98**:37, 1956.

FROMM, G. H. AND PITNER, S. E.: Late progressive quadriparesis due to odontoid agenesis. Arch. Neurol., **9**:291, 1963.

HOLMES, G.: Spinal injuries of warfare. Brit. Med. J., **11**:769, 1915.

ILLINGWORTH, R. S.: Attacks of unconsciousness in association with fused cervical vertebrae. Arch. of Dis. in Child., **31**:6, 1956.

JEFFERSON, G. *et al.*: Discussion of spinal injuries. Proc. Roy. Soc. Med., **21**:625, 1927. Sec. Orthoped.

JEFFERSON, G.: Injuries of the spinal cord. Brit. Med. J., **2**:1125, 1936.

JONES, F.: Compression fracture of the spine, developing delayed symptoms (posttraumatic spondylitis or Kümmel's disease). J.A.M.A., **81**:1860, 1923.

JONES, R. W.: Spontaneous hyperemic dislocation of the atlas. Proc. Roy. Soc., **25**:586, 1932.

KAPLAN, L. I. AND DENKER, P. G.: Acute non-traumatic spinal epidural hemorrhage. Am. J. Surg., **78**:356, 1949.

LOWENTHAL, A. AND MARTIN, F.: Subdural spinal hematoma due to trauma. Monatschr. f. Psychiat. u. Neurol., **117**:30, 1949.

MACKAY, R. M. I.: Spontaneous dislocation of the cervical spine in childhood. Arch. Dis. in Childhood, **32**:505, 1957.

MARTIN, R. C.: Atlas-axis dislocation following cervical infections. J.A.M.A., **118**:874, 1942.

McVEIGH, J. F.: Experimental cord crushes with especial reference to mechanical factors involved and subsequent changes in areas of cord affected. Arch. Surg., **7**:573, 1923.

MIXTER, W. J.: Fracture and dislocation of the spine. Lewis, Practice of Surgery, **12**:4; 1, 1932.

PRATT-THOMAS, H. R. AND BERGER, K. E.: Cerebellar and spinal injuries after chiropractic manipulation. J.A.M.A., **133**:600, 1947.

SASHIN, D.: Intervertebral disc extensions into the vertebral bodies and spinal canal. Arch. Surg., **22**:527, 1931.

SCHULTZ, E. *et al.*: Paraplegia caused by spontaneous spinal epidural hemorrhage. J. Neurosurg., **10**:608, 1953.

SULLIVAN, A.: Subluxation of the atlanto-axial joint. Sequel to inflammatory processes in the neck. J. Pediat., **35**:451, 1949.

SULLIVAN, C. R.: Infection of intervertebral discs. Surg. Clin. North America, **41**:1077, 1961.

PARAPLEGIA DUE TO SEVERE SCOLIOSIS

It is usually taught that scoliosis never causes any injury of the spinal cord no matter how severe it may be, so long as there is no dislocation of the vertebrae. A few cases have been observed, however, in which long-standing kyphosis and scoliosis have resulted in paraplegia or paraparesis.

Elmslie has published two cases of this nature in which tuberculosis of the vertebrae was ruled out by a careful study. At operation the spinal cord was found to be tightly stretched over the kyphos but not compressed. Only a small proportion of the canal was filled by the cord. The dura was under

great tension and when this was split the cord began to pulsate. Some improvement resulted from the operation. Sachs has observed two cases of the same kind in which complete loss of conduction in the spinal cord had developed. In one case great improvement resulted from operation. We have seen several cases of this type. In two of them the paraplegia developed following head traction imposed with the purpose of reducing the spinal curvature.

CASE HISTORY (U. 160788).—*Girl of four years developed progressive scoliosis. Pigmented areas on the skin appeared. Several years later the legs became weak. During traction at the age of 17 years, paraplegia occurred. At operation the cord was found to be stretched over the spinal curvature.*

M. K. was noted to have scoliosis at the age of four years. Despite orthopedic treatment with casts and braces, the deformity slowly grew more pronounced. Brown spots appeared over her body. At about the age of 12 or 15 years, her legs began to grow weak but the significance of this was not recognized and no neurological examination was made. At the age of 17 years she was placed in traction with weights attached to the head and legs. Traction was discontinued after two weeks because the patient vomited repeatedly. It was then discovered that her legs were almost completely paralysed.

Neurological examination revealed an underdeveloped and undernourished girl of 17 years. She was 4 feet 3 inches tall and weighed only 75 lbs. The skin was very dark and there were numerous areas of dark brown pigmentation scattered over her body which ranged from a few mm. to 2 cm in diameter. No subcutaneous tumors were found. There was a severe S shaped spinal curvature with its apex at the midthoracic level. The legs were almost completely paralysed and spastic and the patient could not walk without support. The knee and ankle jerks were increased and ankle clonus and Babinski's sign were present on either side. Cutaneous anesthesia was present up to a level one inch below the umbilicus.

Spinal puncture revealed normal fluid. The Queckenstedt test was positive and lipiodol injection in the cisterna magna stopped at the level of the 7th thoracic vertebra. Exploration revealed no tumor or bony compression but the cord was tightly stretched over the apex of the spinal curve. No improvement followed operation.

Apparently partial paralysis of the legs had developed as a result of stretching the cord over the spinal curvature and this was converted into a complete paraplegia by the traction. The scoliosis was no doubt due to von Recklinghausen's disease.

BIBLIOGRAPHY

ELMSLIE, R. C.: Two cases of scoliosis with paraplegia. Proc. Roy. Soc. Med. London, **18**:25, 1925. Sec. Orthoped.

SACHS, E.: An unusual case of paraplegia associated with marked gibbus and a localized collection of fat at the site of the gibbus. J. Bone & Joint Surg., **7**:709, 1925.

Viets, H. R. and Clifford, M. R.: Paraplegia associated with non-tuberculous kyphoscoliosis. Report of a case and survey of the literature. New England Med. J., **206**:55, 1932.

TRAUMATIC LESIONS OF THE SPINAL NERVES

Etiology.—Among the common causes of nerve injuries in childhood may be mentioned laceration by penetrating wounds, rupture by stretching, compression by scar tissue, by hematomas, by callus formation, by the improper application of a cast, by the use of an inadequately padded crutch and by transient pressure under anesthesia. It is distressing to reflect that most of the nerve lesions described below are the result of careless or incompetent surgery.

Pathological Anatomy.—When a nerve trunk is lacerated as in penetrating wounds, there is hemorrhage in the nerve sheath and surrounding tissue. The distal portions of the fibers which are destroyed degenerate within the next two weeks. Repair then begins. The hemorrhage is absorbed and a connective tissue scar forms at the site of the lesion. The nerve fibers slowly regenerate extending from the proximal portion of the nerve along the course of the degenerated fibers. These regenerating neurons do not necessarily follow their former path so that the nerve pattern may be greatly altered and many fibers apparently reach inappropriate endings so that they never develop any useful function. In some instances, the down growth of nerve fibers is prevented by scar tissue and so forms at the site of the former lesion a bulbous enlargement called a neuroma.

Stretching of the nerve may cause actual rupture of the entire trunk but more often, merely leads to hemorrhage within the nerve sheath and rupture of a few fibers. In some cases in which nerve function has been lost by stretching, no gross lesions can be found when the nerve is exposed.

Long continued pressure on a nerve, by a crutch in the axilla, by a bony deformity or by callus formation, leads to thickening and scar formation with degeneration of the nerve fibers. The scar formation may interfere with regeneration when the pressure is relieved.

Pressure on a nerve such as occurs when the patient is unconscious or under anesthesia probably causes injury to the fibers by ischemia. If mild, there may be no demonstrable anatomical changes but if severe, there is degeneration. In either case, there is practically no scar formation and regeneration is relatively prompt.

Clinical Features.—The common types of traumatic nerve lesions will be taken up in a general way.

Falls on the shoulder are among the most frequent causes of nerve injuries in childhood. The shoulder is violently depressed or perhaps the head is forced to the opposite side so the roots of the brachial plexus are placed under excessive tension and often ruptured or avulsed from the spinal

cord. This gives rise to Erb's upper arm brachial plexus palsy which is more fully described under birth injuries of the brachial plexus. In the same way, the distal plexus palsy of Klumpke may be produced by falls in which the arm is violently abducted and elevated.

Robles points out that when the plexus is avulsed from the cord, a myelogram will usually reveal an empty root sleeve. If in such cases there is no additional damage to the nerve root distal to the posterior root ganglion, the axon reflex is helpful. This is tested by scratching the skin. If the axon reflex is elicited, the red area and wheal which are due to injury to the capillaries are surrounded by a red flare. The flare is absent if the lesion is distal to the posterior root ganglion. *Dislocation* of the head of the humerus into the axilla likewise may cause various nerve lesions. The axillary nerve is not infrequently ruptured. The cords of the brachial plexus may be compressed in the axilla giving rise to paralysis of various muscle groups. The posterior cord is most frequently affected. Crutch paralysis is not common in children, but occurs. The radial nerve may be involved in the axilla causing paralysis of the triceps and the long extensors of the wrist and digits. In some instances the axillary nerve may be involved also. *Fractures* of the bones may cause injury of the nerves in several ways. The nerve trunk may be lacerated or severed by sharp fragments of the bone or compressed by hematoma, scar formation or callus. In one case the radial nerve was pinched between the two fragments of the bone when the fracture was set. The differentiation depends largely upon the time element. Laceration should cause immediate paralysis, hematoma should produce symptoms very promptly and injury from callus or scar formation should be delayed for weeks. A more common cause of nerve injury is the *pressure* of a *cast* or improperly padded *splint*. The nerves which lie over bony prominences such as the ulnar, the radial and the common peroneal are most frequently affected. Fractures of the inner condyle of the humerus give rise to *delayed traumatic ulnar nerve palsies*. The ulnar groove is obliterated or involved by a rough callus and the carrying angle may be altered so as to place the nerve under increased tension. As a result of constant mild trauma, over a period of years, the nerve becomes thickened and fibrosed so that partial or complete loss of function eventually develops. The period between the fracture and the onset of the palsy may be twenty years or more. Transplantation of the nerve anteriorly usually results in partial or complete return of function. A very shallow groove may expose the nerve to constant trauma. In some children, the nerve may be dislocated when the arm is fully flexed. After many years, neuritis may result.

Pressure palsies of the common peroneal nerve due to sitting with the leg crossed over the other knee is rare in children, but I have seen this condi-

tion in a child of 10 years. She recovered rapidly after she was induced to abandon this habit. *Surgical operations* are among the most common causes of nerve injuries. The writer has seen several cases in which the sciatic nerve was injured in operations on the hip joint. The paralysis persisted without signs of recovery for many months. As a rule, the nerve is not actually severed in such cases but is traumatized by pressure of retractors or by pinching with forceps. In some cases, the nerve may be accidentally included in ligatures. The writer has seen several instances in which incisions on the posterior surface of the forearm severed the terminal branches of the radial nerve which were apparently so minute at this point that they were not identified. The use of Esmarch bandages or tourniquets in operations on the extremities may cause paralysis of all muscles below the point at which the band is applied. The same results may follow the constant use of the blood pressure cuff during operation, especially in debilitated patients. In adults pressure palsies frequently occur *under anesthesia* as a result of improper padding of the operating table. The radial nerve is most frequently involved but the ulnar and common peroneal are also often affected. Pressure at the base of the neck may cause Erb's palsy and the writer has seen bilateral paralysis of Klumpke's type in a young girl following operation for appendicitis. Here the pressure must have been in the axillae or was perhaps applied in such a way as to force the shoulders down and compress the lower roots against the first rib. It must be stated that pressure palsies under anesthesia are rare in childhood, perhaps because prolonged operations are uncommon or because the child's body weight is not sufficient to produce great pressure. It is interesting that mild pressure palsies may be associated with no loss of sensibility. The experimental work of Denny-Brown and Brenner has made this clear. Forced abduction and elevation of the arm during anesthesia may cause brachial plexus palsies apparently due to stretching of the nerve roots. I have seen one case in which stretching a boy's hamstrings to relieve contractures caused rupture of both sciatic nerves. Orthopedic correction of knock knees may cause stretching of the peroneal nerve and lasting paralysis. In the same way restoration of flexion of an elbow which has been in full extension for a prolonged period may result in ulnar nerve palsy unless the nerve is transplanted anteriorly. The writer has seen two interesting cases in which the injection of morphine and typhoid vaccine respectively into the radial nerve resulted in severe pain and wrist drop. It is rather remarkable that this accident is not more common since the usual site of hypodermic injections is so close to the radial nerve as it lies on the outer aspect of the humerus. We have seen ten cases in which the injection of penicillin into the buttock resulted in injury to the sciatic nerve with the most disastrous results. In one instance

the sciatic nerves were missed and both pudic nerves were damaged. I have seen one instance in a child of the progressive paralysis of the dorsal interosseus nerve described by Woltman and Learmonth. This case is given in abstract below. The nerve is compressed between the aponeurosis of the common extensor and a fibrous process from the supinator. No doubt a developmental peculiarity is responsible. The long extensor muscles of the digits and wrist become paralysed gradually. The brachioradialis is spared and there is no loss of sensibility in the sensory field of the radial nerve.

I have seen an adolescent boy in whom pain and weakness of the supraspinatus and infraspinatus muscles resulted from pinching of the suprascapular nerve in the suprascapular notch. Operation and freeing of the nerve gave prompt relief.

Jones and Lovett mention cases in which reduction of congenital dislocation of the hip results in injury to the sciatic nerve by stretching or even rupture of the nerve.

Pain attributed to amputation neuromas does not seem to be common in children. Simmel states that phantom limbs rarely follow amputation in children under two years, but almost invariably develop in children over the age of eight years.

I have seen a case in which a small caliber bullet punctured the wall of the subclavian artery and caused a saccular aneurysm. This aneurysm compressed the brachial plexus and caused slowly progressive paralysis. Ligation of the artery gave relief. In another case a similar wound caused an arteriovenous fistula between the subclavian artery and the vein. There was engorgement of all the veins of the arm and neck, edema of the arm and shoulder, a loud bruit and thrill above the clavicle and tachycardia and enlargement of the heart. The lower roots of the plexus were traumatized by the bullet but the aneurysm did not cause increasing loss of function. Dr. Otenasek repaired the aneurysm with end to end anastomosis of the artery and secured a perfect result.

Webb *et al.* describe cases of herniation of lumbar intervertebral discs in childhood. The symptoms do not differ from those seen in adult life. There is pain in the lumbar region and pain radiating into the lumbar dermatomes. The back is rigid and efforts to bend the back increase the pain. I have seen only one case in childhood. The patient was a boy of nine years and operation was performed with complete success. Silverman describes cases of calcification of the intervertebral discs in childhood and mentions that in some instances symptoms of spinal nerve root irritation are present. Calcification of the intervertebral discs may occur in alkaptonuria. Doyle describes infections of the intervertebral discs with narrowing of the interspace and pain and rigidity of the back. Bed rest seems to be the only treatment required. *Spondylolisthesis* may result in damage to the

roots of the cauda. Dr. John Chambers has showed me a case of this kind in a little girl of 10 years.

Logically, the eleventh cranial nerve should be taken up in the discussion of the cranial nerves but its distribution is such that it seems preferable to deal with it here. The accessory nerves is often injured in the neck as a result of incisions into abscesses or removal of infected lymph nodes or neoplasms. I have seen cases in which this nerve was included in the ligature placed around the internal jugular vein during operation for mastoiditis. It may also be injured in operations to relieve torticollis. If the lesion is so placed as to spare the nerve which supplies the sterno-mastoid muscle, the diagnosis is usually missed for only the lower two-thirds of the trapezius are paralyzed and this is not obvious. The second cervical nerve roots do not have proper foramina as the other cervical nerve roots do, but lie between the arches of the atlas and axis. Violent extension of the head may approximate these arches and traumatize the roots with the production of pain and numbness in the back of the head.

If a nerve is completely divided, there are usually no irritative phenomena, but incomplete lesions, especially those which cause extensive scar formation and those in which foreign bodies come to lie near the nerve, may give rise to numerous symptoms of irritative nature. The most common and most severe of these is spontaneous pain, often described as a burning pain. There is also tingling and paresthesias of numerous kinds and sometimes hyperesthesia of the skin and tenderness over the course of the nerve. Trophic changes are very frequently found in such cases. We may find cyanosis and edema of the skin, atrophy of the nails and small bones of the fingers and toes. The skin may be thin and glossy or thick and scaly. It may be very dry or bathed in perspiration. Traumatic nerve lesions are the commonest cause of *causalgia*. This term is applied to incomplete nerve lesions characterized by intractable pain of a burning type which is increased by heat, dryness of the skin and by emotional disturbances. As a rule, causalgia is found almost exclusively in the distribution of the median and sciatic nerves. In my opinion psychological factors play a major role in the more bizarre cases.

Another strange condition is termed *reflex, sympathetic dystrophy* or Sudecks atrophy. It follows a minor injury which, as a rule, does not involve peripheral nerves. One hand may be affected or all extremities may be involved. The affected extremity becomes cold, wet and painful. The patient cannot move it because of pain. The joints become stiff and the muscles and bones become atrophic. I regard this as a psychogenic condition. Disuse plays a major role.

Diagnosis.—A complete diagnosis demands the determination of the cause, the site and the anatomical nature of the lesion. The first question,

namely, the *cause,* is almost always evident from the history. The *location* of the lesion is easily determined, as a rule, by the distribution and extent of the signs and symptoms and by the location of the superficial wound, if any. Frequently, we cannot determine the anatomical nature of the lesion directly and must rely on deduction. As a rule, it is easy to determine whether there is complete loss of function or incomplete paralysis of the nerve, but complete loss of function does not always mean that the nerve is severed. The electric reactions are of considerable value in this respect. If, after two weeks of complete paralysis, we find that the reactions of the muscles are quite normal, we may assume with relative confidence that the nerve fibers have not degenerated and that we are dealing with a physiological loss of function but not anatomical interruption. We cannot distinguish between degeneration due to pressure and degeneration due to division. Again, the history is of the greatest importance.

Two diagnostic tests of some importance may be mentioned at this point. French has shown that if a minute droplet of lipiodol is placed in the sheath of a nerve it will ascend very rapidly. When one is dealing with a nerve lesion of uncertain location, this technique may be helpful. The lipiodol stops at the site of compression or scar formation.

Bonney has pointed out that in dealing with injuries of the brachial plexus due to traction, the axon reaction may be helpful in distinguishing those cases in which the roots are avulsed from the cord from those cases in which the nerve trunks are injured outside the vertebral column. The former condition is hopeless, but regeneration may occur in the latter and suture is sometimes feasible. The histamine cutaneous reaction and the cold vasodilator response are quite normal when the roots have been avulsed and are defective when the damage is distal to the posterior root ganglia.

Prognosis.—The prognosis depends largely upon the anatomical nature of the lesion and upon its severity. *Pressure palsies* almost invariably make satisfactory recoveries. If the electrical reactions indicate degeneration of the nerve fibers, recovery will be delayed until the regenerating nerve fibers can grow downward to the muscles. This growth is estimated to take place at a rate of 1 to 3 mm a day, being somewhat more rapid in children than in adults. If there is no reaction of degeneration after two weeks, recovery will often occur rather suddenly and apparently represents the relief of a physiological block of function rather than regeneration. *If* there is reason to believe that the *nerve trunk is actually severed*, the prognosis is less favorable. We must always consider the possibility that there may be an obstacle to regeneration such as a dense scar, a long unbridged gap in the nerve, foreign bodies or neuromas. In brachial plexus palsies, it is possible that the roots may be avulsed from the cord so that regeneration is impossible.

We can never be sure that the nerve is regenerating satisfactorily until we discover some return of function. The patient's condition should be followed carefully, for if the nerve fails to regenerate, operation should be performed as soon as possible, whereas, operation on a nerve which is regenerating merely delays recovery. We must mention several possible sources of error in this connection. In some cases we may find that voluntary power returns to muscles when faradic irritability is still absent or at least cannot be demonstrated by any reasonable strength of current. Moreover, patients may develop "trick movements," using uninjured muscles for functions, which they do not usually perform. A common example is extension of the wrist in radial nerve paralysis by the use of the long flexors of the fingers. The return of sensibility around the margins of the area of anesthesia, as a rule, does not indicate regeneration but is merely the expression of utilization of the overlap of adjacent nerves. It is only when sensibility returns in that region supplied exclusively by the affected nerve that it may be regarded as evidence of regeneration. Most authorities place little stress on Tinel's sign. This is elicited as follows. The examiner percusses gently with the finger over the course of the affected nerve, beginning at its distal extremity and progressing slowly proximally to the site of the lesion. When the tapping reaches the point to which the regenerating neurons have extended, an intense tingling is felt by the patient and is referred to the area of anesthesia. This is due to the fact that regenerating fibers are very sensitive to pressure. The weakness of this test seems to lie in the fact that it may be elicited by a few fibers which have bridged a gap or escaped from a scar but which have no clinical importance, since the majority of the fibers have been blocked.

Treatment.—A great deal of experience and judgment are required to obtain the best results in the treatment of peripheral nerve lesions. It may be said at once that there is no known way to hasten the growth of the nerve and all we can hope to accomplish is to prevent secondary disabilities such as injury of the affected muscles by stretching, contractures of the opposing muscles and stiffness of the joints. Unfortunately, many physicians neglect these simple measures and pin their hopes on producing rapid regeneration by means of electric treatment or some other magic. The affected limb should be placed in a splint in such a position as to relax the paralyzed muscles and stretch their antagonists. Massage and passive movements should be employed to prevent contractures and stiffness of the joints. These measures are especially helpful in infants since their bones are moulded so quickly by abnormal postures that striking deformities develop in a short time. If we have good reason to believe that regeneration will occur, as, for example, in the common pressure palsies, no other measures are required. If we are relatively certain that the nerve has been severed or

cannot regenerate, operation should be performed at once and end to end suture of the nerve attempted for only in this manner can satisfactory surgical results be attained. Only rarely are grafts successful. If operation is required for brachial plexus injuries, it should be performed promptly for the nerve trunks become bound together by scar tissue after some months so operation is difficult. It is when the prognosis is uncertain that the most difficult problems in treatment arise. Operations should be avoided if possible, but if it is required, it should be done as soon as it is feasible. No rule can be given for such cases, for each is an individual problem. Only surgeons who are familiar with nerve surgery should handle these cases.

CASE HISTORY (Ped. A-54315).

W. G. S., a little boy of three years, was admitted to the Harriet Lane Home on Nov. 28, 1947 for operative repair of cleft palate and hare lip. Operation was performed on the following day under ether anesthesia. The child was placed in the Trendelenburg position and much of his weight was sustained by straps about the shoulders. The operation was long and difficult and much blood was lost. At its conclusion the child was in shock. However, he soon recovered and on Dec. 3 he was up and about. The interns were sure he could use his arm on that day. On Dec. 4 it was discovered that there was complete paralysis and anesthesia of both arms. The tendon reflexes were lost. Marks of the straps were still visible on the shoulders and the anesthesia and paralysis were distal to these marks. There was no weakness of the neck, chest or legs. The spinal fluid was normal. On Dec. 12, a reaction of degeneration was elicited in the long extensors of the forearms and the flexors of the elbows. Faradic responses were secured in the other muscles. On Dec. 29, there was some return of power in the flexors of the fingers and wrists and in the deltoids. Gradual recovery followed.

CASE HISTORY (U-495064).

A boy of 12 years went on a hike with the boy scouts carrying a heavy knapsack which contained so many items that it must have weighed about 50 lbs. After about three hours' march, he stopped to camp. His left arm was found to be completely paralysed and anesthetic. There was no pain at any time. Sensibility began to return within a few hours and on the next day some little power of movement had returned.

On examination seven days after the onset there was found to be profound weakness of the muscles of the left arm which were supplied by the 5th and 6th cervical nerve roots with loss of the biceps and radial tendon reflexes. There was slight weakness of all the other muscles of the arm. No sensory disturbances could be discovered. The electrical reactions were present. Recovery was rapid and complete.

CASE HISTORY (No. 525334).—*Girl of 16 years with slowly progressive paralysis of the muscles supplied by the dorsal interosseus nerves. The*

onset on the right was at age of 12 years; on the left at the age of 15 years. Operation revealed compression by tendon of supinator.

J. W., a girl of 16 years, was examined on Jan. 6, 1950. She stated that some four years before she had noticed that she could not extend the last two fingers of the right hand. Slowly the weakness extended involving the second finger and then the first. Last of all the wrist was affected and wristdrop developed. There was no pain at any time. Approximately two years elapsed before the paralysis was complete. At the age of 15 years, the last finger of the left hand began to get weak in the same way and the process slowly extended as it did in the right hand.

On examination there was pronounced atrophy and complete paralysis of the long extensors of the wrist and fingers on the right. On the left, there was great weakness of the long extensors of the last two digits and slight weakness of the long extensors of the third digit with some atrophy of the affected muscles. No other abnormalities could be found.

Dr. Otenasek exposed the dorsal interosseous nerve on the right and found it to be greatly compressed between a tendinous process from the supinator and the aponeurosis of the common extensor. The nerve was so fibrotic at that point that a segment was removed and end to end suture performed. Exploration on the left revealed the same condition, but here the compression was less severe and no resection was performed. It was believed that the condition at operation was that described by Woltman and Learmonth in 1934.

CASE HISTORY (No. 1095655).—*Girl of seventeen years suffered minor injury to left hand. The hand became cold, wet and painful. Later, the right hand and both feet were affected in the same way in the next two years. Repeated sympathectomies relieved symptoms in the legs and left hand but not in the right hand. Reflex sympathetic dystrophy.*

M. C., an immature, badly adjusted girl of seventeen years who had had an episode of retention of urine which was apparently psychogenic, fell in November 1961, and wrenched the fingers of the left hand. About two hours later, she began to have pain in the left hand. The hand became cold and wet. Sympathectomy at the upper thoracic level was performed with relief of symptoms.

Some time later, after a minimal injury, the right hand became affected in the same way. Again upper thoracic sympathectomy gave relief.

In March 1963, bilateral lumbar sympathectomy was performed because of symptoms already described in both feet. The results were excellent.

In the summer of 1963, a slight injury to the left hand seemed to cause a return of symptoms in both hands. The stellate ganglia were removed. The operation on the left was successful, but the right hand was not improved.

On examination, the right hand was icy cold. There was coldness of the wrist up to a point about four inches above the hand. The fingers were slightly cyanotic. The pulse at the wrist was reduced. Beads of sweat were

evident over the palmar aspect of the hand and fingers. The hand and fingers were tender to pressure and any movement caused pain so the patient did not move them. The joints were somewhat stiff. Slight edema of the hand concealed any atrophy of the muscles which might be present. The pin did not feel sharp over the cold area. There was some limitation of movement at the shoulder. A heating pad made the patient more comfortable and increased the range of movement of the fingers.

The left hand and both feet were warm and dry, and caused the patient no concern. It is of great interest that under psychotherapy, the hand soon became dry and warm.

CASE HISTORY.—*Radical operation for mastoiditis on the right side. Postoperative paralysis of the left vocal cord and Horner's syndrome on the left.*

R. B., a girl of 16 years, had had chronic mastoiditis since early childhood. Operation was performed and a cholesteatoma was removed. The patient was under anesthesia for 6 hours. She was placed on her back with her face rotated to the left so her chin was above her left shoulder. Her neck was strongly extended. When she regained consciousness, it was found that the left eyelid drooped, the left pupil was small and the voice was hoarse. It was found that the left vocal cord did not move. The soft palate lifted well. No evidence of damage to the phrenic nerve was found.

It was concluded that the stretching of the left sternomastoid muscle had caused pressure on the cervical sympathetic nerve and the laryngeal nerve and this pressure in addition to the prolonged anesthesia had led to damage to these nerves. The possibility that the affected nerves were also stretched as a result of the position of the head was also considered. There was evidence of return of function in a few weeks.

CASE HISTORY.—*Congenital dislocation of the hip. Reduction was followed by damage to the sciatic nerve.*

C. Z. was seen at the age of 20 months. The child was found to have congenital dislocation of the left hip. Reduction was accomplished without apparent difficulty. The child began to walk at 10 months, but did not use the left leg properly.

On examination there was atrophy of the left calf muscles. The left foot was held in supination and there was an extensive callus over the outer part of the sole of the left foot. No dorsal movement of the foot or toes was possible. No pronation was present for the supinators were shortened. The ankle jerk was lost but the knee jerk was present. Some loss of sensibility was found over the outer aspect of the foot and ankle.

CASE HISTORY.—*Injury to the sciatic nerve in a child as a result of injection into the buttock. Substantial recovery in 24 months.*

N. T., a little girl, was seen at the age of 7 years. She had been quite healthy until the age of 5 years when her tonsils were removed. Before operation she was given an injection in the left buttock. The operation

was performed without difficulty, but after operation it was found that the child could not walk. There was loss of movement at the left ankle. The child complained of pains in the left leg and pins and needles in the left foot.

The pain ceased after a time and the numbness diminished. The strength slowly returned.

On examination it was found that the left leg was slightly shorter than the right, and the child walked with a limp. The left foot displayed a high arch. The toes were extended at the proximal joints and flexed at the middle joints so the foot was shorter than the right foot. No definite weakness or atrophy of the muscles could be demonstrated and no loss of sensibility could be discovered. The left ankle jerk was lost, but the knee jerk was present. The plantar reflexes were normal.

CASE HISTORY.—*Pinching of the suprascapular nerve in the suprascapular notch on the left side and then on the right side.*

An adolescent boy had had severe pain in the region of the left scapula for 3 weeks. On examination, he was found to have atrophy and partial paralysis of the spinati on the left. Roentgenograms of the cervical spine and a cervical myelogram were negative. At operation, it was found that the suprascapulae nerve was pinched in the supraclavicular notch. The nerve was freed. The pain stopped at once and the muscles rapidly regained their strength.

BIBLIOGRAPHY

BAILEY, G. G. JR.: Nerve injuries in supracondylar fractures of the humerus in children. New England J. Med., 221:260, 1939.

BONNEY, G.: The value of axon responses in determining the site of lesions in traction injuries of the brachial plexus. Brain, 77:588, 1954.

CHILDRESS, H. M.: Recurrent ulnar nerve dislocation at the elbow. J. Bone & Joint Surg., 38, A: 978, 1956.

COMBES, M. A. *et al.*: Sciatic nerve injury in infants. J.A.M.A., 173:1336, 1960.

DENNY-BROWN, D. AND BRENNER, C.: Lesion in peripheral nerve resulting from compression by spring clip. Arch. Neurol. & Psychiat., 52:1, 1944.

DOYLE, J. R.: Narrowing of the intervertebral disc space in children. J. Bone & Joint Surg., 42, A:1191, 1960.

FRENCH, J. D. *et al.*: The mode of extension of contrast substances injected into peripheral nerves. J. Neuropath. & Exper. Neurol., 7:47, 1948.

GILLES, F. H. AND FRENCH, J.: Post-injection sciatic nerve palsies in infants and children. J. Pediat., 58:195, 1961.

HUSTEAD, A. P. *et al.*: Non traumatic, progressive paralysis of the deep radial nerve. Arch. of Neurol. and Psychiat., 79:269, 1958.

JONES, R. AND LOVETT, R. W.: Orthopedic Surgery. William Wood, New York, 1923. p. 560.

KIRK, E. G. AND LEWIS, D. D.: Regeneration in peripheral nerves. Bull. Johns Hopkins Hosp., 28:71, 1917.

LEWIS, DEAN AND HUBER, G. C.: Amputation neuromas. Their development and prevention. Arch. Surg., 1:85, 1920.

LYONS, W. R. AND WOODHALL, B.: Atlas of Peripheral Nerve Injuries. London, W. B. Saunders, 1949.

MAGEE, K. R.: Neuritis of the deep palmar branch of the ulnar nerve. Arch. Neurol. & Psychiat., 73:200, 1955.

MILLER, D. S. AND DE TAKATS, G.: Post-traumatic dystrophy of the extremities. Surg. Gynec. & Obst., **75**:558, 1942.

MILONE, F. P. *etal.:* Childhood intervertebral disc infection. J.A.M.A., **181**:1029, 1962.

MOLDAVER, J.: Tourniquet paralysis syndrome. Arch. Surg., **68**:136, 1954.

Nerve Injury Committee: Peripheral Nerve Injuries. Her Majesty's Stationery Office, London, 1954.

O'CONNELL, J. E. A.: Intervertebral disc protrusions in childhood. Brit. J. Surg., **47**:611, 1960.

PATERSON, F. P. AND MORTON, K. S.: Neurologic defects after pelvic fracture. Surg. Gynec. & Obst., **112**:702, 1961.

PATTERSON, STEWART *et al.:* Orthopedic Surgery of Injuries. Oxford Press, 1921.

PEASE, C. N.: Spondylolisthesis in children. Clin. Orthop., **52**:187, 1967.

PHALEN, G. S.: Spontaneous compression of the median nerve at the wrist. J.A.M.A., **145**:1128, 1951.

POLLOCK, L. J. AND DAVIS, L. E.: Peripheral Nerve Lesions. New York, Paul Hoeber, 1933.

RICHARDS, R. L.: Causalgia. Arch. of Neurol., **16**:339, 1967.

ROBLES, J.: Brachial plexus avulsion. Jour. Neurosurg., **27**:434, 1968.

SILVERMAN, F. N.: Calcification of the intervertebral discs in childhood. Radiology, **62**:801, 1954.

SIMMEL, M. L.: Amputation phantoms in childhood. J. Neurol., Neurosurg. & Psychiat., **25**:69, 1962.

SMITH, R. F. AND TAYLOR, T. K. F.: Inflammatory lesions of intervertebral discs in children. Jour. Bone and Joint Surg., A **49**:1508, 1967.

STAFFORD, J. S. B.: Thermalgia (Causalgia) . Lancet, **11**:195, 1917.

SUNDERLAND, S.: Disturbances of sensibility in an area not innervated by the severed nerve. Brain, **75**:585, 1952.

————: An unusual disturbance of muscular function resulting from severance of peripheral nerves. Brain, **75**:589, 1952.

WEBB, J. H. *et al.:* Protruded lumbar intervertebral discs in children. J.A.M.A., **154**:1153, 1954.

WHITE, H. H.: Pack palsy: a neurological complication of scouting. Pediatrics, **41**:1001, 1968.

WOLTMAN, H. W. AND LEARMONTH, J. R.: Progressive paralysis of the nervus dorsalis interosseus. Brain, **57**:25, 1934.

WOODHALL, B.: Surgical repair of acute peripheral nerve injury. Surg. Clin. North America, **31**: 369, 1951.

WOODHALL, B. AND DAVIS, C.: Changes in the arteriae nervorum in peripheral nerve injuries. J. Neuropath. & Exp. Neurol., **9**:335, 1950.

COMPRESSION OF THE ROOTS OF THE BRACHIAL PLEXUS BY CERVICAL RIBS

Definition.—The essential cause of this condition is an abnormal relationship between the bony structures of the neck and the lower roots of the brachial plexus which leads to stretching, compression and loss of function. Supernumerary ribs are usually responsible but may be present without giving rise to symptoms and, on the other hand, the symptoms of root compression may be due to pressure against a normal first rib.

Pathological Anatomy.—There is a good deal of variation in the anatomical findings. The rib may be well formed or may be a mere bony nodule attached to the transverse process of the seventh cervical vertebra. In most cases, the rib is small and connected with the first rib by a fibrous cord inserted just posterior to the subclavian sulcus. The seventh cervical root usually lies upon the bony process and the eighth root upon the fibrous

cord. If the first thoracic root is present, it usually lies on the cord also. The subclavian artery lies either anterior to the cord or upon it; rarely beneath it. The nerve trunk may be compressed between the bone and the insertion of the scalene muscle. These are merely the most common relations and many other variations are found. Sargent has described a large number of possibilities. Cervical ribs are almost always bilateral, although one rib may be much larger than the other. It has been shown by Sargent and others that cervical ribs are usually associated with a prefixed plexus. That is, there is a large contribution from the fourth cervical segment and little, if any, from the first thoracic. In some cases we find rudimentary first ribs which bear the same relation to the brachial plexus as do cervical ribs and give rise to the same symptoms. These rudimentary ribs are found in association with post-fixed plexuses. The sympathetic fibers which convey vasomotor impulses to the arm lie in the eighth cervical and first thoracic roots in a superficial position, so they may easily be compressed. Sympathetic fibers destined for the head, however, have been given off to the cervical sympathetic ganglia before they reach the neighborhood of the rib and are, therefore, not involved directly.

Clinical Features.—It has been estimated that about 1 per cent of the population have some traces of cervical ribs. These ribs are congenital peculiarities and are, therefore, just as common in children as in adults. As a matter of fact, however, one finds very little mention of cervical ribs in textbooks of pediatrics for symptoms of root compression rarely arise before the age of 20 years and the discovery of supernumerary ribs in childhood must be fortuitous in most cases. Nevertheless, several observers have recorded instances in which cervical ribs in children have given rise to symptoms of spinal root compression identical with those so often seen in adults and it seems probable that the condition is more frequent than it is generally believed to be. Cervical ribs may be found in several members of a family and have, indeed, been traced through the number of generations. Sporadic cases also appear. When the ribs are large, there is a bony tumor at the base of the neck overlying which the subclavian artery may be palpated. Just behind the artery there is usually a tender cord which represents the roots of the brachial plexus. The artery may be dilated distal to the rib and a bruit or even a palpable thrill may be present. In many cases it is impossible to feel the ribs and palpation is, in general, quite unreliable.

Nervous symptoms are present in not more than 10 per cent of cases. Despite the fact that the ribs are almost always bilateral, the symptoms are almost invariably unilateral. The symptoms may develop during childhood as early as the fourth year but are usually not detected before the age of twenty years. Drooping of the shoulders from poor muscular tone, paraly-

sis of the trapezius, anesthesia, or wasting illness may precipitate the symptoms. Females are affected three times as often as males and the right arm is more apt to be involved than the left.

The motor symptoms include weakness of the hand and forearm with atrophy of the intrinsic muscles of the hand and of the superficial flexors of the wrist and fingers. A very typical distribution of the atrophy is that which selects the abductor and opponens pollicis and spares the flexor brevis and adductor as well as the interossei. In other cases, the adductor, flexor brevis and interossei are atrophied and the opponens and abductor are spared.

Pain is present in most cases. This is projected to the hand and forearm. It is worse on exertion and when the arm is allowed to hang down and is relieved by elevation of the arm and by rest. Paresthesias and numbness, as well as loss of cutaneous sensibility, are found over the ulnar half of the hand and inner margin of the forearm. Less frequently the sensory disturbances extend over the radial half of the hand. In many cases, pain and thermal sensibility are reduced without demonstrable loss of tactile sensibility but loss of tactile sensibility may occur alone. Several observers claim that cervical ribs in children may be manifest by recurrent attacks of pain in the neck associated with muscle spasm and with torticollis. I have never been able to understand how such symptoms can be connected with any common type of cervical rib, however.

Various vascular disturbances are common. The pulse may be small or absent. It is often reduced when the shoulder is depressed and grows larger when the shoulder is elevated. In those cases in which the pulse is normal, if the arm is raised above the head and the head turned sharply to the opposite side, the pulse may be obliterated. This is sometimes called the Halsted test. It is claimed that by this maneuver the subclavian artery is compressed between the cervical rib and the scalenus anticus muscle. Occlusion of the artery may occur and gangrene of the fingers is described. It has been claimed that the change in the arteries which leads to occlusion is a proliferation of the intima resulting from vasomotor disturbances, and, indeed, syndromes which simulate Raynaud's disease very closely are seen with cervical ribs. The hand may turn red or blue upon exertion and profuse sweating may occur at the same time. There is sometimes edema.

In some instances, thrombi may form in the subclavian artery due to compression by the rib and may lead to reduction of the circulation in the arm due to narrowing of the lumen or to embolism. If the thrombus extends to the origin of the common carotid artery, emboli may enter the carotid artery and cause contralateral hemiparesis. This can occur only on the right side.

A number of congenital malformations are associated with cervical ribs.

Scoliosis or defects in the cervical spine are, perhaps, most common. Deformities of the thorax and club-hand with absence of the radius or ulnar are also described. Many cases have been reported in which syringomyelia and cervical ribs were present together.

Diagnosis.—The demonstration of cervical ribs in association with slowly developing atrophy of the muscles of the hand, pain and other disturbances of sensibility with or without vasomotor changes is sufficient to establish the diagnosis with a high degree of probability. Unfortunately, one or more of these diagnostic criteria may be absent in certain cases. Sometimes the ribs cannot be clearly visualized in the roentgenograms, for they may be chiefly fibrous or cartilaginous or they may be concealed by the shadow of the transverse processes. In other cases, the pressure may be exerted by a rudimentary or even a normal first rib. In the last analysis, the symptoms depend not so much upon the presence of a bony anomaly as upon an abnormal relation between the nerve roots and the bones. On the other hand, cervical ribs are very common and at least 90 per cent cause no symptoms. It is inevitable, therefore, that they should sometimes be associated with lesions of the certical nerve roots due to entirely different causes.

Syringomyelia is sometimes accompanied by cervical ribs and if the symptoms happen to be confined to the hand, the diagnosis may be in doubt until the extension of the symptoms makes the nature of the process evident. The same statement, of course, applies to other diseases involving the lowest roots of the plexus if they are by chance associated with asymptomatic rudimentary ribs. The neurological signs are most important, for we must be prepared to diagnose bony compression of the lowest roots of the brachial plexus in the absence of cervical ribs and the presence of supernumerary ribs cannot be considered conclusive unless the symptoms are typical.

Southam and Bythell studied a series of 2,000 roentgenograms of children and found cervical ribs, which had given rise to symptoms, in nine. In five cases a clinical diagnosis of caries of the cervical spine had been made and in three cases the diagnosis was torticollis.

Prognosis.—In some cases, the symptoms progress slowly until the hand is almost useless but in the majority of cases, the condition finally becomes arrested before the function of the hand is severely impaired.

Treatment.—If the symptoms are advancing rapidly so it seems probable that the use of the hand will be impaired or if there is severe pain, excision of the rib should be seriously considered. We may anticipate that removal of the rib will stop the progress of the symptoms but if the condition has been present for more than a short time there may be little or no return of function. It is important, therefore, to operate early if at all. In

many cases dissection of the plexus is followed by a material increase in the symptoms although if proper skill is exercised only transient ill effects result. The writer has also observed a return of symptoms after a number of years which may be attributed to constriction of the roots by scar tissue. In order to obviate these disadvantages, an operation has been described in which the insertion of the anterior scalene muscle is severed permitting the first rib to sag down as well as the cervical rib which is usually attached to the first rib. The brachial plexus is not exposed in this operation and the ill-effects enumerated above may be avoided. It is not effective in all cases, however.

BIBLIOGRAPHY

Adson, A. W. and Coffey, J. R.: Cervical rib; method of anterior approach for the relief of symptoms by section of scalenus anticus. Ann. Surg., 85:839, 1927.

Agassiz, C. D. S. and Sykes, K. A. H.: Cervical ribs in children. Brit. Med. J., 1:71, 1925.

Bassoe, P.: The coincidence of cervical ribs and syringomyelia. Arch. Neurol. & Psychiat., 4:542, 1920.

Davis, D. B. and King, J. C.: Cervical rib in early life. Am. J. Dis. Child., 56:744, 1938.

de Villiers, J. C.: The brachiocephalic syndrome. Brit. Med. Jour., ii:140, 1966.

Sargent, P.: Lesions of the brachial plexus associated with rudimentary ribs. Brain, 44:95, 1921.

Shucksmith, H. S.: Emboli from cervical rib damage. Brit. Med. J., 5361:835, 1963.

Southam, A. H. and Bythell, W. J. S.: Cervical ribs in children. Brit. Med. J., 1:844, 1924.

Stopford, J. S. B. and Telford, E. D.: Vascular complications of cervical ribs. Brit. J. Surg., 18:557, 1930-31.

Wilson, S. A. K.: Some points on the symptomatology of cervical rib, with especial reference to muscular wasting. Proc. Roy. Soc. Med. London, 6: Pt. 1, Clin. Sec. p. 133, 1912-13.

INJURIES OF CEREBRAL ARTERIES BY TRAUMA

Carotid Arteries: Frantzen *et al.* report 6 cases in which a blow to the head or neck resulted in thrombosis of a carotid artery. It was suggested that sudden stretching of the artery was probably responsible for the thrombus formation. Boldrey has shown that prolonged or violent turning of the head may cause thrombosis of the contralateral carotid artery as a result of compression of the artery by the transverse process of the axis.

Vertebral Arteries: Suden death may result when fracture or dislocation of one of the cervical vertebrae causes compression of the vertebral arteries. It has been shown that strong rotation of the head will cause compression of these arteries. Chiropractic manipulation may cause softening in the brain stem and cerebellum. I have seen such a case in which the basilar artery was thrombosed. Illingsworth has reported sudden loss of consciousness in children who had congenital fusion of the cervical vertebrae. I have seen a boy of 17 years who had episodes of syncope, nystagmus, vertigo, diplopia, and blurred vision induced by movements of the

head. There was a defect in the odontoid process and the second cervical vertebra was loose. When this vertebra was fused with the adjacent vertebrae, the symptoms ceased. From and Piner describe progressive quadriplegia in children who had agenesis of the odontoid process.

BIBLIOGRAPHY

BOLDREY, E. *et al.:* The role of atlantoid compression in the etiology of carotid thrombosis. Jour of Neursurg., **13:**127, 1956.

FORD, F. R.: Syncope, vertigo, disturbances of vision and diplopia resulting from intermittent obstruction of the vertebral arteries due to a defect in the odontoid process and excessive mobility of the second cervical vertebra. Bull. Johns Hopkins Hosp., **91:**168, 1952.

FORD, F. R. AND CLARK, D.: Thrombosis of the basilar artery with softenings in the cerebellum and brain stem due to manipulation of the neck. Bull. Johns Hopkins Hospital, **98:**37, 1956.

FROM, G. H. AND PITNER, S. E.: Late progressive quadriparesis due to odontoid agenesis. Arch. of Neurol., **9:**291, 1963.

FRANTZEN, E.: Cerebral artery occlusion in children due to trauma to the head and neck. Neurology, **11:**695, 1961.

ILLINGSWORTH, R. S.: Attacks of unconsciousness associated with fused cervical vertebrae. Arch. of Dis. of Childh., **31:**6, 1956.

PRATT-THOMAS, H. R. AND BERGER, K. E.: Cerebellar and spinal injuries after chiropractic manipulations. J.A.M.A., **133:**600, 1947.

GWINN, J. L. AND SMITH, J. L.: Acquired and congenital absence of the odontoid process. Amer. Jour. Roentgen., **88:**424, 1962.

INVOLVEMENT OF THE RADIAL NERVE IN ASSOCIATION WITH SUBCUTANEOUS FAT NECROSIS OF THE NEWBORN

Subcutaneous fat necrosis is sometimes seen in newborn infants. The lesions are marked at first by induration of the subcutaneous tissues but later, the affected areas are represented by shallow depressions. They are found as a rule overlying bony prominences on the shoulders, cheeks and arms. The legs are not affected so frequently. These lesions gradually disappear in the course of a few weeks and then small foci of calcium are seen in roentgenograms. It is believed that the initial induration is due to solidification of the subcutaneous fat which is then absorbed. Obstetrical trauma is thought to play an important role, but the cause of this condition is not entirely clear.

My purpose in mentioning subcutaneous fat necrosis is to call attention to the fact that when the lesion lies on the outer aspect of the arm above the elbow it may be responsible for damage to the radial nerve. Lightwood has reported two cases of this condition. In both cases there was complete recovery within two months. Feldman has studied eight cases. He states that there was abnormal uterine action in all cases and in several a constriction ring was discovered in the uterus. Recovery occurred in all cases.

I have seen only one case by the courtesy of Dr. David Clark. The clini-

cal picture was identical in every respect with that described by Lightwood. There seems to be no reason why other spinal nerves should not be involved in the same way.

BIBLIOGRAPHY

FELDMAN, C. V.: Radial nerve palsy in the newborn. Arch. Dis. Childhood, **32**:469, 1957.
LIGHTWOOD, R.: Radial nerve palsy associated with localized subcutaneous fat necrosis in the newborn. Arch. Dis. Childhood, **26**:436, 1951.

INJURY OF THE NERVOUS SYSTEM BY RADIUM AND BY ROENTGEN RAYS

As a result of the work of Murphy and others, it is now well known that therapeutic irradiation over the pelvis during pregnancy is fraught with great danger to the fetus. Radium and roentgen rays seem to be equally harmful. Murphy has contrasted the fate of 74 children whose mothers received irradiation after conception with that of 402 children whose mothers were treated before conception took place. In the first group of 74, some 38 (51 per cent) were unhealthy or abnormal. Of these 38, 13 showed mild disturbances, such as failure to gain weight or weakness, or died early. Murphy does not stress such conditions since they might occur in any group of unselected babies. Gross deformities were found in 33 per cent or 25 children. In 17 cases (23 per cent) there were microcephaly and idiocy, in 2 hydrocephalus and in 6 cases there were idiocy, blindness, malformation of the head, spina bifida, club-feet or divergent squint. Murphy considers microcephaly and idiocy the characteristic effect of radiation of the fetus. Goldstein and Murphy give a detailed study of a child whose mother was given heavy radium treatment for carcinoma of the uterus at about the sixth month of her pregnancy. At birth, the head was noted to be small. Mental and physical development were defective from the first. At five years he began to walk clumsily but never learned to talk, to feed himself or dress. Cadwalader examined the child at the age of 12 years. The head then measured 48.8 cm in circumference. The cranial nerves were normal. The child was much undernourished. Muscles were small and rigid. Gait was spastic and weak. The tendon reflexes were increased and the plantar reflexes were equivocal. Psychometric tests showed that the child was a low grade idiot. It is claimed that even roentgenograms made for diagnostic purposes during pregnancy may in some instances have an adverse effect on the fetus.

Irradiation of the female pelvis before conception is apparently relatively innocuous. Thus, among 402 children born of mothers who had received irradiation before they became pregnant, only 7 were defective. Microcephaly, anencephaly, parietal bone defect, unnamed deformity, congenital heart defect, tracheal stenosis and absence of right forearm were

all noted once. Only 1.7 per cent were defective in contrast to 33 per cent in the first group in which irradiation took place during pregnancy. Murphy does not feel sure that preconception irradiation can be blamed, for there was no uniformity in the type of defect and the incidence was not much above the average expectation. However, it is known as a result of experimental work that the germ cells are very sensitive to irradiation. Not only does sterility often result but defects have been produced in mice and fruit flies which have been transmitted to subsequent generations, according to Mendelian laws. Anatomical changes have also been found in the chromosomes. It is quite possible, therefore, that even preconception irradiation of the ovaries or testicles may have its effect on the offspring.

Heavy irradiation of the head after birth may also cause destructive changes in the brain. There is an early reaction of inflammatory nature which reaches its maximum within five weeks and then recedes. A late reaction begins from one to seven years after the irradiation and may result in widespread areas of necrosis apparently due to damage to the blood vessels. Scholz and Hsu describe cases in which convulsions, dementia, signs of focal lesions and death resulted. The brain stem and the spinal cord may also be injured as a result of heavy radiation for malignant growths.

Rider describes three cases in which brain damage developed after radiation of the posterior fossa. One patient died four weeks later and the other two patients got well. The symptoms were nystagmus, cerebellar ataxia, dysarthria, dysphagia, nausea and vomiting.

The spinal cord and brain stem may be damaged. I have seen one case in which the spinal cord was liquefied by heavy radiation. There was intense pain for months.

Leach states that irradiation of a neoplasm in the region of the ear may cause loss of hearing and loss of vestibular function. This process may be progressive and may first become apparent 6 months after treatment. Total deafness and loss of vestibular function may develop years later.

I have seen one case in which roentgenotherapy for ring worm of the scalp caused permanent loss of hair on the right side of the scalp. Several years later, the patient developed left hemiparesis with some sensory loss of cortical type. Focal convulsions developed and persisted despite medication. Exploration revealed extensive scarring and atrophy of the cortex just beneath the area of alopecia.

It should also be mentioned that carcinoma may result from heavy radiation especially in middle-aged persons and radiation sarcoma may occur in children. We have seen sarcoma in children who have had large dosage for retinoblastoma. Leukemia is another result of heavy radiation, it seems.

It has been found that children who were subjected to prenatal radiation from the atomic bomb dropped upon Hiroshima between the seventh

and fifteenth weeks of fetal life frequently showed mental defect, microcephaly and often leukemia.

Damage to the genes by atomic radiation is said to lead to an increased incidence of malformed children with mental defects and epilepsy.

> CASE HISTORY (Ped. A-8472).—*Mental deficiency, convulsions, ataxia and weakness in a child whose mother received intensive roentgenotherapy for a malignant abdominal neoplasm during pregnancy.*
>
> M. L. G. was delivered by Caesarian section. Her mother had developed an abdominal tumor during pregnancy. Exploration at the 5th month revealed a malignant growth involving the left kidney. Intensive treatment by deep roentgenotherapy was administered until delivery. At birth, the baby seemed to be normal but, within a few months, it was evident that development was not progressing properly. Generalized convulsions appeared at the sixth month and recurred at irregular intervals afterwards. There were also many minor seizures. At the age of 2 years and 9 months, the child could not stand or walk alone and made no effort to talk.
>
> Examination revealed a small but adequately nourished child of 2 years and 9 months. The head was very small. The cranial nerves seemed to be normal. All movements were ataxic and weak. The gait, when the child was supported, was found to show profound ataxia. Muscle tone was diminished on passive movement. The tendon reflexes were all brisk although no clonus could be elicited. The plantar reactions were variable. Vision could not be tested for the child's attention could not be attracted. Mental development was obviously defective and psychometric tests gave a mental age of 10 months.

BIBLIOGRAPHY

BODEN, G.: Radiation myelitis of the cervical cord. Brit. J. Radiol., **21**:464, 1948.

————: Radiation myelitis of the brain stem. J. Fac. Radiologists, **2**:79, 1950.

Committee on genetic effects of atomic radiation. Genetic effects of atomic radiation. Science, **123**:1157, 1956.

HOLLINGSWORTH, J. W.: Preliminary summary of the atomic bomb casualty commission. New England Med. J., **263**:481, 1960.

LEACH, W.: Irradiation of the ear. Jour. of Laryng., **79**:870, 1965.

LYMAN, R. S., KUPALOV, P. S. AND SCHOLZ, W.: Effect of roentgen rays on the central nervous system. Arch. Neurol. & Psychiat., **29**:56, 1933.

MILLER, R. W.: Delayed effects occurring within the first decade after exposure of young individuals to the Hiroshima atomic bomb. Pediatrics, **18**:1, 1956.

MURPHY, D. P.: The outcome of 625 pregnancies in women subjected to pelvic radium or roentgen irradiation. Am. J. Obst. & Gynec., **18**:179 (references), 1929.

MURPHY, D. P. AND GOLDSTEIN, J.: Microcephalic idiocy following radium therapy for uterine cancer during pregnancy. Am. J. Obst. & Gynec., **18**:189 (references), 1929.

RIDER, W. D.: Radiation damage to the brain. J. Canad. A. Radiol., **14**:67, 1963.

SABANAS, A. O.: Post-radiation sarcoma of bone. Cancer, **9**:528, 1956.

SCHOLZ, W. AND HSU, Y. K.: Late damage from roentgen irradiation of the human brain. Arch. Neurol. & Psychiat., **40**:928, 1938.

WACHOWSKI, T. J. AND CHENAULT, H.: Degenerative effects of large doses of roentgen rays on the human brain. Radiology, **45**:227, 1945.

SUN STROKE, AND HIGH FEVER AND REACTION TO COLD

Definition.—This condition is also termed *heat stroke*. It must be distinguished from *heat cramps* and from *heat exhaustion*. In the former of these last two conditions, we find painful cramps in the muscles of the extremities and abdomen. The temperature is normal. This condition is attributed to loss of sodium chloride as a result of excessive sweating. Injections of saline solution will give relief. In *heat exhaustion*, there is headache, dizziness, sweating, vomiting, dehydration and oliguria. The temperature remains normal. This is attributed to reduction of the blood plasma. *Heat, or sun, stroke* is defined by the following description.

Etiology.—Prolonged exposure to great heat is the essential cause. It has been claimed that direct exposure to bright sunlight is necessary for the production of this condition, but this is probably not true. Recent studies have led to the belief that there is failure of the heat regulating mechanisms with hyperpyrexia and shock, leading to damage to the brain and abdominal viscera.

Pathological Anatomy.—According to Malmud, Haymaker and Custer, the most constant finding is degeneration of the neurons in the cerebellum, the cerebral cortex, and basal ganglia. Hemorrhages in the walls of the third ventricle, around the aqueduct and in the floor of the fourth ventricle are common. Congestion and edema of the brain are found in some instances. Petechial hemorrhages and degenerative changes are found in the abdominal viscera.

Clinical Features.—The onset is abrupt as a rule without prodromata, although in some instances prodromata occur. Among these may be mentioned dizziness, faintness, diarrhea, vomiting and thirst.

Cessation of sweating is often the initial symptom and this is followed by headache, vertigo, and fever which may range up to 106° or even 111°F. The patient soon falls into convulsions and coma ensues. There is rigidity of the muscles and a bilateral Babinski sign is often present. Hemiplegia and aphasia may occur. Cyanosis, tetany, diarrhea, anuria, hematuria, and jaundice are sometimes seen. There are signs of shock in some cases with low blood pressure, rapid thready pulse and shallow respiration.

Baxter and Tescham state that cellular destruction resulting from hyperthermia and extreme tissue hypoxia secondary to shock, extracellular movement of potassium subsequent to hypernatremia and acidosis and destruction of heat-damaged red blood cells probably contribute to hyperkalemia and myocardial potassium intoxication. Renal ischemia and shock may cause acute renal failure. Hypernatremia induces central nervous system symptoms.

In 70 per cent of all fatal cases death occurs in 24 hours and in the re-

maining 30 per cent, in 2 to 12 days. Among patients who survive sun stroke cerebellar ataxia is prominent. Other neurological disturbances may be observed and mental changes may be pronounced.

I have seen a boy of 12 years who developed left hemiparesis and a girl of 18 who had aphasia after exposure to hot sunlight. It seemed that dehydration and concentration of the blood had caused a single local softening due to thrombosis for these patients did not display the high fever or the usual picture of sun stroke.

Hartman states that artificial fever produced by the electric cabinet will cause symptoms not unlike those of sun stroke. He mentions a fatal case which occurred after 14 treatments had been given. The temperature was raised to 107.6°F. The patient collapsed and died. Small areas of necrosis and minute hemorrhages were found in the cerebral cortex.

Stephen describes cases in which hypertherma often severe and fulminant and sometimes irreversible and fatal occurs for no apparent reason during operation under general anesthesia.

Egerton *et al.* state that cerebral damage occurs in cardiac surgery when hypothermia to less than 12°C. is produced. Patients may remain comatose for hours and have convulsions after rewarming. Focal neurological signs may be found and intelligence may be reduced. In some cases, death results.

Stephens states that during operation for congenital heart disease hypothermia of more than thirty minutes may cause sensory or sensory and motor polyneuritis. He mentions eighteen cases of this type. He also mentions one case in which extensive intracranial hemorrhages developed and another in which neuronal ischemic changes occurred.

Shelley and Caro describe a rare congenital condition in which exposure to cold causes muscular spasms, extreme muscular rigidity, diffuse erythema without urticaria and profuse sweating. Touching the skin with ice may cause such symptoms for five minutes even if the ice is applied for only five seconds.

Penner and McNair describe damage to the retinae due to looking at the sun. Vision is blurred at once. In a day or two, a central scotoma can be demonstrated. First a yellow spot is seen in the region of the fovea. Then within 21 days, macular erythema appears and about the 35th day pigmentation appears which may last for months. Vision may be reduced to 20/200. Of 52 eyes studied, 25 had recovered normal vision within 6 months. Another 23 regained vision to between 20/25 and 20/40. The others did not recover good vision. Steroids were used without effect.

Diagnosis.—The diagnosis depends upon the features described above. Heat cramps and heat exhaustion are eliminated at once by the fact that the temperature is not elevated in these conditions.

Prognosis.—In most instances the patient either dies in a short time or makes a complete recovery. Freeman has pointed out that in some rare instances there may be lasting residua. The commonest motor disturbance seems to be cerebellar ataxia but spasticity and athetoid movements are described. Mental changes are probably most frequent of all residua but their incidence is unknown.

Treatment.—Treatment seems to be symptomatic. Sponging with cold water is advised to reduce the fever but ice water baths which have been recommended are probably too drastic. Fluids should be supplied in adequate amounts and efforts to maintain proper levels of the electrolytes made.

Baxter and Tescham advise rapid lowering of the body temperature by immersing the patient in ice water and restitution of the plasma volume by the administration of salt and water.

BIBLIOGRAPHY

BAXTER, C. R. AND TESCHAM, P. E.: Atypical heat stroke with hypernatremia, acute renal failure and fulminating potassium intoxication. Arch. Int. Med., **101:**1040, 1958.

EGERTON, N. *et al.:* Brain damage in profound hypothermia. Ann. Surg., **157:**366, 1963.

FREEDMAN, D. AND SCHENTHAL, J.: A parenchymatous cerebellar syndrome following protracted high body temperature. Neurology, **3:**513, 1953.

FREEMAN, W. AND DUMOFF, E.: Cerebellar syndrome following heat stroke. Arch. Neurol. & Psychiat., **5:**67, 1944.

GORIN, R. *et al.:* A propos des formes graves du coup de chaleur du nourrisson. Sem. Hop. Ann. Pediat., **39:**296, 1963.

HARTMAN, F. W.: Lesions of the brain following fever. J.A.M.A., **109:**2116, 1937.

MALMUD, N., HAYMAKER, W. AND CUSTER, R. P.: Heat stroke: A clinicopathologic study of 125 fatal cases. Military Surgeon, **99:**397, 1946.

PENNER, R. AND MCNAIR, J. N.: Eclipse blindness. Amer. Jour. Ophthal., **61:**1452, 1966.

SHELLEY, W. B. AND CARO, W. A.: Cold erythema. J.A.M.A., **180:**639, 1962.

STEPHENS, J. W.: Neurological sequelae of congenital heart surgery. Arch. Neurol., **7:**450, 1963.

STEPHEN, C. R.: Fulminant hyperthermia during anesthesia and surgery. J. Amer. Med. Ass., **202:**178, 1967.

INJURY OF THE NERVOUS SYSTEM BY LIGHTNING AND ELECTRIC CURRENTS

Etiology.—Occasional cases of paralysis resulting from lightning may be discovered scattered throughout the entire range of medical literature and in recent years a small number of cases have been observed in which definite damage has been inflicted upon the nervous system as a result of accidental shocks derived from high tension currents such as are employed for industrial purposes.

Pathological Anatomy.—The lesions in the nervous system have been studied by Langworthy and others. Petechial hemorrhages are found in the brain and meninges. There are also peculiar cavities around the small blood vessels consisting of a central rarefied zone and a peripheral zone of con-

densation. These, it has been suggested, are due to bubbles of gas formed by heat or electrolysis. Relatively large cavities may be found in the central gray matter of the spinal cord. The neurons may be completely necrotic or less severely injured. Later, secondary degeneration may result and proliferation of the microglia and astrocytes. These lesions have been found in the brains of electrocuted criminals and in experimental animals submitted to electric shocks, as well as in the victims of industrial accidents. Very few anatomical studies have been made upon patients injured by lightning.

Clinical Features.—Jaffe has collected figures to show that from eight to nine hundred deaths occur in the United States every year from electric currents and about two hundred deaths in Europe. The number of persons killed by lightning is also astonishingly large. As a rule, the patient dies almost at once or recovers without any sign of injury to the nervous system. In a small percentage of cases, however, paralysis and other neurological syndromes result and it is with this group of cases that we are particularly concerned in this discussion. The currents of low voltage employed in almost every household at present, apparently rarely, if ever, cause injury to the nervous system although they not infrequently cause fatal fibrillation of the ventricular muscles of the heart.

In case of high voltage shock the patient may die at once as a result of paralysis of respiration or fibrillation of the ventricles of the heart. If the shock is not immediately fatal, the patient may be unconscious for a variable period. In some cases, consciousness is never regained and death may occur in convulsions several days later. If the patient survives, there may be various mental disturbances during convalescence. The site of contact is usually marked by definite lesions. Lightning often causes extensive burns and penetrating wounds. Such burns may have a pattern resembling a tree and are termed arborization burns. In industrial accidents we usually find current markings which are described as grayish-yellow slightly elevated areas containing a central depression. Small metallic granules may be found in such wounds.

Transient cerebral palsies have been mentioned repeatedly in cases in which the electric current passed through the head and a few cases are described in which hemiplegia persisted. When these are due to lightning, they may be associated with necrosis of the skull overlying the lesion. As a rule, of course, such injuries are fatal at once. Lesions of the retinae are sometimes seen and cataracts are well recognized sequels of electrical injuries. Deafness may result and rarely other cranial nerves may be affected.

Transient paraplegia has been described as a result of shocks which are transmitted through the spinal cord but persistent paraplegia is very unusual. As a rule, the paralysis lasts only a few hours and disappears completely. Langworthy, however, has shown that both transient and persisting

paraplegia may be produced in animals by experimental shocks of high voltage. Panse has recently claimed that electrical shocks may give rise to delayed muscular atrophy and flaccid paralysis. He described cases in which the initial symptoms are mild, perhaps no more than slight numbness or weakness of the affected limb. Weeks or months after the accident, however, muscular atrophy begins to develop and may extend eventually so as to involve all four extremities.

Farrell and Starr review the literature and report a case of their own. It seems that the commonest delayed effect of electrical injuries to the nervous system is progressive atrophy and weakness of the arms or legs. Cerebral syndromes, spinal cord damage and injury to peripheral nerves are all reported. The onset may be delayed for a few days or for two years.

The spinal nerves may be affected in electric burns but seem to be no less resistant to electric currents than the other tissues so they usually escape unless there is definite tissue necrosis. Hesser has recently published the case of a man who apparently sustained severe injury to the muscles and blood vessels of one arm.

Coleman states that the cardiac arrest or ventricular fibrillation is the usual cause of death. The damage to the brain may be due to hemorrhage, cortical tears and subdural hematoma. However, patients who survive have only transient paraplegia. Other effects include cataracts, ruptured tympanic membranes, loss of taste and vertigo. Blood pressure may be elevated for several months. Psychotic reactions, myocardial infarctions and leukemia are rare effects.

Thousands of persons in this country have been given electric shock therapy for psychoses though few children are treated in this manner. The results include loss of memory and changes in personality which may eventually recede or persist to some extent. Small hemorrhages and scattered cell degeneration are found in the brains of subjects who succumb soon after treatment.

Diagnosis.—The diagnosis depends upon the history of a violent electrical shock and the physical evidence of injury to the nervous system. Chronic neurological syndromes are very rarely the result of electrical currents. Every case must be taken to rule out hysteria and other diseases of the nervous system. In industrial accidents, compensation neuroses play the major role. Nevertheless, there can be no doubt that electric shocks, especially those of high voltage, may cause serious damage to the nervous system without fatal results. Experimental work has established this fact beyond question.

Prognosis.—In general, injuries which are not fatal at once admit of a favorable prognosis. Paralyses usually last but a very short time and disappear completely.

Treatment.—There is no treatment of established value. If the patient is seen immediately after the accident and respiration is absent, artificial respiration should be administered until recovery occurs or until cooling of the body or the onset of rigor indicates that life is extinct.

Oeconomopoulos states that electric burns in children are best treated by early debridement or excision with immediate repair.

BIBLIOGRAPHY

BAMBRIDGE, W.: Optic atrophy with retinal changes caused by high tension current. Brit. Med. J., 2:955, 1930.

COLEMAN, T. H.: Death by lightning. G. P. Kansas, 37:81, 1968.

CRITCHLEY, McD.: The effects of lightning with especial reference to the nervous system. Bristol Med. Chir. J., 49:285, 1932.

FARRELL, D. F. AND STARR, A.: Delayed neurological sequelae of electrical injuries. Neurology, 18:601, 1968.

HESSER, F. H.: A result of contact with a 2400 volt circuit. Report of an unusual case. Bull. Johns Hopkins Hosp., 68:388, 1941.

JAFFE, R. H.: Electropathology. A review of pathologic changes produced by electric currents. Arch. Path., 5:837, 1928.

JEX-BLAKE, A. J.: The Goulstonian Lectures on death by electric currents and by lightning. Brit. Med. J., 1:425, 1913.

————: Death by electric currents and by lightning. Brit. Med. J., 1:425, etc., 1913.

KENNEDY, F.: A case of pyramidal sclerosis following electric burns. Arch. Neurol. & Psychiat., 4:711, 1920.

LANGWORTHY, O. R.: Abnormalities produced in the central nervous system by electrical injuries. J. Exper. Med., 51:943, 1930.

————: Histological changes in nerve cells following injury. Bull. Johns Hopkins Hosp., 47:11, 1930.

LANGWORTHY, O. AND KOUWENHOVEN, W. B.: An experimental study of abnormalities produced in the organism by electricity. J. Indust. Hyg., 12:31, 1930.

————: Injuries produced in the organism by the discharge of an impulse generator. J. Indust. Hyg., 13:326, 1931.

MORRISON, R., WEEKS, A. AND COBB, S.: Lesions of the brain in electric shocks; histopathology of different types of electric shock on mammalian brains. J. Indust. Hyg., 12:364, 1930.

OECONOMOPOULOS, C. T.: Electric burns in children. Am. J. Dis. Child., 103:35, 1962.

PANSE, F.: Die Schadigungen des Nervensystems durch technische Elecktrizität. S. Karger, Berlin, 1930. (Complete references.)

————: Die Schädigungen des Nervensystems durch technische Elektrizität. Monatschr. f. Psychiat. u. Neurol., 70:193, 1931.

SILVERSIDES, J.: Sequelae of electrical injury. Canad. M.A.J., 91:195, 1964.

INJURY OF THE NERVOUS SYSTEM BY SEVERE BURNS

Alpers has examined the brains of two patients who died of extensive burns and has reviewed the reports of previous studies. He states that there is edema of the cerebral cortex. The perivascular spaces are dilated. There is engorgement of the blood vessels with small ring-like perivascular hemorrhages and occasionally subarachnoid hemorrhage. Some small vessels show swelling or necrosis of the endothelium. Extensive nerve cell changes are

found. The Nissl substance is lost and the nucleus eccentric or extruded. These cell changes are said to be especially severe in the hypothalamus. Two lesions are found in the myelin: small areas of myelin destruction with accumulation of gitter cells and astrocytic reaction and areas in which the myelin is swollen. These lesions are found as a rule around small blood vessels. Alpers thinks that damage to the myelin is found only in the patients who have had the most severe burns. It is pointed out that not all of these lesions are reversible.

Alpers believes that this process suggests a toxic reaction and is probably not due to circulatory disturbances. Shock, dehydration, disturbances of the circulation, anoxia, hepatic and renal damage and infection must all be considered as possible etiological factors, however. Professor Leo Koslowski has reported the demonstration of a burn toxin which seems to be a protein.

A few descriptions of the neurological picture are available. Walker and Shenkin mention disorientation and drowsiness passing into coma as well as muscular twitchings. Five of their six patients died on the fourth day. Sudden failure of respiration was the usual cause of death, and was attributed to involvement of the medulla. Roth reported the case of an eight-year-old girl who became comatose on the twentieth day and had a series of convulsions. She developed aphasia, athetosis and became demented. The ventricles became dilated. Kruse describes the case of a child of fourteen months who developed at the end of a month convulsions, blindness, mental changes and hydrocephalus. Vision returned eventually. Crocco mentions blindness, deafness and choreoathetosis. Morrison describes drowsiness, muscular twitchings and rigidity with elevation of the spinal fluid pressure. She also observed convulsions. Hughes reports the case of a baby of twenty-one months who became spastic and had involuntary movements. There was evidence of a lesion of the spinal cord. Globus and Bender studied a boy of eight years who showed mental deterioration, delusions and profound personality changes before dying. Schachter reports three cases of children who developed seizures after burns and one child who became a problem because of personality changes. Petersen *et al.* state that two thirds of burned children show abnormalities in the electroencephalogram which as a rule disappear when healing occurs. Associated symptoms include delirium, confusion and anxiety. Feller and Pierson advise the use of pseudomonas vaccine and hyperimmune plasma. A case history is given below. This seems to suggest that burns produce a powerful neurotoxin.

CASE HISTORY (U.M.H. 510-0440).—*Girl of three years suffered second degree burns over one tenth of body surface. Did well for four days. Then, on the fifth day, became blind and developed retention of urine.*

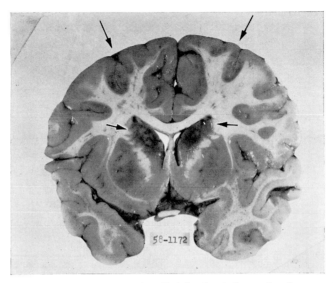

Fig. 276. Brain of a child of one year who died in shock from circulatory collapse following severe burns caused by scalding. Cortical softenings are seen in the border zones of all major cerebral arteries, cerebellar arteries and in both caudate nuclei. (By the courtesy of Dr. Richard Lindenberg.)

On the sixth day, paralysis of legs, loss of reflexes, anesthesia over legs and lower half of body. Stupor and then coma. Cheyne-Stokes respiration and death due to failure of respiration.

K. L. C., a previously healthy girl of three years, suffered second degree burns over the left upper arm, left thigh, and a small area on the left flank, due to boiling water. It was estimated that one tenth of her body surface was involved. She was taken to Union Memorial Hospital. Intravenous fluids and penicillin were given. She seemed to do well for four days. Temperature was 101°F. The pulse was 140.

On the fifth day, the pupils became dilated and the light reflex was lost. The child seemed to be blind. The optic disc showed blurred margins and the retinal veins were dilated. Retention of urine developed requiring a retention catheter. Any noise caused a Moro reflex. The temperature was 102°F. and the pulse 160.

On the sixth day, the child was dull. Her legs jerked at times. It was found that the legs were paralysed and there was anesthesia over the legs and the lower half of the trunk. The knee and ankle jerks were lost, and no abdominal or plantar reflexes could be elicited. Later in the day, Cheyne-Stokes respiration developed. The child sank into coma. Periods of apnea occurred, and finally, respiration ceased. The heart beat for a time. Artificial respiration was not successful.

During this illness, the temperature did not go above 102°F. The pulse varied between 140 and 160. Blood pressure was between 100/58 and

110/70. The white count never rose above 11,700. The hematocrit fell from 47 to 33. The output of urine was well maintained and the blood urea nitrogen was 10. The electrolytes were always normal. The spinal fluid was under a pressure of 210 mm water. There were no cells in the fluid and the total protein was 19 mgs. Blood culture was sterile. No cultures of the burns were made, for there was no obvious evidence of infection. Roentgenograms of the chest and skull revealed nothing of significance.

A post-mortem examination was made, but unfortunately, the spinal cord, optic nerves and peripheral nerves were not examined. The brain and the brain stem were edematous and there was some loss of cells in the cortex. No mention was made of hemorrhage, extensive necrosis or of dural sinus thrombosis.

I am indebted to Dr. Richard Otenasek for these notes.

BIBLIOGRAPHY

ALPERS, B. AND MADOW, L.: Brain changes in patients with extensive body burns. Arch. Neurol. & Psychiat., **72**:440, 1954.

BROUGHTON, A. *et al.*: Magnesium-deficiency syndrome in burns. Lancet, **2**:1156, 1968.

CROCCO, G.: Case of encephalitis following burns. Pediatria, **57**:551, 1949.

FELLER, I AND PIERSON, C.: Pseudomonas vaccine and hyperimmune plasma for burned patients. Arch. Surg., **97**:225, 1968.

GLOBUS, J. H. AND BENDER, M.: Disseminated toxic degenerative encephalopathy secondary to extensive and severe burns. J. Nerv. & Ment. Dis., **83**:518, 1936.

HARBAUER, H.: Neuropsychiatric sequelae after burns in children. Deutsche med. Wchnschr., **88**:1281, 1963.

HUGHES, L.: Burns with cerebral complications. Med. J. Australia, **2**:122, 1917.

KOSLOWSKI, L.: In demonstration of the burn toxin. International Meeting of Medicine of Extensive Burns. Metz, France, July, 1964.

KRUSE, F.: Enzephalitis u. Amaurose nach Verbrennung. Deutsch. med. Wchnschr., **54**:1039, 1928.

MORRISON, B.: Study of burns and scalds in children. Arch. Dis. Child., **22**:129, 1947.

PETERSEN, I. *et al.*: An electroencephalographic and psychiatric study of burn cases. Acta chir. scand., **129**:359, 1965.

PRICE, W. R. AND WOOD, McD.: Treatment of the infected burn with dilute silver nitrate solution. Amer. Jour. Surg., **114**:641, 1967.

ROTH, N: Encephalopathy due to burns. Arch. Neurol. & Psychiat., **45**:980, 1941.

SCHACHTER, M.: Encephalopathies and character disorders following burns in infants. Acta psychiat. et neurol., **25**:285, 1950.

WALKER, J. AND SHENKIN, H.: Studies on toxemia syndrome after burns: Central nervous system changes as a cause of death. Ann. Surg., **121**:301, 1945.

THE EPILEPSIES AND PAROXYSMAL DISORDERS OF THE NERVOUS SYSTEM

THE EPILEPSIES

INTRODUCTION

CONVULSIONS are due to the sudden, violent and disorderly activity of cerebral neurons as Hughlings Jackson stated many years ago. Jackson employed the term *discharge* for such phenomena. Subsequently physiological studies, including electrical stimulation and electroencephalographic investigations, have amply confirmed Jackson's theory.

Many discharges are bilateral and extensive and give rise to a general convulsion. Others are sharply localized and produce a great variety of manifestations depending on the function of the areas of cortex involved. A large number of different seizures are described by Penfield in his book entitled *Epilepsy and Cerebral Localization.* Many of these are mentioned below.

It may be pointed out that discharges may occur at any level of the nervous system. In addition to the cortical discharges, tonic fits are well known

and are attributed to subcortical mechanisms. Discharges of autonomic neurons are described by Penfield and attributed to processes in the diencephalon. In this connection I may mention the oculogyric crises of epidemic encephalitis and also the respiratory tics and the spontaneous emotional reactions seen in the same disease. Gowers described vaso-vagal attacks supposedly due to brain stem reactions. Spinal discharges include certain types of myoclonus and the mass reflex associated with transections of the cord. Even in peripheral mechanisms we observe phenomena which may be attributed to discharges. The lightning pains of tabes dorsalis, the pains of trigeminal neuralgia and the vertigo of Meniere's disease would seem to fall into this grouping. Such conditions are, of course, quite foreign to our concept of epilepsy.

With these facts in mind we may now proceed to define epilepsy as a condition characterized by recurrent, paroxysmal discharges of cerebral neurons. It is necessary to insist upon the qualifying word recurrent for the convulsions which occur in various toxic states such as uremia, tetany, strychnine poisoning, etc., are obviously not apt to occur repeatedly during a number of years and are not regarded as epileptic. Custom decrees that we shall distinguish between secondary or symptomatic epilepsy and primary, essential or idiopathic epilepsy, depending upon whether the cause is known or unknown. Preston Robb has recently written a complete review of the numerous problems encountered in this disease.

Clinical Types of Epilepsy.—It is possible to distinguish different types of epilepsy depending upon the nature of the seizure. Thus, we might separate the children subject to petit mal from those who have only general convulsions, etc. However, this seems to serve no useful purpose since both types of seizures are apt to occur in most cases. It seems to be more useful to distinguish the following groups:

1. Cases of epilepsy beginning early in life which are associated with evidence of congenital defect of development of the nervous system.

2. Cases of epilepsy beginning at any time of life which are associated with evidences of acquired lesions of the brain.

3. Cases of epilepsy beginning at any age which are at first associated with a normal mental condition and in which no clinical evidence of organic disease of the brain can be found. These are of course the so-called essential epilepsies.

GENERALIZED CONVULSIONS

Definition.—In the following pages epileptic seizures, both major and minor, will be discussed.

Etiology.—It has been customary in the past to recognize a *constitutional tendency* to convulsive reactions which is regarded as an inherited peculi-

arity, and a number of *precipitating factors* such as acquired injuries and diseases of the brain. Morbid heredity has always been emphasized, although there is a great deal of difference of opinion about its importance. In a study of epilepsy in twins, Conrad found that in identical (uniovular) twins when epilepsy occurred both were affected in 86 per cent of cases whereas, in non-identical twins both were affected in only 3 per cent of cases. In an excellent review of the subject Cobb states that among a group of 9139 relatives of epileptics, there were 21 cases of epilepsy per thousand; whereas among 1896 relatives of a control group who did not have epilepsy, there was an average of 2.6 cases per thousand. In the general population the incidence of epilepsy is about 3 per thousand so we must have several hundred thousand epileptics in this country. There seems to be little doubt that there is an inherited factor of importance. Electroencephalographic studies have revealed abnormalities of electrical activity which are termed cerebral dysrhythmia in the brains of epileptics and in some instances, in relatives of epileptics and it is probable that this dysrhythmia is an expression of the constitutional factor.

The precipitating factors are very numerous. All types of diseases of the brain, congenital defects, traumatic injuries, inflammatory and toxic processes may be followed by epilepsy. Thus, in congenital spastic diplegia, recurrent convulsions occur in about 25 per cent of all cases and epilepsy is very common in congenital mental defects of various types. In acquired infantile hemiplegia, focal or general convulsions develop in at least 33 per cent. The age of the patient at the time the injury is inflicted is apparently important, for it has been estimated by numerous authors that not more than 5 to 7 per cent of the many thousand soldiers who received wounds of the brain developed epilepsy as a result. Cortical injuries are more apt to be followed by convulsions than lesions situated in other parts of the nervous system but no particular area of the cortex can be held wholly responsible. Lesions in different regions of the cortex give rise to seizures of different types, but all seem capable of causing convulsive reactions. The nature of the injury seems to be quite indifferent for, it has been stated above, congenital defects, traumatic conditions, degenerations, and neoplasms all seem to be efficient in this respect. However, it must be stated that cerebral injuries are not always followed by convulsions no matter where the lesion is placed or how severe it may be and it is for this reason that the underlying constitutional factor has been postulated. Cobb regards the various cerebral injuries as capable of inducing epilepsy only in those in whom there is a latent tendency to the disease. He points out that there is a very high incidence (22 per thousand) of epilepsy among the relatives of patients who have developed epilepsy after traumatic injuries.

In a study of 31 children who had convulsions in the first few days after

birth Schulte found that after one to four years, three had grand mal, three had hypsarhythmia, one had febrile convulsions and 24 had no seizures.

Koch has made a very complete analysis of the many factors which enter into the causation of epilepsy.

Pathological Anatomy.—Post-mortem examinations have revealed no constant anatomical basis underlying the various types of epilepsy. In a few instances no pathological changes whatever are found but in the great majority of cases lesions of some type are present. Evidences of *destructive processes* are often described. For example, Southard and Thom have found only 68 brains which seemed to be normal in the gross out of a total of 205 brains of epileptics who had come to autopsy. Often one finds thickening of the pia-arachnoid, either local or general. Circumscribed or diffuse atrophy of the cortex is another very common observation. There is loss of neurons of the superficial layers of the cortex and proliferation of the fibrous glia. *Developmental defects* of various types are very common. Porencephaly, microgyria, malformation of the cortex, anomalous distribution of cortical blood vessels and many other gross defects are seen. Many writers have emphasized various microscopic evidences of developmental defect such as disordered cortical architecture, displaced cells in the white matter, the presence of immature and atypical cells, and lack of differentiation of the various cortical layers.

If we confine our study to the brains which seem to be normal in the gross examination, we may expect to find both acute and chronic cell changes. These lesions are believed to be a result of the convulsions and not a cause. Spielmeyer has made very careful studies of these lesions. He finds that there are focal areas in the cortex in which the neurons have disappeared and have been replaced by a dense over-growth of neuroglia. These foci he finds most frequently in the cornu Ammonis and in the cerebellar cortex. In brains of patients who have died in status epilepticus, acute changes are found. The ganglion cells are shrunken and disintegrating and stain intensely with eosin. The Nissl substance is broken up. Spielmeyer shows that these changes are exactly the same as those which occur as a result of organic obstruction of the circulation and attributes them to vasomotor spasm of the cerebral vessels. Meyer *et al.* have described especially severe lesions of this type. One must consider the possibility that anoxia may play an important role in the production of such lesions.

Falconer and Taylor state that asphyxial episodes during infancy, especially febrile convulsions, cause sclerosis of the cornu Ammonis which then becomes an eleptogenic lesion leading to convulsions within the first decade in most cases. Such patients respond well to surgery.

A great deal of information about the pathology of epilepsy has been

derived from inspection of the cortex during craniotomy. Dandy has described localized thickening and opacity of the pia-arachnoid with accumulation of fluid in small lakes over the cortex. Palpation reveals areas of induration as well as areas of diminished density. In a number of cases he has discovered malformations of the cortex with anomalous distribution of the blood vessels. Ventriculography and encephalography usually reveal dilatation of the ventricles, both local and general, as well as areas of atrophy over the cortex. By these means, porencephaly and defects of the brain of all types can be demonstrated. Pendergrass has published numerous encephalograms made in various types of epilepsy. He states that he has invariably found some form of atrophy in every case he has studied. It is possible that the lesions described above are in most instances either precipitating factors or results of the seizures and that the basic abnormality is not anatomically demonstrable.

Studies are now being made to determine whether there are any biochemical abnormalities in the epileptic brain. Tower discusses these complex matters.

The Clinical Features: Incidence and Racial Distribution.—Davenport has presented statistics to show that the incidence of epilepsy is subject to a great deal of variation in various racial groups. He states that epilepsy is relatively infrequent among the Maoris, East Indians, natives of the Philippine and Hawaiian Islands, the Japanese, Finns, Germans and Scandinavians. On the contrary, it is more frequent among the Koreans, Italians, French Canadians and inhabitants of England. He states also that there is a high incidence of epilepsy in the State of Maryland. Such figures can scarcely be accepted at their face value, for it seems very unlikely that accurate statistics can be obtained from primitive races and savage tribes. The incidence in the United States seems to be about 3 per thousand.

Inheritance.—Although it is generally agreed that morbid heredity plays some part in the development of epilepsy, most students of the subject have found that direct transmission of the disease from parent to child is rare. In 10 to 15 per cent of cases, however, the history is elicited that some other member of the family, perhaps an uncle, cousin or grandparent was subject to convulsive seizures. Burr and Thom and Walker conclude that a predisposition to nervous or mental disease is transmitted to the offspring of epileptic parents but that the development of convulsions demands some additional exciting factor which might have no ill effect upon a healthy nervous system. It is well known, of course, that certain defects and degenerations of the nervous system whose chief manifestation is convulsions may be inherited. For example, we may mention tuberous sclerosis and myoclonus epilepsy. No doubt, other heredofamilial diseases are re-

garded as essential epilepsies. Certainly, we sometimes encounter a family in which several members are subject to convulsive seizures.

Pre-epileptic Symptoms.—It has been claimed by various psychiatrists that there is a special epileptic personality which is evident before any seizures occur and which is, in fact, the origin of the disorder. These children are said to be egocentric and selfish, to show a rigid resistance to modifying influences and to be abnormally sensitive and irritable. Various psychoanalytic interpretations have been placed upon these observations which need not be discussed, for the writer agrees with Turner that these personality changes develop after the seizures have become established and may be explained by the mental deterioration and the difficult psychological problems which these patients must face. Except for those children whose cases are complicated by extensive organic brain lesions, epileptic children seem to show no characteristic psychic disturbances until the condition is well established.

Patrick and Levy describe a number of recurrent symptoms of various types which they term pre-epileptic attacks and which they regard as premonitory signs of more typical seizures. They distinguish ten groups of symptoms: (1) Attacks of dizziness, faintness and falling without apparent cause. (2) Vomiting, belching, queer feelings in the abdomen, etc. (3) Flushing or pallor of the face. (4) Sudden, strange feelings which are not localized. (5) Throat spasms, asphyxia and thirst. (6) Screaming, crying and laughing. (7) Dreamy states, lonesome feelings, fright, etc. (8) Night terrors, insomnia and abnormal drowsiness. (9) Shivering and jerking of the extremities. (10) Visions, darkness and buzzing in the ears.

These symptoms are of only momentary duration, sudden onset and without apparent cause. Such attacks may slowly increase in frequency and severity. Eventually they become associated with mental confusion or unconsciousness and are then considered petit mal or minor seizures. It must be emphasized that whatever significance these symptoms may have, they do not justify the diagnosis of epilepsy in the absence of more typical seizures.

Onset.—The beginning of definite symptoms is most common in childhood, although it may be deferred until adult life. About 10 per cent of all cases can be traced back to the first three years of life and nearly half develop before the age of ten years. It is often very difficult to determine the exact age of onset for parents often fail to recognize the significance of minor seizures and nocturnal convulsions may continue for years without being observed. A great variety of seizures are described and only the commonest types are mentioned here. When one thinks of the great complexity of the brain, the many regions in which discharges may occur and

the various neural mechanisms which might be involved in the extension of these discharges, it is easy to imagine that an almost endless series of phenomena may result.

Symptoms.—There are two chief varieties of epileptic seizures, the major convulsion or grand mal and the minor attack, often termed petit mal. In most cases both varieties occur but either type may predominate.

GENERAL CONVULSIONS

The *major seizure* may occur without any warning whatever or may follow an *aura*. Innumerable types of aura are described. As a rule in the generalized epilepsies, the aura is either abdominal or cephalic. The patient may complain of dizziness, fullness in the head, a dazed condition or faintness. The abdominal feelings are described as nausea, pain over the heart or stomach, a feeling of distention, a lump in the throat, etc. Such auras have been described as pneumogastric auras. They pass up towards the head and the patient usually becomes unconscious when the feeling reaches the throat or head. Localized auras in the extremities or one side of the body are apt to indicate that there is a focal element in the seizure. At the onset of the convulsion the face becomes pale and the pupils are dilated. The eyes usually roll up but may be directed to one side. Simultaneously there is a violent contraction of the entire bodily musculature and loss of consciousness. The legs are usually rigidly extended, the arms flexed, the fingers clenched, the head retracted and the trunk arched backward. The patient falls forward or backward and not infrequently suffers some injury. The strong contraction of the muscles causes a forced expiration and the air passing through a partially closed glottis causes a hoarse cry. The tongue may be seized between the teeth and badly lacerated and evacuation of the bowels and bladder may occur. As a result of the tonic spasm of the muscles of respiration, the patient may become very cyanotic. After a few seconds to half a minute, the clonic phase of the convulsion develops. The body and extremities jerk and twitch, and there is often foaming at the mouth. After a few minutes, rarely more than ten, the patient's color begins to improve, the muscles relax and the twitching ceases. The patient may remain unconscious for a variable period after the convulsion has ceased and is always confused for a time. There is often severe headache during this period and sometimes vomiting. Usually the patient falls into a deep sleep which may last several hours. Upon awakening the patient has no memory of the seizure, but usually deduces that a seizure has occurred from the headache and aching of the muscles. Severe injuries may occur during convulsions, not only from the fall but from the violent muscular contractions. There may be various strains of the muscles and ligaments and even fractures of the bones and dislocation of the joints. Petechial

hemorrhages in the conjunctiva and about the orbits are not uncommon. In rare cases, lung abscesses have been known to result from the aspiration of saliva into the bronchial tree. Aspiration of vomitus may be fatal. During the stage of stupor immediately following the seizure, the pupils may be dilated and inactive to light, the plantar reflex may be of the extensor type and the abdominal reflexes may be lost.

In some cases the attacks may occur during any part of the twenty-four hours without any rule whatever. In other cases the attacks may occur only at night for many years. There is a strong tendency for the seizures to develop just after the child has fallen asleep or immediately before or after awakening in the morning. In some cases there is a fairly regular periodicity so that the attacks can almost be predicted. In girls who have attained puberty, the seizures may appear every month just before or during menstruation. Laidlaw states that seizures are most common immediately before, during and just after menstruation and least common during the luteal phase four to thirteen days before the menses begin.

STATUS EPILEPTICUS

In some cases, convulsions may occur in series succeeding one another so rapidly that the patient does not regain consciousness in the interval. This is termed *status epilepticus*. One hundred or more convulsions may occur within twenty-four hours. If the seizures cannot be controlled, the patient soon begins to show signs of exhaustion. The stupor grows deeper, temperature rises, respiration becomes labored and signs of circulatory failure become apparent. The heart may become dilated and pulmonary edema is often the cause of death. Some patients seem to have a tendency to status. They may enjoy long periods of freedom from convulsions and then suffer a large number of attacks within a few days. Sooner or later death occurs in such episodes.

Focal Elements in "Essential" Epilepsy.—As a rule, the occurrence of focal signs or symptoms in association with convulsive seizures may be taken to indicate local organic changes and justify placing the case in the group of "symptomatic" epilepsies. However, in some instances such focal symptoms, both transient and persistent may be seen in cases of the so-called "essential" epilepsy. Knapp has made a very careful study of these phenomena. He states that they may occur before the seizure in connection with the aura, after the attack among the post-convulsive phenomena, as an equivalent, during periods of mental confusion and in the intervals between the seizures. He has observed local muscular twitching at the beginning of a general convulsion and also occurring as an isolated phenomenon. Transient local palsies may also be observed following general convulsions. In the same way sensory disturbances referable to injury of the sen-

sory cortex may occur. Knapp has described aphasias of various types, disturbances of vision and signs of involvement of the brain-stem and cerebellum. Probably conjugate deviation of the eyes at the onset of a convulsion is the commonest focal disturbance in such cases. It is important to point out that the symptoms just described do not recur in each successive attack, as they do in true focal epilepsy. If focal symptoms appear a second time in such cases, they are apt to be of a different nature or to involve a different part of the body. It is evident, therefore, that the development of focal disturbances upon one occasion does not necessarily indicate a focal lesion.

Major Atonic Seizures.—In this condition, the patient suddenly falls to the floor and is unconscious. The muscles are relaxed throughout the seizure. No clonic movements are seen. In such cases a diagnosis of syncope is often made. The loss of consciousness persists for several minutes or more. The differentiation from the drop seizures which are also termed minor akinetic seizures or head nodding spells depends upon the duration of the loss of consciousness. In the drop seizures, which are described below, consciousness is either not lost at all or is lost for only a few moments.

PETIT MAL

The *minor attacks* are much less spectacular. The mildest type may easily escape notice. The child may pause for a moment, turn slightly pale or stare rather fixedly for a few seconds and then continue playing as before. In more severe ones, the eyes may turn up and the arms may twitch for a moment. There is no fall or cry. The aura may be present or absent. In certain cases the child may be confused for several minutes and fail to respond when called. Occasional incontinence of urine may be the first evidence of such attacks noted. Older children may state that they are unable to see, hear or talk for a few moments. In some instances there seems to be no more than a brief disturbance of the patient's thoughts or feelings. It is evident that the essential element in these minor seizures is a transient loss of consciousness or at least mental confusion. They occur very frequently as a rule and are usually associated with grand mal. The most characteristic features of the petit mal attacks are their brief duration and frequent repetition. Their recognition is often very difficult in children who are too young to describe their symptoms clearly. The attacks described by Patrick and Levy are probably abortive minor attacks. We must, therefore, be on our guard if the mother states that the child often complains of dizziness, complains of queer feelings in the epigastrium or throat, flushes or turns pale, suddenly laughs or cries without apparent cause or repeatedly awakes from sleep in terror. School children who cannot get along in school

for no apparent reason are often found to have petit mal which has not been recognized by their parents.

Showers of petit mal may result in a kind of status which is manifest chiefly by unconsciousness. The diagnosis depends upon the electroencephalographic study.

It is sometimes very difficult to distinguish between petit mal and the aura of abortive major attacks and mild focal seizures which cause no characteristic signs. Penry and Dreifuss describe a variety of automatisms which occur during petit mal attacks.

It is claimed that children suffering from petit mal excrete in the urine increased amounts of certain amino acids including aspartic acid, glutamic acid, cystine, histadine isoleucine, leucine, lysine and tryptophan.

SEIZURES OF OTHER TYPES

Psychomotor Attacks.—These are manifest by periods of confusion or automatic behavior of variable duration. It is claimed that unpremeditated crimes may be committed during such episodes. Amnesia usually follows. Some of these states are due to seizures and some are probably merely states of confusion following seizures, i.e. post-ictal automatism. Glaser and Dixon have made a careful study of such seizures and state that they are very common in children and require differentiation from behavior disorders. They find the electrographic abnormalities less specific than some other observers.

Jean Holowach *et al.* state that the clinical features fall into five patterns: (1) Dreamy states, with fear and olfactory, visual and auditory hallucinations. (2) Chewing, smacking the lips, drooling, swallowing and choking. (3) Purposeless behavior with fighting, running, laughing, and incoherent speech. (4) Apathy, limpness and arrest of activity preceded by cerebral or epigastric auras.

The so-called *running fits*, or epilepsia cursiva, probably belong in the category of psychomotor epilepsy. The patient becomes confused and starts running. There is evidence that the patient is not completely unaware of the surroundings and is impelled by some vague fear to run away. Occasionally, after running for a time, the patient falls in a convulsion. It has been claimed that all forms of psychomotor epilepsy are due to discharges in the temporal lobes.

Drop Seizures.—This term is applied to a rather unusual type of epileptic attack which is characterized by sudden falls to the ground, without a moment's warning. In infants who cannot stand, one sees only a momentary dropping of the head forward. In older children who can stand, the patient falls forward bruising the knees and cutting the chin. It is possible

that consciousness is lost for a moment but in most instances the patient claims that mental processes are not affected in any way. Unless the patient is dazed as a result of the fall, it is almost always possible for him to arise at once. These attacks may occur in connection with general convulsions. The terms *akinetic* and *static* epilepsy are also employed. Formerly it was believed that the falls were due to relaxation of the muscles, but now we have reason to think that there is sudden involuntary flexion of the extremities. In such cases, the response to medication is often unsatisfactory.

Massive Myoclonic Seizures.—In this condition the head is suddenly flexed, the arms extended and the legs jerked up upon the abdomen. A cry is associated with these movements. As a rule the duration is very brief but the seizures may occur many times a day. They are common in infancy especially between the sixth month and the third year. Some authors speak of these attacks as *infantile spasms*. They are usually, but not always, associated with mental deficiency and often with physical signs of cerebral damage. The character of the seizures may be due to the immaturity of the nervous system for later in life the child is apt to have convulsions or commonplace minor attacks. It is claimed that a characteristic encephalographic pattern known as hypsarhythmia is found. This is manifest by widespread sharp spikes of irregular rates interspersed with high voltage slow waves without any localization.

Such seizures are usually resistant to medication. Pearlstein finds that gemonil, or metharbital is sometimes effective. Cortisone may control the seizures especially in the patients who have no physical signs of cerebral damage. Even if the seizures are controlled, the child is apt to be mentally deficient.

Poser reports cases in which edema and necrosis were found in the brain at post-mortem examination and Sinton and Patterson found status marmoratus with cribiform state and extensive gliosis. The cerebellum was atrophied and there were changes in the cervical cord. These authors were inclined to believe that circulatory disturbances in the basilar system must have occurred at birth. It seems unlikely that any particular pathological condition will be found to be responsible for these seizures.

Myoclonic Twitchings.—Many patients who suffer from generalized convulsive seizures also complain of sudden local twitching and jerking of the muscles. Such attacks most frequently occur in the mornings causing the patient to drop objects out of the hands or even throw them across the room. Any part of the bodily musculature may be affected but the arms are most commonly involved. There is never disturbance of consciousness. In some cases the twitchings may precede the development of convulsions by several years. Cases of epilepsy complicated by such movements must be distinguished from myoclonic epilepsy q.v.

Pyknolepsy.—Goldflam has applied this name to a condition which is sometimes seen between the ages of 4 and 12 years in which very frequent, mild attacks similar to those of petit mal occur. The onset is sudden and the cause entirely obscure. As many as fifty or more attacks may occur in one day. There is never any muscular twitching or lasting confusion and the only distinctive feature of the seizures is their great frequency, mild nature and failure to respond to the usual therapeutic measures. It is stated that this condition has no ill effects whatever upon the child's mental development. The prognosis is good. After a few months or a year they cease and never return.

More recent studies such as those by Owen and Berlinrood throw much doubt on this description. It is clear that in some cases the attacks persist for a number of years and that minor personality changes may occur. Major convulsions are mentioned in a few instances. It is suggestive that in nearly 20 per cent of cases there is a history of more typical epilepsy. On the whole one is somewhat skeptical about the existence of a distinct disease.

Abdominal Epilepsy.—In some instances epileptic children are subject to repeated attacks of severe abdominal pain. Dr. Samuel Livingston has studied a number of these cases. Once a child developed an attack of abdominal pain while the electroencephalogram was being made. Seizure waves appeared at the onset of the pain and ceased just as the pain stopped. One wonders what relation these pains bear to the so-called abdominal migraine.

Latent Epilepsy.—This term may be employed in regard to certain cases in which there is a tendency to convulsive reactions which is not severe enough to lead to spontaneous seizures, but may give rise to convulsions when some complicating factor is present. For example I may mention the febrile convulsions of infancy and the convulsions which occur in some children in association with breath-holding spells. In these cases, there are usually no convulsions after the age of 5 years. I have seen several cases in which seizures occurred in association with syncope or with loss of blood and never at any other time. No doubt, anoxia is responsible. It is well known that some children suffering from tetany or hypoglycemia may have convulsions when the chemical changes in the blood are not sufficient to cause convulsions in most children.

Febrile Convulsions.—Some authorities state that the prognosis is good in febrile convulsions. Others state that from 15 to 75 per cent of children who have febrile convulsions continue to have convulsions and have true epilepsy. Livingston studied 498 cases of febrile convulsions. He found that there were two distinct types. Type 1 he designated as having simple febrile convulsions. Type 2 included those who had true epilepsy and the fever simply precipitated the seizure. There were 57 per cent of the pa-

tients in the type 2 group, and 43 per cent in the type 1 group. In type 1, the onset was usually in the first 3 years. None had an onset after 5 years. The seizures developed soon after a sudden rise in temperature. The fever might be as low as 101°F. It was rare for the seizure to occur later than 6 hours after the fever. It is stated that the electroencephalogram is negative in these patients and there is no history of epilepsy in the family though febrile convulsions in the family are not rare. The convulsion should be generalized and not focal and should not last over 5 minutes. When these criteria were applied, it was found that only 3 per cent of the 201 patients in type 1 were found eventually to have epilepsy.

Course.—The course of epilepsy varies within wide limits. In some patients attacks occur almost every day, in others the average incidence is not more than one in several years. Some patients develop seizures at fairly definite and regular intervals, others can detect no regularity in the distribution of attacks. In a few cases the patient will enjoy long periods of freedom from attacks and then have a large series in quick succession, often dying in status epilepticus. In many cases there are both major and minor attacks, the latter being much more frequent than the former, but in other instances only one or the other type of attack occurs. Occasionally one observes a patient whose seizures have ceased only to be precipitated again following an illness or an injury to the head.

Effects of Convulsions: *Transient Effects.*—Under this head we may include the transient symptoms which often follow severe seizures as well as the mental and physical deterioration which eventually develops in so many epilepsies of long standing. It is difficult to say whether these phenomena are the result of the convulsions per se or whether they are manifestations of the process which gives rise to the convulsions.

States of mental confusion may occur following a series of attacks. As a rule such conditions are of brief duration but they may persist for a number of days. After the patient has recovered, there is usually no memory of events which occurred during this period.

I have mentioned above that during the period immediately following a generalized epileptic convulsion, while the patient is unconscious or stuporous, the light reflex of the pupils may be abolished and the plantar reflex may be of the extensor type. In most instances these signs disappear within a short time but we have observed in a number of children objective signs of widespread damage to the nervous system which followed a series of convulsions and which persisted for several weeks. The children seemed to be very apathetic or stuporous. There was generalized weakness of the extremities, tremors, incoordination, increased tendon reflexes, extensor plantar responses and even apparent blindness and deafness. Speech was always lost. The symptoms persisted for several weeks after the convulsions

had been controlled but after a month or more the children were restored to their former condition. The nature of such disturbances is obscure. They are, perhaps, generalized disturbances comparable to the local palsies which follow focal convulsions. It is possible that they are the result of the acute cell alterations which Spielmeyer has described in the brains of patients dying in status which he attributes to cortical vasoconstriction. I have also seen coma in two instances which developed after a few minor seizures and which persisted for approximately a week in each case. All the usual studies were made without result and eventually the children made complete recoveries.

Local phenomena following focal seizures are well known. The commonest example is probably the transient hemiplegia which appears so often after a unilateral convulsion. This has been termed Todd's paralysis. In the same way we may see transient aphasias of various types and also hemianopia and cortical blindness. These phenomena rarely persist more than a few days and often disappear within a few hours.

Spivak and Conti review 6 cases of myoglobinuria following seizures. In some cases acute renal tubular necrosis resulted. Some such cases are fatal.

Persisting Effects.—Penfield mentions cases in which focal lesions developed during a series of convulsions and persisted thereafter. He also describes cases in which severe and extensive cerebral destruction occurred resulting in decerebrate rigidity and dementia. Atrophy of the brain may be demonstrated in such cases by ventriculography. Fowler reports five cases in which extensive cerebral damage followed prolonged convulsions. The author believes that these were febrile convulsions and that the damage to the brain was due to anoxia. As a rule, however, lasting neurological signs do not appear during the course of epilepsy and the chief evidence of cerebral damage is mental deterioration.

In the secondary epilepsies, due to various injuries and defects of the brain, a great variety of *psychic disturbances* occur which need not be described, for they depend upon the nature of the lesions. Even in the essential epilepsies, however, mental disturbances frequently develop eventually. No satisfactory description of these can be given, for they are profoundly colored by the situation and by the patient's personality. As a rule alterations of the personality appear before there is definite reduction of intelligence. The child becomes irritable and subject to temper tantrums. There are frequent quarrels with playmates due to the child's selfish and unreasonable attitude. The parents cannot secure proper obedience and the child's behavior at school is often a problem. Later the child may fail to make proper progress in learning, school grades fall off and in some cases the child actually becomes demented. The mental changes do not run parallel with the frequency or severity of the seizures in every case, but as a rule

there is an approximate correlation. The occurrence of frequent attacks of petit mal is sometimes followed by rapid mental deterioration, especially if there are prolonged periods of mental confusion. As a rule the earlier in life the attacks begin, the more severe the dementia is apt to be.

We have seen large numbers of infants whose development has been backward from birth, who have had frequent major or minor seizures and who have deteriorated so rapidly that one is inclined to suspect some progressive disease of the brain. They soon lose any motor reactions they may have acquired and eventually sink into a stuporous, vegetative state which is terminated by an intercurrent infection. No treatment seems to be of any avail in these cases. Decoban describes such cases.

Diagnosis.—The diagnosis of epilepsy in infancy is fraught with great difficulty, and a large number of possible causes must be ruled out before it can be made. During infancy convulsions may result from apparently trivial causes. It is very difficult and perhaps impossible in some cases to determine whether infantile convulsions are significant of beginning epilepsy or not. As a rule seizures occurring in relation to definite illnesses have no unfavorable significance. On the other hand, those which occur repeatedly, which are very severe or prolonged, and those which occur without any discoverable cause are more ominous. Focal convulsions are probably more significant than general convulsions. Seizures occurring during the course of acute infectious diseases may be benign or may mark the development of cerebral damage as a result of which "secondary" epilepsy may develop. A well known cause of infantile convulsions is tetany. There are usually signs of latent tetany. Digestive disturbances, fever, acute infectious diseases, lead poisoning, hypoglycemia, syphilis and, in fact, almost any severe illness is a possible cause of convulsions at this age. If careful study reveals no cause for the seizures, the diagnosis of epilepsy should be considered, even if the attacks apparently cease for a time. The existence of other cases of epilepsy in the family may be taken to favor this diagnosis. In early infancy it is very difficult to distinguish the so-called essential epilepsy from symptomatic epilepsy, for a complete neurological examination is impossible. We must, however, always consider the possibility of congenital defects of the brain, birth injury, abscess, brain tumor, progressive degenerative diseases and encephalitis of various types. Vitamin B6, i.e. pyridoxine, deficiency is a cause of convulsions.

The sudden violent, involuntary jerk of an extremity or body which occurs so commonly as the patient is dropping off to sleep is usually termed a *sleep start* or nocturnal jerk. This is regarded as a benign condition quite distinct from epilepsy. Recently Symonds has published evidence to indicate that somewhat similar myoclonic jerks at night are a form of epilepsy.

Masturbation may be mistaken for epilepsy. This habit may develop as early as 18 months. Livingston mentions the case of a child of 3 years who had several "attacks" a day which are described as follows: "She crosses her thighs, holds them very stiff, has a vacant and staring look in her eyes, becomes very red in the face, breaks out in a sweat and remains in this condition for a few minutes going to sleep afterwards."

During the later part of childhood and adolescence, the development of major or minor attacks without other departure from health is presumptive evidence of epilepsy unless some other cause is apparent. Syncope in sensitive young girls may be difficult to distinguish from epilepsy in some instances. It must be kept in mind that some of the circulatory disturbances which cause syncope may also cause convulsions. Fevers rarely cause convulsions after the age of eight years. Every effort should be made to detect gross organic diseases of the nervous system. A careful history and neurological examination will frequently disclose evidence of an organic process. If there are any focal symptoms, a complete study is essential. The Wassermann test should always be performed upon the blood and upon the spinal fluid as well. Roentgenograms of the skull are indicated as a routine and in many cases ventriculography is necessary to rule out tumor of the brain. An electroencephalogram may be helpful.

Liske and Forster describe pseudoseizures and the means by which they may be recognized. If the attacks can be induced, the absence of any seizure discharge in the electroencephalogram is strong evidence against a real seizure. The authors, however, mention the possibility that a discharge in the depths of the brain might not be evident in the electroencephalogram. Seizures in which the pattern changes evolving into more spectacular forms are suspect. Seizures in which the patient shows evidence of being aware of the reaction of the witness are also open to suspicion. Seizures which the patient can develop on request of the physician should usually be rejected.

The Induction of Convulsions for Diagnosis.—It is not uncommon for the seizures to stop when the child is brought into the hospital for observation so that it is frequently impossible for the physician to gain any direct information about them. Several methods have been devised by which seizures may be induced at will in affected children.

Hyperventilation is perhaps the method most commonly employed. The patient is placed on a couch and instructed to breathe deeply and at a rate of 12 per minute. A metronome may be used to control the rate. In many instances, a seizure will result. McQuarrie and Peler have devised a method of inducing seizures by overhydration which is also said to be effective. The administration of small doses of metrazol is recommended for this purpose but it must be kept in mind that large doses will produce convulsions in

healthy subjects. Ajmone-Marsan and Ralston describe their methods of analysing epileptic seizures by means of metrazol and electroencephalography.

Electroencephalography.—The electroencephalograph is now used extensively in the study and diagnosis of epilepsy. For an adequate discussion of this method of examination the reader is referred to articles by Gibbs, Lennox, Jasper and Livingston. At this point, I wish to mention merely some of the more characteristic electroencephalographic patterns which may be found in various types of epilepsy. It should be said first that the normal adult wave pattern, composed of alpha waves of 10 per second and the beta waves of 25 per second, is not found in subjects under the age of 15 years. In infancy there are asynchronous irregular waves of 2 per second. As the child grows older the waves become more rapid and more regular. At the age of 5 years, the dominant rate is 6 to 8 per second and by the age of 10 years, an adult rhythm of 8 to 12 per second may be found in the occipital lobes and slow waves only in the frontal lobes. Runs of slow waves may be found in the frontal region until the age of 15 years.

During a petit mal seizure, it is stated that in all cases there is a generalized outburst of waves of great amplitude at a frequency of 3 per second. Smooth and regular waves are associated with sharp spikes so this is termed the spike and wave pattern or the dart and dome pattern. In grand mal attacks, the alpha waves become larger and faster. As these waves increase, the seizure develops and as the clonic phase sets in, the waves become slower and reach a rate of 5 per second with tall spikes. After such a seizure there is diminished electrical activity during the period of coma. It is stated that

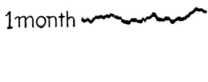

Fig. 277. Electroencephalogram in a normal infant at various ages, illustrating development of the fundamental rhythm. (From Lindsay, J. Gen. Psych., 19:285, 1938.)

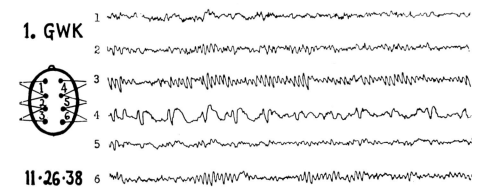

1. GWK

1
2
3
4
5

11·26·38 6

Fig. 278. Electroencephalogram of patient with focal epilepsy and left hemiparesis. The fourth lead from the right frontal area shows abnormal waves. Operation disclosed old scar in cortex. (By the courtesy of Dr. Lyman.)

the psychomotor seizures are manifest by high voltage square topped waves at a rate of about 6 per second. Jacksonian seizures are marked by localized spike and sharp wave discharges. If the discharge spreads and gives rise to a generalized convulsion, the electroencephalogram shows the same pattern mentioned above in connection with grand mal. Jasper states that high amplitude discharges indicate a very large number of cells discharging synchronously and regards this hypersynchrony as a fundamental characteristic of all epileptic seizures.

Since one rarely has an opportunity to make an electroencephalogram during a seizure, one must rely on the *interseizure records* in most instances. In patients suffering from petit mal, one almost always finds short bursts of 3 per second spike and dome forms. In patients suffering from drop seizures (akinetic epilepsy) and myoclonic attacks, spike and dome patterns at a rate other than 3 per second are described. The term petit mal variant is used to describe these waves. In patients subject to grand mal attacks, the interseizure records may show a variety of changes including abnormally fast waves, slow waves, spikes, sharp waves, petit mal variants. In a large percentage of such cases, the record is normal. Normal records are often found in patients subject to nocturnal convulsions. Psychomotor epilepsy is often stated to be usually associated with a focus of spikes in the anterior temporal lobes. In focal epilepsies one may find local foci of abnormal activity or more generalized abnormalities.

Recently it has been shown that records made during natural or induced sleep are more apt to reveal abnormalities than those made when the subject is awake. It must be kept in mind, however, that the normal sleeping record is different from the waking record.

Overbreathing or hyperventilation is routinely employed to bring to light

latent abnormalities in the electroencephalogram. It should be pointed out that children respond more strongly than adults to this procedure and the record must be interpreted in the light of the child's age. In certain cases special stimuli may be employed to bring out abnormalities. Flickering light, i.e., photic stimulation is used and also auditory stimuli.

Pratt *et al.* state that deprivation of sleep for 24 hours will increase the incidence of abnormal recordings.

Various local and generalized disease processes in the brain cause various types of electroencephalographic abnormalities. It is doubtful whether any of these can be recognized by the electroencephalogram. Individuals suffering from migraine often show runs of abnormal waves and it is important in such cases for the electroencephalographer to restrain himself from making a diagnosis of epilepsy.

Some patients who have headaches and abdominal pains show a 14 and 6 spike pattern. Some authorities consider this pattern a manifestation of an epileptic disorder. Others say its significance is still uncertain.

It must be pointed out that between 10 and 15 per cent of apparently normal individuals show abnormal records and a rather large percentage of patients known to have epilepsy show a normal pattern. It is evident, therefore, that the electroencephalogram cannot be relied upon to establish or to exclude the diagnosis of epilepsy without the aid of clinical data.

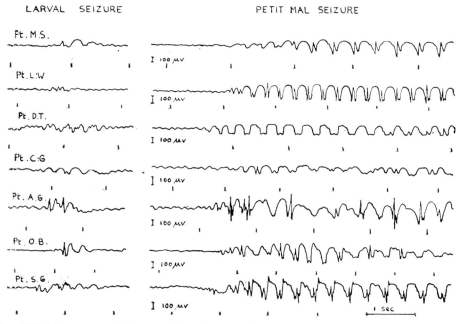

FIG. 279. Electroencephalogram of petit mal and larval seizures (Gibbs, Davis and Lennox. Arch. Neurol. & Psychiat. 34:1133, 1935.)

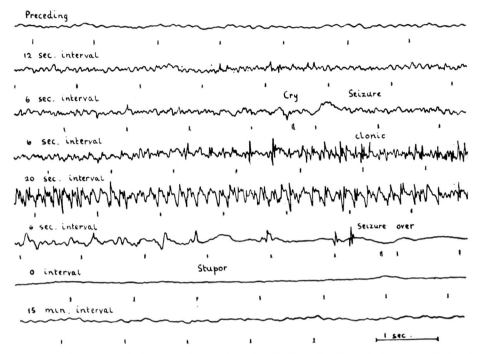

FIG. 280. Electroencephalogram of grand mal. (Gibbs, Davis and Lennox, ibidem.)

Treatment.—If the patient is seen during a convulsive seizure, the clothing should be loosened so as to prevent any possibility of constriction of the neck, and a cork or spool placed between the teeth to prevent biting the tongue. The patient must be prevented from falling out of bed or striking hard objects with the extremities. As a rule, the child is safer on a blanket placed on the floor than on a bed or couch. No special treatment is required and within a few minutes the convulsion will cease, respiration will become regular and color will return to normal. The child should then be allowed to sleep until spontaneous awakening occurs.

If the convulsion persists for a long time or repeated convulsions develop in close succession, i.e. *status epilepticus,* some steps must be taken to control them. Chloral is used very frequently by pediatricians. This is given by rectum through a small catheter. At six months 4 grains are used, at one year 6 grains and at two years, 8 grains. If necessary, the dose may be repeated in an hour. Morphine is sometimes necessary and is recommended when there is evidence of heart failure. The dose is 1/40 grain at six months, 1/20 grain at one year, and 1/16 at two years. If these remedies are not effective or if it seems imperative to stop the convulsions at once, ether may be used. Another remedy frequently used is intravenous phenobarbital. Recently, avertin has been employed with very satisfactory results,

its prolonged action offering obvious advantages over ether and chloroform. Some authorities give sodium pentothal intravenously and follow this by phenobarbital. Others prefer paraldehyde intramuscularly though this is somewhat irritating. Parsonage and Norris advise the use of dizepam. The treatment of epilepsy is still very unsatisfactory despite the introduction of several new methods. The Drug Treatment of Epilepsy by Livingston should be consulted. First we must emphasize that general hygiene is important. Any tendency towards constipation must be treated appropriately. Sleep, rest, exercise and diet should be carefully controlled. Even more important, perhaps, is the elimination of nervous strain and excitement. These children should not be allowed to undertake more than they can accomplish in school work or athletics, but at the same time they should not be prevented from accomplishing as much as they can without undue effort. Discipline should be firm and impersonal as far as possible. The child's attitude to the illness is important. The usual point of view that epilepsy is a disgrace and should be concealed at all costs is very unfortunate. Moreover, the child should not be encouraged to develop the idea of inferiority or invalidism. The parents must impress the idea upon the patient that epilepsy is a common condition which is not hopeless or in any way discreditable and that it must be allowed to interfere with the child's life as little as possible. Food should be simple, easily digested and such as to prevent constipation. Overeating should be avoided.

Barbiturates are important. Phenobarbital is one of the most valuable drugs, and very effective in preventing convulsions. It may be given to infants in doses of $\frac{1}{4}$ grain twice or three times a day and to older children in doses of $\frac{1}{2}$ grain twice or three times a day. Rarely a patient may be sensitive to the drug and develop a morbilliform rash and allergic reactions. It is claimed that if niacin is given with the phenobarbital, these reactions can be prevented. In some cases when the major attacks are controlled by the drug, the child may become very irritable and possibly have very frequent petit mal attacks. *Mebaral* or mephobarbital is closely related to phenobarbital. The dosage is approximately three times as large. Both of these drugs cause drowsiness when given in large doses. Sodium phenobarbital is soluble and may be injected. It is claimed that *gemonil* or methbarbital is especially helpful in seizures due to organic disease of the brain and in the myoclonic spasms or massive myoclonic seizures of infancy. This is barbiturate and is said to be non-toxic.

Hydantoinates such as dilantin and mesantoin are also valuable drugs. Dilantin or diphenylhydantoin may be used in infancy in doses of $\frac{1}{2}$ grain two or three times a day and older children may take up to three grains a day. This drug controls grand mal seizures very effectively and may have some value in psychomotor epilepsy, but is thought to aggravate petit mal.

The list of untoward reactions is a long one but in most instances such reactions occur only as a result of excessive dosage. Skin eruptions of various kinds are common and may be associated with fever. Livingston advises the withdrawal of the drug at once for eruptions may indicate a serious illness. A smooth hyperplasia of the gums is characteristic. Gastric irritation is sometimes troublesome and may require the use of dilute hydrochloric acid to neutralize the alkaline drug. An overgrowth of body hair may result. This may be in the form of an excessive growth of sexual hair of masculine distribution or of a generalized excess of hair over the whole body. Loss of hair also occurs in rare cases and severe alopecia is mentioned. A few cases of polyarthropathy are reported.

Cerebellar ataxia with nystagmus may occur when large doses are given for a long time. Diplopia and blurred vision as well as disturbances of speech are mentioned. These symptoms usually disappear within a week or two when the drug is stopped but I have seen two cases in which the ataxia was still pronounced a year after the drug was withdrawn. Degenerative changes in the cerebellum have been found in the cerebellum by Utterback and by Hoffmann in such cases. I have a strong impression that toxic doses of dilantin may cause tonic seizures. Lovelace and Horowitz find that prolonged administration of dilantin may result in loss of the knee and ankle jerks and sometimes with loss of sensibility in the legs. Significant loss of strength in the legs does not seem to be a problem.

Agranulocytosis and hepatitis are extremely rare. A preparation for intravenous use is now available. Saltzstein *et al.* state that dilantin and related drugs may cause fever, cutaneous eruptions, lymphadenopathy, eosinophilia and hepatosplenomegaly in such a way as to stimulate lymphoma. These symptoms recede when the drug is withdrawn.

Mesantoin, or methylphenyl hydantoin, is used for convulsions and psychomotor attacks. It is not helpful in petit mal. It does not make the gums swell. About 10 per cent of patients are sensitive to this drug. There may be fever, enlargement of the lymph nodes, and a cutaneous eruption. The picture may resemble scarlet fever or Hodgkin's disease. Blood destruction may result. In some cases, irreversible bone marrow damage occurs without warning. Hepatitis is mentioned. Frequent blood counts should be made. The drug is sold in 100 mg tablets. Children may be given from one to four tablets a day.

The *dione drugs* include tridione or trimethyloxyzolidine dione, and paradione or methyloxyzolidine. These drugs are often effective against petit mal; however, in some cases they fail. It is believed that convulsions may be aggravated. If convulsions occur, phenobarbital or mysoline may be added. Dilantin is not effective in such cases for tridione seems to neutralize its effect. Drowsiness is a common effect of these drugs. In some instances,

they cause sensitiveness to light. Bright light is dazzling. Serious leukopenia may occur and frequent blood counts are required. The white count usually returns to normal when the drug is stopped, but fatal cases are described. Rosenblum states that nephrosis may result. Children may start with 150 mgs three times a day of either tridione or paradione.

Phenurone, or phenacetylcarbamide, is said to be effective against convulsions, psychomotor seizures and petit mal. It sometimes controls seizures which are resistant to other drugs. It may aggravate personality disorders which occur in psychomotor epilepsy and cause psychoses. In about four patients in 1,000, it may cause serious damage to the liver.

The *succhinimides* include celontin, or n-methyl-a-a-methylphenyl succinimide, miltonin or methylphenyl succinimide and zerontin or 2-ethyl-2-mcthyl succinimide. It is claimed that these drugs are effective against some cases of petit mal, grand mal, and psychomotor epilepsy. Confusion and abnormal behavior may result. Drowsiness, ataxia and skin eruptions have been observed. Leukopenia is not common. The initial dosage is 300 mgs twice a day.

Diamox, or 2-acetyl-1-3-4 thiadazola 5 sulfonamide, inhibits the carbonic anhydrase enzyme system. It may control petit mal and occasionally convulsions. It may be helpful if added to other drugs. It is supplied in 250 mgs tablets. Children may take half a tablet, twice a day, as an initial dosage. This drug may cause drowsiness, ataxia, nausea and urinary incontinence.

Bromides are effective against convulsions. Livingston states that they may be the most satisfactory drugs for convulsions due to organic disease. They are rarely used now, for it is impossible to control the blood level unless one controls the fluid and salt intake. Acne commonly results, and if the blood level gets too high, bromide delirium may occur.

Only one drug of the *pyrimidine* series is used and this is myosoline. The average dosage for children under six years of age is 125 mgs three times a day. This drug is effective against grand mal attacks but not against petit mal or psychomotor seizures. It may cause nausea and vomiting, somnolence and paranoid trends in certain patients. The last are said to be rare.

Snyder states that valium and mogadon are effective in the treatment of myoclonic epilepsy. Valium is less toxic than mogadon.

Bell states that in status epilepticus the addition of valium to other anticonvulsive drugs usually stops the seizures, but will sometimes cause serious hypotension or respiratory depression.

It is very important for medication to be taken with perfect regularity. Failure to take the medication is very frequently responsible for a return of seizures and is probably the commonest cause of status epilepticus.

A number of diets have been recommended for epilepsy. The only one

which is used at present is the *ketogenic diet*. This involves the use of large amounts of fat and the reduction of carbohydrates with the intention of causing a ketone body acidosis. It is the practice to start treatment with a brief period of fasting of five or six days during which water alone is given. Then a diet is administered containing large amounts of butter, cream, oil dressings, such as mayonnaise, eggs, bacon and meat. The total caloric value of the diet should, of course, be sufficient for the child's needs and there should be at least 1 gram of protein per kilogram of body weight. It is advised to supply 80 to 90 per cent of the calories in the form of fat. Acetone and diacetic acid will appear in the urine soon after this diet is begun. If these bodies are absent, it may be suspected that the child is stealing food. Detailed discussion of the calculation of the diet may be found in Livingston's book. He states that this regimen is most effective in children between the ages of two and five years, that it is especially helpful in minor seizures and akinetic and myoclonic types and in children whose electroencephalogram shows spikes and wave forms. He also states that in a large percentage of patients whose seizures have been controlled by this diet, there is no recurrence of the attacks when the diet is stopped.

It must be kept in mind that the ketogenic diet is not a proper diet and certain untoward effects are to be expected. There is decalcification of the bones and reduction of growth in some cases. Dr. David Clark tells me that he has seen renal rickets result. The child loses weight and is somewhat dehydrated. The blood cholesterol is elevated sometimes to very high levels. We have seen lipemia in a child whose retinal vessels appeared to be full of cream.

Grand mal seizures are best treated with a combination of phenobarbital and dilantin. If these drugs are not effective, mysoline may be added. By such combinations strong protection is secured and untoward effects avoided.

Petit mal attacks are treated with tridione or paradione. If neither drug is effective and both drugs together are also ineffective, ketogenic diet may be tried especially if the child is between 2 and 5 years. In some cases quinacrine is strikingly effective, it is claimed.

Psychomotor seizures are not easily controlled. Livingston advises dilantin or mesantoin. More recently he has found that tegretol, i.e. carbamazopine, is an effective drug in psychomotor epilepsy. For *massive myoclonic seizures* or *infantile spasms,* ACTH is advised and gemonil.

Prognosis.—The prognosis as regards life is not unfavorable as a rule since only a few children die as a direct result of the seizures. The frequency of the attacks seems to be of little importance but tendency to develop seizures in series, that is to *status epilepticus,* is of unfavorable prognostic import in this respect. The writer recalls the case of a child who was

often free from attacks for periods of many months or even a year and then would suddenly develop status epilepticus. Death occurred in the third episode some four years after the onset.

It is very difficult to form any idea of the prognosis in epilepsy in childhood because of the uncertainty about the diagnosis in many cases. If we should include all children who have convulsions for which no cause can be found, we should find that the prognosis is very favorable, since in a large proportion of cases, there are only one or two attacks. If, on the other hand, we restrict the diagnosis to those cases in which repeated seizures occur over long periods of time, we have made the prognosis much more unfavorable by our method of selection. It is customary to include only cases of *repeated seizures* of *unknown origin*. The study of such a group reveals that the prognosis for ultimate recovery is unfavorable but probably not so unfavorable as is generally assumed. Wilkins has reviewed a large series of cases followed for long periods at the Harriet Lane Home and has found that 24 per cent of these children became free from attacks for over one year and 15 per cent for over three years. Certain patients had remained well for ten years or more. Turner's figures are very similar. He found that in those cases of epilepsy which began under ten years of age, freedom from attacks for two years or more occurred in 19 per cent. It seems evident, therefore, that there is a tendency towards recovery or at least to remission during childhood. The subsequent fate of these children is uncertain and we have no significant figures bearing on the probability of recurrence of symptoms later in life. The writer has seen numerous instances, however, in which the seizures returned between the ages of 15 and 25 years.

According to Wilkins' analysis, the most important factor affecting the prognosis for remission is the frequency of seizures. In the groups of cases having attacks less frequent than one a month, the incidence of remissions was 45 per cent, as contrasted with 16 per cent in the group whose attacks were more frequent. It is important to realize that even though a child has had repeated convulsions unassociated with febrile reactions over a number of years, there is a fair possibility of remission provided the attacks have been spaced at long intervals. However, even in the severest cases remissions sometimes occur unexpectedly. The type of seizure affects the prognosis to some extent, apparently. The incidence of remissions was 24 per cent in patients having predominantly grand mal attacks; 27 per cent in patients with focal seizures and 15 per cent in patients with predominantly petit mal seizures.

It is difficult to determine to what extent treatment is responsible for long remissions or recovery. In most instances when the seizures have been

reduced or stopped by the use of drugs, the withdrawal of the drugs causes a return of the seizures. In Wilkins' series, many of the patients had been rendered free of attacks during treatment by drugs or by diet and the treatment had been gradually withdrawn without relapse. In other cases, however, treatment had been administered regularly for long periods without any apparent benefit and then suddenly, without any apparent reason, the attacks had ceased and the patient had remained well for years without treatment. In other cases the remissions occurred when the patient was not being treated. In evaluating the results of treatment, therefore, we should keep in mind the possibility of spontaneous remission.

If the seizures continue at frequent intervals and no tendency to remission is evident, it is not likely that the child will be able to enjoy a normal or even useful life. In severe cases institutional care is often required. Dekaban points out that frequent attacks in early infancy often cause extreme and permanent mental deficiency. Post-mortem study of six such infants failed to reveal any structural basis for the symptoms.

An occasional seizure, however, is not justification for a bad prognosis for I know of a number of patients who have had successful careers despite this handicap.

BIBLIOGRAPHY

General

BRIDGE, E. M.: Epilepsy and Convulsive Disorders. McGraw-Hill Book Co. Inc., New York, 1949.

COBB, S. AND LENNOX, W. G.: Epilepsy. Baltimore, Williams & Wilkins, 1928.

FALCONER, M. A. AND TAYLOR, D. C.: Surgical treatment of drug-resistant epilepsy due to mesial temporal sclerosis. Arch. of Neurol., **19**:353, 1968.

GOWERS, WM.: Epilepsy and Other Chronic Convulsive Diseases. Adlard and Son. London, 1901.

————: The Borderland of Epilepsy. Adlard and Son. London, 1907.

LENNOX, W. G., GIBBS, E. L. AND GIBBS, F. A.: Inheritance of cerebral dysrhythmia and epilepsy. Arch. Neurol. & Psychiat., **44**:1155, 1940.

LIVINGSTON, S.: Living with epileptic seizures. Thomas, Springfield, 1963.

————: The Diagnosis and Treatment of Convulsive Disorders in Children. Springfield, Thomas, 1954.

MUSKENS, L. J.: Epilepsy. New York, Wm. Wood & Co., 1928.

TURNER, A.: Epilepsy; A Study of the Idiopathic Disease. New York, Macmillan & Co., 1907.

Pathological Anatomy

AFIFI, A. K. AND VAN ALLEN, M. W.: Cerebellar atrophy in epilepsy. Jour. Neurol. Neurosurg. and Psychiat., **31**:169, 1968.

COBB, S. AND GILDEA, E. F.: The effect of anemia on the cerebral cortex of the cat. Arch. Neurol. & Psychiat., **23**:876, 1930.

DANDY, W. E.: Impressions of the pathology of epilepsy from operation. Am. J. Psychiat., **6**:519, 1927.

FALCONER, M. A. AND TAYLOR, D. C.: Surgical treatment of drug resistant epilepsy due to mesial temporal sclerosis. Arch. of Neurol., **19**:353, 1968.

NOTKIN, J.: Encephalographic studies in cryptogenic epilepsy. Arch. Neurol. & Psychiat., **26**:115, 1931.

PENDERGRASS, E. P.: Interpretation of encephalographic observations; comments on those found in convulsive states. Arch. Neurol. & Psychiat., **23**:946, 1930.

PENFIELD, W. AND ERICKSON, T. C.: Epilepsy and Cerebral Localization. Springfield, Illinois, Charles C Thomas, 1941.

ROBB, P.: Epilepsy. A review of basic and clinical research. NINDB Monograph No. 1, 1965.

SOUTHARD, E. E. AND THOM, D. A.: Contributions from the State Board of Insanity, Mass. No. 46, 1915.

SPIELMEYER, W.: The anatomic substratum of the convulsive state. Arch. Neurol. & Psychiat., **23**:869, 1930.

WOHLWILL, F.: Ueber akute Pseudolaminäre Ausfalle in der Grosshirn bei Krampfkranken. Monatschr. f. Psychiat. u. Neurol., **80**:139, 1931.

Electroencephalography

ADRIAN, E. D.: The origin of the Berger rhythm. Brain, **58**:323, 1935.

AJMONE-MARSAN, C. AND RALSTON, R. L.: The Epileptic Seizure. A clinical-electrographic analysis of metrazol induced attacks. Springfield, Thomas, 1957.

BUCY, P.: The clinical use of electroencephalography. J. Neurosurg., **14**:442, 1957.

BYERS, R. K.: Electroencephalography. Critical review. J. Pediat., **18**:811, 1941.

FOIS, A.: The Electroencephalogram of the Normal Child. Springfield, Thomas, 1961.

GIBBS, E. L., MERRITT, H. H. AND GIBBS, F. A.: Electroencephalographic foci associated with epilepsy. Arch. Neurol. & Psychiat., **49**:793, 1943.

GIBBS, F. A. AND GIBBS, E. L.: Atlas of Electroencephalography. 2nd Ed. Boston, Addison-Wesley Press, Inc., 1950.

GIBBS, F. A., GIBBS, E. L. AND LENNOX, W. G.: The electroencephalogram in diagnosis and localization of epileptic seizures. Arch. Neurol. & Psychiat., **36**:1225, 1936.

JASPER, H. H.: Electrical signs of cortical activity. Psychol. Bull., **34**:411, 1937.

JASPER, H. AND KERSHMAN, J.: Electroencephalographic classification of the epilepsies. Arch. Neurol. & Psychiat., **45**:903, 1941.

LEMERE, F.: Electroencephalography as a method of distinguishing true from false blindness. J.A.M.A., **118**:884, 1942.

LÖWENBACH, H.: The electroencephalogram in healthy relatives of epileptics. Bull. Johns Hopkins Hosp., **65**:125, 1939.

PENFIELD, W.: Epilepsy and Cerebral Localization. Springfield, Thomas, 1941. (Containing an article by Jasper on Electroencephalography.)

SCHULTE, VON F. J. AND HERRMANN, B.: Elektrencephalographie beim Neugeborenen. Monatash. f. Kinderheilk., **113**:457, 1965.

STEWART, W. A.: Electroencephalographic changes associated with different forms of experimentally produced increased intracranial pressure. Bull. Johns Hopkins Hosp., **69**:240, 1941.

WALTER, W. G.: The localization of cerebral tumors by electroencephalography. Lancet, **ii**:305, 1936.

————: Technique and application of electroencephalography. J. Neurol. & Psychiat., **1**:359, 1938.

Etiology

BACKUS, R. E. AND MILLICHAP, J. G.: The seizure as a manifestation of intracranial tumor in childhood. Pediatrics, **29**:978, 1962.

CHURCHILL, J. A.: The relationship of epilepsy to breech delivery. EEG and Clin. Neurophysiol., **11**:1, 1959.

COBB, S. AND LENNOX, W. G.: The relation of certain physico-chemical processes to epileptiform seizures. Am. J. Psychiat., **8**:837, 1929.

————: The causes of epilepsy. Arch. Neurol. & Psychiat., **27**:1245, 1932.

FAY, TEMPLE: Generalized pressure atrophy of the brain secondary to traumatic and pathologic involvement of the pacchionian bodies. J.A.M.A., **94**:245, 1930.

GAMBLE, J. L. AND HAMILTON, B.: The acid base composition of urine from an epileptic child. Bull. Johns Hopkins Hosp., **41**:389, 1927.

HENDRICK, E. B. AND HARRIS, L.: Post-traumatic epilepsy in children. Jour. Trauma., **8**:547, 1968.

KOCH, G.: Investigationes cromosomicas en las epilepsias. Folia Clinica Internacional, **xv**:6, 1965.

———: Die Erblichkeit der Epilepsien. Psychiat., Neurol. Neurochir., **66**:153, 1963.

LENNOX, W. G.: Metabolism in epilepsy; bicarbonate content of the blood. Arch. Neurol. & Psychiat., **20**:155, 1928.

———: Studies in epilepsy, basal metabolism. Arch. Neurol. & Psychiat., **20**:764, 1928.

———: Studies in epilepsy, chloride content of the blood and spinal fluid. Arch. Neurol. & Psychiat., **23**:525, 1930.

———: Studies in epilepsy, sugar content of the spinal fluid. Arch. Neurol. & Psychiat., **23**:521, 1930.

LENNOX, W. G. AND ALLEN, M. B.: Studies in epilepsy, calcium content of blood and spinal fluid. Arch. Neurol. & Psychiat., **24**:1199, 1930.

LENNOX, W. G., O'CONNOR, M. F. AND WRIGHT, L. H.: Metabolism in epilepsy, non-protein nitrogenous constituents of the blood. Arch. Neurol. & Psychiat., **11**:54, 1924.

LILLIENFELD, A. M.: Association of maternal and fetal factors with development of epilepsy. J.A.M.A., **155**:119, 1954.

McQUARRIE, I.: Experimental studies of the acid base equilibrium in children with epilepsy. Am. J. Dis. Child., **37**:261, 1929.

TOWER, D. B.: Neurochemistry of Epilepsy. Springfield, Thomas, 1960.

WUTH, O.: Blood changes in convulsions especially epilepsy. Bull. Johns Hopkins Hosp., **38**:389, 1926.

Clinical Features: Incidence and Racial Distribution

DAVENPORT, C. B.: Ecology of Epilepsy; racial and geographic distribution of epilepsy. Arch. Neurol. & Psychiat., **9**:554, 1923.

POLOCK, H. M. AND FURBUSH, E. M.: Epileptics in institutions in United States. Ment. Hyg., **11**:369, 1927.

Inheritance

BRAIN, W. R.: The inheritance of epilepsy. Quart. J. Med., **19**:300, 1926.

BURR, C. W.: Heredity in epilepsy. Arch. Neurol. & Psychiat., **7**:721, 1922.

CONRAD, K.: Die Bedeutung der Erbanlage bei der Epilepsie. Untersuchung an 253 Zwillings-paaren. Deutsch. Ztschr. f. Nervenheilk., **139**:76, 1936.

RÜDEN, E.: Der gegenwartige Stande der Epilepsie forschung. IV. Genealogischer Ztschr. f. d. ges. Neurol. u. Psychiat., **89**:368, 1924.

THOM, D. A. AND WALKER, G. S.: Epilepsy in the offspring of epileptics. Am. J. Psychiat., **1**:613, 1922.

Febrile Convulsions

FOWLER, M.: Brain damage after febrile convulsions in children. Arch. of Dis. Child., **32**:67, 1957.

LIVINGSTON, S., BRIDGE, E. M. AND KAJDI, L.: Febrile convulsions; A clinical study with special reference to heredity and prognosis. J. Pediat., **31**:509, 1947.

MORSE, J. L.: Convulsions and epilepsy. Am. J. Dis. Child., **18**:73, 1919.

PATRICK, H. T. AND LEVY, D. M.: Early convulsions in epileptics and others. J.A.M.A., **82**:375, 1924.

SCHMIDT, R. P.: Sequelae of febrile convulsions. Med. Clin. North America. 1958, March, p. 389.

SCHUMAN, S. H. AND MILLER, L. J.: Febrile convulsions in families. Clin. Pediat., **5**:604, 1966.

SHANAHAN, W. J.: Convulsions in infancy and their relation if any to subsequent epilepsy. Am. J. Psychiat., **7**:591, 1928.

THOM, D. A.: Infantile convulsions, their frequency and importance. Am. J. Psychiat., **6**:613, 1927.

TURNER, W. A.: Observations on epilepsy. J. Neurol. & Psychopath., **7**:193, 1927.

Status Epilepticus

BOUTTIER, H.: Questions Neurologiques d'actualité, Paris, 1922.

TUCKER, W. M. AND FORSTER, F. M.: Petit mal epilepsy occurring in status. Arch. Neurol. & Psychiat., **64**:823, 1950.

Focal Elements in Essential Epilepticus

HOLOWACH, J. *et al.*: Petit mal epilepsy in children. Pediatrics, **30**:893, 1962.

KNAPP, A.: Cerebrale Herdsymptome bei genuinen Epilepsie. Ztschr. f. d. ges. Neurol. u. Psychiat., **75**:60, 1922.

Petit Mal

LIVINGSTON, S. *et al.*: Petit Mal Epilepsy. Jour. Amer. Med. Ass., **194**:227, 1965.

MILLICHAP, J. G. AND ULRICH, J. A.: Amino acid excretion in epilepsy. Proc. Staff. Meet. Mayo Clinic, **37**:307, 1962.

————: Evaluation of drug effects and development of a potential new therapy (pyrictal). Neurology, **10**:575, 1960.

————: A critical evaluation of febrile seizures. J. Pediat., **56**:364, 1960.

————: Febrile seizures and the balance of water and electrolytes. Neurology, **10**:312, 1960.

————: Height of the body temperature as a measure of the febrile seizure threshold. Pediatrics, **23**:76, 1959.

————: Studies in febrile seizures. Clinical and electroencephalographic study in unselected cases. Neurology, **10**:643, 1960.

PENRY, J. K. AND DREIFUSS, F. E.: Automatisms associated with absence of petit mal epilepsy. Neurology, **21**:142, 1969.

Psychomotor Attacks

DAVIDSON, G. A.: Psychomotor epilepsy. Canada M. J., **53**:410, 1947.

GIBBS, E. L. AND GIBBS, F. A.: Psychomotor epilepsy. Arch. Neurol. & Psychiat., **60**:331, 1948.

GLASSER, G. H. AND DIXON, M. S.: Psychomotor seizures in childhood. Neurology, **6**:646, 1956.

Effects of Menses

LAIDLAW, M. B.: Catamenial epilepsy. Lancet, **271**:1235, 1956.

Running Fits

SISLER, G. C., LEVY, L. L. AND ROSEMAN, E.: Epilepsia cursiva. Arch. Neurol. & Psychiat., **69**:73, 1953.

Drop Seizures

HUNT, J. R.: On the occurrence of static seizures in epilepsy. J. Nerv. & Ment. Dis., **56**:351, 1922.

Abdominal Epilepsy

LIVINGSTON, S.: Abdominal pain as a manifestation of epilepsy. J. Pediat., **38**:687, 1951.

MOORE, M. T.: Abdominal epilepsy. Rev. Gastroenterol., **15**:381, 1948.

————: Abdominal epilepsy. Am. J. Med. Sc., **220**:87, 1950.

MULDER, D., DALY, D. AND BAILEY, A.: Visceral epilepsy. Arch. Int. Med., **93**:481, 1954.

Post Convulsive Phenomena

FOWLER, M.: Brain damage after febrile convulsions. Arch. Dis. Child., **32**:67, 1957.

PRITCHARD, E.: Case of amaurosis following violent convulsions. Proc. Roy. Soc., **11**:14, 1918.

SPIVAK, J. L. AND CONTI, C. R.: Post-seizure myoglobinuria. Johns Hopkins Medical Jour., 124:18, 1969.

Infantile Spasms

CRAIG, W. S.: Convulsive movements occurring in the first 10 days of life. Arch. of Dis. Child., 35:336, 1960.
POSER, C. M.: Neuropathologic findings in three cases of infantile spasms. Brain Research Foundation. Molecules and Mental Health. Gibbs, F. A. ed. Philadelphia, Lippincott, 1959, p. 150.
SINTON, D. W. AND PATTERSON, P. R.: Infantile spasms. Neurology, 12:351, 1962.

Myoclonic Movements

SCHULTE, F. J.: Neonatal convulsions and their relation to epilepsy in early childhood. Developmental Med. and Child Neurol., 8:381, 1966.
SYMONDS, SIR C.: Nocturnal myoclonus. J. Neurol., Neurosurg. & Psychiat., 16:166, 1953.
WILSON, S. A. K.: Epileptic variants. J. Neurol. & Psychiat., 8:223, 1928.

Pyknolepsy

ADIE, W. J.: Pyknolepsy: A form of epilepsy occurring in children with a good prognosis. Brain, 47:96, 1924.
OWEN, J. W. AND BERLINROAD, L.: Pyknolepsy. J. Pediat., 19:762, 1941.

Mental Disorders

BEARD, A. W. AND SLATER, E.: The schizophrenic-like psychoses of epilepsy. Proc. Royal Soc. Med., 55:311, 1961.
BRIDGE, E. M.: The mental state of the epileptic patient. Arch. Neurol. & Psychiat., 32:723, 1934.
RICHMOND, W.: Psychometric tests in essential epilepsy. J. Abnorm. Psychol., 16:384, 1921.

Pseudoseizures

KEATING, L. E.: Epilepsy and behavior in school children. Jour. Ment. Sci., 107:161, 1961.
LISKE, E., AND FORSTER, F. M.: Pseudoseizures: A problem in diagnosis and management. Neurology, 14:41, 1964.

Spinal Fluid

KULKOFF, A. K.: Die Liquor Cerebrospinalis bei genuinen Epilepsie. Arch. f. Psychiat., 88:114, 1929.
PATTERSON, H. A. AND LEVI, P.: The spinal fluid in epilepsy. Arch. Neurol. & Psychiat., 15:353, 1926.

Urine

NOVICK, N.: The frequency of albuminuria and casts in epileptics following convulsive seizures. Arch. Neurol. & Psychiat., 4:546, 1920.

Diagnosis

JAFFE, J.: Ictal behavior as the only manifestation of a seizure disorder. Jour. of Nerv. and Ment. Dis., 134:470, 1962.
MCQUARRIE, I. AND PEELER, D. B.: The effects of sustained pituitary antidiuresis and forced water drinking in epileptic children. A diagnostic and etiologic study. J. Clin. Invest., 10:915, 1931.
PATRICK, H. T. AND LEVY, D. M.: The diagnosis of epilepsy. J.A.M.A., 79:1009, 1922.
PRATT, K. L. et al.: Electroencephalogram activation of epileptics following sleep deprivation. Electroencephalograph. clin. Neurophysiol., 24:11, 1968.

Treatment

BELL, D. S.: The dangers of treatment of status epilepticus with diazepam (Valium). Brit. Med., i:159, 1968.

CARTER, H. R.: Mesantoin. A new anticonvulsant in management of epilepsy. Rocky Mountain M. J., 14:614, 1947.

DAVIS, J. P. AND LENNOX, W. G.: Effect of tridione on the blood. J. Pediat., 31:24, 1947.

DE JONG, R. N.: Effect of tridione in control of psychomotor attacks. J.A.M.A., 130:565, 1946.

DIETHELM, O.: The bromide treatment for epilepsy in the dispensary. Arch. Neurol. & Psychiat., 21:664, 1929.

DONNER, M. AND FRISK, M.: Carbamazepine (tegretol) treatment of epileptic and psychotic symptoms in children and adolescents. Ann. Paediat. Fenniae., 11:91, 1965.

FAY, T.: The therapeutic effect of dehydration on epileptic patients. Arch. Neurol. & Psychiat., 23:920, 1930.

GRINKER, J.: Further experiences with phenobarbital in epilepsy. J.A.M.A., 79:788, 1922.

HANDLEY, R. AND STEWART, A.: Mysoline, a new drug in the treatment of epilepsy. Lancet, i:742, 1952.

HARRIS, T. H. AND OTTO, J. L.: Hydantoin (mesantoin) as an anticonvulsant drug. Texas State M. J., 43:328, 1947.

KEITH, H. M.: Results of treatment of recurrent convulsive attacks of epilepsy. Am. J. Dis. Child., 74:140, 1947.

KIMBALL, O. P. AND HORAN, T. N.: The use of Dilantin in the treatment of epilepsy. Am. Inst. Med., 13:787, 1939.

LENNOX, W. G.: Petit mal epilepsies: Their treatment with tridione. J.A.M.A., 129:1069, 1945.

LEVY, L. AND FENICHEL, G. M.: Diphenylhydantoin activated seizures. Neurology, 13:195, 1965.

LIVINGSTON, S.: Drug Therapy for Epilepsy. Thomas, Springfield, 1966.

———: Treatment of epilepsy with diphenylhydantoin sodium. Postgrad. Med., 20:584, 1956.

LIVINGSTON, S. AND BOKS, L. L.: The use of the dione drugs in the treatment of epilepsy of children. New England J. Med., 253:138, 1955.

LIVINGSTON, S., KAJDI, L. AND BRIDGE, E. M.: The use of benzedrine and dexedrine sulphate in the treatment of epilepsy. J. Pediat., 32:490, 1948.

LIVINGSTON, S. AND PETERSEN, D.: Primidone (Mysoline) in the treatment of epilepsy. New England J. Med., 254:327, 1956.

LOGAN, W. J. AND FREEMAN, J. M.: Pseudodegenerative disease due to diphenylhydantoin intoxication. Neurology, 21:6, 631, 1969.

LOVELACE, R. E. AND HOROWITZ, S. J.: Peripheral neuropathy in long term diphenylhydantoin therapy. Arch. of Neurol., 18:69, 1968.

MERRITT, H. H. AND PUTNAM, T. J.: Sodium diphenyl-hydantoinate in the treatment of convulsive disorders. J.A.M.A., 111:1068, 1938.

PARSONAGE, M. AND NORRIS, J. W.: Use of diazepam in treatment of severe convulsive status epilepticus. Brit. Med. Jour., 3:85, 1967.

PATRICK, H. T.: Epilepsy in children. Am. J. Dis. Child., 35:653, 1928.

PAULSON, G. W.: Inhibition of seizures. Dis. Nerve Syst., 24:657, 1963.

PETERMAN, M. G.: Ketogenic diet in the treatment of epilepsy. Minnesota Med., 7:708, 1924.

SLOAN, L. L. AND GILGER, A. P.: Visual effects of tridione. Am. J. Ophth., 30:1387, 1947.

SNYDER, C. H.: Myoclonic epilepsy in children. Comparative study of two benzodiazepine derivatives in treatment. Southern Med. Jour., 61:17, 1968.

SPRATLING, W.: Epilepsy and Its Treatment. New York, W. B. Saunders Co., 1904.

TALBOT, F.: The Treatment of Epilepsy. New York, Macmillan & Co., 1930.

THOM, D. A.: Epilepsy and its rational extrainstitutional treatment. Am. J. Psychiat., 10:623, 1931.

WELLS, C. E.: Trimethadione: Its toxicity and dosage. Arch. Neurol. & Psychiat., 77:140, 1957.

WUTH, O.: Rational bromide treatment; new methods for its control. J.A.M.A., 88:2013, 1927.

Prognosis

CHRISTIANSEN, E. AND MELCHOIR, J.: Neuropathologic findings in children with infantile spasms. Danish Med. Bull., 7:121, 1960.

DEKOBAN, A.: Idiopathic epilepsy in early infancy causing undifferentiated type of mental deficiency. Am. J. Dis. Child., 100:181, 1960.

FEINBLATT, T. M. AND FERGUSON, E. A.: Phenobarbital idiosyncrasy. Avoidance by the use of phenobarbital-niacin. New York State J. Med., 62:221, 1962.

HOFFMANN, W. W.: Cerebellar lesions after parenteral dilantin administration. Neurology, 8:210, 1958.

MANLAPAZ, J. S.: Abducens palsy in dilantin intoxication. J. Pediat., 55:73, 1959.

MOORE, M. T.: Pulmonary changes due to hydantoin treatment. J.A.M.A., 171:1328, 1959.

ROSENBLUM, J.: Trimethadione nephrosis. J. Dis. Child., 97:790, 1959.

SALTZSTEIN, S. L. AND ACKERMAN, L. V.: Anticonvulsive drug-induced lymphoma like adenopathy. Cancer, 12:164, 1959.

UTTERBACK, R. A. *et al.*: Parenchymatous cerebellar degeneration with dilantin intoxication. J. Neuropath. Exp. Neurol., 17:516, 1958.

WILKINS, L.: Epilepsy in childhood. J. Pediat., 10:317, 1937.

FOCAL CONVULSIONS

Definition.—From the clinical point of view, focal epilepsy may be defined as a type of epilepsy in which the seizures are of such a nature that they consistently indicate a local origin in some part of the brain. The difference between focal seizures and generalized seizures is in reality one of degree. In some focal epilepsies the seizures are restricted to the segment in which they begin and in others, having begun locally, the seizure may extend over one half of the body or even become bilateral. Some focal seizures involve one whole side of the body simultaneously and extend into the opposite side a few moments later. There is good reason to believe that discharge of certain cortical areas in one hemisphere may cause bilateral movements. Such seizures must appear to be generalized. The more carefully epilepsies are studied, the more focal types are discovered and it is questionable whether truly generalized types exist. It has been shown that secondary epileptogenous foci arise as a result of continuous bombardment from the primary area. These secondary areas develop in a cortical region contralateral and homotopic with the primary area.

Pathological Anatomy.—Focal convulsions may occur in association with almost every known type of disease of the nervous system so it is impossible to offer any adequate description of the anatomical changes. If we exclude the active and progressive diseases, such as neoplasms and inflammatory processes, by our definition, we find most frequently local atrophy, scars, cysts and similar lesions with or without meningeal adhesions. It is no doubt significant that such lesions almost always involve the cerebral cortex. Developmental defects and malformations are not uncommon and numerous writers have described microgyria, pachygyria, distortion of the convolutional pattern and anomalous distribution of the cortical vessels. Ventric-

ulography and encephalography usually reveal asymmetries of the ventricles or lakes of air over the cortex. It must be said however, that similar lesions are found in the brains of the patients who do not have epilepsy and it is not possible to diagnose epilepsy by the examination of the brain.

Clinical Features.—Neurology is greatly indebted to the genius of Hughlings Jackson for his brilliant studies of focal epilepsies which threw so much light on the nature of epilepsy and on the functions of the cerebral cortex. Not a great deal was added to this subject until Foerster and his followers, among whom should be mentioned Penfield, began to make their investigations of traumatic epilepsy. These surgeons have made careful correlations between the nature of the seizures and the site of the lesion in a large number of cases and, by the combined methods of stimulation and ablation of all accessible parts of the cortex, have brought to light a wealth of new and important information. A great deal of the following material is derived from such sources. In recent years electroencephalographic studies have added a great deal to our knowledge.

Stimulation of the cerebral cortex in cases of focal epilepsy under local anesthesia is said to produce definitely abnormal reactions. It is claimed that it is usually possible to find an area in the cortex stimulation of which will induce a seizure more or less identical with those of which the patient complains. Such areas are termed *epileptogenous* or *trigger zones*. They lie, as a rule, in the margin of the anatomical lesion in regions which seem normal on gross inspection. Such zones it is claimed, show a lowered threshold to electrical stimulation and discharges arising within them tend to spread into adjacent parts of the brain in an abnormal fashion. Of course, many parts of the normal cortex respond to electrical stimulation and, by prolonged faradization, extensive discharges may be induced. Quantitative studies must be made, therefore, before we can say that the cortex reacts abnormally. Electroencephalographic studies reveal local abnormalities of various types in contrast to the widespread abnormalities seen in true epilepsy.

Frontal Lobe Discharges.—It is claimed that discharges arising in the frontal lobe anterior to area 4 are initiated by rotation of the head, eyes and the trunk to the opposite side. Consciousness is lost at the onset. Convulsive movements appear in the opposite arm and leg simultaneously. According to Foerster these movements are all due to discharge of area 6 a β. He states that the arm is usually abducted at the shoulder, flexed at the elbow, pronated at the forearm and flexed at the finger and wrist joints. The leg is extended. Less commonly the movements are reversed, the arm is extended and the leg flexed and abducted. These movements are first tonic and then clonic, flexion and extension alternating. Discharges arising in area 8 cause deviation of the eyes to the opposite side. Discharges arising

anterior to areas 6 and 8 are said to cause no movements. Penfield thinks that they may cause loss of consciousness and hence, may be responsible for some of the seizures termed petit mal. Fulton states that discharges arising in area 6 may cause disturbances of gastrointestinal activity and may explain the common epigastric aura. Discharges arising in the motor speech area result in the interruption of speech and are sometimes followed by transient motor aphasia. Ethelberg describes cataplexy as a manifestation of cortical lesions in the frontal lobes.

Precentral Gyrus Discharges.—Discharges arising in area 4 of Brodmann, which contains the giant pyramidal cells giving rise to the corticospinal motor tracts, are manifest by isolated movements of various muscle groups. In certain cases in which the spread of the excitation is very slow it has been possible to observe the sequence in which the various movements develop. In most cases is is found that the movements occur in an order corresponding to that in which they are represented in the cortex. Thus, if we assume that the discharge begins in the area in which movements of the foot are represented and spreads down over the motor cortex, the foot, ankle, knee, abdomen, chest, shoulder, arm, forearm, wrist, fingers, thumb, face and tongue are involved in succession. This rule is not observed in every case, however, and there is a great deal of variation in the sequence in which the movements may occur. Such fits were first described by Jackson and the term Jacksonian fits should be restricted to the seizures in which the various movements appear in the order described above. Deviation of the head and eyes do not always occur at the onset of such attacks. Consciousness is not, as a rule, definitely altered so long as the movements remain localized but, if the seizure becomes generalized, the patient is apt to become unconscious. Following the seizure there may be definite local paresis or even paralysis for a few minutes or hours. Such symptoms may follow every attack and disappear completely in the intervals. The cause is not clear. Some authorities attribute the weakness to exhaustion of the motor cells resulting from the violent discharges and others to vasoconstriction which is believed to be associated with convulsions.

Such seizures may begin in any part of the body but are most apt to begin in the hand or the face. They may remain localized to the part first affected or may spread over that side of the body or even become generalized. I have seen seizures manifest only by involuntary emptying of the bladder without disturbance of consciousness or other symptoms in a girl who was also subject to generalized seizures. These seizures are no doubt due to discharges in the paracentral lobule where control of the bladder is represented.

Ira Ross has reported a well-studied case of paroxysmal involuntary micturition in a boy of nine years. During several days of every month, mictu-

rition would occur every few minutes. In some instances, but not in all, there was loss of consciousness and tonic muscular contractions on the left side. As a rule, micturition was not associated with any other manifestation. Ross concluded that the discharging focus was in the diencephalon.

The term *epilepsia partialis continua* is applied to a persistent local twitching of the muscles of one segment, usually the fingers or wrist. It is regarded as evidence of a local irritative process causing more or less continuous discharge of motor neurons and is, usually, associated with more extensive seizures.

Parietal Lobe Discharges.—Discharges of the posterior central gyrus, i.e. areas 3, 1, 2 of Brodmann, give rise to various sensory disturbances. These are described as tingling, burning, numbness, hot and cold feelings and even at times as pain. Sensations of movement of the opposite arm and leg had been mentioned. In some cases these sensations are the only manifestations of the seizure but, in others, the discharge spreads to adjacent areas and convulsive movements appear. Sittig has made a study of the manner in which the sensory disturbances spread. He finds that in some instances they follow Jackson's law but that, in other cases, they spread irregularly. Such attacks may be followed by temporary loss of sensibility, even by brief analgesia.

Erickson has published a study of a patient who developed nymphomania. Later she had spontaneous orgasms. Then the orgasms were followed by scizures on the left side which were followed by hemiparesis. The ovaries were destroyed by x-ray therapy without result. A tumor was found at the upper end of the rolandic sulcus between the falx and the medial surface of the hemisphere on the right. When this was removed all the symptoms were relieved except for the hemiparesis. Penfield and Rasmussen describe a similar case in which a small glioma was found in the post central gyrus next to the falx.

Alverez states that in certain cases of epilepsy, especially minor seizures, premature ejaculation is often present. Dilantin usually gave relief.

It is stated by Foerster that discharges arising in area 5 are associated with mass movements similar to those described above as arising in area 6 a β the only difference being that in the seizures attributed to area 5 there is a sensory aura referred to the opposite side of the body and the movements spread to the homolateral side of the body very early. The sensory phenomena are projected over the entire body on the opposite side at the same moment.

Temporal Lobe Discharges.—A number of very interesting phenomena due no doubt to discharge of several areas in the temporal lobe are included within this group. Hughlings Jackson was one of the first to draw

attention to seizures of this type. As a rule the first manifestation of the approaching attack is a peculiar emotional disturbance, sometimes termed a "dreamy state." The patient may experience a feeling of terror or apprehension or things may seem changed and yet familiar or there may be the feeling that the patient has been through the same experience before. Usually accompanying these symptoms there is a strange odor or gustatory impression, in most cases a vile or disagreeable smell or taste. These gustatory and olfactory hallucinations may be accompanied by smacking of the lips and sniffing movements. In some cases complex visual hallucinations appear. Elaborate pictures of persons and animals are described. The attack may end without any further symptoms and without loss of consciousness or it may represent merely the prelude to a general convulsion. The olfactory impressions are attributed to discharges of the uncinate gyrus and hence, these attacks are often called *uncinate gyrus fits*. Discharges involving the lateral aspect of the temporal lobe are associated with loud noises in the ears. *Vertiginous seizures* may occur very suddenly. The patient may spin to one side and be thrown down. It is claimed that the mass movements described above in connection with fits arising in areas 5 and 6 occur in discharges of area 22 which includes the superior temporal gyrus. The auditory hallucinations are ascribed to the spread of the excitation into the transverse gyri of Heschl. Micropsia is said to be a feature of some seizures arising in the temporal lobe. We have studied the case of a child who always developed word deafness whenever his seizures, which resembled petit mal, were frequent. When the attacks were controlled by medication this difficulty disappeared.

Psychomotor attacks seem to be episodes of confusion. The patient will often perform some senseless act repeatedly. If addressed, there may be an incoherent reply. The patient may dance, shout, run away or fight. Asocial acts may be performed which are completely unmotivated. In such cases, the diagnosis is of medicolegal importance. Psychomotor attacks may be very brief or may last for hours or possibly days. The patient has no memory of the attack. Personality disorders and even psychoses are common. Anticonvulsive medication is often ineffective. Electroencephalographic studies have led to the belief that in many cases the seizures start in the anterior part of the temporal lobes, but perhaps extend into other areas. One temporal lobe or both may be involved. Bailey states that removal of the anterior part of the temporal lobe is helpful in many cases.

Blumer and Walker point out that temporal lobe epilepsy is associated with loss of interest in sex and after removal of the temporal lobe and control of the seizures, there may be a return of interest in sex or even a great increase in sexual desire.

Falconer *et al.* studied portions of the temporal lobe resected in 100 patients suffering from temporal lobe epilepsy. They found sclerosis in 24 cases, small cryptic tumors in 24 cases, scars and infarcts in 13, subpial and white matter gliosis in 12 and in 6 multiple lesions.

Occipital Lobe Discharges.—In contrast to the elaborate visual hallucinations which may occur in association with lesions of the temporal lobe, lesions which involve the primary visual centers about the calcarine fissure give rise to simple impressions such as flashes of light, splashes of color and scintillating scotomas of various types. These are always projected in the visual fields on the opposite side. Violent discharges in the occipital cortex may be followed by temporary hemianopia or less commonly by total blindness of brief duration.

The Limbic System.—Nelson and Ray state that seizures occurring in the limbic system may cause respiratory arrest. The apnea is of variable duration.

Discharges of Autonomic Mechanisms.—Penfield has described attacks characterized by changes in pulse and respiration, fluctuations of body temperature, sweating, chills, flushing, lacrimation, salivation, gooseflesh, hiccoughs and sometimes loss of consciousness. He suggests that these symptoms represent discharges of autonomic mechanisms in the diencephalon and proposes the term diencephalic autonomic epilepsy for them. In one case such attacks were due to a tumor of the third ventricle.

Fits of *sham rage* are believed to be due to discharges in the hypothalamus. These fits are rare in patients but may be produced in experimental animals by transections which sever the brain from the hypothalamus. Martin has studied cases of *uncontrollable laughter* which he has reason to think are due to lesions in the hypothalamus also. Druckman and Chao state that unprovoked laughter may indicate a discharge in the hypothalamus. Money and Hosta describe cases in which neoplasms or hamartomas of the hypothalamus were associated with laughing seizures and precocious puberty.

Reflex Epilepsy.—A number of cases have been described in which convulsive seizures could be induced by various stimuli. In several cases a sudden loud noise would produce a seizure. Critchley has reported cases in which music was the effective stimulus. Forster *et al.* describe a case in which certain voices induced seizures. Bright light thrown into the eyes will sometimes induce attacks. We have seen several cases of this type. Marshall, Walker and Livingston report a carefully studied case in which seizures could be induced by photic stimuli. We have seen several children who deliberately induced attacks by looking at a bright light and moving their fingers back and forth before their eyes. Several papers mention that look-

ing at television will induce attacks. Pantelakis points out that television induced convulsions are not rare in Britain but are not reported in the United States, where the television system has a much higher flicker threshold.

Green describes seizures induced by closing the eyes. In one case, the seizures occurred even when the patient closed the eyes in a dark room. Flicking the nose, pressure on a gum and stimulating one hand or leg are mentioned in various instances as the precipitating factor. Voluntary movement of an extremity is stated to induce attacks in some patients. We have seen a boy who developed generalized convulsions at the age of nine years. Some time later he got a splinter in the left *fourth* finger. After that movements of the left *fifth* finger would induce a convulsion. This history was verified while an electroencephalogram was being made. The seizure began with a burst of paroxysmal activity in the posterior part of the right hemisphere. The patient's mother refused further study (A. J. U-408076). Emotional reactions may also be effective in this regard. Reading may induce seizures.

Tonic Fits.—No clear definition of this term can be offered for a variety of seizures have been described which have nothing in common except for the fact that the muscular contractions involved are all tonic and no clonic contractions are present.

Hughlings Jackson and other neurologists of his time observed tonic seizures in cases of cerebellar tumor and spoke of cerebellar fits. It has since become clear, however, that these seizures are almost invariably associated with compression of the midbrain by tumors either above or below the tentorium. The attacks are characterized by strong extension of all four extremities and pronation of the forearms. The head may be retracted. There may be repeated brief seizures of this type but if the patient survives long enough, this posture is apt to become constant and is then described as decerebrate rigidity which of course is regarded as evidence of transection of the brain stem. It is very likely, therefore, that this condition is a release phenomenon and not a result of discharge. Penfield has pointed out that opisthotonos may be confused with this reaction. There seems to be no good evidence that discharges of the cerebellar mechanisms occur. Apparently scars due to old cerebellar abscesses do not cause fits.

Gowers and Barnes and Hurst have described tonic seizures in cases of lenticular degeneration. The latter state that the seizures are general and paroxysmal and superimposed on a background of persisting muscular rigidity. Consciousness is preserved. The attacks last about five seconds and occur once in about fifteen seconds. The back is extended, the neck flexed, the arms rigidly extended adducted and pronated, the legs adducted, slightly flexed at hip and knee and extended at the ankle. Any stimulus caused an accentuation of the muscular spasm. There was some fever and profuse

sweating. These attacks occur during an exacerbation of the neurological process. Barnes and Hurst state that the picture is almost identical with that of tetanus. Wimmer and others have described tonic fits in association with epidemic encephalitis. Cases of this type have been ascribed to discharges arising in the lenticular nuclei without entirely convincing evidence.

Lance describes a familial variety of tonic seizures in which there are no physical signs of organic disease. He also mentions sporadic cases in which evidences of damage to the brain are found.

I have observed a small number of cases of tonic fits in disseminated sclerosis. In one instance one side was involved and in others only one extremity was affected, usually one leg. The attacks occurred with considerable frequency during a period of weeks or months. There were gentle tonic muscular contractions causing extension of the extremity and lasting only a few moments. No disturbances of consciousness or other symptoms were associated.

Occasionally one observes a patient with tonic seizures resembling those seen in tetany but there are no signs of latent tetany and no chemical changes in the blood which one would expect to find in tetany. The cause of these is quite obscure.

Diagnosis.—Too much stress must not be placed upon focal signs which appear upon only one occasion, for we have already stated above that transient focal signs may occur in the course of generalized epilepsy. If, however, the attacks are consistently of a focal nature, we may be reasonably sure that there is a local lesion present. Our problem is that of determining the nature and cause of the lesion. Innumerable possibilities exist. For practical purposes we may distinguish two groups of focal epilepsies; those due to congenital defects of the brain, birth injuries, and scars or cysts resulting from injuries or infantile encephalitis, i.e. anatomically static lesions and those due to more active processes such as brain tumors, abscesses, hemangiomas, tuberculomas and syphilis. If the symptoms began early in life and if they have continued for a number of years without the development of additional symptoms, we may conclude with reasonable confidence that the case belongs in the first group. If, on the other hand, the seizures have begun only a short time before the child came under observation, the diagnosis is very much more difficult. The history is perhaps most important and care should be exercised to obtain a full description of the circumstances surrounding the first seizure and of all previous illnesses which may have caused cerebral damage. Physical examination may be negative or reveal no more than the evidences of a local cerebral lesion. If the diagnosis is not evident from the history and examination, we should have as a routine roentgenograms of the skull, tuberculin tests and Wassermann reactions of the blood and spinal fluid. In many cases we are justified in

performing ventriculography or encephalography. Electroencephalographic study is of value in distinguishing truly focal processes from generalized processes in which there are focal phenomena.

Treatment.—The treatment, of course, depends upon the cause and if specific therapy is possible, it should be employed in association with other measures to control the seizures. If the seizures are believed to be the result of a local brain injury, such as a scar or cyst, the attempt should be made to give relief by proper doses of phenobarbital and dilantin. Should these measures be ineffective, ketogenic diet may be tried and all other methods failing, we may consider operation and excision of the lesion. Foerster and Penfield have claimed very good results by a careful dissection of all scar tissue and removal of the epileptogenous focus which they localize by electrical stimulation. Electroencephalographic studies are now being applied to the exact localization of the discharging lesion. During operations under local anesthesia the electrodes may be applied directly to the cortex and the recordings are used to determine what areas should be removed. Metrazol is sometimes used to bring out the abnormal electrical discharges. In the opinion of the writer, operation should be reserved as a last resort. At the moment neurosurgery has little to offer.

In certain cases of infantile hemiplegia in which there is mental deficiency, abnormal behavior and frequent seizures which cannot be controlled by medication, the affected hemisphere is sometimes removed. Grossly destructive lesions are always found. It is claimed that the seizures may be diminished by this operation, behavior may improve and the motor defect is not increased. See Congenital Hemiplegia. Bailey and others remove the anterior part of the temporal lobe when study indicates that the seizures arise in that region. This operation is said to be helpful in many cases.

BIBLIOGRAPHY

ALLEN, I. M.: Observations on cases of reflex epilepsy. New Zealand Med. Jour., **44**:135, 1945.

ALVEREZ, W. C.: Premature ejaculation due to non-convulsive epilepsy. Modern Medicine, **37**:85, 1969.

ANDERMANN, K. *et al.*: Self induced epilepsy. Arch. of Neurol., 7:49, 1962.

BALDWIN, M.: Temporal Lobe Epilepsy. A Colloquim. Springfield, Thomas, 1958.

BARNES, S. AND HURST, E. W.: Hepatolenticular degeneration. Brain, **48**:279, 1925; Hepatolenticular degeneration. Brain, **49**:36, 1926; Hepatolenticular degeneration. Brain, **52**:1, 1929.

BAILEY, P.: Lobectomy for psychomotor epilepsy. South. Med. J., **34**:299, 1961.

BAXTER, D. W. AND BAILEY, A. A.: Primary reading epilepsy. Neurology, **11**:445, 1961.

BICKFORD, R., DALY, D. AND KEITH, H.: Convulsive effects of light stimulation in children. Am. J. Dis. Child., **86**:170, 1953.

BICKFORD, R. G. *et al.*: Hallucinatory epilepsy. Amer. Jour. of Psychiat., **113**:1100, 1957.

BINGLEY, T.: Mental symptoms in temporal lobe epilepsy and temporal lobe gliomas. Acta psychiatrica et neurologica Sup., **120**, vol. 33.

BLUMER, D. AND WALKER, A. E.: Sexual behavior in temporal lobe epilepsy. Arch. of Neurol., **16**:37, 1967.

BOWER, B. D.: Television flicker and seizures. Clin. Pediat., **2**:134, 1963.

BRAY, P. F.: Temporal lobe syndrome in children. Pediatrics, **29**:617, 1962.

CALDERON-GONGALEZ, R. *et al.:* Tap seizures a form of sensory precipation epilepsy. J.A.M.A., **198**:521, 1966.

CHARLTON, M. H. AND HOEFER, P. F. A.: Television-induced epilepsy. Arch. Neurol., **11**:239, 1964.

COBB, S.: Photic driving as a cause of clinical seizures in epileptic patients. Arch. Neurol. & Psychiat., **58**:70, 1947.

CRITCHLEY, M.: Reading epilepsy. Epilepsia, **3**:402, 1962.

DENNY-BROWN, D. AND ROBERTSON, E. G.: Observation on records of local epileptic convulsions. J. Neurol. & Psychopath., **15**:97, 1934.

DRUCKMAN, R. AND CHAO, D.: Laughter in epilepsy. Neurology, **7**:26, 1957.

ERICKSON, T. C.: Erotomania (nymphomania) as an expression of cortical epileptiform discharge. Arch. Neurol. & Psychiat., **53**:226, 1945.

ETHELBERG, S.: Symptomatic cataplexy or chalastic fits in cortical lesions of the frontal lobes. Brain, **73**:499, 1950.

FALCONER, M. A. *et al.:* Etiology and pathogenesis of temporal lobe epilepsy. Arch. of Neurol., **10**:233, 1964.

FOERSTER, O.: The motor cortex in the light of Hughlings Jackson's doctrines. Brain, **59**:135, 1936.

FOERSTER, O. AND PENFIELD, W.: The structural basis of traumatic epilepsy and the result of radical operation. Brain, **53**:99, 1930.

FORSTER, F. M. *et al.:* A case of voice-induced epilepsy treated by conditioning. Neurology, **19**:325, 1969.

FREEMON, F. R. AND NEVIS, A. H.: Temporal lobe sexual seizures. Neurology, **19**:87, 1969.

GOWERS, WM.: The Borderland of Epilepsy. Philadelphia, P. Blakiston's Son & Co., 1907.

GOWERS, W. R.: Epilepsy and Other Chronic Convulsive Diseases, Their Causes, Symptoms and Treatment. Baltimore, Wm. Wood & Co., 1881, p. 90.

GREEN, J. B.: Seizures on closing the eyes. Neurology, **18**:391, 1968.

HOLMES, G.: Savill memorial oration on local epilepsy. Lancet, **1**:957, 1927.

————: Local epilepsy. Lancet, **i**:957, 1927.

HOOSHMAND, H. AND BRAWLEY, B. W.: Temporal lobe seizures and exhibitionism. Neurology, **11**:1119, 1969.

HUTCHISON, J. H., STONE, F. H. AND DAVIDSON, J. R.: Photogenic epilepsy induced by the patient. Lancet, **1**:243, 1958.

INGVAR, D. AND NYMAN, E.: Epilepsia arithmetices. Neurology, **12**:281, 1962.

JACKSON, J. HUGHLINGS: Selected Writings. London, Hodder and Stoughton, 1931.

KENNEDY, R. FOSTER: The symptomatology of temporosphenoidal tumors. Arch. Int. Med., **8**:317, 1911.

LANCE, J. W.: Sporadic and familial varieties of tonic seizures. J. Neurol., Neurosurg. & Psychiat., **26**:51, 1963.

LANDAU, W. AND KLEFFNER, F. R.: Syndrome of acquired aphasia with convulsive disorder in children. Neurology, **7**:523, 1957.

LIVINGSTON, S.: Discussion of paper by H. M. Keith, *et al.* Am. J. Dis. Child., **83**:409, 1952.

MARSHALL, C., WALKER, E. AND LIVINGSTON, S.: Photogenic epilepsy. Arch. Neurol. & Psychiat., **69**:760, 1953.

MARTIN, J. P.: The "discharging lesion" in neurology. Brain, **68**:167, 1945.

————: Fits of laughter (sham mirth) in organic brain disease. Brain, **73**:453, 1950.

MAWDSLEY, C.: Epilepsy and television. Lancet, **1**:190, 1961.

MONEY, J. AND HOSTA, G.: Laughing seizures with sexual precocity. The Johns Hopkins Medical Jour., **120**:326, 1967.

NELSON, D. A. AND RAY, C. D.: Respiratory arrest from seizure discharges in the limbic system. Neurology, **19**:199, 1968.

PALLIS, C., AND LOUIS, S.: Television induced seizures. Lancet, **i**:188, 1961.

PANTELAKIS, S. N.: Television induced convulsions. Brit. Med. J., **5305**:633, 1962.

Penfield, W.: Pitfalls and success in surgical treatment of focal epilepsy. Brit. Med. J., i:669, 1958.

———: Epilepsy and surgical therapy. Arch. Neurol. & Psychiat., 36:449, 1936.

———: Epileptogenous lesions of the brain. Arch. Neurol. & Psychiat., 43:240, 1940.

———: The cerebral cortex and consciousness. Arch. Neurol. & Psychiat., 40:417, 1938.

Penfield, W. and Boldrey, E.: Somatic motor and sensory representation in the cerebral cortex by means of electrical stimulation. Brain, 60:389, 1938.

Penfield, W. and Gage, L.: Cerebral localization of epileptic manifestations. Arch. Neurol. & Psychiat., 30:709, 1933.

Penfield, W. and Keith, H. M.: Focal epileptogenous lesions of birth and infancy with report of eight cases. Am. J. Dis. Child., 59:71, 1940.

Penfield, W. and Rasmussen, T.: The cerebral cortex of man. Macmillan Publishing Co., New York, 1955, p. 26.

Penfield, W. and Steelman, H.: Treatment of focal epilepsy by cortical excision. Ann Surg., 126:740, 1947.

Poskanzer, D. C. et al.: Musicogenic epilepsy caused by a discrete frequency band of church bells. Brain, 85:77, 1962.

Preston, D. N. and Atack, E. A.: Temporal lobe epilepsy. Canad. Med. Ass. Jour., 91:1256, 1964.

Rasmussen, T. et al.: Focal seizures due to chronic localized encephalitis. Neurology, 8:435, 1958.

Robb, P.: Epilepsy. A review of basic and clinical research. NINDB. Monograph No. 1, 1965. National Inst. of Neurological Diseases and Blindness.

Robertson, E. G.: Photogenic epilepsy: Self-precipitated attacks. Brain, 77:233, 1954.

Ross, I. S.: Paroxysmal micturition as a manifestation of focal epileptic discharge. Pediatric Conferences, Babies Hospital Unit, United Hospitals of Newark, New Jersey. 1961, vol. 4, No. 4.

Rothova, N. and Roth, B.: A case of focal reflex epilepsy induced by tactile stimuli. C. S. Neurol., 26:33, 1963.

Russell, W. R.: The anatomy of traumatic epilepsy. Brain, 70:225, 1947.

Schwartz, J. F.: Photosensitivity in a family. Amer. Jour. Dis. Child., 103:90, 1962.

Sittig, O.: Clinical study of sensory Jacksonian fits. Brain, 48:233, 1925.

Sokolansky, G.: Über Anfälle bei der Epidemischen Encephalitis zur Frage der sog. subcorticalen Epilepsie. Ztschr. f. d. ges. Neurol. u. Psychiat. 112:605, 1928.

Spiller, W. G.: Subcortical epilepsy. Brain, 50:171, 1927.

Spiller, W. G. and Martin, E.: Epilepsia partialis continua occurring in cerebral syphilis. J.A.M.A., 52:1921, 1909.

Stevens, Harold: (George Washington University, Washington, D. C.). Reading epilepsy. New England J. Med., 257:165-170, 1957.

Walker, A. E.: Post-traumatic Epilepsy. Springfield, Thomas, 1949.

———: Post-traumatic epilepsy. World Neurology, 3:185, 1962.

Walsh, F. B.: Loc. cit.

Whitty, C. M. W.: Photic and self-induced epilepsy. Lancet, 1:1207, 1960.

Wimmer, A.: Chronic Epidemic Encephalitis. London, 1924.

FAMILIAL PAROXYSMAL CHOREOATHETOSIS

The rarity of this condition justifies only a brief note. Mount and Re-back describe a familial condition characterized by attacks of choreoatheto-sis which last from a few minutes to an hour or more. These attacks are not associated with loss of consciousness or even mental confusion. They are bilateral and generalized. During the attacks speech is difficult or per-haps, impossible. In between the attacks there are no mental or neurologi-cal disorders. The onset is in infancy or early childhood and the symptoms

apparently continue throughout life. Mount and Reback were able to trace the disease back through five generations. Both males and females are affected. In a very complete examination Mount and Reback were able to discover no cause for the seizures in their patient.

Our experience is restricted to one family. The story is given in brief below. The family history would seem to indicate a relation between this disease and common epilepsy. We have found that dilantin and phenobarbital are effective.

Stevens has reported four cases in which the seizures were induced by sudden movements after being still for a time or by being startled. Kertesz describes ten cases in which the seizures were also induced by movement. He distinguishes them from the cases of Mount and Reback by this feature and employs the term kinesigenic choreoathetosis. He states that changes in the sensorium similar to those seen in petit mal occur and last 15 to 30 seconds. The onset in his cases was between 6 and 15 years. Abnormal electroencephalograms were sometimes found and a history of epilepsy in other members of the family was sometimes elicited. He finds that dilantin and phenobarbital usually control the attacks. This condition is regarded as an autosomal recessive trait.

CASE HISTORY (Ped. A-453547).—*Choreoathetosis occurring in sudden paroxysms in a boy of eight years. Older brother and a cousin subject to convulsive seizures. One cousin has seizures identical with those of the patient.*

T. P., a boy of eight years, was born by normal delivery and no evidence of birth injury was noted. No post-natal illnesses were recalled. He was considered a healthy boy in every respect. Shortly before he was brought to the hospital he began to have seizures manifest by generalized irregular movements of the extremities, face and trunk. These movements were of large amplitude and violent enough to make it very difficult for him to stand or walk. They were very similar to those seen in congenital double athetosis. The onset of these seizures was abrupt and the duration varied between two and five minutes. Consciousness was never affected. For a time the child would always have a seizure shortly after arising in the morning and often there would be several more during the day. Examination was completely negative. The child was rather sensitive and emotional but well behaved and of average mentality. His seizures were controlled very well by large doses of dilantin.

A. P. (Ped. A-70959), an older brother of the patient described above, had enjoyed excellent health until the age of 13 years. His school record was a very good one and he often led his class. When he was six months old, he had pneumonia and a generalized convulsion occurred at the onset. At the age of 13 years, he began to have sudden seizures preceded by a peculiar feeling in the toes of the left foot which he described as a sen-

sation of movement of the toes. This was followed at once by a spasm of the left arm which was flexed at the elbow and somewhat abducted. For a moment, the left hand made movements similar to those one would make in "waving goodbye." His face and his eyes would also rotate to the left. At least once, his mother states he was out of contact for a moment. Such attacks occurred on an average of five to six times a month. The electroencephalogram showed no abnormalities. Phenobarbital was found to control the attacks.

The third child in the family, M. P. (Ped.-467319), has had no seizures yet. She is six years old at the present writing.

The mother of these children was subject to fainting spells as a child but has had no symptoms of any type since adolescence. One maternal first cousin has had seizures exactly like those of T. P., i.e. paroxysmal choreoathetosis, since early childhood. Another maternal cousin is subject to generalized convulsions with loss of consciousness.

BIBLIOGRAPHY

HUDGINS, R. L. AND CORBIN, K. B.: Familial paroxysmal choreoathetosis. Brain, **89**:199, 1966.

KATO, M. AND ARAKI, S.: Paroxysmal kinesthetic choreoathetosis. Arch. Neurol., 20:508, 1969.

KERTESZ, A.: Paroxysmal kinesthetic choreoathetosis. One autopsy. Neurology, **17**:680, 1967.

MOUNT, L. A. AND REBACK, S.: Familial paroxysmal choreoathetosis. Arch. Neurol. & Psychiat., 44:841, 1940.

PRYLES, C. V., LIVINGSTON, S. AND FORD, F. R.: Familial paroxysmal choreoathetosis of Mount and Reback. Pediatrics, **9**:44, 1952.

RICHARDS, R. N. AND BARNETT, H. J. M.: Paroxysmal dystonic choreoathetosis. Neurology, **18**:461, 1968.

STEVENS, H.: Paroxysmal choreoathetosis. Arch. of Neurol., 14:415, 1966.

WAGNER, G. S. *et al.*: Familial paroxysmal choreoathetosis. Neurology, **16**:307, 1966.

WILLIAMS, J. AND STEPHENS, H.: Familial paroxysmal choreoathetosis. Pediatrics, 1963, p. 656.

SYNCOPE

Definition.—A condition characterized by loss of consciousness attributed to transient disturbances of the cerebral circulation. The term *fainting* is commonly employed. Weiss and Engel have offered much broader definitions.

Etiology.—Since certain individuals faint repeatedly during their life and others never do so, it seems not unreasonable to assume that these persons must have a constitutional peculiarity. The idea is supported by the fact that the tendency to faint with little provocation is seemingly inherited in certain families.

Among the precipitating causes the upright position must be mentioned first, for syncope rarely occurs in recumbency. In fact, when syncope has occurred recumbency will usually relieve it promptly. Fatigue, especially that due to prolonged standing after exertion, is a common cause. Emotional reactions such as fright, pain, horror and suspense deserve a prominent place

on the list. Hyperventilation, often associated with emotional reactions, may apparently be responsible. Patients often mention overheated and poorly ventilated rooms. Hot baths may provoke this reaction. Lack of food plays a significant role in some instances. Violent coughing and straining against a closed glottis, i.e. the Valsalva maneuver, may cause fainting. In young children breath holding spells seem to be the commonest cause.

So far I have been speaking of individuals who appear to be healthy and of conditions such as everyone encounters in daily life. The list of diseases and physiological disorders which leads to fainting, or to similar reactions, is a long one. I may mention cardiovascular diseases of various types first of all, Stokes-Adams syndrome, exaggeration of the carotid sinus reflex, vagal stimulation of any type, hypotension, especially postural hypotension and anemia. Great heat, dehydration, loss of blood, violent vertigo, prolonged vomiting and vasodilatation are to be included. Hypoglycemia should be mentioned. Undernutrition and wasting illnesses and prolonged recumbency are potent factors. Fainting is not uncommon in the early days of pregnancy.

Mechanisms of Syncope.—One of the commonest types is termed *vasodepressor syncope*. Here we are dealing with a drop in blood pressure. Fatigue and emotional disturbances are usually to blame. Usually no abnormalities can be found on examination between attacks. A special type is due to *postural hypotension*. In such cases the nervous mechanisms which compensate for changes in posture are defective. Fainting tends to occur when the patient assumes the upright position. Another type is due to *abnormalities* of *cardiac action*. In some cases heart block is due to intrinsic disease of that organ, i.e. Stokes Adams syndrome. In other cases reflex vagus inhibition is to blame. The reflex may arise in the pleura, lungs, or gastrointestinal tract but an excessively active carotid sinus reflex is more commonly responsible. Paroxysmal tachycardia should be mentioned at this point. The *Valsalva maneuver,* i.e. straining against a closed glottis as in violent coughing may result in reduction of the cardiac output and syncope. I have seen two cases of *micturition syncope* in adolescent boys. One had swallowing syncope as well. *Hyperventilation* should also be mentioned for loss of consciousness may be produced. Meyer and Gotoh find that cerebral disturbances during over-ventilation are due to cerebral ischemia secondary to the reduction of carbon dioxide. I have seen only one child with the hyperventilation syndrome. This was a very sensitive little girl, of nine years, who would breathe too deeply when emotionally disturbed. She would complain of numbness of the lips and hands. Vision would get blurred and she would feel dizzy. There was some clouding of consciousness. In some of these episodes, she would develop typical carpopedal spasms and signs of tetany.

Anoxia seems to be responsible for the loss of consciousness and in some cases convulsions which may occur in the breath holding spells q.v. of young children. *Congenital heart disease,* especially congenital aortic stenosis, may cause loss of consciousness on exertion. I have seen one case of *swallowing syncope* in an adolescent child. This is due to a cardioinhibitory vagal impulse arising in the esophagus.

Jervell and Lange-Nielson have described four cases in siblings in which congenital deafmutism, prolonged Q T interval, syncopal attacks and sudden death occurred. Some 17 cases are reported. Three children died at 4, 5 and 9 years. One is alive at 15 years. Five post-mortem studies have showed no anatomical changes in the heart. Death is thought to be due to ventricular fibrillation. The onset of cardiac symptoms is usually between 2 and 4 years.

Illingsworth reports a case in which syncopal attacks occurred in a case of the Klippel-Feil syndrome.

Glick and Yu describe vasovagal attacks with slow pulse and drop of blood pressure which they suggest may result from emotional reactions.

Chosy and Graham collected urine from student blood donors shortly before venipuncture. The urine of 21 who fainted and of 42 who did not faint was tested for epinephrine and norepinephrine. These substances were significantly greater in amount in the urine of those who had fainted.

Clinical Features.—Fainting is rare in childhood but more common in adolescence than at other periods of life and probably occurs more often in girls than boys. There are almost always premonitory symptoms. Observers may note that the patient turns pale and begins to sweat. The patient experiences a reduction in the state of consciousness described as a feeling as if "things were far away" and reduction of vision described as "things going black" or as "blacking out." At this point the patient becomes unconscious and falls to the floor. It is not usual for syncope to occur so abruptly that the patient is injured by the fall, but this does occur. During the actual syncope the face is pale, the pupils dilated, respirations are shallow or slow and deep, the pulse is feeble or imperceptible at the wrist and the heart rate slow. Muscular twitchings may be seen which arouse suspicions of a convulsion. As a rule, after the patient has been in a recumbent position for a few minutes, the color begins to return to the face, the pulse grows stronger and consciousness returns. There is only brief confusion after the episode, but the patient is apt to feel weak, exhausted and nauseated for a time. If the patient arises too soon, syncope may occur again. These statements apply to the common vasodepressor type of syncope. Other types may cause somewhat different effects. Heart block may cause very abrupt unconsciousness and occasionally convulsions.

Weiss has studied the physiological mechanisms involved in this reaction

chiefly by the use of vasodilator drugs and the tilting table. He states that as syncope develops, the pulse pressure grows less due to falling systolic pressure, rising diastolic pressure or to both factors. As collapse occurs, i.e. loss of consciousness, there is a precipitous drop of blood pressure and an equally abrupt reduction of pulse rate. He attributes these phenomena chiefly to vagal stimulation. He states that in most persons subject to syncopal attacks the carotid sinus reflex is normal and there is no tendency to postural hypotension between the attacks.

Hyperventilation may occur in both acute and chronic forms. Anxiety and apprehension are the usual causes. The respiratory tics formerly seen in cases of epidemic encephalitis may be mentioned as a type associated with organic disease. The patient often complains of difficulty in breathing, palpitation, tachycardia and a feeling of oppression in the chest but precordial pain is sometimes mentioned. Paresthesias of the lips and the extremities are common. Twitching and tremors of the hands often occur but definite tetany is rare. There may be reduction of consciousness and even syncope. The patient rarely realizes that respiration is too deep. Rebreathing in a paper bag relieves the symptoms promptly.

Diagnosis.—Syncope must be differentiated from (1) Hysterical attacks, (2) Epilepsy.

As regards the first possibility, it may be said that it is not always possible on the basis of the history to distinguish hysterical attacks from true syncope induced by emotional reactions. If the patient is observed in an attack, or can be induced to have one, the absence of changes in the circulation would seem to be strong evidence against most types of true syncope. An electroencephalogram taken during the episode should also be helpful.

The differentiation of epilepsy is not always easy. Engel points out a number of clinical features of differential value. Epilepsy often begins in infancy or early childhood. The epileptic seizures often occur during sleep or soon after awakening. The patient often has seizures of different types such as grand mal and petit mal. The attacks occur in any position. There is often incontinence, tongue biting, burns from falling on a stove and other serious injuries. During the attack the patient is apt to be flushed and cyanotic, not pale. In most instances there is muscular rigidity. There may be prolonged apnea and stertorous breathing. The patient is hot and wet. Post-convulsive confusion, headache, amnesia and aching in the muscles are all typical.

In syncope, onset in childhood or infancy is rare. The attacks do not occur during sleep. The seizures are apt to be steroptyped. They occur only in the upright position. Incontinence, tongue biting and serious injuries are not noted. The patient is pale, not flushed and the skin cool, not warm. There is very little post-seizure confusion and amnesia. Headache is not a

constant sequel of the attack and there is no aching in the muscles such as follows a convulsion. It must be admitted, however, that some seizures of cerebral origin may simulate syncope very closely.

Electroencephalographic study is of great value in differentiating epilepsy from syncope. Patients subject to syncope show scarcely more abnormalities than the normal individual of whom, perhaps, 10 or 12 per cent show some deviations from the normal pattern. During a syncopal attack they display slow waves at a rate of 2 to 4 per second so long as consciousness is in abeyance. In epilepsy, however, definite abnormalities in the encephalogram are evident in about 60 per cent of all cases during the interseizure period but, in some instances, quite normal records are elicited. During an epileptic seizure high voltage rapid waves and spikes are seen in grand mal and petit mal, and slow waves in psychomotor seizures. The last, unfortunately, are similar to those seen during syncope. It is evident, therefore, that the electroencephalogram must be interpreted in the light of the clinical features of the case.

It should be stated that many of the conditions which cause syncope may also cause convulsions. If the cerebral circulation is interrupted for several seconds, syncope may be followed by a seizure. Such reactions are common in Stokes-Adams syndrome and in some cases in which the carotid sinus reflex is exaggerated.

It seems probable that syncope and epilepsy may occur in the same individual, the syncope initiating the convulsion. I have been consulted by a mother in regard to the case of her son. Several members of the family are subject to fainting attacks which are induced by the sight of blood or even by the mention of a surgical operation. One son who is mentally deficient has syncopal attacks as the other children do in response to the same precipitating factors. In this case, however, a violent, generalized convulsion often occurs before the syncope is terminated. His electroencephalogram reveals a pattern typical of epilepsy.

Special methods of examination are often required in the diagnosis of syncope. The reaction of the circulation to change in posture, the reaction to stimulation of the carotid sinus, to hyperventilation and to exercise are all important. An electrocardiogram should be made as well as an electroencephalogram. Often a psychiatric study is required.

BIBLIOGRAPHY

ARONSON, P. R.: Hyperventilation from organic disease. Ann. Int. Med., **50**:554, 1959.

CHOSY, J. J. AND GRAHAM, D. T.: Catecholamines in vasovagal fainting. Jour. psychosom., **9**:189, 1965.

ENGEL, G. L.: Fainting. Physiological and Psychological Considerations. Springfield, Thomas, 1950.

FALSETTI, H. L. *et al.:* Obesity-hypoventilation syndrome in siblings. Amer. Rev. Resp. Dis., **90**:105, 1964.

GILLESPIE, J. B.: The hyperventilation syndrome in childhood. Arch. Pediat., **71**:197, 1954.

GLICK, G., AND YU, P. N.: Spontaneous vasovagal reactions. Am. J. Med., **34**:42, 1963.

ILLINGSWORTH, R. S.: Attacks of unconsciousness in association with fused cervical vertebrae. Arch. Dis. Child., **31**:8, 1956.

JERVELL, A. *et al.:* The surdo-cardiac syndrome. Amer. Heart Jour., **72**:582, 1966.

JERVELL, O. AND LANGE-NIELSON, F.: Congenital deaf-mutism, functional heart disease with prolongation of the Q T interval and sudden death. Am. Heart J., **54**:59, 1957.

LEVINE, S. A. AND WOODWORTH, C. R.: Congenital deafmutism, prolonged QT interval, syncopal attacks and sudden death. New England J. Med., **259**:412, 1958.

LEWIS, B. I.: Hyperventilation syndromes. Postgrad. Med., **21**:259, 1957.

MEYER, J. S. AND GOTOH, F.: Metabolic and electroencephalographic effects of hyperventilation. Arch. Neurol., **3**:539, 1960.

OVERMAN, R. R.: Syncope an analysis of fainting. Modern Medicine, August 15, 1956.

RIVLIN, S.: Fainting on parade. The Practitioner, **176**:541, 1956.

SHARPEY-SCHAFER, E. P. *et al.:* Mechanism of acute hypotension from fear or nausea. Brit. Med. J., **5101**:878, 1958.

THOMAS, J. E. AND ROOKE, E. D.: Diagnostic significance of fainting. Proc. Mayo Clin., **38**:397, 1963.

WEISS, S.: Syncope and related syndromes. Oxford Med., Vol. 2 part 1, p. 250.

YU, P. N.: The hyperventilation syndrome. Medical Science, April 25, 1960, p. 532.

BREATH-HOLDING SPELLS

It is not unusual for small children to hold their breath for a short time when crying. Such episodes are termed breath-holding spells. These are almost invariably induced by an emotional reaction such as anger, fear or pain. The child gives two or three loud cries and then breathing ceases in expiration. In most episodes, the apnea lasts only five to 10 seconds. There may be slight cyanosis. The child then gives a gasp and begins to breathe normally. Such mild episodes are not uncommon even in otherwise well behaved children.

In more severe attacks, the apnea is prolonged and the child falls to the floor in a state of rigidity. Cyanosis may be pronounced. If the apnea lasts more than 30 to 45 seconds, there may be convulsions. According to Bridge *et al.,* convulsions occur in most half of all children who are brought to the hospital because of breath holding spells. No doubt, anoxia is responsible.

Lombroso and Lerman distinguish between cyanotic attacks and pallid attacks. They state the cyanotic attacks are associated with crying and loss of consciousness does not occur at once. The pallid type is characterized by little crying, no cyanosis and prompt loss of consciousness.

It seems to be quite clear that the exciting cause of these seizures is an emotional reaction, usually a temper tantrum. Such children are usually badly spoiled and determined to have their own way. Inadequate training and lack of discipline are responsible.

In differential diagnosis one must consider epilepsy, congenital laryngeal stridor, tumors of the larynx, laryngospasm of tetany and enlargement of the thymus gland. The electroencephalogram may be of value in differen-

tial diagnosis, but a full history or observation of an attack will usually make the nature of the problem clear.

These attacks are said to disappear invariably by the end of the sixth year, usually by the end of the third year. They become less frequent and finally cease. These children's behavior is apt to remain a problem, however. In a small percentage of cases, epilepsy develops. Two of the two hundred and forty-two patients studied by Bridge *et al.* were ultimately found to have epilepsy.

As a rule, proper discipline will prove effective in stopping the attacks. Calm, firmness and purposeful neglect are most important. It must be made clear to the child that such behavior will not secure the desired ends. Phenobarbital may have some symptomatic value.

Holowach and Thurston state that anemia is found in many children with this condition and they may improve when the anemia is relieved.

BIBLIOGRAPHY

BRIDGE, E. M., LIVINGSTON, S. AND TIETZÉ, C.: Breath-holding spells. J. Pediat., 23:539, 1943.
GAUK, E. W. *et al.:* Breath-holding seizures in children. New England J. Med., 268:1436, 1963.
HINMAN, A. AND DICKEY, L. B.: Breath-holding spells. Am. J. Dis. Child, 91:23, 1956.
HOLOWACH, J. AND THURSTON, D. L.: Breath-holding spells and anemia. New England J. Med., 268:21, 1963.
LINDER, C. W.: Breath-holding spells in children. Clin. Pediat., 7:88, 1968.
LOMBROSO, C. T. AND LERMAN, P.: Breath-holding spells (Cyanotic and pallid infantile syncope). Pediatrics, 39:563, 1967.

NARCOLEPSY

Definition.—This term is employed to designate a condition in which paroxysms of irresistible *somnolence* are associated with transient attacks of weakness or *cataplexy*. The sleep attacks may exist alone and in a few cases cataplexy has been observed without any tendency to sleep. Some observers consider narcolepsy a disease sui generis; others regard it as a syndrome.

Etiology.—It may be said at once that in most cases the cause of narcolepsy is obscure and if we regard it as a disease, we must admit that the cause is unknown. Wilson, however, considers it to be a syndrome and gives eight possible etiological factors including trauma, intoxication and infection, epilepsy, neoplasm, circulatory and endocrine disorders, psychopathological conditions and unknown causes. It must be admitted that the last group is the largest. In typical cases it is very difficult to obtain any evidence of cerebral damage other than the essential symptoms and, on the other hand, in cases in which there is abundant evidence of organic disease of the nervous system, the syndrome of narcolepsy is usually incomplete or doubtful.

Daly and Yoss in a study of three generations of a family found twelve

definite cases and three suspected cases of narcolepsy. They suggest that the disease is transmitted as a simple dominant factor with a high degree of penetrance.

It seems unwise to attempt to enter into a discussion of the mechanisms controlling sleep and muscle tone. Our knowledge of these processes is so limited that no clear conclusions could be reached. If we take these reactions for granted, it seems to be fair to say that neither the weakness and relaxation of the muscles during emotional states nor the tendency to sleep when bored are entirely foreign to the behavior of normal individuals. The abnormality seems to lie in the facility with which such reactions occur rather than in their nature. It scarcely seems possible to draw any sharp line of distinction between the normal and abnormal. The writer is not convinced that we are dealing with structural damage of the brain in narcolepsy and is inclined to believe that habit formation and psychological factors play a considerable role in its development.

Pathological Anatomy.—No histological studies have yet been made upon the brains of the victims of this malady, and, indeed, it is not at all certain that such a study would reveal anything significant. It is well known, of course, that lesions in the hypothalamus may be associated with somnolence. This association has frequently been observed in cases of neoplasm and evidence has been presented by Von Economo and others that the striking hypersomnia of epidemic encephalitis is the result of lesions in the floor of the third ventricle and gray matter surrounding the aqueduct of Sylvius. It is very doubtful, however, whether the complete picture of narcolepsy has even been found in such conditions.

Clinical Features.—The onset apparently may occur at any age, most commonly according to medical literature, during the third and fourth decades. In the writer's experience, however, the symptoms have usually appeared during adolescence, especially during the school year. I have discovered no report of cases in infancy.

In some cases, the onset has been preceded by some obscure illness which has often been diagnosed in retrospect as epidemic encephalitis, but it has already been stated above that rarely if ever do we find typical signs of this disease such as the Parkinsonian syndrome in association with the complete picture of narcolepsy. Several cases have followed head injuries and various other conditions affecting the central nervous system. There is little evidence that endocrine disorders are important. However, psychopathological disturbances have been discovered in a number of instances and have probably received less emphasis than they deserve. As a rule, the patient has enjoyed excellent health preceding the onset and the connection of previous illnesses with the narcolepsy is usually uncertain at best.

The attacks of *sleep* may occur under the most unfavorable conditions. The patient may be walking, talking, eating or driving a car. In one case, the child would go to sleep on the back of a pony. Such instances serve merely to emphasize the fact that the urge to sleep may be such that the patient cannot resist. In most cases, however, the attack develops while the patient is relaxed at rest. We have been struck with the frequency with which the history has been obtained that the child began to fall asleep when sitting at the desk at school or when reading or studying at home. In general, such attacks are prone to develop when the child is bored or fatigued. I have employed the term sleep, for these attacks resemble normal sleep very closely. The patient is easily aroused and is quite clear and in full possession of the mental faculties as soon as consciousness is regained. In most cases, the patient feels refreshed. In some instances, the patient falls asleep very suddenly and within a few seconds is quite unconscious. If not disturbed, the sleep may last for a few minutes to a half hour and rarely persists very long. In only a few cases has there been any drowsiness between the attacks. Nocturnal sleep, in a very large percentage of cases, is light and disturbed by unpleasant or even terrifying dreams. One child, whom I have followed for several years, frequently dreams of burglars and awakes screaming. Some authors believe that these vivid dreams are really hallucinations.

The second symptom essential to this disorder, or *cataplexy,* may be very striking or may be so mild that it is elicited only by carefully questioning. The commonest story is that the child grows very weak during emotional reactions. In some cases the patient may fall to the ground and may be unable to move for several seconds or minutes. In other instances, the weakness is so mild that there is merely a consciousness of relaxation of the muscles. It must be said that a certain degree of weakness is always present during hearty laughter in healthy subjects and it is only when the weakness is excessive that we may regard it as pathological. The patient is always quite conscious during the cataplectic attacks although speech may be impossible for a time. It is very exceptional for the sphincters to be relaxed during the attacks. Wilson states that in severe attacks the tendon reflexes may be lost due, no doubt, to loss of muscle tone. In general, laughter or joy is the most efficient cause of cataplexy. One patient in our series has fallen to the ground several times when running joyfully to meet her mother who was returning from a long trip. Fear, sudden frights, anger, mild annoyances and even sexual excitement, however, may bring on the attacks. Some patients can inhibit the attacks voluntarily to a certain degree. One school girl in our series states that if she does not permit herself to laugh out loud at a joke, she experiences merely a feeling of weakness, but

if she laughs heartily she will fall. Palpitation, pallor and feelings of warmth and suffocation may be experienced during the seizure.

In typical cases, the two cardinal symptoms are quite distinct, but in some atypical cases, symptoms have been recorded which seems to show that the somnolence and cataplexy are in reality closely related. Thus, emotional excitement may cause somnolence, or if sleep is prevented, cataplexy may occur. Moreover cataplexy may occur spontaneously without any apparent emotional stimulus. In some patients the sleep states do not involve unconsciousness, for there may be more or less complete awareness of events occurring about them during this period.

Levin points out that *sleep paralysis* is found in some instances. This may occur as the patient awakens or less frequently just as the patient is falling asleep. It lasts a few seconds or minutes as a rule and the patient is entirely helpless though quite conscious during this period. A touch or a word suffices to dispel the difficulty at once. This is a terrifying experience to some patients who feel that they can't breathe. Sleep paralysis may occur without the other symptoms of narcolepsy.

Physical examination is almost invariably quite negative. Indeed, one is often struck by the patient's splendid physical condition. Development in adolescent narcoleptics is usually normal or perhaps slightly precocious. There is often a tendency to obesity due, perhaps, to the inordinate amount of rest the patient usually obtains. This, however, has been ascribed to endocrine disorders. The basal metabolic rate is often low, running from normal to minus twenty or even thirty, but since these patients are almost always asleep during the test, it is doubtful whether this should be regarded as significant of a real disturbance of metabolism. The studies of blood chemistry have been negative. Richter, however, has shown that even during waking periods these patients show a tendency to increase skin resistance to the electric current such as is found in normal sleep.

Very few patients have been followed long enough to determine the eventual outcome of the condition. So far as our information extends at present, however, it may be said that the symptoms vary from time to time and that the condition does not grow progressively worse. Indeed, several children have improved during the course of a few years. It may be said that the absence of a progressive course seems to be against the supposition that epidemic encephalitis plays an important role in this disorder. The writer has studied a case in which the condition persisted from early childhood until the age of 50 years without being associated with any other departure from health.

The electroencephalogram in narcolepsy shows the sleep pattern when the patient is asleep. An abnormal record was found in only 5 of 22 cases when the patient was awake by Dynes and Finley. Cohn and Cruvant, how-

ever, found abnormal waking records in 8 out of 10 of their patients. They state that the patterns are similar to those found in epilepsy.

Diagnosis.—The diagnosis depends upon the discovery of the two cardinal symptoms, but the existence of only one symptom would seem to justify the diagnosis of an incomplete narcoleptic syndrome. We must always make careful investigations of the possibility of neoplasms at the base of the brain and roentgenograms of the sella turcica and study of the visual fields should be performed routinely. We should obtain a careful history and perform a complete neurological examination with epidemic encephalitis in mind. In differential diagnosis we should keep in mind the rare syndrome of *somnolence* and *morbid hunger* q.v.

Prognosis.—In most cases, the symptoms do not greatly interfere with the patient's activities, although progress in school may be somewhat retarded. We are not yet in a position to express an opinion about the eventual outcome. In our experience the disorder runs a chronic course with distinct fluctuations in intensity. It is not at all improbable that the symptoms may cease spontaneously in many cases.

Treatment.—Our concept of narcolepsy is so vague that we cannot claim any rational plan of therapy. Attempts to remedy the low basal metabolic rate by the administration of thyroid substance have given no results. In my own experience, efforts to establish proper habit formation have been most successful. The child is instructed to go to bed early and to take a short nap after meals. At other times the urge to sleep is resisted as strongly as possible. Dexedrine is more effective in my experience than any other drug. It may be given in doses of 10 mgs or more three times a day. In most cases this will reduce the tendency to fall asleep but rarely gives entirely satisfactory results. It does not influence the cataplexy. Retalin is recommended. Ephedrine and caffeine are less effective. Any psychological problems which can be discovered should be fully investigated and treated along psychotherapeutic lines.

Hishikawa *et al.* state that the cataleptic attacks, sleep paralysis and hypnagogic hallucinations are controlled by the use of tofranil and pertofran. Untoward effects are less common when pertofran is used. The sleep attacks are not relieved by these drugs.

BIBLIOGRAPHY

COHN, R. AND CRUVANT, B. A.: Relation of narcolepsy to the epilepsies. A clinical electroencephalographic study. Arch. Neurol. & Psychiat., 51:163, 1944.

DALY, D. D. AND YOSS, R. E.: A family with narcolepsy. Proc. Staff Meet. Mayo Clin., 34:313, 1959.

DYNES, J. B. AND FINLEY, K. H.: The electroencephalograph as an aide in the study of narcolepsy. Arch. Neurol. & Psychiat., 46:598, 1941.

GOODE, G. B.: Sleep paralysis. Arch. Neurol., 6:228, 1962.

HISHIKAWA, Y. *et al.:* Treatment of narcolepsy with tofranil and pertofran. Jour. Neurol. Sci., 3:453, 1966.

LEVIN, M.: Narcolepsy (Gelineau's syndrome) and other varieties of morbid somnolence. Arch. Neurol. & Psychiat., 22:1172, 1929.

————: Cataplexy. Brain, 55:397, 1928.

————: The pathogenesis of narcolepsy. J. Neurol. & Psychopath., 14:1, 1933.

WEIL, A. A.: Electroencephalographic patterns in narcolepsy. Dis. Nerv. Syst., 23:279, 1962.

WILSON, S. A. K.: The Narcolepsies. Modern Problems in Neurology. New York, Wm. Wood & Co., 1928.

————: The narcolepsies. Brain, 51:63, 1928.

YOSS, R. E. AND DALY, D. D.: Narcolepsy in children. Pediatrics, 25:1025, 1960.

———— AND ————: Narcolepsy. Med. Clin. N. Amer., 44:953, 1960.

MIGRAINE

Definition.—This term applies to a type of recurrent headache which occurs at variable intervals throughout the greater part of life, is apt to appear in several members of a family, is often preceded by visual disturbances and accompanied by nausea and vomiting. It is impossible to give an entirely satisfactory definition, since there is no agreement about the proper scope of the term. Some authorities include in this group all cases of chronic recurrent headache for which no adequate cause can be found; others limit the term to such cases as show the complete syndrome. The former definition includes most of the common headaches; the latter embraces a relatively small group.

Etiology.—It may be said at once that the etiology is unknown. Since it is frequently possible to trace the condition through several generations and to find several siblings affected, it seems logical to regard migraine as the expression of some inherited constitutional peculiarity.

Chapman *et al.* have found that a polypeptid which they term neurokinin accumulates in the tissue during severe headaches. This substance is a very powerful vasodilator and seems to lower the pain threshold. It is suggested that the accumulation of this material initiates the vasodilatation and the headache.

Regardless of the cause the symptoms seem to be due to vasomotor disturbances. Wolff and his associates have shown that there is an initial phase of vasoconstriction which seems to be responsible for the disturbances of vision and the paresthesias which may be termed aurae. The pain is due to dilatation of the arteries which occurs during the second phase.

Pathological Anatomy.—No anatomical basis for this disease has ever been established.

Clinical Features.—The following discussion is based upon histories elicited from adolescents, for children cannot give satisfactory descriptions of their symptoms in most cases. There can be no doubt that many victims of migraine are sensitive or unstable, if not actually neurotic persons. It is

usual to elicit a large number of complaints referable to all parts of the body in addition to the headaches and the symptoms directly connected with them. They react excessively to all the troubles and worries which one encounters in life and are especially apt to exhibit labile emotional reactions. In the same way there seems to be a tendency to instability of the more strictly physiological processes. Migrainous patients possess irritable gastrointestinal tracts; they are subject to palpitation and tachycardia, dysmenorrhea, eyestrain, angioneurotic edema, urticaria, asthma, hay fever and a host of other troubles. Whether this statement is true of all patients subject to migraine or not is uncertain. It is undoubtedly true of those who seek medical advice.

A number of cases are found in the same family, as a rule, and patients often are able to trace the disease through several generations. Negative family histories should be investigated, since patients will often attempt to conceal the existence of other cases in the family, for they imagine that if the physician should think it an inherited condition he would regard it as hopeless and would not try to give relief. Some writers claim that females are affected more frequently than males and others state that there is no difference in the incidence in the two sexes. There is no doubt, however, that females seek relief more frequently than males.

The age of onset is apparently variable. In females, the story is frequently elicited that the headaches began at the onset of the menses. Often the child begins to complain of headache when going to school and especially when beginning high school, as increasing demands are made on the eyes and the curriculum becomes more difficult. It is, of course, evident that young children may not be able to let their parents know that they have headache. The writer is convinced from his own experience that migraine begins very early in life in many cases. He has frequently elicited the history that the child did not develop headaches until about the age of ten or twelve years, but that earlier in childhood there were frequent attacks of "indigestion" and "biliousness" during which the child would become fretful and irritable, would cry and finally vomit. After this vomiting the child would seem to be more comfortable and would go to sleep awakening quite well. It seems very probable that such attacks of "indigestion" are in reality nothing but migraine. The so-called *cyclic vomiting* is frequently a manifestation of migraine in childhood.

The headache may begin at any time but it is characteristic for it to start early in the morning, often so early as to awaken the patient from sleep.

In some instances, the headaches occur in unpredictable fashion from time to time, but in certain cases, they occur in series so the patient will have a headache every day at a certain hour during a period of weeks. Then there is apt to be a remission of months before another series begins.

A great variety of *headaches* are described but the most characteristic and most frequent type is the hemicrania which begins over one eye and extends backward over the whole side of the head. It may also begin in the occiput and move forward. Frequently the pain begins locally and eventually becomes generalized or it may move from one side to the other, never involving both sides at the same time. Many patients state that the headache behaves in the same way each time and others describe several types of pain. Sometimes the history is elicited that the pain is always confined to the same spot. Frequently the pain is felt in the eyeballs and in some cases may spread down into the cheek. The fact that the pain is said to be throbbing may lend some weight to the theory of vascular origin. Pulsations of the temporal artery are often visible.

The duration of the headache is variable. Mild attacks may last only half an hour but severe ones may last several days. Many patients find that if they lie down and sleep for a short time or if they even relax completely for an hour or more, the pain will cease. Wolff, who has added so much to our knowledge of migraine, points out that during the headache the temporal arteries may be dilated and their pulsation may be increased. The nasal mucosa may become congested and edematous so the nasal passages are obstructed. The conjunctiva may be congested. Edema of the scalp may develop and the scalp may be tender even after the headache has ceased. Wolff believes that the temporal arteries may become edematous also. In certain cases, especially those in which nervous tension is pronounced, there is increased tone of the muscles of the head and neck which adds another item to the patient's discomfort.

Numerous precipitating factors are mentioned. The writer has elicited the history so many times that nervous strain, fatigue, lack of sleep, worry and stress and strain of all sorts induce the headaches and make them more severe, that he is convinced that this relationship is an essential feature of the condition. Eyestrain no doubt plays a part in inducing headache, but probably a nonspecific part as does any other source of discomfort. It is sometimes difficult to estimate the role of digestive disturbances for the nausea and vomiting which accompany the attack are often confused by the patient with digestive upsets which precede the trouble and might, perhaps, cause it. Most patients believe that constipation is an important factor and that a saline purge or a cathartic will sometimes give relief. Many parents state that the child is apt to have headache after over-loading the stomach, but as a rule the relation of food to headache does not seem to be very clear. In girls about the age of puberty, the attacks of migraine very frequently occur just before or during the first day of menstruation.

Blau and Cumings show that fasting will induce migranious attacks.

Anthony *et al.* have discovered that the total plasma serotonin falls con-

sistently during a migrainous headache and suggest that this may be a significant element in the production of the headache.

In relatively mild headaches there may be no symptoms other than the pain, but frequently there is some degree of *nausea*. This is most apt to occur towards the culmination of the headache when it is most severe. If actual *vomiting* results, there is usually a great deal of relief immediately afterwards, although some patients state that they may vomit for several days without relief. The cause of the vomiting is, of course, not clear. In general it is believed to be the expression of an intracranial disturbance, perhaps vagus stimulation, rather than a local process in the abdomen. Sometimes there is bradycardia of moderate degree which has led to the belief that intracranial pressure may be elevated. Harold Wolff has shown that the intracranial pressure is actually elevated during a migrainous headache probably as a result of dilatation of the intracranial blood vessels.

The patient is often pale and cold in the initial stage of vasoconstriction and flushed and warm in the second phase of vasodilatation. The patient may be disturbed by light and noise and prefers to be in a dark and quiet room. Many patients are conscious of nervous tension and irritability during the headache. They may be unable to lie down and prefer to walk the floor. Some say that the headache is increased by the recumbent position. In some instances there is a feeling of difficulty in thinking and of slowing of mental processes.

Focal symptoms are not rare. The commonest of these is a disturbance of *vision* which develops just before the headache during the phase of vasoconstriction. The term of *ophthalmic migraine* is applied to cases characterized by such symptoms. Intelligent patients describe scintillating scotomas which are confined as a rule to one half of the visual fields. The appearance is that of a fine, gleaming silvery line running a zig zag course. This line may be accompanied by a zone of rainbow colors. Such scotomas move across the fields of vision and seem to oscillate. Associated with the scotomas may be loss of vision on one side or blurring of vision. Transient *hemianopia* is well known in such cases. In some cases the scotomas may extend across the midline. They may also involve the upper fields or lower fields or be confined to the central regions. I have seen cases of transient cortical blindness which I attributed to migraine. Some cases of transient blindness in one eye, sometimes called amaurosis fugax, may be of migrainous origin. I have seen one case in a girl who between the ages of 11 and 16 years had about 60 attacks in which vision of the left eye was obscured for periods lasting from 2 to 28 minutes. Vision was normal in every respect in between these attacks.

Dr. Frank Walsh has showed me a boy of seventeen years who was subject to attacks of amaurosis fugax. His eye was examined, during one of

his episodes, by an ophthalmologist who found severe spasm of the retinal arteries with pallor of the retina. The spasm passed off in about seven minutes as his vision returned.

There seems to be no doubt that prodromatal symptoms, especially the scintillating scotomas, may occur without headache. I have had typical migrainous scotomas for 50 years without a single headache and several of my friends among the medical profession tell me that they have scotomas without headache.

In the same way, *numbness* and *tingling* in one hand or arm and occasionally over one entire side may occur preceding the headache. I have seen two cases in which parietal lobe syndromes developed. The affected extremities seemed to belong to some other person or to be missing. There was apraxia with inability to perform simple acts such as using the telephone or taking a glass of water. Familiar objects could not be recognized by feeling. More complex syndromes are described with micropsia and metamorphosia of various types and distortion of the body image so that the patient seems too tall or too short. Transient *disturbances* of *speech* may occur in the same way before the headache develops. The chief difficulty is in finding words. Rarely, the patient is unable to speak coherently. As a rule, there is numbness of the tongue and lips at such times.

Mitchell Clark, Symonds, Dynes and Whitty mention families in which several members were subject to repeated attacks of *hemiplegia* in associa-

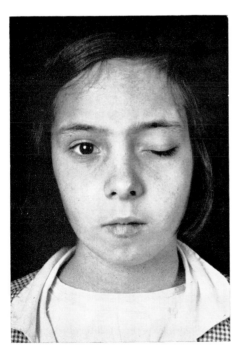

Fig. 281. Third nerve palsy in ophthalmoplegic migraine. Girl of 10 years whose first attack occurred at age of one year. Complete recovery after each attack. Ventriculogram and arteriogram both negative. (By the courtesy of Dr. Woodhall.)

tion with migrainous attacks. It is said that this condition begins in childhood. The onset is marked by hemianopic visual phenomena. Paresthesias develop on one side or the other and the sensory disturbances are followed by paralysis on the same side. Headache and vomiting soon follow. As a rule, the hemiplegia lasts only a few hours but in some instances it lasts several days. It usually clears up completely. I have seen just two cases of this type. One was that of a girl of 13 years and the other in a girl of 15 years. When the right side was involved aphasia occurred in addition to the hemiparesis. Rosenbaum finds that in some instances, the hemiplegia precedes the headache, occurring in the phase of vasoconstriction, and in other cases, follows the headache and occurs, therefore, in the phase of vasodilatation.

The term *ophthalmoplegic migraine* is applied to certain cases in which recurrent unilateral headaches are associated with palsies of the third nerve. Nausea and vomiting are often present as well. The symptoms begin as a rule early in childhood. The headaches seem to be typical of migraine. Brief headaches are not associated with third nerve palsy but if the headache lasts more than twenty-four hours, there will be partial or complete paralysis of the muscles supplied by the third nerve. As a rule all such palsies are found on the same side but in some instances either side is involved. The palsy disappears within a few days or weeks as a rule, but it is stated that it may eventually become permanent. Dr. Norman Dott has told me of a case in which regeneration phenomena developed after many many years. It should be pointed out that these palsies occur twenty-four hours or more after the onset and, therefore, in the phase of vasodilatation. Ophthalmoplegic migraine has been attributed to intracranial aneurysm but in our experiences the arteriogram is always negative. Gynergen will often seem to aid in recovery. Wolff states that injections of norepinephrine will cause prompt clearing of the palsy. It should be said that cases are described in which the fourth and sixth nerves are affected.

Walsh and O'Doherty suggest that swelling of the carotid artery in the cavernous sinus may be responsible for the ophthalmoplegia.

In some instances, after a series of severe migrainous headaches, the patient will display a small pupil and a drooping lid on the side of the pain without reduction of sweating on the face, i.e. the oculosympathetic syndrome. These findings usually disappear gradually during a period of weeks or months. This should be termed Raeder's syndrome rather than Horner's syndrome. Occasionally, the pupil may be contracted for a short time in association with a headache. Rarely the pupil will dilate at the onset of a headache.

In cases in which the symptoms are unilateral, we are probably dealing

with involvement of the carotid system. In some instances, however, the basilar system is probably responsible. The headache is occipital. Bilateral scotomas or cortical blindness may occur. There may be dysarthria, vertigo, tinnitus and paresthesias on both sides of the body. Nystagmus and cerebellar ataxia may occur but are not common. Bickerstaff states that such symptoms occur most frequently in adolescent girls.

Bickerstaff also states that loss of consciousness may occur in migrainous headaches. He found that in eight of twenty-three young girls who had basilar migraine there was loss of consciousness. This occurred during the prodromal visual phenomena. He points out that syncope seems unlikely since during the unconsciousness the pulse remains strong and the color is normal and lying down does not prevent unconsciousness. It is suggested that ischemia in the reticular system is responsible. Sir William Gowers described loss of consciousness in association with a migrainous attack and Engel says that syncope may occur in the early phases of migraine.

The so-called *abdominal migraine* is also a very obscure condition which seems to bear some relation to the headache. Some patients have abdominal pain during each attack of headache. It is claimed that the abdominal pain may also occur apart from the headache as a migrainous equivalent. Whatever may be the nature of these pains, they seem to be of a functional nature for laparotomy reveals nothing abnormal.

The association of convulsions and migraine has been recognized for many years. Since epilepsy and migraine are both very common conditions, it is inevitable that they should both occur in many cases, but it is generally believed that the association is more frequent than the laws of averages would demand. Either of the diseases may precede the other; one may cease while the other continues, and one may begin when the other stops. It has often been stated that a convulsion may represent a migrainous equivalent. Paroxysmal tachycardia is also recognized as a migrainous equivalent by Critchley and Bassoe. It is claimed that scotomata may occur in attacks of tachycardia and that tachycardia and headaches may alternate.

It has been brought to light in recent years that a large percentage of all patients suffering from migraine show abnormal waves in the electroencephalogram. These are usually paroxysms of slow wave activity.

Livingston, S., *et al.* find that the positive spike pattern of 14 and 6 cycles per second is found in 13 out of 28 patients suffering from migraine.

In some instances, *focal symptoms* which develop during the phase of vasoconstriction may *persist* for *years* indicating that organic damage has occurred. I have seen about ten cases in which *hemianopic defects* in the visual fields developed during a migrainous attack and persisted. In most instances, there is complete hemianopia at first and vision then returns in the lower quadrants in the next few years or months. Eventually there is apt

to be a small pie shaped defect near the midline in the upper quadrant. One of my patients who was subject to severe migrainous attacks developed a right homonymous hemianopia at the onset of a severe headache. This persisted. A few days later, a second attack caused left homonymous hemianopia so that he was quite blind for 20 minutes. Vision was then completely restored on the left side but there was only gradual and limited improvement in the right fields of vision. At the patient's death 5 years later there was still a partial upper quadrant defect present. At post-mortem examination the brain was sectioned and examined carefully. No lesions were visible but no histological examination was made. I have seen two cases in which *hemiparesis* persisted after a migrainous attack.

Ohta *et al.* describe persisting cerebellar symptoms following repeated attacks of migraine in a family also subject to migrainous hemiplegia.

Diagnosis.—The diagnosis depends entirely upon the history. The most important features are the family history, the chronic recurrent course, the unilateral distribution of the pain, the nausea, vomiting and scintillating scotomata. In typical cases when a clear history can be elicited, there can be no doubt about the diagnosis but so often only vague and foolish accounts of the symptoms are given and it may be difficult or impossible to form any clear idea of the real situation. In children too young to describe their symptoms, the family history may be of the greatest value. As a rule migraine is most apt to be confused with "neurotic" headaches and hysterical conditions. In fact, it seems to be impossible to make a definite distinction between migraine and such conditions since pyschological factors are so important in the former. I have seen one case in which an angioma of the occipital lobe simulated ophthalmic migraine perfectly and other cases in which a saccular aneurysm of the circle of Willis was found in a patient who suffered from migraine. Some physicians at present make a diagnosis of epilepsy when migrainous headaches are associated with abnormal waves in the electroencephalogram though the patient has never had seizures of any kind. I may say briefly that I am very strongly opposed to this trend.

One must not stress the diagnostic importance of scintillating scotomas too strongly, for occasionally, one encounters a case of intracranial tumor in which scintillating scotomas are associated with the headaches. Presumably, fluctuation of the intracranial pressure cause transient compression of the calcarine arteries as a result of tentorial herniation or some other mechanism.

Having seen massive hemiplegia and other disastrous reactions following arteriography even in young individuals who were healthy except for a tendency to migrainous headaches, I strongly oppose this procedure in patients subject to migraine, if it can possibly be avoided.

Prognosis.—The outlook depends upon the severity of the case, the pa-

tient's economic situation, psychological make-up and the intelligence with which the patient is treated. Unstable individuals, especially if they have been badly advised by their physicians and have had numerous useless operations, are apt to become chronic invalids. Obviously, most victims of migraine are never incapacitated in any way.

Treatment.—The most important element in the treatment is the patient's attitude to the condition. It should be made clear that migraine is not the result of any serious organic disease but a constitutional peculiarity which renders the patient subject to headaches. An increase in the frequency or severity of the attacks should be regarded as evidence of overwork, nervous strain, emotional disturbances or depression which should be treated by appropriate alterations in the mode of living. Proper rest, abundant sleep, adequate recreation and out-door exercise should be insisted upon. The patient must be helped to make an adjustment to the disability, but at the same time must not be over-indulged so as to lead to invalidism. The parents must be cautioned not to be overly sympathetic or to keep the child away from school any more than can be avoided. The diet should be easily digested and such as to prevent constipation.

Any demonstrable abnormalities such as errors of refraction, sinus infections, infected or decayed teeth should receive proper attention, since they constitute a source of discomfort and, therefore, play a role.

No drugs have any value other than their symptomatic effect. Sedatives such as phenobarbital or one of the tranquilizing drugs may be given for a time when the attacks are frequent and seem to have a beneficial effect. It is questionable whether they should be employed for more than a very short time in this way. When an attack is beginning various analgesics such as aspirin, phenacetine, and related drugs are helpful. Morphine should never be given under any circumstances, nor any of its derivatives with the exception of codeine.

Ergotamine tartrate causes a strong and prolonged vasoconstriction of the cerebral arteries and is probably the most helpful drug in the control of a migrainous headache. If the patient cannot retain oral medication because of vomiting, suppositories may be used. In some instances, small doses every day will prevent headaches. I have found this drug of little value when the patient is extremely emotional. Methysergide maleate or sansert is effective in preventing headaches, but it is now believed that it may have serious ill effects including retroperitoneal fibrosis and narrowing of blood vessels.

In some patients, the visual phenomena and the disturbances of speech which precede the headache are very troublesome. Breathing into a paper bag will often give prompt relief of these symptoms. It is believed that

these aurae are due to vasoconstriction and the carbon dioxide which accumulates in the bag no doubt causes vasodilatation.

CASE HISTORY of "Ophthalmoplegic Migraine."—*Recurrent attacks of right frontal headache beginning at the age of three years and associated with nausea, vomiting and transient paralysis of the right third nerve.*

L. F. S. seemed to be healthy and vigorous as a baby. At the age of three years he began to have attacks of violent headache and vomiting which were sometimes associated with paralysis of the right third nerve so the eyelid drooped, the eye turned out and the pupil was enlarged. This paralysis disappeared within three weeks without fail. The attacks continued and even grew more frequent, so that at the age of 8 years he had one every two weeks. He was also subject to milder headaches which were not associated with ptosis of the lid. In such attacks the location and character of the pain were the same and there was also nausea and vomiting. If the headache lasted more than 48 hours, the patient was sure to have paralysis. This would usually appear within 48 hours of the onset of the headache and would then slowly recede during the next few weeks. The headaches were as a rule associated with constipation and drowsiness. The attending physician stated that these phenomena were not due to sedatives. The attacks seemed to be precipitated by emotional upsets and by fatigue.

At the age of 16 years the patient came to the Johns Hopkins Hospital. At that time the headaches were occurring just as frequently as ever. He was just recovering from a third nerve palsy which developed a month previously. Neurological examination was otherwise quite negative, as were roentgenograms of the skull, ophthalmological and laboratory studies. The boy was considered ambitious, intelligent and a bit sensitive. Dr. Dandy advised against exploration at that time.

CASE HISTORY.—*Repeated episodes of amaurosis fugax in a boy of 16 years. Strong history of migraine in family. Boy denied headache.*

A. E. P. was seen at the age of 18 years. At 16 years he began to have episodes of partial or complete loss of vision of the right eye. The onset would be marked by the appearance of complex geometrical figures before the right eye. These would become more opaque so within 2 minutes vision of that eye would be lost. Within 7 minutes, vision would be clear once more. The patient was having one such episode a week.

An ophthalmologist examined the right eye during such an episode. The whole right retinal tree became attenuated. The color of the arteries was almost the same as that of the veins. After a minute or two, the arteries and veins both became engorged and vision was clear again. No evidence of embolism was noted.

The patient's mother and his maternal grandmother had had severe sick headaches, but the patient firmly denied headaches.

Sansert was given and while on this drug the patient had no disturbances of vision.

CASE HISTORY.—*Migrainous hemiplegia. History of severe headaches preceding menses for several years. Mother and maternal grandmother subject to severe headaches. At 16 years began to have hemiparesis just before headache began.*

L. S. was seen at the age of 16 years. She gave a history of headaches for several years. These often occurred on first day of menses. They would also occur between the menses and she had about 3 to 5 headaches a month. Her mother and maternal grandmother were both subject to severe sick headaches.

The pain was located in the frontal and temporal region, but might extend into the occiput. No blurring of vision had been noted. Vomiting was denied.

For several months the patient had had repeated episodes during which she noted numbness of the right arm and right leg. There would also be weakness and clumsiness. These symptoms would last 20 minutes and then clear up just as the headache began.

Neurological examination revealed no physical sign of organic disease of the nervous system. The electroencephalogram was reported to be normal.

CASE HISTORY.—*Severe migraine in a boy of 9 years. Episode of right hemiplegia and aphasia. Recovery from hemiplegia within 2 days. Aphasia still present after 2 months.*

P. J., a boy of 9 years, had had severe morning headaches for more than a year. They were associated with nausea and vomiting. His father had very intense headaches with vomiting and his paternal grandfather had been subject to severe headaches also.

Two months before he was examined, he had headache with vomiting when he got up from bed. After a time, the headache diminished and he was allowed to go to school. Later in the day his mother was called to the school. The child had continued to vomit and the headache had returned. The mother found the boy could not move his right arm or leg and could not talk.

He was taken to a hospital where right hemiplegia and aphasia were found. The spinal fluid was normal. Within 2 days there was some return of power in the right arm and leg, but the aphasia persisted. Neurosurgical studies were performed with negative results.

The child was said by his parents to be a sensitive emotional boy who was easily upset and had never been able to sleep well.

Examination 2 months after the hemiplegia revealed only right facial weakness of central type and deviation of the tongue to the right. Otherwise the examination of the cranial nerves was negative.

No residuum of the right hemiplegia could be found. His articulation was indistinct however, and he could use only a few words. He did not always understand what was said to him.

CASE HISTORY.—*Girl of 14 years with severe headaches with nausea and vomiting and a variety of neurological syndromes.*

D. D., an intelligent little girl of 14 years began to have severe headaches in January 1967. They were associated with nausea and vomiting and unsteadiness which the child said was due to dizziness. The headaches recurred every few weeks.

In March, she was taken to a hospital because of a severe attack of headache and vomiting. This was associated with diplopia for a few days. A very complete neurosurgical study was made with x-rays of the skull and chest, myelogram, electroencephalograms, brain scan, arteriograms and an air study. No evidence of organic disease of the nervous system was found. The symptoms disappeared and she was sent home.

The headaches and other symptoms recurred every few weeks. It is of possible interest that the child had had slight vaginal bleeding termed *spotting* by her mother since the onset of her symptoms but this happened at irregular intervals and no regular menses were established.

In September she had another severe attack. This was the tenth. There was headache, and vomiting as usual. Diplopia was also found which seemed to be due to a partial 3rd nerve palsy on the left. Nystagmus was found on lateral deviation. There was right hemiparesis and ataxia on the left.

Complete neurosurgical studies were performed again. The spinal fluid was normal. The brain scan, electroencephalogram and arteriograms were all normal. The headache soon ceased and the neurological abnormalities were soon gone.

CASE HISTORY.—*Migraine with visual phenomena and loss of consciousness at the age of 13 years.*

K. B. was examined at the age of 20 years. She was a tall slender girl who seemed to be immature and very sensitive. At the age of 13 years, she began to menstruate. At the same time she began to have occasional headaches. They would occur just before her menses or during her menses. There was first blurring of vision and the child claimed she sometimes had loss of vision. Then she would have a headache. She would say she was dizzy. She said she needed more air and would want to go outdoors. She would then sink down on the floor and seem to be unconscious for a few minutes. At such times, her mother stated that she would be very pale and completely relaxed. When she regained consciousness her vision would be blurred for a few minutes. The past history was not helpful. Her father was subject to severe headaches which had been attributed to migraine.

Neurological and neurosurgical examinations were completely negative. The electroencephalogram was normal.

This was regarded as the type of migraine described by Bickerstaff.

BIBLIOGRAPHY

ADIE, W. J.: Permanent hemianopia in migraine and subarachnoid hemorrhage. Lancet, **2**:237, 1930.

ALPERS, B. AND YASKIN, H.: Pathogenesis of ophthalmoplegic migraine. Arch. Ophth., 45:555, 1951. (Arteriograms negative in 2 cases. One post-mortem which revealed no aneurysm.)

ANTHONY, M. *et al.:* Plasma serotonin in migraine and stress. Arch. of Neurol., 16:544, 1967.

BASSOE, P.: Migraine. J.A.M.A., 101:599, 1933.

BELL, E.: Headaches in childhood. Headache, 78/3:127, 1968.

BIANCHINE, J. R. AND SPEED, W. G. III: Treatment of migraine headache. Johns Hopkins Medical Journal, 123:38, 1968.

BICKERSTAFF, E. R.: Impaired consciousness in migraine. Lancet, ii:1057, 1961.

————: Basilar artery disorder in migraine. Lancet, i:15, 1961.

BLAU, J. N. AND WHITTY, C. W. M.: Familial hemiplegic migraine. Lancet, ii:1115, 1955.

BLAU, J. N. AND CUMINGS, J. N.: Method of precipitating and preventing some migraine attacks. Brit. Med. Jour., ii:1242, 1966.

BRADSHAW, P. AND PARSONS, M.: Hemiplegic migraine. Quart. J. Med., 34:65, 1965.

CAMP, W. A. AND WOLFF, H.: The electroencephalogram in migraine. Arch. Neurol., 4:475, 1961.

CHAPMAN, L. F. *et al.:* Humeral agent implicated in vascular headache of migraine type. Arch. Neurol., 3:223, 1960.

CLARKE, J. M.: On recurrent motor paralysis in migraine with a report of a family in which recurrent hemiplegia accompanied the attacks. Brit. Med. J., i:1534, 1910.

CONNON, R. C. R.: Visual and brain damage from migraine. Lancet, ii:1072, 1962.

CRITCHLEY, McD. AND FERGUSON, F. R.: Migraine. Lancet, 1:123, 1933.

DALESSIO, D. J.: Cerebral vasospasm in migraine. Lancet, 87:283, 1967.

DYNES, J. B.: Alternating hemiparetic migraine syndrome. Brit. Med. J., 2:446, 1939.

ELY, F. A.: The migraine-epilepsy syndrome. Arch. Neurol. & Psychiat., 24:943, 1930.

ENGEL, G. L.: Fainting. Thomas, Springfield, Second Edition. 1962.

FISHER, C. M.: Observations on the fundus oculi in transient monocular blindness. Neurology, 9:333, 1959.

FORD, F. R. AND WALSH, F. B.: Raeder's paratrigeminal syndrome. A benign disorder possibly a complication of migraine. Bull. Johns Hopkins Hosp., 103:269, 1958.

FROELICH, W. A. *et al.:* Headache in childhood. Electroencephalographic evaluation of 500 cases. Neurology, 10:639, 1960.

GOWERS, SIR WM.: The Border-Land of Epilepsy. 1907.

HERRAULT, A.: Ann. Pediat., 44:36, 1968.

LEES, F. AND WATKINS, S. M.: Loss of consciousness in migraine. Lancet, ii:647, 1963.

LIPPMAN, C.: Certain hallucinations peculiar to migraine. J. Nerv. & Ment. Dis., 116:346, 1952.

LIVINGSTON, S. *et al.:* Electroencephalographic changes in children with migraine. New England Jour. Med., 276:23, 1967.

MICHAEL, M. I. AND WILLIAMS, J. M.: Migraine in children. J. Pediat., 41:18, 1952.

MOERSCH, F. P.: Psychic manifestations in migraine. Am. J. Psychiat., 3:697, 1924.

OHTA, M. *et al.:* Familial occurrence of migraine with a hemiplegia syndrome and cerebellar syndrome. Neurology, 17:813, 1967.

PHILLIPS, J.: The relation between migraine and epilepsy. J.A.M.A., 78:1960, 1922.

RILEY, H. A.: Migraine. Bull. Neur. Inst. N. Y., 2:429, 1932.

ROSENBAUM, H. E.: Familial hemiplegic migraine. Neurology, 10:164, 1960.

SCHILDKROUT, M. AND SHENKER, I. R.: Headaches and abdominal pains in adolescent. Clin. Pediat., 7/I:55, 1968.

SUTHERLAND, A. M. AND WOLFF, H. G.: Experimental studies on headache. Further analysis of mechanism of headache in migraine, hypertension and fever. Arch. Neurol. & Psychiat., 44:929, 1940.

SYMONDS, C.: Migrainous variants. Med. Soc. Trans. Lond., 68:1, 1950-51.

WALSH, F. B.: *Loc. cit.*

WALSH, J. P. AND O'DOHERTY, D. S.: Possible explanation of mechanism of ophthalmoplegic migraine. Neurology, 10:1079, 1960.

WHITTY, C. W.: Familial hemiplegic migraine. J. Neurol., Neurosurg. & Psychiat., 16:172, 1953.

WOLFF, H. G.: Headache mechanisms. International Arch. of Allergy and Applied Immunology. Separatum Vol. 7, No. 4-6, p. 210, 1955.
WOLTMAN, H. W.: The more common neurologic disorders associated with pain and encountered in general diagnosis. Minnesota Med., 7:193, 1924.

THE SYNDROME OF RECURRENT SOMNOLENCE AND MORBID HUNGER

(Kleine-Levin)

Some 20 cases of this syndrome have been reported. It is most apt to occur in young males, often during adolescence. The history as a rule reveals no cause for the symptoms. The patient has recurrent episodes passing through three phases in each. In the first phase the patient complains of fatigue and lack of energy. There may be severe headache. There is a great increase of appetite especially for carbohydrates. Gastrointestinal disturbances may occur possibly because of overeating. After a few days, the second phase develops. The patient becomes drowsy and goes to sleep. From time to time the patient awakens to go to the toilet or to eat. The large appetite is still present. It is possible to arouse the patient from this sleep, but consciousness is not fully regained for there is apt to be apathy, drowsiness and confusion. After a few days to two weeks, the patient recovers from the somnolence and then usually becomes depressed. There is amnesia for the period of somnolence. The period of depression may last for a week or for months in some instances. It is said that suicidal impulses may be present.

Critchley states that during the state of depression there are symptoms suggestive of schizophrenia. He also states that the episodes grow infrequent and eventually cease. Garland states that uninhibited sexual behavior is characteristic.

Medical and neurological examinations are always negative. The electroencephalogram shows no abnormalities. Laboratory tests in general are negative. The blood sugar levels are within normal limits.

Psychotherapy has been tried without result.

Bonikalo describes the psychiatric background of this condition. Gallinek finds that amphetamine sulphate is helpful in reducing the frequency and severity of the attacks.

BIBLIOGRAPHY

BONKALO, A.: Hypersomnia. Brit. Jour. Psychiat., 114:69, 1968.
CRITCHLEY, MACD.: The hypersomnia syndrome in adolescents. Brain, 85:627, 1962.
GALLINEK, A.: The Kleine-Levin syndrome. World Neurology, 3:235, 1962.
———: The syndrome of hypersomnia, bulimia and abnormal mental states. J.A.M.A., 154:1081, 1954.
GARLAND, H. et al.: The Kleine-Levin syndrome. Neurology, 15:1161, 1965.

GILBERT, G. J.: Periodic hypersomnia and bulimia. Neurology, 14:844, 1964.
KLEINE, M.: Periodische Schlafsucht. Monatschr. f. Psychiat. u. Neurol., 57:285, 1925.
LEVIN, M.: Periodic somnolence and morbid hunger. Brain, 59:494, 1936.

THE EXAGGERATED HEREDITARY STARTLE REACTION

Suhren *et al.* describe the study of 25 persons in 5 generations of a family who were affected. An autosomal dominant inheritance was found. The startle reaction may be manifest by movements more violent than normal or by momentary generalized rigidity of the muscles, loss of voluntary control and falling. Such reactions usually become evident when the child begins to walk. Two patients would lose consciousness. Six patients had histories of epileptic phenomenon. Seven patients had jerking of the muscles as they fell asleep. The startle reactions persisted throughout life.

The electroencephalogram was normal in some cases but showed a variety of abnormalities in other cases. Development was not retarded.

BIBLIOGRAPHY

SUHREN, O. *et al.:* Hereditary startle syndrome. Jour. Neurol. Sc., 3:577, 1966.

Chapter IX

DISEASES OF THE AUTONOMIC SYSTEM

INTRODUCTION.—There are a number of conditions characterized by disordered function of smooth muscle. Many of these are especially frequent in childhood or even peculiar to childhood. It is impossible to say at present whether the muscle itself is at fault or whether the cause of such disorders is to be sought in the nervous system, but it is clear that nervous impulses play important roles. I have classified these conditions among the diseases of the autonomic system for convenience and because this arrangement brings to light some interesting analogies despite the fact that it is open to criticism. Diabetes insipidus and adiposogenital dystrophy are included because it is now believed that they are results of disturbances of function of suprasegmental centers of the autonomic system.

BIBLIOGRAPHY

CASSIRER, R.: Die vasomotorisch Tropischen Neurosen. 2nd Ed. Berlin, S. Karger, 1912.
LIVINGSTON, W. K.: The Clinical Aspects of Visceral Neurology; with Special Reference to the Surgery of the Sympathetic Nervous System. Springfield, Ill., Charles C Thomas, 1935.
MÜLLER, L. R.: Die Lebensnerven, Berlin, Julius Springer, 2nd Ed., 1924.
WHITE, J. C.: The Autonomic Nervous System. New York, Macmillan Co., 1935.

DISORDERS OF THE GASTROINTESTINAL TRACT

Hirschsprung's Disease

Definition.—This term is applied to certain cases of enormous dilatation and hypertrophy of the colon which seem to be of congenital origin.

Etiology.—Whitehouse and Kernohan have made a study of 11 cases of megacolon. They found nerve cells absent in the distal part of the colon in all cases. In the transitional segment of the bowel they were absent in 80 per cent of cases; in the lower sigmoid in 60 per cent and in the upper sigmoid in 20 per cent. Alvord, Stevenson and Dooley found reduction of the lateral horns of the spinal cord in one case.

Clinical Features.—The essential features of this condition are distention of the abdomen and the obstinate constipation. As a rule, the abdomen begins to become enlarged in the first few months of life, although the onset may be somewhat delayed in milder cases. The greatest circumference of the abdomen is usually just above the umbilicus. The stools are hard and dry and may contain blood if there is ulceration. Vomiting is seen from time to time and there may be recurrent attacks of diarrhea. Peristaltic waves are usually visible. In mild cases the condition may be controlled

by diet and lubricants, and there is a tendency to improvement in some cases as puberty approaches. In severe cases all conservative measures seem to be ineffectual. The child is often poorly nourished and well below average size.

Diagnosis.—The diagnosis depends upon the presence of dilatation of the colon and constipation, and the elimination of anatomical obstruction, tuberculous peritonitis, chronic intestinal indigestion and other diseases which may give rise to similar symptoms. Roentgenographic studies of the intestinal tract are important in the diagnosis.

Prognosis.—The outlook depends upon the severity of the condition. In mild cases, there may be improvement or even recovery. In severe cases, the outlook is unfavorable and the child is apt to die from perforation of the intestine, malnutrition or intercurrent infection.

Treatment.—Liquid petroleum should be used with proper diet and enemata as required. The possibility of mechanical obstruction should always be considered and treated if present. Mecholyl, prostigmin and syntropan have been employed with some success. If the child does not improve satisfactorily under these conditions, operation should be considered. Removal of the rectosigmoid and rectum is apparently the operation of choice at present and it is claimed gives good results.

BIBLIOGRAPHY

ALVORD, E., STEVENSON, L. D. AND DOOLEY, S. W.: Developmental anomaly with reduction of lateral horns of the spinal cord in case of congenital megalocolon. J. Neuropath. & Exper. Neurol., **8**:240, 1949.

KLINGMAN, W. O.: The treatment of neurogenic megacolon with selective drugs. J. Pediat., **13**:805, 1938.

LEARMONTH, J. R. AND MARKOWITZ, J.: Studies on the function of the lumbar sympathetic outflow. 1. The relation of the lumbar sympathetic outflow to the sphincter ani internus. Am. J. Physiol., **89**:686, 1929.

SCOTT, W. J. M. AND MORTON, J. J.: Sympathetic inhibition of the large intestine in Hirschprung's disease. J. Clin. Invest., **9**:247, 1930.

SWENSON, O.: Congenital megacolon (Hirschsprung's disease) . Pediatrics, **8**:542, 1951.

TIFFIN, CHANDLER AND FABER: Localized absence of ganglion cells of the mesenteric plexus in congenital megacolon. Am. J. Dis. Child., **59**:1071, 1940.

WHITEHOUSE, F. R. AND KERNOHAN, J. W.: Mesenteric plexus in congenital megacolon. A study of 11 cases. Arch. Int. Med., **82**:75, 1948.

ZUELZER, W. W. AND WILSON, J. L.: Functional intestinal obstruction on congenital neurogenic basis in infancy. Am. J. Dis. Child., **75**:40, 1948.

MEGALOURETER AND DILATED BLADDER

Swenson has made studies of cases in which the bladder and the ureters are greatly dilated. He states that there is a great deficiency of nerve cells in the walls of the bladder and ureters. He points out that megalouterer and dilated bladder are sometimes associated with Hirschsprung's disease

in which deficiency of the nervous plexus in the walls of the intestines is thought to be responsible.

BIBLIOGRAPHY

SWENSON, O. *et al.*: A new concept of the etiology of megaloureters. New England J. Med., **246**:41, 1952.

SPASTIC CONSTIPATION

Definition.—This is a condition in which there is excessive tone of the muscular walls of the large intestines leading to abdominal pains, vomiting and constipation. It seems to be the converse of Hirschsprung's disease.

Clinical Features.—This type of constipation is rare in infancy and not very common at any period of childhood. Holt states that it may occur as early as the third month, however. It is frequently associated with evidences of a neurotic constitution. The characteristic features are the constipation, the presence of abdominal pain, vomiting and anorexia. The stools are either slender and ribbon-like or are small, firm, round scybala. The roentgenological examination reveals several zones in the colon in which the lumen is greatly constricted by strong muscular contractions. Frequently, there may be some dilatation on either side of such constrictions. The entire colon may be affected in this manner. Full doses of atropin usually cause prompt relief from the symptoms. This is so characteristic a feature that it is of diagnostic value. The symptoms are definitely influenced by psychic factors and many authors recommend that psychotherapy be employed in addition to the usual treatment by drugs and diet.

HYPERTROPHIC STENOSIS OF THE PYLORUS

Definition.—In this condition we find spasm and hypertrophy of the circular muscle of the gastric pylorus which seem to be of congenital origin and which cause partial obstruction.

Etiology.—The cause is unknown. There is an obvious analogy between this condition and Hirschsprung's disease.

Pathological Anatomy.—The pyloric muscle is greatly thickened and the lumen very small. The stomach is dilated and the walls thickened. Microscopic examination reveals hypertrophy of the muscles. Friesen *et al.* claim that this condition is due to incomplete maturation of the ganglion cells of the myenteric plexus. They state that the plexus is present but the cells are immature. Under normal conditions, a few mature cells are seen within two weeks after birth and almost all the cells are mature by one to five months of age.

Clinical Features.—The characteristic symptoms are persistent vomiting and distention of the stomach. These may appear within a week of birth or may be delayed for several weeks. The vomiting usually follows meals

and is very violent, almost of projectile type. Bile is usually absent from the vomitus. Constipation is almost always present and usually severe. There is naturally loss of weight and in severe cases, extreme emaciation. The upper part of the abdomen is distended and the lower part may be less prominent than usual. Active peristaltic waves are seen over the stomach which are most easily observed just after feeding. A mass may be palpated in the region of the pylorus which may be felt to contract. In some cases, the vomiting may lead to so much loss of acid that alkalosis and tetany result. The urine is scanty and great dehydration may develop.

Diagnosis.—The diagnosis depends upon the features given above and upon the elimination of other causes of vomiting. We must consider congenital malformations of the intestines, such as atresia of the duodenum, vomiting from increased intracranial pressure, from nephritis and the habitual vomiting which is regarded as a functional condition. Usually it is not difficult to make the diagnosis after a short period of observation.

Prognosis.—This depends upon the severity of the condition and upon the skill with which the child is treated.

Treatment.—In mild cases, medical treatment is advised. Small feedings are given at frequent intervals, the stomach is washed out about three hours after meals, if necessary, and atropine may be used to reduce spasm. If the child is artifically fed, concentrated semi-solid foods are advised. In severe cases, the Rammstedt operation is to be preferred. The circular muscle of the pylorus is incised but the mucosa is not opened. Proper medical care must always be exercised and dehydration prevented.

BIBLIOGRAPHY

BOLLING, R. W.: Congenital hypertrophic pyloric stenosis. J.A.M.A., **85**:20, 1925.

DAVISON, W. C.: Medical treatment of pyloric stenosis in infants. Bull. Johns Hopkins Hosp., **37**:157, 1925.

FRIESEN, S. R., BOLEY, J. O. AND MILLER, D. R.: The myenteric plexus of the pylorus. Surgery, **39**:21, 1956.

HOLT, E.: Hypertrophic stenosis of the pylorus. J.A.M.A., **58**:1517, 1917.

ESOPHAGEAL ACHALASIA

This condition may occur in children of any age. The analogy with hypertrophic pyloric stenosis is obvious. It may follow acute infectious diseases or may appear without apparent cause. The essential feature is difficulty in swallowing. In mild cases, the child can drink liquids and even wash solid foods down with liquids, but in more severe cases, even water is taken with great difficulty. Food often collects in the esophagus and is regurgitated after a time. The regurgitated material, of course, contains no acid or gastric juice. This condition may last only a few weeks or may persist for a long time. In long-standing cases, nutrition is a serious problem.

Fluoroscopy reveals dilatation of the esophagus and constriction of the cardia. Full doses of atropine may give relief but are not always effective. Dilatation of the cardia may be required but is fraught with considerable risk. Rickham advises a longitudinal incision of the esophagus extending through the muscular wall to the mucous membrane. Swenson *et al.* claim that this condition is due to degeneration of Auerbach's plexus in the lower part of the esophagus. It is thus similar to Hirschsprung's disease.

In other cases in which the patient complains of difficulty in swallowing and of regurgitation, the fluoroscope shows only normal conditions. In my experience, psychotherapy has been effective in such cases.

Frank and Gatewood describe transient difficulty in swallowing in the newborn. They state that recovery occurs within 2 weeks.

BIBLIOGRAPHY

BLADES, B. *et al.:* Combined surgical treatment of achalasia of the esophagus and hypertrophic pyloric stenosis. Med. Ann. District of Columbia, **26**:180, 1957.

FRANK, M. M. AND GATEWOOD, O. M. B.: Transient pharyngeal incoordination in the newborn. Amer. Jour. Dis. Child., **111**:178, 1966.

HURST AND RAKE: Achalasia of the cardia. Quart. Jour. Med., **23**:491, 1930.

McCREADY, P. B.: Cardiospasm: Report of two cases with post-mortem observations. Arch. Otol., **21**:633, 1935.

MOERSCH, H. J.: Cardiospasm in childhood. Am. J. Dis. Child., **38**:294, 1929.

RICKHAM, P. P. AND BOECKMAN, C. R.: Achalasia of the esophagus. Clin. Pediat., **2**:676, 1963.

SORSDAHL, O. A. AND GAY, B. B.: Achalasia of the esophagus in childhood. Am. J. Dis. Child., **109**:141, 1965.

SWENSON, O. AND OECONOMOPOULOS, C. T.: Esophageal achalasia in children. J. Thorac. & Cardiovas. Surg., **41**:41, 1961.

DISORDERS OF RESPIRATORY TRACT
Laryngospasm

Definition.—A spasmodic contraction of the laryngeal muscles which may be an expression of tetany or of laryngitis but which also occurs not infrequently in early childhood without apparent cause. It must be distinguished from breath holding spells.

Etiology.—If we omit the cases due to tetany, i.e. laryngismus stridulus and those associated with outspoken laryngitis such as diphtheria of the larynx, we usually find no satisfactory cause for this condition. Exposure to cold and gastrointestinal disorders may play a role but there seems to be a definite constitutional factor involved and in some families there is a predisposition to this condition which suggests that there may be an important hereditary element.

Pathological Anatomy.—No anatomical changes have ever been found.

Clinical Features.—This condition is most common between the ages of six months and four years. The symptoms appear almost invariably at night. About midnight the mother may notice that the child's breathing is

loud and there is stridor on inspiration. This rapidly increases and soon the child is awakened by difficulty in getting the breath. The stridor may be loud enough to be heard at a considerable distance; there is often slight cyanosis and great distress. The supraclavicular fossae and the intercostal spaces are retracted during inspiration. After a few hours the symptoms diminish and the child finally falls asleep. On the following morning, the child usually seems to be quite well or may be slightly hoarse. Such attacks often occur on two or three successive nights with diminishing severity.

Diagnosis.—Tetany and acute laryngitis should be ruled out. Diphtheria of the larynx should never be forgotten. The so-called congenital stridor is easily distinguished since it is not paroxysmal and rarely causes respiratory distress. This condition is attributed to malformations of the larynx or to lack of tone of the vocal cords. It usually disappears before the end of the second year. Breath holding spells are a result of fright or temper tantrums. It is said that there is no stridor and that death never results.

BRONCHOSPASM AND ASTHMA

Definition.—Asthma is a disease characterized by paroxysmal attacks of dyspnea due to obstruction of the bronchioles presumably resulting from spasm of their muscular walls. In early childhood there is a striking tendency to bronchospasm which gives rise to symptoms almost identical with those of true asthma but which seem to be dependent upon entirely different causes. Attacks of this type are termed asthmatic bronchitis or spasmodic bronchitis.

Etiology.—It seems to be generally accepted that true asthma is usually a manifestation of allergy but it must be admitted that this theory cannot be established in a large percentage of cases and that treatment designed to relieve hypersensitization frequently fails to give relief. Some authors speak of "reflex" asthma. It is clear, however, that in many cases the condition is intimately bound up with the patient's personality and that emotional factors are of great importance.

As regards spasmodic bronchitis, two factors seem to be important; the tendency of certain infants to develop bronchospasm with little or no provocation and local irritation or inflammation of the bronchial mucous membrane.

Pathological Anatomy.—No anatomical changes are described except for emphysema and similar lesions which may be regarded as secondary.

Clinical Features.—In asthma the attacks frequently develop at night without apparent cause. Within a short time there may be severe dyspnea with definite cyanosis. Both inspiration and expiration are labored and accompanied by loud, wheezing sounds. The chest is expanded and hyperresonant. Auscultation reveals prolonged expiration and numerous sibilant

rales. The excursion of the chest is limited despite the use of the accessory muscles of respiration. There is often an unproductive cough. In most cases the attack subsides spontaneously within a few hours but some attacks persist for days. Loss of consciousness and convulsions may occur in severe attacks. I have seen transient cortical blindness. No doubt these phenomena are due to anoxia.

Spasmodic bronchitis may give exactly the same picture but there is usually some fever, the condition is more constant than paroxysmal and adrenaline has less effect. Eosinophilia is, as a rule, absent and other signs of allergy are not apparent.

Diagnosis.—The diagnosis depends upon the clinical features described above.

Prognosis.—Bronchitis is not, as a rule, a serious condition in infants unless the child is already in poor condition. In true asthma it is said that the prognosis for spontaneous recovery is relatively good if the symptoms begin in infancy but less favorable if the condition begins later, for the disease usually becomes chronic in such instances.

Treatment.—In asthma, adrenaline and ephedrine are usually more or less effective in relieving the attacks. Cortisone is often very helpful. In preventing the attacks, most stress is placed upon discovering and removing the agent responsible for the allergy, treatment of foci of infection and psychotherapy.

DISORDERS OF THE VASOMOTOR SYSTEM

Raynaud's Disease and Erythromelalgia

Definition.—This condition is characterized by spasmodic contraction of the arterioles of the extremities, causing ischemia and sometimes gangrene. There are no anatomical changes in the vessels which might not be explained by the muscular spasm.

Etiology.—The cause is unknown. There is still some dispute as to whether the condition arises primarily in the muscularis of the vessels or whether a disorder of the autonomic nervous system is responsible. Since it has been shown that section of the sympathetic nerves results in improvement or recovery, the impression has gained ground that we are dealing with an excessive functional activity of the vasoconstrictor fibers. Lewis has advanced numerous arguments against this view, however.

Pathological Anatomy.—Nothing is found except for the changes in the tissues, which result from deficient circulation, and such alterations of the vessels as may result from prolonged spasm.

Clinical Features.—This condition is uncommon in childhood but is known to occur before fifteen years and even in infancy. It is somewhat more frequent in girls than in boys, and in some cases there seems to be a

tendency for the disease to affect several children in one family. The essential symptoms are the same as those of adults. From time to time the tips of the extremities become white and cold. Later there is cyanosis which is followed by hyperemia as the arterioles relax. The first phases are accompanied by numbness and pain, the last by burning and throbbing. Such attacks are induced most commonly by cold, but nervous strain or emotional disturbances are almost as efficient in this regard. Such attacks occur at variable intervals and last for variable periods. In severe cases, prolonged attacks occur which not infrequently lead to gangrene of the tips of the fingers or toes. These disturbances are usually but not always symmetrical. In some cases, patches of gangrene may appear on the tip of the nose, the ears, or even on the proximal portions of the extremities. As a rule, the pulses are not reduced, since the palpable arteries are not affected. Moreover, the color of the extremity is not altered by raising or lowering the limb. Changes in the capillaries of the nail beds may be followed with the microscope. The peripheral nerves are naturally involved as a result of disturbances of the circulation, causing numbness or anesthesia of the affected parts. Moreover, in some cases, convulsions may accompany attacks of cyanosis, and hemiplegia and other cerebral syndromes, which may be due to vasomotor disturbances of the cerebral circulation, have been described. Migraine is frequently associated. Spasms of the retinal arteries may cause transient or persistent amaurosis. Hookman *et al.* have shown that loss of esophageal peristalsis may occur in this condition.

Erythromelalgia is rare in adults and even rarer in children. It is characterized by throbbing pain in the legs associated with redness and increased warmth. The pulses are said to be increased. Catchpole describes a case in a girl of thirteen years who was relieved of symptoms by the use of 4 mgs of methylsergide a day.

Diagnosis.—The most important step in the diagnosis is the elimination of organic disease of the blood vessels, which may, of course, be accompanied by vasomotor disturbances. The history of paroxysmal attacks of pallor, cyanosis and hyperemia is typical. If the circulation is good when the patient is examined, an attack may usually be induced by plunging the hands into cold water. If the affected part is pale or cyanotic most of the time, that is if the condition has reached a chronic stage, injection with novocaine of the nerve supplying the affected area should cause definite relief with elevation of the skin temperature. The reaction may be measured by the thermocouple. In Raynaud's disease we expect to find good pulses in the arteries and, if the pulses are absent or feeble, organic disease of the vessels should be suspected. Moreover, elevation or lowering of the extremity should cause definite changes in the color and temperature of the affected part in organic disease in most cases and no change in Raynaud's

disease. In many cases of paroxysmal hemoglobinuria, symptoms similar to those of Raynaud's disease occur. This condition is usually due to syphilis, and the Wassermann test should always be performed in all cases of this nature. It must be kept in mind that certain cases of polyneuritis are associated with severe vasomotor disturbances which may be mistaken for Raynaud's disease. Acrodynia is always to be considered. Scleroderma, dermatomyositis, rheumatoid arthritis, lupus erythematosis, syringomyelia and cryoglobulinemia cause similar symptoms.

Prognosis.—The disease is usually progressive in most but perhaps not in all cases, and the more severe forms usually lead to gangrene unless operation is performed.

Treatment.—Proper protection against cold, vasodilator drugs and sedatives have some value. Gentle heat is often helpful. In severe cases, operation is indicated. Adson and Brown have shown that removal of the sympathetic ganglia supplying the affected extremities will cause striking benefit, if not complete cure, in all but the most advanced cases. Following operation, the skin temperature becomes elevated and the color returns to normal or is even pinker than normal. Vasomotor reflexes are almost entirely lost and cold causes no pallor except in severe cases, in which some reaction may occur. There is no sweating in the denervated areas when the patient is placed in the sweat box.

BIBLIOGRAPHY

ADSON, A. W. AND BROWN, G. E.: The treatment of Raynaud's disease by resection of the upper thoracic and lumbar sympathetic ganglia and trunks. Surg. Gynec. & Obst., 48:577, 1929.
———: Raynaud's disease. Arch. Neurol. & Psychiat., 26:687, 1931.
CARP, L.: The association of Raynaud's disease with cerebral symptoms, report of a case with migraine, psychoneurotic symptoms, transient hemiplegia and death. Arch. Surg., 22:409, 1931 (no autopsy).
CATCHPOLE, B. N.: Erythromelalgia. Lancet, i:909, 1964.
HOOKMAN, P. *et al.*: The relationship of Raynaud's phenomenon to aperistalsis of the esophagus. Meeting of the American Gastroenterological Ass. May 31, 1963.
DUNPHY, E. B.: Ocular manifestations of Raynaud's disease. Tr. Am. Ophth. Soc., 30:420, 1932.
LEWIS, SIR T.: Raynaud's disease with special reference to the nature of the malady. Brit. Med. J., ii:136, 1932.
MOSES, J. H. M.: Diagnosis of central nervous system involvement in Raynaud's disease. Med. Clin. North America, 11:835, 1928.
WELLINGTON, J. L.: Raynaud's syndrome. Angiology, 20:129, 1969.

THE SYNDROME OF THE CAROTID SINUS

Definition.—A syndrome including pallor, fainting, bradycardia, unconsciousness and convulsions attributed to excessive reflex activity of the carotid sinus. This is apparently rare in children and will be discussed very briefly.

Etiology.—The carotid sinus is a slight dilatation of the internal carotid

artery at its origin close to the bifurcation of the common carotid artery. The artery at this point is rich in nerve endings and receives nerve fibers from the ninth nerve, the tenth nerve and often from the cervical sympathetic nerve. Under experimental conditions it has been shown that raising the blood pressure in this segment of the artery causes reflex bradycardia, fall of blood pressure, disturbances of the cerebral circulation and a general vasodilatation. Conversely, reduction of the pressure in this segment of the vessel causes tachycardia, elevation of the blood pressure and general vasoconstriction. In certain cases, this reflex seems to be abnormally active and even light pressure on the sinus causes such marked bradycardia and fall of blood pressure that the patient may lose consciousness. There is little information about the effects of loss of the sinus reflex. Capps and De Takats state that after bilateral denervation of the sinus, there is tachycardia and hypertension for a few days but that subsequently a moderate degree of postural hypotension is apt to develop.

Pathological Anatomy.—Little is known of the anatomical basis of this condition. In certain cases the sinus has been the site of an aneurysmal dilatation and in others it has been compressed by small tumors such as enlarged lymph nodes. As a rule, however, the sinus has been anatomically normal so far as could be determined.

Clinical Features.—Weiss has collected a series of fifteen patients in whom pressure over the carotid sinus in the neck produced an abnormally pronounced reflex. The patients would turn pale and then cyanotic. There might be feelings of vertigo, faintness or syncope or even violent convulsions. In some cases light pressure would cause convulsions on the contralateral side and heavy pressure would induce general convulsions. These symptoms were due to changes in the circulation. The pulse would slow and there might be transient asystole. There was a general vasodilatation and fall of blood pressure. The cerebral circulation was diminished as measured by study of the oxygen and carbon dioxide content of the jugular vein. Apparently, the bradycardia, the fall of blood pressure and the cerebral symptoms were largely independent of one another for any of the three might occur alone. The existence of a purely cerebral reaction is now doubted. In thirteen of the these cases there were spontaneous attacks of syncope or convulsions which seem to have been identical with the attacks induced by pressure over the sinus. When this syndrome is once established, it is usually persistent, but in two cases the symptoms disappeared after a time. The seizures may be induced by paroxysms of coughing or by pressure on the neck by a stiff collar.

We have seen the case of a little boy whose carotid sinus was denervated by a gunshot wound. The blood pressure fluctuated between 280 and 300

systolic during the next few days. By the end of the week, however, blood pressure was normal again.

Diagnosis.—When the reflex is fully developed pressure over the carotid sinus produces such a striking reaction that the diagnosis is evident at once. Less pronounced reactions must be studied by recording changes in blood pressure and pulse. It is important to massage the sinus rather than exert continuous pressure upon it for mechanical interruption of the carotid circulation may cause misleading symptoms in some subjects.

Treatment.—Atropine will prevent the bradycardia and ephedrine may help to avert the vasodilatation and drop in blood pressure. No drugs are helpful in cases in which the reaction is cerebral. In a number of cases one or both carotid sinuses have been denervated and it is claimed that the results have been satisfactory, but severe hypertension may appear after operation and may be fatal though it does not last long. Greelet *et al.* state that radiation of the carotid sinus gives relief of symptoms in more than 50 per cent of cases and apparently did not observe hypertension.

BIBLIOGRAPHY

BUCY, P. C.: The carotid sinus nerve in man. Arch. Int. Med., **58**:418, 1936.

CAPPS, R. B. AND DE TAKATS, G.: The late effects of bilateral carotid sinus denervation in man. J. Clin. Invest., **17**:385, 1938.

FORD, F. R.: Fatal hypertensive crisis following denervation of the carotid sinus for relief of repeated attacks of syncope. Bull. of Johns Hopkins Hosp., **100**:14, 1957.

GREELEY, H. P. *et al.*: Treatment of carotid sinus syndrome by irradiation. New England Jour. Med., **252**:91, 1955.

HOLTON, P. AND WOOD, J. B.: The effects of bilateral removal of the carotid bodies and denervation of the carotid sinuses in two human subjects. J. Physiol., **181**:365, 1965.

WEISS, S. AND BAKER, J. P.: The carotid sinus reflex in health and disease. Medicine, **12**:397, 1933.

POSTURAL HYPOTENSION

Definition.—This term is applied to the pronounced fall of blood pressure which is included in certain subjects by the sudden transition from a recumbent to an erect posture.

Etiology.—The regulation of the blood pressure is dependent upon a complex neural mechanism, which is represented centrally in the medulla and which is dependant upon the peripheral autonomic nerves to convey impulses to and from the heart and blood vessels. Important sensory mechanisms are believed to lie in the carotid sinus, in the walls of the aorta and, no doubt, in other blood vessels. When a patient assumes an upright position, a readjustment of the circulation is obviously required to compensate for the alterations of the hydrostatic pressure resulting from the change in posture of the body. In normal subjects this adjustment is affected immediately by means of the mechanism described above. In cases in which

this mechanism is defective in any essential part, the proper reflexes fail and the blood pressure falls precipitously with the production of syncope and other symptoms.

Clinical Features.—This syndrome seems to be almost invariably an acquired one. It may occur without apparent cause but it is sometimes found in tabes dorsalis, polyneuritis, diabetes, syringomyelia and in cases in which the cervical cord had been severely injured. Ellis and Haynes found definite postural hypotension in 10 to 17 cases of tabes dorsalis. It is of course well known that various operations on the abdominal and thoracic sympathetic nerves for hypertension result in postural hypotension. The use of drugs to reduce blood pressure is not an uncommon cause of postural hypotension.

The most common symptom is syncope which is usually provoked by suddenly arising from a recumbent to an erect position. This is most apt to occur if the movement is an abrupt one. In milder cases the patient may be merely faint or dizzy and in the most severe cases the patient may fall into convulsions. The history is sometimes elicited that syncope has developed when the patient had been standing for some time and when there had been no recent change in posture. Apparently symptoms never occur when the patient is in a recumbent position. In some instances the patient may be unable to stand or even to sit for days at a time. In other cases the symptoms are so variable and inconstant that they are quite unpredictable. Examination as a rule reveals normal pulse, blood pressure and heart action so long as the patient is lying down. When the patient is placed on the feet or, better still, rotated to an upright position on the tilting table, the blood pressure falls very rapidly and syncope develops. Most descriptions state that the pulse is slow or does not increase as much as one would expect during this reaction, but Gillespie and Barker state that the pulse is accelerated. This has been my experience with few exceptions. The reaction is usually a transient one and, as a rule, the blood pressure slowly rises to an approximately normal level if the patient is maintained in an upright posture. Moreover, if the table is tilted slowly, there may be no reaction even in cases in which rapid tilting causes a severe reaction. Binding the abdomen tightly will prevent the sudden drop in blood pressure. It is also agreed by most observers that ephedrine in full doses exerts a beneficial effect on the patient's condition and often gives substantial relief.

Similar symptoms may occur in patients who have been in bed a long time, in debilitated persons and in states of hypotension of various types.

Diagnosis.—The diagnosis is based upon the presence of the symptoms mentioned above.

Treatment.—The most effective methods of treatment are the use of the

abdominal binder, adequate doses of ephedrine, and such general hygienic measures as are indicated to improve the patient's general health. It is said that 9 alpha-fluorohydrocortisone is also useful but requires careful supervision.

BIBLIOGRAPHY

BRADBURY, S. AND EGGLESTON, C.: Postural hypotension. Am. J. Heart., 1:73, 1925.

CAPPS, R. B. AND DE TAKATS, G.: The late effects of bilateral carotid sinus denervation in man. J. Clin. Invest., 17:385, 1938.

ELLIS, L. B. AND HAYNES, F. W.: Postural hypotension with particular reference to its occurrence in disease of the central nervous system. Arch. Int. Med., 58:773, 1936.

GILLESPIE, D. L. AND BARKER, N. W.: Orthostatic hypotension. J. Pediat., 12:774, 1938.

HICKLER, R. B. *et al.:* The treatment of orthostatic hypotension. New England J. Med., 261:788, 1959.

LEWIS, P.: Familial orthostatic hypotension. Brain, 87:719, 1964.

SCHIRGER, A. AND THOMAS, J. E.: Clinical aspects of orthostatic hypotension. Heart Bull., 15:12, 1966.

SHY, M. AND DRAGER, G. A.: A neurological syndrome associated with orthostatic hypotension. A.M.A. Arch. of Neurol., 2:511, 1960.

STEAD, E. A. AND EBERT, R. V.: Postural hypotension. Arch. Int. Med., 67:546, 1941.

DISORDERS OF SWEAT SECRETION

Congenital Hyperhidrosis

Definition.—This is a condition characterized by excessive sweating which is evident soon after birth and which persists throughout life. Its cause is quite unknown.

Pathological Anatomy.—No anatomical studies have been made.

Clinical Features.—This condition may be illustrated by a brief abstract of one of several cases which we have studied. The patient, S. G. (U65616), was a young girl of Italian parentage. Since infancy it had been observed that her hands and feet were always wet. The sweating was always evident but was increased by nervous strain and activity and reduced to some extent by rest and relaxation. The hands were just as wet in cold weather as in the warmest days of summer. The patient's mother suffered from the same symptoms but in old age the sweating became somewhat less evident.

On examination, the patient was found to be well developed and in excellent general health. The hands and feet were drenched with perspiration and sweat dripped from the finger tips so rapidly that the floor appeared to be covered with rain drops, despite the fact that the room was cool. There were a few fine droplets upon the upper lip and the axillae were moist but the arms, trunk and thighs were quite dry. The hands and feet and especially the fingers and toes were cyanotic and slightly swollen. The skin temperature was definitely below normal. All other examinations were negative and no abnormalities in secretion of saliva, of tears or of the se-

baceous glands were present. Dr. Dandy sectioned the cervical sympathetic nerve and removed the stellate ganglion on either side. There was then complete loss of sweating in the hands and arms.

Diagnosis.—The diagnosis would seem to be obvious when the condition is of congenital origin. If the sweating develops later in life we must rule out various debilitating diseases.

Treatment.—It is claimed that atropine will give some relief and recently drugs such as banthine have been recommended. Bilateral cervical sympathectomy will stop the sweating, but in view of the harmless nature of the symptoms such a procedure seems rather radical.

BIBLIOGRAPHY

PALMER, A. J.: Hyperhidrosis. Study of a case. Arch. Neurol. & Psychiat., **58**:582, 1947.
PEARL, F. L. AND SHAPIRO, N. H.: Ganglionectomy for hyperhidrosis. Ann. Surg., **102**:16, 1935.

CONGENITAL ANHIDROTIC ECTODERMAL DYSPLASIA

This is inherited as an X linked recessive but may also occur as an autosomal recessive and as an autosomal dominant. There is frontal bossing and overhanging brows. The nose is short and the bridge of the nose is depressed. The mandible is small in some cases. The teeth are partly absent or completely absent. Pig shaped teeth are often seen. The lips protrude. The ears may be satyr-like.

The skin is thin and dry. The sweat glands, sebaceous glands and lacrimal glands are absent. As a result the patients develop fever during hot weather, and even convulsions. The lack of lacrimal secretion may cause damage to the corneae. The hair of the scalp is sparce and baldness occurs. Body hair is absent. The nipples may be absent. The fingernails may be imperfectly formed. Skeletal growth may be defective. Mental deficiency is common.

The nose and throat are dry. It is advised that the nose and throat be sprayed with normal saline. Drops of 1 per cent hydroxymethycellulose in each eye help protect the corneae. Damp clothing in hot weather and frequent shower baths are advised.

Gorlin and Sedano describe a condition of hypohidrotic ectodermal dysplasia.

BIBLIOGRAPHY

GORLIN, R. J. AND SEDANO, H.: Hypohidrotic ectodermal dysplasia. Modern Medicine, **37**: No. 6: 202, 1969.
HALPERN, S. L. AND CURTIS, C. M.: Anhidrotic ectodermal dysplasia associated with mental deficiency. Amer. Jour. Ment. Defic., **46**:459, 1942.
HARTWELL, S. W. *et al.*: Congenital anhidrotic ectodermal dysplasia. Clin. Pediat., **4**:383, 1965.
HILL, A. M.: Hereditary ectodermal dysplasia of anhidrotic type; report of a case with results of biopsy. Arch. Dermat. & Syph., **28**:66, 1933.

Vassella, H. M. *et al.:* Congenital sensory neuropathy with anhidrosis. Arch. of Dis. Childh., **43**:124, 1968.

Weech, A. A.: Hereditary ectodermal dysplasia. Am. J. Dis. Child., **37**:766, 1929.

Wilkey, W. D. and Stevenson, G. H.: A family with inherited ectodermal dystrophy. Canad. Med. Ass. Jour., **53**:226, 1945.

ACQUIRED SEGMENTAL HYPOHIDROSIS WITH TONIC PUPILS

Five cases have been described in which localized loss of sweating, orthostatic hypotension, myotonic pupils and loss of tendon reflexes were all associated. The onset of some symptoms was in childhood, but other symptoms appeared later. The patients were all studied in adult life. Biopsy revealed normal sweat glands in the anhidrotic areas.

We have seen a child of 2 years who was brought to the hospital because of recurrent episodes of fever in hot weather. It was found that the fever was due to deficient temperature regulation resulting from deficient sweating over large areas of the body. Normal sweat glands were found in the anhidrotic areas. The pupils were not greatly dilated but did not contract in response to light stimulation or during accommodation and convergence. They contracted strongly when drops of 2.5 per cent mecholyl were instilled. The knee and ankle jerks were absent.

BIBLIOGRAPHY

Lucy, D. D. Jr. *et al.:* Holmes-Adie syndrome with segmental hypohidrosis. Neurology, **17**:763, 1967.

DISORDERS OF THE HEART ACTION

Paroxysmal Tachycardia

Definition.—This term is applied to types of sudden tachycardia ranging between 120 and 250 beats a minute, of abrupt onset and equally abrupt termination, which are not infrequently associated with cerebral symptoms.

Etiology.—In adults paroxysmal tachycardia is not, as a rule, associated with definite evidence of organic heart disease and is regarded as a functional disorder in some instances. Exciting causes such as emotional stress and strain, exertion, over-eating and similar factors seem to be important and an unstable personality is frequently discovered. In children, however, organic factors are probably more important. Myocarditis, endocarditis, congenital heart disease and cardiac decompensation from various causes are mentioned by most authors. Diseases of the nervous system such as encephalitis may be followed by this condition, however, and in a relatively large percentage of cases no evidence of myocardial damage can be found.

Pathological Anatomy.—It may be said very briefly that the anatomical basis of this syndrome is still unknown. In many cases, no anatomical lesions have been found and in others in which organic processes have been

discovered, neither the location nor the character of the lesions has been specific.

Clinical Features.—The onset is always abrupt. For no apparent reason, the pulse suddenly increases up to a rate of 120 to 250 beats per minute. There are frequently dyspnea, precordial distress, nausea and vomiting. If the attack is prolonged, there may be evidences of decompensation such as dilatation of the heart, edema and swelling of the liver. The neurological disturbances are of great interest. At the onset there may be general weakness, vertigo, syncope, blindness or even general convulsions. Brief lapses of consciousness resembling petit mal may occur. These may be regarded as evidence of a sudden reduction of the efficiency of the cerebral circulation. Rarely the symptoms may be of a focal nature suggesting that the circulation is more efficient in certain parts of the brain than in others. Thus, aphasia has been described as well as local paresthesias and hemiparesis. Mental disturbances are not infrequent. Anxiety, depression, confusion and even delirium are perhaps more common than more objective disorders. Barnes found cerebral symptoms in 60 per cent of cases in which the impulse originated in the ventricles, in 41 per cent of cases in which there was nodal tachycardia and in 25 per cent of the auricular tachycardias. The attacks may last from a few moments to several weeks. They may follow excitement, exertion or emotional disturbances or may develop in sleep without apparent cause. They may recur from time to time over a period of many years. Such attacks may be mistaken for epileptic seizures unless the pulse rate is taken during the seizure.

Diagnosis.—This condition may be suspected from the history but can be diagnosed definitely only by examination during an attack. The electrocardiographic study is essential for differentiation of the various types. It is said that nodal tachycardias are most frequently of neurogenic origin and that auricular flutter and ventricular tachycardias are always due to organic changes in the myocardium.

Prognosis.—This depends upon the presence or absence of organic disease and upon the duration of the attacks. The functional tachycardias may recur for many years without endangering the patient's life.

Treatment.—Sedatives and complete rest are recommended. Quinidine may be given. Stimulation of the carotid sinus may be helpful.

BIBLIOGRAPHY

BARNES, A. R.: Cerebral manifestations of paroxysmal tachycardia. Am. J. Med. Sc., **171**:489, 1926.

HORAN, M. AND VENABLES, A. W.: Paroxysmal tachycardia with episodes of unconsciousness. Arch. Dis. Childhood, **37**:81, 1962.

MOERSCH, F. P.: Nervous and mental phenomena associated with paroxysmal tachycardia. Brain, **53**:244, 1930.

SHOKOFF, C., LITVAK, A. M. AND MATUSOFF, I.: Paroxysmal tachycardia in children. Am. J. Dis. Child., **43**:93, 1932.

WILLIUS, F. A. AND AMBERG, S.: Paroxysmal tachycardia with syncope occurring in a child. Am. J. Dis. Child., **38**:551, 1929.

HEART BLOCK WITH STOKES-ADAMS SYNDROME

Definition.—In heart block the contraction of the ventricles no longer follows that of the auricles but occurs independently and at a slow rate usually under 60 beats a minute. Various cerebral disturbances may result, notably syncope and convulsions.

Etiology.—This condition indicates loss of conduction in the auriculo-ventricular bundle of His. This is almost always a result of an organic lesion but there is abundant evidence that a similar condition of brief duration may result from abnormal nervous impulses. An excessively active carotid sinus reflex (q.v.) is one of the causes for heart block.

Pathological Anatomy.—A number of lesions have been found. Among the causes of congenital heart block, a patent intraventricular septum is a common finding but several other defects of the auriculoventricular bundle are described.

Clinical Features.—This condition may result from myocardial damage in severe attacks of diphtheria, from rheumatic myocarditis and other infectious diseases. It may also represent a congenital defect of the heart. Excessive doses of digitalis may cause temporary heart block. Both complete and incomplete forms occur. In the incomplete forms, every second, third or fourth beat of the auricles is followed by a contraction of the ventricles and we speak of a 2 to 1, a 3 to 1 or a 4 to 1 block. The conduction time is increased in such cases. The auricular action may be determined by observing the pulsations of the jugular vein in the neck or by study of the electrocardiogram. In many cases of heart block there are periods of asystole which give rise to sudden symptoms indicative of interruption of the cerebral circulation. The patient may become unconscious and may even have generalized convulsions. Brief lapses of consciousness resembling petit mal may occur. Focal convulsions are relatively rare but may occur. The neurological symptoms are in general not unlike those of paroxysmal tachycardia. Weiss has presented evidence to show that Adams-Stokes syndrome may be due to lesions of the medulla or of the vagus nerve and is inclined to believe that in such cases an abnormally active carotid sinus reflex plays a dominant role.

Diagnosis.—The diagnosis is dependent upon the demonstration of the slow pulse rate and the dissociation of the action of the ventricles and the auricles.

Prognosis.—This is almost always serious since there is usually definite or-

ganic disease of the heart. In the neurogenic type, the outlook is, of course, more favorable.

Treatment.—Exertion and violent exercise should be avoided since these may cause syncope or convulsions. The patient should, of course, be treated for the underlying cause of the condition.

BIBLIOGRAPHY

ALDERSON, A.: Heart block with Stokes-Adams syndrome. Am. J. Dis. Child., **43**:514, 1932. (Abstract.)

NAKAMURA, F. F. AND NADAS, A. S.: Complete heart block in children. New England J. Med., **270**:1261, 1964.

NICHAMIN, S. J.: Stokes-Adams syndrome associated with complete congenital heart block in infancy and childhood. Pediatrics, **1**:327, 1948.

YATER, W. M., LYON, J. A. AND McNABB, P. E.: Congenital heart block. Review and report of a second case. J.A.M.A., **100**:1830, 1933.

DISORDERS OF METABOLISM DUE TO LESIONS IN THE SUPRASEGMENTAL CENTERS OF THE AUTONOMIC SYSTEM

There are two relatively common conditions, which frequently develop without apparent cause and which seem to depend upon dysfunction of the hypothalamus. No doubt congenital defects of the hypothalamus are responsible in some instances. These are adiposo-genital dystrophy, or Fröhlich's syndrome, and diabetes insipidus.

Adiposo-genital Dystrophy.—This is frequently termed Fröhlich's syndrome. It may occur in cases of suprasellar tumors compressing the hypothalamus, internal hydrocephalus, epidemic encephalitis and, indeed, numerous other conditions which injure this part of the nervous system. It appears most frequently, however, without apparent cause in infants or young children who seem to be quite healthy in other respects. In many cases the child gains weight so rapidly in the first few weeks of life that it seems probable that the condition was present at birth. Boys are affected more frequently than girls. The excessive deposits of fat are most evident around the hips, the abdomen and shoulders. The proximal joints of the limbs are more thickly covered with fat than the distal parts. The skin is soft and delicate resembling that of an infant, even after the patient has reached early adult life. There is little or no body hair. The fingers taper to unusually small tips and since the proximal joints are often plump, they seem strikingly pointed. The child is always overweight and, in some cases, is taller than the average, as if the skeletal growth were increased. However, the bones are usually slender. Knock-knees are frequently found, probably as a result of the excessive weight. The cheeks are rosy even in boys, who have a girlish complexion. The development of the penis and

testicles of the boys is almost always defective and the breasts of the girls have small nipples and little glandular tissue although the thickness of the subcutaneous fat may make the breasts appear to be large. The sella turcica is small or normal. This condition may persist throughout life or at puberty or shortly afterwards there may be a striking change towards a more normal appearance. Sometimes the sexual functions may eventually approach normal but they usually remain below par. Thyroid extract has some value but, in general, glandular therapy is ineffective. Proper diet is important since these children often have a craving for carbohydrates.

Diabetes Insipidus. This condition may occur as a feature of Fröhlich's syndrome, or it may occur alone, without any other evidences of disease of the nervous system. A great variety of lesions of the infundibulum are known to cause this condition. Neoplasms, basilar meningitis, trauma, epidemic encephalitis, tuberculosis, sarcoidosis and Schüller-Christian disease may be mentioned. A type is known which is usually inherited as an autosomal dominant trait. Blotner states that in such cases, one finds at post-mortem examination loss of cells in the supraoptic and paraventricular nuclei. The posterior lobe of the pituitary gland may be reduced in size but is otherwise normal.

The child exhibits an abnormal thirst and drinks great quantities of fluid. The polyuria

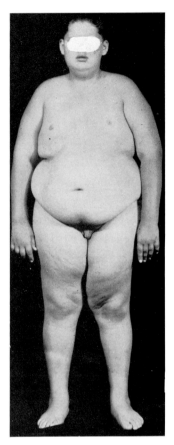

Fig. 282. Adiposogenital dystrophy in a boy of 12 years showing characteristic girdle obesity and absence of genital development. There was polyuria and polydipsia. No evidence of an intercranial tumor.

which results is primary, for the child becomes dehydrated and feverish if the intake of fluid is reduced to a proper level. The patient is unable to concentrate urine above a specific gravity of 1.008. Lozenges of posterior pituitary extract, 30 mgs each, given by mouth every four hours will give symptomatic relief.

Another type of diabetes insipidus is described—the nephrogenic type. In this condition, the posterior pituitary extract has no effect. The distal tubules of the kidneys fail to reabsorb water. This condition is evident as

a rule early in infancy. It is inherited, in some instances, as a sex-linked recessive and is found only in males. Mental retardation is often present and bodily growth may be defective. The patients may die during hot weather, as a result of dehydration. It is stated that if adequate water is given, at frequent intervals, mental deficiency may be prevented.

A third type of diabetes insipidus is apparently psychogenic. I have seen a child who would drink such vast quantities of water that he would lose consciousness and sometimes have convulsions. The serum sodium is reduced. Langgard and Smith have found that the serum osmolarity and urine osmolarity are reduced. There is edema of the brain. If such patients are not permitted to take excessive amounts of water, no dehydration occurs. An intravenous infusion of hypertonic saline will cause an increased output of urine just as in a normal individual.

Familial Dysautonomia.—This condition should be mentioned here for it has been thought that it is due to a disorder of the central autonomic system. The essential features of the syndrome include Jewish ancestry, defective lacrimation, erythematous skin blotching, excessive sweating, drooling, emotional instability, motor disturbances, reduction of the tendon reflexes, and relative indifference to pain which may lead to Charcot's joints as the child grows older. In some cases there are also intermittent hypertension, vomiting, unexplained fever, mental retardation, convulsions and corneal ulceration. Difficulty in swallowing and regurgitation is evident early in life. Breath-holding spells may occur with loss of consciousness. Severe and progressive kyphoscoliosis develops about the eighth year. The mouth is transversely elongated. The fungiform and circumvalate papillae are almost completely absent and taste for sweet and bitter is reduced. The condition is inherited as an autosomal characteristic.

Loss of temperature control was found in one of our cases. Susceptibility to infections, especially pulmonary infections, is evident in some cases. Corneal anesthesia is mentioned. Postural hypotension is stressed by some physicians. Kritchman *et al.* state that these patients react badly to anesthetics. They advise when operation is required, a volatile anesthetic be used after premedication with chlorpromazine and belladonna.

Cohen and Solomon describe the post-mortem findings in two cases. In one, a cyst destroyed the dorsomedial and lateral nuclei of the thalamus and there was also damage to reticular substance in the pons and medulla. In a second case the damage was confined to the reticular substance in the pons and medulla and the myelin sheaths were involved primarily. These authors regard this condition as a familial degenerative process of the central nervous system. Riley, however, prefers to regard dysautonomia as a functional derangement of the nervous system. Hutchinson and Hamilton

suggest that excessive production of acetylcholine may be responsible for the symptoms.

Solitare and Cohen describe lesions in the peripheral autonomic ganglia and plexuses. They point out that there is an increased ratio of homovanillic acid to vanilmandelic acid in the urine of these patients.

Smith and Dancis state that the intradermal injection of histamine in a 1 to 1000 solution is a simple and reliable diagnostic test. In healthy subjects, this injection is followed within five minutes, by a 1.0 cm wheal surrounded by a 1.0 to 3.0 cm zone of erythema. In children suffering from dysautonomia, a wheal at the site of injection is surrounded by an erythematous areola only 1 to 2 mm wide and deeper in color than the normal flare.

Smith *et al.* find an increased excretion of homovanillic acid and a decreased excretion of vanilmandelic acid and suggest that there is a failure of catecholamine precursers to be converted into epinephrine and norepinephrine.

BIBLIOGRAPHY

BLOTNER, H.: Primary or idiopathic diabetes insipidus. Metabolism, **7**:191, 1958.

BRAVERMAN, L. E. *et al.:* Hereditary idiopathic diabetes insipidus. Ann. Int. Med., **63**:503, 1965.

BROWN, W. J. *et al.:* A neuropathological study of familial dysautonomia in siblings. **27**:131, 1964.

CANNON, J. F.: Diabetes insipidus. Arch. Int. Med., **96**:215, 1955.

CHESTER, W. AND SPIEGEL, L.: Hereditary diabetes insipidus. J.A.M.A., **100**:806, 1933.

COHEN, P. AND SOLOMON, N.: Familial dysautonomia. Case report with autopsy. J. Pediat., **46**:663, 1955.

CUTLER, *et al.:* Physiologic studies in nephrogenic diabetes insipidus. Jour. Clin. Endocr., **22**:215, 1955.

DREIFUS, L. S., STAMLER, J. AND LICHTON, I. J.: Production of hypenatremia and hyperosmolarity in diabetes insipidus. Circulation Res., **7**:314, 1959.

FOGELSON, M. H. *et al.:* Spinal cord changes in familial dysautonomia. Arch. of Neurol., **17**:103, 1967.

GORLIN, R. J. AND SEDANO, H.: Familial dysautonomia. Modern Medicine, May 20, 1968, p. 146.

HUTCHISON, J. H.: Acetylcholine in dysautonomia. Lancet, i:1216, 1962.

KIRMAN, B. H. *et al.:* Familial pitressin resistant diabetes insipidus with mental defect. Arch. Dis. Childhood, **31**:59, 1956.

KRITCHMAN, M. M. *et al.:* Experiences with general anesthesia in patients with familial dysautonomia. J.A.M.A., **17**:529, 1959.

LANGGARD, H. AND SMITH, W. O.: Self induced water intoxication without predisposing illness. New England J. Med., **266**:278, 1962.

LEVINGER, E. L. AND ESCAMILLA, F.: Hereditary diabetes insipidus. J. Clin. Endocrinol., **15**:547, 1955.

LIEBMAN, S. D.: Corneal lesions in dysautonomia. Arch. Ophth., **58**:188, 1957.

MINTZER, I. J. AND RUBIN, Z.: Dermatological manifestations of familial autonomic dysfunction (Riley-Day syndrome). Arch Dermat. & Syph., **67**:561, 1953.

MOLOSHOK, R. AND REUBEN, R.: Familial autonomic dysfunction. J. Mt. Sinai Hosp., **21**:137, 1954.

MOSES, S. W. *et al.:* Clinical, genetic and biochemical study of familial dysautonomia. Israel J. M. Sc., **3**:358, 1967.

NIEDERMEYER, E. *et al.:* The electroencephalogram in familial dysautonomia. Electroencephalog. and Clin. Neurophysiol., **22**:473, 1967.

RILEY, C. M.: Familial dysautonomia. Advances in Pediatrics, **9**:157, 1957.

RILEY, C. M. *et al.:* Further observations on familial dysautonomia. Am. J. Dis. Child., **88**:376, 1954.

RILEY, C. M. AND DAY, R. L. *et al.:* Central autonomic dysfunction with defective lacrimation. Pediatrics, **3**:468, 1949.

RILEY, C. M., FRIEDMAN, A. M. AND LANGFORD, W. S.: Further observations on familial dysautonomia. Pediatrics, **14**:475, 1954.

SMITH, A. A. *et al.:* Abnormal catecholamine metabolism in familial dysautonomia. New England Jour. Med., **268**:705, 1963.

SMITH, A. AND DANCIS, J.: Tests for familial dysautonomia. J. Pediat., **63**:889, 1963.

SOLITARE, G. B. AND COHEN, G. S.: Peripheral autonomic nervous system lesions in congenital or familial dysautonomia. Neurology, **15**:321, 1965.

STEWART, E. W.: Pseudohermaphroditism, adiposity, polyuria and hyperglycemia, an infundibulotuberal syndrome. J. Neurol. & Psychiat., **1**:68, 1938, new series.

THIEFFRY, S. *et al.:* Familial dysautonomia. Arch. franc. pediat., **18**:194, 1961.

WARING, A. J., KADJI, L. AND TAPPAN, V.: A congenital defect of water metabolism. Am. J. Dis. Child., **69**:323, 1945.

WARKANY, J. AND MITCHELL, A. G.: Diabetes insipidus in children: A critical review of etiology, diagnosis and treatment with report of four cases. Am. J. Dis. Child., **57**:603, 1939.

WILLIAMS, R. H. AND HENRY, C.: Nephrogenic diabetes insipidus: Transmitted by females and appearing in infancy in males. Ann. Int. Med., **27**:84, 1947.

Chapter X

DISEASES OF THE MUSCLES

INTRODUCTION.—I have attempted to arrange the diseases of the muscles in the same categories as the diseases of the nervous system. Since the cause of a number of these conditions is unknown, the construction of a satisfactory classification is very difficult and the following outline must be regarded as merely tentative. The reader is referred to the splendid monograph, Diseases of Muscles by Adams, Denny-Brown and Pearson, Paul B. Hoeber, Inc., New York, 1953. All of the conditions mentioned in this section and many others are fully discussed by these authors. It should be said that defects of the extraocular muscles, the facial muscles and the muscles of the jaws are discussed in the section on congenital defects of the cranial nerves q.v.

BIBLIOGRAPHY

ENGEL, W. K.: Muscle biopsies in neuromuscular diseases. Pediat. Clin. N. Amer., **14**:963, 1967.
WALSH, F. B.: Clinical Neuroophthalmology, 2nd Ed. Williams and Wilkins, Baltimore, 1957.

CONGENITAL DEFECTS OF MUSCLES

Congenital Absence of Muscles

Definition.—It is well known, of course, that certain muscles are inconstant, such as the palmaris longus, pyramidalis abdominis and plantaris. In such cases we are dealing with anatomical variations which do not in any way incapacitate the patient. In the cases under consideration, however, there is a true defect of development involving a muscle or even several muscles, and often causing pronounced disability. In rare instances several members of a family may present the same peculiarity.

Pathological Anatomy.—Very few histological studies have been made. In some cases, the motor neurons in the corresponding segments of the spinal cord are found to be diminished or absent, but in most cases, no significant changes in the nervous system are discovered. In Bing's case, the nervous system was intact, and sections of affected muscles showed considerable variation in the size of the fibers, increase in the sarcolemma nuclei, and some increase in interstitial tissue. It seems best therefore to regard these conditions at present as primary defects of the muscles and to discuss them in this section.

Etiology.—These conditions seem to represent defects of development which are most probably the expression of an abnormal germ plasm.

Clinical Features.—Bing has made a careful study of one case, and has

1423

collected all the information to be found in medical literature. He finds that the pectoral muscles are affected very much more frequently than any other group, and was able to discover 102 cases in which some part of the pectoralis major or minor was absent. The sterno-costal part of the pectoralis major was most commonly absent. The trapezius was absent or defective in 18 cases, the quadriceps in 16, the serratus magnus in 14, the semimembranous in 7, the abdominals, gemelli, deltoid and latissimus dorsi in 4 cases each, and the sternomastoids, rhomboids, spinati and biceps in 3 cases each. Almost every muscle may be absent or defective at times, but it is evident from the figures given above that there is a definitely selective incidence.

In most cases these defects are unilateral and confined to one muscle or one muscle group, but cases are also well known in which bilateral symmetrical defects involving widely separated groups of muscles are found. Thus, Bing refers to cases in which the trapezius, sternomastoid, and lower half of the pectoralis major were absent on both sides. In another case the deltoid, spinati, serratus magnus, pectorals, biceps and triceps were all absent bilaterally. In a few instances, there have been defects of the facial muscles and absence of the pectorals on one side. Garrod and Davies have described an interesting condition in which the abdominal muscles are absent and the abdominal wall is very thin and wrinkled. Such children cannot cry or make any forced effort of expiration. They often die within a few months as a result of infection of the respiratory tract for they cannot cough up the bronchial secretions. It is the rule to find defects of the ureters, bladder and testicles in such cases. Garrod and Davies found the nervous system normal in their case. Defects of the diaphragm are de-

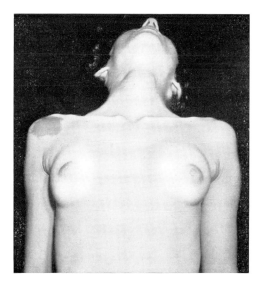

FIG. 283. Child of 11 years showing congenital absence of the sternomastoid muscles. There is also absence of the tibialis anticus and of the lower two thirds of the trapezius on either side. The extensors of the spine are fibrotic and inelastic so the child cannot bend her back. Some thirty years after the patient was first seen, her condition was unchanged.

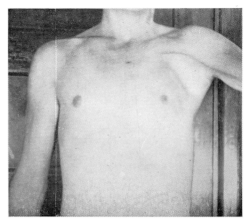

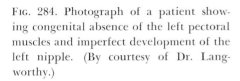

Fig. 284. Photograph of a patient showing congenital absence of the left pectoral muscles and imperfect development of the left nipple. (By courtesy of Dr. Langworthy.)

scribed, causing collapse of the lung and displacement of the abdominal viscera into the thorax.

It is very common for some abnormality of the other tissues to be associated with defects of muscles. Thus, Bing states that when the pectorals are defective it is not unusual for the hand on the same side to be malformed and the fingers webbed. The breast is usually absent in such cases, but polymastia is described. Bony defects in the thorax with lung hernias are also mentioned. Scoliosis and various deformities of the spinal column and malformation or displacement of the scapula are sometimes seen.

The writer's experience may be stated very briefly. If we omit defects in the muscles innervated by the cranial nerves, we have seen 14 cases of congenital deficiency in the skeletal muscles. In 7 cases there was partial or complete absence of one pectoral muscle. In one of these cases there was syndactylism of the corresponding fingers. In 2 cases there was bilateral absence of the external and internal oblique muscles of the abdomen as well as the transversals. This, of course, caused constipation and striking bulging of the abdominal wall. In one case the right trapezius was entirely absent. I have seen isolated defect of the flexors of the hip and defect of the iliopsoas associated with defect of the quadriceps. Another patient showed absence of the tibialis anticus on the left. His father had an indentical condition. In 2 children of the same family, the sternomastoids, part of the pectorals, the trapezii, serrati and anterior tibial muscles were lacking from birth, and the mother had no sternomastoids. In another case, the child lacked sternomastoids, lower two-thirds of the trapezii and the entire anterior tibial group of muscles.

We have observed shortened and fibrotic muscles as well as absence of muscles in certain children. Progressive muscular dystrophy may develop later in life in children who show absence of certain muscles at birth. I

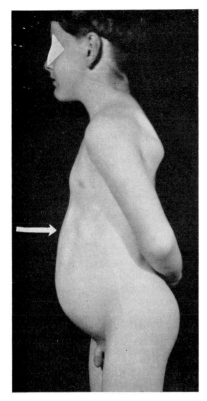

Fig. 285. Congenital absence of the lower abdominal muscles. Above the arrow the recti and oblique muscles seem to be intact; below this point there is no palpable muscle. The ureters and bladder are greatly dilated.

have seen two cases of a peculiar anomaly of the omohyoid muscle. The intermediate tendon which connects the two bellies is not bound down to the posterior aspect of the clavicle. As a result the muscle stands out when the patient swallows and in each instance it was thought that the patient had a goiter. In each case the condition was unilateral and apparently congenital.

CASE HISTORY.—*Congenital absence of both sternomastoids, serrati magni, lower half of the pectorales majores, lower two-thirds of the trapezii, and of anterior tibial group of muscles in a boy and in his sister. Mother lacks sternomastoids.*

J. F. G. (H. 6767) was examined first at the age of 12 years. The history was elicited that he had had weakness of the neck, arms and legs ever since birth, and that his condition had not grown either better or worse. His little sister suffered from identical symptoms.

Examination revealed a well-nourished boy of 12 years, who seemed to be of average intelligence. Both sternomastoid muscles were entirely absent, as were the lower half of the pectorales majores, the serrati magni, and the lower two-thirds of the trapezii. As a result, the scapulae were imperfectly fixed and abduction of the arm was impossible. The head could not be lifted from the couch. The tongue was small and wrinkled, and could not be moved laterally. The anterior tibial group of muscles was lacking on either side, and there was pes cavus and claw toes as well as bilateral foot drop. The patient's little sister, who was eight years old, was also examined and found to show exactly the same condition. The mother of the children stated that there was no similar condition among other members of the family, but it was noticed that her sternomastoid muscles were also absent and that she could not lift her head from the couch. She was examined, but the other muscle groups were found to be well developed. The children have been seen repeatedly during the last 10 years, and it is quite certain that their disability is not increasing.

BIBLIOGRAPHY

BING, R.: Ueber Angeborne Muskeldefecte. Arch. f. Path. Anat. u. Physiol. Virchows Archiv. **170**:175, 1902.

BROWN, J. B. AND DOWELL, F. M.: Syndactylism with absence of the pectoralis major. Surgery, **7**:599-601, 1940.

FRY, F. R. AND KASAK, M.: Congenital facial paralysis. Arch. Neurol. & Psychiat. **2**:638, 1919.

GARROD, A. E. AND DAVIES, L. W.: On a group of associated congenital malformations including almost complete absence of the muscles of the abdominal wall and abnormalities of the genito-urinary apparatus. Med.-Chir. T., **88**:363, 1905.

LE DOUBLE, A. F.: Traite des variations du Systeme musculaire de l'Homme. Paris, Schleicher Freres, 1897.

LICHTENSTEIN, B. W.: Congenital absence of the abnominal musculature: associated changes in the genitourinary tract and in the spinal cord. Am. J. Dis. Child. **58**:339, 1939.

McCLENDON, S. J.: Agenesis of the abdominal muscles. Arch. Pediat., **51**:673, 1934.

RESNICK, E.: Congenital unilateral absence of the pectoral muscles often associated with syndactylism. J. Bone & Joint Surg., **24**:925-928, 1942.

CONGENITAL CONTRACTURES OF THE MUSCLES

Introduction.—We shall consider at this point the congenital deformities which are associated with shortening and fibrosis of muscles. A great variety of such conditions exist, but we need discuss only the more important ones, such as club-foot, torticollis, congenital elevation of the scapula and multiple contractures of the extremities. These all have certain features in common, namely, an abnormal position which is maintained by muscular contracture and accompanied by malformations of the bones and joints, which seem to be secondary. Occasionally progressive muscular dystrophy may develop in patients who have suffered from such contractures.

These conditions have been attributed to intra-uterine pressure and amniotic adhesions or bands, but the evidence for this hypothesis has never been entirely satisfactory. Certainly, not all cases can be explained on this basis. In some instances, the presence of associated deformities, such as the absence of a limb, indicates that we are dealing with a primary developmental defect. Morbid heredity seems to be important in certain cases, for club-foot, for example, has been discovered in several generations of the same family, although, as a rule, the family history is quite negative. Undoubtedly, a number of factors enter into the causation of these conditions.

CONGENITAL TORTICOLLIS

We must distinguish, at least, two types of congenital torticollis: (1) those which are associated with developmental defects of the bones, such as fusion of the atlas and the occipital bone, synostosis of the atlas and the axis, wedge-shaped malformations of the cervical vertebrae and cervical ribs. These may be regarded as the result of primary faults of develop-

ment; (2) the common type, in which only shortening of the muscles is found and the bony abnormalities are such as may be explained by moulding of the plastic bones as a result of long-standing malposition.

The deformity varies somewhat according to the muscles affected and the degree of shortening. In the most common type, the sternomastoid alone is affected. The head is then tilted and somewhat displaced to the same side, and the chin rotated to the opposite side. The chin is a bit elevated as well, and the ear is drawn towards the clavicle. The head cannot be moved passively into normal position, and when the effort is made, it is resisted by the shortened sternomastoid muscle, which is felt as a dense fibrous cord beneath the skin. In many cases, other muscles are involved, such as the deep cervical muscles and trapezius, which results in retraction of the head and elevation of the shoulder. In all but the mildest cases there is soon an asymmetry of the face and cranium. The plane of the face does not intersect the sagittal plane of the skull at a right angle as it should, but at an oblique angle, for the face recedes somewhat on the side of the affected muscle. Moreover, the vertical length of the face on the affected side is diminished. This asymmetry is not very striking so long as the head is seen in its usual position, but when the body is covered, or when the position of the head is corrected, it becomes very obvious. There is, moreover, some lateral curvature of the spine and elevation of the shoulder. In many cases of congenital torticollis a spindle shaped swelling is found in the sternomastoid muscle during the first week of life when there is only a slight inclination of the head. This tumor is said to contain muscle fibers in the process of degeneration and an excess of connective tissue. As the tumor is absorbed during the next few months, fibrous contracture occurs. It is believed by Middleton and others that the tumor is a result of venous obstruction during delivery.

Borchgrevink states that the tumor regresses after one or two months, and disappears after five to eight months. He states that in most instances torticollis does not develop.

The diagnosis is usually apparent at a glance in typical cases, but a number of conditions must be ruled out before treatment is advised. For example, we must always make a careful roentgenological examination to determine whether there is any deformity of the bones, which might render operation useless. It is also necessary to consider several types of acquired torticollis, such as result from cervical infections and arthritis, fractures and dislocations, tuberculous spondylitis, poliomyelitis, tumors of the posterior fossa and defective ocular balance. The so-called spasmodic torticollis q.v. is usually regarded as the result of psychological disturbances, and may be distinguished from congenital torticollis by the fact that the deformity is variable, and that when the spasm is relaxed, the head may be

moved freely. In some cases, torticollis may be the first sign of athetosis or dystonia musculorum deformans.

Mild cases may be treated by manipulations or fixation, but more severe cases require resection of the affected muscles and fixation of the head in an over-corrected position for several weeks. Exercises are then prescribed. It is very important to make a careful study of the case before operation to make sure that the affected muscles are properly identified. Treatment should be begun as early as possible, for the asymmetry of the face develops rapidly, and becomes more pronounced as the child grows older. If the position of the head is corrected early in life, the asymmetry of the face will disappear to a large extent, but in young adults this cannot be expected, and often it becomes so much more conspicuous after operation that the patient is dissatisfied with the results.

BIBLIOGRAPHY

ARMSTRONG, D. *et al.:* Torticollis. Plastic Reconstr. Surg., **35**:14, 1965.
BORCHGREVINK, H. H. C.: Congenital muscular torticollis. Acta chir. scand., **128**:62, 1964.
GRUHN, J. AND HURWITT, E.: Fibrous sternomastoid tumor of infancy. Pediatrics, **8**:522, 1951.
HORTON, C. E. *et al.:* Torticollis. Southern Med. Jour., **60**:953, 1967.
JONES, R. AND LOVETT, R. W.: Orthopedic Surgery. New York, Wm. Wood and Co., 1923, p. 535.
MIDDLETON, D. S.: Pathology of congenital torticollis. Brit. J. Surg., **18**:188, 1930-31.

CONGENITAL CLUBFOOT

There are a number of possible deformities of the feet which fall into this group, such as talipes equinus, the plantar flexed foot; talipes calcaneus, the dorsally flexed foot; talipes varus, the inverted and adducted foot; and talipes valgus, the everted and abducted foot. The most common type, however, is talipes equino-varus, in which the foot is plantar flexed and inverted. In most cases the condition is bilateral. These deformities are maintained by shortening of certain muscles but the actual cause is probably weakness and atrophy of the opposing muscles.

In a small percantage of cases we may obtain a history of other instances in the same or previous generations. Macklin states that this condition is dependent upon a recessive factor or upon multiple factors in most cases. Two-thirds of the cases are in males, suggesting that one of the factors at least is sex-linked. Four sets of identical twins are reported in which both were affected. Clubfoot may occur in otherwise healthy babies or may rarely be associated with hare-lip or other deformities. It has been shown that brief immobilization of a chick embryo *in utero* by injection of curare will result in the production of club feet.

In the common type of talipes equino-varus, the foot is inverted so that the plantar surfaces of the two feet may be brought into contact, and there is, as a rule, some degree of plantar flexion. The attempt to manipulate the

foot into normal position is resisted by the ligaments and by the shortened muscles; in this case the tibial muscles are the chief offenders. The bones are of course moulded by the malposition.

Adams *et al.* state that clubfoot is sometimes due to defects in the spinal cord. In other instances one finds no defects in the cord and no evidence of neurogenic atrophy of the muscles. The atrophic muscles contain fat, connective tissue and a few poorly developed muscle fibers in such cases. The shortened muscles are more normal on histological examination. Possibly we are dealing with primary muscle defects in such cases.

In the differential diagnosis, we must consider defects of the spinal cord, such as are associated with spina bifida, and poliomyelitis, diseases of the bones, fractures of the bones, and progressive paralyses, such as the neural or peroneal type of muscular atrophy and muscular dystrophies. I have seen talipes equino-varus in a pair of identical twins associated with congenital spastic diplegia and mental defect. It must be kept in mind that the normal child often stands or walks on the toes for a short time, usually at about the end of the first year. It would seem unnecessary to mention this, except for the fact the certain orthopedic surgeons have regarded it as an indication for lengthening of the tendo Achilles.

Treatment should be begun at once, while the bones are still plastic. Manipulation and fixation in an over-corrected position are recommended for cases coming under observation during infancy; but in older children, surgical procedures are indicated. Without treatment, the deformity will usually increase.

BIBLIOGRAPHY

JONES, R. AND LOVETT, R. W.: Orthopedic Surgery. New York, Wm. Wood and Co., 578, 1923.

CONGENITAL ELEVATION OF THE SCAPULA

This condition is also called Sprengel's deformity. It is usually unilateral but may be bilateral. The affected scapula is elevated, and is usually rotated so as to bring the lower angle nearer to the spine. The whole shoulder is somewhat advanced. Passive and active rotation of the scapula is diminished or absent, for there are usually fibrous or bony attachments between the scapula and the ribs. Scoliosis is usually present and torticollis is found in about 10 per cent of cases. Roentgenograms reveal that the scapula is shortened so that the transverse diameter is relatively increased. Abduction at the shoulder is limited since the scapula cannot be rotated. The trapezius and perhaps other muscles attached to the scapulae are usually fibrotic and shortened. In certain cases, cervical spina bifida occulta is associated, and the cervical spine may be shortened and the vertebrae fused into a single bony mass. Such cases are discussed under the title of the Klippel-Feil syndrome q.v.

Treatment is operative, and not very satisfactory. There is a tendency for the scapula to ride up after operation, and to prevent this it is often sutured to a rib.

BIBLIOGRAPHY

FAIRBANK, H. A.: Congenital elevation of the scapula: a series of eighteen cases with detailed description of a dissected specimen. Brit. J. Surg., 1:553, 1913-14.
SPRENGEL: Angebornen Verschiebung des Schulterblattes Nach Oben. Arch. f. klin. Chir., 42:545, 1891.

CONGENITAL CONTRACTURES OF THE EXTREMITIES

This condition is also termed amyoplasia congenita, multiple articular rigidity and arthrogryposis multiplex congenita. It may be defined as a condition dating from birth, in which there is immobility of one or more joints associated with absence, or incomplete development, of certain muscles.

Post-mortem examination shows extensive changes in the muscles. Some are well preserved but others may be replaced by fat and connective tissue or may be grossly atrophied containing many small, thin fibers and a few larger ones. Adams *et al.* found extensive loss of motor cells in the spinal cord in one of their cases, which they attribute to a developmental defect or degeneration during foetal life. In some instances no lesions in the spinal cord have been found.

Amick *et al.* found in a study of 10 patients with arthrogryposis, 9 showed evidence of neurogenic atrophy and one seemed to be suffering from myopathy. In addition to myopathy and neurogenic atrophy a third form is described in which fibrosis of the muscles is the only finding. In rare instances the process seems to be progressive.

Pena *et al.* describe a familial type due to nodular fibrosis of the anterior spinal nerve roots with an almost total absence of myelin and axis cylinders. There was no loss of anterior horn motor cells.

The family history is usually negative. Hillman and Johnson describe two pairs of identical twins. One of each pair suffered from arthrogryposis multiplex and the other was normal. Boys are affected more frequently than girls. The rigidity is usually bilateral and symmetrical, but may affect the joints of only one limb or only one joint. The commonest type is that in which all four limbs are fixed in extension, but fixation of the knees in flexion, and of the hips in flexion and abduction, is also common. However, a great variety of combinations may occur. The affected limbs are often shortened. Congenital dislocation of the hips and other deformities may co-exist. The range of movement at affected joints is limited to a few degrees. Creaking may be felt in the joint during movement. The muscles are always affected. If the limb is fixed in extension, the flexors are grossly defective or apparently absent, and, if the position is one of flexion, then

the extensors are deficient. The shortening of the muscles and ligaments seems to be the cause of the immobility, for there is never any bony ankylosis. The reaction of degeneration is never present, but both faradic and galvanic reactions may be sluggish or absent. The tendon reflexes are difficult to elicit. Roentgenograms reveal no bony alterations of the joints or capsules, but the muscle shadows may be very small.

The diagnosis is based upon the clinical characteristics described above. There is little or no spontaneous improvement, but passive movements and manipulations may give some relief. In severe cases, surgical procedures are advised.

BIBLIOGRAPHY

AMICK, L. D. *et al.:* Electromyographic and histopathologic correlations in arthrogryposis. Arch. of Neurol. **16**:512, 1967.

BANKER, B. G., VICTOR, M. AND ADAMS, R. D.: Arthrogryposis multiplex due to congenital dystrophy. Brain, **80**:319, 1957.

BRANDT, S.: A case of arthrogryposis multiplex congenita. Acta Paediat., **34**:365, 1947.

DRACHMAN, D. B.: Arthrogryposis multiplex congenita. Arch. of Neurol., **5**:77, 1961.

HILLMAN, J. W. AND JOHNSON, J. T. H.: Arthrogryposis multiplex congenita in twins. J. Bone & Joint Surg., **34**:211, 1952.

LOWENTHAL, A.: Un groupe heredodegeneratif nouveau: les myoscleroses heredo-familiales. Acta neurol. belg., **54**:155, 1954.

PEARSON, C. M. AND FOWLER, W. G. JR.: Hereditary non-progressive muscular dystrophy inducing arthrogryposis. Brain, **86**:75, 1963.

PENA, C. E. *et al.:* Arthrogyposis multiplex congenita. Neurology, **18**:931, 1968.

SHELDON, W.: Amyoplasia congenita. Arch. Dis. Child. **7**:117, 1932.

CAMPYLODACTYLY

Two types of this rare condition are recognized. In the congenital type the condition is usually recognized in the first few weeks of life. Both boys and girls are affected. It may be associated with other deformities. In some cases it is inherited as a dominant characteristic with variable penetrance and there is in some instances evidence that it may be sex linked. A second type is described which is acquired in childhood or adolescence and is seen almost without exception in girls. This is gradually progressive.

There is a contracture of the little fingers and often of the ring fingers as well. The condition is usually bilateral but may be unilateral. The affected fingers are flexed at the middle and distal interphalangeal joints but not at the metacarpophalangeal joint. The contracture is maintained by shortening of all the soft tissues. The joints are not involved and the fingers may be fully flexed and extended without difficulty within the limited range of movement permitted by the contracture. The affected fingers are cold and sometimes cyanotic. The skin is thin and atrophic. The patients are subject to chilblains.

In contrast to Dupuytren's contracture, which does not occur in children,

there is no thickening of the palmar fascia, no induration of the skin and no flexion of the metacarpophalangeal joints.

It is said that lengthening of the flexor tendons is not helpful. Shortening of the first phalanx by bone excision may permit a greater range of extension. Cervical sympathectomy may improve the circulation.

BIBLIOGRAPHY

OLDFIELD, M.: Campylodactyly flexor contracture of the fingers in young girls. Brit. J. Plast. Surg., 8:312, 1956.

PARKES WEBER, F.: Further Rare Diseases. London, Staples Press. 1949, p. 146.

CONGENITAL LAXITY OF THE LIGAMENTS
(CONGENITAL ATONIA)

This rare condition is manifest by an excessive range of movement of the joints which is believed to be of congenital origin. As a rule, all the joints are affected. Both mild and severe cases are observed. In many instances, the patient is not inconvenienced in any way. In others, pronounced disability results. Fatigue is a very common symptom. Flat feet and low back pain are also frequent complaints. Hernias are often associated. The laxity of the joints may lead to traumatization of the synovial membranes so that effusions into the joints may occur when the patient walks too much. Dislocations are easily produced. Postural curvature of the spine is described. On examination the essential finding is an excessive range of passive movement of the joints. Sometimes subluxation may be produced by gentle traction and it has been pointed out that when released the bone may snap back into place as if the tissues were made of rubber. The muscles seem to present no constant abnormality in strength or bulk. I believe that in most instances they are slender and of somewhat less than average strength. However, I have seen patients who had large muscles and excellent strength and endurance. The tendon reflexes are usually normal. In certain instances the symptoms grow more severe possibly because the ligaments undergo a gradual stretching. I have studied the case of a young woman who was an excellent athlete during adolescence but became disabled during adult life. The condition is sometimes found in several members of a family. The mode of inheritance seems to be irregular and differs in different families.

The anatomical basis of this condition is not entirely clear. Most writers assume that the ligaments and perhaps the capsules of the joints are too lax or perhaps, too elastic. No anatomical studies of the ligaments seem to have been made. Walton believes that in some cases the muscles are responsible and in other cases it is the ligaments which are at fault.

This condition has been regarded as an abortive form of the *Ehlers-*

Danlos syndrome in which we have: (1) Excessive elasticity of the skin. (2) Excessive fragility of the skin. (3) Molluscoid pseudotumors of the skin resulting from trauma. (4) Laxity of the joints. (5) Fragility of the blood vessels. Mental deficiency, congenital heart defects, diaphragmatic hernia, spontaneous rupture of the lung and arterial aneurysm may be associated.

This condition must be distinguished from amyotonia congenita, congenital atonic diplegia, and some of the congenital ataxias and choreas which are associated with loss of muscular tone. Greenfield *et al.* claim that muscle biopsy is important in differential diagnosis.

CASE HISTORY (Ped. A-73659).—*Girl of 7 years who exhibited an abnormal range or movement at all joints from birth without weakness, incoordination or involuntary movements. Normal mentality.*

B. B. was born at full term by normal delivery. It was noticed when she was very young that an abnormal range of movement was possible at the knee joints. Lateral movement and hyperextension were present. It was then noted that all of the joints were extremely flexible. An orthopedist applied casts to her knees which were not removed until she was a year old. As soon as the casts were removed she made rapid progress in learning to walk. She has never seemed to be especially weak or clumsy. Her parents consider her mental development normal. An external squint is apparent at times.

In May, 1948, she developed fever, pains in the legs and abdomen, enlargement of the heart and a systolic murmur. It was suspected that she had rheumatic fever, and she was kept in a hospital for some months. The fever eventually disappeared and all the symptoms ceased.

She was brought to the Johns Hopkins Hospital on Nov. 18, 1949, to see Dr. Taussig for an opinion about possible rheumatic heart disease. She was then 7 years old. No heart disease was found.

On examination the child was well developed and nourished. Her mental condition seemed to be quite normal. There was an inconstant, nonparalytic external squint. The facial muscles showed less spontaneous movement than one would expect in a child of this age, but there was no weakness. Otherwise the cranial nerves were all in order.

The musculature was possibly a little slender but there was no atrophy. The shoulders seemed to sag a little but otherwise the posture seemed to be normal. I could find no definite muscular weakness. No ataxia could be demonstrated. There was no involuntary movements. The tendon reflexes were present everywhere but somewhat sluggish.

The only striking abnormality was the extraordinary range of movement possible at all joints. The child could bring her feet up and place them behind her head. She could also bend her head back until it rested on her sacrum and place her feet on either side of her head. Her thighs

could be abducted to a full 90 degrees. The wrists, ankles and knees permitted an excessive range of movement. At the knee some lateral and anterior movement was possible.

BIBLIOGRAPHY

CATZEL, P.: Congenital laxity of the ligaments with hypotonia. Arch. Dis. Child., **30**:387, 1955.

GREENFIELD, J. G., CORNMAN, T. AND SHY, G. M.: The prognostic value of the muscle biopsy in the floppy infant. Brain, **81**:461, 1958.

KANOF, A.: Ehlers-Danlos syndrome. Report of a case. Am. J. Dis. Child., **83**:197, 1952.

KEY, J. A.: Hypermobility of the joints as a sex-linked hereditary characteristic. J.A.M.A., **88**:1710, 1927.

KING-LEWIS, F. AND POLUNIN, I.: Two cases of Ehlers-Danlos syndrome. Arch. Dis. Child., **22**:170, 1947.

LIDGE, R. T.: Hypotonia. J. Pediat., **45**:474, 1954.

MADISON, W. M. *et al.:* Ehlers-Danlos syndrome with cardiac involvement. Amer. Jour. Cardiol., **11**:689, 1963.

McKUSICK, V.: The Ehlers-Danlos syndrome. J. Chronic Dis., **3**:2, 1956.

REES, T. D. *et al.:* Surgery in Ehlers-Danlos syndrome. Plast. & Reconst. Surg., **32**:39, 1963.

STUKIE, P. D.: Hypermobile joints in all descendants for two generations. J. Heredity, **32**:232, 1941.

SUTRO, C. J.: Hypermobility of the bones due to lengthened capsular and ligamentous tissues. Surgery, **21**:67, 1947.

WALTON, J. N.: The limp child. J. Neurol., Neurosurg. & Psychiat., **20**:144, 1957.

CONGENITAL UNIVERSAL MUSCULAR HYPOPLASIA (KRABBE)

This condition has been described by Krabbe under the title given above and by Gibson as *muscular infantilism*. Dr. W. K. Engle informs me that reexamination of Gibson's material reveals that he was dealing with a form of muscular dystrophy. The skeletal muscles are all small and weak at birth and the patient's condition does not change in any way during life. Strength seems to be proportional to the bulk of the muscles. There is no myotonus, contracture, fasciculation, or alteration of tendon reflexes. So long as the patient's activities do not exceed his muscular strength, there is no undue fatigue. Most patients are able to lead useful lives, though Gibson mentions one patient who was nearly helpless. Amyotonia is often suspected in infancy. The electrical reactions are normal. Biopsy reveals normal muscle fibers or possibly slightly slender fibers. In Gibson's study the disease was traced through four generations among which were found forty-seven individuals with deficient muscular development. Males and females were affected alike and either might transmit the defect. In only one instance did an unaffected individual transmit the disease. Life was not shortened and no special predisposition to any particular disease was noted.

Gibson made some studies of his patient's metabolism. The only finding of interest was an alteration of the creatine-creatinine metabolism which was attributed to the deficiency of muscle fibers.

Schreier and Huperz describe two additional cases in children. These authors made numerous studies and found only creatine metabolism was altered.

Van Wisselingh has studied another case. He emphasizes the fact that biopsy reveals normal muscle fibers.

In differential diagnosis we must distinguish four types of congenital, familial, non-progressive myopathy:

1. The type of Gibson and Krabbe termed congenital, universal, muscular hypoplasia.
2. The central core disease of Shy and Magee.
3. The nemaline myopathy of Shy.
4. The congenital myopathy of Turner (see muscular dystrophy).
5. The distal type of myopathy of Magee and De Jong.

BIBLIOGRAPHY

GIBSON, A.: Muscular infantilism. Arch. Int. Med., **27**:338, 1921.

KRABBE, K. H.: Kongenit. generaliseret muskelaplasi. 338 meeting of the Danish Neurol. Soc., Feb. 27, 1946, p. 264.

MAGEE, K. R. AND DE JONG, R. N.: Hereditary distal myopathy with onset in infancy. Arch. of Neurol., **13**:387, 1965.

SCHREIER, K. AND HUPERZ, R.: Uber die Hypoplasia musculorum generalisata congenita. Ann. Paediat., **186**:241, 1956.

VAN WISSELINGH, C. J.: Een geval van congenitale gegeneraliseerde spierhypoplasia. Maandschr. voor Kindergeneeskunde, **7**:234, 1956.

NEMALINE MYOPATHY OF SHY

In 1963, Shy *et al.* described the case of a little girl of four years whose muscles were poorly developed and very weak. The proximal muscles were most severely involved. The tendon reflexes were lost. Her brother had the same condition but no special studies of his muscles were made. The condition was not progressive. Microscopic study of the muscles revealed no atrophy or degeneration. Rod-like elements were found in a large percentage of the muscle fibers, which as a rule were located just under the sarcolemma, and extended along the length of the fibers. With the Gomori trichrome stain, these structures were colored red and the normal muscle fibrils were stained green. The electron microscope revealed that the rod-like structures were composed of minute fibrils extending transversely across the rod in a kind of palisade formation. Further studies indicated that the rod-like structures were composed of a substance similar to myosin, but not identical with it.

In the same year, Conen *et al.* reported a case of a boy of four years whose muscular development was defective. There was hypotonia as well as weakness. The proximal muscles were most severely affected and his pos-

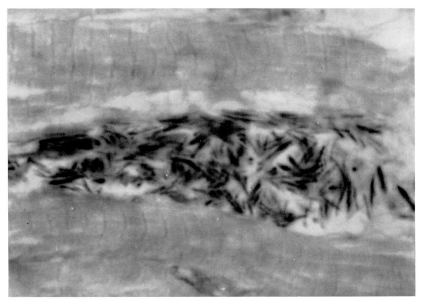

FIG. 286. Section of muscle fibers showing the rod-like structures. (Courtesy, Doctor David Clark and Doctor J. Russel Lindsey.)

ture was that of a patient with muscular dystrophy. The tendon reflexes were present. He was an intelligent child. There was no progression of the weakness. Exactly the same changes in the muscles were found as in the case of Shy.

In 1964, Engel *et al.* reported the study of a girl of sixteen years who had always been weak and whose muscles were very small. Her condition was evident at birth. She showed no increase of her weakness until she was thirteen years old. It then seemed that she was unable to do certain things she had been able to do before. Study of the muscles revealed no evidence of degeneration, but the rod-like structures described by Shy and Conen were present.

Lindsey *et al.* have made a detailed study of the anatomical changes in the muscles of nemaline myopathy and find that fragmentation of the myofibrils is a constant feature.

We have followed, from birth to the age of thirty-seven years, a girl whose muscles have always been extremely small, weak, and atonic. A muscle biopsy at the age of ten years was reported to show only normal muscle fibers and she was thought to suffer from the type of congenital muscular hypoplasia described by Krabbe. Her mother had also displayed the same condition from birth.

Jenis *et al.* report the case of a girl who died at the age of 2 months of

a congenital myopathy. All the evidences of nemaline myopathy were found at post-mortem examination and in addition crystalline inclusions were found in the nuclei.

CASE HISTORY (Ped. 90722).—*Girl of ten years with congenital universal muscular hypoplasia stimulating amyotonia congenita in infancy. Her mother was affected in the same way.*

J. D. was born at full term by normal labor. The child did not breathe well at first and was cyanotic at times for several days. She nursed feebly, and cry was weak. However, there were no convulsions. Her early development was always unsatisfactory. She took food poorly and gained weight slowly. She was subject to infections of the upper respiratory tract which would persist for months at a time. There were numerous digestive dis-

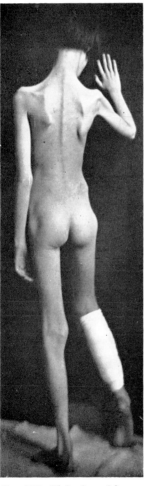

FIG. 287. Girl whose history is given in text at age of 10 years.

turbances. She did not hold up the head until she was almost a year old and could not walk alone until the age of three years. The muscles were always flabby and the limbs would lie where they were placed for a long time. During infancy there was very little spontaneous activity. Her mother took her to many pediatricians all of whom made the diagnosis of amyotonia congenita. Proper diet soon relieved the digestive disorder but no efforts of the physicians produced any effect upon the muscular weakness, which remained unchanged from birth to the age of ten years if one makes allowance for the influence of natural development.

Examination revealed an extraordinary condition illustrated in the accompanying photograph. The child was of about average height for her age but appeared taller because of her slender build. The musculature was reduced to a mere fraction of its proper bulk and even muscles which are usually fleshy appeared to be mere slender ribbons. On palpation the muscles were very soft and on passive movement an increased range of movement was possible so that the feet could be placed behind the head with ease. The shoulders sagged so the neck seemed very long. The abdomen was protuberant as a result of loss of muscle tone. The feet were flat and everted. The lower jaw was narrow and the angle of the jaw was more obtuse than usual. The chest was narrow and there was a deep groove just above the costal margins. Strength was very feeble in general but pro-

Fig. 288. Same patient shown in the preceding photograph at the age of 39 years. Showing defective development of the muscles and bony deformities due to muscular weakness.

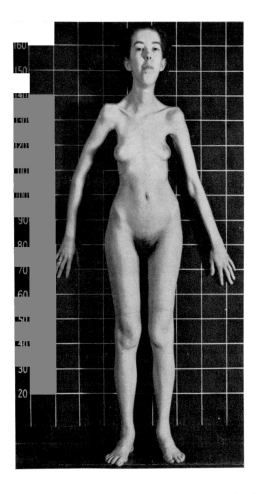

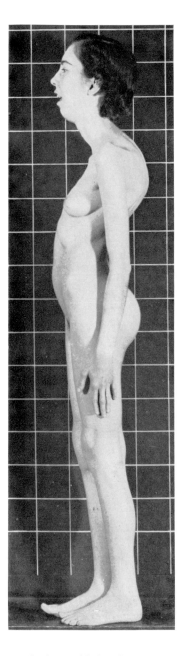

portional to the reduction of muscle tissue. No paralysis could be demonstrated. There were no fibrillary twitchings seen. The tendon reflexes were all present. Control of the sphincters was preserved and sensibility was intact. The child was well behaved and her mental development was quite normal. A bit of muscle was removed from the left calf. This showed nothing to suggest atrophy or degeneration of the muscles. No

"embryonic" fibers were seen and no hypertrophied fibers. There was no excess of fat or of connective tissue.

In 1964, Dr. David Clark was able to demonstrate the rod-like structures of Shy in muscle removed for biopsy in 1937.

The mother's condition was exactly the same as that of her daughter. In early infancy, her muscles were small, weak and atonic. Amyotonia congenita was suspected. The weakness persisted. She did not grow stronger or weaker for many years. She was forced to restrict her activities. Going up stairs was difficult for her. Shortly before she died, at the age of fifty-eight years, there was progressive weakness and loss of sensibility in the arms and hands. At post-mortem examination it was found that the spinal cord had been compressed by bony lipping of the cervical vertebrae. There was damage to the cervical gray matter and some demyelination of the pyramidal tracts. Dr. David Clark demonstrated the same rod-like structures in the skeletal muscles which had been described by Shy.

Engel and Hefferman describe rod myopathies developing late in life.

BIBLIOGRAPHY

CONEN, P. E. *et al.:* Light and electron microscopic studies of myogranules in a child with hypotonia and muscle weakness. Canad. M. A. J., **89**:983, 1963.

ENGEL, A. G.: Late onset rod myopathy. Mayo Clin. Pro., **41**:713, 1966.

ENGEL, W. K. *et al.:* Nemaline myopathy. Arch. Neurol., **11**:22, 1964.

FULTHORPE, J. J. *et al.:* Nemaline myopathy. Neurology, **19**:735, 1969.

GONATAS, N. K. *et al.:* Nemaline myopathy. The origin of nemaline structures. New Eng. Jour. Med., **274**:535, 1966.

HEFFERMAN, L. P. *et al.:* The spectrum of rod myopathies. Arch. of Neurol., **18**:529, 1968.

HOPKINS, I. J., LINDSEY, J. R. AND FORD, F. R.: Nemaline myopathy. A long term clinicopathologic study of affected mother and daughter. Brain, **89**:299, 1966.

HUDGSON, P. *et al.:* Nemaline myopathy. Neurology, **17**:1125, 1967.

JENIS, E. H. *et al.:* New congenital myopathy with crystalline intranuclear inclusions. Arch. of Neurol., **20**:281, 1969.

LINDSEY, J. R., HOPKINS, I. J. AND CLARK, D. B.: Pathology of nemaline myopathy. Bull. of Johns Hopkins Hospital, **119**: 378, 1966.

PRICE, H. M. *et al.:* New evidence for excessive accumulation of Z band material in nemaline myopathy. 1965, Pro. Nat. Acad. Sci., **54**:1398.

SHY, G. M. *et al.:* Nemaline myopathy. A new, congenital myopathy. Brain, **86**:793, 1963.

SPIRO, A. J. AND KENNEDY, C.: Hereditary occurrence of nemaline myopathy. Arch. of Neurol., **13**:155, 1965.

CONGENITAL, FAMILIAL, NON-PROGRESSIVE MYOPATHY OF SHY AND MAGEE OR CENTRAL CORE DISEASE

The authors describe five patients, four males and one female, found in three generations of the same family. Their ages ranged from two years to sixty-five years. The condition seemed to be inherited as a simple dominant trait. The weakness was noted early in infancy and was possibly present before birth for in one instance, fetal movements were less vigorous than

usual. In infancy, muscle tone was reduced though this was not evident later. The patients were unable to walk in most cases until they reached the age of four or five years. The weakness was generalized but most evident in the proximal muscles of the legs and perhaps, in the proximal muscles of the upper extremities. Getting up and going up stairs were especially difficult. In one patient there was weakness of the orbiculares of the eyes and sternomastoids. Hernias were found in some cases. It is of interest that in four patients the bulk of the muscles seemed to be normal though in one muscular development was below average. The tendon reflexes were normal. The condition was not progressive and the patients' condition remained unchanged throughout life. Myotonia is not mentioned. The electrocardiogram was always normal. The excretion of creatine was increased and the excretion of creatinine was reduced.

Biopsy of muscle revealed characteristic changes. There was no excess of small fibers. Some very large fibers up to 240 micra in diameter were occasionally seen and there were also a good many central nuclei. With the Gomori trichrome stain, the central fibrils stained blue and the outer fibrils red. These central fibrils were very compact and their striations were not apparent except under high magnification. Some fibrils were found to turn from the outer layer and enter the central portion of the muscle fiber. The central fibers, or core, contain no mitochondria and there is an abnormality of muscle phosphorylase.

The relation of this condition to congenital universal muscular hypoplasia q.v. is not clear. The deficient bulk of the muscles in the latter would seem to represent a definite difference but it is doubtful that the staining technique of Shy and Magee has been applied to the cases of congenital universal muscular hypoplasia.

BIBLIOGRAPHY

ENGEL, W. K. *et al.:* Central core disease. Brain, 84:167, 1961.

ENGEL, W. K.: The essentiality of histo- and cytochemical studies of skeletal muscle in the investigation of neuromuscular disease. Neurology, 12:778, 1962.

GREENFIELD, J. G., CORNMAN, T. AND SHY, G. M.: Central core disease. Brain, 81:461, 1958.

SHY, M. AND MAGEE, K. R.: A new congenital non-progressive myopathy. Brain, 79:610, 1956.

SHY, G. M. *et al.:* Central core disease. Ann. Intern. Med., 56:511, 1962.

MYOTUBULAR MYOPATHY

Spiro *et al.* have reported the case of an adolescent boy who had defective muscular development and extensive weakness. There was facial diplegia, extraocular palsies and symmetrical muscular weakness. Muscle biopsy showed defective development of the muscles with muscle tubes resembling the fetal state of muscle fibers with myofibrils surrounding a core of clear protoplasm.

Later, Sher *et al.* reported two siblings with the same abnormalities of the muscles. Kinoshita and Cadman have reported a fourth case of the same type in a girl of six years. This patient seems to have differed from the others in that she showed some improvement in strength.

BIBLIOGRAPHY

Kinoshita, M. and Cadman, T. E.: Myotubular myopathy. Arch. of Neurol., **18**:265, 1968.
Mursat, T. L. *et al.*: Centronuclear myotubular myopathy. Arch. of Neurology, **20**:120, 1969.
Sher, J. E. *et al.*: Familial centronuclear myopathy. Neurology, **17**:727, 1967.
Spiro, A. J. and Shy, C. M.: Myotubular myopathy. Arch. of Neurol., **14**:1, 1966.

TYPES OF MYOPATHY ASSOCIATED WITH ABNORMALITIES OF THE MITOCHONDRIA

Luft *et al.* describe a patient of seven years suffering from progressive weakness and wasting of the muscles, profuse sweating and polydipsia. The basal metabolism was estimated at 150 to 200 plus. Thyroid function was normal. The electromyogram showed the picture of myopathy. Histological examination of the skeletal muscles showed a vast increase of the mitochondria. They were increased three to four times in number. Some were of giant size. The authors suggest that there was an abnormal organization of the mitochondrial enzymes resulting in a lowered capacity for respiratory control.

Shy describes a megaconial myopathy manifest by slowly progressive weakness of the proximal muscles and by hypotonia. This was a familial process. It was associated with rectangular inclusions in the mitochondria. It was thought to be due to a defect in the metabolism of the lipids.

Shy also describes pleoconial myopathy with weakness of the proximal muscles. There were episodes of quadriparesis of days or weeks duration. Between these episodes there was no progression of the weakness. Granular material was found between the myofibrils and in the mitochondria. It was believed that this condition was due to a disturbance in cation metabolism. Neither of these two conditions were associated with an increase of metabolism.

D'Agostino *et al.* report two cases of siblings with limb-girdle myopathy and growth retardation. Electron microscopy revealed enlarged mitochondria similar to those found in megaconial and pleoconial myopathy. There was a paucity of myofibrils. No metabolic disorder could be found.

In a study of a large number of muscle biopsies Shaftiq *et al.* found giant mitochondria in four specimens. A different myopathy had been diagnosed in each case.

R. F. Coleman *et al.* describe two patients who developed progressive fatigue, weakness and slight atrophy of the muscles in the first decade. Study

of the muscles revealed large mitochondria with high enzyme oxidative enzyme activities and abnormal accumulations of neutral fat.

BIBLIOGRAPHY

COLEMAN, R. F. *et al.:* New myopathy with mitochondrial enzyme hyperactivity. J.A.M.A., **199:**624, 1967.

D'AGOSTINO, A. N. *et al.:* Familial myopathy with abnormal mitochondria. Arch. of Neurol., **18:**388, 1968.

LUFT, R. *et al.:* A case of severe hypermetabolism of non-thyroid origin with a defect in the maintenance of mitochondrial respiration control. Jour. Clin. Invest., **41:**1776, 1962.

SHY, M.: Rare myopathies. Med. Clin. North America, **47:**1525, 1963.

————: Two childhood myopathies with abnormal mitochondria. Brain, **89:**133, 1966.

SHAFTIQ, S. A. *et al.:* Giant mitochondria in human muscle with inclusions. Arch. of Neurol., **17:**665, 1967.

HEREDOFAMILIAL DISEASES OF THE MUSCLES

The Muscular Dystrophies

Definition.—This term is applied to a common heredofamilial disease which is characterized by progressive wasting and paralysis of the skeletal muscles. There are several types described, which are distinguished by the age of onset, the presence or absence of pseudohypertrophy and the particular muscles first affected, but it is clear that such distinctions are merely artificial, and that all the various types are alike in their essential features.

Pathological Anatomy.—The muscles may be either enlarged and firm, or small and soft. They almost always appear yellowish on section, due to the presence of an increased amount of fat. The microscopic changes are quite uniform, and it is stated that it is impossible to say from the examination of a section whether it was obtained from an atrophic muscle or from one showing pseudohypertrophy. The earliest change is apparently shown by swelling of the muscle fiber, and increase in the sarcolemma nuclei. Such fibers may exceed 200 micra in diameter, and are more nearly round in cross section than the normal fibers. Later there is an increase in the connective tissue septa, and fat is deposited between the muscle fibers. The latter now begin to split longitudinally into a number of smaller fibers each of which is surrounded by a large number of sarcolemma nuclei. Hyaline degeneration and vacuolation may be found in some of the hypertrophied fibers. Gradually the muscle fibers break down and disappear, eventually being replaced by fat and connective tissue. The intrafusal muscle fibers of the muscle spindles may be preserved long after the major portion of the muscle has disappeared. Active phagocytosis by macrophages is very rare and inflammatory cells do not occur except for an occasional small accumulation of mononuclear cells around a small venule. There is no evidence of regeneration. There are always well-marked changes in the

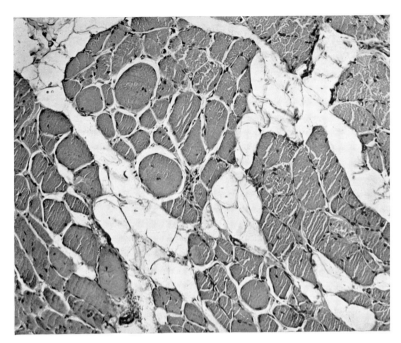

Fig. 289. Section of muscle in case of pseudohypertrophic muscular dystrophy. The muscle was enlarged and firm. In the section one sees some hypertrophic fibers and deposits of fat.

blood vessels, such as thickening of their walls and proliferation of the adventitia. A full description of these changes is given by Adams *et al.*

Roseman and Kukulas found microscopic heterotopias and pachygyria in the brains of patients who had both muscular dystrophy and mental deficiency.

Etiology.—This disease may be regarded as a heredofamilial degenerative process affecting the muscles. Despite many studies it is not yet possible to explain this condition on the basis of any metabolic abnormality.

Whorton *et al.* find that the spectrophotometric absorption curves of metmyoglobin of patients suffering from childhood progressive muscular dystrophy indicate these patients have an abnormal molecular form of skeletal muscle myoglobin. Thus, the study of twelve patients with this condition revealed that the metmyoglobin of their skeletal muscles differed consistently from that of normal adults and from fetal metmyoglobin. Metmyoglobin from cardiac muscle of two children with childhood dystrophy and from the skeletal muscle of a patient with the facioscapulo-humeral type of dystrophy resembled fetal metmyoglobin. The skeletal metmyoglobin of a patient with myotonic dystrophy was similar to that of a normal adult.

Rowland *et al.* however find no proof that abnormalities of the myoglobin are found in muscular dystrophy.

Geiger and Garvin report studies of muscle fibers in tissue culture. Fibers obtained from suffering from muscular dystrophy show certain differences from normal muscle fibers. They have a shorter latent period, more nuclei, are more granular, develop no cross striations, and are larger than normal fibers. Muscle fibers derived from patients suffering from neurogenic muscular atrophy behave in tissue culture as normal fibers do.

W. H. Blahd *et al.* have found by the use of a whole-body radiation counter that patients suffering from muscular dystrophy showed a significant reduction of body potassium. They also found that the apparently healthy parents and siblings of the dystrophic patients had a reduction of body potassium.

Kossmann *et al.* state that whole-body radiation counter shows that reduction of potassium depends upon reduction of muscle mass and is a result of the dystrophic process and not the cause.

Numerous studies of metabolism have been made, and it has been shown that the excretion of creatinine is diminished, and that creatine is present in the urine. The ability to retain ingested creatine is also reduced. The excretion of creatine is abnormal in adults but it is not abnormal in infants so no stress should be placed upon this finding unless the patient has reached the age of puberty. There is still a great deal of difference of opinion about the significance of these findings. Some writers believe that they indicate that muscular dystrophy is the result of a disorder of creatine-creatinine metabolism, but since similar or identical results may be obtained in almost all other diseases associated with general wasting of the muscles, and even in states of weakness without atrophy, such as myasthenia gravis, it seems more likely that the loss of function of the muscles is the cause rather than the result of such disturbances of metabolism. Ribosuria may be found in some instances of muscular dystrophy but it is claimed that this substance may be found in the urine of cases of neurogenic atrophy also. Blahd *et al.* state that there is an increase of the amino acids in the urine of patients suffering from dystrophy.

The measurement of the serum enzymes is of more importance. Aldolase, phosphohexoisomerase, glutamic-oxalacetic transaminase, glutamic-pyruvic transaminase, lactic dehydrogenase, and creatine phosphokinase are present in excessive amounts. The determination of creatine phosphokinase is apparently most helpful. This enzyme is formed chiefly in the muscles. In pseudohypertrophic muscular dystrophy, which is the most rapidly progressive of the dystrophies, this enzyme is constantly found in excessive amounts in the serum especially in the early stages of the disease when the process is most active. It is said that the estimation of this enzyme is of

value in establishing the diagnosis of pseudohypertrophic muscular dystrophy before clinical symptoms are apparent and may also make it possible to detect carriers. It is said that in the facioscapulohumeral type of muscular dystrophy the serum enzyme levels are normal or slightly elevated and this is also true of the limb-girdle type of dystrophy. It is said that the determination of enzymes in the muscles is not reliable but in some instances they are found to be reduced. In neurogenic muscular atrophy, the serum enzymes are not reduced. It is not clear whether the increase of serum enzymes in muscular dystrophy is merely a result of the disease or has some significance as regards the cause of the disease.

Hooshman *et al.* point out that the study of the serum lactate dehydrogenase is of value in the differentiation of diseases of muscle.

Rowland *et al.* state that they were unable to discover phosphofructokinase or myoglobin in the serum of patients suffering from the Duchenne muscular dystrophy.

Clinical Features.—Although the various types of muscular dystrophy differ in certain respects, nevertheless, they all have some features in common, which may be conveniently discussed at this point. There is in most cases a strong hereditary and familial element, and often the disease may be found in several members of a family, and even be traced through a number of generations. On the other hand, sporadic cases are not uncommon, and the absence of a positive family history cannot be regarded as conclusive evidence against the diagnosis. Males and females are affected alike, and either may transmit the disease to their children. Weitz has concluded that the mode of inheritance varies in different families, and may be of at least three different types: simple dominant, simple recessive, and sex-linked recessive. According to Macklin, this disease has been shown to depend upon a dominant characteristic in 9 families, and upon a recessive or sex-linked recessive in 51 instances. In the recessive group, the males numbered 113 and the females only 3.

The onset is very insidious, so that it is often impossible to date the first symptoms with more than approximate accuracy. The onset may occur at

TABLE VII.—SERUM ENZYMES IN MYOPATHIES

	Lactic Dehydrogenase	Creatine Phosphokinase	Glutamic-Oxalacetic Transaminase
Normal	90 to 180	0 to 9	4 to 11
Neurogenic atrophy. Poliomyelitis	100 to 200	1 to 5	7 to 9
Pseudohypertrophic dystrophy	1,000 to 2,500	300 to 2,500	90 to 200
Myotonic dystrophy	100 to 300	3 to 11	10 to 18
Limb girdle dystrophy	160 to 500	10 to 700	10 to 70
Myositis	200 to 500	1 to 7.5	7 to 18

any time during childhood, but definite symptoms are unusual in infancy. The parents usually complain that the child has a clumsy gait, that there is difficulty going upstairs, and, not infrequently, it is noticed that the abdomen is unduly prominent. The essential symptoms include progressive weakness and wasting of certain muscle groups: first, the muscles of the shoulder-girdle and pelvic girdle, and later the muscles of the upper arm and thigh. The wasting may or may not be preceded by pseudohypertrophy. As a result of weakness of these muscle groups, a number of clinical signs may be elicited which are characteristic of the dystrophies, although they all may be produced by any disease causing weakness of the same muscles. Weakness of the muscles which fix the scapula, namely, the serratus magnus, trapezius and rhomboids, results in "winging" of the scapula or displacement of the vertebral border of the scapula from the chest wall, so that it stands out like a wing whenever the child attempts to elevate the arms. If the serratus magnus is very weak, abduction of the arm is impossible, for the action of the deltoid results merely in rotation of the scapula. If the latissimus dorsi is affected in addition to the other muscles, it will be found, when the examiner attempts to lift the child with the hands placed in the axillae, that the shoulders are brought up to the ears, and the child tends to slip through the examiner's hands. As a result of weakness of the pelvic girdle and hip muscles, the posture is strikingly altered. The child stands with the pelvis tilted forward, protuberant abdomen and buttocks, and a marked increase of lumbar lordosis. When sitting, on the contrary, the back is flexed. The gait is also characteristic. The pelvis is swung from side to side in a waddling manner as a result of weakness of the abductors of the thighs, chiefly the glutei medii, which should fix the pelvis on the thigh. It has been pointed out by a number of observers that the gait is not unlike that of double congenital dislocation of the hip. Children who can walk fairly well on level ground experience great difficulty in going upstairs or stepping up on a chair, because of the weakness of extension at the hips and knees. All the textbooks describe the typical manner in which these children get up from the floor. First, the child turns over on the face, draws up the knees and gets up on the hands and knees. Next, the legs are extended so that the child is resting on hands and feet with bent knees. The last maneuver is to work the hands back to the legs and, by grasping the legs at higher and higher levels, the trunk is pushed erect by the arms. These strange antics are necessitated by the weakness of the glutei maximi, which makes it impossible for the child to extend the pelvis on the thigh without the help of the arms. This symptom is representative of a certain stage of the disease, and cannot be expected when the weakness is mild or very severe. When the process extends below the knees, the dorsal

flexors of the ankles are affected before the extensors (so that the foot is maintained in the equinus position). The knee jerks are lost early in most cases, but the ankle jerks persist until late in the course of the disease. In some instances the knee jerks are still present when the quadriceps muscle has become very weak. Severe contractures often develop, especially in the flexors of the hip, and the extensors of the ankles, and even deformities of the bones may occur from the long-standing loss of muscle balance. Sensory disturbances are absent, and there is no disturbance of sphincter control. There are never any fibrillary or fascicular twitchings, the reflexes are never increased, and the Babinski sign is never elicited.

Buchsbaum *et al.* describe papilledema in one patient thought to have the Duchenne type of muscular dystrophy and another who had a type of congenital dystrophy who had only drowsiness. Deficient respiration with retention of carbon dioxide was responsible.

Collis and Engel show that patients suffering from extensive wasting of the muscles may show an elevated oral glucose tolerance test apparently due to decreased functional muscle mass. They suggest that diabetes cannot be diagnosed by this test in such cases.

In advanced cases, the bones show changes with narrowing of the shafts of the long bones, scoliosis, and deformities of the pelvis, scapulae, clavicles and feet. It is believed that these changes are due to disuse and lack of the normal stress and strain on the bones. Prolonged bed rest will cause hypercalcemia with calcium deposits in the kidneys and other tissues simulating a picture of hyperparathyroidism.

Occasionally, mental deficiency is found in association with muscular dystrophy. It has been suggested that this is due to the fact that these children have not been able to attend school, but this explanation is not convincing. Mental deficiency is found more often in the pseudohypertrophic type of dystrophy.

Roseman and Kukulas found microscopic heterotopias and pachygyria in the brains of patients who were mentally defective and had muscular dystrophy.

We may now proceed to discuss the various types of this disease, but it must be kept in mind that many cases are seen which cannot be properly classified, and that the different forms are connected by transitional cases.

The Facioscapulohumeral Type of Landouzy-Dejerine.—This type is characterized by the involvement of the facial muscles. In some cases the face is weak from birth and the shoulder-girdle muscles are not affected until years later, or the disease may begin in the shoulders and involve the face later. The appearance is very typical; the lower lip is pendulous, the nasolabial folds absent, and the whole expression mask-like. The child can-

not nurse properly because of weakness of the orbicularis oris, and cannot close the eyes when asleep because of the weakness of the orbiculares of the eyelids. When crying, there is no movement of the face. There is no weakness of the extraocular muscles, jaws, tongue, pharynx or larynx. Sooner or later, the muscles of the shoulder-girdle are affected. The trapezius, serratus magnus and rhomboids are involved first; then follow the latissimus dorsi, pectorals, biceps and triceps. The deltoids, spinati and forearm muscles are spared until very late. Next the gluteal and pelvic girdle muscles are involved. This type of dystrophy usually begins before the tenth year. It is said that this type of dystrophy is a relatively benign one which advances slowly and may become arrested. It is often inherited as a dominant characteristic, but Minkowski and Sidler found that in a small community it was inherited as a recessive trait.

The Juvenile Scapulohumeral Type of Erb.—The onset is usually between the sixth and tenth years. The process begins in the trapezius and serratus magnus, and later affects the pectorals, rhomboids and latissimus dorsi. The deltoids, spinati, and teres major and minor may be large by comparison, and may even show some pseudohypertrophy. Eventually, the disease extends to the muscles of the pelvic girdle and hips, and to the muscles of the upper arm. This is probably merely a variety of the facioscapulohumeral type and is relatively benign.

The Pseudohypertrophic Type of Duchenne.—The onset is very early in most cases. Frequently there is delay in walking and the child may never be able to go upstairs. In other cases, however, the onset may be delayed until adolescence or even to adult life. The muscles of the thighs and hips are usually affected first. The quadriceps, glutei and hamstrings are atrophied. The vasti often display wasting before the rectus femoris is obviously involved. The gastrocnemius shows pseudohypertrophy and abnormal firmness for a time, eventually undergoing atrophy as the other muscles. The anterior tibial group is atrophied early. The shoulder muscles may be affected simultaneously with the muscles of the lower extremities, or may be spared for a number of years. The pectorals, serratus magnus and biceps are commonly atrophied, and the spinati, triceps and masseters are commonly enlarged. The abdominal muscles may be affected, especially the lower abdominal muscles. In rare cases the tongue may be hypertrophied. It is sometimes claimed that this type is the most rapidly progressive of all. It is often inherited as a sex-linked recessive.

Mabry *et al.* describe 3 types of sex-linked recessive muscular dystrophy. One type begins at 3 to 6 years with pseudohypertrophy and myocardial abnormalities and ends in death before 20 years. Another type begins at 4 to 5 years with atrophic muscles and myocardial abnormalities. The course

is benign but flexion contractures of the elbows and heel cords require surgery. A third type begins at 20 to 30 years. The myocardium is spared. Pseudohypertrophy may occur but the course is benign.

Dubonitz reports the study of pseudohypertrophic muscular dystrophy which is inherited as an autosomal recessive characteristic.

The Femoral Type of Leyden-Moebius.—This type is almost identical with the type of Duchenne. It differs, however, in the absence of pseudohypertrophy. The hip and thigh muscles are usually affected first, and the process subsequently extends to the shoulders, obeying the same topographical laws as the other types. This is regarded as a subvariety of the pseudohypertrophy type of Duchenne and is termed the limb-girdle dystrophy.

Henson *et al.* report a study of eight females suffering from a limb-girdle form of muscular dystrophy in two generations of a family including 53 members. No males were involved. The onset of symptoms was often in childhood.

Adams and Denny-Brown believe that there are only two types, the generalized, severe, form as exemplified by the pseudohypertrophic type of Duchenne and the femoral type of Leyden-Moebius and the mild restricted form including the facioscapulohumeral type and the juvenile scapulohumeral type of Erb.

There are also a number of rare forms which should be mentioned. *Congenital form* is known. Short reports a case and finds seven more in medical literature. This condition is similar to amyotonia congenita. Turners myopathy, the muscular infantilism of Gibson q.v. and the congenital universal muscular hypoplasia of Krabbe q.v. all probably fall into this group. In these cases, little or no progression is said to occur.

De Lange, however, has reported congenital muscular weakness at birth in three siblings with rapid progression and death before the end of the fourth month. Post-mortem examination revealed the changes of muscular dystrophy.

The *distal* form of *myopathy* usually begins in the legs below the knees selecting the anterior tibial muscles as a rule first of all. The tibialis anticus sometimes displays pseudohypertrophy. In some cases the hands may be involved next thus making it difficult to distinguish this condition from the common peroneal atrophy of Charcot-Marie-Tooth. As a rule there is less muscular atrophy than one would expect in a chronic neurogenic process. In other cases, the shoulder girdle muscles are involved shortly after the legs are affected so the diagnosis is not long in doubt. In rare instances the hands may be involved before the legs. The onset is said to occur after the age of 18 years but I have seen this condition in early childhood. Biemond discovered nineteen cases, in five generations of a family, in which myopathy involved the hands and feet at approximately the same time. The age

of onset was between five and fifteen years. Both males and females were affected. The course was very slow so the disease was relatively benign.

In 1966, however, he stated that biopsy showed neurogenic features. Magee and De Jong describe familial cases of myopathy with the onset within two years or earlier and weakness of dorsiflexion of the feet and toes and less pronounced weakness of extension of the fingers, especially the fifth finger. No definite progression is noted after years of observation. The diagnosis of myopathy was established by biopsy and electromyography. Van der Does *et al.* have described the same condition.

The type of *myopathy* described by *Turner* must be very rare. There were six members of his family who displayed the picture of amyotonia congenita in infancy. Later, they gained strength and were able to walk at about the age of five years. There was wasting of the muscles of the neck, shoulders and hands without involvement of the face. No ptosis of the lids, cataracts, myotonia or endocrine disorders are mentioned. The patients were able to lead active lives despite the early onset of symptoms. At postmortem examination of one patient changes in the muscles were found which were characteristic of myopathy. There were rows of central nuclei in the muscle fibers. In 1962, Turner published a fifty-year follow-up of his patients. He stated that the disease was not progressive and that the muscles did not display the histological condition described by Shy as central core disease. Walton and Nattrass mention cases in which the patient displays symptoms of myasthenia gravis and also those of muscular dystrophy and Roland and Eskenazi describe a case of this type.

Progressive dystrophic ophthalmoplegia.—The dystrophic process may begin in the extraocular muscles and remain confined to them for many years. It may also extend from the ocular muscles to the skeletal muscles or may begin in the skeletal muscles and later involve the ocular muscles. See Myopathy of the Extraocular Muscles.

The *oculopharyngeal dystrophy* described by Murphy and Drachman includes difficulty in swallowing and then ptosis of the lids and sometimes facial weakness and wasting of the sternomastoids. It is inherited as an autosomal dominant trait. It usually has a late onset in the fifth or sixth decade.

In some instances progressive muscular dystrophy develops in children who display *congenital absence* of certain *muscles* or *congenital shortening* and fibrosis of *muscles.* See Congenital Defects of Muscles.

Hauptmann and Thannhauser report a study of a family in which an unusual myopathy was found in 9 members and in 3 generations. I have seen a member of the third generation who told me that his daughter is now affected. Early in life these patients display limitation of flexion of the neck and back and also limitation of extension at the elbow and knee. Later weakness develops in the biceps and triceps muscles and then in the

gluteals and quadriceps. The calf muscles may be small and weak. The knee and ankle jerks may be lost. The weakness seems to be very slowly progressive, and the shortening of certain muscles also becomes more pronounced. My examination of a patient examined by Hauptmann and Thannhauser 12 years before makes this progression clear.

Cardiac symptoms are not common in cases of muscular dystrophy though changes in the heart muscles are often found at post-mortem examination. Changes in the electrocardiogram are described, however. We have studied a family of colored children in which five of seven siblings have muscular dystrophy and four of these have died of heart failure before the skeletal muscles had become severely affected. Cardiac symptoms occur in the slowly progressive types of dystrophy as well as in the more rapidly progressive types.

I have seen one family in which three of the eight members who were affected exhibited *unilateral atrophy* of the shoulder girdle muscles. The right shoulder was affected so severely that the scapula was quite loose and could not be rotated; whereas, the left shoulder showed only minimal weakness. Some of these individuals displayed atrophy of the muscles below the knee but strong hips and thighs and the others showed no weakness of the legs.

Diagnosis.—We must distinguish the muscular dystrophies from several conditions which closely resemble them: The Werdnig-Hoffman muscular atrophy, amyotonia congenita, progressive neural muscular atrophy, amyotrophic lateral sclerosis, thyroid disease, dermatomyositis, polymyositis and polyneuritis. The Werdnig-Hoffman muscular atrophy begins somewhat earlier, usually before the end of the first year, and runs a more rapid course, terminating as a rule before the end of the fifth year. If fascicular twitchings are present, or if the reaction of degeneration is obtained, the diagnosis may be made with confidence; but, when these signs are absent, as they frequently are, the diagnosis may require prolonged observation. Amyotonia congenita, which is probably merely a form of the Werdnig-Hoffman muscular atrophy, is present at birth. Progressive neural muscular atrophy may be differentiated by the peripheral distribution of the weakness which begins in the peroneal muscles, and remains distal to the knees and elbows for long periods. Amyotrophic lateral sclerosis, which is very rare in childhood, should be recognized by the wasting and fascicular twitchings of the muscles of the hands and arms and by the spasticity and increase of tendon reflexes in the legs. The changes in the skin should make the diagnosis of dermatomyositis possible, but the differentiation of polymyositis from muscular dystrophy usually requires biopsy. Polyneuritis causes in most cases a peripheral type of weakness with pains, tenderness and sensory loss in the extremities. We have been much confused at times

by unusual cases of polyneuritis in which the weakness involved predominantly the proximal muscle groups, and caused physical signs so similar to those of muscular dystrophy that the diagnosis was not entirely clear until the child began to recover. Thyroid deficiency may cause weakness of the muscles and sometimes enlargement of the muscles. Turner's myopathy simulates amyotonia congenita in infancy and then presents the picture of a very slowly progressive myopathy. The congenital universal muscular hypoplasia resembles amyotonia at birth and thereafter remains static. The central core disease and the nemaline myopathy are manifest by muscular weakness early in life and show little if any increase in weakness in childhood. In general, the most important signs in the diagnosis of muscular dystrophy are the symmetrical and proximal distribution of the weakness, the pseudohypertrophy, the absence of sensory disturbances and the slow course. The myopathy which occurs in association with paralytic myoglobinuria q.v. and also that which occurs with adolescent osteomalacia q.v. should be considered. If the family history is not positive, a muscle biopsy should always be made to establish the diagnosis. Kaeser describes a familial scapuloperoneal atrophy of neurogenic origin. Kugelberg and Welander describe familial juvenile muscular atrophy of proximal distribution q.v. which may be mistaken for muscular dystrophy and adolescent osteomalacia with myopathy q.d. is often thought to be muscular dystrophy.

The electromyogram is important in diagnosis. In early cases, there is an abnormally large number of very rapid action potentials of a duration of only 1 millisecond. Later, when the muscle has become weak, the amplitude of the spikes is reduced and they are also reduced in number. There is an increase of the diphasic and polyphasic potentials. No fibrillations are seen. Abnormalities of the serum and muscular enzymes are important in diagnosis. These are discussed under Etiology.

Prognosis.—The course is usually very slow, and many patients survive for from ten to thirty years after the onset of symptoms. In general, the symptoms are slowly progressive, although cases have been published in which the progress of the disease is said to have been arrested. Outspoken improvement must be very rare if it occurs at all. When recovery is claimed it is probable that the diagnosis is incorrect. Nattrass reviews cases in which recovery has occurred and concludes that they were probably in reality cases of polymyositis or benign congenital dystrophy. It is believed that the prognosis is most favorable in the facioscapulohumeral type, in which the patient often lives to the third or even fourth decade, and is least favorable in the pseudohypertrophic type, which rarely permits survival beyond the second decade.

Treatment.—No treatment is of any value in arresting the progress of

the disease. Exercises and massage are of some aid in improving the efficiency of the muscle tissue remaining, and passive movements and various orthopedic procedures are sometimes indicated to prevent contractures and deformities. The children should not be permitted to grow too fat, but nutrition should be maintained at a high level. The affected muscles are very sensitive. If immobilized in a cast they may waste very rapidly.

CASE HISTORY (No. 500648).—*Boy of 8 years developed signs of progressive muscular dystrophy. At 12 years cardiac symptoms appeared. He died at age of 14 years of heart failure. Two older brothers had died already of heart failure and muscular dystrophy. Two younger brothers showed early signs of dystrophy.*

L. J., a colored boy of 8 years began to have difficulty going up stairs. Soon it was noticed that he fell frequently and found it difficult to get up when he did so. Later there was difficulty in elevating the arms. These symptoms slowly increased. Finally he found that he was unable to get to school.

When he was 12 years old he became short of breath. On May 15, 1950 he was brought to the Johns Hopkins Hospital. On examination he displayed all the signs of well advanced pseudohypertrophic muscular dystrophy. The scapulae were loose and he could not elevate his arms at the shoulder. The strength at the wrist and finger joints was not bad. The large muscles of the thighs and buttocks were grossly wasted and very weak. The patient could not get up out of a chair. He was scarcely able to walk. The calves displayed pronounced pseudohypertrophy and the masseters were very large. The knee jerks were obtained with difficulty.

There were repeated attacks of tachycardia associated with dyspnea. The heart was enlarged. The electrocardiogram showed abnormal T waves and increased amplitude of the Q.R.S. complex.

In June, 1952 the patient was readmitted in severe congestive heart failure. He improved for a time under treatment but got worse again at home and was brought into the hospital in a dying condition on August 24, 1952.

The family consists of 7 siblings. The first, a girl, is quite well. The second, a boy, died at the age of 22 years of heart failure. He also had muscular dystrophy. The third child, a boy, died at the age of 16 years of heart failure and muscular dystrophy. The fourth child is the patient. There are three more boys. The youngest, who is 4 years old, seems healthy at present. The older boys who are 8 and 5 years old show signs of muscular dystrophy but no evidences of heart trouble yet. It is of interest that the mother has had healthy children by a man other than her present husband and the father has also produced healthy children by another woman. Post-mortem examination of the oldest brother (Med. No. 489666-Path. 21668) revealed changes in the heart muscle interpreted as indicative of progressive muscular dystrophy with pseudohypertrophy.

BIBLIOGRAPHY

ADAM, R., DENNY-BROWN, D. AND PEARSON, C.: Diseases of Muscle. New York, Paul Hoeber, Inc. 1953.

ALLEN, J. E. AND RODGIN, D. W.: Mental retardation in association with progressive muscular dystrophy. Am. J. Dis. Child., **100**:208, 1960.

BARNES, S.: A myopathic family with hypertrophic, pseudohypertrophic, atrophic and terminal (distal in upper extremities) stages. Brain, **55**:1, 1932.

BELL, J.: On pseudohypertrophic and allied types of progressive muscular dystrophy. The Treasury of Human Inheritance. London, Cambridge Univ. Press, 4:283 ,1943.

BIEMOND, A.: Symposion uber progressive muskeldystrophie. Berlin, Springer, 1966.

————: Myopathia distalis juvenilis hereditaria. Acta psychiat. Neurol. Scand., **30**:25, 1955.

BLAHD, W. H., BLOOM, A. AND DRELL, W.: Study of the amino acids in the urine of patients with muscular dystrophy. Proc. Soc. Exper. Biol. & Med., **90**:704, 1955.

BRAY, G. M. AND FERRENDELLI, J. A.: Serum creatine phosphokinase in muscle disease. Neurology, **18**:480, 1968.

BUCHSBAUM, H. W. *et al.:* Chronic alveolar hypoventilation due to muscular dystrophy. Neurology, **18**:319, 1968.

COLLIS, W. J. AND ENGEL, W. K.: Glucose metabolism in five neuromuscular disorders. Neurology, **18**:915, 1968.

CORNELIUS, C. E. *et al.:* Plasma aldolase and glutamic-oxalacetic transaminase activities in inherited muscular dystrophy. Proc. Soc. Exp. Biol. & Med., **101**:41, 1959.

DAWSON, D. M. AND FINE, I. H.: Creatine kinase in human tissues. Arch. of Neurol., **16**:175, 1967.

DE LANGE, C.: Studien über angeborene Lähmungen bzw angeborene Hypotonie. Acta paediat., **20**: suppl. 111, 1937.

DREYFUS, J. C. *et al.:* Biochemical study of muscle in progressive muscular dystrophy. J. Clin. Invest., **33**:794, 1954.

DUBONITZ, V.: Progressive muscular dystrophy of the Duchenne type in females and its mode of inheritance. Brain, **83**:432, 1960.

GEIGER, R. S. AND GARVIN, J. S.: Skeletal muscle from muscular dystrophy patients cultured in vitro. Arch. of Neurol. and Psychiat., **78**:585, 1957.

GOTO, I. *et al.:* Creatine phosphokinase in neuromuscular disease. Arch. of Neurol., **16**:529, 1967.

GOWERS, W. R.: A lecture on myopathy and a distal form. Brit. Med. J., **ii**:89, 1902.

HAUPTMAN, A. AND THANNHAUSER, S. J.: Muscular shortening and dystrophy. Arch. Neurol. & Psychiat., **46**:654, 1941.

HENSON, T. E. *et al.:* Hereditary myopathy limited to females. Arch. of Neurol., **17**:238, 1967.

HOOSHMAND, H. *et al.:* The use of serum lactate dehydrogenase isoenymes in the diagnosis of muscle diseases. Neurology, **19**:26, 1969.

JACKSON, C. E. AND CAREY, J. H.: Progressive muscular dystrophy, autosomal recessive type. Pediatrics, **28**:77, 1961.

KAESER, H. E.: Die Familiare scapuloperoneal muskelatrophie. Deutsch. Z. Nervenheilk., **186**:379, 1964.

KOSSMANN, R. J. *et al.:* Total body potassium in muscular dystrophy and related diseases. Neurology, **15**:855, 1965.

KUGELBERG, E.: Electromyography in muscular dystrophy. J. Neurol., Neurosurg. & Psychiat., **12**:129, 1949.

LANDOUZY, L. ET DEJERINE, J.: De la myopathie atrophique progressive; myopathie héréditaire sans neuropathie, débutant d'ordinaire dans l'infance par la face. Paris, F. Alcan, 1885.

LEVIN, S.: The heart in pseudohypertrophic muscular dystrophy. J. Pediat., **55**:460, 1959.

LEWIS, A. J. AND BESANT, D. F.: Muscular dystrophy in infancy. Report of two cases with weakness of the diaphragm. J. Pediat., **60**:376, 1962.

MABRY, C. C. *et al.*: X-linked pseudohypertrophic muscular dystrophy with late onset and slow progression. New Eng. Jour. Med., **273**:1062, 1965.

MAGEE, K. R. AND DE JONG, R. N.: Hereditary distal myopathy with onset in infancy. Arch. of Neurol., **13**:387, 1965.

MARKAND, O. N. *et al.*: Benign sex-linked muscular dystrophy. Neurology, **19**:617, 1969.

MILHORAT, A. T. AND WOLFF, H. G.: Studies in diseases of muscle. Progressive muscular dystrophy of atrophic distal type. Arch. Neurol. & Psychiat., **49**:655, 1943.

MINKOWSKI, M. AND SIDLER, A.: Zur kenntnis der dystrophia musculorum progressiva und ihrer Vererbung Schweiz med. Wchnschr., **9**:1005, 1928.

MONCKTON, G. AND LUDVIGSEN, B.: Identification of carriers in Duchenne muscular dystrophy. Canad. Med. Ass. Jour., **89**:333, 1963.

MONCKTON, G.: Enzyme studies in muscle disease. Modern Medicine, Sept. 13, 1965, p. 288.

MURPHY, S. F. AND DRACHMAN, D. B.: The oculopharyngeal syndrome. J.A.M.A., **203**:1003, 1968.

NATTRASS, F. J.: Recovery from muscular dystrophy. Brain, **77**:549, 1954.

NOTHACKER, W. G. *et al.*: Myocardial lesions in progressive muscular dystrophy. Arch. Path., **50**:578, 1950.

NEVIN, S.: A study of muscle chemistry in myasthenia gravis, pseudohypertrophic muscular dystrophy and myotonia. Brain, **57**:239, 1934.

————: Primary diseases of the voluntary muscles. J. Neurol. & Psychiat., **1**:120, 1938, new series.

OKINAKA, S. *et al.*: Diagnosis of muscular dystrophy. Arch. Neurol., **4**:520, 1961.

PEARSON, C. M.: Serum enymes in muscular dystrophy. New England J. Med., **256**:1069, 1957.

PERLOFF, J. K. *et al.*: Distinctive electrocardiogram in Duchenne's progressive muscular dystrophy. Amer. Jour. Med., **42**:179, 1967.

RICHTERICH, R. *et al.*: Progressive muscular dystrophy. Identification of carrier state in Duchenne type by serum creatine kinase determination. Amer. Jour. Hum. Genet., **15**:133, 1963.

ROLAND, L. P. AND ESKENAZI, A.: Myasthenia gravis with features resembling muscular dystrophy. Neurology, **6**:667, 1956.

ROSEMAN, N. P. AND KUKULAS, B. A.: Mental defect associated with muscular dystrophy. Brain, **89**:769, 1966.

ROWLAND, L. P. *et al.*: Lack of some muscle proteins in serum of patients with Duchenne dystrophy. Arch. of Neurol., **18**:272, 1968.

ROWLAND, L. P. *et al.*: Myoglobin and muscular dystrophy. Arch. of Neurol., **18**:141, 1968.

SHAW, R. F. *et al.*: Serum enzymes in sex linked (Duchenne) muscular dystrophy. Arch. of Neurol., **16**:115, 1967.

SHANK, R. E., GILER, H. AND HOAGLAND, L.: Progressive muscular dystrophy. Arch. Neurol. & Psychiat., **52**:431, 1944 (biochemical studies).

SHORT, J. K.: Congenital muscular dystrophy. Neurology, **13**:526, 1963.

SWAIMAN, K. F. AND SANDLER, B.: Diagnosis of muscular dystrophy. J. Pediat., **63**:1116, 1963.

TURNER, J. W. A.: Congenital myopathy: A 50-year follow-up. Brain, **85**:733, 1962.

TURNER, J. W. A. AND LEES, F.: Congenital myopathy: Follow-up of 50 years. Brain, **85**:733, 1962.

TURNER, J. W. A.: The relationship between amyotonia congenita and congenita myopathy. Brain, **63**:163, 1940.

————: On amyotonia congenita. Brain, **72**:25, 1949.

TYLER, F. H. AND WINTROBE, M. M.: Studies in disorders of muscle. Ann. Int. Med., **32**:72, 1950.

VAN DER DOES DE WILLEBOIS, A. E. M. *et al.*: Distal myopathy with onset in early infancy. Neurology, **18**:383, 1968.

WALTON, J. N. AND NATTRASS, F. J.: On classification, natural history and treatment of the myopathies. Brain, **77**:169, 1954.

WELANDER, L.: Genetic Research in Muscular Diseases in Sweden. Pro. Sec. Intern. Cong. Hum. Genet., **3**:1629, 1963.

————: Homozygous appearance of distal myopathy. Acta Genet. Statist. Med., **7**:321, 1957.

————: Myopathia distalis tarda hereditaria. Acta. Med. Scand. Suppl., **265**:1, 1951.

WHORTON, C. M., HUDGINS, P. C. AND CONNERS, J. J.: Abnormal myoglobin with muscular dystrophy. New England J. Med., **265**:1242, 1961.

ZATUCHNI, J. *et al.*: Heart in progressive muscular dystrophy. Circulation, **3**:846, 1951.

MYOTONIC DYSTROPHY

Definition.—This is a type of heredofamilial degeneration which gives rise to selective atrophy of the muscles, myotonia and various other symptoms, such as cataract, alopecia, atrophy of the sex glands, and premature senility. The term *myotonia atrophica* has also been employed.

Pathological Anatomy.—Microscopic examination of the atrophic muscles reveals that some fibers are very thin and that others are swollen and rounded in cross section. There is a great increase in sacrolemma nuclei around thick and thin fibers alike. Later the large fibers begin to degenerate, and sarcolemma nuclei pass into the center of the fiber where they form long chains of nuclei. In the last stage, the muscle tissue has largely disappeared, and the site of each fiber is marked only by a long row of nuclei. There is a moderate increase in the interstitial connective tissue, and some fat is deposited. It is evident that the pathological process is very similar to that of the dystrophies uncomplicated by myotonia.

Sher *et al.* describe a family whose clinical examination suggested myotonic dystrophy though no myotonus was demonstrated. The muscle fibers showed a larger percentage of central nuclei than in other cases of muscular dystrophy.

Rosman and Rebeiz found in a study of the brain in cases of non-progressive mental deficiency associated with myotonic dystrophy that the brain was small and the brain weight was reduced. There was pachygyria, disordered cortical architecture and heterotopic neurons in the white matter.

Refsum *et al.* state that repeated pneumoencephalograms reveal progressive cerebral atrophy. The testicles display areas of normal spermatogenesis and other areas in which there appears to be arrest of spermatogenesis and varying degrees of hyalinization of the tubules.

Harvey points out that the excretion of creatine is not increased as it is in all other conditions when there is an extensive loss of skeletal muscle. He suggests that there must be a defect in creatine synthesis.

Etiology.—This is believed to be an autosomal dominant characteristic with incomplete penetrance and variable expression.

Fitzgerald and Caughey describe the finding of a small acrocentric supernumerary chromosome in myotonic dystrophy in five cases.

Clinical Features.—It is usual to find more than one case of this disease in a group of siblings, and complete investigations will often reveal some evidence of the same condition in previous generations. Males have been

said to be affected five times as frequently as females but studies of family trees of affected families indicate that the incidence in the two sexes is the same. Often premature cataract or mild myotonic symptoms are noted in the ascendants, and the fully developed syndrome in only one generation, affecting members of several families of the same child rank as regards some common ancestor. The descendants of patients suffering from myotonic dystrophy rarely develop the disease, it is claimed, for about 100 children and a number of grandchildren of these patients have been traced and found to be healthy. The onset is usually between the ages of 20 and 35, but it may occur in childhood and even infancy. The first symptoms may result from wasting of the muscles or from myotonia. The muscles which are first attacked are the facial, especially the orbiculares of the eyelids and the mouth, the masseters and temporals, the sternomastoids, the extensors of the forearms, vasti of the thigh, and the dorsiflexors of the feet. Occasionally one observes complete paralysis of the extraocular muscles, i.e. the clinical picture often termed progressive nuclear ophthalmoplegia. There may be pseudohypertrophy. In some cases, the tongue, soft palate, pharynx, and even the vocal cords are affected. Speech is characteristically low-pitched, monotonous and often nasal. The hard palate is very high and narrow and the face is long and thin.

The myotonus is not constant, but is usually, though possibly not always, present at some time during the course of the disease. Repeated examinations may be necessary before it is demonstrated. It is most easily elicited by asking patient to grip the examiner's hand with maximum force and then open the fingers as rapidly as possible. It will be seen that the flexors do not relax for a second or more after the extensors begin to contract. There may also be difficulty in opening the eyelids after closing them tightly, cramping of the feet on attempting to run, and stiffness of the jaw muscles when chewing. Often repetition of the movement several times will result in disappearance of the myotonus. The phenomenon is most pronounced when the patient exerts the full strength, and it is also accentuated by cold and by emotional reactions. The generalized myotonia in response to a sudden effort or an emotional reaction which is seen in Thomsen's disease does not as a rule occur in this condition.

Percussion of the muscles produces the usual type of contraction in a few fasciculi, but the relaxation is unduly delayed. This mechanical reaction is most easily obtained in the thenar eminence, in the tongue, and in the extensors of the forearm. Myotonus is not observed in the tendon reflexes.

The electrical reactions seem to vary in different cases. The atrophic muscles show, as a rule, diminished reactions to both galvanic and faradic

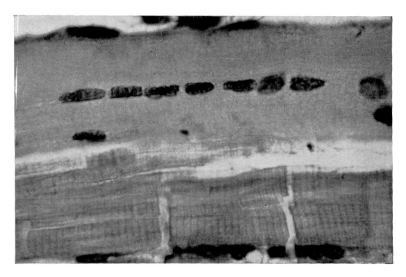

Fig. 290. Case of myotonic muscular dystrophy showing a hypertrophic muscle fiber with a row of centrally placed nuclei.

currents, just as do the wasted muscles in the common dystrophies. In some cases, galvanic stimulation produces a contraction, which persists as long as the current flows, and relaxes slowly after the current is interrupted. This is the myotonic reaction. Adie found the chronaxie to be normal, which he regarded as indicating that the disease is primary in the muscle. The electromyogram shows the standard changes of myopathy and during the delayed relaxation of the muscles bursts of fibrillation-like potentials.

These patients usually are of rather low mentality, and often definitely feeble-minded. It has been said that they are suspicious, unreliable and morose. They show many physical peculiarities besides the muscular atrophy and myotonus. The development of the genital organs is often defective, and males become impotent early. Even young males show atrophy of the testicles. Premature cataract is a very common finding, and is present in at least 30 per cent of these patients. This begins as a star-shaped opacity in the posterior cortical lamellae, and later involves the anterior cortical lamellae as well. There may be some punctiform opacities also. These cataracts ripen quickly, about the same time in each eye. Slit-lamp examination will reveal them long before they may be seen with the ophthalmoscope. Frontal alopecia, atrophy of the skin, loss of subcutaneous fat, salivation, lacrimation and acrocyanosis are all described as common symptoms. Among the ascendants of patients suffering with this disease large families are common, but fertility gradually diminishes, and the patients are often childless. According to Caughey and Brown the endocrine

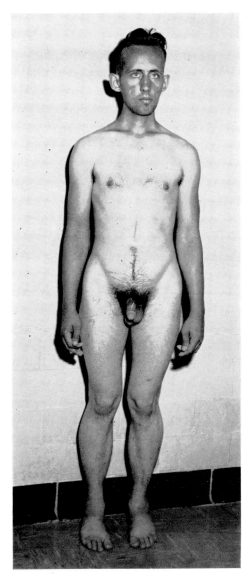

Fig. 291. Myotonic dystrophy with wasting of the temporal muscles, sternomastoids, frontal baldness, narrow jaws, atrophic testicles and pseudohypertrophy of the calves. (By the courtesy of Dr. Harry Butler.)

symptoms are due to atrophy of the androgenic cells of the testes and adrenal cortex. Kaufman and Heckert mention sprue like symptoms due to involvement of the intestinal musculature. Swallowing may be difficult. Cannon describes enlargement of the heart, Stokes-Adams episodes, left ventricular failure, and electrocardiographic abnormalities including heart block, atrial flutter and fibrillation and bundle branch block. Inadequate ventilation may occur and pneumonia is mentioned. Gold found that some patients develop dysfunction of the temporomandibular joint with subluxation and dislocation. This seems to increase with age.

Maas states that he has demonstrated myotonus in children of affected parents between three and twelve years and in seventeen other subjects before the age of adolescence. He states that myotonus is usually present before other symptoms. Vanier reported six cases of myotonic dystrophy in children and infants. Dodge *et al.* report a study of nine children, most of whom were infants. They found five cases in which there was difficulty in sucking, facial weakness and difficulty in swallowing in early infancy. Weakness of the jaws is mentioned. If weakness of the skeletal muscles was present, it was apt to be evident in the proximal muscles rather than in the distal muscles as in adults. In three cases, only myotonia was found. In about one third of all cases, mental deficiency was evident. No endocrine

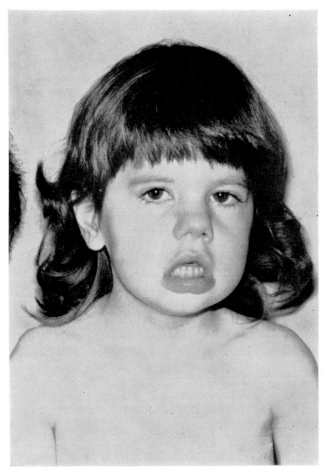

FIG. 292. Girl of 4 years suffering from myotonic dystrophy showing typical V shaped mouth. There is also hollowing of the temples, mild ptosis of the eyelids, and also slender neck with sternomastoid muscle atrophy. (By the courtesy of Dr. Gordon V. Watters and Trevor Williams. Arch. of Neurol. 1967, vol. 17, p. 137.)

abnormalities were found. Eventration of the diaphragm was found in one child.

Watters and Williams report a study of 8 children with myotonic dystrophy in 5 families in which this disease was prevalent. They summarize the findings in 36 patients in whom the onset was before the age of 16 years. In 27 the onset was in infancy. They emphasize the occurrance of bilateral facial weakness and the mouth shaped like an inverted V. They found the immunoglobulin G was reduced in the serum of the affected individuals.

Diagnosis.—This disease is distinguished from the common muscular dystrophy by the distribution of the muscular wasting, the myotonus, the cataracts, the characteristic baldness, the gonadal atrophy, and the appearance of premature senility. From the myotonia congenita of Thomsen it is distinguished by the presence of muscular wasting and by the fact that the myotonus is not congenital. Myotonia may occur in thyroid deficiency. Harvey states that there is only one condition where there is extensive decrease in skeletal muscle mass and no increase of creatinuria and that is myotonic dystrophy.

Prognosis.—The disease is incurable but may permit survival for many years, for in many cases it progresses very slowly. However, it is said to be unusual for patients in whom the syndrome is fully developed to exceed the age of forty-five.

Treatment.—Quinine will relieve the myotonus just as in Thomsen's disease q.v. but no treatment is known which will arrest the progress of the disease. Munsat states that diphenylhydantoin is effective in controlling the myotonia. Thyroid extract will not relieve the myotonia though it will do so in states of thyroid deficiency. Testosterone has some symptomatic value in males.

CASE HISTORY (Ped. A-69395).—*History of immobile face and clubfeet with peroneal muscle weakness at birth in a girl who at seven years showed typical signs of myotonic dystrophy. Mother also showed typical signs. History of same disease in maternal great-aunts.*

A. T. was born with bilateral clubfeet, i.e. pes equinovarus, and casts were applied to her legs early in infancy. The deformity was overcome without great difficulty but the ankles were always weak and her gait awkward. It was noticed very early in life that she showed little change of expression. This fact led to unjustified suspicions that her mental development was deficient. Her speech was never clear. As she grew older it was noticed that she did not go upstairs with proper ease.

On examination at the age of seven years her face was found to be long and narrow. The palate exhibited a high arch. The muscles in general were rather larger than one would expect for her age and sex, but

strength was in general less than the bulk of her muscles would lead one to anticipate. She stood with protuberant abdomen and increased lumbar lordosis. The gluteals were weak so she could not get up from a squatting position without help. The peroneals were very weak and she did not lift her toes properly as she walked. The sternomastoids were also weak and very small. When the arms were outstretched the scapulae winged a bit. The eyelids could be closed fairly well but only the slightest movement was possible in the lower part of the face. The tongue was small and slightly wrinkled but moved well. The jaws moved well but strength was reduced and the muscles were rather small. No myotonic grasp was elicited possibly because the child could not be induced to grip with her full strength, but a good myotonic response was elicted by percussion.

The mother was then examined. She displayed atrophic sternomastoids and muscles of the jaws and a myotonic grip as well as myotonus on percussion. She had had symptomatic relief by the use of quinine. She stated that two maternal great-aunts had suffered from the same disease.

BIBLIOGRAPHY

ADIE, W. J. AND GREENFIELD, J. G.: Dystrophia myotonica (Myotonia Atrophica). Brain, 46:73, 1923. (Full references.)

CANNON, P. J.: The heart and lungs in myotonic dystrophy. Am. J. Med., 32:765, 1962.

CAUGHEY, J. E. AND SAUCIER, G.: Endocrine aspects of dystrophia myotonica. Brain, 85:711, 1962.

CAUGHEY, J. E. AND PACHOMOV, N.: The diaphragm in dystrophia myotonica. J. Neurol., Neurosurg. & Psychiat., 22:311, 1959.

CAUGHEY, J. E. AND BROWN, J.: Dystrophia myotonica. An endocrine study. Quart. J. Med., 19:303, 1950.

CAUGHEY, J. E. AND MYRIANTHOPOULOS, N. C.: Dystrophia Myotonica and Related Disorders. Thomas, Springfield, 1963.

DODGE, P., GAMSDORP, I., BYERS, R. K. AND RUSSELL, P.: Myotonic dystrophy in infancy and childhood. Pediatrics, 35:3, 1965.

DYKEN, P. R.: Extraocular myotonia in families with dystrophia myotonica. Neurology, 16:738, 1966.

FISCH, C.: The heart in dystonia myotonica. Amer. Heart Jour., 41:525, 1951.

FITZGERALD, P. H. AND CAUGHEY, J. E.: Chromosome and sex chromatin studies in cases of dystrophia myotonica. New Zealand Med. J., 61:410, 1962.

GOLD, G. N.: Temporomandibular joint dysfunction in myotonic dystrophy. Neurology, 16:212, 1966.

HARVEY, J. C.: Myotonia dystrophia. Tice-Harvey Practice of Medicine, Vol. VI, p. 539.

KAUFMAN, K. K. AND HECKERT, E. W.: Dystrophia myotonica with associated sprue-like symptoms. Am. J. Med., 16:614, 1954.

KOLB, L., HARVEY, A. M. AND WHITEHILL, M. R.: A clinical study of myotonic dystrophy and myotonia congenita with special reference to the effects of quinine. Bull. Johns Hopkins Hosp., 62:188, 1938.

MAAS, O.: Observations on dystrophia myotonica. Brain, 60:498, 1938.

MUNSAT, T. I.: Therapy of myotonia. A double blind evaluation of diphenylhydantoin, procainamide and placebo. Neurology, 17:359, 1967.

RAVIN, A. AND WARING, J. J.: Studies in dystrophia myotonica. 1. Hereditary aspects. Am. J. Med. Sc., 197:593, 1939.

REFSUM, S. *et al.:* Repeated pneumoencephalographic studies in ten patients with myotonic dystrophy. Neurology, 17:345, 1967.

Roseman, N. P. and Kukulas, B. A.: Mental defect associated with muscular dystrophy. Brain, **89**:769, 1966.

Roseman, N. P. and Rebeiz, J. J.: The cerebral defect and myopathy in myotonic dystrophy. Neurology, **17**:1106, 1967.

Sher, J. H. *et al.:* Familial centronuclear myopathy. Neurology, **17**:727, 1967.

Spillane, J. D.: The heart in myotonia atrophica. Brit. Heart J., **13**:343, 1951.

Thomasen, E.: Myotonia, Thomsen's disease, Paramyotonia and Dystrophia Myotonica. Denmark, Aarhus, Universitetsforlaget., **i**: 1948.

Vanier, T. M.: Dystrophia myotonica in childhood. Brit. Med. J., **ii**:1284, 1960.

Walsh, F. B.: *Loc. cit.*

Watters, G. V. and Williams, T. W.: Early onset myotonic dystrophy. Arch. of Neurol., **17**:137, 1967.

Worster-Drought, C. and Sargent, F.: Muscular fasciculations and reactive myotonia in polyneuritis. Brain, **75**:595, 1952.

MYOPATHY OF THE EXTRAOCULAR MUSCLES

Definition.—This is a slowly progressive external ophthalmoplegia of heredofamilial type.

Pathological Anatomy.—A number of papers have appeared describing histological changes in the extraocular muscles suggestive of myopathy and in one instance absence of any significant changes in the nuclei of the third, fourth and sixth nerves. It seems that this condition is in most instances a myopathy.

Clinical Features.—This is a well known, although rare condition. The onset is usually in infancy or childhood and often occurs before the sixth year. In a few cases, symptoms have been noted within a few days after birth. In most instances, bilateral ptosis of the eyelids is the first evidence of the disease, but in some instances ptosis of the lids is the last manifestation. Later the weakness extends to the superior recti and other muscles which rotate the eyeballs and eventually complete external ophthalmoplegia results. The course of the disease is a very slow one and the paralysis may not become complete until middle age. In the majority of cases, the process is bilateral and symmetrical, but we have seen cases in which the muscles of one eye were affected more severely than those of the other eye, and in rare instances, involvement of only one eye for a long time. The pupils and ciliary muscles are not affected and the optic nerve is never involved. Diplopia is not common. In typical cases the muscles supplied by the other cranial nerves are not affected and, when the ophthalmoplegia has become complete, no further symptoms develop. In a few instances there has been slight weakness of the orbicularis oculi and of the muscles of the forehead, but complete facial paralysis is not seen. The soft palate, muscles of the jaw and pharyngeal muscles may be involved. Dr. Walsh has noted that the anal sphincter may be weak and electromyographic study revealed that myopathy was responsible. At any stage in the course of the

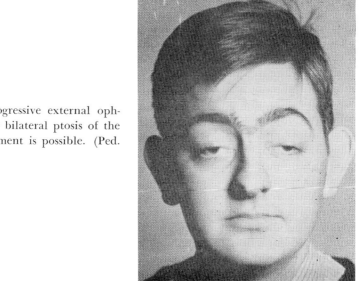

FIG. 293. Case of progressive external oph-thalmoplegia showing bilateral ptosis of the lids. No ocular movement is possible. (Ped. A. 9385.)

disease the symptoms may become arrested. Unfortunately, the process eventually becomes reactivated and continues until it is complete.

As a rule, the process is confined to the extraocular muscles but in some instances, the skeletal muscles are eventually involved. As a rule, the picture then resembles that of progressive muscular dystrophy. We have recently studied the case of a man who developed bilateral ptosis of the lids and complete paralysis of the extraocular muscles during adolescence. When he was 20 years old, wasting of the proximal muscles developed. Biopsy revealed the histological picture of myopathy. In rare instances the skeletal muscles are involved first and the extraocular muscles are affected later. We have seen this in the common muscular dystrophy and in the myotonic dystrophy also.

As a rule, this disease is inherited as an autosomal dominant trait but instances of recessive inheritance are reported.

Kearns and Sayre have found retinitis pigmentosa, external ophthalmoplegia and heart block in two patients. One patient died and it was found that the extraocular muscles showed evidences of muscular dystrophy and the cranial nerve nuclei were intact.

Diagnosis.—This depends upon the clinical picture and upon the family history. Electromyographic study and muscle biopsy help to establish the nature of the process.

Rosenberg *et al.* state that progressive external ophthalmoplegia may be

neurogenic as well as myogenic and that the usual methods of differential diagnosis may be inadequate.

Prognosis.—Unfavorable.

Treatment.—The ptosis of the lids may be relieved by plastic surgery but operation on the extraocular muscles is useless. No other treatment is known.

> CASE HISTORY (No. 1032730).—At fourteen years, generalized weakness of the skeletal muscles began and progressed slowly. At sixteen, ptosis of the eyelids and weakness of the extraocular muscles became evident. Nasal voice and difficulty in swallowing developed. The soft palate did not lift well. There was congenital absence of the pectoralis on the right. Pigmentary degeneration of the retinae was found. Careful tests for myasthenia gravis were negative. No similar symptoms were present in other members of the family or collateral relatives.

BIBLIOGRAPHY

BECKETT, R. S. AND NETSKY, M.: Familial ocular myopathy and external ophthalmoplegia. Arch. Neurol. & Psychiat., **69**:64, 1953.

COGAN, D. G.: Pathology of abiotrophic ophthalmoplegia externa. Bull. Johns Hopkins Hosp., **111**:42, 1962.

FAGIN, I. D.: Chronic ophthalmoplegia externa. Classification of causes. Am. J. Ophth., **25**:968, 1942.

KEARNS, T. P. AND SAYRE, G. P.: Retinitis pigmentosa, external ophthalmoplegia and heart block. Arch. of Ophth., **60**:280, 1958.

KILOH, L. G. AND NEVIN, S.: Progressive dystrophy of the extra-ocular muscles. Brain, **74**:115, 1951.

LEES, F. AND SWERSEDGE: Descending ocular myopathy. Brain, **85**:701, 1962.

MAGORA, A. AND ZAUBERMAN, H.: Ocular myopathy. Archives of Neurology, **20**:1, 1969.

ROSENBERG, R. N. *et al.*: Progressive ophthalmoplegia. Arch. of Neurol., **19**:362, 1968.

SCHWARZ, G. A. AND CHAN-NAO, L.: Chronic progressive external ophthalmoplegia, a clinical and pathological report. Arch. Neurol. & Psychiat., **71**:31, 1954.

WALSH, F. B.: *Loc. cit.*

MYOTONIA CONGENITA OF THOMSEN

Definition.—This may be defined as a heredofamilial condition which becomes apparent very early in life, and is characterized by a tendency to a delayed relaxation of voluntary muscular contractions or myotonia, and often by a bulky musculature as well as by various mental disturbances.

Pathological Anatomy.—The lesions are confined to the muscles, which are often somewhat larger than normal. Grossly, they may seem rather pale, but not fatty. It is claimed that microscopic examination reveals a definite enlargement of the muscle fibers, which are rounded and show indistinct transverse striations. There may be some increase in sarcolemma nuclei, some of which are in the center of the fibers. It is unusual to find any atrophic fibers.

Etiology.—Nothing is known of the cause of this disease beyond the fact that it is inherited.

Clinical Features.—The disease is usually present in several members of a family, and may be traced through a number of generations. It affects males and females alike, and may be transmitted by either sex. This disease may behave as either a dominant characteristic or as a recessive. According to Macklin, in 13 families it has been dominant, and in 9, recessive.

The onset is in most cases early in childhood, and cases are reported in which myotonia of the tongue caused difficulty in nursing soon after birth. It is not unusual for the symptoms to increase in severity about the age of puberty. The patients notice that if they grasp an object firmly it is impossible for them to release it promptly; that upon suddenly rising or starting to run, their muscles become rigid, so that they may be unable to take a step for some seconds, or may even fall helplessly to the ground. After the movement is repeated several times, the rigidity slowly wears off, and they are then able to contract and relax their muscles normally. Emotional factors play a large part in these symptoms, for a sudden fright, a slap on the back; a loud and unexpected noise, or even great anger or mental distress are almost certain to produce general rigidity in affected patients and often a fall. Cold weather also accentuates the myotonia. Percussion of the muscles causes a normal contraction, which is, however, abnormally prolonged, and repeated blows may cause a persisting tetanus. Percussion of the tendons produces a normal reflex without myotonus. The electrical reactions are sometimes characteristic, although many variations are reported. The typical reaction is obtained by a strong galvanic stimulus, which produces a tetanic contraction while the current is flowing. The contraction may also persist a few seconds after the current is interrupted. Faradic stimuli sometimes cause contractions which are unduly prolonged. Useful tests for demonstrating the myotonia are described by Rossett. In addition to the common hand-grasp test, he advises having the patient open and close the hand rapidly, flex and extend the elbow rapidly with the fist firmly clenched, and asking the patient to open the eyelids at once after inducing a sneeze (snuff). The myotonus is not always general, and numerous cases are described in which symptoms were present only in the legs or in the arms alone. The facial, ocular and tongue muscles may be affected, but the pharynx and larynx are usually not involved. Myotonia may be active or latent. In the latter case, it may be elicited only by special tests such as percussion, electrical stimulation or sneezing. In some patients, emotional reactions are the most effective stimuli.

The muscles never show any atrophy, and, on the contrary, they are almost always bulky, even suggesting hypertrophy in some instances. Strength

and endurance are not diminished, and it is possible for these patients to take long walks or to dance for hours. In contrast to the situation in muscular dystrophy the heart is not involved, and there is no evidence of endocrine disease.

It is not unusual to find mental disturbances in families afflicted with myotonia. This may occur in myotonic patients or in relatives who have no disturbance of motility. Seclusiveness, irritability, and recurrent depressions are common. Several authors have emphasized that these patients habitually deny the existence of symptoms in other members of the family, and are untrustworthy about the facts of their own illness. Thomasen denies that there is any significant association of mental disturbances with this disease.

Denny-Brown and Nevin state that there are two separate phenomena involved in myotonia. Electromyographic studies reveal that the delayed relaxation of the prime mover is associated with action potentials of the same order of speed and size as those found in muscular fibrillation indicating that they represent independent incoordinate excitation of single muscle fibers. This reaction may occur after degeneration of the motor nerve and is clearly myogenic. The widespread myotonia which sometimes occurs after a violent effort and which is the cause of much of the disability is associated with an intense discharge of large rhythmical action potentials of motor unit activity. This is therefore a reflex effect.

It is said that in myotonia congenita one finds an increase of creatine tolerance. It is suggested that the hypertrophied muscles have an excessive ability to store creatine and convert it into creatinine.

Diagnosis.—The diagnosis is not difficult if the myotonia is elicited. The absence of atrophy should rule out myotonic dystrophy, although some knowledge of the family history is required to be sure that we are not dealing with a case of the latter in the early stage before atrophy has appeared. Some states of thyroid insufficiency are associated with large muscles and myotonia. The so-called hypertrophia musculorum vera might simulate Thomsen's disease though myotonia is not present in this condition. The effect of quinine in reducing the myotonia is of value in diagnosis.

Prognosis.—This condition rarely causes severe incapacity and does not progress, but it must be considered hopeless so far as recovery is concerned.

Treatment.—Wolf has shown that quinine will abolish the myotonus of myotonia congenita. Adults are given five grains of the hydrochloride and children smaller doses according to their age. The effect of this drug is entirely symptomatic. It is claimed that procainamide will reduce the voluntary contraction myotonia but not the percussion myotonia. Isaacs states that when the administration of cortisone and chlorothiozide has resulted in depletion of potassium, the patients are greatly improved.

BIBLIOGRAPHY

DENNY-BROWN, D. AND NEVIN, S.: The phenomena of myotonia. Brain, **64**:1, 1941.

DRAGER, G. A., HAMMILL, J. F. AND SHY, G. M.: Paramyotonia congenita. Arch. Neurol. & Psychiat., **80**:1, 1958.

GESCHWIND, N.: Procaine amide in the treatment of myotonia. Brain, **78**:81, 1955.

ISAACS, H.: The treatment of myotonia congenita. South Africa Med. Jour., **33**:984, 1959.

MacROBBIE, D. S. AND FRIEDLANDER, W. J.: Treatment of myotonia with procainamide. Arch. Neurol. & Psychiat., **78**:473, 1957.

ROSSETT, J.: A study of Thomsen's disease, based on eight cases in a family exhibiting remarkable inheritance features in three generations. Brain, **45**:1, 1922.

THOMASEN, E.: Myotonia, Thomsen's disease, Paramyotonia, Dystrophia myotonica. Denmark, Universitetsforlaget i Aarhus, 1948.

WOLF, A.: Quinine: An effective form of treatment for myotonia. Arch. Neurol. & Psychiat., **36**:382, 1936.

HYPERTROPHIA MUSCULORUM VERA

This is a rare condition which is manifest by enlargement of the muscles. This usually becomes apparent in childhood and is progressive to some extent. The muscles of the extremities are most apt to be affected but the trunk muscles may also be involved. In some cases the enlargement of the muscles is restricted to one extremity or to one side of the body. The muscles are firm and are said to display increased strength in some instances. In other cases the patient complains of fatigue and weakness and sometimes of dull aching pain in the muscles. The tendon reflexes and the electrical reactions are normal. There is as a rule no myotonia. No changes are seen in the bones, skin or subcutaneous tissues.

Histological studies have revealed muscle fibers which are abnormal only in their increased size. Some studies have led to the belief that the number of fibers is also increased. No degenerative changes are described.

In differential diagnosis one must exclude pseudohypertrophic muscular dystrophy, q.v., Delange's syndrome, q.v. and thyroid deficiency, q.v. Thomsen's disease q.v. is difficult to distinguish. In this connection one should mention the so-called infant Hercules, a condition attributed to congenital adrenal cortical hyperplasia.

BIBLIOGRAPHY

HESSER, F. H.: Hypertrophia musculorum vera associated with hypothyroidism. Bull. Johns Hopkins Hosp., **66**:353, 1940.

MAXWELL, I. L.: Hypertrophia musculorum vera. Brit. Med. J., **2**:656, 1947.

WOODS, A. H.: Muscular hypertrophy with weakness. J. Nerv. & Ment. Dis., **38**:532, 1911.

TRAUMATIC CONDITIONS OF MUSCLES

Volkmann's Ischemic Contracture and Other Conditions

Definition.—Both the muscles and their tendons may be ruptured by violence, and the muscle sheath may be torn. The most serious and one of

the most common types of traumatic injury, however, is the so-called Volkmann's ischemic contracture.

Pathological Anatomy.—Volkmann's contracture is marked at first by edema and necrosis of the muscle fibers. Later, the fibers become shrunken and fissured. The nuclei cannot be demonstrated and the striations are lost. Numerous fibroblasts and phagocytes appear, and the fibers are gradually broken down and replaced by connective tissue, which converts the muscle into a mass of scar tissue. This becomes adherent to the skin, the tendons and bones.

Clinical Features.—Volkmann's contracture occurs more frequently in children than in adults. It is found most frequently in the muscles of the forearm, which flex the fingers and wrist. It almost always follows fracture of the lower end of the humerus, or of the bones of the forearm. Occasionally the leg is affected in the same manner. Thomson and Mahoney mention 9 cases in which the leg was involved as a result of fracture of the femur. They had observed a total of 42 cases, all in children. At present it is generally accepted that circulatory disturbances are responsible, but there is still some difference of opinion about the exact mechanism involved. The application of tight splints is usually held to blame and, no doubt, is a very important factor. Lewis has emphasized the role of hemorrhage and edema in the antecubital space under the fascia which leads to compression of the blood vessels and obstruction of the circulation. In some cases ischemic contracture has followed the application of a tourniquet or occlusion of the large vessels of the arm, so the etiology is not always the same. The development of ischemic contracture is always very painful and marked by pronounced swelling. The fingers are cold and blue. The pulse may be lost for a time. Later, the muscles shrink and become extremely firm and dense. The skin is also drawn tight and is adherent to the subcutaneous tissues. Trophic changes develop in the skin and nails and sometimes ulcerations. The fingers are flexed so strongly at the distal joints that the nails may press into the palm, but the proximal joints are extended. The wrist may be flexed also. The thumb may escape or may be affected in the same way. The muscles lying on the extensor surface of the forearm are usually spared to a large extent, and the greatest atrophy and induration are found in the long flexors and in the intrinsic muscles of the hand. The muscles feel like wood when the condition is fully developed. There is no suggestion of the elasticity of normal muscle, and passive movements are abolished. There may be cutaneous anesthesia over the tips of the fingers and even over part of the hand. This has not the distribution of any one nerve lesion, and is probably due to deficient circulation with injury to the terminal branches of several nerves. The affected muscles usually give no response to electrical

stimulation, or in mild cases show an elevation of the threshold. There is never any reaction of degeneration. The diagnosis depends largely upon the history, the increased density of the muscles, the loss of passive movements, and the absence of reaction of degeneration. The prognosis is bad, since the muscles are actually destroyed and replaced by connective tissue. If the condition is recognized before irreparable damage is done, the splints should be removed at once. If the circulation does not improve satisfactorily, an incision should be made into the antecubital space and the blood clot removed. Myoglobinuria is described in some cases.

Seddon describes methods of treatment. In mild cases, spontaneous recovery may occur and only splinting to prevent deformities is required. In very severe cases nothing can be done. In cases of moderate severity, it is advised that, after six months observation, operation be performed. Excision of all tissues irreparably damaged is advised, nerve grafting is carried out if necessary and tendons lengthened or transplanted. Seddon points out that the flexor digitorum profundus and the flexor pollicis longus are most severely affected.

In addition to the Volkmann's contracture, several other types of traumatic injury may be mentioned. Sudden and violent stretching of a muscle may produce rupture of a tendon. This causes pain, and a sudden snap may be heard. Thereafter, the belly of the muscle may be displaced in the direction of the remaining attachment and, when the muscle contracts, the displacement becomes still more evident. The muscle exerts no motor effect, but can be shown to contract voluntarily and also in response to electrical stimulation. Rupture of the tendon of the long head of the biceps is most common. In the same way, the belly of the muscle may be torn. Here we may palpate a groove in the muscle. When the muscle contracts, a swelling appears on either side of the groove. The so-called rupture of the plantaris is really due to rupture of the medial gastrocnemius Arner and Lindholm state. In some cases, violent exertion may cause rupture of the sheath of a muscle. A muscle hernia develops as a result, which disappears when the muscle contracts.

BIBLIOGRAPHY

ARNER, O. AND LINDHOLM, A.: What is tennis leg? Acta chir. Scandinav., 116:73, 1958.

BRISTOW, W. R.: Myositis ossificans and Volkmann's paralysis. Brit. J. Surg., 10:475, 1922-23.

GOTTLEIB, A.: Muscle tears. Arch. Surg., 9:613, 1924.

GRIFFITHS, D. L.: Volkmann's ischemic contracture. Brit. J. Surg., 28:239, 1940.

LEWIS, D.: Ischemia paralysis. Am. J. Surg., 6:638, 1929, new series.

SEDDON, H. J.: Volkmann's contracture. Treatment by excision of the infarct. J. Bone & Joint. Surg. 38-B: British Vol., 152, 1956.

THOMSON, S. A. AND MAHONEY, L. J.: Volkmann's ischemic contracture and its relation to fracture of the femur. J. Bone & Joint Surg., 33 B, 336, 1951.

TRAUMATIC NECROSIS OF THE PRETIBIAL MUSCLES

About 20 cases of this syndrome have been published in recent years. The patient is almost always an adolescent or a young man. In most instances running, jumping or walking long distances seems to be responsible. In several cases, however, fracture of the tibia or fibula was the cause and in two cases transfusion of blood into a vein of the leg with extravasation into the tissues was blamed.

One or both legs may be affected. Pain is the first symptom and may develop within a few hours after the exertion. The pain is of aching character. The anterior tibial muscles are much swollen and tender. There may be erythema and local increase of temperature. The tibialis anticus, extensor digitorum longus and the extensor hallucis longus are weak or paralysed. Stretching these muscles causes pain. There may be low grade fever and mild leucocytosis. Hypesthesia on the dorsum of the foot has been noted, but it is said that the pulses are present. The affected muscles do not respond to electrical stimulation.

Most of these symptoms subside within a few days but there is usually persisting weakness or paralysis. Fibrosis and contracture gradually develop in the next few months.

If the anterior tibial fascia is incised during the acute stage, the muscles bulge strongly out of the wound. The muscles show swelling, hemorrhages and necrosis. Later, the damaged muscle fibers are replaced by connective tissue.

It has been suggested that the swelling of the muscles due to exertion or other causes is responsible for this condition. Since these muscles are confined by the anterior tibial fascia, the interosseus membrane and the bones of the leg, the circulation is interrupted and ischemic necrosis results. It is evident that there are strong resemblances to Volkmann's contracture. Mild symptoms similar to those described above are not unusual in young athletes in training and are termed "shin splints."

Immediate operation with incision of the anterior tibial fascia is advised. Manipulation of the affected muscles during the acute stage has been followed by collapse and death possibly as a result of myoglobinuria or fat embolism.

BIBLIOGRAPHY

BLUM, L.: The clinical entity of anterior crural ischemia. Arch. Surg., 74:59, 1957.

CARTER *et al.:* The anterior tibial syndrome. Lancet, ii:928, 1949.

FREEDMAN, B. J. AND KNOWLES, C. H. R.: Anterior tibial syndrome due to arterial embolism and thrombosis. Brit. Med. J., 5147:270, 1959.

GRUNWALD, A. AND SILBERMAN, Z.: The anterior tibial syndrome. J.A.M.A., 171:2210, 1959.

PEARSON, C., ADAMS, R. AND DENNY-BROWN, D.: Traumatic necrosis of pretibial muscles. New England Med. J., 239:213, 1948.

PHALEN, G. S.: Ischemic necrosis of the anterior crural muscles. Ann. Surg., 127:112, 1948.

INFLAMMATORY DISEASES OF MUSCLES

Dermatomyositis and Acute Polymyositis

Definition.—This condition may be defined as a disease of unknown origin, which is characterized by a subacute or chronic inflammatory process involving the muscles, skin and subcutaneous tissues.

Pathological Anatomy.—The skin is usually but not always atrophied. The subcutaneous fat is partially replaced by connective tissue. The blood vessels just below the skin are thickened or partially occluded. The muscles are pale, and may be soft and friable or fibrous, depending upon the age of the process. Microscopically, the muscle fibers show hyaline and granular degeneration, vacuolation and fragmentation. Large macrophages ingest the disintegrating material. The sarcolemma nuclei proliferate as the fiber disintegrates. Eventually, the muscle fibers are replaced by connective tissue. Small hemorrhages are often found. The interstitial tissue is increased, and sometimes shows lymphocytic infiltrations. Changes in the blood vessels are constant. The walls of the small arteries are thickened, and their lumina constricted or even occluded. Their adventitia is infiltrated with lymphocytes. Some pathologists regard the process as an interstitial myositis, and some state that it is primary in the parenchyma.

Before the 87th annual meeting of the American Neurological Association, in November 1962, Dr. B. Q. Banker stated that a study of sixty patients suffering from dermatomyositis, between the ages of three and twelve, revealed that the process was essentially a vascular disease. The earliest changes were arteritis and phlebitis of the small vessels in the muscles, connective tissue of the skin, gastrointestinal tract and small nerves. The vessels were occluded by fibrin thrombi and surrounded by cells. Small infarctions resulted. It was suggested that the disease was closely allied to periarteritis and lupus.

Etiology.—The cause is unknown, and it is not at all clear whether this disease is always due to the same cause, or whether it may arise as a result of several different causes.

Clinical Features.—The onset may occur at any age, and a number of cases are described in children. The first symptoms are usually pain, weakness, and swelling with more or less tenderness over the affected muscles. The process may be localized at first, but soon becomes symmetrical and more or less generalized. The proximal muscles of the extremities seem to be first affected in most instances. Evidences of infection are almost always present in the early stages of the disease. The temperature may be only slightly elevated or fever may reach 40°C.; there is leucocytosis; and the spleen and lymph nodes may be enlarged. Tachycardia frequently develops, and, in some cases, seems to be independent of the fever. In some instances

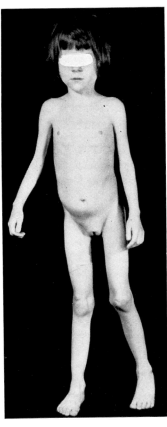

Fig. 294. Dermatomyositis. Late stage showing atrophy of the muscles.

eosinophilia is present. Sweating is frequently pronounced, and is considered very characteristic. Delirium is rare.

A number of cutaneous lesions are described. These may precede or follow the myositis. In some cases the redness suggests erysipelas, but erythema multiforme, morbilliform eruptions, urticaria, purpura and numerous other lesions are mentioned. There is frequently very definite edema of the subcutaneous tissue or a dense infiltration either with or without redness. This is especially apt to overlay the affected muscles, and is, therefore, found chiefly over the proximal segments of the extremities. The fingers form an exception to this rule for they are often conspicuously involved. The skin of the forehead and the eyelids is also frequently involved by a waxy infiltration, giving rise to the characteristic "marble brow." Later, the skin may desquamate and show diffuse or patchy brown pigmentation. In many cases fibrosis of the subcutaneous tissue and thickening of the skin results, producing a picture almost identical with that of scleroderma. There may be redness of the mucous membranes and ulcerations. The cutaneous lesions are apt to appear and disappear during the course of the disease, so that they may be absent at certain stages.

The muscles most affected are those of the shoulders, neck, upper arms and thighs, but in severe cases almost all the skeletal muscles may be affected. At first they are swollen and edematous. Later they are very soft and small. In the active stages of the disease there is almost always tenderness on pressure over the involved muscles, and both active and passive movements cause severe pain. There may be complete paralysis or only mild paresis. Tendon reflexes are normal, diminished or abolished, depending upon the severity of the process. The electrical reactions are not characteristic. Diminution of irritability as regards all types of stimulation is found, but there is never any qualitative change. After some weeks or months, the muscles show very definite atrophy and eventually they may become fibrotic. Passive movements reveal loss of the normal elasticity, and severe contractures fix the limbs in abnormal positions. In some cases the process may in-

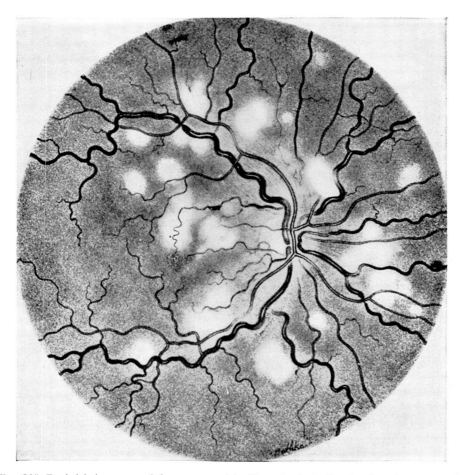

Fig. 295. Retinitis in a case of dermatomyositis (Bruce). A similar fundus picture may be observed in lupus erythematosus, periarteritis nodosa and serum sickness. (From Walsh. Neuro-Ophthalmology, courtesy the Williams and Wilkins Company.)

volve the muscles of respiration, giving rise to dyspnea, or myocarditis may cause decompensation and even death. In some cases the jaw muscles are affected and the patient is unable to chew. In more than half of all cases dysphagia is present and is attributed to involvement of the constrictors of the pharynx which sometimes seem to go into spasm when the patient takes food. The face is sometimes weak and diplopia is mentioned. The tongue may be involved and occasionally the sphincters are paralysed. Tenosynovitis is almost always present to some degree, and in rare cases the joints are affected. Myoglobinuria has been found in some cases. Ross states that in dermatomyositis the terminal capillaries of the nail fold are palisaded. Dilated capillaries are increased in number.

In some cases death occurs in the first acute attack. In other instances a

remission occurs, followed by one or more exacerbations. Sometimes the active acute or subacute symptoms may recede, giving place to a chronic progressive phase. The course may be only a few weeks or may be prolonged for two years or more. The process tends to become inactive eventually.

Severe residua may be found after the active stage of the disease is terminated. The muscles may be atrophic and partially replaced by connective tissue so they feel abnormally dense and inelastic. Severe contractures are common, especially in the flexors. The skin is often deeply pigmented and indurated, so as to resemble scleroderma. Recovery from these changes is slow and frequently incomplete.

Roentgenograms of the muscles sometimes show fine calcareous deposits lying in the superficial layers of the muscle, muscle sheath and subcutaneous tissues in the late stages of the disease. The so-called *neuro-myositis* is distinguished by the fact that the nerve trunks are tender, sensory disturbances are present and the electrical tests reveal reaction of degeneration. This is a rare and doubtful entity.

A rare form of very acute myositis occurs in infancy. This is associated with high fever, pneumonia and pericarditis. Death may occur in a few days. It is said that steroids are helpful. Barrett and Gresham describe an acute local myositis due to streptococci which responds to antibiotics.

Diagnosis.—The chief features of diagnostic importance are the tenderness of the muscles, the edema of the subcutaneous tissues, and the dermatitis; but it is often impossible to establish the diagnosis without biopsy. The electromyogram shows a decrease in the duration and voltage of motor unit potentials. There are many polyphasic potentials. There is an increase in the irritability of the muscle due to the insertion of the needle electrode. The serum enzymes are not reliable in the diagnosis of myositis. Serum electrophoresis may reveal elevation of the alpha 2 and gamma globulin. Trichinosis may be recognized by the history of eating raw pork and by biopsy. Scurvy may simulate acute myositis. It is most easily recognized by the roentgenograms of the bones. Polyneuritis may also simulate polymyositis, and it is probable that many cases of myositis are erroneously diagnosed polyneuritis. The latter should be distinguished by the presence of sensory disturbances, the absence of dermatitis, the restriction of edema to dependent parts, and especially the feet and ankles, the presence of the reaction of degeneration and the tendency for paralysis to be earlier and more severe. Lupus erythematosus must always be considered.

Prognosis.—The outlook is unfavorable but not absolutely bad. In some cases in which the symptoms are mild, the patients often make complete recoveries, and localized processes also have a rather favorable outcome. In

severe generalized cases of dermatomyositis the mortality is high, and, if the patient survives, weakness and atrophy of the muscles often persist. I have mentioned above the tendency for conditions resembling scleroderma to follow polymyositis.

Treatment.—Cortisone is sometimes effective. It is given in large doses at first and then in smaller dosage for maintenance. Christianson *et al.* state that of 62 patients with dermatomyositis treated with cortisone, 28 improved and 9 remained well after the cortisone was withdrawn.

Malaviya states that intravenous methotrexate is effective. After the acute stage is over, massage, passive movements and exercises are indicated. Manipulation under anesthesia or tenotomies may be necessary to overcome contractures.

Recently, potassium paraaminobenzoate has been found to be effective. Adults are given 15 to 20 grams by mouth per day and children smaller doses according to their size. Improvement is evident within three weeks, it is claimed, and in some instances all signs and symptoms disappear after months of treatment.

BIBLIOGRAPHY

BARRETT, A. M. AND GRESHAM, G. A.: Acute streptococcal myositis. Lancet, i:347, 1958.

BOVET, L.: Contribution a l'etude de la myatonie congenitale. Rev. franc pediat., **12**:561, 1936.

CHRISTIANSON, H. B. *et al.*: Dermatomyositis. Arch. Dermat., **74**:581, 1956.

HECHT, M. S.: Dermatomyositis in childhood. J. Pediat., **17**:791, 1940.

HOWARD, F. M. AND THOMAS, J. E.: Polymyositis and dermatomyositis. Med. Clin. North America, **44**:1001, 1960.

JAGER, B. V. AND GROSSMAN, L. A.: Dermatomyositis. Arch. Int. Med., **73**:271, 1944.

JARAMILLO, S. *et al.*: Calcinosis universalis. Arch. Phys. Med., **48**:667, 1967.

KARELITZ, S. AND WELT, S. K.: Dermatomyositis. Am. J. Dis. Child., **43**:1134, 1932.

KARLMARK, E.: Zur Pathologie der Polymyositis. Acta Scand. Med., **72**:59, 1929.

KLINGMAN, W. O.: Dermatomyositis resulting in scleroderma. Arch. Neurol. & Psychiat., **24**:1187, 1930.

MALAVIYA *et al.*: Methotrexate in dermatomyositis. Lancet, **2**:485, 1968.

O'LEARY, P. A. AND WAISMAN, M.: Dermatomyositis. A study of 40 cases. Arch. Dermat. & Syph., **41**:1001, 1940.

RADEMECKER, M. A. AND VAN BOGAERT, L.: Deux observations de polymyosite aigue generalisee. Rev. Neurol., **92**:182, 1955.

ROSS, J. B.: Nail fold capillarocopy. Jour. Invest. Dermatol., **47**:282, 1966.

VAN CREVELD, S.: Ein Fall von Polymyositis acuta. Ztschr. f. Kinderh., **47**:74, 1929; **49**:357, 1930.

WALSH, F. B.: *Loc. cit.*

POLYMYOSITIS

Definition.—This is a condition of unknown origin, which is rare in young children but more common in adolescents. It may be defined as a chronic, low grade, progressive inflammatory process involving the skeletal muscles.

Pathological Anatomy.—The muscles are pale and fibrous on section. The muscle fibers show degeneration, loss of cross striation, and atrophy.

There is an increase of fibrous tissue which replaces muscle fibers. Round cell infiltration is found in isolated foci.

Clinical Features.—The disease may begin without apparent cause or may follow a febrile illness. There is gradually developing weakness of the shoulder girdle muscles and then the pelvic girdle muscles and proximal muscles of the extremities. The muscles of the neck may be affected early but those supplied by the cranial nerves are involved late. Often, the muscles are not swollen or tender and there is usually no pain. No cutaneous eruptions are seen. The picture is similar to that of progressive muscular dystrophy. Myocarditis is sometimes present and may be fatal.

As a rule, there is no fever and systemic symptoms are mild if present at all. The white blood count is usually normal.

Logan *et al.* state that in contrast to polymyositis in adult life, malignancy is not associated.

The process is slowly progressive. Eventually the muscles become atrophic and fibrous contractures develop. Calcium deposits occur in the muscles. The picture then resembles *fibrous myositis,* q.v.

Diagnosis.—The diagnosis is made on the clinical features described above and on the results of muscle biopsy. Often, only the absence of pseudohypertrophy and a history of other cases in the family distinguishes this condition from muscular dystrophy. The electromyogram shows changes similar to those found in dermatomyositis but usually less pronounced. The serum enzymes are usually not increased. Myopathy may result from treatment with certain cortisone derivatives containing fluorine. Byers *et al.* describe myopathy of proximal distribution in children after four to eight weeks treatment with fluorinated steroids for rheumatoid arthritis. He says that recovery is always complete when the drugs are stopped.

Prognosis.—The outlook is gloomy, in most instances, for the disease continues to progress until the patient is helpless.

Treatment.—Cortisone has been employed with unsatisfactory results. Recently potassium paraaminobenzoate has been recommended in the treatment of dermatomyositis. I have found this drug to be dramatically effective in one case of polymyositis.

CASE HISTORY (No. 585427).—*Girl of 16 years developed during a period of 10 months the typical signs and symptoms of progressive muscular dystrophy. Biopsy of muscle, however, revealed myositis. The skin was normal.*

M. S., a previously healthy girl of 16 years, was admitted to Johns Hopkins Hospital on September 26, 1951. She stated that for 10 months she had been growing weak in her legs. This weakness was first evident in going up stairs. Soon she found that she was falling too frequently and getting up from the ground after a fall was very difficult. Later, she noticed

that she could not hold her arms up very long and could no longer reach for things on a shelf. No other symptoms could be elicited. She had had no fever and no eruption on the skin. There had never been any pain in the extremities or abnormalities of sensibility. The family history was entirely negative.

On examination the patient showed severe weakness of the muscles which fix the scapulae so the scapulae winged when she attempted to lift her arms. The muscles which act at the shoulder joints were also weak, whereas, the distal muscles of the arms were intact. The legs were affected in the same manner. The muscles of the thighs and hips were very weak and wasted. The calf muscles were strong. The muscles of the neck were slightly weak. The knee jerks were reduced. No pseudohypertrophy was found. The affected muscles were wasted. The skin was quite normal.

At this point the diagnosis of progressive muscular dystrophy seemed to be evident. Only two items were lacking to complete the evidence, a history of other cases in the family and pseudohypertrophy. Nevertheless, muscle biopsy showed areas of necrosis of muscle fibers associated with foci of lymphocytic infiltration and a diagnosis of myositis was made. A great many laboratory studies were made but these will be omitted since they were not helpful.

BIBLIOGRAPHY

BYERS, R. K. *et al.:* Steroid myopathy in children. Pediatrics, **29**:26, 1962.

EATON, L. M.: Prospective of neurology in regard to polymyositis. Neurology, **4**:245, 1954.

HILL, D. L. AND BARROWS, H. S.: Identical skeletal and cardiac muscle involvement in a case of fatal polymyositis. Arch. of Neurol., **19**:545, 1968.

LOGAN, R. G. *et al.:* Polymyositis: A clinical study. Ann. Int. Med., **65**:996, 1966.

McLEAN, K. AND SCHURR, P. H.: Reversible amyotrophy complicating treatment with fluorocortisone. Lancet, **i**:701, 1959.

WILLIAMS, R. S.: Triamcinolone myopathy. Lancet, **i**:698, 1959.

MYOSITIS FIBROSA

Definition.—A condition of unknown origin in which the muscles develop fibrous contractures. The picture usually represents the terminal state of polymyositis or dermatomyositis but there are cases which, from a clinical point of view, seem to be primary.

Pathological Anatomy.—The muscles are replaced by fibrous tissue and there is little or no evidence of an inflammatory process.

Clinical Features.—The disease may begin early in life. The proximal muscles of the extremities become shortened and inelastic. Eventually, all the muscles of the extremities and trunk are involved. The process is slowly progressive, the extremities become fixed in flexion by contractures and finally the child is helpless. In certain cases, shortening of the muscles appears before weakness is evident. There is no change in the skin and no evidence of infection. The family history is negative.

Diagnosis.—The diagnosis rests upon the clinical picture and the results

of muscle biopsy. Hassin and Levin point out that scleroderma may involve the muscles with little or no involvement of the skin, so it may be mistaken for the type of myositis described above. In fact, these authors suggest that chronic myositis, interstitial myositis and myosclerosis are all forms of scleroderma.

Prognosis.—The outlook is gloomy. The progression of the disease is slow but it is said that remissions are rare.

Treatment.—No proper treatment is available. I am told cortisone has no value. Physiotherapy may be tried.

BIBLIOGRAPHY

ADAMS, R. D., DENNY-BROWN, D. AND PEARSON, C. M.: Disease of Muscle. Paul Hoeber, Inc. 1953.

BLAU, A.: Primary generalized myositis fibrosa. J. Mount Sinai Hospital, New York, 5:432, 1938.

BURTON, J. A. G., COWMAN, J. AND MILLER, H.: Generalized myositis fibrosa. Quart. J. Med., 17: 103, 1923.

HASSIN, G. B. AND LEVIN, P. M.: Sclerodermal muscular atrophy associated with fasciculations. J. Neuropath. & Clin. Neurol., 1:261, 1951.

STEWART, A. M. AND MacGREGOR, A. R.: Myositis fibrosa generalisata. Arch. Dis. Child., 26:215, 1951.

OTHER TYPES OF MYOSITIS

Adams, Denny-Brown and Pearson describe a number of infectious processes involving the muscles.

Rheumatic Fever, Rheumatoid Arthritis, Lupus Erythematosus and *Scleroderma* all may be associated with nodular, interstitial polymyositis, it is said. The essential lesion is a focal infiltration of inflammatory cells in the endomysial and perimysial connective tissue. The muscle fibers adjacent to such foci may undergo degeneration. In lupus there are also small areas of infarction due to vascular occlusion.

Periarteritis nodosa q.v. may change the skeletal muscles in two ways. The occlusion of small blood vessels may cause infarctions and the damage to the nerve trunks may cause neurogenic atrophy.

Pyogenic infections, usually due to streptococci or staphylococci, may occur in the course of septicemia or as result of infected wounds. Direct extension of local infections is another cause. The process may be diffuse at first but usually becomes localized and encapsulated with abscess formation.

Acute streptococcus myositis is described by Barrett and Gresham. It is a fulminating process which may be fatal in a short time. The infection is believed to reach the muscles by way of the blood stream. The muscles are swollen and tender. There may be erythema over the affected extremity. The veins are not engorged as one would expect in thrombophlebitis. Massive antibiotic therapy is required at once.

Clostridial infection or gas gangrene is due usually to the Clostridium

welchii. It causes rapid degeneration of the muscle fibers with formation of gas bubbles and edema. Palpation of the swollen tissues reveal crepitus. Lacerations, compound fractures and deep puncture wounds are usually responsible for the organism thrives only in devitalized tissues. A therapeutic serum is available and the antibiotics are used in treatment. Exposure to oxygen under two atmospheres of pressure is advised.

Sarcoidosis q.v. In this condition many hard tubercles may be found in the muscles. As a rule they do not give rise to any symptoms but in some instances more extensive processes may cause gross destruction of the muscles with weakness and fibrosis.

Tuberculous myositis.—The muscles may be involved by extension of a tuberculous focus and in rare instances a tuberculous process may develop in a muscle as a result of hematogenous infection. The muscles are rarely involved in miliary tuberculosis. A polymyositis characterized by multiple foci of epithelioid cells and lymphocytes as well as giant cells of Langhans is described but may be due to sarcoidosis.

Syphilitic myositis occurs in two forms. Gummata are rare, but may occur in any muscle. Bilateral gumma of the sternomastoid muscle is said to be characteristic. A diffuse syphilitic myositis is also known which may cause extensive weakness, atrophy and contractures.

In *Weil's disease* hemorrhagic lesions are found in the muscles resembling Zenker's hyaline degeneration.

Fungus myositis.—Actinomycosis is usually responsible. The muscle is involved by extension from infection in the skin or pleura.

Among the types of myositis due to parasites, *trichinosis* q.v. is most important. The striated muscles are most favorable for the survival of these organisms. When large numbers of the parasites lodge in the muscles there is pain, tenderness, swelling and gross weakness. The heart may be affected. The muscles may never regain their normal strength.

Toxoplasmosis q.v. may also involve the muscles. Disseminated foci are found which give rise to no symptoms.

Trypanosomyasis cruiz q.v. may cause myositis. The organisms are found in the blood in the form of trypanosomes but in the tissues including the muscles they are in the form of Leishman-Donovan bodies and contained within cysts. Disseminated focal myositis results. This process involves the heart severely and the skeletal muscles as well.

Zenker's hyaline degeneration of the skeletal muscles scarcely belongs in this category for it is believed to be due to toxic or metabolic processes resulting from severe illnesses such as typhoid fever and smallpox. Hyaline degeneration may cause no symptoms but in some cases even slight exertion may cause the damaged muscle fibers to rupture.

BIBLIOGRAPHY

ADAMS, R., DENNY-BROWN, D. AND PEARSON, C. M.: Diseases of Muscle. Paul Hoeber, Inc. 1953.
BARRETT, A. M. AND GRESHAM, G. A.: Acute streptococcal myositis. Lancet, i:347, 1958.

EPIDEMIC MYALGIA

Definition.—This condition has also been termed pleurodynia, devil's grip and the Bornholm disease. The last refers to the name of a Danish island in which the disease has been very prevalent.

Pathological Anatomy.—No post-mortem examinations are yet reported. Lepine has found in a muscle biopsy hyaline degeneration of muscle fibers and focal mononuclear infiltration such as are seen in the muscles of mice infected with the Coxsackie virus.

Etiology.—There is now strong evidence that one of the Coxsackie viruses is responsible for this disease. Thordarson and his associates have isolated this virus from the stools of 9 out of 15 patients whose stools were tested and obtained positive results with the serum neutralization test in 6 to 7 patients tested. Laboratory workers have acquired typical symptoms of Bornholm disease when exposed to the Coxsackie virus.

Clinical Features.—The disease has been known since 1856, and has been most prevalent in Iceland, Finland, Denmark, Sweden, and Norway, but has also occurred in England, Germany and the United States. In this country, it has been reported in Virginia, New York, New Jersey, Pennsylvania, Tennessee, and the New England States. In Denmark, over 4,000 cases were reported in 1932. The various epidemics have all been very much alike. They occur in the summer and early fall. Children between 5 and 15 years are most susceptible. The disease seems to spread by contact, and it is not unusual for all the children in a family to be attacked at the same time. The incubation period seems to be between two and four days.

Pain develops in the muscles of the back, shoulders, abdomen or hips, but most frequently of all in the muscles of the chest and the diaphragm. The affected muscles are tender to pressure, and may show localized swellings. As a rule, there is pain on inspiration and, consequently, respiration is shallow and rapid. Hiccough is present in some cases. Because of the pain in the muscles, the child may assume various abnormal postures, and may be unable to make certain movements. Harvey *et al.* believe that the common cervical myalgia and pleurodynia represent variants of the same disease. There is only slight elevation of temperature, and the blood shows some leucocytosis and an excess of eosinophils. There is no cutaneous eruption. In most cases the internal organs seem to be normal, but the disease may be complicated by dry pleurisy, pneumonia, and otitis media, as well as by orchitis. The more acute pain lasts as a rule one or two days, but ten-

derness may persist somewhat longer. It is said that a mild lymphocytic meningitis occurs in some cases. It is pointed out that relapses after one or two weeks are common and that these patients often have recurrent attacks of the same condition at intervals of months or years. Fever may be quite absent.

Diagnosis.—The diagnosis should be relatively easy if an epidemic is in progress, but the local pain and tenderness have often been mistaken for pleurisy, appendicitis, and other surgical conditions. Dengue fever may cause very similar symptoms.

Prognosis.—Apparently, the disease is never fatal and leaves no residua. Relapses occur in almost one-fourth of all cases, and second attacks are common.

Treatment.—No specific treatment has been developed. Analgesics may be required to relieve the pain, but no other therapeutic measures are indicated.

BIBLIOGRAPHY

Harvey, A. M., Tumulty, P. A. and Bang, F. B.: Epidemic myalgia. South. Med. J., **41**:732, 1948.

Heubner, R. J. *et al.:* Epidemic pleurodynia in Texas. New England J. Med., **248**:268, 1953.

Heubner, R. J. *et al.:* The importance of Coxsackie viruses in human disease particularly herpangina and epidemic pleurodynia. New England Med. J., **247**:285, 1952.

Lepine, P., Desse, G. et Sautter, V.: Myositis in case of Bornhold disease. Bull. Acad. Nat. Med., **5-6**:66, 1952.

Nichamin, S. J.: Pleurodynia in children. J.A.M.A., **148**:1002, 1952.

Payne, G. C. and Armstrong, Charles: Epidemic transient diaphragmatic spasm. J.A.M.A., **81**:746, 1923.

Rector, J. M.: Acute epidemic myalgia or pleurodynia: Clinical course and diagnosis of disease in children. Am. J. Dis. Child., **50**:1095, 1935.

Richter, A. B. and Levine, H. D.: Pleurodynia. J.A.M.A., **102**:898, 1934.

Thordarson, O. T., Sigurdson, B. and Grimsson, H.: Isolation of Coxsackie virus from patients with epidemic pleurodynia. J.A.M.A., **152**:814, 1953.

Tobin, J. O. H.: Coxsackie viruses. Brit. Med. Bull., **9**:201, 1953.

Torrey, R. G.: Epidemic diaphragmatic pleurodynia or "devil's grip." Am. J. Med. Sc., **168**:564, 1924.

Warin, J. F., Davies, J. B., Sanders, F. K. and Vizosa, A. D.: Oxford epidemic of Bornholm disease. Brit. Med. J., **i**:1345, 1953.

TOXIC AND METABOLIC DISORDERS OF MUSCLES

Myasthenia Gravis

Definition.—This name refers to a condition characterized by weakness and by abnormal fatigue of the striated muscles, which is not constantly associated with any demonstrable anatomical lesions. It is also called asthenic bulbar palsy, bulbar palsy without anatomical basis, myasthenia gravis pseudoparalytica, and Goldflam's disease.

Pathological Anatomy.—It seems to be agreed that in perhaps half of all cases of myasthenia gravis, the thymus gland is enlarged and in a very few

cases it is the seat of a malignant growth. In many cases, however, there are no gross changes apparent. A number of histological studies have been made recently. Murray and McDonald state that the thymus tumors are all of essentially the same type and are composed of lymphocytes and large pale cells with indefinite cell boundaries and faintly acidophil cytoplasm. They state that it is not easy to distinguish the malignant from the benign types. Sloan has made a study of the thymus glands which showed no gross changes. He states that the individual lobes of the gland are enlarged, that the cortex is increased in width and density and that the normally sharp differentiation between cortex and medulla is lost. These changes are due to infiltration by large numbers of lymphocytes. In most cases there were also an abnormal number of lymphoid follicles with germinal centers in the medulla. Sloan states that similar changes are found in the thymus glands of patients suffering from acromegaly, Addison's disease and hyperthyroidism.

Another feature of the disease is the presence of clusters of lymphocytes in the striated muscles, which have been called *lymphorrhages*. These are not constant, and even when present, may be found only after hundreds of sections have been made. The same deposits of lymphocytes have been found in cases of hyperthyroidism, where they are often associated with muscular weakness of a somewhat similar type. Numerous studies have been made of the muscle fibers with negative results. Some pathologists have found granular degeneration, hyaline changes and proliferation of the sarcolemmal nuclei, but there seems to be no uniformity in such minor alterations. No convincing lesions have ever been discovered in the nervous system, despite many careful histological studies.

Etiology.—The cause of myasthenia is unknown. There is in most cases no evidence that the disease is inherited though a few instances are reported in which two children in one family were affected. Since complete remissions occur, it is evident that there are no irreversible lesions. It is generally believed that a metabolic disorder is responsible and this interferes with neuromuscular transmission. The high incidence of tumor of the thymus gland must have some significance though removal of this tumor has small value in therapy. There is evidence that disorders of the thyroid gland and possibly the adrenal may play a role. A popular theory is that deficiency of acetylcholine or an excess of cholinesterase is responsible but this theory does not explain all the facts. The old theory that a curare-like toxin is responsible is not completely discredited.

The fact that some newborn infants of mothers who have myasthenia have transient myasthenia seems to lend some weight to this theory.

Clinical Features.—Some textbooks state that myasthenia gravis does not

develop before the age of puberty but this is incorrect for with the aid of the prostigmine test we have found a number of cases of this disease in children between the ages of eighteen months and ten years. Strangely enough most of these children were females and all but two were Negroes. In some instances more than one case is found in a family.

The onset frequently follows an acute infection especially an upper respiratory infection such as influenza or bronchitis. Since it is well known that such infections may cause exacerbations of symptoms in myasthenia, it is probable that they merely bring to light a preexisting condition and are of no etiological significance.

Kimura and Van Allen report a study of 26 cases in which myasthenia gravis developed within days or years following removal of a benign or malignant thymoma.

The essential symptoms are abnormal fatigability, weakness and finally paralysis of the striated muscles. The onset is usually gradual but may be almost apoplectic as in a case given in abstract below. As a rule, the muscles innervated by the cranial nerves are affected first, and later the weakness becomes generalized. Occasionally, the weakness is generalized from the first. Remissions and exacerbations are very characteristic but are found only in a minority of cases. Usually, diplopia is the first symptom, and this is accompanied or followed by the appearance of ptosis of one or of both eyelids, and by some limitation of ocular movement. Usually, upward rotation of the bulb is affected before any other movement, and the palsies do not correspond to the distribution of any single nerve. The pupils react normally. In the mornings the symptoms are least severe and the lidslits may

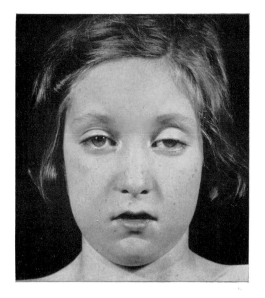

Fig. 296. Myasthenia gravis in a girl of 10 years showing the ptosis of the eyelids, relaxation of the face and sagging jaws. She was then in her third exacerbation, the first and second having occurred at the ages of six and eight years respectively.

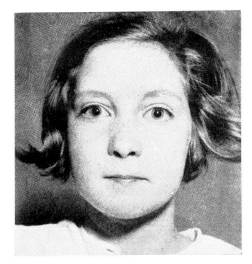

Fig. 297. Same Patient shown in figure 296 showing disappearance of all signs after a few days treatment with prostigmine.

be of normal width. As the day wears on, however, the lid droops more and more, until in the evening the pupil may be partially or completely covered. Mild exophthalmos is observed in rare instances and retraction of one or both upper lids may occur. As a rule, weakness of the bulbar muscles develops shortly after the ocular muscles are affected. The voice becomes weak, and, after the patient has talked for a few minutes, it becomes nasal and hoarse. Swallowing is difficult. The tongue cannot be protruded and articulation becomes indistinct. The jaws grow tired when chewing. The face is relaxed, the eyelids cannot be firmly closed, and the corners of the mouth droop. The neck grows weak relatively early in the course of the disease, and the head cannot be lifted from the pillow. Eventually, the entire bodily musculature is affected, but weakness of the bulbar and oculomotor muscles may be present for long periods before the extremities are affected. The weakness of the skeletal muscles is usually generalized and symmetrical, but it may also seem to select the distal muscles, especially those of the hands and forearms. Occasionally, the large proximal muscles are selected so that the distribution of the weakness is not unlike that seen in the common progressive muscular dystrophy. The patient eventually becomes too weak to walk more than a short distance, then walking and standing are impossible, and, finally, the patient is quite helpless, and respiration becomes difficult. The general weakness is apt to develop rather suddenly, and may lead to death from failure of respiration within a few days or hours. There is no muscular atrophy, except for that due to disuse. No fibrillary twitchings are seen. The tendon reflexes are usually normal even when the muscles are very weak. The electrical reactions of the muscles are usually very characteristic. Faradic stimuli produce strong contractions at first, but

as the stimulus is repeated, the contraction grows less and less, until after a number of shocks, the muscle finally fails to respond. After a short rest, the muscle will respond once more, but each time the test is repeated, the muscle fatigues more and more quickly. This is the so-called myasthenic reaction of Jolly. A muscle which is so fatigued as to be unable to respond to faradism may respond to galvanism. The reaction of degeneration is never observed. It must be emphasized that the myasthenic reaction is not peculiar to myasthenia gravis, although its presence in a typical form is strong evidence for this diagnosis.

It is of interest that smooth muscle is not apparently affected. I have never demonstrated fatigue in the pupillary reactions and the intestines, bladder and sphincters are not affected as a rule. The heart seems to be spared. Neither the special senses nor other modalities of sensibility are altered in any way. Then mental condition is unimpaired.

In some cases only the extraocular muscles are involved. This is termed *ocular myasthenia*. Treatment is usually unsatisfactory. Double vision is rarely relieved. If there is ptosis of one lid the restoration of ability to lift the lid merely causes double vision so the patient may prefer to keep the lid closed.

The course of the disease is variable. In some cases the symptoms advance rapidly and death occurs within a few months. In others when the symptoms have developed to a certain degree there is tendency for them to remain at approximately the same level for long periods. In other cases, the child has recurrent exacerbations with complete remissions between. Such remissions have occurred in only a few of our cases, but a survey of the literature would suggest that a remitting course is more common in children than in adults. Infections play an important role in the acute exacerbations of the disease. Emotional reactions may cause immediate and striking increase of the weakness though such episodes are brief.

No metabolic disturbances have been demonstrated which are constant or significant. In a number of cases there is an abnormal excretion of creatine in the urine and diminished excretion of creatinine which is probably to be regarded as a secondary effect of loss of muscle function, since it is found in other diseases affecting the muscles. Hyperthyroidism is found in a small percentage of cases. In some instances, but not in all, remission follows removal of the thyroid gland.

In some cases, enlargement of the thymus gland can be demonstrated by roentgenography.

As a rule, the child of a myasthenic mother is quite healthy. In a very few instances, however, such children may display severe symptoms of myasthenia. Apparently this type of myasthenia is transient and recovery

may be expected within a short time should the child survive the first few days of life. A total of eighteen cases had been reported in 1954. The myasthenia may disappear suddenly, and, if the child has been treated with prostigmine, toxic reactions may occur as the tolerance to this drug is lost. An abstract of such a case is given below. Levin suggests that the term *myasthenia neonatorum* be employed.

Levin has reported two cases in which myasthenia gave rise to symptoms shortly after birth. These children were born of a normal mother. In contrast to the cases mentioned in the previous paragraph, the symptoms persisted indefinitely. Levin suggests that we speak of this as *congenital myasthenia*. In 1954 a total of six such cases had been reported. In 1958 Dr. Arthur King sent us a family of six children. The four boys had congenital myasthenia but the two girls were normal. The family is described briefly below.

Herman states that in 1969, 82 cases of familial myasthenia were reported. He states that the mode of inheritance is not clear. The incidence of mental deficiency in these familial cases is 7.3 per cent.

Diagnosis.—The diagnosis depends upon: (1) The weakness of the striated muscles, usually beginning in the ocular or bulbar muscles, and finally becoming generalized. (2) The history of remissions and exacerbations. (3) The abnormal fatigue which is shown by increase of symptoms in the evenings and by fatigue in repetition of movements of affected muscles, such as moving the eyes upwards, counting to 100, chewing or gripping. (4) The electrical reactions. (5) The presence of lymphorrhages in bits of excised muscle. (6) It is well known that the injection of 0.5 to 1.5 mgs of prostigmine hypodermically will usually cause a dramatic improvement in myasthenia gravis and that this does not occur in other conditions. It must be admitted, however, that occasional cases of myasthenia are relatively or completely unresponsive to this drug. Disappearance of ptosis of the eyelids is the best indication of a response to prostigmine. Diplopia is rarely relieved even when the drug produces an obvious improvement in ocular movements. It should be said that nothing less than an obvious and unequivocal response is of diagnostic value. The injection of prostigmine is not devoid of danger though patients suffering from myasthenia are as a rule very tolerant of this drug. Merrill reports a case of death resulting from the injection of 0.5 mgs in an adult. Atropine should be given whenever prostigmine is injected. (7) The absence of mental changes, of disturbances of sensibility, of alteration of the special senses, and of significant involvement of smooth muscle. (8) Injection of curare has been used to demonstrate latent myasthenia, but this is a non-specific test, for curare causes weakness in normal individuals. It is not without danger. Quinine

has a more specific effect and will often cause pronounced weakness in myasthenic persons who display no symptoms at the time. It does not cause weakness in normal persons. Severe reactions may occur and facilities for artificial respiration must be available. Ocular myopathy and hyperthyroidism probably simulate this disease most closely but an attack of botulism has a very striking resemblance to an acute exacerbation of myasthenia. During the great epidemic of encephalitis cases were described which simulated myasthenia in some respects. It is most important to distinguish between a myasthenic crisis, i.e. sudden weakness due to the disease and a cholinergic crisis due to over-treatment with prostigmine. Osserman and Kaplan suggest that the intravenous injection of tensilon is of diagnostic value. If the patient is having a myasthenic crisis the injection will cause improvement in strength, whereas, if the crisis is due to over-treatment, there will be transient increase of the weakness. The action of this drug is said to be so brief, that there is little danger of its making a cholinergic crisis worse.

Prognosis.—It has been stated above that the course is variable; that the disease may end fatally in a few months, or run a chronic course. When the diagnosis is established beyond all doubt, the prognosis is unfavorable on the whole. Sudden collapse and failure of respiration may occur at any time. In our experience exacerbations are usually a result of acute infections of the respiratory tract. I don't believe that any of our patients have died early in childhood but a number having developed symptoms early, die about the time of adolescence. In my experience when myasthenia gravis is associated with a malignant thymoma it runs a rapidly fatal course.

Treatment.—It may be said at once that there is no curative treatment at present. The patient's general health should be watched carefully since acute infections may lead to sudden death. Infections of the respiratory tract are especially fatal. Rest is very important, since excessive exertion may cause collapse. Prostigmine is of great value but its effect is purely symptomatic. Given in doses of 5 to 15 mgs by mouth it causes striking increase in strength in most but not in all patients. The effect of each dose lasts about two hours. A total dosage of between 50 and 150 mgs may be given in the course of twenty-four hours. By hypodermic injection the action of prostigmine is more rapid and less lasting. Not more than 0.5 or 1.0 mgs should be given by hypodermic injection. Mestinon, i.e. pyridostigmin, is also a valuable drug and it is claimed has less of a tendency to cause intestinal cramps. Various organic esters of phosphoric acid derivatives have been introduced recently. They produce a powerful effect but their use is not without danger. Over-treatment with these agents as well as over-

treatment with prostigmine may cause weakness and collapse. This condition is termed a "cholinergic crisis." It is not easy to distinguish such a crisis from a myasthenic crisis. Complete thymectomy has been performed in many patients. Recently Blalock has performed complete thymectomy in a number of adults suffering from myasthenia gravis. Half of these patients were improved and a few became free of symptoms. Approximately half were not improved. In one patient who had been improved following operation, the symptoms returned some months later. She died suddenly in an acute exacerbation and at post-mortem examination it was found that the thymus gland had regenerated and regained its former bulk. At present it seems that operative removal of the thymus gland is not a satisfactory method of treatment.

Churchill-Davidson states that if a patient becomes resistant to prostigmine, it may be helpful to cause complete paralysis with d-tubocurarine and employ artificial respiration. After seven days, the d-tubocurarine is withdrawn and the patient may then be free of symptoms for a short time even without prostigmine. Soon the myasthenia recurs, but the patient will then respond to prostigmine for a number of months. Kornfeld *et al.* state that the administration of calcium to patients who do not respond to the standard drugs may cause them to respond more satisfactorily.

Drachman has shown that the symptoms of myasthenia gravis are increased by thyroid deficiency and also by thyrotoxicosis.

Treatment for failure of respiration and bulbar palsy are described in the discussion of bulbar palsy due to poliomyelitis.

CASE HISTORY (795106).—*Four male siblings who have had ocular myasthenia since birth. One shows severe myasthenia of the skeletal muscles and the other three only minimal weakness and fatigue. Two sisters are quite healthy.*

Dr. Arthur King was kind enough to send these patients to Dr. Frank B. Walsh and I saw them in consultation with Dr. Walsh. There are six children in all ranging in age from 18 years to 3 years. The youngest two children are girls and the older children are all boys. The girls and the parents are quite healthy. There is no blood relationship between the parents and no history of any condition similar to that of the boys in ancestors or collateral relatives.

Since early infancy the boys have all displayed identical palsies of the extraocular muscles. There is mild bilateral ptosis of the upper lids. Lateral movements of the eyes are scarcely perceptible. Upward deviation is minimal if present at all, but downward movement is only slightly limited. The orbiculares are weak on both sides. The pupils react normally. The drooping of the lids is easily increased by a few moments' exercise.

The oldest of the boys showed obvious weakness of the skeletal muscles when he was less than two years old, and his weakness slowly increased.

He was once able to walk 100 yards without too much difficulty but now cannot stand without support. He spends most of his time in a wheel chair. The weakness involves all the striated muscles but is most evident in the shoulder and pelvic girdle muscles. He can arise from the floor only with the help of his arms. The muscles are all slender and the muscles about the shoulder are smaller than the others. It is possible that this is due to disuse. Muscle tone is greatly reduced and he can place his feet behind his head with ease. The tendon reflexes are active and easily elicited.

The injection of prostigmine causes an unequivocal and dramatic response. With the help of this drug, he can walk almost normally and can spring up from the floor as a normal young man should. The ptosis of the lids disappears and all the ocular muscles display normal or nearly normal power except for the elevators which show only moderate improvement. Dr. David Grob has made electromyograms with and without prostigmine and states that the results of the tests are typical of myasthenia gravis.

The three younger brothers show only minimal weakness of the skeletal muscles. They have never been able to run more than a short distance, however. They notice fatigue in speech and in chewing. Their symptoms respond in striking fashion to injection of prostigmine.

Case History (Ped. A-66982).—*Baby of myasthenic mother showed signs of myasthenia for some days after birth. Complete spontaneous recovery within three weeks.*

B. A., a colored male, was born on November 24, 1948. His mother had been suffering from myasthenia gravis for several years. In November, 1947, the mother had had the thymus gland removed and thereafter did well and managed to get along without prostigmine as a rule. She was given prostigmine, however, at the time of delivery.

The day after birth when the child was first examined by a pediatrician it was found that the baby could not nurse or swallow. The cry was weak. The eyes were directed down and apparently could not be rolled up. The mouth could not be closed and hung open apparently as a result of weakness of the jaws. There was also weakness of the lips. The eyelids could not be firmly closed. No weakness of the extremities was made out, however. These symptoms were promptly controlled by the administration of prostigmine. On several occasions this drug was withdrawn and the symptoms always returned as before. By the end of the first week of life, however, the symptoms had begun to diminish and there was gradual improvement. The prostigmine was no longer necessary and the child was discharged free from all symptoms on December 17, 1948. Clinical and roentgenographic examinations revealed no evidence of enlargement of the thymus gland.

The mother (U. No. 309888) had had four pregnancies before she developed myasthenia gravis. In three cases the baby was quite healthy. The fourth baby died nine days after delivery of unknown causes.

August 10, 1949, the child was reexamined and found to be in good condition without signs of myasthenia.

CASE HISTORY (Ped. A-25735).—*Boy of five years developed palsy of the bulbar muscles and generalized muscular weakness in the course of an hour. Failure of respiration seemed imminent on the second day but was averted by injection of prostigmine. Prompt recovery.*

J. W., a colored boy of five years, was brought into the Harriet Lane Home on July 6, 1942. A few hours before he had been playing outdoors with the other children seemingly as active and vigorous as ever. Towards noon, he came into the house and asked his mother for a drink. He drank without difficulty. A few minutes later, he asked for a cookie. He could not swallow this and choked and strangled. Shortly after this his mother noticed that his eyes were crossed and his speech had become thick and indistinct. He lay on the floor and could not get up. He vomited once, possibly because of the choking.

When brought to the hospital pulse and temperature were normal but respiration was rapid and weak. There was a variable degree of ptosis of both lids. He complained of double vision. The left external rectus was weak and on the attempt to move his eyes to the right, coarse nystagmoid movements of the eyes were seen which undoubtedly were due to muscular weakness but which were at first mistaken for true nystagmus. There was weakness and relaxation of the face, most evident on the left. The jaws were weak and he could not chew. The tongue could not be fully protruded and articulation was indistinct. He could not swallow. There was also pronounced general weakness of the skeletal muscles for he could not stand or walk and could not sustain the head. The pupils were equal and reacted well.

The next day he was weaker and had several attacks of dyspnea possibly due to getting food or saliva into the bronchi for when he was fed by gavage, the fluid came up into his throat. At this time he seemed to be moribund and it was thought necessary to perform tracheotomy. The nose and throat surgeon, however, suggested that he be given an injection of prostigmine. There was an immediate and dramatic response. Respiration became easy, the eyelids lifted, the articulation became clear and the child could swallow once more. Thereafter, the child made rapid strides towards recovery. The symptoms were controlled by 30 mgs of prostigmine by mouth every three hours. Soon this was reduced to 15 mgs and then stopped. He remained free of symptoms for seven years.

On October 12, 1949 he noticed double vision. His mother noticed that his left eyelid drooped. No other symptoms were present. Examination on October 14 showed merely drooping of the left lid. With brief exercise both lids were easily fatigued so they dropped down over the pupils. No diplopia was present at that time. An injection of prostigmine gave complete relief.

BIBLIOGRAPHY

CELESIA, G. G.: Myasthenia gravis in two siblings. Arch. of Neurol., **12:**206, 1965.

CHURCHILL-DAVIDSON, H. C.: Motor end plate changes in myasthenia gravis. Am. J. Phys. Med., **38:**159, 1959.

DRACHMAN, D. B.: The effect of thyroid status on myasthenia gravis. New England J. Med., **266:**330, 1962.

EATON, L. M. AND CLAGETT, C. T.: Thymectomy in treatment of myasthenia gravis. J.A.M.A., **142:**963, 1950.

GROB, D.: The course and management of myasthenia gravis. J.A.M.A., **153:**529, 1953.

————: Myasthenia gravis. Arch. Int. Med., **108:**615, 1961.

HERMAN, M. N.: Familial myasthenia gravis. Arch. of Neurology, **20:**140, 1969.

HERRMANN, C.: Myasthenia gravis occurring in families. Neurology, **16:**75, 1966.

HOFFER, P. F. A.: Therapy of myasthenia. Bull. New York Acad. Med., **35:**231, 1959.

KIMURA, J. AND VAN ALLEN, M. W.: Post-thymectomy myasthenia gravis. Neurology, **17:**413, 1967.

KORNFELD, P. *et al.:* Role of calcium in myasthenia gravis. Neurology, **21:**466, 1969.

LIEBERMAN, A. T.: Myasthenia gravis—Acute fulminating case in a child five years old. J.A.M.A., **120:**1209, 1942.

LEVIN, P. M.: Congenital myasthenia in siblings. Arch. Neurol. & Psychiat., **62:**745, 1949.

MACKAY, R. I.: Congenital myasthenia gravis. Arch. Dis. Child., **26:**289, 1951.

MACRAE, D.: Myasthenia gravis in early childhood. Pediatrics, **13:**511, 1954.

McKEEVER, G. E.: Myasthenia gravis in mother and newborn son. J.A.M.A., **147:**320, 1951.

MERRILL, G. G.: Neostigmine toxicity. Report of fatality following diagnostic test for myasthenia gravis. J.A.M.A., **136:**362, 1948.

MILLICHAP, J. G. AND DODGE, P. R.: Diagnosis and treatment of myasthenia gravis in infancy, childhood and adolescence. Neurology, **10:**1007, 1960.

MILHORAT, A. T. AND WOLFF, H. G.: III Metabolism of creatine and creatinine in myasthenia gravis. *Ibid.,* **39:**354, 1938.

MURRAY, N. A. AND MACDONALD, J. R.: Tumors of the thymus in myasthenia gravis. Am. J. Clin. Path., **15:**87, 1945.

NEVIN, S.: Primary diseases of the voluntary muscles. J. Neurol. & Psychiat., **1:**120, 1938, new series.

OSSERMAN, K.: The treatment of myasthenia gravis with mestinon. J.A.M.A., **155:**961, 1954.

OSSERMAN, K. AND KAPLAN, L.: Studies in myasthenia gravis. The use of edrophonium in differentiating myasthenic from cholinergic weakness. Arch. Neurol. & Psychiat., **70:**384, 1953.

PERLO, V. P. *et al.:* Myasthenia gravis. Neurology, **16:**431, 1966.

ROTHBART, H. B.: Myasthenia gravis in children. J.A.M.A., **108:**715, 1937.

SCHWAB, R. S. AND TIMBERLAKE, W. H.: Treatment of myasthenia gravis with mestinon. New England J. Med., **251:**271, 1954.

SLOAN, H. E.: The thymus in myasthenia gravis. Surgery, **13:**154, 1943.

STRICKROOT, F. L. *et al.:* Myasthenia gravis in an infant born of a myasthenic mother. J.A.M.A., **120:**1207, 1942.

————: Symposium on myasthenia gravis. Am. J. Med., **19:**655 to 740, 1955.

TUDDENHAM, A. D.: Myasthenia gravis in a boy aged 19 months. Guy's Hospital Reports, **104:** 254, 1955.

VIETS, H. R. AND SCHWAB, R. S.: The diagnosis and treatment of myasthenia gravis with special reference to the use of prostigmine. J.A.M.A., **113:**559, 1939.

WALKER, M. B.: Treatment of myasthenia gravis with prostigmine. Lancet, **1:**1200, 1934.

WALSH, F. B.: Myasthenia gravis and its ocular signs. A review. Tr. Am. Ophth. Soc. 1943. 79th Meeting.

WALSH, F. B. AND HOYT, W. F.: External ophthalmoplegia as a part of congenital myasthenia in siblings. Amer. Jour. Ophthal., **47**:28, 1959.

WYLLIE, W. G., BODIAN, M. AND BURROWS, N.: Myasthenia gravis in children. Arch. Dis. Child., **26**:457, 1951.

ZIEGLER, L. H.: Recurring myasthenia gravis in a boy. Med. Clin. North America, **13**:No. 6, p. 1374, 1930.

PERIODIC FAMILY PARALYSIS WITH LOW SERUM POTASSIUM OR NORMAL SERUM POTASSIUM

Definition.—This is a familial disease which is characterized by recurrent attacks of paralysis of the striated muscles with loss of tendon reflexes and abolition of the electrical reactions. The serum potassium is usually low during attacks.

Pathological Anatomy.—In the early stages of this disease, it is often stated that the muscles show no anatomical changes, though it is claimed that during a paralytic episode, vacuoles may develop in the muscle fibers. Possibly the vacuoles diminish or disappear after strength returns. In the cases in which persistent weakness and atrophy of the proximal muscles develop in the later stages of the disease, Pearson has shown that there is extensive vacuolization of the muscle fibers, with hyalinization and proliferation of the sarcolemmal nuclei. This statement applies to the type associated with reduction of the serum potassium, the type in which the serum potassium is normal and the type in which the serum potassium is elevated.

Etiology.—Until recently nothing was known about the cause of this disease except for the fact that it is inherited. Studies by Aitken *et al.* have now revealed that there is significant fluctuation in the potassium content of the blood. These investigators state that when the patient's blood potassium falls to 12 mgs per 100 cc, there is marked weakness and when it reaches 10 mgs there is paralysis. By giving glucose or by injecting insulin, it was found to be possible to cause this reduction in potassium of the blood. This reaction is found in healthy persons, but is exaggerated in persons subject to this disease. The investigators suggest that when glucose is stored in the tissues, potassium is removed from the blood stream. The observation that a heavy meal would bring on an attack is thus supported by the experimental work. More recent investigations have led to the belief that there is no constant correlation between the level of the serum potassium and the presence or absence of paralysis. In some cases, but not in all, the administration of potassium will relieve the paralysis even when the serum potassium is within normal limits. Vastola and Bertrand, as a result of analyses of serum and muscle during attacks of paralysis, find that there is an increase of extracellular and intracellular water and also an increase of intracellular potassium.

Conn *et al.* have shown that the attacks of paralysis are preceded by large

increases in urinary aldosterone and retention of sodium. As the level of the potassium falls, the serum sodium rises to an abnormally high level. It is stated that when a diet very low in sodium is given, attacks of periodic paralysis cannot be induced.

Evidences of abnormalities of carbohydrate metabolism have been found including diabetic glucose tolerance curves.

Engel *et al.* describe a very complete biochemical study of this disease and conclude that the metabolic error is still undefined.

Clinical Features.—In most instances, the history reveals that a number of relatives are affected in the same manner, and the disease may often be traced through five or six generations. It may skip a generation, and then reappear in the next. Obviously, it may be transmitted by persons who are apparently unaffected. In some cases no family history is obtained. Males are affected as frequently as females, and either may convey the disease to their children. However, Macklin states that the mode of inheritance suggests a dominant factor. Myers suggests that we are dealing with a dominant trait with incomplete penetrance.

The onset is on an average at about the age of 14 years, but symptoms may develop as early as the fifth or sixth years, or be deferred to the twenty-fifth year. The attacks may be frequent and severe, or a patient may have only one or two attacks during a long life.

As a rule, the paralysis develops at night when the patient is in bed asleep. Sometimes the patient may experience drowsiness, numbness and tingling in the legs the preceding evening; an excessive appetite or thirst; or a sense of heaviness or fatigue. Such prodromata enable some patients to predict an attack with considerable accuracy. They may, however, pass off without further incident. Many patients have no warning of an impending attack whatever. Early in the morning the patient awakens and finds that he is paralyzed. The weakness begins, as a rule, in the legs, then extends to the arms, and finally involves the trunk and neck. In general, the proximal muscles are affected first, and the fingers and toes may be moved freely after the hips and shoulders are paralyzed. The cranial nerves are not affected except in a few exceptional cases. Several times weakness of the facial muscles has been described, and in one case there was ptosis of both eyelids. The intercostals and accessory muscles of respiration are always paralyzed in severe attacks, but the diaphragm is rarely affected. Disturbances of speech and swallowing are mentioned, but such symptoms may be due in part, at least, to the respiratory distress. There is never any disturbance of sphincter control or loss of sensibility. No disturbance in consciousness has ever been described. The weakness may be mild and the patient may be able to continue his work; but in severe attacks the patient may be completely helpless and unable to move a single joint for many

hours. Holtzapple describes local attacks in which the paralysis is confined to a single extremity or to one half of the body. In some instances, the paralysis may be complete in some muscles and only partial in other muscle groups.

The duration is variable. Mild attacks may last for three or four hours, and severe ones may last several days. When improvement once begins, it is very rapid and recovery is complete. Holtzapple states that patients are able to perform hard work on a farm a few hours after they have been completely paralyzed. In a few cases, relapses have occurred soon after the patient began to improve.

The intervals between the attacks are subject to great variation. In many cases, attacks are infrequent at first, but gradually occur at shorter and shorter intervals until paralysis may appear every week. Later in life, they again become less frequent. There is no invariable rule, however.

The most striking feature of the paralysis is the complete loss of irritability of the muscles. Neither faradic nor galvanic reactions can be obtained from paralyzed muscles. Likewise, mechanical stimuli are ineffective. The tendon and cutaneous reflexes are abolished. These changes are proportional to the loss of voluntary power, and develop coincidently with the weakness. In intervals between attacks electrical reactions are normal. In severe attacks, the heart is dilated and functional murmurs may occur. The pulse is sometimes feeble, slow or irregular. Respiration may be shallow and rapid. In one of Goldflam's cases, there was dangerous asphyxia, so that artificial respiration was necessary for several hours. Evidently the diaphragm may be involved, as well as the intercostal muscles. The bowels never move during an attack, but Holtzapple has observed diarrhea and vomiting during recovery. Urine is not passed, despite the fact that sphincter control is preserved. Profuse sweating is described during the attacks, and this may play some part in the partial suppression of urine. The temperature is normal or subnormal. According to the work of Aitken *et al.* one would expect to find the blood potassium below 12 mgs per 100 cc whenever the patient is suffering from definite weakness. Stoll and others have shown that the electrocardiogram shows a flattening of the T wave during an attack of paralysis. This is regarded as characteristic of a reduction of the potassium content of the blood.

Myers reports attacks in two children in which paralysis was associated with rigidity of the muscles and pain on passive movement. The tendon reflexes were present. These children afterwards had typical attacks with flaccidity of the muscles. Their father also was subject to typical attacks with flaccidity. Myers found that there were 25 cases of the typical disease in this family. It was shown that six generations were affected. Holtzapple

had studied the same family earlier. Myers points out that the disease seems to be dying out in this family for one third of the first generation was affected but only one twelfth of the fifth generation.

The patients are usually quite healthy between attacks, and examination reveals no abnormality. They seem to be able to endure fatigue as well as other people. After a number of years, wasting and weakness of the proximal muscles develops in some patients. This process may continue even when the paralytic episodes are infrequent.

Various factors have been stated to play some part in exciting attacks of paralysis. Fatigue and excessive exertion are often mentioned. Holtzapple emphasizes the danger of over-eating.

Diagnosis.—The recurrent attacks of weakness or paralysis occurring over a period of many years are almost pathognomonic. The diagnosis is greatly strengthened if a positive family history is obtained, and if the electrical reactions are lost during an attack, the classification of the disease cannot be questioned. Failure of the muscles to respond to percussion is possibly just as significant as loss of electrical reactions. The reduction of potassium in the serum is characteristic as is the electrocardiogram. In some cases, but not in all, an attack may be induced by the injection of glucose and insulin. The differentiation from Gamstorp's disease which is described in the following pages, would seem to require determination of the serum potassium during an attack of paralysis. Diffuse weakness of the skeletal muscles and sometimes even paralysis may occur in various conditions in which the serum potassium is reduced. We may mention Cushing's syndrome, prolonged diarrhea, excessive vomiting, over-treatment of Addison's disease with desoxycorticosterone, and over-treatment of diabetic coma with insulin. It may also occur in some cases of renal failure. The electrocardiogram shows depression of the S-T segment and diminution, disappearance or inversion of the T wave. The administration of potassium will give relief. Certain adenomas of the adrenal cortex may produce an excess of aldosterone which may cause reduction of serum potassium with muscular weakness or paralysis, changes in the electrocardiogram, polyuria, elevation of the serum sodium, alkalosis, tetany resistant to calcium, hypertension and chronic renal failure. Conn describes the clinical features and methods of diagnosis of primary aldosteronism.

E. Satoyoshi *et al.* describe a type of hyperthyroidism associated with periodic paralysis and low serum potassium. Treatment of the thyroid disease prevented the paralytic attacks.

Camachio and Blizzard describe a familial type of hypokalemic alkalosis with onset in early infancy.

Tyler and Poskanzer and Kerr have studied families in which the plasma

potassium level is normal during attacks of paralysis. This is termed a third type of periodic paralysis. The muscles show the same vacuoles that are found in the other types of periodic paralysis. Poskanzer and Kerr state that sodium chloride is helpful in treating attacks and that a combination of 9-α-fluorohydrocortisone and acetazolamide is effective in preventing attacks.

Prognosis.—It is generally agreed that the attacks grow less frequent after middle life, although this rule is subject to exceptions. Death is infrequent in the attacks, but in the seventeen cases described by Holtzapple, six deaths occurred during the twenty-year period of observation. Talbot estimates that death had occurred in paralytic episodes in about 10 per cent of the 400 cases which had been described in 1941. In a number of cases, weakness and atrophy of the proximal muscles develop after a number of years so the clinical picture resembles that of progressive muscular dystrophy.

Treatment.—In view of the work of Aitken *et al.* one would imagine that the patient should take a diet low in carbohydrates and high in potassium. In acute attacks of paralysis Aitken has given 12 grams of potassium chloride by mouth and has reported improvement within 10 minutes and recovery within an hour. Potassium salts may be taken by mouth every day to prevent paralysis.

Sotoyoshi *et al.* gave thiamine to his patients who were subject to frequent attacks of paralysis associated with reduction of serum potassium and found that the paralytic episodes were always reduced in frequency, and, sometimes, were completely prevented. They also found that the intensive administration of thiamine to subjects who always reacted to the injection of insulin and glucose by the development of paralysis protected them completely from this paralytic reaction.

CASE HISTORIES (B-43000 and B-42999).—*Two little girls, Sharon G. and Karen G., were identical twins. They had always been healthy in every way and their development was quite normal.*

In January, 1957 at the age of one year and eight months, they began to have recurrent attacks in which they were very weak or paralysed. Such attacks lasted for several hours as a rule and when the twins were seen in August at the age of two years and three months, they were having on an average two attacks a week. It should be said that there was no history of any condition in the family resembling that of the twins.

On examination the children were well developed and nourished and medical and neurological examinations were completely negative. No alteration of the serum electrolytes was found.

Injection of insulin and glucose caused paralysis of the extremities in one child and great weakness in the other. In the paralysed child the ten-

don reflexes were lost. The electrocardiogram showed changes characteristic of potassium deficiency and the serum potassium was estimated at 2.4
mEq. The administration of potassium resulted in prompt recovery. Repetition of this test gave identical results.

BIBLIOGRAPHY

AITKEN, R. S., ALLOTT, E. N., CASTLEDEN, L. AND WALKER, M.: Observations on a case of familial periodic paralysis. Clin. Sco., **3**:47, 1937.

BRADY, I. A. AND DUDLEY, A. W. JR.: Thyrotoxic hypokalemic periodic paralysis. Arch. of
Neurol., **21**:1, 1969.

BREMOND, A. AND DANIELS, A. P.: Family periodic paralysis and its transition into spinal muscular atrophy. Brain, **57**:91, 1934.

CAMACHIO, A. M. AND BLIZZARD, R. M.: Congenital hypokalemia. Am. J. Dis. Child., **103**:535, 1962.

CONN, J. W.: Evolution of primary aldosteronism as a highly specific clinical entity. J.A.M.A.,
172:1650, 1960.

CONN, J. W.: Primary aldosteronism. Ann. Int. Med., **44**:1, 1956.

CONN, J. W. *et al.:* Intermittent aldosteronism in periodic paralysis: Dependence of attacks
on retention of sodium and failure to induce attacks by restriction of dietary sodium.
Lancet, **i**:802, 1957.

DANOWSKI, T. S.: Newer concepts of the role of potassium in disease. Am. J. Med., **7**:525, 1949.

DYKEN, M. *et al.:* Hypokalemic periodic paralysis: Children with permanent myopathic paralysis. Neurology, **19**:691, 1969.

ELKINTON, J. R. AND TARAIL, R.: Present status of potassium therapy. Am. J. Med., **9**:200, 1950.

ENGEL, A. G. *et al.:* Studies on carbohydrate metabolism and mitochondrial respiratory activities in primary hypokalemic periodic paralysis. Neurology, **17**:329, 1967.

ENGEL, A. G. *et al.:* Clinical and electromyographic studies in patient with primary hypokalemic
periodic paralysis. Amer. Jour. Med., **38**:626, 1965.

HOLTZAPPLE, G. E.: Periodic paralysis. J.A.M.A., **45**:1224, 1905.

KRETCHMER, N., DICKINSON, A. AND KARL, R.: Aldosteronism in a nine year old child. Am. J. Dis.
Child., **94**:452, 1957.

MACLACHLAN, T. K.: Familial periodic paralysis. Brain, **55**:47, 1933.

McQUARRIE, I. AND ZIEGLER, M. R.: Hereditary periodic paralysis. Metabolism, **1**:129, 1952.

MYERS, W. A.: Familial periodic paralysis traced in one family for five generations. (Note about
atypical episodes with rigidity) Pennsylvania M. J., **52**:1060, 1949.

OLIVER, C. P., ZIEGLER, M. R. AND McQUARRIE, I.: Hereditary periodic paralysis in a family showing varied manifestations. Am. J. Dis. Child., **68**:308, 1944.

PEARSON, C. M.: The periodic paralyses. Differential features and pathology in permanent
myopathic weakness. Brain, **87**:1964.

POSKANZER, D. C. AND KERR, D. N.: Third type of periodic paralysis with normokalemia. Am. J.
Med., **31**:328, 1961.

SATOYOSHI, E. *et al.:* Periodic paralysis in hyperthyroidism. Neurology, **13**:746, 1963.

SATOYOSHI, E. *et al.:* Periodic paralysis. A study of carbohydrate and thiamine metabolism.
Neurology, **13**:24, 1963.

STOLL, B. AND NISNEWITZ, S.: Electrocardiographic studies in a case of periodic paralysis. Arch.
Int. Med., **67**:755, 1941.

TALBOTT, J. H.: Periodic paralysis. Medicine, **20**:85, 1941.

TYLER, F. H. *et al.:* Clinical manifestations and inheritance of a type of periodic paralysis
without hypopotassemia. J. Clin. Invest., **30**::492, 1951.

VAN'T HOFF, W.: Familial myotonic periodic paralysis. Quart. J. Med., **31**:385, 1962.

VASTOLA, E. F. AND BERTRAND, C. A.: Intracellular water and potassium in periodic paralysis.
Neurology, **6**:523, 1956.

FAMILIAL PERIODIC PARALYSIS AND MYOTONIA WITH ELEVATION OF SERUM POTASSIUM

Definition.—A heredofamilial condition characterized by recurrent attacks of weakness or paralysis of the skeletal muscles and myotonia associated in most instances with elevation of the serum potassium.

Pathological Anatomy.—See Familial Periodic Paralysis with Low Serum Potassium.

Clinical Features.—Gamstorp has studied 138 patients with this condition. She states that the disease is inherited as a dominant characteristic with almost complete penetrance. It is equally prevalent in the two sexes and either sex may transmit it.

The attacks begin before the age of 10 years in 90 per cent of cases. They occur during rest after exertion. In mild attacks there may be merely weakness of one extremity, but in severe attacks, there is generalized weakness so the patient may be unable to sit up or even roll over in bed. Respiration is seldom involved. The muscles innervated by the cranial nerves are mildly involved in about half of the patients. The tendon reflexes are reduced in some attacks. Chvostek's sign is found during less than half of the attacks. The weakness lasts an hour or less as a rule. In three fourths of the patients the attacks occur on an average once a week. It is said that the attacks are frequent and brief in childhood, longer and more severe at puberty and most troublesome up to the age of 30 years. After the age of 30 years, there is usually improvement. Only two patients showed slight weakness between attacks and only one patient displayed atrophy of the muscles.

Egan and Klein studied three families and found evidence that thirty members had this disease. Some eleven patients were interviewed and five were studied. The onset of symptoms was often two and three years. They found that epinephrine and glucagon would relieve the symptoms.

Between attacks the serum electrolytes and the electrocardiogram are normal. During an attack, the serum potassium is elevated but there is no change in the urinary potassium excretion. The electrocardiogram reveals changes characteristic of increased serum potassium. Attacks of paralysis are produced by the oral administration of potassium in amounts which would not produce symptoms in normal individuals. Calcium administered during an attack usually terminates it promptly. The administration of glucose with or without insulin, has a beneficial effect. The electromyogram shows signs of loss of muscle fibers in some cases.

Buchtal *et al.* state that during the attacks the mechanical irritability of the muscles is increased in contrast to the cases of periodic paralysis in

which the serum potassium is diminished in which the muscle irritability is reduced or lost.

In 1886, Eulenberg described paramyotonia congenita, an inherited condition in which exposure to cold caused myotonia. He also mentioned that weakness might result from exposure to cold. Less stress was placed on the weakness, however. In 1957, French and Kilpatrick studied a patient with paramyotonia who was subject to attacks of weakness. They found that a dose of potassium by mouth would cause weakness of several days duration. Articles by Drager *et al.,* Van der Meulen *et al.,* Van't Hoff, McArdle and Gamstorp describe the same findings. Exposure to cold would produce myotonia of the face, eyelids, tongue and thenar muscles and the administration of potassium salts would give rise to weakness.

Layzer *et al.* published a study of 12 patients among 35 affected individuals who came from 4 families. Of the 12 patients studied, 6 had attacks of weakness and myotonia, 3 had myotonia but no weakness and 3 had no complaints but had myotonia on examination. The condition was an autosomal dominant. Paralysis was apt to occur after exercise and sleep. Fasting seemed to induce some attacks and eating seemed to help. The paralysis was apt to be brief in the day, but nocturnal attacks might last several days. The administration of potassium induced weakness in all 4 patients tested. All patients had myotonia on examination which could be induced by percussion of the tongue, thenar muscles or extensors of the wrist. Some patients said that cold increased the myotonia. Electromyography was effective in demonstrating myotonia in all patients. It was concluded that hyperkalemic periodic paralysis and paramyotonia congenita are identical. Diamox, diuril and hydrodiuril were all helpful in some patients but not in all.

Diagnosis.—The diagnosis seems to rest upon the clinical features and laboratory findings described above. The family history is important.

It must be kept in mind that potassium intoxication may result from renal failures, excessive administration of potassium, concentration of body fluids, diabetic coma and Addison's disease. Pollen and Williams describe cases of Addison's disease complicated by renal failure in which great elevation of the serum potassium occurred with extensive paralysis, weakness of respiration, myocardial failure, sensory disturbances, loss of reflexes and apparent involvement of the cranial nerves. Transfusion of blood that has been kept in the blood bank too long should be mentioned. Hypoaldosteronism also results in elevation of the serum potassium. In such cases, it is stated that cardiac arrest may occur without paralysis of the skeletal muscles, but in some instances paralysis of the skeletal muscles oc-

curs without heart failure. The electrocardiogram shows first an elevation of the T wave, then decrease in size of the R wave with increase of the S component, then disappearance of the P wave and obliteration of the S-T segment. Finally there is a series of very large, biphasic S-T complexes. The proper treatment is the administration of sodium chloride or calcium.

Prognosis.—It seems that the condition is never fatal and does not prevent the patient from leading an active life. There is said to be improvement after the age of 30 years.

Treatment.—Gamstorp states that except for symptomatic treatment during an attack, no therapy has been devised.

BIBLIOGRAPHY

ARMSTRONG, F. S.: Hyperkalemic familial periodic paralysis. Ann. Int. Med., **57**:455, 1962.

BELL, H. *et al.:* Hyperkalemic paralysis due to adrenal insufficiency. Arch. of Int. Med., **115**:418, 1965.

BROOKS, J. E.: Hyperkalemic periodic paralysis. Archives of Neurology, **20**:13, 1969.

BUCHTAL, F. *et al.:* Paresis and hyperexcitability in adynamia episodica hereditaria. Neurology, **8**:347, 1958.

BULL, G. M. *et al.:* Hyperpotassemic paralysis. Lancet, **ii**:60, 1953.

DRAGER, G. A. *et al.:* Paramyotonia congenita. Arch. of Neurol. and Psychiat., **80**:1, 1958.

DUNLOP, D.: Eighty-six cases of Addison's disease. Brit. Jour. Med., **2**:887, 1963.

EGAN, T. AND KLEIN, R.: Hyperkalemic familial period paralysis. Pediatrics, **24**:761, 1959.

FRENCH, E. B. AND KILPATRICK, R.: A variety of paramyotonia congenita. Jour. of Neurol., Neurosurg. and Psychiat., **20**:40, 1957.

GAMSTORP, I.: Adynamia episodica hereditaria and myotonia. Acta neurol. Scandinav., **39**:41, 1963.

GAMSTORP, I.: Adynamia Episodica Hereditaria. Acta paediat., **45**:supp. 108, 1956.

GAMSTORP, I. *et al.:* Adynamia episodica hereditaria. Am. J. Med., **23**:385, 1957.

HELWEG-LARSON, H. F. *et al.:* Hereditary transient muscular paralysis in Denmark. Acta Genet., **5**:263, 1955.

HUDSON, J. B. *et al.:* Hypoaldosteronism. New England Jour. Med., **257**:529, 1957.

LAMBREW, C. T. *et al.:* Hypoaldosteronism. Amer. Jour. Med., **31**:81, 1961.

LAYZER, R. B. *et al.:* Hyperkalemic periodic paralysis. Arch. of Neurol., **16**:455, 1967.

MACDONALD, R. D. *et al.:* Myopathy of hyperkalemic periodic paralysis. Arch. of Neurol., **19**:274, 1968.

MCARDLE, B.: Adynamia episodica hereditaria. Brain, **85**:121, 1962.

PEARSON, C. M.: The periodic paralyses. Differential features and pathology in permanent myopathic weakness. Brain, **87**:341, 1964.

POLLEN, R. H. AND WILLIAMS, R. H.: Hyperkalemic neuromyopathy in Addison's disease.

POSNER, J. B. AND JACOBS, D. R.: Primary analdosteronism. Clin. Res., **10**:94, 1962.

SAMAHA, F. J.: Hyperkalemic paralysis. Arch. Neurol., **12**:145, 1965.

VAN DER MEULEN, J. P. *et al.:* Hyperkalemic paralysis with myotonia. New England J. Med., **264**:1, 1961.

VAN'T HOFF, W.: Familial myotonic periodic paralysis. Quart. Jour. Med., **31**:385, 1962.

THE MYOGLOBINURIAS

It is believed that myoglobinuria is a result of damage to the muscle fibers and it is assumed that increased permeability of the cell membrane must also occur to permit the myoglobin to escape. Myoglobin seems to

damage the renal tubules so nephritis is usually associated. Several types of myoglobinuria are recognized. (1) The *Haff disease* which is best known in East Prussia. It is attributed to the ingestion of fish and eels, but the mechanism is obscure. (2) It is claimed that *dermatomyositis* may cause myoglobinuria. (3) Extensive *crushing* injuries of the muscles. (4) *Carbon monoxide* poisoning. (5) Injury to the muscles by *high voltage currents*. (6) *vascular occlusion* with ischemic necrosis of the muscles as in Volkmann's contracture. (7) *Paroxysmal, familial, paralytic myoglobinuria* which is described below. There seem to be two types: In one there is no persisting muscular damage and in the other, there are muscular changes suggestive of progressive muscular dystrophy. (8) *March hemoglobinuria* may be related to this last condition for it is claimed that some of the pigment in the urine is myoglobin. The name refers to the fact that the pigment was first found in the urine of soldiers after a long march. Greenberg and Aronson found in a study of 586 young men undergoing training in an officers training school 23 cases of myoglobinuria. Some had swelling of the muscles, brown urine and weakness of the muscles. The serum transaminase was frequently elevated. When training was more gradually increased and rest periods were allowed, such cases ceased to occur. Thus it seems possible that normal individuals may develop myoglobinuria if forced to exercise beyond their endurance. (9) *McArdle's disease.* (10) *Larsson's disease.*

BIBLIOGRAPHY

Assmann *et al.*: Beobachtungen und Untersuchungen bei der Haffkrankheit. Deutsch. Med. Wchnschr., 59:122, 1933.

Biörk, G.: On myoglobin and its occurrence in man. Acta med. Scandinav. 133:Suppl. 226, 1949.

Bywarters, E. G. *et al.*: Myohaemoglobin in the urine of air raid casualties with crushing injury. Biochem. J., 35:1164, 1941.

Gilligan, D. and Blumgart, H.: March hemoglobinuria. Medicine, 20:341, 1941.

Greenberg, J. and Arneson, L.: Exertional rhabdomyolysis with myoglobinuria in a large group of military trainees. Neurology, 17:216, 1967.

SPONTANEOUS, FAMILIAL, PARALYTIC MYOGLOBINURIA
With and Without Evidences of Muscular Dystrophy

This rare condition is inherited and several cases may be found in one family. It effects both males and females. The onset of symptoms usually occurs in childhood. Schaar reviews 17 cases but in some of these the presence of myoglobin in the urine was not actually proven.

The disease is characterized by repeated episodes associated with fever, chills, nausea and vomiting. There is pain, swelling, tenderness and sometimes cramps or contractures of the skeletal muscles. Muscular weakness or paralysis soon appears. The calves are apt to be involved first and most severely, but in our fatal case the muscles of respiration were selectively af-

fected. The tongue and pharynx may be involved. Cardiac weakness is mentioned. When these symptoms appear, the urine becomes dark red or black. Renal function is impaired and uremia may result. Such attacks may be mild or severe. In severe attacks the patient may die of failure of respiration, of uremia or circulatory failure. The active phase of the episode is a matter of days. Repeated attacks are to be expected throughout life.

It is usually stated that the attacks are induced by excessive exertion. Our patient found that by taking a large lunch on a hunting trip, he could avert the attack which would otherwise occur. Hed finds that exertion without food is the most effective method of precipitating an attack. Infection is apparently responsible for some episodes.

The diagnosis depends upon the clinical features described above and upon the demonstration that the pigment in the urine is really myoglobin. Other types of myoglobinuria must be ruled out. The spectroscopic examination is essential. It is stated that two spectroscopic bands characteristic of oxyhemoglobin are observed, but these are shifted 50 Angstrom units to the left. Ultracentrifugation and electrophoretic study of the urine may also make it possible to identify myoglobin. It has been shown that the values of serum enzymes, glutamic-oxalacetic transaminase and aldolase increase during a paralytic episode and then gradually return to normal.

In one group of cases such as that of Debre *et al.,* Hed's 3 cases and our 3 cases, there is no persisting weakness between the acute episodes, no wasting of the muscles or enlargement of the muscles. There is no history of muscular dystrophy in relatives and no disturbances of creatine-creatinine metabolism are found on examination.

In another group of cases, in which the same acute episodes occur, there may be evidence of progressive muscular dystrophy. These patients may show wasting of the shoulder girdle muscles and hypertrophy of the calves. The process seems to advance very slowly however. Wasting of the muscles may be a residuum of the damage sustained in an acute attack but Bowden states that it may occur without acute attacks. Changes in the creatine-creatinine metabolism are present as in progressive muscular dystrophy. It is of interest that relatives of these patients are claimed to have evidences of progressive hypertrophic muscular dystrophy without secretion of dark urine. Acheson and McAlpine describe these cases and review the cases of Meyer-Betz, Louw and Nielson, Wissler and Kreutzer in which evidences of dystrophy were also present.

Post-mortem examination reveals that the striated muscles are pale. Scattered degenerated muscle fibers are found. The striations of such fibers are lost. The process is said to be essentially an acute necrosis of sarcoplasmic substance with preservation of the sheath and supporting tissues. Such le-

sions admit of some degree of repair. There is tubular degeneration in the kidneys with deposits of pigment in the lumen of the tubules. The cause of the damage to the muscles is completely obscure. Bowden states that the smooth muscle and the heart muscle are spared.

Larsson *et al.* describe a type of myoglobinuria which may be different from other types. They found 14 cases in 5 families. It seemed to be an autosomal recessive characteristic. The onset is early in life. Even moderate exercise causes tachycardia and dyspnea. Continued exertion causes cramps in the muscles, necrosis of muscle fibers and myoglobinuria. The muscle fibers regenerate so persistent atrophy does not occur. In one family the calves were hypertrophied. Studies revealed that the muscles did not utilize oxygen properly. The blood lactate and pyruvate levels were above normal level. The cause was not established, but it was suspected the myoglobin might be abnormal.

CASE HISTORY (No. 658102-Path. 24736).—*Father and two sons were subject to repeated attacks of fever, chills, dark discoloration of the urine, muscular pains and weakness. One son died in a severe attack. Pigment in the urine proved to be myoglobin. Post-mortem findings typical of paralytic myoglobinuria.*

R. F. was admitted to Johns Hopkins Hospital on November 24, 1953. The patient, his brother and his father had all been subject to exactly the same symptoms since early childhood. When the patient was old enough to run and play with the other children, he began to have repeated illnesses initiated by fever and chills and pains in the muscles which were followed by darkening of the urine and by muscular weakness which was so severe he could not walk. It is mentioned that breathing might be difficult and the jaws might be weak. Such illnesses would last for from two to four days and during this time the patient would be confined to bed. During childhood there were on an average three or four such attacks a year. After an attack the patient would recover his strength rapidly. There was no persistent weakness. Muscular exertion seemed to provoke the attacks. During childhood outdoor games were apparently responsible, but later in life, hunting trips were the usual cause. The patient might be carried home from the hunt. Evidently the weakness would develop within a few hours after the exertion. Later, the patient discovered that if he took a good lunch on the hunt, the weakness would not occur. The family believed that exertion without proper food was responsible for the attacks and took proper precautions to prevent them. Possibly these precautions were effective for when the present illness began the patient had had no symptoms for 2 years. His brother had had little trouble in recent years and his father had been free of paralytic attacks for a long time. No history of similar symptoms in collaterals or ancestors could be elicited.

The patient had been working hard just prior to his admission to the hospital and a week before he had had an illness with fever, coryza, cough and diarrhea. A few hours before he was brought into the hospital, he developed chills and the familiar pains in his muscles. The pains were chiefly in the chest and back. The urine was found to be dark brown. Muscular weakness developed rapidly. His breathing became difficult. He was brought to the hospital. He was then 29 years old.

On examination the temperature was normal. The pulse was 100. The blood pressure was 108/80. The patient was mentally clear. Respiration was rapid and labored. There was a moderate degree of cyanosis. It was evident that the intercostal muscles were not contracting and the diaphragmatic action was not vigorous. The neck was so weak the head could not be lifted from the pillow. The muscles of the extremities and those innervated by the cranial nerves were still strong. There was no atrophy of the skeletal muscles and no hypertrophy. The patient described a dull aching pain in the extremities as well as in the chest and back. The muscles were not tender and there was no muscle spasm. The tendon reflexes were all lost except the ankle jerks which were feeble. No loss of sensibility could be found.

Respiration slowly became weaker and the cyanosis deepened. The patient was placed in a respirator and seemed to do well for a short time. Soon it was found that he could not breathe at all outside the respirator. The output of urine diminished and then ceased. On November 27, just 3 days after he was admitted to the hospital, he became confused and excited. The temperature rose to 103°F., the blood pressure fell to 74 systolic, the pulse rose to 120, the cyanosis became extreme and the patient expired.

Laboratory investigations gave the following results. The non-protein nitrogen rose during the illness from 55 mgs. to 98 mgs. The electrocardiogram showed merely sinus tachycardia. The spinal fluid contained only 3 cells and a normal amount of protein. The blood counts showed only a terminal leucocytosis. The urine contained a dark brown pigment. Spectroscopic and electrophoretic studies led to the conclusion that this was myoglobin.

On post-mortem examination the significant findings were restricted to the muscles and the kidneys. The skeletal muscles were pale but not atrophic. Microscopic examination revealed scattered necroses of the muscle fibers and hyaline degeneration. These were, of course, fresh lesions. A few atrophic muscle fibers containing calcium deposits were also found which were attributed to lesions which had occurred in previous attacks. The heart showed focal necroses of muscle fibers surrounded by round cells and polymorphonuclear cells. The kidney tubules were dilated and showed focal necroses. Dark rusty casts were found in the tubules and purple crystals were noted.

BIBLIOGRAPHY
Cases with Muscular Dystrophy

ACHESON, D. AND MCALPINE, D.: Muscular dystrophy associated with myoglobinuria and excessive excretion of ketosteroids. Lancet, ii:372, 1953.

FARMER, T. A., HAMMACK, W. J. AND FROMMEYER, T. A.: Idiopathic recurrent rhabdomyolysis with myoglobinuria. New England J. Med., 246:60, 1961.

GILLETT, R. L.: Primary myoglobinuria. New England J. Med., 260:1156, 1959.

HAASE, G. R. AND ENGEL, A. G.: Paroxysmal recurrent rhabdomyolysis. A.M.A. Arch. Neurol., 2:410, 1960.

KONTOS, H. A. *et al.*: Exertional idiopathic paroxysmal myoglobinuria. Am. J. Med., 35:283, 1963.

KOREIN, J. *et al.*: Clinical syndrome of paroxysmal paralytic myoglobinuria. Neurology, 9:767, 1959.

KREUTZER, F. L. *et al.*: Spontaneous myohemoglobinuria in man. Arch. Int. Med., 81:249, 1948.

LOUW, A. AND NIELSEN, H. E.: Paroxysmal paralytic hemoglobinuria. Acta med. Scandinav., 117:424, 1944.

MEYER-BETZ, F.: Beobachtungen an einem eigenartigen mit Muskellähmungen verbindenen Fall von Hämoglobinurie. Deutsch. Arch. klin. Med., 101:85, 1910.

ROWLAND, L. P. *et al.*: Diagnosis of myoglobinuria. Arch. Neurol., 10:537, 1964.

WISSLER, H.: Paroxysmal Myoglobinurie. Helvet. paediat. acta, 3:334, 1948.

Cases without persistent weakness

BOWDEN, D. H.: Acute recurrent rhabdomyolysis. Medicine, 36:335, 1957.

DEBRE, R. *et al.*: Crises Myopathiques paroxystiques avec hemoglobinurie. Bull. et mem. Soc. med. hos. Paris., 54:725, 1938.

HED, R.: Myoglobinuria. Arch. Int. Med., 92:825, 1953.

LARSSON, L. E. *et al.*: Hereditary metabolic myopathy with paroxysmal myoglobinuria due to abnormal glycolysis. Jour. Neurol., Neurosurg. Psychiat., 27:361, 1964.

Cases without note about state of muscles

BUCHANAN, D. AND STEINER, P.: Myoglobinuria with paralysis. Proc. Chicago Neurol. Soc., Jan. 9, 1951.

ELEK, S. D. AND ANDERSON, H. F.: Paroxysmal paralytic myoglobinuria. Brit. Med. J., ii:533, 1953.

SCHAAR, F. E.: Paroxysmal myoglobinuria. Am. J. Dis. Child., 89:23, 1955.

SCHAAR, F. E., LABREE, J. W. AND GLEASON, D. F.: Paroxysmal myoglobinuria with fatal renal injury. Proc. Central Soc. Clin. Research, 22:71, 1949.

SEVERE MYOPATHY ASSOCIATED WITH ADOLESCENT OSTEOMALACIA SIMULATING VITAMIN D DEFICIENCY (DENT AND HARRIS)

The infantile rickets due to vitamin D deficiency, which has largely disappeared from many countries, is associated with weakness and loss of muscle tone, but the muscular condition is not stressed as a rule for the bony deformities are much more impressive.

McCance and Dent and Harris have described a type of osteomalacia which develops during adolescence in which gross muscular weakness is one of the most striking features. McCance reports one case with onset at 15 years and Dent and Harris report four cases. In one of their cases the on-

set was at 12 years and in another, at 19 years. In our case, given in abstract below, the onset was at 14 years. No evidence of morbid inheritance has yet been discovered.

In McCance's case the patient could not stand without support and could not get out of a chair without help. Dent and Harris state that the weakness may be so severe the patient may be confined to bed, unable to lift the head and scarcely able to move the limbs. Tetany never occurs. Our patient was rapidly becoming helpless when first seen and was able to walk only with crutches. A diagnosis of progressive muscular dystrophy is almost invariably made unless the patient is carefully studied. One expects bony deformities in cases of advanced dystrophy.

The bony changes are manifest by pains in the bones, deformities and loss of height. Roentgenographic study reveals extensive osteoporosis with pseudofractures and true fractures. The changes are such as one finds in juvenile rickets.

The biochemical study reveals plasma calcium between 9 and 10 mgs per cent, plasma phosphorus between 1 and 2 mgs and elevation of the alkaline phosphatase. There is a moderate reduction of the bicarbonate level. No sign of renal damage is found. The excretion of calcium is diminished and that of phosphorus is increased. There is no glycosuria. The basic defect is believed to be inadequate reabsorption of phosphorus by the renal tubules. The myopathy would seem to be due to phosphorus deficiency.

Very large doses of vitamin D are given. The effort is made to keep the serum calcium below 11.5 mgs. and the phosphorus up to 2.5 mgs. Hypercalcemia with ectopic calcification may result from excessive dosage of vitamin D. It is stated that the muscular weakness disappears with this treatment and it is possible to control the bony process to a great extent.

CASE HISTORY (No. 747049).—*Great muscular weakness and failure of growth beginning at the age of 14 years. Slowly progressive course. Diagnosis of progressive muscular dystrophy. At 18 years nearly helpless. Diagnosis of adolescent osteomalacia made.*

J. F. was examined on August 14, 1956 when he was 18 years old. He was a vigorous boy who enjoyed athletic games until the age of 14 years. At that time he developed pain in the left leg. A diagnosis of osteomyelitis was made but later this was changed to a malignant growth of the left femur. Amputation was advised. The lesion was explored, however. The family was told that neither infection nor neoplasm was found.

After this it was noted that the boy was getting weak and his muscles were becoming wasted. The process was progressive. He gave up outdoor games. Then his gait became affected. During his seventeenth year, he started to use a cane and soon was forced to use crutches. A diagnosis of progressive muscular dystrophy was made.

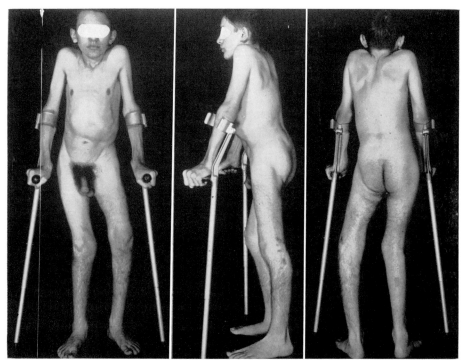

FIG. 298. (No. 747049) Showing beading of ribs, deformity of chest, scoliosis, shortening of the trunk, and extremities, deformities of the knees, relatively large hands and feet and wasting of the muscles. The weakness of the muscles which fix the scapulae is obvious.

His father was a large man of six feet four inches, but the boy ceased to grow and, indeed, became shorter. The left knee bent outward. At 16 years his height was 62 inches and his weight 110 pounds. At 18 years, his height was 59 inches and his weight 90 pounds.

The patient had had no illness except for the usual childhood diseases. There was no history of any symptoms resembling his in any other member of the family.

On examination the patient's mental condition seemed to be quite normal. His body stature was much reduced. The head and face were normally formed. There was a gross thoracic scoliosis. The chest was narrow laterally and the anterior-posterior diameter was increased. The shoulders were very small and narrow and the extremities were also shortened. The shortening seemed to be more pronounced in the proximal segments. The hands and feet, however, were large and well formed, suitable for a large boy of 18 years. The epiphyses were enlarged at the wrist and ankle. The ribs were beaded. When standing the left knee deviated to the left and the right knee also slightly to the left.

The muscles supplied by the cranial nerves were not definitely involved.

The neck was rather small but strength was fairly good. The scapulae were loose and would wing in certain movements. There was gross weakness at the shoulders and elbow joints involving all muscles which act at these joints. The long flexors and extensors of the forearms were also weak but the intrinsic muscles of the hands seemed to be stronger. The patient could stand only with the aid of crutches. He could walk only a short distance with much effort. He could not arise from a chair without help of his arms. There was diffuse weakness of all muscles of the legs which seemed to be somewhat greater in the proximal muscles. Plantar movement at the ankle was still fairly strong. There was gross wasting of all the muscles of the extremities except for those of the hands and feet. No twitchings of the muscles were seen. The tendon reflexes were all within normal limits. Plantar responses were normal. There was no myotonia and no signs of latent tetany. No sensory changes of any kind were present. His genital organs were well developed. Blood pressure was 100/75.

Biochemical studies were made by Dr. John E. Howard. The serum phosphorus varied between 1.1 and 1.3 mgs per cent. The serum calcium was estimated at 10.5 mgs and 10.2 mgs. The non-protein nitrogen was 30 mgs and the blood sugar 104 mgs. The alkaline phosphate was 25.5 and 31.0 units. The carbon dioxide combining power was 22.5. The urine contained neither sugar nor albumin. There was no excess of amino acids in the urine. The excretion of phosphorus in the urine in 24 hours was 400 mgs but only 50 mgs of calcium was excreted in 24 hours.

Roentgenograms of the bones were of great interest. The chest showed deformities due chiefly to scoliosis with pseudofractures of the ribs. At the knees there was defective osteogenesis which was more severe on the left than the right. There were changes in the epiphyseal lines in the femurs, tibiae and fibulae. Evidences of an old fracture were seen in the left femur. The thoracic spine showed scoliosis, osteoporosis and narrowing of the bodies of the vertebrae. In general all the bones showed osteoporosis. There were no deposits of calcium in the kidneys.

The patient was given increasing doses of vitamin D. With 400,000 units of vitamin D a day, the serum phosphorus rose to a level between 1.9 and 2.2 mgs. On December 10, the patient's muscular strength was greatly increased and he could get about with ease. There were no evidences of vicarious calcification.

In June, 1957 the patient could walk as far as he wished. The muscles had increased greatly in bulk and in strength. Roentgenograms of the bones showed healing of the lesions. The deformities were not altered in any way but were not increasing. He was able to lead an active life.

BIBLIOGRAPHY

DENT, C. E. AND HARRIS, H.: Hereditary forms of rickets and osteomalacia. J. Bone & Joint Surg., 38-B:British Vol., 211, 1956.

McCANCE, R. A.: Osteomalacia with Looser's nodes (Milkman's syndrome) due to raised resistance to vitamin D acquired at the age of 15 years. Quart. J. Med., 16:33, 1947.

Winters, R. W. *et al.:* A genetic study of familial hypophosphatemia and vitamin D resistant rickets. Medicine, 37:97, 1958.

STEROID MYOPATHY

A variety of corticosteroids may be responsible for myopathy though there is some evidence that the incidence is higher when those with 9-alpha-fluorine configuration are used. This condition may occur in either sex and at any age. Myopathy may become evident after a few weeks of treatment or after more than a year. It may occur when small doses are given or when the dosage is large. However, it seems to be more frequent when large doses are given over a long period.

There is gradual increasing weakness chiefly in the proximal muscles of the legs. The arms may be affected and even the muscles of the neck and face. There is wasting of the involved muscles. No loss of reflexes is found as a rule and no loss of sensibility is usually present. Sphincter control is not lost.

Pathological changes in the muscles include an increase in glycogen, increase in the sarcolemal nuclei, vacuolation of the muscle fibers and even necrosis. With the electron microscope it may be seen that the mitochondria are increased and later are enlarged and degenerated.

Treatment consists in withdrawal of the steroid, reduction of dosage and substitution of the steroid with another steroid. With such treatment improvement may begin within a few days and as a rule within 2 to 3 weeks. Complete recovery is expected within 2 months or a year.

BIBLIOGRAPHY

Afifi, A. K. *et al.:* Steroid myopathy. Johns Hopkins Med. Jour., 123:158, 1968.

PROGRESSIVE MYOSITIS OSSIFICANS

Definition.—Bony deposits in the muscles may develop as a result of a number of causes. Hematomas and granulation tissue resulting from inflammatory processes may eventually become ossified. Bits of periosteum torn from the bones as a result of trauma give rise to new bone formation wherever they chance to lodge. Long-continued trauma of a milder type may also lead to bony deposits in the muscle or tendons. For example, I may mention the plaques of bone which are found in the adductors of the thighs in persons who ride horseback continually. Extensive bony processes sometimes appear in the muscles of the lower extremities in severe spastic paraplegias of long duration. All of these conditions, however, are localized, and do not progress beyond a certain point.

There is a rare condition in which a generalized ossification of the skeletal muscles develops which seems to be dependent upon some inborn defect of metabolism. This is termed myositis ossificans progressiva.

Pathological Anatomy.—The pathological process has been studied by Munchmeyer and others. At first, there is merely edema and infiltration with round cells. Hemorrhages may occur. Later, granulation tissue develops, and in the center of this tissue large cells resembling those of cartilage appear. Ossification begins in the region of these cells. The bone is identical with normal bone and shows periosteum and Haversian canals.

A number of studies have been made of the calcium and phosphorus metabolism. So far, no conclusive results have been obtained. It has been claimed that during attacks the phosphates of the urine are diminished. Calcium in the urine may be normal or diminished.

Etiology.—The cause is obscure, but most writers regard this disease as the expression of an inherent defect in metabolism.

Clinical Features.—The disease has been found in three generations of one family, but in most cases it has been impossible to discover any evidence of morbid heredity. The onset is usually before the tenth year, and, often, before the age of five. One case is described in which symptoms appeared in the fifth month of life. A local swelling is first noted. This is usually situated in the muscles of the trunk, and very often in the back, especially the back of the neck. The swelling is firm and may or may not be tender. A little edema of the subcutaneous tissues may be found about the margins of the swelling, and the skin may be slightly red. A mild fever may occur at the same time. After two to four weeks, the swelling slowly disappears, leaving in many cases a firm small area in the muscle, which eventually becomes bone. After a variable interval, additional swellings develop, each making a small contribution to the bony deposits. The disease, therefore, advances by a series of local reactions. The bony tumors are at first small and confined to the muscles. Later, they coalesce and form long irregular branching processes, extending throughout the muscles of the trunk and proximal segments of the extremities. Soon these become attached to the bones of the skeleton. As a result, limitation of movement eventually develops. The neck and scapulae are first to be immobilized. The whole spine becomes rigid. Later, the hips and shoulder joints are fixed. Eventually, the jaws are involved, and food must be given through a tube. In one case, thin sheets of bone appeared in the skin. The disease runs a slow course, and the patient is usually not completely helpless until middle age.

It is of great interest that several peculiarities of development are frequently associated. The great toes and thumbs are usually shortened, and roentgenograms reveal that the first metatarsal and metacarpal bones respectively are absent or reduced to a minimum. In a few cases the trunk has seemed to be shortened as well. The development of the sexual organs is often defective. Males show a rudimentary penis or small testicles, and females often fail to menstruate.

Diagnosis.—When the disease is fully developed it can scarcely be confused with any other condition. The roentgenographic appearances are quite characteristic. However, the diagnosis may be difficult in the early stages, when only localized bony tumors are to be found. Osteogenic sarcoma may be distinguished by its origin from the epiphysis of the bone and its progressive course without the tendency of the initial swelling to recede. Local bony deposits resulting from trauma or inflammation should be recognized by the history. Multiple cartilaginous exostoses have a characteristic appearance in the roentgenograms, and are found attached to the epiphyses of the bones, not in the muscles. Subcutaneous calcification does not have the appearance of true bone and, moreover the deposits are very superficial, and often cause ulceration of the overlying skin. In some instances, however, calcium may be laid down in the muscle sheath; thus offering at least a superficial resemblance to myositis ossificans. None of these conditions are associated with congenital shortening of the thumbs or great toes, which is so common in true progressive myositis ossificans.

Prognosis.—All patients eventually become quite helpless, and die from inanition or fixation of the respiratory apparatus.

Treatment.—No treatment has been of any value. Lockhart and Burke review recent methods of treatment and report that they secured some slight improvement when corticotropin was used.

BIBLIOGRAPHY

BAUER, W., MARPLE, A. AND BENNETT, G. A.: Further studies in a case of calcification of the subcutaneous tissues in a child. Am. J. Med. Sc., **182**:237, 1931.

FREJKA, B.: Heterotopic ossification and myositis ossificans progressiva. J. Bone & Joint Surg., **11**:157, 1929.

KOONTZ, A. R.: Myositis ossificans progressiva. Am. J. Med. Sc., **174**:406, 1927.

LOCKHART, J. D. AND BURKE, F. G.: Myositis ossificans progressiva. Report of a case treated with corticotropin. Am. J. Dis. Child., **87**:626, 1954.

MAIR, W. F.: Myositis ossificans progressiva. Edinburgh Med. J., **39**:13, 1932.

RILEY, H. D. AND CHRISTIE, A.: Myositis ossificans progressiva. Pediatrics, **8**:753, 1951.

NEOPLASMS OF THE MUSCLES

Adams, Denny-Brown and Pearson describe a number of tumors composed of muscle cells. A well known type is the rhabdomyoma of the heart. This occurs as an isolated lesion and also in cases of tuberous sclerosis and in von Gierke's disease. It is composed of large vacuolated cells which display striations between the vacuoles. Surgeons are now able to remove some of these. They are always benign.

Teratomatous rhabdomyomas are also described. These arise in various tissues such as the uterus, bladder, and prostate and not as a rule in the skeletal muscles. Rhabdomyosarcomas may arise in the middle ear as well as in the orbits. When the growth arises in the middle ear, it may be mis-

taken for otitis. We have seen lesions of the 7th and 8th nerves result from such a growth in the middle ear. The adenomyosarcoma of the kidney, or Wilms' tumor, is placed in this group. Most of these are malignant.

BIBLIOGRAPHY

ADAMS, R., DENNY-BROWN, D. AND PEARSON, C. M.: Diseases of the Muscle. Paul Hoeber, Inc., 1953.
PINKEL, D. AND PICKREN, J.: Rhabdomyosarcoma in children. J.A.M.A., **175**:293, 1961.

Chapter XI

PSYCHOGENIC DISORDERS SIMULATING ORGANIC DISESASES OF THE NERVOUS SYSTEM

A T THIS point, I wish to discuss those disorders of psychic origin which simulate organic diseases of the nervous system. I shall make no distinction between the various types since their neurological manifestations are essentially the same. The cases mentioned below are those in which the symptoms were relieved by suggestion or persuasion, and therefore chiefly of hysterical nature. I shall use the term hysteria in this loose sense below. No effort will be made to discuss the psychological aspects of these conditions.

Whatever opinion we may hold about the origin of hysteria we must admit that hysterical episodes may occur at a very early age and that there is a striking tendency for various manifestations to recur from time to time throughout life. It seems to be generally believed that these episodes represent the reaction of a special type of personality to some provoking factor. It should be said that this hysterical personality exists in varying degrees and that it would scarcely be an exaggeration to state that none of us is quite free from it.

Among the inciting factors of hysterical episodes *suggestion* is always given first place but it is clear that emotional disturbances are also important. Frights, shocks, disappointments and emotional stress and strain seem to play a major role in provoking the reaction, and the form which the reaction takes seems to be determined by suggestion. Unfortunately hysterical phenomena are not infrequently found in association with organic diseases so that one is led to believe that the suggestion may be due to the symptoms of an organic process. This association is especially common in early disseminated sclerosis but I have observed it also in syringomyelia and in neurosyphilis. The litigation or compensation neuroses, which are common in adults, are fortunately rare among children.

From a theoretical point of view it might seem to be impossible to offer any description of the possible manifestations of hysteria since they are determined by psychological laws and not by those functions of the nervous system with which we deal in clinical neurology. However, in most instances, hysterical reactions take certain well known forms. I have observed the following types:

Paralysis.—I have seen apparent paralysis of one arm, of one or both legs and of both the arm and the leg on the same side of the body. There

may be apparent loss of tone so the extremity is quite relaxed, or it may be rigid and held in strange postures. When there is rigidity, there is also often cyanosis and edema, which, in my experience, are absent in the flaccid palsies. Wasting of the muscles and retardation of development may be striking when the condition is of long standing. The case of a young woman who was examined many years ago may be mentioned in this connection. When she was a child of six years, she suddenly developed complete paralysis of the left leg for no apparent reason. The child was taken to Weir Mitchell who found complete analgesia up to the hip and who made a diagnosis of hysteria. The patient remembered that he would tip-toe into her room at night and stick pins in her leg. Despite his best efforts, the child could not be induced to move the leg but, suddenly, one afternoon at the age of 10 years, the full power of movement and normal sensation returned. In the following years there were numerous episodes which could be explained only on the basis of hysteria. At the age of 20 years, examination revealed that the affected leg was 2 inches shorter than the right leg and was somewhat smaller in circumference. Sensibility, motility and the reflexes were all in order. The long period of disuse during a period of active growth had left a permanent defect of development. One of the most impressive peculiarities of hysterical palsies is the calm indifference of the patient. A patient who is completely disabled shows usually no sign of alarm and may smile cheerfully during the examination. It should also be said that it is rare for such palsies to persist for more than a few months although they may for many years.

Several tests may be mentioned at this point which are useful in distinguishing these conditions from true paralysis. The tendon and plantar reflexes are always normal although they may be modified by the tension of the muscles and so it is sometimes difficult to compare them on the two sides. There may be a pseudoclonus which is not easy to distinguish from a true clonus. As a rule it is ill-sustained. The electrical reactions of the muscles are always normal. If rigidity is present it is not that of true spasticity and feels more like that of voluntary resistance. A number of tests are employed to demonstrate that the patient is actually able to make use of the affected muscles. One of the best known is *Hoover's sign,* which is found in hysterical hemiplegia. The patient is placed on the couch in the supine position, and the examiner's hands are placed under the heels. The patient is then told to raise the normal leg from the couch; if the paralysis is hysterical, the examiner will feel that the heel of the paralysed leg is pressed down upon his hand since this is a normal associated movement. When the patient is told to try to elevate the paralysed leg from the couch, the examiner will feel no such movement of the normal leg for the patient is not really making any effort. I have found it helpful to test the *movement of*

adduction in the legs and arms. When the patient is told to press the hands or feet firmly together, and the examiner suddenly pulls them apart, it is easy to feel that the adductors are contracting with equal force on the two sides for it is very difficult for us to adduct one extremity strongly without adducting the other at the same time. The *Japanese illusion* may be used in the same way. With the forearms pointing upward the patient's fingers are interlocked in such a way that the left hand is on the right and the right hand on the left. The examiner points to one finger and says, "move that finger"; it is difficult for the patient to decide at once whether the indicated finger is right or left and if a prompt response is required many mistakes are made, and the paralysed finger is often moved.

Abnormalities of Gait.—Sometimes a child may seem to be unable to walk normally although there is no disturbance of motility in the legs when lying down on the couch. There is usually inability to stand as well. The term *astasia abasia* is frequently applied to this condition. When the child is placed on the feet the legs may give way so as to let the child down or the child may tremble and shake, showing signs of fear or of pain. In other cases the child may be willing to try to walk but advances by skips and jumps and other strange contortions.

Muscular Spasms.—We have seen numerous cases in which the extremities are held in distorted postures by powerful and persistent contractions of certain muscles. Often such spasms persist for periods of months and eventually become associated with circulatory disturbances causing edema and cyanosis and with true contractures of the muscles and fibrous changes in and about the joints. There may be alterations of the skin and nails. Babinski has described these phenomena in detail and claims that they are not entirely explained by immobilization. After the primary disorder has disappeared, these changes may be relieved by exercises, passive movements and massage. It is claimed that hysterical spasms always disappear during sleep. We have seen several cases in which there was strong fixation and adduction of the fingers and often flexion of the wrist. In one case there was fixation of the elbow and shoulder joints with freedom of movement at finger and wrist joints. Inversion of the foot with flexion of the toes and sometimes flexion of the knee and hip are not uncommon. The right hand is affected more often than the left but the right and left legs are affected with about equal frequency. Some of the cases of spasmodic torticollis seem to be of hysterical origin but this can scarcely be said of the majority of cases. Rarely one sees cases of spasm of the tongue and face. Blepharospasm is not uncommon in association with hysterical disturbances of vision but since it may also occur among the sequels of epidemic encephalitis there is often great difficulty in making a correct diagnosis. One adolescent girl exhibited a powerful spasm of the adductors of the thighs which

caused her to walk into the hospital with a "scissor gait." It was learned that she had run away from home to be married the previous day and that the spasm had developed that night when her husband had attempted to have sexual relations. This case illustrates the usual teaching that spasms are often protective, for one can scarcely doubt that the spasm represented an attempt to protect her virginity.

Spasms are never confined to one muscle for they obey the laws of voluntary motility and may be simulated more or less exactly by the examiner. The resistance to passive movements is similar to that produced voluntarily and is quite unlike that due to spasticity or Parkinsonian rigidity. The distorted postures which occur in dystonia musculorum deformans and also sometimes in epidemic encephalitis may be mistaken for hysteria.

Tremors and Other Abnormal Movements.—As a rule tremors are coarse and fairly rhythmical. They are apt to be found in the right arm but may appear in the left arm. The examiner can usually imitate them very closely. We have seen several cases in which movements very similar to those of Sydenham's chorea seemed to be psychologically determined. These movements were found in young unmarried girls who had become pregnant and would naturally be attributed to chorea gravidarum. However, in two instances the movements ceased within a few minutes after the girl had been informed of her parents' forgiveness.

The repetitive movements of mentally defective children should be mentioned. They seem to be different from habit spasms. The commonest such movement is rocking back and forth when in a seated position. This may occur for hours every day for years. As a result, there may be hypertrophy of the sacrospinalis and abdominal muscles.

In this connection it is necessary to mention the elaborate tic-like movements which are not uncommon in *epidemic encephalitis* and which are profoundly modified if not determined by psychological factors. These are discussed in connection with encephalitis. Other repetitive movements, such as facial grimaces, winking, blinking, shrugging the shoulder or twisting the neck, seem to be dependent upon habit formation and are commonly termed *habit spasm.* They may persist for long periods despite every method of treatment and seem to distress parents more than more serious disorders. Torup reexamined 220 patients who had had tics in childhood, usually before the age of ten years. Ages on reexamination ranged between six and twenty-six years. Half of the patients were free from tics and recovery usually occurred at about ten or twelve years. In 6 per cent of all cases, the tics persisted unchanged into adult life. In the remaining cases, the tics had become less severe or even insignificant. In 30 or 40 per cent of cases, tics were present in more than one member of the family. Conflicts in the home seemed to be the usual cause. The patients were sensitive, restless,

lacking in self-confidence and immature. Various elaborate tics associated with explosive utterances are found in *obsessions* and *compulsions*. These were described by *Gilles de la Tourette* many years ago. The case of a young girl who had just entered a nunnery may serve to illustrate this type. Having read the lives of the saints and their temptations by the devil she developed strange seizures which were induced by contact with holy water and other blessed objects. At such moments she would experience a terrible feeling as if a great beast had fastened his fangs in her back and was shaking her as a dog does a rat. She would strike out at anybody who happened to be near and at the same time would shout a few obscene or profane words. A moment later she would be her smiling and affable self once more. She claimed that she was forced against her will to perform these distressing acts. Such patients often utter strange sounds and may bark like a dog. It is often possible to discover that the inarticulate sounds are modifications or substitutes for obscene words. Complex motor reactions are frequently associated. It is said that the patient performs these acts because of a feeling of compulsion in contrast to the patient with the common habit spasm who is largely unconscious of the movements. Eisenberg *et al.* have studied a number of cases and point out that psychotherapy is not often effective. They suggest that organic processes may play a role. The prognosis is rather unfavorable.

Stevens and Blachly state that haldol, i.e. butyophenone haloperidol, is an effective treatment in this condition though they apparently treated only one patient.

Spasmodic torticollis is in my opinion a psychogenic condition though there is no general agreement about its nature. It is manifest as a rule by turning of the face to one side or the other, and often by tilting the head. These vicarious positions may be maintained by a persistent muscular spasm or may occur from time to time as a result of tonic contractions of the neck muscles. Occasionally, there are tremulous movements. The condition is usually confined to the muscles of the neck but the shoulder may be elevated and facial spasm may be seen. After a time the sternomastoid may be hypertrophied. This condition is aggravated by nervous tension and is often abolished by lying down and relaxing. The patient may be able to hold the head in proper position by placing the finger on the chin. This condition is rare in adolescence and even rarer in children.

In differential diagnosis we must exclude involuntary movements due to epidemic encephalitis, progressive athetosis and dystonia musculorum which may begin in the neck. Congenital torticollis q.v. and ocular torticollis q.v. must also be ruled out. Bony malformations of the neck and inflammatory processes in the joints and muscles should also be considered. Posterior fossa neoplasms may cause head tilting.

Occasionally, there is a spontaneous remission or apparent recovery. In some instances, skillful psychotherapy may result in apparent cure, but these patients are stubborn and have rigid personalities so they may be unwilling or unable to respond. I am opposed to operation on the cervical muscles or cervical nerve roots though the patients are sometimes pleased with the results.

Kinsbourne reports that strange contortions of the head and neck in childhood may indicate hiatus hernia. They are apt to occur during and immediately after eating. He has observed five such cases in all of which operation gave relief.

Disorders of Speech.—There may be sudden loss of voice with the retention of ability to whisper, or all forms of speech may be lost at the same time. Often the patient can sing, whistle and read and write and there is never, in my experience, any difficulty in understanding spoken speech. In some cases the speech is tremulous and in other cases it is halting or interrupted, so it has some resemblance to stuttering. In one unusual case a little girl spoke with a nasal voice after tonsillectomy. She had apparently developed the ability to relax her soft palate for, after the laryngologist had pretended to apply some drug to the mucous membrane, she spoke quite normally.

In cases resembling motor aphasia it is significant that there is no palsy of the lips or tongue and no inability to read, write or to understand. As a rule such patients refuse to vocalize at all and are therefore mute rather than aphasic. When the voice is lost, the vocal cords move well during respiration and there is no stridor or difficulty in swallowing.

Fits and Seizures.—In my experience these are relatively uncommon and of unpredictable form. I have seen only one of the dramatic major seizures described by Charcot in which the patient becomes rigid with the head retracted and the body arched backwards, so that only the head and heels touch the couch. More frequently we see states of apparent unconsciousness or of apparent confusion which are preceded or followed by screaming and weeping. I have seen one child who would act at times as if she were in a frenzy of anger and would try to bite everyone who came near as she apparently believed a rabid animal would do.

It is rarely difficult to distinguish such seizures from true convulsions. Hysterical fits are not associated with biting of the tongue or with changes in the plantar response or loss of the light reflex of the pupils. There is rarely cyanosis. I have never seen incontinence. The patient does not pass into a stupor as a rule at the end of the fit and is not sleepy afterwards. If one attempts to open the eyelids or to move the limbs, the patient usually resists in a purposeful manner. It must be kept in mind, however, that hys-

terical states may follow epileptic convulsions or petit mal and the co-existence of hysteria and epilepsy is not very rare.

Sensory Disturbances.—Anesthesia is one of the commonest and most typical of hysterical symptoms. It is often seen in one or both extremities in the glove or stocking distribution, terminating abruptly at a line running transversely around the limb often where the limb joins the body at the shoulder or groin. Hemianesthesia is another common finding. Universal anesthesia is less common but very typical. In most cases the anesthesia is complete and involves all modalities of sensibility, though it may be selective. Anesthesia is frequently associated with paralysis or other symptoms. As a rule the patient makes no complaint of anesthesia for it is discovered during the examination, and probably produced in most cases at the same time. The distribution of the anesthesia usually gives a clue to its nature and it is usually easy to find discrepancies on further examination. For example, if a tuning fork is placed upon the anesthetic side of the forehead or sternum, the patient will state that its vibrations are not felt although they are of course transmitted by the bones well beyond the midline. In the same way a patient who has apparently no postural sense in one extremity can always find that extremity easily with the opposite finger when the eyes are closed. The absence of the pharyngeal reflex is not so important as some writers have claimed, for it is sometimes absent in healthy subjects. Complete anesthesia of the pharynx is more significant however.

Hysterical pains, tenderness and hyperesthesia are all seen. They are apt to be elaborated upon a basis of some minor organic trouble and are usually associated with paralysis or other symptoms.

Disorders of Vision.—Blindness in one or both eyes is sometimes seen. More commonly, however, the patient complains of partial loss of vision. In such cases one finds, on examination, concentric constriction of the visual fields, with either normal or reduced central vision. Often the fields grow progressively smaller as the examination proceeds, so that one can observe the constriction developing. Such fields are termed helicoid fields. Occasionally there is merely general reduction of vision without changes in the fields or local defects. I have never seen homonymous hemianopia or central scotomas. Photophobia and blepharospasm are often associated with hysterical disturbances of vision. We have seen two cases in which there was apparent loss of accommodation. In one case the near vision returned to normal within a few minutes after a brief talk with the patient and in the other, recovery followed discussion of some domestic problems. Spasms of convergence and accommodation are well known. Diplopia may occur and is sometimes of monocular type. True ptosis of the lid does not occur, but spasm of the orbicularis is often mistaken for ptosis.

Ophthalmologists have a number of methods for detecting hysterical disorders of vision. It may often be shown, for example, that when dealing with concentric constriction of the fields, the absolute size of the fields remains the same no matter how close the patient is placed to the perimeter. When the patient claims that one eye is blind, he may be required to look at a chart containing red and green letters. If the sound eye is covered with red glass, the red letters should be invisible unless the patient is using the supposedly blind eye. In the same way, the patient who claims to be quite blind, may be confronted with a lighted candle. When a prism of 6° is placed before one eye with the base out, and the eye deviates outwardly and then deviates inwardly when the prism is removed, the patient must have vision in that eye.

Deafness.—Hysterical deafness is described but I have never seen it.

Gastrointestinal Disorders.—We have seen several cases in which the child claimed to be unable to swallow. Almost all of these cases followed some illness, the nature of which did not seem to be important. In each case the child was easily cured by isolation from the parents. Vomiting seems to be commonly produced by emotional disturbances. Air swallowing with great distention and belching is also well recognized as hysterical in some cases. Retention of feces, leading to severe constipation, is often described as an hysterical phenomenon.

Altschule states that globus hystericus occurs with strong emotional reactions. Barium studies reveal spasm along the entire length of the esophagus. This is believed to be due to strong vagal discharges.

Anorexia Nervosa.—This rare condition occurs as a rule in adolescent girls. They refuse to eat and when parents insist that they take proper nourishment, will pretend to eat and put the food in the garbage can. Emaciation often becomes extreme. Amenorrhea develops. Farquharson and Hyland state that the condition often results from a pathological fear of obesity but there are other psychological factors. These authors have published a paper describing the course of 15 patients who had been treated by psychotherapy 20 to 30 years previously. Ten of the patients remained well, three had no recurrence of the anorexia but had other neurotic symptoms, one remained thin but seemed to be well adjusted and one developed paranoid schizophrenia.

Respiratory Disturbances.—Coughing is sometimes psychologically determined. In one case, I recall a little girl of 9 years who had to care for her mother and two sisters, all of whom were ill with influenza. The child began to cough constantly and continued this for three days. She was cured by psychotherapy in the course of a brief, but very difficult interview. Deep breathing and breath holding seem to be hysterical phenomena at times, though they are probably more often simple expressions of emotions, espe-

cially in infants. They may be very alarming at times and we have recently seen a child who very nearly died on two occasions. Frequent and prolonged sneezing has been cured by the use of a device which administers an electric shock whenever the child sneezes.

Retention of Urine.—I have seen two hysterical girls who would retain vast quantities of urine at times, although their bladder function was repeatedly studied by cystometric methods and found to be normal.

Enuresis.—This is sometimes due to organic causes and sometimes due to emptying the bladder so frequently during the day that the bladder never develops a proper capacity.

Invalid Reaction.—We have seen a number of children, in most cases girls, who claim to have innumerable pains and disabilities including hemiplegia, paraplegia, contractures, retention of urine, blindness and anesthesias. They spend their whole time in bed attended by a devoted mother and a well meaning but ignorant physician who usually prescribes unwisely and frequently performs many unwarranted operations. In most of these cases there has been mild, but definite, mental defect in addition to a very childish personality.

Somnambulism.—Kales *et al.* present a study of sleepwalking. They state that it occurs during deep sleep. The personalities are sometimes healthy and sometimes disturbed. They are not disturbed by the sleepwalking. They are not as a rule psychotic, schizophrenic or paranoid. Some show anxiety and depression. Brain damage and epilepsy are rarely present. The somnambulistic periods last from 5 to 30 minutes. During such periods, they have a low level of awareness and motor skill. Their activities are random and not purposive. They are glassy eyed and dazed. They are hard to awaken and do not remember what happened.

Trophic Lesions.—A large number of "trophic" lesions have been described, which seem to be regarded as indicating some mysterious influence of the state of mind upon the tissues. It is claimed, for example, that hemorrhages may occur from the mucous membranes or under the skin. Tears of blood are mentioned and other occult phenomena of great interest. Unfortunately, I have never had the pleasure of observing such cases. I have seen cases of "bloody" tears and "bloody" sweat both due to infections with B. prodigiosus. I have observed cyanosis and edema in paralysed extremities and if such conditions are prolonged there may be contractures and wasting of the muscles and fibrotic changes in the joints, but none of the more bizarre manifestations have presented themselves to me. I have, however, seen a number of cases in which patients have mutilated themselves in various manners. Most commonly phenol or household lye is employed to burn "ulcers" into the skin. Knitting needles may be thrust under the skin so as to suggest the presence of a burrowing parasite of some kind.

Belladonna may be instilled into the eye to dilate the pupil and destroy its reflexes. Dr. Walsh has told me of the case of a girl who destroyed her vision by causing ulcers of the corneae.

Diagnosis.—The diagnosis rests upon the following points: (1) The absence of the physical signs which should be present were the disability due to organic disease. We might term this negative evidence from the objective point of view. (2) Evidence that the symptoms followed emotional stress or suggestion and that the patient has an hysterical personality. This might be termed positive evidence from the psychiatric point of view. (3) The *only conclusive proof* of the diagnosis is the *cure of the symptoms by suggestion or persuasion*. It must be kept in mind that hysteria and organic disease may coexist, and it is best to rely upon objective methods as far as possible in making a differential diagnosis. An hysterical personality does not protect the subject against disease of the nervous system.

Prognosis.—In giving a prognosis every aspect of the case must be taken into consideration and this of course demands an intelligent psychiatric investigation. It does not seem proper to offer a prognosis on the basis of a neurological examination alone. In my experience it is only in those cases which are complicated by mental defect and in a few cases in which the patient holds the unusual tenacity to the symptoms that significant physical disability persists for more than a short time.

Treatment.—There are two chief problems: (1) The removal of the symptoms. (2) The treatment of the underlying psychological disorder. The first step is to make a correct and definite diagnosis, and to accomplish this it is often necessary to remove the symptoms by some form of psychotherapy. In many cases in young children it is necessary only to isolate the child from the parents for a few days and the symptoms will disappear, for they flourish, as a rule, only in the most sympathetic atmosphere. In older children, isolation not only from the parents but from other physicians, is sometimes wise. A quiet talk with reassurance that there is no real loss of function and the firm insistence that the child try to overcome the trouble, will often be effective. Such methods are termed *persuasion*. If this is not effective, one may proceed to suggestion. In cases characterized by anesthesia or by paralysis this is most easily accomplished by the use of electrical stimulation. The strong contractions of the muscles and the disagreeable shocks soon convince the child that the extremity is neither anesthetic nor paralysed. In using such methods one should be careful not to make any false or misleading statements or to lead the child to think that the shocks are actually curing a real disability. It is very important not to antagonize or to frighten the child. Hypnosis may be used in the same way as a method of suggestion. In some cases it seems best to ignore the symp-

toms and to proceed at once to the second step in the problem, i.e. the treatment of the psychological disorder.

When the symptoms have been removed or when the diagnosis is firmly established by other means, we must consider what can be done to remedy the mental condition which gives rise to such symptoms. This is a psychiatric problem and if the neurologist is not prepared to undertake this responsibility he should place the patient and the parents in the hands of the best psychiatrist available. It is my custom to follow this course and to wish both the patient and the psychiatrist the best of luck.

BIBLIOGRAPHY

ALTSCHULE, M. D.: Globus hystericus. Medical Science. April 10, 1960, p. 471.

ARKONAC, O. AND GUZE, S. B.: Familial background of hysteria. New England J. Med., **268**:239, 1963.

CREAK, M.: Hysteria in children. Brit. Jour. Child. Dis., **35**:85, 1938.

EISENBERG, L., ASCHER, E. AND KANNER, L.: A clinical study of Gilles de la Tourette's disease in children. Am. J. Psychiat., **115**:715, 1959.

FARQUHARSON, R. F. AND HYLAND, H. H.: Anorexia nervosa. Canad. Med. Ass. Jour., **94**:411, 1966.

FEILD, J. R. *et al.*: Gilles de la Tourette's syndrome. Neurology, **16**:453, 1966.

KALES, A. *et al.*: Sonambulism: psychophysiological correlates. Arch. Gen. Psychiat., **14**:586, 1966.

KANNER, L.: Child Psychiatry. Thomas, Springfield, 1935.

KINSBOURNE, M.: Neck contorsions with hiatus hernia. Lancet, **i**:1058, 1964.

MILLER, P. R. *et al.*: Imipramine in the treatment of enuretic school children. Amer. Jour. Child., **115**:17, 1968.

PERLEY, M. J. AND GUZE, S. B.: Hysteria a distinct syndrome. New England Jour. Med., **266**:421, 1962.

STEVENS, H.: Conversion hysteria. Mayo Clin. Proc., **43**:54, 1962.

STEVENS, J. R. AND BLACHLY, P. H.: Successful treatment of maladie des tics. Amer. Jour. Dis. Child., **112**:541, 1967.

TORUP, E.: Follow-up study of children with tics. Acta paediat., **51**:261, 1962.

WALSH, F. B.: Clinical Neuroophthalmology. 2nd Ed., Baltimore, Williams and Wilkins, 1957.

WOLFF, E. AND LACHMAN, G. S.: Hysterical blindness in children; report of 2 cases. Am. J. Dis. Child., **55**:743, 1938.

YASUNA, E. R.: Hysterical amblyopia in children. Am. J. Dis. Child., **106**:558, 1963.

NAME INDEX

SUBJECT INDEX